THE PUZZLERS™

Complete
Crossword
Puzzle
Dictionary

Compiled by
Jane Shaw Whitfield

SWEET WATER PRESS

THE PUZZLERS™ COMPLETE CROSSWORD PUZZLE DICTIONARY

Sweetwater Press

P.O. Box 531127
Birmingham, AL 35253

Library of Congress Cataloging-in-Publication Data

Whitfield, Jane Shaw
        [Webster's New World crossword puzzle dictonary]
        The puzzlers complete crossword puzzle dictionary / compiled by Jane Shaw Whitfield.
        p.   cm.
        Originally published: Webster's New World crossword puzzle dictionary, New York: Simon and Schuster, c1975.
        ISBN 1-889372-02-1 (hardcover) – ISBN 1-889372-01-3 (pbk.)
        1. Crossword puzzles–Glossaries, vocabularies, etc.   I. Title.
GV1507.C7W485   1997
793.73'2'03–dc21
                                                                                        97-20382
                                                                                        CIP

Cover design by Southern Lights Custom Publishing
Manufactured in the United States of America

FOREWORD

This reference work has been compiled especially for the millions who enjoy solving crossword puzzles and for those who construct them. But because of its comprehensive coverage of rare, arcane, technical, and dialectal terms, as well as of many proper names from geography, literature, the Bible, and the like, it is also an invaluable aid to those who enjoy solving other kinds of word puzzles or playing word games. And its listings of synonyms and of identifying facts about persons, places, and things make it as well a useful thesaurus and general reference book for the home library.

Unlike some other puzzle dictionaries on the market, this one is not merely a mechanical listing of words of six letters or fewer, offering no clue as to meanings. This list contains answers actually found in a survey of thousands of puzzles, and so you will discover here words from two to fourteen or more letters, as well as phrases and compounds of two or more words, of the kind frequently encountered in puzzles today, such as "in a trice" for "instantly" or "black eye" for "contusion."

A special feature of this book is the arrangement of the materials. All clue words are in bold-face type, alphabetically arranged, with subcategories, where these exist, in italic type, also in alphabetical order. The answer terms for each clue are arranged by the count of letters in each word (or phrase), in numerical order. Each group of answers with the same letter count are then arranged alphabetically to help you find quickly the solution to your problem fill-in.

For example: you need the six-letter name of a Greek sun god. You turn to **Greek god of**, find the subcategory *sun*, and discover after the numeral **6** the two names "Apollo" and "Helios." If you have even one letter of the answer already filled in, you know immediately which is the correct name.

In general, words are shown with their prevailing spellings, but certain rarer variants that commonly appear in puzzles are also given. Although upper-case and lower-case distinctions, and accents on foreign words, are insignificant in crossword puzzle practice, the other uses to which this book will undoubtedly be put made it desirable to observe these orthographic conventions.

So to all enthusiasts of crossword puzzles and to their creators, I hereby dedicate this WEBSTER'S NEW WORLD™ CROSSWORD PUZZLE DICTIONARY.

Jane Shaw Whitfield

ABBREVIATIONS USED IN THIS WORK

Abbr — Abbreviation	Gen — General	Philol — Philolo
abdom — abdominal	Geog — Geography	Philos — Philosop
aborig — aboriginal	Geol — Geology	Phonet — Phonet
Acad — Academy	Geom — Geometry	Phys — Physi
adj — adjective	Ger — German	pl — plu
adm — admitted	Gov — Governor	PO — Post Off
Afr — African	Govt — Government	poet — poe
Agric — Agriculture	Gr — Greek	Polit — Politics, Politi
Alex — Alexander	Gram — Grammar	Polyn — Polynes
Am Ind — American Indian	Gr Brit — Great Britain	ppty — prope
Anat — Anatomy		pref — pre
anc — ancient	Haw — Hawaiian	P Rico — Puerto Ri
Anglo-Ir — Anglo-Irish	Heb — Hebrew	Pros — Proso
Anthrop — Anthropology	Hem — Hemisphere	
Antiq — Antiquity	Her — Heraldry	R — Rom
Arab — Arabian	Hind — Hinduism	RCCh — Roman Catholic Chur
Arch — Architecture	Hindu — Hindustani	Rd — Ro
Archaeol — Archaeology	Hist — Historical	ref — referri
Astrol — Astrology	Holl — Holland	Relig — Relig
Astron — Astronomy	Horol — Horology	R Estate — Real Est
Austral — Australia(n)	Hung — Hungarian	Rev War — Revolutionary W
		Rhet — Rheto
Babyl — Babylonia	illeg — illegal	Riv — Riv
Belg — Belgium	Ind — India, Indian	Rom — Rom
Bib — Bible, Biblical	Indo-Chin — Indo-China	rr — railro
Biol — Biology	Ins — Insurance	Rum — Ruma
Bot — Botany	Internat — International	Russ — Russi
Braz — Brazil(ian)	Ir — Irish	
Brit — Britain, British	irreg — irregular	S — Sou
Brit Col — British Columbia	Isl(s) — Island(s)	Scot — Scotland, Scotti
Buddh — Buddhism	It — Italian	Scand — Scandinavi
Bus — Business		Shakesp — Shakespe
	Jap — Japanese	sing — singu
Can — Canada, Canadian	Jew — Jewish	sl — sla
Capt — Captain		Slav — Slavo
Caucas — Caucasian	L — Latin	So Afr — South Afr
Celt — Celtic	Legislat — Legislature	So Am — South Ameri
Cent — Central, Century	Lit — Literature	Sp — Spani
Cent Am — Central America	Log — Logic	Surg — Surgi
Chem — Chemistry		sym — symb
Chin — Chinese	Maced — Macedonia	
Chr — Christian	Malay — Malayan	Tag — Taga
coll — colloquialism	Math — Mathematics	Tahit — Tah
comb form — combining form	MD — Doctor of Medicine	Terat — Teratolo
Confed — Confederation	Med — Medical	terr — territo
Constell — Constellation	Mex — Mexican	Teut — Teuton
contemp — contemporary	Mil — Military	Theat — Theatri
Criminol — Criminology	Mohamm — Mohammedan	Theol — Theolo
	Mt(s) — Mountain(s)	Theos — Theosop
Dan — Danish	Mus — Music	triang — triangu
Dept — Department	Myth — Mythology	TID — Ter in d
derog — derogatory		Trop — Tropi
dial — dialectal	Nat'l — National	Turk — Turki
div — division	Naut — Nautical	TV — Televisi
Du — Dutch	Nav — Naval, Navy	
	neg — negative	U — Uni
E — East	New Test — New Testament	Univ — Univers
East Ch — Eastern Church	NZ — New Zealand	USS — United States S
Eccl — Ecclesiastical	No — North	USSR — Union of Sov
Educ — Education	No Am — North American	Socialist Republi
Egypt — Egyptian		
Elec — Electricity	obs — obsolete	Vet — Veterina
Eng — England, English	Old Test — Old Testament	
Episcop — Episcopal	opp — opposite	W — We
equiv — equivalent	Orient — Oriental	WAC — Women's Army Cor
Esk — Eskimo	Oxf Univ — Oxford University	W Indies — West Indi
est — established		WWI — World Wa
Eur — Europe(an)	Penol — Penology	
exclam — exclamation	Pers — Persian	Yidd — Yiddi
ext — extinct	pert — pertaining	YMCA — Young Men's Christi
	Petrol — Petrology	Associati
FDR — Franklin D. Roosevelt	Pg — Portuguese	yr — ye
Fem — Feminine	Pharm — Pharmaceutical	
Finan — Finance, Financial	Philat — Philately	Zool — Zoolo
Flem — Flemish	Phil I — Philippine Islands	
Fr — France, French		

A

A... **5.** alpha, first **7.** article
A 1... **5.** prime **6.** symbol **8.** superior **10.** first–class
aa (Haw)... **4.** lava
aal... **8.** morindin (dye), mulberry
aam (Du)... **7.** measure (liquid) **11.** water bucket
Aani (Egypt)... **3.** ape (sacred) **6.** baboon **12.** cynocephalus
aardvark... **3.** pig **6.** farrow **8.** anteater
aardwolf... **5.** hyena **8.** Proteles
Aaron (pert to)...
  ally (Bib).. **3.** Hur
  brother.. **5.** Moses
  burial place.. **3.** Hor
  leader (Jew).. **9.** Levitical **10.** High Priest
  rod.. **4.** wand (magic) **7.** molding, mullein
  sister.. **6.** Miriam
  son.. **5.** Abihu, Nadab
Aaru (Egypt Relig)... **12.** fields of Aaru **14.** abode of the dead
aasvogel... **7.** vulture
abaca... **4.** hemp **5.** lupis **6.** linaga
abacus... **4.** slab **8.** cupboard **10.** calculator **11.** compartment
Abaddon... **3.** pit (bottomless) **4.** Hell **5.** Sheol **8.** Apollyon (angel) **11.** destruction
abaft... **3.** aft **5.** after **6.** astern, behind
abalone... **5.** awabi, ormer, uhllo (ullo) **6.** sea ear **8.** ear shell
abandon... **4.** quit **5.** cease, leave, remit, waive, yield **6.** abjure, depart, desert, disuse, give up, maroon, reject, resign, vacate **7.** cast off, discard, forsake, freedom, neglect **8.** abdicate, forswear, renounce **9.** surrender, turpitude **10.** relinquish **11.** abandonment, discontinue, unrestraint **12.** carelessness, heedlessness
abandoned... **4.** left, lost **7.** disused, forlorn, given up **8.** derelict, deserted, forsaken **9.** desolated, discarded, neglected **11.** surrendered **12.** relinquished, unredeemable, unrestrained
abase... **5.** lower, shame **6.** bemean, depose, humble, reduce **7.** degrade, mortify **8.** cast down, disgrace **9.** humiliate **10.** depreciate
abash... **5.** shame **6.** appall, dismay **7.** astound, confuse, disturb, mortify **8.** bewilder, confound **9.** discomfit, embarrass, humiliate **10.** disconcert, put to shame
abate... **3.** ebb **4.** lull, wane **5.** let up, relax, remit **6.** deduct, lessen,

reduce **7.** abolish, nullify, qualify, slacken, subside **8.** decrease, diminish, discount, moderate
abatement... **5.** letup **6.** myosis (miosis), rebate **8.** decrease **9.** lessening, reduction **10.** diminution, mitigation, moderation
abb... **4.** wool, yarn **6.** fleece (pert to)
Abba... **5.** abbot, title **6.** Father
abbe... **4.** monk **6.** cleric, curate, priest
abbess... **4.** amma **15.** spiritual mother
abbreviate... **7.** abridge, curtail, shorten **8.** compress, condense, contract, simplify **9.** epitomize **11.** make briefer
abbreviation... **5.** brief, lapse **6.** digest **8.** abstract **9.** reduction **10.** abridgment, compendium, shortening **11.** contraction **12.** condensation
abdicate... **4.** cede, quit **5.** demit, leave **6.** depose, disown, resign, retire **7.** lay down **8.** disclaim, renounce, withdraw **9.** surrender **10.** disinherit, relinquish
Abdiel (Heb)... **5.** angel **12.** servant of God
abdomen... **3.** pot (sl) **4.** wame **5.** belly, tharm (obs) **6.** paunch, venter **7.** stomach **8.** potbelly **12.** pelvic cavity
abdominal... **7.** coeliac, gastric, ventral **11.** ventricular
abdominal limb (crustacean)... **7.** pleopod
Abel's brother... **4.** Cain, Seth
aberration... **5.** mania, wrong **6.** lunacy, oddity **7.** errancy, madness **8.** dementia, insanity **9.** departure, deviation, variation, wandering **10.** alienation, digression, divergence **11.** abnormality, derangement, distraction, peculiarity **12.** eccentricity, irregularity **14.** disorientation
abet... **3.** aid, egg **4.** back, help **5.** egg on **6.** assist, foment, incite, second, succor, uphold **7.** connive, endorse, support, sustain **8.** advocate **9.** encourage, instigate **11.** countenance
abeyance... **4.** rest, stay **5.** lapse, pause **7.** waiting **9.** inertness **10.** expectancy, suspension
abhor... **2.** ug **4.** hate, shun **6.** detest, loathe **7.** despise, dislike **8.** execrate **9.** abominate
abhorrence... **5.** odium **6.** hatred, horror **7.** dislike **8.** aversion, loathing **9.** antipathy, disliking, repulsion

10. repugnance

abide... 4. bide, live, stay, wait
5. await, dwell, pause, tarry
6. endure, remain, reside 7. sojourn
8. continue, submit to, tolerate
9. acquiesce, withstand

abide by... 3. own 4. avow, heed
5. admit, allow, yield 6. accept,
follow, regard 7. concede, respect
8. adhere to 9. conform to
11. acknowledge

abiding... 7. durable, lasting
8. constant, enduring 9. permanent,
steadfast 10. continuing, indwelling,
persisting

Abies... 4. firs 5. pines 8. conifers
10. evergreens

abigail... 4. ayah, maid 5. bonne
7. servant 9. soubrette

Abijah's son (Bib)... 3. Asa

ability... 4. gift 5. force, might,
power, skill 6. genius, talent
7. caliber, faculty, fitness, potency
8. aptitude, capacity, strength
10. capability, competence, efficiency
11. proficiency, sufficiency
13. qualification

abiosis... 11. without life

abject... 3. low 4. base, mean, meek,
vile 6. humble, menial, supine
7. hangdog, ignoble, servile, slavish
8. beggarly, contrite, cringing,
degraded, wretched 9. groveling,
miserable 10. despicable, obsequious

abjuration... 6. denial 8. palinode
(song), yielding 9. disavowal,
rejection, surrender 10. abjurement,
retraction, withdrawal
11. abandonment, forswearing,
recantation, repudiation
12. disclamation 14. relinquishment

abjure... 4. deny, wave 6. disown,
recant, reject, revoke 7. abandon,
disavow 8. disclaim, forswear,
renounce 9. disaffirm, repudiate

able... 3. can, fit 5. adept, smart
6. clever, fitted, suited 7. adapted,
capable, learned, solvent 8. adjusted,
literate, powerful, skillful (skilful),
vigorous 9. competent, effective,
efficient, qualified 10. omnipotent,
proficient

able (pert to)...
suffix.. 7. capable, fitness
to pay.. 7. moneyed, solvent
8. affluent 10. prosperous
to read and write.. 8. lettered, literate
10. book taught

ablepsia... 9. blindness

ably... 7. capably 11. competently,
effectively, efficiently

abnormal... 6. albino 7. erratic,
unusual 8. aberrant 9. deviative,
eccentric, irregular, unnatural
11. exceptional 13. extraordinary

aboard... 4. onto 6. across 7. athwart
9. alongside

abode... 3. dar, hut 4. cell, cote,
Eden, home 5. delay, house, lodge
7. habitat, Olympus, sojourn
8. dwelling, tenement 9. apartment,
residence 10. habitation

abode of the dead... 3. Dar 4. Aalu,
Aaru, Hell 5. Aralu, Hades, limbo,
Orcus, Sheol 6. Asgard, heaven,
Naraka 7. Abaddon, Elysium, Nirvana
8. paradise, Valhalla 9. perdition,
purgatory 11. Pandemonium

abolish... 4. undo 5. annul, quash
6. cancel, recall, repeal, revoke,
vacate 7. destroy, nullify, rescind,
retract, reverse 8. abrogate, withdraw
10. annihilate, invalidate
11. countermand

abominable... 4. base, dire, foul, vile
5. awful, gross 6. odious, wicked,
woeful 7. beastly, hateful 8. dreadful,
grievous, infamous, shocking, terrible,
wretched 9. execrable, loathsome,
obnoxious 10. despicable, detestable,
outrageous, unpleasant
12. disagreeable, disreputable

Abominable Snowman... 4. Yeti

abominate... 4. hate 5. abhor
6. detest, loathe 8. execrate

abomination... 3. woe 4. evil
5. odium, wrong 6. hatred, horror,
plague 7. disgust, outrage
8. aversion, loathing, vexation
9. grievance 10. abhorrence,
defilement, odiousness, repugnance

aboriginal... 5. first, natal 6. binghi,
native 7. ancient 8. original
9. beginning, primitive
10. autochthon, indigenous

aborigines... 4. Ainu (Aino), Toda
5. lubra, Sakai, Vedda 7. cave men,
Indians, natives, savages
9. indigenes, old–timers
10. Dravidians 11. preadamites

abortion... 6. arrest 7. failure
11. embryoctomy, miscarriage,
miscreation 13. misconception

abound... 4. flow, teem 5. swarm
8. overflow 9. exuberate, plentiful

abounding... 4. rife 5. ample, flush
7. copious, teeming 8. abundant
9. exuberant, luxuriant, plentiful

abounding in...
blossoms.. 7. flowery
forests.. 6. sylvan
grass.. 6. cressy
snow.. 5. nival

about... 2. of, on, re 3. amb (pref)
5. anent, astir, circa 6. almost,
around, nearly 8. circiter
10. concerning 13. approximately

about to happen... 8. imminent

above... 2. on, up 3. o'er, sur (pref)
4. atop, over, upon 5. aloft, super,
supra (pref)

abrade... 3. rub 4. file, fret, gall
5. chafe, grate 6. scrape
9. excoriate

Abraham (pert to)...
birthplace.. 2. Ur
concubine.. 5. Hagar
father.. 5. Terah
grandfather.. 5. Nahor
grandson.. 4. Esau
nephew.. 3. Lot
son.. 4. Shua (Shuah) 5. Isaac,
Medan 7. Ishmael
wife.. 5. Sarah (Sara, Sarai)

7. Keturah

abrasion... 4. flaw, gall, hurt 5. scuff
6. lesion, scrape 8. limation
9. attrition

abrasive... 4. file, sand 5. emery
6. garnet, polish, pumice 7. erodent
8. abradant, corundum 9. attritive,
sandpaper

abraxas... 3. gem 5. charm, stone

Abraxas (pert to)...
god (anc Gnostic).. 12. Supreme
Deity
source of mind.. 4. Nous
the Word.. 5. Logos

abreast... 4. even (with) 6. beside
8. opposite 10. alongside

abrege... 7. epitome 10. abridgment

abri... 4. shed 6. cavity, dugout
7. shelter

abridge... 5. brief, razee (rasee)
7. curtail, shorten 8. abstract,
condense, diminish, retrench
9. epitomize 10. abbreviate

abridgment... 6. digest 7. compend,
epitome, summary 8. abstract,
syllabus, synopsis 9. lessening,
reduction 10. compendium,
diminution 11. deprivation

abroad... 4. away 5. forth 6. astray,
widely 7. at large, broadly, distant
8. away from 9. spread out
11. widely apart

abrogate... 5. annul, quash 6. cancel,
repeal, revoke 7. abolish, rescind
8. set aside 10. put an end to

abrogation... 8. quashing 9. annulling,
cessation 10. rescinding, rescission
11. dissolution

abrupt... 4. curt, rude 5. blunt, hasty,
quick, sharp, sheer, steep, terse
6. broken, craggy, sudden
7. brusque 8. headlong, vertical
9. broken off, impetuous
10. unexpected 11. precipitous
12. disconnected 13. perpendicular,
unceremonious

abruptly... 7. briefly, in brief
8. suddenly

Absalom (pert to)...
father.. 5. David (King)
host's captain.. 5. Amasa
sister.. 5. Tamar
slayer.. 4. Joab

abscond... 3. run 4. bolt, flee, hide
5. elope 6. decamp, desert, eloine,
levant 8. steal off

absence... 4. AWOL, lack, void, want
5. exeat, leave 6. vacuum 7. silence
10. deficiency, withdrawal
13. nonappearance, nonattendance

absence of... (see also *without*)
animal, plant.. 8. lipotype
hair.. 6. acomia
pain.. 8. anodynia
pigment.. 8. alphosis
self-worth.. 7. modesty
taste.. 7. ageusia

absent... 3. off, out 4. away, gone,
lost 6. dreamy, musing, truant
7. lacking 8. absorbed 9. engrossed
10. abstracted 11. preoccupied
12. nonattendant

absinthe... 5. green (color) 6. ajenjo,
liquor

absolute... 4. alod, dead, pure, real,
true, very 5. freed, sheer, total,
utter, whole 6. empery, simple
7. certain, elative, perfect, plenary
8. absolved, complete, positive
9. arbitrary, downright, unlimited
10. autocratic, disengaged,
peremptory 11. categorical,
independent 13. unconditional
15. plenipotentiary

absolute (pert to)...
dominion.. 6. empery
property.. 4. alod 7. alodium
sovereign.. 8. autocrat
superlative.. 7. elative
time.. 9. Greenwich, universal

absolutely... 3. yea, yes 5. stark
6. wholly 7. utterly 8. entirely
10. altogether, positively, thoroughly
13. unequivocally 15. unconditionally

absolution... 6. pardon, shrive
7. penance 9. acquittal, remission
11. exculpation, forgiveness

absolve... 4. free 5. remit 6. acquit,
finish, pardon 9. discharge, exonerate
10. accomplish

absonant... 8. contrary 10. discordant
12. unreasonable

absorb... 3. eat 4. soak, suck
5. drink, eat up, learn, use up
6. corner, digest, engulf, imbibe,
soak up, sponge 7. consume,
swallow 10. assimilate, monopolize,
understand 11. incorporate

absorbed... 4. deep, lost, rapt, sunk
6. buried, intent, lost in
7. bemused, devoted, engaged
8. occupied 9. engrossed
11. monopolized, preoccupied

absorbent... 5. fomes 6. spongy
7. blotter 9. adsorbent
10. imbibitory

absorption... 10. imbibition

abstain... 4. deny, fast, hold, shun
5. avoid, cease, forgo, waive
6. eschew 7. forbear, refrain
8. restrain, teetotal, withhold

abstemious... 5. sober 7. sparing
8. moderate 9. abstinent, temperate
11. abstentious

abstinence... 6. disuse 7. encraty
8. sobriety 9. restraint, sacrifice
10. abstention, continence,
desistance, moderation, self-denial,
temperance 11. abandonment,
forbearance, self-control
13. self-restraint
14. abstemiousness, discontinuance

abstract... 4. deed, part, take 5. brief,
steal 6. deduct, noetic (purely),
remove 7. abridge, epitome, shorten,
summary 8. argument, condense,
syllabus, withdraw 9. capsulize,
statement 10. abridgment,
compendium 12. nonobjective

abstract being... 3. ens 6. entity

abstruse... 4. deep 6. hidden
7. obscure 8. esoteric, profound
9. concealed, recondite
10. acroamatic (acroatic)

16. incomprehensible

absurd ... 4. wild 5. droll, inept, silly
6. stupid 7. asinine, foolish
8. fabulous 9. ludicrous
10. impossible, irrational, ridiculous
11. incongruous, nonsensical
12. inconsistent, unbelievable, unreasonable

absurdity ... 7. twaddle 8. nonsense
10. absurdness 11. foolishness
13. contradiction, impossibility
14. ridiculousness 16. inconceivability

abundance ... 4. mass, much, rife
5. ample 6. galore, plenty, riches,
volume 8. fullness (fulness),
opulence, overflow, quantity
9. affluence 10. exuberance
11. copiousness, superfluity
12. extravagance, generousness
13. plenteousness

abundant ... 4. lush, much, rich, rife,
teem 5. ample 6. galore, plenty
7. copious, profuse 9. abounding,
exuberant, luxuriant, plentiful
10. sufficient

abundant, not ... 5. spare 6. lenten,
meager (meagre)

abuse ... 4. gali, harm, hurt, maul, rail,
rape 5. crime, curse, scold, snash
6. berate, ill use, injure, insult,
malign, misuse, ravish, revile
7. calumny, deceive, obloquy,
offense, pervert, traduce, upbraid
8. dishonor, maltreat, misapply,
reproach 9. contumely, disparage,
invective, violation 10. opprobrium,
revilement, scurrility
11. debauchment, malediction,
objurgation 12. mistreatment,
vituperation

abusive ... 3. mud (throw)
10. scurrilous 12. catachrestic

abut ... 4. butt, join 5. touch
6. adjoin, appose, border, rest on
7. conjoin, connect 8. adjacent,
neighbor

abutment ... 4. arch, pier, wall
6. alette 7. abuttal, sea wall
8. buttress, shoulder 13. fortification

abysmal ... 4. deep 7. yawning
8. profound, unending 9. plumbless
10. bottomless, fathomless

abyss ... 3. pit 4. Absu, gulf, hell,
hole, void, well 5. abysm, chaos,
chasm, cleft, shaft 6. cavity, vorago
15. infernal regions

Abyssinia, Ethiopia ...
capital .. 10. Addis Ababa
city .. 5. Aduwa, Aksum (Axum)
6. Gondar 7. Ankober, Gambela,
Magdala
dialect .. 4. Geez
Empire (old) .. 7. Axumite
Hamite .. 4. Afar
King .. 13. Haile Selassie
kingdom (former) .. 4. Shoa 5. Tigre
6. Amhara
population .. 7. Hamites, Semites
8. Negroids
river (famed) .. 5. Abdai (Blue Nile)
sea .. 3. Red
title (anc) .. 12. Negusa Nagast

Abyssinian (pert to) ...
fly .. 4. zimb
gold (artificial) .. 5. talmi
lyre .. 6. kissar
tea leaves .. 3. kat
wolf .. 6. kaberu

Academe, The ... 14. Academy of Plato
(Athens)

academic ... 5. ideal, rigid 6. formal
7. classic, elegant 8. abstract,
pedantic, Platonic 9. scholarly
10. Ciceronian, scholastic
11. educational, impractical,
speculative, theoretical
12. conventional, hypothetical
13. institutional

academy ... 5. école 6. lyceum,
manège, school, Schule 7. college,
escuela, society 8. academie,
seminary 9. accademia, institute
10. university 11. institution

Acadia ... 6. Acadie 10. Nova Scotia

acarpous ... 7. sterile 9. fruitless

acaudal ... 7. anurous 8. tailless

accede ... 5. agree, enter, grant, yield
6. assent, attain, comply, concur,
relent, submit 7. conform, consent
9. acquiesce 11. acknowledge

accelerate ... 4. rush 5. speed
6. hasten, step up 7. advance,
forward, further, quicken 8. activate,
dispatch, expedite

acceleration ... 5. haste 6. pickup
8. velocity 9. catalysis, hastening
10. expedition, quickening
11. advancement

accelerator ... 6. muscle 7. speeder
8. throttle 9. quickener

accent ... 4. beat, mark, tone 5. breve,
ictus, pitch, twang 6. brogue, stress
7. cadence, dialect 8. emphasis
9. emphasize 10. accentuate,
expression, inflection, modulation
12. accentuation

accent (pert to) ...
Irish .. 4. blas 6. brogue
on last syllable .. 7. oxytone
Scot .. 4. birr
unaccented syllable .. 5. arsis

accept ... 2. OK 3. buy, own 4. avow,
fang, take 5. admit, adopt, agree,
allow, grant, trust, yield 6. assent,
comply, credit, expect, ratify
7. approve, believe, certify, condone,
confess, consent, embrace, receive,
swallow (coll) 8. accredit, tolerate,
validate 9. undertake
11. countenance

accept (as one's own) ...
12. nostrificate (of foreign degrees)

acceptable ... 2. OK 6. worthy
7. welcome 8. eligible, passable,
pleasant, pleasing, suitable
9. agreeable, allowable, desirable,
expedient, qualified, tolerable
10. admissible 11. comfortable
12. satisfactory

accepted ... 6. chosen, deemed
7. adopted, assumed, popular,
reputed, trusted 8. admitted,
approved, believed, credited,
embraced, espoused, inferred,

orthodox, received, standard,
supposed 9. customary, prevalent
10. accredited, understood,
undertaken 11. traditional
12. conventional, unquestioned
13. authoritative

access... 3. way 4. adit, door, gain
5. entry 6. avenue, entree, ingate,
tunnel 7. ingress 8. approach,
entrance, entryway, increase
9. accession, accretion, admission
10. admittance 11. entranceway
13. accessibility, attainability
15. approachability

accessible... 4. open 5. handy
6. open to, public 7. getable
8. amenable, pervious 9. admissive,
available, permeable, reachable,
receptive 10. attainable, obtainable,
open–minded, penetrable, procurable
11. persuasible 12. approachable
13. communicative

accession... 6. access, assent, attack,
growth 7. adjunct, consent, joining,
uniting 8. addition, increase
9. accretion, agreement, increment
10. acceptance, affixation,
annexation, attainment, compliance,
concession, coronation
12. acquiescence 13. reinforcement
14. aggrandizement

accessory, accessary... 5. extra, party
7. abettor 8. addition, litigant
9. adjective, appendage, assistant,
attendant, auxiliary, obbligato
10. accomplish, additional, collateral,
subsidiary 11. appurtenant,
concomitant, participant
12. accompanying, appurtenance,
contributory, nonessential, participator
13. accompaniment, supplementary

accident... 3. hap 4. luck 6. chance,
hazard, mishap 8. calamity, casualty,
disaster 9. adventure, befalling,
mischance 10. misfortune
11. catastrophe

accidental... 6. casual, chance
9. unwitting 10. contingent,
unforeseen, unintended

acclaim... 4. hail, laud 6. praise
7. applaud 8. applause
11. acclamation, approbation

acclamation... 3. cry, joy 5. shout
7. acclaim, ovation, plaudit
8. applause, approval 9. unanimity

acclimate... 5. adapt, inure 6. adjust,
season 8. accustom 9. condition,
habituate 10. naturalize
11. acclimatize, familiarize

acclivity... 4. bank, brow, hill, rise
5. climb, slope, talus 6. ascent
7. upgrade 9. ascendant (ascendent)
11. inclination

accolade... 4. fold, rite 5. award,
brace, clasp, Oscar 6. praise, reward
7. embrace, tribute 8. encomium
9. panegyric 10. enfoldment

accommodate... 3. fit 4. help, lend,
meet, suit 5. adapt, favor, lodge,
shape, yield 6. adjust, afford,
comply, invest, oblige, orient, settle,
supply 7. conform, furnish

9. reconcile 10. correspond

accommodation... 3. aid 4. loan,
room 5. limit, space, terms
6. giving, volume 7. advance,
lodging, service 8. capacity
9. advantage, provision
10. adaptation, adjustment,
attunement, conformity, settlement
11. convenience, integration,
orientation, subsistence
12. coordination 13. harmonization
14. reconciliation

accompaniment... 7. adjunct, descant,
support 8. ornament 9. attendant,
obbligato 11. concurrence
12. concomitance

accompany... 4. join 6. attend,
convoy, escort, follow, squire
7. conduct 11. synchronize
12. contemporize

accomplice... 3. pal 4. aide, ally,
chum 6. stooge 7. abettor
9. accessory, assistant, associate
11. confederate, conspirator

accomplish... 2. do 3. win 4. make,
work 5. enact, equip 6. attain, effect
7. achieve, compass, execute,
furnish, operate, perfect, produce,
realize, succeed 8. contrive, engineer
9. negotiate 10. consummate,
effectuate

accomplishment... 4. deed, feat
5. skill 8. dispatch 9. discharge,
execution 10. attainment, completion
11. achievement, acquirement,
fulfillment, performance, proficiency,
transaction 12. effectuation

accord... 5. award, grant, unity
6. accede, unison 7. comport,
concede, concert, concord, harmony,
rapport 8. diapason, symphony
9. agreement, harmonize, reconcile,
unanimity 10. accordance, conformity,
uniformity 11. concurrence

accordant... 7. attuned 8. agreeing,
suitable 9. agreeable, assenting,
consonant 10. concordant,
concurrent, consenting, consilient,
consistent 11. conformable,
homogeneous 13. corresponding

accordingly... 2. so 4. then, thus
9. therefore 12. consequently

according to... 3. a la, aux 4. alla,
fact, true 5. datal 7. a la mode
8. pursuant

accost... 4. hail, meet 5. greet, speak
6. halloo, salute 7. address
8. approach

accoucheuse... 7. midwife

account... 3. sum, tab 4. bill, cast,
sake, tale, word 5. debit, honor,
score, tally 6. assign, credit, esteem,
profit, reckon, regard, report
7. compute, memoirs, recital
9. narration, reckoning, rehearsal,
statement, summation
10. numeration, recitation
11. description, explanation,
information 13. communication

accountable... 6. liable 8. amenable,
knowable 9. divinable, traceable
10. answerable, ascribable,

assignable, calculable, explicable,
fathomable 11. explainable,
predictable, responsible
12. attributable, intelligible
13. apprehensible
14. comprehensible

accountant . . . 5. clerk 7. actuary,
auditor 8. reckoner 9. defendant,
registrar 10. bookkeeper, calculator

accouter, accoutre . . . 3. fit, rig
4. deck, gird, suit 5. array, dress,
equip, habit 6. attire, fettle, outfit
7. appoint, costume, furnish, provide

accouterment, accoutrement . . .
5. dress, sword 6. attire 8. trapping
9. equipment, haversack

accoy . . . 4. tame 5. daunt 6. soothe,
subdue

accredit . . . 5. trust 6. accept, affirm,
credit, depute, ratify 7. approve,
ascribe, believe, certify, confirm,
empower, endorse 8. deputize,
sanction, validate 9. authorize
10. commission

accrete . . . 3. add 6. attach

accretion . . . 4. gain 6. growth
8. addition, adhesion, increase
9. coherence, increment
10. concretion 11. coagulation,
enlargement 12. accumulation,
augmentation 13. amplification

accrue . . . 4. grow 5. arise, ensue,
issue 6. mature, result 7. acquire,
collect, redound 8. accresce
10. accumulate

accumulate . . . 4. grow, heap, mass,
save 5. amass, hoard, store
6. accrue, garner, gather, muster
7. advance, collect, store up
8. increase 9. aggregate

accumulation . . . 4. fund, gain, mass
5. hoard, store 7. accrual
8. gleaning, increase, treasure
9. accession, accretion, extension,
gathering 10. acervation, assemblage,
collection 11. acquisition, serendipity
12. augmentation 13. amplification
14. aggrandizement

accuracy . . . 6. nicety 9. exactness,
fussiness, precision, rightness
11. correctness 14. meticulousness,
scrupulousness

accurate . . . 4. just, nice, prim 5. close,
exact, right 6. proper, strict
7. correct, perfect, precise 8. faithful
9. syntactic 10. meticulous, particular
11. grammatical

accursed . . . 6. cursed, damned,
doomed 9. execrable, execrated
10. detestable 13. anathematized

accusation . . . 5. blame 6. attack,
charge, taxing 7. calumny
8. reproach 9. complaint
10. imputation, indictment
11. impeachment 12. denunciation

accuse . . . 3. tax 5. blame 6. attack,
charge, delate, indict 7. arraign,
censure, impeach 8. denounce
9. criminate 11. incriminate,
recriminate

accuser . . . 7. delator 8. accusant,
libelant (libellant) 9. plaintiff

10. prosecutor 11. complainant
12. incriminator

accustom . . . 3. use 4. wont 5. enure,
habit, inure, train 6. addict
7. educate, toughen 9. habituate
11. familiarize

accustomed . . . 4. used, wont 5. usual
6. enured, inured 8. familiar
9. customary, sedentary (to sit)

ace . . . 3. jot, one, pip, tib 4. atom,
card, dole, dram, unit, whit
5. monad, pilot, point, shark (sl)
7. aviator 8. particle, pittance,
superior 10. crackajack (sl), proficient
11. crackerjack (sl)

ace (pert to) . . .
ace–queen . . 6. tenace
of clubs . . 5. basto

acedia (Gr) . . . 5. sloth 6. torpor

acedia (Sp) . . . 8. flatfish

Aceldama, Akeldama (Bib) . . . 12. Field
of Blood, potter's field

acemila . . . 8. pack mule

acephalous . . . 8. headless
10. leaderless

acephalus . . . 15. headless monster

acerb . . . 4. sour 5. harsh, sharp
6. bitter, unripe 7. acerbic, austere,
pungent

acerbity . . . 7. acidity 8. acridity,
acrimony, asperity, mordancy,
pungency, severity 9. harshness
10. bitterness, causticity
11. astringency

acetic acid . . . 7. vinegar 8. vesicant
9. corrosive

Achaean, Achaian . . . 5. Greek (a)
6. Greece

ache . . . 4. burn, long, pain, pang
5. throb 6. grieve, sorrow, twinge
7. agonize, longing 10. suffer pain

achieve . . . 2. do 3. get, win 4. gain,
kill 6. arrive, attain, effect, finish
7. compass, execute, fulfill, perform,
produce, realize, succeed
8. complete, conclude, contrive
10. accomplish, consummate,
effectuate

achievement . . . 3. act 4. deed, feat
5. doing, stunt 6. action, record
7. arrival, exploit 8. dispatch
9. adventure 10. attainment,
escutcheon (Her) 11. fulfillment,
performance, transaction
12. effectuation 14. accomplishment,
implementation

Achilles (pert to) . . .
advisor . . 6. Nestor
dipped into . . 9. River Styx
father . . 6. Peleus
friend . . 9. Patroclus
horse . . 7. Xanthus
mother . . 6. Thetis
slayer . . 5. Paris
slayer of . . 6. Hector
son . . 7. Pyrrhus 11. Neoptolemus
vulnerable spot . . 4. heel

achromatic . . . 4. gray 8. achromic
9. achromous, colorless, uncolored
13. free from color

achropsia . . . 14. color blindness

acid . . . 4. keen, sour, tart 5. acrid,

amino, boric, malic, mucic, pyrol
6. acetic, arabic, biting, bromic,
nitric, oxalic, tannic 7. acetose,
caustic, chloric, racemic, stearic,
terebic, vinegar 9. corrosive
11. acrimonious
acid, removing ... 12. edulcoration
acidity ... 4. acor, sour 8. acrimony,
mordancy, sourness, tartness, verjuice
9. sharpness 10. bitterness
13. acidulousness
acknowledge ... 3. nod, own, pay, say
4. avow, sign 5. admit, allow, grant,
own up, reply, swear, thank, vouch,
yield 6. accede, accept, answer,
assent, attest, redeem 7. certify,
concede, confess, testify 8. disclose
9. recognize
acknowledgment ... 5. favor, reply
6. answer, avowal, avowry, shrift,
thanks 7. apology, epistle, receipt,
voucher, warrant 8. rescript
9. admission 10. acceptance,
concession, confession, disclosure,
owning up to 11. recognition
12. thanksgiving
acme ... 3. top 4. apex 5. limit
6. apogee, climax, crisis, heyday,
summit, tip–top, vertex, zenith
7. ceiling, maximum 11. culmination
12. consummation
acology, science of ... 8. remedies
acolyte ... 7. patener 8. altar boy
9. assistant
acomia ... 8. alopecia, baldness
12. hairlessness
aconite ... 8. Cammarum, Eranthis
9. monkshood
acorn ... 3. nut 4. duck 6. camata
10. meadowlark (color)
acosmic ... 11. unorganized
acquaint ... 4. tell 6. advise, impart,
inform 7. apprise 9. enlighten,
introduce 11. familiarize
acquaintance ... 3. ken 5. amigo
6. friend 7. privity 8. familiar,
intimacy, intimate 9. companion,
knowledge 10. fellowship
11. familiarity, information,
sympathizer 15. familiarization
acquainted ... 6. au fait 7. versant
8. familiar 9. cognizant
10. conversant
acquiesce ... 3. bow 5. abide, agree,
chime, yield 6. accede, assent,
comply, concur, relent, resign, submit
7. conform, consent, succumb
acquire ... 3. buy, get, win 4. earn,
gain, reap 5. adopt, catch, incur,
learn, steal 6. attain, effect, obtain,
secure 7. procure, receive
8. contract 9. cultivate
acquire (pert to) ...
beforehand .. 7. pre–empt
feathers .. 6. fledge
immunity .. 14. serum injection
knowledge .. 5. clear, study
9. ascertain
acquit ... 4. free 5. clear 6. excuse,
pardon, pay off 7. absolve, fulfill,
release, requite 9. exculpate,
exonerate

acquittal ... 7. freeing, payment, release
8. clearing, requital 9. clearance,
discharge 10. observance
11. exculpation, fulfillment
12. satisfaction
acquittance ... 7. payment, quietus,
receipt 9. discharge, quittance
acre ... 5. field 6. arpent 7. measure
8. farmhold
acre (pert to) ...
half .. 3. erf (S Afr)
hundred .. 7. hectare (metric)
quarter .. 4. rood (Brit)
acres ... 5. lands 6. estate, ground
acrid ... 4. acid, bask (dial), keen, sour,
tart 5. harsh, rough, sharp 6. acetic,
biting, bitter 7. acetose, caustic,
mordant, pungent, reeking
8. unsavory, virulent 9. acidulous,
corrosive 10. escharotic, irritating
11. acrimonious
acrimonious ... 4. acid, keen 5. acrid,
angry, gruff, harsh, irate, sharp
6. bitter 7. caustic 8. stinging
9. rancorous, resentful
acrimony ... 5. venom 6. rancor 7. ill
will, vitriol 8. acerbity, acridity,
asperity, mordancy, pungency,
rudeness, severity, sourness, tartness
9. animosity, virulence 10. bitterness,
causticity, resentment
11. astringency, crabbedness
acroamatic ... 4. oral 5. parol
6. arcane, occult, secret, verbal
8. abstract, abstruse, anagogic,
esoteric, profound 9. recondite,
unwritten 11. nuncupative
acrobat ... 7. gymnast, tumbler
8. balancer 10. ropedancer,
ropewalker 11. funambulist
13. contortionist, schoenobatist
acrochordon ... 4. wart (small)
Acrocorinth, Acrocorinthus ...
9. acropolis (Corinth) 12. Pirene
Spring (site)
acromegaly ... 7. disease
11. enlargement (head, hands, feet)
acronical, acronichal (opp of
cosmical) ... 10. rising star
11. setting star
acronyx ... 13. ingrowing nail
acrophobia ... fear of 7. heights
acropolis ... 6. refuge 7. citadel
Acropolis (pert to) ...
Argos .. 7. Larissa
Corinth .. 11. Acrocorinth
Thebes .. 6. Cadmea
across ... 4. over, span 5. cross
6. thwart 7. athwart 8. crossway,
traverse 9. crossways, crosswise
10. crisscross, transverse
across (pref) ... 3. dia 4. tran 5. trans
acrostic ... 4. agla, game, poem
6. puzzle 7. erratic 8. wordplay
9. crosswise, jeu de mots, telestich
act ... 2. do 3. jus, law, lex 4. deed,
feat, play, skit, turn, work 5. actus,
emote, favor, of God, stunt
6. action, behave, demean, motion
7. comport, measure, perform,
pretend, process 8. function,
kindness, simulate 9. enactment,

represent 10. enterprise, exert power, theatrical 11. impersonate, legislation, performance, transaction
act (pert to)...
a part.. 8. simulate 9. dissemble
causing ruin.. 11. Kiss of Death
criminal.. 8. villainy
detestable.. 11. abomination
formal.. 10. instrument
game.. 7. charade
illegal.. 4. tort 5. crime 6. delict
nonsense.. 10. tomfoolery
planned.. 12. premeditated
pompously.. 11. pontificate
suffix.. 3. ure
acting... 5. doing 6. action, posing
7. playing, serving 8. pretense
9. dramatics, execution, operating
10. masquerade, performing, simulating 11. make–believe
13. impersonating, impersonation
acting with force... 8. vehement
action... 2. re 3. act, res 4. deed, feat, play, stir, suit, work 5. award, doing, order, works 6. battle, decree, motion, praxis, ruling 7. conduct, contest, lawsuit, verdict, working
8. activity, behavior, demeanor, exercise, movement, sentence
9. mechanism, operation
10. automation, enterprise
11. performance 13. pronouncement
active... 4. spry 5. acute, agile, alert, brisk, quick, ready, smart, yauld
6. breezy, dapper, lively, nimble, prompt, strong 7. dynamic, intense, kinetic, vibrant 8. animated, forceful, spirited, vigorous 9. assiduous, effective, effectual, energetic, energized, operating, pragmatic, sprightly, vivacious 11. industrious
active, not... 6. static 7. dormant
11. inoperative
activity... 3. ado, gog, pep, vir 4. stir, work 5. vigor 6. action, energy
7. agility, bristle 8. business, movement 9. athletics, briskness, operation, quickness 10. activeness, employment, nimbleness, occupation
act of...
cutting.. 4. kerf 8. shearing
endearment.. 4. kiss 6. caress
God.. 8. accident
kindness.. 5. favor
leaving.. 6. congee, egress
respect.. 6. curtsy, homage
ruling.. 5. regle
self–examination.. 13. introspection
sharing.. 13. participation
witnessing.. 11. attestation
working together.. 13. collaboration
worship.. 6. prayer 8. devotion
actor... 3. ham 4. doer, hero, mime, star, supe 5. agent 6. mummer, player, worker 7. Roscius, trooper
8. aisteoir, comedian, histrion, Thespian 9. performer, portrayer, pretender, tragedian 10. comedienne, dramatizer, pantomimic, personator
11. barnstormer, entertainer, pantomimist, protagonist, tragedienne
12. impersonator

actor (personage)... 4. Lunt, Ward
5. Booth 7. Skinner 8. Warfield
9. Faversham
actors' group... 4. cast 6. troupe
actor's hint... 3. cue 12. teleprompter
actress (personage)... 5. Adams, Bates, Hayes, Terry 6. Robson, Scheff
7. Marlowe, Russell 8. Fontanne, Modjeska 9. Bernhardt
actual... 4. real, true 5. posit
7. factual, genuine, present
8. absolute, positive, tangible
9. practical, veritable 11. substantial
actual being... 4. esse
actuality... 4. fact 6. verity 7. reality
8. realness 9. existence
10. factuality 14. substantiality
actually... 5. quite, truly 6. indeed, really, verily 8. actively 9. assuredly, certainly
actuary... 5. clerk 9. registrar
10. accountant, bookkeeper, calculator 13. arithmetician, mathematician
actuate... 3. egg 4. move 5. force, impel, rouse 6. arouse, induce, prompt, propel 7. animate
8. motivate 9. stimulate
acuate... 7. sharpen
12. needle–shaped, sharp–pointed
acumen... 7. insight 8. gumption, keenness, sagacity 9. acuteness, sharpness 10. astuteness, perception, shrewdness 11. discernment
12. perspicacity 14. discrimination
acute... 4. high, keen, tart, thin
5. canny, sharp, smart, vivid
6. accent, biting, crafty, fierce, severe, shrewd, shrill, subtle
7. crucial, cutting, dynamic, intense, knowing, painful, pointed, violent
8. critical, deep–felt, forceful, incisive, piercing, poignant, rigorous, stabbing, stinging, vigorous 9. energetic, ingenious, sensitive 11. sharp–witted
13. perspicacious 14. discriminating
acuteness of...
sight.. 7. oxyopia 10. oxyblepsia
taste.. 9. oxygeusia
touch.. 8. oxyaphia
Adam (pert to)...
grandson.. 4. Enos
son.. 4. Abel, Cain, Seth
wife.. 3. Eve 6. Lilith (legend)
Adam's...
ale.. 5. water
apple.. 6. larynx 10. pomum Adami
herb.. 7. mullein
needle.. 5. yucca
adapt... 3. fit, set 4. suit 6. adjust, attune, comply, modify, orient, season 7. arrange, conform, prepare, qualify 8. accustom, regulate
9. acclimate, condition, habituate, harmonize, reconcile
11. accommodate
adaptable... 7. elastic, pliable
9. tractable, versatile 10. adjustable, responsive 11. conformable
13. accommodative
adaptation... 7. fitting 10. adjustment, attunement, conformity, regulation

11. arrangement, habituation,
orientation 12. conditioning,
coordination, modification
13. accommodation, harmonization,
orchestration, qualification
15. familiarization
add... 3. eke, tot 4. foot, give, join,
plus, tote 5. affix, annex, sum up,
total, unite 6. append, attach, reckon
7. accrete, augment, compile,
compute, put with, subjoin
8. increase 9. calculate
10. supplement
adda... 5. skink (scink) 6. lizard
7. reptile
addax... 6. pygarg (Bib) 8. antelope
added... 3. and 4. plus 5. extra
6. joined, united 7. affixed, annexed
8. appended, attached 9. appendant
13. supplementary
adder... 3. asp 5. Bitis, krait, snake,
viper 6. nedder 7. machine, serpent
13. mathematician
addict... 4. buff 5. fiend 7. adjudge,
devotee, hophead 9. habituate
15. apply habitually
addicted... 4. wont 5. prone
8. attached, disposed, inclined
9. devoted to 10. accustomed,
habituated 11. given over to
addiction... 5. habit 9. surrender
10. attachment 11. enslavement
Addison's signature... 4. Clio (The
Spectator) 7. Atticus (by the Pope)
addition... 3. and, ell, too 4. also,
gain, plus, wing 5. farse (Relig), rider
6. addend, augend, lean–to
7. additum, adjunct, joining, uniting
8. addendum, additory, increase
9. accession, accretion, amendment,
appendage, extension, reckoning
10. annexation 11. calculation,
computation, enlargement
12. augmentation
additional... 3. new 4. else, more
5. added, extra, fresh, spare
7. besides, further 9. auxiliary,
extrinsic 12. supervenient,
supplemental 13. supplementary
additional (pert to)...
explanation.. 10. epexegesis
11. elucidation
grant.. 3. ann 5. bonus
specimen.. 6. cotype
address... 3. air, wit, woo 4. call, hail,
mien, pray, tact, talk 5. abode,
court, grace, greet, guise, place,
skill, speak 6. accost, direct, eulogy,
salute, sermon, speech 7. arrange,
conduct, consign, declaim, finesse,
lecture, manners, oration, prepare,
prowess, request 8. behavior,
demeanor, greeting, harangue,
inscribe, perorate, petition, presence
9. dexterity, diplomacy, direction,
discourse, ingenuity, readiness
11. comportment, destination,
inscription, savoir–faire
14. sophistication, superscription
addressee... 8. occupant 10. inhabitant
12. communicator 13. correspondent
adduce... 4. cite, name 5. argue,

infer, offer, plead, quote 6. allege,
assign 7. advance, mention, present,
produce
Adelphi... 7. theater (Strand, London)
13. London Quarter
adeps... 4. lard 9. animal fat
adept... 3. ace, apt 4. whiz (coll)
6. adroit, artist, expert, versed
7. capable, dabster, mahatma, skilled
8. skillful (skilful) 9. alchemist
(formerly), occultist 10. conversant,
proficient 11. crackerjack
adequate... 3. due, fit 4. able, full
5. ample, digne, equal 6. enough
7. capable 8. all right, equalize,
suitable 9. competent, effective,
effectual, sufficing, tolerable
10. sufficient 12. commensurate,
satisfactory 13. proportionate
adhere... 4. cleg, glue, hold 5. cling,
stick 6. cleave, cohere 7. accrete,
observe, persist
adherent... 4. ally 6. adnate, sticky,
votary 7. dangler, sequela
8. adhesive, clinging, disciple,
faithful, follower, hanger–on, partisan,
sticking, upholder 9. appendage,
dependent, supporter
adherent to the Crown... 4. Tory
adhesive... 3. gum, wax 4. glue
5. paste 6. cement, mastic, sticky
8. adherent, mucilage 9. tenacious
adhesiveness... 4. stay 8. tenacity
12. cohesiveness 13. tenaciousness
16. stick–to–itiveness
adhibit... 3. use 5. admit, affix, apply
6. attach, devote 7. bring in
10. administer
adieu... 4. vale 5. adios, aloha
6. good–by, so long (sl) 7. cheerio,
good–bye, good day 8. au revoir,
farewell 11. leave–taking
adipose... 3. fat 4. oily 5. fatty,
plump, pursy, squab 9. sebaceous
adit... 3. way 4. duct 5. entry, stulm
6. access, ingate, intake, tunnel
7. channel, conduit, haulage, ingress,
passage 8. approach, drainage,
entrance 9. admission
11. entranceway, ventilation
adjacent... 4. abut, near, nigh
5. close, handy 6. next to
7. meeting, nearest 8. abutting,
touching 9. adjoining, bordering
10. contiguous, juxtaposed
11. neighboring 12. conterminous
adject... 3. add 4. join 5. annex
adjective... 3. the 6. adnoun
7. epithet (significant) 8. modifier
9. accessory, dependent
adjective (pert to)...
demonstrative.. 4. that, this 5. these,
those
suffix.. 2. ic, il 3. ent, ial, ian, ile,
ish, ist, ite, ive, ous
verbal.. 9. gerundive
adjoin... 3. add 4. abut, butt, join
5. unite 6. attach, border 7. conjoin
8. neighbor
adjourn... 3. end 5. close, defer, delay
6. recess 7. suspend 8. dissolve,
postpone, prorogue 11. discontinue

adjudge, adjudicate . . . 3. try 4. deem,
doom, find, hold, pass 5. award,
judge, order 6. assign, decree,
esteem, ordain, reckon, regard, settle
7. condemn 8. consider, sentence
9. determine

adjunct . . . 4. ally, word 5. added
6. device 7. additum, annexed,
consort 8. addition, appanage
(apanage) 9. appendant, associate,
auxiliary, colleague, companion,
component, qualifier 11. confederate
12. appurtenance, nonessential

adjuration . . . 4. oath, plea 6. appeal,
avowal, charge 8. entreaty, swearing,
vouching 10. deposition
11. beseechment, obsecration,
obtestation

adjure . . . 3. ask, beg, bid 4. bind, pray
5. plead 6. appeal, charge
7. beseech, command, entreat,
implore, swear in

adjust . . . 3. fit, fix, set 4. meet, size,
suit, trim, true 5. adapt, align,
amend, frame, group, match, right,
shape 6. accord, attune, orient,
remedy, settle, square 7. arrange,
conform, correct, justify, mediate,
rectify, redress 8. accustom,
organize, regulate 9. condition,
habituate, harmonize, reconcile
10. compromise, coordinate,
straighten 11. accommodate,
systematize

adjuster, adjustor . . . 6. fitter
8. arranger 11. coordinator

adjustment . . . 4. gear 5. means, terms
7. fitting, suiting 8. bearings,
disposal 9. bundobust
10. adaptation, attunement,
compromise, concession, conclusion,
conformity, regulation, settlement
11. arrangement, disposition,
habituation, orientation
12. assimilation, coordination,
organization 13. harmonization,
methodization, rectification
14. naturalization, reconciliation

adjutant . . . 4. aide, ally 6. helper
7. officer 9. assistant, auxiliary

adjutant bird . . . 5. stork 6. argala
7. hurgila, marabou

ad lib, ad libit, ad libitum . . .
6. make up 7. cadenza
9. extempore, impromptu, improvise
10. at pleasure 11. play it by ear
13. accompaniment

administer . . . 4. give 5. apply, issue
6. bestow, direct, govern, manage,
supply, tender 7. adhibit, conduct,
dispose, execute, fulfill, furnish, give
out, husband, perform 8. dispatch,
dispense, transact 9. discharge
10. distribute 12. administrate

administer extreme unction . . .
5. anele 6. anoint

administration . . . 3. use 4. rule
6. employ, giving, policy 7. conduct,
regimen 8. bestowal, disposal,
issuance, ministry 9. direction,
execution 10. employment,
government, management, regulation
11. application, directorate,
disposition 12. dispensation,
ministration 13. apportionment

administration of justice . . .
10. judicatory, judicature

administrator . . . 2. fu 5. dewan
7. alcalde, manager, provost, trustee
8. director, executor 9. dispenser,
executive 12. entrepreneur

admirable . . . 5. sweet 6. worthy
7. likable (likeable), winning, winsome
8. adorable, laudable 9. estimable,
excellent, marvelous, wonderful
10. creditable 11. commendable,
meritorious 12. praiseworthy

admiration . . . 6. esteem, liking, regard,
wonder 7. respect 8. surprise
9. adoration, amazement, reverence
10. wonderment 11. astoundment,
idolization 12. appreciation,
confoundment

admire . . . 4. like, love 5. adore, honor
6. esteem, regard, revere
7. approve, idolize, respect
8. venerate

admissible . . . 3. fit 4. just, sane
5. sound 6. worthy 7. apropos,
germane, logical 8. apposite, eligible,
rational, relevant, suitable
9. admissory, agreeable, allowable,
desirable, pertinent, qualified,
receptive, tolerable 10. acceptable,
applicable, legitimate, reasonable
11. justifiable, permissible,
warrantable 12. satisfactory

admission . . . 4. adit 5. entry
6. access, assent, avowal, entree,
shrift 8. entrance 9. agreement,
allowance, inclusion, letting in,
receiving, reception, testimony
10. accordance, admittance,
allegation, avouchment, compliance,
concession, confession, initiation,
permission 11. affiliation, affirmation,
declaration 12. acquiescence,
assimilation 14. acknowledgment,
naturalization 15. enfranchisement

Admission Day holiday . . . 6. Nevada
(Oct 31) 7. Arizona (Feb 14)
10. California (Sept 9)

admit . . . 3. own 4. avow 5. adopt,
allow, enter, grant, let in, own up,
trust, yield 6. accept, credit,
embody, permit 7. adhibit, believe,
concede, confess, embrace, include,
profess, receive 8. initiate 9. affiliate
10. naturalize 11. acknowledge,
incorporate

admittance . . . 6. access 8. entrance,
sanction 9. admission, letting in
10. initiation

admitted . . . 6. indeed 8. believed,
conceded 12. acknowledged

admixture . . . 5. alloy, blend 6. fusion
7. mixture 8. compound, infusion
10. minglement 11. combination,
composition

admonish . . . 4. warn 5. chide, scold
6. advise, enjoin, exhort, preach,
rebuke, remind 7. caution, monitor,
reprove, upbraid 8. dissuade
9. reprimand 11. expostulate,

remonstrate, give warning

admonition... 6. advice 7. caution, censure, reproof, warning 8. reminder 10. counseling (counselling), dissuasion 11. exhortation 12. remonstrance, reprehension

ado... 4. fuss, stir 5. doing, hurry 6. bustle, flurry, hubbub, pother, rumpus, tumult 7. trouble, turmoil 9. commotion 10. excitement 11. disturbance

adobe... 4. clay, silt 5. brick, house (clay)

adolescent... 3. lad 5. minor, youth 6. nonage 9. pubescent, youngster 10. developing

Adonis (pert to)...
beloved by.. 9. Aphrodite
festival.. 6. Adonia
modern youth.. 6. a dandy
mother.. 5. Myrrh
slain by.. 8. wild boar

adopt... 4. take 5. admit, usurp 6. accept, assume, borrow, choose, father, mother, select 7. embrace, espouse, receive, welcome 9. affiliate 10. assimilate, naturalize 11. appropriate

adoption... 6. choice 8. espousal 9. admission, borrowing, reception 10. acceptance, assumption, conversion, redemption, usurpation 11. embracement 13. appropriation 14. naturalization

adore... 4. love 5. enjoy, honor 6. esteem, regard, revere 7. idolize, worship 8. venerate

adorn... 4. clad, deck 5. array, begem, drape, grace, primp, prink 6. attire, bedeck, clothe, enrich 7. bedight, bejewel, dignify, garnish 8. beautify, decorate 9. embellish

adorn (with)...
color.. 4. gild 5. paint 7. emblaze
feathers.. 7. implume
needlework.. 9. embroider
ornaments.. 6. tinsel 7. imagery

adorned... 4. clad 6. ornate 7. clothed, prinked 9. decorated 16. chryselephantine

adornment... 5. decor, frill 6. frills, tinsel 10. decoration, embroidery 13. embellishment 14. beautification

ad patres... 4. dead 12. to his Fathers

Adriatic (pert to)...
city.. 5. Fiume 6. Venice 7. Lagosta, Trieste 8. Brandisi
island.. 7. Lagosta
peninsula.. 6. Istria
wind (cold).. 4. bora

adrift... 4. asea, free, lost 5. at sea, loose 6. afloat, astray, aweigh, undone 7. aimless, unfixed 8. aberrant, derelict, floating, insecure, straying, unmoored, unstable 9. erroneous 10. bewildered, unanchored, unfastened, without aim

adroit... 4. neat 5. quick, ready, smart 6. clever, expert, habile, nimble 7. cunning 8. skillful (skilful)

9. dexterous, ingenious

adroitness... 4. tact 5. knack, skill 7. address 9. dexterity, ingenuity, readiness, smartness

adsorbent, absorbent... 6. spongy 7. osmotic, soaking 8. blotting 12. assimilative

adulation... 6. praise 8. flattery 9. adoration 10. compliment

adulterate... 3. mix 5. alter, taint 6. debase, defile 7. corrupt 8. denature 11. contaminate

adulterated... 6. impure 7. debased 8. spurious 9. denatured 11. counterfeit 12. contaminated

adust... 3. tan (color) 4. burn 5. burnt, dried, fiery 6. singed 7. parched 8. scorched 9. blistered

advance... 2. go 3. aid 4. gain, inch, loan, move, near, nose, pass, push, rise (in price) 5. ahead, boost, creep, march, raise 6. better, stride 7. elevate, process, promote, propose 8. approach, heighten, increase, progress 9. aforehand, elevation, promotion, upgrading 10. accelerate, beforehand, preferment 11. advancement, development, furtherance, improvement, progression

advanced... 3. old 4. aged 6. modern 7. elderly, forward 8. bettered, enhanced, enriched, foremost, unproved 9. venerable 10. in the front, precocious, senectuous 11. enlightened, progressive

advanced (pert to)...
equally.. 7. abreast
study.. 7. seminar
time.. 6. modern 8. up–to–date 12. contemporary

advantage... 3. use 4. boot, bote (bot), edge, gain, good, hold, odds 5. avail, favor, start, stead 6. behalf, behoof, profit 7. benefit, further, promote, service, vantage 8. facility, interest, purchase 9. appliance 10. expedience 11. convenience, superiority 13. accommodation, vantage ground

advantageous... 5. handy 6. aidful, useful 7. helpful 8. edifying, salutary 9. expedient, favorable 10. auspicious, beneficial, convenient, profitable, propitious, worthwhile 11. encouraging

advent... 6. coming 7. arrival 8. approach 11. forthcoming

Advent (Eccl)... 14. Coming of Christ

adventitious... 4. rale 6. casual 8. acquired 9. extrinsic 10. accidental, incidental 12. nonessential

adventure... 3. act (heroic), hap 4. bout, dare, deed, feat, gest, risk 5. event, quest, stunt 6. action, hazard 7. episode, exploit, fortune, venture 8. escapade, incident (novel), maneuver, occasion 9. happening 10. enterprise, experience, occurrence 11. performance, undertaking 12. happenstance 13. striking event

14. accomplishment
adventurer... 4. goer 5. sport
7. bounder, gambler, Hessian,
parvenu, soldier, upstart 8. gamester,
hazarder, merchant, traveler
9. sportsman 10. speculator
16. soldier of fortune
adventuress... 7. demirep 10. gold
digger
adventurous... 4. rash 5. risky
6. daring 8. reckless 9. dangerous,
foolhardy, hazardous, venturous
11. venturesome 12. enterprising,
presumptuous
adversary... 3. foe 5. enemy, Satan
6. foeman 8. opponent 9. archfiend,
assailant 10. antagonist, competitor,
Philistine
adverse... 3. ill 4. anti 5. loath
7. opposed 8. contrary, converse,
opposing, sinister, untoward
9. reluctant, unwilling 10. afflictive,
calamitous, indisposed 11. conflicting,
disinclined, unfavorable
12. antagonistic, unpropitious
adversity... 6. misery 7. trouble
8. calamity, distress, hardship
9. suffering 10. affliction, misfortune,
opposition 11. destitution
advert... 5. recur, refer 6. allude,
return
advertent... 7. heedful 9. attentive
advertise... 4. plug, warn 5. boast,
boost 6. notify 7. promote, publish
8. announce, ballyhoo, proclaim
9. publicize 10. promulgate
advertisement... 2. ad 4. bill, copy,
Neon, plug, sign 6. notice, poster,
spread 7. placard 10. commercial
(TV)
advice... 4. rede 5. aviso 6. caveat,
wisdom 7. counsel, opinion, warning
8. prudence, reminder 9. knowledge
10. admonition, suggestion
11. exhortation, information,
instruction 12. consultation,
deliberation, intelligence
13. consideration
14. recommendation
advice, containing... 9. mentorial
advisable... 6. proper 7. prudent
9. befitting, desirable, expedient
11. commendable
13. recommendable
advise... 4. rede, tell, warn 5. coach
6. exhort, impart, inform, remind
7. apprise, bethink, caution, counsel,
suggest 8. acquaint, admonish,
advocate 9. enlighten, recommend
11. communicate, familiarize, take
counsel
adviser, advisor... 5. guide 6. Egeria,
nestor 7. monitor 8. appriser, kibitzer
(sl) 9. counselor (counsellor),
informant 10. admonisher
advisers, advisors... 7. Cabinet,
Council 10. councilors, counselors,
informants
advocate... 3. pro 4. urge 6. advise,
backer, defend, deputy, lawyer
7. endorse, espouse, pleader,
support 8. attorney, champion,

defender, exponent, plead for
9. barrister, counselor, justifier,
paraclete, proponent, recommend,
solicitor, supporter 11. protagonist
advocate of the simple life...
14. simplicitarian
adytum... 6. shrine 7. chamber (inner),
sanctum 9. sanctuary
Aeetes (pert to)...
daughter.. 5. Medea
keeper of.. 12. Golden Fleece
king of.. 7. Colchis
Aegean Island group...
10. Dodecanese (including twelve)
aegis, egis... 4. care 5. guard
6. screen, shield, symbol (anc)
7. backing, defense 8. guidance
9. fosterage, patronage
10. protection
Aello (Gr)... 5. Harpy 7. monster
Aeneid... 4. poem (Vergil)
aerage... 11. ventilation
aerate... 6. aerify 7. freshen, inflate,
refresh 9. ventilate
aerial... 3. ear 4. aery, airy, mast
5. aeric, lofty 6. unreal 7. airlike,
antenna 8. ethereal, fanciful,
vaporous 9. pneumatic 10. chimerical
12. aeronautical 13. unsubstantial
aerie, eyrie... 4. nest 5. brood (birds)
6. family 9. penthouse
aeriform... 6. unreal 7. gaseous
aeroplane... 8. airplane
Aesir, Norse Gods... 3. Tyr (Tiu), Ull
4. Odin (Woden), Thor (Donar), Vali
5. Bragi 6. Balder, Hoenir 7. Forseti
8. Heimdall
Aeson's son... 5. Jason (Gr Myth)
affability... 6. comity 8. civility,
courtesy, urbanity 9. geniality
10. amiability, cordiality, politeness
11. sociability 12. conviviality
14. gregariousness
16. companionability
17. communicativeness
affable... 4. mild 5. civil, suave
6. benign, fluent, social 7. amiable
8. gracious, sociable 9. convivial,
courteous 10. accessible, gregarious
11. complaisant 13. communicative
affair... 4. duel, love 5. fight, issue,
thing, topic 6. action, gadget,
matter, object, soiree 7. concern,
problem 8. business, interest,
question, sociable 9. gathering,
reception, something 10. proceeding
11. get–together, transaction
12. circumstance
affect... 4. melt, move, stir 5. feign,
grate, haunt, touch 6. assume,
excite, regale, relate, soften, thrill
7. concern, involve, operate, pretend,
qualify 8. frequent, interest, simulate
9. influence 11. counterfeit,
hypothecate
affectation... 3. air 4. pose, sham
7. display, foppery, pietism
8. elegance, pretense 9. mannerism
12. affectedness 13. artificiality
14. grandiloquence
15. pretentiousness
affected... 4. airy, sham 5. faked,

moved, posey, put–on 6. fal–lal,
formal 7. assumed, beloved, elegant,
feigned, gushing, stilted 8. disposed,
mannered 9. impressed, pretended,
unnatural 10. artificial, euphuistic
11. pretentious 12. ostentatious
13. counterfeited, grandiloquent
affected by...
   age.. 6. senile
   love.. 4. smit 7. smitten
   pain.. 4. pang 6. twinge
   paralysis.. 7. paretic
   wonder.. 6. marvel 9. convulsed
affectedly languid... 13. lackadaisical
affectedly shy... 3. coy, mim 4. prim
   6. demure 10. coquettish
affection... 4. amor, love 6. animus,
defect, storge (animal) 7. disease,
emotion, feeling, illness, leaning,
passion 8. devotion, fondness,
tendency 9. attribute, infirmity,
sentiment 10. affliction, attachment,
disability, proclivity, propensity,
tenderness 11. disposition,
inclination, temperament
affectionate... 4. fond, soft, warm
6. ardent, loving, tender 7. adoring,
devoted, earnest, zealous
8. attached, friendly, parental,
romantic 10. headstrong
13. demonstrative
afferent... 6. esodic (nerves), inward
7. sensory 11. centripetal
affiance... 5. faith, troth, trust
6. belief, pledge, plight 7. betroth,
promise 8. credence, reliance
9. assurance, betrothal
10. confidence, engagement
affiche... 6. poster 7. placard
affidavit... 4. oath 9. statement
10. deposition 11. affirmation,
certificate, declaration
affiliation... 4. body, sect 5. group,
union 6. church, fusion, hookup,
league 7. faction, lineage
8. adoption, alliance, espousal,
relation 9. admission, alignment,
coalition 10. connection, federation,
fellowship, persuasion
11. association, cooperation
12. denomination, organization
13. confederation, consanguinity
14. naturalization
affinity... 3. kin 6. accord, family,
liking 7. kinship, rapport 8. relation,
soul mate 9. agreement
10. attraction, connection, similarity
11. propinquity, resemblance
12. congeniality, relationship
13. compatibility, rapprochement
affirm... 3. say 4. aver, avow 5. posit,
state, swear, vouch 6. allege, assert,
attest, avouch, ratify 7. assever,
certify, confirm, declare, endorse,
profess, testify, warrant 8. sanction,
validate 9. predicate, pronounce
10. asseverate 12. authenticate,
substantiate
affirmation... 3. vow 4. amen, oath,
word 5. basis 6. ground 7. premise
8. averment 9. admission, assertion,
statement, testimony 10. affirmance,

allegation, avouchment, deposition,
foundation, profession
11. declaration, proposition
12. confirmation, ratification
affirmative... 3. aye (ay), nod, yea,
yes 8. dogmatic, positive, thumbs up
(coll) 10. cataphatic (rare)
11. affirmation, declarative,
predicative
affirmatory... 9. assertive
11. affirmative, assertional
affix... 3. add, fix, pen, tag 4. seal
5. annex, stamp 6. anchor, append,
attach, fasten, impose 7. connect,
subjoin 9. increment
11. superimpose
afflict... 3. ail, try, vex 4. hurt, pain
5. upset, wound 6. grieve, harass,
sicken 7. agitate, chasten, derange,
disturb, oppress, torment, trouble
8. disorder, distress, lacerate
9. overthrow, persecute
afflicted... 3. sad 5. ailed 6. pained
7. smitten, wounded 8. troubled
9. depressed, suffering 10. distressed
affliction... 3. woe 4. airs, bane, evil,
pain, pest 5. curse, grief 6. misery,
plague 7. illness, scourge, torment,
trouble 8. calamity, distress, hardship
9. adversity 10. misfortune, visitation
12. wretchedness
afflictive... 6. severe 11. causing pain,
distressing
affluence... 4. ease, flow 6. afflux,
influx, plenty, riches, wealth
8. opulence, richness 9. abundance,
concourse, plenitude, profusion
10. prosperity
affluent... 4. rich 5. flush 6. fluent
7. copious, moneyed, opulent,
wealthy 8. abundant, well–to–do
9. luxuriant, pecunious, plenteous
10. prosperous
afford... 4. bear, cost, give, lend
5. allow, endow, grant, spare, stand,
yield 6. accord, confer, invest, supply
7. furnish, provide, support, undergo
affray... 3. war 4. feud, fray, riot
5. brawl, fight, melee, scrap (sl),
set–to (coll) 6. battle, combat, tumult
7. assault, contest, quarrel, scuffle
9. encounter 11. disturbance
affright... 5. alarm, scare 6. appall
(appal), dismay 7. confuse, startle,
terrify 8. frighten
affront... 4. defy, face, meet, slap
5. abuse 6. harass, insult, offend,
oppose 7. offense, outrage, provoke
8. confront, dishonor, envisage,
ill–treat, irritate 9. encounter,
humiliate, indignity 11. provocation
afghan (pert to)...
   fox.. 6. corsac
   language.. 11. Afghanistan
   prince.. 4. amir (ameer), emir (emeer)
   rug.. 5. Herat 6. carpet
   stitch.. 7. crochet
   wrap.. 7. blanket (woolen)
Afghanistan...
   capital.. 5. Kabul
   city.. 5. Herat 8. Kandahar
   language.. 6. Pushtu 7. Persian

mountain.. 9. Hindu Kush
Pass (famed).. 6. Khyber
people.. 6. Durani 7. Sistani
pony.. 4. yabu (yaboo)
religion.. 5. Islam
river.. 5. Indus
tribe.. 4. Safi, Ulus
Africa... see also *African*
desert.. 6. Libyan, Sahara 8. Kalahari
gulf.. 4. Aden 5. Gabes, Sidra
island (largest).. 10. Madagascar
lake.. 6. Nyassa 8. Victoria
   10. Tanganyika
Mt.. 5. Kenya, Natal 8. Cameroon
   9. Ruwenzori 11. Kilimanjaro
river.. 4. Nile 5. Congo, Niger
   7. Senegal, Zambezi
size (in world).. 6. second
African (pert to)...
charm, fetish.. 4. juju 6. grigri
drum.. 8. bamboula
enclosure.. 4. boma 5. kraal
garment.. 4. haik, tobe 6. kaross
grass.. 7. esparto
grassland.. 4. veld (veldt) 8. bushveld
harp (Nubian).. 5. nanga
hemp.. 3. ife
herb.. 4. ocra
instrument.. 4. gora (gorah) 5. nanga,
   rebab 6. balafo
language.. 3. Ibo 4. Zulu 5. Bantu,
   Sotho, Tonga 6. Somali, Yoruba
   7. Ashanti (Ashantee)
palm.. 6. ronier 7. palmyra
secret society.. 4. Egbo (Negro)
   8. Bachichi (cannibal)
soldier.. 5. spahi 6. askari
sorcery.. 5. obeah
spiritual power.. 4. ngai
thong (rawhide).. 4. riem
tree.. 3. oak 4. akee, baku, cola,
   etua, shea 5. artar, sassy, siris
   6. baobab
African people (pert to)...
Islamitic sect.. 9. Almohades
Natal.. 4. Zulu 6. kaffir 7. Amazulu
Negro society.. 4. Egbo 6. Ogboni
pygmy.. 4. Akka, Doko 5. Afifi, Batwa
   7. Bambute
race, tribe.. 4. Arab, Boer, Copt, Kafa
   (Kaffa), Zulu 5. Bantu, Fulah, Negro
   6. Berber, Kabyle, Kaffir, Nubian,
   Semite, Somali 7. Ashanti (Ashantee),
   Bushman, Swahili 8. Bechuana
   9. Hottentot
African wildlife (pert to)...
antelope.. 3. gnu 4. oryx 5. addax,
   eland, oribi 6. impala, rhebok
   7. blaubok (small), blesbok, gemsbok
   10. duikerbuck, hartebeest
bird.. 4. lory, taha 6. weaver
   8. umbretti 9. beefeater, hammerkop
fly.. 4. kivu 6. tsetse
goat.. 5. Capra
horse disease.. 5. surra
mammal.. 8. anteater, pangolin
monkey.. 4. mona, waag 6. baboon,
   grivet, guenon 7. guereza 8. talapoin
peacock.. 5. paauw
rhinoceros.. 6. borele 7. keitloa
rodent.. 4. jird 5. ratel
sheep.. 4. zenu 5. oudad (udad)

squirrel.. 5. xerus
stork.. 6. simbil 7. marabou
toad.. 7. Xenopus
worm.. 3. loa
aft, after... 4. anon, past, rear
   5. abaft, later, since 6. astern,
   behind 9. posterior 10. subsequent,
   succeeding
after (pert to)...
all.. 11. considering 12. nevertheless
awhile.. 4. anon 5. later
breast (Zool).. 10. metathorax
date.. 8. postdate
dinner.. 12. postprandial
dinner coffee.. 9. demitasse
prefix.. 4. meta, post
aftermath... 4. crop 5. rowen
   9. afterglow 12. consequences
aftermost... 4. last 7. aftmost
   8. hindmost, rearmost
afterpiece... 3. act 4. heel 5. epode,
   exode 8. postlude 9. aftercome,
   afterpart, tailpiece
after song... 5. epode
afterthought... 6. regret, sequel
   10. reflection 13. arrière–pensée,
   second thought
afterward, afterwards... 4. next
   5. after, later, since 6. ensues 7. by
   and by 9. afterhand 10. thereafter
   11. in the future 12. subsequently
aga, agha... 5. chief, title
   9. commander
agacant, agacante... 8. exciting
   11. provocative
agacella (Her)... 8. antelope
again... 2. re (pref) 3. yet 4. anew,
   anon, back, over, then 5. ditto,
   newly, often, recur 6. afresh, de
   novo, encore, rather 7. freshly
   8. eftsoons (eftsoon), likewise,
   moreover, once more 9. twice over
   10. repeatedly, second time
   11. furthermore
against... 2. on, to, vs 3. con, non
   4. agin (dial), anti, upon 6. contra,
   versus 7. counter, opposed, towards
   8. averse to, converse, opposite
against the...
clock.. 4. race, time 7. in haste
grain.. 6. across 7. oblique
   9. backwards 10. contrarily
   11. unwillingly
law.. 7. illegal, illicit 8. wrongful
   12. illegitimate
sun.. 16. counterclockwise
agal... 4. cord (Bedouin head wrap)
agalloch... 4. agar 5. aloes 7. linalon
   8. calambac 9. eaglewood, lignaloes
agama, agamoid... 6. iguana, lizard
Agamemnon (pert to)...
brother.. 8. Menelaus
daughter.. 7. Electra 9. Iphigenia
father.. 6. Atreus
king of.. 7. Mycenae
rival.. 9. Aegisthus
son.. 7. Orestes
wife.. 12. Clytemnestra
wife's paramour.. 9. Aegisthus
agape... 4. agog, ajar 6. aghast,
   gaping 7. curious, yawning
   8. open–eyed 9. expectant, love

feast (Chr) 10. astonished, bewildered, breathless

agate . . . 3. taw 4. onyx, ruby, type 5. color 6. achate, rnarble (game), pebble, quartz 10. birthstone, chalcedony

agave . . . 4. aloe 5. datil 6. maguey, mescal, pulque 8. henequen

age . . . 3. eon, era, old 4. aeon, date, eral, eval, time 5. cycle, epoch, major, minor, older, ripen 6. junior, mature, mellow, modern, period, remote, senior 7. century, grow old 8. eternity, lifetime, maturity 9. antiquate, senectude 10. generation

Age . . . 3. Air, Ice, Jet 4. Iron, Jazz, Yuga 5. Azoic, Kalpa, Space, Steel, Stone 6. Atomic, Bronze, Copper, Eocene, Gilded, Golden, Heroic, Silver 7. Glacial, Homeric, Miocene 8. Cambrian, Cenozoic, Mesozoic 10. Geological, Supersonic 11. Elizabethan

aged . . . 3. eld, old 5. anile, hoary, olden 6. feeble, infirm, senile 7. ancient, elderly, Ogygian 8. gerontic 9. Nestorian 10. senectuous

agency . . . 5. means 6. action, medium, office 8. function 9. operation 10. collection, commission, efficiency, management 14. intermediation 15. instrumentality

Agency, News . . . 2. AP, UP 3. DNB, INS, UPI 4. Tass 5. Domei 7. Reuters 13. International

agenda . . . 5. slate 7. agendum (sing), program 9. memoranda 14. memorandum book, things to be done

agent . . . 3. spy 4. doer, test, tool 5. actor, buyer, envoy 6. author, broker, deputy, factor, medium 7. creator, proctor, reagent, scalper 8. aumildar, emissary, operator, salesman 9. canvasser, comprador, consignee, go–between, operative 10. instrument, originator 11. facilitator 12. intermediary 14. representative

Ages . . . 4. Dark 6. Middle

aggrandize . . . 5. add to, exalt 6. extend 7. advance, enhance, enlarge, glorify, magnify, promote 8. increase 10. exaggerate

aggravate . . . 3. irk, nag, vex 4. miff, rile, twit 5. anger, annoy, chafe, pique, sting, taunt, tease, worry 6. nettle, pester, ruffle, worsen 7. bedevil, disturb, incense, magnify, provoke 8. heighten, increase, irritate 9. infuriate, intensify 10. exasperate

aggravation . . . 6. bother 7. anguish, torment, trouble 8. vexation 9. annoyance, worsening 10. affliction, excitement, irritation, resentment 11. displeasure, provocation 12. exasperation 15. intensification

aggregate . . . 3. all, sum 4. mass 5. total, whole 6. amount, volume

8. compound, ensemble 9. accretion 10. collection 11. combination 12. accumulation

aggregate (pert to) . . .
definable member . . 4. unit
fruit . . 7. etaerio
in the . . 7. en masse, totally 8. together 12. collectively
of plants . . 5. flock, flora 7. cluster

aggregation . . . 4. heap 5. group, union 9. congeries 10. assemblage, collection 11. combination 12. accumulation, amalgamation 13. consolidation

aggression . . . 6. attack, injury 7. assault, offense 8. invasion 9. hostility, intrusion, offensive 10. enterprise, initiative 11. provocation 12. encroachment 14. aggressiveness

aggressive . . . 7. hostile, pushing 9. assertive, attacking, bellicose, combative, offensive 10. assaulting, pugnacious 11. belligerent, contentious, provocative 12. enterprising

aggrieve . . . 4. pain 6. grieve 7. afflict, oppress, trouble 9. displease, persecute, tyrannize

aggrieved . . . 6. pained, woeful 7. doleful 8. mournful 9. sorrowful 10. displeased

aghast . . . 4. agog 5. agape 6. afraid 8. appalled, dismayed 9. astounded, horrified, terrified 10. astonished

agile . . . 4. fast, spry 5. alert, brisk, quick, ready, swift 6. active, lively, nimble, prompt, supple 7. lissome, springe 11. expeditious

aging . . . 6. doting, fading 8. maturing, ripening 9. mellowing, senescent 10. senescence

agio . . . 7. premium 8. discount, exchange 9. brokerage 13. money changing

agitate . . . 3. fan, jar, wey 4. fret, move, plot, rile, stir 5. alarm, churn, rouse, shake, upset 6. debate, devise, excite, foment, incite, ruffle 7. canvass, perturb, revolve, trouble 8. disquiet, distract, distress 10. discompose

agitated . . . 7. anxious, excited, ruffled 8. alarming, troubled 9. disturbed, perturbed, turbulent 10. distressed 11. discomposed, overwrought

agitation . . . 4. fury, rage, stir 5. alarm, storm 6. debate, dither, foment, frenzy, furore, hubbub, tumult, unrest, uproar 7. anxiety, flutter, shaking, turmoil 8. disorder, distress, upheaval, vexation 9. commotion, trepidity 10. discussion, excitement, incitement, turbulence 11. disturbance, fomentation, trepidation 12. deliberation, perturbation, restlessness

agnate . . . 3. sib 4. akin 6. allied 7. connate, kindred, related (father's side) 10. equiparent 11. correlative 14. consanguineous

agnomen . . . 4. name 5. alias, nomen

7. epithet, surname 8. nickname
agnus castus (Eccl)... 4. lamb
   6. chaste 14. tree of chastity
Agnus Dei, Lamb of God... 4. disk
   6. anthem, prayer 7. the Mass (part)
ago, agone... 2. by 4. erst, gone,
   over, past, yore 5. since 6. bygone,
   passed 7. extinct
agog... 4. avid, keen 5. agape, astir,
   eager 6. lively, wonder 7. all eyes,
   curious, excited, zestful
   8. open—eyed, vigilant 9. expectant,
   impatient 10. astonished, breathless
agonize... 4. pain, rack 6. grieve,
   harrow, strive 7. crucify, torture
   8. struggle 10. excruciate
agony... 4. pain, pang, rack 5. grief,
   gripe, panic, throe 7. anguish,
   torment, torture 8. distress
   9. suffering 11. crucifixion
agrarian... 5. rural 6. rustic, sylvan
   (silvan) 7. bucolic, hoosier
   8. agrestic, Arcadian, frontier,
   pastoral 10. campestral, hinterland,
   provincial 11. countrified
   12. agricultural
agree... 3. fit 4. give, jive, make,
   rime, side 5. chime, ditto, grant,
   match, rhyme, tally 6. accede,
   accord, assent, commit, comply,
   concur, engage, submit 7. bargain,
   comport, concede, conform, consent,
   promise 8. coincide, contract
   9. acquiesce, harmonize, stipulate
   10. coordinate, correspond
agreeable... 4. nice 5. amene, sapid,
   suave 6. comely, dulcet, savory
   7. amiable, likable, welcome, willing
   8. charming, friendly, obliging,
   pleasant, pleasing 9. accordant,
   compliant, desirable, indulgent
   10. acceptable, compatible,
   concordant, consenting, euphonious,
   harmonious 11. conformable,
   considerate 12. reconcilable,
   satisfactory
agreement... 4. mise, pact 5. terms
   6. accord, assent, cartel, parity,
   treaty, unison 7. bargain, compact,
   concord, consent, entente, promise,
   rapport 8. contract, covenant, identity
   9. accession, consensus
   10. accordment, comparison,
   compliance, conformity, similarity
   11. coincidence, concurrence,
   parallelism, stipulation
agrestic... 5. rural 6. rustic 7. bucolic
   8. pastoral 10. provincial
agriculture... 7. culture, farming, tillage
   8. agrology, agronomy 9. husbandry
   10. agrotechny 11. cultivation
   13. sharecropping
agriculture (pert to)...
   goddess of.. 3. Ops 4. Gaea (Gaia)
   5. Ceres, Flora 6. Pomona, Vacuna
   7. Demeter
   god of.. 4. Nabu, Nebo 6. Faunus
   8. Dionysus
   means of.. 3. hoe 4. plow (plough)
   6. harrow, header, reaper, seeder
   7. combine, planter, tractor
   8. thrasher 10. cultivator

11. caterpillar
ref to.. 7. georgic
science, crop growing.. 11. arviculture
terms.. 5. arado, grove, ranch, thorp
   6. garden, hamlet 7. cropper,
   orchard 8. haymaker, vineyard
   9. homestead
agriculturist... 6. farmer 7. planter
   10. agricolist, husbandman
Agrippina's son... 4. Nero
agrise... 5. abhor, dread 6. loathe
   7. shudder, terrify, tremble 8. affright
agronomy, study of... 11. agriculture
aground... 5. stuck 6. ashore
   7. swamped, wrecked 8. grounded,
   stranded 10. high and dry
agrypnia... 5. vigil 8. insomnia
   13. sleeplessness
agua... 4. toad 5. water
aguacate... 7. avocado
ague... 5. chill, fever 7. disease,
   malaria, shaking, shivers 9. shivering
ague tree... 9. sassafras
agueweed... 7. boneset, gentian
Ahab (pert to)...
   daughter.. 7. Athalie
   king of.. 6. Israel
   wife.. 7. Jezebel
ahead... 2. on 3. pre (pref) 4. fore
   5. afore, early 6. before, onward
   7. advance, forward, leading
   10. successful, surpassing
ahoy... 4. hail, yo—ho 5. hello 8. ship
   ahoy 9. attention
ahu... 5. mound 7. gazelle
   8. memorial
ai... 5. sloth 11. exclamation
aid... 4. abet, aide, help, pony
   5. allay, devil (printer's), favor, serve
   6. assist, helper, incite, relief,
   remedy, succor 7. benefit, service,
   stipend, subsidy, support 8. befriend,
   ministry 9. alleviate, allowance,
   assistant 10. assistance, benefactor
   11. countenance 13. accommodation
aim... 3. end, fix, way 4. bent, goal,
   plan 5. point, scope 6. aspire,
   direct, intend, intent, object, strive
   7. bearing, current, meaning,
   purpose 8. endeavor 9. direction,
   intention, objective 11. destination
aimful... 8. aspiring 10. purposeful
aimless... 4. idle 5. blind, loose
   6. chance, random 8. drifting
   9. desultory, orderless, senseless
   10. designless, unarranged,
   undirected 11. meaningless,
   purposeless, unorganized
aine... 5. elder 6. senior
air... 3. gas, oam, sky 4. aria, aura,
   mien, tune, wind 5. draft, ether,
   ozone, vapor 6. aerate, aerial,
   aspect, breath, breeze, bubble,
   manner, melody, oxygen 7. aerator,
   bearing, climate, display, hyaline,
   posture, publish, refresh 8. attitude,
   aviation, behavior, buoyance,
   demeanor, hydrogen, presence
   9. lightness, publicize, ventilate
   10. appearance, atmosphere,
   deportment, navigation
   11. haughtiness 12. stratosphere

air (pert to) . . .
disease . . 5. bends 7. caisson
  12. aeroembolism
music . . 4. aria, lilt, solo, tune
  6. melody 7. arietta, sortita
passage . . 4. duct, flue, vent
  7. pharynx 9. ventiduct
pressure unit . . 8. millebar
stone . . 8. aerolite 9. meteorite
term . . 5. aural 6. flight, flying 9. jet
  stream, katabatic 11. aeronautics
tight . . 5. close, proof 6. sealed
  7. compact 8. hermetic 9. resistant
  11. impermeable
travel . . 6. jet lag 7. skyjack
aircraft . . . 3. jet 4. kite, link 5. avion,
  blimp 6. bomber, glider 7. airship,
  aviette, balloon, biplane, chopper
  8. airplane, jetliner, triplane, turbojet,
  zeppelin 9. amphibian, dirigible,
  fixed–wing, monoplane, orthopter,
  simulator, spaceship, transport,
  turboprop 10. helicopter, hydroplane,
  whirlybird
aircraft (pert to) . . .
carrier . . 7. flattop
designer . . 8. Sikorsky
formation . . 5. fleet 7. echelon
inventor . . 6. Wright (Brothers)
motorless . . 6. glider
part . . 3. fin, pod 4. keel, tail, wing
  5. rotor 6. cabane 7. aileron,
  cockpit, nacelle 8. fusilage
  9. empennage (tail)
airily . . . 5. gaily 6. thinly 7. lightly,
  loftily 8. jauntily 10. delicately
  13. pretentiously 14. ostentatiously
airiness . . . 6. rarity 7. tenuity
  8. delicacy 9. gauziness, gustiness,
  lightness, loftiness, unreality, windiness
  10. breeziness, jauntiness
  16. lightheartedness, unsubstantiality
airing . . . 4. walk 8. exposure
airport (pert to) . . . 4. beam, dock, gate,
  shed, taxi 5. apron, pylon, tower
  6. hangar, runway, skycap 7. airpost,
  fairway, jetport, taxiway 8. airfield,
  airstrip, heliport 9. aerodrome
  (airdrome), helidrome
airy . . . 3. gay 4. aery, cool, rare, thin
  5. foamy, light, lofty, merry, windy
  6. aerial, breezy, drafty, frothy, jaunty,
  lively 7. gaseous, haughty, soaring
  8. animated, aspiring, delicate,
  ethereal, fanciful, feathery, flippant,
  towering, volatile 9. gossamery,
  vivacious 10. chimerical, phantasmal
  11. atmospheric 12. lighthearted,
  ostentatious
aiseweed . . . 8. goutweed
aisle . . . 4. lane, nave 5. alley 6. artery,
  avenue 7. passage 8. corridor
  10. passageway
ait, eyot . . . 3. oat 4. holm, isle, reef
  5. atoll, islet 6. island
aitu . . . 3. god 5. demon 6. spirit
Aix . . . 4. duck
aizle . . . 4. soot 5. ember, spark
Ajax (pert to) . . .
called . . 11. Ajax the Less (next
  swiftest to Achilles)

father . . 7. Telamen
hero of . . 8. The Iliad (Homer)
ajonjoli . . . 6. sesame
akimbo . . . 4. bent 6. angled, hooked
  7. angular, crooked
akin . . . 3. sib 4. like, near 5. close
  6. agnate, allied 7. cognate,
  germane, kindred, related, similar
  9. connected 10. correlated
  14. consanguineous
ala . . . 4. wing 8. winglike
a la . . . 2. so 4. thus 11. identically
  13. in the manner of
Alabama . . .
capital . . 10. Montgomery
Capitol, Confederate (2 months) . .
  10. White House (1st 1861)
carnival . . 11. Azalea Trail
city . . 6. Mobile 7. Gadsden
  10. Birmingham
monument . . 11. Russell Cave
museum . . 22. George Washington
  Carver
native woman (famed) . . 11. Helen
  Keller
President, Confederate . . 5. Davis
  (Jefferson)
State admission . . 12. Twenty–second
State bird . . 12. yellowhammer
State flower . . 8. camellia
State motto . . 21. We Dare Defend
  Our Rights
State nickname . . 12. Heart of Dixie
statue (huge) . . 6. Vulcan
alabaster . . . 6. gypsum, marble
  7. mineral
alacrity . . . 4. zest 7. avidity
  9. briskness, eagerness, immediacy,
  quickness, readiness, swiftness
  10. promptness 11. promptitude,
  punctuality, willingness
  13. sprightliness
Aladdin (pert to) . . .
possessor of (magic) . . 4. lamp, ring
spirit (of magic) . . 4. jinn
window . . 4. task (impossible)
youth (character) . . 13. Arabian Nights
á la diable . . . 7. deviled (devilled)
  8. seasoned
alameda . . . 4. mall, walk 5. prado
  9. esplanade, promenade
Alamo . . . 6. poplar (tree) 7. Mission
  (San Antonio, Tex)
a la mode . . . 4. mode 5. smart
  6. modish, spruce 7. fashion, stylish,
  voguish 8. up–to–date 9. stylishly
  11. fashionably 12. with ice cream
alan . . . 3. dog (Her)
alar (pert to) . . . 4. wing 6. pteric
  8. axillary, shoulder
alarm . . . 3. din 4. call, fear, flap
  5. alert, broil, clock, daunt, panic,
  scare 6. alarum, arouse, dismay,
  fright, terror, tocsin 7. startle, terrify,
  warning 8. affright, frighten
  11. trepidation 12. apprehension
  13. consternation
alarmist . . . 6. scarer 9. pessimist,
  terrorist 10. frightener
  11. scaremonger
alas . . . 2. ah, ay, oh 3. ach, heu, och

4. oime 5. alack, ohone 7. woe is
me 8. lackaday
Alaska ... see also *Alaskan*
capital .. 6. Juneau
city .. 4. Nome 5. Sitka 7. Skagway
9. Anchorage, Fairbanks, Ketchikan
discoverer .. 11. Vitus Bering
fish .. 6. salmon, wachna 7. inconnu
glacier .. 4. Muir
highway .. 5. Alcan 6. Alaska
island .. 6. Kodiak, Unimak 7. Diomede
(Little), Nunivak 9. Aleutians, Probilofs
mountain .. 3. Ada 7. Foraker
8. McKinley (highest in N Am),
Wrangell
northernmost point .. 11. Point Barrow
peninsula .. 5. Kenai 6. Seward
rapids .. 10. Whitehorse
river .. 5. Yukon 9. Kuskokwim
State admission .. 10. Forty-ninth
State bird .. 9. (willow) ptarmigan
State flower .. 11. forget–me–not
State symbol .. 9. bald eagle
strait .. 6. Bering
volcano .. 6. Katmai 8. Wrangell
Alaskan (pert to) ...
boat .. 5. kayak, umiak 7. bidarka
(bidarkee)
codfish .. 6. wachna
liquor .. 9. hoochinoo
native .. 3. Aht 5. Aleut, Haida, Tinna
6. Ahtena, Eskimo 7. Tlingit
8. Aleutian 9. Tsimpsean
10. Athapascan
albacore ... 4. tuna 5. tunny 6. bonito,
germon
Albania ...
capital .. 6. Tirana
city .. 5. Berat 6. Durres, Valona
7. Scutari 8. Elbasani
dialect .. 4. Gheg, Tosk
lake .. 6. Prespa 7. Scutari
mountain .. 5. Koreb 6. Pindus
river .. 4. Drin 6. Bojana
soldier .. 7. palikar
triba .. 4. Cham
albatross ... 5. nelly (sooty) 6. burden
7. pelican 9. mallemuck
albe (anc) ... 5. album
albert (pert to) ...
jewelry .. 10. watch chain
medal .. 4. gold (for bravery)
Albion ... 7. England (Poet)
albumin ... 5. glair 7. protein
9. endosperm
alcazar ... 6. palace 8. fortress
alchemy ... 5. magic 6. change
7. sorcery 10. changeover,
conversion
alcohol ... 5. drink 6. liquor
7. ethanol, spirits, talitol, terpene
8. beverage 9. aqua vitae, firewater
10. intoxicant
alcoholic beverage ... 3. gin, rum
4. beer, brew, grog, malt, mead, wine
5. booze, hooch, negus, punch, vodka
6. arrack (arrak), brandy, mao–tai,
whisky (whiskey) 7. bourbon, cordial,
liqueur, tequila 8. champers (Brit sl),
cocktail, highball 9. applejack,
champagne, moonshine
alcoholism ... 9. addiction, oenomania

10. dipsomania 11. drunkenness
12. intoxication
Alcott character ... 2. Jo 3. Amy,
Meg 4. Beth
alcove ... 3. bay 4. cove, nook
5. arbor, bower, kiosk, niche, oriel
6. carrel, recess 7. cubicle, dinette,
pergola 8. alhacena
alder (pert to) ...
chief .. 5. ruler 6. prince
fishing .. 3. fly (artificial)
tree .. 8. sagerose (yellow)
ale ... 3. mum 4. beer, flip 5. stout
6. alegar, liquor (malt) 8. festival
alee ... 7. leeward (opp of windward)
Aleppo (pert to) ...
city .. 5. Syria
grass .. 7. Johnson
stone .. 3. gem 5. agate 8. eye agate
alert ... 4. keen, warn, wary 5. agile,
alarm, alive, aware, brisk, peart (pert),
quick, ready, sharp 6. active, bright,
lively, nimble, prompt 7. guarded
8. vigilant, watchful 9. attentive,
observant, sprightly, wide–awake
11. circumspect
Aleut ... 4. Atka 6. Eskimo
7. Unungun 8. Unalaska
Aleutians ...
islands (chain) .. 8. volcanic
native of .. 5. Aleut
site .. 4. Alaska 9. Bering Sea
alewife ... 4. fish 7. herring, pompano,
walleye 9. gaspereau
Alexander the Great (pert to) ...
birthplace .. 5. Pella (Macedonia)
conqueror of .. 6. Persia
expedition .. 10. Hellespont
horse .. 10. Bucephalus
Alexandria, Egypt ...
bishop .. 5. Arius 10. Athanasius
12. Eratosthenes
island .. 6. Pharos
obelisks .. 17. Cleopatra's Needles
'(now in NY City & London)
ruler .. 7. Ptolemy
world wonder .. 10. Lighthouse
(Pharos)
alfa ... 5. grass 7. esparto
alfalfa ... 3. hay 5. medic 6. clover,
fodder 7. lucerne (lucern)
alforja ... 3. bag 5. pouch 6. wallet
9. saddlebag
alfresco ... 4. airy 7. open–air, outside
alga, algae ... 4. cell, moss, nori
5. Dasya, fungi 6. Alaria, diatom,
fungus 7. seaweed 8. plankton
9. spirulina, stonewort
Algeria ...
capital .. 7. Algiers
Mohammedan saint .. 8. Marabout
monastery .. 5. ribat
mountain .. 5. Atlas (Range)
native .. 5. Arabs 7. Berbers, Kabyles
ruler .. 3. bey, dey
ship .. 5. xebec
soldier .. 5. spahi (spahee) 6. Zouave
algid ... 3. icy 4. cold 5. brisk, crisp,
nippy 6. frigid, frosty, wintry
7. ice–cold
algodon ... 6. cotton
algology, study of ... 5. algae

8. seaweeds
Algonquian spirit... 6. manito
(manitou)
Algonquian tribe... 4. Cree, Sauk
5. Miami 6. Ottawa 7. Arapaho,
Ojibway, Shawnee 8. Cheyenne,
Delaware 9. Blackfoot
Alhambra (pert to)...
architecture.. 7. Moorish
palace, alcazar of.. 12. Moorish Kings
site.. 7. Granada (Spain)
alias... 6. anonym 7. epithet
8. cognomen, nickname 9. otherwise,
pseudonym, sobriquet
Ali Baba (pert to)...
adventurer.. 4. cave (Forty Thieves)
password to cave.. 6. Sesame
tale.. 13. Arabian Nights
alien... 3. ger 5. fremd 6. exotic,
remote 7. adverse, foreign, hostile,
opposed, strange 8. outsider,
stranger 9. foreigner, peregrine,
unrelated 10. extraneous, unfriendly
11. incongruous
alienate... 4. part, wean 6. demise,
detach, devest, divest, divide
8. disunite, estrange, separate
alienation... 4. outs 5. split 6. breach
8. disfavor 10. conveyance,
falling–out, withdrawal
12. amortization, disaffection,
estrangement
alienist... 12. psychiatrist
aliform... 8. winglike 10. wing–shaped
alight... 4. land, rest, stop 5. ditch,
lodge, perch 6. settle 7. burning,
descend, lighted 8. dismount
align, aline... 4. true 5. level, match
6. equate, line up 7. arrange,
marshal 10. collineate, straighten
11. parallelize
alike... 3. iso (comb form) 4. akin,
like, same, twin 7. similar, uniform
8. selfsame 9. duplicate, identical
10. homonymous
17. indistinguishable
aliment... 4. food, keep 5. broma,
manna 7. nurture, pabulum, support
9. nutriment, nutrition, refection
10. sustenance 11. nourishment,
refreshment
alimentary canal, part... 5. mouth
7. pharynx, stomach 9. esophagus,
intestine
alimony... 7. stipend 8. estovers
9. allotment
aline... see *align*
alipin... 5. slave (Phil)
alipod... 3. bat 10. wing–footed
aliquid... 8. somewhat 9. something
aliquot... 4. part 5. prime 7. decimal,
digital, divisor, partial 10. fractional,
reciprocal 11. submultiple (opp of
aliquant)
alive... 3. vif 4. keen 5. alert, awake,
brisk, vital 6. extant, lively, loving,
zoetic 7. animate, current, topical
8. animated, existent 9. breathing,
conscious, sensitive, sprightly
11. clear–witted, unforgotten
alkali... 3. lye 4. salt, soda
8. saltwort

alkaline... 3. reh 4. usar 6. alkali
7. antacid, nonacid
alkaline forming... 10. kaligenous
alkaloid... 6. codein, conine, eserin
7. aricine, caffein, cocaine, codeine
8. atropine, morphine 10. strychnine
13. physostigmine
alkaloid (pert to)...
bark.. 7. aricine
bean.. 13. physostigmine
beverage.. 8. caffeine (caffein)
drug.. 7. cocaine, codeine
8. morphine 10. strychnine
extract.. 6. curare (curari) 11. arrow
poison
hemlock.. 7. coniine
ipecac.. 7. emetine
lupine.. 8. lupinine
mustard seed.. 7. sinapin
all... 3. pan (pref), sum 4. omni (pref),
only, toto 5. alone, every, sum of,
total, tutti, whole 6. entire, wholly
7. perfect 8. ensemble, entirely,
totality 9. aggregate, everybody
10. altogether, completely,
everything, thoroughly 11. exclusively
all (pert to)...
absorbing.. 4. main 5. chief, prime
6. ruling 7. capital, leading, primary
8. foremost 9. paramount, principal
11. controlling
around.. 5. handy 9. versatile
devouring.. 6. greedy 9. rapacious
10. gluttonous
in all.. 9. generally 10. on the whole
inclusive.. 6. global 7. omneity
8. catholic, ecumenic, pandemic
9. universal 12. cosmopolitan
knowing.. 4. wise 6. divine
10. omniscient
powerful.. 6. divine 7. all–wise,
supreme 8. absolute, almighty
9. all–seeing 10. all–knowing,
omnipotent, omniscient, ubiquitous
the same.. 9. identical 10. equivalent
12. nevertheless
Allah... 3. God 5. deity 12. Supreme
Being
allay... 4. cool, ease 5. abate, check,
slake 6. pacify, soothe, subdue
7. appease, assuage, compose,
relieve, repress, satisfy 8. moderate
9. alleviate
allée... 4. mall, walk 5. aisle
6. avenue 7. passage
allege... 4. aver, cite 5. offer, plead,
quote, state 6. adduce, affirm,
assert, assign 7. advance, ascribe,
declare, present, pretend, profess,
propose 8. maintain 9. attribute
allegiance... 3. tie 4. bond 5. faith,
liege 6. fealty, homage 7. loyalty
8. devotion, fidelity, firmness
9. adherence, constancy
12. faithfulness 13. steadfastness
allegory... 5. fable, story 6. emblem
7. parable 8. apologue
alleviate... 4. ease 5. abate, allay,
erase, quiet, salve, slake 6. lessen,
pacify, reduce, soften, solace, soothe
7. assuage, compose, lighten, relieve
8. mitigate, moderate, palliate

9. extenuate 11. tranquilize

alley... 3. mig (marble), way 4. lane, mall, path, slum 5. aisle, byway, tewer 6. arcade, artery, byroad 8. cul–de–sac

alliance... 4. pact 5. union 6. fusion, league, treaty 7. compact, entente 8. affinity, agnation, covenant 9. coalition 10. federation 11. association, combination, confederacy 13. confederation

allied... 4. akin 6. agnate, linked, united 7. cognate, germane, kindred, leagued, related, similar 10. associated, correlated

alligator... 5. gator, niger 6. Caiman, cayman, jacare (yacare) 7. lagarto 9. crocodile

alligator pear... 7. avocado 8. aguacate

alliteration... 4. rime 5. rhyme 6. jingle 9. assonance 10. repetition

allocate... 4. deal, mete 5. allot 6. assign, locate, ordain 7. appoint, arrange, consign, reserve 9. apportion 10. distribute

allocation... 8. disposal 9. billeting 11. collocation, disposition 12. distribution

allot... 3. fix 4. cast, dole, mete 5. grant 6. assign, billet, design, intend, ordain, ration, select 7. appoint, destine, specify 9. apportion, attribute, prescribe 11. appropriate

allotment... 5. cavel, share 6. ration 7. subsidy 10. allocation, assignment, ordainment 13. apportionment

allow... 3. let 4. bear, give 5. admit, think 6. endure, permit, rebate, suffer 7. approve, concede, suppose 8. consider, discount, tolerate 9. authorize 11. acknowledge

allowance... 3. fee 4. tare, tret 5. arras, grant 6. ration 7. pension, scalage, stipend 8. appenage (prince's), discount, granting, sanction 9. admitting, allotment, conceding, tolerance 10. permission 11. scholarship 13. authorization

allowing for... 2. if 8. provided

allow to pass... 5. lapse 6. expire, revert

alloy... 3. mix 4. asem 5. blend, mokum 6. billon, fusion, oroide 7. amalgam, bullion, corrupt, mixture 8. compound 9. composite 10. adulterate, amalgamate

alloys...
iron, carbon.. 5. steel
iron, nickel.. 6. Calite (trademark)
lead, tin.. 6. pewter, solder
nickel, steel.. 5. Invar

allspice tree... 7. pimento

alltud... 5. alien, slave 9. foreigner

allude... 4. hint 5. imply, point, refer 6. relate 7. mention, suggest 8. indicate, intimate 9. insinuate

allure... 3. win 4. bait, draw, lead, lure, tice, tole 5. charm, decoy, snare, tempt 6. entice, entrap, invite, seduce 7. attract, prevail 8. inveigle, persuade 9. captivate, fascinate, influence

allurement... 4. bait, lure 5. bride 7. glamour (glamor) 8. agacerie, coquetry 10. attraction, enticement, inducement, temptation 12. inveiglement

allusion... 4. clue, hint 7. inkling 8. innuendo, instance 9. reference 11. implication

alluvial deposit... 3. mud 4. silt 5. delta, geest 6. placer

ally... 3. pal 4. aide, join 5. union 6. fellow, friend, league 7. comrade, consort, kinsman, partner 8. adherent, relative 9. associate, attendant, colleague 10. accomplice 11. confederate 12. collaborator

Alma (It)... 4. soul 6. spirit 10. cherishing, nourishing

alma... 6. fabric (silk)

almacen... 4. shop 8. magazine 9. warehouse

Alma Mater... 6. school· 7. college 9. goddesses 10. university

almanac... 5. fasti 6. record 7. calends (kalends) 8. calendar, register 9. ephemeris (obs)

almighty... 5. great 6. divine 10. omnipotent 11. all–powerful 12. irresistible

almost... 4. most, nigh 5. anear, close 6. all but, nearly 8. well–nigh 9. nearabout 13. approximately

alms... 4. dole, mite 6. aumous, bounty, corban, relief 7. charity, handout 8. donation, gratuity, pittance 12. contribution, philanthropy

alms (pert to)...
box.. 4. arca 5. chest
giver.. 5. donor 7. almoner 11. contributor 14. philanthropist
man.. 5. donee 6. pauper 7. feoffee 9. pensioner

alodium... 4. land 6. tenure 8. freehold 10. real estate

aloe, aloes... 4. drug 5. agave, plant 6. tambac 7. incense 8. agalloch

aloft... 2. up 4. high, over 5. aloof 7. skyward 8. overhead

aloha... 4. hail, love 7. good–bye 9. affection, greetings 11. salutations

Aloha State... 6. Hawaii

aloin... 4. drug 5. aloes 8. nataloin 9. barbaloin (Barbados) 12. isobarbaloin

alone... 4. solo 5. apart, solus 6. single, singly, solely, unique 8. desolate, homeless, isolated,

alloys...
copper, aluminum.. 9. duralumin
copper, sulphur.. 5. niello
copper, tin.. 6. bronze
copper, white metal.. 6. oroide
copper, zinc.. 5. brass 6. tombac
copper, zinc, iron.. 4. Aich (Chin)
copper, zinc, nickel.. 4. iron 7. paktong (packtong)
copper, zinc, nickel, iron.. 7. rheotan
German silver.. 6. albata
gold, silver.. 4. asem

separate, solitary 9. exclusive,
matchless 10. unassisted
12. single–handed
13. companionless, independently,
unaccompanied
along . . . 2. on 3. via 4. with
6. beside, onward 7. forward
8. together
alongside . . . 2. by 4. near 6. beside
7. abreast 8. parallel
aloof . . . 6. offish, remote 7. distant,
haughty 8. reserved 10. unsociable
11. indifferent, standoffish
15. uncommunicative
aloofness . . . 7. reserve 10. offishness,
remoteness 11. haughtiness
12. indifference 13. unsociability
alopecia . . . 6. acomia 8. baldness
12. hairlessness
aloud . . . 4. oral 6. loudly 7. audibly,
plainly
alp . . . 3. tor 4. peak, pico, pike
6. summit 8. mountain 9. bullfinch
alp (Teut Folklore) . . . 5. demon, witch
9. nightmare
alpaca . . . 4. coat, paco 5. llama
7. garment
Alph . . . 11. sacred river (Kubla Khan)
alpha . . . 4. star 5. prime 6. letter
7. initial, numeral 9. beginning
alphabet . . . 4. ABC's 5. Sarada
(Kashmir) 9. abecedary
10. Davanagari (Sanskrit)
alphabet characters (Teut) . . . 4. ogam,
rune
alphabetize . . . 4. file 5. group, index
6. codify, letter 8. classify, tabulate
9. catalogue (catalog) 10. categorize
alpha test (Army) . . . 12. intelligence
alpine . . . 5. alpen, hilly 6. knobby
10. alpestrine 11. mountainous
Alpine (pert to) . . .
climber . . 10. alpestrian
dance . . 7. gavotte (gavot)
dress . . 6. dirndl
dwelling . . 6. chalet
goat . . 4. ibex
herdsman . . 4. senn
peak . . 5. Blanc 9. Monte Rosa
10. Matterhorn
plant . . 9. edelweiss
province . . 5. Tyrol
shelter . . 7. hospice
snowfield . . 4. firn, neve
tunnel . . 7. Simplon 10. St Gotthard
wind . . 4. bise 5. foehn
Alps . . . 5. Blanc, Tirol (Tyrol) 6. Julian
7. Dinaric 8. Jungfrau 9. Dolomites,
Monte Rosa (peak) 10. Matterhorn
already . . . 3. ere, yet 5. afore
6. before 7. earlier 8. hitherto
10. heretofore 11. theretofore
also . . . 2. as, et, so 3. and, too, yet
4. more, plus 7. besides, further
8. likewise, moreover 9. similarly
11. furthermore
altar (pert to) . . .
boy . . 7. acolyte
cloth . . 6. dossal (dossel) 7. haploma
9. ependytes
constellation . . 3. Ara
curtain . . 6. riddel

end of church . . 4. apse 7. chancel
Greek . . 5. bomos 6. hestia
7. eschara
Latin . . 7. scrobis
ledge . . 7. retable
platform . . 8. predella
screen . . 7. reredos
shelf, table . . 6. gradin 7. retable
8. credence
step . . 8. predella
top slab . . 5. mensa
alter . . . 4. geld, vary, veer 5. amend,
emend, reset, shift 6. adjust,
change, immute, modify, mutate,
revise 7. falsify 8. castrate
9. transform
alteration . . . 6. change 9. diversity,
variation 10. castration, correction
12. modification 13. interpolation
15. diversification
altercation . . . 3. row 4. feud, spat, tiff
5. fight, snarl 6. fracas, strife
7. dispute, quarrel, wrangle
8. squabble, vendetta 9. imbroglio
10. contention 11. controversy
alter ego . . . 4. mate, self, twin
7. oneself 10. complement
11. counterpart
alternate . . . 4. vary 5. proxy
6. change, deputy, rotate, seesaw
7. reverse, stand–in 8. delegate
9. oscillate 10. substitute
11. alternative, interchange,
reciprocate
alternate writing mode (anc) . . .
13. boustrophedon
alternative . . . 2. or 3. nor 5. other
6. choice, either, option, switch
7. dilemma 8. election, loophole
9. secondary 10. nip–and–tuck,
preference, substitute
11. replacement
although, altho . . . 4. even, when
5. while 6. albeit, though 7. despite,
whereas 15. notwithstanding
altimetry . . . 6. height 10. hypsometry
11. measurement
altitude . . . 6. height (highth) 7. heroics,
stature 8. eminence, highness,
tallness 9. elevation, loftiness
altogether . . . 5. fully, quite 6. bodily,
wholly 7. utterly 8. entirely, outright
9. generally 10. completely,
thoroughly 12. collectively
alto horn . . . 7. althorn, saxhorn
10. mellophone
altruism . . . 7. charity, concern
8. kindness 11. beneficence,
benevolence 12. philanthropy
alumnus (alumni) . . . 4. grad 5. pupil
6. alumna (alumnae) 8. graduate,
postgrad 12. postgraduate
alveary . . . 4. hive 6. apiary 7. beehive
alveola . . . 3. dip, pit 4. pore, sink
6. crater, pocket
alveolar . . . 6. pitted, pocked
7. notched 8. indented 9. depressed
always . . . 2. ay 3. aye, e'er 4. ever
6. anyway, semper 7. forever
8. evermore 9. eternally, uniformly
10. constantly, invariably
11. continually, everlasting,

perpetually, universally

ama... 4. tree 5. amula (Bib) 6. vessel

amabile... 6. gentle, tender
9. agreeable

Amadis de Gaul (Arthurian)... 4. hero
5. lover

amadou... 4. punk 6. tinder 7. styptic

amah... 5. nurse 7. servant
9. nursemaid 11. maidservant

amain... 5. apace 7. hastily, quickly,
swiftly 9. posthaste

amalgamate... 3. mix 4. fuse, join,
weld 5. blend, merge, unite
6. commix 7. combine 8. coalesce,
compound, intermix 11. consolidate

amalgamation... 6. fusion, merger
7. mixture 11. combination

Amalkite... 4. Agag (King) 5. nomad
7. Bedouin

amant... 5. lover 6. amante

amaryllis... 4. bulb, lily 5. agave, plant
6. flower 8. mistress 10. sweetheart
11. shepherdess

amass... 4. save 5. hoard, stack, store
6. gather 7. collect 8. assemble
10. accumulate

amate... 5. daunt 6. subdue
10. dishearten

amateur... 3. ham 4. tyro 6. novice
7. dabbler, fancier 8. beginner,
virtuoso 10. aficionado, apprentice,
dilettante 15. nonprofessional

amateurish... 5. inapt 9. unskilled,
untrained, untutored 10. unfinished
15. nonprofessional

Amati... 6. family, violin

amatory... 4. fond 6. ardent, erotic,
loving, tender 7. amorous, philter
9. loverlike 10. passionate

amaze... 3. awe 4. stun 7. astound,
perplex, stagger, startle, stupefy
8. astonish, bewilder, confound,
surprise 9. dumbfound, overwhelm

amazement... 3. awe 5. alarm
6. wonder 8. surprise 10. perplexity
12. bewilderment 13. consternation

Amazon... 5. Queen (Myth), river
6. virago 9. androgyne
10. warrioress 11. Penthesilea

Amazon river (pert to)...
cetacean.. 4. Inia
discoverer.. 6. Pinzon (1500)
mouth.. 4. Para
rain forest.. 5. selva
tributary.. 3. Apa 4. Napo

ambary... 2. da 4. hemp 5. fiber
6. Nolita

ambassador... 5. envoy 6. legate,
nuncio 8. diplomat, emissary,
minister 9. messenger
12. intermediary 14. representative
15. plenipotentiary

amber... 6. yellow 8. electrum

ambidextrous... 7. capable
8. two-faced 9. two-handed,
versatile 11. ambidextral, treacherous
13. double-dealing

ambiguous... 6. double 7. dubious
9. equivocal, uncertain, unsettled
10. indefinite, indistinct, mistakable
12. questionable 13. indeterminate

ambit... 5. orbit, scope 6. extent,
sphere 7. circuit 8. precinct

ambition... 4. goal, spur 6. desire
10. aspiration

amble... 4. pace, rack, trot 7. piaffer

ambrosia... 4. food 5. honey, manna
6. nectar 7. perfume 8. delicacy,
libation

ambulate... 4. hike, move, walk

ambush... 4. trap 5. snare 6. hiding,
waylay 7. mantrap 9. ambuscade
10. subterfuge 11. concealment

ameliorate... 4. ease, mend 5. emend
6. better 7. improve 8. progress
9. meliorate

amelioration... 10. betterment
11. improvement, restoration

amenable... 6. liable, pliant
7. movable 9. receptive
10. answerable, open-minded,
responsive 11. accountable,
persuadable, responsible

amend... 4. beat (dial), beet (beete)
5. alter, atone, emend 6. reform,
repeal 7. convert, correct, improve,
rectify, redress, restore

amendment... 5. rider 8. addition
10. conversion, correction
11. improvement, reformation

amends... 7. redress 8. reprisal
9. atonement 10. recompense,
reparation 11. restitution

amenities... 5. mores 7. decorum,
manners 9. etiquette 10. civilities,
courtesies 11. formalities, gentilities,
proprieties

ament... 6. catkin 7. cattail

American (pert to)...
bear.. 7. musquaw (black)
buffalo.. 5. bison
cactus.. 4. bleo 7. saguaro
carnivore.. 4. puma
cataract.. 7. Niagara (Falls)
cedar (red).. 5. savin
elk.. 6. wapiti
Japanese.. 5. Nisei 6. Kibbei
leopard.. 6. ocelot
marsupial.. 7. opossum
merganser.. 4. duck (fish-eating)
Mexican.. 6. gringo
mink.. 5. vison
moth.. 2. io
nickname.. 6. Yankee (Yank)
ostrich.. 4. rhea
palm.. 5. Sabal 8. palmetto
quail.. 5. colin
rail.. 4. sora
squirrel.. 9. chickaree (red)
vulture.. 5. urubu 6. condor

American, famed...
artist.. 5. Flagg, Peale 6. Stuart
7. Sargent 8. Rockwell, The Eight
astronomer.. 11. Rittenhouse
chemist.. 6. Carver (G Washington)
crusader (Temperance).. 12. Carrie
Nation
discoverer.. 4. Eric (The Red)
5. Cabot, Votan 8. Columbus
doctor, surgeon.. 4. Mayo 6. Schick
7. Cushing
educator.. 4. Hume, Mann 5. Eliot
10. Washington (Booker T)
explorer.. 4. Byrd 5. Boone, Clark,

Lewis, Peary 6. Carson (Kit)
9. Ellsworth
musician.. 6. Foster 8. Damrosch,
Gershwin 9. Bernstein, MacDowell,
Stokowski
naturalist.. 4. Muir 5. Beebe
7. Audubon, Burbank
patriot.. 4. Clay, Hale, Otis 5. Dawes,
Henry (Patrick), Paine (Thomas)
6. Revere
physicist.. 6. Teller (H–bomb)
pianist.. 6. Duchin, Levant
8. Horowitz, Liberace, Williams
(Roger) 10. Van Cliburn
pirate.. 4. Kidd (Capt)
poet.. 4. Nash 5. Benet, Eliot, Frost
6. Kilmer, Lowell, Millay 8. Sandburg
10. Longfellow
Red Cross organizer.. 6. Barton (Clara)
Scouts (Girl) organizer.. 3. Low
(Juliette)
sculptor.. 6. Calder 7. Borglum
singer.. 4. Pons 5. Jones, Moore
6. Farrar, Peerce 7. Kirsten, Merrill,
Tibbett 8. Anderson (Marian)
statesman.. 4. Clay, Root 6. Baruch,
Dulles 8. Harriman
suffragette.. 4. Catt (Carrie Chapman)
violinist.. 7. Menuhin
writer, novelist.. 6. Ferber 8. Faulkner
9. Hemingway
American Indian (pert to)...
chief.. 5. brave 6. sachem
child.. 7. papoose
conference.. 6. powwow
girl.. 7. Nokomis (Myth)
9. Minnehaha, Sacagawea
(Sakajawea) 10. Pocahontas
hero (Myth).. 8. Hiawatha
magician.. 6. shaman, wabeno
(Ojibway)
shelter.. 4. tent 5. hogan, tepee
(teepee) 6. wigwam 7. wickiup
(wikiup)
American Indian tribe... see also
Indian 3. Fox, Oto (Otoe), Ree, Sac,
Ute 4. Cree, Crow, Erie, Hopi, Iowa,
Pima 5. Creek, Kansa, Osage, Piute,
Sioux 6. Cayuga, Dakota, Mohawk,
Oneida, Pueblo, Seneca 7. Arapaho,
Choctaw, Mohican, Ojibway, Siksika
8. Cherokee, Chippewa, Iroquois,
Onondaga, Seminole 9. Algonquin,
Blackfoot, Chickasaw 10. Athapascan,
Muskhogean
ami... 5. lover 6. friend (law)
amiable... 6. kindly 7. lovable
8. charming, friendly, pleasant,
pleasing 9. agreeable, indulgent
10. hospitable
amicable... 4. kind 8. friendly, sociable
9. congenial, peaceable
10. harmonious
amicus curiae... 5. judge 6. deputy,
lawyer 16. friend of the court
amid, amidst... 2. in 5. among
7. amongst, between
amigo... 6. friend 8. neighbor
amiss... 3. ill 5. badly, fault, wrong
6. astray, sinful 8. faultily, improper
10. disorderly 11. erroneously

amity... 4. love 5. peace 7. harmony
10. friendship 11. sociability
12. congeniality, friendliness
amma... 6. abbess, mother (spiritual)
ammonia... 9. hartshorn 10. fertilizer
11. refrigerant
ammoniac plant... 5. oshac
ammunition (pert to)...
box.. 9. bandoleer
chest.. 7. caisson
type.. 4. arms, bomb, shot 7. bullets
8. grenades, missiles, munition,
shrapnel 10. explosives
wagon.. 7. caisson
amnesty... 6. pardon 8. oblivion
9. acquittal 13. forgetfulness
amoeba, ameba... 3. olm 4. cell
7. proteus 10. protoplasm
13. microorganism
among, amongst... 2. in 3. mid
4. amid, with 5. midst 6. amidst,
imelle 7. between
among nations... 13. international
Amor... 4. Eros 5. Cupid
AMORC... 11. Rosicrucian
amorous... 4. fond 6. ardent, erotic,
loving, tender 7. adoring, devoted
8. enamored 10. passionate
12. affectionate
amorous looks... 4. ogle 5. stare
8. coquetry 10. come–hither,
flirtation
amorphous... 8. abnormal, formless
9. deviative, shapeless, subnormal
14. uncrystallized
amorphous mineral... 4. opal
amort... 8. dejected, lifeless
9. inanimate 10. spiritless
amortize... 5. clear 6. convey, payoff,
settle 9. discharge, negotiate
amount... 3. lot, sum 4. cost, rate,
rise, unit 5. chunk, price, ratal,
store, total 6. ascend, degree
7. quantum, signify 8. quantity
amount (pert to)...
due.. 5. price 6. arrear 7. default,
deficit
mean.. 7. average
realized.. 4. take 6. intake
8. proceeds
small.. 6. morsel 7. modicum
smallest.. 5. least
to.. 3. all 4. even 5. equal, match,
total 10. correspond
amour... 6. affair 7. liaison, romance
8. intrigue, triangle 10. flirtation
ampere... 3. amp 4. unit 6. ohmage
7. current, voltage
ampersand... 3. and 4. also
Amphibia... 5. Anura, frogs, toads
7. Aglossa 8. tadpoles 9. Salientia
11. salamanders
amphibious... 5. mixed 9. adaptable
10. fifty–fifty 11. half–and–half, mixed
nature (land and water)
amphibole... 7. edenite, mineral, uralite
8. aluminum, nephrite
amphigory, amphigouri... 5. rhyme
6. jingle, poetry 8. doggerel
9. rigmarole
amphilogism, amphilogy...
9. ambiguity, duplexity (meaning)

10. equivocacy
Amphion (pert to)...
  capturer of.. **6.** Thebes
  husband of.. **5.** Niobe
  son of.. **4.** Zeus
  twin of.. **6.** Zethus
amphitheater... **4.** bowl **5.** arena,
cavea, scene, stage **6.** circus, cirque
7. stadium **8.** coliseum, platform
10. hippodrome
amphora... **3.** jar, urn **4.** vase
5. diota, prize **7.** measure
8. ornament
ample... **4.** full, rich, wide **5.** broad,
large, roomy **6.** enough, plenty
7. liberal **8.** abundant **9.** bountiful,
capacious, extensive, plenteous,
plentiful, unstinted **10.** munificent
12. satisfactory
ampliation... **5.** flare **9.** expansion,
extension **11.** enlargement
12. postponement **13.** amplification
14. aggrandizement
amplify... **3.** pad **5.** widen **6.** dilate,
extend **7.** develop, enlarge
8. increase **9.** aggravate, expatiate
10. exaggerate, overstress
amplitude... **4.** size **6.** amount
7. breadth **8.** fullness **9.** greatness,
plenitude **12.** spaciousness
amputate... **4.** trim **5.** prune, sever
6. cut off **8.** mutilate, retrench,
truncate
amuck, amok... **3.** fit **4.** rage
6. attack, frenzy, malady
12. corybantiasm
amulet... **3.** gem **5.** charm **6.** fetish,
scarab, voodoo **7.** periapt
8. ornament, talisman **10.** protection
amuse... **3.** wow **6.** divert, please,
regale, tickle **7.** beguile, gratify
8. recreate **9.** entertain, titillate
10. exhilarate
amusement... **3.** fun **4.** play **5.** farce,
mirth, sport **7.** pastime **9.** avocation,
diversion **10.** recreation, relaxation
13. divertisement, entertainment
amusement place... **4.** club, park
6. casino, midway **7.** cabaret, theater
ana... **5.** books **6.** events **8.** analecta,
excerpts **9.** Americana **10.** collection
11. collectanea, compilation,
memorabilia
anachronous... **8.** misdated, mistimed
10. beforehand, behindhand
anaglyph... **5.** cameo, carve **6.** chisel,
plaque, relief **10.** embossment
Anak (Eccl)... **5.** giant (Canaan)
6. Anakim
analogous... **4.** like **7.** similar
8. parallel **10.** comparable, equivalent
11. correlative
analogue... **8.** parallel **11.** resemblance
13. correspondent
14. correspondence
analogy... **8.** likeness, sameness
9. agreement **10.** accordance,
comparison, similarity
14. correspondence
analysis... **5.** assay, logic **6.** biopsy,
theory **9.** breakdown, diagnosis
10. compendium, discussion,

dissection **11.** examination
14. classification
analyze... **5.** assay, parse, study
7. discuss, dissect, examine
8. classify, describe, diagnose,
separate
Ananias (Bib)... **4.** liar **8.** disciple
(Damascus), Shadrack (Sidrack)
10. high priest **12.** prevaricator
anarch, anarchist... **3.** red **7.** radical
8. nihilist **9.** socialist, terrorist
13. revolutionist
anarchy... **4.** riot **5.** chaos **6.** acracy
7. license, misrule **8.** disorder
9. confusion, mobocracy, rebellion
10. ochlocracy
anathema... **3.** ban **5.** curse
9. damnation **11.** abomination,
imprecation, malediction
Anatolian rug... **4.** Kurd **5.** Tuzla
anatomy... **4.** body **5.** build, frame
7. carcass **8.** analysis, skeleton
9. formation, structure
11. arrangement
anatomy of animals... **7.** zootomy
ancestor... **4.** Adam, sire **5.** elder,
stock **6.** atavus, family, parent
8. forebear **9.** patriarch, precursor
10. antecedent, forefather,
forerunner, progenitor
11. grandfather, predecessor
ancestral... **4.** aval **6.** avital, lineal
7. atavism **8.** maternal, paternal
9. atavistic, primitive **10.** hereditary
11. patrimonial
ancestral spirits... **5.** lares, manes
7. lemures, penates
ancestry... **4.** race, rank **5.** birth,
blood **7.** descent, lineage
11. antecedents **14.** progenitorship
anchor... **3.** fix, tie **4.** hook, moor,
rest, stop **5.** affix, clamp, kedge
6. attach, batten, fasten, secure
7. grapnel, killick
anchor (pert to)... **3.** arm, cat, pee
4. cast, palm, tore (ring) **5.** fluke
7. capstan
anchorite, anchoret... **6.** hermit,
shut–in **7.** ascetic, eremite, recluse,
stylite **8.** homebody
anchor–shaped... **8.** ankyroid
10. hook–shaped
anchovy... **4.** alec **5.** sauce, sprat
7. herring
ancienne noblesse... **5.** elect, elite
7. royalty **8.** nobility **11.** aristocracy
ancient... **3.** eld, old **4.** aged, auld,
wise **5.** adept, early, hoary, olden
7. antique **8.** historic, obsolete,
outdated, primeval, pristine
9. grandeval, primitive, venerable
10. aboriginal, antiquated, preadamite
12. antediluvian
ancient (pert to)...
  chariot.. **5.** essed
  city.. **4.** Elis, Tyre **5.** Argos, Sedon
  6. Athens, Sparta, Thebes
  drink.. **5.** morat
  empire.. **4.** Gaul **5.** Roman **6.** Lydian
  7. Persian **8.** Assyrian, Athenian,
  Chaldean, Hellenic **10.** Babylonian,
  Phoenician

god.. 4. Esus (Gaulish)
isles.. 5. Chios, Crete, Samos
 6. Aegina, Ionian, Ithaca, Lemnos,
 Lesbos, Rhodes 7. Salamis
 8. Cyclades
language.. 4. Pali 5. Latin 6. Celtic,
 Gaelic 7. Cornish, Gaulish
mariner.. 4. Rime (of) 5. rover
 6. roamer, sailor, seaman
 8. seafarer, wanderer 9. navigator
soldier.. 7. peltast
theater.. 5. odeum
and... 2. et 4. also, plus 8. et cetera
 9. ampersand, including
 12. additionally
andante... 5. largo, tempo 6. slowly
Andean (pert to)...
camel.. 5. llama
deer.. 4. pudu
region, wind.. 4. puna
term.. 5. grand, lofty
andiron... 3. dog 7. firedog, Hessian
andrenid... 3. bee 10. Andrenidae
androgyny... 9. sissiness
 10. effeminacy 11. unmanliness
 15. hermaphroditism
android... 5. robot 9. automaton
anecdote... 4. tale, yarn 5. story
 7. account 9. chronicle, narrative
anecdotes... 3. ana 7. sayings, stories
anemone... 7. actinia 10. windflower
anent... 2. of, on, re 4. upon, with
 5. about 8. opposite 10. concerning
anesthesia, anaesthesia...
 8. deadness, numbness
 13. insensibility
anesthetic... 3. gas 5. ether
 8. freezing, Novocain, procaine
 9. pentothal 10. chloroform
 13. refrigeration
anesthetize... 4. dull, numb, stun
 6. benumb, deaden, freeze 7. stupefy
 8. etherize, paralyze 9. narcotize
 10. chloroform 11. desensitize
anew... 5. again, newly 6. afresh, de
 novo 8. recently
angel... 6. cherub, genius, seraph
 (seraf) 7. Madonna, prophet
angel (pert to)...
Arab (apostate).. 5. Eblis
archangel.. 5. Uriel 7. Gabriel,
 Michael, Raphael
Biblical.. 6. bishop, pastor
Fallen.. 6. Belial, Mammon
financial.. 6. backer, patron
 7. sponsor 8. promoter
fish.. 5. shark 9. spadefish
Hebrew.. 6. Abdiel 8. cherubim,
 seraphim
Jewish.. 6. Azrael (of death)
 7. Zadkiel (of planet Jupiter)
 8. Metatron
Mohammedan (Mus).. 7. Israfil
 (Israfeel)
Moslem.. 5. Nakir (Repudiating)
 6. Munkar (Unknown)
angelic... 5. godly 7. lovable, saintly
 8. cherubic, heavenly, seraphic,
 virtuous 9. celestial 10. beneficent
angelica... 4. herb 6. lovely 7. liqueur
Angelus... 4. bell, call 6. prayer
 8. devotion

anger... 3. ire, vex 4. fume, rage, rile
 5. annoy, chafe, wrath 6. choler,
 dander, enrage, nettle, offend,
 temper 7. dudgeon, emotion,
 inflame, madness, passion, trouble
 8. vexation 9. infuriate 10. affliction,
 enragement, irritation, resentment
 11. displeasure, indignation
 12. exasperation
angered... 3. mad 5. irate, wroth
 8. incensed, wrathful 9. indignant,
 irascible
angle... 3. ell, tee, zig 4. axil, coin,
 fish, fork, hade, nook 5. acute,
 ancon, arris, right, slant, story
 6. akimbo, distal, epaule, obtuse,
 octant 7. bastion, outlook, ravelin,
 salient 8. attitude 9. incidence,
 rectangle, viewpoint
angler... 6. fisher 7. dibbler, trawler,
 troller 8. piscator 9. fisherman,
 Waltonian
angler's basket... 5. creel
Anglican... 7. English
Anglo—Celtic... 7. British
 10. Anglo—Saxon
Anglo—Indian (pert to)...
Empire founder.. 5. Clive
measure.. 3. ser 4. tola
pageant.. 7. tamasha
peasant.. 4. ryot
princess.. 5. begum
wealthy.. 5. nabob
Anglo—Saxon (pert to)...
armor.. 7. hauberk
assembly.. 4. moot 5. gemot
 (gemote)
attendant.. 5. thane
consonant.. 3. edh, eth
council.. 9. heptarchy
councilman.. 5. witan
epic (heroic).. 7. Beowulf
native.. 7. English 11. Anglo—Celtic
prince (heir apparent).. 8. atheling
slave.. 4. esne
tenant.. 6. geneat
warrior.. 5. thane
Angora...
capital of.. 6. Turkey
garment.. 5. shawl
goat.. 6. chamal
wool fabric.. 6. mohair
angry... 3. hot, mad 4. sore 5. cross,
 grame, irate, irked, vexed 6. ireful,
 stormy 7. enraged, painful
 8. inflamed, wrathful 9. indignant,
 irascible, resentful, turbulent
 10. passionate
anguish... 3. woe 4. bale, pain, pang
 5. agony, dolor, grief, throe
 6. misery 7. remorse, sadness,
 torment, torture 8. distress
 9. heartache 10. desolation
 11. lamentation
angular... 4. bent, bony, edgy
 5. gaunt, sharp 6. abrupt, akimbo,
 forked 7. crooked, pointed, scrawny
 8. cornered, crotched
ani... 8. keelbill (keelbird) 9. blackbird
animadversion... 7. censure, comment,
 obloquy 8. judgment, reproach
 9. aspersion, criticism

10. imputation, reflection
12. condemnation
animadvert ... 4. note 5. watch
   6. notice, regard, remark 7. censure,
   comment, observe 9. criticize
   (criticise)
anima humana ... 4. mind, self, soul
   5. heart, human 6. psyche, spirit
animal (pert to) ...
   anatomy .. 7. zootomy
   back, spine .. 4. nota 5. chine
   body .. 4. soma
   castrated .. 3. seg (segg)
   coat .. 6. pelage
   cud .. 5. rumen
   disease .. 8. enzootic
   enclosure .. 3. pen, sty 4. cage, coop,
      cote, reem, yard 5. hutch, kraal, stall
      6. corral 7. pasture
   fabulous .. 7. griffin
   group .. 3. gam, pod 4. herd
      5. drove, flock, pride 9. menagerie
   hairless .. 5. pelon
   hindleg part .. 4. crus
   hornless .. 7. pollard
   hybrid .. 4. mule 5. hinny
   hypnosis .. 9. cataplexy
   male .. 3. tom 4. bull, jack, stag
      5. steer 8. stallion
   many–egged .. 5. zooid
   many–footed .. 7. polyped
   molt .. 8. exuviate
   mother .. 3. dam
   no feet .. 4. apod
   nose .. 5. snout
   oar–footed .. 7. remiped
   one–egged .. 4. zoon
   one–footed .. 6. uniped
   pet .. 4. cade
   reference to .. 4. wild 6. carnal
      7. bestial, fleshly, kingdom
      8. domestic 12. ferae naturae
      14. domitae naturae
   regional .. 5. fauna
   small .. 10. animalcule
   symbolic .. 5. totem
   track, trail .. 4. rack 5. piste, spoor
   web–footed .. 8. pinniped
   wing–footed .. 6. aliped
   worship .. 8. zoolatry
   young .. 3. cub, kid, pup 4. calf, colt,
      fawn, foal, lamb 5. filly, puppy
      6. kitten
animal family ...
   bear .. 6. ursine
   cat .. 6. feline
   cow .. 6. bovine
   deer .. 7. cervine
   dog .. 6. canine
   fox .. 7. vulpine
   horse .. 6. equine
   pig .. 7. porcine
   sheep .. 5. ovine
   wolf .. 6. lupine
animal stomach ...
   1st .. 5. rumen 6. paunch
   2nd .. 5. tripe 9. honeycomb,
      reticulum
   3rd .. 6. omasum 9. manyplies
   4th .. 4. read (reed) 8. abomasum
animate ... 3. act 4. fire, live, move
   5. alive, cheer, imbue, impel, liven

6. arouse, ensoul, spirit, vivify
   7. enliven, inspire, organic, refresh
   8. energize, vitalize 9. stimulate
   10. exhilarate
animated ... 3. gay 5. alive, brisk
   6. active, lively, living, minded
   8. disposed (in mind), prompted
   9. energetic, refreshed
animated spirit ... 6. animus
animation ... 3. pep 4. brio, dash, life
   5. ardor 6. energy, gaiety, spirit
   8. airiness, buoyancy, vivacity
   10. excitement, liveliness, motivation
   11. earnestness, inspiration
   12. invigoration, vivification
   13. sprightliness
animation suspended ... 6. apathy,
   torpor 8. dormancy, lethargy
animé ... 6. bright 8. animated
animosity ... 5. clash, spite 6. enmity,
   hatred, rancor 7. ill will 8. conflict
   9. antipathy, hostility
   10. antagonism, opposition,
   repugnance
animoso ... 6. lively 8. animated
   9. energetic
animous ... 3. hot 8. resolute,
   vehement
animus ... 4. mind, will 6. desire,
   spirit, temper 8. attitude, volition
   9. intention 10. discretion
   11. disposition, inclination
ankh (Egypt) ... 3. tau 4. life 5. cross
   6. emblem, symbol
ankle ... 4. tali (pl) 5. joint, pivot, talus
   6. tarsus 8. astragal 9. ginglymus
   10. astragalus 11. diarthrosis
ankle cover ... 4. spat 6. gaiter
ankylostoma ... 7. lockjaw
annalist ... 6. writer 8. recorder
   9. historian 10. chronicler
   11. memorialist 12. chronologist
annals ... 5. diary 6. record 7. history,
   journal 8. register 9. chronicle
   11. publication
Annam ... 5. Hanoi 6. Tonkin
   (Tongking)
Annamese ... 7. Chinese 8. Buddhist
   9. Mongolian
anneal ... 4. fuse, heat 6. harden,
   temper 7. inflame, toughen
   8. indurate
Anne Hathaway's home ... 8. Shattery
annelid ... 3. lug 4. lurg, naid, worm
   6. phylum 7. lugworm
annex ... 3. add, ell 4. join, wing
   5. affix 6. append, attach, fasten
   7. acquire, subjoin 8. addition
   9. extension
annexation ... 7. adjunct 8. addition
   9. accession 10. affixation
   13. appropriation
Annie Oakley ... 4. pass 6. ticket
   (free)
annihilate ... 4. undo, void 5. erase,
   wreck 6. quench, reduce, stifle
   7. abolish, destroy, expunge, nullify,
   smother 8. decimate 9. extirpate
   10. extinguish, obliterate
   11. exterminate
annihilation ... 5. death 6. demise
   7. passing 10. extinction

11. destruction, dissolution
13. extermination 14. extinguishment
anniversary... 5. cycle 6. course
7. jubilee, wedding 8. birthday
10. centennial, regularity
13. commemoration
annotation... 4. note 5. gloss
7. apostil, comment 8. exegesis,
notation, rescript, scholium
9. reference 10. commentary
annotator... 6. critic 7. analyst
9. expositor, expounder, publicist,
scholiast 10. glossarist
11. commentator
announce... 3. bid 4. call, tell 5. bruit
6. affirm, assert, herald, notify
7. declare, forerun, gazette, presage
8. proclaim 9. advertise, broadcast,
pronounce 10. annunciate,
promulgate
announcement... 4. fiat 5. blurb, edict
6. decree, notice 8. bulletin
9. manifesto 10. commercial
11. affirmation, declaration
12. notification, proclamation
13. advertisement
announcer... 4. page 5. crier, emcee
6. nuncio 9. harbinger, informant
10. newscaster, proclaimer
11. broadcaster
annoy... 3. irk, nag, try, vex 4. bore,
rile 5. anger, devil, harry, peeve,
spite, tease 6. bother, harass,
molest, offend, pester, ruffle
7. disturb, trouble 8. irritate
9. displease 13. inconvenience
annoyance... 4. bore, pest
8. nuisance, vexation 10. resentment
11. molestati̇n 13. inconvenience
annoying... 4. sore 7. galling
9. vexatious 11. distressing
annual... 4. book 5. plant 6. yearly
7. etesian 10. periodical
11. publication
annuity... 5. rente, trust 6. income
(life) 7. pension, subsidy, tontine
9. allotment 10. investment, life
income
annul... 4. cass, undo, void 5. avoid,
blank, quash 6. cancel, repeal,
revoke 7. abolish, nullify, rescind
8. abrogate, derogate, overrule,
withdraw 9. disaffirm 10. invalidate,
neutralize, obliterate 11. countermand
annular... 6. banded, cyclic, ringed
8. cingular, circular
annulet... 4. ring (Her) 6. fillet
7. circlet, ringlet
annulment... 6. repeal 7. erasure,
vacatur 9. abolition 10. abrogation,
defeasance, revocation
12. invalidation 14. neutralization
annunciate... 6. affirm, assert
8. announce, proclaim
annunciation... 11. affirmation
12. announcement, proclamation
13. pronouncement
anoa... 2. ox (wild) 8. sapiutan
anode... 8. terminal (positive)
9. electrode (opp of cathode)
anodic... 12. turned toward
anodyne... 4. balm 6. opiate

7. soother 8. antalgic, narcotic,
pacifier, sedative 9. analgesic
10. depressant, palliative
anoesia... 6. idiocy
anoint... 3. oil 4. balm, cere, nard
5. anele, bribe, smear 6. chrism,
grease, spread 7. moisten
8. medicate 9. embrocate, lubricate
10. consecrate
anoli, anole... 6. lizard
anomalous... 3. odd 7. erratic,
strange, unusual 8. aberrant,
abnormal, peculiar 9. eccentric,
irregular 10. dissimilar
11. exceptional 13. unconformable
anomaly... 6. oddity, rarity
11. abnormality, nondescript
12. irregularity
anomy... 7. miracle
anon... 4. soon 5. again, later
6. mañana, thence 7. by–and–by
8. tomorrow 10. eventually
11. straightway
anonymous (opp of onomatous)...
7. unknown 8. nameless, unavowed
9. undefined
anoöpsia... 10. strabismus (upward)
Anopheles... 10. mosquitoes
anophthalmia... 13. absence of eyes
(congenital)
anopia... 15. defective vision
anorak... 12. hooded jacket (Arctic)
anorexia... 10. no appetite
anorthopia... 15. distorted vision
anosmia... 11. loss of smell
another... 3. new 4. more 5. alias,
extra, other 6. second 7. further
10. additional
another time... 5. again
10. otherwhile
ansa... 4. loop 6. handle
anserine... 6. stupid 9. gooselike
answer... 2. do 3. say 4. echo
5. avail, reply, sauce, serve
6. oracle, retort 7. defense, epistle,
respond, riposte 8. conclude,
reaction, repartee, response, solution
9. rejoinder 10. correspond,
responsory 11. acknowledge
16. counterstatement
answerable... 6. liable 8. amenable,
solvable 11. responsible
12. commensurate 13. proportionate
answer the purpose... 2. so 3. fit
4. suit 5. avail, serve 6. become
7. benefit, satisfy, suffice
ant (pert to)...
family.. 10. Formicidae, Myrmicidae
11. Formicoidea (super),
Hymenoptera
feeding on.. 13. formicivorous
genus.. 6. Eciton, Termes 7. Formica
killer.. 9. formicide
male.. 8. macraner (large), micraner
(small)
nest.. 9. formicary
ref to.. 6. formic
type.. 5. emmet 7. formica, pismire
white.. 4. anay (anai) 7. termite
wingless.. 8. ergatoid
worker.. 6. ergate 9. harvester
antacid... 6. alkali, remedy 8. medicine

9. absorbent 11. neutralizer
12. counteragent 13. counteractant
Antaeus, Antaios (Gr)... 5. giant
6. Libyan 8. wrestler
antagonism... 3. war 5. clash
8. conflict 9. antipathy, hostility
10. opposition, repugnance
11. contrariety 12. disagreement
13. counteraction
antagonist... 3. foe 5. enemy, rival
6. foeman 8. opponent 9. adversary
antagonistic... 7. hostile, opposed
8. contrary, converse, inimical,
opposite 9. repugnant 10. unfriendly
11. belligerent, disagreeing
13. counteractive
Antarctic...
Circle.. 4. Pole 6. region
continent.. 10. Antarctica
explorer.. 4. Byrd, Ross
islands.. 11. Archipelago
rel to.. 8. subpolar 9. antipodal,
South Pole
sea.. 4. Ross 7. Weddell
seal (brown) discoverer.. 7. Weddell
volcano.. 6. Erebus
ante... 3. pay, pot 4. bank, fund, pool
5. kitty, stake 7. jackpot
anteater... 5. Manis 7. echidna
8. aardvark, edentate, pangolin,
tamandua
antecede... 4. head 5. front 6. prefix
7. outrank, precede, preface
antecedent... 4. fore 5. prior, scout
6. former 7. pioneer 8. ancestor,
previous 9. foregoing, precedent,
preceding, precursor 10. forerunner,
precedence 11. voortrekker (Dutch)
12. avant–courier
antecedents... 7. fathers 9. ancestors,
forebears 10. ascendants
(ascendents) 11. forefathers
12. predecessors 13. prerequisites
antechamber... 4. hall 5. lobby
6. lounge 7. chamber 8. anteroom
9. vestibule
antedate... 7. precede, predate
8. datemark, pre–exist 10. anticipate
antelope... 3. gau, gnu, kob, nil
4. guib, koba, oryx, roan 5. addax,
bovid, eland, goral, oribi, peele,
saiga, serow 6. cabree, dzeren,
impala, nilgai, pygarg 7. blaubok,
blesbok, bubalia, chamois, gazella,
gazelle, gemsbok, sassaby
8. agacella, bontebok, steinbok
9. duikerbok, pronghorn
10. hartebeest
antenna... 4. horn, mast, palp
5. clava (Zool), tower 6. aerial, feeler
7. scanner
antepast... 6. canape, repast
8. aperitif 9. antipasto, appetizer,
foretaste 11. hors d'oeuvre,
prelibation
anteroom... 4. hall 5. lobby 6. lounge
7. chamber 9. vestibule
11. antechamber
anthem... 3. lay 4. hymn, song
5. motet, music, psalm 7. chorale
8. doxology 9. antiphony, offertory
10. responsory

anthill... 5. mound 9. formicary
anthology... 3. ana 5. album
6. corpus 7. omnibus, prayers
8. analects 9. potpourri
10. collection 11. collectanea,
compilation
Anthozoa... 6. corals, polyps
8. anemones
anthropoid... 3. ape, lar, man
6. gibbon 7. gorilla, primate,
siamang 9. orangutan (orangoutang)
10. chimpanzee, troglodyte
12. Anthropoidea (suborder)
anthropophagi... 9. cannibals,
man–eaters
anti... 6. contra 7. adverse, counter,
opposed 8. contrary, converse
13. contradictory
antiaircraft artillery... 4. guns
6. ack–ack, Archie, cannon
7. weapons 8. cannonry, ordnance
10. skysweeper
antibiotics... 5. drugs 7. vaccine
10. penicillin 12. streptomycin
antic... 4. dido 5. caper, prank, stunt
6. frolic, gambol 7. bizarre, buffoon,
gambado 9. grotesque
11. merry–andrew, monkeyshine
anticipate... 4. hope 5. await, dread
6. expect 7. foresee, obviate,
portend, prevent 8. preclude
9. forestall, foretaste, forethink
11. contemplate
anticipation... 4. hope 9. foresight,
foretaste, intuition, prolepsis
10. foreboding 11. expectation,
forethought 12. presentiment
13. preoccupation
anticlimax... 6. bathos 8. comedown,
decrease
antidote... 6. remedy 10. corrective,
preventive 11. neutralizer
12. counteragent, prophylactic
13. counteractant
Antioch... 7. capital (Syria)
antipathy... 6. hatred, nausea
7. dislike 8. aversion, loathing
9. disrelish, hostility 10. abhorrence,
antagonism, opposition, reluctance,
repugnance 11. contrariety,
detestation, inimicality
13. counteraction 14. disinclination
antipodal... 5. polar 7. counter (global)
8. contrary, opposite
14. contrapositive
antiquated... 4. aged 5. passé
6. bygone, voided 7. antique,
archaic, elderly 8. absolute, medieval
9. Victorian 10. fossilized
12. old–fashioned 13. superannuated
antique... 3. old 5. hoary, relic
7. ageless, ancient 8. dateless,
outmoded 9. venerable
12. old–fashioned
antiquities... 5. codex, ruins 6. relics
7. fossils, papyrus, remains, tablets
9. archaisms, artifacts, monuments
11. manuscripts, palimpsests
antiquity... 3. ago, eld 4. past, yore
7. oldness 9. paleology
11. ancientness, elderliness
13. aboriginality, primitiveness

antisepsis ... 7. asepsis
  11. prophylaxis 12. disinfection,
  immunization 13. sterilization
antiseptic ... 5. Salol 6. cresol, iodine
  (iodin), phenol 7. alcohol, aristol,
  aseptic 8. creosote, peroxide
  9. germicide 12. disinfectant,
  formaldehyde, prophylactic
antispasmodic ... 7. anodyne
  8. sedative 9. asadulcis (deadly
  carrot), asafetida (asafoetida)
  10. depressant 12. tranquilizer
antithesis (opp of thesis) ... 8. contrast,
  opposite 9. antipodes 10. opposition
  11. contrariety 14. contraposition
antitoxin ... 5. serum 7. vaccine
  8. antibody 9. antivenin (antivenene)
  10. antibiotic 11. antipyretic,
  immunotoxin
antler ... 3. dag 4. horn, snag, tine
  5. dague, point, prong, spike
  6. bosset, rights 8. advancer
  9. caducicorn
Antony & Cleopatra characters ...
  4. Eris, Iras 6. Caesar 7. Octavia
  9. Demetrius
antonym (opp of synonym) ...
  7. reverse 8. contrary, opposite
antrum ... 3. pit 5. sinus 6. cavern,
  cavity, hollow 10. depression
Anu ... 3. god (sky, heavens)
Anubis ... 3. god (Necropolis)
  6. Hermes
Anura ... 4. Rana 6. frogs, toads
  9. Salientia 10. amphibians
anvil ... 5. block, incus, teest 6. stithy
  7. bickern, incudes (pl) 8. beakiron
  (horned)
anxiety ... 4. care, fear 5. angst,
  dread, worry 7. concern, trouble
  8. disquiet, distress, neurosis,
  suspense 9. eagerness, misgiving
  10. foreboding, perplexity, solicitude,
  uneasiness 12. apprehension,
  restlessness
anxious ... 4. cark 5. antsy, eager
  6. uneasy 7. fearful, unquiet
  8. watchful 9. concerned, disturbed,
  expectant, impatient 10. disquieted
any ... 3. all, ary (dial), one, oni (dial)
  4. some, that, this 5. aught, every
  8. quantity 9. unlimited
  10. unmeasured 12. undetermined
anybody ... 3. any, one 5. aught
  6. anyone 7. someone, whoever
  15. no–account person
anything ... 3. any 4. some 5. at all,
  aught 7. anywise 8. no choice,
  whatever 9. something
  14. choicelessness
anything (pert to) ...
  existing .. 6. entity 8. quiddity
  of value .. 5. asset
  of value, least .. 5. plack
  puzzling .. 4. crux 11. mind–boggler
  remote .. 6. forane
  small .. 3. tot 5. minim
  spiral .. 4. gyre 5. helix
  terrifying .. 5. ghost 9. scarecrow
  true .. 4. fact 9. certitude
  worthless .. 4. mean 7. useless
  9. valueless

aoudad ... 5. sheep 7. chamois
apa ... 7. wallaba
Apache (pert to) ...
  French .. 4. thug 5. dance 8. assassin
  Indian .. 5. nomad
  Indian Chief (famed) .. 8. Geronimo
  Indian jacket (deerskin) .. 6. bietle
  State .. 7. Arizona
apart ... 3. dis (pref) 4. away 5. alone,
  aloof, aside, solus, split 6. singly
  7. asunder, distant 8. secluded,
  separate, unjoined 9. severally,
  unrelated 10. separately
apartheid ... 4. bias 5. twist 7. bigotry
  9. prejudice 11. segregation
  13. provincialism 14. discrimination
apartment ... 3. pad (sl) 4. flat
  5. condo, suite 7. chamber
  8. tenement 11. compartment,
  condominium
apathetic ... 4. dull 5. inert 6. torpid
  7. passive 8. listless, sluggish
  10. insouciant, phlegmatic
  11. indifferent, unconcerned
apathy ... 6. acedia (in a monastery),
  torpor 7. languor 8. neurosis
  9. lassitude, unconcern
  12. indifference, sluggishness
  13. insensibility, unfeelingness
ape ... 4. copy, dupe, fool, mime
  5. mimic 6. alalus, mocker, monkey,
  parrot 7. barbary, copycat, emulate,
  imitate, portray 8. imitator, mimicker,
  simulate 10. anthropoid
  11. impersonate
ape (pert to) ...
  anthropoid .. 6. pongid
  10. chimpanzee, troglodyte
  Egypt Relig .. 4. Aani
  genus .. 5. Cebus, Simia
  India .. 3. kra
  kind .. 6. simian 7. macaque
  largest .. 6. baboon 7. gorilla
  Malay .. 3. lar 5. orang 6. gibbon
  9. orangutan (orangoutang)
  nocturnal .. 5. lemur
aperitif ... 5. drink 6. canape
  8. antepast 9. antipasto, appetizer
  11. hors d'oeuvre
aperture ... 3. gap, vue 4. hole, leak,
  pore, rift, rima, slit, slot, vent
  5. chasm, chink, cleft, inlet, mouth,
  stoma 6. hiatus, window 7. fissure,
  foramen, opening, orifice, osteole
  8. fenestra 10. passageway
apex ... 3. tip, top 4. acme, cone,
  cusp, noon 5. point, spire 6. apogee,
  height, macron, summit, tittle, vertex,
  zenith 7. cacumen 8. pinnacle
  11. culmination
apex ornament ... 6. finial
aphid ... 5. Aphis, louse 6. insect
  7. puceron
aphorism ... 3. saw 5. adage, axiom,
  gnome, maxim, moral 6. dictum,
  saying 7. proverb 8. apothegm
Aphrodite (pert to) ...
  consort .. 4. Ares 10. Hephaestus
  father .. 4. Zeus
  goddess of .. 4. love 6. beauty
  Roman equivalent .. 5. Venus
  sacred birds .. 5. doves 8. sparrows

statue.. 17. Aphrodite of Cnidus (by Praxiteles)
zoology.. 9. butterfly
Apis... 4. bull (sacred)
aplomb... 5. poise 6. surety
7. balance 8. fastness, firmness, security, solidity 9. assurance, erectness, plumbness, restraint, soundness, stability 10. confidence, equanimity 11. equilibrium
apocalypse... 8. prophecy, teaching 9. discovery, scripture
10. revealment, revelation
a poco... 6. little, slowly 9. gradually
apocryphal... 4. mock, sham
5. bogus, false 6. mythic, unreal
8. doubtful, mythical, spurious
9. imitative 10. fictitious, unorthodox
11. counterfeit 15. unauthoritative
apod... 8. footless
Apodes... 4. eels 6. morays
apogee (opp of perigee)... 4. acme, apex, peak 6. climax, summit, zenith
11. culmination
apograph... 4. copy 5. tenor
7. tracing 8. transfer 9. recording
10. transcript 13. transcription
Apoidea... 4. Apis, bees 9. honeybees
11. Hymenoptera
Apollo (pert to)...
birthplace.. 5. Delos
father.. 4. Zeus
festival.. 5. Delia
god.. 3. sun (personified)
mother.. 4. Leto 6. Larona
oracle.. 6. Delphi
sage follower.. 6. Abaris
sister (twin).. 5. Diana (Rom)
7. Artemis
son.. 3. Ion 5. Hymen, Linos
apologetic... 5. sorry 7. apology
8. excusing 10. excusatory, justifying, remorseful 11. vindicative
12. propitiatory 13. justification
apologue... 4. myth 5. fable, story
6. legend 7. fantasy, parable
8. allegory
apology... 4. plea 6. excuse
7. pretext, regrets 9. makeshift
11. explanation, vindication
13. justification 14. acknowledgment
aport... 8. larboard, leftward
9. sinistrad
apostasy... 5. lapse 9. desertion, recreancy 11. backsliding
apostate... 6. bolter 7. pervert, runaway, seceder 8. deserter, recreant, renegade, turncoat, turntail
10. unfaithful
apostle... 5. saint 8. disciple, follower
10. evangelist
Apostle (Bib)... 4. John, Jude, Paul
5. James, Judas, Peter, Silas, Simon
6. Andrew, Philip, Thomas
7. Matthew 8. Barnabas, Matthias
11. Bartholomew
Apostle of...
France (Gauls).. 5. Denis
Franks.. 4. Remi
Gentiles.. 4. Paul
Germany.. 8. Boniface
Goths.. 7. Ulfilas

Indies.. 6. Xavier
Ireland.. 7. Patrick
Rome.. 4. Neri
Apostle to the Indians... 5. Eliot
apostolic... 5. faith, papal 6. gospel
8. Biblical 9. evangelic 10. pontifical, scriptural
apostrophe... 8. squiggle 9. soliloquy
apothecary... 8. druggist, gallipot
9. dispenser 10. pharmacist, posologist 13. pharmaceutist
14. pharmacologist
apothecary measure... 4. dram, pint
5. minim, ounce
apothecary weight... 4. dram
5. grain, ounce, pound 7. scruple
apothegm... 3. saw 4. dict 5. adage, axiom, gnome, maxim 6. dictum, saying 7. precept 8. aphorism
apotheosis... 5. ideal 10. exaltation
11. deification, ennoblement, idolization 12. resurrection
13. dignification, glorification, magnification 14. aggrandizement
apotheosize... 5. deify, exalt
7. ennoble, glorify, idolize 8. enshrine
11. immortalize
appall, appal... 3. awe 5. shock
6. dismay
appalling... 4. grim 5. awful
7. awesome, fearful 8. dreadful, shocking, terrible, terrific 9. frightful
10. remarkable
appalto... 8. monopoly
appanage... 7. adjunct, pendant
8. property 9. appendage, endowment 10. perquisite
11. prerogative 12. appurtenance
apparatus... 4. gear, tool 6. outfit
7. machine, rigging, trapeze
8. recorder 9. appliance, equipment, mechanism, trappings 10. instrument
13. paraphernalia
apparatus (pert to)...
distillation.. 7. alembic
dyeing.. 4. ager
heating.. 4. etna 5. stove 6. boiler
7. furnace 8. radiator
hoisting.. 3. pry 4. jack 5. davit, lever, lewis 7. capstan, derrick
planetarium.. 6. orrery
steering.. 4. helm 5. wheel 6. rudder, tiller
water.. 4. pump 5. noria 6. faucet, siphon, tremie
apparel... 3. alb 4. deck, duds, garb, gear, togs, wear 5. dress, equip, habit 6. attire 7. clothes, costume, garment, raiment, toggery, vesture
8. clothing, fatigues 10. garmenture
11. habiliments
apparent... 4. open 5. clear, overt, plain 6. patent, visual 7. certain, evident, obvious, seeable, seeming, visible 8. distinct, illusory, manifest, specious 9. notorious, plausible
10. ostensible 11. discernible, indubitable, perceivable, superficial
12. recognizable
apparently... 7. visibly 9. evidently, obviously, seemingly 10. manifestly, presumably, speciously

11. perceptibly

apparition... 4. bogy, form 5. ghost, shade, spook 6. shadow, spirit, sprite, vision, wraith 7. eidolon, fantasy, phantom, specter (spectre) 8. illusion, phantasm, revenant 9. hobgoblin 10. appearance, phenomenon, revelation

appassionato... 9. emotional 11. impassioned

appeal... 3. beg, cry 4. call, cite, plea, pray, suit 5. charm, plead 6. avouch, invoke, prayer 7. address, beseech, entreat, implore, request, solicit 8. entreaty, petition 9. importune 10. lovability, loveliness, supplicate 11. winsomeness 12. supplication

appealing... 4. nice 7. winsome 8. alluring, charming, engaging, pleasant 9. agreeable, glamorous, imploring 10. attractive, beseeching, bewitching, delightful, enchanting, entreating 11. fascinating, interesting

appear... 4. loom, seem 5. occur 6. arrive, attend, emerge 11. materialize

appearance... 3. air 4. form, look, mien 5. front, guise, looks, phase 6. aspect, format, manner, ostent 7. arrival, feature, specter (spectre) 8. illusion, presence, pretense 9. emergence, semblance 10. apparition, disclosure, revelation 11. resemblance 13. manifestation

appearance (pert to)...
book.. 6. format
false.. 8. disguise
first.. 4. dawn 5. debut 8. premiere
frontal.. 6. facade
surface.. 6. patina
truth (appearance of)..
  14. verisimilitude
white.. 6. pallid

appease... 4. calm 5. allay, atone, mease, quiet, salve 6. pacify, soothe 7. content, placate, relieve, satisfy 8. mitigate 10. conciliate 11. tranquilize

appeasement... 6. relief 7. salving 8. easement 10. compromise, mitigation, palliation 12. pacification

appellation... 3. tag 4. name 5. label, style, title 7. calling, epithet 8. cognomen, nickname 9. sobriquet 11. designation 12. denomination, nomenclature 14. identification

append... 3. add 4. hang 5. affix, annex 6. adjoin, attach 7. subjoin 11. superimpose

appendage... 3. arm, awn, cue, tab, tag 4. barb, flap, lobe, tail 5. cauda, queue 6. ligule (Bot), palpus 7. adjunct, pigtail 8. addition, hanger–on, pendicle 9. accessory, tailpiece 10. dependency 12. appurtenance 13. accompaniment

appendix... 6. sequel 7. codicil, process 8. addendum, addition 9. accessory, appendage 10. dependency 12. augmentation

appertain... 4. bear 5. apply 6. affect, belong, regard, relate 7. involve, pertain

appetite... 4. zest 5. taste 6. desire, hunger, orexis, thirst 7. longing, passion 8. cupidity 9. appetency 10. hungriness, propensity

appetizer... 4. fish (sauce) 6. canape 8. antepast, aperitif 9. antipasto, foretaste 11. hors d'oeuvre

appetizing... 6. savory 7. piquant 8. tempting 9. appealing, desirable 10. attractive 11. captivating, provocative, tantalizing

applaud... 4. clap, hail, laud, root, yell 5. cheer, extol, shout 6. hurrah, praise 7. acclaim, approve, commend, endorse 10. compliment

applauders (paid)... 6. claque 8. clappers 9. claqueurs

applause... 4. clap, hand 5. bravo, éclat, huzza 6. encore, praise 7. acclaim, ovation 8. plaudits 11. acclamation 12. commendation

apple... 3. May, Spy 4. crab, pome 6. annona, pippin, rennet, russet 7. Baldwin, codling (codlin), costard, Newtown, Roxbury, winesap 8. Greening, Jonathan, Mandrake, McIntosh, queening 9. astrachan, Delicious 10. bellflower, Rome Beauty 11. Gravenstein, Northern Spy

apple (pert to)...
acid.. 5. malic
crushed.. 6. pomace
dessert.. 10. brown betty
disease.. 7. stippen
genus.. 5. Malus
juice.. 5. cider 9. applejack
love.. 6. tomato
seed.. 3. pip
shaped.. 8. pomiform

Apple of Discord (Gr Myth)... 4. Eris

apple of one's eye... 3. pet 4. idol 5. jewel, pupil 7. darling, desired 8. favorite 10. preference

applesauce... 4. bunk, pooh 5. tripe 6. phooey 7. baloney, hogwash 8. malarkey, nonsense, tommyrot 12. fiddlesticks 13. horsefeathers

appliance... 3. dam (dental) 4. tool 6. device, gadget 7. utensil 8. facility 9. commodity, implement 10. instrument 11. application, contraption, convenience

applicable... 3. apt, fit 6. usable 7. pliable 8. apposite, relative, relevant 9. compliant, pertinent 11. appropriate

application... 3. use 6. appeal, effort 7. bearing, concern, request 8. petition, recourse 9. attention, constancy, diligence, relevance, relevancy 10. connection, employment, pertinence 11. attribution, disposition, engrossment, persistence, requisition 12. perseverance 14. administration

application (body)... 4. balm 5. salve, stupe (hot) 7. plaster 8. cosmetic, poultice

apply... 3. use 4. suit 6. appose,

bestow, comply, devote, employ,
relate 7. solicit, utilize 9. associate,
attribute 10. administer
11. appropriate

appoggiature ... 9. grace note
13. embellishment

appoint ... 3. fix 4. name 5. equip
6. assign, decree, depute, detail,
ordain 7. destine, prepare
8. delegate, deputize 9. designate,
establish, prescribe 10. constitute

appointment ... 4. date 5. order, tryst
7. command 8. position 9. direction,
equipment, ordinance
10. engagement 11. designation
13. establishment

appointments ... 6. things 8. fittings,
fixtures 9. equipment, furniture
10. belongings, upholstery
11. acquirement, furnishings
12. accumulation, conveniences
13. accouterments, paraphernalia

apportion ... 3. fix, lot 4. deal, dele,
mete, part 5. allot, carve, share
6. assign, budget, divide 7. arrange,
dispose 8. allocate 9. collocate,
partition 10. distribute

appose ... 4. abut 5. audit, liken, place
6. adjoin 7. compare, examine
9. juxtapose

apposite ... 3. apt 4. like 5. close,
match 6. timely 7. fitting, germane
8. position, relative, relevant
9. pertinent 11. appropriate

appraise ... 4. mark, rank, rate
5. assay, gauge, judge, price, value
6. assess, evalue, praise 7. apprise,
commend, measure 8. consider,
estimate, evaluate 10. adjudicate,
appreciate

appraiser (tax) ... 5. rater 6. lister
8. assessor

appreciable ... 3. any 8. tangible
9. estimable 11. perceptible

appreciate ... 4. feel, grow, know
5. enjoy, prize, savor, value
6. admire, esteem 7. advance,
amplify, approve, augment, realize,
respect 8. estimate, increase,
treasure

appreciation ... 7. respect 9. appraisal,
awareness, gratitude 10. estimation
11. realization, recognition, sensibility
12. gratefulness, thankfulness

apprehend ... 3. ken, see 4. know,
take 5. dread, grasp, pinch (sl),
savvy, sense 6. arrest 7. capture,
imagine, realize 8. conceive, perceive
10. anticipate, comprehend,
understand

apprehensible ... 8. knowable
9. scrutable 10. explicable,
fathomable 11. accountable
12. discoverable, intelligible
14. comprehensible, understandable

apprehension ... 4. fear, idea 5. alarm,
doubt, dread, qualm 6. arrest
7. anxiety, capture, concern, opinion,
seizure 8. distress, distrust, suspense
9. misgiving, suspicion
10. foreboding, solicitude, uneasiness
11. fearfulness, premonition

12. intelligence 13. understanding

apprehensive ... 5. smart 6. uneasy
7. alarmed, fearful, knowing, nervous,
worried 8. troubled 9. cognizant,
concerned, conscious, perturbed
10. perceptive, solicitous

apprentice ... 4. tyro 6. novice
7. amateur, trainee 8. beginner

apprize, apprise ... 4. rate, tell
5. price, value 6. advise, assess,
impart, inform, reckon 8. acquaint,
appraise 9. enlighten
11. communicate

apprized ... 5. aware 8. informed
9. cognizant

approach ... 3. way 4. adit, come,
near, road 5. stalk, verge 6. access,
accost, advent, impend 7. arrival,
nearing, sea gate 8. entryway,
likeness, nearness, overture, resemble
11. approximate, entranceway

approachable ... 4. open 8. gettable,
passable 9. reachable 10. accessible,
attainable 13. communicative

approbation ... 5. favor, proof 6. praise
7. plaudit 8. applause, approval,
sanction 10. acceptance, admiration
12. commendation, confirmation

appropriate ... 3. apt, fit 4. akin, meet,
take 5. allot, steal, usurp 6. borrow,
pirate, proper, timely, worthy
7. condign, germane, related, special
8. deserved, relevant, suitable
9. befitting, expedient, favorable,
opportune, pertinent 10. assimilate,
monopolize, plagiarize
11. conformable

appropriately ... 4. duly 5. aptly
6. timely

appropriation ... 5. theft 6. corner,
taking 8. monopoly 9. allotment
10. assignment, possession,
usurpation

approval ... 6. assent 7. consent,
support 8. sanction 10. admiration
11. approbation, endorsement
12. ratification

approve ... 2. OK 4. like, okay, pass,
sign, test 6. attest, ratify 7. applaud,
betoken, certify, confirm, endorse
(indorse), signify 8. accredit,
sanction, validate 9. authorize,
undersign 10. appreciate
11. countenance 12. authenticate

approve of ... 5. favor 6. accept
7. endorse (indorse) 8. sanction
11. countenance

approximate ... 4. near 5. about, circa,
match 8. approach, draw near,
parallel, resemble 10. correspond

approximately ... 5. about, circa
6. around, nearly 11. thereabouts

appui ... 4. prop, stay 6. bridle
(manège) 7. support

appulse ... 6. syzygy 7. impinge
8. approach 9. collision
11. conjunction (Astron)

appurtenance ... 4. gear 7. adjunct
8. addition 9. accessory, apparatus,
appendage, belonging, component

appurtenant ... 7. annexed 8. incident,
relevant 9. appendant, belonging

11. appropriate
après... 5. after 10. afterwards
apricot (pert to)...
African.. 6. meebos (dried)
beverage.. 7. cordial, liqueur, persico
color.. 9. red–yellow
confection.. 6. meebos (mebos)
Japanese.. 3. ume 4. ansu
vine.. 6. maypop
a priori (opp of posteriori)...
9. deductive 11. conditional,
presumptive 12. hypothetical
13. presumptively
apron... 3. bib 4. boot, brat, tier
5. smock 6. barvel (barvell), runway
7. garment, tablier 8. airstrip,
lambskin (Masonic), pinafore
9. appendage
apropos, a propos... 3. apt, pat
7. germane, purpose 8. by the way,
relevant, suitably 9. pertinent
10. applicable, seasonable
11. appurtenant, opportunely
12. incidentally
apt... 3. fit, pat 4. deft 5. adept,
prone, ready, smart 6. clever, expert,
likely, prompt, suited 7. capable,
elegant, subject 8. apposite,
disposed, inclined, skillful, suitable
9. competent, dexterous, ingenious,
masterful, pertinent, qualified,
teachable 10. proficient
11. appropriate
apteral... 8. apterous, wingless
Apteryx... 3. moa (extinct) 4. kiwi
aptitude... 3. art 4. bent, gift, turn
5. flair, skill 6. genius, talent
7. ability, aptness, fitness, leaning
8. penchant, tendency 9. liability
10. likelihood, proclivity
11. inclination 12. suitableness
15. appropriateness
aptly... 7. exactly, readily 8. suitably
11. pertinently
aptness... 5. skill 7. fitness
8. tendency 9. smartness
11. suitability 12. teachability
aqua... 3. eau 4. agua 5. water
aquatic... 6. natant, wading, watery
8. natatory, swimming 12. grallatorial
13. water–dwelling
Aquila... 6. eagles 13. constellation
(Milky Way)
aquiline... 6. hanate, hooked
7. curving 8. aduncous, unciform
10. Roman–nosed
ara... 5. macaw 7. goddess
(vengeance) 8. aracanga 9. screw
pine 13. constellation
Arab... 4. waif 5. gamin, horse,
nomad 6. Semite 7. Bedouin,
Saracen 8. wanderer, Yemenite
9. Caucasian
araba... 3. cab 5. coach 6. monkey
(howling)
Arabia... see *Saudi–Arabia*
Arabian (pert to)...
antelope.. 5. addax
beverage.. 4. boza (bosa) 5. leban
(lebban)
bird.. 7. phoenix
chief.. 5. sheik

cloth (shoulder).. 6. cabaan (caban)
demon.. 5. Eblis, jinni (jinnee)
6. afreet
father.. 3. Abu (Ab, Abou) 4. Abba
garment.. 3. aba 4. haik 8. burnoose
gazelle.. 4. cora, oryx 5. ariel
horse.. 4. Kohl 8. kadischi, palomino
jasmine.. 4. bela
judge.. 4. cadi
juniper (Bib).. 5. retem
nomad.. 7. Saracen
peasant.. 6. fellah
physician.. 8. Avicenna
poet.. 5. Antar
prince.. 4. amir (ameer) 5. sheik
6. sherif, sultan
romance.. 5. Antar (Antara)
ruler.. 6. caliph (calif)
Satan.. 5. Eblis, Azazel
scripture.. 7. Alcoran
seaport.. 4. Aden 5. Mocha
state of bliss.. 3. kef (kaif)
street urchin.. 5. gamin
tambourine.. 4. taar
tribe.. 3. Aus (anc)
vessel.. 4. dhow 6. boutre, sambuk
winds (hot).. 6. simoom (simoon)
arable land... 4. farm 5. arada, arado
6. plowed, tilled 10. cultivated
arachnid... 4. mite, tick 6. spider
8. scorpion 9. Arachnida
Aralu... 5. Hades
Aram (Bib)... 6. Rimmon (deity)
7. Aramaic, Semitic 8. language
araneous... 4. thin 7. weblike
8. delicate 10. cobweblike
arapunga... 8. bellbird 9. campanero
Arawak... 5. Guana 6. Indian
arbeit... 4. work 8. research
arbiter... 3. ump 5. judge 6. umpire
7. arbiter, referee 8. mediator
9. moderator 10. arbitrator
arbitrary... 6. thetic 8. absolute,
despotic, dogmatic 9. imperious,
unlimited 10. autocratic, capricious,
high–handed, peremptory, tyrannical
11. determinate, dictatorial
13. discretionary
arbitrate... 6. decide 7. bargain,
mediate 9. determine, intervene,
negotiate 12. intermediate
arbitrator... 5. judge 6. umpire
7. arbiter, referee 8. mediator
9. moderator 11. conciliator
arbor, arbour... 5. bower, kiosk
6. alcove, garden, pandal 7. pergola,
retreat, trellis 11. latticework
summerhouse
arboreal... 6. ramous 8. branched,
treelike 10. arboriform
arboreal mammal... 2. ai 4. unau
5. lemur, sloth 6. aye–aye, monkey
arc... 3. bow 5. curve 6. radian
7. azimuth, rainbow
arca... 3. box 5. chest, paten
9. reliquary
arcade... 3. orb 4. arch, hall
6. arches, avenue 7. gallery, portico
8. arcature, corridor 9. colonnade,
peristyle 10. passageway
Arcadia...
composition.. 4. poem 5. prose

7. romance
district .. **6.** Greece
huntress .. **8.** Atalanta
pert to .. **5.** rural **8.** pastoral
poetic .. **6.** Arcady
priestess .. **4.** Auge
woodland spirit .. **3.** Pan
arcanum ... **6.** elixir, enigma, remedy, secret **7.** mystery
arch ... **3.** arc, sly **4.** ogee **5.** chief, hance (part), ogive, vault **6.** fornix, instep **7.** cunning, eminent, roguish **8.** greatest, memorial, monument **9.** principal **11.** mischievous
arch (pert to) ...
enemy .. **5.** devil, Satan **9.** adversary
inner curve .. **8.** intrados
memorial .. **6.** pailou (pailoo)
stone .. **8.** keystone
title .. **4.** duke **6.** bishop, deacon **7.** duchess
archaic ... **3.** old **8.** obsolete, old-world **10.** antiquated **12.** old-fashioned
archangel (celestial) ... **5.** Uriel **7.** Gabriel, Michael, Raphael
archangel plant ... **4.** mint **8.** angelica
archbishop ... **6.** bishop (chief), exarch **9.** patriarch
arched ... **6.** curved **7.** embowed
Archer (Astron) ... **11.** Sagittarius
archery ... **3.** bow **4.** vane **5.** arrow, clout **6.** quiver **8.** fistmele, shooting **10.** ballistics
archetype ... **4.** idea **5.** model **7.** pattern **8.** standard **9.** prototype
Archie (sl) ... **3.** gun **12.** antiaircraft
Archipelago (pert to) ...
Alaska .. **9.** Alexander
Australia .. **8.** Bismarck
Indonesia (largest) .. **5.** Malay
Italy .. **6.** Aegean
architect ... **6.** artist, author **7.** builder, planner **8.** designer **9.** artificer, draftsman **11.** constructor, enterpriser
architectural (pert to) ...
arch .. **8.** keystone, voussoir
base .. **5.** socle **6.** plinth
construction .. **8.** tectonic
ornament (part) .. **5.** gutta **6.** bezant, finial, frieze **8.** acanthus, dosseret, fretwork **10.** chambranle
pier .. **4.** anta
space (triang) .. **8.** pediment
style .. **5.** Doric, Greek, Ionic, Tudor **6.** Gothic **7.** Baroque, Cape Cod, Moorish, Spanish **8.** Colonial, Etruscan, Georgian **9.** Byzantine, Palladian **10.** Corinthian, Romanesque **11.** Renaissance **13.** Mediterranean
archives ... **6.** annals **7.** records **8.** chancery, registry **9.** documents, registers **10.** chronicles
arch traitor ... **6.** Arnold (Benedict), Brutus **8.** Quisling **13.** Judas Iscariot
archway ... **6.** pailou (pailoo)
arctic ... **5.** polar **6.** boreal, frigid, galosh **7.** Alaskan **8.** hibernal, Northern, Siberian **11.** hyperborean
Arctic (pert to) ...
base .. **4.** Etah (Greenland)
bird .. **3.** auk **4.** xema **6.** falcon

cetacean .. **7.** narwhal
current .. **8.** Labrador
dog .. **5.** Husky (Siberian) **8.** Malemute
food .. **8.** pemmican (pemican)
jacket (hooded) .. **5.** parka (parkee) **6.** anorak
native .. **5.** Aleut **6.** Eskimo, Indian
polar .. **6.** Circle
sea .. **7.** Barents **8.** Beaufort
arctoid ... **6.** ursine **8.** bearlike
Arctoidea ... **4.** bear **6.** weasel **7.** raccoon
ardent ... **3.** hot **4.** avid, keen, warm **5.** eager, fiery, rethe **6.** fervid, fierce **7.** amorous, cordial, fervent, flaming, glowing, intense, shining, violent, zealous **8.** eloquent, vehement **10.** passionate **12.** affectionate, enthusiastic
ardilla ... **8.** squirrel
ardor ... **4.** élan, fire, heat, love, zeal **5.** estro, flame, gusto, verve **6.** fervor, fougue, spirit, warmth **8.** fervency **9.** affection, eagerness, eloquence, intensity **10.** enthusiasm **11.** impetuosity
arduous ... **4.** hard **5.** steep **6.** trying **7.** onerous **8.** toilsome **9.** difficult, laborious, strenuous, wearisome **10.** burdensome, exhausting
area ... **4.** belt, loci (pl), size, zone **5.** areal, basin, field, locus, range, scope, space, tract **6.** extent, locale, region, sector, sphere **7.** circuit, compass, environ, expanse **8.** province, vicinity **9.** bailiwick, territory **12.** neighborhood
Areca ... **4.** palm
arena ... **4.** bowl, oval, ring, rink **5.** court, field **6.** campus, circus **7.** cockpit, stadium, theater **8.** coliseum, platform **9.** gymnasium **10.** hippodrome **12.** amphitheater
arenose ... **5.** sandy **6.** grainy, gritty **8.** sabulous
areola ... **4.** halo, ring **5.** space **6.** armlet, wreath **7.** aureole, garland **10.** interstice
Ares (pert to) ...
consort .. **9.** Aphrodite
father .. **4.** Zeus
god .. **3.** war
Roman name .. **4.** Mars
argala ... **7.** marabou **8.** adjutant (bird)
argent ... **5.** white **6.** silver **7.** shining, silvery **9.** whiteness
Argentina ...
capital .. **11.** Buenos Aires (1535)
city .. **5.** Lanus **6.** Paraná **7.** Cordoba, Mendoza, Rosario
Indian .. **4.** Lule
mountain .. **5.** Andes **9.** Aconcagua (peak) **10.** Cordillera (Range)
native .. **7.** Mestizo
Plains .. **6.** Pampas **9.** Gran Chaco
plateau .. **9.** Patagonia
poet .. **7.** Andrade **10.** Echeverria
river .. **5.** Plata **6.** Chubut, Paraná
Argentine (pert to) ...
color .. **7.** silvery **8.** art brown
cowboy .. **6.** gaucho
dance .. **5.** tango

Argonauts (pert to) . . .
destination . . 7. Colchis (anc)
heroes (50) . . 6. Jason's
objective . . 12. Golden Fleece
of '49 . . 6. miners (gold)
ship . . 5. Argos
Argos . . . 3. dog (of Odysseus)
argosy . . . 4. ship 5. fleet 6. armada,
  vessel 8. flotilla
argot . . . 4. cant, jive 5. lingo, slang
  6. jargon, patois 7. dialect
  10. vernacular
argue . . . 3. rap 4. moot, spar
  5. plead, prove 6. bicker, debate,
  evince, reason 7. contend, contest,
  discuss, dispute, wrangle 8. indicate,
  maintain, persuade 10. controvert
  11. expostulate, ratiocinate,
  remonstrate
argument . . . 4. case, plea, spar
  5. cavil, lemma, proof, theme
  6. debate, hassle 7. defense, dispute,
  fallacy, polemic, premise, sophism
  8. brouhaha, squabble 9. dialectic,
  discourse, enthymeme, pro and con
  10. discussion 11. altercation,
  disputation 13. consideration,
  ratiocination
argumentative . . . 7. eristic 8. forensic
  10. indicative, rhetorical
  11. belligerent, contentious,
  presumptive, quarrelsome
  12. disputatious 13. controversial
Argus (Gr Myth) . . . 7. monster (founder
  of Argos)
Argus–eyed . . . 8. vigilant 9. observant
  11. hundred–eyed 12. sharpsighted
argute . . . 5. acute, sharp 6. astute,
  shrewd, shrill, subtle 9. sagacious
aria . . . 3. air, lay 4. solo, song, tune
  5. canto 6. cantus, melody, strain
  7. ariette, sortita
arid . . . 3. dry 4. dull 6. barren, jejune,
  vacant 7. parched, sterile, thirsty
  9. anhydrous, waterless
  13. unimaginative
Arid Austral zone . . . 7. Sonoran
Ariel . . . 5. angel, sylph 6. spirit
  7. lioness 9. Jerusalem
ariel . . . 7. gazelle
Aries (Astron) . . . 3. ram 4. sign
  6. meteor 13. constellation
aries . . . 12. battering–ram (anc)
aright . . . 4. fine, well 7. exactly
  8. directly, straight 11. straightway
aril . . . 3. pod 7. arillus, coating
  8. arillode (false), covering
Arion . . . 4. poet (of Lesbos) 5. horse
  (talking)
arioso . . . 7. melodic, tuneful
  9. melodious
arise . . . 4. lift, rise, soar, stem, zoom
  5. begin, issue, mount, occur, rebel,
  surge, tower, waken 6. appear,
  ascend, emerge, revolt, spring
  7. emanate 9. originate
Aristarch . . . 6. critic 10. grammarian
Aristides . . . 7. The Just 9. statesman
  (Athens)
aristocracy . . . 5. elite 7. peerage,
  royalty 8. nobility 10. government,
  patriciate, upper class

aristocrat . . . 4. lord, peer 5. noble
  7. aristos, Brahman, Brahmin,
  grandee, parvenu 8. cavalier, eupatrid
  (Athens), nobleman 9. blueblood,
  patrician 12. silk–stocking
aristology, science of . . . 6. dining
Aristotle (pert to) . . .
birthplace . . 6. Thrace 7. Stagira
  (Macedonia)
famed as . . 9. scientist
  11. philosopher 12. The Stagirite
school . . 6. Athens
teacher . . 5. Plato
wife . . 7. Pythias
arithmetic . . . 4. sums 7. numbers
  11. computation, enumeration,
  mathematics
arithmetic terms . . . 5. prime 6. result
  7. divisor, product 8. dividend,
  multiple, quotient 9. remainder
  10. multiplier 12. multiplicand
Arizona . . .
capital . . 7. Phoenix
city . . 4. Yuma 5. Tempe 6. Bisbee,
  Tucson
famed site . . 9. Hoover Dam
  11. Grand Canyon 13. Painted
  Desert 15. Petrified Forest
Indian . . 4. Hano, Hopi, Pima
  6. Apache, Navaho (Navajo)
river . . 4. Gila 8. Colorado
State admission . . 11. Forty–eighth
State bird . . 10. cactus wren
State flower . . 6. cactus 7. saguaro
State motto . . 9. Ditat Deus 11. God
  Enriches
State nickname . . 11. Grand Canyon
ark . . . 3. vat 4. boat, ship 5. chest,
  haven 6. asylum, refuge, vessel
  8. flatboat 9. broadhorn, sanctuary
  (Ararat)
Arkansas . . .
capital . . 10. Little Rock
city . . 8. El Dorado 9. Fort Smith
famed for . . 8. diamonds (found in
  Murfreesboro)
famed newspaper . . 7. Gazette (1819)
mountain . . 6. Ozarks 9. Ouachitas
Park (Nat) . . 10. Hot Springs
river . . 5. White 11. Mississippi
State admission . . 11. Twenty–fifth
State bird . . 11. mockingbird
State flower . . 12. apple blossom
State motto . . 13. Regnat Populus
  16. Let the People Rule
State nickname . . 19. Land of
  Opportunity
arm . . . 4. limb 5. equip, saber, sword
  6. branch, member, pistol, tappet,
  weapon 7. forearm, fortify, protect,
  quillon (of sword), support 8. revolver
  9. appendage 10. projection
  12. ramification
arm (pert to) . . .
armpit . . 5. oxter 6. axilla
bone . . 4. ulna 6. radius 7. humerus
hole . . 4. scye (of sleeve)
muscle . . 6. biceps 7. triceps
projection . . 6. tappet
sea . . 4. gulf, mere 5. bayou, firth,
  inlet 7. estuary
sundial . . 6. gnomon

walk arm in arm.. 5. oxter
armada... 5. fleet 6. argosy
   8. armament, flotilla, squadron,
   warships 10. escadrille
Armada (famed)... 7. Spanish (1588)
   10. Invincible
armadillo... 4. apar, peba (peva)
   5. apara, poyou, tatou (tatu)
   6. mulita, peludo (giant) 7. tatouay
   10. pichiciago, Tolypeutes
   11. quirquincho (hairy)
Armageddon... 3. war 7. Megiddo
   (Bib) 8. conflict, world war
armed... 6. fitted, rigged 7. clothed,
   endowed 8. equipped, invested,
   prepared, provided, supplied
   9. furnished, outfitted 10. laquearian
   (with noose)
armed (pert to)...
  conflict.. 3. war 6. combat 7. warfare
   11. hostilities
  forces.. 4. army, host 5. ranks
   6. troops 8. military 9. besiegers
  vessel.. 3. HMS, sub, USS 5. U–boat
   9. destroyer, submarine
   10. battleship 11. battlewagon
Armenia...
  anc name.. 9. Armenenak
  capital.. 6. Erivan
  founder.. 4. Haik
  herb.. 5. cumin 7. caraway
  highlanders.. 5. Gomer
  mountain.. 6. Ararat, Taurus
  river.. 3. Kur 5. Cyrus 6. Araxes,
   Tigris 9. Euphrates
  worshiper.. 7. Yesidio (Yesdi)
   9. Gregorian
armistice... 5. peace, truce
   9. cessation 12. pacification
armoire... 5. ambry 8. cupboard,
   wardrobe 10. repository
armor... 4. arms, bard (barde), egis,
   jamb, mail, tace 5. acton, aegis,
   plate, seton, tasse 6. cuisse, gorget,
   graith, greave, helmet, lorica, sconce,
   shield, tasset, tuille 7. ailette,
   cuirass, hauberk, jambeau, panoply
   8. aventail, brassort, ordnance,
   pallette, solleret 9. cubitiere,
   epauliere, gardebras, mainferre,
   rerebrace 10. cataphract
armor–bearer... 6. squire 7. armiger,
   esquire
armored... 6. mailed 8. equipped,
   ironclad, mailclad 9. cuirassed,
   loricated, panoplied
armpit... 5. oxter 6. axilla
arms... 7. weapons 8. armament,
   ordnance 9. munitions
arms depository... 5. depot 6. armory
   7. arsenal
army... 3. mob 4. host, unit 5. array,
   crowd, horde, posse 6. forces,
   galaxy, legion, rabble, throng, troops
   9. multitude, Salvation
army (pert to)...
  brown.. 7. rosario
  commission (special).. 6. brevet
  trader.. 6. sutler
army unit... 4. ROTC 5. corps, guard
   (Nat) squad 7. brigade, cavalry,
   company, militia, platoon, Sabaoth

   (Bib) 8. division, infantry, Landwehr,
   regiment, reserves 9. artillery,
   minutemen 10. volunteers
Arnold's co–conspirator... 5. Andre
   (Maj)
aroma... 4. musk, odor, tang 5. attar,
   balmy, nidor, savor, scent, smell,
   spice 6. flavor 7. bouquet, feature,
   incense, perfume 9. fragrance,
   muskiness, redolence 11. peculiarity,
   singularity
aromatic... 5. spicy 6. savory
   7. odorous, pungent 8. fragrant,
   redolent 11. fluorescent
aromatic (pert to)...
  gum.. 5. myrrh 12. frankincense
  herb.. 4. mint 5. clary, nondo
  oil.. 4. balm 6. balsam 9. sassafras
  seed.. 4. anis 6. nutmeg 7. aniseed
  tree.. 5. aromo 6. balsam
   7. champac 8. huisache
around... 4. near, peri (pref) 5. about,
   circa 9. bordering, somewhere
   11. thereabouts 13. approximately
arouse... 4. fire, stir, wake 5. alarm,
   anger, evoke, raise, rally, roust
   6. awaken, elicit, excite, incite,
   kindle, summon 7. animate
arpa... 4. harp
arpeggio... 5. chord 7. roulade
   8. division, flourish
arraign... 4. cite 6. accuse, charge,
   indict 7. impeach 8. denounce,
   reproach 9. prosecute
arrange... 3. fix 4. cast, cite, file,
   plan, plot, sort 5. adapt, aline,
   besee, drape, ettle, frame, grade,
   preen, range, stack 6. adjust, deploy,
   design, devise 7. dispose, mediate,
   prepare, provide, seriate 8. classify,
   contract, contrive, laminate, organize,
   tabulate 9. catalogue (catalog),
   negotiate 10. distribute, paniculate
   11. alphabetize, systematize
arranged... 5. fixed, timed 6. ranked,
   sorted 7. aligned, grouped, ordered,
   orderly, planned, settled, uniform
   9. regulated 10. contracted
arranged in...
  fives.. 7. quinate
  fours.. 11. tetramerous
  hours.. 9. staggered
  rays.. 9. radial
  threes.. 7. ternate
arrangement... 3. art, rig (sails)
   4. plan, rank 5. order, setup
   6. series, syntax, system 7. echelon
   (troops), musical 8. disposal,
   neatness, trimness 9. agreement,
   condition, structure 10. adaptation,
   engagement, settlement
   11. collocation, combination,
   permutation, preparation
   12. distribution
arrant... 3. bad 6. wicked 8. rascally
   9. confirmed, shameless
   11. unmitigated 12. disreputable
array... 3. don 4. deci, robe 5. adorn,
   align, dress, order 6. clothe, muster,
   series, throng 7. arrange, dispose,
   envelop, marshal 8. clothing,
   garments 9. adornment

11. arrangement
arrears... 3. due 4. debt 5. short
7. wanting 9. arrearage, deficient
10. behindhand, defaulting
arrest... 4. halt, hold, stop 5. check,
delay, seize 6. detain, hinder,
impede, retard 7. custody, seizure
8. obstruct, restrain, stoppage
9. apprehend, hindrance, intercept,
restraint 11. retardation
arrested... 6. behind 7. checked,
delayed, impeded, stopped
8. detained, retarded 10. restrained
11. intercepted
arrested development... 6. simple
7. dwarfed, idiotic, moronic
8. backward, retarded 10. half–witted
13. unintelligent
arrival... 5. comer (anc) 6. advent,
coming 7. landing 8. approach,
reaching 10. attainment, homecoming
11. achievement
arrive... 4. come 5. debus, reach
6. alight, debark, happen 7. detrain
9. disembark
arrogance... 5. pride 7. conceit,
disdain, hauteur 8. audacity,
rudeness, snobbery 9. brashness,
insolence, loftiness 10. effrontery
11. haughtiness 12. impertinence
arrogant... 4. bold, pert 5. cocky,
lofty, proud 6. lordly, uppish
7. forward 8. impudent, insolent
9. audacious, insulting, masterful,
presuming 10. disdainful
11. domineering, high–falutin,
impertinent, overbearing
12. contemptuous, contumelious,
presumptuous, supercilious
arrogate... 5. seize, usurp, wrest
6. assume 11. appropriate
arrow... 4. barb, dart, reed, vire
(feathered) 5. guide, shaft 6. finger
7. missile, pointer 10. guideboard
arrow (pert to)...
astronomy.. 7. Sagitta
bows.. 6. bowyer (maker, seller)
case.. 6. quiver
end.. 4. nock 9. arrowhead
feather (to).. 6. fletch
handle.. 5. stele
head.. 4. dart
poison.. 4. inee, upas 5. urali
6. curare, uzarin
poisoned.. 6. sumpit 8. sumpitan
propeller.. 3. bow
shape.. 6. beloid 9. cuneiform,
sagittate
stone.. 9. belemnite
variety.. 4. self 6. footed 7. chested
9. bobtailed
arrowroot... 3. pia 5. araru 6. ararao,
starch 7. Maranta
arroyo... 5. brook, creek 6. ravine,
stream 11. watercourse
arroz... 4. rice
arse... 4. butt, rump (vulgar)
8. buttocks 10. posterior
arsenal... 4. dump 5. depot, plant
6. armory 7. factory 8. magazine
10. depository, storehouse
arsis... 5. ictus 6. accent, stress (opp

of thesis), upbeat
arson... 7. burning, cautery
9. pyromania 12. incendiarism
art... 4. wile 5. cameo, craft, knack,
skill, taste, trade 6. design
7. calling, cartoon, cunning, drawing,
science 8. aptitude, artifice, artistry,
business, ceramics, drafting, intaglio,
painting, vocation 9. dexterity,
duplicate, engraving, ingenuity,
readiness, sculpture, sketching
10. adroitness, decoration, profession
11. contrivance, photography,
portraiture 12. architecture
art (pert to)...
addict.. 8. aesthete (esthete)
decoration.. 9. sgraffito
design.. 7. graphic
fancier.. 10. dilettante
gallery.. 5. salon
grotesque.. 11. incongruous
mystic.. 6. cabala
of assaying.. 8. docimasy
of discourse.. 8. rhetoric
of embossing.. 9. toreutics
of government.. 8. politics
of horsemanship.. 6. manège
of imitation.. 7. mimicry
of manual craft.. 5. sloyd
of memory.. 10. mneumonics
of metal inlay.. 6. niello
primitive.. 9. artifacts
realistic.. 5. genre
rhyming.. 5. poesy 6. poetry
self–defense.. 6. boxing 7. fencing,
jujitsu (jiujitsu)
style.. 6. cubism, purism 7. baroque,
Dadaism, Fauvism 8. futurism
9. modernism 10. surrealism
13. impressionism
theme.. 5. motif
tooling.. 10. diesinking
transmutation.. 7. alchemy
Artemis (pert to)...
brother (twin).. 6. Apollo
epithet (Homeric).. 6. Phoebe
father.. 4. Zeus
goddess of.. 4. moon 6. nature
7. the Hunt 8. Olympian
Mother.. 4. Leto
religion.. 4. Upis
Roman equivalent.. 5. Diana
artery... 4. tube, vein 6. avenue,
street, vessel 7. channel, highway,
passage 8. ligament 10. passageway
artery (Anat)... 4. tube, vein 5. aorta
6. vessel 7. anonyma, carotid,
trachea 9. capillary, pulmonary
10. innominate
artery pulsation... 4. beat 5. ictus
artful... 3. sly 4. foxy, wily 5. cagey
6. adroit, clever, crafty, shrewd,
subtle, tricky 7. crooked, cunning,
knowing, politic 8. skillful, stealthy
9. deceitful, deceptive, designing,
dexterous, imitative 10. artificial
Artful Dodger... 3. fox 6. rascal
7. slicker 8. deceiver 11. John
Dawkins (Dickens tale) 12. crafty
person
artfulness... 5. skill 7. finesse
8. artifice, subtlety, wiliness

9. stratagem 10. cleverness,
refinement, shrewdness
arthron... 5. hinge, joint, pivot
12. articulation
Arthurian abode... 6. Avalon
9. Lyonnesse (Leonnoys)
Arthurian character... 6. Arthur (King),
Elaine, Merlin 7. Geraint 8. Lancelot
9. Percivale
artichoke... 6. canada, Cynara
7. chorogi, thistle 9. Jerusalem
article... 3. mat 4. item, news, term
5. scoop, story, thing 6. belief,
clause, detail, gadget, object, treaty
7. camelot, feature (news), grammar,
integer 8. treatise 9. commodity,
editorial 10. particular
11. composition, stipulation
article (Gram)...
English.. 1. a 2. an 3. the
French.. 2. la, le, un 3. les, une
Spanish.. 2. el, un 3. las, los, una
article (of)...
agreement.. 8. contract
apparel.. 5. smock, tunic 6. duster,
gaiter, mantle 8. pinafore
faith.. 5. canon, creed, dogma, tenet
6. belief 7. precept
property.. 7. chattel
virtu.. 5. curio, relic 6. rarity
7. antique
articulation... 4. tone 5. hinge, joint,
sound, voice 7. voicing 8. locution,
sonation 9. phonation, utterance
11. enunciation 12. vocalization
13. pronunciation
artifact... 5. curio, relic, virtu 6. fossil
7. antique, remains 8. archaism
artifice... 4. plot, ruse, wile 5. blind,
chest, craft, dodge, fraud, guile,
shift, trick 6. deceit 7. cunning,
evasion, finesse, knavery, sleight
8. intrigue, maneuver, trickery
9. chicanery, collusion, deception,
expedient, imposture, stratagem
10. connivance, imposition,
subterfuge 11. contrivance,
machination, skulduggery
artificer... 5. smith 6. artist, framer
7. artisan, creator, deviser, workman
8. Daedalus, inventor, mechanic
9. architect, carpenter, craftsman,
goldsmith 11. coppersmith,
silversmith
artificial... 4. fake, mock, sham
5. bogus, dummy, false, phony
6. ersatz, forged, unreal 7. assumed,
bastard, elegant, feigned 8. affected,
fabulous, spurious 9. imaginary,
imitation, pretended, unnatural
11. adulterated, counterfeit,
unauthentic 12. supposititious
artificial (pert to)...
butter.. 4. oleo 13. oleomargarine
channel.. 3. gat 4. leat 5. canal,
flume 6. sluice
gum.. 7. dextrin
language.. 2. ro 3. Ido 5. Arulo
7. Volapuk 9. Esperanto
10. Occidental
silk.. 5. nylon, rayon
surface.. 4. rink

voice.. 8. falsetto
artillery... 4. army, guns 5. bombs
6. cannon, slings 7. cavalry,
gunners, gunnery, mortars
8. ordnance 9. arbalests, catapults
10. ballistics
artillery (pert to)...
emplacement.. 7. battery
fire.. 5. salvo 6. rafale
man.. 6. gunner 8. rifleman, topechee
9. cannoneer, musketeer
11. artillarist
wagon.. 7. battery
artiodactyl... (opp of perissodactyl)
2. ox 3. pig 4. deer, goat 5. camel,
sheep 6. artiad 7. giraffe
12. hippopotamus
artisan... 6. artist, limner 7. painter,
workman 8. mechanic, virtuoso
9. artificer, craftsman
artist... 5. rapin (Fr pupil) 6. etcher,
limner, potter 7. artisan, painter
8. designer, sculptor 9. architect,
decorator 10. cartoonist, ceramacist
11. illustrator 12. photographer
artist (pert to)...
equipment.. 5. easel 7. palette
8. maquette
sleight of hand.. 4. mage 5. Magus
8. magician 9. alchemist
artiste... 5. actor, adept 6. dancer,
singer 7. artisan 8. musician
9. performer
artistic... 4. pure 6. ornate 7. classic
8. graceful, skillful, tasteful
9. aesthetic (esthetic), art—minded,
beautiful, exquisite
artistic (pert to)...
ardor.. 5. verve 6. spirit
dance.. 6. ballet
quality.. 6. virtue
symbol of the dead.. 5. orant
temperament.. 7. caprice, emotion
artless... 4. naif, open, rude 5. frank,
naive 6. candid, simple 7. natural,
sincere 8. ignorant 9. guileness,
ingenuous, unskilled 10. inartistic,
unaffected, uncultured
11. undesigning 15. unsophisticated
artlessness... 6. candor 7. naiveté
9. frankness, innocence
11. naturalness 13. ungenuousness
arts (pert to)...
liberal.. 7. trivium 10. quadrivium
quadrivium.. 5. music 8. geometry
9. astronomy 10. arithmetic
trivium.. 5. logic 7. grammar
8. rhetoric
aru... 6. indeed, really
arui... 5. oudad, sheep 7. chamois
(Bib)
arum... 4. taro 5. calla (lily) 6. starch
9. arrowroot
arx... 7. citadel
Aryan (pert to)...
God of Fire.. 4. Agni
invader.. 4. Pict
people.. 4. Mede 5. Hindu
9. Caucasian 11. Indo—Iranian
as... 3. qua 4. como, than, thus
5. since, while 7. because, equally,
similar 9. similarly

Asa... 11. King of Judah
asafetida... 8. medicine
   13. antispasmodic
Asa's son... 11. Jehoshaphat
ascend... 3. fly 4. rise, soar, upgo
   5. arise, climb, mount, scale, tower
   6. aspire, uprise 7. clamber, upsurge
ascendancy... 4. sway 7. control,
   mastery 8. dominion, prestige,
   priority 9. authority, influence,
   supremacy 10. domination
   11. sovereignty, superiority
   12. predominance 13. preponderance
ascendant, ascendent... 5. elder
   6. father 7. supreme 8. ancestor,
   forebear, superior 9. governing,
   patriarch 10. antecedent, decoration
   (Arch)
ascended... 4. rose 5. arose, risen
   6. uprose
ascending... 6. anodic, rising
   7. scaling, sloping 8. mounting,
   racemose 9. emanating
ascending signs... 5. Aries 6. Gemini,
   Pisces, Taurus 8. Aquarius
   9. Capricorn
ascenseur... 8. elevator
Ascension Day... 8. Thursday (Holy),
   (40 days after Easter)
Ascension lily... 7. Madonna
ascertain... 4. find 5. learn, prove,
   solve 6. decide 7. certify
   9. determine
ascetic... 4. yati, yoga, yogi 5. fakir,
   stoic 6. Essene, hermit, strict
   7. austere, eremite, puritan, recluse
   8. anchoret, Diogenes, solitary
   9. abstainer, anchorite, mendicant
   10. abstemious
asceticism... 4. Yoga 9. austerity,
   nephalism 10. abstention, abstinence,
   puritanism 11. anchoritism,
   teetotalism
ascribable... 3. due 9. traceable
   10. assignable 11. attributive
   12. attributable
ascribe... 5. count, refer 6. assign,
   attach, credit, impute, reckon
   7. ascribe 8. accredit 9. attribute
ascus fruit... 8. truffles
asepsis... 6. purity 7. clarity 9. sterility
   13. taintlessness
ash... 4. sorb, tree 5. rowan
   6. samara (fruit) 8. Fraxinus
ashes... 4. dust, lava, lees, slag
   5. dregs, ruins 6. embers
   7. cinders, residue
ash tree symbol (Norse Myth)...
   10. Yggdrasill (horse of Yggr)
Asia... 4. East 6. Orient, region 7. Far
   East 8. Old World 9. continent
Asia Minor...
  city (anc).. 4. Myra, Teos, Troy
   5. Ilium, Issus, Lydia 6. Nicaea,
   Sardes 7. Ephesus
  district.. 4. Aria 5. Ionia, Troad (The
   Troad) 6. Aeolis
  island.. 6. Lesbos
  language (anc).. 6. Lycian, Lydian
   8. Etruscan
  mountain.. 3. Ida
  old name.. 8. Anatolia

sea.. 5. Black 6. Aegean 7. Marmosa
   13. Mediterranean
Asiatic (pert to)...
  barbarian (anc).. 3. Hun 6. Vandal
  desert.. 4. Gobi
  gulf.. 4. Aden, Oman, Siam 6. Tonkin
   7. Persian
  island.. 4. Java 5. Luzon, Malay
   7. Celebes, Diomede (Big), Formosa,
   Sumatra 8. Japanese, Mindanao,
   Sakhalin 11. Philippines
  mountain.. 4. Ural 5. Altai, Sayan
   7. Everest 8. Caucasus, Himalaya
   9. Hindu Kush
  native.. 4. Arab, Turk, Yuit 5. Tatar
   6. Indian, Innuit (Esk), Syrian
   7. Chinese, Malayan 8. Annamese,
   Japanese 9. Mongolian
  nomad.. 4. Arab
  river.. 2. Ob 4. Amur, Lena
   5. Hwang, Indus 6. Ganges
   7. Yangtze, Yenisei 9. Euphrates,
   Irrawaddy 11. Brahmaputra
  sea.. 4. Azov (Azof) 5. Black, China,
   Japan 6. Bering, Yellow 7. Caspian,
   Okhotsk
Asiatic animal...
  antelope.. 5. goral
  ass.. 6. onager
  camel.. 8. Bactrian 9. dromedary
  carnivore.. 5. panda, tiger
  cattle.. 4. zobo
  deer.. 4. axis 10. chevrotain
  elephant.. 7. Elephas
  fox.. 6. corsac
  gazelle.. 3. ahu
  goat.. 5. serow
  lemur.. 5. loris 6. macaco
  lynx.. 7. caracal
  mongoose.. 4. urva
  monkey.. 6. langur (long–tailed)
  ox.. 3. yak
  rodent.. 4. pika
  sheep.. 3. sha 5. uriel 6. argali
  squirrel.. 8. jelerang 10. polatouche
Asiatic bird...
  finch.. 9. brambling
  jay.. 7. sirgang
  owl.. 4. utum
  partridge.. 6. seesee
  plover.. 8. dotterel
  songless.. 5. Pitta
  talking.. 4. myna (mynah)
Asiatic snake... 3. asp 5. cobra
   8. ringhals
Asiatic storm (pert to)...
  sand.. 6. simoom (simoon) 7. tebbard
  snow.. 5. buran
  wind.. 5. buran 7. monsoon
aside... 4. away 5. apart, hence
   6. aslant, astray, beside 7. whisper
   8. sidewise 9. alongside, privately,
   sotto voce 12. interjection
asinine... 4. dumb 5. inane, inept, silly
   6. mulish, stupid 7. doltish, foolish,
   idiotic 9. obstinate
ask... 3. beg 4. quiz 5. claim, exact,
   query, speer 6. assess, demand,
   invite 7. beseech, entreat, implore,
   inquire, request, require, solicit
   8. petition, question 9. catechize,
   obsecrate (Relig) 11. interrogate

askance / assertiveness 40

askance . . . 4. awry 5. askew
7. asquint, crooked 8. sideways
9. obliquely
askew . . . 4. agee, alop, awry 5. agley,
amiss 6. faulty 7. askance, asquint,
crooked 8. deranged 9. distorted,
obliquely 10. catawampus, disorderly
aslant . . . 5. atilt 6. tilted, tipped
7. athwart, leaning, listing, pitched,
sloping 8. inclined 9. careening,
obliquely
asleep . . . 4. dead, dull, numb
7. dormant, unaware 8. deadened,
sleeping, unarisen 9. oblivious,
senseless, unruffled 10. motionless
11. inattentive, insensitive,
unconscious
Asoka's Empire (anc Ind) . . . 5. Patna
asp . . . 5. cobra, snake, viper 6. uraeus
(sacred sym)
aspect . . . 3. air 4. look, mien, pose,
side, view 5. angle, decil, facet,
guise, phase, shape, sight, state
6. decile, facies, status, visage
7. bearing, posture, scenery
8. attitude 9. astrology, component,
influence, seaminess, situation
10. appearance 11. countenance
aspen . . . 4. tree, wood 6. poplar
7. quaking 9. quivering, shivering,
trembling, tremulous, vibrating
asperge . . . 3. wet 4. damp 5. spray,
water 7. baptize 8. humidify, sprinkle
asperge . . . 9. asparagus
Asperges . . . 4. rite 6. anthem
10. sprinkling (altar)
aspergillum . . . 5. brush 7. sprayer
8. baptizer 9. sprinkler
asperity . . . 5. rigor 7. raucity
8. acerbity, acrimony, hardship,
severity, tartness 9. bleakness,
roughness 10. causticity, difficulty,
inclemency, moroseness, resentment
asperse . . . 4. slur 5. abuse, decry, libel
6. defame, malign, revile, vilify
7. blacken, slander, traduce
8. besmirch 9. bespatter, discredit
10. calumniate
aspersion . . . 4. rite, slur 6. insult
7. affront, baptism, calumny, outrage,
wetting 8. innuendo 9. indignity
10. defamation, sprinkling
12. calumniating, calumniation
13. disparagement
asphalt . . . 4. pave 5. pitch 7. bitumen,
mineral 8. blacktop, pavement,
uintaite 9. gilsonite 10. macadamize
asphyxia . . . 5. apnea (apnoea)
7. choking 11. suffocation
12. smotheration
aspic . . . 3. asp (poet) 5. jelly
6. cannon 8. lavender 9. galantine
aspiration . . . 3. aim 4. hope, wish
5. ideal 6. breath, desire
7. pumping, sucking, suction
8. ambition, staccato 9. breathing
10. exhalation 11. inspiration
aspire . . . 4. long, plan, rise, soar
5. tower 6. attain, desire, expect,
intend 7. breathe, propose
ass . . . 3. ono (comb form) 4. dolt,
dope, fool, jack 5. burro, jenny

assail . . . 4. pelt 5. beset, stone
6. attack 7. assault 9. implicate
11. incriminate
assailant . . . 3. foe 5. enemy 7. invader
8. assailer, attacker, opponent
9. adversary, aggressor
10. antagonist, challenger
Assam . . .
capital . . 8. Shillong
native . . 4. Ahom 8. Assamite
11. Indo–Chinese
province of . . 5. India
river . . 11. Brahmaputra
tribe . . 2. Ao 3. Aka 4. Garo, Naga
assassin . . . 4. Cain, thug 5. bravo
6. apache, cuttle, gunman, killer,
slayer 7. gorilla, ruffian 8. murderer,
sicarian 9. manslayer 11. slaughterer
assassination . . . 5. purge 6. murder
7. killing 8. regicide 11. liquidation
12. manslaughter
Assassin Order . . . 8. Ismalian
10. Mohammedan
assault . . . 5. onset, storm 6. assail,
attack, charge 7. descent, seizure
8. invasion 9. incursion
13. incrimination
assay . . . 3. try 4. test 5. prove, trial
6. accost 7. attempt 8. analysis,
docimasy (art), endeavor
10. experiment 12. verification
assay cup . . . 5. cupel
assemblage . . . 3. all 4. herd 6. throng
8. assembly, entirety 9. gathering
12. congregation
assemblage (pert to) . . .
cattle . . 5. drove, rodeo 7. roundup
fashionable . . 5. salon
mob . . 4. rout 6. rabble
splendid . . 6. galaxy
tents . . 4. camp 10. encampment
assemble . . . 3. pod 4. mass, meet
5. amass, piece, rally, unite
6. couple, gather, muster 7. cluster,
collect, convene, convoke, recruit
10. congregate
assembly . . . 4. bevy, diet, moot
5. agora, gemot, group, synod, troop
6. assize, sabbat 7. company,
council, landtag, meeting 8. auditory,
conclave (secret), folkmoot (Hist)
9. concourse, gathering
10. collection, convention
11. convocation 12. congregation
assent . . . 3. aye, nod, yea, yes
4. amen 5. admit, agree, grant
6. accede, accord, concur
7. consent 8. sanction 9. acquiesce,
agreement 10. compliance
12. acquiescence
assert . . . 3. say 4. aver, pose 5. claim,
plead, posit, state, voice 6. affirm,
allege, avouch, relate, uphold
7. contend, declare, profess, protest,
support 8. advocate 9. pronounce,
vindicate 10. asseverate
assertion . . . 5. claim 6. remark, thesis
7. premise 8. averment 9. statement
10. assumption, hypothesis
11. affirmation, declaration,
maintenance, proposition, vindication
assertiveness . . . 10. pragmatism

14. aggressiveness
assertor... 8. affirmer, defender
9. supporter 10. vindicator
assess... 3. ask, tax 4. cess, levy,
mise, rate 5. price, value 6. charge
7. measure 8. appraise, estimate
assessment... 3. fee, tax 4. levy, rate,
scot 5. ratal, stock, value 6. surtax
7. pricing, scutage 8. estimate
9. appraisal, valuation 10. evaluation
11. measurement
assets... 5. funds, means 6. wealth
7. capital 8. accounts, property
9. resources
asseverate... 3. say, vow 4. aver
5. state, swear 6. affirm, allege,
assert 7. contend, declare, profess,
protest 8. maintain 9. pronounce
asseveration... 3. vow 4. oath
(solemn) 8. averment 9. assertion
11. affirmation, declaration
13. pronouncement
assiduity... 8. industry 9. diligence
11. painstaking, persistence
12. perseverance
assiduous... 4. busy 6. active
7. intense, zealous 8. diligent,
sedulous 9. energetic, laborious,
unwearied 11. industrious,
perseverant 13. indefatigable,
unintermitted
assign... 3. fix, set 4. cast, cede, seal
5. allot, refer 6. allege, commit,
detail 7. address, adjudge, appoint,
ascribe, consign, empower
8. accredit, allocate, delegate,
nominate, transfer 9. attribute
10. commission 11. appropriate
assignment... 3. job 4. task 5. chore,
stint 6. lesson 7. mission
8. exercise, transfer 9. allotment
10. allocation, commission,
commitment 11. attribution
13. specification
assimilate... 5. adapt, learn, liken
6. absorb, digest, imbibe 7. convert
10. understand 11. approximate
assimilation... 8. imbibing, learning
9. anabolism, digestion, ingestion,
reduction 10. absorption, adaptation,
comparison, conversion
14. naturalization
assist... 3. aid 4. abet, back, help
5. avail, boost, favor 6. attend,
prompt, second, succor 7. benefit,
relieve, support, sustain 8. befriend
9. accompany, subsidize
assistance... 3. aid 4. help 5. grant
6. relief, succor 7. service, subsidy,
support 10. logrolling (Polit)
11. furtherance
assistant... 4. aide, ally 5. tutor
6. deputy, helper 7. abettor,
famulus, servant, teacher
9. associate, attendant, auxiliary
11. subordinate 12. right-hand man
assize... 3. fix 4. rate 5. edict, trial,
value 6. assess, decree 9. ordinance
10. regulation 11. instruction,
measurement
associate... 3. mix, pal 4. ally, chum,
mate 5. buddy, crony 6. fellow,

friend, hobnob, mingle 7. combine,
comrade, consort, partner
9. colleague, companion
10. accomplice 11. concomitant,
confederate
associated... 6. allied, banded, joined,
united 7. coupled, leagued, related
9. connected 10. affiliated,
concurrent
associates... 4. crew 5. force, staff
7. retinue 9. personnel
12. constituency
association... 4. body, club 5. artel,
cabal, guild, hanse (Hist), union
6. league, lyceum, symbol
7. company, society 8. alliance,
relation, sodality, sorority 9. syndicate
10. fellowship, fraternity
11. affiliation, combination,
comradeship, concurrence, corporation
13. communication, interrelation
assonance... 3. pun 4. rime 5. rhyme
8. paragram 9. agreement
11. paronomasia, resemblance
12. alliteration
assort... 4. sort, suit 5. adapt, class,
grade, group 7. consort (with)
8. classify, separate 9. associate
(with) 10. categorize, distribute
assortment... 3. mix, set 4. hash,
mess, olio 5. class, group 6. jumble,
medley 7. mélange, mixture, sorting
9. potpourri 10. collection,
hodgepodge, miscellany
11. arrangement 14. conglomeration
assuage... 4. calm, ease 5. allay, slake
6. lessen, mellow, pacify, quench,
soften, solace, soothe 7. appease,
comfort, gratify, qualify, relieve,
satisfy 8. mitigate, palliate
9. alleviate
assuasive... 5. balmy 6. easing
8. remedial, soothing 9. relieving,
softening 10. mitigating, palliative
11. alleviative 13. tranquilizing
assume... 3. don 4. deem, sham, take
5. adopt, feign, guess, imply, infer,
judge, think, usurp 6. affect, allege,
betake, borrow, deduce 7. believe,
imagine, premise, presume, pretend,
suppose, surmise 8. arrogate,
conclude, simulate 9. undertake
11. appropriate, counterfeit
assume (pert to)...
character.. 11. impersonate
different forms.. 7. protean
unduly.. 5. usurp 8. arrogate
without proof.. 11. theoretical
12. hypothetical
assumed... 6. deemed 7. alleged,
implied, thought 8. affected, inferred,
presumed, supposed 9. fictional,
pretended 10. fictitious, understood,
undertaken 11. conjectured,
make-believe, presumptive,
presupposed, theoretical
12. appropriated, hypothetical,
supposititious
assuming... 5. lofty 8. arrogant,
superior 9. presuming
10. assumptive 11. overweening,
pretentious 12. presumptuous

assumption... 8. adoption
9. arrogance, postulate, reception
10. usurpation 11. implication,
proposition, supposition
13. appropriation, incorporation
14. presupposition
assurance... 4. hope, oath 5. poise,
trust 6. aplomb, belief, pledge,
surety 7. comfort, courage, promise
8. security, sureness 9. certainty,
guarantee, impudence, insurance
10. confidence, steadiness
11. assuredness, intrepidity
12. cocksureness 14. self–confidence
assure... 4. aver 5. vouch 6. assert,
avouch, depose, ensure, insure,
secure 7. confirm, declare, protest,
satisfy 8. convince, embolden,
persuade, reassure 9. encourage,
guarantee 10. asseverate
Assyria...
capital.. 7. Nineveh
city.. 5. Calab (Bib) 9. Khorsabad
(ruins)
empire (anc).. 5. Assur (Ashur)
language.. 6. Semite 9. cuneiform
(written)
people.. 6. Semite 7. Amorite (Bib)
Assyrian god...
atmosphere.. 5. Hadad
fire.. 5. Nusku
hunt.. 7. Ninurta
moon.. 3. Sin
storm.. 2. Zu
sun.. 7. Shamash
war.. 6. Nergal 7. Ninurta
winds.. 4. Adad 5. Hadad
Assyrian goddess... 5. Nanai
6. Allatu, Ishtar 9. Sarpanitu
(Zirbanit)
Assyriology, science of... 8. language
11. antiquities
aster... 4. star 9. asterwort, karyaster
10. Carduaceae
asterisk... 4. mark (reference), star
6. accent, figure (star) 9. highlight
10. asteriskos (Eccl)
astern... 3. aft 4. baft, rear 5. abaft,
after 6. behind 8. hindward,
rearward, tailward
asteroid... 5. Ceres (largest) 6. planet
8. starlike 9. planetoid
Asteroidea... 8. starfish
astir... 2. up 5. about, afoot, eager
6. active, moving 8. stirring
11. forthcoming
as to... 7. apropos, suppose
9. regarding 10. concerning,
respecting
astonish... 4. stun 5. amaze, appal
7. astound, stagger, startle
8. bewilder, confound, surprise
9. overwhelm
astonishing... 7. amazing 8. fabulous
9. appalling, marvelous, wonderful
10. incredible, remarkable
astound... 4. stun 5. abash, amaze,
shock 6. appall (appal), dismay
7. stagger, stupefy 8. astonish,
surprise 10. disconcert
astounding... 8. horrible, shocking
9. appalling, frightful 10. horrendous,

horrifying 11. astonishing
astraddle... 7. astride 9. horseback,
pickaback (piggyback) 10. straddling
astral... 6. spirit, starry 7. stellar
8. sidereal, starlike 9. celestial
11. star–studded
astray... 4. lost 5. amiss, wrong
6. adrift, afield, erring 8. aberrate,
mistaken 9. erroneous 10. bewildered
astray, to go... 3. err, sin 4. mang,
rove 5. drift, lapse, stray 6. wander
7. deviate, digress 8. miscarry
9. backslide 10. misbelieve
astriction... 4. bond 7. binding
8. thirlage 9. fastening 10. litigation
11. confinement, contraction
12. constipation
astride... 8. straddle 9. astraddle,
horseback, pickaback (piggyback)
astringent... 4. acid, alum, sloe, sour
5. acerb, acrid, harsh, sapan, stern
6. tannin 7. austere, bitters, caustic,
pungent, rhatany (root), styptic
9. vitriolic 10. antiseptic
11. acrimonious, argentamine
12. constrictive
astrologer... 8. Chaldean 9. stargazer
11. astrologian, astromancer,
Nostradamus
astrology (pert to)... 5. house, signs
6. aspect, zodiac 7. mansion,
mundane 8. siderism 9. horoscope,
planetary 11. horoscopist
astronaut... 7. Martian 8. spaceman
9. cosmonaut, rocketeer
astronomer... 9. stargazer
11. uranologist 12. uranographer
13. meteorologist, uranographist
astronomer, famed... 6. Kepler
7. Galileo 12. Eratosthenes
astronomical... 4. huge, vast 5. large
6. cosmic, uranic 7. immense,
mammoth, Uranian 8. colossal,
empyreal, heavenly 9. celestial
10. prodigious, stupendous,
tremendous
astronomy (pert to)... 4. coma (the)
5. apsis, saros (Bab) 6. syzygy
7. almanac, apsides, azimuth,
gibbous 8. sidereal 9. idiometer,
insulated 11. debilissima
astute... 3. sly 4. keen, wily 5. acute,
canny, smart 6. artful, clever, crafty,
shrewd 7. cunning, skilled
9. insidious, sagacious 10. discerning
14. discriminating
asunder... 5. apart, cleft, split
6. atwain, halved 7. divided
9. disjoined, separated
as yet... 8. hitherto
asylum... 3. ark 4. home, jail, port
5. haven 6. harbor, refuge
7. retreat, shelter 9. hospitium,
infirmary, sanctuary 10. stronghold
11. institution
asymmetrical... 6. uneven, warped
7. twisted, unequal 9. contorted,
distorted 11. zygomorphic
16. disproportionate
at... 2. by, in 4. near, nigh 5. there
8. location, position 9. direction,
situation

at (pert to)...
great length.. 7. on and on
　9. tediously
home.. 2. in 4. here 9. en famille
last.. 3. end 7. finally 9. extremely
　10. ultimately
once.. 3. now 7. readily
the same time.. 6. coeval
　10. coetaneous 12. contemporary
atabal... 4. drum 5. tabor
　10. kettledrum
atabeg... 5. title 6. vizier
Atalanta (pert to)...
defeated in romantic race by..
　10. Hippomenes 17. three golden
　apples (Gr Myth)
famed.. 8. huntress
foe.. 9. Aphrodite
husband.. 8. Milanion
legend.. 8. Arcadian, Boeotian
atalaya... 10. watchtower
atap... 4. nipa, palm
atavism... 8. heredity 9. reversion
　10. regression
ate... 5. dined, fared 6. dieted,
　gnawed, supped
Ate... 7. goddess (of infatuation)
atelier... 5. easel 6. studio
　8. workshop
a tempo... 4. time
Aten (Egypt)... 9. solar disk
ates... 8. sweetsop
athanasia... 8. athanasy
　11. immortality 13. deathlessness
　15. imperishability
athanor (Fr)... 7. furnace (alchemist's)
Athapascan Indian... 5. Tinne
　6. Apache, Navaho (Navajo)
atheist... 5. pagan 7. heathen, infidel,
　nastika 8. agnostic 10. unbeliever
　11. disbeliever, unchristian
　13. antichristian
Athena (pert to)...
attributes.. 3. owl 5. aegis 7. serpent
festival.. 11. Panathenaea
Rom equivalent.. 7. Minerva
shrine.. 9. Parthenon (Athens)
Athena, goddess of...
arts, crafts.. 6. Ergane
health.. 6. Hygeia
horses, tamer of.. 6. Hippia
light.. 4. Alea
maid of Athens.. 12. Pallas Athene
poetry.. 6. Pallas
victory.. 4. Nike
wisdom.. 8. Palladis
Athenian (pert to)...
assembly.. 4. Pnyx
Bee.. 5. Plato
general.. 8. Xenophon
lawgiver.. 5. Draco, Solon
sculptor.. 7. Phidias
statesman.. 8. Pericles 9. Aristides
　(The Just) 10. Alcibiades
temple.. 11. Nike Apteros
Athens...
capital of.. 6. Attica (anc), Greece
citadel.. 9. Acropolis
magistrate.. 5. Draco, Solon
rival.. 6. Sparta (anc)
senate.. 5. boule
temple.. 9. Parthenon

Athens of...
America.. 6. Boston 9. Nashville (The
　South)
Ireland.. 4. Cork 7. Belfast
North.. 9. Edinburgh 10. Copenhagen
Switzerland.. 6. Zurich
West.. 7. Cordoba
athlete... 7. acrobat, gymnast, tumbler
　11. funambulist, palaestrian,
　pancratiast 13. contortionist
athlete (pert to)...
foot disease.. 15. dermatophytosis
of Christendom.. 10. Scanderbeg
portico (Gr, Rom).. 6. xystus (xyst)
athletic... 5. lusty, thewy, yauld
　6. brawny, robust, sinewy, strong
　8. muscular, stalwart, vigorous
　9. acrobatic, agonistic, gymnastic
　10. palaestral (palestral)
　15. broad–shouldered
athwart... 6. across, aslant
　8. sideways, sidewise, traverse
　9. crosswise, obliquely
　10. crisscross, perversely
atimon... 9. muskmelon
Atlantean... 6. strong 7. titanic
　8. gigantic 9. Atlaslike
　10. Gargantuan
atlantes (opp of caryatids)...
　7. columns (carved men)
　9. telamones
Atlantic Sisters (Gr)... 8. Pleiades
　(stars)
Atlas (pert to)...
converted into.. 7. Mt Atlas
daughter.. 7. Calypso 8. Pleiades
famed as a.. 5. giant, Titan
king of.. 10. Mauretania
mother.. 4. Asia 7. Clymene
supporter of.. 5. earth 10. the
　heavens
Atman (Hind)... 3. ego 4. Self, Soul
　6. Brahma
atmosphere... 3. air 4. aura, mood
　5. ether, ozone 7. climate
　10. aerosphere, background
　11. environment, hydrosphere
atmosphere (pert to)...
condition.. 9. epedaphic
density.. 8. isostere, isoteric
disturbance.. 5. storm 6. static
　9. tornadoes, whirlwind
pressure.. 10. barometric
shooting star.. 6. meteor
spectrum.. 7. rainbow
atole... 5. gruel 8. porridge
atoll... 4. belt, reef (coral) 6. island
atom... 3. ace, bit, ion, jot 4. gram,
　iota, mite, whit 5. monad
　8. molecule, particle 9. corpuscle
atomic... 3. Age, ray 4. beam, bomb,
　tiny 5. power 6. energy, minute,
　number, radius, weight 7. nuclear
　9. atomistic, molecular, radiation
　10. intangible 11. microscopic
　13. infinitesimal
atomic submarine... 5. Skate 6. Triton
　8. Nautilus, Thresher 9. Sea Dragon
atomize... 4. fume 5. smash, spray
　6. aerate, gasify 7. fission, perfume,
　shatter 8. dissolve, fumigate, nucleize
　9. carbonate, decompose, evaporate,

micronize, pulverize 11. disorganize
12. disintegrate
atomy... 4. atom, mote 5. dwarf,
pygmy 6. droich, midget 8. skeleton
10. micromorph
atonement... 6. amends 7. apology,
penance, redress 8. requital
10. recompense, redemption,
reparation 11. reclamation, restitution
12. propitiation 15. indemnification
Atreus (pert to)...
brother.. 8. Thyestes
father.. 6. Pelops
king of.. 7. Mycenae
mother.. 10. Hippodamia
slayer of.. 12. Thyestes' sons
son.. 8. Menelaus 9. Agamemnon
wife.. 6. Aerope
atrium... 4. hall, room 5. court (inner)
6. cavity (Anat) 7. chamber
9. peristyle
atrocious... 4. rank, vile 5. awful,
cruel, grave 6. brutal, savage, sinful,
wicked 7. heinous, vicious, violent
8. dreadful, flagrant, horrible,
infamous, ruthless, shocking, terrible,
wretched 9. monstrous, nefarious
10. abominable, deplorable,
detestable, outrageous
atrociousness... 8. baseness, vileness
12. dreadfulness, shamefulness
13. nefariousness 15. Schrecklichkeit
atrocity... 4. evil, harm 5. abuse,
havoc, wrong 7. misdeed, outrage
8. enormity 9. indignity
12. mistreatment
atrophy... 5. tabes 7. disease
8. marasmus 10. emaciation
11. attenuation
Atropos (Gr)... 7. goddess (Fate)
attach... 3. add, fix, pin, put, tag, tie
4. bind, glue, join, vest 5. affix,
annex, hitch, paste, seize, unite
6. append, assign, fasten 7. ascribe,
connect, postfix, subjoin 9. associate,
attribute 11. superimpose
attached... 4. fond 6. adnate, welded
7. annexed, devoted, engaged,
sessile (Bot), smitten 8. cemented,
enamored
attachment... 4. bond, love 5. fancy
6. liking, regard 7. adjunct, fixture
8. addition, devotion, fidelity,
fondness 9. accession, adherence,
affection, fastening, increment
10. annexation 11. attribution
12. augmentation
attack... 3. fit 4. pang, raid 5. beset,
blitz, drive, feint, ictus, onset, sally,
siege, spasm 6. affret, assail, charge,
onrush, oppugn, sortie 7. aggress,
assault, bowling, descent, offense,
seizure 8. camisado (anc), paroxysm,
sickness 9. offensive, onslaught
10. aggression 11. enunciation
13. incrimination
attain... 2. do 3. get, win 4. earn,
gain 5. enact, reach 6. accede,
arrive, effect, obtain 7. achieve,
acquire, compass, fulfill, perform,
realize 9. discharge 10. accomplish,
consummate

attainable... 8. gettable 9. available
10. achievable
attainment... 5. skill 7. arrival
8. learning 9. accession
11. acquirement, acquisition,
cultivation, edification, realization
14. accomplishment
attar... 4. otto 5. scent 6. parfum
7. essence, perfume, rose oil
attempt... 3. aim, jab (sl), try 4. dare,
seek, stab 5. assay, ensue, essay,
fling, offer, onset, siege, trial
6. attack, effort, result 7. venture
8. endeavor 9. undertake
attend... 4. hark, heed, help, mind,
note, tend, wait 5. ensue, nurse,
serve, treat, visit 6. doctor, escort,
follow, foster, listen, result
7. conduct, hearken, nurture, observe
9. accompany
attendance... 4. draw 5. court
7. service, turnout 8. presence,
tendance 9. following
13. accompaniment
attendant... 4. maid, page 5. nurse,
staff, usher 6. caddie, escort, gillie,
porter, waiter 7. bellboy, orderly
8. follower 9. associate, attending,
companion 10. subsequent
11. concomitant, ministering
attendants, train of... 5. suite
7. cortege, retinue 9. entourage
attention... 3. ear 4. care, heed, hist,
note 6. notice, regard 7. concern,
hearing, respect, thought 8. courtesy
11. mindfulness 13. concentration,
consideration
attentive... 5. alert, awake, eared
6. intent 7. careful, heedful, mindful
8. obedient, vigilant, watchful
9. courteous, listening, observant,
wide–awake 10. meticulous,
respectful 11. circumspect,
considerate, surveillant
attenuated... 3. cut 4. fine, rare, slim,
thin 6. svelte, wasted 7. diluted,
gracile, reduced, slender, thinned,
watered 8. lessened, rarefied,
weakened 9. decreased, emaciated
attest... 4. seal 5. vouch 6. adjure,
affirm, avouch, depose 7. certify,
testify, witness 8. evidence, indicate,
manifest 9. testimony 10. deposition
12. authenticate
attestation... 4. oath (solemn) 5. proof
6. avowal 8. swearing 9. assertion
10. allegation 11. affirmation,
certificate, declaration, testimonial
13. testification 14. authentication
attic... 3. top 4. dome, head, loft,
wall 6. belfry, garret 8. cockloft
Attic... 5. salty, witty 6. simple
7. elegant, refined 8. academic,
Athenian, tasteful 9. classical
10. Ciceronian
Attic (pert to)...
Bee.. 9. Sophocles (poet)
bird.. 11. nightingale (Milton)
Muse.. 8. Xenophon
native.. 8. Athenian
school.. 9. sculpture
Attica (pert to)...

capital of.. 6. Athens
state of.. 6. Greece (anc)
famed as.. 15. world's first city
Attila... 3. Hun (leader) 5. Etzel
(fabled) 12. Scourge of God
attitude... 3. air, set 4. pose, view
5. angle, slant, stand 7. bearing,
feeling, opinion, outlook, posture,
thought 8. position, reaction
9. arabesque (dance), sentiment,
viewpoint 10. estimation, impression
attitude (reverent)... 6. salaam
8. kneeling 9. obeisance
12. genuflection (genuflexion)
attorney... 6. lawyer 7. counsel,
pleader 9. barrister, counselor
(counsellor) 11. intercessor
attract... 4. bait, draw, lure, pull
5. charm, tempt 6. appeal, beckon,
enamor, engage, entice, invite
8. interest 9. captivate, fascinate,
influence, magnetize
attraction... 4. lure, pull, star
6. appeal 7. gravity 8. affinity,
headline, interest, penchant
9. magnetism, seduction
10. allurement 11. fascination
attractive... 4. cute 6. lovely, pretty,
taking 7. winsome 8. alluring,
engaging, fetching, graceful, magnetic
9. allicient, appealing, beauteous,
beautiful, desirable 10. attracting,
delightful 11. captivating, interesting
attractive and repellent...
10. ambivalent
attrahent... 6. magnet 7. drawing
8. sinapism (Med) 10. attracting
attribute... 3. owe 5. refer, trait
6. impute, nature, symbol 7. ascribe,
feature, quality 8. property
9. adjective, qualifier, specialty
attrition... 4. wear 5. grief (Theol)
7. massage 8. abrasion, friction,
limation 9. detrition 10. contrition
attune... 4. tune 5. chime 6. accord,
adjust 7. concord, harmony, syntony
9. melodious 10. symphonize
11. concordance
atwain... 7. asunder
atweel... 5. truly 6. surely
aubade (Fr)... 3. lay 4. poem, song
6. ballad 7. concert (morning)
8. serenade
auberge... 3. inn
aubergiste... 9. innkeeper
auction... 3. bid 4. cant, roup, sale
5. block 6. vendue 7. bidding
auction (game)... 4. pool 5. pitch
6. bridge, euchre, hearts 8. pinochle
audacious... 4. bold 5. saucy
6. brazen, daring 7. defiant
8. impudent, insolent, intrepid,
spirited 9. barefaced, foolhardy,
insulting 11. adventurous,
challenging, impertinent, presumptive,
venturesome
audacity... 5. cheek, crust, nerve
6. daring 7. courage 8. defiance,
temerity 9. assurance, hardihood,
impudence, insolence, sauciness
10. effrontery, enterprise
11. presumption 12. impertinence

13. audaciousness, foolhardiness,
shamelessness
audible... 5. aloud, clear 8. distinct,
hearable 10. articulate
audible respiration... 4. sigh
audience... 3. ear 5. house, trial
6. parley, tryout 7. hearing, theater
8. audition, auditory, congress
9. interview, listeners 10. conference
12. congregation
audit... 5. check 6. reckon, verify
7. certify, collate 10. accounting
11. examination
auditor... 5. clerk 6. censor, hearer
7. actuary, apposer 8. examiner,
listener 10. accountant, bookkeeper
11. comptroller
auditorium... 4. hall, nave (anc)
5. house 7. theater 8. auditory,
building 9. Guildhall
auditory... 4. otic 5. audio, aural
6. phonic 7. hearers 8. audience
9. accoustic, auricular
12. congregation
au fait... 4. able 6. expert 7. equal to
8. informed, skillful 9. qualified
10. conversant (with)
au fond... 9. basically, primarily
11. essentially 13. fundamentally
auger... 3. bit 4. bore, tool 5. borer,
drill 6. gimlet, wimble 10. perforator
aught... 3. any 4. none, some, zero
5. ought 6. cipher 7. nothing
8. anything
augment... 3. add, eke 5. affix, annex,
exalt, swell 6. expand, extend
7. amplify, broaden, develop,
enhance, enlarge 8. increase
9. reinforce
Augsburg Church... 8. Lutheran
augur... 4. bode, omen, seer 5. sibyl,
vates (Gauls) 6. oracle 7. betoken,
presage 8. forebode, forecast,
foretell, forewarn, haruspex (Rom),
indicate, prophesy 10. anticipate,
astrologer, conjecture, soothsayer
13. prognosticate 14. prognosticator
augury... 4. omen, rite 7. auspice,
portent 8. ceremony
august... 5. awful, grand, novel, regal
6. sedate, solemn 7. courtly,
eminent, stately 8. imposing, majestic
9. dignified, honorable, important,
venerable 11. magnificent, ritualistic
12. aristocratic
August... 6. Lammas 8. Sextilis
10. First month (Rom year)
August meteor (11th of month)...
7. Perseid
auk... 4. Alca, Alle, bird (sea), falk
5. murre, noddy 6. auklet, rotche
(rotch) 7. Alcidae, dovekie
9. guillemot, razorbill
Auk... 6. Indian 7. Alaskan, Tlingit
(tribe) 9. Koluschan
aula... 4. hall, room 5. court
6. emblic (E Ind tree) 9. ventricle
aulos... 5. flute 8. woodwind
9. woodwinds (collectively)
aura... 3. air 4. halo, ring 6. astral,
circle, fringe (Psychol), nimbus
7. aureola 9. effluvium, emanation

10. atmosphere, exhalation
aureole... 4. halo 5. glory 6. circle, nimbus
auricle... 3. ear 4. lobe 5. pinna 6. atrium (heart) 9. appendage
auricular... 4. otic 5. aural, eared 6. phonic 8. acoustic, auditory
aurifex... 9. goldsmith
aurochs... 3. tur 4. goat, urus 5. bison
aurora... 3. eos 4. dawn 5. sunup 7. sunrise 8. borealis, daybreak, daylight 9. australis 11. polar lights
aurora borealis... 14. northern lights
auroral... 4. dawn, eoan, rosy 7. eastern, radiant, roseate
auspices... 3. aid 4. care, sign, wing 5. aegis (egis) 6. charge 7. backing, custody 8. guidance 9. patronage 10. management, protection 11. sponsorship, supervision
auspicious... 4. good 6. timely 9. favorable, fortunate, opportune 10. convenient, propitious, prosperous, seasonable 12. advantageous
Aussie... 6. digger 10. Australian
Auster... 9. southland, south wind
austere... 4. dour, hard 5. acrid, harsh, rigid, rough, stern 6. bitter, severe, strict 7. ascetic, pungent 8. exacting 10. astringent
Australasia... 7. Oceania 15. South Sea Islands
Australasian bird... 8. lorikeet 9. pardalote
Australia... see also *Australian*
capital.. 8. Canberra
desert.. 10. Great Sandy 13. Great Victoria
First Englishman (1688).. 14. William Dampier
holiday.. 13. Foundation Day (Jan 26)
island.. 8. Tasmania
mountain peak.. 9. Kosciusko
ocean.. 6. Indian
river.. 6. Murray
sea.. 5. Coral 6. Tasman
Tropic (southern).. 9. Capricorn
Australian (pert to)...
bee.. 5. karbi
bedroll.. 6. bindle 7. matilda
candy.. 5. lolly
feast.. 10. corroboree
fish.. 4. mako (shark) 5. yabby
flag.. 13. Southern Cross
flower.. 7. waratah (tulip) 9. rhodanthe
hut.. 6. miamia
native.. 5. myall 6. Aussie, binghi 8. kangaroo, warragal 9. aborigine, Dravidian
reptile.. 6. elapid, goanna, lizard (barking, frilled)
soldier.. 5. Anzac 6. digger
Australian animal...
dog (wild).. 5. dingo
horse (wild).. 6. brumby
sheep dog.. 6. kelpie
mammal.. 7. daysure 8. duckbill, platypus 9. blind mole
marsupial.. 4. tait 5. koala 6. wombat

7. echidna 8. anteater, kangaroo 9. phalanger, teddy bear 10. kookaburra 14. Tasmanian Devil
Australian bird... 3. emu, owl 4. lory, titi 5. arara, ariel, galah 6. leipoa, petrel 7. boobook, bustard, corella (parrot), grinder, rosella (parakeet) 8. ganggang, lorikeet, lyrebird, morepork, nightjar, paradise 9. bowerbird, cassowary, pardalote 10. flycatcher, goatsucker 11. budgereegah (parakeet)
Australian State capitals... 5. Perth 6. Darwin, Hobart, Sydney 8. Adelaide, Brisbane, Canberra (chief) 9. Melbourne
Australian tree... 4. teak, toon 5. belah, penda 6. jarrah, mallee, marara, she–oak, wattle 7. gunnung (mahogany) 8. Alstonia (dogbane), ironbark (eucalypt) 9. boobyalla (willow)
Austria...
capital.. 6. Vienna
city.. 4. Graz, Linz 8. Salzburg 9. Innsbruck
forest belt.. 10. Wiener Wald
monarchy.. 14. Austria–Hungary
mountain.. 4. Alps 6. Otztal 9. Dolomites
mountain peak.. 10. Wildspitze 13. Gross–Glockner
Pass (famed).. 7. Brenner
river.. 3. Inn, Mur 4. Enns 6. Danube
Austrian (pert to)...
botanist.. 6. Mendel (Mendel's Law)
composer.. 6. Mozart 7. Strauss
inventor.. 8. Welsbach
pianist.. 8. Kreisler
ruler (former).. 6. Kaiser
scientist.. 5. Adler, Freud
soldier.. 5. jager
theaterman.. 9. Reinhardt (Max)
autarch... 6. despot, tyrant 8. autocrat
authentic... 4. pure, real, true 5. valid 6. native 7. certain, correct, genuine, natural 8. bona fide, credible, official, original, orthodox, reliable 9. firsthand 11. trustworthy 13. authoritative
authenticate... 6. affirm, attest, ratify 7. certify, confirm, warrant 8. validate 12. substantiate
authenticity... 11. genuineness, reliability 13. dependability 15. trustworthiness
author... 4. doer, poet 5. ghost, maker 6. parent, penman, writer 7. creator, inditer 8. annalist, begetter, compiler, composer, essayist, inventor, novelist, producer 9. dramatist, scribbler 10. originator 13. encyclopedist (encyclopaedist)
authoritative... 4. wise 5. valid 6. potent, ruling, strong 7. weighty 8. approved, forceful, official, oracular, orthodox, positive, powerful 9. authentic, imperious 10. commanding, peremptory 11. dictatorial, influential 13. determinative
authoritative (pert to)...

command.. 4. fiat 5. usage
6. decree, dictum 7. mandate
example.. 9. precedent
10. antecedent
letter.. 4. writ 5. breve
authority... 5. judge, power, right
6. critic, expert, oracle, regent
7. command, warrant, witness
8. dominion, validity 9. influence,
testimony 10. commission,
competency 11. connoisseur,
prerogative 12. jurisdiction
13. authorization
authorize... 6. accept, permit, ratify
7. certify, charter, empower, endorse,
entitle, justify, license, warrant
8. accredit, delegate, sanction,
validate 10. commission
11. enfranchise 12. legitimatize
authorless... 8. nameless
9. anonymous
autobiography... 7. journal, letters,
memoirs 11. memorabilia
autochton... 6. binghi, native
8. indigene 9. primitive
10. aboriginal
autocracy... 8. monarchy 9. despotism
10. absolutism 15. totalitarianism
autocrat... 4. czar (tsar) 5. mogul
6. despot 7. arbiter, monarch
8. dictator 9. sovereign
10. taskmaster
autodidactic... 8. self–made
10. self–taught 12. self–educated
autograph... 4. seal, sign 5. cross
9. signature 11. John Hancock
automatic... 7. machine
10. mechanical, self–acting
11. instinctive, involuntary,
spontaneous
automatic device... 3. gun 4. gear
5. drill, pilot, rifle, robot 6. pistol,
switch 8. computer, revolver
10. six–shooter
automaton... 5. golem, robot
6. puppet 7. android, machine
automobile... 3. cab, car 4. auto, taxi
5. coupe 6. jalopy 7. autocar,
flivver, machine, taxicab, vehicle
8. motorcar
autosuggestion... 7. therapy
8. hypnosis 9. hypnology, mesmerism
10. psychology 14. self–suggestion
autumn... 4. fall 6. mature, old age,
season (yearly) 7. equinox, harvest,
October 8. maturity, November
9. September
auxiliary... 4. ally, plus 5. extra
6. aiding, helper 7. adjunct, helping
9. accessory, ancillary, assistant,
attendant, coadjutor, colleague,
companion, secondary 10. additional,
subsidiary, supporting
11. confederate, cooperating,
subordinate, subservient
12. nonessential, supplemental
13. supplementary
auxiliary army... 6. relief 7. support
8. Landwehr, recruits, reserves
11. contingents 14. reinforcements
auxiliary verb... 3. can, had, has, may
4. hast, have, will 5. could, shall,

would 6. should
avail... 3. use 4. good, help 5. value
6. inform, profit 7. benefit, service,
utility 9. advantage, expedient
availability... 7. utility 9. usability
10. usefulness 13. acquirability,
attainability 14. serviceability
available... 4. free, open 5. handy,
ready, valid 6. on hand, usable,
vacant 8. unfilled 9. securable
10. accessible, attainable, convenient,
obtainable, unoccupied
avalanche... 5. slide 7. descent
(sudden) 8. slippage
avant–garde... 3. van 8. vanguard
avant–propos... 7. preface
12. introduction (remarks)
avarice... 4. lust 5. greed 7. avidity
8. avidness, cupidity, grasping,
rapacity, voracity 10. greediness
12. covetousness
avarice demon... 6. Mammon
avaricious... 5. close 6. grabby,
greedy 7. miserly 8. covetous,
grasping 9. niggardly, penurious,
rapacious, voracious 12. parsimonious
avatar... 8. epiphany 10. embodiment
11. incarnation 14. transmigration
avatars of Vishnu (Hind Relig)...
11. incarnation (deity to man)
avaunt... 4. away 5. allez, boast,
scram, vaunt 6. begone, depart
7. advance, vamoose
ave... 4. hail, viva, vive 8. farewell
Ave Maria... 4. bead (rosary), song
6. prayer 10. devotional
Avena... 4. oats 7. grasses
avenge... 7. requite 9. retaliate,
vindicate
Avenging Angels... 8. nickname (Polit
1858) 10. Danite Band (Mormons)
Avenging Spirit... 4. Fate, Fury
6. Erinys 7. Alastor, Atropos
avenue... 3. rue 4. land, pike, road,
vent 5. alley 6. arcade, artery, defile,
egress, outlet, street 7. channel,
freeway, highway, opening
8. corridor, turnpike 9. boulevard,
concourse 10. passageway
12. thoroughfare
aver... 3. say 5. state 6. affirm,
allege, assert 7. declare, profess,
protect 10. asseverate
average... 2. go 3. par, run 4. mean,
rule 6. common, medial, medium,
normal 7. balance 8. mediocre
10. generality
averment... 6. dictum, remark
7. witness 9. assertion, statement,
testimony, utterance 10. allegation
11. affirmation, attestation
12. verification 13. pronouncement
Avernus... 4. lake (poison vapors)
5. Hades
averse... 5. loath 7. adverse
9. reluctant, unwilling 11. disinclined
aversion... 4. hate 5. odium
6. hatred, horror 7. disgust, dislike
9. antipathy, repulsion
10. abhorrence, repugnance
11. abomination 12. estrangement
13. indisposition, unwillingness

aversion to ... see also *fear of*
novelty .. 9. neophobia
society .. 14. anthropophobia
strangers .. 10. xenophobia
wine .. 10. oenophobia
avert ... 4. fend, save 5. check, deter,
evade, repel 6. forbid, retard, switch,
thwart 7. deflect, prevent 8. alienate,
prohibit 9. forestall, sidetrack
aviary ... 4. cage 5. house 7. dovecot
(dovecote) 8. ornithon 9. birdhouse,
columbary, enclosure
11. columbarium
aviation ... 6. flight, flying 7. winging
9. skyriding 10. airplaning
11. aeronautics
aviation maneuver ... 9. Immelmann
(Ger)
aviator ... 3. Ace 5. flier (flyer), pilot
6. airman, Icarus (fabled first)
7. wingman 8. aeronaut, aviatrix,
operator 9. astronaut, birdwoman,
Immelmann
avichi (Buddh) ... 4. Hell 5. Hades
9. depravity, perdition 10. underworld
avid ... 4. agog, keen 5. eager
6. grabby, greedy 7. anxious,
craving, zestful 8. grasping
9. rapacious, voracious 10. avaricious
avidity ... 4. lust 5. greed 7. avarice
8. cupidity, grasping 9. eagerness
10. greediness 12. covetousness
avion ... 5. plane 8. airplane
avisa ... 4. news 6. advice, caveat
7. tidings, warning 11. information
Avis Indica (Astron) ... 4. Apus
13. constellation
avital ... 9. ancestral
avoid ... 4. shun, snub 5. annul,
dodge, elude, evade 6. escape,
eschew, repeal, revoke, vacate
7. abstain, forbear 10. invalidate
avoidance ... 6. outlet 7. evasion,
removal 8. emptying, shunning,
vacating 9. annulment 10. withdrawal
avoirdupois ... 4. beef 6. weight
7. gravity, tonnage 8. poundage
9. heaviness
avoirdupois weight ... 3. ton 4. dram
5. grain, ounce, pound
13. hundred–weight
avow ... 3. own, vow 5. admit, swear,
vouch 6. allege, assert, pledge
7. confess, declare, profess, promise
10. avouchment 11. acknowledge
avulsion ... 7. removal 9. severance
10. extraction, separation (ppty),
withdrawal
awabi ... 7. abalone
awaft ... 6. adrift, afloat, wafted
await ... 4. bide, come, heed, loom,
pend, wait 5. abide, tarry, watch
6. ambush, attend, expect, impend,
waylay 8. approach 9. forthcome
awake ... 5. alert, alive, astir, rouse
6. arouse, excite, waking
8. open–eyed 9. attentive, conscious,
sleepless, wide–awake
awaken ... 5. awake 6. arouse, excite,
stir up 8. roust out
award ... 4. gift, give, meed, mete
5. allot, grant, medal, Oscar, prize

6. reward, trophy 7. adjudge,
present, verdict 8. accolade
9. medallion
aware ... 3. hep 4. know 5. sense
7. mindful 8. apprized, sensible
9. cognizant, conscious
11. intelligent
awareness ... 5. sense 7. feeling
9. sensation 10. impression,
perception 11. mindfulness, sensibility
13. consciousness
away ... 2. on 3. awa, far, fro, off, out
4. gone 5. aside, hence 6. abroad,
absent, begone, onward, thence
7. escaped 8. vanished 9. elsewhere
away from ...
body center .. 5. ectad 6. distal
mouth .. 6. aborad, aboral
wind .. 4. alee
awe ... 3. cow 4. fear 5. dread
6. regard, terror, wonder 7. emotion,
respect 8. astonish, frighten, surprise
9. reverence 10. admiration,
veneration, wonderment
13. consideration
aweather ... (opp of alee) 8. windward
11. weatherward
awe–inspiring ... 5. eerie (eery)
7. awesome, ghostly 8. glorious,
imposing, splendid, terrific
9. wonderful 10. impressive
11. magnificent
awe–struck ... 4. awed 9. terrified
10. astonished, fear–struck,
spellbound 12. wonder–struck
13. thunderstruck
awful ... 4. awed, ugly 5. dread, great,
gross 6. sacred, silent, solemn,
woeful 7. awesome, fearful, hideous
8. dreadful, infamous, reverent,
shocking, terrible 9. appalling,
atrocious, deathlike, ludicrous,
venerable, wonderful 10. deplorable,
impressive, outrageous, unpleasant
11. exceedingly
awkward ... 5. gawky, inapt, inept
6. clumsy, gauche 7. froward,
loutish, unhandy 8. bungling,
clownish, lubberly, perverse, ungainly,
unwieldy 9. graceless, inelegant,
lumbering, maladroit, ponderous
10. backhanded, blundering,
ungraceful 12. embarrassing,
incommodious, inconvenient
awkward age ... 4. teen 5. teens
awkward fellow ... 6. galoot
11. hobbledehoy
awless, aweless ... 4. bald 6. brazen
8. fearless, unafraid 9. bold–faced,
dauntless 10. irreverent
11. unsurprised 12. unastonished
awn ... 4. barb 5. beard (plant)
6. arista, papous 7. bristle
awning ... 6. canopy, screen, shield
7. shelter 8. velarium (anc)
AWOL ... 5. hooky 7. truancy
9. truantism 11. absenteeism
awry ... 4. agee 5. agley, amiss, askew
6. faulty 7. askance, asquint,
crooked, oblique 9. distorted
10. disorderly 11. disarranged
12. disorganized

ax, axe... 3. adz (adze), ask (dial)
　4. tool 6. hammer, poleax (poleaxe)
　7. hatchet (small) 8. axhammer
　9. discharge, dismissal
ax (pert to)...
　ancient.. 4. celt 6. chisel
　blade.. 3. bit
　execution.. 10. guillotine
　handle.. 5. helve
axial... 7. central, midmost, pivotal
axilla... 3. ala 4. axil 5. oxter
　6. armpit 8. shoulder
axiom... 3. law, saw 4. rule 5. adage,
　maxim, motto, truth 6. byword,
　dictum, saying, truism 7. dictate,
　precept, proverb, theorem
　8. aphorism, apothegm 9. principle
　11. proposition
axiomatic... 10. aphoristic, proverbial
　11. self–evident, sententious
　12. epigrammatic
axis... 3. hub 4. axle, bloc, nave,
　stem 5. pivot, stalk 6. caulis, center,
　league 7. fulcrum 8. alliance,
　vertebra 9. coalition
axle... 3. pin 4. axis 5. pivot, shaft
　6. swivel 7. spindle 8. axletree
axle tooth... 5. molar
ayal... 4. amah, maid 5. mammy
　9. governess, nursemaid
　11. maidservant
aye... 2. ay 3. pro, yea, yes 4. ever,
　vote 5. voice 6. always, assent
　8. thumbs up, viva–voce

aye–aye... 5. lemur (Madagascar)
ayes... 10. all in favor
Azazel... 5. Eblis, Satan 9. scapegoat
Azerbaijanian... 4. Turk
　14. Transcaucasian
azimuth... 3. arc 4. dial 6. circle
　7. compass, horizon 8. distance,
　magnetic 10. North point
Azores...
　capital.. 5. Angra
　city.. 5. Horta
　group (islands).. 6. St Mary 8. St
　George 9. St Michael
　locale.. 8. Atlantic (Ocean)
　owner.. 8. Portugal
Aztec (pert to)...
　calendar.. 7. Mexican
　capital (anc).. 12. Tenochtitlan
　emperor.. 9. Montezuma
　god.. 4. Xipe (sowing)
　　12. Quetzalcoatl (peace)
　hero.. 4. Nata (Myth) 6. Cortez
　language.. 7. Nahuatl
　locale (anc).. 6. Aztlan
　Noah (Mex).. 6. Coxcox
　stone.. 12. chalchihuitl
　temple.. 8. teocalli
　tribe.. 9. Nahuatlan
azure... 4. blue 7. celeste, sky–blue
　8. bice blue, cerulean 9. blue vault,
　cloudless 11. lapis lazuli
azygous... 3. odd 4. only, sole
　6. single, unique 8. singular
　10. unrepeated
azymous... 10. unleavened

B

B... 4. beta 6. letter (2nd)
ba (Egypt)... 3. khu 4. soul
baa... 5. bleet
baahling... 4. lamb
Baal... 4. idol 5. deity 6. Baalim (pl)
　7. Baalath 8. false god 9. fertility
baba (pert to)...
　India.. 4. baby 5. child
　Malaya.. 4. male
　Slavic.. 5. nurse 7. midwife 8. old
　　woman
　Turkey.. 5. title (of respect)
babacoote... 5. lemur (Madagascar)
Babbar... 3. Utu (Utug) 6. sun god
babbo... 5. daddy 6. father
babel... 5. clang 6. jargon, tumult
　7. discord 9. confusion
　11. pandemonium
Babel (pert to)...
　Bible.. 5. Tower 8. ziggurat
　presently.. 14. Temple of Marduk
　site (ancient).. 6. Shinar (land of)
　site (present).. 7. Babylon
babirusa, babiroussa... 9. quadruped
　(hoglike)

Babism (Persia)... 4. sect
baboon... 3. ape 5. Papio 6. chacma
　7. babuina, monster 8. mandrill
babushka... 11. grandmother
baby... 4. babe, doll 6. coward, infant,
　puppet, weanie 7. bambino, chicken
　8. juvenile, weakling 9. miniature,
　youngling, youngster 10. diminutive
baby carriage... 4. pram 5. wagon
　6. go–cart 8. stroller
　12. perambulator
babyish... 6. simple 7. dollish, puerile
　8. childish 9. childlike, infantile
Babylon... see also *Babylonian*
　capital of.. 9. Babylonia
　kingdom.. 4. Elam 5. Akkad (Accad)
　meaning.. 9. Gate of God
　mountain.. 6. Ararat
　river.. 6. Tigris 9. Euphrates
　World Wonder.. 14. Hanging Gardens
Babylonian (pert to)...
　abode of the dead.. 5. Aralu
　chaos.. 4. Apsu
　deity.. 5. Alalu (Alala), Siris
　earth mother.. 6. Ishtar

god.. 2. Ea, Zu 3. Anu, Bel 4. Adad,
Apsu, Irra 5. Dagan, Enlil 6. Nergal
7. Shamash
goddess.. 3. Aya 4. Nina 5. Belit
(Beltis)
hero (Myth).. 5. Adapa, Etana
9. Tilgamesh
king.. 6. Sargon 9. Habonidus,
Hammurabi 10. Nabonassar
14. Nebuchadnezzar (Nebuchadrezzar)
temple, tower.. 8. ziggurat
bacach... 6. beggar 7. cripple
bacalao... 7. codfish, grouper
bacalao bird... 3. auk 5. murre
9. guillemot
Bacardi... 3. rum
bacca... 5. berry
baccalaureate... 6. degree (college),
sermon 8. bachelor
baccate... 5. pulpy 9. berrylike
bacchanal... 7. reveler 8. carouser
Bacchanalia... 4. orgy 5. feast
7. debauch 8. festival (Bacchus)
bacchante... 6. maenad 7. bacchae
Bacchus... 4. wine 9. god of wine
baccivorous... 11. berry–eating
bachelor... 4. male 6. degree (Acad),
garçon 8. benedict, celibate
10. misogamist
bacillus... 9. bacterium
Bacis... 2. Ra 4. bull (sacred)
back... 3. aft, aid, fro 4. abet, hind,
past, rear 5. stern 6. behind,
second, uphold 7. finance, sponsor,
support, sustain 8. extrados, intrados,
resource 9. encourage, posterior
10. background
back (Anat)... 4. loin, nape 5. notum
6. dorsal, dorsum, lumbar, tergal,
tergum 7. occiput 8. backbone,
notalgia 10. opisthenar (hand)
backbone... 4. grit, guts 5. nerve,
pluck, spunk 6. mettle, spirit
7. courage, stamina, support
8. firmness, gameness, mainstay
10. dependence
backbone (Anat)... 4. axis 5. brace,
chine, spine 6. column, spinal
7. spinule, support 8. ossicles
9. vertebrae
backer... 5. angel 6. patron
7. abettor, sponsor 8. financer,
promoter, upholder 9. supporter,
sustainer 10. maintainer
background... (opp of foreground)
4. rear 5. stage 6. offing 7. horizon,
setting 8. backdrop, distance,
practice, training 9. education
10. experience 11. savoir–faire
backhanded... 6. clumsy 7. awkward,
devious 9. insincere, insulting,
sarcastic 10. circuitous
backslider... 8. apostate, deserter,
recreant 10. unfaithful
back–to–back... 7. dos–à–dos
backward... 4. back, dull, late
5. arear, loath, tardy 6. averse,
modest, stupid 7. bashful, belated,
reverse 8. arrested, dilatory, perverse,
rearward, retarded, reticent, retrorse,
reversed 9. hindwards, recessive,
reluctant, subnormal, unwilling

10. behindhand, hesitating,
regressive, retrograde 11. unfavorable
13. retrogressive, retrospective
bacon... 4. lard, pork, side 5. prize
6. flitch, gammon, rasher
8. Canadian, sowbelly
Bacon's Rebellion... 6. revolt (Va
1676)
bacteria... 5. cocci, germs 7. aerobes,
aerobia, bacilli 8. microbes, spirilla
9. organisms
bacteriologist culture... 4. agar
Bactrian camel... 9. two–humped
bad... 3. ill, mal (pref) 4. evil, fell,
foul, poor, vile 5. drole, fetid, nasty,
wrong 6. arrant, in pain, putrid,
rotten, sinful, wanton, wicked
7. corrupt, hurtful, naughty, noxious,
spoiled, tainted, unlucky, unmoral,
unsound, vicious 8. annoying,
criminal, improper, inferior, iniquity,
sinister 9. dangerous, defective,
offensive, perverted, worthless
10. iniquitous, malodorous, unsuitable
11. inexpedient, inopportune
12. disagreeable, inauspicious
bad (pert to)...
blood.. 4. feud 6. rancor 7. ill will
10. bitterness, resentment
custom.. 9. cacoethes
legislation.. 7. dysnomy
luck.. 5. deuce 7. ambsace
man´s oatmeal.. 7. hemlock (poison)
11. wild chervil
badge... 3. pin 4. mark, sign, star
5. index, token 6. emblem, ensign,
plaque, shield, symbol 7. earmark
8. insignia 14. identification
badger... 3. nag, rag 4. bait 5. harry,
tease, worry 6. bother, extort,
harass, hawker, heckle, hector, pester
8. huckster
badger (animal)... 5. Meles (anc),
pahmi, ratel 6. bauson, mammal,
teledu, wombat 9. bandicoot,
mistonusk
Badger State... 9. Wisconsin
badinage... 4. fool 5. joker, sport
6. banter 8. raillery 9. badinerie,
simpleton 10. persiflage, pleasantry
badly... 3. bad, ill 4. sick 5. amiss,
wrong 6. poorly, unwell 8. faultily,
wickedly 9. viciously 11. exceedingly,
imperfectly 12. disagreeably,
unskillfully 13. unfortunately
badly off... 3. sad 7. hapless, unblest,
unhappy, unlucky 8. luckless
11. impecunious, unfortunate
12. unprosperous 14. unprovidential
baff... 4. beat, blow, thud 6. strike,
stroke (golf)
baffle... 4. balk, foil 5. cheat, elude,
evade, spike 6. defeat, delude,
muffle, puzzle, thwart 7. mystify,
nonplus 8. bewilder, confound
9. bamboozle, frustrate
10. disconcert
baffling... 7. elusive, evasive
8. puzzling 9. bothering, confusing,
dismaying 10. mystifying, perplexing,
perturbing 11. frustrating
13. disconcerting

baft... 3. aft 4. baff 5. abaff, cloth, shaft 6. astern

bag... 3. net, pac, pot, sac, sag 4. etui, grip, load, poke, sack, trap 5. ascus, belly, catch, droop, pouch, purse, seize, snare, steal 6. entrap, sachet, valise 7. bladder, capture, distend, handbag, pannier, satchel 8. reticule, suitcase 9. Gladstone, haversack, sac de nuit 10. pocketbook 11. portmanteau

bag and baggage... 10. completely 11. impedimenta

bagatelle... 3. toy 4. game 6. bauble, geegaw, trifle 7. trinket 10. knickknack, triviality 12. fiddle–faddle

Bagdad, Baghdad...
capital of.. 4. Iraq
character.. 6. Sinbad (The Sailor)
city.. 6. Moslem
founder (762).. 8. Almanzor
kingdom (anc).. 11. Mesopotamia
Oriental term.. 8. lambskin (raw)
river.. 6. Tigris
transportation (famed).. 7. Railway

bagpipe, bagpipes... 5. drone, pipes 7. musette 9. Dudelsack 10. doodlesack, sordellina

bagpipe (pert to)...
music variations.. 7. pibroch
parts.. 4. lill, oboe 5. drone 7. chanter 9. chalumeau
player.. 5. piper
tube.. 6. drones 7. chanter
tune.. 4. port

Bahamas, Bahama Islands...
capital.. 6. Nassau
discoverer.. 8. Columbus
native.. 5. conch
naval base (US).. 9. Mayaguana
San Salvador (now).. 14. Watlings Island (Watling Island)

bahan... 6. poplar, willow (Bib)

bahay... 5. house

bahi... 7. fortune (gypsy)

bail... 3. dip 4. bond, hoop, lade, lave, ring, rynd 5. court, ladle, throw 6. bucket, dipper, handle, pledge, secure, surety 8. replevin, security 9. guarantee

bailiff... 5. agent, bobby, reeve, staff 6. deputy, staves (pl) 7. marshal, officer, sheriff, shrieve, steward 8. bluecoat, gendarme, overseer 9. constable 12. understeward

bailiwick... 6. canton, county, domain 7. commune, diocese 8. precinct, province 12. municipality

bain... 4. near 5. lithe, ready, short 6. direct, limber, supple 7. forward, willing

bairn... 3. kid, tot 4. mite 5. child 6. urchin

bait... 3. fly 4. feed, hook, lure, trap 5. bribe, decoy, snare 6. badger, harass, hockle 7. fulcrum, torment 8. inveigle 9. persecute 10. enticement, exasperate, temptation

bait... 3. dap, dib 4. fish, hook 6. dibble

bakal (Orient)... 9. tradesman 10. shopkeeper

bake... 3. dry 4. cake, cook, fire, kiln 5. roast 6. anneal, harden 8. clambake 9. dehydrate

bakehead... 4. rail 5. guard, shack 6. stoker 7. fireman 8. trainman

baken... 4. buoy 6. beacon 8. landmark

baker's dozen... 4. long 6. devil's 7. inbread 8. thirteen

baksheesh... 3. sop, tip 5. bribe 7. largess (largesse) 8. gratuity 12. compensation

bal... 4. ball, mine, prom

balance... 4. even, rest, rule 5. poise, ratio, scale, weigh 6. adjust, aplomb, normal, offset, reason, rhythm, sanity 7. average, ballast, compare, euphony, measure, remains, surplus 8. equality, equalize, leftover, residual, saneness, serenity, symmetry 9. composure, equipoise, remainder, stability 10. equanimity, neutralize, proportion, symmetrize 11. equilibrium 12. counterpoise

balanced... 4. even, just 6. poised 7. equable 8. measured 9. equitable 10. euphonious 11. symmetrical 13. self–possessed

balancer... 7. acrobat, gymnast 10. ropedancer 11. equilibrist

balcony... 4. dais 5. stage 6. podium 7. estrade, gallery, rostrum 8. brattice, platform

bald... 4. bare, dull, mere, open 5. crude, naked, plain 6. simple 7. epilose 8. depilous, hairless 9. bald–pated 11. unconcealed

baldachin, baldaquin... 6. canopy (St Peter's, Rome), fabric

Balder (pert to)...
father.. 4. Odin
god of.. 5. light, peace
mother.. 5. Frigg
slain by.. 9. mistletoe (dart)
wife.. 5. Nanna

balderdash... 3. rot 4. bosh 5. trash 6. bunkum, jargon 7. bombast 8. buncombe, falderal, nonsense, tommyrot 9. poppycock

baldness... 6. acomia 8. alopecia 11. phalacrosis 12. hairlessness

baldric... 4. belt (ornament) 6. zodiac 7. support (sword)

bale... 3. woe 4. bind, load, pack 5. truss 6. ballot, bundle, burden, misery, packet, seroon 7. anguish, package 11. encumbrance

Balearic Islands... 5. Iviza 7. Cabrera, Majorca, Minorca 10. Formentera

baleful... 3. bad, sad 4. dire 6. woeful 7. baneful, harmful, malific, noisome, noxious 8. damaging 9. ill–omened, malignant 10. pernicious 12. inauspicious

balk... 4. foil 5. check, ridge 6. baffle, defeat, fallow, rafter, signal (fishing), thwart 7. blunder, faux pas, stickle 9. frustrate, hindrance 10. bafflement, disappoint

14. disappointment
Balkan Peninsula...
native.. 4. Serb
river.. 3. Une 5. Saave 6. Danube
sea.. 5. Black 6. Aegean 7. Marmosa
  8. Adriatic 13. Mediterranean
State.. 6. Greece, Serbia, Turkey (Eur)
  7. Albania, Rumania 8. Bulgaria
balky... 7. restive 9. faltering,
  obstinate, shrinking, stickling
ball... 3. bal, fly, hop, lob, orb
  4. bead, clew (yarn), pill, shot
  5. dance, globe, pearl, pinda (rice)
  6. pellet, pelota, sphere 7. rissole
  8. conglobe, snowball 9. eight ball
  10. cannonball 12. medicine ball
ball (of games)... 4. golf, hand, polo,
  soft 6. basket, tennis, volley
  7. bowling, cricket, croquet, jai alai
  8. baseball, billiard, ping–pong
ballad... 3. lay 4. lied, poem, song
  5. derry, rhyme, verse 6. sonnet
  7. ballade, canzone
ballast... 5. poise 6. aplomb, steady,
  weight 7. balance 9. kentledge,
  saburrate, stabilize 10. equanimity,
  equivalent 14. counterbalance
balled up... 7. complex, mixed up,
  muddled 8. confused, fouled up
  9. befuddled, entangled, snarled up
  10. disordered 11. complicated
ballet (pert to)...
arrangement.. 12. choreography
dance.. 6. adagio 9. pantomime
dancer.. 8. coryphee, danseuse
  9. ballerina
jump.. 4. jeté 5. coupé
lover.. 11. balletomane
music.. 5. opera 6. comedy
  7. d'action 14. divertissement
balloon... 3. bag 4. ball, tire 5. barge
  (Siam), blimp, swell 6. aviate, ballon,
  dilate, expand, gasbag 7. distend,
  nacelle 8. aerostat, aircraft
  9. dirigible
balloon (type)... 4. free, kite 5. pilot
  7. captive 8. sounding
  11. montgolfier, observation
ballot... 4. bale, poll, vote 5. elect,
  slate, voice 6. select, ticket
  8. suffrage
ballyhoo... 4. plug 5. boost, noise
  6. fracas, hoopla, hubbub, ruckus,
  rumpus 7. promote 9. advertise,
  publicity 10. hullabaloo
balm... 3. oil 4. bito, calm 5. cream,
  salve 6. balsam, elixir, lotion, pacify
  7. anodyne, cushion, Melissa,
  perfume, relieve, unction, unguent
  8. liniment, mitigate, ointment
  9. calmative, fragrance, mitigator
  10. palliative
balm (pert to)... 5. Vicks 6. arnica,
  zachun 7. camphor, lanolin, menthol
  8. glycerin, ointment, vaseline
  10. petrolatum
Balm of... 6. Gilead
balmy... 4. mild 5. batty, daffy, dippy,
  drunk, goofy, moony, spicy, sweet
  6. dreamy, insane, savory 7. healing
  8. aromatic, fragrant, lenitive,
  redolent, soothing 9. ambrosial,

assuaging, emollient 10. palliative,
  refreshing 11. odoriferous
  12. sweet–scented
balsam... 3. fir 4. riga, tolu 5. resin
  6. embalm, poplar, storax
  7. benzoin, perfume 8. bdellium
  (Bib), medicine 9. oleoresin
  12. Balsam of Peru, Balsam of Tolu
Baltimore...
Belle.. 4. rose
bird.. 6. oriole
butterfly.. 7. phaeton
city of.. 8. Maryland
hemp.. 4. flax
history of.. 18. Star Spangled Banner
  (1814)
baluster... 4. post 7. support, upright
  8. banister
bam... 4. fake, hoax, mock, sham
  5. cheat, spoof, trick 6. deceit
  7. wheedle 8. flimflam 9. deception,
  imitation
bambino... 4. babe, baby, icon
  5. child, Pietà 6. infant (Christ)
bamboo (pert to)...
curtain.. 8. frontier
English.. 10. Philippine
genus.. 7. Bambuss
sacred.. 6. nandin
sprouts (pickled).. 5. achar
stems.. 4. cane
sugar.. 6. silica 9. tabasheer
bamboozle... 4. dupe, hoax 5. trick
  6. baffle, cajole, humbug 7. beguile,
  deceive, mystify, perplex 9. victimize
ban... 4. coin, tabu, veto 5. curse,
  edict, taboo, title (anc) 6. muslin,
  outlaw 7. embargo, exclude, kokumin
  8. anathema 9. interdict, ostracism,
  ostracize 10. injunction, kokumingun
  11. malediction, prohibition
  12. proscription 15. excommunication
banal... 4. flat 5. corny, stale, trite
  6. cliché, common, old hat
  11. commonplace, stereotyped
  13. platitudinous
banana... 4. Musa, saba 6. ensete
  8. Musaceae, plantain
banana (pert to)...
Bananaland.. 10. Queensland
bananalike.. 8. plantain
bird.. 4. quit 6. oriole
boa.. 5. snake
color.. 7. sunbeam
fish.. 8. ladyfish
freckle.. 7. disease
leaf.. 5. frond
oil.. 7. lacquer
Philippine.. 7. saguing
shrub.. 9. evergreen
band... 3. bar, tie 4. belt, body, crew,
  hoop, line, pack, ring, sash, zone
  5. bunch, corps, group, patte, strap,
  stria, strip, tribe, unite 6. cohort,
  collar, fascia, fillet, girdle, ligula,
  outfit, pledge, radula (Zool), tether
  7. bandage, company 8. cincture,
  encircle, ensemble, neckband, striping
  9. frequency (radio), orchestra,
  striation
bandage... 3. gag 4. bind, tape
  5. sling, spica, truss 6. ligate,

swathe 7. wrapper 8. compress,
dressing, ligature 9. accipiter,
blindfold 10. tourniquet
bandicoot... 3. rat 9. Perameles
bandit... 4. thug 5. thief 6. dacoit,
outlaw, robber 7. bandido, brigand,
footpad, ladrone 8. marauder,
picaroon 9. bandolero
10. highwayman
bandmaster... 5. Sousa 6. leader
7. maestro 8. choragus, director
9. conductor 13. Kapellmeister
bandolero... 5. thief 6. robber
10. highwayman
bandy... 4. beat, cart, game 5. bowed
6. curved, strive, stroke (tennis)
7. contend, embowed 8. carriage
(Ind), exchange, to and fro
9. bowlegged 11. bandy–legged,
reciprocate
bandy words... 5. argue 6. bicker,
parley 7. contend, wrangle
8. converse
bane... 3. woe 4. evil, harm, kill, pest,
ruin 5. curse, venom 6. injury,
plague, poison, slayer 7. disease
(sheep), scourge 8. murderer,
vexation 9. grievance 10. affliction,
pestilence, visitation
baneful... 3. ill 4. vile 7. harmful,
noxious 9. injurious 10. pernicious
11. detrimental
bang... 3. hit, rap 4. beat, blow,
dash, drub, kick, lift, shut, slam
5. crack, knock, pound, punch,
smack, thump, verve, whack
6. energy, report, strike, thrash, thrill
7. collide 8. coiffure
bangle... 5. charm 7. circlet
8. bracelet
banish... 3. ban 4. oust 5. exile, expel
6. deport, dispel, outlaw, punish
7. condemn, dismiss, exclude
8. relegate 9. ostracize, proscribe
10. expatriate 13. excommunicate
banister... 4. post, rail 8. baluster
10. balustrade
banjo... 7. samisen
bank... 3. row 4. brae, edge, heap,
quay, ripa 5. brink, flock, hurst
(sandy), marge, shoal, shore, slope,
table 6. aviate, margin, quarry,
rivage, series, stakes, strand
7. anthill, barrier, deposit, incline
8. buttress, treasury 9. acclivity,
riverside 13. fortification
bank account... 5. funds, means
6. assets, moneys 8. finances
9. exchequer
banker... 4. game 6. broker, lender
9. financier 11. moneylender
12. money–changer
bankrupt... 4. bust, ruin 5. broke,
smash 6. failed, quisby (sl) 7. failure
9. destiture, insolvent, moneyless,
penniless 12. impoverished
banner... 4. fane, flag 6. ensign,
poster 7. leading, pennant, placard
8. foremost, headline, standard,
streamer 9. exemplary 10. surpassing
banns, marriage... 6. notice
7. sibrede 12. proclamation

banquet... 4. fete 5. diffa, feast, festa
6. fiesta, junket, regale, repast,
spread 8. festival, jamboree
10. regalement
Banquo... 9. character (Shak)
banshee, banshie... 4. shee 5. fairy,
Geist, sidhe 6. spirit, sprite
bantam (pert to)...
cock.. 3. fop 5. dandy, sport
7. peacock 8. strutter 9. swaggerer
12. swashbuckler
Java.. 4. duck, fowl 5. breed
6. Brahma, Cochin
slang.. 4. runt 6. peewee, shrimp
sports.. 6. weight
bantamweight... 5. boxer (118 lbs)
7. fighter 8. pugilist 9. contender
10. contestant
banter... 4. jest, josh, mock, twit
5. borak, chaff, sport, tease, trick
6. delude, deride, satire 7. asteism,
wheedle 8. badinage, raillery, ridicule
10. persiflage, pleasantry
Bantu, South Africa...
language.. 3. Ila 8. Kongoese
people.. 5. Duala 6. Basuto
tribe.. 4. Vili, Zulu 6. Damara, Kaffir
7. Negroid, Swahili 8. Bechuana
banzai... 4. hail 5. hello, hullo
6. attack, charge 9. greetings
11. salutations
baobab tree (pert to)...
bark.. 4. rope 5. cloth, paper
fruit.. 11. monkey bread
genus.. 9. Adansonia
pulp.. 8. beverage
baptism... 4. rite 6. naming 7. wetting
8. ablution 9. aspersion, immersion,
sacrament 10. initiation, sprinkling
11. christening 12. consecration,
purification, regeneration (spiritual)
baptism (pert to)...
cloth.. 7. chrisom
dead (RCCh).. 5. Blood 6. Desire
fire.. 9. fuertaufe
place.. 4. font 10. baptistery (anc)
receptacle.. 5. basin 7. piscina
water.. 5. laver
bar... 3. ban, dam, fid, pry, rod
4. bolt, deny, fess, joke, line, rack,
rail, sess, type 5. betty
(thieves'slang), block, court, deter,
easer, estop, ingot, lever, shoal,
space, staff 6. except, forbid, hinder,
ripper, saloon, stitch, stripe
7. barrier, barroom, bass–bar,
chevron, counter, crowbar, exclude,
prevent, railing, sandbar, trapeze
8. blockade, disallow, obstacle,
obstruct, preclude, prohibit
9. barricade, hindrance
10. impediment, profession,
singletree 11. obstruction,
whippletree 12. underscoring
barb... 3. jag 4. clip, flue, harl, herl,
seta 5. horse, point, ramus, scarf
(nun's), speed 6. setula, striga
7. bristle, feather, pinnula 8. kingfish
9. arrowhead 10. projection
Barbados Island...
capital.. 10. Bridgetown
drink.. 3. rum

government.. 7. British
location.. 8. Antilles (Lesser) 10. West
  Indies
native.. 3. Bim (nickname)
barbarian... 3. hun 4. Goth, rude
  5. beast, brute 6. savage, vandal
  8. cannibal, man—eater 9. untutored,
  vulgarian 10. extraneous, Philistine,
  unlettered 11. uncivilized
  15. anthropophagite
barbaric... 5. cruel 6. brutal, Gothic,
  savage 7. foreign, inhuman, vicious
  8. non—Greek, non—Latin, ruthless
  9. barbarous, primitive
  10. extraneous 11. uncivilized
  12. non—Christian
barbarism... 6. ferity 8. rudeness,
  solecism 9. barbarity, crudeness,
  Gothicism, ignorance, vulgarism
  10. coarseness, corruption,
  foreignism 11. impropriety
Barbarossa... 7. emperor (Rom) 8. red
  beard
Barbary ape... 5. magot
Barbary State (former)... 5. Tunis
  7. Algiers, Morocco 12. Tripolitania
barbate... 7. bearded, stubbly
  9. whiskered 11. barbigerous
barbecue... 5. feast, roast 6. animal
  (whole), picnic 7. brazier, hibachi
  9. Dutch oven 10. shish kebab
  13. entertainment (out—of—doors)
barber... 5. shave 6. figaro, shaver,
  tonsor 7. tonsure 10. haircutter
  12. tonsorialist
Barber of Seville character...
  6. Figaro, Rosina
Barcelona, Spain...
  building (famed).. 6. palace (Kings of
  Aragon) 9. Cathedral (Gothic)
  port.. 13. Mediterranean
  street (famed).. 6. Rambla
bard... 4. muse, poet, scop (Hist)
  5. druid, runer, vates 8. minstrel,
  musician (wandering) 10. Parnassian
Bard of...
  Avon.. 11. Shakespeare
  Ayrshire.. 5. Burns
  Rydal Mount.. 10. Wordsworth
bare... 3. raw 4. bald, mere, nude,
  open 5. alone, empty, naked, plain,
  shear, sheer, stark, strip 6. barren,
  denude, divest, expose, reveal,
  simple, vacant 7. exposed, unarmed,
  uncover 8. desolate, disclose,
  stripped 9. destitute, unadorned,
  uncovered 10. stark—naked,
  threadbare 11. defenseless,
  unconcealed
barefaced... 4. bare, bold 6. brassy,
  brazen 8. impudent 9. audacious,
  shameless 11. undisguised
barely... 4. jimp, only 5. faint
  6. hardly, merely, nudely, poorly,
  simply 7. nakedly 8. narrowly,
  scantily, scarcely 14. insufficiently
bargain... 3. buy 4. deal, pact, prig,
  sell 5. trade 6. barter, chisel, dicker,
  haggle 7. chaffer, compact, mediate
  8. contract, covenant, purchase
  9. agreement, Bon Marché,
  cheapness, negotiate 10. engagement

11. stipulation, transaction
barge... 3. ark, hoy 4. raft, scow, ship
  5. ferry, float, praam, scold
  6. berate, lumber, rebuke, tender
  7. birlinn (birling) 9. transport
barge in... 5. enter 6. bungle, butt in,
  invade, push in 7. blunder, intrude
barghest... 6. goblin
bargoose... 4. duck 9. merganser,
  sheldrake
bark... 3. bay, yap, yip 4. bang, bast,
  husk, peel, rind, ross, ship, skin,
  tapa, yelp 5. cough, niepa, shout,
  strip, youff 6. bowwow, clamor,
  cortex, outcry, packet, scrape
  7. canella 8. ballyhoo, periderm
  9. sassafras
barker... 4. tout 6. pistol 7. spieler
  9. solicitor 10. ballyhooer,
  theaterman
barking... 7. latrant 8. hylactic
Barlaam and Josaphet (Joasaph)...
  11. Buddha story (Christian version)
barley... 4. bigg, food, seed 5. grain
  6. ptisan, tsamba 7. Hordeum
barley (pert to)...
  bird.. 6. siskin 7. wagtail (yellow),
  wryneck 11. nightingale
  bree.. 3. ale 6. liquor
  shaped.. 10. hordeiform
barlow... 9. jackknife (one—bladed)
barm... 5. froth, yeast 6. leaven
  7. ferment
barn... 3. bay, mow 4. loft
barnacle... 4. bray (Her) 5. acorn,
  goose, leech 6. animal, sucker
  8. adherent, parasite 9. sycophant
  10. Cirripedia, crustacean
barnstormer... 5. actor 7. aviator
  11. entertainer
baron... 4. peer 5. mogul, noble
  6. daimio, tycoon 7. freeman
  8. nobleman, somebody 9. financier,
  personage 10. capitalist
  13. industrialist
baroque... 6. ornate, quaint, rococo
  7. bizarre 9. irregular 11. extravagant
barracks... 4. camp, huts 6. casern,
  laager 9. barracoon 10. encampment
barraclade... 7. blanket (homemade)
barracuda... 4. fish, spet 5. barry
  (Bahamas) 6. sennet
barrage... 3. dam 4. weir 5. blitz
  6. strafe 7. barrier, gunfire, milldaw
  9. cannonade, roadblock
  11. obstruction
barrage (military)... 3. box 5. mines
  6. normal 7. balloon 8. creeping,
  standing 9. emergency
  12. anti—aircraft
barranca... 4. bank 5. bluff 6. ravine
barratry... 6. breach, simony 8. bad
  faith, mala fide 10. infidelity
  11. dereliction
barred... 6. cooped, fenced, grated,
  ribbed 7. striped 8. confined,
  debarred, excluded, streaked
barrel... 3. box, keg, tun 4. cade,
  cask, drum, knag 5. quill, speed
  6. runlet, tierce 7. calamus (Zool),
  rundlet 8. cylinder 9. kilderkin
barrel (pert to)...

maker.. **6.** cooper
miscellaneous.. **3.** gun, pen **4.** pipe
6. pencil
sling.. **9.** parbuckle
stopper.. **4.** bung
barren... **3.** dry **4.** arid, bare, dull
5. blank, empty, heath, inane
6. desert, effete, jejune, karroo,
meager, Sahara, stupid **7.** sterile
8. desolate, impotent, unpoetic
9. infertile **10.** unfruitful, unprolific
12. unproductive, unprofitable
barricade... **3.** bar **4.** bolt, rail, seal,
stop **5.** block, close, fence **6.** abatis
7. barrier, padlock **8.** blockade,
obstacle, obstruct **11.** obstruction
13. fortification
barrico... **3.** keg **4.** cask
barrier... **3.** Alp, bar, dam **4.** clog,
door, gate, wall, weir **5.** block,
fence, hedge, panel **6.** screen
7. parapet, railing **8.** blockade,
boundary, fortress, obstacle, stockade,
stoppage **9.** partition, restraint
10. impediment, portcullis
11. obstruction
barrikin (Eng sl)... **6.** jargon
9. gibberish
barrister... **6.** lawyer **7.** adviser,
pleader **8.** advocate, attorney
9. counselor (counsellor), solicitor
barroom... **3.** bar, pub, tap **6.** saloon,
tavern **7.** cantina, taproom
8. alehouse **11.** rathskeller
barrow... **3.** hod, hog (male) **4.** brae,
fell, hill, knap, moor **5.** grave (anc),
mound **7.** tumulus **8.** mountain
11. wheelbarrow **12.** Reihengräber
bartender... **5.** mixer **6.** barman, bistro
7. barkeep, tapster **8.** publican
barter... **4.** deal, sell, swap **5.** trade,
truck **7.** bargain, permute, traffic
8. commerce, exchange
Bartholomew (pert to)... **4.** Fair, Play
(Shak) **5.** Saint **6.** martyr **7.** Apostle
(one of 12) **8.** Massacre
Bartimeus (Bib)... **6.** beggar (blind)
barton... **4.** farm **5.** abode, manor
6. grange **7.** demesne **8.** farmyard,
hacienda **9.** homestead
baru... **4.** tree (fiber) **7.** majagua
base... **3.** bed, low **4.** dado, evil, foot,
foul, mean, root, seat, site, sole
5. basis, basso, cause, petty, radix,
socle, voice **6.** abject, bottom,
center, factor, patten, plinth, podium,
singer, sordid, vulgar, wicked
7. servile, station **8.** basement,
cosmetic, degraded, infamous,
inferior, pedestal, shameful, standard
9. principle, worthless
10. despicable, foundation, villainous
12. contemptible, dishonorable,
headquarters
baseball (terms)... **3.** bag, bat, box,
fan, fly, hit, lob, out, RBI, run
4. ball, base, bunt, deck, foul,
home, nine, pill, sack, save, walk,
wild **5.** bench, clout, coach, count,
curve, drive, error, field, first, force,
glove, homer, liner, mound, pitch,
plate, pop–up, score, slide, sport,

swing, third **6.** assist, batter, bungle,
double, dugout, fumble, ground,
putout, rubber, runner, screen,
second, series, single, sinker, stance,
strike, string, target, triple, windup
7. battery, bullpen, diamond, fielder,
floater, rhubarb (sl), squeeze, stretch
8. backstop, grounder, keystone,
knuckler, outfield, pinch–hit,
powdered, spit ball **9.** sacrifice,
strikeout **10.** ballplayer
baseborn... **3.** low **4.** mean **5.** lowly,
plain **6.** common, humble **7.** bastard,
ignoble, lowborn **8.** plebeian,
spurious **11.** commonplace
12. illegitimate
based on...
evidence.. **7.** damning **8.** decisive
10. conclusive
experience.. **7.** empiric **9.** empirical
numbers.. **5.** hexad **6.** nonary, senary
7. tertial
baseness... **6.** infamy **7.** badness
9. servility, vulgarity **10.** wickedness
11. inferiority **13.** dastardliness,
subordination
bash... **3.** bat, jab, lam **4.** beat, belt,
biff, blow, conk, mash, slug, sock
5. clout, paste, punch, smack, whack
6. bruise, strike, wallop **7.** clobber
Basham's King... **2.** Og
bashful... **3.** coy, shy **5.** heloe, mousy,
timid **6.** demure, modest
8. blushing, retiring, sheepish,
timorous, verecund **9.** diffident
13. self–conscious
basic... **4.** root **5.** basal, basis
7. essence, primary **8.** alkaline,
original **9.** essential **10.** underlying
11. fundamental
Basilian... **3.** art **4.** monk, rule
6. bishop **7.** liturgy, St Basil (The
Great) **8.** precepts **10.** Cappadocia
basilica... **5.** major, minor, title
6. canopy, church, shrine, temple
11. patriarchal
Basilican (pert to)...
books.. **5.** sixty **6.** Digest
century.. **5.** Tenth
empire.. **9.** Byzantine
laws.. **9.** Justinian
basin... **3.** bed (water), cup, pit, tub
4. bowl, cock, font, hole, sink, tank
5. laver, plain, playa, stoup **6.** cavity,
chafer, coulee, ground, lavabo,
marine, valley, vessel **7.** lowland,
piscina **8.** curvette **9.** washbasin
10. depression
basis... **4.** base, fond, root **5.** cause,
start **6.** bottom, factor, motive,
reason, thesis **7.** premise, warrant
9. assertion, principle **10.** foundation,
groundwork **13.** justification
bask... **3.** sin, tub **4.** warm **5.** bathe,
revel **7.** suffuse **8.** apricate
9. luxuriate
basket... **3.** bin, box, car (balloon),
net, ped, pod **4.** caba, cage, kish,
skep, trug **5.** cabas **6.** dosser,
gabion, vessel, wisket **7.** corbeil,
hanaper, pannier, scuttle, wattage
9. container

basket (pert to)...
coal mine.. 3. tub 4. corf
fig.. 5. frail 6. tapnet
fire.. 5. grate 7. cresset
fishing.. 3. pot 4. buck (eel), caul,
weel 5. crail, crate, creel 6. hamper
making.. 5. slath 6. slarth
wicker.. 3. cob 5. cesta, osier
6. hamper 7. hanaper 8. bassinet
Basque (pert to)...
ancestors.. 8. Iberians
cap.. 5. beret
home.. 5. Spain 8. Pyrenees
bas–relief... 7. carving, relievo
12. basso–relievo (basso–rilievo)
bass... 4. fish 5. fiber, voice (low)
6. singer 8. weakfish 13. basso
profundo
bassoon... 4. oboe 6. fagott 7. fagotto
bast... 4. bass 5. fiber
Bast (Egypt)... 4. Ptah 7. goddess
10. lady of life
bastard... 3. odd 4. heel (sl), sham
5. false, louse (sl) 7. batarde
8. abnormal, bantling, spurious
9. scoundrel 10. adulterate
12. illegitimate 13. nullius filius
baste... 3. hit, sew 4. cook, lard, lash,
tack, whip 6. stitch, thrash
7. trounce 8. lambaste
bastion... 5. redan 8. fastness
10. stronghold 13. fortification
bat... 3. hit, jag, lam, rap 4. belt,
blow, clip, club, slug, sock, swat,
wink 5. binge, clout, paste, smack,
spree, stick, whack 6. bender,
cudgel, racket, wallop 7. clobber
bat (mammal)... 6. aliped, fox bat,
kalong 7. noctule, vampire
8. serotine 9. flying fox, pipistrel
(pipistrelle), reremouse 10. Chiroptera
batch... 3. lot 4. heap, lump, mess,
slew 5. bunch, group, stack
6. amount, baking 7. mixture
8. quantity 10. collection
bath... 3. dip, tub 4. sitz 5. steam,
sweat, vapor 6. plunge, shower,
sponge 7. Finnish, mineral, sulphur
bath (pert to)...
Eccl.. 8. ablution
house.. 6. bagnic, cabana 8. balneary
10. natatorium
photography.. 5. toner 9. developer
Roman.. 7. balneum 11. Warm
Springs
sitz.. 5. bidet
warm.. 5. therm
bathe... 3. tub, wet 4. bask, lave,
swim, wash 5. flush 6. drench
7. immerse, moisten, pervade,
suffuse 8. medicate, permeate
baton... 3. rod 4. mace, wand
5. staff, stick 6. baston, cudgel,
fasces 7. scepter, support
9. truncheon
Batrachia... 5. Anura, frogs, toads
7. Surinam 8. Salienta
Battalion of Death (Russ)...
13. legion of women
batten... 5. close, gloat 6. fasten,
fatten, secure, thrive, timber
battered... 6. beaten, pasted

7. bruised 8. impaired 9. shattered,
weathered
battery... 3. set 4. guns, pack
6. cohort, series 7. assault, platoon
8. baseball (term) 9. artillery
battery (Elec)... 4. cell, grid, pole
5. anode, plate 6. Leyden
7. storage, voltaic 9. electrode
battle... 3. war 4. fray, meet, tilt
5. brush, fight, joust, scrap
6. action, affray, barney, combat,
tussle 7. contest, scuffle, warfare
8. conflict, skirmish, struggle
9. challenge, encounter
10. engagement
Battle (pert to)...
Bib.. 8. Aceldama 12. potter's field
Civil War.. 7. Bull Run 15. Lookout
Mountain
formation.. 4. line 5. herse, order
Great.. 10. Armageddon
Hundred Years (1346).. 5. Crecy
Revolution.. 10. Bunker Hill
slogan.. 8. aux–armes 9. battle cry
World War I.. 6. Verdun (1916)
World War II.. 11. Pearl Harbor
(1941)
battologize... 6. repeat 7. iterate,
recount, restate 9. reiterate
12. recapitulate
bauble... 3. toy 4. gaud 6. doodad,
geegaw, trifle, trivia 7. bibelot, trinket
8. falderal (folderol) 9. bagatelle,
plaything 10. knickknack
Bavaria...
capital.. 6. Munich
city.. 8. Augsburg, Wurzburg
9. Nuremburg 12. Ludwigshafen
freeway.. 8. autobahn
government.. 10. Third Reich
king (former).. 10. Maximilian
prince.. 6. Rupert
river.. 4. Eger, Isar
bawdry... 6. filthy 8. ribaldry, salacity,
unchaste 9. obscenity
11. pornography
bawl... 3. cry, say, sob 4. bark, howl,
roar, wail, weep, yell 5. blare, shout
6. bellow, boohoo, plaint 8. proclaim
10. vociferate
bay... 3. ria 4. cove, howl, roan, wail
5. bight, horse, inlet, oriel, sinus
6. recess, window 7. ululate
bay (pert to)...
antler.. 9. stag's tine (2nd)
bird.. 5. snipe 6. curlew, godwit,
plover
color.. 4. roan
tree.. 6. laurel
Bayard... 5. horse, steed (Rinaldo's)
bayonet... 5. lance, saber, spear,
sword 6. dagger, weapon 7. poniard
bayou... 5. creek, marsh 6. slough,
stream 7. channel 11. watercourse
Bayou State... 11. Mississippi
Bay State... 13. Massachusetts
bazaar... 4. fair, shop 6. market
7. canteen (army) 10. exposition
be... 2. am 3. are 4. live 5. exist
7. prevail
beach... 5. coast, plage, playa, praya,
sands, shore 6. shilla, strand

9. waterside
beachcomber... 4. wave 6. loafer
8. vagabond
beacon... 4. beam, flag, sign, vane
5. fanal, light, radar, radio
6. marker, pharos, signal 7. cresset,
lantern, seamark 10. lighthouse,
watchtower
bead... 4. ball, drop 5. bugle, pearl,
sight (firearm) 6. rondel 8. ornament
beads... 5. grain, sewan 6. rosary
7. chaplet, granose (antennae),
jewelry, prayers
beak... 3. neb, nib 4. bill, lora, nose,
peck, prow 5. judge, mouth, spout,
tutel 10. magistrate 11. stipendiary
beaker... 3. cup 6. vessel (Chem)
beakless... 9. erostrate
beam... 3. ray 4. emit, grin, sile, sill,
stud 5. caber, gleam, joist, shaft,
shine, smile, tonka, trave 6. girder,
mantel, rafter, timber 7. radiate,
support, trimmer 8. trabeate
bean... 4. buck, faba, gram, lima,
mung, navy, seed, soya 5. black,
coral, pinto, Sieva 6. adzuki, castor,
frijol (frijole), kidney, legume, lentil,
string 7. calabar 9. Phaseolus
bean (pert to)...
eye of.. 5. hilum
game.. 7. beanbag
licorice seed.. 9. jequirity
lima.. 4. haba
seed (string bean).. 7. haricot
shaped.. 8. fabiform
slang.. 4. buck, head 5. brain
6. dollar, noodle, trifle
bear... 3. aim, cub, lug 4. dubb, tote,
turn, ursa 5. bring, brown, bruin,
carry, clack, crank, koala, polar,
press, short, sloth, stand, ursus, yield
6. animal, endure, grouch, harbor,
Kodiak, stress, suffer, Syrian, uphold
7. Ephraim (nickname), furnish,
grizzly, incline, musquaw, produce,
support 8. cinnamon, fructify,
maintain, Melursus, sorehead, tolerate
10. speculator 11. short seller
(Finan)
bear (pert to)...
cat.. 5. panda 9. binturong
class.. 6. ursine 7. Ursidaw
color.. 6. yellow
constellation.. 9. Ursa Major, Ursa
Minor
flag.. 10. California (State)
head.. 4. hure
The.. 6. Russia
beard... 3. awn 6. arista, goatee
7. stubble, Vandyke 8. whiskers
bearded... 5. awned 7. barbate,
pappose 8. aristate 9. whiskered
beards, science of... 10. pogonology
bearer... 3. boy 5. macer, usher
6. porter, tender 7. carrier
8. cargador, conveyor, escudero
9. attendant 10. khidmatgar,
pallbearer
bearing... 3. air 4. mien, port
5. poise 6. bel air, regard
7. concern, conduct, dignity,
meaning, posture 8. behavior,

carriage, demeanor, relation, tendency
9. direction, influence, relevance
10. connection, deportment,
supporting 12. significance
bearing (Her)... 4. enté, orle 5. bevel,
pheon 6. billet
bear witness... 6. attest 7. testify
beast... 4. bête, game, lion, pard
5. brute, camel, demon, fiend, horse,
spado, tiger 6. animal, cattle,
dragon, savage 7. carrier, critter,
leopard, monster 8. behemoth,
creature 9. dromedary
beastly... 5. gross 6. animal, bloody,
carnal, odious 7. bestial, brutish,
hideous, inhuman, leonine, theroid,
ungodly 8. dreadful 9. execrable
10. abominable, disgusting
beat... 3. hit, lam, tan, taw, wap
4. bang, bash, best, cane, drub,
drum, flog, lace, lash, maul, pelt,
tund 5. baste, excel, pound, pulse,
route, scoop, throb, thump 6. bruise,
cudgel, defeat, larrup, pommel,
punish, rhythm, strike, stroke, swinge,
thrash, thresh 7. baffled, belabor,
cadence, clobber, conquer, flutter,
musical, pulsate, routine, surpass,
trounce 8. chastise, fatigued,
lambskin, overcome, vanquish
9. exhausted, pulsation
beat (pert to)...
back.. 7. repulse
black and blue.. 9. suggilate
down.. 6. haggle 7. cheapen
into plate.. 8. malleate
slang.. 4. blow 5. scoot, scram
6. beat it, skidoo 7. vamoose
traverse.. 6. patrol
beatify... 5. bless, cheer, saint
6. hallow 7. gladden, glorify
8. enshrine, sanctify
beatnik... 8. Bohemian, maverick,
sulphite 13. nonconformist
beau... 3. fop 5. blade, dandy, flame,
lover, spark, swain 6. escort, squire
7. admirer, courter 9. caballero,
inamorato 10. beau–garçon
beautiful... 4. fair, fine 5. bonny,
kalon (Gr) 6. comely, lovely, poetic,
pretty 7. elegant, Tempean
8. graceful, handsome, stunning
9. aesthetic (esthetic), exquisite
15. pulchritudinous
beautify... 4. deck, trim 5. adorn,
grace 6. bedeck, doll up, enrich
8. decorate, prettify 9. embellish,
glamorize
beauty... 5. belle, charm, glory, grace
8. elegance 10. loveliness, prettiness
11. pulchritude
beauty, famed...
Egypt.. 9. Cleopatra
Greek.. 4. Hebe 6. Graces
9. Aphrodite 11. Helen of Troy
Historical.. 4. Lais
Persian.. 4. peri 5. houri
Norse.. 5. Freya
Roman.. 5. Venus
Becken... 7. cymbals
beckon... 4. beck 5. court 6. invite,
summon 7. gesture 11. gesticulate

becloud... 5. bedim, cloud, shade, smoke 6. bemist, darken, opaque 7. conceal, encloud, obscure 8. nubilate, overcast 9. adumbrate

become... 2. go 3. fit, get, wax 4. grow, rise, suit 5. befit, grace 6. befall, beseem, mature, mellow 7. behoove, benefit 8. befuddle 9. originate

becoming... 3. fit 6. comely, decent, fitted, likely, proper, seemly, suited 7. decorum, suiting 8. decorous, pleasing, suitable, tasteful 9. befitting, expedient 11. appropriate

bec–scie... 4. duck 9. merganser

becuna... 9. barracuda

bed... 3. cot, kip, tye (feather) 4. bunk, crib, doss, lair, nest 5. basin, berth, couch 6. billet, bottom, flower, litter, pallet 7. channel, feather, stratum 8. bassinet 9. stretcher 10. foundation

bed (pert to)...
canopy.. 4. ceil 6. tester
coverlet.. 5. quilt 6. spread 7. blanket 9. comforter 11. counterpane
famed.. 15. bed of Procrustes

bedaub... 3. dab 4. blur, daub, soil 5. paint, smear, stain 6. belaud, smudge 7. bedizen, besmear 8. besmudge, ornament

bedazzle... 4. daze, stun 5. blind, shine 6. dazzle 7. astound, confuse 8. astonish, bewilder

bedeck... 3. gem 4. trim 5. adorn, array, grace, prink 6. clothe, rag out 7. bedrape 8. ornament

bedevil... 3. hex 4. foul, ride 5. abuse, tease 6. befoul, muddle, needle, pester, plague 7. bewitch, confuse, torment 8. demonize 9. diabolize, tantalize 10. complicate

bedight... 5. adorn, array, equip

bedikah... 6. ritual

bedim... 3. dim, fog 4. blur, fade 5. blear, cloud 6. bemist, darken 8. bedarken

bedlam... 3. din 6. clamor, tumult, uproar 8. madhouse 9. charivari 11. pandemonium

Bedlam (London)... 6. priory (1247) 8. Hospital (St Mary of Bethlehem)

Bedouin... 4. Arab, Moor 5. gypsy, nomad 7. Saracen, vagrant

Bedouin head cord... 4. agal

bedroll... 6. bindle 7. matilda

bee... 3. dor 4. apis 5. drone, karbi, queen 6. insect, worker 8. andrenid, angelito, honeybee 9. bumblebee 12. carpenter bee

bee (pert to)...
fear of.. 9. apiphobia
glue.. 8. propolis
hive.. 4. butt, scap, skep (straw) 6. apiary 7. alveary 8. workshop
keeper.. 8. apiarist, skeppist
sociable.. 7. husking, raising 8. quilting, spelling
study.. 10. apiculture 11. melittology
wax.. 7. beeswax, ceresin, cerotic

9. cera flava

Beebe, William... 13. ichthyologist

beef... 4. heft, kine, thew 5. brawn, sinew, steer 6. buccan (dried), cattle, muscle 8. poundage 10. brawniness 11. muscularity

Beelzebub (pert to)...
Bible.. 5. deity 6. oracle 14. prince of demons
literature.. 5. demon (Prince), devil 11. fallen angel
zoology.. 6. monkey

beer... 3. ale 4. bock, flip, hops, suds 5. lager, weiss 6. liquor, porter, swipes

beer (pert to)...
cask.. 4. butt
inventor.. 9. Gambrinus (Myth king)
mug.. 4. toby 5. stein 8. schooner
vessel.. 6. tanker 9. blackjack

beet... 4. Beta 5. chard 6. mangel 8. beet root 9. sugar beet

Beethoven, Ludwig Van (pert to)...
birthplace.. 4. Bonn (Ger)
composed.. 7. Fidelio 10. symphonies
famed as.. 7. pianist 8. composer

beetle... 3. bat, bug, dor, jut, ram 4. June, rose 5. Amara, gogga, Hispa, meloe, snout 6. chafer, elater, golach, goloch, hammer, masher, sawyer, scarab, weevil 7. ladybug, prionid 8. circulio, sharnbud, skipjack 9. cockroach, dorbeetle 10. cockchafer, Elateridae

beetlehead... 5. stupe 6. plover (bird), stupid 8. bonehead 9. blockhead 10. loggerhead

befall... 3. hap 4. come 5. occur 6. betide, chance, happen 9. eventuate, transpire

befit... 4. suit 5. serve 6. become, beseem, please

befitting... 3. fit 4. meet 6. filial, proper, seemly, timely 7. ethical, fitting, suiting 8. becoming, decorous, suitable 9. expedient 10. seasonable 11. appropriate

befog... 3. dim, fog 5. blind, cloud 6. bemist 7. becloud, conceal, confuse, mystify, obscure

before... 3. ere 5. afore, ahead, avant, early, prior 6. anteal, facing, openly, sooner 7. already, earlier, forward, yestern 8. anterior, foremost, formerly, hitherto 9. foregoing, preceding 10. beforehand, face to face, heretofore, previously 11. theretofore

before (pert to)...
birth.. 8. prenatal
long.. 4. soon
mentioned.. 4. said, same, such 5. named 6. former 10. aforenamed
others.. 5. first
this.. 3. ere 5. prior 6. erenow

before (pref)... 3. pre, pro 4. ante, prae

befoul... 4. soil 5. taint 6. bemire, defile, muddle 7. bedevil 8. entangle 10. complicate 11. contaminate

befriend... 3. aid 4. abet, help 5. favor 6. assist, foster, succor

7. benefit, support, sustain
11. countenance
befuddle... 3. fog 5. addle, besot
6. fuddle, muddle 7. becloud,
confuse 9. inebriate 10. intoxicate
beg... 3. ask, sue, woo 4. pray, sorn
5. cadge, crave, mooch, plead,
touch (sl) 6. appeal 7. beseech,
entreat, implore, solicit 8. petition
9. importune 10. supplicate
beget... 3. ean 4. sire 5. breed,
hatch, spawn 6. father 7. develop
8. engender, generate 9. procreate,
reproduce
begetter... 4. sire 5. pater 6. author,
father, mother, parent 7. creator
10. procreator, progenitor
beggar... 3. bum 4. hobo, waif
5. fakir (Moslem), gamin, lazar, rogue
6. loafer, pauper, wretch
7. almsman, dervish, vagrant, wastral
8. indigent, vagabond 9. mendicant,
suppliant 10. panhandler, ragamuffin
14. tatterdemalion
beggarly... 3. low 4. base, mean,
poor, rank 5. petty 6. abject,
meanly, paltry, vulgar 7. hangdog,
ignoble 8. bankrupt, indigent,
infamous, wretched 9. miserable,
niggardly 10. despicably, obsequious
12. contemptible
Beggars, King of (Eng)... 5. Carew
beggary... 4. want 6. penury
9. indigence, mendicity, pauperism
10. mendicancy 11. destitution,
panhandling
begin... 4. open 5. enter, start
6. attack 8. commence, initiate, take
rise 9. institute, introduce, originate
10. inaugurate
begin again... 5. renew 6. resume
10. recommence
beginner... 3. dub 4. tyro (tiro)
5. chela 6. infant, novice
7. amateur, entrant, recruit
8. begetter, freshman, neophyte
9. debutante, fledgling, initiator,
novitiate 10. catechumen, originator,
tenderfoot 11. inaugurator
beginning... 4. head, rise, root
5. alpha, birth, debut, onset, start
6. origin, outset, source 7. genesis,
infancy, opening 8. entrance,
inchoate, nascency, outstart, starting
9. inception, threshold 10. derivation,
foundation, incomplete, initiation
12. commencement, introduction
begone... 3. out 4. away, scat, shoo
5. allez, scram 6. aroint, avaunt,
depart 7. vamoose
begrudge... 4. envy 5. covey, stint
6. grudge, refuse 7. grumble
beguile... 4. dupe, lure, vamp
5. amuse, charm, cozen, elude,
spend, trick 6. delude, divert, regale
7. bewitch, deceive, ensnare, mislead
8. enthrall, intrigue 9. bamboozle,
captivate, deception, entertain,
fascinate, victimize 11. double–cross
14. disappointment
begum (Hind)... 5. queen 7. heiress
8. princess

begunk... 4. jilt 5. trick
behalf... 4. gain, good, part, sake,
side 5. avail, stead 6. affair, matter,
profit 7. benefit, defense, service,
support, welfare 8. interest
9. advantage
behalf of... 3. for 6. lieu of, rather
7. defense (of), instead
behave... 2. do 3. act 4. bear
5. carry 6. demean, deport, manage
7. conduct 8. regulate, restrain
behavior, behaviour... 3. air 4. mien
6. action, manner 7. actions,
address, bearing, conduct, decorum,
manners 8. carriage, demeanor,
maintien 10. deportment
11. comportment
behavior (pert to)...
good.. 7. decorum, P's and Q's
riotous.. 7. rampage
wicked.. 10. wrongdoing
behead... 7. execute 9. decollate
10. decapitate, guillotine
Behemoth (Bib)... 5. beast
12. hippopotamus
behest... 3. vow 5. order 7. bidding,
command, mandate, promise
10. injunction 11. commandment
behind... 3. aft 4. late, past, rear,
rump (vulgar), slow, tail 5. abaff,
abaft, after, ahind, arear, later, tardy
6. astern 7. delayed, impeded
8. arrested, backward, retarded 9. in
the past, posterior, remaining
behindhand... 4. late 5. tardy
7. arrears, belated, overdue
8. backward, dilatory, misdated,
mistimed 10. defaulting, delinquent
behind the times... 5. passé
behold... 2. lo 3. see 4. ahoy, ecce,
ecco, espy, look, scan, view 5. voilà
6. descry, regard, retain 7. discern,
observe, witness 8. maintain,
perceive
beholden... 5. bound 7. bounden,
obliged 8. grateful, indebted, thankful
9. obligated
beholder... 5. gazer 7. watcher,
witness 8. looker–on, observer,
onlooker 9. spectator
beige... 4. ecru, hopi 5. grège
6. dorado 13. reddish–yellow
being... 3. ego, ens, man, one
4. bion, body, esse, home, life, self
5. entia, gnome, human, thing, wight
6. actual, animal, entity, extant,
mortal, person 7. Adamite, essence,
present, reality 8. creature, existent,
existing, organism, presence
9. actuality, existence, personage,
something 10. individual
11. subsistence
being (pert to)...
celestial.. 4. deva 5. angel 6. cherub,
seraph
imaginary.. 4. pixy (pixie) 5. fairy,
sylph
science of.. 8. ontology
supernatural.. 6. Garuda (Hind)
Supreme.. 3. God 7. Creator
belaud... 4. laud 5. extol 6. praise
7. glorify

belay ... 4. halt, quit, stop 5. beset,
cease, cover, halte 6. fasten, invest,
waylay 7. besiege, silence 8. encircle
belch ... 4. burp, emit, vent 5. eject,
eruct, erupt, spout, vomit 7. gush out
8. disgorge, eructate 9. small beer
(vulgar) 10. eructation
beldam, beldame ... 3. cat, hag
4. fury 5. crone, frump, shrew, vixen,
witch 6. virago 7. she–wolf, tigress
8. ancestor (fem), harridan
9. termagant 11. grandmother
Belgian (pert to) ... see also *Belgium*
anthem .. 13. La Brabanconne
hare .. 8. leporide
horse .. 9. Brabancon
marble .. 5. rance
resort .. 6. Ostend
sheep dog .. 8. Malinois
11. Groenendael
violinist .. 5. Ysaye
Belgian Congo ... see *Zaire*
Belgium ...
capital .. 8. Brussels
city .. 5. Ghent, Liege 6. Bruges
7. Antwerp, Louvain 9. Charleroi
commune .. 3. Ath
forest .. 8. Ardennes
king .. 6. Albert 7. Leopold
8. Baudouin
native .. 7. Fleming (of Flanders),
Flemish, Walloon
nickname .. 15. cockpit of Europe
World War II Battle of .. 8. The Bulge
Belgravia (London) ... 8. district
(fashion)
Belial ... 5. devil, Satan (New Test)
10. wickedness (Old Test) 11. Fallen
Angel
belie ... 4. deny 6. belong, defame,
oppose, oppugn 7. besiege, falsify,
gainsay, pertain, slander 8. disclaim,
disprove, surround 9. encompass
10. calumniate 12. misrepresent
belief ... 3. fay (anc), ism 4. cult, rule,
sect, view 5. credo, creed, dogma,
faith, maxim, tenet 7. opinion,
precept 8. credence, doctrine,
reliance, religion, teaching
9. assurance, certainty, principle
10. confidence, conviction,
persuasion 13. Apostles' Creed
believe ... 3. buy 4. deem, feel, trow,
ween 5. think, trust 6. accept, credit,
reckon 7. suppose, swallow
8. conceive, consider
believer (pert to) ...
all religions .. 6. omnist
facts .. 7. realist
religion .. 5. deist 6. theist
9. Adventist, Calvinist
13. particularist
Belit (Bab) ... 8. goddess (wife of Bel)
belittle ... 4. slur 5. decry, dwarf,
scoff, scorn 6. debase, demean,
deride, impugn 7. detract, run down
8. minimize 9. discredit, disparage,
underrate 10. depreciate
13. underestimate
bell ... 4. gong 5. codon, knell
6. curfew, tocsin 7. campana,

cowbell 8. carillon, doorbell 9. ship's
bell 10. dinnerbell, schoolbell
12. glockenspiel 13. tintinnabulum
bell, bells (pert to) ...
bird .. 9. campanero 10. wood thrush
botany .. 7. corolla
evening .. 6. curfew 7. Angelus
flat .. 4. gong 6. tam–tam (Chin),
tom–tom
funeral .. 5. knell
nautical .. 8. half hour
ringer .. 6. toller
ringing .. 7. peeling 14. tintinnabulism
science of .. 11. campanology
set of .. 6. chimes 8. carillon
shaped .. 11. campaniform
specialist .. 9. campanist
13. campanologist
tongue .. 7. clapper
tower .. 6. belfry 9. campanile
warning .. 6. tocsin
belle ... 4. lady (fine) 5. toast
6. beauty 7. charmer 8. handsome
10. grande dame
belles–lettres ... 8. classics
10. humanities (The), literature
bellflower ... 8. daffodil
belligerent ... 7. hostile, scrappy,
warlike 8. choleric, militant
9. bellicose, irascible, litigious,
offensive, wrangling 10. aggressive,
pugnacious 11. contentious,
quarrelsome 12. disputatious
belligerent's right (Internat law) ...
6. angary
bellow ... 3. cry, low, moo, say
4. bawl, roar, wail, yawp 5. blare,
shout 6. clamor 7. thunder
9. vociferate
bellows ... 4. fish 5. gills, lungs
6. blower, lights (Zool), rotary
8. ctenidia (Zool)
bellwether ... 5. sheep 6. leader,
wether (with bell)
belly ... 3. bag, pot 4. crap, wame
5. bulge, front, tummy 6. bottom,
paunch, venter 7. abdomen, stomach
8. potbelly, swell out 9. ingluvies
belong (to) ... 6. answer, inhere
7. pertain, related 9. appendant,
ingrained, possessed (by)
10. correspond
belonging (to) ...
collector, hobbyist .. 10. collection
11. collectible (collectable)
dean .. 7. decanal
era .. 7. epochal
Fall .. 8. autumnal
pencil (a) .. 6. desmic
people .. 7. endemic
present (the) .. 7. current
Spring .. 6. vernal
Summer .. 7. estival
Winter .. 6. hiemal
belongings ... 4. duds, gear 5. goods,
traps 6. family, things 7. baggage,
effects, kinsmen 8. chattels, property
9. homefolks, relations, trappings
11. connections, perquisites,
possessions 13. accouterments,
appurtenances

beloved... 3. pet 4. dear 6. prized
7. darling 8. precious, truelove
9. cherished, inamorata
beloved physician... 6. St Luke
below... 4. alow, here, less 5. Hades,
neath, sotto, under 6. aneath, in hell
7. beneath, short of 10. downstairs
11. belowstairs
Belshazzar (Bib)... 11. crown prince
Bel's wife... 5. Belit (Beltis)
belt... 3. bar, bat, hit 4. area, band,
beat, blow, cest, mark, pelt, ring,
sash, sock, whip, zone 5. apron,
Libya, strap, whack, zonar 6. cestus,
cingle, cordon, fascia, fasten, fillet,
girdle, region, strait, streak, stripe
7. baldric, kurbash, sjambok,
stratum, terrain 8. cincture, encircle,
surround 9. encompass
10. cummerbund
Belteshazzar (Bib)... 6. Daniel
belt of heaven... 6. zodiac 7. circuit
beluga... 5. whale (white)
Belus (pert to)...
father of.. 4. Dido
king of.. 4. Tyre 7. Assyria
son of.. 5. Libya
sons.. 7. Cepheus, Phineus
8. Aegyptus
belvedere... 5. cigar 7. cypress (mock)
10. watchtower 11. summerhouse
bema... 8. platform 9. sanctuary
bemoan... 4. pity, wail 5. mourn
6. bewail, grieve, lament, regret,
repine 7. deplore 10. sympathize
bemuse... 4. daze 5. addle, besot
6. absorb, muddle 7. stupefy
8. befuddle, distract 10. intoxicate
ben... 2. in 3. oil, son 4. tree
(Moringa) 6. within
bench... 3. pew 4. banc (judge's),
seat 5. chair, court, siege, staff,
stand, stool, table 6. exedra, settee,
settle 7. terrace 8. platform,
woolsack 9. committee
bend... 3. bow, nod, ply, sag, sny
4. bias, flex, genu, kink, knot, sway,
turn, warp 5. crimp, crook, curve,
drink, kneel, prone, squat, stoop,
twist, yield 6. buckle, crouch, curtsy,
direct, divert, humble, inflex, kowtow,
pleach, relent, salaam, strain, swerve
7. bendlet (Her), chevron (Her),
incline, refract, retract 9. genuflect,
introvert, sinuosity 10. inflection
bend (pert to)...
an ear.. 4. hear, heed 6. listen
one's will.. 4. bias, move, sway
the elbow.. 5. drink
the knee.. 5. kneel 6. kowtow,
salaam 9. genuflect
the mind.. 5. think
bends... 7. caisson, disease
8. blackout (aeronaut)
beneath... 4. alow 5. below, lower
(than), 'neath, under 6. aneath,
nether 7. in Hades 11. underground
beneath one's dignity... 8. infradig
15. infra dignitatem
benedict... 7. husband
10. bridegroom, married man (newly)
benediction... 4. rite 6. praise, prayer,

thanks 7. benison 8. blessing
10. invocation 12. thanksgiving
benefaction... 4. alms, boon, gift,
good 5. favor 7. benefit, present
8. courtesy, donation, gratuity,
kindness 9. beau geste
11. beneficence, benevolence
benefactor... 5. angel, donor
6. backer, helper, patron 8. promoter
10. befriender
beneficence... 7. charity 8. goodness,
kindness 11. benefaction,
benevolence 12. philanthropy
beneficial... 4. good 6. benign, useful
7. helpful 8. edifying, salutary
9. favorable, healthful, lucrative,
wholesome 10. profitable, salubrious
11. serviceable 12. advantageous,
remunerative
beneficiary... 4. heir 5. donee
6. vassal 7. devisee, feoffee, grantee,
legatee 8. assignee 9. annuitant
benefit... 3. aid, use 4. boon, gift,
good, help, vail 5. avail, favor, trust
6. profit, relief, succor 7. advance,
concert, improve, service, welfare
8. blessing, kindness 9. advantage
11. benefaction, convenience,
performance
benevolence... 3. tax 4. gift, good
6. bounty, giving 7. charity
8. altruism, bestowal, blessing,
donation, kindness 10. generosity,
liberality 11. munificence
12. contribution, philanthropy
14. charitableness
benevolent... 4. free, good, king
6. benign 7. liberal 8. generous,
princely 9. benignant, bountiful
10. altruistic, charitable, munificent
11. magnanimous 13. philanthropic
Bengal, Indian State...
capital.. 8. Calcutta
gentleman.. 5. baboo (babu)
language.. 7. Bengali
native.. 3. Kol (Kohl) 6. banian
7. Bengali
negro.. 3. Ibo (Ebo)
river.. 6. Ganges 11. Brahmaputra
river boat.. 7. bauleah
benign... 4. mild 5. bland 6. genial,
humane, kindly 7. benefic (Astrol),
liberal 8. gracious, salutary
9. benignant, favorable, healthful,
wholesome 10. propitious, salubrious
benignity... 5. favor 7. benefit
8. blessing, goodness, mildness
9. salubrity 10. kindliness
11. benevolence 12. graciousness
benison... 3. benefaction, benediction
10. invocation 11. benediction
benjamin... 6. jacket 7. benzoin
8. overcoat 9. spicebush
Benjamin (Bib, pert to)...
father.. 5. Jacob
history.. 5. tribe
mother.. 6. Rachel
Benjamin's mess... 6. big end
10. lion's share
benjy (Brit sl)... 3. hat (straw)
9. waistcoat
benne... 6. sesame

bennet... 4. herb 5. daisy 7. hemlock
bent... 3. aim, way, wry 4. bias, turn,
warp 5. drift, grass, slant, tenor,
trend, twist 6. course, curved,
desire, minded, nature, swayed
7. angular, aptness, crooked,
heather, leaning, stooped 8. aptitude,
penchant, tendency 9. obliquity,
prejudice, proneness 10. propensity
11. disposition, inclination
12. idiosyncrasy, predilection
13. prepossession 14. predisposition
Benthamism... 9. welfarism
14. utilitarianism
benthonic... 7. benthal, deep sea
benthonic plant... 6. enalid
benthos... 5. deeps 6. depths
8. ocean bed 16. Davy Jones's
locker
benumb... 3. nip 4. drug, numb, stun
5. chill 6. deaden, freeze 7. stupefy
8. paralyze 11. anesthetize,
desensitize
Beowulf... 4. poem (oldest in Teutonic
language)
bequeath... 4. give, will 5. endow,
leave 6. bestow, demise, devise,
invest, will to 7. bequest 8. transmit
bequest... 4. will 6. devise, legacy
8. heritage 9. patrimony, testament
10. birthright 11. inheritance
berate... 3. jaw, nag 4. lash, rail
5. chide, scold, slate 7. censure,
reprove, upbraid
Berber... 4. Riff 6. Hamite, Kabyle,
Taureg
berceau... 4. walk (leaf–covered)
5. arbor, bower 6. cradle
berceuse... 10. cradlesong
11. composition
bereave... 3. die, rob 5. leave, strip
6. divest, orphan, sadden 7. deprive,
despoil 10. disentitle, dispossess
bereavement... 4. loss 5. death
9. privation 10. divestment
bereft... 4. lorn 7. denuded, fleeced,
shorn of, witless 8. bereaved,
divested, orphaned, stripped
9. senseless 10. parentless,
pauperized
Bereshith (Jew)... 7. Genesis
9. Beginning
beret... 3. cap, tam 7. biretta
bergamot... 4. pear 5. snuff 6. orange
7. essence 9. fragrance
beriberi... 5. kakke 7. disease
Berkeleianism (pert to)...
  founder.. 8. Berkeley (Bishop)
  science.. 10. philosophy
  system.. 8. idealism 13. immaterialism
Berlin, Germany...
  avenue.. 14. Unter den Linden
  capital.. 7. Germany
  garden (Zool).. 10. Tiergarten
  gate.. 11. Brandenburg
  government.. 9. Reichstag
berm, berme... 4. mall, path 5. prado
6. runway 7. terrace 8. shoulder
(road)
Bermuda...
  capital.. 8. Hamilton
  color.. 12. geranium pink

  discoverer.. 8. Bermudez
  government.. 7. British
  grass.. 5. decil
  ocean site.. 8. Atlantic
Bernardine Order... 11. Cistercians
Berne, Bern (Switz)... 7. capital
berry... 3. haw 4. buck, seed
5. bacca, cubeb, fruit, grain, money
6. acinus, kernel
berry, fruit... 5. grape, salal
6. banana, tomato 7. currant
8. bilberry, dewberry, hagberry,
mulberry 9. bearberry, blueberry,
cranberry, raspberry 10. blackberry,
elderberry, gooseberry, loganberry,
strawberry 11. boysenberry,
huckleberry 12. checkerberry,
whortleberry
berserk... 4. amok, bunk, dock, post,
room 5. house, roost 6. billet,
marina, office, reside 8. quarters
9. situation 11. appointment
bertha... 4. cape 6. cannon, collar
7. Perchta (goddess) 9. Big Bertha
(Ger gun)
beseech... 3. beg, sue 4. pray
5. crave, plead 6. obtest 7. entreat,
implore, solicit 9. obsecrate
10. supplicate
beset... 3. dun, ply, vex 4. stud
5. harry, haunt, hem in, siege, worry
6. attack, harass, infest, invade,
obsess, plague, ravage 7. besiege
8. blockade, surround 9. beleaguer,
importune, infatuate
beset with danger... 5. risky
6. chancy 8. perilous 9. dangerous
10. jeopardous
beset with hairs... 7. barbate,
bearded
beside, besides... 2. by 3. too, yet
4. also, else, near, nigh, para (pref)
5. about, along 6. nearby
8. likewise, moreover 9. other than
11. furthermore 12. over and above
beside oneself... 3. mad 4. wild
5. crazy, rabid 6. beserk, raging,
raving 7. frantic, ranting 8. frenzied
9. desperate, overjoyed
10. distracted, distraught
11. overwrought
besiege... 5. beset 6. attack, harass,
obsess, plague 7. torment
8. blockade, surround 9. beleaguer
besmear... 3. dab 4. coat, daub,
mark, soil, spot 5. paint, smear,
stain, taint 6. bedaub 7. tarnish
8. besmudge
besmirch... 4. blot, soil 5. smear, sully
6. defile, smirch, smudge, vilify
7. besmear, blacken, tarnish
8. discolor
besom... 5. broom, hussy
besotted... 4. dull 5. drunk
7. muddled, sottish 8. obsessed
9. senseless, stupefied 10. infatuated
11. intoxicated
bespangled... 5. aglow 7. lighted,
studded, trimmed 8. spangled
9. decorated, garnished
10. glittering, ornamented
11. embellished, illuminated

bespatter... 3. wet 4. blot, spot
5. dirty, slosh, smear, stain, sully
6. splash, vilify 7. asperse, scatter,
spatter, tarnish 8. besmirch, splatter,
sprinkle 9. denigrate 10. stigmatize
bespeak... 4. mean, show 5. imply
6. ask for, attest, engage, evince
7. address, betoken, connote, exhibit,
suggest, testify 8. foretell, indicate,
manifest 11. demonstrate
best... 4. aces, beat, most, tops
5. cream, elite, queen 6. choice,
finest 7. largest 8. champion,
outstrip 9. nonpareil, overmatch
11. superlative
bestial... 3. low 4. vile 5. cruel
6. brutal, filthy, savage 7. beastly,
brutish, inhuman, sensual
8. depraved, ruthless 9. barbarous
bestow... 4. deal, give 5. allot, apply,
award, grant, spend 6. accord,
confer, convey, demise, devote,
donate, impart, render, tender
7. deposit, present 8. transmit
10. administer
bestow honor upon... 5. adorn, exalt,
grace 7. dignify, ennoble, glorify
10. aggrandize 11. distinguish
bestride... 4. pass 5. mount 7. climb
on, protect, support 8. straddle
10. bestraddle
bet... 3. bas (roulette), pot 4. play
5. stake, wager 6. gamble, hazard,
pledge
beta test (army)... 12. intelligence
bête... 5. beast, silly 6. stupid
7. foolish
betel (pert to)...
leaf.. 3. pan 4. buyo, paun (pan)
palm.. 5. areca
pepper.. 4. itmo (ikmo)
bête noir... 4. ogre 7. bugbear
10. black beast, frightener,
mumbo–jumbo, Mumbo Jumbo
bethel... 4. kirk 6. chapel, church
8. Bethesda (Jerusalem)
12. meetinghouse
bethink... 5. think 6. recall 7. reflect
8. cogitate, remember 9. cerebrate,
recollect
betide... 3. hap 4. fall 5. occur
6. befall, happen 7. betoken,
presage 9. come about, eventuate,
transpire
betimes... 4. anon, soon 5. early
7. ere long, shortly 8. directly,
speedily 9. forthwith, presently
10. beforehand, seasonably
12. occasionally
betise... 5. folly 9. asininity, silliness,
stupidity 11. foolishness
betoken... 4. mark, mean, note
5. augur 6. denote, typify
7. bespeak, connote, express,
portend, presage, purport, signify
8. evidence, indicate 9. foretoken,
symbolize
betray... 4. blab, dupe, hoax, sell
5. bluff, peach, trick 6. reveal,
seduce, tattle 7. beguile, deceive,
divulge, mislead, sell out 8. disclose,

inform on 9. bamboozle, victimize
11. double–cross
betrayal... 4. ruse 5. trick 7. sellout,
treason 8. giveaway 9. Judas kiss,
seduction, treachery 10. disclosure
betrayer... 5. Judas 6. Arnold, Brutus
7. seducer, traitor 8. derelict,
informer, Quisling, turncoat
10. treasonist 13. double–crosser,
Judas Iscariot
betroth... 4. affy, earl 5. tryst
6. engage, pledge, plight
7. espouse, promise 8. affiance,
contract, espousal 10. engagement
better... 3. top 4. more 5. amend,
emend, excel, raise (poker), safer,
wiser 6. bigger, exceed, outwit,
reform 7. advance, choicer, greater,
improve, promote, surpass, victory
8. improved, superior 9. advantage,
meliorate 10. ameliorate, preferable
11. superiority
betting term... 4. ante, odds, tout
6. parlay 7. pyramid 10. parimutuel
11. sweepstakes
between... 5. among, mesne
6. atween 7. average, betwixt
bevel... 4. edge, ream 5. angle, bezel,
slant, slope, snape, splay 6. square
7. incline, oblique 9. obliquity
beverage... 3. ade, opo (comb form),
pop, tea 4. coke, malt, maté, mead,
milk, soda 5. cider, cocoa, drink,
leban, morat (anc), punch, water
6. coffee, eggnog, frappé, nectar
7. Seltzer 8. Adam's ale, Coca–Cola,
lemonade, root beer, sourdook
9. ginger ale, orangeade, phosphate
10. buttermilk, grape juice
12. sarsaparilla
beverage (alcoholic)... 3. ale, gin, rum
4. beer, brew, grog, kava, port, raki
5. booze, cider, hooch, julep, lager,
negus, punch, smash, vodka
6. arrack, bishop, brandy, cognac,
eggnog, kumiss, kummel, likker,
porter, posset, sherry, tiswin, whisky
(whiskey), zythum (anc) 7. Bacardi,
bootleg, bourbon, cordial, liqueur,
martini, tequila 8. absinthe, aleberry,
Burgundy, cocktail, highball, muscatel,
sauterne, vermouth 9. applejack,
aqua vitae, firewater, Manhattan
10. shandygaff, Tom Collins
11. Benedictine, boilermaker,
grasshopper, mountain dew
bevy... 4. bund, gang, herd, host
5. covey, flock, group, party, troop
6. galaxy, throng 7. company
8. assembly 10. collection
bewail... 3. rue 4. keen, mean
5. mourn 6. bemoan, grieve, lament,
regret, repine, sorrow 7. deplore
bewilder... 3. fog 4. daze 5. addle,
amaze 6. baffle, dazzle, puzzle
7. buffalo, confuse, fluster, mystify,
nonplus, perplex 8. astonish,
confound, distract 9. bamboozle,
embarrass
bewilderment... 3. awe, fog 4. maze
6. wonder 9. confusion
10. perplexity 11. distraction

12. perturbation 13. disconcertion, embarrassment

bewitch... 3. hex 5. charm, witch
6. enamor, entice, hoodoo, voodoo
7. beguile, delight, enchant
8. enthrall 9. captivate, enrapture, ensorcell, fascinate, infatuate

bewitching... 5. siren 6. hexing, lovely
7. magical 8. alluring, charming, enticing 10. enchanting
11. captivating, fascinating

bey (Turk)... 5. title 8. governor

beyond... 2. by 3. too, yet 4. meta (pref), past, plus, well 5. above, extra, ultra 6. yonder 7. besides, farther, further, yonside 8. moreover
9. exceeding, Hereafter (The)
11. furthermore 12. additionally, ultraliminal

beyond hope... 9. desperate

bezant (pert to)...
architecture.. 4. disc 8. ornament
coin (anc).. 7. solidus (gold)
heraldry.. 4. disc (gold)
offering (Eng king).. 4. gold

bezel... 4. edge 5. crown (gem), facet
6. chaton, flange 8. pavilion, template (templet) 9. obliquity

bezonian... 6. mucker, wretch
7. budmash, caitiff, recruit
8. blighter 9. pilgarlic, scoundrel

bhikshu... 6. gelong 7. ascetic
8. sannyasi 9. mendicant

bhut (Dravidian)... 5. demon, ghost
6. goblin

bias... 3. ply 4. awry, bent, turn, warp
5. amiss, slant, twist 6. desire
7. leaning, oblique 8. diagonal, slanting, tendency 9. obliquity, prejudice 10. favoritism, partiality, prepossess, transverse 11. disposition

biased... 4. bent 6. narrow, swayed
7. bigoted, partial 8. diagonal, partisan, slanting 10. prejudiced

bib... 3. sip, sup 4. swig 5. apron, drink, quaff 6. guzzle, imbibe, tipple, tucker 7. tablier 8. pinafore

bibacious... 6. toping 7. drunken, sottish 8. bibulous, drinking, tippling

Bible... 7. The Book, The Word, Vulgate 10. Scriptures, Testaments (Old, New)

Bible (pert to)...
battle site.. 10. Armageddon
city.. 2. Ur 5. Joppa, Sidon, Sodom
6. Hebron 9. Bethlehem, Jerusalem
coin.. 6. talent
Commandments.. 9. Decalogue
Holy Land.. 9. Palestine
interpretation.. 7. anagoge
introduction.. 9. Isagogics
kingdom.. 4. Elam 6. Basham, Canaan 7. Chaldea
land of plenty.. 6. Goshen
language.. 7. Aramaic
mountain.. 4. Ebol, Zion 5. Horeb, Sinai 6. Ararat, Gilead, Moriah, Olives (Olivet), Pisgah
pause.. 5. selah
pool.. 6. Siloam
precious stone.. 6. ligure (jacinth)
Promised Land.. 6. Canaan

sea.. 3. Red 4. Dead 7. Galilee
Sermon on the Mount..
10. Beatitudes
sheep.. 7. chamois
town.. 4. Edar 5. Babel
Wells of.. 5. Hagar, Jacob

Bible character...
archangel.. 7. Raphael
giant.. 4. Anak 7. Goliath
High Priest.. 3. Eli
hunter.. 6. Nimrod
liar.. 7. Ananias
patriarch.. 5. Jacob 6. Israel
prophet.. 4. Amos, Joel 5. Hosea, Jonah, Micah, Nahum 6. Daniel, Haggai, Isaiah, Joseph, Joshua, Samuel 7. Ezekiel, Malachi, Obadiah
8. Habakkuk, Jeremiah 9. Zachariah, Zephaniah

Bible version... 5. Douay, Reims
6. Geneva 7. Bishop's, Luther's, Revised, Targums, Vulgate
8. Cranmer's, Matthew's, Peshitta, Tyndale's, Wartburg, Wycliffe 9. King James, Maccabees 10. Great Bible, Septuagint 15. American Revised

bicker... 5. argue, cavil 6. hassle, quiver, strife 7. dispute, flicker, flutter, quarrel, quibble, rhubarb (sl), wrangle 8. argument, pettifog
9. scrimmage, tremulous
10. contention 11. altercation

bicuspid... 5. bifid, tooth, valve
6. cuspid 8. premolar
10. two–pointed 13. double–pointed

bid... 3. beg 4. pray 5. offer, order, utter 6. charge, direct, enjoin, invite, reveal, tender 7. command, declare, entreat, offered, summons
8. overture, proclaim 9. quotation
12. presentation

biddy... 3. hen 4. dame 5. skirt
6. female 7. chicken, Partlet
8. bedmaker 11. maidservant

bide... 4. bear, stay, wait 5. abide, await, tarry 6. endure, remain, suffer
8. continue, tolerate 9. encounter, withstand

bield... 3. den 4. cozy 7. comfort, courage, hearten, shelter 8. boldness, embolden 9. sheltered
10. confidence, habitation

bien... 4. fine, good, snug

bienseance... 7. decorum, manners
9. propriety 11. correctness, proprieties (the) 12. mannerliness
17. conventionalities

bier... 6. coffin, litter 10. catafalque

Bier... 4. beer

biff... 4. bash, blow, slug, sock
5. paste, punch

bifold... 4. dual 5. duple 6. binary, binate, double 7. twofold

bifurcate... 3. wye (letter) 4. fork
7. forking, furcate 8. biforked, branched, forklike 9. two–forked

big... 4. huge 5. bulky, grand, great, grown, jumbo, large 6. august, famous, mighty 7. massive, pompous, teeming 8. boastful, powerful, pregnant, swelling
9. momentous 10. tremendous

11. magnanimous, pretentious
big (pert to)...
shot.. 3. VIP
stick.. 5. power (T Roosevelt)
toe.. 6. hallux
top.. 6. circus
wig.. 3. VIP (humorous)
Big (pert to)...
Ben.. 5. clock 13. Tower of London
Bend State.. 9. Tennessee
Bertha.. 3. gun 5. Krupp (factory)
Board.. 6. Bourse 8. Exchange
   11. stock market 13. stock exchange
House.. 3. pen 6. prison (State)
   12. penitentiary
Push (WWI).. 5. Somme
bight... 3. bay 4. bend, gulf, loop
   5. angle, noose, point 6. corner,
   hollow 7. estuary
bigot... 3. bug, nut 6. zealot
   7. fanatic 9. dogmatist, hypocrite,
   illiberal 10. enthusiast, opinionist,
   positivist
bigoted... 5. petty 6. little, narrow
   10. intolerant, prejudiced
   12. narrow—minded
bijou... 5. jewel 7. trinket
bilbi, bilby... 8. kangaroo
bilbo... 5. sword 6. rapier
bilingual... 6. diglot 12. linguistical
bilious... 3. ill 8. choleric, liverish
   9. dyspeptic, jaundiced
   11. ill—tempered
bilk... 2. do 3. gyp 4. balk, hoax, sell
   5. cheat, cozen, trick 6. delude,
   fleece, illude 7. deceive, defraud,
   swindle 8. flimflam 11. hornswoggle
bill... 3. dun, neb, nib, pee, tab, Vee
   ($5) 4. beak, deed, list, menu, sign
   5. carte, money 6. docket, pickax,
   poster, ticket 7. account, invoice,
   mattock, placard, program, receipt,
   statute, voucher 8. billhook, schedule
   9. publicize, statement
   10. prospectus 11. legislative
   13. advertisement
billet... 3. bar, log 4. note, pass
   5. berth, stick, strap 6. assign,
   docket, letter, notice, ticket
   7. bearing (Her), epistle, missive,
   molding 8. dispatch, document,
   insignia, position, quarters
   11. appointment
billiard shot... 5. carom, masse
   6. cannon
Billingsgate... 4. Gate (London)
   10. fish market 12. vituperation
billow... 3. sea 4. roll, toss, wave
   5. eagre, heave, surge, swell
   6. dilate 7. distend 10. undulation
billowy... 4. wavy 5. surgy 7. surging
   8. swelling 10. undulating
bin... 3. box 4. crib, loft, vina
   5. frame, kench, pungi (Hind flute)
   6. manger 8. elevator
binary... 4. dual 6. bifold, binate,
   double, duplex 9. duplicate
bind... 3. jam, tie 4. ally, frap, gird,
   gyve, hold, lace, lash, rope, tape
   5. chain, leash, stick, truss, withe
   6. engage, fasten, fetter, pinion,
   pledge, secure 7. confine, shackle

8. obligate 10. constipate
binding... 4. tape 5. valid 6. binder,
   edging 7. girding, joining, liaison
   8. trimming, trussing, wrapping
   9. bordering, fastening, stringent
   10. astringent, compulsory, obligatory
   11. restraining, restrictive
binding (agreement)... 4. bond, pact
   7. bargain, promise 8. contract
binding (book)... 4. yapp 5. cover
   6. jacket 10. bibliopegy
binge... 4. bout 5. spree 6. bender
   8. carousal 11. celebration
bingo... 3. pop 4. bang, keno
   5. lotto, socko 6. brandy
biographer... 8. annalist 9. historian
   10. chronicler 11. biographist,
   memorialist
biography... 4. life 6. memoir
   7. history, memoire, recount
   8. memorial 11. hagiography
biological... 4. gene 5. class, genus,
   order, vital 6. biotic, family
   7. animate, organic, paracme,
   species
biology, science of... 6. botany
   7. ecology, zoology 8. eugenics,
   genetics 9. bionomics, organisms
   10. embryology, morphology,
   physiology
biopsy (Med)... 8. analysis (tissue)
   9. diagnosis 11. examination
   (microscopic)
biped... 3. man 9. two—legged
birch... 4. flog 5. stick 6. switch
birch tree (pert to)...
family.. 10. Betulaceae
genera.. 5. alder, birch, hazel
order.. 7. Fagales
product.. 16. oil of wintergreen
variety.. 5. paper, river, sweet, white
   6. cherry, yellow
bird (pert to)...
best swimmer.. 4. loon 6. gannet
cage.. 6. aviary 7. paddock
   8. dovecote
Class.. 4. Aves
crested.. 7. hoatzin 9. stinkbird
fabled, sacred.. 3. roc 4. ibis
fastest flyer.. 4. hawk 5. eagle, swift
   6. falcon
fastest runner.. 7. ostrich
feathers.. 5. remix (sing) 7. remiges
first.. 13. archaeopteryx
footless.. 4. apod
greatest traveler.. 4. tern
greatest wingspread.. 9. albatross
halcyon.. 10. kingfisher
highest flyer.. 5. goose
immortal.. 7. phoenix
killing.. 7. avicide
largest.. 6. condor 7. ostrich
   13. whooping crane
Latin.. 4. avis
life.. 5. ornis
longest—lived.. 5. macaw
lover.. 12. ornithophile
most dangerous.. 9. cassowary
naked hatched.. 11. gymnogenous
of prey (prized).. 6. falcon
oldest known.. 13. archaeopteryx
one year old.. 8. annotine

Order.. 7. Rasores 8. Raptores
smallest.. 14. bee hummingbird
smartest.. 4. crow
study.. 6. oology
young.. 4. eyas 8. birdikin, nestling
9. fledgling
bird, anatomy (pert to)...
beak.. 3. neb, nib 4. bill, lora
5. ceral 7. rostrum
eye process.. 6. pecten
head.. 4. lore 6. pileum
jaw.. 4. mala
leg (featherless).. 9. cnemidium
wing part.. 5. alula
bird, Arctic... 3. auk 4. gull, skua
5. brant 6. dunlin, fulmar, jaeger
7. penguin 9. ptarmigan
bird, colorful... 3. kea 5. egret,
macaw 6. magpie, parrot, trogon
7. peacock, quetzal (quezal)
8. lyrebird 10. kingfisher 14. bird of
paradise
bird, common... 3. ani, daw, owl
4. chat, dove, lark, pisk, wren
5. finch, pipit, robin, vireo 6. dunlin,
linnet, martin, oriole, phoebe, pigeon,
shrike, siskin, thrush, towhee 7. blue
jay, bunting, catbird, cowbird, flicker,
grackle, kinglet, sparrow, swallow,
tanager, warbler, waxwing
8. blackcap, bluebird, bobolink,
cardinal, grosbeak, kingbird, redstart,
starling, titmouse 9. chickadee,
goldfinch, nighthawk, sandpiper
10. flycatcher, meadowlark,
turtledove, woodpecker
11. hummingbird, mockingbird,
nightingale, pyrrhuloxia
12. whippoorwill, yellowhammer
14. scarlet tanager
bird, crow family... 4. crow, rook
5. crake, raven 6. chough, magpie
7. corvine, jackdaw
bird, duck family... 4. clee, coot,
lory, smew, teal, wood 5. eider,
goose 6. scoter 7. gadwall, mallard,
Muscovy, pintail, pochard
8. baldpate, redshank, shoveler
9. merganser 10. bufflehead,
canvasback
bird, flightless... 3. emu, moa
4. dodo (ext), kiwi, rhea, weka
7. apteryx, ostrich, peacock, penguin
8. Notornis 9. cassowary
bird, foreign...
Africa.. 4. taha 5. crane 6. cuckoo
7. ostrich 8. umbrette
10. weaverbird
Arctic.. 3. auk 4. gull, skua 5. brant
6. dunlin, falcon, jaeger 7. penguin
8. grayling 9. gyrfalcon, ptarmigan
Asia.. 4. myna 5. pitta 6. bulbul,
linnet 7. boobook, peacock, sirgang
8. dotterel, leaf bird 9. brambling,
muted swan
Australia.. 3. emu 4. kiwi, lory
5. lowan 6. leipoa 7. boobook,
grinder 8. ganggang, lorikeet,
lyrebird, morepork, parakeet, platypus
9. bowerbird, cassowary, pardalote
Central America.. 6. barbet, toucan
7. quetzal (quezal) 8. puffbird

Cuba.. 6. trogon 8. tocororo 14. bee
hummingbird
England.. 4. kite, rook 9. cormorant
11. carrion crow
Europe.. 4. merl 5. pipit, stilt
(3–toed), stork (white), swift, tarin
6. godwit, hoopoe, merlin, roller,
siskin 7. bittern, ortolan, skylark,
starnel 8. bee eater, dotterel,
garganey, nuthatch, redstart
9. brambling, chaffinch, gallinule,
sheldrake 10. lammergeir, turtledove
11. nightingale, wallcreeper
12. capercaillie (grouse)
Hawaii.. 2. io, o–o 3. ava, iwa, poe
4. iiwi, mamo 6. parson 7. frigate
India.. 5. shama 8. amadavat,
pheasant 11. red hornbill
Java.. 7. sparrow 8. rice bird 9. fruit
dove
New Guinea.. 9. cassowary 14. bird
of paradise
New Zealand.. 3. ihi, kea, moa, tui
4. kuku, weka
So America.. 4. guan 5. macaw
6. barbet, motmot, toucan
7. jacamar, tinamou, warrior
8. boatbill, caracara 9. trumpeter
11. scarlet ibis
bird, game... 4. teal 5. brant, goose,
quail, snipe 6. grouse, pigeon,
plover, turkey (wild) 7. bustard,
gadwall, mallard 8. bobwhite,
pheasant, woodcock 9. partridge,
ptarmigan 10. canvasback 14. prairie
chicken
bird, group...
partridge.. 5. covey
pheasant.. 3. nye 4. nide
quail.. 4. bevy
bird, long–legged... 4. ibis, rail, sora
5. crane, egret, heron, stilt, stork
6. avocet, curlew, jacana 7. seriema
8. flamingo 9. sandpiper
10. demoiselle
Bird of...
Freedom.. 9. bald eagle
Jove.. 5. eagle
June.. 7. peacock
Minerva.. 3. owl
Wonder.. 7. phoenix
bird, pet... 4. myna (mynah)
6. canary, parrot 8. cockatoo,
lovebird, parakeet
bird, poultry... 4. duck 5. goose
6. pigeon, turkey 7. chicken
8. pheasant
bird, shore... 4. swan 5. egret, heron,
stork 6. avocet, curlew, plover, willet
7. frigate, pelican 8. dotterel, killdeer
10. demoiselle
bird, sky... 4. erne (ern), gier (Bib),
hawk, kite 5. Buteo, eagle, saker
6. condor, falcon, gannet, jaeger,
merlin, osprey 7. buzzard, harrier,
kestral, vulture 8. caracara, ringtail
9. Accipiter 10. lammergeir
bird, water... 3. auk 4. coot, gull,
ibis, loon, rail, shag, skua, swan
5. cahow, crane, grebe, heron, stork
6. curlew, cygnet, gannet, jabiru,
jacana, petrel, plover 7. bittern,

bustard, dovekie, pelican, seriema,
skimmer 8. dabchick, flamingo,
umbrette 9. albatross, cormorant,
gallinule, guillemot, phalarope,
spoonbill 10. kingfisher, yellowlegs
biretta ... 8. skullcap 9. headdress
birl ... 4. spin 6. rattle 7. resolve
birth ... 3. nee 4. line 5. blood, breed
  6. origin 7. descent, genesis, lineage
  8. heritage, nativity, nobility
  9. beginning 10. derivation,
  extraction, renascence
  11. inheritance, Renaissance
birthday (pert to) ...
  astrology .. 7. casting, lineage (the
  gods)
  nativities .. 9. genethlic 10. genethliac
  poems .. 12. genethliacon
birth flower (by months) ...
  Jan .. 9. carnation
  Feb .. 8. primrose
  Mar .. 6. violet
  Apr .. 5. daisy
  May .. 15. lily of the valley
  June .. 4. rose
  July .. 8. sweet pea
  Aug .. 9. gladiolus
  Sept .. 5. aster
  Oct .. 6. dahlia
  Nov .. 13. chrysanthemum
  Dec .. 5. holly 10. poinsettia
birthmark ... 4. mole 5. nevus (naevus)
birthright ... 6. rights 8. heritage
  9. privilege 10. possession
  11. inheritance
birth seniority ... 9. first—born
  13. primogeniture
birthstone (by days) ...
  Sun .. 5. topaz 7. diamond
  Mon .. 5. pearl 7. crystal
  Tues .. 4. ruby 7. emerald
  Wed .. 8. amethyst 9. loadstone
  Thurs .. 8. sapphire 9. carnelian
  Fri .. 7. cat's eye, emerald
  Sat .. 7. diamond 9. turquoise
birthstone (by months) ...
  Jan .. 6. garnet
  Feb .. 8. amethyst
  Mar .. 6. jasper
  Apr .. 7. diamond 8. sapphire
  May .. 5. agate 7. emerald
  June .. 7. emerald 11. alexandrite
  July .. 4. onyx, ruby
  Aug .. 8. sardonyx 9. carnelian
  Sept .. 8. sapphire 10. chrysolite
  Oct .. 4. opal 10. aquamarine
  Nov .. 5. topaz
  Dec .. 4. ruby 9. turquoise
bis ... 5. again, ditto, twice 6. encore,
  repeat 7. replica 8. repetend
  9. duplicate 10. repetition
biscuit ... 3. bun, doe 4. rusk
  5. bread, cooky, scone, wafer
  6. pommel 7. cracker 8. biscotin,
  zwieback
bise ... 4. wind (cold) 6. winter
  7. Norther
bisect ... 4. fork 5. cross, halve, split
  6. cleave, divide
bishop ... 4. Abba 7. pontiff, prelate
  8. chessman, director, overseer
  9. churchman, clergyman, inspector

  14. superintendent
bishop (pert to) ...
  Bible .. 10. Great Bible
  cap .. 4. hura 5. miter
  revenue .. 7. annates
  staff .. 7. baculus, crosier (crozier)
  throne .. 3. see 4. apse
  vestment .. 4. cope 5. stole 6. rochet
  7. gremial, pallium 8. dalmatic
  10. omophorion
bishopric ... 3. see 4. seat 7. diocese
  10. episcopacy, episcopate
bison ... 2. ox 4. gaur, urus
  7. aurochs, buffalo 9. quadruped
bisque (pert to) ...
  ceramics (unglazed) .. 7. biscuit
  color .. 9. red—yellow
  food .. 4. soup 8. ice cream
  term (sports) .. 4. turn 5. point
  6. stroke
bissext (pert to) ...
  calendar .. 6. Julian (Rom)
  day .. 5. sixth (intercalary)
  year .. 8. Leap Year
bistro ... 6. tavern 7. barroom 8. wine
  shop 10. restaurant
bit ... 3. ace, jot, ort 4. bite, coin,
  iota, mite, mote, part (acting), role,
  snip, tool, tube, whit 5. check,
  crumb, hitch, money, piece, scrap,
  speck 6. morsel, smidge, tittle
  7. portion, smidgen, traneen
  8. somewhat 9. something
bit (harness) ... 4. curb 6. bridle,
  Pelham 7. snaffle 9. Liverpool
bit (money) ...
  two bits .. 7. quarter 9. ninepence
  (Bahamas)
  four bits .. 10. half dollar
bitch ... 6. female (animal) 8. slattern,
  strumpet (vulgar)
bite ... 3. cut, eat, nip, zip 4. food,
  gnaw, grip, hold, knap, pang, tang,
  zest 5. champ, smart, snack, sting,
  taste 6. morsel, nibble, pierce
  8. pungency
biting ... 4. acid, tart 5. acerb, acrid,
  sharp 6. bitter, rodent 7. caustic,
  cutting, mordant, nipping, painful,
  piquant, pungent 8. piercing,
  poignant, scathing, stinging
  9. sarcastic, trenchant, vitriolic,
  withering 10. astringent, irritating
  11. acrimonious, penetrating
biting nails ... 12. phaneromania
bito (pert to) ...
  bark .. 10. fish poison
  seeds .. 6. zachun (oil)
  tree .. 7. hajilij
bitter ... 4. acid, cold, keen, sore, sour
  5. acerb, acrid, irate, sharp
  6. severe 7. cutting, hostile, pungent
  8. grievous, stinging, virulent
  9. rancorous, resentful
  10. embittered, unpleasant
  11. acrimonious, distressful,
  reproachful
bitter (pert to) ...
  apple (herb) .. 9. colocynth
  chemical .. 4. alum
  earth .. 8. magnesia
  gentian .. 9. baldmoney

grass.. 9. colicroot
herb.. 3. rue 4. aloe 5. aloin
  8. centaury
plant.. 10. bitterroot 11. bittersweet
  (poisonous)
prefix.. 5. picro
salts.. 5. Epsom
suffix.. 6. picrin
vetch.. 3. ers
waters (Bib).. 5. Marah
wintergreen.. 10. pipsissewa
wormwood.. 8. de Gaulle (said of)
bitterness... 3. rue 5. venom
  6. rancor 7. remorse 8. acerbity,
  acrimony, tartness, wormwood
  9. animosity, poignancy, virulence
  10. causticity, resentment
bivalve... 4. clam, spat, Unio 5. pinna
  6. Anomia, mussel, oyster, Teredo
  7. mollusk, pandora, scallop
  10. brachiopod (fossil form)
bivocal... 9. diphthong (dipthong)
bivouac... 4. camp 6. encamp, laager
  7. camping, leaguer (Hist)
  10. encampment
biwa... 6. loquat
bizarre... 3. odd 5. dedal, outré, queer
  6. absurd, exotic, quaint, rococo
  7. baroque 8. fanciful 9. eccentric,
  fantastic, grotesque, highflown
  11. extravagant, sensational
Bizen... 7. pottery (unglazed)
Bizet... 8. composer (Carmen)
bizzarro (Mus)... 7. bizarre
  9. whimsical
blab... 6. gossip, reveal, snitch, tattle,
  tell on 7. blabber, chatter
  8. informer, squealer, telltale
  10. taleteller, tattletale 11. taletelling
blabber... 4. blab 6. babble, gabber,
  gossip, tattle 7. chatter, twaddle
  8. informer, nonsense
black... 3. ink, jet 4. ebon, evil, foul,
  inky, noir 5. color, cruel, ebony,
  murky, negro, niger, raven, sable,
  tarry 6. dismal, filthy, gloomy, pitchy,
  somber, sullen, wicked 7. hateful,
  melanic, nigrine, nigrous, ominous,
  unclean 8. atrament, menacing,
  mournful, sinister 9. atrocious,
  lightless, nigricant 10. calamitous,
  disastrous, forbidding
black (pert to)... see also *Black*
African.. 10. blackamoor
alloy.. 6. niello
and blue.. 5. livid 7. bruised
  10. discolored, ecchymosed,
  ecchymosis 11. bluish–black,
  lead–colored
art.. 5. magic 7. alchemy 8. wizardry
  10. black magic
ball.. 7. exclude 9. ostracize
bird.. 2. Zu (Myth) 3. ani, daw, pie
  4. crow, merl, rook 5. amsel, ouzel,
  raven 6. thrush 7. jackdaw
  10. Melanesian, Polynesian
bottom.. 9. clog dance
coffee.. 8. café noir
diamond.. 4. coal
duck.. 6. Cayuga
earth.. 4. mold 9. Chernozem (Russ)
face.. 4. type 5. sheep 8. minstrel

fish.. 6. tautog
garnet.. 8. melanite
gibbon.. 7. siamang
guard.. 5. drole, gamin, knave, rogue,
  scamp 6. rascal 7. vagrant, villain
  8. criminal, scalawag, scullion,
  vagabond 9. scoundrel
  11. rapscallion
Harry.. 7. sea bass
jack.. 4. flag (pirate) 6. coerce,
  cudgel, hijack 9. strong–arm
  10. Jolly Roger
partridge.. 9. francolin
rhinoceros.. 7. borelle
sheep.. 10. scapegrace
smith.. 5. smith 6. forger, smithy
  7. farrier
spruce.. 7. yewpine
strap.. 8. molasses
widow spider.. 6. pokomo
Black (pert to)...
Bess.. 4. mare (Dick Turpin's)
Current.. 5. Japan
Death.. 6. Plague (bubonic)
Foot.. 6. Indian (Siksika)
  10. Algonquian
Friar.. 4. monk 9. Dominican
  (mendicant Order)
Friday.. 10. Good Friday 14. public
  disaster (day)
Hand.. 7. anarchy, Camorra, Society
  (secret) 9. blackmail
Hawk.. 3. War (1831) 11. Indian
  Chief
Hole.. 8. Calcutta
Jack (General).. 5. Logan (Civil War)
  8. Pershing (WWI)
Maria.. 7. vehicle (prisoner's)
  14. explosive shell
Monday.. 12. Easter Monday (1630)
Monk.. 11. Benedictine
Plague.. 7. bubonic
Prince.. 6. Edward
Republic.. 5. Haiti
Rood.. 8. crucifix, Holy Rood (anc)
Sea (Asia).. 6. Euxine (anc)
Sea (Russia).. 11. Chernoe More
Shirt.. 7. Fascist 8. Fascisti
Watch.. 16. Royal Highlanders
Water State (nickname).. 8. Nebraska
blacken... 5. sully 6. defame
  9. denigrate
bladder... 3. bag, sac 4. sack
  5. pouch 6. bubble, pocket
  7. blister, globule
blade... 3. arm, bit, fop 4. beau,
  dude, edge, epee, foil, leaf, vane
  5. blood, dandy, frond, knife, spark,
  spear, spire, sport, sword 6. cutter,
  rafter (roof), runner, Toledo (sword)
  7. gallant, sabreur, scapula, traneen
  9. swordsman
blague... 6. humbug 8. claptrap
blah... 4. bunk 8. contempt, nonsense
blain... 4. bleb, sore 5. bulla
  7. blister, inflame, pustule
  8. swelling 9. chilblain
Blake's symbolic figure... 3. Zoa
blame... 5. chide, curse, shend
  6. accuse, charge, revile 7. accusal,
  censure, obloquy, reproof, reprove
  8. denounce, reproach 9. criticism,

damnation, reprehend 10. accusation,
imputation 11. attribution, reprobation
12. condemnation, denunciation,
reprehension 14. responsibility
blameless... 7. sinless 8. innocent
9. faultless, guiltless 12. sans
reproche
blameworthy... 8. culpable
10. censurable, reprovable
11. impeachable 13. reprehensible
blanch... 4. fade, pale 5. gloss, scald
6. whiten 8. etiolate 9. whitewash
blanc mange... 7. dessert, pudding
bland... 4. glib, mild, oily, smug, soft,
tame 5. suave 6. gentle, smooth
7. affable 8. soothing (manner),
unctuous 9. temperate 10. flattering
12. hypocritical, ingratiating,
mealy–mouthed, smooth–spoken
blandishment... 7. amenity, coaxing,
palaver 8. cajolery, flattery
9. wheedling 10. allurement,
inducement
blank... 4. arid, bare, dash, dull, form,
nude, null, void 5. empty, naked,
verse 6. closed, hollow, jejune,
poetry, stupid, vacant, vacuum
8. bull's–eye, document, spotless
(domino) 9. fruitless, unadorned,
untrimmed 10. instrument (law),
tabula rasa 11. empty–headed,
thoughtless 13. unembellished,
unintelligent 14. expressionless
blank book... 5. album 6. tablet
8. memo book, notebook
10. memorandum, pocketbook
blanket... 3. rug 4. robe 5. bluey,
cloak, cotta, cover, manta, quilt,
throw 6. afghan, shroud, spread
7. lap robe 8. covering, coverlet
10. barraclade (homespun)
blankness... 7. vacancy, vacuity
8. negation 9. emptiness
blare... 4. bawl, blow, bray, honk,
peal, toot 5. blast, blaze, glare
6. bellow 7. fanfare, tantara
9. tantarara
blarney... 6. bunkum 7. wheedle
8. buncombe, cajolery, flattery,
soft–soap 9. adulation
Blarney Stone site... 13. Blarney
Castle (Cork, Ir)
blart... 4. blab, roar 5. bleat 6. bellow
blasé... 5. bored, sated 6. casual
9. easygoing, sans souci, surfeited
10. hard–boiled, nonchalant
11. indifferent, self–assured,
unconcerned, worldly–wise
12. disenchanted 13. disillusioned,
disinterested, lackadaisical
blaspheme... 4. damn 5. abuse, curse,
swear 6. revile, vilify 10. calumniate
blasphemy... 7. cursing, impiety
8. anathema, swearing 9. profanity,
sacrilege 10. execration
11. desecration, imprecation,
irreverence, malediction
blast... 3. jet, pop 4. bang, blow,
gust, ruin, shot, toot 5. curse, stunt
6. blight, flurry, onrush, wither
7. blowout, explode 9. discharge,

explosion, explosive, frustrate
10. detonation, propulsion
11. fulmination
blasted... 5. blown 6. blamed, cursed,
danged (sl), darned, ruined
7. wrecked 8. blighted
10. confounded
blatant... 5. crude, noisy 6. garish,
puling, vulgar 7. flaring, glaring,
howling, ululant, wailing 8. brawling
9. clamorous, turbulent
10. blustering, uproarious, vociferous
12. obstreperous
blate... 4. blab, dull, slow 5. bleat,
blunt, prate, timid 7. bashful
8. sheepish 9. diffident 10. spiritless
blaw... 4. blow, brag 5. boast
blaze... 4. fire, gash, mark (trail), sign
5. flame, flare 6. luster 7. bonfire,
flare–up 8. eruption, outburst,
radiance, splendor 9. explosion,
firebrand 10. effulgence
11. resplendent
blazer... 6. jacket
blazon... 4. deck, show 5. adorn,
blaze, grace, paint 6. enrich, shield
7. display, étalage, exhibit, furbish
8. proclaim 9. embellish 10. coat of
arms, exhibition 11. publication
blazoning arms... 8. bearings, heraldry
bleach... 3. lye, sun 4. lime
6. blanch, purify, whiten 7. decolor,
lighten 8. chemical, chlorine, etiolate,
peroxide 9. whiteness 10. dealbation,
decolorant 11. decolorizer
bleaching vat... 4. kier 5. kieve
bleak... 3. dry, raw 4. arid, bare,
cold, pale 5. gaunt, sharp 6. bitter,
desert, dismal, dreary, frigid, pallid,
severe 7. cutting, exposed
8. desolate, rigorous 9. cheerless,
wind–blown, wind–swept
10. depressing
blear... 3. dim, fog 4. blur, dull, film
6. bleary 7. blurred 10. indistinct
bleat... 3. baa 4. blat 5. blate, whine
7. blather
bleb... 5. bulge, bulla 6. bubble
7. bladder, blister, globule, pustule,
vesicle
bleed... 3. cup, tap 4. milk, soak
5. drain 6. fleece, grieve, let out,
suffer 7. agonize, despoil, exploit,
overtax 8. let blood, transude
9. surcharge 10. hemorrhage,
overcharge
bleeding... 7. cupping 9. hemorrhea
10. hemorrhage, phlebotomy
11. venesection 12. bloodletting
blemish... 3. mar 4. blot, blue, dent,
flaw, mole, mote, pock, rift, scar,
spot, wart 5. crack, fault, nevus,
sully, taint 6. breach, macula,
macule, stigma 7. failing, fissure,
freckle, lentigo 8. cicatrix, pockmark
9. birthmark, cicatrice, deformity,
disfigure 10. defacement, deficiency
12. imperfection 13. disfigurement
blench... 4. duck, pale, wile 5. blink,
dodge, quail, trick, wince 6. bleach,
cringe, flinch, recoil, shrink, whiten
9. stratagem 10. disconcert

blend... 3. mix 4. fuse, melt
5. merge, shift, unite 6. fusion,
mingle 7. combine, mixture, scumble
8. coalesce, compound, tincture
9. commingle, composite, harmonize
10. amalgamate 11. combination,
incorporate
blended... 5. fondu, mixed 6. merged
7. mingled 9. confluent
blending... 6. crasis 11. inheritance
blessing... 4. boon, gift, good, luck,
rite 5. favor, grace 7. benefit,
benison, fortune, godsend, service,
welfare 8. good turn, kindness
9. advantage 10. benedicite, good
wishes 11. benediction, benevolence
12. felicitation 13. beatification
blight... 3. mar, nip 4. dash (hope),
ruin, rust, seer, smut 5. blast, crush,
spoil 6. freeze, mildew, wither
7. destroy, shatter 9. frustrate
10. disappoint
blighter... 4. chap 6. beggar (anc),
fellow
blimp... 6. ballon 7. airship, balloon
8. potbelly, zeppelin 9. dirigible
10. bureaucrat 12. Graf Zeppelin,
stuffed shirt
blind... 3. dim 4. ante (poker), mask,
peed, ruse, seel, slat, veil, wile
5. ciego, guise, trick 6. ambush,
scheme, screen 7. benight, conceal,
dim—eyed, eyeless, gimmick, obscure,
pretext, shutter 8. artifice, hoodwink,
jalousie, purblind, unseeing
9. dead—drunk, senseless, sightless
10. ableptical, dim—sighted,
subterfuge 11. inattentive
12. undiscerning 13. stalking—horse
blind (pert to)...
alley.. 7. impasse 8. cul—de—sac
fear.. 5. panic
girl (of Pompeii).. 5. Nydia
gut.. 6. caecum, window
10. persiennes
one eye.. 4. peed
printing for.. 7. braille
blindness... 7. anopsia, meropia (part)
8. ablepsia 9. achropsia, amaurosis
10. bleariness, nyctalopia 11. gutta
serena, hemeralopia
13. achromatopsia
blink... 4. wink 5. light, quail, wince
6. cringe, flinch 7. flicker, glimmer,
glimpse, glitter, nictate, shimmer,
twinkle 9. nictitate 10. bat the eyes
blink at... 6. accept, ignore
7. condone 8. overlook, tolerate
9. be blind to, disregard
bliss... 3. joy 4. Eden 6. heaven
7. delight, harmony, rapture
8. felicity, gladness 9. beatitude,
happiness 11. blessedness
12. spirituality 14. blithesomeness
blissful... 4. holy 5. seely 6. Edenic
7. blessed, Elysian, Utopian
8. ecstatic 9. beatified, glorified
blister... 4. bleb, blob, burn, flay
5. blain, bulge, bulla, roast 6. beat
up, bubble, oyster, scorch (with
words), thrash 7. bladder, blemish,
pustule, trounce, vesicle 9. criticize

10. vesicatory
blistered... 6. seared, singed
7. parched 8. scorched 9. vesicated
blithe... 4. airy, glad 5. merry
6. cheery, joyous 7. jocular
8. cheerful 10. blithesome
blitz... 5. shell 6. strafe 7. bombard
10. blitzkrieg
blizzard... 4. blow, wind 5. purga
7. tornado 9. snowstorm 10. snow
squall 11. white squall
Blizzard State... 11. South Dakota
bloated... 5. cured (herring), proud,
tumid 6. sodden, turgid 7. dilated,
pompous, swollen 8. inflated, puffed
up, tumefied 9. distended, flatulent,
plethoric 10. incrassate
13. emphysematous
bloated plutocrat... 9. bourgeois
10. capitalist
blob... 3. wen 4. bleb, blot, daub,
drop, lump, mark 5. bulge
6. bubble, pimple 7. blister, globule,
pustule, splotch
bloc (political)... 4. axis 5. cabal, union
6. league 7. faction 8. alliance
9. coalition 11. combination
block... 3. bar, dam, set 4. cake,
clog, cube, mass, peck, plot, stop
5. check, parry, shape, solid
6. hamper, hinder, impede, oppose,
shares, stymie 7. auction, barrier,
outline 8. blockage, obstacle,
obstruct 9. barricade 10. impediment
11. obstruction
block (pert to)...
architecture.. 5. socle 6. dentil,
mutule, plinth 7. tessera
blacksmith's.. 5. anvil
coal (Eng).. 3. jud
executioner's.. 10. guillotine
falconry.. 5. perch
finance.. 6. shares
football.. 4. clip
glacier.. 5. serac
insulating.. 6. taplet
land.. 4. city 5. tract 7. section
medicine.. 10. anesthesia
railroad.. 6. signal
sandstone (Eng).. 6. sarsen
blockade... 3. bar, dam 5. hem in,
siege 6. shut in 7. closure, exclude,
fortify 8. obstacle, obstruct
9. exclusion 11. obstruction
blockhead... 3. oaf 4. dolt, fool,
mome (anc) 5. dunce, idiot
7. half—wit, tomfool 8. bonehead,
lunkhead 11. knucklehead
blockhouse... 4. fort 7. shelter 8. log
cabin 10. stronghold
bloke... 3. man 4. bird, chap, tuff
6. fellow 9. personage
blond, blonde... 4. fair 5. color, light
6. flaxen 10. goldilocks
blood... 4. cell, clot, type, vein
5. aorta, fluid, group, grume, hemad
(haemad), hemal, hemic, ichor
(gods'), lymph, serum 6. artery,
factor, fibrin, haemal, plasma, Rhesus
(type) 7. blister, carotid 8. platelet
9. corpuscle, hemamoeba, leucocyte
10. hemachrome, hemoglobin,

hemorrhage, phlebotomy
11. erythrocyte, transfusion
12. bloodletting
blood (pert to) . . .
clotted . . 4. gore 5. cruor 8. thrombus
color . . 7. crimson, para red 8. blood
red, sanguine 11. sanguineous
13. sanguinaceous
disease . . 6. anemia 8. leukemia
(leukaemia, leucemia)
feud . . 8. vendetta
flower . . 5. hippo 9. blood lily
horse . . 7. blooded 12. thoroughbred
hound . . 4. lyam (lyme)
money (anc) . . 3. cro 4. eric
7. galanas, wergild 9. bloodwite
particle (foreign) . . 7. embolus
poisoning . . 6. pyemia (pyaemia)
pressure . . 12. hypertension
pudding . . 7. sausage
relationship . . 3. sib 6. agnate
7. cognate, kinship, kinsman, progeny,
sibship
shed . . 6. murder 7. killing, slaying
9. slaughter
stone . . 10. chalcedony
sucker . . 5. leech 8. parasite
10. sanguisuge
thirsty . . 5. cruel 8. sanguine
9. ferocious, murderous
10. sanguinary 11. ensanguined
vessel . . 3. vas 4. vein 6. artery
9. capillary
blood, kinship . . . 4. race, ties 5. birth,
breed, stock 6. strain 7. descent,
kinsman, lineage, royalty, sibship
8. heredity, nobility, relation 9. blue
blood, lifeblood, life force
10. extraction 13. consanguinity
bloodless . . . 4. pale 5. ashen, faint
6. anemic (aenemic) 7. ghastly,
inhuman 8. lifeless, peaceful
9. unfeeling 11. cold of heart
bloody . . . 4. gory 5. cruel, wound
6. cruent (obs), cursed 7. smeared
8. infamous 9. murderous
10. sanguinary 11. ensanguined
12. bloodstained, bloodthirsty
Bloody (pert to) . . .
Angle . . 11. battlefield (Spotsylvania,
1860)
Mary . . 5. Queen (Eng) 8. cocktail
bloom . . . 3. dew 4. glow, posy
5. blush, flush, youth 6. beauty,
flower, health, heyday, thrive
7. blossom 11. healthiness
bloomer . . . 5. boner, error 6. bobble,
boo-boo 7. blooper, blunder, failure,
faux pas, mistake, trouser
blossom . . . 4. bell, blow, grow, posy
5. bloom, ripen 6. floret, flower,
mature, thrive 7. develop, prosper
8. flourish, floweret, progress
10. effloresce 13. efflorescence
blossoming . . . 4. rise 6. growth
8. anthesis, blooming 9. flowerage,
flowering 10. florescent, unfoldment
11. development, florescence,
flourishing, progressing
13. efflorescence, inflorescence

blot . . . 3. dry, mar 4. blur, soil, spot
5. erase, error, fleck, smear, speck,
stain, sully 6. absorb, blotch, damage,
impair, smutch, soak up, sponge,
stigma 7. blacken, blemish, erasure,
expunge 9. bespatter 10. obliterate,
stigmatize 12. obliteration
blot out . . . 3. fix 4. dele, kill 5. purge
6. absorb, cancel, delete, efface,
excise, rub out 7. bump off, destroy,
expunge, obscure, wipe out 8. black
out 10. obliterate
blotch . . . 4. bleb, mark, soil, spot
5. patch, stain 6. macula, mottle,
stigma 7. blemish
blotched . . . 4. pied 5. pinto 6. spotty
7. mottled 8. speckled
blouse . . . 4. blou, sark 5. bluey, middy,
shift, shirt, smock, tunic, waist
6. basque 7. casaque 10. shirtwaist
blow . . . 3. dab, hit, rap, tap 4. brag,
bump, coup, gust, pant, puff, slap,
toot, waft, wind 5. bloom, devel,
feint, impel, knock, shock, sound, utter
6. expand, puff up 7. beating,
bluster, whiffle 8. calamity, disaster,
disclose, lambskin (obs)
14. disappointment
blow . . . 4. flee, over, rant, slog
5. boast, clout, scram 6. beat it,
betray, buffet, depart, wallop
8. squander 10. blow me down
blow (pert to) . . .
hard . . 6. blower 7. windbag
8. braggart 11. braggadocio
hot and cold . . 4. vary 5. shift, waver
6. seesaw 7. quibble 9. fluctuate,
vacillate 12. shilly-shally
out . . 5. douse, snuff 10. extinguish
blower . . . 4. blow, gale, wind 5. whale
6. puffer (fish), squall 7. bellows,
bloomer, blowgun, boaster, monsoon,
tornado 8. braggart 9. hurricane,
whirlwind, windstorm
11. braggadocio
blow up . . . 4. fail, rage 5. blast, bloat,
burst, fluff 6. berate, dilate, excite,
expand, forget, praise 7. blow out,
enlarge, explode, inflate 8. demolish,
detonate, disprove 9. fulminate
blowzy . . . 5. dowdy, ruddy, tacky
6. coarse, frowzy, sloppy, untidy
7. unkempt 8. careless, frumpish,
slovenly 10. disheveled, slatternly
blubber . . . 3. fat 4. weep 6. bubble
7. whimper 8. whale fat
blubbery . . . 3. fat 7. swollen
9. quivering 10. gelatinous
bludgeon . . . 3. bat, hit 4. beat, club,
mace 5. billy, bully, stick 6. coerce,
cudgel, menace 8. browbeat,
bulldoze, threaten 9. truncheon
10. intimidate, shillelagh (shillalah)
blue . . . 4. anil, baby, bice, bleu, navy
5. azure, beryl, Ching, email, king's,
merle, perse, royal, smalt 6. cobalt,
cyanic, French, indigo, powder
7. aniline, azarite, cesious, Dresden,
Dumont's, gobelin, lobelia, mesange,
peacock, Persian 8. caesious,

calamine, cerulean, Coventry, electric,
lavender, midnight, pavonine,
sapphire, wisteria 9. turquoise
10. aquamarine, cornflower

blue (pert to)... see also *Blue*
  baby.. 8. cyanotic
  bonnet.. 3. cap 4. Scot 6. flower
  (Texas State) 8. Scotsman, titmouse
  china.. 7. Nanking
  circle (archery).. 6. target
  day.. 6. Monday
  emblem of.. 6. Oxford 9. Cambridge
  grass.. 3. poa
  ground.. 10. kimberlite
  hero.. 9. Bluebeard
  melancholy.. 3. sad 6. gloomy
  7. pensive, wistful 8. tristful
  9. cheerless, depressed, penseroso
  10. atrabiliar 11. atrabilious,
  melancholic 13. hypochondriac
  nose.. 4. snob 5. prude 7. Puritan
  10. goody—goody 11. Nova Scotian
  pencil.. 4. dele, edit 6. delete, excise,
  revise
  print.. 4. plan, plot 5. graph
  6. layout 7. diagram, program
  8. schedule 9. cyanotype 10. master
  plan, photograph, photoprint
  ribbon.. 5. award, badge 10. cordon
  bleu, decoration
  skin.. 5. livid
  sky.. 5. ether, vault 6. caelum,
  heaven, welkin 7. the blue
  8. empyrean 9. firmament 10. blue
  yonder, the heavens
  stocking.. 4. blue 6. pedant 7. bas
  bleu 8. Gamaliel (Bib) 9. formalist,
  pedagogue 10. Parliament

Blue (pert to)...
  Boy.. 8. painting (Gainsborough)
  Grass State.. 8. Kentucky
  Grotto site.. 5. Capri
  Law State.. 11. Connecticut
Bluebeard's wife... 6. Fatima
blue—gray... 7. cesious (caesious)
blue—green... 8. calamine
bluff... 4. bank (steep), crag, curt,
dupe, fool, rude, wall 5. brash, cliff,
frank, gruff, krans, sheer, short
6. abrupt, crusty 7. beguile, blinder,
blinker, bluffer, bluster, brusque,
deceive, pretend, uncivil 8. impolite
9. bamboozle, blusterer, charlatan,
falseness, four—flush, precipice
11. four—flusher 13. unceremonious
bluffer... 5. quack 9. blusterer,
charlatan 10. mountebank
11. four—flusher
bluffness... 6. candor 9. bluntness
10. abruptness 11. brusqueness
blunder... 3. err, mix 4. bull, goof,
slip 5. boner, botch, error, misdo
6. boo—boo, bungle, fumble 7. faux
pas, mistake, stumble 8. flounder,
solecism (speech) 9. mismanage
blunt... 4. curt, dull, open 5. bluff,
frank, gruff, plain 6. benumb, candid,
deaden, obtund, obtuse, snippy,
stupid, weaken 7. artless, brusque,
sincere 8. hebetate 9. ingenuous
13. unceremonious
blur... 3. bog, dim, hum 4. blob, blot,

film, mist, soil, spot 5. blear, cloud,
smear, stain 6. blotch, darken,
mackle 7. blemish, dimness, obscure,
splotch 9. disfigure
blurb... 2. ad 4. plug 5. boost, brief
6. notice 7. write—up 8. ballyhoo
9. publicity 12. announcement
commendation 13. advertisement
blurt out... 4. blab, bolt 7. blunder
9. ejaculate
blush... 4. glow, look 5. bloom, color,
flush 6. glance, mantle, redden
7. modesty, redness 9. suffusion
blushing... 4. meek 5. ruddy
6. modest 7. roseate 8. flushing,
sheepish 9. reddening, rubescent
10. erubescent
bluster... 4. blow, bray, fume, rage,
rant, roar 5. broil, bully, furor, noise
6. flurry, hoopla, hubbub, squall,
tumult 7. roister, swagger, turmoil
8. boasting, bullying, threaten
9. agitation, confusion
10. swaggering, turbulence
11. rodomontade
blusterer... 5. bully 7. boaster
8. blowhard, braggart 9. roisterer,
swaggerer 11. braggadocio
12. swashbuckler
bo... 4. hobo 5. buddy, tramp
9. sundowner 10. landlouper
11. bindle stiff
bo, boh (Burma)... 5. chief 6. leader
7. captain
boa... 5. aboma, scarf (feather), snake
8. anaconda
boar... 3. hog, sus 4. apex, hure
(head) 5. swine 6. barrow, hogget
(2—year) 9. hoggaster (3—year)
board... 4. deal, doll, feed, lath, side,
slat, wood 5. curia (anc), enter,
forum, meals, plank, table 6. border,
lumber, timber 7. binding (book),
council, lodging 8. approach,
exchange (Finan), tribunal
9. committee, provision
11. accommodate, bed and board,
directorate, refreshment
14. accommodations
boast... 4. brag, crow 5. extol, exult,
glory, pride, vapor, vaunt 6. menace
7. bluster, swagger 8. braggart,
flourish 9. gasconade
boastful... 4. vain 8. bragging
9. conceited, overproud, presuming
11. thrasonical 12. vainglorious
13. self—important
boat... 3. ark, bac, gig, tub, tug
4. brig, dhow, dory, junk, punt, saic,
scow, ship, trow, yawl 5. aviso,
balsa, barge, canoe, craft, dandy,
dhoni, dingy, ferry, kayak, ketch,
liner, oolak, praam, scull, skiff,
U—boat, umiak, xebec, yacht
6. argosy, baidak, bateau, convoy,
cutter, dinghy, dogger, launch,
mistic, oomiac, packet, randan,
sampan, settee, tanker, vessel,
whaler 7. bidarka, caravel, coracle
(anc), cruiser, gondola, masoola,
piragua, pirogue, rowboat, scooter,
shallop, trawler, tugboat, warship

8. dahabeah, man–of–war, palander,
sailboat, seaplane 9. catamaran,
destroyer, steamship, submarine
10. brigantine, windjammer
11. side–wheeler, treckschuyt
boat (pert to)...
boatswain.. 5. bosun 6. serang
captain.. 4. rais (reis) 6. master
7. skipper
deck.. 4. poop 6. flight 9. promenade
man.. 5. rower 6. bargee 7. ferrier,
oarsman 9. gondolier, yachtsman
sail.. 3. jib 4. main, reef 6. lateen,
mizzen
shaped.. 9. navicella, navicular
side.. 7. gunwale
song.. 7. chantey 9. barcarole
bob.. 3. bow, cut, nod, rap, tap
4. bend, jeer, jerk, jest 5. cheat,
filch, float, flout, plumb, shake, taunt,
trick 6. bobble, curtsy, delude,
hairdo, kowtow, sinker, weight
7. haircut 8. coiffure, greeting,
shilling 9. obeisance, oscillate
bobac... 5. pahmi 6. marmot
bobber... 4. duck (ruddy) 5. float
6. bobfly 7. dropper 8. deadhead
bobbin... 3. pin 4. coil, cord, pirn,
reel 5. braid, spool 7. spindle
bobble... 3. bob, dib (angling) 4. muff
5. shake 6. boggle, bungle, fumble
7. blunder 9. oscillate
bobby... 6. peeler 9. policeman
Boche... 6. German (a)
bodach... 5. churl, clown 7. bugaboo
bodacious... 4. bold 8. insolent,
reckless 9. audacious, bumptious,
insulting 12. contumelious
bode... 5. augur 6. divine 7. portend,
presage 8. forebode, foreshow,
foretell 13. prognosticate
bodhisattva... 8. Buddhism
13. Enlightenment
bodice... 4. belt 5. stays, waist
6. basque, girdle 7. corsage,
garment
bodily... 6. carnal 7. fleshly, somatic
8. corporal, material, physical
9. corporeal 10. completely
boding... 7. ominous 10. foreboding,
portentous, prediction, prognostic
12. apprehension
bodkin... 3. awl 4. dagger, needle
7. hairpin, poniard 8. stiletto
9. eyeleteer
body... 3. man 4. deha (Theos), homo,
soma 5. being, human, trunk
6. corpse, entity, licham, mortal,
person 7. carcass 8. creature,
organism 9. substance 10. individual
13. corpus delicti 14. substantiality
body (pert to)...
armed.. 5. corps, posse
business.. 7. company
11. cooperation 12. organization
celestial.. 3. sun 4. luna, star
5. comet 6. meteor, planet
church.. 4. nave
dead.. 6. corpse 7. cadaver
division (mollusk).. 7. prosoma
injury.. 6. mayhem, trauma
petrified.. 6. fossil

political.. 4. weal 6. senate 7. cabinet
11. legislature
small.. 6. nanoid 8. dwarfish
body of...
people.. 3. mob 4. band, bevy, gang,
host 5. bunch, crowd, flock, group,
horde 6. rabble, throng 9. multitude
singers.. 5. choir 6. chorus
soldiers.. 4. file 5. corps, squad,
troop 7. brigade, company, platoon
8. division
water.. 3. bay, sea 4. lake, pond,
pool 5. fiord (fjord), inlet, ocean
6. lagoon 9. reservoir
Boeotian (pert to)...
city.. 5. Ionia (Dist) 6. Thebes
figurine.. 7. Tanagra
king (Myth).. 6. Ogyges
Boer (pert to)...
General, statesman.. 5. Botha
language.. 4. Taal 9. Afrikaans
War site.. 9. Ladysmith (S Afr)
bog... 3. bug, fen 4. blei, bold, holm,
mire, moor, moss, ooze, quag, sink
5. jheel, marsh, saucy, swamp
6. morass, slough 8. quagmire
9. everglade
bogey, bogie, bogy... 3. par 5. Devil
6. goblin 7. bugaboo, bugbear
boggle... 3. shy 4. foil, quip 5. botch,
cavil, demur, parry, pause, start
6. bicker, bungle, falter, object,
shrink 7. dispute, quibble, scruple
8. hesitate, sidestep 9. dissemble,
objection 10. difficulty, equivocate
bogglebo... 5. bogle 7. bugaboo,
specter 9. hobgoblin, scarecrow
bogus... 4. fake, mock, sham
5. phony, queer 8. spurious
10. apocryphal, factitious, fictitious
11. counterfeit
bohawn... 3. hut 5. cabin 7. cottage
Bohemia...
capital.. 6. Prague
city.. 5. Praha 6. Aussig, Pilsen
7. Budweis, Teplitz 11. Reichenberg
dance.. 6. redowa
measure.. 5. stopa 6. merice
mineral.. 6. egeran
reformer.. 4. Huss
river.. 4. Elbe, Iser 6. Moldau
tribe (anc).. 4. Boii
vagabond.. 5. gypsy (gipsy)
bohunk... 6. Slovak 7. laborer
8. Bohemian, Croatian (formerly)
boil... 3. sty (styr) 4. buck, cook,
fume, stew 5. churn, steam
6. bubble, pimple, seethe 7. bristle
8. furuncle
boiling... 5. angry 7. cooking, flushed,
stewing 8. seething, sizzling
9. agitating, ebullient 10. smoldering
bois (Fr)... 4. wood
boisterous... 4. loud 5. noisy, rough,
rowdy 6. stormy 7. blatant, excited,
furious, roaring, violent 8. brawling
9. clamorous, turbulent
10. blustering, roisterous,
tumultuous, unyielding
12. obstreperous
Bokhara (pert to)...
fur.. 9. astrakhan, broadtail

rug .. **8.** Turkoman
sheep .. **7.** karakul (caracul)
site .. **4.** Asia (Russ)
bola ... **4.** tree (fiber) **6.** weapon
bold ... **4.** deep, pert, rash, rude, snug
5. steep, stout **6.** abrupt, brazen,
daring, heroic, raised **7.** dashing,
defiant, eminent, forward, salient,
valiant **8.** fearless, immodest,
impudent, in relief, intrepid, powerful,
repoussé, stalwart **9.** audacious,
confident, dauntless, shameless,
unabashed **10.** courageous
11. lionhearted, outstanding,
precipitous, venturesome
12. presumptuous, stouthearted
boldness ... **5.** valor **6.** defial, virtue
7. bravery, courage **8.** audacity,
defiance, salience, temerity
9. assurance, gallantry, hardihood,
immodesty, impudence
10. brazenness, confidence,
effrontery, prominence, resolution
11. forwardness, intrepidity,
obviousness **12.** protuberance
13. dauntlessness
14. courageousness
bolero ... **5.** dance, music, waist
6. jacket
boliche ... **3.** inn **5.** bowls
Bolivia ...
capital .. **5.** La Paz (Polit), Oruro (anc),
Sucre (law)
hero .. **5.** Sucre **7.** Bolivar, Pizarro
Indian tribe .. **3.** Uro **4.** Iten, Moxo
lake .. **8.** Titicaca (world's highest)
mountain .. **5.** Andes **6.** Sorata
8. Illimani
product .. **3.** tin **8.** tungsten
river .. **4.** Beni **6.** Blanco
bolo ... **5.** knife **7.** machete **8.** pacifist
(Bolo Pasha, traitor) **9.** defeatist
Bolshevik, bolshevik ... **7.** Marxian,
radical (Bolsheviki) **9.** Communist
(1918), Socialist **13.** revolutionist
14. Social Democrat **18.** Third
International
Bolshevist (Communist) leader ...
5. Lenin **6.** Stalin **7.** Kosygin
8. Bulganin **9.** Krushchev
bolster ... **3.** pad **4.** bear, hold
5. boost **6.** pillow **7.** cushion,
support, sustain **8.** maintain
bolt ... **3.** bar **4.** flee, lock, roll,
sift **5.** arrow, rivet, scram, screw,
shaft, speed **6.** decamp, devour,
faster, flight, pintle, secede, staple,
toggle **7.** missile, padlock **8.** firebolt,
separate **10.** projectile **11.** eat
greedily, fulguration, thunderbolt
bolus ... **4.** bite, clay, clod, food
(chewed), mass, pill **6.** tablet, troche
8. mouthful
bomb ... **3.** dud, egg **5.** shell **6.** petard
7. grenade, missile **8.** divebomb,
fireball, surprise **9.** bombshell,
pineapple **10.** projectile
bomb (type of) ... **4.** time **5.** stink
6. aerial, atomic, rocket **7.** nuclear,
tear gas **8.** hydrogen **10.** demolition
bombard ... **3.** zap **5.** blitz, shell
6. assail, attack, strafe **7.** atomize,

barrage **9.** cannonade
bombardier ... **5.** jager **6.** bomber,
gunner **9.** cannoneer, musketeer
12. artilleryman
bombast ... **4.** blow, brag, rage, rant,
rave **5.** boast **7.** fustian **8.** boasting,
inflated, stuffing (hist) **9.** bombastic,
turgidity **11.** rodomontade
12. magniloquent **13.** grandiloquent
bombastic ... **5.** tumid **7.** orotund,
pompous, stilted **8.** boastful, inflated
12. high–sounding **13.** grandiloquent
Bombay ...
capital of .. **11.** Maharashtra (state)
college .. **11.** Elphinstone
duck .. **10.** lizard fish
hemp .. **4.** sunn **6.** ambary
merchant .. **4.** Arab
seaport of .. **5.** India
bomber ... **5.** stuka **10.** bombardier
Bombyx ... **4.** eria, moth **8.** silkworm
bona fide ... **4.** real **7.** genuine
9. authentic **10.** constantly, faithfully,
legitimate
bona mano ... **3.** tip **8.** gratuity
bon ami ... **5.** lover **6.** friend
10. good friend, sweetheart
bonanza ... **6.** riches **8.** El Dorado
(Myth), gold mine (US)
Bonanza State ... **7.** Montana
bond ... **3.** tie, vow **4.** duty, gyve, link,
mise, pact, yoke **5.** chain, nexus,
rente **6.** fetter, league **7.** entente,
manacle, shackle **8.** contract,
covenant, relation, security (Finan)
9. agreement, captivity
10. allegiance, connection
11. association, certificate
bondage ... **4.** yoke **6.** chains
7. serfdom, slavery **9.** captivity,
restraint, servitude, thralldom
11. enslavement, subjugation
bondman, bondsman ... **4.** esne, serf
5. churl, helot, slave **6.** thrall, vassal
7. servant **8.** bailsman **9.** guarantor
bone ... **2.** os **4.** chip **5.** boner
6. dollar, osteon **7.** blunder, counter
(game), ossicle **8.** skeleton, wishbone
9. funny bone (humerus), pygostyle
(bird's), whalebone
bone (Anat) ... **3.** rib **4.** ulna **5.** femur,
ilium, incus (ear), malar, skull, spine,
talus, tibia **6.** carpus, coccyx, fibula,
tarsus **7.** humerus, maxilla, patella,
scapula, sternum **8.** astragal, clavicle,
mandible, phalange, vertebra
9. calcaneus, occipital
10. metacarpus, metatarsus
bone (pert to) ...
bonelike .. **6.** osteal **7.** osteoid
cell .. **10.** osteoblast
china .. **7.** English
curvature .. **8.** lordosis
divination .. **10.** osteomancy
fish .. **9.** operculum
marrow .. **7.** medulla
process .. **7.** mastoid **8.** alveolar
9. apophysis
science .. **9.** osteology
surgery .. **9.** osteotomy **11.** osteoclasis
12. osteoplastic
tissue .. **6.** ossein

tumor.. 7. osteoma
bones... 4. body, dice, form, ossa
5. cubes, frame, money, torso, trunk
6. end man, refuse 7. carcass,
ivories 8. skeleton 11. rattlebones
boneyard... 4. bank (game)
8. golgotha 9. graveyard
10. necropolis 11. polyandrium
bonhomie... 8. pleasant 9. good
humor 10. affability, amiability
Bonhomme Richard... 4. ship
8. man–of–war (1779), (opponent of
Serapis)
bonito, bonita... 4. nice 6. pretty
8. mackerel, skipjack
bon mot... 9. witticism 10. jeu
d´esprit 11. smart saying
bonne... 5. mammy 9. nursemaid
10. baby sitter 11. maidservant
bonnet... 3. cap, hat 4. coif, hood,
poke 5. toque 7. chapeau
9. headdress
bonnetman... 10. Highlander
bonny, bonnie... 3. bon 4. good
5. plump 6. comely, lively, pretty
7. healthy, très bon 8. handsome
9. beautiful
Bontok... 7. Malayan (Luzon)
10. Indonesian
bonus... 3. tip 4. cash, gift 5. batta,
bribe, extra, share, stock (Finan)
7. cumshaw, douceur, premium,
rake–off, subsidy 8. dividend, gratuity
9. Trinkgeld 10. honorarium
bon vivant... 7. epicure, gourmet
8. gourmand, hedonist, sybarite
10. boonfellow, good fellow,
voluptuary 12. Heliogabalus (anc)
bony... 4. hard, thin 6. osteal, skinny
7. osseous 8. rawboned, skeletal
bonze (Far East)... 2. bo 4. monk
boo... 4. hoot, jeer, razz 7. catcall,
feather (ostrich) 9. raspberry
10. Bronx cheer
boob... 4. dupe, fool, goon, jerk
5. chump, dunce 6. nitwit
7. fathead 9. schlemiel, simpleton
boobook... 3. owl 8. morepork
booby hatch... 3. can, jug 4. jail
6. asylum, cooler, prison
8. hoosegow, madhouse
11. institution (mental)
boodle... 3. sop 4. loot, swag
5. booty, bribe, bunch, crowd, graft,
money (hush) 6. spoils 8. caboodle
10. pork barrel 11. counterfeit
boohoo... 3. rob 4. bawl, hoot, weep
5. shout 8. sailfish
book... 2. mo (abbr) 3. day 4. hire,
opus, tome 5. album, atlas, Bible,
canto, diary, folio, liber, novel
6. agenda, engage, ledger, manual,
missal, primer, record, sign up,
volume 7. diurnal, journal, mystery
8. brochure, libretto, register,
schedule, songbook, whodunit
9. paperback, storybook
10. literature, memorandum
11. publication
book (pert to)...
announcement.. 5. blurb
back.. 5. spine

binder.. 12. bibliopegist
binding devise.. 7. trindle
collector.. 10. bibliothec
12. bibliomaniac 14. bibliothecaire
cover.. 5. recto 6. jacket
destroyer.. 11. biblioclast
division.. 7. chapter
lore.. 10. bibliology
lover.. 11. bibliophile
one versed in.. 11. bibliognost
page.. 5. folio
seller.. 10. bibliopole (rare books)
sheath.. 5. forel
size.. 6. quarto
stealer.. 11. biblioklept
style.. 6. Aldine 8. Etruscan
9. Arabesque
treatise.. 8. isagogue
worshiper.. 11. bibliolater
writer.. 13. bibliographer
book (religious)... 4. Ordo 5. Bible,
Kells, Tobit 6. Esdras, Mormon
7. Psalter 8. Holy Writ
9. Apocrypha, Catechism, Testament
10. Pentateuch, Scriptures
Book of...
award (Harvard).. 5. detur
Concord.. 8. Lutheran
Discipline.. 12. Presbyterian
Hours.. 5. Horae
Moses (Laws).. 10. Pentateuch
Psalms.. 7. Psalter
the Dead.. 12. Pyramid Texts
boom... 3. hum 4. gain, peal, raft,
roar, spar, zoom 5. boost, cable,
speed, sprit, withe 6. thrive, upturn
7. pontoon, resound, thunder
8. bowsprit, flourish, increase
9. cannonade, Golden Age, outrigger
10. navigation, prosperity
boomerang... 6. resile 7. rebound
8. backfire, ricochet
Boomer State... 8. Oklahoma
boon... 3. gay 4. bene, gift, good,
nice 5. favor, jolly 6. jovial, kindly
7. benefit, gleeful, godsend, present
8. blessing 9. convivial
11. benefaction
boor... 3. cad, oaf 4. hick, lout
5. churl, clown, yokel 6. rustic
7. bumpkin, cauboge, peasant, ruffian
9. roughneck, vulgarian
10. clodhopper, husbandman
boorish... 4. rude 5. gawky, surly
6. clumsy, rustic, sullen 7. awkward,
crabbed, loutish, uncouth 8. churlish,
inurbane, lubberly, ungainly
9. farmerish, unrefined
11. countrified
boost... 4. help, hike, lift, plug, push
5. heist, raise, shove 6. assist,
thrust 7. commend, hearten, inspire,
promote, upswing 8. advocate,
increase 9. promotion, publicize
10. assistance 11. advancement
12. commendation
boot... 3. pac 4. kick, pack, sack,
shoe 5. armor, bonus, jemmy, kamik,
wader 6. buskin, fumble, rookie,
sheath 7. dismiss, recruit, trainee
8. balmoral, enlistee, inductee,
napoleon 9. discharge

booth... 3. hut, pew 4. crib, loge
  5. stall, stand, store 6. manger
  11. compartment
booty... 4. gain, loot, pelf, swag
  5. graft, prize, spoil 6. spoils
  7. pillage, plunder
booze... 4. bout 5. drink, spree
  6. liquor 8. potation
boozer... 3. pub, sot 5. toper
  6. barfly, bibber, saloon 7. guzzler,
  reveler, tippler 8. drunkard
  9. alcoholic, inebriate
  11. dipsomaniac
Bordeaux, France...
  capital.. 7. Gironde
  entrance gate.. 16. Porte de
  Bourgogne
  Roman name.. 9. Burdigala
  wine.. 5. Cotes, Medoc, Palus
  6. claret (best–known), Graves
border... 3. hem, rim, tip 4. abut,
  brow, dado, edge, line, rand, rund
  5. bound, brink, flank, limit, marge,
  shore, skirt, touch, verge, wings
  6. adjoin, fringe, margin, ruffle
  7. bordure, confine, flounce, selvage,
  valance 8. boundary, frontier,
  neighbor 9. periphery 10. borderland,
  sidepieces
border (pert to)...
  heraldry.. 4. orle 7. bordure
  lace.. 5. picot 9. hemstitch
  picture.. 3. mat 4. orle
  stamps (PO).. 8. tressure
  wall.. 4. dado
Border Country (Russ)... 6. Latvia,
  Poland 7. Estonia, Finland, Romania
  9. Lithuania
bordering... 4. near 6. edging
  7. binding 8. abutting, adjacent,
  marginal, skirting, trimming
  9. adjoining, immediate
  10. contiguous
Border State (Civil War Era)...
  8. Arkansas, Delaware, Kentucky,
  Maryland, Missouri, Virginia
  9. Tennessee 13. North Carolina
bore... 3. irk, tap 4. drip, hole, pest,
  pill, ream 5. auger, drill, eagre (tidal
  wave), weary 6. bother, cavity, pierce
  7. caliber, carried 8. diameter,
  nuisance, ordnance (anc), puncture,
  terebate 9. penetrate, perforate, tidal
  wave, worriment 10. capability
  11. perforation
boredom... 5. ennui 6. tedium
boring... 3. dry 5. yawny 6. tiring
  7. irksome, tedious 8. piercing,
  tiresome, wearying 11. penetrating
boring tool... 3. awl, bit 4. rime (Eng)
  5. auger, drill 6. gimlet, reamer,
  wimble
born... 3. ean, nee 4. bred, foal, lamb
  5. calve, hatch, issue 7. hatched,
  quicken 9. originate
born (pert to)...
  after father's death.. 10. posthumous
  again (Theos).. 7. renewed
  high.. 8. imperial 11. to the purple
  14. porphyrogenite
  in the country.. 10. rurigenous
  nature.. 6. inborn

  well.. 7. eugenic
borne... 4. held 6. eolian, upheld
  7. aeolian, carried, endured
  8. produced 9. cherished, supported
  10. maintained
borné... 6. narrow 7. limited
  12. narrow–minded
Borneo...
  aborigine.. 4. Dyak (Dayak), Iban
  5. Dusun, Malay
  ape.. 9. orangutan (orangoutang)
  island of.. 11. Archipelago (Malay)
  mountain.. 8. Kinibalu
  pirate tribe (anc).. 5. Bajau 9. Samal
  Laut
  protectorate.. 6. Brunei 7. Sarawak
  river.. 6. Rejang
  rubber.. 9. gutta susu
  sea.. 4. Java, Sulu 10. South China
  tree (antproof).. 7. billian
borough... 4. burg, town, ward
  5. burgh, manor 6. suffix
  8. precinct, township 10. municipium
  11. corporation 12. municipality
borrow... 4. copy, take 5. adopt,
  steal, touch 8. simulate
  10. plagiarize, substitute
  11. appropriate
borsch, borscht... 4. soup (beet juice)
  6. ragout
borzoi... 9. wolfhound
Bos... 2. ox 3. cow 4. beef, calf, neat
  6. cattle 8. ruminant 9. quadruped
bosh... 4. bull, bunk 5. trash
  6. humbug, piffle 7. baloney
  8. buncombe, falderal, nonsense
  9. poppycock 10. balderdash
bosky... 5. braky, bushy, shady, tipsy,
  woody 6. woodsy 7. fuddled,
  shadowy 11. intoxicated (Eng)
Bosnia...
  capital.. 8. Sarajevo
  native.. 5. Croat 8. Adriatic, Croatian
  race.. 4. tall 14. Slavic–speaking
  republic (present).. 10. Yugoslavia
  site.. 15. Balkan Peninsula
bosom... 4. bust 5. chest 6. breast,
  dickey, spirit 7. cherish, embrace
  8. inner man, interior 9. enclosure
  (loving), innermost 10. affections
  12. heartstrings
boss... 4. dean 6. manage, master
  7. foreman 8. director 9. supervise
  14. superintendent
boss (pert to)...
  architecture.. 4. knob, stud
  12. protuberance
  politics.. 4. whip 6. leader 7. cacique
  (W Indies) 8. dictator
  sculpture.. 5. chase, raise 6. emboss,
  relief 7. relievo 8. ornament
  shield.. 4. umbo
bosthoon (Anglo–Ir)... 4. boor, dolt
  5. clout
Boston...
  building (Hist).. 11. Faneuil Hall
  14. Old North Church
  capital of.. 13. Massachusetts
  famed names.. 6. Holmes, Lowell
  7. Emerson 8. Whittier 9. Hawthorne
  10. Longfellow
  hero.. 10. Paul Revere

history .. 8. Massacre (1770), Tea
Party (1773)
Puritan leader .. 8. Winthrop (Gov)
river .. 7. Charles
botany (pert to) ...
development (plant) .. 7. peloria
10. craticular
research terms .. 7. ecology
8. cytology, taxonomy 9. pathology
10. morphology
science .. 7. biology 9. plant life
Botany Bay ...
colony (original) .. 5. penal
discoverer .. 4. Cook (1770)
settlers .. 8. convicts (Eng)
site .. 9. Australia
botch ... 3. fix, mar 4. hash, mend,
mess, mull 5. patch, spoil 6. boggle,
bungle, fiasco, goof up, muddle
7. blunder, failure
both ... 3. two 4. duad, pair 5. twain
6. as well 7. equally
bother ... 3. ado, ail, nag 4. fuss,
to–do 5. annoy, tease 6. badger,
bustle, harass, molest, pester, pother
7. concern, confuse, fluster, torment,
trouble 8. bewilder, distress, irritate,
nuisance 9. commotion
10. discommode, excitement,
perplexity 11. botheration,
disturbance 13. inconvenience
bothersome ... 6. trying 7. galling,
irksome, onerous 8. annoying
9. difficult, worrisome 10. disturbing
11. troublesome
both sexes ... 7. epicene, sexless
10. effeminate
bo tree (Buddh) ... 5. pipal 6. sacred
(at Buddh Gaya)
bottle ... 3. pig 4. lota, vial 5. cruet,
flask, gourd, phial 6. carafe, carboy,
flagon, lagena, matara, vacuum
7. ampoule (ampule), ampulla (anc),
costrel, enclose 8. borachio,
calabash, decanter, preserve
9. aryballus (anc)
bottom ... 3. bed (water) 4. base, glen,
hulk, less, root, rump, vale, vlei
5. basin, fanny, floor, marsh, nadir
6. coulee, hopper (RR) 7. bedrock,
channel 9. underside 10. nethermost
bottomless ... 7. abysmal, abyssal
8. baseless 9. plumbless, soundless
10. fathomless 12. unfathomable
boudoir ... 7. bedroom, cabinet,
chamber 10. bedchamber
bouffant ... 4. full 7. bulging 9. puffed
out
bough ... 4. fork, limb, spur, twig
5. shoot, spray, sprig 6. branch
8. offshoot
bought ... 8. boughten (dial)
9. purchased (see also *buy*)
bouillabaisse ... 7. chowder (fish)
boulevard ... 4. pike 7. highway
8. highroad, turnpike
12. thoroughfare
bounce ... 3. hop 4. bang, brag,
bump, jump, kick, leap, snap
5. bound, burst, carom, eject, shake,
thump, verve 6. levity, recoil, spring
7. bluster, bravado, rebound

8. buoyancy, outburst, ricochet
9. discharge, lightness 10. resilience
11. fanfaronade, ostentation,
springiness 16. lightheartedness
bouncer ... 4. liar 5. bully 6. fibber,
ouster 7. boaster, chucker, whopper
8. braggart, fanfaron 9. falsehood
bound ... 3. hop, run 4. jump, leap,
skip, tied 5. ambit, limit, speed,
taped, tiled (secrecy), vault, verge
6. border, bounce, bourne, domain,
hurdle, spring, sprint 7. barrier,
certain, confine, cramped, limited,
obliged, pledged, rebound, secured,
trussed 8. beholden, boundary,
confined, enclosed, frontier, precinct,
promised, resolved, surround
9. committed, duty–bound,
encompass (incompass)
10. borderland, determined,
restrained, restricted 11. termination
12. circumscribe
boundary ... 3. end, rim 4. edge, mere
(obs), mete, term, wall 5. ambit,
bourn, fence, limit, march, verge
7. barrier 8. terminus 9. perimeter
11. conterminal, termination
13. circumference
bounder ... 3. cad 4. snob 6. rotter
7. epicier, parvenu, upstart
bounding (Mus) ... 8. saltando
boundless ... 4. vast 7. endless
8. infinite, termless 9. limitless,
unlimited 10. unconfined
11. illimitable 12. interminable,
unfathomable
bounds ... 4. pale 6. frames, limits,
skirts 7. borders, margins
8. confines, outlines 9. outskirts
10. delineated 11. limitations
bounteous ... 5. ample 6. freely, lavish
7. liberal 8. generous, prodigal
9. bountiful, plentiful 10. munificent
11. extravagant
bountiful ... 4. rich 7. copious, fertile,
liberal, teeming, uberous
8. abundant, fruitful, generous,
prolific 9. bounteous, exuberant,
luxuriant, plentiful
bounty ... 3. fee 4. gift 5. bonus
6. reward 7. largess, premium,
subsidy 8. gratuity, solatium, sportula
9. pourboire 10. generosity, liberality
11. beneficence 12. compensation
bouquet ... 4. odor, posy 5. aroma,
cigar, spray 7. corsage, flowers,
incense, nosegay, perfume
9. fragrance, redolence
10. compliment
Bourbon, bourbon ...
ancient .. 7. Reunion (Isl)
dynasty .. 5. Spain 6. France, Naples
famed personage .. 4. Duke
13. French General
famed ruins .. 7. castles (Dukes')
liquor .. 6. whisky (whiskey)
rose .. 9. Le Phoenix
bourd ... 3. fun 4. jest 7. mockery
bourdon ... 4. stop (organ) 5. baton,
music (bagpipe), spear, staff
6. burden (Fr), cudgel
bourgeois ... 4. type (size)

8. commoner 9. common man,
plutocrat 10. capitalist
11. middle–class, proletarian
bourn, bourne ... 3. aim 4. goal, port
5. bound, brook, limit, realm
6. arroyo, stream 7. rivulet
8. boundary 11. destination
bourock ... 3. hut 4. heap (stone)
5. crowd, mound 7. cluster
Bourse ... 5. Board 8. Exchange
13. Stock Exchange
bouse ... 3. cup 4. haul (Naut), swig,
tope 5. booze, drink, heave
6. beaker 7. carouse
bouser ... 5. toper 6. boozer, bursar
7. fuddler, swigger
bout ... 2. go 3. act, war 4. coup,
fray, game, spar, turn 5. cycle, fight,
match, revel, round, scrap, set–to,
spree, trial 6. fracas, inning, series,
stroke 7. attempt, circuit, contest,
exploit 8. conflict, maneuver, rotation
9. encounter 10. enterprise, prize
fight 11. celebration
boutade ... 4. whim 5. dance, prank
7. caprice 8. outbreak
11. composition (Mus)
boutonniere ... 6. flower 7. bouquet,
nosegay 8. incision 10. buttonhole
bovine ... 2. ox 3. Bos, cow, yak
4. bull, dull, goat, kine, zebu
5. bison, dogie, steer, stirk, zebus
6. catalo, cattle, oxlike, stolid, stupid
7. bullock, cattalo, taurine, vaccine
8. maverick, sluggish 10. complacent
11. beef–brained
bow ... 3. arc, bob, nod 4. arch, beak,
bend, knot, node, prow 5. bulge,
curve, debut, embow, kneel, stoop,
yield 6. assent, convex, curtsy,
encore, kowtow, salaam, submit,
weapon 7. curtain (Theat), incline,
rainbow 8. crossbow, greeting
9. obeisance 11. fiddlestick 12. bow
and scrape
bow (out) ... 4. exit 6. depart
7. concede, dismiss
Bow Bells (pert to) ...
area .. 10. cockneydom
bells of .. 9. Bow Church (St Mary le
Bow)
city .. 6. London
bowels ... 3. pit 4. guts 5. abyss,
chasm, depth 7. innards, insides,
viscera 8. entrails, interior (earth)
10. compassion (Shak), tenderness
bower ... 5. abode, arbor, cards
(game), kiosk 6. alcove, pandal
7. retreat, shelter 11. summerhouse
bowfin ... 4. Amia 7. mudfish
bowhead (Arctic) ... 10. Right whale
Bowie, bowie (pert to) ...
instrument .. 5. knife
knife inventor .. 5. Bowie (James)
Scottish .. 3. tub 4. cask 8. milk pail
State nickname .. 8. Arkansas
bowkail ... 4. kale (kail) 7. cabbage
bowl ... 3. cup, jug 4. ball, roll, vase
5. arena, basin, kitty (poker), mazer,
rogan 6. cavity, crater, hollow, patina
(anc), vessel 7. stadium 8. washbowl
9. washbasin 10. hippodrome,

receptacle 12. amphitheater
Bowl (sports) ...
Abilene .. 5. Pecan
Atlanta .. 5. Peach
Dallas .. 6. Cotton
El Paso .. 3. Sun
Honolulu .. 4. Hula
Houston .. 10. Bluebonnet
Jacksonville .. 5. Gator
Memphis .. 7. Liberty
Miami .. 6. Orange
Mobile .. 6. Senior
New Orleans .. 5. Sugar
Orlando .. 9. Tangerine
Pasadena .. 4. Rose
Sacramento .. 8. Camellia
bowlegged ... 6. valgus
bowler ... 3. hat 5. derby 6. kegler
7. trundle
bowling ... 4. ball, rink 5. alley, green,
spare 6. strike 7. rolling, tenpins
8. ninepins 10. greensward,
playground
Bowling Green ... 4. Park (Ky, NY)
bowsprit ... 3. jib 4. boom 6. steeve
box ... 2. ro (Jap) 3. bin, pew, pyx
4. arca (alms), cage, case, cist, cuff,
kist, kite, loge, safe, spar, tray
5. brace (faro), caddy (tea), cheat,
crate, stall, vault 6. buffet, carton,
casket, coffin, encase 7. confine,
enclose 8. bungalow 9. fisticuff
11. compartment
box (pert to) ...
alms .. 4. arca
bed .. 7. springs
cosmetic .. 4. inro
floating .. 3. car (for fish)
lifesaving .. 9. faking box
railroad .. 6. boxcar 8. box wagon
resistance .. 8. rheostat
sewing .. 5. plait, pleat
sleigh .. 4. pung
sports .. 5. score
tea .. 5. caddy 8. canister
theater .. 4. loge, seat
tree .. 8. Buxaceae
boxer ... 3. dog, pug 5. champ
6. miller 7. bruiser, fighter, sparrer
8. derby hat, pugilist 11. fisticuffer
12. prizefighter 13. militia member
(Chin)
boxer weight ... 3. fly 5. heavy, light
6. bantam, middle, welter 7. feather
10. light heavy
boxing ... 4. bout 5. match, set–to
7. contest, crating 8. pugilism,
sparring 10. encasement, fisticuffs
12. shadowboxing
boy ... 2. bo 3. bat, bus, lad, tad, tot
4. nino, page, puer 5. child, gamin,
knave, rogue, water, youth
6. garçon, laddie, master, rascal,
shaver, urchin, varlet 7. callant,
gossoon 8. muchacho
boy (pert to) ...
book author .. 5. Alger, Henty
errand .. 4. page 9. messenger
friend .. 4. beau 10. sweetheart
interjection .. 5. Oh boy
organization .. 6. Scouts
Scout founder .. 11. Baden–Powell

street.. 4. Arab 6. urchin
boycott... 3. ban 6. oppose, strike
  9. blackball, ostracize
brace... 3. leg, tie, two 4. bind, cord,
  gird, pair, prop, span, stay, yoke
  5. spale, staff, stave, strut 6. couple
  7. bandage, bracket, fulcrum, refresh,
  rigging, support 8. encircle
  9. reinforce, stimulate 10. invigorate,
  recuperate, strengthen
bracelet... 5. armil, armor, chain
  6. sankha 7. armilla 8. handcuff,
  vambrace 10. calombigas
bracer... 4. prop 5. tonic 7. reviver,
  support 8. pick–me–up, roborant
  9. stimulant
bracing... 5. crisp, tonic 10. salubrious
  11. stimulating 12. invigorating
bracken... 4. fern 5. brake, plaid
bracket... 4. mark 5. ancon, angle,
  group, strut 6. corbel, sconce
  7. fixture 11. electrolier
brackish... 4. foul 5. salty 7. saltish
  8. nauseous 11. distasteful
bract... 4. leaf 5. glume, palea, palet
  6. spathe 8. bractlet 9. bracteole
brad... 3. pin 4. nail 5. sprig
brae... 4. bank, down, hill, moor
  5. slope 6. valley 8. hillside
brag... 4. crow 5. bluff, boast, vaunt
  6. flaunt 7. blow off, bluster,
  deceive, roister, swagger 8. braggart
  9. gasconade 11. braggadocio
braggart... 4. brag 6. crower
  7. boaster 8. boastful, fanfaron
  9. blusterer, swaggerer
  11. braggadocio 12. swashbuckler
bragging... 11. thrasonical
Brahma... 3. God 4. fowl 5. Hindu
Brahman (pert to)...
  learned.. 6. pundit
  precept.. 5. sutra 8. netineti
  sacred book.. 4. Veda
  Sanskrit scholar.. 6. pundit
  Supreme soul.. 6. Brahma
  title.. 3. Aya
  Trinity.. 4. Siva 6. Brahma, Vishnu
  woman created by.. 6. Alalya
Brahmin... 4. prig, snob 7. egghead
  8. highbrow 10. high–hatter
  12. intellectual
braid... 3. cue 4. cord, gimp, hair,
  plat, trim 5. lacet, orris, plait, pleat,
  queue, tress, twist, weave 6. oxreim,
  sennit 7. entwine, outline, pigtail,
  topknot 8. ornament, soutache
  9. interlace 10. interweave
brain... 4. head, mind, nous
  6. psyche, reason 9. intellect,
  mentality 10. encephalon, vital organ
brain (pert to)...
  canal.. 4. iter
  case.. 3. pan 5. skull 7. cranium
  division.. 8. cerebrum 10. cerebellum
  11. pons Varolii 16. medulla
  oblongata
  matter.. 4. alba, dura, tela
  operation.. 6. trepan 8. trephine
  term.. 4. lobe, lura 6. sulcus
  7. fissure 9. ventricle
  11. convolution
  tumor.. 6. glioma

X–ray.. 14. encephalograph
brainless... 4. dumb 5. dizzy, giddy,
  silly 6. unwise 7. asinine, foolish,
  witless 9. senseless 10. unthinking
  11. thoughtless 14. scatterbrained
brainy... 5. smart 6. bright, clever
  9. brilliant
brake... 4. cage, curb, drag, fern, reef,
  skid, trap 5. check, delay, snare
  6. bridle, retard 7. dilemma, thicket
  9. canebrake 10. decelerate
bramble... 4. burr 5. berry, brier,
  shrub (prickly), thorn 6. nettle
  7. prickle, thicket 9. brierbush
  10. blackberry 12. brambleberry
branch... 3. arm, set 4. axil, fork,
  limb, rame, stem, twig, wing
  5. bough, class, frond, ramus, shoot,
  spray, sprig, vimen, withe 6. divide,
  member, ramify, sprout, stolon,
  stream, switch 7. descent, diverge,
  lineage 8. category, division, offshoot
  9. affiliate, bloodline, filiation
  10. department, descendant,
  triskelion (three branches)
Branchiata (Group)... 6. fishes
  9. Crustacea 10. Amphibians
brand... 4. burn, iron, kind, mark,
  sear, smit 5. label, stamp, sword,
  torch 6. smirch, stigma 7. earmark,
  feature, hot iron, quality 8. gridiron
  (Hist), hallmark 9. trademark
  10. stigmatize
brandish... 5. shake, swing, wield
  6. flaunt 7. flutter, glitter 8. flourish
brandy... 6. cognac 7. rosolio (cordial)
  8. rossolis 11. aguardiente
brash... 4. dash, rain, rash 5. gruff,
  saucy, storm 6. scurry 7. brittle
  (lumber) 8. impudent, tactless
  9. impetuous
brass... 4. cash, gall 5. alloy, braze,
  cheek, money, nerve, plate 6. latten,
  ormolu, platen 8. brass hat, officers,
  sisterce (anc coin) 9. impudence
  10. instrument (wind)
brass (wind instrument)... 5. bugle
  6. cornet, lituus (anc) 7. althorn,
  brasses, clarion, saxhorn, trumpet
  8. trombone 9. saxophone
  10. flügelhorn, French horn
brasserie... 6. saloon 7. brewery
  8. beer shop
brassy... 4. bold 6. aerose, brazen
  8. impudent
brat... 3. bib, elf, imp 4. film, minx,
  scum 5. apron, bairn, child, cloak,
  minor 6. mantle 7. garment
  8. clothing 9. offspring 14. enfant
  terrible, whippersnapper
brattice... 7. support 9. partition
  (mining) 10. breastwork
bravado... 6. bounce, daring, defial
  7. bluster, bombast, bravery, bravura
  8. defiance 11. braggadocio
brave... 4. bold, buck, dare, game,
  hero, meet 5. boast, bravo, bully,
  front, manly, showy, stout 6. daring,
  endure, heroic, Indian 7. Amerind,
  gallant, soldier, spartan, valiant,
  warrior 8. confront, fearless, intrepid,
  valorous 10. courageous, untimorous

12. stouthearted

bravery... 5. valor 7. bravado, bravura, courage

bravo... 3. mug 4. good, thug
5. rough, tough 6. bandit 7. gorilla, ruffian 8. assassin 9. blusterer, cutthroat, roisterer, roughneck, swaggerer 11. exclamation

bravura... 4. dash 5. macho 6. daring 7. bravado, bravery 10. brilliance (Mus), confidence

brawl... 3. row 4. fray, fury, rage, riot 5. broil, fight, furor, scold 6. affray, clamor, fracas, hubbub, rumpus, shindy, tumult, uproar 7. dispute, quarrel, rampage, turmoil, wrangle 10. hullabaloo, turbulence 11. altercation, embroilment

brawny... 5. beefy, burly, lusty, thewy 6. fleshy, robust, sinewy, strong, sturdy 7. callous 8. muscular, powerful, stalwart 9. corpulent

bray... 4. beat 5. blare, bleat, grind, neigh 6. heehaw, powder, thrash, whinny 9. pulverize, triturate 12. disintegrate

braze... 4. weld 5. plate (with metal) 6. solder

brazen... 4. bold, pert 5. brass, brave, harsh 6. brassy, cheeky, harden 7. aweless, callous 8. immodest, impudent, indurate, insolent, metallic 9. bold–faced, shameless, unabashed 10. unblushing 13. bronze–colored, harsh–sounding

brazier... 5. grill 6. brazer 7. hibachi 8. barbecue, gridiron 10. money chest (anc)

brazil... 3. red 4. wood (hard) 8. dyestuff

Brazil... see also *Brazilian*
capital.. 8. Brasilia 12. Rio de Janeiro (old)
city.. 5. Bahia, Belem 6. Recife, Santos 8. Sao Paulo 9. Horizonte 11. Porto Alegre, Sao Salvador
discoverer.. 6. Cabral (1500)
Falls (world wonder).. 6. Iguacu
lake.. 12. Lago dos Patos
product.. 6. coffee
river.. 5. Negro 6. Amazon, Branco, Paraná 7. Madeira, Orinoco 8. Paraguay 9. Tocantins

Brazilian (pert to)...
aborigine.. 5. Carib
ant (powerful).. 9. tucandera
bird.. 3. ani, ara 5. arara, macaw 6. cuckoo, darter, tiribo 7. maracan, sierema
crab (land).. 8. horseman
dance.. 5. samba 6. maxixe
drink.. 5. assai
flycatcher.. 6. yetapa
Indian.. 4. Anta 5. Arara, Araua, Guana 6. Tupian 8. Araquayu, Arawakan (tribe)
mammal.. 5. tapir
parrot.. 3. ara 5. macaw 6. tiriba
plant.. 4. yaje 5. caroa 7. ayapana (Med)
tree.. 3. apa 4. anda (oil), jara 5. assai (palm) 6. embuia, satiné

7. araroba, gomavel, seringa (rubber), wallaba 8. bakupari 10. barbatimao
weight.. 4. onza 5. libra 6. arroba 7. quintal

breach... 3. gap 4. rent, rift 5. break, burst, chasm, cleft, split 6. schism 7. caesura, dispute, quarrel, rupture 8. fracture, solecism 9. violation 10. disruption, falling–out, infraction, separation 12. infringement, interruption 16. misunderstanding

bread... 4. cush, food, gelt, loaf, pain (obs), pita, pone, rusk 5. azyme, miche, panis, toady, toast, tommy 6. damper, panada, sippet 7. chapati, hoecake, matzoth 8. tortilla 9. eucharist (part of), sourbread 10. livelihood

bread (pert to)...
basket.. 7. stomach
bread and butter.. 5. plate 6. letter (of thanks), pickle, staple 7. prosaic 8. juvenile
fruit.. 3. nut 4. tree 7. castana 8. chestnut
winner.. 6. earner, toiler, worker 7. workman 10. wage earner

break... 3. gap 4. dash, knap, luck, lull, rent, rift, ruin, rush, slip, snap, stop 5. blank, burst, cleft, lapse, letup, pause, smash, train 6. breach, chance, change, depose, escape, hiatus, injury, lacuna, market (Finan), recess, subdue, weaken 7. blunder, caesura (cesura), disrupt, getaway, respite, rupture, shatter, violate 8. bad break, bankrupt, breakage, breather, fracture, interval 9. interlude, jail break, violation 10. depreciate, falling–out, infraction, suspension 11. fragmentize 12. intermission, interruption 13. discontinuity

break down... 3. cry, sob 4. bawl, raze, weep 5. crush 6. boohoo, divide, master, reduce, revolt, subdue 7. analyze, crack up, dissect, resolve, unnerve 8. classify, collapse, separate 9. decompose, overwhelm, subdivide

breakdown... 7. debacle, failure 8. analysis 9. cataclysm 10. dissection, impairment, revolution

breakfast... 6. brunch (late) 8. dejeuner 10. chota hazri

break in... 4. open, tame 5. enter, force, train 6. butt in, subdue 7. barge in, intrude, prepare 9. interrupt 10. housebreak

break up... 4. cure, rift, ruin 5. decay, leave, smash, spall, split, upset 7. adjourn, atomize, crumble, disband, relieve, scatter, shatter 8. disperse, dissolve, separate, unsettle 9. decompose 10. demobilize, dispersion, disruption 11. disorganize, dissolution 12. disintegrate

breakwater... 4. dike, mole, pier 5. jetty, jutty 6. refuge, riprap 7. sea wall 8. buttress 10. embankment 11. obstruction

bream... 4. fish, scup 5. clean (Naut)

breast... 4. bust, soul, teat 5. bosom, cheat, gland (mammary), heart 6. spirit, thorax 8. inner man 9. encounter

breast (pert to)...
absence of.. 7. amastia
bone.. 6. ratite 7. sternum
breastlike.. 7. mastoid
plate.. 4. Urim 5. armor, ephod 6. gorget, lorica 7. poitrel 12. breastsummer
works.. 7. defense, parapet, railing (Naut), ravelin 8. mantelet 9. banquette

breath... 3. air 4. fume, life, odor, pant, puff, wind 5. draft, pause, prana, scent, smell, touch, vapor, whiff 6. breeze, caress, flatus, pneuma, spirit 7. halitus, respite, whisper 8. breather 9. emanation, ozostomia, utterance 10. exhalation 11. respiration

breathe... 3. say, tip 4. gulp, live, mean, pneo (comb form), rest, sigh, tell 5. exist, imbue, imply, scent, smell, snuff 6. evince, exhale, infuse, inhale, let out, reveal 7. bespeak, divulge, emanate, instill (instil), pervade, respire, suspire, whisper 8. aspirate, indicate

breathe (pert to)...
comb form.. 4. pnea, pneo
convulsively.. 4. sigh
hard.. 4. pant
one's last.. 3. die 6. expire, perish 7. decease, succumb
vengeance.. 9. retaliate

breather... 4. lull, rest 5. break, pause, truce 6. recess 7. interim, respite 9. interlude 12. intermission

breathing... 5. alive, vital 6. living, zoetic 7. animate, panting, respite 8. animated 9. conscious, phonation, utterance 10. aspiration 11. respiration, respiratory, ventilation 12. articulation

breathing (pert to)...
apertures.. 5. stoma 8. spiracle
morbid.. 4. rale 7. stridor 8. rhonchus
painful.. 8. dyspnoea
pause.. 7. caesura
smooth.. 4. lene

breathless... 4. awed, dead, gone, keen 5. eager 6. ardent, fervid, winded 7. airless, demised, fervent 8. deceased, lifeless, windless, wordless 9. impatient 10. astonished, speechless, spellbound

bred... 6. hybrid, inbred, reared, tablet (compressed) 7. lowbred, mongrel 8. exogamic, purebred 9. autogamic, crossbred, endogamic, half–caste, interbred 11. half–blooded, impregnated, inseminated 12. thoroughbred

bree... 4. brow 5. broth, scare 6. liquor 7. eyebrow 9. commotion 11. disturbance

breech... 4. doup, rump, tall 5. fanny, stern 6. bottom 8. buttocks 9. posterior, underside

breeches... 5. chaps, jeans, pants, trews 8. britches, jodhpurs, trousers 10. pantaloons 12. galligaskins (jocular)

breed... 3. ilk 4. kind, race, rear, sort 5. beget, brood, caste, class, mixed, raise, stock, train, tribe 6. family 7. descent, educate, lineage, mongrel, produce 8. engender, generate, instruct 9. originate, posterity, procreate, propagate 10. crossbreed

breeding... 6. polish 7. culture, decorum, exogamy, manners, raising, rearing 8. autogamy, endogamy, hatching, training 9. education, fostering, gentility 10. deportment, upbringing 11. instruction, procreation, propagation

breeding place... 4. nest 5. nidus 7. brooder 8. hatchery 9. incubator 10. birthplace

breeze... 3. air, row 4. aura, pirr, snap, stir, wind 5. cinch, rumor 6. squall, zephyr 7. ill wind, whisper 8. duck soup, pushover 9. commotion 11. disturbance

breezy... 4. airy, spry 5. blowy, brisk, gusty, windy 6. drafty, jaunty, lively 7. squally 8. animated, blustery, spirited 9. vivaceous 12. lighthearted

Brehon Law... 4. eric (anc) 10. Senchus Mor 12. Book of Aicill

breve... 4. note (Mus), writ 5. brief, order 7. compose

brevet... 4. fiat 5. ukase 6. decree 7. warrant 10. commission 11. certificate (teaching)

breveté... 8. patented

breviary... 6. manual, ritual 7. compend, epitome

brevity... 9. briefness, shortness, terseness 11. conciseness, transience 12. succinctness

brew... 3. ale, mix 4. grog, plot 5. hatch, steep 6. cook up, foment, gather, menace, scheme 7. concoct, distill (distil) 8. contrive, threaten 9. aqua vitae

brewer's grain... 4. corn, malt 6. barley

brewer's yeast... 4. barm 6. leaven

bribe... 3. oil, sop 5. bonus 6. boodle, buy off, grease, suborn 9. hush money

bric–a–brac... 6. curios 7. artware 8. antiques, trinkets 9. artifacts, objet d'art 11. knickknacks

bric–a–brac cabinet... 7. étagère, whatnot

brick... 3. bat 4. dobe, tile 5. adobe, stone 6. pament (pamment) 7. clinker 8. hardness

brick (pert to)...
color.. 3. red 7. Saravan
kiln.. 5. clamp
layer.. 3. cad (helper) 5. mason
laying.. 8. toothing
slang.. 3. pip 4. lulu 5. dilly, peach 6. corker, winner 8. jim–dandy 10. sweetheart 11. crackerjack 12. lollapaloosa

unburned.. 5. samel
brickbat... 4. rock 5. stone 7. affront, missile, offense 9. indignity
bridal (pert to)...
  chest.. 9. trousseau
  flower.. 13. orange blossom
  ode, song.. 9. Brautlied
    11. Epithalamon (anc)
  portion.. 3. dot 5. dower, dowry (dowery)
  rite.. 7. wedding 8. marriage, nuptials
bridge... 3. tie 4. arch, bond, link, pons, pont, span 5. unite
    7. connect, passage (Mus), pontoon, viaduct 9. structure
    13. steppingstone
bridge (pert to)... 4. deck, game, nose 5. magas, truss 6. phoebe (bird)
    7. bascule, trestle 9. dentistry
    10. ponticello (Mus)
bridge, historic...
  Bridge of Boats.. 10. Hellespont
  Bridge of Sighs.. 6. Venice (Doge's Palace) 7. Al Sirat (Moslem, over infernal fire)
  Norse Myth.. 7. Bifrost (rainbow)
  Old Bridge.. 12. Ponte Vecchio (Florence It, 1345)
Bridge game... 3. bid 4. pass, ruff, slam 6. honors, points, renege, tenace 7. finesse 9. part—score
bridle... 3. bit 4. cord (kite), curb, rein 5. check, guide, smirk 6. fetter, govern, halter, master, simper, subdue 7. harness, manacle, repress, shackle, snaffle 8. cavesson, headgear, noseband, restrain, suppress 9. hackamore, headstall, restraint
brief... 4. curt, plan, writ 5. breve, charm, pithy, short, terse 6. report 7. compact, concise, laconic, summary 8. fleeting, instruct, succinct 9. condensed, ephemeral, summarize, transient
    10. compendium, short—lived, transitory 11. compendious
    14. inconsiderable
brier, briar... 4. burr, pipe 5. heath, shrub, spine, thorn 7. bramble, bruyère, clotbur, prickle, sticker, thistle 8. adherent 11. French brier
brig... 4. boat 6. vessel
    10. guardhouse
brigade... 4. unit 6. troops 7. company 8. regiment
brigand... 5. rover, thief 6. bandit, dacoit, pirate, robber 7. bedouin, cateran, ladrone 8. picaroon
    10. highwayman
bright... 3. apt, gay 4. naif, rosy 5. alert, beamy, fresh, lucid, nitid, palmy, sleek, smart, sunny, vivid, witty 6. brainy, clever, florid, garish, golden 7. halcyon, radiant, shining, unfaded 8. cheerful, colorful, flashing, gleaming, luminous, lustrous, splendid 9. brilliant, effulgent, refulgent, sparkling 10. auspicious, epiphanous, glistening, glittering, optimistic 11. intelligent, resplendent
brightness... 5. sheen 6. luster

7. sparkle 8. radiance, splendor 9. alertness, clearness, smartness
    10. brilliance 12. cheerfulness, colorfulness, pleasantness
brilliance, brilliancy... 5. éclat, glory 6. luster 7. glitter, oriency, success 8. radiance, splendor 9. smartness, vividness 10. brightness, cleverness
brilliant... 5. smart, vivid, witty 6. bright 7. eminent, radiant, shining 8. gorgeous, meteoric, splendid 9. refulgent, sparkling 10. glittering 11. illustrious
brilliant group... 6. galaxy
brim... 3. hem, lip, rim 4. edge 5. brink, marge, verge 6. border, margin 7. selvage
brine... 3. sea 4. main, salt 5. brack, ocean, tears 6. pickle 7. the deep 12. preservative
bring... 3. get 4. bear, cost, haul, lead 5. carry, fetch, go get, yield 6. convey, entail, induce, obtain 7. contain, involve, require 8. comprise 9. transport
bring about... 2. do 4. make 5. cause 6. create, effect 7. achieve, produce 8. generate 9. instigate 10. accomplish, consummate, effectuate
bring around... 4. cure, heal, ween 5. renew, sober 6. revive 7. convert, restore, win over 8. persuade 10. rejuvenate
bring back... 5. fetch 6. recall, return, revive 7. restore 8. rekindle, remember, retrieve 9. recollect, resurrect
bring forth... 3. ean 4. bear, rise 5. beget, breed, cause, educe, hatch, spawn, yield 6. adduce, elicit, reveal 7. develop, produce 8. disclose, fructify, generate, manifest
bring forward... 4. cite 5. offer 6. adduce, broach, submit 7. advance, improve, promote, propose 8. manifest 9. introduce
bring into...
  bondage.. 7. enslave
  court.. 7. arraign
  harmony.. 6. attune
  position.. 5. align, aline
  union.. 9. correlate
bring together... 5. amass, group 6. gather 7. cluster, compile, reunite 8. assemble 9. harmonize, reconcile 10. accumulate
bring to light... 4. find 5. trace 6. elicit, expose, reveal 7. uncover, unearth 8. disclose, discover
bring to mind... 6. recall, remind 8. look like, remember, resemble
bring to pass... 2. do 5. cause 6. author, father 9. originate 10. accomplish, effectuate
bring up... 4. rear, spew 5. drill, raise, train, vomit 6. foster, muster 7. advance, educate, nurture, propose 9. challenge, condition, cultivate 10. discipline 11. regurgitate

bring up to date ... 4. post 6. update
9. modernize 10. streamline
brink ... 3. lip, rim 4. bank, brow,
edge, near 5. ditch, marge, skirt,
verge 6. border, margin
briny ... 3. sea 4. salt 5. salty
6. saline 8. brackish
Brisbane, capital of ... 10. Queensland
(Austral)
Brisbane tree ... 3. box 8. quandong
brisk ... 3. gay 4. cold, fast, keen,
racy, spry, yern 5. agile, alert, alive,
crisp, fresh, peart, quick, sharp,
tangy, zippy 6. breezy, lively, nimble,
snappy 7. caustic, pungent
8. animated, forceful, spirited,
vigorous 9. energetic, sprightly,
vivacious 11. stimulating
bristle ... 4. barb, hair, seta 5. anger,
seton 6. chaeta, palpus, ruffle,
rumple, see red, setula, setule
7. acicula, prickle, stubble
bristling ... 5. angry 6. horrid (anc)
7. horrent 9. offensive
bristly ... 5. rough, setal 6. hispid,
setose, thorny 7. prickly, scopate,
unshorn 8. acicular, echinate
11. bristlelike
Bristol ...
church (England's finest) .. 15. St
Mary Redcliffe
fashion .. 6. ataunt 9. shipshape
library .. 6. oldest (British Isles)
milk .. 6. sherry
Britain ...
name, ancient .. 6. Albion
name, modern .. 12. British Isles,
Commonwealth, Great Britain
13. United Kingdom
name, Roman .. 9. Brittania
native .. 5. Iceni (tribe), Jutes, Picts,
Scots 6. Angles 7. Britons, Silures
native (sl) .. 5. limey (limy), tommy
7. Blighty
sea .. 5. Irish, North 8. Atlantic,
Hebrides
British (pert to) ... see also *English*
battle .. 8. Hastings
boat (anc) .. 7. coracle
cavalry .. 8. yeomanry
earldom (Egypt) .. 7. Khartum (1898)
emblem .. 4. lion
fish .. 8. dragonet (gobylike)
oak .. 5. robur
Order of .. 9. The Garter
prison .. 4. gaol
pudding .. 4. suet 9. Yorkshire
tavern .. 3. pub 9. beerhouse, jerry
shop
thief (wharf) .. 6. tosher
Z (letter) .. 3. Zed
British people ...
author .. 6. Austen, Barrie, Jonson
7. Dickens
buccaneer .. 4. Kidd 6. Morgan
explorer .. 4. Cook, Ross 6. Baffin
7. Stanley 9. Vancouver
11. Livingstone
hero (sea) .. 6. Nelson
king (legend, Myth) .. 3. Lud 4. Beli,
Bran, Brut 7. Belenus
painter .. 8. Rossetti

philosopher .. 7. Russell (Bertrand)
physicist .. 5. Boyle
poet .. 7. Chaucer 8. Browning,
Tennyson 9. Masefield
soldier .. 7. Redcoat (Hist)
Brittany ... 7. Armoric 8. Bretagne
brittle ... 4. weak 5. brash, candy,
crisp, frail 6. feeble, infirm, slight
7. fragile, friable 8. delicate, insecure
9. breakable, frangible
11. shatterable
broad ... 4. free, girl, lake (Eng), wide
5. ample, large, roomy, thick, wench
7. breadth, diffuse, general, liberal
8. spacious, strumpet, sweeping,
tabulate, tolerant 9. expansive,
extensive 10. collective, commodious,
indefinite, voluminous
13. comprehensive
broad (pert to) ...
arrow .. 5. pheon (Her) 6. stigma
8. insignia
footed .. 8. platypod
hearted .. 8. generous
11. magnanimous
minded .. 7. liberal 8. tolerant
9. receptive
broaden ... 5. swell, widen 6. dilate,
expand, extend, spread 7. augment,
enlarge, ennoble 8. increase
broadly ... 3. far 6. widely 10. far and
wide 11. extensively 12. indefinitely,
right and left
broadside ... 4. guns, side 6. folder
7. gunfire, quarter, surface
8. enfilade, sideways 10. broadsheet,
floodlight 11. breadthwise
broadsword ... 7. cutlass, Ferrara
8. claymore, scimitar
Brobdingnagian ... 5. giant, titan
8. colossal, gigantic 10. gargantuan
brocade ... 6. broché, fabric
8. baudekin 9. baldachin
brochan ... 7. oatmeal 8. porridge
brochure ... 5. tract 6. folder
7. booklet, leaflet 8. chapbook,
pamphlet
brod ... 3. awl 4. goad, pike, urge
5. thorn 6. sprout 9. incentive
brode, brodee ... 11. embroidered
brodyaga ... 7. vagrant 8. vagabond
brogan, brogue ... 4. shoe
brogue ... 4. burr 5. twang 6. accent
7. dialect
broil ... 4. cook, fray, fume 5. brawl,
grill, melee 6. affray, braise (braize),
scorch 7. contest, discord, dispute,
quarrel 8. conflict, grillade, scramble
10. contention, dissension, turbulence
11. altercation, embroilment
broke ... 4. flat 6. busted, ruined
8. bankrupt, strapped 9. destitute,
insolvent, penniless
broken ... 4. tame 5. broke, bumpy,
burst, rough, tamed 6. chined,
ruined, shaken, uneven, zigzag
7. crushed, décousu, severed,
subdued 8. bankrupt, detached,
impaired, ruptured, sporadic,
weakened 9. conquered, dispersed,
irregular, shattered, unsettled
10. incoherent, incomplete

11. fragmentary, housebroken,
interrupted 12. disconnected,
domesticated, intermittent
13. discontinuous
broken pottery (anc)... 5. shard
(sherd) 8. potsherd
broker... 5. agent 6. dealer, jobber
7. cambist, scalper (ticket)
8. marriage 9. go—between,
insurance, middleman, schatchen
10. pawnbroker, real estate
11. internuncio, stockbroker
12. intermediary
brokerage... 3. fee 4. agio 6. charge
8. agiotage, business 9. exactment
10. commission
brolly... 5. chute 8. umbrella
9. brollyhop, parachute
bromide... 4. corn 5. trite 6. Babbit,
cliché, halide, old hat 8. banality,
sedative 9. conformer, criticism,
platitude 10. conformist, Philistine
15. conventionalist
bronco, broncho... 4. pony 5. horse
6. cayuse 7. mustang
10. broomstick
bronco, bucking... 9. estrapade
broncobuster, bronchobuster...
6. cowboy 7. trainer, vaquero
Bronx cheer... 3. boo 4. hiss, razz
9. raspberry
bronze... 3. aes (anc), tan 5. alloy,
color 6. ormolu, patina, suntan
9. sculpture
Bronze Age... 9. Neolithic
11. Aeneolithic
Bronze Plaques (pert to)...
called.. 14. Eugubine Tables (Iguvine
Tables, 1444)
number.. 5. Seven
site.. 6. Gubbio (It)
brooch... 3. bar, pin 4. boss, ouch
5. cameo, clasp 6. fibula (anc),
shield 8. pectoral 9. breastpin
brood... 3. fry, nye, set 4. kind, mope,
mull, muse, nide, race 5. breed,
covey, folks, hatch, pride (lions),
young 6. clutch, family, farrow (pigs),
litter, ménage, people, strain
7. lineage, progeny, reflect
8. cogitate, incubate, meditate,
ruminate, soredium 9. household,
offspring 11. contemplate
brood over... 4. fret, mope 5. hover
6. grieve, ponder 7. agonize
8. remember
brook... 3. run 4. bear, beck, burn,
rill, sike 5. abide, bourn, creek, crick
6. arroyo, endure, rillet, runlet, suffer
7. freshet, rivulet 8. brooklet
9. arroyuelo, streamlet
broom... 5. besom, shrub, spart,
sweep, whisk
broth... 4. soup 5. stock 6. brewis
8. bouillon, consommé
brother... 3. fra 4. mate, monk
5. friar, title 6. frater, friend,
member, oblate 8. alter ego, relative
9. associate 11. counterpart
brotherhood... 5. lodge 7. kinship,
society 8. sodality 10. fellowship,
fraternity 11. association

12. fraternalism 13. confraternity
brotherly... 4. kind 6. tender
8. friendly 9. fraternal
11. sympathetic 12. affectionate
Brothers... 7. Danites (Mormon)
9. Christian (RCCh)
brothers and sisters (same family)...
8. siblings
brow... 3. cap, rim, tip, top 4. brae
5. brink, crest, crown 6. border,
summit, tiptop, visage 7. eyebrow,
feature 8. boldness, forehead
9. gangplank 10. effrontery
11. countenance
browbeat... 3. cow 5. bully 7. buffalo,
henpeck 8. bulldoze, domineer
10. intimidate
brown... 4. dark 5. cheat, dusky
6. august, braise, tanned
9. red—yellow (class)
brown... 3. bay, dun, nut, tan
4. ecru, faon, fawn, roan, rust, seal
5. acorn, cocoa, hazel, henna, khaki,
mocha, olive, otter, sepia, snuff,
sumac, tawny, tenné, toast, topaz
6. auburn, bister, bronze, burnet,
coffee, copper, loutre, oriole, russet,
sienna, sorrel, titian, walnut
7. asphalt (smoke), gazelle, perique,
rosario (army) 8. chestnut, cinnamon,
mahogany 9. buckthorn, chocolate
10. café au lait, terra cotta
brown (pert to)...
Bess.. 6. musket
betty.. 5. daisy 7. pudding
10. coneflower
earth.. 5. umber
ebony.. 6. wamara 10. coffeewood
browned in deep fat... 7. rissole
Brownian movement (Bot)...
7. pedesis
brownie... 3. elf 4. cake 5. dwarf,
gnome, nisse, pixie, Scout, urisk
6. camera, goblin 9. sandpiper
Brownism (Eng)...
17. Congregationalism
browze... 4. brut (obs), read, scan
5. graze 6. nibble
bruckle... 5. frail 7. brittle
9. breakable 10. changeable,
inconstant
bruin... 4. bear
bruise... 4. bash, beat, hurt, maul
5. abuse, crush, dinge, pound,
wound 6. batter, buffet, injury
7. contuse 8. abrasion, black eye
9. contusion, pulverize, triturate
bruiser... 3. mug, pug 5. boxer,
bravo, tough 7. fighter, ruffian,
sparrer 8. pugilist 11. fisticuffer
bruit, bruit about... 3. din 4. fame,
hawk, tell 5. bandy, noise, rumor
6. clamor, report 9. advertise
brujo... 8. magician, sorcerer
11. witch doctor
brumal... 4. cold 6. hiemal, wintry
8. hibernal 10. winterlike
brune... 6. brunet (brunette)
11. Melanochroi
Brunhild... 5. Queen (wife of Siegfried)
8. Valkyrie (Myth)
brunt... 3. rub 4. crux 5. pinch, shock

6. stress 7. squeeze
brush... 3. art 4. bush, comb, tail
(fox), tuft 5. besom, briar, broom,
clash, graze, groom, sweep, touch
6. artist, forest, pappus, stroke,
teazel 7. painter, scuffle, thicket
8. conflict 9. brushwood, encounter
10. paintbrush 11. undergrowth
brush aside... 5. spurn 6. reject
7. dismiss 8. shrug off 9. disregard
brush wolf... 6. coyote
brusque... 4. curt 5. bluff, blunt,
brash, brusk, frank, gruff, rough,
sharp, short 6. abrupt, candid,
snippy
brutal... 5. cruel, gross 6. animal,
carnal, coarse, savage 7. bestial,
inhuman 8. ruthless 9. barbarous
brutality... 7. cruelty 9. barbarian,
carnality 12. ruthlessness
brute... 5. beast, gross, harsh, rough
6. animal 7. beastly, bestial, sensual,
varment 8. soulless 9. barbarian,
inanimate 10. unpolished
11. uncivilized
brutish... 4. rude 5. cruel, gross
6. brutal, carnal, fierce, savage,
stupid 7. bestial, inhuman, sensual,
vicious 9. barbarous, ferocious,
insensate, unfeeling 10. insensible,
irrational
Brutus... 3. wig 6. hairdo, peruke
7. traitor (Julius Caesar)
13. chrysanthemum
Bryan's speech (1896)... 11. Cross of
Gold 13. Crown of Thorns
bryology, science of... 6. mosses
10. bryophytes, liverworts
Brython... 4. Celt 6. Briton
8. Welshman
Brythonic god... 3. Ler 4. Bran
Brythonic goddess... 9. Arianrhod
bubble... 4. bead, bleb, blob, boil,
foam 5. bulge, empty, fancy, tumor
6. burble, gurgle, murmur, ripple,
scheme, trifle 7. chimera (chimaera),
globule, trickle 8. bubbling, delusive,
illusion 9. ephemeron, intumesce,
lightness 10. effervesce
16. unsubstantiality
buccal... 4. oral 5. cheek, mouth
buccaneer... 4. Kidd (Capt) 5. rover
6. Morgan, pirate, rifler, viking
7. corsair, Lafitte, spoiler
8. marooner, picaroon 9. privateer
10. Blackbeard (Capt Teach),
freebooter
Bucephalus... 5. horse, steed
7. charger 8. war horse (Alex the
Great)
buck... 3. man, ram, rat 4. bunt, butt,
deer, goat, hare, jump, male, sore
(4–yr deer) 5. fight, sasin 6. animal,
combat, dollar, Indian, oppose
7. contest, launder, pricket
8. antelope, sawhorse 10. fallow
deer
buckaroo... 6. cowboy 7. trainer,
vaquero 8. horseman
12. broncobuster (bronchobuster)
bucket... 3. tub 4. bail, bowk, pail,
ship 5. chest, cozen, scoop, skeel

6. bailer, bushel, drench, sityla
10. bucket shop
Buckeye State... 4. Ohio
Buckingham Palace... 9. residence
11. St James Park (London)
buckle... 3. bow 4. bend, curl, kink,
warp 5. tache 6. fasten 8. marriage
9. fastening
buckthorn... 4. tree 5. brown, shrub
7. cascara, Rhamnus
buckwheat... 4. cake, coal, herb,
seed, titi 5. flour
bucolic... 4. idyl, poem, poet 5. idyll,
local, rural 6. farmer, poetic, rustic
7. eclogue, georgic 8. agrestic,
pastoral 9. bucoliast
bud... 3. deb 4. bulb, cion, germ,
grow, knop, stem 5. brier, buddy,
gemma, graft, plant, shoat, youth
6. embryo, sprout 7. blossom,
brother, burgeon, develop
8. rudiment, soredium 9. debutante,
germinate
Buddha (Gautama)... 2. Fo 4. sage
(Shakya) 5. amita, deity 7. ascetic,
teacher 8. Daibutsu 10. Blessed One
Buddhism (pert to)...
church.. 4. tera
city (sacred).. 5. Lassa (Lhasa)
evil spirit.. 4. Mara
fate.. 5. Karma
festival.. 3. Bon
friar, monk.. 2. Bo 5. arbat, bonze
6. bhikku, gelong 7. Mahatma
8. poonghia 9. Dalai Lama
goal.. 13. Enlightenment
hell.. 6. Naraka
language (sacred).. 4. Pali 5. sutra
9. Tripitaka
liberation.. 7. Nirvana
mountain (sacred).. 4. Omei (Chin)
paradise.. 4. Jodo 8. gokuraku
sect.. 3. Zen
shrine (Ind).. 4. tope 5. stupa
6. dagoba
temple.. 4. rath, Tera 6. vihara
temple column.. 3. lat
term.. 6. nidana
buddy... 3. pal 4. chum, mate
5. crony 7. brother, comrade
8. tentmate 9. bedfellow, companion
budge... 3. fur (lambskin) 4. grog,
move, stir 5. booze, brisk, stiff
6. guzzle, jocund, liquor, solemn,
tipple 7. austere, pompous
8. movement 11. nervousness
budget... 3. bag 4. bulk, plan, sack
5. funds, pouch, purse, store
6. agenda, assets, bundle, moneys,
packet, parcel, ration, wallet
7. program, stipend 8. finances,
quantity, schedule 9. allowance,
statement 12. accumulation
Buenos Aires (pert to)...
avenue (famed).. 13. Avenida de
Mayo
bourse.. 5. Bolsa
capital.. 9. Argentina
river.. 7. La Plata
buff... 3. rub 4. hide (animal) 5. color,
scour 6. polish 7. burnish, leather
buffalo (animal)...

American.. 5. bison
Asian, African.. 2. ox 4. arna, Cape,
gaur 8. seladang
European.. 7. aurochs
hybrid.. 7. cattalo (catalo)
Indian.. 4. arna
Philippines.. 7. carabao, timarau
buffalo (pert to)...
grass.. 5. grama 6. guinea 11. St.
Augustine
pea.. 4. plum 5. vetch
10. bluebonnet
slang.. 3. cow 5. bully 7. perplex
8. bulldoze, confound
Buffalo Bill... 11. William Cody
buffer... 4. buff 5. guard, wheel
6. bumper 7. bulwark, cushion
8. backstop, polisher
buffet... 3. bar, box, hit 4. beat,
blow, cuff, slap, toss, whip
5. abuse, smite, stool 6. bruise,
oppose, strike 12. chastisement
14. disappointment
buffet... 6. supper 7. counter, hassock
8. cupboard 9. sideboard
buffo... 7. buffoon 10. bass singer
(comic opera), buffo–basso
buffoon... 4. fool, mima (fem), mime,
zany 5. actor, clown, droll, mimer
6. jester, mummer 8. humorist,
ridicule 9. Hanswurst, harlequin
12. Eulenspiegel (Tyll)
13. pickel–herring (pickle–herring)
buffoonery... 6. japery, pranks
7. fooling 8. clownery, drollery,
trickery 9. slapstick 10. buffoonism
12. harlequinade
bug (insect)... 3. fly, sow 4. flea, gnat,
moth, pill, tick 5. Anasa, aphid,
Aphis, cimex, louse 6. beetle, cicada,
earwig, locust, mantis, needle,
scarab, slater, spider, weevil
7. firefly, hexapod, katydid, ladybug,
Ranatra, termite 8. chilipod,
diplopod, mosquito, myriapod
9. arthropod (jointed), centipede,
cockroach, lightning, millipede,
tarantula 10. silverfish
11. grasshopper
bug (slang)... 3. nut 4. bogy, flaw,
rage 5. craze, fault, manis 6. defect,
zealot 7. bugaboo, bugbear, fanatic,
passion 9. energumen
bugaboo... 4. bogy, ogre, trap (golf)
bugan... 5. ghost 6. spirit (evil)
9. hobgoblin
bugger... 3. guy, rat 4. chap, heel
6. booger, jasper, wretch
buggy... 3. bus 4. ga–ga, shay
5. wagon 6. cuckoo 7. caboose,
foolish, haywire, vehicle 8. carriage,
demented, infested, stanhope
9. insectile 10. insectlike
bug juice... 6. liquor (strong), whisky
(inferior)
bugle... 3. iva (ragweed) 4. bead, call
(mating), honk, horn, nose, toot
7. clarion, trumpet 9. schnozzle
10. instrument
bugle call... 4. taps 6. alerte, sennet
(Hist) 7. retreat, tantara 8. last post,
reveille

build... 4. form, rear 5. edify, erect,
found, frame, raise, shape 6. create,
evolve, figure, nidify 7. fashion,
stature 8. increase, physique
9. construct, establish
building... 4. barn, casa, crib, shed,
wing 5. annex, tower 6. casino,
castle, lean–to, making, museum
7. edifice, factory, forming, rookery,
rotunda, theater 8. creation, dwelling,
erecting, erection, tenement
9. apartment, structure
10. fashioning, production,
skyscraper, storehouse 11. fabrication
build–up... 5. boost 9. promotion
11. advertising 12. commendation
built... 4. made 6. formed, shaped
7. crested, erected 9. fashioned
10. fabricated 11. constructed
bulb... 3. bud 4. corm, lily, root,
sego, stem 5. onion, swell, tuber,
tulip 6. bulbil, camass, crocus, dahlia
7. bulblet, globule, rhizome
8. earthnut
bulbous... 5. round 7. bulbose,
bulging 8. swelling, tuberous
Bulgaria...
capital.. 5. Sofia
city.. 5. Varna 6. Plevna, Sliven
7. Ruschuk
native.. 6. Bulgar
origin.. 4. Slav 9. Mongolian
river.. 6. Danube, Marica (Maritsa),
Struma
bulge... 3. bow 4. bump, edge, hump,
jump, knob, odds 5. bilge, bloat,
flash, pouch, swell 6. convex, wallet
7. vantage 9. advantage
10. projection 12. protuberance
bulk... 3. sum 4. loom, mass, most,
size 6. extent, staple, volume
7. bigness, quantum 8. majority,
quantity 9. dimension, largeness,
substance, thickness 11. massiveness
12. accumulation 13. preponderance
bulky... 5. heavy, hulky, stout, thick
6. clumsy 7. awkward, lumpish,
massive 8. unwieldy 9. corpulent,
policemen (Eng sl), ponderous
10. cumbersome, unwielding
11. substantial
bull... 4. fiat, seal 5. edict, error,
large, ukase 6. brevet, decree,
firman, humbug, letter (papal), market
(Finan), rising, Taurus 7. blunder
8. nonsense, solecism 9. Irish bull,
policeman 10. speculator
bull (male animal)... 2. ox 3. cow
4. Apis (sacred), stot, toro, zebu
5. moose, steer, whale 6. walrus
7. bullock 8. elephant, Minotaur,
terrapin
bull (slang)... 4. blah, bosh, bunk
5. hokum 6. hot air 7. baloney
8. buncombe, flimflam
bulla... 4. bleb, boss, case (leather),
knob, seal (papal), stud 6. button
7. blister, globule, pendant, vesicle
8. ornament
bulldog... 3. ant 4. pipe 5. leech
7. courage, forceps 8. barnacle,
stubborn, tenacity 9. newspaper

(early), tenacious
bulldoze . . . 3. cow 5. bully, grade,
level 6. coerce, harass 7. buffalo
8. browbeat 10. intimidate
bullet . . . 4. ball (cannon), shot, slug
6. dumdum, pellet, sinker (angling),
tracer 7. missile
bulletin . . . 5. brief, flash 6. notice,
record 7. account, message
8. newsbill 9. statement
10. newsletter, periodical
11. publication 12. announcement
bullfighter . . . 6. torero 7. matador,
picador 8. capeador, toreador
bullfinch . . . 3. alp 4. nope 5. hedge
11. pyrrhuloxia 12. gray grosbeak
Bull Moose . . . 16. Progressive Party
bullpen (pert to) . . .
  camp . . 8. barracks 9. enclosure
  ice hockey . . 5. bench (penalty)
  ring cell . . 5. toril
  Western US . . 6. corral
Bull Run (battle) . . . 8. Manassas
bully . . . 4. beef 6. hector, jovial
7. gleeful, ruffian 8. browbeat,
bulldoze 9. bulldozer, tormentor
10. browbeater, intimidate
bulwark . . . 4. bank 6. buffer, sconce
7. barrier, parapet, rampart
8. abutment, buttress 10. protection
13. fortification
bum . . . 3. beg 5. idler, revel, rummy,
souse, spree 6. beggar, loafer,
tipple, wretch 7. budmash, moocher,
wastrel 8. blighter, drunkard,
vagabond 9. lazzarone, schnorrer
10. panhandler
bump . . . 3. hit, jog 4. bang, clop, jolt,
lump, meet, push, thud 5. bulge,
cahot, crash, crump, knock, lower,
plunk, tumor 6. demote, impact,
reduce, strike 7. collide 8. demotion,
dilation, swelling 9. air pocket,
collision, downgrade
bumpkin . . . 4. boor, clod, gawk, hick,
lout, rube, tike 5. yokel 6. farmer,
rustic 7. cauboge, hayseed, hoosier,
lumpkin 9. chawbacon
10. clodhopper
bumptious . . . 8. insolent 9. audacious,
insulting 12. contumelious
bunch . . . 3. bob, lot, mop, set
4. pack, tuft, wisp 5. batch, clump,
covey, crowd, flock, grist, group
6. bundle 7. cluster, company
8. assemble, quantity 9. multitude
10. congregate
bundle . . . 3. lot, wad 4. bale, bolt,
hank, pack, send 5. bluey, bunch,
fagot, sheaf, shook 6. bindle, fardel,
fascis, packet, parcel, seroon
7. fascine, package, rouleau
10. collection
bung . . . 3. tap 4. cork, plug, stop
5. spile 6. bruise 7. contuse,
stopper, stopple, tampeon, tampoon
8. bankrupt, bunghole 15. falsehood
bungle . . . 3. err 4. muff 5. botch,
fudge 6. bobble, foozle, fumble, tailor
(hunting) 7. blunder
bungling . . . 5. fudgy 6. clumsy
7. awkward, unhandy 8. botchery

9. unskilled 10. blundering, unskillful
bunion . . . 12. hallux valgus
bunk . . . 3. bed, kip, rot 4. blah, brag
5. abide, berth, couch, dwell,
hokum, hooey, sleep 6. humbug,
kibosh 7. baloney, hogwash
8. nonsense, tommyrot
9. cross–beam (logging)
Bunker Hill (Mass) . . . 6. battle (1775)
bunkum . . . see *buncombe*
Bunsen . . . 4. cell, disk 5. flame, valve
6. burner 9. Professor (Ger)
bunt . . . 3. bat, dig, jab, jog, tap
4. blow, bump, butt, pike, push, tail
(Scot) 5. knock, shove 7. bunting
10. propulsion
bunting . . . 4. flag, hood 5. flags
6. banner, pennon 7. pennant
8. streamer
bunting (bird) . . . 3. red 4. cirl, corn,
crow, lark, pape (Creole) 5. finch
6. indigo, towhee 7. cowbird, ortolan
8. bobolink 12. yellowhammer
buoy . . . 3. dan 4. bell 5. float
6. marker 7. can buoy, nunbuoy
8. bell buoy, deadhead, life buoy,
spar buoy 11. mooring buoy
12. breeches buoy 13. whistling
buoy
buoyance, buoyancy . . . 4. hope, snap
5. verve 6. bounce 7. flotage
9. lightness 10. levitation, resilience
12. floatability 16. lightheartedness
buoyant . . . 5. light 7. elastic
8. cheerful, floating, levitate, volatile
11. supernatant 12. lighthearted,
recuperative
bur, burr . . . 3. nut 5. thorn
8. adherent (see also *burr*)
burble . . . 6. muddle 7. confuse, trouble
8. disorder
burbot . . . 4. ling, Lota 7. eelpout
burden . . . 3. key, tax 4. birn, care,
cark, clog, lade, load, note, onus,
task, tone 5. cargo, cross, music,
tenor, voice 6. charge, cumber,
hamper, saddle, weight 7. bourdon,
freight, oppress, payload, refrain
8. capacity, overload, pressure
10. impediment, imposition
11. encumbrance
burdensome . . . 5. heavy 7. arduous,
massive, onerous, weighty
8. unwieldy 9. difficult, laborious,
ponderous 10. cumbersome,
oppressive 11. troublesome
12. impedimental
bureau . . . 4. desk, shop 6. office
7. dresser 8. chambers
10. chiffonier, department
bureaucracy . . . 10. government
11. directorate, officialdom, officialism
burgeon . . . 3. bud 4. grow 5. gemma,
shoot, sprit 6. sprout
burglar . . . 4. yegg 5. thief
9. cracksman 11. safecracker
12. housebreaker
burglary . . . 5. theft 6. burgle
7. larceny, robbery 8. stealage
13. housebreaking
burgle . . . 3. rob 8. burglary
10. burglarize

burgomaster... 5. mayor 7. alcalde
10. magistrate 11. burghmaster
burgoo, burgout... 4. stew 5. gruel
7. pudding (oatmeal) 8. porridge
burial... 5. inurn 7. funeral
9. interment, sepulture
10. engulfment, inhumation,
submersion 11. concealment,
submergence
burial ground... 4. pyre 5. grave
6. barrow 7. tumulus 8. bone yard,
catacomb, cemetery, golgotha
9. graveyard 10. churchyard,
necropolis 11. polyandrium
12. potter's field
burlesque... 3. fun 4. jest 5. farce,
comic 6. parody, review, satire
7. mimicry, mockery, overact,
take–off 8. burletta, doggerel,
ridicule, travesty 9. charivari,
imitation, travestie 10. caricatura,
caricature 13. entertainment
Burlingame Treaty... 11. Immigration
(Chin 1868)
burly... 3. fat 5. bulky, large, noble,
obese, stout 6. brawny 7. stately
8. imposing, stalwart 9. corpulent,
excellent
Burma, Burmese...
alphabet.. 4. Pali
capital (anc).. 3. Ava 4. Pegu
capital, present.. 7. Rangoon
city.. 8. Mandalay
dagger.. 3. dah (dhao)
gibbon.. 3. lar
girl.. 4. mima
monk.. 2. bo
native.. 3. Lai
relation.. 5. Thais (Tais) 6. Malays
7. Chinese 8. Tibetans
10. Mongolians
religion.. 8. Buddhism
robber.. 6. dacoit
shed (public).. 5. zayat
tribe.. 3. Mon, Tai 4. Laos, Shan
7. Siamese
viol.. 4. turr (3–stringed)
Burma Road... 6. Lashio (to China,
1938–1942, replaced by Ledo Rd)
burn... 3. dry, tan 4. char, fire, glow,
hurt, pain, sear, sere 5. blaze,
brand, brook, cense, flame, scald,
singe 6. ignite, injury, scorch
7. cremate, encauma, flicker,
sunburn, swelter, torrefy 9. cauterize,
sacrifice 10. incandesce, incinerate
burner... 3. jet 4. lamp 5. torch
6. Bunsen, candle, censer (incense)
7. cresset 9. blowtorch
10. lucubrator 11. incinerator
burning... 3. hot 4. fire, pain, sore
5. afire, angry, ardor, arson, blaze,
fiery, flame 6. ablaze, ardent, fervid
7. blazing, cautery, excited, fervent,
flaming, glowing, shining, zealous
8. eloquent, feverish, inustion
9. cremating, cremation, execution
10. combustion, ustulation
13. conflagration
burning place... 4. ghat 9. crematory
10. cinerarium
burnish... 3. rub 4. buff 5. glaze,

gloss, shine 6. patina, polish
burnt... 3. red 5. dried 6. burned,
seared, singed 7. charred
8. hardened, scorched, sunburnt
9. blistered, sunburned
burnt (pert to)...
art.. 11. pygrography, pyrogravure
color.. 4. rose 5. ocher, topaz
6. almond, orange, russet, sienna
8. amethyst
sugar.. 7. caramel
burn with anger, excitement...
4. fume 5. smoke 6. seethe,
simmer, sizzle 7. smolder
burp... 5. belch, eruct 8. eructate
burr... 3. cut, hem 4. buzz, whir
5. brier, drone, gnarl, knurl, thorn
6. brogue, corona (moon), meatus
(ear) 7. bramble, clotbur, prickle,
silique, sticker 8. excavate, follicle
9. cocklebur, whetstone
burro... 3. ass 4. jack 5. cuddy,
neddy 6. dickey, donkey 7. jackass
burrow... 3. dig 4. abri, hide, hole,
lair, mine 5. couch (otter's), lodge
(beaver's) 6. search, tunnel 7. shelter
burrowing... 9. effodient, fossorial
11. lithodomous (in rock)
burrowing animal... 4. mole, peba
5. poyou 6. peludo 8. suricate
9. armadillo
burst... 3. pop 4. bang, rend 5. blast,
blaze, break, broke, erupt, flare,
flash, shots, spurt 6. volley
7. explode, flare–up, gunfire, implode
8. outbreak, outburst, ruptured
9. discharge, explosion, fractured
10. detonation 11. dissiliency
burst (forth)... 4. grow 5. erupt, sally
6. sprout
burst (pert to)...
applause.. 5. éclat, hands 7. ovation,
plaudit 8. clapping
cheers.. 5. salvo
gunfire.. 6. rafale
laughter.. 3. fit 4. peal, roar
10. convulsion
temper.. 4. rage 5. scene, storm
7. passion 8. explosion
bursting... 4. full 7. brimful, crammed,
excited, replete 8. overfull, thrilled,
volcanic 9. explosive, surfeited
10. detonating 11. impassioned,
overflowing, overwhelmed
bury... 4. hide, sink 5. cache, cover,
inter, inurn, plant, stash 6. engulf,
entomb, inhume 7. conceal,
embosom, repress, secrete
8. submerge 9. overwhelm, sepulture
bus... 6. jitney 7. omnibus 10. motor
coach
bush... 3. tod 4. shag (hair) 5. brush,
plain, shrub, wahoo, wilds 6. branch,
lining 7. boscage, bushing
8. bushveld, woodland 10. hinterland
bushed... 4. beat 5. all in 6. pooped
7. baffled 8. dog–tired 9. exhausted,
nonplaced, perplexed, played out
10. nonplussed
bushel... 3. foo 4. full 6. basket,
vessel 7. measure (dry) 8. imperial,
standard 10. Winchester

Bushido (Jap)... 11. code of honor
bushing... 4. bush 6. lining, sleeve
(mach) 7. bearing, padding (piano)
Bushman... 3. San 4. Saan 5. nomad,
pygmy 6. Abatua, rustic
8. woodsman 9. aborigine
bushmaster... 5. snake
bushwhacker... 7. pioneer 8. guerilla
10. forerunner 11. bushfighter,
voortrekker 12. frontiersman
bushy... 5. hairy, thick, woody
6. dumose, shaggy, woodsy
7. hirsute, scrubby, shrubby
business... 3. job 4. firm, game, line,
work 5. craft, house, trade 6. affair,
career, matter, racket 7. calling,
company, concern, pursuit
8. commerce, industry, interest,
practice, vocation 10. enterprise,
occupation, proceeding, profession
11. transaction 13. establishment
business (pert to)...
  agreement.. 6. cartel
  businesslike.. 11. pragmatical
  customer.. 6. patron
  cycle.. 9. recession 10. depression,
  prosperity 11. liquidation
  deal.. 4. turn 9. operation
  11. negotiation, transaction
  Exchange.. 4. bank 5. Bolsa
  6. Bourse 11. stock market
  man.. 6. tycoon 8. salesman
  9. solicitor
  place.. 4. mart, shop 5. store
  6. office, shoppe 8. Exchange
bust... 4. bang, fail, hand (Bridge),
tame (bronco) 5. burst, chest, crash,
flunk, spree 6. breast, figure
7. degrade, explode, failure
8. collapse, demotion, fracture
9. sculpture 10. bankruptcy
bustard... 4. bird (Old World), kori,
Otis 5. goose, paauw 6. curlew
8. Otididae
busted... 4. flat 5. broke 6. broken,
failed, ruined 7. severed 8. bankrupt,
ruptured, strapped 9. insolvent,
penniless 10. stone–broke
bustle... 3. ado 4. fuss, stir, to–do
5. haste, whirl 6. flurry, hubbub,
hustle, pother, scurry, tumult
7. bluster, ferment, fluster, scamper,
turmoil 8. activity 9. agitation,
commotion 10. excitement,
hurly–burly 11. disturbance
bustling... 6. active 7. hurried, rushing
8. eventful, stirring
busy... 4. nosy, work 5. drive
6. active, devote, employ, engage,
occupy 7. engaged, on the go,
operose 8. diligent, employed,
meddling, occupied, on the run,
sedulous 9. assiduous, attentive,
laborious, officious 10. meddlesome
11. industrious, inquisitive,
persevering
busy... 4. dick 6. gossip 7. gumshoe,
meddler 8. busybody, flatfoot
9. detective
busybody... 6. gossip 8. quidnunc
9. pragmatic
but... 2. ma 3. yet 4. even, just,

mere, save 5. hence, outer, still
6. except 7. however, without
10. regardless 12. nevertheless
15. notwithstanding
butcher... 3. fly (angling), mar 4. kill,
slay 5. botch, spoil 6. killer, vendor
7. croaker, meatman 8. merchant,
train–boy 9. slaughter 11. slaughterer
12. bloodshedder
butchery... 6. murder 7. carnage
8. business, massacre, shambles
9. slaughter 14. slaughterhouse
butt... 3. aim, end, jut, pit, ram, tun,
tup 4. buck, bunt, cart, cask, goat,
rump, stub 5. cigar, hinge, joint,
mound, piece, stump 6. target
(archery), thrust (fencing) 7. buttock,
parapet, project 8. flatfish
9. cigarette 13. laughingstock
butter... 3. pat 4. coat, ghee (ghi),
oleo 5. smear 6. bedaub, spread
7. butyric 8. flattery 9. margarine,
suaveness 10. semiliquid
13. oleomargarine
butter–and–eggs... 8. flaxweed,
ranstead, toadflax
buttercup fruit... 6. achene
7. crowtoe
butterfingered... 6. clumsy
7. awkward, unhandy 8. bungling,
careless 9. all thumbs 10. blundering
butterflies (slang)... 6. nerves
7. fidgets, jitters
butterfly (pert to)...
  American.. 7. viceroy
  family.. 10. Agapetidae
  11. Rhopalocera
  genus.. 7. Lycaena 11. Lepidoptera
  large.. 7. monarch
  larva.. 11. caterpillar
  lily.. 4. sego 8. mariposa
  peacock.. 2. io 7. buckeye
  swallowtail.. 5. black, tiger, zebra
  type.. 4. moth 5. satyr 10. fritillary,
  silverspot
buttocks... 4. butt (vulgar), hips, rear,
rump, seat 5. fanny, podex
6. bottom 8. haunches, maneuver
(wrestling) 9. backsides, posterior
buttress... 4. pier, pile, prop, stay
5. brace, tower 7. shelter, support
8. abutment 10. projection,
strengthen 11. counterfort
13. fortification
buttress (Arch)... 4. pier 6. flying
7. hanging
buxom... 3. gay 4. boon, rosy 5. jolly,
plump 6. blithe, jocund, jovial
7. gleeful
buy... 5. bribe 6. accept, redeem
7. bargain, expiate 8. purchase
buy back... 6. redeem
Buyer Beware... 12. Caveat Emptor
buzz... 3. hum, saw 5. rumor, snore
6. bustle, murmur, rumble
7. ferment, whisper 9. fricative,
murmuring 10. sibilation
buzzard... 4. aura (turkey), hawk, pern
5. buteo 6. osprey, stupid 7. harrier
9. dorbeetle, senseless
10. cockchafer
buzz bomb... 9. doodlebug

10. bumblebomb
14. Chase–Me–Charlie
bwana (Afr)... 4. boss 6. master
by... 2. at, in, on 3. ago, bei, par,
per, via 4. away, gone, near, over,
pass (bridge), past, with 5. after,
aside 6. beside, beyond, nearby,
toward 7. abreast, close by, through
9. in reserve
by–and–by... 4. anon, soon 5. later,
sweet 6. mañana 7. betimes,
bientôt, ere long, shortly 8. directly
9. presently 11. tout à l'heure
by birth... 3. nee
bygone... 3. ago 4. lost, over, past
6. buried, bypast, gone by, passed
7. elapsed, extinct 8. departed,
preterit (preterite)
byname... 6. eponym 7. babyism,
epithet, surname 8. cognomen,
monicker, nickname 9. sobriquet
10. patronymic 11. appellation
bypass... 4. go by, miss 5. byway,
elude 6. byroad, detour, escape
7. deviate, digress 8. side path

10. circumvent, roundabout
By the Grace of God... 9. Dei Gratia
byword... 3. mot, saw 5. adage,
maxim 6. byname, phrase, saying,
slogan 7. adagium, parable, proverb
8. aphorism, nickname, reproach
9. catchword, sobriquet
10. shibboleth
by word of mouth... 4. oral 5. parol
(parole)
Byzantine Empire...
architecture.. 7. St Marks (Venice)
9. elaborate
bookbinding.. 9. unadorned (earlier)
10. bejewelled (later)
church.. 7. Eastern
city.. 14. Constantinople (Istanbul)
creator.. 11. Constantine (the Great)
historian.. 9. Procopius 11. Anna
Comnena
poetry.. 5. hymns
scepter.. 6. ferula
writer.. 6. Prazes 7. Priscus, Romanus
Byzantium... 14. Constantinople
(Istanbul)

C

C... 4. clef 7. cedilla, century,
hundred, keynote
caama... 3. fox 4. asse 10. hartebeest
cab... 4. pony, taxi 7. measure,
purloin, shelter, taxicab, vehicle
8. carriage (anc) 9. cabriolet
10. locomotive (part) 11. translation
cabal... 4. clan, plot 5. group, junta,
party 7. chatter, complot, coterie,
dispute, faction 8. intrigue
9. camarilla, collusion, Committee
10. complicity, conspiracy
cabala... 7. mystery 9. mystic art,
occultism
cabalessou... 9. armadillo (giant)
cabalistic... 6. occult 7. cabalic
8. abstract, anagogic, esoteric,
mystical 10. mysterious
caballeria... 7. measure (land)
8. chivalry 10. knighthood
caballero... 5. lover, rider 6. knight
8. cavalier, horseman 9. chevalier,
gentleman 10. equestrian
caballo... 5. horse
cabaret... 3. inn 4. cafe 6. hostel,
posado, tavern 7. barroom 9. night
club, roadhouse 11. café dansant
13. entertainment
cabbage... 3. kos (cos) 4. cole, kale,
palm 5. colza, savoy 7. collard
8. colewort, kohlrabi 11. cauliflower
15. Brussels sprouts
cabbage (pert to)...
curly leaf.. 5. savoy
daisy.. 11. globeflower

fermented.. 5. kraut
headless.. 4. kale
salad.. 4. slaw
seed.. 5. colza
slang.. 4. crib, fool 6. pilfer
7. fathead, purloin 9. numbskull
11. cabbagehead, knucklehead
species.. 8. Brassica
tree.. 4. palm 7. angelin 8. palmetto
white.. 9. butterfly
yellows.. 7. disease (destructive)
caber... 4. apar, beam, pole 6. rafter,
timber
cabin... 3. hut 4. shed 5. booth,
coach (Naut), house, hovel, lodge,
shack 6. cabana, saloon 7. caboose
10. blockhouse
cabinet... 3. box, den 4. Body, buhl,
case 6. bureau, closet, office
7. almirah, boudoir, council, étagère,
whatnot 8. cellaret, cupboard,
ministry 9. committee
cable... 4. boom, cord, rope, wire
5. chain, twine 6. fasten, hawser
7. coaxial, measure, molding,
ropeway 8. telegram 9. cablegram
cable (pert to)...
car.. 7. telpher
holder (Naut).. 7. wildcat 10. cable
wheel
post.. 4. bitt
cabling... 9. rudenture
cabochon... 5. jewel, stone (uncut),
style (convex cut) 8. ornament
caboodle... 3. all, kit, lot 5. bunch,

whole 10. collection 14. kit and caboodle
caboose... 3. car (RR) 5. buggy 6. galley 7. kitchen 9. deckhouse
cabotin... 5. actor (strolling) 9. charlatan
cachaca... 3. rum (white)
cache... 4. hide, hole 5. stash, store 7. conceal, hide—out, retreat 8. hideaway 10. storehouse
cachet... 4. seal 5. sigil, stamp, wafer 6. signet 7. capsule
cachilla... 8. white man
cachot... 7. dungeon
cackle... 3. gab 4. cank, chat, crow, talk 5. clack, laugh, prate 6. babble, gabble, giggle, gossip, jabber 7. chatter, prattle 8. laughter
cacodemon... 4. deva 5. devil, fiend, Indra 10. evil spirit
cacology... 10. bad diction, corruption (speech) 16. mispronunciation
cacophonous... 7. raucous 8. jangling, strident 9. diaphonic, dissonant 10. discordant 11. unmelodious
cacophony... 5. clash 6. jangle 7. discord 8. diaphony (Mus) 9. harshness 10. dissodence
cactus... 4. bleo 5. agave 6. chaute, cholla, mescal 7. Opuntia, saguaro 8. fishhook 9. Turk's—head 11. prickly pear 12. Echinocactus
cad... 4. boor, chum, heel, hick 5. yokel 6. mucker 7. bounder, servant 8. townsman 9. scoundrel, vulgarian
cadaver... 4. body (dead) 5. stiff 6. corpse 7. carcass 8. skeleton
cadaverous... 4. pale 5. gaunt, lurid 6. sickly, wasted 7. ghastly, haggard 9. emaciated 10. attenuated, corpselike
caddis (pert to)...
　bait.. 3. fly 4. worm 5. cadew
　material.. 4. yarn 5. twill 6. crewel 7. worsted
　worm.. 5. larva (aquatic)
caddle... 4. fuss 5. annoy, worry 6. gossip 7. confuse, trouble 8. disarray 9. confusion
cade... 3. keg, oil (Med), pet 4. cask, lamb (orphan) 6. barrel, coddle, petted
cadeau... 4. gift
cadence... 4. beat, lilt, tone 5. meter 6. rhythm 7. balance 9. free verse, vers libre 10. modulation
cadence... 4. half 5. trill 6. plagal 7. perfect 9. authentic, deceptive, imperfect, suspended 11. interrupted
cadency (Her)... 4. rose 5. label 6. mullet 7. annulet, martlet 8. crescent 10. fleur—de—lis 11. cross moline
cadenza... 7. cadence 8. flourish
cadet... 3. son 4. pleb 5. color (blue), youth 6. junior 10. midshipman
cadge... 3. beg 4. hawk 5. fakir, mooch 6. beggar, hawker, mumper, peddle, sponge, vendor 7. carrier, moocher, sponger 8. huckster, sannyasi

cadgy... 6. wanton 7. lustful 8. cheerful, mirthful
Cadmus (pert to)...
　daughter.. 3. Ino 6. Semele
　father.. 6. Agenor
　founder of.. 6. Thebes (Boetia)
　sister.. 6. Europa
　wife.. 8. Harmonia
cadre... 4. list, unit 5. frame, panel 6. line—up, roster, scheme 8. cadastre, register, schedule, skeleton 9. framework
caduceus (Gr Antiq).. 4. wand (Hermes') 5. staff 6. symbol 8. insignia (Med Corps)
Caesar (pert to)...
　betrayer.. 6. Brutus
　colleague.. 7. Bibulus
　death site.. 4. Nola
　Emperor, Dictator of.. 4. Rome
　fatal day.. 4. Ides (of March) 11. Ides of March
　language.. 5. Latin
　rival.. 6. Pompey
　river.. 7. Rubicon
　sister.. 4. Atia
　uncle.. 11. Caius Marius
　wife.. 8. Cornelia
caesura, cesura... 4. rest 5. break, colon, comma, pause 8. interval 12. interruption
cafard... 5. bigot, blues 6. humbug 9. hypocrite 10. depression
café... 5. coffe 6. coffee 10. restaurant 11. coffeehouse
café (pert to)...
　au lait.. 5. brown 6. alesan 10. French nude
　creme.. 5. suede (color)
　noir.. 4. musk (color) 11. black coffee
　parfait.. 8. beverage
cafetière... 9. coffeepot 10. percolator
caffeine... 6. coffee, theine (in tea) 8. alkaloid 9. stimulant
cafila... 7. caravan (camel)
cage... 3. mew, pen 4. coop 6. corral 7. confine, goal net, impound 8. goal post
cagey... 3. sly 4. foxy, wary, wily 5. canny, leery 6. artful, crafty, shifty, shrews 7. cunning, evasive. knowing
Cain (pert to)...
　brother.. 4. Abel
　founder of.. 5. Enoch (1st city)
　Land of.. 3. Nod
　slayer of.. 4. Abel
　son.. 5. Enoch
cairn... 4. heap (stones) 6. menhir 8. catstone (catstane), landmark, memorial, monument
Cairo...
　capital.. 5. Egypt
　city gate (famed).. 9. Bab—el—Nasr
　mosque.. 12. Sultan Hassan
　resident.. 7. Cairene
　river.. 4. Nile
　seaport.. 10. Alexandria
　tomb.. 10. Mehemet Ali
　warrior.. 9. Rameses II
caisson... 3. box 4. case 5. chest, wagon 7. chamber

C
E

caitiff... 4. base, mean, vile
  6. coward, wicked, wretch
  7. budmash, captive 10. despicable
cajole... 4. coax, urge 5. cheat, jolly
  6. delude 7. flatter, palaver,
  sweeten, wheedle 8. blandish
  9. importune 10. honeyfogle
Cajun (pert to)...
  descent.. 6. French (Canadian)
  dialect.. 5. Cajun
  home (present).. 9. Louisiana
  native of.. 6. Acadia (Nova Scotia)
cake... 3. bun, wig 4. bake, food,
  lump, mass, wigg 5. batty, block,
  crust, solid, torte, wafer 6. gateau,
  harden 7. bannock, congeal, oatcake,
  pancake 8. corn pone, solidify
  9. charlotte, simpleton
  11. griddle–cake
cake (pert to)...
  almond paste.. 7. ratafia
  corn.. 4. pone
  flat.. 7. placent
  fried.. 7. cruller 8. doughnut
  Lenten.. 6. cimbal, simnel
  Scotch.. 4. farl (farle) 5. scone
  unleavened.. 8. tortilla
Cake Day (Scot)... 8. hogmanay (New
  Year's)
calabar bean... 6. myotic, ordeal
  7. eserine 8. alkaloid
  13. physostigmine
calabash... 5. gourd 6. baobab, bronze
  (color)
calaboose... 4. gaol, jail 5. choky,
  clink 6. bagnio, lockup, prison
  8. bastille, calabozo 9. Bridewell
calamitous... 3. sad 4. dire, evil
  5. black 6. tragic, woeful 7. adverse,
  baleful, ruinous, unhappy 8. grievous,
  tragical, wretched 10. afflictive,
  deplorable, disastrous
  11. cataclysmic, destructive,
  distressful, unfortunate
  12. catastrophic
calamity... 4. blow, evil, ruin 5. wrack
  6. mishap 7. tragedy 8. casualty,
  disaster, distress, fatality 9. adversity
  10. affliction, misfortune
  11. catastrophe, direfulness,
  unhappiness 12. wretchedness
calathiform... 9. cup–shaped
calcarea... 5. coral 7. sponges
calceiform... 10. orchidlike
  13. clipper–shaped
calcitrant... 8. stubborn
  12. recalcitrant
calcitrate... 4. boot, kick 6. oppose
calculate... 3. aim 4. deem, rate, tell
  5. allow, count, frame, judge, score,
  tally, think 6. cipher, deduce, figure,
  gather, number, reckon 7. average,
  compute, suppose 8. conclude,
  estimate 9. determine, enumerate
calculated... 7. advised, studied,
  weighed 8. measured
  10. considered, deliberate
  11. intentional 12. contemplated
calculating... 8. plotting, scheming
  9. computing, designing, judicious
  10. estimating, numerative, reflecting,
  thoughtful 11. circumspect,

  considerate 14. discriminative
calculator... 5. table 6. abacus
  7. suan pan (swan pan, Chin)
  8. computer 9. estimator, tabulator
  10. parimutuel 11. Comptometer,
  totalizator
caldron, cauldron... 3. pot, red
  (color), vat 6. boiler, kettle, mortar,
  retort 7. alembic 8. crucible
Caleb (pert to)...
  daughter.. 7. Achsaph
  literally.. 3. dog
  son.. 3. Hur, Iru
  spy of.. 6. Canaan
calèche... 7. vehicle (Quebec)
Caledonia (anc)... 8. Scotland
Caledonia bird... 4. kagu
Caledonian... 5. brown 6. Scotch
  8. Scotsman, Scottish
calefacient... 4. warm 6. remedy
  7. heating 11. calefactory
calendar... 4. list, Ordo 5. index, slate
  6. docket, line–up, record
  7. almanac, calends (kalends),
  program 8. register, schedule
  9. catalogue, ephemeris
  10. chronology, prospectus
calendar (type)... 5. Roman, Swiss
  6. Jewish, Julian 7. Chinese
  9. Cotsworth, Gregorian, perpetual
  13. International (fixed)
calenture... 4. glow 5. ardor, fever
  7. passion, pyrexia 9. febrility,
  sunstroke
calepin... 4. book (ref) 7. lexicon
  10. dictionary
calf... 3. leg (part) 4. dolt, fool, skin
  6. bovine, island, weaner 7. iceberg,
  leather 9. youngling
calf (pert to)...
  flesh.. 4. veal
  hide.. 3. kip
  leg (part).. 5. sural
  motherless.. 5. dogie 8. maverick
  sweetbread.. 9. ris de veau
  time.. 5. youth
Caliban (pert to)...
  character.. 5. brute, slave (The
  Tempest)
  deity.. 7. Setebos
  mother.. 7. Sycorax (witch)
caliber, calibre... 4. bore 7. ability
calico... 4. dame 5. cloth 6. salloo
  8. goldfish 12. multicolored
calico (pert to)...
  bird.. 9. turnstone
  bush.. 6. laurel
  horse, pony.. 5. pinto 7. piebald
  printing.. 4. teer 7. topical
calid... 3. hot 4. mild, warm 6. genial
  7. burning, thermal
California...
  bay.. 8. Monterey
  capital.. 10. Sacramento
  city.. 6. Fresno 7. Oakland 8. San
  Diego, Stockton 9. Long Beach
  10. Los Angeles 12. San Francisco,
  Santa Barbara
  desert.. 6. Mojave 8. Colorado
  discoverer.. 6. Cortez (1535)
  flower.. 5. poppy
  history.. 8. Gold Rush (1848),

Missions 11. Sutter's Mill
lake.. 5. Tahoe 8. Elsinore 9. Salton
Sea
lowest point.. 11. Death Valley
mountain.. 6. Lassen, Shasta
7. Whitney
oldest living thing.. 8. redwoods
14. General Sherman (tree)
15. bristlecone pine
river.. 4. Kern 7. Feather, Russian
10. Sacramento
pageant.. 10. Rose Parade
17. Tournament of Roses
State admission.. 11. thirty–first
State motto.. 6. Eureka
State nickname.. 6. Golden
caliph, calif... 3. Ali (4th) 4. Imam
(Imaum), Omar 6. Othman 7. Abu
Bekr 8. Islamite
Caliph Ali's descendants... 5. Alids
(Alides)
caliphate... 7. Omniads, Shiites
(Sectaries) 8. Idrisids 9. Fatimites
calk, caulk... 4. copy, plug, stop
5. close, sleep (Naut sl) 6. calque,
catnap, chinse, plug up, stop up
7. occlude
call... 3. bid, cry, dub, hip, nod
4. ahoy, beck, dial, name, plea, ring,
soho, sook (hog), taps, term, yell
5. alarm, basis, cause, clepe, rally,
rouse, shout, style, visit, waken
6. appeal, demand, ground, invoke,
motive, muster, option, reason,
sennet, signal, slogan, summon
7. appoint, bidding, collect, convoke,
fanfare, summons, trumpet
8. assemble, nominate, occasion,
reveille 9. battle cry, challenge,
designate, induction, telephone,
watchword 10. denominate, invitation
11. recruitment, requisition
12. conscription 13. justification
call (pert to)...
attention.. 6. direct, remind 8. point
out
back.. 6. recall, recant, repeal, revive,
revoke 7. retract 8. remember
9. recollect
down.. 6. invoke 7. bawl out,
reprove, tell off
evil upon.. 8. execrate
forth.. 5. evoke, rouse 6. elicit,
excite, induce, prompt, summon
names.. 4. cite 5. abuse, curse
6. insult, revile, vilify 8. besmirch
10. vituperate
together.. 6. muster, summon
7. convoke
to mind.. 4. cite 8. remember
9. visualize
callant, callan... 3. boy, lad 4. chap
5. youth 6. fellow, garçon, laddie
8. customer, muchacho
11. hobbledehoy
calle... 6. street
called.. 5. named 6. dubbed, y–clept,
yermed 7. y–cleped
calling... 3. art, nod 4. beck, lure,
name, work 5. trade 6. career,
metier, naming, outcry 7. bidding,
mission, pursuit, styling, summons

8. biddance, business, labeling
(labelling), practice, vocation
9. condition, evocation
10. employment, invitation,
occupation, profession
13. circumstances
calling crab... 7. fiddler
calling hare... 4. pika
Calliope... 4. Muse (poet) 5. organ
8. asteroid
Calliope's son... 7. Orpheus
callous, calloused... 4. horn, sear
5. horny, inure 6. harden, seared
8. hardened 9. heartless, indurated,
unfeeling 10. impervious
11. hardhearted 12. thick–skinned
14. pachydermatous
callow... 5. crude, green 6. tender,
unripe, vernal 7. budding
8. immature, unformed 9. unfledged
10. unseasoned 11. undeveloped
15. unsophisticated
callus... 6. tyloma
calm... 3. lay 4. cool, dill, fair, lull,
mild 5. allay, balmy, peace, quiet,
sober, still 6. becalm, hushed, pacify,
placid, sedate, serene, smooth,
soothe, steady 7. appease, compose,
halcyon, orderly, pacific, placate,
restful, unmoved 8. peaceful, tranquil
9. quiescent, unruffled
10. phlegmatic 11. tranquilize,
undisturbed 13. dispassionate,
imperturbable
calmant, calmative... 7. anodyne,
soother 8. lenitive, pacifier, sedative,
soothing 10. depressant, palliative
11. alleviative 12. tranquilizer
calmato (Mus)... 4. calm 8. tranquil
calmness... 4. calm, lull 5. peace,
poise, quiet 6. repose 8. quietude,
serenity 9. composure, placidity
10. equanimity, quiescence
11. restfulness, self–control
calor... 4. heat 5. therm 7. thermal
calorifics... 4. heat 7. heating
calumniate... 4. slur 5. belie, libel
6. accuse, revile 7. asperse, slander,
traduce 9. blaspheme
calumnious... 7. abusive 8. derisive,
insolent, libelous 9. insulting
10. defamatory, derogatory,
slanderous 11. maledictory,
opprobrious
calumny... 5. abuse 7. lampoon,
slander 9. contumely 10. detraction,
scurrility 11. malediction
12. vilification
calvary... 8. crucifix
Calvary (Bib)... 8. Damascus, Golgotha
9. Jerusalem
Calvinism (pert to)...
author.. 6. Calvin
doctrine.. 5. Grace 9. Atonement,
Depravity (total) 12. Perseverance (of
Saints) 14. Predestination
site.. 6. Geneva
Calvinistic Methodist... 5. Welsh
10. Whitefield 14. Lady Huntingdon
Calypso... 6. Ogygia (home)
8. Cytherea, sea nymph (The
Odyssey)

calyx... 3. cup 4. husk 5. galea, sepal
6. corona 7. corolla 8. epicalyx,
perianth
camarada... 7. comrade, partner
9. companion
camaraderie... 8. good will
11. familiarity 14. good–fellowship
camarilla... 5. cabal 6. clique
7. council
camata... 6. acorns 8. oak fruit
cambist... 6. banker, broker
9. financier 11. moneylender
12. money–changer
Cambodia...
capital.. 6. Angkor 8. Pnom–Penh
language.. 5. Khmer 9. Cambodian
religion.. 8. Buddhism
seaport.. 6. Kampot
Cambria... 5. Wales
Cambridge University (pert to)...
English examination.. 6. tripos
English student.. 5. sizar 6. optime
(honor)
Massachusetts.. 3. MIT 7. Harvard
camel... 4. oont 5. llama 6. deloul,
mammal, vicuna 7. Camelus
8. Bactrian (2–humped)
9. Camelidae, dromedary
camel hair shawl... 8. cashmere
camelopard... 7. giraffe
13. constellation
Camelot... 6. legend 10. King Arthur,
palace site, Round Table
cameo... 4. onyx 7. relievo
8. anaglyph
camera type... 5. Kodak 7. Brownie
10. Rollieflex
Cameroon...
capital.. 7. Yaounde (Afr)
native.. 4. Sara
river.. 5. Shari
seaport.. 6. Douala
tribe.. 3. Abo 5. Bantu
Camino Real (Calif)... 9. Royal Road
12. El Camino Real, King's Highway
Camorra (It)... 12. organization (secret)
camouflage... 7. falsify 8. disguise
9. dissemble 10. false front
12. misrepresent
camp... 3. clan, tent 5. abode, etape,
junto, tabor 6. campoo, clique,
laager 7. bivouac, faction
10. encampment
campaign... 5. serve 7. crusade
9. operation
camphorated tincture of opium...
9. paregoric
campus... 4. quad 5. field (academic)
can... 3. jar, may, tin 6. hopper,
vessel 7. capable 8. canister,
conserve 9. competent
10. receptacle
can... 5. skill 7. ability 9. competent
10. receptacle
can (sl)... 3. jug, tin 4. boot, bump,
fire, jail, john, kick 6. bounce,
cooler, toilet 7. dismiss 9. discharge
11. give the gate
Canaan... 9. Palestine 12. Promised
Land
Canada... see also *Canadian*
capital (Federal).. 6. Ottawa

city.. 7. Toronto 8. Hamilton,
Montreal, Winnipeg 9. Vancouver
discoverer.. 9. John Cabot (1497)
Hudson's Bay Co.. 8. fur trade
native.. 6. French 7. English
nickname.. 6. Canuck
park.. 6. Jasper
peninsula.. 5. Gaspé
police.. 8. Mounties 12. Royal
Mounted (7,000)
river.. 5. Peace, Slave 6. Fraser,
Nelson, Ottawa 8. Gatineau
9. Athabasca, Churchill, Mackenzie
10. St Lawrence
Canadian (pert to)...
flour.. 6. Shorts (milling) 8. canaille
jay.. 9. moose bird 10. whisky jack
lynx.. 5. pishu
plum.. 6. cheney
porcupine.. 5. urson 7. cawquaw
squaw.. 6. mahala
canaille... 3. mob 4. ruck 6. rabble,
ragtag, Shorts 8. riffraff
10. roughscuff
canal... 4. duct, iter (brain), pipe, tube
5. drain 6. meatus 7. acequia,
channel 10. waterspout
11. watercourse
Canal... 4. Erie, Kiel, Suez 6. Panama
13. Sault Ste Marie (Soo)
Canal Zone Lock... 5. Gatun
10. Miraflores
canard... 4. duck, hoax 5. rumor
6. humbug 9. falsehood
canary... 6. yellow 8. song–bird,
songster, weakling
Canary Islands...
capital.. 9. Santa Cruz (Teneriffe)
city.. 9. Las Palmas (Grand Canary)
commune.. 4. Icod
owner.. 5. Spain
cancel... 4. blot, dele, kill, omit, undo
5. annul, erase 6. delete, excise,
recall, repeal, revoke 7. abolish,
destroy, nullify, rescind, retract
8. write off 10. invalidate, neutralize,
obliterate 11. countermand
cancellation... 6. repeal 7. erasure
8. deletion, write–off 10. moratorium
12. obliteration
cancer... 4. evil 5. tumor 6. canker,
growth 7. sarcoma 8. neoplasm
9. carcinoma
Cancer... 4. crab 7. mansion (moon)
10. zodiac sign 13. constellation
cancion... 4. song 5. lyric
Candia... 5. Crete (Isl)
candid... 4. fair, just, open, pure
5. frank 6. direct, honest 7. sincere
9. guileless, impartial, ingenuous
10. impersonal 13. dispassionate
15. straightforward
candidate... 6. seeker 7. aspirer,
electee, nominee 8. aspirant, selectee
9. applicant, appointee, postulant
10. solicitant
candidate list... 4. leet 5. slate
6. roster
Candide (pert to)...
hero, title.. 5. novel
novel, author.. 8. Voltaire
philosophy.. 8. optimism

candied... 5. sweet 7. honeyed
   9. congealed, incrusted, preserved
   10. flattering, granulated
   12. crystallized
candied sea holly... 6. eryngo (eringo)
candle... 3. dip, wax 5. light, power,
   taper 6. bougie, cierge, tallow, votive
   7. paschal 8. bayberry 9. chandelle
candlestick (pert to)...
   Bib.. 6. lampad
   branched.. 9. girandole
   ornamental.. 10. candelabra
   Scot.. 6. crusie
   spike.. 7. pricket
   three—branched.. 9. tricerion
   torch type.. 8. flambeau
   wall.. 6. sconce
candlewood... 6. flower 8. ocotillo
candor... 8. fairness, openness
   9. frankness, sincerity, unreserve
   10. directness 11. artlessness,
   unrestraint 13. outspokenness
candy... 5. sweet 6. penide (pulled),
   sweets 7. sweeten 8. crystals
   9. granulate, sweetmeat
   10. confection 11. crystallize
   13. confectionary
candy (type)... 4. mint 5. fudge, taffy
   6. bonbon, nougat, toffee 7. brittle,
   caramel, fondant, panocha, penuche,
   praline 8. licorice, lollipop
   9. chocolate 11. marshmallow
candytuft... 6. iberis
cane... 3. rod 4. beat, club, reed,
   stem, whip 5. crook, sorgo, staff,
   stick, sugar 6. bamboo, rattan
   7. bagasse, bourdon, sorghum,
   sucrose 9. handstaff, truncheon
   12. swagger stick
canescent... 5. hoary, white 7. grizzly,
   silvery, whitish 9. snow—white
Canfield... 9. solitaire
canine... 3. cur, dog, fox, pug, pup
   4. lobo, mutt, tike 5. dingo, pooch,
   puppy, whelp 6. animal, coyote
   7. Canidae, doggish, laniary, mastiff,
   mongrel, reynard 8. dogtooth,
   eyetooth
canis... 3. dog
Canis Majoris... 13. Constellation (with
   Dog Star, Sirius)
cannibalism... 9. barbarity, endophagy
   10. perversion 11. blood thirst
   13. anthropophagy
cannon... 3. gun 5. crash 6. mortar
   7. firearm, robinet 8. dog of war,
   howitzer, ordnance 9. artillery,
   collision
cannon (pert to)...
   ball.. 6. pellet 7. missile
   bore.. 6. breech
   fire.. 7. barrage
   handle.. 4. anse
   nautical.. 5. chase
   part.. 8. cascabel
   pivot.. 8. trunnion
   platform.. 10. terreplein
   plug.. 7. tampion
   shot.. 5. grape
   shoulder part.. 7. rimbase
cannonade... 4. boom, peal, roar
   5. blitz, shell 6. rumble, strafe

   11. bombardment
canny... 3. sly 4. foxy, wary, wily
   6. artful, frugal, shrewd, subtle
   7. cunning, knowing, prudent, thrifty
   8. cautious 9. sagacious
canoe... 4. kiak, pahi, proa, waka
   5. bongo, bungo, kayak, umiak,
   waapa 6. corial, dugout, oomiak,
   pitpan 7. almadia, buckeye (bugeye),
   coracle, piragua, pirogue
   12. pambanmanche
canon... 3. law 4. code, list, rule,
   type 5. model, nodus (Mus)
   6. belief, clergy, decree, ritual
   7. measure, precept 8. decision
   9. catalogue, criterion 10. regulation
   11. composition 12. constitution
canonical... 4. None (hour), Sext
   (hour) 5. Lauds, Prime 6. Matins
   7. creedal 8. dogmatic, orthodox
   9. doctrinal 10. scriptural
   11. theological 14. ecclesiastical
canonization... 8. sainting
   10. ordainment, ordination
   12. consecration, enshrinement
canopy... 3. sky 4. ceil, cope, dais,
   tent 5. cover, shade, vault
   6. awning, tester 7. blanket,
   marquee, shelter 8. caponier
   (caponiere), ciborium, pavilion
   9. baldachin, firmament
canorous... 5. clear 8. sonorous
   9. melodious 10. euphonious
cant... 3. tip 4. lean, list, sing, song,
   sway, tack, tilt 5. angle, argot,
   chant, lingo, pitch, slang, slope,
   whine 6. careen, intone, jargon,
   patois, snivel 7. auction, incline,
   mummery 8. pretense 9. hypocrisy
   10. intonation, sanctimony
   17. sanctimoniousness
cantabank... 6. singer (ballad)
cantador... 6. singer (folk songs)
cantankerous... 8. perverse
   9. malicious 10. contention,
   ill—natured 12. cross—grained
cantata... 5. motet 8. serenata
   9. pastorale
canter... 4. gait, lope 6. gallop
   (Canterbury) 8. vagabond
Canterbury...
   archbishop.. 7. Cranmer, Primate
     13. Thomas à Becket (murdered)
   capital (Eng).. 14. ecclesiastical
   famed building.. 9. Cathedral
   gallop.. 5. aubin 6. canter
   Tales, author.. 7. Chaucer
canticle... 3. lay, ode 4. hymn, lied,
   song 5. carol, ditty 6. Te Deum
Canticle of Canticles (Bib)...
   11. Song of Songs 13. Song of
   Solomon
cantilena... 6. legato, melody
   8. graceful
cantina... 3. bag 6. pocket, saloon
   7. canteen
cantle... 4. nook, part 5. crown, slice
   6. corner, saddle (part) 7. segment
   11. cornerpiece
canto... 4. book, song 5. poems (div
   of), tenor, verse 6. cantus, melody,
   poetry 7. descort

canton... 3. Uri (Switz) 6. county
7. commune, quarter 8. district,
insignia (Her), mofussil (Ind)
9. bailiwick, partition
cantor... 6. leader, singer 7. soloist
8. melodist, vocalist 9. precentor
cantoria... 7. balcony, gallery (choir)
cantrip... 5. charm, magic, spell, trick
canty... 6. lively 7. chipper 8. cheerful
9. sprightly
Canuck... 8. Canadian
canvas... 4. sail, tent, tuke (tewke)
5. cloth 6. circus 7. picture, tentage
8. covering, likeness, pavilion
9. tarpaulin 14. representation
canvasback... 4. duck
canvass... 4. poll 5. study 6. survey
7. examine, inquiry, solicit
8. campaign, consider 10. scrutinize
11. electioneer 12. solicitation
13. questionnaire
canyon, cañon... 4. abra (mouth)
5. chasm, dalle (wall), gorge, gulch
6. arroyo, coulee, ravine, violet
7. couloir
canzone, canzonetta... 4. poem, song
6. ballad, melody 8. canzonet,
madrigal
caoba... 8. mahogany, muskwood
caoutchouc... 3. ule 6. caucho, rubber
cap... 3. fez, hat, lid, taj, tam 4. atef,
coif, hood, kepi 5. beret, boina,
busby, shako, toque 6. barret,
biggin, bonnet, calpac, cloche, pileus,
turban 7. biretta (beretta), calotte,
calpack, chapeau 8. Balmoral,
havelock 9. headdress, headpiece,
shtreimal, sou'wester, zucchetto
10. cervelière 11. mortarboard,
tam—o'—shanter
cap (outer part)... 3. lid, tip, top
4. dome, fuze, peak, type 5. cover,
crown, excel, match, spire, trump
6. summit, top off 7. capital (Arch),
overlie, patella 8. complete
9. copestone, detonator
capa... 5. cloak 6. mantle 7. tobacco
capability... 5. power, skill 6. genius
7. ability, caliber, faculty, potency
8. ableness, adequacy, capacity
10. competence 13. qualification
capable... 3. apt, can, fit 4. able
5. adept, expert 7. equal to,
skilled 8. adequate 9. competent,
effective, efficient, qualified
10. proficient 12. accomplished
capable of...
boring.. 10. zylotomous
carrying.. 9. portative
flying.. 6. volant
growing.. 6. viable
living in harmony.. 10. compatible
penetration.. 8. pervious
suffering.. 8. passible 9. sensitive
capable of being...
ascertained.. 12. determinable
cultivated.. 6. arable
cut.. 7. sectile
defended.. 7. tenable
done.. 10. effectible
heard.. 7. audible
prevented.. 9. avertible

proved.. 8. testable 12. demonstrable
regulated.. 12. controllable
separated.. 9. divisible
spread.. 10. infectious
12. communicable
thrown.. 7. missile
uttered.. 7. effable
capacious... 4. full, much, wide
5. ample, broad, large, roomy
8. generous, spacious 9. expansive,
extensive 10. commodious,
voluminous 12. considerable
13. comprehensive
capacity... 4. role, room, size 5. limit,
power, skill, space 6. extent, spread,
status, talent, volume 7. caliber,
content, faculty, fitness, measure
8. adequacy, aptitude, function,
position, relation, strength
9. character 10. capability, efficiency
11. capacitance (Elec)
12. intelligence 13. accommodation
capacity for knowing... 9. intellect
cap and bells... 6. bauble, comedy
(symbol), motley 7. costume, marotti
9. headdress
caparison... 3. rig 4. tack 5. armor,
dress, get–up 6. livery 7. harness,
housing, panoply 10. horsecloth
12. horse blanket
cape... 3. ras 4. hood, mino, naze,
ness, spur 5. amice, cappa, cloak,
fichu, orale, point, sagum, talma
6. mantle, sontag, tippet 8. pelerine
(fur) 9. Inverness
cape (pert to)...
gooseberry.. 4. poha
hen.. 4. skua 6. petrel
pigeon.. 7. pintado
polecat.. 5. zoril
ruby.. 6. garnet, pyrope
sheep.. 9. albatross (Naut term)
Cape Cod turkey... 7. codfish (humor)
Cape Dutch... 9. Afrikaans (language)
Cape of Good Hope discoverer...
4. Diaz (1488)
caper... 3. tea 4. dido, leap, romp,
skip 5. antic, berry, dance, frisk,
prank 6. cavort, frolic, gambol,
prance 8. capriole, marigold
9. privateer (Hist)
capercaille... 6. grouse 13. cock of
the wood
caper herb family... 6. Cleome
8. Capparis 9. Polanisia
10. clammyweed 13. Capparidaceae
Cape Town... 7. capital (U of S Afr)
Cape Verde Island (Afr)... 3. Sal
Cape Verde negro... 5. Serer
capias... 4. writ 6. caveat 7. process,
warrant 8. mandamus 9. nisi prius
capillary... 4. fine, tube 6. minute,
vessel 7. slender 8. hairlike, trichoid
capilliform... 7. thready 8. hairlike
capillus... 4. hair
capistrate... 6. cowled, hooded
capital... 3. top 4. city, main, rare,
seat, type 5. chief, crest, crown,
funds, major, means, prime, vital
6. assets, letter, ruling, supply
7. leading, primary, serious, weighty
8. cardinal, dominant, foremost,

splendid 9. excellent, financial, important, paramount, principal, prominent **10.** commanding, preeminent, shoestring
capitalism . . . **8.** politics **10.** government **11.** bourgeoisie **14.** free enterprise
capitalist . . . **5.** baron **6.** tycoon **7.** rich man **8.** investor **9.** bourgeois, financier, plutocrat
capital letter . . . **6.** uncial **9.** majuscule
capital punishment . . . **5.** noose **7.** gallows, hanging **8.** shooting, the chair **9.** beheading, execution, fusillade **10.** guillotine **12.** decapitation **13.** electrocution
capitano . . . **3.** don **4.** capo **5.** chief **7.** captain, headman
capitate . . . **7.** globose **8.** enlarged, headlike
Capitol (pert to) . . .
Federal . . **10.** Washington (DC)
State . . **10.** Statehouse
capitulate . . . **4.** cede, fall **9.** surrender
capitulation . . . **6.** resumé, review, treaty **7.** recount, summary **9.** agreement, reckoning, rehearsal, statement, summation, surrender **10.** compendium **11.** enumeration, stipulation **14.** relinquishment
capon . . . **3.** hen **4.** cock, fowl **6.** pullet, rabbit (castrated) **7.** chicken, poulard, poultry, rooster
caporal . . . **4.** boss **7.** foreman, tobacco **8.** overseer
capote . . . **4.** hood **5.** cloak **6.** bonnet, mantle, piquet **8.** overcoat
capped . . . **7.** crested, pileata, pileate
Capri . . .
beverage . . **4.** wine (white)
color . . **4.** blue **9.** blue–green
island site . . **11.** Bay of Naples
ruins (famed) . . **7.** palaces (Tiberius) **8.** grottoes **10.** Blue Grotto
caprice . . . **3.** fad, toy **4.** kink, mood, whim **5.** fancy, freak, humor, prank, quirk **6.** vagary **7.** whimsey (whimsy) **8.** crotchet, escapade, flimflam
capricious . . . **5.** moody **6.** fickle, fitful **7.** erratic, wayward **8.** fanciful, freakish, humorous, notional, sporadic, unsteady **9.** arbitrary, crotchety, eccentric, fantastic, whimsical **10.** inconstant **12.** inconsistent **13.** temperamental
Capricorn . . . **4.** goat **7.** mansion (of Saturn) **10.** zodiac sign **13.** constellation
capriole . . . **4.** leap **5.** caper **6.** cavort, curvet, gambol
capsicum . . . **4.** herb **5.** chili **6.** pepper
capsize . . . **5.** spill, upset **7.** subvert, tip over **8.** overturn **9.** overthrow **10.** turn turtle
capsule . . . **3.** sac **4.** pill **5.** ascus, brief, theca, wafer **6.** précis, sheath **7.** enclose, epitome **8.** abstract, envelope, pericarp, seedcase, synopsis **10.** compendium
capsulize . . . **5.** brief **7.** abridge, outline **8.** abstract, condense **9.** epitomize, summarize

captain . . . **4.** skip **5.** chief, ruler **6.** leader, master, patron, police **7.** headman, officer, skipper **8.** overlord **9.** commander **10.** shipmaster
Captain Kidd . . . **6.** pirate
Captains Courageous (pert to) . . .
author . . **7.** Kipling
setting . . **9.** Grand Bank (Newfoundland)
tale of . . **7.** romance
caption . . . **5.** title **6.** legend, rubric **7.** capture, seizure **8.** headline, subtitle
captious . . . **6.** severe **7.** carping, cynical, peevish **8.** caviling, critical **9.** bickering, paltering, quibbling **12.** equivocatory, faultfinding **13.** hypercritical
captivate . . . **4.** lure, vamp **5.** charm, snare **6.** allure, enamor, ravish, seduce **7.** attract, becharm, beguile, bewitch, capture, delight, enchant **8.** enthrall **9.** enrapture, fascinate, infatuate, transport
captive . . . **4.** bond, serf **5.** helot **6.** détenu, thrall, unfree, vassal **7.** hostage **8.** conquest, enslaved, prisoner **10.** subjugated
captivity . . . **6.** duress **7.** bondage, durance, serfdom, slavery **9.** detention, servitude, thralldom **10.** internment, subjection **11.** confinement, impoundment **12.** imprisonment **13.** incarceration
captor . . . **5.** taker **7.** catcher **8.** capturer
capture . . . **3.** beg, nab, net, win **4.** gain, haul, take **5.** catch, pinch, raven, snare **6.** arrest, collar **7.** caption, seizure **9.** apprehend, detention **12.** apprehension
capuche (Eccl) . . . **4.** cowl, hood
capuchin . . . **3.** sai **5.** Cebus **6.** monkey, pigeon
caput . . . **3.** cap, top **4.** head **5.** crest, crown **7.** chapter, section **9.** paragraph
car . . . **4.** auto, cart, jeep, tram **5.** coupe, motor, sedan, truck, wagon **6.** hot rod, jalopy, wheels (sl) **7.** caboose, chariot, clunker (sl), compact, flivver, machine, Pullman, vehicle **8.** carriage **9.** dune buggy, hatchback **10.** automobile, subcompact
carabao . . . **5.** mango **7.** buffalo
carabinieri . . . **9.** policeman **10.** carabineer
caracal . . . **3.** fur **4.** lynx, pelt
caracara . . . **4.** hawk **8.** carancha
caracole . . . **5.** caper (manège) **9.** staircase
caract . . . **5.** charm **6.** symbol (magic)
carafe . . . **6.** bottle
carafon . . . **8.** decanter
carapace . . . **5.** plate, shell (turtle) **6.** chitin, lorica, shield **7.** carapax
caravan . . . **3.** van **5.** wagon **6.** cafila (camel) **9.** cavalcade, motorcade **10.** expedition, procession
caravansary . . . **3.** inn **4.** khan (chan)

5. hotel, serai 6. hostel, imaret,
posado 8. hostelry 9. resthouse,
roadhouse
carbine... 5. rifle 6. musket 7. escopet
carbohydrate... 5. sugar 6. starch
7. dextrin, glucose, lactose, maltose,
sucrose 8. dextrose, glycogen,
nutrient 9. cellulose 10. saccharide,
saccharose
carbon... 4. coke, copy, fuel, lead,
soot 7. diamond, residue 8. graphite
carbonate... 3. ore 5. trona 6. aerate,
natron 9. carbonize 11. chemicalize
carbon dioxide... 3. gas 6. dry ice
7. seeding (cloud) 11. refrigerant
Carborundum... 5. emery 8. abrasive
14. silicon carbide
carcass... 4. body 5. bones, kreng
(whale) 6. corpse 7. cadaver,
remains 8. skeleton
carcer... 5. stall (Rom circus) 6. prison
card... 3. map, tum 4. comb, menu,
post, rove 6. docket, domino, oddity,
postal, record, ticket 7. calling,
program 8. calendar, schedule
9. character 13. communication
card game... 3. gin, hoc, loo, pan
4. bank, faro, keno, skat 5. cinch,
comet, monte, pitch, poker, rummy,
stuss, tarot, whist 6. bridge, casino,
écarté, hearts, piquet, rounce
7. auction, bezique, canasta, cassino,
cayenne 8. baccarat, contract,
cribbage, pinochle 9. solitaire
10. panguingui
card game term... 3. ace 4. meld,
pass, pone, slam, trey, vole 5. joker,
pedro, tarot 6. cathop, misère,
tenace, tricon 7. declare 9. mistigris
cardinal... 3. red 4. bird, fish, main
5. chief 6. bishop, deacon, number,
priest, ruling 8. crowning, dominant,
foremost 9. paramount, principal
10. preeminent
cardinal (pert to)...
astrology.. 5. nadir 6. zenith
astronomy.. 10. solstitial
11. equinoctial
biology.. 7. maximum, minimum,
optimum
compass point.. 4. east, west
5. north, south
number.. 7. primary (one, two, three)
office.. 6. datary 7. dataria
virtues.. 7. justice 8. prudence
9. fortitude 10. temperance
virtues (Theol).. 4. hope 5. faith
7. charity
cardinal's hat... 3. red 4. rank
6. office
care... 4. duty, fret, heed, reck, task,
tend, wish 5. aegis, worry 6. desire,
regard 7. anxiety, caution, cherish,
concern, custody, keeping
9. attention, patronage 10. affliction,
protection, solicitude 11. carefulness,
heedfulness, supervision, thriftiness
12. jurisdiction 13. consideration
careen... 3. tip 4. cant, heel, keel,
lean, list, tilt 5. slant, slope
career... 3. set 4. flow, flux, line, work
6. course, stream 7. calling, mission,

passage, pursuit 8. business,
practice, progress, vocation
10. occupation, profession
care for... 4. help, like, love, mind,
reck, tend 5. fancy, guard, nurse,
prize, watch 6. attend, dote on,
foster, mother, relish, wait on
7. nurture 10. appreciate
carefree... 5. happy 6. jaunty
8. debonair 10. insouciant
12. lighthearted
careful... 4. wary 5. canny, chary,
exact 7. anxious, guarded, heedful,
mindful, prudent, thrifty 8. cautious,
discreet, gingerly, vigilant
9. advertent, attentive
10. meticulous, scrupulous,
solicitous, thoughtful 11. circumspect,
considerate, painstaking, punctilious
careless... 3. lax 5. loose 6. rakish,
remiss, sloppy 8. heedless, mindless,
reckless, slipshod, slovenly
9. impulsive, negligent, unheeding,
unmindful 10. nonchalant, regardless,
unthinking 11. inadvertent,
thoughtless, unconcerned
13. inconsiderate
carelessness... 8. bungling, disorder
9. disregard, unconcern
10. blundering, negligence
11. nonchalance 12. heedlessness,
indifference, recklessness
13. impulsiveness
15. inconsideration, thoughtlessness
caress... 3. pat, pet 4. bill, kiss
5. touch 6. coddle, cosset, dandle,
fondle, pamper, stroke
10. endearment
caressing... 7. hugging, kissing
8. fondling 9. endearing
cargo... 4. load 5. goods 6. burden,
charge, lading 7. carload, freight
8. boatload, shipload 9. truckload
cargo (pert to)...
afloat.. 7. flotsam
cast overboard.. 6. jetsam
loader, unloader.. 9. stevedore
Carib... 6. Indian
caribou... 4. deer 8. reindeer
caricature... 5. comic 6. overdo,
parody 7. cartoon, picture 8. satirize,
travesty 9. burlesque 10. caricatura,
distortion 12. exaggeration
caricaturist... 6. artist 8. humorist,
parodist 10. burlesquer
caries... 5. decay (Dent) 10. ulceration
carillon... 4. lyra 5. bells (fixed)
6. chimes 12. glockenspiel
cark... 3. vex 4. care, heed, load
5. pains, worry 6. burden, charge,
harass 7. trouble 8. distress
carl, carlot... 4. boor 5. churl
6. rustic 7. peasant, villein
8. bondsman 10. husbandman,
pinchpenny
Carmelite... 3. nun 4. monk 5. friar
8. White Nun 10. White Friar
carmen... 4. poem, song
11. incantation
Carmen... 5. gypsy, opera (1875)
7. heroine, romance
carmine... 3. red 5. color, stain

7. crimson, scarlet
carnage... 8. butchery, massacre
9. bloodshed, slaughter
10. decimation
carnal... 4. lewd 6. bodily, fleshy
7. earthly, mundane, sensual, worldly
9. corporeal 11. unspiritual
12. bloodthirsty
carnation... 3. red 4. pink, self
7. bizarre, picotee 8. Dianthus
carnelian... 4. sard 9. copper red
10. chalcedony
carnival... 4. fair, show 6. circus
7. revelry 8. feasting, festival
9. amusement, Mardi Gras
11. merrymaking 12. masquerading
carnivore... 3. cat, dog 4. bear, lion,
puma, seal 5. civet, coati, genet,
hyena, otter, panda, ratel, sable,
tiger, ursus 6. badger, mammal,
marten, weasel 7. meerkat, raccoon
8. mongoose 9. ichneumon
10. cacomistle
carnivorous... 10. meat–eating,
predaceous 11. omophageous
carol... 3. lay 4. lied, lilt, noel, sing,
song 5. dance (anc) 6. ballad,
warble 7. rejoice
Caroline Islands (coral)... 3. Yap
5. Parao 6. Ponape
carom... 4. bump 6. bounce, cannon,
strike 8. ricochet
carousal... 4. lark, orgy, romp
5. binge, feast, fling, revel, spree
6. frolic 7. banquet, carouse, revelry,
wassail
carouse... 4. birl 5. bouse, drink,
spree, toast 9. dissipate
carpet... 3. mat, rug 4. Agra, Kali,
Kuba 5. Herat (Herati), namda, tapis
6. nammad, Wilton 7. drugget
8. Brussels, flooring, moquette
9. Axminster, broadloom
11. Baluchistan
carpetbagger... 8. swindler
10. politician
carriage... 3. air 4. mien, pose
7. bearing, posture 8. attitude,
demeanor, presence 10. deportment
carriage (pert to)...
English.. 6. waggon 7. growler
8. dormeuse, stanhope
French.. 6. fiacre 7. caliche, voiture
general.. 3. bus, cab, car, gig, rig,
van 4. baby, hack, pram, shay, trap
5. buggy, coach, wagon 6. calssh,
chaise, cisium, dennet, go–cart,
hansom, landau, surrey, tandem
7. cariole, chariot, omnibus, phaeton,
tallyho, vehicle 8. carryall, clarence,
dearborn, rockaway, victoria
9. kittereen, landaulet
10. conveyance, shandrydan
12. perambulator
history.. 7. tumbrel, vis-à-vis, whiskey
8. curricle
Indian.. 4. okka 5. tonga 6. gharry
7. hackery
Italian.. 7. vettura
one–horse.. 3. gig 4. shay 5. sulky
Orient.. 4. sado 10. jinrikisha

Philippines.. 9. carromata
Russia.. 5. araba 6. troika 7. droshky
9. tarantass
carried... 5. borne, giddy, toted
6. carted, lugged 8. conveyed,
ravished 11. transported
carrier... 3. boy 4. mail, mule, rail,
ship, wave 5. crate 6. bearer, coolie,
pigeon, porter, redcap, runner, vessel
7. courier, drayman, express
8. cargador, conveyor, teamster
9. messenger, stevedore
carrier (pert to)...
disease.. 3. fly, rat 7. typhoid
8. mosquito
Indian.. 5. Tinne (Brit)
staff.. 5. macer
carrion... 4. vile 6. corpse, rotten
7. carcass, corrupt 9. loathsome
carrion (pert to)...
bug.. 6. beetle
buzzard.. 4. hawk 7. vulture
8. caracara
flower.. 5. morel
fungus.. 9. stinkhorn
carrot... 5. drias (deadly) 6. Daucus
(Old World) 9. Ammiaceae
10. nivernaise (glazed), umbellifer
carrousel... 9. whirligig
10. roundabout, tournament
12. merry–go–round
carry... 3. lug 4. bear, cart, hold,
take, tote, wart 5. ferry 6. convey
7. conduct, publish 8. transfer,
transmit 9. transport
carry away, off... 3. win 6. abduct,
eloign, enamor, remove 7. succeed
9. fascinate 10. accomplish
carry on... 4. rage, wage 6. endure,
frolic, manage 7. conduct, operate
8. continue 9. misbehave, persevere
carry out, through... 2. do 5. apply
6. ravish 7. execute, perform, sustain
8. complete, continue, transact
10. accomplish
cart... 4. dray, wain 5. carry, sulky,
wagon 6. convey, reckla, telega
7. morfrey (morphrey), tumbrel (anc),
vehicle (2–wheeled)
carta, Charta... 4. deed 5. Magna
(Eng) 7. charter 9. parchment
cartage... 7. drayage, portage
8. carriage, teamster, truckage
10. expressage 14. transportation
carte... 3. map 4. card, list, menu
5. chart 7. diagram 10. bill of fare
cartel... 4. bloc (Polit), defy, pact, pool
5. paper, truce, trust 6. letter
7. compact, entente 8. covenant
9. agreement, challenge, syndicate
10. convention 11. arrangement
Carthage... see also *Carthaginian*
capital.. 13. Vandal Kingdom
destroyer.. 6. Romans
queen.. 4. Dido
rebuilt by.. 8. Augustus
Carthaginian (pert to)...
apple.. 11. pomegranate
foe.. 4. Cato
general.. 6. Xerxes 8. Hannibal
god.. 6. Moloch 8. Melkarth
language.. 5. Punic

Lion .. 8. Hannibal
magistrate .. 7. suffete
name (later) .. 15. Justinianopolis
wars (three) .. 5. Punic
Carthusian Order (pert to) ...
founder .. 7. St Bruno
monastery .. 7. Certosa (It, 1396)
site .. 8. Grenoble (Fr)
cartilage ... 4. bone (ossified) 6. tissue
7. gristle
cartload ... 6. fother
cartograph ... 3. map 4. plat 5. chart
cartoon ... 6. design, sketch 7. pattern,
picture 10. caricature
cartoonist ... 4. Arno, Capp, Ding, Nast
6. Disney
cartouche ... 5. shell 6. corbel, design,
shield (Her), tablet 7. console
9. cartridge 10. cantilever (Arch)
cartwheel ... 4. coin 6. dollar
8. somerset 10. handspring,
somersault
carve ... 3. cut, hew 4. form, make
5. chase, grave, sever, shape
6. chisel, cleave, furrow, incise
7. engrave, fashion 9. apportion,
fabricate, sculpture
carving ... 5. cameo 8. diaglyph,
intaglio 9. anaglyphy, embossing,
sculpture 11. anaglyptics
caryatid ... 6. column, figure (fem)
8. pilaster 11. priestesses (temple)
casa ... 5. adobe, cabin, house
8. building
cascade ... 4. fall, linn 5. Falls, Sault
7. Niagara 8. cataract 9. waterfall
case ... 3. box 4. etui, file 5. cover,
crate, crush (sl), event, folio
6. carton, coffer, pillow, sheath,
victim 7. attaché, cabinet, example,
holster, lawsuit 8. argument,
covering, cupboard, instance
9. condition, portfolio 10. receptacle
12. circumstance
case (in any) ... 3. yet 4. even
6. anyhow, anyway 7. anywise,
however 8. possibly, provided
10. regardless 15. notwithstanding
case (pert to) ...
arrow .. 6. quiver
book .. 5. forel
bottle (liquor) .. 8. cellaret
cigar .. 7. humidor
conscience (Sci) .. 9. casuistry
grammar .. 6. dative 8. ablative,
genitive, vocative 10. nominative
history (disease) .. 6. record
9. anamnesis
image (Bib) .. 5. ephod
jewel, relics .. 3. tye 4. apse
spore .. 5. ascus
surgeon's .. 7. trousse
cash ... 4. coin, dust (gold) 5. darby,
funds, money 6. silver, specie
7. capital, coinage, mintage
8. currency 9. spondulix
cashmere ... 4. goat, wool 5. shawl
6. fabric
casino ... 6. tavern 7. cabaret, cassino
(game) 8. ballroom, gambling
9. roadhouse 11. summerhouse
cask ... 4. butt, case, drum, pipe

5. terce 6. bareca, barrel, casket,
firkin, tierce 8. puncheon 9. kilderkin
cask (pert to) ...
amt when not filled .. 6. ullage
bulge .. 5. bilge
oil .. 4. rier
part .. 3. lag 4. hoop 5. stave
rim .. 5. chime (chimb)
support .. 8. stillage
casket ... 3. box, pyx, tye (jewel)
4. cist, kist, tomb 5. chest
8. cassette 11. sarcophagus
casserole ... 4. dish, mold 5. brown
(color) 6. vessel 8. saucepan
cassine ... 4. game (card)
cast ... 3. hue 4. form, hurl, kind, look,
mold, role, shed, tone, toss, type
5. eject, fling, heave, model, pitch,
sling, throw 6. glance, matrix, squint,
troupe 7. pattern 8. template
9. facsimile 10. impression,
strabismus 16. dramatis personae
cast (pert to) ...
aside .. 4. jilt, junk, shed 5. scrap
6. reject 7. discard
away .. 5. eject, wreck 6. unmoor
9. shipwreck
blame .. 6. accuse 7. censure
8. reproach 9. reprehend
off .. 4. doff, knit, molt, shed 5. untie
6. unmoor 7. discard 9. eliminate
castaway ... 6. pariah 7. outcast
8. derelict 9. reprobate
caste ... 4. race, rank 5. breed, class,
stock 6. status 7. lineage, society
8. standing
caste (Ind) ... 3. Dom, Meo 4. Ahir,
Jati, Koli, Magi, Mali, Pasi, Teli
5. Gaddi, Sudra, Varna 6. banian,
pariah, Vaisya 7. Brahman
9. Kshatriya
caster, castor ... 4. vial 5. cruet, horse
(old), wheel 6. roller, vessel
(condiment)
castigate ... 5. emend 6. punish,
revise, strafe 7. chasten, correct,
reprove 8. chastise, penalize
9. criticize 10. discipline
Castile ... 4. soap 7. kingdom
Castilian ... 7. Iberian, Spanish
castle ... 4. fort, keep 5. house, tower,
villa 6. donjon 7. chateau, citadel
8. fortress 10. stronghold
13. fortification
Castor (pert to) ...
brother (twin) .. 6. Pollux
constellation .. 6. Gemini
mother .. 4. Leda
stars .. 6. Castor, Pollux
castrate ... 4. geld, spay 5. alter,
prune 10. emasculate
castrated (pert to) ...
bull .. 5. steer
cat .. 3. gib
horse .. 7. gelding
man .. 6. eunoch
rooster .. 5. capon
casual ... 5. stray 6. chance, random
9. offhanded 10. contingent,
fortuitous, incidental, occasional,
unforeseen 11. indifferent
14. unpremeditated

casual observation... 6. remark
casualty... 6. chance, hazard, injury,
mishap 7. payment, tragedy
8. accident, calamity, disaster, fatality
9. mischance 10. misfortune
11. contingency, contretemps
12. misadventure
casus (pert to)...
act of God.. 14. casus fortuitus
common law.. 12. casus omissus
conscience.. 17. casus conscientiae
Latin.. 4. case 5. event 8. occasion
treaty.. 13. casus foederis
war.. 10. casus belli
cat... 3. gib 4. balu, eyra, lynx, pard,
puma 5. alley, civet, Felid, Felis,
genet, hyena, manul, ounce, tabby,
tiger 6. caffre, cougar, feline, jaguar,
margay, ocelot, pajero, rasset, serval
7. cheetah, dasyure, leopard,
panther, wildcat 9. catamount,
grimalkin
cat (pert to)...
fear of.. 12. ailurophobia, aleurophobia
fish.. 4. pout, raad 6. hassar, tandan
7. eelpout
game.. 6. tipcat
gut.. 5. tharm 6. string (violin)
slang.. 6. hepcat
term.. 5. kitty, shrew, tabby, vixen
6. kitten 8. ailuroid 9. chessycat,
Mehitabel (Mehetabel)
cat (species)... 4. Manx 5. Manul,
Tibet 6. Angora, Caffre, Margay
7. Burmese, Maltese, Persian,
Siamese, Turkish 8. Cheshire,
Egyptian 10. Abyssinian, Chinchilla
13. tortoise–shell (black and yellow)
cataclysm... 4. ruin 6. deluge
7. debacle 8. calamity, disaster, The
Flood, upheaval 10. convulsion,
inundation, revolution 11. catastrophe
catacomb... 4. tomb 5. crypt, vault
6. grotto, locule 8. cemetery
(underground) 9. Appian Way
catalepsy... 6. trance 8. hypnosis
9. cataplexy 10. thanatosis
catalogue... 4. book, file, list 5. index,
tally 6. codify, digest, record
8. calendar, classify, pamphlet,
register, schedule, tabulate
11. enumeration
catamaran... 4. boat, raft 5. balsa,
float 6. vessel 7. jangada
catamount... 3. cat 6. cougar
12. catamountain
catapult... 4. hurl 5. shoot, sling
6. engine, onager 7. robinet
8. arbalest, ballista, scorpion
9. slingshot
cataract... 4. fall, linn 5. Falls, flood,
sault (soo) 6. deluge 7. cascade,
disease, Niagara, opacity (eye),
torrent 8. downpour, Victoria
9. cachoeira, waterfall
cataria... 6. catnip
catasta... 5. stage (slave traffic)
6. stocks 8. scaffold
catastrophe... 4. doom, ruin 6. finale,
mishap, payoff 7. tragedy
8. calamity, disaster 9. cataclysm

10. denouement, misfortune,
revolution 11. termination
catastrophic... 4. dire 5. black
7. ruinous 10. calamitous,
deplorable, disastrous
catawba... 4. wine 5. color (red),
grape 6. Indian
catch... 3. get, nab 4. draw, hear,
hold, hook, take, trap 5. fault, ketch,
prize, reach, rondo, seize, snare,
trick, troll 6. detent (clock), engage,
entrap, ignite 7. attract, capture,
seizure 8. overtake 9. intercept
catch (pert to)...
a likeness.. 4. draw 6. depict
7. portray
a ride.. 4. hook 5. hitch, thumb
9. hitchhike
sight of.. 3. see 4. espy 6. behold,
descry 7. discern, glimpse
catchword... 3. cry, cue 6. byword,
phrase, slogan 7. formula
10. shibboleth
cate... 4. food 6. viands 8. dainties
10. delicacies, provisions (bought)
catechism... 5. guide 6. belief, manual
9. questions (set of) 11. instruction
(oral)
catechumen... 5. chela, pupil
6. layman, novice 7. convert
8. disciple, neophyte
categoric, categorical... 6. direct
7. crucial, logical 8. absolute,
explicit, positive 9. arbitrary,
pragmatic 10. convincing
11. dictatorial, unequivocal,
unqualified
category... 4. head 5. class, genre,
genus, group, order, state 6. branch,
family, specie 7. bracket, species
8. division 12. denomination
14. classification
catena... 5. chain 6. series
8. sequence 10. continuity
catenary... 5. curve (Math) 9. chainlike
cater, cater to... 4. feed 5. favor,
humor, serve, toady 6. oblige,
pander, please, purvey 7. indulge,
procure, provide, satisfy 10. minister
to 11. diagonalize 13. cater–cornered
caterpillar... 4. grub, weri 5. aweto,
eruca, larva 7. tractor
caterwaul... 3. woo (derog) 4. meow,
wail 5. court, miaow 7. screech
cathedral... 3. dom 4. fane (anc)
5. duomo 6. church 8. official
10. ex cathedra 13. authoritative
Cathedral...
England.. 6. Durham 9. Salisbury
France.. 5. Reims (Rheims) 6. Amiens
9. Notre Dame
Istanbul (Constantinople).. 8. St
Sophia
Italy.. 7. Lateran, St Mark's
Rome.. 8. St Peter's
Scotland.. 7. St Giles
cathedral (pert to)...
chair (Bishop's).. 8. cathedra
chapter member.. 10. capitulary
church.. 3. dom 7. Lateran (Rome)
city.. 3. Ely (Eng)
passage.. 5. slype

catholic... 4. wide 5. broad 6. church, global 7. general, liberal 8. orthodox, pandemic 9. Christian, universal 10. ecumenical 12. cosmopolitan
Catholic publication... 4. Ordo
catkin... 5. ament, spike 7. cattail
catlike... 5. catty 6. feline 8. stealthy 9. noiseless
catling... 3. cat (little) 6. kitten, string (violin)
Cato (pert to)...
  author of.. 13. De Agri Cultura
  famed as.. 7. General 9. statesman 10. ambassador (to Carthage)
  nickname.. 8. The Elder 11. Cato of Utica
Catoism... 9. austerity, harshness
cats... 8. Kilkenny
cat's cradle... 3. hei 4. game 7. ribwort
cat's-paw... 4. dupe, gull, loof, pawn, tool 5. cully, hitch (knot) 6. breeze (Naut), puppet, stooge 10. instrument
cattail... 4. musk, reed, tule 5. ament, raupo, teree 6. catkin, totora 7. matreed 9. Typhaceae
cattle... 3. Bos 4. cows, kine, neat, oxen, stot, yaks 5. asses, goats, mules, sheep, stock, swine 6. bovine, camels, horses, llamas, niatas, rabble, Taurus 7. banteng, chattel 8. bullocks, property 9. livestock
cattle (breed)... 4. Zebu 5. Angus, Devon, Kerry, Niata, Welsh 6. Brahma, Durham, Jersey, Sussex 7. Dishley 8. Guernsey, Hereford, Holstein, Longhorn 9. Charolais, Leicester, Shorthorn 14. Santa Gertrudis
cattle (pert to)...
  collection.. 4. herd 5. drove
  disease.. 7. murrain 10. rinderpest
  driver.. 6. drover
  food.. 5. agist 6. forage
  herder.. 6. cowboy, drover
  hybrid.. 4. Zobo 7. cattalo 9. cattleyak
  motherless.. 6. dogies
  pen.. 4. crew 5. barth, reeve
  shed.. 6. hemmel
  stealer.. 7. abactor, abigeus, rustler
  unbranded.. 9. mavericks
catty... 6. feline, weight 7. catlike, cattish 8. spiteful, stealthy 11. treacherous
cauboge... 4. boor 7. bumpkin
Caucasian... 4. race, Slav, Svan, Turk 5. gypsy, Latin, Norse, Osset, Pshav, white 6. Hebrew, Semite, Teuton, Viking 8. Armenian, Bohemian, Georgian, White Man 10. Anglo-Saxon 11. Xanthochroi
Caucasian (pert to)...
  blond.. 6. Teuton 8. Estonian 11. Xanthochroi
  brunette.. 7. Iberian 8. Armenian 11. Melanochroi
  Chinese.. 4. Lolo, Nosu
  dialect.. 4. Andi, Avar, Svan
  European.. 8. Japhetic

goat (wild).. 3. tur
liquor.. 5. kefir
Moslem.. 3. Laz (Laze, Lazi) 7. Sunnite
mountain.. 8. Caucasus
peak.. 6. Elbrus (Elbruz), Kazbek
cauchemar... 9. nightmare
caucus... 7. meeting (Polit), primary 8. assembly
cauda... 4. scut, tail 9. appendage
caudata... 5. newts 8. Amphibia 11. salamanders
caught... see also *catch* 5. treed 7. latched 8. cornered
caught (pert to)...
  napping.. 7. unready 8. unprimed 10. unprepared
  sight of.. 3. saw 6. espied 8. descried
  up in.. 4. tied 7. engaged, tangled 8. absorbed, intent on, involved 10. implicated
caul... 3. net 6. basket 7. netting, network, omentum 8. membrane
cause... 5. aetio (comb form), agent, basis, drive, greed 6. create, factor, ground, induce, motive, reason, source 7. crusade, produce, provoke 8. campaign, etiology, movement, occasion 9. originate 10. mainspring 13. justification
cause (pert to)...
  approach.. 7. attract
  be done.. 4. writ 11. fieri facias
  bring about.. 6. effect
  buy and sell.. 7. whipsaw
  coagulate.. 4. curd 6. curdle 7. congeal, thicken
  contract unevenly.. 6. pucker
  face East.. 6. orient
  harm.. 4. bane
  irritate.. 6. rankle
  raise in relief.. 6. emboss
  remember.. 6. remind
  roll.. 7. trundle
  speed up.. 10. accelerate
  take root.. 8. radicate
causerie... 4. chat, talk 6. parley 7. article 8. converse, treatise 9. paragraph 10. discussion 12. conversation
causes, science of... 8. etiology
causeuse... 4. sofa 9. tête-à-tête
causeway... 4. dike 7. highway 10. embankment
causing...
  destiny.. 5. fatal
  emotion.. 7. emotive
  forgetfulness.. 8. nepenthe
  laughter.. 8. risorial
  motion.. 6. motile
caustic... 4. acid, tart 5. acrid, curve (optic), sharp 6. biting, bitter, severe 7. burning, cutting, erodent, mordant, pungent, pyrotic 8. snappish, stinging, virulent 9. corrosive, satirical, vitriolic 10. astringent, escharotic 11. acrimonious, penetrating
caustic agent... 3. lye 4. alum, lime 7. erodent 9. quicklime
causticity... 7. acidity 8. acerbity,

acrimony, asperity, pungency, tartness
9. mordacity 10. bitterness
11. astringency 13. corrosiveness
cautel ... 5. trick 7. caution
8. prudence 9. direction (Eccl)
10. precaution
cauterize ... 4. burn, char, sear
5. brand, singe 7. torrefy
cautery ... 7. burning, searing
8. inustion 10. instrument
13. cauterization
caution ... 4. card (coll), care, heed,
warn 5. aviso 6. advice, caveat,
notice, oddity 7. anxiety, counsel,
precept, proviso, warning 8. forecast,
prudence, wariness 9. chariness,
vigilance 10. admonition, providence,
solicitude 11. exhortation,
forethought, mindfulness
12. cautiousness, notification,
watchfulness 14. circumspection
cautious ... 4. wary 5. canny, chary
6. Fabian 7. careful, guarded,
heedful, mindful, prudent
11. circumspect
cautiously ... 6. cagily, warily
7. cannily, charily 8. gingerly
9. carefully, guardedly, heedfully,
mindfully, prudently 10. discreetly
13. circumspectly
cavalcade ... 4. raid, ride 5. march
6. parade, review 7. caravan,
pageant 9. motorcade 10. procession
cavalier ... 3. gay 4. coin (Fr), curt
5. brave, frank, lover, rider 6. escort,
knight, squire 7. admirer, brusque,
esquire, gallant, haughty, soldier
8. horseman, Royalist 9. caballero,
cavaliere, chevalier, Roundhead
10. disdainful, equestrian
12. high–spirited, supercilious
cavalry ... 4. army 6. horses, yellow
(color) 8. horsemen 10. knighthood
cavalry (pert to) ...
horse .. 6. lancer
man .. 5. spahy, uhlan 6. Hussar,
lancer 7. dragoon, trooper
unit .. 5. troop
weapon .. 5. lance, saber 9. demilance
cave ... 3. den, mew 4. abri, cove,
grot, hole, lair 5. antre, cover, lodge
(beaver), speos 6. antrum, cavern,
cellar, covert, dugout, grotto,
subway, tunnel 7. chamber, shelter,
spelunk 10. subterrane
cave (pert to) ...
fish .. 9. blindfish
man .. 11. Paleolithic
nature of .. 9. speluncar
study of .. 10. speleology
cave canem ... 11. Beware of Dog
cave dweller ... 10. troglodyte
Cave of Adullam ... 9. Seceeders
(1866)
caviar, caviare ... 3. roe 5. garum
6. relish 8. delicacy, fish eggs
cavil ... 4. cark, carp, marl, quip
5. dodge, evade, parry, shift
6. bicker, boggle, haggle, palter
7. quibble, shuffle 9. criticize,
pussyfoot 10. equivocate
caviler ... 5. momus 6. critic, hedger

8. frondeur, quibbler 10. criticizer
11. equivocator, faultfinder
cavity ... 3. dip, pit, sac, vug (voog)
4. aula, bore (gun), cava, hole, sink,
well 5. abyss, antra, atria, bursa,
chasm, fossa, fosse, geode, lumen,
shaft, sinus 6. antrum, areole,
atrium, caries, coelom, crater, hollow
7. cochlea, loculus 10. depression
11. compartment
cavort ... 4. dido, romp, skip 5. antic,
caper, cut up, frisk, prank 6. curvet,
gambol, prance 7. flounce, gambade,
gambado
cavy ... 3. pig 4. paca 5. stray
6. agouti, rodent 8. capybara
(capibara) 9. guinea pig
caw ... 3. cry 5. croak, quark, quawk
11. exclamation
cay ... 3. kay 5. islet
cease ... 3. end 4. quit, rest (law),
stop 5. avast, pause, stint 6. desist,
perish 7. abandon, fade out, refrain
8. intermit, leave off, shutdown
9. disappear, pretermit
11. discontinue
ceaseless ... 7. endless, nonstop
8. constant, unbroken, unending
9. continued, incessant, perennial,
perpetual, unceasing 10. continuous
12. interminable 13. round the
clock, uninterrupted
ceaselessness ... 9. constancy
10. continuity, incessancy, perpetuity
11. endlessness 14. successiveness
cease to be ... 3. die 6. expire, perish
8. dissolve 9. disappear
cease to please ... 4. pall
Cebus ... 3. sai 6. monkey 8. capuchin
cecils ... 10. croquettes
cecity ... 9. blindness
Cecrops (pert to) ...
daughter .. 5. Herse 8. Aglauros
founder of (tradition) .. 6. Athens
king of .. 6. Attica
symbol .. 7. half man 10. half dragon
cedar (pert to) ...
bird .. 7. waxwing
class .. 7. conifer
fruit .. 6. cedron
genus .. 5. Thuja, Toona 6. Cedrus
9. Juniperus
green .. 5. cedre
moss .. 8. hornwort
type .. 5. savin 6. deodar, sabine
7. incense, juniper, Lebanon (Bib),
Spanish 10. arborvitae
11. cryptomeria
cede ... 5. grant, waive, yield 6. assign,
confer 7. abandon 8. renounce
9. surrender 10. capitulate, relinquish
cedula ... 3. tax 6. permit 8. schedule,
security (Finan) 10. obligation
11. certificate
ceil ... 4. line 5. cover 7. overlay
8. wainscot
ceiling ... 4. acme, roof 5. astel, limit,
price, trave 6. apogee, lining, screen,
utmost 7. curtain, lacunar, maximum,
plafond 8. covering 9. lacunaria
10. planchment, visibility
12. consummation

celebrant . . . 6. priest (Eucharist)
   9. worshiper (worshipper)
   11. communicant
celebrate . . . 4. keep, laud, sing
   5. extol, honor, revel 6. herald,
   praise 7. glorify, maffick, observe,
   roister 8. emblazon, proclaim
   9. solemnize 11. commemorate,
   memorialize
celebrated . . . 5. famed, noted
   6. famous 7. feasted, honored,
   popular 8. far–famed, observed,
   renowned 9. distingué, well–known
   11. illustrious 13. distinguished
celebration . . . 4. bout, fete, rite
   5. fling, revel, spree 6. bender
   7. fanfare, jubilee 8. ceremony,
   function 9. epinicion, festivity,
   rejoicing 10. observance
   13. commemoration
celebrity . . . 3. VIP 4. fame 5. éclat,
   glory 6. notary 7. notable
   8. luminary, somebody
   10. famousness, popularity
   11. recognition
celerity . . . 5. haste, speed 8. dispatch,
   rapidity, velocity 9. swiftness
   10. speediness
celery . . . 4. ache 8. smallage (wild)
   9. Ammiacaea
celestial . . . 6. astral, divine, uranic
   7. angelic, sky blue 8. ethereal,
   heavenly 12. paradisaical
Celestial (pert to) . . .
   being . . 5. angel 6. cherub, seraph
   body . . 4. star 5. comet 6. nebula
   city . . 6. heaven, utopia 9. Jerusalem
   empire . . 7. Chinese, Tien Chu
   equator . . 8. meridian
   mind elevation . . 7. anagoge
   teacher . . 6. Taoist
celibate . . . 4. monk 6. single
   8. bachelor, monastic, Platonic,
   spinster 9. abstinent, continent,
   unmarried
cell . . . 3. egg, kil 4. cyst, germ, ovum
   5. cnida, crypt 6. cytode, prison
   7. alveola, cellule, dungeon
   11. compartment
cell (pert to) . . .
   animal . . 6. amoeba (ameba) 7. rotifer
   8. protozoa
   biology . . 7. energid, meiosis, mitosis,
   nucleus, spireme
   cell–like . . 9. celliform
   division . . 5. linin 7. spireme
   8. amitosis
   eating . . 9. cytophagy
   Egyptian (tomb) . . 6. serdab
   honeycomb . . 8. alveolus
   Irish . . 3. kil (kill)
   locomotive . . 5. sperm, zooid
   Roman . . 4. alla, naos
   study . . 8. cytology
   substance . . 5. linin
   walls . . 9. cellulose
cellaret . . . 4. case 8. tantalus
   9. sideboard
Celt . . . 4. Erse, Gael, Manx, Scot
   5. Welsh 6. Breton 7. Cornish
Celtic (pert to) . . .
   abbot . . 5. coarb

bard . . 6. Ossian
cattle . . 2. ox
church . . 9. Christian
deity . . 7. Taranis
foot soldier . . 4. kern
horse . . 4. pony (Shetland)
Island . . 4. Manx
language . . 4. Erse
minstrel . . 4. bard
Mother of Gods . . 3. Ana (Anu)
mountain . . 3. ben
Neptune . . 3. Ler
nickname . . 10. Turtleback
Order . . 5. Druid
people . . 5. Gauls, Irish, Scots, Welsh
   7. Bretons, Britons
perfume . . 4. nard 9. spikenard
sun god . . 3. Lug (Lugh)
cembalo . . . 8. dulcimer 11. harpsichord
   12. clavicembalo
cement . . . 4. bind, fuse, glue, join,
   paar, pave 5. putty, stick, unite
   6. cohere, fasten, mastic, mortar,
   solder 8. adhesive, concrete,
   pavement, solidify
cemetery . . . 6. litten 7. Calvary
   8. boneyard, catacomb, Golgotha,
   lich gate (entrance), mortuary
   9. graveyard, mausoleum
   10. churchyard, necropolis
   11. polyandrium 12. potter's field
cenobite . . . 4. Monk 5. Order (anc)
   6. Essene 7. recluse
cenotaph . . . 4. tomb (empty)
   7. memento 8. memorial, monument
censer bearer . . . 7. acolyte 8. altar
   boy, thurifer
censor . . . 5. judge 6. critic 7. monitor
   8. censurer, reviewer, superego
   11. faultfinder
censure . . . 4. flay 5. blame, chide,
   slate, targe 6. accuse 7. chasten,
   condemn, impeach, inveigh, reprove,
   slating 8. reproach 9. damnation,
   expurgate, reprimand 11. reprobation
   12. condemnation, denunciation,
   reprehension
cent . . . 4. coin, game (old) 5. penny
   6. copper, trifle 7. hundred, red cent
centaur (Myth) . . . 4. race (Thessaly)
   6. Nessus 8. Lapithae, man–horse
   (half man) 9. bucentaur, Centaurus
   (Astron)
centennial . . . 4. game (dice)
   9. hundredth, red–yellow
   11. anniversary
Centennial State . . . 8. Colorado
center . . . 3. cor, hub 4. base, core,
   nave 5. axial, focus, heart, midst
   6. kernel, marrow, middle
   7. midmost, nucleus, pivotal, seaport
   8. emporium
center (pert to) . . .
   away from . . 6. distal
   bull's–eye . . 5. clout 6. target
   line . . 6. axiate, cesura
center of . . .
   attention . . 8. cynosure
   earth . . 9. epicenter
   gravity . . 6. kernel 7. centrum
   nervous system . . 5. brain
   sail . . 4. bunt

target .. **3.** eye **8.** bull's–eye
centerpiece ... **4.** bowl **7.** epergne
centipede ... **4.** rope (Naut) **6.** earwig,
    insect **8.** chilipod, myriapod
central ... **3.** mid **4.** arch, main
    5. axial, basic, chief, focal, prime
    6. master, middle **7.** capital, centric,
    leading, midmost, pivotal, primary
    8. cardinal, dominant, foremost
    9. principal **11.** equidistant
Central America ...
    bird .. **7.** jacamar **8.** puffbird
    boat .. **6.** cayuco, pitpan
    country .. **6.** Panama **8.** Honduras
    9. Costa Rica, Guatemala, Nicaragua
    10. El Salvador
    Indian .. **4.** Maya **5.** Carib
    monkey .. **4.** mono
    rodent .. **4.** paca
    snake .. **10.** bushmaster
    tree .. **3.** ebo, ule **5.** amate
    9. sapodilla
Central Asia (pert to) ...
    gazelle .. **3.** ahu
    wild horse .. **6.** tarpan
    wind storm .. **5.** buran
Central State ... **6.** Kansas
centuries (ten) ... **7.** chiliad
century ... **3.** Age **4.** aeon (eon)
    7. centred (anc), hundred **8.** eternity
    9. centenary **10.** centennial
century plant ... **4.** aloe **5.** agave
    6. maguey
ceorl (Eng Hist) ... **5.** churl, thane
    7. freeman, villein
cepa ... **5.** onion
cephalon ... **4.** head (Zool)
cephalopod ... **3.** ink (secretion)
    5. sepia **6.** cuttle **7.** octopus
    10. cuttlefish
ceramics ... **4.** tile **5.** china, delft,
    spode **6.** mosaic **7.** pottery, Satsuma
    8. crockery, majolica, Wedgwood
    9. porcelain
ceramics term ... **4.** clay, kiln, laun
    5. adobe, stove, wheel **6.** sleeve (silk)
    7. furnace **8.** ceramist **10.** ceramicist
    12. ceramography
ceratoid ... **5.** horny **8.** hornlike
    10. horn–shaped
cere ... **3.** wax **4.** wrap (dead body)
    6. anoint **12.** protuberance (bird's)
cereal ... **4.** bran, mush, rice **5.** grits,
    gruel, maize, wheat **6.** farina, hominy
    7. granola, oatmeal **8.** porridge
    10. corn flakes
cereal grass ... **3.** oat, rye **4.** ragi
    5. grain, maize, wheat **6.** barley,
    raggee
cereal spike ... **3.** ear
cerebellum ... **5.** brain (part)
cerebral (pert to) ... **4.** lobe **5.** brain
    6. speech **8.** arteries, peduncle
    9. consonant (Phonet) **11.** crus
    cerebri, hemispheres
cerebrum ... **5.** brain **10.** encephalon
cere cloth ... **7.** wrapper (corpse)
    8. cerement, chrismal **12.** grave
    clothes
ceremonial ... **4.** prim **5.** stiff
    6. custom, formal, ritual **7.** precise,
    service, studied **8.** ceremony,

function, liturgic **9.** formality
    11. punctilious **12.** conventional
ceremonial (pert to) ...
    chamber .. **4.** kiva
    departure .. **6.** congee
    splendor .. **9.** pageantry
ceremonious ... **6.** formal, polite
    7. precise **8.** gracious **9.** attentive,
    courteous **10.** ceremonial, respectful
    11. deferential, ritualistic
ceremony ... **4.** form, pomp, rite, show
    6. parade, review, ritual **8.** function
    9. formality, solemnity
    10. observance **11.** performance
ceremony, without ... **6.** humbly,
    meekly, simply **7.** quietly **8.** casually,
    modestly **9.** sans façon
    10. informally **15.** unceremoniously
Ceres, Rom (pert to) ...
    astronomy .. **8.** asteroid (lst found)
    father .. **6.** Saturn
    Feast .. **8.** Cerialia (Apr 19)
    Goddess of .. **4.** Corn **5.** Grain
    9. Fertility **11.** Agriculture
    Greek name .. **7.** Demeter
    mother .. **3.** Ops
Cereus ... **6.** cactus **7.** saguaro
    13. night–blooming
cerise ... **5.** color **7.** blue–red, fuchsia
    10. cherrylike
ceroplastics ... **8.** modeling, waxworks
certain ... **3.** one **4.** sure **5.** clear,
    exact, fixed, plain **7.** assured,
    decided, insured, precise **8.** absolute,
    definite, positive **9.** certified,
    confident, exclusive, indubious,
    undoubted, warranted
    10. guaranteed, inevitable,
    undeniable, undoubting
    11. determinate, trustworthy
    14. unquestionable
    16. incontrovertible
certainly ... **3.** yea, yes **4.** amen
    5. truly **6.** indeed, really, surely, verily
    7. clearly, in truth, utterly **8.** actually,
    of course **9.** assuredly, precisely
    10. absolutely, by all means,
    definitely, inevitably, positively
certainty ... **6.** pledge, shoo–in, surety
    8. sureness **9.** assurance, certitude
    13. inevitability, infallibility
certificate ... **5.** check, money
    6. ticket **7.** diploma, voucher
    10. credential **11.** testimonial
certificate (pert to) ...
    financial .. **3.** IOU **5.** draft, scrip
    9. debenture
    India .. **5.** hundi
    medical (Eng college) .. **8.** aegrotat
certification ... **2.** OK **3.** fix **5.** proof
    8. sanction **10.** validation
    11. affirmation, attestation, certificate,
    endorsement **12.** confirmation,
    ratification **13.** ascertainment,
    authorization **14.** substantiation
certify ... **5.** prove, swear, vouch
    6. assure, attest, avouch, ratify, verify
    7. approve, confirm, endorse, witness
    8. accredit, validate **9.** ascertain,
    determine, establish, guarantee
    11. acknowledge, corroborate
cerulean ... **4.** blue **5.** azure

7. sky–blue
cerumen... 6. earwax
cervine... 8. deerlike
cess... 3. bag, tax 4. cede, duty, levy, toll 5. yield 6. assess, impost, tariff 7. revenue 9. surrender 10. assessment
cessation... 3. end 4. lull, stay 5. letup, truce 7. respite 8. abeyance, desition 9. interlude 10. suspension 12. intermission, interruption 14. discontinuance
cetacea, cetacean... 3. orc 4. apod, orca, susu (blind) 5. whale 6. whales 7. cowfish, finback, grampus, narwhal (narwal), rorqual
Cete... 5. whale 10. The Cetacea
Cetus... 8. The Whale 13. constellation (Equator)
Ceylon...
capital.. 7. Colombo
city.. 5. Galle, Kandy (famed Buddhist Temple) 6. Jaffna
mountain peak.. 14. Pidurutalagala
ocean.. 6. Indian
old name.. 9. Taprobane
people.. 5. Tamil 6. Malays, Veddas 8. Malabars 10. Singhalese
Ceylon (pert to)...
boat.. 5. dhoni (doni)
canoe.. 5. balsa
Festival.. 8. Perahera
garment.. 6. sarong
hill dweller.. 4. Toda
monkey.. 4. maha 6. langur, rillow
moss.. 4. alga 6. Jaffna 7. gulaman 8. agar–agar
palm.. 7. talipot
rat.. 9. bandicoot
sand (sea bottom).. 4. paar
tree.. 4. doon
chabouk, chabuk (Ind)... 4. whip 9. horsewhip
chacma... 6. baboon
chafe... 3. cut, irk, rub, vex 4. fret, fume, fuss, gall, heat, rage, skin, warm 5. anger, annoy, grate, grind, pique, scuff, worry, wound 6. abrade, banter, excite, harass, injure, nettle, rankle 7. inflame 8. irritate
chaff... 3. hay 4. bran, husk, quiz, twit 5. dregs, fluff, husks, palea, straw, trash, waste 6. banter, cobweb, glumes, refuse, scraps 7. remains, residue, tailing 8. raillery, ridicule, riffraff
chaffer... 5. trade, wares 6. buying, dicker, haggle, higgle, market 7. bargain, chaffer, chatter, selling 9. negotiate 11. merchandise
chafing dish... 7. cresset
chagrin... 7. anxiety, mortify 8. distress, troubles, vexation 13. mortification
chain... 4. bind, bond, boom, gyve, reef, torc 5. cable, range 6. catena, fasten, fetter, secure, series, tether, torque 7. creeper, sorites 15. contravallation (fort series)
chair... 4. seat, sill 5. bench, sedan 6. rocker, throne 7. enchair, speaker

chair (pert to)...
back.. 5. splat 7. upright
collegiate.. 10. fellowship 13. professorship
cover.. 4. tidy 12. antimacassar
India.. 6. musnud
Japan.. 4. kago
maker.. 5. caner 6. reeder
chair (type of)... 4. camp, deck, easy, high, lawn, wing 6. lounge, Morris, swivel 7. contour, folding, steamer, Windsor 8. armchair, captain's, electric, fauteuil, straight 10. ladder–back 11. overstuffed
chairman... 7. officer, speaker 8. director 9. moderator
chalcedony... 4. onyx, opal, sard 5. agate 6. jasper, quartz 7. opaline 9. carnelian 11. chrysoprase
Chaldean (pert to)... 2. Ur 4. seer 6. Semite 10. astrologer, soothsayer 13. Neo–Babylonian (language)
chalice... 3. ama, cup 5. amula (anc), calix, grail 6. goblet 8. daffodil
chalice pall... 4. veil 8. animetta
chalk... 4. draw, mark, pale, tick 5. score 6. blanch, bleach, crayon, credit, pastel, whiten 7. account, drawing 9. limestone, reckoning
chalker... 7. milkman (Eng sl)
chalklike... 10. calcareous
chalky... 5. white 7. crumbly, friable, powdery 10. cretaceous
challenge... 4. dare, defy, gage 5. claim, doubt, query 6. accost, cartel, defial, demand, impugn 7. dispute, protest 8. question, reproach 10. accusation, controvert 11. questioning
chamal... 4. goat (Angora)
chamber... 4. cave, hall, kiva, room 5. court 6. camera, cavity 7. bedroom, boudoir, cabinet, chambre, cubicle 10. bedchamber 11. compartment
chamber (pert to)...
harem.. 3. oda
heart.. 7. auricle 9. ventricle
King's.. 9. camarilla
music.. 14. sonata da camera
chambers... 4. flat 5. suite 6. office 9. apartment, bicameral (Legis) 14. Inns of Chancery (Eng)
chameleon... 6. lizard 10. vacillator 13. changeability, constellation
chamfer (to)... 5. bevel, carve, flute, score 6. chisel, groove
chamois... 5. Gemse, izard 8. antelope
champ... 4. bite, chew, mash 5. gnash 6. victor 7. trample 11. battlefield
champagne... 4. wine 9. red–yellow 13. chrysanthemum
champaign... 5. field, plain 7. expanse 11. battlefield
champion... 3. Ace 4. best, hero 5. champ 6. defend, expert, victor, winner 7. espouse, fighter, titlist 8. advocate, defender 9. combatant, conqueror 10. unexcelled
champion (pert to)...
Christian (anc).. 3. Cid

constellation.. 7. Perseus
knight (legend).. 7. Paladin
Spanish.. 12. conquistador
chance... 3. die, hap, lot 4. fate, luck,
 odds, risk, turn 6. casual, gamble,
 happen, mishap, tossup 7. fortune,
 lottery, tychism 8. fortuity, Lady
 Luck, occasion 9. happening,
 mischance 10. likelihood
 11. opportunity, possibility, probability
 12. happenstance
chancel (pert to)...
 part.. 4. bema
 screen.. 4. jube
 seats.. 7. sedilia
change... 4. flux, move, turn, vary,
 veer 5. alter, amend, break, coins,
 money, shift 6. modify, mutate,
 switch 7. caprice, convert, deviate,
 variety 8. transfer 9. diversity,
 transform, transmute, variation
 10. alteration, fickleness, modulation
 11. inconstancy, vicissitude
 12. substitution 13. metamorphosis
 14. transformation 15. diversification
change (pert to)...
 color.. 3. dye, wan 4. fade, pale
 5. blush 6. blanch, redden
 medicine.. 11. heterotopia
 mind.. 6. repent 12. tergiversate
 music.. 4. muta
 order of.. 9. metabolic, rearrange,
 transpose
changeable... 6. fickle, fitful, mobile
 7. erratic, flighty, mutable, protean
 8. freakish, notional, unstable,
 variable, volatile, weathery
 9. alterable, chameleon, metabolic,
 uncertain, unsettled, whimsical
 10. capricious, inconstant
 15. interchangeable
changeling... 3. oaf 4. dolt 5. idiot
 7. waverer 8. imbecile, renegade,
 turncoat 9. simpleton 10. substitute
 (child)
channel... 3. bed, cut, gat, way
 4. dike, duct, gate, gurt, lane, leat,
 pass, vein 5. basin, canal, ditch,
 drain, flume, flute, fosse, radio, river,
 sinus, stria 6. alveus, avenue, coulee,
 groove, gutter, outlet, sluice, trench,
 trough 7. conduit, tideway
 8. aqueduct, tailrace 9. broadcast
 10. passageway
Channel Islands... 4. Sark (Sercq)
 6. Jersey 8. Alderney
chanson... 4. song 5. lyric 6. ballad
chant... 3. say 4. sing 6. intone,
 melody, warble 7. introit, singing
 8. canticle 10. intonation
 11. composition
chanter... 6. cantor, singer 7. bagpipe
 (part), intoner, sparrow (hedge)
 8. songster, vocalist 9. chanteuse,
 chorister
chanticleer... 4. cock 7. rooster
 11. cock–a–doodle
 14. cock–a–doodle–doo
chaos... 2. Nu (Egypt) 3. pie (type)
 4. gulf, mess 5. abyss, babel, chasm
 7. anarchy 8. disorder 9. confusion,
 imbroglio 10. unruliness

 13. orderlessness
Chaos (pert to)...
 daughter.. 3. Nox, Nyx
 parent of.. 5. earth 6. heaven
 8. Creation
 son.. 6. Erebus
chaotic... 6. muddle 8. confused,
 formless 12. disorganized
chap... 3. boy, buy, guy, lad, man
 4. kibe (sore) 5. buyer, chink, cleft,
 crack, scout, split, youth 6. barter,
 choose (Scot), fellow, galoot
 7. chapman 8. customer
chapeau... 3. cap, hat, lid 5. beret
chapel... 4. cape, cope, cowl, hood
 5. altar, choir 6. bethel 7. chantry,
 galilee, oratory, service, Sistine
 8. sacellum (anc) 9. reliquary
chaperon... 4. hood 6. attend,
 duenna, escort 8. guardian
 9. attendant 10. gooseberry
chaplet... 4. band 5. beads
 6. anadem, wreath 7. garland,
 prayers 8. beadroll, insignia, necklace
chappaul... 9. squawfish
chaps... 8. overalls 10. chaparajos
chapter... 4. Sura 5. topic 6. clause
 7. council, meeting, passage,
 section, Society 8. division
 9. capitular 10. fraternity
 12. organization
chaptrel... 6. impost
char... 4. burn 5. trout 6. scorch
 8. charcoal, sandbank
character... 4. hero, kind, mark, role,
 sign, star 5. trait 6. cipher, letter,
 nature, repute, status, symbol
 7. quality 8. function 9. reference
 10. reputation 11. temperament
 14. characteristic
character (pert to)...
 giver.. 5. toner
 Hebrew.. 3. Tav, Taw
 Irish.. 5. Ogham
 musical.. 3. bar 4. clef, rest
 5. neume
 of people.. 5. ethos
 real.. 7. essence
 science of.. 8. ethology
 Teutonic.. 4. rune
characteristic... 4. mark 5. habit, trait
 7. feature, impress, quality, typical
 8. peculiar, symbolic 9. attribute,
 character, idiopathy, lineament,
 specialty 11. distinctive, peculiarity,
 singularity, symptomatic
 13. individualism
characteristic (pert to)...
 descent.. 6. racial
 peculiar.. 9. idiopathy
 spirit.. 5. ethos
 tone (Mus).. 7. seventh
characterization... 4. role 5. drama
 9. depiction, portrayal
 11. description, distinction
 13. impersonation 14. identification,
 representation
characterize... 4. mark, name 5. enact
 7. engrave, imprint, portray
 8. describe, inscribe 9. delineate,
 designate, epitomize, represent
 11. distinguish

characterized by...
abstinence.. 7. ascetic
bacteria exclusion.. 7. asepsis
cruelty.. 7. Neronic
exact thinking.. 13. ratiocinative
melody.. 6. ariose
poison (bloodstream).. 6. sepsis
pomposity.. 13. grandiloquent
characterless... 5. inane 9. colorless,
pointless
charcoal... 4. coke, fuel, lave, peat
5. black, chark 6. carbon, fusain
7. drawing, residue 9. boneblack,
briquette
charge... 4. bill, cost, dues, fill, load,
onus, rate, task, toll, ward 5. blame,
chore, debit, onset, order, price,
trust 6. accuse, advice, advise,
allege, amount, attack, client,
commit, credit, demand, dictum,
impute, indict 7. assault, command,
concern, custody, expense, impeach,
keeping, mandate, precept, primage,
protégé 8. guidance, insignia,
instruct, tutelage 9. dependent,
electrify, exactment 10. accusation,
commission, imposition, impregnate,
injunction, management
11. arrangement, attribution,
instruction, supervision
13. incrimination 14. responsibility
charge of affairs... 8. diplomat
15. chargé d'affaires
charge off... 5. debit 6. forget
7. dismiss, forgive 8. discount
charges (law)... 4. dues, fees 5. costs
9. retainers
charge with...
crime.. 6. indict 7. impeach
11. incriminate
debt.. 5. debit
gas.. 6. aerate
offense.. 6. accuse
to.. 5. blame 7. ascribe 9. attribute
charily... 6. cagily, warily 8. frugally
9. carefully, thriftily 10. cautiously
12. economically, suspiciously
chariness... 7. caution 8. caginess,
distrust, wariness 9. frugality
11. heedfulness, thriftiness
chariot... 3. car 4. biga, cart, rath
(ratha), wain 5. essed (anc), wagon
7. vehicle 8. quadriga
charioteer... 6. Auriga (Astron), Ben
Hur
charitable... 3. big 4. kind 6. kindly
7. lenient, liberal 8. generous,
tolerant 9. forgiving, indulgent
10. altruistic, benevolent, bighearted
11. beneficent 12. eleemosynary,
humanitarian 13. compassionate,
philanthropic
charity... 4. alms, dole 6. bounty,
virtue 7. handout, largess
8. lenience, pittance 9. tolerance
10. almsgiving, liberality
11. benevolence 12. philanthropy
charity dispenser... 7. almoner
charivari... 5. babel 6. medley, uproar
8. serenade (mock) 10. callithump
charlatan... 5. faker, fraud, phony,
quack 6. humbug 7. empiric

8. impostor 9. pretender
10. medicaster, mountebank
Charlemagne, Emperor (pert to)...
brother.. 8. Carloman
emperor of.. 7. The West
father.. 5. Pepin (the Short)
name also.. 15. Charles The Great
nephew.. 7. Orlando
charm... 3. obi 4. lure, mojo, play,
song 5. grace, magic, oomph, spell
6. allure, amulet, appeal, beauty,
enamor, entice, fetish, glamor, scarab
7. beguile, bewitch, cantrip, delight,
enchant, glamour, periapt
8. breloque, elegance, entrance,
ornament, talisman 9. captivate,
fascinate, sex appeal, sweetness
10. allurement, attraction, brimborion
(brimborium), lovability
11. captivation, conjuration,
incantation, pulchritude, winsomeness
12. antinganting 14. attractiveness,
delightfulness
charmer... 5. siren 6. beauty
7. enticer 8. exorcist, magician,
sorcerer 9. bewitcher
charming... 7. winsome 8. alluring,
pleasing 10. bewitching, delightful
11. captivating, fascinating
chart... 3. map 4. list, plat, plot
7. diagram
charter... 4. hire 5. carta, grant
6. charta, firman, treaty 7. license
9. privilege (special), purwannah
chartreuse... 4. mold (cookery)
5. color 7. liqueur
Chartreuse... 9. monastery 18. La
Grande Chartreuse (Grenoble)
chary... 4. wary 5. cagey 6. frugal,
skimpy 7. thrifty 8. cautious
10. suspicious 12. parsimonious
Charybdis... 6. Scylla 8. Galofaro
9. whirlpool (Messina)
chase... 3. gun (Naut), set (gem)
4. hunt, park, race 5. chevy (chivy),
raise, sport, track 6. emboss, follow,
furrow, groove, hasten, pursue,
shikar, stroke (tennis) 7. engrave,
pursuit, repulse 8. ornament
12. steeplechase
Chase (The), goddess of... 5. Diana
chasm... 3. gap, pit 4. gulf, hole, rift,
well 5. abyss, cleft, shaft 6. breach,
canyon, cavity, hiatus 7. fissure,
opening 8. crevasse
chasma... 7. yawning
chasse... 4. step (dance) 6. shrine
9. reliquary
chaste... 4. pure 6. modest, simple
8. innocent, virtuous 9. continent,
uncorrupt, undefiled, unmarried
10. immaculate
chasten... 4. rate 5. smote 6. punish,
refine 7. correct 8. chastise,
penalize, restrain 9. castigate
10. discipline
chastened... 4. meek 5. smote
7. subdued 8. punished, purified,
tempered 10. restrained
chastise... 4. beat, slap, whip
5. amend, blame, scold, spank, taunt
6. punish, rebate, rebuke, swinge

7. correct, reprove 9. castigate
10. discipline
chastity . . . 6. purity, virtue
9. cleanness 10. chasteness
12. virtuousness
chat . . . 3. gab, rap, yak 4. chin, coze,
jist, talk, tove 5. prate 6. babble,
confab, gabble, gibber, gossip, jabber
7. chatter, prattle 8. causerie,
chitchat, converse 12. conversation
14. chitter–chatter
chatelaine . . . 3. pin 4. etui, hook
5. clasp, purse, watch 6. brooch,
torque
chattels . . . 4. naam 5. goods, money,
wares 6. estate 7. effects
8. holdings, property 9. livestock,
principal 11. possessions
chatter . . . 3. gab, yap 5. clack, prate
7. clatter, prattle
chatterer . . . 3. jay, mag 4. bird, piet
6. magpie 10. chatterbox
chatty . . . 3. pot (earthen) 4. glib
5. gabby 7. affable 8. sociable
9. garrulous, prattling, talkative
14. conversational
Chaucer (pert to) . . .
  author of . . 15. Canterbury Tales
  Inn . . 9. (The) Tabard
  pilgrimage city . . 10. Canterbury
  style of work . . 7. novella
chauvinist . . . 5. jingo 6. Rajput
7. chauvin, patriot 8. jingoist
9. warmonger 10. militarist
cheap . . . 5. small, tacky, tinny, trade,
value 6. cheesy, paltry, plenty, sleazy
7. abashed, bargain, chintzy, cut–rate,
reduced, schlock 9. niggardly
11. inexpensive
cheat . . . 2. do 3. ban, con, fob, gyp
4. bilk, fake, flam, hoax, liar, rook,
scam, sell, sham 5. cozen, elude,
guile, phony, scalp 6. deceit, fleece,
humbug, hustle, illude, rip–off
7. deceive, finesse, sharpen, swindle
8. artifice, impostor 9. bamboozle,
overreach, stratagem, victimize
10. thimblerig 12. bait–and–switch
check . . . 3. nip, tab 4. balk, curb,
damp, mark, rein, stem, stop, test
5. agree, brake, count, delay, limit,
money, plaid, repel, stunt, tally
6. bridle, cheque, detain, detent,
impede, oppose, rebuff, retard, ticket,
verify 7. counter, examine, inhibit,
measure, monitor, pattern, repress
9. hindrance, restraint 12. verification
check (pert to) . . .
  in . . 3. die 6. arrive 8. register
  out . . 3. die 5. croak, leave 6. assess
    8. withdraw
  pattern . . 11. houndstooth
  game, term . . 5. chess 8. gambling
checkered . . . 4. vair 5. diced, plaid
6. mosaic, tartan, varied 7. checked
10. changeable, tesserated,
variegated 11. diversified
checkers, chequers . . . 4. game
8. draughts (Brit)
cheek . . . 4. gall, gena, jowl 5. brass,
bucca, crust, malar, nerve 8. audacity,
chutzpah 9. impudence

10. buccinator
cheer . . . 3. rah 4. yell 5. bravo, elate,
huzza, liven, mirth, salvo 6. gaiety,
hurrah, regale, repast, salute, solace
7. animate, applaud, console, gladden,
hearten, jollity, refresh, rejoice
8. applause, inspirit, pleasure, vivacity
9. encourage, merriment
10. exhilarate 12. conviviality
cheerful . . . 3. gay 4. gleg (Scot), rosy
5. happy, peart, sunny 6. blithe,
cheery, genial, hearty, jocund, joyful
8. gladsome, homelike 9. contented,
lightsome 12. lighthearted
cheerfulness . . . 3. joy 4. glee
5. cheer, mirth 6. gaiety 7. jollity
8. gladness, hilarity 9. happiness,
merriment 12. exhilaration
cheerio . . . 5. adios, aloha, skoal, toast
6. hurrah, prosit 8. au revoir,
farewell, Godspeed 9. greetings
cheerless . . . 3. sad 4. cold, drab
5. drear 6. dismal, dreary, gloomy
7. forlorn, joyless, unhappy
8. dejected 9. unsmiling
10. depressing, melancholy
11. dispiriting 12. disconsolate
cheese . . . 3. pot 4. bleu, brie, edam,
feta, jack 5. cream, Gouda, Swiss
6. barrie, Dunlop, mysost, Romano,
zieger 7. Cheddar, cottage, fromage,
Munster, sapsago 8. American,
Monterey (jack), Parmesan
9. Camembert, Limburger, Roquefort
10. Gorgonsola, Neufchatel
cheese dish . . . 6. fondue, omelet,
quiche, strata 7. rarebit, soufflé
cheesy . . . 3. bad 6. paltry 8. inferior
9. worthless 12. disreputable
cheetah . . . 3. cat 5. youse (youze)
7. guepard (gueparde)
cheilos . . . 3. lip
chela . . . 4. claw 6. novice 8. disciple
Chelonia . . . 7. reptile, turtles
9. tortoises
chemical (pert to) . . .
  analysis . . 5. assay
  cleanser . . 6. kryton
  etching . . 11. chemigraphy
  strength . . 5. titer (titre)
  term . . 3. gas 4. acid, atom, base, salt
    5. imine 6. alkali, eluate 7. hormone,
    nonacid, organic, radical, valence
    8. catalyst, compound 10. bathoflore
    11. bathochrome
  vessel . . 4. etna 6. aludel, retort
    7. alembic 8. crucible, reductor
chemical suffix . . . 2. ac, el, yl 3. ane,
ene, ile, ine, ole, ose 4. enol, olic,
osan
chemin de fer . . . 7. railway
8. baccarat, railroad
chemist . . . 7. analyst 8. druggist
9. alchemist 10. apothecary,
biochemist 12. iatrochemist (anc)
cherish . . . 3. aid, hug, pet, woo
4. love 5. adore, cheer, nurse, prize
6. caress, faddle, fondle, foster
7. care for, comfort, nourish, nurture,
protect, support 8. enshrine,
remember, treasure 9. cultivate,
encourage, entertain

cherry . . . 3. pin 4. Bing, bird, gean,
ming 5. black 6. egriot, Prunus
7.. capulin, marasca, mazzard, Morello,
oxheart 8. Napoleon 9. amarelles,
bigarreau, Queen Anne
11. chokecherry, Montmorency
cherub . . . 5. angel, child, saint
6. seraph, spirit 7. darling, eudemon
8. cherubim, seraphim
chess (pert to) . . .
chessman . . 4. king, pawn, rook
5. piece, queen 6. bishop, castle,
knight
Italian . . 7. scacchi
term . . 4. dual, move 5. debut
6. chassé, fidate, gambit 7. end
game, opening, problem
9. checkmate, en passant, rook's
tour, stalemate 10. fianchetto
chesslike . . . 8. scacchic
chest . . . 3. ark, box 4. arca, cist, kist
5. bahut 6. breast, cajeta, coffer,
coffin, locker 7. highboy, wanigan
(wangan) 10. chiffonier
11. gardeviance
chest (pert to) . . .
ammunition . . 7. caisson
animal . . 7. brisket
human . . 6. thorax 7. midriff
sound . . 4. rale
sepulchral . . 6. larnax
Chester (Eng), inhabitant . . . 8. Cestrian
chesterfield . . . 4. sofa 5. divan
8. overcoat 9. cigarette, davenport
chestnut . . . 4. ling, rata 5. horse,
water 6. marron 7. buckeye
8. Aesculus, Castanea 10. breadfruit,
chinquapin
chestnut . . . 4. joke 6. cliché
7. bromide 8. banality
chestnut color . . . 4. roan 5. brown
6. sorrel 12. reddish–brown
chevalier . . . 5. cadet (nobility), noble
6. knight 7. gallant 8. cavalier,
horseman 10. greenshank (bird)
chevron . . . 4. beam 5. glove 6. rafter,
stripe, zigzag 8. insignia
chevrotain . . . 4. napu 7. deerlet,
kenchil, meminna 9. Tragulina
chevy . . . 3. cry (hunting) 4. game, hunt
5. chase 6. flight, harass, pursue
7. torment
chew . . . 3. cud 4. bite, chaw, gnaw,
quid 5. champ, chomp, grind, munch
6. chavel, ponder 8. meditate,
ruminate 9. masticate
chiasma . . . 11. decussation
12. intersection
chiasmus . . . 9. inversion (of words)
chib (Gypsy) . . . 6. tongue 8. language
chic . . . 4. trig, trim 5. natty, smart
6. modish, spruce 7. stylish
Chicago's nickname . . . 9. Windy City
chicanery . . . 4. ruse, wile 5. feint,
trick 6. deceit 7. knavery 8. artifice,
trickery 9. stratagem 11. skulduggery
chickadee . . . 8. titmouse
10. Pebthestes
chicken . . . 3. hen 4. cock, fowl, girl
5. biddy, capon, chick, deedy, fryer,
poult, young 6. coward, pullet

7. broiler, rooster 8. cockerel,
weakling 9. youngling
11. chanticleer, milquetoast
chickenhearted . . . 5. timid
8. cowardly 12. fainthearted
chicory . . . 6. endive 7. succory
12. Cichoriaceae
chide . . . 4. rate 5. blame, scold
6. berate, rebuke 7. censure, reprove,
wrangle 8. admonish, reproach
9. reprimand
chief . . . 3. dux, top 4. arch, head,
main, rais (reis) 5. first, forte, major,
mogul 6. leader, primal, staple, syndic
7. kingpin, supreme 9. directing,
governing, paramount, potentate,
principal, prominent 11. predominant
chief (pert to) . . .
African . . 3. dey 4. kaid 5. negus
6. induna
Am Indian . . 6. sachem 7. Osceola
8. sagamore
Arab . . 5. sheik
Chinook . . 4. tyee
Cossack . . 6. ataman, hetman
Egypt . . 3. Min (Panopolis)
Europe . . 6. syndic
Germany . . 6. Führer (Fuehrer), Kaiser
Iran . . 9. ayatollah
Italy . . 4. doge, duce
Japan . . 6. mikado, shogun
Mexico . . 7. cacique
Nepal . . 4. Rais
Oriental . . 4. kahn 6. sirdar
Persia . . 4. shah
Russia . . 4. czar (tsar)
Spain . . 7. alcalde
Tibet . . 9. Dalai Lama
Turkey . . 3. aga (agha) 6. vizier
chilblain . . . 6. pernio
child . . . 3. imp, tad, tot 4. babe, baby,
bata, brat, teen, tike 5. bairn, cupid,
elfin, fetus 6. cherub, childe (anc),
infant, urchin 7. adoptee, nestler,
preteen, progeny 9. offspring
10. descendant
childish . . . 4. weak 5. naive, petty,
young 6. senile, simple 7. babyish,
kiddish, puerile, unmanly 8. immature
9. infantile, kittenish
children (pert to) . . .
doctor . . 12. pediatrician
mythology . . 6. Titans
Patron Saint . . 5. Santa
slain by Herod . . 12. The Innocents
study of . . 8. pedology 10. pediatrics
Chile . . . see also *Chilean*
cape . . 4. Horn
capital . . 8. Santiago (1541)
city . . 4. Lota 5. Arica 8. Valdivia
10. Concepcion, Valparaiso (1543)
conqueror . . 7. Pizarro 8. Valdivia
desert . . 7. Atacama
explorer . . 8. Magellan (1520)
mountain . . 5. Andes
river . . 3. Loa 6. Biobio
settlement (southernmost) . . 8. Navarino
(Isl) 14. Puerto Williams
Chilean (pert to) . . .
coconut . . 7. coquito
evergreen . . 6. pepino 10. arborvitae

shrub (poison).. 5. lithi
wind.. 5. sures 11. sures pardos
workman.. 4. rote
chiliad... 8. thousand 9. millenium
   13. thousand years
chill... 3. ice, raw 4. ague, cold,
   damp 5. algor, frost, rigor
   6. damper, formal, shiver 7. malaria
   8. coldness, coolness, dispirit
   10. depressing 11. refrigerate
chilly... 3. raw 4. ague, cold 5. gelid
   6. aguish, freeze, frosty
   12. refrigerated
chiloplasty... 10. lip surgery
   12. mouth surgery
chime... 4. bell, peal, ring, suit
   5. agreé, bells, prate, rhyme
   6. accord, concur, cymbal, jingle
   7. harmony
chimera... 5. dream, fancy, vapor
   6. bubble, utopia 7. monster
   8. illusion, paradise (fool's)
chimerical... 4. vain 7. utopian
   8. delusive, fanciful, romantic
   9. fantastic, imaginary, unfounded
chimney... 3. lum 4. flue 5. cleft,
   stack, tewel 10. smokestack
chimpanzee... 6. gibbon, nchega
   7. gorilla
chin... 4. talk 5. genio (comb form)
   6. mentum, weight (Chin)
   8. converse 10. chew the rag
   11. genioplasty (Surg), mentoplasty
   (Surg)
china... 7. Dresden, pottery
   8. crockery 9. porcelain
   11. earthenware
China... see also *Chinese*
  Buddha.. 2. Fo
  capital.. 7. Nanking
  capital, former.. 7. Peiping (Peking)
  city.. 4. Amoy, Tsin, Wuhu 6. Canton,
   Hankow, Ningpo 7. Foochow,
   Nanking, Soochow 8. Hangchow,
   Shanghai, Tientsin
  dynasty.. 3. Han, Kin, Sui 4. Chou,
   Hsia (BC), Ming, Tsin, Yuan 5. Ching
   6. Mongol (Kublai Khan's)
  island.. 5. Matsu 6. Quemoy, Taiwan
   (Formosa)
  magistrate.. 5. tupan 6. tuchun
   8. mandarin
  Mainland.. 15. People's Republic
  Military Academy.. 7. Whompoa
  Mongol.. 3. Hun
  mountain.. 7. Kuen–lun 9. Himalayas
  nickname.. 14. Flowery Kingdom
  philosopher.. 6. Laotse 9. Confucius
  poet.. 4. Li Po 7. Li Tai Po
  race.. 9. Mongoloid
  religion.. 6. Taoism 8. Buddhism
   9. Confucian 12. Confucianism
  river.. 5. Peibo 7. Hwanglo, Yangtze
  sea.. 5. China 6. Yellow
  treaty port.. 4. Amoy
  Chinese (pert to)...
  antelope.. 6. dzeren
  boat.. 4. junk 5. tanka 6. sampan
  cabbage.. 7. pakchoi
  card game.. 6. fantan
  carpet.. 6. Khotan 7. Kashgar,
   Yarkand 9. Samarkand, Turkestan

Catholic Church.. 11. Tien Chu T'ang
  12. Tien Chu Chiao
chestnut.. 4. ling
confection.. 8. chowchow
deer.. 8. elaphure
defense.. 4. Wall (2,000 mi long)
desert.. 4. Gobi 5. Shamo
dragon.. 6. chi–lin
fabric.. 3. sha 7. nankeen
festival (Spring).. 9. Ch'ing Ming
flute.. 4. tche (che)
fruit.. 6. litchi (nut)
ginger.. 9. galingale
God.. 4. Shen (Chr) 7. Shangti, Tien
  Chu (RCCh)
gong.. 6. tam–tam, tom–tom
grass.. 5. ramee
idol.. 4. joss 6. pagoda (pagod)
instrument.. 3. che, kin 4. tche
  5. sheng (cheng)
jade.. 2. yu
jute.. 7. chingma
laborer.. 6. coolie
lily.. 9. narcissus
liquor.. 6. samshu (rice)
literary degree.. 8. hsiu tsai
monkey.. 4. douc
nurse.. 4. amah
officer.. 4. kwan
oil.. 4. tung
ox.. 4. zebu
pagoda.. 3. taa
paradise (Buddh).. 4. Jodo
  7. Ching–tu 8. Gekuraku
philosophy.. 10. Yang and Yin
religion.. 6. Taoism 8. Buddhism
  12. Confucianism
residence (official).. 5. yamen
screen (folding).. 10. Coromandel
silkworm.. 4. sina 9. ailanthus
sky.. 4. tien
society (secret).. 3. hui (hoey) 4. tong
vessel.. 4. junk 6. lorcha
Chinese Wall, Great (pert to)...
  builder.. 15. Ch'in Shih Huang Ti
  composition.. 7. granite (blocks)
  length in miles.. 11. two thousand
  time.. 2. BC
chink... 4. rent, rift, rima, rime, ring
   5. cleft, crack 6. cranny, furrow
   7. bunting (bird), fissure
   10. interstice
chinook... 4. herb, wind 6. salmon
   7. quinnat
Chinook (pert to)...
  chief.. 4. tyee
  tribe.. 8. Flathead
  State (nickname of).. 10. Washington
chinquapin... 3. oak 6. bonnet (water)
   8. chestnut
chip... 3. cut, hew 4. coin 5. break,
   carve, flake, piece, scrap, token
   6. chisel, gallet (stone) 7. counter
chipmunk... 6. hackee
chipped stone (instrument)...
   9. paleolith
chipper... 5. chirp 6. babble, chisel,
   hammer, lively 7. chirrup, twitter
   8. cheerful
chirognomy... 9. palmistry
   10. chiromancy
chironomy... 7. gesture (hands)

9. pantomime
chiropter... 3. bat 6. aliped
chirp... 3. pew (pue) 4. peep
5. cheep, chirl, tweet 7. chirrup,
twitter
chisel... 3. cut, gad, hew 4. celt
(anc), form, pare 5. bruzz, burin,
carve, cheat, drove, gouge, grave
6. furrow, jagger, mallet, peeker,
pommel 7. engrave, swindle
9. sculpture
chit... 4. note, runt, wisp 5. child,
shoot 6. sprout 10. memorandum
14. recommendation
chitarra, chitarrine... 6. guitar
chiton... 7. garment (anc), mollusk
chivalrous... 5. brave 6. gentle, heroic
7. gallant, valiant 8. knightly
9. courteous 11. magnanimous
chive... 4. stab 5. onion, plant
6. garlic
chloride... 3. ore 4. salt 5. ester
7. calomel
chlorine... 2. Cl 7. bromine, halogen,
radical 8. cyanogen, fluorine
chloroform... 4. dope, kill 6. poison
7. stupefy 9. narcotize
11. anesthetize
chlorophyll... 5. ester, green 7. etiolin
9. deodorant
chocolate... 5. brown, cacao, candy,
cocoa, color 6. pinole 8. beverage
13. Sterculiaceae
choice... 4. beat, rare, will 5. prime
6. dainty, option, select, tidbit
8. election, free will, uncommon
9. recherché, selection
10. preference, well–chosen
11. alternative
choir... 6. chorus 7. singers
choir leader... 6. cantor 9. precentor
choke... 3. gag, jam, ram 4. clog
5. burke, check 6. hinder, impede,
muffle, stifle 7. garrote, repress,
smother 8. obstruct, strangle, throttle
9. constrict, suffocate
choler... 3. ire 4. bile, foam, gall,
rage 5. anger, wrath 6. spleen
10. resentment 11. biliousness
12. irascibility
choleric... 5. angry, testy 7. bilious,
enraged, iracund 8. wrathful
9. dyspeptic, irascible 10. passionate
chololith... 9. gallstone
choose... 3. opt 4. cull, like, list, pick,
want 5. elect 6. desire, optate,
prefer, select
choosing... 6. optant 8. eclectic,
elective 9. selecting
chop... 3. axe, cut, hew, jaw, lop
4. dice, fell, hack, jowl, meat, raze,
seal 5. cheek, mince, prune, sever,
stamp 8. griskin 8. noisette (eye of)
choppy... 5. bumpy, rough 6. uneven
7. jolting 8. unstable, variable
9. irregular 10. changeable,
incoherent 13. discontinuous
chord... 4. rope 6. radius, secant,
string, tendon 7. concord, harmony
8. arpeggio, concento, filament
chord (terms)... 5. major, minor, tonic,
triad 6. broken, common, tetrad

7. seventh 8. dominant, unbroken
10. enharmonic
chords... 4. tune 7. cadence, cantata
chore... 3. job (odd) 4. task, work
5. stint 10. assignment
chorography... 5. chart 7. diagram
10. topography 11. cartography,
description (region), ichnography
chortle... 5. laugh, snort 7. chuckle,
snortle
chorus... 4. echo 5. choir 6. accord,
outcry, unison 7. refrain, singers
8. chanters 9. unanimity
chorus (pert to)...
girl.. 7. chorine, chorist
leader.. 8. choragus 9. conductor
small.. 7. octette
Chosen (anc)... 5. Korea
Chosen People... 10. Israelites
chrism... 7. unction, unguent
10. anointment 12. confirmation
christen... 4. name 6. launch
7. baptize 10. denominate,
inaugurate 12. Christianize
Christian (pert to)...
Eastern.. 5. Uniat
feast.. 5. agape (anc) 8. Epiphany
9. Christmas
martyr (first).. 7. Stephen
philosopher (anc).. 6. Jesuit
9. Schoolman 10. Scholastic
sect.. 7. Docetae
symbol.. 5. orant (fem)
Christmas (pert to)...
bag.. 6. piñata
carol.. 4. Noel
decoration.. 6. crèche
feast.. 4. Yule
mummer.. 6. guiser
plant.. 5. holly 9. evergreen, mistletoe
term.. 4. Noel, Xmas 8. Nativity,
Yuletide 11. Weihnachten
Christ's–thorn... 4. nabk
chromosome... 2. id 5. idant
8. biophore, germ cell
chronic... 7. abiding 8. constant,
enduring, habitual 9. confirmed
10. continuous, inveterate, persistent
14. valetudinarian
chronicle... 4. sard 5. annal, diary
6. record 7. account, archive, history
8. register 9. narrative
10. chronology
chronicler... 6. writer 8. annalist,
compiler, recorder 9. historian
12. chronologist
chronology error... 9. prolepsis
chronometer... 5. clock, timer, watch
6. ghurry 7. sundial 9. hourglass,
metronome, timepiece
chrysolite... 5. green (color) 7. olivine,
peridot
chthonian... 4. gods (underworld)
7. hellish, worship 9. diabolist
11. demonolater
chub... 4. bass, dace, dolt, fool, lout
6. shiner, tautog 8. fallfish
9. hornyhead, squawfish
chubby... 3. fat 5. plump, pudgy,
round 6. stocky, stubby 9. corpulent
chuck... 4. beef, cast, food, hurl, jerk,
toss 5. fling, heave, pitch, throw

9. eliminate
chuckle... 5. cluck, laugh 6. cackle, wabble 7. chortle
chuff... 3. fat 4. boor 5. churl, clown, cross, proud, sulky, surly 6. chubby, elated, rustic 9. conceited 11. ill–tempered
chum... 3. pal 4. bait, pard 5. buddy, crony 6. fellow, hobnob 7. company, comrade, consort, partner 8. playmate, roommate 9. associate, classmate, colleague, companion
chump... 3. ass 4. dolt, dupe, fool, head 5. block, booby 8. endpiece
chunk... 3. dab, gob, pat, wad 4. hunk, junt, lump, slug (metal) 5. stick, stump, throw 8. fragment
chunky... 3. fat 4. game (Am Ind), junt 5. lumpy, stout, tubby 6. chubby, portly, stocky, stodgy, stubby 8. thickset
church... 3. dom 4. fane (anc), kirk, sect 5. abbey 6. bethel, temple 7. Lateran, minster, templet 8. basilica, conclave 9. cathedral 10. House of God, worshipers 11. Christendom 12. denomination
church (pert to)...
assistant.. 5. Elder
attendant.. 6. sexton, verger
calendar.. 4. Ordo
Court.. 10. Consistory
dignitary.. 4. dean 6. bishop, priest 7. prelate, primate 8. benefice, minister
dissenter.. 7. sectary 10. anti–Nicean, anti–Nicene
doctrine (State, church).. 8. Erastian
dominion.. 10. sacerdotum
doorkeeper.. 7. ostiary
Elder.. 9. Presbyter
feast.. 4. utas (octave of) 6. Easter
governing body.. 7. classis
law.. 5. canon, synod 7. council
part.. 4. apse, bema, nave 5. altar, canon 7. narthex 8. transept 10. clerestory
peace device.. 8. irenicon
property.. 5. glebe
Roman.. 7. Lateran 8. basilica
seats.. 4. pews 7. sedilla
service (part).. 3. pax 4. Mass 5. crede 7. epistle, introit, sanctus 8. Agnus Dei, blessing 9. communion
stipend.. 7. prebend
traffic (preferments).. 6. simony
vessel.. 3. ama, pyx (pix) 6. lavabo 8. ciborium
vestry.. 8. sacristy
churl... 3. cad, oaf 4. boor, carl, hind, lout, serf 5. ceorl, knave 6. rustic 7. bondman, freeman, peasant, villain 9. vulgarian 10. countryman
churlish... 4. mean 5. gruff, rough, surly 6. rustic, sordid, sullen, vulgar 7. boorish, crabbed, knavish 9. gruffness, niggardly 10. ill–humored 11. countrified
churn... 4. beat, kirn, stir, whip 5. mixer, shake 6. beater, seethe, vessel 7. agitate 8. agitator, emulsify

chute... 4. tube 5. flume, scarp, slide 6. trough 7. channel, incline, passage 9. parachute
cibel... 5. chive, onion 7. shallot
ciborium... 3. pyx 6. canopy, coffer, vessel
cicada... 6. dog–day, locust 9. Cicadidae
cicatrix... 4. mark, scar 7. blemish
Cid... 3. Ruy 4. hero, poem 5. Chief 6. leader (Christian) 7. Rodrigo
cider (weak)... 6. perkin
Cid's sword... 6. colada
cienaga... 5. marsh, swamp
cigar... 4. rope, toby 5. claro 6. concha, corona, Havana, stogie 7. cheroot, culebra, londres 8. cigarite, colorado, panatela 9. belvedere, cigarillo
cigarette... 3. fag 4. pill 5. cubeb 6. gasper, reefer 9. cigarillo
cilium... 4. hair, lash 7. eyelash 8. barbicel, ciliolum, filament 9. eyewinker
cimarron... 6. maroon 7. bighorn, wild dog 8. district (Okla)
cimex... 6. bedbug
Cimmerian, Homer Myth... 4. dark 5. Nomad (anc) 6. gloomy (abode) 8. Cimmeria
cinch... 4. game (cards), grip, sure 5. girth 6. fasten 7. harness (part) 9. certainty, sure thing
cinders... 3. ash 4. lava, slag 5. ashes, dross 6. embers 7. residue 8. clinkers
cinerarium... 8. mortuary
cinerator... 7. furnace 9. crematory 11. crematorium, incinerator
cingular... 7. annular 8. circular
cinnamon... 5. brown, spice 6. cassia 8. ishpingo (S Am) 10. Cinnamomum
cinque... 4. dice, five
cipher... 3. nil 4. code, zero 5. aught 6. figure, nobody, number, symbol 7. compute 9. calculate, character, nonentity
circa... 5. about 6. around 13. approximately
Circe (pert to)...
brother.. 6. Aeetes
father.. 6. Helios
Island abode.. 5. Aeaea
role, Odyssey.. 5. siren 7. charmer 9. sorceress, temptress
sister.. 5. Medea
circle... 3. orb 4. halo, hoop, loop, ring 5. ambit, orbit, rhomb, rigol, round, wheel 6. clique, cordon, girdle, rotate, sphere 7. annulus, aureole, circuit, compass, enclose, revolve 9. circulate, encompass 13. circumference
circle (pert to)...
astronomy.. 6. tropic
celestial.. 6. colure 10. almucantar
Japan.. 4. maru
luminous.. 6. corona
of hell (8th).. 9. Malebolge
of monoliths.. 8. cromlech 9. cyclolith
part.. 3. arc 6. areola, octant, radius,

sector 7. sextant 8. diameter
circuit... 3. lap, orb 4. bout, gyre,
loop, tour, zone 5. ambit, cycle,
orbit, relay, round, route 6. circle,
detour 7. compass 9. round trip
10. revolution
circuit court... 4. eyre
circuitous... 4. mazy 6. curved
7. crooked, devious, sinuous, twisted,
vagrant, winding 8. circular, flexuous,
indirect, tortuous 9. deceitful,
deviating, underhand, wandering
10. roundabout, serpentine
12. disingenuous, labyrinthine
14. circumlocutory
circular... 5. round 6. ringed
7. annular, discoid, program
8. cingular, coronary, ringlike
9. crownlike, orbicular 10. circuitous,
roundabout 13. advertisement
circular (pert to)...
enclosure.. 3. lis (liss)
indicator.. 4. dial
letter.. 10. encyclical
ornament.. 6. patera
circulate... 4. pass 5. issue 6. circle,
rotate, spread 7. diffuse, publish
8. monetize 9. propagate
11. disseminate
circumference... 4. girt 5. ambit,
bound, girth 6. bounds 7. circuit,
compass 8. encircle, surround
9. outskirts, perimeter, periphery
circumscribe... 5. bound, fence, limit
6. define 7. enclose, environ
8. encircle, restrict 9. encompass
circumscribed... 6. finite, narrow
9. definable 10. restricted
circumspect... 4. wary 5. chary
7. careful, politic, prudent
8. cautious, discreet 9. judicious
10. thoughtful 11. considerate
circumstance... 4. fact, item, pomp
5. event, state 7. proviso
8. incident, occasion, position
9. condition, provision, situation
10. occurrence, particular
11. arrangement, opportunity,
stipulation
circumstantial... 5. exact 6. minute
7. precise 8. detailed 10. evidential,
incidental, particular 11. conditional
12. nonessential
circumvent... 5. cheat, evade
6. delude, entrap, outwit, thwart
7. capture, circuit, deceive
8. surround 9. encompass, frustrate
circus... 4. hawk, ring, show 5. arena
6. big top, circe, cirque 7. harrier,
theater 8. carnival, side show
12. amphitheater
circus (pert to)...
concessionaire.. 7. grifter
hawk.. 15. circus assimilis
rider.. 8. desultor
Roman.. 13. Circus Maximus
sideshow.. 6. freaks
superintendent.. 10. ringmaster
cirque... 6. circle, corrie 7. circlet
cis (pref)... 8. this side
cist... 3. box, pit 5. chest 7. chamber
8. cistvaen (kistvaen)

Cistercian... 4. monk, Rule
(Benedictine) 5. Order 8. Trappist
cistern... 3. bac, sac, tub, vat
4. back, tank, well 7. cuvette,
raintub 9. impluvium, reservoir
citadel... 3. arx 4. fort 5. Alamo,
tower 6. castle 7. bastion, bulwark
8. fastness, fortress 9. acropolis
10. stronghold 13. fortification
14. propugnaculum
citation... 5. honor 6. eulogy, notice
7. mention, summons 8. subpoena
9. quotation 11. enumeration
12. verification
cite... 5. quote 6. adduce, allege,
repeat, summon 7. extract
8. indicate
citizen... 3. cit 6. native 7. citoyen,
denizen (of beasts), dweller
8. civilian, townsman 10. inhabitant
citizenship... 10. citizenism
15. enfranchisement
citron... 5. melon 6. cedrat (cedrate),
citrus, yellow
citrus fruit... 4. lime 5. lemon
6. orange 7. kumquat 8. citrange,
shaddock 10. grapefruit
cittern, cithern... 4. lute (anc)
6. zither 7. cithara, gittern
city... 4. town 8. township
10. metropolis 12. municipality
city (parts)... 4. ward 5. civic, urban
8. district, precinct
City of...
Bells.. 10. Strasbourg
Bridges.. 6. Bruges
Brotherly Love.. 12. Philadelphia
Churches.. 8. Brooklyn
David.. 9. Jerusalem
Dead (The).. 8. cemetery
10. Necropolis
Elms.. 8. New Haven
Gods.. 6. Asgard (Asgarth)
Golden Gate (The).. 12. San Francisco
Great King.. 9. Jerusalem
Hundred Towers.. 5. Pavia
Kings.. 4. Lira
Lilies.. 8. Florence
Magnificent Distances..
10. Washington (DC)
Masts.. 6. London
Palms (Bib).. 7. Jericho
Prophet (The).. 6. Medina
Rams.. 6. Canton
Saints.. 8. Montreal
Seven Hills.. 4. Rome
Straits.. 7. Detroit
Sun (the).. 7. Baalbek 10. Heliopolis
Victory.. 5. Cairo
Violated Treaty.. 8. Limerick
Violet Crown.. 6. Athens
civet... 5. fossa, genet, rasse
6. foussa, musang 7. nandine
10. paradoxure
civic... 5. civil, urban 6. public
7. burghal, oppidan 9. municipal
12. metropolitan
civil... 4. hend (hende) 5. suave
6. decent, polite, public, urbane
7. affable, courtly, elegant, secular
8. discreet, gracious, obliging,
polished, well-bred 9. courteous,

political 10. respectful
11. complaisant 13. condescending
civil (pert to) . . .
  dress . . 5. mufti 7. civvies
  fraud (Rom) . . 11. stellionate
  process . . 4. writ
  strife . . 6. stasis
  wrong . . 4. tort
civility . . . 6. comity 7. amenity
  8. courtesy, urbanity 9. attention,
  etiquette, gentility 10. affability,
  politeness
civilization . . . 6. kultur, polish
  7. culture 10. refinement
  11. cultivation
civilize . . . 4. tame 6. polish
  8. humanize, urbanize 9. cultivate
  11. domesticate
clad . . . 5. robed 6. decked, garbed
  7. arrayed, attired, clothed, dressed
  9. appareled, garmented
claim . . . 3. hak (hakh) 4. case, lien,
  name 5. right, title 6. assert,
  demand 7. preempt, profess, require
  8. arrogate, maintain, pretense
  (pretence), proclaim 9. postulate
  10. pretension
claimant . . . 7. claimer 9. applicant,
  plaintiff, pretender 10. solicitant
clairvoyance . . . 3. ESP 7. insight
  8. lucidity, sagacity 9. intuition
  10. divination 11. penetration
clairvoyant . . . 4. seer 7. prophet,
  seeress 9. sagacious 12. clearsighted
clam . . . 3. Mya 5. Chama, razor, Solen
  6. gweduc, Mactra, quahog
  7. mollusk 10. veneriform (shape)
clam destroyer . . . 6. winkle
  10. periwinkle
clammy . . . 4. cool, damp, dank, soft
  5. moist, mucid 6. sticky, sweaty
clamor . . . 3. cry, din, hue 4. roar, wail
  5. decry, noise, vocal 6. hubbub,
  outcry, racket, uproar 10. hullabaloo
clamorous . . . 4. loud 5. noisy
  7. blatant, clamant, excited
  8. brawling 9. demanding, insistent,
  turbulent 10. blustering, uproarious,
  vociferous
clamp . . . 4. vise 6. fasten 9. appliance
clan . . . 3. set 4. camp, club, cult,
  gens, race, sept 5. group, party,
  tribe 6. circle, clique, family
  7. coterie, society
clan (quarrel) . . . 4. feud 8. vendetta
clandestine . . . 3. sly 5. privy 6. covert,
  secret 7. furtive, illicit 8. stealthy
  9. concealed, underhand
  10. frandulent, undercover
  11. unobtrusive 13. surreptitious
clang . . . 4. ding, ring 5. clank, sound
  6. jangle 7. ringing
clang color . . . 6. timbre 8. tonality
clangor . . . 3. din 4. ring 5. clang,
  noise 6. fracas, hubbub, jangle,
  racket, ruckus, rumpus, tumult,
  uproar 7. discord, ringing
clank . . . 4. ring 5. clang 7. ringing
clapper . . . 4. bell, clap 5. bones
  (minstrel)
claque . . . 8. chaqueur, opera hat

9. applauder
clarify . . . 5. clear 6. filter, purify,
  refine, render, strain 7. cleanse,
  explain, rectify
clash . . . 3. jar 4. bang, bump 5. crash
  6. impact, jangle, tussle 7. collide,
  scuffle 8. conflict, disagree, skirmish
  9. collision, encounter, hostility
  10. dissonance
clasp . . . 3. hug 4. belt, grip, hasp,
  hold, ouch (anc), tach 5. grasp,
  morse (priest's), seize, stick, tache
  (anc) 6. buckle, enwrap, fasten,
  secure 7. agraffe (agrafe), embrace,
  tendril 8. fastener 10. chatelaine
class . . . 3. ilk 4. rank, sect 5. caste,
  genus, grade, order, tribe 6. brevet
  (mil), status 7. station 8. category,
  classify, division 9. catalogue
  14. classification
class (learned) . . . 8. literate, literati
  14. intelligentsia
classical . . . 4. pure 5. Attic 6. chaste
  7. classis, elegant 8. academic,
  literary, tasteful 10. Ciceronian
classification . . . 4. rank, sort 5. genus,
  grade 6. rating, system 7. species
  8. analysis, category, grouping
  12. distribution
classify . . . 4. list, rank, rate, sort, type
  5. grade, label, range 6. assort,
  digest, ticket 7. aggroup, arrange
  8. register 9. catalogue
clatter . . . 3. din, jar 5. noise, rumor
  6. babble, gabble, hubbub, racket,
  rattle, rumpus, tattle, uproar
  7. chatter, prattle 9. commotion
  11. disturbance
clause . . . 5. rider 6. phrase
  7. passage, proviso, section
claustral . . . 9. cloistral 10. cloistered
claw . . . 4. hand, nail, unce 5. chela,
  cloof, clufe, talon 6. nipper, unguis
claw . . . 3. dig 4. grab, grip, pull, tear
  5. grasp, seize 6. clutch, scrape,
  snatch 7. grapple, scratch
clay . . . 3. mud 4. marl, mire, soil
  5. argil, earth 6. corpse, kaolin
clay (pert to) . . .
  baked . . 4. tile 5. brick
  box . . 6. sagger
  covered . . 6. lutose
  mix . . 3. pug
  mold . . 3. dod
  molded . . 7. fictile
  nodule . . 10. eaglestone
  pipe . . 2. TD 10. meerschaum
  plug . . 4. bott
  polish . . 5. rabat
  softening . . 8. malaxage
  variety . . 4. bole, loam, marl 5. gault,
  ocher, tasco 8. petuntse
clayey . . . 4. soft 5. adobe, bolar
  6. earthy 12. argillaceous
clean, cleanse . . . 4. dust, swab, wash,
  wipe 5. brush, purge, rinse, scrub
  6. kosher, purify, refine 7. cleanse,
  deterge, launder 8. absterge,
  depurate, renovate 9. disinfect,
  elutriate, expurgate
cleanness . . . 6. purity (of life) 7. clarity
  8. chastity, elegance, neatness,

pureness, tidiness 10. immaculacy
13. impeccability
clear . . . 3. net, rid 4. free, gain, over,
pure 5. clean, lucid, plain 6. acquit,
excuse, exempt, hurdle, limpid,
pardon, purify 7. absolve, concise,
crystal, evident, explain, graphic,
lighten, release 8. apparent, distinct,
incisive, luculent 9. cloudless,
exonerate, extricate, vindicate
clear land . . . 7. thwaite (Eng)
clearsighted . . . 4. keen 10. discerning
13. perspicacious
cleat . . . 4. bitt 5. level, strip, wedge
7. joinery
cleave . . . 3. cut 4. part, rend, rive,
tear 5. clave, cling, clove, crack,
sever, shear, split 6. adhere, bisect,
cohere, divide, pierce 7. dispart
8. separate
cleek . . . 5. marry, pluck, seize
6. clutch, snatch
clef . . . 1. C, F, G 4. alto, bass
6. treble 7. descant, soprano
9. character
cleft . . . 3. gap 4. reft, rent, rift, rima
5. chasm, chink, crack, notch, riven,
split 6. chappy, cranny, gaping,
recess 7. crevice, fissure 8. scissure
cleft palate operation . . .
13. staphyloraphy (staphylorrhaphy)
clemency . . . 5. favor, grace, mercy
6. lenity 7. quarter 8. kindness,
leniency, mildness 10. compassion,
indulgence 11. forbearance
Clemens (Samuel) pen name . . .
9. Mark Twain
clench . . . 4. fist, grip, grit, hold
5. grasp 6. clinch, clutch
8. purchase 9. interlock
Cleopatra (pert to) . . .
attendant . . 4. Iras
downfall . . 3. asp
lover . . 6. Antony (Marc), Caesar
obelisk (two) . . 6. Needle
queen of . . 5. Egypt
river . . 4. Nile
clepe . . . 3. bid 4. call, name 6. invite,
invoke 7. address 8. christen
clergy . . . 5. cloth 6. pulpit
9. clergymen, clericals 10. priesthood
clergyman . . . 4. abbé, dean 5. canon,
vicar 6. cleric, curate, divine, parson,
pastor, priest, rector 7. dominie,
prelate 8. minister, preacher, sky
pilot 9. presbyter 12. ecclesiastic
clergywoman . . . 3. nun 8. minister
9. parsoness, priestess 10. religieuse
cleric, non . . . 4. laic
clerical . . . 7. scribal 11. ministerial
clerical (pert to) . . .
attire . . 3. alb 5. amice, cloth, fanon,
orale, stole
collar . . 5. rabat
hat . . 7. biretta
clerk . . . 3. nun 4. monk 5. write
6. cleric, hermit, layman, scribe
7. scholar (anc) 8. salesman
9. assistant, clergyman
12. ecclesiastic
cleronomy . . . 8. heritage
11. inheritance

clever . . . 3. apt 4. able, cute, deft
5. handy, slick, smart, witty
6. adroit, astute, brainy, bright,
expert, habile, nimble 7. amiable,
cunning, parlous 8. pleasing, skillful,
talented 9. brilliant, dexterous,
ingenious 11. good–natured
cleverness . . . 4. tact, wits 5. skill
6. esprit 7. cunning 9. ingenuity,
smartness, wittiness 10. adroitness,
astuteness, shrewdness
clew, clue . . . 3. key 4. ball, loop
(Naut) 5. rope 5. globe 6. cocoon,
tackle (see also *clue*)
cliché . . . 4. joke 5. banal, trite 6. old
saw 7. bromide 8. banality, chestnut
9. Joe Miller, platitude
click . . . 3. rap 4. snap 5. clack 6. go
over 7. prosper, succeed
click beetle . . . 3. dor (dorr) 6. elater
cliff . . . 3. gat 4. crag, klip, rock, wall
5. bluff, cleve, crest, scarp, slope
6. rocher 7. clogwyn 8. palisade
9. precipice 10. escarpment
climax . . . 3. cap, epi (Arch) 4. acme,
near, peak, shut 5. tight 6. apogee,
result, summit 7. heights
11. culmination 12. consummation
climb . . . 3. fly, gad 4. shin 5. grimp,
scale, speel 6. ascend, ascent
7. clamber, upgrade 9. acclivity
climbing . . . 7. scaling 8. scandent
10. scansorial
climbing plant . . . 3. hop, ivy 4. bine,
nito, vine 5. betel, liana 6. bryony
clime . . . 4. zone 5. realm, tract
6. region 7. climate
clinch . . . 4. bind, grip, hold, seal
5. grasp, prove, seize 6. clutch,
fasten, secure 7. confirm, grapple
8. conclude, purchase 9. establish
cling . . . 4. hold 5. stick 6. adhere,
cohere
clingfish . . . 6. testar
clink . . . 4. rime, slap 5. rhyme
6. jingle, lockup, prison, strike
9. assonance
clinquant . . . 4. gold, sham 6. tinsel
8. frippery, tinseled 10. glittering
clip . . . 3. bob, lop, mow 4. barb,
blow, dock, gaff, snip, trim 5. clasp,
prune, shear 6. clutch, fasten
7. curtail, scissor, shorten
8. ornament 10. instrument
clique . . . 3. set 4. cell, clan, club, ring
5. group, Junta, junto 6. circle
(people) 7. coterie
Cloaca Maxima (anc Rome) . . .
5. sewer 10. repository
cloak . . . 3. aba 4. cape, mask, pall,
wrap 5. cover, grego, jelab, manta,
sagum 6. abolla, capote, dolman,
mantle, mantua, screen, serape,
shield 7. chlamys (anc), conceal,
galabia, manteau, paenula (anc),
paletot, pelisse, pretext, protect
8. disguise 9. dissemble, new–market
10. witzchoura
clobber . . . 3. hit 4. beat, conk, poke,
swat 5. clout, punch, whack
6. defeat, strike, wallop
clock . . . 3. nef (ship's) 4. dial, time

5. knock 6. record 7. digital
8. recorder, sidereal 9. clepsydra,
metronome, timepiece 10. isochronon
11. chronometer
clockwise . . . 6. deasil (dessil)
11. withershins 14. dextrorotation,
dextrorotatory
clog . . . 4. stop 5. choke, dance
6. daggle, hamper, impede
8. encumber, obstruct, restrain
clog shoe . . . 4. geta 5. sabot
6. chopin, cobcab (Orient), patten
7. chopine
cloister . . . 4. stoa 5. abbey 6. arcade,
friary, immure, priory 7. confine,
convent, nunnery, retreat
9. anchorage, hermitage, monastery,
peristyle 10. passageway
cloistered . . . 7. recluse 8. enclosed,
monastic 11. sequestered
close . . . 2. at, by 3. end 4. near, nigh,
seal, shut, slam 5. dense, finis, stivy
6. finale, finish, period, secret, stingy,
sultry 7. airless, extreme, occlude,
related 8. complete, conclude,
familiar, imminent, intimate, stifling
9. extremity, secretive, terminate
11. approximate, termination
13. juxtaposition
close (pert to) . . .
eyes (the) . . 4. seel 5. blink
fasten . . 6. batten
of day . . 8. eventide 9. nightfall
poetic . . 4. nigh 5. anear
tightly . . 3. bar 4. bung, seal
6. clench, enseal 8. obturate
closely . . . 4. just 6. almost, barely,
nearly 8. narrowly
closely allied . . . 6. chummy
7. germane 8. intimate
closeness . . . 7. density, secrecy
8. fidelity, intimacy, likeness,
nearness, sameness 9. tightness
10. chumminess, narrowness,
similarity, stinginess, strictness,
sultriness 11. airlessness,
compactness, conciseness, familiarity,
resemblance 14. oppressiveness
closet . . . 5. ambry, cuddy, emery
6. locker, pantry 7. cabinet
8. cupboard, wardrobe 9. cloakroom,
storeroom
closing device . . . 3. key 4. lock, snap
5. clasp, hinge, latch 6. Velcro (tm),
zipper
closing measure (Mus) . . . 4. coda
clot . . . 4. lump, mass 5. grume
7. thicken 8. coagulum, concrete
9. coagulate 12. crassamentum
cloth . . . 3. net, tat 4. brin, crea, drap,
felt, lamé, silk, tapa, wool 5. adati,
baize, bezan, bluet, carda, crash,
crepe, denim, khaki, linen, manta,
nylon, orlon, rayon, satin, scrim,
surat, tamis, terry, tulle, twill, voile
6. alpaca, burlap, calico, canvas,
chintz, cotton, damask, dimity,
dowlas, duffel, faille, jersey, madras,
mohair, muslin, nankin, pongee,
poplin, samite (gold), sateen, velour
7. acetate, baracan, brocade,
bunting, cambric, challis, chiffon,

drap d'or, flannel, foulard, gingham,
nankeen, organdy, organza, percale,
sacking, spandex, taffeta, ticking,
worsted 8. cashmere, chambray,
corduroy, cretonne, drilling,
nainsook, Shantung 9. crinoline,
gabardine, polyester, sailcloth,
tarpaulin, tricotine 10. broadcloth,
seersucker 11. cheesecloth, drap
d'argent (silver), marquisette
cloth (pert to) . . .
checkered . . 5. plaid
finisher . . 7. beetler
piece . . 4. bolt 5. scrap
ridge . . 4. wale
selvage . . 4. roon 6. border 7. listing
twilled . . 5. denim, serge
weaving . . 4. warp, weft, woof
clothe . . . 3. tog 4. deck, garb, gird,
robe, vest 5. array, drape, dress,
endue, indue 6. afford, enrobe, invest
7. empower, provide, sheathe
8. accouter
clothes . . . 3. rig 4. duds, garb, togs
5. guise, habit, jeans, Levis 6. attire,
bikini, briefs 7. apparel, costume,
raiment, regalia, threads (sl)
8. clothing, garments, leotards,
swimsuit 9. dungarees
10. bedclothes, garmenture
11. habiliments, investiture
cloud . . . 3. fog, low 4. dust, film, haze,
mist, rack, scud 5. nepho (comb
form), nubia, stain, sully, taint, vapor
6. cirrus, damage, darken, defame,
defect, nebule, nimbus, shadow,
stigma 7. blacken, blemish, cumulus,
nubilus, obscure, pea-soup, stratus,
tarnish, tornado 8. cat's-tail, cocktail,
overcast 10. horizontal
clouds (pert to) . . .
astronomy . . 4. coma 9. nubeculae
kind . . 6. cirrus, nimbus 7. cumulus,
fractus, stratus 9. mare's-tail
luminous . . 5. nimbi
Magellanic . . 5. Major, Minor
photography . . 9. nephogram
science of . . 9. nephology
seeding . . 10. nucleation
vapory . . 4. rack
cloudy . . . 4. dark, hazy 5. filmy, foggy,
misty, murky, shady, vague 6. gloomy,
lowery, opaque 7. nebular, obscure
8. confused, overcast, vaporous
9. cloudlike 10. indistinct, lackluster
clout . . . 3. hit, jab, rag 4. blow, bump,
clod, mend, nail, swat 5. patch,
power, shred, smack 9. influence
12. handkerchief
clove . . . see also *cleave* 5. spice
clover . . . 3. red 4. bush 5. lotus, snail,
white 6. alsike 7. crimson, melilot,
prairie, spotted 9. Melilotus
clown . . . 3. oaf 4. boor, fool, lout,
mime, mome, zany 5. comic, Kelly
(Emmet), mimer, yahoo 6. jester,
rustic 7. buffoon 9. harlequin
10. countryman 11. merry-andrew
clownish . . . 4. rude 5. gawky, rough
6. clumsy, coarse, rustic 7. awkward,
boorish, ill-bred, loutish, uncivil
8. churlish, ungainly

9. untutored 10. buffoonish
11. countrified
cloy . . . 4. clog, glut, pall, sate
   5. gorge, stuff 6. accloy 7. satiate,
   satisfy, surfeit
club . . . 3. bat, hit 4. beat, join, mace
   5. billy, clout, staff, unite, yokel
   6. cudgel, league, weapon 7. society
   8. bludgeon, spontoon
   9. boomerang, espantoon
   10. nulla–nulla, pogamoggan
   11. association
club (pert to) . . .
  actors . . 6. Friars
  historic . . 5. Whigs 8. Jacobins
   10. Cordeliers
  Service . . 7. Kiwanis
  Women's (first) . . 7. Sorosis
clubfoot . . . 7. talipes 9. deformity, pes
   valgus 13. talipes valgus
club–shaped . . . 7. clavate
clue, clew . . . 3. key, tip 4. data, hint
   5. scent 6. thread 7. inkling
   8. evidence 9. suspicion
   11. fingerprint
clump . . . 3. tod 4. heap, lump, thud,
   tuft 5. bunch, chunk, group, motte
   (mott), patch, stamp 6. growth,
   trudge 7. cluster, thicket
clumsy . . . 4. ugly 5. bulky, gawky,
   inapt, inept, unfit 6. gauche, oafish
   7. awkward, uncouth, unhandy
   8. slipshod, ungainly, unwieldy
   9. inelegant, lumbering, maladroit,
   misshapen 10. blundering,
   cumbersome, left–handed
   13. inappropriate
clumsy person . . . 4. gawk 5. jumbo,
   staup 7. bungler
clupeoid fish . . . 7. herring
cluster . . . 4. crop, cyme, gang, tuft
   5. bunch, clump, group 6. huddle
   8. fascicle 9. glomerule
cluster (pert to) . . .
  bean . . 4. guar 6. legume
  fibers . . 3. nep
  flowers . . 6. raceme 7. rosette
   8. anthemia, panticle
  fruit . . 6. grapes
  spores . . 5. sorus
  stars . . 8. Globular, Pleiades (The)
clustery . . . 8. racemose
clutch . . . 3. nab 4. claw, grip, hold,
   nest 5. brood, catch, clasp, grasp,
   seize 6. clench, cletch, crisis
clyster . . . 5. enema 6. lavage
   9. injection
Clytemnestra's mother . . . 4. Leda
cnemis . . . 4. shin 5. tibia
coach . . . 3. car, rig 5. prime, stage,
   train, tutor 6. direct, fiacre, jarvey
   7. adviser, prepare, tallyho, teacher
   8. carriage, equipage, instruct,
   preparer 9. charabanc 10. instructor
coach dog . . . 9. Dalmatian
coachman . . . 3. fly (angling) 4. fish,
   jehu, whip 5. driver
coagulate . . . 3. gel, jel, set 4. cake,
   clot, curd, lump 6. curdle, posset
   7. congeal 8. solidify
coagulator . . . 6. enzyme, rennet
coagulum . . . 4. clot, curd 5. grume

7. clabber
coal . . . 4. fuel 5. black, ember
   6. carbon, cinder 7. lignite, residue
coal (pert to) . . .
  bin . . 6. bunker
  car . . 3. dan 4. corf, tram 6. hopper
  dust . . 4. coom (coomb), culm, smut
  gas . . 7. Pintsch 9. acetylene
  miner . . 7. collier
  miner's disease . . 11. anthracosis
  oil . . 8. kerosene
  tar . . 5. lysol, pitch 6. cresol, decane,
   phenol 7. toluene
  tunnel . . 4. adit
  type . . 3. egg, nut, pea 4. dant, hard,
   peat, soft 6. broken, cannel
   8. charcoal, chestnut 9. buckwheat
   10. anthracite, bituminous
coalition . . . 5. trust, union 6. fusion,
   hookup, league, merger 7. society
   8. alliance 10. federation
   11. affiliation, combination,
   confederacy, conjunction
coalition advocate . . . 9. fusionist
coals . . . 5. gleed 6. embers 7. cinders
coarse . . . 3. fat, low 4. dank, lewd,
   rude, vile 5. broad, crass, gross,
   thick 6. carnal, earthy, impure,
   ribald, rustic, vulgar 7. goatish,
   obscene, sensual 8. granular,
   immodest, indecent, inferior, unchaste
   9. inelegant, offensive, unrefined
   10. unfinished, unpolished
coarse (pert to) . . .
  grain . . 4. meal
  grass . . 4. reed 5. sedge 6. quitch
  hominy . . 4. corn, samp
coast . . . 4. sail 5. beach, glide, shore,
   slide 6. rivage 7. seaside
   8. seaboard, seashore
coast (pert to) . . .
  dweller . . 7. orarian
  live oak . . 6. encina
  projection . . 4. cape, ness
coat . . . 4. jupe 5. cloak, frock, parka,
   tunic 6. blazer, capote, duster,
   jacket, raglan, reefer, trench, tuxedo,
   ulster 7. cassock, cutaway, paletot,
   slicker 8. gossamer, Mackinaw,
   tegument 9. newmarket, redingote
coat (pert to) . . .
  fastener . . 4. frog 6. zipper
  of animal . . 3. fur 4. pelt, wool
   6. pelage 8. feathers
  of arms . . 5. crest 8. blazonry
   10. escutcheon
  of mail . . 6. byrnia 7. hauberk
  of the eye (inner) . . 6. retina
coati . . . 5. Nasua 6. narica 7. raccoon
coating (pert to) . . .
  cake . . 5. glacé, icing 8. frosting
  copper, bronze . . 6. patina
  grain . . 4. bran
  medical . . 9. collodion
  metal . . 5. plate
  seed . . 5. testa 6. tegmen
   10. endopleura
  tin, lead . . 5. terne
  vitreous . . 6. enamel
coax . . . 3. beg, ply 4. lure, urge
   5. press, tease 6. cajole, entice,
   exhort 7. beguile, flatter, implore,

wheedle 8. blandish, inveigle,
persuade 9. importune
10. manipulate

cob... 4. axis, blow, gull, loaf, mole,
pier, swan 5. block, chief, horse
6. basket, leader, muffin, spider
7. beating, corncob 8. dumpling
10. breakwater

cobbler... 3. pie 5. coler, sutor
6. bungle, repair, souter 7. botcher,
crispin 9. fortescue (fortesque),
shoemaker

cobbra... 4. head 5. skull

cobby... 5. stout 6. hearty, lively,
stocky 10. headstrong

cobra... 3. asp 4. Naga (Myth), Naja
5. mamba, snake, viper 8. ringhals

cobweb... 3. net 4. trap 5. snare,
wevet 7. fiction, network 8. filament,
gossamer 9. intricacy

cobweblike... 8. araneous 9. arachnoid

cocaine... 4. coca, snow (sl)
8. narcotic 9. mydriatic
10. anesthetic

coccus... 4. cell 5. spore
9. bacterium, cochineal

cochleate... 6. spiral 11. shell–shaped

cock... 3. nab, tap 4. bird, heap,
kora, pile, vane (weather) 5. strut,
valve 6. faucet, grouse, leader,
muckna 7. rooster, swagger

cockade... 4. knot 7. rosette

Cockade State... 8. Maryland

cockatoo... 3. ara 5. arara (palm),
galah 6. parrot 8. ganggang

cockle... 4. boat, gith, kiln, oast
5. shell, stove 6. pucker 7. mollusk,
wrinkle

cockpit... 3. pit 4. well 5. arena,
cabin (airplane) 7. gallera

cockscomb (coxcomb)... 5. crest, plant

cocktail... 5. cloud, drink, horse
6. beetle 9. appetizer

cocky... 4. pert 5. saucy 6. jaunty
7. stuck–up 9. conceited

cocoa... 5. broma, cacao 8. beverage
9. chocolate 11. theobromine

coconut (pert to)...
fiber.. 4. coir, kyar
India.. 6. nargil (narghile)
meat.. 5. copra

cocoon... 3. pod 4. bave (silk), clew,
kell, pupa 9. chrysalis

cod... 3. bib, cor 4. fish, ling
5. scrod, sprag 6. burbot, cultus,
gadoid 7. bacalao

coddle... 3. pet 4. baby, cook
5. humor, spoil 6. caress, fondle,
pamper 11. mollycoddle

code... 3. law 5. canon, codex, Morse,
salic 6. digest, equity, signal, symbol
7. pandect, precept
12. Commandments

codfish (pert to)...
Alaska.. 6. wachna
genus.. 5. Gadus
ready for cooking.. 5. scrod
type.. 3. cod, red 4. cusk, rock
6. Murray, tomcod 7. buffalo

codger... 5. crank, miser 6. oddity

codicil... 4. will 5. rider 6. sequel
8. addition, appendix 10. instrument

Cody (William)... 11. Buffalo Bill

coerce... 4. curb 5. force 6. compel
7. dragoon, enforce, repress
9. blackjack, strong–arm, terrorize
10. intimidate

coercion... 5. force 6. duress
8. violence 10. compulsion,
constraint

coffee (pert to)...
bean.. 3. nib
container.. 8. canister
cup holder.. 4. zarf
extract.. 8. caffeine
kind.. 3. Rio 4. Java 5. Milds,
Mocha 6. Bogota, Brazil, Santos
7. Sumatra, Turkish 8. Medellin
9. Maracaibo
mix.. 7. chicory
pot.. 6. biggin 10. percolator

coffin... 3. box, urn 4. bier, case, kist,
mold 5. chest, crust 6. basket,
casing, casket 11. sarcophagus

coffin (pert to)...
cloth.. 4. pall 5. cloak
litter.. 4. bier
nail.. 9. cigarette
prehistoric.. 4. cist 5. chest

cog... 3. cam 4. boat (fishing), gear
5. catch, cheat, cozen, tenon, tooth
7. ratchet, wheedle 8. sprocket
9. deception

cogent... 5. valid 6. potent, strong
7. telling 8. powerful 9. effective
10. compelling, conclusive,
convincing, persuasive

cogitate... 4. mull, muse, plan
5. think 6. ponder 8. meditate
9. cerebrate

cognizance... 3. ken 4. heed, plea
5. badge (knight's) 9. knowledge
11. recognition 12. apprehension

cognizant... 5. aware 7. knowing
8. sensible 9. conscious
10. perceptive 11. intelligent

cognomen... 4. name 5. title
6. y–clept 7. surname 8. nickname
10. patronymic 11. appellation

coheir... 5. joint 8. parcener

cohere... 5. agree, cling, serry, stick,
unite 6. adhere, cleave 9. glutinate

coherence... 5. cling 8. adhesion,
cohesion, sticking 9. adherence,
connected 11. consistency

coil... 4. ansa, clew, curl, loop, mesh,
wind 5. querl, twine, twist 6. spiral
7. haycock 8. encircle
11. convolution

coiled... 7. tortile, twirled

coin... 3. rin, sou, yen 4. cash, cent
5. money, penny, stamp 6. specie

coin (pert to)...
Bib.. 6. talent
brass.. 13. Rosa Americana (1722)
gold.. 3. lev 4. ryal (rial) 5. daric,
eagle 6. guinea
minor.. 4. doit
parts of.. 4. flan 5. field, tails, verso
6. legend 7. exergue, obverse (front),
reverse
silver.. 4. batz, obol, ryal (rial)
5. crown, ducat, sceat 6. tester
tester.. 6. shroff (saraf)

coincide . . . 5. agree, check, chime, match, tally 6. concur 7. consent 10. correspond 11. synchronize

coincident . . . 9. consonant 10. concurrent 12. contemporary

coiner . . . 8. inventor 9. neologist (words) 10. fabricator 13. counterfeiter

coins (pert to) . . .
roll of . . 7. rouleau
science of . . 11. numismatics
specialist . . 11. numismatist

colander . . . 5. sieve 6. filter, sorter 8. strainer

Colchis King . . . 6. Aeetes

cold . . . 3. icy, nip, raw 4. dank, dead, drow, dull, frio, sure 5. algid, bland, bleak, frore (anc), gelid 6. chilly, frigid, frosty 7. chilled, cinched 8. chilling, reserved, unheated 9. heartless 10. lackluster 11. indifferent, passionless, unconscious

cold (pert to) . . .
blooded . . 9. heartless, unfeeling 13. dispassionate, heterothermal 14. poikilothermal
feet . . 9. cowardice
infection . . 4. post 5. rheum 6. coryza 7. catarrh
sore . . 6. herpes 7. simplex, vesicle 14. herpes labialis
steel . . 5. sword 7. bayonet, weapons
term . . 8. frigoric
wind . . 4. bise

Coleoptera . . . 7. beetles, insects

Coleridge's sacred river . . . 4. Alph (Kubla Khan)

colewort . . . 4. kale 7. cabbage

colic . . . 4. pain 5. gripe, spasm 7. tormina 10. enteralgia 11. stomachache

coliseum . . . 4. bowl 5. arena 6. circus 7. stadium, theater 9. Colosseum 10. hippodrome 12. amphitheater

collaborate . . . 3. aid 6. co–work 8. coauthor 9. cooperate 10. fraternize

collage . . . 6. gluing 7. montage 8. abstract, adhesive 9. cyclorama

collapse . . . 4. cave, fail, fall 5. crash, slump 6. cave–in, defeat 7. crack–up, debacle, deflate, failure 8. downfall 9. breakdown, shrinking 10. bankruptcy, exhaustion 11. prostration

collar . . . 4. band, grab, ruff 5. chain, rabat, ruche 6. arrest, bertha, rabato, tackle, torque 7. barghan, capture, harness (part), shackle 8. carcanet, neckband 10. pickadilly

collate . . . 5. audit, check 6. verify 7. certify, compare, examine

collateral . . . 4. extra 6. margin 7. related 8. indirect, relation (folks), security 9. accessory, secondary 10. contingent, obligation, subsidiary 11. subordinate 12. nonessential

collation . . . 3. tea 4. meal 5. lunch 6. repast, sermon 7. address, reading 8. luncheon, treatise 10. collection, comparison,

conference 12. consultation, contribution

colleague . . . 6. fellow 7. compeer, comrade, consort, partner 8. camarada, confrere 9. associate, companion 11. confederate

collect . . . 3. bag, tax 4. levy, mass 5. amass, glean, raise, rally 6. deduce, forage, garner, gather, muster, prayer, sheave 7. compile, procure 8. assemble, mobilize 9. aggregate 10. accumulate, congregate

collection . . . 3. ana, bag, set 4. book, olio 5. group, hoard, store 6. rosary, sorite 8. assembly, donation, offering 9. aggregate, congeries, gathering, repertory 10. assemblage, repertoire 11. acquisition

collection (pert to) . . .
anecdotes . . 3. ana 4. data 8. analecta
animals (wild) . . 3. zoo 9. menagerie
bubbles . . 4. foam
curiosities . . 6. museum
documents . . 4. Veda 6. corpus 7. dossier
fruit . . 7. syncarp
implements (Surg) . . 7. trousse
of four . . 6. tetrad
of twenty–four . . 5. quire
poems . . 5. sylva 9. anthology
proper names . . 11. onomasticon
type . . 4. font
writing . . 10. literature

collector (pert to) . . .
bird eggs . . 8. oologist
books . . 10. bibliothec 11. bibliophile 12. bibliomaniac
coins . . 11. numismatist
rent . . 8. landlord
stamps . . 11. philatelist

colleen . . . 4. girl, lass, maid 6. damsel, maiden 7. girleen

college . . . 6. school 7. academy, society 9. Alma Mater, institute 10. université, university 11. corporation, institution

college (pert to) . . .
campus . . 4. lawn, quad 7. grounds
graduate . . 6. alumna 7. alumnus
license for absence . . 5. exeat
official . . 4. dean 5. prexy 6. beadle, bursar, regent 7. proctor

collegiate . . . 8. academic 9. collegian, scholarly 11. college–bred

collide with . . . 3. hit, ram 5. clash, crash 6. hurtle, strike 7. contend 8. conflict, disagree

collier . . . 5. miner 6. plover

collieshangie . . . 3. row 7. quarrel 8. squabble 11. disturbance (noisy)

collision . . . 4. bump 5. clash, crash 6. impact 7. smashup 8. accident 9. hostility 11. composition, impingement 12. interference

colloquial . . . 6. common 8. everyday, familiar, informal 9. unstudied 10. vernacular 11. undignified 14. conversational

colloquy . . . 4. chat, talk 6. parley 9. discourse 10. conference

12. conversation
Cologne Kings (legend)... 4. Magi
  6. Gaspar 8. Melchior 9. Balthasar
Colombia...
  capital.. 6. Bogota (1538)
  city.. 4. Cali 5. Pasto 6. Medellin
    9. Cartagena 10. Santa Marta
  Falls.. 10. Tequendama
  Liberator.. 7. Bolivar (Simon)
  mountain.. 5. Andes 11. Cordilleras
  river.. 9. Magdalena
colonize... 6. gather, people, settle
  8. populate 9. establish
colonizer... 3. ant 6. oecist
  7. planter, settler
colonnade... 3. row (columns) 4. stoa
  6. arcade 7. columns, pillars, portico
  8. cloister 9. peristyle
colony... 4. body 5. group, swarm
  8. dominion 9. community
  10. dependency, settlement
colophon... 4. logo 6. emblem
  9. bookplate 11. inscription (book)
color... 3. dun, dye, hue 4. tint, tone
  5. blush, paint, shade, stain, terne,
  tinge 6. flaxen, nuance, pastel, sallow,
  timbre 7. piebald, pigment 8. tincture
  (Her) 10. complexion
color (pert to)...
  application (paste).. 7. impasto
  blending.. 4. teer 5. fondu
    9. scumbling
  blind.. 13. achromatopsia
  clouded.. 9. nebulated
  colorful.. 9. chromatic
  colorless.. 4. drab, dull, pale 6. pallid
    7. whitish 8. blanched
    10. achromatic
  irregularity.. 5. fleck 6. streak
    10. rivulation
  material.. 5. eosin, morin, smalt
    7. pigment 11. chlorophyll
  off color.. 6. risqué 8. improper
  organ.. 8. clavilux
  paint, rouge.. 6. ruddle 7. blusher
  science of.. 10. chromatics
    11. spectrology
  variegated.. 7. rainbow, The Flag,
    vibgyor 8. spectrum 11. iridescence
Colorado...
  canyon.. 5. Black 10. Royal Gorge
  capital.. 6. Denver
  city.. 5. Aspen, Lamar 6. Pueblo
    7. Boulder, Manassa, Manitou
  Indian.. 7. Arapaho
  lake (highest).. 10. Frozen Lake
  Mt peak.. 6. Elbert 9. Pike's Peak
  park.. 5. Estes 15. Garden of the
    Gods
  river.. 4. Gila 6. Platte 8. Arkansas
  State admission.. 12. Thirty–eighth
  State bird.. 11. lark bunting
  State flower.. 9. columbine
  State motto.. 13. Nil Sine Numine
    (Nothing Without God)
  State nickname.. 10. Centennial
colossal... 4. huge 5. great, large
  6. absurd, superb 7. mammoth
  8. gigantic 9. monstrous
colossal beast... 8. behemoth (Bib)
colt... 3. gun 4. foal 5. filly, horse
  8. yearling

Columbus (pert to)...
  birthplace.. 5. Genoa (It)
  companion.. 5. Ojeda
  discoverer.. 7. America (1492)
  landing site.. 11. San Salvador
  sailing site.. 5. Palos (Sp)
  vessel.. 4. Nina 5. Pinta 10. Santa
    Maria
column... 3. lat (Buddh) 4. anta
  5. pylon, shaft, stele (stela) 6. pillar
  7. telamon 8. baluster, caryatid,
  pilaster
column (pert to)...
  base.. 5. socle 6. plinth 9. stylobate
  military.. 4. unit 9. formation
  Order (Arch).. 5. Doric, Ionic
    6. Tuscan 9. Composite
    10. Corinthian
  ref to.. 5. train 7. cortege
    8. cylinder, memorial, monument
    10. procession
  shaft.. 4. fust 5. scape 8. apophyge
  term.. 5. bague, galbe, shank
    7. capital, entasis
coma... 4. daze, tuft 5. carus, sleep,
  sopor 6. stupor, trance 9. catalepsy
  12. sluggishness 13. insensibility
  15. unconsciousness
comatose... 6. drowsy, torpid
  9. apathetic, lethargic 10. cataleptic,
  insensible 11. unconscious
comb... 4. card, wave 5. cock's, crest,
  curry, groom, scour, tease 6. search
  7. rummage 8. caruncle
combat... 3. war 4. cope, duel, fray,
  tilt 5. fight, joust (anc), repel
  6. action, battle, karate, kung fu,
  oppose, strife 7. contest, jujitsu,
  scuffle 8. argument, conflict
  9. withstand 10. antagonize,
  contention, engagement
combat (pert to)...
  challenge.. 6. cartel 8. gauntlet
  code.. 6. duello
  scene.. 5. arena 8. coliseum
combatant... 6. dueler 7. battler,
  fighter 8. disputer 9. contender
  10. competitor, contestant
combative... 8. militant 9. agonistic,
  bellicose 10. aggressive, pugnacious
  11. belligerent, contentious
combination... 4. gang, pact, pool
  5. blend, combo, party, trust, union
  6. clique, fusion, hookup, league,
  merger 7. amalgam, combine, faction,
  mixture 8. alliance, coalesce,
  ensemble, junction 9. camarilla,
  coalition, synthesis 10. embodiment
  11. aggregation, association,
  confederacy, unification
  12. undergarment 13. incorporation
combine... 3. add, mix 4. join, pool
  5. merge, unite 6. concur, mingle
  7. machine 10. synthesize
combining form...
  above, beyond.. 3. sur 5. ultra
  across.. 4. tran 5. trans
  bad.. 3. dys, mal
  black.. 4. mela
  earth.. 3. geo 5. terra
  equal.. 3. iso 4. homo, pari
  far.. 3. tel 4. tele

good.. 2. eu
hundred.. 4. cent
inner, within.. 4. ento (ent)
kidney.. 4. reni
middle.. 4. medi 5. medio
mountain.. 3. oro
needle.. 3. acu
new.. 3. neo
not.. 2. un 3. non
old, ancient.. 5. paleo
one.. 3. uni 4. mono
outside, without.. 3. ect, ext 4. ecto
personal.. 4. idio
soft.. 4. leni
stone.. 4. lith
thought.. 4. ideo
thrice.. 3. ter
tooth.. 6. odonto
touch.. 3. tac
up, upward.. 3. ano
watery.. 4. sero

comblike... 7. ctenoid 8. pectinal
combustible... 5. fiery, quick
   7. piceous 8. volcanic 9. irascible
   10. accendible 11. hot–tempered,
   inflammable
combustion... 4. fire 6. tumult
   7. blazing, flaming 8. ignition
   9. agitation, confusion, cremation
   12. inflammation 13. conflagration
come... 3. hop 4. near 5. issue, occur
   6. appear, arrive, happen
   8. approach 9. transpire
come (pert to)...
across.. 3. pay 4. meet 7. confess
   10. contribute
back.. 6. answer, retort, return
   7. rebound, recover 8. remember,
   repartee
before.. 4. lead 7. precede, prevene
   8. antecede
between.. 8. estrange, interlie
   9. interpose, intervene
by.. 3. get 4. gain 6. obtain
   7. acquire, inherit, receive
forth.. 3. jet 4. gush, spew 5. hatch,
   issue, occur 6. appear, emerge,
   spring 7. emanate 9. originate
together.. 4. join, knit, meet 5. clash
   7. collide, convene 8. assemble,
   converge
come (to)...
light.. 7. develop
maturity.. 5. ripen
pass.. 5. occur 6. befall, betide,
   happen 9. eventuate
rest.. 3. sit 5. light 6. settle
comedian, comedienne... 4. buff
   5. actor, comic 6. player 7. farcist
   8. funnyman 9. dramatist
comedy... 5. drama, farce, revue
   7. comedie 8. travesty 9. burlesque,
   slapstick
comestibles... 4. food 5. manna
   8. eatables, victuals
comfort... 4. ease 5. cheer, quilt
   6. relief, solace, soothe, succor
   7. confirm, console, enliven, fortify,
   refresh, relieve, support, sustain
   8. inspirit, nepenthe (drug)
   9. enjoyment 10. invigorate,

strengthen 11. consolation
   12. satisfaction
comfortable... 4. cozy, easy, snug
   5. scarf 8. adequate, cheerful,
   homelike, wristlet 9. contented,
   endemonic 10. complacent,
   prosperous 11. consolatory,
   encouraging
comforter... 5. quilt 6. tippet
   7. solacer 8. pacifier 9. Paraclete
comfortless... 7. forlorn 8. desolate
   9. cheerless, heartsick 10. despairing
   11. distressing 12. disconsolate,
   inconsolable
comic, comical... 3. odd 5. cutup,
   droll, funny, queer, witty 6. absurd,
   quaint 7. cartoon, risible
   8. comedian, farcical, humorous
   9. burlesque, laughable, ludicrous,
   quizzical, whimsical 10. capricious,
   outlandish
coming... 3. due 6. access, advent,
   future 7. arrival, forward, looming
   8. eventual, expected, imminent
   9. imminence 11. approaching,
   forthcoming
coming into being... 7. genesis,
   nascent
comity... 7. amenity, suavity 8. civility,
   courtesy, urbanity 10. affability
command... 3. bid, gee, haw, hup
   4. bade, beck, fiat, hest, rule, sway
   5. avast, check, edict, exact, grasp,
   order, power, ukase 6. behest,
   charge, compel, decree, direct,
   enjoin, govern 7. control, dictate,
   mandate, mastery 8. dominion,
   restrain 9. authority, prescribe
   10. domination 11. commandment
   12. jurisdiction
commander... 3. cid 5. chief, ruler
   6. leader 7. admiral, captain, skipper
   8. dictator, governor, myriarch,
   overlord
commander, Eastern... 3. ras 4. amir,
   emir, Imam, khan, rani 5. ameer,
   begum, dewan, emeer, nawab, Nizam
   6. caliph, regent, Sultan
commanding... 8. dominant
   9. imperious 10. imperative
   13. authoritative
commandments... 4. laws 6. orders,
   tables 8. mandates, precepts
   9. Decalogue (Ten)
comme il faut... 8. properly
   9. correctly 10. decorously 12. as it
   should be
commemoration... 7. service
   8. Encaenia (Oxford Univ)
   10. observance 11. anniversary,
   celebration, remembrance
   13. solemnization
commence... 4. open 5. arise, begin,
   start 6. spring 8. initiate 9. originate
commencement... 4. rite 6. source
   8. ceremony, nascency 9. beginning,
   formality, inception, novitiate
   10. initiation
commend... 4. plug 5. boost, extol,
   offer 6. assign, commit, praise,
   remand, resign 7. approve, deliver,
   entrust 8. advocate, delegate

9. recommend 10. compliment
commendation ... 4. hype, plug, puff
5. boost, kudos 8. approval
10. assignment, commitment,
compliment, delegation
11. approbation, consignment,
entrustment
comment ... 4. note, talk 6. gossip,
postil, remark, report 7. descant,
discuss, explain, mention 8. annotate,
critique 9. criticism, discourse
commentary ... 5. gloss 6. memoir
7. remarks 8. treatise 9. memoranda
10. annotation 11. explanation
commerce ... 5. trade 7. traffic
8. dealings 9. communion
11. interchange 13. communication
commis ... 5. agent, clerk 6. deputy
commiserate ... 4. pity 7. condole,
console 10. sympathize
commiseration ... 4. pity, ruth
5. mercy 6. sorrow 7. empathy,
feeling 8. sympathy 10. compassion,
condolence
commission ... 4. duty, task 5. allot,
board, share, trust 6. brevet, depute,
office, ordain 7. empower, mandate,
mission, payment, rake–off, warrant
8. delegate 9. authority
10. assignment, constitute,
delegation, deputation
11. performance 12. perpetration
commissioned ... 8. allotted, assigned,
breveted 9. delegated
10. accredited, authorized
commissioner ... 5. envoy 6. dubash,
legate 7. steward 8. delegate,
emissary, official 9. commissar
commissure ... 4. seam 5. cleft, joint,
mitre, raphe 6. stitch, suture
7. closure 8. juncture 10. interstice
commit ... 2. do 3. con 4. game
(cards) 5. refer 6. remand 7. confide,
consign, entrust, promise
8. memorize, relegate
10. commission, perpetrate
commode ... 3. cap 5. chest
8. fontange 9. washstand
10. chiffonier
commodious ... 3. fit 5. ample, roomy
6. proper 8. suitable 9. capacious,
expansive, opportune 10. convenient
11. comfortable, serviceable
13. accommodating
commodity, commodities ... 5. goods,
wares 6. profit 7. staples
common ... 4. park 5. cheap, plain,
stale, trite, usual 6. mutual, paltry,
vulgar 7. average 8. familiar,
frequent, mediocre, ordinary, plebeian
9. customary, household, universal
11. commonplace
common (pert to) ...
ancestor .. 4. Adam 10. progenitor
funds .. 4. pool 7. tontine
gender .. 6. unisex 7. epicene
informer .. 7. delator
people .. 3. mob 5. demos, gente
6. vulgus 7. demotic 8. populace
commonly accepted ... 7. vulgate
commonly thought ... 8. putative
commonplace ... 5. banal, daily, stale,

theme, trite, usual 6. truism
7. humdrum, prosaic 8. ordinary,
workaday 9. platitude
commonwealth ... 5. group, State
7. society 8. Kentucky, Virginia
9. Australia, community
12. Pennsylvania 13. Massachusetts
commotion ... 3. ado 4. fray, riot,
to–do, whir 5. flare, tizzy 6. flurry,
fracas, hubbub, rumpus, tumult, unrest
7. turmoil 8. foofaraw, uprising
9. agitation, confusion
10. concussion (med), excitement,
turbulence 12. perturbation
commune ... 4. area, soil 5. realm,
share 6. confer, impart 7. kibbutz
8. converse 9. communion
10. commonalty 11. intercourse
(spiritual) 12. conversation
Commune of Paris (1871) ...
10. government
communicate ... 3. say 4. give, join
5. share 6. bestow, impart, inform
7. apprize 8. converse, transmit
9. communion
communication ... 4. word 5. radio
6. letter, report 7. account, contact,
epistle, message 8. buzzword,
feedback 9. statement
10. communique, connection
11. computerese, impartation,
information, intercourse 12. body
language 14. word processing
communion ... 5. share 6. church
7. concord, rapport 8. converse
9. agreement 11. intercourse
12. denomination 13. participation
Communion ... 9. Eucharist, Sacrament
10. intinction, Last Supper
communion (pert to) ...
bread (blessed) .. 4. host 5. wafer
7. eulogia 9. antidoron
cloth .. 8. corporal, corporas
plate .. 5. paten 12. processional
table .. 5. altar
vessel .. 3. ama, pyx
communique ... 4. word 7. message
8. dispatch 13. communication
comose ... 5. hairy 6. tufted
compact ... 4. etui, firm, pact, plot,
snug, trim 5. brief, close, dense,
pithy, press, solid, terse, tight
6. treaty, united, vanity 7. concise,
crowded, entente, leagued, serried
8. alliance, compress, contract,
covenant, succinct 9. agreement,
condensed 10. compressed,
conspiracy 11. compendious,
sententious, stipulation
companion ... 3. pal 4. ally, fare, mate,
twin 5. amigo, crony 6. fellow,
shadow 7. Achates, compeer,
comrade, consort 8. alter ego,
co–worker 9. associate
11. confederate, counterpart
companionship ... 5. amity 7. society
10. fellowship, fraternity
11. comradeship, sociability
13. accompaniment
company ... 3. set 4. band, bevy,
body, crew, gang, ging, host
5. crowd, flock, group, party, troop

6. circle, cohort, throng, troupe
9. concourse, gathering
company (pert to)...
detachment.. 5. posse
people, players.. 4. bevy, crew, gang,
team 5. troop 6. galaxy, guests,
troupe 9. cavalcade
ships.. 5. fleet 6. armada
8. squadron
soldiers.. 5. corps, squad 7. brigade,
phalanx, platoon 9. battalion
travelers.. 7. caravan 8. pilgrims,
tourists 9. merchants
comparative... 5. equal, rival
8. relative 10. comparable, relational
compare... 4. even 5. liken 6. confer,
semble 7. collate, examine
8. contrast
comparison... 6. simile 7. parable
8. likening, metaphor
10. accordance, similarity
11. parallelism
compartment... 3. bin 4. cell, part
5. stall 6. alcove 7. cellule,
chamber, quarter 8. district, division
10. department
compass... 3. arc 4. area, plot, ring
5. guide, range (Mus), reach, solar,
sweep 6. attain, bounds, circle,
curved, degree, extent 7. circuit,
divider, enclose, imagine 8. circular,
distance, surround
compass (pert to)...
housing.. 8. binnacle
part.. 3. pen 6. needle
point.. 4. airt 5. rhumb 7. azimuth
sight.. 4. vane
suspender.. 6. gimbal
compassion... 4. pity, ruth (anc)
5. mercy 8. humanity, sympathy
10. condolence 13. commiseration
compassionate... 6. gentle, humane
7. clement, pitiful 8. merciful
11. sympathetic, warmhearted
12. sympathizing
compatible... 8. affinity, suitable
9. accordant, agreeable, congruous
10. consistent, harmonious
12. congeniality
compeer... 4. mate, peer 5. equal,
match, rival 7. comrade
9. companion
compel... 4. urge 5. drive, force,
impel, press 6. coerce, incite, oblige,
obsess 7. actuate, dragoon, require
9. constrain, influence, instigate
compelling... 6. urgent 7. driving
8. pressing 9. insistent, necessary,
obsessing 10. compulsory
motivating, obligatory, persuasive
compelling assent... 6. cogent
compelling attention... 9. insistent
compendious... 5. brief, short, terse
7. compact, concise 8. abridged,
succinct 9. condensed
10. summarized
compendium... 5. brief 6. abrégé,
digest 7. capsule, epitome, medulla,
pandect, summary 8. abstract,
syllabus, synopsis 9. comprisal
10. abridgment 11. compilation,
contraction 12. abbreviation

compensate... 3. pay 5. atone, repay
6. reward 7. redress, requite
9. indemnify 10. recompense,
remunerate 14. counterbalance
compensation... 3. pay 4. hire
5. bonus, wages 6. manbot
(manbote), reward, salary 7. penalty,
stipend 8. gratuity, pittance, requital,
solatium 9. atonement, indemnity
10. reparation 12. remuneration,
satisfaction 15. indemnification
compete... 3. vie 4. cope 5. match
6. outvie, strive 7. contend, contest,
emulate
competence... 5. means, skill
7. ability, fitness 8. adequacy,
capacity, property 10. capability
efficiency 11. proficiency, sufficiency,
suitability 13. effectiveness,
qualification
competent... 3. apt, can, fit 4. able
5. capax, smart 7. capable
8. adequate, suitable 9. effective,
effectual, efficient, qualified
10. catechumen, sufficient
12. appertaining (to)
competition... 5. match, trial 6. strife
7. contest, rivalry 8. ambition,
concours 9. emulation 10. corrivalry
compilation... 5. cento 6. digest
9. Americana 10. collection
compile... 3. add 4. edit 5. amass
6. gather 8. assemble
complacent... 4. smug 6. bovine
7. fatuous 9. contented, satisfied
11. considerate 13. self–satisfied
complain... 4. beef, carp, fret, kick,
pule, wail 5. gripe, growl, whine
6. accuse, bewail, grieve, grouse,
lament, murmur, mutter, repine,
squawk, yammer 7. deplore, grumble,
protest 9. bellyache
complaint... 6. charge, lament, malady
7. ailment, disease, illness, protest
8. disorder, repining, reproach
9. grievance, murmuring
10. accusation, imputation
11. declaration, lamentation
complaisance... 6. regard 7. amenity,
concern, suavity 8. civility, courtesy,
urbanity 10. indulgence, solicitude,
submission, toleration
13. consideration
complaisant... 4. easy, kind 5. civil
6. polite 7. lenient 8. gracious,
obliging 9. compliant, courteous
complement... 4. crew 7. adjunct
8. addition, complete
10. correspond, supplement
11. counterpart
complete... 3. all, end 4. dead, fill,
full, sole 5. stark, total, utter, whole
6. effect, entire, finish, intact, mature
7. achieve, execute, germane,
perfect, plenary, realize 8. absolute,
conclude, detailed, outright
9. terminate 10. accomplish,
complement, consummate
11. unqualified
completely... 3. all 5. fully, quite,
stark 7. solidly, totally, utterly
8. entirely

completeness... **9.** entelechy, integrity
complex... **4.** mazy **5.** mixed
6. knotty **7.** twisted **8.** involute,
involved **9.** entangled, intricate,
perplexed **10.** interlaced
11. complicated
complexion... **4.** blee, mode, tone
5. color, guise, tinge **10.** appearance
compliance... **6.** assent **7.** consent
9. accession, obedience
10. concession, conformity,
observance, submission
11. willingness **12.** acquiescence
compliant... **6.** docile **7.** duteous,
dutiful, willing **8.** obedient
10. submissive **11.** acquiescent,
complaisant, conformable
complicated... **6.** daedal **7.** complex,
Gordian, snarled, tangled **8.** involved
9. difficult, embroiled, intricate
11. embarrassed **12.** labyrinthine
complication... **4.** node (drama)
5. nodus **7.** illness **9.** complexus
10. complexity **11.** combination
compliment... **6.** praise **7.** adulate,
commend, flatter **8.** encomium,
flattery **12.** blandishment,
commendation **14.** congratulation
comply... **4.** obey **5.** agree, yield
6. accede, accord, assent, submit
7. conform, observe **9.** acquiesce
compone... **6.** settle **7.** arrange,
compose **8.** compound
component... **3.** ion **4.** part **5.** basis
6. factor **7.** element **8.** integral
10. ingredient **11.** constituent
comport... **3.** act **6.** accord, behave
7. conduct **10.** correspond
comportable... **8.** suitable
10. consistent
compose... **3.** pen **4.** calm, form,
make **5.** order, score, write
7. arrange, fashion, prepare
8. compound, melodize **9.** reconcile
10. constitute **11.** orchestrate,
tranquilize
composed... **4.** calm, cool **5.** quiet,
sober, wrote **6.** sedate, serene
7. consist **8.** arranged, tranquil
9. collected **11.** unflappable
composed of...
flat plates.. **9.** lamellate
lobes.. **6.** lobate
composer... **6.** author **7.** idylist
(idyllist) **10.** compositor, typesetter
composer of...
Aida.. **5.** Verdi
Carmen.. **5.** Bizet
Faust.. **6.** Gounod
La Boheme.. **7.** Puccini
Merry Widow.. **5.** Lehar
Mikado.. **8.** Sullivan
Naughty Marietta.. **7.** Herbert
Stars and Stripes Forever.. **5.** Sousa
composition... **4.** opus **5.** piece,
theme **6.** make–up **7.** melange
9. formation, synthesis
12. constitution, construction
composition (pert to)...
literature.. **5.** cento, essay, poesy,
prose **6.** poetry, satire, thesis
8. treatise **10.** brainchild

music.. **2.** op **4.** aria, glee, hymn,
opus **5.** drama, étude, motet, nonet,
opera, rondo, suite **6.** anthem,
septet (septuor), sextet (sestet),
sonata **7.** duetino, quartet
8. concerto, oratorio, postlude,
symphony
composure... **6.** repose **8.** calmness,
coolness, serenity **9.** placidity
10. equanimity, quiescence,
sedateness **11.** tranquility
compound... **3.** mix **4.** olio **5.** agree,
amide, ester, oxide, pyran, unite
6. anisil, elixir, iodide, ketone
7. ammonia, combine, farrago,
metamer **8.** tincture **9.** composite
comprehend... **3.** see **4.** know
5. grasp, sense **6.** embody, fathom
7. enclose, imagine, include, involve,
realize **8.** comprise, conceive
10. understand
comprehensible... **8.** exoteric,
included, knowable **9.** comprised
11. conceivable, discernible,
perceptible **12.** intelligible
comprehensive... **4.** full, wide
5. large **7.** generic, knowing
8. thorough **9.** extensive, inclusive,
universal **11.** compendious
compress... **4.** firm **5.** cling, crowd,
pinch, press, stupe **7.** compact,
densify, embrace, squeeze **8.** astringe,
condense, contract, decrease
comprise, comprize... **5.** imply
6. number **7.** contain, embrace,
enclose, include, involve **8.** perceive
10. comprehend, constitute
compromise... **4.** bind **6.** adjust
8. compound, trade–off **9.** agreement
10. adjustment, concession,
settlement **11.** appeasement,
arbitration
compulsion... **5.** drive, force
6. duress, urging **7.** impulse
8. coaction, coercion **9.** necessity,
obsession **10.** compelling
compulsory... **7.** driving **9.** mandatory,
necessary **10.** compelling, imperative,
obligatory **11.** involuntary
compunction... **3.** rue **5.** guilt, pangs,
qualm **6.** regret **7.** remorse
8. pricking **9.** penitence
11. impenitence **13.** regretfulness
compute... **5.** count, score, tally
6. cipher, figure, number, reckon
8. estimate **9.** calculate, enumerate
computer terms... **3.** bit **4.** byte,
GIGO **5.** BASIC, COBOL, coder, input,
modem **6.** access, analog, glitch
7. digital, FORTRAN **8.** data base
(bank), hard copy, printout, software,
terminal **9.** mainframe, videodisc
10. floppy disc **11.** computerese
12. minicomputer
13. microcomputer, word processor
14. cathode–ray tube
comrade... **3.** pal **4.** ally, chum, mate,
peer **5.** buddy, crony **6.** fellow, frater
7. compeer **8.** camarada, sidekick
9. associate, colleague, companion
con... **2.** no **3.** nay **4.** know, read
5. cheat, learn, steer, study

6. peruse 7. convict, deceive,
swindle 8. memorize, negative
10. understand 13. confidence man

conceal... 4. dern, hide, mask, palm,
veil 5. cloak, cover, derne, eloin,
feign 6. eloign, pocket, screen
7. secrete 8. bescreen, disguise,
enshield

concealed... 5. doggo 6. covert,
hidden, latent, perdue, secret, veiled,
velate 7. covered, larvate, obscure,
unknown, velated 9. disguised,
incognito, insidious 11. clandestine

concede... 3. own 5. admit, agree,
allow, grant, yield 6. accord
7. confess, consent 8. consider
9. surrender 11. acknowledge

conceit... 3. ego 4. idea 5. fancy,
pride 6. vagary, vanity 7. caprice,
egotism, foppery, tympany 8. priggery
12. boastfulness

conceited... 4. smug, vain 5. proud
7. foppish 8. arrogant, boastful,
priggish 9. egotistic, pragmatic
11. egotistical, opinionated
12. stuffed shirt

conceivable... 7. tenable 8. credible
9. plausible 10. believable,
imaginable 12. intelligible

conceive... 5. dream, fancy, think
6. create, devise, ideate 7. imagine,
produce, realize, suppose, suspect
9. originate 10. understand

concentrate... 4. mass 5. focus
6. center 7. compact, densify,
extract 8. condense, converge
9. intensify 10. centralize
11. consolidate

concept... 4. idea 5. image
7. opinion, thought 8. category

conception... 4. idea 5. image, savvy
6. notion 7. conceit, opinion
9. pregnancy 12. apprehension
13. comprehension, understanding

concern... 4. care, firm, sake 5. event,
grief 6. affair, affect, import, matter
7. anxiety, pertain 8. business,
interest, salience 9. relevance
10. importance 12. consequence
12. significance 13. consideration

concerning... 2. of, on, re 3. for
4. over, upon 5. about, anent
9. regarding 10. respecting

concert... 6. aubade 7. recital
9. agreement, unanimity
11. co–operation, performance

concert hall... 5. odeum (odeon)
6. lyceum 7. theater 9. music hall,
playhouse

concession... 5. grant 6. market
7. consent 8. discount
10. compromise, confession
13. qualification

concierge... 6. porter, warden
7. ostiary 8. chokidar 10. doorkeeper

conciliate... 4. ease 6. pacify
7. appease, mollify, placate
9. reconcile 10. propitiate

conciliatory... 6. assent, irenic
8. irenical 9. appeasing, forgiving
10. mollifying

concise... 4. curt, neat 5. brief, crisp,

pithy, terse 6. précis 7. laconic,
pointed, serried, summary 8. succinct
11. compendious, sententious
13. comprehensive

conclude... 3. end 4. rest 5. close,
infer 6. deduce, endeth, finish, settle
7. arrange, presume, resolve,
suppose 8. complete 9. determine,
terminate

conclusion... 3. end 4. last 5. close,
finis 6. finale, finish, result
8. decision, epilogue 9. deduction,
diagnosis, inference 10. completion
13. determination

conclusive... 5. final, valid 8. decisive,
ultimate 9. mandatory
10. convincing, evidential
11. irrefutable, sockdologer (answer)
12. unanswerable

concoct... 3. mix 4. brew, cook, make
6. devise, digest, invent, scheme
7. perfect, prepare 9. fabricate

concoction... 4. dish, plan, plot
6. device 7. mixture 8. compound
9. falsehood, invention
11. combination, fabrication,
preparation

concomitant... 9. accessory, attendant,
co–operant 10. coincident, concurrent
11. synchronous 12. accompanying,
simultaneous

concord... 4. tune 5. chord, peace
6. accord, treaty, unison 7. concert,
harmony, rapport 8. symphony
9. agreement, unanimity

concordant... 8. agreeing, harmonic,
unisonal 9. consonant, unanimous
10. harmonious 11. conformable
13. correspondent

concrete... 4. hard, pave 5. béton,
solid 6. cement 7. congeal, plaster
8. hardness, pavement, solidify
11. substantial

concur... 5. agree, chime, unite
6. accede, assent 7. approve,
combine, consent 9. acquiesce,
co–operate 11. synchronize

concurrence... 6. united 7. joining
9. adherence, concourse, unanimity
11. coincidence, conjunction,
convergence, co–operation, parallelism

concurrent... 5. joint 6. united
7. meeting, uniting 8. parallel,
syndrome 9. unanimous
10. associated, coincident, synergetic
11. co–operative, synchronous
12. accompanying, simultaneous

concussion... 5. clash, shock, smash,
wound 6. injury, trauma 9. collision

condemn... 3. ban 4. doom 5. blame,
decry 7. adjudge, censure, convict
8. penalize, sentence

condense... 3. mix 5. unite 6. absorb,
decoct, deepen, harden, lessen,
narrow, reduce 7. abridge, combine,
compact, densify, enhance, shorten,
squeeze, thicken 8. compress,
contract, diminish, heighten, solidify
9. constrict, intensify
11. concentrate, consolidate

condensed... 7. compact, concise,
cramped, tabloid 9. shortened

10. compressed, contracted
12. concentrated

condenser (anc) . . . 9. Leyden jar

condescend . . . 5. deign, stoop
6. submit, unbend 7. concede,
descend 9. patronize, vouchsafe

condign . . . 3. fit 4. just 6. severe,
worthy 7. fitting 8. adequate,
deserved, suitable

condiment . . . 3. soy 4. dill, mace,
mint, sage, salt 5. chili, clove, curry,
sauce, spice 6. catsup, garlic,
ginger, nutmeg, pepper, relish
7. cayenne, ketchup, mustard,
paprika, vinegar 9. seasoning
10. peppermint

condition . . . 2. if 4. case, haze, rank,
term 5. covin, limit, stage, state
6. estate, fettle, health, plight, status
7. posture, proviso, quality, station
8. capacity, position, standing
9. requisite, situation 10. limitation
11. predicament 12. circumstance

condition (pert to) . . .
favorable . . 4. odds
flushed . . 4. rosy
habitual . . 5. tenor
hypnotic . . 4. daze 6. stupor, trance
7. narcose
made . . 7. premise
murk . . 3. fog 4. haze, mist 5. gloom
proper . . 6. kilter
stipulation . . 7. proviso

conditionally . . . 2. if 8. provided
11. tentatively 13. provisionally

condone . . . 5. remit 6. accept, excuse,
pardon 7. absolve, forgive 8. tolerate
11. countenance

condor . . . 6. falcon 7. vulture

conduce . . . 4. lend, tend 5. serve
6. effect 7. advance, dispose,
incline, redound 10. contribute

conducive . . . 6. useful 7. helpful
11. implemental, serviceable
12. instrumental

conduct . . . 3. act, run 4. lead, mien,
rule 5. guide, usage, usher
6. action, convey, convoy, direct,
escort, govern, manage 7. bearing,
comport, control, manners
8. behavior, demeanor, regulate
9. operation, supervise
10. deportment, management
11. comportment, superintend

conduct (pert to) . . .
a cause . . 5. plead
breach . . 6. guilty
doctrine of . . 6. morals
one's self . . 6. behave, demean
7. comport

conducting inward . . . 9. afference

conductor . . . 5. guide 6. escort, leader
7. cathode, maestro, manager
8. cicerone, director, operator,
trainman

conduit . . . 3. way 4. adit, duct, pain,
pipe, tube 5. canal, sewer 6. course
7. channel 8. aqueduct

cone (pert to) . . .
conelike . . 5. conic 6. pineal
7. conical
pine . . 8. strobile

silver . . 4. pina
tree . . 5. larch 7. conifer

confab, confabulation . . . 4. chat, talk
7. palaver, prattle 8. chinfest, talkfest
12. conversation

confection . . . 3. jam 5. candy, dulce,
icing, jelly 6. cimbal, comfit, nougat,
sweets 7. caramel, fondant, praline,
succade 8. preserve 9. sweetmeat
11. bittersweet, marshmallow

confederacy . . . 5. cabal, hanse, union
6. fusion, league 8. alliance,
covenant 9. coalition 10. complicity,
conspiracy, federation 11. affiliation,
association, combination
13. consolidation

confederate . . . 3. pal, reb 4. ally
5. stall 7. abettor 9. accessory,
assistant, associate, auxiliary
10. accomplice

confer . . . 4. give 6. advise, bestow,
invest, parley 7. collate, commune,
consign, consult, counsel 8. ordinate
(knighthood) 10. deliberate

conference . . . 5. trust 6. huddle,
parley, powwow 7. council, palaver
9. interview 10. discussion
12. consultation

conferring respect . . . 9. honorific

conferring title . . . 9. ennobling

confess . . . 3. own, rue 4. avow
5. admit, own up 6. regret, repent,
reveal, shrive 7. concede
11. acknowledge

confession . . . 5. credo (of faith), creed
6. avowal, shrift 9. admission,
communion 10. profession
14. acknowledgment
(acknowledgement)

confetti . . . 5. paper 6. ribbon
7. bonbons 9. cascarons (in
eggshells) 10. sweetmeats
11. confections

confidant . . . 6. friend 8. intimate

confide . . . 4. hope, rely 5. trust
6. commit, depend, repose

confidence . . . 5. faith, poise 6. belief,
morals, secret 7. courage
8. credence, sureness 9. assurance,
impudence 10. effrontery
12. impertinence

confident . . . 4. smug, sure 6. secure
7. assured, certain, hopeful, reliant
8. cocksure, positive, sanguine,
unafraid 9. convinced 10. determined

confidential . . . 5. privy 6. secret
7. private 8. esoteric, intimate
9. auricular 10. unquotable
11. trustworthy

confidentially . . . 7. sub rosa

configuration . . . 4. form 5. shape
6. figure 7. contour, Gestalt, pattern
8. asterism 13. constellation

confine . . . 3. dam, hem, mew, pen,
sty, tie 4. bind, cage, coop, jail,
lock 5. bound, limit, stint 6. border,
immure, intern, secure, strain
7. compass 8. imprison, restrain
9. enclosure 11. incarcerate,
restriction 12. circumscribe

confined . . . 4. pent 5. bound, caged
6. shut–in 7. cribbed, endemic,

limited 8. esoteric, impended,
interned 9. bedridden, impounded,
invalided, parochial
confinement... 5. limbo 7. durance,
lying–in 9. detention, isolation,
restraint 10. cabin fever, childbirth
12. accouchement, imprisonment
13. incommunicado
15. circumscription
confirm... 4. seal 5. prove 6. assure,
attest, ratify, settle, verify 7. approve,
fortify, sustain 8. convince, sanction,
validate 9. establish 11. corroborate
12. substantiate
confirmed... 6. proved 7. chronic
8. habitual, ratified 10. encouraged,
inveterate 11. established
confiscate... 5. seize, usurp
7. impound 11. appropriate
conflagrant... 5. afire 6. ablaze,
aflame 7. blazing, burning
conflagration... 4. fire 5. blaze, fever
8. wildfire 9. holocaust
12. inflammation
conflict... 3. war 4. bout, duel, fray
5. clash, fight, run–in 6. action,
battle, combat, oppose, strife, tussle
7. contend, contest, discord
8. clashing, struggle 9. antipathy,
collision, encounter, hostility
10. contention, donnybrook,
opposition 11. competition
confluence... 4. flow 5. crowd
6. stream 7. flowing (together),
meeting 8. junction 10. assemblage
11. concurrence, convergence
12. assimilation
conform... 2. go 3. fit 4. lean, obey,
suit 5. adapt, agree 6. adjust,
concur, settle 7. compose, consent,
observe 8. coincide, fine–tune
9. reconcile 11. accommodate
conformity... 6. dharma 7. harmony
8. legality, symmetry 9. agreement,
congruity 10. compliance
15. conventionality
confound... 3. mix 5. abash, amaze
6. baffle, dismay, puzzle, thwart
7. astound, buffalo, mystify, nonplus,
perplex 8. astonish, bewilder
9. dumbfound, embarrass, frustrate
10. complicate, contradict, disconcert
11. intermingle
confront... 4. face, meet 5. front
6. oppose 7. compare 9. encounter
confrontation... 6. crisis 7. face–off
8. showdown 9. encounter
10. opposition
confuse... 3. mix 4. maze 5. abash,
addle, upset 6. baffle, flurry, jumble,
muddle 7. derange, fluster
8. befuddle, bewilder, disorder,
distract, entangle 9. embrangle
10. complicate, disarrange,
discompose, disconcert
confused... 7. chaotic, jumbled, rattled
8. deranged 9. chagrined, flustered,
perplexed, uncertain 10. indistinct
confusion... 3. ado, din 4. mess, moil
5. babel, chaos 6. jumble, pother,
welter 7. anarchy, clutter, turmoil
8. disarray, disorder 9. abashment,

agitation 10. perplexity
11. derangement 12. bewilderment
13. embarrassment
confute... 4. deny 5. rebut 6. answer,
expose, refute 7. dismiss
8. confound, overcome, redargue
9. overwhelm (by argument)
congeal... 3. gel, ice, set 4. rime
6. freeze 7. pectize, thicken
congenial... 4. boon 7. kindred
8. friendly 9. accordant, agreeable
10. affinitive, compatible
11. sympathetic
congenital... 6. inborn, innate
7. connate, genetic, natural
14. constitutional
conger... 3. eel 8. cucumber
13. Leptocephalus
congeries... 4. heap 9. amassment
10. collection 11. aggregation
congestion... 3. jam 4. heap
8. fullness, stoppage 9. gathering
11. obstruction 12. accumulation
Congo...
  capital.. 11. Brazzaville
  city.. 6. Makoua 7. Louboma
  port.. 11. Pointe Noire
  river.. 5. Congo (Zaire) 6. Sangha
congratulate... 4. laud 5. bless
6. salute 7. rejoice 8. macarize
10. compliment, felicitate
congregate... 4. herd, mass, meet
5. group, troop 6. gather, muster
7. collect 8. assemble 9. forgather
congregation... 4. mass 5. house,
laity 7. council 8. assembly, audience
9. gathering 10. collection
11. churchgoers
congress... 4. diet 5. synod
6. durbar, indaba, soviet 7. council,
meeting 8. assembly, conclave
9. Sanhedrin 10. convention,
parliament 11. convergence,
convocation, legislature
12. congregation
congruous... 3. fit 4. meet 6. proper
7. fitting 8. agreeing, becoming,
suitable 9. consonant
conic, conical... 8. parabola
9. pyramidal 10. cone–shaped,
funnellike
conifers... 4. yews 5. pines 6. cedars
7. larches, Pinales, Sabines, spruces,
Torreys 8. hemlocks, Soledads
9. Coniferae, Corsicans
10. evergreens
conjecture... 3. aim 5. ettle, guess,
opine, think 6. divine 7. conjoin,
imagine, presume, suppose, surmise,
suspect 8. supposal 9. inference
10. assumption, hypothesis
11. supposition
conjoin... 4. join, link, yoke 5. hitch,
unite 6. adjoin, concur 7. combine,
connect 8. corelate 9. correlate
conjoined parts... 6. adnexa
conjointly... 10. hand–in–hand
conjugal... 7. marital, nuptial
9. connubial 11. matrimonial
conjugate... 4. join 5. yoked
6. couple, united 7. coupled, related
8. bijugate, combined

10. paronymous 12. etymological
conjugation... 5. union 6. fusion
7. duality, joining, uniting
10. assemblage 11. combination
13. juxtaposition
conjunct... 6. united 8. combined
9. conjoined, corporate
conjunction... 2. as, et, if, or 3. and,
but, nor 4. than, that 5. since,
union 6. casual, though 7. whether
10. connection 11. adversative,
association, combination, concurrence,
correlative
conjure... 4. pray 5. charm 6. adjure,
enjoin, invoke, juggle, summon
(magic) 7. beseech, enchant, entreat,
implore 10. supplicate
conjure (up)... 5. raise 6. call up
8. exorcise (exorcize), remember
9. visualize
conjurer, conjuror... 4. mage
6. voodoo, wizard 7. juggler
8. exorcist, magician
conk... 4. head, nose 5. decay (tree)
conk out... 4. fade, fail 5. stall
6. fizzle, perish, weaken
connate... 4. akin 6. allied 7. cognate,
related, similar 9. congenial
10. congenital
connect... 3. tie 4. ally, join, link,
meet 5. unite 6. adjoin, attach,
couple, enlink, fasten, relate
7. bracket, succeed 9. associate,
hyphenate
connected... 3. met 5. telic
6. adnate, joined 7. serried, similar
8. coherent, inlinked, syndetic
10. continuous, correlated
Connecticut...
capital.. 8. Hartford
city.. 6. Darien, Mystic 7. Meriden
8. Hartford, New Haven 9. Waterbury
10. Bridgeport
college (famed).. 4. Yale (1701)
historic site.. 10. Charter Oak (1687,
Hartford)
museum.. 6. Barnum (P T)
river.. 6. Thames 9. Naugatuck
10. Hoosatonic 11. Connecticut
State admission.. 5. Fifth
State Motto.. 21. Qui Transtulit
Sustinet (He Who Transplants
Sustains)
State nickname.. 6. Nutmeg
12. Constitution
connecting link... 3. tie 4. bond
6. connex 7. kiaison 8. ligament,
vinculum 11. intermedium
12. intermediary
connection... 4. bond 5. nexus, union
6. clevis, family, series 7. kinship,
passage 8. alliance, commerce,
junction, relation 9. coherence,
go—between, relevance 10. continuity
11. association, intercourse
12. intermediary, relationship
13. communication, juxtaposition
conner... 5. pilot 6. balker, tester
7. peruser 8. examiner 9. inspector
connive... 4. plot, wink 5. blink
6. scheme 7. collude, complot,
finagle 8. conspire, contrive,

maneuver, overlook
conniving... 8. scheming 9. collusive,
deceitful 10. conspiring
11. calculating
connoisseur... 5. judge 6. expert
7. epicure, gourmet 8. gourmand
11. cognoscente, connaisseur
connotation... 5. sense 6. import,
intent 7. meaning, purport
10. denotation 11. implication
12. significance 13. comprehension
connubial... 7. martial, nuptial
8. conjugal 11. matrimonial
12. epithalamium (song)
conquer... 3. win 4. beat, best
5. crush 6. defeat, humble, master,
reduce, subdue 7. subject
8. overcome, overturn, surmount,
vanquish 9. discomfit, overpower,
overthrow, subjugate
conqueror... 4. hero 6. captor, Cortez,
victor, winner 7. subduer
10. subjugator 12. conquistador
conquest... 6. Norman (1066)
7. mastery, triumph, victory
consanguinity... 5. nabob 7. kinship,
sibship 8. affinity, relation (blood)
12. relationship
conscience... 4. mind, self 6. psyche
8. superego 9. casuistry
conscientious... 7. dutiful, servile
8. faithful 10. fastidious, meticulous,
scrupulous 11. punctilious
conscientious objection... 7. scruple
conscious... 4. keen 5. alive, awake,
aware, vital 7. animate, feeling
8. sensible, sentient 9. breathing,
cognizant 13. self—conscious
consecrate... 4. sain 5. bless, exalt
6. anoint, devote, hallow, ordain
7. glorify 8. dedicate, sanctify
consecrated (pert to)...
bread.. 4. host 5. wafer
oil.. 6. chrism
thing.. 6. sacrum
consent... 4. give 5. agree, grant,
yield 6. accede, accord, assent,
concur, permit 8. approval
9. acquiesce 10. compliance,
permission 11. concurrence
13. understanding
consequence... 3. end 5. event
6. course, effect, result, weight
7. dignity, outcome 8. pursuant (in),
sequence 9. aftermath, inference,
influence, loftiness, outgrowth
10. importance, notability
11. distinction
consequential... 7. pompous
8. eventual 9. important
13. self—important
consequently... 2. do 4. ergo, then
5. hence 9. as a result, therefore,
wherefore 12. subsequently
13. consecutively
conservative... 4. Tory 5. staid
7. die—hard, fogyish, old—line
8. moderate 10. long—haired
11. reactionary 12. preservative
13. unprogressive
conserve... 3. jam 4. save 5. guard,
uvate 6. defend, secure, shield,

uphold 7. protect, sustain
8. maintain 9. preserves, sweetmeat
consider... 3. ain, see 4. care, deem,
heed, muse, rate 5. judge, think,
treat, weigh 6. esteem, intend,
ponder, regard 7. discuss, examine,
reflect, revolve 8. cogitate, meditate,
ruminate 10. deliberate
11. contemplate
considerable... 5. great, large
7. notable, several 8. numerous
9. important 10. noteworthy,
remarkable 13. authoritative
considerate... 4. kind 6. gentle
7. careful, heedful, prudent, serious
8. obliging 9. attentive, judicious
10. deliberate, reflective, solicitous,
thoughtful
consideration... 4. self 5. study
6. esteem, regard 7. respect,
thought 9. attention, deference,
incentive, influence 10. cogitation,
importance, meditation, reflection,
reputation, rumination
11. examination 12. compensation,
deliberation
considering... 2. if 5. since 8. after
all, inasmuch, in view of
consign... 5. allot 6. assign, commit,
devote, remand, resign 7. deliver,
entrust 8. transfer 11. subscribe to
consignee... 6. factor 7. awardee
8. assignee 9. committee
consign to...
a place.. 8. allocate
prison.. 6. commit, send up
ruin.. 4. doom
unimportance.. 8. relegate
consistent... 5. equal, solid, stiff
7. equable, logical, uniform
8. coherent 9. agreement,
consonant, steadfast 10. persisting
consisting of...
cavities.. 9. cellulose
layers (thin).. 8. laminate
names.. 8. onomatic
one word.. 7. monepic
pages.. 7. paginal
three measures.. 8. trimeter
three spots.. 4. trey
three styles (Bot).. 10. tristylous
two parts.. 6. binary
consist of... 5. imply 6. embody
7. contain, embrace, enclose, involve
8. comprise (comprize)
consolation... 6. solace 7. comfort
10. condolence
console... 4. desk 5. cheer, organ,
table 6. solace, soothe 7. bracket,
cabinet, comfort, support, sustain
9. alleviate, encourage
consolidate... 4. knit, mass 5. merge,
unify, unite 7. combine, densify
8. coalesce, compress, organize,
solidify 9. intensify 10. strengthen
consonant... 4. lene, surd 5. lenis,
nasal, velar 6. dental, labial
7. lingual, palatal, spirate 8. gutteral
9. accordant, congruous
10. compatible, concordant,
consistent
consonant (pert to)...

hissing.. 8. sibilant
rustling.. 9. fricative
voiceless (breathed).. 6. atonic
7. spirate
consort... 4. Devi (of Siva), mate, wife
5. group, Sakti 6. mingle, spouse
7. husband, partner 9. associate,
colleague, companion, harmonize
11. combination, confederate,
conjunction
conspicuous... 6. famous, signal
7. eminent, glaring, obvious, salient,
visible 8. distinct, lionized, manifest,
striking 9. important, prominent
10. celebrated, noticeable, remarkable
11. illustrious, outstanding
13. distinguished
conspiracy... 4. plot 5. cabal, unite
6. scheme 8. intrigue 9. collusion
10. connivance 11. confederacy,
machination
conspire... 4. plot 5. unite 6. concur,
scheme 7. collude, complot, finagle
9. fainaigue 11. confederate
constable... 3. cop 5. staff 6. beadle,
keeper, warden 7. bailiff 8. tipstaff
9. policeman
constabulary... 6. bureau (police)
10. constables
constancy... 4. zeal 5. ardor, faith,
truth 6. fealty, garnet (symbol)
7. honesty, loyalty 8. devotion,
fidelity 9. adherence, continual,
eagerness, integrity, stability
10. allegiance, attachment,
permanence, perpetuity, uniformity
11. devotedness, earnestness
12. faithfulness
constant... 4. firm, true 5. fixed
7. regular, uniform 8. faithful,
resolute 9. continual, invariant,
parameter (Math), perpetual, steadfast
10. continuous, invariable, persistent
12. unchangeable
constant desire... 4. itch 9. hankering
Constantine (pert to)...
birthplace.. 4. Nish (Nis) 7. Naissus
(now Yugoslavia)
known as.. 8. The Great
title.. 7. Emperor (Rome)
Constantinople...
official name.. 8. Istanbul
patriarch.. 9. Nestorius
site.. 6. Turkey (Eur)
constellation... 5. stars 6. galaxy
8. asterism 10. luminaries
13. configuration (stars)
Constellations (partial list)...
arrow.. 7. Sagitta
bears (Dipper).. 9. Ursa Major, Ursa
Minor
Bird of Paradise (S Pole).. 4. Apus
bull.. 6. Taurus
crab.. 6. Cancer
crane.. 4. Grus
dog.. 5. Canis
dragon.. 5. Draco
eagle.. 6. Aquila
fishes.. 6. Pisces
goat.. 9. Capricorn
goldfish.. 6. Dorado
hunter.. 5. Orion (most conspicuous)

lion.. 3. Leo
Noah's Ark.. 4. Argo
Northern Crown.. 14. Corona Borealis,
  Northern Lights
peacock.. 4. Pava
scorpion.. 7. Scorpio
serpent (sea).. 5. Hydra
Southern Cross.. 4. Crux
swan.. 6. Cygnus
Twins.. 6. Gemini
virgin.. 5. Virgo
water bearer.. 8. Aquarius
whale.. 6. Cestus
winged horse.. 7. Pegasus
wolf.. 5. Lupus
Constellations' brightest star...
  3. Cor
Constellations of the Zodiac...
  3. Leo 5. Aries, Libra, Virgo
  6. Cancer, Gemini, Pisces, Taurus
  7. Scorpio 8. Aquarius
  11. Capricornus, Sagittarius
constituent... 5. voter 6. factor,
  matter 7. elector, element, essence
  8. elective 9. component
  10. ingredient 11. determinant
  (Math)
constituent of...
blood serum.. 7. opsonin
coal.. 6. carbon
coffee, tea.. 8. caffeine
hair, nails.. 7. keratin
oil of cloves.. 7. eugenol
constitute... 4. form 5. enact, found
  6. create, depute 7. appoint,
  compose 8. legalize 9. determine,
  establish
constitution... 3. law 6. crasis,
  custom 7. passage 8. creation
  9. enactment, essential, ordinance,
  structure 11. composition, institution
  12. organization
Constitution (ship)... 12. Old Ironsides
constitutional... 5. legal, valid
  6. innate 9. essential, healthful
  12. governmental 13. dispositional
constitutional (pert to)...
health.. 4. walk 8. exercise
right.. 9. franchise
temperament.. 6. crasis
vigor.. 5. nerve
Constitution State... 11. Connecticut
constrain... 4. curb, urge 5. chain,
  check, drive, force, impel, press
  6. compel, oblige 7. confine, repress
  8. restrain 11. necessitate
constrained... 6. forced, modest
  7. cramped 8. moderate, reserved
  9. obligated
constraint... 4. bond, urge 5. force
  6. duress, stress 7. modesty, reserve
  8. coercion, pressure 9. restraint,
  stiffness 10. compulsion, moderation
  11. confinement
constrict... 3. tie 4. bind 5. cramp
  6. narrow, shrink 7. squeeze, tighten
  8. astringe, condense, contract
  10. constringe
constriction... 9. narrowing, stricture,
  tightness 11. contraction
  13. strangulation
constrictor... 3. boa 5. snake

7. serpent, styptic 9. sphincter
10. compressor
construct... 4. make, rear 5. build,
  erect, frame 6. create 7. compose
  9. establish, fabricate, originate
constructive... 7. virtual 8. creative,
  implicit 9. anabolism 10. suggestive
  14. interpretation, interpretative
construe... 5. parse 6. deduce, render
  7. explain 9. interpret, translate
consuetude... 5. habit, usage
  6. custom
consuetudinary... 6. manual (customs),
  ritual 9. customary
consult (with)... 6. advise, confer, take
  up 7. discuss 10. deliberate
consultation... 7. counsel 8. audition,
  congress 9. interview 10. conference,
  discussion 12. deliberation
consume... 3. eat, use 4. burn
  5. spend, waste 6. absorb, devour,
  expend 7. destroy (fire) 8. squander
  9. dissipate 12. disintegrate
consumed... 3. pau
consummate... 3. end, top 4. ripe
  5. ideal 6. finish, utmost 7. achieve,
  perfect 8. complete 10. accomplish
consumption... 3. use 4. loss
  5. decay, waste 6. eating
  7. disease, using up 8. phthisis
  9. decrement 11. destruction
  12. tuberculosis 13. deterioration
contact... 4. meet 5. touch, union
  6. impact, syzygy (Astron)
  7. meeting, oscnode (Math)
  8. junction, tangency, touching
  10. contiguity 13. communication
contain... 4. have, hold, keep 5. cover
  6. embody, number, retain
  7. embrace, enclose, include, involve,
  subsume 8. comprise, restrain
  9. divisible (by) 10. comprehend
container... 3. bag, bin, box, can,
  cup, jug, lug, pan, pod, pot, tin,
  tub, urn, vat 4. case, crib, ewer,
  pail, sack, vase 5. crate, cruet,
  pouch 6. basket, bottle, carboy,
  carton, hamper, hatbox 7. capsule,
  hanaper 8. canister, decanter
containing...
air.. 9. pneumatic
antimony.. 8. stibiate
boron.. 5. boric 7. boracic
carbon.. 7. organic 13. carboniferous
copper.. 6. cupric
fire.. 7. igneous
gold.. 4. doré 5. auric
iron.. 6. ferric
silver.. 5. lunar
slag.. 6. drossy
ten.. 6. denary
tin.. 7. stannic
containing maxims... 6. gnomic
contaminate... 4. slur, soil 5. stain,
  sully, taint 6. befoul, defile, infect,
  poison 7. corrupt, debauch, degrade,
  pollute, vitiate 8. dishonor
  9. desecrate 10. adulterate
contemn... 4. defy, hate 5. scorn,
  spurn 6. reject 7. despise, disdain
contemplate... 4. muse, plan, scan,
  view 5. study 6. design, expect,

intend, ponder 7. examine, foresee,
propose 8. consider, envision,
meditate
contemplation... 5. study 6. musing
7. theoria, thought 8. scrutiny
9. foresight, intuition 10. expectancy,
reflection 11. examination,
expectation, speculation
contemplative... 6. sedate 7. pensive
10. meditative, reflective, ruminative,
thoughtful 11. speculative
13. retrospective
contemporary... 6. coeval 7. present
10. coetaneous, coexistent,
coincident 11. concomitant,
synchronous 12. simultaneous
15. contemporaneous
contempt... 4. fico, geck 5. scorn,
shame, sneer 7. despect, disdain
8. defiance, derision, ridicule
9. arrogance, contumely
10. disrespect 12. disobedience
contemptible... 3. low 4. base
5. cheap, petty, sorry 6. abject,
paltry, sordid 7. pitiful 8. beggarly,
inferior, unworthy 9. groveling,
worthless 10. despicable
13. insignificant
contemptuous... 6. sneery 7. haughty
8. insolent, scornful 10. disdainful
12. contumelious, supercilious
contemptuous action... 9. indignity
10. incivility
contend... 3. vie, war 4. cope, deal,
race 5. argue, fight 6. assert, bicker,
insist, strive 7. compete, contest,
grapple, quarrel, wrangle 8. contrive,
maintain, militate
content, contents... 4. list, room
5. index, space 6. amount, please,
volume 7. filling, gratify, makings,
satisfy, suffice 8. capacity
9. contented, happiness, satisfied
10. components, dimensions
11. ingredients
contention... 3. war 4. feud
6. combat, debate, strife 7. quarrel,
rivalry 8. argument, conflict, struggle,
variance 9. emulation 10. dissension,
litigation 11. altercation, competition,
controversy 12. disagreement
contentious... 7. peevish 8. perverse
9. combative, litigious, wrangling
10. pugnacious 11. belligerent,
dissentious, quarrelsome
13. argumentative
contentment... 4. ease 5. bliss
8. pleasure 11. peace of mind
12. satisfaction 13. contentedness,
gratification
conterminous... 4. next 8. abutting,
adjacent, proximal 9. adjoining
contest... 3. sue, vie 4. agon, bout,
cope, deny, game, race, tilt
5. argue, set—to, trial 6. debate,
oppose, strife, strive, tryout
7. contend, dispute, tourney, wrangle
8. argument, disclaim, litigate,
skirmish, struggle 9. emulation
10. engagement 11. altercation,
competition
contest (pert to)...

art of.. 10. agonistics
draw.. 9. stalemate
log hurling.. 5. roleo
prize.. 5. stake
undecided.. 4. draw
contestant... 5. rival 6. player
7. athlete, entrant 8. opponent
9. candidate, combatant, contender
10. competitor
contiguous... 4. near, next
8. adjacent, touching 9. adjoining,
immediate, proximate 11. neighboring
Continent... 4. Asia 6. Africa, Europe
7. Eurasia, Lemuria 8. Atlantis (lost),
Cascadia 9. Australia, Greenland
10. Antarctica 12. North America,
South America
contingency... 4. case 5. event
6. chance 8. accident, casualty,
exigency, juncture 9. emergency,
liability 11. eventuality, possibility,
uncertainty
contingent... 6. casual 8. eventual
9. dependent (law), provisory
10. accidental, fortuitous, incidental
11. conditional, provisional
continual... 7. endless, eternal, regular,
undying, uniform 8. constant,
enduring, frequent, unbroken
9. ceaseless, connected, continued,
incessant, perennial, permanent,
perpetual, unceasing 10. continuous,
invariable 11. everlasting, intermitted,
unremitting 12. imperishable
13. uninterrupted
continually... 3. aye 4. ever 5. often
7. eternal 9. eternally 10. constantly
11. perpetually, unceasingly
12. continuously
continuation... 6. sequel 8. addition,
sequence 10. continuity
11. continuance, propagation,
protraction 12. postponement,
prolongation
continue... 3. run 4. go on, last, stay
5. abide 6. endure, extend, remain,
resume 7. perdure, persist, proceed,
sustain 8. protract 9. persevere,
steadfast (be)
continuing... 5. still 7. chronic,
durable, lasting 9. permanent
10. continuous 11. persevering
continuous... 7. chronic, endless,
uniform 8. unbroken 9. continued,
perpetual 13. uninterrupted
contorted... 3. wry 4. bent 6. coiled,
warped 7. garbled, gnarled, twisted,
wristed 8. deformed 9. perverted
contour... 4. form, line 5. curve,
graph 6. figure 7. isobase, outline,
profile 9. lineament, periphery
13. configuration
contra... 6. offset 7. against, counter,
reverse 8. contrary, opposite 9. vice
versa 10. conversely 12. contrariwise
contraband... 7. bootleg, illegal, illicit
8. unlawful 9. moonshine
10. prohibited
contract... 4. hale, knit, pact 5. incur,
lease 6. cartel, engage, pledge,
reduce, shrink 7. bargain, compact,
promise, shorten, shrivel 8. covenant

9. agreement, constrict, indenture
10. convention, obligation, straighten
11. arrangement 13. understanding
contraction... 3. tic 4. coup, fist
5. spasm 7. elision, systole
8. decrease 9. reduction, short—hand,
stricture 11. compression
contrada... 3. way 4. ward 6. street
7. quarter
contradict... 4. deny 5. belie, rebut
6. impugn, negate, oppose, refute
7. gainsay 10. counteract
contradiction... 6. denial 7. paradox
10. opposition, refutation
11. contrariety 13. counteraction
contradictory... 7. denying 8. contrary,
opposite 10. refutatory
12. inconsistent
contrary... 7. adverse, counter,
froward, opposed, reverse
8. captious, inimical, opposite,
perverse, refutive 9. different,
repugnant 10. discordant, unorthodox
12. antagonistic
contrast... 7. compare 8. opposite
11. contrariety
contravene... 4. defy 6. hinder,
oppose, refute, thwart 7. violate
8. infringe 9. disregard
contravention... 6. denial 9. violation
10. opposition, refutation
contribute... 3. aid 4. give 6. donate
7. benefit, conduce, provide
9. subscribe
contribution... 3. tax, tip 4. boon,
gift, scot 6. tariff 7. payment, tribute
8. donation 12. subscription
13. participation
contrite... 6. abject, humble
8. penitent 9. repentant, sorrowful
10. remorseful 11. penitential
contrition... 7. remorse 9. attrition,
penitence 11. compunction
contrivance... 3. art 5. means, shift
6. design, devise 7. coinage,
machine, measure, project 8. artifice,
intrigue 9. expedient, invention,
makeshift 11. contraption
contrive... 4. plan, plot 5. frame,
hatch, weave 6. design, devise,
invent, manage, scheme 7. fashion,
project 9. fabricate
control... 4. hold, rein, rule, sway, test
5. check, gripe, guide, leash, power,
wield 6. direct, govern, manage,
subdue 7. conduct, mastery, preside,
regimen 8. dominate, dominion,
ironhand, regulate, restrain
9. direction, influence, regulator,
restraint 10. management, regulation
11. self—control, superintend
controller, comptroller... 7. auditor
8. governor 9. dominator, regulator
controversial... 7. eristic, polemic
9. eristical, polemical, pro and con
11. contentious 12. disputatious,
questionable 13. argumentative
controversy... 6. debate 7. dispute,
quarrel, wrangle 8. argument
10. contention 11. altercation
12. disagreement, disputatious
controvert... 4. deny, moot 5. argue

6. debate, oppose, refute 7. discuss,
dispute 10. contradict
contumacious... 6. unruly 7. riotous
8. mutinous, perverse 9. seditious
10. headstrong, rebellious, refractory,
unyielding 11. disobedient, intractable
12. ungovernable 13. insubordinate
contumelious... 7. haughty 8. insolent
9. insulting 10. derogatory,
despiteful, disdainful
12. contemptuous
contumely... 5. scorn 8. contempt
9. indignity, insolence 10. revilement
11. humiliation, malediction
contusion... 4. blow 6. bruise, injury
8. black eye 13. discoloration
conundrum... 5. rebus 6. enigma,
puzzle, riddle 7. charade
convalesce... 5. rally 7. recover,
recruit 10. recuperate
convene... 3. sit 4. come, meet
5. unite 6. summon 8. assemble
10. congregate, foregather
convenient... 5. handy, ready 6. fitted,
nearby, suited, timely 7. adapted
8. suitable 9. agreeable, available,
opportune 10. accessible,
commodious, seasonable
11. comfortable
convent... 4. meet 6. concur, friary,
priory 7. convene, nunnery
8. cloister, lamasery 9. monastery,
sanctuary
convention... 4. rule 5. usage
6. accord, custom 7. meeting
8. assembly 9. gathering, tradition
10. assemblage, compliance,
conformity
conventional... 5. fixed, nomic, usual
6. formal, modish 7. correct
8. accepted, orthodox 9. customary
10. ceremonial 11. established,
traditional
converge... 4. meet 5. focus, unite
conversant (with)... 5. adept 6. expert,
versed (in) 7. skilled 8. familiar
9. practiced 10. acquainted,
proficient
conversation... 4. chat, talk 7. trialog
8. causerie, converse, dialogue
9. communion, discourse
10. conference 11. association
13. conversazione, interlocution
conversationalist... 6. talker
9. converser 10. discourser
12. confabulator
convey... 4. cede, deed, pass, send
5. bring, carry, eloin, grant
6. assign, convoy, demise, devise,
impart, import 7. dispone 8. transfer,
transmit 9. transport 10. commission
11. communicate
conveyance... 3. bus, car, van
4. auto, sled, taxi, tram 5. plane,
train 6. demise, litter 7. cession,
norimon, trailer, vehicle 8. airplane,
carriage 10. automobile
conveyer, conveyor... 6. bearer,
coolie, pigeon (homing), porter
7. bheesty, carrier 8. cargador
9. stevedore
convict... 4. damn 5. felon, lifer

6. refute, termer, trusty 7. condemn, culprit 6. refute 8. criminal, prisoner 10. malefactor

conviction ... 4. hope 6. belief 7. opinion 9. certainty 10. persuasion 12. condemnation

convince ... 6. assure, subdue 7. confute, jawbone 8. overcome, persuade 9. overpower

convincing ... 5. proof 6. cogent, potent 7. telling 8. assuring 10. conclusive, persuasive, satisfying

convivial ... 3. gay 4. gala 5. jolly, merry 6. festal, jovial, joyful, joyous, social 7. festive, jocular 9. hilarious

convocation ... 4. diet 5. synod 7. bidding, council, meeting, summons 8. assembly, congress 10. convention 12. congregation

convoke ... 4. call 6. summon 7. convene 8. assemble

convoy ... 5. guard, guide 6. attend, escort 7. conduct 8. navigate 9. accompany, conductor

convulse ... 5. amuse, shake 6. regale 7. agitate, disturb, torture 9. entertain 10. discompose

convulsion ... 5. cramp, spasm, throe 6. tumult, uproar 8. laughter, paroxysm 9. agitation, commotion 10. revolution 12. disturbance

cony, coney ... 3. das, fur 4. dupe, hare, pika 5. daman, hyrax 6. burbot, rabbit

cony catcher ... 5. cheat 7. sharper 8. swindler

coo ... 4. bill (and), curr 5. chirr 6. murmur, mutter

cook ... 4. bake, boil, chef, stew 5. broil, roast, sauté, spoil (chess), steam, trill 6. braise, seethe 7. parboil, stir-fry 8. barbecue, magirist 9. charbroil, cuisinier

cookie ... 5. scone 7. biscuit, brownie 8. macaroon 10. gingersnap, ladyfinger, shortbread

cooking (pert to) ...
art .. 8. magirics
device .. 3. wok 4. etna, olla 5. grill, plate, stove 6. spider 7. griddle 9. autoclave, microwave (oven)
room .. 6. galley 7. cuisine, kitchen 8. scullery 11. kitchenette
scent .. 4. reek 5. nidor

cool ... 3. fan, ice 4. calm 5. chill, fresh, nervy, sober, tepid 6. chilly, freeze, sedate, temper 7. unmoved 8. careless, composed, impudent, mitigate, reserved, tranquil 9. apathetic, collected, unruffled 10. nonchalant, unfriendly, unsociable 11. indifferent, levelheaded, unconcerned 13. dispassionate, imperturbable, self-possessed

cooler ... 4. icer, jail 6. icebox, lockup, prison 7. chiller 10. ventilator 11. refrigerant 12. refrigerator

coolness ... 4. cold 5. nerve 6. aplomb 7. reserve 12. indifference 14. unfriendliness

coop ... 3. mew, pen 4. cage, cote, yard 5. court, hutch 7. confine

9. enclosure

cooper ... 5. drink 6. vessel 8. grogshop (floating) 11. barrel maker 12. wine retailer

cooperate ... 4. join, tend 5. agree, coact 6. concur 7. combine, conduce, connive 8. conspire 9. interface, synergize 10. contribute 11. collaborate

coordinate ... 5. talky 6. adjust 7. syntony (radio) 8. classify, equalize, organize, regulate 9. harmonize, integrate 10. proportion 11. systematize

copious ... 4. full, rich 5. ample 7. diffuse, profuse 8. abundant, numerous 9. exuberant, plenteous, plentiful 11. overflowing

copper ... 2. Cu 3. aes 4. cent, coin 5. metal, penny 6. cuprum 9. policeman 12. reddish-brown

copper (pert to) ...
alloy .. 5. brass 6. bronze, oroide
brass .. 6. chalco
cup .. 3. dop
engraving .. 9. mezzotint
film .. 6. patina
kettle (anc) .. 5. lebes
pewter .. 7. rheotan

Copperfield characters ... 4. Dora 6. Dartle 8. Micawber 9. Uriah Heep 11. Little Emily

coppice ... 4. bosk, holt 5. copse, grove 6. growth 7. boscage, thicket 9. brushwood, underwood

Coptic (pert to) ...
church .. 8. Egyptian
color .. 7. oxblood
title .. 4. anba

copy ... 3. ape 4. news 5. model, Xerox (tm) 6. ectype, follow 7. edition, estreat, imitate, pattern, replica, reprint, tracing 8. protocol, revision 9. duplicate, imitation 10. transcribe, transcript 11. counterfeit 12. reproduction

coquet, coquette ... 4. vamp 5. flirt 7. amorous 11. hummingbird

coquille ... 5. shell 7. ruching

Coquille ... 6. Indian 10. Athapascan

coquin ... 5. knave, rogue 6. rascal

coral ... 3. red 6. polyps, porite 8. Anthozoa 9. madrepore, millepore

coral (pert to) ...
branch .. 7. ramicle
division .. 7. Aporosa
formation .. 5. palus
island .. 3. key 5. atoll
ridge .. 4. reef 5. shoal
snake .. 5. Elaps 6. garter 7. Micurus
worm .. 6. palolo

cord ... 3. guy, rib 4. lace, line, rope, welt, wood 5. sinew, twine 6. lariat, sennet, spinal, string, tendon 7. measure (cubic), skirreh 8. corduroy, shoelace 9. hamstring 11. clothesline

cordage ... 5. ropes 7. rigging 8. ropework

cordelle ... 6. hauler 7. towline, towrope

cordial ... 4. real, warm 6. ardent,

elixir, genial, hearty, liquor 7. fervent, liqueur, sincere, zealous 8. friendly, vigorous 9. unfeigned 10. hospitable
cordial (liqueur)... 5. shrub 6. kummel 8. anisette, periscot 9. Cointreau 11. Benedictine, crème de moka 13. crème de menthe
cordiality... 4. zeal 5. ardor 6. fervor 7. ardency 8. kindness, warmness 9. geniality 11. hospitality 12. empressement, friendliness
core... 3. ame, hub, nub, nut 4. gist, nave, pith 5. heart, nowel 6. center, kernel, matrix 7. nucleus 9. substance
Corinthian (pert to)...
Age.. 5. plush 11. extravagant
color.. 3. red 4. pink 6. purple
Epistles (Bib).. 12. New Testament
General (Rom).. 9. Flaminius
King.. 8. Polybius
Spring.. 14. Pirene Fountain
Temple.. 5. Doric 7. Minerva
cork... 3. ork 4. bark, bung, plug 5. float, shive, suber (oak) 7. blacken, stopgap, stopper, stopple
corm... 4. bulb (flower)
cormorant... 4. bird, shag 5. norie, scart, urile 8. ravenous 9. snakebird, voracious 13. Phalacrocorax
corn... 4. joke 5. grain, grist 6. cliché, kaffir, kernel, liquor
corn (pert to)...
bread.. 4. pone 8. dumpling 10. corndodger
goddess.. 5. Ceres
hulled.. 4. samp 6. hominy
Indian.. 3. Zea 5. maize
lily.. 4. Ixia 8. bindweed 10. wandflower
liquor.. 6. whisky (whiskey)
meal.. 4. masa 7. hoecake
porridge.. 5. atole
salad.. 8. fetticus
Corn Belt... 4. Iowa, Ohio 6. Dakota, Kansas 7. Indiana 8. Illinois, Missouri, Nebraska 9. Minnesota
Corncracker State... 8. Kentucky
corner... 2. in 4. nook, pose, trap, tree 5. angle, coign (coigne), herne, ingle, niche, quoin
cornered... 5. cater (diagonal), sharp 7. angular, up a tree 10. cornerwise
cornerstone... 4. coin 5. quoin 8. keystone 10. foundation
Cornhusker State... 8. Nebraska
cornice... 4. drip, eave 7. antefix 8. astragal
Cornish... 3. elm 4. fowl 5. heath 7. dialect, diamond (Cornwall)
Cornwallis surrender site... 4. York (Va)
corolla... 5. galea (Her), petal 8. perianth
corollary... 6. effect, porism, result 7. adjunct 8. addition 9. deduction 11. proposition
corona... 4. coin, halo 5. cigar, crown 6. circle 7. aureole, circlet, garland, scyphus 8. Borealis 11. corona lucis
Corona Australis... 13. Southern Crown

Corona Borealis... 13. Northern Crown
coronet... 5. crown, tiara 6. anadem, circle, diadem, wreath 8. insignia, ornament
corporate... 5. joint 6. united 7. leagued 8. conjoint 10. associated
corporeal... 5. hylic, somal 6. bodily 7. fleshly, somatic 8. corporal, material, physical, tangible
corpse... 4. body 7. cadaver, carcass 9. endowment (Eccl)
corpulent... 3. fat 5. bulky, obese, stout 6. fleshy
corpuscle... 11. poikilocyte, schistocyte 12. erythroblast
corral... 3. mew, pen, sty 4. coop, herd 5. atajo, pound, tambo 7. impound 8. stockade 9. enclosure, inclosure
correct... 2. OK 4. edit, okay, true 5. amend, emend, right 6. better, proper, punish, reform, remedy, revise, strict 7. chasten, improve, perfect, rectify, regular, retouch 8. accurate, definite, orthodox, rigorous 9. faultless 10. particular, scrupulous 11. grammatical, punctilious 12. conventional
correlative... 2. or 3. nor 6. mutual 7. similar 8. conjoint 10. reciprocal 11. conjunction, counterpart 13. corresponding
correspond... 3. fit 4. suit 5. agree, equal, match, tally 6. accord 7. comport 8. assonate (sound), coincide, parallel 9. analogous, harmonize 11. parallelize
correspondence... 4. mail 8. homology (Biol), identity, symmetry 10. conformity, epistolary, similarity 11. equivalence, intercourse
corresponding... 8. balanced 9. analogous, homologic, isometric 10. coinciding 11. paralleling
corridor... 4. hall 5. aisle 6. airway, arcade 7. gallery 10. passageway
corrige (obs)... 6. punish 7. correct
corrigible... 8. amenable 10. submissive 11. rectifiable
corroborate... 5. prove 7. certify, confirm, support 8. calidate, roborate 9. establish 12. adminiculate, substantiate
corroborative... 11. adminicular
corrode... 3. eat 4. bite, etch, gnaw, rust 5. erode, waste 11. deteriorate 12. disintegrate
corrosive... 4. acid 7. caustic, erodent, erodine, mordant 9. corroding 10. escharotic 14. disintegrative
corrugate... 5. crimp 6. rugate 7. crumble, wrinkle 8. crumpled, furrowed, wrinkled
corrupt... 3. rot 5. bribe, taint, venal 6. Augean, debase, putrid, rotten 7. attaint, crooked, defiled, deprave, putrefy, vitiate 8. polluted 9. dishonest 11. adulterated 12. contaminated
corruption... 5. taint 6. pidgin

(language) 8. impurity 9. chicanery,
pollution 10. debasement, defilement,
distortion 11. depravation,
putrescence 12. adulteration
13. contamination

corsage . . . 5. waist 6. bodice
7. bouquet (boquet), flowers

corsair . . . 5. rover 6. pirate
7. Saracen 8. picaroon, rockfish
9. buccaneer, privateer
10. freebooter

Corsica . . .
capital . . 7. Ajaccio
birthplace of . . 8. Napoleon
feud (blood) . . 8. vendetta
seaport . . 6. Bastia

cortege . . . 5. train 6. parade
7. funeral, retinue 10. procession

Cortes palace site . . . 8. Coyoacan
(Mexico)

cortex . . . 4. bark, peel, rind

corundum . . . 3. gem 5. emery
7. mineral 8. abrasive

corundum colors . . .
blue . . 5. white 8. sapphire
brown . . 14. adamantine spar
green . . 7. emerald
purple . . 8. amethyst
red . . 4. ruby
topaz . . 6. yellow

coruscate . . . 5. gleam, shine 7. glitter,
radiate, sparkle 11. scintillate

cosmetic . . . 5. cream, henna, paint,
rouge 6. enamel, lotion, make–up
7. blusher, mascara 8. lipstick,
toiletry 11. beautifying

cosmic . . . 4. vast 5. great 7. orderly
8. catholic, infinite 9. grandiose,
universal 10. harmonious

Cosmic Order . . . 4. Rita (Vedic law)

Cossack (pert to) . . .
chief . . 6. ataman, hetman
district . . 6. Voisko
native . . 5. Tatar 7. Russian
squadron . . 6. sotnia
village . . 8. stanitsa (stanitza)
whip (knotted) . . 5. knout

cosset . . . 3. pet 4. lamb 6. caress,
coddle, cuddle, fondle, pamper

cost . . . 4. loss, rate 5. price
6. amount, charge, figure, outlay,
rental 7. expense 9. detriment,
suffering 11. deprivation, expenditure

costa . . . 3. rib 4. vein (Bot) 5. ridge
6. border, midrib

Costa Rica . . .
capital . . 7. San José
crater (world's greatest) . . 4. Poas
discovered . . 8. Columbus (4th visit)
export . . 6. coffee 7. bananas
port . . 5. Limon 10. Puntarenas

costate . . . 6. ribbed (Bot)

costermonger . . . 6. coster, hawker
7. peddler 9. costerman 11. apple
seller

costly . . . 4. dear, rich 8. gorgeous,
splendid 9. expensive, sumptuous
10. high–priced 11. extravagant

costume . . . 3. rig 4. garb, suit
5. dress, habit 6. attire, tights
7. apparel, raiment 8. clothing

cot . . . 3. bed, hut, pen, set 4. boat (Ir),

coop, cote 5. cabin, cover, house
6. cabana 7. charpoy, cottage,
shelter 8. bedstead

cote . . . 3. hut, pen 4. coop 5. house
7. cottage, shelter 9. sheepfold

coterie . . . 3. set 4. clan, club, ring
5. cabal, group, junto 6. circle, clique
9. camarilla (secret)

cottage . . . 3. cot, hut 4. shed
5. cabin, house, villa 6. cabana
7. shelter 8. bungalow

cottager . . . 6. cottar (cotter) 7. cottier,
laborer, peasant

cotton (pert to) . . .
cloth . . 4. jean, lawn 5. denim, khaki,
scrim, surat, terry 6. calico, dimity,
madras, nettle 7. batiste, percale
fiber . . 4. lint 6. staple 7. viscose
gin inventor . . 7. Whitney (Eli)
knot . . 3. nep
layer . . 7. batting
medical . . 5. gauze 6. sponge
raw . . 5. bayal
roll . . 4. slub
seed . . 4. bole, boll
seed sugar . . 9. raffinose
staple . . 6. upland (short) 8. Egyptian
(long) 14. Sea Island (long)
twisted . . 5. lisle 6. thread

Cotton State . . . 7. Alabama

couch . . . 3. bed, cot 4. lair, sofa
5. divan 6. canapé, canopy, litter,
lounge, pallet, phrase 8. loveseat
9. embroider (with gold), stretcher

cougar . . . 3. cat 4. lion, puma
7. panther 9. catamount

cough . . . 4. bark (sl), hack 6. tussis

council . . . 4. diet, rede 5. cabal, synod
6. senate 7. cabinet 8. assembly,
conclave, tribunal 10. conference,
parliament 12. consultation
15. League of Nations

council table cover . . . 5. tapis

counsel . . . 4. rede 6. advice, advise,
confer, lawyer 8. guidance
9. recommend 10. suggestion
11. instruction 12. deliberation

counselor, counsellor . . . 4. sage
6. lawyer, mentor, nestor 7. adviser,
advisor, counsel 8. attorney
9. barrister, solicitor

count . . . 3. sum, tot 4. tale, tell
5. check, judge, relay, tally
6. number, reckon, rely on
7. compute, summary 8. nobleman,
quantify 9. calculate, enumerate,
reckoning, summation 12. capitulation

Count (pert to) . . .
Mayence . . 3. Gan 7. Ganelon
Monte Cristo . . 6. Dantes
Rousillon . . 7. Bertram

countenance . . . 3. aid 4. abet, brow,
face, mien 6. aspect, permit, visage
7. approve, endorse, support
8. approval, sanction, tolerate
9. composure, encourage
10. appearance, permission

counter . . . 4. chip 5. table, token
7. adverse 8. computer, contrary,
opposite 9. retaliate 10. calculator

counteract . . . 6. offset, oppose, thwart
7. nullify 8. antidote 10. neutralize

11. countermand
counter current... 4. eddy 5. swirl
  6. vortex 9. whirlpool
  12. counterforce
counterfeit... 4. base, fake, mock,
  sham 5. bogus, false, feign, forge,
  phony, queer 6. assume, forged,
  unreal 7. falsify, forgery, imitate
  8. simulant, spurious 10. artificial,
  fictitious 11. unauthentic
counterirritant... 4. moxa 5. seton
  6. arnica, iodine, pepper 7. mustard
countermand... 5. annul 6. cancel,
  forbid, recall, revoke 7. abolish,
  reverse 8. prohibit 9. frustrate
  10. counteract 12. counterorder
counterpane... 5. quilt 6. bedcover,
  coverlet 9. comforter 10. counterpin
  11. comfortable
counterpart... 4. copy, like, twin
  5. image 6. double, eponym (name)
  8. parallel 9. duplicate
  10. complement, equivalent
counterpoise... 6. offset 8. equalize
  10. compensate, counteract
  12. counterforce 14. counterbalance
countersign... 4. sign 6. signal
  7. tessera 8. password 9. signature,
  watchword 10. mot de passe, open
  sesame 12. counterstamp
countersink... 4. ream 5. bevel
  6. deepen 7. chamfer
countertenor... 4. alto (male)
  8. falsetto
counterthrust (fencing)... 7. riposte
  (ripost) 12. return thrust
countless... 8. infinite 10. numberless,
  unnumbered 11. innumerable
  12. incalculable
countrified... 5. rural 7. boorish,
  hickish, uncouth 8. inurbane
  10. unpolished
country... 4. land, pais (law), vale
  5. rural, state, weald 6. nation,
  region 9. territory 10. fatherland
  12. commonwealth
country (pert to)...
  alien.. 7. enclave, exclave
  ancient.. 4. Aram, Elis, Gaul
  bumpkin.. 4. clod, jake, rube
    5. churl, yokel 9. greenhorn
  gallant.. 5. swain
  mythical.. 2. Oz
  native (earliest).. 9. aborigine
  Roman.. 8. campagna
  term.. 5. rural, urban 6. rustic
    8. agrestic, pastoral, praedial (predial)
countryman... 4. rube 5. yokel
  6. rustic 7. hayseed, patriot, peasant
  10. compatriot, home towner
county... 4. seat 5. shire 6. domain,
  parish 8. district
coup... 3. buy 4. blow, move (games)
  5. scoop, upset 6. barter, strike,
  stroke (master) 8. overturn, strategy
  9. trump card
coup de grâce... 9. deathblow
coup de main... 6. attack (sudden)
  8. strategy 9. stratagem
coup d'état... 6. stroke (political)
  8. strategy
couple... 3. duo, tie, two 4. bond,

dyad, join, link, mate, pair, span,
team, twin, yoke 5. brace, marry,
twain, unite 6. Gemini 7. bracket
coupled... 5. gemel, mated 6. braced,
  joined, linked, paired, teamed, united
  7. leagued, married
couplet... 3. two 4. pair 5. brace,
  verse 7. distich, doublet
coupon... 5. scrip, stock, token
  6. ticket 11. certificate (Finan)
courage... 4. grit, sand, will 5. heart,
  metal, nerve, pluck, valor 7. bravery,
  heroism, prowess 8. audacity,
  boldness, firmness 9. fortitude,
  gallantry, hardihood 11. intrepidity
  12. fearlessness 13. dauntlessness
courageous... 4. bold, game 5. brave,
  hardy, manly, stout 6. daring, heroic,
  spunky 7. gallant, spartan, valiant
  8. fearless, intrepid, knightly,
  resolute, stalwart, valorous
  11. adventurous 12. enterprising,
  stouthearted
courant... 4. romp 5. caper 6. letter
  7. gazette, running (Her)
  9. messenger, newspaper
courier... 5. guide 8. dragoman,
  horseman 9. attendant, messenger
course... 3. run 4. flow, line, mode,
  path, road, rote, tack 5. route,
  study, trend 6. career, manner,
  method, policy, series, stream
  8. progress 9. direction, procedure
  10. succession
course (pert to)...
  college.. 7. seminar
  direct.. 7. beeline
  regular.. 4. rote 6. regime 7. routine
  roundabout.. 6. detour 11. indirection
course of...
  action.. 5. habit 7. routine
    9. procedure
  eating.. 4. diet
  instruction.. 6. lesson
  procedure.. 4. rule
  thought.. 5. tenor
courser... 5. horse, steed 6. hunter,
  plover 7. charger 8. war horse
court... 3. see (papal), woo 4. area,
  eyre, fawn (upon), rota 5. atria,
  curia, dairi, gemot, patio, spark
  6. palace, parvis, street 7. council,
  tribune 8. tribunal 10. attendance,
  curry favor, quadrangle
court (Eng)... 3. soc 4. eyre, leet
  8. woodmate 10. court–baron
court (pert to)...
  assistant.. 5. staff 6. elisor
  crier, cry.. 4. hear, oyez (oyes)
    6. beadle
  criminal.. 6. assize
  exemption, excuse.. 6. essoin
  game.. 6. tennis 9. badminton
  hearing.. 4. oyer
  minutes.. 4. acta
  order.. 4. writ 5. arret 6. capias
    7. summons 8. subpoena
  public.. 5. forum 8. forensic
  sitting.. 7. session
courteous... 5. civil 6. gentle, polite,
  urbane 7. affable, gallant
  8. debonair, gracious 9. attentive

10. respectful

courtly... 4. hend (hende) 5. aulic,
civil 7. elegant, gallant, stately
9. dignified 10. obsequious
11. ceremonious

courtship... 4. suit 6. plight, wooing
7. romance 8. courting

covenant... 4. bond, pact 6. engage
7. bargain, compact, entente,
promise 8. contract 9. agreement,
stipulate, testament 11. undertaking

Covenant of God to Noah...
7. rainbow

cover... 3. cap, lap, lid 4. coat, cozy,
hide, mask, pale, pave, roof, span,
veil 5. blind, crust, drape, tapis
6. canopy, mantle, purdah, screen,
shield, thatch 7. elytron, overlay,
shelter 8. chrismal, coverlet
9. tarpaulin 10. overspread

cover (pert to)...
alloy.. 5. terne
cork.. 9. corticate
crumbs.. 5. bread
dots.. 7. stipple
figures (Her).. 4. seme
straw.. 6. thatch
turf.. 3. sod
up.. 4. bury 5. inter 7. conceal
8. submerge 10. camouflage
with wax.. 4. cere

covering... 3. mat, rug 4. caul, film,
hull, tile 5. apron, armor, shell, testa
6. awning, carpet, cestus, lorica,
pelage, screen, shroud 7. epeiric,
shelter, tegumen, wrapper
8. lineolum, pericarp 9. caparison
10. integument, protection
11. smoke screen

covering (head)... 3. cap, hat, wig
4. hood 5. beret, scarf, snood
6. bonnet, peruke, toupee
7. chapeau 10. fascinator

coverlet... 5. quilt 6. afghan, spread
7. blanket, lap robe 11. counterpane

covert... 3. den, lie 4. abri, lair
6. hidden, refuge, secret 7. covered,
private, thicket 9. concealed,
disguised, insidious, sheltered

covet... 4. envy 5. crave, yisse (obs)
6. aspire, desire, grudge, hanker
7. long for 8. begrudge

covetousness... 5. greed 7. avarice

covey... 4. bevy, pack 5. brood, flock,
hatch 6. flight 7. company
9. multitude

cow... 3. awe 5. abash, daunt
7. overawe, terrify 8. browbeat,
frighten 10. intimidate

cow (animal)... 3. Bos 4. calf, kine,
moil 5. Angus, bossy, brock (obs),
Kerry, vache 6. bovine, heifer
7. pollard 8. Ayrshire, maverick,
moulleen

cow (pert to)...
barn.. 4. byre, shed 5. reeve, stall
6. stable 7. vaccary, vachery
food (chewed).. 3. cud 5. rumen
hornless.. 6. mulley 7. pollard
8. moulleen
sea.. 6. dugong, walrus 7. manatee,
Sirenia 12. hippopotamus

tether.. 4. rope 6. baikie
unbranded.. 8. maverick
young.. 4. calf 6. heifer

coward, cowardly... 3. shy 5. sneak
6. afraid, craven, scared 7. caitiff,
chicken, dastard, milksop 8. poltroon,
recreant, weakling 9. dastardly,
fraidy–cat, jellyfish 12. uncourageous
13. pusillanimous

cowboy... 5. roper 6. herder
7. llamero, puncher, vaquero
8. jackaroo, neatherd
12. broncobuster (sl)

cowboy breeches... 5. chaps
8. jodhpurs

cower... 4. fawn 5. crawl, quail, stoop
6. cringe, crouch, grovel

cowfish... 3. ray 4. toto 7. dolphin,
grampus, manatee 8. porpoise

cowled... 9. cucullate

coxcomb... 3. fop 4. dude, fool
5. cleat (Naut), dandy 8. popinjay

coy... 3. shy 4. arch 5. timid
6. demure, modest 7. bashful
10. coquettish 13. self–conscious

coyote... 4. wolf (prairie)

Coyote State... 11. South Dakota

coypu... 6. nutria, rodent

cozen... 5. cheat, trick 7. beguile,
deceive, defraud

cozy... 4. easy, snug 6. chatty
8. cheerful, familiar, homelike,
sociable 9. contented, talkative
11. comfortable

crab... 3. Uca 4. king, Maia (genus)
5. ayuyu (Guam) 6. partan, spider
7. fiddler, limulus, mollusk, Ocypode
8. Lithodes 9. horseshoe
10. crustacean

crabbed... 5. cross 6. bitter, crusty,
morose, trying 7. bilious, peevish
8. abstruse, liverish 9. difficult,
fractious, irascible, irregular
10. perplexing

crab claw... 5. chela 6. metope,
nipper

crab eater... 4. seal 5. heron
7. opossum, raccoon

crachoir... 8. cuspidor, spittoon

crack... 4. blow, chap, clap, flaw,
kibe, leak, quip, rift, rime, snap
5. brack, break, chink, craze, spang,
split 6. breach, cleave, cranny
7. crackle, crevice, fissure, rupture
8. fracture

Cracker State... 7. Georgia

crackle... 4. snap 5. craze (art), crink
9. crepitate

crackman... 4. yegg 7. burglar

cradle... 4. slee (ship's) 7. infancy,
nursery 8. bassinet, cunabula
10. beginnings, incunabula

cradle book... 11. incunabulum

Cradle of Liberty... 11. Faneuil Hall
(Boston)

cradle song... 7. lullaby 8. berceuse
13. Schlummerlied

craft... 3. art 4. boat 5. skill, trade
6. device, tender 7. cunning, finesse,
know–how, prowess 8. aptitude,
vocation 9. dexterity
10. employment, handicraft,

occupation, watercraft 12. skillfulness

craftsman... 6. artist, writer
7. artisan, workman 9. artificer

crafty... 3. sly 4. foxy, slim, wily, wise
6. artful, astute, shifty, shrewd, subtle,
tricky 7. cunning 8. skillful (skilful)
9. deceitful, ingenious, underhand
10. fraudulent 13. Machiavellian
15. Mephistophelean

crag... 3. tor 4. spur 5. arête, cliff
7. nunatak 9. precipice

craggy... 5. rough 6. cliffy, clifty,
jagged, knotty, rugged

cram... 4. fill 5. choke, crowd, drive,
force, gorge, press, study, stuff
9. overstuff 10. gluttonize

cramp... 4. pain 5. stunt 6. hamper
7. confine, seizure 8. compress,
restrict 9. hindrance, paralysis
(muscle) 11. restriction

cranberry... 3. red 9. sourberry

cranberry center of trade...
10. Barnstable (Mass)

crane... 3. gib, jib 5. davit, jenny,
titan 7. derrick, machine

crane... 4. Grus 5. heron, sarus
7. Gruidae 9. cormorant
10. Gruiformes 13. constellation

cranial nerve... 5. radix, vagus

cranium... 5. skull 8. cerebrum

crank... 3. wit 4. bear, crab 5. crook,
winch 6. griper, grouch, handle
7. fanatic, growler, hothead
8. frondeur, grumbler, sorehead
9. eccentric 10. bellyacher,
crosspatch, monomaniac

cranny... 4. hole, nook 5. chink, cleft,
crack 6. corner, furrow 7. crevice,
fissure 8. crevasse

crash... 4. bank, fail 5. smash
7. debacle, failure, intrude, shatter
8. accident 9. collision
10. bankruptcy

crate... 3. box 4. case 6. basket,
cradle, encase, hamper 8. airplane
9. container 10. automobile

crater... 3. pit 6. cavity 7. caldera
13. constellation (The Cup)

cravat... 3. tie 4. teck 5. ascot, stock
7. bandage, bolo tie, necktie
9. neckcloth 10. four-in-hand

crave... 3. ask, beg 4. long, seek
5. covet, yearn 6. desire, hanker
7. beseech, entreat, implore, request,
solicit 10. supplicate

craven... 6. afraid, coward 7. caitiff,
dastard 8. cowardly, poltroon,
recreant 12. fainthearted
13. pusillanimous

craving... 4. pica 6. desire, thirst
7. longing 8. appetite, yearning

craw... 3. maw 4. crop 6. gebbie
7. gizzard, stomach 9. ingluvies

crawfish... 5. yabby (yabbie) 7. back
out, crawdad, lobster, retreat
8. crayfish

crawl... 4. fawn, inch, shug 5. creep
6. cringe, grovel, recant

crayon... 5. chalk 6. pastel, pencil
8. charcoal

craze... 3. fad 4. flaw, maze 5. crack
(ceramics), crush, furor, mania, vogue

6. defect, whimsy 7. crackle, fashion
9. infirmity 11. infatuation

craze (for)... see also *madness, mania*
foreign customs.. 9. xenomania
freedom.. 14. eleutheromania
love (erotic).. 10. erotomania
music.. 9. melomania
setting fires.. 9. pyromania
shopping.. 9. oniomania
single subject.. 9. monomania
stamps (postage).. 11. timbromania
stealing.. 11. kleptomania
wandering.. 10. dromomania
wealth.. 10. plutomania

crazed... 4. amok 6. insane, marked
(with crazes) 7. severed 8. deranged
10. distraught

crazy... 3. mad 4. amok, loco, luny
6. dottle, insane 7. damaged, foolish,
unsound 9. deficient

cream... 4. best, ream 5. elite
6. lotion 8. sillabub (with wine)

cream of tartar... 5. argol

crease... 4. fold, ruck 5. crimp, pleat
7. wrinkle 9. plication

create... 4. make 5. build, cause,
clone, hatch 6. invent 7. fashion,
produce 8. generate 9. originate

creation... 3. art 5. virtu, world
6. cosmos, making 7. classic, fantasy,
forming, product 8. artifact, universe
9. objet d'art 10. providence
11. composition, fabrication,
manufacture, masterpiece

creator... 5. maker 6. author
8. designer, inventor, producer
10. originator

Creator... 3. God 5. Maker
7. Jehovah 8. Almighty, Demiurge
11. King of Kings

creature (pert to)...
civetlike.. 3. cat
duplicate.. 5. clone
elflike.. 4. peri 6. hobbit
evil.. 7. hellcat 8. hellicat
fire.. 10. salamander
folklore.. 3. elf 4. Yeti 5. dwarf, fairy,
pixie 9. sasquatch
ghost.. 11. poltergeist
minute.. 10. animalcule
outer space.. 5. alien
sentient.. 6. animal
timid.. 4. deer 5. sheep
underground.. 5. gnome
water.. 5. sylph 6. undine
winged (Myth).. 6. wivern
10. cockatrice

credence... 5. trust 6. belief, credit
8. affiance, reliance 10. acceptance,
confidence, dependence
15. trustworthiness

credential... 7. voucher
11. certificate, testimonial
14. recommendation

credible... 6. likely 7. tenable
8. probable 9. plausible
10. believable 11. well-founded

credit... 5. faith, honor, trust 6. belief,
esteem, impute 7. account, believe
8. accredit, credence 10. estimation,
regulation 15. trustworthiness

creditor... 5. agent (collection)

6. debtee, dunner, usurer 7. Shylock (greedy)

creed ... 5. credo, dogma, tenet
6. belief, Nicene 8. Apostles'
9. Catechism 10. Athanasian, confession

creek ... 3. rio 4. burn, slue, wick
6. arroyo, estero, slough, spruit, stream

creel ... 4. rack, trap 6. basket (fish)

creep ... 5. crawl, prowl, skulk, slink, sneak, steal (away) 6. grovel
8. scramble 9. pussyfoot

creeping ... 4. slow 7. reptant
8. crawling 10. slithering
11. reptatorial

Cremona, famed names ... 5. Amati
6. violin 10. Guarnerius
12. Stradivarius

crena ... 4. gash, kerf, nick 5. cleft, notch 7. scallop 10. depression
11. indentation

creole ... 6. French 7. mestizo
9. half–breed, janissary

Creole State ... 9. Louisiana

crepitate ... 4. snap 7. crackly

crescent ... 4. cusp, horn, lune
5. curve 8. meniscus

crescent–shaped ... 4. horn, lune
6. bicorn, lunate 7. lunular
8. lunulate 9. horseshoe, meniscate, semilunar

crest ... 3. top 4. comb, peak, tuft
5. arête, crown, ridge 6. copple, crista, height, summit 7. panache, topknot, wave top 8. feathers, insignia, pinnacle 9. cockscomb
11. mountaintop

crested ... 6. capped, topped, tufted
7. coppled, cristed, crowned, pileate

creta ... 5. chalk

Crete ...
capital .. 5. Canea
city .. 6. Candia, Khanis
civilization (anc) .. 6. Aegean, Minoan
king (anc) .. 5. Minos (Gr)
monster .. 8. Minotaur (man, bull)
mountain .. 3. Ida 9. Theodoros
priests .. 7. Curetes

cretin ... 5. idiot 8. imbecile

crevice ... 3. gap 4. rift 5. chink, cleft
6. cranny 7. fissure, opening
8. peephole 10. interstice

crew ... 3. men 4. band, body, gang, pack 5. force, staff 7. company
9. employees, personnel

crib ... 3. bed, bin, den (gambling)
5. cheat, stall, steal 6. Cratch (stars), manger, pilfer 7. brothel
8. Praesepe

cricket ... 4. game, grig 6. acheta, cicada, locust 7. katydid 9. footstool
10. Orthoptera 11. grasshopper

cricket (pert to) ...
game term .. 3. bye, run 6. yorker
noise .. 5. chirp 7. stridor
symbol (Myth) .. 4. tice 5. ashes

cried ... 4. wept 6. bawled, called, wailed, yelled 7. shouted, uttered
8. lamented, screamed, shrieked
9. exclaimed 10. proclaimed

crime ... 3. sin 4. evil 5. guilt, wrong

6. delict, felony, mayhem 7. offense
8. delictum, iniquity 9. violation
10. illegality, wickedness, wrongdoing
11. malfeasance

crime (pert to) ...
benefice (Eccl) .. 6. simony
goddess (Myth) .. 3. Ate
of 1873 .. 12. Silver Dollar
scene .. 5. venue

Crimea ...
city .. 5. Kerch, Yalta 10. Sevastopol
isthmus site .. 8. Black Sea
Russian .. 4. Krim
sea (Russ) .. 4. Azof

criminal ... 4. thug, yegg 5. crook, felon, thief 6. nocent 7. convict, yeggman 8. swindler 9. desperado, dishonest, felonious 10. malefactor, recivist 11. blameworthy, disgraceful
13. reprehensible

criminal refuge ... 7. Alsatia
11. Whitefriars (London)

criminology ... 8. penology

crimp ... 4. curl, fold 5. frizz, notch, plait 6. ruffle, thwart 7. crinkle, wrinkle 8. Shanghai

cringe ... 4. fawn 5. cower, quail, sneak, wince 6. flinch, grovel, shrink, submit 7. truckle

crinkle ... 4. curl, kink, turn, wind
5. twist 6. rustle 7. wrinkle

crinose ... 5. hairy 7. hirsute
11. barbigerous

cripple ... 4. halt, hock, lame, maim
6. injure, weaken 7. amputee, disable 8. handicap 9. hamstring
12. incapacitate

crisis ... 5. cycle, peril 8. exigency, juncture 9. criterion, emergency
11. climacteric

crisp ... 4. cold 5. curly, flaky, sharp, short, spalt 7. brittle, concise, crackle, crinkle, friable 8. clear–cut
9. frangible

criterion ... 4. norm, rule, test, type
5. canon, model 7. measure
8. standard 9. yardstick

critic ... 5. judge, Momus (Myth)
6. censor, slater, Zoilus 8. collator, reviewer 9. literator 11. connoisseur, criticaster, faultfinder

critical ... 4. edgy 7. carping, crucial, cynical, Zoilean 8. captious, caviling, exacting 10. censorious, particular
12. faultfinding 13. hairsplitting
14. discriminating

Critical system of philosophy ...
10. Kantianism

criticism ... 3. rap 5. cavil, roast
6. report, review 7. censure, Zoilism
8. critique, judgment 9. aspersion
10. commentary

criticize, criticise ... 3. pan 4. carp, flay 5. cavil, judge, knock, slate
6. review 7. censure, comment
9. castigate 10. animadvert

Croatian ... 4. Slav 5. Croat
11. Yugoslavian

Croatian capital ... 6. Zagreb

crock ... 3. ewe (old), jug, pot, urn
4. smut, soil, soot 5. horse (old)
7. ceramic 8. potsherd

11. earthenware
crocodile... 3. goa 5. nakoo 6. gavial, mugger 7. reptile, sophism 9. Niloticus 10. Crocodilia, Crocodilus
crocus... 4. bulb, herb, iris 6. flower, yellow 7. saffron
croft... 5. crypt, field, vault 6. carafe, cavern 7. hillock
crone... 3. ewe (old), hag 5. witch 6. beldam (beldame)
Cronus (pert to)...
god of .. 8. Harvests
father .. 6. Uranus
son .. 4. Zeus
wife .. 4. Rhea
crony... 3. pal 4. chum 5. buddy 6. friend 9. companion 10. playfellow
crook... 4. bend, warp 5. angle, curve, staff, thief 6. akimbo 7. crosier 8. criminal, insignia 10. camshachle
crooked... 3. wry, zag 4. agee, awry, bent 5. agley, askew, false 6. aslant, curved, hooked, zigzag 7. angular, askance, asquint, oblique 8. deformed 9. dishonest, distorted 10. circuitous, fraudulent 12. dishonorable
crooked legs... 8. rhebosis (rhaebosis) 10. tortuosity
croon... 3. hum 4. boom, sing, wail 5. whine 6. bellow, lament, murmur 8. complain
crop... 3. lop, maw 4. clip, craw, dick, reap, whip 5. belly, shear, yield 6. gebbie, growth, sheave 7. harvest, produce, soilage, stomach 11. cultivation
cross... 2. go 3. tau 4. crux, ford, rood 5. bless, corse, irate, staff 6. oppose, thwart, touchy 7. athwart, fretful, oblique, peevish, pettish 8. crucifix, insignia, monument, obstruct, petulant, snappish, swastika (swastica), traverse 9. hybridize, intersect, irritable 10. disappoint, transverse 11. crucifixion
cross (pert to)...
archaeology .. 4. ankh
astronomy .. 13. Southern Cross
barred .. 11. trabeculate
beam .. 5. spale, trave 6. girder
bow .. 8. arbalest
breed .. 5. Husky (dog) 6. hybrid
British .. 6. Celtic
Egypt .. 10. life symbol
eye .. 9. esotropia 10. strabismus
heraldry .. 6. pattée 7. erminee, patonce
Latin .. 12. crux commissa
palm .. 5. bribe (gypsy)
St Anthony's .. 3. tau
stroke .. 5. serif
tau–shaped .. 10. crux ansata
crossing... 6. voyage 7. chiasma, fording, passage 8. cheating, opposing 9. hybridism 10. traversing 13. crossbreeding
crossing (famed)...
Alps .. 8. Hannibal, Napoleon
Hellespont .. 6. Xerxes

Pyrenees .. 8. Hannibal
Rubicon .. 6. Caesar
crouch... 4. bend, fawn 5. cower, squat, stoop 6. cringe, grovel, hunker
crow... 3. daw 4. brag, rook 5. aylet, boast, crake, raven, vaunt 6. chough, Corvus, Indian (Sioux) 7. corvine, jackdaw 8. laughter 13. constellation
crowbar... 5. jimmy, lever 7. gablock
crowberry... 5. shrub 8. bilberry 9. cranberry
crowd... 3. jam, mob 4. bike (Scot), cram, host, pack, push, ruck, urge 5. crush, drive, drove, horde, press, serry, swarm, three, wedge 6. galaxy, hasten, legion, masses, throng 7. squeeze 8. compress 9. multitude 10. assemblage
crowded... 6. packed 7. compact, crammed, serried, teeming 8. numerous, populous 9. congested, jampacked
crown... 3. cap, top 4. atef, coin, pate, peak, poll, tiar 5. crest, miter (mitre), tiara 6. anadem, circle, corona, diadem, fillet, reward, summit, trophy, wreath 7. chaplet, coronet, garland, glorify, install 8. coronate, enthrone, ornament, pinnacle, surmount
crowning glory... 8. last word
crucial... 5. final 6. severe, trying, urgent 7. crossed 8. critical, decisive 9. cruciform 13. demonstrative
crucible... 3. pot 4. etna, test 6. retort, vessel 10. conversion
crucifix... 3. pax 4. rood 5. cross 6. emblem
crucifixion... 5. death (on a cross) 7. torture 9. execution, suffering 11. persecution
crude... 3. raw 4. rude 5. crass, green, rough 6. callow, coarse, common, garish, savage, vulgar 8. unseemly 9. inelegant, rough–hewn, tasteless, uncourtly, unrefined 10. outlandish, unpolished 13. inexperienced
crudity... 7. rawness 9. crassness, harshness, roughness, vulgarity 10. immaturity
cruel... 4. fell, hard 5. harsh 6. brutal, savage, severe, unkind 7. inhuman, painful, unhuman 8. dreadful, fiendish, pitiless, ruthless, tyrannic 9. ferocious, heartless, merciless, murderous, truculent 11. remorseless
cruelty... 9. brutality 10. inclemency, inhumanity 12. ruthlessness 13. heartlessness 15. remorselessness
cruelty, lover of... 6. sadist 9. masochist
cruet... 3. ama 4. vial 6. bottle, caster (castor), vessel 7. ampulla, urceole
cruller... 7. olycook (olykoek) 8. doughnut 9. friedcake
crumb... 3. bit 5. break, piece 6. little 8. fragment
crumble... 5. decay 6. molder, powder

7. friable 9. pulverize
12. disintegrate
crumple... 4. ruck 6. crease, raffle, rumple 7. wrinkle 9. corrugate
cruor... 4. gore 5. blood, ichor
crusade... 5. cause, drive, issue, jihad (jehad) 7. crusado 8. campaign 10. expedition
Crusades... 8. Holy Land 9. Children's (1212)
crush... 3. jam 4. bray, mash, sink 5. crash, crowd, grind, press, smash 6. bruise, crunch 7. conquer, mortify, oppress, shatter, squeeze 8. compress, suppress 9. humiliate, pulverize 11. infatuation
crushed sugar cane... 7. bagasse
crust... 4. rind 5. shell 8. dumpling, exterior 9. impudence 11. lithosphere 14. aggressiveness
crustacean... 4. crab 5. prawn 6. huitre, isopod, limpet, mussel, oyster, shrimp 7. limulus, lobster, scallop 8. barnacle, crawfish, starfish 9. shellfish, trunkfish 10. coquillage, periwinkle
crustacean (pert to)...
extinct.. 5. Eryon
footless.. 4. apod, apus
fossil.. 9. trilobite
genus.. 5. Hippa 6. Triops 7. Caridea (Carida) 8. Copepoda, Decapoda 10. Notostraca
larva.. 5. alima
limb.. 6. endite, podite
crutch... 5. brace, staff, stave 6. crotch 7. support
cry... 3. baa, caw, cri, hue, mew, olé, sob 4. alas, barr, call, evoe, home, hoot, mewl, pish, pule, wail, weep, yell, yelp 5. alack, avast, bleat, crook, miaou, yoick 6. bellow, boohoo, clamor, outcry, scream, shriek, slogan, snivel, squawk 7. tantivy (hunting), trumpet, weeping 8. entreaty, jeremiad, lackaday, proclaim 10. shibboleth 11. lamentation
cry (out)... 5. crake, decry, shout 6. accuse, clamor, object, scream, suffer 7. censure, exclaim 8. complain, denounce 10. vociferate
crying... 6. puling, urgent 7. clamant, heinous, howling, sobbing, weeping 9. insistent, notorious
crying bird... 6. Aramus 7. courlan, limpkin 8. raillike
cryptic... 4. Rite (Freemasonry) 6. hidden, occult, secret 8. puzzling 9. concealed, enigmatic 10. mysterious 11. problematic 12. hieroglyphic
cryptogram... 4. code 5. agama 7. writing (secret) 8. symbolic
crystal... 4. dial 5. clear, glass, lucid 6. argent (Her), quartz 7. diamond 8. pellucid 9. glassware, snowflake 11. crystalline, transparent
crystal (pert to)...
diamond.. 7. glassie
gazer.. 4. seer 7. diviner 8. presager 10. soothsayer 13. fortuneteller

gazing.. 4. scry
twin.. 5. macle
crystalline... 4. pure 8. pellucid 11. transparent 12. crystal–clear
crystalline (pert to)...
colorless.. 7. orcinol
compound.. 5. oscin 6. anisil, dulcin
mineral.. 4. spar 7. apatite 8. elaterin, feldspar
rock.. 7. diorite, greisen
salt.. 5. borax 8. analgene (analgen)
cub... 3. bin, boy, fox, pen, pup 4. bear, coop, crib, lion, shed 5. shark, stall, tiger, whale, whelp 8. boy scout, cupboard 9. youngling
Cuba...
capital.. 6. Havana
castle.. 5. Morro
city.. 8. Santiago 10. Bahia Honda, Guantánamo
discoverer.. 8. Columbus (1492)
island.. 11. Isle of Pines (Isla de Pinos)
mountain.. 8. Camaguey 9. Las Villas 12. Pico Turquino
nickname.. 18. Pearl of the Antilles
province.. 7. Oriente
Cuban (pert to)...
asphalt.. 9. chapapote
bird.. 6. trogan 8. tocororo
dance.. 5. rumba
fish.. 4. bobo
rodent.. 5. hutia (jutia) 6. pilori
rum.. 7. Bacardi
cube... 3. die 4. dice 5. solid 6. triple 7. tessera (marble) 10. third power
cubic (pert to)...
body.. 3. die 4. dice
decimeter.. 5. litre
math.. 9. isometric
measure.. 4. cord
meter.. 5. stere
shape.. 6. cuboid 8. cubiform
cubicle... 4. cell, room, tomb 7. bedroom, chamber, roomlet 9. cubiculum
cuckoo... 5. mimic 8. imitator, songbird
cuckoo (pert to)...
ally.. 3. ani
American.. 8. Coccyzus
bees.. 9. Nomadidae
bird (Orient).. 4. coel (koel)
cap.. 9. monkshood
family.. 9. Cuculidae
fool.. 7. wryneck
pint.. 4. arum 10. cuckoo spit
cucumber... 4. cuke, pepo 6. pedata (sea), pepino
cucurbit... 5. flask, gourd 7. matrass
cud... 4. bite, quid 5. rumen 8. merycism
cuddle... 3. hug, pet 6. fondle, nestle 7. snuggle
cudgel... 3. bat, hit 4. beat, club, drub 5. baste, staff, stave, stick 6. alpeen 7. belabor 9. fustigate, shillalah (shillelagh)
cue... 3. nod, rod, tip 4. ball, clue, hint, role, tail 5. braid, queue, twist 6. prompt 8. billiard (term), function 9. catchword 10. intimation

cuerpo... 4. body, hulk 5. naked, torso
10. dishabille (in)
cuff... 3. hit 4. band, blow, slap
5. clout 6. strike 8. chastise,
gauntlet, handcuff 12. chastisement
cuirass... 4. mail 5. armor 6. lorica
11. breastplate
cul–de–sac... 5. alley (blind)
7. impasse 14. pouch of Douglas
cull... 4. pick 6. assort, choose, select
8. separate
culmination... 3. end 4. acme, apex,
auge, noon 6. ascent, climax, result,
vertex, zenith 10. perfection
12. consummation
culpability... 5. blame, fault, guilt
11. criminality 15. blameworthiness
culpable... 6. faulty, guilty 7. immoral
8. criminal 9. accusable, imputable
10. censurable, indictable
11. blameworthy 12. reproachable
13. reprehensible
cultivate... 3. ear (dial), hoe 4. farm,
grow, plow, teel, till 5. court, train
6. excite, foster, harrow, plough,
refine 7. educate, improve
8. approach, civilize
cultivated... 4. grew, hoed 6. seeded,
tilled, urbane 7. genteel, refined
8. cultured, polished, well–bred
cultivation... 5. tilth 7. culture,
farming, tillage 9. husbandry
10. refinement 12. civilization
culver... 4. dove 6. pigeon 10. wood
pigeon
cumbersome... 5. bulky 6. clumsy
8. cumbrous, unwieldy
10. burdensome
cummer... 4. lass 5. witch 6. friend
(girl) 7. midwife 9. companion,
godmother
cummerbund... 4. band, belt, sash
6. cestus, girdle
cumshaw... 3. tip 5. bonus 6. thanks
7. present 8. gratuity
cunning... 3. sly 4. cute, foxy, wile,
wily 5. sharp, skill 6. artful, clever,
crafty, dainty, shrewd, subtle, tricky
7. politic, shyness 8. dextrous,
foxiness, skillful, stealthy, trickery
9. designing, dexterity, ingenious,
ingenuity, insidious 13. Machiavellian
cunningly formed... 6. daedal (dedal)
cup... 3. ama, can, dop, mug, tyg
4. tass, teet, Toby 5. calyx, chark,
cruse, cupel, cylix, grail, jorum, ladle,
stein 6. beaker, goblet, noggin,
trophy 7. chalice, tumbler
cupbearer... 4. Hebe, saki
8. Ganymede
cupboard... 3. kas 5. ambry (anc)
6. buffet, closet, larder, pantry
7. armoire, dresser 8. aparador
9. sideboard
Cupid... 3. boy, Dan 4. amor, Eros,
Kama, love 5. Freya 7. Amorino,
cupidon
Cupid (pert to)...
mother.. 5. Venus
sweetheart.. 6. Psyche
title.. 3. Dan
cupidity... 4. lust 5. greed 6. desire

7. avarice, avidity, longing
8. appetite, avidness, rapacity
cuplike (pert to)...
calyx.. 9. calicular
stone.. 5. geode
vessel.. 4. zarf
cupola... 4. dome, kiln 5. tower
6. concha (Arch) 7. ceiling, furnace
(foundry)
cur... 3. dog 4. mutt 7. gurnard (fish),
mongrel 9. goldeneye
curare, curari... 5. urali 7. extract
9. Strychnos 11. arrow poison
curate... 4. abbé 6. cleric, parson,
pastor, priest 7. dominie
9. clergyman
curator... 6. keeper 7. manager,
steward 8. guardian 9. custodian,
librarian, treasurer
curb... 3. bit 4. rein 5. check, limit
6. arrest, border, bridle, market
(Finan) 7. control, inhibit, repress
8. restrict 9. hindrance, restraint
curd... 4. crud 6. casein
curds and whey... 7. clabber
cure... 4. balm, heal, salt 5. smoke
6. elixir, remedy, rizzor 7. nostrum,
panacea, restore, therapy 8. preserve
10. corrective
curio... 8. artifact 9. bric–a–brac,
curiosity
curiosity... 5. curio 6. gabion (rare),
oddity, prying, wonder 8. interest
9. exception, spectacle
14. meddlesomeness
15. inquisitiveness
curious... 3. odd 4. rare 5. nosey
(nosy), outre, queer 6. prying, quaint
7. careful, strange, unusual
8. cautious, meddling, singular
9. inquiring, intrusive 10. meticulous
11. inquisitive
curl... 4. coil, kink, lock, roll 5. crimp,
crisp, frizz, tress, twirl, twist
6. marcel, spiral 7. crinkle, frizzle,
ringlet 8. curlicue 9. corkscrew
11. convolution
curled... 5. curly, spiry 6. coiled
7. crimped, savoyed, twisted
8. wrinkled (Bot)
curlew... 4. bird, fute 5. kioea, snipe,
whaup 6. marlin 7. bustard
8. whimbrel
curlewlike... 6. godwit 9. sandpiper
curly... 4. wavy 5. kinky, oundy (obs)
6. crispy, frizzy, kinked 8. crinkled
curmudgeon... 4. crab 5. churl, miser
7. niggard 8. tightwad 9. skinflint
currant... 3. red 5. berry, Ribes
6. raisin, rizzar (rizzart)
currency... 5. money, scrip 6. dinero
9. publicity 10. greenbacks,
popularity, prevalence
15. fashionableness
current... 4. eddy, flow, race (water),
rife, tide 5. draft, going, rapid,
trend, usual 6. course, stream
7. present, topical 8. existent
9. direction, prevalent
11. fashionable
current regulator...
electric.. 9. rheometer

12. galvanometer
physiology.. 11. hematometer
curriculum... 7. courses, studies, Three R's 8. curricle
curry... 4. comb, cook, drub 5. dress, groom 6. cajole 9. condiment
curry favor... 6. cajole 7. flatter, smoodge (smooge), wheedle
curse... 3. ban 4. bane, damn, oath 5. swear 7. bewitch, malison 8. anathema, execrate 9. blaspheme 10. affliction 11. imprecation, malediction 13. excommunicate
cursed... 6. damned, odious, wicked 7. hateful 8. damnable, shrewish 9. execrable 12. cantankerous
Cursores... 5. birds (long–legged) 7. spiders (wolf)
Cursoria... 6. mantes (mantis) 10. Orthoptera 11. cockroaches
cursory... 5. hasty 6. fitful, roving, slight 7. passing 8. careless, rambling 9. desultory, irregular 10. evanescent 12. disconnected, unmethodical
curt... 4. buff 5. bluff, brief, brusk, gruff, short, terse 6. abrupt 7. brusque, concise, curtate, laconic 9. condensed
curtail... 3. lop 4. crop, dock, pare, slip 5. short 6. lessen, reduce 7. abridge, shorten 8. compress, decrease, diminish, retrench
curtain... 4. mask, veil 5. drape, shade 6. coster (altar), encore, purdah, riddel, screen, shadow, shield 7. drapery, secrecy, shelter, vitrage 8. portiere
curtsy, curtsey... 3. bow, nod 4. bend 6. kowtow, salaam 12. genuflection
curvature... 3. arc, bow 4. arch, bend 5. plane, sinus 6. camber 7. arching, curving, evolute 8. aduncity, cyrtosis, lordosis, vaulting 9. curvation 11. convolution
curve... 3. arc, bow, ess 4. arch, bend, ogee, turn 5. crook, polar 6. spiral, toroid 7. cissoid, evolute, flexure 8. extrados, parabola, sinusoid 9. curvature, sinuosity
curved (pert to)...
arch.. 8. arciform, arcuated
glass.. 4. lens
inward.. 5. adunc 8. aduncous
molding.. 4. ogee
planking (ship's).. 3. sny
process.. 5. hamus (Zool)
roundabout.. 10. circuitous
staircase.. 8. caracole
wedge.. 3. cam
curvet... 4. leap 5. bound, caper, frisk, prank 6. frolic, gambol
cush... 3. cow 5. money 7. cookery, sorghum
Cush (pert to)...
father.. 3. Ham
land of.. 8. Ethiopia 10. land of Cush
son.. 4. Seba 6. Nimrod
cushion... 3. pad 4. mute, seat 6. ignore, pillow, sachet 7. brioche, conceal, dashpot, muffler 8. plantula,

pulvinus, suppress, swelling (Queen Mary's) 9. pulvillus 10. pincushion
cusk... 4. fish (codlike), tusk 5. torsk 6. burbot
cusp... 3. end, tip 4. apex, peak 5. crown, point 6. cantle, corner 8. paracone
custard... 4. flan 7. charlet, pudding
custard apple... 4. tree 5. papaw 8. sweetsop
custodian... 5. guard 6. bailee, jailer, keeper, warden, warder 7. curator, janitor 8. curatrix, guardian
custody... 4. care, keep 5. trust 6. charge 8. guidance 10. protection 12. guardianship, jurisdiction
custom... 3. fad, law, mos, use 4. mode, wont 5. habit, mores, usage, vogue 7. fashion 8. practice 9. patronage, tradition 10. consuetude, consuetudo
customary... 5. usual 6. wonted 7. general, usitate 8. habitual, orthodox 11. traditional 12. conventional
customs... 4. duty 5. mores, taxes
cut... 3. bob, lob, lop, mow, nip, rip 4. blow, chop, crop, dock, edit, fell, gash, hack, make, mode, nick, open, pain, pare, reap, slit, snee, snip, snub, trim 5. canal, carve, cleft, lance, notch, piece, plate, scarp, sever, share, shear, shorn, slash, slice, slish (Shak), snick, split, vogue 6. dilute, furrow, injury, mangle, reduce, trench 7. affront, curtail, engrave, offense, sectile, serrate, truancy, whittle 8. discount, excision, incision 9. engraving, indignity, reduction 10. adulterate
cut (pert to)...
and furrow.. 7. chamfer
and polish.. 8. lapidate
and weave.. 5. plash
back.. 6. polled 7. shorten
capable of being.. 7. sectile
down.. 5. razee
fine.. 5. mince
in.. 7. intrude 9. interpose, interrupt, introduce
in half.. 9. dimidiate
in squares.. 4. dice
into.. 6. incise
jaggedly.. 4. snag
out.. 6. excide, excise
up.. 6. frolic, grieve 9. apportion, misbehave
vertically.. 5. scarp, slice
with shears.. 4. snip 5. shirl
cutaneous... 4. skin 6. dermal, dermic
cute... 4. keen 5. peart, sharp 6. brainy, clever, dainty, pretty, shrewd 7. cunning 10. attractive 11. picturesque
cuticle... 4. skin 5. cutin, cutis 8. membrane, pellicle 9. epidermis, scarfskin 10. integument
cut of beef... 4. loin, ribs, rump 5. chine, roast, steak 6. corned, cutlet, rosbif, saddle 7. brisket, icebone 8. shoulder 9. aitchbone, roundbone

cut off... 3. bob 4. crop, dock, drib,
snip 5. elide, pared, roach (Naut)
6. bereft, bobbed, divest, lopped,
screen 7. abscind, abscise, clipped,
deprive, severed 8. amputate
9. amputated, apocopate, intercept
10. disinherit
cut off (pert to)...
by bits.. 4. drib
edges (coins).. 3. nig
on slant.. 4. bias 5. bevel, miter
short.. 3. bob 4. crop
syllable.. 5. elide
with die.. 4. dink
wool.. 3. dod (dodd)
cut short... 3. bob, lop 4. crop, dock,
halt, stop 5. check 6. arrest
7. clipped, cropped, curtail, shorten
9. terminate
cutter... 4. boat 5. knife, sloop, tooth
6. sleigh, vessel 7. incisor
cutting... 4. cold, slip, tart 5. piece,
scion, sharp 6. biting, secant, severe
7. caustic, incisal, satiric, sectile
8. chilling, piercing 9. sarcastic,
severance, trenchant 10. separating
11. penetrating 12. adulteration
cutting (pert to)...
diamonds (imperfect).. 4. bort
edge.. 5. blade
in two.. 6. secant
last letter of word.. 7. apocope
off.. 7. apocope 10. abscission,
amputation
tool.. 3. axe (ax), bit 4. adze 5. razor
6. chisel
wit.. 6. satire
cuttle... 4. thug 5. knife 7. ruffian
8. assassin 9. swaggerer
cuttlebone... 7. osselet
cuttlefish... 5. Sepia, squid
7. mollusk, octopus
cuttlefish secretion... 3. ink (black)
cuttyhunk... 11. fishing line
Cyclades Islands (Gr)... (200 in all)
3. Ios 5. Delos (smallest), Melos,
Naros, Paros, Tenos, Thera 6. Andros
7. Amorgos, Myconus
cycle... 3. Age, eon, era 4. aeon
5. orbit, recur, saros (Astron), wheel
6. course, period, series 7. bicycle,
circuit 8. electric, tricycle
9. Arthurian 10. revolution
12. Carlovingian (Charlemagne)
cyclone... 5. storm 6. baguio
7. tornado, twister, typhoon
9. hurricane
cyclopean... 4. huge, vast 7. massive,
one–eyed 8. gigantic
Cyclops (pert to)...
assistant to.. 6. Vulcan (Fire God)
father.. 6. Uranus
forger of.. 12. thunderbolts
home.. 6. Sicily (Mt Etna)
oddity.. 7. one–eyed
race (Myth).. 6. giants
cygneous... 8. swanlike
cygnet... 4. swan
cylinder... 4. drum, pipe, roll, tube
5. inker, stele 6. barrel, gabion,

platen, record, roller, rounce, terete
10. cylindroid
cylindrical... 5. conic 6. terete
7. tubular
cymbal, cymbals... 3. tal, zel
6. Becken, piatti 7. potlids
8. doughnut
Cymric... 5. Welsh 9. Brythonic
Cymric (pert to)...
bard.. 6. Merlin 7. Aneurin
god of the dead.. 5. Pwyll
god of the sky.. 7. Gwydion
god of the sun.. 4. Lleu
god of the waves.. 5. Dylan
cynic... 5. Timon 7. ascetic, doglike,
egotist, snarler 9. pessimist
11. misanthrope
Cynic (pert to)...
pupil.. 8. Socrates
school.. 10. Philosophy
teacher.. 8. Diogenes
teaching.. 6. virtue
cynical... 7. currish 8. captious,
snarling 9. sarcastic 11. pessimistic
12. misanthropic
cynosure... 5. guide 8. lodestar
(loadstar), polestar 9. celebrity, North
Star 13. constellation
cyprinoid (fish)... 2. id 3. ide, orf
(orfe) 4. bass (black), carp, chub,
dace 6. chevin, shiner 7. herring
(lake) 8. fallfish 9. hornyhead,
squawfish
Cyprus...
capital.. 7. Nicosia (Sicily)
colonizer (anc).. 11. Phoenicians
history.. 11. New Stone Age
mountain.. 7. Troodos
port.. 7. Lornaca 8. Limassol
9. Famagusto
Cyrenaic (pert to)...
city.. 6. Cyrene
country.. 9. Cyrenaica (Afr)
division of.. 5. Libya
harbor.. 6. Tobruk 7. Bengazi
philosophy.. 8. hedonism, pleasure
Cyrene... 4. city (anc) 5. nymph
7. goddess
cyrus... 5. crane, sarus
Cyrus the Elder (pert to)...
conqueror of.. 7. Babylon
founder of.. 6. Persia (Empire)
king of.. 5. Lydia, Media
subduer of.. 9. Palestine
cyst... 3. box, sac, wen 5. chest,
pouch 7. vesicle
Czar... 4. Ivan, tsar, tzar 5. Peter
8. Nicholas
Czechoslovakia...
capital.. 6. Prague (Praha)
city.. 5. Praha 6. Pilsen 7. Ostrava
10. Bratislava
empire (anc).. 7. Bohemia, Moravia
8. Slovakia
forest.. 12. Great Bohemia
mountain, peak.. 3. Ore 6. Tatras
11. Carpathians
people.. 6. Czechs 7. Slovaks
river.. 4. Elbe (Labe), Iser, Oder
6. Vltava
czigany... 5. gypsy

D

D... 3. 500 6. letter (4th)
dab... 3. hit, tap 4. blow 5. paint,
 smear 6. expert, lizard, smooth
 7. dabster 8. flatfish
dabble... 4. mass 5. dally 6. befoul,
 meddle, paddle, potter, splash,
 tamper, trifle 7. spatter 8. sprinkle
dabbler... 7. trifler 8. sciolist
 10. dilettante
dabchick... 5. grebe 9. gallinule
dacha (Russ)... 5. villa 12. country
 house
dacoit... 6. bandit, robber
dacry, dacryo (comb form)... 5. tears
dactyl... 3. toe 4. foot 6. finger
 8. dactylus
dactyliomancy... 17. divination by
 rings (finger)
dactylogram... 11. fingerprint
dactylology... 12. sign language
Dadaism... 4. cult 8. negation
daddy–longlegs... 5. stilt 6. curlew,
 spider, Tipula 7. spinner
daedal, dedal... 4. rich 6. varied
 8. artistic, skillful (skilful)
 9. ingenious, intricate 10. variegated
Daedalus (Gr Myth)... 9. artificer
daffodil... 6. yellow 9. narcissus
 10. bellflower
daffy, daft... 3. gay, mad 4. wild
 5. batty, crazy, giddy, goofy, loony
 6. insane 7. foolish, idiotic
Dagda (pert to)...
 children.. 6. Aengus (Angus), Brigit
 famed as.. 7. harpist
 Gaelic name.. 7. Jupiter
 god of.. 10. pagan Irish
dagger... 4. dirk, kris, snee 5. kalar
 6. anlace, bodkin, creese 7. bayonet,
 poniard 10. misericord
Daibutsu (pert to)...
 famed image.. 6. Buddha
 Japanese Bronze.. 11. Great Buddha
 site.. 8. Kamakura (near Tokyo)
daily... 4. a day 7. diurnal, journal
 9. hodiurnal, newspaper, quotidian
 11. day in day out
daily food... 4. fare 5. bread
 10. livelihood 11. subsistence,
 substenance
dainties... 5. cates, estes 7. titbits
 (tidbits)
dainty... 4. fair, fine, rare 5. frail,
 small 6. choice, pretty, select
 8. elegance 9. exquisite, toothsome
 10. fastidious
dairy... 4. farm 8. creamery
 9. lactarium
dairymen caste (Ind)... 4. Ahir

dais... 5. stage, table 7. estrade
 8. platform
daisy... 5. gowan, oxeye 6. morgan,
 Shasta 7. Gerbera 9. Whiteweed
dale... 4. dell, dene, vale 5. spout
 6. dingle, ravine, trough, valley
dalles... 5. dells 11. canyon walls
dalliance... 4. chat 5. delay 6. gossip,
 trifle 8. fondling, trifling 10. flirtation
dally... 3. toy 5. tarry 6. dawdle,
 linger 13. procrastinate
Dalmatia...
 capital.. 7. Spalato (Yugoslavia)
 cherry.. 7. marasca
 coast.. 8. Adriatic
 dog.. 5. coach 8. carriage
 home of.. 10. Diocletian
 people.. 5. Serbs 8. Adriatic
 9. Yugoslavs
 product.. 4. lace
dam... 4. stay, stem, stop, weir
 5. Aswan, block, check, choke,
 Gatun (CZ) 6. Hoover (Boulder),
 mother, Norris, parent 7. barrier
 8. millpond, obstruct, Oroville,
 restrain 9. Roosevelt 10. Bull Shoals,
 Glen Canyon 11. Grand Coulee
damage... 3. mar 4. harm, hurt, loss,
 noxa 6. impair, injury, mayhem,
 scathe, strafe 8. disserve, sabotage
 9. detriment, vandalism
 10. impairment
daman... 4. cony (Bib) 5. Hyrax
 6. mammal 8. Procavia
Damascus, Syria (pert to)...
 Bib scene.. 20. Street Called Straight
 division.. 6. Jewish, Moslem
 9. Christian
 history.. 16. world's oldest city
 (inhabited)
 mosque (renowned).. 7. Ommiade
 river.. 5. Abana 6. Barada
damask... 3. red (color) 5. cloth, steel
 (Damascus) 8. to deface (the Great
 Seal, Eng)
dame... 4. lady, Miss 5. Madam, title
 6. matron, Nature, parent
damn... 4. cuss, ruin 5. abuse, curse
 6. shucks 7. accurse, condemn,
 swear at
damsel... 4. girl, lass 5. Rhoda (Bib),
 wench 7. colleen 10. damoiselle
dance... 4. jazz, prom, skip, trip
 5. frisk, glide 6. cavort, frolic,
 gambol 7. flicker, flutter, rejoice,
 saltate 10. tripudiate
dance (pert to)...
 art.. 12. choreography
 clumsily.. 6. balter
 mimetic (Rom).. 5. Salii 7. Luperci

146

8. Curetics
movement.. 6. chassé, gestic
7. saltant 9. pirouette
step.. 3. pas 5. coupe 6. chassé
7. gambado (gambade), shuffle
8. glissade 9. arabesque, grapevine
10. pigeonwing
dance (type)... 3. bal, hop, jig, toe
4. ball, clog, haka, kolo, polo, reel,
shag 5. gavot (gavotte), pavan,
polka, tango, waltz 6. althea, apache,
ballet, bolero, cancan, corant, maxixe,
minuet, morris, redowa, rhumba
(rumba), shimmy, square, watusi
7. beguine, coranto (old), courant,
foxtrot, gavotte, hoedown, mazurka,
one–step, ridotto, tempete, two–step
8. bunny hug, cakewalk, courante,
fandango, halliard (anc), hornpipe,
lanciers, rigadoon 9. allemande (anc),
butterfly, farandole, polonaise,
quadrille 10. Charleston, tarantella
11. schottische (schottish)
dancer... 6. hoofer 7. danseur
8. coryphee, danseuse, stripper
9. ballerina, ecdysiast, jitterbug
11. terpsichore 13. choreographer
dancer (pert to)...
Bib.. 6. Salome
Egyptian.. 4. alme (almeh) 7. ghawazi
8. Baramika
Japanese.. 6. geisha (girl)
Oriental.. 4. hula 6. nautch
8. bayadere
dancing (pert to)...
arrangement.. 12. choreography
Muse of.. 11. Terpsichore
term.. 6. ballet, chassé, gestic
7. hoofing, saltant
dandelion... 4. herb 5. plant 6. yellow
9. Taraxacum
dandified... 7. foppish
dandify... 6. spruce 7. adonize,
smarten 8. titivate (tittivate)
dandy... 3. fop 4. beau, dude, good,
toff 5. daisy 6. Adonis 7. coxcomb
9. exquisite 11. Beau Brummel
dangerous... 3. bad 4. dire 5. feral,
risky 6. chancy 7. ominous, parlous
8. alarming, critical, insecure,
perilous 9. hazardous 10. jeopardous,
precarious
dangle... 3. lop 4. hang, loll, yawl
5. droop, swing 6. flaunt, mizzen
Daniel (pert to)...
Bib.. 4. Book (Old Test) 7. prophet
(Heb)
form of verse.. 7. lyrical, sestina
verse adopted by.. 5. Dante
8. Petrarch
Danish... see also *Denmark*
capital.. 10. Copenhagen
council (anc).. 8. Rigsraad
country.. 7. Denmark
doctor.. 6. Finsen
export.. 8. cryolite
fiord.. 3. Ise
flag.. 9. Dannebrog
island.. 3. Als (Alsen) 5. Faroe
9. Greenland
King (anc).. 6. Canute
native.. 4. Dane 12. Scandinavian

parliament.. 7. Rigsdag
prince (legend).. 6. Hamlet
settlers in Ireland.. 6. Ostmen
dank... 3. wet 4. damp 5. humid,
moist, muggy
Dan McGrew... 11. Hound of Hell
danseuse... 7. danseur 8. coryphee
9. ballerina
Dante (pert to)...
birthplace.. 8. Florence
famed as.. 4. poet 6. lyrist
famed poem.. 12. Divine Comedy
poem's companion.. 6. Vergil (Virgil)
poem's division.. 4. Hell 6. Heaven
9. Purgatory
poem's love.. 8. Beatrice
Danube River (pert to)...
end.. 8. Black Sea
source.. 11. Black Forest
tributary.. 4. Isar, Raab 5. Drava
6. Morava
Danubian (pert to)...
color.. 5. green
fish.. 6. huchen (huch)
goose.. 10. Sevastopol
Danzig...
Polish name.. 6. Gdansk
river site.. 7. Vistula
Sea.. 6. Baltic
territory of (now).. 6. Poland
dap... 3. bob, dab, dib, dip
6. bounce, dibble, guddle 7. rebound
Daphne (pert to)...
Bib.. 4. Park (Antioch, Syria)
father.. 5. Ladon 6. Peneus
lover.. 6. Apollo
transformation.. 10. laurel tree
dapper... 4. braw, neat, pert, trim
5. natty, sleek 6. jaunty, little, lively,
spruce 7. dashing, finical
dappled... 6. dotted 7. flecked,
piebald, spotted
dare... 4. daze, defy, face, osse, risk
5. brave 6. assume, dazzle
7. venture 8. confront, defiance,
paralyze 9. challenge, undertake
daring... 4. bold, rash 5. brave, manly
8. boldness, defiance 9. audacious,
foolhardy 11. adventurous,
venturesome 12. enterprising
dark... 3. dim, mum, sad 4. ebon
5. black, blind, dense, faint, mirky,
murky, night, unlit, vague 6. closed,
gloomy, occult, opaque, secret,
wicked 7. joyless, melanic, obscure,
stygian 8. abstruse, ignorant,
moonless 9. ambiguous, atrocious,
Cimmerian (realm), lightless, nightfall,
tenebrous, uncertain 10. foreboding,
indistinct
dark (pert to)...
Ages.. 6. Middle 8. Medieval
9. Neolithic
Continent.. 6. Africa (formerly)
10. unexplored
horse.. 7. unknown 9. candidate
hue.. 5. dusky, swart 6. somber
7. swarthy
moon area.. 4. mare
darken... 3. dim 4. dull 5. blind,
umber 6. darkle, sadden, shadow
7. becloud, blacken, confuse, eclipse,

enshade 8. bewilder 9. obfuscate

darkness... 4. dark, dusk, mirk, murk
5. shade 6. Erebus, shadow
7. dimness, tenebra 9. blackness,
blindness, ignorance, obscurity
10. opaqueness

darling... 2. jo 3. pet 4. dear, idol,
lief 5. cheri, sweet 6. minion
7. acushla, beloved 8. favorite
9. mavournin 10. mavourneen,
sweetheart 13. cushlamochree
(cushlamachree)

darnel... 4. tare, weed 5. grass
6. Lolium

dart... 4. barb, bolt, flit, leap, vire
5. arrow, bound, lance, scoot, shoot,
start, throw 6. dartle, elance, glance,
spring, weapon 7. javelin, missile,
stinger 8. jaculate

Darwinism... 9. Evolution (theory,
1858) 12. Evolutionism

das, dasse... 6. badger

dash... 4. code, élan, gift, race, ruin,
rush, slam 5. ardor, crash, haste,
onset, plash, smash, speed, swash
6. energy, obelus (anc), spirit, sprint,
strike, stroke 7. bravura, spatter,
splurge 8. confound, gratuity
9. animation 11. punctuation

dashing... 3. gay 4. fast 5. showy
6. dapper, jaunty, sporty 7. stylish

dastardly... 4. base, foul 6. craven
8. cowardly

data... 5. facts, logic 7. grounds (for
facts) 11. information

date... 3. age 4. line (newspaper),
time 5. fruit, tryst 6. person
10. engagement 11. appointment

date (pert to)...
birth.. 5. natal
coin line.. 7. exergue
error.. 11. anachronism
fruit of.. 4. palm
plum.. 6. sapote

daub... 3. dab 4. blob, gaum, soil,
teer 5. paint, smear, stain, sully
6. bedaub 7. besmear, picture (art),
plaster 8. scribble

daughter... 5. child 7. cadette
9. offspring 10. descendant

daughter of...
Inachus (river god).. 2. Io
Night.. 5. Nemesis
the moon.. 7. Nokomis
the Spanish king.. 7. infanta

daunt... 3. awe, cow 4. faze 5. amate
(anc) 6. dismay, subdue 7. overawe,
repress 10. discourage, dishearten,
intimidate

dauntless... 4. bold 7. aweless
(awless) 8. fearless, intrepid, resolute
9. dreadless 11. unfaltering

davenport... 3. bed 4. desk, sofa
5. divan 12. Chesterfield

David (Bib)...
daughter.. 5. Tamar
father.. 5. Jesse
helpers.. 4. Igal 5. Abner
7. Shammah
king of.. 6. Israel (40 years)
slayer of.. 7. Goliath
son.. 7. Solomon

wife.. 7. Abigail

davit... 4. spar 5. crane

dawdle... 3. lag 4. idle, poke, toit
5. dally 6. linger, loiter, potter, trifle
9. vacillate 10. dillydally
13. procrastinate

dawn... 2. eo (comb form) 3. Eos
(goddess), red 4. morn 5. sunup
6. appear, aurora, sink in 7. sunrise
8. daybreak 9. beginning, penetrate

day (pert to)...
Athenians, Jews.. 6. sunset
Babylonians.. 7. sunrise
blindness.. 10. nyctalopia
11. hemeralopia
divisions.. 5. lunar, solar 8. sidereal
dream.. 4. muse 5. fancy 7. fantasy,
reverie 8. phantasy
Egyptians, Romans.. 8. midnight
god.. 5. Horus
nursery.. 6. crèche
scholar.. 7. externe

Day of...
Atonement.. 9. Yom Kippur
Brahma.. 9. Maha Yugas
doom.. 8. Judgment

day's march... 5. étape

day's work... 4. darg (dargue)

daze... 3. fog 4. asea, maze, stun
5. sopor, swoon 6. benumb, dazzle,
stupid, trance 7. confuse, stupefy
8. bewilder 9. dumbfound
12. razzle–dazzle

dazzling... 6. bright, garish 7. glaring
8. blinding, gorgeous 9. beautiful,
brilliant 11. bewildering

dead... 3. fey 4. flat, numb, obit
5. amort, blind, inert, napoo, passé
6. active, barren, lapsed 7. defunct,
expired, insipid, tedious 8. ad patres,
complete, deceased, inactive, lifeless,
obsolete 9. apathetic, inanimate
10. lusterless, motionless, spiritless,
unexciting 11. nonexistent

dead (pert to)...
Dead Sea apple.. 12. Apple of
Sodom
Dead Sea country.. 4. Moab
5. Sodom 8. Gomorrah
language.. 5. Latin
rise from the.. 7. resurge
9. reanimate, resurrect
set (slang).. 8. full tilt, hell–bent
tree.. 7. rampike (rampick)

deaden... 4. damp, dull, mute, numb
6. muffle, obtund, opiate, weaken
7. relieve, repress 8. enfeeble
10. devitalize

deadly... 4. dire, mort 5. fatal
6. lethal, mortal 7. deathly
8. venomous 10. implacable,
lifelessly 11. destructive, internecine

deaf... 4. surd 7. earless
10. intolerant 11. inattentive,
preoccupied

deaf alphabet... 11. dactylology
12. sign language

deaf and dumb... 9. surdomute
10. deaf–mutism 11. surdimutism

deafness... 6. amusia (tone) 7. surdity
13. insensibility

deafness operation... 8. fenestra

deal... 3. lot 4. dole, give, mede,
mete, sale, sell 5. allot, share, trade,
treat 6. parcel 7. dispose, portion,
wrestle 8. business, dispense,
quantity 9. apportion, entertain
10. administer, distribute
dealer (pert to)...
  cattle.. 6. drover, herder
  cloth.. 6. draper, mercer
  drug.. 8. druggist 10. apothecary,
  pharmacist 14. pharmacopolist
  retail.. 6. grocer, monger 8. merchant
  9. tradesman
  stock exchange.. 6. broker, jobber,
  trader 11. stockbroker
dean, dene... 4. dell 6. valley
dean... 4. head, Inge 5. decan, doyen
6. fellow (Educ), master, senior,
verger 7. officer 9. churchman,
principal
dear... 5. chere, cheri, deary, lover,
sugar, sweet 7. beloved, darling
8. precious 9. expensive
10. sweetheart
dearth... 4. want 6. famine, rarity
7. paucity, poverty 8. rareness,
scarcity, sparsity
death... 4. doom, mort, obit 5. sleep
(eternal) 6. demise 7. decease,
passing, quietus, release
10. euthanasia (mercy), expiration
11. evanishment
death (pert to)...
  after.. 10. posthumous
  eternal.. 9. perdition
  foreboding.. 6. funest 7. doleful
  lawless.. 8. lynching
  notice.. 4. obit 5. orbit 8. obituary
  of a deity.. 4. Mors
  rattle.. 4. rale
  stoning (by).. 8. lapidate
deathlessness... 9. athanasia
11. immortality 15. everlastingness
debacle... 4. rout 5. crash, flood
7. washout 8. collapse, stampede
9. breakdown, cataclysm
11. catastrophe, destruction
debar... 3. bar 4. deny 5. estop
6. forbid, hinder, refuse 7. exclude
8. obstruct, preclude, prohibit
debark... 4. land 8. go ashore
9. disembark
debase... 5. abase, alloy, lower
6. demean, demote, reduce
7. corrupt, degrade, deprave
8. disgrace 10. adulterate, depreciate
11. deteriorate
debasement... 8. demotion
9. abasement, abjection, reduction,
vitiation 11. degradation
13. deterioration
debatable... 4. moot 9. refutable
10. disputable 11. contestable
13. controversial
debate... 4. agon (anc), moot
5. argue, forum, plead, weigh
6. reason 7. analyze, closure,
cloture, dispute, wrangle
8. argument, consider, forensic,
militate 9. quodlibet 10. deliberate,
discussion 11. controversy
12. deliberation, dissertation

13. argumentation
debauch... 4. bout, orgy 5. broil,
spree, taint 6. defile, seduce, splore
7. mislead 8. carousal, escapade
9. disaffect, dissipate
11. contaminate
debauchee... 4. rake, roué 5. satyr
7. rounder 9. libertine 10. profligate
debenture (Finan)... 4. bond 5. claim
6. pledge 7. voucher 10. instrument
11. certificate
debilitated... 4. weak 5. seedy
6. feeble, infirm, sapped, sickly
7. languid 8. asthenic, impaired,
weakened 9. enfeebled, langorous
11. devitalized
debility... 5. atony 7. languor
8. adynamia, asthenia, cachexia,
weakness 9. infirmity, lassitude
10. feebleness, sickliness
debit... 4. debt 5. entry 6. charge
debonair, debonaire... 4. airy
5. suave 6. breezy, jaunty, urbane
7. affable, buoyant 8. carefree
debris... 4. junk 5. attle, ruins, scrap,
talus, trash 6. litter, refuse, rubble
7. deposit, remains, rubbish
8. detritus 10. clamjamfry
debt... 3. due, IOU, sin (Bib)
7. arrears, default 8. trespass
9. arrearage, liability 10. obligation
debut... 3. bow 8. entrance (formal)
9. coming out 12. introduction,
presentation
debutante... 3. bud, deb 6. subdeb
9. socialite
decade... 3. ten 9. decennium
decadence... 5. decay 7. decline
13. deterioration, retrogression
decamp... 4. flee 6. depart
7. abscond, vamoose
12. absquatulate
decanter... 4. ewer 5. croft 6. bottle,
carafe, vessel (liquors)
decapod... 4. crab 5. prawn 6. shrimp
7. Homarus, lobster 8. Decapoda
10. crustacean
decay... 3. rot 4. blet, doty 5. spoil,
waste 6. caries, wither 7. crumble,
mortify, putrefy 8. spoilage
9. decadence, decompose
11. deteriorate, dissolution
13. decomposition, deterioration
deceased... 4. dead, gone, late 6. at
rest 7. defunct, demised
8. decedent, departed
deceit... 5. covin, craft, fraud, guile,
guise 7. cunning 8. artifice,
cozenage, intrigue, subtlety, trickery,
wiliness 9. chicanery, deception,
duplicity, imposture, mendacity,
sophistry, treachery 10. craftiness,
sneakiness 13. deceitfulness,
dissimulation 14. tergiversation
15. treacherousness
deceitful... 4. wily 5. false 6. artful,
crafty, sneaky, tricky 8. guileful,
scheming, trickish 9. deceptive,
gnathonic, insincere 10. fraudulent
11. treacherous 13. Machiavellian
deceive... 3. cog, lie 4. bilk, dupe,
flam, fool, gull, hoax, sile 5. cheat,

cozen, elude, hocus, trick, troil
6. baffle, delude, illude, seduce
7. beguile, mislead 8. hoodwink
deceiver . . . 3. gay 5. cheat 6. hoaxer,
trepan (trapan) 8. betrayer, impostor
9. trickster
decency . . . 7. decorum, fitness,
modesty 8. chastity, niceness
9. propriety 10. seemliness
12. tastefulness
decent . . . 4. kind 6. comely, kindly,
proper, seemly 7. clothed
8. adequate, gracious, suitable,
tasteful 9. tolerable
deception . . . 3. lie 4. hoax, wile
5. cheat, fraud, guile 6. deceit,
misled 7. fallacy 8. artifice, deceived,
flimflam, illusion 9. duplicity,
imposture
deceptive . . . 5. vague 8. illusive,
illusory 9. deceiving, sirenical (sirenic)
10. fallacious
decide (upon) . . . 3. opt 4. vote
5. adapt, elect, judge 6. choose,
settle 7. referee, resolve 9. arbitrate,
ascertain, determine, influence
decima . . . 4. stop (organ) 5. tenth,
tithe 8. interval
decimal . . . 3. ten 5. tenth 7. tenfold
8. repetend
decimate . . . 3. few 4. kill, slay
5. burke, tenth 6. divide 7. destroy
8. subtract 9. devastate, slaughter
decipher . . . 4. read 5. crack
6. decode, detect 7. unravel
8. discover 9. translate
decision . . . 4. grit 5. arret, nerve,
pluck 6. mettle, report 7. verdict
8. firmness 10. conclusion,
resolution, settlement
12. announcement 13. determination
decisive . . . 3. end 5. final 7. certain,
crucial 8. critical, resolute
9. mandatory 10. conclusive,
convincing
decisive moment . . . 6. crisis
deck (ship's) . . . 3. gun 4. main, poop
5. orlop, upper 6. bridge 7. scupper
(gutter) 8. hatchway, platform
9. promenade 10. forecastle
deck . . . 4. gild 5. adorn, array, cards
(playing), equip 6. blazon, clothe,
enrich 7. bedizen, dress up
8. emblazon
declaim . . . 4. rant, rave 5. orate, spiel,
spout 6. herald, recite 8. denounce,
harangue, perorate 9. discourse
11. declamation
declamation . . . 7. lecture 9. elocution
10. recitation
declaration . . . 3. vow 4. oath
6. avowal, decree, oracle 8. pleading
(law) 9. assertion, manifesto,
testimony 10. confession (of faith)
11. affirmation 12. proclamation
13. pronouncement
declare . . . 3. say 4. aver, avow, meld
5. bruit, state 6. affirm, allege,
assert, blazon, herald, spread
7. publish 8. announce, indicate,
maintain 9. advertise
declare (pert to) . . .

against . . 6. indict
as fact . . 5. posit
innocent . . 6. acquit
declension . . . 4. drop, fall 5. slope
7. decline, descent, refusal
10. inflection 13. deterioration
decline . . . 3. dip, ebb, set 4. fade, fail,
fall, flag, sink, wane 5. droop, repel,
slope, slump, stoop 6. refuse, reject,
weaken 7. dwindle 8. decrease,
downhill 9. decadence, declivity,
repudiate 10. retrograde
12. depreciation
declivity . . . 3. dip 4. drop, hill
5. scarp, slope 7. descent
8. downgate 9. downgrade
decoction . . . 4. sapa (sape) 6. apozem,
cremor, tisane 7. boiling
10. extraction 11. preparation
decompose . . . 3. rot 4. frit 5. decay
7. resolve 10. photolysis
12. disintegrate
decorate . . . 4. deck, trim 5. adorn,
honor 6. emboss 7. bedizen,
brocade, miniate 8. beautify,
ornament 9. scrimshaw
decorated . . . 5. fancy 6. ornate
7. adorned 8. nielloed 9. sigillate
(pottery) 11. embellished
decoration . . . 4. buhl 5. gutta (anc),
medal 6. plaque, purfle, ribbon
7. epergne, festoon, garnish 8. gold
star, ornament, trimming
9. adornment, garniture, sgraffito
10. cordon bleu, emblazonry,
embroidery
decorous . . . 4. calm, prim 5. grave,
quiet, staid 6. decent, demure,
modest, proper, sedate, seemly,
serene 7. fitting, regular, settled
8. becoming, composed, suitable,
tasteful 9. unruffled 12. conventional
decorticate . . . 4. bark, flay, husk, pare,
peel, skin 5. strip 9. excoriate
decoy . . . 4. bait, lure, tole 6. capper,
entrap 8. by—bidder 9. come—on man
11. stool pigeon
decrease . . . 3. ebb 4. drop, sink, wane
5. abate, waste 6. decess, lessen,
reduce, shrink 7. decline, dwindle,
shorten, slacken, subside
8. compress, diminish, moderate
9. abatement, deduction, deflation,
lessening 10. diminution
11. contraction 12. depreciation
decree . . . 3. act, law 4. bull, fiat, rede
(anc), will 5. arret, canon, edict,
enact, irade, order, ukase 6. dictum,
ordain 7. command, mandate, verdict
8. decision, rescript 9. ordinance
decree beforehand . . . 7. destine
decree nisi . . . 7. divorce
decrepit . . . 3. old 4. aged, lame, weak
6. infirm, senile, wasted (with age)
7. worn out 8. unstable, unsturdy
decry . . . 3. boo 4. slur 5. lower
7. condemn, degrade, detract
8. belittle, denounce, derogate
9. discredit, disparage, underrate
10. depreciate, undervalue
dedal . . . see *daedal*
dedicate . . . 6. devote, hallow

7. address 8. inscribe
10. consecrate
deduce ... 5. infer 6. deduct, derive,
elicit, evolve 7. suppose
deduct ... 4. bate, faik, take 6. remove
8. discount, retrench, separate,
subtract
deduction ... 6. rebate 7. reprise
8. discount, illation 9. allowance,
corollary, induction, inference,
reasoning, syllogism
deed ... 3. act, ado 4. feat, fiat, gest
(geste) 5. actum, actus, stunt, title
6. action, doings 7. exploit
8. contract, tenendum
11. achievement, malefaction,
performance
deem ... 5. judge, opine, think
6. esteem, regard 7. believe,
presume, suppose 8. conclude,
consider 10. adjudicate
deemed ... 7. assumed, reputed
8. adjudged, inferred, presumed,
supposed 10. considered
deep ... 3. low, pit 4. rich, wide, wise
5. great 6. hidden, remote, solemn
7. learned, obscure, serious
8. immersed, involved, powerful,
profound 9. engrossed, entangled,
sagacious 10. deep–seated,
mysterious
deep (pert to) ...
dish pie .. 7. cobbler
sea .. 6. depths
seated .. 8. habitual 9. ingrained
11. established
sleep .. 5. sopor
sound .. 4. bell, gong
deepen ... 5. lower 6. dredge
7. broaden, enhance 9. aggravate,
intensify 10. strengthen
deer ... 3. elk, red, roe 4. buck, fawn,
hart, hind, maha, stag 5. eland,
moose, ratwa 6. fallow, sambar,
wapiti 7. caribou, deerlet, roebuck
8. reindeer, ruminant
deer (pert to) ...
antler .. 3. dag 4. snag 8. tres–tine
(royal)
Asiatic .. 6. sambar
barking .. 7. muntjac (muntjak)
deerlike .. 10. chevrotain
female .. 3. doe, roe 4. hind
genus .. 4. Dama 6. Cervus
8. Cervidae
Japanese .. 4. sika
Java .. 4. napu 7. muntjac (muntjak)
Lapland .. 8. reindeer
male .. 4. buck, hart, stag 6. havier
7. brocket (brok), pricket
meat .. 7. venison
mouse .. 7. plandok
Oriental .. 4. axis, Rusa 5. kakar
6. chital, rativa, sambar 7. kanchil,
muntjac (muntjak)
Russian .. 4. olen
S American .. 4. pita 6. guemal
(guemul) 7. brocket, spitter
Tibet .. 4. shou
tiger .. 6. cougar
tracks .. 3. run 4. slot
type .. 3. red, roe 4. mule 6. fallow

11. black–tailed, white–tailed
deface ... 3. mar 4. ruin, scar 5. spoil
6. damage, injure 7. blemish, distort
9. discredit, disfigure
defamation ... 5. libel 7. calumny,
slander, spatter 8. disgrace, dishonor
9. aspersion 10. defilement,
detraction
defame ... 5. libel 6. accuse, charge,
infamy, malign, vilify 7. asperse,
blacken, detract, slander, traduce
8. dishonor 10. calumniate
default ... 4. fail, lack, loss, mora
7. deficit, failure, neglect
9. deficient, denigrate, oversight
10. nonpayment 11. delinquency
14. nonfulfillment
defeat ... 4. beat, best, lose, rout
5. worst 6. baffle, derout, master,
refute 7. beating, clobber, confute,
conquer, failure, mastery, repulse,
triumph (over), undoing 8. Waterloo
9. frustrate, overthrow 10. disappoint
11. subjugation 12. discomfiture
14. disappointment
defeating ... 7. beating, routing
10. anatreptic, conquering
11. vanquishing
defeatism ... 6. malism 7. Boloism
10. retreatism
defect ... 4. flaw, lisp, lock, quit, want
5. fault 7. blemish, forsake
8. withdraw 9. discredit
10. deficiency, inadequacy
12. imperfection, irregularity
defection ... 4. loss 7. failing, failure
9. desertion 10. abjurement
11. abandonment
defective ... 3. bad 4. lame 5. idiot
6. cretin, faulty 7. half–wit, lacking
8. crippled 9. deficient, imperfect,
subnormal 10. incomplete
defective vision ... 6. anopia, myopia
defend ... 4. save, ward 5. guard,
plead, shend, watch 6. screen,
secure, shield, uphold 7. contest,
justify, protect, shelter, support,
sustain 8. enshield, preserve
10. controvert
defendant ... 4. reus 7. accused,
libelee, suspect 8. appellee
10. respondent
defender ... 8. advocate, champion
9. justifier, protector 10. vindicator
defense ... 4. boma, fort, plea 5. alibi,
guard 6. abatis (abattis), glacis
(slope) 7. bulwark, rampart, ravelin
8. estacade (dike), sepiment,
stockade 10. protection
12. counterscarp 13. justification,
machicolation
defenseless ... 7. aidless, forlorn,
unarmed 8. helpless 9. unarmored,
unguarded 10. undefended,
unshielded 11. unfortified,
unprotected
defer ... 3. bow 4. wait 5. delay
6. retard 7. adjourn, suspend
8. postpone, protract, stave off
13. procrastinate
defer (to) ... 5. yield 6. admire, regard,
submit 7. concede, respect

9. recognize 11. acknowledge

deference... 5. honor 6. esteem, fealty, homage, regard 7. respect 8. courtesy 9. reverence 10. politeness, submission 12. complaisance 13. consideration

deferential... 8. obeisant 9. attentive, courteous 10. respectful, submissive 11. ceremonious

defiance... 6. defial 8. audacity, boldness 9. challenge, disregard, insolence

deficiency... 4. lack, want 6. dearth, ullage 7. aneuria, deficit 8. scarcity, shortage 10. inadequacy 13. insufficiency 14. incompleteness

deficient... 5. minus, short 6. faulty, meager (meagre), scarce 7. lacking, missing, wanting 8. inferior 9. defective, imperfect 10. inadequate, incomplete 12. insufficient

defile... 4. file, pass (Mt), soil 5. dirty, gorge, notch, sully, taint 6. befoul, debase, ravine, vilify 7. corrupt, debauch, deprave, pollute, tarnish 8. dishonor 10. passageway

define... 3. fix 4. name 5. bound, limit 6. decide 7. delimit, explain, outline 8. boundary 9. delineate, determine, stipulate 11. distinguish 12. characterize, circumscribe

defined (sharply)... 8. clear–cut 9. trenchant

defined track... 3. rut 4. slot

definite... 4. sure 7. certain, limited, precise 8. absolute, distinct, explicit, manifest, positive 10. undeniable 11. determining, unqualified 12. unmistakable 14. unquestionable

definitely... 10. explicitly, positively 12. conclusively, unmistakably

definition... 6. naming 7. clarity, meaning 9. sharpness 11. description, explanation 12. delimitation, distinctness 14. interpretation

deflation... 7. decline 8. collapse 9. reduction 10. cheapening 11. devaluation, humiliation 12. depreciation

deflect... 4. bend, warp 5. avert 6. divert 7. deviate

deformed... 5. varus 7. taliped 8. formless 9. amorphous, distorted, grotesque, loathsome, malformed, misshapen, monstrous 10. clubfooted

defraud... 3. gyp, rob 4. bilk, gull 5. cheat, cozen 6. fleece 7. swindle

deft... 3. apt, fit, pat 4. meet, trim 5. adept, handy, quick 6. adroit, clever, expert 8. skillful (skilful) 9. dexterous, masterful

defunct... 3. die 4. dead, gone 6. depart, finish 7. extinct 8. deceased 11. nonexistent

defy... 4. dare 5. beard, brave, stump 6. cartel 7. disdain, disobey 9. challenge

degenerate... 6. debase, wicked, worsen 7. atrophy, corrupt, degrade, deprave 8. decadent 10. retrogress

11. deteriorate

degeneration... 7. decline 9. decadence, turpitude 10. degeneracy 11. degradation 13. deterioration, retrogression

degradation... 5. shame 7. censure, decline 8. demotion, disgrace, ignominy 9. reduction, turpitude 10. debasement, punishment 11. humiliation 13. deterioration

degrade... 5. abase, lower 6. debase, demean, demote, depose, humble 7. corrupt 8. disgrace, dishonor 9. humiliate 10. depreciate

degrade (socially)... 8. declassé

degree... 4. rank, step, tate 5. class, grade, order, point, scope, shade, stage, stair 6. extent 7. station 8. capacity, relation 9. intensity

degree (pert to)...
academic.. 8. bachelor 9. doctorate, masterate 11. engineering 13. baccalaureate
highest.. 13. summa cum laude
slight.. 5. shade 9. gradation
to what.. 9. howsoever 10. howsomever

dehydrate... 3. dry 5. dry up 6. wither 8. preserve 9. anhydrate, dessicate, evaporate, exsiccate

deify... 5. exalt 7. ennoble, glorify, idolize 8. enshrine 11. apotheosize, immortalize

deign... 7. consent 9. vouchsafe 10. condescend

deity... 2. El 3. Dea, God 4. Deus, deva 5. numen 6. Elohim 7. goddess, godhead, godhood 8. Almighty, Divinity, Immortal 12. Supreme Being

deity (aboriginal)... 4. mana, Zemi 5. huaca, wakan 6. manito (manitou), nagual, orenda, pokunt 8. tamanoas

deity (pert to)...
avenging.. 6. Erinys 7. Alastor, Anteros
destroying.. 4. Siva (Shiva)
evil.. 5. Sebek (crocodile–headed)
hearth.. 5. Vesta
household.. 3. Lar 7. Penates
human sacrifice.. 6. Moloch
judge of the dead.. 4. Yama
love.. 4. Amor, Eros 5. Cupid
mockery.. 5. Momus
music.. 6. Apollo
solar.. 5. Mentu (Ment, falcon–headed)
sun.. 2. Ra
supreme.. 6. Ormazd
two–faced.. 5. Janus
underworld.. 3. Dis 4. Gwyn 5. Pluto 6. Osiris
war.. 4. Ares
woodland.. 3. Pan 4. faun 5. satyr 7. silenus

dejected... 3. sad 5. amort 6. abased, droopy 7. à la mort, lowered 8. downcast 9. depressed, prostrate 10. despondent 11. downhearted, low–spirited

dejection... 7. lowness, sadness

10. depression, melancholy
11. despondency
Delaware...
beach.. 8. Rehoboth
capital.. 5. Dover
church (oldest Prot).. 9. Old Swedes
city.. 5. Lewes 9. New Castle
  10. Wilmington (Fort Christina,
  1638)
corporation.. 6. DuPont
product.. 9. chemicals 13. Blue Hen
  chicks
river.. 8. Delaware 10. Brandywine
State admission.. 5. first
State motto.. 22. Liberty and
  Independence
State nickname.. 5. First 7. Diamond
delay... 3. lag 4. halt, mora, stay,
  wait 5. block, check, dally, defer,
  demur, pause, tarry 6. arrest, detain,
  hinder, impede, loiter, retard
  7. confine, setback 8. lateness,
  obstruct, postpone, reprieve,
  slow—down 9. detention, hindrance
  10. cunctation, moratorium
  13. procrastinate 15. procrastination
delayed... 4. late, slow 5. tardy
  7. belayed, overdue 10. behindhand
delectable... 6. savory 8. luscious,
  pleasing 9. ambrosial, delicious
  10. delightful 11. scrumptious
delegate... 4. name, send 6. assign,
  commit, depute, deputy, legate
  7. appoint, consign, entrust
  8. deputize 9. authorize
  10. commission 12. commissioner
  14. representative
delete... 4. dele 5. erase 6. cut out,
  excise, remove 7. edit out, expunge
  9. eradicate 10. obliterate
deleterious... 7. harmful, hurtful,
  noxious 9. injurious 10. pernicious,
  prejudiced 11. destructive,
  detrimental, prejudicial
deletion... 4. stet 7. apocope
  8. excision 9. expunging
delf, delft... 3. pit 4. mine 6. quarry
Delhi... 7. capital (Ind)
deliberate... 4. cool, muse, pore, slow
  5. study, think, weigh 6. ponder
  7. discuss, reflect, studied
  8. consider, measured, prepense
  9. calculate, leisurely, speculate,
  unhurried, voluntary 11. contemplate,
  intentional, premeditate
  12. premeditated 13. dispassionate
deliberately... 6. slowly 7. tardily
  8. by design 9. expressly, purposely,
  willfully 13. intentionally
delicacy... 4. cate, tact 5. snack, taste
  6. caviar, luxury, nicety, tidbit
  7. finesse, frailty, tenuity 8. fineness,
  niceness, softness, subtlety
  9. exactness, fragility, precision
  10. daintiness, refinement, slightness
  11. sensitivity
delicate... 3. sly 4. fine, lacy, nice,
  soft 5. frail, light 6. dainty, mignon,
  petite, pretty, queasy, subtle, tender
  7. elegant, fragile, minikin, refined,
  tenuous 8. araneous, graceful,
  luscious, tasteful 9. exquisite,

sensitive 10. fastidious, meticulous,
  scrupulous 11. considerate
delicious... 5. tasty 8. luscious
  9. ambrosial, nectarean
  10. delightful, nectareous
delight... 3. joy 4. glee 5. amuse,
  bliss, charm, exult, mirth 6. divert,
  please, ravish, regale, relish
  7. enchant, gratify, overjoy
  8. pleasure 9. delectate, enrapture,
  happiness 13. gratification
delightful... 6. lovely, savory
  7. amusing, winsome 8. charming,
  engaging, pleasant 9. appealing,
  delicious, enjoyable 10. enchanting
  11. fascinating
delineate... 3. map 4. draw, limn, line
  5. trace 6. define, depict 7. outline,
  picture, portray 8. describe
  9. represent
delinquency... 7. default, failure
  8. omission 9. violation
  10. nonpayment 11. malfeasance,
  misdemeanor, misfeasance
  13. nonobservance
deliquesce... 4. give, melt 6. ramify
  7. liquefy 8. diminish, dissolve
delirious... 6. insane, raving 8. frenzied
  9. wandering (mental)
  14. disorientation
delirium... 4. fury, rage 6. frenzy,
  lunacy 7. madness, passion
  8. insanity 9. phrenitis
  10. aberration, excitement,
  unsaneness 11. derangement
  13. hallucination
deliver... 4. free, give, save 5. speak
  6. commit, impart, ransom, redeem,
  render, resign 7. consign, release,
  relieve 8. transfer 9. discharge,
  enunciate, extradite, surrender
deliver of evil spirits... 8. exorcise
deliver oration... 7. declaim
dell... 4. dale, dene, vale 5. slade
  6. dalles (pl), dingle, ravine, valley
Delos...
famed for.. 5. ruins 10. Stone Lions
island group.. 8. Cyclades
sea.. 6. Aegean
Delphi, Delphoi (Gr)...
modern name.. 6. Kastri
oracle.. 7. Delphic 8. Delphian
priestess.. 6. Pythia
delude... 3. jig 4. dupe, flam, fool,
  hoax 5. elude, trick 6. befool
  7. beguile, deceive, mislead
  9. bamboozle, frustrate, victimize
  11. double—cross
deluge... 5. flood 6. drench 7. freshet,
  Niagara, torrent 8. cataract, flooding,
  inundate, overflow, submerge, The
  Flood 9. cataclysm, overwhelm
  10. oversupply 14. superabundance
delusion... 4. ruse 6. mirage
  7. fallacy, fantasm 8. illusion,
  phantasm 9. deception
  10. misleading 13. hallucination
delve... 3. dig 4. mine, till 5. gouge,
  scoop, spade 6. exhume 8. excavate
demand... 3. ask, COD, cry, dun, fee
  4. call, need 5. claim, query 6. elicit
  7. require 8. exaction, question

9. requisite, ultimatum
11. requirement, requisition
demeanor, demeanour... 4. mien
7. bearing, conduct, posture
8. behavior, carriage
11. comportment
demented... 3. mad 4. daft, loco, luny
5. crazy, loony 6. crazed, insane
7. cracked 8. deranged
10. unbalanced 11. disoriented
Demeter... 7. goddess (Agric)
demigod... 4. hero 5. satyr (sylvan)
6. Triton 7. godling, half—god
10. semidivine
demise... 5. death, lease 6. convey
7. decease 8. bequeath
10. alienation, conveyance
demit... 4. quit 5. leave 6. resign,
vacate 8. abdicate 10. relinquish
11. resignation
demiurgic... 8. creative 9. formative
demivolt... 4. jump 5. vault (half)
6. curvet 8. capriole
Democrat (Polit slang)... 6. Hunker
demoded... 5. passé 6. passed
10. out of style
demolish... 4. rase, raze, ruin, undo
5. wreck 7. destroy, shatter
9. devastate, dismantle, overthrow
11. disassemble
demon, daemon... 3. hag, imp, nat
4. atua, jinn, Mara, ogre, Rahu
5. asura, devil, Eolis, fiend, genie,
jinni (jinnee), lamia, Satan 6. afreet
7. Amaimon, villain 8. Asmodeus
9. cacodemon (cacodaemon)
demoniac... 8. devilish, fiendish
demons (pert to)...
adjurers.. 9. exorcists
assembly of.. 6. sabbat
charm against.. 10. demonifuge
possessed of.. 8. demoniac
theory of.. 10. demonology
worship of.. 11. demonolatry
demonstrate... 4. show 5. prove
6. evince, typify 7. display, explain,
portray 8. manifest 9. exemplify
demonstrative... 7. gushing 8. effusive
9. emotional 10. indicative
11. explanatory 12. affectionate,
illustrative
Demosthenes (Gr)... 6. orator
(greatest)
demur... 4. stay 5. delay, pause, tarry
6. linger, object (to) 7. scruple
8. demurrer, hesitate 9. objection
12. irresolution
demure... 3. coy, mim, shy 4. prim,
smug 5. grave, staid, timid
6. sedate, solemn, stuffy 7. bashful,
prudish, serious 8. decorous
den... 4. cave, dell, lair, nest, room
5. cavea (anc), group (scouts), haunt,
study 6. cavern, grotto, hollow,
ravine 7. retreat 8. hideaway
denial... 5. cross 7. refusal
8. demurrer, negation 9. disavowal,
disowning, rejection 10. refutation
11. deprivation 12. disallowance
13. disaffirmance
denizen... 3. cit 6. native 7. citizen,
dweller, hellion (of hell) 9. indweller

10. inhabitant 11. cosmopolite
Denmark... see also *Danish*
anc name.. 5. Thule
capital.. 10. Copenhagen
city.. 6. Nyborg (Fyn Isl), Odense
7. Aalborg 8. Elsinore
founder.. 7. Absalon (Axel)
Hamlet's grave.. 8. Elsinore
island possession.. 6. Faroes
9. Greenland
peninsula.. 7. Jutland
river.. 5. Guden
ruler (anc).. 6. Canute (Kanute)
denomination... 3. ism 4. cult, name,
sect 5. class, party, value 6. church,
number, school 7. society
8. category 10. persuasion
11. appellation, designation,
stipulation
denote... 4. mark, mean, note, show
5. imply 6. convey 7. bespeak,
betoken, connote, express, purport,
signify 8. indicate 10. denominate
denoting (pert to)...
equal pressure.. 8. isobaric
final end (Gram).. 5. telic
usual action.. 9. usitative
denouement... 3. end 5. issue
6. result 7. outcome (plot)
8. solution 10. revelation
denounce... 4. damn 6. accuse, assail,
scathe 7. arraign, censure, condemn,
upbraid 9. reprobate 10. denunciate,
stigmatize
de novo... 3. new 4. anew 5. fresh,
newly 6. afresh
dense... 4. dewy, firm 5. close, crass,
gross, heavy, solid, thick 6. opaque,
stupid 7. compact, crowded
8. populous, thickset 11. thickheaded
density... 4. dord (Chem) 8. dumbness
9. stupidity 11. compactness
dent... 3. pit 4. dint 5. dinge, notch,
tooth 6. batter, hollow, indent
7. imprint 10. depression, impression
11. indentation
dentagra... 7. forceps 9. dentalgia,
toothache
dental (pert to)...
appliance.. 3. dam 6. scaler
7. forceps
drill.. 8. cavitron
filling.. 5. inlay
measure.. 10. dentimeter
toothache.. 8. dentagra 9. dentalgia
dentate... 7. serried, toothed
dentine... 5. ivory
dentist... 10. exodontist
12. orthodontist 14. prosthodontist
denude... 4. bate 5. scalp, strip
6. divest, expose, unrobe 7. uncover
denunciation... 6. menace, threat
7. inveigh 8. reproach
10. accusation 11. arraignment
deny... 4. nego 5. debar 6. abjure,
impugn, negate, recant, refuse,
renege 7. confute, disavow, dispute,
gainsay 8. disclaim, forswear,
traverse 9. repudiate 10. contradict,
contravene, controvert
deodar (species)... 5. cedar
depart... 2. go 3. die 4. exit, quit

5. leave, mosey 6. decamp, demise, egress, perish 7. abscond, vamoose 8. separate (Chem), withdraw
depraved . . . 4. evil, vile 6. shrewd, wicked 7. corrupt, immoral, vicious 8. vitiated 9. debauched, dissolute, perverted 10. degenerate
depravity . . . 8. depraved 9. turpitude 10. corruption, wickedness 15. incorrigibility
depreciate . . . 4. fall 5. lower, slump 6. debase, lessen, reduce, shrink 7. cheapen, deflate 8. belittle, discount, pejorate, vilipend 9. disparage 10. undervalue
depreciation . . . 8. decrease, discount 9. deflation 10. cheapening, pejoration 12. belittlement 13. disparagement 14. undervaluation
depredator . . . 5. thief 6. looter, robber 7. spoiler 8. marauder, ravisher 9. despoiler, plunderer
depress . . . 4. dent, sink 5. lower 6. dampen, deepen, deject, indent, reduce, sadden 7. flatten, imprint, oppress 8. dispirit, enfeeble 10. discourage
depressed . . . 3. low, sad 4. dire, sunk 6. dismal, oblate 8. dejected, downcast 9. debruised (Her), flattened (vertically) 10. dispirited 11. downhearted 12. disheartened
depressing . . . 5. chill 6. dismal, dreary, gloomy, somber 7. joyless 9. saddening 10. melancholy
depression . . . 3. col, dip, pit 4. dent, fall 5. blues, fossa (Anat), gloom, gully 6. cavity, crater, ravine, trough, vapors 10. melancholy 11. despondency, humiliation
deprivation . . . 4. loss, want 7. deposal, ousting, removal 9. privation, unseating 10. divestment 11. bereavement
deprive . . . 3. rob 4. take 5. debar, mulct, strip 6. divest, remove 7. bereave, despoil 10. dispossess
deprived of . . .
authority . . 9. dethroned
life . . 5. slain 6. killed 12. exterminated
limb . . 6. maimed
natural qualities . . 9. denatured
possessions . . 12. expropriated
professional standing . . 8. laicized
rank . . 7. deposed
reason . . 8. demented
vigor . . 6. sapped 8. deadened, unnerved 9. enervated, enfeebled
depth . . . 5. abyss, midst 6. extent 9. intensity 10. profundity
depths . . . 3. sea 5. adyta (spiritual), ocean 16. Davy Jones's locker
depute . . . 6. assign, devote 7. appoint 8. delegate, deputize
deputy . . . 5. agent, envoy, proxy, vicar 6. legate 8. alter ego 9. alternate 10. substitute
deracinate . . . 6. evulse, unroot, uproot 7. extract (forcibly)
deride . . . 3. pan 4. dupe, geck, gibe, jeer, mock, razz 5. cheat, fleer, flout,

scoff, scorn, trick 6. insult 8. ridicule
derision . . . 5. fleer, scorn 7. asteism, mockery 8. contempt, ridicule
derivation . . . 6. effect, origin, source 7. descent, lineage 9. deduction, education, evolution 10. derivative 12. transmission
derivation of . . .
descent . . 7. lineage 8. pedigree 9. genealogy
name (race, tribe) . . 7. eponymy
word . . 9. etymology
derivative of . . .
bauxite . . 8. aluminum
benzine . . 6. phenol
coal tar . . 8. creosote
flax . . 5. linen
mercury . . 11. quicksilver
milk . . 6. lactic
morphine . . 6. heroin
pitchblende . . 6. radium 7. uranium
sorrel . . 10. oxalic acid
derogate . . . 5. annul, decry 6. repeal 7. detract 8. restrict, withdraw 9. disparage
derogatory . . . 10. detracting, detractory, pejorative 11. deprecatory, disparaging 12. depreciatory
derrick . . . 3. rig 4. spar 5. crave, hoist, tower 6. lifter, steeve, tackle 7. hangman, staging
dervish . . . 4. monk 5. fakir, friar 6. beggar, fakeer 7. ascetic 11. religionist
dervish cap . . . 3. taj 4. atef
dervishes . . .
howling . . 8. Rufaiyah
wandering . . 12. Kalandariyah
whirling, dancing . . 10. Maulawiyah
descend . . . 4. fall, sink 5. deign, stoop 6. alight, unbend 7. decline 9. gravitate 10. condescend
descendant . . . 3. son 5. child, scion 8. daughter, offshoot 9. offspring
descendants . . . 5. breed 7. progeny 9. posterity
descent . . . 4. drop, fall, root 5. birth, issue, scarp, slope, stock 7. assault, decline, lineage 8. ancestry, downfall, invasion (sea), pedigree 9. declivity, incursion, posterity 10. extraction 11. degradation
describe . . . 4. name 5. paint, parse, state 6. define, depict, relate 7. explain, express, narrate, outline 9. delineate, designate, represent 12. characterize
description . . . 4. idyl, kind, sort 5. idyll 7. account, version 8. features, relation 9. discourse, narration, narrative, portrayal 10. definition 11. delineation, explanation 14. representation 18. descriptio personae
descry . . . 3. see 4. espy, view 6. behold, detect, reveal 7. discern, observe, witness 8. discover 9. determine 11. distinguish
Desdemona's husband . . . 7. Othello
desecrate . . . 5. abuse 6. misuse 7. profane, violate 8. misapply
Deseret . . . 4. Utah (1849)

desert ... 3. due 4. bolt, fail 5. merit, oasis 6. defect, renege, reward 7. abandon, forsake 8. desolate 10. apostatize, relinquish, wilderness
desert (pert to) ...
Africa .. 5. El Erg 6. Karroo
Algeria .. 3. Erg
Australia .. 10. Great Sandy 13. Great Victoria
beast .. 5. camel
dweller .. 4. Arab
Mongolia (Asia) .. 4. Gobi
phenomenon .. 6. mirage
prospector .. 3. rat
ship .. 5. camel
shrub .. 5. ratem 6. Alhagi 7. juniper (Bib)
train, travelers .. 7. caravan
wind (hot) .. 6. simoom (simoon) 7. sirocco
deserter ... 3. rat 6. bolter 8. apostate, recreant, renegade, turncoat, turntail
deserved ... 3. due 4. fair, just 5. rated 6. earned, worthy 7. condign, merited 8. rightful 9. justified, warranted 11. appropriate
deserving ... 6. worthy 8. laudable 10. creditable, entitled to 11. commendable, meritorious 12. praiseworthy
desiccated ... 3. dry 4. arid, sere 5. dried 6. seared 7. parched 9. preserved 10. dehydrated, exsiccated
design ... 3. aim, art, end 4. draw, form, idea, mean, plan, plot 5. ettle 6. intent, layout, motive, object, scheme, sketch 7. destine, drawing, meaning, outline, pattern, propose 8. artifice, artistry, contrive 11. arrangement
design (pert to) ...
carved .. 4. seme 5. cameo 8. intaglio
metal, glass .. 4. etch 6. niello
ornamental .. 9. medallion 10. needlework
pattern .. 5. batik 6. mosaic
skin .. 6. tattoo
designate ... 3. fix, set 4. call, mark, name, show 5. state, style, title 6. select 7. appoint, entitle, specify 8. describe, indicate, nominate 9. determine, stipulate 10. denominate 11. distinguish 12. characterize
designation ... 4. name 7. meaning 9. selection 10. indication 12. denomination 13. signification
desire ... 3. yen 4. care, urge, want, wish 5. covet, crave, yearn 6. aspire, hunger, prefer, thirst 7. craving, longing, passion, request 8. appetite 9. appetency, eagerness 10. desiderium 11. inclination
desire (pert to) ...
expectant .. 4. hope
greatly .. 6. aspire
liquid .. 6. thirst
ungovernable .. 5. mania
desirous ... 4. avid 5. eager 6. ardent 7. envious, lustful, willing

8. covetous, spirited 9. ambitious 10. solicitous
desist ... 2. ho 3. end 4. don't, halt, quit, stay, stop 5. cease 6. lay off 7. forbear, refrain 8. cut it out 11. discontinue
desk ... 4. ambo, dais 5. board, table 6. pulpit 7. lectern, rostrum 8. kneehole 9. monocleid (monocleide), secretary 10. escritoire
desolate ... 3. sad 4. arid, lorn, ruin 5. alone, bleak, drear, gaunt 6. barren, dismal, gloomy, lonely, ravage 7. forlorn 8. deserted, forsaken, solitary, wretched 9. destitute 10. depopulate 11. comfortless, uninhabited
desolation ... 3. woe 4. ruin 5. gloom, grief, havoc, waste 6. ravage 7. sadness 10. gloominess, loneliness, melancholy 11. destitution, destruction, devastation, forlornness 12. depopulation, solitariness, wretchedness
despair ... 11. desperation, despondency, forlornness 12. hopelessness
desperado ... 5. brave 6. outlaw 7. ruffian 8. criminal 10. lawbreaker
desperate ... 3. mad 4. rash, wild 7. frantic, furious 8. headlong, heedless, hopeless, reckless 10. despairing, desponding, distraught, infuriated 11. extravagant, precipitate 13. irretrievable
despicable ... 4. base, vile 6. odious, shabby 8. terrible, unworthy, wretched 9. miserable 12. contemptible, contemptuous, disreputable, vilipendious
despise ... 4. defy, hate 5. scorn, scout, spurn 6. detest, slight 7. contemn, disdain 8. vilipend 9. disregard
despised being ... 6. pariah 7. outcast
despoil ... 3. rip, rob 4. riot 5. reave, rifle, strip 6. divest, fleece, injure, ravage, ravish 7. bereave, debauch, deprive, disrobe, pillage, plunder 9. depredate
despondency ... 7. despair 10. depression 11. desperation 13. heartlessness
despot ... 4. czar (tsar), lord 6. master, satrap, tyrant 8. autocrat, dictator 9. patriarch
despotic ... 8. arrogant 9. arbitrary, tyrannous 10. autocratic, tyrannical 11. dictatorial, patriarchal 12. governmental
dessert ... 3. ice, pie 4. cake 5. fruit, glacé, sweet 6. mousse, pastry, sweets 7. parfait, pudding, sherbet, strudel 8. ice cream 10. shoofly pie
destination ... 3. end 4. goal, port 5. bourn (bourne) 7. address, destiny 9. objective
destine ... 4. doom, fate 5. allot 6. design, devote, intend, ordain 7. appoint 8. set apart 9. designate 10. foreordain, predestine 12. predetermine

destiny . . . 3. end, lot, ure (anc)
4. bahi, doom, eure, fate, goal
5. karma, stars 6. Kismet 7. fortune
11. destination
destitute . . . 4. void 5. needy 6. bereft,
devoid 7. forlorn, lacking
8. bankrupt, forsaken, homeless
9. abandoned, penniless
10. down–and–out
destitution . . . 6. penury 7. poverty
11. deprivation 12. helplessness
destroy . . . 3. end 4. kill, rase, raze,
root, ruin, sack, slay, undo 5. abash,
annul, erase 6. ravage 7. abolish,
consume, nullify, unbuild
8. decimate, demolish, overturn
9. dismantle, eradicate
10. annihilate, neutralize
11. exterminate
destroyer . . . 3. hun 6. ruiner, vandal
7. marplot, wrecker 8. nihilist,
saboteur 9. iconclast (of images)
11. torpedo boat
destroying angel . . . 6. Danite
7. Abaddon, Amanita (fungus)
8. Apollyon
destruction . . . 4. loss, ruin 5. havoc,
waste 7. killing 8. downfall,
genocide, ravaging, sabotage,
shambles 9. holocaust, overthrow,
perdition, ruination 10. decimation,
demolition, desolation, extinction,
subversion 11. devastation,
dissolution, extirpation
13. extermination
destructive . . . 5. fatal 6. deadly, mortal
7. baleful, fateful, ruinous 8. aneretic
(anaeretic), ravaging 10. calamitous,
catawampus, pernicious, subversive
desuetude . . . 6. disuse, nonuse
9. cessation 12. obsolescence
13. nonemployment
14. discontinuance
desultory . . . 4. idle 5. hasty 6. roving,
wanton 7. aimless, cursory, wayward
8. rambling, unsteady, wavering
9. deviative, orderless, unsettled
10. discursive, inconstant
detach . . . 4. part, wean 5. sever
7. disjoin, isolate 8. disunite,
separate, withdraw 9. disengage
detached . . . 4. free 5. alone, aloof,
scarp 7. detaché, retired, severed
8. isolated, secluded, separate,
solitary 9. unrelated, withdrawn
11. unconnected 12. disconnected
detachment . . . 8. disunion
9. aloneness, aloofness, isolation,
seclusion, unconcern 10. separation
11. disjunction 14. demobilization
detail . . . 4. item, unit 6. assign
7. appoint, itemize, minutia, narrate,
specify 9. enumerate, narrative
10. particular 12. technicality
details . . . 6. trivia 8. minutiae
11. particulars
detain . . . 4. hold, keep, stop 5. check,
delay 6. arrest, hinder, intern, retard
8. imprison, restrain, withhold
detect . . . 3. see, spy 4. show, spot,
tail 6. accuse, descry, reveal
7. discern, find out, uncover

8. discover, perceive 9. recognize
detective . . . 4. dick 6. beagle, sleuth,
tailer, tracer 7. gumshoe, spotter
8. exposing, flatfoot, Hawkshaw,
mouchard 9. operative
12. investigator
detent . . . 3. dog 4. pawl 5. catch,
click, fence 6. tongue 7. ratchet
detention . . . 5. delay 6. duress
7. detinue 9. captivity, hindrance
10. detainment, internment
11. restraining, retardation,
withholding 12. imprisonment
deter . . . 5. daunt, delay, repel
6. divert, hinder 7. prevent
8. restrain 10. discourage, disincline
deterge . . . 5. purge 6. purify
7. cleanse 8. depurate 9. elutriate
detergent . . . 4. soap 7. cleaner,
purging, saponin (saponine), smectic,
solvent 8. cleanser, medicine, purifier
9. cleansing 10. abstergent, lixiviator
deteriorate . . . 4. wear 6. impair,
weaken, worsen 10. degenerate,
retrogress
deterioration . . . 5. decay 7. decline
9. decadence 10. debasement,
declension, impairment, perversion
11. degradation 12. degeneration
13. retrogression
determinate . . . 5. fixed 6. cymose
7. certain, special 8. definite,
resolute, resolved, specific 9. arbitrary
10. definitive, invariable
11. established, unqualified
determination . . . 4. will 5. limit, proof
6. choice 7. purpose, resolve, verdict
8. decision, firmness, judgment
9. impulsion 10. conclusion,
definition, discussion, resolution,
settlement 11. disputation,
measurement, termination
12. decisiveness, dijudication,
resoluteness 13. specification
determine . . . 3. end 5. impel, learn,
prove, state 6. assess, choose,
decide, define, direct, ordain, settle
7. delimit, resolve, specify
8. conclude, discover 9. arbitrate,
ascertain, stipulate, terminate,
variously 10. dijudicate, foreordain
determined . . . 3. set 4. sure 5. fixed
6. mulish 7. assured, cinched,
decided, settled 8. foregone,
perverse, resolute, stubborn
9. obstinate, pigheaded
detest . . . 4. hate 5. abhor 8. execrate
9. abominate
detestable . . . 6. odious 7. hateful
8. accursed, terrible 9. abhorrent,
execrable, loathsome, obnoxious
10. abominable 12. contemptible
dethrone . . . 6. depose, disbar, divest
7. uncrown 8. disbench
detonation . . . 4. bang, boom 5. blast
7. blowout 8. backfire 9. discharge,
explosion 10. combustion
detract . . . 6. deduce, deduct, vilify
7. asperse, traduce 8. belittle,
derogate, distract, subtract, withdraw
9. disparage 10. depreciate
detraction . . . 5. delay 7. calumny,

slander 9. aspersion 10. belittling
11. distraction, subtraction
detriment... 4. hurt, loss 6. damage,
injury 8. mischief, weakness
10. impairment, impediment
12. disadvantage
detrimental... 7. baleful, baneful,
harmful, hurtful, noxious 9. injurious
10. pernicious 11. deleterious,
mischievous, prejudicial
15. disadvantageous
Deus Fidius... 7. Jupiter
Deus vobiscum... 12. God be with
you
Deus vult... 8. God wills (anc cry)
deuterogamy... 6. digamy
Deuteronomy (pert to)...
comprising.. 10. law of Moses
Fifth Book of.. 10. Pentateuch
meaning.. 11. repeated law (of
Moses)
devastate... 4. rape, ruin, sack
5. havoc, strip, waste 6. ravage
7. destroy, pillage, plunder, scourge
8. demolish, desolate 10. depopulate
devastation... 4. ruin 5. havoc, waste
6. ravage 7. scourge
develop... 4. grow 5. arise, ripen,
train 6. appear, detect, evolve,
expand, mature, reveal 7. advance,
convert, enlarge, expound, further,
improve, perfect, promote
8. discover, generate 9. elaborate
(details)
developed... 4. ripe, zoon 5. adult
6. mature, mellow 7. grownup
8. improved 9. perfected
10. precocious
development... 6. growth 7. changes,
endysis 8. increase, maturity
9. evolution, expansion, formation,
unfolding 10. maturation
11. elaboration, improvement,
ontogenesis 12. phylogenesis
devest... 5. strip 6. denude, divest
7. deprive, undress 8. alienate
Devi (Hind)... 3. Uma 4. Kali
5. Durga, Gauri 6. Chandi, Shakti
7. heroine, Parvati 8. divinity
9. Haimavati
deviate... 3. err, yaw 4. hade, miss,
slew, vary, veer 5. sheer, stray
6. change, depart, swerve, wander
7. deflect, digress, diverge
deviation... 3. yaw 5. lapse 6. change
7. circuit, synesis 8. aberrant
9. aberrance, deformity, departure,
diverging, obliquity, variation
10. deflection, difference, digressing,
digression, distortion, divergence
11. abnormality 12. eccentricity
device... 4. plan, tool 5. motto, shift,
trick 6. design, desire, gadget,
scheme 7. adjunct, compass, project,
purpose 8. artifice, insignia
9. appliance, expedient, implement,
invention, stratagem 10. instrument
11. contrivance
device (pert to)...
bark peeling.. 8. stripper
clamping.. 4. vise 7. pincers
distilling.. 7. alembic

fabric stretching.. 7. stenter
heating.. 4. etna 5. stove
hoisting.. 5. crane, davit, lewis
6. garnet 7. derrick 8. elevator
9. parbuckle
leveling.. 6. gimbal
measuring.. 4. gage, tape 5. chain,
gauge, meter, ruler 9. ergometer,
yardstick 10. micrometer
nautical.. 4. bitt 5. cleat, otter
6. becket 8. paravane
regulating.. 5. valve 9. remontoir
spraying.. 8. atomizer 9. sprinkler
steering.. 4. helm 5. wheel 6. rudder,
tiller
stopping.. 5. brake, sprag
devil... 3. imp 4. deil, deva, evil, haze
5. annoy, demon, error, fiend, grill,
ruler (of Hell), Satan, tease
7. hellion, serpent, tempter, torment
8. printer's 9. archenemy, daredevil,
dust devil
devil (pert to)...
dog.. 6. marine
bird.. 3. owl 5. swift 10. goatsucker
fish.. 3. ray 5. manta, whale (gray)
7. octopus
grass.. 7. Bermuda
lore.. 10. demonology
tree.. 4. dita
Devil, the... 5. Deuce, Eblis, Satan
6. Azazel, Belial, Diablo, Teufel
7. Ahriman, Amaimon (Amammion),
diavolo, Evil One, Lucifer, Old Nick,
Sammael, Shaitan (Sheitan)
8. Apollyon, Asmodeus, Diabolos
9. Archenemy, Archfiend, Beelzebub
11. Auld Clootie 14. Mephistopheles
devilish... 5. cruel 6. daring, rakish,
wicked 7. extreme, hellish, satanic
8. fiendish, infernal 9. chthonian
10. demoniacal 11. mischievous
deviltry... 6. malice 7. cruelty, devilry
8. mischief 9. diablerie, diabolism
10. black magic, wickedness
12. fiendishness
devious... 6. errant, erring, roving,
sinful 7. oblique, vagrant, winding
8. rambling, tortuous 9. deviative,
eccentric 10. circuitous
11. out—of—the—way
14. unconventional
devise... 3. aim 4. form, plan
5. array, build, frame 6. create,
divide, evolve, invent, scheme, will to
7. appoint, arrange, bequest,
concoct, fashion 8. bequeath,
contrive 9. fabricate 10. distribute,
excogitate 11. distinguish
deviser of IQ test... 5. Binet
devoid... 4. free, void 5. empty
6. faulty, vacant 7. without
9. destitute 11. nonexistent
devoid of...
feeling.. 9. apathetic, insensate
interest.. 6. jejune
devote... 3. use, vow 5. apply
6. employ, hallow, resign 7. address
consign, destine 8. dedicate, set
apart 10. consecrate 11. appropriate
devoted... 5. loyal, pious, vowed
6. doomed, loving 7. zealous

8. addicted, constant, faithful,
friendly, obedient 9. dedicated,
engrossed, patriotic
devotee... 3. fan, ist, nun 4. monk
6. votary 7. epicure, fanatic, Pietist
8. aesthete (esthete), partisan
devotion... 4. love, zeal 5. ardor, piety
6. novena, prayer 7. pietism, worship
9. addiction, adoration, constancy
10. attachment, dedication,
devoutness, friendship
11. devotedness, earnestness,
engrossment 12. consecration
13. appropriation, religiousness
devour... 3. eat 4. bolt, gulp, wolf
5. gorge, use up, waste 6. absorb,
engulf 7. consume, engorge, swallow
(up) 8. prey upon 9. devastate
10. annihilate
devout... 4. holy, warm 5. godly,
pious 6. hearty, solemn 7. cordial,
devoted, saintly, sincere, zealous
8. reverent 9. religious, righteous
10. worshipful
dew... 4. rime 5. bedew, bloom, roris
dewy... 5. roral, roric
dexterity... 3. art 5. knack, magic,
skill 7. ability, address, aptness,
finesse, sleight 8. aptitude, deftness,
facility 9. smartness 10. adroitness
15. right–handedness
dexterous... 3. apt 4. deft, yare
5. adept, handy, quick, ready
6. adroit, artful, clever 7. skilful
8. skillful 11. right–handed
dextral... 5. right (to the) 9. favorable
diabolical... 5. cruel 6. wicked
7. beastly, demonic, hellish, satanic,
ungodly 8. damnable, demoniac,
devilish, fiendish, infernal
diacritic... 4. mark 5. point
7. symptom 10. diagnostic
14. distinguishing
diacritical mark... 5. breve, tilde
6. tittle 9. diaeresis (dieresis)
diadem... 5. crown, tiara 6. anadem,
circle, emblem, empire, fillet
7. coronet 8. headband, insignia,
ornament 11. sovereignty
diaeresis, dieresis... 4. mark 5. break
8. division 10. resolution
diagnose... 7. analyze 8. construe
9. interpret
diagnosis... 8. analysis, decision,
nosology 9. prognosis
14. interpretation
diagonal... 4. bias 7. oblique
8. bendwise (Her) 10. transverse
11. cater–corner 13. cater–cornered
diagram... 4. draw, icon, plan, plot,
tree 5. chart, epure, gamut, graph
6. design 7. drawing 9. blueprint
dial... 4. disk 5. plate 8. horologe
9. indicator, timepiece
11. chronometer
dialect... 5. idiom, lingo 6. patois,
speech 7. diction 8. language,
locution, parlance 10. vernacular
dialect (pert to)...
Afrikaans.. 4. Taal
Aramaic.. 6. Syriac

Aryan.. 4. Pali
provincial.. 6. patois
Semitic.. 4. Geez
diameter... 2. pi (3.1416) 4. bore
5. width 6. module, radius
7. breadth, caliber (calibre)
9. thickness
diametric, diametrical... 6. averse
7. adverse 8. antipode, opposite
9. antipodal, diametral
diamond... 3. gem, ice 5. cards, field
(baseball), jager, jewel, plane
6. carbon 7. adamant, infield,
lozenge, rhombus 8. treasure
diamond (pert to)...
crystal.. 7. glassie
cutting.. 4. bort
cutting cups.. 3. dop
famed.. 4. Pitt 5. Sancy 6. Orloff
7. Lesotho (601 carat) 8. Cullinan,
Koh–i–noor 9. Excelsior 10. Great
Mogul 14. Star of the South
surface.. 5. facet
weight.. 5. carat (karat)
Diamond State... 8. Delaware
diaphanous... 4. fine, thin 5. filmy,
gauzy, lucid, sheer 6. flimsy
9. gossamery 11. translucent,
transparent
diaphragm... 4. wall 6. middle,
septum 7. midriff 9. partition
diary... 3. log 6. record 7. journal
8. register 9. chronicle
13. autobiography
diaskeuast... 6. editor 7. reviser
diatribe... 6. screed, tirade 7. lecture
8. berating, harangue 9. invective,
philippic 10. discussion (prolonged)
dice... 3. cog, die (sing) 4. cube,
game, sice (6's) 5. bones, craps,
cubes 7. ivories, tessera
Dickens characters... 3. Tim 4. Dora,
Nell 5. Fagin, Miggs, Sikes 6. Cuttle
7. Barnaby 9. Pecksniff
10. Chuzzlewit 11. Oliver Twist
Dickens pseudonym... 3. Boz
dictate... 3. law 4. rule 5. maxim,
order, utter 6. advise, dictum, enjoin,
impose 7. command, deliver, require,
suggest 9. prescribe 10. injunction
dictatorial... 5. bossy 6. lordly
7. pompous 8. absolute, arrogant,
despotic, dogmatic, oracular, positive
9. imperious, masterful, pragmatic
10. autocratic, dogmatical,
imperative, peremptory
11. categorical, domineering,
magisterial, opinionated, overbearing
13. authoritative
diction... 5. style 8. language,
parlance, phrasing 9. elocution
10. vocabulary 11. enunciation,
phraseology 14. expressiveness
dictionary... 5. words 7. calepin,
lexicon 8. wordbook 9. reference
10. vocabulary 11. terminology
dictionary compiler... 7. Webster
(Noah) 13. lexicographer
dictum... 3. saw 5. adage, maxim
6. saying 7. opinion, precept,
proverb 8. aphorism, apothegm
11. declaration

didactic... 8. teaching 9. mentorial
10. preceptive 11. instructive
dido... 5. antic, caper, prank, trick
6. frolic
Dido (also Elissa)... 5. Queen (of
Carthage) 8. Princess (Tyrian)
die... see also *dice* 4. fade, mold,
pass, seal, wane 5. stamp 6. expire,
perish, recede, vanish, wither
7. decease, succumb 8. languish
12. extinguished (to be)
die–hard... 4. Tory 11. British Army
12. Conservative
dies... 3. day
dies atri... 9. black days
dies faustus... 13. favorable omen
(day of)
diet... 4. fare 5. board 6. Hoftag,
ration, viands 7. Council, Landtag,
regimen 8. assembly, Kreistag
9. allowance, nutrition, Reichstag
10. Parliament
Diet (of)... 5. Worms (1521)
6. Speyer (1529), Spires
8. Augsburg (1530)
dietetics... 8. sitology 9. nutrition
12. biochemistry, dietotherapy
differ... 4. vary 5. clash 7. dispute,
dissent, quarrel 8. disagree
difference... 3. sum 5. shade
6. nuance 8. variance 10. inequality,
unlikeness 11. contrariety, distinction,
distinguish 12. disagreement,
discriminate 13. differentiate,
dissimilarity
different... 4. many 5. novel, other
6. divers, sundry, unlike 7. diverse,
several, unequal, unusual, variant
8. assorted, contrary, distinct,
manifold, opposite, separate, variform
9. divergent, otherwise 10. dissimilar,
variegated 11. diversified
13. heterogeneous
different place... 9. elsewhere
10. otherwhere
difficulty... 3. bar, rub 4. clog, crux,
knot, snag 5. cavil, check, demur,
nodus 6. plight, scrape, strait
7. barrier, problem, trouble
8. obstacle 9. hindrance
10. impediment, ruggedness
11. obstruction 12. disagreement
difficulty in swallowing...
9. dysphagia
diffidence... 5. doubt, qualm
7. anxiety, modesty 8. distrust,
humility, timidity 10. hesitation
11. bashfulness 12. apprehension
diffident... 3. coy, shy 5. timid
6. modest 7. anxious 8. doubtful,
reserved, retiring 9. shrinking,
unwilling 11. distrustful
12. apprehensive
diffuse... 4. full, shed 5. strew
6. expand, extend, prolix 7. copious,
perplex, pervade, publish, radiate,
refract, verbose 8. disperse
9. redundant 10. widespread
diffused... 5. loose 6. sparse
7. flowing 9. dispersed
diffusion... 7. osmosis 9. pervasion,
radiation 10. dispersion, refraction

dig... 3. jab 4. find, grub, mine, open,
pion, prod, root 5. delve, dwell,
spade 6. exhume, loosen, pierce,
plunge, search, thrust 7. extract,
unearth 8. excavate 10. understand
digamy... 11. deuterogamy 12. twice
married (legally)
digest... 4. code 5. brief 6. abrégé,
codify 7. epitome, Pandect
8. abstract, classify, synopsis
10. assimilate, compendium
digestion... 6. pepsis 8. eupepsia
9. dyspepsia, ingestion
10. absorption 12. alimentation,
assimilation
digestive secretions... 4. bile, gall
6. pepsin, rennin 7. chalone, gastric,
glucase, hormone, maltase
8. salivary, thyroxin 9. endocrine
10. intestinal, pancreatic
digestive tract... 7. enteron
15. alimentary canal
digger... 3. loy, pal 4. plow, wasp
5. spade 6. Indian, sapper
7. comrade, soldier 8. Levelers
9. excavator 12. New Zealander
digit... 3. toe 4. unit 5. thumb
6. finger, number (under 10)
7. dewclaw, integer, measure
digits repeated... 8. repetend
digitus... 6. finger, tarsus 8. dactylus
dignified... 5. grand, lofty, manly,
sober, staid 6. august, graced,
sedate 7. courtly, pompous, togated
8. decorous, ennobled, imposing,
majestic 9. venerable
11. ceremonious 12. aristocratic
dignify... 5. exalt, grace, honor
7. elevate, ennoble 9. solemnize
11. distinguish
dignitary... 3. don 4. rank 5. mogul
6. priest, sachem 7. magnate,
notable, prelate 9. clergyman
dignity... 4. rank 5. grace, honor
6. status 7. decorum, majesty
8. nobility, prestige, standing
9. loftiness, nobleness
10. excellence, sedateness
digraph... 8. ligature 9. diphthong
digress... 4. veer 5. shift 6. swerve,
wander 7. deviate, diverge
8. divagate 9. turn aside
10. transgress
digression... 4. loop 6. ecbole
7. circuit, episode 8. excursus
9. deviation, excursion, obliquity
10. discussion
digressive... 8. rambling 9. deviative,
excursive, wandering 10. circuitous,
discursive
dike, dyke... 3. bar, dig, gap 4. bank,
gulf, ha–ha, mole, pond, pool
5. ditch, levee, mound 7. barrier,
channel 8. causeway, estacade
9. earthwork 10. embankment
11. watercourse 13. fortification
diked land... 6. polder
dike rock... 7. odinite
dilapidation... 4. ruin 5. decay, waste
7. breakup 9. disrepair
10. impairment 11. dissolution
13. decomposition 14. disintegration

dilate... 5. bulge, swell, widen
6. expand 7. distend, enlarge, inflate
9. expatiate
dilation... 7. ectasia, ectasis
8. swelling 9. expansion
10. dilatation, distension
dilatory... 3. lax 4. slow 5. slack,
tardy 6. fabian, remiss 8. backward,
delaying, inactive, sluggish
10. behindhand 13. lackadaisical
15. procrastinating
dilemma... 4. trap 5. brike (obs),
snare 8. argument, quandary
10. perplexity 11. alternative,
predicament
dilettante... 7. amateur, dabbler,
devotee, esthete (aesthete)
diligence... 4. care, heed 6. effort
7. caution 8. industry, sedulity
9. assiduity, attention, constancy
10. stagecoach 11. application,
earnestness, painstaking
12. heedlessness, perseverance,
sedulousness 15. industriousness
diligent... 4. busy 6. active 7. operose
8. sedulous 9. assiduous, attentive,
laborious 11. industrious, persevering
dill, dill seed... 4. anet, herb 5. anise
(Bib) 6. fennel
dillydally... 3. lag 6. linger, loiter,
trifle 9. vacillate 12. shilly–shally
13. procrastinate
dilute... 3. cut 4. thin 6. debase,
rarefy, reduce, weaken 8. lengthen
9. attenuate 10. adulterate
12. denaturalize
diluted... 4. thin, weak 7. reduced,
thinned, watered 10. attenuated
dim... 4. dull, fade, pale 5. bleak,
blear, faint 6. darken 7. darkish,
dimness, eclipse, obscure 8. overcast
10. caliginous, indistinct, mysterious
dimension... 4. size 6. extent, height,
length 7. breadth 9. magnitude,
thickness 11. measurement
13. circumference
diminish... 3. ebb 4. bate, fade, pare,
ploy, wane 5. abase, abate, lower,
peter, taper 6. lessen, recede,
reduce, weaken 7. curtail, dwindle
8. decrease, subtract 9. disparage
diminution... 5. abate, taper 7. litotes
8. decrease, lowering 9. decrement,
lessening, reduction 10. moderation
diminutive... 3. wee 4. runt, slip
5. minny, small 6. bantam, little,
peewee, petite 7. bendlet
diminutive suffix... 2. el, ie 3. ole,
ule 4. ette
dimmer... 8. rheostat
din... 4. ding 5. clang, noise
6. clamor, hubbub, racket, rattle,
tumult, uproar 7. clatter, turmoil
9. commotion
dingle... 4. dale, dell, glen, ring, vale
6. jingle, tingle, tinkle, valley
7. tremble 9. storm door
dining room... 4. hall 5. salon
6. spence 7. cenacle 8. mess hall
9. refectory 12. salle à manger
dining science... 10. aristology
dinosaur... 7. reptile 8. sauropod

9. Sauropoda 10. Diplodocus,
Morosaurus 11. Ornithopoda,
Stegosaurus 12. Brontosaurus,
Ceratosaurus, Megalosaurus,
Palaeosaurus 13. Atlantosaurus,
Tyrannosaurus
diocese... 3. see 6. parish 8. district,
province 9. bishopric 12. jurisdiction
Diocletian martyr (Rome)... 5. Agnes
Dionysus (pert to)...
  birthplace.. 6. Thebes
  father.. 4. Zeus
  festival.. 8. Dionysia
  god of (Gr).. 4. wine (Bacchus, later)
  10. vegetation
  lover.. 6. Selene
  mother.. 6. Semele
Dioscuri, The (Gr Myth)... 4. cult
5. twins (Castor and Pollux)
8. Castores 10. Polydeuces
dip... 3. dap, dib, sop 4. bail, dunk,
lade 5. merge, merse, pitch, rinse,
scoop, slope, souse 6. candle,
plunge 7. baptize, immerse
9. declivity 10. pickpocket 11. hors
d'oeuvre
diphthong, dipthong... 5. sound
7. digraph 8. ligature
diploma... 4. testamur 9. sheepskin
10. credential 11. certificate,
testimonial
diplomacy... 4. tact 7. address,
cunning 9. dexterity 10. artfulness,
discretion 11. arbitration,
diplomatism, negotiation, savoir–faire
diplomat... 5. doyen (head), envoy
6. consul 7. attaché 8. emissary,
minister 10. ambassador, politician
15. chargé d'affaires, plenipotentiary
diplomatic... 6. crafty 7. cunning
8. consular 11. mediatorial
diplomatic corps, staff... 7. embassy
8. legation 17. corps diplomatique
dipsomania... 9. addiction, oenomania,
potomania 10. alcoholism
15. delirium tremens
dipthong... see *diphthong*
dire... 3. bad 4. base, evil, rank, want
5. awful, fatal, needy 6. deadly,
dismal, funest, odious 7. baneful,
doleful, fearful, ghastly 8. dreadful,
horrible, terrible, ultimate
10. oppressive 12. inauspicious,
overpowering
direct... 3. ain, bid, con 4. bend,
boss, head, lead, turn 5. order,
pilot, refer, steer, teach 6. govern,
manage 7. avigate, command,
conduct, marshal 8. instruct, straight
9. influence
direction... 3. way 4. airt, bent, care,
east, west 5. avast, belay, north,
route, south, trend 6. advice, course
7. address, command, pointer
8. guidance 10. management
11. instruction 15. superintendence
directly... 4. soon 6. pronto 7. shortly
8. as soon as, promptly 9. forthwith,
instantly, presently 11. immediately
directly opposite... 9. antipodal,
diametric 10. intipodean
director... 4. boss 5. aimer (gunner)

6. conner, leader 7. manager, teacher 8. governor, producer 14. superintendent

direful... 4. dire 6. woeful 8. dreadful, terrible 10. calamitous

dirge... 4. keen, Mass, song 5. psalm, rites 6. lament 7. requiem 8. coronach

dirigible... 4. Roma 5. blimp 7. balloon 10. Shenandoah 12. Graf Zeppelin

Dirigo... 5. I Lead 7. I Direct (Maine motto)

dirk... 4. snee, stab 5. knife, sword 6. dagger

dirt... 3. mud 4. dust, foul, land, muck, soil 5. earth, filth, grime, stain 6. gossip, refuse 7. scandal, slander 9. obscenity

dirty... 4. foul, mean 5. dingy, foggy, gusty, mucky, nasty 6. bemire, filthy, soiled, stormy, untidy 7. clouded, muddied, squalid, sullied

dis (pert to)...
Greek.. 5. Pluto
Norse.. 5. Freya 7. spirits 9. Valkyries 11. superhumans
prefix.. 5. twice 6. double
Roman.. 3. Dis 8. Dis pater 12. realm of Pluto

disable... 4. main 5. unfit 6. impair, weaken 7. cripple 9. disparage, hamstring 10. disqualify 12. incapacitate

disadvantage... 3. out 4. harm, hurt 6. damage, injury 7. penalty, trouble 8. drawback, handicap 9. detriment, liability, prejudice 12. inexpedience 13. inconvenience

disagreeable... 4. edgy 5. cross, nasty 7. fulsome 8. unsavory 9. dissonant, invidious, irritable, offensive, repugnant 10. ill–humored, unpleasant 11. displeasing, ill–tempered, incongruous 13. uncomfortable

disagreement... 5. clash 7. detente, discord, dispute, dissent, wrangle 8. variance 9. diversity 10. contention, difference, dissension, unlikeness 11. contrariety, controversy, discrepancy, incongruity 13. nonconformity 16. misunderstanding

disappear... 3. die 4. face, pass 5. cease 6. be lost, perish, vanish 7. dwindle 8. evanesce 9. evaporate

disappoint... 4. balk, bilk, fail, fall, foil 6. baffle, thwart 7. let down 9. frustrate 10. disenchant, dissatisfy 11. disillusion

disappointment... 3. rue 6. defeat 7. failure 10. bafflement 11. frustration 15. dissatisfaction

disapprobation... 5. odium 11. disapproval 12. condemnation 13. disparagement

disapproval... 3. boo 4. hiss, veto 7. censure, protest 9. objection, rejection 12. condemnation 14. disapprobation

disarrange... 4. muss 5. upset 6. foul up, jumble 7. disturb 8. disorder, unsettle 10. discompose 11. disorganize

disarray... 5. strip 6. unrobe 7. despoil, undress, unkempt 8. disorder 9. confusion, ungarment 10. disarrange, dishabille 12. discomposure, dishevelment

disaster... 4. evil, ruin 6. mishap 8. accident, calamity, casualty, fatality 9. cataclysm, mischance 10. misfortune 11. catastrophe 12. misadventure

disastrous... 4. dire 7. unlucky 8. ill–fated 9. ill–boding 10. calamitous 11. destructive, unfortunate 12. unpropitious

disavow... 4. deny 6. abjure, disown, recant, refuse 7. decline, retract 8. disclaim, renounce 9. disaffirm, repudiate

disbeliever... 5. pagan 7. atheist, heathen, heretic, infidel 8. agnostic

disburse... 5. spend 6. defray, expend, pay out

disbursement... 5. outgo 6. outlay 7. payment 8. spending 11. expenditure

disc... see also *disk* 3. man 4. dial, puck 5. medal, plate, quoit, wheel 6. circle, record 7. discoid 8. artifact 9. gyroscope, medallion

discard... 4. drip, shed 5. scrap, sluff 6. disuse, reject, remove 7. abandon, cast off, dismiss, forsake 9. eliminate, eradicate, throw away

discern... 3. see, spy 4. espy, know, read, view 5. sight 6. behold, descry, detect 7. witness 8. discover, perceive 10. understand 11. distinguish 12. discriminate 13. differentiate

discernible... 7. evident, obvious, visible 8. apparent, distinct, knowable, manifest 11. conspicuous, perceptible 15. distinguishable

discerning... 4. sage 5. acute, sharp 6. astute, shrewd 9. sagacious 14. discriminating, discriminative

discernment... 4. tact 6. acumen 7. insight 8. sagacity 9. sharpness 10. astuteness, perception, shrewdness 12. perspicacity 14. discrimination

discharge... 2. do 4. bang, cass, fire, sack, shot 5. blast, egest, eject, erupt, expel, exude, flash, salvo, shoot, speed 6. acquit, bounce, defray, exempt, pay off, report, unload, volley 7. dismiss, execute, explode, payment, quietus, release 8. emission, eruption 9. acquittal, dismissal, excretion, execution, explosion, fusillade 10. accomplish, detonation, observance 11. performance

disciple... 5. chela, Judas, pupil 7. apostle, convert, learner, scholar, student 8. adherent, believer, follower

disciples (Bib)... 6. twelve (72, Vulgate) 10. Christians

disciplinarian... 7. Puritan, teacher,

trainer 8. martinet

discipline... 4. rule, whip 6. govern, punish 7. chasten, control, culture, educate, penance, scourge 8. training 9. education, restraint 10. correction, punishment 11. castigation, instruction, self—control 12. chastisement 13. regimentation

disclaim... 4. deny 6. abjure, cry out, disown, recant, refuse, reject 7. disavow 8. abnegate, disallow, renounce 9. repudiate

disclose... 4. bare, open, show, tell 5. utter 6. expose, impart, reveal, unmask, unveil 7. divulge, uncloak, unclose 8. discover, indicate

disclosure... 6. exposé 8. exposure 9. discovery, revealing, unmasking, unveiling 10. appearance, revealment, revelation

discolor... 4. spot 5. stain 6. bruise 7. distain (anc), tarnish 9. ecchymose (by blood)

discolored... 4. doty (by decay) 5. faded 7. altered 8. ustulate 10. variegated

discomfit... 4. balk, rout 5. upset 6. baffle, defeat, dismay 7. confuse 9. embarrass, frustrate, overthrow 10. disconcert

discomfiture... 4. rout 6. defeat, flurry 7. letdown 9. confusion, overthrow 10. bafflement 11. frustration 13. embarrassment, inconvenience 14. disappointment

discomfort... 4. pain 6. sorrow 7. misease 8. distress 9. annoyance 10. uneasiness 11. displeasure 13. embarrassment, inconvenience

discommode... 6. bother, molest, put out 7. trouble 9. incommode 13. inconvenience

discompose... 4. fret 5. upset 6. excite, flurry, rubble 7. agitate, confuse, derange, disturb, fluster 8. unsettle 9. embarrass 10. disarrange, disconcert

disconcert... 5. abash, alarm 6. rattle, thwart 7. confuse, disturb, fluster, nonplus 8. bewilder 9. discomfit, embarrass 10. disarrange

disconnect... 5. sever 6. detach, unyoke 7. disjoin 8. disunite, separate, uncouple

disconnected... 6. broken 8. detached, rambling 9. desultory, scattered 10. disjointed, incoherent 11. unconnected

disconsolate... 3. sad 6. gloomy, woeful 7. forlorn 8. desolate, hopeless 9. sorrowful 10. despairing, despondent, melancholy 12. inconsolable

discontent... 6. misery, unrest 8. disquiet 10. inquietude, uneasiness 11. displeasure, unhappiness 14. discontentment 15. dissatisfaction

discontinue... 3. end 4. drop, quit, stop 5. cease 6. desist, give up 7. abandon, refrain 8. intermit 9. terminate

discord... 3. din 5. noise 6. strife 7. dissent 8. disunity, variance 9. cacophony, Discordia, harshness 10. antagonism, contention, difference, discordant, disharmony, dissension, dissonance 11. altercation 12. disagreement

discord (goddess of)... 3. Ate 4. Eris

discordant... 5. harsh 7. grating, jarring 8. contrary, jangling 11. cacophonous, disagreeing, incongruous, quarrelsome, unmelodious 12. inconsistent, inharmonious 14. irreconcilable

discordant (pert to)...
music.. 8. scordato
serenade.. 9. charivari 10. callithump
sound.. 6. jangle

discount... 3. cut 4. agio 6. rebate 9. abatement, allowance, reduction 10. concession, percentage

discourage... 4. damp 5. check, daunt, deter 6. deject, dismay, oppose 7. depress 8. dispirit, dissuade 10. dishearten

discourse... 4. talk, tell 5. essay, paper (written), prose, speak, spiel 6. homily, lesson, screed, sermon 7. account, address, article, declaim, discant, dissert, expound, lecture, narrate, oration 8. converse, treatise 9. expatiate, narrative 10. exposition, recitation 12. conversation, dissertation

discourteous... 4. rude 7. uncivil 8. impolite, insolent 9. ungallant 10. ungracious 13. disrespectful

discover... 3. see 4. espy, find 5. learn 6. descry, detect, expose 7. exhibit, find out, uncover, unearth 9. apprehend, ascertain

discoverer... 3. spy 5. scout

discoverer of...
America.. 4. Eric (the Red) 7. Vikings 8. Columbus (1492)
blood circulation.. 6. Harvey
electric light.. 6. Edison
North Pole.. 5. Peary (1909)
radium.. 5. Curie (Madame)
South Pole.. 8. Amundsen (1911)
telegraph.. 5. Morse (Samuel)
telephone.. 4. Bell (Alexander)
vaccination.. 6. Jenner

discovery, logic of... 8. heuretic

discredit... 5. doubt 7. asperse, falsify, scandal 8. disgrace, dishonor, disprove, distrust 9. disbelief, disparage, disrepute, misgiving, suspicion 10. invalidate 11. discredence

discreet... 4. wary 5. civil 6. polite 7. careful, mindful, politic, prudent 8. cautious 9. judicious, selective 11. circumspect 12. noncommittal 13. discretionary

discrepancy... 8. variance 9. disaccord, disparity, diversity 10. difference 11. contrariety 12. disagreement 13. inconsistency 15. incompatibility

discretion... 4. tact, will 6. option 7. caution, reserve 8. judgment, prudence, wariness 11. disjunction

12. cautiousness, discreetness
13. discontinuity, judiciousness,
secretiveness 14. circumspection,
discrimination
discretionary ... 7. politic, prudent
8. discreet 9. arbitrary, judicious,
voluntary 10. prudential
11. considerate 14. discriminating
discriminate ... 6. divide, screen,
secern 8. separate, set apart
11. distinguish 13. differentiate
discrimination ... 5. taste 6. acumen,
option 9. prejudice 10. discretion
11. discernment, distinction,
penetration, segregation
discursive ... 6. roving 7. cursory
9. desultory, diffusive, wandering
10. circuitous, digressive
discus ... 4. disk 5. plate, quoit
discuss ... 3. air, rap 4. moot
5. argue, treat 6. confer, debate,
parley 7. bargain, canvass, dispute,
dissert, mention 9. discourse
discus thrower ... 10. discobolus
disdain ... 5. pride, scorn 7. askance,
contemn, despise 8. contempt
9. arrogance 11. haughtiness
16. contemptuousness
disease ... 6. malady 7. ailment, illness,
trouble 8. disorder, sickness
9. affection, infirmity 10. affliction,
disability 11. derangement
disease (of) ...
animals (Afr) .. 5. nenta
apoplexy .. 4. esca
apples .. 7. stippen 9. bitter pit
blood .. 6. anemia 8. leukemia
(leukaemia, leucemia)
cattle .. 5. hoose (hooze) 6. nagana,
wheeze 7. anthrax
chickens .. 3. pip 4. roup
diet .. 7. rickets 8. pellagra, rachitis
divers .. 5. bends 7. caisson
dog .. 5. lyssa 6. rabies
11. hydrophobia
eye .. 6. caligo 7. pinkeye 8. cataract,
glaucoma, trachoma 9. amaurosis
14. conjunctivitis
fungus .. 6. mildew 9. elm blight
Oriental .. 8. beriberi
painful .. 7. lumbago 9. arthritis
plant .. 4. rust, smut 5. ergot, scald
6. Panama (banana) 7. erinose (grape)
potato, tomato .. 8. dartrose
skin .. 5. hives, psora 6. eczema,
herpes, tetter 7. scabies 8. impetigo,
shingles 9. psoriasis, urticaria
10. erysipelas
stonecutter's .. 9. silicosis
sugar cane .. 5. sereh
disease (pert to) ...
classification .. 8. nosology
10. nosography
decline .. 9. catabasis
determination of .. 9. diagnosis
germ transfer .. 7. vection
native to .. 7. endemic
outlook .. 9. prognosis
science of .. 8. etiology, medicine
spread of .. 8. epidemic
suffix .. 4. itis, osis
treatment .. 7. therapy 12. kinesiatrics

disembark ... 4. land 6. alight, debark
7. deplane, detrain, pile out (sl)
disembowel ... 3. gut 10. eviscerate
disengage ... 5. clear 6. detach,
loosen 7. release 8. liberate, unfasten
9. extricate 11. disencumber,
disentangle 12. disembarrass
disentangle ... 4. card, comb 5. clear,
loose, ravel, solve 6. evolve, sleave,
sleeve 7. unravel, unsnare, untwine,
untwist 8. simplify 9. disengage,
extricate 10. disinvolve, unscramble
disfavor ... 7. dislike 8. distaste
9. detriment, disrepute 10. alienation
11. disapproval, displeasure
14. discountenance
disfigure ... 3. mar 4. scar 6. deface,
deform, injure, mangle, uglify
7. blemish 8. mutilate
disgorge ... 4. barf (sl), spew, vent
5. eject, eruct, erupt, expel, heave,
vomit 7. exhaust 9. discharge
10. relinquish 11. regurgitate
disgrace ... 5. abase, odium, shame,
shend, sully 7. attaint, degrade,
distain, obloquy, upbraid 8. dishonor,
ignominy, reproach 9. discredit,
disesteem, disrepute, humiliate
10. opprobrium 11. abomination,
humiliation 13. disparagement
disguise ... 3. mum (mumm) 4. mask,
veil 5. cloak, feign 6. covert, masque
7. conceal, costume, falsify, pretend
9. dissemble, incognito, inebriate
10. camouflage, masquerade
11. dissimulate 12. misrepresent
disgust ... 6. nausea 7. offense,
quarrel 8. aversion, loathing, nauseate
9. animosity, annoyance, antipathy,
revulsion 10. abhorrence, repugnance
11. abomination
disgusting ... 5. nasty 6. filthy, odious
9. loathsome, obnoxious, offensive,
repellent, repulsive, revolting,
sickening
dish ... 3. jar, pot 4. boat (gravy)
5. cruse, nappy, paten, plate
6. patera, saucer, tureen 7. charger
(anc), platter, ramekin 9. casserole
dish (food) ... 5. kibbe (kibbeh), pilaf,
pilau, salmi 6. hachis, haslet, omelet,
potage, ragout 7. bok choy, chowder,
falafel (felafel), pudding, soufflé
10. egg foo yong, shish kabob
11. ratatouille
dishabille ... 6. kimono 7. neglige,
undress 8. bathrobe, negligee,
peignoir 9. housecoat, nightgown
dishearten ... 5. amate (anc), appal,
daunt, deter, unman 6. deject, dismay
7. depress, unnerve 8. dispirit
10. disconcert, discourage
disheveled ... 5. tousy 6. frowzy,
mussed, shaggy, untidy 7. ruffled,
tousled, tumbled, unkempt
8. deranged, uncombed
10. disarrayed, disordered
11. disarranged
dishonest ... 4. base 5. false 6. crafty,
unjust 7. corrupt, crooked, knavish
8. rascally, scheming 9. deceitful,
truthless 10. fraudulent, perfidious

untruthful 12. dishonorable
dishonor... 5. shame 6. defame,
infamy 7. debauch, degrade, obloquy
8. disgrace, ignominy, reproach
9. desecrate, disrepute, improbity
10. disrespect, opprobrium
13. disparagement
dishonorable... 7. ignoble 8. infamous,
shameful 9. dishonest 10. inglorious
11. disesteemed, disgraceful
12. disreputable
disillusion... 10. disquixote
disillusioned... 8. thwarted
12. disappointed, disenchanted
disinclination... 7. dislike 8. aversion,
distaste 10. reluctance, repugnance
12. disaffection 13. indisposition
disinclined... 6. averse 8. indolent
9. reluctant, unwilling 10. indisposed
disinfectant... 5. Lysol 6. cresol,
iodine, phenol 7. alcohol
9. germicide 10. antiseptic
12. formaldehyde
disintegrate... 5. decay, erode
7. break up, corrode, crumble,
disband, resolve 8. dissolve
9. decompose 11. disorganize
disjoin... 4. part, undo 5. sever, untie
6. detach, sunder, unhook 7. unhitch
8. disunite, separate, unbutton
9. disengage 10. disconnect,
dissociate
disk, disc... 4. puck 5. medal, paten,
plate, quoit, wafer, wheel 6. harrow,
record, sequin 7. discoid, medalet
9. faceplate, gyroscope, medallion
dislike... 4. mind 5. odium 6. detest
8. aversion, distaste 9. antipathy,
disrelish 12. disaffection
dislike of children... 9. misopedia
dislike of home... 9. ecophobia
disloyal... 5. false 6. fickle, untrue
9. faithless 10. inconstant,
perfidious, unfaithful 11. treacherous
dismal... 3. sad, wan 4. dark
5. black, bleak, drear, lurid
6. dreary, gloomy, somber 7. doleful,
joyless, Stygian, unhappy, unlucky
8. dolorous, dreadful, funereal,
lonesome, mournful, overcast, sinister
9. ill—omened, sorrowful
10. calamitous, depressing,
lugubrious 11. pessimistic,
unfortunate
dismantle... 4. raze, undo 5. strip
6. divest 7. deprive, destroy, disrobe,
uncloak 8. demolish 11. disassemble
dismay... 4. fear 5. alarm, daunt
6. appall, fright, terror 8. affright,
bewilder 9. dejection 10. depression,
disconcert 12. apprehension
13. consternation
14. discouragement
dismiss... 4. drip, fire 5. amand,
amove, eject, exile, remue 6. acquit,
bounce, depose, recall, refute, shelve
7. forgive, release 8. relegate
9. discharge, disregard 10. relinquish
dismount... 6. alight 7. descend,
unhorse, unmount 11. disassemble
disobedient... 7. forward, froward,
wayward 8. mutinous 10. rebellious,

refractory 11. intractable
12. contumacious
disorder... 3. tic 4. mess, riot
5. chaos, deray, snarl 6. malady,
tumult 7. ailment, anarchy, derange,
illness, misdeed 8. disarray, paranoia,
sickness 9. confusion, craziness,
distemper, paranomia
10. discompose, revolution
11. lawlessness, misdemeanor
12. irregularity 13. indisposition
14. disarrangement
15. disorganization
disorderly... 3. bad 5. mussy, rowdy
6. unruly 7. chaotic, naughty, violent
8. confused, rowdyish, slipshod
9. irregular, offensive, turbulent
12. ungovernable, unmanageable
disorganization... 5. decay 7. anarchy,
breakup, split–up 8. disorder
10. separation 11. destruction,
dissolution 13. disbandonment
14. disarrangement, disintegration
disown... 4. deny 5. expel 6. recant,
reject 7. disavow 8. disclaim,
renounce 9. disaffirm, repudiate
10. disinherit
disparage... 4. slur 5. decry, lower (in
rank) 6. slight 7. degrade, detract
8. dishonor, minimize 10. depreciate,
disapprove, discourage, undervalue
11. incongruity
disparagement... 7. diasyrm
8. disgrace 9. indignity
10. detraction 12. depreciation
disparaging... 8. decaying
10. defamatory, pejorative
11. unfavorable
dispart... 4. open, rend, rive 5. break,
sever, split 6. cleave, divide
dispassionate... 4. cool, fair 6. serene
8. composed, moderate 9. collected,
impartial, temperate, unruffled
11. unemotional 12. unprejudiced
dispatch... 4. kill, mail, post, send,
slay 5. haste, speed 6. hasten
7. message 8. celerity, conclude,
expedite 9. diligence 10. accelerate,
accomplish, promptness
dispatch boat... 5. aviso 6. packet
Dis pater (Rom)... 3. god (underworld)
5. Pluto (Gr) 12. realm of Pluto
dispel... 6. vanish 7. scatter
8. disperse 9. dissipate
dispensation... 6. scheme 7. economy
9. exemption, remission
10. dispersion, management,
misericord (misericorde)
11. arrangement 12. distribution
13. apportionment 14. administration
dispense... 4. deal, dole, give, vend
6. effuse, excuse, exempt 7. absolve
8. disperse 9. apportion
10. administer
dispenser of alms... 7. almoner
disperse... 3. sow 4. rout 5. strew
6. branch, spread, vanish 7. diffuse,
refract, scatter 9. apportion, dissipate
10. distribute 11. disseminate
dispirit... 3. cow 4. damp 5. daunt
6. deject 7. depress 10. discourage,
dishearten, intimidate

displace ... 6. depose, mislay, remove 8. misplace 9. discharge, dislocate, supersede 10. substitute

display ... 3. air 4. pomp, show, wear 5. array 6. evince, flaunt, parade, set out 7. exhibit, pageant, splurge 8. emblazon 9. advertise 10. appearance 11. demonstrate, ostentation 13. manifestation

display (pert to) ...
case .. 10. show window
in public .. 5. stage
of emotion .. 10. enthusiasm
of force (distant) .. 9. telenergy
of temper .. 5. scene 9. spectacle

displease ... 3. vex 4. miff 5. anger, annoy, pique 6. offend 7. provoke 8. irritate 10. dissatisfy

displeasure ... 5. anger 7. disgust, dislike, offense, trouble 8. disfavor, distaste 10. resentment, uneasiness 11. indignation, unhappiness 14. disapprobation 15. dissatisfaction

dispose (of) ... 3. set 4. give, mind, sell, tend 5. order, place 6. adjust, assign, bestow, settle 7. arrange, destroy, discard, testate 8. give away, regulate 9. eliminate 10. distribute, relinquish

disposed ... 5. prone 7. settled, willing 8. arranged, assigned, inclined 11. distributed

disposed (pert to) ...
favorably .. 7. propend
to cling together .. 8. clannish
to doubt .. 9. skeptical
to please .. 11. complaisant

disposition ... 3. use 4. bent, bias, mood, turn 6. animus, giving, morale, nature, temper 7. control 8. tendency 9. character 10. management, settlement 11. arrangement, elimination, temperament 12. organization 13. apportionment

dispossess ... 5. eject, evict 6. divest, refute 8. disseize

dispossessed ... 6. bereft, ousted 7. ejected, evicted 8. deprived, divested

disproof ... 6. answer, denial 8. negation, rebuttal 10. refutation 11. confutation 12. invalidation

disprove ... 5. belie, rebut 6. refute 7. confute 9. discredit 10. invalidate

disputation ... 6. debate 7. polemic 8. argument 10. contention 11. controversy 12. conversation

disputatious ... 7. eristic, polemic 11. contentious, quarrelsome 13. argumentative, controversial

dispute ... 4. deny, feud, moot, spar 5. brawl, broil 6. bicker, debate, haggle, higgle, naggle 7. contest, dissent, protest, quarrel, wrangle 8. argument, squabble 11. altercation, controversy

disqualify ... 5. debar 9. indispose 10. invalidate 12. incapacitate

disquiet ... 3. vix 4. fret 5. alarm 6. excite 7. agitate, concern, disturb 8. distress, frighten 12. apprehension

disquisition ... 5. essay 10. discussion 12. dissertation

disregard ... 4. snub 6. ignore, slight 7. neglect 8. defiance 9. unconcern 11. inattention

disreputable ... 3. low 4. base 5. seamy 7. raffish 8. shameful, unworthy 13. discreditable 15. persona non grata

disrespect ... 7. affront 9. disesteem, insolence 10. incivility 11. discourtesy

disrespectful ... 7. uncivil 8. impudent, insolent 10. irreverent 12. discourteous

disrupt ... 4. part (forcibly), rend, tear 5. upset 6. thwart 11. disorganize

dissatisfaction ... 8. vexation 10. discontent 11. displeasure, unsatisfied

dissect ... 3. cut 6. divide 7. analyze 8. separate 9. anatomize

disseize (law) ... 4. oust 5. evict 6. depose 10. dispossess 11. expropriate

dissemble ... 4. hide 5. cloak, feign 7. conceal 8. disguise 9. disregard 11. counterfeit

disseminate ... 3. sow 6. effuse, spread 7. publish, scatter 8. disperse 9. circulate, propagate

dissension ... 7. discord 8. brouille, friction 10. dissidence 12. disagreement

dissent ... 3. nay 8. apostasy, disagree 10. separation 12. disagreement, nonagreement 13. nonconformity 14. nonconcurrence

dissenter ... 7. heretic, Sectary 8. apostate, recusant 9. protester 10. Protestant 13. nonconformist

dissertation ... 5. essay, tract 6. debate, thesis 7. article, lecture 8. treatise 9. discourse 10. discussion, exposition 12. disquisition

dissidence ... 7. dissent 8. variance 9. cacophony 10. difference, dissension 12. disagreement

dissimilarity ... 7. variety 9. disparity, diversity 10. difference, unlikeness, unsameness 13. dissimilation, heterogeneity 17. heterogeneousness

dissipate ... 5. spend, waste 6. dispel, expend 7. consume, scatter, shatter 8. dispense, dissolve, squander 9. disappear

dissipation ... 4. loss 9. decrement, diffusion 10. dispersion, profligacy 11. consumption, prodigality 12. intemperance 13. disappearance, dissoluteness 14. disintegration

dissolute ... 3. lax 4. lewd, wild 5. loose 6. loosed, rakish, wanton, wicked 7. lawless, vicious 8. reckless, uncurbed 9. abandoned, debauched, unbridled 10. dissipated, licentious, profligate 11. demoralized 12. unrestrained

dissolve ... 4. fuse, melt 5. solve 7. adjourn, liquefy 9. decompose, disappear 11. disorganize

12. disintegrate
dissolved... 6. solute 7. soluble
dissonant... 5. harsh 7. grating, jarring
8. jangling 9. deviative, different,
differing 10. discordant, discrepant
11. disagreeing, unmelodious
12. inconsistent, inharmonious
13. contradictory
dissuade... 5. deter 6. advise, dehort,
divert 8. admonish 10. discourage,
disincline 11. expostulate
distaff side... 5. women 6. female
distain... 5. stain, tinge 6. define
7. tarnish 8. discolor
distance... 4. step, yond 5. depth,
range, space 6. offing 7. mileage,
reserve, yardage 8. coldness, outstrip
9. aloofness, antiquity, dimension
10. remoteness
distant... 3. far, tel, yon 4. afar, cold,
tele (pref) 5. aloof 6. remote,
utmost, yonder 7. foreign 8. ulterior
distaste... 7. disgust 8. aversion
9. disrelish 10. repugnance
11. displeasure 14. disinclination
15. dissatisfaction
distasteful... 7. hateful 8. nauseous,
unsavory 9. loathsome, offensive
10. disgusting, unpleasant
11. displeasing, unpalatable
12. disagreeable
distemper... 3. vex 4. soak 5. anger,
color, steep 6. dilute, malady, ruffle
7. ailment, disease, disturb
8. painting (process), sickness
13. indisposition
distend... 4. grow 5. bulge, swell
6. dilate, expand, spread 7. enlarge,
inflate, stretch 8. lengthen
distended... 5. tumid 7. bloated,
swollen 8. inflated, patulous, puffed
up
distich... 7. couplet 8. two lines
distill, distil... 4. leak 6. decoct,
infuse 7. extract, squeeze, trickle
8. vaporize
distilling device... 5. flask 6. retort
7. alembic 10. distillery
distinct... 4. fair 5. clear 7. audible,
obvious, precise, several 8. explicit,
manifest 9. different 10. individual
13. distinguished
distinction... 4. rank 5. honor
6. repute 8. nobility 9. clearness,
greatness, variation 10. difference
14. discrimination 15. differentiation
distinctive... 7. typical 8. peculiar
9. prominent 14. characteristic,
discriminative
distinctive mark... 4. sign 5. badge
6. cachet, emblem, symbol
distinctive quality... 6. genius, talent
9. specialty
distinguish... 6. secern 7. discern
8. perceive, separate 9. recognize
12. discriminate 13. differentiate
distinguished... 5. great, noted
6. famous, marked 7. defined,
eminent, honored, special 8. laureate,
renowned, superior 9. different,
egregious, prominent 10. celebrated
11. conspicuous, illustrious

13. extraordinary 14. characteristic
distort... 4. warp 5. screw, twist,
wrest 6. deform 7. contort, falsify,
pervert 10. camshackle
12. misrepresent
distorted... 4. awry 6. rubato
7. twisted
distortion... 5. loxia 10. perversion
12. malformation
distract... 5. craze 6. divert, harass,
madden, puzzle 7. confuse, perplex
10. distraught
distracted... 3. mad 7. frantic
8. distrait, diverted, rambling
9. disturbed 10. distraught
11. overwrought
distraction... 6. frenzy, tumult
7. despair, madness 8. disorder
9. agitation, confusion, diversion
10. dissension, perplexity
11. derangement, disturbance,
inattention 12. perturbation
distress... 3. ail 4. pain 5. agony,
annoy, grief, worry 6. danger, grieve,
harrow, misery 7. anguish, anxiety,
perplex, poverty, trouble 8. distrain,
vexation 9. necessity 10. affliction,
discomfort
distress call... 3. SOS
distribute... 3. dot, sow 4. deal, dole,
mete 5. allot, share 6. assign,
assort, divide, spread 7. deal out,
prorate, scatter 8. allocate, classify,
dispense, disperse 9. apportion,
broadcast 10. administer
distribution... 8. disposal 9. allotment
10. dispersion 11. arrangement,
disposition 12. dispensation
13. apportionment 14. classification
distribution of favors... 9. patronage
11. benefaction
distributor... 5. agent 6. agency
8. merchant 11. broadcaster
district... 4. pale, slum, ward 5. realm
6. canton, domain, ghetto, region
7. circuit, demesne, quarter
8. province 9. bailiwick, territory
District of Columbia... see
Washington, DC
distrust... 5. doubt, qualm 8. jealousy,
mistrust, wariness 9. misgiving,
suspicion, treachery
disturb... 3. vex 4. riot, roil 5. alarm,
annoy, rouse, roust, upset 6. excite,
molest, ruffle 7. agitate, derange,
fluster, perturb, trouble 8. disorder,
distract 9. interrupt 10. discompose,
disconcert
disturbance... 5. alarm, brawl
6. hubbub, rumpus, static, tumult,
uproar 7. anxiety, clatter 8. stramash
9. agitation, annoyance, commotion,
confusion 10. excitement, turbulence
11. derangement 12. perturbation
disturbed... 6. uneasy 7. annoyed,
excited, inquiet, unquiet 8. agitated
10. bewildered 12. disconcerted
disunion... 9. severance 10. alienation,
detachment, dissension, separation
11. disjunction 13. disconnection
disunite... 3. rip 4. part 5. sever,
untie 6. divide, sunder, unteam,

unyoke 7. discerp, disjoin, unravel
8. alienate, separate 9. dismember
disuse... 6. misuse, nonuse
7. abandon, discard 8. disusage
9. desuetude 11. antiquation,
discontinue 12. obsolescence
ditch... 3. sap 4. dike, hole, moat,
rine 5. canal, evade, fossa, fosse,
rhine 6. escarp, furrow, relais, trench
7. abandon, acequia, channel
dithyramb... 3. ode 4. hymn 6. poetry
7. epithet (of Dionysus)
ditty... 3. lay 4. poem, sing, song
5. carol 6. saying 7. canzone
8. canticle
diurnal... 5. daily 8. everyday
9. quotidian
divan... 4. sofa 5. couch 6. leewan,
settee 9. davenport 12. Chesterfield
dive... 4. swim 6. plunge, resort,
saloon 7. brothel, descend, descent,
explore 8. submerge
divergence... 7. theorem 9. deviation,
obliquity 10. difference, separation
12. disagreement, divarication
divers... 5. cruel 6. sundry 7. several,
various 8. perverse 9. different
diver's disease... 5. bends 7. caisson
diverse... 6. sundry, unlike 7. several,
various 8. distinct, separate
9. different, multiform
diver's gear... 8. flippers
12. respirometer
diversify... 4. vary 6. change
7. variate 9. variegate 10. distribute
13. differentiate
diversion... 4. game, play 5. hobby,
sport 6. change 7. pastime
8. apostasy 9. amusement
10. deflection, recreation
11. distraction 13. entertainment
diversity... 7. variety 10. difference
11. variegation 12. multiformity
divert... 5. amuse, avert, parry
7. deflect, delight 8. dissuade,
distract, recreate 9. entertain
10. disincline
divest... 4. doff, reft, tirl 5. strip
6. debunk, depose 8. unclothe
10. dispossess
divide... 3. lot 4. fork, part 5. cleft,
halve, sever, share, slice, space, split
6. bisect, cleave, septum, sunder
7. prorate 8. alienate, classify,
separate 9. apportion, bifurcate,
calculate, dismember, partition,
segregate, watershed 11. distinguish
divide (pert to)...
areas (small).. 8. areolate
feet.. 4. scan
four parts.. 4. paly (Her) 7. quarter
many parts.. 8. fraction 9. multisect
seven parts.. 9. septimole
steps.. 8. graduate
transversely.. 12. cross–section
two parts.. 6. bisect
divided... 4. enté (Her), reft 5. bifid,
split, zoned 6. halved, parted
7. partial, partite, septate
8. aerolate, bifidate, unjoined
9. alienated, disunited 11. distributed
dividend... 5. bonus, share 6. number

7. payment
divination... 3. art (magic) 4. omen,
sors 6. augury, sortes 7. presage
9. intuition
divination by...
ashes (sacrificial).. 11. tephromancy
cards.. 10. cartomancy
dead spirits.. 10. necromancy
dreams.. 11. oneiromancy
eggs.. 7. oomancy
fig leaf.. 9. sycomancy
figures.. 8. geomancy
fire.. 9. pyromancy
footprints.. 10. ichnomancy
forehead.. 11. metapomancy
fountains.. 9. pegomancy
letters of a name.. 7. nomancy
8. onomancy
mice.. 8. myomancy
moon.. 10. seleomancy
neighing horse.. 10. hippomancy
oracles.. 9. theomancy
palmistry.. 10. chiromancy
pebbles.. 9. thrioboly
romantic medium.. 5. daisy
salt.. 9. halomancy
serpents.. 10. ophiomancy
smoke (sacrificial).. 10. capromancy
stars.. 11. sideromancy
straws (burning).. 11. sideromancy
sword.. 13. machairomancy
verses.. 13. rhapsodomancy
wands, rods.. 11. rhabdomancy
water.. 10. hydromancy
weather.. 9. aeromancy
wild animals.. 11. theriomancy
wine.. 9. oenomancy
divine... 5. divus, guess, pious
6. priest, sacred, superb 7. foresee,
godlike, predict 8. forebode, foretell,
heavenly, minister, prophecy
9. beautiful, celestial, clergyman,
religious 10. anticipate, superhuman,
theologian 12. supernatural
divine (pert to)...
being.. 4. deva
breath.. 4. soul
force.. 5. deity, numen 6. spirit
gift.. 8. blessing
inspiration.. 8. afflatus
messenger.. 7. apostle
opinion.. 14. theologoumenon
power.. 7. entheos (obs)
utterance.. 8. prophecy
wisdom.. 8. theogamy
word.. 5. grace, logos
work.. 7. theurgy
divining rod... 4. wand 6. dowser
9. doodlebug
divinity... 3. God, Ler 4. Deus, Lord
5. Allah, deity, Khuda, Mazda
6. Brahma, Christ 7. Jehovah,
Saviour, Taranis, Trinity 8. Almighty
division... 4. part, sect, unit 5. share
6. schism, sector 7. faction, section
8. cleavage, disunion, variance
9. allotment, bisection, partition
10. alienation, department, separation
11. compartment, disjunction
12. distribution 13. apportionment,
disconnection, dismemberment
14. classification

14. classification
division (pert to) . . .
center (Biol) . . **9.** centriole
city . . **4.** ward **5.** block **8.** precinct
French . . **6.** canton **7.** Commune
　10. department **14.** arrondissement
mankind . . **4.** race
poem . . **5.** canto, verse **6.** stanza
time . . **3.** Age, Eon (Aeon), Era
　6. Eogaea (Zool)
zone (earth) . . **6.** frigid, torrid, tropic
　9. temperate
divorce, Mohammedan law . . . **5.** talak
divot . . . **3.** sod **4.** clod, turf
divulge . . . **4.** tell **6.** expose, impart,
　reveal **7.** confide, publish, uncover
　8. disclose, discover, proclaim
　11. communicate
Dixie, Dixieland . . . **4.** song **6.** utopia
　7. Sunbelt **8.** The South (US)
dizziness . . . **5.** whirl **7.** vertigo
　9. giddiness **10.** fickleness
dizzy . . . **5.** crazy, giddy, tipsy **6.** fickle,
　stupid **7.** foolish **8.** confused,
　swimming, unsteady **9.** delirious
　10. capricious **11.** vertiginous
Djibouti, east Africa . . .
city . . **5.** Obock **6.** Dikkil
gulf . . **4.** Aden
do . . . **2.** ut (Mus) **3.** act, pay **4.** dost,
　fare, make, suit, work **5.** avoid, cause,
　cheat, exert, serve, solve **6.** answer,
　effect, finish **7.** achieve, deceive,
　execute, perform, produce, prosper,
　suffice **8.** transact **9.** discharge
　10. administer
docile . . . **4.** calm, tame **6.** gentle
　7. duteous **9.** compliant, teachable,
　tractable
dock . . . **4.** clip, pier, slip **5.** basin, jetty,
　plant, wharf **6.** cut off, deduct,
　hangar **7.** curtail, shorten
　8. waterway **9.** anchorage
　12. witness stand
docket . . . **4.** list, mark **6.** record, ticket
　8. calendar, schedule **11.** certificate
docking post . . . **7.** bollard
dock worker . . . **6.** loader **7.** laborer
　9. stevedore **12.** longshoreman
doctor . . . **3.** cut, fly (angling) **4.** dose
　5. spike, title, treat **6.** degree, dilute,
　healer, intern (interne) **7.** surgeon,
　teacher **9.** physician **10.** adulterate,
　veterinary **12.** psychiatrist
doctrine . . . **3.** ism, ist **4.** rule **5.** credo,
　creed, dogma, logic, maxim, tenet
　6. gospel **7.** article, opinion, precept
　8. position **9.** principle
doctrine (pert to) . . .
existence (Philos) . . **6.** henism
finality (Theol) . . **11.** eschatology
good . . **8.** agathism
inevitability . . **8.** fatalism
philosophy . . **10.** pragmatism
secrecy . . **6.** cabala **8.** esoteric
selfishness . . **6.** egoism
doctus . . . **7.** learned
document . . . **4.** deed, writ **5.** paper,
　proof, scrip **6.** escrow **7.** archive
　11. corroborate
document (pert to) . . .
copy (true) . . **5.** Xerox **7.** estreat

8. syngraph **9.** duplicate, photostat
depository . . **8.** archives
file, report . . **7.** dossier
hamper . . **7.** hanaper
dodecade . . . **5.** dozen **6.** twelve (series)
dodge . . . **4.** duck, jouk, snub **5.** avoid,
　cheat, elude, evade, parry, trick
　6. escape, palter **7.** deceive
　8. artifice **9.** expedient
dodger . . . **7.** biscuit, shirker
　8. deceiver, handbill
dodo . . . **3.** moa **4.** bird (extinct)
doe . . . **3.** tag, teg **4.** deer, hind
doer . . . **5.** actor, agent, maker
　6. author, factor, worker **7.** manager
　8. attorney, executor, producer
　9. performer
doff . . . **4.** vail **5.** strip **6.** divest,
　remove **7.** take off, undress
dog . . . **3.** cur, pug **4.** foot, lyam (lyme)
　5. canis, hound, pooch, whelp
　6. canine, fallow, shadow, wretch,
　yelper **7.** mongrel **9.** carnivore
　13. constellation
dog (breed) . . . **3.** pom **4.** chow, Dane
　5. boxer, husky **6.** basset, beagle,
　collie, lucern, nootka, poodle, Saluki,
　setter, Sussex **7.** bulldog, griffon,
　mastiff, pointer, Samoyed, Shih Tzu,
　spaniel, terrier, whippet **8.** Airedale,
　Doberman, Keeshong, Labrador,
　Malemute, Pekinese, Sealyham,
　shepherd **9.** Chihuahua, dachshund,
　Dalmatian, greyhound, Pekingese,
　retriever, schnauzer, St Bernard,
　wolfhound **10.** bloodhound,
　Pomeranian, schipperke **11.** Skye
　terrier **12.** gazelle hound **13.** Boston
　terrier
dog (pert to) . . .
Buster Brown . . **4.** Tige
Cape (hunting) . . **8.** cynhyena
days . . **8.** canicule
F D R's . . **4.** Fala (Falla)
ferocious . . **7.** agouara
fictional . . **4.** Asta, Toby
house . . **6.** kennel
howl . . **9.** ululation
like . . **6.** cynoid
mythical . . **7.** Cerebus
part . . **5.** flews **7.** dewclaw
short–eared (Her) . . **4.** alan (aland)
star . . **6.** Sirius **8.** Canicula
Victor records . . **6.** Nipper (His
　Master's Voice)
wild . . **5.** dhole, dingo **6.** bandog,
　kolsun **8.** cimarron
Doge's barge . . . **9.** Bucentaur
dogfish . . . **5.** shark **6.** burbot
　9. blackfish **10.** nursehound
dogma . . . **4.** code **5.** tenet **6.** belief,
　dictum, ritual **7.** precept **8.** doctrine
　9. Levitical, principle
dogmatic . . . **7.** certain **8.** absolute,
　positive **9.** assertive, canonical,
　doctrinal, pragmatic **11.** dictatorial,
　doctrinaire, magisterial, opinionated
dogmatism . . . **10.** pragmatism
　11. intolerance
dogwood . . . **5.** osier **6.** cornel
　7. boxwood
do it again . . . **5.** itero

dole... 4. alms, mete 5. grief
6. sorrow 8. pittance 9. allotment
10. distribute, misfortune
12. distribution
doleful... 3. sad 4. dree 5. drear
6. dismal, dreary, rueful, woeful
8. doloroso, dolorous, grievous,
jeremiad, mournful 10. lugubrious,
melancholy
doll... 3. toy 4. baby (toy), girl
6. moppet, puppet 9. miniature,
plaything
dolphin... 4. fish, inia 5. bouto
6. dorado, dugong, sea pig
8. Cetacean, porpoise 9. goosebeak
10. bottlenose
dolt... 3. ass, oaf 4. clod, dope, loon,
lout, moke 5. dunce, idiot 7. dullard
8. clodpate, dumbbell, numskull
9. blockhead, dumb bunny
10. ignoramous
domain... 5. realm 6. empery, empire,
sphere 7. country, demesne
8. dominion
dome... 4. arch, head, roof (Astron)
5. spire, tower 6. cupola, turret
Domesday, doomsday... 4. Book (Eng
Hist) 11. Judgment Day 13. Great
Domesday 14. Little Domesday
17. Domesday of St Paul's
domestic... 4. tame 5. domal
7. servant 9. enchorial, home–grown,
intestine (not foreign)
domestic establishment... 6. ménage
9. household
domicile... 5. abode, house 7. habitat
8. dwelling 9. residence
10. habitation
dominant... 5. chief, chord 6. ruling
7. regnant, supreme 8. superior
9. ascendant, governing, imperious,
paramount, principal
10. pre–eminent, prevailing
11. influential, outweighing,
overtopping 12. preponderant
13. authoritative, overbalancing
dominate... 4. boss, rule, sway
5. reign 6. govern 7. command,
control, overtop, possess
11. predominate
domineering... 6. lordly 7. haughty
8. arrogant, blustery 9. imperious,
masterful 10. oppressive
11. overbearing
Dominican Republic...
capital.. 12. Santo Domingo
city.. 14. Ciudad Trujillo
discoverer.. 8. Columbus
island site.. 10. Hispaniola
oldest city (W Hem).. 12. Santo
Domingo (1496)
dominion... 4. rule, sway 5. realm
6. empery, empire, sphere 7. control
9. authority, hierarchy (celestial)
12. jurisdiction
domino... 3. pip (spot) 4. game (in
pl), hood, mask 5. amice, cloak,
ivory 7. costume
dominoes, galloping... 7. ivories
donate... 3. tip 4. give 6. bestow
7. present
done... 4. fini 5. baked, ended, finis

6. agreed, cooked 7. through
8. finished, tired out 9. completed,
concluded, exhausted
done (pert to)...
by stealth.. 13. surreptitious
by word of mouth.. 5. parol
for pay.. 9. mercenary
with effort.. 5. labor
Don Juan's girl (novel)... 6. Haidee
donkey... 3. ass 4. moke 5. burro,
neddy 6. onager
donna... 4. Dona, lady, wife
5. madam, woman 8. mistress
Don Quixote's steed... 9. Rosinante
doom... 3. fey, lot 4. fate, ruin
5. death 7. condemn, destine,
destiny 8. sentence 11. destruction
doomed... 3. fey 5. death, fated,
goner 9. sentenced
doomsday... 8. Ragnarok
11. Judgment Day (see *Domesday*)
door... 4. gate 6. portal 7. doorway,
opening, passage, postern
11. entranceway 12. porte–cochere
doorframe... 3. dar 4. jamb, rail,
sash, sill 5. janua, panel, stile
6. lintel 9. threshold
doorkeeper... 4. hasp 5. tiler 6. porter
7. durwaum, ostiary 8. chokidar
9. concierge
dope... 3. hop, LSD 4. hemp
6. mescal, opiate, peyoti (peyote)
7. fathead 8. narcotic 9. marijuana
Dorian Festival (Sparta)... 6. carnea
(carneia)
Dorian magistrates... 6. ephors
Doric Order (Gr Arch)...
capital.. 6. abacus
frieze fillet.. 6. taenia
frieze space.. 6. metope
history.. 6. oldest 8. simplest
dormant... 5. inert 6. asleep, latent,
torpid 7. resting 8. inactive, sleeping
9. quiescent
dormer window... 5. oriel 6. gablet
7. dormant (obs), lucarne
dormeuse... 5. couch 8. carriage
(sleeping), nightcap
dormouse... 4. Glis, loir 5. lerot
6. rodent
dorsal (pert to)...
back.. 5. notal, notum 6. dorsum,
lumbar, neural, tergal, tergum
column.. 6. spinal
dose... 5. bolus, draft, treat 6. potion
7. portion
dot... 3. jot 4. clot, code, lump
5. dowry, fleck, point, speck, telia
(fungus) 6. period 7. stipple
dote... 3. rot 5. decay, dowry
6. babble, dotage, dotard, drivel,
stupor 7. portion (marriage)
8. imbecile
dotted... 5. pinto 7. piebald, specked,
studded 8. stippled 9. sprinkled
11. diversified
Douay Bible... 4. Aree
double... 2. di (pref) 4. dual, fold,
twin 5. duple, plait, twice 6. binary,
binate, duplex, folded 7. twofold
8. artifice, two–faced 9. deceitful,
duplicate, insincere, intensify

11. counterpart
double (pert to)...
bars (Her).. 5. gemel
cross.. 7. deceive, two–time
dagger.. 6. diesis
edged.. 9. ancipital
ghost (live person).. 11. counterpart
12. Doppelgänger, doubleganger
meaning.. 9. equivocal
doubt... 5. demur, waver 8. hesitate,
mistrust, question 9. misgiving,
suspicion 10. Pyrrhonism, skepticism
11. uncertainty
doubter... 5. cynic 6. Humist
7. skeptic 10. Pyrrhonist
doubtful... 7. dubious 8. wavering
9. ambiguous, equivocal, uncertain,
undecided 10. hesitating, improbable,
precarious 11. distrustful, vacillating
12. questionable, unbelievable,
undetermined 13. problematical
doubtful authority... 6. mythic, unreal
10. apocryphal
dough... 4. cash, mash 5. money,
paste 6. leaven, noodle
doughnut... 6. sinker 7. cruller, simball
9. friedcake
dour... 5. harsh, stern 6. gloomy,
severe 9. obstinate 10. inflexible
dove... 3. nun 4. blue (color), Inca
5. color 6. culver, pigeon
7. Columba, tumbler
Dove, the... 6. symbol (Relig)
10. Holy Spirit
dovefoot... 8. geranium (wild)
dovekey, dovekie... 3. auk 4. Alle
6. rotche 9. guillemot
dowdy... 3. pie (deep–dish) 6. pastry,
shabby, untidy 7. pudding 8. slovenly
10. slatternly
dowel... 3. pin 4. coak 5. tenon
6. fasten, pintle
dower... 3. dos 5. dowry, endow,
grant 6. dotate 7. bequest
8. dotation, jointure
down... 2. de (pref) 3. nap 4. fuzz,
hair 5. adown, below, floor
7. descent 8. softness
downcast... 3. low, sad 7. lowered
8. dejected 9. bowed down,
depressed 10. despondent, dispirited
11. discouraged, downhearted
downright... 4. flat 5. blunt, plain,
sheer, stark, utter 6. arrant, candid
8. positive, thorough 10. absolutely,
forthright 11. unqualified
13. unceremonious
downy... 4. soft, wary 5. nappy, pilar,
quiet 6. placid 7. villous 8. feathery
10. flocculent, lanuginose, lanuginous
dowry... 3. dos, dot 4. gift 5. dower,
sulka 6. talent 9. endowment
dowser's tool... 4. wand 6. willow
Doxology... 4. hymn 6. praise
7. Kaddish
doze... 3. nap, nod 5. sleep
6. catnap, drowse, snooze 7. stupefy
(obs)
draft, draught... 3. map, nip 4. dose,
dram, draw, plan, pull, swig
5. drink, epure 7. current, diagram,
drawing, outline 8. protocol, recruits,

traction 9. conscript 10. money
order
drag... 3. lag, lug, tow, tug 4. clog,
draw, hale, haul, pull, sing, tump
5. drawl, scent (hunt), smoke, trail
6. drogue, harrow 7. grapnel
8. dragrope, linger on, obstacle
10. conveyance
dragoman... 11. interpreter (official)
dragon... 4. lung 5. drake, Rahab (Bib)
6. animal, duenna, lizard, musket
(anc), pigeon 7. dragoon, monster
(Her), serpent 10. earthdrake
14. Dragon of Komodo
drain... 3. gaw, sap 4. lade, loss,
sink, sump 5. ditch, dreen, empty,
rhine, sewer, siver 6. filter, trench
7. acequia, alberca, channel,
consume, exhaust, outflow
11. watercourse
dram... 3. nip 4. mite, slug 5. draft,
drink 6. drachm 8. potation
11. indifferent
drama (pert to)...
beginning.. 8. Dyonysia (anc)
form.. 4. play 5. opera 6. comedy
7. tragedy 10. peripeteia
11. composition
parts.. 8. epitasis, protasis
12. introduction
scenery.. 8. diorama
dramatic... 4. wild 5. stagy, vivid,
vocal 6. poetic, scenic 8. thespian
10. histrionic, theatrical
11. pretentious, spectacular
12. melodramatic
dramatic piece... 4. skit
drastic... 5. stern 6. fierce, severe
7. intense, radical 8. rigorous
draught... see *draft*
Dravidian (pert to)...
country (anc).. 5. India
ghost.. 4. bhut
language.. 5. Tamil 8. Kanarese
12. Dravido–Munda
native.. 5. Croat 8. Croatian
people.. 4. Nair 6. Slavic
soldier.. 8. Croatian
draw... 3. lug, tie, tow, tug 4. drag,
etch, haul, limn, lure, plot, pull, tole
5. draft, smoke 6. allure, arroyo,
convey, entice 7. attract, conduct,
extract, lottery 9. delineate
10. attraction
draw (pert to)...
away.. 6. abduce, divert 7. detract
close.. 4. loom, near 5. hover
8. approach
forth.. 5. educe 6. elicit, ferret
7. extract
off.. 6. siphon 7. extract 8. abstract,
withdraw
through an eye.. 4. rove
together.. 4. coul, frap, lace, rake
8. assemble
drawback... 5. fault, wince 6. defect,
resile, retire 8. obstacle 9. objection
12. disadvantage
drawing... 3. art 5. draft 7. diagram,
hauling, picture, pulling 8. doodling
9. animation 10. attracting,
extracting

drawing back... 9. retrahent
drayage... 6. charge 7. cartage,
  haulage 8. truckage
  14. transportation
dread... 3. awe 4. fear 5. timor
  6. dismay, horror, terror 7. anxiety
  8. affright, disquiet 9. reverence
  12. apprehension
dreadful... 4. dire 6. horrid
  7. awesome, fearful, hideous
  8. horrible, terrible, terrific 9. frightful
  10. formidable, outrageous
dreadnaught, dreadnought... 5. cloth
  7. garment 8. fearless 10. battleship,
  fearnought
dream... 4. muse, rêve 5. fancy
  6. bubble, vision 7. imagine,
  reverie, romance, suppose
  8. illusion, stargaze
  11. contemplate
dream (pert to)...
  interpretation.. 10. oneirology
  interpreter.. 12. oneirocritic
  tranquility.. 3. kef (keef) 7. reverie
dreamer... 4. seer 7. fantast
  8. idealist, puffbird 9. visionary
  11. romanticist 13. castle–builder
dreamy... 3. kef (keef) 6. poetic
  7. languid 8. soothing 9. visionary
  11. imaginative
dreary... 3. sad 4. dull, gray 5. bleak,
  ourie 6. dismal, elenge, gloomy,
  remote 7. doleful, tedious
  9. cheerless 10. depressing,
  foreboding, melancholy, monotonous
  11. comfortless
dredge... 4. tong (for oysters)
  5. scoop 6. burrow, deepen, grains,
  tunnel 8. excavate
dregs... 4. faex, lees, marc, silt
  5. draff, dross, magma 6. refuse,
  scoria, sludge 7. grounds, hogwash,
  residue 8. riffraff, sediment
  9. settlings 10. faex populi
drench... 4. hose, soak 5. douse,
  draft, imbue, purge, scour, souse
  6. potion 7. immerse 8. inundate,
  permeate, saturate, submerge
drenched... 4. asop 5. asoak
  6. doused, soaked 9. saturated
dress... 3. rig, tog 4. deck, garb,
  gown, suit, trim 5. getup, mufti,
  preen 6. attire, clothe, enrobe, livery,
  toilet 7. apparel, threads (sl)
  8. clothing, decorate, negligee
  10. habiliment 13. mother hubbard
dress (pert to)...
  flax.. 3. ted
  gaudily.. 5. prank 7. bedizen, spangle
  leather.. 3. taw, tew 5. curry
  of Mecca pilgrims.. 5. ihram
  riding.. 5. chaps, habit 7. hacking
  (jacket) 8. jodhpurs 10. chaparajos
  stone.. 3. dab, nig 5. nidge
  surgically.. 5. dight, panse 7. bandage
  8. ligature
  up.. 4. dude 5. preen, primp
  6. spruce 8. titivate
dressed loosely... 8. discinct,
  ungirded
dressing... 4. lint 5. sauce
  7. bandage, pledget, raiment, reproof

8. attiring, scolding 9. condiment,
  neatsfoot (leather) 11. castigation
drew... see *draw*
dried... 4. sere 5. wiped 6. seared,
  wasted 7. drained, parched, wizened
  9. shriveled 10. dehydrated,
  desiccated, exsiccated
dried meat... 7. biltong (biltongue),
  charqui 8. pemmican 10. jerked beef
dried tubers (orchids)... 5. salep
drift... 3. aim, sag 4. idle, pile, sail,
  soar, tide, tool 5. float, stray, tenor,
  trend 6. course, intent 7. deposit,
  impetus, meaning 8. crescent
  (sidewise), movement, seaweeds,
  tendency 9. deviation
drill... 3. gad, row (seeds), tap 4. bore
  5. auger, borer, train 6. baboon,
  pierce 7. machine 8. excavate,
  exercise, practice, rehearse
  9. perforate
drilling... 5. denim 7. nurture
  8. training 11. inculcation
drink... 3. ade, ale, bib, lap, nip, pop,
  rum, sip, tea, tot 4. flip, fram, grog,
  shot, slug, soda, soma, swig, tope
  5. bouse, draft, julep, negus, posca,
  punch, quaff, skink, toast, toddy,
  water 6. caudle, coffee, imbibe,
  liquor, mai tai, mao–tai, posset, potion,
  ptisan, tipple 8. beverage, cocktail,
  highball, sillabub 9. decoction
  10. intoxicant, mixed drink
drink (pert to)...
  ancient.. 5. morat
  Arabian.. 4. boza
  English.. 7. wassail 8. champers
  fond of.. 8. bibulous
  frozen.. 6. frappé
  gods (of the).. 6. nectar
  honey.. 4. mead 5. morat
  hot.. 5. salep, toddy 6. posset, saloop
  Irish.. 10. shandygaff
  Japanese.. 4. sake
  mix.. 5. setup 8. vermouth
  9. grenadine
  rum.. 5. bumbo
  Russian.. 5. vodka 6. kumiss (koumiss)
  Spanish.. 7. tequila
  together.. 9. symposium
  tropical.. 7. sangria 8. sangaree
  Turkish.. 4. raki 5. airan, arrak
drinking salutation... 5. skoal, toast
  6. prosit 7. propine, slainte
drinking vessel... 3. mug 4. bowl,
  tass 5. cylix (anc), glass, gourd, jorum,
  mazer, stein 6. goblet, rhyton
  7. tankard 8. schooner 10. Vaphio
  cups (gold)
drip... 4. bore, drop, leak 5. droop
  7. dribble, falling, trickle
drive... 3. caa 4. herd, ride, slog, urge
  5. force, guide, impel, pilot, press,
  rouse 6. attack, compel, energy,
  propel, thrust 7. crusade, operate
  8. campaign 10. compulsion
drive (pert to)...
  away.. 4. rout 5. chase, exile, expel,
  repel 6. banish, dispel, rebuff
  7. repulse 8. disperse
  down.. 4. tamp
  frantic.. 4. loco 6. madden 7. bedevil

obliquely .. 3. toe 5. slice
stakes .. 4. camp, park 6. locate,
  settle
drivel ... 4. dote 5. drool 6. slaver
  7. slobber, twaddle 8. nonsense
driveler ... 4. fool 5. doter, idiot
  6. dotard, prater 8. jabberer
  9. blatherer, chatterer
driver ... 4. club (golf), jehu 6. drover,
  hammer, mahout, sarwan 7. speeder
  8. coachman, engineer, motorist,
  operator, overseer, reinsman
  9. propeller 10. charioteer,
  taskmaster
drizzle ... 4. mist, rain, smur 6. mizzle
  (misle)
droll ... 3. odd 4. zany 5. comic,
  merry, queer, witty 6. jester
  7. amusing, buffoon, waggish
  8. farcical, humorous 9. diverting,
  laughable, whimsical 10. ridiculous
  11. merry–andrew
drollery ... 3. wit 4. jest 5. farce,
  humor 6. puppet 9. absurdity
  10. buffoonery
dromedary ... 4. oont 5. camel
  (one–hump) 6. hageen 7. Camelus
  8. Bactrian (two–hump)
drone ... 3. bee, dor, hum 4. male
  (bee) 5. idler, snail 7. bagpipe,
  humming 8. sluggard 9. non–worker,
  slow mover
drool ... 6. drivel, slaver 7. dribble,
  slabber, slobber
droop ... 3. lop, sag 4. flag, hang, loll,
  pine, sink, tire, wilt 6. nutate, slouch
  7. decline 8. languish
drooping ... 4. alop, weak 5. loose
  7. hanging, nodding, sinking
  8. dejected, fatigued 11. languishing
drooping eyelids ... 6. ptosis
drop ... 4. bead, blob, dose, dram,
  drib, drip, fall, omit, shed, sink, slot,
  stop, tear 5. candy, dreep, droop,
  gutta, lower, minim, remit 6. letter,
  plunge 7. abandon, descent, distill
  (distil), earring, globule, pendant,
  trickle 8. ornament, trapdoor
  9. declivity 10. relinquish
drop (pert to) ...
anchor .. 4. moor
by drop .. 7. guttate 9. guttation
measure .. 7. pipette 11. stactometer
nautical .. 5. hance
serene .. 9. amaurosis (Med)
vowel .. 5. elide
dropsy ... 5. edema 8. hydropsy,
  swelling
dross ... 4. lees, scum, slag 5. chaff,
  dregs, scobs, sprue, waste 6. refuse,
  scoria, sinter (iron)
drove ... 4. herd 5. crowd, drive, flock
drover ... 4. boat 6. dealer (cattle),
  driver 8. herdsman
drowse ... 3. nid, nod 4. doze 5. dover
  (Eng), sleep 6. snooze
drowsiness ... 7. languor 8. dullness,
  lethargy 9. lassitude, oscitance
  10. narcolepsy, sleepiness
  12. listlessness, sluggishness
drowsy ... 4. logy 6. sleepy 8. oscitant,
  soothing 9. somnolent, soporific

drudge ... 3. fag 4. grub, hack, mail,
  plod, toil 5. labor, slave 6. toiler
  7. plodder
drug ... 4. alum, dope, dull, numb
  6. opiate 7. stupefy 8. narcotic,
  sedative 10. medication
  11. anesthetize
drug (pert to) ...
action .. 7. synergy
addict .. 6. junkie
analgesic .. 6. Anacin 7. aspirin
  10. acetanilid, phenacetin
anesthesia .. 3. gas 5. ether
  8. Novocain 10. chloroform
dangerous .. 11. thalidomide
emetic .. 6. ipecac 11. ipecacuanha
eye .. 8. atropine 10. belladonna
forgetfulness .. 8. nepenthe
narcotic .. 3. hop, kif 4. hemp
  5. bhang, daggo, opium 6. codein
  7. cocaine 9. marijuana
sedative .. 7. bromide, Seconal,
  Veronal 8. barbital, Nembutal
  11. scopolamine 13. phenobarbital
drugget ... 3. mat, rug 5. cloth
druggist ... 8. gallipot 10. apothecary,
  pharmacist
Druids (anc) ... 5. Order (Relig)
  9. conjurers 12. philosophers
drum ... 4. beat 5. naker, snare, tabor,
  tombe 6. atabal, barrel, tambor
  (tambour), tom–tom, tympan
  7. taboret, timbrel, timpany
  8. cylinder, tympanum (ear)
drum (pert to) ...
call .. 4. dian (diana) 6. rappel, tattoo
  8. rataplan
Indian .. 6. nagara
nautical term .. 7. capstan
Oriental .. 6. tom–tom 7. anacara
drunkard ... 3. sot 4. soak 5. souse,
  toper 6. addict, barfly, boozer
  7. guzzler, tippler 9. alcoholic,
  inebriate 11. dipsomaniac
dry ... 3. sec, ted 4. arid, blot, brut,
  dull, keen, seco, sere, wipe 5. drain,
  parch, vapid 6. aerify, barren, jejune,
  shrewd 7. insipid, sterile, thirsty,
  xerotic 8. solidify, tiresome
  9. dehydrate, fruitless, pointless
  12. unprofitable 13. uninteresting
dryad ... 5. deity, Napea, nymph, oread
duck ... 3. dip 4. flee, fowl 5. dodge,
  douse 6. plunge 7. bob down
duck (breed) ... 4. Anas, coot, pato,
  skua, smee, smew, teal 5. Anser,
  eider, scaup 6. Aythya, Nyroca,
  Peking, scoter 7. mallard, Muscovy,
  pintail, pochard, Spatula, widgeon
  8. Anatinae, bluebill, shoveler
  (shoveller) 9. harlequin, merganser,
  sheldrake 10. bufflehead, canvasback,
  ring–necked
duck (pert to) ...
baby .. 8. duckling
class .. 3. sea 5. river 7. Muscovy
disabled .. 4. lame
ducklike .. 5. decoy 8. duckbill
fabric .. 5. cloth
flock (mallards) .. 4. sord
flower .. 12. lady's slipper
game .. 6. tenter

hawk .. **6.** falcon **7.** harrier
litter .. **4.** team
male .. **5.** drake
ruddy .. **5.** noddy
duct ... **3.** vas **4.** main, pipe, race,
  tube **5.** canal **7.** channel, passage,
  trachea **8.** aqueduct
ductile ... **6.** docile, facile, pliant
  7. elastic, plastic, tensile **8.** flexible,
  tractile, yielding **9.** compliant,
  complying, malleable, tractable
  10. manageable
dude ... **3.** fop **5.** dandy **7.** coxcomb,
  Johnnie **10.** tenderfoot
dudeen ... **4.** pipe (tobacco)
due ... **4.** debt, duty, just, meed, owed
  5. owing **6.** charge, lawful **7.** exactly
  8. adequate, directly, expected,
  rightful **9.** appointed **10.** ascribable,
  sufficient
duel ... **4.** tilt **5.** fence **6.** combat
  7. contest **8.** conflict **9.** monomachy
  12. satisfaction
duelist's aide ... **6.** second
duet ... **3.** duo **8.** duettino
dug ... see *dig*
dugong ... **7.** manatee, Sirenia
  8. Halicore
dugout ... **4.** abri, cave, shed **5.** canoe
  6. cavity **7.** pirogue, shelter
dulcet ... **5.** sweet **6.** ariose **7.** tuneful
  8. pleasant, soothing **9.** agreeable,
  melodious **10.** harmonious
dulcimer ... **6.** citole **7.** bagpipe,
  cembalo **8.** psaltery **10.** instrument
dull ... **3.** dim, dry, dun **4.** dead, drab,
  gray, logy, poky **6.** barren, cloudy,
  deaden, dismal, dreary, drowsy,
  jejune, leaden, muffle, obtund,
  obtuse, sleepy, somber, stupid
  7. doltish, irksome, prosaic, tedious
  8. lifeless, listless, overcast, sluggish,
  stagnant, tiresome **9.** apathetic,
  inanimate, saturnine, unfeeling
  10. insensible, lackluster, melancholy,
  slow-witted **13.** unimaginative
dull (pert to) ...
finish .. **3.** mat (matte)
heavy .. **4.** logy **5.** leady **6.** stodgy
of cloth .. **6.** starry (Eng)
statement .. **9.** platitude
dullard ... **3.** oaf **4.** dope, mope
  5. dunce **8.** dumbbell, numskull
  9. dumb bunny
dumb ... **4.** mute **6.** aphony, silent,
  stupid **7.** aphonia **8.** ignorant,
  taciturn **9.** inanimate, irregular
  10. speechless **12.** inarticulate
dumbfounded ... **6.** amazed **7.** crabbed
  9. staggered, surprised
  10. astonished, bewildered
  11. overwhelmed **13.** flabbergasted
dummy ... **3.** pel **4.** copy, dolt, mort
  (cards), sham **5.** model **6.** pontic,
  silent **9.** imitation, mannequin,
  nonentity **10.** figurehead, substitute
  11. counterfeit
dump ... **3.** tip **4.** bump, game (Eng),
  jail, sell, thud, tune **5.** empty, hovel
  6. plunge, unload **7.** discard
  10. rendezvous

dumpling ... **7.** biscuit, gnocchi
  10. appleberry
dupe ... **3.** fox **4.** bilk, cull, tool
  5. cheat, fraud, trick **6.** delude,
  sucker **7.** cat's-paw, deceive, mislead
duplicate ... **4.** copy, game (cards),
  twin **6.** double, duplex **7.** estreat,
  mislead, replica, twofold **8.** likeness
  9. analogous, facsimile, identical,
  replicate **10.** transcript
  11. counterpart **12.** reproduction
duplicated ... **7.** dittoed **8.** repeated
  10. repetitive
duplicity ... **5.** fraud, guile **6.** deceit
  7. duality **9.** deception, duplexity,
  falsehood, treachery
  13. dissimulation, double-dealing
durable ... **4.** firm **5.** stout, tough
  6. staple **7.** lasting **8.** constant,
  enduring **9.** permanent
  10. continuing, persistent
  11. everlasting, substantial
duration ... **3.** age **4.** date, span, term,
  time **6.** period **8.** eternity, lifetime
  10. durability, permanence
  11. continuance
during ... **4.** time **5.** while **6.** whilst
  7. pending, through **10.** throughout
dusk ... **4.** dark **5.** dusky, gloom, slate
  (color) **8.** gloaming, twilight
dusky ... **3.** dim, sad **4.** dark, dusk
  5. murky, tawny, umbra **6.** gloomy,
  somber **7.** swarthy **8.** blackish
  10. melancholy
dust ... **4.** cash, coom (coomb), dirt,
  gold, pilm, soil **5.** briss, brush, chaff,
  clean, color, earth, money, stive,
  stour (dial), trash **6.** corpse, pollen,
  powder **7.** dryness, turmoil
  9. commotion, confusion, sweepings
dust (pert to) ...
flax .. **5.** pouce
flour .. **5.** stive
glacier .. **10.** kryokonite
reduce to .. **4.** mull
speck .. **4.** mote
Dutch (pert to) ... see also *Netherlands*
cheese .. **4.** Edam **7.** cottage
country .. **7.** Germany, Holland
  11. Netherlands
man .. **10.** Hogen-Mogen
news agency .. **5.** Aneta
painter .. **4.** Hals
poet .. **7.** Da Costa
pottery .. **4.** delf (delft) **9.** delftware
river .. **3.** Eem **4.** Maas **5.** Meuse
scholar .. **7.** Erasmus (Humanist)
woman, wife .. **4.** frow
uncle .. **3.** eme (dial), oom
Dutch East Indies (Indonesia) ...
capital .. **7.** Batavia (former), Jakarta
  (Djakarta)
islands (3,000), largest .. **4.** Bali, Java
  6. Borneo (part) **7.** Celebes, Sumatra
  8. Malaysia (part) **9.** New Guinea
  (part)
renamed .. **9.** Indonesia
Dutch Guiana (Netherlands Antilles) ...
capital .. **10.** Paramaribo
mountain .. **10.** Tumuc Humac
renamed .. **7.** Surinam
dutiful ... **6.** devout, docile **7.** duteous

8. obedient, reverent 9. compliant
10. respectful, submissive
11. deferential, reverential
duty . . . 3. job, tax 4. care, onus, rite,
task, toll 5. chore, stint, trick
6. devoir, dharma, excise, heriot
(anc), impost, tariff 7. payment,
respect 9. reverence 10. imposition,
obligation
dwale . . . 5. sable (Her) 6. opiate,
potion 9. soporific 10. belladonna,
nightshade
dwarf . . . 3. elf, urf 4. grig, puny, runt
5. crile, gnome, midge, pygmy
(pigmy), small, stunt, troll 6. droich,
durgan, midget 7. manikin, Pacolet,
stunted 9. dandiprat, micrander
10. diminished, homunculus
dwarfish . . . 6. nanoid
dwarfishness . . . 6. nanism
Dwarfs, The Seven . . . 3. Doc
5. Dopey, Happy 6. Grumpy, Sleepy,
Sneezy 7. Bashful
dwell . . . 4. bide, harp, live, stay
5. abide, delay, lodge, pause, tarry
6. linger, remain, reside
dwelling . . . 3. hut 4. flat 5. abode,
hotel, house, hovel 6. duplex, shanty
7. trailer 8. abidance, domicile,
tenement 9. apartment, residence
10. habitation
dwelling (pert to) . . .
house (law) . . 8. messuage
in field . . 10. arvicoline
in groves . . 10. nemoricole
of dead (Bab) . . 5. Aralu
of souls (Polyn) . . 2. Po
Oriental . . 3. dar
dwindle . . . 4. melt, wane 5. taper,
waste 6. lessen, shrink, sicken

8. decrease, diminish 10. degenerate
dyad . . . 3. two 4. duad, pair
6. couple, dyadic
Dyak, Dayak . . . 5. tribe (Borneo)
7. blowgun 8. sumpiter 9. aborigine
dye . . . 4. anil 5. color, imbue, stain,
tinge 7. pigment 8. colorant
dye stuff (pert to) . . .
blue . . 4. woad (wad, wade)
brown . . 5. erika, sumac
indigo . . 4. anil
mulberry . . 3. aal
red . . 4. chay 5. aurin, eosin, henna
6. isatin, madder, relbun 7. annatto,
magenta 8. morindin 9. rhodamine
10. orseilline
violet . . 5. murex 6. archil
yellow . . 7. xanthic 8. luteolin,
orpiment 10. quercitron
dyke . . . see *dike*
dynamic . . . 4. keen 5. acute, vivid
6. potent 7. intense, kinetic
8. forceful, forcible 9. energetic,
strenuous
dynamite inventor . . . 5. Nobel (1866)
dynamo (pert to) . . .
attachment . . 10. commutator
inventor . . 7. Faraday
machine . . 9. generator
part . . 5. rotor 8. armature
dynast . . . 5. ruler 6. prince 8. governor
dynasty . . . 4. race 8. dominion,
lordship 10. succession
11. sovereignty
dynasty (pert to) . . .
Chinese . . 2. Fo 3. Han, Yin 4. Isin,
Ming, Sung, Tang
Spanish . . 6. Ommiad
dysphoria . . . 7. illness 8. debility
dyvour . . . 6. beggar 8. bankrupt
dzeren . . . 8. antelope

E

E . . . 7. Epsilon (Gr)
Ea (Bab) . . . 3. God 5. deity
each . . . 3. all, per 5. alike, every
6. apiece, singly 10. separately
12. individually 14. distributively
eager . . . 3. apt 4. agog, avid, keen,
yare 5. agasp, sharp 6. ardent,
greedy, intent 7. anxious, burning,
excited, thirsty, willing, zealous
8. desirous, spirited 9. strenuous
eager beaver . . . 7. hustler 8. go—getter
10. enthusiast
eagerness . . . 4. élan, zeal 5. ardor
6. fervor 7. avidity 8. alacrity,
cupidity, fervency 9. alertness,
readiness 10. enthusiasm, impatience
13. impetuousness
eagle . . . 4. erne (ern), gier (Bib), seal
6. bergut, eaglet, emblem

8. standard (Rom) 13. constellation
(Milky Way)
eagle (pert to) . . .
American . . 4. bald
brood . . 5. aerie, eyrie
coin . . 4. gold
European . . 3. sea 5. harpy 6. golden
8. imperial
genus . . 6. Aquila
heraldry . . 8. allerion
male . . 6. tercil
sacred to Jupiter . . 9. Jove's bird
S America . . 9. eagle hawk
scout badge . . 5. merit
Eagles . . . 14. Fraternal Order
eagre (acker) . . . 4. bore, flow, wave
5. flood (tidal)
ear . . . 4. head 5. auris 7. auricle,
hearing 8. orillion 9. appendage,

attention, orecchion (obs)
ear (pert to)...
anvil.. 5. incus
bone.. 6. stapes, tegman 7. stirrup
canal.. 7. cochlea 9. labyrinth
10. Eustachian, scala media
external.. 6. concha
grain.. 3. epi 5. spica 6. mealie,
rizzom (ressum)
hammer.. 7. malleus
inflammation.. 6. otitis
middle.. 8. tympanum
part.. 5. helix, pinna 6. tragus
science.. 7. otology
shell.. 5. ormer 7. abalone
specialist.. 6. aurist 9. otologist
stone.. 7. otolith
term.. 4. otic 5. aural
wax.. 7. cerumen
earache... 6. otalgy 7. otalgia
early... 4. soon 7. ancient, betimes,
matinal 9. premature, primitive
10. beforehand, beforetime
earn... 3. get, win 4. gain 5. ettle,
merit 7. acquire, deserve
earnest... 5. arles (pledge), grave,
sober, staid 6. ardent, hearty, pledge,
sedate, solemn 7. handsel (money),
serious, sincere, zealous 8. resolute
9. heartfelt, important 10. thoughtful
12. wholehearted
earnestly... 8. solemnly 9. intensely,
zealously 10. resolutely
earphone... 7. trumpet (double)
8. otoscope 9. auriphone, topophone
(double) 11. stethescope
earring... 4. hoop 6. earbob, pendle
7. earstud, pendant 9. girandole
(girandola)
earth... 3. erd 4. clay, clod, dirt, land,
marl, muck, sand, soil, vale 5. geest,
loess, sloam, terra 6. ground, planet,
rideau 7. topsoil 8. alluvium
earth (pert to)...
center.. 10. geocentric
12. centrosphere
comb form.. 3. geo
deformation.. 10. epeirogeny
formed beneath.. 8. hypogene,
plutonic
formed by ores.. 9. supergene
formed on surface.. 7. epigene
god (Egypt).. 3. Geb (Keb)
goddess.. 4. Erda, Gaea (Gaia), Tari
6. Semele 7. Demeter
produced by.. 6. mortal
11. terrigenous
satellite.. see *satellite*
volcanic.. 5. trass
earthdrake... 6. dragon
earthly... 7. mundane, secular, terrene,
worldly 8. temporal 11. terrestrial,
universally, unspiritual
13. materialistic
earthmover... 6. digger 7. backhoe,
leveler 9. bulldozer, excavator
10. steam shovel
earth pig... 8. aardvark
earthquake... 5. quake, seism
7. temblor 12. diastrophism

earthstar... 6. fungus 7. Geaster
earthworm... 7. annalid, dew worm,
ipokoea 9. Lumbricus
earthy... 3. low 5. gross 6. coarse
7. worldly 8. material 9. unrefined
ease... 4. calm, rest 5. abate, allay,
peace, quiet, relax 6. pacify, relief,
repose, soothe 7. assuage, comfort,
content, leisure, relieve, slacken
8. facility, mitigate 9. alleviate,
disburden, enjoyment 10. prosperity,
relaxation, solicitude 11. informality,
tranquilize 12. tranquillity (tranquility)
easily... 4. eath (eith) 6. gently, slowly,
softly 7. readily 8. smoothly
11. comfortably, dexterously
12. effortlessly
easily (pert to)...
broken.. 6. shelly 7. fragile, friable
frightened.. 8. skittish
managed.. 6. docile
moved.. 6. mobile
offended.. 9. sensitive
split.. 8. schistic
understood.. 5. lucid
east... 4. Asia, dawn 6. Levant, Orient
7. sunrise 8. eastward
East Africa...
hartebeest.. 4. tora
house (mud).. 5. tembe
republic.. 5. Kenya 7. Somalia
island.. 8. Zanzibar
tribes.. 3. Luo 4. Embu, Teso
5. Bantu, Masai 6. Kikuyu, Mau Mau
7. Nilotes
vessel.. 4. dhow
East India... see also *East Indian*
drink.. 4. nipa
fan.. 6. punkah (punka)
gateway (temple).. 5. toran (torana)
hat, helmet.. 5. topee (topi)
money of account.. 4. anna
mountain pass.. 4. ghat (ghaut)
musical instrument.. 4. vina 5. ruana,
saron
police station.. 5. thana (tanna)
sailing vessel.. 5. dhoni (doni)
7. patamar
sugar, molasses.. 3. gur
10. massecuite
water vessel (brass).. 4. lota (lotah)
East Indian animal...
antelope.. 5. bongo, takin 6. impala,
nilgai 8. axis deer
cattle.. 4. gaur, zebu 5. gayal, tsine
7. banteng
civet.. 6. musang 10. paradoxure
goat (wild).. 4. tahr 7. markhor
lemurlike.. 7. tarsier
raccoonlike.. 3. wah 5. panda
rat.. 9. bandicoot
swine.. 8. babirusa (babiroussa)
East Indian bird...
broadbill.. 4. raya
bulbul.. 4. kala
falcon.. 5. besra
fruit pigeon.. 6. treron
thrush.. 5. shama
weaverbird.. 4. baya
East Indian people...

boatswain .. 6. serang
chief .. 6. sirdar
groom .. 4. syce
harem .. 6. zenana
native sailor, soldier .. 5. sepoy
  6. lascar
nurse .. 4. amah, ayah
peasant .. 4. ryot
poet .. 6. Tagore
princess .. 4. rani (ranee)
robber .. 6. dacoit
title .. 4. raja 5. rajah, sahib
warrior .. 5. singh
East Indian tree, plant ...
bark .. 4. lodh 5. niepa
cedar .. 6. deodar
cotton .. 5. simal
fiber .. 4. jute
fruit .. 3. bel 6. lanseh (lansa)
gum .. 4. kino
herb .. 5. tikor 6. sesame 7. roselle
mahogany .. 4. toon
mulberry .. 4. tapa
palm .. 4. tal (fiber) 4. nipa (thatch)
  5. sural (juice), toddy 7. palmyra
pea .. 4. dhak 5. Butea
rubber .. 3. saj
shade .. 6. banyan
timber .. 3. saj, sal (saul) 4. poon, teak
  5. siris 6. sissoo
walnut .. 6. lebbek
east wind ... 5. Eurus
easy ... 4. calm, slow 5. loose, suave
  6. cinchy, facile, gentle, simple
  7. natural 8. gullible, informal,
  moderate, tranquil, unforced
  9. leisurely, unhurried
  10. manageable, nonchalant,
  unaffected 11. comfortable,
  complaisant, unconcerned
easy–going ... 4. calm 11. unflappable
easy job ... 8. sinecure
easy mark ... 4. dupe, gull 6. sucker,
  victim 7. cat's–paw
eat ... 3. sup 4. dine, etch, feed, gnaw
  5. board, erode 6. devour, ravage
  7. consume, corrode, destroy
eat (pert to) ...
between meals .. 4. nosh 5. bever,
  snack
by rule .. 4. diet
earth, clay .. 8. geophagy
  12. chthonophagy
greedily .. 3. lab 4. glut 5. gorge,
  scarf (down) 6. gobble, pig out (sl)
  7. edacity 8. voracity
eatable ... 6. edible 8. esculent,
  gustable 10. comestible
eater ... 5. diner 7. epicure, glutton,
  gourmet 8. gourmand
eating (pert to) ...
alone .. 9. monophagy
comb form .. 7. phagous
decay .. 12. saprophagous
fish .. 11. piscivorous
  13. icthyophagous
flesh, raw .. 9. omophagia
flesh–eating .. 9. creophagy
  10. zoophagous 11. carnivorous
man–eating .. 12. androphagous
  13. anthropophagy
nuts .. 10. nucivorous

  11. nuciphagous
plants, herbs .. 11. herbivorous
  12. phytophagous
roots .. 12. rhizophagous
eavesdrop ... 3. bug 4. drip 6. harken,
  listen 7. wiretap 10. stillicide
  14. listen secretly
ebb ... 3. low 4. neap, sink, tide, wane
  5. abate, decay 6. recede, reflux,
  retire 7. decline, dwindle, shallow,
  subside 8. decrease
ebb and flow ... 5. surge 6. aestus
  (estus) 11. alternation
ebb tide ... 8. low water
ebullition ... 7. boiling, ferment
  8. bubbling 9. agitation, commotion
  12. fermentation 13. effervescence
eccentric ... 3. cam (shaft), odd
  5. flaky, kinky 6. weirdo 7. erratic,
  strange 8. abnormal 9. erratical,
  irregular 13. nonconformist
  15. idiosyncratical
eccentricity ... 6. oddity 9. queerness
  10. aberration, erraticism
  11. abnormality, peculiarity,
  strangeness 12. idiosyncrasy,
  irregularity 13. nonconformity
  17. unconventionality
Ecclesiastes ... 8. Koheleth (Gr)
echidna ... 7. monster (Gr Myth)
  8. anteater
echinoderm ... 8. starfish 9. sea urchin
echo ... 4. mute, stop (organ) 5. nymph
  (Myth), reply 6. repeat 7. imitate,
  resound, respond 8. resemble,
  response 9. duplicate 10. repetition
  13. reverberation
echoism ... 12. onomatopoeia
Eciton ... 4. ants (legionary)
eclipse ... 5. cloud, sully 6. darken
  7. obscure, surpass 10. extinguish
ecliptic term ... 5. lagna, orbit
  6. circle 9. penumbral
ecology, oecology ... 4. sere 6. botany
  7. biology 9. bionomics, sociology
  10. bioecology
economical ... 5. canny, chary
  6. frugal, saving 7. careful, thrifty
  8. domestic 9. provident
  12. parsimonious
economics terms ... 5. T–bill
  7. bailout 8. bankable, cash flow,
  rollover 9. plutology 10. monetarism,
  production (wealth)
economize ... 4. save 5. skimp, stint
  6. scrimp 7. husband, utilize
  8. retrench
economy ... 4. care 6. saving, thrift
  7. cutback 8. prudence 9. canniness,
  husbandry 10. providence
ecstasy ... 5. bliss 6. trance
  7. emotion, rapture 9. enrapture
ecstatic ... 4. rapt 7. rapture
  9. rapturous, rhapsodic
ectad ... 7. outward
ecto (comb form) ... 7. outside, without
  8. external
Ecuador (pert to) ...
capital .. 5. Quito
export .. 7. bananas
hat .. 6. Panama 8. 'Jipijapa'
island .. 9. Galapagos

mountain . . 5. Andes
reptile . . 6. iguana 8. tortoise
volcano . . 10. Chimborazo
ecumenical . . . 7. general, liberal
8. catholic, tolerant 9. universal,
world–wide 12. cosmopolitan
eczema . . . 6. herpes, tetter 8. eruption
9. salt rheum
edacity . . . 5. greed 7. avarice
8. appetite, gulosity, voracity
10. greediness
eddy . . . 4. bore, gulf 5. gurge, surge,
swirl, whirl 6. vortex 7. current,
wreathe 9. whirlpool
Edentate (Zool) . . . 6. sloths
7. mammals 9. aardvarks, anteaters
10. armadillos
edge . . . 3. hem, jag, lip, rim 4. brim,
brow, side 5. arris, brink, crest,
marge, sharp, sidle (to), splay, verge
6. border, flange, labrum, margin
7. ambitus, selvage 8. acrimony,
pungency, selvedge 9. advantage,
sharpness 10. escarpment
edged . . . 5. erose 7. crenate
8. bordered, invected (Her)
edging . . . 3. hem 4. lace, welt 5. frill,
ruche 6. border, fringe, ruffle
7. binding, bordure (Her), flounce,
tatting
edgy . . . 5. sharp 7. angular, nervous
8. critical, snappish 9. excitable,
impatient 13. sharp–cornered
edict . . . 3. act, ban 4. Bull (Pope's),
fiat 5. arret, dicta (pl), irade, order,
ukase 6. assize, decree, dictum,
firman 7. command, mandate
8. decretal 9. ordinance
12. proclamation
edification . . . 8. learning 9. knowledge
11. improvement, instruction
edifice . . . 5. house 6. church, palace,
temple 7. Capitol 8. building
9. structure 10. tabernacle
edify . . . 5. build, teach 7. educate,
improve 8. instruct, organize
9. construct, enlighten, establish
Edinburgh . . .
burgh . . 5. Leith
capital of . . 8. Scotland
county . . 10. Midlothian
famed street . . 9. Royal Mile
Gaelic name . . 7. Dun Edin (Dunedin)
nickname . . 16. Athens of the North
site . . 12. Firth of Forth
edit . . . 5. emend 6. direct, excise,
redact, revise, reword 7. arrange,
correct, prepare
edition . . . 4. copy 5. issue 6. number
7. version
editions (Bib) . . .
eight texts . . 7. octapla
four texts . . 8. tetrapla
six texts . . 7. hexapla
style and type . . 7. Elzevir (1583)
editor . . . 7. analyst, newsman, reviser
8. arranger, redactor 9. annotator,
gazetteer 10. journalist, supervisor
11. commentator 12. newspaperman
Edom . . . 5. Teman (Bib) 7. Idumaea
Edomite . . . 4. Esau 5. Isaac, Jacob
8. Idumaean

educate . . . 4. rear 5. teach, train
6. inform 7. develop 8. instruct
9. cultivate, enlighten 10. discipline
12. indoctrinate
educated . . . 6. taught 7. erudite,
learned, trained 8. cultured,
informed, lettered, literate
11. enlightened
education . . . 8. breeding, literacy,
training 9. opsimathy (late in life),
schooling 10. discipline
educe . . . 4. draw 6. deduce, elicit,
evolve, obtain, secure
eel (pert to) . . .
colorful . . 5. moray 7. Muraena
genus . . 8. Anguilla 13. Leptocephalus
marine . . 5. elver 6. conger
mud . . 5. siren
sand . . 4. grig
young . . 5. elver
eellike . . . 4. lant, ling 7. eelpout,
lamprey 8. Ophidion 10. anguilloid
11. Lepidosiren
eels, fishing for . . . 7. sniggle
eels, migration of . . . 7. eelfare
eelworm . . . 4. nema 8. Nematoda
9. roundworm 10. vinegar eel
eerie, eery . . . 5. scary, timid, weird
6. gloomy, spooky 7. awesome,
fearful, uncanny 9. deathlike,
unearthly 10. frightened
efface . . . 5. erase 6. cancel, delete
7. blot out, expunge 10. obliterate
effect . . . 4. does 5. close, éclat, force,
mneme 6. mirage, obtain, result
7. achieve, compass, conjure,
execute, fulfill, meaning, operate,
outcome, perform, reality, realize
8. complete 9. discharge, execution,
influence 10. accomplish,
appearance, consummate, impression
11. consequence, performance
effective . . . 4. able 6. active, actual,
cogent 7. capable, telling
8. adequate, eloquent, equipped,
striking 9. brilliant, competent,
effectual, efficient, operative,
trenchant 11. efficacious, influential
effects . . . 5. goods, wares 8. movables,
property
effeminate . . . 3. sop 5. sissy
6. female, tender 7. cockney,
epicene, womanly 8. feminine,
womanish 9. Sybaritic
11. mollycoddle 12. overdelicate
13. overemotional
effervescent . . . 5. fizzy 6. bubbly, lively
7. boiling, hissing 8. bubbling,
mousseux 9. ebullient, sparkling
10. boisterous
effete . . . 4. aged, idle 5. spent
6. barren 7. worn out 9. exhausted,
fruitless 11. ineffectual
efficacious . . . 4. able 5. valid
6. potent 9. effective, effectual,
operative 11. influential
efficacy . . . 4. dint 5. force, power
6. virtue 7. ability, potency
10. efficiency
efficiency . . . 5. power, skill 7. ability,
utility 8. efficacy 10. capability,
competence 11. proficiency

12. productivity 13. effectiveness
15. efficaciousness
efficient... 4. able 7. capable, operant
9. competent, effective, effectual,
operative 10. productive
12. businesslike
effigy... 4. copy, icon 5. image
8. likeness 9. facsimile, jackstraw,
semblance 11. resemblance
effluvium... 4. aura, fume, odor
9. ectoplasm, emanation
efflux... 3. end 6. expiry, runoff
7. outflow 8. effusion 9. effluence,
emanation
effodient... 9. burrowing, fossorial
effort... 3. try, tug 4. dint, jump, toil,
will, work 5. assay, burst, labor,
nisus, pains, trial 6. strain
7. attempt, conatus, trouble
8. endeavor, exertion, struggle
11. application
effrontery... 5. brass 8. audacity,
boldness 9. arrogance, impudence,
sauciness 11. presumption
effulgence... 5. aglow, glory 6. luster
8. radiance, rutilant, splendor
10. brightness, brilliance
effusive... 7. gushing 9. exuberant,
rhapsodic 13. demonstrative
eft... 4. evet, newt 6. lizard, triton
7. urodele 10. salamander
egest... 4. emit, void 7. excrete
9. discharge, ejaculate, eliminate
egg... 3. nit, ova (pl), ove 4. goad,
ovum, prod, urge 5. ovule 6. incite
9. instigate
egg (pert to)...
bird's.. 7. chalaza (white of), treadle
(embryo)
case.. 6. ovisac
comb form.. 2. oo 3. ovi
part.. 7. latebra
shaped.. 4. ooid, oval 5. ovate, ovoid
6. ooidal 9. ovaliform
shell.. 5. shard 6. ovisac
undeveloped.. 5. addle
white.. 5. glair 7. albumen
yolk, yelk.. 7. liaison 8. lecithin
eggplant... 9. melongena
eggs (pert to)...
feeding on.. 9. ovivorous
fish.. 3. roe 5. berry, spawn
preserved.. 5. pidan
tester of.. 7. candler
two at a time.. 8. ditokous
egis, aegis... 4. care 5. guard
6. shield, symbol (anc) 7. backing,
defense 8. advocacy, auspices,
guidance, tutelage 9. fosterage,
patronage 10. protection
11. sponsorship
ego... 3. man 4. self 5. atman (Hind)
6. psyche, spirit 7. conceit, jivatma
(Hind) 11. selfishness
egress... 4. exit 5. issue 6. outlet
8. issuance 9. departure
egret... 5. heron, plume 8. aigrette
Egypt, UAR... see also *Egyptian*
capital.. 5. Cairo
Christian.. 4. Copt
city (ruined).. 5. Luxor, Tanis
6. Karnak, Thebes

dam.. 5. Aswan
desert.. 5. Dakla
gulf.. 4. Suez 5. Aqaba
language (anc).. 6. Coptic
lighthouse (anc).. 6. Pharos
mother.. 3. Mut
peninsula.. 5. Sinai
philosopher.. 8. Plotinus
port.. 4. Said, Suez 10. Alexandria
queen.. 9. Cleopatra
river.. 4. Nile
ruler.. 5. pasha 6. caliph 7. khedive
ruler.. 6. Farouk 7. Busiris (Myth),
Pharaoh, Ptolemy, Rameses
sea.. 3. Red 13. Mediterranean
Egyptian (pert to)...
abode of dead.. 4. Aaru (fields of)
6. Amenti
antelope.. 7. bubalis
ape (sacred).. 4. Aani
beetle.. 6. scarab
bird (crocodile).. 6. sicsac
bird (sacred).. 4. Benu, ibis
7. phoenix
bull.. 4. apis
cobra.. 4. haje
cross.. 3. tau 4. ankh (emblem of
life) 10. crux ansata
crown.. 4. atef
dancing girl.. 4. alma (alme, Almeh)
7. ghawazi 8. Baramika
dog.. 6. saluki (gazelle hound)
headdress of ruler.. 6. Uraeus
heaven.. 4. Aaru
lizard.. 4. adda 5. skink
lute.. 5. nable
paper.. 7. papyrus
solar disk.. 4. aten
soul.. 2. Ba 4. khet, sahu
stone (famed).. 7. Rosetta
symbol.. 3. asp 6. scarab (beetle)
tomb.. 6. serdab (cell) 7. mastaba
watchman.. 6. ghafir (ghaffir)
writing.. 13. hieroglyphics
Egyptian god of...
day.. 5. Horus
earth.. 3. Geb, Keb
life.. 4. Ptah
pleasure.. 3. Bes
primeval fluid.. 2. Nu
sea.. 5. Aegir
sun.. 3. Ra 3. Tem (Tum) 4. Atmu
5. Mentu (Ment) 7. Khepera
11. Harpocrates
supreme.. 4. Amen (Amon)
underworld.. 6. Osiris 7. Hershef
unknown.. 2. Ka
wisdom.. 5. Thoth 6. Dhouti
Egyptian goddess of...
arms.. 4. Anta
fertility.. 4. Isis
gods.. 4. Sati
motherhood.. 4. Apet
sea.. 3. Ran
truth.. 4. Maat
eidolon... 5. image 7. phantom
8. illusion 10. apparition
eight, eighth (pert to)...
day (every).. 5. octan
feast day.. 4. utas
group.. 5. octad, octet 6. octave
7. octette

heaven.. **5.** stars (fixed)
number.. **4.** ocho **6.** ogdoad
philosophy.. **8.** Diagrams
sided.. **9.** octagonal
tone, note.. **4.** unca **6.** quaver (8th)
8. diatonic
eighteen inches... **5.** cubit
Eire... **4.** Erin **7.** Ireland
ejaculate... **4.** emit, oust, void
5. blurt, eject, evict, expel
7. exclaim **8.** dislodge
eject... **4.** emit, oust, spew, void
5. evict, expel, spout, spurt
6. banish **7.** extrude **9.** discharge,
eliminate
ejection... **6.** ouster **8.** eviction
9. expulsion **11.** elimination
eke (out)... **3.** add, imp, tab **4.** also,
etch **8.** addition, appendix (dial),
increase, piece out **10.** postscript
El... **3.** God **5.** deity
elaborate... **6.** ornate, refine
7. develop, improve, perfect, studied
9. embellish, perfected, superfine
11. complicated, high–wrought
Elam capital... **4.** Susa (anc)
élan... **4.** dash **5.** ardor **6.** spirit
9. eagerness **10.** enthusiasm
elapse... **2.** go **3.** die, fly, run **4.** flit,
pass, slip **5.** lapse **6.** expire
elastic... **6.** pliant, rubber **7.** buoyant,
ductile, springy **8.** flexible, stretchy
9. expansive, resilient
12. recuperative
elasticity... **4.** give **6.** elater, spring
7. pliancy, rebound **9.** ductility
10. resilience
elated... **6.** jovial **7.** gleeful
8. exultant, jubilant **9.** overjoyed
Elbe tributary... **4.** Eger, Iser
elbow... **5.** ancon, joint, nudge
6. jostle **8.** chelidon (hollow of)
El Camino Real... **9.** Royal Road
12. King's Highway (Pac Hwy)
elder... **3.** iva **4.** ainé, blue (color)
5. berry, judge, ruler **6.** Mormon,
senior **7.** ancient **8.** ancestor
10. forefather
eldest... **5.** eigne **6.** oldest **8.** earliest
9. firstborn
eldritch... **4.** wild **5.** eerie (eery), weird
9. frightful
elect... **3.** ort **4.** name **5.** elite
6. choose, select **9.** designate
election... **6.** choice **11.** alternative
13. determination **14.** discrimination
electric (pert to)...
atom.. **8.** electron
condenser (anc).. **9.** Leyden jar
conductor.. **6.** ohmage
current.. **2.** AC, DC **7.** circuit
force.. **4.** elod
generator.. **6.** dynamo
light.. **3.** arc **4.** neon
12. incandescent
meter.. **7.** ammeter **9.** voltmeter,
wattmeter
particle.. **3.** ion **6.** cation (kation)
power.. **7.** wattage
safety device.. **4.** fuse
unit.. **3.** ohm, rel **4.** volt, watt
5. farad, henry, joule **6.** ampere,

proton **7.** coulomb, oersted
8. kilowatt
electrical wonders... **6.** Venus V
9. Surveyor V **11.** Oroville Dam
12. nuclear plant
electricity... **5.** juice, power
10. illuminant
eleemosynary... **4.** alms, free
7. charity **10.** almsgiving
elegance... **5.** charm, grace, taste
6. beauty, polish **9.** propriety
10. ornateness, politeness, refinement
13. sumptuousness
elegant... **4.** rich **6.** dressy, ornate,
soigné, urbane **7.** courtly, genteel,
refined **8.** graceful, handsome,
polished, tasteful **9.** admirable,
beautiful, excellent **10.** fastidious
11. fashionable **13.** grandiloquent
element... **3.** air **4.** fire **5.** earth,
water
elementary... **5.** basic **6.** simple
7. primary **8.** inchoate, original
9. beginning **11.** fundamental
elephant... **3.** cow **4.** bull, calf
5. hathi, rogue **6.** tusker
8. behemoth **9.** pachyderm
elephant (pert to)...
apple.. **7.** Feronia
boy.. **4.** Sabu
call, cry.. **4.** barr **7.** trumpet
enclosure, trap.. **6.** keddah
goad.. **5.** ankus
keeper.. **6.** mahout
seat.. **6.** howdah
tusk.. **5.** ivory **9.** scrivello
young.. **4.** calf
elevate... **4.** lift, rear **5.** elate, exalt,
raise **6.** refine, uplift **7.** advance,
dignify, ennoble, glorify, inspire,
promote **10.** exhilarate
elevated... **2.** el **5.** lofty, risen
6. elated **7.** exalted, sublime
8. eminence
elevation... **4.** hill **6.** height (highth)
9. promotion **10.** exaltation
11. composition (Eccl), distinction
13. glorification
elevation of the mind... **7.** anagoge
elevator... **3.** bin **4.** cage, lift, silo
9. ascenseur
eleven... **7.** hendeca (comb form)
elf... **3.** fay, hob, imp, nix **4.** peri
5. fairy, gnome, ouphe, pixie
6. goblin, sprite **7.** brownie
elfish... **5.** elfin **6.** elvish, impish
7. elflike, tricksy **8.** eldritch
11. mischievous
Elgin Marbles... **10.** sculptures (by
Phidias)
elicit... **3.** get **4.** draw, pump
5. claim, educe, evoke, exact, wrest,
wring **6.** deduce, demand, entice,
extort, induce, obtain **7.** extract
elide... **4.** dele, omit **5.** annul
6. ignore **7.** destroy, nullify, shorten
8. demolish, suppress **9.** eliminate
eligible... **3.** apt, fit **4.** meet
6. worthy **8.** entitled, suitable
9. competent, desirable, qualified
10. acceptable, admissible
Elijah... **7.** prophet **8.** oratorio

14. John the Baptist (Bib)
eliminate... 3. rid 4. kill 5. erase,
expel 6. detach, remove 7. discard,
divulge, exclude, excrete, release
8. evacuate, separate 9. segregate
11. exterminate
Elisha... 7. prophet 8. disciple (of
Elijah)
elision... 7. syncope 9. severance
10. abridgment, shortening
11. suppression (vowel)
elite... 5. stars 6. flower, galaxy
7. fashion, society 9. beau monde
10. upper crust
elixir... 6. remedy 7. cure–all, essence,
extract, heal–all, panacea
8. medicine, tincture 10. catholicon
12. quintessence
elixir of life... 11. elixir vitae
Elixir of Love... 13. L'Elisir d'Amore
elk... 4. deer 5. Alces, eland, moose
6. sambar, wapiti
ellipse, elliptical... 5. curve, ovoid,
ovule
elm (pert to)...
borer.. 6. beetle, lamiid
fruit.. 6. samara
genus.. 5. Ulmus
rock, wing (kinds).. 5. wahoo
Elm City... 8. New Haven
Elmo... 11. patron saint (sailors)
elocution... 7. oratory 8. rhetoric
9. eloquence 10. expression
elocutionist... 6. reader 7. reciter
11. elocutioner 13. recitationist
eloge... 6. eulogy 7. address, oration
8. encomium, eulogium
eloign... 6. convey, remove 7. conceal
elongate... 6. extend, remove
7. stretch 8. continue, lengthen,
protract
elongated... 4. lank, long 6. linear,
oblong 7. prolate, slender
8. extended 9. stretched
10. attenuated
elope... 6. decamp 7. abscond, skip
out 8. slip away
eloquence... 7. fluency, oratory
9. discourse, elocution
14. expressiveness
eloquence, teacher of... 6. rhetor
eloquent... 5. vivid 10. Ciceronian,
expressive, meaningful, oratorical
11. significant
else... 2. or 4. ense (ens) 5. if not,
other 9. otherwise 10. additional
12. accompanying
elsewhere... 4. away 5. alibi (law)
elucidate... 5. clear, lucid 7. clarify,
clear up 8. simplify 9. interpret
10. illustrate
elude... 4. flee, foil, mock, shun
5. avoid, dodge, evade 6. baffle,
befool, escape 10. circumvent
elusive... 4. eely 6. subtle 7. elusory,
evasive 8. baffling 9. equivocal
10. impalpable
elves... see *elf*
Elysium (Myth)... 8. paradise
em... 2. en (half) 4. unit (Elec)
emaciated... 4. lean 5. gaunt
6. peaked, wasted 7. pinched

10. attenuated, cadaverous
emanation... 4. aura, odor 5. light,
niton (radium), vapor 7. outcome
8. creation, effluvia 9. ectoplasm,
radiation 10. exhalation, generation
11. consequence
emancipation... 6. rescue 7. freedom,
release 10. liberation
11. manumission
15. enfranchisement
emasculate... 4. geld, spay 5. unman
6. soften 8. castrate 9. expurgate,
sterilize 10. effeminize
embalmer... 5. cerer 9. mortician,
preserver 10. undertaker
embankment... 3. dam 4. bund, dike
5. levee, revet, shore 7. barrier,
pilapil (rice field) 8. buttress
10. breakwater 13. fortification
embargo... 5. edict, order 7. exclude
8. blockade, prohibit, stoppage
9. exclusion 10. impediment
11. prohibition, requisition
embark... 4. sail, ship 6. depart,
invest, unmoor 7. cast off, entrain
embarrass... 5. abash, shame
6. hamper, hinder, impede
7. confuse, fluster, involve, mortify,
nonplus 8. bewilder, confound,
encumber, handicap 9. discomfit,
dumbfound 10. complicate,
disconcert
embarrassment... 5. shame
9. abashment, confusion
11. involvement, predicament
12. discomfiture, entanglement
13. inconvenience, mortification
embellish... 3. gem 4. deck, gild
5. adorn, array, dress, gouge, grace
6. bedeck, enrich 7. bedrape,
enhance, garnish 8. beautify,
emblazon, furbelow, ornament
9. embroider 10. exaggerate
embellishment... 9. garniture
10. decoration, furbishing
12. exaggeration 13. ornamentation
ember... 3. ash 4. coal (live), izle
5. gleed 6. cinder 7. residue
embers... 5. ashes 8. emotions (past),
memories
embezzle... 5. steal, swipe 6. lessen,
thieve, weaken (obs) 7. purloin
8. peculate, squander 9. dissipate
11. appropriate
embitter... 4. sour 5. anger
7. envenom 8. acerbate
10. antagonize, exacerbate
emblazon... 4. laud 5. color, extol
6. praise 7. display, exhibit, glorify
9. celebrate, embellish
emblem... 3. rue 4. mace, sign, type
5. badge, crown, image, token,
totem 6. device, figure, symbol
7. balance (justice), coronet, sceptor
9. prototype
emblematic... 5. typal 7. typical
8. symbolic 10. figurative
14. characteristic
embodiment... 4. Apis 6. avatar,
matter 7. epitome 9. inclusion
10. enfoldment 11. combination,
composition, incarnation

12. organization 13. incorporation
14. representative 15. personification
embolden ... 5. nerve 6. assure
7. hearten 8. reassure 9. encourage
embosom ... 6. foster 7. cherish,
embrace, enclose 8. surround
embrace ... 3. hug 4. fold, gain, hold,
love, wrap 5. adopt, clasp, cling,
grasp, inarm, seize 6. accoll (obs),
caress, enfold 7. cherish, contain,
enclose, espouse, include, involve,
welcome 8. comprise, encircle,
greeting, surround 9. encompass
embroider ... 7. falsify 8. decorate,
ornament 9. embellish
10. exaggerate
embroidery ... 8. appliqué 9. hardanger
embroidery frame ... 7. taboret
(tabouret)
embroil ... 5. upset 6. jumble
7. agitate, disturb, perplex, trouble
8. convulse, disorder, distract
9. commingle, implicate
10. complicate, discompose
eme ... 5. uncle 6. friend, gossip
emend ... 4. edit, mend 5. amend,
right 6. better, remedy, revise
7. correct, improve, rectify
emerald ... 5. beryl, color, green
7. smaragd
Emerald Isle ... 4. Erin 7. Ireland
emerge ... 3. dip 4. pend, rise
5. hatch, issue 6. appear
7. debouch, emanate
10. disembogue
emergency ... 5. pinch 6. clutch, crisis,
strait 8. exigency, juncture
9. extremity, necessity 10. substitute
emery ... 6. pumice 8. abradant,
abrasive, corundum 9. sandpaper
emesis ... 6. puking 7. spewing
8. vomiting 12. disgorgement
13. regurgitation
emeute ... 4. riot 6. Putsch
8. outbreak 10. insurgence
12. insurrection
emigrant ... 6. emigré 7. migrant,
outgoer, settler 8. colonist, stranger
9. immigrant, migratory (of birds)
eminence ... 4. hill 5. title 6. height,
rideau 7. dignity 9. authority,
elevation, greatness, loftiness
10. famousness, importance,
projection 11. superiority
13. transcendency
eminent ... 4. arch, high 5. great,
lofty, noted 6. famous, marked,
signal 8. renowned, superior,
towering 9. important 10. celebrated,
protruding 11. illustrious
13. distinguished
emissary ... 3. spy 5. agent, scout
8. delegate, diplomat
emit ... 4. glow, reek, shed 5. eject,
eruct, exude, issue, pluff, voice
6. exhale 7. distill (distil), emanate,
publish, radiate 8. opalesce (colors),
transmit 9. discharge, irradiate
emmet ... 3. ant 7. pismire 8. formicid
emollient ... 4. balm 8. ointment,
soothing 9. lubricant, softening
emolument ... 4. fees, gain 5. wages

6. profit, salary 7. stipend, tribute
9. allowance 12. compensation
emotion ... 5. agony, stoic 6. pathos
7. feeling, passion 9. agitation,
gratitude, sensation, sentiment
10. excitement 11. disturbance,
sensibility
emotionless ... 9. apathetic, impassive,
unfeeling 10. spiritless
11. unemotional 12. unresponsive
emperor ... 4. czar, tsar 5. Mogul
7. monarch 9. commander,
imperator, sovereign
emphasis ... 6. accent, stress
7. cadence 8. salience
10. insistence 14. impressiveness
emphasize ... 6. accent, insist, stress
7. point up 9. punctuate
10. accentuate
emphatic ... 7. earnest 8. forcible,
positive, striking 9. energetic,
insistent 10. expressive
11. significant
empire ... 4. rule, sway 5. green
(color), reign, state 6. domain
7. control, country
Empire (pert to) ...
of the Rising Sun .. 5. Japan
State .. 7. New York
State of the South .. 7. Georgia
empiric ... 4. fake 5. cheat, quack
8. impostor 9. charlatan
10. mountebank
employ ... 3. use 4. busy, coax, hire
5. apply, exert 6. devote, occupy
7. concern, entrust, service
10. occupation
employees ... 4. crew, gang, help
5. force, hands, staff 9. personnel
10. associates
employer ... 4. user 5. hirer 6. master
8. consumer 12. entrepreneur
employment ... 3. use 4. work
5. trade 7. calling, purpose, service
8. business, vocation 10. occupation,
profession
emporium ... 4. fair, mart 5. store
6. bazaar, market 10. exposition
empower ... 6. enable 7. entitle
8. delegate, deputize 9. authorize
10. commission
empty ... 4. idle, toom, vain, void
5. blank, clear, drain, inane
6. hollow, hungry, jejune, vacant,
vacate 7. deplete, foolish, vacuous
8. evacuate, unfilled 9. insincere
10. unburdened, unoccupied
empusa (Gr Myth) ... 5. fungi
7. specter 9. hobgoblin
empyrean ... 3. sky 5. ether 6. Caelus,
welkin 7. heavens, the blue
emulate ... 5. equal, outdo, rival
7. compete, imitate, vie with
11. competition
emulsion ... 9. demulcent
10. semiliquid, suspension
enable ... 5. equip 6. clothe
7. empower, qualify 9. authorize
10. capacitate
enact ... 4. pass, play 6. decree,
enjoin, ordain, record 7. actuate,
appoint, perform 9. legislate,

represent 10. constitute
11. impersonate
enactment... 3. law 4. veto 5. canon,
edict, usage 6. decree 7. statute
9. ordinance 11. legislation
encamp, encampment... 4. camp, tent
5. siege 7. bivouac, camping
enchant... 5. charm 6. delude
7. bewitch, delight 8. ensorcel
9. captivate, enrapture, fascinate
enchantment... 5. charm, magic, spell
7. sorcery 8. witchery
10. allurement, necromancy,
witchcraft 11. bewitchment,
fascination, incantation
enchantress... 5. Circe, Medea
7. charmer 9. bewitcher, sorceress,
temptress
encina... 7. live oak
encircle... 3. orb 4. gird, ring, zone
5. belay, inorb, twist 6. enfold
7. besiege, circuit, enclose, environ,
include, wreathe 8. surround
12. circumscribe
encircled... 4. girt 5. orbed, paled,
zoned 6. belted, forded, hooped,
ringed 7. enlaced 8. enclosed,
enfolded, wreathed 10. surrounded
enclose... 3. hem, mew 5. bound,
fence 6. corral, encase, engulf
7. enclave, envelop, harness, include
8. imprison, surround 9. encompass
12. circumscribe
enclosed... 4. pent, sept (area)
7. encased 8. confined
10. surrounded
enclosure... 3. pen 4. bawn, cage,
yair (yare), yard 5. carol (cloister),
kraal (craal), sekos 6. corral
8. contents, poundage, stockade
encomium... 4. hymn 5. eloge
6. eulogy, praise 7. tribute
8. accolade 9. panegyric
encompass... 4. ring 5. hem in
6. begird, effect 7. besiege, circuit,
compass, contain, enclose, environ,
include 8. encircle, surround
10. accomplish 12. circumscribe
encompassing... 7. ambient
13. circumambient
encore... 3. bis 4. echo, over 5. again
8. applause, once more
encounter... 4. bout, meet 5. brave,
brush, fight, incur, onset 6. attack,
breast, oppose 7. collide, meeting
8. conflict 10. engagement,
experience
encourage... 4. abet, urge 5. boost,
cheer, impel, nerve, rally 6. assure,
exhort, foster, incite 7. advance,
comfort, console, hearten, inspire,
promote 8. embolden, inspirit
9. instigate, stimulate
11. countenance
encouragement... 3. aid 7. comfort
9. fosterage, incentive
10. inducement 11. emboldening
encroach upon... 5. poach 6. invade,
trench 7. impinge, intrude
8. infringe, overstep, trespass
encumber... 4. clog, load 5. check
6. burden, hamper, hinder, retard,

saddle 7. involve, oppress
8. entangle, handicap, obstruct,
overload 9. embarrass
10. overburden
encumbrance... 5. alien (law), claim
6. burden 9. dependent
10. impediment
encyclic... 6. letter 7. pandect
8. circular, treatise 10. encircling
13. comprehensive
encyclopedic learning, person of...
10. polyhistor 13. encyclopedist
end... 3. aim, neb, tip, toe 4. fate,
kill, ruin, tail 5. amend, close, death,
finis, limit, omega, point, telos,
upend 6. expire, finale, finish, result,
thirty 7. destroy, purpose
8. complete, conclude, dissolve
9. cessation, determine, extremity,
intention, objective, terminate
10. completion 11. termination
end (pert to)...
  arrow.. 4. nock
  boundary.. 5. bourn 7. abuttal
  cloth.. 5. remnant
  game.. 4. goal
  man.. 8. minstrel
  news.. 6. thirty
  timber.. 5. tenon
endanger... 4. risk 6. expose, hazard
7. imperil 10. compromise,
jeopardize
endeavor... 3. aim, try, vie 4. seek
5. essay, ettle, nisus, tempt
6. effort, strive 7. attempt
8. struggle
endemic... 6. native 10. indigenous
14. characteristic
ending... 5. death 6. result
9. cessation, desinence
10. completion, conclusion
11. destruction, termination
endless... 4. many 6. eterne
7. eternal, undying 8. eternity,
infinite, numerous, unending
9. boundless, continual, incessant,
perpetual, unceasing, unstinted
10. continuous 11. everlasting
12. interminable 13. uninterrupted
endorse, indorse... 4. sign 6. attest,
second 7. approve, support
8. sanction 9. authorize, guarantee
endorsement... 4. fiat, visa (vise)
8. approval, sanction 9. provision,
signature 10. acceptance, validation
12. ratification 14. authentication
endow... 3. dow, due 4. dote, vest
5. dower, endue, indue 6. bestow,
clothe, enrich, give to, invest
7. empower, furnish, provide
endowment... 4. gift 5. dower, grant
7. talents 8. appanage (apanage)
9. insurance, provision
11. empowerment, instruction
(Mormon)
endue... 5. endow, teach 6. clothe,
digest, invest, supply 7. empower
endurable... 8. bearable 9. tolerable
10. sufferable 11. supportable
endurance... 7. stamina 8. patience,
strength 9. fortitude, suffering
10. durability, permanence, sufferance

11. continuance, resignation
12. perseverance
endure... 4. bear, bide, dree, last, live, tide, wear 5. abide, allow, brook, stand 6. afford, remain, suffer 7. condone, persist, sustain, undergo 8. continue, tolerate 9. persevere, withstand
enduring... 7. durable, lasting, patient 9. permanent 11. persevering, substantial, unforgotten 13. long–suffering
enemy... 3. foe 5. devil, force, fremd (frenne), hater, rival, Satan 6. foeman 8. opponent 9. adversary 10. antagonist
energetic... 5. fresh 6. active 8. forceful, forcible, vigorous 9. strenuous 11. industrious
energy... 2. go 3. erg, pep, vim 4. bent 5. force, nerve, power, vigor 6. spirit 7. potency, sthenia 8. strength 9. animation
energy (pert to)...
lack of.. 5. atony 6. anergy 7. aneuria, inertia 8. asthenia
mental.. 9. psychurgy
personified.. 6. Shakti
potential.. 5. ergal
unit.. 3. erg 5. ergon
enervate... 3. sap 5. drain, unman 6. weaken 7. exhaust, unnerve 8. enfeeble 10. debilitate
enfeeble... 4. numb 6. sicken, soften, weaken 7. depress 8. enervate 9. attenuate 10. debilitate
enfilade... 4. rake 5. vista 7. barrage 9. broadside 11. arrangement (in rows)
enfold, infold... 4. fold, wrap 5. clasp, cover 6. infold 7. embrace, envelop 8. surround
enforce... 5. drive 6. assail, compel 7. execute, inspire 9. constrain, encourage, intensify, reinforce 10. invigorate
enfranchise... 4. free 5. admit 7. deliver, set free 8. liberate 10. emancipate
engage... 4. bind, draw, hire, rent 5. lease 6. absorb, embark, employ, enlist, induce, occupy, pledge 7. attract, betroth, engross, involve, promise 8. contract, entangle 9. interlock, intermesh
engaged... 4. busy 5. hired 6. bonded, meshed 7. earnest, entered, pledged, versant 8. embedded, employed, involved, occupied, promised 9. affianced, betrothed, engrossed 10. contracted
engaged in controversy... 9. disputant
engagement... 4. date 6. battle 7. promise 9. betrothal, encounter 10. attachment 11. appointment, involvement
engaging... 5. sapid 6. taking 8. alluring, duelling 10. attractive, delightful 11. interesting
engender... 3. sow (seeds) 5. beget, breed, cause 6. excite 7. develop, produce 8. generate, occasion 9. call

forth, procreate, propagate
engine... 3. gin, ram 5. mogul, motor 6. onager 7. machine, robinet, turbine 10. locomotive
engine (type)... 3. gas 5. motor, solar, steam 6. Diesel, rocket 8. gasoline 10. combustion
engineer... 4. plan 7. manager 8. computer, contrive, designer, inventor, maneuver, operator, therblig 9. construct 11. constructor, superintend
engineer (type)... 5. civil, corps, sales 6. driver, mining 7. planner 8. chemical, geodetic, military, railroad, research, sanitary 9. hydraulic 10. electrical, industrial, mechanical, structural 11. electronics 12. aeronautical, construction 14. administrative
engird... 6. begird, circle, girdle 7. envelop 8. encircle, ensphere
England... see also *English*
called.. 6. Albion (anc) 7. Britain 9. Britannia
capital.. 6. London
city.. 3. Ely 4. Hull, York 5. Derby, Leeds 6. Exeter 7. Bristol, Croydon 8. Brighton, Coventry, Hastings, Plymouth 9. Liverpool, Sheffield 10. Birmingham, Epsom Downs, Manchester, Nottingham, Portsmouth 11. Southampton
college (famed).. 4. Eton 6. Harrow, Oxford 9. Cambridge, Sandhurst (military)
conqueror.. 5. Danes 6. Angles, Saxons 7. Normans
constitution.. 10. Magna Carta (1215) 12. Bill of Rights (1688)
county.. 4. Kent 5. Devon, Essex 6. Dorset, Sussex 9. Yorkshire
emblem.. 4. lion, rose
House of.. 4. York 5. Blois, Tudor 6. Stuart 7. Hanover, Windsor 8. Normandy 9. Lancaster 11. Plantagenet
island.. 5. Wight 6. Scilly, Virgin 7. Bahamas, Bermuda, Channel, Solomon 8. Falkland, Windward 9. Isle of Man
king (anc).. 6. Arthur (legend), Egbert 8. Ethelred 9. Ethelwulf
native (anc).. 4. Celt, Dane, Jute 5. Saxon 8. Anglican 9. Sassenach 10. Anglo–Saxon
river.. 3. Exe 4. Avon, Ouse 5. Trent 6. Thames
royal residence.. 7. Windsor
street (London).. 10. Piccadilly 12. Threadneedle
English (pert to)...
bride's gift.. 3. dos
court.. 4. eyre (circuit), leet (anc)
dislike of.. 11. Anglophobia
district.. 4. Soho
estate (feudal).. 4. fief
excuse (legal).. 6. essoin
festival (country).. 3. ale
field.. 5. croft
forest.. 5. Arden 8. Sherwood
freeman.. 5. ceorl, thane, thegn

hamlet.. **4.** dorp
heather.. **4.** ling
lawyer.. **9.** barrister, solicitor
leave of absence (school).. **5.** exeat
lover of.. **10.** Anglophile
Marbles.. **6.** Oxford **7.** Arundel
money of account.. **3.** ora
news agency.. **6.** Reuter
Parliament process.. **7.** Hansard
political party.. **4.** Tory, Whig
   8. Laborite **12.** Conservative
porcelain.. **5.** Spode **8.** Wedgwood
prehistoric site.. **8.** Piltdown
race course.. **5.** Ascot **9.** Newmarket
   10. Epsom Downs
races (famed).. **5.** Derby **7.** The Oaks
sheep (blackface).. **4.** Lonk
song (mock).. **12.** lillibullero
stolen article (on thief).. **7.** mainour
symbol.. **4.** bull, lion, rose
thicket.. **5.** copse **7.** spinney
tract (sandy).. **4.** dean (dene)
trolley.. **4.** tram
uplands.. **5.** downs
wren.. **6.** tomtit
English Channel... **8.** La Manche
English, famed...
composer.. **6.** Handel **7.** Stainer
diarist.. **5.** Pepys
engraver.. **3.** Pye **7.** Hogarth
essayist.. **4.** Elia (Charles Lamb), Lang
   6. Steele **7.** Addison
explorer.. **4.** Ross **5.** Cabot **6.** Baffin,
   Beatty, Hudson **7.** Raleigh
   10. Shackleton
financier.. **7.** Gresham
historian.. **4.** Bede **7.** Spelman,
   Toynbee **8.** Macaulay
humorist.. **4.** Lear (Edward)
mathematician.. **5.** Hooke **6.** Gunter
murderer (famed).. **4.** Aram
navigator.. **4.** Cook **5.** Drake
   6. Nelson
painter.. **4.** Lear **6.** Turner
   7. Hogarth, Lutyens, Millais
philosopher.. **7.** Spencer
physicist.. **7.** Faraday
poet.. **5.** Noyes **8.** Browning,
   Tennyson **9.** Masefield, Swinburne
printer.. **6.** Caxton
reformer.. **4.** Owen **6.** Spence
saint.. **6.** George (patron saint)
   7. Alphege, Swithin
scientist.. **6.** Newton
spy (in Am Rev).. **5.** André
statesman.. **4.** Peel, Pitt **7.** Baldwin,
   Balfour, Walpole **8.** Cromwell,
   Disraeli, Thatcher **9.** Churchill
   11. Chamberlain, Lloyd George
surgeon.. **5.** Haden, Paget **6.** Lister
theologian.. **5.** Booth **6.** Becket
   7. Tyndall **8.** Wycliffe **10.** Whitefield
thesaurus compiler.. **5.** Roget
engrave... **3.** cut **4.** etch, rist
   5. carve, chase, hatch, infix **6.** chisel,
   incise **7.** enchase, impress, imprint,
   stipple **9.** sculpture
engraver's tool... **5.** burin
engraving... **3.** cut **5.** print
   7. etching, chasing, tooling
   8. celature, incising, intaglio
   9. stippling **10.** xylography (wood)

   11. lithography **12.** glyptography
engross... **6.** absorb, engage
   10. monopolize **11.** concentrate
engrossed... **4.** busy, rapt **6.** intent
   8. absorbed, employed **10.** interested
engulf... **4.** gulf, gulp **5.** swamp
   6. absorb **7.** swallow **8.** inundate,
   submerge **9.** overwhelm
enhance... **4.** lift **5.** exalt, extol, raise
   7. advance, augment, elevate, enlarge,
   magnify **8.** increase **9.** aggravate
   10. exaggerate
enigma... **3.** why **5.** rebus **6.** puzzle,
   riddle **7.** charade, mystery
   9. conundrum **11.** mind-boggler
enigmatic... **6.** arcane, mystic
   8. puzzling **12.** inexplicable
enjoin... **3.** bid **5.** order **6.** advise,
   charge, decree, direct, forbid
   7. command **8.** admonish, prohibit
enjoy... **4.** bask, have **5.** savor
   6. relish **10.** appreciate
enjoyment... **4.** ease, zest **6.** relish
   7. delight **8.** felicity, fruition, pleasure
   9. amusement, happiness
enlarge... **3.** eke **4.** ream **5.** swell
   6. dilate, expand, extend, spread
   7. amplify, augment, develop, distend
   8. increase **9.** expatiate
   10. exaggerate
enlargement... **8.** increase
   9. expansion, extension
   12. augmentation **13.** amplification
enlighten... **5.** teach **6.** inform
   7. educate, explain **8.** enkindle,
   instruct **10.** illuminate **11.** disillusion
enlightened person... **10.** illuminate
enlist... **4.** join, list **6.** engage, enroll,
   induce, muster
enliven... **5.** amuse, cheer, rouse
   7. animate, comfort, inspire, refresh
   8. brighten, energize, inspirit
   9. encourage, stimulate
   10. exhilarate, invigorate
enmity... **3.** war **4.** feud **6.** hatred,
   malice, rancor **7.** discord **8.** aversion
   9. antipathy, disaccord, hostility
   10. antagonism, repugnance
   11. malevolence **14.** unfriendliness
ennead... **4.** gods (nine), nine
   18. Ennead of Heliopolis (famed)
ennoble... **5.** exalt, honor, raise
   6. uplift **7.** elevate, glorify, promote
ennui... **4.** bore **5.** bored **6.** tedium
   7. boredom, fatigue, languor
   9. weariness **15.** dissatisfaction
enormous... **4.** huge, vast **5.** great
   6. wicked **7.** immense, massive,
   titanic **8.** abnormal, colossal, gigantic,
   infamous **9.** atrocious, excessive,
   monstrous **10.** inordinate, prodigious,
   stupendous
Enos' father... **4.** Seth
enough... **4.** enow **5.** ample, basta,
   fully, quite **6.** plenty **8.** adequate
   9. amplitude **10.** sufficient
   12. satisfactory
enounce... **5.** state, utter **8.** proclaim
   9. enunciate, pronounce
enow... **9.** presently
enrage... **5.** anger **6.** madden
   7. incense, inflame **9.** infuriate

enraged... 5. irate 7. angered
8. maddened 10. infuriated

enraptured... 6. enrapt 8. ecstatic
9. delighted, entranced
10. enravished

enravished... 4. rapt 9. enchanted,
entranced, rapturous 10. enraptured

enrich... 4. lard 5. adorn, endow
6. fatten 7. improve 8. increase,
ornament 9. embellish, fertilize

enroll... 4. coil, join, list, roll 5. enter
6. enlist, induct, unfurl, wrap up
7. engross, impanel 8. initiate,
register 11. matriculate

ens... 5. being 6. entity 7. essence

ensconce... 4. hide 5. cover 6. settle
7. conceal, protect, shelter
9. establish

ensemble... 3. all 5. decor, group,
whole 7. costume

enshroud... 4. wrap 6. clothe, swathe
7. conceal, enclose 8. enshrine

ensiform... 12. xiphisternum

ensign... 4. flag 6. banner 7. officer
8. gonfalon, standard 9. oriflamme
(oriflamb, anc)

ensign of Othello... 4. Iago

enslave... 8. enthrall

ensnare... 3. web 4. trap 5. benet,
catch, innet, noose 6. allure,
enmesh, entrap, seduce 7. involve

ensorcell, ensorcel... 7. bewitch,
enchant

ensue... 6. follow, pursue, result
7. imitate, succeed 8. come next

ensuing... 4. next 9. resultant
10. subsequent, succeeding

ensure... 6. assure, insure, secure
7. protect, warrant 9. guarantee

entad... 6. inward (opp of ectad)

ental... 5. inner (opp of ectal)

entangle... 3. mat, web 4. mesh, mire
5. afoul, ravel, snarl, twist 6. enlace,
enmesh, puzzle, raffle 7. confuse,
ensnare, involve, perplex 8. bewilder
9. embarrass 10. interweave

entanglement... 4. knot 5. snare, snarl
6. abatis 8. obstacle 9. barricade,
imbroglio 10. barbed wire, complexity
11. involvement

enter... 4. join, list 5. begin, start,
train 6. engage, enlist, enroll, insert,
record 8. initiate, inscribe, register
9. introduce, penetrate
11. participate

enter (pert to)...
career.. 6. incept
legal objection.. 5. demur
with hostility.. 6. invade
without permission.. 7. intrude
8. encroach, infringe

enterprise... 4. firm 5. essay 6. daring
7. attempt, crusade, exploit, venture
10. initiative 11. undertaking

enterprising... 4. bold 6. daring
9. energetic 11. up—and—coming

entertain... 4. fete 5. amuse, treat
6. divert, regale 7. beguile, cherish
8. interest

entertainer... 5. actor 6. dancer,
singer 7. actress, speaker
8. magician 9. performer

11. pantomimist 12. impersonator

entertainment... 4. play 5. party,
revue, sport 6. kermis (kermess),
repast 7. pastime, ridotto, theater
8. entr'acte, musicale 9. amusement,
diversion, reception, wayzgoose
10. recreation 12. Roman holiday

enthusiasm... 4. élan, fire, zeal, zest
5. ardor, craze, estro, furor (furore),
mania, verve 6. fervor 7. ecstasy
8. interest 9. animation, eagerness,
transport 10. exaltation

enthusiast... 3. fan 5. bigot 6. rooter,
zealot 7. devotee, fanatic

enthusiastic... 5. eager, nutty, rabid
6. active, ardent 7. zealous
10. interested

entice... 4. bait, coax, lure, tole
5. decoy, tempt 6. allure, cajole,
incite, seduce 7. attract, wheedle
8. inveigle, persuade

enticement... 9. seduction
10. allurement, attraction, incitement,
inducement, persuasion, temptation
12. inveiglement

entire... 3. all 5. cover (Philat), sound,
total, utter, whole 6. intact
7. perfect, sincere, upright
8. complete, faithful, stallion
9. integrate, undivided
10. unimpaired 11. unqualified
12. undiminished

entirely... 3. all 5. clean, fully, stark
6. solely, wholly 7. totally 9. every
inch, perfectly, sincerely
10. completely

entitle... 3. dub 4. call, name, term
5. style 6. assign, enable, impute
7. empower, qualify 9. authorize,
designate 10. denominate

entity... 3. ens 4. soul, unit 5. being,
entia, thing 7. integer 8. infinity
(Math) 9. existence

entomb... 4. bury 5. inter, inurn
6. hearse, inhume 7. confine
9. sepulture

entourage... 5. suite, train 7. retinue
10. associates, attendants
12. surroundings

entr'acte... 3. act 5. dance, music
7. interim 9. interlude

entrails... 4. guts 6. bowels
7. insides, viscera 8. interior
10. intestines

entrance... 3. way 4. adit, door, gate
5. entry, inlet 6. access, portal
7. gateway, ingress, postern
9. admission, insertion, threshold,
vestibule 10. admittance

entrance (pert to)...
church (Eastern).. 5. Great 6. Little
formal.. 5. debut 12. introduction
hostile.. 9. incursion
temple (Buddh).. 5. toran (torana)

entranced... 4. rapt 8. dreaming
9. delighted, overjoyed
10. fascinated, hypnotized, spellbound
11. overpowered

entrap... 3. net 4. trap 5. catch,
decoy, noose, snare 6. tangle
7. beguile, ensnare 8. entangle,
inveigle

entreat... 3. ask, beg, woo 4. pray
5. crave, halse (obs), plead
6. adjure, appeal 7. beseech,
implore, solicit 8. petition
9. importune 10. supplicate
entreaty... 4. plea, suit 6. appeal,
prayer 7. request 8. petition
10. invitation 11. importunity
12. solicitation, supplication
entree, entrée... 4. dish 6. access
7. ingress, opening 9. admission
10. permission (to enter)
entrench... 6. invade 7. enter on,
fortify, intrude 8. encroach, trespass
9. establish
entrenchment... 7. defense, parapet
9. intrusion 10. protection
12. encroachment, infringement
13. establishment
entrepot... 5. depot, store
9. warehouse 10. depository
entrepreneur... 7. provost 9. executive
10. impresario 13. administrator
entrust... 6. commit 7. confide,
consign 8. delegate 10. commission
entry... 4. hall, item, lane, post
7. ingress 8. entrance, register
9. admission, vestibule
10. contestant, memorandum
12. introduction
entwine... 4. lace 5. clasp, twine,
twist, weave 6. enlace 7. wreathe
9. interknit
enumerate... 4. list, tell 5. count
6. detail, number, reckon, relate
7. compute 8. estimate, name over,
rehearse 9. calculate, catalogue
(catalog) 12. recapitulate
13. particularize
enumeration... 4. list 5. count
6. census 10. numeration
14. recapitulation
enunciate... 3. say 5. utter 6. affirm
7. declare 8. announce, proclaim
9. postulate, pronounce
10. articulate
enunciation... 9. statement, utterance
11. affirmation, attestation,
declaration 12. announcement
13. pronouncement, pronunciation
envelop... 4. case, wrap 5. cover
6. clothe, encase, enwrap, infold,
invest, sheath, shroud 7. conceal,
enclose, sheathe 8. encircle,
surround 9. encompass, enwreathe
10. integument
envelope... 3. bur (burr) 5. cover,
curve 6. jacket 7. conceal, rampart,
vesicle, wrapper 8. membrane
10. integument
enveloped... 6. amidst 7. covered
10. surrounded
envenom... 5. taint 6. poison
8. embitter
envious... 7. jealous 8. covetous,
grudging, spiteful 9. green–eyed
10. begrudging
environ... 3. hem 6. suburb
7. compass, envelop, hedge in,
involve, purlieu 8. encircle, outskirt,
surround 9. encompass
environment... 4. area 6. medium,

milieu 7. setting, suburbs, terrain
8. environs 10. background
12. neighborhood, surroundings
13. encompassment
envisage... 4. face 8. confront
9. visualize 11. contemplate
12. meet squarely
envision... 5. dream 7. picture
9. visualize 11. contemplate
12. meet squarely
envoy... 5. agent 6. legate, l'envoi,
stanza 7. refrain 8. ablegate,
delegate, diplomat 9. messenger
10. ambassador, postscript
12. commissioner
envy... 5. covet 6. grudge 8. jealousy
12. covetousness
enwrap, inwrap... 4. roll, wrap
6. clothe, enfold, infold 7. engross
8. surround
enzyme... 3. ase (suff) 5. bread (Eccl)
6. lotase, olease, pepsin, rennin,
urease 7. amylase, ferment, laccase,
ptyalin, trypsin 8. diastase, protease
9. digestant
enzyme activator... 11. biocatalyst
eoan... 7. auroral 8. daybreak, easterly
eon, aeon... 3. age, era 4. time
5. cycle 8. eternity 10. generation
ephemeral... 7. diurnal 8. chickweed,
deciduous, transient 10. short–lived
ephemeris... 5. diary 7. almanac,
journal 8. calendar 10. periodical
11. publication
Ephesus (pert to)...
city of.. 6. Greece (anc)
famed for.. 5. ruins 12. Christianity
site.. 9. Aegean Sea
temple.. 7. Artemis
visitor (early).. 6. St Paul
Ephraim... 4. bear (grizzly) 5. tribe
8. fruitful
epi... 6. finial
epic... 3. cid 4. epos, poem, saga
5. epode 6. Aeneid (by Vergil),
epopee, heroic 9. narrative
epicene... 7. neutral, sexless
10. effeminate
epicure... 6. friand (obs) 7. glutton,
gourmet 8. gourmand, Sybarite
10. voluptuary 11. connoisseur
epidemic... 4. pest 6. plague
8. pandemic 9. prevalent, spreading
10. contagious, pestilence
epidermis... 4. skin 7. cuticle
8. ectoderm 9. scarfskin
epigram... 3. mot, saw 4. poem, quip
5. adage, maxim 6. dictum, saying
7. distich 11. inscription (obs)
epigraph... 5. motto, title 9. quotation
11. inscription
Epiphany (Eccl)... 5. Feast (Jan 6)
Epirus, oracle of... 6. Dodona (Mt
Tomarus, Gr)
episode... 5. event, story 8. incident
10. digression (Mus), occurrence
epistle... 4. note, post 6. billet,
lesson, letter 7. message, missive,
writing 8. dispatch, rescript
13. communication
epitaph... 7. writing (monument) 8. hic
jacet 11. inscription

epithet... 4. name, term 5. label
6. byname 7. agnomen 9. sobriquet
11. appellation (significant)
epitome... 6. digest 7. summary
8. abstract 9. comprisal
10. abridgment, compendium
epitomize... 7. abridge, curtail
8. abstract, compress, condense,
contract, diminish 9. capsulize
epoch... 3. age, day, eon, era 4. date,
time 5. event 6. period
epopee... 4. epic, epos, poem
5. genre (epic) 6. poetry (epic)
epoptic... 6. mystic, secret
equable... 4. even 6. steady
7. uniform
equal... 3. iso (pref), par, tie 4. both,
even, fere (obs), just, pari (pref),
peer, same 5. match, rival
7. compeer, emulate, equable,
uniform 8. adequate, parallel
9. equitable, identical 10. coordinate,
equivalent, substitute 11. counterpart
12. commensurate 13. proportionate
equal day and night...
11. equidiurnal, equinoctial
equal density (atmospheric)...
8. isoteric
equality... 3. par, tie 6. equity, owelty
(payment), parity 7. egalite, isonomy
(law) 8. adequacy, evenness, fairness,
identity, sameness 10. uniformity
12. impartiality
Equality State... 7. Wyoming (first
with Woman Suffrage)
equalize... 4. even 5. equal, level,
match 6. equate, smooth 7. balance
10. symmetrize
equally... 2. as 4. equi (pref) 5. alike
6. evenly, justly 11. identically
15. correspondingly
equanimity... 5. poise 6. aplomb
7. balance 8. calmness, evenness,
serenity 9. assurance, composure
10. confidence, equability
11. tranquility 12. tranquillity
equilibrium... 5. poise 7. balance
8. equality 9. stability 10. equanimity
equine... 3. ass 4. colt, foal, mare
5. filly, horse, steed, zebra 6. donkey
equine cry... 5. neigh 6. whinny
equip... 3. arm, fit, imp, rig 4. deck,
gear, gird 5. dress, endow
7. costume, furnish, qualify
8. accouter
equipment... 4. gear 5. armor
6. outfit, tackle, traits (personal)
7. ability, panoply (warriors)
8. equipage 9. apparatus
11. preparation 12. accouterment,
accoutrement
equitable... 4. fair, just 5. right
6. honest 7. upright 9. impartial
10. bonitarian (Rom law), reasonable
equity... 4. laws 6. rights 7. honesty,
justice 8. fairness 9. rectitude
11. uprightness
equivalence... 3. par 7. valence
8. equality, sameness 10. relativity
11. correlation
equivalent... 5. alike, equal
9. identical 10. tantamount

equivocal... 7. dubious, obscure
8. doubtful, puzzling 9. ambiguous,
enigmatic, uncertain 10. amphibolic,
mysterious, perplexing
13. indeterminate, problematical
equivocate... 3. lie 5. dodge, evade,
fence, shift 6. palter, trifle
7. quibble, shuffle 11. prevaricate
12. tergiversate
era... 2. AD, BC 3. age, eon 4. date,
time 5. cycle, epoch 6. period
10. Anno Domini 12. Before Christ
eradicate... 4. dele, root, weed
5. annul, erase 6. remove, uproot
7. abolish, destroy, epilate, extract,
root out 9. eliminate, extirpate
10. annihilate 11. exterminate
erase... 4. dele, kill 5. arase (obs)
6. cancel, delete, efface, excise
9. expunge, relieve 10. obliterate
Erasmus (Dutch)... 6. lovely 7. scholar
Erastus (Swiss)... 9. physician
10. theologian
ere... 4. also, soon 5. early, prior
6. before, erenow, sooner 7. earlier,
ere long 8. erewhile, formerly
10. before long, previously, sooner
than
Erebus (pert to)...
brother.. 3. Nox
father of.. 3. Day 6. Aether
Greek myth.. 8. darkness (nether)
native of.. 5. Hades
son.. 5. Chaos
erect... 4. lift, rear, stay 5. build,
found, raise, stand, upend 6. raised
7. elevate, upright 8. uplifted,
vertical 9. construct, establish,
institute 13. perpendicular
eremite... 6. hermit 7. recluse
8. anchoret, solitary 9. anchorite
erenow... 5. prior 8. erewhile, formerly
10. heretofore
ergo... 5. hence 9. therefore
Erin... 4. Eire 7. Ireland
Eritrea, Africa...
capital.. 6. Asmara
coastline of.. 8. Ethiopia
ruler.. 7. England (formerly It)
site.. 6. Red Sea
ermine... 3. fur 4. robe (emblem)
5. stoat (stot) 6. clothe, lasset,
weasel 7. ermelin
erode... 3. eat 4. gnaw, wear
7. corrode, decline, destroy
11. deteriorate 12. disintegrate
erotic... 6. loving, sexual 7. amative,
amatory, amorous 8. doctrine (of
love)
err... 3. sin 4. miss, slip 5. stray
6. bungle 7. blunder, deviate
10. transgress 12. miscalculate,
misinterpret
Er Rai... 5. stars 8. shepherd
errand... 4. task, trip 7. journey,
mission 8. business (special)
10. commission
errand boy... 4. page 7. bellboy,
bellhop, courier 9. messenger
errant... 6. erring, roving 7. peccant
8. fallible 9. deviating, erroneous,
itinerant, wandering 10. journeying

erratic... 5. queer, rogue 6. whacky
7. nomadic, strange 8. abnormal
9. eccentric, irregular, planetary,
wandering 10. capricious, changeable
erroneous... 5. false, wrong 6. untrue
7. peccant 8. illusory, mistaken
9. wandering
error... 3. sin 4. flub, muff, slip
5. boner, lapse 6. errata (pl), miscue
7. blunder, falsity, misstep, mistake
8. iniquity 11. anachronism,
misjudgment 14. miscalculation
ersatz... 5. proxy, token 9. vicarious
10. equivalent, substitute
11. alternative, replacement
12. substitution
Erse... 4. Irish 6. Celtic, Gaelic
erst, erstwhile... 4. also, once 5. first
6. former, sooner 8. earliest, formerly
10. heretofore, previously
erudite... 4. wise 7. learned
8. cultured, educated, literate
9. scholarly
erudition... 4. lore 6. finish, wisdom
7. letters 8. learning, pedantry
9. knowledge
eruption... 4. rash 6. geyser
7. volcano 8. ejection, outbreak,
outburst 9. commotion, exanthema
10. nettlerash 13. efflorescence
Esau (pert to)...
 Bible ref.. 7. Genesis
 brother.. 5. Jacob
 father.. 5. Isaac
 home.. 4. Seir
 mother.. 7. Rebekah
 name (later).. 4. Edom
escape... 4. flee 5. dodge, elope,
elude, evade, spill 7. evasion
9. avolation 13. circumvention
escargot... 5. snail
escarpment... 5. cliff, slope
9. precipice 13. fortification
eschar... 4. scab, sore 5. crust
6. slough
escharotic... 7. caustic, mordant
8. stinging 9. corrosive
escheat... 4. fall 5. lapse 6. revert
(land) 7. forfeit 9. reversion
10. forfeiture
eschew... 4. shun 5. avoid 7. abstain,
refrain
escolar... 4. fish 8. mackerel (like)
escort... 3. see 4. beau 5. guard
(honor), usher 6. attend, convoy,
gigolo, squire 7. conduct, retinue
8. chaperon 9. accompany
13. accompaniment
escritoire... 4. desk 6. bureau
7. dresser 9. secretary 10. secretaire
escrow... 4. bond, deed (deposit)
9. muniments
esculent... 6. edible 7. eatable
8. gustable 10. comestible
escutcheon... 4. fess (band), orle
(voided) 5. crest 6. shield
esker, eskar... 2. os 4. osar (pl)
5. drift, hills, mound, ridge
Eskimo... 3. Ita 4. Yuit 5. Aleut
6. Innuit 10. skraelling 11. Yikirgaulit
(Diomede Isles)
Eskimo (pert to)...

 boat, canoe.. 5. kayak, umiak
 (oomiac)
 boot (sealskin).. 5. kamik
 coat (bird skin).. 5. parka 6. temiak
 color.. 5. brown (rustic)
 dog.. 5. Husky 8. Malemute
 family.. 9. Eskimauan
 fish.. 4. Atka 8. mackerel
 hut, house.. 5. igloo, tupek (tupik)
 jacket.. 6. temiak
 knife (woman's).. 3. ulu
 memorial post.. 3. xat
 settlement.. 4. Etah
 totem.. 4. pole, post 6. symbol
esne... 4. serf 5. slave 8. hireling
esophagus, oesophagus... 4. crop,
gula 6. gullet, throat 7. pharynx
esoteric... 5. inner 6. occult, secret
7. private 8. abstruse, initiate,
personal 9. recondite 12. confidential
esoteric doctrine... 6. cabala
esoteric wisdom... 6. gnosis
espalier... 7. epaulet, railing, trellis
Español... 7. Spanish
especial... 5. chief 7. special
8. peculiar, uncommon
Esperanto... 3. Ido 8. language
(Internat)
espionage... 4. espy 6. spying
11. observation (secret)
14. reconnaissance
esplanade... 4. walk 5. drive, level,
Prado, praya 6. strand 7. walkway
espousal... 7. wedding 8. adoption,
ceremony 10. acceptance
11. embracement
espouse... 3. wed 4. bind, mate
5. adopt, marry 6. defend, pledge
7. betroth, embrace, support
8. maintain, plead for
esprit de corps... 3. wit 6. spirit
8. devotion 10. enthusiasm,
fellowship 11. partisanism
esprit fort (Relig)... 11. freethinker
espy... 3. see 5. watch 6. behold,
descry, detect 7. discern 8. discover
9. look about
esquire... 5. title 6. escort, gentry
7. armiger 8. escudero, nobleman
11. armor–bearer 12. shield–bearer
essay... 3. try 4. test 5. assay, chris
(Rhet), paper, theme, tract, trial
6. effort, thesis 7. attempt
8. endeavor, treatise 11. composition
12. disquisition, dissertation
esse... 5. being (real) 9. existence
essence... 3. ens 4. gist, odor, pith
5. attar, being, scent 6. nature
7. element, extract, perfume
9. principle, substance
12. quintessence
essential... 5. vital 6. mortal
7. needful 8. existent, inherent
9. necessary, necessity
13. indispensable
essential oil... 8. volatile 12. attar of
roses
essential part... 4. core, crux, gist,
pith 7. element 8. inherent
10. inwardness
establish... 3. fix 4. base, seat
5. build, enact, erect, found, plant,

prove, set up 6. create, ground, locate, ordain, settle 7. confirm, pre—empt 8. ensconce, legalize, radicate (rare) 9. ascertain, originate

established ... 5. fixed 6. proved, rested, stable 11. naturalized, traditional 12. conventional

established (pert to) ...
church .. 9. Episcopal (Eng)
rule .. 8. standard
thing .. 4. fact
truth .. 8. verified

establishment ... 4. mill 5. plant 6. custom, menage 7. factory 9. structure 12. organization

establishment of cordial relations ... 13. rapprochement

establishment of new plant home ... 6. ecesis

estate ... 4. alod, fief (feudal), rank (social) 5. manor, title 6. assets, equity 7. alodium, demesne, fortune 8. interest, property 9. situation

esteem ... 4. dear 5. adore, honor, judge, pride, value 6. admire, regard, repute, revere 7. respect 8. appraise, venerate 10. appreciate 13. consideration

ester of ...
silicic acid .. 8. silicate
stearic acid .. 7. stearin 8. stearate
tropic acid .. 7. tropate
vinegar .. 7. acetate

esthetic, aesthetic ... 6. essene 8. artistic, tasteful 9. beautiful

estimable ... 6. worthy 8. valuable 9. admirable, honorable, reputable, venerable 10. measurable 12. praiseworthy

estimate ... 3. aim, set 4. gage, rank, rate 5. audit, gauge, guess, prize, think 6. assess, repute 7. adjudge, compute, measure, opinion 8. appraise, judgment 9. calculate, statement, valuation

Estonia ...
capital .. 5. Revel 7. Tallinn
industry .. 3. oil
island .. 5. Oesel
peasant (rich) .. 5. kulak
ruler .. 4. USSR

estop ... 3. bar 4. fill, halt, plug, stay 6. impede, stop up 7. prevent 8. prohibit

estrange ... 4. part, wean 6. divert, divide 8. alienate, disunite, separate

estreat ... 4. copy 6. amerce, sconce 7. extract 9. duplicate, penalties (law)

estuary ... 3. bay 4. Pará 5. firth, frith, Plata

etch ... 3. cut 4. bite 5. infix 7. corrode, engrave, impress (upon)

eternal ... 6. eonian 7. aeonian, ageless, endless, lasting 8. enduring, immortal, timeless 9. boundless, ceaseless, immutable, incessant, unceasing 10. unchanging 11. everlasting 12. imperishable, interminable, unchangeable

Eternal City ... 4. Rome

eternal death ... 9. perdition

eternal home ... 6. heaven 12. The Hereafter

eternity ... 3. eon 4. aeon, ages, olam 8. Olam haba

etesian ... 4. wind (Aegean Sea) 6. annual 8. seasonal 10. periodical

ether ... 3. air, sky 5. ester, space 6. anisol, heaven (anc) 8. empyrean 10. anesthetic

ethereal ... 4. rare 5. aerie (aery), light 7. fragile, slender, tenuous 8. delicate, heavenly, vaporous 9. celestial 10. atmosphere (earth's), spiritlike 11. phantomlike 13. unsubstantial

ethereal (pert to) ...
being .. 5. sylph
color .. 7. sky blue
fluid .. 5. ichor (icor)
poetic .. 4. aery
salt .. 5. ester

ethical ... 5. moral, right 7. upright 8. virtuous

ethics ... 6. morals 8. hedonics 10. principles (moral) 11. highest good, summum bonum 12. Magna Moralia (Aristotle)

Ethiopia (Abyssinia) ...
capital .. 10. Addis Ababa
city .. 5. Adowa
colony .. 7. Eritrea
empress .. 7. Zauditu
king (Myth) .. 5. Negus 6. Memnon
native .. 5. Negro 6. Hamite 10. Abyssinian, black—a—moor
river .. 3. Omo 4. Juba 5. Abbai (Blue Nile)
ruler .. 7. Menelik 13. Haile Selassie
tribes (anc) .. 5. Bejas, Galla 7. Hamites, Semites

Ethiopian (pert to) ...
ape .. 6. gelada
banana .. 6. ensete
dialect .. 4. Geez
lily .. 5. calla
Torah .. 5. tetel

ethnic ... 5. pagan 6. racial 7. gentile, heathen

ethnology ... 5. races (Man)

ethology ... 7. manners 9. bionomics, character

ethos (opp of pathos) ... 9. attitudes (moral), esthetics

etiquette ... 4. form 5. label, mores 6. ticket 7. decorum, manners 9. amenities, propriety 10. civilities

etiquette, breach of ... 8. solecism

Etruria, Italy ... see *Etruscan*

Etruscan (pert to) ...
bookbinding (anc) .. 9. classical
deity .. 3. Lar, Uni
pottery .. 8. bucchero (black)
race .. 7. Rasenna 8. Tursenoi, Tyrrheni
soothsayer .. 8. haruspex (a)
soothsayer's function .. 8. extispex

ettle ... 3. try 4. plan 6. aspire, design, intent 8. consider, endeavor

etui, etwee ... 4. case 7. trousse

etymology ... 10. word origin

eucalyptus ... 4. lerp (laap, juice) 7. gum tree 8. eucalypt

Eucharist (pert to) . . .
administer to . . 6. housel 8. viaticum
(dying)
plate . . 5. paten
rite . . 9. Communion (Holy) 11. Lord's
Supper
wafer . . 4. host
wafer vessel . . 8. ciborium
wine . . 5. krama
wine vessel . . 3. ama 5. amula
Euclid (Gr) . . . 8. geometer (BC)
eulogist . . . 9. encomiast 10. panegyrist
eulogize . . . 4. laud 5. boost, extol
6. praise 7. commend, glorify
9. celebrate 10. panegyrize
eulogy . . . 5. eloge 6. hesped (Heb),
praise 7. oration 8. citation,
encomium 9. laudation, panegyric
euphony . . . 5. meter 6. melody,
rhythm, speech (ease of) 7. harmony
Eurafrica . . . 5. Egypt 6. Europe
7. Algeria 9. Abyssinia (anc)
Eurasia . . . 4. Asia 6. Europe 7. Scythia
(anc)
Eurasian (pert to) . . .
herb . . 6. yarrow 7. gosmore
mint . . 6. Nepeta
people . . 5. Finns 7. Ugrians
9. Armenians, Turanians
eureka . . . 11. exclamation 12. I Have
Found It (Calif motto)
Euripedes (Gr) . . . 4. poet (BC)
Europe . . . see also *European*
basin (coal) . . 4. Saar
battlefield . . 5. Marne 6. Verdun
8. Normandy, Waterloo 11. Belleau
Wood
capitals . . 4. Bonn, Oslo, Riga, Rome
5. Berne, Paris, Sofia 6. Athens,
Berlin, Lisbon, Madrid, Moscow,
Prague, Warsaw 8. Belgrade,
Budapest, Helsinki 9. Amsterdam,
Bucharest, Stockholm
10. Copenhagen, Monte Carlo
country (anc) . . 4. Elis (Gr) 7. Etruria
(It)
country (modern) . . 5. Italy, Spain
6. France, Greece, Latvia, Monaco,
Norway, Poland, Russia, Sweden
7. Denmark, Finland, Germany,
Hungary, Rumania 8. Bulgaria,
Portugal 10. Yugoslavia
11. Netherlands, Switzerland
14. Czechoslovakia
gulf . . 4. Riga 7. Bothnia
health resort . . 5. Baden 10. Baden
Baden (Ger)
invaders . . 4. Huns 5. Arabs, Turks
7. Mongols
kingdom (anc) . . 5. Arles 6. Aragon
8. Burgundy
lake . . 9. Zuider Zee (Holland)
lancer . . 5. uhlan 6. hussar
mountain region . . 4. Alps 5. Tyrol
race (anc) . . 5. Goths 7. Teutons
9. Visigoths 10. Ostrogoths
river . . 4. Elbe, Isar 5. Loire, Meuse,
Rhine, Rhone, Seine, Volga
6. Danube 7. Dneiper, Moselle
sea . . 4. Aral, Azov 5. North 6. Baltic
strait . . 8. Bosporus
valley . . 4. Ruhr

European (pert to) . . .
antelope . . 7. chamois
bat . . 8. serotine
bird . . 3. ani, mew (gull) 4. kite, stag
5. glede, mavis, ousel, serin
6. godwit, linnet, marten, merlin
(falcon) 7. bittern, ortolan, starnel
8. dotterel, garganey 9. brambling,
gallinule 10. turtledove
11. lammergeier 12. capercaillie
bison . . 7. aurochs
clover . . 6. alsike
dog . . 7. griffin
fish . . 3. gar 4. dace, rudd, spet, tope
(shark) 5. sprat 6. allice, barbel,
brasse, morgay, turbot
grape . . 6. muscat
linden . . 4. teil
mint . . 6. hyssop 9. horehound
mouse . . 4. loir, vole 5. lerot
polecat . . 7. fitchew
rodent . . 3. erd 4. loir 5. stoat
(ermine) 6. leriot 7. hamster
sandpiper . . 4. ruff 5. terek
squirrel . . 5. sisel 10. polatouche
tree . . 4. cade (juniper), sorb (apple)
5. carob 9. terebinth
wheat . . 5. emmer (speltz) 7. einkorn
evacuant . . . 6. emetic 8. diuretic
9. cathartic, purgative
evacuate . . . 4. void 5. empty, expel
6. depart, vacate 7. deprive, exhaust
8. withdraw 9. discharge
evade . . . 3. gee 4. foil, shun 5. avoid,
dodge, elude, parry, shirk, shunt
6. baffle, escape, illude 7. beguile,
quibble 8. slip away 10. circumvent
evanescent . . . 8. fleeting 9. ephemeral,
transient, vanishing 11. impermanent
12. disappearing 13. infinitesimal
evangelical . . . 7. Gospels 8. orthodox
10. Protestant, scriptural
Evangeline (pert to) . . .
home . . 6. Acadia
lover . . 7. Gabriel
poem by . . 10. Longfellow (1847)
evangelist . . . 6. Graham, Sunday (Billy)
7. apostle, Roberts 9. McPherson
evaporate . . . 3. dry 5. steam
6. escape, exhale 7. avolate
8. vaporize 9. cease to be,
dehydrate, disappear
evasion . . . 5. dodge, shift 6. escape
8. avoiding 9. avoidance, quibbling,
shuffling 12. equivocation
13. circumvention, secretiveness
evasive . . . 3. sly 4. eely 6. shifty
7. elusive, elusory 9. deceitful,
quibbling, secretive
eve . . . 3. iva (herb), wet 4. dusk, thaw
6. sunset 12. on the brink of, on
the verge of
even . . . 3. e'en, tie 4. just, tied
5. equal, exact, level, match, plane
6. placid, smooth, square, steady
7. abreast, balance, equable, neutral,
regular, uniform 8. directly, parallel
9. impartial, precisely
11. symmetrical
even (if) . . . 8. although
12. nevertheless 15. notwithstanding
even (so) . . . 3. yes 12. nevertheless

evener... 9. equalizer 10. doubletree
evenglow... 3. red (color) 8. twilight
evening... 5. Abend 6. sunset
evening dress... 4. gown 6. jewels,
tuxedo 8. slippers (high heel) 9. full
dress, headdress 10. dinner coat
11. tie and tails 17. swallow–tailed
coat
event... 4. fate (obs), game 5. drama,
issue 6. result 7. contest, episode,
scandal 8. incident 9. adventure,
happening, milestone 10. conclusion,
occurrence 11. consequence,
termination 12. circumstance
event (pert to)...
extraordinary.. 10. phenomenon
supernatural.. 7. miracle
theater.. 6. opener 8. premiere
turning point.. 6. crisis 8. decision,
landmark
eventide... 4. dusk 6. sunset, vesper
7. evening, sundown 8. twilight
9. nightfall
eventually... 3. yet 6. lastly 7. finally
10. ultimately
ever... 3. e'er 4. anon 5. at all
6. always 7. forever 10. constantly
11. perpetually
Everest peak... 6. Lhotse (28,100 ft)
evergreen shrub... 4. Ilex, moss, Olax,
titi 5. heath, holly, savin, toyon
6. laurel 7. baretta, jasmine
9. perennial 12. rhododendron
evergreen tree... 3. fir, yew 4. pine
5. carob, cedar, larch, olive, Taxus
6. balsam, deodar, spruce, tarata
7. conifer, hemlock, madrona,
redwood
everlasting... 6. eterne 7. aeonian,
agelong, durable, endless, eternal,
forever, lasting, tedious 8. enduring,
evermore, immortal, infinite
9. continual, incessant, perpetual,
unceasing, wearisome 10. immortelle,
indefinite 11. never–ending,
strawflower 12. Eternal Being,
imperishable 13. unintermitted,
uninterrupted
every... 3. all, any, ilk 4. each, ilka
6. entire 8. complete
every one, everyone... 3. all 4. each
9. everybody 10. individual
everything... 3. all, sum 5. total
evict... 4. oust 5. eject, expel, prove
6. remove 7. confute 8. force out
eviction... 6. ouster 9. ejectment
11. dislodgment 13. dispossession
evidence... 4. clue, sign 5. proof,
token 6. attest, evince 7. constat
(law), probate, support 8. argument,
manifest, rebuttal 9. testimony
10. indication 15. circumstantiate
evident... 5. clear, plain 6. patent
7. obvious, visible 8. apparent,
manifest, palpable 9. notorious
11. indubitable
evil... 3. bad, ill, mal (pref) 4. bane,
vile 6. injury, sinful, wicked
7. adverse, baleful, corrupt, hurtful,
immoral, malefic, misdeed, satanic,
unsound, vicious 8. depraved,
iniquity, sinister 9. injurious,

malignant, offensive 10. calamitous,
malevolent, pernicious, wrongdoing
12. unpropitious
evil (pert to)...
child.. 3. imp
deed.. 3. sin 4. harm
devil (little).. 9. deevilick (Scot)
doer.. 5. cheat 9. miscreant,
wrongdoer 10. malefactor
omen.. 5. knell
spirit.. 5. bugan, demon, devil, ghoul,
Satan 6. Belial 7. Ahriman, Amaimon
8. Asmodeus 9. cacodemon,
demonkind, lost souls
evils... 4. ills, mala
evince... 4. show 7. display, exhibit,
express, provoke 8. convince,
evidence, indicate, manifest
evoke... 4. call (out) 5. educe, voice
6. elicit, prompt, summon 7. conjure
evolution... 7. biogeny, cosmism
8. heredity, maneuver, movement
9. Darwinism, phylogeny, unfolding,
unrolling 10. evolvement
11. development 13. manifestation,
Spencerianism
evolve... 4. emit 5. educe 6. create,
deduce, derive, unfold, unroll
7. develop, grow out 9. disengage,
expatiate, extricate 11. disentangle
ewe... 3. keb 4. lamb 5. crone (old),
sheep 6. theave
ewer... 3. jug 5. crock 7. pitcher
exacerbate... 5. anger 6. incite
8. embitter, irritate 9. aggravate
exact... 4. just, levy, nice 6. assess,
demand, elicit, extort, formal, minute,
oblige, strict 7. careful, correct,
literal, precise, regular, require
8. accurate 10. methodical,
meticulous
exact (pert to)...
opposite of.. 8. antipode 9. antipodal
penalty.. 4. fine 7. estreat
thinking.. 13. ratiocination
vengeance.. 6. avenge
exacting... 6. severe, strict 7. arduous
8. critical 9. demanding, elicitory
10. fastidious 12. extortionate
exacting devotion (exclusive)...
7. jealous
exactly... 3. due 5. spand 6. nicely
7. quite so 8. as you say
9. precisely 10. accurately
exaggerated... 5. outré 8. enhanced,
enlarged, overdone, romanced
9. excessive, increased, magnified
10. overstated 11. exceptional
13. overestimated 14. misrepresented
exaggerated comedy... 5. farce
exalt... 5. elate, extol, raise 6. praise
7. elevate, ennoble, glorify, inspire,
promote, worship 8. enthrone,
increase, sanctify 10. aggrandize
exalted... 5. grand, noble, sheen
6. elated 7. refined, sublime
8. elevated, extolled 9. dignified
11. illustrious
examination... 4. test 5. audit, trial
7. inquiry 8. research, scrutiny,
specimen 10. discussion, inspection
11. inquisition 13. investigation

examine... 3. pry, spy, try (law)
4. pore, scan, sift, test 5. audit,
probe, quest 6. censor, debate,
ponder 7. analyze, collate, discuss,
explore, inspect 8. consider
10. scrutizine 11. interrogate
examiner... 6. censor, conner, tester
7. auditor, officer (court) 9. inspector
example... 4. case, norm, type
5. bysen (obs), model 6. sample
7. pattern, warning 8. instance,
paradigm, specimen 9. exemplify,
precedent 12. illustration
15. exemplification
ex animo... 9. sincerely 12. from the
heart
excavate... 3. dig 4. cave, mine
5. dig up, scoop, stope 6. dredge,
exhume, quarry 9. hollow out
excavation... 3. pit 4. hole, mine
5. stope 6. cavity, dugout 7. digging
8. opencast
exceed... 3. top 4. pass 5. excel,
outdo 6. outvie, overdo 7. eclipse,
outrank, surpass 8. outstrip, overstep
9. overshoot, transcend
11. predominate
exceedingly... 4. many, very
9. extremely 13. extraordinary
excel... 3. cap, top 4. beat, best
5. outdo, outgo, rival 6. better,
exceed, precel 7. surpass
8. dominate, outshine 9. transcend
excellence... 4. meed 5. merit
6. desert, virtue 7. classic, probity
9. supremacy 13. inimitability
excellent... 4. A-one, best, fine, good
5. bravo, prime, super 6. choice,
select, tiptop, worthy 7. capital,
corking 8. skillful (skilful), stunning,
valuable 9. admirable, exquisite,
first-rate 12. transcendent
except... 3. bar, but 4. omit, save
6. exempt, reject, unless 7. besides
9. eliminate, other than
exception... 4. plea 5. cavil, doubt
6. oddity 7. dissent 8. demurrer
9. condition, exclusion, exemption,
objection, rejection 11. restriction
exceptional... 4. rare 7. notable,
unusual 8. superior, uncommon
9. exclusive, wonderful
10. remarkable 11. outstanding
13. extraordinary
excerpt... 4. cite 5. quote, scrap
6. choice 7. extract, passage
(selected) 9. selection
excess... 3. too 4. over, plus 5. luxus
7. nimiety, overage, profuse, surplus
10. indulgence (undue), redundancy
11. superfluity 12. intemperance
14. immoderateness, superabundance
excess (solar over lunar month)...
5. epact
excessive... 3. too 5. undue 6. overly
7. extreme, profuse 8. overmuch
9. fanatical, plethoric 10. exorbitant,
immoderate, inordinate, redundancy
11. exaggerated, extravagant
12. unreasonable
excessive (pert to)...
development.. 11. hypertrophy

fear.. 5. panic 6. phobia
gushing.. 8. effusion
waste.. 12. extravagance
excessively... 3. too 5. enorm
6. unduly 12. exorbitantly,
inordinately 13. intemperately
exchange... 4. swap 5. bandy, trade
6. barter, resale, rialto 7. dealing,
traffic 9. transpose 10. substitute
11. interchange, reciprocate
exchange (pert to)...
discount.. 4. agio
for money.. 4. cash, sell
letters.. 10. correspond
place.. 4. mart 5. store 6. bourse,
market, shoppe
premium.. 4. agio
visits.. 3. gam
exchequer... 4. fisc (fisk) 5. funds,
purse 8. finances, treasury
11. possessions (money)
excise... 3. tax 4. toll 6. impost
exciseman... 5. gager 7. officer
8. revenuer
excision... 7. erasure, removal
10. cutting off, cutting out, mutilation
11. destruction, extirpation
excite... 4. fire, roil, spur, stir, urge
5. elate, impel, rouse 6. arouse,
awaken, bestir, incite, kindle, prompt,
stir up 7. agitate, animate, inflame,
provoke, psych up 8. energize,
interest 9. electrify, impassion,
instigate, stimulate
excited... 4. agog 6. hoopla
7. aroused, fevered, keyed up
8. agitated, startled 10. interested
11. impassioned
excited, not easily... 6. stolid
7. stoical 9. impassive
excitement... 3. ado 4. stir 5. fever
6. furore 7. emotion, ferment
9. agitation, commotion
10. incitement, irritation
11. disturbance, stimulation
exciting... 5. kicky 6. gung-ho, hectic
7. parlous 8. alluring 9. desirable,
thrilling 10. delightful 11. interesting,
provocative
exciting compassion... 7. piteous
exclamation... 2. ah, lo, oh, so
3. aha, bah, boo, fic, hep, oho, tut,
ugh, yah 4. ahem, alas, drat, egad,
evoe, phew, pish, rats, yech 5. bravo,
humph, pshaw 6. indeed, shezam
7. kerwham 9. alackaday
11. ejaculation 12. interjection
exclude... 3. bar 4. omit 5. debar,
eject, expel 6. banish 7. shut out
8. disallow, preclude, prohibit
9. eliminate 13. excommunicate
exclusive... 5. aloof, ritzy 6. select
7. special 8. limiting, snobbish
9. seclusive 10. definitive, unsociable
11. prohibitive, restrictive
exclusive right... 6. patent
10. concession 11. restriction
excoriate... 4. flay, gall, peel 5. strip
6. abrade 9. criticize
excrescence... 4. boss (Arch), lump
6. growth, nodule 9. appendage,
outgrowth 10. protrusion

excrete... 5. egest 9. discharge, eliminate

excruciating... 7. painful, racking 9. agonizing, torturing 11. distressing

excursion... 3. row 4. ride, sail, tour, trek, trip 5. jaunt, sally, junket, outing, ramble 7. circuit, journey, outlope 8. circuity 10. expedition

excusable... 6. venial 9. allowable, justified 10. defensible, exemptible, pardonable, remissible 11. justifiable

excuse... 4. plea 5. alibi, remit 6. acquit, essoin, pardon 7. absolve, apology, condone, forgive, pretext 8. overlook 9. exonerate, extenuate

execrable... 7. impious 9. nefandous

execute... 2. do 3. act 4. hang, kill, vest 6. direct, effect, finish, manage 7. conduct, enforce, perform 8. carry out, complete, transact 10. accomplish, administer

execution... 4. writ 7. hanging 10. production, punishment 11. achievement, performance, transaction 14. accomplishment

exegate... 6. leader 7. adviser 8. dragoman 11. interpreter

exegesis... 7. explain 9. interpret 10. exposition, expounding

exemplar... 5. ideal, model 7. example, paragon, pattern 8. specimen 9. archetype

exemplary... 8. laudable, monitory 11. commendable 12. exemplifying, praiseworthy 14. representative

exemplify... 4. copy 6. typify 7. explain 10. illustrate, transcribe

exempt... 4. exon 5. clear 6. immune 7. absolve, release 8. dispense, excepted, excluded, released, set apart 10. privileged

exemption... 6. essoin 7. freedom 8. immunity, impunity, navicert 12. dispensation

exercise... 3. ply, ure (anc), use 4. task, yoga 5. drill, étude, exert, train 6. action, employ, lesson, praxis, school, tai chi 7. display, jogging, problem, workout 8. activity, aerobics, ceremony, practice, training 9. athletics 10. exhibition, gymnastics, isometrics

exertion... 5. essay, trial 6. effort 7. attempt 8. endeavor

exhalation... 4. aura, fume 5. steam 6. breath 7. halitus 8. effluvium, emanation 10. expiration 11. evaporation 12. vaporization

exhale... 4. emit 6. vanish 7. exhaust, respite 9. transpire 10. breathe out

exhaust... 3. fag, sap 4. emit, jade, tire 5. drain, empty, spend, waste, weary 6. exhale, overdo, weaken 7. consume, deplete, fatigue 9. discharge 10. impoverish

exhausted... 4. done, worn 5. spent, tired 6. used up 7. emptied, petered (out) 8. dog-tired, forspent

exhaustion... 6. effete 7. burnout, fatigue 9. depletion, lassitude 11. prostration 14. impoverishment

exhibit... 3. air 4. fair, shew (anc), show, wear 5. stage, state 6. evince, expose, flaunt, parade, reveal 7. display 8. disclose, evidence, manifest 9. spectacle 11. demonstrate 15. circumstantiate

exhibit (pert to)...
colors (change of).. 8. iridesce, opalesce
pleasure.. 5. gloat, revel (in)
taste (refined).. 6. ostent 7. elegant

exhibition... 4. fair, show 9. spectacle 10. exposition 11. ostentation 13. manifestation

exhibition room... 10. panopticon

exhilaration... 6. gaiety 7. jollity 8. gladness, hilarity 9. animation, merriment 10. excitement, joyousness 11. gleefulness, refreshment 12. cheerfulness, invigoration

exhort... 4. urge, warn 6. advise, dehort, incite, preach 7. caution 9. encourage, stimulate

exhume... 3. dig 5. delve 7. unearth 8. disinter, exhumate

exigeant... 8. exacting 11. importunate

exigency... 4. need, urge 6. crisis 7. demands, urgency 8. juncture, pressure 9. emergency, extremity, necessity 12. requirements

exigent... 4. writ 6. strict, urgent 8. critical, exacting, pressing 9. demanding, necessary 10. compelling 13. indispensable

exile... 6. banish, deport 7. outcast 8. outlawry, relegate 9. expulsion 10. banishment, expatriate 12. expatriation, proscription

exist... 2. am, be, is 3. are 4. live 5. alive 6. abound 9. be present

existence... 3. ens 4. esse, life 5. actus, being, entia 6. extant 7. essence, reality 8. presence 9. actuality 13. manifestation

existing (pert to)...
fancifully.. 9. imaginary 10. transitory
name only (in).. 7. nominal, titular
now.. 6. extant 7. current, present 9. immediate
same time.. 15. contemporaneous
way of.. 9. lifestyle

exit... 3. die 4. door, gate, vent 5. going, go out, issue 6. egress, outlet 7. leaving, passage (out), walkout 9. departure

exitus... 5. death, issue 6. exodus, outlet 7. outcome

exlex... 6. outlaw

ex libris... 8. colophon 9. bookplate

exodus... 4. Book (Bib), exit 5. going 6. flight, hegira 9. departure

exonerate... 4. free 5. clear 6. acquit 7. absolve, release, relieve 9. disburden (obs), exculpate

exorbitant... 5. undue 9. excessive 10. high-priced

exorbitant interest... 5. usury

exorcism... 5. spell 7. formula 9. expulsion (of evil spirits) 11. conjuration, incantation

exordium... 5. proem 7. preface,

prelude 8. overture 9. beginning
12. introduction
exoteric... 8. exterior, external, outsider
14. comprehensible
exotic... 5. alien 7. foreign, strange
8. colorful, ulterior 9. not native,
peregrine, unrelated 10. extraneous,
outlandish
expand... 4. grow, open 5. sheet,
splay, tract 6. dilate, spread
7. broaden, develop, distend, enlarge
9. expatiate, intumesce
expanse... 3. sea 4. main (broad)
5. ocean, plain, reach, tract
6. desert, extent, spread 7. stretch
8. eternity (time) 9. expansion
expansion... 4. size 6. extent, growth,
spread 8. dilation, increase
10. distention 11. development,
enlargement, expatiation
expansive... 4. wide 5. broad, large
7. elastic, liberal 8. effusive,
spacious 9. bombastic, grandiose
11. extensional, sympathetic
12. unrestrained 13. comprehensive
expatiate... 5. dwell 6. dilate
7. descant, enlarge 10. widespread
expatriate... 5. exile, expel 6. banish,
outlaw 7. exclude, outcast
9. ostracize 13. excommunicate
expect... 4. deem, hope, wait
5. await, think 6. intend 7. suppose
10. anticipate
expectation... 4. hope 9. imminence,
intention 12. anticipation
expedience... 6. wisdom 7. fitness
10. adaptation, timeliness
11. suitability
expedient... 4. wise 5. shift 6. timely
7. fitting, politic, ressort, stopgap
8. artifice, resource 9. advisable
10. profitable 12. advantageous
expedite... 3. hie 4. easy, free
5. hurry, light, speed 6. hasten
7. further, quicken 8. dispatch
10. accelerate, facilitate
expedition... 5. drave, foray, haste,
speed 6. safari 7. Crusade, entrada,
journey 8. Crusades 9. excursion,
hastening
expel... 4. oust, void 5. eject, evict,
exile 6. banish, exhale 7. extrude
9. discharge, eliminate
10. dispossess
expend... 3. pay, use 5. spend, waste
7. consume 8. disburse
10. distribute
expenditure... 5. outgo, price 6. outlay
7. expense, payment
11. consumption 12. disbursement
expense... 4. cost 5. price 6. outlay
9. allowance 11. consumption
12. disbursement
expensive... 4. dear, high 5. fancy,
steep 6. costly, lavish 7. liberal
10. high–priced 11. extravagant
experience... 3. see, try 4. feel, have,
know, test 5. maxim, sense, skill
6. ordeal, suffer, wisdom 7. emotion,
undergo 8. facility 9. knowledge,
sensation 10. occurrence

experience (pert to)...
  pleasure.. 5. enjoy
  regret.. 6. repent
  suffering.. 7. calvary
  worldly.. 14. sophistication
experiment... 3. try 4. test 5. essay,
proof, prove, trial 6. verify
11. observation
expert... 3. ace 4. deft 5. adept
6. adroit, clever, habile, master
7. casuist (in conscience) 8. artistic,
skillful 10. proficient 11. connoisseur,
experienced 12. professional
expiate... 5. atone, purge 6. purify,
shrive (anc)
expiation... 4. rite 6. amends
7. redress 8. piacular 9. atonement
10. redemption 12. compensation,
propitiation
expire... 3. die, end 4. pass 5. cease,
lapse 6. elapse, perish 7. breathe
(out) 9. terminate
explain... 5. clear, solve 6. define
7. expound, premise 8. describe
9. elucidate, interpret
11. demonstrate
explanation... 6. theory 7. meaning
8. exegesis, scholium, solution
10. exposition 11. description,
explication 13. clarification
14. interpretation 15. exemplification
explanatory description... 5. title
7. titulus
expletive... 3. gee 4. egad, gosh,
oath 5. curse, there, voilà 6. behold
8. addition 9. added word
11. exclamation
explicit... 4. open 5. exact, fixed
6. candid 7. express, precise
8. absolute, distinct, implicit,
manifest, positive 9. outspoken
11. unambiguous, unequivocal,
unqualified 13. unconditional
14. discriminating
explode... 3. pop 4. fail 5. blast,
burst 6. blow up 7. implode
8. backfire, detonate
exploit... 3. act (heroic) 4. dare, deed,
feat, gest, milk 5. bleed 7. heroism
9. advantage 10. overcharge
11. achievement
exploration, modern... 10. space
probe
explore... 4. look, view 5. probe
6. search 7. examine 8. discover
9. penetrate 11. investigate
explorer... 5. diver 7. pioneer
10. discoverer
explorer... 4. Byrd, Eric, Gama
7. Johnson (Osa), Wilkins (Hubert)
8. Amundsen, Magellan 9. Ellsworth
explosion... 3. pop 4. bank 5. blast,
noise 6. report 7. failure 8. outburst
10. detonation
explosive... 3. cap, TNT 4. mine
5. niter, shell 6. amatol, petard,
powder, tittle, tonite 7. cordite,
grenade, lyddite 8. dynamite
9. cartridge, cellulose, fulgurite,
guncotton, pyroxylin 11. firecracker
13. nitroglycerin 15. trinitrotoluene
exponent... 4. note 5. index

7. symptom 9. explainer, expounder
10. explaining 11. interpreter
expose... 3. air 4. bare, open
6. divest, reveal, unmask 7. exhibit,
unearth 8. disclose, discover,
endanger 9. ventilate 10. exposition
expose to danger... 11. periclitate
expose to scorn... 6. satire 7. pillory
exposition... 4. fair 6. bazaar, exposé,
lesson 7. display 8. exposure,
treatise 9. discourse, spectacle
10. disclosure, exhibition
11. abandonment, explanation
12. dissertation 14. interpretation
expostulate... 5. orate 6. advise,
demand 7. call for, discuss, protest
8. complain, dissuade
11. remonstrate
exposure... 8. disproof, jeopardy,
openness, snapshot 9. liability
10. appearance, disclosure,
exposition, visibility
express.. 3. say 4. mean, show
5. exude, speak, state, train, utter,
voice 6. depict, evince, extort,
phrase 7. betoken, carrier, declare,
exhibit, expound, extract, signify,
testify 8. describe, dispatch, indicate,
intimate, manifest 9. delineate,
messenger, posthaste, utterance
11. declaration
express (pert to)...
censure.. 10. animadvert
disapproval.. 9. deprecate
fervor.. 7. enthuse
gratitude.. 5. thank
indirectly.. 5. imply
in words.. 6. phrase
numerically.. 8. evaluate
regard.. 6. praise 10. compliment
regret.. 9. apologize
sympathy.. 7. condole, console
10. grieve with 11. commiserate
expressing...
doubt.. 10. dubitative
extra phrase (Gram).. 12. periphrastic
feeling.. 7. emotive
past tense.. 11. preteritive
pique.. 5. pouty
praise.. 9. laudatory
expression... 4. grin, show, term
5. scowl, smile 6. aspect, oracle,
phrase 7. diction, meaning
8. locution 9. statement, utterance
10. extraction, indication
11. delineation 13. manifestation
14. representation
expression (pert to)...
mathematics.. 8. equation
of approval.. 4. clap 7. ovation
8. applause
of contempt.. 3. fie 5. pshaw, sneer
of disapproval.. 6. rebuke
of ideas.. 4. mode 5. style 7. fashion
of politics.. 4. vote
of weariness.. 4. sigh
peculiar.. 5. idiom
without.. 7. deadpan
expressive motion... 7. gesture
13. gesticulation
expulsion... 5. exile 10. banishment,
expiration 11. elimination

expunction... 4. blot 7. erasure
10. effacement 12. obliteration
expunge... 4. dele 5. erase 6. cancel,
delete, efface, excise, rub out 7. blot
out, destroy 9. strike out
10. annihilate, obliterate
expurgate... 5. bathe, purge
6. censor, excise, purify 7. cleanse
exquisite... 4. fine, rare 6. dainty,
superb 7. perfect, refined 8. delicate
9. beautiful, delicious, matchless
10. delightful, fastidious
exsanguine... 6. anemic 9. bloodless
exsiccate... 3. dry 4. arid, sear 5. dry
up, parch 7. exhaust 9. evaporate
extant... 5. being 7. in vogue,
present, visible 8. existent, existing
extempore... 5. ad lib 7. offhand
9. impromptu 13. improvisation
14. unpremeditated
extend... 2. go 3. eke, jut, lie, run
4. give, span 5. bulge, reach,
renew, steal, widen 6. deepen,
deploy, expand, spread 7. amplify,
broaden, draw out, proffer, prolong,
radiate, stretch 8. continue, increase,
lengthen, postpone, protract, protrude
10. exaggerate, straighten
extended... 4. open 5. broad
6. valued 7. assured, diffuse
8. expanded, spacious
10. lengthened 12. outstretched
extended view... 8. panorama
extension... 4. area 5. range, scope
6. extent 8. addition, duration,
increase, sequence 9. expansion
10. denotation 11. continuance,
enlargement, lengthening
12. augmentation 13. extensiveness
extension of time... 4. stay 7. respite
extensive... 4. vast, wide 5. broad,
large 7. immense, titanic
8. expanded, spacious 9. expansive,
wholesale 10. widespread
11. far-reaching
extent... 4. area, bulk, room, side, writ
5. areal, range, reach, scope
6. amount, degree, length
7. breadth, compass, expanse,
measure 8. distance, frontage
9. dimension 10. assessment (Hist),
denotation, proportion
extenuate... 4. thin 6. excuse, lessen,
reduce, sicken, weaken 7. justify
8. diminish, palliate 9. attenuate
extenuating... 10. justifying, qualifying
exterior... 5. ectad (toward), ectal,
outer 7. outside 8. external
10. extraneous
exterminate... 4. kill 5. expel
7. abolish, destroy 8. get rid of
9. eradicate, extirpate 10. annihilate
extermination... 9. expulsion
11. destruction, eradication
extern... 7. outward 8. exterior,
external 9. extrinsic
external... 4. ecto 5. outer, outre
6. nonego 7. outside 8. cortical
10. extraneous
external appearance... 5. guise,
image, looks 6. aspect 8. features
9. semblance

extinct... 4. dead, past 5. passé
7. defunct, died out, expired
8. quenched 11. nonexistent
12. extinguished
extinct bird... 3. moa 4. dodo
extinction... 5. death 9. quenching
11. destruction 12. annihilation
extinct reptile... 11. pterodactyl
extinguish... 5. annul, choke, douse,
quell 6. quench, stifle 7. destroy
8. suppress
extirpate... 4. dele, root, stub
5. erase, expel 6. excise, uproot
7. destroy 9. eradicate
11. exterminate
extol... 4. laud 5. exalt, kudos
6. praise 7. applaud, commend,
elevate, glorify 8. emblazon
9. celebrate
extort... 5. bleed, exact, steal, wrest,
wring 6. compel, elicit, wrench
7. extract 10. overcharge
extortion... 7. robbery, seizure
8. exaction, rapacity 10. extraction,
oppression, overcharge
extortionist... 5. harpy 7. vampire,
vulture 9. profiteer 11. blackmailer
extra... 3. bye 4. over 5. added,
spare, super 7. surplus 8. superior
9. accessory 10. additional
extra cache... 5. stock, store
7. reserve 9. reservoir
extract... 4. cite, pull 6. deduce, elicit,
select 7. essence, estreat, excerpt
8. withdraw
extract (pert to)...
balsam.. 7. toluene
Bible.. 7. passage 8. pericope
forcibly.. 6. evulse
newspaper.. 8. clipping
orchid (climbing).. 7. vanilla
extraction... 5. birth, stock 6. origin
7. essence, excerpt 8. tincture
9. parentage 10. withdrawal
extraneous... 5. outer 6. exotic
7. foreign 9. extrinsic, separated,
unrelated 11. unessential
extraordinary... 3. odd 4. rare, unco
5. great 7. notable, special, unusual
8. singular 9. irregular, marvelous,
wonderful 10. noteworthy, remarkable
11. exceptional 13. distinguished
extravagance... 5. waste 6. excess
8. wildness 9. abundance
10. fanaticism, lavishness
11. exorbitance, prodigality
12. exaggeration, intemperance,
recklessness
extravagant... 3. E la 4. ee la (Mus),
high (priced) 5. outré 6. absurd
7. baroque, bizarre, diffuse, fanatic
8. boastful, prodigal, wasteful
9. excessive, fanatical, fantastic,
luxurious, plentiful 10. digressive
11. intemperate 12. unrestrained
extreme... 3. end 4. last, sore
5. final, great, ultra 6. excess,
severe, utmost 7. drastic, intense,
outward, radical 8. farthest, greatest,
ultimate 9. excessive, extremity,
fanatical, outermost 10. conclusive,
immoderate

extreme fear... 5. panic 6. horror
extreme unction... 5. anele 9. last
rites, sacrament
extremist... 7. radical 8. ultraist
extremity... 3. end, tip 4. foot, limb
(body), pole 5. verge 6. border,
crisis, summit 8. terminal
9. necessity 11. termination
extricate... 4. free 5. loose 6. evolve,
rescue, wangle 7. extract 8. liberate
9. disengage 10. disembroil
11. disentangle 12. disembarrass
extrinsic... 7. foreign, outward
8. external 9. objective
10. accidental (Log), contingent,
extraneous, incidental
12. adventitious, nonessential
extrovert... 11. personality (opp of
introvert)
exuberance... 6. excess, plenty
8. overflow, rankness, vivacity
9. abundance, animation, profusion
10. friskiness, liveliness, luxuriance
11. copiousness 14. superabundance
exuberant... 6. frisky, lavish 7. fertile,
profuse 8. effusive, fruitful, thriving
9. luxuriant, plentiful 11. overflowing
13. superabundant
exudation... 3. gum, lac, tar 5. pitch,
resin 6. oozing 8. emission, sweating
9. discharge, excretion
exude... 4. emit, ooze, reek 5. sweat
7. excrete, give out 9. discharge
exult... 3. joy 4. crow, leap (obs), rave
5. boast, elate, ovare, pride
7. rejoice 8. jubilate
exultant... 5. ovant 6. elated
exultation... 3. joy 7. delight
8. boasting 9. jubilance, rejoicing
10. jubilation
exults... 5. leaps 7. glories, springs
9. jubilates
eye... 2. ee 3. orb, see 4. auge, glim,
hole, ogle 5. optic, organ (human),
sight, watch 6. look at, peeper
7. observe, witness 10. scrutinize
eye (pert to)...
absence of pupil.. 6. acorea
black.. 5. mouse 6. shiner
brow.. 4. arch 6. eebree
11. supercilium
cavity.. 5. orbit 6. hippus, socket
disease.. 8. cataract, glaucoma,
hypopyon, trachoma 9. amblyopia
14. conjunctivitis
disorder.. 6. squint 7. walleye
9. exotropia 10. strabismus
dropper.. 7. pipette
glass.. 4. lens 7. lorgnon, monocle
8. pince–nez 10. spectacles
inflammation.. 6. ititis 7. uveitis
lash, lashes.. 5. cilia (pl) 6. cilium
lid.. 8. palpebra
part.. 4. iris, uvea 5. pupil 6. cornea,
retina
to blind (falconry).. 4. seel
eyelet... 7. cringle, grommet, ocellus
8. loophole, peephole
eyetooth... 6. cuspid 8. dogtooth
eyot... 3. ait 4. holm 5. islet
eyra... 7. wildcat
eyrie, eyry... 4. nest 5. aerie, nidus

F

F... 6. letter (6th)
fabes... 10. gooseberry
fabian... 7. caution 8. dilatory, inaction
  15. procrastination
Fabian... 7. General (Rom), Society
fable... 3. lie 4. myth 5. story
  6. legend 7. fabliau, fantasy, fiction,
  Marchen, parable 8. allegory,
  apologue, folk tale 9. falsehood
fable (pert to)...
  being.. 5. troll
  king.. 3. Log
  monster.. 4. ogre 7. centaur
  narrator.. 10. parabolist
  writer.. 5. Aesop
fabric... 5. build, cloth 6. tissue
  7. texture 8. erection, material
  9. framework 11. workmanship
  12. construction
fabric (types of)... 3. rep 4. alma,
  duck, felt, gros, jean, lawn, leno, silk
  5. baize, batik, beige, crash, crepe,
  denim, linen, nylon, pekin, rumal,
  satin, scrim, serge, suede, tulle,
  tweed, twill, voile, wigan 6. agaric,
  alpaca, burlap, calico, canvas, chintz,
  cotton, dimity, étoile, madras,
  mohair, moreen, muslin, penang,
  pongee, poplin, ratiné, sateen, tricot
  7. batiste, brocade, bunting, challis,
  chiffon, delaine, elastic, etamine,
  flannel, galatea, gingham, hernani,
  paisley, percale, satinet, ticking,
  worsted 8. cashmere, chambray,
  chenille, corduroy, cretonne, drilling,
  prunella, sarcenet, Shantung,
  sheeting, whipcord 9. crinoline,
  gabardine, grenadine, lansdowne,
  matelassé, paramatta 10. broadcloth,
  seersucker, terry cloth
fabric (pert to)...
  dealer.. 6. mercer
  ornamental.. 4. lace 8. fagoting
  silk, watered.. 5. moiré
  silk and gold.. 4. acca (anc)
  7. brocade
  twill.. 6. caddis (cadis)
  velvet.. 5. panne, terry 6. velure
  7. velours
  waste.. 5. mungo
  window shade.. 7. Holland
  woven.. 6. tricot
fabricate... 4. coin, form, make, mint
  5. build, frame, weave 6. create,
  devise, invent, scheme 7. falsify,
  fashion, produce, trump up
  9. construct 11. manufacture
fabrication... 3. lie, web 5. guile
  6. cogger, deceit, making 7. fiction,
  forging, untruth 9. falsehood,

invention 12. construction
fabulist... 4. liar 5. Aesop
  11. storyteller
fabulous... 6. absurd 7. feigned
  8. mythical 9. fictional, imaginary,
  legendary 10. fictitious, remarkable
  11. astonishing 12. mythological
fabulous (pert to)...
  animal.. 7. unicorn 9. rosmarine
  (walrus)
  beast.. 4. lung 6. dragon, wivern
  7. griffon, serpent 10. earthdrake
  being.. 6. Lapith, Nessus 7. centaur
  bird.. 3. moa, roc 4. rukh
facade... 4. face 5. facia, front
  7. frontal
face... 3. mug 4. dare, defy, dial, line,
  meet, moue, phiz 5. brave, cover,
  front 6. answer, obvert, oppose,
  phizog, visage 7. grimace
  8. boldness, confront, envisage,
  exterior, features, pretense
  9. encounter, impudence
  10. effrontery 11. countenance,
  physiognomy, self–respect
face (pert to)...
  bone.. 6. zygoma (cheek) 7. maxilla
  (jaw)
  east.. 9. orientate
  gem.. 5. facet
  lifting.. 13. rhytidoplasty
  masonry.. 5. revet
  nose.. 11. rhinoplasty
  pains.. 4. ague 13. tic douloureux
  surgery.. 14. blepharoplasty (eyelid)
  to face.. 6. afront 7. vis-à-vis
  value.. 3. par
faces (twelve)... 12. dodecahedron
facet... 4. face 5. bezel, culet
  6. aspect, collet 8. exterior
facetious... 5. droll, funny, witty
  6. facete, jocose 7. comical, jesting
  8. laughter 9. whimsical
facia... 5. plate 6. tablet
facial pain... 3. tic 4. ague
  9. neuralgia 13. tic douloureux
facient... 4. doer 5. agent
  10. multiplier
facile... 4. easy 5. quick, ready
  6. expert, fluent, gentle, pliant
  7. affable, lenient, pliable
  9. compliant, teachable
facilitate... 3. aid 4. ease, help
  6. assist
facility... 3. art 4. ease, help 5. éclat,
  means, skill 7. address, pliancy
  8. easiness 9. readiness
  10. adroitness, expertness, pliability
  11. convenience, furtherance
  13. accommodation

facing... 6. lining, veneer 7. coating,
surface 8. opposite
facing (pert to)...
glacier direction.. 5. stoss
inward.. 8. introrse
outward.. 8. extrorse
facsimile... 4. copy 5. match
7. replica 9. duplicate
11. counterpart
fact, facts... 4. data, deed, feat, fiat
5. datum, event, posit, truth
6. really 7. keynote, lowdown,
paradox 9. actuality
fact collector... 7. statist
12. statistician
faction... 4. bloc, camp, sect, side
5. cabal, junto, party 6. clique
7. machine (Polit) 11. combination,
partisanism
factious... 9. demagogic, seditious,
turbulent
factitious... 4. made (by art), mock,
sham 5. phony 9. unnatural
10. artificial 11. make–believe
factor... 4. ager, gene 5. agent, cause
6. detail 9. component
11. constituent
factotum... 4. maid 5. do–all
7. servant 8. busybody
faculties... 4. wits 6. senses
7. talents 9. abilities, aptitudes
12. capabilities
faculty... 3. art 4. body, ease, gift
6. talent 7. ability, know–how
8. aptitude, teachers 9. endowment
(mental) 12. professorate
fad... 4. rage, whim 5. craze, fancy,
hobby 6. custom 7. caprice, fashion
faddist... 10. monomaniac
fade, fade out... 3. age, dim, dow,
wan 4. flat, pale, wilt 5. daver,
decay, peter 6. perish, vanish,
weaken, wither 7. decline, insipid
8. discolor, dissolve, languish
9. disappear 11. deteriorate
faded... 3. dim 4. dull, pale 5. faint,
passé 8. impaired
Faerie Queene (pert to)...
author.. 7. Spenser
character.. 3. Ate, Una 5. Guyon,
Truth 7. Acrasia 8. Gloriana
theme.. 8. chivalry 10. knighthood
type work.. 4. poem 8. allegory
fag... 4. flag, hack, jade, tire, toil,
work 5. droop, slave, weary
6. drudge, menial 7. exhaust,
fatigue, untwist (rope end)
8. drudgery 9. cigarette
fag end... 3. end 4. tail 6. scraps,
tag end 7. remnant 8. last part,
leavings
Fagin... 3. Jew (Oliver Twist)
Fagin's pupil... 12. Artful Dodger
(John Dawkins)
fagot, faggot... 4. bind 5. bunch
6. bundle, emblem (Her) 8. firewood,
slattern
fail... 3. ebb, err 4. flop, lack, miss,
sink 5. decay, flunk, lapse 6. defect,
desert, weaken 7. decline, exhaust
8. unbetide 9. fall short
10. disappoint, go bankrupt

11. deteriorate
failed admission... 11. blackballed
failed to follow suit... 7. reneged
failure... 3. dud 4. flop, foil, lack,
lose, miss 5. decay, fault, lapse
6. defeat, fiasco 7. default
10. bankruptcy, deficiency, insolvency,
nonsuccess, suspension
11. delinquency
faint... 3. din, ill 4. pale, soft, weak
5. swelt, swoon, timid 6. feeble,
sickly 7. languid 8. cowardly,
fatigued, listless, timorous
10. indistinct, oppressive
faintness... 5. qualm (sudden)
7. dimness, syncope 8. paleness,
weakness 10. feebleness
fair... 4. just, mart 6. bazaar, blonde,
comely, honest, kermis 8. festival,
mediocre, rainless, unbiased
9. impartial 10. auspicious,
reasonable 12. unprejudiced
13. dispassionate
fairy, faery... 3. elf, fay 4. peri, pixy
5. genie, magic, nymph, ouphe, pixie
6. elfkin, sprite 7. brownie, gremlin
8. illusion
fairy (pert to)...
abode (Scot).. 4. shee (sidhe)
death spirit.. 7. banshee
evil.. 4. ogre, puck 9. hobgoblin
fort.. 3. lis (liss)
German.. 6. kobold
Irish.. 10. cluricaune, leprechaun
king.. 6. Oberon
Persian.. 4. peri
queen.. 3. Mab, Una 7. Titania
Scandinavian.. 5. nisse
tale.. 3. fib 7. Marchen 8. allegory
9. narrative
faith... 4. hope 5. creed, piety, troth,
trust 6. belief, credit, verily, virtue
7. loyalty 8. credence, fidelity
9. assurance, authority, orthodoxy
10. confidence 11. credibility
faithful... 4. fast, feal, leal, true
5. liege, loyal, pious 6. devout,
steady, trusty 7. devoted, sincere,
staunch 8. constant, obedient,
reliable 9. believers, steadfast,
veracious
faithful friend... 7. Achates (Vergil's
Aeneid)
faithless... 5. false, punic 6. fickle,
untrue 8. apostate, disloyal, shifting
9. deceptive, mercurial, skeptical
10. perfidious, unfaithful
11. incredulous, irreligious,
treacherous, unbelieving
12. falsehearted
fake... 3. rob 4. sham 5. cheat, fraud,
trick 7. trump up 8. doctor up
9. deception, fabricate, imitation
11. counterfeit
faker... 5. cheat, fraud 7. bluffer
8. impostor 9. hypocrite, pretender
fakir... 4. sect (Moslem, Islam), yogi
7. dervish 9. mendicant
falcon... 4. hawk 5. besra, saker
6. laggar, lanner, luggar, merlin,
shahin (shaheen), sorage, tercel
7. kestrel, sakeret 8. lanneret,

Raptores 9. gyrfalcon (gerfalcon),
peregrine
falcon, military... 8. ordnance
falconry term... 4. hood, jess, lure,
seel 6. rebate 7. hawking
fall... 3. ebb 4. bang, drop, plop,
ruin, sink, slip 5. crash, spill
6. autumn, defeat, perish, plunge,
tumble 7. descend, descent, devolve,
failure, plummet, relapse 8. collapse,
commence, downfall, rainfall
9. abatement, overthrow, surrender,
waterfall 10. depreciate, subversion
11. degradation, precipitate
fall (pert to)...
back.. 6. recede, recoil 7. relapse,
retreat 10. retrogress
behind.. 3. lag 4. lose 7. regress
guy.. 5. patsy
in.. 4. cave 5. agree, lapse
6. concur, line up 8. collapse
9. terminate
rhythmical.. 6. cadent
short.. 4. lack, want 10. disappoint
fallacious... 4. wily 5. false 6. crafty,
untrue 8. delusive, guileful
9. deceitful, deceptive, erroneous,
illogical, insidious 10. fraudulent,
misleading 13. disappointing
fallacy... 5. error 6. idolum
7. sophism 9. deception, falseness,
sophistry 13. deceitfulness
false... 4. sham, tale 5. bogus, paste
6. betray, impugn, pseudo, untrue
7. mislead 8. apostate, spurious
9. deceitful, deceptive, erroneous,
faithless, incorrect, insincere,
pretended, unfounded 10. fictitious,
mendacious, traitorous, unfaithful,
unreliable, untruthful 11. counterfeit
12. illegitimate
false (pert to)...
friend.. 5. Judas 7. traitor
front.. 8. disguise 11. affectation
fruit.. 10. pseudocarp
god.. 4. idol
hearted.. 9. deceitful 10. perfidious
11. treacherous
items.. 6. spuria
jewelry.. 5. paste 6. strass
reasoning.. 10. paralogism
report.. 5. rumor 6. canard 7. slander
show.. 6. tinsel
wing (bird's).. 5. alula
falsehood... 3. lie 4. tale 7. falsity,
fiction, perjury, untruth 9. imposture,
mendacity 11. counterfeit, fabrication
12. exaggeration
falseness... 5. error 8. illusion
9. deception, falsehood 10. infidelity
falsetto... 5. voice (false) 10. artificial
11. high–pitched
falsify... 3. lie 5. belie, forge
7. distort, pervert 8. disprove
10. adulterate 11. counterfeit
12. misrepresent
Falstaff... 5. opera (Verdi) 9. character
(Shak)
falter... 3. lag 4. fail 5. demur, pause,
waver 6. flinch, quaver, totter
7. stagger, stammer, stumble,
tremble 8. hesitate, lose hope

fame... 4. note 5. éclat, glory, kudos
6. renown, repute
famed... 7. eminent, honored, popular
8. renowned 9. notorious
10. celebrated
familiar... 4. easy 5. usual
6. common, versed 7. affable
8. domestic, frequent, friendly,
habitual, informal 9. companion,
customary, well–known
10. accustomed, colloquial,
conversant 12. domesticated,
presumptuous 13. unconstrained
familiarity... 8. intimacy 9. awareness,
knowledge, liberties 10. affability
12. acquaintance (close), friendliness
familiarize... 6. inform 8. accustom
9. habituate
family... 3. ilk, kin 4. clan, line, race
5. class, group, house, tribe
6. stirps 7. kindred, lineage
9. community, household, posterity
10. kith and kin
family (pert to)...
bees.. 5. apina 7. Apoidea
favoritism.. 8. nepotism
herbs.. 7. Ranales
Italians (famed).. 4. Este
kings.. 7. dynasty
name.. 7. surname
famous... 5. named, noted 7. eminent,
namable, notable 8. renowned
9. excellent, notorious
10. celebrated, remarkable
13. distinguished
famous murderer... 4. Aram, Cain
9. Bluebeard
famous pirate... 4. Kidd (Capt)
fan... 4. blow, cool, vane, whip
5. punka (punkah) 6. blower, foment,
incite, rooter, spread, thresh, winnow
7. admirer, devotee, refresh
9. stimulate, strike out (baseball),
ventilate 10. enthusiast
fanatic, fanatical... 3. mad 5. bigot,
crank, crazy, rabid 6. maniac, zealot
7. devotee, frantic, lunatic 8. frenzied
9. energumen, phrenetic
10. enthusiast, unbalanced
11. extravagant, overzealous
12. enthusiastic 13. nonconformist,
overreligious
fanatical partisan... 6. zealot
fancied... 6. unreal 7. dreamed,
ideated 8. favorite, imagined
9. well–liked 10. ornamental
fanciful... 3. odd 5. queer 7. bizarre,
strange 9. fantastic, grotesque,
visionary, whimsical 10. capricious,
chimerical 11. imaginative
12. grandiloquent
fancy... 3. fad 4. idea, like, love,
ween, whim 5. dream, freak
6. design, desire, devise, humour,
ideate, megrim, notion, ornate,
vagary 7. caprice, conceit, fantasy,
imagine, impulse, suppose, thought
8. illusion, phantasy, superior
9. expensive 10. conception,
impression 11. extravagant,
imagination, inclination
12. ostentatious

fandango... 3. hop 4. ball, prom
5. dance 7. cantico
fandango bird... 7. manakin
Faneuil Hall (1742)... 4. hall
6. market (Boston) 15. Cradle of
Liberty
fanion... 4. flag 6. guidon, marker
fanon... 4. cape (Pope's) 5. orale
6. banner 7. maniple
fan–shaped... 10. flabellate
fan sticks (radiating)... 4. brin
7. panache
fantastic... 3. odd 5. outré, queer
6. absurd, rococo, unreal
7. baroque, bizarre, caprice, foppish,
unusual 8. fanciful, freakish, illusory
9. eccentric, grotesque, visionary
10. capricious, chimerical, irrational
11. extravagant, imaginative
12. phantastical
fantastic imitation... 6. parody
8. travesty
fantasy... 5. dream, fancy, story
6. vision 7. caprice, phantom,
romance 8. illusion 10. apparition
13. hallucination
far... 3. tel (pref) 4. afar, long, tele
(pref) 6. marked, remote
9. separated 10. abstracted
farce... 4. mime, play 5. drama
(humorous), exode, humor, stuff
6. comedy 7. mockery 8. stuffing
9. burlesque, forcemeat
farceur... 5. joker 8. comedian
9. dramatist
fare... 3. eat 4. diet, food, rate
5. crowd, going, swarm, table
7. conduct, journey, passage,
prosper, succeed 9. passenger
10. expedition
farewell... 3. ave 4. vale 5. adieu,
adios, aloha, congé (formal)
7. good–bye, leaving, parting 8. au
revoir, Godspeed 9. bon voyage
11. leave–taking
farinaceous drink... 6. ptisan
farinaceous food... 4. sago 5. flour,
grain, salep, wheat 7. cereals
farm... 4. plot, till, torp 5. croft, ranch
6. grange, rancho 7. acreage,
cotland 9. cultivate
farm (pert to)...
English.. 6. barton
laborer.. 4. hind 6. farmer, tiller
prefix.. 4. agro
repairer.. 10. plowwright
Spanish.. 8. hacienda
steward.. 7. granger
tenant.. 6. cotter
farmer... 4. ryot 5. kulak 6. grower,
tiller 7. cropper, metaver, peasant,
planter, rancher 10. agronomist,
cultivator 13. agriculturist
faro term... 4. bank 5. monte, stuss
6. cathop, layout
Faroe (Faeroe) Islands...
called also.. 12. Sheep Islands
capital.. 9. Thorshavn
magistrate.. 4. foud
rule.. 5. Norse (anc) 7. Denmark
whirlwind.. 2. oe
far–reaching... 4. deep, long 5. scope

7. intense 9. extensive
farrow... 3. pig 6. litter
farsighted... 6. shrewd 9. provident,
sagacious 10. presbyopic
11. foresighted 12. clearsighted
farther, further... 4. also 7. thither
8. moreover 10. additional
farthest... 5. final 6. inmost, utmost
7. endmost, extreme, longest
fascia... 4. band, sash 6. fillet, ribbon
7. bandage
fascinate... 5. charm 6. allure,
enamor, thrill 7. bewitch, delight,
enchant 8. entrance, interest
9. captivate, enrapture
fascinating... 5. siren 8. alluring,
charming 10. attractive, bewitching,
delightful 11. interesting
Fascist (1919)... 6. Pareto
9. Mussolini 10. Black Shirt
fashion... 3. fad, fit, ton, way
4. make, mode, mold, rage
5. adapt, carve, craze, feign, forge,
frame, guise, model, shape, style,
vogue 6. create, custom, invent
7. compose 8. contrive 9. construct,
fabricate, smartness 10. appearance
fashionable... 5. smart 6. formal,
modish 7. a la mode, in vogue,
stylish 8. up–to–date 10. conforming
13. well–appearing
fast... 5. agile, fixed, fleet, hasty,
quick, rapid, sound, space, stuck,
swift 6. lively, speedy, staple
7. abiding, soundly 8. enduring,
securely 10. profligate, stationary,
unyielding 11. expeditious
fasten... 3. bar, pin, tie 4. bind, clip,
lace, lash, moor, nail, rope, seal,
tack, wire 5. affix, belay, chain,
clamp, clasp, latch, paste, rivet
6. attach, secure, solder, staple,
tether, toggle 7. padlock
fastening... 5. desmo (comb form)
fastest (pert to)...
animals.. 6. coyote 7. cheetah
8. antelope
birds.. 5. eagle, goose 7. ostrich
fast horse... 6. pelter
fastidious... 4. nice 6. dainty
7. elegant, finical, precise 8. critical,
delicate, exacting, overnice
9. squeamish 10. meticulous,
particular, scrupulous
fastness... 4. fort 6. fixity 7. citadel
8. celerity, firmness, velocity
9. stability 10. profligacy, stronghold
fat... 4. lard, oily, suet 5. adeps, fatty,
lipin, obese, olein, stout 6. axunge
(goose), grease, portly, steato (pref),
stocky, tallow 7. adipose, lanolin,
opulent, paunchy, stearin, wealthy
9. corpulent, plentiful 10. profitable
fatal... 5. fated 6. deadly, doomed,
lethal, mortal 7. fateful, ominous
8. destined 9. condemned, prophetic
10. calamitous, disastrous
11. destructive
fatality... 4. fate 5. death 8. disaster
10. deadliness
fatally... 8. mortally 9. ruinously
fate... 3. end, lot 4. doom, luck, ruin

5. karma 6. chance, kismet
7. destiny, fortune 8. disaster,
downfall 13. inevitability
fateful... 5. fated 6. deadly
9. momentous 10. inevitable,
portentous 11. destructive,
predestined
Fates (Gr)... 6. Clotho, Moirae (group
of Three) 7. Atropos 8. Lachesis
Fates (Norse)... 4. Urth 5. Norns
(group of three), Skuld 9. Verthandi
Fates (Rom)... 4. Fata, Mona 5. Morta
6. Decuma, Parcae (group of three)
father... 2. pa 3. Abu, dad 4. abba,
papa, père, sire 5. adopt, friar,
padre, pater, vater 6. priest, senior
7. creator 8. generate 9. confessor,
procreate 11. acknowledge
Father (of)...
Ajax.. 7. Telamon
Christmas.. 10. Santa Claus
English learning.. 4. Bede
engraving.. 3. Pye
Evil.. 5. Satan
his country.. 6. Cicero (Rom), Medici
(It) 10. Washington (US)
history.. 9. Herodotus
Mankind (Myth).. 7. Iapetus
New York.. 13. Knickerbocker
Ocean.. 7. Neptune
the Gods.. 6. Amen–Ra
Time.. 10. Methuselah
Waters.. 11. Mississippi
father (pert to)...
land.. 6. native
land, love of.. 10. philopater
term.. 6. agnate 8. paternal
wise.. 6. mentor
fatherless... 6. orbate 7. forlorn
8. helpless, orphaned
fathom... 3. try 4. test 5. delve,
plumb, solve, sound 7. measure,
plummet 8. encircle 9. penetrate
10. understand 13. take soundings
fatigued... 5. bored, faint, jaded,
spent, tired, weary 6. fagged
7. languid, wearied 9. exhausted
Fatima (pert to)...
character in.. 14. Arabian Nights
father.. 8. Mohammed
husband.. 9. Bluebeard
fatten... 4. feed 6. batten, enrich
7. improve, prosper 8. pinguefy
fatty... 5. suety 6. greasy 7. adipose
9. aliphatic
fatty (pert to)...
acid.. 6. adipic 7. valeric
degeneration.. 8. adiposis
substance, sheep.. 5. suint
tumor.. 6. lipoma
fatuous... 4. vain 5. inane, silly
6. vacant 7. foolish, idiotic, witless
8. demented, illusory, imbecile
9. insensate 11. thoughtless
faucet... 3. peg, tap 4. cock 6. spigot
7. fixture, hydrant, petcock
fault... 4. hade, lode, slip, vice
5. cavil, cleft, culpa (law), error,
lapse, tache (anc) 6. defect, foible
7. blemish, blunder, demerit, failing,
frailty, misdeed, offense 8. fracture
10. peccadillo 11. delinquency

12. imperfection
faultfinder... 6. carper, nagger
7. caviler 10. complainer, criticizer
faultfinding... 7. carping, nagging
8. captious, caviling, critical
9. censorial
faultless... 4. pure 5. right 7. correct,
paragon, perfect 8. flawless, innocent
9. blameless 10. impeccable
13. unimpeachable 14. irreproachable
faultlessness... 8. accuracy
9. innocence 10. perfection
11. preciseness
faulty... 3. ill 5. amiss, unfit 6. guilty
8. culpable 9. blemished, defective,
deficient, erroneous, imperfect
11. blameworthy
faun... 3. Pan 5. deity, satyr
6. Faunus 10. Praxiteles
Faust... 4. hero 5. drama (Goethe),
opera
faux pas... 5. error, gaffe 6. booboo
7. blunder, misstep, mistake
favor, favour... 3. aid 4. boon, gift,
help 5. bless, grace, token
6. esteem, letter, regard 8. good
will, kindness, leniency, resemble
9. patronage, patronize, privilege
10. assistance, concession,
favoritism, partiality, permission
11. approbation
favorable... 4. good, kind, rosy
6. benign, timely 7. helpful, hopeful,
popular 8. friendly, gracious, pleasing
9. approving, opportune
10. auspicious, beneficial, propitious
11. complaisant 12. advantageous
favorite... 3. pet 4. lamb (pet)
6. minion 7. darling 10. preference
favoritism... 4. bias 7. leaning
8. nepotism 10. partiality
12. predilection
fawn... 3. doe 4. buck, coax, deer,
faon (color) 5. color, cower, crawl,
creep, toady 6. cringe, grovel, shrink
7. truckle 10. ingratiate
fawning... 7. servile 8. toadyish
9. truckling 10. obsequious
11. bootlicking, sycophantic
fawnskin (classic art)... 6. nebris
fay... 3. elf 5. fairy 6. sprite
fealty... 4. duty 6. homage 7. loyalty,
respect 8. fidelity 9. constancy
10. allegiance, obligation
fear... 3. awe 5. alarm, dread, panic
6. dismay, fright, horror, phobia,
terror 7. anxiety 8. venerate
9. apprehend, cowardice, reverence
11. nervousness 13. consternation
fear (of)...
animals.. 9. zoophobia
bees.. 9. apiphobia
being alone.. 10. autophobia,
monophobia
blood.. 10. hemophobia
cats.. 12. aelurophobia
crossing streets.. 11. dromophobia
crowds.. 11. ochlophobia
darkness.. 11. nyctophobia,
scotophobia
death.. 11. necrophobia
disease.. 10. nosophobia

enclosures .. 14. claustrophobia
fire .. 10. pyrophobia
food .. 10. cibophobia
heights .. 10. acrophobia
   11. hypsophobia
holy things .. 11. hagiophobia
men .. 11. androphobia
new things .. 9. neophobia
open spaces .. 11. agoraphobia
pain .. 10. algophobia
places (certain) .. 10. topophobia
poison .. 10. toxiphobia
reptiles .. 13. herpetophobia
sea .. 14. thalassophobia
strangers .. 10. xenophobia
sunlight .. 11. heliophobia
thirteen .. 13. tridecaphobia
weeds .. 11. runcophobia
fearful ... 4. dino (pref), dire 5. awful,
   pavid, timid 6. afraid, craven
   7. anxious, nervous 8. dreadful,
   horrible, timorous 9. appealing,
   frightful 11. distressing, frightening
   12. apprehensive
fearless ... 4. bold 5. brave 6. daring
   7. impavid 8. harmless, intrepid
   9. audacious, confident, dauntless,
   undaunted 10. courageous
feast ... 4. fete, meal 5. agape, epulo,
   revel 6. junket, picnic, regale, repast
   7. banquet, gratify 8. carousal,
   festival 9. carrousel
Feast (of) ...
Lanterns (Jap) .. 3. Bon
Lots .. 5. Purim
Nativity .. 9. Christmas
Pentecost (weeks) .. 8. Shabuoth
Tabernacles .. 7. Succoth
feasting ... 6. dining 9. epulation
feat ... 3. act 4. deed 5. stunt
   7. exploit 11. achievement,
   performance 14. accomplishment
feather ... 4. deck, flaw (jewel), tuft
   5. adorn, penna, plume, quill
   6. clothe, fletch, hackle, trifle
   7. plumage 9. lightness
feather (pert to) ...
an arrow .. 6. fledge, fletch
barb .. 7. pinnula 8. barbicel
bird (area) .. 7. pteryle
featherlike .. 7. pinnate
filament .. 4. dowl
key (machine) .. 6. spline
molt .. 3. mew
repair (falconry) .. 3. imp
shaft .. 5. scape
feathered ... 5. swift 6. plumed,
   winged 7. fledged 8. pennated,
   plumaged 10. ornamented
feature ... 4. face 5. motif, trait
   6. aspect 7. special 8. headline,
   resemble 9. component, lineament
   10. appearance, comeliness
   11. countenance 14. characteristic
features ... 3. mug 4. face 5. looks
   6. visage 7. outline 9. geography
February birthstone ... 8. amethyst
federation ... 5. union 6. league
   8. alliance 10. government
   11. affiliation 13. confederation
fed up ... 5. bored, jaded 7. wearied
   8. satiated 9. surfeited

fee ... 3. feu, tip 4. fief, rate, wage
   5. bribe 6. charge, estate (law)
   8. gratuity, retainer 9. emolument
   10. honorarium
feeble ... 4. aged, lame, puny, weak
   5. dotty 6. infirm 10. indistinct
   11. debilitated
feeble–minded ... 5. anile 9. infirmity
   10. irresolute, weak–willed
   11. vacillating
feed ... 4. dine, meal, sate 5. stoke
   6. fodder, gavage 7. engorge,
   foldage, furnish, indulge, nourish,
   nurture, pannage (swine)
   9. encourage, provision
feel ... 3. ail, air 4. palp 5. grope,
   sense, touch 6. handle, suffer
   7. examine, explore, quality, texture
   8. perceive 10. atmosphere,
   experience
feel (pert to) ...
compunction .. 6. repent
dejection .. 6. repine
fear .. 2. ug
melancholy .. 6. grieve
worth of .. 10. appreciate
feeler ... 4. palp, test 6. barbal, palpus
   7. antenna 8. question, tentacle
feeling ... 4. feel, tact, view 5. hunch,
   touch 7. emotion, opinion, passion
   8. attitude 9. sensation, sentiment
   10. atmosphere, experience,
   perception 11. sensibility
   13. consciousness
feeling (pert to) ...
capable of .. 5. emote 8. sentient
   9. sensitive
displeasure .. 9. resentful
hostility .. 6. animus 9. animosity
ill .. 7. malaise 10. discomfort
impassive .. 8. stoicism
joyful .. 6. jocund
offense .. 5. pique
superiority .. 9. arrogance
without .. 6. apathy, steely 7. callous
   8. numbness 9. unfeeling
   13. insensibility
feet ... see also *foot*
designating .. 5. podal
having .. 6. pedate
number .. 7. footage
two (Pros) .. 6. dipody 7. dimeter
   9. ditrochee
without .. 4. apod 6. apodal
   8. footless
feign ... 3. act 4. sham 5. fable
   6. affect, assume, gammon, garble,
   invent 7. connive, imagine, pretend
   8. malinger (illness), simulate
   9. dissemble 11. counterfeit,
   make–believe
feint ... 5. appel (fencing), blind, shift,
   trick 6. attack (mock), thrust
   7. mislead, pretext 8. artifice,
   pretense
Felicia ... 7. thistle 9. happiness
felicitate ... 4. laud 5. bless
   8. macarize 10. compliment
   12. congratulate
felicity ... 5. bliss, grace 7. aptness,
   success 8. aptitude 9. happiness,
   well–being 11. achievement (happy),

blessedness 12. blissfulness

Felidae... 4. cats, lion, lynx, pard,
puma 5. tiger 6. jaguar 7. cheetah,
leopard, wildcat

feline... 3. sly 5. Felis 6. animal
7. catlike, furtive 8. stealthy
11. treacherous

Felis... 3. cat

fell... 3. cut, hem, hew 4. beat, hill,
kill, pelt, ruin, skin 5. cruel, level
6. fierce, fleece, lay low, mighty,
savage 7. brutish, tumbled
9. barbarous, ferocious, overthrow,
prostrate

fellow... 3. lad, man 4. beau, chap,
peer 5. equal 6. member, person
7. comrade 8. neighbor 9. associate,
companion 10. sweetheart
11. confederate

fellow (pert to)...
accomplice.. 7. abettor 9. accessory
11. confederate
awkward.. 4. boor, gawk
clumsy.. 3. oaf 4. lout, pleb 5. yahoo
7. bumpkin
coward.. 3. cad, fop 4. drip
7. bounder 8. spalpeen
droll.. 3. wag 4. card
old.. 6. geezer 7. callant
small.. 6. shaver
smart.. 5. aleck
young.. 4. chap 5. blade, youth
7. younker 9. stripling

fellowman... 7. brother 11. fellow
being

fellowship... 4. sect 5. guild, union
7. company 8. alliance, sodality
9. communion 10. membership
11. affiliation, comradeship,
partnership, scholarship
12. friendliness 13. companionship

felon... 3. bum 4. wild 5. cruel
6. wicked 7. convict, culprit, outcast,
villain, whitlow 8. criminal, disloyal
9. infection, malignant, murderous
10. malefactor, paronychia, traitorous

felony... 3. sin 5. crime, wrath
6. daring, deceit 8. baseness,
burglary, outlawry 9. treachery
10. illegality, wickedness
11. misdemeanor

female... 4. bibi, dame, doña, girl,
gyne, lady, miss 5. donna, femme,
rhyme, squaw, woman 6. maiden,
matron 7. distaff, dowager, fair sex,
Sahibah 8. mistress 9. weaker sex

female (pert to)...
architecture.. 8. Caryatid
comb form.. 5. gyneo, thely
erudite.. 10. pedantress
fox.. 5. vixen
government.. 8. gynarchy
hormone.. 8. estrogen
monster.. 6. gorgon
prayerful.. 5. orant
spirit.. 7. banshee
suffix.. 4. ette
term.. 8. gynecoid
warrior.. 6. Amazon

feminine... 4. soft, weak 6. female,
gender, tender 7. womanly
8. maidenly 10. effeminate

femme fatale... 4. vamp 5. siren
7. Lorelei, vampire

femur... 3. hip (bone) 4. bone (thigh),
coxa

fen... 3. bog 4. moor, pool 5. marsh,
swale 7. The Fens

fence... 3. aha 4. bank, duel, ha–ha,
pale, rail, wall 5. close, ditch, fight,
hedge, stile 6. paling, picket, secure
7. barrier, confine, enclose, fortify,
protect, railing 8. palisade, prohibit
9. enclosure, swordplay
11. self–defense

fencing (pert to)...
breastplate.. 8. plastron
defense.. 5. carte, parry, prime, sixte
6. octave, quinte, tierce 7. seconds,
septime
master.. 7. lanista
position.. 9. pronation 10. supination
sword.. 4. epee, foil, tuck 5. extoc
6. rapier
term.. 4. volt 7. corrida 8. estocado
thrust.. 6. remise 7. riposte

fend... 4. ward 5. avert, parry, shift
6. defend, resist 7. prevent, repulse,
ward off

fender... 5. guard 6. buffer, bumper,
shield, sluice 7. cushion 9. fireguard
10. firescreen 11. splashboard

fenestra... 6. window 7. foramen,
opening, orifice

Fenian... 5. Irish 11. Brotherhood

fennel... 4. herb 6. Seseli 7. Azorian,
Nigella

feral... 4. wild 6. deadly, ferine,
savage 7. bestial, untamed
8. funereal, unbroken 9. malignant
12. uncultivated

feretory... 4. bier 6. chapel, shrine
(saint's) 8. feretrum

ferment... 4. barm, brew, fret, sour,
stum, zyme 5. anger, fever, yeast
6. enzyme, foment, leaven, rennin,
seethe, uproar 7. glucase, maltase
8. diastase, disorder 9. agitation
10. effervesce, turbulence

fermentation... 6. unrest 9. agitation,
chemistry, leavening 10. ebullition
13. effervescence

fermenting vat... 4. gyle

fern... 4. tara 5. brake, heath, holly
6. osmund, spider 7. bracken
8. polypody 10. maidenhair
11. elephant–ear

fern (pert to)...
family.. 12. pteridophyte
genus.. 6. Anemia
leaf.. 5. frond
scale.. 8. ramentum

ferocious... 4. grim, wild 5. cruel,
feral 6. bloody, brutal, fierce, savage
7. acharne, inhuman 8. pitiless,
ravenous, ruthless 9. barbarous,
malignant, merciless, murderous,
rapacious, truculent 10. implacable,
malevolent, relentless, sanguinary
11. remorseless 12. bloodthirsty

ferret... 3. hob 4. hunt, jill, tape
5. worry 6. badger, harass, search,
weasel 7. polecat

ferrotype... 7. tintype 10. photograph

ferrum... 2. Fe (sym) 4. iron
ferry... 7. traject 9. transport 10. sail across
ferryboat... 3. bac 4. pont 6. wherry
ferryman... 6. Charon (River Styx) 7. ferrier
fertile... 4. rank, rich 7. teeming 8. abundant, fruitful, prolific 9. exuberant, inventive, plenteous, plentiful 10. productive
fertilizer... 4. marl 5. guano 6. pollen 7. compost, nitrate 8. dressing 9. phosphate
ferule... 3. rod 5. ruler 6. fennel 10. punishment
fervency... 4. heat, keen, zeal 5. ardor, eager, fiery, gusto, verve 6. fervor, warmth 7. ardency, passion 9. eloquence, vehemence 12. empressement 15. impassionedness
fervent... 3. hot 4. keen, warm 5. eager, fiery 6. ardent, fervid 7. excited, intense, zealous 8. eloquent, vehement 10. passionate 11. impassioned
fervid... 3. hot 5. fiery 6. ardent, tropic 7. boiling, fervent, zealous 8. vehement 11. impassioned
fervor... 4. rage, zeal, zest 5. ardor 7. ecstasy, passion 11. earnestness
fester... 6. rankle 7. abscess, pustule, putrefy 9. suppurate
festival... 3. ale, bal 4. fete, gala 5. Delia (Apollo), feast, revel, Seder 6. Easter, Kermis 7. holiday, uphelya 8. apodosis (Church) 9. Christmas, Mardi gras 10. Parentalia, Saturnalia
festive... 3. gay 4. gala 5. merry 6. joyous 8. mirthful, sportive 9. convivial
festivity... 3. joy 4. fete, gala 5. mirth, revel 6. gaiety 7. jollity, whoopee 8. festival, jamboree 10. joyfulness 11. celebration, merrymaking 12. conviviality
fetch... 3. get 5. bring, reach 6. attain, deduce, revive 7. achieve 8. go and get, retrieve
fetching... 8. alluring, charming, pleasing 10. attractive, delightful 11. fascinating
fete... 4. gala 5. feast, party 6. fiesta 8. carnival, festival 10. Saturnalia 13. entertainment
fetid... 4. olid, rank 5. fusty 7. noisome 10. malodorous 11. ill-smelling
fetish... 3. obi 4. idol, joss, juju 5. charm, image, totem 6. amulet, avatar, mascot 7. Dahoman 8. talisman
fetter... 4. band, bond, gyve, iron 5. chain 6. hamper, hobble, hopple, thrall 7. enchain, manacle, shackle
feud... 4. fief, fray 5. broil 6. affray, estate, strife 7. contest, dispute, quarrel 8. vendetta 9. hostility
feudal (pert to)...
 estate.. 3. fee 4. fief, soke
 French.. 4. feod

lord.. 6. tenure 8. overlaid, suzerain
payment.. 6. socage
service.. 5. banal
tenant.. 4. leud 6. vassal
tribute.. 6. heriot
fever... 4. ague 5. ardor 6. frenzy 8. delirium, sickness 9. calenture 10. excitement
fever (pert to)...
 heat.. 9. sunstroke
 intermittent.. 5. octan 7. quartan
 malarial.. 4. ague
 marsh.. 6. elodes 7. helodes
 subsidence.. 12. defervescent
 term.. 7. febrile, pyretic
 tropical.. 6. dengue 9. calenture
feverish... 5. hasty 7. excited, febrile, fervent, fevered 8. restless 9. delirious, overeager 10. disordered
fey... 4. dead 5. dying, elfin, fatal, spell 9. enfeebled, visionary 12. otherworldly
fez... 3. cap 5. busby, shako 8. tarboosh 9. headdress
fiat... 3. act 5. edict, order 6. decree 7. command 8. decision, sanction
fiber... 3. nap, nep, tal 4. bast, eruc, imbe, lint, pile, pita, silk, yarn 5. datil, istle, kapok, linen, nerve, rayon, sisal 6. fibril, raffia, staple, thread 7. filasse, texture 8. fibrilla, filament
fiber plant... 4. hemp, imbe, palm 5. abaca, agave 6. ambary, cotton, linaga
fibers... 5. hairs 7. strands 9. filaments
fibula... 4. bone (arm) 5. class 6. brooch (anc), buckle 9. safety pin
fickle... 5. false 6. mobile 7. mutable 8. unstable, unsteady, variable, wavering 9. changeful, deceitful, faithless, unsettled 10. capricious, changeable, inconstant, irresolute, unfaithful 11. vacillating
fiction... 4. tale 5. false, fancy, novel, story 6. legend 7. coinage, figment, forgery, romance 9. falsehood, invention 11. fabrication
fictitious... 5. false 6. poetic, pseudo (pref) 7. assumed, feigned 8. chimeric 9. imaginary, imitative, pretended 10. artificial
fictitious name... 5. alias 6. anonym 7. pen name 8. nickname 9. pseudonym, stage name 10. nom de plume 11. nom de guerre
fidelity... 5. topaz, troth, truth 6. fealty 7. honesty 8. accuracy, devotion, veracity 9. adherence, constancy, exactness 10. allegiance 12. faithfulness
fidget... 4. fuss 5. worry 6. twitch 9. dysphoria 10. uneasiness 12. restlessness
fidgety... 5. jerky 6. uneasy 7. nervous, restive, twitchy 8. bustling, restless 9. excitable, impatient
fiducial... 4. firm 5. solid, sound 6. secure, stable 7. trusted 8. trustful 9. confident

11. trustworthy
fiduciary . . . 4. held (in trust) 5. trust
7. founded, holding, in trust, trustee
12. confidential
fief . . . 3. fee 4. feud 6. estate
field . . . 3. lea, lot 4. acre, ager, land,
mead, rand 5. croft, glebe, range,
tract 6. campus, ground, meadow,
sphere 7. compass, diamond,
expanse, pasture, savanna (savannah),
terrain 8. clearing, gridiron
11. battlefield
field (pert to) . . .
athletic . . 4. oval 5. arena, court, track
6. course, sphere 7. diamond,
stadium 8. gridiron
bloodshed . . 8. Aceldama (Akeldama)
13. Ager Sanguinis
duck . . 7. bustard
god of . . 4. Faun
mouse . . 4. vole
snow . . 4. neve
stubble . . 5. rowen
term . . 5. agral 8. agrarian
10. campestral
fiend . . . 3. foe 5. demon, devil, enemy,
Satan 6. addict, wizard 7. Amaimon
(Amamon) 9. archfiend 10. evil spirit
fiendish . . . 5. cruel 6. wicked
7. Avernal, demonic 8. demoniac,
devilish, diabolic
fierce . . . 4. grim 5. cruel, eager
6. raging, savage 7. furious, racking,
violent 9. ferocious, impetuous,
truculent 10. catawampus, forbidding,
passionate 11. belligerent,
overwrought 12. overpowering
fierceness . . . 7. cruelty 8. violence
10. truculence
fiery . . . 3. hot, red 4. sore 5. angry
6. ardent 7. burning, excited,
fervent, flaming, glowing, igneous,
parched, violent 8. choleric, feverish,
inflamed, spirited, vehement
9. impetuous, irascible
10. mettlesome, passionate
11. hot–tempered, inflammable
fiery cross . . . 5. alarm 6. emblem,
signal, symbol 8. crantara 10. call to
arms
fiesta . . . 5. color 7. holiday 8. festival
9. festivity
fifish . . . 6. cranky 9. half crazy
Fifteenth Amendment . . . 16. Negro
Citizenship (1870)
fig . . . 4. fico 5. eleme, gruit 6. Carica,
Fiscus, Smyrna, trifle
fig basket . . . 5. cabas, seron
fight . . . 3. row, war 4. bout, duel, fray,
mell, tilt 5. brawl, melee, scrap
6. affray, attack, barney, battle,
combat, oppose, strife, strike, strive
7. contest, quarrel, warfare
8. conflict, struggle 9. pugnacity
13. combativeness
fighter . . . 7. battler, duelist, soldier,
warrior 8. champion, pugilist,
scrapper 9. combatant
fighting . . . 3. war 4. game 6. plucky
7. warlike 8. militant 10. contention,
pugnacious 11. belligerent
fig leaf . . . 6. symbol (modesty)

8. clothing (Bib), covering
figment . . . 5. fancy 6. fiction
9. falsehood, invention
figurative . . . 6. florid 7. flowery, typical
8. allusive 9. numerical
12. emblematical, metaphorical
figure . . . 4. body, dash, dope, form,
nude, rank, type 5. digit, image,
judge, price, shape, solve 6. aspect,
emblem, entail, number, symbol
7. diagram, numeral, outline, pattern
8. ornament, phantasm 9. calculate,
celebrity, character, personage
10. appearance, impression,
similitude 11. distinction
figure (pert to) . . .
column . . 6. elamon 7. telamon
8. Atlantes, Caryatid, pilaster
geometric . . 4. cone, lune 5. prism,
rhomb 6. isagon, isogen, isogon
(rare) 7. ellipse, rhombus
8. pentagon, triangle
13. parallelogram, quadrilateral
16. parallelepipedon
praying . . 5. orant
repeated digits . . 8. repetend
speech . . 5. trope 6. aporia, simile
8. metaphor
star–shaped . . 8. pentacle
figured . . . 4. rich 6. ornate 7. façonné
10. ornamented
figurine . . . 4. doll 7. carving, tanagra
9. sculpture, statuette
Fiji Island, Viti Levu . . .
capital . . 4. Suva
export . . 5. sugar
mountain . . 8. Victoria
natives . . 9. cannibals (anc)
11. Melanesians
ruler . . 7. British
filament . . . 4. barb, dowl (dowle), hair
5. fiber (fibre), harle 6. strand,
thread
filament lamp . . . 12. incandescent
filbert . . . 3. nut 5. brown, hazel
7. Corylus 8. hazelnut
filch . . . 3. nim, rob 4. beat 5. steal,
theft 6. pilfer 7. purloin
file . . . 3. row 4. list, rasp, rate
5. enter, march, store 6. abrade,
smooth 7. sharpen 8. classify
9. catalogue 10. pickpocket
11. triggerfish (filefish)
file (combmaking) . . . 5. grail (graille)
6. carlet 7. quannet
filibeg . . . 4. kilt 5. skirt
filibuster . . . 6. pirate 7. impeder
8. thwarter 9. legislate
10. freebooter, obstructer
14. obstructionist
filicide . . . 6. murder (child by parent)
filigree . . . 4. lace 5. adorn (with)
7. pattern 8. fanciful 10. decorative
13. unsubstantial
Filipino, Filipina (pert to) . . .
homeland (mostly) . . 5. Luzon
native of . . 11. Philippines
tribe . . 5. Bikol (Bicol) 7. Malayan
(Christian), Tagalog (Tagal), Visayan
(see also *Philippine*)
fill . . . 3. pad 4. calk, feed, glut, hold,
plug 5. block, close, gorge, stuff

6. occupy, stop up 7. execute, fulfill,
pervade, satiate, satisfy, suffuse
8. complete, compound, permeate
10. accomplish 11. superabound

fille... 4. girl 8. daughter

filled... 5. dated 7. replete 8. suffused
9. saturated

filled with crevices... 7. areolar

fillet... 4. band, orle, ring, tape
5. snood, tiara 6. anadem, border,
ribbon, taenia 7. bandage
8. headband, insignia 9. lemniscus,
scantling 10. tenderloin

fillet (Arch)... 5. stria 6. cimbia, listel,
reglet, regula, taenia 7. chaplet,
molding (part)

filly... 4. colt, foal, girl, mare

film... 4. brat, haze, scum, skin, veil
5. cover, layer 6. lamina, patina
7. coating 8. pellicle 10. photograph

filmy... 3. dim 4. fine 5. gauzy, misty
6. cloudy, opaque 7. clouded
9. laminated 10. indistinct

fils... 3. son

filter... 4. ooze 5. clean, drain
6. purify, strain 7. trickle 8. colature
9. percolate

filth... 4. dirt, muck, slut 5. lucre
6. vermin 7. squalor 9. excrement,
obscenity, scoundrel

filthiness... 8. cenosity 9. fetidness,
obscenity 10. odiousness

filthy... 3. low 4. foul, vile 5. dirty,
fetid, gross 6. impure, odious, putrid
7. obscene, squalid, unclean
9. polluting 10. licentious

filthy lucre... 4. gain (shameful)
5. money

fimbriated... 5. edged 7. fringed
8. bordered (Her), margined

fin... 3. arm 4. five, keel

fin (pert to fish)...
median.. 4. anal 6. caudal, dorsal
paired.. 6. pelvic 7. ventral
8. pectoral

final... 3. end 4. last 5. be-all, telic
7. dernier 8. decisive, definite,
eventual, ultimate 9. mandatory,
ultimatum 10. conclusive, definitive
11. unqualified 13. determinating

final argument... 11. ultima ratio

finale... 3. end 4. coda 5. close
6. result 8. swan song
10. completion, conclusion
11. termination

finality... 5. finis 6. finale, finish,
windup 10. conclusion
11. termination 12. decisiveness
14. conclusiveness

finally... 10. eventually, ultimately
12. conclusively

final outcome... 5. issue 6. upshot
10. denouement

financial... 6. fiscal 8. monetary
9. pecuniary

finch... 4. moro 5. Junco, serin, spink,
tarin 6. burion, linnet, siskin, towhee
7. chewink, redpoll 9. brambling,
chaffinch, Fringilla

find... 3. get 4. gain 5. learn
6. detect, locate, summon, supply

7. procure, provide 8. discover, meet
with, perceive 9. determine,
discovery, good thing 10. experience
11. acquisition

find fault... 4. beef, carp 5. cavil
8. complain 9. criticize

finding... 7. verdict 8. solution
9. discovery 11. serendipity

find out... 5. learn, solve 6. detect
8. discover 9. ascertain

fine... 3. fit 4. good, lacy, pure, rare,
thin 5. dandy, filmy, frail, gaudy,
noble, sharp, sheer 6. ornate, slight,
smooth 7. elegant, fragile, healthy,
perfect, powdery, precise, slender
8. absolute, ethereal, handsome,
polished, skillful, superior 9. beautiful,
excellent, sensitive 10. fastidious,
pulverized, surpassing

finery... 6. beauty 7. clothes, gaudery,
gewgaws 8. elegance, fineness,
frippery, ornament 10. decoration,
lavishness 11. refinements

finesse... 5. skill 6. purity, serene
7. cunning 8. artifice, card play,
subtlety, thinness 9. clearness, good
taste, stratagem 10. refinement
14. discrimination (subtle)

finger... 3. toy (with) 4. hook 5. digit,
touch 6. dactyl, handle, pilfer
7. measure, purloin

finger (pert to)...
alphabet.. 11. dactylology
cymbal.. 8. castanet
fish.. 8. starfish
flower.. 8. foxglove
fore.. 5. index 7. pointer
little.. 6. pinkie 7. minimus
9. auricular
middle.. 6. medius
ring.. 7. annular
stall.. 3. cot
term.. 7. digital

fingernail moon... 6. lunule

fingernail overgrowth...
10. onychauxis

fingerprint (term)... 4. arch, loop
5. whorl 9. composite
11. dactylogram 12. dactyloscopy

finial... 3. epi, tee

finical... 4. nice 5. fussy 6. dainty,
dapper, jaunty, spruce 7. finicky,
foppish, mincing, prudish 8. delicate
9. finicking, squeamish
10. fastidious, meticulous
11. overprecise 14. overscrupulous

finis... 3. end 4. goal 6. finale
8. finality 10. conclusion
11. culmination

finish... 3. end 4. kill 5. chare, close,
matte (mat), style 6. enamel, polish
7. destroy, perfect, surface, texture
8. complete, conclude 9. terminate
10. completion, consummate,
perfection

finished... 3. o'er 4. done, fine, over,
ripe 5. ended 6. closed 7. refined,
stopped 8. climaxed, complete,
lustered, polished 9. completed,
concluded, perfected 10. terminated

finite... 7. fleshly, limited 9. definable
10. restricted, terminable

11. conditional
fink ... 3. spy 4. scab 5. finch
8. informer 13. strikebreaker
Finland ... see also *Finnish*
capital .. 8. Helsinki (Helsingfors)
Finnish for Finland .. 5. Suomi
government .. 8. republic
island .. 5. Aland
language .. 6. Magyar 7. Swedish
8. Estonian
legislature .. 9. Eduskunta
port .. 3. Abo 5. Turku 9. Mariehamn
Finnish (pert to) ...
bath .. 5. sauna
dramatist .. 4. Kivi 7. Waltari
people .. 5. Finns, Suomi 9. Karelians
10. Tavastians
fire ... 4. heat, zeal 5. blaze, fever,
flame 6. excite, fervor, igneus, ignite,
incite, kindle 7. barrage, explode,
inspire 8. detonate, illumine
9. discharge, eloquence
11. inspiration 12. inflammation
13. conflagration
fire (pert to) ...
basket .. 5. grate 7. cresset
comb form .. 4. igni
cracker .. 6. petard
dog .. 7. andiron
fear of .. 10. pyrophobia
god .. 6. Vulcan
opal .. 7. girasol (girasole)
power over .. 10. ignipotent
worshiper .. 5. Parsi 9. pyrolater
10. ignicolist
firearm ... 3. gat, gun 5. piece, rifle
6. musket 7. demihag, rimbase (part)
8. ordnance, revolver 9. harquebus
(arquebus)
firearms discharge ... 9. fusillade
fired ... 3. lit 4. shot 5. baked 6. on
fire (Her) 7. excited 8. inspired
10. discharged
fireman ... 4. vamp 6. fueler, stoker
8. trainman 9. fire–eater
11. firefighter
fireplace ... 5. fogon, forge, ingle
6. hearth 9. inglenook 13. Franklin
stove
fireside (home) ... 11. hearthstone
firewood ... 6. billet
fireworks ... 4. caps, gerb 6. flares
7. fizgigs, gunfire, rip–raps, rockets
8. serpents 9. pinwheels, sparklers,
torpedoes 10. girandoles
12. firecrackers, Roman candles
firm ... 4. fast, hard, safe, sure, trig
5. dense, fixed, rigid, solid, sound,
stout, tight 6. secure, stable, stanch,
steady, strict, strong 7. compact,
company, decided, devoted, staunch
8. faithful 9. immovable, steadfast
10. determined, unslipping, unyielding
11. substantial
firmament ... 3. sky 5. vault 6. Caelus,
welkin 7. heavens 8. empyrean
firmly set ... 5. fixed, solid 6. rooted
10. inveterate
firmness ... 8. fidelity, rigidity, solidity,
strength, tenacity 9. constancy,
stability 10. immobility, steadiness
11. reliability 15. indissolubility

firmness, want of ... 5. loose 6. laxity
8. weakness 11. instability, vacillation
firn ... 3. ice 4. neve, snow
firs ... 5. Abies, pines
first ... 5. chief, front, prime 6. maiden,
primal, primus 7. highest, initial,
leading, primary 8. earliest, foremost,
original 9. beginning, elemental,
principal 10. primordial
first (pert to) ...
appearance .. 5. debut 8. premiere
born .. 5. eigne 6. eldest
Christian martyr .. 7. Stephen
coin (silver) .. 8. sesterce
days of Rom month .. 7. calends
(kalends)
fruits (Eccl) .. 7. annates
letter .. 4. Alif 5. Aleph
stages .. 8. inchoate 9. rudiments
world navigator .. 8. Magellan
fish ... 3. dib 4. food 5. angle, drail,
seine, troll 6. Pisces
13. constellation
fish (types of) ... 2. id 3. cat, cod, gar,
ray 4. bass, carp, char, chub, cusk,
dace, goby, hake, ling, opah, parr,
peto, pike, ruff, scup, shad, sisi,
sole, tuna, ulua 5. bream, cisco,
fluke, guppy, perch, porgy, shark,
skate, smelt, snook, sprat, trout,
tunny, wahoo 6. barbel, bonito,
bowfin, burbot, conger, darter,
marlin, minnow, puffer, redfin,
salmon, shiner, sucker, tarpon,
tautog, turbot 7. alewife, anchovy,
catfish, crappie, croaker, dogfish,
garfish, grouper, haddock, halibut,
herring, hogfish, jewfish, lamprey,
mudfish, oquassa, pollack, pompano,
redfish, sardine, sawfish, sunfish,
torpedo, walleye 8. albacore, blue
fish, bluegill, bonefish, bullhead,
chimaera, filefish, flatfish, flounder,
goldfish, grayling, kingfish, lumpfish,
mackerel, menhaden, pickerel,
pilchard, sailfish, sergeant, sting ray,
sturgeon, toadfish, weakfish
9. barracuda, cigarfish, devilfish,
jellyfish, namaycush, sheatfish,
whitefish 10. barramunda, butterfish,
candlefish, hammerhead, yellowtail
11. muskellunge (see also *mammal*)
fish (pert to) ...
adhering .. 4. pega 6. remora
ascending rivers .. 7. anadrom
10. anadromous
bait .. 4. chum 5. chack 6. minnow
9. killifish (killy)
basket .. 4. caul 5. creel, slath (slarth)
bivalve, mollusk .. 4. clam, slug
5. snail, whelk 6. limpet, mussel,
oyster 7. abalone, Ocypode (crab),
scallop
caviar–yielding .. 7. sterlet
climbing, jumping .. 5. saury
6. anabas 7. skipper
club .. 6. muckle
codfish .. 4. cusk 5. torsk 7. bacalao,
buffalo
comb form .. 7. ichthyo
crustacean .. 3. Uca 4. crab 6. shrimp
7. lobster 8. Decapoda

devil.. 3. ray 5. manta
eaters.. 12. ichthyophagi
eating.. 11. piscivorous
  14. ichthyophagous
fabled (Pers).. 4. Mahi (Mah)
gaff (through ice).. 5. ching
game.. 4. tuna 5. chiro, sword, trout
  6. marlin, salmon, tarpon 8. grayling
  11. muskellunge
genus.. 4. Amia (bowfin), Mola
  (sunfish) 5. Elops (tarpon), Perca
  (perch) 8. Haliotis (abalone),
  Octopoda (octopus)
hook.. 5. Kirby, snell (part)
  8. Aberdeen, barbless, Carlisle,
  Limerick
largest (freshwater).. 8. arapaima
like.. 8. ichthyic
line.. 6. nossel (norsel) 7. spillet
living by.. 9. piscatory
living on.. 12. ichthyophagy
man–eating.. 6. caribe 7. piranha
mollusk.. see *bivalve*
nest building.. 5. acara
net.. 4. fyke 5. seine, snell, trawl
  7. boulter, spiller
pond.. 7. piscina 8. aquarium
roe.. 6. caviar
salmon.. 3. fog 4. masu, parr
  5. sprod 6. alevin 7. gilling
sauce.. 4. alec
spear.. 3. gig
taboo.. 13. ichthyophobia
treatise.. 11. ichthyology
worship.. 12. ichthyolatry
young brood.. 3. fry
fisherman... 6. angler 8. piscator
fishery... 7. piscary
fishing... chug (through ice)
  8. snelling 9. halieutic, piscation
fishing vessel... 5. smack 6. seiner
  7. trawler
fishy... 4. dull 6. vacant 8. fishlike
  9. deceptive, dishonest
  10. improbable, lusterless, suspicious,
  unreliable 11. extravagant
  14. expressionless
fissure... 3. gap 4. leak, lode, open,
  rent, rift, rima, seam, slit, vein
  5. break, chasm, chine, chink, cleft,
  crack, sever, split 7. crevice
fissured... 5. cleft 6. rimate, rimose
fist... 4. duke, hand (closed) 5. nieve
  6. clench 8. tightwad
  11. handwriting
fit... 3. due, fay, pat 4. able, gear,
  meet, mesh, ripe, suit, whim
  5. adapt, equip, fancy, ready, spasm,
  train 6. attack, enmesh, frenzy,
  proper, stroke, suited 7. adapted,
  caprice, conform, healthy, prepare,
  tantrum 8. disposed, dovetail,
  eligible, outbreak, suitable
  9. competent, qualified
  11. accommodate, appropriate
fit (pert to)...
an arrow (archery).. 4. nock
fury.. 4. rage
groove (Arch).. 4. dado
resentment.. 4. huff, mood 5. pique
  7. tantrum
to eat.. 6. edible

to till.. 6. arable
fitchew... 5. skink, zoril 7. foumart,
  polecat
fitful... 8. restless, unstable, variable
  9. impulsive, irregular, orderless,
  spasmodic 10. capricious, convulsive
  12. intermittent
fitly... 4. duly 5. right 6. timely
  8. properly, suitably 10. decorously
fitness... 7. decorum 9. congruity
  10. expedience, timeliness
  11. eligibility, suitability
  12. preparedness
fitting... 3. apt, pat 4. just, meet
  6. proper, seemly, timely
  8. adapting, suitable 9. expedient
  11. appropriate
five (pert to)...
Books of Moses.. 10. Pentateuch
children (born at once)..
  11. quintuplets
Civilized Tribes (Ind).. 5. Creek
  7. Choctaw 8. Cherokee, Seminole
  9. Chickasaw
comb form.. 5. penta
cornered.. 11. pentagonous
divided by.. 11. quinquesect
dollar bill.. 1. V 3. fin 5. fiver
feet.. 10. pentameter
five–year period.. 6. pentad 7. lustrum
  (census) 12. quinquennial
fold.. 9. quintuple
group.. 6. pentad 8. fivesome
lines (nonsense).. 8. limerick
Nations (Ind Confed).. 7. Cayugas,
  Mohawks, Oneidas, Senecas
  9. Onondagas
trump card (auction pitch).. 5. pedro
fix... 3. peg, pin, set 4. mend, moor,
  nail 5. amend, brace, bribe, imbed,
  limit, stamp 6. adjust, anchor,
  cement, define, fasten, ossify, punish,
  repair, settle 7. arrange, confirm,
  delimit, dilemma, prepare, rectify
  8. organize, solidify 9. condition,
  establish, stabilize, stipulate
  10. prearrange
fixed... 3. set 4. firm 5. rigid
  6. formal, intent, nailed, static
  7. assured, limited, settled, special
  8. arranged, habitual 9. immovable,
  permanent, unwinking
  11. established, prearranged,
  traditional
fixed (pert to)...
allowance.. 4. diet 6. ration
  7. stipend 10. remittance
beforehand.. 13. predetermined
by choice.. 8. elective
manner.. 9. immovably
star.. 4. Veda
time.. 3. era 4. date, fast
fizgig... 9. fireworks, whirligig
flabellate... 9. fan–shaped
flabrum... 3. fan 9. flabellum
flaccid... 4. limp, weak 6. flabby
  8. yielding
flag... 3. sag 4. fail, fane, iris, pave,
  pine, sign, weak, wilt 5. Roger
  (pirate) 6. banner, burgee, colors,
  cornet, ensign, fanion, flower, guidon,
  pennon, signal 7. bunting, calamus,

decline, pennant 8. gonfalon,
masthead, standard, streamer,
vexillum 9. banderole 16. Quincunx
of Heaven

flagging... 4. weak 7. languid
8. pavement 10. flagstones, spiritless
11. languishing

flagging in energy... 9. lassitude

flagitious... 6. wicked 7. corrupt,
heinous 8. criminal, flagrant
10. scandalous, villainous

flagon... 3. jug 4. ewer 5. stoup
6. bottle, carafe 7. canteen
8. demijohn

flagpole standard... 7. bracket
9. bracciale

flagrant... 4. rank 5. great 6. absurd,
wanton, wicked 7. glaring, hateful,
heinous, obvious, scarlet, violent
8. infamous, terrible 9. abandoned,
atrocious, monstrous, nefarious
10. profligate, villainous

flail... 4. beat, flag, whip 6. thrash,
weapon (anc) 7. swingle

flam... 4. hoax 5. cheat, spoof, trick
6. cajole 7. pretext 8. drumbeat,
flimflam 9. deception, falsehood

flambeau... 5. torch (flaming)
7. cresset 11. candlestick

flamboyant... 4. wavy (Arch) 6. florid,
ornate 9. brilliant, flamelike
11. resplendent

flame... 3. arc 4. beam, burn, fire,
glow, leye (obs), love, zeal 5. ardor,
blaze, flare, flash, glare, ingle, light,
lover 6. redden 7. scarlet
8. flammule (small) 10. brightness,
sweetheart

flamen... 6. priest (anc)

flamenco... 5. dance (gypsy)

Flaminian Way... 4. Rome

Flanders, Belgium...
brick.. 4. Bath
capital.. 5. Ghent (East) 6. Bruges
(West)
city.. 5. Alost 6. Ostend 7. Dixmude
(Dixmuide)
people (anc).. 5. Celts 6. Franks
11. Burgundians
poppy.. 9. corn poppy

flap... 3. tab 4. blow, slap, sway,
wave 5. skirt 6. dangle, lappet,
stroke 7. flapper, flutter
9. appendage

flare... 5. blaze, flame, flash, fusee,
glare, light 6. signal, spread
7. display, flicker 8. outburst
10. illuminate

flaring... 5. gaudy 6. spread
7. burning, glaring 8. dazzling,
flashing

flash... 4. show 5. blaze, burst, gleam,
glint, shine, spark 6. glance, signal
7. display, glimmer, glisten, glitter,
instant, shimmer, sparkle 8. dispatch
9. telegraph

flashing... 5. showy 6. flashy
8. meteoric, snapping 9. transient

flashy... 3. gay 5. fiery, gaudy, showy
6. frothy, garish, sporty 7. raffish
8. vehement 9. flaunting, impetuous
13. grandiloquent

flask... 4. ewer, olpe 5. betty
6. flagon 7. ampulla, canteen
9. aryballus (aryballas, anc)

flask–shaped... 10. lageniform

flat... 3. low 4. palm 5. banal, blunt,
level, molle, plain, plane, prone,
stale, suite, tract, vapid 6. boring,
dreary, wholly 7. insipid, uniform
8. tenement, unbroken 10. horizontal

flat (pert to)...
boat.. 3. ark 4. punt, scow 5. barge
breastbone.. 6. ratite
canopy.. 6. tester
flatfoot.. 9. pes planus 13. talipes
planus
iron.. 7. sadiron
nosed.. 6. simous
piece.. 4. slab
surface.. 4. area 6. pagina 7. tabular
worm.. 9. planarian, trematode

flatfish... 3. dab 4. sole 5. brill, fluke
6. acedia, turbot 7. halibut
8. flounder

flatten... 4. even 5. level 6. deject,
smooth 7. depress 8. dispirit
9. prostrate 10. discourage,
dishearten

flattened... 6. evened, oblate
7. leveled 8. smoothed 9. applanate

flatter... 3. oil 4. coax, palp 5. charm,
float 6. cajole, caress, please, praise,
smooge, soothe 7. adulate, beguile,
blarney, flutter 8. blandish
9. encourage 10. compliment,
ingratiate

flatterer... 6. flunky, glozer 7. Jenkins
8. adulator, courtier, parasite
9. sycophant

flattering... 9. adulatory, gnathonic,
insincere 10. obsequious
13. complimentary

flattery... 5. gloze, taffy 6. praise
7. blarney, eyewash, fawning, palaver
8. cajolery 9. adulation
10. compliment, sycophancy
14. obsequiousness

flaunt... 4. wave 5. boast, vaunt
6. parade 7. display, flutter
8. brandish

**Flavian, House of Flavius,
Emperors**... 5. Titus 8. Domitian
9. Vespasian

Flavian Amphitheater... 9. Colosseum
(Rome)

flavor... 4. gust, odor, tang, zest
5. aroma, imbue, sapid, sapor,
sauce, savor, scent, taste 6. season
7. perfume 8. piquancy 9. flavoring
14. characteristic

flaw... 3. gap, mar 4. rase, rift
5. cleft, fault 6. breach, defect
7. blemish, fissure, sophism
8. fracture 12. imperfection

flax... 3. lin, tow 5. linen

flax (pert to)...
capsule.. 4. boll
dust.. 5. pouce
filaments.. 4. harl
process plant.. 7. rettery
refuse.. 3. pob, tow 5. hurds
seed.. 7. linseed
soak.. 3. ret

weed.. 8. toadflax
flaxweed... 8. toadflax
flay... 4. peel, skin 6. fleece
7. censure, reprove, scarify
9. criticize, excoriate
flea... 4. puce 5. pulex 6. beetle,
chigoe 7. chigger, cyclops
8. reminder 13. Ctenocephalus
fleam... 6. lancet, stream
10. millstream
fleck... 4. flea, mark, spot 5. flake
6. blotch, dapple, streak, stripe
7. freckle, speckle, stipple 8. particle
9. variegate
flection, flexion... 7. bending, turning
flee... 3. fly, run 4. shun 5. avoid,
elope, evade, speed 6. vanish
7. abandon, forsake 9. disappear
fleece... 3. abb, nap 4. flay, pile, skin,
wool 5. fleck, mulct, sheer, strip
6. divest 7. despoil, swindle
10. overcharge
fleer... 4. gibe, jeer, mock 5. flout,
scoff, sheer, taunt
fleet... 4. fast, flit, flow, navy, sail,
swim 5. drift, group, quick, rapid,
swift 6. armada, hasten, nimble,
speedy 9. transient 10. evanescent,
transitory
fleeting... 7. passing 9. transient
10. evanescent, transitory
Fleet Street... 5. Fleta (book written
in prison) 6. prison (London)
11. London press
Flemish painter... 5. David 6. Rubens
7. Van Dyke
flesh... 3. kin 4. body, meat, pink,
pulp, race (human) 6. family, fatten,
muscle 7. kindred, kinsmen, mankind
8. humanity 9. mortality
10. sensuality
flesh (pert to)...
eating.. 8. omophagy (raw)
9. omophagia 10. omophagous,
zoophagous 11. carnivorous,
creophagous
fond of.. 12. sarcophilous
like.. 7. carnose
lust for.. 9. carnality
resembling.. 7. sarcoid
slain animals.. 7. carnage
fleshpots... 6. plenty, wealth 10. high
living, prosperity 12. fat of the land
fleshy... 3. fat 5. beefy, human,
obese, plump, pulpy, stout 6. carnal
7. adipose, carnose 9. corpulent
fleshy fruit... 4. pear, pome 5. bacca,
berry, drupe
fleur–de–lis... 3. lis (Her) 4. iris, lily,
luce 6. emblem
flew... see *fly*
flexible... 4. limp 5. lithe 6. limber,
pliant, supple 7. elastic, lissome
flexion, flection... 7. anaclasis
flexure... 4. genu 5. crook 7. bending
flicker... 4. burn, flit 5. blaze, glare,
waver 7. flutter, high–hoe
10. woodpecker
flickering... 7. burning, lambent
8. flickery 9. irregular
flier, flyer... 3. ace 4. bird 5. pilot,

train 6. airman, gamble, insect
7. aviator, speeder, sunfish, venture
11. speculation
flight... 3. hop 4. rout 5. arrow
(volley), flock, skein (wild fowl), speed
6. exodus, fletch (arrows), flying,
hegira, perron, stairs, throng
7. soaring 8. escapism, mounting,
stampede, swarming 9. excursion,
formation, migration 10. volitation
flighty... 5. barmy, swift 6. fickle, fitful
7. foolish 8. fanciful, freakish, volatile
9. frivolous 10. capricious
flimflam... 5. freak, hocus, trick
6. humbug 7. caprice, swindle
8. nonsense, trifling 9. deception,
deceptive 11. nonsensical
flimmer... 7. flicker, glimmer
flimsy... 4. limp, rare, thin, vain, weak
5. frail 6. feeble, paltry, sleazy,
slimsy 7. flaccid, shallow, trivial
9. illogical 11. superficial
13. unsubstantial
flinch... 4. game 5. quail, start, wince,
wonde 6. blench, cringe, falter,
flense, recoil, shrink, swerve
fling... 3. shy 4. dart, dash, gibe,
hurl, toss 5. cheat, dance, flock
(sandpipers), revel, sling, sneer, throw
6. baffle, spirit 7. cast off, sarcasm
9. prostrate
flint... 5. chert, clint, silex 6. quartz
7. lighter 8. hardness 9. firestone,
skinflint
flip... 3. hop, tap 4. flap, glib, snap,
toss 5. drink (spiced), flick, flirt,
throw 6. fillip 8. flippant, turn over
10. somersault 11. impertinent
flippant... 4. flip, glib, pert 5. cocky
6. chatty, fluent 8. impudent
10. persiflate 11. impertinent
flipper... 3. arm, fin, paw 4. hand
5. panel 8. flapjack
flirt... 3. toy 4. dart, fike, flip, jerk,
jilt, mash, play, toss 5. dally
6. coquet, fillip, masher, trifle
7. trifler 8. coquette 11. philanderer
flirtation... 5. dance 8. coquetry,
trifling 10. love affair
flit... 3. fly 4. dart 5. glide, hover
6. nimble 7. flicker, flutter, migrate
flitter... 3. rag 5. hover, piece
6. tatter 7. flicker, flutter, fritter
8. fragment
flittermouse... 3. bat
float... 4. buoy, cork, hove, lure, raft,
ride, sail, soar, swim, waft 5. balsa,
drift, hover, ladle 6. launch
7. support 8. navigate, undulate
9. transport 10. inaugurate
floating... 4. free 5. awash, loose
6. adrift, natant 7. buoyant,
movable, rumored 8. changing,
drifting, shifting 9. launching,
wandering
floating herb... 7. frogbit
16. Hydrocharitaceae
flock... 4. bevy, fold, herd, pack, raft
6. flight, hirsel 7. company
9. multitude 10. assemblage,
collection 11. aggregation
flock (pert to)...

bees.. 4. hive 5. swarm 6. colony
cattle.. 4. herd
fish.. 5. shoal
geese.. 5. skein 6. gaggle
herons.. 5. sedge
insects.. 5. swarm
like.. 6. gregal
lions.. 5. pride
partridge...5. covey
pheasants.. 4. nide (nid)
sandpipers.. 5. fling
walrus.. 3. pod
flocks, god of... 3. Pan
floe... 3. ice 4. berg
flog... 3. cat, tan 4. beat, cane, goad,
lash, wale, welt, whip 6. larrup,
punish, strike, thrash 8. chastise
flogging... 4. toco (toko) 7. beating
8. whipping 9. thrashing
10. punishment 12. chastisement
flood... 3. sea 5. eagre, spate
6. deluge, drench, excess 7. freshet,
torrent 8. cataract, inundate, overflow
9. cataclysm 10. oversupply
14. superabundance
flood (pert to)...
disaster.. 9. Galveston (1900),
Johnstown (1889)
gate.. 4. gool, lock, slow 6. sluice
8. penstock
lights.. 5. klieg
tidal.. 5. eagre
floor... 4. base, pave, sill 5. chess
(pontoon), story 6. baffle, bottom,
defeat 7. coaming, silence
9. overthrow 10. substratum
floor leader... 4. whip
flora... 6. plants 11. florilegium
flora and fauna... 5. biota
Florence gallery... 5. Pitti 6. Uffizi
Florentine (pert to)...
color.. 7. scarlet
family (famed).. 6. Medici
lily.. 6. giglio
school.. 6. Tuscan
sculptor.. 8. Ammanati, Ghiberti
florid... 3. red 5. ruddy 6. ornate,
rococo 7. flowery, flushed
8. enriched, rubicund 10. figurative,
melismatic, rhetorical 11. embellished
13. grandiloquent
Florida...
capital.. 11. Tallahassee
city.. 5. Miami, Tampa 7. Key West
8. Sarasota 9. Pensacola 11. St
Augustine (1565) 12. St Petersburg
discoverer.. 11. Ponce de Leon
(1513)
fish.. 6. mullet, shrimp, tarpon, testar,
tetard 8. blue crab
flower.. 13. orange blossom
Indian.. 8. Seminole
lake.. 10. Okeechobee
museum.. 10. Circus Hall (Ringling)
plant.. 7. coontie
river.. 8. Suwannee
State admission.. 13. twenty–seventh
State motto.. 22. Liberty and
Independence
State nickname.. 8. Sunshine
swamp, park.. 10. Everglades
trail.. 7. Tamiami

flounce... 4. flap, fold, jerk, trim
5. caper, frill, twist 6. edging, frolic
8. flounder, struggle
flounder... 4. roll 6. bungle, muddle,
welter 7. stumble 8. struggle
9. fluctuate
flounder (fish)... 3. dab 5. fluke
6. plaice, turbot 8. flatfish
flour... 4. bran, meal 6. farina, pinole,
powder 9. middlings, pulverize
flour (pert to)...
diabetic.. 9. aleuronat
gravy.. 4. roux
maker.. 6. miller
pudding.. 4. duff
flourish... 4. grow, show, wave
5. vaunt 6. flaunt, paraph (signature),
thrive 7. display, fanfare, prosper,
roulade 8. arpeggio, brandish,
ornament 9. embellish, luxuriate
11. ostentation
flout... 4. defy, gibe, jeer, mock
5. fleer, scoff, scout, sneer, taunt
6. insult 8. ridicule
flow... 3. jet, run 4. bore, flow, flux,
gush, ooze, pour, roll, teem 5. glide,
issue, river, spout 6. abound, afflux,
course, stream 7. current, fluency,
flutter 9. streaming 10. outpouring
flow (pert to)...
along.. 4. lave
back.. 7. redound
jet.. 4. gush 5. spurt
out.. 5. exude, issue, spill
over.. 5. slosh, spill 6. deluge, engulf
8. inundate 9. overwhelm
tide.. 3. ebb 4. flow, neap
flower... 3. bud 4. best, blow
5. bloom 6. unfold 7. blossom,
develop, essence, produce
8. choicest, ornament 11. Four
Hundred (Society)
flower (types of)... 3. gul (rose) 4. iris,
ixia, lily, pink, rose 5. aster, calla,
canna, daisy, pansy, peony, phlox,
poppy, stock, tulip 6. azalea,
cosmos, crocus, dahlia, lupine,
maypop, orchid, oxalis, violet, zinnia
7. arbutus, begonia, fuchsia, gentian,
passion, petunia, rhodora, verbena
8. amaranth, arethusa, camomile,
cyclamen, daffodil, geranium,
hepatica, hyacinth, larkspur, magnolia,
marigold, Mariposa (lily), primrose,
sweet pea 9. amaryllis, calendula,
carnation, edelweiss, gladiolus,
hollyhock, mayflower, narcissus, water
lily 10. cornflower, delphinium,
fleur–de–lis, marguerite, mignonette,
nasturtium, periwinkle, poinsettia,
snapdragon 11. forget–me–not,
strawflower 13. chrysanthemum
15. lily of the valley
flower (pert to)...
arranging.. 7. ikebana
bed, garden.. 8. floretum, parterre
bloom (full).. 8. anthesis
bud (sauce).. 5. caper
bunch.. 4. posy 7. bouquet, corsage,
nosegay
bursting into.. 12. efflorescent
cluster, clustered.. 4. cyme 5. umbel

8. racemose 9. glomerule
10. paniculate
largest.. 9. rafflesia (3–ft diameter)
like.. 7. anthoid
meadow–grown.. 6. pratal
part.. 4. stem 5. bract, calyx, petal,
sepal, torus 6. carpel, pistil
7. corolla, petiole 8. epicalyx,
peduncle, perianth
poet's.. 8. asphodel 9. narcissus
sacred.. 5. lotus
seed.. 5. ovule
shaped.. 7. fleuron
small.. 7. fleuret
stand.. 7. epergne
flower, shrub... 5. lilac 6. azalea,
laurel 7. dogwood, heather, jasmine,
spiraea, syringa 8. bayberry,
hawthorn 9. jessamine, mistletoe,
sagebrush 10. bitterroot
12. rhododendron
flower, vine... 8. clematis, wisteria
11. honeysuckle 12. morning glory
flower, wild... 5. bluet, daisy
6. cactus, clover, myrtle, pasque
7. anemone, cowslip 8. bluebell,
camellia 9. buttercup, goldenrod,
mayflower, sunflower 10. bluebonnet
12. lady's–slipper
flowering again... 9. remontant
flowers... 9. flowerage
flowers, goddess of... 5. Flora (Rom)
Flowery Kingdom... 5. China
flowing... 5. fluid 6. afflux, fluent
7. copious, cursive, emanant, fluxing
8. coursing, eloquent 9. streaming
10. transitive
flowing (pert to)...
from source.. 6. rising 9. emanating
together.. 9. confluent
veil.. 5. colet (anc)
well.. 6. gusher
fluctuate... 4. roll, vary, veer 5. waver
7. vibrate 8. intermit, undulate,
unsteady 9. oscillate, vacillate
10. irresolute 12. undetermined
flue... 4. barb 5. fluke 6. funnel,
tunnel 7. chimney
fluent... 4. glib 5. fluid, ready
6. facile, smooth, solute 7. copious,
elegant, flowing, gliding, verbose,
voluble 8. eloquent 9. talkative
10. loquacious
fluff... 4. down, girl, lint, yarn 5. floss
6. bungle 8. softness 9. lightness
fluffy... 4. soft 5. downy, drunk, fuzzy,
linty 8. feathery 9. forgetful
12. undependable
fluid... 3. gas, ink, oil 4. bile, milk
5. ichor, serum, water 6. fluent,
liquid, plasma, watery 7. flowing
8. floating, nonsolid
fluke... 4. fish, worm 5. blade (whale)
8. accident, flatfish, flounder
flume... 5. shoot 6. raving, sluice
7. channel, conduit
flunk... 4. fail, miss, slip 5. shirk
6. flinch 7. back out
flunky, flunkey... 4. snob 5. toady
6. cookee, lackey 7. footman,
servant 8. henchman 9. stagehand
flurry... 3. ado 4. fret, gust 5. haste,

hurry 6. bustle, squall 7. bluster,
fluster, flutter 8. snowfall
9. agitation, commotion, confusion
10. excitement
flush... 3. hot, jet 4. full, glow, gush,
rush 5. blush, cards, color, drunk,
fever, rinse, ruddy 6. drench, lavish,
redden, thrill 7. healthy, wealthy
8. abundant, affluent, prodigal,
rosiness, squarely, unbroken
10. prosperous
flushed... 3. hot, red 4. ruby
5. aglow, drunk 6. elated, florid
7. excited, fervent 8. blushing,
exultant, feverish, reddened
fluster... 4. move 5. shake 6. bustle,
excite, flurry, pother 8. distract
10. excitement 11. distraction
flute... 5. crimp, twill 6. furrow,
groove 7. magadis 8. organ stop,
wineglass 10. instrument
flute (pert to)...
bagpipe part.. 7. chanter
nose.. 3. bin 5. pungi
player.. 6. aulete 7. tootler
shrill.. 7. piccolo
stop.. 7. ventage
transverse.. 4. fife
fluting... 5. strix 7. gadroon, shading
10. decoration
flutter... 4. flap, flit, wave 5. float,
haste, hover, waver 6. bustle, ruffle
7. agitate, pitapat 8. disorder
9. agitation, confusion, palpitate
flux... 4. flow, fuse, melt 5. flood,
purge, resin, rosin, smalt, smear
6. course 7. flowing, liquefy, outflow,
solvent
fly... 3. hop 4. flee, flit, leap, melt,
soar, wave, whir, wing 5. alate,
float, glide, speed 6. aviate, elapse,
escape, insect, spring, vanish
7. avigate, avolate 8. fishhook
9. cease to be, disappear
fly (types of)... 3. bot 4. gnat
5. cadew, horse, house, midge
6. Asilus, caddis, gadfly, punkie,
tsetse 7. Diptera, nosee–um
8. dipteron, lacewing, mosquito
11. caterpillar
fly (pert to)...
African.. 4. zimb (zebub) 6. tsetse
agaric.. 8. mushroom (poisonous)
artificial.. 4. harl 5. alder, sedge
6. Cahill, claret 7. grannom
blow.. 4. eggs 5. larva
catcher.. 4. tody 6. peewee (pewit),
phoebe 8. kingbird
flying... 5. a–wing, brief, hasty, yarak
(falcon) 6. volant, waving 7. fleeing
8. fleeting, floating 9. temporary,
transient 12. aeronautical
flying (pert to)...
adder.. 9. dragonfly
boat.. 8. airplane, seaplane
9. amphibian
cat.. 5. lemur 6. marmot
Dutchman.. 5. opera 7. mariner
(fabled) 8. wanderer
fox.. 3. bat 6. kalong
island.. 6. Laputa (Gulliver's Travels)
machine.. 9. gyroplane, orthopter

foal... 4. colt 5. filly 8. Equuleus
(Astron) 9. youngling
foam... 4. barm, boil, fume, rage,
scum, suds 5. froth, spume, yeast
6. trivia 7. bubbles
foaming... 7. spumous 8. bubbling
10. fermenting, infuriated
11. overwrought
fob... 4. sham 5. cheat, trick
6. impose, pocket 7. palm off
8. ornament
focal point... 8. omphalos
focus... 6. center 8. converge,
omphalos 10. adjustment
11. concentrate
fodder... 3. hay 4. corn, feed
5. straw, vetch 6. forage, silage,
stover 7. stubble 8. ensilage
9. pasturage, provender
fodder (pert to)...
 pit.. 4. silo
 storage.. 6. haymow
 store.. 6. ensile
 stored.. 6. silage
foe... 4. army 5. enemy, rival
8. opponent 9. ill–wisher
fog... 4. blur, daze, haar, haze, mist,
roke, smog 5. brume, cloud, vapor
6. nebula, opaque, stupor 7. aerosol,
confuse, pogonip (Sierras)
9. confusion
fogdog... 5. stubb 8. fogeater
foggy... 3. dim 4. dull, hazy, roky
5. dense, misty, vague 6. cloudy,
opaque 7. muddled, obscure
8. confused, nubilous 9. beclouded,
uncertain 10. indistinct
12. muddleheaded
foghorn... 5. siren, voice (hoarse)
6. signal
fogle... 12. handkerchief (thieves')
fogy... 4. dull, slow 6. dotard, fogram,
Hunker 8. mossback 10. Barnburner
12. conservative, old–fashioned
16. overconservative
foible... 5. blade (part), fault 7. failing,
frailty 8. weakness 9. infirmity
12. imperfection
foil... 4. balk 5. actor, metal, sheet,
stump, sword 6. defeat, offset,
outwit, stooge, thwart, weapon
7. failure, repulse 9. frustrate
10. disappoint 11. frustration
Foism... 8. Buddhism
foist... 4. palm 5. cheat 7. intrude
9. interpose 11. interpolate
fold... 3. end, lap, pen, ply 4. coil
(serpent), fail, furl, loop, pile, reef,
ruga, sile, tuck, wrap 5. clasp, close,
crimp, drape, laity, plait, pleat, plica
6. crease, dewlap, double, infold,
lamina, lappet, rimple, suffix
7. entwine, envelop, plicate (fanlike)
8. collapse 9. plicature 10. go
bankrupt
folded, not... 8. eplicate
folder... 7. booklet, leaflet 8. pamphlet
13. advertisement
foliage... 5. spray 6. leaves, ramage
7. bouquet, leafage, umbrage
8. ornament (Arch)
folio... 4. case, leaf 5. paper (folded)

6. folder, number (serial)
folk... 4. race 5. tribe 6. nation,
people 8. servants 9. followers,
relatives, retainers 11. aggregation
folk (pert to)...
 learned.. 7. pedants
 lore.. 6. legend 9. mythology,
 tradition 12. superstition
 song.. 4. fado, lied 7. art song,
 lullaby 9. Kunstlied, Volkslied
 tale.. 4. myth, saga 5. fable, Nancy
 6. legend, mythos, mythus
 7. fantasy, parable
follow... 3. dog, tag 4. heed, heel,
next, nose, obey, seek, tail 5. after,
ensue, trace, trail 6. pursue, result,
shadow 7. conform, draggle,
emulate, imitate, observe, replace,
succeed 8. come next, practice,
supplant 9. persevere, supervene
10. understand
follower... 3. fan, ist (suff), ite (suff),
son 4. aper 5. lover (of) 6. copier,
ensuer, votary, zealot 7. devotee,
pursuer, sequent 8. adherent,
believer, disciple, henchman, partisan
9. Christian, dependent, satellite
10. enthusiast 11. cuadrillero
follower of...
 Arius.. 5. Arian
 Buddha.. 8. Buddhist
 Confucius.. 9. Confucian
 Falstaff.. 3. Nym
 Mohammed.. 6. Moslem 8. Islamite
following... 4. next, sect 5. suant
7. ensuing, pursuit, sequent
8. trailing 9. resultant
10. subsequent, succeeding,
successive 13. accompaniment
following (pert to)...
 exact words.. 7. literal
 one's death.. 10. posthumous
 stories.. 6. sequel, series
folly... 3. sin 5. crime 6. levity, lunacy
7. blunder, foolery, madness
8. lewdness, unwisdom 9. silliness
10. desipience, imprudence,
wantonness 11. foolishness
12. indiscretion
foment... 3. egg 4. abet, brew, spur
5. bathe, rouse 6. arouse, excite,
incite 7. agitate, cherish
9. encourage, instigate
fomentation... 6. lotion, stupes
10. excitement 11. instigation
13. encouragement
Fomoriana (Celt Myth)... 10. sea
robbers (race of)
fonda... 3. inn 5. hotel 6. fonduk
fondle... 3. pet 4. neck 5. ingle
6. caress, coddle, cosset, foster,
pamper 7. cherish 8. blandish
fondling... 3. pet 4. fool 5. ninny
9. caressing, simpleton
10. love–making
fondly... 6. dearly 8. tenderly
14. affectionately
fondness... 3. gra 4. love 6. desire,
doting, liking, relish 8. appetite
9. affection 10. attachment,
propensity
fond of...

hunting .. **7.** venatic
sea .. **15.** thalassophilous
wife (overly) .. **8.** uxorious
font ... **3.** jet **4.** fons, lava **5.** stoup
   6. source, spring **7.** piscina
   8. fountain **9.** reservoir
food ... **3.** cud, pap **4.** cate, chow,
   diet, eats, fare, grub, junk (food), meat,
   tofu **5.** bread, manna, scran **6.** bulgur
   (wheat), cereal, gluten, quiche, snacks,
   Tex–Mex, viands **7.** aliment, cuisine,
   edibles, tapioca **8.** chili dog,
   fast–food, kreplach, munchies, victuals
   9. nutriment, nutrition, provender
   10. sustenance **11.** charcuterie,
   comestibles, nourishment
food (pert to) ...
animal .. **6.** forage **9.** provender
bit .. **4.** bite **6.** morsel **7.** munchie
devotee .. **7.** epicure, gourmet
digestant .. **5.** chyle
digested (partly) .. **5.** chyme
dislike of .. **9.** sitomania
   10. cibophobia
element .. **7.** protein, vitamin
fasting (Lenten) .. **9.** xerophagy
gods, the .. **6.** amrita **8.** ambrosia
heavenly .. **5.** manna
impure .. **4.** tref
provide .. **5.** cater, scaff **6.** tucker
room .. **5.** ambry **6.** pantry, spence
   7. butlery, pantler
fool ... **3.** ass, toy **4.** butt, dolt, dupe,
   jerk, nerd, nizy, raca (Bib), simp
   5. clown, idiot, moron, ninny
   6. dotard, jester, noodle, trifle, turkey
   7. buffoon, deceive, dingbat, fathead
   9. ignoramus, simpleton
foolhardy ... **4.** rash **7.** Icarian
   8. reckless **11.** adventurous
fool hen ... **6.** grouse
foolish ... **3.** mad **4.** daft, raca, rash,
   zany **5.** inane, inept, silly **6.** absurd,
   harish **6.** palty **6.** simple, stupid,
   unwise **7.** asinine, fatuous, idiotic,
   puerile, witless **9.** brainless, desipient,
   imprudent, ludicrous, senseless
   10. illadvised, irrational, ridiculous
   12. preposterous **13.** insignificant
foolish fancy ... **7.** chimera (chimaera)
foolishness ... **5.** folly **6.** levity
   9. absurdity, stupidity **10.** triviality
fool's bauble ... **7.** marotte
fool's gold ... **6.** pyrite
foot ... **3.** pad **6.** paw pes (pref)
   4. base, hoof, inch (part), sole, step,
   walk **5.** sum up, tread **6.** reckon
   7. residue **9.** calculate, extremity
foot (pert to) ...
bone .. **6.** tarsus **10.** metatarsus
care of .. **8.** pedicure, podiatry
   9. chiropody **11.** chiropodist
lever .. **5.** pedal **7.** treadle
like .. **8.** pediform
measure .. **4.** inch
part .. **3.** toe **4.** arch, heel, sole
prefix .. **4.** pedi
race course (anc) .. **7.** diaulos
reference to .. **5.** pedal, podal
rest .. **4.** rail **7.** cricket, hassock,

ottoman, support **8.** footrail
   9. footstool
sole .. **7.** plantar
unstressed part (Pros) .. **5.** arsis
foot, feet (metric) ... **4.** iamb, mora,
   unit **6.** dactyl, dipody, iambus
   7. anapest, dimeter, pyrrhic, spondee,
   tripody **8.** trimeter **9.** hexameter
   10. heptameter, pentameter
football terms ... **3.** end **4.** trap
   5. guard, slant **6.** center, safety,
   tackle **7.** flanker, lineman **8.** goalpost,
   receiver **9.** touchdown
   10. linebacker, yard marker
   11. quarterback
footed ... **5.** biped **7.** bipedal,
   megapod (large), metered
footing ... **4.** lace, rank **5.** basis,
   dance, tread **6.** status **7.** support
   8. foothold, progress, standing
   9. condition **11.** calculation
footman ... **6.** varlet, walker **7.** servant
   9. attendant **10.** pedestrian
footprint mold ... **7.** moulage
footway ... **7.** catwalk (Naut)
fop ... **3.** nob **4.** Adon, buck, dude
   5. dandy, puppy, sport, swell
   6. Adonis, masher **7.** coxcomb,
   gallant **9.** exquisite, pretender
   12. boulevardier
foppish ... **6.** dapper, spruce **7.** finical,
   foplike **8.** dandyish **9.** conceited,
   dandified
for ... **2.** to **3.** pro **5.** spite
   7. because, instead **8.** behalf of
   9. intending **10.** indicating
   11. preparation
for (pert to) ...
each .. **3.** per
example .. **2.** as, eg **4.** vide
   13. exempli gratia
fear .. **4.** lest
most part .. **6.** mostly **7.** chiefly,
   usually **9.** generally
nothing .. **6.** gratis, naught
   9. lagniappe (lagnappe)
this reason .. **4.** ergo **5.** hence
forage ... **4.** food, mast, raid **5.** spoil
   6. browse, ravage **7.** plunder
   9. pasturage
foramen ... **4.** pore **7.** opening, orifice,
   passage **8.** fenestra
foray ... **4.** raid **6.** ravage, sortie
   7. pillage **9.** incursion
forbear ... **4.** lose, shun **5.** avoid
   6. desist, endure **7.** abstain, decline,
   refrain **8.** part with **9.** be patient
forbearance ... **5.** mercy **6.** disuse,
   lenity **8.** leniency, mildness, patience
   9. tolerance **10.** abstinence,
   temperance **11.** forgiveness,
   placability
forbid ... **3.** ban **4.** deny, tabu, veto
   5. debar, taboo **6.** disbar, hinder,
   impede, oppose **7.** exclude, inhibit,
   prevent **8.** disallow, preclude, prohibit
   9. interdict, proscribe
   11. countermand
forbiddance ... **3.** ban **4.** veto
   11. unallowable **12.** illiberality,

interdiction, proscription
forbidden city... 5. Lhasa (Tibet),
    Pekin (walled, now Peiping)
forbidden food (Bib)... 4. tref
    8. terephah
forbidding... 4. grim, ugly 5. plain,
    stern 6. fierce, odious 9. offensive,
    revolting 10. prevention, unpleasant
    11. displeasing, prohibitive
force... 3. vim, vis 4. dint, make, urge
    5. drive, impel, power, press, repel,
    staff, vigor 6. coerce, compel, effect,
    energy, extort, hasten, strain
    7. impetus, meaning 8. eloquent,
    momentum, pressure, validity,
    violence 9. constrain, influence,
    puissance 10. compulsion, constraint
    11. necessitate
force (pert to)...
    alleged.. 2. od
    armed.. 4. army 5. posse
    by seizure.. 5. usurp
    down.. 7. detrude
    full.. 5. amain
    substance.. 8. catalyst
    unit.. 4. dyne 5. staff, tonal
    7. poundal
forced... 7. labored 9. reluctant,
    unwilling 10. artificial, compulsory,
    farfetched 11. constrained
forced feeding... 6. gavage
forceful... 5. valid 6. mighty, potent,
    strong 7. dynamic 8. eloquent,
    emphatic, vigorous 9. effective,
    energetic 10. compulsory
forces... 4. army 5. armed 6. troops
forcible... 6. cogent, mighty, potent
    7. violent, weighty 8. eloquent,
    emphatic, positive, puissant
    9. energetic 10. compulsory,
    impressive 11. influential
forcible entry... 10. effraction
forciform... 6. forked 7. furcate
    11. forficulate 14. scissors–shaped
ford... 4. wade 5. cross 6. stream
fore... 3. way 5. front, prior, track
    6. former 7. journey
forebear... 4. sire 5. elder 6. parent
    8. ancestor 10. antecedent,
    forefather, progenitor
forebode... 5. augur 7. betoken,
    portend, predict, presage 8. foretell
    15. prognostication
foreboding... 6. augury 8. croaking,
    sinister 11. pessimistic, presagement
    12. apprehension, presentiment
forecast... 4. bode, plan 6. scheme
    7. foresee, fortune, predict
    8. foretell, prophecy 9. calculate,
    foresight, foretoken 10. foreordain,
    prediction 12. predetermine
forecaster... 4. seer 5. vates 6. oracle
    7. diviner, palmist, prophet
    8. dopester, presager 10. astrologer,
    soothsayer 11. Nostradamus
    13. meteorologist 15. prognosticator
foreclose... 5. debar 6. hinder
    7. prevent, shut out 8. preclude
    10. dispossess
foredoom... 4. doom 7. predict
    12. predestinate

foredoomed... 3. fey 5. fatal
    8. accursed
forefather... 4. sire 5. elder 6. parent
    8. ancestor, forebear 10. progenitor
forefinger... 5. index
foregather... 4. meet 7. convene
    8. assemble 9. encounter
forego, forgo... 6. pass by 7. neglect,
    precede 8. renounce
foregoing... 4. past 5. above
    6. former, prefix 7. leading
    10. antecedent
foregone... 4. past 8. previous
    11. predestined, preordained,
    preresolved 13. predetermined
foregone conclusion... 9. certainty
forehead... 4. brow 8. calvaria,
    glabella, sinciput 9. assurance
    10. effrontery
forehead, divination by...
    11. metopomancy
forehead, frontal... 7. metopic
foreign... 4. xeno (comb form)
    5. alien, fremd 6. exotic, remote
    7. distant, outside (of country),
    strange 8. excluded 9. extrinsic,
    peregrine, unrelated 10. extraneous,
    outlandish 11. incongruous
    12. adventitious
foreign (pert to)...
    accent.. 4. burr 6. brogue, patois
    7. dialect
    crystals (Geol).. 7. epigene
    disease.. 7. ecdemic
    insertion.. 13. interpolation
    place.. 6. forane
    quarter.. 4. Para 5. Latin 6. French
    7. enclave
    service residence.. 9. consulate
foreigner... 5. alien 6. gringo
    8. outsider, stranger 9. outlander,
    uitlander 10. tramontane
    12. ultramontane
foreland... 8. headland 10. promontory
forelock... 4. bang 7. cowlick, fetlock
    8. linchpin 9. cotter pin, fastening
    (armor)
foreman... 4. boss 5. chief 6. leader
    7. juryman, overman 10. supervisor
    14. superintendent
foremost... 5. chief, first, front
    7. leading, supreme 8. headmost
    13. most important
forensic... 10. rhetorical
    13. argumentative
foreordain... 7. destine 9. predicate,
    preordain 12. foreordinate,
    predestinate, predetermine
forerun... 6. herald 7. advance,
    prelude, presage 8. announce,
    antecede 9. forestall, introduce,
    prefigure 10. anticipate, foreshadow
forerunner... 4. omen, sign 6. augury,
    herald 8. ancestor 9. harbinger,
    messenger, precursor 10. forefather,
    foreganger, progenitor, prognostic
    11. predecessor
foreshadow... 6. shadow (beforehand)
    7. presage 9. adumbrate, prefigure
foresight... 8. sagacity 9. prevision
    10. precaution, prediction,
    prescience, prevoyance, providence

11. omniscience 13. foreknowledge
forest... 4. wold, wood 5. grove, woods 6. jungle, timber 8. woodland 9. greenwood 10. timberland, wilderness
forest (pert to)...
deity.. 3. Pan 7. Aegipan
fire.. 5. crown, stand 6. ground 7. surface
fire–finding instrument.. 7. alidade
glade.. 6. camass (camas, cammas)
love of, lover of.. 9. nemophile, nemophily
regarding.. 6. sylvan 7. nemoral
tilled.. 7. thwaite
warden.. 6. ranger
forestall... 6. hinder 7. exclude, head off, prevent 9. intercept 10. anticipate, monopolize
foretell... 4. bode, spae 5. augur, insee 7. portend, predict, presage 8. forebode, forecast, prophesy 10. vaticinate 13. prognosticate
foretelling... 6. augury 7. fatidic 9. fatidical, prophetic 10. vaticinant
forethought... 8. prepense, prudence 9. foresight, provident 10. deliberate, precaution 12. aforethought, anticipation 13. premeditation
foretoken... 4. omen 7. presage 8. foreshow, indicant 10. presignify 13. preindication, prognosticate
foretooth... 5. biter 6. cutter 7. incisor 9. milk tooth
forever... 3. ake (Maori), aye (ay) 4. olam, ever 6. always, eterne 7. endless 8. infinity 9. continual, perpetual 10. constantly, invariably 11. ceaselessly, continually, incessantly, perpetually, unceasingly 12. interminably, unchangeably 13. everlastingly
forewarning... 4. omen 7. caution, portent 9. informing 10. admonition, foreboding
foreword... 5. proem 7. preface, prelude 8. exordium, preamble, prologue 12. introduction
forfeit... 4. fine, lose, loss 5. forgo, mulct 6. forego, pledge 7. deodand, penalty
forfeiture... 4. fine, loss 5. dédit, mulct 7. penalty 10. amercement
forfend... 5. avert 6. forbid 7. prevent, protect 8. preserve, prohibit
forfex... 6. shears
forgather... 4. meet 7. consort, convene 8. assemble 9. encounter 10. fraternize
forge... 4. coin, form, mint 5. feign 6. create, smithy, stithy, swinge 7. falsify, imitate 8. bloomery, smithery 11. counterfeit
forgery... 4. sham 6. fiction 9. falsehood, invention 11. counterfeit, fabrication 13. falsification
forget... 4. omit 5. lapse, remit 6. slight 7. neglect 9. disregard 11. disremember
forgetfulness... 5. Lethe (Myth), lotus (legend) 7. amnesia, amnesty

8. Manassah, oblivion 12. carelessness, heedlessness 13. obliviousness
forgive... 5. remit, spare 6. acquit, excuse, pardon 7. condone
forgiveness... 6. pardon 9. remission 10. absolution 11. condonation, exoneration, magnanimity
forgiving... 6. humane 8. merciful, placable 9. remissive 11. magnanimous
forgo... 4. quit 5. leave, waive 6. give up, resign 7. abstain, forbear, forfeit, forsake, neglect, refrain 8. overlook, renounce 9. do without 10. relinquish
forhoo... 7. abandon, despise
fork... 4. tine 5. prong 6. expend, pay out 7. dilemma, diverge 10. divaricate, divergence, headstream 11. bifurcation
fork (pert to)...
garden.. 5. graip
pickle.. 13. runcible spoon
table.. 5. salad 6. dinner, oyster 7. dessert 8. ice–cream
forked... 5. bifid 6. horned, ramous 7. divided, furcate 8. branched, crotched 9. ambiguous, equivocal 10. bifurcated, branchlike
forlorn... 4. reft 5. alone 6. abject, bereft 8. deserted, desolate, forsaken, helpless, pitiable 9. abandoned, destitute, miserable 10. friendless 12. disconsolate
form... 4. body, cast, idea, mold, rite 5. build, guise, model, shape 6. beauty, create, figure, invent, ritual 7. compose, contour, formula, outline, pattern, profile, species, variety 8. ceremony, conceive, document 9. establish, formality 10. appearance 11. arrangement 12. conformation 13. configuration, questionnaire 15. conventionality
form (pert to)...
bust.. 6. taille
chainlike.. 8. catenate
deceptive.. 5. ghost 7. specter 8. phantasm
display.. 4. rack
good.. 4. chic 6. fettle
government.. 6. polity
hollow.. 5. shell
into fabric.. 4. knit, spin 5. weave
primitive.. 9. prototype
spiral.. 5. helix
suffix.. 5. shape 10. resembling
formal... 4. prim 5. exact, stiff 6. solemn 7. orderly, outward, precise, regular, stilted 8. affected, apparent, starched 9. formative 10. ceremonial, methodical 11. pharisaical, ritualistic, superficial 12. conventional
formal introduction... 5. debut 12. presentation
formalities... 5. rites 9. etiquette 10. ceremonies
formal warning... 5. alarm 6. caveat 12. caveat emptor
format... 4. size 5. shape, style

formation... 4. form 5. order
9. structure 11. arrangement,
composition 12. construction
formation (pert to)...
chain (twisted).. 9. torquated
geologic.. 7. terrain, terrane
military.. 4. line 5. herse 7. echelon
sand.. 4. dene, dune
formed... 4. made 5. built 7. created,
decided, matured, settled 8. arranged
9. fashioned, organized
11. constructed
formed (pert to)...
by law.. 9. corporate
by lips.. 6. labial
mountain foot.. 8. piedmont
on earth's surface.. 7. epigene
plates (two).. 11. bilamellate
formed into...
chain.. 8. catenate 9. torquated
fabric.. 4. spun 5. woven 7. knitted
mass (hard).. 4. iced 5. caked
6. frozen 9. congealed
mosaic.. 9. tessellar 11. tessellated
former... 2. ex 3. old 4. erst, late,
once, past 5. front, prior 6. passed,
whilom 7. ancient, earlier 8. previous
9. foregoing, preceding
10. antecedent
former days... 3. eld, old 4. yore
formerly... 3. nee 4. erst, once, then
6. before, whilom 7. one–time
8. sometime 9. aforetime, erstwhile
10. heretofore, previously
formicary... 7. anthill 8. ant's nest
formicid... 3. ant 5. emmet
7. Formica
formidable... 7. fearful 8. alarming,
dreadful, menacing, terrible
9. difficult 11. redoubtable,
threatening
formless... 5. arupa 7. anidian, chaotic
9. amorphous, shapeless
13. indeterminate
Formosa, Taiwan...
capital.. 6. Taipei
city.. 6. Tainan 7. Hualien, Keelung
9. Kaohsiung
group.. 6. Penghu (64 Isls)
island.. 5. Matsu 6. Quemoy
formula... 3. law 4. form, rule
5. axiom, creed, lurry, maxim, model
6. method, recipe, ritual
12. prescription
forsake... 4. deny, quit, shun 5. avoid,
leave 6. depart, desert, refuse, reject
7. abandon 8. renounce, withdraw
9. surrender
forsaken... 4. lorn 6. vacant 7. forlorn
8. deserted, lovelorn, rejected
9. abandoned
forspeak... 5. curse 6. forbid
7. asperse, bewitch 8. renounce
9. relinquish
fort... 5. redan, tower 6. abatis,
castle, escarp, glacis (bank of)
7. bastion, bulwark, castlet
8. bastille, fastness, fortress
10. stronghold 13. fortification,
propugnaculum
Fort (Fr Ind War)... 9. Necessity
forth... 3. out 4. away 6. abroad,

onward 7. forward, outward
forthright... 5. ahead 7. frankly
8. forwards 9. downright
11. immediately, straightway
13. straightforth
forthwith... 3. now 6. pronto
8. promptly 9. summarily
11. immediately, straightway
fortification... 4. wall 5. redan
6. abatis 7. bastion, citadel, defense,
parados, ravelin, redoubt 8. barbette
(part), fortress 10. stronghold
13. corroboration, strengthening
fortify... 3. arm, man 4. gird 5. add
to, spike, stank 6. defend, secure
7. confirm, refresh 8. embattle
10. adulterate (drink), invigorate,
strengthen, vitaminize 11. corroborate
fortitude... 6. virtue 7. bravery,
courage 8. strength 9. endurance
10. resolution 12. resoluteness
14. impregnability
fortress... see *fort*
fortuitous... 3. hap 6. chance
10. accidental 12. unexpectedly
fortunate... 5. happy, lucky 6. timely
7. favored 10. auspicious,
prosperous, successful
12. providential
fortune... 3. hap, lot 4. doom, fate,
luck 6. chance, estate, riches, wealth
7. destiny, success 8. accident
10. prosperity 13. circumstances
fortune (pert to)...
gypsy.. 4. bahi
ill.. 9. mischance
planet (Astrol).. 5. Venus 7. Jupiter
teller.. 4. seer 5. sibyl, Tyche
6. oracle 7. spaeman
forward... 2. on, to 3. aid 4. abet,
bold, fore, help, pert, send, ship,
vain 5. ahead, along, eager, front,
impel, ready, relay, saucy, ultra
6. active, bright, hasten, onward
7. deliver, earnest, extreme, further,
radical, willing 8. advanced,
immodest, impudent, transmit
9. audacious, encourage
10. precocious 11. progressive
12. presumptuous
forward moving (Zool)... 5. proal
(digestion) 11. mastication
fosse, foss... 3. pit 4. moat 5. canal,
ditch, fossa, grave 6. cavity, trench
10. depression
fossil, fossils... 5. relic, stone
7. antique, remains
fossil (pert to)...
egg.. 7. ovulite
footprint.. 7. ichnite
resin.. 5. amber
shell.. 6. dolite 8. ammonite
site.. 8. Badlands (Dakota, Nebraska)
study of.. 12. paleontology
toothlike.. 8. conodont
worm track.. 7. nereite
foster... 4. rear 5. breed, nurse
7. cherish, gratify, indulge, promote
9. cultivate
fosterage... 7. nurture
11. development
foster child... 4. dalt 5. norry (nurry)

7. stepson 8. nursling
12. stepdaughter
fought... see *fight*
foul... 3. bad 4. olid, ugly 5. dirty,
fetid, grimy, nasty, reeky, spoil, sully
6. defame, filthy, malign, odious,
putrid, rotten, thwart, unfair
7. abusive, confuse, noisome,
obscene, profane, unclean
8. entangle, indecent, infamous,
shameful, stagnant, stinking
9. dishonest, obnoxious
10. complicate, malodorous,
scurrilous 11. contaminate,
ill–smelling, unfavorable
12. inauspicious, unpropitious
foul play... 6. murder, unfair (play)
7. perfidy 8. violence 9. deception,
treachery 10. unfairness
found... 3. fix 4. base, cast 5. endow,
set up 6. attach, create 9. establish,
institute, originate
foundation... 3. bed 4. base, plot, sill
5. basal, basis 6. legacy, riprap
7. bedding, charity, premise, support
8. cosmetic, creation, donation,
pedestal 9. placement
11. corporation 13. justification
found by chance (thing)...
11. serendipity
founded on...
base.. 10. predicated
evidence.. 10. evidential
experience.. 7. empiric 9. empirical
imagination.. 7. Utopian
founder... 4. fail, fall, sink 6. author
7. capsize, creator, stumble
8. miscarry 9. break down, organizer
10. originator
foundling... 3. oaf 4. waif 5. child
(unclaimed) 6. orphan 8. derelict,
nursling
fountain... 3. jet, spa 4. font, head,
well 6. spring 9. reservoir
11. scuttlebutt (ship's)
12. fountainhead
fountain (pert to)...
god of.. 4. Fons
Muse (Gr).. 8. Aganippe
nymph.. 5. naiad 6. Egeria
of Lions.. 8. Alhambra (Granada, Sp)
four (pert to)...
bits.. 7. quarter (silver)
Books.. 8. Classics (Chin)
footed.. 8. tetrapod
genii, of Amenti.. 13. Horus' children
group.. 6. tetrad
Hundred.. 5. elect, elite 7. society
letters, word of.. 9. tetragram
seas.. 13. Great Britain's
senses (Bib).. 15. interpretations
four–flusher... 5. cheat, fraud
7. bluffer 8. impostor 9. pretender
fourth (pert to)...
Caliph.. 3. Ali
century martyr.. 8. St Blaise
estate.. 5. press 10. newspapers
part.. 6. fardel 7. quarter
stomach (cow).. 8. abomasum
fowl... 3. hen 6. bantam, Gallus
7. Blue Hen, broiler, chicken,
Dorking, leghorn, Minorca, poultry,

rooster, seafowl 8. pheasant
9. guinea hen, waterfowl
11. chanticleer
fox... 3. cub, tod 4. stag 5. vixen
fox (pert to)...
African.. 4. asse
Asian.. 5. adive 6. corsac
female.. 5. vixen
genus.. 6. Vulpes
hedge (hunter's).. 4. oxer
foot.. 3. pad
Indian.. 10. Algonquian
Russian.. 6. corsac 7. karagan
foxglove... 9. digitalis
foxy... 3. sly 6. artful, crafty
7. cunning
foyer... 5. lobby 8. anteroom, entrance
9. greenroom
fracas... 3. row 5. brawl, melee,
set–to 6. uproar 7. quarrel
9. commotion 11. disturbance
fraction... 3. bit 4. part 5. piece,
scrap 6. sector 7. element, ruction
8. division, fragment 9. commotion
fractious... 4. ugly 5. cross 6. unruly
7. peevish, waspish 8. perverse,
snappish 9. irritable 10. ill–humored
11. disobedient
fracture... 4. rend 5. break, cleft,
crack 6. breach, injury 7. rupture
fragile... 4. weak 5. brash, frail
6. frough (obs), infirm, slight
7. brittle 8. delicate, slattery
9. frangible
fragment... 3. bit, ort 4. chip, grot,
part, snip 5. groat, piece, relic,
scrap, shard, sherd, shred, torso (art)
6. morsel, sippet 7. flinder
8. fraction
fragments... 3. ana 6. fardel, groats,
rubble 8. buttings, excerpts, flinders
10. miscellany 11. smithereens
fragrance... 4. odor 5. aroma, elemi,
smell 7. incense, perfume
9. redolence
fragrant... 4. nard 5. balmy, olent,
spicy, sweet 7. odorous 8. aromatic,
redolent 9. ambrosial 11. odoriferous
12. sweet–scented
13. sweet–smelling
frail... 4. girl, thin, weak 5. woman
6. basket (fig), feeble, sickly, slimsy
7. brittle, fragile 8. strumpet,
unchaste 10. weak–willed
12. destructible
frailty... 5. fault 6. defect 7. failing
8. thinness, weakness 9. fragility,
infirmity 12. imperfection
frame... 4. body, make, plan, rack,
sess, sill 5. build, easel, grate,
herse, knape 6. abacus, border,
charge (falsely), direct, tenter
7. carcass, chassis, cresset (torch),
fashion, prepare, setting, taboret
8. conceive, skeleton 9. construct
10. prearrange
framework... 4. rack, sill 5. cadre,
shell 6. cradle 7. trestle 8. skeleton
11. scaffolding
France... see also *French*
anc name.. 4. Gaul 6. Gallia
Bay.. 6. Biscay

Botanical Gardens.. 16. Jardin des Plantes
capital.. 5. Paris
city.. 4. Nice 5. Lyons 7. LeHavre 8. Bordeaux, Toulouse 9. Marseille 10. Strasbourg
dread of.. 11. Gallophobia
island.. 6. Comoro (Afr), Tahiti 7. Corsica, Réunion 10. Guadeloupe (Leeward), Martinique (Windward) 12. New Caledonia
lover of.. 10. Gallophile
mountain.. 4. Alps, Jura 5. Pelat 8. Pyrenees 9. Mont Blanc 11. Pic Montcalm
port.. 4. Caen 5. Brest, Havre 6. Calais, Toulon 8. Bordeaux 9. Dunkerque (Dunkirk)
resort.. 3. Pau 5. Vichy 6. Cannes, Menton (Mentone) 7. Riviera 11. Aix–les–Bains (anc)
river.. 3. Lys 4. Yser 5. Aisne, Eiser, Loire, Meuse, Rhône, Seine
Southern.. 4. Midi
Verdun battle site.. 4. Vaux
franchise... 4. vote 5. right 6. patent 7. freedom, license 8. immunity, suffrage 9. exemption
frank... 4. free, mail, open 5. blunt, naive, plain 6. candid, direct, honest 7. artless, liberal, sincere 8. generous 9. ingenuous, outspoken 10. unreserved 11. frankfurter 15. straightforward, unsophisticated
frankincense... 4. thus 8. gum resin, olibanum 9. fragrance
Frankish (pert to)...
dynasty.. 11. Carolingian, Merovingian
king.. 5. Pepin 6. Clovis
law.. 5. Salic
site.. 4. Gaul
tribe (anc).. 6. Salian
Franklin, Benjamin... 11. Poor Richard
frantic... 3. mad 4. mang 5. moved, rabid 7. furious 8. frenetic, frenzied 9. delirious, desperate, turbulent 10. distracted, distraught 11. overwrought
frappé... 3. ice 5. chill 6. freeze 7. dessert, mixture (sweet) 8. beverage
fraternal... 4. kind 5. order, twins 7. society 8. friendly 9. brotherly
fraud... 4. fake, sham, wile 5. cheat, covin, craft, guile 6. deceit, ringer 7. defraud, roguery 8. artifice, cozenage, impostor, subtlety, swindler, trickery 9. deception, imposture, stratagem 10. imposition 13. circumvention
fraudulence... 9. improbity 10. subreption
fraudulent... 4. fake, wily 5. snide 6. crafty, quacky 7. cunning, knavish 8. cheating, guileful, spurious 9. deceitful, deceiving, deceptive, designing, dishonest, insidious 10. fallacious 11. counterfeit, treacherous
fraught... 4. lade, load 5. cargo, equip, laden 6. burden, filled

7. freight 9. freighted, transport
fray... 4. fret (cloth), wear 5. broil, dread, melee, panic, ravel 6. affray, combat, fright, hassle, terror, tumult 7. contest, frazzle, ruction 9. commotion 12. apprehension
freak... 4. flam, lune, whim 5. fancy, prank, sport 6. streak, vagary 7. caprice, checker, crochet, monster 9. eccentric, variegate 11. monstrosity 12. whimsicality
freakish... 7. curious 9. eccentric, fantastic, whimsical 10. capricious, changeable
freck... 4. bold, hale 5. eager, frack, lusty, ready, stout 6. strong 7. forward 8. desirous
freckle... 4. mark, spot 7. blemish, ephelis, lentigo, speckle 10. ferntickle
free... 3. rid 4. easy, open 5. clear, frank, loose 6. acquit, candid, exempt, gratis, immune, vacant 7. absolve, inexact, manumit, not busy, release, relieve, unbound 8. liberate 9. extricate, footloose, voluntary 10. autonomous, gratuitous, unconfined, unhampered 11. emancipated 12. uncontrolled, unrestrained, unrestricted
free (pert to)...
bacteria.. 7. aseptic, sterile
difficulty.. 9. extricate
doubt.. 7. resolve
flesh (dietary).. 6. maigre
knots.. 7. enodate, unravel
reproach.. 9. blameless
slavery.. 7. manumit 10. emancipate
suspicion.. 5. clear, purge 6. acquit 7. absolve 9. exculpate, exonerate
sweetness.. 3. sec
freebooter... 5. rover 6. pirate 8. pillager 9. plunderer 10. filibuster
freed... 3. rid 6. loosed, spared, untied 8. released 9. delivered, liberated 10. manumitted 11. emancipated
freedom... 6. candor 7. leisure, liberty, license 8. latitude 9. exemption, privilege 11. manumission 12. emancipation, independence
freedom (pert to)...
abused.. 7. liberty (excess), license
from doubt.. 9. assurance, certitude
from sepsis.. 7. asepsis
Freedom Our Rock (motto)... 7. Tammany (1789)
free enterprise... 6. policy 8. commerce 10. capitalism 15. noninterference
freely... 6. gratis 7. largely, readily 9. bountiful, copiously, liberally, willingly 10. abundantly, generously 11. bounteously, plenteously, plentifully, voluntarily 12. gratuitously
freeze... 3. ice 5. be–ice, chill 6. steeve 7. congeal, terrify 8. preserve, solidify 9. stabilize 11. anesthetize, refrigerate
freezing, science of... 10. cyrogenics
freight... 4. load, ship 5. cargo, laden, train 6. burden, charge, lading 7. fraught, rattler 8. shipment

9. transport 14. transportation
freight boat... 5. barge 9. freighter
freit, freet... 4. omen 5. charm
fremd (obs)... 5. alien 7. foreign,
  hostile 9. unrelated
French (people)...
  artist, painter.. 4. Doré 5. Corot,
  David, Monet 6. Gervex, Greuze,
  Renoir 7. Gauguin, Lemoine, Matisse
  8. Daubigny, Rousseau
  author.. 4. Hugo, Loti, Zola
  5. Dumas, Renan, Verne (Jules)
  6. Balzac, Proust
  caricaturist.. 7. Gavarni
  chemist.. 7. Gautier, Holbach, Pasteur
  composer.. 4. Lalo 5. Bizet, Ravel
  6. Gounod 7. Debussy
  conqueror (anc).. 6. Clovis
  crusader.. 7. Godfrey (of Bouillon)
  dramatist.. 6. Favart 8. Quinault
  dynasty.. 5. Caput 6. Valois
  Foreign Legion creator, 1831..
  8. Philippe (Louis)
  impressionist.. 5. Monet 8. Pissarro
  marshal.. 3. Ney 4. Foch, Niel, Saxe
  5. Murat
  naturalist.. 8. Audebert
  navigator.. 9. Freycinet
  pantomimist.. 7. Pierrot
  patron saint.. 5. Denis 6. Martin
  philosopher.. 5. Bayle, Camus
  6. Pascal 7. Abelard 8. Rousseau
  9. Descartes
  physician.. 7. Laveran
  physicist.. 5. Binet 6. Ampere
  poet.. 6. Villon 7. Gilbert, Mistral
  8. Rousseau 9. Deschamps
  radical.. 7. Jacobin
  scientist.. 5. Curie 7. Pasteur
  sculptor.. 4. Etex 5. Barye, Rodin
  6. Gerome, Millet
  statesman.. 4. Coty 5. Laine, Laval,
  Morny 6. Carnot 7. Briande, Herriot
  8. DeGaulle
  therapist.. 4. Coué
French (pert to)...
  academic rank.. 6. agrégé
  Academy.. 12. The Institute
  and.. 2. et
  annuity.. 5. rente
  anthem.. 12. Marseillaise
  article.. 2. la, le, un 3. les, une
  beast.. 4. bête
  calender (Rev).. 6. Nivose 7. Ventose
  champagne.. 2. Ay
  cheese.. 4. Brie 6. Chevre
  9. Camembert
  chorus (male).. 7. orpheon
  coach.. 6. fiacre
  coat–of–arms.. 10. fleur–de–lis
  coffee (black).. 8. café noir
  company (Bus).. 3. cie
  crown (gold coin).. 3. ecu
  cult (art).. 7. Dadaism
  daisy.. 10. marguerite
  dance.. 3. bal 5. gavot 6. cancan
  decree, edict.. 5. arrêt
  dialect.. 6. patois
  dugout.. 4. abri
  father.. 4. père
  fortification.. 7. parados
  fugitive.. 6. émigré

God.. 4. Dieu
hairdresser.. 7. friseur
hat.. 5. beret 7. chapeau
here.. 3. ici
inn.. 6. hostel
lace.. 5. Cluny
language (Provence).. 9. Provençal
laugh.. 3. ris
liquor.. 8. absinthe (banned 1915)
mask.. 4. loup
morning.. 5. matin
mountain peak.. 3. pic
narcissus.. 10. polyanthus
native.. 8. Gallican
nursemaid.. 5. bonne
ornaments (set of).. 6. parure
outcast.. 5. Agote, Cagot 6. pariah
pancake.. 5. crepe
parliament.. 5. Sénat
pastry.. 7. dariole, galette
plane.. 4. avion
poem, poetry.. 3. dit 6. aubade,
  rondel
police.. 6. Sûreté 8. gendarme
political club.. 7. Jacobin
porcelain.. 6. Sèvres 7. Limoges
priest.. 4. abbe, père
racecourse.. 7. Auteuil
restaurant.. 4. café 6. bistro
sauce.. 8. ravigote 9. allemande
school.. 5. école, lycée
school of painting.. 8. Barbizon
securities.. 6. rentes
smoking room.. 9. estaminet
soldier.. 5. poilu 6. Zouave
stable.. 6. écurie
stock exchange.. 6. Bourse
storm.. 5. orage
street.. 3. rue
summer.. 3. été
theater.. 16. Comédie Française
verse.. 3. lai 4. alba 6. rondel
  7. ballade, virelay
wall.. 3. mur
water.. 3. eau
wind.. 7. mistral
wine.. 5. Medoc 6. Barsac, brandy,
  claret, Cognac, masdeu 8. Bordeaux,
  Burgundy, sauterne 10. Beaujolais
world.. 5. monde
Frenchman... 4. frog, Gaul 6. froggy,
  Picard (of Picardy) 8. Parisian
  9. frogeater
Frenchy... 6. Gallic
frenzied... 4. amok 5. rabid
  7. enraged, frantic, madding
  8. maddened 9. turbulent
  11. overwrought
frenzy... 3. mad 5. furor, mania
  7. frantic, madness 8. delirium
  9. agitation 10. excitement,
  turbulence
frequent:.. 3. oft 5. haunt, often,
  usual 6. common 7. current
  8. familiar, habitual, intimate (with)
  9. recurrent 10. persistent
frequenter... 7. habitué, visitor
  8. attender
frère... 5. friar 7. brother
fresh... 3. new 4. good, lush 5. relay,
  ruddy, sound, sweet 6. florid, lively,
  strong, unused 7. healthy, unfaded,

untried 8. impudent, original
10. additional, refreshing, unimpaired
13. inexperienced
freshen... 4. cool 5. renew 6. revive
7. refresh, sweeten
freshet... 4. gush 5. flood, spate
6. stream 7. outflow, torrent
10. inundation (sudden)
freshman... 5. frosh 6. novice
7. student
freshness... 7. newness, novelty
8. verdancy 9. impudence
11. originality
freshwater fish... 2. id (ide) 4. chub,
dace, inid (porpoise) 6. anabas
7. herring 8. drumfish
fret... 3. eat, nag, orp, rub, vex
4. fray, fume, gall, gnaw, stew
5. adorn, annoy, chafe, grate, tease,
worry 6. abrade, grieve, harass,
plague, strait 7. agitate, consume,
disturb, network, roughen
8. diminish, irritate, ornament
fretful... 5. angry 6. repine 7. peevish,
pettish 8. captious, petulant
9. impatient, irascible, irritable,
plaintive, querulous 10. ill—humored,
ill—natured
friable... 5. crisp, frail, mealy, short
7. brittle 8. fragible
friar... 3. fra 4. fish (small), monk
5. abbot, Minor 6. lister (obs)
7. brother 8. cenobite, Minorite,
Teresian (anc) 9. Carmelite,
Dominican 10. Franciscan
11. Augustinian
friction... 7. erasure, rubbing
8. clashing 9. attrition, disaccord
10. resistance 12. disagreement
13. counteraction
friend... 3. ami, pal 4. ally, amie,
chum, kith, sect 5. amigo, crony
7. comrade 8. promoter
9. associate, attendant, companion,
supporter 10. benefactor, sweetheart,
well—wisher
Friend... 6. Quaker
friendless... 5. alone 7. forlorn
8. helpless 9. destitute (friends)
friendly... 3. sib 4. kind 7. affable
8. amicable, homelike, sociable
9. favorable 10. harmonious,
hospitable 11. comfortable
Friendly Islands... 5. Tonga
friendship... 4. kelt 5. amity
7. harmony 8. good will, relation
9. affection, right hand
10. attachment 12. friendliness
frieze... 4. band (sculptured) 5. adorn,
chase 6. taenia (Doric) 8. ornament,
trimming 10. decoration, embroidery
Frigga, Norse Myth (pert to)...
goddess.. 3. sky
maid.. 5. Fulla
named for.. 6. Friday
wife of.. 4. Odin
fright... 3. awe 4. fear, ogre 5. alarm,
panic, scare, shock 6. terror
7. eyesore 13. consternation
frighten... 3. cow 5. alarm, appal,
scare 7. startle, terrify 10. intimidate
frightened... 3. rad 5. eerie, timid

6. afraid 8. skittish
frightful... 5. awful, great 6. horrid
7. hideous 8. alarming, dreadful,
horrible, shocking, terrible, terrific
11. frightening
frightfulness... 13. atrociousness
15. Schrecklichkeit
frigid... 3. icy 4. cold 5. stiff
6. formal 8. freezing, impotent,
reserved
frijol, frijole... 4. bean
frill... 4. purl 5. jabot, ruche (rouche)
6. border, edging, ruffle 8. furbelow
9. frillback (pigeon) 11. superfluity
fringe... 4. lace, loma, tuft 5. thrum
6. border, edging, margin 8. ciliella,
trimming
frisk... 4. skip 5. brisk, caper 6. frolic,
gambol, lively, search 7. disport,
rejoice
frisky... 3. gay 6. lively 7. playful
8. sportive 10. frolicsome
frisson... 5. chill 6. quiver, shiver, thrill
7. shudder 10. excitement
frivolous... 5. giddy, petty 6. fickle,
slight 7. fatuous, trivial 9. worthless
13. shallow—witted
frock... 4. gown, wrap 5. dress, tunic
6. jersey, kirtle (anc), mantle
7. garment, soutane
frog... 3. pad (horse's) 4. Rana, toad
5. Anura 6. peeper 7. croaker,
paddock, tadpole 8. Amphibia,
pollywog 9. Batrachia, Frenchman,
Salientia 10. hoarseness
froglike... 6. ranine
frogman... 5. diver 6. seaman
7. swimmer 9. Frenchman
frog pond... 8. ranarium
frolic... 3. fun 4. lark, ogle, play,
ramp, romp 5. binge, caper, frisk,
prank, spree, trick 6. gambol, shindy
7. disport, marlock, shindig, wassail
8. carousal
frolicsome... 3. gay 5. merry 6. frisky
7. playful, waggish 8. sportive
from... 2. at, de (pref), of 3. apo
(pref) 4. away 5. above, out of
6. source 8. away from, downward
from (pert to)...
beginning to end.. 4. over 7. through
egg to apple.. 16. ab ovo usque ad
mala
head to foot.. 7. cap—a—pie
slang.. 10. soup to nuts 11. stem to
stern
front... 3. bow, van 4. face, fore
5. aface, afore, blind (false), forne
(obs) 6. before, façade 7. obverse
8. confront, mediator 9. forefront
10. appearance, figurehead
11. affectation 12. intermediary
frontier defense... 11. arcifinius
frontiersman... 5. Boone 6. Carson
(Kit)
frost... 3. ice, mat 4. cold, foam, rime
5. chill 6. freeze, whiten 7. failure
8. severity (manner)
14. unfriendliness
frosty... 3. icy 4. cold, gray, rimy
5. chill, hoary, white 6. frigid
8. freezing, inimical 10. unfriendly

froth . . . 4. foam, scum, suds 5. spume,
yeast 6. lather 7. bubbles
frothy . . . 5. foamy, light, sudsy
7. spumous 8. sillabub
frow . . . 4. froe (tool), wife 5. woman
6. maenad 8. slattern
froward . . . 5. cross 7. peevish,
wayward 8. perverse, petulant,
scolding, shrewish, untoward
9. obstinate 10. refractory, unyielding
11. disobedient 12. ungovernable
frowl . . . 9. guillemot
frown . . . 5. gloom, lower, scowl
6. glower
frowsey, frowzy . . . 5. musty
7. unkempt 8. slovenly 9. offensive
10. discordant, disordered
frozen . . . 4. cold 5. frore (anc), froze,
gelid, glacé 6. chilly, mousse
7. chilled 9. congealed, terrified,
unfeeling, unmovable 10. unyielding
11. coldhearted 12. refrigerated
frugal . . . 5. chary 6. meager, saving
7. careful, sparing, thrifty
9. provident 10. economical,
unwasteful 11. inexpensive
12. parsimonious
frugality . . . 6. thrift 7. economy
9. parsimony
fruit (types of) . . . 3. fig 4. lime, pear,
plum, pome 5. apple, berry, drupe,
grape, guava, lemon, mango, melon,
olive, peach, pomum 6. banana,
cherry, orange, papaya, pawpaw,
pomelo 7. apricot, azarole, genipap,
tangelo 8. shaddock 9. persimmon,
tangerine 10. grapefruit, watermelon
11. pomegranate
fruit . . . 4. diet, food 5. yield, young
7. benefit, product 9. offspring,
outgrowth, posterity 11. consequence
fruit (pert to) . . .
 aggregate . . 7. etaerio
 astringent . . 4. sloe
 basket . . 6. pottle
 buttercup . . 6. achene 8. achenium
 class . . 6. simple 9. aggregate
  10. collective
 cordial . . 7. ratafia (ratafee)
 decay . . 4. blet
 dried . . 6. raisin 7. apricot
 drink . . 3. ade 6. nectar
 Goddess . . 6. Pomona
 gourd . . 4. pepo 7. chayote
 grapefruit . . 6. pomelo
 imperfect . . 6. nubbin
 jelly substance . . 6. pectin
 Jove's . . 9. persimmon
 part . . 7. epicarp 8. mesocarp,
  pericarp 9. sarcocarp
 preserve . . 7. compote 9. marmalade
 pulpy . . 3. uva
 rose . . 3. hip
 study of . . 9. carpology
 tree . . 4. date, nuts 5. regma
  6. camato, samara (winged)
 tropical . . 3. fig 4. date 5. guava,
  mango, papaw (pawpaw) 6. papaya
fruitful . . . 7. fertile, uberous
8. abundant, prolific 9. plenteous
fruitfulness, goddess of . . .
7. Demeter

fruitless . . . 4. vain 6. barren 7. sterile,
useless 10. profitless 11. ineffectual
12. unprofitable, unsuccessful
frump . . . 3. vex 4. mock, snub
5. crone, flout, shrew 6. gossip,
insult 7. provoke 8. irritate
frustrate . . . 4. balk, bilk, foil 5. block,
cross, elude 6. baffle, blight, defeat,
outwit, thwart 7. nullify 8. confound
9. checkmate 10. circumvent,
disappoint, disconcert
frustrater . . . 7. marplot 8. thwarter
frustration . . . 4. balk 6. defeat, fiasco
13. circumvention
14. disappointment
15. disillusionment
fry . . . 4. cook 5. brood (fish), group,
saute, young 7. stir-fry 9. offspring
frying pan . . . 6. spider 7. skillet
fubsy . . . 5. plump, short 6. chubby
fuddle . . . 4. bout (drinking) 5. drink
(strong), spree 6. muddle, tipple
7. confuse 9. confusion, inebriate
fudge . . . 4. fake 5. candy, cheat
6. bungle, humbug 7. trump up
8. nonsense 9. makeshift
10. substitute 11. counterfeit
Fuegian . . . 3. Ona 5. tribe 6. Indian,
Yakgan 8. Alikuluf 14. Tierra del
Fuego (pert to)
fuel . . . 3. gas, log, oil 4. coal, coke,
peat 6. diesel, elding 7. gasohol,
nuclear, synfuel 8. gasoline
9. petroleum 11. combustible
fugie . . . 4. cock (nonfighter) 6. coward
fugient . . . 7. fleeing 8. retiring
fugitive . . . 5. exile 6. outlaw, roving
7. fleeing, refugee, roaming, runaway
8. fleeting, unstable, vagabond,
volatile 9. fugacious, strolling,
uncertain 10. evanescent
fugue . . . 5. theme, tonal 7. amnesia,
stretto (stretta) 9. psychosis, ricercare
fulcrum . . . 4. axis, bait, prop 5. pivot,
scale (fish), thole 7. support
fulfill . . . 4. meet 6. finish, redeem
7. execute, satisfy 8. complete
10. accomplish, effectuate
fulfillment . . . 8. fruition 9. execution,
flowering 10. completion
11. performance 14. accomplishment
full . . . 3. fat 4. fill 5. drunk, sated
6. entire, filled, rotund 7. perfect,
plenary, replete, satiety 8. abundant,
adequate, complete, occupied,
resonant, satiated, thorough
9. satisfied
full (pert to) . . .
 blooded . . 6. virile 8. rubicund
  12. thoroughbred
 bloom . . 8. anthesis, blooming, maturity
 control . . 7. mastery 10. domination
 force . . 5. amain
 house . . 3. SRO
full of . . .
 cracks . . 6. rimose
 hollows . . 8. lacunose
 love . . 7. amative, amatory
 meaning . . 5. pithy 10. meaningful
 openings (tiny) . . 6. porous
 sand . . 7. arenose 8. sabulous
 substance . . 5. meaty

suffix .. 3. ose
thorns .. 6. briary
vigor .. 5. lusty
fulness, fullness ... 4. much
  7. orotund, pleroma, satiety, surfeit
  9. abundance, greatness, plenitude,
  repletion, resonance 10. perfection
  12. completeness
fulsome ... 3. bad, fat 4. base, foul,
  full 5. nasty, plump, suave
  7. copious, overfed 8. abundant
  9. offensive, overgrown, repulsive
  10. disgusting
Fulton's Folly ... 8. Clermont
fumble ... 5. grope 6. bungle, huddle,
  mumble 7. confuse
fume ... 4. odor, rage, rant, reek
  5. anger, smoke, steam, vapor
  8. outburst 10. excitement,
  exhalation
fun ... 4. gell, jest, joke, play 5. chaff,
  sport 9. amusement, merriment
function ... 3. act, use 4. duty, rite,
  role, work 5. party 6. office
  7. calling, operate, purpose, service
  8. ceremony, province
  10. providence
function (pert to) ...
  math .. 4. sine 6. cosine
  mind .. 8. ideation
  social .. 3. tea
functional ... 8. official 9. operative
  11. ceremonious, utilitarian
fund ... 5. basis, money 6. bottom,
  supply 7. capital, provide, revenue
  10. foundation, groundwork
fundamental ... 4. tone 5. basal, basic,
  vital 7. basilar, organic, primary,
  radical 8. original, rudiment
  9. elemental, essential, principle
  10. elementary
Fundamental Orders (US Hist) ...
  8. document (1639) 12. Constitution
  (first, 1639 Conn)
funds ... 5. means 6. assets, moneys
  8. finances
funeral ... 5. rites 6. burial 8. exequies
  9. obsequies 10. procession
funeral (pert to) ...
  bell .. 5. knell
  ceremony .. 6. exequy
  hymn, song .. 5. dirge, éloge, elogy
    7. requiem 8. threnody
  oration, poem .. 5. elegy
  pile .. 4. pyre
  procession .. 6. exequy 7. cortege
  vase .. 3. urn
funereal ... 3. sad 4. dark 6. dismal,
  solemn 8. exequial, mournful
  9. dirgelike
fungi ... 5. rusts, Uredo 6. mildew
  7. Boletus
fungoid ... 6. fungal, fungus
fungus ... 4. bunt, mold, rust, smut
  5. ergot, morel, uredo 6. agaric,
  mildew 7. aminita, blewits, boletus,
  geaster, truffle 8. mushroom, puffball
  9. toadstool
fungus, edible ... 5. morel 7. truffle
  8. mushroom
funguslike ... 6. agaric
funk ... 4. kick, odor, rage 5. panic,

smell (bad), smoke, spark 6. flinch,
  fright, shrink, terror 8. frighten
  9. cowardice, touchwood
funnel ... 4. cone, flue, pipe, tube
  6. hopper 7. channel
funnel–shaped ... 8. choanoid
funny ... 3. odd 5. comic, droll, queer,
  witty 7. comical, rowboat (Eng),
  strange 8. humorous 9. eccentric,
  laughable
fur ... 3. fox 4. mink, pelt, seal, vair
  5. coypu, fitch, genet, otter, sable,
  skunk 6. badger, ermine, martin,
  nutria 7. miniver (anc) 8. squirrel
  10. chinchilla
fur (pert to) ...
  collective .. 6. peltry
  cover .. 4. pelt 6. pelage
  garment .. 4. robe 5. stole 6. tippet
    7. pelisse
  tippet .. 8. palatine
furbish ... 3. rub 4. vamp 5. clean,
  scour 6. polish 7. burnish, touch up
  8. renovate 9. embellish
Furies ... 5. Dirae 6. Alecto, ghosts,
  Semnae 7. Erinyes (Erinys), Magaera,
  spirits (avenging) 9. Eumenides,
  Tisiphone
Furies, The Three ... 6. Alecto
  7. Magaera 9. Tisiphone
furious ... 5. angry, hasty 6. fierce
  7. frantic, violent 8. frenzied,
  vehement 9. impetuous, turbulent
  10. boisterous, passionate,
  tumultuous 11. overwrought
furl ... 4. roll, wrap 6. bundle, inroll
furlough ... 5. leave 14. leave of
  absence
furnace ... 4. etna, kiln, oven 5. forge,
  stove 7. caldron, reactor, rotator,
  smelter
furnish ... 3. fit 4. bear, give, lend
  5. adorn, cater, endow, equip, indue
  6. afford, fit out, render, supply
  7. appoint, provide
furnishing ... 7. fitting 8. fixtures,
  ornament 9. adornment, apparatus,
  furniture, provision 10. enrichment
furnish with ...
  funds .. 5. endow
  meals .. 5. board, cater
  Mil equipment .. 8. accoutre
  tapestry .. 5. arras
  wings .. 3. imp
furniture ... 5. goods 6. Empire, graith,
  outfit 7. Regency (Regence)
  8. hardware, Sheraton, supplies
  9. equipment 10. decoration,
  housewares 11. Chippendale,
  Renaissance
furor ... 4. fury, rage 5. anger, craze
  6. fervor, flurry, frenzy, furore, tumult
  7. madness 10. excitement,
  turbulence
furrow ... 3. rut 4. plow 6. groove,
  gutter, trench 7. channel, wrinkle
furrowed ... 5. rutty 6. rivose
  7. grooved
further ... 3. aid, and, new, yet
  4. abet, more 7. advance, develop,
  improve, promote, remoter, thither
  10. additional

furtherance ... 3. aid 4. help 6. relief,
  succor 8. progress 9. promotion
  11. advancement, development
furtherer ... 7. abettor 8. promoter
furthermore ... 3. and, yet 4. then
  5. again 7. au reste, besides
  8. moreover 10. in addition
  12. additionally
furtive ... 3. sly 4. wary 6. covert,
  secret, sneaky, stolen 8. skulking,
  stealthy 9. deceitful 11. clandestine
fury ... 3. ire 4. rage 5. anger, wrath
  6. frenzy 7. madness 8. violence
  10. excitement, turbulence
  13. desperateness
Fury ... 6. Erinys, Spirit (avenging)
  7. Atropos
furze ... 4. Ulex, whin 5. gorse, shrub
fuse ... 4. flux, frit (partly), melt
  5. blend, smelt, unite 6. anneal,
  mingle, solder 7. combine, liquefy
  8. dissolve 9. detonator
fusee ... 5. flair, torch 6. signal
fusion ... 5. alloy, blend, union
  7. melting, mixture, nuclear 8. fluidity

  9. coalition
fuss ... 3. ado 4. spat, to–do 5. busle
  6. bother, bustle, pother, tumult
  7. bombast, dispute, quarrel, trouble
  8. brouhaha 9. confusion
fussy ... 7. finical 8. overnice
  10. fastidious, meticulous
fustian ... 4. rant 5. cloth, tumid
  7. bombast, pompous 8. claptrap,
  inflated 9. bombastic, worthless
fustic ... 3. dye 5. amber, morin
  7. dyewood
futile ... 4. idle, vain 6. otiose
  7. trivial 8. hopeless 11. ineffectual
futility ... 8. nugacity 10. invalidity
  11. uselessness 12. bootlessness
future ... 3. yet 4. to be 5. later, still,
  tense 6. fiancé 8. expected,
  intended 9. hereafter
  11. prospective
fuzzy ... 5. downy, hairy 6. fluffy
  7. blurred, frizzly 9. imperfect
  10. indistinct
fyke ... 3. net 6. bag net
fylfot ... 8. swastika 9. gammadion

G

G ... 4. tone (scale) 6. letter (7th)
gab ... 3. lie 4. mock, talk 5. boast,
  mouth, prate, scoff, taste 6. tongue
  7. chatter, deceive 9. utterance
gabardine ... 6. cotton, woolen
gabble ... 4. chat 6. babble, jabber,
  mumble 7. chatter 8. nonsense
gabelle ... 3. tax 5. likin (imports)
  6. excise, impost
gaberdine ... 4. gown 5. frock
  6. mantle 7. garment (loose)
  8. covering, pinafore 9. gabardine
gable ... 4. roof (part) 7. aileron (half)
  8. pediment
gablock ... 4. gaff, spur 5. spear
  6. gaffle 7. crowbar 8. gavelock
Gabon, Africa ...
  capital .. 10. Libreville
Gabriel (pert to) ...
  astrology .. 10. moon spirit
  New Test .. 6. herald 11. good tidings
  Old Test .. 5. angel
  tradition .. 9. archangel (one of seven),
  messenger
gaby ... 4. fool 9. simpleton
gad ... 3. bar, God (oath), rod 4. goad,
  roam, rove, whip 5. ingot, spear, staff
  6. billet, chisel, wander 7. on the go,
  run wild, traipse (trapes) 8. gadabout
  9. gallivant
Gad (pert to) ...
  Bib .. 7. prophet
  deity (Bib) .. 7. Fortune
  father .. 5. Jacob
  tribe .. 6. Gadite, Israel (one of seven)

gadabout ... 3. gad 6. roving
  7. dogcart, gadding, on the go
Gaddang, Gaddan ... 7. Malayan
  8. language (Indonesia)
gadfly ... 6. botfly, insect 8. horsefly
gadget ... 6. device, jigger 7. gimmick
  8. gimcrack 11. contrivance,
  thingumajig
Gadsden Purchase (1853) ... 5. tract
  7. Arizona 9. New Mexico
gadwall ... 4. duck
Gaea, Gaia ... 12. Earth Goddess
Gael ... 4. Celt, Kelt, Manx, Scot
  10. Highlander
Gaelic (pert to) ...
  for John .. 3. Ian
  hero .. 6. Ossian
  language .. 4. Erse
  native .. 4. Erse 5. Irish 6. Celtic,
  Keltic, Scotch
  pagan god .. 5. Dagda (harpist)
  sea god .. 3. Ler
  spirit .. 7. banshee
  warriors .. 7. Fenians
gaff ... 4. hoax, hook, scam, spar, spur,
  talk 5. fraud, spear, trick 6. deceit,
  fleece, gamble 7. chatter, prating
  8. trickery 9. spearhead
gaffer ... 4. hick, rube 6. old man
  11. electrician (TV)
gag ... 4. hoax, joke 5. choke, retch
  7. closure, prevent, shackle
  8. obstruct, one–liner, restrain,
  silencer 9. imposture 10. instrument
  13. interpolation

gage, gauge ... 4. rule, test 5. scale
6. device, pledge 7. measure
8. capacity, defiance, diameter
(firearm), mortgage, security
9. challenge 11. measurement
gaggle ... 5. flock (geese), group
(women) 6. cackle
gaiety, gayety ... 4. gala, glee, show
5. mirth 6. finery 7. jollity
8. vivacity 9. festivity, merriment,
showiness 10. liveliness
12. colorfulness, conviviality
gain ... 3. get, net, win 4. earn, pelf,
reap 5. booty, clear, lucre, reach
6. attain, come by, obtain, profit,
secure, trover 7. acquire, benefit,
procure, realize 8. addition, arrive at,
increase 9. advantage 11. acquisition
12. accumulation 13. amplification
gainsay ... 4. deny 6. forbid, impugn,
oppose, refute 7. dispute
10. contradict, controvert
gait ... 3. run, way 4. lope, pace, trip,
trot, walk 5. amble, order, strut, tread
6. canter, gallop 8. slowness, velocity
gaiter ... 4. boot, spat 5. strad
6. puttee 7. legging 8. overshoe
11. galligaskin
gala ... 4. fete, pomp 6. festal, fiesta,
gaiety 8. festival 9. festivity
11. celebration
Galago ... 5. lemur
Galatea ... 7. heroine 8. sea nymph
9. sculpture (Pygmalion)
11. shepherdess
galaxy ... 6. throng 8. Milky Way
10. assemblage 11. celebrities
gale ... 4. gust, wind 5. storm
8. outburst 9. hurricane
galea ... 6. helmet
galeate ... 12. helmet-shaped
Galen (Gr) ... 9. physician
Galilean (pert to) ...
astronomer .. 7. Galileo
province .. 9. Palestine
religion .. 9. Christian
town .. 4. Cana 8. Tiberias
gall ... 3. vex 4. bile, fret 5. annoy,
chafe, grate, spite 6. bitter, harass,
rancor 8. irritate 9. impudence,
secretion, virulence
gallant ... 4. hero 5. dandy, lover,
noble, spark, swain 6. escort, suitor
7. stately 8. cavalier, cicisbeo
9. attentive, courteous
10. chivalrous, courageous
gallantry ... 7. bravery, courage,
display 8. courtesy 9. courtship
11. intrepidity
galleon ... 6. vessel (sailing)
gallery ... 3. poy 4. hall 5. salon
6. dedans, loggia, museum
7. passage, veranda 8. audience,
corridor, platform 9. promenade
10. ambulatory 11. observatory
galley ... 4. boat, tray 6. vessel
7. caboose, caravel (caravelle),
dromond, kitchen 8. cookroom
galley, Roman ...
one-bank oared .. 7. unireme
two-bank oared .. 6. bireme
three-bank oared .. 7. trireme

six-bank oared .. 7. hexeris
slave .. 5. rower 6. drudge
Gallic ... 4. Gaul 6. French 7. Frenchy
Gallic chariot ... 5. essed
gallimaufry ... 4. hash, olio, stew
6. medley, ragout 9. potpourri
10. hodgepodge
gallipot ... 6. vessel (Medit) 8. druggist
gallo ... 7. rooster 12. fighting cock
gallop ... 3. run 4. lope, ride 6. canter
7. tantivy
gallopade ... 5. dance, galop 6. curvet
gam ... 3. leg 4. herd 5. visit
6. school
Gambia, Africa ...
capital .. 6. Banjul
gambit ... 4. move 7. comment,
opening (chess) 8. maneuver
9. launching 10. concession
gamble ... 3. bet 4. dice, game, risk
5. stake, wager 6. chance, exacta,
hazard, plunge 8. perfecta
9. speculate, totalizer 10. parimutuel,
superfecta 11. daily double,
uncertainty
gambler ... 5. shill 7. sharper
gambol ... 3. hop 5. bound, caper,
prank 6. cavort, curvet, frolic
Gambrinus (King) ... 6. brewer (1st)
game ... 4. lark, play, prey 5. brave,
dodge, prank, sport 6. frolic, gamble,
gritty, plucky, quarry 7. contest,
pastime 8. resolute 9. amusement,
diversion 10. courageous
game, ball ... 4. golf, polo, pool
5. rugby 6. hockey, pelota, soccer,
squash, tennis 7. cricket, croquet
8. baseball, football 11. racquetball
game, beans ... 6. fan-tan
8. beanbags
game, board ... 4. keno 5. bingo,
chess, lotto 7. pachisi (parchesi)
8. checkers, cribbage, Monopoly
10. backgammon
game, card ... 3. gin, pam 4. bank,
faro, skat 5. pitch, poker, rummy,
whist 6. bridge, écarté, flinch, hearts
7. bezique, canasta, cassino, old
maid, seven-up
game, club ... 4. golf 6. hockey
7. cricket
game, court ... 6. pelota, squash,
tennis 7. jai alai 9. badminton
game, parlor ... 5. jacks 7. marbles
8. charades, dominoes
11. tiddlywinks
game plan ... 6. scheme 8. strategy
game, ring ... 6. quoits
gamin ... 3. tad 4. serf 6. urchin
7. mudlark 10. street Arab
gamut ... 5. orbit, range 6. extent
7. compass
gamy ... 4. game 7. lustful 8. sporting
12. high-flavored
gander ... 5. goose 6. stroll
9. simpleton
Gandhi (Hind) ... 6. Indira, leader
7. Mahatma (Mohandus)
gang ... 3. mob, set 4. band, crew,
pack, team, walk (cattle) 5. group,
horde, sheet (Print), shift 6. clique
7. company 9. pasturage

gangling... 5. lanky 9. spindling
gangrene... 5. decay 6. slough
　8. necrosis 9. sphacelus
　13. mortification
gangster... 4. thug 5. thief 6. bandit
　7. mobster 8. criminal, hireling
　9. racketeer
gannet... 4. ibis, Sula 5. booby,
　goose, solan 6. gander
gap... 3. col 4. hole, pass 5. break,
　chasm, cleft, fault, meuse, shard,
　space, split 6. breach, hiatus,
　lacuna, lacune, ravine 7. opening
gaping... 5. agape 6. chappy
　7. ringent, yawning 9. expectant
garb... 5. array, dress, habit, style
　6. clothe 7. apparel, costume,
　fashion, raiment, uniform 8. clothing
　10. appearance, habiliment
garbed... 4. clad 7. attired, dressed,
　habited
garble... 5. alloy 6. mangle 7. distort,
　falsify, pervert 8. mutilate
　12. misinterpret, misrepresent,
　sophisticate
garden... 3. bed 4. yard 5. hardy,
　patch 6. jardin, verger 7. topiary
　8. outfield 9. arboretum, cultivate,
　enclosure, herbarium
garden (pert to)...
　Berlin.. 10. Tiergarten
　Bible.. 4. Eden
　city.. 4. Kent 6. Sicily 7. Chicago
　　8. Touraine
　colony.. 5. Natal
　Colorado.. 9. of the Gods
　Kansas.. 9. of the West
　kind of.. 5. truck 8. kaleyard
　　9. botanical 10. zoological
　State.. 9. New Jersey
garden implement... 3. hoe 4. fork,
　rake 5. graip, mower 6. scythe,
　sickle, trowel, weeder
Garfield's death site... 7. Elberon
　(NJ)
Gargantua (pert to)...
　character.. 4. King (Rabelais romance)
　son.. 10. Pantagruel (giant)
gargantuan... 4. huge 7. titanic
garish... 5. gaudy, showy 7. flighty,
　glaring 8. dazzling
garland... 3. lei 6. anadem, circle,
　corona, fillet, rosary, trophy, wreath
　7. chaplet, coronal, festoon
　8. headband 9. anthology
　11. compilation
garlic... 4. herb, moly 5. clove
　6. ramson
garment... 4. cape, coat, gown, robe,
　suit, vest, wrap 5. cloak, dress,
　frock, shift, simar, smock, stole, tunic
　6. coatee, duster 7. pelisse, raiment,
　surcoat, topcoat 8. overcoat,
　vestment
garment (pert to)...
　African.. 6. kaross
　ancient.. 5. burel
　Arab.. 3. aba
　clerical.. 3. alb 5. amice 6. chimer
　　7. cassock, zimarra 8. surplice
　cover.. 5. apron 8. overalls, pinafore
　　9. coveralls

　Eskimo.. 5. parka
　Jewish.. 5. ephod
　knight's.. 6. tabard
　patchwork.. 5. cento
　thin.. 8. gossamer
garner... 4. reap 5. amass, store
　6. gather 7. collect 10. accumulate
garnet... 3. gem, red 5. color
　6. aplome, pyrope 7. olivine (green)
　8. cinnamon (stone), essonite
　(yellow), melanite (black)
　9. almandine (almandite, dark red),
　uvarovite (green)
garnish... 4. trim 5. adorn 6. attach,
　bedeck 7. fetters 8. decorate,
　ornament
garnishment... 4. lien 7. summons
　8. ornament 10. attachment,
　decoration
garret... 4. loft 5. attic 6. turret
　8. cockloft 10. watchtower
garrot... 9. goldeneye (duck)
　10. tourniquet
garrote, garrotte... 8. strangle
　9. execution 10. throttling
　13. strangulation
garrulous... 5. gabby, wordy 6. chatty
　7. diffuse 9. talkative 10. loquacious
gas... 4. brag, talk 5. vapor 6. poison
　7. chatter 8. gasoline, nonsense
　10. anesthesia, asphyxiate, illuminant
　11. anesthetize
gas... 3. air 4. neon 5. argon, ether,
　ozone, radon, xenon 6. arsine,
　butane, ethane, helium, ketene,
　nebula (luminous), oxygen 7. methane
　8. chlorine, cyanogen, etherion,
　hydrogen, nitrogen 9. butadiene
gascon... 7. boaster 8. braggart
　11. braggadocio 12. swashbuckler
gasconade... 4. brag 5. boast
　7. bluster, bravado 11. fanfaronade,
　rodomontade
gaseous... 4. smog, thin 5. smoke
　7. tenuous 8. vaporous
　13. unsubstantial
gash... 3. cut 5. cleft, notch, sever,
　slash 6. furrow, gossip, injury, tattle
　8. incision
gasp... 3. say 4. pant, yawn 5. utter
　7. breathe
gasping... 5. agasp 7. panting
gastropod... 4. slug 5. Harpa, Murex,
　Oliva, snail, whelk 6. Nerita, volute
　7. abalone, mollusk 8. sea snail
gat... 3. gun, rod 7. channel, passage
　8. revolver
gate... 3. dar 4. door, hole, pass
　5. start (racing), toran, valve
　6: defile, portal 7. barrier, opening,
　postern 8. Lion–Gate 9. floodgate,
　turnstile 10. Needle's Eye
　(Jerusalem), portcullis
gateau... 4. cake
gather... 4. bale, brew, fold, meet,
　reap 5. amass, glean, pleat, rally,
　shirr 6. bundle, deduce, garner,
　muster, pucker 7. acquire, collect,
　compile, convene, convoke, harvest,
　procure, suppose 8. assemble
　10. accumulate
gatherer, collector of...

coins.. 11. numismatist
money.. 5. miser
news.. 8. reporter 10. journalist
stamps.. 11. philatelist
gathering... 3. sum 4. stag 5. crowd,
   party, troop 6. galaxy, smoker
   7. abscess, meeting 8. swelling
   10. assemblage, harvesting
   11. contraction 12. accumulation,
   congregation 14. conglomeration
gaucho... 6. cowboy (pampas)
   8. herdsman, horseman
gaucho weapon... 4. bola
gaud... 4. jest, joke 5. adorn, fraud,
   paint, sport, trick 6. finery, flashy,
   gewgaw 7. trinket 8. artifice,
   ornament
gaudy... 4. fine, loud 5. cheap, feast,
   showy 6. flashy, flimsy, garish,
   tawdry, tinsel 7. glaring, trinket
   9. flaunting 11. pretentious
   12. meretricious, ostentatious
   13. overdeveloped
gaufre... 4. iron (waffle) 6. waffle
gauge, gage... 4. norm, rate, rule, size
   5. judge, scale, value 6. assess
   7. measure 8. estimate
gauge (pert to)...
airplane.. 10. tachometer
distance.. 10. micrometer
miles.. 8. odometer
pointer.. 3. arm
rain.. 8. udometer
velocity.. 11. speedometer
wind.. 10. anemometer
Gaul... 5. Aedui 6. France, Gallia
   9. Frenchman
Gauls... 4. Remi 5. Celts, Cymry
gaunt... 4. bony, lank, lean, thin, ugly
   5. spare 7. haggard 8. desolate
gauntlet... 4. cuff 5. armor (part),
   glove 7. bandage
gaur... 5. gayal 7. buffalo
gauss... 4. unit (Elec)
Gauss... 13. mathematician
gauze... 4. haze, leno 5. crape, lisse,
   marli (marly) 6. barege, filter, tissue
   8. dressing
gauze film on wine... 8. beeswing
gavage... 7. feeding
gave... see *give*
Gavia... 4. loon
gavial... 11. crocodilian
gaw... 4. gape 5. drain 6. trench
gawk... 4. dolt, gowk, left, lout
   5. booby, stare 9. simpleton
gawky... 6. clumsy, cuckoo, stupid
   7. awkward, foolish 8. clownish
gay... 4. airy, glad 5. drunk, gaudy,
   jolly, merry, riant, showy 6. blithe,
   cheery, jovial, joyful, joyous, lively
   7. dashing, festive, gleeful
   8. cheerful, colorful, rory–tory,
   sportive 9. convivial, sprightly,
   vivacious 10. frolicsome, profligate
   12. lighthearted
gay time... 4. lark 5. spree
   8. jamboree
gazabo, gazebo... 4. cony 6. rabbit,
   turret 7. balcony, blunder, whopper
   11. summerhouse
gaze... 3. con, eye 4. gape, look,

moon, peer, pore, scan 5. glare,
   gloat, stare 6. glower, regard
gazelle... 3. ahu, goa 4. admi, cora,
   dama, kudu, mohr, oryx 5. ariel,
   brown, korin 7. chikara (4–horn),
   corinne, dibatag 8. antelope
   9. springbok
gazette... 7. journal, publish
   8. announce 9. newspaper
   15. Arkansas Gazette (1819)
gazetteer... 7. newsman 9. newspaper
   10. dictionary
gear... 3. cam, rig 5. equip, goods,
   tools, wheel 6. things 7. baggage,
   conform, harness, rigging 8. adjust
   to, clothing, cogwheel, garments
   9. equipment, mechanism, trappings,
   vestments 10. appliances, implements
gecko... 6. lizard 7. tarente
geese... 5. brant, quink, solan
geese (pert to)...
fat.. 6. axunge
flock.. 4. raft 6. gaggle
genus.. 4. Chen 5. Anser 6. Branta
Gekko... 6. lizard
gelatin, gelatine... 4. agar, food, jell
   5. jelly 6. collin 7. protein
   8. agar–agar
gelid... 3. icy 4. cold 6. frozen
gem... 4. jade, onyx, opal, ruby, sard,
   type 5. agate, beryl, jewel, pearl,
   stone, topaz 6. garnet, ligure, spinel,
   zircon 7. cat's–eye, diamond,
   emerald, jacinth 8. amethyst,
   hawk's–eye, sapphire 9. carnelian,
   moonstone 10. aquamarine
   11. alexandrite, lapis lazuli 12. star
   sapphire
gem (pert to)...
artificial.. 5. paste
carver.. 8. lapidary
Egyptian.. 6. scarab
flaw.. 8. gendarme
food.. 6. muffin
imperfect.. 5. loupe
semiprecious.. 5. cameo 8. intaglio
six rays.. 7. asteria
surface.. 5. bezel, facet
weight.. 5. carat
gemel... 4. bars (Her), twin 6. paired
   7. coupled, doubled
gemsbok... 4. goat, oryx 7. chamois
Gem State... 5. Idaho
gendarme... 4. blue, flaw (gem)
   5. guard 6. police 7. soldier, trooper
   9. policeman 10. cavalryman
gender... 3. sex 5. breed, genus
   7. grammar (term) 8. engender
genealogy... 4. tree 5. order (of
   descent) 6. family 7. account,
   history, lineage, peerage, progeny
   8. pedigree, register 9. offspring
genealogy of the gods... 8. theogony
gener... 8. son–in–law
general... 5. gross, usual, vague,
   whole 6. common, public 7. officer
   8. catholic, communal 9. extensive,
   prevalent, universal, well–known
   10. encyclical, indefinite
   11. approximate
general (pert to)...
agreement.. 5. chief, court

aspect.. 6. facies
chief.. 6. Führer, Il Duce 9. president
  10. Grand Mogul 13. Generalissimo
court.. 5. Synod
direction.. 5. tenor, trend 6. course
favor.. 7. popular 10. popularity
feature.. 5. motif
group.. 8. ensemble
orders.. 7. routine
rule.. 5. canon
summary.. 8. synopsis
type.. 7. average
generalize... 5. widen 6. extend,
  reason, spread 7. broaden
  12. universalize
General Sherman (pert to)...
  Civil War march.. 15. Atlanta to the
  Sea
  giant trees.. 8. sequoias
  tree.. 10. eucalyptus
generate... 5. beget, breed, cause
  6. create 7. develop, produce
  8. engender 9. originate, procreate,
  propagate
generation... 3. age 7. descent
  8. lifetime 9. epigonous (later),
  formation, genealogy 10. production
  11. abiogenesis, procreation
generosity... 10. liberality
  11. hospitality, magnanimity,
  munificence
generous... 4. free 5. large 7. liberal
  8. tolerant 9. indulgent, plentiful,
  unstinted 10. hospitable
  11. magnanimous
genesis... 4. Book 5. birth 6. origin
  (of races) 8. nascency 9. beginning,
  ethnology, etymology, inception
  10. generation
genet... 3. fur 5. civet
genethliac... 5. stars (influence)
  9. birthdays
Geneva Cross... 8. Red Cross
genial... 4. warm 5. bland 6. jovial,
  kindly 7. amiable, festive, nuptial
  8. cheerful, friendly, pleasant
  9. expansive 10. enlivening
geniculate... 5. kneel
genie... 4. jinn 6. genius
genius... 5. deity, jinni 6. talent
  7. ability, prodigy 9. endowment
  (supreme) 11. inspiration
  12. intelligence
Genoa lace... 4. tape 6. bobbin
  7. macramé 13. gold and silver
genos... 4. clan, gens, race
genre... 3. art (style) 4. kind, sort
  5. genus 6. gender 7. species
  8. category
genteel... 6. polite 7. refined
  8. wellborn, well-bred
Gentiles... 6. goyims 10. Christians,
  non-Moslems
  14. non-Mohammedans
gentle... 4. calm, easy, meek, mild,
  soft, tame 5. bland, quiet 6. docile,
  humane, kindly, tender 7. amabile
  (Mus), clement, genteel, refined,
  subdued 8. moderate, peaceful,
  soothing, tranquil, wellborn
  9. courteous, honorable, temperate,
  tractable 10. chivalrous

  11. considerate 13. compassionate
gentleman... 3. sir 6. knight
  7. esquire, shoneen (would-be),
  younker 8. nobleman
gentleness... 6. lenity 8. elegance,
  leniency, meekness, softness
  9. lightness 10. kindliness,
  moderation 11. genteelness
genuflect... 5. kneel 6. curtsy
genuine... 4. pure, real, true 5. frank,
  pucka (pukka) 7. germane, sincere
  8. existent 9. authentic, simon-pure,
  unalloyed, veritable 10. unaffected
  13. unadulterated
genus... 4. kind, sort 5. class, order
genus, animal life...
  animals (one-celled).. 6. Amoeba
  8. Protozoa 9. Rhizopoda
  ants.. 6. Eciton
  apes.. 5. Simia
  armadillos.. 9. Glyptodon
  auks.. 4. Alle
  bears.. 5. Ursus
  bees (honey).. 4. Apis
  beetles.. 10. Coleoptera
  birds.. 7. Ratitae
  bivalve mollusks.. 6. Anomia
  8. Estheria
  bugs (long-legged).. 5. Emesa
  cats.. 5. Felis
  cattle.. 3. Bos
  crabs.. 4. Maia
  dogs.. 5. Canis
  ducks.. 3. Aix 4. Anas 7. Harelda
  8. Clangula
  elks.. 5. Alces
  fish.. 6. Cybium, Remora 7. Girella,
  Muraena
  flies.. 6. Asilus 8. Glossina (tsetse)
  frogs.. 4. Rana 5. Anura 8. Amphibia
  9. Batrachia
  geese.. 4. Chen 5. Anser
  goats.. 5. Capra
  gulls.. 5. Xema
  herons.. 7. Egretta
  hogs.. 3. Sus
  horses.. 5. Equus
  insects.. 10. Coleoptera
  lemurs.. 6. Galago
  lizards.. 3. Uta 5. Agama
  mammals.. 4. Homo
  Man.. 11. Homo sapiens
  marten.. 7. Mustela
  mice.. 3. Mus
  monkeys (spider).. 6. Ateles
  moose.. 5. Alces
  moths.. 5. Tinea
  oysters.. 6. Ostrea
  peacocks.. 4. Pavo
  pigeons (crowned).. 5. Goura
  porcupines.. 7. Hystrix
  porpoise.. 4. Inia
  rats.. 6. Spalax
  roadrunners.. 9. Geococcyx
  scorpions.. 4. Nepa
  seabirds.. 4. Sula
  sloths.. 11. Megatherium
  slugs.. 5. Arion
  snails.. 5. Mitra 6. Nerita, Triton
  8. Geophila
  snakes.. 4. Eryx (sand) 7. Ophidia
  spiders.. 7. Agalena

squirrels.. 7. Sciurus
swans.. 4. Olar 6. Cygnus
ticks.. 6. Ixodes
tortoises.. 4. Emys
turkeys.. 9. Meleagris
wasps.. 5. Vespa
whales.. 4. Orca 5. Areta
  9. Sibbaldus (blue)
genus, plant life...
algae (blue–green).. 10. Gloeocapsa
apple trees.. 5. Malus
cabbage.. 3. Cos
currant.. 5. Ribes
elms.. 5. Ulmus
evergreen, heaths.. 5. Erica
fern.. 6. Anemia
fungi.. 7. Boletus 10. geoglossum
grasses.. 3. Poa (blue) 5. Avena
  6. Elymus 7. Setaria
herbs.. 4. Arum 6. Asarum, Asitis
  (mustard), Cassia, Seseli
  7. Hedeoma, Linaria 8. Solidago
holly.. 4. Ilex
ipecac.. 4. Evea
ivy.. 11. Hedera helix
lily.. 7. Bessera
maples.. 4. Acer
olives.. 4. Olea
orchids.. 5. Vanda 7. Listera
palms.. 5. Areca, Assai 6. Bacaba
poplar.. 5. Alamo
rhubarb.. 5. Rheum
vines (woody).. 6. Hedera
geode... 3. vug (vugg, vugh, voog)
  5. druse 6. nodule
geological (pert to)...
division.. 3. eon, era
era.. 6. Eocene 7. Miocene
  8. Cenozoic, Mesozoic 9. Paleozoic
  11. Archaeozoic
period.. 4. Dyas, Lias 5. Trias
prelife.. 5. Azoic
zone (fossil).. 6. assise
geologist... 6. Strabo (anc Gr)
  8. geognost 12. mineralogist
geometric (pert to)...
angle.. 9. incidence
axis.. 8. abscissa
contact.. 10. osculation
curve.. 6. spiral 7. evolute
pottery.. 7. Dipylon (anc)
geometric figure... 4. cone, cube,
  lune 5. prism 6. gnomon, oblong,
  square 7. hexagon, octagon, polygon,
  rhombus 8. heptagon, pentagon,
  triangle 9. rectangle, trapezoid
  10. quadrangle 13. parallelogram
geometric proposition (pert to)...
ratio.. 2. pi (3.1416)
surface.. 4. tore 5. nappe
term.. 4. sine 5. locus 6. secant
  7. tangent 11. asses' bridge
geometry (pert to)...
figure.. 6. conoid 9. ellipsoid
  10. paraboloid
mathematician.. 6. Euclid, Pascal
proposition.. 6. porism
geoponic... 5. rural 6. rustic
Georgia...
capital.. 7. Atlanta
city.. 5. Macon 7. Augusta

  8. Columbus, Marietta, Savannah
  9. Brunswick
holiday.. 10. Georgia Day (Feb 12)
memorial.. 11. Warm Springs
  16. Little White House (FDR)
mountain.. 7. Lookout 9. Blue Ridge
  11. Alleghenies
peak.. 9. High Point 13. Brasstown
  Bald
river.. 8. Savannah, Suwannee
settler (1st).. 10. Oglethorpe
State admission.. 6. Fourth
State nickname.. 5. Peach 7. Cracker
  16. Empire of the South
swamp.. 10. Okefenokee
Georgian of the Caucasus... 4. Svan
georgic... 4. poem (rural)
geosphere... 5. earth
Geraint, Sir... 6. Knight (Round Table)
germ... 3. bud 4. ovum, seed
  5. spore 6. embryo, origin
  7. microbe 8. bacteria (pl)
  9. bacterium 13. microorganism
germ (free)... 7. aseptic 10. antiseptic
German... 3. Hun 5. Boche, jerry
  6. Almain (Alman), Teuton
  9. Deutscher
German (pert to)... see also *Germany*
air force.. 9. Luftwaffe
airplane.. 5. Gotha, Stuka 7. Dornier,
  Heinkel, Junkers 13. Messerschmitt
article.. 3. das, der, ein
battleship.. 8. Graf Spee (1939)
beverage.. 5. lager
cake.. 5. torte
castle.. 7. schloss
Christmas.. 11. Weihnachten
dance.. 9. allemande
drinking salute.. 6. prosit
folklore.. 5. gnome 6. kobold
gun.. 6. Bertha (Big)
hail.. 4. heil
highway.. 8. autobahn
knight.. 6. Ritter (title)
language.. 7. Deutsch
law.. 5. Salic
league.. 4. Bund 6. Verein
  9. Hanseatic 10. Turnverein
letter.. 4. rune
lyric poems.. 6. lieder
mister.. 4. Herr
ox (wild).. 4. urus
parliament.. 9. Bundestag, Reichstag
people.. 5. Quadi 6. Franks, Saxons
  7. Teutons, Vandals 8. Lombards
  9. Prussians 10. Herminones
police.. 7. Gestapo
prison.. 6. stalag
society.. see *league* (above)
song.. 4. lied
student set.. 7. Kommers
teacher.. 6. docent 12. privatdocent
title.. 3. Von 4. Graf, Herr 6. Ritter
tribal group.. 3. gau
union.. 9. Auschluss
vowel change.. 6. umlaut
wheat.. 5. spelt
wine.. 4. wein 5. Rhine 7. Moselle
woman.. 4. frau 8. fraulein
yes.. 2. ja
germane... 4. akin 6. allied 7. kindred
  8. relevant 11. appropriate

German people (famed)...
actor.. 8. Jannings (Emil)
astrologer.. 5. Faust
astronomer.. 5. Galle 6. Kepler
author.. 4. Dahn 5. Ebers
  8. Brentano
bacteriologist.. 4. Koch (Nobel Prize,
  1905)
biographer.. 6. Ludwig
chemist.. 6. Bunsen
composer.. 3. Abt 4. Bach 5. Hasse
  6. Handel, Wagner
deity.. 5. Donar (thunder)
educator.. 5. Grimm 6. Beneke
  7. Francke
Egyptologist.. 5. Ebers
general.. 6. Rommel
geographer.. 6. Ritter
Gestapo chief.. 7. Himmler
goldsmith (anc).. 5. Faust
historian.. 4. Dahn 5. Moser
  7. Neander (Eccl)
inventor.. 6. Diesel
metaphysician.. 4. Kant 5. Lange
mystic.. 7. Eckhart
naturalist.. 9. Ehrenberg
neurologist.. 5. Ebing 6. Krafft
painter.. 5. Durer 6. Lessing
pathologist.. 6. Eberth
philologist.. 5. Grimm, Heyne
philosopher.. 4. Elze 5. Groos, Hegel,
  Weber 6. Ritter 8. Spengler
  9. Feuerbach
physician.. 8. Hufeland
physicist.. 3. Ohm 5. Weber
  6. Franck 7. Doppler 10. Fahrenheit
pianist.. 5. Bauer
poet.. 4. Elze 5. Heine 6. Goethe,
  Uhland 7. Lessing 8. Schiller
president (first).. 5. Ebert
sculptor.. 5. Begas
Socialist.. 10. Liebknecht
theologian.. 5. Bauer 6. Spener
  (Pietist) 7. Francke
Germany...
capital.. 4. Bonn 6. Berlin
cathedral town.. 5. Essen
city.. 3. Ulm 4. Bonn, Gera
  5. Baden, Emden, Essen, Gotha
  6. Munich
coal region.. 4. Ruhr, Saar 6. Aachen
East.. 10. Third Reich
empire.. 14. Deutsches Reich
kingdom.. 6. Saxony 7. Bavaria,
  Hanover
lake.. 9. Constance
leader.. 6. Hitler (Fuehrer), Kaiser
  13. von Hindenburg
mountain.. 4. Harz
port.. 5. Emden
river.. 3. Aar 4. Elbe, Iser, Oder,
  Ruhr 5. Rhine, Saale
steel region.. 5. Essen
West.. 15. Federal Republic
wine (white).. 4. hock
germicide... 6. iodine (iodin), phenol
  10. antiseptic 12. disinfectant
germinate... 3. bud 4. grow 5. beget
  6. sprout 7. develop 8. vegetate
  10. effloresce
Geronimo... 6. Apache (Chief)
gerrymander (Polit)... 6. divide (unfairly)

  10. manipulate
gesticulation... 6. motion 7. gesture
gesture... 3. act 4. gest (geste), sign
  5. sanna 6. beckon, behave, motion
  7. perform, pretext 8. carriage (body)
  11. gesticulate 13. gesticulation
get... 3. pen, win 4. earn, hear, pain,
  take, trap 5. beget, fetch, incur,
  learn 6. attain, become, derive,
  induce, obtain, profit, secure
  7. achieve, acquire, capture, prepare,
  procure, receive 8. contract, contrive,
  discover 9. ascertain, determine
  10. understand
get along... 3. age 5. hurry
  6. begone, depart, manage, move on
  7. advance, prosper
get around... 5. evade 6. cajole,
  outwit, spread 7. deceive 9. circulate
  10. circumvent
get off... 5. start, utter 6. alight,
  depart, escape, go free 8. dismount
get out... 4. exit 5. scram 6. elicit,
  escape, reveal 7. draw out, leak out,
  publish 8. evacuate 9. extricate
get over... 4. move 5. cover
  6. bridge, finish 7. recover
  8. surmount 9. make clear
Ghana, capital of... 5. Accra (Gold
  Coast)
ghastly... 3. wan 4. grim, pale
  5. lurid 6. dismal, grisly, pallid
  7. deathly, hideous 8. gruesome,
  horrible, shocking, terrible
  9. deathlike, frightful 10. cadaverous
ghost... 3. Ker 5. larva (Rom Relig),
  lemur, shade, spook 6. daemon,
  spirit, wraith 7. banshee (banshie),
  eidolon, phantom, specter
  8. phantasm, revenant
  10. apparition, glimmering, substitute
  11. ghostwriter, poltergeist
ghostly... 5. eerie (eery) 8. spectral
  9. spiritual
giant... 4. huge, ogre 5. Titan
  6. afreet, nozzle, thurse 7. monster
  8. colossus 9. monstrous
  10. gargantuan, prodigious,
  tremendous
giant (pert to)...
Biblical.. 7. Goliath, Rephaim
classic.. 5. Atlas
crafty.. 5. Cacus
Greek.. 5. Mimas
hundred–armed.. 9. Enceladus
land, country.. 9. Utgarthar
  10. Jotunnheim 11. Brobdingnag
Norse.. 4. Ymir (Ymer) 5. Mimir
  6. Jotunn (Jotun) 12. Utgartha–Loki
one–eyed.. 5. Arges 7. Brontes,
  Cyclops 10. Polyphemus
primeval.. 4. Ymir 5. Titan
  12. Utgartha–Loki
rock.. 9. Gibraltar 13. Stone Mountain
  (Atlanta)
sea god.. 5. Aegir
seer.. 5. Mimir
strong.. 6. Samson, Targan
  7. Antaeus 8. Hercules
Teutonic.. 4. Wade 5. Aegir
thousand–armed.. 4. Bana
three–hundred handed, many–handed..

8. Briareus
giantess (Teut Myth)... 4. Norn
gibbed... 9. castrated (cat)
gibber... 4. chat, hump, talk (rapid)
   5. stone (loose) 6. mumble
   7. boulder, chatter 8. swelling
gibberish... 4. talk 5. lingo 6. jargon,
   patois, patter 8. nonsense
gibbet... 3. jib 4. hang 7. gallows
   9. execution
gibbon... 3. ape, lar 6. wou–wou
   7. hoolock, siamang 10. anthropoid
gibe... 4. jape, jeer, jibe, quip 5. fleer,
   flirt, flout, scoff, sneer, taunt
   6. heckle
Gibraltar...
  named for (legend).. 5. Gobir
  ruled by.. 12. Great Britain
  site.. 5. Spain (coast)
giddy... 4. reel 5. dizzy, tipsy, whirl
   6. fickle 7. flighty 8. gyratory,
   heedless 9. delirious
   14. scatterbrained
gift... 4. alms, bent, boon, dole, free
   5. bribe, grant, knack, token
   6. legacy, talent 7. aptness, faculty,
   largess (largesse), present
   8. aptitude, blessing, donation,
   gratuity 9. endowment, lagniappe
   (lagnappe), readiness 11. serendipity
   12. contribution
gifted... 7. endowed 8. talented
gigantic... 4. huge 5. giant, large,
   titan 7. immense, mammoth
   8. colossal, enormous 9. colossean,
   monstrous 10. prodigious
giggle... 5. laugh (silly), te–hee
   6. tee–hee, titter 7. chuckle, snicker,
   snigger
Gila monster... 4. Gila 6. lizard
gild... 4. coat, lure 5. adorn, paint,
   tempt 7. aureate, falsify 8. brighten
   9. embellish
gilding... 4. gilt, gold 6. ormolu
   7. coating 8. ornament, painting
gill... 5. brook, leach, organ, penny
   6. tipple, valley, wattle 7. measure
   10. sweetheart
gimcrackle... 3. fob, toy 5. showy
   6. bauble, gewgaw, paltry, trifle
   7. trinket 8. trumpery, whimwham
   15. Jack–of–all–trades
gimlet... 3. awl 4. tool 5. drink
   (mixed) 6. wimble
gimp... 5. orris (upholstery) 6. fabric,
   thread 7. galloon 8. fishline,
   trimming
gin... 4. game, sloe, tool, trap, whim
   5. snare, trick 6. device, liquor,
   scheme, thresh 7. machine
   8. artifice, schnapps 11. contrivance
ginger... 3. pep 5. color 6. Asarum,
   energy, lively, mettle, spirit
   8. pungency, Zingiber 9. rootstalk
gingerbread... 4. cake 5. money
   6. flimsy, frills, wealth 8. ornament
   (tawdry) 11. superfluity
gingerly... 6. warily 7. charily
   9. carefully, finically, guardedly
   10. cautiously 12. fastidiously
gingham... 5. cloth 8. umbrella
   (cheap)

gipsy... see *gypsy*
giraffe... 5. okapi 6. mammal, spinet
   10. camelopard 13. constellation
girasol, girasole... 4. opal
   9. artichoke, sunflower
gird... 4. belt, bind, gibe, girt, sill
   5. brace, equip, scoff, sneer
   6. fasten, girdle, secure 7. enclose,
   environ 8. surround 10. strengthen
girder... 4. beam 5. truss 6. timber
   7. support
girdle... 3. obi 4. band, belt, cest,
   ring, sash 6. cestus, cingle, circle,
   corset 8. cincture, encircle
   10. cummerbund
girdle bone... 12. sphenethmoid
Girdle of Venus (pert to)...
  bridal.. 11. power of love
  palmistry line.. 8. hysteria
   11. nervousness
girl... 3. sis 4. bint, chit, dame, lass,
   minx, miss 5. filly, sissy, skirt
   6. damsel, female, giglet, hoyden
   (hoiden), lassie, maiden, shiver, thrill,
   tomboy 7. colleen, damosel, fillock,
   ingénue, roebuck 10. sweetheart
   11. maidservant
girlish... 4. pert 5. sissy 7. artless
   8. immature, maidenly 10. flapperish
girt... 4. band 6. fasten, saddle
   7. besiege 9. encircled
girth... 4. band, hoop, size 5. brace,
   strap 6. girdle, saddle 7. measure
   8. encircle 13. circumference
gist... 3. nub 4. core, crux, meat, pith
   5. point (main) 7. essence, meaning
give... 3. gie 4. hand 5. endow,
   grant, yield 6. accord, afford,
   bestow, confer, devote, donate,
   impart, remise, render, supply
   7. present, proffer, provide
   9. attribute, vouchsafe
   10. administer, elasticity
give (pert to)...
  and take.. 11. reciprocity
  authority.. 7. empower
  away.. 5. break, grant, marry, yield
   6. bestow, betray 7. discard, divulge,
   succumb 8. disclose 9. sacrifice
   10. relinquish
  back.. 4. echo 5. remit 6. recede,
   remand, remise, retire, return
   7. replace, restore, retreat
  birth to.. 4. foal 5. calve 6. farrow,
   mother 9. originate
  expectation.. 7. promise
  forth.. 4. emit 5. blaze 6. afford,
   exhale 7. publish
  information.. 4. tell 6. inform, report
   7. divulge, publish 8. disclose
   9. advertise
  out.. 4. deal, emit 5. exude, issue,
   print, utter (publicly) 6. report,
   weaken 7. declare, publish, release
   8. announce 9. apportion, circulate
  prominence.. 4. star 7. feature
   8. headline
  up.. 4. cede, emit, fail, quit 5. demit,
   waive, yield 6. betray, disuse, resign,
   vacate 7. abandon, despair, succumb
   8. abdicate, part with, renounce,
   swear off 9. sacrifice, surrender

10. relinquish

given... 5. dated, datum, fixed
6. stated 7. assumed, granted
8. accorded, addicted, bestowed,
inclined, set forth 10. determined,
disposed to

given (pert to)...
by word of mouth.. 4. oral 5. parol
name.. 7. surname
particularly.. 9. specified

given (to)...
experiment.. 7. empiric
expression.. 13. demonstrative
meditation.. 13. contemplative
suspicion.. 9. querulent

giving... 6. ceding 7. largess (largesse)
9. bestowing 10. conferring, liberality
12. philanthropy, presentation
13. administering

giving name to a country...
8. eponymic

giving up... 8. yielding
10. abandoning, despairing
11. sacrificing 12. surrendering
13. relinquishing

glacial (pert to)...
deposit.. 6. placer 7. moraine
direction.. 5. stoss (opp to lee)
drift.. 8. diluvium
dust.. 10. kryokonite
erosion wall.. 6. cirque
mill.. 6. moulin
ridge.. 4. kame (Scot) 5. esker (eskar)
snow.. 4. neve

glaciarium... 4. rink (skating)

glacis... 5. slope 7. incline
13. fortification

glack... 4. fork (road) 6. defile, ravine,
valley

glad... 3. gay 4. fain 5. merry
6. elated, joyful, joyous 8. animated,
cheering, pleasing 9. animating,
beautiful, delighted, gratified
11. exhilarated, well–pleased
12. exhilarating

gladden... 5. cheer, elate 6. please
7. gratify

gladdy... 12. yellowhammer

glade... 4. dell, nemo (comb form),
vale 5. laund 6. valley 8. clearing
9. everglade, open space

gladiator... 6. fencer 7. lanista

gladiator's arena... 4. ludi

gladly... 4. fain, lief 5. fitly 6. freely
7. eagerly, readily 8. joyfully, properly
9. willingly 10. cheerfully, preferably

gladsome... 4. glad 6. blithe, joyful
7. festive, jocular, pleased
8. cheerful

Gladstone... 3. bag (travel) 4. wine
7. Liberal (Party) 8. carriage,
Irishman 11. portmanteau

glad tidings... 3. joy 6. gospel
7. evangel

glamorous... 8. alluring, charming
10. bewitching 11. fascinating

glance... 3. eye 4. hint, leer, look,
ogle, scry, skew 5. flash, gleam,
glint, touch 6. allude, signal
7. glimpse

gland... 5. gonad, liver, lymph, ovary
6. spleen, thymus 7. adrenal,

carotid, parotid, thyroid 8. pancreas,
salivary 9. pituitary 10. suprarenal

gland (pert to)...
enlargement.. 6. ademia
full of.. 7. adenose
glandlike.. 7. adenoid 9. glandular
inflammation.. 8. adenitis
secretion.. 7. hormone
tumor.. 7. adenoma

glaring... 5. clear, plain 6. bright,
garish 7. evident, flaring, obvious,
staring, visible, vividly 8. apparent,
distinct, flagrant, manifest
9. barefaced 11. conspicuous

glass... 4. lens, pony 5. glaze, purex
6. goblet, liquor, mirror, seidel
7. binocle, crystal, reflect, tumbler
9. barometer, binocular, hourglass,
telescope 10. microscope, opera
glass 11. stactometer, thermometer

glass (pert to)...
blue.. 5. smalt
device.. 7. ironman
flask.. 7. matrass (mattrass)
French for.. 5. verre
furnace, oven.. 4. lehr (leer) 5. bocca,
siege, tisar 7. drosser (part)
like.. 6. vitric 8. vitreous
material.. 4. frit (fritt)
mineral.. 7. hyalite 8. feldspar
molten.. 7. parison
mosaic.. 7. tessera
paste (jewelry).. 6. strass
red.. 7. schmelz (schmelze)
refuse.. 4. calx
rod.. 5. punty (pontil)
sheet.. 4. pane 5. slide 7. platten
showcase.. 7. vitrine
volcanic.. 6. pumice 8. obsidian
worker.. 7. glazier

glass (type of)... 3. cut 4. milk
6. safety 7. hobnail, Lalique, plastic,
stained, Swedish 8. Fostoria,
Sandwich, Venetian 9. Fiberglas,
Plexiglas, Vitaglass

glass blowing (pert to)...
annealing term.. 4. fuse, heat
glass content.. 4. sand, zinc
6. potash, temper 7. soda ash
oven.. 4. lehr (leer)
rod.. 5. punty (pontil)

glazier's diamond... 5. emery (emeril)

glazing machine... 8. calender

gleam... 3. ray 4. glow 5. flash, glint,
gloze, light 7. glimmer, shimmer
8. radiance 9. coruscate
10. brightness

glean... 4. reap 5. sheaf (of hemp)
6. bundle, deduce, gather 7. collect,
harvest, procure

glee... 3. joy 4. club, song 5. mirth
7. delight 8. pleasure 9. merriment
12. cheerfulness

glen... 4. dale, dell, vale 6. dingle,
ravine, valley 10. depression

glib... 4. easy, oily 5. suave 6. facile,
fluent, smooth 8. castrate, flippant,
slippery 9. talkative 10. loquacious

glide... 4. sail, skid, slip, soar
5. coast, slide

gliding over... 7. lambent
10. slithering

glimmer... 3. bit 4. hint, leam
5. blink, flash, gleam, glint
7. glimpse, glitter 10. perception
(slight)
glimpse... 4. view (quick) 5. flash,
tinge, trace 6. glance, luster
7. glimmer, inkling
glisten... 5. flash, shine 7. glister,
sparkle 9. coruscate
glitter... 5. glare, gleam, shine
7. glimmer, glisten, sparkle
9. coruscate, showiness
14. attractiveness
gloaming... 4. dusk 8. twilight
9. darkening 11. candlelight
globe... 3. map, orb 4. ball, moon
5. earth 6. sphere 10. hemisphere
(half)
Globe, The... 7. Theater (London, first
to play Shakespeare)
globular... 5. beady 7. globose
9. orbicular, spherical 10. orbiculate
11. globe–shaped
globule... 4. bead, blob, drop, pill,
tear 5. minim 6. bubble 8. spherule
glochis... 4. hair (barbed) 7. bristle
glockenspiel... 4. lyra, stop (organ)
8. carillon 10. instrument
gloom... 5. cloud, frown, scowl
7. dimness, sadness 8. darkness
9. dejection, heaviness, obscurity
10. cloudiness, depression,
melancholy, sullen look
gloomy... 3. dim, sad, wan 4. dark,
dour, glum 5. drear, eerie, lurid,
moody, murky 6. cloudy, droopy,
lowery, morose 7. obscure
8. darkling, dejected, dolesome,
downcast 9. darkening, depressed,
tenebrous 10. depressing, foreboding,
tenebrific 11. pessimistic
12. disheartened
Gloomy Dean... 4. Inge
gloomy person... 7. killjoy
Gloria... 4. rite 8. doxology
glorification... 6. praise 7. worship
8. doxology, honoring 9. festivity
10. apotheosis 13. jollification
14. sanctification
glorify... 4. laud 5. adore, bless, exalt,
extol, honor 6. praise 7. elevate,
worship 8. beautify, sanctify
9. celebrate
glorious... 3. sri 5. grand, noble
6. elated, superb 7. eminent, radiant
8. ecstatic, renowned, splendid
9. beautiful, hilarious 10. celebrated,
delightful 11. illustrious, magnificent,
resplendent 12. praiseworthy
glory... 4. fame, halo 5. bliss
(celestial), boast, éclat, honor
6. heaven, nimbus (cloud of), praise,
renown 8. grandeur 10. admiration,
brilliancy, effulgence 11. distinction
13. glorification
gloss... 4. glow 5. color, sheen, shine
6. enamel, luster, polish, remark
7. burnish, pretext 8. glossary,
palliate 9. extenuate 10. brightness,
commentary 14. interpretation
gloss over... 4. fard (obs), wink
5. blink, color 6. excuse 8. palliate

glossy... 5. glacé, nitid, shiny, sleek
6. luster, sheeny, smooth 7. radiant,
shining 8. lustrous, polished
10. reflecting
glove... 3. mit 4. mitt 5. trank
(shaped) 6. boxing, ceatus, mitten
7. gantlet 8. gauntlet
12. mousquetaire
glow... 4. burn 5. ardor, flame, flush,
glean, shine 6. beauty, redden
7. redness 9. eloquence
10. luminosity 13. incandescence
glower... 4. gaze 5. glare, scowl, stare
glowing... 3. red 4. warm 5. drunk
6. ardent, cadent 7. burning,
excited, fervent, flushed 8. eloquent,
luminous 9. beautiful 10. enthusiastic
glucose... 5. rutin, sugar 8. dextrose
glue... 3. fix 4. join 5. paste, stick
6. adhere, cement, fasten, sizing
7. gelatin 8. adhesive, fastener
9. viscosity
glum... 3. sad 5. moody 6. dismal,
gloomy, sullen 8. frowning
glut... 4. cloy, fill, sate 5. gorge, stuff
6. pamper 7. engorge, satiate,
satisfy, surfeit 8. overfill, overload,
plethora, saturate
gluten... 3. gum 4. glue 6. fibrin
7. gliadin 8. adhesive
glutinous... 4. sizy 5. gluey 6. viscid
8. adhesive
glutton... 6. rascal, wretch 7. epicure
8. gourmand 9. cormorant,
scoundrel, wolverine 11. gormandizer,
greedy eater
gluttony... 5. greed 7. edacity
8. voracity 12. intemperance
13. voraciousness
glycerine machine man... 8. effetman
gnar, gnarr (of dogs)... 5. growl, snarl
gnarl... 4. knot 5. growl, snarl, twist
6. tangle 7. contort, distort, roughen
10. contortion 12. protuberance
(tree)
gnarled... 5. rough 6. knotty, rugged
7. complex, knotted, twisted
12. cross–grained
gnash... 4. bite 5. grate, grind (teeth)
gnat... 3. fly 5. nidge 6. insect
8. mosquito
gnaw... 3. eat 4. bite, chew 5. grind,
waste 6. rankle 7. corrode 8. wear
away
gnede... 6. scanty 7. lacking, miserly,
sparing
gnib... 5. ready, sharp 6. clever
gnome... 3. elf, imp, saw 5. bodie,
bogey, dwarf, maxim, nisse
6. goblin, kobold, sprite 8. aphorism
gnomic... 8. didactic 10. aphoristic
gnomic poets (Gr)... 5. Solon
8. Theognis (of Megara)
10. Phocylides (of Miletus)
gnostic... 4. wise 6. shrewd
7. knowing 9. sagacious
Gnostic... 6. Ophite 7. Abraxas
(Abrasax), Sethite
gnu... 6. kokoon 8. antelope
go... 3. act, die, gae, run 4. fail, fare,
game, move, pass, turn, walk, wane,
wend, work 5. leave, sally 6. betake,

decamp, depart, elapse, embark,
energy, extend, result, retire, travel,
weaken **7.** advance, entrain, journey,
proceed **8.** continue, diminish,
withdraw **9.** eventuate, harmonize

go (pert to)...
around.. **6.** detour **7.** circuit
8. surround
ashore.. **4.** land **9.** disembark
astray.. **3.** err
at.. **6.** attack **9.** undertake
away.. **4.** exit, scat, shoo **5.** scoot,
scram **6.** begone, depart
9. disappear
back.. **3.** ebb **6.** recede, repass,
retire, return, revert **7.** regress,
retrace
before.. **7.** precede **8.** antecede
11. participate
down, under.. **4.** fail, sink **7.** capsize,
descend, founder, succumb, undergo
8. submerge **11.** deteriorate
easily.. **4.** lope **5.** amble
furtively.. **5.** steal **6.** tiptoe
over.. **5.** renew **6.** revise **7.** retrace
8. rehearse, traverse **9.** backtrack,
re–examine
through.. **4.** pass **5.** spend **6.** suffer
7. exhaust (fortune), persist, undergo
9. persevere **10.** experience
up.. **4.** fail, rise **5.** arise, raise
6. ascend
with.. **4.** suit **5.** agree, court
6. accord **8.** coincide **9.** accompany
10. understand

goa... **5.** Tribe (Queensland) **6.** mugger
7. gazelle

goad... **3.** egg **4.** poke, prod, prog,
spur, urge **5.** ankus (elephant),
decoy, impel, prick, sting, thorn,
valet (manège) **6.** incite **7.** inflame
8. irritate, stimulus **9.** incentive

goal... **3.** aim, end **4.** base, fate,
home, mark **5.** bourn (bourne),
Mecca, reach, score, Thule (Myth)
6. object **7.** purpose **9.** objective
11. destination

goanna... **6.** iguana, lizard **7.** monitor

goat... **4.** buck, dupe **5.** brown
6. engine, lecher **9.** scapegoat
13. laughingstock

goat (pert to)...
astronomy.. **9.** Capricorn
fig.. **8.** caprifig
fish.. **6.** mullet
get one's.. **3.** irk, vex **4.** rile **5.** pique
6. nettle
god.. **3.** Pan
haircloth.. **5.** Tibet (Thibet) **6.** camlet
hair cord (Bedouin).. **4.** agal

goat (type of)... **3.** kid, ram, tur, zac
4. ibex, tahr, urus **5.** Capra, goral,
pasan (pasang), serow, takin
6. Alpine, Angora, chamal, Jemlah,
mammal **7.** aurochs, markhor
8. Cashmere, ruminant

goatsucker... **4.** bird **7.** dorhawk,
grinder **9.** nighthawk
12. whippoorwill

gob... **4.** lump, mass **5.** choke, mouth
6. sailor **8.** mouthful, quantity

goby... **4.** fish, mapo

go–by... **4.** snub **7.** evasion, passing
13. circumvention

god (Myth, Relig)...
Babylonian.. **2.** Zu **3.** Anu, Sin
4. Adad, Enzu, Nama, Nebo (Nebu)
5. Aruru, Cirru, Dagan, Nintu
8. Ningirsu **10.** Ninkhursag
11. Ningishzida
Celtic.. **6.** Aengus
Cymric.. **4.** Lleu (Llew)
Egyptian.. **2.** Ra **3.** Bes, Dis, Geb
(Keb), Min, Seb **4.** Amen, Amon,
Ptah **5.** Horus, Thoth **6.** Dhouti,
Osiris
false.. **4.** Baal, idol **6.** Mammon
Greek.. **4.** Ares, Zeus **5.** Comus,
Hymen, Momus, Pluto **6.** Hermes,
Somnus **7.** Bacchus **8.** Dionysus
Hebrew.. **3.** Jah **7.** Jehovah
Hindu.. **4.** Agni, Deva, Kama, Siva
(Shiva) **6.** Varuna
household.. **3.** Lar **5.** Lares **6.** Penate
Irish.. **5.** Dagda (pagan)
love of, for.. **5.** piety **6.** bhakti
9. theophile
Norse.. **2.** Er, Ve **3.** Tyr, Ull, Van
4. Loki, Odin, Thor, Ymir **5.** Aesir,
Donar, Vanir, Wodin
Roman.. **4.** Jove **5.** Comus, Janus,
Orcus **7.** Bacchus, Mercury **8.** Dis
pater
Semitic.. **5.** Hadad **6.** Nergal
Supreme.. **3.** Dei, Deo, Dio **4.** Deus,
Soul, Zeus **6.** Elohim, Spirit
12. Infinite Mind, Supreme Being
Teutonic.. **3.** Tiu **4.** Hoth

god (of)...
agriculture.. **4.** Nebo **6.** Faunus
beauty.. **6.** Aengus (Oengus)
beginnings, creation.. **4.** Ptah, Zeus
5. Janus **6.** Varuna
commerce.. **5.** Vanir **7.** Mercury
darkness, evil.. **3.** Set, Sin **6.** Nergal
day.. **5.** Horus
dead.. **5.** Orcus **6.** Osiris
discord.. **4.** Loki
earth.. **3.** Geb (Keb), Seb **5.** Dagan
east wind.. **5.** Eurus
evil.. **2.** Zu **3.** Set, Sin **6.** Nergal
fate.. **5.** Moira (Moera)
fire.. **4.** Agni **5.** Girru **6.** Vulcan
flocks.. **3.** Pan
January.. **5.** Janus
joy.. **5.** Comus
justice.. **7.** Forseti (Forsete)
law.. **4.** Zeus
lightning.. **4.** Agni
love.. **4.** Amor, Ares, Eros, Kama
5. Bhaga, Cupid **6.** Aengus (Oengus)
March.. **4.** Mars
marriage.. **5.** Hymen
medicine.. **11.** Ningishzida
mountains.. **5.** Atlas **7.** Olympus
music.. **6.** Apollo
Northmen.. **5.** Aesir
oceans.. **7.** Oceanus
poetry.. **5.** Bragi
ridicule.. **5.** Momus
sea.. **7.** Neptune, Proteus
sky.. **3.** Anu
sleep, dreams.. **6.** Somnus
8. Morpheus

storm.. 2. Zu 6. Teshup
sun.. 2. Ra (Re) 6. Apollo, Nergal
thunder.. 4. Thor 7. Jupiter
Thursday.. 4. Thor
Tuesday.. 3. Tiu, Tyr
underworld.. 3. Dis 5. Pluto 6. Osiris
  7. Serapis 8. Dis pater
  11. Ningishzida
war.. 3. Ira, Tyr 4. Mars 5. Woden
  8. Ningirau
wealth.. 5. Bhaga 6. Plutus
Wednesday.. 5. Woden
wind.. 4. Adad 5. Eolus, Eurus,
  Hadad 6. Aeolus, zephyr 8. Favonius
wine.. 7. Bacchus 8. Dionysus
wisdom.. 4. Nebo 5. Thoth 6. Dhouti
woods.. 7. Silenus
youth.. 6. Apollo
goddess... 3. Ate, Dea, Eir, Eos, Nox,
  Nyx, Ops, Pax, Uni 4. Apet, Eris,
  Fury, Gaea, Hera, Isis, Leda, Maat,
  Nike, Nina, Sati 5. Aruru, Damia,
  Diana, Doris, Epona, Freya, Hygea,
  Irene, Pakht, Salus, Venus, Vesta
  6. Allatu, Athena, Aurora, Cybele,
  Hecate, Hestia, Ningal, Pietho,
  Selene, Semele, Tellus, Vacuna
  7. Artemis, Demeter, Minerva, Parvati
  9. Aphrodite, Eumenides, Mnemosyne
  10. Persephone, Proserpina
goddess of...
agriculture.. 3. Ops 7. Demeter
arts.. 6. Athena, Pallas
beauty.. 3. Sri 5. Freya, Venus
  7. Lakshmi
dawn.. 3. Eos 5. Ushas 6. Aurora,
  Matuta
destiny.. 4. Fate 5. Moira, Parca
discord.. 3. Ate 4. Eris
earth.. 4. Gaea 5. Aruru 6. Ishtar,
  Tellus
Eskimos.. 5. Sedna
fertility.. 7. Demeter
fire.. 6. Hestia
fortune.. 5. Tyche
freedom.. 7. Feronia
fruit.. 6. Pomona
grain, harvest.. 3. Ops 5. Ceres
Hawaiians.. 4. Pele
healing.. 3. Eir 4. Gula
health.. 5. Damia, Hygea, Salus
hearth.. 5. Vesta
history.. 4. Saga
horses.. 5. Epona
hunt.. 5. Diana 6. Vacuna
infatuation.. 3. Ate
justice.. 7. Nemesis
light.. 6. Lucina
love.. 5. Venus 6. Ishtar 9. Aphrodite
magic, witchcraft.. 6. Hecate
marriage.. 4. Hera
maternity.. 4. Apet
mischief.. 3. Ate 4. Eris
moon.. 4. Luna 5. Diana 6. Phoebe,
  Selene (Selena)
mother of the gods.. 4. Rhea
nature.. 4. Rhea 5. Nymph 6. Cybele
night.. 3. Nox, Nyx
peace.. 3. Pax 5. Irene 6. Athena
poetry.. 5. Erato
rainbows.. 4. Iris

sea.. 5. Doris
seasons.. 5. Horae
summer.. 6. Aestus
sun.. 5. Pakht (Pacht)
trees.. 6. Pomona
truth.. 4. Maat
underworld.. 4. Fury 6. Allatu
  10. Persephone, Proserpina
vengeance.. 3. Ara, Ate 7. Nemesis
victory.. 4. Nike
virtue.. 5. Fides
war.. 5. Anath, Bella
wealth.. 3. Sri 7. Lakshmi
wisdom.. 6. Athena 7. Minerva
youth.. 4. Hebe
Godforsaken... 6. vacant 7. forlorn
  8. desolate, wretched 9. neglected
godly... 5. pious 6. devout, divine
  7. saintly 9. religious, righteous
godmother... 6. cummer (kimmer)
  7. sponsor
God's...
abode.. 7. Olympus
acre.. 10. churchyard
board.. 14. communion table
country.. 4. home 8. homeland
  9. Vaterland 10. fatherland
cupbearer.. 8. Ganymede
fluid (vein).. 5. ichor (icor)
food.. 8. ambrosia
gods, The (pert to)...
death of.. 9. theoktony
marriage of.. 8. theogamy
messenger of.. 6. Hermes
mother of.. 4. Rhea
Twilight of.. 8. Ragnarok
worship of.. 9. theolatry
Goetae... 7. wizards (anc) 9. sorcerers
  14. thaumaturgists
Goethe (pert to)...
home.. 6. Weimer (Ger)
masterpiece.. 5. Faust
talent.. 4. poet 8. novelist
  9. dramatist
goffer, gauffer... 5. crimp, flute, plait
  (lace, paper)
gog... 3. bog 4. stir 9. agitation
Gog (Bib)... 5. Ruler (of Magog), tribe
goggle... 3. eye 4. roll 5. state
  6. squint 11. roll the eyes
goggler... 4. fish (oceanic)
goggles... 6. screen 7. glasses
  8. blinkers, eyeshade 10. spectacles
going... 6. moving, travel 7. current,
  working 9. departure 10. obtainable
  11. in operation
gola... 7. granary 9. storeroom
  11. Indian caste
golach, goloch... 6. beetle, earwig
  9. centipede
Golconda... 6. wealth 8. rich mine
gold... 2. Au 3. oro 4. gelt, gilt
  5. aurum, color, lucre, metal, money
  6. riches, wealth 7. bullion
gold (pert to)...
alloy.. 4. asem 6. oroide
artificial.. 8. Mannheim
assayer cup.. 5. cupel
bar.. 5. ingot
braid, lace.. 5. orris
brick.. 7. swindle
coin (US).. 5. eagle

compound.. 6. auride
containing.. 4. doré
discoverer (US).. 6. Sutter (1849)
field (Bib).. 5. Ophir
fish.. 9. shubunkin
fool's.. 6. pyrite
gilding.. 6. ormolu 9. imitation
Heraldry.. 2. or
King (Myth).. 5. Midas
land of (Bib).. 5. Ophir
like.. 5. auric 7. aureate
measure.. 5. carat
Rush.. 8. Klondike (1897)
   10. California (1849)
seekers (Calif).. 9. Argonauts (1849)
   11. Forty–Niners
symbol.. 2. Au
vein.. 4. lode
washing pan.. 5. cupel
gold and silver... 11. noble metals
golden... 4. gilt 5. auric, blest
   6. blonde, yellow 7. aureate,
   aureous, halcyon 8. metallic,
   precious, valuable 9. Pactolian
   10. auspicious 11. flourishing
golden (pert to)...
Age.. 9. Saturnian, siècle d'or
apple.. 3. bel 4. Eris (goddess)
   5. Paris (giver) 6. tomato
bird.. 6. oriole
bough.. 9. mistletoe
Fleece seeker.. 5. Jason 8. Argonaut
Fleece ship.. 5. Argos
rod.. 8. solidago
goldenrod (pert to)...
genus.. 8. Solidago
State Flower of.. 7. Alabama
   8. Kentucky, Nebraska
goldfish... 4. carp 9. shubunkin
Goldfish (Astron)... 6. Dorado
golf (pert to)...
club.. 4. iron 5. baffy, spoon
   6. driver, mashie, putter 7. brassie,
   midiron, niblick
hazard.. 4. trap 5. stymy 6. bunker
   11. restriction
score.. 3. par 4. bogy (bogie)
   5. eagle 6. birdie
stroke.. 4. baff, chip, hook, loft, putt
   5. drive, slice
term.. 3. ace, par, tee 4. baff, fore
   5. bogey, divot, eagle, green, slice
   6. birdie, dormie, sclaff, stymie
   (stimy) 7. gallery
Golgotha... 7. Calvary 8. cemetery
goliath... 4. frog 5. crane, giant,
   heron
Goliath (pert to)...
Bib.. 5. giant (Philistine)
death site.. 4. Elah
home.. 4. Gath
slayer.. 5. David
Gomorrah (Bib)... 5. Sodom
   13. wicked country
Gomuti palm... 5. areng
gondola race (Venice)... 7. regatta
gone... 3. ago, off 4. dead, left, lost,
   past, yore 5. since 6. absent,
   passed, ruined 8. departed, past
   hope, vanished 9. forgotten
   10. infatuated
goober... 6. peanut

good... 2. eu (pref) 3. bon, fit 4. able,
   full, gain, just, kind 5. ample, godly,
   moral, nifty, pious, sound, valid
   6. benign, devout, expert, profit,
   savory 7. genuine, helpful, liberal,
   trained, upright 8. decorous, interest,
   pleasing, salutary, suitable, virtuous
   9. admirable, competent, enjoyable,
   estimable, excellent, favorable,
   honorable, indulgent, reputable
   10. auspicious, beneficial,
   courageous, gratifying, profitable,
   sufficient 11. commendable,
   well–behaved 12. considerable,
   satisfactory, stouthearted
good (pert to)...
bye.. 4. ta–ta 5. adieu, adios, ciaou
   6. so long 7. cheerio 8. farewell
for nothing.. 4. mean 5. idler
   6. wretch 7. useless 8. indolent
   9. worthless 11. rapscallion
health.. 5. skoal 6. prosit
management.. 6. eutaxy
mighty.. 7. skookum
ordinarily.. 8. mediocre
spirit.. 6. daemon 8. Eudaemon
   12. agathodaemon
tidings.. 6. gospel 7. evangel
will.. 5. favor 9. affection, readiness
   11. benevolence 12. friendliness
goodness... 5. piety 6. virtue
   8. kindness, validity 9. godliness,
   propriety 10. excellence, generosity,
   savoriness
goods... 5. wares 7. ability 8. chattels,
   property 11. information, merchandise
goods cast overboard, sunk...
   5. lagan (lagend) 6. jetsam
   7. flotsam 10. contraband
goose... 4. bean, dupe, fool, gull, iron,
   snow, tule 5. Anser, brant, solan
   6. Canada, gander, gannet, goslet
   7. gosling, graylag (greylag)
   8. barnacle 12. white–fringed
goose (pert to)...
grease.. 6. axunge
pygmy.. 6. goslet
relating to.. 8. anserine
story character.. 5. ganza
gooseberry... 5. fabes (color)
   6. escort, groser (groset), thapes
   8. chaperon, feaberry
gopher... 5. snake 6. rodent 7. burglar
   8. squirrel, tortoise 10. salamander
Gopher State... 9. Minnesota
gore... 3. mud 4. dirt, dung, stab
   5. blood, cloth (triang), filth, slime
   6. pierce 8. heraldry 9. bloodshed,
   penetrate
gorge... 3. eat 4. bolt, glut, sate
   5. chasm, gully 6. canyon, coulee,
   defile, nullah, ravine, valley 7. choke
   up, overeat, pitcher, satiate 8. overfill
gorgeous... 5. grand, showy
   8. colorful, dazzling 9. beautiful
   10. delightful 11. magnificent,
   resplendent
gorgon... 4. ogre, ugly 7. Jezebel
   (Bib), monster
Gorgons (Gr Myth)... 6. Medusa,
   Stheno 7. Euryale 9. sentinels
gorilla... 3. ape 4. thug 5. brute

6. monkey 8. assassin
gorilla man... 9. Du Chaillu (brought ape from Africa)
gormandizer... 9. chowhound 11. trencherman
gorse... 5. furze 7. juniper
goshawk... 5. Astur 6. tercel
gospel... 5. faith, truth 6. belief 7. epistle, evangel 8. doctrine 9. orthodoxy, selection (Bib) 10. revelation 11. glad tidings 12. proclamation
Gospels (Four)... 11. diatessaron
gossip... 3. cat, eme, gup 4. chat, news, talk 5. on–dit 6. claver, gabble, norate, report, tattle 7. clatter 8. idle talk, quidnunc 9. chatterer 10. newsmonger, talebearer
gossoon... 3. boy, lad (serving) 5. youth 6. garçon
got... see *get*
Gotham... 9. Newcastle (Eng) 11. New York City
Gothamite... 9. New Yorker
Gothic (pert to)...
alphabet.. 11. Moeso–Gothic
architecture.. 6. French
design.. 7. writing 12. architecture
era.. 10. Middle Ages
people.. 4. rude 5. Goths 6. fierce 7. Teutons
printing type.. 5. Doric 9. square–cut
gouge... 4. tool 5. cheat 6. chisel, groove 7. defraud, swindle 8. impostor 10. imposition
Gounod's opera... 5. Faust
gourd... 4. pepo 5. color, flask, melon 6. squash 8. calabash, cucurbit 9. Cucurbita 11. calabazella
gourmand... 5. eater (luxurious) 6. taster 7. epicure, glutton, gourmet 10. fastidious, gluttonous, voluptuary 11. connoisseur
gourmet... 7. epicure 8. gourmand 11. connoisseur
gout... 4. clot, drop 6. blotch 7. disease 9. arthritis
govern... 3. run 4. curb, lead, rein, rule 5. reign 6. bridle, direct, manage 7. conduct, control, preside 8. dominate, regulate, restrain 9. influence, supervise
governess... 4. ayah 5. nurse 6. abbess, duenna 8. guardian 12. instructress
government... 4. rule, sway 6. polity 7. control, regimen 10. management 12. jurisdiction 14. administration
government (pert to)...
agent.. see *representative* below
centralized.. 12. totalitarian
church.. 9. hierarchy 10. hierocracy
foe.. 3. Red 9. anarchist, mercenary, terrorist
form.. 6. polity
grant.. 6. patent
in exile.. 7. de facto
lands.. 5. amani
levy.. 3. tax 6. impost
official.. 10. bureaucrat
representative.. 6. consul 8. diplomat,

minister 10. ambassador
science of.. 8. politics
strong.. 5. power
system.. 6. regime
vicarious.. 7. regency
without.. 6. acracy
government by...
church.. 9. hierarchy 10. hierocracy
few.. 9. oligarchy
God.. 8. theonomy
holy body.. 9. hagiarchy 10. hagiocracy
inner control.. 8. endarchy
law.. 9. nomocracy
men.. 9. andocracy
mob.. 10. ochlocracy
no one.. 6. acracy
rich.. 10. plutocracy
seven.. 9. heptarchy
six.. 12. sextumvirate
slaves.. 10. doulocracy
ten.. 8. decarchy (dekarchy)
three.. 8. triarchy 11. triumvirate
women.. 11. gynecocracy
worst men.. 12. kakistocracy
governor... 4. woon 5. chief, nabob, ruler 6. dynast, regent 7. alcalde, decarch (of 10 men), viceroy 8. decurion, director 9. mechanism 10. magistrate
gown... 4. robe, toga 5. cloak, dress, frock 6. chiton, clothe, cyclas, invest, kimono, mantle 7. cassock, college, garment, matinee, soutane (Eccl), sultane 8. negligee, peignoir 9. nightgown
gozell, gozill... 10. gooseberry
gozzard... 9. gooseherd
gra... 4. love 5. agrah 6. liking 8. fondness 10. sweetheart
grab... 3. nab 4. game (cards), take 5. grasp, seize 6. arrest, clutch, snatch, vessel
grabble... 4. feel 5. grope 6. grovel, sprawl 7. harvest 11. appropriate
grace... 4. fate, luck, note, tact 5. adorn, charm, favor, honor, mercy, title 6. beauty, become, bedeck, polish, prayer, virtue 7. dignify, enhance 8. clemency, easiness, elegance, kindness, reprieve 10. comeliness, refinement, seemliness 12. graciousness, thanksgiving
graceful... 4. airy, easy, feat 6. comely, seemly 7. elegant, fitting, tactful 8. charming, debonair 9. beautiful, courteous, sylphlike 11. appropriate
Graces, The Three (Gr Myth)... 5. Aegle (Mother) 6. Aglaia (Brilliance), Thalia (Bloom) 10. Euphrosyne (Joy)
gracile... 4. slim, thin 6. slight 7. slender
gracious... 4. kind 5. suave 6. benign, urbane 7. affable 8. generous 9. courteous, favorable
grackle... 3. daw 4. bird, myna 7. jackdaw 9. blackbird
gradation... 4. step 5. scale, steps 6. ablaut, nuance, series, stages

7. degrees 10. graduation,
succession
grade... 4. even, rank, rate, size, sort,
step 5. level, order 6. assort,
degree, school, smooth 7. arrange,
incline 8. classify, gradient, graduate
gradual... 4. easy, slow 6. gentle
9. leisurely
graduate... 4. pass, size 5. grade,
taper 6. alumna 7. alumnus,
promote, student 8. shade off
graffito (scratched crudely)...
7. drawing 10. scratching
11. inscription
Graf Spee blown up... 7. Uruguay
(1939)
graft... 3. dig 4. cion (scion), join,
toil, work 5. ditch, fraud, labor,
spade, unite 6. boodle, fasten,
inarch, trench 7. bribery, implant,
joining
grafted (Her)... 4. enté
Grail... see *Holy Grail*
grain... 3. jot, rye 4. atom, bran,
corn, dram, food, grit, iota, malt,
meal, mite, oats, rice, whit 5. fiber,
maize, scrap, spark, trace, wheat
6. barley, millet, sesame 8. particle
grain (pert to)...
Bible.. 4. ador
bundle.. 5. sheaf 7. sheaves
chaff.. 4. bran, grit
cracked.. 6. groats
ear of.. 5. spike 6. ressum (rizzom)
exchange (Finan).. 3. pit
feeding on.. 11. granivorous
fungus, disease.. 4. rust, smut
5. ergot 6. mildew
goddess of.. 5. Ceres
ground.. 4. meal 5. flour, grist
husks.. 4. bran 5. straw
measure.. 6. thrave
mill.. 5. quern
mixture.. 6. fodder 7. farrage
9. bullimong
small.. 7. granule
spike.. 3. ear 6. rizzom
stack.. 4. rick
storage, warehouse.. 3. mow 4. silo
5. hutch 8. elevator
grammar (pert to)... 5. parse
6. gender, simile, syntax 7. diction,
parsing, prosody, synesis, wordage
8. enallage, language, metaphor,
paradigm 9. accidence, etymology,
phonology 10. conformity, declension,
inflection 11. conjugation
grammatical case... 6. dative
8. ablative, genitive, vocative
9. objective 10. accusative,
nominative
grampus... 3. arc 4. orca 5. whale
6. killer 7. dolphin 8. cetacean
granada... 11. pomegranate
Granada Moorish Castle site...
8. Alhambra (Sp)
granary... 3. bin 6. grange 8. cornloft
10. repository, storehouse (grain)
grand... 4. epic 5. great, large, lofty,
money, noble, piano 6. august,
epical, famous, superb, swanky
7. eminent, sublime 8. gorgeous,

majestic, splendid, thousand
9. dignified, grandiose, important,
sumptuous 11. illustrious, magnificent
Grand Canyon State... 7. Arizona
grandchild... 2. oe, oy
grandchild, great... 5. ieroe
grandee... 7. magnate 8. nobleman
10. clarissimo
grandeur... 5. glory 7. dignity, majesty
8. elegance, eminence, vastness
9. greatness, immensity, sublimity
10. augustness 11. stateliness
grandeval... 4. aged 7. ancient
grandfather... 4. aiel (obs), avus
6. atavus 8. gudesire
grandiloquent... 5. grand, lofty
6. turgid 7. pompous 9. bombastic
12. magniloquent
grandiose... 4. epic 5. grand 6. turgid
8. imposing 9. bombastic, flaunting
12. ostentatious
Grandma Moses... 17. Anna Mary
Robertson
grandmother... 6. beldam (beldame),
granny, gudame 7. grandam
(grandame), grandma 8. babushka
grandparent (pert to)... 4. aval
grandson... 6. nepote
Grand Teton peak... 7. Wyoming
grange... 4. farm 7. granary
9. farmhouse 11. association (1867)
18. Patrons of Husbandry
granite... 4. rock 5. stone 6. aplite,
marble, quartz 8. feldspar
9. pegmatite
Gran Quivira... 5. ruins (mission)
16. National Monument (N M)
grant... 4. cede, deed, enam, gift,
give, lend, loan, mise 5. admit,
allow, bonus, jagir (jaghar), spare
6. accord, bestow, confer, demise,
permit, remise 7. appease, concede,
confess, subsidy 8. appanage,
sanction, transfer 10. conveyance
11. acknowledge
granulated... 5. rough 6. coarse
7. grained 8. granular, hardened
12. crystallized
grape... 3. fox, uva 5. Tokay
6. Malaga, Muscat 7. Catawba,
Concord, Hamburg, Mission, Niagara
8. Delaware, grenache, Isabella,
Thompson 9. Chasselas, muscadine
10. sweetwater 11. scuppernong
grape (pert to)...
cluster.. 6. raceme
color.. 7. blue–red 9. cathedral
conserve.. 5. uvate
cultivation.. 11. viticulture
dried.. 4. pasa 6. raisin
family, genus.. 5. Vitus 8. Vitaceae
juice.. 4. dibs, must, sapa, stum
military.. 4. shot
pomace.. 4. marc, rape
preserve.. 7. raisine
residue.. 4. marc, rape 6. pomace
seed.. 6. acinus
sugar.. 7. maltose 8. dextrose
grapefruit... 6. pomelo 8. shaddock
12. Citrus Maxima
grapevine... 4. caro 5. rumor
6. canard, report 8. maneuver

(wrestling), pipeline 9. dance step
11. information, underground

graph... 5. chart 7. contour, diagram,
drawing

graphic... 5. clear, drawn, vivid
7. written 8. engraved 9. pictorial
11. descriptive, picturesque,
significant 12. diagrammatic

grasp... 4. grip, hent (obs), hold, take
5. catch, clasp, gripe, seize
6. clinch, clutch, gowpen (gowpin)
7. control 8. handgrip 9. apprehend
10. comprehend, understand

grasping... 4. avid 5. close 6. greedy
7. holding, miserly 8. covetous
9. rapacious 10. avaricious,
prehensive 11. acquisitive
13. comprehending, understanding

grass... 3. eel, hay, Poa, rye 4. cane,
Coix, crab, gama, herb, oats, reed,
rice, rush, tare, wire 5. ankee,
Avena, Briza, brome, chess, goose,
grain, grama, hedge, otate, spart,
spear 6. bamboo, barley, darnel,
fescue, marram, millet, redtop,
sesame, switch 7. alfalfa, Bermuda,
buffalo, esparto, Hordeum, Poeceae,
timothy 8. mesquite 9. blue–grass,
Boutelous

grasshopper... 4. grig 6. cicada, locust
7. katydid

grassland... 3. lea, sod 4. mead, veld
(veldt) 5. llano, range, sward
7. pasture, prairie, savanna
(savannah)

grate... 3. rub 4. fret, grid, grit, rasp
5. annoy, chafe, grind 6. abrade,
scrape 7. network 8. irritate

grateful... 7. cumshaw (beggar's
phrase), welcome 8. pleasing,
thankful 10. gratifying
12. appreciative

gratification... 6. relish, reward
8. gratuity, pleasure 10. indulgence,
recompense

gratified... 4. glad 7. pleased

gratify... 5. favor, grace, humor
6. arride, foster, pamper, please
7. appease, delight, flatter, indulge,
requite, satisfy 10. remunerate

grating... 4. grid 5. grate, grill, harsh,
raspy 6. grille 7. lattice, network
8. strident 10. irritating
11. latticework 12. nerve–racking

gratis... 4. free 6. freely 9. on the
cuff 10. for nothing, gratuitous, on
the house 12. gratuitously

gratitude... 5. grace 6. praise, thanks
12. appreciation, gratefulness,
thankfulness

gratuitous... 4. free 5. given 6. gratis,
wanton 7. assumed 8. baseless,
needless 9. voluntary 10. groundless
11. superfluous, unwarranted

gratuity... 3. fee, tip 4. dole, gift,
give, vail 5. bonus, bribe 6. bounty
7. cumshaw, pension, present
9. baksheesh (bakshish), buonamano,
lagniappe (lagnappe), pourboire

grave... 3. pit, urn 4. bier, tomb
5. fosse (foss), sober, staid
6. sedate, solemn, trench 7. earnest,

engrave, serious 8. sermonic
9. important, momentous, ponderous,
sculpture, sepulcher

grave (pert to)...
   cloth.. 6. shroud 8. cerement
   9. cerecloth
   coffin.. 4. pall
   comb form.. 5. serio
   mound (anc).. 6. barrow 7. hillock,
   tumulus
   person.. 10. sobersides
   robber.. 5. ghoul

gravel... 5. geest, grain, stone
6. baffle, defeat, refute 7. calculi,
erratic (boulder), pebbles
10. meerschaum (color)

graven... 6. etched 7. infixed
8. engraved 10. sculptured

gravestone... 5. stele (stela) 6. cippus,
marker, pillar 8. monument
9. tombstone 11. sarcophagus

gravitation... 7. descent, gravity
10. attraction

gravity... 6. weight 7. dignity, sadness
8. enormity, grimness, sobriety
9. formality, solemnity 10. attraction,
importance 11. earnestness,
seriousness, weightiness
12. significance 13. momentousness

gravity law, discoverer... 6. Newton

gray, grey... 3. dim, old, sad 4. aged,
dark, dull, gris, obex 5. dingy, hoary,
polio (comb form), sober 6. animal
(gray), dismal, somber 7. hueless,
neutral, silvery 9. cheerless
10. achromatic

gray, grey (color)... 3. ash, bat, dun
4. ashy, dove, iron, lead, mole, zinc
5. acier, ashen, dusty, mouse, pearl,
slate, smoke, steel, taupe 6. French,
Oxford, Quaker, reseda, silver
7. cesious, dappled, grizzle
8. charcoal, cinereal, gunmetal
10. battleship, dapple–gray
13. pepper–and–salt

graze... 3. eat, rub 4. drab, rase, skim
5. brush, shave 6. browse, feed on,
scrape 7. scratch

grease... 3. fat, oil, tip 4. daub, lard,
mort, saim, soil 5. bribe, smear,
suint 6. axunge 7. fatness, fawning,
lanolin 8. flattery 9. lubricate

greasy... 4. oily 5. dirty, gross, thick
6. smooth 8. slippery, unctuous
10. indelicate

great... 3. big 4. good, huge, vast
5. ample, chief, large, major, stout,
whole 6. famous, grande 7. drastic,
eminent, extreme 8. intimate,
numerous 9. elaborate, important
11. magnanimous 12. considerable
13. distinguished

great (comb form)... 5. macro, megal

Great (pert to)...
   Barrier (NZ).. 4. Otea (Isl) 9. coral
   reef
   Beyond.. 5. grave 9. afterlife,
   hereafter 10. after world, The
   Unknown 11. eternal home
   14. beyond the grave
   Cham of Literature.. 13. Samuel
   Johnson (Dr)

Circle sailing .. 10. orthodromy
Commoner .. 4. Clay, Pitt 7. Stevens (Thaddeus) 9. Gladstone
Divide .. 7. Rockies 8. Rocky Mts 9. watershed (US) 14. Rocky Mountains 17. Continental Divide
Fire .. 6. London (1666) 7. Chicago (1871)
Lakes .. 4. Erie 5. Huron 7. Ontario 8. Michigan, Superior
Mogul .. 5. Akbar (Hind) 7. diamond
Names .. 6. Hector 8. Hercules, Lysander 9. Alexander
Pyramid .. 6. Cheops
Spirit (Ind) .. 4. Mana, Zemi 5. Wakan 6. Manito (orenda), Pokunt
White Way .. 8. Broadway (NY)
Great Britain ... 5. Wales 7. England 8. Scotland 12. Commonwealth 13. United Kingdom 15. Northern Ireland
greatest ... 6. utmost 7. extreme, noblest
greatness ... 9. largeness 10. importance 11. magnanimity
Greco, Graeco (comb form) ... 5. Greek 7. Grecian
Greece ... see also *Greek*
ancient .. 4. Elis 5. Argos, Doris, Ionia 6. Attica, Epirus, Hellas 7. Argolis, Boeotia
cape .. 5. Melea 7. Matapan
capital .. 4. Elis (anc) 6. Athens
citadel .. 9. Acropolis
city .. 6. Patras, Sparta 7. Corinth, Piraeus 8. Salonika, Thessaly
island .. 5. Chios, Corfu, Crete, Samos 6. Lesbos 10. Dodecanese, Samothrace
mountain .. 3. Ida 5. Athos 6. Peleon, Pindus 7. Olympus 9. Parnassus
peninsula .. 6. Balkan
river .. 4. Arta 7. Hellada 9. Archelous
sea .. 6. Aegean, Ionian
seaport .. 4. Enor, Volo 5. Corpu, Pylos 8. Salonika 9. Gallipoli
Greek, Grecian (pert to) ...
abbess .. 4. amma
alphabet .. see *Greek alphabet*
altar .. 7. eschara
architecture .. 5. Doric, Ionic 6. xystus (part) 10. Corinthian
assembly .. 4. pynx 5. agora
avenging spirit .. 3. Ate, Ker 6. Erinys
boat .. 6. caique
bowl (golden) .. 5. depas
breath .. 6. pneuma
chariot .. 4. biga
church section .. 6. andron, bemata
citadel .. 9. Acropolis
city (Greek for) .. 5. polis
commander (anc) .. 7. navarch
commune .. 4. deme, nome
contest .. 4. agon (anc) 6. Delian 7. Pythian, Olympic 8. marathon
courtesan (Athen) .. 5. Thais
culture, literature .. 7. classic 9. classical
cup, bowl .. 5. depas 6. cotula
cupid .. 4. Eros
dance (anc) .. 6. hormos 7. pyrrhic, strophe 9. dithyramb

department .. 8. nomarchy
dish .. 5. gyros 9. souvlakia
early .. 5. Arius 6. oecist
epic .. 5. Iliad 7. Odyssey
female worshipper .. 5. orant
garment .. 5. tunic 6. chiton, peplos
gravestone .. 5. stele
horse (talking) .. 5. Arion
hospitality .. 5. zenia
judge .. 6. dicast
language .. 6. Romaic
lawgiver .. 5. Minos, Solon
magistrate .. 6. archon, eparch 7. nomarch
mistress .. 7. hetaera (hetaira)
monster .. 8. Typhoeus (100–headed)
note .. 4. nete 5. neume 6. pneuma 9. hexachord 10. tetrachord
Old Testament .. 10. Septuagint
platform .. 4. bema 7. logeion
poem .. 5. Iliad 7. Odyssey
portico .. 4. stoa, xyst
sacred enclosure .. 5. sekos
sacred object .. 6. sacrum
sacrificial offering .. 5. hiera 8. sphagion
school .. 7. Eleatic
serpent .. 4. seps 6. Python
slave .. 5. Baubo, helot, iambe 6. penest
soldier .. 7. hoplite
song .. 5. melos
sorceress .. 5. Circe
spirit .. 5. Momus (evil)
temple .. 4. naos 5. cella (part)
theater .. 5. odeon
war cry .. 5. alala
youth (would–be citizen) .. 7. ephebus
Greek alphabet ... 2. Mu, Nu, Pi, Xi 3. Chi, Eta, Phi, Psi, Rho, Tau 4. Beta, Iota, Zeta 5. Alpha, Delta, Gamma, Kappa, Omega, Sigma, Theta 6. Lambda 7. Digamma (obs), Epsilon, Omicron, Upsilon
Greek Furies ... 6. Alecto, Erinys 7. Magaero 9. Tisiphone
Greek god of ...
atmosphere .. 5. Hadad
chief .. 4. Zeus
dreams .. 8. Morpheus
fire .. 6. Vulcan
flocks .. 3. Pan
heavens .. 6. Uranus
love .. 4. Eros
lower world .. 5. Hades
ridicule .. 5. Momus
river .. 8. Eridanus
sea .. 6. Nereus
storm .. 6. Teshup 7. Hittite
sun .. 6. Apollo, Helios 7. Phoebus
vegetation .. 8. Dionysus
war .. 4. Ares 8. Enyalius
winds .. 5. Eurus 6. Aeolus
youth .. 6. Apollo, Pothos (winged)
Greek goddess of ...
agriculture .. 7. Artemis, Demeter
beauty .. 9. Aphrodite
chase .. 7. Artemis
clouds .. 5. Niobe
dawn .. 3. Eos 7. Alcmene, Ariadne
discord .. 4. Eris
earth .. 2. Ge 4. Gaea

fate.. 5. Moira
fortune.. 5. Tyche
heaven.. 4. Hera
infatuation.. 3. Ate
magic.. 6. Hecate (3–headed)
memory.. 9. Mnemosyne
moon.. 2. Io 5. Diana 6. Selene
nature.. 7. Artemis
night.. 3. Nyx 4. Leto 6. Hecate
peace.. 5. Irene
phallus.. 5. Baubo
retribution.. 7. Nemesis
underworld.. 6. Hecate (Hekate)
vengeance.. 3. Ara 7. Nemesis
victory.. 4. Nike
wisdom.. 6. Pallas 7. Minerva
youth.. 4. Hebe

Greek Myth...
character.. 5. Niobe, Sinon 6. Adonis,
   Gorgon, Rhesus 7. Calchus, Icarius,
   Pandora, Phrixos 8. Atalanta,
   Endymion, Meleager, Tantalus
   12. Erichthonius
deity.. 5. Satyr, Titan 6. Cronus
enchantress.. 5. Circe, Medea
giant.. 7. Antaeus 9. Enceladus
   (100–armed)
huntress.. 8. Atalanta
monster.. 8. Typhoeus (100–headed)
nymph.. 5. Oread 6. Nereid
serpent.. 6. Python
spirit (evil).. 5. Momus

Greek personalities...
astronomer.. 12. Eratosthenes
author.. 6. Lucian
biographer.. 8. Plutarch
counselor.. 6. Nestor
dramatist.. 9. Aeschylus (Poet),
   Euripedes, Sophocles
   12. Aristophanes
fabulist.. 5. Aesop
geographer.. 6. Strabo
hero.. 4. Ajax 5. Talos 6. Nestor,
   Thesus 7. Cecrops 10. Hippolytus
historian.. 8. Xenophon 9. Dionysius,
   Herodotus 10. Thucydides
mathematician.. 6. Euclid
   10. Archimedes
painter.. 7. Apelles, El Greco
patriarch.. 5. Arius
philosopher.. 5. Galen, Plato, Timon
   6. Nestor 8. Diogenes 9. Aristotle
   10. Heraclitus, Parmenides,
   Pythagorus, Xenophanes
   11. Anaximander
physician.. 5. Galen
poet.. 5. Arion, Homer 6. Pindar
   7. Thespis 8. Anacreon 9. Aeschylus
poetess.. 6. Erinna, Sappho
   7. Corinna
sage.. 6. Thales
sculptor.. 5. Myron 7. Phidias
statesman.. 8. Pericles 9. Aristides
green... 3. raw 4. vert 5. fresh, mossy
   6. callow, praseo (comb form),
   unripe 7. emerald, verdant
   9. malachite, unskilled, untrained
   11. flourishing 13. inexperienced
   15. unsophisticated
green (pert to)...
back.. 4. frog 11. legal tender (US)
blue.. 4. cyan, saxe 7. sistine

comb form.. 6. praseo
eyed.. 7. jealous
famous.. 6. Gretna (Scot)
film.. 6. patina
gray.. 5. olive 6. reseda
pale.. 7. celadon
pigment.. 10. terre–verte
quartz.. 5. prase
sickness.. 9. chlorosis
tea.. 5. Hyson
green–back herring... 5. cisco
Greenland...
Bay.. 6. Baffin
capital.. 8. Godthaab
Danish word.. 8. Crönland
explorer.. 9. Frobisher (1576)
   10. Eric the Red
natives.. 6. Eskimo (mostly)
settlement.. 4. Etah
strait.. 5. Davis
whale.. 5. right
Green Mt Boys' leader... 10. Ethan
   Allen (1775)
Green Mt State... 7. Vermont
greenness... 5. color 8. sourness
   9. ignorance 10. immaturity
   11. gullibility 12. inexperience
Greenwich time (London)...
   8. absolute, standard 16. Royal
   Observatory
Greenwich Village... 9. Manhattan
   11. New York City
greeting... 3. ave, how 4. hail 5. hallo
   6. accoil, halloa, salute 7. address,
   welcome 8. saluting 9. reception
   10. compliment, salutation
   14. correspondence
gregarious... 6. common, social
   7. affable 8. sociable
   12. social–minded 13. communicative
grego... 5. cloak 6. jacket 9. greatcoat
Gregory... 4. Code (Rom law), Pope,
   year 5. chant, staff (Mus) 6. church
   8. calendar
grenier... 5. attic
grey... see *gray*
grid... 5. grill 7. grating, griddle,
   network 8. gridiron 13. football field
grief... 3. rue, woe 4. care, pain, ruth
   5. abuse, dolor, trial 6. mishap,
   sorrow 7. anguish, offense, remorse,
   sadness 8. disaster, distress,
   document 9. grievance, suffering
   10. affliction 11. bereavement,
   lamentation
grieve... 3. cry, rue 4. erme, pain
   5. mourn, wound 6. lament, sorrow
   7. afflict 8. complain, distress
   10. discomfort
grievous... 4. sore 6. bitter, severe
   7. doleful, heinous, intense
   8. terrible 9. sorrowful
   10. disastrous, oppressive
   11. distressing, gravaminous
griff... 4. claw, glen 6. griffe, ravine
griffe... 4. spur (Arch) 7. mulatto
griffin, griffon... 6. charge (Her)
   7. monster 10. decoration
grig... 3. eel 5. annoy, dwarf
   7. cricket, heather 8. irritate
   9. tantalize 11. grasshopper
grill... 4. cook 5. broil 7. griddle,

network, torture 8. gridiron
10. restaurant 11. interrogate
12. cross—examine
grille... 6. window (ticket) 7. grating,
network
grilse... 6. salmon 7. botcher
grim... 4. dour, sour 5. gaunt, harsh,
stern 6. grisly, horrid, savage, sullen
7. ghastly, hideous 8. horrible,
pitiless, ruthless, sinister 9. ferocious,
frightful, merciless, repellent
10. forbidding, inexorable, relentless,
unyielding
grimace... 3. mop, mow, mug 4. face,
mock, moue, pout, sham 8. pretense
10. distortion 11. affectation
grimalkin... 3. cat 5. vixen 6. feline
8. old woman
grime... 4. dirt, smut, soot 5. sully
9. blackness
grin... 5. fleer, smile, smirk
grind... 3. dig, rub, vex 4. bray, grit,
mull, whet 5. crush, gnash, grate,
study 6. abrade, drudge, harass,
polish, powder, satire, school, squash
7. operate, routine, sharpen
8. drudgery 9. comminute, masticate,
pulverize, triturate
grinder... 5. molar, tooth, tutor
8. sideshow 9. announcer
10. flycatcher, goatsucker
grinding... 6. boning 7. grating
9. attrition 10. burdensome,
irritating, tyrannical 12. excruciating
grinding (pert to)...
mental.. 6. boning 8. cramming,
studying
stone.. 4. mano 6. metate, muller
9. millstone
substance.. 5. emery 8. abrasive
gringo... 5. alien 8. American
9. foreigner 10. Englishman
grip... 3. bag 4. hold 5. clasp, cleat,
ditch, drain, grasp, seize, spasm
6. clench, clutch, furrow, grippe,
handle, obsess, trench, valise
7. control, illness 8. gripsack,
handfast
gripe... 4. grip, hold, pain 5. annoy,
brake, colic, grasp, pinch, spasm
6. clutch, harass 7. afflict, control,
mastery, vulture 8. complain, distress
9. complaint 10. affliction,
oppression
griskin... 4. chop, loin 5. steak
grisly... 4. grim 5. harsh 7. ghastly,
hideous 8. gruesome, terrible
9. deathlike 10. forbidding
grist... 3. lot 4. malt 5. grain, grind
8. quantity (bees)
grit... 4. sand 5. nerve, pluck
6. gravel 7. bravery, courage, Liberal
9. sandstone 11. persistence
12. perseverance
grivet... 4. tota, waag 6. monkey
grizzly bear... 7. Ephraim (hunter's)
15. Ursus horribilis
groats... 5. grain, wheat (cracked)
6. cereal
grog... 3. rum 5. rumbo 8. beverage
9. firewater
groggy... 5. dazed, drunk, shaky, tipsy

8. unsteady, wavering 9. tottering
groin... 4. lisk 6. inguen
groom... 4. syce, tidy 5. brush, curry,
dress, preen, train 7. hostler,
servant, shopboy 9. assistant,
stableman 10. bridegroom,
manservant
groove... 3. rut 4. dado 5. chase,
croze, flute, scarf, stria, track
6. furrow, rabbet, raggle, scrobe,
sulcus 7. channel, rifling, routine
8. philtrum 10. excavation
11. canaliculus
grooved... 6. fluted 7. striate, sulcate
11. canalicular 12. canaliculate
grope... 4. feel 6. fumble, search
7. grabble, grubble
groper... 4. fish 7. grouper
grosbeak... 5. finch 8. hawfinch
gros point... 4. lace (Venetian)
6. stitch (Aubusson) 8. tapestry
(Gobelin) 11. cross-stitch
gross... 3. fat 5. obese 6. brutal,
coarse, earthy, greasy, impure, vulgar
7. brutish, massive, obscene,
sensual, witless 8. flagrant, indecent,
receipts 9. aggregate, unrefined
10. indefinite, indelicate, scurrilous
grotesque... 3. odd 5. antic, clown,
freak 6. unique 7. awkward, baroque,
bizarre 8. deformed, fanciful
9. fantastic 11. incongruous
grotesque figure (Chin)... 5. magot
grotto... 3. den 4. blue, cave, grot
5. crypt, speos, vault 6. cavern,
recess 8. catacomb
ground... 3. bog 4. acre, area, base,
clay, clod, farm, land, moor, park,
plot, root, soil 5. basis, cause, earth,
field, hurst, marsh, ridge, solum,
swale, train 6. belief, bottom, milled,
region 7. country, gritted, opinion,
premise, terrain (terrane) 8. initiate,
instruct 9. establish, territory,
viewpoint 10. background,
foundation, substratum
ground (pert to)...
beetles.. 5. Amara
berry.. 9. cranberry 12. checkerberry
grain.. 4. bran, meal 5. flour, grist
nut.. 5. chufa, gobbe 6. goober,
peanut
squirrel.. 5. Xerus 6. gopher, hackee,
rodent 8. chipmunk 11. spermophile
groundhog (pert to)...
American.. 6. marmot
day.. 9. Candlemas (Feb 2)
home.. 8. Puxatori
termed.. 6. marmot, rodent
8. aardvark, whistler 9. woodchuck
10. whistlepig
groundless... 4. idle 5. false
8. baseless 9. unfounded
11. unwarranted 13. unsubstantial
grounds... 4. lees, park 5. basis,
dregs 7. residue 8. scruples
group... 3. set 4. band, bevy, clan,
crew, gang, herd, pack, sect, sept,
team, unit 5. batch, bunch, class,
clump, corps, flock, genus, order,
panel, shift, tribe 6. legion, troupe
7. arrange, bracket, cluster,

company, species 8. assemble,
category, classify, division
10. assemblage 11. aggregation
group (pert to) . . .
actors . . 6. troupe
animals . . 3. gam, nid, nye, pod
4. herd, nide 5. covey, drove, pride
(lions)
birds . . 4. Pici (woodpeckers)
brilliant . . 6. galaxy
far out . . 6. hippie 7. hipster
laymen . . 5. laity
political . . 4. bloc, ring 5. party
7. machine
singer . . 4. duet 5. choir, octet
6. chorus 7. chanter, quartet
(quartette)
students (graduate) . . 7. seminar
trees . . 4. tope 5. copse, grove,
woods 7. alameda, orchard, pinetum
(pines)
group (quota of) . . .
eight . . 5. octad, octet (octette)
five . . 6. pentad
four . . 4. tetrad 7. quartet (quartette)
nine . . 6. ennead
seven . . 6. heptad, septet (septette)
six . . 6. sextet (sextette)
ten . . 5. decad 6. decade
three . . 4. trio 5. triad, trine 7. Trinity
two vowels . . 6. digram 7. digraph
9. diphthong
grouped . . . 7. classed 8. agminate,
arranged, gathered 9. assembled,
collected, organized 10. classified
grouper . . . 4. fish 5. guasa 6. groper
8. rock hind
grouse . . . 4. bird 6. repine 7. grumble
8. complain 9. ptarmigan
12. capercaillie
grouse (pert to) . . .
courtship . . 3. lak
red . . 7. Lagopus
ruffed . . 6. Bonasa
grouty . . . 5. cross, sulky 6. crabby,
grumpy 7. grouchy
grove (pert to) . . .
living in . . 7. nemoral
mango . . 4. tope
pine . . 7. pinetum
poplar . . 7. alameda
sacred . . 5. Altis (Gr), Nemus (to
Diana)
small trees . . 5. copse
grovel . . . 4. fawn, roll 5. crawl, creep
6. cringe, crouch, shrink, tumble,
wallow, welter 7. debauch, truckle
8. flounder
groveling, grovelling . . . 6. abject
7. fawning 9. prostrate, truckling
11. bootlicking
grow . . . 3. bud, wax 4. come 5. raise
6. accrue, expand, mature, thrive
7. augment, develop, enlarge,
improve, produce 8. increase,
vegetate 9. cultivate
grow (pert to) . . .
dark . . 6. darkle
dim . . 5. blear
intense, profound . . 6. deepen
thin . . 8. emaciate
tiresome . . 4. bore, pall

together . . 7. accrete
worse . . 11. deteriorate
growing (pert to) . . .
angry . . 8. irascent
from without . . 9. ectogenic
10. ectogenous
in . . 6. linose
on trees . . 10. epidendral, epidendric
11. xylophilous (fungus)
out from . . 3. bud 4. stem 5. enate
6. sprout
spontaneously . . 9. adventive
together . . 7. accrete, joining
8. adhering
growing in . . .
clusters . . 8. racemose
fields . . 8. agrestal 9. agrestial
10. campestral
ground . . 9. geogenous
mud . . 9. uliginose
pairs . . 6. binate
rubbish . . 7. ruderal
snow . . 5. nival
water . . 7. aquatic
growl . . . 4. girn, gnar, rome 5. snarl
6. mutter 7. grumble 8. complain
growler . . . 3. cab, can 4. bass (black)
7. iceberg, pitcher 8. clarence
growth . . . 3. bud, wen 4. rise 5. felon,
shoot, tumor 6. effect, result
8. increase, swelling 9. expansion
10. vegetation 11. consequence,
development, enlargement
12. augmentation
growth (pert to) . . .
from within . . 8. endogeny
from without . . 9. ectogenic
10. ectogenous
fungus . . 4. mold, moss 6. mildew
marine . . 7. seaweed
of wood . . 5. copse 7. coppice
9. brushwood
premature . . 9. precocity
process of . . 8. nascency
retarding . . 9. paratonic
grub . . . 3. dig 4. food, plod, root,
spud 5. larva, mathe, slave, stump
6. assart, drudge, maggot, search
7. plodder 8. victuals
grubby . . . 5. dirty, grimy, small
8. dwarfish, infested, slovenly,
toadfish
grudge . . . 4. envy 5. covet, spite
6. hatred 7. grumble 8. begrudge
10. resentment
grudging spender . . . 8. tightwad
gruel . . . 4. diet 6. cereal, liquid
7. disable 8. porridge
grueling, gruelling . . . 6. trying
9. demanding, punishing, weakening
10. exhausting
gruesome . . . 4. ugly 6. grisly, horrid,
sordid 7. ghastly, hideous, macabre
9. deathlike
gruff . . . 4. deep, rude, sour 5. bluff,
harsh, surly 6. clumsy, hoarse,
morose, severe 7. austere, bearish,
brusque
grum . . . 4. glum, sour 6. sullen
8. gutteral 13. harsh—sounding
grumble . . . 4. fret, hone, kick 5. growl,
snarl 6. grouse, mumble, mutter,

repine, rumble 7. maunder
8. complain
guacharo... 6. owlish 7. oilbird
10. goatsucker
Guam...
capital.. 5. Agana
discoverer.. 8. Magellan (1521)
idol, fetish.. 5. anito
island.. 7. Mariana
mountain peak.. 6. Lamlam
port.. 4. Apra
guanaco... 5. llama (like) 6. alpaca
guarantee... 6. avouch, ensure, insure,
surety 7. endorse, promise, warrant
8. guaranty, security, warranty
9. agreement
guaranty... 4. bond 6. pledge
8. security, warranty 9. agreement,
assurance, guarantee
guarapucu... 5. wahoo
guard... 3. van 4. care, curb, keep,
tend, tile 5. tiler, watch 6. bantay,
bridle, convoy, defend, escort, fender,
gaoler, jailer, keeper, patrol, picket,
police, shield, warden 7. defense,
protect 8. restrain, sentinel,
watchman 9. attention, protector
10. cowcatcher, precaution,
protection
guarded... 4. wary 7. careful
8. cautious, defended, discreet,
vigilant, watchful 9. protected
10. restrained 11. circumspect,
sentinelled
guardhouse... 4. brig
guardian... 5. angel, tutor 6. helper,
keeper, patron, warden 7. trustee
8. defender, tutelary 9. custodian,
protector 10. mystagogue (Church
relics)
guardian (Gr)... 5. Argus (100–eyed)
8. Cerberus (3–headed)
guardianship... 4. care 6. charge
7. custody, tuition 8. guidance,
tutelage 13. protectorship
Guatemala...
ant.. 5. kelep
bird (sacred).. 7. quetzal (quezal)
capital.. 13. Guatemala City
coin (gold).. 7. quetzal
fruit (avocadolike).. 4. anay
Indian tribe.. 4. Inca
port.. 7. San José 10. Champerico
13. Puerto Barrios
ruins.. 5. Mayan
volcano.. 4. Agua 5. Fuego
gudgeon... 4. bait, dupe, goby
9. killifish 10. allurement
gue... 5. rogue 7. sharper
guenon... 6. monkey (long–tailed)
guerdon... 5. crown, prize 6. reward
8. requital 10. recompense
guereza... 6. monkey
Guernsey... 6. brandy, cattle, Island
(Channel) 7. garment
guess... 5. fancy, think 6. divine
7. imagine, presume, surmise,
suspect 8. estimate 10. conjecture
guest... 6. caller, inmate, lodger,
patron 7. visitor 9. inquiline (insect)
Guiana...
British capital.. 10. Georgetown

Dutch (Surinam) capital..
10. Paramaribo
French capital.. 7. Cayenne
guide... 3. con, key 4. clew, clue,
lead, rein, sign, sley 5. order, pilot,
steer, teach, tutor, usher 6. advise,
direct, dirigo, govern, guidon
7. adviser, conduct, courier, marshal
8. Baedeker (book), cicerone,
director, polestar, regulate
9. regulator
Guido (scale)... 2. ut 3. alt, A re, B
mi, E la (highest) 5. E la mi, gamut
7. alamire
guild... 5. hanse 7. society
10. fellowship 11. association,
brotherhood
Guildhall statue (London)... 3. Gog
5. Magog (1708)
guile... 5. craft 6. deceit 9. duplicity,
falseness, treachery 11. furtiveness
guileless... 5. naive 6. simple
7. artless, natural, sincere
8. innocent
guillemot... 3. auk 4. coot 5. murre
guilt... 3. sin 4. sake 5. culpa
8. iniquity, peccancy 10. guiltiness,
wickedness 11. criminality, culpability
14. impeachability
guilty... 6. nocent 8. culpable
Guinea, W Afr...
capital.. 7. Conakry (Konakri)
city.. 4. Boke, Labe
export.. 7. bananas 10. pineapples
government.. 8. republic
mineral.. 4. gold 7. bauxite
8. diamonds
tree.. 4. akee
tribe.. 6. Fullah 7. Malinke, Soussou
guinea fowl... 3. hen 4. keet
6. turkey 7. pintado 8. pheasant
guinea pig... 4. boar, cavy 5. Cavia
8. capybara
guise... 3. way 4. form, garb, mask,
mien, mode 5. cloak, cover
6. aspect, custom 7. fashion, pretext
8. behavior 9. semblance
10. appearance
guitar (pert to)...
Hindu.. 4. vina
like.. 4. lute 7. bandore
octaves.. 5. three
Oriental.. 5. sitar
pitch (term).. 5. dital
ridge.. 7. samisen
small.. 7. ukulele
strings, number.. 3. six
gula... 4. cyma, neck, ogee 6. gullet
7. cavetto, molding
gulch... 5. cleft, gorge 6. arroyo,
coulee, ravine
gulf... 3. bay, pit, sea (landlocked)
4. eddy 5. abyss, basin, chasm,
cleft, inlet 6. vorago 7. opening
9. whirlpool 10. separation (wide)
gull... 4. dupe, fool, gray 5. brick,
cheat, cully, fraud 7. cheater,
deceive, defraud, mislead 8. impostor
gull (bird)... 3. cob (cobb), mew
4. Lari, pirr, skua, tern, Xema
5. pewit (laughing) 7. Larinae
8. seedbird 9. kittiwake

gullet... 3. maw 4. tube 5. gully
6. throat 7. channel, harness (part)
9. esophagus
Gulliver, Lemuel (pert to)...
brutes.. 6. Yahoos (race of)
character, story by.. 5. Swift
romance.. 16. Gulliver's Travels
voyage.. 6. Laputa 8. Lilliput
9. Houyhnhnm 11. Brobdingnag
gully... 3. gut 4. wadi (wady) 5. drain,
gorge, gulch 6. arroyo, gutter, ravine
7. couloir 11. watercourse
gum... 3. ase 4. chew, lerp (larp,
laarp) 5. elemi, myrrh, xylan
6. acacia, arabic, chicle, conima,
thwart, tupelo 7. camphor, deceive,
elastic, gingiva 8. bdellium (Bib),
mucilage 12. frankincense
gum (pert to)...
Africa.. 4. kino 7. catechy
Asia.. 6. Storax 8. galbabum
Australia.. 5. tuart
Central America.. 6. chicle
Egypt.. 5. kikar
India.. 5. amrad
Philippines.. 8. galagala
United States.. 5. Nyssa 6. tupelo
gumbo... 3. mud 4. okra (ocra), sail,
soup 6. patois
gumboil... 7. abscess, parulia
gummy... 5. lumpy 6. viscid
7. viscous 8. adhesive, resinous
gumption... 8. sagacity 10. enterprise,
initiative, shrewdness
gums... 3. ula 6. resins 8. gingivae
gun... 3. gat, rod 4. iron, pump, roer
5. Maxim, rifle, thief, tommy
6. ack–ack, Archie, barker, Bertha,
cannon, mortar, pistol, Rodman
7. bazooka, carbine, firearm, Gatling,
machine, shotgun 8. amusette,
ordnance, revolver
gun (pert to)...
blow.. 8. sumpitan
caliber.. 4. bore
case (leather).. 7. holster
chamber.. 5. gomer
cleaner.. 6. ramrod
cotton.. 5. nitro 9. explosive, pyroxylin
mount.. 6. turret
platform.. 11. emplacement
gunfire... 5. salvo 6. strafe 8. enfilade
gunner... 10. bombardier
12. artilleryman
guppy... 6. minnow 8. Lebistes
9. killifish
gurnard... 4. fish 6. rochet, Trigla
8. dragonet, sea robin
guru (Ind)... 7. teacher
gush... 3. jet 4. flow, pour 5. emote,
spurt 7. chatter 10. outpouring
14. sentimentalize
gushing... 7. flowing 8. diffused,

effusive, spurting 9. exuberant
11. sentimental 13. demonstrative
gusset... 4. gore 7. bracket
9. abatement (Her)
gust... 4. blow, gale, scud, wind
5. berry, blast, storm 6. flurry, squall
8. outburst 10. excitement
gusto... 4. élan, zest 5. savor, taste
6. fervor, liking, relish 9. eagerness
12. appreciation
gut... 3. sac (silkworm) 5. gully
6. bowels, catgut, defile, strait
7. destroy, plunder 8. entrails
9. intestine 10. disembowel,
eviscerate
guts... 5. belly, force, pluck 6. vitals
7. courage, insides, stamina,
stomach 8. backbone, gluttony
10. intestines
gutta... 4. drop, spot 5. latex
7. campana, marking 8. ornament
guttate... 7. spotted 8. droplike
gutter... 4. rone 5. brook, ditch, drain,
eaves, gully, siver 6. cullis, groove
7. channel, conduit, scupper
11. watercourse
gutteral... 3. dry 4. burr 5. husky,
velar 6. hoarse 7. rasping, throaty
guttersnipe... 4. Arab 5. gamin
6. poster 9. ragpicker, sandpiper,
vulgarian
guy... 3. rod 4. flee, rope, stay, vang
5. chaff, chain, guide 6. banter,
decamp, effigy (Guy Fawkes), fellow,
person
Guy Fawkes Day... 13. Gunpowder
Plot (Eng, Nov 5,1605)
guzzle... 3. tun 4. tope 5. drain,
drink, spree 6. gutter, liquor, throat,
tipple 7. debauch, swallow
gymnast... 7. acrobat, athlete, teacher
gymnastics... 9. exercises
10. acrobatics 12. calisthenics
gypsy (pert to)...
book.. 3. lil
devil.. 5. theng
Dutch.. 8. Heidenen
horse.. 3. gri (gry)
Hungarian.. 7. Czigany
husband.. 3. rom
India.. 7. Bazigar
language.. 6. Romany
man.. 4. chal
sea.. 6. Selung
Spanish.. 6. gitano 7. Zincalo
Syrian.. 5. Aptal
term.. 4. calo 5. nomad
woman.. 4. chai (chi)
gyrate... 4. spin 5. twirl, whirl
6. rotate 7. revolve
gyre... 5. demon, whirl 10. revolution
gyves... 5. irons 6. chains 7. fetters
8. shackles

H

H... 5. aitch, zygal (shaped) 6. letter (8th), symbol 8. aspirate
haab... 8. calendar (Mayan)
haar... 3. fog
haba... 4. bean 8. lima bean
Habakkuk... 4. Book (Old Test) 7. prophet
habble... 5. brawl 6. gabble, hobble, uproar 9. confusion 10. difficulty
habeas corpus... 4. writ 7. summons (you have the body)
habile... 3. apt, fit 4. able 6. adroit, clever, expert 8. skillful (skilful), suitable 9. dexterous
habiliment... 4. garb 5. dress, habit 6. attire 7. apparel, costume, raiment 8. clothing, vestment 11. furnishings
habilitate... 5. dress, equip 6. clothe, fit out 7. entitle, qualify (for teaching)
habit... 3. rut, use 4. garb, suit, vice, wont 5. array, dress, haunt, usage 6. attire, clothe, custom, joseph (riding), nature 7. costume 8. clothing, habitude, practice 9. mannerism 10. deportment, habiliment
habitat... 4. home 5. abode, house, hovel 6. harbor, reside 7. exhibit (museum), lodging, station
habitation... 4. ecad, home 5. hovel 6. ghetto, warren (rabbit) 7. lodging 8. domicile, dwelling, tenement 9. occupancy, residence
habitual... 5. usual 6. common, wonted 7. orderly, regular 9. customary 10. accustomed, inveterate
habituate... 5. enure, inure 6. addict, inborn, season, settle 8. accustom, frequent, inherent 9. acclimate 11. acclimatize, familiarize
habitué... 8. attender 10. frequenter
hacendero... 6. farmer 10. proprietor
hache... 2. ax 7. hatchet
hacienda... 4. farm 5. abode, croft 6. estate 7. revenue 13. establishment
hack... 3. cut, hew 4. chop, jade, rent 5. coach, cough, devil, horse (rented), sever 6. drudge, mangle, writer 8. carriage, mutilate 9. mercenary 11. chronometer
hackberry... 6. Celtis 8. hapberry, oneberry 10. sugarberry
hackee... 8. chipmunk
hackle... 3. fly (angling) 4. comb, hack 6. shiner, temper 7. feather, hatchel, plumage 11. stickleback
hackneyed... 3. saw 5. banal, corny,

trite 6. cliché 8. timeworn 10. threadbare 11. commonplace, stereotyped 13. platitudinous
Hades... 3. pit 4. hell 5. abyss, limbo 7. inferno 9. perdition 10. lower world, underworld 11. netherworld
Hades (pert to)...
Babylonian.. 5. Aralu
capital.. 11. Pandemonium
god.. 5. Pluto
Greek.. 8. Tartarus
Hebrew.. 5. Sheol 7. Abaddon, Gehenna 8. Apollyon
Hindu.. 6. Naraka
mother.. 4. Rhea
river.. 4. Styx 5. Lethe 7. Acheron
Roman.. 3. Dis 5. Orcus
hadj... 10. pilgrimage
haft... 4. ansa, grip, hold 6. handle 8. dwelling
hag... 4. Fury, goad 5. crone, ghost, Harpy, vixen, witch 6. beldam (beldame), goblin 8. harridan, old woman 9. hobgoblin
hageen, hagein... 9. dromedary
hagfish... 5. borer 6. Mysine 7. lamprey (lowest existing craniate vertebrate)
haggard... 4. bony, lank, lean, pale, thin, wild 5. gaunt, spare 6. wanton 7. anxious, untamed 8. harrowed, unchaste, wild—eyed 9. deathlike, suffering, untrained 10. cadaverous 11. intractable, overwrought
haggle... 3. cut, hew 4. hack, prig 5. cavil 6. chisel, dicker, higgle, palter 7. bargain, chaffer, stickle, wrangle
Hague, The... 7. capital (Neth)
Haida (pert to)...
famed for.. 6. totems 7. carving 10. seamanship
Indian.. 15. British Columbia
tribe.. 11. Skittagetan
hail... 3. ave, ice 4. ahoy, call 5. avast, greet, skoal 6. accost, health, signal 7. acclaim, address, graupel, pellets
hair... 3. cue, fur, mop 4. lock, mane, seta, shag 5. pilus, plume, tress 6. thread 7. bristle 8. filament 10. narrowness
hair (pert to)...
accessory.. 3. net, pin 8. barrette
Angora.. 6. mohair
band.. 5. snood 6. fillet
braid.. 3. cue 4. fall 5. queue 7. pigtail
cell.. 12. Organ of Corti
cloth.. 3. aba 5. shirt 6. cilice

247

comb form .. **4.** pilo
curly .. **10.** cymotrichy
disease .. **8.** dandruff, psilosis
dresser .. **7.** friseur (Fr), stylist
dryness .. **7.** xerasia
excessive growth .. **7.** pilosis
flaxen .. **5.** linus
horse's foot .. **7.** fetlock
intestinal .. **6.** villus
liquid for .. **3.** set **5.** spray **6.** lotion
   7. relaxer
lock .. **5.** tress **7.** earlock, ringlet
   8. lovelock **9.** dreadlock
loss of .. **8.** alopecia, baldness
of the .. **6.** crinal
remover .. **9.** decalvant, epilatory
   10. depilatory
straight .. **10.** leiotrichy
style .. **3.** set **4.** Afro, tete, updo
   6. hairdo **7.** chignon, cornrow
   8. coiffure
tuft .. **4.** coma **5.** beard **6.** goatee
   7. cirrose, Galways, Vandyke
   8. whiskers **9.** sideburns
wave .. **4.** perm **6.** marcel
wig .. **6.** peruke **7.** periwig
wooly .. **9.** ulotrichy
hairiness ... **7.** villous **9.** villosity
hairless ... **4.** bald **5.** acoma
   7. acomous, epilose **8.** depilous,
   glabrous
hairpin ... **6.** bodkin **8.** bobby pin
hairsplitting ... **9.** quibbling
   11. distinction **13.** hypercritical
   14. hypercriticism, overparticular
hairy ... **4.** noil **5.** pilar **6.** comate,
   comoid, comose, crinal, pilose, shaggy
   7. bristly, crinose, hirsute **8.** trichoid
Haiti, Haitian ...
bandit .. **4.** caco
capital .. **12.** Port–au–Prince
dance .. **5.** mambo
discoverer .. **8.** Columbus (1492)
evil spirit .. **4.** baka (boko)
island .. **10.** Hispaniola **15.** Greater
   Antilles
language .. **6.** Creole, French, patois
liberator .. **9.** Toussaint
product .. **6.** coffee
sweet potato .. **6.** batata
hake ... **4.** fish **5.** idler, tramp **6.** loiter
   7. handgun **8.** kingfish
halberd ... **4.** bill **5.** frame (flogging)
   6. glaive, weapon (Mil)
halcyon ... **4.** bird, calm **8.** peaceful,
   tranquil **10.** auspicious, kingfisher
Halcyone (pert to) ...
changed to .. **10.** kingfisher
daughter of .. **6.** Aeolus
wife of .. **4.** Ceyx (Gr)
hale ... **3.** tug **4.** drag, draw, haul, pull,
   well **6.** hearty, robust, strong
   7. healthy **8.** vigorous **9.** strapping
half ... **4.** demi, hemi, part, semi, term
   5. share **6.** moiety **7.** divided, partial
   8. division, semester **9.** equal part,
   bisection **11.** imperfectly
half (pert to) ...
and half .. **5.** equal, mixed **6.** halved
   7. neutral
boot .. **3.** pac (pack) **6.** buskin
man, half bull .. **8.** minotaur

man, half horse .. **7.** centaur
mask .. **6.** domino
moon–shaped .. **9.** semilunar
nelson (wrestling) .. **4.** hold
stem to stern .. **8.** midships
turn (manège) .. **8.** caracole (caracol)
wit .. **4.** dolt **5.** dunce **9.** blockhead
Half Moon ship (pert to) ...
captain .. **11.** Henry Hudson
country .. **11.** Netherlands
first to sail .. **11.** Hudson River (1609)
Halicarnassus, famed for ...
Historians (Gr) .. **9.** Dionysius,
   Herodotus
monument .. **9.** Mausoleum (Tomb of
   Mausolus, 325 BC)
hall ... **3.** aula, room, sala **5.** entry,
   foyer, odeum (odeon) **6.** atrium,
   lyceum **7.** hallway, passage, theater
   8. corridor **9.** vestibule
   10. auditorium, passageway
hallow ... **5.** bless **8.** dedicate,
   sanctify, venerate **9.** celebrate
   10. consecrate
hallowed place ... **4.** fane, holy
   5. altar **6.** bethel, church, shrine,
   temple **9.** cathedral, synagogue
hallucination ... **6.** mirage **7.** chimera,
   fantasy **8.** delusion **9.** nightmare
hallux ... **3.** toe **5.** digit
halo ... **3.** arc **4.** aura, glow, nimb, ring
   5. glory, light **6.** areola, brough,
   circle, corona, nimbus **7.** aureole
   (aureola) **8.** encircle, halation
halt ... **3.** end **4.** camp, lame, limp,
   stop **5.** cease, check, pause, stand
   6. arrest, hold up, maimed **7.** limping
   8. blockage, crippled, lameness
   9. mutilated **10.** standstill
halter ... **4.** hang, rope **5.** noose, strap
   6. hamper **7.** shackle **8.** cavesson,
   restrain **9.** hackamore
halting ... **4.** lame **6.** maimed
   7. limping **8.** spavined
   10. hesitating, stammering
halting place ... **4.** camp **5.** étape
   7. bivouac **10.** encampment
halved ... **9.** dimidiate
Hamburg, Germany ...
color .. **5.** white **6.** yellow **7.** carmine
   11. carmine lake
fowl .. **11.** Leghornlike
fruit .. **5.** grape
lace .. **6.** edging
root (edible) .. **7.** parsley
steak .. **4.** beef
hamiform ... **6.** curved, hooked
   7. hamulus **8.** aquiline
   10. hook–shaped
Hamilton (pert to) ...
dynamics .. **8.** equation
famed as .. **9.** statesman
   11. philosopher **13.** mathematician
math .. **10.** quaternion
Hamite (N Afr) ... **5.** Fulah **6.** Berber,
   Somali (Somal)
hamlet ... **4.** dorp, vill **5.** aldea (aldee),
   casal (casale), thorp (thorpe)
   7. grouper (fish), village
Hamlet (pert to) ...
character .. **11.** Shakespeare
country .. **7.** Denmark

friend.. 7. Horatio
site.. 8. Elsinore
hammer... 4. beat, claw, jack, maul, peen, tack, tamp 5. gavel, kevel, madge, pound 6. beetle, martel, oliver, sledge, strike, swinge 7. belabor 8. malleate
hammer (pert to)...
bird.. 8. umbrette
blacksmith's.. 6. fuller, oliver
bricklayer's.. 6. scutch
end.. 4. poll
face.. 4. trip
head.. 4. peen 5. shark
medical.. 6. plexor 7. plessor
out.. 5. anvil, forge
smite.. 5. skite
stone.. 5. kevel, spall
hamper... 3. ped 4. clog, curb, load, slow 5. cramp, crate, maund 6. basket, burden, fetter, hinder, hopple, impede, seroon 7. confine, hanaper, manacle, shackle, trammel 8. encumber, restrain, restrict 9. container, embarrass 10. impediment
Ham's son... 4. Cush
hamster... 6. rodent 8. Cricetus
hamus... 4. hook 7. process (Zool)
hanaper... 6. basket, hamper
hand... 3. paw 4. fist, give, mano, palm, part, pass, side, till 5. claut, grasp, index, manus, power, share, skill 6. agency, worker 7. ability, pointer, workman 8. applause, tendency, transmit 9. craftsman, handiwork, signature 10. metacarpus 11. handwriting, performance 15. instrumentality
hand (pert to)...
back of.. 10. opisthenar
bag.. 4. etui, grip 5. cabas, purse 8. reticule
book.. 4. tome 5. codex 6. manual 9. vade mecum
cuffs.. 7. darbies 8. manacles 9. bracelets
handful.. 4. kirn 6. gowpen 7. maniple 8. quantity
measure.. 8. fistmele
me–down.. 4. used, worn 5. cheap 9. ready–made 10. secondhand
of the.. 6. chiral, manual
palm.. 4. loof 6. thenar
picked.. 5. eleme 6. choice 8. selected
script.. 6. Neskhi (Neski)
stone (grinding).. 4. mano
without.. 7. amanous
writing.. 11. chirography
writing on walls.. 4. doom, mene (Bib), omen 8. graffito
handicap... 4. lisp, race 6. burden, hamper, hinder, impede 8. encumber, equalize, penalize 9. advantage 10. impediment, stuttering 11. encumbrance 12. disadvantage
handicraftsman... 7. artisan
handkerchief... 7. malabar 8. mouchoir 9. neckcloth 11. neckerchief

handle... 3. ear, paw, ply, use 4. ansa, bail, deal, feel, haft, hilt, knob, maul, name, toat, tote 5. helve, pilot, snath, swipe, title, touch, treat, wield 6. deal in, direct, manage, rounce, second, sneath, tiller 7. control, operate
handle (pert to)...
awkwardly.. 6. fumble, mumble
carelessly.. 6. cajole 7. tweedle
roughly.. 4. maul 6. bruise, injure, mangle
shaped.. 6. ansate
skillfully.. 6. manage 7. control 10. manipulate
hands (pert to)...
nautical.. 4. crew, gang
off.. 4. don't, quit, stop 5. taboo 6. desist 9. interdict
on hips.. 6. akimbo
without.. 7. amanous
handsome... 5. ample 6. comely, heppen (dial) 7. elegant, gallant, liberal 8. generous, gracious, pleasing, suitable 9. agreeable, beautiful 10. jimpricute 11. appropriate, magnanimous 12. considerable
handwriting on the wall... 4. mene (Bib) 8. graffito, upharsin
handy... 4. deft 5. adept, ready 6. adroit, heppen, nearby, wieldy 8. skillful (skilful) 9. dexterous, versatile 10. accessible, convenient
hang... 3. sag 4. pend, rest, sway 5. cling, drape, droop, hover, knack 6. cleave, dangle, depend 7. execute, meaning, suspend
hang (pert to)...
around.. 4. loaf, wait 6. loiter 8. frequent
back.. 3. lag 5. demur, loath 6. falter 9. reluctant
down.. 3. lop 4. lave 5. droop 6. depend
loosely.. 3. lop 4. flag, loll 6. bangle, dangle
on, onto.. 5. cling 6. adhere, depend 9. persevere
over.. 6. impend
together.. 4. loin 6. cohere 9. co–operate
hanger–on... 3. bur 5. toady 6. heeler 8. follower, loiterer, parasite 9. appendage, dependent, sycophant, toadeater (menial) 10. blackguard
hanging... 5. arras, drape, loose 7. curtain, pendant (pendent), pensile, valance 8. downcast, pendency 9. execution, suspended
hanging (pert to)...
Eccl.. 6. dorsal, dossal (dossel)
Gardens of Babylon, builder.. 14. Nebuchadnezzar (Nebuchadrezzar)
ornament.. 6. bangle 7. pendant
stage.. 7. scenery
hangman... 8. carnifex 9. Jack Ketch 11. executioner
hangman's noose... 4. rope 6. hempen
hangnail... 6. agnail 7. whitlow
hangout... 5. joint 10. rendezvous

hank... 3. ran (twine) 4. coil 5. skein
hanker after... 5. crave, yearn
   6. aspire, desire, hunger 7. long for
Hannibal (pert to)...
   accomplishment.. 8. Punic War (2nd)
   father.. 13. Hamilcar Barca
   native of.. 8. Carthage
   rank.. 7. General (genius)
   victory at.. 6. Cannae
Hanover, House of... 8. Victoria
Hanukkah, Hanukka... 7. holiday
   (Jew) 16. Festival of Lights (Bib)
   17. Feast of Dedication (Jew)
haphazard... 6. chance, random
   8. accident, careless 9. orderless
haply... 9. perchance
happen... 4. come, fall, fare 5. evene
   (obs), occur 6. arrive, befall, betide,
   chance, mayhap 9. eventuate,
   transpire
happening... 4. fact 5. event (chance)
   6. tiding 7. episode 8. incident,
   periodic, sporadic 10. occurrence
happily... 5. fitly, haply 6. gladly
   9. tactfully, willingly 10. blissfully,
   cheerfully, gracefully 11. contentedly,
   opportunely 12. auspiciously,
   felicitously, prosperously, successfully
   13. appropriately
happiness, science of...
   11. eudaemonics
happy... 3. apt 4. cosh, glad 5. blest,
   faust, lucky, ready, seely, sunny
   6. joyful, timely 7. blessed, content,
   fitting 8. cheerful 9. contented,
   fortunate, pertinent 10. auspicious,
   felicitous, propitious, prosperous
Happy Valley... 8. paradise (of
   Rasselas, Andrew Jackson)
hara–kiri (Jap)... 7. seppuku, suicide
harangue... 3. nag 4. rant 5. orate,
   spiel, spout 6. screed, speech, tirade
   7. address, declaim, expound,
   lecture, oration
harass... 3. din, fag, nag, try, vex
   4. bait, fret, gall, haze, jade, raid,
   tire 5. annoy, beset, bully, chafe,
   grind, harry, tease, weary, worry
   6. badger, bother, heckle, hector,
   molest, pester, plague 7. agitate,
   disturb, hagride, perplex, provoke,
   torment, trouble 8. distress, irritate
   9. persecute, tantalize
harbinger... 4. host, omen 5. usher
   6. herald 7. presage, shelter
   8. fourrier, harborer 9. informant,
   messenger, precursor 10. forerunner
harbinger of Spring... 5. robin
   6. crocus
harbor, harbour... 3. bay 4. cave,
   port 5. haven 6. covert, foster,
   refuge 7. lodging, outport, retreat,
   shelter
hard... 3. fit 4. cold, dour, firm, iron,
   mean 5. close, harsh, rigid, stern,
   stony 6. knotty, robust, steely, stingy,
   strict, strong 7. callous, onerous
   8. diligent, rigorous, toilsome
   9. difficult, heartless, intricate,
   strenuous, stringent, wearisome
   10. inflexible, relentless, unyielding
   12. impenetrable, incorrigible

   13. unsympathetic
hard (pert to)...
   boiled.. 4. hard 5. tough 6. strict
   7. callous 8. hardened 10. solidified
   13. sophisticated
   coal.. 10. anthracite
   money.. 6. silver 8. metallic
   prefix.. 3. dys
   question.. 5. poser
   rubber.. 7. ebonite 9. vulcanite
   shell.. 6. lorica
   stone.. 7. adamant (diamond)
   wood.. 4. mabi, teak 5. maple
   6. walnut 8. mahogany
harden... 3. gel, set 4. cake, kern
   5. enure, inure, steel 6. freeze,
   ossify, temper 7. toughen
   8. indurate, solidify 9. habituate
   10. strengthen
hardened... 4. hard 5. caked
   6. frozen, wicked 7. callous, steeled
   8. indurate, obdurate, ossified
   9. heartless, reprobate, unfeeling
   10. impenitent, impervious,
   inveterate, solidified 12. impenetrable
hardening of the arteries...
   16. arteriosclerosis
hardening of the eyeball...
   8. glaucoma
hardheaded... 5. boche (Boche)
   6. German, shrewd, strict
   9. obstinate, sagacious
hardhearted... 4. mean 5. cruel
   7. callous 8. pitiless 9. unfeeling
   13. unsympathetic
hardship... 5. rigor 6. injury 7. trouble
   8. hardness 9. adversity, privation
hardtack... 5. bread 7. galette
   10. sea biscuit
hardwood... 3. ash, oak 4. ipil, mabi,
   teak 5. maple 6. walnut
   8. mahogany
hardy... 4. bold, hale, rash 5. brave,
   lusty, stout 6. daring, strong
   7. healthy, spartan 8. intrepid,
   resolute 9. audacious, confident
   10. courageous
hare... 3. doe, wat (watt) 4. buck,
   cony, pika (tailless) 5. lapin, Lepus
   6. rabbit, rodent, tapeti 7. leveret
hare (pert to)...
   constellation.. 5. Lepus
   harelike.. 6. agouti 8. leporine
   tail.. 4. scut
   track.. 4. slot
   type.. 10. cottontail, jack rabbit
harem... 5. serai 6. purdah, zenana
   8. seraglio 9. gynaeceum
harem room... 3. oda (odah)
harem slave... 9. odalisque (odalisk)
hark... 4. heed, hist 6. listen
   7. hearken, whisper 9. attention
harkened... 5. heard 6. heeded
   8. listened 9. hearkened
harlequin... 4. duck (sea) 5. clown,
   color 7. buffoon 9. fantastic, trickster
   11. masquerader 12. multi–colored,
   parti–colored
Harlequin (comedy)... 11. pantomimist
harm... 3. mar 4. bane, dere, evil,
   hurt, pain 5. grief, wrong
   6. damage, impair, injure, injury,

scathe (scath), sorrow
10. misfortune, wickedness
12. disadvantage
harmful ... 3. bad 4. evil, upas
6. nocent 7. baneful, hurtful, malefic,
noisome, noxious 8. damaging,
sinister 9. injurious 10. pernicious
11. deleterious, detrimental
12. insalubrious
harmless ... 5. seely 6. unhurt
8. dehorned, unharmed
9. innocuous, undamaged, uninjured
11. unoffending
harmonious ... 6. syntax 7. harmony,
musical, orderly, spheral, tuneful
9. accordant, agreeable, congruous,
consonant, eurythmic (eurhythmic),
melodious 10. compatible,
concordant, euphonious
11. conformable, symmetrical
harmonize ... 2. go 3. gee 4. tone
5. agree, blend, chime 6. attune
7. conform, consist 9. reconcile
10. correspond, symmetrize,
sympathize
harmony ... 4. tone, tune 5. music,
order, triad, unity 6. accord, cosmos,
melody, unison 7. concord, euphony
8. symmetry 9. agreement,
harmonics 10. conformity,
consonance
harness ... 4. gear 5. armor, equip
6. graith, tackle 7. uniform
8. accouter, ornament 9. caparison,
parachute
harness part ... 3. tug 4. hame, rein
5. trace 6. collar, halter, terret
7. apparel 9. hackamore
10. breastband, martingale
harp ... 4. arpa, koto, lyre, Lyra (Astron)
5. nanga 8. Irishman 11. clairschach
harp (pert to) ...
key .. 5. C Flat
octaves (number) .. 11. six and a half
pedals .. 5. seven
star .. 12. Harp of Arthur
strings .. 8. forty-six
harping ... 7. humdrum, tedious
9. iterating, repeating 11. repetitious
harpoon ... 5. spear 7. javelin 8. lily
iron
harpsichord ... 6. spinet 8. clavecin
9. lyrichord 12. clavicembalo
harpy ... 3. bat 5. eagle, fiend
9. plunderer 12. extortionist
Harpy (Myth) ... 5. Aello, ghoul
7. Celaeno, monster (part bird,
woman), Ocypete, Podarge (The Iliad)
harridan ... 3. hag 5. vixen, witch
6. virago 7. Jezebel 8. strumpet
9. termagant
harrier ... 3. dog 4. hawk 5. bully,
hound 7. heckler 8. badgerer
9. tormentor
harrow ... 4. dish, pain 5. harry, herse
(Hist), wound 7. oppress, torment,
torture 8. distress, lacerate
9. cultivate, formation (geese),
implement
harrowing ... 7. painful, racking, tilling
9. agonizing, torturous

11. cultivating, distressing
12. heart-rending
harry ... 3. vex 4. sack 5. annoy,
hound, worry 6. harass, hector,
plague, ravage, ravish 7. agitate,
besiege, pillage, plunder, violate
8. lay waste 9. persecute
Harry ... 5. Devil (Shak)
harsh ... 3. raw 4. dure, grim
5. acerb, acrid, asper, crude, gruff,
raspy, stern, stiff 6. bitter, coarse,
severe, unkind 7. drastic, painful,
pungent, rasping 8. clashing,
gutteral, jangling, rigorous, strident
9. inclement, offensive, repellent
10. discordant, relentless
11. acrimonious, disagreeing
harshness ... 5. rigor 7. raucity
8. acrimony, pungency, severity
9. gruffness 11. raucousness
hart ... 4. deer, stag 5. spade
hartebeest ... 4. asse, tora 5. caama
(kaama) 6. lecama 7. bubalis
8. antelope 10. Alcelaphus
Harvard College honor ... 4. book
5. detur 12. let it be given
harvest ... 4. crop, gain, rabi, reap
5. fruit, yield 6. autumn, gather,
reward 7. acquire, produce
harvest (pert to) ...
god .. 6. Cronus, Saturn
goddess .. 3. Ops 5. Ceres
home .. 4. kirn, mell 6. hockey
moon .. 4. full 15. autumnal equinox
second .. 9. aftermath
tick .. 6. acarid
hash ... 4. food 5. mince 6. jumble,
medley, ragout 7. mixture
10. hodgepodge 11. gallimaufry, olla
podrida
hashish ... 4. hemp 5. bhang (bang)
8. cannabis, narcotic
hassle ... 4. fray 5. brawl, melee
hasten ... 3. hie 4. scud, urge
5. amain, apace, hurry, scamp,
speed 7. further 8. expedite
10. accelerate 11. precipitate
hastened ... 3. ran 4. hied, sped
5. raced 6. rushed 7. hurried,
scooted 8. galloped 9. expedited
11. accelerated 12. precipitated
hasty ... 4. fast, rash 5. brash, eager,
fleet, quick, swift 6. speedy, sudden,
urgent 7. cursory, hurried 8. reckless
9. impetuous, impulsive, premature
11. expeditious, precipitate
hasty pudding ... 4. mush 9. stirabout
hat ... 3. fez, tam, top 4. felt, hood,
silk 5. beret, derby, gibus, opera,
straw, terai, toque 6. bonnet, cloche,
cocked, fedora, Panama, sailor,
topper, turban 7. chapeau, picture,
pillbox, porkpie, tricorn 8. sombrero
9. headdress, sou'wester, stovepipe,
ten-gallon 11. mortarboard
13. three-cornered
hat (pert to) ...
antique .. 7. bycoket (bycocket),
petasos (petasus)
covering .. 8. havelock
crown .. 4. poll
defensive .. 4. coif

Eccl.. 7. biretta 9. Cardinal's
military.. 5. shako
opera.. 4. tile 5. gibus 6. topper
pass (the hat).. 10. collection
slang.. 4. plug 5. dicer
stovepipe.. 8. caroline
under one's.. 6. secret 9. to oneself
hatch... 4. door, gate, line (art), plot
   5. breed 6. invent 7. concoct,
   produce 8. contrive, hatchway,
   incubate 9. floodgate, originate
   10. bring forth, sluice gate
hatchet... 2. ax (axe) 3. adz (adze)
   4. mogo 8. tomahawk
hate... 4. miso (comb form) 5. abhor,
   odium 6. detest, hatred, loathe,
   rancor 7. despise, dislike
   9. abominate, antipathy
hateful... 6. odious 7. heinous
   8. terrible 8. abhorrent, execrable,
   invidious, loathsome, malicious,
   obnoxious, offensive, revolting
   10. abominable, detestable,
   disgusting 11. distasteful
   12. disagreeable
hater of...
   children.. 10. misopedist
   mankind.. 11. misanthrope
   marriage.. 10. misogynist
   mathematics.. 8. misomath
   newness.. 9. misoneist
   sights.. 11. misoscopist
   strangers.. 8. misoxene
   work.. 11. ergophobiac
hatred... 5. odium 6. enmity, rancor
   8. aversion 9. animosity, malignity
   10. abhorrence, repugnance
   11. detestation, malevolence
hatred of...
   argument.. 8. misology
   change.. 9. misoneism
   children.. 9. misopedia
   God, gods.. 10. misotheism
   mankind.. 11. misanthropy
   marriage.. 8. misogamy
   strangers.. 8. misoxeny
   10. xenophobia
   war.. 9. polemical 11. misopolemic
   wisdom.. 9. misosophy
   women.. 8. misogyny
hauberk... 5. armor 9. habergeon
haughty... 4. airy, bold, high 5. lofty,
   noble, proud 6. snooty 7. fatuous,
   stately 8. arrogant, cavalier, orgulous,
   scornful 10. disdainful, hoity–toity
   11. domineering, highfalutin
   12. contemptuous, supercilious
haul... 3. lug, tow, tug 4. cart, drag,
   draw, pull 5. booty, bouse, catch,
   check, shift 9. reprimand, transport
haul down a flag... 6. strike
haunch... 3. hip 4. huck 10. leg and
   loin 12. hindquarters
haunch bone... 10. innominate
haunt... 3. den 4. dive, nest 5. ghost,
   habit 6. infect, obsess, resort
   7. torment 8. frequent, practice
hautboy... 4. oboe
have... 3. get, hae, own 4. hold,
   keep, know 5. beget, trick 6. accept,
   effect, retain 7. cherish, perform,
   possess, swindle 10. experience,

understand, suffer from
have (pert to)...
   ambition.. 6. aspire
   charge.. 4. tend
   on.. 4. wear
   thoughts of.. 6. ideate
   to do with.. 4. deal
   weight.. 8. militate
haven... 3. bay 4. port 5. hithe
   (small), inlet 6. asylum, harbor,
   recess, refuge 7. shelter 9. sanctuary
havier... 4. deer
having (pert to)...
   blind end.. 6. caecal
   branches.. 6. ramose
   clamp, pincers.. 7. chelate
   dignity.. 8. majestic
   equal sides.. 9. isosceles
   eyes.. 7. oculate
   faith.. 8. trusting
   featherlike petals.. 7. pinnate
   feelers.. 9. antennate
   fingers.. 8. digitate
   foreknowledge.. 9. prescient
   four feet.. 11. quadrupedal
   harmful quality.. 9. innocuous
   leaves.. 6. foliar 7. foliate
   limits.. 6. finite
   local designation.. 7. topical
   lumps.. 7. noduled
   more than one mate.. 9. polyandry
   no angles.. 6. agonic
   no interest.. 6. supine
   no teeth.. 7. edental 8. edentate
   nothing to do.. 6. otiose
   one foot.. 6. uniped
   pits, depressions.. 7. foveate
   9. foveolate
   plane surfaces.. 7. faceted
   pointed end.. 6. peaked 7. cuspate
   8. aristate
   power over fire.. 10. ignipotent
   power to believe.. 9. creditive
   reflecting surface.. 8. specular
   same ending.. 11. conterminal
   same parents.. 7. germane
   sawlike edge.. 7. serrate
   scales.. 8. perulate
   scalloped edge.. 7. crenate
   taste.. 5. sapid
   thorns.. 7. spinate
   three broods yearly.. 11. trigoneutic
   two feet.. 5. biped 7. bipedal
   two horns.. 6. bicorn
   two meanings.. 9. ambiguous
   unequal sides.. 7. scalene
   web feet.. 8. pinniped
   wings.. 4. alar
having a...
   backbone.. 10. vertebrate
   beak.. 8. rostrate
   beard.. 8. aristate
   handle.. 6. ansate
   large nose.. 6. nasute
   shield.. 9. clypeated
   stem.. 9. petiolate
   tail.. 7. caudate
   tuft.. 6. comose
   veil.. 6. velate
   will.. 7. testate
havoc... 4. harm 5. botch, waste
   7. destroy 11. destruction,

devastation 12. annihilation
haw . . . 4. sloe 5. fence, hedge
  6. eyelid (3rd) 7. stammer
  8. hawthorn, messuage, turn left
  9. enclosure 11. exclamation
Hawaii . . . see also *Hawaiian*
  capital . . 8. Honolulu
  city . . 4. Hilo 7. Wailuku
  district . . 7. Lahaina
  explorer . . 4. Cook (Capt)
  harbor . . 5. Pearl (bombed 12/7/41)
  islands (major) . . 4. Maui, Oahu
    5. Kauai, Lanai 6. Hawaii, Niihau
    7. Molokai 9. Kahoolawe
  lake . . 5. Waiau
  native . . 10. Polynesian
  old name . . 15. Sandwich Islands
  peak . . 8. Mauna Kea, Mauna Loa
    9. Waialeale
  resort . . 7. Waikiki
  Southernmost point (US) . . 5. Ka Lae
  State admission . . 8. Fiftieth
  State bird . . 13. Hawaiian goose
  State flower . . 8. hibiscus
  State nickname . . 5. Aloha
    20. Paradise of the Pacific
  volcano . . 7. Kilauea 8. Mauna Loa
    (largest active)
Hawaiian . . . 6. Kanaka
  10. Melanesian, Polynesian
  16. South Sea islander
Hawaiian (pert to) . . .
  banquet, feast . . 7. ahaaina
  basket . . 2. ie
  beverage . . 4. kava 8. kavakava
  bird . . 2. io, o–o 3. iwa 4. iiwi, mamo
    (ext), noio, o–o–a–a 6. olomao (thrush)
    8. drepanis
  canoe . . 5. waapa
  chant . . 4. mele
  cloth, clothes . . 4. kapa, tapa
  coffee . . 4. kona
  dance . . 4. hula
  fern . . 4. pulu
  fibre (pine) . . 2. ie
  fish . . 3. awa 4. ulua 5. akule, lania
  flower wreath, garland . . 3. lei
  food . . 3. poi 4. kalo, taro
  garment . . 6. holoku, muumuu
  god . . 5. Wakea 7. Kanaloa (Pantheon)
  goddess . . 4. Pele (volcanoes, fire)
  gooseberry . . 4. poha
  grass . . 6. emoloa
  greeting . . 5. aloha
  herb . . 3. pia (starch root)
  king (first) . . 10. Kamehameha
  lava . . 2. aa 8. pahoehoe
  loincloth, girdle . . 4. malo
  musical instrument . . 7. ukulele
  pepper . . 3. ava 4. kava 8. kavakava
  precipice . . 4. pali
  Queen . . 8. Kamamalu
  royalty . . 4. alii
  seaweed (edible) . . 4. limu
  shampoo, massage . . 8. lomi–lomi
  shrub . . 3. pia 4. akia, pulu 5. olona
  temple . . 5. heiau
  tern . . 4. noio
  veranda . . 5. lanai
  windstorm . . 4. kona
  woman . . 5. haole 6. wahine
  yam . . 3. hoi

hawfinch . . . 8. grosbeak
hawk . . . 3. cry 4. hunt, sell, vend
  6. peddle 7. canvass 9. plunderer,
  warmonger
hawk (bird) . . . 2. io 3. hen 4. eyas,
  kahu, kite, nyas, seel (blind) 5. Astur,
  Buteo 6. falcon, osprey, tercel (tiercel)
  7. buzzard, Cooper's, goshawk,
  harrier, kestrel, puttock, sparrow,
  vulture 8. caracara 9. Accipiter,
  red–tailed
hawker of fruit (Eng) . . . 6. coster
  12. costermonger
hawk–eyed deity . . . 2. Ra
Hawkeye State . . . 4. Iowa
hawking . . . 7. hunting, vending
  8. falconry
hawk moth . . . 6. sphinx 8. sphingid
hawksbill . . . 4. pawl 6. turtle
  8. tortoise
hawkshaw . . . 6. sleuth 9. detective
  11. sleuthhound
hawk's nest . . . 5. aerie (aery)
hawser . . . 4. line, rope
hawser post . . . 4. bitt 7. bollard
hawthorn . . . 3. may 5. hazel (fruit)
  6. red haw 7. haw tree 9. mayflower
Hawthorne, Nathaniel . . . 6. author
  8. novelist
hay . . . 6. fodder 7. timothy
hay (pert to) . . .
  bird . . 7. hay jack 8. black cap
    9. sandpiper (pectoral)
  bundle . . 3. mow 4. bale, cock, rick
    5. stack
  fork . . 5. pikel (pikle), pitch
  herb . . 8. sainfoin
  mown . . 5. swath
  second cutting . . 5. rowen
  spreader . . 6. tedder
  stack . . 4. rick 7. hayrick
  storage site . . 3. mow 4. barn, loft,
    silo
hazard . . . 3. fog 4. dare, game, jump,
  risk 5. peril 6. gamble, sanger, stroke
  7. imperil, jeopard, presume, venture
  8. cabstand, casualty, endanger,
  jeopardy 11. restriction
hazardous . . . 5. hairy (sl), jumpy, risky
  6. chancy, queasy, unsafe 7. unsound
  8. perilous 9. uncertain, venturous
  10. fortuitous 11. speculative,
  venturesome
haze . . . 3. fog 4. beat, film, glin (at
  sea), mist, smog 5. scold, smoke,
  vapor 7. dimness, drizzle 8. frighten
hazy . . . 3. dim 5. filmy, foggy, misty,
  smoky, thick, vague 6. cloudy,
  opaque, stupid 7. muddled, nebular,
  obscure 8. overcast 9. invisible,
  uncertain 10. indistinct
he . . . 2. il 3. man 4. ipsi, male 6. any
  one, letter 7. pronoun
head . . . 3. aim, nob 4. lead, pate, poll,
  tete 5. caput, chief, skull 6. noggin,
  noodle (sl), source 7. cranium
head (pert to) . . .
  abbey . . 5. abbot 6. abbess
  back of . . 7. occiput
  bald . . 6. acomia 9. pilgarlic
  bone . . 8. parietal 9. occipital
  Gorgon . . 6. Medusa (Myth)

hard.. **5.** boche
of hair.. **5.** crine
pert to.. **8.** cephalic
proportion.. **14.** mesitacephalic
shaven.. **7.** tonsure
shrunken.. **7.** tsentsa
headache... **6.** megrim **8.** migraine
11. cephalalgia
head covering... **3.** cap, hat, tam, wig
4. hair, hood, veil **5.** beret, miter,
scalp **6.** bonnet, peruke, toupee,
wimple **7.** biretta **8.** sombrero
10. fascinator
headdress... **3.** wig **4.** pouf, tête
5. busby, miter, shako, tiara
6. coiffe, diadem, hennin, peruke,
pinner **7.** bandore, buzz wig, coronet,
periwig **8.** coiffure, headtire
headdress (Egypt)... **6.** uraeus (with
sacred asp)
headhunters (Luzon)... **7.** Igorots
heading... **3.** top **5.** front, title, topic
6. pillow **7.** bolster, caption
8. headline **9.** direction
12. decapitation
headland... **4.** cape, mull, ness
5. morro, ridge **10.** promontory
headless... **6.** stupid **7.** acephal,
topless **9.** acephalus (monster)
10. acephalous
headline... **6.** banner **7.** caption,
display, heading
headliner... **4.** star **7.** feature
8. composer
headlong... **4.** rash **5.** hasty, steep
6. head–on, sudden **8.** reckless
9. headfirst, impetuous, impulsive
10. recklessly **11.** impulsively,
precipitate, precipitous
headpiece... **3.** cap, hat, top **4.** atef
5. crown **6.** halter, helmet, lintel
7. fitting **8.** covering, ornament, skull
cap **9.** headboard, headdress,
headstall
head–shaped... **8.** capitate
headstrong... **4.** rash **6.** entêté, unruly
7. violent, wayward **9.** obstinate
11. intractable, opinionated
12. contumacious, ungovernable
heal... **4.** cure, knit, mend **6.** doctor,
pacify, remedy, repair **7.** correct,
restore **9.** cicatrize
healing (pert to)...
agent.. **6.** balsam
compound.. **4.** balm
goddess.. **3.** Eir
magic.. **6.** powwow
process.. **4.** scar **8.** cicatrix
remedy.. **8.** curative, sanative
science.. **9.** iatrology
suffix.. **7.** iatrics
health (pert to)...
care.. **7.** welfare
comb form.. **4.** sani
conditions.. **8.** sanitary
goddess.. **5.** Salus **6.** Hygeia
7. Minerva
Latin.. **5.** salus
neurotic.. **13.** hypochondriac
resort.. **3.** spa **7.** springs
symbol.. **5.** pansy

healthful... **7.** healthy **8.** curative,
salutary, sanatory **9.** medicinal
10. salubrious
healthy... **4.** hale, sane, well
6. hearty, robust **8.** salutary,
vigorous **9.** healthful, wholesome
10. salubrious
heap... **3.** cop **4.** dess, load, lump,
pile, pyre, raff, raft **5.** amass, cairn,
crowd, stack **6.** plenty, sorite, throng
7. cumulus **9.** multitude
10. accumulate
heaped... **5.** piled **7.** stacked
8. acervate **9.** collected
hear... **3.** see **4.** feel, heed, oyez
(oyes) **5.** favor, judge, learn
6. attend, listen **7.** hearken (harken)
8. listen to, perceive **9.** attention
10. adjudicate
hearer... **7.** audient, auditor
8. disciple, listener **9.** hearkener
(harkener) **12.** eavesdropper
hearing (pert to)... **3.** act, aid, ear
4. otic, oyer **5.** aural, sense
(special), sound, trial **6.** otosis, tryout
7. earshot **8.** audience, audition,
auditory **9.** attention, auricular,
interview, knowledge
hearken, harken... **4.** hear, heed
6. attend, listen **7.** give ear, inquire
hearsay... **4.** talk **5.** bruit, rumor
6. gossip, report **8.** evidence
heart... **3.** cor **4.** card, core, gist, life,
love, mood, soul **5.** cheer, organ
6. center, depths, kardia, middle,
spirit, vitals **7.** courage, emotion,
essence, feeling **9.** affection,
substance **10.** conscience
11. temperament
heart (pert to)...
ache.. **5.** grief **6.** sorrow **7.** anguish
active.. **7.** sthenic
beat.. **5.** pulse, throb **7.** systole
8. diastole **9.** pulsation
10. palmoscopy
bleeding (flower).. **8.** dicentra
burn.. **4.** envy **6.** enmity **7.** burning,
pyrosia **8.** jealousy **10.** cardialgia,
discontent, heartscald (heart–scaud)
cavity.. **6.** atrium
chamber.. **6.** atrium **7.** auricle
9. ventricle **11.** ventriculum
contraction.. **7.** systole
disease.. **14.** angina pectoris
Egypt.. **2.** Ab **4.** hati
expansion.. **8.** diastole
felt.. **4.** dear, deep, real, true
7. genuine, sincere
shaped.. **7.** cordate
valve.. **6.** mitral **8.** bicuspid
9. tricuspid
hearten... **5.** cheer **7.** comfort
8. embolden, inspirit, reassure
9. encourage
hearth... **4.** home **5.** ingle **6.** astrer
(pert to) **8.** fireside **9.** fireplace
hearth goddess... **5.** Vesta **6.** Hestia
hearty... **4.** hale, real, rich, warm
5. heavy, lusty **6.** active, robust,
stanch **7.** cordial, earnest, fervent
8. friendly, vigorous **9.** convivial,
energetic, unfeigned **10.** nourishing

11. substantial
heat... 4. fire, race, warm, zeal
  5. ardor, calor, cauma, fever, tepor
  6. degree, warmth 7. inflame,
  passion 10. excitement
  11. temperature
heat (pert to)...
  heating.. 9. calorific
  measure.. 5. therm (therme) 7. calorie
    (calory) 10. centigrade, Fahrenheit
  pert to.. 7. thermic
  plaster.. 4. mull 7. steatin
  principle.. 7. caloric
  white.. 13. incandescence
heater... 4. etna, kiln, oven 5. forge,
  stove, tisar 6. boiler, retort
  7. brazier, furnace 8. annealer,
  register 12. electron tube
heath... 4. moor 5. Erica, plain, savin,
  waste 8. tamarisk 10. underbrush
heathen... 5. pagan 6. ethnic, paynim
  7. gentile, godless, infidel
  10. unbeliever 11. irreligious
  13. unenlightened
heathen deity... 4. idol 5. image
  6. symbol
heather... 5. color, Erica, plant
  9. crowberry 12. poverty plant
heaume... 6. helmet (armor)
heave... 4. cast, draw, hurl, lift, toss
  5. fling, hoist, pitch, raise, retch,
  scena, throw 11. rise and fall
heaven... 3. sky 4. ciel, Eden 5. ether
  6. utopia, welkin 7. arcadia, Elysium,
  Nirvana 8. empyrean, Paradise,
  Valhalla (Valhall) 9. firmament
heavenly... 5. godly 6. divine, sacred
  7. angelic, blessed, uranian
  8. supernal 9. beautiful, celestial
  10. delightful
heavenly (pert to)...
  being.. 5. angel, saint 6. cherub,
    seraph 7. Madonna 8. cherubim, Dei
    Mater, seraphim
  belt.. 6. galaxy, zodiac
  body.. 3. sun 4. luna, moon, star
    5. comet 6. planet 8. luminary
  city.. 4. Zion 12. New Jerusalem
  path.. 5. orbit
  solar apparatus.. 6. orrery
  sphere.. 8. empyrean
  twins (Gemini).. 6. Castor, Pollux
heavens... see *heaven*
heaves... 9. emphysema
heavy... 3. sad 4. deep, dull, hard,
  role 5. actor, dense, grave, great,
  inert, massy 6. coarse, gloomy,
  leaden, sleepy, strong, viscid
  7. doleful, onerous, serious, villain,
  violent, weighty 8. burdened,
  grievous, overcast, pregnant, profound
  9. difficult, ponderous 10. afflictive,
  burdensome, encumbered, oppressive
  11. substantial 13. consequential
heavy (pert to)...
  handed.. 6. clumsy 7. awkward,
    unhandy 8. bungling 9. maladroit
    10. oppressive
  headed.. 4. dull, logy 6. drowsy,
    stupid
  hearted.. 3. sad 10. despondent,

melancholy
  laden.. 6. loaded 8. careworn
    9. oppressed 12. weighted down
  with moisture.. 6. sodden
Hebrew... 3. Jew 4. Zion 6. Habiri,
  Habiru, Semite 7. Semitic
Hebrew (pert to)...
  abode of the dead.. 5. Sheol
  acrostic.. 4. agla
  amulet.. 4. agla
  demon.. 8. Asmodeus
  eternity.. 4. Olam 8. Olam haba
  excommunication form.. 5. herem
  festival.. 5. Purim, Seder 8. Passover
  flute (Bib).. 8. nehiloth
  forbidden.. 4. tref
  God.. 2. El 5. Eloah 6. Adonai,
    Elohim 7. Jehovah
  grammar.. 7. stative
  greeting.. 6. Shalom
  instrument (lyrelike).. 4. asor
  kinsman.. 4. goel
  law book.. 5. Torah (Tora) 6. Talmud
    7. Mishnah (Mishna) 8. Tosephta
    10. Pentateuch
  lesson (Nebiim).. 9. haphtarah
  marriage custom.. 8. levirate
  month (Spring).. 4. Abib 5. Nisan
  Order (Cenobite).. 6. Essene
  plural ending.. 2. im
  prayer shawl.. 7. tallith
  proselyte.. 3. ger
  psalm of praise.. 6. hallel
  quarters.. 6. ghetto
  rabbis, teachers.. 6. sabora
    7. amoraim, tannaim 8. saboraim
  sacred objects.. 4. Urim 7. Thummin
  school.. 5. heder (cheder)
  spice (anc).. 6. stacte
  town.. 6. Mizpah (Mizpeh)
  trumpet.. 7. shophar (shofar)
  underworld.. 5. Sheol
Hebrew alphabet... 2. he, pe
  3. mem, nun, sin, tav, vau 4. ayin,
  beth, caph, koph, resh, shin, yodh
  5. aleph, cheth, gimel, sadhe, zayin
  6. daleth, lamedh, samekh
Hebrides, New...
  administrators.. 6. French 7. British
  church.. 6. Celtic (early)
  islands.. 4. Iona, Skye 5. Banks
    6. Torres
  people.. 10. Melanesian
  type rule.. 11. Condominium
hecatomb... 9. sacrifice 11. hundred
  oxen
hecco... 8. hickwall 10. woodpecker
heckle... 4. gibe 6. badger, hackle,
  harass
hectic... 5. fever, flush 7. excited
  8. feverish, restless 9. reddening
  11. consumptive
hector... 5. bully, worry 6. harass
  7. bluster, swagger 8. browbeat
  9. roisterer 10. intimidate
Hector (pert to)...
  character in.. 5. (The) Iliad
  companion.. 8. Diomedes
  father.. 5. Priam
  mother.. 6. Hecuba
  slain by.. 8. Achilles
  wife.. 10. Andromache

heddle ... 4. loom 5. blade (with eyelet) 7. weaving

hedge ... 3. bar, haw, hem, pen 4. boma 5. fence 6. hinder, raddle 7. barrier, enclose, quibble 8. boundary, obstruct, sidestep, surround

hedgehog ... 6. animal, tenrec, urchin 7. dredger, echidna, echinus, pudding (fruit) 8. herisson, hurcheon 9. porcupine 11. transformer

hedge trimmer ... 7. plasher, topiary

hedonism (pert to) ... *advocate* .. 8. Cyrenaic 9. Epicurean *doctrine of* .. 8. pleasure

heed ... 3. ear 4. care, hear, mind, note, obey 6. attend, listen, notice, regard 7. caution, observe 8. consider 9. attention, be careful, diligence 10. cognizance, solicitude 11. observation

heedful ... 4. wary 5. alert 6. attent 7. careful, mindful 8. cautious, vigilant 9. advertent, attentive 11. considerate

heedless ... 6. remiss 8. careless 9. desperate, impulsive, negligent 10. insouciant, regardless 11. improvident, inadvertent, inattentive, thoughtless, unobservant, without heed 13. inconsiderate

heel ... 3. cad, tip 4. cant, foot (part), knob, tilt 5. stern 6. careen, follow 7. bounder, deviate, incline 9. scoundrel 12. protuberance

Heidi author ... 12. Johanna Spyri

heifer ... 3. cow 4. quey 5. stirk, woman 6. bovine 8. terrapin (fem) 10. colpindach

height ... 3. alt, top 4. apex 5. crest, pitch 6. summit 7. stature 8. altitude, eminence, highness 9. elevation 10. The Heavens

heighten ... 5. raise 7. augment, elevate 8. increase 9. aggravate, intensify 10. exaggerate

height of action, drama ... 10. catastasis

heimlich ... 10. reticently 12. mysteriously

Heimweh ... 9. nostalgia 12. homesickness

heinous ... 3. bad 6. odious, wicked 7. beastly (Brit), hateful 8. flagrant, infamous, terrible 9. atrocious, malicious 10. outrageous

heir ... 5. scion 7. heritor, legatee 8. atheling (apparent), parcener (joint) 9. firstborn, inheritor, successor 11. beneficiary

Hejaz ... *city* .. 5. Islam, Mecca 6. Medina *monument* .. 14. Tomb of Mohammed (Mosque of the Prophet) *district* .. 11. Saudi Arabia *shrine* .. 5. Kaaba

helcos ... 5. ulcer

helcos (pert to) ... *repair* .. 11. helcoplasty *science* .. 9. helcology *ulceration* .. 8. helcosis

held ... see *hold*

Helen of Troy (pert to) ... *abductor, lover* .. 5. Paris *brother–in–law* .. 9. Agamemnon *famed for* .. 6. beauty *husband* .. 8. Menelaus (King) *mother* .. 4. Leda *sister of* .. 11. The Dioscuri

helical ... 5. helix (formed) 6. spiral

helical year ... 6. Sothic

helicoid ... 6. curved, ear rim (like) 10. snail shell (like)

helicon ... 4. tuba

helicopter (pert to) ... 5. rotor 7. chopper 8. autogiro (autogyro), heliport 9. eggbeater 10. whirlybird

helicopter developer ... 8. Sikorsky

heliophobia ... 14. fear of sunlight 16. sensitivity to sun

Heliopolis ... 12. City of the Sun (Egypt)

Helios ... 3. Sol 6. sun god 16. Colossus of Rhodes

helix ... 4. coil 5. snail 6. spiral

hell ... 5. grave, Hades, limbo 7. dungeon, inferno 9. perdition, purgatory 10. underworld

hell (pert to) ... *bottomless pit* .. 9. barathrum *capital of* .. 11. Pandemonium *Hebrew* .. 5. Sheol *Hindu* .. 6. Naraka *Iliad* .. 8. Tartarus *Jewish* .. 6. Tophet 7. Gehenna *Norse* .. 7. Niflhel (Neflheim) *Queen* .. 3. Hel *Roman* .. 3. Dis 5. Orcus

hellbent ... 7. dead set, like mad 8. full tilt, reckless 10. determined, recklessly 12. determinedly

Hellene ... 5. Greek

Hellenistic school (Sculp) ... 9. Pergamene

Hellespont, Turkey ... *ancient name* .. 9. Gallipoli (Strait of) *city* .. 6. Abydos (legend), Sestos *legend* .. 4. Hero 7. Leander (swimmer) *modern name* .. 11. Dardanelles (The)

helm ... 5. wheel 6. helmet, rudder, summit, tiller 7. control 10. management 12. steering gear

helmet ... 5. armet, armor, galea, topee (topi) 6. casque, heaume, morion, sallet, sconce 7. basinet, hard hat

helmet (pert to) ... *flap* .. 8. aventail *lower part* .. 6. beaver *nose guard* .. 5. nasal *opening* .. 3. vue *part* .. 4. bell 5. crest, visor (vizor) 7. ventail 8. aventail *shaped* .. 7. galeate

helmet of Hades ... 5. magic 8. Tarnhelm 9. invisible, Tärnkappe

helminth ... 4. worm

helmsman ... 5. pilot 6. conner, guider 8. coxswain 9. steersman

helot ... 4. esne, serf 5. slave 6. thrall, vassal 7. servant

help ... 3. aid 4. abet, back, cure

5. avail, boost, serve, stead 6. assist,
relief, remedy, succor 7. benefit,
forward, further, improve, prevent,
relieve, servant, serving, subsidy,
support, sustain
helper ... 3. aid (aide) 8. teammate
9. assistant, paramedic
10. apprentice, benefactor
helpful ... 6. useful 7. helping
8. salutary 10. beneficial, tiding over
12. contributory, instrumental
helpless ... 4. limp, weak 7. forlorn
8. impotent, unaiding 9. destitute,
powerless, spineless 10. bewildered,
unsupplied 11. defenseless,
unprotected 12. irremediable
helpmate ... 4. wife 5. spouse
6. helper 7. husband 8. helpmeet
9. assistant, companion
Helsinki, Finland ... 7. capital
helter–skelter ... 5. haste, hurry
7. hastily 8. disorder 9. confusion
10. carelessly, recklessly
helve ... 5. lever 6. handle
hem, hem in ... 3. pen 4. edge
5. beset 6. border, margin
7. environ, stammer 8. hesitate,
surround 9. hem and haw
11. circumscribe, exclamation
hemal, haemal (pert to) ... 5. blood
12. blood vessels
hemeralopia ... 12. day blindness (opp
of nyctalopia)
hemi ... 4. half, semi (pref)
hemiplegia ... 9. paralysis (body half)
hemlock ... 3. kex 5. Tsuga 6. conium
(fruit) 9. evergreen, poisoning
hemophilia ... 8. bleeding
10. hemorrhage (uncontrollable)
hemp ... 3. ife, kef 4. flax, keef, kief,
rine, sunn 5. abaca, bhang, istle, sisal
(sizal) 6. fennel, Manila 7. hashish,
lhiamba (liamba) 8. cannabis
hemp (pert to) ...
bagasse .. 6. linaga
cannabis .. 5. ganja (smoking)
fabric .. 6. burlap
filament .. 4. harl
leaves .. 5. sabzi
like .. 9. cannabine
loose .. 5. oakum
resin (narcotic) .. 6. charas
seed .. 5. rogue, scamp
short .. 3. tow
hen ... 4. fowl, wife 6. pullet
hen (pert to) ...
Chaucer character .. 7. Partlet
clam .. 4. surf 5. pismo
hawk .. 7. buzzard, harrier
heath .. 4. gray 6. grouse (black)
poison .. 7. hebenon, henbane
water .. 9. gallinule
hence ... 2. so 4. away, ergo, thus
8. away from 9. therefore
henchman ... 4. page 5. groom
6. gillie, squire 7. mafioso
8. follower, hanger–on 9. attendant,
supporter 12. right–hand man
hend, hende ... 4. fair, kind, near
5. civil 6. clever, comely, gentle,
kindly 8. gracious, pleasant, skillful
(skilful) 9. dexterous 10. convenient

heortology, science of ... 14, liturgical
year
hepar ... 5. liver 8. compound (Chem)
hepatitis ... 12. liver disease
Hephaestus (Gr Relig) ... 9. god of Fire
Hepplewhite ... 9. furniture
heptad ... 5. seven (group of)
Hera (pert to) ...
husband .. 4. Zeus
mother of .. 4. Ares, Rhea
rival .. 2. Io 4. Leto
herald ... 5. crier 6. tabard
7. presage, usher in 8. announce,
point man, proclaim 9. harbinger,
messenger 10. forerunner
heraldic (pert to) ...
balls .. 5. palle (6 balls of Medici)
band .. 3. bar 4. fess, fill
barnacle .. 4. brey
bearing .. 4. ente, gore, orle 5. pheon
6. charge 8. tressure
boss .. 5. rumbo
charge .. 5. fusil, gyron 7. bearing,
humetty (humettee)
circle (gold) .. 6. bezant
cross .. 4. nowy, paty, urde 6. cleche,
pattée (patté), raguly 7. patonce,
saltier (saltire)
decoration .. 4. seme 5. crest
design (fur) .. 4. pean, vair
division .. 4. ente, paly 5. barry
6. canton 7. compone
11. counterpaly
embattled .. 8. bretessé
end (metal) .. 7. boterol (boteroll)
large .. 5. pavis
lozenge (voided) .. 6. mascle
opening .. 6. rustre
panel .. 9. hatchment (death)
sardonyx .. 8. sanguine
scalloped, edged .. 8. invected
segment .. 6. flanch
ship .. 7. lymphad
star .. 6. mullet 7. estoile
stripe .. 4. pale
swallow .. 10. hirondelle
winged .. 4. aile
wreath .. 5. torse 7. chaplet, garland
heraldic (pert to animals) ...
head .. 8. caboshed (caboched)
bear .. 5. grise
beast, running .. 7. courant
beast, sitting .. 5. assis 6. sejant
beasts .: 6. enurny
beast's leg .. 4. gamb (gambe)
bird .. 7. issuant (half visible), martlet
9. half eagle
duck (footless) .. 6. cannet (cannette)
fish, swimming .. 6. naiant
headless .. 5. etète
heraldic (pert to color) ...
black .. 5. sable
blue .. 5. azure
brown .. 5. tenne
gold, yellow .. 2. or
green .. 4. vert
purple .. 7. purpure
red .. 5. gules
heraldic shield (pert to) ...
back .. 8. aversant
back to back .. 8. addorsed
bent .. 9. debruised

broken.. **5.** rompu
Danes.. **5.** raven
England.. **14.** lilies of France
facing each other.. **8.** affronté
savages.. **6.** tattoo
toward spectator.. **4.** gaze **7.** gardant
tribe of Judah.. **4.** lion
herb... **3.** pia, rue **4.** aloe, anet, balm,
dill, hemp, mint, moly, sage, woad,
yamp **5.** anise, basil, nondo, sedge,
senna, tansy, thyme **6.** arnica,
borage, catnip, cicely, clover, endive,
fennel, hyssop, jacoby, madder,
yarrow **7.** boneset, caraway, chervil,
chicory, figwort, gentian, ginseng,
henbane, parsley, ragwort
8. abelmosk, licorice, marjoram,
rosemary, samphire, tarragon
9. coriander, digitalis, spikenard
10. elecampane, pennyroyal,
turtlehead
herb (pert to)...
bitter.. **3.** rue **4.** aloe **5.** tansy
7. boneset **8.** centaury **9.** snakehead
10. turtlehead
dill.. **4.** anet
genus.. **3.** Iva **4.** Arum, Ruta
5. Galax, Inula, Lemna, Rubia
6. Cassia, Mentha, Oxalis, Sagina
7. Alpenia, Anemone, Freesia,
Hedeoma, Tellima, Tovaria
8. Hepatica, Psorales **9.** Grundelia
living on.. **11.** herbivorous
12. phytophagous
mythical.. **4.** moly
narcotic.. **4.** hemp
onionlike.. **5.** chive
poisonous.. **4.** loco **6.** conium
7. hemlock, henbane **9.** hellebore
salad.. **6.** endive **7.** chicory
10. watercress
Hercules (pert to)...
father.. **4.** Zeus
hero of.. **8.** strength **12.** twelve
labors
mother.. **7.** Alcmene
statue.. **7.** Farnese
stone.. **9.** loadstone
sweetheart.. **4.** Iole
wife.. **4.** Hebe
herd... **3.** mob **5.** crowd, drive, drove,
flock, guard **6.** gregis, rabble
7. shelter **11.** aggregation
herd's grass... **7.** timothy
herdsman... **4.** senn **6.** drover
7. vaquero (vaciero) **8.** Damoetas,
ranchero, wrangler
herdsman's god... **5.** Pales
here... **3.** ici, now **6.** hereat, hither
7. present **8.** vicinity **9.** this place
11. in this place
here and now... **8.** thisness
9. haecceity **11.** specificity
here and there... **5.** about **6.** passim
10. everywhere
hereditary... **6.** inborn, innate, lineal
8. heirship **9.** ancestral, descended,
lineality **11.** inheritable, inheritance,
patrimonial
heredity... **4.** gene **5.** birth **7.** atavism
8. heritage **10.** Mendel's law
11. inheritance

heretic... **9.** dissenter, sectarian
10. schismatic **13.** nonconformist
heretofore... **6.** erenow **7.** prior to
8. formerly, hitherto, previous
heritage... **3.** lot **9.** cleronomy
10. birthright **11.** inheritance
heritrix, heretrix... **7.** heiress
herl, harl... **3.** fly (angling) **4.** barb
hermeneutics... **14.** interpretation
(Scriptures)
Hermes (pert to)...
birthplace.. **7.** Cyllene
character.. **6.** herald **9.** messenger
father.. **4.** Zeus
god of.. **5.** youth **7.** science
9. eloquence, invention
mother.. **4.** Maia
Roman equivalent.. **7.** Mercury
shoes (winged).. **7.** talaria
hermetic... **6.** closed, sealed
7. magical **8.** airtight **10.** alchemical
hermetic art... **7.** alchemy
hermit... **4.** monk **5.** cooky **7.** ascetic,
eremite, recluse, stylite (Hist)
8. headsman **9.** anchorite, pillarist
11. hummingbird
hermitary... **3.** hut **4.** cell
hern, herne... **4.** hers, hook **5.** heron
6. corner
hero... **4.** idol, star **5.** model
7. demigod, warrior **8.** champion
9. celebrity, conqueror
11. protagonist
hero (pert to)...
American.. **5.** Allen (Ethan), Bowie
6. Bonham, Travis **8.** Crockett
Babylonian.. **5.** Etana
deified.. **7.** demigod
genealogy.. **9.** heroogony
Greek.. **3.** Ion **4.** Ajax
legendary.. **6.** Amadis, Roland
7. Paladin, Tancred
lore.. **9.** heroology
Persian.. **6.** Rustam (Rustum)
romantic.. **4.** Erec **6.** Amadis
7. Leander
Russian.. **4.** Igor
heroic... **4.** bold, epic, huge **5.** brave,
great, noble **6.** epical, poetic, viking
7. extreme, gallant, valiant
8. fearless, intrepid, powerful
10. courageous **11.** magnanimous,
venturesome
heroic poem, story... **4.** epic, epos
6. epopee
heroine... **4.** Tess **5.** actor **6.** Esther,
Europa **8.** Atalanta **9.** celebrity
11. demigoddess
heroism... **5.** valor **7.** bravery, courage
9. fortitude **11.** magnanimity
13. unselfishness
heron... **5.** Ardea, crane, egret, herle
7. Bittern **8.** Ardeidae, heronsew
9. Great Blue **10.** Great White, Little
Blue
heron flock... **5.** sedge
herpes... **6.** eczema **8.** cold sore,
shingles
herring... **3.** cob **4.** alec, brit, raun
(fem), sile **5.** cisco, matie, sprat
7. alewife, anchovy, shadine
8. scuddawn

herring (pert to) . . .
barrel . . 4. cade, cran
bone . . 7. pattern 11. arrangement
fry . . 4. sile
herringlike . . 5. cisco 7. anchovy
young . . 4. brit 5. sprat (sprot)
Herse (Gr) . . . 7. goddess (dew)
Hershef (Egypt) . . . 5. deity (tutelary)
hesitate . . . 3. haw, hem 4. wait
5. delay, demur, pause, stall
6. falter, loiter 7. stammer
13. procrastinate
hesitation . . . 5. doubt, pause, waltz
9. faltering, hesitancy 10. reluctance,
stammering 11. uncertainty,
vacillation 15. procrastination
hesped (Heb) . . . 6. eulogy 7. funeral
Hesperides (pert to) . . .
group name . . 10. Atlantides
guards of . . 12. golden apples (Hera)
nymph . . 5. Aegle 6. Hestia
7. Hespera 8. Arethusa, Erytheia
Hesperus . . . 4. poem (Wreck of the
Hesperus) 5. Venus 6. Hesper
11. evening star
Hessian . . . 3. fly 5. boots, Hesse
6. German 9. mercenary
10. adventurer
hest . . . 6. behest 7. command,
precept, promise 10. injunction
Hestia (pert to) . . .
goddess of . . 6. hearth
guard of . . 12. golden apples
mother . . 4. Rhea
hetaera, hetaira (Gr) . . . 4. Lais
6. Phryne 8. mistress, paramour
hetaerocracy, governed by . . .
8. hetaerae 10. college men
Heterodontus . . . 5. shark
heterodox . . . 9. heretical
10. unorthodox 11. nonorthodox
heterogeneous . . . (opposed to
homogeneous) 5. mixed 6. unlike
7. diverse 9. different 10. dissimilar
11. diversified 13. miscellaneous
hew . . . 3. cut 4. chop, fell, hack
5. carve, sever
hex . . . 3. hag, six 4. jinx 5. lamia,
spell 7. bewitch 9. sorceress,
witchwife
hexad . . . 3. six 6. sestet
hexameter verse . . .
meter . . 7. six feet
terms . . 4. iams 8. dipodies, trochees
9. anapaests
hexapod . . . 7. six feet 9. six–footed
hexarchy . . . 9. six States (group)
hexastich, poem or stanza . . . 8. six
lines 9. six verses
heyday . . . 3. joy 4. acme 8. wildness
11. high spirits 12. highest vigor
14. frolicsomeness
heyrat . . . 8. kinkajou (obs)
Hezekiah (pert to) . . .
Biblical . . 4. King (12th)
kingdom . . 5. Judah
mother . . 3. Abi
hiatus . . . 3. col, gap 5. break, chasm,
pause, space 6. lacuna 7. fissure,
opening 8. interval 12. interruption
Hiawatha (pert to) . . .
character, poem by . . 10. Longfellow

grandmother . . 7. Nokomis
mother . . 7. Wenonah
tribe (Ind) . . 8. Iroquois
hibernate . . . 6. hole up (summer in
torpor), winter 8. estivate
10. latibulize
Hibernia . . . 4. Erin 7. Ireland
Hibernian (pert to) . . .
color . . 5. green
native . . 8. Irishman
secret society (US 1832) . .
24. Ancient Order of Hibernians
hickory . . . 4. cane 5. Carya, pecan
6. switch 8. kiskatom 9. shellbark
hidalgo . . . 5. title 8. nobleman (lower
class)
hidden . . . 4. dern, lurk 5. inner, perdu
6. arcane, buried, cached, closed,
covert, latent, masked, occult, secret
7. covered, cryptic, obscure,
unknown 8. abstruse, screened,
secluded, secreted 9. concealed,
latescent 10. mysterious
11. clandestine
hide . . . 3. kip 4. bury, cyst, dern
(derne), lurk, mask, pelt, skin, veil
5. cache, cloak, cover, skulk
6. screen, shroud 7. conceal,
eelskin, rawhide, secrete 8. carucate,
disguise, ensconce, suppress
9. dissemble 10. camouflage
hidebound . . . 5. bound, petty 6. little,
narrow 7. bigoted 9. barkbound
10. restrained (opinion)
11. strait–laced 12. conventional,
narrow–minded 13. hyperorthodox
hideous . . . 4. grim, ugly 6. grisly,
horrid, odious 7. ghastly 8. scabrous,
terrible 9. frightful, revolting
10. detestable, terrifying
hiding place . . . 3. mew 4. lair
5. cache 9. latibulum
hi–fi devotee . . . 10. audiophile
high . . . 3. alt, dry, ela (note) 4. tall
5. aloft, drunk, great, noble, steep
6. costly, shrill 7. eminent, haughty
8. elevated, foremost, stranded,
towering 9. excessive, expensive
high (pert to) . . .
and mighty . . 8. arrogant 9. imperious
brow . . 4. snob 7. Brahmin, egghead,
high–hat, learned 12. intellectual
14. intelligentsia
flown diction . . 8. euphuism
flying . . 7. Icarian 9. visionary
11. extravagant, pretentious
12. ostentatious 13. grandiloquent
handed . . 9. arbitrary 10. autocratic,
imperative 11. domineering,
overbearing
hat . . 8. snobbish 12. aristocratic
priest . . 3. Eli (Israel) 11. Melchezedek
(Mormon)
sounding . . 4. loud 7. fustian
9. high–toned 13. grandiloquent
spirited . . 4. edgy 5. fiery 6. lively
9. excitable 10. mettlesome
11. high–mettled
strung . . 4. taut 5. tense 7. nervous
9. excitable
time . . 3. fun 5. binge, spree
8. carousal 11. opportunity

toned .. 5. tense 7. stylish 8. elevated
9. dignified 11. fashionable
highest ... 3. top 4. best 6. utmost
7. maximum, supreme, topmost
8. bunemost, dominant 9. nth
degree, uppermost
highest (pert to) ...
comb form .. 4. acro
dice number .. 3. six 4. sise (sice)
point .. 3. top 4. acme, apex 5. crest
6. apogee, climax, summit, vertex,
zenith 7. ceiling, noonday
8. meridian, noontide, pinnacle
11. ne plus ultra
highway ... 3. via, way 4. bahn, iter,
path, pike, road, toby 6. artery,
course, street 7. beltway, freeway,
parkway, thruway, (throughway)
8. arterial, autobahn, turnpike
9. boulevard, concourse
10. expressway 12. thoroughfare
highwayman ... 5. thief 6. bandit,
robber 7. brigand, footpad, ladrone
8. hijacker 9. bandolero
10. bushranger, highjacker
hike ... 4. jerk, toss, walk 5. hitch,
march, raise, throw, tramp
8. backpack, increase
hilarious ... 3. mad 5. merry, noisy
7. festive 8. mirthful 9. ludicrous
hilarity ... 4. glee 5. mirth 6. gaiety,
levity 7. jollity, whoopee 8. laughter
9. joviality 10. jocularity, joyousness
12. cheerfulness, exhilaration
hill ... 3. kop, tor 4. dene, dune, heap,
holt, kame, knob, loma, mesa, paha,
rath 5. bargh, butte, esker, morra,
mound 6. barrow, summit
9. acclivity, elevation, monadnock
hill myna ... 8. starling
hillside ... 4. bank, brae, hill, knop,
ramp 5. cleve (cleeve), cliff, knoll,
scarp, slope 6. glacia
hilt ... 4. haft 6. handle
hilum ... 3. eye (bean) 5. hilar, notch
7. opening (kidney)
Himalaya (pert to) ...
antelope .. 5. goral, serow
bear .. 5. bhalu
bearcat .. 5. panda
bird .. 5. monal (pheasant) 6. chough
(crow)
cat .. 5. ounce
dweller .. 8. Nepalese
formations .. 7. Siwalik
goat .. 4. ibex, kail, tahe
kingdom .. 5. Hunza
mountain peak .. 3. Api 7. Everest,
The Hump
pass .. 7. Nathula
plant .. 4. nard (Med)
sheep (wild) .. 6. bharal, nahoor
swamp .. 5. Terai
tree .. 3. fir (silver) 5. Neoza (pine)
6. Bhutan, deodar (cedar)
himself .. 4. ipse
hind ... 3. doe 4. back, deer, rear, stag
6. caudal, haunch, rustic 7. peasant,
servant 8. domestic 9. posterior
11. hindquarter
hind (red fish) ... 7. grouper 8. cabrilla
hinder ... 3. bar 5. block, check,

cramp, debar, delay, deter, embar
6. cumber, hamper, impede, retard
7. prevent 8. restrain 9. posterior
hindrance ... 3. bar, rub 4. clog, snag,
stop 5. check, delay 8. obstacle
9. deterrent, restraint, stricture
10. impediment 11. obstruction
12. interruption
Hindu, Hindoo ... 4. Koli, Sikh
5. Tamil 6. Indian 9. Hindustan
Hindu (pert to) ...
alphabet .. 6. Sarada
apartment .. 5. mahal
ascetic .. 4. yati, yogi 5. sadhu
atheist .. 7. nastika
author of law .. 4. Manu (Code)
bird .. 5. Munia 6. garuda
Buddha's mother .. 4. Maya
caravansary .. 8. choultry
carriage .. 6. gharry (gharri)
caste .. 4. Bhil 5. Palli, Sudra, Tamil
7. Brahman
ceremony .. 7. sraddha
city (sacred) .. 5. Mecca 7. Benares
9. Allahabad
coin .. 4. anna
cymbals .. 3. tal
dancing girl .. 8. bayadere
darkness (spiritual) .. 5. tamas
deity .. 4. Deva, Rama, Siva (Shiva),
Yama 5. Ahura, Asura 6. Brahma,
Vishnu 7. Krishna 8. Trimurti
deity consort .. 5. sakti
dialect .. 5. Tamil
division .. 5. Patti, Taraf 6. zillah
7. Pargana
Dravidian .. 5. Tamil
drink (sacrificial) .. 4. soma
evil spirit .. 4. Mara 5. asura
6. yaksha
festival .. 4. Holi, tali 6. Dewali, Pongal
9. Dashahara
first mortal to die .. 4. Yama
flute .. 3. bin 5. pungi
garment .. 4. sari (saree)
Gautama's wife .. 6. Ahalya
gentleman (Mr) .. 5. baboo (babu), sahib
giant .. 4. Bana (thousand–armed)
government .. 6. sircar
guitar .. 4. vina 5. sitar
hero .. 4. Nala
incarnation .. 4. Rama 5. asura
6. yaksha
jackal .. 4. kola
king .. 5. Rajah
language (oldest) .. 5. Tamil
language (sacred) .. 4. Pali
loincloth .. 5. dhoti
magic .. 4. jadu (jadoo), maya
magician .. 4. yogi 5. fakir
meal (wheat) .. 4. atta (ata)
mendicant .. 4. naga 8. sannyasi
merchant .. 6. banian (banya)
7. goladar
mind .. 5. manas
monkey god .. 7. Hanuman
mountain .. 4. Meru
mystic .. 4. yogi
nursemaid .. 4. ayah
paradise .. 7. Nirvana
patriarch .. 5. Pitri
peasant .. 4. ryot

philosophy.. **4**. yoga, Yuga **5**. tamas
physicist.. **5**. Raman (Nobel 1930)
pillar.. **3**. lat
poet.. **5**. rishi **6**. Tagore (Nobel
   1913)
reign.. **3**. raj
sage.. **5**. rishi **6**. Dharma
   7. Gautama, Mahatma
savant.. **5**. swami
scarf.. **4**. sari (saree)
serpent (semi–human).. **4**. Naga
servant.. **5**. hamal
slave.. **4**. dasi (fem)
soldier.. **4**. sikh **5**. sepoy
supernatural being.. **6**. Garuda
swan.. **5**. hansa
syllable of assent.. **2**. om
Taraf ruler.. **8**. tarafdar
title.. **3**. Sri **4**. Raja, Rana, Rani
   5. Rajah, Ranee **6**. sirdar
   8. maharaja (maharajah)
tree (sacred).. **5**. pipal **6**. bo tree
tribesman.. **4**. Naga
tunic.. **4**. jama (jamah)
underworld (series).. **6**. Patala
village.. **5**. abadi
virtue.. **6**. sharma
widow (cremation).. **6**. suttee
woman (first).. **6**. Ahalya
Hindu Ages, Yoga ...
1st.. **5**. Krita
2nd.. **5**. Treta
3rd.. **7**. Dvapara
4th.. **4**. Kali
end.. **7**. Pralaya
total.. **4**. Maha **10**. Manvantara
Hindu goddess ... **3**. Sri, Uma **4**. Devi,
   Kali **5**. Durga, Gauri **6**. Chandi,
   Shakti **7**. Lakshmi, Parvati
   9. Haimavati (Durga)
Hindu god of ...
ancestors.. **5**. Pitri
dead.. **4**. Yama
fire.. **4**. Agni
love.. **4**. Kama
spirit.. **5**. Asura
unknown.. **2**. Ka
wisdom (elephant–headed).. **6**. Ganesa
   (Ganesha)
Hindu religion ...
abode of gods.. **4**. Meru
call to prayer.. **4**. azan (adan)
ceremony, rite.. **7**. araddha
congregation.. **5**. samaj
convert (to Islam).. **6**. shaikh
creator.. **6**. Brahma
cremation.. **4**. sati **6**. suttee
doctrine, destiny.. **5**. karma
first human to die (deified).. **4**. Yama
hell.. **6**. Naraka
Hinduism.. **5**. Agama **6**. Tantra
   7. Jainism **8**. Buddhism
   10. Brahmanism
holy man.. **5**. Sadhu (Sadh)
image worship.. **5**. arati
incarnation.. **4**. Rama **6**. avatar
   11. Ramachandra
literature (sacred).. **4**. Veda **7**. Shastra
lord of the world.. **9**. Jagannath
   (Jagannatha)
monastery.. **4**. math
philosophy (life).. **5**. artha, atman,

prana **6**. tattva
prayer, call to.. **4**. azan (adan)
prayer rug.. **5**. asana, Melas
religion.. **5**. Agama **6**. Tantra
   7. Jainism **8**. Buddhism
   10. Brahmanism
scripture.. **4**. Veda **5**. Agama
   6. Tantra **7**. Shastra
sect.. **4**. Jain (Jaina), Sikh **6**. tantra
Shastra (4 parts).. **5**. aruti **6**. purana,
   smriti, tantra
Siva worshiper.. **5**. Saiva
Supreme Spirit.. **5**. atman **7**. jivatma
teacher.. **4**. guru **5**. swami
Trimurti (Triad).. **4**. Siva **6**. Brahma,
   Vishnu
trinity, triad.. **8**. Trimurti (Siva,
   Brahma, Vishnu)
unorthodox.. **7**. Jainism
widow (cremation).. **6**. suttee
Hindustan (pert to) ...
dialect.. **4**. Urdu **10**. Hindustani
people.. **9**. Dravidian
poet.. **5**. Siraj (Beng)
rice.. **7**. aghanee
tribesman.. **4**. toda
hinge ... **3**. pan (part) **4**. axis, axle,
   hang, knee, turn **5**. joint, pivot,
   stand **6**. depend, fasten, lamina,
   pintle
hint ... **3**. cue **5**. imply, refer, tinge,
   trace **6**. allude, glance **7**. eyewink,
   inkling, suggest **8**. allusion, innuendo,
   intimate, reminder **9**. insinuate
   10. intimation, suggestion
   11. insinuation, supposition
hip ... **3**. hop, pod **4**. coxa, limp, miss,
   skip **6**. haunch **8**. greeting
hip, hips (pert to) ...
bone.. **4**. coxa **5**. ilium **7**. os coxae
   10. innominate
muscle.. **9**. iliopsoas
nerve.. **7**. sciatic (largest)
rose fruit.. **10**. pseudocarp
Hippocrates (pert to) ...
drug.. **5**. mecon (possibly opium)
famed as.. **9**. physician (Gr)
oath.. **11**. Hippocratic
hippopotamus ... **5**. hippo **6**. seacow,
   zeekoe **8**. behemoth (Bib)
hippopotamus, thong of hide ...
   7. chicote
Hiram ... **9**. most noble **10**. King of
   Tyre (Bib)
hire ... **3**. let, use **4**. hack, rent
   5. bribe, lease, price, wages
   6. employ, engage, reward, salary
   7. charter, stipend **9**. allowance
   12. compensation
hireling ... **4**. esne, serf **5**. slave, venal
   8. employee **9**. mercenary
hirmos ... **4**. hymn **8**. canticle
   9. troparion
hirondelle (Her) ... **7**. swallow
hirsel ... **4**. herd **5**. flock **7**. pasture
hirsute ... **5**. hairy, rough **6**. coarse,
   shaggy **7**. boorish, bristly, uncouth
Hispania (anc) ... **16**. Spain and
   Portugal
hispid ... **5**. rough **7**. grooved
   8. strigose
hiss ... **3**. boo, tst **4**. fizz **7**. condemn

8. derision, sibilate 10. effervesce, sibilation
historian ... 5. actor 6. writer 8. annalist 10. chronicler
history ... 5. drama 6. events, memoir 7. account 8. relation, treatise 9. chronicle, narrative
history (pert to) ...
development .. 8. ontogeny
Father of .. 9. Herodotus
muse of (Gr Myth) .. 4. Clio
period .. 3. era
personal .. 7. memoirs 9. biography, genealogy 13. autobiography
study, knowledge of .. 10. historical 12. historiology
histrio ... 5. actor
histrion ... 5. actor
histrionics ... 6. acting, actors 9. theatrics 11. theatricals
hit ... 3. bop, lob, rap, tap 4. blow, bunt, slam, slap, slog, suit, swat 5. flick, knock, shoot, smite 6. buffet, larrup, please, strike 7. succeed, success 9. collision
hitch ... 3. hop, tie, tug 4. halt, jerk, knot, limp, pull, yoke 5. catch, cling, crick, marry, unite 6. enlist, fasten, hobble 8. obstacle 9. hindrance 10. enlistment
hitherto ... 3. ago, yet 5. as yet 7. prior to 8. formerly, until now
hit or miss ... 6. casual 8. at random, by chance, careless 9. haphazard
Hittite (pert to) ...
ancestor (Bib) .. 4. Heth
city .. 6. Hamath, Pteria (ruins)
country .. 6. Khatti (Asia Minor)
people (anc) .. 8. Hittites 10. aborigines
storm god .. 6. Teshup (Teshub)
hoar ... 4. aged, gray, rime 5. hoary, white 7. ancient 9. hoarfrost, venerable
hoard ... 5. amass, lay up, store 6. garner, supply 7. husband 8. treasure, treasury 10. accumulate, collection
hoarder ... 5. miser 6. storer 9. treasurer
hoarfrost ... 3. rag 4. hoar, rime 7. needles (ice) 9. Jack Frost
hoarse ... 3. old 4. aged, gray 6. remote (in time) 7. ancient 9. canescent
hoatzin, hoactzin ... 4. anna 5. hanna 8. pheasant 9. stinkbird 11. Opisthocomi (group)
hoax ... 3. bam 4. bilk, ruse, sham 5. bluff, cheat, trick 6. canard 7. deceive 8. artifice 9. deception
hob ... 3. elf, hub, peg, pin 4. game, mark 5. clown, fairy, havoc 6. ferret, rustic, sprite 7. hobnail 8. mischief 9. fireplace, hobgoblin
hobble ... 4. clog, gait (unequal), halt, limp 5. dance 6. fetter, tether, wabble 7. dilemma, pastern, shackle 11. predicament
hobbledehoy ... 4. gawk 5. youth
hobbler ... 5. pilot 7. boatman, hoveler, laborer, soldier 8. retainer

hobby ... 3. fad, nag 5. dolly, horse 6. falcon 7. bicycle, pastime 9. avocation, plaything 10. hobbyhorse 12. rocking horse
hobgoblin ... 3. elf, imp 4. bogy, pixy, Puck 5. scrat 6. sprite 7. bugaboo 9. coltpixie 10. apparition 15. Robin Goodfellow
hobnob ... 9. associate (with), drink with, hit or miss
hobo ... 3. bum 5. tramp 6. beggar 7. vagrant 8. vagabond
hock ... 3. ham 4. pawn 5. ankle, joint, thigh (man) 6. pledge 7. disable 9. hamstring
hockey (pert to) ...
ball, disk .. 3. nur 4. knur, puck
cup .. 7. Stanley (prize)
goal .. 4. cage
stick .. 6. shinny 7. cammock
team number .. 5. seven
hocus ... 4. drug 5. cheat 6. liquor (drugged) 7. deceive, falsify 8. cheating, trickery 10. adulterate
hocus–pocus ... 5. cheat, trick 6. bunkum, humbug 7. juggler 8. flimflam, nonsense, quackery 9. deception, trickster 11. incantation 12. charlatanism 13. sleight of hand 15. juggler's formula
hod ... 3. tub 4. hide 6. barrow, trough 7. scuttle
hodgepodge ... 4. mess, olio, stew 5. cento 6. medley 7. mélange, mixture 10. miscellany 11. gallimaufry, olla–podrida
hog ... 3. pig, sow, Sus 4. bene, boar, galt, gilt 5. sheep (unshorn), shoat, swine 6. barrow 8. babirusa (babiroussa), javelina 9. boschvark, razorback
hog ... 4. corner (the market) 7. glutton 8. slattern 9. take it all 10. locomotive, monopolist
hog (pert to) ...
breed .. 5. Essex 9. Hampshire
food .. 4. mast
ground .. 6. marmot
hoglike .. 7. porcine
salted side .. 5. bacon 6. flitch
shears (snout) .. 7. snouter
thigh (cured) .. 3. ham
hogfish ... 7. capitan, pigfish 8. scorpene
hoggerel ... 5. sheep 6. hogger
hoggery ... 4. hogs 5. greed 11. beastliness 14. hoggish manners
hoggish ... 6. filthy, greedy 7. porcine, selfish, swinish 10. gluttonous
hogshead ... 4. cask 6. barrel 7. measure
hogwash ... 5. swill, waste
hoi polloi ... 3. mob 5. herde 6. masses, rabble 7. the many 8. populace 9. multitude
hoist ... 4. lift, sail 5. boost, heave, hoise, raise 7. elevate 8. elevator
hoisting device ... 3. gin 4. jack 5. crane, davit, lewis 7. capstan, derrick 8. elevator, windlass 9. parbuckle
hoity–toity ... 5. giddy, proud 6. snooty

7. flighty, haughty 8. arrogant
11. exclamation, harum–scarum,
patronizing, thoughtless
13. irresponsible
hold . . . 3. own 4. bind, have, keep,
lien, seat, stow 5. avast, cling,
delay, grasp, judge 6. adhere, arrest,
cleave, clench, defend, detain,
endure, harbor, regard, retain
7. contain, control, custody
8. consider, foothold, maintain,
thurrock (ship's), treasury
9. anchorage, constrain, entertain,
prosecute 11. compartment
hold (pert to) . . .
  back . . 3. dam 4. last, stem 5. delay,
deter, stint 6. detain, hinder, refuse,
retard 7. abstain, inhibit, repress
8. restrain
  belief . . 7. suppose
  dear . . 7. cherish
  fast . . 5. cling 6. adhere 9. persevere
  forth . . 5. offer, speak 7. declaim,
descant, exhibit, expound
8. continue, maintain, propound
  off . . 5. avert, delay 7. repulse, ward
off 9. stay aloof, temporize
  on . . 4. stop, wait 6. endure, retain
7. forbear 8. continue
  opinion . . 4. deem
  out . . 4. last 6. endure, refuse, resist
7. exclude 8. continue
  session . . 3. sit 7. convene
8. assemble
  together . . 6. adhere, cohere 8. be
joined 9. co–operate
  up . . 3. rob 4. buoy, halt, lift, rein
5. check, delay, raise 6. hinder,
resist, retard 7. display, exhibit,
pillory (to scorn), robbery, support,
sustain
  water . . 5. sound 10. consistent
holder . . . 3. cop (yarn) 4. file
5. owner, payee 6. bearer, binder,
lienor, tenant 7. trustee 8. endorsee
9. mortgagor, possessor, recipient
10. receptacle
hold in . . .
  check . . 4. curb, rein 6. arrest, bridle
7. control 8. restrain
  custody . . 4. jail 6. detain, intern
  hand . . 6. assure 7. control, promise,
toy with
  mind . . 6. harbor 7. cherish
9. entertain
holding . . . 5. asset, claim, stake, tenet,
title, trust 6. belief, equity, estate,
tenure 8. interest, property
9. retention 10. possessing,
possession, supporting
holding fast . . . 9. tenacious
10. persistent
holding sway . . . 7. regnant
8. dominant, reigning
hole . . . 3. den, pit 4. bore, cave, cove,
dive, flaw, gulf, lair, nook, slot, vent
5. abyss, chasm, fault, hovel, place,
shaft 6. burrow, cavern, cavity,
cellar, hollow, prison 7. impasse,
opening, orifice, ostiole
10. excavation 11. predicament
hole (pert to) . . .

bowling ball . . 4. grip
cable (ship's) . . 5. hawse
enlarger . . 6. reamer
implement . . 3. awl, eye 4. bore
5. drill 8. stiletto
metal mold . . 5. sprue
mud . . 6. wallow
wall . . 5. niche
water . . 5. oasis
whirlpool . . 5. gourd (obs)
Holi (or Hoolee) . . . 8. festival (Hind)
holia . . . 6. salmon (humpback)
holiday . . . 4. fete 5. feria, merry
6. fiesta, jovial, outing 7. festive,
playday 8. festival, vacation
9. convivial, festivity 10. recreation
holiness . . . 5. piety, title (Pope)
8. sanctity 9. godliness
10. sacredness 11. saintliness
13. righteousness
Holland . . . 11. Netherlands (which see)
Holland . . .
  capital . . 8. The Hague (Court)
9. Amsterdam
  city . . 3. Ede 5. Doorn 6. Leyden
9. Amsterdam, Rotterdam
  government . . 8. monarchy
  liquor . . 3. gin 8. schnapps
  oddity . . 5. dikes 6. canals, tulips
  painter . . 6. Rubens 7. Van Eyck
  people . . 5. Dutch
  port . . 4. Edam
  pottery . . 5. delft (delf)
  province . . 4. Edam 7. Drenthe,
Zeeland
  river . . 3. Ems, Lek 5. Meuse, Rhine
7. Scheldt (Schelde)
  sea . . 5. North
  village . . 3. Ede
hollow . . . 3. den, pit 4. thin, void
5. bight, empty, false, gaunt, sinus
6. cavern, cavity, cirque, corrie,
groove, hungry, socket, sunken,
vacant 7. concave, unsound
8. capsular, specious 9. cavernous,
depressed, faithless, insincere,
worthless 10. sepulchral
12. unsatisfying
hollowed . . . 6. cavate 7. concave,
glenoid
holly . . . 4. holm, hull, Ilex 5. yapon
6. hulver, laurel 8. Eryngium
9. blackjack, Ilicaceae 10. Sapindales
hollyhock . . . 5. color 7. Althaea,
blue–red 9. perennial
holm . . . 3. oak 5. holly, islet, marsh
7. bottoms, low land
holobaptist . . . 12. immersionist
holocaust . . . 9. sacrifice (by fire)
11. destruction 13. burnt offering
holy . . . 5. godly, pious 6. chaste,
devout, sacred 7. epithet (Relig),
sainted 8. hallowed 9. venerated
Holy, holy (pert to) . . .
  carpet . . 5. kiswa (kiswah)
  comb form . . 5. hagio
  Joe . . 8. sky pilot 9. clergyman
  oil . . 6. chrism 7. unction
  Ones . . 9. Innocents (slain by Herod)
  pilgrim . . 6. palmer
  receptacle . . 5. cruet, stoup
  Rood . . 5. cross 8. crucifix

water sprinkler.. 11. aspergillum
Holy Grail (pert to)...
  castle.. 9. Monsalvat (Mt)
  guardian.. 8. Amfortas
  knight.. 7. Galahad
  legend.. 8. Sangraal (Sangreal)
  quest by.. 4. Bors 7. Galahad
    9. Percivale
  terms.. 7. platter, wine cup
homage... 5. dulia, honor, liege
  6. fealty, latria 7. loyalty, ovation,
  respect, worship 9. deference,
  obeisance, reverence 10. allegiance
  12. commendation
homard... 7. Homarus, lobster
hombre... 3. man 4. homo, male
  6. fellow
home... 4. care, goal (games), kern
  (kirn), nest 5. abode, astre, grave,
  heart 6. asylum, estate, hearth
  7. habitat, village 8. domicile,
  dwelling 9. residence 10. fatherland,
  habitation
home (pert to)...
  base.. 3. den 5. plate
  dislike.. 9. ecophobia
  Home Sweet Home author.. 5. Payne
    (John Howard 1823)
  Irish King's.. 4. Tara
  of the gods.. 7. Olympus
  of the Golden Fleece.. 7. Colchis
homely... 4. ugly 5. plain 6. humble,
  kindly, simple 7. plainly 8. domestic,
  homelike, informal, plebeian,
  uncomely 9. unsightly 10. intimately
  11. comfortable 13. unpretentious
homemade... 5. plain 6. simple
  8. domestic, handmade, homespun
Homer (pert to)...
  birthplace.. 5. Chios (claimed)
  book.. 5. Iliad 7. Odyssey
  burial place.. 3. Ios (Isl)
  hero.. 6. Aeneas
Homer's poems (pert to)...
  rhapsodists.. 9. Homeridae
  student, reciter of.. 7. Homerid
    8. Homerist
  study of.. 10. Homerology
  style.. 7. Homeric
homesickness... 7. Heimweh 9. mal
  du pays, nostalgia
homespun... 5. cloth, plain, rough
  6. coarse, russet 8. domestic,
  homemade 10. not elegant,
  unpolished (person)
homicide... 5. morth 6. murder
  7. killing 12. manslaughter
homily... 5. adage 6. sermon
  8. assembly, converse
  9. communion, discourse
homing pigeon... 13. carrier pigeon
hominy... 4. samp 5. maize 10. hulled
  corn
Homo sapiens... 3. man 4. homo
  9. anthropos
Honduras...
  capital.. 11. Tegucigalpa
  city.. 4. Tela 6. Roatan 8. Trujillo
    12. Puerto Cortes
  discoverer.. 8. Columbus
  gulf.. 7. Fonseca
  Indian tribe.. 5. Lenca

  language.. 7. Spanish
  people.. 6. Indian 7. Spanish
  river.. 4. Ulua 5. Negro 6. Patuca
hone... 4. long, pine 5. delay, dress,
  stone (sharpening), strop, yearn
  6. lament 7. grumble, sharpen
  8. oilstone 9. whetstone
honest... 4. open 5. frank 6. candid,
  chaste 7. genuine, up and up,
  upright 8. faithful, suitable, virtuous
  9. guileless, honorable, ingenuous,
  integrity 10. creditable
  13. unadulterated 15. straightforward
honesty... 5. honor 6. equity
  7. justice 8. fairness 9. integrity,
  rectitude 11. genuineness,
  uprightness 12. truthfulness
  15. trustworthiness
honey... 3. mel 5. melli (comb form),
  sweet 6. nectar 7. sweeten
  10. endearment
honey (pert to)...
  bear (sloth).. 8. Melursus
  bearing.. 11. melliferous
  bee.. 4. Apis 6. dingar 7. deseret
    9. mellifera
  bird.. 3. iao 6. manuao 10. honey
    eater
  buzzard.. 4. kite, pern
  comb.. 4. raat 5. favus 8. alveolus
  drink.. 4. mead 5. morat
  flowing.. 11. mellifluent, mellifluous
  pert to.. 8. melissic
  sucking.. 11. mellisugent, mellivorous
  yellow.. 6. dorado 10. melichrous
Hong Kong...
  capital.. 8. Victoria
  government.. 11. Crown Colony
  island.. 12. Stonecutters
  peninsula.. 7. Kowloon
Honolulu...
  capital of.. 6. Hawaii
  island site.. 4. Oahu
  port.. 11. Pearl Harbor
  suburb.. 3. Ewa
honorable, honourable... 5. moral,
  title 7. upright 8. honorary
  9. estimable, reputable, venerable
  10. creditable 11. commendable,
  illustrious, meritorious, respectable
honorably... 5. nobly 6. fairly, justly
  8. worthily 9. equitably, reputably,
  uprightly
honorarium... 7. douceur
honored... 5. famed, feted 6. graced
  7. awarded, revered 8. knighted
  9. accoladed
hood... 4. corf, cowl, hide, mail
  (armor) 5. amice, blind, cloak
  6. bonnet, camail, capote
  7. capuche (capouch) 8. babushka,
  burnoose (burnous), capsheaf,
  covering, liripipe, mozzetta, tapadera
  12. strong—arm man
hood (suff)... 9. condition
hooded... 9. cucullate
hooded seal... 11. bladdernose
hoodwink... 4. dupe, fool, hide, wile
  5. blear, blind, cheat, cover, cozen
  6. befool, delude 7. deceive, mislead
  9. blindfold
hooey... 4. blah, bunk 5. tripe

7. baloney, hogwash 8. buncombe, malarkey, nonsense 13. horsefeathers

hoof... 4. clee, frog, walk 5. cloof (clufe, cluve) 6. ungula 7. pastern (part) 8. periople (part), pododerm

hoof–paring tool... 8. butteris

hoof–shaped... 8. ungulate

hoof track... 5. piste

hook... 4. gaff, lure 5. catch, chape, cleek, crome, curve, hamus, snare, steal 6. anchor, clevis, fasten, hangle, tenter 7. hamulus

hookah, hooka... 4. pipe 8. narghile

hooked... 6. curved, hamate 7. angular, cleeked 8. aduncous (adunc), anchoral, aquiline, uncinate

Hooker (Thomas)... 9. clergyman 18. Luther of New England

hooks (group)... 5. Party (Neth) 9. pulldevil, scrodgill 10. Kabbeljaws (Nobles)

hookworm... 7. Necator 9. Uncinaria

hooligan... 6. loafer 7. gorilla, hoodlum, ruffian 8. larrikin

hoop... 4. bail, band, ring 5. clasp 6. circle, wicket 7. circlet 8. surround

hoop skirt... 9. crinoline 11. farthingale

Hoosier poet... 5. Riley (J Whitcomb)

Hoosier State... 7. Indiana

hop... 3. fly 4. drug, halt, jump, leap, limp, trip, vine 5. bound, caper, dance, frisk, opium 6. flight, gambol, spring 8. narcotic

hope... 3. bay 4. opal, spes, Spes (Goddess) 5. haven, inlet, trust 6. aspire, desire, expect 7. cherish, promise 8. optimism, reliance 11. expectation 12. anticipation

hoped for... 7. sperate

hopeful... 8. probable, sanguine 9. confident, expectant 10. propitious

hopeless... 4. vain 6. futile 7. forlorn, useless 8. downcast 9. desperate, incurable 10. despairing, despondent 11. ineffectual 12. disconsolate, irremediable 13. irrecoverable, irretrievable

hopelessness... 7. despair 8. futility 13. impossibility

hop kiln... 4. oast (ost)

hoplite... 7. soldier

hopper... 3. box 5. chute 6. dancer, jumper, leaper 7. penguin (rock) 10. receptacle 11. grasshopper

hopscotch... 6. pebble, peever 7. pallall

Horace... 4. poet 10. Ars Poetica

Horae (Gr Relig)... 4. dike (justice) 6. Eirene (peace) 7. Eunomia (wisdom) 9. goddesses 11. Book of Hours

horal... 6. hourly

horde... 4. army, camp, clan, pack 5. crowd, swarm, tribe, troop

Horde, Golden... 6. Tatars (Mongol)

Horde, Great (Anthrop)... 5. Kazak 7. Kirghiz

horizon... 4. blue 5. limit, range 6. circle, sea rim 7. azimuth, sea line, sky line 8. junction (earth and sky), boundary

horizon glass... 7. sextant

horizontal... 4. flat 5. level 8. parallel (to horizon)

hormone... 8. estrogen 9. cortisone

horn... 4. Cape, cusp, gore, peak, tuba 5. alarm, bugle, cornu, keras, siren 6. antler, beaker, cornet, vessel 7. buccina, process (animal), trumpet 8. tentacle 9. appendage

horn (pert to)...
blare.. 4. toot 7. fanfare, tantara 9. tantarara
comb form.. 5. kerat 6. kerato
crescent moon.. 4. cusp
drinking (anc).. 6. rhyton
insect's.. 7. antenna
Jewish.. 7. shophar (shofar)
player.. 6. bugler 9. cornetist, trumpeter
producing.. 11. keratogenic
trumpet.. 6. kerana (kerrana)
unbranched (antler).. 3. dag 7. pricket

hornbill... 4. bird, tock 6. homrai, toucan 7. Buceros

horned animal (Myth)... 7. Unicorn 9. Monoceros

horned rattlesnake... 3. asp 5. viper 8. cerastes 10. sidewinder

horned toad... 6. lizard 9. Iguanidae

hornet... 4. wasp 5. Vespa 6. crabro

horny tissue... 7. keratin 8. keratoid (ceratoid), keratose (ceratose)

horologe... 4. dial 5. clock, watch

horoscope... 3. map 5. chart 6. scheme 7. diagram

horrendous... 7. fearful 8. horrible

horrible... 4. dire, grim 6. grisly, horrid, odious 7. ghastly, hideous 8. dreadful, shocking, terrible 9. atrocious, frightful, revolting 10. detestable, horrendous

horror... 3. awe 4. fear 5. dread 6. aghast, terror 8. aversion, distress 10. abhorrence 11. abomination, detestation 13. consternation

hors d'oeuvre... 6. canapé, relish 8. aperitif 9. antipasto, appetizer

horse... 3. cob, nag 4. colt, foal, mare, mule, plug, pony, prad, race, stud 5. beast, burro, draft, filly, genet (jennet), hobby, mount, pacer, steed 6. bronco (broncho), cheval, dobbin, donkey, equine, garran, hippos, maiden, pelter, rouncy 7. caballo, cavalry, charger, courser, Equidae, gelding, hackney, harness, mustang, prancer, quarter, stepper, trotter 8. roadster, stallion, trotting 9. broomtail

horse (pert to)...
ankle.. 4. hock
arena.. 10. hippodrome
Australian.. 5. dingo, myall 8. warragal, yarraman
breastplate.. 7. poitrel (peytrel)
broken–down.. 6. garran, gleyde
buyer (of nags).. 5. coper 7. knacker
calico.. 5. pinto
collar.. 7. bargham
comb form.. 4. hipp 5. hippo 6. hippus

command . . 3. gee, haw, hup
4. whoa 6. giddap
covering . . 9. caparison
cry . . 5. neigh 6. whinny
dealer . . 7. chanter, scorser
disease . . 5. surra (surrah) 6. heaves,
lampas, spavin 7. founder, lampers
draft . . 9. Percheron
family . . 7. Equidae 9. Miohippus,
Orohippus
fast . . 6. pelter
feed box . . 6. manger
female . . 4. mare, yaud 5. filly
fly . . 4. cleg (clegg) 6. botfly
foot . . 4. frog, hoof 7. fetlock, pastern
forehead . . 8. chanfrin
gait . . 3. run 4. lope, pace, trot, walk
6. canter, gallop
genus . . 5. Equus
giant (Norse) . . 7. Goldfax
goddess . . 5. Epona
gray . . 8. schimmel
hide . . 8. cordovan
hired . . 4. hack
hoof (part) . . 7. caltrop 8. periople
laugh . . 5. snort 6. guffaw, heehaw
leap . . 6. curvet, hurdle 9. ballotade
lover . . 10. hippophile
mackerel . . 5. atule, tunny 6. bonita
male . . 4. stud 7. gelding 8. stallion
manège term . . 5. longe, mount
6. pesade 7. piaffer, saccade
8. caracole 9. estrapage
measure . . 4. hand
miracle (Myth) . . 5. Arion
monster (fabled) . . 11. Hippocampus
old . . 4. jade, yaud 5. skate
8. harridan, old paint
opera . . 7. Western
pace . . 4. lope, trot 5. amble
6. canter
pack . . 7. sumpter
pair . . 4. span, team
pasturage right . . 9. horsegate
piebald . . 5. pinto
pole . . 5. poler, wheel
prehistoric . . 8. Eohippus
10. Mesohippus, Pliohippus
13. Protorohippus
racer . . 4. pony 6. mudder, plater,
staker
ref to . . 6. equine, equoid, hippic
9. caballine
relay (remounts) . . 6. remuda
riding . . 3. cob
rope . . 5. longe 6. halter
roundup . . 5. rodeo
saddle . . 3. cob 5. mount 7. palfrey
shoer . . 7. farrier 10. blacksmith
slang . . 3. nag 4. hack, plug
6. dobbin 8. bangtail
small . . 3. cob, tit 4. pony 5. bidet,
genet (jennet) 8. Galloway, Shetland
sorrel . . 4. roan 8. chestnut
spirited . . 4. Arab 5. steed 6. rearer
7. courser
stable of . . 6. string
study of . . 9. hippology
swift . . 6. pelter 7. Pacolet
talking (Myth) . . 5. Arion
three (harnessed) . . 6. tandem

7. unicorn
track, arena . . 10. hippodrome
trappings . . 5. manta 6. tackle
7. harness 9. caparison
trotting . . 6. Morgan
turn . . 7. passade
war . . 5. steed 7. charger 8. destrier
(anc)
white–streaked face . . 4. shim
wild . . 6. bronco, tarpan 7. mustang
8. warragal (warrigal)
winged . . 7. Pegasus
horse, breed . . . 4. Arab, Barb 5. Shire,
Waler 6. Cayuse, Morgan 7. Arabian,
Belgian, Hackney, Mustang, Suffolk
8. Galloway, Normandy, Palomino,
Shetland 9. Appaloosa, Miohippus,
Percheron 10. Clydesdale
horse, color . . . 3. bay, tan 4. pied,
roan 5. cream, pinto 6. calico, sorrel
7. brindle, dappled, piebald
8. chestnut, palomino, schimmel,
skewbald 10. flea–bitten
horse, famed (and rider) . . . 4. Tony
(Tom Mix) 5. Grani (Sigurd)
6. Bayard (Rinaldo), Rienzi (Gen
Sherman), Silver (Lone Ranger),
Trojan (legend), Whitey (Zachary
Taylor) 7. Alborak (Mohammed),
Morengo (Napoleon), Pegasus (Gr
Myth), Trigger (Roy Rogers), Xanthus
(Achilles) 8. Comanche (Gen Custer),
Sleipnir 8–legged (Odin), Soapsuds
(Will Rogers) 9. Black Bess (Dick
Turpin), Houyhnhnm (Gulliver's
Travels), Incitatus (Caligula), Rosinante
(Don Quixote), Traveller (Gen Robt E
Lee) 10. Bootlegger (Will Rogers),
Bucephalus (Alexander the Great),
Cincinnati (Gen Grant), Copenhagen
(Wellington at Waterloo), King Philip
(Gen Forrest) 11. Black Beauty
(legend), Vegliantino (Orlando)
12. Little Sorrel (Stonewall Jackson)
horseman . . . 5. rider 6. cowboy
7. centaur, vaquero 8. buckaroo
10. cavalryman, equestrian
12. broncobuster
horsemanship . . . 6. manège
horseradish tree . . . 3. ben (oil)
5. behen (behn) 7. Moringa
Horus (pert to) . . .
bird . . 6. falcon
father . . 6. Osiris
hawk–headed god of . . 3. day
mother . . 4. Isis
slayer of . . 4. Seth
hospice . . . 3. inn 6. asylum, imaret
9. hospitium, infirmary
hospitable . . . 6. kindly 7. cordial
8. friendly, gracious 9. receptive,
welcoming 10. neighborly
hospital . . . 6. crèche, refuge
9. ambulance (mobile), infirmary
10. nosocomium, sanatorium
sanitarium 11. institution,
xenodochium 12. ambulatorium
hospitality . . . 7. accueil, welcome
8. open door 9. open house,
xenodochy 10. cordiality
13. receptiveness
host . . . 3. sum (obs) 4. army 5. swarm

6. legion, throng 8. assemble,
landlord 9. multitude, sacrifice
11. entertainer
hostel... 3. inn 5. hotel, motel
6. tavern 8. lodgings 9. residence
(student)
hostelry... 3. inn 5. hotel 6. hostel,
tavern 11. caravansary
hostile... 5. enemy 7. adverse (law),
opposed 8. contrary, inimical
10. malevolent, unfriendly
11. belligerent 12. antagonistic
13. unsympathetic
hostilities... 3. war 5. feuds, raids
hostility... 5. anger 6. animus, enmity,
hatred, rancor 7. ill will, warfare
8. opponent 9. animosity, antipathy
10. antagonism, bitterness,
opposition, resentment 11. contrariety
13. antisocialism 14. unfriendliness,
vindictiveness
hostler... 5. groom 7. equerry
9. innkeeper, stableboy, stableman
Host vessel... 3. Pyx 5. paten
hot... 3. red 5. calid, eager, fiery
6. fervid, raging, recent, torrid,
urgent 7. burning, calidus, excited,
fervent, glowing, peppery, violent
8. feverish, sizzling, vehement
10. hot–blooded, passionate
hot cakes... 8. kneepads (army sl)
hotel... 3. inn 5. lodge 6. hostel,
tavern 7. albergo 11. caravansary
hot–tempered... 5. angry, breth, fiery
7. enraged, iracund 8. choleric,
wrathful 10. hot–blooded
Hottentot, S Africa (pert to)...
cloak.. 6. kaross
hut.. 5. kraal
mixed native.. 6. Griqua
musical instrument.. 4. gora (gorah)
nickname.. 9. Khoi–Khoin (Koi–Koin)
(men of men)
purest tribe.. 5. Namas 7. Namaqua
race.. 6. Bantus 7. Bushmen
tribe.. 6. Damara, Herero
9. Ovahehero
hound... 4. hunt 5. chase, track
6. follow, pursue 7. devotee
9. scoundrel
hound (animal)... 4. alan 6. Afghan,
basset, beagle, setter 7. harrier,
skirter 8. Cerberus (Myth), elkhound,
foxhound 9. boarhound, dachshund,
deerhound, greyhound, staghound,
wolfhound 10. bloodhound,
otterhound
hounds, relay of... 8. avantlay
hour (pert to)...
astrology.. 7. inequal 9. planetary
by the.. 5. horal 6. horary
Eccl.. 4. sext 9. canonical
Latin.. 4. hora 5. Horae (Book of
Hours)
measure.. 9. hourglass
term.. 4. time 6. period 7. measure
8. interval
houri... 5. nymph (Moham)
Hours, Book of... 5. Horae
house... 3. eco (comb form) 4. casa,
firm, home 5. abode, cover, lodge,
tribe 6. billet, family 7. cottage,

enclose, lineage, mansion, quarter,
shelter, theater 8. audience,
bungalow, Congress, domicile,
dwelling 9. playhouse, residence,
workhouse 10. habitation, Parliament
house (pert to)...
astrology.. 7. mansion, mundane
9. planetary
boarding.. 3. inn 5. hotel 6. tavern
9. dormitory
comb form.. 3. eco 4. oeco, oiko
correction.. 9. Bridewell (Eng)
11. reformatory
dog.. 6. kennel
government.. 5. Lords 7. Commons
15. Representatives
ranch.. 4. casa 6. casita 8. hacienda
roof.. 9. penthouse
small.. 3. hut 4. nest 5. cabin, shack
stately.. 5. villa 6. palace 7. mansion
summer.. 6. casino, gazebo
9. belvedere
warming.. 6. infare
household (pert to)...
deity.. 5. Lares 7. Penates
domestic.. 6. family, menage
fairy.. 4. Puck
linen.. 6. napery
housekeeping... 8. oikology
10. management 11. hospitality
House of... 4. Keys (Isle of Man)
5. David, Lords, Peers 7. Bishops,
Commons, Windsor 11. Seven
Gables
housewarming... 6. infare
11. merrymaking
Houston, Texas...
capital.. 8. Republic (Texas, 1837)
college.. 4. Rice
named for.. 10. Sam Houston (Gen)
nickname.. 12. Space City USA
site.. 11. Ship Channel
site of.. 4. NASA
hovel... 3. den, hut 4. shed 5. cabin,
hutch, shack 6. dugout 7. shelter
hover... 4. flit, soar 5. brood, drift,
float 6. linger 7. shelter 9. hang
about 12. be irresolute
however... 3. but, how, tho, yet
6. anyhow, though 7. at least
8. although 11. at all events
12. nevertheless 15. notwithstanding
howl... 3. bay, cry 4. wail, yell, yowl
6. lament 7. ululate
howling monkey... 5. araba
hoyden, hoiden... 4. rude 5. a romp
6. tomboy 7. ill–bred
Hoyle (Edmond)... 6. writer
12. encyclopedia (of games)
hub... 3. hip 4. axle, nave 6. center
(centre) 7. hummock
12. protuberance (rough)
Hub (The)... 6. Boston
hubbub... 3. ado, din 4. game (US
Ind), stir 6. bustle, clamor, outcry,
racket, rumpus, tumult, uproar
8. rowdy–dow 9. agitation,
commotion, confusion 10. turbulence
hubristic... 8. arrogant, insolent
12. contemptuous
hubshi... 5. Negro
huck... 3. hip 4. hook, howk

6. haunch, higgle, hollow 7. bargain
huckleberry... 5. bacca 9. blueberry
   12. Vacciniaceae
huckleberry endocarp... 6. pyrene
huckster... 6. broker, hawker, vendor
   7. peddler 8. pitchman, retailer
   9. middleman
huddle... 3. hug 5. crowd 6. bustle,
   confer, jumble, mingle 7. confuse
   8. assemble, disorder, grouping
   (football) 9. confusion, skinflint
   10. conference 14. conglomeration
Hudson (pert to)...
  boat.. 8. Half Moon (Henry Hudson's)
  explorer.. 11. Henry Hudson
  River School.. 8. Painters (19th Cent)
  River seal.. 7. muskrat
hue... 4. form, tint, tone 5. color,
   guise, shade, shout, swart, tinge
   6. outcry 7. swarthy 8. shouting
   10. complexion
huff... 4. puff 5. anger, bully, swell
   6. offend 7. inflate
hug... 4. hold 5. clasp, seize
   6. adhere 7. embrace, welcome
   8. greeting
huge... 3. big 4. vast 5. giant, great,
   large 7. immense, mammoth,
   massive, monster, titanic 8. colossal,
   enormous, gigantic 9. monstrous
   10. gargantuan
Huguenot... 10. Protestant
Huguenot leader... 6. Adrets (Baron)
hui (Chin)... 4. firm 5. guild 7. society
   (secret) 11. partnership
huisache... 4. wabe (wabi) 5. shrub
   7. popinac
huissier... 5. usher 7. bailiff, sheriff
   10. doorkeeper
huitre... 6. oyster
hulky... 5. bulky, large 6. clumsy
   7. hulking, loutish
hull... 3. pod 4. free, husk 5. calyx,
   frame (ship), shell, shoot, strip
   8. covering
hullabaloo... 3. din 6. clamor
   (clamour), hubbub, outcry, racket,
   tumult, uproar 9. confusion
hulled corn... 4. samp 5. maize
   6. hominy
hulver... 5. holly
hum... 4. buzz, sing (with closed lips)
   5. croon, drone 6. murmur
   7. deceive
human... 3. man 4. homo, kind
   6. humane, mortal 7. Adamite
   8. merciful
human (pert to)...
  being.. 3. man 6. mortal, person
   7. Adamite 8. creature
  bondage.. 7. slavery
  race.. 3. man 7. mankind
  skull.. 10. death's–head
  structure.. 7. anatomy
  trunk.. 5. torso
humble... 3. low 4. mean, meek, mild,
   poor 5. abase, abash, demit, lower,
   lowly, plain 6. modest, simple,
   subdue 7. degrade, mortify
   8. chastise, deferent, disgrace,
   plebeian, reverent 9. humiliate
   10. unassuming 12. unpretending

humbug... 4. bosh, fake, flam, guff,
   hoax, sham 5. cheat, fraud, guile,
   trick 7. deceive, mislead 8. pretense
   9. deception, imposture, stratagem
humid... 4. damp, dank 5. moist
   6. sultry 8. vaporous
humiliate... 5. abase, abash, shame
   6. humble, nither 7. affront, degrade,
   mortify 8. disgrace
humiliation... 7. subdual 9. abasement
   11. disgraceful 13. mortification
humility... 6. humble (spirit)
   7. modesty 8. meekness, mildness
   9. lowliness (mind) 10. humbleness
hummingbird... 3. ava 4. star
   5. sylph, topaz 6. rufous, Sappho
   7. colibri, Lucifer 8. calliope
   9. sheartail, thornbill, thorntail
   10. rackettail 11. Trochilidae
humor, humour... 3. fun, wit 4. baby,
   mood, whim 5. blood, cater, fancy,
   fluid, freak, quirk 6. comedy, levity,
   nature, please 7. caprice, gratify,
   indulge 8. drollery 10. comicality
   11. inclination, temperament
humorist... 3. wag 5. comic, droll
   8. comedian 11. entertainer
humorous... 5. funny, humid, moist,
   witty 6. jocose 7. amusing, jocular
   9. facetious, laughable, whimsical
   10. capricious
hump... 4. arch, hunk, lump 5. bulge,
   exert, hurry, mound, sulks
   7. hummock 8. shoulder
   12. protuberance
humpbacked... 6. humped, kyphos
   8. deformed, kyphosis 9. camel back
   11. hunchbacked
humpbacked fish... 5. whale
   6. salmon, sucker 9. whitefish
humus... 4. mold, soil 5. humin,
   mulch
Hun... 6. Attila, vandal 7. soldier
   9. barbarian 10. Ephthalite
hunch... 4. bend, hump, lump
   5. crook, fudge, shove 6. chilly,
   crouch, frosty, thrust 9. intuition
   12. protuberance
Hunchback of Notre Dame (pert to)...
  character.. 9. Esmeralda (gypsy),
   Quasimodo (The Hunchback)
  French name.. 16. Notre Dame de
   Paris
  literature (famed).. 5. novel
hunched... 7. gibbous
hundred (pert to)...
  comb form.. 5. centi, hecto
   7. hecaton
  eyed being.. 5. Argus
  fold.. 8. centuple 12. centuplicate
  historian (of centuries)..
   11. centuriator
  Latin.. 6. centum
  men, soldiers.. 7. century
   12. centumvirate
  number.. 7. ten tens 9. five score
  symbol.. 1. C
  victim sacrifice.. 8. hecatomb
  weight.. 6. cental 7. centner
  years.. 7. century 9. centenary,
   centurial
Hundred Days (pert to)... 8. Napoleon,

Waterloo (Battle 1815)
hundred percent... 5. quite 8. entirely
10. altogether 14. unquestionable
hundredth of a right angle... 4. grad
Hundred Years War... 5. Crecy
(Cressy)
hung... see *hang*
Hungarian (pert to)... see also *Hungary*
  army.. 6. Honvéd 9. Honvédség
  cavalryman.. 6. Hussar
  dance.. 7. czardas
  gypsy.. 7. tzigane
  hash.. 7. goulash
  legislature.. 8. Felsohaz
  measure.. 5. antal, itcze
  partridge.. 6. Perdix
  physicist.. 6. Teller
  poet.. 5. Arany
  Pretender to the throne.. 4. Otto
  racial unit.. 3. Hun 6. Magyar
  surgeon.. 6. Schick
  turnip.. 8. kohlrabi
  wine.. 5. Tokay
Hungary (People's Republic of)...
  capital.. 8. Budapest (Budapesth)
  city.. 6. Szeged (Szegedin)
  8. Debrecen 9. Kecskemet
  government.. 9. Communism
  lake.. 7. Balaton 10. Neusiedler
  mountain.. 5. Tatra 11. Carpathians
  Plain (fertile).. 6. Alfold
  port.. 5. Fiume
  river.. 4. Raab 5. Drava (Drave)
  6. Danube, Theiss 7. Vistula
hunger... 4. long, want 6. acoria,
  desire, famine, thirst 7. craving
  8. appetite, coveting, voracity
  9. esurience
hungry... 4. avid, poor 5. eager
  6. barren, hollow, jejune 7. starved
  8. esurient, famished, indigent
  10. avaricious
Hung Society (secret)... 5. Triad (Man,
  Earth, Heaven) 6. Deluge
hunt... 3. dig 4. seek 5. chase, delve,
  hound, probe, quest, track, trail
  6. ferret, follow, pursue, search,
  shikar
hunter... 3. dog 5. green, horse,
  jager, Jason, Orion 6. cuckoo,
  Nimrod 7. shikari (shikaree), stalker,
  trapper, venerer 8. huntsman
hunting (pert to)...
  act of.. 6. venery 7. pursuit
  10. cynegetics
  coyotes.. 7. wolfing
  dog.. 5. dhole 6. basset, beagle,
  setter 7. pointer
  Dogs (Astron).. 13. Canes Venatici
  expedition.. 6. safari
  fond of.. 7. venatic
  horn.. 5. bugle
  leopard.. 7. cheetah
hurdy–gurdy... 4. lire, rota 5. organ
  (street) 7. sambuke 10. instrument
  (lutelike), waterwheel
hurl... 4. cast, pelt, rush, toss
  5. fling, pitch, sling, throw 6. elance
  (dart), hurtle 9. overthrow
hurlbarrow... 11. wheelbarrow
hurled... 4. cast, sent 5. flung, slung,

threw 6. pelted, tossed 7. hurtled,
  twisted 8. betossed
hurly–burly... 5. storm 6. tumult,
  uproar 9. agitation, confusion
  10. excitement
huron... 6. grison (animal) 9. black
  bass
Huron... 4. lake 6. Indian 9. Iroquoian
hurrah... 3. joy 4. viva 5. cheer,
  huzza, shout 7. triumph 8. applause
  10. hallelujah 11. exclamation
  13. encouragement
hurricane... 5. storm 6. baguio
  7. cyclone, Hurakan (god), tornado,
  typhoon (in China Sea)
hurry... 3. hie 4. rush, scud 5. chase,
  haste, impel, sessa, speed 6. hasten,
  scurry, tumult, urge on 7. quicken
  8. dispatch, expedite 9. agitation,
  commotion 10. expedition
  11. disturbance, precipitate
hurst... 4. hill, wood 5. copse, grove,
  knoll 7. hillock (wooded)
hurt... 4. harm, maim, pain 5. lesed,
  parry 6. damage, grieve, impair,
  injure, injury, offend 8. distress,
  mischief 9. detriment 10. impairment
hurtful... 6. malign, nocent 7. baneful,
  harmful, malefic, nocuous, noisome,
  noxious, painful 9. injurious
  10. pernicious 11. destructive,
  detrimental, prejudicial
  15. disadvantageous
hurtle... 4. dash, push 5. clash, fling
  6. assail, jostle 7. collide, resound
  8. brandish
husband... 3. eke 4. mate, save
  5. marry, store 6. direct (frugally),
  farmer, spouse, tiller 7. espouse,
  granger, manager, steward
  8. conserve 9. cultivate, economize
  10. husbandman
husbandry... 6. thrift 7. economy,
  farming, tillage 10. management
  (domestic) 11. agriculture, cultivation
husband's brother... 5. levir
hush... 3. tut 4. calm, hist, lull
  5. allay, quiet, still 6. soothe
  7. appease, silence 10. keep secret
husk... 4. bran, leam, rind 5. shood,
  shuck, straw
husky... 3. dry 5. burly, harsh
  6. hoarse, strong 7. raucous
  8. powerful
Husky... 3. dog 6. Eskimo
  8. Malemute
huss... 7. dogfish
hussar... 4. fish (banded) 6. dolman
  (jacket) 10. cavalryman, skirmisher
hussy... 4. girl, jade 8. strumpet
  9. housewife
hustings... 5. court 8. platform
  (Guildhall)
hut... 3. cot 4. cote, isba, shed, skeo
  (fisherman's) 5. cabin, hogan, hovel,
  igloo, jacal, scale 6. lean–to, shanty,
  wigwam
hutch... 3. bin, box, car, hut, pen
  4. coop 5. chest, hoard, hovel
  6. coffer, humped, shanty, warren
hyacinth (pert to)...
  color.. 5. tenne 7. blue–red

genus.. 10. Hyacinthus
mineral.. 6. zircon
myth.. 4. iris, lily (Turk's cap)
of Peru.. 9. Cuban lily
precious stone.. 8. sapphire (legend)
wild.. 6. camass
hybrid... 7. mongrel 9. half–breed
hybrid (pert to)...
buffalo.. 7. cattalo
dog.. 5. Husky 7. mongrel
fruit.. 7. plumcot, tangelo 8. citrange
horse.. 4. mule 5. hinny, jenny
vegetable.. 6. pomato
zebra.. 7. zebrass, zebrula 8. zebrinny
hydra... 4. evil 6. polyps
11. thermometer
Hydra (Gr)... 6. island 7. serpent
13. constellation
hydraulic (pert to)...
brake.. 8. cataract
element.. 5. water
engine.. 3. ram 6. tremie
product.. 5. power
hydria... 3. jar 6. kalpis
hydrocarbon... 5. tolan (tolane)
6. ethane, octane, pinene, pyrene,
tolane, toluol 7. benzene, methane,
terpene 9. acetylene
hydrocarbon radical... 4. amyl
6. pentyl
hydrocyanic acid... 7. cyanide, prussic
8. fumigant
hydrogen... 1. H 3. gas 7. element
(univalent)
hydroid... 9. polyplike
hydrophobia... 5. lyssa 6. rabies
Hydrus... 12. water serpent (fabled)
13. constellation
hyena... 6. mammal 8. aardwolf
9. earthwolf 13. Tasmanian wolf
hygienic... 7. sterile 8. sanitary
9. healthful 10. uninfected
12. prophylactic
hylophagous... 10. wood–eating
hymenopter, hymenopteron... 3. ant,
bee, fly 4. wasp 9. ichneumon
hymn... 3. ode 4. song (of praise)
5. dirge, music, paean (pean)
6. anthem, hirmos, Te Deum
7. chorale 8. doxology 9. Trisagion
11. recessional

hymn (pert to)...
book.. 6. hymnal
composer.. 7. hymnist
12. hymnographer
science of.. 9. hymnology
singing of.. 7. hymnody
victory.. 9. epinicion
hypnotic... 6. opiate, sleepy
8. mesmeric, narcotic, sedative
9. soporific 12. somnifacient
13. sleep–inducing
hypnotist... 6. Mesmer 9. mesmerist
10. hypnotizer
hypnotize... 5. charm 6. dazzle
8. entrance 9. fascinate, mesmerize,
spellbind
hypochondriac... 4. hypo 6. insane
7. invalid (imaginary) 8. dejected,
neurotic 9. depressed, psychotic
10. nosomaniac
hypocrisy... 4. cant 6. deceit
8. feigning 9. falseness
10. sanctimony, simulation
11. outward show
hypocrite... 4. fake 5. cheat 7. tartufe
(tartuffe) 8. deceiver 10. dissembler
hypocritical... 5. false 8. specious
9. insincere 11. pharisaical
13. sanctimonious, self–righteous
hypodermic glass vessel...
7. ampule (ampule)
hypodermic injection... 4. shot
11. inoculation
hypothesis... 3. ism 6. theory
7. premise, theorem 8. proposal
9. condition, postulate
10. assumption 11. proposition,
supposition
hypothetical... 8. academic
11. conditional, conjectural,
speculative, theoretical
hypothetical (pert to)...
being.. 3. ens 5. entia (pl) 6. entity
biological unit.. 2. id
force.. 2. od
medium.. 5. ether
hyrax... 8. procavia
hyssop... 4. mint 11. aspergillum
hysteria... 7. anxiety 12. emotionalism
hysterical... 7. frantic 8. frenzied,
wild–eyed 9. emotional
12. uncontrolled

I

I ... **2.** me **3.** eye **4.** iota (Gr), self **6.** letter (9th), myself **7.** pronoun
I (pert to) ...
big .. **3.** ego
excessive .. **8.** iotacism
love .. **3.** amo
Iago ... **7.** villain (Othello)
iambus ... **4.** foot, iamb
iatrics (comb form) ... **11.** treatment of
iatrology ... **7.** healing **8.** treatise
Iberia ... **5.** Spain **7.** Georgia (anc)
ibex ... **3.** sac, tur, zac **4.** kail (kyl) **6.** sakeen **8.** antelope
ibid ... **6.** lizard **7.** monitor
ibidem ... **4.** ibid **9.** same place
ibis ... **5.** guara, stork **9.** gourdhead
Ibsen (pert to) ...
famed as .. **4.** poet **9.** dramatist
native of .. **6.** Norway
story character .. **3.** Ase **4.** Gynt, Nora
ice ... **4.** rime **5.** frost, glacé, glaze **6.** freeze **7.** congeal, diamond, jewelry **11.** refrigerant, refrigerate
ice (pert to) ...
bartender's .. **5.** rocks (sl)
cream dish .. **4.** cone, soda **6.** frappé, mousse, sundae **7.** parfait
dessert .. **5.** glacé **6.** frappé **7.** sherbet
fine, slushy .. **4.** grue, hail, sish, snow **5.** flake, frost, sleet
fishing .. **4.** chug
glacier .. **4.** neve **5.** serac
mass .. **4.** berg, calf, floe **5.** serac **6.** icecap **7.** glacier, growler
pendent .. **6.** icicle
sea .. **6.** sludge
Iceland ...
airport .. **9.** Kopavogur
assembly .. **7.** Althing
bird .. **4.** gull **6.** falcon **10.** gyrofalcon
capital .. **9.** Reykjavik
city .. **3.** Hof **8.** Akureyri
dramatist .. **12.** Siguryonsson
epic .. **4.** Edda
first discoverer .. **8.** Norseman (about 870)
giant .. **4.** Atli
glacier .. **6.** Jökull **11.** Orafajökull
god .. see *Norse god(s), goddess*
government .. **8.** republic (1944)
legends .. **5.** Eddas, Sagas **12.** Volsunga Saga
Parliament .. **7.** Althing (world's oldest)
product .. **7.** herring
sculptor .. **9.** Sveinsson
volcano .. **5.** Askja, Hekla, Katla
ichneumon ... **3.** fly **8.** mongoose **9.** Herpestes **10.** hymenopteron
ichor ... **5.** fluid (of the gods)

ichthus ... **4.** fish **6.** amulet, symbol **8.** talisman
ichthyophagy ... **10.** fish eating
icicle ... **7.** shoggle **10.** stalactite, stalagmite
icing ... **8.** frosting, meringue
icterus ... **6.** oriole **7.** disease **8.** jaundice **10.** yellowness
ictus ... **4.** beat (rhythm), blow **6.** accent, stress, stroke
icy ... **4.** cold **5.** algid, gelid **6.** frigid, frosty, frozen **7.** glacial **8.** chilling
id ... **4.** idem, unit **5.** idant **6.** libido, psyche, suffix **7.** the same
Idaean (pert to) ...
dweller of .. **5.** Mt Ida
goddess .. **4.** Rhea (Crete) **6.** Cybele (Asia Minor)
nature goddess .. **6.** Cybele **11.** Great Mother
Idaho ...
capital .. **5.** Boise
city .. **7.** Orofino **9.** Pocatello
crop (famed) .. **8.** potatoes
dam .. **3.** Oxbow **8.** Brownlee
famed citizen .. **5.** Borah (Sen)
monument .. **16.** Craters of the Moon
mountain .. **8.** Sawtooth **11.** Bitterroots
river .. **5.** Snake
salmon (landlocked) .. **7.** kokanee
State admission .. **10.** Forty–third
State bird .. **8.** bluebird
State flower .. **7.** syringa
State motto .. **11.** Live Forever **12.** Esto Perpetua
State nickname .. **8.** Gem State
ide (id) ... **3.** orf (orfe) **4.** fish **7.** the same
idea ... **4.** clue, idée, ideo (comb form) **5.** ethic, motif **6.** belief, notion **7.** concept, meaning, opinion, wrinkle **10.** impression **11.** supposition
ideal ... **4.** type **5.** dream, model, Thule (Myth) **6.** unreal **7.** paragon, pattern, perfect, typical, Utopian **8.** complete, exemplar, fanciful **9.** faultless, imaginary, visionary **10.** conceptual, consummate, idealistic **11.** mental image, theoretical **12.** intellectual
idealist ... **7.** dreamer **8.** romancer **9.** visionary **11.** illusionist
idealistic ... **9.** fictional, visionary **10.** starry–eyed **13.** philosophical
ideate ... **5.** think **6.** invent **7.** imagine **8.** conceive **9.** prefigure
identical ... **4.** same, self, twin **5.** alike, equal **10.** equivalent, tantamount
identification ... **3.** tag **4.** disk, sign

5. badge, brand 6. naming
7. earmark 11. recognition,
unification
identify... 4. name 5. place, prove
8. coalesce 9. designate, establish
13. associate with
identity... 5. unity 7. oneness
8. equality, sameness 9. exactness
11. homogeneity 13. individuality
ideologist... 7. dreamer 8. theorist
9. visionary
idiocy... 7. amentia, anoesia, fatuity,
idiotry 10. deficiency (mental)
11. foolishness
idiograph... 9. trademark
idiom... 6. phrase 7. diction
8. language 11. peculiarity
idiosyncrasy... 9. mannerism
11. peculiarity 12. eccentricity
14. characteristic
idiot... 3. oaf 4. dolt, fool 5. booby,
dunce, moron 6. cretin, nitwit
7. dullard, half–wit 8. imbecile
9. blockhead, simpleton
idiotic... 4. daft 5. crazy 7. foolish
9. senseless 12. feeble–minded
idle... 4. laze, lazy, loaf, sorn, vain
5. drone, empty, inert 6. loiter,
otiose, tiffle, truant, unused, vacant
7. leisure, loafing, trivial, useless
8. baseless, inactive, indolent,
slothful, trifling 9. unfounded,
worthless 10. groundless,
unemployed, unoccupied
11. ineffectual, unwarranted
idleness... 5. folly, sloth 6. vanity
7. inertia 8. delirium, faniente,
laziness 9. silliness 10. inactivity,
triviality 15. lightheadedness
idler... 4. hobo 5. drone 6. loafer
7. dawdler, lounger 8. loiterer
idol... 3. god (sacred) 4. Baal, icon,
zemi 5. afgod, deity (heathen), eikon,
satyr 6. effigy, fetish, idolum, statue
7. darling, fallacy, phantom, picture
8. impostor 9. pretender
idolater... 5. pagan 6. adorer
7. admirer, Baalist, Baalite, heathen
8. idolizer 9. worshiper
idolize... 6. adore 6. esteem, revere
7. worship 10. idolatrize
idyl, idyll... 4. poem 5. image
7. bucolic, eclogue, picture
8. pastoral
i. e... 5. id est 6. that is
if... 2. si 3. gif 8. granting, provided
9. supposing
if ever... 4. once
if not... 4. else, nisi (law) 6. unless
igneous rock... 4. boss, dike, trap
5. magma 6. basalt 7. peridot
10. granophyre 11. molten magma
ignis... 4. fire
ignite... 4. burn, fire, heat 5. light
6. kindle 7. blaze up, flare up 9. set
fire to
ignoble... 3. low 4. base, mean, vile
6. menial 8. plebeian, shameful
11. disgraceful 12. dishonorable,
disreputable
ignoramus... 4. dolt, fool 5. dunce
6. nitwit, no bill (law)

11. know–nothing
ignorance... 5. tamas (Hind)
9. nescience 12. inexperience
ignorant... 7. unaware 8. nescient
9. unknowing, untutored
10. illiterate, unlettered
13. inexperienced, unintelligent
ignore... 3. cut 4. omit, snub
7. condone, disobey, neglect
8. overlook 9. disregard, eliminate
Igorot... 6. Bontok 7. Nabaloi
8. Kankanai 10. Indonesian
iguana... 6. goanna (goana), lizard
7. monitor, tuatara 9. Iguanidae
10. lace lizard
I Have Found It... 6. Eureka (Calif
motto)
ihi (Maori)... 7. skipper 8. halfbeak
10. stitchbird
IHS... 5. Jesus 6. symbol 10. In hoc
signo
iiwi... 4. bird
ikbal... 7. arrival 8. prestige
10. prosperity
Iknaton... 9. Amenhotep, Amenophis
(IV)
ikona... 9. greenhorn, simpleton
ileum... 9. intestine (small)
ilex... 5. holly 7. holm oak
11. Paraguay tea
Iliad (pert to)...
founder (anc).. 4. Troy 5. Ilium
poem author.. 5. Homer
poem character.. 4. Ajax 6. Hector
7. Stentor 8. Achilles, Brisseis
9. Agamemnon, Cassandra
ilium... 4. bone (pelvic)
Ilium... 4. Troy (anc)
ill... 3. bad, mal (comb form) 4. evil,
hard, poor, rude, sick 5. badly,
wrong 6. ailing, malice, poorly,
savage, unkind 7. noxious, painful,
unlucky 9. dangerous, difficult
10. disastrous, indisposed, iniquitous,
malevolent, unpolished, unskillful
11. unfavorable, unfortunate,
unwholesome 12. disagreeable,
inauspicious
ill (pert to)...
at ease.. 7. awkward 9. graceless,
maladroit
bred.. 4. rude 7. uncivil 8. impolite
9. bourgeois
hap.. 10. misfortune
humored.. 5. cross, moody
natured.. 4. dour 5. cross, moody,
surly 6. morose, sullen 7. crabbed
10. crosspatch
tempered.. 7. bilious 8. choleric
timed.. 5. inapt 8. untimely
9. premature 10. malapropos
11. inexpedient, inopportune
will.. 6. enmity, malice
11. malevolence
illegal... 4. foul 7. illicit 8. outlawry,
unlawful, wrongful 10. contraband,
unofficial 12. illegitimate,
unauthorized
illegal entry... 6. ringer
illimitable... 4. vast 8. infinite
9. boundless 11. measureless
12. immeasurable, unrestricted

Illinois...
airport.. 5. O'Hare
capital.. 8. Vandalia (first)
  11. Springfield
city.. 5. Elgin 6. Peoria 7. Chicago,
  Decatur 8. Evanston, Waukegan
  9. Centralia
lake.. 8. Michigan
slogan.. 13. Land of Lincoln
State admission.. 11. Twenty–first
State nickname.. 7. Prairie
illiterate... 6. unread 8. ignorant,
  untaught 9. inerudite, unlearned,
  unrefined, untutored, unwritten
illness... 6. malady 8. cachexia,
  sickness 9. complaint, distemper
  10. affliction 13. indisposition
illuminant... 3. gas 4. lamp
  9. petroleum 10. Kleig light
illuminate... 5. adorn, color, light
  6. illume 7. explain, lighten, miniate
  8. emblazen, illumine 9. elucidate,
  enlighten, irradiate, rubricate
  10. illustrate
illumination, unit of... 3. lux 4. phot
illusion... 5. fancy 6. mirage
  7. chimera, fallacy, mockery,
  phantom 8. delusion, phantasy
  9. deception, false show
  10. apparition 13. hallucination,
  misconception
illusive... 5. false 6. unreal 8. spectral
  9. deceitful, deceptive, imaginary
  10. phantasmal, transitory
illusory... 5. false 6. delusory, illusive
  9. deceptive, erroneous, imaginary,
  unfounded 10. fallacious
illustrate... 4. cite, draw 5. adorn
  7. explain, picture 8. beautify
  9. elucidate, exemplify, represent
  10. illuminate
illustrious... 5. noble, noted
  6. famous, heroic 7. eminent,
  exalted, radiant 8. glorious, luminous,
  renowned, splendid 9. brilliant,
  honorable 10. celebrated
image... 3. god 4. copy, icon, idea,
  idol, ikon, type 6. alraun, aspect,
  effigy, idolon, mirror, recept, sphinx,
  statue, typify 7. eidolon, phantom,
  picture, portray 8. illusion, likeness,
  phantasm 9. semblance
  10. apparition, conception,
  simulacrum 11. counterpart
  12. reproduction
imaginary... 5. ideal 7. fancied
  8. fanciful, illusory, mythical
  10. fictitious
imaginary disease... 9. nosomania
imagination... 5. dream, fancy
  8. phantasy, poetical
imagine... 5. dream, fancy, opine,
  think 6. ideate 7. suppose
  8. conceive 10. conjecture
imam... 6. caliph, priest (Moham)
imbecile... 4. dolt, weak 5. anile,
  idiot, inane, moron 6. cretin, dotard,
  feeble, stupid, witlet 7. fatuous,
  idiotic, witling 9. driveling
  10. half–witted 12. feeble–minded
imbed... 5. embed, inset 6. cement
  9. establish

imberbe... 9. beardless
imbibe... 4. soak 5. drink, imbue,
  learn 6. absorb, inhale 8. saturate
  10. assimilate
imbroglio... 5. brawl 11. embroilment,
  predicament 16. misunderstanding
imbrue... 3. fig, wet 4. soak 5. color,
  stain (with blood), steep 6. defile,
  drench 7. moisten 8. saturate
imbue... 3. dye 5. steep, teach, tinge
  6. infuse, leaven 7. ingrain, inspire
  8. permeate, saturate, tincture
  9. inculcate 10. impregnate
imitant... 9. imitation 11. counterfeit
imitate... 3. ape 4. copy, mime, mock
  5. mimic 6. borrow 7. emulate
  8. pastiche, resemble, simulate
  9. dissemble, reproduce
imitation... 4. copy, echo, sham
  5. apery, apism, paste 6. ectype,
  olivet (pearl), parody 7. mimesis,
  mimicry 8. travesty 9. burlesque
  10. caricature, simulation
  12. onomatopoeia
imitative... 5. apish 8. apatetic
  9. emulative, imitation 10. simulative
  11. counterfeit
immaculate... 4. pure 5. clean
  6. chaste 8. spotless, unsoiled
  9. faultless, undefiled, unstained,
  unsullied
immanence... 7. inbeing 9. inherence
  10. indwelling, innateness
immanent... 5. inner 6. inward
  8. internal 9. intrinsic 10. indwelling
immaterial... 6. slight 8. trifling
  9. spiritual 10. impalpable, intangible
  11. disembodied, incorporeal,
  unimportant 12. supernatural
  13. insignificant, unsubstantial
immature... 5. crude, green 6. callow,
  unripe 7. untried 8. untimely,
  youthful 9. premature 10. unfinished
  11. undeveloped
immeasurable... 7. endless 8. infinite
  9. boundless, unlimited 10. indefinite
  11. illimitable, innumerable
  12. immensurable, incalculable,
  unfathomable 13. indeterminate
  16. incomprehensible
immediacy... 9. awareness, closeness
  10. directness 11. punctuality
immediate... 4. next 6. direct, prompt
  7. instant, nearest, present
  10. continuous, succeeding
immediately... 3. now 4. anon
  7. closely 8. directly, promptly
  9. instantly, therewith 11. straightway
  12. without delay
immemorial... 3. old 7. ageless,
  ancient 8. dateless 9. out of mind
  11. prehistoric, traditional
immense... 4. huge, vast 5. grand,
  great 6. superb 7. mammoth, titanic
  8. enormous, infinite 9. monstrous
  10. prodigious, unmeasured
immerge... 3. dip 4. sink 5. merge
  6. engulf, plunge 7. immerse
  8. inundate, submerge
immerse... 3. dip 4. bury, dunk, sink
  5. douse, souse 6. absorb, plunge
  7. baptize, engross 9. overwhelm

imminent . . . 7. nearing 8. menacing,
upcoming 9. impending 10. near at
hand 11. approaching, forthcoming,
overhanging, threatening
immobile . . . 3. set 5. fixed, inert
6. stable 8. moveless 9. immovable,
obstinate, unfeeling 10. inflexible,
motionless, stationary
immoderate . . . 5. ultra, undue
7. extreme 9. excessive
10. exorbitant, inordinate
11. extravagant, intemperate
12. unreasonable
immolation . . . 8. oblation, offering
9. sacrifice
immoral . . . 3. bad 6. wicked
7. corrupt, vicious 8. depraved,
indecent 9. dissolute 10. licentious,
misconduct
immortal . . . 6. divine 7. abiding,
endless, eternal, godlike, undying
8. enduring 9. ambrosial, ceaseless,
celebrity, perpetual 10. superhuman
11. amaranthine, everlasting
12. imperishable 13. incorruptible
Immortal (Taoism) . . . 8. Chang Kuo
immortality . . . 4. fame 6. amrita
(conferring) 9. anathasia 11. lasting
fame 13. deathlessness
15. everlastingness
immovable . . . 3. pat 4. fast, firm
5. fixed, rigid 6. stable 7. adamant
8. immobile, obdurate 9. obstinate,
unfeeling 10. inflexible, stationary
immunity . . . 7. freedom 8. impunity
9. exemption 10. resistance (power
of) 11. unrestraint
immure . . . 4. wall 6. entomb
7. confine 8. imprison, surround
9. encompass 11. incarcerate
immutable . . . 4. firm 6. stable
7. eternal 8. constant 9. obstinate
10. inflexible, invariable
12. unchangeable 13. unadulterated
imp . . . 3. bud, elf, fay 4. brat, cion,
pixy, slip 5. child, demon, devil,
fairy, graft, rogue, scion, shoot, youth
6. repair (falconry), spirit, sprite
7. progeny 9. offspring
impact . . . 4. pack, slam 5. brunt,
force, shock, wedge 6. effect, stroke
7. contact, impulse, meaning
8. striking 9. collision, fix firmly,
impinging
impair . . . 3. mar 4. harm, hurt, ruin,
rust, wear 5. break, spoil
6. damage, debase, injure, lessen,
reduce, weaken 7. vitiate
8. decrease, enfeeble 11. deteriorate
impairment of . . .
capital . . 4. loss 7. deficit
character . . 6. injury 10. defamation
11. degradation 13. deterioration
nerve (a) . . 11. anerethisia
impale . . . 4. edge, gore, join (Her),
spit, stab 5. hem in, spike
6. border, pierce, punish 7. confine,
torture 8. encircle, surround
impalement . . . 5. calyx 8. stabbing
10. punishment 11. coats of arms
(united)
impalpable . . . 4. fine 10. immaterial,

intangible 13. infinitesimal
impart . . . 3. say 4. give, lend, tell
5. grant, share, yield 6. confer,
convey, inform, reveal 7. divulge
8. disclose, discover 9. partake of
10. distribute 11. communicate
impartial . . . 4. even, fair, just
7. neutral 8. unbiased 9. equitable
12. unprejudiced 13. disinterested,
dispassionate
impartiality . . . 7. justice 8. fairness
10. neutrality 11. unprejudice
17. disinterestedness
impassable . . . 6. stolid 9. impassive
10. impervious, unpassable
11. impermeable, unnavigable
12. impenetrable
impasse . . . 8. cul–de–sac 9. stalemate
10. blind alley
impassible . . . 9. impassive, unfeeling
impassioned . . . 6. ardent 7. amorous,
zealous 8. eloquent, vehement
10. passionate
impassive . . . 4. calm 6. serene
7. passive 9. apathetic
10. impassable 12. invulnerable
13. insusceptible
impatient . . . 5. eager, testy 6. uneasy
7. anxious, fretful, itching, peevish,
restive 8. choleric, petulant, restless
9. impetuous, irascible, irritable
10. intolerant
impavid . . . 8. fearless
impeach . . . 4. harm 6. accuse, charge,
hinder, impair, impede, indict
7. arraign, censure, prevent
9. challenge, criminate, discredit,
disparage
impeccable . . . 8. flawless, innocent
9. faultless 10. immaculate
impede . . . 3. bar, let 4. clog 5. block,
debar, estop 6. hamper, hinder,
retard, stymie (stimy) 8. encumber,
obstruct, restrict
impediment . . . 3. bar, rub 4. snag
5. hitch 6. defect, malady
7. baggage, barrier 8. obstacle
9. hindrance 10. difficulty
11. encumbrance, obstruction
impel . . . 3. put 4. move, urge 5. drive,
force, forge 6. compel, incite,
induce, obsess, prompt, propel
7. actuate 9. constrain, influence
impel a boat . . . 3. oar, row 4. pole
5. scull
impelling force . . . 7. impetus
8. momentum
impending . . . 7. nearing 8. awaiting,
imminent, menacing 9. hindering
11. overhanging, threatening
impenetrable . . . 5. dense
10. impervious 11. impregnable,
inscrutable 12. inaccessible,
unfathomable 13. unimpressible
14. unintelligible
impenitent . . . 8. obdurate
10. uncontrite 11. unrepentant,
unrepenting
imperative . . . 4. mood (Gram)
6. needed, urgent 7. binding
8. pressing 9. directive, imperious,
mandatory, necessary

10. compulsory, obligatory,
peremptory 13. authoritative
imperceptible... 6. subtle 9. invisible
10. insensible 13. inappreciable,
indiscernible, infinitesimal
14. unintelligible
imperfect... 3. mal (pref) 4. cull
5. frail 6. faulty, second 7. errable
8. fallible, immature, impaired
9. blemished, defective
10. inadequate, incomplete
imperfection... 4. flaw, vice 5. fault
6. defect 7. blemish, failing
8. fraility, weakness 10. deficiency
11. shortcoming 14. incompleteness
imperfectly... 8. slightly
12. inadequately
imperial... 5. regal, royal 6. kingly,
lordly, purple 8. majestic
9. imperious, masterful, monarchal,
sovereign
imperial (pert to)...
Academy.. 6. Han–lin (Chin)
blue.. 5. smalt
cap.. 5. crown
city (anc).. 4. Rome
domain.. 6. empire
legislature.. 4. Diet (Jap)
officer.. 8. palatine
imperil... 4. risk 6. expose
8. endanger 10. jeopardize
imperious... 6. lordly 7. haughty
8. arrogant, despotic, dominant,
pressing 10. commanding,
compelling, tyrannical 11. dictatorial,
domineering, overbearing
imperishable... 7. eternal, undying
8. enduring, immortal 11. everlasting
14. indestructible
impermanent... 8. fleeting, temporal,
unstable 9. ephemeral, momentary,
temporary, transient 10. evanescent,
short–lived
impersonate... 3. ape 4. pose 6. pose
as, typify 7. portray 9. exemplify,
personate (law), personify, represent,
symbolize
impertinence... 4. sass 9. impudence,
insolence, unfitness 10. incivility
11. impropriety, irrelevance
impertinent... 4. rude 5. saucy
7. ill–bred 8. impudent, insolent
9. frivolous, officious 10. inapposite,
irrelevant 12. inapplicable,
inconsequent 13. disrespectful
imperturbability... 8. ataraxia (ataraxy),
serenity
imperturbable... 4. calm, cool
6. placid, serene, steady 8. tranquil
9. impassive 10. phlegmatic
13. dispassionate
impervious... 5. tight 6. opaque
7. callous 10. impassable
12. impenetrable, inaccessible
impetuosity... 5. ardor 6. fougue
8. rashness
impetuous... 3. hot 4. rash 5. eager,
hasty, heady, sharp 6. ardent, bensel
(motion), fervid, sudden 7. furious,
violent 8. forcible, headlong, reckless,
vehement 9. impulsive
10. passionate 11. precipitate

impetus... 4. birr 7. impulse
8. momentum, stimulus 9. incentive
impi (Zulu)... 8. armed men, warriors
impignorate... 4. pawn 6. pledge
8. mortgage
impious... 7. godless, profane
9. nefandous, undutiful 10. irreverent
11. irreligious
impish... 5. elvan 6. elfish 7. puckish
9. malignant 11. mischievous
implacable... 6. enmity
11. immitigable 12. unappeasable
14. uncompromising
implant... 4. root 5. infix, inset, plant
6. enroot, infuse, insert 7. enforce,
engraft, impress, inspire, instill
9. establish, inculcate, inoculate,
insinuate, introduce
implement... 3. kit 4. peel, tool
5. dolly, knife, means, scoop, tongs
6. pestle, petard 7. fulfill, utensil
8. carry out, complete, material,
scissors 9. equipment
10. accomplish, instrument
implement (pert to)...
ancient.. 4. celt 6. eolith 9. paleolith
(stone)
cleaning.. 3. mop 5. broom, brush
6. vacuum 7. sweeper
hide flesher.. 6. slater
holding.. 5. tongs 6. pliers
8. tweezers
lifting.. 3. pry 5. crane, lever, tongs
lumbering.. 4. tode 6. peavey (peavy)
nap.. 6. teasel
printing.. 5. biron, press 6. brayer
reaping.. 5. mower 6. reaper, scythe,
shears, sickle
surgical.. 7. scalpel 9. tenaculum
threshing.. 5. flail
implicate... 5. imply 7. embroil,
entwine, involve 8. entangle
10. interweave 11. incriminate
implicit... 5. tacit 7. implied, virtual
8. complete, inherent 9. entangled,
potential 11. unqualified
12. constructive 13. unquestioning
implied... 5. tacit 11. inferential
12. not expressed
implore... 3. ask, beg 4. pray 5. crave
7. beseech, entreat, solicit
8. petition 10. supplicate
imply... 4. hint, mean 5. argue
6. infold 7. connote, involve,
suggest, suppose 9. predicate
impolite... 4. rude 5. crude, rough
7. uncivil 10. ill–behaved,
mannerless, ungracious, unmannerly,
unpolished 12. discourteous
13. disrespectful
impolitic... 6. unwise 9. untactful
10. indiscreet 11. inexpedient
12. undiplomatic
import... 5. drift, sense, value
6. denote, weight 7. betoken,
meaning, signify 8. commerce,
indicate 9. introduce, of concern
10. importance 11. consequence,
implication, importation, merchandise
importance... 6. moment, stress,
weight 8. prestige 9. influence
10. famousness 11. consequence,

importunity 12. solicitation
important... 5. grave 6. famous,
urgent 7. pompous, weighty
8. material 9. momentous
11. considerate, influential,
significant, substantial
12. considerable, ostentatious
13. consequential
import tax... 4. duty 6. tariff
importune... 3. beg, ply, tax, woo
4. coax, push, urge 5. beset, impel,
plead, press 6. appeal, cajole
7. entreat, press on
importunity... 11. importunate,
pertinacity 12. solicitation
impose... 3. tax 4. duty, levy
6. burden, entail 7. command,
confirm (Eccl), exploit, inflict, intrude,
obtrude, penalty, presume
10. discommode
imposing... 5. noble, regal 6. august
7. stately 9. dignified, grandiose
10. commanding, impressive
11. ceremonious 13. grandiloquent
impossible... 6. absurd 8. hopeless,
terrible 9. insoluble 10. outlandish
11. unthinkable 12. unimaginable
13. contradictory, impracticable
impost... 3. tax 4. levy, task, toll
5. abwab 6. custom, excise, surtax,
tariff, weight 7. tribute 8. handicap
impostor... 4. fake 5. fraud, phony,
quack 6. humbug 7. empiric
9. charlatan, pretender
10. mountebank
imposture... 5. fraud, trick 8. delusion,
quackery 9. deception 10. imposition
impotent... 4. weak 6. barren
7. cripple, sterile 9. deficient,
incapable, powerless 13. uninfluential
impound... 5. pen in, seize, store
6. freeze 7. collect 8. imprison
9. reservoir 10. confiscate
11. appropriate
impoverish... 4. ruin 6. beggar
7. despoil, exhaust 8. bankrupt,
make poor 11. make sterile
imprecation... 4. oath 8. anathema
10. execration 11. malediction
impregnable... 4. hard 10. inviolable
12. inexpugnable, invulnerable
13. unconquerable
impregnate... 5. imbue 6. infuse
8. fructify 9. fertilize, inculcate
impresa... 5. maxim, motto 6. device,
emblem
impresario... 7. manager 9. conductor,
projector (opera) 12. entrepreneur
impress... 3. awe, fix 4. bite, dent,
levy, mark, seal 5. press, print,
stamp 6. affect, effect, enlist, indent
7. engrave, imprint 8. printing,
shanghai 9. conscript, engraving,
inculcate 10. commandeer,
impression 11. indentation
14. characteristic
impressed... 4. awed 7. infixed,
stamped 8. affected, engraved
9. imprinted
impression... 4. form, idea, mark
5. hunch, print, stamp 6. macule,
signet 7. emotion, opinion 8. printing

9. engraving, sensation
10. appearance 11. inculcation,
indentation, supposition
impressionable... 6. pliant 7. plastic
9. sensitive, teachable 10. responsive
11. suggestible, susceptible
impressive... 6. solemn 8. dramatic,
eloquent 9. arresting, grandiose
10. convincing
imprint... 3. fix 4. dint 5. infix, press,
stamp 6. indent 7. edition, engrave
8. printing 9. engraving
imprison... 4. bond, cage, gaol, jail
5. limit 6. arrest, detain, immure,
intern, lock up 7. confine, impound
8. restrain 11. incarcerate
imprisonment... 4. band 6. duress
8. coercion 9. restraint
10. constraint, immurement,
internment 11. confinement,
impoundment 13. incarceration
impromptu... 6. extemp 7. offhand
11. extemporary 13. improvisation
14. extemporaneous
15. autoschediastic
improper... 3. ill, pah 4. evil 5. amiss,
wrong 6. vulgar 7. illegal, naughty
8. indecent, unseemly, unsuited,
untoward 9. incorrect, inelegant
10. inaccurate, indecorous, indelicate,
unbecoming, unsuitable
impropriety... 5. wrong 8. solecism
9. indecency, vulgarity
11. malapropism, misbehavior
improve... 4. mend 5. amend, edify,
emend, moise, train 6. better,
employ, uplift 7. advance, augment,
correct, enhance, perfect, promote,
recover, rectify, upgrade 9. cultivate,
get better, intensify, meliorate
10. ameliorate, recuperate
improvident... 4. rash 8. prodigal,
wasteful 9. negligent 10. thriftless
11. thoughtless
improvise... 5. ad lib 6. invent 7. ad
libit 9. ad libitum 11. extemporize
13. autoschediaze
imprudence... 5. brass 8. rashness
9. hardihood 12. indiscretion,
recklessness
impudence... 5. cheek 8. rudeness
9. flippancy, indecency, insolence
10. brazenness, disrespect
12. impertinence 13. shamelessness
impudent... 4. bold, pert, rude
5. brash, saucy 6. brazen
8. flippant, insolent, malapert
9. audacious, shameless
11. impertinent 13. disrespectful
impugn... 4. deny 5. blame 6. assail
(by words), oppose, refute
7. asperse, censure, gainsay
impulse... 3. ate 4. rush, urge
5. force 6. motive 7. impetus
8. instinct 9. incentive
11. instigation
impulsive... 5. hasty, quick 6. moving
9. impellent, impetuous
10. motivating 11. instinctive
13. ill—considered
impure... 4. foul, lewd 5. dirty, mixed
6. filthy, unholy 7. bastard, defiled,

obscene, unclean 8. unchaste
10. inaccurate, unhallowed
11. adulterated, unwholesome
impure metal ... 5. alloy, matte
6. speiss
impure rock ... 5. chert 9. flintlike
imputation ... 7. censure 8. charging
9. aspersion, criticism
10. accusation, ascription
11. attribution, insinuation
impute ... 6. accuse, charge, credit,
impart, reckon, regard 7. arraign,
ascribe 8. consider 9. attribute
impy ... 11. mischievous
in ... 2. at 4. amid, into 5. among
6. at home, inside, within
in (pert to) ...
abundance .. 5. store 6. galore
accordance .. 8. pursuant
addition .. 3. too, yet 4. also, more,
plus 11. furthermore
all directions .. 8. everyway
12. everywhither
an undertone .. 9. sotto voce
as much as .. 3. for 5. since
6. seeing 7. because, insofar
back .. 3. aft 5. arear 6. astern
7. postern
behalf of .. 3. for, pro 7. favor of
camera .. 9. in private 10. in
chambers
common .. 4. same 5. alike
concert .. 8. together
contact .. 8. touching 9. attingent
current style .. 3. a la 7. alamode,
popular
existence .. 6. extant
fact .. 5. truly 6. indeed 7. de facto
favor of .. 3. aye, pro, yea
good health .. 3. fit 4. hale 7. healthy
love .. 7. smitten 9. enamoured
need .. 7. straits 8. distress
open air .. 7. outdoor 8. al fresco
passing .. 9. en passant
place of .. 3. for 5. stead 7. instead
possession .. 5. title 6. seizin
private .. 8. in camera
regard to .. 5. anent
rows .. 4. arow 6. serial 7. aligned
(alined)
so far as .. 3. qua
spite of .. 6. mauger 7. despite,
however 11. nonetheless
standing position .. 7. statant
store .. 5. ready 7. waiting 8. awaiting
straight lines .. 8. e regione
succession .. 6. series 8. serially,
seriatim
the future .. 5. hence, later 6. mañana
12. subsequently
the know .. 3. hep
the same place .. 4. ibid 6. ibidem
the year of .. 4. anno
truth .. 6. certes, indeed, verily
8. forsooth
what way .. 3. how 7. quo modo
inability ... 9. impotence
10. inadequacy, incapacity
12. incapability, incompetence
inability to ...
articulate .. 7. inaudia
chew .. 8. amasesis

comprehend .. 11. acatalepsia
move .. 7. apraxia
name objects .. 9. paranomia
read .. 6. alexia
stand erect .. 7. astasia
swallow .. 7. aphagia
inaccessible ... 8. reserved
10. unsociable 11. out–of–the–way
12. unattainable 14. unapproachable
inaccurate ... 5. loose 6. faulty
7. inexact 9. defective, erroneous,
imperfect, incorrect
13. ungrammatical
inaction ... 6. torpor 7. inertia
8. abeyance, idleness 9. inertness
10. suspension
inactive ... 4. idle 5. inert 7. abeyant,
neutral, not busy 8. sluggish
9. sedentary 10. indisposed
inadequacy ... 9. inability
10. deficiency, inequality
11. inferiority 12. incompetence
13. insufficiency 14. incompleteness
inadvertence ... 5. error 7. neglect
11. inattention 12. carelessness,
heedlessness 15. thoughtlessness
inadvertent ... 9. negligent, unwitting
11. inattentive
inadvertently ... 10. heedlessly
11. unwittingly 12. neglectfully
inane ... 4. vain, void 5. empty, inept,
silly 6. famous 7. fatuous, foolish,
puerile, trivial 8. trifling 9. frivolous
11. ineffectual, thoughtless
13. characterless
inappropriate ... 5. inept, undue
8. untimely 10. irrelevant, unsuitable
11. inexpedient
inapt ... 5. inept 10. unsuitable
inattentive ... 3. lax 6. absent, remiss
8. careless, heedless 9. negligent,
unheeding, unmindful 10. distracted,
regardless 11. inadvertent
inaugurate ... 5. admit, begin, start
6. induct 7. install, instate, usher in
8. initiate 9. auspicate, institute,
introduce 10. consecrate
inauspicious ... 7. adverse, ominous,
unlucky 8. sinister, untimely
9. ill–omened 12. unpropitious
inborn ... 6. allied, inbred, innate,
native 7. cognate, natural 8. inherent
10. connatural
inbred ... 6. inborn, innate
9. endogamic 10. bred within 15. to
the manner born
Inca (pert to) ...
descent .. 6. the sun
empire .. 4. Peru (11th cent)
government .. 11. communistic
king .. 9. Atahualpa (15th cent)
prince .. 7. Huascar (16th cent)
incalculable ... 8. infinite 9. boundless,
uncertain, very great 11. illimitable
12. immeasurable 13. unforeseeable
incandescent ... 5. clear, light, white
7. glowing, shining
incantation ... 5. magic, spell
6. powwow 7. sorcery 8. exorcism
10. hocus–pocus, mumbo jumbo
incapable ... 6. unable 8. impotent
11. incompetent, inefficient,

unqualified 12. disqualified
incapacitate... 7. cripple, disable,
    invalid 10. disqualify 11. render unfit
incapacitated... 8. crippled, disabled
    9. hamstrung, paralyzed
    11. invalidated 12. disqualified
    13. superannuated (retired)
incarcerate... 5. hem in 6. immure,
    intern, lock up, retire 7. confine,
    impound 8. imprison 10. disqualify
incarnate... 4. rosy 6. embody
    9. enshrined 11. incorporate,
    personified 12. impersonated
incarnation... 6. avatar, Christ
    10. embodiment
Incarnation of Vishnu (eight)...
    4. Apis, Rama 7. Krishna (8th)
incase... 3. box, can 4. pack 5. box
    up, cover, crate 6. carton
    7. enclose, package 8. surround
incaution... 4. rash 6. unwary
    8. careless, heedless, reckless
    9. impolitic, imprudent 10. indiscreet
incendiarism... 5. arson 9. pyromania
incendiary... 5. firer 7. exciter
    8. agitator, arsonist, incitive
    9. seditious 10. instigator
    12. inflammatory
incense... 3. ire 5. anger 6. arouse,
    enrage, incite 7. inflame, provoke
    8. irritate 9. instigate
incense (pert to)...
    burner.. 6. censer 8. thurible
    9. incensory
    carrier.. 8. thurifer
    Hebrew for.. 7. keturah
    pert to.. 5. aroma, spice 7. perfume
    9. fragrance, redolence
    product.. 5. matti, myrrh 6. storax
    7. linaloa 8. gum resin, olibanum,
    pastille, thurible 9. lignaloes,
    tacamahac 12. frankincense
    sacrifice.. 8. oblation
    spice.. 6. balsam, stacte
    tree bearing.. 7. linaloa 8. agalloch,
    calambac 9. Boswellia
    vessel.. 6. censer 7. navette
incensed... 3. mad 5. angry, irate,
    vexed, wroth 6. peeved, piqued
    7. angered, enraged, nettled
    8. wrathful 11. exasperated
incentive... 4. brod, call, goad, spur,
    urge, whet 5. spark 6. motive
    7. impulse, rousing 8. inciting,
    stimulus 9. influence 10. incitement,
    inducement 11. provocation,
    stimulative 13. encouragement
inception... 6. origin, source
    9. reception 10. inchoation, initiation
    12. commencement
    15. intussusception
inceptive... 9. beginning 10. inchoative
incessant... 7. endless 8. constant
    9. ceaseless, continual, perpetual
    10. continuous 11. unremitting
    13. unintermitted
inch (pert to)...
    barometric.. 6. degree
    forward.. 4. edge 7. crowhop
    inch by inch.. 9. gradually, piecemeal
    meal.. 9. gradually
    three parts.. 11. barleycorns (anc)

twelve parts.. 5. lines
twelve seconds.. 6. a prime (anc)
verb.. 5. creep 7. measure
inches... 4. hand (4), nail (2 1/4),
    span (9)
inchoate... 6. partly 8. initiate, recently
    9. beginning, incipient
    10. incomplete
inchpin... 10. sweetbread
incident... 5. event 7. episode, subject
    8. accident, casualty 9. befalling,
    happening 10. incidental, occurrence
    11. contingency 12. circumstance,
    slight matter
incidental... 3. bye 6. casual, chance,
    liable 8. episodic 9. accessory,
    extrinsic 10. accidental, contingent,
    fortuitous, occasional 11. subordinate
    12. nonessential 13. parenthetical
incidentally... 6. obiter 8. by chance,
    by the way 9. en passant, in passing
incinerate... 4. burn 7. consume,
    cremate
incipient... 4. seat 6. induct 7. initial
    8. inchoate 9. beginning, embryonic
    10. commencing, inaugurate
    11. rudimentary
incise... 3. cut 4. open 5. carve,
    lance, sever 6. furrow 7. engrave
incised... 6. carved 7. notched
    8. engraved, furrowed 9. laciniate
    10. laciniated
incision... 3. cut 4. gash, slit 5. cleft
    6. furrow, injury 7. cutting
    9. engraving 10. laceration,
    separation 11. penetration
incite... 3. egg, tew 4. abet, fire,
    goad, prod, spur, urge 5. impel,
    sting 6. arouse, foment, stir up,
    suborn 7. agitate, animate, inflame,
    provoke 9. encourage, stimulate
inclemency... 4. cold 5. rigor
    8. coldness, severity, violence
    9. bleakness, frigidity, harshness
    13. mercilessness
inclination... 3. dip, nod 4. bent,
    bias, love, urge 5. fancy, grade,
    slant, slope, taste, trend 6. animus,
    bowing, desire, liking, nature
    8. aptitude, penchant, tendency
    9. affection, attention, deviation,
    direction, intention, obeisance,
    proneness 10. attachment, proclivity,
    propensity 11. disposition
    12. predilection 13. prepossession
incline... 3. dip, tip 4. bend, cant,
    heel, lean, tend, tilt 5. alist, bevel,
    grade, slant, slide, slope, trend 9. be
    willing, gravitate
inclined... 3. apt, dip 4. wont
    5. prone 6. sloped 7. leaning,
    pronate, willing 8. disposed
    11. predisposed
inclined (pert to)...
    plane.. 4. ramp 7. oblique
    to believe.. 9. credulous
    to droop.. 3. sag
    to sin.. 13. transgressive
inclose... see also *enclose* 3. hem,
    pen, pin 4. case, mure 5. embar
    6. encase, encave, incase
    7. enclose, environ

inclosure . . . 3. pen, ree, sty 4. cage,
cote, sept 5. hutch, kraal 6. corral
8. sepiment 9. enclosure
10. impalement
include . . . 6. shut up 7. confine,
contain, embrace, enclose, inclose,
involve 8. comprise 9. encompass
including . . . 8. covering
10. comprising, containing
12. encompassing 13. comprehensive
incognito . . . 6. veiled 7. feigned
8. disguise, not known
10. camouflage
incoherent . . . 5. loose 6. broken
8. detached, inchoate 9. delirious,
illogical 11. incongruous
12. disconnected, inconsequent,
inconsistent
income . . . 4. gain 5. rente, wages
6. profit, return, usance 7. annuity,
pension, produce, revenue, tontine
8. interest, proceeds, receipts
9. emolument
incommensurate . . . 7. unequal
12. insufficient 14. unsatisfactory
16. disproportionate
incommode . . . 3. vex 5. annoy
6. molest, plague, put out
7. disturb, trouble 8. disquiet
13. inconvenience
incomparable . . . 7. eminent, unalike
8. peerless 9. matchless, unrivaled
10. surpassing 11. superlative
12. transcendent, without equal
incompatible . . . 9. differing
10. intolerant 11. disagreeing
12. inconsistent, inharmonious
13. contradictory, unsympathetic
14. irreconcilable
incompetence . . . 9. inability, unfitness
10. disability, inadequacy
13. insufficiency 15. unqualification
incompetent . . . 5. inept, unfit
7. wanting 8. impotent 9. incapable
10. unskillful 11. inefficient
12. disqualified, insufficient
14. incommensurate
incomplete . . . 5. crude 6. undone
7. lacking 8. immature, inchoate
9. defective, deficient, imperfect,
partially 10. unfinished
incomprehensible . . . 8. infinite
9. wonderful 10. miraculous,
mysterious, unreadable
11. unthinkable 12. unfathomable,
unimaginable 13. inconceivable,
unconceivable 14. unintelligible
incongruity . . . 9. inharmony
10. dissonance 11. incoherence
12. disagreement, inexpedience
13. inconsistency 14. unsuitableness
incongruous . . . 5. alien 6. absurd,
motley 8. off–color 9. differing,
illogical 10. solecistic, unsuitable
12. disagreeable, inconsistent,
inharmonious 13. inappropriate
inconsequent . . . 7. invalid 8. unproved
9. illogical 10. irrelevant
11. impertinent, unimportant
12. inconsistent 13. inconsecutive
inconsiderate . . . 4. rash 5. hasty
6. unkind 8. careless, heedless

9. imprudent, impulsive
10. ill–advised, incautious, indiscreet,
neglectful 11. improvident,
injudicious, thoughtless
inconsistent . . . 9. differing, dissonant,
fanatical, illogical 10. discordant,
discrepant, incoherent, inconstant
11. incongruous 12. incompatible,
inharmonious 13. contradictory
14. irreconcilable
inconspicuous . . . 9. unseeable 10. out
of sight, unapparent 12. not
prominent 13. imperceptible,
indiscernible
incontestable . . . 7. certain
10. undeniable 11. indubitable,
irrefutable 13. unimpeachable
14. unquestionable
inconvenience . . . 6. bother 8. disquiet
9. incommode 10. uneasiness
11. awkwardness, disturbance
12. disadvantage, untimeliness,
unwieldiness
inconvenient . . . 5. unfit 7. unhandy
8. annoying, improper, unwieldy
10. unsuitable 11. inexpedient,
inopportune, troublesome
12. unreasonable 15. disadvantageous
incorporate . . . 3. mix 4. fuse 5. blend,
merge, unite 6. embody 7. combine,
include 8. embodied 10. assimilate
incorporation . . . 5. union 9. inclusion
10. embodiment 11. affiliation,
association, combination, composition,
incarnation 12. assimilation
incorporeal . . . 7. phantom 8. bodiless
9. spiritual 10. immaterial
13. unsubstantial
incorrect . . . 5. wrong 6. faulty
8. improper 9. erroneous, inelegant
10. inaccurate, solecistic,
unbecoming 13. ungrammatical
incorrect naming of objects . . .
9. paranomia
incorruptible . . . 4. just 7. upright
8. immortal 11. trustworthy
14. indestructible
increase . . . 3. add, eke, wax 4. gain,
grow, rise 5. add to, amass, raise,
swell 6. accrue, dilate, enrich,
expand, extend 7. accrete, advance,
augment, enhance (inhance), inflate,
promote, upswing 8. heighten,
multiply 9. accession, aggravate,
crescendo, expansion, extension,
increment, intensify 10. accelerate
11. aggravation, enlargement
13. amplification 15. intensification
incredible . . . 8. fabulous, unlikely
9. fantastic, marvelous, wonderful
10. improbable, remarkable
12. unbelievable
increment . . . 6. growth 8. addition,
increase 11. enlargement
12. augmentation
incriminate . . . 6. accuse 7. involve
9. implicate, inculpate
incubator . . . 8. couveuse, isolette
incubus . . . 4. ogre 5. demon, dream
6. burden 9. nightmare 10. evil
spirit 13. hallucination

inculcate... 5. imbue, infix 7. implant, impress, instill (instil) 12. indoctrinate
incumbent... 5. vicar 6. rector 8. resident 9. clergyman, impending, overlying 10. burdensome, obligatory (upon) 11. threatening 12. superimposed
incumbents... 3. ins
incunabula... 7. infancy 10. beginnings
incur... 5. bring 6. accrue, entail 7. bring on 8. be liable, contract, fall into 10. be involved
incurable... 8. hopeless 9. apathetic 11. inattentive, indifferent, unconcerned, uninquiring 12. uninterested 13. uninquisitive
incur hostility... 10. antagonize 11. contend with
incursion... 4. raid 5. foray 6. attack, influx, inroad 8. invasion 9. intrusion
incus... 4. bone (ear) 5. anvil 6. hammer
indecency... 8. impurity 9. immodesty, indecorum, obscenity, vulgarity 10. indelicacy, unchastity
indecent... 5. gross 6. impure, vulgar 7. obscene 8. immodest, improper, uncomely 9. offensive 10. ill–looking, indecorous, indelicate 11. inexpedient
indecision... 5. doubt 10. hesitation 11. uncertainty, vacillation 12. irresolution
indecisive... 7. dubious 8. formless 9. uncertain 10. hesitating, indefinite, indistinct, irresolute 11. unsupported, vacillating 12. inconclusive
indecorous... 4. rude 5. wrong 6. coarse, vulgar 7. uncivil 8. impolite, improper, indecent, unseemly 9. inelegant 10. out of place, unbecoming 11. inexpedient
indefatigable... 6. active 8. sedulous, tireless, untiring 9. unwearied, weariless 10. unwearying 11. persevering
indefinite... 5. loose, vague 7. general, inexact, neutral 8. formless 9. ambiguous, equivocal, uncertain 10. inexplicit, unmeasured 12. undetermined 13. indeterminate
indefinite amount... 3. any 4. some 5. about 10. more or less
indehiscent (pert to)...
fruit.. 3. uva 4. pepo (gourd) 5. apple, grape 6. orange, samara 9. sunflower
legume.. 3. pea 4. bean 6. loment
vegetable.. 5. melon 6. squash, tomato 7. pumpkin 8. cucumber
indelible... 4. fast 5. fixed 8. deepfelt 9. permanent 10. inerasable 12. ineffaceable, ineradicable, inexpungible 13. unforgettable
indelicate... 5. gross 6. coarse, vulgar 7. fulsome 8. impolite, improper, indecent, unseemly 9. offensive, unrefined 10. indecorous, unbecoming
indemnification... 9. atonement 10. recompense 11. restitution 12. compensation 13. reimbursement

indemnify... 3. pay 6. recoup, secure 8. make good 9. reimburse 10. compensate, recompense
indent... 3. cut, jag 4. dent 5. inlay, notch, press, stamp, tooth 6. emboss, furrow, recess, zigzag 7. impress, imprint, press in 8. contract, covenant, draw upon 9. indenture 11. requisition
indentation... 3. jab 4. dint, nick 5. choil, notch 6. crenel, furrow, hollow, recess 7. imprint 8. crenelet 10. depression, impression
indented... 6. dented, jagged, milled 7. notched, sinuous 8. serrated (Her) 9. impressed 10. undulating
indenture... 4. dent 5. notch 8. contract, document 9. agreement 10. depression 11. indentation
independence... 7. freedom 9. exemption 10. competency, neutralism, Urania blue 13. unrelatedness 14. nonpartisanism 15. self–subsistence
independent... 4. free 5. Party (Polit) 7. neutral, wealthy 8. separate 9. competent, exclusive, free–lance, isolative, sovereign, uncoerced, unrelated 12. irrespective, uncontrolled, unrestricted 13. self–governing
independent land... 7. alodium (law)
indescribably... 9. ineffably 11. wonderfully
indeterminate... 5. vague 7. apeiron, general, neutral, obscure 8. formless, infinite
index... 4. face, file, fist, list 5. guide, ratio, table 6. gnomon 7. pointer 8. exponent 9. indicator 10. forefinger, indication
India... see also *Indian*
anc.. 9. Hindustan
Bay.. 6. Bengal
Cape.. 7. Comorin
capital.. 4. Agra (anc) 5. Simla (summer) 8. New Delhi
city.. 4. Agra, Gaya 5. Dacca, Delhi, Poona, Surat 6. Bombay, Jaipur, Lahore, Madras, Madura, Nagpur, Nysore 8. Calcutta, Kolhapur, Mandalay, Mirzapur, Shahpura 10. Darjeeling
city, sacred.. 5. Nasik 7. Benares
kingdom.. 5. Asoka, Nepal
mountain.. 5. Ghats 8. Sulaiman (Throne of Solomon) 9. Himalayas, Hindu Kush 12. Vindhya Hills
Persian name (anc).. 9. Hindustan
region.. 3. Goa 5. Assam, Surat 6. Baroda 7. Benares, Kashmir
relics (famed).. 8. Taj Mahal (Agra) 10. Kutab Minar 11. Ajanta Caves
river.. 6. Kistna
State.. 4. Rewa 5. Delhi 6. Baroda, Indore, Jaipur, Madras, Marwar, Punjab, Rampur, Sakkim 7. Manipur
Indian (pert to)...
aeon.. 5. kalpa
animal.. 4. zebu 5. sasin 6. nilgai
apartment.. 6. zenana
army officer.. 4. naik (naig)

7. jemadar
attorney.. 6. muktar
bandit.. 6. dacoit
bard.. 4. bhat
bird.. 4. baya, kala, koel, kyak
   5. sarus, shama 6. seesee, shahin
   8. amadavat
boat.. 5. dhoni (doni)
book (sacred).. 6. Avesta
bracelet.. 6. sankha
bread (unleavened).. 8. chapatty
breakfast.. 5. hazri
buffalo.. 4. arna (arnee)
carpet.. 4. Agra
carriage.. 4. ekka 5. tonga 6. gharry
   (gharri)
caste.. 3. Jat, Meo 4. Ahir 5. Sudra,
   Varna 6. Lohana, Rajput, Vaisya
   7. Brahman (Brahmin) 9. Kahatriya
cavalryman.. 5. sowar 7. ressala
charm.. 6. mantra
chief.. 4. Raja 5. Rajah 6. sirdar
   7. Gaekwar
cigarette (cheap).. 4. biri
claim (legal).. 3. hak (hakh)
college (Sanskrit).. 3. tol
Court, Supreme.. 6. Sudder
crocodile.. 6. gavial, mugger (muggar,
   muggur)
cymbal.. 3. tal
dagger.. 5. katar
dam.. 6. anicut (annicut)
dancer (fem).. 8. bayadere
dancing girls.. 6. nautch
deer.. 4. axis 5. kakar 6. sambur
deity.. 4. Deva
demon.. 4. bhut 5. asura 6. daitya
devil's tree.. 4. dita
dialect.. 4. Urdu 5. Hindi, Tamil
   7. Prakrit
disciple.. 5. chela
dog.. 5. dhole 6. pariah
drama.. 6. nataka
drink.. 4. soma 5. bhang (bang)
   6. arrack
dust storm.. 7. peesash, shaitan
   (sheitan)
elephant.. 5. hathi
elephant driver.. 6. mahout
elephant trappings.. 5. jhool
epic.. 8. Ramayana 11. Mahabharata
falcon.. 6. shahin (shaheen)
father.. 4. babu
festival.. 4. Holi, Mela 6. Dewali
   10. Rathayatra
fig tree (sacred).. 5. pipal 6. banian,
   banyan
garment.. 4. sari 7. luhinga
gateway.. 5. toran
ghost.. 4. bhut
god.. 4. Deva, Yama 5. Shiva
goddess.. 4. Amma
governor.. 5. nazim
grove.. 5. Sarna
guard.. 7. daloyet
hall.. 6. durbar
handkerchief.. 7. malabar
harem.. 5. serai 6. zenana 8. seraglio
heiress.. 5. Begum
herb.. 6. sesame 7. curcuma,
   tumeric, zeodary

holy.. 3. sri (shri)
holy powder.. 4. abir (perfumed)
hunt.. 6. shikar
intoxicant.. 4. soma
jungle.. 5. shola
king.. 4. Shah
king of serpents (Myth).. 6. Shesha
   (Sesha)
king's son.. 8. shahzada
knife.. 3. dah 5. kukri
lady.. 7. sahibah
language.. 4. Urdu 5. Hindu, Tamil
   8. Sanskrit (anc)
leader.. 13. Mahatma Gandhi
legal claim.. 3. hak (hakh)
leopard.. 7. cheetah
licorice.. 9. jequirity (bean)
loincloth.. 5. dhoti
lover of.. 9. Indophile
mahogany.. 4. toon
mail.. 3. dak (dawk)
medicine man.. 6. Shaman
mendicant.. 5. fakir
merchant.. 8. soudagar
midwife.. 4. dhai
Minister of Finance.. 5. Dewan
mountain pass.. 4. ghat
musical instrument.. 5. ruana
narcotic.. 4. bang 5. bhang
   7. hashish
native.. 5. Hindu, Sepoy, Tamil
   8. Assamese 10. Hindustani
Negro.. 6. hubshi
palanquin (conveyance).. 6. palkee
   (palhi)
palm.. 7. Calamus, malacca
peasant.. 4. ryot
pheasant.. 5. monal (monaul)
philosopher.. 4. Yogi
pillar.. 3. lat
pipe.. 6. hookah
police.. 4. peon 5. sepoy
police station.. 5. thana
priest.. 5. mobed 6. shaman
prince.. 4. rana
princess.. 4. rani (ranee) 5. Begum
queen.. 4. rani (ranee) 8. maharani
religious body.. 5. samaj 7. ajivika
   (anc)
resort.. 3. Abu 5. Mt Abu
rope dancer.. 3. nat
rubber.. 10. caoutchouc
ruler.. 4. rana 5. nabob, nawab,
   nizam
sage.. 6. pundit
sailor.. 6. lascar
sarsaparilla root.. 7. nunnari
servant.. 3. par 4. amah, maty
sheep.. 5. urial 6. nahoor
shrine.. 6. dagoba
silkworm.. 3. eri
snake.. 5. krait 6. bongar, katuka
soldier.. 4. peon 5. sepoy, singh
split pea.. 3. dal
study of.. 8. Indology
sugar (crude).. 3. gur 9. tabasheer
   (bamboo)
Supreme Court.. 6. Sudder
sword (short).. 5. kukri
syllable of assent.. 2. om
tapir.. 8. saladang

tariff .. **6.** zabeta
teacher .. **6.** mullah (mulla)
temple .. **4.** rath **12.** Seven Pagodas
   (of Madras)
title of respect .. **3.** sri (shri) **4.** mian
tower .. **5.** minar, sikar **7.** sikhara
tree .. **3.** saj **4.** dita, teak **5.** dhava
   6. banyan, sissoo
umbrella .. **6.** chatta
water carrier .. **7.** bheesty (bheestie)
wheat .. **4.** suji
wine .. **5.** shrab
yellow (color) .. **5.** piuri **7.** majagua
Indian, American (pert to) ...
   chief .. **5.** Logan **6.** Joseph, Philip,
      sachem **7.** Cochise, Pontiac
      8. Geronimo, Red Cloud, Tecumseh
      9. Massasoit **10.** Crazy Horse
      11. Sitting Bull, Spotted Tail
   dance .. **7.** cantico
   festival .. **8.** potlatch
   hatchet .. **8.** tomahawk
   hero .. **4.** Rama (S Am)
   largest tribe .. **6.** Navaho (Navajo)
   lodge .. **5.** hogan, igloo, tepee
      6. wigwam **7.** wickiup
   married .. **5.** squaw (fem) **6.** sannup
      (male)
   Mexico .. **4.** Maya **5.** Aztec
      7. Tehueco
   money .. **5.** sewan (beads) **6.** wampum
   Newfoundland .. **6.** Micmac
   pipe (peace) .. **7.** calumet
   pony .. **6.** cayuse
   richest tribe .. **5.** Osage
   S America .. **3.** Ona **4.** Cara (anc),
      Inca, Peru, Tupi **5.** Carib **6.** Arawak,
      Aymara **7.** Quechua
   Spirit, Great .. **6.** Manito **7.** Manitou
      12. Gitchi Manito
   squaw .. **6.** mahala
   symbol .. **5.** totem
   tax, impost .. **5.** abwab
   village .. **6.** pueblo
   water lily .. **5.** wokas (wocas)
Indiana ...
   capital .. **12.** Indianapolis
   city .. **4.** Gary **6.** Muncie **7.** Hammond
      9. Vincennes **10.** Terre Haute
   industrial region .. **7.** Calumet
   monument (Hist) .. **7.** Lincoln
      12. Indian Mounds **13.** Wyandotte
      Cave
   post office (famed) .. **10.** Santa Claus
   river .. **6.** Maumee, Wabash
      10. Tippecanoe
   State admission .. **10.** Nineteenth
   State bird .. **8.** cardinal
   State flower .. **5.** peony
   State motto .. **19.** Crossroads of
      America
   State nickname .. **7.** Hoosier
Indian tribes ... **3.** Aht, Fox, Oto
   (Otoe), Ree, Sac, Ute **4.** Cree, Crow,
   Erie, Hano, Hopi, Iowa, Maya, Mono,
   Sauk, Yuma, Zuni **5.** Aleut, Cadoo,
   Carib, Coree, Creek, Haida, Huron,
   Miami, Moqui, Omaha, Osage, Piute,
   Ponca, Sioux, Sooke, Teton, Yazoo
   6. Ahtena (Alaska), Apache, Biloxi,
   Cayuga, Dakota, Eskimo, Isleta,
   Lenape, Mohawk, Mojave, Navaho,

Nootka, Oneida, Paiute (Piute),
Pawnee, Santee, Seneca, Siwash
7. Amerind, Bannock, Catawba,
Chinook, Ojibway, Tlingit, Yavanai
8. Arapahoe, Cherokee, Chippewa,
Comanche, Iroquois, Kickapoo, Nez
Percé, Onondaga, Sagamore,
Seminole, Shoshone **9.** Algonquin,
Athabasca, Blackfoot, Chickasaw,
Winnebago **10.** Muskhogean
12. Narragansett
indicate ... **4.** cite, hint, mark, mean,
   show **5.** point **6.** denote, evince,
   reveal, sketch **7.** bespeak, betoken,
   connote, declare, display, signify,
   specify **8.** disclose, evidence,
   intimate, manifest, point out, register
   9. designate, foretoken
indicated ... **6.** marked, signed
   7. denoted, implied **8.** presumed
   9. betokened, portended, suggested
indicating succession ... **7.** ordinal
indication ... **4.** clue, hint, mark, note,
   omen, sign **5.** proof, token, trace
   6. signal **7.** reading (a) **8.** evidence
   10. suggestion **13.** manifestation
indicative ... **7.** ominous
   10. evidential, indication, meaningful,
   suggestive **11.** connotative
   13. significative
indicator ... **4.** dial, hand, sign, vane
   5. arrow, gauge, index, level
   6. gnomon **7.** indices (pl), pointer
   9. grape fern (belief) **10.** instrument
   11. annunciator, thermometer
   15. telethermometer
indicia (sing **indicium**) ... **5.** marks,
   signs **6.** tokens **8.** markings (PO)
   11. appearances, indications, metered
   mail
indict ... **6.** accuse, charge, decree
   7. arraign, impeach **8.** proclaim
indictive ... **8.** declared **9.** appointed
   10. proclaimed
indictment ... **6.** charge
   10. accusation, imputation
   11. arraignment
indifference ... **5.** shrug **6.** apathy
   7. inertia **8.** coldness **9.** unconcern
   10. mediocrity, negligence, neutrality
   12. carelessness, heedlessness,
   unimportance **13.** insensibility
   14. insignificance
indifferent ... **3.** ill **4.** cold, cool, sick
   5. blasé **6.** casual, poorly
   7. neutral, stoical, uneager
   8. careless, heedless, listless,
   mediocre **9.** apathetic
   10. nonchalant, regardless
   11. adiaphorous, unimportant
   12. nonessential, uninterested
indigence ... **4.** lack, need, want
   6. penury **7.** poverty **10.** deficiency
indigene ... **6.** native **8.** habitant
   9. primitive **10.** autochthon
indigenous ... **6.** inborn, innate, native,
   rooted **7.** edaphic, endemic, natural
   8. endemism, inherent
   13. autochthonous
indigent ... **4.** free, poor, void
   5. needy **6.** bereft **7.** lacking,
   wanting

8. beggarly 9. destitute, penniless
10. pauperized 11. impecunious,
necessitous 15. poverty–stricken
indigestion... 8. disorder, phthisis
9. dyspepsia 10. immaturity
indignant... 3. hot 5. angry, irate,
wroth 7. annoyed 8. incensed,
wrathful 9. resentful 11. exasperated
indignation... 3. ire 4. base, fury
5. .anger, wrath 7. disdain
8. contempt
indignity... 7. affront, dudgeon
10. uncivility
indigo... 3. dye 4. anil, blue
indigo (pert to)...
  bale of.. 6. seroon
  compound.. 6. isatin
  plant.. 4. anil
  source.. 7. indican 9. indigotin
  wild.. 8. Baptisia
indirect... 7. devious, oblique
9. deceitful, dishonest 10. circuitous,
contingent, misleading, roundabout
indirect expense... 8. overhead
indiscreet... 4. rash 5. hasty, silly
6. unwise 7. foolish, witless
8. careless, heedless 9. imprudent
10. incautious 11. injudicious
12. undiscerning 13. inconsiderate
indiscriminate... 5. mixed 7. mingled
9. extensive, haphazard, orderless,
wholesale 13. heterogeneous
indispensable... 5. basic, vital
6. needed 7. exigent 8. integral
9. essential, requisite, right–hand
10. imperative 13. irreplaceable
indisposed... 3. ill 4. sick 6. averse
9. unwilling 10. disordered, unfriendly
11. disinclined
indisposition... 7. ailment, illness,
malaise 10. averseness, reluctance
13. unwillingness
indisputable... 4. sure 7. certain,
evident 8. positive 10. undeniable
11. indubitable 12. irrefragable
13. incontestable
indistinct... 3. dim 4. hazy 5. vague
7. blurred, obscure, unclear
8. confused 9. ambiguous, undefined
10. indefinite 16. undiscriminating
17. indistinguishable
indite... 3. pen 5. write 6. phrase
7. compose 8. describe, inscribe
individual... 3. man, one 4. bion, idio
(comb form), self, sole, unit, zoon
6. egoist, person, single 7. special
8. organism, selfsame 9. identical
11. inseparable, personality
individuality... 5. being, seity
6. nature 7. oneness 8. ethology,
identity, selfness
individually... 9. severally
10. personally 12. each by itself
14. distributively
Indo–Aryan (pert to)...
  deity.. 5. Indra
  native of.. 5. India
  speech.. 5. Aryan
  type.. 4. Jats 7. khatris, Rajputs
Indo–Chinese (pert to)...
  language.. 3. Tai (Thai)
  mammal.. 4. zebu

  river.. 6. Mekong
  State (former French).. 4. Laos
  7. Vietnam 8. Cambodia
indoctrinate... 5. coach, edify, imbue,
teach 8. instruct 12. rehabilitate
indolence... 5. scorn, sloth 7. inertia,
languor 8. inaction, laziness
10. ergophobia 11. lotus–eating,
spring fever 13. indisposition
indolent... 4. idle, lazy 5. inert
6. otiose 8. inactive, slothful,
sluggish 10. unemployed
indomitable... 10. invincible
11. intractable, "never say die"
13. unconquerable
Indonesia...
  capital.. 7. Jakarta (Djakarta)
  formation.. 11. archipelago (once
  world's largest)
  former name.. 7. Batavia 15. Dutch
  East Indies
  government.. 8. Republic (1950)
  islands (3,000 in all).. 4. Bali, Java
  7. Sumatra 8. Sulawesi (Celebes)
  9. New Guinea (W half)
  10. Kalimantan (W Borneo)
  president.. 7. Sukarno
  race.. 5. Dyaks (Dayaks) 7. Battaks
  (Bataks), Igorots 8. Balinese,
  Javanese
  religion.. 6. Moslem
  shrine.. 6. dagoba
indorse, endorse... see *endorse*
indorsement, endorsement... 4. visa,
visé (passport)
Indra (Hindu)... 3. God 5. Deity, Sakra
(Sakka)
indubitable... 4. fact, sure 7. evident
10. infallible, undeniable
11. irrefutable 12. irrefragable,
unanswerable 13. incontestable
14. unquestionable
16. incontrovertible
induce... 4. lead, move, urge
5. cause, impel, infer 6. allure, elicit,
entice, incite 8. persuade
9. influence, instigate, prevail on
inducement... 6. motive, reason
8. stimulus 9. incentive, influence
10. persuasion 13. consideration
induct... 6. enroll 7. bring in, install
8. initiate 9. conscript, introduce
inductance unit... 5. henry
inductile... 10. inflexible, unyielding
induction... 5. logic 7. causing
8. entrance 9. accession, beginning,
deduction 10. conclusion, initiation,
production 12. commencement,
conscription, installation, introduction
indue... 5. endow 6. assume, clothe,
draw on, invest, supply (spiritual)
7. furnish
indulge... 3. pet 5. grant, humor, yield
6. pamper 7. cherish, gratify
indulgences... 8. excesses
10. tolerances
indulgent... 4. easy 7. lenient, patient
8. tolerant, yielding 9. compliant
10. permissive 11. considerate,
intemperate
indurate... 6. harden 7. callous
10. solidified

indurated... 3. set 5. fixed
9. calloused 10. solidified
industrial magnate... 6. shogun,
tycoon
industrious... 4. busy 6. active
7. zealous 8. diligent, sedulous
9. assiduous 11. intentional,
painstaking 13. indefatigable
industry... 4. toil, work 5. labor, trade
7. concern 8. commerce 9. diligence
12. perseverance, sedulousness
indweller... 6. native 7. denizen
8. indigene
indwelling... 7. inbeing 8. immanent,
inherent 9. immanence, inherence
10. inhabiting
inearth... 5. inter 6. inhume
inebriacy... 11. drunkenness
12. intemperance
inebriate... 3. sot 5. addle, drunk,
toper 7. stupefy, tippler 8. drunkard
10. exhilarate (by liquor), intoxicate
ineffable... 4. surd 6. sacred
9. wonderful 11. unspeakable,
unutterable 13. indescribable,
inexpressible 15. unpronounceable
ineffaceable... 9. indelible
10. inerasable 12. ineradicable
ineffectual... 4. vain, weak 6. futile
7. useless 9. fruitless 10. unavailing
11. inefficient 12. unsuccessful
13. inefficacious, uninfluential
inefficient... 6. unable 10. indisposed
11. incompetent 12. unproficient
inelegant... 6. clumsy, vulgar
8. indecent 9. deficient (in beauty)
11. unbeautiful
inept... 4. null, void 5. silly, unfit
6. absurd 7. foolish 8. unsuited
10. out of place, unbecoming,
unskillful, unsuitable 11. inexpedient
inequality... 9. disparity, diversity
10. inadequacy, unevenness
12. disagreement, variableness
13. disproportion
ineradicable... 7. lasting 9. indelible,
permanent 12. ineffaceable
inerrant... 8. unerring 10. infallible
inert... 4. dead, lazy 6. latent, stupid,
supine, torpid 7. passive 8. inactive,
lifeless, listless, slothful, sluggish
9. apathetic, inanimate, lethargic
10. motionless, phlegmatic
inertia... 9. indolence, inertness
10. immobility
inesculant (rare)... 9. indelible
inestimable... 9. priceless
10. invaluable 12. incalculable
inevitable... 3. due 5. fated
7. nemesis 9. necessary
11. unavoidable
inexorability... 5. rigor 9. obstinacy
10. strictness
inexorable... 6. strict 9. obstinate
10. inflexible, relentless, unyielding
inexpedience, inexpedient... 6. unwise
8. untimely 9. ignorance, impolitic,
imprudent, unfitting 10. indiscreet,
unwiseness 11. inadvisable
15. disadvantageous
inexperience... 6. unwise 9. ignorance,
imprudent 10. immaturity, indiscreet

11. inadvisable 12. unprofitable
14. unskillfulness
15. disadvantageous
inexperienced... 3. raw 4. naif
5. green, naive 6. callow
8. ignorant, immature, prentice
9. unskilled 10. amateurish
11. unpracticed
inexplicable... 11. undefinable
12. supernatural 13. preternatural,
unaccountable, unexplainable
inextricable... 4. mazy 5. stuck
8. involved 9. intricate 10. insolvable
infallible... 4. sure, true 6. gospel
7. certain 8. inerrant, unerring
9. inerrable 11. indubitable
infamous... 4. base 6. odious, wicked
8. shameful, terrible 9. negarious
10. detestable 11. ignominious
12. contemptible, disreputable
infamy... 5. shame 8. disgrace,
dishonor, ignominy, reproach
9. disrepute 10. opprobrium
11. abomination
infancy... 8. babyhood, minority
9. beginning
infant... 4. babe, baby 5. child, minor
6. novice 8. bantling 9. foundling
infantryman... 6. Zouave 7. dog–face
8. chasseur 9. musketeer
11. footslogger, foot soldier
14. gravel agitator
infatuated... 7. foolish, smitten
8. enamored, obsessed 9. bewitched
10. captivated, enraptured
12. enthusiastic
infatuation... 3. ate, mad 4. love
5. craze, folly 10. enthusiasm
11. foolishness
infeasible... 8. unlikely 10. improbable,
unsuitable 13. impracticable
infect... 5. taint 6. defile, excite,
poison 7. corrupt, deprave, pollute
11. contaminate
infection... 7. disease 8. epidemic
9. pollution 11. implication (law),
inspiration 13. contamination
infelicity... 6. misery 9. inaptness
10. misfortune 11. unhappiness
12. inexpedience, untimeliness,
wretchedness
infer... 4. hint 5. drive, guess, imply
6. deduce 7. presume, suppose,
surmise 8. conclude, construe
inference... 5. truth 8. illation
9. corollary, deduction
10. assumption, conclusion
11. implication, proposition
inferential... 8. illative 9. deductive,
inducible 10. deductible, suggestive
15. inconsequential
inferior... 3. bad 4. less, poor
5. baser, lower, minor, petit, petty
6. lesser, menial, nether 7. humbler,
unequal 8. anterior, mediocre
10. inadequate, low–blooded
11. subordinate
inferior lawyer... 9. leguleian
11. pettifogger
infernal... 6. cursed, plaguy, wicked
7. hellish, satanic 8. damnable,
devilish 9. chthonian, execrable,

malignant, Tartarean 10. demoniacal,
detestable, outrageous
inferno (pert to)...
 Bib.. 4. Hell 5. abyss, limbo
 Buddah.. 6. Naraka
 Egypt.. 6. Amenti
 ferry to.. 4. Styx
 Hebrew.. 5. Sheol 7. Abaddon,
 Gehenna
 myth.. 5. Aralu, Hades, Orcus
 7. Acheron, Niflhel 8. Tartarus
infest... 3. vex 5. annoy, beset
 6. assail, molest, plague 7. overrun,
 torment 8. frequent
infidel... 5. deist, pagan 6. Kaffir
 7. atheist, Saracen, skeptic
 8. agnostic 10. unbeliever
 11. freethinker 12. non–Christian
 13. non–Mohammedan
infidelity... 6. deceit 7. perfidy
 8. unbelief 9. misbelief, treachery
 10. disloyalty 11. incredulity
 13. faithlessness
infinite... 4. vast 5. vague 6. divine
 7. endless, eternal, immense, perfect
 9. boundless, limitless, unlimited
 10. indefinite 11. illimitable,
 interminate, omnipresent, The
 Absolute 12. all–embracing,
 interminable, undetermined
 13. inexhaustible, The Omnipotent
 16. all–comprehensive
Infinite Being... 3. God
Infinite knowledge... 11. omniscience
infinitesimal... 5. small 7. minimum
 9. invisible, molecular 10. evanescent
 11. microscopic
infirm... 4. weak 5. anile, frail
 6. senile 7. fragile 8. decrepit
 9. doddering 10. irresolute
 11. vacillating
infirmity... 6. defect, foible, malady,
 old age 7. disease, failing, frailty,
 illness 8. debility, weakness
 10. feebleness
inflame... 4. burn, fire 5. anger
 6. arouse, enrage, excite, ignite,
 kindle, madden, rankle, redden
 7. incense 8. irritate 10. exasperate
inflammable... 5. fiery 6. tinder
 7. piceous 8. burnable 9. excitable,
 irascible, irritable 10. accendible
 11. combustible
inflammable substance... 6. ethane,
 tinder 7. acetone, bitumen
inflammation... 8. ignition, soreness
 10. congestion, excitement,
 incitement
inflammation (pert to)...
 bladder.. 8. cystitis
 bone.. 7. rickets 8. osteitis
 13. osteomyelitis
 ear.. 6. otitis
 eye.. 6. iritis 7. uveitis
 joints.. 4. gout 9. arthritis
 10. rheumatism
 spinal cord.. 13. poliomyelitis
 stomach.. 9. gastritis
 suffix.. 4. itis
 vein.. 9. phlebitis
inflect... 3. bow 4. bend 5. curve
 7. decline, deflect 8. modulate

inflection, inflexion... 4. tone
 5. angle, curve 7. bending
 8. paradigm 9. accidence
 10. modulation
inflexible... 4. iron 5. rigid, stiff
 6. strict 8. obdurate, rigorous
 9. immovable, immutable, obstinate,
 unbending 10. implacable, inexorable,
 relentless, unyielding 11. unalterable
 14. uncompromising
inflict... 3. add 4. deal 5. wreak
 6. impose, punish
inflorescence... 4. cyme 5. whorl
 6. cymose 7. budding, flowers
 8. racemose 9. flowerage, flowering
 10. unfoldment 13. efflorescence
inflow... 6. influx 9. inpouring
 11. inspiration
influence... 3. win 4. lead, move, pull,
 sway 5. aegis (egis), bribe, force,
 impel, lobby 6. affect, effect, induce,
 influx, leaven, obsess 7. control,
 inspire, mastery 8. dominate,
 effusion, persuade, prestige
 9. authority, determine
influence (world–wide)... 8. ecumenic
influenced... 6. biased 7. induced,
 pliable (easily) 8. affected
 10. prejudiced
influential... 6. potent, strong
 7. weighty 8. momentus, powerful
 9. effective 13. authoritative
influx... 4. tide 5. firth, mouth (river)
 6. import, inflow 7. estuary, illapse
 9. influence, inpouring
 11. debouchment
infold... see *enfold*
inform... 4. tell 5. teach, train
 6. advise, notify, report 7. animate,
 apprise, inspire 8. instruct
 9. enlighten
informal... 7. offhand 9. irregular
information... 3. air, tip 4. data, lore,
 news 5. aviso, datum, facts
 6. digest 7. advices, tidings
 9. knowledge 10. annotation
 11. instruction 12. intelligence
informed... 2. up 3. hep 4. up on,
 wise 6. posted 8. apprised,
 educated, versed in 10. instructed
 11. enlightened
informer... 3. spy 4. tout 6. gossip,
 snitch, teller 7. delator 8. affirmer,
 betrayer, mouchard, reporter, telltale
 9. informant, spokesman
 10. talebearer, tattletale
informer (sl)... 4. fink, nark 6. canary,
 snitch 7. stoolie 8. snitcher, squealer
 9. blabberer 11. stool pigeon
 12. blabbermouth
infraction... 6. breach 8. fracture,
 trespass 9. intrusion, violation
 12. encroachment, infringement,
 overstepping 13. transgression
infrequency... 6. rarity 7. fewness
 8. rareness, solitude 9. isolation
 12. uncommonness
infrequent... 4. rare 6. scarce,
 seldom, sparse 8. uncommon
 9. spasmodic 10. occasional
infrequently... 6. rarely, seldom 8. not
 often, sparsely

infringe... 6. defeat, refute 7. confute, destroy, violate 8. encroach, overstep, trespass 9. frustrate

infringement... 6. breach, piracy (copyright) 9. intrusion, violation 10. infraction 12. overstepping 14. nonfulfillment

infundibulum... 4. cone, lura 10. gray matter (brain)

infuriate... 5. anger 6. enrage, incite, madden 8. irritate 10. antagonize

infuscate... 6. darken 7. obscure

infuse... 4. fill, shed 5. steep 6. drench 7. implant, instill 9. insinuate, introduce

infusion... 3. tea 4. wort 8. affusion, tincture 9. admixture, decoction, inpouring 12. instillation

ingang... 5. porch 8. entrance 10. intestines

ingenious... 5. sharp, smart, witty 6. adroit, clever, daedal, gifted, shrewd, subtle 8. skillful, talented 9. Daedalian, deviceful 11. intelligent, resourceful

ingenuity... 5. skill 6. candor, genius 10. adroitness 11. originality 13. inventiveness

ingenuous... 4. naif, open 5. frank, naive, noble, plain 6. candid, innate 7. artless, sincere 8. freeborn, innocent 9. guileless 10. unreserved 15. unsophisticated

ingest... 3. eat 5. learn 6. take in 7. consume, swallow

ingot... 3. gad, pig 4. mold 5. metal 7. bullion

ingratiate... 4. fawn 7. commend, flatter 9. insinuate, introduce

ingredient... 6. factor 7. element 9. component 11. constituent

ingress... 4. go in 5. entry 6. access, portal 8. entrance 9. reception 11. entranceway

ingrowing nail... 7. acronyx

inhabitant... 3. cit 6. inmate, people, tenant 7. citizen, denizen 8. resident

inhabitant (pert to)...
Alaska.. 9. sourdough
desert.. 4. Arab 5. nomad
earliest.. 9. aborigine
foreign.. 5. alien
Maine.. 10. down–easter
moon.. 8. selenite
northern.. 6. Yankee 11. Septentrion (Lowell)

inhabitants, equator's other side... 8. antiscii 10. antiscians

inhabited... 5. lived 7. dwelled, peopled 8. occupied, tenanted 9. populated

inhabiting (pert to)...
caves.. 8. spelaean (spelean) 10. troglodyte
ground.. 9. terricole 11. terricolous
groves.. 7. nemoral 10. nemoricole
islands.. 7. nesiote
lakes.. 9. lacustral
sea.. 7. pelagic 15. thalassophilous
seashore.. 8. littoral

inhale... 4. suck 5. smell, smoke, sniff 7. breathe, inspire, respire

inharmonious... 7. jarring 9. differing, dissonant, unmusical 10. discordant 11. conflicting, disagreeing

inherent... 6. inborn, innate 7. infixed 8. immanent 9. immanence, intrinsic 10. indwelling, subsistent 11. instinctive 13. indispensable

inheritance... 6. legacy 7. bequest, legitim 8. heirship, heredity, heritage, Salic law 9. cleronomy 10. birthright

inheritance diminisher... 6. abator

inheritor... 4. heir 6. coheir 7. heiress, legatee 10. coparcener 11. beneficiary

inhibit... 5. check 6. forbid, hinder 8. prohibit, restrain 9. interdict

inhibition... 3. ban, bar 4. writ 7. embargo 8. checking 9. hindrance, restraint 10. impediment 11. prohibition 12. interdiction

inhuman... 4. fell 5. cruel 6. brutal, savage 7. bestial, brutish 8. devilish, nonhuman 9. barbarous, ferocious 10. demoniacal, diabolical

inhumation... 6. burial 9. arenation, interment

inhume... 4. bury 5. inter, inurn 7. deposit, inearth

inimical... 7. adverse, hostile, opposed 8. contrary 10. unfriendly 11. belligerent, unfavorable

iniquity... 3. sin 4. evil, vice 5. crime 7. misdeed 9. injustice 10. immorality, wickedness

initial... 6. paraph 9. incipient 11. large letter 12. commencement

initiate... 4. open 5. admit, begin, epopt (anc) 6. induct 7. install, instate 8. inchoate 10. inaugurate 11. preinstruct

initiation... 8. ceremony 9. admission 10. admittance 12. inauguration, introduction

injection... 4. hypo 5. enema 7. clyster 9. immission

injudicious... 4. rash 6. unwise 9. impolitic, imprudent 11. inexpedient

injunction... 3. ado 4. writ 5. order, union 6. behest 7. mandate, precept 9. direction 11. prohibition

injure... 3. mar 4. harm, hurt, lame, maim 5. wound, wrong 6. assail, damage, grieve, impair, scathe 7. affront, slander, tarnish

injurious... 3. bad 4. evil 7. abusive, harmful, hurtful, noxious 10. defamatory, slanderous 11. detrimental, mischievous

injury... 3. ill, mar 4. dere (obs), evil, harm, hurt, loss, pain, tort 5. wound, wrong 6. damage, lesion, mayhem, trauma 7. slander 9. detriment, indignity, injustice 10. impairment

injustice... 5. wrong 6. injury 7. umbrage 8. hardship, inequity, iniquity 10. imposition, unfairness

ink... 3. jet 5. black 7. blacken 8. atrament, blacking

ink (pert to)...

bag . . 3. sac (fish)
berry . . 5. holly 6. indigo
black . . 10. atramental
  11. atramentous
cap . . 8. mushroom
fish . . 5. squid 6. cuttle
pad . . 7. tompion (tampion)
ref to . . 10. atramental
source . . 7. inkweed, oak gall
  8. inkstone, pokeweed 9. gallberry
spreader . . 6. brayer
inkle . . . 4. hint, tape, yarn 5. braid,
  twist 6. thread 8. intimate
inkling . . . 4. hint 5. rumor 6. desire,
  report 10. intimation 11. supposition
inlaid . . . 6. mosaic 7. adorned, set into
  9. champleve, decorated
inlay . . . 4. buhl, line 5. inset 6. insert,
  mosaic, niello, tarsia 7. filling,
  implant 8. buhlwork, intarsia
  9. champleve
inlet . . . 3. bay, ria, voe 4. cove, slew,
  sump 5. admit, bayou, bight, creek,
  fiord (fjord), firth, inlay 6. estero,
  recess, strait 7. estuary, orifice
  8. entrance, waterway
inn . . . 3. pub 4. khan 5. abode, fonda,
  hotel, motel, serai 6. hostel, imaret,
  posada, tavern 7. albergo, cabaret,
  hospice, locanda, osteria, pension,
  shelter 8. alehouse, hostelry
  9. roadhouse 11. caravansary
innate . . . 4. born 6. inborn, inbred,
  native 7. natural 9. ingrained,
  inherited, intrinsic 10. congenital,
  hereditary, inveterate 11. instinctive
  14. constitutional
innate ability . . . 6. genius, talent
innate idea (Philos) . . . 11. immortality
inn courts . . . 11. Inner Temple
inner . . . 4. ento (comb form) 5. ental
  6. inside, inward, secret 7. obscure
  8. esoteric, interior, internal
  9. intestine 10. indistinct
  14. intramolecular
inner circle . . . 3. set 4. clan, club,
  ring 5. group, junta, junto 6. clique
inner man . . . 4. mind, self, soul
  6. psyche 7. stomach
innermost coating . . . 6. intima
Inner Temple . . . 11. Inns of Court
Innisfail . . . 4. Eire, Erin 7. Ireland
  15. Island of Destiny
innocence . . . 6. purity 7. diamond
  11. sinlessness 12. harmlessness
  13. guiltlessness, innocuousness
innocent . . . 4. Holy, pure 5. idiot,
  naive, seely 6. benign, lawful
  7. artless, sinless, upright 8. spotless
  9. destitute, guiltless, ingenuous,
  permitted, simpleton, stainless,
  unsullied 10. unblamable
  12. simple–minded 13. free from
  guilt
innocuous . . . 8. harmless, hurtless,
  innocent 9. innoxious 11. inoffensive,
  unoffending
innovation . . . 3. new 6. change
  7. novelty 13. prolification
innuendo . . . 4. hint, slur 6. change
  7. meaning 9. aspersion
  10. intimation 11. implication,

indirection, insinuation
Innuit . . . 4. Yuit (Eskimo)
innumerable . . . 6. legion, myriad
  8. infinite, numerous 9. countless
  10. numberless
inodorous . . . 8. odorless 9. scentless
inopportune . . . 8. ill–timed, untimely
  10. malapropos, unsuitable
  11. contretemps, inexpedient
  12. embarrassing, unseasonable
inordinate . . . 5. undue 9. excessive,
  fanatical 10. disordered, disorderly,
  exorbitant, immoderate
  11. unregulated 12. unrestrained
inorganic . . . 7. mineral 9. inanimate
  13. nonbiological
inquest . . . 4. jury 5. quest, trial
  6. assize, search 7. inquiry
  11. examination 13. investigation
inquire . . . 3. ask 4. seek 5. query
  7. examine 8. question
  11. interrogate, investigate
inquirer . . . 6. seeker 7. querier,
  student, zetetic 8. searcher
inquiry . . . 5. query 6. examen, tracer
  7. examine, seeking 8. question,
  research 11. examination
  13. investigation
inquisition . . . 5. trial 6. search
  7. inquiry 8. tribunal 11. examination
  13. investigation
Inquisition . . . 6. French (1772)
  7. Spanish (1480–1834)
inquisitive . . . 4. nosy 5. peery
  6. prying 7. curious 8. meddling
  10. meddlesome
inquisitor . . . 6. tracer 7. coroner,
  sheriff 8. examiner
in re . . . 10. concerning 13. in the
  matter of
inroad . . . 4. raid 5. foray 8. invasion,
  trespass 9. incursion, intrusion,
  irruption 12. overstepping
  13. transgression
insane . . . 3. mad 4. daft, loco, luny
  5. batty, crazy, loony 6. crazed
  7. cracked, foolish, frantic, rammish,
  touched, witless 8. demented,
  deranged 9. non compos 15. non
  compos mentis
insane urge to steal . . .
  11. kleptomania
insanity . . . 5. mania 6. frenzy, lunacy,
  trance 7. madness 8. delirium,
  dementia 10. alienation
  11. derangement 16. mental
  deficiency
inscribe . . . 4. draw, etch 5. infix,
  stamp, write 6. blazon, enroll
  7. address, engrave, impress
  8. dedicate, depencil
inscribed . . . 5. runed 7. written
  8. engraved, recorded 10. registered,
  rupestrian (on rocks)
inscription . . . 4. text 5. motto, title
  6. legend 7. epitaph, writing
  8. colophon, epigraph, graffito
  9. lettering, sgraffito 10. dedication
  14. superscription
inscrutable . . . 6. secret 8. abstruse
  10. mysterious 12. impenetrable,
  inexplorable, unfathomable

16. incomprehensible

insect . . . 3. ant, bee, bug, dor, fly
4. flea, gnat, lerp, lice, mite, moth,
tick, wasp 5. aphid, borer, cadew,
emmet, leech, louse, roach, Vespa
6. acarid, beetle, cicada, earwig,
hornet, locust, mantis, sawfly, scarab,
spider 7. ant lion, chigger, firefly,
gallfly, katydid, ladybug, pismire,
termite 8. bullhead, glowworm,
mosquito, stinkbug, turicata
9. bumblebee, butterfly, caddis fly,
centipede, cockroach, dragonfly,
ichneumon, tsetse fly, tumblebug
10. silverfish 11. caterpillar,
grasshopper 12. yellow jacket

insect (pert to) . . .
adult . . 5. imago
aquatic . . 7. Ranatra
arboreal . . 7. katydid
back . . 5. notum
Bible . . 7. ant lion
butterfly . . 11. Lepidoptera
egg . . 3. nit
eyes . . 6. ocelli 7. stemmas
feelers . . 5. palps 8. antennas
9. tentacles
fly . . 4. zimb 7. Diptera
hymenopterous . . 3. ant, bee 4. wasp
6. sawfly 7. gallfly
immature . . 4. grub, pupa 5. larva
6. maggot 9. chrysalis
immature covering . . 6. cocoon
leg . . 6. proleg
like . . 8. entomoid
long–legged . . 5. emesa
10. harvestman 13. daddy–longlegs
mature . . 5. imago
molting . . 6. instar 7. ecdysis
parasitic . . 4. lice 5. louse
plant . . 5. aphid, aphis, borer, thrip
plate . . 6. scutum
praying . . 6. mantis
reference to . . 11. entomologic
relationship to host . . 7. metochy
10. parasitism
science . . 10. entomology
sound . . 5. chirr 7. stridor
stage . . 4. pupa 5. imago, larva
6. instar 9. chrysalis
stinging . . 3. ant, bee 4. wasp
6. hornet 7. sciniph (Bib) 12. yellow
jacket
wingless . . 4. flea 6. aptera
wing vein . . 5. media
Insectivora (mammals) . . . 5. moles
6. shrews 7. desmans, tenrecs
7. hedgehogs
insecure . . . 5. risky, shaky 6. infirm,
unsafe, unsure 7. dubious, rickety,
unsound 8. unstable 9. dangerous,
hazardous 10. precarious
insensate . . . 5. blind, harsh 6. brutal,
unwise 7. fatuous, foolish 8. lifeless
9. inanimate, unfeeling, untouched
10. insensible, insentient
11. insensitive 13. unintelligent
insensibility . . . 4. coma 8. neurosis
9. analgesia 13. lack of feeling
insensible . . . 4. slow 7. gradual,
unaware 9. apathetic, inanimate,
insensate, senseless 11. indifferent,

unconscious 13. inappreciable

insert . . . 4. gore 5. foist, graft, immit,
inset, panel, wedge 7. ingraft
8. interact, ornament 9. interface,
interpose, introduce 11. intercalate,
interpolate
insertion . . . 5. inset 9. injection
10. embroidery, needlework
insertion (pert to) . . .
cords in cloth . . 5. shirr
day in calendar . . 13. intercalation
newspaper . . 2. ad 13. advertisement
phrases, words . . 11. parenthesis
sound in a word . . 9. anaptyxis
10. epenthesis
inset . . . 5. panel 6. inflow, influx
10. phenocryst
inside out, turning . . . 5. evert
8. aversion 9. evertible
insidious . . . 4. deep, wily 7. cunning
8. guileful 9. deceitful, dishonest
11. full of plots, treacherous
insight . . . 3. ken 6. acumen
9. intuition 11. discernment,
penetration 12. clairvoyance
13. understanding
insignia . . . 3. bar 4. ankh, flag
5. badge, cross, crown 6. banner,
emblem, symbol 7. chevron, regalia,
scepter 8. caduceus, swastika
15. hammer and sickle
insignificance . . . 6. trifle 9. smallness
10. slightness 12. unimportance
insignificant . . . 4. puny 5. minor,
petit, petty, small, zilch 6. paltry
7. trivial 8. inferior 9. senseless
11. meaningless, unimportant
12. contemptible 13. inconsiderate
insignificant object . . . 8. molehill
insincere . . . 5. false 8. affected
9. deceptive 12. hypocritical
insinuate . . . 4. hint 5. enter, imply
6. allude, infuse 8. intimate
9. penetrate 10. ingratiate
insinuation . . . 4. hint 5. sneer
8. innuendo 9. aspersion, insertion,
intrusion 10. intimation
12. ingratiation, interjection
insipid . . . 3. dry 4. dead, dull, flat,
tame 5. heavy, prosy, stale, vapid,
wimpy (sl) 6. jejune 7. prosaic
8. lifeless, mediocre 9. tasteless
10. monotonous, namby–pamby,
spiritless, unanimated, wishy–washy
11. indifferent 13. uninteresting
insisted . . . 5. urged 6. held to
7. pressed 8. demanded 9. persisted
10. maintained, stipulated
insnare . . . see *ensare*
insolence . . . 5. serve 6. insult
8. defiance 9. arrogance, contumely,
impudence 11. haughtiness
insolent . . . 4. pert, rude 7. abusive,
defiant 8. arrogant, impudent
9. insulting 10. disdainful
11. extravagant, impertinent,
overbearing 12. contemptuous,
contumelious 13. disrespectful
insouciant . . . 8. carefree
11. indifferent, unconcerned
inspect . . . 3. pry, spy 4. view
5. grade 7. examine 10. scrutinize

inspector... 4. ager 6. conner, grader, police, sealer, tester 8. examiner, overseer
inspiration... 6. sprite 8. afflatus, hiccough 9. influence, intuition 10. exhalation, inhalation, motivation
inspire... 4. fire 5. cheer, exalt 6. infuse, inhale 7. animate, breathe, enliven 8. motivate 9. encourage, infatuate 11. communicate (to the spirit)
inspired power... 7. entheos
inspiring... 8. cheering, eloquent 11. provocative
inspiring (pert to)...
awe.. 4. fear 5. awful, eerie
confidence.. 11. encouraging
favor.. 13. prepossessing
horror.. 6. grisly
inspirit... 5. cheer, elate, rouse 7. animate, enliven, hearten, inspire, quicken 9. encourage 10. ingratiate, invigorate
instability... 8. weakness 10. changeable, insecurity, mutability, unsafeness 11. inconstancy 12. irresolution, unsteadiness 13. changeability, unreliability
install... 4. seat 6. induct, ordain 7. instate 8. initiate 9. establish 10. inaugurate
instance... 4. case, suit 6. motive 7. example, request, urgency 8. occasion 10. suggestion 11. instigation
instant... 3. pop 4. time, urge 5. flash, trice 6. direct, minute, moment, second, urgent 7. current, solicit 8. pressing 9. immediate, importune 11. importunate
instantly... 3. now 8. directly, in a flash, in a trice
instate... 5. admit, endow 6. invest 7. install 9. establish
instead of... 4. else 5. stead 6. in lieu, rather 10. equivalent, substitute
instigate... 3. egg 4. abet, goad, move, prod, spur, urge 5. impel 6. foment, incite, suborn 7. provoke 8. motivate 9. stimulate
instigator... 5. urger 7. abettor, exciter, inciter 8. agitator, fomenter, inflamer, provoker 10. ringleader
instill, instil... 5. imbue 6. impart, infuse, pour in 7. pervade 9. inculcate, insinuate
instinct... 5. knack 6. libido, talent 7. impulse 8. aptitude 11. instigation, orientation
instinctive... 6. innate 7. natural 8. inherent, original 9. automatic, intuitive 11. involuntary, spontaneous
institute... 5. erect, found 6. create, ordain, school 7. academy, college, precept, society 8. initiate, organize, seminary 9. originate, principle 10. inaugurate 12. organization
Institute (The)... 5. Gaius 6. France 8. Politics 10. Technology
institute a suit... 3. sue 7. go to law 8. litigate 9. prosecute
Institution, International (maritime)...

7. Veritas 13. Bureau Veritas
instruct... 4. show 5. coach, edify, order, teach, train 6. advise, direct, inform 7. command, confirm, educate, nurture 9. enlighten 10. discipline 12. indoctrinate
instruction... 3. act 4. lore, news 6. lesson, report 7. precept, tuition 8. pedagogy, teaching, tutorage 9. paideutic 11. information 13. propaedeutics
instructive... 8. didactic, sermonic 10. commanding, preceptive 11. educational, informative 12. propaedeutic
instructor... 5. tutor 6. mentor 7. adviser, teacher, trainer 8. lecturer 9. preceptor, professor
instrument... 4. barb, bill, deed, tool, writ 5. agent, means 6. medium 7. utensil, writing 8. document 9. implement 11. contrivance
instrument, musical (pert to)...
ancient.. 4. asor, lyre 5. rebab, rocta, shawn 7. cithern, theorbo 8. penorcon, psaltery
brass.. 4. horn 6. cornet 7. helicon
keyboard.. 5. organ, piano 6. spinet 10. clavichord 11. harpsichord
percussion.. 4. drum, gong 5. bells 6. chimes 7. cymbals, marimba 8. carillon 9. castanets, xylophone 10. vibraphone 12. glockenspiel
sacred (Mormon).. 4. Urim 7. Thummim
stringed.. 4. asor, harp, lute, lyre, rota' 5. banjo, cello, ribec (ribeck), viola 6. fiddle, guitar, violin 7. ukulele 8. dulcimer, mandolin 10. hurdy–gurdy
stringed (anc).. 7. bandora
supplementary.. 7. ripieno
wind.. 3. sax 4. horn, oboe, reed, tuba 5. flute, organ 6. cornet 7. althorn, bassoon, ocarina, piccolo, trumpet 8. clarinet, trombone 9. accordion, flageolet, harmonica, saxophone
instrument, others (pert to)...
astronomical.. 5. armil
Biblical.. 4. Urim
butcher's.. 5. steel 7. cleaver
communication.. 9. telegraph, telephone 10. hydrophone
cooking (eggs).. 7. oometer
cutting.. 5. knife, razor 6. scythe, shears, sickle 7. cutlery 8. scissors, strickle
drawing.. 10. pantograph
gripping.. 4. vise 5. clamp, tongs 7. pincers 8. tweezers
legal.. 4. deed, writ 6. escrow
mathematics.. 6. abacus 8. mesolabe
measure.. 7. ammeter 8. odometer, otoscope, rheostat 9. barometer, koniscope, rheometer 11. pyrometer
medical.. 6. trocar (trochar) 7. dilator, levator, ligator, scalpel 8. trephine
mining.. 6. jumper
music.. 4. bell 9. ergograph, metronome

navigating.. 7. pelorus, sextant
optical.. 7. alidade (alidad)
  9. periscope, telescope
pointed.. 3. awl 6. stylet, stylus
  8. stiletto
time.. 11. chronometer, chronoscope
two–pronged.. 6. bident
instrumental... 6. useful 7. helpful
  9. conducive, promoting, symphonic
  10. orchestral 11. implemental,
  serviceable
instrumental (pert to)...
composition.. 5. fugue, rondo
  6. sonata 7. cantata 8. symphony
grammar.. 4. case
introduction.. 7. intrada
instrumentality... 5. means 6. agency,
  medium 7. organon 9. mechanism
insubordinate... 8. mutinous
  10. unresigned 11. disobedient
  12. contumacious, unsubmissive
insubstantial... 5. frail 6. flimsy
  9. illogical 10. unreliable
  12. apparitional
insufficient... 5. short 6. scanty,
  scarce 7. unequal, wanting
  9. deficient 10. inadequate
  14. incommensurate, unsatisfactory
insular... 5. alone 6. narrow
  7. nesiote 8. detached, islander,
  isolated, secluded 9. illiberal,
  insulated, sclerosis, separated,
  unrelated 10. contracted 12. Island
  of Reil (Anat)
insulated... 5. isled, taped 8. isolated
  9. separated 10. segregated
insulating material... 4. tape 5. kapok
  6. balata, Kerite 7. okonite 10. fiber
  glass 12. friction tape
insult... 3. cag 4. mock, slur 5. flout
  6. offend, revile 7. affront, assault,
  offense, outrage 8. contempt
  9. contumely, indignity
insulting... 8. arrogant, insolent
  9. offensive 10. affrontive
  13. disrespectful
insurance... 4. risk 7. annuity, promise
  8. guaranty, security, warranty
  9. assurance 10. protection
insurance group... 7. tontine
insurance personnel... 5. agent
  6. broker 7. actuary 8. adjuster
insurgent... 5. rebel 8. agitator,
  mutineer, revolter 10. rebellious
  13. insubordinate
insurmountable... 10. impassable,
  invincible 11. insuperable 13. beyond
  control
insurrection... 4. riot 6. mutiny, revolt
  8. sedition, uprising 9. rebellion
  10. insurgence, revolution
intact... 5. sound, whole
  9. unchanged, undefiled, undivided,
  uninjured, untouched 10. unimpaired
intaglio... 3. die, gem 6. relief
  7. carving 9. engraving
intangible... 5. vague 7. phantom
  10. immaterial, impalpable
  13. imperceptible, insubstantial,
  unsubstantial
integer... 3. one 5. whole 6. entity,
  number 8. integral

integral... 3. all 5. inner, whole
  8. totality 9. component, essential
integration... 5. whole 10. adjustment
  11. unification 12. coordination,
  equalization 13. accommodation
integrity... 5. unity 6. purity, virtue
  7. honesty, probity 9. innocence,
  soundness 12. completeness
integument... 4. aril, coat, derm, skin
  5. testa 8. covering, envelope
  10. investment
intellect... 3. wit 4. mind, nous
  5. inwit, mahat 6. genius, noesis,
  reason 7. noetics, wise man
  9. mentality 12. intelligence
  13. understanding
intellectual... 6. brainy, mental, noetic,
  sophic 7. egghead, learned
  8. highbrow 11. intelligent
intelligence... 4. mind, news 5. sense,
  spies 6. acumen, spirit 8. capacity
  9. intellect, knowledge
  11. information 13. understanding
intelligent... 3. apt 4. sane 5. acute,
  aware, smart 6. astute, bright,
  versed 7. knowing, skilled 8. rational,
  sensible 9. cognizant
  13. understanding
intelligentsia... 8. literati 10. illuminati
  11. the educated 13. intellectuals
intelligible... 5. clear, plain
  8. knowable 10. cognizable,
  conceptual, explicable, fathomable
  11. perspicuous 13. suprasensuous
  14. comprehensible, understandable
intelligibly... 6. simply 7. clearly,
  lucidly, plainly 13. unequivocally
  14. comprehensibly, understandably
intemerate... 4. pure 9. inviolate,
  undefiled
intemperance... 6. excess 8. bibacity,
  gluttony, severity, tippling
  10. debauchery, inclemency
  11. drunkenness 12. inabstinence,
  incontinence
intemperate... 6. Frigid (Zone), severe,
  Torrid (Zone) 7. extreme 8. addicted,
  bibulous 9. excessive, inclement,
  indulgent 10. gluttonous,
  immoderate, inordinate
  12. ungovernable, unrestrained
intend... 3. aim 4. mean, plan
  5. serve 6. design, direct, expect,
  regard, set out, strive 7. proceed,
  propose 8. aspire to, attend to,
  consider
intended... 5. meant 8. designed,
  purposed, remedial 9. affianced,
  betrothed, meditated 10. calculated,
  considered 11. deliberated, intentional
  12. contemplated
intense... 4. deep 5. great, vivid
  6. strong 7. violent 8. powerful
  9. energetic 10. high degree
intensely... 4. very 5. quite 7. acutely
intensify... 6. deepen 7. enhance
  8. condense, heighten, increase
  9. aggravate
intensity... 5. depth 6. deepen,
  degree, energy 7. density
  8. loudness, softness, strength
  9. greatness, vehemence

12. colorfulness
intent... 4. rapt 5. eager, tense
  6. design 7. earnest, meaning,
  purpose 9. intention
intention... 3. aim, end 4. will
  6. animus, design, motive, object
  7. concept, healing, meaning,
  purpose 8. intentio 13. determination
intentional... 5. aimed, meant
  7. knowing 8. designed, intended
  9. voluntary 10. calculated, deliberate
  12. contemplated
intently... 7. eagerly, fixedly
  9. earnestly, zealously 10. diligently,
  sedulously 11. attentively, steadfastly
inter (pref)... 5. among, intra
  6. mutual, within 7. between
  10. reciprocal
inter (verb)... 4. bury 5. inurn
  6. entomb, inhume 7. inearth
intercalary month... 6. Veadar 8. leap
  year 10. bissextile
intercalate... 6. insert 11. interpolate
intercede... 6. umpire 7. bargain,
  mediate, referee 9. arbitrate, go
  between, interpose, intervene
intercessor... 5. agent, front
  6. bishop, Christ 8. mediator
  9. middleman 10. interceder
  11. internuncio
interchange... 5. trade 6. barter
  7. permute 8. commerce, exchange
  9. alternate 10. transposal
  11. alternation, reciprocate, retaliation
intercourse... 7. dealing 8. commerce
  10. connection, fellowship
  12. conversation 13. communication
interdependence... 9. mutuality
  13. interrelation 16. interaffiliation
interdict... 3. ban 4. veto 5. debar,
  taboo (tabu) 6. forbid 7. inhibit
  8. prohibit 9. proscribe
interest... 4. hold, weal 5. savor,
  share, usury 6. behalf, engage
  7. attract, concern 9. entertain
interested... 4. rapt 7. partial 8. a
  party to, involved, partisan
  9. attentive 10. prejudiced
interesting... 8. exciting 10. attractive
  11. provocative
interfere... 5. clash 6. hinder, meddle,
  molest, tamper 7. intrude
  9. interpose, intervene
  11. intermeddle
interim... 7. respite 8. interval,
  meantime 9. interlude, meanwhile
  12. intermission
interior... 5. inner 6. center, inland,
  inside, secret 8. internal 9. enclosure
interjection... 2. eh, lo 3. bah
  4. ahem, alas, egad, haha, whew
  7. heavens 11. ejaculation,
  exclamation
interlace... 3. mix 5. braid, unite
  9. alternate, interlink 10. intertwine,
  interweave 11. interpolate, intersperse
interlock... 4. knit, mesh 5. unite,
  weave 6. device, engage 7. connect
  9. interjoin, interlace 11. interrelate
interlope... 6. insert 7. intrude,
  obtrude 9. interfere, intervene
  11. intermeddle, interpolate

interloper... 8. intruder 10. trespasser
  11. gate crasher
interlude... 5. farce, pause, truce
  6. verset 7. interim, respite
  8. entr'acte, overture, versicle
  10. intermezzo 11. performance
  13. entertainment
intermediary... 5. agent 6. medium,
  middle 8. mediator 9. go−between
  10. interagent 11. intervening,
  mediatorial
intermediate... 5. mesne 6. grades,
  medial, medium, middle 7. aniline
  (dye), mediate 8. mediator
  9. naphthols 11. interjacent,
  intervening 12. intermediary
interminable... 4. aeon, long
  7. endless, eternal 8. infinite,
  unending 9. boundless, limitless,
  perpetual, unlimited 10. continuous,
  protracted
intermission... 4. rest 5. pause
  6. recess 7. respite 8. entr'acte,
  interval 9. cessation 10. suspension
  12. interruption
intermit... 4. stop 5. cease, recur
  7. suspend 9. interpose, interrupt
  11. discontinue
intermittent... 6. broken, fitful
  8. periodic 9. irregular, recurrent,
  spasmodic 11. alternating
internal... 5. inner 6. inside, inward,
  mental, within 7. revenue
  8. domestic, esoteric, interior
  9. intrinsic, spiritual
internal organs... 6. vitals 7. viscera
international (pert to)...
  agreement.. 4. pact 6. accord, treaty
  7. entente 9. suzerain
  business combine.. 6. cartel
  fixed calendar.. 9. Cotsworth
  language.. 2. Ro 3. Ido 5. Arulo
  7. Volapük 9. Esperanto
  10. Occidental 11. Interlingua
interpolate... 5. alter 6. insert
  7. corrupt, implant 11. intercalate
interpose... 7. intrude, mediate
  9. intercede, interfere, interject,
  intervene, introduce
interpret... 4. read, rede, scan
  6. define 7. explain, expound
  8. construe, diagnose, exegesis
  9. elucidate, translate
interpretation... 5. sense 8. solution
  9. rendering 10. definition
  11. explanation, translation
interpretation, science of...
  7. anagoge (Bib) 8. exegesis
  9. dittology 12. hermeneutics
interpreter... 5. ulema 6. gnomon
  7. exegete, latiner 8. dragoman,
  exponent 9. catechist, exegetist,
  explainer, go−between, hermeneut
  12. oneirocritic (dreams)
interrogate... 3. ask 4. pump, quiz,
  test 5. query 7. examine, inquire
  8. question 9. catechize
interrogation... 7. eroteme (question
  mark) 8. erotisis, question, quizzing
  11. examination, questioning
interrupt... 4. stop 5. break, check
  6. arrest, hinder, thwart 7. break in,

intrude 8. obstruct 9. intercept
11. interpolate
interrupter (electric)... 8. rheotome
interruption... 3. gap 5. pause
6. hiatus 7. interim 8. interval
9. cessation, hindrance
10. suspension 11. obstruction
12. intermission, intervention
13. interposition
intersect... 3. cut 4. meet 5. cross
6. divide, pierce 9. decussate
10. intercross
intersperse... 6. insert, thread
7. scatter 9. diversify
interstice... 4. mesh, pore 5. chink,
crack, space 6. areola 7. crevice
8. interval 10. interspace
intertwine... 5. unite, weave
8. entangle 9. interknit, interlace
10. intertwist
interval... 3. gap 4. rest 5. break,
lapse, pitch, space 6. degree, period,
recess 7. diastem, interim, respite
8. diastema, distance, half step
10. interspace 12. intermission,
interruption
intervals, at... 8. brokenly, fitfully
11. haphazardly, irregularly
12. occasionally 14. intermittently
15. longo intervallo
intervene... 7. intrude, mediate
9. interlude, interpose 10. lie
between 11. come between
intervening (pert to)...
between, among.. 11. interjacent
law.. 5. mesne
space.. 8. distance
time.. 7. interim 9. interlude
interweave... 3. mat 4. plat 5. braid,
plait, plash 6. enlace, raddle, splice,
wattle 8. intermix 9. interlace
13. twist together
intestinal... 7. enteric 8. visceral
intestine (pert to)...
coating.. 4. caul
comb form.. 6. entero
part.. 5. colon, ilium, large, small
6. caecum, rectum 7. jejunum
8. appendix, duodenum
15. alimentary canal
intestines... 4. guts 6. bowels
8. entrails
intimacy... 9. closeness
10. connection, friendship
11. association, familiarity, sociability
intimate... 3. sib 4. hint, near
6. friend, united 8. familiar, friendly,
informal, personal, sociable
9. confidant, innermost
12. confidential
intimation... 3. cue 4. clue, hint
5. trace 7. inkling 9. reference
10. foreboding, indication, suggestion
11. supposition 12. announcement,
notification
intimidate... 3. awe, cow 5. abash,
bully, daunt, deter 7. overawe, terrify
8. browbeat, frighten, threaten
intolerance... 7. bigotry 9. dogmatism,
prejudice 10. impatience, narrowness
12. illiberality
intolerant... 6. narrow 7. bigoted

8. dogmatic 9. impatient
10. prejudiced 11. not enduring
intolerant person... 5. bigot 7. fanatic
intone... 4. sing 5. chant, croon,
sound 7. introit
intoxicated... 3. lit, sot 4. tosy
5. drunk, heady, tipsy 6. boiled
7. fervent, fuddled, maudlin
8. besotted, temulent 9. befuddled
10. inebriated
intractable... 5. tough 6. sullen, unruly
7. restive, willful (wilful) 8. indocile,
perverse, stubborn 9. obstinate,
unbending, unpliable 10. headstrong,
inflexible, refractory 11. unteachable
12. ungovernable
intransitive... 6. neuter, verbal
8. confined 10. in transitu
intrenchment... 2. pa (pah) 4. fort
7. defense, parapet 8. stockade
12. encroachment, infringement
intrepid... 4. bold 5. brave 6. heroic
7. doughty, valiant 8. fearless,
resolute 9. dauntless, undaunted
10. courageous
intrepidity... 5. nerve, valor
7. courage, prowess 8. boldness,
valiancy 9. gallantry
intricacy... 9. sinuosity 10. complexity,
involution, perplexity 11. complexness
12. complication, entanglement
intrigue... 4. plot 5. amour, cabal
6. brigue, scheme 8. artifice,
cheating 9. fascinate 10. conspiracy
11. machination
intrinsic... 4. real, true 5. inner
6. inborn, inbred, inward, native
7. genuine, natural 8. immanent,
implicit, inherent 9. essential,
necessary 11. inseparable
13. indispensable
intrinsically... 5. truly 6. really
10. internally 11. essentially
intrinsic being... 7. essence
introduce... 5. immit, start, usher
6. broach, herald, infuse, insert,
submit 7. bring in, preface, present,
sponsor 8. acquaint, approach,
initiate, innovate 10. inaugurate
11. preinstruct
introduced from foreign country...
6. exotic 10. extraneous
introduced serum... 10. inoculated
introduction... 5. debut, guide, proem
7. introit, isagoge, preface
8. exordium, foreword, preamble
9. insertion 10. innovation
11. instruction, preparation
12. inauguration, presentation
introduction (pert to)...
Biblical.. 9. isagogics
drama (anc).. 8. protasis
new words.. 7. neology
spurious matter.. 13. interpolation
introductory... 9. prefatory, prelusive
11. preliminary
introit... 4. hymn, rite 5. psalm
8. entrance 12. introduction
introrse... (opp of extrorse) 12. facing
inward
introversion... (opp of extroversion)
9. inversion, reticence

intrude... 5. enter 6. invade, meddle
8. encroach, infringe, overstep,
trespass 9. interfere, interlope
intruder... 7. invader 8. outsider
9. buttinsky 10. interloper, trespasser
intrust, entrust... 6. commit
7. confide, consign 8. delegate
10. commission
intuition... 5. hunch 6. noesis, regard
7. insight 9. knowledge, reference
13. contemplation
intuitive... 6. noetic, seeing 7. sensing
10. perceiving 11. instinctive
inulase... 6. enzyme
inunction... 7. unguent 8. inunctum,
ointment
inundate... 3. dip 4. dunk 5. douse,
drunk, flood 6. deluge, engulf
7. baptize, immerse 8. overflow,
submerge 9. overwhelm
10. oversupply
inure... 6. harden, season 7. benefit,
callous, toughen 8. accustom
9. habituate
inurn... 4. bury 5. inter 6. entomb
invade... 4. raid 5. enter (foeman),
usurp 6. attack, infest 7. intrude,
overrun, violate 8. encroach, trespass
invader... 4. Pict 8. attacker, intruder
9. aggressor, assailant 10. trespasser
invalid... 4. null, sick, void, weak
5. frail 6. feeble, infirm, sickly
8. nugatory 11. ineffectual
14. valetudinarian
invalidate... 4. undo 5. annul, quash
7. abolish, nullify, vitiate 8. disprove
10. disqualify, neutralize
invalidism... 13. indisposition
17. valetudinarianism
invaluable... 6. useful 8. precious
9. priceless, worthless
11. inestimable
invariable... 7. uniform 8. constant
10. unchanging 12. unchangeable
invasion... 4. raid 5. foray 6. attack,
breach, inroad 8. entrance (hostile)
9. incursion, intrusion, irruption
10. infraction 11. infestation
invective... 5. abuse, curse 6. tirade
7. inveigh, railing 8. diatribe
10. revilement 11. malediction
12. vituperation
inveigle... 4. lure, rope 5. snare
6. allure, entice, entrap, seduce
7. deceive, wheedle 10. lead astray
invent... 4. coin 5. frame 6. create,
design, devise 7. concoct 8. discover
9. fabricate (mentally), originate
inventive... 6. adroit 7. fertile
8. creative, original 9. ingenious
inventor... 7. creator 8. imaginer
10. discoverer, originator
inventor, discoverer of...
airplane.. 6. Fokker, Wright (Bros)
baseball.. 9. Doubleday
brake (safety).. 4. Otis
cotton gin.. 7. Whitney
dynamite.. 6. Nobel
electric light.. 6. Edison
elevator.. 4. Otis
gun.. 4. Colt 5. Maxim 9. Remington
harp (Bib).. 5. Jubal

lamp (safety).. 4. Davy
phonograph.. 6. Edison
printing.. 9. Gutenberg
radio.. 8. De Forest
sewing machine.. 4. Howe
steamboat.. 5. Fitch 6. Fulton
steam engine.. 4. Watt
telegraph.. 5. Morse
wireless.. 7. Marconi
X–ray.. 8. Roentgen
inventory... 4. list 5. index 7. account
8. register 9. catalogue (catalog)
10. tally sheet
inverse... 8. inverted, opposite,
reversed
inversely club–shaped... 9. obclavate
inversely oval... 7. obovate
inversion... 8. overturn, reversal
9. overthrow, reversion
10. conversion 12. introversion
invert... 7. capsize, convert, pervert
(obs), reverse, tip over 8. overturn
9. transpose 10. turn turtle
invertebrate... 5. polyp 6. insect,
sponge 7. mollusk 9. spineless
10. weak–willed
invest... 3. don 4. vest, wrap
5. array, dress, endow, indue, spend
6. clothe 7. empower, envelop,
instate 8. surround
invest (pert to)...
authority.. 8. accredit, sanction
ministry.. 6. ordain
sovereignty.. 8. enthrone
investigate... 3. pry 4. sift 5. probe,
study, track 6. excuse, search
7. discuss, explore 8. indagate
10. scrutinize
investigation... 6. examen 7. inquiry,
zetetic 8. research 9. discovery,
heuristic 10. discussion
11. examination
investiture... 7. clothes, vesture
8. clothing, covering 9. induction
10. holy orders, investment (money),
ordination 11. instatement
12. installation 15. enfranchisement
investment... 5. siege 7. finance,
garment 8. blockade, clothing,
covering, purchase, vestment
9. endowment 11. empowerment
investment list... 9. portfolio
inveterate... 3. old 6. rooted
7. chronic 8. habitual, hardened
9. confirmed, ingrained
10. deep–rooted 11. established,
traditional 15. long–established
invidious... 6. odious, ornery
7. envious, hateful 9. malignant
14. discriminating (unjustly)
invigorate... 3. pep 5. brace, cheer,
nerve, renew 6. vivify 7. animate,
enliven, fortify, refresh 8. energize
9. stimulate 10. exhilarate,
strengthen
invigorating... 4. cool 5. tonic
8. cheering 10. energizing,
life–giving, refreshing 11. stimulating
invincible... 10. unbeatable
11. indomitable 13. unconquerable
inviolate... 6. sacred, secret
8. faithful, unbroken 9. unchanged,

undefiled, unstained 10. inviolable,
unimpaired, unprofound
13. incorruptible
invisible... 3. hid 6. hidden
10. indistinct, unapparent
13. infinitesimal, undiscernible,
unperceivable
Invisible, The... 3. God
11. Rosicrucian 16. German
Protestant
invisible emanation... 4. aura
invitation... 3. bid 4. call 7. bidding,
summons 10. allurement, inducement
12. solicitation
invite... 3. ask, beg, bid, try 4. bade
5. court, order, tempt 6. allure,
entice, induce 7. request, solicit
9. encourage
invocation... 4. call, plea, rite
6. appeal, prayer, sermon
7. summons 8. entreaty
11. conjuration, incantation
12. supplication
invoice... 4. bill 7. account (written)
8. manifest 9. reckoning 12. bill of
lading
invoke... 3. beg 4. pray 6. appeal
7. address, conjure, entreat, implore,
solicit 8. draw down 10. supplicate
involuntary... 9. not willed, reluctant,
unwilling, unwitting 11. instinctive,
spontaneous 13. unintentional
involve... 3. lap 4. coil, wind, wrap
5. imply 6. employ, entail, evince,
infold 7. concern, ensnare, entwine,
envelop, include 8. interest
9. embarrass, implicate
10. complicate 11. incriminate
involved... 7. complex, implied
8. involute, tortuous 9. engrossed
10. implicated
involving punishment... 8. punitive
invulnerable... 10. invincible
11. impregnable, insuperable
12. impenetrable, unassailable
inward... 4. into 5. entad, inner
6. inside 7. ingoing, muffled
8. interior, internal 9. spiritual
10. internally
inwards... 8. entrails 10. intestines
Io... 7. goddess (Gr) 9. butterfly,
satellite (of Jupiter)
iodine, iodin (pert to)...
comb form.. 3. iod 4. iodo
compound.. 6. iodide
containing.. 5. iodic 6. iodous
poisoning.. 6. iodism 9. iododerma
source.. 4. kelp 8. sea water 9. salt
peter 12. thryoid gland
standard.. 9. idiometry
substitute.. 7. Aristol
ion... 5. anion 6. cation (kation)
8. electron, particle (Elec)
Ionian (pert to)...
city.. 4. Teos (birthplace of Anacreon)
islands.. 5. Greek 9. Asia Minor
mode (Mus).. 6. Lydian
Ionic (pert to)...
architecture.. 5. Order
dialect.. 5. Greek
poetry.. 4. foot 5. meter
printing.. 4. type

iota... 3. ace, jot 4. atom, mite, star
(9th brightest), whit 6. letter (Gr),
tittle 8. particle
Iowa...
capital.. 9. Des Moines
city.. 4. Ames 8. Waterloo
9. Davenport, Fort Dodge,
Marquette, Sioux City 10. West
Branch 11. Cedar Rapids
famed attractions.. 10. Hoover home
12. Effigy Mounds 17. Little Brown
Church
famed first.. 12. apple orchard (1799)
famed names.. 6. Joliet 7. Dubuque
9. Marquette
flower.. 8. wild rose
locale.. 8. farm belt (Midwest)
river.. 8. Missouri 11. Mississippi
State admission.. 11. twenty–ninth
(1846)
State nickname.. 7. Hawkeye
ipecac... 4. evea 6. emetic 7. emetive
9. purgative
irade... 6. decree (Turk)
Iran... see also *Iranian*
capital.. 7. Teheran (Tehran)
city.. 6. Abadan, Shiraz 7. Isfahan
conqueror.. 6. Darius 9. Alexander
founder.. 5. Cyrus (the Great)
lake.. 7. Rezaieh
mountain.. 6. Elburz, Zagros
8. Damavand (peak)
parliament.. 6. Majlis (Mejlis)
people.. 3. Tat 7. Indians
ruins.. 10. Persepolis (Shiraz)
Iranian (pert to)...
almond.. 5. badam
books.. 5. Koran, Yasma 6. Avesta
country.. 4. Elam 5. Media
demigod.. 4. Yima
demon.. 7. Ahriman
diadem.. 3. taj
dynasty.. 6. Safavi, Seljuk
10. Sassanidae
fire worshiper.. 5. Parsi (Parsee)
god.. 6. Ormazd (Supreme) 7. Mithras
Koran student.. 5. hafiz
poet.. 4. Omar 5. Saadi
Relig founder.. 9. Zoroaster
tapestry.. 7. susanee
tentmaker.. 4. Omar
Iraq, Mesopotamia...
capital.. 6. Bagdad (Baghdad)
culture (anc).. 8. Sumerian
historic city.. 2. Ur 5. Eridu
7. Babylon, Nineveh
historic Valley.. 15. Tigris–Euphrates
port.. 5. Basra (Busrah)
product.. 3. oil 4. date 5. sheep
river.. 6. Tigris 9. Euphrates
irascibility... 3. ire 6. choler
9. crossness, testiness 10. perversity
11. waspishness 12. churlishness,
irritability
irate... 3. hot 5. angry, wroth
7. enraged 8. incensed 9. irascible
ire... 5. anger, wrath 7. madness
8. vexation 9. vehemence
10. enragement, resentment
12. exasperation
ireful... 5. angry, wroth 7. iracund
9. irascible 10. passionate

Ireland... 4. Eire, Erin 5. Irena 6. Old
    Sod, Ulster 8. Hibernia 9. Innisfail
    11. Emerald Isle, Erin go brath
    14. Ireland Forever
Ireland (pert to)... see also *Irish*
    Bay.. 6. Bantry, Dingle, Galway
        7. Donegal
    capital.. 4. Tara (old) 6. Dublin
    channel.. 5. North 9. St George's
    city.. 4. Cobh (Queenstown), Cork,
        Tara 6. Galway, Tralee, Ulster
        7. Belfast, Donegal, Kildare, Wexford
        8. Kilkenny, Limerick 9. Tipperary
    island.. 4. Aran
    legislature.. 4. Dail
    mountain.. 7. Errigal 13. Carrantuohill
    river.. 3. Lee 4. Erne, Suir 6. Liffey
        7. Shannon
    sea.. 5. Irish
    seaport.. 4. Cobh 6. Tralee
    seat of archbishops.. 6. Armagh
irenic... 7. henotic 8. peaceful
    11. harmonizing 12. conciliatory
iridescent... 7. opaline 9. prismatic
    10. opalescent
iris... 4. flag 6. flower 7. rainbow
iris (pert to)...
    astronomy.. 8. asteroid (7th)
    color.. 11. reddish–blue
    eye part.. 4. uvea 5. irian
    Florentine.. 5. orris (orrice)
    inflammation.. 6. iritis
    mineral.. 6. quartz (iridescent)
Iris, goddess... 7. rainbow
Irish (pert to)...
    alphabet (early).. 4. ogam (ogham)
    battle cry.. 3. abu (aboo) 9. To
        Victory 11. Erin go brath
    cattle.. 5. Kerry
    churchman.. 7. erenach (herenach)
    club, cudgel.. 10. shillalagh (shillalah)
    convention (anc).. 4. Feis 10. Feis of
        Tara
    cordial.. 10. usquebaugh
    dagger (anc).. 5. skean
    dance.. 3. jig 4. rink 10. rinkafadda
    emblem.. 8. shamrock
    exclamation.. 3. aru 5. arrah
    fairy, spirit.. 4. shee (sidhe)
        7. banshee (banshie) 10. leprechaun
    festival.. 4. feis
    goblin.. 5. pooka
    god.. 3. Ler (sea)
    goddess.. 4. Dana
    king's home.. 4. Tara
    landholding.. 7. rundale
    legislature.. 10. Oireachtas (House)
        11. Dail Eireann (Chamber)
        13. Seanad Eireann (Senate)
    liquor house (illegal).. 7. shebeen
    love, sweetheart.. 3. gra
    moss.. 9. carrageen
    peasant.. 4. kern (lerne)
    pig.. 5. bonav
    policeman.. 8. spalpeen
    potato city.. 7. Youghal
    queen (folklore).. 4. Medb
    Society (secret).. 6. Fenian
    soldier.. 4. kern (kerne) 10. galloglass
    tenant.. 4. saer
    tribal lord.. 6. tanist
    verse.. 4. rann

whisky, whiskey (illegal).. 6. poteen
    (potheen)
Irish (people)...
    ancestor (fabled).. 3. Mil 6. Miledh
    author.. 4. Shaw 5. Wilde
    chemist.. 5. Boyle
    composer.. 7. Herbert
    Irishman.. 4. Aire, Celt, Gael
        6. Teague 8. Milesian 9. Hibernian,
        Orangeman 10. Eireannach
    lawyer.. 6. brehon
    Nuns (Order).. 15. Ladies of Loretto
    patriot.. 5. Emmet, Tandy 6. Oakboy
    poet.. 5. Colum, Moore, Wilde, Yeats
        7. Russell (George)
    refugee.. 7. fuidhir
    saint (patron).. 7. Patrick
    Saxon.. 8. Sasanach
    sea robbers (Myth).. 9. Fomorians
    surgeon.. 6. Colles
    tribe (family).. 4. sept 5. cinel
irk... 3. vex 4. bore, tire 5. annoy,
    weary 6. nettle 7. disgust, trouble
    10. exasperate
irksome... 5. vexed, weary 7. operose,
    painful, tedious 8. annoying
    9. fatiguing, vexatious, wearisome
    10. burdensome, exhausting,
    monotonous 12. disagreeable
iron... 2. Fe (symbol) 5. harsh, metal,
    power, press 6. ferrum, fetter,
    mangle, pistol, severe 7. firearm,
    manacle, shackle, sideros
    8. firmness, handcuff, hardness,
    strength 10. inflexible, unyielding
    11. unrelenting
iron (pert to)...
    casting.. 5. mitis
    comb form.. 5. ferro 6. sidero
    compound.. 5. steel
    containing.. 6. ferric
    dog.. 7. firedog
    dross.. 6. sinter
    herb.. 8. Vernonia 9. ironweeds
    lump.. 3. pig
    magnet.. 8. armature
    meteoric.. 8. siderite
    ore.. 7. turgite 8. hematite, siderite
        11. sesquioxide
    ref to.. 6. ferric 7. ferrous
        8. siderous
    rod.. 5. punty (puntee)
    salts of.. 10. chalybeate
    sand.. 7. iserine
    science of.. 10. siderology
    symbol.. 2. Fe
    tailor's.. 5. goose
    tool.. 6. lifter
    vessel, basket.. 7. cresset
ironclad... 6. severe 7. armored,
    Monitor (ship) 8. exacting, rigorous
    9. stringent
ironic, ironical... 3. dry 7. cynical,
    satiric 9. sarcastic 10. figurative
    11. Rabelaisian
irons... 5. gyves 6. chains 7. fetters
    8. manacles, shackles 9. handcuffs
Ironsides... 7. cavalry (Cromwell's)
    8. Cromwell
ironwood... 4. acle 5. olive 6. colima
    7. breakax 8. hornbeam
    9. stavewood

irony... 6. banter, satire 7. lampoon, sarcasm 8. ridicule
Iroquoian Indian... 4. Erie 5. Huron 6. Cayuga, Mohawk, Oneida, Seneca 7. Wyandot 8. Cherokee, Onondaga 9. Conestoga, Tuscarora
Iroquois (pert to)...
   famed.. 11. Five Nations
   native of.. 7. New York 9. Wisconsin
   tribes (Five).. 6. Cayuga, Mohawk, Oneida, Seneca 8. Onondaga
irrational... 6. stupid 9. fanatical, illogical, senseless 10. ridiculous 11. impractical 12. preposterous, unreasonable 13. unintelligent
irregular... 4. wild 5. erose, rough 6. fitful, rugged, uneven 7. atactic, crooked, devious, erratic, mutable, styptic, unequal 8. aberrent, abnormal, atypical, informal, variable 9. anomalous, desultory, distorted, eccentric, haphazard, orderless, unsettled 10. changeable, immoderate, inconstant 11. intemperate 12. unsystematic
irregularity... 6. ataxia (muscular) 7. anomaly 8. disorder 9. deviation 10. distortion 11. abnormality, informality 12. eccentricity
irrelevant... 7. foreign 9. unrelated 10. extraneous 11. impertinent, unessential 12. inconsequent 13. insignificant
irreligious... 5. pagan 7. godless, impious, profane 11. unreligious
irreparable... 4. gone, lost 6. ruined 11. irrevocable 12. incorrigible, irremediable 13. irrecoverable, irretrievable
irrepressible... 7. Homeric (laughter) 12. ungovernable, unrestrained
irrepressible conflict... 8. civil war
irreproachable... 7. perfect 9. blameless 10. impeccable, inculpable
irresolute... 6. fickle, unsure 8. doubtful, unstable 9. uncertain, undecided 10. capricious, changeable, inconstant 12. undetermined
irresolution... 10. fickleness, indecision 11. fluctuation, uncertainty, vacillation 14. capriciousness
irresponsible... 6. fickle, lawless 8. carefree 9. insolvent 12. independable 13. unaccountable, untrustworthy
irretrievable... 8. hopeless 9. incurable 11. irreparable 12. irremediable, unchangeable 13. irrecoverable
irreverence... 7. impiety 8. dishonor 9. profanity 10. disrespect
irrevocable... 3. end 4. past 5. final 10. inevitable, past recall 11. unalterable 12. beyond recall, unchangeable
irrigate... 3. wet 5. water 6. dilute, sluice 7. moisten, refresh
irritable... 4. edgy 5. cross, techy, testy 6. cranky, ornery, touchy 7. fretful, iracund, peevish, tempery,

twitchy 8. snappish
irritate... 3. irk, nag, vex 4. fret, gall, rasp, rile 5. anger, annoy, chafe, cross, grate, peeve, pique, rouse, sting, tease 6. excite, incite, madden, needle, nettle, rankle 7. incense, provoke 10. exacerbate, exasperate 14. rub the wrong way
irritated... 4. sore 5. afret, testy 6. peeved 7. annoyed, nettled, rankled 8. provoked
irritation... 4. itch 5. pique 6. temper 9. annoyance 10. resentment 12. exasperation
irruption... 5. foray 6. inroad 8. invasion 9. incursion
Irving pseudonym... 13. Knickerbocker (Diedrich)
is... 6. exists 10. represents 11. personifies
Isaac (pert to)...
   Bib.. 9. patriarch (Heb)
   father of.. 4. Esau 5. Jacob
   grandfather of.. 4. Edom
   husband of.. 7. Rebekah
   son of.. 5. Sarah 7. Abraham
Ishmael (pert to)...
   ancestor.. 11. Ishmaelites
   Bib.. 6. pariah 7. outcast
   father of.. 8. Nebaioth
   son of.. 5. Hagar 7. Abraham
isinglass... 4. huso, mica 7. gelatin 8. agar–agar
Isis (pert to)...
   daughter of.. 3. Geb, Nut
   goddess of.. 9. fertility 10. motherhood
   identified with.. 7. Dog Star
   mother of.. 4. Sept (Horus)
   represented (at times).. 9. cow–headed
   shrine of.. 5. Iseum (Iseium)
   wife of.. 6. Osiris
Islam, religion (pert to)...
   founder.. 7. Mahomet
   God.. 5. Allah
   people.. 7. Moslems
   prophet.. 8. Mohammed
Islamic (pert to)...
   convert.. 5. ansar
   holy city.. 5. Mecca 6. Medina
   mosque.. 6. masjid
   pilgrimage.. 5. Kaaba (Caaba) 10. Black Stone
   Supreme Being.. 5. Allah
   teacher.. 4. alim 5. ulema 6. mullah (mulla)
island... 3. ait, cay, ile, key 4. calf, cayo, eyot, holm, isle, reef 5. atoll, islet 7. isolate 8. insulate
island (pert to)...
   city.. 8. Montreal
   coral.. 5. atoll 8. Zanzibar
   enchanted.. 4. Bali
   fabled.. 4. Meru 6. Avalon, Bimini 8. Atlantis
   fabulous.. 7. Zangbar
   group.. 8. Antilles, Marshall 11. archipelago
   inhabitant, native.. 7. nesiote 8. islander
   universe (Astron).. 6. galaxy

Island of ...
Langerhans .. 8. pancreas
Odysseus .. 6. Ithaca
Reil .. 5. brain
Saints .. 4. Erin
Isle of Man ...
Celtic name .. 4. Manx
city .. 4. Peel 6. Ramsey 7. Douglas
division .. 5. Treen
judge .. 8. deemster (dempster)
legislature .. 7. Tynwald
mountain peak .. 8. Snaefell
Northern point .. 4. Ayre
site .. 8. Irish sea
Isle of Wight ...
Queen's summer home .. 12. Osborne
   House
site .. 10. English Sea
sport (famed) .. 9. yacht race
town .. 7. Newport
watering place .. 4. Ryde
Isles of Galway Bay ... 4. Aran
ism ... 4. cult 5. dogma, ideal, tenet
   6. belief, school, system 8. doctrine,
   practice 11. abnormality
isochromatic ... 9. same color
isochronal ... 9. equal time
   11. uniform time
isocracy ... 9. equal rule 10. equal
   power
isodont (Zool) ... 10. alike teeth
isogonal ... 11. equal angles
isolate ... 4. isle 6. enisle 7. seclude
   8. insulate, separate 9. segregate,
   sequester 10. quarantine
isolation ... 8. escapism, solitude
   9. seclusion 10. insulation, loneliness,
   separation 11. segregation
isomer ... 7. metamer 8. compound
   (Chem)
isonomy ... 11. equal rights
isonym ... 7. paronym 8. same name
isosceles ... 10. equal sides (triangle)
Israel (Bib) ... 4. Jews 5. Jacob, Zions
   13. Hebrew Kingdom
Israel (pert to) ... see also *Israelite*
appellation .. 8. Jeshurun
capital .. 9. Jerusalem
city .. 4. Acre 5. Elath, Haifa, Jaffa
   7. Galilee, Jericho, Tel Aviv
desert .. 5. Negev
dust storm .. 7. khamsin
lawgiver .. 5. Moses
Plain of .. 6. Sharon
priest .. 3. Eli
river .. 6. Jordan
sea .. 4. Dead 7. Galilee
song (Zionist) .. 8. Hatikvah
statesman .. 4. Meir 5. Begin
Israelite (pert to) ...
hero .. 6. Gideon
judge .. 4. Elon 8. Jephthah
king .. 4. Ahab, Jehu, Saul (1st)
   5. David (2nd) 7. Solomon
lawgiver .. 5. Moses
priest .. 3. Eli
tribe .. 3. Dan 5. Asher 6. Reuben
tribe, priestly .. 4. Levi
issue ... 3. son 4. come, emit, flow,
   gush 5. arise, child, sally, spout,
   stock, topic, utter 6. effect, emerge,
   escape, sortie, source, upshot
   7. edition, emanate, proceed, product,
   progeny 8. question 9. emergence,
   offspring, posterity 11. consequence,
   publication
Istanbul (Constantinople) ...
ancient name .. 9. Byzantium
capital of .. 6. Turkey (to 1923)
foreign quarter .. 4. Pera
Greek quarter .. 5. Fanar
site .. 8. Bosporus 10. Golden Horn
isthmus (pert to) ...
American .. 6. Panama
anatomy .. 6. fauces
Greek (anc) .. 7. Corinth
Siam .. 3. Kra
it ... 5. charm, thing 6. itself, person
   7. egotist, pronoun
Ita ... 4. Acta 7. Negrito
Italian (pert to) ... see also *Italy*
card game .. 5. tarot
carriage .. 7. vettura
cathedral .. 5. duomo
cheese .. 6. Romano 8. Parmesan
   10. mozzarella
condiment .. 6. tamara (tamarind)
deity .. 4. faun
dish .. 5. pizza 7. calzone 8. braciola
   11. saltimbocca
dome, peak .. 4. cima
entertainment .. 5. festa 7. ridotto
food .. see *pasta*
grape .. 6. verdea
hamlet .. 5. casal
house .. 4. casa 6. casino (summer)
inlay .. 6. tarsia
inn .. 7. locanda
innkeeper .. 7. padrone
lady .. 5. donna 7. signora
lake .. 4. lago
law .. 6. Latium 8. Jus Latii
lover .. 7. amoroso
magistrate (anc) .. 8. podesta
marble .. 4. Neri 7. carrara, cipolin
marsh .. 7. maremma
opera house .. 7. La Scala (1778)
peasant .. 7. paesano 9. contadino
photographers .. 9. paparazzi (press)
pottery .. 8. majolica
secret society .. 6. Maffia (Mafia)
   7. Camorra
sheep .. 6. merino
vessel .. 9. trabacolo
wind (hot) .. 7. sirocco
wine .. 4. Asti 5. Capri 7. Chianti,
   Orvieto 12. Asti Spumante
Italian (pert to people) ...
anti–Fascist .. 6. Sforza
architect .. 8. Bramante
astronomer .. 6. Secchi 7. Galileo
author .. 5. Dante
deity .. 6. Faunus
dictator .. 9. Mussolini
educator .. 10. Montessori
explorer .. 8. Columbus, Vespucci
   9. Marco Polo
family (princely) .. 4. Este 5. Doria
   6. Medici
family (violin) .. 5. Amati
friend (outside) .. 10. Italophile
geographer .. 8. Amoretti
goddess .. 3. Ops 4. Juno 5. Diana
hero .. 7. Orlando

historian.. **4**. Dion **5**. Cantu
king.. **7**. Umberto
musician.. **5**. Guido, Verdi **7**. Puccini,
  Rossini **9**. Scarlatti
naturalist.. **4**. Poli
noblewoman.. **8**. Marchesa
  11. Marchioness
painter.. **5**. Lippi **6**. Giotti **7**. da
  Vinci, Raphael **10**. Botticelli
  11. Della Robbia **12**. Michelangelo
patriot.. **7**. Foscolo **9**. Garibaldi
people.. **7**. Italici **8**. Umbrians
  9. Etruscans, Ligurians
philosopher.. **7**. Rosmini
physician.. **5**. Abano **9**. Eustachio
physicist.. **5**. Volta **7**. Galvani,
  Marconi
poet.. **4**. Redi **5**. Dante, Tasso
  7. Manzoni **8**. Annunzio, Casanova,
  Petrarch **9**. Boccaccio
saint.. **4**. Neri **7**. Aquinas (Thomas)
sculptor.. **5**. Dupre, Leoni
  8. Ammanati **12**. Michelangelo
singer.. **5**. Patti **6**. Caruso
statesman.. **5**. Rossi **8**. Gioberti
  11. Machiavelli
theologian.. **7**. Peronne
tribe (anc).. **5**. Aequi
Italy...
  Alps.. **5**. Cozie **6**. Carnac, Julian
  7. Atesine, Letiche, Pennine
  8. Maritime **9**. Lepontine
  capital.. **4**. Rome
  city.. **4**. Lodi, Pisa **5**. Anona, Fiume,
  Genoa, Milan, Padua, Pavia, Trent,
  Turin **6**. Mantua, Modena, Naples,
  Spezia, Venice, Verona **7**. Messina,
  Palermo, Pompeii, Ravenna, Trieste
  8. Brandisi, Florence, Sorrento
  commune.. **6**. Rivoli (Hist) **7**. Trieste
  country (anc).. **7**. Etruria, Lucania,
  Tuscany
  gulf.. **7**. Salerno
  historical site.. **10**. Blue Grotto
  18. Leaning Tower of Pisa
  island.. **4**. Elba **5**. Capri, Leros
  6. Eschia, Sicily **8**. Sardinia
  lake.. **4**. Como **6**. Albano, Lugano
  8. Maggiore
  mountain.. **4**. Alps, Rosa **5**. Blanc
  12. Gran Paradiso
  port (fishing).. **6**. Amalfi
  resort.. **4**. Lido **5**. Capri **6**. Agnone
  7. Riviera
  river.. **2**. Po **4**. Arno **5**. Tiber
  sea.. **6**. Ionian **8**. Apennine

  10. Tyrrhenian
  strait.. **7**. Messina, Obranto
  volcano.. **4**. Etna **8**. Vesuvius
  9. Stromboli
itch... **4**. reef, riff **5**. mange, psora
  6. desire, eczema **7**. scabies, sycosis
  9. cacoethes, hankering, psoriasis,
  sensation **10**. irritation
ite... **8**. adherent, disciple, follower
item... **3**. bit **4**. news **5**. asset, entry,
  scrap, topic **6**. detail **7**. article,
  integer **9**. commodity
  10. memorandum **11**. information
iter... **4**. eyre, road (Rom) **7**. circuit
iterate... **6**. recite, repeat, retell,
  review **7**. recount **8**. rehearse
iteration... **5**. recap **10**. repetition
  11. restatement
ithand... **8**. constant, diligent
  14. unintermittent
itinerant... **5**. mover, nomad **6**. roamer
  7. nomadic **8**. gadabout **9**. traveling,
  unsettled, wandering, wayfaring
itinerary... **4**. gest (royal), plan
  5. route **6**. prayer, record
  8. register, roadbook **9**. directory,
  guidebook
Ivanhoe (pert to)...
  author.. **5**. Scott
  character.. **5**. Boeuf **6**. Cedric,
  Rowena, Ulrica
  hero.. **7**. Ivanhoe
ivories (pert to)...
  anatomy.. **5**. teeth
  game.. **4**. dice
  piano.. **4**. keys
ivory (pert to)...
  anatomy.. **5**. tooth **7**. dentine
  block.. **4**. dice **7**. tessera
  carving.. **9**. toreutics
  color.. **5**. white (off)
  Latin.. **4**. ebur
  mixture (dust, cement).. **7**. eburine
  plum.. **11**. wintergreen
  tower.. **7**. retreat
ivy... **5**. Rheus, sumac **11**. Hedera
  helix
iwa... **11**. frigate bird
IWW... **6**. sab–cat (emblem), wabbly
  (Chin), wobbly
Izaac Walton... **9**. fisherman
izar (Hind)... **4**. star **7**. garment **9**. loin
  .cloth
izle... **4**. root **5**. ember, spark
Izmir... **6**. Smyrna
izzat... **5**. honor **6**. credit **8**. prestige
  10. reputation

J

J... 3. Jay 6. letter (10th)
ja (Ger)... 3. yes
jaal goat... 4. ibex 5. beden
jab... 3. dig, hit, jag 4. poke, prod,
  stab 5. punch 6. strike, thrust
jabber... 4. chat 5. prate 6. babble,
  gabble, jargon 7. chatter, twaddle
  8. nonsense 9. gibberish
Jabberwock... 6. Jubjub 7. monster
  (Through the Looking Glass)
Jabberwocky... 4. poem 6. prolix
  8. nonsense 10. double talk
jabble... 6. splash 7. dashing
  8. rippling 9. agitation, confusion,
  splashing
jabiru... 5. stork
jack... 3. can, jug, man 4. card, coat,
  flag, male, pump 5. hoist, knave,
  money 6. lifter, sailor 7. mariner
  8. nickname
jackal... 3. dog (wild) 4. dieb, kola,
  Thos 7. cat's–paw 8. henchman
jackass... 3. ass 4. deer (mule), dolt,
  fool, hare, nerd 6. clover, donkey,
  rabbit 7. morwong, penguin, witling
  9. blockhead
jackdaw... 3. daw, kae 4. crow
  7. grackle
jacket... 4. coat, Eton, pelt 5. cover
  (book) 6. blazer, blouse, bolero,
  casing, jerkin, jumper, reefer
  7. garment, Mae West, wrapper
jacket (pert to)...
  Arctic .. 6. anorak
  armor .. 5. acton
  Eskimo .. 6. temiak
  horseback riding .. 7. hacking (jacket)
  knitted .. 6. jersey, sontag 7. sweater
  8. cardigan
  Levant .. 5. grego
  Scottish .. 4. jupe
  Spanish .. 8. chaqueta
Jack Ketch... 7. hangman (Eng)
  11. executioner (public)
jackknife... 6. barlow 8. penknife
  11. toadstabber, toadsticker
jackstones... 4. dibs, game
  7. pebbles
Jacob... 6. Israel 9. patriarch
Jacob (pert to)...
  brother .. 4. Edom, Esau
  daughter .. 5. Dinah
  father–in–law .. 5. Laban
  parents .. 5. Isaac 7. Rebekah
  retreat .. 5. Haran
  son .. 3. Gad, Dan 4. Levi 5. Asher,
  Judah 6. Reuben (oldest)
  wife .. 4. Leah 6. Rachel
Jacobin... 4. Club 5. Friar (Dominican)
  7. plotter, radical, Society

8. Democrat (Fr 1789)
Jacob's ladder... 4. herb 8. hyacinth
  10. belladonna 11. bittersweet
  12. Solomon's seal
jade... 4. bore, tire 5. green, horse,
  stone, wench 7. fatigue 8. strumpet
jaded... 8. fatigued, shopworn
  9. dissolute 10. bedraggled
jaeger (jager)... 4. gull (like), skua
  6. teaser
jager... 6. hunter 7. diamond
  8. huntsman, rifleman
jagged... 5. erose, rough, sharp
  6. barbed, pinked, ragged, rugged
  7. cutting, notched, pointed, slashed
  8. serrated 10. saw–toothed
jagua... 4. palm 7. genipap
jaguar... 3. cat 4. puma 5. ounce
  6. cougar 7. panther 11. snow
  leopard
Jah (Heb)... 3. God 7. Jehovah
jai alai... 4. game 5. cesta 6. pelota
  7. fronton
jail... 3. jug 4. brig, gaol 5. clink
  6. cooler, lockup 7. slammer (sl)
  8. hoosegow 9. Bridewell (London),
  calaboose 11. incarcerate
jailer, jailor... 5. guard 6. gaoler,
  keeper, warden 7. alcaide, turnkey
jail sentence... 3. rap
jalousie... 5. blind 7. shutter
Jamaica...
  beverage .. 3. rum 4. jake
  capital .. 8. Kingston
  cucumber .. 7. gherkin
  ebony .. 10. crocuswood
  island .. 10. West Indies
  pepper .. 8. allspice
  tree (drug) .. 7. quassia
jangle... 5. brawl, chide, noise, prate
  6. babble, gossip 7. chatter, grate on,
  quarrel, ringing, whimper
Janizary (anc)... 5. slave 7. soldier
Janus (Rom)... 3. god (two–faced)
Japan... 5. Jipun (Chin), Nihon, Nisei
  6. Nippon 7. Cipango (of Marco
  Polo)
Japan... see also *Japanese*
  capital .. 4. Nara (anc) 5. Kyoto (anc),
  Tokyo
  city .. 4. Kobe 7. Sapporo
  8. Kawasaki, Kumamoto, Nagasaki,
  Yokohama, Yokosuka 9. Hiroshima
  10. Kitakyushu
  current .. 8. Kuroshio
  islands .. 6. Honshu, Kyushu
  7. Shikoku 9. Haikkaido (Yezo)
  mountain .. 8. Fujiyama
  naval base .. 8. Yokosuka
  port .. 4. Kobe 5. Osaka 6. Nagoya

J N

8. Yokohama
protectorate .. **9**. Manchukuo
river .. **4**. Yalu (Annock)
shrine .. **7**. Toshogu (at Nikko)
spring (hot) .. **6**. Hakone
volcano .. **9**. Asamayama
Japanese (pert to) ...
airplane .. **4**. Zero
annals, chronicles .. **7**. Nihongi
apricot .. **3**. ume
army (conscription) .. **6**. geneki
army officer .. **7**. samurai
art of self–defense .. **4**. judo **7**. jujitsu
   (jujutsu, jiujutsu)
badge (family) .. **3**. mon
banjo .. **7**. samisen
battle cry .. **6**. banzai
brazier .. **7**. hibachi
button (carved) .. **7**. netsuke
cape .. **4**. mino
cedar .. **4**. sugi
chess .. **5**. shogi
church (Buddhist) .. **4**. tera
circle, ship (suffix) .. **4**. maru
deer .. **4**. sika
dog .. **6**. tanate
drama .. **4**. no **6**. no–gaku
drink .. **4**. sake
entertainer .. **6**. geisha
festival .. **3**. Bon **15**. Feast of Lanterns
fish .. **3**. ayu, tai **4**. fugu
flower arranging .. **7**. ikebano
flower design .. **10**. Shin, Soe, Tai
   (Heaven, Man, Earth)
game (forfeits) .. **3**. ken
gateway .. **5**. torii
girdle .. **3**. obi
girdle box .. **4**. inro
greeting .. **6**. banzai
herb (edible) .. **3**. udo
legislature .. **4**. Diet
litter (covered) .. **7**. norimon
news agency .. **5**. domei
newspaper (Tokyo) .. **12**. Asahi
   Shimbun
outlaw .. **5**. ronin
pagoda .. **3**. taa
painting school .. **4**. Kano
palanquin, litter .. **4**. pago **7**. norimon
persimmon .. **4**. kaki
plant .. **3**. udo (edible) **6**. sugamo
porgy .. **3**. tai (fish)
pottery .. **7**. Satsuma
prefecture .. **2**. fu
radish .. **6**. daikon
religion .. **6**. Shinto **8**. Buddhism
   9. Shintoism
robe .. **6**. kimono
salmon .. **4**. masu
screen (partition) .. **5**. shoji
seaweed .. **4**. nori
self–defense, art of .. **4**. judo **7**. jujitsu
   (jujutsu, jiujutsu)
ship suffix .. **4**. maru
shout (greeting) .. **6**. banzai
shrine .. **7**. Toshogu (at Nikko)
silk .. **7**. habutai **8**. chirimen (crepe)
silkworm .. **4**. eria **7**. yamamai
sock (separate big toe) .. **4**. tabi
song .. **3**. uta
suicide .. **7**. seppuku **8**. hara–kiri
   (hari–kari)

tree .. **5**. akeki, kiaki **7**. camphor,
   hinooki
verse .. **5**. hokku, tanka **6**. haikai
wrestling .. **4**. sumo
Japanese people ...
aborigine .. **4**. Ainu (Aino)
admiral .. **3**. Ito **4**. Togo
admirer .. **11**. Japanophile
American–born .. **5**. Issei, Nisei
army officer .. **7**. samurai
baron .. **6**. daimio
Buddha, Great .. **8**. Daibutsu
caste (nobility) .. **7**. kwazoku
clan .. **7**. Satsuma **8**. Fujiwara,
   Minamoto
deity .. **5**. Amita (Amida) **8**. Amitabba
Emperor .. **8**. Hirohito
Emperor, founder .. **5**. Jimmu (660
   BC)
Emperor, title .. **5**. Tenno **6**. Mikado
God of Happiness .. **7**. Jurojin
   10. Fuku–roku ju
nobility (caste) .. **7**. kwazoku
outlaw .. **5**. ronin
paradise (of Amita) .. **4**. Jodo
race .. **4**. Ainu
jape ... **4**. fool, jeer, jest, jipe, mock
   5. fraud, trick **6**. banter, deride
japery ... **4**. jest, joke **7**. jesting
   8. trickery **10**. buffoonery
jar ... **4**. jolt **5**. grate, shake **6**. incase,
   rattle **7**. startle, vibrate **8**. preserve
   9. vibration
jar ... **3**. jug, urn **4**. ewer, lute
   (rubber), olla **5**. cadus (anc), crock,
   cruse **6**. dolium, goglet, hydria
   7. amphora, terrine **10**. jardiniere
jararaca ... **7**. serpent **10**. fer–de–lance
   11. jararacussu
jardiniere ... **3**. jar, jug, urn **4**. vase
   5. stand (plant) **9**. flowerpot
jargon ... **4**. cant **5**. argot, idiom, lingo,
   slang **6**. drivel, patois, patter, zircon
   7. Chinook, Yiddish **8**. nonsense
   9. gibberish **10**. vocabulary (secret)
jasmine, jasmin ... **4**. bela **5**. color,
   papaw **7**. jessamy **9**. jessamine
Jason (pert to) ...
friend, sweetheart .. **5**. Medea
heroes .. **9**. Argonauts
quest .. **12**. Golden Fleece
ship .. **4**. Argo
son .. **5**. Aeson
uncle .. **6**. Pelias
jaundice ... **7**. disease, icterus
   8. jealousy **9**. prejudice
   10. yellowness
jaunt ... **4**. ride,. trip **6**. ramble
   7. journey **9**. excursion
jaunty ... **4**. airy **5**. perky, showy, smart
   6. dapper, rakish **7**. finical, stylish
   12. lighthearted
Java ... see also *Javanese*
city .. **7**. Batavia, Jakarta (Djakarta)
   8. Samarang, Surabaya **9**. Surakarta
island group .. **10**. East Indies
Java Man (anc) .. **15**. Pithecanthropus
   (erectus)
location .. **7**. equator **16**. Malay
   Archipelago
Javanese (pert to) ...
arrow poison .. **4**. upas

badger.. 5. ratel 6. teledu
carriage.. 4. sado (sadoo)
cotton.. 5. kapok
dancers.. 6. bedoyo
dog (wild).. 5. adjag
ox (wild).. 7. banteng
pantomime.. 6. topeng
plum.. 5. jambo (jambul) 6. lomboy
puppet show.. 6. wajang (wayang)
rice field.. 5. sawah
squirrel.. 8. jelerang
temple.. 6. chandi (candi)
tree.. 4. upas 5. ligas 7. gondang
javelin... 3. bat 4. dart, pike 5. lance,
  spear 6. jereed (jirid) 7. assagai
  (assegai)
javelina... 4. boar 7. peccary
jaw... 3. maw 4. chop 5. scold
  6. berate, splash 7. chatter, orifice
  8. scolding
jaw (pert to)...
angle of.. 6. gonion
bone.. 7. maxilla 8. mandible
comb form.. 6. gnatho
disease.. 7. lump jaw
  13. actinomycosis
formation.. 8. gnathism
Greek for.. 7. gnathos
muscle.. 8. masseter
ref to.. 5. malar 7. gnathic
without.. 8. agnathic
jawab... 5. reply 6. answer, mosque
  (false Arch)
jay... 3. gae 4. bird, blue, dupe
  9. chatterer
jayhawker... 6. Kansan, spider
  7. soldier 8. guerilla
Jayhawker State... 6. Kansas
jazz... 4. jive 5. dance, music, swing
  9. syncopate 11. syncopation
jealous... 7. envious, zealous
  8. doubtful, grudging, vigilant,
  watchful 9. jaundiced 10. solicitous
  11. distrustful 12. apprehensive
jealousy... 4. envy 5. doubt 7. rivalry
  8. distrust, jaundice, mistrust
  12. covetousness
jeans... 8. overalls, trousers
jeer... 4. gibe, hoot, jape, mock
  5. flout, scoff, sneer, taunt 6. deride
  8. ridicule
Jehovah... 3. God, Jah 4. Lord
  6. Yahweh (Yahwe) 8. Almighty (The)
  12. Supreme Being
Jehovah's comfort... 8. Nehemiah
jehu (humorous)... 8. coachman
  10. fast driver
Jehu's father (Bib)... 11. Jehoshaphat
jejune... 3. dry 4. arid 5. banal,
  empty, stale, trite 6. barren, hungry,
  meager 7. insipid 8. foodless
  12. unproductive
jelly... 3. jam, rob (rhob) 4. food,
  sapa 5. aspic 6. pectin 7. gelatin
  8. gelatine, Kei Apple 10. semiliquid
jellyfish... 5. quarl 6. coward, medusa
  7. acaleph 8. weakling 9. Acalephae
jellyfish (pert to)...
class.. 9. Acalephae
group.. 10. discophora
part.. 6. pileus 8. umbrella
  10. exumbrella

stinging.. 9. sea nettle
swim organ.. 5. stene
jemmy... 4. boot (riding) 5. jimmy,
  lever 7. crowbar 9. greatcoat
Jena (Ger)... 5. glass 6. battle (1806)
jenna... 8. Paradise (Moham)
jennet... 3. ass 5. horse 6. donkey
jenny... 3. ass 5. crane (moving)
  6. female 8. airplane 13. spinning
  wheel
jenny (pert to)...
billiards.. 6. hazard
folklore.. 4. wren
howlet.. 3. owl 5. owlet
machine.. 13. spinning wheel
spinner.. 3. fly (angling)
jeopardize... 4. risk 6. expose, hazard
  7. imperil 8. endanger
jeopardy... 4. risk 5. peril 6. hazard,
  menace
jeremiad... 3. woe 6. lament, plaint,
  tirade 9. complaint
jerk... 3. tic 4. flip, jolt, push, yank
  5. shake, tweak 6. chorea, thrust,
  twitch 7. charqui
jerkin... 4. coat 6. jacket, salmon
  9. gyrfalcon, waistcoat
jeroboam... 4. bowl 6. battle, goblet
Jeroboam... 4. King (of Israel)
jerry... 5. aware 6. flimsy, Geremy,
  German 7. knowing 9. beer house,
  conscious
jersey... 5. cloth 6. cattle, jacket
Jersey Red... 5. swine
  11. Duroc–Jersey
Jersey tea... 11. wintergreen
  12. checkerberry
Jerusalem... 5. Ariel, Salem 8. Holy
  City 11. City of David
Jerusalem (pert to)...
artichoke.. 7. girasol 10. topinambou
capital of.. 6. Israel
corn.. 5. durra
Garden.. 10. Gethsemane
haddock.. 4. opah
hill.. 6. Olivet 13. Mount of Olives
historic site.. 11. Wailing Wall
  12. Mosque of Omar 13. Mount of
  Olives (Olivet) 18. Garden of
  Gethsemane
mosque.. 4. Omar
pool.. 6. Siloam 8. Bethesda
region.. 5. Perea 6. Gilead
Relig.. 7. Judaism 12. Christianity
  13. Mohammedanism
spring.. 5. Gihon 6. Siloam
star.. 7. salsify
Sunday.. 11. Refreshment
thorn.. 7. catechu 12. Christ's–thorn
willow.. 8. oleaster
jess... 5. strap (hawk's leg) 6. ribbon
jessamy... 3. fop 5. dandy 7. jasmine
jessant (Her)... 7. issuing 9. lying over
jessur... 5. viper (Russell's)
jest... 3. fun, mot, wit 4. fool, jape,
  jeer, joke, quip 5. droll, prank, sport,
  taunt, trick 6. banter, rail at, trifle
  8. ridicule
jester... 4. fool, mime 5. clown
  7. buffoon, goliard 8. humorist
  11. merry–andrew
jester's cap... 7. coxcomb

Jesuit... 5. Order 7. casuist, sectary
8. explorer 9. intriguer
10. missionary 14. Society of Jesus
(S J)
jet... 3. jut 4. gush, spew 5. black,
ebony, ladle, raven, spout, spray,
spurt 6. burner, nozzle, stream
7. mineral, outpour 8. spouting
9. black onyx
jet coal... 6. cannel
jetty... 4. mole, pier 5. wharf
8. buttress
Jew... 6. Essene, Hebrew, Semite
9. Israelite
jewel... 3. gem 4. naif, opal, ruby
5. beryl, stone 6. garnet 7. bearing,
diamond, emerald 8. ornament
9. bespangle, brilliant 10. rhinestone
13. precious stone, precious thing
jewel cutter... 10. lapidarist
jeweler's glass... 5. loupe
jeweler's weight... 4. tola 5. carat
(karat, kerat)
jewelry... 3. ice 4. ring 5. paste
6. parure, strass 7. costume
10. bijouterie
Jewish... 6. Hebrew 7. Yiddish
9. Israelite
Jewish (pert to)...
academy (Talmudic).. 8. Yeshinah
adherent.. 7. Zionist
benediction.. 5. Shema
Bible.. 5. Torah (Tora) 6. Gemara,
Talmud 7. Haggada, Halakah
10. Pentateuch
calendar.. 4. Adar, Ahab, Elul, Iyar
5. Nisan, Sivan, Tebet 6. Kislev,
Shebat, Tammuz, Tishri, Veadar (leap
year) 7. Heshvan
Day of Atonement.. 9. Yom Kippur
Dispersion.. 8. Diaspora
divorce.. 3. get (gett)
doctrine.. 7. Mishnah (Mishna)
enemy (Bib).. 5. Haman
faction.. 7. Zealots
father, patriarch.. 7. Abraham
festival.. 5. Purim, Seder (Sedar)
7. Sukkoth
greeting, peace.. 6. Shalom
high priest.. 3. Eli 4. Ezra 5. Aaron,
Annas 8. Caiaphas
high priest costume.. 4. urim
5. abnet 7. petalon, tallith, yamilke
historian.. 8. Josephus
holiday.. 7. Sukkoth 8. Hanukkah
(Hannukka), Tishabov 11. Rosh
Hashana (Rosh Hashonoh)
horn.. 7. shophar (shofar)
lawgiver.. 5. Moses
leader.. 8. Nehemiah
liturgy.. 6. minhah (PM) 9. shaharith
(AM)
loaves (unleavened).. 9. shewbread
(showbread)
mystical writing.. 6. atbash
patriots.. 9. Maccabees
prayer book.. 6. siddur
prophet.. 6. Elijah
psalms of praise.. 6. hallel
quarter (living).. 6. ghetto
ram's horn.. 7. shophar (shofar)
slaughter (Relig).. 8. shehitah

song (Zionist anthem).. 8. Hatikvah
(Hattikvah)
jew's harp... 8. guimbard
9. crembalum
Jezebel (pert to)...
epithet.. 5. vixen 6. virago
8. strumpet
father.. 7. Ethbaal
husband.. 4. Ahab (King)
murdered (caused to be).. 6. Naboth
jib... 3. gib, jaw 4. balk, boom, sail,
spar, tack 5. crane, shift 6. fleece
8. underlip
jibe... 3. fit 4. gibe 5. agree, shift
9. harmonize
jiff, jiffy... 5. trice 6. moment
7. instant, quickly 9. instantly,
twinkling
jig... 4. jerk, jolt 5. dance 6. ballad,
twitch 8. fishhook
jigger... 4. club, dram
jiggle... 5. sauce, shake
jimmy... 3. pry 5. handy, smart
6. spruce 7. coal car, crowbar, pry
open 10. sheep's head
jimson weed... 6. dature
10. stramonium, thorn apple
11. apple of Peru
jingle... 4. poem, rime 5. clink, rhyme
6. tinkle 13. two-wheeled car
jinn, jinnee... 5. demon, Eblis, genie
6. afreet 8. jenniyeh
jinx... 3. hex 5. Jonah 6. hoodoo,
whammy
jitters... 6. nerves 7. dithers, fidgets
8. trembles
jittery... 4. edgy 5. jumpy 7. nervous
jivatma (Hind)... 4. soul 9. life force
10. life energy 11. human spirit
Joan of Arc's appellation...
7. pucelle 13. Maid of Orleans
job... 3. act 4. hire, task 5. chare,
chore, stint 8. position, sinecure
Job (pert to)...
Book.. 8. patriarch 12. Old Testament
friend.. 6. Zophar
home.. 2. Uz
literally.. 9. afflicted 10. persecuted
jockey... 3. pad 5. cheat, racer, rider
6. outwit 7. cushion 8. cavalier,
horseman, minstrel, vagabond 9. Earl
Sande (famed)
jocose... 3. dry 5. droll, lepid, merry
7. jocular 8. humorous 9. facetious
jocular... 3. gay 4. airy, loco 5. droll,
funny, merry, witty 6. elated, jocund,
lively, ribald 7. comical, festive,
gleeful, jesting, playful, waggish
8. animated, mirthful 9. convivial,
facetious, hilarious, laughable,
vivacious 10. frolicsome
jocund... 3. gay 4. airy 5. merry
6. lively 7. jocular 8. cheerful,
sportive
jog... 4. gait, jolt, lope, plod, push,
trot, walk 6. canter, notify, remind,
trudge 8. slow pace 9. suggest to
John... 3. Ian 4. Ivan, Jack, Juan
8. Chinaman, Johannes 9. policeman
John (pert to)...
Bull.. 10. Englishman
Company.. 9. East India

Crow . . **7.** buzzard (turkey)
Doe (law) . . **7.** a nobody **9.** false name
Hancock . . **9.** autograph, signature
Q Public . . **6.** people **8.** populace
johnnycake . . . **4.** pone **7.** hoecake
   9. corn bread
join . . . **3.** add, mix, pin, tie, wed
   4. ally, fuse, link, lock, meet, pair,
   seam, team, weld, yoke **5.** annex,
   blend, enter, graft, group, hitch, marry,
   merge, unite **6.** adjoin, attach,
   cement, concur, couple, engage,
   enlist, fasten, mingle, solder, splice,
   suture, syzygy **7.** combine, conjoin,
   connect **8.** assemble, coalesce,
   compound **9.** associate
   11. incorporate
joint . . . **3.** ell, hip **4.** dive (sl), knee,
   node, seam **5.** alula, elbow, hinge,
   miter, nexus, tenon, wrist **6.** rabbet,
   resort **7.** hangout, pastern
   8. coupling, dovetail **12.** articulation
joint (pert to) . . .
cavity . . **5.** bursa
firs . . **7.** ephedra
fluid . . **7.** synovia **8.** synovial
grass stem . . **4.** culm
pert to . . **5.** nodal **9.** articular
put out of . . **6.** lucate **9.** dislocate
without . . **10.** acondylous
joke . . . **3.** fun, gag, pun **4.** fool, hoax,
   jape, jest, quip **5.** prank, rally, sport
   6. banter, humbug **7.** bromide
   8. chestnut, one–liner
joker . . . **3.** dor, wag, wit **4.** card
   7. buffoon, farceur, gagster
   8. humorist **9.** mistigris
jollity . . . **4.** jest **5.** mirth **6.** gaiety
   8. hilarity **9.** enjoyment, festivity,
   joviality, merriment **12.** conviviality
jolly . . . **6.** banter, jovial, joyful, mellow
   7. flatter, jocular **9.** make merry
Jolly Roger . . . **5.** Roger **10.** pirate flag
jolt . . . **3.** jar, jig, jut **4.** blow, butt, stun
   5. shake, shock **6.** jostle, jounce
   7. startle **8.** astonish, jail term
   (thieves')
Jonah (pert to) . . .
Bib . . **7.** prophet (Heb)
Book . . **12.** Old Testament
slang . . **4.** jinx
swallowed by . . **5.** whale
Jordan . . .
capital . . **5.** Amman
city . . **7.** Jericho, Samaria
   9. Bethlehem
historic trove . . **14.** Dead Sea Scrolls
official name . . **9.** Hashemite (The)
people (anc) . . **7.** Essenes
region . . **5.** Perea **6.** Basham
river . . **6.** Jordan
Jorth (pert to) . . .
goddess . . **5.** Earth
husband . . **4.** Odin
named also . . **6.** Forgyn
son . . **4.** Thor
Joseph (pert to) . . .
Bib . . **9.** patriarch
buyer of . . **8.** Potiphar
called also . . **17.** Joseph of Arimathea
coat of . . **10.** many colors
father . . **5.** Jacob

mother . . **6.** Rachel
son . . **5.** Jesus **7.** Ephraim
josh . . . **3.** guy, kid **5.** chaff, spoof,
   tease **6.** banter
Joshi (Ind) . . . **10.** astrologer,
   astronomer
Joshua (pert to) . . .
associate . . **5.** Caleb
Book . . **12.** Old Testament
burial place . . **5.** Gaash
successor to . . **5.** Moses
tree . . **5.** yucca
jostle . . . **4.** jolt, push, rush **5.** crowd,
   elbow, joust, shake, shove **6.** hustle,
   joggle, jounce, thrust
jot . . . **3.** ace, bit **4.** atom, iota, item,
   mite, whit **5.** minim, point, speck
   6. tittle **7.** smidgen **8.** particle
jouk . . . **4.** dart, duck, fawn, hide
   5. cheat, dodge, evade, perch, roost,
   skulk **6.** cringe **9.** obeisance
Joule, James P . . . **9.** physicist
journal . . . **3.** log **5.** diary, paper
   6. record **7.** daybook, diurnal,
   logbook, support **8.** magazine, register
   9. chronicle **10.** periodical
   11. account book
journalist . . . **6.** editor, legman
   7. newsman **8.** reporter **9.** columnist,
   gazetteer **11.** interviewer
   13. correspondent
journey . . . **3.** run **4.** fare, iter, ride,
   tour, trek, trip, wend **5.** jaunt
   6. travel, voyage **7.** odyssey
   8. traverse **9.** excursion
   10. expedition, pilgrimage
   13. peregrination
journey (pert to) . . . **4.** eyre (circuit)
   6. viatic **8.** anabasis (upward)
   9. itineracy, itinerary, traveling
   10. travelling
joust . . . **4.** bout, spar, tilt **6.** combat
   10. tournament
Jove . . . **7.** Jupiter
jovial . . . **5.** jolly, merry **6.** elated,
   joyous **7.** festive, jocular **8.** Jovelike
   9. convivial, hilarious
   14. mirth–inspiring
jowl . . . **3.** jaw **4.** chop **5.** cheek
   6. dewlap, wattle **7.** jawbone
joy . . . **3.** gee **4.** glee **5.** bliss, exult, gelid
   6. gaiety **7.** delight, ecstasy, rapture,
   rejoice **8.** felicity, gladness, hilarity,
   pleasure **9.** beatitude, happiness,
   merriment, transport **10.** exultation
   12. exhilaration
joyous . . . **3.** gay **4.** glad **5.** happy,
   merry **6.** blithe, elated, festal, joyful
   7. festive, gleeful, jocular **8.** cheerful,
   mirthful
jubilant . . . **6.** elated **8.** exultant,
   exulting **9.** overjoyed, rejoicing
   10. triumphant
Judah (pert to) . . .
ancestry . . **12.** tribe of Judah
brother . . **4.** Levi **6.** Reuben, Simeon
father . . **5.** Jacob
kingdom . . **9.** Palestine
son . . **2.** Er **6.** Shelah
translation (Heb) . . **10.** celebrated
Judas (pert to) . . .
Bible . . **7.** apostle, traitor **8.** betrayer,

deceiver, disciple
called.. 8. Iscariot
historic.. 13. Paschal candle
kiss.. 8. betrayal 11. double–cross,
  treacherous
priest.. 4. oath
suicide site.. 8. Aceldama
Judea (pert to)...
governor.. 6. Pilate
king.. 3. Asa 5. Herod 7. Jehoram
  11. Jehoshaphat
location.. 5. Berea
people.. 4. Jews
province of.. 9. Palestine
judge... 3. try 4. deem, rate 5. opine,
  think 6. critic, puisne 7. arbiter,
  referee, suppose 8. deemster,
  estimate, mediator, sentence
  9. arbitrate, criticize 10. adjudicate,
  magistrate 11. connoisseur
judge (pert to)...
bench.. 4. banc (bancus)
chamber.. 6. camera
circuit.. 4. iter
gavel.. 4. mace
group.. 5. bench 9. judiciary
of the dead.. 6. Osiris
opinion.. 12. obiter dictum
sittings.. 7. assizes
summary.. 6. postea
judgment... 4. doom 5. arrêt, award,
  sense, taste 7. censure, opinion
  8. decision, judicium, sentence
  9. criticism 10. conclusion,
  discretion, persuasion (Relig),
  punishment 11. arbitration, sensibility
judgment (pert to)...
creditor.. 13. quasi contract
day.. 7. last day 8. Dies Irae,
  doomsday
left to one's.. 13. discretionary
note.. 10. promissory
seat.. 3. bar 5. mercy 8. tribunal,
  woolsack
judicial... 5. legal 8. critical
  9. judicious 10. judicatory
judicial (pert to)...
council.. 5. cabal, junta, junto
  7. coterie
hearing.. 5. trial
order.. 4. writ 6. elegit, venire
  7. precept
security.. 7. custody
judicious... 4. wise 7. politic, prudent
  8. cautious, discreet 9. sagacious
  10. discerning 11. circumspect,
  well–advised
jug... 4. ewer, jail, olpe, toby
  5. askos, buire, cruse, gotch
  6. flagon, gomlah, lockup, prison,
  tinaja, urceus 7. pitcher
  13. Schnabelkanne
Juggernaut... 6. Vishnu (Hind)
juggler... 5. cheat, trick 7. buffoon
  8. deceiver 13. sleight of hand
  14. legerdemainist
Jugoslavia, Yugoslavia...
area.. 6. Kosovo 8. Dalmatia
brandy.. 5. rakia 9. slivovitz
capital.. 8. Belgrade
language.. 7. Slovene
  10. Macedonian, Serbo–Croat

leader.. 4. Tito
monarch.. 5. Peter
money.. 5. dinar
organization.. 9. Comitadji
people.. 4. Cerb 5. Croat 7. Slovene
juice... 3. rob, sap 4. milk (plant),
  must, stum 5. fluid, latex, syrup
  (sirup) 7. essence, hebenon, moisten
  10. succulence 11. electricity
jujitsu, jiujitsu... 11. self–defense
juju... 5. charm, magic 6. amulet,
  belief, fetish, voodoo
jujube... 3. ber 5. fruit, jelly
  7. lozenge 8. Zizyphus
Jules Verne's captain... 4. Nemo (the
  Nautilus)
Julian Emperors (first Five)... 4. Nero
  8. Augustus, Caligula, Claudius,
  Tiberius
jumble... 2. pi 3. mix 4. cake, hash,
  heap, mess, raff, stir 5. blend,
  botch, chaos, shake 6. medley,
  muddle 7. agitate, confuse, mixture
  8. disorder, riffraff
jumble type... 3. pie (pi)
jump... 3. hop, lep 4. leap, move
  (checkers) 5. bound, caper, halma,
  salto, scold, start, vault 6. chorea,
  escape, hurdle, spring, twitch
  7. saltary, saltate 8. increase
  9. advantage 10. transition
jumping (pert to)...
adjective.. 7. saltant
Frog, tale by.. 9. Mark Twain
music.. 7. saltato
rodent.. 5. mouse 6. jerboa
  11. kangaroo rat
stick.. 4. pogo, pole
junction... 4. axil, seam 5. union
  6. suture 7. joining, meeting
  11. combination, concurrence
juncture... 4. pass 5. joint, pinch
  6. crisis, strait 8. exigency, quandary
  9. emergency 10. connection
  11. conjuncture, predicament
  12. articulation
June bug... 3. dor 6. beetle, May bug
  8. figeater
jungle... 4. camp 7. thicket
  8. woodland 11. dense growth
  12. complication
jungle (pert to)...
dweller.. 5. beast 6. savage
fever.. 7. malaria
grass.. 3. poa
ox.. 4. gaur 5. gayal 7. timarau
sheep.. 7. muntjac
junior... 5. cadet, petty 6. puisne,
  recent 7. student, younger 8. inferior
  9. unskilled
juniper... 4. cade, puny 5. cedar,
  gorse, retem (raetem), savin
junket... 4. dish (milk), food, meal
  5. feast 7. banquet 8. festival
  9. excursion, sweetmeat
Juno (pert to)...
consort.. 7. Jupiter
goddess (Rom).. 3. sky 5. light
identified with.. 4. Hera
messenger.. 4. Iris
junta, junto... 5. cabal 6. circle,
  clique 7. coterie, council, faction

8. intrigue 11. combination
jupe... 4. coat 5. jupon, shirt, skirt,
  tunic 6. bodice, jacket
Jupiter (pert to)...
  angel.. 7. Zadkiel
  astronomy.. 6. planet (largest)
  daughter.. 4. Bura
  deity.. 4. Jove 9. Father Sky
  festival.. 14. Vinalis sustica
  god of.. 7. Heavens
  heraldry.. 5. azure
  lover.. 2. Io
  son.. 6. Castor, Pollux
  triad.. 4. Juno 7. Minerva
  wife.. 4. Juno
Jupiter, god of...
  law.. 6. Fidius 10. Dius Fidius
  lightning.. 6. Fulgur
  rain.. 7. Pluvius
  thunder.. 6. Tonans
jurat... 5. juror 8. recorder
  10. magistrate (Channel Isls)
jure... 3. jus (ius), law 5. right
  13. jurisprudence
jurisprudence... 3. law, soc 4. soke
  5. power (legal) 6. charge, sphere
  7. control, custody, emirate
  9. authority, consulate
  10. government, judicature, patriarchy
juror... 6. dicast 7. assizer, juryman
  9. venireman
jury... 5. panel, tales (additions)
  6. venire
jus... 3. law 5. gravy, juice 10. legal
  power, legal right
just... 4. fair, tilt 5. equal, exact, valid
  7. logical, upright 8. provided,
  unbiased 9. equitable, righteous
  10. legitimate

just begun... 8. inchoate
justice... 4. doom 5. right 6. equity,
  virtue 8. fairness, fair play, justness
  9. rectitude 10. judicature 11. give
  and take 12. rightfulness
justice of the peace... 6. squire
  10. magistrate
justification... 7. apology, defense
  11. vindication
justify... 5. clear 6. defend, excuse
  7. absolve, support, warrant
  8. maintain, sanction, underpin
  9. authorize, exculpate, vindicate
  12. substantiate
justly... 5. truly 6. fairly 7. equally
  8. honestly 9. equitably
  10. deservedly
justness... 7. fitness, justice
  8. accuracy, validity 9. exactness
  11. correctness
Justus... 4. just
jute... 5. fiber, gunny 6. burlap
  7. sacking
Jute... 4. Dane 9. Jutlander
jutty... 4. mole, pier 5. jetty
  7. project 8. buttress, protrude
juvenile... 5. actor, young, youth
  8. immature, youthful 9. youngling,
  youthlike 11. undeveloped
juvia... 9. Brazil nut
juxta... 4. near 6. nearby
juxtaposition... 5. touch 7. contact
  8. nearness 9. proximity
  10. contiguity, side by side
jynx... 5. charm, spell 7. wryneck
  10. woodpecker
Jynx... 11. woodpeckers
J'y suis, j'y reste... 18. I am here;
  here I remain

K

K... 5. kappa (Gr) 6. letter (11th)
Ka... 3. God (Hind)
Kaaba, Caaba (pert to)...
  content.. 10. Black Stone (of Mecca)
  location.. 11. Great Mosque (Mecca)
  pilgrimage.. 7. Islamic
  praying direction.. 6. Kiblah
  shape.. 7. cubical
kaama... 10. hartebeest
Kaddish... 8. Doxology
Kadiak, Kodiak, bear... 5. brown
  7. Alaskan
Kaffir (pert to)...
  club weapon.. 10. knobkerrie
  country.. 11. South Africa
  creed.. 10. unbeliever
  13. non–Mohammedan
  race.. 5. Bantu
  servant.. 6. umfaan
  tribes (world's tallest).. 4. Xosa, Zulu
  5. Pondo, Temby

  warriors.. 4. impi
  weapon.. 4. keri 10. knobkerrie
Kaiser brown... 6. ginger
Kaiser's residence... 5. Doorn
kaka... 6. parrot
kakapo... 6. parrot 9. owl parrot
kakar... 7. muntjac
kakariki... 6. lizard
kaki... 5. stilt (bird) 9. persimmon
kakkak... 5. heron 7. bittern
kakke... 8. beriberi
kala... 6. bulbul (bird)
kale... 4. cole 5. money 7. cabbage,
  collard 8. colewort, corecole
kaleidoscopic... 7. varying
  10. changeable, variegated
Kali (pert to)...
  Hindu.. 10. evil genius
  Persian.. 6. carpet
  Vedic Myth.. 12. tongue of Agni
  (fire–god)

kallah... 5. bride (Jew)
kamavachara... 6. heaven (Buddh)
Kamchatka...
  capital.. 13. Petropavlovsk
  peninsula.. 7. Siberia
  people.. 7. Russian 9. Mongolian
  sea.. 6. Bering 7. Okhotsk
Kamehameha Day... 7. holiday (Haw)
Kamerad... 7. comrade 9. surrender
kamik... 12. sealskin boot
Kammerspiel... 5. drama 7. theater
Kanaka... 3. man 8. Hawaiian
  10. Melanesian, Polynesian
  16. South Sea islander
Kanaloa... 3. God (Pantheon)
kangaroo (pert to)...
  class.. 9. marsupial
  family.. 12. Macropodidae
  female.. 3. doe, gin, 'roo
  giant.. 8. forester
  leaping.. 6. jeroba 7. bettong
    (bettonga)
  male.. 5. bilby (bilbi)
  rat.. 7. pototoo
  reference to.. 7. wallaby
    11. macropodine
  small.. 7. wallaby
  young.. 4. joey
kangaroo court... 9. mock court, moot
  court 14. irregular court
Kansas...
  capital.. 6. Topeka
  city.. 5. Dodge 7. Abilene, Wichita
  10. Hutchinson, Kansas City
  11. Leavenworth
  Eisenhower home.. 7. Abilene
  military post.. 9. Fort Riley
  penitentiary.. 11. Leavenworth
  State admission.. 12. Thirty–fourth
  State motto.. 16. Ad Astra per
    Aspera (To the Stars Through
    Difficulties)
  State nickname.. 9. Sunflower
kapok tree... 7. God tree 9. Ceiba
  tree 10. silk–cotton
kappa... 1. K (Gr) 4. star 6. letter
  (10th)
karakul, karakule... 5. sheep
  9. astrakhan, broadtail
karma... 4. fate 7. destiny 8. casualty
Kartvelian people... 4. Svan (Svane)
  9. Georgians 10. Imeritians,
  Svanetians
kasha... 4. mush (Russ)
Kashmir, India...
  alphabet.. 6. Sarada
  capital.. 8. Srinagar
  deer.. 6. hangul
  official.. 6. pundit
Kashyapa (Vedic Myth)... 8. tortoise
Kaskaskia... 5. epoch 6. Indian
  10. Algonquian
kat... 5. shrub 8. narcotic
katar... 6. dagger
katchung... 6. peanut
katogle... 8. eagle owl
kava, kavakava... 6. Kawaka, pepper
kayak... 5. canoe
kea... 6. parrot
Keat's poem... 8. Endymion, Hyperion
keek... 3. spy (of rival fashions)
  6. peeper

keel... 4. cool, seel, ship, skeg, tilt
  6. careen, ruddle, timber (ship's)
  7. capsize 8. overturn, red ocher,
  turn over 10. guinea fowl
keelbill, keelbird... 3. ani
keeling... 7. codfish
keel–shaped... 6. carina 7. carinal
keen... 4. avid, cute, gare, good, nice,
  tart 5. acute, alert, eager, sharp,
  smart, snell, vivid, witty 6. astute,
  bitter, clever, shrewd, shrill
  7. caustic, fervent 9. sensitive,
  trenchant 11. acrimonious,
  penetrating
keenness... 4. edge 5. acies (of sight),
  nifty 6. acumen 8. acrimony,
  pungency 9. acuteness, eagerness,
  sharpness, smartness, wittiness
keep... 4. save 6. detain, retain
  7. confine, custody, fulfill, husband,
  reserve 8. conserve, maintain,
  preserve, restrain, withhold
  14. accommodations
keep (pert to)...
  account.. 5. score
  afloat.. 4. buoy
  apart.. 7. seclude 8. separate
  back, out.. 3. bar, dam 4. save
    5. debar, delay 6. detain, except,
    hinder, retard 7. exclude, reserve
    8. restrain, withhold
  from.. 5. avoid, delay 7. abstain,
    boycott, prevent
  hidden.. 7. secrete
  in.. 6. retain
  off.. 4. fend 7. prevent, repulse, ward
    off
  on.. 6. endure 9. persevere
keeper... 5. guard 6. warden
  9. constable, custodian, possessor
  10. maintainer
keeper of...
  birds.. 8. aviarist
  borders.. 8. margrave
  door.. 5. tiler
  elephant.. 6. mahout
  golden apples (Myth).. 6. Ithunn
    (Ithun)
  parks.. 6. ranger
  prison.. 6. gaoler, jailer, jailor, warden
    7. turnkey
keeping... 4. care 5. board, guard,
  trust 7. custody 8. tutelage
  9. retention 10. caretaking,
  conformity, possession, preserving,
  protection 11. maintenance
  12. guardianship
keeve... 3. tub 4. tuft 5. knoll, plume
  8. haystack
kef... 6. dreamy 7. languor
  12. tranquillity (tranquility)
keg... 3. tun, vat 4. cade, cask
  6. firkin
kelly... 5. derby, killy (fish)
kelp... 4. game 5. sight, wrack
  7. insight, seaweed 9. water lily
ken... 4. lore 9. recognize
  10. cognizance, prescience
  13. understanding
Kentish freedman... 4. laet
Kentucky...
  bluegrass.. 3. poa

capital .. 9. Frankfort
city .. 7. Paducah 9. Lexington
  10. Louisville 12. Bowling Green
famed road .. 15. Wilderness Trail
famed sights .. 7. Obelisk (J Davis)
  8. Fort Knox, Log Cabin (Lincoln)
  11. Federal Hill (My Old Ky Home),
  Mammoth Cave
famed sport .. 13. Kentucky Derby
  (Churchill Downs)
mountain .. 4. Pine 10. Cumberland
pioneer .. 11. Daniel Boone
river .. 4. Ohio 10. Cumberland
State admission .. 9. Fifteenth
State name meaning (Indian) ..
  8. tomorrow
State nickname .. 9. Bluegrass
Kenya, E Africa ...
capital .. 7. Nairobi
product .. 3. tea
tribe .. 4. Embu
kept ... see *keep*
Ker (Gr) ... 4. doom, fate 5. ghost
  6. spirit
kermis, kermess ... 4. fair 8. festival
kernel ... 3. nut 4. core, gist, meat,
  pith, seed 5. grain, heart 6. acinus,
  nutmeg 7. nucleus
ketch ... 4. Jack, saic, ship 6. vessel
ketone ... 5. irone 6. carone
  7. acetone, camphor 8. deguelin
kettle ... 3. pot 4. drum, pail 6. kibble
  7. caldron 8. cauldron 9. teakettle
  10. kettledrum
kettledrum ... 4. drum 5. naker, tabor
  6. atabal 7. anacara 8. tympanon
key ... 4. clue, crib, isle, quay, reef,
  tone 5. islet, pitch, tasto 6. clavis,
  cotter, fasten, island, opener, switch,
  tapper 7. digital 8. mainstay, solution
  11. explanation, fundamental,
  translation
keyed up ... 4. agog 5. eager, fired
  7. aroused, stirred 8. hopped up,
  worked up 10. stimulated
Keys, House of ... 9. Isle of Man,
  officials
Keystone State ... 12. Pennsylvania
khan ... 3. inn 4. lord 6. prince
  9. resthouse 11. caravansary
kiang ... 5. diver 6. onager 7. wild ass
kick ... 4. blow, boot, funk, punt
  6. energy, object, thrill 7. grumble,
  protest 8. complain, pungency,
  sixpence 9. complaint 10. calcitrate,
  enthusiasm
Kickapoo ... 6. Indian 10. Algonquian
kickshaw ... 3. toy 6. trifle 7. trinket
  8. delicacy
kid ... 3. guy 4. fool, goat, hoax, joke,
  josh, twit 5. child, jolly, suede
  6. banter, humbug 8. antelope
  (young), yeanling 9. youngling
kidang ... 4. deer 7. muntjac
kidney ... 4. neer 5. gland, reins
  7. nephros
kidney (pert to) ...
comb form .. 6. nephro
disease .. 7. nephria 9. nephritis
pyramid .. 9. reniculus
reference to .. 4. reni 5. renal
  6. vitals 7. nephric

shaped .. 8. reniform
stone .. 6. pebble 8. nephrite
kiki ... 14. castor oil plant
kill ... 4. slay, veto 5. blast, creek
  6. defeat, murder 7. channel,
  destroy, execute, silence 8. dispatch,
  immolate, lapidate, massacre,
  overbeat 9. slaughter
  11. assassinate, exterminate
killer ... 4. Cain 6. gunman, slayer
  7. butcher 8. cannibal, man–eater,
  mongoose, murderer 9. cutthroat
  12. assassinator
killer whale ... 3. orc 4. orca
  7. grampus
killing ... 5. fatal 6. deadly, murder
  7. amusing, carnage, cleanup
  (speculation), garrote 8. homicide
  9. execution 10. euthanasia
  11. captivating 12. overpowering
killing of ...
brother .. 10. fratricide
cats .. 8. felicide
father .. 9. patricide
man .. 8. homicide
mother .. 9. matricide
old men (tribal) .. 8. senicide
self .. 7. suicide 9. martyrdom
sister .. 10. sororicide
wolf .. 8. lupicide
kiln ... 4. oast, oven 5. clamp, stove,
  tiler 7. furnace
kilo (pref) ... 8. thousand
kind ... 3. ilk 4. good, race, sort, type
  5. class, genre, genus, order, seely,
  style 6. benign, gender, humane,
  loving, strain 7. kindred, lenient,
  species 8. gracious 9. benignant
  10. benevolent 11. sympathetic
  12. well–disposed
kindle ... 4. burn, fire 5. brood, light,
  rouse, young 6. excite, ignite, incite,
  litter 7. animate, inflame, provoke
kindly ... 4. mild 6. benign, blithe,
  genial, humane 7. natural
  8. benignly, heartily 9. agreeably,
  benignant, indulgent 10. beneficent,
  legitimate, pleasantly 11. sympathetic
kindness ... 5. favor 8. clemency,
  goodness, humanity, mildness
  9. benignity 10. compassion,
  generosity, gentleness, indulgency,
  tenderness
kindred ... 3. sib, tie 4. akin, clan, kith
  5. blood 6. allied, family 7. cognate,
  descent, kinship, kinsmen, related
  8. kinsfolk 9. relations
  12. relationship 14. consanguineous
kine ... 4. cows 6. cattle
kinetic ... 6. active, moving
king ... 3. rex, rey, roi 4. rank 5. chief,
  ruler 6. master 7. regulus
  8. chessman 9. potentate, sovereign
king (pert to) ...
beasts .. 4. lion
birds .. 5. eagle
chamber .. 9. camarilla
cheeses .. 4. Brie
child .. 6. prince 8. princess
dwarfs .. 8. Alberich (Ger)
fairies .. 6. Oberon
family .. 7. dynasty

gods.. 7. Jupiter
heaven.. 3. God 6. Christ
herrings.. 4. opah 7. oarfish
  8. chimaera
mackerel.. 4. cero
March (The).. 5. Sousa
metals.. 4. gold
monkeys.. 7. guereza
murder of.. 8. regicide
myth.. 4. Atli 5. Midas
myth (classical).. 4. Zeus 7. Jupiter
rivers.. 6. Amazon
serpents (race of).. 6. Shesha (Sesha)
symbol.. 7. scepter (sceptre)
vultures.. 4. papa
waters.. 7. Neptune, Pacific
Woods (The).. 13. Rex Nemorensis
King Arthur (pert to)...
abode.. 6. Avalon 7. Camelot
battleground (fatal).. 6. Camlan
home.. 8. Caerleon (on the Usk)
Knights of the Round Table..
  6. Gawain 7. Galahad 8. Lancelot,
  Tristran 9. Percivale
Queen.. 9. Guinevere
quest of.. 9. Holy Grail (The)
shield.. 7. Pridwin
sword.. 9. Excalibur
kingdom... 5. realm 6. empire, estate
  8. dominion, kingship, monarchy
kingdom (pert to)...
ancient.. 4. Elam, Moab
Asia.. 5. Nepal
between Spain, France.. 7. Navarra
  (Navarre)
confusion.. 5. Babel
divisions.. 6. animal 7. mineral
  9. vegetable
Indo–China.. 5. Annam (Anam)
kingfish... 4. cero, haku, opah
  7. kingpin, pintado 8. big wheel
  9. threadfin
kingly... 5. grand, noble, regal, royal
  6. august 7. leonine 8. imperial,
  majestic, princely 9. dignified,
  sovereign 11. monarchical
King of...
Albania.. 3. Zog
Bashan.. 2. Og
Bulgaria.. 5. Boris
Greece (anc).. 9. Agamemnon
Israel.. 4. Ahab, Jehy, Saul 5. David
  7. Solomon 8. Jeroboam
Judea.. 3. Asa
Kings.. 3. God 6. Christ
Men.. 4. Odin, Zeus 7. Jupiter
Oriental.. 11. King of Kings
Persia (Iran).. 5. Cyrus 6. Xerxes
Troy.. 5. Priam
Tyre.. 5. Hiram
Visigoths.. 6. Alaric
Kipling, Rudyard (pert to)...
award.. 10. Nobel Prize (1907)
birthplace.. 6. Bombay
poem (for Queen Victoria)..
  11. Recessional
kissing, science... 13. philematology
knee (pert to)...
bend.. 9. genuflect
bent.. 10. geniculate
bone.. 6. rotula 7. kneepan, patella
britches.. 6. smalls 8. knickers

on bended.. 7. humbled 8. obeisant
  10. submissive, worshipful
  12. supplicatory
kneeling desk... 8. prie–dieu
knew... see know
Knickerbocker, Father... 9. New
  Yorker (Hist)
knickknack... 3. toy 6. bauble,
  gewgaw, trifle 7. trinket 8. gimcrack
knife... 4. bolo, snee, stab 5. corer,
  prune 6. cutter, weapon
knife (pert to)...
Burmese.. 3. dah
Hindu.. 5. kukri
Irish.. 5. skean 8. skean dhu
Malay.. 4. kris 6. barong, creese
New Zealand.. 4. patu
one–bladed.. 6. barlow
Scottish.. 4. dirk
Spanish.. 7. machete
surgical.. 7. scalpel 10. greffotome
Turkish.. 8. yataghan (yatagan)
US Navy.. 7. cutlass
knife maker... 6. cutler
knife–throwing game...
  11. mumbletypeg
  12. mumble–the–peg
knight (pert to)...
adventure.. 8. errantry
adventurer.. 8. cavalier 9. caballero,
  chevalier
cloak.. 6. tabard
combat.. 5. joust
ensign.. 8. gonfalon, gonfanon
errant.. 7. Paladin
hero.. 7. Paladin
servant.. 4. page 6. varlet
title.. 3. Sir 8. banneret
wife.. 4. Dame, Lady
wreath (with crest).. 4. orle
Knight of the Round Table... 3. Kay
  6. Gawain 7. Galahad, Paladin
  8. Lancelot, Tristram 9. Percivale
Knight of the Rueful Countenance...
  10. Don Quixote
knit... 4. bind, heal, join, seam
  5. plait, unite, woven 6. cement,
  couple, fasten 7. conjoin, connect,
  wrinkle 8. contract 9. interlace
  11. consolidate
knitting machine guide... 4. sley
knitting stitch... 4. knit, purl
knob... 3. nub 4. boss, head, hill,
  lump, node, stud, umbo 5. bulge,
  knurl 6. croche (antler), pommel
  8. tubercle 12. protuberance
knobkerrie... 4. club, kiri 5. stick
knock... 3. hit, rap, tap 4. bang,
  bash, beat, bump, dash, glow, hill,
  pass, slay, snop 5. pound, thump
  6. hammer, jostle, strike 7. collide
  9. criticism, criticize, disparage
  12. faultfinding
knock (pert to)...
about.. 6. travel, wander
down.. 4. fell, raze 6. deject, strike
  8. vanquish
off.. 3. die 6. deduct, recess
  9. improvise
out.. 2. KO 4. kayo
knocking... 6. rat–tat 7. rapping,
  tapping 9. rat–tat–tat

knock–knee... 6. in–knee
knoll... 4. bank, clod, hill, knap, knob, lump 5. bunch, hurst, knell, mound 7. hillock
knot... 3. bow, nep, tie 4. burl, knar, knob, knur, lump, node, noil, snag 5. gnarl, noose 6. clique, nodule, tangle 7. dilemma, lanyard, problem, rosette 9. sandpiper 10. sheepshank 12. complication, protuberance
knotted... 3. nep 5. noded, nowed (Her) 6. knotty 7. clotted, complex, gnarled, knitted, nodated 8. abstruse, puzzling 9. difficult, entangled
knotty... 5. nodal, rough 7. gnarled, knarred, knobbed, knurled, nodular 9. difficult, entangled, intricate 10. perplexing
know... 3. ken, wis, wot 5. sense 6. regard, reveal 8. perceive 9. apprehend, be certain, recognize 11. be cognizant, distinguish
knowing... 3. hep 6. artful, crafty, scient, shrewd 7. cunning 8. informed 9. cognitive, conscious, wide–awake 10. perceptive 11. intelligent, intentional 12. familiar with 13. comprehension
know–it–all... 6. gossip 8. quidnunc, wiseacre
knowledge... 3. ken 4. kith, lore 5. ology 6. wisdom 7. science 8. learning, scientia 9. erudition 11. familiarity, information, instruction 12. acquaintance
knowledge (pert to)...
acquisition of.. 7. organon
ancestral.. 9. tradition
epithet of Muses.. 7. Pierian
exhibition of.. 6. pedant
instrument.. 7. organon
lack of.. 9. ignorance, nescience
object of.. 7. scibile
pert to.. 7. gnostic 8. instinct 9. epistemic, intuition, sciential 12. epistemology
pretender to.. 7. aeolist (eolist) 8. sciolist
seeker of.. 10. philonoist
slight.. 7. inkling, smatter 10. smattering
summarized.. 12. encyclopedia

(encyclopaedia)
superficial.. 9. sociology
system.. 7. science
universal.. 9. pantology
without.. 8. atechnic
know–nothing... 5. dunce 8. agnostic 9. ignoramus
kobird... 6. cuckoo
kobold... 3. elf, imp 5. gnome 8. folklore 9. hobgoblin
Kodiak, Kadiak bear... 7. Alaskan
Kohinoor... 7. diamond (700 carats)
kohl... 5. horse 8. antimony, cosmetic
kola... 3. nut 6. jackal
kooky... 7. offbeat
kopje... 5. mound 7. hillock
Koran, Alcoran (pert to)...
author.. 8. Mohammed
division.. 4. Sura (chapter)
learned man.. 5. ulema
recording angel.. 6. sijill (sijil)
scriptures.. 10. Mohammedan
teacher.. 5. ulema 7. alfaqui (alfaquin)
Korea...
capital.. 5. Keijo, Seoul
city.. 6. Gensan
mountain peak.. 6. Paekdu
old name.. 6. Chosen 13. Hermit Kingdom
peninsula.. 6. Ongjin
province.. 5. Fusan (Fuzan)
river.. 4. Yalu 5. Tuman 7. Naktong
kosher... 5. clean 8. kashruth 10. sanctioned
kra... 3. ape (long–tailed)
krimmer... 8. lambskin
Krishna (Hind)... 5. deity (of Vishnu) 6. avatar (8th), Goloka
Krupp steel works, site... 5. Essen (Ger)
kudu... 8. antelope 9. gray–brown
kusimansel... 6. mangue 8. mongoose
Kwantung capital... 6. Dairen
kwazoku (Jap)... 8. nobility (modern)
kyah... 9. partridge
kyaung... 9. monastery
kymatology, science of... 5. waves 10. wave motion
kyphosis... 8. humpback 9. hunchback 15. spinal curvature
kyte... 5. belly 7. stomach
Kyushu (Jap)... 6. Island (southernmost)

L

L . . . 5. fifty (Rom num) 6. lambda, letter (12th) 7. lammedh
laager, lager . . . 4. camp
laagte . . . 6. bottom, valley 8. riverbed
Laban (pert to) . . .
  daughter . . 4. Leah 6. Rachel
  father . . 7. Bethuel
  son–in–law . . 5. Jacob
label . . . 3. tab, tag 4. band, name 6. fillet, lappet, tassel, ticket 8. insignia 9. designate
labellum . . . 3. lip 6. labium, labrum
labia . . . 4. lips
labial stop . . . 9. organ stop
labial teeth . . . 6. canine 7. incisor
labile . . . 8. shifting, unstable
labium . . . 3. lip
La Boheme . . . 4. Mimi 7. Puccini
labor, labour . . . 4. moil, task, toil, work 5. sweat 6. strive 7. travail, work for 8. drudgery, endeavor, exertion, industry
labored . . . 5. heavy 6. forced, strove 7. not easy, operose 8. strained 9. difficult, elaborate, laborious 11. painstaking
laborer . . . 4. hind, peon, toty 5. navvy 6. coolie, toiler, worker 7. bracero, wetback, workman
laborious . . . 4. hard 7. arduous, operose 8. toilsome 9. difficult 11. hard working, industrious, painstaking
labor leader . . . 5. Hoffa, Lewis, Meany 7. Gompers (1st), Reuther 8. Petrillo
Labrador (pert to) . . .
  Arctic flow . . 7. Current
  dog . . 9. retriever 12. Newfoundland
  missionary . . 8. Grenfell (Dr)
  part . . 12. Newfoundland
  tea . . 5. Ledum 8. gowiddie
labyrinth . . . 4. maze 7. circuit, cochlea 10. perplexity 12. complication
labyrinthe . . . 7. complex 8. involved 9. intricate 10. circuitous 11. complicated
lac . . . 4. milk 5. resin 7. lacquer, shellac
lace . . . 3. net, tat, tie, web 4. band, beat, cord, flog, lash, line, trim 5. braid, filet, lacis, snare 6. fasten, string, tissue 7. network 9. embroider 10. intertwine, shoestring 13. dash of spirits
lace (pert to) . . .
  Antwerp . . 7. pot lace
  bobbin . . 3. val 12. Valenciennes
  cape, scarf . . 8. mantilla
  edge . . 5. picot
  Flemish . . 7. malines, Mechlin

  French . . 5. filet 7. guipure
  frill . . 5. ruche
  front . . 5. jabot
  gold, silver . . 5. orris
  make . . 3. tat 5. weave 7. crochet, entwine
  needlepoint . . 7. Alençon
  opening . . 6. eyelet
  patterned . . 7. guipure
lacerate . . . 3. cut, rip 4. pain, rend, tear 6. harrow, injure, mangle 7. afflict, torture
lachryma . . . 4. tear 5. fluid 8. teardrop
lachrymal, lachrymose . . . 5. teary, weepy 7. tearful 8. tearlike
lack . . . 4. need, want 6. dearth 7. absence, lacking, missing, require 8. have need, scarcity 9. fall short, neediness 10. deficiency
lack (pert to) . . .
  blood cells (red) . . 6. anemia
  correspondence . . 13. nonconformity
  energy . . 5. atony, tepid 6. energy 7. aimless, sapless
  feeling . . 10. insensible 13. insensibility
  firmness . . 4. limp 8. boneless 9. spineless
  interest . . 6. apathy 9. apathetic
  knowledge . . 9. ignorance, nescience
  melody . . 6. atonic 9. atonality
  preparation . . 8. unfitted
  reasoning . . 7. idiotic
  refinement . . 5. gross 9. grossness, inelegant 10. inelegance
  vigilance . . 6. unwary
lackadaisical . . . 7. languid 8. listless 10. spiritless
Laconia (anc) . . .
  capital . . 6. Sparta
  clan . . 3. obe
  inhabitant . . 5. Lacon
  location . . 12. Peloponnesus
  race . . 6. Dorian
laconic . . . 5. brief, pithy, short, terse 7. concise, pointed, summary 8. succinct, taciturn
lacquer . . . 3. lac, red (color) 5. japan, resin 6. enamel 7. shellac, varnish
lacrimando . . . 9. lamenting, plaintive
lactarium . . . 5. dairy
lacteal . . . 5. milky
lacune, lacuna . . . 3. gap, pit 5. break 6. hiatus 7. opening (small) 10. depression
ladder . . . 3. run, sty 5. scale 7. scalade 8. escalade 10. stepladder
lade . . . 3. dip 4. bail, draw, fill, load, ship 5. drain, ladle 6. burden
laden . . . 6. loaded 8. burdened

9. freighted
lading... 4. load 5. cargo 6. burden
7. freight
ladle... 3. dip 4. bowl 5. scoop,
spoon 6. dipper
lady... 4. burd (anc), dame 5. donna
6. domina, female, senora 7. signora
8. ladylove 13. harlequin duck
lady (pert to)...
  bird.. 6. beetle 7. Vedalia
  fish.. 6. wrasse
  killer.. 4. wolf 5. shiek 7. Don Juan
  8. Casanova
  like.. 6. female, polite 7. genteel
  8. feminine
Lady Godiva's town... 8. Coventry
Lady of the Lake character
(legend)... 6. Merlin, Vivian
Lady's Book author... 5. Godey
lady's–slipper... 6. balsam, orchid
8. Noah's ark 9. nerveroot
lady's–thumb... 9. peachwort, persicary
lag... 4. slow 5. delay, tardy
6. dawdle, linger, loiter 7. belated
10. dillydally, fall behind
lagarto... 9. alligator 10. lizard fish
laggard... 4. slow 5. idler 7. lagging
8. backward, dilatory, indolent,
loiterer, sluggish 9. loitering, straggler
La Gioconda... 8. Mona Lisa
lagniappe, lagnappe... 5. pilon
7. largess (largesse), present (trifling)
8. gratuity
lagoon... 4. lake, pond, pool 5. atoll
laic... 3. lay 5. civil 6. layman
7. secular 8. temporal
lair... 3. bed, den, pen 4. cave, shed,
trap 5. abode, couch 6. cavern
7. retreat
Lais (Gr)... 7. hetaera (of Corinth)
8. mistress 14. beautiful woman
laissez faire, laisser faire... 5. let go
7. let pass 8. inaction, inactive
9. do–nothing, passivism, unconcern
12. indifference 15. noninterference
Laius' son... 7. Oedipus (of Thebes)
lake... 4. loch, mere, pond, pool, tarn
5. lacus 6. lagoon 7. carmine (color)
lake (pert to)...
  bass.. 4. rock 6. calico
  deposit.. 5. trona
  duck.. 5. scaup 7. mallard
  dweller.. 10. lacustrian
  dwelling.. 7. crannog
  growing in.. 10. lacustrine
  Hades (of).. 7. Avernus
  highest.. 8. Titicaca
  pert to.. 9. lacustral
  poet (Eng).. 6. lakist 7. Southey
  9. Coleridge 10. Wordsworth
  State.. 8. Michigan
lama... 4. monk 5. Dalai
Lamaism... 8. Buddhism
Lamaism, Buddhism (pert to)...
  convent.. 8. lamasery
  dignitary.. 8. hutukhtu
  palace site.. 5. Lhasa
  priest, monk.. 4. lama 6. Getsul
  9. Dalai Lama, Grand Lama
  reliquary, stupa.. 7. chorten
lamb... 3. ean, ewe 4. cade, yean
5. gigot, sheep 6. cosset 7. eanling,

lambkin 8. yearling 9. youngling
10. endearment
Lamb, Charles... 4. Elia (pen name)
lambaste... 4. beat, whip 6. thrash
7. reprove
lambent... 7. glowing, radiant
8. wavering 10. flickering 11. gliding
over
Lambeth (London)... 6. palace (of
Archbishops) 15. religious center
Lamb of God... 7. paschal 8. Agnus
Dei
lame... 4. halt 7. halting, limping
8. crippled, disabled, hobbling
9. defective 11. inefficient
lame (pert to)...
  brains.. 9. balminess, daffiness,
  goofiness, wackiness
  duck.. 7. session 9. insolvent
  10. politician, speculator
Lamech (pert to)...
  descendant of.. 4. Cain
  father of.. 5. Jabal, Jubal
  9. Tubal–cain
lament... 3. rue 4. keen, moan, sigh,
wail, weep 5. mourn 6. bemoan,
bewail, grieve, plaint, regret, repine,
yammer 7. condole, deplore, elegize,
weeping 8. jeremiad
lamentation... 3. cry, woe 5. dolor,
grief, tears 6. sorrow 7. anguish,
wailing
Lamentations... 4. Book (Old Test)
lamia... 5. witch 7. monster, vampire
(Myth) 8. cub shark 9. sorceress
lamina... 4. obex (brain) 5. blade,
flake, hinge, layer
lamp... 4. davy, etna 5. light, torch
6. crusie 7. lantern, lucigen
9. veilleuse
lamp (pert to)...
  black.. 4. soot
  holder.. 11. candelabrum
  lighter.. 5. spill
  safety.. 4. davy 7. Geordie
  slang.. 6. look at
  waving of.. 5. arati
lampadedromy (Gr)... 8. foot race
(with torch)
lampoon... 4. skit 5. squib 6. iambic
8. ridicule, satirize 10. pasquinade
lampoon writer... 8. satirist
lamprey... 3. eel 6. ramper
Lamps of the Lord... 5. yucca
(blooms)
Lancashire (Eng)... 6. Eccles
lance... 3. cut 4. dart, hurl, stab
5. blade, spear 6. incise, launch,
pierce, weapon 7. javelin
lance (pert to)...
  battle.. 5. joust
  head.. 5. morne
  knight.. 10. lansquenet (Hist)
  officer.. 4. Jack
  surgical.. 6. lancet
Lancelot... 6. Knight 13. Lancelot du
Lac
Lancelot's beloved... 6. Elaine
lancer... 5. uhlan 6. Hussar
7. cossack, soldier, spearer
land... 3. lot 4. acre, farm 5. arada,
downs, field, range, tilth 6. alight,

debark, ground, region 7. country,
pasture 9. disembark
land (pert to)...
absolute ppty.. 4. alod 7. alodium
alluvial.. 5. delta
ancestral.. 5. ethel
assessor.. 8. cadastre (cadaster)
church.. 5. glebe
heritable.. 4. odal, udal
holding.. 6. tenure 9. leasehold
leasehold.. 5. feoff
locked in.. 13. mediterranean
mythical.. 4. Eden 6. Utopia
9. Shangri–La
northernmost.. 5. Thule (Greenland)
open.. 4. moor, wold 5. heath
pile.. 5. cairn
prefix.. 4. agro
reversion.. 7. escheat
sandy.. 4. dene
surveyor.. 9. arpenteur
Sussex tract (Eng).. 5. laine
treeless.. 5. llano 6. steppe 7. prairie
verb.. 3. win 4. gain 5. catch
6. secure 7. capture
waste.. 5. heath
landed estate... 5. manor 7. demesne
landing place... 4. deck, dock, pier,
quay 5. field, levee, strip, wharf
7. airport 8. platform 9. staircase
landmark... 4. copa, tree 5. senal
Land of (the)...
bondage.. 5. Egypt
Cush.. 8. Ethiopia
Eden (East of).. 3. Nod
Enchantment.. 9. New Mexico
Leal.. 6. Heaven
Little Sticks (Canada).. 19. Barren
Islands border
Midnight Sun.. 6. Alaska, Norway
O'Cakes.. 8. Scotland
Opportunity.. 8. Arkansas
Plenty.. 6. Goshen
Promise.. 6. Canaan
Regrets.. 5. India
Rising Sun.. 5. Japan
Rose.. 7. England
Shamrock.. 4. Eire 7. Ireland
sleep.. 3. Nod
Steady Habits.. 11. Connecticut
Thistle.. 8. Scotland
Thousand Lakes.. 7. Finland
White Elephant.. 4. Siam
landscape... 7. paysage, scenery,
topiary
landslide... 9. avalanche
10. éboulement
Landsmaal, Landsmal... 8. language
(Norway)
Landstag... 4. Diet 8. assembly
11. legislature
lane... 4. path, road 5. alley, route,
track 6. airway, course, gullet, throat
7. channel, red land 8. footpath
10. passageway
language... 6. langue, speech, tongue
7. dialect, diction 8. parlance
9. utterance 11. linguistics
language (pert to)...
acquiring.. 12. chrestomathy
ancient.. 4. Pali 5. Aryan, Greek,
Latin 6. Hebrew 7. Chinese

8. Sanskrit
artificial.. 2. Od, Ro 3. Ido
7. Volapük 9. Esperanto
classical.. 5. Greek, Latin
conversant in.. 9. pantoglot
dead.. 4. Pali
deaf–mute.. 11. dactylology
expression, peculiar.. 5. idiom, lingo
6. jargon 7. dialect 13. colloquialism
international.. 2. Od, Ro 3. Ido
7. Volapük 9. Esperanto
pert to.. 8. semantic
pretentious.. 7. bombast
11. highfalutin'
Romance.. 5. Latin 6. French
7. Catalan, Italian, Spanish
9. Provençal 10. Portuguese
sacred.. 4. Pali
sign.. 11. dactylology
thieves'.. 5. argot
languid... 4. slow, weak 5. faint, inert,
weary 6. dreamy, feeble, sickly,
supine, torpid 7. passive 8. careless,
drooping, flagging, heedless, indolent,
sluggish 9. apathetic 10. spiritless
languish... 3. die 4. fade, fail, flag,
pine, wilt 5. droop, faint 6. repine,
sicken, weaken, wither 7. decline
languor... 3. kef (kief) 7. fatigue
8. dullness, weakness 9. indolence,
lassitude 10. dreaminess, drowsiness,
stagnation 12. listlessness,
sluggishness
lanky... 4. lean, tall, thin 5. gaunt,
spare 12. loose–jointed
lanner... 6. falcon
Lanterns, Feast of (Jap)... 3. Bon
Laodicean... 8. lukewarm 9. apathetic
11. indifferent
Laos...
aborigine.. 3. Kah
capital.. 9. Vientiane 12. Luang
Prabang
native.. 7. Chinese
14. Thai–Indonesian
religion.. 8. Buddhism
river.. 6. Mekong
tribesman.. 3. Yun
lap... 3. sip 4. fold, lick, wrap 5. drink
6. ripple, tipple 7. circuit
lapel... 4. fold 5. rever 6. facing,
lappet
lapicide... 11. stonecutter
lapidate... 4. kill (by stoning), pelt
5. stone
lapin... 6. rabbit
lapis lazuli... 4. blue 5. stone
8. lazurite, sapphire 10. azure stone
Lapland...
people.. 5. Lapps 10. Laplanders
11. Ural–Altaics 12. tent–dwellers
sledge (traveling).. 5. pulka (pukk)
sledge puller.. 8. reindeer
town.. 6. Kiruna
waterfalls.. 11. Harspranget
lappet... 4. flap, fold, lobe 5. lapel
6. wattle 9. appendage
lapse... 3. err 4. fall, slip 5. error,
fault, pause 6. expiry 7. decline,
misstep, relapse 8. apostasy
9. reversion
lapsus... 4. slip 5. error

12. inadvertence
lapsus calami ... 10. lipography
12. slip of the pen
lapsus linguae ... 15. slip of the
tongue
lapwing ... 4. gull 5. pewee, pewit
6. plover
larceny ... 5. theft 7. robbery
8. burglary, stealage 10. scrounging
larch ... 5. Larix 8. tamarack
lard ... 3. fat 4. line, pork 5. adeps,
bacon, baste, enarm 6. axunge,
cerate, enrich, fatten, grease
7. garnish 8. saindoux 9. lubricate
larder ... 6. pantry 7. buttery
8. cupboard 12. commissariat
lares (Rom) ... 4. gods (household)
7. spirits
large ... 3. big, nth 4. bold, huge,
much, vast 5. ample, bulky, burly,
giant, great, loose, scads 7. copious,
immense, leonine, liberal, massive,
titanic, weighty 8. colossal,
enormous, gigantic, spacious
9. excessive, extensive, plentiful
11. exaggerated 12. considerable
13. comprehensive
large (pert to) ...
artery .. 5. aorta
comb form .. 5. macro
fish .. 4. opah, tuna 9. swordfish
intestine .. 5. colon 6. caecum, rectum
knife .. 4. bolo, snee
lettered .. 6. uncial
number .. 4. slew 6. myriad
pulpit .. 4. ambo
volume .. 4. tome
largess, largesse ... 4. gift 6. bounty
7. charity, present 10. generosity,
liberality 11. beneficence
largest bird ... 6. condor 7. ostrich
13. whooping crane
largest fish (freshwater) ... 8. arapaima
larghetto ... 9. slow tempo
larghissimo ... 8. very slow
lariat ... 4. rope 5. honda (part), lasso,
noose, reata, riata
lark ... 5. ghost (anc), prank, revel
6. frolic 7. skylark, titlark 8. songbird
9. adventure, Alaudidae, parchment
(color)
larrigan ... 8. moccasin
larrikin ... 5. rough, rowdy 6. loafer
10. street Arab
larrup ... 3. hit 4. beat, blow, flog,
whip
larva ... 3. bot (bott) 4. grub, pupa
5. redia 6. embryo, maggot
7. atrocha 8. cercaria 9. chrysalis,
doodlebug 11. caterpillar
lascivious ... 4. lewd 5. bawdy
6. erotic, wanton 7. lustful, sensual
9. lecherous, salacious 10. libidinous,
licentious
laser ... 9. light beam
lash ... 3. tie 4. beat, bind, flag, whip
5. scold, smite 6. splice, strike
7. scourge
lass ... 4. girl 6. lassie, maiden
7. colleen 11. maidservant
lassitude ... 7. languor 8. debility,

lethargy, weakness 9. weariness
lasso ... 4. lash, rope 5. noose, reata
(riata), snare 6. lariat 8. cabestro
last ... 3. end 5. final, omega
6. endure, latest, lowest, newest,
penult, ultima, utmost 7. extreme,
supreme 8. eventual, rearmost,
terminal, ultimate 9. penultima
10. antepenult, conclusive, most
recent
last (pert to) ...
at last .. 6. Eureka
but one .. 6. penult
cry .. 10. dernier cri
evening .. 9. yesterday
long .. 7. outwear, perdure
9. perendure
month .. 3. ult 6. ultimo
offer .. 9. ultimatum
person in contest .. 4. mell
shoe .. 5. block
syllable but one .. 6. penult
syllable but two .. 10. antepenult
Last (pert to) ...
Assize .. 11. Last Inquest 12. Last
Judgment
Days of Pompeii character .. 4. Ione
5. Nydia 7. Glaucus
Gospel .. 4. Mass
of the Gothic Kings .. 8. Roderick
of the Mohicans .. 5. Uncas (Chief)
Supper .. 6. Christ 9. disciples
lasting ... 4. long 6. stable 7. abiding,
durable, eternal 8. constant
9. continual, lingering, permanent,
steadfast 11. substantial, unforgotten
lasting briefly ... 9. ephemeral,
temporary
lat .. 6. column, pillar
latchet ... 3. tap 4. lace (leather)
5. strap, thong 9. fastening
late ... 3. neo (comb form), new
4. sero 5. tardy 6. former, recent
7. belated, overdue 8. neoteric
10. behindhand
latent ... 5. inert 6. hidden 7. dormant
9. disguised, potential, quiescent,
suspended 10. underlying
later ... 4. anon, soon 5. after
6. future, mañana, puisne
9. posterior, presently
12. subsequently
lateral ... 5. flank, raphe 8. indirect,
sideward
lath ... 4. slat 9. wood strip
lathe ... 4. tool 7. mandrel
lather ... 4. foam, suds 5. froth
Latin (pert to) ...
alphabet letters .. 9. twenty–one
and .. 2. et
bath .. 7. balneum
behold .. 4. ecce
booth .. 7. taberna
bowl .. 6. patina
bronze .. 3. aes
church .. 8. Catholic
couch .. 9. accibutum
country .. 6. French 7. Italian, Spanish
dish .. 4. lanx 6. patina
foot .. 3. pes
God .. 3. Dei, Deo 4. Deus
7. Mercury

goddess.. 3. Dea
grammar (case).. 6. dative 8. ablative, genitive, vocative 10. accusative, nominative
historian.. 6. Justin
holidays.. 5. feria
hymn.. 13. Adesti Fideles
javelin.. 5. aclys, pilum
land.. 4. ager
law.. 6. Latium
life.. 4. vita
people.. 6. Romans
poet.. 4. Ovid 6. Horace
pronoun.. 2. tu 3. ego, hic 4. ille, ipse, iste
quarter (section).. 5. Paris 10. New Orleans
ram.. 5. aries
rite.. 4. orgy 5. sacra
seat.. 5. sella
trumpet.. 4. tuba 7. buccina
Way.. 9. Via Latina
latite... 4. lava
latitude... 4. zone 5. scope, width 6. extent 7. breadth, freedom 8. distance 10. liberality
latrant... 7. barking
latter... 4. last 5. final 6. latest 9. foregoing 10. more recent
Latter–day Saint... 6. Mormon
lattice... 6. grille 7. trellis 8. cancelli 9. crossbars, framework 12. crossed slats
latticelike... 7. grating 8. espalier 9. clathrate 10. cancellate
Latvia...
capital.. 4. Riga
city.. 6. Dvinsk, Libava (Libau)
money unit.. 3. lat (gold)
people.. 5. Letts
river.. 2. Aa
laud... 4. sing 5. extol 6. praise 7. applaud, commend, glorify, magnify 8. eulogize
laudable... 9. admirable, estimable 11. commendable, meritorious 12. praiseworthy
laudatory... 9. panegyric 10. flattering 11. approbatory, encomiastic 12. commendatory
laugh... 4. roar 5. fleer, smile, snort 6. cackle, deride, giggle, guffaw, hawhaw, tee–hee 7. chortle, chuckle 8. ridicule 10. cachinnate
laughable... 3. odd 5. droll, funny, merry, queer, witty 7. amusing, comical, jocular, risible, strange, waggish 8. humorous, sportive 9. burlesque, diverting, facetious, ludicrous 10. ridiculous
laughing... 3. gay 5. merry, riant 6. rident
laughing (pert to)...
bird.. 4. loon 10. woodpecker
falcon.. 4. hawk
gas.. 12. nitrous oxide
jackass.. 10. kingfisher, kookaburra
pert to.. 8. gelastic
laughter... 4. gelo (comb form) 5. gelos, mirth, risus 6. guffaw 12. cachinnation
launch... 4. hurl 5. begin, float, lance,

shove, start, throw 6. plunge 7. descant 9. undertake 10. inaugurate
laureate... 4. poet 6. decked (with laurel) 7. drowned, honored 13. distinguished
laurel... 3. bay, ivy, oak, oil 6. daphne, Kalmia, salmon 8. magnolia 9. sassafras, spoonwood
laurel wreath... 7. Iresine
lava... 2. aa, oo 3. ash 5. ashes 6. coulee, latite, scoria 8. lapillus, pahoehoe
lava field... 8. pedregal
lavaliere, lavalier... 7. pendant 8. ornament
lavatory... 5. basin 7. piscina 8. washroom 9. washbasin
lave... 4. lade, pour, wash 5. bathe, rinse 6. drench 8. absterge
lavender... 4. mint 6. purple 7. blue–red, perfume 9. fragrance
laver... 4. bowl 5. basin 6. trough, vessel 7. cistern, seaweed
Lavinia (pert to)...
father.. 7. Latinus
husband.. 6. Aeneas
mother.. 5. Amata
myth.. 5. Roman
lavish... 4. free, lush, rank, wild 5. spend 7. profuse 8. abundant, generous, prodigal, reckless, squander 9. bountiful, exuberant, impetuous, luxuriant, plentiful, unstinted 10. immoderate 11. extravagant 12. unrestrained 13. superabundant
law... 3. act, jus, lex 4. bill, code, jure, nisi, rule 5. axiom, canon, droit, edict, mercy, mesne 6. decree, equity, Latium, police 7. justice, precept, statute 9. enactment 12. constitution 13. jurisprudence
law (pert to)...
action.. 3. res 4. suit 5. actus 6. trover 7. impeach, implead 8. gravamen, replevin 9. ademption
Bible.. 6. Mosaic 12. Old Testament
claim.. 4. lien
code.. 9. Hammurabi 10. codex juris 16. Codex Justinianus
decree.. 4. nisi 5. edict
degree.. 3. LLD
divine.. 11. commandment
document.. 4. deed, writ 6. capias, elegit
drafting.. 10. nomography
evidence.. 7. constat
expert (US).. 5. Moore (John B)
for fourth offender (NY).. 6. Baumes
German Franks.. 5. Salic
goddess.. 4. Maat (Egypt)
heredity.. 8. Gresham's
Manu.. 5. sutra
mathematics.. 7. formula
morals.. 7. conduct
Moses.. 5. Torah (Tora) 10. Pentateuch
offender.. 5. felon 6. sinner 8. criminal 9. wrongdoer
offense.. 4. tort 5. crime, malum 6. delict
pert to.. 3. res 9. judiciary

philology.. 6. Grimm's
science.. 8. nomology
13. jurisprudence
student.. 8. stagiary
thought.. 7. noetics
warning.. 6. caveat
within the.. 5. licit 8. judicial
wrong.. 4. tort
lawful... 3. due 5. legal, licit, valid
9. permitted 10. legitimate
11. permissible
lawgiver... 5. Moses
lawless... 4. lewd 6. unruly 7. illegal
10. anarchical, disorderly
lawlessness... 4. riot 6. mutiny
7. anarchy, license 12. disobedience
lawmaker... 5. solon 7. senator
10. legislator 11. congressman
lawn... 5. green 7. batiste 9. grassplot
12. village green
lawyer... 5. agent 6. jurist, legist
7. abogado, shyster 8. advocate,
attorney, lawgiver 9. barrister,
counselor (counsellor), leguleian,
solicitor 11. intercessor, pettifogger
lax... 4. dull, free, limp, open, slow
5. loose, slack, tardy 6. remiss
7. lenient 8. backward, dilatory,
inactive, indolent, not tense
9. dissolute, scattered 10. licentious,
unconfined 12. unrestrained
lay... 3. bet, put 4. lair, pave, poem,
song 5. allay, ditty, place, quiet,
stake, still 6. ballad, hazard, impose,
impute, pacify 7. appease, ascribe,
deposit, relieve, store up 9. direction
10. profession
lay (pert to)...
aside.. 5. table 6. remove, shelve
7. dismiss, reserve 8. postpone
9. segregate
away.. 4. heap, hive 5. amass,
cache, hoard, store 7. husband
8. treasure 10. accumulate
bare.. 5. strip 6. denude, expose,
reveal 7. uncover
down.. 3. bet, set 5. level 6. give up
7. declare, deposit 9. postulate,
prescribe, stipulate, surrender
off.. 4. don't, stop 5. cease
6. recess 7. dismiss, measure
out.. 4. plan 5. set up 6. design
7. pattern
waste.. 6. ravage 7. destroy
8. desolate 9. depredate, devastate
layer... 3. bed 4. coat, derm, tier,
uvea 5. sloam (earth) 6. lamina
7. stratum (strata, pl)
10. substratum
lazar... 5. leper 9. loathsome
lazaretto, lazaret... 8. hospital 9. pest
house 10. lazar house
laziness... 7. inertia 8. oisivity,
vagrancy 9. indolence
10. ergophobia, remissness
12. slothfulness 13. shiftlessness
lazy... 3. lax 4. idle, slow 5. slack
6. otiose, remiss 7. dronish, laggard
8. dilatory, inactive, indolent, slothful,
sluggish 9. shiftless 13. lackadaisical
lazy man... 3. bum 4. lusk 5. drone,
idler 6. rotter 9. lazybones

11. Weary Willie
lea... 4. mead 5. haugh 6. meadow
7. pasture 9. grassland
leach... 3. wet 7. moisten 9. lixiviate,
percolate
lead... 3. cue, key, van 4. cart, clue,
head, lode 5. begin, guide, pilot,
plumb, usher 6. direct, entice,
escort, govern, induce 7. conduct,
pioneer, precede 8. antecede,
guidance 9. direction, influence,
precedent 10. precedence
lead (mineral)... 4. came (rod), gray,
shot 6. ceruse, fother, galena,
leaden, strass (glass) 7. bullets,
plummet 8. graphite, litharge,
plumbago
lead astray... 4. lure, mang 6. allure,
delude, entice, induce 7. deceive,
pervert 8. inveigle
leader... 4. head 5. chief, guide,
sinew 6. cantor, tendon 7. special
8. choragus, director 9. chieftain,
conductor 10. forerunner
leader (Eccl)... 3. fra 4. pope 5. rabbi
6. bishop, priest 8. cardinal,
minister, preacher 10. evangelist
leading... 5. chief, first 6. ruling
7. guiding 8. foremost, in the van
9. directing, governing
11. controlling
leaf... 3. ola 4. gear, page 5. blade,
frond, petal, sepal 6. areola, ligula,
spathe 7. tendril
leaf (pert to)...
book.. 5. folio
bud.. 5. gemma
curvature.. 8. epinasty (down)
9. hyponasty (upward)
floating.. 3. pad
green.. 11. chlorophyll
heart–shaped.. 9. obcordate
mold.. 5. humus
network.. 6. areola
part.. 5. bract, costa, stoma
6. pagina, stipel 7. petiole
9. petiolule
point, pointed.. 5. mucro
9. mucronate 13. mucroniferous
pore.. 8. lenticel
secretion.. 4. lerp
stalk.. 7. petiole 8. petiolus
vein.. 3. rib 5. costa
leafless... 9. aphyllous
leaflet... 5. pinna, tract 6. folder
7. booklet 8. pamphlet
13. advertisement
league... 4. band, Bund 5. Hanse,
union 7. combine 8. alliance
9. coalition 10. federation
11. affiliation, combination
13. confederation
League of Nations site... 5. Paris
(1920) 6. Geneva (Secretariat)
League of the Iroquois... 11. Five
Nations
Leah's sister... 6. Rachel
leak... 4. drip, hole, seep 5. crack
6. escape, run out 7. crevice, fissure
10. be revealed
leal... 4. just, real, true 5. legal, loyal
6. lawful 7. correct, genuine

8. accurate, faithful

lean... 4. bare, cant, lank, poor, rely, slim, tend 5. gaunt, slope, spare 6. barren, meager 7. scraggy, slender 8. not plump 9. deficient, gravitate

lean (pert to)...
animal, person.. 4. ribe (Scot)
emaciated.. 6. marcid
make.. 8. macerate
towards.. 6. prefer

Leander's love... 4. Hero

leaning... 5. slope 6. desire 7. pronate, tending 8. aptitude, enclitic, penchant, tendency 9. prejudice 10. partiality

Leaning Tower... 4. Pisa 6. Venice 7. Bologna 8. Zaragoza

lean–to... 4. roof, shed, wing 5. shack 9. extension (bldg)

leap... 4. dive, jump, ramp, skip 5. bound, caper, lunge, salto, spang, vault 6. spring 7. saltary 8. capriole

leaping... 7. jumping, salient, saltant 8. bounding, salience 9. saltation

learn... 4. lere (anc) 6. master 8. memorize 9. ascertain, determine

learned... 3. wot 4. read, sage 6. legist 7. erudite 8. lettered, literate, schooled 9. scholarly 12. well–informed

learned man... 6. pundit 7. scholar, teacher 8. mastered 9. professor

learning... 3. art, ken, wit 4. lore 7. culture 8. pedantry 9. education, erudition, knowledge, philology (love of), philomath 11. scholarship

lease... 3. let 4. hire, rent 5. weave 6. demise, remise, tenure 8. contract

leasehold... 6. rental, tenure

leash... 4. bind, cord, lash, lune (hawking) 5. reins, three 6. fasten, string, tierce 9. restraint 11. subjugation

leash hound... 5. limer

least... 5. grain 6. little, lowest, merest 7. minimum 8. minority, shortest, simplest, smallest 9. slightest

leather... 4. hide, skin 5. aluta, leder (old spelling) 6. vellum 7. canepin 8. cheveril (cheverel) 9. toughness

leather (kinds)... 3. kid, kip 4. calf, napa, vici 5. Mocha, suede 6. patent, saddle, skiver 7. chamois, Morocco 8. cordovan 9. sheepskin

leather (pert to)...
artificial.. 7. keratol
bookbinding.. 4. roan 6. levant
bottle.. 4. olpe 6. matara
cuirass.. 6. lorica
glove.. 5. suede, trank 8. capeskin
pare.. 5. skive
patch.. 5. clout
piece of.. 5. strap, thong 6. latigo
pouch (Highlander's).. 7. sporran
process.. 3. tan, taw
strap.. 5. thong 6. latigo
term.. 8. efflower
tool.. 6. skiver
worker.. 6. chamar, tanner 8. chuckler

leatherneck... 6. marine

leave... 2. go 4. quit 6. depart, retire, vacate 7. liberty 9. allowance 10. permission

leave (pert to)...
desolate.. 7. bereave
empty.. 6. vacate
isolated.. 6. desert, maroon
of absence.. 5. exeat 8. furlough
off.. 4. don't, stay 5. cease 6. desist
out.. 4. omit, skip 8. pass over
taking.. 5. adieu 6. congee 7. vamoose 9. departure

leaven... 4. barm 5. imbue, yeast 6. enzyme 7. corrupt (implied), ferment, pervade 10. impregnate

leaves... 5. pages, shaws 6. sepals 7. foliage

leaves, feeding on...
13. phyllophagous

leavings... 4. left, orts, rest 5. culls, dregs, dross, waste 6. refuse 7. remains, residue 8. remnants

leban, lebban... 5. drink 8. beverage, sour milk

Lebanon capital... 6. Beirut

Lebanon city... 7. Tripoli

lech (anc)... 4. slab 8. capstone, monument

lecher... 7. glutton 8. gourmand, parasite 9. debauchee, libertine

lectern... 4. ambo, desk 6. pulpit 10. escritoire

lecture... 4. jobe, rate 5. scold 6. lesson 7. declaim, expound, lection, reproof, reprove 8. instruct, scolding 9. discourse 10. admonition

lecturer... 6. docent, reader 7. teacher 9. prelector

Leda (pert to)...
geology.. 4. clay (marine)
husband.. 4. Zeus
mother of.. 6. Castor, Pollux 11. Helen of Troy
zoology.. 7. mollusk

ledge... 4. berm, edge, lode, reef, sill 5. shelf 7. retable, stratum

leechlike... 8. bdelloid

lees... 5. draff, dregs 8. sediment

leeward... (opp of windward) 9. protected, sheltered

Leeward Islands... 5. Nevis 7. Antigua, Barbuda, Redonda 8. Anguilla, Sombrero 10. Montserrat 13. St Christopher

Leeward Islands group... 6. Virgin 7. Society

leeway... 10. enough rope

left... see also *leave* 3. haw, kay 8. departed, larboard 9. abandoned, remaining

left (pert to)...
aground.. 6. neaped 8. beneaped
animal (motherless).. 4. cade 5. dogie
comb form.. 8. sinistro
hand (Mus).. 8. sinistra
hand page.. 5. verso
hand pitcher.. 8. southpaw
out.. 7. omitted 8. excluded 10. eliminated
spirally.. 11. sinistrally
to one's judgment.. 13. discretionary
toward the.. 5. aport 9. sinistrad,

sinistral 12. levorotatory (Chem)
left–handed... 6. clumsy, gauche
  7. oblique 8. southpaw 9. insincere,
  insulting 14. sinistromanual
  16. counterclockwise
left–handed marriage...
  10. morganatic
leftist... 7. liberal, radical
  10. left–winger, liberalist
  11. progressive
leg (pert to)...
  armor.. 4. jamb 6. greave 7. jambeau
  bone.. 4. shin 5. tibia 6. fibula
  calf.. 5. sural
  insect.. 4. coxa
  joint.. 4. hock, knee 5. thigh
  longest bone.. 5. femur
  of lamb (cooked).. 5. gigot
  term.. 4. crus 5. jambe 6. crural
legacy... 4. gift, will 6. devise
  7. bequest, codicil 9. testament
  10. bequeathal
legal... 4. leal 5. licit, valid 6. lawful
  10. authorized, legitimate
legal (pert to)...
  abstract.. 6. précis
  act, thing.. 5. actus
  action.. 3. res 4. case 7. detinet,
  lawsuit, summons
  case, postponed.. 7. remanet
  claim.. 4. lien
  confirmation.. 10. validation
  contestant.. 6. suitor 8. litigant
  9. plaintiff
  critic.. 6. censor
  decree, divorce.. 10. decree nisi
  defense.. 5. alibi
  delay.. 4. mora
  denial, stoppage.. 8. estoppel
  extract.. 7. estreat
  order.. 4. writ
  paper.. 4. deed, writ 5. lease
  6. escrow
  possession.. 6. seizin (seisin)
  power (to take).. 7. prender (prendre)
  process.. 6. caveat 7. detinet
  right, by.. 6. ex jure
  security.. 4. bond
  surrender.. 6. remise
legally competent... 5. capax
legate... 5. envoy 8. bequeath,
  delegate 10. ambassador, diplomatic
legend... 4. Edda, myth, saga, tale
  5. fable 7. history 9. narrative,
  tradition 11. inscription
legendary... 8. fabulous 9. imaginary,
  narrative 11. traditional
  12. mythological
legendary (pert to)...
  goddess (slave).. 5. Baube, Iambe
  primate.. 6. Dubric
  water sprite.. 6. undine
legendry... 7. legends (collectively)
leggings... 5. chaps, spats 6. strads
  7. gaiters, greaves, puttees
  8. gamashes, gambados
  12. galligaskins
legislate... 3. act 5. elect, enact
  8. pass laws 10. put through
legislative (pert to)...
  agent.. 8. lobbyist
  assembly.. 4. diet 6. assize, senate

8. congress 10. parliament
  group.. 4. bloc
legislator... 5. solon 7. senator
  8. lawgiver, lawmaker 9. statesman
  11. congressman 14. representative
legislature... 4. Diet 5. House
  6. Senate 8. Congress 9. bicameral
  (2 branches)
legitimate... 4. real, true 5. legal, licit,
  valid 6. cogent, lawful 7. genuine
  9. permitted 11. efficacious,
  justifiable
legman... 8. newshawk
legume... 3. pea, pod, uva 4. bean,
  soya 6. clover, lentil, loment
  7. alfalfa
leisure... 4. ease, time, toom 5. otium
  6. otiose 7. freedom 9. spare time
  11. convenience, opportunity
lemming... 4. maki, vari 5. mouse
  6. rodent
lemur... 5. indri, loris, makis, potto
  6. anguid, aye–aye, colugo, galago,
  macaco, monkey 7. tarsier
  8. Anguidae, mongoose
  10. angwantibo
Lenape... 6. Indian (Del)
lend... 4. loan 5. grant 6. devote (to)
  7. advance
length (pert to)...
  measure.. 4. area 5. gauge 6. linear,
  volume
  ten meters.. 9. decameter
  three–quarters inch.. 5. digit
  time.. 3. age, eon, era 6. moment,
  period
  two and 1/4 inches.. 4. nail
  unit.. 6. micron, parsec (Astron)
lengthen out... 7. prolong, stretch
  8. continue, elongate, protract
lengthwise... 5. along 12. horizontally
  14. longitudinally
lenient... 3. lax 4. easy, mild
  7. clement, patient 8. merciful,
  relaxing, tolerant 9. assuasive,
  emollient, softening
Lenin (pert to)...
  birthplace.. 9. Ulyanovsk
  famed as.. 8. Dictator (Russ)
  real name.. 7. Ulianov
Leningrad (Russ)... 9. Petrograd
  12. St Petersburg 15. Window on
  the West
lenis... 4. soft 6. gentle, smooth
lenitive... 4. mild 6. gentle
  8. mitigant, ointment, remedial
  9. assuasive, emollient, mitigator,
  relieving, softening 10. palliative,
  qualifying
lens... 5. toric 7. bifocal, lentoid
  8. meniscus, sunglass 9. lenticula
  10. anastigmat 13. apochromatism
Lent... 6. carême 9. Forty days, Great
  Fast 12. Quadragesima
lentamento... 6. slowly
lentando... 9. retarding 14. becoming
  slower
lenticula... 7. freckle, lentigo (freckly)
lento... 4. slow
Leo constellation star... 7. Regulus,
  the Lion
leopard... 4. pard 5. ounce 6. jaguar,

ocelot 7. cheetah, panther
leper... 5. lazar, mesel 6. Naaman
   (Bib)
Lepontine Alps... 10. Monte Leone
   (peak)
lepra... 7. leprosy 14. Hansen's
   disease
Lesbos... 5. Assos (Aristotle's)
   6. Island (Sappho's) 8. Mytilene
Les Miserables author... 4. Hugo
   (Victor)
lessen... 4. bate, wane 5. abate,
   lower, peter, relax 6. impair, minify,
   narrow, reduce, shrink, weaken
   7. cut down, relieve 8. decrease,
   diminish, mitigate, moderate, palliate
   11. deteriorate
lesser... 4. less 5. minor (Mus)
   7. smaller 8. inferior
Lesser Bear (Astron)... 9. Ursa Minor
Lesser Dog (Astron)... 10. Canis Minor
Lesser Lion (Astron)... 8. Leo Minor
let... 4. hire, rent 5. allow, lease,
   leave 6. hinder, impede, permit
   7. prevent
let (pert to)...
   down.. 5. lower 8. comedown,
      drawback, relaxing 10. slackening
      14. disappointment
   fall.. 4. drop, slip 5. spill 7. mention
   in.. 5. admit, enter 6. insert
   it be given.. 5. detur
   it stand.. 3. sta (Mus) 4. stet
   up.. 4. rest 5. cease, pause, relax
      6. slow up 7. slacken 8. decrease
lethal... 5. fatal, feral 6. deadly, mortal
   7. deathly, killing 11. destructive
   12. death–dealing
lethargic... 4. dull 5. heavy, inert
   6. drowsy, sleepy, torpid
   8. comatose, listless 9. apathetic
lethargy... 4. coma 5. sleep, sopor
   6. apathy, stupor, torpor 7. languor
   8. hebetude, neurosis 9. lassitude
   10. drowsiness (morbid)
Lethe... 5. abyss, Hades, river
   8. oblivion 13. forgetfulness
lethiferous... 6. deadly 11. destructive
Leto (pert to)...
   mother of.. 6. Apollo 7. Artemis
   Roman name.. 6. Latona
   wife of.. 4. Zeus
letter... 4. note, type 7. epistle,
   message 9. character
   13. communication
letter (pert to)...
   bright star.. 4. Beta
   carrier.. 6. correo 7. mailman,
      postman
   cross stroke.. 5. serif
   first.. 7. initial
   letter for letter.. 9. literatim
   marks.. 5. breve
   of advice.. 11. lettre d'avis
   of challenge.. 6. cartel
   representation.. 10. literation
   short.. 4. line, note 6. billet
   sloping.. 6. italic
   sound loss (last).. 7. apocope
   two letters (one sound).. 7. digraph
      9. diphthong

writer.. 13. correspondent
letters (pert to)...
   decorate with.. 7. miniate
      10. illuminate
   man of.. 9. literatus
   ref to.. 8. literary
lettuce... 3. cos 4. head 7. Lactuca,
   romaine
leukocyte... 9. corpuscle (white)
Levant... 4. East 6. Orient 7. leather
   (Morocco) 8. East wind
Levantine (pert to)...
   country.. 13. Mediterranean
   garment.. 6. caftan
   herb.. 6. madder
   ketch.. 3. bum 4. jerm, saic 5. xebec
      6. settee 8. levanter
   valley.. 4. wadi (wady)
   wind.. 7. Morocco
levee... 4. bank, dike, pier, quay
   5. ridge 6. durbar, trench
   8. assembly 9. reception
   10. embankment
level... 4. even, fell, flat, just, raze
   5. equal, grade, plane, plani (comb
   form), point 6. peavey (peavy),
   smooth, steady, topple 7. flatten,
   terrace, uniform 8. demolish,
   equalize, parterre 12. well–balanced
lever... 3. bar, lam, pry 5. crank,
   jimmy, pedal, prise 6. peavey
   (peavy), tappet, tiller 7. crowbar,
   treadle
leviathan (pert to)...
   animal (Bib).. 5. whale 6. dragon
      9. crocodile
   embroidery.. 6. canvas
      11. cross–stitch
   political.. 12. (the) commonwealth
   size.. 4. huge 7. titanic
      10. formidable
Levi's father (Bib)... 5. Jacob
Levite... 5. tribe 10. descendant
Levitical... 7. Aaronic 9. Aaronical
   10. priesthood (Mormon)
Leviticus... 10. Pentateuch
levity... 6. gaiety 8. buoyancy
   9. frivolity, lightness 10. triviality,
   volatility
levy... 3. tax 4. fine, wage (war)
   5. rally, stent 6. assess, impose
   7. collect, estreat 9. recruital
lex... 3. law 7. statute
lexicon... 4. book (of words)
   10. dictionary, vocabulary
lex loci... 13. law of the place
lex non scripta... 12. unwritten law
liability... 4. debt 5. debit 8. cessavit
   9. proneness 10. likelihood,
   obligation 11. possibility
   14. responsibility
liable... 3. apt 5. bound 6. likely
   7. exposed, subject 10. answerable,
   chargeable 11. responsible
liable (pert to)...
   likely to.. 3. apt 5. prone
      11. predisposed
   not liable.. 6. exempt
   to objection.. 13. exceptionable
   to penalty.. 6. guilty
Lia Fail... 12. Stone of Scone
   15. Coronation Stone (Ir)

liaison... 4. link 7. joining 8. intimacy, intrigue 11. co–operation 18. intercommunication
liana... 4. cipo 5. vines (woody) 9. wild grape
liar... 5. cheat 6. fibber 7. Ananias, wernard (obs) 8. deceiver, fabulist, perjurer 12. prevaricator
Lias system... 8. Jurassic
libation... 5. drink 8. oblation, offering, potation
libel... 4. bill 6. defame 7. lampoon, request, slander 8. circular (obs), handbill, roorback 10. defamation 11. certificate, declaration 12. supplication
liberal... 4. free, Whig 5. ample, frank 7. copious, profuse 8. eclectic, generous 9. bountiful, extensive, plentiful 10. hospitable, munificent 11. broad–minded, magnanimous 12. uncontrolled
liberate... 4. flee, free 5. loose 6. redeem 7. deliver, manumit, release 8. separate, unfetter 9. disengage 10. emancipate
Liberia...
capital.. 8. Monrovia
city.. 8. Buchanan 10. Greenville
gulf.. 5. Sidra
language.. 3. Kru 7. English
people.. 3. Vai (Vei) 5. Negro
liberty... 4. ease, free 5. leave 7. freedom, license 9. exemption, privilege 10. permission 11. opportunity
librarian... 7. bookman 10. bibliosoph, bibliothec 13. bibliothecary
Libya, Africa...
astronomy.. 4. Mars (portion)
capital.. 7. Tripoli 8. Benghazi
district.. 6. Fezzan 9. Cyrenaica 12. Tripolitania
language.. 7. Hamitic
oasis (saline).. 6. Sebkha (Sebka)
people.. 5. Arabs
sea.. 13. Mediterranean
Libya, Gr (pert to)...
children.. 5. Belus 6. Agenor
heroine of.. 5. Libya
husband.. 8. Poseidon
license... 5. right 6. bandon, permit 7. dismiss, freedom, liberty 8. sanction 9. approbate, authority, authorize, privilege 10. permission 11. lawlessness 13. authorization
licentious... 3. lax 4. lewd 5. loose 7. immoral, lawless 9. debauched, dissolute 10. lascivious, profligate 12. uncontrolled, unrestrained
licet... 6. lawful 7. granted 12. it is conceded
lichens (pert to)...
abounding in.. 9. lichenose
derivative.. 4. moss 5. usnic 6. litmus
genus.. 5. Usnea 7. Evernia
study of.. 11. lichenology
licit... 3. sue 4. just 5. legal 6. lawful 9. permitted
lick... 3. lap, win 4. flog, whip 5. lap up, taste 6. baffle, defeat, thrash

7. conquer 8. overcome, vanquish
licorice... 5. abrin 9. jequirity
lid... 3. cap, hat 4. bred, case, roof 5. cover 6. eyelid 7. stopper 9. operculum
lid, put on the... 3. end 6. hush up 7. license 8. complete, suppress
lie... 3. fib 4. rest 7. falsify, falsity, recline, untruth 9. deception, falsehood, mendacity 10. equivocate 13. prevarication
lie (pert to)...
at ease.. 4. loll 5. droop 6. dangle
face down.. 7. pronate
hidden, in ambush.. 4. lurk, plot 6. in wait 9. insidiate 11. concealment
in warmth.. 4. bask 9. luxuriate
low.. 6. abased 9. prostrate
prostrate.. 4. flat 5. creep 6. grovel
Liebestraum composer... 5. Liszt
Liechtenstein, Europe...
capital.. 5. Vaduz
government.. 12. principality
language.. 6. German
religion.. 8. Catholic
lief (anc)... 4. dear, fain, glad 7. willing 8. disposed 9. agreeably, favorably
lieutenant... 6. deputy 10. substitute 11. locum tenens
life... 3. vie 4. bios 5. being 6. always, energy, spirit 8. vitality, vivacity 9. animation, existence
life (pert to)...
after death.. 8. Olam–haba
animal.. 4. bios 5. biota (flora, fauna)
biology.. 4. bios
comb form.. 3. bio
giving.. 9. animative 11. procreative
god of.. 6. Faunus
insurance.. 7. tontine
jacket (sl).. 7. Mae West
later, older.. 8. autumnal
lifelike.. 5. alike, vital 6. biotic 9. realistic
plant.. 4. bios 5. biota
principle.. 5. atman, prana, tenet 6. spirit
prolonger.. 6. elixir
science of.. 7. anatomy, biology, zoology 12. paleontology
sea.. 5. coral 8. plankton
staff of.. 5. bread
without.. 4. dead 5. azoic 8. lifeless 9. inanimate
lifeless... 4. abio (comb form), dead, dull, flat 5. amort, azoic, heavy, inert, vapid 6. jejune, torpid 8. inactive, listless 9. bloodless, exanimate, inanimate, powerless, tasteless 10. lackluster, spiritless, unanimated
lifetime... 3. age, day, eon (aeon) 6. always 8. duration 10. generation
lift... 3. aid, pry 4. jack, perk 5. boost, exalt, heave, hoist, raise, steal, theft 6. puff up, thrill 7. derrick, elevate, improve, inspire 8. elevator 11. inspiration
lifting device... 4. jack, pump

5. crane, davit, lever, tongs
7. capstan, derrick, erector
8. elevator, heighten, windlass
lifting muscle . . . 7. erector, levator
ligament . . . 4. bond, cord 6. tendon
  7. bandage
ligan, lagan . . . 6. debris, jetsam
  7. flotsam
ligature . . . 3. tie 4. band, bond, cord,
  note 6. amulet, binder, taenia
  7. bandage
light . . . 3. arc, gay, sun 4. dawn, easy,
  glim, lamp, lume, mild, pale, soft
  5. flare, flood, klieg, laser, taper
  6. alight, aspect, blonde, bright,
  candle, gentle, ignite, illume, medium,
  window 7. cresset, fragile, glimmer,
  glowing, trivial 8. buoyancy, daylight,
  delicate, illumine, lambency, radiance,
  trifling 9. effulgent 10. brightness,
  luminosity, weightless 11. information
  12. incandescent
light (pert to) . . .
apparatus . . 9. holophote
circle . . 4. halo, nimb 6. corona,
  nimbus 7. aureola, aureole
cloud . . 6. nimbus
coating . . 4. film
footed . . 4. fast 5. agile
globe . . 4. bulb
god . . 6. Balder (Baldr)
handed . . 4. deft
headed . . 5. dizzy 6. fickle
  9. beeheaded
image . . 8. spectrum
leading . . 8. luminary
reflector . . 4. lens 6. mirror
refractor . . 5. prism
science . . 6. optics
source . . 3. sun
touch . . 3. dab
unit . . 3. lux, pyr 4. phot, watt
  5. lumen 6. carcel, Hefner
without . . 4. dark 7. aphotic, obscure
  8. starless 9. pitch–dark
  10. caliginous
yellow . . 5. amber
light and airy . . . 7. tenuous
  8. delicate, ethereal
light and quick . . . 6. nimble, volent
light dress fabric . . . 6. merino
  8. cashmere 9. bombazine, paramatta
  (parramatta)
lighten . . . 4. ease 5. allay, cheer, clear
  6. reduce 7. gladden, relieve
  8. brighten, illumine, jettison
  9. alleviate, disburden 10. illuminate
lighter . . . see also *light* 4. scow
  5. barge 7. gabbard, igniter, pontoon
  8. chopboat (Chin)
lighthearted . . . 3. gay 6. upbeat
  7. buoyant 8. carefree, cheerful,
  jubilant 9. vivacious
Light Horse Harry . . . 3. Lee (Gen
  Henry Lee)
lighthouse . . . 5. tower 6. beacon,
  pharos 7. seamark 10. watchtower
lightness . . . 6. gaiety, levity
  8. airiness, buoyancy, sobriety
  9. flippancy, frivolity, giddiness
  10. fickleness, triviality, volatility,
  wantonness 11. flightiness,

inconstancy, instability
  12. unsteadiness 14. weightlessness
  15. thoughtlessness
lightning . . . 4. lait 5. flash, levin
  6. stroke 8. flashing 9. discharge
lightning (pert to) . . .
bug . . 6. beetle 7. firefly
discharge . . 4. bolt 11. thunderbolt
form . . 4. fork 5. chain, sheet
reference to . . 8. fulgural
rod . . 8. arrester
stone . . 9. fulgurite
war . . 10. blitzkrieg
lightsome . . . 3. gay 4. airy 5. agile,
  clear, light, lucid, merry 6. fickle,
  nimble 7. lighted 8. cheerful,
  cheering, graceful, luminous, unsteady
  9. frivolous 12. lighthearted
lights out . . . 4. taps
ligneous . . . 5. woody 6. wooden,
  xyloid 8. firewood
lignite . . . 4. coal
like . . . 2. as 4. copy, love 5. enjoy,
  equal, liken, savor 6. admire, desire
  7. similar 10. comparable
  11. counterpart, homogeneous
like (pert to) . . .
bone . . 6. osteal
fern . . 8. frondose, frondous
gland . . 7. adenose
gold . . 7. aureate
house, dome . . 5. domal
kneecap . . 7. rotular 10. rotuliform
sea lion . . 7. otarian, otarine
suffix . . 2. ar, ic 3. ine, oid, ose
likeable, likable . . . 6. genial
  8. charming, pleasant
likelihood . . . 8. prospect 10. good
  chance 11. possibility, probability
  14. apparently true
likely . . . 3. apt, fit 5. prone 6. comely
  8. credible, feasible, probable, suitable
  9. promising 11. verisimilar
likeness . . . 4. copy, icon, twin
  5. clone, guise, image 6. effigy,
  statue 7. parable, picture, replica
  8. parallel, portrait 9. imitation,
  semblance 10. comparison,
  photograph, similarity 11. counterfeit
  12. reproduction 14. representation
likewise . . . 3. too 4. also 5. ditto
  8. moreover 11. furthermore
liking . . . 4. like, love, lust 5. fancy
  6. comely 7. delight 8. pleasing
  10. preference 12. predilection
lilac . . . 5. lilas, mauve 6. purple
  7. syringa
lilac throat . . . 11. hummingbird
Lilliputian . . . 4. tiny 5. dwarf, minim
  6. midget 7. dwarfed 10. diminutive
lilt . . . 3. air 4. song, tune 5. swing
  6. poetic, rhythm 7. rejoice
lily . . . 2. ti 3. lis 4. aloe, ixia, sego
  5. calla, lotus, onion, water, wokas
  (wocas), yucca 6. Allium, Nuphar
  8. daffodil, mariposa, martagon,
  soaproot 9. narcissus
lily (pert to) . . .
family, genus . . 4. aloe 6. Tulipa
  7. Bessera 9. Liliaceae
  10. Hyacinthus
grass . . 10. cuckoopint

iron.. 7. harpoon
of France.. 10. fleur–de–lis
shaped.. 7. crinoid 9. crinoidal
water.. 8. Castalia, Nymphaea
lily of the valley (pert to)...
bud.. 3. pip
Cape Cod.. 13. barney–clapper
English.. 6. mugget
family.. 15. Convallariaceae
liliaceous plant.. 5. yucca
shrub.. 10. fetterbush
tree.. 6. sorrel
lima bean disease... 6. mildew
9. yeast spot
liman... 5. marsh 6. lagoon
limb... 3. arm, fin, imp, leg 4. wing
5. bough, scamp 6. branch, member
7. flipper 9. anaclasis
limber... 4. limp, weak 5. agile, lithe,
loose 6. flabby, pliant, supple
7. flaccid, lissome 8. flexible, yielding
limbo... 4. hell, jail 6. prison
9. purgatory
limbs, absence of... 6. amelia
7. acolous
lime... 4. calx 5. color, fruit
8. chlorine, fumigant 9. deodorant,
quicklime 11. green–yellow
12. linden yellow
limen... 9. threshold
limestone... 4. calp, malm 5. chalk
6. marble, oolite 8. pisolite
lime tree... 6. linden, tupelo
limey... 6. sailor 7. soldier
limit... 3. end, fix, ori (comb form)
4. term 5. allot, bourn 6. summit
7. confine 8. boundary, capacity,
restrain, restrict, terminal
11. restriction, termination
12. consummation
limited... 3. few 5. local, scant
6. finite, narrow, scanty 7. bounded,
topical 8. confined, reserved
9. astricted, parochial 10. restricted
11. conditional, topopolitan
13. circumscribed
limiting... 7. hedging 10. qualifying,
relational 11. restraining, restricting,
restrictive
limn... 4. draw 5. paint 6. depict
7. portray 8. decorate 9. delineate
10. illuminate
limp... 3. hop, lax 4. halt, soft, thin,
weak 5. loose 6. flabby, limber
7. flaccid 8. drooping, flexible
9. inelastic 13. unsubstantial
limpid... 4. pure 5. lucid 6. bright
7. crystal 8. pellucid 11. translucent,
transparent 12. intelligible
Lincoln, Abraham (pert to)...
assassin.. 15. John Wilkes Booth
birthplace.. 8. Kentucky (1809)
debater.. 7. Douglas (Stephen A)
dog.. 4. Fido
mother.. 10. Nancy Hanks
Secy of State.. 6. Seward
Secy of War.. 7. Stanton
son.. 10. Robert Todd
wife.. 8. Mary Todd
Lincoln (pert to)...
color.. 9. Carthamus 11. yellow–green
sheep (breed).. 7. English

Lindbergh, Charles A (pert to)...
birthplace.. 7. Detroit (1902)
flight field.. 9. Roosevelt (LI)
flight to (1927).. 5. Paris (1st)
retreat.. 10. Illiec Isle (Fr)
wife.. 10. Anne Morrow
linden... 3. lin 4. lime, teil 5. Tilia
line... 3. row 4. arrow, axis, cant, ceil,
clew, cord, face, mark, race, rail,
rein, rule, seam, side 5. agone,
align, raphe, ridge, route, stria, track
6. crease, isobar, policy, series,
streak, stripe 7. engrave, outline
8. boundary, vocation, wainscot
9. delineate
line (pert to)...
adjusting.. 9. alinement
central.. 4. axis
comb form.. 4. lino
conceptual, geological.. 6. agonic,
isotac, tropic 7. equator 8. isothere,
isotherm, latitude, meridian
9. longitude
equidistant.. 8. parallel
fine (type).. 5. leger, serif
fishing.. 5. snell 7. ratline (ratlin)
imaginary.. 7. equator, Maginot
mathematics.. 4. sine 5. agone
6. secant 7. tangent
measure.. 3. gry 4. rule
meteoric.. 6. isobar
nautical.. 6. earing 7. halyard,
hawsing
poetic.. 5. stich, verse
racing.. 4. wire
raised.. 4. weal, welt 5. ridge
selling.. 11. merchandise
soldiers.. 4. file, rank 6. cordon
transport.. 5. stage 7. carrier
8. carriage
type.. 5. agate, serif
up, lineup.. 4. plan 5. align
6. muster 7. arrange 8. schedule
9. formation 11. arrangement,
parallelize
lineage... 3. kin 4. race 5. birth,
blood, stock, tribe 6. family, strain
7. descent 8. pedigree 9. offspring
10. extraction, progenitor
lineal... 6. racial 10. continuous,
delineated 12. genealogical
lineman... 3. end 5. guard 6. center,
tackle 7. wireman 11. electrician
linen... 4. crea, duck, lawn, lint
5. crash, gulix, inkle (tape), toile
6. barras, damask, dowlas, napery,
sheets 7. cambric, Holland, lockram
ling... 4. fish, hake 5. heath 6. burbot
7. eelpout, Gidadae, heather
8. chestnut
linger... 3. lag 4. drag, idle, wait
5. dally, defer, delay, dwell, hover,
tarry 6. dawdle, go slow, loiter,
remain 8. continue, hesitate
13. procrastinate
lingerie... 9. underwear 10. underlinen
11. underthings 14. unmentionables
lingering... 5. delay 7. chronic
8. dilatory, slowness 10. protracted
lingo... 4. cant 6. jargon, lingua,
patois, patter, tongue 8. language
lingua... 5. lingo 6. jargon, tongue

11. hypopharynx
lingual... 7. glossal 9. lingulate
  10. linguiform, tonguelike
linguistics... 6. syntax 7. grammar
  8. language 9. phonology, semantics
  10. lexicology
link... 3. tie 4. bond, join, loop, yoke
  5. annex, nexus, torch, unite
  6. couple, member, relate
  7. connect, liaison, passage
  8. catenate 12. intermediary
linkage... 5. tie–up, union 6. hookup
  7. joinder, joining 8. junction
  11. conjunction
linking... 7. liaison 9. annectent
links in a chain... 7. hundred
lion... 3. cat, cub, leo 4. puma
  5. simba 6. cougar, Lionel, lionet
  8. Felis leo 9. celebrity 12. King of
  Beasts
Lion (pert to)...
  England.. 8. heraldry
  God.. 3. Ali
  Lucerne.. 11. Switzerland (Sculpture)
  St Mark.. 6. Venice (winged)
  the North.. 6. Sweden (King
  Adolphus)
lionlike... 6. feline 7. catlike, leonine
lip... 3. jib, rim 4. edge, kiss, talk
  5. cheil, words 6. flange, labium,
  labrum, speech 7. cheilos
  8. labellum 10. mouthpiece
  12. impertinence
lip (pert to)...
  comb form.. 5. chilo, labio
  formed.. 6. labial
  inflammation.. 9. cheilitis
  ornament.. 6. labret
  service.. 9. hypocrisy 10. sanctimony
  12. unctuousness
  surgery.. 9. chilotomy 11. chiloplasty
  tumor.. 7. chiloma
lipped... 6. labial 7. labiate
liquefy... 4. fuse, melt, thaw
  6. reduce 8. dissolve, fluidify
  10. deliquesce
liqueur... 5. crème, noyau, sirup
  6. cognac, genepi, kummel
  7. cordial, curaçao, ratafia
  8. absinthe, anisette 9. Cointreau
  11. Benedictine
liquid... 5. clear, fluid 6. watery
  7. flowing 8. beverage, manifest, not
  solid
liquid (pert to)...
  assets.. 4. cash 5. money
  9. resources
  chemical.. 7. acetone 8. furfural
  inflammable.. 3. gas 5. ether
  7. alcohol 8. gasoline
  oily.. 5. olein 7. aniline, picamar
  soap.. 6. napalm
  thick.. 3. tar 4. dope 5. syrup (sirup)
  weak.. 5. blash
liquidate... 4. kill 6. depose, pay off,
  settle 8. amortize 9. discharge
  11. exterminate
liquor... 3. ale, dew, gin, rum, rye
  4. beer, brew, grog, lush, sake, wine
  5. hooch, kefir, punch, stout, vodka
  6. arrack (arak), arrope, elixir, whisky
  (whiskey) 8. cocktail, highball

9. applejack, moonshine
  10. chasse–café
liquor container... 3. keg 5. flask
  6. barrel, bottle 8. cellaret, decanter
liquor maker... 6. abkari (Ind), brewer
  7. vintner 9. distiller
liquor server... 6. barman 7. barmaid,
  skinker (anc), tapster
liquor shop... 3. bar 6. saloon, tavern
  7. barroom, cabaret, shebeen (Scot),
  taproom 8. alehouse 9. groghouse,
  honky–tonk 11. rathskeller (ratskeller)
liripipe, liripoop (Hist)... 4. hood
  5. scarf 6. dotard, tippet
lissom... 5. layer 7. stratum
  8. platform 12. strand of rope
lissome... 5. agile, lithe 6. limber,
  nimble, supple 7. willowy 8. flexible
list... 3. tip 4. edge, file, roll, rota,
  rote 5. index, limit, panel, table
  6. careen, edging, enlist, record,
  roster, stripe 7. catalog, incline
  8. calendar, classify, manifest,
  register, schedule, tabulate
  9. catalogue, enclosure, inventory,
  repertory 10. repertoire
  11. enumeration
list (pert to)...
  actors.. 4. cast
  competitors.. 5. entry, slate
  foods.. 4. menu 5. carte
  investments.. 9. portfolio
  memoranda.. 5. scrip
  officers.. 6. roster
  references.. 5. index
listen... 3. ear 4. hear, heed 6. attend
  7. give ear, hearken (harken)
  8. overhear 9. eavesdrop
listening... 7. audient 9. attentive
listing... 4. list 6. strips 7. selvage
  10. enlistment, enrollment
listless... 4. dull 6. abject, drowsy,
  moping, supine 7. languid
  8. careless, heedless, sluggish
  9. apathetic 10. spiritless
  11. unconcerned 13. uninteresting
litchi nut... 8. rambutan
literary... 6. versed 8. lettered
  9. classical 11. book–learned
literary (pert to)...
  composition.. 5. cento, essay, opera
  8. rhetoric
  criticism.. 9. epicrisis
  drudge.. 4. grub, hack
  extracts.. 9. anthology
  fragments.. 3. ana 5. notes
  8. analecta, analects
  laws.. 9. copyright
  piracy.. 10. plagiarism
  selection.. 7. excerpt
  style.. 5. prose 6. purism 8. pedantic
literature... 4. book, epic, Veda
  5. drama, lyric, novel 6. ballad,
  poetry 7. fiction, writing
  10. nonfiction 13. belles–lettres
lithe... 4. slim 6. limber, supple, svelte
  7. lissome, slender 8. flexible
Lithuania...
  capital.. 5. Vilna (Vilnius) 6. Kaunas
  (Kovno)
  Jew.. 6. Litvak
  people.. 5. Balts, Letts 6. Aestii

port .. **8.** Klaipeda (Memel)
river .. **6.** Niemen
litigant ... **6.** suitor **9.** defendant,
    disputant, litigator, plaintiff
litigation ... **4.** suit **7.** contest, dispute,
    lawsuit **10.** contention, discussion
litigious ... **10.** disputable
    11. belligerent, contentious
litten ... **7.** lighted **8.** cemetery
    10. churchyard
litter ... **3.** bed, hay **4.** bier, mess
    5. couch, dooly (doolie), mulch,
    straw, young **6.** coffin, jumble
    7. clutter, rubbish **9.** palanquin,
    stretcher
litter of pigs ... **6.** farrow
little ... **3.** sma, wee **4.** puny, tiny,
    weak **5.** brief, petit, petty, scant,
    short, small **6.** dapper, petite, slight
    7. not much **8.** trifling **9.** niggardly
    11. unimportant **12.** narrow–minded
    14. inconsiderable
little (pert to) ...
    bethel .. **6.** chapel (seaman's), church
    by little .. **6.** slowly **7.** peu à peu
    9. piecemeal, poco a poco
    comb form .. **5.** steno
    devil .. **3.** imp **4.** minx **5.** rogue
    7. ruffian **13.** mischief–maker
    fellow .. **6.** shaver
    finger, toe .. **7.** minimus
    flag .. **9.** banderole
    music term .. **4.** poco
    ring .. **7.** annulet
Little Rhody ... **11.** Rhode Island
Little Women, author ... **6.** Alcott
    (Louisa)
littoral ... **4.** zone (marine) **5.** shore
    7. coastal **9.** bordering
liturgical ... **10.** ceremonial
    11. ritualistic
liturgy ... **4.** rite **6.** ritual **8.** ceremony
    14. consuetudinary
live ... **5.** dwell, exist **6.** reside
    7. breathe **8.** continue, have life
live (pert to) ...
    by sponging .. **5.** cadge
    by stratagems .. **5.** shark
    by wits .. **5.** cheat **7.** deceive, falsify
    13. Machiavellize
    earlier .. **8.** pre–exist
    in .. **7.** inhabit
    in tents .. **5.** nomad **7.** scenite
    in the country .. **9.** rusticate
live ... **5.** alert, alive, vital, vivid
    6. bright, lively, living, virgin (mineral)
    7. charged, not dead **8.** vigorous
    9. energetic **11.** electrified
lively ... **3.** gay, vif **4.** airy, grig, keen,
    pert, spry, yare **6.** active, blithe,
    bright, snappy **7.** animate, buoyant,
    pungent, tittupy (tittuppy) **8.** spirited
    9. energetic, sprightly, vivacious
    10. enlivening, rebounding
    11. interesting **12.** effervescent
liver (pert to) ...
    comb form .. **6.** hepato
    disease .. **9.** cirrhosis, hepatitis
    duct .. **4.** bile
    pert to .. **5.** hepar **7.** hepatic
    resembling .. **8.** hepatoid
Liverpool native ... **12.** Liverpudlian

liverwort ... **6.** Riccia **8.** agrimony,
    hepatica **9.** bryophyte
living ... **4.** life **5.** alive, being, quick
    6. extant **7.** animate, organic, topical
    8. benefice, existent, lifelike
    10. livelihood **11.** subsistence
living (in, on, near) ...
    currents .. **5.** lotic
    ground .. **7.** epigeal
    holes .. **11.** latebricole
    leaves .. **13.** phyllophagous
    oxygen .. **7.** aerobic
    plane (same) .. **8.** coplanar
    poverty .. **11.** necessitous
    river bank .. **9.** riparious
    rivers, streams .. **9.** rheophile
    seas (deep) .. **8.** bathybic
    shores .. **8.** littoral
    solitude, seclusion .. **10.** eremitical
    11. eremiticism
    tents .. **7.** scenite
    together .. **11.** contubernal
living (pert to) ...
    again .. **6.** Buddha **7.** revived
    8. Hutukhtu **9.** redivivus
    being .. **5.** wight **6.** animal
    8. organism
    capable of .. **6.** viable
    dull .. **10.** vegetation
    individual .. **4.** bion
    near the ground .. **7.** epigeal
    together .. **8.** intimate **11.** contubernal
    (contubernial)
lixivium ... **3.** lye **6.** bleach **8.** cleanser
lizard ... **3.** dab, eft **4.** adda, gila,
    newt, seps, uran **5.** agama, anoli,
    gecko, skink, varan **6.** dragon,
    hardim, iguana, moloch **7.** monitor,
    saurian, tuatera **8.** basilisk
    9. chameleon **10.** chuckwalla,
    salamander
llama ... **6.** alpaca, vicuna **7.** guanaco
load ... **3.** jag **4.** fill, lade, onus
    5. cargo **6.** burden, charge, weight
    7. fraught, freight, oppress, prepare
    8. contents, encumber **10.** imposition
    11. encumbrance
loaded ... **5.** drunk, flush, laden, ready
    7. charged, fraught **8.** burdened,
    weighted **10.** in the chips
loader of vessels ... **9.** stevedore
loadstone, lodestone ... **6.** magnet
    8. terrella **9.** magnetite
loaf ... **4.** idle, lump **5.** bread **6.** loiter,
    lounge **9.** Eucharist
loafer ... **5.** idler **6.** beggar **7.** lounger
    8. vagabond
loam ... **3.** rab **4.** clay, lime, silt, soil
    5. chalk, loess, regur
loan ... **4.** lend **6.** borrow **7.** advance
    10. provisions **13.** accommodation
loath ... **6.** averse **7.** hostile
    9. disliking, reluctant, unwilling
loathe ... **4.** hate **5.** abhor **6.** detest
    7. despise, dislike **9.** abominate
loathsome ... **4.** foul, vile **5.** nasty
    6. odious **7.** cloying, hateful
    9. abhorrent, offensive, repellant
    10. abominable, disgusting
lob ... **3.** box, cop **4.** step, till, toss,
    vein **5.** stair, throw **7.** lugworm,
    pollack **9.** chandelle

lobby ... 4. hall, room 5. foyer
8. anteroom, corridor, coulisse
9. enclosure, vestibule 10. wirepuller
13. pressure group
lobe ... 5. alula 6. earlap, lappet, lobule
7. pendant
lobster (pert to) ...
claw .. 5. chela 6. nipper, pincer
eggs .. 3. roe 5. coral
French .. 6. homard
genus .. 7. Homarus, Macrura
8. Nephrops
part .. 6. thorax
tail .. 6. telson
trap .. 3. pot 4. corf 5. creel 6. bow
net
local ... 7. edaphic, topical 8. regional
9. parochial 10. epichorial (epichoric)
13. autochthonous
local court ... 5. gemot (gemote)
locale ... 4. site 5. place, scene, venue
locality ... 4. area, spot 5. place, situs
7. endemic, habitat 8. position
locate ... 4. find, spot 6. settle
7. situate 9. establish
locatio ... 7. leasing, letting
location ... 4. seat, site, spot 5. locus,
place, situs 6. ubiety 7. habitat
8. district 9. situation
12. neighborhood
locator of forest fires ... 7. alidade
loch ... 3. bay 4. lake, pond 5. inlet,
lough
lock ... 4. bolt, hasp, hold 5. Gatun,
latch 6. cotter, detent, fasten, fetter
8. fastener 9. floodgate
lockjaw ... 7. tetanus, trismus
11. ankylostoma
lockman ... 8. summoner (Isle of Man)
11. executioner
lock of hair ... 4. curl 5. tress
6. berger 7. daglock, ringlet
8. lovelock, spit curl
lockup ... 3. jug 4. jail 5. clink
6. cooler 8. hoosegow (hoosgow)
9. calaboose
loco ... 3. mad 4. daft 5. craze, crazy
6. crazed 7. disease 10. moonstruck
15. non compos mentis
locomotion ... 6. lation (Astrol), moving,
travel 7. transit 8. progress
locomotive ... 3. hog 4. dolly, mogul
6. diesel, dinkey, engine, mikado
9. iron horse
locomotive cowcatcher ... 5. pilot
locus ... 4. area, drug, site 5. place
8. locality
locus (pert to) ...
in quo .. 5. where 12. place in which
sigilli .. 14. place of the seal
locust ... 4. weta 6. beetle, cicada,
cicala, kowhai 7. Locusta
9. wetapunga 11. grasshopper
locust (pert to) ...
berry .. 5. drupe 9. glamberry
bird .. 4. dial 7. grackle 8. starling
10. white stork
like .. 6. mantis
plant .. 5. senna
sound .. 7. stridor 10. stridulate
tree .. 5. carob, honey 6. acacia
lode ... 3. vug (vugg) 4. path, road,

vein 5. canal, drain, ledge 6. course
7. deposit 8. waterway
lodestar ... 8. cynosure, polestar
11. guiding star
lodestone, loadstone ... 6. magnet
8. terrella 9. magnetite
lodge ... 3. hut, lie 4. camp, tent
5. cabin, hovel 6. billet, encamp,
reside 7. deposit, quarter
11. brotherhood
lodge doorkeeper ... 5. tiler
lodging ... 3. inn 4. gite, room
5. abode, hotel, roost 6. billet,
harbor (harbour), tavern 8. barracks,
dwelling, hostelry, quarters
9. dormitory, harborage (harbourage)
10. habitation
loess ... 4. loam, silt, soil
lof ... 6. praise 7. measure
loft ... 3. bin 4. balk 5. attic
loftiness ... 6. height 7. dignity
8. eminence 9. eloquence
11. distinction, magnanimity
lofty ... 4. high, tall 5. proud 6. aerial,
Alpine, Andean 7. eminent, exalted,
haughty, stately, sublime 8. arrogant,
elevated, eloquent, majestic, towering
9. dignified 11. magisterial,
magnanimous 13. distinguished
lofty place ... 4. peak 5. aerie, eyrie
(eyry) 6. summit 8. eminence,
pinnacle
log ... 4. birl, slab 5. diary 6. record
8. firewood, mountain, puncheon,
register 11. speedometer
log (pert to) ...
cock .. 10. woodpecker
gin .. 6. jammer
hauler (sled) .. 4. tode
implement .. 6. nigger, peavey (peavy),
rosser
measure .. 7. scalage
noser .. 6. sniper
rolling .. 7. birling
section .. 5. spalt
support .. 3. nog
logarithmic terms ... 3. bel 5. curve
6. spiral 7. ellipse, tangent
9. decrement
logarithm inventor ... 6. Napier
loge ... 3. box 5. booth, stall
loggerhead ... 4. tool 6. turtle
7. fathead 8. bonehead, numskull
9. blockhead 10. thickskull
loggia ... 7. gallery
logging (pert to) ...
boots .. 4. pacs
rock .. 6. loggan
sled .. 4. tode 7. travois (travoise)
wheels .. 7. katydid
logic ... 9. reasoning 13. argumentation
logic (pert to) ...
fallacy .. 6. idolum
induction .. 7. epagoge
proposition .. 5. lemma 7. ferison
9. enthymeme, obvertend
specious .. 7. sophism
term .. 5. Darii, Ferio 8. Celarent
logical ... 4. sane 5. sound, valid
8. coherent, credible, rational
9. plausible 10. consistent,
reasonable

logician... 8. reasoner
logograph... 5. rebus 6. riddle
  7. anagram 8. logogram
logy... 4. dull 6. drowsy 8. sluggish
Lohengrin (pert to)...
  character.. 4. Elsa 8. Parsifal
  composer.. 6. Wagner (1850)
  Knight.. 15. Knight of the Swan
loin (pert to)...
  beef.. 10. tenderloin
  mutton.. 4. rack 5. chump
  pork.. 7. griskin
loincloth... 5. dhoti, pagne 7. G–string
  11. breechcloth
loir... 8. dormouse
Loire, France...
  Dept capital.. 12. Saint Etienne
  river's old name.. 5. Liger
  town.. 6. Nantes
  tributary.. 5. Indre
loiter... 3. lag 5. dally, delay, tarry
  6. dawdle, linger 7. saunter
loiterer... 4. slug 5. drone, idler
  6. lagger 7. dawdler, laggard
  8. sluggard
Loki (pert to)...
  god.. 7. Discord 8. Mischief
  wife.. 5. Sigyn
loll... 4. hang 5. droop 6. dangle,
  frowst (froust), lounge, repose, sprawl
  7. recline
loma, lomita... 4. hill
Lombard (pert to)...
  ancient.. 6. cannon
  historic.. 4. bank, loan
  Italy.. 5. tribe
  King.. 6. Alboin (legend)
  school.. 11. Renaissance
  street.. 6. London
Lombardy province... 4. Como
lomboy... 8. Java plum
lomilomi (Haw)... 3. rub 7. massage,
  shampoo
London, England...
  art gallery.. 4. Tate
  bank.. 27. Old Lady of Threadneedle
  Street
  borough.. 6. Ealing
  bridge.. 6. Thames
  bridle path.. 9. Rotten Row
  brown.. 9. carbuncle
  clock.. 6. Big Ben
  club (Whigs).. 6. Kit–Kat
  district.. 4. Soho 7. Alsatia, Lambeth,
  Mayfair (fashion) 9. Wimbledon
  10. Marylebone
  hawker.. 6. coster
  monument (Guildhall).. 3. Gog
  5. Magog
  Opera Company.. 12. Sadler's Wells
  porter.. 6. George
  prison.. 7. Newgate 9. Bridewell
  quarter.. 8. Vauxhall
  roisterer (Hist).. 3. mum
  Roman name.. 6. Agusta
  stables.. 4. mews
  stock exchange.. 17. Throgmorton
  Street
  street.. 9. Cheapside, Whitehall
  10. Piccadilly 11. Throgmorton
  12. Threadneedle
Londoner... 7. Cockney

Londres... 5. cigar
lone... 3. one 5. alone 6. lonely,
  single 7. forlorn 8. solitary
  9. unmarried 12. unfrequented
loneliness... 8. loneness, solitude
  9. aloneness, dejection, isolation
  10. depression, desolation
  12. lonesomeness
lonely... 4. lorn 6. dreary 8. desolate,
  lonesome, secluded, solitary
  10. friendless 11. sequestered
  12. unfrequented
Lone Star State... 5. Texas
long... 3. yen 4. pine 5. crave, wordy,
  yearn 6. aspire, prolix, thirst
  7. lengthy, tedious 8. tiresome
  9. prolonged, wearisome
  10. protracted
long (pert to)...
  ago, since.. 3. eld 4. yore
  beard.. 9. graybeard 10. bellarmine
  (jug)
  discourse, speech.. 6. screed, tirade
  7. descant 9. philippic, rigmarole
  dog.. 9. dachshund, greyhound
  dozen.. 8. thirteen
  established.. 8. habitual 10. inveterate
  11. traditional
  for.. 4. hope, pine 5. covet, crave
  horn.. 6. cattle (Tex)
  inlet.. 3. ria
  journey.. 4. trek 7. odyssey
  jump.. 5. halmo
  letters.. 7. screeds
  life.. 9. longevity
  limbed.. 9. rangy
  lived.. 9. macrobian
  periods.. 4. ages, eons
  scarf.. 4. sari
  suffering.. 7. patient 10. forbearing
  Tom.. 3. gun 8. titmouse
  windedness.. 9. garrulity, prolixity
  13. longiloquence
longing... 3. yen 6. desire, pining
  7. craving, wistful 8. yearning
  9. hankering, nostalgia
longitudinal... 10. euthytatic (stress),
  lengthwise
longshoreman... 6. docker, loader,
  lumper, stower 9. stevedore
  10. roustabout
loo... 3. pam 4. game
look... 3. con, ken, pry, see 4. haze,
  heed, leer, peep, scry, seek, seem
  5. point, stare, watch 6. appear,
  expect 7. examine, inspect, observe
  8. indicate, perceive 9. search for
look (pert to)...
  after.. 4. tend 5. serve 6. follow
  7. care for 9. keep vigil, supervise
  at.. 3. eye 4. face, scan, upon
  6. regard 7. examine
  back.. 6. recall 7. retrace
  8. remember 9. recollect 10. call to
  mind
  down upon.. 4. leer, snub 5. fleer,
  gloat 7. askance, despise
  forward to.. 5. await 6. expect
  7. foresee 10. anticipate
  like.. 8. resemble
  obliquely.. 4. skew
  slyly.. 4. leer, ogle, peer

sullen.. 5. frown, lower 6. glower
toward.. 4. face
upon.. 2. at 4. deem 6. behold
  11. contemplate
lookout... 4. view 5. guard, watch
  6. conner 7. outlook 9. vigilance
looks... 4. cons, face, kens, sees
  5. peers, pores, pries, seeks, seems
  6. visage 8. features 9. resembles
  10. appearance 11. countenance
loom... 3. auk 4. loon, tool 6. appear,
  puffin, vessel, weaver 7. machine
  9. guillemot, implement
  10. receptacle
loom part... 3. lam 4. caam, leaf, sley
  5. easer, lathe, lever 6. heddle
loon... 5. diver (great Northern), Gavia,
  grebe, wabby 10. Gavia immer
loon... 4. dolt 6. menial (anc), rascal
  7. lunatic
loop... 3. eye, tab 4. ansa, clew, kink
  5. bight, bride, honda, noose, picot,
  sling, wootz (iron) 6. becket
  7. folding 8. doubling
loophole... 4. hole, plea 5. mense,
  oilet 6. escape, eyelet, outlet
  7. opening, pretext 8. aperture
loop–shaped... 9. fundiform
  11. sling–shaped
loose... 3. lax 4. free, limp 5. slack
  6. detach, remiss, unlash, wanton,
  wobbly 7. escaped, immoral,
  movable, relaxed, slacken, unbound,
  unleash 8. insecure, unstable
  9. discharge (gun, arrow)
  10. unconfined 11. improvident
  12. loose–moraled
  14. unconventional
loose (pert to)...
ends.. 4. dags 5. slack 7. tagrags
  8. restless
garment.. 5. simar 6. banion, chimar,
  kimono 7. zimarra 8. peignoir
jointed.. 5. lanky, rangy 6. wobbly
  7. rickety 10. ramshackle
loosely dressed... 8. discinct
loosen... 4. ease, free, undo 5. pried,
  relax 6. soften 7. slacken
looseness... 7. laxness 8. limpness
  9. slackness, vagueness
  10. remissness, wantonness
loot... 3. rob 4. gelt, haul, sack, swag
  5. booty 6. spoils 7. pillage,
  plunder, seizure 10. contraband
looter... 6. rifler, sacker 7. ravager,
  spoiler 8. marauder, pillager
lop (off)... 3. bob, cut 4. oche, sned,
  trim 5. droop, prune 6. cut off,
  snathe 8. truncate
lopsided... 4. alop 7. leaning
  8. top–heavy 10. unbalanced
  13. unsymmetrical
loquacious... 4. glib 6. chatty
  7. voluble 9. garrulous, talkative
  10. chattering
loquacity... 7. fluency, leresis
  8. glibness 9. gabbiness, garrulity
  12. effusiveness
lord... 3. aga (agha), bey, God 4. earl,
  peer, rule, tsar 5. liege, ruler, title
  6. master, prince 7. Jehovah,
  marquis, Saviour 8. governor,

nobleman, seignior, suzerain, viscount
  10. proprietor 11. Jesus Christ
Lord (pert to)...
Buddhism.. 6. Buddha
Jacobite.. 3. Mar
of Heaven.. 7. Tien Chu (Chin)
of Lords.. 8. Demiurge (Plato)
  11. King of Kings 13. Prince of
  Peace
of Wisdom.. 5. Mazda 6. Ormazd
Lord have mercy upon us...
  12. Kyrie eleison 14. Christe eleison
lordly... 6. uppish 8. arrogant,
  despotic 9. dignified, masterful
  10. tyrannical 11. domineering,
  overbearing
Lord's Prayer... 11. Pater Noster
lore... 4. lear 6. advice, wisdom
  7. counsel 8. learning 9. erudition,
  mythology, tradition 12. superstition
lorgnette... 7. lorgnon 8. eyeglass
  10. opera glass
lorica... 5. shell 7. cuirass
  11. Breastplate (St Patrick's)
lorikeet... 6. lories, parrot
loris... 5. lemur
lorn... 6. bereft 7. forlorn 8. deserted,
  desolate, forsaken 9. abandoned
  11. Godforsaken
loro... 10. monk parrot, parrot fish
lose... 4. fail, miss, omit 5. leese
  (obs), spill, waste 6. forget, mislay,
  perish 7. forfeit, let slip 8. estrange,
  squander 9. incur loss 10. wander
  from
lose (pert to)...
balance.. 4. trip 7. stumble
courage.. 7. despair, despond
flesh.. 8. emaciate
freshness.. 4. fade, wilt 6. wither
ground.. 7. regress 8. slow down
  9. fall short 10. fall behind
luster.. 7. tarnish
vigor.. 3. fag, sag 4. fail, flag, pine
  6. weaken 7. decline
loser... 6. victim 8. also ran
  8. defeatee, underdog
loss... 4. ruin, weak 6. damage, injury
  9. decrement, detriment, privation
  10. forfeiture 11. bereavement,
  destruction
loss of...
commodities.. 6. ullage
eyebrows, lashes.. 9. madarosis
feeling.. 7. agnosia 10. anesthesia
  (anaesthesia)
hair.. 8. alopecia
loved one.. 11. bereavement
memory.. 7. amnesia
reason.. 7. amentia
smell.. 7. anosmia
speech.. 4. mute 6. alalia 7. aphasia
  10. laloplegia
voice.. 7. aphonia
willpower.. 6. abulia
lost... 4. asea, gone, lorn 5. unwon
  6. hidden, ruined, sinful, wasted
  7. mislaid 8. absorbed, confused,
  defeated, obscured, vanished
  9. abandoned, forfeited, forgotten,
  perplexed, reprobate, subverted
  10. abstracted, bewildered,

dissipated, overthrown, parted with
11. preoccupied 13. irreclaimable,
irretrievable
lost (pert to) . . .
cause . . 8. Civil War
color . . 5. faded, paled
consciousness . . 7. fainted, swooned
life fluid . . 4. bled
to view . . 5. perdu
tribes (ten) . . 10. Israelites
lot . . . 3. tax 4. doom, fate, luck,
much, plat 5. share 6. chance,
hazard, studio 7. destiny, fortune,
portion 9. allotment, great deal
13. apportionment
Lot (pert to) . . .
father . . 5. Haran
penalty . . 12. pillar of salt
sister . . 6. Milcah
son . . 4. Moab
uncle . . 7. Abraham
lots, divination by . . 9. sortilege
lottery . . . 4. game 5. bingo, lotto
6. chance, raffle 7. Genoese, grab
bag 11. sweepstakes
lottery prize . . . 4. tern (from three
numbers)
lotus . . . 7. nelumbo 10. chinquapin
lotus (pert to) . . .
bird . . 6. jacana
eaters . . 9. indolents, Lotophagi
11. daydreamers
tree . . 4. sadr 6. jujube, nettle
9. persimmon
loud . . . 5. crass, gaudy, noisy, showy
6. coarse, flashy, garish, vulgar
7. blatant, booming 8. vehement
9. clamorous, turbulent, unrefined
10. blustering, boisterous,
tumultuous, vociferous
11. stentorious 12. obstreperous
loudmouthed . . . 10. scurrilous,
stentorian 11. thersitical
Louise de la Ramée (novelist) . . .
5. Ouida (pen name)
Louisiana . . .
bird . . 7. pelican
capital . . 10. Baton Rouge
city . . 10. New Orleans, Shreveport
county . . 6. parish
dialect . . 6. Creole
dish (cooked) . . 9. jumbalaya
flower . . 8. magnolia
hero . . 6. De Soto, de Vaca, Pineda
7. La Salle
native . . 5. Cajun 6. Creole, French
7. Acadian, Spanish
purchased from . . 8. Napoleon (1803)
river . . 5. Pearl 6. Sabine
11. Mississippi
State admission . . 10. Eighteenth
State motto . . 22. Union, Justice,
Confidence
State nickname . . 7. Pelican
tradition . . 10. pirate lore
Louis Viaud (author) . . . 10. Pierre Loti
(pen name)
lounge . . . 4. loaf, loll, sofa 5. divan
6. frowst, repose 7. recline
louse . . . 5. aphis 6. cootie, insect,
slater 8. Anoplura, arachnid
9. Hemiptera, scoundrel

lout . . . 3. oaf 4. boor, clod, dolt
6. lubber, rustic 7. bumpkin
loutish . . . 4. rude 7. awkward, boorish,
ill–bred 8. clownish 11. countrified
lovable . . . 7. amiable 8. adorable,
charming 9. desirable, endearing
love . . . 3. amo, gra, woo 4. like
5. adore, amore, fancy 6. liking
7. charity 8. fondness, good will
9. affection 10. endearment,
sweetheart
love (pert to) . . .
affair . . 7. liaison, romance
10. flirtation
apple . . 6. tomato
bird . . 6. parrot
call . . 3. coo
feast . . 5. agape
flower . . 4. lily
full of . . 4. dote 6. doting, erotic
7. amative 9. idolizing
god of . . 4. Amor, Ares, Eros, Kama
5. Bhaga, Cupid
goddess of . . 5. Athor, Freya (Freyja),
Venus 6. Ishtar 9. Aphrodite
intrigue . . 5. amour
knot, token of . . 6. amoret
meeting . . 5. tryst 10. rendezvous
of . . 5. phile (comb form)
parental . . 6. storge
potion . . 7. philter
science . . 9. erotology
song . . 6. serena (evening) 8. madrigal
lover . . . 4. beau 5. amant, Romeo
6. minion 7. amorist, Don Juan
8. paramour 9. enamorato
10. sweetheart
lover of . . . see also *craze for*
animals . . 10. zoophilist
beauty . . 8. aesthete (esthete)
wealth . . 9. plutocrat
work . . 9. ergophile
Lover's Leap . . . 10. Cape Ducato
Lovers' Quarrels . . . 12. amantium Irae
loving . . . 4. fond 5. phile (comb form)
6. ardent, erotic 7. adoring, amative,
amatory, amorous, devoted
8. charming, enamored, romantic
11. sentimental 12. affectionate
loving cup . . . 3. tyg (tig)
low . . . 3. bas, moo 4. base, deep,
neap, orra 5. faint 6. humble,
menial, sneaky, vulgar, wicked
8. dejected, indecent, infamous,
inferior, plebeian 9. inelegant
11. unfavorable
low (pert to) . . .
born . . 4. rude 5. lowly 6. common
7. lowbred 8. plebeian
bred . . 5. crude 6. coarse, vulgar
brow . . 9. ignoramus
church . . 11. evangelical
comedy . . 8. travesty
country . . 7. Belgium, Holland
9. Luxemburg 11. Netherlands
German . . 5. Saxon 8. Frankish
12. Plattdeutsch
in spirits . . 4. blue 6. megrim
8. dejected, downcast 10. dispirited,
melancholy 11. crestfallen
Roman wall . . 5. spina
shrubs, plants . . 4. moss 5. Erica

syllable (Mus).. 2. ut
tide.. 3. ebb 4. neap 8. low water
lower... 3. dip 4. vail, vase 5. abase,
demit, frown, neath 6. bemean,
debase, deepen, demean, demote,
humble, lessen, meaner, nether,
reduce 7. cheapen, degrade, depress,
descent 8. diminish, inferior
10. depreciate
lower (pert to)...
case letter.. 5. small
Empire.. 9. Byzantine
geology.. 5. Chalk (Eng) 6. strata
7. stratum
most.. 6. bottom, lowest 7. bedrock
10. nethermost
world.. 4. hell 5. earth, Hades, limbo,
orcus, Sheol 7. Abaddon, Gehenna
8. Cerberus 9. perdition, purgatory
lowering... 4. dark 6. gloomy, sullen
7. ominous 8. frowning 9. deepening
10. cheapening 11. threatening
lowery... 6. cloudy, gloomy 8. lowering
lowest (pert to)...
animal life.. 6. amoeba (ameba)
deck.. 5. orlop
least.. 5. minim 6. bottom
7. minimum
pedestal member (Arch).. 6. plinth,
quadra
peer (ranking).. 5. baron
point.. 5. depth, nadir 6. bottom
10. nethermost
point, planet.. 7. perigee
lowing... 6. mooing 7. mugient
9. bellowing
lowland... 4. flat, holm, spit 5. plain,
terai 6. bottom 8. molehill
lowly... 4. mean, meek 6. humble,
humbly, meekly, menial, modest
8. inferior, modestly, plebeian
12. unpretending
loxia... 7. wryneck 9. crossbill
loy... 5. slick (tool), spade
loyal... 4. feal, leal, true 5. liege
6. stanch 7. staunch 8. constant,
faithful, obedient
loyalty... 5. faith 6. fealty, homage
8. devotion, fidelity 9. constancy
10. allegiance, stanchness
(staunchness) 12. faithfulness
13. steadfastness
Loyolite... 6. Jesuit
lozenge... 5. candy, facet 6. jujube,
tablet, troche 7. diamond, molding
8. pastille (pastil, pastile)
11. perforation
lubber... 4. boor, dolt, gawk, lout
5. churl, drone, idler, thick 6. sailor
8. landsman 11. grasshopper
lubricity... 8. lewdness
10. smoothness 12. slipperiness
lubricous... 4. lewd 6. tricky, wanton
7. elusive 8. unstable 10. lascivious
lucban... 8. shaddock
luce... 4. pike 10. fleur—de—lis
lucent... 5. clear 6. bright 7. shining
11. translucent, transparent
lucern... 3. dog 4. lynx
lucerne... 4. herb 6. fodder 7. alfalfa
11. purple medic
lucet, luce... 4. pike (fish)

Lucia's home... 10. Lammermoor
lucid... 4. sane 5. clear, vivid
6. bright, lucent 7. shining
8. luminous, pellucid 11. translucent
12. intelligible
luck... 3. hap 4. cess 5. deuce
6. chance 7. ambsace 8. fortuity
11. good fortune
lucky... 5. canny, happy 6. timely
9. fortunate 10. auspicious 11. good
fortune
lucky animal... 6. mascot
lucky token... 4. mojo 5. charm
6. amulet 7. periapt 8. talisman
9. alectoria 10. rabbit foot
12. antinganting
lucrative... 3. fat 6. paying 7. gainful
10. productive, profitable, worthwhile
12. remunerative
lucre... 4. gain, pelf 6. profit, riches
9. emolument 11. acquisition
lucubrate... 18. burn the midnight oil
ludicrous... 5. antic, comic, droll,
funny 6. absurd 7. amusing, comical,
jesting, risible 9. burlesque, laughable
10. ridiculous
Ludolphian... 2. pi (3.14159)
14. Ludolph's number
Luftpost... 7. airmail, air post
lug... 3. box, ear, hug 4. drag, hale,
haul, loop, pull, tote 5. carry
6. basket 9. container
lugs... 4. airs 7. clothes (showy),
tobacco 10. affections
lugubrious... 3. sad 6. woeful
7. doleful 8. grievous, mournful
9. plaintive 10. lamentable
lugworm... 3. lob 7. annelid
9. Arenicola
luhinga... 9. petticoat
lukewarm... 4. cool 5. tepid 6. tepefy
8. tepidity 9. not ardent
10. irresolute 11. indifferent
lumber... 4. wood 6. bungle, litter,
refuse, rumble, timber, trudge
7. lombard 9. rough wood
10. pawnbroker 11. impedimenta
lumberman... 6. logger, sawyer, scorer
9. timberman 10. lumberjack,
woodcutter
lumberman's half boot... 3. pac
lumberman's sled... 4. tode
7. go—devil, travois (travoise)
luminary... 3. sun 4. fire, star 5. light
7. wise man 9. celebrity
12. illumination, leading light
luminescence... 7. foxfire
12. fluorescence
15. phosphorescence
luminous... 5. clear, lucid 6. bright
7. shining 9. brilliant
11. enlightened, illuminated,
intelligent, transparent
14. phosphorescent
luminous circle... 4. halo
luminous impression... 9. phosphene
10. afterimage
lummox... 4. boor, dolt, lout 5. yahoo
7. bumpkin, bungler 12. clumsy
fellow
lump... 3. gob, lob, wad 4. beat,
blob, clot, hunk, loaf, mass 5. bulge

6. nodule, nubble, nugget, thresh
7. cluster 8. swelling
12. protuberance

lump (pert to) ...
butter .. 3. pat
clay .. 4. clag, clod
metal .. 3. pig 5. ingot

lumpish ... 4. dull 5. bulky, inert
6. clumsy, stolid, stupid 7. boorish
8. sluggish 9. heaviness, inertness,
ponderous 11. countrified
13. shapelessness

lumpy ... 5. drunk, rough 6. choppy
7. gnarled, nodular

lumpy jaw ... 6. big jaw
13. actinomycosis

luna ... 6. silver 11. moon goddess

lunacy ... 4. moon 5. mania
7. madness 8. insanity 9. craziness
11. derangement, foolishness

lunar ... 5. orbed 6. lunate
8. crescent, moonlike 9. celestial,
satellite 10. moon–shaped

lunar (pert to) ...
appulse .. 7. eclipse
bone .. 7. lunatum
cycle .. 7. Metonic 9. Callippic
deity .. 6. Selene (Selena)
halo .. 6. corona, nimbus 7. aureola

lunatic ... 3. mad 5. crazy, idiot, loony
6. insane, madman 8. demoniac
9. moonstruck

lunatic asylum ... 9. Bethlehem
(London)

lunch ... 5. snack 6. brunch, repast,
tiffin 8. brown–bag, luncheon,
nuncheon 9. collation
11. refreshment

lunchroom ... 6. eatery 10. coffee
shop, restaurant 12. luncheonette

lundyfoot ... 5. snuff (by Lundy Foot)

lunge ... 3. cut, jab 4. grab, pass, stab
5. feint, swing 6. thrust

lungs (pert to) ...
ailment .. 9. emphysema 10. chalicosis
12. tuberculosis
having .. 9. pulmonate
part .. 5. lobes 6. lights 7. bronchi,
trachea
sound .. 4. rale 6. rattle

lurch ... 4. joll, roll, sway 5. lunge
6. careen, topple 7. deceive
8. flounder 10. disappoint

lure ... 4. bait, trap 5. decoy, snare,
tempt 6. allure, entice, invite
7. attract, beguile, trumpet, tweedle
10. enticement

lurid ... 3. wan 4. dark, pale 5. color,
vivid 6. dismal, gloomy 7. ghastly,
obscene 9. deathlike 11. sensational

lurk ... 4. hide, lote (obs) 5. creep,
prowl, skulk, slink, sneak 9. lie in
wait, pussyfoot

luscious ... 4. rich 5. sweet
6. creamy, wanton 7. cloying,
honeyed 8. sensuous 9. delicious
10. lascivious, voluptuous

lush ... 4. soft 5. drink, drunk, juicy
6. lavish, limber, liquor, mellow
7. verdant 8. flexible 9. luxuriant,
succulent 11. intoxicated

lusory ... 7. playful 8. sportive

lust ... 5. greed 6. desire, libido
7. craving, longing, passion 8. virility
14. lasciviousness

luster, lustre ... 4. naif 5. glory, gloss,
sheen, shine 6. beauty, polish
7. glitter, lustrum 8. radiance,
schiller, splendor 10. brightness
11. distinction, iridescence

lusterless ... 3. dim, mat 4. dead, dull,
flat 14. expressionless

lustful ... 4. lewd 5. randy
9. lecherous 10. lascivious

lustrous ... 4. naif 5. nitid 6. agleam,
bright 7. radiant, shining
11. illustrious, transparent

lustrous mineral ... 4. spar

lustrum (Roman) ... 6. census, luster
12. purification (5 yrs), quinquennium

lusty ... 6. active, robust, strong, sturdy
7. healthy 8. vigorous 9. corpulent

lute ... 4. clay, ring (rubber), seal
6. cement

lute, lutelike ... 4. asor 6. guitar
7. bandore, pandore, theorbo, ukulele
8. archlute (archilute)

lute tablature ... 7. lyraway

lutjanoid fish ... 4. sesi 7. snapper

Luxembourg ...
capital .. 10. Luxembourg
government .. 10. Grand Duchy
language .. 6. French, German
13. Letzeburgesch
river .. 7. Moselle

luxuriant ... 4. lush, rank, rich
6. ornate, uberty 7. fertile, opulent,
profuse, teeming 8. abundant, prolific
9. bounteous, Sybaritic

luxuriate ... 4. bask 5. revel
8. flourish

luxurious ... 5. plush, ritzy 6. ornate,
superb 8. imposing 9. expensive,
grandiose, sumptuous 10. impressive
11. extravagant

luxury ... 4. lust 7. lechery
8. elegance, pleasure, richness
10. prosperity, sensuality
11. superfluity 12. extravagance
13. gratification, sumptuousness
14. voluptuousness

luxury lover ... 7. reveler 8. Sybarite

Luzon ...
dialect .. 6. Itaves
mountain .. 3. Iba 6. Pagsan (Sicapoo)
people .. 5. Malay 7. Tagalog
8. Tinggian (Tinguian)
savage .. 6. Igorot (Igorrote)
seaport .. 5. Vigan 6. Aparri, Cavite
volcano .. 5. Mayon

lyam ... 5. leash (Her) 10. bloodhound

lycanthrope ... 8. werewolf
9. loup–garou

Lycia (pert to) ...
citizen .. 6. Lycian
city .. 4. Myra
district of .. 9. Asia Minor
language .. 5. Greek 6. Lycian

Lydia ...
capital .. 6. Sardis
dynasty of .. 5. Gyges 7. Croesus
13. Cyrus the Great
name, later .. 6. Persia
name, old .. 5. Ionia

queen.. 7. Omphale
river.. 8. Pactolus
ruins.. 6. temple
lye... 4. buck 6. bleach, potash
   8. lixivium
lying... 5. false 6. deceit 7. fudging
   9. decumbent, mendacity, reclining,
   recumbent 10. untruthful
lying (pert to)...
across.. 10. transverse
at mountain base.. 8. piedmont
hidden.. 6. latent 11. delitescent
in.. 12. accouchement
near earth's axis.. 5. polar
on the back.. 5. prone 6. supine
   7. passive
lymph... 3. sap 5. chyle, fluid, serum,
   water 6. plasma 7. cassein
lynch... 4. hang 6. murder, punish
   (lawlessly) 7. execute
lynx... 6. bobcat, lucern 7. caracal,
   wildcat 8. carcajou 13. constellation

lynx–eyed... 7. oxyopia
lyre... 4. asor, harp 6. kissar, sabeca,
   trigon, zither 7. cithara, cittern,
   testudo 8. phorminx
lyre (pert to)...
bird.. 6. Menura 8. lyretail, pheasant
shaped.. 6. lyrate
tree.. 5. tulip
turtle.. 11. leatherback
lyric (pert to)...
Arabic.. 5. gazel
Muse.. 5. Erato 10. Polyhymnia
music, poetry.. 3. lay, ode 4. epic,
   poem 5. epode, melic, rhyme (rime),
   verse, vocal 6. epopee, poetic
   7. canzone, musical, rondeau
   8. operatic, palinode 9. dithyramb
poet.. 5. odist
lyrical... 6. epodic
lyrichord... 11. harpsichord
lyssa... 6. rabies 11. hydrophobia
lyssophobia... 17. fear of hydrophobia

M

M... 2. Mu (Gr) 6. letter (13th)
   8. thousand
Ma (Ma Bellona)... 7. goddess
   (fertility)
maarib (Jew)... 7. liturgy
Maat (Egypt)... 7. goddess (justice)
Mab (Queen Mab)... 4. poem 10. fairy
   queen
mabolo... 4. plum 7. camagon
macabre... 4. grim 5. lurid, weird
   6. grisly 7. ghastly 8. gruesome
   12. Dance of Death
macaco... 5. lemur 6. Macaca
   7. macaque 10. Barbary ape
macan... 4. rice
macao... 4. game (gambling)
Macao... 6. Island 7. seaport
macaque... 6. machin, monkey
Macassar... 7. seaport (Celebes)
macaw... 3. ara 5. arara 6. parrot
   7. maracan 8. aracanga (blue and
   red), ararauna (blue and yellow)
Macbeth (pert to)...
author.. 11. Shakespeare (1605)
character.. 4. Duff, Ross 5. Angus
   6. Hecate, Lennox 7. Macduff
murder victim.. 6. Duncan
play type.. 7. tragedy
rival.. 7. Macduff
McBurney's Point (Med)...
   13. abdominal wall
Maccabees... 11. Hasmonaeans
   14. fraternal order, Jewish patriots
maccaboy... 5. snuff
mace... 4. maul 5. baton, gavel, spice
   (nutmeg), staff 6. ensign, mallet
   7. scepter (sceptre)
mace bearer... 5. macer 6. beadle

Macedonia, Balkans...
capital (anc).. 5. Pella
city.. 5. Berea 6. Edessa 8. Salonika
people.. 6. Greeks 8. Serbians
   9. Albanians 10. Bulgarians
ruler.. 6. Philip 9. Alexander (the
   Great)
site.. 15. Balkan Peninsula
macerate... 3. ret, vex 4. soak
   5. steep 6. soften 7. mortify,
   oppress, torture 8. emaciate
   9. waste away
machete... 4. bolo, fish 5. knife
   6. guitar 11. cutlass fish
Machiavellian, Machiavelian... 4. wily
   6. crafty 7. cunning 8. guileful,
   scheming 9. deceitful
   12. falsehearted
machila... 7. hammock
machin... 6. monkey 7. macaque
machinate... 4. plan, plot 6. scheme
   8. contrive, maneuver
machination... 6. design, device,
   scheme 7. machine 8. intrigue
   9. stratagem 10. conspiracy
machine... 3. car 4. auto 6. device,
   engine 7. vehicle 9. apparatus,
   automaton 10. automobile
   11. association, standardize
machine (pert to)...
cloth maturing.. 4. ager
cloth stretching.. 6. tenter
cotton.. 3. gin 4. mule, 5. baler
glazing.. 8. calender
hay.. 5. baler 6. tedder
hoisting.. 3. gin, pry 4. pump
   5. crane, davit, lever, tongs
   7. derrick
hummeling.. 5. awner

hydraulic .. 9. telemotor
imitating .. 9. automaton
military .. 3. ram 6. onager
mixing .. 9. malaxator
ore .. 6. vanner
planing .. 8. surfacer
planting .. 6. seeder
political .. 5. party 6. system
   7. faction
reckoning .. 6. abacus 9. tabulator
   10. calculator
rubber shaping .. 8. extruder
stage effect .. 13. deus ex machina
tool .. 5. drill, lathe
machine gun ... 4. nest (hidden place)
   5. Maxim 6. cannon 7. Gatling
   9. Hotchkiss 10. chatterbox
machine–made ... 11. stereotyped
machine power, energy ... 5. input
   6. output
machinist ... 7. artisan 8. mechanic
mackerel ... 5. atule, spike, tunny
   6. sierra, tinker
mackerel (pert to) ...
bait .. 9. jellyfish
bird .. 7. wryneck 9. kittiwake
genus .. 7. Scomber
goose .. 9. phalarope
like .. 4. cero 6. bonito 7. escolar
net .. 7. spiller
shark .. 9. porbeagle
sky .. 6. clouds 9. striation
small (allowable size) .. 5. spike
   6. tinker 7. blinker
mackle ... 4. blur, spot 6. blotch,
   macule
macrobiotic ... 9. long–lived
mad ... 4. vain, wild 5. angry, crazy,
   irate, rabid, vexed 6. insane, maniac
   7. enraged, foolish, frantic, furious
   8. demented, frenetic, maniacal,
   reckless 9. hilarious, turbulent
   10. distraught, infatuated, infuriated
   12. arreptitious
Madagascar, Malagasy ...
animal .. 5. indri, lemur 6. aye–aye,
   tenrec (tendrac) 9. babacoote
capital .. 10. Tananarive
cattle .. 4. zebu (humped)
city .. 7. Majanga 8. Tamatave
civet .. 7. fossane
govenment .. 8. Republic (1960)
language .. 16. Malayo–Polynesian
native .. 4. Hova 8. Sakalava
palm .. 6. raffia
religion .. 7. Animist 9. Christian
Madam ... 3. Mrs 4. Frau, lady,
   Ma'am 5. donna, hussy 6. Madame,
   Señora 8. goodwife, mistress
   9. courtesan
madcap ... 3. wag 4. rash, wild
   5. blood 6. madman 7. hotspur,
   violent 8. reckless 9. daredevil,
   foolhardy
madden ... 3. vex 5. craze 6. enrage,
   incite 7. incense 9. infuriate
   10. antagonize
madder ... 2. al 3. aal, red 4. herb,
   rose (color) 5. brown, Rubia
   6. orange, violet, yellow 7. crimson,
   xanthin 9. turkey–red
made ... 5. built 7. created, trained

   8. invented, prepared, produced,
   rendered 10. artificial, successful
   11. constructed 12. enfranchised,
   manufactured
made (pert to) ...
accurate .. 5. trued
believe .. 7. feigned 9. pretended,
   simulated
blind .. 6. seeled
clear .. 9. explained 10. elucidated
destitute .. 6. bereft
fun of .. 6. jeered, mocked 7. derided
   9. ridiculed
hard, obdurate .. 7. steeled
light of .. 7. dwarfed 9. belittled
   10. disparaged
over .. 8. reformed, revamped
   9. remodeled
plain .. 9. evidenced, exhibited
   10. manifested
public .. 5. aired 7. accused, delated
   8. reported
scalloped edges .. 6. pinked
sound .. 7. bleated, rumbled, swished
tart .. 7. euchred
up .. 9. composite 10. artificial,
   fabricated 12. manufactured
up mind .. 7. decided
valid .. 6. proved 9. confirmed
   13. authenticated
whole again .. 7. renewed
   10. reconciled 13. redintegrated,
   re–established
Madeira Islands ...
capital .. 7. Funchal
embroidery .. 6. eyelet
nut .. 6. walnut
owner of Islands .. 8. Portugal
wind .. 5. leste
wine .. 4. bual 5. tinta (red)
   7. malmsey, sercial 8. verdelho
wood .. 8. ironwood (white), mahogany
madhouse ... 5. chaos 6. asylum,
   bedlam 8. nuthouse
madman ... 3. nut 4. coot, loon
   6. maniac 7. lunatic 9. phrenetic
madness ... 3. ire 4. fury, rage
   5. anger, mania 6. frenzy, lunacy
   8. insanity 9. agitation, theomania
   (Relig) 11. foolishness, inspiration
Mad Parliament (1258) ...
   18. Provisions of Oxford
Madras, India ...
capital .. 6. Madras
city .. 5. Adoni, Arcot 7. Calicut
export .. 4. lace 7. fabrics 9. kerchiefs
   (for turbans)
government .. 10. presidency
madrepore ... 5. coral 6. fossil, marble
   8. Acropora 12. Madreporaria
Madrid, Spain ...
architecture .. 7. Moorish
boulevard .. 5. Prado 12. Salon de
   Prado
noted buildings .. 7. Armeria
   11. Prado Museum, Royal Palace
madrigal ... 3. ode 4. glee, poem
   5. lyric, music 6. verses
maduro ... 5. cigar 6. mature
   11. dark–colored
maelstrom ... 5. churn 6. foment
   7. turmoil 9. whirlpool (Norway)

maestro... 6. master 7. teacher
8. composer, musician 9. conductor
13. Kapellmeister
maestro–di–cappela... 11. choirmaster
Mae West... 8. life belt
Maffia... 9. syndicate 10. underworld
12. organization (Sicilian)
maffle... 6. muddle, mumble
7. confuse, stammer 8. squander
mafoo, mafu (Chin)... 5. groom
9. stable boy
mag... 6. magpie 7. chatter
8. titmouse 9. halfpenny
magadis... 5. flute 9. monochord
magazine... 4. shop 5. depot, store
6. review 7. arsenal, chamber (gun),
tabloid 8. ephemeris, reservoir,
warehouse 10. periodical, repository,
storehouse
magazine rifle... 6. Mauser
8. repeater
mage... 5. Magus 6. Merlin 7. Houdini
8. conjurer, magician
magenta... 3. dye 7. fuchsia
maggot... 4. grub, mawk 5. larva,
mathe 6. notion 7. caprice, Diptera
12. eccentricity
Magi (Three Wise Men)... 6. Gaspar
8. Melchior 9. Balthasar
magic... 3. art 4. juju, mana, maya,
rune, show 5. charm, fairy, spell
6. voodoo 10. necromancy
11. conjuration, enchantment,
legerdemain
magic (pert to)...
art (black).. 7. demonry 9. diablerie,
diabolism
art (white).. 5. turgy 7. theurgy
ejaculation.. 2. om (um) 6. sesame
goddess.. 5. Circe 6. Hecate
image.. 5. sigil 8. sigillum
lantern.. 11. epidiascope
12. stereopticon
lantern slide.. 6. tinter
staff, wand.. 6. rhabdo 8. caduceus
symbol.. 5. charm 6. caract, fetish
8. pentacle 9. pentalpha
word.. 2. om (um) 6. presto, sesame
10. abacadabra
magical... 6. goetic (goety)
8. charming
magician... 4. mage 5. magus
6. Merlin, wizard 7. Houdini, juggler
8. conjurer, mandrake, sorcerer
9. archimage, charlatan, enchanter
11. entertainer, necromancer,
thaumaturge 13. thaumaturgist
15. prestidigitator
magician (pert to)...
attendant.. 7. famulus
command.. 6. presto 11. abracadabra
manual.. 8. grimoire
magirics... 7. cookery
magirist... 4. cook
magisterial... 5. lofty, proud
6. august, lordly 7. haughty, stately
8. arrogant, dogmatic, judicial, official
9. dignified, imperious, masterful
10. commanding 11. dictatorial,
domineering, overbearing
13. authoritative
magistrate... 4. doge 5. ephor, judge

6. aedile (edile), archon, bailli,
puisne, syndic 7. alcaide (alcaid),
alcalde, bailiff
magistrate's orders... 4. acta
magma... 5. dregs 8. sediment
10. molten rock, suspension (Pharm)
magna cum laude... 14. with great
honor
magnanimous... 4. free 5. lofty, noble
7. exalted, liberal 8. generous
9. honorable, unselfish, unstinted
10. high–minded 11. great of mind
13. disinterested
magnate... 4. lord 5. baron, mogul,
noble 6. bashaw, bigwig, tycoon
7. grandee, richman 9. personage
11. millionaire
magnesium (pert to)...
limestone.. 8. dolomite
nitrate.. 9. saltpeter
silicate.. 4. talc
sulphate.. 10. Epsom salts
magnet... 7. terella 8. solenoid
9. loadstone, lodestone
magnet (type)... 3. bar 9. horseshoe
10. artificial
magnetic... 10. attractive, electrical
14. attractiveness
magnetism... 5. oomph 8. polarity
magnificence... 5. glory 8. grandeur,
splendor 15. superexcellence
magnificent... 5. grand, regal
6. lavish, superb 7. exalted,
pompous, sublime 8. imposing,
palatial, splendid, striking 9. brilliant,
grandiose, sumptuous 10. munificent
magnify... 4. laud 5. exalt, extol
6. expand, praise 7. enlarge, glorify,
worship 8. increase 9. intensify,
overstate 10. exaggerate
magnitude... 4. size 6. extent
7. bigness 8. grandeur, nobility
9. extension, greatness
Magnolia State... 11. Mississippi
magnum... 4. bone (wrist) 6. bottle
9. capitatum
magnum opus... 9. great work
11. achievement
magpie... 3. daw, mag, pie 4. Pica,
piet (pyet) 5. madge, scold
6. pigeon, talker 9. chatterer
10. chattermag
magpie type...
diver.. 4. smew
shrike.. 7. tanager
maguari... 5. stork
magus... 8. magician 9. one of Magi
Magyar... 3. Hun 9. Hungarian
Mah (Persian)... 9. moon angel
maha... 10. sambar deer
Mahabharata (blind king, Hind)...
13. Dhritarashtra
mahajan, mahajun (Ind)... 8. great
man 11. moneylender
mahal... 8. Taj Mahal 9. residence
(summer) 10. apartments, Natal
brown
mahala... 5. squaw
maharaja, maharajah... 5. ruler
6. prince
maharani, maharanee... 5. queen
mahatma... 4. sage 7. wise man

9. great soul, occultist 21. Great
White Brotherhood (member)
mahogany... 3. roe (burl) 4. toon,
wood 5. brown 6. totara 7. ratteen
maholi... 5. lemur
Mahomet... see *Mohammedan*
Mahound... 5. Devil 8. Mohammed
mahout... 6. driver (elephant), keeper
Mah to Mahi... 10. Fish to Moon
Maia (pert to)...
mountain nymph.. 7. Arcadia
son.. 6. Hermes
star.. 8. Pleiades
maid... 4. girl, lass 5. bonne, woman
6. damsel, maiden, virgin 7. abigail,
servant 8. spinster 9. tirewoman
Maid (of)...
Astolat.. 6. Elaine
Athens.. 12. Theresa Macri
Lydia.. 7. Arachne (changed to a
spider)
Orléans.. 9. Joan of Arc
Zeus.. 2. Io (changed to heifer)
maidenhair... 4. fern 8. Adiantum
10. Venus's hair
maidenhair tree... 6. gingko
maidenly... 6. gentle, modest 7. girlish
9. unmarried
maigre... 4. diet, fish
mail... 3. dak (dawk) 4. post 5. armor
7. consign, letters, plumage
8. dispatch
mail, coat of... 5. armor 6. byrnie
(brinie) 7. broigne, cuirass (part),
hauberk, panoply
mail boat... 6. packet
maim... 6. injure, mangle, mayhem
7. disable 8. mutilate 9. tear apart
main... 3. sea 4. duct 5. chief, first,
great, prime, sheer, utter 6. mighty,
potent 7. chiefly, conduit, leading
8. foremost 9. conductor, essential,
principal 10. on the whole
11. essentially 13. most important
main (pert to)...
act (drama).. 8. epitasis
beam.. 6. girder 7. walking
part.. 4. body
point.. 3. jet, nub 4. crux, gist, pith
post.. 9. sternpost
sea (poet).. 11. Spanish Main
(Caribbean Sea)
Maine...
bay.. 5. Casco 13. Passamaquoddy
capital.. 7. Augusta
city.. 4. Saco 5. Hiram, Orono
6. Bangor 8. Lewiston, Portland
11. Millinocket
college.. 5. Bates, Colby 7. Bowdoin
Easternmost city.. 8. Eastport
Easternmost point.. 19. West Quoddy
Head Light
Easternmost town.. 5. Lubec
lake.. 6. Sebago 9. Moosehead
mountain.. 5. Kineo 8. Cadillac,
Katahdin
resort.. 9. Bar Harbor
resort island.. 8. Mt Desert
river.. 8. Kennebec 9. Penobscot
State admission.. 11. Twenty-third
State motto.. 6. Dirigo 7. I Direct
State nickname.. 8. Pine Tree

trout.. 7. oquassa
Maine, The... 10. battleship (Sp–Am
War)
maintain... 4. aver, hold, keep
5. claim 6. affirm, allege, assert,
avouch, defend, endure, insist, retain
7. justify, support, sustain
8. continue, preserve
maintainable... 7. tenable
maintenance... 3. aid 6. upkeep
7. alimony, defense, support
9. retention 10. livelihood,
sustenance 11. continuance
12. conservation, preservation,
sustentation
maison... 5. house
Maison Carrée... 12. Norman Temple
(Nimes)
maison de santé... 6. asylum
8. hospital 10. sanatorium
maître d'hôtel (famed)... 5. Oscar
maize... 3. Zea 4. corn 7. mealies
maja, majo... 5. belle, dandy
majestic... 5. grand, great, lofty,
noble, regal, royal 6. august, kingly
7. stately, sublime 8. elevated,
eloquent, imperial, splendid
9. dignified, grandiose
11. ceremonious, magnificent
majesty... 5. title 7. crowned (Her),
dignity 8. grandeur 9. eloquence,
greatness, loftiness, sceptered (Her)
major... 3. dur (Mus) 6. course
(study), ditone 7. greater, officer
8. legal age, majority
major–domo... 6. butler 7. bailiff,
steward 9. seneschal
majority... 3. age 4. most 6. quorum
7. greater 8. maturity 9. majorship,
plurality, seniority 12. more than half
make... 2. do 4. earn, form, gain,
kind 5. shape 6. compel, create,
induce, render 7. compose, execute,
produce 8. contrive, generate
9. structure 10. accomplish
11. composition, manufacture
make (pert to)...
affidavit.. 4. affy
allowance.. 5. abate, admit
7. concede
allusion to.. 7. mention
amends.. 5. atone 7. redress
as if.. 7. pretend 8. as though
bare.. 5. strip 6. balden, denude
believe.. 4. sham 5. feign 7. pretend
8. pretense
better.. 5. widen 6. soften
7. broaden, improve 9. meliorate
10. ameliorate
book.. 10. record bets
buoyant.. 8. levitate
calm.. 5. allay, quiet 6. serene
7. appease, compose
certain.. 6. assure, ensure
cheerful.. 6. solace 7. comfort,
console
choice.. 3. opt 4. cull 6. choose,
select 7. pick out
clean breast of.. 7. confess
8. disclose
clear.. 7. explain 9. elucidate
coins.. 4. mint

countercharge.. 11. recriminate
crisp.. 9. embrittle
deduction.. 6. rebate
desolate.. 5. strip 7. bereave
diminutive.. 9. bantamize
do.. 3. eke 5. get by 8. piece out
  9. improvise
eccentric.. 8. decenter
edging.. 3. tat 7. crochet
effective.. 6. compel 7. enforce
enduring.. 6. anneal, temper
equal.. 6. equate
evident.. 6. evince
familiar.. 8. accustom
famous.. 8. eternize 11. immortalize
fast.. 4. snub 5. belay 6. batten,
  secure
faulty.. 6. impair 7. vitiate
  11. contaminate
firm.. 3. fix 5. brace 6. cement
fit.. 4. suit 5. adapt 6. adjust
  7. conform
foolish, stupid.. 4. daff 8. stultify
  10. ridiculous
fun of.. 3. rib 5. scoff 8. ridicule
glass.. 7. platten
good.. 7. absolve, justify, succeed
  9. indemnify, vindicate
happy.. 5. elate 7. beatify 8. felicify
  (obs)
hard, harsh.. 5. steel 6. freeze
  7. roughen
harmonious.. 6. attune
headway.. 4. gain 7. advance
  8. progress
holy.. 5. bless 6. hallow
  10. consecrate
honorable.. 5. exalt 6. uplift
  7. ennoble
ineffective.. 4. void 5. annul
insensible to pain.. 11. anesthetize
  (anaesthetize)
into law.. 5. enact 9. legislate
known.. 6. impart, reveal 7. divulge,
  publish, uncover 8. disclose,
  discover, proclaim
lace.. 3. tat 7. crochet
less dense.. 4. thin 6. rarefy
less smooth.. 7. roughen
level.. 4. true
light.. 6. jetsam 8. illumine, jettison
lively.. 8. energize
love.. 3. coo, woo 5. court
merry.. 5. laugh 6. banter 7. disport
mild.. 8. mitigate, modulate
moral.. 8. ethicize
much of.. 6. praise 7. enthuse, lionize
  10. exaggerate
muddy.. 4. roil
notes.. 8. annotate
out.. 4. know 5. solve 6. decode,
  draw up 7. analyze, discern
  8. contrive, decipher 10. understand
over.. 4. redo 6. revamp 7. convert
  9. refashion, reproduce
pale, sickly.. 8. etiolate
possible.. 6. enable
pottery.. 7. spattle
precious.. 6. endear
pretentious.. 7. buckram
public.. 3. air 5. bruit, noise
  6. delate 7. publish 9. divulgate

  11. acknowledge
ready.. 4. gear 5. coach, prime
  7. prepare
reparation.. 5. atone
resistance.. 5. rebel 6. mutiny, revolt
secure.. 3. fix, pin 4. nail, snub
  5. belay 6. batten, fasten
shift.. 9. temporary
short work of.. 6. hasten 7. destroy
  10. accomplish
shrill noise.. 10. stridulate
smooth.. 4. buff, iron 5. sleek, slick
  6. scrape
spruce.. 4. perk 7. smarten
strong.. 7. stouten
thin.. 9. attenuate
three–cornered.. 11. triangulate
unhappy.. 8. embitter 10. exacerbate
up.. 5. atone, build 6. invent, settle
  7. compose, concoct, prepare
  8. assemble, cosmetic 9. construct,
  improvise, reconcile 10. compensate
use of.. 5. apply 6. borrow, employ
  7. utilize 11. appropriate
waste (law).. 7. estrepe
watertight.. 4. calk, seal
white.. 6. blanch, bleach
worse.. 9. aggravate
zealous.. 7. enthuse
maker of...
  arrows.. 8. fletcher
  barrels.. 6. cooper
  bundles.. 5. baler
  infusion.. 7. steeper
  knives.. 6. cutler
  pottery.. 6. potter 8. ceramist
makeshift... 7. stopgap
maki... 5. lemur
mal (comb form)... 3. bad, ill 5. badly
  7. disease 8. sickness
Malabar (pert to)...
  bark.. 5. ochna
  nutmeg.. 10. Bombay mace
  palm.. 7. talipot
  rat.. 9. bandicoot
Malacca... 7. seaport (Malaya)
Malachi... 4. Book (Old Test)
  7. prophet
malachite... 4. bice 5. green
  6. copper 7. pigment
maladroit... 6. clumsy 7. awkward,
  unhandy 8. bungling 9. all thumbs,
  graceless 10. blundering, left–handed,
  ungraceful
maladventure... 6. mishap
  8. escapade 12. ill adventure
malady... 4. amok 7. ailment, disease,
  illness 8. disorder, sickness
  9. complaint, distemper
  13. indisposition
mala fide... 10. in bad faith
Malaga... 4. city (Sp), wine
  10. oxblood red
Malagasy lemur... 6. aye–aye
Malagasy region... 10. Madagascar
malaise... 4. pain 10. discomfort,
  uneasiness
malapert... 4. bold, pert 5. saucy
  8. impudent
malaria... 5. miasm 6. miasma
  10. strophulus
malaxation... 7. massage 9. softening

Malay Archipelago . . .
animal . . **4.** mias **5.** tapir, tsine
  6. gibbon, taguan **7.** banteng
apparel . . **4.** baju **5.** banju **6.** sarong
buffalo . . **4.** gaur **7.** carabao, seldang
canoe . . **4.** proa **5.** prahu
chief (tribal) . . **4.** dato (datto)
crane . . **5.** sarus
dagger, knife . . **6.** creese (kris), parong
disease (jumping) . . **4.** Lata (Latah)
gentleman . . **3.** sir **4.** tuan
island . . **4.** Bali, Java **5.** Timor
  7. Celebes, Sumatra **9.** New Guinea
  11. Philippines
isthmus . . **3.** Kra
language . . **7.** Tagalog
native . . **5.** Bajau **6.** Ifugao **8.** Filipino
  9. Samal Laut **10.** sea gypsies
palm . . **6.** Arenga, gomuti (gomuto)
  8. Saguerus
pygmy . . **4.** Aeta
rice field . . **5.** sawah
seaport . . **7.** Malacca
state . . **5.** Kedah, Perak **6.** Jahore
tree . . **4.** upas **5.** kapur, niepa, terap
  6. durian (fruit)
vessel . . **4.** toup **6.** lugger
Malaysia . . .
capital . . **11.** Kuala Lumpur
malcontent . . . **5.** rebel **6.** Fenian,
  uneasy **7.** repiner **8.** agitator,
  grumbler **10.** rebellious
  12. discontented
male . . . **2.** he **3.** cob, him, tom **4.** bull,
  dude, galt, jack, stud **5.** andro (comb
  form), macho, manly **6.** tercel, virile
  7. rooster **8.** stallion **9.** masculine
male (pert to) . . .
column (Arch) . . **7.** Telamon
  8. Atlantes
One Hundred eyes . . **5.** Argus
malediction . . . **5.** curse **6.** threat
  7. malison, slander **8.** anathema
  11. imprecation **12.** denunciation
malefaction . . . **5.** crime **7.** offense
  9. malum in se
malefactor . . . **5.** felon **7.** culprit
  8. criminal, evildoer **9.** wrongdoer
malevolence . . . **4.** hate **5.** pique, spite
  6. grudge, malice, rancor **7.** ill will
  8. inimical **9.** animosity, malignity
  10. bitterness
malevolent . . . **4.** evil **6.** hating
  7. envious, hateful **8.** spiteful
  9. malicious, rancorous
  11. ill–disposed
malfeasance . . . **7.** misrule **8.** impolicy
  10. wrongdoing **11.** evil conduct,
  illegal deed
malfeasant . . . **8.** criminal, evildoer
malgré . . . **9.** in spite of
  15. notwithstanding
malheur . . . **10.** misfortune
Mali, Africa . . .
capital . . **6.** Bamako
malice . . . **4.** envy, evil **5.** malum,
  pique, spite, wrong **6.** rancor **7.** ill
  will **9.** animosity, malignity, malintent
  10. bitterness **11.** malevolence
malicious . . . **4.** evil, mean **6.** bitter,
  malign, ornery **7.** hateful **8.** sinister,
  spiteful **9.** rancorous, resentful,

vitriolic **11.** ill–disposed
  12. cantankerous, unpropitious
malicious (pert to) . . .
destruction . . **5.** arson **8.** sabotage
  9. vandalism
gossip . . **4.** dirt **7.** scandal, slander
intention . . **6.** animus
maliform . . . **11.** apple–shaped
malign . . . **4.** evil **5.** abuse, libel
  6. deadly, defame, revile, vilify
  7. asperse, baleful, harmful, slander,
  traduce **8.** badmouth, virulent
  10. calumniate **12.** unpropitious
malignancy . . . **6.** malice **9.** virulence
  10. deadliness **11.** harmfulness,
  noxiousness
malignant . . . **3.** ill **4.** evil **5.** felon
  6. deadly, wicked **7.** harmful,
  heinous, vicious **8.** spiteful, virulent
  9. felonious, invidious, malicious,
  poisonous, rancorous **10.** rebellious
  11. deleterious
maligner . . . **8.** libelist **9.** slanderer
malignity . . . **4.** evil, hate **5.** spite,
  venom **11.** harmfulness, heinousness
maline(s) . . . **3.** net **11.** Mechlin lace
malingerer . . . **6.** truant **7.** quitter,
  shirker, slacker, welsher
malison . . . **5.** curse **11.** malediction
malkin . . . **3.** cat, mop **4.** drab, hare
  6. sponge **8.** slattern **9.** scarecrow
mall . . . **4.** gull, walk **5.** alley, plaza,
  prado **6.** arcade, mallet **7.** alameda
  8. assembly **9.** esplanade, promenade
  14. shopping center
mallongong . . . **8.** duckbill
mallard . . . **4.** Anas, duck **5.** drake
malleable . . . **4.** soft **6.** pliant
  7. ductile, plastic **9.** teachable
mallemuck . . . **6.** fulmar, petrel
  9. albatross
mallet . . . **3.** tup **4.** club, mace, maul
  5. gavel, madge **6.** beater, beetle,
  driver, hammer
malm . . . **4.** marl **5.** chalk
malmsey . . . **4.** wine
malodorous . . . **4.** rank **5.** fetid
  6. rotten **7.** noisome, odorous
  11. ill–smelling, odoriferous
malt (pert to) . . .
froth . . **4.** barm
ground . . **5.** grist
infusion . . **4.** wort **9.** sweetwort
liquor . . **4.** beer, suds **6.** swipes
material . . **5.** grain **6.** barley
mixture . . **6.** zythum **7.** maltate
vinegar . . **4.** wort **6.** alegar
Malta, Mediterranean Isle . . .
capital . . **8.** Valletta
fever . . **8.** undulent
group island . . **4.** Gozo **6.** Comino
Maltese . . . **3.** cat **5.** cross **6.** Knight,
  native (of Malta)
maltreat . . . **5.** abuse **6.** misuse **8.** ill
  treat **9.** do wrong by
malty . . . **5.** drunk
malum . . . **4.** evil **5.** wrong **7.** offense
malversation . . . **9.** extortion (in office)
  10. corruption **11.** evil conduct,
  fraudulence, misbehavior
mammal . . . **3.** ape, man **4.** homo
  5. whale **10.** vertebrate

mammal ... 2. ai, ox 3. ape, bat, cat, cow, dog, hog, orc, pig, rat, yak 4. bear, bull, deer, lion, mink, mole, paca, seal, tait, zebu 5. camel, coati, daman, koala, lemur, llama, moose, mouse, okapi, otter, ounce, panda, ratel, rhino, sable, shark, sheep, swine, tapir, tayra, whale 6. alpaca, badger, desman, dugong, marten, monkey, ocelot, rytina (ext), tenrec (tendrac), walrus, weasel 7. dolphin, manatee, opossum, peccary, raccoon 8. aardvark, anteater, antelope, elephant, kangaroo, mongoose, reindeer 10. chevrotain, rhinoceros 12. hippopotamus

mammal (pert to) ...
coat.. 4. hide, skin 6. pelage
cud–chewing.. 8. ruminant
edentate.. 8. anteater, pangolin, tamandua (anteater)
extinct.. 6. rytina 8. mastodon 9. Glyptodon
flying.. 3. bat
largest.. 5. whale
man.. 6. Bimana (group)
meat–eating.. 9. carnivore
nipple.. 4. teat 8. mammilla
omnivorous.. 3. hog, pig 5. swine
Order.. 7. Cetacea 8. Edentata, Rodentia
Order, highest.. 7. Primata 8. Mammalia
Order, lowest.. 9. Marsupial
plantigrade.. 7. raccoon
primate (except Man).. 10. Quadrumana
scaled.. 8. pangolin
shelled.. 9. armadillo
smallest.. 5. shrew
snake–eating.. 8. mongoose
toothless.. 8. edentate
web–footed.. 6. aliped
wing–footed.. 6. aliped
zebralike.. 6. quagga

mammock ... 4. tear 5. break, scrap 8. fragment

mammon ... 5. money 6. riches, wealth 11. fallen angel (Bib) 15. demon of cupidity

mammoth ... 5. giant, large (very) 7. titanic 8. behemoth, elephant, gigantic, mastodon 9. pachyderm 11. Dinotherium 12. hippopotamus

man ... 3. arm, fit, rig 4. homo, male 5. adult, equip, fit up, human, staff 6. outfit, person 7. fortify, furnish, mankind, prepare, someone 9. human race 10. human being

man (of) ...
all work.. 4. mozo 6. Friday 8. factotum 9. assistant
Blood and Iron.. 8. Bismarck
Destiny.. 9. Bonaparte (Napoleon)
Galilee.. 11. Jesus Christ
God.. 5. saint 6. priest 9. clergyman 12. ecclesiastic
law.. 6. lawyer 7. counsel 8. attorney 9. counselor (counsellor)
learning.. 6. pundit, savant 7. scholar 9. literatus 11. litterateur
quackery.. 7. buffoon 9. trickster
10. mountebank
the sea.. 3. tar 6. merman, sailor
the signs.. 12. homo signorum
the woods.. 6. rustic 8. silvanus, woodsman 9. orangutan
the world.. 6. layman 11. cosmopolite 12. sophisticate
war.. 7. frigate, soldier, warrior

man (pert to) ...
aged.. 3. vet 9. patriarch 12. octogenarian
bachelor.. 4. stag 8. celibate
bald.. 9. pilgarlic
conceited.. 7. coxcomb
cunning.. 5. rogue 6. rascal 7. shyster 10. mountebank
dissolute.. 4. roué
eccentric, elderly.. 4. sire 5. uncle 6. codger, gaffer 11. grandfather
effeminate.. 9. androgyne
entire (soul and body).. 3. ego
fashionable.. 3. fop 4. dude 5. dandy 11. Beau Brummel 12. boulevardier
fungus.. 9. earthstar (the)
handsome.. 6. Adonis
hardheaded.. 5. Boche
hard–pressed.. 3. Job
important.. 4. hero, lion 5. chief, nabob 6. tycoon 7. mugwump
Isle of, capital.. 7. Douglas
lady's.. 4. beau 6. fiancé
lawless.. 7. ruffian
learned.. 6. pundit, savant 7. erudite, scholar 9. literatus 11. philologist
like.. 7. android 10. anthropoid
little.. 6. mankin, shrimp, squirt 10. homunculus
loud–voiced.. 7. stentor
lowbred.. 4. serf 5. churl 6. rustic 7. peasant 8. plebeian
medicine, magic.. 6. shaman
millionaire.. 7. Croesus 10. capitalist, Corinthian
newspaper.. 6. editor 8. reporter 10. journalist
old.. 5. elder 7. veteran 12. octogenarian
prehistoric.. 4. cave 6. Ice Age 8. eolithic, Grimaldi, Piltdown 9. neolithic 11. paleolithic
red.. 6. Indian
strong.. 6. Samson 8. ironside
wise.. 4. sage, seer 5. solon 6. nestor 7. Solomon
without a country.. 5. Nolan (Philip)

manacle ... 4. gyve, iron 5. chain 6. fetter 7. shackle 8. handcuff 9. restraint

manada ... 4. herd 5. drove, flock

manage ... 3. man, run 4. boss, head, lead, tend 5. cater, dight, guide, pilot, wield 6. direct, govern 7. control, husband, operate 8. contrive, engineer 10. administer, manipulate

manageable ... 4. easy, tame, yare 6. docile, wieldy 7. ductile 9. compliant, tractable 10. governable 12. controllable

management ... 4. care 6. charge, menage 7. conduct, control, gestion 9. direction 10. government

11. negotiation
manager... 4. boss 6. gerent
   7. steward 8. director, governor,
   operator, overseer 9. economist
   12. entrepreneur 13. administrator
managery... 7. cunning 8. artifice
   9. frugality, husbandry
   10. management 12. manipulation
   14. administration
mañana... 8. tomorrow 10. before
   long
manas (Hind)... 3. ego 4. mind
Manasseh... 5. tribe (Israel) 11. King
   of Judah
Manchuria...
   capital.. 6. Mukden (old)
     9. Changchun
   government.. 9. Communist (Chin)
   Japanese name.. 9. Manchukuo
   native.. 9. Mongolian
   river.. 4. Amur, Liao, Yalu
manciple... 5. slave 7. servant,
   steward 8. purveyor
mandarin (pert to)...
   bird.. 4. duck
   city.. 9. Chungking
   color.. 3. red
   dialect.. 7. Chinese
   figure in Chiness dress, seated..
     9. grotesque
   fruit.. 6. orange 9. tangerine
   official.. 8. governor 10. bureaucrat
   residence.. 5. yamen
   ware.. 9. porcelain
mandate... 5. edict, order 6. behest,
   charge, decree, mandat 7. bidding,
   command, precept 9. direction
   10. injunction, referendum
mandatory... 10. imperative, obligatory,
   preceptive
mandible... 3. jaw 4. beak 5. chops,
   molar (part) 9. chelicera
mandrel, mandril... 3. hob 4. axle,
   pick (miner's) 5. arbor 7. spindle
mandriarch... 9. monk ruler
mandrill... 6. baboon
mane... 4. hair, juba, shag 6. thatch
manege... 6. school (riding)
   7. academy (riding) 8. cavesson
   (halter)
manes (Rom)... 4. gods (lower world)
   7. spirits
maneuver, manoeuvre... 4. ruse
   5. trick 6. device, jockey, scheme,
   tactic 7. operate 8. artifice, intrigue,
   strategy 9. stratagem 10. manipulate
   13. Immelmann turn
mangabey... 6. monkey
manger... 3. bin 4. crib, meal, rack
   6. bunker, trough 7. banquet
mangle... 3. cut, mar 4. hack
   5. press 6. bruise, injure, ironer
   8. calender, demolish, lacerate,
   mutilate 9. dismember
mango (pert to)...
   bird.. 6. oriole 11. hummingbird
   fish.. 9. threadfin
   fruit.. 5. amini, bauno, drupe, melon
     9. muskmelon
   grove.. 4. tope
mangy... 4. mean 5. itchy, seedy

6. ronyon, scurvy, shabby 7. squalid
   12. contemptible
manhandle... 4. maul 5. abuse
   7. rough up 8. maltreat, mistreat
mania... 4. rage 5. craze, furor
   6. frenzy, furore, lunacy 7. madness,
   passion 8. delirium 10. alienation
   11. fascination, infatuation
mania (for)...
   buying.. 9. oniomania
   drink.. 9. potomania 10. dipsomania
   foreign customs.. 9. xenomania
   narcotics.. 10. narcomania
   religion.. 9. theomania
   stealing.. 10. erotomania
     11. kleptomania
   wandering.. 10. dromomania
   work.. 9. ergomania
manifest... 4. list, open, show
   5. clear, index, overt 6. evince,
   liquet, patent 7. declare, evident,
   express, obvious, visible 8. apparent,
   disclose 11. indubitable
   12. indisputable, unmistakable
manifestation... 4. aura 5. phase
   7. display 8. evidence
   10. appearance, disclosure,
   exhibition, indication, revelation
   13. demonstration
manifestation of...
   deity.. 4. Apis 7. serapis
   divinity.. 6. Christ 8. Epiphany
   Vishnu.. 6. avatar
manifesto... 5. edict 6. decree
   8. evidence, rescript 11. declaration
   (public) 12. announcement
   13. demonstration
manikin... 5. dwarf, model, pygmy
   6. figure 7. phantom 9. mannequin
Manila...
   boat.. 6. bilalo
   capital of.. 11. Philippines
   hemp.. 5. abaca
   hero.. 5. Dewey (Adm)
   island site.. 5. Luzon
   native.. 7. Chinese, Tagalog
     9. Filipinos
maniple... 5. fanon, orale 7. handful,
   phalanx, platoon
manipulate... 3. rig, use 4. work
   5. pilot, treat, wield 6. handle,
   manage 7. operate
manipulation... 5. using 8. handling,
   intrigue 9. operation, stratagem
   10. management, use of hands
Manitoba, Canada...
   capital.. 8. Winnipeg
   Indian.. 4. Cree
   lake.. 8. Manitoba
   river.. 3. Red
mankind... 3. man 4. Adam, folk
   7. menfolk 8. humanity 9. human
   race
mankind (pert to)...
   division.. 4. race 5. tribe
   group (kindred).. 6. ethnos, socius
   hater.. 11. misanthrope
   science.. 9. ethnogeny, ethnology
     12. anthropology
manly... 4. bold 5. adult, brave, hardy,
   noble 6. daring 8. resolute
   9. honorable, masculine, undaunted

10. courageous

manna... 4. food (miracle), lerp (laap, laarp) 7. godsend 10. gazangabin

manner... 3. air, way 4. kind, mien, mode, sort 5. guise, style 6. aspect, custom, method 7. fashion 8. behavior 10. appearance, deportment

manner (pert to)...
frenzied.. 4. amok 5. amuck, huffy 7. haughty
law.. 5. modus
like.. 4. thus 6. in kind 8. parallel
meddlesome.. 9. officious
meditative.. 13. contemplative
rough.. 7. brusque 10. irreverent

mannerism... 4. mode 8. elegance 11. affectation

mannerly... 4. nice 5. moral, suave 6. seemly 8. decorous, politely 9. courteous 10. well–spoken 12. ingratiating

manner of...
making something.. 7. facture
pronouncing.. 6. accent, brogue
speaking.. 7. grammar

manners... 5. mores 8. behavior 9. amenities, etiquette

Mannheim gold... 5. brass

mano (comb form)... 4. hand

manoc... 4. fowl (jungle) 7. chicken, rooster

manor... 4. hall 5. abode 6. estate 7. demesne, mansion

manred... 6. homage 9. vassalage 10. leadership (in war)

mansion... 4. seat 5. house, manor, manse 8. dwelling 9. astrology

manta... 3. ray (fish) 4. wrap 5. cloak, cloth 7. blanket 8. mantelet (mantlet) 9. devilfish

mantilla... 4. cape, veil 5. cloak

mantis... 9. Cagn (deity) 6. insect 7. mantoid 9. rearhorse

mantis crab... 7. squilla

mantle... 4. cape, cope, robe 5. cloak, cover 6. capote, kittel 7. garment 8. filament, insignia, mantelet, mantling (Her), vestment 10. witzchoura 11. mantelletta

manto... 3. ore 4. gown 5. cloak 6. mantle, mantua

mantoid... 6. mantis

Mantua (pert to)...
birthplace of.. 6. Vergil (Virgil)
capital.. 7. Mantova
walled by.. 11. Charlemagne

Manu (Myth)...
laws.. 8. creation, religion
progenitors of.. 3. Man
Seventh Age, author of.. 10. Code of Manu (Hind laws)

manual... 4. book 7. clavier (Mus), didache 8. exercise, handbook 14. consuetudinary

manual (pert to)...
alphabet (deaf).. 11. dactylology
arts.. 6. crafts
crafts.. 5. sloyd (sloid, slojd) 10. handicraft
digit.. 3. toe 5. thumb 6. finger 8. dactylar

ritual.. 7. rituale 8. breviary 9. formulary

manufacture... 4. make 6. invent 7. produce, trump up 9. fabricate

manufacturer of drugs, liquors... 6. abkari (abkary)

manumission... 7. freeing 10. liberation (slave) 12. emancipation

manumit... 4. free 5. let go 6. unhand 7. dismiss, release 8. liberate

manuscript (Ms, Mss)... 4. copy (author's), opus 5. codex, folio 7. writing 8. document 11. composition, handwriting 13. written by hand

manuscript (pert to)...
back.. 5. dorso
blank space.. 6. lacuna
copier.. 6. scribe
mark (old).. 6. obelus

many... 6. divers 7. diverse, several, various 8. frequent, manifold, numerous 9. different, multitude 10. multiplied

many (pert to)...
footed.. 8. multiped
prefix.. 4. poly, vari 5. multi
sided.. 9. versatile 12. multilateral
times.. 5. often 10. frequently

manyplies... 12. third stomach (ruminant)

mao... 7. peacock

Maori (pert to)...
Adam, ancestor.. 4. Tiki
bird.. 3. tui 4. weka (flightless)
canoe, raft.. 4. moki, waka
charm (grotesque).. 7. heitiki
compensation.. 3. utu
fish.. 4. hiku 7. rainbow 9. trumpeter
hero.. 4. Maui
people.. 9. cannibals (anc) 10. aborigines
priest.. 7. tuhunga
sect.. 7. Ringatu
tatooing.. 4. moko
tree.. 5. mapau
tribe.. 3. Ati 4. Hapu
village.. 4. kaik (kaika)
weapon.. 4. mere, patu, rata 6. marree

Maoriland... 10. New Zealand

map... 4. plat 5. chart, image 6. charte, design, isobar (weather line), sketch, survey 7. diagram, epitome, explore, picture 9. delineate 10. embodiment 14. representation

maple (pert to)...
bowl.. 5. mazer, rogan (sap)
flowering.. 8. abutilon
genus.. 4. Acer 9. Aceraceae
insect scale.. 10. pulvinaria
seed.. 6. samara
sugar tube.. 5. stile
tree.. 8. box elder 9. moosewood

map maker... 4. Eric (Father) 7. charter 8. Mercator 12. cartographer

mapo... 4. goby (fish)

mar... 4. ruin, scar 5. botch, spoil 6. damage, deface, impair, mangle

7. blemish 8. mutilate 9. disfigure
Mar... 4. Lord (Jacobite)
marabou, marabout... 5. stork
6. argala, covert 8. adjutant
maracan... 5. macaw
maranon... 6. cashew
marasca, maraschino... 6. cherry
marasma... 5. waste 7. disease
10. emaciation 12. malnutrition
maraud... 3. rob 4. loot, raid, rove,
sack 6. forage 7. brigand, cateran,
pillage, plunder 10. plundering
marble... 3. mib, mig, taw 4. cold,
hard 5. agate, white 6. basalt,
marmor 7. pattern (mottled)
8. dolomite 9. limestone, sculpture,
unfeeling
marble (pert to)...
Belgian.. 5. rance
Catalonia.. 8. brocatel (brocatelle)
cork (tree).. 9. tambookie
famous.. 6. Parian 7. Carrara
8. Pentelec
game.. 3. taw 5. alley
group (famed).. 5. Elgin (Marbles)
made of.. 9. marmoreal
mosaic.. 7. tessera
Roman.. 7. cipolin
slab.. 5. dalle
marbled... 9. marmorate
Marbles... 5. Elgin 7. Arundel
marc... 6. refuse, spirit 7. residue
14. eau de vie de marc
marcato (Mus)... 6. marked
8. accented, emphatic
march... 4. fill, hike, step, trek
5. troop 6. border, parade
7. advance, proceed 8. boundary,
drumbeat, frontier, lockstep,
movement, progress, smallage
9. cavalcade, quickstep
March King... 5. Sousa (John Philip)
marcid... 4. weak 7. decayed, tabetic
8. withered 9. exhausted
10. emaciating
Marcobrunner... 4. wine (White Rhine)
Mardi Gras... 8. carnival 10. fat
Tuesday (literal) 13. Shrove Tuesday
Mardi Gras King... 3. Rex
mare... 4. yaud 5. filly, horse
6. goblin, grasni (gypsy) 7. incubus,
specter, trestle 8. the blues
9. nightmare 10. blue devils,
melancholy
marge, margent... 3. rim 4. brim,
edge, side 5. brink, shore 6. border,
fringe, margin 8. marginal
margin... 3. rim 4. brim, edge, rand,
room, side 5. brink, limit 6. amount,
border, reward 10. collateral
margin (pert to)...
business.. 5. gross
notched.. 5. erose
note.. 7. apostil 8. scholium
10. annotation
scalloped.. 7. crenate
set in.. 6. indent
straighten (to).. 5. align
marginal note... 4. kere (kri, keri)
7. apostil 8. scholium 10. annotation
marigold... 5. aster, boots, caper,
finch 6. orange (cadmium)

7. cowslip, Tagetes
marijuana... 3. hay 4. hemp 6. reefer
7. tobacco (wild) 8. locoweed
9. cigarette
marikina... 7. tamarin 8. marmoset
marimba... 9. xylophone
marina... 4. dock 5. basin
9. esplanade, promenade (seaside)
marinal... 6. marine, sailor, saline
marine... 3. tar 5. jolly, naval
7. mariner, oceanic, pelagic
8. maritime, nautical 11. leatherneck
marine (pert to)...
animal.. 3. orc 4. brit, seal 5. coral,
polyp 6. dugong, Otaria, teredo,
walrus 7. manatee, mollusk, octopus
clam.. 8. shipworm
crustacean.. 4. brit 8. barnacle
fauna, flora.. 7. benthos
fish.. 5. shark 8. menhaden
gastropod.. 5. conus (snail), murex
7. terebra
growth.. 4. kelp 5. algae 6. enalid
7. seaweed 10. ditch grass
individual.. 6. merman 7. mermaid
skeleton.. 5. coral
slogan.. 6. gung–ho
mariner... 3. gob, tar 4. salt 5. Jacky
6. sailor, seaman 8. waterman
mariner's card... 5. chart
mariner's compass points...
6. rhumba
marionette... 4. doll, duck 6. figure,
puppet
maritime... 5. naval 6. marine
7. oceanic 8. nautical
marjoram... 3. dot 4. mint 6. origin
8. origanum 9. flavoring
mark... 3. aim, tee 4. heed, line,
note, rist, seal, sign 5. brand, label,
notch, score, stain, stamp, trait
6. denote, symbol, target
7. betoken, blemish, earmark,
engrave, impress, imprint, insigne
8. evidence, identify, insignia,
landmark 9. emphasize, objective,
punctuate, signature, trademark
10. indication 11. distinction,
distinguish 14. characteristic
mark (pert to)...
bad.. 7. demerit
bounds.. 7. delimit 9. demarcate
contest (in a).. 5. bogey (bogie)
critical.. 6. obelus
diacritical.. 5. tilde 6. tittle 7. cedilla
disgrace.. 6. stigma
fingerprint.. 5. whorl
logic.. 11. differentia
misconduct.. 7. demerit
off.. 4. plot 6. assign 7. measure
12. characterize, circumscribe
of homage.. 7. ovation
of whip.. 4. wale, welt
out.. 6. cancel 10. obliterate
possessive.. 10. apostrophe
printing.. 4. dele, stet 5. caret
6. dagger, diesis, obelus 7. obelisk
10. apostrophe
pronunciation.. 5. breve 6. macron
proofreading.. 4. dele 5. caret
prosody.. 7. caesura, triseme
9. diaeresis, tetraseme

punctuation.. 4. dash 5. colon,
  comma 6. period 9. diaeresis
  (dieresis), semicolon 10. apostrophe
question.. 7. eroteme (erotema)
reference.. 4. star 6. dagger, diesis
  8. asterisk
with bars.. 5. grill
with dots, spots.. 6. dapple 7. stipple
with pointed instrument.. 6. scrive
with ridges.. 3. rib
marked by...
dispute.. 13. controversial
maneuvering.. 8. tactical
nicety.. 7. elegant
small areas.. 9. areolated
time.. 5. dated
marked with...
colors.. 7. mottled 10. variegated
  11. psychedelic
depressions.. 7. dimpled
furrows.. 6. rivose
grooves.. 6. lirate
lines.. 5. ruled 6. linear, notate
sables (Her).. 8. pelleted
spots.. 6. notate 7. mottled
stripes.. 7. lineate
zones.. 6. zonate
marker... 4. buoy 5. pylon 6. scorer,
  signal 7. brander, counter, monitor
  8. bookmark, marksman, monument,
  recorder 9. indicator
market... 4. mart, sale, sell, shop
  5. forum, trade 6. rialto, square
  9. clientele
market (pert to)...
bonds.. 5. float
day (Rom).. 7. nundine
French.. 8. débouché
place.. 4. sook 5. agora, plaza, store
  6. bazaar, rialto 8. emporium,
  exchange
marketable... 6. staple 7. salable
  8. in demand, vendible
  12. merchantable
markhor... 4. goat
marking (crescent)... 6. lunula, lunule
  7. lunulet 9. engraving
markings... 7. rasceta
marksman... 4. shot 6. gunner, sniper
  7. shooter 9. Orangeman
Mark Twain (pert to)...
category.. 8. humorist
character.. 9. Tom Sawyer
  15. Huckleberry Finn
name.. 13. Samuel Clemens
tale.. 9. Gilded Age 10. Roughing It
  15. Innocents Abroad
marl... 4. malm 5. earth, fiber
  6. manure 7. deposit (earthy), marlite
  9. greensand 10. fertilizer,
  overspread
marli... 4. lace 5. gauze, tulle
  6. border (raised on dish)
marlin... 6. curlew, godwit 8. sailfish
  9. spearfish
marlinspike... 3. fid 4. bird, tool
  6. jaeger 8. skua gull
marmalade... 3. jam 6. Achras, sapote
  8. plum tree, preserve 12. mammee
  sapota
marmit... 6. kettle 7. soup pot
marmite (Mil)... 4. bomb (soup kettle)

  5. shell
marmor... 6. marble
marmoset... 4. mico (black–tailed)
  6. monkey, sagoin 7. tamarin
marmot... 5. bobac 6. rodent
  7. Marmota 8. Arctomys, whistler
  9. ground hog, woodchuck
maroon... 5. slave 7. abandon, cast
  off, forsake, isolate 8. chestnut
  13. leave helpless
marquee... 4. tent 6. canopy
marriage... 5. union 7. wedding,
  wedlock 9. matrimony 10. nuptiality
  11. espousement
marriage (pert to)...
absence of.. 5. agamy
age.. 6. mature, nubile
broker.. 9. schatchen 10. matchmaker
forswearer.. 8. celibate
god.. 5. Hymen
goddess.. 4. Hera
hater.. 10. misogamist
intermarriage.. 13. miscegenation
late in life.. 8. opsigamy
more than one.. 6. bigamy, digamy
  8. polygamy 9. polyandry, tetragamy
  (4th) 11. deuterogamy
notice.. 5. banns
of the gods.. 8. theogamy
outside the tribe.. 7. exogamy
pert to.. 7. marital, spousal
  8. hymeneal 9. connubial, endogamic
portion.. 3. dot 5. dotal, dowry
promise.. 7. betroth 8. affiance
secret.. 9. elopement
married... 5. wived 6. wedded
  8. espoused 9. connubial
married (pert to)...
more than once at a time..
  9. polyandry (woman)
once at a time.. 8. monandry
person.. 4. wife 6. spouse
  7. husband 8. benedict
twice.. 6. bigamy, digamy
  11. deuterogamy
marrow... 4. pith 6. center
  7. essence, medulla 9. substance
Mars... 3. god (of War) 4. Ares
  6. planet, war–god
Mars (pert to)...
altar.. 13. Campus Martius (field of
  Mars)
constellation.. 3. Ara
festival.. 5. March 7. October
pert to.. 5. Arean 7. Martian
priests.. 5. Salii
red.. 5. totem
satellites.. 6. Deimos, Phobos
ship.. 8. moon ship 9. spaceship
sons (twin).. 5. Remus 7. Romulus
spot.. 5. oasis
Marseillaise... 4. song (1792)
Marseille, France...
capital of Dept.. 14. Bouches du
  Rhone
church.. 9. Notre Dame
fort.. 11. Rue Noailles 13. Rue
  Cannebière
old name.. 8. Massilia
seaport site.. 13. Mediterranean
marsh... 3. bog, fen 4. meer, mire,
  moor, slue 5. liman, swale, swamp

6. morass, saline, slough
7. maremma
marsh (pert to)...
bird.. 4. sora 5. snipe, stilt
crocodile.. 3. goa
elder.. 3. Iva
fever.. 7. helodes
gas.. 7. methane 8. firedamp
grass.. 5. sedge, spart
hawk.. 5. harpy 7. harrier
hen.. 4. rail
inhabiting.. 12. limnophilous
mallow.. 5. altea
marigold.. 5. boots, calla 7. cowslip
pert to.. 8. paludine
shrub.. 4. reed 5. sedge 7. bulrush,
cattail 8. moorwort 12. pickerelweed
marshal... 3. Ney (Fr) 4. lead 5. align,
aline, array, groom, guide, range,
usher 6. direct, parade 7. farrier,
officer 8. official
Marshall Islands...
chains (two).. 6. Ralick (eleven isls)
7. Rattach (13 isls)
government.. 11. trusteeship
WWII scene.. 6. Bikini 8. Eniwetok
9. Kwajalein
marshberry, marshwort... 9. cranberry
marshy... 3. wet 5. boggy, fenny,
liman 7. moorish 8. morassey,
paludine
marsupial... 4. frog, tait 5. kaola
6. wombat 7. opossum, wallaby
8. kangaroo 9. bandicoot, phalanger,
tapoatafa 10. Diprotodon
11. Marsupialia
marsupium... 5. pouch
martel (Hist).. 6. hammer
martel–de–fer... 6. weapon
12. hammer of iron
marten... 3. fur 4. pelt 5. sable
6. mammal 7. Mustela
martial... 4. Mars (pert to) 5. brave
7. warlike 8. fighting, militant,
military
Martinique...
capital.. 8. St Pierre (former) 12. Fort
de France
formation.. 8. volcanic
mountain peak.. 9. Mont Pelée
martyr... 4. kill 5. title 7. Stephen
(Christian), torture 8. sufferer
marvel... 4. gape 6. wonder
7. miracle, portent, prodigy
8. astonish
marvelous... 6. superb 7. strange
9. wonderful 10. improbable,
incredible, remarkable 11. astonishing
13. extraordinary
Maryland...
bay.. 10. Chesapeake
capital.. 9. Annapolis
city.. 9. Baltimore
Hist site.. 8. Antietam 10. State
House (nation's oldest) 11. Fort Mc
Henry
mountain.. 8. Backbone, Piedmont
11. Appalachian
race (famed).. 9. Preakness
12. Steeplechase
race track.. 5. Bowie 6. Butler, Laurel
7. Pimlico

school.. 9. Annapolis (Acad)
12. Johns Hopkins
settler.. 7. Calvert (Leonard)
State admission.. 7. Seventh
State motto.. 22. Manly Deeds,
Womanly Words
State nickname.. 4. Free 7. Old Line
mash... 4. feed, ogle, pulp 5. crush,
flirt, press, smash, steep 6. jumble,
soften 7. mixture 9. pulverize
11. infatuation
mashal... 7. parable, proverb
masher... 5. dandy, flirt, ricer
7. utensil 10. pulverizer
11. philanderer
masjid... 6. mosque
mask... 4. ball, loup, veil 5. cloak,
cover, dance, drama, onkos
6. domino, screen 7. conceal,
pretext 8. disguise 10. subterfuge
masked... 6. comedy, cowled, hidden,
veiled 7. larvate, obscure
8. shrouded 9. concealed, disguised
masker... 5. mimer 6. mummer
11. masquerader
maslin... 5. brass 6. kettle 7. mixture
(grain) 9. potpourri
Masonic doorkeeper... 5. tiler
masonry... 6. ashlar 9. revetment
mass... 3. cob, dab, gob, mop, pat,
wad 4. blob, body, bulk, load, loaf,
lump, roll, size 5. solid 8. quantity
9. large part, magnitude 11. large
amount 12. accumulation,
congregation
mass (pert to)...
book.. 6. missal
collection.. 9. aggregate
directory (RCCh).. 4. ordo
for dead.. 7. requiem
matter.. 5. molar
molten glass.. 7. parison
nerve tissue.. 8. ganglion
tangled.. 3. mop 4. shag
vestment (Eccl).. 5. amice
Massachusetts...
capital.. 6. Boston (1630)
city.. 5. Salem 7. Concord
8. Plymouth 9. Cambridge, Lexington
10. Gloucester, New Bedford
12. Provincetown
college (oldest, US).. 7. Harvard
explorer.. 5. Cabot 7. Gosnold
9. Capt Smith (John)
hero.. 10. Paul Revere
island.. 9. Nantucket 15. Martha's
Vineyard
mountain.. 3. Tom 8. Greylock
10. Berkshires
river.. 10. Housatonic 11. Connecticut
school (first free).. 6. Dedham (1649)
settlers.. 8. Pilgrims, Puritans
State admission.. 5. Sixth
State nickname.. 8. Bay State 9. Old
Colony
massacre... 5. havoc 6. pogrom
7. carnage 8. butchery, decimate,
genocide 9. slaughter
massage... 3. rub 5. knead 6. stroke
7. therapy
massive... 3. big 4. bold 5. bulky,
large, massy 7. weighty 8. imposing

9. ponderous 10. impressive
11. substantial

mast... 3. cue, fid 4. pole, spar
5. stick, stuff (oneself)

master... 3. man, rab 4. lord, mian,
rule 5. chief, judge, rabbi, tutor
6. expert, humble, subdue
7. captain, conquer, maestro,
padrone, subject, teacher
8. dominate, overcome, regulate,
surmount, vanquish 9. commander,
conqueror, craftsman, preceptor,
subjugate

master (pert to)...
African.. 5. bwana
Eton.. 4. beak
fencing.. 7. lanista
hard.. 6. despot
Indian.. 5. sahib
music.. 7. maestro
of a house.. 13. paterfamilias
of ceremonies.. 2. M C 5. emcee
of Heaven.. 16. Celestial Teacher
of the horse.. 7. equerry
stroke.. 4. coup

masterful... 6. lordly 7. haughty
8. arrogant, skillful 9. arbitrary,
imperious 10. commanding
11. dictatorial, domineering,
magisterial, overbearing
13. authoritative

mastery... 4. gree 5. power, skill
7. control, victory 8. dominion
10. ascendancy 11. proficiency
12. vanquishment

mastic... 3. asa, gum 5. resin
6. liquor 8. adhesive 9. red–yellow

masticate... 4. chew 5. crush, grind
8. macerate

mastiff... 3. dog 5. burly, matin
7. massive

mastodon... 5. giant 6. animal,
Mammut 7. mammoth 8. behemoth
9. dinothere 10. Dinotheres,
Mammutidae 11. Dinotherium

mat... 3. rug 4. dull (finish) 5. doily,
platt, twist 7. webbing 8. entangle,
material 10. interweave, lusterless

matador (pert to)...
garment.. 4. cape
staff.. 6. muleta (with red flag)
sword.. 7. estoque

matagasse... 11. butcherbird

match... 3. pit 4. copy, game, mate,
pair, peer, sort 5. equal, fusee,
marry, tally, vesta 7. compare,
contest, lighter, lucifer 8. coincide,
marriage, parallel 10. correspond
11. counterpart

matched... 5. mated 6. paired, pitted,
teamed 7. equaled (equalled)

matchless... 5. alone 6. unlike
7. unequal 8. peerless 9. unequaled
10. inimitable 12. incomparable

matchlock... 3. gun 7. gunlock

mate... 4. pair, wife 5. equal, marry,
match 6. seaman, spouse
7. comrade, husband, mariner,
partner 9. companion
11. confederate, counterpart

matelassé... 6. fabric 8. quilting
(imitation) 13. ornamentation

material, materiel... 4. data 5. goods,
stuff 6. fabric, matter, plasma,
staple, swatch 7. weighty
8. relevant, supplies, tangible
9. apparatus, corporeal, equipment,
essential 11. substantial
12. nonspiritual 13. materialistic

material (pert to)...
building.. 4. frit, lime, tile, wood
5. adobe, brick, rabat, tapia
6. cement, thatch 7. plywood
8. asbestos, Masonite 9. wallboard
discard.. 4. slag 5. scrap 6. refuse
7. rubbish
dress.. 4. silk, wool 5. crepe, linen,
satin, surah, tulle, tweed 6. baleen,
faille, sennit, tricot, velvet
8. corduroy
household.. 5. scrim 6. carpet,
damask, lampas, mohair, napery
7. drapery 8. tapestry
needlework.. 4. lace, yarn 6. thread
8. arrasene, chenille
paper.. 3. wax 4. bond, news, note,
rice 6. letter, tissue, vellum
7. drawing, writing 8. wrapping
9. cardboard, onionskin, parchment
11. papier–mâché
polishing.. 11. rottenstone

materia medica... 7. acology
10. leechcraft

maternal... 7. enation 8. motherly
10. motherlike

math... 6. mowing 9. aftermath,
monastery

mathematician... 6. Euclid 7. actuary
9. physicist, Whitehead

mathematics (pert to)...
abbreviation.. 3. QED
arbitrary.. 5. radix 9. parameter
deduction.. 8. analysis
diagram.. 5. graph
element.. 4. cube, root 6. factor
7. decimal, divisor, formula, minuend
8. dividend, fraction, quotient,
repetend 10. multiplier, subtrahend
12. multiplicand
equation.. 2. pi 4. cosh, sine, surd
6. cosine
factor.. 10. quaternion
instrument.. 6. sector 7. compass
8. arbalest
number.. 5. digit
operation, operator.. 5. nabla
6. scalar 7. operand 10. quaternion
proposition.. 7. theorem
quantity.. 6. addend, augend, scalar
sheets of.. 4. cone 5. nappe
symbol.. 5. digit 7. facient, operand
12. multiplicand
type.. 4. pure 6. higher 7. algebra,
physics 8. abstract, calculus,
geometry 10. arithmetic, elementary,
quadratics 12. trigonometry

mathemeg... 7. catfish

matie... 7. herring

matin... 6. aubade (song) 7. morning,
service 8. watchdog 11. morning
song 13. morning prayer

matinee... 5. levee, party, salon
6. soiree 8. negligee 9. reception
13. conversazione, entertainment

matipo... 4. wood (fuel) 5. napau
matka, matkab... 4. seal
matlow... 6. sailor
matrass... 4. tube 5. flask 6. bottle,
carafe 8. bolthead
matriculate... 4. list 5. admit, adopt,
enter 6. enroll 8. register
10. naturalize
matrimonial... 7. marital, nuptial,
spousal 8. conjugal, hymeneal
9. connubial
matrimony... 7. wedlock 8. marriage
matrix... 3. bed 4. cast, form, mold,
womb 5. cutis 6. gangue
10. foundation, impression
matron... 4. dame, wife 5. widow
11. housekeeper
matter... 3. gas, pus 4. body, gear,
malm, pith 5. atoms, fluid, vapor
6. affair, amount, solids 7. problem,
trouble 8. business, elements,
material 10. importance
11. constituent 12. circumstance
matter (pert to)...
alluvial.. 5. geest
celestial.. 6. nebula
coloring.. 5. eosin 10. endochrome
fatty.. 5. sebum
noxious.. 6. miasma
of doubt.. 7. dubiety
of fact.. 7. literal, prosaic 9. practical,
pragmatic
of law.. 3. res
of note.. 8. notandum
particle.. 4. atom
perfume.. 7. essence
spinal cord.. 4. alba
uniform (physics).. 7. inertia
volcanic.. 2. aa, oo 4. lava
mature... 3. age, due, old 4. ripe
5. adult, grown, ripen 6. digest,
mellow, season 7. develop, fall due,
grow old, perfect 8. complete
9. full-grown, perfected, ratheripe
maturity... 8. ripeness 9. adulthood,
readiness 10. falling due
11. development
matutinal... 5. early, matin 7. morning
12. antemeridian
maty... 7. servant
maud... 3. rug 5. plaid, shawl
maudlin... 5. beery, drunk, silly, tipsy
7. tearful, weeping 10. lachrymose
11. sentimental (overly)
maul, mall... 4. beat, bung, club,
mace, mall, moth 5. abuse, gavel,
staff 6. beetle, bruise, mallet
maumet... 3. god (false), guy 4. doll,
idol 5. image 6. puppet
9. scarecrow
maund, maun... 3. beg 6. basket,
hamper 7. begging, measure
Maundy... 4. alms 8. ceremony
10. Last Supper
Maundy Thursday (Bib)... 8. Holy
Week 13. washing of feet
Mauritius, Ile de France...
capital.. 9. Port Louis
government.. 7. British
product.. 5. coral, sugar
site.. 11. Indian Ocean
Mauser... 5. rifle 7. firearm

mauve... 5. lilac 6. mallow, purple,
violet 10. atmosphere (color)
maverick... 4. calf (orphan) 5. dogie
6. animal 8. newcomer
13. nonconformist
mavis, mavie... 6. thrush
maw... 4. craw, crop 6. gullet, mallow
7. gizzard, stomach
mawk... 6. maggot
mawkish... 5. vapid 6. sickly
8. nauseous 9. squeamish
10. disgusting 11. sentimental
maxilla... 7. jawbone
maxim... 3. saw 4. dict, rule
5. adage, axiom, gnome, motto,
tenet, truth 6. saying 7. precept,
proverb 8. aphorism, apothegm
10. apophthegm
maxims... 5. logia 9. moralisms
maximum... 4. most 5. limit
7. highest, supreme 8. greatest
12. consummation
maximus... 7. largest
may... 3. can 6. be able 9. be
allowed 11. in one's power,
opportunity
May (pert to)...
apple.. 8. mandrake
bird.. 6. thrush
cock.. 5. melon 6. plover
curlew.. 8. whimbrel
Duke.. 6. cherry
festival.. 7. Beltane (anc)
First.. 7. Beltane 14. May-day festival
fish.. 9. killifish
flower.. 7. arbutus 8. hawthorn,
marigold 9. calla lily 10. stitchwort
12. cuckooflower
fly.. 3. dun 7. shad fly 9. ephemerid
goddess.. 4. Maia
gowan.. 5. daisy
Maya... 3. Mam (tribe) 6. Indian
8. Pokonchi
Mayan calendar...
five added days.. 5. uayeb
no leap year.. 5. solar
twenty-day month.. 5. uinal
year.. 4. haab
Mayan underworld... 7. xibalba
maybe... 2. if 7. perhaps 8. possibly
9. perchance 11. conceivably,
possibility, uncertainty
Mayfair... 6. London (fashionable)
Mayflower (pert to)...
boat of.. 8. Pilgrims (1620)
Compact.. 9. agreement (1620)
sister ship.. 9. Speedwell
mayhap... 7. perhaps 12. peradventure
mayor... 5. maire 7. alcalde
10. magistrate 11. burgomaster
mazarine... 4. blue (color from Cardinal
Mazarin)
maze... 5. fancy 7. stupefy
8. confound, delirium, delusion
9. confusion, deception, labyrinth
12. bewilderment, complication
mazed... 4. lost 7. in a maze
9. stupefied 10. bewildered
mazuma... 7. money
mead... 5. drink 6. meadow
8. hydromel 9. metheglin
meadow... 3. lea 4. mead 5. field,

haugh, pampa, swale 7. pasture,
savanna (savannah) 9. grassland
10. agostadero
meadow (pert to) . . .
chicken . . 8. sora rail
crocus . . 7. saffron
crowfoot . . 9. buttercup
hen . . 4. coot, rail 7. bittern
mouse . . 4. vole 8. arvicole
part . . 5. swale
sage . . 6. salvia
saxifrage . . 6. seseli
sweet . . 7. Spiraea
meager, meagre . . . 4. arid, bare, lank,
poor, slim 5. gaunt, scant, spare
6. barren, jejune, lenten, narrow,
sparse 7. starved, sterile, trivial
9. emaciated 10. inadequate
meal . . . 3. tub 4. bran, dune, mess
5. feast, grout, salep, snack
6. bucket, fodder, powder, ration,
repast, tiffin 7. banquet 8. sandbank
9. collation, pulverize
mealy . . . 4. pale 7. friable, powdery
10. soft–spoken 11. farinaceous
12. mealymouthed
mealy (pert to) . . .
Amazon . . 6. parrot
back . . 6. cicada
bird, duck . . 5. squaw
bug . . 4. pest 5. scale 10. pear blight
mouth . . 7. warbler
tree . . 9. arrowwood, wayfaring
mealy–mouthed . . . 5. suave
10. flattering 12. hypocritical
13. sanctimonious
mean . . . 3. low 4. base 5. petty,
small, snide, solar (time), sorry
6. common, denote, design, humble,
intend, medium, menial, middle,
midway, paltry, shabby, sordid, stingy
7. average, ignoble, purport, purpose,
servile, squalid 8. beggarly, ordinary,
plebeian, shameful, wretched
9. difficult, malicious, niggardly,
penurious 10. despicable,
ill–humored, spiritless 11. closefisted,
disgraceful 12. contemptible,
dishonorable, narrow–minded,
parsimonious
mean clef (Mus) . . . 5. C clef
meaning . . . 4. null (without) 5. sense
6. import, intent, spirit 7. purport
8. semantic 9. intending, intention,
knowledge 10. understand
12. significance 13. signification
14. interpretation
meaningless . . . 4. rote 5. banal, derry
7. aimless 9. senseless
10. designless 11. purposeless
13. insignificant
meanness . . . 6. infamy, malice
8. baseness, ill–humor 9. servility
10. humbleness, paltriness,
sordidness, stinginess 11. inferiority
means . . . 5. funds 7. capital
8. averages 9. resources
11. wherewithal
means of . . .
access . . 4. adit 5. inlet 7. ingress
8. aperture
communication . . 4. note 5. flags,

phone, radio, smoke 6. letter, postal,
tom–tom 8. telegram 9. telegraph,
telephone
livelihood . . 4. work 5. labor, trade
8. vocation 10. profession
outlet . . 4. door, exit 6. egress
8. aperture
support . . 5. funds 6. assets
7. aliment 11. maintenance
meantime . . . 5. while 7. interim
8. interval, same time 9. meanwhile
measles . . . 7. rubella, rubeola
8. morbilli
measure (pert to) . . .
area . . 2. ar 3. are, rod 4. acre, area,
mile, rood 6. square 7. geodesy,
hectare, section 8. township
Bible . . 3. cab (kab), kor, log 4. epha
5. cubit, homer
gauge . . 3. erg, lea (yarn) 5. ergon,
level, plumb, scale, stone 6. denier,
square 7. calorie (calory), compass,
sextant 8. calipers, quadrant
length . . 3. ell, mil, rod 4. foot, hand,
inch, knot, mile, nail, pace, rule,
tape, yard 5. chain, cubit, meter
6. league 7. furlong 9. kilometer,
yardstick 10. centimeter, micrometer,
millimeter
nautical . . 4. knot 6. fathom, league
paper . . 4. page, ream 5. quire, sheet
poetry . . 6. dipody, iambic, rhythm,
sestet 7. anapest, couplet, distich,
tripody 8. quatrain 9. hexameter
10. ottava rima, pentastich,
tetrameter, tetrastich 11. Alexandrine
printer . . 2. em, en 4. pica 5. agate
volume, weight . . 3. ton, tun (wine)
4. bale, butt, cord 5. carat, liter,
minim, ounce, pound, quart
6. barrel, bushel, finger, gallon,
magnum, pottle 8. hogshead,
teaspoon 9. kiloliter 10. tablespoon
measurement . . . 4. size 6. amount,
alnage, extent, metage 7. azimuth
8. abscissa, capacity, quantity
9. substance 11. calculation,
mensuration
measuring instrument . . . 6. stadia
7. alidade, caliper 8. odometer
12. perambulator (surveyor)
meat . . . 4. beef, fish, food, lamb, pork
5. flesh 6. fillet, kernel, mutton,
quarry 7. brisket 9. aitchbone
(icebone), spareribs
meat (pert to) . . .
ball . . 7. rissole 9. croquette,
hamburger
cured, dried . . 3. ham 5. bacon
6. flitch, jerked 7. biltong (biltongue)
8. pemmican
jellied . . 5. aspic
minced, roll . . 7. rissole
roasted . . 5. cabob (kabob)
9. barbecued
slaughterhouse . . 8. abattoir
smoking place . . 6. buccan (bucan)
stew . . 8. mulligan 9. lobscouse
meatus . . . 4. burr (ear) 5. canal
7. opening, passage
meaty . . . 5. pithy, solid 11. substantial
Mecca, Arabia . . . 8. Holy City 16. City

of the Prophet
Mecca (pert to)...
birthplace of.. 8. Mohammed
capital.. 5. Hejaz
color.. 11. Tuscan brown
famed for.. 5. Kaaba (Caaba, Kaabeth)
   10. Black Stone 11. Great Mosque
governor.. 6. sherif (shereef)
pilgrimage.. 4. hadj
pilgrim's dress.. 5. ihram
rug.. 6. Shiraz
mechanic... 7. artisan, workman
   8. operator 9. artificer, craftsman,
   machinist, operative
mechanical... 8. machinal
   9. automatic, practical, technical
   11. involuntary, stereotyped
mechanical (pert to)...
adjustment.. 9. tentation
drawing.. 8. drafting
law, motion.. 8. dynamics, kinetics
lever.. 6. tappet
part.. 5. rotor 6. stator
mechanics... 9. technique
   11. mechanology
mechanism... 4. gear, tool 5. means
   6. tackle 7. control, rigging
   9. apparatus, machinery, technique
medal... 4. coin, disk (disc) 5. badge
   6. plaque 9. medallion
   10. decoration
medallion... 4. coin 5. cameo, medal,
   panel 6. tablet 8. ornament
meddle... 3. pry 4. nose 6. dabble,
   tamper 7. obtrude 9. interfere
meddler... 8. busybody 9. pragmatic
meddlesome... 7. Paul Pry 8. meddling
   9. officious 11. inquisitive,
   pragmatical
Mede... 6. Median 7. Persian
medial, median.. 4. mean 5. mesne,
   raphe (valve) 6. medium, middle
   7. average 11. intervening
   12. intermediate
Median... 4. Magi, Mede 5. Medic
mediate... 5. opine 9. intercede,
   interpose, reconcile
mediator... 5. muser 7. arbiter
   9. go–between 10. interagent
   11. intercessor
medic... 3. doc 6. clover, doctor,
   median, medico 9. physician
medical (pert to)...
comb form.. 3. oma 4. itis 6. iatric
   7. iatrics
compound.. 5. hepar
fluid.. 5. blood, lymph, serum
man.. 5. medic 6. shaman, voodoo
monster.. 5. teras
officer.. 7. coroner
practitioner.. 2. MD 6. doctor, intern
   (interne) 7. surgeon 8. sawbones
system.. 7. therapy 9. allopathy
   10. homeopathy, psychiatry
term.. 8. curative 9. medicinal
medical terms...
chicken pox.. 9. varicella
flat feet.. 9. pes planus
headache.. 11. cephalalgia
heartburn.. 7. pyrosis
hives.. 9. urticaria
measles.. 7. rubella, rubeola

mumps.. 9. parotitis
whooping cough.. 9. pertussis
medicinal (pert to)...
agent.. 3. tea 6. tisane 9. decoction
bark.. 6. cartex
dropper.. 7. pipette
equal parts.. 3. ana
herb, plant.. 3. rue 4. aloe 5. ergot,
   jalap, orris, senna, tansy 6. arnica,
   cohosh, ipecac 7. boneset, chirata,
   comfrey 8. licorice, valerian
pain allaying.. 7. anodyne 8. sedative
   9. goofballs, paregoric
   11. barbiturate
patent.. 7. nostrum
remedy.. 5. drops, salve 6. elixir,
   iodine 7. panacea 8. antidote,
   ointment
science.. 7. biology 10. physiology,
   psychology
tablet.. 4. pill 6. troche 7. lozenge
term.. 4. drug 11. therapeutic
mediety... 6. loiety 10. moderation,
   temperance
medieval, mediaeval... 7. archaic
   10. Middle Ages
medieval (pert to)...
galley (ship's).. 3. nef 5. xebec
   6. bireme, galiot (galliot) 7. dromone
   (dromon), trireme, unireme
garment.. 6. tabard
headdress.. 6. abacot
helmet.. 5. armet
instrument (stringed).. 5. rebec
   (rebeck)
money of account.. 3. ora
monster.. 5. golem 9. automaton
   12. Frankenstein
shield.. 3. ecu 6. scutum
title, teacher.. 8. magister
weapon, club.. 4. mace 5. oncin
Medina, Saudi Arabia (pert to)...
anc name.. 9. Lathrippa
Mohammed supporters.. 6. ansars
sacred city of.. 5. Islam
tombs.. 4. Omar 6. Fatima
   8. Mohammed
mediocre... 4. mean, so–so 6. medium
   7. average 8. middling, ordinary,
   passable 9. tolerable 11. indifferent
meditate... 4. muse, plan, pore
   5. brood, study, watch, weigh
   6. ponder 7. purpose, reflect, revolve
   8. cogitate, consider 11. contemplate
meditation... 4. yoga 7. thought
   8. devotion 10. rumination
   11. thanatopsis 13. contemplation
   14. omphaloskepsis
mediterranean... 6. inland 7. midland
   10. landlocked
Mediterranean (pert to)...
boat.. 3. nef 4. saic 5. xebec (zebec)
   6. galiot (galliot), mistic (mistico),
   settee (setee) 7. felucca, hexeris
cat.. 5. genet
coast.. 7. Riviera
falcon.. 6. lanner
fish.. 6. remora
fowl.. 7. leghorn
fruit.. 5. olive 7. azarole
gulf.. 5. Tunis
herb.. 4. Ammi

inland.. 3. sea
island.. 4. Elba, Gozo 5. Crete, Malta
 6. Candia, Cyprus, Ebusis, Sicily
 7. Majorca 8. Belearic (group),
 Sardinia
island, volcanic.. 6. Lipari, Salina
 7. Vulcano 9. Stromboli
port.. 5. Tunis 7. Tunisia
storm.. 7. borasca (borasco, borasque)
tree.. 5. carob 7. azarole
wind.. 6. solano 7. etesian, gregale,
 mistral, sirocco 8. levanter
 10. euroclyden
medium... 4. agar (cultured), doer,
 mean 5. color, organ 6. degree,
 medial, oracle 7. average, psychic
 8. mediator, mediocre
 10. instrument, interagent
 11. environment 12. intermediary,
 spiritualist
medley... 4. olio 5. relay 6. jumble
 7. ferrago, mélange, mixture
 8. fantasia, mingling 9. potpourri
 10. hodgepodge, salmagundi
medrick... 4. gull (Bonaparte's), tern
 (Wilson's)
medulla... 4. pith 6. marrow
 7. summary 9. oblongata
 10. compendium
Medusa (Myth)... 6. Gorgon, Stheno
 (sister) 9. gorgoneum
Medusa's head (pert to)...
constellation (cluster).. 7. Perseus
star.. 5. Algol
vegetable.. 8. mushroom
Zool.. 10. basket fish
meed... 5. bribe, merit, repay, share
 6. desert, reward 7. bribery
 10. recompense
meek... 4. mild 6. docile, gentle,
 humble, modest 7. pacific, patient
 8. moderate, yielding 10. spiritless,
 submissive
meerkat... 6. monkey
meerschaum... 4. pipe 6. gravel
 (color) 7. seafoam 9. sepiolite
meet... 3. fit 4. face, game, join
 5. equal, match, touch 6. battle,
 combat, concur 7. collide, conform,
 contact, contest, convene, fulfill,
 satisfy 8. assemble, confront
 9. encounter 10. congregate,
 experience, rendezvous
meet halfway... 7. mediate
 10. compromise
meeting... 4. mall, race 5. court,
 gemot (gemote), joint, synod, tryst,
 union 6. caucus, powwow, séance
 7. contact, joining 8. assembly,
 conclave, junction 9. encounter,
 gathering, in contact 10. conference,
 convention, converging, rendezvous
 11. convergence 12. congregation,
 intersection
mega, meg (comb form)... 5. great
 6. mighty
megalith... 5. stone (huge) 6. dolman
 7. boulder 8. monument (Prehist)
megapode, megapod... 6. leipoa
 9. mound bird 10. jungle fowl
 11. brush turkey
megascope... 12. magic lantern

megaseism... 10. earthquake
megrim, megrims... 4. whim 5. fancy,
 freak, humor 8. headache
 9. dizziness 12. hypochondria
Mehitabel, Mehetabel... 3. cat
Mekong River tribe... 3. Moi (Asian)
mel... 5. honey
melancholia... 7. sadness 8. neurosis
 9. nostalgia, psychosis
 10. depression
melancholy... 3. sad 4. blue, dark,
 glum 5. drear, gloom 6. sombre,
 sorrow 7. doleful, sadness
 8. atrabile, liverish, tristful
 9. dejection 10. depressing,
 depression, dispirited, lamentable
 11. despondency, downhearted,
 pensiveness 12. hypochondria,
 mournfulness
Melanesia... 14. Pacific Islands
Melanesian (pert to)...
island.. 4. Fiji 7. Solomon 11. New
 Hebrides
native.. 4. Fiji 6. Papuan
 10. Polynesian
superbeing.. 5. adaro
mélange... 4. olio 6. jumble, medley
 7. mixture 9. pasticcio
 10. miscellany 14. conglomeration
melee... 3. row 4. fray 5. fight
 6. affray 7. contest, diamond (small
 cut) 8. skirmish 9. commotion
melicocca... 5. genip 9. soapberry
melicratum... 4. mead 8. beverage,
 hydromel
melilotus... 6. clover
meliorate... 6. soften 7. improve
 10. ameliorate
melisma... 6. melody 7. cadenza
Melissa... 4. balm 12. Old World mint
mell... 3. mix 4. maul 5. grain (last
 cut), honey 6. beetle, hammer,
 mallet, meddle, mingle
mellow... 4. rich, ripe, soft 5. drunk
 6. genial, jovial, mature, tender
 7. amiable, matured 9. melodious
melodic... 6. ariose 7. cadenza,
 melisma 9. melodious
melodious... 6. ariose, arioso, dulcet
 7. musical, tunable, tuneful
 10. harmonious
melodist... 6. singer 8. composer,
 musician 9. harmonist
melodramatic... 8. dramatic, romantic
 11. sensational
melody... 3. air 4. aria, tune 5. canto,
 charm, dirge, melos, music
 6. rhythm, strain 7. harmony,
 melisma, rosalia 9. cantilena,
 cantilene 11. tunefulness
melon... 4. musk, pepo 6. casaba
 7. Persian 8. honeydew
 9. muskmelon, red–yellow
 10. cantaloupe, paddymelon,
 watermelon
melon (pert to)...
financial.. 4. plum 8. dividend
like.. 5. gourd
pear.. 6. pepino
political.. 5. graft 6. spoils
melongena... 7. brinjal (brinjaul)
 8. eggplant

melos... 4. song 6. melody
melt... 3. run 4. frit, fuse, thaw
   5. smelt, swale 6. render, soften
   7. liquefy 8. diminish, dissolve
   9. disappear 12. disintegrate
member... 4. limb, part 5. organ
   6. branch, fellow, joiner 7. section
   8. belonger, district, enlistee, enroller
   9. associate
member (pert to)...
   boy's club.. 3. cub 5. scout
   Caliph dynasty.. 6. Omniad
   chapter (Eccl).. 9. capitular
   crew.. 4. hand
   diplomatic staff.. 6. consul 7. attaché
      8. minister 10. ambassador
   Jewish brotherhood.. 6. Essene
   laity.. 6. layman
   literary club.. 9. academist
      11. academician
   oldest.. 4. dean
   regiment.. 8. legioner 9. grenadier,
      legionary 11. legionnaire
   religious sect.. 5. Amish 6. Quaker,
      Shaker
   Roman Catholic society.. 6. Jesuit
   State.. 7. citizen
   swing band.. 6. hepcat 7. swinger
membrane... 4. caul, skin, tela
   5. lemma 6. lamina 8. ectoderm,
   striffin
membrane (pert to)...
   brain.. 13. meninges mater
   diffusion.. 7. osmosis
   ear.. 7. eardrum
   fold.. 5. plica
   optical.. 6. retina
   weblike.. 4. tela
memento... 5. relic, token 6. trophy
   8. keepsake, memorial, souvenir
   11. remembrance
Memnon (pert to)...
   famed statue.. 11. vocal Memnon
   father.. 8. Tithonus
   Greek name.. 9. Amenhotep
   king of.. 8. Ethiopia
   mother.. 3. Eos (Aurora)
   war hero.. 6. Trojan
memoir... 4. hint, note 5. éloge, essay
   6. record, report 7. account, history
   9. biography, narrative, reminding
   10. memorandum 12. dissertation
   13. autobiography
memorabilia... 3. ana 5. notes
   6. record 7. memoirs 8. memories
memorable... 7. namable, notable
   9. reminding 11. reminiscent
memorandum... 4. chit, note 5. diary
   6. minute, record 7. tickler
   8. protocol, reminder
memoria... 4. tomb 6. chapel, church,
   shrine 8. monument 9. reliquary
memorial... 6. memoir, memory,
   record, trophy 8. mnemonic,
   monument 10. memorandum
   11. celebrative, remembrance
   12. recollection 13. commemorative
memorial mound... 5. cairn (stone),
   totem (carved)
memory... 4. mind 6. recall
   9. retention 11. remembrance
   12. recollection, reminiscence

   13. commemoration
memory (pert to)...
   aid.. 10. anamnestic
   book.. 5. diary 9. scrapbook
   jog.. 6. remind
   loss of.. 5. lethe 7. amnesia, aphasia
      (partial) 13. forgetfulness
   term.. 6. mnesic 8. mnemonic
Memphis, Egypt (pert to)...
   deity.. 2. Ra (Re) 3. Shu, Tem
   dynasty.. 8. Memphite
   god, chief.. 4. Ptah
men (pert to)...
   armed body.. 5. posse
   gymnasts.. 8. acrobats
   learned.. 8. erudites, literati
   mechanical.. 6. robots
   of same tongue.. 6. langue
   old.. 7. gaffers 10. patriarchs
   party of.. 4. stag 6. smoker
   section, Gr Church.. 6. andron
   single.. 5. stags 9. bachelors,
      celibates
   slang.. 6. blokes
   Three Wise.. 4. Magi (Gaspar,
      Melchior, Balthazar)
   wild.. 7. savages 9. cannibals
menace... 6. threat 8. forebode,
   threaten 10. intimidate
   11. fulmination
menacing... 7. ominous 8. imminent
   11. threatening
menage... 4. club 7. society
   9. homestead, household, husbandry
   10. management 12. housekeeping
menagerie... 3. zoo 10. collection,
   Tiergarten
menald (said of horses)... 8. speckled
   10. variegated
Menaspis... 5. shark (crescent–shaped)
mend... 3. fix, sew 4. cure, darn,
   heal, knit 5. alter, amend, botch,
   emend, moise, patch 6. better,
   cobble, reform, repair 7. correct,
   improve 9. reconcile 10. ameliorate
mendacious... 5. false, lying 6. untrue
   7. in error 9. truthless 10. fallacious
mendacity... 3. lie 5. lying 6. deceit
   7. falsity, fibbery, untruth
mendicant... 5. fakir 6. beggar
   7. begging
mendicant order... 10. Carmelites,
   Dominicans 11. Franciscans
   12. Augustinians
mendole... 4. fish 8. cackerel
Menelaus' wife... 11. Helen of Troy
menhaden... 4. pogy 7. sardine
   8. bonyfish 10. mossbunker
menhir... 5. stone (standing)
   8. monolith
menial... 6. flunky, varlet 7. servant,
   servile, serving, slavish
meninges membrane... 8. pia mater
   9. arachnoid, dura mater
meniscus... 4. lens 8. crescent
   12. crescent moon
Mennonite leader... 11. Menno
   Simons
Mennonite sect... 5. Amish
meno... 4. less 5. month (comb form)
menology (Eccl)... 8. calendar, register
Menominee, Menomini... 5. Falls

(Wis), river 6. Indian 9. whitefish
Menorah... 11. candelabrum (Jew)
  12. organization
mensk... 5. adorn, favor, grace, honor
  6. credit 8. ornament 9. reverence
  12. graciousness
mental... 7. phrenic 9. of the mind,
  psychotic 11. intelligent
  12. intellectual
mental (pert to)...
  alienation.. 8. insanity
  deficiency, deficient.. 5. ament, idiot,
  moron 6. idiocy 8. imbecile
  discipline.. 8. mathesis
  disorder.. 7. aphasia 8. insanity,
  neurosis, paranoia 9. psychosis
  11. megalomania 12. hypochondria
  13. forgetfulness, schizophrenia
  faculties.. 4. mind, wits
  feeling.. 7. emotion
  image, picture.. 4. idea 6. idolus
  8. phantasm 10. conception
  peculiarity.. 12. idiosyncracy
  science, study.. 10. New Thought,
  psychiatry
  state.. 6. morale 7. doldrum
  (doldrums) 8. euphoria
  strain.. 7. tension
mentality... 4. mind 5. sense
  6. acumen, sanity 9. endowment,
  intellect 11. mental power
  12. intelligence
mention... 4. cite, mind, name
  5. refer, speak, trace 6. denote,
  notice, record, remark 7. specify,
  vestige 8. citation, indicate 9. make
  known, statement 10. indication
mentor... 7. adviser, teacher, wise
  man 10. instructor
mentum... 4. chin
menu... 4. card, list 5. carte
  8. schedule 10. bill of fare
Mephistopheles... 5. devil, Faust,
  Satan
mephitis... 4. odor 5. skunk, smell
  6. stench 7. polecat 10. exhilation
  (earth)
mercantile... 5. trade 7. trading
  10. commercial, industrial
mercenary... 4. hack 5. hired, venal
  6. sordid 7. Hessian 8. hireling,
  salaried, vendible
merchandise... 4. ware 5. goods,
  wares 7. effects 9. vendibles
  10. emporeutic (pert to)
  11. commodities 12. stock in trade
merchant... 5. buyer 6. trader
  7. vintner 10. shopkeeper, trafficker
  11. storekeeper
merchant (pert to)...
  group.. 5. guild, hanse 6. cartel
  Indian.. 4. seth
  League.. 9. Hanseatic
  ship.. 6. argosy 8. Indiaman
  wine.. 7. vintner
Merchant of Bagdad... 7. Sindbad
Merchant of Venice character...
  6. Portia 7. Antonio, Shylock
merci... 6. thanks
merciful... 4. kind, mild 6. humane,
  tender 7. clement, lenient
  9. benignant 10. charitable

13. compassionate
merciless... 5. cruel 8. pitiless
  9. unsparing 10. relentless
  13. unsympathetic
mercurial (pert to God Mercury)...
  4. fast 5. swift 6. active, clever,
  fickle 8. metallic 9. saturnine
  11. money–making
mercurous chloride... 7. calomel
mercury... 5. azoth, guide, metal
  7. chibrit, element 9. barometer
  11. quicksilver, temperature,
  thermometer
Mercury (pert to)...
  astronomy.. 6. planet (smallest)
  god of.. 8. commerce
  Greek name.. 6. Hermes
  staff.. 8. caduceus
  statue, image.. 5. herma
  winged cap.. 7. petasos (petasus)
  winged shoes.. 7. talaria
mercy... 4. pity, ruth 5. grace
  6. blithe, lenity 7. charity
  8. clemency, lenience, leniency
  9. tolerance 10. compassion,
  indulgence 11. forbearance
mercy killing... 10. euthanasia
mercy seat... 5. bench 11. golden
  plate (on the Ark), Throne of God
  12. judgment seat 13. seat of
  justice
mere... 3. sea 4. bare, lake, only,
  pool, sole, such, wisp 5. bound,
  limit, sheer, small 6. divide, simple
  8. absolute, boundary, landmark, only
  this
mère... 6. mother
merely... 4. also, just, only 5. quite
  6. barely, purely, simply, singly,
  solely 7. utterly 8. entirely, scarcely
  9. unmixedly 10. absolutely
mere show... 4. airs 5. front
  8. pretense 9. formality
  10. pretension 11. affectation
mere taste... 3. nip, sip 4. gulp
  7. draught
merganser... 3. nun 4. duck, smee,
  smew 6. Mergus 7. bec–scie
  8. Merginae 9. goosander
merge... 4. sink 5. blend, unite
  6. mingle 7. combine, immerse
  8. coalesce 11. consolidate
merger... 4. pool 5. union 6. cartel,
  fusion 8. monopoly 10. absorption
  12. amalgamation
meridian... 3. top 4. apex, noon
  5. plane 6. midday, summit, zenith
  8. latitude, southern 9. celestial
  11. culmination 12. highest point
meringue... 5. icing 8. egg white,
  frosting
Merino... 4. wool, yarn 5. sheep
merit... 4. earn, meed 5. worth
  6. desert, reward 7. deserve
  10. excellence
merited... 3. fit 4. just 6. worthy
  8. adequate, deserved, suitable
  9. warranted
meritorious... 5. valid 6. worthy
  7. merited 9. deserving, honorable
  12. praiseworthy
merlin... 6. falcon

Merlin... 7. prophet, romance
  8. magician
mermaid... 5. siren 6. merrow
  7. Oceanid, swimmer 8. sea nymph
  9. sea spirit 14. marine creature
mermaid's hair... 4. alga
mero... 4. fish 5. guasa 7. grouper
  8. rock hind
merogenesis... 12. segmentation
meropia... 9. blindness (partial)
meros... 5. thigh 10. meropodite
merriment... 3. fun 4. glee 5. mirth
  6. gaiety (gayety) 8. laughter
  9. amusement, diversion
  11. merrymaking
merrow... 7. mermaid
merry... 3. gai, gay 4. glad 5. funny,
  happy 6. blithe, bonnie, jocose,
  jovial, joyous 7. comical, festive,
  gleeful, jocular 8. cheerful, mirthful,
  sportive 9. favorable, hilarious,
  sprightly 13. sweet–sounding
merry–andrew... 4. mime, zany
  5. antic, clown, joker 6. jester
  7. buffoon 8. merryman
merry–go–round... 9. carrousel
  (carousal) 17. revolving platform
merrymaking... 4. reel 5. momus,
  revel 7. festive, wassail 9. festivity,
  merriment 12. conviviality
merrythought... 8. wishbone
merrytrotter... 5. swing 6. seesaw
merrywing... 4. duck 9. goldeneye
  10. bufflehead
merse... 3. dip 5. marsh 6. plunge
  7. immerse
merycism... 7. chewing 10. rumination
mesa... 7. mesilla, oakwood (color),
  terrace 14. flat–topped hill
mesel... 5. leper
mesh... 3. net, web 5. catch 6. areola
  7. complex, ensnare, netting, network
  10. crisscross 11. interaction
mesial plane... 5. meson (Zool)
  6. median, middle
mesmeric... 11. fascinating, hypnotizing
  12. irresistible, spellbinding
mesmeric force... 2. od
Mesopotamia...
  ancient city.. 2. Ur 5. Eridu
    7. Babylon, Ninevah
  city.. 5. Basra, Mosul 6. Edessa
  colloquialism.. 6. Mespot
  culture.. 8. Sumerian
  export.. 3. oil
  language.. 6. Arabic
  people (anc).. 8. Aramaean (Aramean)
  river.. 6. Tigris 9. Euphrates
  wind.. 6. shamal
Mesopotamian... 5. Iraqi
Mesozoic era... 7. reptile 8. dinosaur
  10. evergreens, ganoid fish
mesquin... 4. mean 6. shabby, sordid
mesquita... 6. mosque
mesquite... 5. pacay 7. thicket
  8. Prosopis 9. algarroba
mesquite bean flour... 6. pinole
mess... 4. meal 5. batch, share, spoil
  6. bungle, jumble, litter 7. eyesore,
  failure, mixture 8. disorder
  9. confusion 11. predicament
  12. kettle of fish

mess (up)... 5. botch, spoil 6. muss
  up 7. clutter, derange, shuffle
  10. disarrange
message... 4. news, note, wire, word
  5. cable 6. brevet, letter, notice
  7. epistle, evangel, tidings
  8. dispatch, telegram
  10. communiqué 13. communication
message medium... 5. Ouija
messenger... 4. Iris, page, sand, toty
  5. angel, envoy 6. herald, nuncio,
  Revere (Paul) 7. apostle, carrier,
  courier, prophet, totyman
  8. delegate, minister 9. estafette
  (estafet) 10. forerunner
messenger bird... 9. secretary
Messenger of the Gods... 6. Hermes
  (Gr) 7. Mercury (Rom)
Messiah... 6. Christ 7. Saviour (Savior)
  8. Oratorio (Handel) 9. deliverer
Messina Rock... 6. Scylla
messy... 5. dirty 6. untidy 7. jumbled
  8. slovenly 10. disordered
mestive... 8. mournful
mesto... 3. sad 7. pensive
met... 3. sat 7. equaled, measure
  11. measurement (see also *meet*)
metabolism... 9. anabolism
  10. catabolism 12. assimilation
  13. dissimilation, metamorphosis
  14. transformation
metacarpus... 4. bone
metad... 3. rat
metagnomy... 10. divination
metagnostic... 10. unknowable
metal... 3. tin 4. gold, iron, lead, zinc
  5. steel 6. cobalt, copper, erbium,
  nickel, radium, silver, sodium
  7. cadmium, calcium, element,
  gallium, iridium, lithium, mercury,
  terbium 8. cast iron 9. potassium
  11. quicksilver
metal... 6. mettle, spirit 8. material
  9. substance
metal (pert to)...
  bar.. 3. gad 5. ingot
  cake.. 4. slag
  casting.. 3. pig
  cement.. 6. solder
  clippings.. 7. scissil
  coarse.. 5. matte
  coat.. 6. patina
  color.. 9. pearl blue
  content.. 3. ory
  crude.. 5. matte
  deposit.. 4. lode
  disc.. 5. paten
  dross.. 4. slag
  electric.. 6. magnet
  filings.. 5. lemel
  forging term.. 5. sprue
  goldlike.. 6. oroide
  impurity.. 7. regulus
  layer.. 4. seam, vein 5. stope
  lightest.. 7. lithium
  lump.. 3. pig 4. slug 6. nugget
  patch.. 6. solder
  plate.. 4. foil, shim
  rare.. 6. erbium 7. iridium, terbium,
    yttrium 8. platinum
  refuse.. 4. slag 5. dross 6. scoria
  rock.. 3. ore

science of .. 10. metallurgy
tag .. 5. aglet (aiglet)
test .. 5. assay
tool .. 5. swage 7. stemmer
ware .. 4. tole 6. Revere
worker .. 6. welder 7. riveter
   9. goldsmith 11. silversmith
metamerism ... 12. segmentation (Zool)
metamorphosis ... 6. change
   9. oxidation 10. hydrolysis
   12. degeneration, ossification
   14. transformation
metaphor ... 5. trope 6. simile
   10. comparison 11. tralalition
metaphysics ... 5. being 6. nature
   8. ontology, theology 9. cosmology
   10. psychology
mete ... 4. give, goal 5. award
   7. measure 8. boundary 9. apportion
   10. distribute
meteor ... 5. bolis 6. Bielid, bolide,
   Leonid, Lyraid 7. Arietid, Perseid
   8. fireball 9. Andromede
meteorite (pert to) ...
iron .. 10. siderolite
shower .. 6. Leonid 9. Andromede
   (Andromedid)
stony .. 8. aerolite
meteor mark ... 6. crater
meteorology ... 9. astronomy
   10. atmosphere 11. climatology
meter, metre ... 5. gauge 6. rhythm
   7. cadence, measure 8. measurer
meter (pert to) ...
cubic .. 5. stere
measure .. 5. litre
millionth .. 6. micron
prosody .. 4. mora
square .. 7. centare
ton .. 5. tonne
unit term .. 3. are 6. decare
   9. decameter, decastere
weight .. 4. gram
methane ... 8. paraffin
metheglin ... 4. mead 8. beverage
mether ... 3. cup
method ... 3. way 4. mode, plan, rule
   5. means, order, usage 6. course,
   manner, system 7. fashion, process
   9. procedure 11. arrangement
   14. classification
methodic, methodical ... 6. formal
   7. orderly, regular 10. systematic
Methuselah (pert to) ...
Bib .. 7. aged man 9. Patriarch
father .. 5. Enoch
metic ... 5. alien 7. settler
   9. immigrant
meticulous ... 4. nice, prim 5. fussy
   7. careful, fearful, precise 8. exacting
   9. selective 10. fastidious, scrupulous
   14. discriminating
métier ... 4. line 7. calling 8. business
   10. occupation, profession
metis, metisse ... 7. mulatto
   8. octoroon 9. half–breed
Metis ... 8. asteroid 9. Zeus's wife
metrical ... 8. measured, poetical,
   rhythmic
metrical composition ... 4. poem
   5. poesy 6. poetry

metrical foot ... 4. iamb 6. iambus
   7. anapest, spondee, trochee
   8. choriamb
metrical stress ... 4. scan 5. arsis,
   ictus 6. thesis
metronome (Maelzel's) ... 5. timer
metropolis ... 4. city, seat, town
   6. center 8. district 9. metropole
metropolitan ... 5. chief, urban
   6. bishop, center 7. leading
   9. principal
mettle ... 5. ardor, honor, nerve, pluck,
   spunk 6. spirit 7. courage
   9. fortitude 11. temperament
meuse, muse ... 3. gap 4. hole
   7. opening 8. loophole
Meuse River ... 4. Maas
mew ... 3. cob, den 4. cage, cast,
   coop, gull, molt, shed 5. miaow,
   miaul 6. change 7. seagull, stables
   8. spicknel 11. concealment,
   confinement
mewl ... 3. cry, mew 6. squall
   7. whimper
Mexican (pert to) ... see also *Mexico*
agave .. 5. datil 6. zapupe
   8. henequen
almond .. 7. Malabar
American .. 6. gringo
ancient .. 4. Maya 5. Aztec, Nahua
   6. Mixtec, Toltec 7. Zapotec
antelope .. 9. pronghorn
asphalt .. 9. chapapote
bean .. 6. frijol 7. frijole
bedbug .. 8. conenose
beverage (alcoholic) .. 6. mescal,
   pulque 7. tepache
bird .. 6. jacana, towhee 7. jacamar,
   tinamou 8. zopilote
blanket .. 6. serape
brigand .. 7. ladrone
bull .. 4. toro
cactus .. 6. chaute, mescal
cape .. 6. serape
cat .. 6. margay
cherry tree .. 7. capulin
chief .. 4. jefe 12. jefe politico
cloak .. 5. manta
cockroach .. 9. cucaracha
common land (law) .. 6. ejidos
coral drops (lily) .. 7. Bessera
cottonwood .. 5. alamo
dance (solo) .. 8. guaracha
dish .. 5. atole, chili (chile), tacos
   6. tamale 8. frijoles, tortilla
   9. enchilada 13. chili con carne
dog .. 9. Chihuahua
dollar .. 4. peso 5. adobe
dove .. 4. Inca
drug .. 7. damiana
elm .. 6. mezcal 8. Ulmaceae
estate, farm .. 8. hacienda
fever .. 10. tabardillo
fish (food) .. 6. salema 7. totuava
game (card) .. 4. frog
grass .. 3. mat 5. otate 6. petate
   8. henequen
herdsman .. 8. ranchero
hog .. 7. peccary
hut, house .. 5. jacal
insect .. 8. turicata
labor system .. 7. peonage

landmark.. **5**. senal
masonry.. **5**. adobe
moon god (Aztec).. **6**. Meztli
mullet.. **4**. bobo
musical instrument.. **6**. clarin (anc)
    7. maracas
Noah.. **6**. Coxcox
onyx.. **6**. tecali
orange.. **7**. Choisya
peasant.. **4**. peon
persimmon.. **7**. chapote
phlox.. **6**. cobaea
plant, shrub.. **4**. pita **5**. agave,
    amole, datil, istle, sisal, sotol, yucca
    6. maguey **8**. ocotillo
    10. candlewood, Dasylirion
rose.. **9**. portulaca
saloon.. **7**. cantina
sandal.. **8**. huaracho (huarache)
sauce.. **7**. Tabasco
scarf.. **6**. tapalo
shawl.. **6**. serape
stirrup.. **7**. estribo
stirrup hood.. **8**. tapadera (tapadero)
sugar.. **7**. panocha
tea.. **6**. basote **7**. apasote
thong.. **5**. romal
throwing stick.. **6**. atlatl
tree.. **3**. ule **5**. alamo, ocote
    6. colima, poplar **7**. capulin
    10. cottonwood
war god.. **7**. Mexitli
yucca.. **5**. izote (isote)
Mexican people...
composer.. **6**. Chavez
conqueror.. **6**. Cortez
Dictator.. **4**. Diaz
historian.. **6**. Orozco
painter.. **6**. Rivera
Mexico...
battleground.. **6**. Puebla
capital.. **10**. Mexico City
city.. **6**. Merida, Puebla **7**. Durango,
    Tampico **8**. Mazatlan, Monterey, Vera
    Cruz **11**. Guadalajara
conqueror.. **6**. Cortes (Cortez)
hero.. **6**. Juarez **11**. Poncho Villa
lake.. **7**. Chapala
mountain.. **12**. Popocatepetl
peninsula.. **4**. Baja **7**. Yucatan
people.. **5**. Mayas **6**. Aztecs
    7. Toltecs **10**. Cuitlateco
river.. **9**. Rio Grande
volcano.. **6**. Colima **7**. Jorullo, Orizaba
    12. Ixtaccihuatl, Popocatepetl
mezzanine... **8**. entresol, low story
miaow, miaou... **3**. mew
mias... **9**. orangutan
miasma... **4**. fume **6**. poison
    7. malaria, malodor **9**. contagion
mib... **7**. a marble
mica... **4**. talc **5**. glist **7**. biotite
    8. chlorite, silicate **9**. damourite,
    hydromica, isinglass, muscovite
    10. lepidolite
Micah... **4**. Book (Old Test) **7**. prophet
mice... **3**. Mus **5**. voles **7**. rodents
miche... **5**. skulk, sneak **6**. lie hid
    7. conceal
micher... **5**. sneak, thief **6**. truant
Michigan...
capital.. **7**. Lansing

city.. **5**. Flint **7**. Detroit, Lansing
    8. Ann Arbor **9**. Marquette
explorer.. **7**. Jolliet, Nicolet
    9. Marquette **13**. Sault Ste Marie
river.. **4**. Cass **5**. Huron
State admission.. **11**. Twenty–sixth
State motto.. **6**. Tuebor **11**. I Will
    Defend
State nickname.. **9**. Wolverine
mickey finn... **5**. drink **8**. narcotic
Micky... **8**. Irishman
mico... **6**. monkey **8**. marmoset
micraner... **3**. ant (small)
micro (comb form)... **4**. moth **5**. petty,
    small
microbe... **4**. germ **5**. virus
    8. organism **9**. bacterium
    13. microorganism
microcosm... **4**. body (humerous)
    5. world (small) **8**. universe
microscopic (pert to)...
algae.. **6**. amoeba, diatom
anatomy.. **9**. histology
size.. **5**. small **6**. minute **9**. very
    small **13**. infinitesimal
microspores... **6**. pollen
Midas (Gr)... **13**. King of Phrygia
midday... **4**. noon **7**. noonday
    8. meridian, noontide
midday nap... **6**. siesta
middle... **5**. mesne, midst **6**. center,
    centry, median, medium, mesial
    7. central **8**. interior **11**. intervening
    13. intermediator
middle (pert to)...
Age.. **8**. Medieval
class.. **9**. bourgeois **11**. proletarian
comb form.. **3**. mes **4**. medi, meso
finger.. **6**. medius **10**. third digit
ground.. **4**. mean **7**. average
    9. mid–course
man.. **5**. agent **6**. broker, medium
    8. mediator **9**. go–between
    11. intercessor **12**. intermediary
middling... **4**. fair **6**. medium, middle
    7. average, between, midland
    8. mediocre, moderate, ordinary
    10. middle–aged
midge... **3**. fly **4**. gnat **6**. midget,
    punkie **7**. minutia
Midi... **8**. The South (France)
Midian king... **3**. Evi **4**. Reba
Midian priest... **6**. Jethro
midriff... **9**. diaphragm
midshipman... **5**. cadet **6**. reefer
    8. toadfish
Midsummer Night's Dream (play)...
    4. Puck, Snug **6**. Bottom, Oberon
    7. Titania
midwife... **4**. baba, dhai **6**. cummer
    (kimmer) **11**. accoucheuse
mien... **3**. air, eye **4**. look **5**. guise
    6. aspect, manner, ostent
    7. bearing, posture **8**. behavior,
    carriage, demeanor **10**. appearance,
    deportment
miff... **3**. vix **4**. tiff **5**. anger **6**. offend
    7. dudgeon, quarrel **9**. displease,
    sulkiness **10**. sullenness
mig... **4**. duck **7**. a marble
might... **3**. arm **5**. force, power
    7. ability **8**. efficacy, strength

9. greatness
mighty ... 4. huge, vast, very
  6. potent, strong 7. eminent, violent
  8. enormous, forcible, powerful,
  puissant 9. extremely 10. omnipotent
  11. efficacious 13. authoritative
migniard ... 6. dainty, minion
  7. mincing 8. delicate, mistress
mignon ... 5. small 6. dainty, petite
  7. blue-red 8. delicate, graceful
mignonette (pert to) ...
  color .. 5. green 6. reseda
  emblem of .. 6. Saxony
  herb .. 6. reseda
  tree .. 5. henna
  vine .. 7. Madeira, tarweed
migraine ... 6. megrim 8. headache
  10. hemicrania
migrate ... 4. move, trek 8. resettle,
  transfer 12. transmigrate
migration ... 4. trek 5. exode
  6. exodus 7. passage 8. shifting
  (Chem) 10. relocation
migratory ... 6. moving, roving
  7. nomadic 9. peregrine, wandering
migratory (pert to) ...
  ant .. 6. driver
  cell .. 9. leucocyte
  thrush .. 5. robin
mihrab ... 4. slab 5. niche 7. chamber
  (mosque)
Mikado ... 5. dairi, opera, title
  9. red-yellow, sovereign
Mikado character ... 4. Ko-Ko
  6. Yum-Yum 7. Pooh-Bah
Mikania ... 7. dogbane, thistle
  11. Willugbaeya (Willugheia)
  12. Ancylocladus
mike ... 4. loaf 6. loiter
  10. microphone
mil ... 5. mille 8. thousand
milady ... 5. woman 6. madame
  10. noblewoman 11. gentlewoman
Milan (pert to) ...
  hat .. 5. straw
  opera house .. 5. Scala
  point .. 10. bobbin lace 12. point de
  Milan
mild ... 4. calm, kind, meek, soft, warm
  5. bland 6. benign, gentle
  7. clement, insipid, lenient
  8. benedict, gracious, lenitive,
  moderate, soothing, tranquil
  9. assuasive, indulgent, temperate
  10. mollifying 11. considerate
mildew ... 4. mold, must, rust, smut
  6. blight, fungus 8. honeydew
mild expression ... 9. euphemism
mild offense ... 6. delict
mile (term) ... 3. sea 7. statute
  8. nautical 9. Admiralty
  12. geographical
Miledh ... 8. ancestor (fabled)
Milesian ... 4. Celt 8. Irishman
  10. Miledh's son
milestone ... 5. stele 7. waymark
  8. landmark, milepost
milfoil ... 4. herb 6. yarrow
milieu ... 7. ecology 8. ambience
  11. environment 12. surroundings
militant ... 7. hawkish, warlike
  8. battling, fighting 9. combating,

combative 11. contentious
military ... 7. martial 8. soldiers
military (pert to) ...
  advance .. 8. anabasis
  aide .. 7. attaché
  base .. 4. camp 5. depot, field
  7. billets 8. barracks, firebase,
  quarters 10. encampment
  call .. 6. tattoo 8. reveille
  cap .. 4. kepi 5. busby, shako
  cap, hat cover .. 8. havelock
  cloak .. 5. sagum (anc)
  commission .. 6. brevet
  defense .. 4. fort 6. abatis
  depot .. 4. base
  division .. 4. unit 5. corps, squad
  7. company, platoon 8. regiment
  engine .. 6. onager 7. robinet
  expedition to Holy Land .. 7. Crusade
  force .. 4. army 5. ranks, troop
  6. legion 7. reserve 8. soldiery
  guard .. 6. patrol
  horsemen .. 7. cavalry, hussars
  infraction .. 4. AWOL
  inspection .. 5. drill 6. parade, review
  instrument .. 5. bugle 7. althorn
  landing point .. 9. beachhead
  maneuver .. 6. tactic
  messenger .. 7. estafet
  night attack .. 8. camisade
  obstruction .. 6. abatis
  officer .. 5. major 7. captain, colonel,
  general 8. corporal, sergeant
  9. brigadier, subaltern 10. lieutenant
  operations .. 8. campaign, strategy
  order .. 7. command
  organization .. 5. cadre
  pit .. 10. trou-de-loup
  police .. 2. MP 9. gendarmes
  12. constabulary
  punishment .. 4. brig 9. strappado
  quarters .. 4. camp 7. billets
  8. barracks 10. cantonment
  salute (artillery) .. 5. salvo
  science .. 3. war 7. war game
  8. warcraft 9. logistics
  service stripes .. 9. hashmarks
  signal .. 7. chamade (anc)
  staff .. 5. cadre
  storehouse .. 5. étape 7. arsenal
  supplies .. 8. materiel, ordnance
  survey .. 11. reconnoiter
  testament, will .. 11. nuncupative
  tool (hook-shaped) .. 4. croc (anc)
  truck (cannon) .. 6. camion
  vehicle .. 4. jeep, tank 6. camion
  7. caisson
militate ... 5. fight 6. debate, rebuff
  7. contend 8. conflict
milk ... 3. lac 5. cream, drain, fluid
  6. elicit, suckle 7. despoil, draw out,
  exploit, extract 8. beverage
milk (pert to) ...
  beverage .. 4. whig 10. buttermilk
  coagulator .. 4. ruen 6. rennet
  curd .. 5. zeiga 6. casein
  curdled .. 6. yogurt 7. clabber
  fermented .. 5. kefir 6. kumiss
  (koumiss) 7. matzoon
  fish .. 3. awa 6. Chanos, sabalo
  food (fasting) .. 10. lacticinia
  glass .. 7. opaline 8. cryolite

mouse.. 6. spurge
pail.. 5. bowie, eshin
pert to.. 6. lactic 7. lactary, lacteal
product.. 6. cheese, yogurt
sap.. 5. latex
sop.. 5. sissy 11. mollycoddle
sour.. 4. curd, whey, whig 6. blinky
store.. 5. dairy 9. lactarium
strainer.. 6. milsey (milsie)
sugar.. 7. lactose
watery part.. 4. whey
with (milk).. 6. au lait
milkweed... 6. spurge 7. dogbane
   10. sow thistle 14. Asclepiadaceae
milkwood... 8. Moraceae 9. paperbark
milky... 4. mild, tame, weak 5. timid,
   white 6. gentle, liquid 7. lacteal
   8. emulsion, emulsive, lactesce (to
   become), timorous 10. effeminate
Milky Way... 6. Galaxy 9. Via Lactea
   14. galactic circle
Milky Way black spaces...
   9. Coalsacks
mill... 3. box 4. beat, coin (to)
   5. crush, dress, fight, grind, knurl,
   quern, shape 6. finish, powder,
   thrash 7. factory, machine, serrate
   8. arrastra, snuffbox, vanquish,
   workshop 9. comminute, pulverize,
   transform 10. move around
   12. housebreaker
mill (pert to)...
beetle.. 9. cockroach
bill.. 3. adz
clapper.. 10. chatterbox
course.. 4. lade 8. millrace, tailrace
end.. 7. remnant
run of.. 7. average 8. millrace,
   ordinary
millefleurs... 7. perfume
millenarian... 8. chiliast
millennium... 6. period, utopia
   9. millenary 13. thousand years
millepede... 6. insect 8. myriapod
millepore... 5. coral 9. madrepore
miller... 3. ray 4. moth 5. boxer
   7. harrier 8. pugilist 10. flycatcher
miller's thumb... 4. bird, fish
   7. warbler 8. titmouse (long–tailed)
   9. goldcrest
millesimal... 10. thousandth
millet... 4. moha 5. bajra, grass,
   hirse, milly 6. cenchrus
   9. broomcorn 10. hirse grass
   14. non–Moslem group
millimeter... 6. micron 14. thousandth
   part
millions, one thousand... 7. billion
millions of millions... 9. trillions
Mills grenade... 4. bomb
milo... 5. durra 12. grain sorghum
Milvus... 4. kite
Milwaukee... 21. German Athens of
   America
mime... 3. ape 4. aper, copy 5. actor,
   clown, mimic 6. jester, mummer
   7. buffoon, imitate
mimesis... 7. mimicry 9. imitation
mimic... 3. ape 4. aper, copy, mime,
   mimo, mock 5. actor 6. mummer,
   parrot 7. buffoon, copying, imitate,
   mimetic 8. imitator 9. imitative

   11. counterfeit
mimicry... 5. apery, apism 7. mimesis,
   mockery 8. parrotry
mimic thrush... 11. mockingbird
Mimidae, Miminae... 7. catbird
   8. thrasher 11. mockingbird
Mimir... 5. giant
mimsey... 4. prim 7. prudish
min... 5. ruler 6. memory, prince,
   remind 8. remember
   11. remembrance
Min (Egypt)... 3. god (procreation)
   5. deity
Minar... 4. myna 5. Kutab (Delhi),
   tower
minaret... 4. lamp 5. tower
   10. lighthouse
minaway... 6. minuet
mince... 3. cut 4. chop, dice, hash
   5. slash 8. diminish, prim step
   9. subdivide 10. short steps
minced meat... 7. rissole
minced oath... 4. drat, egad
minchen... 3. nun
minchery... 7. nunnery
minchiate... 5. tarot
mind... 4. care, heed, mens, obey,
   reck, tend, will 6. desire, memory,
   psyche 7. opinion 9. intellect,
   intention 11. remembrance
   12. intelligence
mind (pert to)...
development.. 13. psychogenesis
jubilant.. 7. elation
peace of.. 8. ataraxia, calmness
   16. imperturbability
pert to.. 6. mental 7. phrenic
picture.. 4. idea 5. image
split.. 13. schizophrenic
Mindanao...
language.. 3. Ata
site.. 11. Philippines
town.. 4. Dapa 5. Davao
   9. Zamboanga
tribe.. 3. Ata 4. Moro 5. Lutao
   6. Bagobo, Illano
volcano.. 3. Apo 9. Malindany
mindful... 8. disposed 9. observant,
   regardful 11. remembering
mine... 2. my 3. bal, dig, mio, pit,
   sap 4. meum 5. stope 6. cavity,
   quarry 7. gallery, passage
   10. excavation 12. entrenchment
mine (pert to)...
basket, tub.. 4. corf
ceiling.. 5. astel
coal.. 3. rob
deviation (lode).. 4. hade
device (sweeper).. 3. gad 8. paravane
entrance, passage.. 4. adit 5. stulm
excavation.. 5. stope
floor.. 4. sill
guardian (Myth).. 5. gnome
holes.. 7. gophers
prop.. 5. sprag, stull
reservoir.. 4. sump 8. standage
shack.. 3. doe
shaft.. 4. sump 6. upcast
signalman.. 5. cager 7. cageman
step.. 7. stemple (stempel)
surface.. 6. placer
thrower.. 6. minnie 11. minenwerfer

tunnel .. 5. stulm
vein .. 4. lode
waste .. 3. gob 4. goaf
worker .. 5. cager, miner 8. onsetter
miner (pert to) ...
disease .. 8. phthisis
instrument .. 4. dial
lamp .. 4. davy
pick .. 3. gad 7. mandrel
sieve .. 6. dillue
worm .. 8. hookworm
mineral ... 3. ore, tin 4. alum, iron
5. pitch 6. barite, egeran, gangue,
iolite, pinite, quartz 7. apatite,
asphalt, ataxite, bullion, epidote,
felsite, felspar 8. danalite, edentite,
misenite 9. uraninite
mineral (ore) ...
black .. 3. jet 6. cerine, yenite (Elba)
7. niobite 8. graphite 10. minguetite
blue–green .. 5. beryl
brittle .. 7. euclase
brown .. 6. cerine, egeran, rutile
9. elaterite
calcium, plus .. 7. calcite 8. calespar,
diopside
crosslike .. 10. staurolite
dark .. 7. minette
fibrous .. 8. asbestos (abeston)
flaky .. 4. mica
gray white .. 5. trona
green .. 7. alalite, erinite 9. malachite
gunpowder .. 5. niter 7. thorite
hard .. 4. ruby 6. spinel (spinelle)
7. adamant
jelly .. 8. vaseline
jewelry .. 8. diopside
lustrous .. 4. spar 7. blendes
magnetic .. 9. lodestone (loadstone)
nonmetallic .. 5. boron 6. iodine
plaster of Paris .. 6. gypsum
rare, brittle .. 7. euclase, thorite
red .. 4. ruby 6. garnet
soft .. 4. talc
waxlike .. 9. ozocerite 11. hatchettine
white, colorless .. 6. barite, gypsum
yellow .. 5. topaz 6. pyrite 7. epidote
mineral (pert to) ...
cavity .. 3. vug (vugg, vugh, voog)
dark spot .. 5. macle
deposit .. 4. lode 6. placer
greasy .. 7. atopite
oil .. 5. colza
pitch .. 7. asphalt
pocket .. 4. nest
salt .. 4. alum
spring .. 3. spa 4. well
tallow, wax .. 9. ozocerite
11. hatchettine
tar .. 6. maltha
water .. 6. lithia 7. Seltzer 8. alkaline
Minerva (pert to) ...
feast .. 11. Quinquatrus
flower, plant .. 6. azalea
goddess of .. 5. civic 6. health
11. handicrafts
shield .. 5. aegis (egis)
temple site .. 8. Aventine (Rome)
ming ... 6. remind 7. mention, recount
8. remember
Ming (Chin) ... 7. dynasty
mingle ... 3. mix 4. fuse, meld

5. admix, blend, merge, unite
7. combine, concoct 8. coalesce,
intermix 9. associate 10. amalgamate
11. consolidate
mingle–mangle ... 6. jumble, medley
7. mixture 9. potpourri
10. hodgepodge, miscellany
minhag (Jew) ... 6. custom, manner
7. liturgy
miniate ... 5. paint 8. decorate,
luminate 9. rubricate
minikin ... 4. type 5. baize 6. dainty
7. elegant, mincing 8. affected,
delicate 10. diminutive
minim ... 3. jot 4. drop 5. Order
(RCCh) 6. minute 8. smallest
11. small amount
minimize ... 6. reduce 7. detract
8. belittle 9. disparage
10. depreciate 13. underestimate
minimum ... 3. jot 5. least 6. lowest
minion, minionette ... 4. idol, neat
5. lover 6. dainty, pretty 7. darling,
elegant 8. delicate, favorite, ladylove,
mistress, paramour
minister ... 4. tend 5. angel, cater,
serve 6. afford, attend, curate,
parson, pastor, priest, supply
7. furnish 8. diplomat, executor,
preacher 9. clergyman, officiate
ministerial ... 7. serving 9. executive
12. instrumental 14. administrative,
ecclesiastical
minister's home ... 5. manse
9. parsonage
Minnesota ...
capital .. 6. St Paul
city .. 6. Duluth 11. Minneapolis
hero .. 14. Father Hennepin
lake .. 3. Red 10. Minnewaska
land of .. 16. Ten Thousand Lakes
mountain .. 6. Cayuna, Mesabe
9. Vermilion
river .. 3. Red 10. St Lawrence
11. Mississippi
State admission .. 12. Thirty–second
State motto .. 13. L'Etoile du Nord
14. Star of the North
State nickname .. 6. Gopher 9. North
Star
Minoan ... 6. Cretan 7. culture (Prehist)
8. language
minor ... 3. key 4. less, mode 5. friar
(Franciscan), petit, petty, scale, youth
6. course, infant, league, lesser
7. smaller 8. inferior, interval,
underage 9. youngling
minority ... 3. few 6. nonage
7. smaller 8. underage
10. immaturity 11. inferiority
Minos (pert to) ...
daughter .. 7. Ariadne
father .. 4. Zeus
king of .. 5. Crete
mother .. 6. Europa
Minotaur (Gr) ... 7. monster (half man,
half bull)
minster ... 6. church 9. monastery
minstrel ... 3. lay 4. bard, poet, show
6. end man, troupe 7. gleeman,
goliard 8. jongleur, musician
9. troubador 11. entertainer

minstrel show (pert to) . . .
　end man . . 5. bones
　middleman . . 12. interlocutor
　part . . 4. olio
mint . . . 3. aim 4. blow, coin, sage
　5. basil, feint, money 6. hyssop,
　intend, invent, mentha, ramona
　7. attempt, purpose, venture
　8. endeavor 9. fabricate
mint (pert to) . . .
　charge, levy . . 8. brassage
　11. seigniorage
　drink . . 5. julep
　family . . 5. basil 6. catnip 8. calamint
　9. Lamiaceae
　genus . . 6. Ramona 7. Melissa
　geranium . . 8. costmary
　hog . . 8. shilling
　sauce . . 5. money
minuet . . . 5. dance 7. scherzo
minus . . . 4. lack, less 6. absent, bereft,
　defect 7. short of, without
　8. subtract 10. deficiency
minuscule . . . 4. type 5. petty, small
　6. letter (lower case) 10. diminutive
minute . . . 3. jot, wee 4. mite, note,
　tiny 5. draft, petty, small 6. atomic,
　little, moment, period, record, slight,
　tittle 7. instant 8. atomical, trifling
　10. memorandum 11. unimportant
　12. sixty seconds 14. circumstantial
minute (pert to) . . .
　animal . . 10. animalcule
　details . . 11. particulars
　difference . . 5. shade
　glass . . 9. hourglass
　Jack . . 10. timeserver
　opening . . 4. pore 5. stoma
　organism . . 5. monad, spore
　8. zoospore
　part . . 6. tittle
　particle . . 4. atom, iota, mote
　record . . 8. protocol
minutely . . . 9. continual, unceasing
　11. every minute
minutes . . . 4. acta 6. record
minutia . . . 6. detail, minute 11. minor
　detail, petty matter
minx . . . 4. brat, doll, miss 6. pet dog
　7. colleen 8. pert girl 9. saucy girl,
　saucy jade 13. mischief–maker
minyan . . . 6. quorum 7. pottery
Miohippus . . . 5. horse
miqra . . . 9. Bible text (Heb)
mir (Pers) . . . 4. head 5. chief, title
　9. president
miracle . . . 4. feat, play 5. anomy
　6. marvel, wonder 10. occurrence,
　phenomenon 17. supernatural event
miracle scene . . . 4. Cana
miracle wheat . . . 7. poulard
miracle worker . . . 8. magician
　11. thermaturge
miraculous . . . 9. marvelous, wonderful
　12. supernatural 13. wonder–working
mirador . . . 5. brown, oriel 6. loggia,
　turret 7. balcony 9. bay window
　10. watchtower
mirage . . . 5. serab 7. chimera, reflect
　8. illusion 10. phenomenon
mire . . . 3. bog, mud, wet 4. glar, moil,
　ooze, slud 5. addle, dirty, marsh,

slush, stall 7. sludder
mirror . . . 5. glass 7. crystal, paragon,
　pattern, reflect 8. exemplar,
　speculum 9. reflector 11. image
　worker 12. looking glass
mirror iron . . . 12. spiegeleisen
mirth . . . 3. fun, joy 4. glee 6. gaiety
　(gayety), levity, spleen 7. delight,
　jollity 8. gladness, hilarity
　9. happiness, merriment, rejoicing
　10. joyousness 12. cheerfulness
mirthful . . . 3. gay 5. happy, jolly
miry . . . 4. oozy 5. boggy, muddy, slimy
　6. filthy, lutose
mis (comb form) . . . 5. amiss, wrong
misadventure . . . 6. mishap 8. accident,
　calamity, casualty, disaster
　9. mischance 10. misfortune
misandry (opp of misogyny) . . .
　12. dislike of man (by woman)
misanthrope . . . 5. cynic, Timon (Shak)
　8. man hater 9. pessimist
　12. mankind hater
misapply . . . 5. misdo 6. misuse
　12. misinterpret
misapprehend . . . 7. mistake
　8. misapply 11. misconceive
　13. misunderstand
misbegotten . . . 8. deformed
　12. illegitimate
miscalculate . . . 3. err 8. misjudge
　9. misreckon, overshoot
miscall . . . 5. abuse 6. revile
　7. misname 9. read amiss
　12. mispronounce
miscarriage . . . 5. lapse 6. mishap
　7. failure, misdeed, mistake
　8. abortion 9. mischance
　11. misdemeanor
　13. mismanagement 14. premature
　birth
miscegenation . . . 8. marriage
　13. interbreeding, intermarriage
miscellaneous . . . 5. mixed 6. medley,
　varied 7. blended, diverse, mingled
　8. combined 12. conglomerate
　13. heterogeneous 14. indiscriminate
miscellany . . . 6. medley 7. mixture
　8. excerpts 9. anthology
　10. collection 11. odds and ends
mischance . . . 6. mishap 8. calamity,
　disaster 10. misfortune
　12. misadventure
mischief . . . 3. ill 4. evil, harm
　5. wrack 6. damage 7. trouble
mischief (pert to) . . .
　god . . 4. Loki
　goddess . . 3. Ate 4. Eris
　maker . . 8. agitator 12. troublemaker
mischievous . . . 4. arch 6. elfish
　(elvish), impish 7. harmful, mocking,
　naughty, parlous, roguish, waggish
　8. sportive
misconduct . . . 7. offense
　10. wrongdoing 11. delinquency,
　misbehavior, misdemeanor
　13. mismanagement
miscreant . . . 6. rascal, wretch
　7. heretic, villain 8. polisson
　9. reprobate 10. unbeliever, villainous
　11. fallen angel, misbeliever
　12. unscrupulous

miscue... **3.** err **4.** miss, slip **5.** error
   6. bungle **7.** mistake
misdeed... **5.** crime, wrong **7.** offense
   8. wrongful **11.** misdemeanor
misdemeanor... **3.** sin **4.** tort
   5. crime **7.** misdeed, offense
   10. illegality, wrongdoing
   11. misbehavior
mise... **4.** levy **5.** grant **6.** layout,
   treaty **8.** expenses (law), immunity
   9. privilege
miser... **5.** hunks, Nabal (Bib)
   6. nipper, wretch **7.** boarder, niggard
miserable... **3.** sad **6.** abject, paltry
   7. forlorn, pitiful, unhappy
   12. disconsolate, disreputable
misericord, misericorde... **4.** hall, pity
   5. mercy **6.** dagger **9.** refectory
   10. compassion **12.** dispensation
miserly... **4.** mean **5.** close, tight
   6. stingy **7.** chintzy (sl) **8.** churlish,
   covetous, niggardly, penurious
   10. avaricious **12.** parsimonious
misery... **3.** woe **5.** grief **7.** anguish,
   avarice, poverty, sadness **8.** calamity,
   distress **9.** heartache, privation
   10. affliction, misfortune
   11. despondency, Pandora's box,
   unhappiness **12.** covetousness,
   wretchedness **13.** niggardliness
misfeasance... **5.** wrong **8.** trespass
   10. wrongdoing
misfortune... **3.** ill **4.** evil, harm
   6. mishap **7.** bad luck, reverse,
   setback **8.** calamity, disaster
   9. adversity, holocaust, mischance
   11. catastrophe **12.** misadventure
misgiving... **5.** doubt, qualm
   7. anxiety **10.** foreboding
   12. apprehension
mishap... **4.** slip **8.** accident, casualty
   10. misfortune **11.** contretemps,
   miscarriage **12.** misadventure
Mishnah, Mishna... **4.** Moed **5.** tenet
   6. Nashim **7.** Nezikim **8.** doctrine,
   Halakoth, Kodashim, Tohoroth
   9. tradition
misinterpret... **3.** err **4.** warp
   7. distort, misread **8.** misjudge
misjudge... **3.** err **11.** misconstrue
   12. miscalculate
misky... **5.** foggy, misty
mislay... **4.** lose **8.** displace, misplace
misle... **4.** mist, rain **6.** mizzle
   7. drizzle
mislead... **4.** fool **5.** blear **6.** delude,
   seduce **7.** deceive **8.** misguide
   9. deception, misbehave, misinform
misleading... **5.** false **7.** crooked
   8. illusory **9.** deceptive
   10. fallacious, fraudulent
   12. misinforming **14.** misinformation
mislippen... **6.** delude **7.** neglect,
   suspect **10.** disappoint
mismanage... **5.** blunk, misdo
   6. bungle, misuse **9.** mishandle
misogynist... **8.** celibate **10.** woman
   hater
misplace... **4.** lose **6.** mislay, misset
   8. displace **9.** dislocate, mislocate
   11. anachronism

misplay... **3.** err **5.** error **6.** renege
   7. mismove **9.** wrong play
misprise, misprize... **5.** scorn
   6. slight **7.** despise, disdain, mistake
   8. contempt **9.** underrate
   10. misprision, undervalue
   13. underestimate
misprision... **5.** scorn **7.** mistake
   8. contempt, misprize
   10. misconduct **11.** misdemeanor
   12. depreciation
   16. misunderstanding
mispronunciation... **8.** cacology
   10. bad diction
misrepresent... **5.** belie **7.** deceive,
   distort, falsify **8.** disserve
miss... **2.** Ms. **3.** err **4.** chit, fail, girl,
   lack, lose, omit, skip **5.** evade, lapse,
   title **7.** failure, mistake **8.** mistress
   9. fall short **10.** prostitute
   12. mademoiselle
missal... **4.** book (Eccl) **8.** breviary
missel... **9.** mistletoe
misshapen... **4.** ugly **8.** deformed
   9. distorted, monstrous, unshapely
missile... **2.** MX **4.** ICBM, Nike, Thor
   5. Atlas, Snark, Titan **6.** rocket
   7. grenade, matador **8.** Redstone
   9. Minuteman
missing... **3.** out **4.** gone, lost
   6. absent **7.** lacking, wanting
   8. vanished **11.** nonexistent
mission... **3.** job **4.** body, duty, task
   5. Alamo **6.** charge, church, errand
   7. calling, embassy **8.** legation,
   outreach **10.** assignment, commission,
   delegation, deputation, missionary
missionary... **7.** apostle **8.** emissary,
   preacher **10.** evangelist
Missionary Ridge... **11.** Chattanooga
   (Tenn)
Mississippi...
   capital.. **7.** Jackson
   city.. **6.** Biloxi **7.** Natchez **8.** Gulfport
   9. Vicksburg **13.** Pass Christian
   explorer, colonizer.. **6.** De Soto
   9. Iberville
   festival.. **9.** Mardi gras (Biloxi)
   king crop.. **6.** cotton
   kite (bird).. **9.** everglade
   mountain.. **6.** Woodal
   river.. **5.** Yazoo **11.** Mississippi
   State admission.. **9.** Twentieth
   State bird.. **11.** mockingbird
   State flower.. **8.** magnolia
   State motto.. **14.** Virtute et Armis (By
   Valor and Arms)
   State nickname.. **5.** Bayou
Mississippian (Geol)...
   15. Eocarboniferous (system)
Mississippi River head... **10.** Lake
   Itasca (Minn)
Mississippi River nickname...
   10. Great River **14.** Father of Waters
missive... **4.** note **6.** billet, letter
   7. message, missile **8.** document
Missouri...
   capital.. **13.** Jefferson City
   city.. **7.** Sedalia, St Louis **8.** Hannibal,
   St Joseph
   famed native.. **6.** Carver (G W),

Truman (Pres) **9.** Mark Twain
10. Jesse James
gourd .. **11.** calabazilla
mountains .. **6.** Ozarks
river .. **8.** Big Muddy, Missouri
11. Mississippi
skylark .. **13.** Sprague's pipit
State admission .. **12.** Twenty–fourth
State bird .. **8.** bluebird
State flower .. **8.** hawthorn
State nickname .. **6.** Show Me
sucker (fish) .. **10.** black horse
misspelling ... **10.** cacography
misspend ... **4.** lose **5.** waste
8. squander **10.** spend amiss
misstep ... **4.** slip, trip **7.** faux pas
mist ... **3.** dim, fog **4.** blur, film, gray,
haze, rain, smur **5.** bedim, brume,
cloud **7.** droplet **9.** obscurity
11. uncertainty
mistake ... **3.** err **4.** bull, goof, slip
5. boner, botch, error, fault, folly
7. blooper, blunder, erratum, violate
8. miscount, solecism
11. anachronism **12.** inadvertence
13. misconception
15. misapprehension
mistaken ... **5.** wrong **9.** erroneous
12. misconceived **13.** misunderstood
14. judging wrongly
mistletoe ... **6.** emblem (Okla), missel,
Viscum **9.** Loranthus
mistonusk ... **6.** badger
mistress ... **4.** bibi (beebee) **5.** title,
woman **6.** matron **7.** control, teacher
8. Dulcinia, ladylove **9.** concubine,
governess, patroness **10.** proprietor,
sweetheart
Mistress of ...
Adriatic .. **6.** Venice
Charles II .. **4.** Nell
Seas .. **12.** Great Britain
World .. **4.** Rome (anc)
misty ... **3.** dim **4.** hazy, roky **5.** foggy,
rouky, vague **6.** blurry, cloudy, hoarse
7. obscure, shadowy **10.** indistinct
13. unenlightened, unilluminated
misuse ... **5.** abuse **6.** revile **7.** pervert
8. maltreat, misapply, wrong use
9. misemploy **12.** misrepresent
misuse of words in speech ...
11. heterophemy, malapropism
mite ... **3.** bit, jot **4.** atom, coin, mote
5. child, speck **6.** acarus, insect
7. bdellid, chigger, smidgen (smidge)
8. acaridan, particle
miter, mitre ... **4.** belt **5.** frank, joint,
tiara **6.** fillet, girdle, gusset, tavern
7. petalon (Eccl) **8.** dovetail,
headband, insignia **9.** headdress
mithridate ... **8.** antidote **9.** electuary
12. alexipharmic
mitigate ... **4.** ease, tone **5.** abate,
allay, mease, relax, remit, slake
6. lessen, reduce, soften, temper
7. appease, mollify, qualify, relieve
8. diminish, lenitive, moderate, palliate
9. alleviate, extenuate, meliorate
mitigation ... **6.** relief **9.** abatement
10. diminution, moderation
11. extenuation **13.** mollification
mix ... **3.** pug (clay) **4.** ease, join,

meng, stir **5.** addle, blend, cross,
knead, unite **6.** jumble, mingle,
muddle **7.** combine, fluster
8. coalesce **9.** associate
10. complicate
mixable ... **8.** miscible
mixed (pert to) ...
breed .. **7.** mongrel
type .. **2.** pi
with water .. **6.** slaked
with yeast .. **6.** barmed, frothy
mixer ... **5.** whisk **6.** beater **7.** mingler
9. eggbeater, (food) processor
mixture ... **4.** hash, mash, olio
5. blend, chaos, mixed **6.** batter,
medley, miscue **7.** amalgam, mélange
8. compound, solution
9. admixture, potpourri
10. hodgepodge **11.** combination,
preparation
mixture (pert to) ...
beverage .. **5.** clary **10.** shandygaff
cement .. **5.** putty
medicinal .. **5.** hepar **6.** potion
12. prescription
metallic .. **6.** speiss
sand and clay .. **4.** loam
mix–up ... **5.** melee, snafu **6.** muddle,
tangle **8.** conflict **9.** confusion
Mizar ... **4.** Zeta (Great Dipper)
mizmaze ... **9.** confusion
12. bewilderment
mizzenmast ... **9.** aftermast, third mast
mizzle ... **4.** mist, rain **5.** misle
6. decamp **9.** slink away
mizzy ... **3.** bog **8.** quagmire
Mnenosyne (pert to) ...
ancestor .. **5.** Titan
goddess .. **5.** memory
mother of .. **8.** The Muses
moa ... **6.** ratite (flightless) **8.** Dinornis
moab ... **3.** hat (anc)
Moabite (pert to) ...
dwelling (Bib) .. **7.** Dead Sea
language .. **7.** Semitic
mountain .. **4.** Nebo
people .. **4.** Emim
stone (Bib) .. **11.** black basalt
moan ... **3.** cry **4.** suum, wail
5. groan, sough **6.** bemoan, bewail,
grieve, lament, suffer **9.** complaint
11. lamentation
moat ... **4.** foss (fosse) **5.** ditch
6. trench **13.** fortification
mob ... **3.** set **4.** gang, herd, mass
5. crowd, drove, flock, group, Mafia,
taunt **6.** clique, rabble, throng
7. company **8.** canaille, populace
mobile ... **7.** movable **8.** not fixed
9. versatile **10.** changeable
Mobile Bay hero ... **8.** Farragut (Adm)
mobile home ... **3.** van **6.** camper
7. caravan (Brit), trailer
mob member ... **6.** rioter **7.** Mafioso
8. criminal, mobocrat **9.** roisterer
mobocracy ... **7.** mob rule
Moby Dick (pert to) ...
author .. **8.** Melville (Herman)
character .. **4.** Ahab **5.** Peleg
theme .. **7.** whaling **10.** White Whale
moccasin ... **3.** pac **4.** shoe **5.** snake
6. Flower (Minn State), orchid

8. larrigan 10. argus brown
11. cottonmouth
moch . . . 4. moth
mocha . . . 4. bark, town (Arab)
6. coffee, dollar 7. leather 9. moss
agate
mock . . . 3. ape 4. defy, gibe, jape,
jibe, sham 5. feign, fleer, flout,
mimic, scoff, sneer, taunt 6. delude,
deride 7. imitate, mockery, pretend
8. ridicule 10. disappoint
11. counterfeit
mock (pert to) . . .
brawn . . 10. headcheese
cucumber . . 11. balsam apple
duck . . 4. meat 8. pork chop
hero . . 5. comic
jewelry . . 5. logie, paste 9. imitation
lead, ore . . 10. sphalerite
moon . . 10. paraselene
nightingale . . 7. warbler 8. blackcap
olive . . 9. axbreaker 12. cherry laurel
orange . . 7. syringa (seringa)
plane . . 8. sycamore
sun . . 9. parhelion
turtle . . 9. calf's head
mockage . . . 7. mimicry, mockery
9. imitation
mocker . . . 5. mimic 7. scoffer
8. deceiver 11. mockingbird
mockernut . . . 7. hickory
mockery . . . 5. farce 6. satire
7. mimicry, sarcasm 8. derision
9. imitation 11. counterfeit
mockingbird . . . 5. Mimus
mode . . . 3. fad, way 4. form 5. flair,
style, vogue 6. manner, method
7. fashion, variety
mode (pert to) . . .
expression . . 10. vernacular
government . . 6. regime, system
logic . . 7. Ferison (3rd figure)
procedure . . 5. order 6. system
speech . . 8. parlance 11. phraseology
standing . . 4. pose 6. stance
7. posture 8. position
model . . . 3. act 4. form, idea, mold,
norm, plan, plat, pose 5. ideal,
image, shape 7. example, manikin,
measure, paragon, pattern, templet
8. ensample, paradigm, standard,
template 9. archetype, mannequin,
precedent 11. meritorious
12. reproduction
model (of) . . .
a word . . 8. paradigm
a work . . 9. archetype
excellence . . 7. paragon 8. exemplar
solar system . . 6. orrery
11. planetarium
moderate . . . 4. bate, ease, slow, some
5. abate, lower, slake 6. frugal,
lessen, soften, temper 7. control,
lenient, mediate, modesto
8. mediocre, modulate, slow down
9. temperate 10. reasonable
11. inexpensive 12. conservative
14. inconsiderable
moderation . . . 7. control 9. abatement,
restraint 10. diminution, governance,
limitation, mitigation 11. restriction
13. temperateness

moderator . . . 5. judge 6. umpire
7. arbiter 8. mediator 10. arbitrator,
controller
modern . . . 3. neo (pref), new 4. late
6. latter 7. present 8. neoteric
modernize . . . 6. update 10. streamline
Modern School of Art . . . 4. Dada
7. Dadaism (1920)
modern Syriac script . . . 5. serta
8. peshitta
modest . . . 3. coy, mim, shy 6. chaste,
demure, humble, seemly 8. reserved,
retiring, virtuous 9. diffident
11. well–behaved 13. unpretentious
14. inconsiderable
modesty . . . 7. decency, reserve,
shyness 8. chastity, humility, pudicity
10. diffidence, humbleness
11. self–control
modicum . . . 3. bit 4. drop 5. minim,
share 6. little 11. small amount
12. small portion
modification . . . 4. tone 6. change,
umlaut 9. variation 10. adaptation,
alteration, limitation 13. qualification
15. differentiation
modify . . . 4. vary 5. alter, limit
6. change, master, temper
7. assuage, qualify 8. attemper,
mitigate, moderate, quantify
9. influence 13. differentiate
modish . . . 4. chic, trim 5. smart 7. in
vogue, stylish 8. vogueish (voguish)
11. fashionable
modiste . . . 8. milliner 9. couturier
10. couturière, dressmaker
modulated . . . 5. toned 6. merged
7. adapted, attuned, changed,
intoned 8. softened, tempered
9. inflected, regulated
modulation . . . 4. tone 6. change
8. shifting 9. tempering
10. alteration, inflection, moderation
moggan . . . 8. stocking 10. knit sleeve
moggy . . . 3. cat, cow 4. calf 7. pet
name 8. slattern 9. scarecrow
mogo . . . 7. hatchet
mogul . . . 4. lord 5. nabob 6. tycoon
7. magnate 8. autocrat 9. dignitary
10. locomotive, panjandrum
14. great personage
Mogul . . . 6. Empire, Mongol 7. dynasty
9. Mongolian
Mohammed (pert to) . . .
birthplace . . 5. Mecca
daughter . . 6. Fatima
flight to Mecca . . 6. hegira
horse . . 5. Fadda (white mule)
7. Alborak
names . . 7. Mahomet, Mahound
son–in–law . . 3. Ali
Mohammedan (pert to) . . .
angel of death . . 6. Azrael
ascetic . . 4. Sufi 5. fakir (fakeer)
8. Marabout
caliph . . 3. Ali 4. Omar 6. Othman
7. Abu Bekr
chief . . 3. aga (agha) 4. dato (datto)
5. sayid 6. Caliph
crier (for prayer) . . 7. muezzin
crusader's enemy (Moslem) . .
7. Saracen

deity.. 5. Allah 9. Termagant
demon.. 5. afrit, eblis, jinni (jinnee)
  7. Shaitan (Sheitan)
Malay (Javanese).. 6. Sassak
Moslem.. 5. hanif 9. Mussulman
noble.. 4. amir (ameer), emir
nymph.. 5. houri
officer.. 3. aga 5. diwan 6. vizier
  (vizir)
princess, queen.. 5. begum
saint.. 3. pir 6. santon
scholars, body of.. 5. ulema
sect.. 6. Wahabi (Wahabee, Wahhabi)
student (Theol).. 5. softa
successor.. 6. Caliph (Calif)
teacher.. 5. mufti 6. mullah (mollah)
unbeliever.. 6. Kaffir (Kafir)
Mohammedanism (pert to)...
  Bible, book.. 5. Koran 7. Alcoran
  bier, tomb.. 5. tabut
  cap.. 3. taj
  caravansary.. 6. imaret
  crusade.. 5. jihad (jehad)
  custom, tradition.. 6. sunnah
  divorce.. 5. talak 7. mubarat
  dome, over tomb.. 6. turbeh
  Easter.. 3. Eed
  Fast (annual).. 7. Ramadan
  festival.. 6. Bairam
  garment.. 4. izar 6. jubbah
  house (men's part).. 8. selamlik
  instrument.. 5. rebab
  marriage custom.. 5. iddat
  marriage settlement.. 4. mahr
  Messiah, priest.. 4. Imam (Imaum)
    5. Mahdi
  monastery.. 5. ribat
  platform, porch.. 7. mastaba
  prayer.. 4. azan (adan) 5. namaz
  property (law).. 6. mushaa
  religion.. 6. Moslem 8. Islamism
  saber.. 8. yataghan (yatagan)
  salutation.. 6. salaam (salam)
  shrine (Mecca).. 5. Kaaba (Caaba,
    Kaabeh) 10. Black Stone
  veil.. 7. yashmak (yashmac)
  war (Relig).. 5. jihad (jehad)
moho... 4. rail 9. gallinule 10. honey
  eater
mohr... 7. gazelle
moider... 4. toil 5. crowd, worry
    6. wander 7. smother 8. bewilder,
    encumber
moiety... 4. half, part (small)
    7. portion
moil... 4. spot, tire, toil 5. labor, taint
    6. seethe 7. torment, trouble,
    turmoil 8. drudgery 9. confusion
    10. defilement
moiré... 7. clouded, watered
moist... 3. wet 4. damp, dank, dewy,
    uvid 5. humid, rainy 7. tearful
moisten... 3. wet 4. hose, moil
    5. bedew, spray 6. anoint, dampen,
    sparge 8. humidify, sprinkle
moisture... 3. dew, fog 5. vapor,
    water 6. liquid 8. dampness,
    dankness, dewdrops, humidity
moisture (pert to)...
  body.. 6. humors 9. exudation
  condensed.. 4. drip, drop
  excess, swelling.. 5. edema

expose to.. 3. ret
remove.. 4. wipe 5. wring
mojo... 4. Moxo 5. charm (voodoo)
    6. amulet 7. majagua
moke... 4. dolt, mesh 5. horse
    6. donkey 7. network 8. minstrel
    9. performer
moki... 4. raft
moko... 9. tattooing
moky... 5. foggy, misty
molar... 5. tooth 6. molary
    7. chopper, grinder 8. grinding
molarimeter... 11. thermometer
molasses... 5. sirup 7. treacle
    8. theriaca
mold, mould... 3. die 4. cast, form,
    must 5. humus, knead, nowel,
    plasm, sprue 6. blight, growth
    (fungus), matrix, mildew 7. moulage
    9. sculpture 12. reproduction
Moldavia, Rumania...
  balm.. 4. mint
  capital.. 5. Balta 8. Tiraspol
  govt.. 9. Socialist
molding... 3. ess 4. bead, beak,
    cyma, ogee, reed, tori 5. conge,
    gulla, ovolo, splay, torus 6. fascia,
    fillet, listel, reglet, scotia 7. cavetto,
    cornice, reeding, shaping 8. astragal,
    bezantee 12. reproduction
molding (pert to)...
  convex.. 5. torus
  decoration.. 4. dado
  egg and dart.. 9. arrowhead
  series.. 7. surbase
  suit of.. 8. ledgment (ledgement)
moldy, mouldy... 5. fusty, mucid,
    musty, stale 8. mildewed
mole (rat)... 4. gray 5. fault, nevus
    (naevus), shrew, snake, Talpa, taupe
    6. rodent 7. blemish, Nesokia
    9. birthmark 12. imperfection
molecule... 3. ion 4. atom, unit
    6. steric 8. particle
molest... 4. harm 5. annoy, tease
    6. bother, harass, pester 7. disturb
    8. mistreat 9. incommode
    13. interfere with
Molière (pert to)...
  author of.. 5. drama, plays
    6. comedy, L'Avare, satire 8. Tartuffe
  character (story).. 5. Damis 6. Eraste,
    Scapin 7. Dorante
mollify... 4. calm 5. allay, relax, sleek
    6. pacify, relent, soften, temper
    7. appease, lighten, qualify, relieve
    9. alleviate 10. conciliate
mollitious... 8. sensuous 9. luxurious,
    softening
mollusk... 3. asi 4. clam, pipi, slug,
    spat 5. chama, snail, squid, whelk
    6. cockle, limpet, mussel, oyster
    7. abalone, bivalve, octopus, scallop,
    veliger 8. univalve 10. cuttlefish
mollusk... 5. Anoma, Chama, Murex
    6. Chiton 7. Astarte, Etheria
    8. Buccinum, Mollusca, Nautilus
mollusk (pert to)...
  bait.. 6. limpet
  eight–armed.. 7. octopus
  freshwater.. 7. etheria
  marine.. 7. abalone, scallop

8. nautilus
shell.. 4. test 5. testa 6. cockle,
cowrie (cowry)
shell, without.. 4. slug
shell concretion.. 5. pearl
teeth.. 6. radula
ten–armed.. 5. squid
young.. 4. spat
mollycoddle... 6. coddle, pamper
8. weakling 12. spoiled child
13. effeminate boy
Moloch (pert to)...
Bible.. 5. deity
doctrine.. 4. evil
zoology.. 6. agamid, lizard
Molotov cocktail... 4. bomb
molt, moult... 3. mew 4. cast, mute,
shed 7. ecdysis 8. exuviate
molten rock... 2. aa
Moluccas, Spice Islands...
capital.. 7. Amboina
island.. 5. Banda
product.. 5. spice
site.. 9. Indonesia
moly... 4. herb (fabled) 6. garlic
momble... 6. jumble, tangle
mome (anc)... 4. fool 7. buffoon
9. blockhead
moment... 4. time 5. avail, flash,
nonce, point, trice, value 6. crisis,
minute, second, weight 7. impetus,
instant 9. influence, twinkling
10. importance 11. consequence
13. consideration, signification
momentary... 9. ephemeral, transient
10. transitory 13. instantaneous
momentous... 7. weighty 8. eventful
9. important 11. influential
13. authoritative
momo... 3. owl
Momus (Gr)... 3. god (of ridicule)
6. critic 11. faultfinder
mon... 5. badge (imperial) 7. kikumon
13. chrysanthemum
monachal... 8. celibate, monastic
9. claustral
monad... 3. one 4. atom, unit
5. deity, monas 8. particle
10. individual 12. Supreme Being
monadnock... 4. hill 8. mountain (NH)
Mona Lisa (pert to)...
famed for.. 5. smile (subtle)
named also.. 10. La Gioconda
painter.. 7. da Vinci
site (of picture).. 6. Louvre (The)
monandry... 10. one husband (at a
time)
monarch... 4. czar, king, shah
5. chief, queen, ruler 6. dynast,
kaiser, sultan 7. czarina, emperor
9. potentate, sovereign 13. royal
highness
monarch... 9. butterfly
13. constellation
monastery... 5. abbey 6. friary, priory
7. convent, hospice, nunnery
8. cloister
monastery (pert to)...
head.. 3. dom 5. abbot
Pavia.. 10. Carthusian
room.. 4. cell
Tibet.. 8. lamasery

monastic... 4. monk 5. friar
7. monkish 8. celibate 9. claustral
monde... 5. globe, world (fashion)
6. circle (fashion) 7. coterie, société,
society 9. beau monde
monetary... 7. coinage 8. currency
9. financial, pecuniary
money... 3. wad 4. cash, coin, grig,
mina, pelf 5. frank, funds, lucre,
maneh, uhllo (ullo) 6. mazuma,
talent, wampum, wealth 8. currency
10. spondulics (spondulix) 11. legal
tender
money (pert to)...
ancient.. 3. aes
bank (Eur).. 5. banco
box, chest.. 4. arca, safe, till, tray
5. chest 6. drawer 7. brazier
8. register
changer.. 6. banker, broker, shroff
(saraf), usurer 7. cambist
coinage.. 4. mint
English slang.. 7. ooftish (oof)
found.. 5. trove
gamblers'.. 6. barato
gift.. 4. alms 7. bequest
9. endowment
lender.. 6. banker, usurer 7. Shylock
10. pawnbroker
luck.. 6. barato 7. handsel
maker.. 6. coiner, minter
13. counterfeiter
manual.. 7. cambist
matters.. 6. fiscal 9. economics
of account.. 3. ora
paper.. 4. bill, kale 7. lettuce
pledge.. 5. arles
premium.. 4. agio
roll (coins).. 7. rouleau
shell.. 5. uhllo (ullo) 6. cowrie (cowry)
slang.. 4. gilt, jack, lour 5. rhino
6. boodle, wampum
spinner.. 6. usurer 10. speculator
to coin.. 4. mint
wildcat.. 9. yellow dog
worthless.. 4. pelf
moneyed... 4. rich 5. flush 7. opulent,
wealthy 8. affluent, well–to–do
10. prosperous, well–heeled
monger... 6. dealer, mercer, trader,
vendor 7. peddler 8. merchant
9. tradesman
mongler... 9. sandpiper
Mongol... see also *Mongolian*
5. Asian, Tatar 9. yellow man
Mongolian (pert to)...
ass (wild).. 8. chigetai
capital.. 4. Urga
conjurer.. 6. shaman
conqueror.. 9. Tamerlane
desert.. 4. Gobi
dynasty.. 4. Yuan
monk, priest.. 4. lama
religion.. 9. Shamanism, Shintoism
12. Confucianism
river.. 3. Pei 4. Onon
tribe.. 3. Lai 4. Lapp 5. Ordos
7. Khalkas, Tsaktar 9. Ouryalag
mongoose... 4. urva 5. lemur
9. ichneumon
mongrel... 3. cur 5. mixed 6. hybrid
10. crossbreed 14. stilt sandpiper

mongrel fish... 5. skate (angelfish)
8. tullibee (whitefish)
monial... 3. nun
moniker... 4. name 8. nickname
monition... 6. advice, notice
7. summons, warning
10. admonition, dissuasion, intimation
11. forewarning
monitor... 4. ship (Civil War), uran
5. varan 6. lizard, manual, mentor,
nozzle 7. adviser, student, warning
8. conenose (bug), director, recorder,
reminder 9. informant
monk... 3. fra 4. bede, lama, saki
5. fakir, friar, padre 6. ferret,
monkey 7. ascetic, caloyer, dervish
8. anchoret, capuchin, celibate,
cenobite 9. anchorite, bullfinch,
touchwood
monkey (pert to)...
African.. 4. waag 5. potto 6. grivet,
vernet
American.. 4. saki 5. acari 6. ouakari
8. marmoset 9. beelzebub
bearded.. 8. entellus
bonnet.. 4. zati 5. toque
bread.. 6. baobab
chimpanzee.. 6. nchega
crying.. 4. kaha
cups.. 9. nepenthes 12. pitcher plant
family.. 10. Catarrhina
flower.. 7. mimulus (herb)
genus.. 5. Cebus 6. Ateles
7. Colobus, Saimiri, Tarsius
8. Alouatta
handsome.. 4. mona
house.. 5. apery
howling.. 4. mono 5. araba 7. stentor
8. alouatte
large.. 5. sajou
Madagascar.. 8. mangabey (mangaby)
organ grinder.. 5. Cebus 8. capuchin
Oriental.. 7. macaque
puzzle.. 5. piñon
small.. 8. marmoset
South American.. 4. titi 6. grison
9. beelzebub
spider.. 7. sapajou
squirrel.. 7. saimiri
tailless.. 3. ape
wrench.. 7. spanner
monk's hood... 4. cowl
monkshood... 4. atis 7. aconite
9. dandelion
monoceros... 4. fish (one–horned)
7. sawfish, Unicorn 9. swordfish
13. Constellation
monochord... 7. concord, harmony
9. sonometer 10. clavichord,
instrument
monocle... 8. eyeglass
monocleid, monocleide... 4. desk (one
key) 7. cabinet
monocracy... 9. autocracy
13. undivided rule
Monodelphia... 7. mammals
8. Eutheria
monody... 3. ode 4. poem (lament),
song 5. dirge 6. melody
9. homophony
monogamy... 11. one marriage
monogram... 6. cipher, sketch

7. outline 8. initials 9. character
monolith... 5. stone 6. menhir, pillar,
statue 8. monument
monologue... 6. speech 9. soliloquy
monomachy... 4. duel 6. combat
monopoly... 5. grant, right, trust
6. corner 7. charter, control
9. privilege, syndicate 10. possession
(exclusive)
monotonous... 4. dead, drab, dull
5. drone, thrum 6. dreary, samely
7. humdrum, tedious 8. singsong
9. wearisome 11. repetitious
monotony... 6. tedium 8. sameness
9. wearisome 10. sameliness,
uniformity 15. repetitiousness
monoxylon, monoxyle... 4. boat
5. canoe
monseigneur... 5. title 6. My Lord
monster... 4. ogre 5. fiend, harpy,
teras 6. dragon, ellops, geryon,
gorgon, sphinx 8. behemoth,
Cerberus 11. monstrosity
monster (pert to)...
classic.. 8. minotaur
comb form.. 6. terato
eight–headed.. 6. Scylla
fabled.. 5. harpy 6. kraken, sphinx
7. centaur 9. bucentaur
flame–breathing.. 7. chimera
(chimaera)
half man, half bull.. 8. minotaur
headless.. 9. acephalus
like.. 8. teratoid
man–eating.. 4. ogre 5. lamia
medical.. 5. teras
three–bodied.. 6. Geryon (slain by
Hercules)
twin.. 10. xiphopagus
two–bodied.. 7. disomus
two–headed.. 10. dicephalus,
opodidymus
winged.. 5. harpy
monstrous... 4. huge, ugly, vast
5. enorm (anc) 6. absurd, wicked
7. strange, titanic 8. deformed,
gigantic, infamous 9. fantastic,
monstrous, unnatural 10. prodigious,
stupendous 12. overpowering,
overwhelming 13. extraordinary
Montana...
capital.. 6. Helena
city.. 5. Butte 8. Anaconda, Billings
10. Great Falls
Historic site.. 14. Custer Cemetery
lake.. 8. Flathead
mountain.. 7. Rockies 17. Continental
Divide
park.. 7. Glacier 11. Yellowstone
peak.. 7. Granite
reservation (Ind).. 4. Cree, Crow
5. Sioux 8. Cheyenne, Chippewa
9. Blackfeet
State admission.. 10. Forty–first
State motto.. 13. Gold and Silver
State nickname.. 8. Treasure
montanto... 6. rising 10. broadsword
Monte Cristo, Count of (pert to)...
author.. 5. Dumas (Alexandre)
hero.. 6. Dantès
Montenegro... 10. Yugoslavia
montero... 3. cap (hunter's) 6. ranger

8. forester, huntsman, mountain
Montezuma (pert to)...
  Chief of.. 6. Aztecs
  cypress.. 9. ahuehuete
  hero of.. 6. Mexico
  prisoner of.. 6. Cortez
  ruins, site of.. 6. Pueblo
month (pert to)...
  astronomy.. 5. lunar, solar
  half.. 9. fortnight
  revolution.. 8. sidereal 9. synodical
  term.. 5. epact 6. ultimo 7. proximo
  twelfth part.. 8. calendar
monticule... 4. cone (volcano)
  5. mount 7. hillock 10. prominence
  (small)
montilla... 6. sherry
Montmorency... 6. cherry
monture... 5. frame, horse (saddle),
  mount
monument... 4. tomb 5. cairn, stele
  (stela), tower, vault 6. bilith, dolmen
  7. obelisk 8. cenotaph, cromlech,
  monolith 9. sepulcher 10. gravestone
  11. commemorate, remembrance
monumental... 4. high 5. great
  7. mammoth, massive, notable
  8. colossal 10. impressive, sculptural,
  stupendous
Monumental City... 9. Baltimore
moo... 3. low (of a cow) 6. lowing
mooch... 4. loaf 5. skulk, sneak, steal
  6. loiter, pilfer 7. vagrant
moocha... 6. girdle 9. loincloth
mood... 3. tid 4. tone, vein, whim
  5. freak, humor 6. nature 7. caprice
  11. disposition
moody... 3. sad 4. glum 5. sulky
  6. gloomy, sullen 7. pensive
  9. whimsical 10. capricious
mool... 4. bury, mold, soil 5. earth,
  grave 6. mingle 7. crumble
mools... 10. chilblains
moon... 4. idle, Luna 5. Diana
  6. Phoebe, wander 7. Cynthia
  8. crescent 9. satellite 13. celestial
  body
moon (pert to)...
  age (first of year).. 5. epact
  area.. 4. mare
  Astrol.. 6. Cancer (mansion), planet
  autumn.. 7. harvest
  beam.. 3. ray 9. pearl blue
  bird.. 11. goldencrest
  blindness.. 10. nyctalopia
  calf.. 4. dolt 7. monster 8. born fool,
  imbecile
  comb form.. 5. selen
  fern.. 8. moonwort
  festival.. 8. neomenia
  fish.. 4. opah 6. minnow 7. sunfish
  9. spadefish
  flower.. 10. oxeye daisy
  gazing.. 16. absent–mindedness
  geographer.. 13. selenographer
  god.. 3. Sin 6. Nannar
  heraldry.. 6. argent
  inhabitant.. 8. Selenite
  instrument.. 11. selenoscope
  lighter.. 9. serenader 10. moonshiner
  11. night worker
  lily.. 10. moonflower

mad.. 7. lunatic
mock.. 10. paraselene
month.. 5. lunar
new.. 6. phasis
phase.. 7. gibbous, horning
picture of.. 11. selenograph
point.. 4. cusp, horn 5. apsis
  6. apogee 7. perigee
position.. 6. octant
raker.. 10. stupid lout
  12. woolgatherer
stone.. 3. gem 8. feldspar
  10. hecatolite
struck.. 7. lunatic 8. obsessed
Uranus's.. 5. Ariel
valley.. 4. rill (rille) 5. cleft
moon goddess...
  Greek.. 6. Hecate, Phoebe 7. Artemis,
  Cynthia
  Italian.. 5. Diana
  Phoenician.. 6. Tanith (Tanit)
  7. Astarte
  Roman.. 3. Dea 5. Virgo 9. Caelestis
moonish... 7. flighty 10. capricious
moonshine... 5. empty 6. liquor,
  poteen, whisky (whiskey) 7. bootleg
  8. egg sauce, nonsense
  10. balsamweed
moony... 5. round 6. dreamy
  9. moonlight 10. abstracted
  14. crescent–shaped
moor... 3. bog, fen 4. hill, root
  5. heath, marsh, swale 6. anchor,
  fasten, secure 9. fix firmly
Moor... 6. Berber, Moslem
  7. Moorman, Saracen 8. goldfish
  (black), Moroccan
moor (pert to)...
  berry.. 9. cranberry
  bird.. 6. grouse
  blackbird.. 5. ouzel
  buzzard.. 5. harpy 7. harrier
  cock.. 9. blackcock
  dance.. 7. morisco
  grass.. 5. heath 6. sundew
  hen.. 4. coot 9. gallinule
  monkey.. 7. macaque
  stone.. 7. granite
Moorish... 6. Moslem 8. Moresque
Moorish (pert to)...
  garment.. 5. jupon
  horse.. 4. barb (Barbary)
  judge.. 4. cadi
  kettledrum.. 5. tabor 6. atabal
  Order.. 7. Alcazar 8. Alhambra
  9. horseshoe, Saracenic
  palace.. 7. Alcazar
moose... 3. elk 4. alce 5. eland
  7. society (Loyal Order)
moose bird... 9. Canada jay
moot... 4. pose 5. argue, plead, speak
  6. debate 7. discuss, propose
mop... 4. swab, wipe 5. scrub
  6. merkin 7. drink up, grimace
  9. blindfold, implement
mope... 4. sulk 5. dumps, idler
  6. grieve
moppet... 3. tot 4. baby, doll, tike
  7. darling, toddler 9. youngster
mora... 4. tree (Trinidad) 5. delay,
  stool 7. default 8. syllable
  9. footstool 11. Spartan army

12. postponement
moral... 4. good, pure 5. maxim
   6. lesson 7. epimyth, ethical,
   upright, virtual. 8. likeness, virtuous
   9. righteous
moral (pert to)...
   excellence.. 6. virtue
   fault.. 4. vice
   law.. 9. Decalogue
   obligation.. 4. duty
   poem.. 3. dit
   principle.. 7. precept
   story.. 5. fable 7. parable
   8. apologue
morale... 4. hope, zeal 6. morals,
   spirit 8. morality 10. confidence
moralist... 4. prig 7. teacher
   9. moralizer 10. sermonizer
morality... 6. amoral, ethics, virtue
   13. righteousness
morals... 8. morality 10. ethography
morass... 3. bog, fen 4. moor
   5. marsh, swamp 6. slough
   8. quagmire 9. everglade
moratorium... 5. delay 10. suspension
Moravia, capital... 5. Brünn (Brno)
Moravian... 9. Christian 10. Herrnhuter
   13. Unitas Fratrum 19. Church of
   the Brethren
moray... 3. eel 6. hamlet 7. Muraena
   8. food fish 10. Muraenidae
morbid... 4. sick 6. gloomy 7. ghastly,
   unsound 8. diseased 9. unhealthy
   11. unwholesome
morbid (pert to)...
   appetite.. 10. adephagous
   complex.. 11. inferiority
   condition.. 8. ochlesis
   desire for music.. 9. melomania
   displacement.. 7. ectopia
morbus... 7. disease, illness
morceau... 3. bit (Mus) 6. morsel
mordant... 4. acid, keen 6. biting
   7. burning, caustic, pungent
   8. scathing 9. corrosive, sarcastic
   11. acrimonious
more... 3. yea 4. also, mair, plus,
   some 5. again, extra 6. plural
   7. greater 10. additional
   13. approximately
more (pert to)...
   cunning.. 5. slyer 6. tricky
   difficult.. 6. harder
   distant.. 8. ulterior
   mature.. 5. older, riper
   miserly.. 6. closer, meaner, nearer
   not any.. 4. dead, past 8. vanished
   11. nonexistent
   or less.. 4. some 8. somewhat
   13. approximately
   over.. 3. and 4. also, else
   7. besides, further, thereto
   precious.. 6. dearer
   relative.. 11. comparative
   severe.. 7. sterner
   so.. 3. yea
   than.. 4. over 5. above 6. beyond
   9. exceeding 10. in excess of
   than enough.. 3. too
   than one.. 4. many 6. plural
   7. several
   than this.. 3. yes

   unusual.. 5. rarer
   vapid.. 6. staler
morel... 6. fungus 8. mushroom
morello... 4. ruru 6. cherry
   7. boobook 8. morepork, mulberry
   (color)
morena... 8. brunette
mores... 7. customs, manners
   9. etiquette 11. conventions
Moreton Bay... 9. Australia
Morgan... 5. horse 10. sea dweller
morganatic marriage...
   10. left–handed (royal)
morgay... 7. dogfish
morglay... 5. sword
morgue... 8. mortuary 9. deadhouse,
   stolidity 11. haughtiness, impassivity
Morgue (The)... 17. Library of
Congress
moribund... 4. sick 5. dying 9. near
death
moriform... 14. mulberry–shaped
morindin dye... 2. al
morion... 6. helmet, quartz 8. cabasset
Mormon Church (pert to)...
   Band (Polit).. 6. Danite (1837)
   cricket.. 11. grasshopper
   emblem.. 3. bee
   Indian.. 8. Lamanite
   instrument.. 4. Urim 7. Thummin
   officer.. 5. Elder
   official name.. 36. Church of Jesus
   Christ of Latter Day Saints
   patriarch.. 11. Joseph Smith
   12. Brigham Young
   prophet.. 6. Moroni
   State.. 4. Utah
   tea plant.. 7. Brigham
   tree.. 11. black poplar
morning (pert to)...
   clouds.. 4. velo
   coat.. 7. cutaway
   concert.. 6. aubade
   glory.. 3. nil 7. ipomoea
   14. Convolvulaceae
   goddess.. 3. Eos
   performance.. 7. matinee
   prayer.. 5. matin
   reception.. 5. levee
   star.. 4. Mars 5. Venus 6. Saturn
   7. Daystar, Jupiter, Lucifer, Mercury
   8. Phosphor
   term.. 4. dawn 5. matin, wight
   6. Aurora 7. sunrise 9. matutinal
moro... 5. finch
moro (comb form)... 6. stupid
Moro... 6. Moslem
Morocco...
   capital.. 5. Rabat
   city.. 7. Tangier 10. Casablanca
   color.. 3. red
   enclave.. 4. Ifni
   famed site.. 5. Casba
   hat.. 3. fez
   island.. 7. Madeira
   Jewish quarter.. 8. El Millah
   language.. 6. Arabic
   leather imitation.. 4. roan
   military expedition.. 5. harka
   millet.. 12. Johnson grass
   people.. 4. Arab, Moor 6. Berber
   plateau.. 6. mesata

ruler.. 4. king 5. malek 6. sultan
soldier.. 5. askar
morology... 5. folly 8. nonsense
moron... 4. dull 5. ament, idiot, zombi
6. nitwit, stupid 8. imbecile, sluggish
12. stupid person
morose... 4. blue, dour, glum, grum,
sour 5. moody, surly 6. crusty,
gloomy, sullen 7. crabbed, unhappy
9. splenetic 10. embittered
Morpheus (Gr)... 10. god of Sleep
11. god of Dreams
morphine... 6. heroin 8. hypnotic
9. analgesic, calmative
morphology... 7. anatomy 8. cytology
9. histology 10. embryology
12. organography
morris... 4. game 5. chair, dance
morro... 4. hill 6. Castle (Havana)
7. hillock 11. point of land
Mors (Rom)... 5. Death, deity
Morse... 4. code, lamp 8. alphabet
morsel... 3. ort 4. bite, chip 5. piece,
scran (sl), scrap, snack 6. tidbit,
titbit 7. morceau 8. delicacy,
fragment 11. small amount
mort... 4. dead, lard 5. death, fatal
6. deadly, grease, salmon
9. abundance
mortacious... 4. very 9. extremely
mortal... 5. fatal, human 6. deadly,
lethal 10. perishable
mortally... 5. amort 6. deadly 7. à la
mort, deathly, fatally 9. extremely
10. grievously
mortar... 3. rab 4. bowl 5. putty
6. cannon 7. mortier 10. night light
(Hist)
mortarboard... 3. cap (Acad)
mortgage... 4. bond, pawn 6. pledge
mortician... 8. embalmer
10. undertaker 15. funeral director
mortification... 5. decay, shame
7. chagrin 8. gangrene, vexation
11. humiliation
mortify... 5. abase, abash, abuse,
shame, spite 6. ashame, deaden,
humble 7. chagrin 9. embarrass,
humiliate
mortis causa... 15. by reason of
death
mortise, mortice... 6. cavity, insert
8. amortize 10. foundation
mortuary... 4. gift (burial) 6. morgue
7. funeral 8. funereal 9. deadhouse,
sepulcher 10. cinerarium
12. corsepresent (offering, Hist)
mosaic... 5. virus 6. design
7. ceramic, picture 10. decoration,
variegated 11. tessellated
mosaic (pert to)...
apply.. 7. incrust
gold.. 6. ormolu
law.. 5. Torah (Moses)
piece.. 7. tessera
Moscow...
capital of.. 6. Russia
citadel.. 7. Kremlin
river.. 6. Moskva
shrine.. 9. Lenin Tomb, Red Square
Third Internat.. 9. Comintern
Moselle... 4. Saar, wine 5. river,

Ruwer 9. Rhine wine
Moses (pert to)...
Bible.. 7. prophet 8. lawgiver
brother.. 5. Aaron
emissary.. 5. Caleb
father.. 5. Amram
father–in–law.. 6. Jethro
law.. 5. Torah (Tora) 10. Pentateuch
mother.. 8. Jochebed
mountain.. 4. Nebo
sister.. 6. Miriam
successor.. 6. Joshua
wife.. 8. Zipporah
mosey... 6. depart, stroll 7. shuffle
Moslem... 5. Hanif, Islam, Salar
7. Saracen 9. Mussulman
10. Mohammedan
Moslem (pert to)...
ablution.. 4. wudu (widu, wuzu)
cap.. 3. fez, taj
capturer of Jerusalem.. 4. Omar
caste.. 5. mopla (moplah)
chief.. 4. dato (datto), rais
city (holy).. 5. Mecca
college, school.. 8. madrasah
(madrasa, madrasseh)
dagger.. 7. khanjar
deity.. 5. Allah, Eblis
devil.. 5. Eblis
devotee.. 6. santon 7. dervish
Easter.. 3. Eed
guide (spiritual).. 3. pir
interpreter.. 5. ulema
invocation.. 9. bismillah
javelin.. 6. jereed
judge.. 4. cadi
lawyer.. 5. mufti
market, booth.. 4. sook
monastery.. 5. ribat 7. khankah
mosque.. 6. masjid
noble.. 4. amir (ameer), emir
officer.. 5. dewan (diwan)
pilgrimage to Mecca.. 4. hadj
prayer.. 4. azan (adan)
priest.. 4. imam (imaum)
saint.. 3. pir 6. santon 8. Marabout
sect.. 5. Senusi (Senousi, Senussite)
shrine, Mecca.. 5. Kaaba (Caaba,
Kaabeh)
teacher.. 4. Alim 8. mujtahid
title.. 3. Sid 5. Sayid (Said)
tradition.. 7. Al Sirat (Bridge to
Paradise)
tribesman.. 4. Moro
Turkish.. 5. Salar
university.. 8. madrasah (madrasa)
viceroy.. 7. Saracen
mosque... 4. Omar 5. Kaaba (Caaba)
6. masjid 11. Great Mosque
mosque tower... 7. minaret
mosque warden... 5. nazir
mosquito (pert to)...
bite preventive.. 10. culicifuge
coast.. 8. Honduras 9. Nicaragua
comb form.. 6. culici
destroyer.. 8. culicide
disease.. 7. malaria 11. yellow fever
family.. 7. Culicidae
fish.. 8. gambusia
genus.. 5. Aedes, Culex 7. Diptera
8. Mansonia 9. Anopheles, Culicidae
10. Psorophora

hawk .. **9.** dragonfly, nighthawk
Indian drink .. **6.** mushla
larvae .. **8.** wigglers
plant .. **4.** mint **10.** pennyroyal
shaped .. **10.** culiciform
term .. **7.** culicid **11.** gallinipper
moss ... **3.** bog, rag **4.** agar **5.** Maium,
money, Musci, swamp **6.** lichen,
morass **7.** skeeter **8.** agar–agar
9. treebeard
moss (pert to) ...
back .. **4.** dodo, fogy (fogey) **9.** old
turtle **10.** fuddy–duddy, Southerner
(1861) **12.** conservative
berry .. **9.** cranberry
capsule .. **9.** operculum
color .. **5.** green
coral .. **8.** bryozoan
duck .. **7.** mallard **8.** moss–head
9. merganser
fish .. **8.** menhaden **10.** mossbunker
grown .. **10.** antiquated
kind .. **4.** peat **7.** Spanish
like .. **6.** mnioid
mossy ... **4.** dull **5.** boggy, downy
6. marshy, stupid **9.** crumbling
most ... **7.** highest, maximum
8. greatest, main part, majority
9. nearly all
most favorable ... **7.** optimum
Most High ... **3.** God **12.** Supreme
Being
most northerly land ... **5.** Thule
mot ... **5.** adage, maxim, motto
7. opinion **9.** witticism
mote ... **4.** atom, hill, iota **5.** match,
speck, squib **6.** barrow, height, trifle
7. tumulus **8.** eminence, particle
mote nut ... **5.** carap
motet ... **4.** hymn **6.** anthem, choral
moth ... **2.** io **5.** egger, tinea
6. lappet, miller **7.** noctuid, Tineina
8. forester (8–spotted), Tineidae
9. Tineoidea **11.** Lepidoptera
moth (pert to) ...
hawk .. **10.** goatsucker
kind .. **5.** gypsy **6.** carpet **9.** browntail
spot (Med) .. **8.** chloasma
spot (wing) .. **8.** fenestra
mother ... **2.** ma **3.** dam **4.** amma
5. adopt, mamma, mater **6.** abbess,
parent **7.** care for, creator
8. ancestor, begetter, genetrix,
producer **10.** procreator
mother (pert to) ...
church .. **9.** cathedral **16.** Christian
Science
goddess .. **6.** matris **7.** Shaktis
10. sapta–matri (7 mothers)
goddess of motherhood (Egypt) ..
4. Isis
godmother .. **4.** Rhea **6.** cummer
(kimmer) **9.** Brigantia
Goose character .. **5.** Simon, Sprat
6. Bo–peep
Govt .. **10.** matriarchy, metrocracy
house .. **7.** convent **9.** monastery
Hubbard .. **4.** gown **5.** dress
Maid .. **10.** Virgin Mary
Mother Carey's chickens .. **7.** petrels
(stormy)
Myth (Gr) .. **5.** Niobe

related .. **6.** enatic
spiritual .. **4.** amma
Tagalog .. **3.** Ina
motherly ... **8.** maternal
mother of ...
Castor .. **4.** Leda
gods .. **4.** Rhea **9.** Brigantia
Graces .. **5.** Aegle
Nature .. **6.** Cybele
Night .. **3.** Nox, Nyx
pearl .. **5.** nacre **7.** abalone
presidents .. **8.** Virginia
States .. **8.** Virginia
the month .. **4.** Moon
motif ... **5.** theme, topic **6.** edging
7. subject
motion ... **3.** bob **4.** lipe, move
5. impel, trend **6.** seesaw, travel,
tremor, unrest **7.** gesture, propose,
request, suggest **8.** kinetics, mobility,
movement, petition
motionless ... **5.** inert, rigid, still
6. static **8.** immobile, stagnant
10. stationary, stock–still
motion picture terms ... **4.** film, show
5. flick, klieg (light), movie, rerun
6. cinema **7.** cartoon, feature
9. filmstrip, videotape **11.** golden
oldie **12.** silver screen
motivate ... **4.** move **5.** force, impel
6. compel, incite, induce, propel
7. actuate, animate, promote, trigger
9. stimulate
motive ... **4.** sake, spur **5.** cause,
motif, topic **6.** reason **7.** pretext
8. stimulus **9.** incentive, influence,
intention **10.** incitement, inducement
11. instigation **13.** consideration
motley ... **5.** mixed **6.** fabric
7. diverse, mixture, mottled
9. checkered, diversity **10.** variegated
12. parti–colored **13.** heterogeneous
motor ... **5.** mover, rotor **6.** Diesel,
dynamo, engine **7.** turbine **8.** motor
car **9.** locomotor **10.** automobile
motor speed control ... **8.** governor,
rheocrat
mottled ... **3.** roe **4.** pied **5.** pinto
6. calico **7.** dappled, marbled,
piebald, spotted **13.** pepper–and–salt
mottled soap ... **7.** castile
motto ... **3.** mot **5.** adage, axiom,
gnome, maxim **6.** advice **7.** empresa
(impresa), precept **8.** aphorism
9. principle **11.** inscription
motto of ...
Boy Scouts .. **10.** Be Prepared
Coast Guard .. **11.** Always Ready
13. Semper paratus
Order of the Garter .. **20.** Honi soit qui
mal y pense
Queen Elizabeth .. **11.** Semper Eadem
13. Always the Same
mouche ... **5.** patch (black)
mouchoir ... **12.** handkerchief
mouflon, moufflon ... **5.** sheep
mould, mold ... **5.** knead **6.** matrix
moulrush ... **7.** pollack (food fish)
mound ... **3.** dam, dun, tee **4.** bank,
dene, doon, dune, heap, hill, terp,
tomb, tump **5.** knoll **6.** bounds
7. barrier, bulwark, rampart, tumulus

8. boundary 9. elevation
10. embankment 13. fortification
mound (pert to) . . .
bird . . 8. megapode
City . . 7. St Louis
lily . . 5. yucca
memorial . . 5. cairn
of light . . 8. Kohinoor (diamond)
Polynesian . . 3. ahu
prehistoric . . 5. matte
Scottish . . 5. toman
mount . . . 3. fly, set (jewel) 4. glue,
hill, lift, pony (polo), rise 5. arise,
climb, horse, paste 6. ascent
7. elevate 8. increase, mountain
10. promontory
Mount (pert to) . . .
Etna city . . 7. Catania
Everest peak . . 6. Lhotse
Parnassus fountain, spring . . 8. Castalia
mountain . . .
Africa . . 11. Kilimanjaro
Alaska . . 8. McKinley
Asia . . 7. Everest
Babylonia . . 6. Ararat
California . . 6. Shasta 7. Whitney
Crete . . 3. Ida
Europe . . 4. Ural 8. Pyrenees
fabled . . 4. Meru
Greek (Myth) . . 7. Helicon
Japan . . 8. Fujiyama
legendary . . 3. Kaf, Qaf (Moslem)
4. Meru
Mexico . . 12. Popocatepetl
Montana . . 6. Tetons
Switzerland . . 4. Alps 10. Matterhorn
Thessaly . . 4. Ossa 6. Pelion
U S Chain . . 5. Rocky 7. Sawback,
Sierras 9. Blue Ridge
11. Appalachian
Yukon . . 5. Logan
mountain (pert to) . . .
ash . . 5. rowan
badger . . 6. marmot
balsam . . 3. fit
banana . . 3. fei
barometer . . 8. orometer
beaver . . 8. sewellel
blackbird . . 5. ouzel
cat . . 4. lynx 6. bobcat, cougar
10. cacomistle
comb form . . 3. oro
cowslip . . 8. auricula
crest, spur . . 5. arête
curassow (pheasant) . . 10. oreophasis
defile . . 3. gap 4. gate, ghat (ghaut),
pass 5. gorge
depression . . 3. col
dew . . 6. whisky
eagle . . 6. golden
goat . . 4. ibex
highest . . 7. Everest
ice . . 4. berg 7. glacier
ivy . . 6. laurel
lake . . 4. tarn
lion . . 4. puma 6. cougar
lodge . . 4. gite
low . . 5. butte
nymph . . 5. oread
oak . . 8. chestnut
peak . . 3. tor
raspberry . . 10. cloudberry

rose . . 6. laurel
sheep . . 7. bighorn 13. Rocky
Mountain
shrub . . 10. fetterbush
sickness . . 7. soroche
State . . 7. Montana
sunset . . 9. alpenglow
Tatars . . 5. Tauli
witch . . 9. quail dove
mountaineer . . . 7. climber
11. backsettler
mountains, science of . . . 7. orology
9. orography
mountant . . . 6. raised, rising
8. mounting 9. ascendant
mountebank . . . 4. gull 5. cheat, quack
7. buffoon, empiric 8. impostor
9. charlatan, pretender 11. quack
doctor
mounted men . . . 7. knights
mounting . . . 6. ascent 7. rimbase,
seating, setting 9. adjusting,
equipment 13. embellishment
mourn . . . 3. rue 4. erme, long, sigh,
wail, weep 6. bemoan, bewail,
grieve, lament, murmur, repine,
sorrow 7. deplore
mourner . . . 6. keener, wailer 7. griever
8. lamenter
mournful . . . 3. sad 6. repine 7. elegiac
8. grievous 9. elegiacal, plaintive,
saddening, sorrowful, threnodic,
woebegone
mournful poem . . . 5. elegy
mourning . . . 3. sad 4. garb 5. crape,
weeds (dress) 6. lament, sorrow
7. drapery 9. sorrowing 10. black
badge 11. lamentation
mourning dress . . . 5. weeds 6. sables
mouse . . . 3. erd, Mus 4. buck, vole
5. prowl, shrew 6. jerboa, migale
7. harvest, toy with
mouse (pert to) . . .
bird . . 4. coly 6. shrike
color . . 4. gray
deer . . 7. plandok 10. chevrotain
ear . . 8. hawkweed 9. bloodwort,
chickweed 11. forget–me–not
fish . . 9. sargassum
hare . . 4. pika
hound . . 6. weasel
kind . . 6. pocket 7. harvest, jumping
leaping . . 6. jerboa
milk . . 6. spurge
mouselike . . 6. murine
web . . 6. cobweb, phlegm
8. gossamer
mousse . . . 7. dessert 9. moss green
12. gelatine dish
moutan . . . 5. peony
mouth . . . 2. os 3. mow, mun 4. boca,
dupe, lade, lick 5. inlet, stoma
6. cavity, rictus 7. declaim, opening,
orifice 8. aperture, lorriker
9. impudence
mouth (pert to) . . .
away from . . 6. aboral
deformity . . 7. harelip
disease . . 6. canker 10. stomatitis
furnace . . 5. bocca
glands . . 8. salivary
muscle . . 7. caninus

organ.. **4.** harp **7.** Pandean
  8. jew's–harp **9.** crembalum,
  harmonica
part.. **3.** lip **5.** uvula **6.** palate
  7. pharynx
pert to.. **4.** oral **6.** rictal, stomal
  8. stomatic
piece (Mus).. **10.** embouchure
through the.. **7.** peroral
tissue.. **3.** gum
toward.. **4.** orad
wide, gaping.. **6.** rictus
mouthed, loud... **11.** thersitical
mouton... **5.** sheep **9.** prison spy
movable... **6.** mobile **10.** changeable
  12. transferable
movable property... **8.** chattels
move... **3.** act, gee, mog, say
  4. goad, sell, spur, stir **5.** budge,
  cause, impel, rouse, shift **6.** excite,
  incite, induce, kindle, motion,
  prompt, travel **7.** actuate, advance,
  animate, propose, provoke
  9. instigate, recommend, stimulate
move (pert to)...
about.. **8.** locomote
along.. **5.** mosey, scram **7.** maunder
back.. **3.** ebb **6.** recede, retire, revert
  7. retreat **10.** retrogress
back and forth.. **6.** teeter, wigwag
  7. shuttle **9.** oscillate
clumsily.. **4.** joll
false.. **4.** balk **5.** feint
forward.. **4.** edge, scud **5.** drive
  7. advance **8.** progress
furtively.. **5.** slink, sneak
heavily.. **3.** lug **6.** fidget, lumber,
  trudge
in circles.. **4.** purl
place to place.. **7.** migrate
  8. emigrate
quickly.. **3.** ply **4.** dart, dash, scud,
  shot **5.** scoot, spank **6.** bustle,
  gallop, hurtle
restlessly.. **6.** kelter
rhythmically.. **5.** dance
sideways, sidewise.. **4.** slue **5.** sidle
slowly.. **3.** jog, lag **4.** edge, inch,
  pant
smoothly.. **4.** slip **5.** glide, skate,
  slide
spasmodically.. **6.** twitch
to and fro.. **3.** wag **4.** flap, sway
together.. **5.** unite **8.** converge
towards each other.. **8.** converge
towards the east.. **9.** orientate
unsteadily.. **4.** reel **6.** wabble
  7. stagger
up and down.. **3.** bob **6.** teeter
with exertion.. **5.** heave
with measured tread.. **5.** march
moved by entreaty... **8.** exorable
moved easily... **5.** loped **6.** mobile
  8. affected **9.** emotional
movement... **5.** cause, trend **6.** action,
  motion, rhythm, travel **7.** emotion,
  gesture, impulse **8.** activity,
  maneuver, progress
movement (pert to)...
backwards.. **13.** retrogression
dance step.. **4.** lilt **6.** chassé
  9. pirouette

music.. **4.** moto **7.** con moto
of ships.. **5.** heave, pitch, scend
of waves.. **4.** roll, toss **5.** surge
  6. tumble, welter
vibratory.. **6.** tremor
moving... **6.** active, motile **7.** nomadic
  8. eloquent, exciting, pathetic
  9. affecting, impelling, traveling
  10. motivating
moving stairway... **9.** escalator
mow... **3.** cut, lay, mew **4.** dess, fell,
  heap, mass, math, mock, raze, stow
  5. mouth, stack **6.** garner, smooth
  7. cut down, grimace, harvest,
  shorten **9.** cornfield
mowana... **6.** baobab
mowing... **7.** cutting, mockery
  8. derision **9.** grimacing
  10. harvesting, meadowland
mowing machine... **5.** mower
  6. scythe, sickle
moxieberry... **9.** snowberry
moy... **4.** mild **6.** demure, gentle
  8. affected
moyen... **3.** way **5.** means **6.** agency,
  course **8.** property **9.** influence
Mozambique...
Bay.. **8.** Mossuril
capital.. **15.** Lourenco Marques
native.. **3.** Yao
port.. **10.** Mozambique
mozo... **10.** manservant
Mrs... **5.** madam **8.** goodwife, Mistress
mucaro... **3.** owl
much... **3.** lot **4.** high, many **5.** great
  7. greatly **8.** abundant, uncommon
  9. great deal **10.** indefinite
  12. considerable
muchacha... **4.** girl, lass
muchacho... **3.** boy, lad **7.** servant
mucid... **5.** musty, slimy **6.** clammy,
  mucous **8.** muculent
mucilage... **3.** gum **5.** paste
  6. mucago **8.** adhesive **9.** lubricant
mucilaginous... **5.** moist **6.** sticky,
  viscid
muckender... **12.** handkerchief
mucker... **4.** fall (from a horse), mess
  6. muddle, wretch **8.** disorder
  9. confusion, vulgarian
muckle... **4.** club, fret **6.** bother,
  putter
muckraker... **7.** defamer **8.** vilifier
  9. slanderer
mud... **4.** mire, muck, silt, slop
  5. abuse, gumbo, limus, shine
  6. gobbet, sludge **12.** offscourings
  14. abusive charges
mud (pert to)...
bath.. **10.** illutation
dab.. **8.** flounder
dauber.. **4.** wasp
devil.. **10.** hellbender
eel.. **5.** siren
hole.. **6.** puddle **8.** quagmire
lark.. **5.** gamin, horse **6.** magpie,
  urchin
like.. **7.** luteous
living in.. **10.** limicolous
peep.. **9.** sandpiper **11.** meadow pipit
pike.. **5.** saury
puppy.. **10.** hellbender, salamander

rake .. **5.** claut
shoveler .. **13.** spoonbill duck
snipe .. **8.** woodcock
sunfish .. **4.** bass **8.** warmouth
teal .. **9.** greenwing
volcano .. **5.** salse
Mudcat State ... **11.** Mississippi
muddle ... **3.** mix **4.** daze, mess, soss,
  stir **5.** addle, botch, snafu **6.** bemuse,
  bollix, jumble **7.** confuse, perplex,
  stupefy **8.** befuddle, bewilder,
  confound, disorder, squander
  10. intoxicate **11.** predicament
muddled ... **3.** ree **5.** drunk, muzzy,
  tipsy **7.** burbled, fuddled **8.** confused
  9. befuddled, entangled
muddlehead ... **4.** dolt **9.** blockhead
muddy ... **4.** base, miry **5.** dingy, dirty,
  roily, slaky **6.** lutose, opaque, slushy,
  turbid **7.** clouded, obscure
  8. confused **9.** besmeared
muddy places ... **7.** wallows
muezzin ... **4.** azan (adan) **5.** crier
  (Moham)
muff ... **5.** beard, cover **6.** bungle
  7. bungler, failure **8.** feathers
  11. mollycoddle, whitethroat
muffed ... **5.** vexed **7.** crested
  9. irritated
muffet ... **11.** whitethroat
muffetee ... **7.** muffler **8.** wristlet
muffin ... **3.** cob, gem **5.** bread, hazel,
  plate, scone **7.** biscuit, crumpet,
  English, popover
muffle ... **3.** gag **4.** damp, dull, mute,
  wrap **6.** deaden, mumble, shroud,
  stifle **7.** conceal **8.** decorate,
  envelope **9.** blindfold, soft-pedal
muffler ... **3.** gag **4.** mute **5.** scarf
  6. muzzle, tippet **8.** silencer
  10. suppressor
mufflin ... **8.** titmouse
mufti ... **5.** dress (civilian)
mufti (Moham) ... **4.** alim **5.** judge
  6. priest **8.** assessor, official
mug ... **3.** cup **4.** cram, dupe, face,
  fool, Toby **5.** mungo, pulse, sheep,
  study **6.** noggin **9.** drizzle, grimace
  8. quantity **10.** photograph
muga ... **4.** moth, silk **11.** caterpillar
mugger ... **3.** goa **6.** robber, tinker
  7. peddler **9.** crocodile
mugget ... **8.** woodruff **15.** lily of the
  valley
muggins (game) ... **5.** cards **7.** penalty
  8. dominoes
muggy ... **4.** damp, warm **5.** humid,
  moist, moldy **6.** sticky, stuffy, sultry
  10. sweltering **11.** whitethroat
mug house ... **6.** tavern **7.** barroom
  8. alehouse, pothouse
mugient ... **6.** lowing **9.** bellowing
mugwump ... **5.** chief **8.** apostate,
  objector **11.** independent, nonpartisan
  16. Republican bolter
Muhammed ... see *Mohammed*
muir ... **4.** wall
muirfowl ... **9.** red grouse
muishond ... **5.** zoril **6.** weasel
mujer ... **4.** wife **5.** woman
mulberry ... **2.** al **5.** Morus **6.** murrey
  10. blackberry **12.** thimbleberry

mulberry (pert to) ...
bark (paper) .. **4.** tapa (tappa)
beverage .. **5.** morat
bird .. **8.** starling
dye .. **3.** aal **8.** morindin
fig .. **8.** sycamore
purple .. **7.** blue–red **8.** camerier
tree .. **5.** Morus
wild .. **7.** yawweed
mulch ... **5.** straw **6.** ground, leaves
  7. sawdust
mulct ... **4.** fine, scot **6.** amerce,
  defect, punish **7.** blemish, deceive,
  penalty, swindle **10.** amercement
mulcter ... **7.** amercer
mule ... **4.** mewl, mool, mute **5.** coble,
  hinny, jenny **6.** acemia, hybrid
  7. slipper, tractor **9.** chilblain
  10. crossbreed, locomotive
  15. obstinate person
mule (pert to) ...
chair .. **7.** cacolet
driver .. **7.** skinner **8.** muleteer
drove .. **5.** atajo
killer .. **6.** mantis
leading .. **8.** cencerro
skinner .. **6.** driver
untrained .. **9.** shavetail
muleteer ... **4.** peon **6.** driver
mulga ... **6.** acacia, shield
muliebria ... **8.** feminine
muliebriety ... **9.** womanhood
  10. femininity **11.** womanliness
mulier ... **4.** wife **5.** woman **6.** mother
mulish ... **6.** hybrid, sullen **7.** asinine,
  sterile **8.** stubborn **9.** obstinate
mull ... **3.** cow **4.** crag, dust, heat,
  mess, mold **5.** crush, grind, snout,
  spice **6.** fumble, muddle, muslin,
  muzzle, ponder **7.** failure, rubbish,
  squeeze, steatin, sweeten **8.** cogitate,
  consider, ointment, ruminate, snuffbox
  9. pulverize **10.** promontory
  11. contemplate
mullah ... **6.** priest **7.** teacher (Moham)
mullet ... **4.** bobo, fish, star **6.** puffin
mullet hawk ... **6.** osprey
mulligan ... **4.** stew
mulligatawny ... **4.** soup
mulligrubs ... **5.** blues, colic, sulks
mullock ... **5.** spoil, waste **6.** refuse
  (mine) **7.** rubbish
mulloway ... **7.** jewfish
multi (comb form) ... **4.** many
multifarious ... **8.** manifold
  9. multifold, multiplex **10.** multiphase
multifold ... **7.** diverse **8.** manifold,
  multiple, numerous
multilingual ... **8.** polyglot
multiped ... **10.** many–footed
multiplier ... **6.** bulbil **7.** facient
  8. operator
multiply ... **5.** breed **6.** spread
  7. amplify, magnify **8.** increase
  9. calculate, pluralize, procreate
multitude ... **3.** mob **4.** host, many,
  mass, much **5.** crowd, horde, shoal,
  swarm **6.** legion, throng **7.** myriads
  8. populace **9.** profusion
  11. bourgeoisie **12.** numerousness
multitudinous ... **6.** myriad
mum ... **3.** ale **4.** mute **6.** silent

8. taciturn 11. not speaking
mumble ... 4. chew, mump 6. chavel, fumble, mutter, patter
mumbo jumbo ... 6. genius 7. bugaboo 12. superstition 13. awesome person
mummer ... 5. actor 6. guiser 7. buffoon 9. performer
mummy ... 5. brown, Congo (color), relic 6. corpse, mother 7. cadaver, carcass
mummy apple ... 6. papaya
mump ... 3. beg 5. cheat, sulks 6. mumble, sponge 7. deceive, grimace 10. impose upon
mumpish ... 4. dull, glum 5. sulky 6. sullen
mumruffin ... 8. titmouse
mundane ... 6. cosmic 7. earthly, horizon, secular, terrene, worldly 8. temporal 11. unspiritual
mundatory ... 9. cleansing 11. purificator
mundil ... 6. turban (embroidered)
mungo ... 4. herb, wool (reclaimed) 8. mongoose, mung bean 13. mongoose plant
municipal ... 5. civic, urban 7. oppidan 9. political 10. municipium
munificence ... 6. bounty 7. largess (largesse) 10. generosity, liberality 13. bounteousness, unselfishness
muniment ... 6. record 7. defense 8. evidence, writings 9. valuables 10. furnishing 13. fortification
munity ... see *immunity* 9. privilege
munshi (Hind) ... 6. writer 7. teacher 9. secretary 11. interpreter
muntjac, muntjak ... 5. kakar, ratwa 6. kidang
mura (Jap) ... 7. village 9. community
Mura ... 6. Indian
mural ... 4. wall (pert to) 5. crown 8. painting
murder ... 4. kill, slay 7. carnage 8. homicide 9. slaughter 11. assassinate 12. manslaughter
murder of ...
brother .. 10. fratricide
father .. 9. patricide
king .. 8. regicide
mother .. 9. matricide
own child .. 9. prolicide
parent .. 9. parricide
prophet .. 8. vaticide
sister .. 10. sororicide
spouse (by the other) .. 10. mariticide
wife .. 9. uxoricide
woman .. 8. femicide
murderous ... 4. gory 5. cruel 6. bloody, deadly, savage 7. killing 10. sanguinary 12. bloodthirsty
mure ... 4. meek, soft, wall 6. gentle, immure, modest 8. imprison
murk, mirk ... 3. fog 4. dark, mist 5. gloom 6. opaque 7. blacken 8. darkness 9. dark color 11. dark-colored
murky, mirky ... 4. dark 5. dense, foggy, thick 6. gloomy, opaque 7. obscure, stained 11. dark-colored 12. impenetrable

murmur ... 3. coo, hum 4. blow, curr, fret, purl 6. babble, mutter, repine 7. trickle, whisper 8. complain
muscle ... 4. beef, thew 5. brawn, sinew, teres 6. flexor, lacert, tensor 8. lacertus, retentor
muscle (pert to) ...
affection .. 5. crick 6. ataxia
bending .. 6. flexor
chemistry .. 6. inosic 8. inosinic
column .. 10. sarcostyle
contracting .. 7. agonist
expander .. 7. dilator
extending .. 8. extensor
eyeball .. 6. rectus
lifting .. 7. levator
loin, tenderloin .. 5. psoas
lower .. 9. depressor
raising .. 7. deltoid, erector, levator
recording .. 8. ergogram 9. ergograph
round .. 5. teres
segment .. 8. myocomma
sense .. 11. kinesthesia
separating .. 11. divaricator
spasm .. 5. tonus
stretching .. 6. tensor
sugar .. 8. inositol
trapezius .. 10. cucullaris
triangular .. 7. deltoid
turning .. 7. evertor, rotator
two-headed .. 6. biceps
muscovite ... 4. mica 11. yellow-green
Muscovite ... 7. Russian
muscular ... 4. wiry 5. beefy, thewy 6. brawny, mighty, sinewy, strong, torose 8. athletic, stalwart, vigorous
muscular (pert to) ...
contraction (involuntary) .. 3. tic 5. spasm
co-ordination .. 7. synergy
in-co-ordination .. 6. ataxia 15. locomotor ataxia
non-co-ordination in walking .. 6. abasia
spasm .. 5. tonus
stomach .. 7. gizzard
muse ... 4. mull, poet, rune 5. dream 6. ponder 7. bagpipe, reverie 8. cogitate, consider, meditate, ruminate
Muse of ...
astronomy .. 6. Urania
choral song .. 11. Terpsichore
comedy .. 6. Thalia
dancing .. 11. Terpsichore
eloquence .. 8. Calliope
history .. 4. Clio
joy .. 4. Tara
music .. 7. Euterpe
poetry .. 5. Erato (lyric) 6. Thalia (bucolic) 8. Calliope (heroic)
tragedy .. 9. Melpomene
Muses ... 4. Clio 5. Erato 6. Thalia, Urania 7. Euterpe 8. Calliope, Polymnia (Polyhymnia) 9. Melpomene 11. Terpsichore
Muses (pert to) ...
epithet .. 7. Pierian
fountain .. 8. Aganippe (near Thebes)
mother of .. 9. Mnemosyne
mountain .. 6. Pierus 7. Helicon 9. Parnassus

number .. 4. nine
sacred place .. 5. Aonia (Boeotia)
spring .. 7. Pierian
The Muses (Gr) .. 8. Pierides
musette ... 3. air, bag 4. oboe
   7. bagpipe, gavotte
museum ... 6. Louvre 7. gallery
   8. Ptolemy I 10. Pinakothek
   11. glyptotheca, pinakotheke
   14. Madame Tussaud's
museum keeper ... 7. curator
   9. custodian
mush ... 3. cut 4. call, face, pulp
   5. atole, march (over snow), notch
   6. cereal, indent, sepawn 8. flattery,
   umbrella 12. hasty pudding
   14. sentimentality
mushroom ... 5. morel, plant 6. agaric,
   anchor, fungus 7. parvenu, upstart
   8. umbrella 11. beaver brown
mushroom (pert to) ...
disease .. 5. flock
edible .. 5. morel 11. chanterelle
poisoning .. 8. mycetism
poisonous .. 7. amanita 9. toadstool
stem .. 5. stipe
umbrella top .. 6. pileus
music (pert to) ...
abridgment .. 7. ridotto
accompaniment .. 9. obbligato
aftersong .. 5. epode
all voices .. 5. tutti
as written .. 3. sta
chapel .. 9. a cappella
character .. 3. bar, key 4. clef, rest,
   slur 5. cleft, neume, segno
chord .. 8. arpeggio
clear–cut .. 8. staccato
closing measure .. 4. coda
comic .. 6. bouffe
do .. 2. ut
drama .. 5. opera
duet .. 3. duo
encore .. 3. bis
flourish .. 7. cadenza
half note .. 5. minim
half tone .. 8. semitone
impassioned, emotional ..
   12. appassionato
interlude .. 6. verset
interval .. 6. octave 7. tritone
introduction .. 7. prelude
it proceeds .. 2. va
knowledge .. 10. musicology
lead cue .. 5. presa
left–handed .. 8. sinistra
light notes .. 6. ottava
low pitch .. 5. grave
lutelike .. 10. hurdy–gurdy
major .. 3. dur
major third .. 6. ditone
melodious .. 6. arioso
melody .. 5. melos
nine–piece composition .. 5. nonet
one performer (choral) .. 4. soli
opera (comic) .. 6. bouffe
organization .. 4. band 5. Ascap, choir
   6. chorus 8. symphony 9. orchestra
organ stop .. 6. dulcet, tromba
   7. celesta
performance .. 7. recital
phrase .. 9. leitmotiv (leitmotif)

pick .. 8. plectrum
pitch C .. 2. du
pompous .. 7. orotund
refrain .. 5. epode 8. repetend
repetition .. 5. rondo
scale .. 5. gamut
sestet .. 7. sestuor
sextuplet .. 7. sestole (sestolet)
soprano part .. 5. canto
speaking part .. 8. parlando
study .. 5. étude
tenor part .. 5. canto (original)
theme .. 4. tema
third .. 6. tierce
three–chord note .. 5. triad
thrice .. 3. ter
time .. 4. temp 6. giusto
timing device .. 9. metronome
twice .. 3. bis
variations, set of .. 7. partita
whimsical .. 8. bizzarro 9. capriccio
musical direction (pert to) ...
accented .. 8. sforzato 9. sforzando
bold .. 6. audace
brisk .. 5. tanto 7. animato
detached .. 8. spiccato, staccato
dying away .. 7. calendo
emphatic .. 7. marcato
evenly .. 10. egualmente
fantastic .. 11. carpiccioso
fast .. 4. vivo 5. tosto 6. presto,
   vivace 10. tostamente
faster .. 7. stretto
fluctuating .. 6. rubato
gay .. 7. giocoso 10. brilliante
gentle .. 5. dolce
half .. 5. mezzo
held firmly .. 6. tenuto
high .. 3. alt
hurried .. 7. agitato
less .. 4. meno
let it stand .. 3. sta
lightly .. 10. con agilita
little by little .. 9. poco a poco
lively .. 6. vivace 7. allegro, animato
loud .. 5. forte 10. fortissimo
louder .. 9. crescendo
lutelike .. 10. hurdy–gurdy
more rapid .. 7. stretto (stretta)
movement (with) .. 7. con moto
muted .. 5. sorda, sordo
narrating .. 8. narrante
one by one .. 7. uno a uno
quick .. 6. presto
quickening .. 11. affrettando
quicker than .. 7. andante 9. andantino
repeat .. 3. bis 6. da capo 7. ripresa
sadly .. 7. dolente 8. doloroso
shake .. 5. trill
silent .. 5. tacet
sliding .. 9. glissando
slow .. 5. largo, lento, molto, tardo
   6. adagio 7. andante
slow (very) .. 5. molto
slowing .. 9. allentato 10. ritardando
   11. rallentando
smooth .. 6. legato
soft .. 5. dolce, piano
softer .. 10. diminuendo
spirited .. 7. con moto
strict tempo .. 6. giusto
sustained .. 6. tenuto 9. sustenuto

tenderly .. **10.** affettuoso, con affetto
turn .. **5.** verte **9.** gruppetto
vivacious .. **7.** con brio
musical form ... **3.** jig, ode **4.** aria,
   jazz, jive, olio, opus, punk (rock), scat,
   song, soul **5.** derry, dirge, disco,
   elegy, fugue, melos, motet, opera,
   salsa **6.** arioso, ballad, medley,
   melody, minuet, reggae, sonata
   7. ragtime, toccata **8.** carillon (bells),
   hornpipe, operetta, oratorio, serenade,
   symphony **9.** barcarole, bluegrass,
   interlude, polonaise **11.** rock and roll
   12. boogie woogie
musical instruments ... **3.** sax
   4. asor, drum, fife, harp, horn, lute,
   lyre, oboe, pipe, reed, tuba, viol
   5. banjo, bugle, cello, Dobro, flute,
   organ, piano, rebec (rebeck), rocta,
   tabor, viola **6.** atabal, cither, citole,
   cornet, fiddle, guitar, spinet, tabret,
   violin, zither **7.** althorn, bagpipe,
   bandore, bassoon, celesta, clarion,
   clavier, gittern, helicon, marimba,
   musette, ocarina, pandora, theorbo,
   trumpet, ukulele **8.** castanet, clarinet,
   dulcimer, keyboard, mandolin,
   trombone **9.** flageolet, saxophone
   10. concertina, sousaphone (tuba),
   tambourine **11.** harpsichord,
   synthesizer, violoncello
musical instruments (foreign) ...
   Africa .. **5.** nanga **7.** kalimba (thumb
     piano), sistrum
   China .. **3.** kin
   E Indies .. **4.** bina
   Egypt .. **7.** sistrum
   Greece .. **7.** cithara (anc)
   Hindu .. **4.** vina (anc)
   India .. **5.** ruana
   Italy .. **6.** tromba
   Japan .. **7.** samisen (shamisen)
     10. shakuhachi
   Java .. **8.** gamelang (gamelan)
   Mexico .. **6.** clarin **7.** maracas
   Spain .. **6.** atabal **9.** castanets
musician ... **4.** bard **5.** piper
   6. hepcat, lyrist, singer **7.** chorist,
   crooner, drummer, fiddler, flutist,
   pianist, yodeler **8.** bandsman,
   composer, minstrel, organist
   9. conductor, serenader, troubador,
   violinist **10.** prima donna, trombonist
   11. clarinetist, keyboardist,
   minnesinger, saxophonist
   12. interlocutor **13.** Kapellmeister
musicians' group ... **4.** band, duet, trio
   5. nonet **6.** septet, sextet **7.** nonetto,
   quartet **8.** ensemble, septette,
   sextette, symphony **9.** orchestra,
   quartette
musicians' patron saint ... **7.** Cecilia
musk ... **4.** deer **7.** perfume
musk (pert to) ...
   beaver .. **7.** muskrat
   cat .. **5.** civet
   cattle .. **4.** oxen
   cucumber .. **11.** cassabanana
   deer .. **10.** chevrotain
   duck .. **7.** Muscovy
   hog .. **7.** peccary
   melon .. **10.** cantaloupe

okra .. **8.** abelmosk
shrew .. **6.** desman
weasel .. **5.** civet
muskellunge ... **4.** fish, pike
musket ... **4.** hawk **5.** rifle **7.** firearm
   9. flintlock
Musketeers, Three ... **5.** Athos
   6. Aramis **7.** Porthos **9.** D'Artagnon
muskmelon ... **6.** atimon, casaba
   10. cantaloupe
muskrat ... **5.** shrew **6.** desman
   7. ondatra
Muslim ... see *Moslem*
muslin ... **3.** ban, cap **4.** mull **5.** doria,
   shela **6.** canvas, gurrah **7.** organdy
   8. nainsook, sheeting, tarlatan
muss ... **4.** mess, soil **5.** chaos, dirty
   6. bitter, muddle, rumple, tousle
   7. confuse, wrinkle **8.** dishevel,
   scramble, squabble **10.** disarrange
mussel ... **4.** food, naid, unio **5.** horse,
   moule, naiad **6.** byssus, mucket, nerita
   7. mollusk, Mytilus
Musselman ... **6.** Moslem **7.** Saracen
   10. Mohammedan
must ... **4.** mold, musk, sapa, stum
   5. juice, ought, shall **6.** blight,
   mildew, refuse **7.** malodor
   9. necessity **10.** obligation
mustang ... **5.** horse, pinto **6.** bronco,
   sphinx
mustard ... **5.** nigra, senvy **7.** sinapis
   8. charlock
mustard (pert to) ...
   chemistry .. **8.** sinapine
   gas .. **7.** yperite
   genus .. **7.** Sinapis **8.** Brassica
   plaster .. **8.** sinapism
Mustelidae ... **5.** minks **7.** badgers,
   martens, weasels
muster ... **4.** levy **5.** erect **6.** gather,
   summon **7.** collect, marshal
   8. assemble, comprise
   10. assemblage
muster out ... **7.** disband
musty ... **3.** bad, old **4.** damp, hoar,
   rank **5.** fetid, fusty, moist, moldy,
   rafty, stale, trite **6.** rancid **7.** pungent
mutable ... **6.** fickle **7.** erratic
   8. variable **9.** alterable, changeful
mute ... **3.** mum **4.** dumb, lene, surd
   6. muffle, silent **8.** deadener, silencer,
   taciturn **9.** voiceless **10.** speechless
mutilate ... **3.** mar **4.** geld, hack, maim
   6. deface, deform, garble, injure,
   mangle **7.** cripple, destroy **8.** castrate
   9. dismember, tear apart
mutinous ... **6.** unruly **9.** seditious,
   turbulent **10.** rebellious, refractory
   11. intractable
mutiny ... **6.** Putsch (Swiss), revolt,
   strife, tumult **9.** commotion, rebellion
   12. insurrection **15.** insubordination
mutter ... **5.** growl **6.** murmur, patter,
   plaint **7.** grumble, maunder
   8. complain **9.** mussitate
mutton ... **4.** meat **5.** cabob (kabob),
   gigot, sheep **6.** candle
muttonfish ... **4.** sama **5.** pargo
   7. abalone, eelpout, mojarra, snapper
mutual ... **4.** plan **5.** joint **6.** common

8. intimate 9. symbiotic
10. reciprocal, responsive
15. interchangeable
mutual understanding ... 9. agreement,
unanimity 12. consentience,
co-ordination 13. interrelation
17. interrelationship
mux ... 4. mess 5. batch
muy ... 4. very 7. greatly
muzhik, muzjik ... 7. peasant
muzzle ... 3. gag 4. cope, maul, nose
5. mouth, snout 6. clevis, thrash
7. shackle, sheathe, silence
8. restrain 10. respirator
my ... 3. mes, mon 4. mine 7. due to
me 11. exclamation
myall ... 4. wild, wood (fragrant)
6. acacia 11. uncivilized
mycoderma ... 5. fungi 6. mother
(formed on wine) 8. membrane
(ferment)
mycophagy ... 11. eating fungi
15. eating mushrooms
myna, mynah ... 4. bird 7. grackle
8. starling
Mynheer ... 8. Dutchman
myo (comb form) ... 6. muscle
myomancy, divination by ...
14. muscle movement
myopic ... 11. nearsighted
myriad ... 11. innumerable, ten
thousand 13. multitudinous
myriapod ... 9. centipede
myrmicid ... 3. ant
myrtle ... 8. ramarama 10. periwinkle
11. candleberry
mysterious ... 4. dark 6. arcane,
mystic, occult, secret 7. cryptic
8. abstruse, esoteric 9. recondite,
sphinxian 10. cabalistic
12. inexplicable, unfathomable
mystery ... 4. cult, rune 6. arcane,
cabala, enigma, puzzle, secret
7. arcanum, esotery, miracle
8. whodunit 9. sacrament
13. inexplainable
19. incomprehensibility
mystic ... 4. seer, yogi 5. magic, runic
6. occult, orphic, secret 7. cryptic,

Mahatma 8. cabalist, esoteric,
symbolic 9. enigmatic, recondite
10. cabalistic, mysterious
mystic (pert to) ...
cry .. 4. evoe
doctrine .. 5. cabal 7. esotery
8. esoteric
initiate .. 5. epopt (Gr Antiq)
ocean isle .. 6. Avalon
theosophy .. 6. cabala
word .. 2. om 7. abraxas
11. abracadabra
mystical ... 6. muddle, puzzle
7. confuse, cryptic, furtive, obscure
9. enigmatic, obfuscate
mystical (pert to) ...
character (Teut Myth) .. 8. Eckehart
meaning .. 7. anagoge
word .. 11. abracadabra
mystify ... 5. befog 6. muddle, puzzle
7. becloud, confuse, perplex
8. befuddle, bewilder 9. bamboozle,
obfuscate
myth ... 4. tale 5. fable, fancy, story
6. legend 7. figment, parable
9. apocrypha, falsehood
mythical ... 7. fancied 8. fabulous
9. fictional, imaginary, legendary
10. fictitious 12. mythological
mythical (pert to) ...
being .. 6. Garuda, Icarus 7. centaur,
griffin
bird .. 3. roc
deity .. 6. Moloch (tyrant)
demon .. 4. Rahu (tail called Kehu)
hero .. 4. Ajax 8. Achilles
heroine .. 4. Leda 6. Europa
8. Atalanta
hunter .. 5. Orion
island .. 8. Atlantis
king (Hind) .. 4. Nala
monster .. 4. ogre 7. chimera
mother .. 5. Niobe
river .. 4. Styx
serpent .. 5. Apepi
winged creature .. 7. Alborak
woman .. 6. Gorgon, Medusa, Stheno
7. Euryale
mythogony, science of ... 5. myths
mythologist ... 9. mythmaker

N

N ... 2. en, Nu 8. nitrogen (symbol)
nab ... 4. grab 5. catch, seize
6. arrest, nibble, snatch 7. capture
9. apprehend
Nabal's wife (Bib) ... 7. Abigail
nabob ... 5. nawab 6. bigwig, tycoon
7. viceroy 8. governor 9. plutocrat
10. viceregent
nacelle ... 4. boat 7. shelter
nacket ... 3. boy 4. cake 5. lunch

6. caddie 8. saucy boy
nacre ... 9. shellfish 10. conchiolin
13. mother-of-pearl
Nadab (Bib) ... 12. King of Israel
nadir ... 4. pole 11. lowest point (opp
zenith)
nag ... 4. pony, twit 5. annoy, cobra,
horse, scold, snake, tease 6. heckle,
hector, peck on, pester, plague
7. henpeck 8. harangue

nagor... 8. antelope, reedbuck
nahoor... 5. sheep 6. bharal
naiad... 5. nymph 6. mussel, Nereid
    7. limniad, Oceanid
nail... 3. cut, hob 4. brad, claw, spad,
    stud, tack, wire 5. clout, spike,
    sprig, talon 6. fasten, secure, unguis,
    ungula 7. capture, measure
    8. sparable 9. finishing, intercept
    12. upholstering
nail (pert to)...
    headless.. 5. sprig
    ingrowing.. 7. acronyx
    marking, fingernail.. 6. lunule
    size.. 8. tenpenny
    slanted.. 4. toed
naissance... 5. birth 6. origin
naive... 5. frank 6. simple 7. artless,
    ingenue 8. childish, gullible, untaught
    9. guileless, ingenuous, unworldly
    10. simplicity 13. unphilosophic
    15. unsophisticated
naked... 4. bald, bare, mere, nude,
    open 5. clear, plain 6. barren,
    meager 7. exposed, literal, obvious
    8. manifest, stripped 9. unadorned,
    uncovered 11. defenseless,
    unprotected, unsupported
nakoo... 6. gavial 9. crocodile
namaycush... 5. togue, trout
namby–pamby... 5. inane, silly, vapid
    7. insipid 10. wishy–washy
    11. sentimental
name... 3. dub, nom 4. call, cite,
    term 5. clepe, nomen, style, title
    6. y–clepe 7. appoint, entitle,
    mention 8. cognomen, identify
    9. celebrity, enumerate, personage
    10. denominate, reputation
    11. appellation, designation
    12. denomination
name (pert to)...
    added.. 7. agnomen
    assumed.. 3. pen 5. alias 7. John
        Doe 9. incognito, pseudonym,
        sobriquet 10. nom de plume
    bad.. 7. caconym
    binomial.. 8. teutonym
    by location.. 7. toponym
    derivation.. 7. eponymy
    family (father's).. 7. eponymy
        9. patronymy
    fictitious.. 9. pseudonym
    first.. 9. baptismal, Christian,
        praenomen
    Japanese.. 4. maru
    known.. 9. onomatous
    nickname.. 7. moniker (monicker)
        8. cognomen
    nominate.. 9. designate
    secret.. 9. cryptonym
    spelled backwards (real name)..
        6. ananym
    surname.. 7. eponymy
    technical.. 4. onym
    unknown.. 9. anonymous
    wrong.. 8. misnomer
name as agent... 6. depute
named... 5. cited 6. called, y–clept
    (y–cleped)
named for a god... 10. theophorous

nameless... 7. bastard, obscure 8. not
    known 9. aforesaid, anonymous,
    unnamable 10. unrenowned
    12. illegitimate 13. indescribable,
    inexpressible 15. undistinguished
namelessness... 9. anonymity
namely... 5. to wit 9. expressly,
    nominally, videlicet (viz)
names, divination by... 8. onomancy
names, science of... 11. onomatology
namesake... 6. eponym 7. homonym
nanga... 4. harp
nanism... 12. dwarfishness (opp of
    gigantism)
Nanking...
    capital.. 5. China (1932–1937)
    color.. 12. Naples yellow
    province.. 7. Kiangsu
    river site.. 7. Yangtze
nanoid... 8. dwarfish
nanpie... 6. magpie
naos... 5. cella 6. shrine, temple
Naos... 4. star
nap... 3. nod 4. doze, pile, shag, wink
    5. fluff, grasp, seize, sleep, steal
    6. duffel, siesta, snooze
nape... 5. nucha, nuque, scrag
    6. scruff, turnip 7. niddick
    9. auchenium
napellus... 9. monkshood
napery... 5. linen (table)
napiform... 12. turnip–shaped
napkin... 5. doily, towel 6. diaper
    8. kerchief 9. serviette
    11. neckerchief
Naples...
    biscuit.. 10. ladyfinger
    famed building.. 9. Cathedral (Gothic,
        1272)
    red.. 5. ochre 6. Indian
    site.. 11. Bay of Naples
napoleon... 4. game 6. pastry 7. top
    boot 11. reddish–blue, sweet cherry
    13. crimson clover
Napoleon I (pert to)...
    birthplace.. 7. Ajaccio (Corsica)
    brother–in–law.. 5. Murat
    death site.. 8. St Helena
    exiled to.. 4. Elba
    father.. 7. Charles
    island.. 5. Capri
    marshal.. 3. Ney (executed)
    title.. 7. Emperor (of France)
    warfare site.. 5. Ligny, Malta
        7. Marengo 8. Waterloo
        10. Alexandria
napped (short)... 3. ras
nappy... 3. ale 4. dish 5. downy,
    heady, wooly 6. liquor, shaggy,
    sleepy 7. foaming 10. inebriated
napu... 10. chevrotain
Naraka (Hind)... 4. hell
Narcissus (Gr)... 6. egoist 14. beautiful
    youth
narcosis... 5. sleep 10. drowsiness
narcotic... 4. dope, drug, hemp, junk
    5. bhang (bang), ether, opium
    6. heroin 7. anodyne, cocaine,
    hashish 8. hypnotic, mandrake,
    morphine 9. soporific 10. belladonna,
    hyoscyamus, stramonium
narcotic (pert to)...

dose.. 3. fix 5. locus
package.. 6. bindle
seller.. 6. pusher 7. peddler
user (group).. 6. love–in 9. snow
 party
nard... 6. anoint 8. matgrass,
 ointment, rhizomes
nardoo, nardu... 6. clover
nares... 8. nostrils
narghile, nargile, nargileh... 4. pipe
 6. hookah
nargil... 7. coconut
nark... 3. spy 5. annoy 8. informer
 11. stool pigeon
Narragansett... 3. Bay 5. horse
 6. Indian, turkey
narrate... 4. tell 6. detail, recite, relate
 7. recount 8. describe
narration... 4. tale 5. drama (acted),
 story 6. detail 7. account, recital
 8. relation 9. discourse, narrative,
 rehearsal
narrative... 4. epic, epos, myth, poem,
 saga, tale 5. conte, drama, fable,
 story 6. legend 7. account, episode,
 history, parable 8. allegory, anecdote
 9. narration, statement
narrator... 9. raconteur 11. storyteller
narrow... 4. mean, poor 5. inlet,
 scant, taper 6. linear, strait
 7. closely, slender 8. strictly
 9. confining, illiberal, niggardly
 10. restricted, straighten
 11. reactionary 12. parsimonious
 13. circumscribed
narrow (pert to)...
comb form.. 4. sten 5. steno
leather strip.. 5. thong
minded.. 5. petty 6. biased
 7. bigoted 10. intolerant, prejudiced
opening.. 4. rima, slot 9. stenopaic
souled.. 10. ungenerous
narrowly incised... 9. laciniate
narrows... 5. sound 6. strait
narthex... 7. portico 9. asafetida
 (asafoetida)
narwhal, narwal... 5. whale
 8. cetacean
nasab (Moham Law)... 7. kinship
 13. consanguinity
nasal... 4. nose 5. sound 6. narine,
 rhinal, twangy 11. inspiratory
nascency... 5. birth 6. origin
 7. genesis 9. beginning
naseberry... 9. sapodilla
Nasi... 6. prince 8. Gamaliel
 9. patriarch
Nasicornia... 10. rhinoceros
nasology... 9. nose study
Nassau...
capital.. 7. Bahamas
hamlet.. 7. grouper
sports.. 4. golf
nastika... 7. atheist
nasty... 4. foul, mean 5. dirty 6. filthy,
 odious 7. obscene 8. indecent,
 unsavory 9. offensive
 12. disagreeable, dishonorable
Nasua... 5. coati 6. coatis
nasute... 10. large–nosed
nasutiform... 8. noselike
natal... 6. inborn, native 7. gluteal,

nascent 9. from birth
Natal... 7. seaport (Braz) 8. Province
 (S Afr)
natator... 7. swimmer
natatorium... 4. pool 6. plunge
 12. swimming hole
natchbone... 9. aitchbone
Natchez... 4. city (La) 6. Indian
nation... 4. host, race 5. caste, class,
 state 6. people, polity 7. country
 9. community, multitude
national... 4. blue 6. racial 7. citizen,
 federal
nationality... 4. race 6. nation
 8. nativity 9. statehood
 11. nationalism
national salute... 13. Twenty–one
 guns
native... 3. ite, son 5. natal 6. innate,
 normal, simple 7. genuine, natural,
 primary 8. inherent, original, primeval
 9. unbranded 10. aboriginal,
 indigenous, unaffected 11. not
 acquired
native (pert to)...
agent.. 9. comprador (compradore)
bear.. 5. koala
cat.. 7. dasyure
dog.. 5. dingo
Indian.. 4. Arab
juniper.. 9. blueberry
Madagascan.. 4. Hova
naturalized person.. 7. denizen
plant, animal.. 8. indigene
salt.. 6. halite
nativity... 5. birth 9. beginning,
 horoscope, sculpture
Nativity, The... 8. festival
 9. Christmas 13. birth of Christ
natterjack... 4. toad
natty... 4. chic, neat, tidy, trim
 6. spruce 10. fastidious
Natty Bumppo's alias... 7. Hawkeye
 15. Leatherstocking
natural... 3. raw 4. born 5. flesh,
 usual 6. common, cretin, expert,
 inborn, inbred, innate, normal
 7. genuine, regular, typical
 8. informal, inherent, lifelike, ordinary
 9. character (Mus), dice throw,
 unassumed, unfeigned 10. unaffected
natural (pert to)...
capacity.. 9. endowment
condition.. 4. norm
group.. 4. race 6. ethnic, family
location, position.. 4. site 5. situs
not (natural).. 5. alien 8. acquired
 10. artificial
philosophy.. 7. physics
science.. 10. physiology
voice (Mus).. 7. dipetto
naturalist... 4. Muir (John) 7. animist,
 Burbank (Luther) 9. biologist, scientist
 11. taxidermist
naturalize... 5. adapt 8. accustom
 9. acclimate 11. domesticate,
 familiarize
nature... 4. kind, self, sort, soul, type
 6. cosmos 7. essence 8. tendency,
 universe 11. naturalness,
 temperament 14. characteristic
nature (pert to)...

concealed.. 7. latency
divinity of.. 5. dryad, naiad, nymph
god.. 3. Pan
goddess.. 6. Cybele 7. Artemis
in the raw.. 6. nudity
of the case.. 9. ipso facto
worship.. 11. physiolatry
natus... 4. born
nausea... 4. pall 5. qualm 8. loathing,
mal de mer 10. queasiness
11. seasickness
nauseous... 7. fulsome, mawkish
9. loathsome, offensive, sickening,
squeamish 10. disgusting
nautical... 5. naval 6. marine
7. oceanic 8. maritime
nautical (pert to)...
almanac.. 9. ephemeris
direction.. 5. avast, belay
hail.. 4. ahoy
instrument.. 3. aba 7. compass,
pelorus, sextant
measure.. 3. ton 4. knot 6. fathom
7. sea mile
nautilus... 7. mollusk 8. argonaut
9. submarine 10. diving bell
Navaho, Navajo... 5. hogan 6. Indian
7. blanket 9. red–yellow
naval... 6. marine 8. nautical
naval (pert to)...
brigade.. 7. militia
commander.. 7. navarch
depot.. 4. base
device.. 6. dolter
officer.. 5. bosun 6. ensign, yeoman
7. admiral, captain 9. boatswain
(bosun), commander 10. lieutenant
nave... 3. hob, hub, nef 4. apse, fist
5. nieve 7. apsidal
navel... 6. middle, orange 8. omphalos
9. umbilicus 10. depression
navigate... 4. keel, sail 7. avigate
11. ship science
navigator... 5. navvy 12. third
command (or 4th)
navy (fleet)... 7. tankers 8. cruisers,
flattops, gunboats 10. destroyers,
submarines 11. battleships 12. mine
sweepers 13. hospital ships
16. aircraft carriers
navy (pert to)...
bean.. 6. kidney
coffee.. 3. mud
color.. 4. blue 10. marine blue
drinking fountain.. 11. scuttlebutt
fleet.. 6. armada 13. combat vessels
plug.. 7. tobacco
ships, collectively.. 5. fleet 6. armada
song.. 13. Anchors Aweigh
training camp.. 8. boot camp
underwear.. 8. skivvies
nawab, nabob... 5. ruler, title
7. viceroy
nay... 2. no 4. deny 5. flute, never
6. denial, naysay, refuse 7. refusal
8. negative 11. prohibition
nayaur... 5. sheep
nayword... 6. byword 7. proverb (of
reproach) 9. watchword
Nazarene (pert to)...
artist.. 8. Overbeck (of Rome)
disciple.. 9. Christian

native.. 11. Jesus Christ
native of.. 8. Nazareth
Nazi... 9. Hitlerite
Nazi emblem... 6. fylfot 8. swastika
nchega... 6. monkey 10. chimpanzee
neanic... 6. immature, youthful
neap... 4. tide 6. tongue (vehicle)
7. low tide 8. low water
Neapolitan (pert to)...
dance.. 10. tarantella
fever.. 8. undulent
Italian.. 6. Naples
medlar.. 5. fruit 7. azarole
music.. 5. chord (6th)
ointment.. 9. mercurial
yellow.. 6. Naples
near... 2. at 4. nigh 5. about, close,
handy 6. around, within 7. closely,
related 8. adjacent, approach,
imminent, intimate 11. approximate
13. propinquitous
nearby, near–by... 3. gin 4. nigh
5. anent, handy 6. beside, nearly
7. close by, close to, vicinal
8. adjacent 9. adjoining
10. convenient
Nearctic... 9. Greenland, Holarctic
11. Palaearctic 13. Arctic America
Near East... 7. Balkans 12. Balkan
States
Near East valley... 4. wadi (wady)
5. oasis 6. ravine
nearest... 4. next 7. closest
9. proximate
nearly... 5. about 6. almost 7. closely
8. narrowly 10. similarity
13. approximately
nearness... 8. affinity, intimacy,
likeness, relation 9. closeness
11. propinquity
near of kin... 7. germane
nearsighted... 6. myopic 8. purblind
12. narrow–minded, shortsighted,
undiscerning
neat... 3. pat 4. prim, smug, snod,
tidy, trig, trim 5. natty 6. adroit,
dapper, spruce 7. orderly, perjink,
precise 9. shipshape 10. meticulous,
perjinkety 12. spick–and–span
neatherd... 7. cowherd 8. herdsman
neathmost... 6. lowest
neb... 3. tip 4. beak, bill, face, kiss,
nose 5. point, snout
Nebo, Nebu... 8. mountain (Bib)
11. god of wisdom
Nebraska...
capital.. 7. Lincoln
city.. 5. Omaha 8. Hastings
11. Scottsbluff
Indian.. 4. Otoe 5. Omaha 6. Pawnee
meaning.. 11. water valley
railroad (1865).. 12. Union Pacific
river.. 6. Nemaha, Platte 8. Missouri
State admission.. 13. Thirty–seventh
State motto.. 20. Equality Before the
Law
State nickname.. 4. Beef
10. Cornhusker
nebula... 3. sky 4. mist 5. cloud,
vapor 10. atmosphere
Nebula of... 4. Lyra 5. Orion
9. Andromeda

nebulous... 4. hazy 5. misty, vague
  6. cloudy 7. clouded, nebular
  8. nebulose
nebulous envelope... 4. coma
  9. chevelure
necessarily... 8. perforce
  11. unavoidably 12. consequently
  13. indispensably
necessary... 5. vital 7. needful
  9. essential, mandatory, requisite
  11. requirement, unavoidable
  13. indispensable
necessitate... 5. force, impel
  6. compel, entail, oblige 7. require
  9. constrain
necessity... 4. food, need, want
  5. drink 7. aliment, poverty, urgency
  9. neediness 10. constraint
  14. inevitableness
neck... 4. hals (halse) 5. crane, scrag,
  swire 6. cervix, fondle, strait
  7. channel, embrace, isthmus
neck (pert to)...
  armor.. 6. gorget 8. gorgerin
  artery.. 7. carotid
  back of.. 4. nape 5. nucha, nuque
    6. scruff
  frill.. 5. jabot, ruche 6. wimple
  land.. 6. strake 9. peninsula
  muscle.. 8. scalenus
  pendant.. 6. locket 9. lavaliere
  piece.. 3. boa 5. amice, rabat, scarf,
    stole 6. collar
  water.. 6. strait
  zoology.. 4. gula 6. wattle 7. withers
neckcloth... 6. cravat 7. muffler
  9. barcelona 11. neckerchief
neckerchief... 7. belcher 8. kerchief
  12. handkerchief
necklace... 5. beads 6. torque
  7. baldric, chaplet, rivière
  11. shark's-teeth
neckpiece... 3. boa 5. ascot, rabat,
  scarf, stole 6. collar 8. kerchief
necktie... 3. tie 4. band 5. ascot,
  scarf 6. cravat 10. four-in-hand
necrology... 9. death roll 13. death
  register 14. obituary notice
necromancy... 5. goety, magic
  7. sorcery 9. sortilege
  11. conjuration, enchantment
necropolis... 8. cemetery
necropsy... 7. autopsy
  10. post-mortem
nectar... 3. red 5. drink, honey
  8. beverage
nectar of the gods... 8. ambrosia
neddy... 6. donkey 13. life preserver
need... 4. lack, poor, thar, want
  7. poverty, require, urgency
  8. exigency 9. extremity, necessity
  10. compulsion, deficiency
  11. requirement
needle... 3. sew 4. acus, goad, sail
  5. tease, thorn 6. bodkin, pierce
  7. darning, obelisk 9. astatizer
  10. upholstery
needle (pert to)...
  bath.. 3. jet 9. sprinkler
  bird.. 9. phalarope 10. needlebill
  bug.. 4. Nepa 7. Ranatra
  case.. 4. etui (etwee)

fish.. 3. gar 8. pipefish
gun.. 11. Dreyse rifle
kind.. 5. blunt, sharp 7. between,
  crochet, darning 8. knitting
long-eyed.. 10. embroidery
medical.. 10. hypodermic
needlelike body.. 7. spicule
needlework.. 7. crochet, sampler
  8. knitting 10. embroidery
record.. 10. phonograph
shaped.. 6. acuate 7. acerose
  8. acicular
under the skin.. 5. seton
needy... 4. poor 7. almoner
  8. indigent 9. necessary, penniless,
  requisite 10. distressed
neel-bhunder... 8. wanderoo 10. blue
  monkey
neep... 6. turnip
ne'er-do-well... 5. idler 6. wretch
  8. poltroon 9. schlemiel
  14. good-for-nothing
nef... 4. nave 5. clock (ship-shaped)
nefarious... 6. wicked 7. heinous,
  impious 8. horrible, infamous, terrible
  9. atrocious 10. detestable,
  iniquitous, villainous
nefas... 6. sinful
negate... 4. deny 6. refuse, refute
  7. nullify 8. disprove 10. counteract
negative... 2. ir, ne, no 3. nay, non,
  nor, not 4. deny, film, veto 5. minus
  6. refuse 7. neutral 8. disprove,
  negation 9. privative
  13. contradiction
negative (pert to)...
  electrode, pole.. 7. cathode (kathode)
  eyepiece.. 8. Campani's 9. Huygenian
  ion.. 5. anion
  sign.. 5. minus
neglect... 4. fail, omit, slip, snub
  5. shirk 6. slight 7. failure
  8. omission 9. disregard, negligent,
  pretermit 11. inattention
negligee... 4. gown, robe 6. attire
  8. peignoir
negligence... 7. laxness 9. oversight,
  unconcern 10. remissness
  11. inattention 12. carelessness,
  inadvertence
negligent... 3. lax 4. lash 6. remiss,
  supine 8. careless, heedless
  10. neglectful 11. unconcerned
negotiate... 4. deal, pass 5. treat
  6. manage, treaty 7. bargain,
  mediate 8. transact
Negrito (pert to)...
  African.. 4. Akka 5. Batwa, Pygmy
    7. Bambute, Bushman
  Dutch New Guinea.. 6. Tapiro
  Indonesian.. 3. Ata 4. Aeta (Ita)
  Malay.. 6. Semang
Negro (pert to)...
  dance.. 4. juba
  dish.. 9. jambalaya
  Egyptian.. 6. Nubian
  friend of.. 10. negrophile
  magic (anc).. 6. voodoo
  spiritual.. 8. Swing Low
neigh... 4. akin 6. whinny 7. whicker
neighborhood... 7. purlieu 8. environs,
  vicinity 9. proximity 10. thereabout

neighborhood law... 5. venue
neither masculine nor feminine...
   6. neuter 7. sexless
neither right nor wrong...
   11. adiaphorous, indifferent
Nemesis... 7. avenger, goddess,
   penalty
nemoral... 6. sylvan 14. living in a
   grove
neology... 8. new words 9. neologism
   11. new doctrine 14. new
   expressions
neonatus... 7. new baby, newborn
neophobia *(fear of)*... 6. the new
neophyte... 4. tyro 6. novice
   7. convert 8. beginner 9. proselyte
   10. catechumen
neosology *(study of)*... 10. young birds
neoteric... 3. new 4. late 6. modern,
   recent
nep... 6. catnip
Nepal...
   aborigines.. 10. Mongolians
   capital.. 8. Katmandu
   district.. 7. Mustang
   mountain.. 7. Everest 9. Himalayas
   ruler.. 9. Maharajah
nepesh... 4. soul 10. animal soul
   12. divine breath
nephew... 4. neve 6. nepote
nephrite... 4. jade 7. mineral
   11. kidney stone
nephroid... 8. reniform
   12. kidney–shaped
nephros... 6. kidney
nepote... 6. nephew 8. grandson
nepotism... 9. patronage
   10. favoritism, preference
Neptune... 3. sea 5. ocean 6. sea
   god
Neptune (pert to)...
   Astron.. 6. planet (3rd largest)
   Celtic.. 3. Ler
   consort.. 7. Salacia
   emblem.. 7. trident
   Greek.. 8. Poseidon
   Roman.. 6. sea god
   son.. 6. Triton
   wife.. 6. Medusa
Nereid (Gr)... 8. sea nymph
Nero (pert to)...
   excesses.. 7. cruelty 13. burning of
   Rome (64 AD)
   mother.. 9. Agrippina
   Roman title.. 7. Emperor
   wife.. 6. Sabina 7. Octavia
nerve... 4. pulp 5. cheek, fiber, pluck,
   sinew 6. aplomb, energy, tendon,
   tissue 7. courage, nervure
   8. audacity, coolness, strength
   10. resolution
nerve (pert to)...
   action.. 9. neurergic
   cell.. 4. axon 6. neuron
   center.. 8. ganglion
   comb form.. 5. neuro
   fiber.. 5. motor 7. sensory
   8. afferent, efferent
   force.. 7. neurism
   gray matter.. 7. cinerea
   inflammation, medical.. 8. neuritis,

neurosis 9. neurotomy
   10. neurectasy, neurolysis, neuropathy
   11. neurologist 13. tic douloureux
network.. 4. rete 6. plexus
of Wrisberg.. 6. facial
operation.. 10. neurolysis
passage.. 4. rete 5. hilum 8. ganglion
ref to.. 6. neural, neuric 7. neuroid
   8. neurotic
root.. 5. radix
science.. 9. neurology
sheath.. 9. medullary
tissue.. 7. cinerea, neurine
   9. neuroglia
tumor.. 6. glioma 7. neuroma
nerveless... 4. dead 5. inert
   9. foolhardy, powerless
   10. courageous
nervous... 5. tense, timid 6. neural,
   touchy 7. fearful, jittery 8. eloquent,
   neurotic, timorous 9. excitable,
   sensitive 10. high–strung
   12. apprehensive
nervous (pert to)...
   affliction.. 3. tic 6. ataxia, chorea
   7. aphasia 8. neurosis
   energy deficiency.. 7. aneuria
   seizure.. 4. amok (amuck)
   system, center.. 5. brain, spine
   system, description.. 11. neurography
   system, name.. 9. neuronymy
   system, science.. 9. neurology
   system, specialist.. 12. neuropathist,
   psychiatrist
   tissue tumor.. 11. neurocytoma
ness... 4. cape 8. headland
   10. promontory
nest... 3. bed, den, nye, web 4. inro
   5. abode, aerie, eyrie, group, haunt,
   nidus 6. cuddle, series (graduated)
   7. lodging, retreat 9. residence
   10. nidificate 13. breeding place
nest (pert to)...
   boxes.. 4. inro
   eagle's.. 5. aerie, eyrie (eyry)
   pheasant's.. 4. nide
   spider's.. 3. web
   squirrel's.. 4. dray (drey)
   swallow's.. 9. nidus avis
   to build.. 6. nidify
nestle... 3. pet 4. nest 6. cuddle,
   pettle, settle 7. protect, shelter,
   snuggle
nestling... 4. bird 5. child 9. fledgling,
   youngling
Nestor (pert to)...
   famed for.. 6. wisdom
   King of.. 5. Pylos
   known as.. 4. sage 7. adviser 8. The
   Elder 9. Patriarch
net... 3. gin, web 4. mesh, toil, trap,
   weir 5. clear, lacis, score, seine,
   snare, weave 6. profit 7. enclose,
   network, trammel 8. receipts
   9. reticulum
net (pert to)...
   fishing.. 4. fyke 5. seine, trawl
   7. trammel
   hair.. 5. snood
   lacemaking.. 5. lacis
   silk.. 5. tulle 6. maline
   winged (lacy).. 12. neuropteroid

Netherlands... see also *Dutch, Holland*
capital.. 9. Amsterdam
cheese.. 4. Edam
city.. 5. Delft 7. Utrecht
  9. Eindhoven, Rotterdam
gin.. 8. schnapps
government.. 8. monarchy
government seat.. 8. The Hague
inhabitant.. 5. Dutch 7. Flemish
lake.. 7. Haarlem
legislative body.. 4. Raad
low land.. 6. polder
port.. 9. Rotterdam
possession.. 7. Surinam (Dutch
  Guiana) 8. Antilles (W Ind)
river.. 3. Eem 5. Meuse, Rhine
  6. Ijssel (Yssel), Kromme
sea (inland).. 9. Wadden Sea, Zuider
  Zee 10. Ijssel Lake, Ijsselmeer
nettle... 3. vex 4. fret, herb, line,
  whip 5. anger, annoy, pique, rouse
  6. incite, Urtica 7. provoke 8. irritate
  10. Parietaria, Urticaceae
nettle (pert to)...
bird.. 11. whitethroat
geranium.. 6. coleus
rash.. 5. hives, uredo 9. urticaria
sea.. 5. cnida
network... 3. web 4. caul, fret, kell,
  lace, mesh, moke, rete 5. chain
  6. cobweb, plexus, reseau, sagene
  7. webwork
neume... 5. neuma 6. pneuma
neurad... 12. to neural side
neural... 6. dorsal, nerval 7. ventral
  9. posterial
neuralgia... 3. tic 4. pain 8. face
  ague 13. tic douloureux
neuter... 6. gender 7. neither, neutral,
  sexless 9. impartial
neutral... 7. antacid 8. mediocre,
  middling, negative, unbiased
  10. achromatic 11. indifferent,
  nonpartisan 12. noncombatant,
  noncommittal
neutral equilibrium... 7. astatic
neutralize... 5. annul 6. offset
  7. nullify, vitiate 9. frustrate
  10. counteract 11. countervail
  14. counterbalance
Nevada...
capital.. 10. Carson City
city.. 3. Ely 4. Elko 6. Sparks
  7. Boulder 8. Las Vegas
lake.. 4. Mead 6. Mohave
  7. Pyramid
mine (famed).. 12. Comstock Lode
  (1859)
mountain.. 7. Rockies, Wasatch
  13. Sierra Nevadas
native Indian.. 6. Digger
resort.. 4. Reno 8. Las Vegas (The
  Meadows) 9. Lake Tahoe
State admission.. 11. Thirty–sixth
State motto.. 16. All For Our Country
State nickname.. 6. Silver
  9. Sagebrush
neve... 4. firn, snow 6. nephew
  7. glacier
nevel, nevell... 9. fisticuff
never... 4. nary 6. nowise 7. not ever
  8. at no time, not at all 9. by no

means, nevermore
nevertheless... 3. but, yet 5. still
  6. anyhow 7. however
  15. notwithstanding
nevus... 4. mark, mole 5. tumor
  7. blemish 9. birthmark
new... 3. neo (pref) 4. anew, late,
  nova (star) 5. fresh, novel 6. growth,
  modern, recent 8. neoteric, original,
  untested 9. recreated, renovated
  12. unaccustomed 13. inexperienced
New Brunswick...
capital.. 11. Fredericton
city.. 6. St John
gulf.. 10. St Lawrence
new but yet old... 10. novantique
New England (pert to)...
book.. 6. Primer
explorer.. 13. Capt John Smith
native.. 6. Yankee
theology.. 9. Calvinism
Newfoundland...
city.. 7. St John's 9. Grand Bank
discoverer.. 9. John Cabot (1497)
gulf.. 10. St Lawrence
New Guinea, Papua Island...
capital.. 6. Rabaul
hog (wild).. 4. bene
island size (world).. 5. third
native.. 6. Papuan
parrot.. 4. lory
port.. 4. Daru 7. Moresby
region.. 10. Melanesian
river.. 3. Fly
New Hampshire...
capital.. 7. Concord
city.. 6. Durham 7. Hanover
  8. Merrimac 10. Manchester,
  Portsmouth
cog rail (first).. 12. Mt Washington
lake.. 13. Winnipesaukee
mountains.. 5. White
Our Town.. 13. Grover's Corner
park.. 13. Crawford Notch, Dixville
  Notch
range.. 12. Presidential
river.. 8. Merrimac 11. Connecticut
sculpture.. 14. Great Stone Face
  (Profile Peak)
State admission.. 5. Ninth
State motto.. 13. Live Free or Die
State nickname.. 7. Granite
New Jersey...
capital.. 7. Trenton
city.. 6. Camden, Newark 7. Raritan
  9. Montclair 12. Fort Monmouth,
  New Brunswick
college.. 9. Princeton (1746)
inventor.. 6. Edison
naval air station.. 9. Lakehurst
poet.. 11. Walt Whitman
resort.. 7. Cape May 8. Wildwood
  9. Ocean City 10. Asbury Park
  12. Atlantic City
river.. 7. Raritan
State admission.. 5. Third
State motto.. 20. Liberty and
  Prosperity
State nickname.. 6. Garden
New Mexico...
capital.. 7. Santa Fe
city.. 4. Taos 7. Roswell
  11. Albuquerque

Fort .. **5.** Tejon
Indian Reservation .. **5.** Acoma (Sky City) **11.** Chaco Canyon
peak .. **7.** Wheeler
river .. **4.** Gila **5.** Pecos **8.** Canadian
space center .. **6.** Sandia **8.** Holloman, Kirtland **9.** Los Alamos **10.** White Sands
State admission .. **12.** Forty–seventh
State bird .. **10.** road runner
State flower .. **5.** yucca
State motto .. **12.** Crescit Eundo **15.** It Grows as It Goes
State nickname .. **17.** Land of Enchantment
State wonder .. **15.** Carlsbad Caverns
new moon festival ... **8.** neomenia
news ... **5.** flash, scoop **6.** report **7.** courier, evangel, tidings
news agency ... **2.** AP **3.** DNB, UPI **4.** Tass **5.** Aneta, Domei **7.** Reuters **9.** syndicate
newspaper (pert to) ...
editor .. **7.** reviser **8.** redactor
file .. **6.** morgue
popular name .. **7.** gazette
writer .. **8.** reporter **9.** columnist **10.** newscaster **13.** correspondent
newsstand ... **5.** booth, kiosk, stall
new star ... **4.** nova
newt ... **3.** eft **6.** lizard, triton **10.** salamander
New Testament ... **6.** Gospel **8.** Epistles **15.** Pauline Epistles
new wine ... **4.** must
new word, usage ... **7.** neology **9.** neologism, neoterism
New York ...
borough .. **5.** Bronx **6.** Queens **8.** Brooklyn, Richmond **9.** Manhattan
buyer (for $24) .. **11.** Peter Minuit
capital .. **6.** Albany
city .. **5.** Utica **7.** Buffalo, New York **8.** Saratoga **9.** Rochester **11.** Schenectady **12.** Poughkeepsie
college .. **7.** Colgate, Cornell **8.** Columbia **9.** West Point
Falls .. **7.** Niagara
Indian .. **6.** Oneida, Seneca **8.** Iroquois
Irving's home .. **9.** Tarrytown
island .. **6.** Staten **9.** Manhattan
monument .. **7.** Obelisk **10.** Grant's Tomb **15.** Statue of Liberty
mountains .. **9.** Catskills
name, old .. **12.** New Amsterdam
nickname .. **6.** Gotham **8.** Big Apple
river .. **4.** East **6.** Harlem, Hudson
river channel .. **8.** Hell Gate
section (famed) .. **4.** SoHo **16.** Greenwich Village
State admission .. **8.** Eleventh
State bird .. **8.** bluebird
State flower .. **4.** rose
State motto .. **9.** Excelsior **10.** Ever Upward
State nickname .. **6.** Empire
New Yorker ... **8.** Dutchman **9.** Gothamite **13.** Knickerbocker
New Zealand ...
capital .. **10.** Wellington
city .. **7.** Dunedin **8.** Auckland, Hamilton **12.** Christchurch

discoverer .. **6.** Tasman
explorer .. **4.** Cook (Captain James)
location .. **12.** South Pacific
native .. **5.** Maori **10.** Polynesian
peak .. **6.** Mt Cook
sect .. **7.** Ringatu
soldier .. **5.** Anzac
tribe .. **3.** Ati **5.** Maori
volcano .. **7.** Ruapehu
New Zealand (pert to) ...
bird ... **3.** kea, moa, poe **4.** titi, weka, kiwi **7.** apteryx, boobook, wrybill, Xenicus
caterpillar .. **5.** aweto
club, weapon .. **4.** mere
mahogany .. **6.** totara
mollusk .. **4.** pipi
myrtle .. **8.** ramarama
morepork .. **4.** peho, ruru
palm .. **5.** nikau
parrot .. **6.** kakapo **9.** owl parrot
pigeon .. **4.** kuku
reptile .. **7.** tuatara
white pine .. **5.** kauri (kaury)
next ... **4.** then **5.** aware, neist **7.** closest, nearest, proximo **9.** adjoining, immediate **10.** contiguous, succeeding
next to ... **6.** almost, beside, nearly **8.** adjacent
next to last syllable ... **6.** penult **11.** penultimate
nexus ... **3.** tie **4.** bond, link **5.** group **6.** series **10.** connection **15.** interconnection
Nez Percé ... **6.** Indian **11.** pierced nose
Niagara ... **5.** flood, grape (green)
Niagara Falls (pert to) ...
cataract .. **8.** American, Canadian **9.** Horseshoe
division between .. **10.** Bridal Veil, Goat Island
point of interest .. **14.** Cave of the Winds
nib ... **3.** end **4.** beak, bill **5.** point (pen), prong **6.** tongue
nibble ... **3.** eat, nab, nip **4.** gnaw, peck **5.** champ, munch **6.** browse
Nicaragua ...
capital .. **7.** Managua
city .. **7.** Granada
lake .. **7.** Managua
mountain range .. **10.** Cordillera
river .. **4.** Coco, Tuma **7.** San Juan
nice ... **4.** fine, good, kind, neat **6.** dainty, proper, queasy, subtle, tickle **7.** elegant, finical, genteel, prudish, refined **8.** exacting, pleasant, pleasing, suitable **9.** agreeable, squeamish **10.** appetizing, delightful, fastidious, particular, scrupulous **11.** considerate, punctilious, well–behaved **13.** hypercritical **14.** discriminating, discriminative
Nicene Creed ... **10.** Confession
nicety ... **7.** finesse, modesty **8.** accuracy, delicacy **9.** precision **11.** preciseness **13.** squeamishness
niche ... **4.** apse, nook **5.** space (recessed) **6.** alcove, covert, recess **7.** retreat, secrete **10.** tabernacle

nick ... 3. gap 4. dent, dint, slit
5. notch, steal 7. swindle
nickel (pert to)...
alloy .. 5. Invar
bronze .. 11. cupranickel
coin .. 13. five–cent piece
color .. 4. gray 6. nimbus
compound .. 8. argenton
11. maillechort
silver .. 6. German
symbol .. 2. Ni
nickelodeon ... 4. juke 7. jukebox,
theater (5–cent)
nickname ... 3. pun 6. monica
7. agnomen, epithet, misname,
moniker (monicker), pet name
8. cognomen, misapply
10. soubriquet
nicknaming pun ... 12. prosonomasia
nictate ... 4. wink 5. blink 7. twinkle
9. nictitate
nid ... 3. nod 10. bend and bob
nide ... 4. nest 5. brood
nidge ... 3. nig 5. shake 6. quiver
nidificant ... 12. nestbuilding
nidology, science ... 10. birds' nests
nidor ... 5. aroma, scent
nidus ... 4. nest 5. abode 7. nucleus
13. breeding place
Nietzsche ... 11. philosopher
nieve ... 4. fist, hand
niffer ... 7. bargain 8. exchange
niffy–naffy ... 7. finical 8. trifling
Niflheim, Nifelheim (Norse Myth)...
8. Universe (division of) 10. Nine
Worlds
nifty ... 5. smart 7. stylish 8. very
good
Nigeria ...
capital .. 5. Lagos
city .. 3. Ede 6. Ibadan
export .. 5. cocoa
plains .. 5. Bornu
tribe .. 4. Eboe 5. Benin
niggardly ... 5. scant 6. paltry, sordid,
stingy 9. penurious, scrimping
10. avaricious 12. parsimonious
nigh ... 2. at 3. nei 4. left, near
5. about, anear, close 6. almost,
direct, nearly 8. adjacent
10. contiguous 11. neighboring
night ... 4. nuit 5. death 7. evening
8. darkness, wee hours 9. adversity,
nightfall 11. concealment
night (pert to)...
bird .. 5. potoo 8. nightjar
9. nighthawk 10. goatsucker,
nightchurr, owl swallow, shearwater
11. nightingale
blindness .. 10. nyctalopia
cap .. 6. biggin
club .. 4. café 5. disco 6. bistro
7. cabaret 11. discotheque
goddess .. 3. Nox, Nyx
jasmine .. 10. hursinghar
Norse .. 4. Nott
sight (only) .. 11. hemeralopia
wandering .. 11. noctivagant
nightfall, at ... 6. sunset 9. acronical
(achronical) (opp of cosmical)
nightingale ... 6. thrush 8. philomel
9. bed jacket

night jar ... 5. potoo 10. goatsucker
nightmare ... 3. alp 4. Mara, ogre
5. dream 7. incubus 9. cauchemar
13. hallucination
nightshade ... 5. morel (moril)
7. henbane 10. belladonna
11. bittersweet
nigrescent ... 8. blackish
nihil ... 7. nothing, no value
nihil debet ... 13. he owes nothing
nihil ex nihilo ... 7. nothing (comes)
11. from nothing
Nihilist ... 9. anarchist, Socialist
Nile (pert to)...
bird .. 4. ibis 7. wryneck
boat .. 5. baris 6. nuggar 8. dahabeah
city .. 7. Rosetta
color .. 3. boa 5. green
dam .. 5. Aswan
Falls .. 5. Ripon
fish .. 5. bagre 8. mormyrid (sacred)
god .. 4. Hapi
headstream .. 6. Kagera
houseboat .. 8. dahabeah
island .. 4. Roda (Rhoda)
waste .. 4. sudd
nilgai ... 8. antelope
nimble ... 4. deft, fast, flit, gleg, lish,
spry 5. agile, alert, brisk, fleet, quick,
smart, swift 6. active, adroit, clever,
lively, prompt, volant
nimbose ... 6. cloudy, stormy
7. clouded 8. nebulous, nubilous,
overcast
nimbus ... 4. disk, halo 5. cloud, vapor
6. fabric, gloria, nickel 7. aureole
10. atmosphere
nimiety ... 6. excess 10. redundancy
niminy–piminy ... 7. mincing, refined
10. effeminate
nimmer ... 5. thief
Nimrod (Bib) ... 5. ruler 6. hunter
8. Cush's son
nimshi ... 4. fool 7. half–wit 11. silly
person
Nimshi's son (Bib) ... 11. Jehoshaphat
nine (pert to)...
angles .. 7. nonagon
banded armadillo .. 4. peba
based on .. 8. novenary
Books of nine chapters .. 7. Enneads
comb form .. 6. ennead
composition for nine .. 5. nonet
days' devotion .. 6. novena
eyes .. 7. lamprey
gems .. 7. Vikrama
gods .. 9. Etruscans
group .. 6. ennead, nonary 18. Ennead
of Heliopolis
headed monster .. 5. Hydra
inches .. 4. span
number .. 5. ennea, nueve
pert to .. 8. enneadic
players .. 8. baseball
poetic .. 8. ninefold
Nineteenth amendment ...
14. Woman's Suffrage
Nineveh (Bib)...
capital .. 7. Assyria
famed for .. 11. excavations (1814)
Nine Worlds (Norse) ... 3. Hel
6. Asgard 7. Alfheim, Midgard

8. Niflheim, Vanaheim
10. Jotunnheim 12. Muspellsheim
13. Svartalfaheim
Nine Worthies ... 5. David, Judas
6. Arthur, Caesar, Hector, Joshua
7. Godfrey 9. Alexander
11. Charlemagne
ninny ... 4. clod, dolt, fool, nerd
9. blockhead, simpleton
ninth ... 5. nones (day before Ides)
8. enneatic, ninefold
11. ennea–eteric (year)
Ninth of Ab (Jew) ... 7. fast day
ninut ... 6. magpie
Niobe (pert to) ...
  changed by Zeus to .. 5. stone
  father .. 8. Tantalus
  husband .. 12. King of Thebes
nip ... 3. bit, cut, sip 4. bite, clip,
dram, peck 5. blast, cheat, check,
chill, clamp, draft, drink, hurry, pinch,
seize, sever, steal, thief 6. benumb,
blight, catnip, cut off, freeze, snatch,
tipple 7. shorten, squeeze
8. compress 10. pickpocket
nipa (pert to) ...
  drink .. 9. alcoholic
  mat .. 6. thatch
  palm .. 4. atap
  palm sap .. 5. sugar 7. alcohol
nipcheese ... 5. miser 6. purser
nipper ... 3. boy, lad 4. claw, grab
5. biter, drink, miser, thief 6. cunner,
mitten, urchin 7. gripper, incisor,
pincers 12. costermonger
nippers ... 6. pliers 7. pincers 8. leg
irons, pince–nez 9. handcuffs
nipple ... 3. pap 4. teat 7. mamelon,
papilla 8. mammilla 10. projection
12. protuberance
nippy ... 4. cold 5. brisk 6. active,
biting 7. nipping, pungent
8. grasping, vigorous
Nirvana ... 4. rags 6. heaven
8. oblivion 12. emancipation
Nisan (Jew calendar) ... 10. first month
(Mar–Apr)
nisi ... 5. if not 6. unless
nissen ... 6. goblin, kobold 7. brownie
nisus ... 7. impulse 8. endeavor,
striving
nit ... 3. egg 4. mite 8. parasite
nitency ... 6. luster 10. brightness
niter, nitre ... 6. natron 9. saltpeter
13. sodium nitrate 16. potassium
nitrate
nither ... 5. blast 6. debase, shiver
7. oppress, tremble 9. humiliate
nithing (anc) ... 6. coward 7. niggard
nitid ... 3. gay 6. bright 8. lustrous
nitric acid ... 10. aqua fortis
nitrogen ... 3. azo (comb form), gas
5. azote 7. element 10. atmosphere
nitrogen compound ... 7. ammonia
nitroglycerin, nitroglycerine ...
8. dynamite (1846) 9. explosive,
guncotton
nitrous oxide ... 3. gas 10. anesthetic
11. laughing gas
nitty–gritty ... 4. base, crux, gist
7. essence
Niue, Pacific island ...

  territory of .. 10. New Zealand
niveau ... 5. level
niveous ... 5. snowy, white (shining)
nix ... 2. no 5. no one 6. forbid,
nobody, sprite 7. nothing
Njorth, Njord (Norse) ... 3. god
(fertility) 5. Vanir
Njorth's daughter ... 5. Freya (Freyja)
7. goddess (love and beauty)
Njorth's son ... 3. god 4. Frey
no ... 3. naw, nay, nit 4. baal, dead,
gone, none 5. not so 6. denial,
no–gaki, not any 8. not at all
Noah, Bib (pert to) ...
  boat .. 3. Ark
  dove .. 7. Columba
  father .. 6. Lamech
  flood .. 6. Deluge
  Genesis .. 9. patriarch
  grandson .. 4. Aram
  landing, the Ark .. 6. Ararat
  raven .. 6. Corvus
  son .. 3. Ham 4. Shem 7. Japheth
nob ... 4. head, nave 6. hobnob
8. nobleman 9. personage
nobby ... 4. boat 5. smart 7. stylish
Nobel powder ... 10. Ballistite
noble ... 4. epic, fine, peer 5. ducal,
grand, lofty, manly 6. epical
7. eminent, grandee, liberal, stately,
sublime 8. elevated, generous,
imposing, renowned, splendid
9. dignified, high birth, honorable
10. impressive 11. illustrious,
magnanimous, magnificent
12. aristocratic
nobleman ... 3. sir 4. duke, earl, lord,
peer 5. baron 6. barony, flaith, thakur
7. baronet, grandee, marquis
8. margrave, optimate, viscount
9. blueblood, patrician 10. aristocrat,
chess piece
nobleness of birth ... 6. eugeny
noblewoman ... 4. lady 5. begum
7. duchess, peeress 8. baroness,
contessa, countess, marquise
11. marchioness
nobody ... 4. none 5. no one
7. nebbish 8. no person
9. jackstraw, nonentity 10. not
anybody
nocent ... 6. guilty 7. harmful, hurtful
8. criminal (opp of innocent)
nocturnal ... 5. night 7. nightly
8. darkness, nocturne
nocturnal (pert to) ...
  animal .. 3. bat 4. coon 5. lemur, ratel
  6. possum 7. opossum
  astronomy .. 9. astrolabe
  bird .. 3. owl
  signs .. 8. zodiacal
nocturne ... 7. lullaby 8. serenade
10. night scene (art)
nocuous ... 7. hurtful, noxious
nod ... 3. bow 4. bend, bock, doze,
tend, wink 6. beckon, signal
7. bidding 8. greeting
Nod (Bib) ... 9. Land of Nod 10. East
of Eden
nodding ... 6. nutant 7. annuent,
weeping (as a willow) 8. cernuous,
drooping

noddy... 3. auk 4. fool 6. drowsy, fulmar, noodle, sleepy 7. foolish, hackney 9. simpleton
node... 4. knob, knot, knur, plot 5. joint, nodus 7. dilemma 8. swelling 10. difficulty 12. complication, protuberance
nodule... 4. auge, bump, knot, lump, mass 5. geode 7. granule, nablock 8. tubercle 12. complication
nodus... 4. knot, node 10. difficulty 12. complication
noel... 5. carol (Xmas), shout 9. sign of joy
Noel... 6. Natale 9. Christmas
noeud... 3. bow 4. knot
nog... 3. peg, pin 5. block 6. eggnog, noggin 8. treenail 9. brickwork
nogada... 10. pecan candy
nogal... 5. pecan
noggin... 3. cup, mug 4. head, pate
noise... 3. din, pop, rap 4. bang, boom, klop, roar, rout 5. blare, blast, bruit, chang, clang, click, rumor, sound 6. clamor, outcry, racket, report, strife, uproar 7. brattle, chortle, discord, quarrel, rapping 9. shoutings
noise (pert to)...
ghost.. 11. poltergeist
harsh.. 4. bray 7. stridor 9. caterwaul
respiration.. 4. rale
rustling.. 5. swish
Scotch.. 5. chang
water.. 5. plash 6. ripple, splash
whirring.. 4. burr
noised... 6. dinned 7. rumored 8. reported
noisemaker... 4. horn 5. siren 6. rattle 7. clacker, whistle 8. whiz–bang
noisome... 3. bad 4. foul 5. fetid, nasty 7. harmful, noxious 8. stinking 9. offensive 10. malodorous, pernicious 11. destructive, unwholesome 12. insalubrious
noisy... 4. loud 7. blatant 8. brawling, clattery 9. clamorous, turbulent 10. blustering, boisterous, vociferous 12. obstreperous, rattlety–bang
nom... 4. name
nomad... 4. arab 5. gypsy 6. roamer, Romany 7. Bedouin, Saracen, scenite, zingaro 8. wanderer
nomadic... 9. itinerant
nomarchy (Gr)... 4. nome 8. province 10. department
nom de plume... 7. pen name 9. pseudonym
nomen... 4. gens, name 7. agnomen 8. cognomen 9. praenomen
nomenclature... 4. name 5. onymy 8. glossary, onymatic, register 10. dictionary, Latin names, vocabulary 11. designation, terminology
nominal... 3. par 6. unreal 7. not real, titular, topical 8. so–called
nominal recognizance (law)... 3. Doe
nonage... 6. neanic 8. immature, minority, pupilage, youthful
nonary... 9. nine group 10. base of

nine 11. group of nine
nonbeliever... 5. pagan 7. atheist, heathen, infidel 8. agnostic 11. disbeliever 12. non–Christian
nonce... 3. now 8. meantime 11. temporarily
nonchalant... 4. cool 6. casual 8. careless 10. insouciant 11. indifferent, unconcerned 13. imperturbable
noncompliance... 7. refusal 12. disobedience 13. recalcitrance
non compos mentis... 7. unsound 8. demented, deranged 11. disoriented
nonconformist... 7. heretic, sectary 8. objector, recusant 9. dissenter, protester
nondescript... 11. exceptional 13. indescribable 14. indeterminable
none... 2. no 4. nary 5. nones, no one 6. nobody, not any, not one 10. nobody else
nonentity... 7. a nobody, nullity 8. nihility, nonbeing 9. res nihili 11. nothingness 12. nonexistence
nonessential... 8. needless 9. extrinsic 10. adiaphoron, incidental, irrelevant 11. superfluous 12. adventitious
non licit... 8. unlawful
non–Mahometan... 5. Kafir 6. giaour 9. non–Moslem
nonmetallic... 4. spar 5. argon, boron 6. carbon, helium, iodine, oxygen 7. bromine 8. chlorine, nitrogen
nonpareil... 4. type 7. paragon 8. nonesuch, peerless 9. unrivaled 11. unsurpassed 14. painted bunting
nonplus... 4. stop 5. blank, stump 6. baffle, puzzle, thwart 7. mystify, perplex 8. quandary
nonproductive... 6. barren 7. sterile 9. fruitless
nonprofessional... 3. ham, lay 4. laic 5. laity 7. amateur 10. apprentice
nonsense... 3. bah 4. bosh, bunk, tosh 5. folly, stite 6. drivel, humbug, jargon 7. blarney, foolery, trifles, twaddle 8. falderal, flimflam, trumpery 9. absurdity, frivolity, poppycock, senseless, silliness 10. balderdash, tomfoolery, triviality 11. monkeyshine 12. fiddle–dee–dee
nonsense verse... 9. amphigory (amphigouri), rigmarole
non tanto (Mus)... 9. non troppo, not as much
noodle... 4. fool, head 5. brain, ninny 9. blockhead, simpleton 12. stupid person
nook... 4. cant, cove 5. angle, herne, niche 6. corner, cranny, recess 7. crevice 10. promontory
noon... 6. midday, summit 8. meridian, noontide 9. ninth hour 11. noon of night (poet)
noonday rest... 6. siesta
noose... 3. tie 4. bond, hang, loop 5. snare 6. circle, halter 7. laniard (lanyard) 12. hangman's rope
Nootka... 3. Aht, dog 6. Indian
norati... 5. noise 6. gossip

Norbertine... 12. Premonstrant
Nordic... 8. Germanic
   12. Scandinavian
norie... 9. cormorant
norm... 4. rule, type 5. model, norma
   7. average, measure, pattern
   8. standard, template
norma... 4. rule 5. gauge, model
   6. square 7. pattern 8. standard,
   template 13. constellation
normal... 3. par 4. just, mean, sane
   5. usual 6. common 7. average,
   logical, natural, orderly, regular, typical
   8. everyday, ordinary 9. customary
Norman... 6. French 7. crimson
   8. Northman 10. Romanesque
   17. conquest of England (1066)
Normandy...
   beach.. 5. Omaha
   capital.. 4. Caen 5. Rouen (old)
   city.. 5. Havre 6. Dieppe 7. Alençon
   9. Cherbourg
   conqueror.. 5. Rollo 8. William I
   governed by.. 6. France (1940)
   Viking duke (anc).. 5. Rollo
Norn (Teut Myth)... 4. Urth, Wyrd
   5. Skuld 9. Verthandi
Norse... 9. Norwegian
   12. Scandinavian
Norse (pert to)...
   abode of gods.. 6. Asgard 8. Valhalla
   alphabet.. 6. runics
   ash tree, universe.. 10. Yddgrasill
   bard.. 5. scald (skald) 7. sagaman
   collected songs, myths.. 4. Edda
   demon (Fire).. 4. Surt (Surtr)
   earth.. 7. Midgard
   epic.. 4. saga
   explorer.. 11. Leif Ericson
   first man.. 4. Askr
   giant.. 4. Loki, Ymir (Ymer) 5. Jotun
   6. Fafnir
   horse.. 8. Brimfaxi 9. Skinfaksi
   horse (Odin's).. 10. Yggdrasill
   king.. 4. Atli
   language (old).. 9. Icelandic
   maidens (Odin's).. 8. Valkyrie
   man.. 8. Northman
   monster.. 6. kraken 7. Midgard
   patron saint.. 4. Olaf
   poem.. 4. rune
   toast.. 5. skoal
   warrior.. 8. berserker
   watchdog (Hel's).. 4. Garm (Garmr)
   wolf.. 6. Fenrir
Norse goddess of...
   death, underworld.. 3. Hel, Ran
   fate.. 4. Norn, Urth, Wyrd
   flowers.. 5. Nanna
   giantess.. 4. Nott
   love, beauty.. 5. Freya
   peace, healing.. 3. Eir
   sky.. 5. Frigg (Frigga)
Norse God of...
   day.. 3. Dag
   evil.. 4. Loki
   fertility.. 4. Frey (Freyr) 6. Njorth
   (Njord)
   giants.. 4. Ymir
   justice.. 4. Frey 7. Forseti
   light.. 6. Balder
   night.. 4. Nott

   poetry.. 4. Odin 5. Bragi
   primeval (the world).. 4. Ymir (Ymer)
   sea.. 5. Aegir
   thunder.. 4. Thor
   war, wisdom.. 4. Odin (Wodin)
   watchfulness.. 8. Heimdall
Norse gods, chief... 3. Tyr (Tiu)
   4. Frey, Jarl, Loki, Odin (Othin,
   Wodin), Thor (Donar), Vali, Ymir
   5. Aesir (group) 6. Balder, Njorth
   7. Asynjur (group), Forseti
   8. Heimdall
North (far)... 6. Arctic
North Africa... see also *Africa*
   country.. 7. Algeria, Tunisia
   fruit.. 3. fig 4. date
   people.. 4. Moor 6. Berber, Hamite,
   Libyan
   port.. 4. Sfax
North America... see also *America*
   Indian blanket.. 6. stroud
   mountain, highest.. 8. McKinley
   orchid.. 8. arethusa
   owl.. 7. wapacut
   rail.. 4. sora
   reindeer.. 7. caribou
   river, longest.. 5. Yukon 8. Missouri
   11. Mississippi
   snake.. 5. adder
North Atlantic (pert to)...
   cape.. 5. Sable
   island.. 7. Britain, Iceland, Ireland
   9. Greenland, Manhattan
   sea gull.. 4. skua
North Carolina...
   cape.. 4. Fear 7. Lookout 8. Hatteras
   capital.. 7. Raleigh
   city.. 6. Durham 9. Asheville
   explorer.. 6. De Soto 9. Verrazano
   famed person.. 12. Virginia Dare
   16. Sir Walter Raleigh
   first flight.. 9. Kitty Hawk
   mountain.. 10. Mt Mitchell
   pine.. 8. loblolly
   river.. 3. Tar 5. Neuse 6. Peedee
   (Yadkin)
   State admission.. 7. Twelfth
   State bird.. 8. cardinal
   State flower.. 7. dogwood
   State motto.. 14. Esse Quam Videri
   20. To Be Rather Than To Seem
   State nickname.. 7. Tarheel 8. Old
   North
North Dakota...
   capital.. 8. Bismarck
   city.. 5. Fargo, Minot
   fort.. 6. Mandan 7. Lincoln
   11. Abercrombie
   historic site.. 24. International Peace
   Garden
   mountain.. 10. White Butte
   reservoir.. 8. Garrison
   State admission.. 8. Fortieth (or
   Thirty-ninth)
   State bird.. 10. meadowlark
   State flower.. 11. prairie rose
   State nickname.. 5. Sioux
   11. Flickertail
northeaster... 4. gale, wind 5. storm
Northern... 6. boreal 11. hyperborean
   13. septentrional
Northern constellation... 3. Cor

9. Andromeda
northernmost world (inhabitable)...
  5. Thule 9. Trondheim
North Pole... 10. boreal pole
North Sea... 6. Baltic, German
North Sea arm... 8. Kattegat
  9. Skagerrak (Skager–Rak)
North Sea canal... 4. Kiel
North Star... 7. Polaris 8. Cynosure,
  lodestar (loadstar), polestar
north wind... 6. Boreas
  10. tramontane
Norway... see also *Norwegian*
  capital.. 4. Oslo 11. Christiania (old)
  city.. 6. Bergen 7. Drammen
    9. Trondheim
  county.. 5. fylke
  inlet.. 5. fiord (fjord)
  mountain.. 6. Kjolen
  parliament.. 8. Storting (Storthing)
  patron saint.. 4. Olaf (Olaus)
  phenomenon.. 11. midnight sun
    14. Northern Lights
  plateau.. 5. fjeld
  river.. 2. Oi 4. Tana 7. Glommen
Norwegian (pert to)...
  bird.. 4. rype 9. ptarmigan
  cart.. 11. stolkjaerre
  dance.. 7. halling
  duck.. 7. widgeon
  embroidery.. 9. hardanger
  goblin.. 5. Nisse 6. kobold
  guardian spirit.. 6. fylgja 8. hamingja
  haddock.. 8. rosefish
  language.. 5. Norse 8. Rigsmaal
    9. Landsmaal
  liquor.. 7. akevitt
  sea monster.. 6. kraken
  tales.. 4. Edda
Norwegian people...
  author, explorer.. 8. Sverdrup
  composer.. 5. Grieg
  dramatist.. 5. Ibsen
  explorer.. 6. Nansen (Nobel Prize)
  king.. 6. Harold (The Fairhaired)
    15. Harold Hardraade
  philologist.. 5. Assen
  raiders.. 7. Vikings
  saint.. 4. Olaf (Olaus)
  violinist.. 7. Ole Bull
  zoologist.. 4. Sars
nose... 3. neb, pry 4. conk, prow
  5. nasus, scent, smell, snout
  6. meddle, muzzle, nuzzle 8. olfactor
  9. detective, proboscis
  11. investigate
nose (pert to)...
  ailment.. 6. coryza 8. rhinitis
  bees, birds.. 4. lore 5. lorum
  bleeding.. 9. epistaxis
  cartilage.. 6. septum
  glasses.. 8. pince–nez
  large.. 6. nasute
  muscle.. 7. nasalis
  opening.. 5. naris (nares, pl) 7. nostril
  partition.. 5. vomer
  plug.. 12. rhineurynter
  relating to.. 5. nasal 6. narial, rhinal
  snub.. 6. simous
  surgery.. 11. rhinoplasty
noseband (bridle)... 6. misrol
nosegay... 4. posy 7. bouquet,

perfume 9. fragrance 10. frangipani
  (tree)
nosocomium... 8. hospital
nosography, nosology *(science of)*...
  7. disease
nostalgia... 8. yearning 11.. wistfulness
  12. homesickness 14. sentimentality
nostology *(study of)*... 8. senility
  10. geriatrics 11. gerontology
Nostradamus... 4. seer 7. prophet
  10. astrologer
nostril... 5. naris (nares, pl) 6. narial
  9. olfactory
nostril–shaped... 8. nariform
nosy... 5. nasal 6. prying 7. curious
  8. fragrant 10. malodorous
  11. inquisitive
Nosy, Old (nickname)... 16. Duke of
  Wellington
not (pert to)...
  any.. 2. no 4. nane, nary, none
    7. no trace
  at all.. 5. nohow 6. nowise
  easy.. 7. labored
  either.. 7. neither
  feral.. 4. tame
  harmed.. 9. unscathed
  having a will.. 9. intestate
  hollow.. 5. solid
  in motion.. 5. fixed 6. stable, static
    7. stabile 10. stationary
  in the least.. 6. nowhit
  moral.. 6. amoral 7. immoral
  open (fruit).. 11. indehiscent
  prefix.. 2. il, im, in, ir, un 3. non
  professional.. 4. laic 7. amateur
  qualified.. 5. unfit
  running (stream).. 8. stagnant
  separable.. 11. indivisible
  settled.. 4. moot
  subjugated.. 7. unbowed
  suitable.. 5. inept
  the same.. 5. other 9. different
  to know.. 5. unken 10. unfamiliar
notable... 6. famous 8. historic
  9. celebrity, important, memorable,
  notorious 10. noteworthy, remarkable
  13. distinguished, extraordinary
notandum... 4. note 5. entry
  10. memorandum
notary... 5. notar 8. attestor,
  notebook, official 9. scrivener
  12. notary public, stenographer
notation... 4. memo, note 5. entry
  7. comment, marking 9. etymology
  10. annotation
notator... 5. noter 8. recorder
  9. annotator
notch... 3. gap, jap 4. dent, dint,
  kerf, nick, nock 5. cleft, crena, score
  6. defile, dentil (Her), indent
  7. passage 8. undercut 9. indenture
  11. indentation
notched bar (door)... 4. risp
notched opening (Anat)... 5. hilum
note... 2. ut 3. jot 4. chit, heed,
  mark, memo, sign, sole, song, tone,
  tune 5. breve, gloss, sound, token
  6. billet, notice, postil, record,
  remark, report 7. apostil (apostille),
  comment, epistle 8. dispatch,
  eminence, indicate, marginal,

scholium 9. character 10. annotation,
importance, indication, memorandum,
reputation 11. certificate, observation
note (pert to)...
death sound.. 4. mort
explanatory.. 5. gloss 8. scholium
half.. 5. minim
high.. 3. alt, E la
marginal.. 6. postil 7. apostil
(apostille)
musical.. 5. breve 6. ecbole
7. punctus
stem of.. 5. filum
notebook... 6. street 7. estreat
8. ratebook 10. adversaria,
memorandum
noted... 4. seen 5. famed 6. famous,
marked 7. eminent, notable
8. far–famed, renowned 9. distingué,
prominent, well–known 10. celebrated
notes... 5. duole 6. strain 7. tiralee
11. solmization
nothing... 3. nil, nox 4. luke, rien,
void, zero 5. nihil 6. naught, nichil,
nought, trifle 7. a nobody
9. nonentity 11. empty–handed
12. nonexistence
nothing doing... 4. calm 6. hushed,
no dice, no soap, placid 7. I refuse
9. by no means, God forbid,
quiescent
notice... 2. ad 3. see 4. heed, idea,
mark, mind, news, note, sign
5. blurb, edict, quote 6. advice,
espial, notion, regard, remark
7. affiche, mention, observe, warning
8. bulletin, citation 9. attention
10. commentary 11. information,
observation 12. announcement,
intelligence 13. advertisement
notice (pert to)...
advance.. 8. ballyhoo
death.. 4. obit 8. obituary
marriage.. 4. bans 5. banns
notify... 4. cite, page, tell, warn
6. inform, remind 7. apprise,
declare, publish 8. announce
notion... 4. idea, view, whim 5. freit
6. belief, theory, vagary 7. caprice,
impulse, opinion 9. intention
10. conception, denotation,
knickknack 11. supposition
notionable... 8. fanciful 9. whimsical
notional... 6. unreal 9. imaginary,
visionary, whimsical
notions... 5. goods, wares
11. commodities, merchandise
notoriety... 4. fame, plug 5. éclat
8. ballyhoo 9. limelight, publicity,
spotlight
notorious... 5. known, noted 6. arrant,
famous, notour 8. flagrant, infamous,
talked of 10. recognized
11. conspicuous
notorious character... 5. James
(Jesse) 7. Cochise, Younger
8. Geronimo, Jennings, Murietta
9. Jack Ketch, Wyatt Earp 11. Billy
the Kid, Poncho Villa, Sitting Bull
12. Calamity Jane 13. John Dillinger
14. Wild Bill Hickok
notum... 4. back

notus... 4. back (comb form)
notwithstanding... 3. but, yet 5. still
6. mauger (maugre), though
7. despite, however 8. although
9. in spite of 12. nevertheless
nought, naught... 3. bad, nil 4. zero
5. wrong 7. nothing, useless
9. worthless
noughty... 3. bad 9. worthless
noumenal... 4. real 5. ontal (opp of
phenomenal)
noun... 7. subject
noun (pert to)...
gender, common.. 7. epicene
indeclinable.. 6. aptote
irregular.. 5. pecus 11. heteroclite
suffix.. 2. et, ia 3. ent, ery, ier, ion,
ior, ist, ite 4. ence
verbal.. 6. gerund
nourish... 4. feed, grow 5. nurse
6. foster, suckle, supply 7. support,
sustain 9. cultivate 13. promote
growth
nourishing... 6. alible 8. nutrient
9. nutritive 10. alimentary
nourishment... 3. aid 4. food
5. manna, meats 7. aliment,
pabulum 9. nutriment, nutrition
10. sustenance 13. nutritiveness
14. nutritiousness
nous... 4. mind 8. ready wit
9. intellect 11. world spirit
Nova... 4. star
Nova Scotia...
bay.. 5. Fundy 10. Chedabucto
cape.. 5. Canso
capital.. 7. Halifax
greens.. 11. sea plantain
island.. 10. Cape Breton
lake, salt.. 7. Bras d'Or
native.. 7. Acadian 8. Bluenose
poetic name.. 6. Acadia (Acadie)
settlement, first.. 9. Port Royal
novel... 3. new 4. book, rare 5. fresh,
story 7. fiction, romance, strange,
unusual 8. original
novelty... 3. fad 7. newness
9. freshness 10. innovation,
recentness 11. originality
novice... 3. nun 4. puny, tyro (tiro)
5. chela, rooky 6. tyrone 7. amateur,
convert, learner 8. beginner,
freshman, initiate, neophyte,
newcomer 9. fledgling, greenhorn,
postulant 10. apprentice, catechumen
11. abecedarian 13. alphabetarian
novitiate... 6. novice 9. probation
14. apprenticeship
now... 3. noo 4. here 6. at once
7. present 9. at present, forthwith,
instantly 10. very lately 12. at this
moment
nowhere... 5. limbo 6. absent 7. no
place 8. oblivion 9. nowhither
11. nonexistent, not anywhere,
nullibicity
nowhere else... 5. there
nowise... 8. not at all
Nox (pert to)...
brother.. 6. Erebus
daughter.. 10. Hesperides
goddess (Rom).. 5. Night

husband .. 5. Chaos
noxious ... 4. evil 5. nasty, yucky (sl)
6. nocent, odious 7. baneful, harmful,
hurtful, noisome 9. injurious,
miasmatic 10. corruptive, pernicious
11. destructive, unwholesome
12. insalubrious
nozzle ... 3. tew 4. nose, vent
5. giant, snout 6. nuzzle, outlet,
tuyère 7. conduit 9. sprinkler
nuance ... 5. shade 9. gradation,
variation 10. refinement
nub ... 4. gist, knob, knot, knub, lump,
neck, snag 9. main point
12. protuberance
Nubia (pert to) ...
afterglow .. 14. second twilight
animal .. 4. goat 5. horse
autonym .. 6. Berber 7. Barabra
harp .. 5. nanga
tribe .. 4. Nuba
nubia ... 4. wrap 5. cloud
nucha ... 4. nape, neck
nuclear complex ... 7. Oedipus
nuclear energy (terms) ... 4. mass
6. fusion, ionize 7. fission, neutron,
reactor, tokamak 8. hydrogen,
meltdown
nuclear network fiber ... 5. linin
nucleus ... 4. core 5. cadre, focus,
umbra 6. center, kernel 8. rudiment
nude ... 4. bare 5. color, naked
6. Season (color) 7. denuded
8. stripped, undraped 9. unadorned,
unclothed, undressed
nudge ... 3. jog, nog 4. knub, lump,
poke, prod, push 5. block, elbow
6. jostle, remind, signal
nudibranch ... 7. mollusk
nugatory ... 4. vain 7. invalid, trivial
8. trifling 9. worthless
11. ineffectual
nuisance ... 4. bane, bore, harm, hurt,
pest 6. injury 9. annoyance
nuit ... 5. night
null ... 4. void 6. vacant 7. invalid
8. nugatory 11. nonexistent
13. inefficacious, insignificant
nullifidian ... 7. skeptic 9. nullibist,
skeptical 10. unbeliever
11. disbeliever
nullify ... 4. undo, void 5. annul
6. cancel, negate 7. abolish, destroy
8. abrogate 10. counteract, neutralize
numb ... 6. clumsy, freeze, stupid,
torpid 8. benumbed, deadened,
helpless 9. apathetic, incapable,
rigescent 10. insensible
12. anesthetized
number ... 3. sum 5. count, digit, limit
7. integer, numeral 8. quantity
9. aggregate, enumerate
10. complement 11. information
number (pert to) ...
added .. 6. encore
again .. 10. renumerate
by tens .. 7. decimal
cardinal .. 7. primary (one, two)
consecutively .. 5. folio
copies (printed) .. 7. edition
describable .. 6. scalar
irrational .. 4. surd

least whole .. 4. unit
lucky .. 5. seven
many .. 4. herd 6. myriad 7. several
9. multitude 12. considerable
ordinal .. 5. first 6. second (etc)
third power .. 4. cube
votes .. 4. poll
whole .. 7. integer
numbles, nombles ... 6. umbles
7. inwards 8. entrails
numbness ... 6. torpor 10. rigescence
numeral ... 5. Roman 6. Arabic, figure
9. character
numerous ... 4. lots, many 7. copious,
crowded 8. abundant, measured,
thronged 9. plentiful
Numidia (pert to) ...
city .. 5. Hippo
crane .. 10. demoiselle
language (written) .. 5. Punic 6. Tuareg
7. Hamitic
modern kingdom .. 7. Algeria
numskull ... 4. dolt, nerd 5. dunce
nun ... 4. moth, smew 5. Clare
(Franciscan), Vesta 6. monial, pigeon,
sister 8. titmouse, votaress
9. priestess 13. Lady of Loretto
nun bird ... 6. Monasa 8. puffbird
nunciate ... 9. announcer, messenger
nuncio ... 6. legate 8. delegate
9. messenger 11. internuncio
nuncupate ... 7. declare 8. dedicate,
inscribe, proclaim 9. designate
nuncupative ... 4. oral 9. unwritten
(will) 11. designative
nun headdress ... 6. wimple
nunnari root ... 12. sarsaparilla
nunnery ... 5. abbey 7. convent
8. cloister
nunnery head ... 6. abbess
nunni ... 7. blesbok (blesbuck)
8. antelope
Nuphar ... 12. spatterdocks 16. yellow
pond lilies
nuptial ... 6. bridal 7. marital
9. connubial 11. matrimonial
nurse ... 4. amah, ayah, feed, rear, tend
5. bonne, mammy 6. caress, suckle
7. care for, cherish, nourish, nurture,
nutrice 9. nursemaid
nursed ... 3. fed 6. tended 7. cradled,
suckled 8. nurtured 9. nourished
nursery ... 6. crèche, school 7. day
care (center)
nurse shark ... 4. gata
nurture ... 3. aid 4. feed, rear
5. nurse 6. foster 7. care for,
cherish 8. breeding, training
9. education, encourage, nutriment
nut ... 4. anta, kola (cola) 5. acorn,
betel, pecan, piñon 6. almond, Brazil,
cashew, litchi, peanut, walnut
7. filbert, hickory, maranon
8. beechnut, chestnut 9. butternut
nut (pert to) ...
bearing .. 10. nuciferous
brown .. 5. hazel 6. walnut
8. chestnut
coal .. 10. anthracite
collectively .. 4. food 5. shack
9. beechnuts
confection .. 8. marzipan

cracker.. **4**. crow
eating.. **10**. nucivorous
  11. nuciphagous
edible part.. **6**. kernel
grass.. **5**. sedge
Med.. **4**. kola **5**. bichy **9**. gourounut
odd.. **9**. eccentric
palm.. **5**. betel, lichi **7**. coconut
ref to.. **5**. nucal
shell.. **4**. case, hull **6**. trifle
Nut (pert to)...
  consort of.. **3**. Geb
  daughter.. **4**. Isis **8**. Nephthys
  goddess of.. **5**. earth
  son.. **2**. Ra
nutation... **3**. nod **7**. nodding
nuthatch... **4**. bird **5**. sitta **6**. xenops
  8. titmouse **9**. nutpecker
nutmeg... **4**. mace **5**. drupe **6**. beaver
  (color)
nutmeg (pert to)...
  bird, finch.. **5**. cowry **10**. weaverbird
  family.. **13**. Myristicaceae
  tree.. **6**. camara
Nutmeg State... **11**. Connecticut
nutpecker... **8**. nuthatch
nut quad... **6**. en quad
nutria... **3**. fur **5**. grège **10**. beaverlike
nutria fur bearer... **5**. coypu
nutrice... **5**. nurse
nutriment... **4**. food **7**. aliment,
  pabulum **9**. nutrition **11**. nourishment
nutritious... **9**. alimental
  10. alimentary, nourishing
nuts... **4**. food, mast **5**. shack
  9. beechnuts
nutty... **4**. gaga, zest **5**. queer, smart,
  spicy **7**. amorous, piquant
  10. unbalanced **11**. fascinating
  14. cracker–brained
nuzzle... **5**. nurse **6**. burrow, cuddle,
  foster, nestle **7**. cherish **8**. make
  snug
nyctalopia... **14**. night blindness

nye... **4**. eyas, nest, nide **5**. brood
nymph... **4**. nais **5**. deity, dryad,
  naiad, oread, siren, sylph **6**. Nereid
  7. Oceanid **9**. hamadryad
nymph (pert to)...
  Arcadian.. **6**. Syrinx
  beloved of Narcissus.. **4**. Echo
  color.. **4**. pink
  Cretan.. **8**. Cynosura
  fountain, river.. **4**. nais **5**. naiad
    6. Egeria
  German legend.. **7**. Lorelei
  Greek.. **4**. Echo **6**. Daphne
    8. Arethusa
  Hesperides (one of).. **5**. Aegle
    7. Hespera
  hills, mountain.. **5**. oread
  laurel tree.. **6**. Daphne
  Messina Strait.. **6**. Scylla
  Mohamm paradise.. **5**. houri
  monster.. **6**. Scylla
  Mt Ida.. **6**. Oenone
  ocean.. **5**. siren **6**. Nereid **7**. Galatea,
    Oceanid **10**. Callirrhoe
  pursued by Apollo.. **6**. Daphne, Syrinx
    8. Arethusa
  Queen.. **3**. Mab
  sea bird.. **6**. Scylla
  tree.. **5**. Dryad **9**. Hamadryad
  water.. **5**. Naiad **6**. Undine **7**. Hydriad
  woods.. **5**. Dryad **8**. Arethusa
    9. Hamadryad
  young.. **7**. nymphet
Nymphaea... **8**. Castalia **11**. water
  lilies
nymphs... **10**. Atlantides, Hesperides
nystagmus... **14**. eyeball disease
Nyx, Nox (pert to)...
  daughter.. **4**. Eris
  father.. **5**. Chaos
  goddess of.. **5**. Night
  mother of.. **11**. Day and Night
Nzambi... **7**. goddess (Afr) **11**. earth
  mother

O

O (pert to)...
  interjection.. **11**. exclamation
  letter.. **5**. tenth
  mathematics.. **4**. zero **6**. cipher
  pref (family).. **5**. Irish
oaf... **4**. boor, dolt, lout **5**. idiot,
  ouphe, yokel **9**. blockhead, simpleton
  10. changeling
oafish... **6**. simple, stupid
oak... **4**. club **5**. brave, color, oaken,
  stout **6**. strong **7**. Quercus
  8. hardness, strength **13**. artificial fly
oak (pert to)...
  apple.. **4**. gall **10**. she–oak cone
  beauty.. **4**. moth
  California.. **5**. roble **6**. encina

  comb form.. **6**. querci
  evergreen.. **4**. holm, ilex **5**. holly
  family.. **8**. Fagaceae
  fern.. **8**. polypody
  fruit., **5**. acorn **6**. camata
  fungus.. **10**. armillaria
  gall.. **8**. oak apple
  Jerusalem.. **7**. ambrose
  kinds.. **3**. bur, red **5**. black, white
    6. ground, poison, willow
    8. chestnut **10**. canyon live
  plantation.. **9**. quercetum
  resembling.. **9**. roboreous
  tannin.. **7**. quercic **9**. quercinic
  thicket.. **9**. chaparral
  Turkey.. **6**. cerris

O
Q

web.. 10. cockchafer
young.. 8. flittern
oam... 5. steam 7. warm air
Oannes (Bab)... 5. deity (part man, part fish)
oar... 3. row 5. blade, remus, rower, scull 6. paddle, propel 7. oarsman
oar (pert to)...
blade.. 4. palm, peel
feather.. 5. remex
fulcrum, lock.. 5. pivot, thole
lop.. 6. rabbit
shaft.. 4. loom
shaped.. 7. remiped 8. remiform
oars (pert to)...
collective.. 6. oarage, sculls
one bank.. 7. unireme
reverse.. 6. sheave
three banks.. 7. trireme
two banks.. 6. bireme
oasis... 3. ojo 4. wadi (wady) 5. Gafsa 6. Dakhla 11. fertile spot
oast... 4. kiln, oven
oat (pert to)...
cake.. 5. caper
ear (Old World).. 4. bird 7. wagtail
fowl.. 11. snow bunting
genus.. 5. Avena 6. oathay
grass.. 4. ulla 9. chaparral
husks.. 5. shood (shude)
like.. 10. avenaceous
rent (paid as).. 7. avenage
oath... 3. God 4. aith, drat, egad 5. bedad, curse 6. pledge 7. serment 9. affidavit, holy smoke, profanity 10. deposition 11. affirmation
Obadiah (Bib)... 6. Quaker 7. prophet
obbligato... 8. required 13. accompaniment, indispensable
obduction... 7. autopsy 8. covering
obdurate... 4. firm, hard 5. rough, stony 6. mulish, rugged 7. adamant, callous 8. stubborn 9. heartless, obstinate, unbending, unfeeling 10. impenitent, inflexible, insensible, unyielding 11. hardhearted, intractable
obedient... 6. docile 7. duteous, dutiful, orderly 8. amenable, yielding 9. attentive, compliant 10. submissive 11. conformable
obeisance... 3. bow 5. binge, congé 6. curtsy, fealty, homage 9. deference 10. respectful 14. obsequiousness
obeisance, to make... 3. bow 6. congee, curtsy, salaam
obelisk... 5. pylon 6. guglia (guglio), needle, obelus, pillar 16. Cleopatra's Needle
Oberon (pert to)...
Astron.. 9. satellite
character of.. 11. Shakespeare
classic.. 4. poem 5. opera
husband of.. 7. Titania
Myth.. 13. King of Fairies
obese... 3. fat 5. puffy, pursy, squab, stout 6. fleshy, turgid 8. liparous 9. corpulent
obey... 3. ear 4. hear, mind 5. yield 6. comply, submit

obfuscate... 3. dim 6. darken, opaque 7. confuse, perplex 8. bewilder
obi... 4. sash 6. girdle
obit... 4. rest 5. death 6. notice 7. decease, release 8. obituary 9. obsequies 10. necrologue 11. Requiem Mass 12. mortuary roll
obiter... 9. in passing 12. incidentally
obiter dictum... 7. opinion (of judge)
object... 3. aim, end 4. goal, hulk 5. cavil, demur, scoff, thing 6. appose, expose, motive, oppose 7. article, grammar, protest, purpose 9. intention
object (pert to)...
bulky.. 4. hulk
circular.. 7. trundle
cloudlike.. 6. nebula
illustrative.. 6. realia (pl)
rare.. 5. curio 7. antique
rational.. 8. noumenon
sacred.. 4. Urim 7. Thummim
small.. 4. mite
object for...
devotion, worship.. 4. icon, idol 5. totem 6. fetish
dread.. 5. bogey (bogie) 6. goblin 8. the Devil
going and coming.. 6. errand
greed.. 5. lucre, money 6. wealth
knowledge.. 7. scibile
objection... 3. bar 5. cavil 7. protest, quarrel 8. demurrer, obstacle 9. exception 11. disapproval
objectionable... 9. offensive 11. exceptional, inexpedient 13. uncommendable
objective... 3. aim, end 4. goal 6. motive, target 7. purpose
objector, conscientious... 6. conchy
objects (Bib)... 4. Urim 7. Thummim
objects (floating)... 7. flotsam
objurgate... 5. abuse, chide, scold 6. rebuke 7. reprove, upbraid 9. reprimand
oblate... 5. oblat 7. devoted 9. dedicated, flattened (opp of prolate)
obligated... 5. bound 6. in debt 7. obliged 8. beholden 9. obstringe
obligation... 3. tie, vow 4. bond, debt, duty, oath, onus 7. promise 8. civility, contract 9. agreement, necessity 10. compulsion 11. obstriction
obligatory... 7. binding 8. imposing, required 9. mandatory, necessary 10. compulsory
oblige... 4. bind, pawn 5. favor 6. compel, engage 7. gratify 8. obligate 9. constrain, obstringe 11. accommodate
obliged... 7. favored 8. beholden, grateful 9. duty bound
obliging... 4. kind 7. helpful 9. agreeable, courteous, indulgent 11. complaisant, considerate 13. accommodating
oblique... 4. cant, skew 5. bevel, slant, slope 7. obscure, scalene 8. inclined, perverse, sidelong, sidewise, sinister, slanting

9. underhand 10. circuitous, collateral, transverse 12. disingenuous
oblique angle... 5. acute 6. obtuse
obliquely... 4. skew 6. aslant
  7. askance 8. sideways, sidewise
  9. on the bias 10. slantingly
obliterate... 4. blot, dele 5. erase
  6. cancel, delete, efface, sponge
  7. expunge
obliteration... 6. rasure 7. erasure
  8. deletion 10. extinction
oblivion... 7. nirvana, silence
  9. unfeeling 13. forgetfulness
  15. unconsciousness
oblivion, producing... 8. nepenthe
oblivion, river of... 5. Lethe
oblivious... 6. asleep 8. heedless
  9. forgetful, unfeeling 10. abstracted
  11. unconscious
oblong... 8. elliptic 9. elongated
  11. rectangular 12. quadrangular
obloquy... 5. abuse 6. infamy
  7. calumny 9. criticism
  11. malediction 12. reprehension
obnoxious... 4. vile 5. nasty
  6. odious, rancid 7. hateful
  8. amenable, infamous, terrible
  9. offensive 13. objectionable
oboe... 4. reed 5. shawm (anc)
  7. hautboy, musette 8. schalmei
  (schalmey) 9. chalumeau
obscuration... 7. eclipse 9. darkening, vagueness
obscure... 3. dim, fog 4. dark, hazy, slur 5. bedim, blind, mirky, misty, murky 6. cloudy, darken, delude, mystic, opaque, remote 7. becloud, conceal, eclipse, shadowy, unknown 8. darkling, formless, nameless, nubilous, obstruse, oversile (obs)
  9. enigmatic, undefined
  10. indistinct, unrenowned
obscurity... 3. fog 5. gloom
  7. dimness, opacity, unknown
  8. darkness 9. nonentity, vagueness
  12. formlessness 13. imperspicuous
  14. insignificancy, uncomprehended
obsecrate... 7. beseech, entreat
  10. supplicate
obsequies... 5. wakes 8. funerals
  9. last rites
obsequious... 5. slick 6. abject
  7. devoted, dutiful, fawning, servile, slavish 8. cringing, funereal, obedient, toadying 9. attentive, compliant 11. subservient
observance... 3. act 4. form, rite
  6. custom 8. behavior, ceremony, practice 9. attention, deference, sacrament, vigilance 10. conformity
  11. celebration
observant... 7. careful, heedful, mindful
  8. faithful, vigilant, watchful
  9. attentive, regardant, regardful
observation... 4. idea 6. espial, remark
  7. opinion 9. attention
observatory... 4. Lick 6. Yerkes
  7. lookout, Palomar 8. Mt Wilson
  11. planetarium
observe... 2. lo! 3. eye, see, spy
  4. espy, heed, keep, nark, note, obey, tout 6. behold, notice, remark

7. conform, examine, witness
  8. preserve 9. celebrate, solemnize
observed, to be... 8. notandum
  10. memorandum
observer... 4. eyer, nark 7. aviator, student, witness 8. beholder, informer, looker–on, onlooker
  9. spectator 11. stool pigeon
obsess... 5. beset, haunt 6. harass
  7. bewitch, possess 8. demonize
  9. influence, preoccupy
obsession... 5. mania 8. impelled
  11. bewitchment 13. spirit control
obsignate... 4. seal 5. stamp 6. ratify
obsolete... 3. old 5. passé 6. effete
  7. archaic, disused, effaced, outworn, worn out 9. out of date
  10. antiquated 12. old–fashioned
obstacle... 3. dam 4. snag 6. hurdle
  9. hindrance 10. difficulty, impediment 11. obstruction
obstetrician... 6. doctor
  10. accoucheur
obstetrix... 7. midwife
obstinate... 3. set 5. balky, tough
  6. dogged, mulish, sullen 7. willful
  8. perverse, stubborn 9. pigheaded
  10. determined, headstrong, self–willed 11. opinionated
obstreperous... 5. noisy 6. unruly
  7. blatant 9. clamorous, turbulent
  10. vociferous 11. disobedient
  12. ungovernable
obstruct... 3. bar, dam, dit 4. clog, ditt, stop 5. beset, block, check, choke, delay 6. arrest, hamper, oppose, stop up 7. occlude
  9. barricade, embarrass, interfere, interrupt
obstruction... 3. ban, dam 4. clog, reef, snag 7. barrier 8. obstacle
  9. hindrance 10. difficulty, filibuster, impediment 11. retardation
obtain... 3. buy, eke, get, win
  4. earn, fang, gain 5. fetch, reach
  6. attain, derive, elicit, secure
  7. achieve, acquire, capture, prevail, procure, receive
obtain (pert to)...
  by intimidation.. 9. blackmail
  by threats.. 6. extort
  control of.. 6. corner 8. overcome
  equivalent.. 6. recoup
obtest... 6. beg for 7. beseech
  10. supplicate
obtrude... 5. eject, expel 6. impose
  7. intrude
obtrusive... 7. forward, pushing
  9. intrusive, officious
obtund... 4. dull 5. blunt, quell
  6. deaden 8. moderate
obtuse... 4. dull 5. blunt, crass, dense
  6. stupid 9. unfeeling 11. insensitive
obvelation... 7. veiling 10. concealing
obverse... 5. front 8. converse
  10. complement 11. counterpart
obviate... 7. head off, rule out
  8. preclude 9. forestall 10. anticipate
obvious... 5. clear, gross, plain
  7. evident, patient 8. apparent, distinct, manifest, palpable
  11. conspicuous, open and shut

obvolute ... 7. twisted 9. contorted, convolute 11. overlapping

occasion ... 4. sele, time 5. cause, event, nonce 6. excuse, motive 7. pretext 8. ceremony, exigency, function, incident 9. condition, happening 11. opportunity 12. circumstance

occasional ... 3. odd 4. orra 5. stray 6. casual 10. incidental, infrequent

occasionally ... 7. at times 9. sometimes 10. now and then 11. at intervals 12. sporadically

occasive ... 8. westward 10. setting sun

Occident ... 4. West 6. sunset 17. Western Hemisphere (opp of Orient)

Occidental ... 6. ponent 7. The West, Western 9. Hesperian

occiput ... 10. back of head 11. back of skull

occlude ... 3. dam 4. shut 5. close 6. shut up 8. obstruct

occult ... 5. magic 6. hidden, mystic 7. alchemy, cryptic 8. esoteric 9. concealed, recondite 10. mysterious, necromancy 11. supernormal 12. supernatural

occultation ... 4. gone, lost 7. eclipse 11. concealment

occultism ... 6. cabala 7. mystery

occult science ... 9. esoterics

occupant ... 6. inmate, tenant 10. inhabitant

occupation ... 3. job 4. call, note, work 5. hobby, trade 6. career, tenure 7. calling, pursuit 8. business, vocation 9. avocation 10. employment, habitation, possession, profession 11. engrossment

occupied ... 3. sat 4. busy, held 6. filled 7. engaged 8. employed, pervaded 9. engrossed, inhabited

occupy ... 3. use 4. fill, hold 6. employ, engage, expend, invest 7. engross, inhabit, oversit, pervade, possess 8. interest

occur ... 4. come, fall, meet 5. clash 6. appear, befall, betide, happen

occurrence ... 3. hap 5. event 8. incident, presence, scenario 9. existence, happening 10. appearance 11. eventuality 12. circumstance

occurring (pert to) ...
after death .. 10. posthumous
at nightfall .. 9. acronical
often .. 8. frequent 10. frequently

ocean ... 3. sea 4. brim, deep, main 5. brine 6. depths, pelago 8. great sea

ocean (pert to) ...
approach .. 7. sea gate
bottom .. 3. bed
crop cultivation .. 11. mariculture
deep .. 7. bathyal
deepest, lowest .. 5. hadal 8. bathybic 12. bathypelagic
division .. 6. Arctic, Indian 7. Pacific 8. Atlantic 9. Antarctic

floating matter .. 5. algae 7. flotsam
geography .. 12. oceanography
mammal .. 4. seal 5. whale
on (the ocean) .. 4. asea
periodic motion .. 4. tide
person .. 8. aquanaut, oceanaut 9. skin diver 10. scuba diver
ref to .. 7. pelagic 9. Neptunian
route .. 4. lane
sealing .. 7. pelagic
vessel .. 6. Sealab 9. submarine 10. bathyscaph 11. bathysphere

Oceania, Oceanica ... 9. Melanesia, Polynesia 10. Micronesia 12. Pacific lands

Oceanids (Gr Myth, pert to) ...
father .. 7. Oceanus
mother .. 6. Tethys
nymphs .. 13. three thousand

Oceanus (Gr Myth, per to) ...
children .. 5. Doris 8. Eurynome (goddess), Oceanids
god of .. 6. rivers
wife .. 6. Tethys

ocellus ... 3. eye 6. stemma 7. eyespot

ocelot ... 3. cat 7. leopard

ocher, ochre (pert to) ...
red .. 5. tiver 7. almagra 8. hematite 9. faded rose
yellow .. 3. sil 7. Chinese 8. limonite 9. ochrolite

ochlocracy ... 7. mob rule

ochlophobia (fear of) ... 6. crowds

ocotillo ... 5. shrub 10. candlewood

ocracy ... 9. group rule

octad ... 5. eight (group)

octaemeron ... 12. eight–day fast

octagon ... 8. octangle 11. eight angles

octahedron ... 10. eight faces

octameter ... 8. octapody 9. eight feet

octarchy ... 11. rule by eight

octastich ... 6. octave 10. eight lines 11. eight verses

Octateuch (Old Test) ... 10. Eight Books (1st)

octave ... 4. utas 5. eight 6. eighth 8. wine cask 10. eight notes

Octavia (pert to) ...
sister of .. 8. Augustus
wife of .. 10. Mark Antony

Octavian ... 7. Library (Rome's 1st) 16. committee of eight (one of)

octet, octette ... 7. huitain 12. group of eight

October (pert to) ...
bird .. 8. bobolink
birthstone .. 4. opal 5. beryl
Club .. 9. political
drink .. 3. ale
month .. 5. tenth

octogenarian ... 13. eighty–year–old

octopod ... 9. eight arms, eight legs

Octopoda (Roder) ... 8. mollusks (8–armed) 9. argonauts, octopuses

octopus ... 5. poulp (poulpe)

octroi, octroy ... 3. tax 9. privilege 10. concession

ocular ... 3. eye (pert to) 5. optic, sight 6. visual 10. ophthalmic

oculus ... 3. eye 14. Corona Borealis

odd... 4. orra, rare 5. droll, extra, outré, queer 6. uneven, unique 7. azygous, bizarre, strange, unequal, unusual 8. unpaired 9. eccentric, remaining, unmatched 10. occasional

oddity... 9. queerness 11. peculiarity, singularity 12. eccentricity, idiosyncrasy

odds... 6. gamble 7. dispute, quarrel 8. gambling, variance 9. advantage 10. difference, dissension, inequality 11. probability 12. disagreement 13. probabilities

odds and ends... 4. orts 6. refuse, scraps 7. mixture, remains 8. remnants 10. miscellany

ode... 4. like (suff), poem 5. psalm 8. canticle, serenata

ode (type)... 7. Lesbian, regular 8. Horatian, Pindaric 9. irregular

odeon... 4. hall 7. gallery, theater

Odin (pert to)...
  attendants.. 9. Valkyries
  god of.. 3. war 6. poetry, wisdom
  hall.. 8. Valhalla
  horse.. 8. Sleipner
  son.. 4. Tyre, Vali 6. Balder
  Teutonic name.. 5. Woden
  wife.. 5. Frigg

odious... 4. foul, vile 5. nasty 7. hateful 8. infamous, terrible

odium... 6. hatred, infamy 9. antipathy 10. abhorrence, opprobrium 11. detestation

odontist... 7. dentist

odontology *(science of)*... 5. teeth 9. dentistry

odor, odour... 4. fume, funk, nose 5. aroma, fetor, nidor, scent, smell 6. flavor 7. essence, malodor, perfume 9. fragrance, redolence

odor, meat cooking... 5. fumet (fumette)

odorous... 8. aromatic, fragrant, redolent, smelling

Odysseus (pert to)...
  chieftain.. 9. Trojan War
  dog.. 5. Argos
  father.. 7. Laertes
  hero of.. 10. The Odyssey (Homer)
  king of.. 6. Ithaca (Gr)
  magic herb.. 4. moly
  modern name.. 7. Ulysses
  wife.. 8. Penelope

oecist... 9. colonizer

oecodomic... 13. architectural

Oedipus (pert to)...
  daughter.. 8. Antigone
  father.. 5. Laius (King of Thebes)
  mother.. 7. Jocasta

oeno (comb form)... 4. wine

oenomancy... 12. wine prophecy

oenophilist... 9. wine lover

oenopoetic... 10. wine making

oestrus... 4. fury 5. sting 6. desire, frenzy 7. impulse 8. stimulus

of... 2. in, on 4. over, upon, with 5. about, avent 10. indication

of (pert to)...
  a chamber.. 7. cameral
  a class (related).. 7. generic
  a father.. 6. agnate
  a flock.. 6. gregal
  a forefather.. 9. ancestral
  a grandfather.. 4. aval
  all.. 3. ava
  a mother.. 7. cognate
  an epoch.. 4. eral
  an order.. 7. ordinal
  a wife.. 7. uxorial
  common gender.. 7. epicene
  each.. 3. ana
  earth.. 4. geal
  equal value.. 10. comparable
  French.. 2. du 3. des
  great importance.. 7. capital 9. momentous
  high standing.. 8. sterling
  little importance.. 5. petty 7. trivial
  morning.. 5. matin 7. matinal
  New Stone Age.. 9. Neolithic
  no avail.. 6. futile
  nostrils.. 6. narine
  old age.. 8. gerontal
  planet's path.. 7. orbital
  recent times.. 6. lately 9. latter–day
  reign.. 6. regnal
  river banks.. 8. riparian
  same family.. 7. cognate, germane
  sound.. 5. tonal
  summer.. 7. estival
  tears.. 8. lacrimal
  the country.. 5. rural
  the mouth.. 4. oral
  the third degree.. 7. cubical
  the throat.. 5. gular
  the tongue.. 7. glossal
  the wrist.. 6. carpal
  this day.. 9. hodiernal
  thread color.. 7. ficelle
  winter.. 6. hiemal
  yore.. 5. olden

off... 3. ill 4. agee, away, doff 5. aside 6. begone, insane, remote 7. distant, tainted 9. dissonant, erroneous, imperfect, right–hand 10. unemployed

offal... 5. filth 6. ordure, refuse 7. carrion, garbage, rubbish

offbeat... 14. unconventional

off–color... 6. risqué 7. dubious 8. inferior

offend... 3. cag, sin, vex 4. miff 5. anger, annoy, pique, wound 6. assail, insult, revolt 7. affront, do wrong, mortify 9. displease

offender... 6. sinner 8. criminal 9. wrongdoer 10. malefactor 12. transgressor

offense... 3. sin 5. crime, delit, fault, grief, malum 6. delict, felony, insult 7. outrage, umbrage 8. trespass 9. indignity 10. resentment 11. delinquency, misdemeanor, stellionate

offensive... 4. foul, ugly 6. attack, odious, ribald, vulgar 7. abusive, eyesore, fulsome, harmful, obscene 8. invading, shocking 9. assailant, attacking, insulting, obnoxious, repugnant, revolting 10. aggressive, malodorous, scurrilous 11. approbrious, displeasing, distasteful 12. disagreeable

13. transgressive
offer... 3. bid 6. adduce, tender
7. proffer, propine, propose
8. immolate, overture 9. ultimatum
offered for sale... 6. vended
9. auctioned
offering... 4. gift 6. corban
7. deodate, present 8. oblation
9. sacrifice
offering resistance... 8. renitent
offhand... 8. careless, informal,
slapdash 9. extempore, impromptu
10. carelessly, nonchalant
11. extemporary 12. nonchalantly
15. autoschediastic
office... 4. duty, post, rite, wike (obs)
5. place, trust 7. station
8. ceremony, function, position
9. situation 11. appointment
office (pert to)...
chief.. 7. manager
divine.. 9. akoluthia
for the dead.. 7. trental
holder.. 8. placeman
of a datary (Roman Curia).. 7. dataria
of a ruler.. 7. regency
relinquish (to).. 5. demit
third hour.. 6. tierce
officer... 6. tindal 7. bailiff, command,
conduct, general, manager, marshal,
sheriff 8. adjutant, avigator, director
9. constable, policeman, president
officer (pert to)...
assistant.. 4. aide
Brit Royal Guard.. 4. exon
chief executive.. 3. dey 4. czar
5. mayor 7. emperor, monarch,
premier 8. governor 9. president
10. chancellor
church.. 5. elder 6. sexton
civil law.. 6. notary, police 7. bailiff,
marshal, sheriff 9. constable,
policeman 10. magistrate
club.. 7. steward
corrupt.. 7. grafter
despotic.. 6. satrap
diplomatic.. 7. attaché
Jewish Relig.. 6. parnas
King's stables.. 6. avener
monastic.. 5. prior
naval.. 6. ensign, yeoman
parish.. 6. beadle, bedral
ship's.. 9. boatswain (boson)
weights, measures.. 6. sealer
official... 6. formal 9. authentic
10. functional 13. authoritative
official (pert to)...
command.. 5. edict
despotic.. 6. satrap
game.. 5. judge 6. umpire 7. referee
government.. 10. bureaucrat
insurance.. 7. actuary 8. adjuster
itinerant (Hist).. 6. missus
mark.. 5. stamp
order (RCCh).. 8. rescript
proclamation.. 5. ukase 6. decree
record.. 5. actum
state.. 8. governor 9. secretary
officious... 4. cool, pert 5. saucy
6. formal 8. arrogant, impudent,
official 9. pragmatic 10. meddlesome
11. efficacious, impertinent,

pragmatical 12. contemptuous
officiousness... 10. pragmatism
offing... 10. background
offshoot... 3. rod 5. scion 6. branch,
member 8. addition 9. by–product
10. descendant 12. organization
offspring... 3. son 4. brat, seed
5. child, fruit, issue, sprig 6. origin,
result 7. produce, product, progeny
8. fountain 9. posterity
10. descendant
oficina... 5. works 6. office 7. factory
10. laboratory
often... 3. oft 9. many times
10. frequently, repeatedly 11. over
and over 13. time after time
ogdoad... 5. eight 10. eight group
ogee... 4. gula 5. talon 7. molding
9. cyma recta 11. cyma reversa
ogle... 3. eye 4. gaze, leer 5. stare
7. examine
Ogpu... 8. Gay–Pay–Oo (Russ secret
service)
O Henry... 6. Porter (Wm Sydney)
Ohio...
capital.. 8. Columbus
city.. 5. Akron 6. Dayton, Toledo
9. Cleveland 10. Cincinnati
first settlement.. 8. Marietta
hero.. 12. Anthony Wayne (Gen)
lake.. 4. Erie
name meaning (Indian).. 14. Beautiful
River
State admission.. 11. Seventeenth
State motto.. 27. With God All Things
are Possible
State nickname.. 7. Buckeye
oil... 3. ben, fat 4. balm, ghee
5. bribe, oleum 6. aceite, anoint,
asarum, grease, olanin 8. flattery,
medicate, painting 9. lubricant,
lubricate, petroleum 10. illuminant
oil (pert to)...
beetle.. 5. meloe
berry.. 5. olive
bird.. 8. guachare
cask.. 4. rier
class.. 5. fatty, fixed 6. animal
7. mineral 8. volatile 9. essential,
vegetable
cloth.. 8. linoleum
coal.. 8. photogen
comb form.. 2. ol 3. ole
fish.. 7. escolar
flask.. 4. olpe
gauge.. 9. oleometer
glands (birds).. 9. uropygial
11. elaeodochon
lamp.. 7. lucigen
mineral.. 7. naphtha
plant.. 6. sesame 9. castor–oil
prefix.. 2. ol
rock.. 5. shale 9. limestone
seed.. 3. til (teel) 6. sesame
7. linseed 8. rapeseed 10. castor
bean, cottonseed
skin.. 5. sebum
stone.. 4. hone 9. whetstone
term.. 5. oleic
tree.. 4. eboe (ebo), tung 5. mahua
6. illupi 7. oil palm 9. candlenut,
castor–oil

tube .. **5.** vitta
whale .. **5.** sperm
oil of ...
　cloves .. **7.** eugenol
　myrcia .. **6.** bay oil
　orange blossoms .. **6.** neroil
　roses .. **4.** otto **5.** attar (atar)
　salt .. **7.** bittern
oils ... **10.** elaeoptene (elaeopten) (opp
　of stearoptene)
oily ... **3.** fat **4.** glib **5.** bland, oleic,
　suave **6.** olease, supple **7.** pinguid
　8. unctuous **9.** compliant, plausible
　10. flattering, oleaginous
　11. insinuating, subservient
　12. hypocritical
oily liquids ... **3.** tar **6.** cresol, octane
　7. aniline, picamar **8.** creosote
oily tissue ... **3.** fat
ointment ... **4.** balm, cere, lard, nard
　5. salve **6.** balsam, carron, cerate,
　ceroma, grease **7.** pomatum, unguent
　8. liniment **9.** spikenard, xeromyron
　10. petrolatum **11.** embrocation
Oise (France) ... **5.** Aisne (tributary),
　river **10.** department
Ojibway secret order ... **4.** mide
　(meda) **9.** midewiwin
ojo ... **5.** oasis
OK ... **6.** righto **7.** correct
Okinawa ...
　capital .. **4.** Naha
　island group (64) .. **6.** Ryukyu
　prefecture of .. **5.** Japan
Oklahoma ...
　capital .. **12.** Oklahoma City
　city .. **3.** Ada **4.** Enid **5.** Tulsa
　6. Lawton **8.** Muskogee
　9. Claremore **12.** Bartlesville
　Five Civilized Tribes .. **5.** Creek
　7. Choctaw **8.** Cherokee, Seminole
　9. Chickasaw
　lake .. **6.** Texoma
　migrant from .. **4.** Okie
　mountain .. **5.** Ozark **8.** Ouachita
　museum .. **6.** Indian **8.** Woolaroc
　native son (famed) .. **10.** Will Rogers
　old name .. **15.** Indian Territory
　State admissison .. **11.** Thirty–third
　State bird .. **10.** flycatcher
　State flower .. **9.** mistletoe
　State motto .. **16.** Labor Omnia Vincit
　(Labor Conquers All)
　State nickname .. **6.** Sooner
okra ... **5.** bendy, gumbo **6.** mallow
old ... **3.** ald, eld **4.** aged **5.** anile
　6. infirm, senile **7.** ancient, antique,
　archaic **8.** obsolete **9.** doddering,
　senescent, venerable **10.** antiquated
old (pert to) ...
　age .. **6.** senile **7.** geratic **8.** gerontic,
　senility **10.** geriatrics (Med),
　senescence **11.** gerontology
　ancient (very) .. **7.** Ogygian
　billy, granny .. **5.** squaw
　fashioned .. **4.** fogy **7.** antique
　9. primitive **12.** conservative
　hat .. **5.** trite **9.** out–of–date
　maid .. **5.** prude **10.** fussbudget
　man .. **5.** elder, timer **6.** codger,
　gaffer, geezer, Nestor **8.** kangaroo
　10. fuddy–duddy

sailor .. **3.** tar **4.** salt
saying .. **3.** saw **5.** adage, maxim
time .. **3.** eld **4.** syne
woman .. **3.** hag **4.** fogy **5.** crone
　6. dotard, gammar
womanish .. **5.** anile **6.** senile
　10. effeminate
Old (pert to) ...
　Bailey .. **12.** English court
　Bay State .. **13.** Massachusetts
　Dominion .. **8.** Virginia
　Empire .. **4.** Maya
　English alphabet .. **10.** Anglo–Saxon
　Faithful .. **6.** geyser
　Franklin State .. **9.** Tennessee
　Gentleman Harry .. **5.** Devil
　Gooseberry .. **5.** Devil, Satan
　Glory .. **15.** Stars and Stripes
　Guard (Waterloo) .. **9.** Napoleon's
　Hickory .. **13.** Andrew Jackson
　Ironsides .. **15.** USS Constitution
　Kingdom .. **7.** Memphis (Egypt)
　Lady of Threadneedle Street ..
　　13. Bank of England
　Line State .. **8.** Maryland
　Man of the Mountain .. **7.** Profile (The)
　Noll .. **14.** Oliver Cromwell
　North Church .. **12.** Christ Church
　North State .. **13.** North Carolina
　Rough and Ready .. **16.** (Gen) Zachary
　　Taylor
　Serpent .. **5.** Satan
　Sod .. **4.** Erin **7.** Ireland
　Sol .. **3.** sun
　Stone Age .. **11.** Paleolithic
　Three Stars .. **8.** (Gen) Grant
　World .. **7.** Eastern
olden ... **6.** bygone
older ... **5.** elder **6.** senior **8.** ancestor
oldest ... **4.** dean **6.** eldest **7.** stalest
Old Testament (pert to) ...
　Books (number) .. **10.** Thirty–nine
　Elohim .. **3.** God (The Hexateuch)
　Hexateuch .. **13.** first Six Books
　Land of riches .. **5.** Ophir
　objects (sacred) .. **4.** Urim
　　7. Thummim
　Pentateuch .. **10.** Law of Moses
　　14. first Five Books
　writer .. **7.** Elohist (The Hexateuch)
Old World (pert to) ...
　ape .. **7.** Primate **10.** Catarrhina
　carnivore .. **5.** genet
　falcon .. **5.** saker
　herb .. **5.** tansy
　lizard .. **5.** Agama
　shrub .. **4.** Olax
oleaginous ... **4.** oily **5.** oleic
　8. unctuous
oleander ... **6.** Nerium
　11. rhododaphne **12.** rhododendron
oleoresin ... **5.** anime, elemi **6.** balsam
　7. copaiba
oleum ... **3.** oil
olfaction ... **7.** osmesis **8.** smelling
　12. sense of smell
olfactory organ ... **4.** nose **8.** olfactor
olid ... **4.** foul **5.** fetid **6.** rancid, smelly
　. malodorous **11.** strong smell
oligarchy ... **10.** rule by a few
olinda bug ... **6.** weevil
olio ... **4.** olla, stem **6.** medley

7. mixture 8. chowchow
9. burlesque, potpourri
10. collection, hodgepodge
11. olla–podrida
oliphant... 8. elephant 9. ivory horn
oliprance... 4. romp, show 7. jollity
11. merrymaking, ostentation
olive (pert to)...
   branch.. 5. child, peace 6. symbol
   (peace)
   color.. 11. yellow–green
   dun.. 3. fly (fishing)
   enzyme.. 6. olease
   family.. 8. Oleaceae
   fly.. 3. dun 4. gnat 5. quill
   gray.. 10. Scotch gray
   gum.. 6. olivil
   overripe.. 5. drupe
   stuffed.. 6. pimola
   true.. 4. Olea
   wild.. 8. oleaster
   yard.. 6. olivet
   yellow.. 9. moss green 10. chartreuse
olla... 3. jug, pot 4. olio 8. palm leaf
   (palmyra) 11. olla–podrida
olla–podrida... 4. hash, olio 6. medley
   10. hodgepodge
oloroso... 6. sherry
olpe... 5. flask 8. oenochoë 11. wine
   pitcher
olycook, olykoek... 7. cruller
   8. doughnut
Olympia... 4. ship 7. capital (Wash)
   8. heavenly 9. sanctuary (anc)
Olympiad... 14. four–year period
Olympian god... 4. Ares, Zeus
   6. Apollo, Hermes 8. Dionysus,
   Hercules, Poseidon 10. Hephaestus
Olympian goddess... 4. Hera
   6. Athena, Hestia 7. Artemis,
   Demeter 9. Aphrodite
Olympic cupbearer... 8. Ganymede
Olympic Games (pert to)...
   honor of.. 4. Zeus
   period.. 14. four years apart
   revival site.. 6. Athens (1896)
   site (first).. 4. Elis 7. Olympia
   time of games.. 8. four days
Olympieion, Olympium... 6. temple
   (Athens)
Olympus (Gr)... 3. sky 5. Mount
   6. heaven 8. mountain
Olympus (Hind)... 4. Meru
Omaha... 4. city (Neb) 5. Sioux
   6. Indian
Omar Khayyam (pert to)...
   country.. 4. Iran 6. Persia
   fish (fabled).. 3. mah
   poem.. 8. Rubaiyat
omasum... 9. manyplies 10. psalterium
   12. third stomach
ombro (comb form)... 4. rain
ombrometer... 9. rain gauge
omega... 3. end 4. last 5. final
   6. letter (Gr)
omen... 4. bode, sign 5. abode, knell,
   token 6. augury 7. auspice, portent,
   presage 8. forebode, foreshow
   9. abodement 10. divination
   15. prognostication
omer... 5. ephah, sheaf 9. fifty days
   (Passover to Pentecost)

ominous... 4. dour, trim 8. sinister
   9. ferocious 10. inexorable,
   portentous 12. inauspicious
omission... 4. want 5. caret, error
   7. neglect 9. oversight
   10. deficiency, leaving out
   13. nonobservance
omission of end syllables...
   7. apocope
omission of words... 8. ellipsis
omit... 4. dele, pass, skip 5. elide
   6. delete, ignore 7. exclude
   11. leave undone
omitting... 7. elision 9. excepting,
   excluding 10. precluding
omneity... 7. allness
   16. all–comprehensive
omnipotent... 6. divine 8. almighty
   9. unequaled, unlimited
   11. all–powerful
omniscient... 4. wise 6. divine
   7. learned 10. all–knowing
omnitude... 7. allness 8. totality
   12. universality
omnivorous... 6. greedy 9. all–eating
   10. gluttonous
omoplate... 7. scapula
omphalos... 3. hut 4. knob 5. altar,
   navel 6. center 9. umbilicus
on... 2. at 4. atop, upon 5. above,
   ahead, along 6. toward 7. against,
   forward 10. concerning
   13. juxtaposition
On (Bib)... 7. Baalbek 8. holy city
   10. Heliopolis (Egypt) 12. City of the
   Sun
on (pert to)...
   account of.. 3. for
   all sides.. 5. about 6. around
   and on.. 7. forever, tedious
   9. tediously
   behalf of.. 3. for
   dit.. 5. rumor 6. report
   going.. 7. forward 10. proceeding
   grand scale.. 4. epic
   hand.. 5. here 7. present 9. available
   high.. 5. aloft
   other side.. 4. over 6. across
   sheltered side.. 4. alee
   this side.. 3. cis (pref) 9. cisalpine
   10. cismontane, cispontine
   windward side.. 8. aweather
onager... 3. ass 5. kiang 8. catapult
once in a while... 9. erstwhile
   10. now and then 12. occasionally
once upon a time... 6. one day
   7. the past, time was 8. formerly
   10. the long ago
Oncorhynchus... 6. salmon
ondoyant... 4. wavy (art)
one... 2. an, un 3. ace, ain, ein
   4. unit 5. alone, unity, whole
   6. person, single 9. unmarried
   10. individual
one (pert to)...
   after the other.. 8. serially, seriatim
   12. successfully
   bearing heraldic arms.. 7. armiger
   behind the other.. 8. tandem
   born in serfdom.. 4. neif
   bringing good luck.. 6. mascot
   by one.. 6. apiece, singly 10. one at

a time 12. individually
comb form.. 3. uni 4. mono
curious.. 6. gossip 8. quidnunc
despondent in views.. 9. pessimist
fond of women.. 11. philogynist
footed.. 6. uniped
frantic for freedom..
  15. eleutheromaniac
gigantic in size.. 5. giant, titan
happy in views.. 8. optimist
horse.. 5. petty 6. little 8. inferior
  10. second–rate 13. insignificant
in a thousand.. 6. oddity 7. paragon,
  prodigy
in second childhood.. 6. dotard
instructed in secret system.. 5. epopt
  8. initiate
living on another.. 8. parasite
moving stealthily.. 7. prowler
sided.. 5. askew 7. partial
  10. prejudiced, unilateral
thousand.. 3. mil
time.. 7. quondam 8. formerly
undergoing change.. 6. mutant
oneberry... 9. hackberry
  14. partridgeberry
one devoted to...
deviltry.. 7. hellion
fast driving.. 4. jehu 7. speeder
indolence.. 10. daydreamer,
  lotus–eater
own opinion.. 5. bigot
physical feats.. 7. athlete
pursuit.. 3. ist (suff)
table delicacies.. 7. epicure
onefold... 6. simple, single 7. sincere
  9. guileless
onegite... 8. amethyst
Oneida... 6. Indian 8. Iroquois
  9. Community (NY)
oneiros... 5. dream
oneirotic... 6. dreams (pert to)
oneism... 6. egoism, monism
oneness... 5. union, unity 7. concord
  8. identity, sameness 9. agreement,
  aloneness, constancy 10. loneliness,
  singleness, uniformity, uniqueness
  11. singularity 13. undividedness
one of...
ancient race.. 4. Mede 7. Iberian
Buddhist precepts.. 6. nidana
Persian dynasty.. 8. Sassanid
religious sect.. 10. Anabaptist
the Bears.. 4. Ursa
the Greek Wise Men.. 6. Thales
the initiated.. 5. epopt
twins.. 5. gemel (Her)
onerous... 4. load 5. heavy 6. burden
  7. onerose 9. difficult, laborious,
  ponderous 10. burdensome,
  oppressive 12. impedimental
one versed in...
children's diseases.. 12. pediatrician
law.. 6. legist
literature.. 6. savant 9. literatus
memory.. 9. mnemonist
politics.. 9. statesman
religious law.. 8. canonist
resources, wealth.. 9. economist
one who...
absconds.. 6. eloper 8. decamper,

deserter
appropriates.. 9. pre–emptor
attacks.. 9. aggressor
believes in all religions.. 6. omnist
believes in personal God.. 5. deist
believes in self.. 9. solipsist
beseeches.. 7. pleader
brings meat to royal table.. 7. dapifer,
  steward
cherishes.. 8. fosterer
collects voluntary taxes.. 6. tither
conveys property.. 7. alienor
dies for a cause.. 6. martyr
differs.. 4. anti 9. dissenter, dissident
disowns.. 10. repudiator
displays learning.. 6. pedant
disposes by will.. 7. devisor
edits.. 7. reviser
feigns illness.. 10. malingerer
fights for cause.. 8. crusader
forsakes faith principles.. 8. apostate
frustrates a plan.. 7. marplot
gives up.. 9. abnegator
grants by deed.. 7. remiser
hates argument.. 10. misologist
hates people.. 11. misanthrope
holds office.. 2. in 9. incumbent
inculcates.. 7. infuser 9. instiller
inflicts retribution.. 7. nemesis
misuses authority.. 6. satrap
plunders.. 6. sacker 8. pillager
practises palmistry.. 11. chiromancer
prevents entrance.. 5. hajib
quarrels.. 5. rowdy
removes nuisance.. 6. abator
rules, manages.. 6. gerent
sells provisions to troops.. 6. sutler
shoots from ambush.. 6. sniper
sponges.. 6. cadger 8. parasite
stays.. 5. bider
summons spirits.. 8. evocator
testifies.. 8. deponent
transfers property.. 7. alienor
ongall... 5. onset 6. attack
onion... 3. set (bulbs) 4. boll, bulb,
  cepa, leek 5. chive, cibol, pearl,
  reeve 6. Allium 7. Bermuda, onionet,
  shallot 8. eschalot, rareripe, scallion
onkos (Gr)... 7. topknot
only... 4. just, lone, mere, sole
  5. chief 6. lonely, merely, simple,
  simply, single, singly, solely
  8. uniquely 11. exclusively
  13. companionless 14. above all
  others
onocentaur... 3. ape 5. demon
  (fabled)
onomasticon... 7. lexicon
  10. dictionary, vocabulary (Gr)
onomatology *(science of)*... 5. names
  11. terminology
onomatopoeic... 6. echoic 9. imitative
  (of natural sound)
onset, onslaught... 6. attack
  7. assault 11. rushing upon, setting
  upon
Ontario...
Bay.. 6. Hudson
capital.. 7. Toronto
city.. 6. Ottawa 7. Timmins
  8. Hamilton
lake.. 9. Great Lake (one of five)

province.. 6. Canada
river.. 6. Ottawa, Thames 7. Niagara
  10. St Lawrence
ontogeny... 9. evolution
ontology *(science of)*... 5. being
  7. reality
onus... 4. duty, load 6. burden, charge
  10. impediment, imposition,
  obligation
onus probandi... 13. burden of proof
onward, onwards... 5. ahead, forth
  6. future, moving 7. forward
  8. forwards, progress 9. in advance
onychauxis... 14. nail overgrowth
onyx... 6. nicolo (niccolo), tecali
ooid... 9. egg–shaped
oology *(science of)*... 8. bird eggs
oomancy *(divination by)*... 4. eggs
oont... 5. camel 13. beast of burden
oop... 4. join 5. unite
oopak, oopack... 3. tea (black)
oorial... 3. sha 5. sheep, urial
ooze... 3. bog 4. drip, leak, seep,
  sipe, soak 5. exude, marsh 6. be
  damp 7. leather 8. transude
  9. percolate
oozy... 4. miry 5. muddy, slimy
opah... 4. fish, soko 8. kingfish
  9. Lampridae
opal... 3. gem 4. blue 5. stone
  7. hyalite 10. pearliness
opal, variety of... 4. wood 5. black,
  noble, pitch, resin 6. common
  7. girasol, hyalite 8. menilite,
  precious 9. cacholong, geyserite,
  harlequin 10. chalcedony
opalescent... 6. pearly 7. opaline
  8. irisated 10. iridescent
opaque... 4. dark 6. obtuse, stupid
  7. obscure 8. eyeshade 10. not
  shining 13. unilluminated 14. not
  transparent
open... 3. ope 4. ajar, bare, free,
  undo 5. agape, begin, clear, frank,
  overt, plain, start, untie 6. candid,
  honest, patent, public, reveal, unbolt,
  unfold, unfurl, unlock, unseal, unstop,
  vacant 7. artless, evident, exposed,
  natural, obvious, sincere, unbosom,
  unclose 8. apparent, commence,
  disclose, expanded, initiate, patulous,
  revealed, unclosed, unfasten
  9. spreading, uncertain, uncovered,
  unfeigned 10. accessible, unreserved
  11. unprotected 12. questionable
open (pert to)...
acknowledgment.. 6. avowal
air.. 8. alfresco
and shut.. 7. assured, obvious
  11. prearranged
bursting.. 10. dehiscence
cabinet.. 7. étagère
country.. 5. veldt, weald
court.. 4. area 5. patio
door.. 6. policy 11. hospitality
eyed.. 7. curious 8. vigilant
  9. attentive, expectant
for discussion.. 4. moot
fully.. 4. wide 9. dehiscent, full–blown
land.. 4. moor 5. heath 6. desert,
  plains
out.. 6. deploy (Mil)

partly.. 3. mid 4. ajar
passage in forests.. 5. glade
to scorn.. 9. derisible
to view.. 5. overt
opening... 2. os 3. bay, gap 4. door,
  gate, hole, loop, pore, rift, slot, vent
  5. cleft, mouth, sinus, start
  6. breach, eyelet, hiatus, outlet,
  portal 7. display, foramen, initial,
  orifice, vacancy 8. aperture, fenestra,
  position 9. admission, beginning
  10. passageway, unfoldment
  11. entranceway, opportunity
opening (pert to)...
chess.. 6. gambit
ear.. 4. burr
enlarge.. 4. ream
from 3rd ventricle (Anat).. 4. pila
having.. 10. fenestrate
in a mold.. 6. ingate
minute.. 5. stoma
narrow.. 4. rima, slot 7. crevice
  9. stenopaic
nasal.. 4. nare
small.. 4. pore 5. chink 6. cranny,
  eyelet, lacuna 7. foramen, orifice,
  pinhole
wide (Bot).. 9. dehiscent
openings... 3. ora 7. stomata
openwork... 6. eyelet 7. Madeira,
  tracery 10. decoration
opera (pert to)...
comic (singer).. 5. buffa, buffo
  7. buffoon
glass.. 7. binocle 9. binocular,
  lorgnette
hat.. 5. crush, gibus 6. topper
kind.. 4. soap 5. horse 8. burletta
singer.. 4. bass, diva 5. buffa, buffo,
  tenor 7. buffoon, soprano 10. basso
  buffo, coloratura
solo.. 4. aria 5. scena
star.. 4. diva 10. prima donna
text.. 8. libretto
opera, composer... 5. Bizet, Gluck,
  Verdi 6. Glinka, Gounod, Handel,
  Hayden, Mozart, Wagner 7. Puccini,
  Rossini 9. Donizetti 11. Deems
  Taylor 14. Rimski–Korsakov (Korsakoff)
opera, drama... 4. Aida 5. Boris,
  Faust, Orfeo, Thais, Tosca
  6. Bohême, Carmen, Coq d'or,
  Daphne, Isolde 7. Alceste
  9. Lohengrin, Pagliacci, Rigoletto
  10. Magic Flute, Prince Igor,
  Tannhäuser 11. Don Giovanni, Il
  Travatore 13. Peter Ibbetson
  14. Tales of Hoffman 15. Hansel
  and Gretel, Madame Butterfly
  16. Marriage of Figaro
operation... 6. action, agency
  7. surgery 8. creation 9. influence
  11. functioning, transaction
operation, surgical... 5. major, minor
  6. trepan 8. excision 9. resection
  10. amputation, castration
  11. exploratory 12. appendectomy,
  hysterectomy 13. tonsillectomy
operative... 6. worker 7. artisan,
  working 8. mechanic 9. detective
operative, become... 5. inure (enure)
operator... 5. agent, quack 6. dealer,

worker 7. creator, handler, surgeon
10. mountebank, speculator
operculum (Bot)... 3. cap, lid
7. stopper 8. covering
operose... 4. busy 8. diligent
9. difficult, laborious 11. painstaking
Ophidia... 6. snakes 8. reptiles,
serpents 9. Serpentes
ophidian... 5. snake, viper 7. serpent
ophiolatry... 12. snake worship
ophthalmic... 6. ocular 7. optical
9. eye region
ophthalmology, science... 6. the eye
opiate... 4. drug, hemp, snow
5. opium 6. heroin 7. anodyne,
cocaine, hashish (hasheesh), soother
8. narcotic 9. analgesic, paregoric
11. somniferous 12. somnifacient
opine... 4. deem 5. judge, think
6. remark 7. opinion, suppose
10. conjecture
opinion... 4. idea, view 6. belief,
esteem, notion, report 7. feeling
8. judgment 9. sentiment
10. estimation, impression, ober
dictum, reputation
opinion (pert to)...
expert.. 9. expertise
expression, common.. 5. theme
expression, formal.. 4. vote
religious, unorthodox.. 6. heresy
opinions (pert to)...
collection.. 9. anthology, symposium
professed.. 5. credo
opium... 4. drug 8. narcotic
10. intoxicant
opium (pert to)...
concentrate.. 6. heroin
derivative (Chem).. 7. meconic
Egyptian.. 8. thebaine
extract.. 7. chandoo (chandu), codeine
8. morphine 9. narcotine
10. papaverine
overuse.. 8. opiumism
poppy seed.. 3. maw
source.. 5. poppy
tincture.. 9. paregoric
variety.. 6. Indian, Smyrna, Turkey
7. Chinese, Persian
opodeldoc... 7. plaster 8. liniment
opodidymus... 7. monster (two–headed)
opossum... 7. Marmosa 9. didelphid,
marsupial, phalanger
opossum (pert to)...
S America.. 5. quica 7. sarigue
variety.. 5. mouse, water, wooly
water.. 5. yapok (yapock)
wood.. 10. silver bell
opponent... 3. foe 4. anti 5. enemy,
rival 7. adverse 8. opposite
9. adversary, combatant
10. antagonist
opportune... 3. fit, pat 5. ready
6. timely 7. apropos 8. suitable
9. expedient, well–timed
10. convenient 11. appropriate
opportunist... 10. politician, vacillator
opportunity... 4. turn 6. chance
7. opening 8. occasion
12. circumstance 16. suitable
occasion
oppose... 3. pit 4. deny, face 5. fight,

rebel 6. expose, oppugn, refute,
resist 7. contest, exhibit, gainsay
8. confront 10. antagonize,
contradict, contravene, counteract
opposed... 3. met 4. anti, vied
5. coped 6. averse, pitted
7. adverse, fronted 8. contrary,
renitent, resisted 9. contested,
withstood 12. oppositional
opposed (pert to)...
against.. 6. pitted
lee.. 5. stoss
to change.. 7. die–hard
11. reactionary 12. conservative
to entad (inward).. 5. ectad
zenith.. 5. nadir
opposite... 5. polar 6. facing
7. adverse, antonym, hostile,
opposed, reverse 8. contrary,
converse 9. different, repugnant
10. opposition 12. antagonistic
13. contradictory 14. contrapositive
opposite (pert to)...
directly.. 10. antipodean
exact.. 8. antipode
in action, in nature.. 5. polar
7. inverse
prefix.. 6. contra
science.. 3. art
to spring tide.. 4. neap
opposition... 9. hostility, opponency
10. antagonism, antithesis, refutation,
resistance 11. contrariety, disapproval
13. contradiction
oppress... 4. rape 5. crush 6. burden,
harass, nither (Scot), ravish
7. depress, swelter 8. distress,
macerate, suppress 9. overpower,
overwhelm, persecute, tyrannize
10. extinguish
oppressive... 5. harsh 6. severe,
stuffy, sultry 7. onerous 8. rigorous
9. ponderous 10. burdensome,
depressing, tyrannical
oppressor... 4. czar (tsar), Nero
6. despot, tyrant 8. autocrat,
burdener 11. Simon Legree
opprobrious... 7. abusive 8. despised,
infamous 9. insulting, offensive
10. scurrilous 11. disgraceful
12. contumelious
opprobrium... 5. odium 6. infamy
8. disgrace 11. malediction
oppugn... 6. assail, oppose
10. controvert, counteract
oppugnant... 7. hostile, opposed
8. contrary 12. antagonistic
13. counteractive
Ops (pert to)...
called also.. 10. Ops Consiva
consort of.. 6. Consus, Saturn
Festival.. 6. Opalia
Greek counterpart.. 4. Rhea
Roman goddess of.. 7. Harvest
opsigamy... 14. old–age marriage
opt... 4. pick 5. elect 6. choose
11. make a choice
optic... 6. ocular, visual 11. optological
optical (pert to)...
device.. 9. stenopaic
glass.. 4. lens
illusion.. 6. mirage

instrument.. 5. prism 7. alidade,
reticle 9. eriometer, optometer
10. microscope
membrane.. 6. retina
organ.. 3. eye
optic defect... 6. myopia
optimistic... 4. rosy 7. hopeful,
roseate 8. cheerful, sanguine
9. expectant 10. auspicious
optimum... 4. best 7. maximum
13. most favorable
option... 6. choice, future (Finan)
7. refusal 8. free will 11. alternative
13. right to choose
optional... 8. elective 9. voluntary
10. permissive 13. not compulsory
opulence... 6. plenty, riches, wealth
9. abundance, affluence, amplitude,
profusion
opulent... 4. rich 6. lavish 7. profuse,
wealthy 8. abundant, affluent
9. luxuriant
opulus... 11. guelder–rose
13. cranberry tree
opus... 4. work 5. étude
10. embroidery, needlework
11. composition
oquassa... 5. trout
oracle... 4. seer 5. sibyl 6. Dodona,
medium, mentor 7. prophet, wise
man 8. Delphian (Delphic)
10. revelation
oracular... 4. wise 5. vatic (vatical)
9. prophetic 10. predictive
11. forecasting
orage... 5. storm 7. tempest
oral... 5. parol, vocal 6. spoken, verbal
10. not written 11. nuncupative
orang... 9. orangutan (orangutang)
orange (pert to)...
Bowl site.. 5. Miami
bird.. 7. tanager
color.. 5. ocher, peach 6. carrot
7. apricot 8. mandarin
flower oil.. 6. meroli
genus.. 6. Citrus
heraldry.. 5. tenné
kind.. 4. mock 5. hedge, navel,
Osage 8. bergamot, mandarin,
Valencia 9. tangerine
leaf.. 6. karamu
marigold.. 9. tangerine
membrane.. 4. zest
mock.. 7. seringa
seed.. 3. pip
Orangeman... 14. North Irelander
orangutan... 4. mias 5. orang, Pongo,
satyr, Simia
orate... 5. plead, speak, spiel
8. harangue
oration... 5. éloge 6. eulogy, prayer,
sermon, speech 7. lecture
8. encomium, petition 9. discourse
orator... 6. rhetor 7. speaker
9. perorator 10. petitioner
11. rhetorician, spellbinder
orator, famed... 5. Bryan (Wm
Jennings) 6. Cicero 9. Churchill
11. Demosthenes
oratory... 6. chapel 7. chantry
9. elocution, eloquence
orb... 3. eye, sun 4. ball, moon, star

5. earth, globe, world 6. bereft,
circle, planet, sphere 7. enclose
8. encircle, insignia, surround
orbed... 5. lunar, round
orbit... 4. path 5. globe, route
6. sphere 7. circuit 10. trajectory
orbit (pert to)...
cavity.. 9. eye socket
curve.. 10. trajectory
of a planet.. 7. ellipse
point.. 5. apsis
point, farthest.. 6. apogee
orc, Orca... 5. whale 7. grampus
orchestra (pert to)...
bells.. 12. glockenspiel
circle.. 7. parquet 8. parterre
small.. 11. symphonette
orchestra instrument group...
brass.. 4. horn, tuba 6. cornet
7. trumpet 8. trombone
percussion.. 4. drum 7. cymbals,
timpani (tympani) 8. triangle
strings.. 5. cello, viola 6. violin
10. contrabass 11. violoncello
wind.. 4. oboe 5. flute 7. bassoon
8. clarinet
orchid... 4. Disa 5. vanda 6. Ophrys
7. Listera, lycaste, pogonia
8. arethusa, Cattleya, Oncidium
9. cymbidium, puttyroot 10. letterleaf
orchid (pert to)...
appendage.. 8. caudicle
handsomest.. 4. Disa
largest.. 10. letterleaf
meal.. 5. salep
petal.. 8. labellum
tuber, root.. 5. salep 7. cullion
Orcus... 3. God (Rom) 5. Hades, Pluto
(Gr) 10. lower world
ordain... 4. plan 5. allot, enact, equip
6. decree 7. appoint, arrange,
command, destine, install 8. canonize
9. institute 10. predestine
ordeal... 4. gaff, test 5. trial
7. sorcery 8. judgment
10. experience (painful)
order... 3. bid 4. fiat, ordo, rank, rule,
sect, will 5. array, class, edict,
genus, money 6. cosmos, decree,
direct, enjoin, genera (pl), manage,
system 7. arrange, command,
dispose, mandate, prepare, verdict
8. regulate, sequence 9. condition,
procedure 10. injunction
11. arrangement
order (pert to)...
back.. 6. remand
connecting.. 6. in turn 8. seriatim
cosmic.. 3. tao 4. rita
for writ.. 7. precipe
good.. 6. eutaxy
grammar.. 5. taxis
judicial.. 4. fiat, writ 7. summons
proper.. 6. kilter
written.. 8. billet
Order, architecture... 5. Doric, Ionic
6. Tuscan 8. Etruscan 10. Corinthian
Order, association... 4. Club 5. Guild
7. DeMolay, Society, St Clare
8. Sodality, Sorority 9. The Garter,
Trappists 10. Fellowship, Fraternity,
Sisterhood 11. Brotherhood, Eastern

Star, Purple Heart 12. The Rising
Sun

ordered... 4. bade, trim 7. regular
8. arranged, measured, ordained
9. regulated

orderly... 4. neat, tidy, trim 7. regular,
uniform 8. obedient, peaceful
9. attendant, regularly, shipshape
10. methodical, systematic

order of...
amphibians.. 5. Anura
aquatic animals.. 7. Cetacea
holy beings.. 9. hierarchy
insects.. 7. Diptera
mammals.. 8. Edentata, Primates
mites.. 6. acarid
the day.. 8. schedule 12. instructions
whales.. 4. Cete

ordinal... 6. number, ritual, serial
10. succession 11. Book of Rules
(Eccl), categorical

ordinance... 3. law 4. rite 5. bylaw,
edict 6. assize, decree 7. control,
statute 8. decretum 9. allotment,
direction, enactment, sacrament
10. management, regulation

ordinarily... 7. plainly, usually
8. commonly 9. generally, naturally
11. customarily

ordinary... 4. ruck, so–so 5. judge,
nomic, plain, prosy, usual
6. common, normal, tavern
7. average, natural, prosaic, vulgate
8. everyday, habitual, mediocre,
plebeian, workaday 9. of the Mass
10. table d'hôte

ordinate... 6. ordain 7. appoint,
orderly, regular 8. moderate
9. harmonize 10. co–ordinate

ordination... 5. order 11. appointment,
arrangement, disposition
12. organization

ordnance... 4. guns 5. armor, orgue
7. petards, rabinet, weapons
8. armament, firearms, supplies
9. artillery, torpedoes
10. ammunition 14. apparatus belli

ordo... 5. order 11. publication

ore... 3. tin 4. gold, iron, lead, paco
5. brass, metal, ochre 6. copper,
silver, speiss 7. mercury, mineral,
seaweed, uranium 8. cinnabar,
tungsten 9. loadstone (lodestone)
11. quicksilver

ore (pert to)...
box.. 6. sluice
deposit.. 4. lode, mine 7. bonanza
fuser.. 7. smelter
horizontal layer.. 5. stope
impure.. 6. speiss
iron.. 5. ocher 8. hematite
9. magnetite
lead.. 6. galena
loading platform.. 4. plat
machine separator.. 6. vanner
refuse.. 6. scoria 8. tailings
roller.. 9. edgestone
silver.. 5. noble (metal)
sluice.. 5. trunk
stirrer.. 5. dolly
tin.. 5. scove
trough.. 6. strake

vein.. 4. lode 5. scrin, stope
worthless.. 5. matte

oread... 5. nymph 7. seamaid

Oregon...
capital.. 5. Salem
caves.. 11. Marble Halls
city.. 6. Eugene 7. Astoria, Medford
8. Portland 12. Klamath Falls
crab apple.. 7. powitch
emigrant route.. 11. Oregon Trail
famed persons.. 4. Gray (Capt)
5. Astor, Clark, Lewis
Indian.. 5. Modoc 7. Chinook,
Klamath 8. Nez Percé
mountain.. 4. Hood 5. Coast
8. Cascades
native nickname.. 7. webfoot
river.. 5. Rogue 7. Klamath
8. Columbia 10. Willamette
State admission.. 11. Thirty–third
State motto.. 8. The Union
State nickname.. 6. Beaver
13. Sawdust Empire
wind.. 7. chinook

oremus... 9. let us pray

Oreortyx... 5. quail

Orestes (pert to)...
father.. 9. Agamemnon
friend.. 7. Pylades
mother.. 12. Clytemnestra
sister.. 7. Electra
wife.. 8. Hermione

orf, orfe... 3. ide 4. fish

orfevrerie... 7. jewelry 9. gold plate

organ (pert to)...
anatomy.. 3. ear, eye 4. lung, nose
5. brain, heart, liver 6. kidney,
syrinx, tongue, tonsil 7. viscera (pl)
bristlelike.. 4. seta
desk.. 7. console
fish.. 8. drumfish
honey–secreting.. 7. nectary
plant.. 5. stoma 7. tendril
motion.. 6. muscle
respiratory.. 4. lung
secretion.. 5. gland
spider's spinner.. 9. spinneret
stop (music).. 8. register
tactile.. 6. feeler 8. tentacle

organic... 5. state, vital 6. innate
8. inherent 9. organized
10. structural 11. fundamental
14. constitutional

organic (pert to)...
compound.. 5. amine 6. enzyme,
ketone
disease.. 11. organopathy
memory.. 5. mneme
radical.. 5. ethyl
remains.. 5. azoic
soil.. 5. humus

organism (pert to)...
bacterial.. 4. germ 7. microbe
body of.. 4. soma
elementary.. 5. monad
minute.. 5. spore 6. amoeba
pelagic.. 6. nekton
plant.. 5. spore
potential.. 7. idorgan
sea.. 6. nekton 7. benthos
8. plankton
type.. 5. plant 6. animal 9. vegetable

vegetable.. 4. tree 5. plant
organization... 4. bloc, sect, unit
  5. cadre, guild, party, setup
  6. empire 11. association,
  corporation 12. constitution
  13. establishment 14. classification
organized body... 5. corps, posse
organized matter... 5. fauna, flora
  6. living, nekton 7. animate, benthos
  8. plankton
organology, science... 10. phrenology
  13. splanchnology
organoscopy... 10. phrenology
orgueil... 5. pride 11. haughtiness
orgy... 4. lark, romp 5. binge, revel,
  rites (anc), spree 6. frolic, ritual,
  shindy 7. debauch, revelry, shindig,
  wassail 8. carousal 11. celebration,
  merrymaking
oribi... 7. bleebok, Ourebia 8. antelope
oriel... 3. bay 6. recess, window
  7. balcony, gallery, portion
  8. corridor 10. moucharaby
  11. meshrabiyeh (Moham)
orient... 4. dawn 5. eastern, shining,
  sunrise 8. oriental, pellucid
  11. resplendent
Orient... 4. Asia, East 6. Levant
oriental (pert to)...
  abode, gateway.. 3. dar
  animal.. 4. zebu
  archangel.. 5. Uriel
  beverage.. 6. arrack
  building.. 6. pagoda
  burden bearer.. 5. hamal
  cap (sheepskin).. 6. calpac (calpack)
  caravansary.. 4. khan 5. serai
  6. imaret
  carpet.. 4. kali
  carriage.. 10. jinrikisha (jinricksha)
  cart, wagon.. 5. araba
  chief.. 4. Khan 6. Mikado
  Christian.. 5. Uniat
  corn.. 4. para
  cosmetic.. 4. kohl
  council.. 5. Divan
  cymbals.. 4. zels
  deity.. 3. Bel
  destiny.. 6. Kismet
  disease.. 8. beriberi
  dish.. 4. rice 5. pilau (pilaw) 6. pilaff
  8. chop suey, chow mein
  drug.. 5. opium 6. heroin 7. hashish
  (hasheesh)
  drum.. 6. tom–tom
  dulcimer.. 6. santir
  fan.. 3. ogi
  food.. 4. rice 5. salep
  garment.. 3. aba 6. sarong
  guitar.. 5. sitar
  head cover.. 6. turban
  hospice.. 6. imaret
  inn.. 5. serai
  instrument (Mus).. 7. samisen
  laborer.. 6. coolie (cooly)
  leader.. 4. amir (ameer)
  liquor.. 4. sake, saki
  litter.. 5. dooly (doolie) 9. palanquin
  lute.. 3. tar
  maid.. 4. amah, ayah, eyah
  manservant.. 5. hamal 6. coolie
  marketplace.. 6. bazaar

monkey.. 7. macaque
nurse.. 4. amah, ayah (governess)
obeisance.. 6. salaam (salam)
pagoda.. 3. taa
people.. 4. Sere (anc) 5. Asian, Malay
  6. Indian 7. Chinese, Eastern, Tartars
  (Tatars) 8. Japanese
  10. Mohammedan
pipe.. 8. narghile
rice paste.. 3. ame
rug.. 8. sedjadeh 11. Baluchistan
ruler.. 4. Khan, Shah 5. sahib (saheb)
  6. caliph (calif), sultan
sabre.. 8. scimitar
sailor.. 6. lascar
sash.. 3. obi
tambourine.. 5. daira
taxi.. 7. ricksha (rickshaw)
  10. jinrikisha
trousers (women).. 9. shaksheer
vessel (sailing).. 4. dhow, saic
wagon.. 5. araba
warehouse.. 6. godown
wind.. 7. monsoon
worker.. 6. coolie (cooly)
orifice... 4. hole, lura, pore, vent
  5. inlet, mouth, porus, stoma
  6. outlet, porule 7. chimney,
  opening, ostiole 8. aperture,
  bunghole, spiracle
origin... 3. nee 4. rise, root, seed
  5. alpha, birth, cause, start
  6. nature, parent, source 7. genesis
  9. beginning, etymology, inception,
  parentage 10. inconabula, provenance
  11. provenience 12. commencement,
  fountainhead
original... 3. new 5. basic, first, novel
  6. fontal, native, primal, primer,
  unused 7. genuine, pattern, primary
  8. pristine 9. aborigine, beginning,
  inventive, primitive 10. inimitable
  11. fundamental, origination
  12. commencement
original copy... 6. ectype
originate... 4. coin, open, rise, stem
  5. arise, begin, breed, start
  6. author, create, derive, invent
  7. emanate, produce 8. generate,
  initiate 11. etymologize
originator... 5. cause, maker
  7. creator 8. inventor, producer
  9. contriver 10. discoverer
oriole... 5. pirol 6. golden, hooded,
  loriot, Mimeta 7. orchard
  8. Bullock's 9. Baltimore, Icteridae
Orion (pert to)...
  Astron.. 7. Dog Star 10. Canis Major
  11. Orion's Hound 13. constellation
  color.. 11. Holland blue
  Gr Myth.. 6. hunter
  Jacob's Staff.. 10. Yard and Ell
  13. Golden Yardarm
  slain by.. 7. Artemis
  star.. 5. Rigel
orison... 6. prayer
Orkney Islands, Scotland...
  capital.. 8. Kirkwall
  Firth.. 8. Pentland
  fishing grounds.. 4. haaf
  island, largest.. 6. Pomona
  President, Supreme Court.. 4. foud

stone tower (Prehist).. 5. broch
orle (Her)... 6. border, fillet, wreath
  7. bearing, chaplet 10. escutcheon
  (voided)
Orloff... 5. horse 7. diamond (Russ,
  194 3/4 carats)
orlop... 4. deck (lowest)
Ormazd (Pers)... 5. deity (supreme)
ormer... 7. abalone 8. ear shell
ornament... 4. ouch, semé 5. adorn,
  decor, gutta, honor 6. amulet,
  brooch, emboss, finery, sequin
  7. antefix 8. appliqué, decorate
  9. embellish 10. decoration
  13. embellishment
ornament (pert to)...
  apex.. 6. finial
  ball.. 6. pompon
  bell–shaped.. 9. clochette
  Bible.. 4. Urim
  boat–shaped.. 3. nef
  brilliant.. 4. gaud 5. spang 6. sequin,
    tinsel 7. spangle
  circular.. 7. rosette
  delicate.. 7. tracery
  diamond–shaped.. 11. epigonation
  dress.. 5. jabot 9. stomacher
    10. embroidery
  egg–shaped.. 3. ove
  hair, head.. 4. comb 5. tiara
    8. barrette
  indented.. 5. chase
  Japanese girdle.. 4. inro
  leaves and grapes.. 6. pampre
  magical.. 6. amulet
  mantel.. 7. bibelot, trinket
  pendant.. 6. bangle, tassel 7. earring
    9. lavaliere (lavalier)
  pretentious.. 6. rococo
  protuberant.. 4. boss
  raised design.. 7. brocade
  scroll–like.. 6. volute
  set of.. 6. parure
  setting in.. 5. inlay 7. emblema
  silverware.. 7. gadroon
  spiral.. 5. helix
  terminal.. 6. finial
  wall.. 6. plaque, sconce
ornamental (pert to)...
  bottle.. 8. decanter
  button.. 4. stud
  description.. 5. fancy 10. decorative
  lace edge.. 5. picot 7. tatting
  metal.. 6. niello
  raised.. 7. brocade
  stand.. 7. étagère
  vase.. 3. urn
ornamented... 6. chased, etched,
  tooled 8. engraved
ornate... 3. gay 5. fancy 6. florid,
  tawdry 7. adorned 9. decorated
ornery... 8. perverse, stubborn
  9. malicious 11. ill–tempered
ornithoid... 8. birdlike
ornithology (study of)... 5. birds
ornithon... 6. aviary
oro... 4. gold 5. money
Oro... 3. God (Tahiti)
oro (comb form)... 5. month, serum
  8. mountain
orology (science of)... 9. mountains
orotund... 7. pompous 9. bombastic

orp... 4. fret, weep
Orpheus (pert to)...
  astronomy.. 6. Cygnus
  eighteenth century.. 6. Handel
  father.. 6. Apollo
  mother.. 8. Calliope
  poet.. 8. Thracian
  reference.. 6. Orphic
  river.. 6. Hebrus
  wife.. 8. Eurydice
Orphic... 3. egg (Creation's) 5. hymns
  7. tablets (gold) 13. Book of the
  Dead (rites)
orphrey... 10. embroidery (gold)
orpit (Scot)... 7. fretful
orra... 3. odd 5. oddly 10. not
  matched, occasional, unemployed
  13. miscellaneous
ort... 3. end 4. bits 5. scrap
  6. refuse, scraps 7. remnant
  8. leavings, leftover
orthodox... 7. Trinity 8. accepted,
  approved, believer, standard
  9. canonical, customary
  12. conventional
Orthodox Moslem... 5. hanif
orthography... 8. spelling
ortolan... 7. bunting 8. bobolink, sora
  rail, wheatear
Oryx... 5. beisa 7. gazelle, gemsbok
  8. antelope, leucoryx
os... 4. bone 5. mouth, osker (Geol)
  7. opening
Osage... 5. river 6. Indian (Sioux)
  10. orange tree
Osaka, Japan... 7. capital
  10. prefecture
oscillate... 3. wag 4. rock, sway, vary
  5. swing, waver, weave 7. vibrate
  9. fluctuate
Oscines... 12. singing birds
oscitancy... 6. gaping 7. yawning
  8. dullness, lethargy 10. drowsiness
oscitant... 4. dull 6. drowsy, gaping,
  sleepy 7. yawning 8. careless,
  sluggish 9. apathetic
osculate... 4. buss, kiss
osculation... 4. kiss 7. contact, kissing
osier... 3. rod 4. wand 6. sallow,
  willow 7. dogwood
Osiris, Egypt (pert to)...
  brother.. 3. Set (Seth)
  crown.. 4. atef
  enemy.. 3. Set 7. brother
  father.. 3. Geb
  god.. 9. fertility 10. underworld
  god (Gr).. 8. Dionysus
  husband of.. 4. Isis
  king of.. 5. Egypt
  mother.. 3. Nut
  seat.. 6. Abydos
  son.. 5. Horus 6. Anubis
Osmanli... 4. Turk 8. language
osmesis... 8. smelling 9. olfaction
osmosis... 10. absorption
  12. infiltration
osprey... 4. hawk 7. feather (hat)
  8. fish hawk 9. ossifrage
  10. breakbones
ossature... 8. skeleton 9. framework
  (Arch)
osse... 4. dare 7. attempt, presage,

promise 8. prophecy
osseous... 4. bony, hard 10. ossiferous
ossifrage... 5. eagle 6. osprey
　　11. lammergeier
ossuary... 3. urn 4. tomb
　　10. depository 12. charnel house
　　13. burial chamber
ostend... 6. reveal 7. exhibit
　　8. manifest 11. demonstrate
ostensible... 5. shown 6. avowed
　　7. alleged, seeming 8. apparent,
　　declared, specious 9. exhibited,
　　plausible, professed
ostent... 3. air 4. mien 5. token
　　7. portent 10. appearance
ostentatious... 4. arty, vain 5. dashy
　　6. sporty 7. pompous
　　11. conspicuous, pretentious
ostiole... 4. pore 5. stoma 7. orifice
　　8. aperture
ostler... 7. hostler 9. stableman
ostracize... 5. exile, expel 6. banish,
　　deport 7. cast out, exclude
　　9. extradite 10. expatriate
ostrich... 3. emu 4. Rhea 5. nandu
　　8. Struthio 9. cassowary
ostrichlike... 11. struthiform
ostrich tail feather... 3. boo
Otaheite... 6. Tahiti
otalgia... 7. earache
Othello (pert to)...
　　opera by.. 5. Verdi
　　tragedy by.. 11. Shakespeare
　　villain.. 4. Iago
　　wife.. 9. Desdemona
other... 2. or 5. alter, ither 6. either,
　　second 8. one of two 9. different
　　10. additional
others... 7. the rest 9. remaining
otherwise... 2. or 5. alias, ossia, other
　　6. or else 9. different 10. contrarily
　　11. differently
Othman... 4. Turk 5. Osman 6. sultan
　　7. Osmanli, Ottoman, Turkish
Othman's successor... 3. Ali
otiant... 4. idle 8. in repose
　　10. unemployed
otiose... 4. idle 6. at ease, futile
　　7. sterile, useless 8. indolent
　　12. functionless
otium... 7. leisure
otkon... 4. okee (oki) 5. demon
　　(Iroquois)
otologist... 6. aurist 9. ear doctor
ottava... 6. eighth, octave
ottava rima... 15. eight–line stanza
ottavino... 7. piccolo
ottoman... 4. seat 5. couch, stool
　　7. cricket 9. footstool
Ottoman (pert to)... see also *Othman*
　　color.. 9. vermilion
　　court.. 5. Porte 12. Sublime Porte
　　Empire.. 7. Turkish
　　fabric.. 6. ribbed 10. corded silk
　　governor.. 3. bey, dey 5. pasha
　　leader.. 5. Osman
　　native.. 4. Turk
　　poetry (couplet).. 4. beyt
　　province.. 6. eyalet (former) 7. vilayet
　　Turkish.. 7. Osmanli
oubliette... 7. dungeon (top opening)

ouch... 5. bezel, clasp, jewel
　　6. brooch 8. ornament
　　11. exclamation
ought... 4. duty, must, zero 5. at all,
　　aught, owned 6. cipher, should
　　7. behoove, nothing 8. anything, in
　　need of 9. possessed 10. obligation
Ouija board... 10. planchette
ouk... 4. week
ouphe... 3. elf 6. goblin
Our (pert to)...
　　Father.. 11. Lord's Prayer
　　French.. 5. notre
　　Lady.. 10. Virgin Mary
　　Lady's–mint.. 9. spearmint
　　Lady's Wand (Astron).. 10. Orion's
　　Belt
　　Lady's Way.. 6. Zodiac
ourie... 4. cold 5. dingy 6. dreary
ousia... 6. nature 7. essence
　　9. substance, true being
oust... 3. bar 5. eject, evict
　　6. depose, remove 7. turn out
out... 3. odd 4. away 5. drunk
　　6. absent, beyond, excuse, issued,
　　outlet 9. published 10. dislocated,
　　extinguish 11. unconscious
　　12. extinguished, not available
out and out... 8. absolute, complete,
　　outright, thorough 9. downright
　　13. thoroughgoing
outbreak... 4. rash, riot 5. burst, spurt
　　6. emeute, tumult 7. outcrop,
　　ruction 8. eruption, hysteria, outburst
　　12. insurrection 13. recrudescence
outburst... 4. gale 5. blast, flare, flash
　　8. ejection, eruption 9. explosion
　　10. ebullition
outcast... 5. exile, leper, ronin
　　6. pariah 7. quarrel 8. castaway,
　　derelict, vagabond 10. expatriate
outclass... 5. excel, outdo 6. outvie
　　7. outrank, surpass 8. outshine
　　10. outperform
outcome... 5. issue 6. effect, outlet,
　　result, sequel, upshot 7. emanate,
　　product 8. solution 10. denouement
　　11. consequence
outcry... 4. wail, yell 5. alarm, shout
　　6. clamor, plaint 7. suction
　　8. proclaim 11. exclamation
outdo... 5. excel 6. defeat, exceed,
　　outwit
outdoor game... 4. polo 6. hockey,
　　tennis 7. cricket, croquet
outer... 5. ectad, ectal 7. outside,
　　outward 8. exterior, external
　　9. objective 10. extraneous
outer (pert to)...
　　boundary.. 9. perimeter
　　coat.. 4. coat, hull 5. testa 6. extine,
　　jacket 8. tegument
　　garment.. 4. suit, wrap 5. cloak,
　　dress 7. paletot, sweater
　　8. mackinaw, mantilla, overcoat,
　　raincoat
　　layer of roots.. 7. exoderm
　　opposed to.. 5. ental
　　shell.. 4. test
　　skin.. 9. epidermis
Outer Mongolia...
　　capital.. 4. Urga 14. Ulan Bator

Khoto

desert .. 4. Gobi

outermost ... 6. utmost 7. extreme, outmost 8. far–flung, farthest

outfit ... 3. kit, rig 4. gear, suit, unit 5. equip, group 7. company, costume 8. wardrobe 12. organization 13. paraphernalia

outflow ... 4. gush, teem 6. deluge, efflux 7. freshet, outflux, outpour 8. effusion 10. ebullience

outgate ... 4. exit, vent 6. egress, outlet 7. outcome

outknee ... 6. bowleg

outlander ... see *outsider*

outlandish ... 3. odd 6. remote 7. bizarre, foreign, strange, uncouth 8. freakish 9. barbarous, inelegant, unrelated 10. extraneous, impossible, tramontane

outlaw ... 5. horse, ronin 6. bandit, banish 7. brigand, outcast 8. criminal, fugitive 9. ostracize, proscribe

outlet ... 4. exit, vent 5. bayou 6. stream 7. culvert, opening, outcast, passage

outline ... 3. map 5. chart, draft, frame, shape 6. sketch 7. contour, drawing, summary 8. scenario 9. adumbrate, delineate, lineament, perimeter, summarize 10. compendium 11. delineation 13. configuration

outlook ... 5. scope, vista, watch 7. purview 8. frontage, prospect 9. viewpoint 10. perception 11. probability 12. watchfulness

outmoded ... 5. passé 7. offbeat 8. outdated 10. superseded

outmost ... 5. final, utter 6. remote, utmost 8. farthest 9. extremest, outermost, uttermost 15. farthest outward

out of ...

agreement .. 6. dehors

danger .. 4. safe

date, style .. 3. old 5. passé 10. antiquated

place .. 5. inept

sorts .. 5. nohow 7. peevish

the ordinary .. 7. unusual

the question .. 10. impossible

the way .. 5. aside 6. afield

outpeer ... 5. excel 7. surpass

output ... 3. cut 5. expel, power, yield 6. amount, energy 7. turnout 10. production

outraged ... 6. abused, harmed 8. insulted, offended 9. affronted 10. infuriated, mistreated

outrageous ... 6. absurd 7. furious, heinous, obscene 8. flagrant 9. atrocious, excessive, monstrous 10. exorbitant, scandalous 11. disgraceful, unwarranted

outré ... 3. odd 6. absurd 7. bizarre 10. immoderate 11. extravagant

Outre–Mer ... 13. Book of Travels (Longfellow, 1835)

outremer ... 12. beyond the sea,

foreign parts

outrigger ... 4. proa, spar 5. canoe

outright ... 8. thorough 10. completely 11. unqualified 12. unreservedly

outrival ... 5. excel 6. outvie 7. eclipse, outrank 8. outclass, outshine, outsmart, outstrip

outside ... 3. exo (pref) 4. ecto (comb form) 8. exterior, external, outdoors 10. extraneous 11. superficial

outsider ... 5. alien 8. stranger 9. auslander, foreigner, Uitlander

outspoken ... 4. free 5. blunt, frank 6. candid, direct 10. unreserved 13. communicative

outstanding ... 3. due 5. famed, noted 6. famous, unpaid 7. eminent, obvious 8. exterior 9. important, principal, prominent 10. projecting 11. conspicuous, uncollected

outstrip ... 4. best, lead 5. excel, outdo 7. surpass 8. outrival

outward ... 5. ectad, evert, outer, overt 6. formal, spiral 8. apparent, exterior, external, manifest 9. extrinsic 11. superficial

outwit ... 4. balk, best, foil 5. block, check, cross 6. baffle, thwart 9. checkmate, frustrate 10. circumvent, disappoint

outwork (Fort) ... 7. ravelin 8. tenaille (tenail)

ouvrage ... 4. work

ouzel, ousel ... 4. piet 6. thrush 8. whistler 9. blackbird

oval ... 5. ovate, ovoid 6. circle 7. ellipse 10. elliptical 11. ellipsoidal

ovale ... 3. egg

ovate ... 4. bard, oval 7. obovate (inversely)

oven ... 3. umu 4. kiln, oast (oste) 7. furnace 8. hot place 9. microwave 12. brick chamber

oven (pert to) ...

glass annealing .. 4. lehr (leer)

hop drying .. 4. oast

mop .. 6. scovel

over ... 3. o'er, too 4. also, anew, atop 5. above, again, ended, super, supra 8. finished

overact ... 3. haw 5. emote, spout

overalls ... 5. chaps 8. trousers 10. chaparajos

overbearing ... 7. haughty 8. arrogant, cavalier, snobbish, subduing 9. imperious 10. highhanded 11. domineering 12. overpowering

overcast ... 3. dim 4. dark 6. cloudy, darken, gloomy 10. overturned (Geol)

overcoat ... 5. benny, parka 6. capote, raglan, slip–on, ulster 7. paletot, surtout, topcoat 9. greatcoat, inverness (sleeveless)

overcome ... 3. awe, win 4. beat 5. crush 6. beaten, defeat, exceed 7. conquer 8. outstrip, overbear, overturn, persuade, surmount, unnerved, vanquish 9. overpower, overthrow, overwhelm, prostrate

overcrowded ... 9. congested

overdue ... 4. late 5. tardy 7. belated

8. mistimed

overfeed... 4. glut 6. agrote, pamper
7. satiate, surfeit 8. overfill
9. crapulate, overstuff

overflow... 4. teem 5. spate
6. abound, deluge, outlet 7. copious,
overrun 8. inundate, opulence,
overload, plethora, teem with
9. abundance, pour forth
10. ebullience

overfond of... 4. dote 5. silly

overfull... 8. inflated, satiated
9. plethoric 10. overloaded

overhang... 3. jut 6. beetle 7. project,
suspend 9. advantage 11. over and
over

overlapping... 8. obvolute 9. imbricate,
syphering

overloaded... 6. turgic 8. inflated,
overfill 9. bombastic, plethoric

overlook... 4. face, miss, scan, skip,
snub 6. acquit, excuse, ignore,
slight, survey 7. absolve, condone,
forgive, neglect, overtop 9. disregard,
oversight, rise above, supervise

overlord... 6. master 8. domineer,
governor 9. tyrannize

overly... 3. too 8. careless
9. negligent 11. overbearing,
superficial 12. supercilious

overmodest... 7. prudish 8. priggish
11. puritanical, strait-laced

overnice... 5. fussy 6. purist
7. elegant, finicky 8. affected
10. fastidious

overpower... 3. awe 4. rout, stun
5. crush 6. dazzle, defeat, master,
subdue 7. conquer 8. overbear,
overcome, vanquish 9. overthrow,
overwhelm

overpowering... 6. fierce 8. exciting
12. overwhelming

overreach... 4. dupe 5. cheat
6. exceed, nobble, outwit, overgo,
strain 7. deceive 10. circumvent

overrun... 5. crush, swarm 6. abound,
desert, exceed, infest, outrun, ravage,
spread 7. destroy, pervade, run over,
trample 8. overflow 9. overwhelm
11. superabound

overscrupulous... 7. prudish
9. overexact 10. overstrict
14. overfastidious

overshadow... 5. excel 6. darken
7. eclipse, obscure, shelter
8. dominate 9. overcloud

overshoe... 3. gum 6. arctic, galosh
(galoshe)

oversight... 4. care 5. error, lapse,
watch 6. charge 7. control, neglect
8. omission 9. direction
10. inspection 11. supervision
12. guardianship, surveillance
13. nonobservance

overskirt... 7. pannier (anc) 10. upper
skirt

oversleeve... 6. armlet

overspread... 5. cover 6. infest
7. overrun, pervade 8. disperse,
suffused

overt... 4. open 6. patent, public
7. obvious 8. apparent, manifest

10. open to view

overtake... 5. catch, reach, seize
6. detect, rejoin 7. ensnare
9. apprehend, captivate

overthrow... 4. down, rout, ruin
5. worst 6. defeat, depose, refute,
unseat 7. conquer, deposal, destroy,
ruinate, unhorse 8. demolish,
disprove, overcome, overturn,
vanquish 9. prostrate 10. revolution

overthrown... 6. fallen, ruined
8. defeated 9. disproved

overtones... 5. tones 8. partials
9. harmonics

overtop... 5. dwarf, excel 7. obscure,
surpass 8. go beyond, overhead,
override 9. transcend 10. tower
above

overture... 5. offer, proem 7. opening,
prelude 8. aperture, proposal
11. composition, proposition
13. peace offering

overturn... 3. tip 4. tilt 5. throw,
upset 6. topple 7. capsize, conquer,
destroy, overset, reverse, subvert
9. overthrow, overwhelm

overweight... 7. obesity
11. overbalance 13. preponderance

overwhelm... 4. bury, rout 5. crush
6. defeat, deluge, engulf 7. confute,
conquer, engross, immerse, oppress
8. overturn, submerge 9. overpower,
overthrow

Ovidae, Ovinae... 5. goats, sheep

oviparous... 11. ovoviparous 12. egg
producing (opp of viviparous)

ovoid, ovoidal... 7. egglike
9. egg-shaped

ovule... 3. egg 4. seed 6. embryo,
ovulum

ovum... 3. egg 4. seed 5. spore
6. gamete 8. germ cell

owe... 3. due, own 7. possess 9. be
obliged 10. be indebted

ower... 6. debtor

owl (pert to)...
barn.. 4. lulu 5. padge
breed.. 6. pigeon
eagle.. 7. katogle 14. Tiger of the
Wood
eye.. 4. disc
family.. 9. Strigidae
female.. 3. hen
genus.. 4. Bubo 5. Ninox, Strix
7. Syrnium
horned.. 4. Bubo 6. aziola (small)
8. Hush-wing
light.. 4. dusk
like.. 4. owly 8. strigine
parrot.. 6. kakapo
Puerto Rican.. 6. mucaro
short-eared.. 8. marsh owl
tawny.. 8. billywix
term.. 4. hoot 11. bird of night
13. bird of Minerva
white.. 7. wapacut
young.. 4. utum 5. owlet

own... 4. have 5. admit 7. confess,
possess 11. acknowledge

owner... 6. master 7. planter
(plantation) 8. landlady, landlord
10. proprietor

ownership... 4. oadl (anc law)
   5. claim 7. tenancy 8. dominium,
   interest, property 10. possession
   11. seigniorage 12. seignioralty
   14. proprietorship
ox... 5. beeve, steer 6. bovine
   8. strength 13. beast of burden
ox (pert to)...
  Celebes.. 4. anoa
  genus.. 3. Bos
  harness.. 4. yoke
  horned.. 4. reem
  India.. 4. gaur
  like.. 5. bison 6. bovine 7. taurine
  stall.. 5. boose
  Tibetan.. 3. yak
  type.. 4. zebu
  wild.. 4. urus 7. banteng
  working.. 4. aver
  yoke.. 4. span
oxeye... 4. boce (fish) 5. daisy
   6. dunlin, plover
oxford... 4. gray, shoe 5. cloth
Oxford (pert to)...
  college accts.. 6. battel
  color.. 4. blue, gray

  Marbles.. 7. Arundel
  Museum.. 9. Ashmolean (1683)
  officer.. 6. beadle (bedel at Oxford)
   (bedell at Cambridge)
  scholarship.. 6. Rhodes
  school.. 10. University (1570)
  sheep (hornless).. 4. Down
oxide of iron... 4. rust
oxide of sodium... 4. soda
oxidize... 4. rust 5. erode 9. sulphuret
  (Philat)
oxter... 3. arm 6. armpit 7. embrace
oxtongue... 5. plant 7. biltong,
  bugloss
oxwort... 9. butterbur
oxygen... 3. gas 5. oxide, ozone
  7. element
oxyopia... 10. extra sight
oyster... 6. huitre 7. bivalve, mollusk
oyster (pert to)...
  gatherer.. 7. tongman
  rake.. 5. tongs
  shell.. 4. husk, test 5. shuck
  spawn.. 6. cultch
  young.. 4. spat
Ozark State... 8. Missouri
ozone... 3. air 6. oxygen

P

P... 2. Pi 6. letter (16th)
pa... 4. Papa 6. father
pa, pah... 4. fort 7. village
  10. settlement (fortified)
paauw... 7. bustard
pabulum... 4. food, fuel 7. aliment,
  support 9. nutriment 10. sustenance
  11. nourishment
pac, pack... 8. half boot, moccasin
paca... 4. rodent 9. Cuniculus
pace... 3. run 4. gait, lope, rate, step,
  trot, walk 5. speed 7. measure
  8. movement, velocity
pace (L)... 5. peace
Pace... 5. Pasch 6. Easter
pachyderm... 8. elephant
  10. rhinoceros 12. hippopotamus,
  Pachydermata
pachydermous... 11. thick–walled
  12. thick–skinned
pacific... 4. calm 6. irenic, serene
  8. irenical, peaceful, tranquil
  9. peaceable, quiescent
  12. conciliatory
Pacific (pert to)...
  Coast tree.. 7. madrona 8. knob pine
  Highway.. 10. Camino Real
  island bird.. 4. kagu
  island shark.. 4. mako 11. blue
  pointer
  island tree.. 4. ipil
  islands.. 4. Guam, Wake 5. Samos
  7. Oceania 8. Caroline, Tasmania

  9. Melanesia, Polynesia
  10. Micronesia
  shrub.. 5. salal
  States.. 6. Oregon 10. California,
  Washington
  stepping stones.. 9. Aleutians (Russia
  to America)
Pacific Ocean discoverer... 6. Balboa
pacifier... 3. sop 4. ring (baby's)
  6. nipple 7. soother 8. sedative
  10. peacemaker
pacify... 4. calm, ease, lull 5. abate,
  allay 6. soften, soothe 7. appease,
  assuage, mollify, placate 8. mitigate,
  palliate 9. alleviate 10. conciliate,
  propitiate 11. tranquilize (tranquillize)
pack... 3. ram, set, wad 4. cram, fill,
  load, stow, tamp 5. carry, flock,
  horde, steve, truss 6. bundle, embale
  8. assemble, encumber, quantity,
  send away
pack (pert to)...
  animal.. 3. ass 5. burro, camel, llama
  6. donkey
  back.. 8. knapsack
  horse.. 7. sumpter
  horse bag.. 5. kyack 7. pannier
  of hounds.. 6. kennel
package... 3. pad 4. bale 5. fadge
  6. bundle, packet, parcel, robbin
  (peppers), seroon 11. combination
packing... 4. lute, seal 7. stowage
  9. packaging 10. rubber ring

paco... 3. ore 6. alpaca
Pacolet... 10. swift horse
pact... 6. pactum 7. bargain
    8. contract 9. agreement
Pactolian... 6. golden
Pactolus, Myth (pert to)...
    famed for.. 5. Midas 11. gold–bearing
    river (Asia Minor).. 5. Lydia
pad... 3. mat, paw 4. fill, foot, frog,
    line, path, walk 5. quilt, stuff, track,
    tramp 6. tablet, trudge 7. bedding,
    bolster, cushion, footpad
    8. notebook, protract, saturate
    9. footprint, pulvillus 10. highwayman
pad (pert to)...
    cloth.. 7. housing 11. saddlecloth
    hair.. 3. rat
    harness, part.. 5. panel 6. terret
    7. housing 10. horsecloth
    perfume.. 6. sachet
padding... 6. lining 7. wadding
    8. softness, stuffing 11. superfluity
paddle... 3. oar, row 4. beat, stir,
    wade, whip 5. blade, board, scull,
    spank, spoon 6. dabble, propel
    7. flipper 8. lumpfish
paddle (pert to)...
    English.. 7. trample 8. lumpfish
    9. tread upon 10. paddlecock
    Scotch.. 3. hoe 4. spud
paddock (pert to)...
    paddockstool.. 9. toadstool
    piper.. 9. horsetail
    stone.. 10. greenstone
paddy... 4. rice, soft 7. padlike
    8. cushiony 9. rice field 10. hod
    carrier
Paddy... 7. Patrick 8. Irishman
paddymelon... 7. wallaby
Paddy's hurricane (Naut)... 4. calm
paddywhack... 4. beat, blow
    6. temper 9. ruddy duck, thrashing
padge... 7. barn owl
padmasana... 11. cross–legged
    (Buddha style), lotus–shaped
padre... 4. monk 6. Father, priest
    8. chaplain, minister
padrona... 8. landlady, mistress
padrone... 6. master, patron
    8. landlord 9. innkeeper
paedarchy... 14. rule by children
pagan... 6. ethnic, paynim 7. heathen
    10. heathenism, idolatrous, unbeliever
    11. irreligious
Paganalia... 8. festival (Rom)
pagan god... 4. idol
page... 3. boy 4. leaf 5. child, folio
    6. summon 9. attendant, messenger
page (pert to)...
    beginning.. 7. flyleaf
    book.. 5. folio 6. cahier, sheets
    lady's.. 7. esquire 8. escudero
    left–hand.. 5. verso
    number.. 5. folio
    right–hand.. 5. recto
    title.. 5. unwan 6. rubric
    12. frontispiece
pageant... 4. pomp, show 5. drama
    6. parade 7. tableau 8. aquacade
    9. spectacle 10. exhibition
    11. ostentation
pages... 7. paginal 8. paginate

Pagliacci... 5. opera 9. character
pagne... 9. loincloth, petticoat
pagoda... 2. ta 3. taa 4. idol
    5. booth 6. temple
    11. summerhouse
pagoda (pert to)...
    finial.. 3. tee
    sleeve.. 12. funnel–shaped
    stone.. 12. Agalmatolite
    tree.. 6. banyan 10. frangipani
paha... 4. hill 5. ridge (glacial)
pahi... 4. ship 5. canoe (seagoing)
pahmi... 5. bobac 6. marmot
paho... 7. pahutan 11. prayer stick
pahutan... 5. mango
paid... 5. hired 6. cashed 7. content,
    settled, yielded 9. satisfied
    10. discharged
paideutics... 8. pedagogy, teaching
paid office (without work)...
    8. sinecure
paid out... 5. spent 8. expended
    9. disbursed
paigle... 7. cowslip 8. crowfoot
    10. stitchwort 12. cuckooflower
pail... 3. can, pan 4. beat 6. bucket,
    harass, situla, thrash, vessel
    8. cannikin
paillasse, palliasse... 3. bed (masonry)
    8. mattress (straw)
pailles... 6. straws (cookery)
paillou, pailoo... 7. archway
    (memorial)
pain... 3. ail 4. ache, agra, pang
    5. agony, labor, thraw, throb, wound
    6. grieve, stitch 7. afflict, ailment,
    gnawing, torture, trouble 8. disquiet,
    distress 9. suffering 10. affliction,
    punishment
painful... 4. sore 7. careful 8. diligent
    9. difficult, laborious 10. afflictive,
    unpleasant 11. industrious,
    painstaking
painkiller... 7. anodyne 8. medicine,
    sedative 9. analgesic, calmative
    10. depressant
painstaking... 5. fussy 7. careful,
    labored 8. diligent, thorough
    9. assiduity, assiduous, laborious
paint... 4. coat, draw, limn 5. adorn,
    color, rouge, stain 6. depict, parget,
    sketch 7. picture, pigment, portray
    8. cosmetic, describe 9. delineate,
    embellish 11. application (Med)
paint (pert to)...
    blue, green.. 4. bice
    comb form.. 5. picto
    face.. 4. fard
    glossy.. 6. enamel
    Latin.. 6. pinxit
    spreader.. 7. spatula
    through pattern.. 7. stencil
    with vermilion.. 7. miniate
paintbrush... 8. hawkweed 10. painted
    cup 11. St John's wort
painted... 6. coated 7. colored,
    feigned 9. disguised, portrayed
    10. artificial, variegated
painted (pert to)...
    bat.. 11. Vespertilio
    beauty.. 9. butterfly
    bunting.. 5. finch

duck.. 8. mandarin 9. harlequin
enamel.. 7. Limoges
hyena.. 14. Cape hunting dog
lady.. 7. thistle 8. sweet pea
  9. butterfly
process.. 7. scumble
trillium.. 9. wake–robin
turtle.. 8. carapace
painter... 4. puma 6. cougar
  7. panther
painter... 4. Dali 5. Monet 6. Millet,
  Rubens 7. da Vinci, El Greco,
  Picasso, van Gogh 8. Reynolds,
  Whistler 9. Rembrandt
  12. Gainsborough, Grandma Moses,
  Michelangelo
Painter's Easel... 6. Pictor
  (constellation)
painting... 3. oil 5. genre, mural, Pietà
  (sacred), secco 6. fresco, marine
  7. impasto, tempera 9. encaustic,
  grisaille, landscape 10. cerography
  11. portraiture 12. illustration
pair... 3. duo, two 4. dyad, mate,
  span, team, yoke 5. brace, unite
  6. couple
paired... 5. gemel (Her) 7. coupled,
  leagued
pairs, growing in... 6. binate, double
paisano... 7. peasant 10. countryman,
  road runner
pal... 4. chum, pard 5. buddy, crony
  6. cobber 7. partner 9. companion
  10. accomplice
palace... 5. court, Doges, house
  (Astrol) 6. palais 7. palazzo
  10. praetorium (pretorium)
paladin... 4. hero 6. knight (Round
  Table)
Paladins of France... 9. The Twelve
palais... 6. palace 10. courthouse
Palamedes... 4. hero (Trojan War)
palampore... 7. hanging (cotton)
  8. bedcover
palanquin, palankeen... 4. kago
  5. dooly (doolie), palki 6. litter,
  palkee 10. conveyance
palanquin bearer... 5. hamal 6. sirdar
palas... 4. dhak, tree (yellow dye)
palatable... 5. sapid, tasty 6. savory
  8. pleading, seasoned 10. acceptable
palate... 4. cion 5. taste, uvula, velum
  6. relish 10. epipharynx
palatine... 4. bone 6. artery, county
  8. palatial
Palatine Confession... 10. Heidelberg
palaver... 4. talk 6. confer 7. chatter
  8. converse, flattery 10. conference
  12. conversation
pale... 3. dim, wan 4. ashy, fade, lily
  5. ashen, fence, lurid, pasty, stake,
  white 6. blanch, bounds, paling,
  pallid, pallor, sallow, sickly, sphere
  7. haggard, obscure, whitish
  8. palisade 9. deathlike 10. indistinct
palea, palet... 4. fold 5. bract, scale
  6. dewlap 8. ramentum
paleo (comb form)... 3. old 7. ancient
paleolithic culture... 8. Stone Age
Paleozoic... 10. Appalachia
Palestine (pert to)...
  ancient name.. 6. Canaan

animal.. 4. cony (Bib) 5. daman
conqueror.. 5. David, Turks
  11. Constantine
country (anc).. 4. Edom 5. Endor
  (Indur) 8. Nazareth 9. Philistia
lake.. 7. Dead Sea, Galilee
language.. 7. Aramaic
mountain (Bib).. 4. Zion 6. Carmel,
  Gilead, Hermon 13. Mount of Olives
plain, steppe.. 5. Negeb 6. Sharon
river.. 6. Jordan
town, district.. 4. Gaza 5. Haifa
  7. Samaria 9. Jerusalem
paletot... 4. coat 8. overcoat
pali... 9. precipice 10. steep slope
pali (comb form)... 5. again
  8. backward
Pali... 7. dialect (anc) 12. dead
  language
palimpsest... 9. parchment, rewritten
  10. re–engraved 15. codex rescriptus
palindrome (same backward, forward)...
  8. wordplay 9. inversion
paling... 5. fence, limit, palis, stake
  6. fading, picket 7. fencing
  9. enclosure
palisade... 5. cliff, fence, stake
  6. picket 7. defense, enclose, fortify
  8. espalier, palisado, surround
  9. precipice 10. impalement
  13. fortification
pall... 4. pale 5. cloak, cover, faint,
  qualm 6. coffin, mantle, nausea
  7. secrecy 12. graveclothes
pallall... 9. hopscotch
palle... 5. balls 8. six balls (Medici)
pallet... 3. bed 4. pate 5. quilt
  7. blanket 8. mattress 9. headpiece,
  paillasse
palliard... 6. beggar, lecher, rascal
  8. vagabond
palliate... 4. hide 5. abate, cloak,
  cover, gloss 6. excuse, lessen, soften
  7. conceal, qualify, relieve, shelter
  8. disguise, mitigate, moderate
  9. alleviate, extenuate
pallid... 3. wan 4. gray, pale 5. pasty,
  white 6. anemic, sallow
Pallu... 10. Reuben's son (Bib)
palm... 4. hand (part) 5. areca, bribe,
  steal 6. bacaba, handle, rattan,
  stroke, trophy
palm (pert to)...
  civet.. 6. musang
  cockatoo.. 5. arara
  down.. 7. pronate
  drink.. 5. assai
  drink (alcoholic).. 4. beno, nipa
  hand.. 6. palmus, thenar
  handlike.. 7. palmate
  house.. 8. palmetum
  lily.. 2. ti
  mat.. 6. petate
  off.. 5. foist
  ref to.. 10. palmaceous
  sap (fermented).. 5. toddy
  starch.. 4. sago
  sugar.. 7. jaggery
  thatch.. 4. nipa
palm (tree)...
  African.. 7. palmyra (sugar, wine)
  Arab.. 4. doum (doom)

Asiatic.. 4. atap, nipa
betel.. 5. areca, bonga 6. pinang
book.. 4. tara 7. taliera
Brazil.. 7. urucuri (urucury)
bussu, thatching.. 7. troolie (trooly)
cabbage.. 5. Sabal 8. palmetto
Ceylon.. 4. tala 7. talipot (fanleaf)
climbing, flexible.. 6. rattan
dwarf.. 5. Sabal
E Indies.. 4. atap, nipa 7. jaggery
   (sugar), tokopat (hat)
fan.. 7. talipot 8. palmetto
fiber.. 3. tal 6. raffia 8. piassava
   (piassaba)
Florida.. 5. royal
gingerbread tasting.. 4. doum (doom)
leaf.. 3. tal 4. olla (ola)
   12. chiquichiqui
Malayan, feather.. 4. irok 6. gomuti
palmyra.. 4. brab, olla 6. ronier
Philippine (coconut).. 4. niog
pinnate.. 5. assai, nikau 7. calamus,
   feather
S America.. 5. bussu, datil 6. tooroo
   12. chiquichiqui
spiny.. 6. grugru
palmate... 6. antler, webbed
   10. hand—shaped
palmer... 6. ferule 7. pilgrim (Holy
   Land) 8. date palm
   15. prestidigitator
Palmetto State... 13. South Carolina
palmistry... 10. chirognomy,
   chiromancy
palmodic (Med)... 5. jerky
palp... 6. feeler, palpus 8. tentacle
palpable... 5. plain 6. patent
   8. manifest, tangible 9. touchable
   10. noticeable, ponderable
palpebra... 6. eyelid
palpebrate... 4. wink
palpitate... 4. beat, drum 5. throb
   7. flutter, pulsate
palpitation... 7. flutter, tremble
   9. pulsation, quivering, throbbing
   10. excitement
palsied... 5. shaky 9. paralyzed,
   tottering
palter... 5. shift 6. babble, haggle,
   mumble, parley 7. bargain, chatter,
   quibble 9. vacillate 10. equivocate
   11. prevaricate
paltry... 4. mean, vile 5. petty, trash
   6. trashy 7. pitiful, rubbish
   8. picayune, trifling 9. worthless
   10. despicable 12. contemptible
pampas... 5. Pampa 6. plains (treeless)
pamper... 3. pet 4. cram, glut
   5. humor, spoil 6. caress, coddle,
   cosset, cuddle, dandle, posset
   7. gratify, indulge 11. mollycoddle
pamphagous... 10. omnivorous
pamphlet... 5. tract 6. folder
   7. booklet, leaflet 8. brochure
pan... 3. tab 4. part, tina (mining),
   wash 5. basin, roast, title (nobility)
   6. frying, lappet, spider, vessel
   7. cranium, hardpan, portion, skillet,
   subsoil 8. ridicule, saucepan
   9. criticize 10. acetabulum
pan (comb form)... 3. all 5. every

Pan (pert to)...
animal.. 3. ape 10. chimpanzee
god (Gr).. 6. flocks
instrument.. 4. pipe, reed
music.. 9. Pan's pipes
Pipes of.. 6. syrinx 8. Panpipes
Roman identity.. 6. Faunus
seat of worship.. 7. Arcadia
son.. 7. Silenus
panacea... 4. cure 6. elixir, remedy
   7. allheal (plant), cure—all
   8. nepenthe 10. catholicon
   11. panchreston
panache... 4. tuft (feathered) 5. plume
   7. swagger
Panama...
bay.. 5. Limon
capital.. 10. Panama City
city.. 5. Colon 6. Balboa 9. Cristobal
engineer.. 8. Goethals
gulf.. 6. Darien
Indian.. 4. Cuna
isthmus of.. 6. Darien (old name),
   Panama 7. San Blas
redwood.. 5. quira
river.. 7. Chagres
Panama Canal Lock... 5. Gatun
   10. Miraflores
panarchy... 13. universal rule
panaris... 5. felon 7. whitlow
   10. paronychia
panary... 5. bread 11. breadmaking
panatela... 5. cigar
pancake... 6. froise (fraise) 7. fritter
   11. griddlecake
Pancake Day... 13. Shrove Tuesday
pancreas... 5. gland 10. sweetbread
   16. Isle of Langerhans
panda... 7. bearcat
pandemonium... 4. hell 5. noise
   6. tumult, uproar
Pandemonium (pert to)...
abode of.. 6. demons
capital of.. 4. Hell
palace of.. 5. Satan
pert to.. 15. infernal regions
pander... 4. bawd, pimp 5. cater,
   serve 7. toady to 12. administer to
pandle... 7. a shrimp
Pandora's Box... 6. plague 9. human
   ills
Pandora's husband... 10. Epimetheus
panegyric... 5. éloge, elogy 6. eulogy
   7. oration, writing 8. encomium
   9. discourse, laudation
pang... 3. fit 4. pain 5. throe
   6. twinge 8. paroxysm
pangolin... 5. Manis 8. anteater
   9. Pholidota
panhandle... 3. beg
Panhellenic... 5. games (Isthmian)
   6. Greece 10. fraternity (Greek—letter)
panic... 4. fear, fray 5. alarm, chaos,
   scare 6. fright 8. stampede
pannier... 6. basket, dosser (dorser)
   7. corbeit 9. overskirt
panoply... 7. defense 11. suit of
   armor
panorama... 4. view 5. scene
   7. picture, scenery 9. cyclorama
pant... 4. beat, gasp 5. heave, throb
   7. breathe, pulsate 11. palpitation

Pantagruel (pert to)...
  character (romantic).. 5. giant
  companion.. 7. Panurge
  father.. 9. Gargantua
pantaloon, pantaloons... 5. pants
  6. dotard, old man 8. breeches,
  trousers 11. Patron Saint (Venice)
Pantheon (pert to)...
  aggregate.. 4. gods 7. deities
  builder.. 7. Hadrian (120 AD)
  building.. 6. shrine, temple 10. le
  Pantheon (Paris) 16. Westminster
  Abbey
  Rome.. 15. Temple of the Gods
panther, painter... 4. pard, puma
  6. cougar, jaguar, ocelot 7. leopard
pantler... 6. butler 7. servant
pantry... 5. ambry 6. larder 7. buttery,
  pannier, pantler 8. cupboard
pants... 5. chaps 7. drawers
  8. trousers 10. chaparajos
  (chaparejos), pantaloons
panuelo... 6. collar 8. kerchief
  9. neckcloth
pap... 4. teat 6. nipple 8. mammilla,
  soft diet
papa... 3. dad 4. clay, Pope
  6. baboon, father, potato, priest
  7. vulture
papal... 9. apostolic 10. pontifical
papal (pert to)...
  book of decrees.. 8. decretal
  chancery.. 6. datary
  Court.. 3. See 5. Curia
  envoy.. 8. ablegate
  letter.. 4. bull
  reformer.. 7. Gregory
  seal.. 5. bulla
  vestment.. 5. fanon, orale
paper (pert to)...
  absorbent.. 7. blotter
  broken.. 5. casse
  brown.. 6. manila
  coated.. 6. charta
  collection.. 7. dossier
  copy.. 6. carbon
  crinkled.. 5. crepe
  crisp.. 6. pelure
  currency.. 5. scrip
  cutlet wrap.. 8. papilote
  damaged.. 5. casse, salle 6. retree
  design.. 9. watermark
  fine.. 5. linen 6. vellum 9. parchment
  flower.. 11. strawflower
  folded.. 5. folio
  for pounding gold sheets.. 7. cutches
  gummed.. 5. label, stamp 7. plaster,
  sticker
  legal.. 4. writ 5. title
  measure.. 4. page, ream 5. quire,
  sheet
  nautilus.. 8. argonaut
  official.. 5. targe 8. document
  pad.. 6. tablet
  postage stamp.. 6. pelure
  size.. 3. cap 4. copy, demy, pott,
  quad 5. atlas, crown, folio, legal
  6. octavo 8. foolscap, imperial
  9. colombier
  small piece.. 5. scrip
  thin.. 4. rice 6. pelure, tissue
  9. onionskin

  transfer.. 12. decalcomania
  untrimmed.. 6. deckle (deckel)
  10. deckle edge 11. deckle–edged
  writing size.. 3. cap
paper chase... 13. hare and hounds
papilla... 6. nipple 10. projection
papule... 6. papula, pimple
papyra (comb form)... 5. paper
papyrus... 4. pith, reed 5. paper,
  sedge 6. scroll
par... 2. by 5. value 7. average, by
  way of, strokes, through 8. equality,
  superior
parable... 4. myth, tale 5. fable, story
  8. allegory, apologue
  10. comparison, similitude
parabola... 5. curve
parade... 4. pomp, show 5. march
  6. flaunt 8. flourish, grandeur,
  splendor 9. pageantry, promenade,
  spectacle 10. pretension, procession
  11. ostentation 12. magnificence
  13. formal display
paradigm... 5. model 7. example,
  pattern
paradisaic... 6. Edenic
Paradise... 4. Eden 5. Jenna
  6. Aidenn, heaven, Utopia 7. Elysium
Paradise (pert to)...
  apple.. 5. dwarf
  Arabic form.. 6. Aidenn
  Buddhist, Western.. 4. Jodo
  fool's.. 5. limbo
  grosbeak.. 9. cutthroat (bird)
  Mohammedan.. 5. Jenna
  plumage.. 14. bird of paradise
  poem (Milton).. 12. Paradise Lost
  16. Paradise Regained
  river.. 5. Gihon (Bib)
  tree.. 9. China tree
paragon... 4. type 5. ideal, match,
  model 7. diamond (100 carats),
  paladin, pattern 8. parallel
  9. nonpareil
paragram... 3. pun
Paraguay...
  capital.. 8. Asunción
  city.. 9. Paraguari 10. Concepcion,
  Villarrica
  language.. 7. Guarani, Spanish
  river.. 6. Paraná 8. Paraguay
  tea.. 4. maté 5. yerba 11. yerba de
  maté
parakeet... 5. green 6. parrot, puffin
  11. budgereegah (budgerygah)
paralysis... 5. palsy 7. paresis
  10. hemiplegia, paraplegia 11. loss
  of power
paralyze... 5. scram 6. benumb,
  deaden 7. astound, terrify, unnerve
paramount... 3. top 5. chief, liege
  6. ruling 7. supreme 8. dominant,
  superior 9. principal 10. preeminent
  13. most important
paramour... 5. amour, leman, lover,
  wooer 8. mistress 9. gallantry
  10. sweetheart
paranoia... 9. catatonia, monomania,
  nosomania
parapet... 5. redan 7. barrier, bulwark,
  rampart
parasite... 3. bur, sug 5. drone, toady

6. Gnatho, insect, sponge 7. entozoa
8. hanger–on 9. entophyte,
sycophant
parasite (pert to) . . .
animal . . 6. cuckoo 7. cowbird,
entozoa
external . . 12. ectoparasite
internal . . 7. entozoa
marine . . 6. remora, sponge
plant . . 9. entophyte
slang . . 6. flunky
trout . . 3. sug
parasitic (pert to) . . .
fish . . 6. remora
fungus . . 4. rust 6. lichen
worm . . 8. trichina (larva)
parcel . . . 3. lot 4. mete, part 5. piece,
solum (law) 6. bundle, packet
7. package, portion 8. fragment
parch . . . 3. dry 4. burn 5. dry up,
roast, toast 6. scorch 7. shrivel,
torrefy
parched . . . 4. sere 5. burnt, dried
7. thirsty 8. withered
parchment (pert to) . . .
bookcover . . 5. forel (forrel)
fine . . 6. vellum
manuscript . . 10. palimpsest
roll . . 4. pell 6. scroll
school . . 7. diploma
pard . . . 4. chum 5. tiger 7. comrade,
leopard, panther, partner
10. camelopard 11. confederate
pardesi (Hind) . . . 9. foreigner, outlander
pardie, parde, pardi (anc) . . . 4. oath
6. indeed, surely, verily 9. certainly
pardon . . . 5. mercy, remit, spare
6. acquit, excuse 7. absolve,
amnesty, condone, forgive 8. tolerate
9. acquittal, remission
10. absolution, indulgence (Eccl)
11. forgiveness
pardonable . . . 6. venial 8. expiable
9. excusable 10. forgivable
pardon chair, stall . . . 12. confessional
pare . . . 3. cut 4. peel, skin 5. shave
6. cut off, remove, resect
parent . . . 3. dad 4. sire 5. pater
6. father, mother, source 7. genitor
8. begetter 10. progenitor
parental affection (animal) . . . 6. storge
parget . . . 4. coat 5. paint 7. plaster
8. decorate, ornament 9. whitewash
parhelion . . . 3. sun (mock)
pariah . . . 3. dog (half–wild) 7. outcast
8. commoner, low caste
parian . . . 6. marble, market
Parian . . . 5. Paros 6. marble
(sculptural) 9. porcelain
parimutuel machine . . . 9. totalizer
11. totalizator
Paris (pert to) . . .
blue . . 6. cobalt 8. Prussian
daisy . . 10. marguerite
Garden (London) . . 10. bear garden
green . . 11. insecticide
Paris, France . . .
anc name . . 7. Lutetia (Lutice)
capital of . . 6. France
criminal . . 6. apache
famed sites . . 6. Louvre 8. Pantheon
9. Notre Dame 10. Montmartre

11. Eiffel Tower 13. Champs Elysées,
Napoleon's Tomb
native . . 8. Parisian
patron saint . . 5. Denis (Denys)
racecourse . . 7. Auteuil
river . . 5. Seine
subway . . 5. Metro
Paris, Gr legend . . .
brought about . . 9. Trojan War
10. Fall of Troy
father . . 5. Priam (King of Troy)
killer of . . 8. Achilles
mother . . 6. Hecuba
wife . . 6. Oenone
parish . . . 5. laity 7. diocese 8. district
9. parochial
paristhmion . . . 6. tonsil
park . . . 4. area (enclosed) 5. place,
tract 6. claire, common, settle
7. pasture (Eng) 8. woodland
9. grassland, pleasance
10. playground 11. reservation, set
and leave
Park, Highway . . .
Avenue . . 9. Manhattan
Lane . . 6. London
Row . . 9. Manhattan
Park, Historical . . . 6. Shiloh 8. Pea
Ridge, Saratoga 9. Minute Man
10. Gettysburg, Morristown
12. Harper's Ferry, Independence
Park, US . . . 4. Zion 7. Glacier,
Olympic (rain forests) 8. Sequoyah
(Sequoja), Yosemite 9. Haleakala,
Mesa Verde 10. Everglades, Mt
McKinley, Shenandoah 11. Grand
Canyon, Kings Canyon, Yellowstone
12. Harper's Ferry 15. Petrified
Forest
parlay, parley . . . 4. chat 5. parle, treat
6. confer 7. discuss 8. converse
10. conference, discussion
11. arbitration
parliament . . . 4. Diet 8. Congress
11. legislature
parlous . . . 4. keen 5. risky 6. shrewd
7. cunning 8. shocking 9. dangerous
Parnassian . . . 4. muse, poet
9. butterfly 10. Parnassius
Parnassus, Greece . . .
mountain . . 6. Phocis
site of . . 6. Delphi 8. Castalia
(fountain) 13. Delphic Apollo
symbol of . . 6. poetry
parody . . . 5. farce 6. satire 7. mockery,
take–off 9. burlesque, imitation
10. caricature
paroemia . . . 7. proverb
parol, parole . . . 4. oral, word
6. speech 7. freedom, promise,
release 8. pleading 11. word of
mouth
paronomasia . . . 3. pun 7. punning
8. wordplay 9. assonance
12. agnomination
paroxysm . . . 3. fit 4. pang 5. throe
6. access, attack, frenzy 7. illness
9. agitation 10. fit of anger
12. exacerbation
paroxysm of grief . . . 5. agony
parricide (*murder of*) . . . 7. kinsman
parrot . . . 3. ara, hia, kea 4. jako, kaka,

loro, lory 5. arara, cagit, macaw, polly
6. kakapo, tiriba 7. corella, lorilet
8. cockatoo, lorikeet, lovebird,
parakeet 9. Psittacus (Old World)
14. Psittaciformes
parrot (pert to)...
disease.. 11. psittacosis
genus.. 6. Nestor 9. Psittacus
gray.. 4. jako
green.. 5. cagit
hawk.. 3. hia
long–tailed.. 5. macaw
monk.. 4. loro
New Zealand.. 4. kaka
owl.. 6. kakapo
parrot fish.. 4. loro, scar 5. lauia
6. scarid 7. labroid 8. Labridae,
Scaridae
parrotlike (tongued).. 12. anthropoglot
sheep–killing.. 3. kea
short–tailed.. 7. lorilet
parry... 4. fend, ward 5. avert, avoid,
elude, evade, shift 6. refute, thwart
pars... 4. part
Parsee Bible... 10. Zend Avesta
Parsei, Parsi... 6. Gheber (Ghebre)
11. Zoroastrian 13. fire worshiper
Parsifal (pert to)...
character.. 6. Knight
healer of.. 8. Amfortas
son.. 9. Lohengrin
parsimonious... 4. near 5. close
6. frugal, meager, skimpy, sordid,
stingy 7. miserly, sparing
8. covetous, grasping 9. illiberal,
mercenary, penurious 10. avaricious
parsley... 4. herb 5. cumin 7. garnish
9. Ammiaceae, flavoring
parsley camphor... 6. apiole
parson... 6. rector 8. minister,
preacher, reverend 9. clergyman
parsonage... 5. gleve, manse, tithe
7. rectory 8. benefice, vicarage
9. pastorate 10. presbytery
parson bird... 3. tui
part... 3. cut, die 4. open, role, twin
5. allot, break, piece, sever, share
6. depart, divide, member, sunder
7. analyze, disband, disjoin, divorce,
portion, section, segment 8. dissever,
disunite, division, fragment, function,
separate 9. component
part (pert to)...
basic.. 4. core, pith 7. essence,
nucleus
choice.. 5. cream, elite 6. marrow
coarse.. 5. dregs
composite.. 7. section
corresponding.. 7. isomere
essential.. 4. core, gist, pith 5. heart
extra.. 5. spare
greater.. 4. bulk
hardest.. 5. brunt
infinitesimal.. 4. atom, mite
insignificant.. 3. bit 4. iota 6. trifle
kept.. 6. retent
main.. 4. body 5. trunk
narrow.. 4. neck
proportional.. 5. quota
rootlike.. 7. radicle
sawlike.. 5. serra
segment.. 5. tmema

small.. 3. bit, jot 4. iota 6. detail
7. snippet
smallest.. 4. whit 5. minim
solo accompaniment.. 8. obbligato
tenth.. 5. tithe
unpaid.. 6. arrear 9. arrearage
uppermost.. 3. top 4. peak 6. upside
7. topside
winglike.. 3. ala
with.. 7. discard 10. relinquish
partage... 4. part 5. share 7. portion
8. division
partake... 3. eat 5. share 7. receive
11. participate
partan... 4. crab
parted... 5. cleft 6. cloven 7. divided,
severed 8. separated
11. apportioned
parterre... 10. level space 12. theater
boxes, theater space 17. ornamental
gardens
parthogenesis... 7. apogamy
10. thelyotoky 12. reproduction
partial... 6. biased, unfair, unjust
7. limited 8. not total, one–sided,
partisan 9. imperfect 10. fractional,
incomplete, prejudiced
11. predisposed 13. foolishly fond
partiality... 4. bias 6. desire
9. injustice, prejudice 10. preference
11. inclination, partisanism
12. partisanship, predilection
participant... 6. sharer 7. entrant
8. partaker 9. accessory, colleague
12. participator
particle... 3. ace, bit, ion, jot 4. atom,
drop, iota, mite, mote, whit 5. grain,
piece, shred, spark 6. tittle
7. globule, granule, smidgen
particle (pert to)...
electric.. 3. ion 5. anion 6. proton
least possible.. 5. minim
minute.. 3. jot, ray 4. atom, iota
5. grain, speck 7. granule
negative.. 3. nor, not
nuclear.. 5. gluon, meson, quark
6. baryon, hadron
parti–colored... 4. pied, roan 5. pinto
6. motley 7. piebald 9. harlequin
10. variegated 11. polychromic
particular... 4. item, nice, part, sole
5. event, fussy 6. detail 7. precise,
special, topical 8. detailed, especial,
peculiar, separate, specific
9. attentive 10. fastidious, individual,
overminute 11. persnickety
12. circumstance, technicality
partisan, partizan... 4. pike 5. staff
6. zealot 7. partial 8. adherent,
advocate, follower 9. supporter
10. fractional, prejudiced
partition... 4. wall 5. allot 6. divide,
screen, septum 7. scantle 8. set
apart 9. apportion, severance
10. distribute, separation
13. apportionment
partitioned... 7. septate
partly... 6. in part 9. partially
partly illuminated... 6. shaded
8. adumbral 9. penumbral
partly open... 4. ajar
partner... 3. pal 4. ally, mate, wife

6. sharer, spouse 7. comrade,
husband 9. associate, coadjutor,
colleague 10. accomplice
11. confederate, participant
partnership... 4. firm 7. cahoots,
co–mated 8. business, contract
10. fellowship 11. affiliation
13. participation
part of...
anchor.. 4. palm
bird wing.. 5. alula
cannon.. 5. chase
church.. 4. apse, nave 5. altar
7. chancel 8. transept
circle.. 3. arc 6. degree 7. segment
compass.. 6. needle
ear.. 4. lobe 5. pinna 6. tragus
8. tympanum 9. labyrinth
eye.. 4. iris, uvea 5. pupil 6. cornea,
retina
flower.. 4. stem 5. calyx, petal, sepal
foot lever.. 5. pedal 7. treadle
fort.. 5. redan 7. bastion
head.. 4. pate 5. scalp, skull
7. cranium
minstrel show.. 4. olio 5. bones
6. end man 12. interlocutor
newspaper.. 3. ear 4. item, page
6. by–line 9. editorial
optical measure.. 7. alidade
printing press.. 6. platen
rifle (anc).. 4. tige
ship.. 3. bow 4. brig, deck, helm,
keel, mast 5. stern, wheel 6. anchor,
bridge, rudder 8. steerage
step.. 5. riser, tread 6. nosing
theater.. 3. box 4. loge 5. foyer,
stage 7. balcony, curtain, gallery,
parquet 8. parterre 9. orchestra
turtle.. 7. calipee 8. calipash
partridge... 4. hill, snow, yutu
5. covey (flock) 6. bamboo, chukar
(chukor), Perdix, seesee 7. cinerea,
tinamou 8. raw umber 9. francolin
11. Francolinus 12. ruffed grouse
party... 3. tea 4. ball, drum, sect,
side 6. clique, fiesta, person
7. company, faction 8. sociable
9. reception 10. detachment
11. association, combination
12. participator
party (pert to)...
deserter.. 6. bolter
evening.. 6. soiree
lawn.. 4. fete
man.. 8. partisan
member.. 8. Democrat, Federate
9. Communist, Dixiecrat, Greenback
(Hist), Socialist 10. Republican
11. Independent
men's.. 4. stag 6. smoker
Parvati (pert to)...
consort.. 4. Siva
father.. 7. Himavat
goddess.. 8. mountain
parvenu... 4. snob 7. upstart
12. nouveau riche
Pasch, pasch... 4. lamb, moon
6. candle, Easter, supper 8. Passover
10. Good Friday 11. candlestick,
celebration
pascual... 8. pascuage, pastures

pasear... 4. walk 6. parade, stroll
9. promenade 11. perambulate
pasha, pacha... 3. dey 4. emir 5. title
6. bashaw (early) 8. nobleman
10. magistrate
pashalik (pashalic)... 9. territory
(pasha's) 12. jurisdiction
pashm... 6. fleece (Tibetan goat)
pasigraphy... 6. system (Universal)
7. symbols 8. language
Pasiphae (pert to)...
mother of.. 7. Ariadne
son.. 8. minotaur (monster)
wife of.. 5. Minos
pasquinade.:. 5. squib 6. satire
7. lampoon, pasquil
pass... 2. go 3. die, end, gap
4. ghat, hand, lane, pace, step
5. canto, enact, gorge, lapse, occur,
relay, spend, throw 6. convey, crisis,.
defile, elapse, exceed, happen,
passus, perish, permit, ratify, ticket
7. excrete, passage 8. hand over,
passport, surmount, transfer
10. permission 11. Annie Oakley
13. complimentary
pass (pert to)...
Alpine.. 3. col
around.. 5. skirt 6. detour
as genuine.. 5. cheat, foist
11. interpolate
away.. 3. die, end 6. perish, vanish
9. cease to be, disappear, obsolesce
by.. 4. cote, omit, skip, snub
6. elapse, forego, ignore 7. proceed
8. overlook 9. disregard
hurriedly.. 7. scamper, skitter 9. skim
along
into.. 5. glide, merge 6. become
7. get to be 9. penetrate
judgment.. 4. rule 6. decree, ordain
8. sentence
on.. 3. die 6. confer, ratify
7. advance 8. bequeath, continue
out.. 3. die 4. exit 5. faint 7. be
dazed 9. disappear 11. be dead
drunk 13. be unconscious
over.. 4. omit, skip 5. cross
6. elapse, excuse, exempt, ignore,
slight 7. condone, exclude, neglect
8. overlook, transfer, traverse
sudden.. 5. lunge
through.. 5. cross, reeve (cringle)
6. pierce 7. pervade, undergo
8. traverse 9. penetrate
10. comprehend, experience
up.. 4. snub 5. evade 6. reject
7. decline 9. disregard
without touching.. 5. clear
passable... 4. so–so 7. current
8. mediocre, moderate, traveled
9. navigable, tolerable, traversed
10. acceptable, accessible, admissible
12. satisfactory
passado (fencing)... 6. thrust
passage... 4. adit, exit, flue, ford,
gang, hall, iter 5. aisle, allay, allée,
canal, death 6. atrium, avenue,
egress, travel, voyage 7. channel,
excerpt, journey, transit 8. corridor,
incident, progress, sanction
9. enactment, migration

10. transition 11. altercation, negotiation, preterition
12. thoroughfare

passage (pert to) . . .
book . . 4. excerpt
brain . . 4. iter
closed end . . 7. impasse 8. cul–de–sac
covered . . 4. pawn
history . . 5. alure
mine . . 4. sill 5. stope
narrow . . 3. gut 5. aisle, alley, gully, slype 6. defile, strait
river . . 7. estuary

passageway . . . 4. hall, lane, ramp, slip 5. aisle, alley, lumen 6. access, arcade, avenue, defile, outlet, strait, tunnel 7. gangway 8. corridor

passant . . . 7. cursory, walking (Her) 8. passer–by 9. ephemeral, excelling 10. surpassing, transitory

passé . . . 4. aged, past, worn 5. faded 6. gone by 8. obsoléte 10. antiquated 13. superannuated

passed (pert to) . . .
by . . 6. bygone, former 8. preterit (preterite)
over . . 7. fleeted 11. preterition
through pores . . 7. osmosed 8. dialyzed 9. permeated, transuded

passenger . . . 4. fare 6. pigeon, trekku 7. pilgrim, tourist 8. commuter, traveler, wayfarer 9. sightseer, transient

passerine bird . . . 5. finch 7. sparrow 8. songbird

passing . . . 7. cursory 8. elapsing, fleeting 9. departing, enactment, ephemeral, exceeding, happening, transient, vanishing 10. surpassing, transitory 11. preterition

passion . . . 3. ire, yen 4. love, lust, rage, zeal 5. anger, craze, wrath 6. desire 7. emotion, feeling 9. eloquence, martyrdom 10. enthusiasm, excitement

passion (pert to) . . .
flower . . 6. maypop 11. passionwort
flower family . . 10. Passiflora
for doing great things . . 11. megalomania
music . . 8. oratorio
Play . . 14. Christ's Passion (Oberammergau)
Week . . 8. Holy Week

passionate . . . 3. sad 5. angry 6. ardent 7. amorous, excited, fervent, pitiful, violent 8. agitated, eloquent, vehement 9. emotional, irascible 10. passionato 11. hot–tempered, impassioned

passionless . . . 4. calm 8. painless 9. heartless, unfeeling 10. spiritless 11. unemotional 13. dispassionate

passive . . . 5. inert, quiet, stoic 6. stolid 7. languid, patient 8. inactive 9. apathetic 10. submissive 11. acquiescent, indifferent, unresisting

Passover (pert to) . . .
festival . . 5. Seder 6. Jewish
lamb . . 7. paschal
psalm . . 6. hallel 14. Egyptian Hallel

sacrifice . . 11. paschal lamb
The (Passover) . . 5. Pasch

passport . . . 4. pass, visa (vise) 5. congé 6. congee, permit 8. document 11. safe conduct

passus . . . 5. canto

password . . . 9. watchword 10. mot de passé, open sesame 11. countersign

past . . . 2. by 3. ago 4. date, dead, gone, over, yore 5. after, since 6. beyond, ultimo 7. elapsed, outworn 9. foregoing, yesterday

pasta . . . 7. gnocchi, lasagna, ravioli 8. linguini, macaroni 9. fettucini, manicotti, spaghetti 10. vermicelli

paste . . . 3. pap, poi 4. glue, sham 5. dough, stick 6. mastic, strass 8. adhesive, frippery, mucilage 10. confection 13. stick together

pastel . . . 5. light 6. crayon, sketch 9. pale color

pastille . . . 6. troche 7. lozenge

pastime . . . 4. game 5. hobby, sport 9. amusement, diversion 10. recreation 13. entertainment

pastor . . . 5. rabbi 6. curate, divine, keeper, parson, priest, rector 8. chaplain, guardian, minister, Reverend, shepherd

pastoral . . . 4. poem 5. drama, rural 6. poetic 7. romance 14. ecclesiastical

pastoral (pert to) . . .
cantata . . 8. serenata
crook, staff . . 5. pedum 7. crosier
god . . 3. Pan
oboe . . 7. musette
pert to . . 6. rustic 8. agrestic, herdsman, shepherd
pipe . . 3. oat 4. reed
poem . . 4. idyl 7. bucolic, eclogue

pastry . . . 3. pie 4. tart 6. Danish, éclair 7. dariole, strudel 8. napoleon, pandowdy, turnover 9. cream puff, shortcake 10. pâtisserie

past tense . . . 8. preterit (preterite)

pasturage, right of . . . 9. horsegate

pasture . . . 3. ham, lea 4. feed, food 5. agist, grama, grass, graze 6. meadow 9. grassland 10. agostadero

pasture bird . . . 6. plover 7. sparrow

pat . . . 3. dab, fit, paw, tap 4. blow, lump 5. fixed, impel, known, throw 6. caress, smooth, stroke 7. flatten 9. immovable 10. seasonable

Patagonia (S Am) . . .
city . . 11. Punta Arenas
deity . . 7. Setebos
Indian tribe . . 9. Tehuelche
nearby island . . 14. Tierra del Fuego
race (said of) . . 6. giants 7. Big Feet, tallest 9. Patagones
rodent . . 4. cavy 8. capybara, Caviidae
strait . . 8. Magellan (Magallanes)

patamar (pattamar) . . . 6. vessel (Naut) 7. courier 9. messenger

patata . . . 6. potato 11. sweet potato

patch . . . 4. mend, vamp 5. bodge, botch, clump, cover, field 6. blotch 8. appliqué

cobble, parcel 8. addition
9. reconcile
patch (pert to)...
cloth.. 5. clout
imprinting.. 5. friar
metal.. 6. solder
of trees.. 4. mott
patcher (humorous)... 6. sartor
patchwork... 5. quilt 6. jumble, pillow,
scraps 7. mixture 9. checkered,
fancywork, fragments
10. hodgepodge
pate... 3. pie, top 4. head 5. brain,
crown, pasty, patty 6. badger
pâté de foie gras... 5. patty (goose
liver and truffles)
patella... 3. pan 4. bone, dish, vase
7. kneecap, kneepan
paten... 4. disc, dish, disk 5. plate
7. patener (bearer of)
patent... 4. open 5. berat (Turk), right
7. license, warrant 8. document,
manifest 9. available, copyright,
privilege, trademark 10. accessible,
protection, university
12. unobstructed
pater... 6. father, priest
Pater Noster... 11. Lord's Prayer
Paternoster Row... 6. street (London)
Pater Patriae... 18. Father of his
country (Cicero, Marius, Trajan,
Washington, etc)
path... 3. way 4. lane, line 5. piste,
route, swath, track, trail 6. course
7. footway
path (pert to)...
along a slope.. 4. berm (berme)
animal.. 5. piste, spoor 6. roddin
7. rodding
of energy.. 7. ergodic
of moving parts.. 5. locus
of planets.. 5. orbit
Spanish.. 6. camino, comino
pathetic... 3. sad 5. teary 8. dolorous,
grievous, stirring 9. affecting
10. lamentable
pathological... 6. morbid 9. unhealthy
pathological reaction... 7. allergy
patience... 9. endurance, fortitude,
solitaire, tolerance 10. submission,
sufferance 11. forbearance,
resignation 12. acquiescence,
perseverance
patient... 4. calm, meek 6. client
8. tolerant 9. unsettled
11. persevering 13. long–suffering
patio... 5. court 9. courtyard
patriarch... 4. Noah, sire 5. elder,
pater 6. bishop, father 7. aged man,
veteran 9. churchman
10. Methuselah 13. paterfamilias
patrimonial... 9. inherited
10. hereditary
patrimony... 8. heritage 10. birthright
11. ancient rite, inheritance
patriot... 4. Cato (Rom), Otis (Am)
5. jingo 7. chauvin 9. flag–waver
10. chauvinist, countryman
patriotism... 10. chauvinism
11. nationalism 13. love of country
patrol... 5. guard 7. protect
8. traverse 9. keep guard

13. perambulation
patron... 5. buyer, guest 6. backer,
seller, trader 8. customer, guardian
9. financier, protector, supporter
10. benefactor
patronage... 5. aegis (egis), favor
6. defend 7. support 8. auspices
9. clientele, fosterage 10. assistance
13. condescension, encouragement
patronizing... 8. deigning 9. financing,
revealing 10. sponsoring
13. condescending
patrons (group)... 7. backers, masters
9. clientele, customers
Patron Saint of...
beggars.. 5. Giles
boys.. 8. Nicholas
England.. 4. Anne 6. George
fishermen.. 5. Peter
France.. 5. Denis
Ireland.. 7. Patrick
lawyers.. 4. Ives
motherhood.. 6. Gerard
musicians.. 7. Cecilia
Pueblo Indians.. 7. Stephen
sailors.. 4. Elmo
Scotland.. 6. Andrew
shoemakers.. 7. Crispin
swineherds.. 7. Anthony
Venice.. 4. Mark 9. Pantalone
Wales.. 5. David
patten... 4. clog 5. skate 8. footgear,
overshoe, snowshoe
pattern... 4. norm, seme 5. habit,
model 6. design, format 7. diagram,
paragon 8. paradigm, parterre,
template
pavilion... 4. tent 5. cover, kiosk
6. canopy 8. covering 9. gloriette
10. tabernacle
pavis... 5. cover 6. screen, shield
7. protect
paw... 3. pad, pud 4. foot, hand
5. patté, pedal 6. handle, stroke
7. foreleg (Her) 8. forefoot
10. manipulate
pawl... 4. bolt, sear, trip 5. click
6. detent, pallet, tongue 7. ratchet
9. mechanism
pawn... 4. gage, hock, tool 6. pledge
7. counter, peacock 8. chessman,
guaranty, hockshop 9. put in pawn
10. pawnbroker
Pawnee... 6. Indian
pawnie... 7. peacock
pay... 3. aby (abye), fee, tip 4. ante,
meet, wage 5. remit, repay
6. defray, reward, salary, suffer
7. requite, satisfy 9. indemnify,
reimburse, retaliate 10. compensate,
punishment, recompense, remunerate
11. retribution 12. compensation
pay (pert to)...
attention.. 4. heed 6. listen
back.. 6. rebate, refund 9. reimburse,
retaliate
dirt.. 3. ore
envelope.. 5. wages 6. salary
7. stipend
extra.. 5. bonus 8. kickback
for.. 3. aby (abye) 5. atone 6. suffer
off.. 6. punish 7. requite 9. pay in

full, retribute 10. compensate
out.. 5. spend 6. expend, settle
   7. hand out 8. disburse
   10. distribute 12. exorbitantly
   14. through the nose
up.. 4. ante 6. settle 9. liquidate
paymaster... 6. burser, purser
   7. cashier
payment... 3. cro, fee 4. dues, mail
   6. return 8. defrayal, requital
   10. punishment, recompense
   12. chastisement, compensation
payment (pert to)...
for homicide, murder.. 3. cro 4. eric
   (Brehon Law) 7. galanas (Welsh),
   wergild (weregild)
immediate.. 4. cash
upon delivery.. 3. COD 14. cash on
   delivery
paynim... 5. pagan 7. heathen, infidel
   8. Pagandom 10. Mohammedan
payong... 8. umbrella (golden)
paysage... 7. picture (landscape)
   9. landscape
pea (pert to)...
bird.. 6. oriole
chick.. 4. gram 5. Cicer
everlasting (Bib).. 9. vetchling
family.. 8. Fabaceae
flour (seasoned).. 9. Erbswurst
heath.. 7. carmele
pigeon.. 3. dal 5. arhar
sausage.. 9. Erbswurst
shaped.. 8. pisiform
soup.. 3. fog (dull yellow)
split.. 3. dal
tree.. 8. laburnum
tropical.. 4. dove 7. Zenaida
   12. mourning dove
vine.. 8. earthpea
peace... 3. pax 5. amity, quiet, truce
   6. accord, repose 7. harmony,
   Nirvana, silence 8. ataraxia (ataraxy),
   serenity 9. stillness 10. quiescence
   11. tranquility
peaceable... 5. quiet, still 6. irenic,
   silent 7. henotic, pacific 8. amicable,
   tranquil 9. quiescent 10. concordant,
   harmonious 11. undisturbed
peaceful... 4. calm 5. irene 6. irenic,
   placid, serene 7. halcyon, pacific
   8. tranquil 11. comfortable
peace pipe... 7. calumet
peach... 5. fruit 6. accuse, betray,
   brandy, indict, inform 7. impeach
   8. quandong 9. red–yellow
peach (pert to)...
cordial.. 7. persico 8. persicot
family.. 12. Amygdalaceae
French.. 8. persicot
grafted (quince).. 9. melocoton
like.. 6. almond
origin.. 5. China
stone.. 7. putamen
variety.. 7. Elberta 8. Crawford
   9. freestone, nectarine 10. clingstone
peacock... 3. mao 4. Pavo (Astron),
   pawn, pose 5. strut 9. swaggerer
peacock (pert to)...
blue (color).. 4. paon
butterfly.. 2. io
fan.. 9. flabellum

feather part.. 4. marl
female.. 6. peahen
fish.. 6. wrasse
flower.. 9. poinciana
heron.. 7. bittern
ref to.. 7. peafowl 8. pavonine
tail spot.. 3. eye
peak... 3. alp, epi, pic, top, tor
   4. acme, apex, cone, crag, cusp,
   dent, dolt 5. crown, piton, slink,
   sneak, steal 6. finial, shrink, summit
   8. headland, mountain 9. simpleton
   10. promontory
Peak... 5. Borah, Logan 7. Everest, St
   Elias 8. McKinley 9. Mont Blanc
   10. Matterhorn 11. Kilimanjaro
   12. Popocatepetl
peal... 4. boom, clap, echo, ring, toll
   6. appeal, shovel 7. resound,
   summons, thunder 8. carillon
peanut... 5. pinda (pindal, pindar)
   6. goober, trifle 8. earthnut,
   earthpea, katchung
pear (pert to)...
alligator.. 7. avocado
cider.. 5. perry
Latin.. 5. pirum
prickly.. 4. tuna 5. nopal 7. Opuntia
shaped.. 8. pyriform
shaped vessel.. 6. aludel
squash.. 7. chayote
type.. 4. Bosc 8. Bartlett
pearl... 3. gem 4. drop 5. nacre,
   tooth, white 9. margarite
pearl (pert to)...
bird.. 10. guinea fowl
color.. 4. blue 13. mother–of–pearl
eye.. 8. cataract
imitation.. 6. olivet
of great luster.. 6. orient
opal.. 9. cacholong (opaque)
oyster.. 7. Avicula
seed.. 7. aliofar (obs)
vegetable.. 5. onion
pearly... 5. milky, quick, smart
   7. opaline, whitish 8. pellucid
   10. opalescent 11. flourishing
Pearly Gates (Bib)... 6. heaven, twelve
peasant... 4. boor, hind, peon, serf
   5. clown, knave, swain 6. carlot,
   cotman, cottar, rascal, rustic
   10. countryman
peasant (pert to)...
Arab, Syria.. 6. fellah
cropsharer.. 7. metayer
English.. 4. hind 5. churl
Indian.. 4. ryot
Irish.. 4. kern (kerne) 7. cottier
like.. 4. base, rude 8. clownish
Russian.. 5. kulak (rich)
Scottish.. 4. tyke (tike) 6. cotter
   (cottar)
pease... 5. quiet 6. pacify 7. appease
   9. reconcile
peasecrow... 4. tern
peat... 3. bog, pet 4. coal, fuel, moor,
   moss, turf 6. minion 7. darling
   8. favorite 11. combustible
peat (pert to)...
cutter.. 5. piner
moss.. 8. sphagnum
turf spade.. 5. slave

wood.. 11. loosestrife

peau... 4. skin (silks) 6. fabric

peba... 9. armadillo

pebble... 5. scree, stone, talus
6. quartz 7. chuckie (chucky), crystal, psephos 11. gravelstone, pebblestone

peccadillo... 4. slip 5. error, fault, lapse 12. indiscretion

peccant... 3. bad 5. wrong 6. guilty, morbid, wicked 7. corrupt, sinning, spoiled 9. incorrect, unhealthy 12. insalubrious

peccary... 6. mammal (piglike)
7. Tagassu, Tayassu 8. javelina

pech... 4. pant 11. breathe hard

pecht (Scot)... 5. fairy, gnome, pygmy

peck... 3. dab, dot, eat, nag 4. food, hole, jerk, kiss 5. pitch, prick, throw 6. peggle, stroke 7. measure 8. quantity 11. large amount

peck at... 3. nag 4. carp, twit
5. tease 6. attack, harass

pectase... 6. enzyme

peculiar... 3. odd 4. idio (comb form)
5. queer 6. oddish, unique 7. curious, special, strange, typical 8. distinct, separate, singular 9. different, eccentric 10. particular 14. characteristic

peculiar expression... 5. idiom

peculiarity... 4. kink 5. quirk, trait
6. oddity 7. oddness 9. mannerism 10. partiality 11. singularity 12. eccentricity 14. characteristic

peculiar to a district... 7. endemic

pecuniary... 6. fiscal 8. monetary
9. financial

pedagogue... 5. tutor 6. pedant
7. teacher 12. schoolmaster

pedal... 4. foot 5. lever 6. driver
7. treadle 9. propeller

pedant... 4. prig 5. tutor 6. dorbel, purist 9. formalist, pedagogue 10. conformist 12. bluestocking, precisionist, schoolmaster

peddle... 4. hawk, sell, vend 6. piddle, retail 11. disseminate

peddler, pedlar... 6. cadger, coster, hawker, mugger, sutler 7. chapman 8. huckster 9. vivandier 12. costermonger

peddler's French... 6. jargon (thieves')
9. gibberish

pedestal... 7. support 10. foundation

pedestal part... 3. die 4. base, dado
5. socle 6. plinth, quadra

pedestrian... 3. ped 4. dull, slow
5. hiker 6. hoofer, walker 11. commonplace 12. foot traveler 13. unimaginative

pedicel... 3. ray (of an umbel) 4. stem
5. stalk 8. peduncle

pediculosis... 9. lousiness

Pediculus... 4. lice

pedigree... 6. stemma 7. descent, lineage 8. ancestry, register 9. genealogy 10. family tree

pedio (comb form)... 4. sole 6. instep

pedology... 9. soil study 10. child study

pedometer... 5. watch 8. odograph
10. instrument, passometer

pedregal... 9. lava field

pedum... 5. crook, staff (pastoral)

peduncle... 4. stem 5. scape, stalk
7. pedicel, pedicle, sessile

peek... 3. pry 4. peep 5. chirp, flash
6. glance 7. glimpse 9. look slyly

peekaboo... 4. game 6. bopeep

peel... 4. bark, pare, rind, skin
5. slipe, stake, strip 6. cut off, lamina, shovel 8. car blade, palisade, stockade

peel (off)... 4. harl, pare, tear 7. come off 8. get loose 11. decorticate

peeler... 4. crab (shedding), yarn
5. corer 7. hustler 8. pillager 9. policeman

peep... 3. pry 4. peek, peer, pule, skeg 5. cheep, chirp, pipit, sight (firearms) 6. glance, squeak 7. crevice 8. peephole 9. sandpiper

peephole... 4. hole 6. eyelet
8. aperture 9. sighthole

peer... 4. duke, earl, fere, gaze, mate
5. baron, equal, match, noble, stare, stime (styme) 7. marquis 8. nobleman, superior, viscount

Peer Gynt (pert to)...
drama, poem by.. 5. Ibsen
mother.. 3. Ase
music suite by.. 5. Grieg

peerless... 9. matchless, nonpareil, paper size, unequaled, unmatched 10. unexcelled 11. ne plus ultra, superlative

peesweep, peeseweep... 7. lapwing
10. greenfinch

peetweep... 9. sandpiper (spotted)

peeved... 4. sore 7. annoyed, nettled
9. irritated

peevish... 3. coy 4. sour 5. cross, sulky, techy, testy 6. crusty, morose, touchy 7. fretful, pettish, spleeny, waspish 8. captious, choleric, contrary, perverse, petulant, snappish 9. irascible, irritable, querulous, splenetic

peg... 3. hob, leg, nob, nog, pin
4. dram, skeg 5. drink, stake, tooth 6. drudge, fasten, reason 7. pretext, support 9. persevere, recognize

peg (pert to)...
cribbage.. 4. game
iron.. 5. piton
out.. 7. croquet
shoe.. 5. cleat
wood.. 5. spill, thole 8. treenail

pega... 5. shark 6. remora

Pegasus... 5. horse (winged), steed
13. constellation

Pegasus's rider... 11. Bellerophon

pegomancy, divination by...
7. springs 9. fountains

peho... 8. morepork

peignoir... 8. negligee 12. dressing gown, dressing sack

pejorative... 11. disparaging
12. depreciatory

Peking, Pekin... 4. blue, city, duck
7. spaniel

pelagic... 6. marine 7. oceanic
9. underseas

pelagic organism... 6. nekton

7. benthos 8. plankton
Pele... 7. goddess (volcanoes)
pêle–mêle... 8. pellmell
Peleus (pert to)...
　father.. 6. Aeacus
　King of.. 9. Myrmidons
　son.. 8. Achilles
　wife.. 6. Thetis
pelf... 3. fur, rob 4. gain 5. booty,
　lucre, money, spoil, trash 6. pilfer,
　profit, refuse, riches, wealth
　7. rubbish 10. ne'er–do–well
Pelias (pert to)...
　daughter.. 5. Medes
　King of.. 6. Iolcus
　nephew.. 5. Jason
　son.. 7. Acastus
pelican (pert to)...
　heraldry.. 10. in her piety
　symbolic of.. 6. Christ 7. charity
Pelican State... 9. Louisiana
pell... 3. fur 4. hide, pelt, skin
　5. hurry 6. hasten 13. parchment
　roll
pellagra... 5. zeism
pellar, peller... 6. wizard 8. conjurer
pellet... 4. ball, pill 6. bullet
　7. granule, missile, pallion
pellicle... 4. film, scum 6. lamina
　7. coating 8. membrane
pell–mell, pellmell... 10. vehemently
　12. furious haste 13. helter–skelter
pellock... 8. porpoise
pellucid... 5. clear 6. bright, limpid
　8. luminous 11. translucent,
　transparent 12. intelligible
pelmet... 7. valance (short)
Peloponnesus...
　capital.. 7. Corinth
　city.. 7. Argolis
　League.. 11. Confederacy
　peninsula (Gr).. 5. Morea
　　12. Peloponnesos (old), Peloponnesus
　　(modern)
　race (anc).. 6. Dorian 7. Spartan
　School.. 6. Dorian 9. Sculpture
　War.. 12. Athens–Sparta (BC)
Pelops (pert to)...
　father.. 8. Tantalus
　son.. 6. Atreus 8. Thyestes
　wife.. 10. Hippodamia
pelota... 4. ball, game 5. cesta
　7. fronton, jai alai
pelt... 3. fur 4. blow, fell, hide, push,
　skin 5. stone 6. hurl at, pelage,
　refuse, strike, thrust 7. apparel (of
　skins), rubbish 8. woolfell
peltry... 4. furs, pelt 5. skins
peludo... 9. armadillo (six–banded)
pelvic bone... 5. ilium 7. ischium
　8. seat bone
pelvic–shaped... 11. basin–shaped
pemmican... 4. meat (dried) 7. buffalo,
　venison
pen... 3. cot, sty 4. bolt, coop, gaol
　5. abode, hutch, quill, write
　6. fasten, indite 7. confine
　9. enclosure 12. penitentiary
pen (pert to)...
　like.. 7. styloid
　name.. 6. anonym 9. pseudonym
　　10. nom de plume

point.. 3. neb, nib 4. stub
text.. 5. ronde
penalize... 4. fine 5. mulct 6. punish
　8. handicap
penalty... 4. fine, loss 7. forfeit
　8. handicap, hardship
　10. punishment, repentance
Penang Islands capital...
　10. Georgetown
penchant... 4. bent 6. desire, liking
　7. leaning 8. tendency 10. attraction
　11. inclination 12. decided taste
pendant... 3. bob, tag 4. tail 5. aglet
　(aiglet), queue 6. tassel 7. eardrop,
　earring, hanging 8. appendix,
　pendulum 9. lavaliere 10. chandelier
pendent... 3. lop 4. pend 7. hanging
　8. appended 9. impending,
　pendulous 11. jutting over,
　overhanging
pendent cone (limestone)...
　10. stalactite
pendulous fold, skin... 6. dewlap
Penelope (pert to)...
　father.. 7. Icarius
　husband.. 7. Ulysses 8. Odysseus
　island.. 6. Ithaca
　suitor.. 7. Agelaus
penetrate... 4. bore, gore, stab
　5. delve, elbow, enter 6. pierce
　7. pervade 8. permeate 9. perforate
　10. move deeply
penetrating... 4. cold, deep 5. acute,
　sharp 6. shrill, subtle 7. caustic,
　odorous 8. incisive 9. pervading,
　sagacious, searching
penetration... 6. acumen 7. ingress,
　insight 9. acuteness, sharpness
　11. discernment, perforation
　14. discrimination
Peneus (pert to)...
　father of.. 6. Daphne
　genus of.. 6. prawns
　god of.. 11. Peneus River (Thessalia)
penguin... 3. auk 6. Johnny 10. rock
　hopper
penguin (pert to)...
　aviation.. 13. training plane
　duck.. 12. Indian Runner (duck)
　genus.. 8. Eudyptes
　nest.. 7. rookery 10. penguinery
　type.. 4. king 6. Adelie 7. emperor,
　jackass
peninsula... 4. neck 6. penile
　10. chersonese
Peninsula...
　Asia.. 5. Malay
　Cimbrian, Cimbric.. 7. Jutland
　Iberia.. 5. Spain
　Seward.. 6. Alaska
　Tauric.. 6. Crimea
　Thracian.. 9. Gallipoli
penitent... 5. sorry 8. contrite
　9. repentant
penitential discipline... 7. penance
penitential period... 4. Lent
pennant... 4. fane, flag, whip
　6. banner, burgee (yacht), ensign,
　pennon, pinion 9. banderole
pennant fish... 11. cobblerfish
pennate... 6. winged 7. pinnate
　9. feathered, penniform

pennon... 4. flag, wing 6. banner, pinion 8. streamer

Pennsylvania...
capital.. 10. Harrisburg
city.. 4. Erie 7. Reading 8. Scranton 10. Pittsburgh 12. Philadelphia
famed site.. 10. Gettysburg 11. Liberty Bell, Valley Forge 16. Independence Hall
founder.. 11. William Penn
mountain.. 5. Davis 11. Alleghenies
named, first.. 10. Penn's Woods
river.. 4. Ohio 8. Delaware 10. Schuylkill 11. Susquehanna
State admission.. 6. second
State motto.. 28. Virtue, Liberty and Independence
State nickname.. 8. Keystone

penny... 4. cent, coin 5. pence 6. copper, stiver 8. denarius (Bib)

penologist, famed... 5. Lawes

penology, study of... 11. criminology 18. punishment for crime

pensive... 3. sad 5. mesto, sober 6. dreamy, musing 7. wistful 10. meditative, melancholy, reflective, thoughtful 13. contemplative

pentastich... 4. poem 6. stanza 7. strophe 10. five verses

Pentateuch... 5. Torah (Tora) 10. Law of Moses 14. First Five Books (Old Test) 16. Five Books of Moses

Pentecost... 8. festival 10. Whitsunday

Pentheus (pert to)...
grandson of.. 6. Cadmus
King of.. 6. Thebes
mother.. 5. Agave

penthouse... 6. lean–to 7. leaning, pentice 9. apartment (roof) 11. overhanging

penury... 4. want 7. poverty 9. indigence, privation 10. scantiness 11. destitution, miserliness

peon... 4. pawn (chess), serf 7. laborer, peasant, soldier 9. attendant, constable, messenger, policeman

peony... 4. piny 6. moutan 7. Paeonia 11. Burmese ruby

people... 3. kin, men 4. folk, ones, race, Rais 5. demos, laity 6. family, nation, public 7. kinsmen, persons 8. populace, subjects 9. citizenry 10. population

people (pert to)...
Am Indian, Eskimo.. 7. Amerind
ancient.. 5. Medes 6. Greeks, Romans 7. Sabines 9. Egyptians, Etruscans
class, lowest.. 8. canaille
common.. 6. vulgar 7. tilikum (tilicum)
headless (Myth).. 8. Acephali
old–fashioned.. 6. prudes 7. squares 13. antediluvians
ref to.. 4. laic 6. ethnic 7. demotic
Spanish.. 5. gente
wild young.. 10. rantipoles

people (of)...
culture (earliest).. 8. Grecians
gentle birth.. 6. gentry
one government.. 6. nation
rank.. 11. aristocracy, aristocrats

the people.. 6. ethnic

peopled... 5. abadi (Ind village) 8. occupied, populous 9. populated

pep... 2. go 3. vim 4. dash 6. energy 7. quicken 9. stimulate 10. initiative, liveliness

pepper... 4. pelt 5. shoot 6. energy 7. bombard 8. sprinkle 9. condiment

pepper (pert to)...
betel.. 4. siri (sirih)
black.. 11. Piper nigrum
box.. 5. tower 8. spitfire
Capsicum, source of.. 7. cayenne, chilies (chili), paprika
climbing.. 5. betel 6. nigrum
condiment.. 7. cayenne, paprika
dulse.. 7. seaweed (red)
genus.. 8. Capsicum
grass.. 5. crass 8. pillwort
sauce.. 7. Tabasco
turnip.. 15. jack–in–the–pulpit

pepper (pert to country)...
Australia.. 4. kava (cava) 8. kavakava
Borneo.. 4. kava (cava)
Guinea.. 5. chili 8. Capsicum
Malay.. 4. siri (sirih)
Spain.. 7. paprika, pimento 8. allspice, pimiento

pepper–and–salt... 4. gray 17. harbinger–of–spring

peppermint... 3. oil 4. herb 6. spirit 7. essence, gum tree, lozenge, menthol (camphor)

peppery... 5. fiery 7. piquant, pungent 8. choleric, spirited, stinging 10. passionate 11. hot–tempered

per... 2. by 7. for each, through 9. by means of 11. according to

peradventure... 3. hap 5. doubt 7. it may be 8. possibly 11. uncertainty

perambulate... 4. walk 6. ramble, stroll 8. traverse 9. promenade, walk about

perceive... 3. see 4. hear, know, note 5. sense 6. behold, descry, detect, divine, notice, remark 7. discern, observe, sensate 9. apprehend 10. comprehend, understand 11. distinguish 12. discriminate

perceptible... 5. faint 7. tactile, visible 8. knowable, manifest, tangible 10. cognizable 11. appreciable, discernible, perceivable

perception... 3. ear 4. tact 5. sense, taste 6. acumen, seeing 8. sagacity 9. awareness, sensation 10. cognizance 11. discernment 13. consciousness 14. discrimination

perceptive... 7. knowing 8. sensible 9. sagacious 14. discriminative

perch... 3. bar, peg, rod, sit 4. fish, pole 5. aerie, barse, roost, sit on, staff 6. alight, aviary, sauger, settle, weapon 7. measure 9. trumpeter

Percheron... 5. horse 15. Percheron Norman

perchers... 5. birds 7. candles 8. Passeres 10. Insessores

percolate... 4. ooze, seep, sift, silt, sipe 5. exude, leach, steep 6. filter, strain 7. trickle 8. permeate, transude

percussion... 9. collision
10. concussion, detonation
percussion instrument... 4. drum,
gong 5. bells, bones, traps
6. Becken, chimes, tom–tom
7. celesta, cymbals, marimba, potlids
8. carillon, clappers, triangle
9. castanets, xylophone
10. tambourine, vibraphone
12. glockenspiel
perdition... 4. hell, loss (soul), ruin
5. wreck 9. damnation
11. destruction
peregrinate... 6. travel, wander 7. go
about, sojourn
peregrine... 5. alien 6. exotic, falcon
7. foreign, pilgrim, strange
9. foreigner
perempt... 5. quash 6. defeat
7. destroy
peremptory... 5. final 7. express
8. absolute, arrogant, decisive,
dogmatic, positive, resolute
9. arbitrary, mandatory
10. compulsory, conclusive,
imperative, obligatory 11. dictatorial
13. authoritative 16. incontrovertible
perennial... 7. lasting 8. constant,
enduring 9. continual, evergreen,
permanent, perpetual, unceasing
10. continuous 12. never–failing
perennial (pert to)...
climbing.. 5. liana (liane)
grass.. 4. lyme 6. Elymus (genus)
7. wild rye
herb.. 4. Geum 5. avens
weed.. 8. toadflax
perfect... 4. holy, pure, sole 5. ideal,
model, teleo (comb form), whole
6. entire 7. correct, develop, improve
8. finished 9. blameless, faultless,
inviolate, righteous 10. consummate,
satisfying 11. unqualified
perfection... 4. acme 5. ideal
7. paragon 8. accuracy, maturity
10. completion, excellence
13. faultlessness
perfectly... 5. quite 7. ideally, rightly,
utterly 9. correctly 10. absolutely,
accurately, altogether, completely,
flawlessly, thoroughly
perfecto... 5. cigar (tapering)
perficient... 6. actual 9. effective,
effectual
perfidious... 6. shifty 8. disloyal
9. faithless 11. disaffected,
treacherous 12. falsehearted
perfidy... 7. treason 8. apostasy
9. duplicity, treachery 10. disloyalty
13. faithlessness
perforate... 4. bore, dock 5. drill,
punch 6. pierce, pounce, riddle
9. penetrate 10. umbilicate
perforated...
block.. 3. nut
initials (Philat).. 10. stamp marks
nozzle.. 4. rose
space.. 5. brain
sphere.. 4. bead
perforation... 4. bore, hole 6. eyelet
8. aperture, piercing, punching
perform... 2. do 3. act 4. play

5. enact, exert 6. effect 7. execute,
fulfill, produce 8. complete, transact
9. officiate 10. accomplish, bring
about, perpetrate
performance... 3. act 4. test, work
6. action 7. exploit 8. ceremony
9. operation 10. completion
exhibition, observance, production
12. consummation
14. accomplishment
performance (pert to)...
clumsy.. 6. bungle
daytime.. 7. matinee
for one.. 4. solo
notable.. 4. feat
of duty.. 8. feasance
performer... 4. doer 5. actor
6. dancer, worker 8. magician,
musician, thespian 9. pretender
15. prestidigitator
perfume... 4. balm, odor 5. aroma,
attar, orris, savor, scent, smell
7. bouquet, cologne, essence, rose
oil 9. fragrance, redolence
10. frangipani
perfume (pert to)...
base.. 4. musk 9. ambergris
cherry.. 7. mahaleb
essence.. 8. bergamot
medicated.. 8. pastille (pastil)
musky.. 5. civet
oriental.. 5. myrrh 7. incense
12. frankincense
scent.. 7. jasmine 8. lavender
10. heliotrope
toilet.. 6. bay rum 12. eau de
Cologne
unguent.. 6. pomade
violet.. 5. irone
pergola... 5. arbor, bower, kiosk
6. pandal 7. balcony, trellis
9. colonnade 11. summerhouse
perhaps... 5. maybe 6. ablins (Scot),
belike, mayhap 8. doubtful, possibly,
probably 9. perchance 10. contingent
peri... 3. elf 5. about (pref), fairy
6. beauty
periapt... 5. charm 6. amulet
pericarp... 3. pod 5. berry, shell
8. seedcase
Pericles (Gr)... 9. statesman
periculum (Rom law)... 4. risk 5. peril
6. danger
perigee (Astron)... 12. nearest earth
(opp of apogee)
peril... 4. risk 6. danger, hazard,
menace 8. jeopardy
perilously high... 7. Icarian (flying)
perimeter... 5. ambit 6. border
7. outline 8. boundary 9. periphery
period... 3. age, day, dot, end, eon,
era, eve 4. stop, term, time, year
5. cycle, epoch, limit, spell
6. degree, moment, season
8. duration, sentence 10. conclusion
11. termination
period (pert to)...
historical.. 4. eral 6. Eocene
7. Neocene
penitential.. 4. Lent
statutory.. 10. limitation
Tertiary.. 6. Eocene 7. Miocene,

Neocene 8. Pliocene
periodic... 4. eral 6. annual 7. etesian
8. seasonal 9. recurrent
10. rhythmical 12. intermittent
periodic (pert to)...
sea motion.. 4. tide
wind.. 2. oe 7. chinook, etesian,
monsoon
windstorm.. 2. oe 7. tornado
9. whirlwind
periodical... 5. paper 6. review
7. etesian, journal 8. magazine
9. recurring 11. publication
periodical cicada... 6. locust (17 yrs)
period of...
delay.. 10. moratorium
dryness.. 7. drought
evolution.. 6. hemera
fifty days.. 13. quinquagesima
five years.. 6. pentad
holding.. 6. tenure
instruction.. 7. session
possession.. 5. lease
probation.. 6. parole
prosperity.. 4. boom 6. golden
recovery.. 13. convalescence
14. reconstruction
sleep.. 11. hibernation
ten years.. 6. decade
time.. 3. age, day, eon 4. span
work.. 4. turn 5. shift, spell, watch
youth.. 6. nonage
peripatetic... 7. walking 8. rambling
Peripatetic (pert to Aristotle)...
6. school 8. disciple 10. Philosophy
peripheral... 6. distal 7. outmost
8. external 9. outlinear 10. round
about
periphery... 3. lip, rim 4. brim
5. ambit 6. areola, border
8. confines 9. perimeter
10. borderland 13. circumference
perique... 7. tobacco (strong) 10. otter
brown
perish... 3. die, rot 4. fade 5. decay,
waste 8. pass away, squander
9. cease to be, disappear 11. be
destroyed
perissodactyl... 15. odd-numbered
toes
peristyle... 7. columns (range of)
8. corridor 9. colonnade
10. peripteral
peritoneum fold... 7. omentum
periwig... 3. wig 6. frizzy, peruke
9. shellfish 10. periwinkle
periwinkle... 4. blue 5. snail
6. mussel, myrtle 9. evergreen
perjink... 4. neat, nice 7. precise
perjure... 7. violate 8. forswear
perjury... 9. violation 12. breech of
oath 13. false swearing
perk... 5. preen, prink 7. smarten
9. percolate 10. perquisite
perkin... 5. cider
perk up... 7. cheer up, improve, raise
up, refresh 11. recuperate
permanent... 5. fixed 6. innate, stable
7. abiding, durable, lasting
8. constant, enduring, inherent
9. perpetual 10. changeless,
continuing 12. unchangeable

permeate... 5. imbue 7. pervade
8. saturate
permission... 5. grace, leave
7. consent, license 9. allowance
10. sufferance 13. authorization
permissive... 8. optional 9. allowable,
permitted, tolerated 10. consenting,
permitting 13. power of choice
permit... 3. let 4. leve 5. allow, grant,
leave 6. suffer 7. consent, license,
warrant 8. tolerate 9. authorize
10. permission
permit to live... 5. spare 8. reprieve
permutate... 6. change 9. rearrange
11. interchange
permutation... 6. barter
11. interchange 13. transmutation
14. transformation
pern... 6. Pernis 7. buzzard (honey)
pernicious... 4. bane 5. fatal
6. anemia, deadly, malign, wicked
7. baleful, baneful, harmful, hurtful,
noisome, noxious, ruinous, vicious
10. villainous 11. deleterious
pernio... 9. chilblain
perorate... 5. speak (at length)
7. declaim 8. harangue 9. expatiate
perpendicular... 4. sine 5. erect,
plumb, sheer, steep 7. apothem,
upright 8. binormal, vertical
9. rectitude 10. standing up
11. precipitous
perpetrate... 6. commit 7. perform
12. carry through
perpetual... 7. endless, eternal
8. constant, unending 9. continual,
perennial, permanent, unceasing
10. continuous 11. everlasting
perpetually... 9. endlessly, eternally
11. ceaselessly 12. interminably
perpetuity... 7. annuity 8. eternity
11. endless time
perplex... 3. vex 4. cark 5. amaze
6. puzzle, riddle 7. confuse
8. bewilder, entangle 9. obfuscate
10. complicate
perplexity... 3. fog 6. tangle
7. anxiety, dilemma, problem
8. question 9. confusion, situation
10. complexity 11. distraction
12. bewilderment, complication
perquisite... 3. tip 4. gain 6. boodle
8. appanage, gratuity
perquod... 7. whereby
per se... 6. itself 8. directly
11. essentially 13. intrinsically
perse... 4. blue
persecute... 5. annoy, harry, hound
6. harass 7. afflict, oppress, torment
8. hunt down 9. martyrize
persecution... 9. treatment
10. harassment, oppression
12. mistreatment
Persephone (pert to)...
abductor.. 5. Hades
Attica, name.. 4. Kore (Cora)
deity of.. 11. agriculture
father.. 4. Zeus
Greek name.. 11. Persephassa
mother.. 7. Demeter
Orphic literary name.. 8. Despoina
queen of.. 15. infernal regions

Roman name.. 10. Proserpine
(Proserpina)
Perseus (pert to)...
Astron.. 13. Constellation
father.. 4. Zeus
mother.. 5. Danae
slayer of.. 6. Medusa
perseverance... 8. patience
  9. constancy 10. resolution,
  steadiness 11. persistence, pertinacity
  13. steadfastness
persevere... 5. abide 6. endure, insist,
  keep on 7. carry on, persist
  8. continue
Persia (Iran, Irani)... see also *Persian*
capital.. 7. Teheran (Tehran)
city.. 5. Niriz 6. Abadan, Shiraz,
  Tabriz 7. Hamadan, Ispahan
country (anc).. 4. Elam 7. Chaldea
gulf.. 4. Oman 7. Persian
gulf port.. 7. Bushire 9. Mohamerah
gulf province.. 6. Kuwait
gulf wind.. 6. shamal
lake.. 7. Rezaieh, Urumidh (Salt)
mountain.. 6. Ararat, Elburz, Zagros
  9. Hindu Kush
pert to.. 6. Persic
river.. 5. Safid 9. Euphrates
ruins.. 10. Persepolis (Shiraz)
Persian (pert to)... see also *Iranian*
blue.. 10. regimental
calendar reformer.. 9. Jalalaean
  (Jalalian)
carpet, rug.. 4. kali 5. Herat (Herati),
  Senna 6. Kerman, Tabriz
  11. Baluchistan
cushion.. 6. musnud
diadem.. 3. taj
door.. 3. dar
evergreen.. 4. olax
grass.. 6. millet
gum.. 10. tragacanth
hat.. 3. fez 6. turban
idiom.. 7. persism
javelin.. 6. jereed (jerid)
rose.. 3. gul
rug.. see *carpet* (above)
screen.. 6. purdah
Persian animals, birds, fruit...
apple.. 6. citron
bird.. 6. bulbul
cat.. 6. Angora
deer.. 5. maral 6. fallow
gazelle.. 4. cora
lamb.. 9. astrakhan, broadtail
lynx.. 7. caracul
tick (venomous).. 8. Miana bug
Persian Myth, Religion...
angel.. 3. Mah
deity.. 6. Ormazd (Supreme)
demigod, hero.. 4. Yima
demon.. 7. Apaosha
fairy.. 3. elf, fay 4. peri
fire worshiper.. 5. Parsi (Parsee)
god of light.. 7. Mithras
mystic.. 4. sufi
nymph.. 5. houri
religion founder.. 9. Zoroaster
religious doctrine.. 6. Babism
  (Babiism)
sacred books (Zoroastrian).. 6. Avesta

scriptures (Moham).. 5. Koran
spirit.. 7. Ahriman
Persian people, government...
assembly (1906).. 6. Majlis (Mejlis)
caste (priestly).. 4. Magi 7. Wise Men
chief.. 3. mir 4. Shah
chief's wife, lady.. 4. bibi
civil officer.. 4. khan
dynasty.. 5. Kajar 7. Arsacid
  8. Selencid 10. Sassanidae
  (Sassanid)
governor (anc).. 6. satrap
King.. 4. Shah 5. Cyrus 6. Darius,
  Xerxes
language (anc).. 4. Zend 7. Pahlavi
  (Pahlevi)
natives.. 5. Kurds, Medes, Mukri,
  Perse 6. Aryans
New Year's Day.. 7. Nowroze
people.. 7. Hadjemi, Iranics
  8. Iranians
poet.. 4. Omar 5. Hafiz, Saadi
ruler.. 4. Shah 6. atabeg (atabek),
  Sultan
student (Koran).. 5. hafiz
trader.. 4. Sart
tribe.. 4. Leks, Lurs 5. Arabs, Kurds,
  Turks 7. Gypsies 8. Baluchis
Wise Men.. 4. Magi
persiflage... 6. banter 8. raillery
persimmon... 4. kaki 7. chapote
persist... 4. last, urge 6. endure
  7. prevail 9. persevere
persistent... 7. durable 8. constant,
  habitual 10. determined, inveterate
  11. persevering 13. indefatigable
persistently opposed... 8. renitent
  9. obstinate 12. recalcitrant
person... 3. one 4. body, soul
  5. being, wight 6. figure 8. creature
  9. character 10. individual
person (pert to)...
accuser, challenger.. 9. appellant
acting for another.. 5. proxy
  9. alternate
baptized (anc).. 11. illuminatus
base.. 7. caitiff, hangdog
bringing bad luck.. 4. jinx 5. Jonah
bringing good luck.. 6. mascot
canonized.. 5. saint
careless.. 7. trifler 11. pococurante
charged with high mission.. 7. apostle
charitable.. 9. samaritan
cheerful.. 8. optimist
clumsy.. 3. oaf 5. staup 6. lummox
  7. bungler
common.. 3. lay 8. roturier
conceited.. 4. prig
contemptible.. 3. cad 4. heel, toad
  7. bauchle (Scot)
crazed.. 6. maniac 10. monomaniac,
  psychopath
credulous.. 5. Simon
cruel.. 5. fiend
dishonorable.. 6. rotter
dissolute.. 4. roué
drunken.. 4. lush
dull.. 4. dolt 5. dunce, moron, stock
  6. dorbel 9. blockhead
dwarf.. 5. shurf
educated.. 6. pedant, pundit, savant
  7. erudite, learned, student

8. cultured, highbrow 9. literatus
12. intellectual
emitting smoke .. 7. whiffer
enterprising .. 8. go-getter
fabulously rich .. 5. Midas
foolish .. 3. sop 4. zany 5. clown,
idiot, nutty 6. dotard 7. bonkers,
buffoon 9. simpleton
gigantic .. 5. giant, titan 7. monster
gloomy .. 7. killjoy 10. crosspatch
good luck .. 6. mascot
grotesque .. 9. golliwogg
guilty .. 7. culprit, transgressor
held as pledge .. 7. hostage
image of .. 4. doll, idol 5. clone
6. poppet, puppet
impatient .. 6. fidget 7. hotspur
important .. 3. VIP 5. mogul
7. magnate, notable 9. personage
indifferent .. 5. stoic
inexperienced .. 9. greenhorn
insignificant .. 5. sprat 6. little, nobody
lazy .. 5. drone 8. sluggard
learned .. see *educated* (above)
left-handed .. 6. clumsy 8. sinister
9. portsider
loud-voiced .. 7. stentor 8. blowhard
low-bred .. 3. cad 6. vulgar
miserly .. 9. skinflint 10. curmudgeon
non-Jewish .. 5. Aryan 7. Gentile
overmodest .. 5. prude 8. bluenose
perfidious .. 5. snake 7. traitor
9. faithless
rapacious .. 4. wolf 5. harpy
relaxed .. 4. calm 8. laid-back
representing another .. 5. proxy
7. stand-in 9. alternate
respondent to appeal .. 8. appellee
rich .. 7. wealthy 9. plutocrat
10. capitalist 11. millionaire
rude, ill-mannered .. 4. boor 5. yahoo
scatterbrained .. 6. madcap
self-centered .. 6. egoist 7. egotist
9. extrovert, introvert
self-righteous .. 8. pharisee
sharp-eyed .. 5. alert, Argus
sick .. 9. aegrotant, bedridden
skilled .. 6. artist, master 7. artisan
8. mechanic
staff (Mil) .. 10. aide-de-camp
stupid .. 3. ass 4. dolt, gump, nerd
5. moron, stock
supercilious .. 4. snob 9. conceited
thankless .. 7. ingrate
unclassified .. 11. nondescript
unique .. 4. oner
unknown .. 7. inconnu 8. inconnue
unmarried .. 6. maiden, single
8. bachelor, celibate, spinster
untidy .. 5. messy 6. grungy
8. slipshod, slovenly 9. litterbug
valorous .. 4. hero 8. champion
violent-tempered .. 6. tartar
wealthy .. 5. nabob, pluto (comb form)
10. capitalist 11. millionaire
who reads, writes .. 8. literate
witty .. 3. wag 7. punster
8. comedian 10. comedienne
worthless .. 5. lorel, losel
writ serving .. 6. elisor
young .. 9. stripling
14. whippersnapper

personage ... 5. image, mogul
7. bearing, stature 8. great man,
one's body, portrait
13. impersonation
persona grata ... 13. welcome person
16. acceptable person
personal (pert to) ...
appearance .. 8. presence
comb form .. 4. idio
history .. 6. memoir
ornament .. 6. parure
ownership, land .. 6. estate
7. demesne 8. chattels, property
personality ... 3. ego 5. being
6. person 8. identity 13. individuality
15. distinctiveness
persona non grata ...
18. unacceptable person
personate ... 5. enact 7. feigned
9. represent 10. personated
11. counterfeit
personification ... 3. Una (truth)
10. embodiment 11. attribution
14. representation
person of ...
age .. 5. major
courage .. 7. Spartan
eighty years .. 12. octogenarian
encyclopedic learning .. 10. polyhistor
fifty years .. 15. quinquagenarian
forty years .. 14. quadragenarian
great intellect .. 6. genius
nervous disorders .. 8. neurotic
ninety years .. 12. nonagenarian
one hundred years .. 11. centenarian
seventy years .. 14. septuagenarian
sixty years .. 12. sexagenarian
skill .. 6. master, talent 7. magnate
persons of ...
a familiar set .. 7. coterie
a family tree .. 6. stirps
groups .. 4. army, band, team
6. chorus, troupe 7. company
8. assembly 9. orchestra
organized bodies .. 5. corps, posse
perspicacity ... 6. acumen, vision
8. sagacity 9. acuteness
11. discernment, penetration
perspicuity ... 8. lucidity, sagacity
12. translucency, transparency
perspiration ... 5. sudor, sweat
7. sudoric 8. hard work
11. evaporation, saline fluid
13. transpiration
persuade ... 4. coax, sway, urge
6. entice, induce, reason 7. convert,
suasion 8. convince, inveigle
9. influence, plead with, stonewall
persuasible ... 6. pliant
11. persuadable
14. open-mindedness
persuasive ... 8. eloquent 9. impelling
10. convincing, persuading
pert ... 3. gay 4. bold, keen 5. brash,
sassy, saucy 6. clever, comely,
dapper, daring, lively, nimble
7. forward 8. handsome, skillful
9. exquisite, officious, sprightly
11. impertinent 12. presumptuous
pert (girl) ... 4. chit, minx
pertain ... 5. belie 6. belong, relate
7. adjunct 8. function, peculiar

9. accessory, appendage, appertain, attribute
pertaining to ...
act of rising .. 6. ortive 7. eastern
agriculture .. 7. georgic
ancestral type .. 9. atavistic
ancient Nile city .. 4. Sais (Saite)
ancient Troy .. 5. Iliac
anything remote .. 6. forane
apostles .. 7. Petrine
Asiatic (old) .. 8. Chaldean
Asiatic mountain .. 6. Altaic
Athens .. 5. Attic
authorized doctrine .. 8. dogmatic
   10. dogmatical
birthmark .. 6. nevoid (naevoid)
body .. 5. somal
body of land .. 11. continental
book description .. 13. bibliographic
both ears .. 8. binaural
both sexes .. 6. unisex 7. epicene
breadmaking .. 6. panary
breastbone .. 7. sternal
bristles .. 5. setal
bunch .. 5. comal
canonical hours .. 7. matinal
carving .. 6. glypic 7. glyptic
cheek .. 5. malar
church, part .. 7. apsidal
city .. 5. civic, urban
cod family .. 6. gadoid
coins .. 12. numismatical
colors .. 9. chromatic
construction .. 8. geodesic, tectonic
cork .. 7. suberic
cough .. 7. tussine
court .. 5. aulic 9. judiciary
crown .. 7. coronal
dance .. 6. gestic 13. terpsichorean
daughter .. 6. filial
dawn .. 4. eoan
day (ordinary) .. 6. ferial
desert wastes .. 6. eremic
diaphragm .. 7. phrenic
dogma .. 9. levitical
doves .. 9. columbine
downward air .. 9. katabatic
downy .. 5. dotal
dreams .. 7. oneiric 9. oneirotic
ducks .. 7. anatine
early church .. 9. patristic
early culture .. 8. eolithic
earth .. 4. geal 5. terra 7. teluric
   9. planetary
earthquake .. 7. seismic
east .. 4. dawn, eoan 7. auroral
elms .. 9. ulmaceous
engraving .. 7. glyptic
equal rights .. 3. ERA 6. libber
essence .. 5. basic
exhaustion .. 7. burnout 9. tiredness
fallow deer .. 6. damine
fashion .. 5. modal 6. preppy, trendy
fasting .. 8. anorexic 9. abstinent
fats .. 6. adipic, sebaic 9. cellulite
feet .. 5. pedal
fields .. 8. agrarian
fine arts .. 9. aesthetic (esthetic)
fingers .. 7. digital
first principles .. 9. elemental
fissure .. 5. rimal
flood .. 7. diluvian

flowers .. 9. floscular 10. florescent
forehead .. 7. metopic
frogs .. 6. anuran, ranine
funeral music .. 10. threnodial
funerals .. 8. exequial
gospel .. 9. evangelic
gulls .. 6. larine
gums (Anat) .. 8. gingival
hair .. 5. pilar 7. blow–dry
hands .. 6. chiral, manual
head .. 8. cephalic
heaths .. 8. ericetal
holiday .. 6. ferial (Eccl), festal
honey .. 10. melaginous
horse .. 6. equine
house .. 5. domal (Astrol)
hypothetical force .. 4. odic
infernal regions .. 7. avernal
ink .. 10. atramental
insects .. 11. entomologic
intellect .. 6. noetic
iron .. 6. ferric
islands .. 7. insular
jaw .. 10. mandibular
kidney .. 5. renal
knots .. 5. nodal
land .. 8. praedial (predial)
language meaning .. 8. semantic
laughter .. 8. risorial
leg .. 6. crural 7. fibular
lips .. 6. labial
liver .. 7. hepatic
living organism .. 13. parasitologic
lockjaw .. 7. tetanic
love .. 6. erotic 7. amatory 8. erotical
male .. 5. macho, manly 7. agnatic
marriage .. 7. marital 8. hymeneal
marsh .. 8. paludine
meaning, in language .. 8. semantic
medicine .. 6. iatric 8. iatrical
medulla oblongata (brain) .. 6. bulbar
memory .. 6. mnesic 7. mnestic
   8. mnemonic 13. retrospective
midday .. 8. meridian
milk .. 7. lactary, lacteal
mind .. 6. mental 7. phrenic
money matters .. 5. T–bill 7. bailout
   8. economic
morning .. 5. matin, sunup 7. matinal
   9. matutinal
motion .. 7. kinetic
mouth .. 4. oral 7. oscular, palatal
   8. stomatic
mustard family .. 11. cruciferous
nephew .. 7. nepotal
north wind .. 6. boreal
nose .. 5. nasal 6. narial, rhinal
nut .. 5. nucal
ocean .. 7. pelagic
old age .. 6. senile 7. geratic
   8. gerontic 9. geriatric
Old World .. 13. gerontogenous
peacock .. 8. pavonine
people .. 4. laic 7. demotic
pigs .. 7. porcine
pleasure .. 7. hedonic
priests .. 10. sacerdotal
prophecy .. 9. vaticinal
public .. 7. cameral
public prayer .. 8. liturgic 10. liturgical
punishment .. 5. penal 8. punitive
queen .. 7. reginal

rainbow.. **6**. iridal
reason.. **6**. noetic
region without earthquakes..
  11. peneseismic
rhubarb.. **7**. rheumic
river.. **5**. amnic
river bank.. **8**. riparian
rock.. **7**. petrean
royal court.. **5**. aulic
salvation.. **8**. soterial **9**. soterical
sarcasm.. **8**. ironical
school of philosophy.. **7**. Eleatic
sea.. **6**. marine **7**. oceanic, pelagic
  9. thelassic
seacoast.. **8**. littoral
sense of taste.. **9**. gustatory
sepulchral mound.. **7**. tumular
shin, shinbone.. **7**. cnemial
ship's sails.. **5**. velic
singing birds.. **6**. oscine
skull.. **5**. inial
sole of foot.. **7**. plantar
spring.. **6**. vernal
stars.. **6**. astral **7**. stellar **8**. sidereal
state affairs.. **9**. pragmatic
stepmothers.. **8**. novercal
storks.. **7**. pelagic
summer.. **7**. estival (aestival)
  8. festival
sun.. **5**. solar **6**. heliac
tail.. **6**. caudal
teaching.. **9**. pedagogic
tears.. **8**. lacrimal
tempo.. **6**. agogic
the plague.. **6**. loimic
the skin.. **5**. deric **6**. dermic
thread.. **5**. filar
tile.. **7**. tegular
time.. **7**. chronic
tin.. **7**. stranic
tissue.. **5**. telar
tongue.. **7**. glossal, lingual
tortoises.. **9**. chelonian
touch.. **7**. tactile
travel.. **6**. viatic
trees.. **8**. arboreal
verse stress.. **5**. ictic
walls.. **5**. mural **8**. parietal
wax.. **5**. ceral
weight.. **5**. baric **8**. ponderal
whales.. **5**. rotal
wife.. **7**. uxorial
wine.. **5**. vinic
wine making.. **10**. oenopoetic
wings.. **5**. alary
winter.. **6**. hiemal
womanhood.. **9**. muliebral
woods.. **6**. sylvan
wrist.. **6**. carpal
pertaining to country...
Asiatic.. **8**. Chaldean
Asiatic mountain.. **6**. Altaic
Athens.. **5**. Attic
Carthage.. **5**. Punic
Celts.. **4**. Erse
Cretan language.. **6**. Minoan
Dissenters' meeting house.. **7**. pantile
  (from the roofing)
England.. **8**. Anglican
Ethiopian religion.. **6**. Coptic
France.. **6**. Gallic
Franks.. **5**. Salic

Gentiles.. **6**. ethnic
German State.. **8**. Bavarian
Greek epic.. **9**. Homerical
Greek philosophy.. **7**. Eleatic
  8. Platonic
Greek race (anc).. **6**. Aeolic
Greek valley.. **6**. Nemean **8**. Argolian
Hindu books, writing.. **5**. Vedic
  7. Tantric
Hindu philosophy, inertia.. **5**. tamas
Irish.. **6**. Celtic, Gaelic
Isle of Man.. **4**. Manx
Mars.. **5**. Arean
Mediterranean.. **6**. Levant
Moses.. **6**. Mosaic
Nile city (anc).. **4**. Sais (Saite)
Norse poem.. **5**. runic
Passover.. **7**. Paschal
Red Sea colony.. **8**. Eritrean
Rhine.. **7**. Rhenish
Scotch Highlander.. **6**. Gaelic
Spice Islands.. **7**. Molucca
Troy (anc).. **5**. Iliac **6**. Trojan
Vulcan.. **11**. Mulcibirian
West Indies.. **9**. Antillean
pertenencia... **10**. concession
  11. mining claim
Perth... **6**. Atholl (Athole) **7**. Ontario
  9. Australia
pertinacious... **4**. firm **8**. adhering,
  resolute **9**. tenacious **10**. determined,
  inflexible, persistent, unyielding
  11. persevering
pertinacity... **9**. obstinacy
  11. persistency
pertinence... **7**. fitness **9**. relevancy
  10. timeliness **12**. appositeness
perturb... **5**. alarm **6**. excite
  7. agitate, derange, disturb, fluster,
  trouble **8**. bewilder, disorder, distress
  9. confusion
perturbation... **5**. alarm **7**. anxiety,
  fluster **9**. agitation, confusion
  10. excitement **11**. fearfulness
  12. bewilderment, irregularity
pertusion... **8**. piercing, punching
  11. perforation, punched hole
pertussis... **5**. cough **13**. whooping
  cough
Peru... see also *Peruvian*
capital.. **4**. Lima **5**. Cuzco (Inca)
  14. City of the Kings
hero.. **7**. Bolivar, Pizarro
lake.. **8**. Titicaca
mountain.. **5**. Andes **10**. Cordillera
port.. **6**. Callao **7**. Iquitos
  8. Mollendo
river.. **4**. Sama **5**. Santa **6**. Amazon
  7. Maranon, Ucayali **8**. Urubamba
ruins.. **4**. Inca **5**. huaco (relics)
Peruvian (pert to)...
animal.. **4**. paco **5**. llama **6**. alpaca
bark.. **8**. cinchona
goddess of fertility.. **4**. Mama
inn, tavern.. **5**. tambo
king (petty).. **7**. cacique
plant.. **3**. oca
rodent.. **10**. chinchilla
tinamou.. **4**. yutu
tree.. **8**. cinchona
university.. **9**. San Marcos
volcano.. **7**. El Misti

wind (cold) . . 4. puna
pervade . . . 4. fill 5. imbue 6. extend
  8. permeate, traverse 9. penetrate
pervading . . . 9. prevalent, universal
perverse . . . 3. awk 4. awry, wogh
  5. wrong 6. cranky, erring
  7. corrupt, forward, froward,
  wayward, willful (wilful) 8. contrary,
  petulant 9. obstinate 10. ill–humored
perversion . . . 5. error 6. misuse
  8. apostasy 9. sophistry
  10. corruption, distortion
  13. falsification 17. misinterpretation,
  misrepresentation
perversion of taste . . . 7. malacia
pervert . . . 4. ruin 5. upset 6. divert,
  misuse 7. corrupt, distort, falsify,
  heretic 8. apostate, overturn,
  renegade 9. turn aside
  10. degenerate, lead astray
  12. misinterpret, misrepresent
pervulgate . . . 7. publish
Pesach, Pesah . . . 8. Passover (Feast)
pesante . . . 5. heavy 10. impressive
peshkash . . . 3. tax 7. present, tribute
  8. offering
peskar . . . 5. agent 7. steward
  8. minister 10. accountant
pesky . . . 6. plaguy 7. teasing
  9. harassing 10. tormenting
pes planus . . . 8. flatfoot 13. talipes
  planus
pess . . . 7. hassock (church)
pessimist . . . 5. cynic 6. malist
  9. defeatist, worrywart
pessimistic . . . 6. gloomy 7. cynical
  8. cowardly, hopeless 10. despairing,
  foreboding, uncheerful
pest . . . 3. nag 4. bane 6. plague
  7. ragweed 8. epidemic, nuisance
  9. annoyance 10. pestilence
pester . . . 3. nag, rib 5. annoy, tease,
  worry 6. badger, harass, impede,
  infest 7. torment 8. entangle
  9. importune 10. overburden
pestilence . . . 4. bane 7. disease,
  scourge 8. epidemic 13. bubonic
  plague
pestilent . . . 6. deadly 7. noxious
  8. annoying 9. pestering, poisonous
  10. contagious, infectious, pernicious
  11. mischievous, troublesome
pestle . . . 4. club 6. muller 7. crusher,
  pounder
pes valgus . . . 9. bowlegged 13. talipes
  valgus
pet . . . 4. dear, tiff 5. humor 6. caress,
  coddle, cosset, dandle, fondle,
  pamper 7. darling, dudgeon, indulge
  8. cade lamb, favorite
  10. endearment
petals (pert to) . . .
  flower . . 7. corolla
  having . . 8. petalous
  orchid . . 8. labellum
  ref to . . 5. whorl 8. petaline, petaloid
  without . . 9. apetalous
petard . . . 9. explosive 11. firecracker
peteman (thieves' sl) . . . 5. thief
  7. burglar 8. peterman
  9. cracksman, fisherman (Hist)
  10. safeblower

Peter (pert to) . . .
  Bell . . 4. poem
  Bible . . 5. Simon (also called)
  7. epistle (New Test)
  Ibbetson . . 5. novel
  Pan . . 3. boy 4. play
  Pan dog . . 4. Nana
  the Great . . 4. Czar
  the Great's father . . 6. Alexis
  the Hermit . . 8. Crusader (1st)
peter out . . . 4. fade, fail, tire, wane
  6. weaken 7. dwindle 9. cease to
  be
petiole . . . 4. stem 5. stalk 8. peduncle
  9. leafstalk 10. mesopodium
petit . . . 4. mean 5. petty, small
  6. little 13. insignificant
petite . . . 5. small 6. demure, little
petite (pert to) . . .
  bourse . . 6. Market (Finan)
  marmite . . 4. soup
  noblesse . . 8. nobility (lesser)
petition . . . 3. ask, beg, sue 4. plea,
  pray 5. apply, plead 6. prayer
  7. entreat, relator, request, solicit
  8. entreaty 10. supplicate
peto . . . 5. wahoo
petrified . . . 8. hardened 9. terrified
  15. carved from stone
petrified body . . . 6. fossil
petrify . . . 4. numb 6. deaden, harden
  7. astound, stupefy 8. paralyze
  11. become stone
petroglyph . . . 11. rock carving 15. rock
  inscription
Petrograd . . . 9. Leningrad
petroleum product . . . 6. butane, diesel
  7. naphtha, propane 8. gasoline
petrology *(science of)* . . . 5. rocks
petrosal . . . 4. bone 5. sinus, stony
  7. petrous 8. ganglion
petticoat . . . 4. girl, kilt 5. jupon,
  pagne, woman 6. kirtle 8. basquine
  9. undercoat, waistcoat
  10. fustanella, underskirt
petticoat tails . . . 7. teacake
  9. shortcake
pettifogger . . . 4. tyro 5. quack
  6. lawyer 7. shyster 8. attorney
pettish . . . 7. fretful, peevish 9. irritable
pettle . . . 6. cuddle, nestle, potter
  7. cherish
petto . . . 12. in one's breast 15. in
  contemplation
petty . . . 4. mean, orra 5. minor, small
  6. paltry 7. trivial 8. childish,
  inferior, nugatory, trifling 9. miniscule
  10. diminutive 11. small–minded,
  subordinate, unimportant
  12. narrow–minded 13. insignificant
  14. inconsiderable
petty (pert to) . . .
  captain . . 9. centurion
  fault . . 10. peccadillo
  larceny . . 10. scrounging
  mullein . . 7. cowslip
  objection . . 5. cavil
  prince . . 6. satrap
petulance . . . 8. ill humor, pertness
  9. insolence, sauciness
  10. wantonness 11. peevishness,
  pettishness

petulant... 4. pert 5. cross, huffy,
saucy, testy 6. wanton 7. forward,
fretful, peevish, wayward, willful
8. contrary, immodest, insolent
9. querulous

peu à peu... 9. by degrees 14. little
by little

pewee... 5. pewit 6. phoebe
8. woodcock 10. flycatcher

pewit... 5. pewee 7. lapwing
12. laughing gull

Pfefferkuchen... 11. gingerbread

Phaëthon, Class Myth (pert to)...
bird.. 4. swan
car.. 3. sun
father.. 6. Helios
sun god.. 6. Helios

phagomania... 3. insanity
16. insatiable hunger

Phalacrocorax... 5. coots
10. cormorants

phalacrosis... 8. alopecia, baldness

phalanger... 5. tapoa 9. marsupial

phalanx... 4. bone 5. pawns 6. troops
7. company (Mil) 8. infantry

phalera.. 4. boss 5. cameo

phantasm... 5. dream, fancy, ghost
6. idolum, spirit 7. eidolon, fantasy,
phantom, specter (spectre)
8. delusion, illusion 10. apparition

phantasy, fantasy... 5. fancy, image
6. autism 8. daydream
11. imagination

phantom... 5. fairy, ghost 7. eidolon,
specter (spectre) 10. simulacrum

Pharaoh (Bib).. 4. faro, king

Pharaoh (pert to)...
ancestor.. 2. Ra
chicken, hen.. 7. vulture (Egypt)
fig.. 8. sycamore
mouse.. 9. ichneumon

phare... 6. beacon, pharos
10. lighthouse

pharisee... 7. pietist 9. hypocrite

pharmacology... 5. drugs 13. materia
medica

pharos... 5. cloak 6. beacon
10. chandelier (Eccl), lighthouse,
watchtower

phase... 5. facet, stage 6. aspect
7. caprice, chapter, horning (moon)

phases, having many...
11. Hydra–headed

phasm... 6. meteor 7. phantom

pheasant... 5. cheer, monal 6. pukras
7. kallege 8. tragopan 12. ruffed
grouse

pheasant (pert to)...
brood.. 3. nye 4. nide (nid) 5. flock
cuckoo.. 6. coucal
duck.. 7. pintail 9. merganser
finch.. 7. waxbill
genus.. 10. Oreophasis
wren.. 7. emu wren

pheasant species... 5. argus, blood
6. golden, silver 7. kallege
8. curassow 9. Mongolian
10. ring–necked 12. Lady Amherst's

phenomenal... 7. unusual 8. eventful,
sensible 9. objective, wonderful
13. extraordinary

phenomenon... 4. fact 5. event

(unusual) 7. prodigy

phial... 3. cup 4. bowl, vial 6. bottle,
vessel

phiale... 5. laver 6. vessel 8. fountain
(Eccl)

Phi Beta Kappa (pert to)...
badge.. 8. watch key
founding.. 21. William and Mary
College (1776)
meaning.. 24. Philosophy the guide of
life
society.. 11. Greek–letter (oldest)

philabeg (filibeg)... 4. kilt

Philadelphia...
city.. 12. Pennsylvania
fleabane.. 7. skevish
lawyer.. 6. shrewd
meaning.. 3. brother–loving
ref to.. 12. Philadelphus (Ptolemy II)

philander... 5. flirt, lover 7. opossum
10. flirtation, love–making, lover of
men

philanthropic... 6. humane
10. benevolent 12. eleemosynary

philanthropist... 5. donor 8. altruist,
do–gooder 9. Robin Hood
10. benefactor, benevolist,
Montefiore, Rothschild
12. humanitarian

philanthropy... 7. charity 8. good will
10. almsgiving 11. beneficence,
benevolence (opp of misanthropy)

Philippic... 6. screed, tirade 7. oration
8. diatribe 9. Philippus

Philippine, Philippines...
archipelago.. 4. Sulu 5. Malay
bay.. 6. Manila
capital.. 6. Baguio (summer), Manila
10. Quezon City
city.. 5. Albay, Davao 6. Cavite
7. Dagupan
district.. 7. Lepanto
fort.. 4. Gota 10. Corregidor
island.. 4. Cebu 5. Leyte, Luzon,
Panay, Samar, Ticao 6. Negros
7. Palawan, Paragua 8. Mindanao
mountain.. 3. Apo, Iba 5. Mayon
river.. 4. Abra, Agno 5. Pasig
8. Mindanao, Pampanga
university.. 10. Santo Tomas (1611)
volcano.. 3. Apo 5. Mayon

Philippine (pert to)...
animal.. 5. civet, lemur
ant, termite.. 4. anay (anai)
barracks.. 7. cuartel
boat, canoe, raft.. 5. balsa, banca
breadfruit.. 7. camansi
buffalo.. 7. carabao, timarau (timerau)
chair (on poles).. 7. talabon
dagger.. 4. itac
drink.. 4. beno 5. bubud
fabric.. 4. pina 9. pineapple
fetish, idol.. 5. anito
food.. 3. poi 4. Musa, saba, taro
hemp.. 5. abaca 6. Manila
house.. 5. bahay
knife.. 4. bolo
litter, pole chair.. 7. talabon
lizard.. 4. ibid (monitor)
mango.. 5. bauno 7. pahutan
market day.. 7. tiangue
melon.. 6. atimon

mudfish .. **5.** dalag
palm .. **4.** nipa **6.** anahau (anahao)
parrot (green) .. **5.** cagit
reptile .. **6.** python
rice .. **4.** paga **5.** macan
rice field bank .. **7.** pilapil
river .. **4.** ilog
shrub .. **4.** alem
sweetsop .. **4.** ates
town .. **4.** agoa
tree .. **3.** tui **4.** ipil (ypil) **5.** asana,
   ligas, narra, yacal **6.** molave
   7. Eugenia, tindalo **8.** macaasim
turnip .. **7.** cincoma
vehicle (public) .. **9.** carromata
water jar .. **5.** banga
wood .. **4.** teak **5.** ebony **6.** sandal
   8. mahogany
Philippine people (pert to) . . .
discoverer .. **8.** Magellan (1521)
farmer .. **3.** tao
headman .. **4.** datu
language .. **4.** Moro **7.** Tagalog (Tagal)
   8. Pilipino
Luzon savage .. **4.** Aeta **6.** Igorot
   (Igorrote)
Muslim, Moslem .. **4.** Moro
native .. **3.** tao **4.** Moro, Sulu
native race .. **3.** Lao **4.** Aeta (dwarf)
   7. Tagalog, Visayan
native worker .. **7.** polista
Negrito .. **3.** Ati **4.** Aeta
patriot .. **5.** rizal
peasant .. **3.** tao
priest (Moro) .. **7.** pandita
servant .. **4.** bata **5.** alila
tribe (Chr) .. **5.** Bikol (Bico, Vicol)
tribe (pagan) .. **6.** Italon
Philistine . . . **5.** enemy **7.** prosaic
   9. philister **10.** conformist,
   uncultured **12.** antagonistic
   13. prosaic person, unenlightened
Philistine (pert to) . . .
anc name .. **9.** Palestine, Philistia
assimilated by .. **7.** Semites
city .. **4.** Gaza **5.** Ekron (Bib)
god .. **4.** Baal **5.** Dagon
philo (comb form) . . . **6.** fond of, loving
philogeant . . . **12.** lover of earth
philogyny . . . **11.** love of women
philology . . . **11.** linguistics **14.** love of
   learning
Philomela (pert to) . . .
father .. **7.** Pandion (King of Athens)
sister .. **6.** Procne
turned into .. **7.** swallow
   11. nightingale
philosopher . . .
American .. **7.** Emerson **9.** Santayana
Chinese .. **9.** Confucius
Dutch .. **7.** Spinoza
English .. **5.** Bacon
French .. **5.** Renan **8.** Rousseau,
   Voltaire
German .. **4.** Kant **9.** Nietzsche
   12. Schopenhauer
Greek .. **4.** Zeno **8.** Socrates
Scottish .. **4.** Hume
Seven Sages (7 Wise Men of Greece) ..
   4. Bias **5.** Solon **6.** Chilon, Thales
   8. Pittacus **9.** Cleobulus
   10. Epimenides (or Periander)

Philosopher of . . .
Farney .. **8.** Voltaire
Malmesbury .. **6.** Hobbes
Sans Souci .. **17.** Frederick the Great
Syracuse .. **4.** Dion
Wimbledon .. **14.** John Horne Tooke
philosopher's school . . . **7.** Eleatic
philosophical . . . **4.** wise **7.** erudite,
   logical, sapient **8.** rational
   9. temperate, unruffled
philosophical being . . . **6.** entity
philosophy (pert to) . . .
choice of .. **11.** eclecticism
of law .. **13.** jurisprudence
of pantheists .. **5.** Stoic
sublimated .. **17.** Transcendentalism
theory .. **4.** yoga **9.** pantheism,
   Platonism, solipsism **12.** epistemology
phlegmatic . . . **4.** calm, dull, slow
   5. inert **6.** mucous, watery
   7. viscous **8.** sluggish **9.** apathetic
phlogistic . . . **5.** fiery **6.** heated
   7. burning **11.** impassioned
   12. inflammatory
Phoebad . . . **7.** seeress **9.** priestess
   (Delphian) **10.** prophetess
Phoebe (pert to) . . .
daughter .. **4.** Leto
epithet of .. **7.** Artemis
mother .. **4.** Gaea (earth goddess)
poetic .. **4.** moon
phoebe . . . **4.** fish **5.** craps, pewit
   6. peewee **9.** satellite (Saturn)
   10. flycatcher
Phoebus . . . **3.** Sol **6.** sun god
Phoenicia . . .
capital city .. **4.** Tyre **5.** Sidon
Colony .. **5.** Hippo **8.** Carthage
deity .. **4.** Baal
famed for .. **9.** purple dye
   10. navigation
goddess of fertility .. **6.** Baltis
   7. Astarte
god of healing .. **6.** Eshmun (Eshmoun)
king .. **6.** Agenor
region .. **5.** Syria
Phoenix . . . **4.** bird (fabled), palm
   7. capital (Ariz)
phonetic (pert to) . . .
science .. **9.** phonology
sound .. **7.** phoneme
stop .. **9.** occlusive
system .. **5.** romic
phonic . . . **6.** spoken, voiced
   7. sounded **8.** auditory **9.** accoustic,
   vibration
phony (comb form) . . . **5.** sound, voice
phony . . . **4.** fake **9.** contrived,
   simulated **11.** counterfeit
photograph . . . **4.** film **5.** image, photo
   7. picture **8.** likeness, portrait
   9. ferrotype, pictorial, portrayal
   10. centerfold, heliograph
   12. photogravure
photographic bath . . . **5.** toner
   7. reducer **9.** developer
photography, science of . . . **5.** light
   6. optics **7.** photics
photography inventors . . . **4.** Land
   6. Niepce, Talbot **8.** Daguerre
photometric unit . . . **3.** pyr, rad
phrase . . . **5.** idiom **6.** remark, saying,

slogan 7. diction, epigram, epithet,
passage 8. flattery 9. catchword
10. expression 11. phraseology
phraseology... 5. style 6. jargon
7. diction, wording 8. parlance
phratry (Hist)... 4. clan 5. group
phrenetic... 3. mad 5. crazy
6. madman 7. fanatic, frantic, violent
9. delirious 10. passionate
phrenology, science of... 5. skull
10. craniology
Phrygia, Asia Minor...
cap (comical).. 10. liberty cap
deity.. 5. Attis
Eccl Hist.. 9. Montanist
founder.. 7. Gordius (800 BC)
King.. 5. Midas
marble (anc).. 9. pavonazzo
(pavonazzetto)
music.. 4. mode
river.. 7. Meander
phylactery (Eccl)... 4. case 5. charm,
chest, miter 6. amulet, infula, record,
scroll
phylarchy... 12. rule by tribes
phyletic... 6. racial 7. descent, species
12. phylogenetic
phyllophagous... 15. feeding on leaves
physical... 6. bodily 7. natural, somatic
8. material 9. corporeal
physical force... 10. attraction
physical unit... 3. erg
physician... 5. medic 6. doctor,
healer, intern 7. coroner 8. restorer
physician (pert to)...
ancient.. 5. Galen
comb form.. 5. iatro
French Nobel Prize.. 7. Laveran
Greek (anc).. 5. Galen
11. Asclepiades
quack.. 10. medicaster
symbol.. 8. caduceus
physicist... 7. Faraday, Galvani,
Marconi 10. naturalist
physiognomy... 3. mug 4. face
11. countenance 14. external aspect,
interpretation
physique... 4. body 6. figure
physis (Gr)... 6. nature
phytology, science of... 6. botany,
plants
piacle... 3. sin 5. crime, guilt
7. offense 15. sacrificial rite
17. expiatory offering
pian... 5. tumor 9. frambesia
piano (pert to)...
direction.. 10. pianissimo (softly)
duet, upper part.. 5. primo
dumb keyboard.. 10. digitorium
early.. 6. spinet
Italian.. 10. Cristofori
keyboard.. 7. clavier 8. pedalier
pedal.. 7. celeste
pianolike.. 7. celesta
player.. 7. pianola
slang.. 11. eighty–eight
small.. 8. pianette
piatti... 7. cymbals
piazza... 5. campo, porch 6. square
7. gallery, portico, veranda
pic... 4. peak 8. picayune
picacho... 4. hill 5. butte

picador... 3. wit 6. jester 7. debater
8. horseman (with lance), toreador
11. bullfighter
picaro... 5. knave, rogue 7. sharper
8. vagabond 10. picaresque
picaroon... 5. rogue, thief 6. pirate,
rascal 7. brigand, corsair 8. prey
upon
pick... 4. cull, gaff, peck, sort
5. elect, pluck, strum 6. assort,
choose, indent, pickax, pierce, select
7. diamond (card), harvest, the best
8. plectrum, the elite 9. toothpick
pick (pert to)...
flaws.. 5. cavil
out.. 6. pilfer, select 7. acquire,
procure, specify 9. eliminate,
segregate 11. distinguish
pick–me–up.. 5. tonic 6. bracer
9. kittiwake, stimulate 11. restorative
up.. 4. tidy 6. arrest 7. improve
9. stimulant 10. recuperate
picked... 4. trim 5. piked, spiny
6. choice, chosen, culled, dainty,
peaked, spruce 7. adorned, plucked,
pointed 8. stripped 10. fastidious
pickerel... 4. fish, pike 9. Esox niger
12. walleyed pike
picket... 3. peg 4. pale, post, tern
5. fence, guard, stake 6. bullet,
fasten, paling, sentry, tether
7. enclose, fortify, shackle 8. sentinel
10. go on strike
pickle... 4. alec, peck 5. achar, brine
6. dawdle, nibble, piddle, pilfer, trifle
7. chutney, vitriol
pickled... 5. drunk 6. soused
9. marinated
pickled pig's feet... 5. souse
pickle fork... 8. runcible
pickle–herring... 7. buffoon
11. merry–andrew 12. Pickelhering
pickpocket... 4. wire 5. thief 6. bulker
picnic... 3. fun 4. camp, play
6. junket, outing 9. festivity
Pict (anc)... 4. Scot 5. Aryan
9. aborigine
Pictland... 8. Scotland
pictorial... 8. painting 11. illustrated,
picturesque
Pict's house (Archaeol)... 8. dwelling
(subterranean)
picture... 3. oil 4. copy, draw, icon
5. image, print, scene 6. chromo,
depict, pastel 7. diorama, etching,
portray, porture, tableau 8. describe,
likeness, painting, portrait
9. engraving, paintings, represent,
visualize 10. photograph
11. description 14. representation
picture (pert to)...
mounting, border.. 3. mat 5. frame
8. kakemono, makimono (scroll)
moving.. 4. film 5. movie 6. cinema
positive.. 5. print
puzzle.. 5. rebus
small.. 5. cameo 9. miniature
stand.. 5. easel
viewer.. 11. alethoscope, stereoscope
12. magic lantern, stereopticon
picturesque... 5. vivid 6. scenic
7. graphic 9. pictorial

picuda... 9. barracuda (great), picudilla (small)
picudo... 6. weevil 10. boll weevil
piddle... 3. toy 4. pick, play 6. putter, trifle 9. waste time
pie... 4. food, mess 5. chaos, patty 6. jumble, magpie, pastry 7. cobbler, dessert, measure 9. confusion
piebald... 4. pied 5. mixed, pinto 6. motley 7. mongrel, mottled, pintado 10. variegated 13. heterogeneous
piece... 3. bit 4. join, part, role 5. crumb, drama, piece, scrap, shred 6. sample 7. measure, portion, writing 8. chessman, fragment, specimen, treatise
piece (pert to)...
  armor.. 5. tasse (tace) 8. corselet
  de résistance.. 6. entrée 8. main dish
  door, jamb.. 6. lintel
  eccentric.. 3. cam
  fastening.. 3. gib
  fitted.. 4. shim 5. tenon
  flat.. 4. slab, slat 5. flake, strip
  meal.. 9. by degrees, fragments 12. piece by piece 14. little by little
  metal.. 3. sow
  neck.. 3. boa 5. rabat, scarf, stole 8. kerchief
  of one's mind.. 6. rebuke 7. reproof 13. candid opinion
  out.. 3. eke 6. cantle
  preventing slippage.. 5. cleat
  short.. 4. skit
  side.. 3. rib 5. stave
  split off.. 6. sliver, splint 8. splinter
  tapering.. 4. gore 6. gusset
  work (art).. 4. pavé 6. mosaic, niello
pieces of...
  eight.. 6. dollar, escudo
  meat.. 5. cabob
  silk waste.. 4. noil
pied... 4. foot 5. pinto 7. colored (2 or more colors), dappled, piebald 10. variegated 12. parti–colored
pied (pert to)...
  blackbird.. 6. thrush
  brant.. 5. goose
  diver.. 4. smew
  duck.. 8. Labrador
  Friar (Eccl Hist).. 9. mendicant
  monk.. 10. Bernardine, Cistercian
  Piper of Hamelin.. 8. musician 10. rat charmer
  widgeon.. 8. garganey 9. goldeneye
Piedmont, Italy... 7. capital (Turin)
pieplant... 7. rhubarb
pier... 4. anta, dock, mole, quay 5. groin, wharf 6. pillar 7. landing 8. buttress, gatepost 9. promenade 10. breakwater
pierce... 4. bore, cold, gore, pain, tart 5. enter, gride, lance, probe, spear, spike, sting, wound 6. riddle, tunnel 7. discern 8. puncture 9. penetrate, perforate 10. comprehend
piercing... 4. keen, loud 5. acute 6. shrill 7. caustic, clearly, painful, piteous, pungent, sharply, shrilly, spiking, violent 8. deep–felt, poignant, spearing, stabbing

9. searching
Pieria, Macedonia (pert to)...
  epithet of.. 5. Muses
  native.. 7. Pierian
  reference to.. 6. poetry 9. knowledge
  seat of.. 5. Muses
piet... 5. ouzel 6. magpie 7. piebald 10. chatterbox, chattering 11. saucy person
Pietà (It)... 9. sculpture 10. Virgin Mary
pietose (Mus)... 11. sympathetic 13. compassionate
piety... 4. pity, zeal (worship) 6. filial 8. devotion, holiness, religion 9. reverence 10. compassion, devoutness, sanctimony 11. dutifulness
pig... 3. car (RR), ham, hog, sow 4. boar, pork 5. bacon, crosk, flask, swine 6. farrow 7. casting, dogboat, glutton 8. pressman, sixpence, slattern 9. policeman 11. stoolpigeon
pig (pert to)...
  bed.. 3. pen, sty 5. reeve 6. pigsty
  female.. 3. sow 4. gilt
  guinea.. 4. cavy
  headed.. 6. stupid 9. obstinate
  iron.. 5. ingot
  iron, ballast (Naut).. 9. kentledge
  iron, cast.. 9. kentledge (Mil)
  last of litter.. 4. runt
  lead, weight.. 6. fother
  litter.. 6. farrow
  piglike.. 7. hoglike, porcine, suiform
  piglike animal.. 7. peccary 8. babirusa
  potato.. 7. cowbane
  rat.. 9. bandicoot
  skin.. 6. saddle 8. football
  yoke.. 7. sextant 8. quadrant
  young.. 5. grice, shoat 6. farrow, piglet 9. gruntling
pigdan... 8. spittoon
pigeon... 3. nun 4. barb, dove, dupe, fowl, girl, gull, ruff 5. heart, piper, pluck, sweet 6. coward, fleece, pouter, roller, turbit 7. fantail, jacobin, pintail, tumbler 9. trumpeter
pigeon, pidgin (pert to)...
  Australia.. 5. wonga 10. wonga–wonga
  berry.. 7. dogwood 9. Juneberry, wild elder
  blood.. 6. garnet
  carrier.. 5. homer 6. homing 10. scandaroon
  extinct.. 4. dodo
  food.. 7. saltcat
  genus.. 5. Goura 7. Columba
  hawk.. 6. falcon, merlin
  house.. 7. dovecot 9. columbary
  ref to.. 12. peristeronic
  short–beaked.. 4. barb
  wood.. 6. cushat 8. ringdove
  young.. 5. piper
pigment... 3. red 4. blue, gray, pink 5. black, brown, color, green, ocher (ochre), paint, white 6. orange, purple, yellow 8. colorant
pigment (pert to)...
  arsenic, yellow.. 8. orpiment
  black.. 3. tar 5. sepia 7. melanin

blue.. **5.** smalt
blue–green.. **4.** bice
brown.. **5.** sepia, umber **6.** bister
(bistre), sienna (burnt) **7.** cypress
brownish yellow.. **6.** sienna
calico yellow.. **7.** canarin (canarine)
coal tar.. **7.** aniline
cuttlefish.. **5.** sepia
madder root.. **7.** rubiate
orange red.. **7.** realgar
oxide of lead.. **8.** massicot
red.. **7.** turacin
yellow.. **5.** ocher (ochre) **7.** etiolin
pigmy... see *pygmy*
pignus... **4.** pawn **6.** pledge
pig's feet... **9.** pettitoes
pigtail... **5.** braid, queue **7.** tobacco
(rolled) **8.** rope's end (Naut)
pika... **6.** rodent
pike... **3.** ged (gedd) **4.** fish, luce, pick
6. beacon, pickax
pike (pert to)...
North American.. **11.** muskellunge
perch.. **6.** sauger
pikelike.. **3.** gar **4.** luce **5.** lucet
6. robalo **8.** robalito **9.** barracuda
walleyed.. **4.** doré
pikel, pikle... **7.** hayfork **9.** pitchfork
pikelet... **7.** crumpet
piker... **5.** thief, tramp **6.** coward
7. gambler, quitter, shirker, vagrant
8. tightwad
pilar... **5.** downy, hairy
pilaster... **4.** anta **6.** alette (part),
column
Pilate (Bib)... **10.** procurator (Judean)
pilchard... **7.** sardine
pile... **3.** awn, mow, nap **4.** heap,
load, mole, pier, rick, shag
5. amass, slack, spile, stake **6.** heap
up, pillar, wealth **7.** fortune, store
up, texture
pile (pert to)...
burning.. **4.** pyre
defense.. **8.** estacade
driver.. **7.** fistuca
of hay.. **3.** mow **4.** dess, rick
5. stack
up.. **4.** heap **7.** smashup, store up
9. shipwreck **10.** exaggerate
pilfer... **3.** rob **4.** lift, loot **5.** filch,
steal, swipe **6.** rustle (cattle), snitch
7. purloin
pilgrim... **5.** exile (Relig) **6.** palmer
8. crusader, newcomer, traveler,
wanderer, wayfarer **9.** immigrant,
sojourner **10.** tenderfoot
12. peregrinator
Pilgrim (pert to)...
father.. **9.** John Alden
Fathers.. **11.** Separatists (1620)
garment.. **5.** ihram (Mecca)
landing.. **12.** Plymouth Rock (1620)
Scotch.. **6.** palmer
ship.. **9.** Mayflower, Speedwell
pilgrimage to Mecca... **4.** hadj
Pilgrim's bottle... **7.** ampulla, costrel
Pilgrim's Progress... **8.** allegory
(Bunyan)
pill... **3.** rob **4.** ball, bore, pare, pell,
pool **5.** bolus, creek **6.** bullet, pellet,
pilule **8.** medicine **9.** cigarette

11. decorticate
pillage... **4.** flay, loot, prey, sack
5. booty, harry, spoil, strip **6.** rapine,
ravage **7.** despoil, plunder, robbery
9. depredate, extortion **10.** spoliation
pillar... **4.** post, slab **5.** shaft, stele
(stela), tower **6.** column **7.** support
8. mainstay, monument, pedestal
pillar (pert to)...
airfield.. **5.** pylon
Buddhist.. **3.** lat
carved.. **9.** totem pole
little.. **8.** pillaret
of society.. **9.** personage
pillarlike.. **6.** stelar
saint.. **7.** recluse, stylite
tall, slender.. **7.** obelisk
with front figure.. **7.** osiride
Pillars of Hercules site... **5.** Abila,
Calpe **17.** Strait of Gibralter
pillbox... **3.** cap, hat **8.** brougham,
fortress **13.** fortification
pillory... **4.** yoke **5.** stock, trone
6. cangue, punish
pillow... **3.** pad **5.** block **7.** cushion,
support
pillow (pert to)...
case, cover.. **4.** sham, slip
long.. **7.** bolster
stuffing.. **5.** kapok **8.** feathers
pilose... **5.** hairy **6.** pilous
pilot... **4.** lead **5.** flyer, guide, steer
6. aviate, direct, leader **8.** director,
helmsman, preacher **9.** clergyman,
navigator **10.** cowcatcher
pilot (pert to)...
bird.. **6.** plover
expert.. **3.** ace
fish.. **6.** remora **9.** amberfish,
whitefish
house.. **10.** wheelhouse
jacket.. **9.** pea jacket
sky.. **8.** preacher **9.** clergyman
snake.. **10.** copperhead
weed.. **9.** rosinweed
whale.. **9.** blackfish
Piltdown, England (pert to)...
Hist yield.. **7.** Dawn Man, fossils
Prehist station.. **6.** Sussex
piltock... **8.** coalfish
pilum... **6.** pestle **7.** javelin
pilus... **4.** hair
Pima... **5.** Opata **11.** Indian tribe
pimento... **6.** pepper **7.** paprika
8. allspice, pimiento
pin... **3.** hob, peg, pen **4.** axle, bolt,
coak (coag), join **5.** affix, badge,
dowel, rivet, thole **6.** brooch, cotter,
fasten, secure, trifle **7.** confine,
enclose, gudgeon, jewelry, spindle,
stopper, trenail **10.** linchpin, ornament,
transfix **10.** chatelaine
pin (pert to)...
axle.. **8.** linchpin
dial.. **5.** style
fish.. **11.** stickleback
game.. **7.** skittle
grass.. **9.** alfilaria (forage)
jackstraw (game).. **8.** spilikin (spillikin)
meat fastener.. **6.** skewer
quoits.. **3.** hob
sailmaker's.. **3.** fid

small.. **3.** peg **4.** lill
with looped head.. **7.** eyebolt
pinafore... **5.** apron, smock **7.** tablier
　8. sun dress
Pinafore... **5.** opera (Gilbert & Sullivan)
pinag... **4.** lake (rain season)
piñata... **5.** globe (swinging, with gifts)
pinax... **4.** dish **5.** table **6.** plaque,
　scheme, tablet **7.** picture
　9. catalogue
pinbone... **7.** hipbone
pince–nez... **7.** glasses, nippers
　10. eyeglasses
pincers... **3.** tew **5.** chela, tongs
　6. pliers **7.** forceps, pinette
pinch... **3.** nip, rob **4.** pain, raid
　5. cramp, gripe, pugil (anc), steal,
　stint, tweak **6.** arrest, crisis, extort,
　scrimp, snatch, snitch, strait, twinge
　7. afflict, confine, squeeze, urgency
　8. compress, contract, exigency,
　straiten
pinchbeck... **4.** sham **5.** alloy (cheap
　jewelry) **8.** frippery, spurious
　11. counterfeit
pinched... **4.** poor, thin **8.** squeezed
　10. compressed, contracted,
　distressed, straitened
pinchem... **8.** titmouse
pinda... **6.** peanut
Pindar... **4.** poet (lyric)
pindaric... **3.** ode **9.** irregular
　12. unrestrained
pine... **4.** flag **5.** waste, yearn
　6. grieve, lament, needle, repine,
　sicken, weaken, wither **8.** languish
　11. deteriorate
pine (pert to)...
　Brazil.. **6.** paraná
　chemical.. **5.** pinic
　exudation.. **5.** resin, rosin
　family.. **3.** fir **5.** larch, piñon
　　6. spruce
　finch.. **6.** siskin
　fir.. **6.** balsam **12.** Balm of Gilead
　fruit.. **4.** cone
　genus.. **5.** Pinus
　gum.. **8.** sandarac
　knot.. **7.** dovekie
　leaf.. **6.** needle
　low–growing.. **5.** piñon
　mahogany.. **6.** totara
　New Zealand.. **5.** kauri (kaury)
　Pacific coast.. **8.** knobpine
　Philippine.. **7.** Amboina **8.** galagala
　screw.. **3.** ara **6.** pandan
　tar extract.. **6.** retene
　tulip.. **10.** pipsissewa
pineal... **5.** brain, gland **8.** pine cone
pineapple... **4.** bomb, pina **5.** fiber,
　fruit **6.** ananas **8.** pine cone
　12. Bromeliaceae
pineapple (pert to)...
　cheese.. **7.** Cheddar
　cloth.. **4.** pina
　segment.. **3.** pip
　weed.. **8.** marigold
Pine Tree State... **5.** Maine
pinguescent... **9.** fattening
pinguid... **3.** fat **4.** oily, rich **5.** fatty
　8. unctuous
pinguitude... **7.** fatness, obesity

8. oiliness **10.** greasiness
pink... **3.** cut, Red **4.** deck, rose, stab
　5. adorn, blink, color, coral, smart,
　wound **6.** flower, indent, minnow,
　pierce, salmon, vessel **7.** radical,
　serrate **8.** decorate, grayling
　9. carnation **11.** fashionable
pink (pert to)...
　coat.. **10.** foxhunter's
　eye.. **4.** duck **14.** conjunctivitis
　family.. **7.** Campion **9.** Carnation
　　15. Caryophyllaceae
　fish.. **8.** gobylike
　genus.. **6.** Silene
　lady.. **3.** fly (fishing) **8.** cocktail
　needle.. **9.** alfilaria
　Pearl.. **6.** azalea
　pill.. **7.** cure–all
　root.. **8.** wormroot
pinkeen... **6.** minnow **19.** insignificant
　person
pinna... **3.** fin **4.** wing **7.** auricle,
　feather, leaflet
pinnace... **4.** boat **5.** woman **6.** tender
　(Naut) **9.** procuress **10.** prostitute
pinnacle... **3.** epi, tee, tor **4.** acme,
　apex, peak **5.** crest, crown, serac,
　spire **6.** finial, needle, summit
pinnate... **11.** featherlike
pinniped... **4.** seal **6.** walrus
pinochle term... **3.** dix **4.** meld
piñon... **4.** pine, seed **8.** pignolia
　12. monkey puzzle
pintado... **4.** cero, fish, sier (fish)
　5. pinto **6.** chintz, pigeon, sierra
pintail (pert to)...
　duck.. **4.** smee **5.** river, ruddy
　grouse.. **4.** sand **11.** sharp–tailed
pinto (horse)... **4.** pied **6.** calico
　7. mottled, painted, piebald, spotted
Pinto... **6.** Indian (Pakawa tribe)
pinwing... **7.** penguin
pioneer... **4.** lead **5.** guide, miner
　6. digger, open up **7.** settler
　8. colonist, explorer **9.** excavator
　10. forerunner
Pioneer's Day... **4.** Utah (July 24)
　5. Idaho (June 15)
pious... **5.** godly, loyal **6.** devout,
　worthy **8.** excellent, religious
　11. reverential **13.** sanctimonious
pip... **3.** ace **4.** paip, peep, roup,
　seed, spot, trey **7.** disease
　12. officer's star
pipe... **2.** TD **3.** see, tee **4.** blow,
　clay, duct, reed, tube **5.** spout, voice
　6. convey, dudeen, hookah (hooka),
　outlet **7.** channel **9.** brierwood
pipe (pert to)...
　connection.. **3.** ell, tee **5.** cross,
　　elbow
　dream.. **8.** illusion **10.** bemusement
　end.. **4.** taft **6.** nozzle
　line.. **9.** grapevine
　Oriental.. **8.** narghile (nargile)
　pastoral, shepherd's.. **3.** oat **4.** reed
　　7. larigot **9.** flageolet
　peace.. **7.** calumet
　player.. **5.** fifer **8.** shepherd
　short.. **6.** dudeen
　smoke.. **5.** tewel
　steam.. **5.** riser

tobacco.. 10. meerschaum
wood.. 5. brier (briar) 9. brierwood
wrench.. 8. Stillson
pipette... 6. taster, tubule 7. dripper
pipit... 7. titlark
piquancy... 4. zest 5. spice
    8. pungency, raciness, tartness
    11. conciseness
piquant... 4. racy, tart 5. salty, sharp,
    spicy, zesty 7. concise, cutting,
    pungent 11. interesting, provocative
pique... 4. dive, fret, goad 5. anger,
    annoy, sting, tempt 6. grudge, incite,
    nettle, offend 7. dudgeon, offense,
    provoke, umbrage 8. irritate
    9. displease 10. irritation, resentment
    11. displeasure
pir (Moham)... 4. tomb 5. guide, saint
pirate... 6. robber 7. corsair, mariner
    8. marauder, picaroon 9. buccaneer
    10. freebooter 11. appropriate
pirate (famed)... 4. Kidd 6. Morgan
    7. Lafitte 10. Blackbeard (Capt
    Teach)
pirate (pert to)...
    bird.. 10. jaeger gull
    flag.. 5. Roger
    gallows.. 7. yardarm
    perch.. 8. Xenarchi
    weapon.. 4. snee
piraya... 6. caribe (fish) 7. piranha
pirogue... 5. canoe 7. piragua
pirol... 6. oriole
Pisa, Italy...
    capital of.. 7. Tuscany
    famed for.. 9. campanile 12. Leaning
    Tower
    river.. 4. Arno
pis aller... 10. last resort
piscary... 7. fishery 12. fishing place
    13. fishing rights
piscatology *(science of)*... 7. angling,
    fishing 10. halieutics
Pisces... 4. fish 6. fishes
    13. constellation
piscina... 4. tank 5. basin (Eccl)
    8. fishpond 9. reservoir
Piscis Volans... 10. flying fish
    13. constellation
Pisgah (pert to)...
    site.. 4. Nebo 8. mountain (top)
    view.. 12. Land of Canaan 13. Land
    of Promise
    viewer.. 5. Moses
pismire... 3. ant 5. emmet
pistachio... 3. nut 5. green
piste... 4. path 5. spoor, track, trail
    10. racecourse
pisteology, pistiology... 5. faith
    6. belief
pistil... 5. ovary 6. carpel
    9. gynoecium
pistol... 3. dag 7. firearm 9. derringer
pistol (pert to)...
    case.. 7. holster
    lock.. 5. rowet
    slang.. 3. gat, rod 6. barker, cannon,
    heater
pistology (Theol)... 5. faith
piston... 7. plunger
pit... 4. cave, hole, mine, pool, sump,
    tomb, trap, well 5. abyss, arena,

grave, sluig, snare 6. cavity, slough
    7. alveola, cockpit, dungeon
    8. audience 9. waterhole
    10. excavation 13. Stock Exchange
pit (pert to)...
    anatomy.. 5. fossa, fovea
    botany.. 7. alveola, pitamen
    8. endocarp
    bottomless.. 7. Abaddon
    fodder.. 4. silo
    Hades.. 4. hell
    Hawaiian.. 3. imu
    theater.. 7. parquet
    viper.. 9. Viperidae 11. rattlesnake
pitch... 3. key, tar 4. camp, hurl, tilt,
    tone, toss 5. black, color, erect,
    fling, heave, lurch, resin, sense,
    slope, throw 6. degree, encamp,
    plunge, settle, topple 7. incline
    8. flounder 9. sales talk
pitch (pert to)...
    high.. 6. shrill
    identity.. 6. unison
    inflammable.. 7. piceous
    mineral.. 7. asphalt, bitumen
    music.. 4. flat 6. accent, stress
    8. paranete 9. tonometer
    pitchlike.. 7. piceous
pitchblende... 6. radium 7. uranium
pitched ball, curving away...
    8. outshoot
pitcher... 3. jug 4. ewer, olla, olpe,
    toby 5. gorge 8. cruisken (cruiskeen),
    oenochoe (wine), southpaw
    (left–handed)
pitcher (pert to)...
    plant, genus.. 9. Nepenthes
    10. Cephalotus, Sarracenia
    plus catcher.. 7. battery
    shaped.. 9. urceolate
    shaped vessel.. 8. aiguière
piteous... 5. pious 6. devout, paltry,
    tender 7. pitiful, pitying 8. pitiable
    13. compassionate
pitfall... 3. pit 4. lure, trap 5. decoy,
    snare 6. danger 10. difficulty
pith... 3. jet, nub 4. gist, meat, pulp
    6. center, kernel, marrow
    7. essence, meaning, nucleus
    9. substance
pith helmet... 3. cap, hat 5. topee
    (topi)
pith tree (Nile)... 7. ambatch (ambash)
pithy... 4. soft 5. crisp, meaty, pulpy,
    terse 7. laconic 10. meaningful
    12. epigrammatic
pithy (pert to)...
    expression.. 7. epigram
    saying.. 3. mot
    sentence.. 5. motto
pitiable... 3. sad 6. woeful 7. piteous
    8. grievous, terrible 9. miserable,
    sorrowful 10. lamentable
pitiful... 4. mean 6. paltry 7. piteous
    8. pathetic, shameful 10. despicable
    12. contemptible 13. compassionate,
    tenderhearted
pitiless... 5. cruel 8. ruthless
    9. merciless 10. relentless
    13. unsympathetic
pitpit... 8. guitguit 12. honey creeper
Pitri, Hindu (pert to)...

ancestor of.. **4.** gods **6.** demons
10. four castes
Prajapatis, one of.. **10.** progenitor
(human race)
semidivine.. **6.** father **9.** patriarch
10. forefather
pittance... **4.** alms, dole, gift, scat
7. bequest **8.** donation **9.** allowance
11. small amount
pity... **4.** ruth **5.** mercy, yearn
7. remorse **8.** clemency, sympathy
10. compassion, condolence,
repentance **13.** commiseration
pivot... **3.** toe **4.** slew, slue, turn
5. hinge **6.** pintle, swivel
pivotal... **4.** crux **5.** polar **7.** turning
pixy, pixie... **3.** elf, imp **5.** fairy
6. goblin, sprite **13.** mischief–maker
Pizarro (pert to)...
adventurer.. **7.** Spanish
conqueror of.. **4.** Peru
founder of.. **4.** Lima (capital)
placable... **8.** peaceful **9.** agreeable,
forgiving, peaceable **10.** appeasable
placard... **4.** bill, post **5.** edict
6. notice, poster **7.** affiché
9. manifesto, stomacher
12. proclamation
placate... **4.** calm **6.** pacify, soothe
7. appease **10.** conciliate
11. tranquilize
place... **3.** put **4.** lieu, site, spot
5. abode, locus, posit, situs, stead
6. locale, locate, region, street
7. arrange, demesne, deposit
8. classify, location, position
9. recognize, situation
place (of)...
amusement.. **4.** park **6.** casino,
midway
bliss.. **4.** Eden **8.** paradise
confinement.. **3.** pen **4.** brig, cage,
coop, gaol, jail, stir **6.** asylum,
corral, prison **7.** dungeon
9. calaboose **12.** penitentiary
confusion.. **5.** Babel
content.. **7.** Arcadia
darkness.. **6.** Erebus
exit.. **6.** egress
honor.. **9.** right hand
origin.. **6.** cradle, source
refuge.. **3.** ark **4.** port **5.** haven
resort.. **7.** purlieu
rest.. **3.** bed, den **4.** lair, nook
5. chair, couch, grave, niche
sleep.. **3.** bed **4.** doss **5.** berth,
couch **6.** pallet **7.** hammock
suffering.. **10.** Armageddon,
Gethsemane
trial.. **5.** venue
place (pert to)...
apart.. **6.** enisle **7.** isolate
9. sequester
beneath.. **9.** infrapose
between.. **9.** interpose
burial.. **5.** grave **8.** catacomb,
cemetery **9.** graveyard **10.** necropolis
by itself.. **7.** isolate
camping.. **5.** étape
confidence in.. **7.** entrust
different.. **10.** otherwhere
for boats.. **7.** portage

for candles.. **9.** chandlery
forest (open).. **5.** glade
for keeping animals.. **3.** zoo **4.** barn
7. pasture **9.** menagerie
frequented.. **4.** dive **5.** haunt
6. resort
from which jury is taken.. **5.** venue
hallowed.. see *sacred* below
hiding.. **3.** mew **4.** lair **5.** niche
high.. **7.** eminent **8.** eminence
horse training.. **4.** ring **5.** longe
in a row.. **5.** align, aline
in bondage.. **7.** enslave
in order.. **7.** arrange **11.** systematize
in statu quo.. **7.** put back, replace,
restore
interpretation on.. **8.** construe
landing.. **4.** dock, pier **5.** wharf
7. airport
market.. **4.** mart **5.** agora **6.** rialto
meeting.. **5.** tryst
of.. **4.** lieu **5.** stead
on mound.. **3.** tee
opposite.. **6.** appose
over.. **11.** superimpose
sacred.. **4.** fane **5.** altar **6.** chapel,
church, shrine, temple **9.** synagogue
10. tabernacle
side–by–side.. **9.** collocate, juxtapose
sleeping.. **3.** bed **4.** bunk **5.** berth,
couch **6.** pallet **7.** hammock
under.. **9.** infrapose
under restraint.. **6.** arrest, intern
value upon.. **5.** price **6.** assess
8. appraise, estimate
wet.. **4.** slew **5.** marsh **6.** slough
wrestling.. **5.** arena **9.** palaestra
(palestra)
placed... **3.** put **7.** located
8. arranged, situated **10.** classified
placed in lodgings... **6.** roomed
8. billeted
placid... **4.** calm **5.** quiet, suant
6. demure, gentle, serene
8. composed, peaceful **9.** agreeable,
quiescent, unruffled **11.** undisturbed
pladaroma... **5.** tumor (eyelid)
plafond... **7.** ceiling **14.** contract
bridge
plage... **5.** beach
plagiarism... **6.** piracy **8.** cribbing,
stealing **10.** purloining
13. appropriation
plague... **3.** dun, vex **4.** bane, pest,
twit **5.** harry, tease, worry **6.** harass,
hector, infest **7.** scourge, torment
8. epidemic, nuisance **10.** Black
Death, pestilence **11.** infestation
plaguy... **6.** vexing **8.** annoying
9. difficult, harassing **10.** tormenting
11. troublesome
plaice... **8.** flatfish, flounder
plaid... **4.** maud **6.** tartan
plain... **3.** lea **4.** chol, mesa, moor,
wold **5.** blunt, camas, clear, frank,
heath **6.** lenten **7.** artless, evident,
genuine, legible, obvious, prairie
8. apparent, distinct, explicit, ordinary
9. downright, primitive, unadorned
10. unaffected
plain (pert to)...
clothes.. **10.** unofficial

dealing.. 4. open 5. frank
knitting.. 12. garter stitch
of Mars.. 9. palmistry
spoken.. 15. straightforward
Plains (pert to)...
  Arctic.. 6. tundra
  Europe.. 6. steppe
  Florida.. 7. savanna (savannah)
  Italy.. 8. campagna
  Russia.. 6. steppe, tundra
  S African.. 9. pampas
  Sp American.. 4. vega 5. llano
  6. salada (salt–covered)
Plains Indians... 6. Kiowan, Siouan
  7. Caddoan 10. Algonquian,
  Athapascan, Uto–Aztecan
plainsman... 6. cowboy 7. llanero
  8. herdsman
Plains of Abraham... 10. Quebec City
plaint... 6. bewail, lament 9. complaint
  11. lamentation
plaintiff... 4. suer 6. orator 7. accuser
  8. claimant, libelant (libellant)
  10. complainer 11. complainant
plaintive... 3. sad 5. cross 7. elegiac,
  fretful, peevish, pettish, wailful,
  wistful 8. mournful, petulant, repining
  9. lamenting, sorrowful
  10. melancholy 11. complaining
  12. discontented
plait... 4. fold, hair, knit, lace, plat
  5. braid, pleat, weave 6. pleach,
  wimple 9. corrugate, interlace
  10. interweave
plaited... 5. Milan (straw) 6. folded,
  kilted, sennit (palm leaves)
  8. pleached 10. interlaced
  11. intertwined
plan... 3. map, way 4. form, idea,
  line, plat, plot 5. chart, draft, ettle,
  frame, setup 6. design, devise,
  intend, layout, method, scheme
  7. arrange, diagram, outline, pattern,
  project 8. engineer, strategy
  9. calculate, procedure
  11. arrangement, contemplate,
  preconceive, premeditate
plan (pert to)...
  architecture.. 5. draft, épure
  frustrator of.. 7. marplot
  preliminary.. 4. idea 6. map out
  8. proposal
  secretly.. 4. plot 7. connive
  8. conspire
planate... 5. plane 9. flattened
plancher... 3. bed 5. board (occult),
  floor, plank 6. pallet 8. planking,
  platform
plancier... 6. soffit 7. cornice
plandok... 9. mouse deer
plane... 3. fly 4. even, flat, ramp,
  scar, tool 5. level 6. degree, smooth
  7. jointer, surface 8. airplane
  10. smoothness
plane (pert to)...
  block.. 5. stock
  boundary.. 9. perimeter
  four-angled.. 6. square 7. rhombus
  8. tetragon 10. quadrangle
  handle.. 4. tote (bench plane)
  inclined.. 4. ramp 5. chute
  iron.. 5. blade

kind.. 3. mig 5. stuka 6. router
measure.. 10. planimeter
smoothing, chamfering.. 5. howel
tree.. 6. chinar (Orient) 8. Platanus
type.. 5. bench, block, stock
  6. trowel 7. jointer, routing
planet... 4. Mars, star 5. Earth, Pluto,
  Venus 6. Saturn, Uranus 7. Jupiter,
  Mercury, Neptune 8. wanderer
planet (pert to)...
  astrology.. 9. alfridary
  brightest.. 5. Venus
  cone.. 8. strobile
  course.. 5. orbit
  minor.. 9. satellite
  nearest sun.. 7. Mercury
  orbit.. 7. ellipse
  red.. 4. Mars
  remotest.. 5. Pluto (1930)
  resembling.. 8. asteroid
  ringed.. 6. Saturn
  satellite.. 4. moon
  shadow.. 5. umbra
  small.. 8. asteroid
  sphere.. 6. oblate
planet (solar system) *by size*...
  7. Jupiter 6. Saturn 7. Neptune
  6. Uranus 5. Earth, Venus, Pluto
  4. Mars 7. Mercury
planetarium... 5. Zeiss 6. orrery
planetary... 7. earthly, erratic
  9. celestial, wandering, worldwide
planetology *(study of)*... 7. planets
  10. satellites
plangor... 4. wail 11. lamentation
planisphere... 7. sextant 9. astrolabe
plank... 3. sny 4. deal, slab 5. board,
  shole, stone 6. timber 7. pay down
  8. planking 10. gravestone
plank down... 3. pay 7. advance,
  deposit
planner... 8. designer, engineer,
  gardener 9. architect, projector
plant... 3. fix, sow, spy 4. ache, bury,
  herb, seed, trap 5. cache, decoy,
  shrub 6. clover 7. falsify 8. colonize,
  workshop 9. deception, detective,
  equipment, vegetable
plant (pert to)...
  abnormal environs.. 4. ecad
  adjustment.. 6. ecesis
  air.. 8. epiphyte
  appendage.. 7. stipula
  biggest.. 10. Aspidistra
  body.. 6. cormus 7. thallus
  bud.. 4. cion 5. scion
  climbing.. 4. vine 5. liana
  coloring matter.. 11. chlorophyll
  crossbred.. 6. hybrid
  cross–fertilization.. 9. phytogamy
  disease.. 4. gall, rust, smut 5. ergot
  7. blister 8. ramentum
  embryo.. 8. plantule
  enchantment–proof.. 7. haemony
  (Milton's Comus)
  flowerless.. 4. fern 6. lichen
  9. cryptogam 11. Cryptogamia (opp
  of phanerogam)
  growing on rock.. 6. lichen
  growing on sea bottom.. 6. enalid
  growing wild.. 9. agrestial
  history.. 12. phytogenesis

legendary, forgetfulness . . 5. lotus
male . . 3. mas
mosslike . . 6. orpine
mushroom type . . 6. fungus
native . . 8. indigene
orifice . . 5. stoma
pigment lacking . . 6. albino
poisonous . . 4. atis 6. datura
   7. amanita 8. oleander
poisonous to cattle . . 4. loco
   8. locoweed
pore . . 8. lenticel
round–leaved . . 9. pennywort
science of . . 6. botany
seedless . . 6. agamic
stem, stalk . . 4. bine 5. haulm
   6. caulis
tequila–yielding . . 5. agave
tissue . . 7. tapetum
without chlorophyll . . 6. albino
without petals . . 9. apetulous
woody . . 6. xyloid
plant (type of) . . .
aconite . . 4. bikh
agave, century plant . . 4. aloe, pita
   9. amaryllis
ammoniac . . 5. oshac
anise . . 4. dill
aquatic . . 5. sugamo 7. frogbit
   8. plankton
aromatic . . 4. mint, nard 5. basil,
   tansy, thyme 8. tarragon
arum . . 4. sago 6. starch 9. arrowroot
aster family . . 5. daisy 8. fleabane
bitter . . 3. rue
bitter vetch . . 3. ers
box . . 5. Buxus 7. boxwood
broom . . 5. spart 6. Canary 7. genista
bryophytic . . 4. moss
burdock . . 5. elite 8. Xanthium
burning bush . . 5. wahoo
butter–and–eggs . . 8. ranstead
cactus . . 5. dildo 6. cereus, chaute,
   mescal 7. saguaro 9. xerophyte
century . . 4. aloe 5. agave 6. maguey
dill . . 4. anet
evergreen . . 3. ivy 5. holly 6. laurel
   8. conifers 9. mistletoe
everlasting . . 6. orpine 11. live–forever
furze . . 4. ulex 5. gorse
garlic (wild) . . 4. moly
leguminous . . 3. pea 4. bean
   6. Cassia, clover, lentil
lilaceous . . 4. aloe, iris, leek 5. lotus,
   onion, tulip, yucca
linen . . 4. flax
medicinal . . 4. alem, aloe 5. anise,
   wahoo 6. arnica, cacoon, catnip,
   ipecac 7. aconite, boneset, gentian,
   lobelia, rhatany 8. camomile
pea family . . 7. Cytisus
perennial . . 4. Geum 5. avens
   10. sneezewort
poisonous . . 6. datura 8. oleander
poisonous to cattle . . 8. locoweed
poisonous to fowl . . 7. henbane
prickly, thorny . . 5. brier 6. cactus,
   nettle, teasel 7. thistle
satinpod (transparent) . . 7. honesty
soap . . 5. amole
tapioca . . 7. cassava
thorny . . see *prickly* 6. fatsia

trifoliate . . 6. clover 8. shamrock
plant, typical of . . .
Africa . . 5. argel (arghel)
Alps . . 9. edelweiss
Arabia . . 3. kat (stimulant)
Australia . . 5. Hakes, lilac 6. Correa
   7. columba, fuchsia 8. Rutaceae
China . . 5. ramie
Egypt . . 5. anise, cumin 7. aniseed
   8. nepenthe
Hawaii . . 5. olona
Japan . . 3. tea 5. acuba 6. quince
   7. cydonia 8. japonica
Japan (vine) . . 8. Bignonia 14. trumpet
   creeper
Mexico . . 4. chia 5. datil 6. salvia
   9. sabadilla
Peru . . 3. oca 7. rhatany
Philippines . . 4. alem (Med) 6. agamid
Spain . . 3. aji 6. pepper 8. Capsicum
Syria . . 5. cumin
tropical vine . . 8. redwithe
   10. tillandsia
tropics . . 4. arum, palm, taro
   5. agave, zamia 7. dasheen, hamelia
   8. mangrove
plantain . . . 6. banana
plantation pines . . . 7. pinetum
plantation trees . . . 4. holt 6. forest
   7. nopalry (cactus), orchard
planters, Govt of . . . 11. plantocracy
plantigrade mammal . . . 5. panda
plaque . . . 5. medal, patch 6. brooch,
   tablet 8. ornament, platelet (Anat)
plash . . . 4. plop, pool 5. swash
   6. puddle, ripple, splash
plasm . . . 4. mold 6. matrix
plasma . . . 4. cell, whey 5. blood (fluid)
   10. protoplasm
plaster . . . 4. teer 5. gesso, grout, salve
   6. gypsum, parget, stucco
   8. adhesive, poultice 9. inebriate
plastered . . . 5. drunk 7. crocked,
   smeared 8. mortared
plasterer . . . 5. mason
plaster of Paris . . . 5. gesso
   6. gypsum 15. calcium sulphate
plastic . . . 3. pug 5. gesso, vinyl
   6. slurry 7. ductile, fictile, pliable,
   viscose 8. creative 9. compliant,
   formative, teachable
   14. impressionable
plastic, commercial . . . 6. Lucite
   7. Formica 8. Bakelite, Vinylite
   9. Plexiglas
plasty (pert to) . . .
comb form . . 7. molding
eyelid . . 14. blepharoplasty
face lift . . 13. rhytidoplasty
nose . . 11. rhinoplasty
plat . . . 3. map 4. flat, plan, plot
   5. braid, chart, field, level, plain,
   plait, pleat 6. flatly, scheme
   7. outline, plateau 8. absolute,
   directly, straight 9. tableland
   10. interweave 15. straightforward
platanist . . . 4. fish, susu
plate . . . 3. gib 4. disc, dish, shoe
   (horse) 5. paten 6. lamina, patera
   7. coating, denture, overlay
   9. bookplate, engraving
   10. receptacle

plate (pert to)...
  armor.. 6. cuisse (cuish)
  battery.. 4. grid
  bone (Anat).. 7. scapula
  cooking.. 4. grid
  culture.. 8. bacteria
  Eccl.. 5. paten 6. patina
  graduated.. 4. dial
  holder.. 8. cassette
  horny.. 5. scute
  horse.. 6. plater
  insect (bony).. 6. scutum
  mark.. 8. hallmark 9. engraving
  numbered.. 4. disc
  of glass.. 5. slide
  perforated metal.. 3. dod
  ship–shaped.. 3. nef
plateau... 4. dish, mesa, puna 5. plain
  6. plaque, salver 9. tableland
platform... 3. map 4. dais, deck,
  k'ang, plan 5. arena, chart, plank,
  stage 6. lissom, lyceum, podium,
  policy, pulpit, scheme 7. estrade,
  outline, rostrum, soapbox, tribune
  8. hustings 9. bandstand 14. public
  speaking
platform (pert to)...
  fort.. 8. barbette
  gun.. 11. emplacement
  mining.. 6. sollar (soller)
  nautical.. 7. foretop, maintop
  9. gangplank
  scaffold (funeral).. 10. catafalque
  wheeled.. 5. float
platic (Astrol)... 8. not exact
  9. imperfect
plating... 5. armor 6. lamina
  7. shoeing
platinum wire... 4. oese
platitude... 6. cliché, old hat, truism
  7. bromide 8. banality 9. staleness,
  triteness 11. commonplace
  15. commonplaceness
Plato (pert to)...
  famed for.. 9. Dialogues
  10. philosophy
  founder of.. 7. Academe, academy
  name, real.. 10. Aristocles
  pupil of.. 8. Socrates
platoid... 4. flat 5. broad
Platonic (pert to)...
  idea.. 5. eidos
  love.. 4. pure 5. ideal 6. chaste
  8. virtuous 10. idealistic
  11. comradeship
  philosophy.. 8. idealism 9. Platonism
  11. theoretical
  solids.. 10. hexahedron, octahedron
  11. icosahedron, tetrahedron
  12. dodecahedron
platoon... 3. set 4. unit 5. squad
  7. company, coterie 11. subdivision
platoon school... 4. Gary (Ind)
platter... 4. dish, lanx 5. grail, plate
  6. record 9. scutellum
platter–shaped... 10. scutellate
platyfish... 8. moonfish
platypus... 8. duckbill
plaudit... 5. cheer, éclat 6. encore
  8. applause, approval, clapping,
  encomium 10. plaudation
  11. acclamation, approbation

plausible... 8. credible, probable,
  specious 10. applausive, believable,
  ostensible, plauditory, reasonable
  11. conceivable
plausible excuse... 5. alibi
play... 3. act, fun, toy 4. game, jest,
  romp 5. dally, drama, enact, feign,
  sport, wager 6. affect, frolic
  7. disport, operate, pretend
  9. amusement, diversion, melodrama,
  pantomime 10. recreation
  11. impersonate 13. entertainment
play (pert to)...
  exhibit a.. 5. stage
  for time.. 5. stall
  house.. 5. movie 6. cinema
  7. theater 9. dollhouse
  musical.. 5. opera 8. burletta,
  operetta
  outline.. 8. scenario
  part.. 4. role 7. prelude 8. epilogue,
  epitasis, prologue
  pranks.. 4. haze
  silent.. 9. pantomime
  story.. 8. scenario
  stupid.. 5. boner
  the bagpipe.. 5. skirl 6. doodle
  the buffoon.. 5. droll
  the coquette.. 5. flirt
  tricks.. 4. hoax, shab
  truant.. 5. miche
  unskillfully.. 5. strum
  upon words.. 3. pun 11. paronomasia
playa... 5. beach, shore 7. salt pan
playboy... 4. fool 5. clown, cutup
  7. buffoon, reveler 8. carouser
  10. merrymaker 12. Jack of Trumps
  (Spoilfive)
player... 3. dub 4. star 5. actor, idler,
  piper 7. gambler, trifler 8. gamester,
  musician, stroller, thespian
  9. frolicker, performer
  11. barnstormer
player on words... 7. punster
playful... 3. gay 6. lusory 7. jocular
  8. humorous, playsome, sportive
  9. facetious, kittenish
  11. mischievous
playing cards... 4. deck, pack
  6. tarots
playlet... 4. skit 9. short play
plaything... 3. die, toy 4. dupe
  6. bauble 7. cat's–paw
plea... 4. suit 5. claim 6. abater,
  appeal, excuse, prayer 7. apology,
  defense, pretext 8. argument,
  entreaty, pretense 10. advocation,
  allegation 13. nolo contendre
plead... 3. beg, sue 5. argue
  6. adduce, allege 7. entreat, implore
plead (for)... 7. entreat, justify, solicit
  10. supplicate
pleader... 4. suer 6. lawyer
  8. advocate 9. entreater, justifier
  11. intercessor
pleading... 4. oyer 8. advocacy,
  demurrer, entreaty 9. imploring,
  objection 10. litigation
  12. intercession, supplication
pleasant... 3. fun, gay 4. nice
  5. merry, sweet 6. genial 7. affable,
  amusing, leesome, winsome

8. cheerful, friendly, humorous, pleasing, sportive 9. agreeable, diverting, laughable, sprightly

pleasant (pert to) . . .
manners . . 9. amenities
sound . . 6. dulcet 8. euphonic 9. melodious 10. harmonious
to peruse . . 8. readable
weather . . 4. fair, fine 6. bright 8. rainless 9. cloudless

please . . . 4. like, suit 5. fancy 6. arride 7. appease, content, delight, gratify, indulge, placate, satisfy 9. vouchsafe

pleased . . . 4. fain, game, glad 5. happy 9. contented, gratified

pleasing . . . 4. cool, lief, nice 5. sooth 6. comely, eesome, savory 7. amiable, roseate, welcome 8. pleasant 9. agreeable, desirable 10. delectable 11. pleasureful

pleasurable . . . 7. hedonic 8. pleasant 10. gratifying

pleasure . . . 3. joy 4. gree, will, wish 5. mirth, sport 6. choice, gaiety 7. delight, purpose 8. gladness, hedonism, hilarity 9. amusement, diversion, enjoyment, happiness, merriment 11. delectation 12. satisfaction 13. gratification

pleasure (pert to) . . .
god . . 3. Bes
ground . . 4. park 9. pleasance
pert to . . 7. hedonic
philosophy . . 8. Hedonism
seeker . . 5. sport 7. epicure, playboy 8. hedonist

pleat . . . 4. fold 5. braid, plait

pleater . . . 8. plicator

plebeian . . . 4. pleb (Rom) 6. common, vulgar 7. ignoble, ill–bred, lowborn 8. ordinary

plebiscite . . . 4. vote 6. decree 10. referendum

pleck . . . 4. plot (ground), spot 5. speck, stain 9. enclosure

plectrum . . . 4. pick 5. uvula 6. tongue 7. malleus 8. plectron

pledge . . . 3. bet, vas, vow 4. bond, gage, gate, oath, pawn, seal, wage 5. swear, toast, troth 6. engage, parole, plight 7. chattel, earnest, promise 8. guaranty, mortgage, obligate, security 9. assurance 10. collateral 11. impignorate

pledget . . . 4. swab 8. compress

Pleiad (pert to) . . .
Alexandria . . 10. Seven Poets
French . . 10. The Pléiade
lost Pleiad . . 6. Merope 7. Electra
philosophical (Gr) . . 12. Seven Wise Men

Pleiades (pert to) . . .
Seven Daughters of Atlas . . 10. Atlantides
star . . 4. Maia 7. Sterope 8. Asterope
star cluster . . 8. in Taurus (Constellation)

plenary . . . 4. full 5. great 6. entire 7. perfect 8. absolute, complete 9. unlimited 11. unqualified

plenipotentiary . . . 5. envoy 8. diplomat, minister 10. ambassador

plenteous . . . 6. plenty 7. copious, fertile, liberal 8. abundant, fruitful, generous 9. bounteous, bountiful, plentiful 10. productive

plentiful . . . 4. full, rich, rife 5. ample 6. lavish 7. copious, fertile, liberal, opulent, profuse 9. abounding, bounteous, bountiful 13. superabundant

plentifully . . . 6. galore 9. abounding, abundance

plenty . . . 4. enow 6. enough, galore, uberty 8. fullness 9. abundance, plenitude 10. perfection 11. copiousness 12. completeness, considerable 14. superabundance

plenum . . . 5. space 8. assembly, fullness (of space) (opp of vacuum)

pleon . . . 6. telson 7. abdomen

pleonasm . . . 8. fullness 10. redundancy 11. diffuseness, reiteration

plethora . . . 4. glut 6. excess 9. repletion 14. superabundance

plethoric . . . 6. turgid 8. inflated, overfull 9. bombastic 10. overloaded

plexiform . . . 4. rete 7. network 11. complicated

plexus . . . 4. rete 5. solar 7. network

pliable . . . 4. limp 6. limber, pliant, supple 7. plastic 8. flexible, suitable 9. compliant, teachable

pliant . . . 7. bending, pliable, tensile, willowy 8. flexible, workable, yielding 9. adaptable, compliant

plicate . . . 4. fold 5. pleat 6. folded 7. plaited

plight . . . 4. fold 5. braid, plait 6. status 7. embrace, promise 8. position 9. condition, situation (bad) 11. predicament

plinth . . . 4. orlo 7. subbase

Pliosaurus (extinct) . . . 7. reptile

plod . . . 3. dig, mog 4. slog, toil, tore 6. drudge, trudge

plodder . . . 3. fag 4. grub, hack 5. slave 6. drudge

plot . . . 3. lot, map 4. acre, area, brew, burn, pack, plan, plat 5. cabal, frame, tract, trick 6. design, scheme, scorch, secret 7. diagram, project 8. conspire, intrigue 10. conspiracy, prearrange 11. machination

plot (of ground) . . . 3. lot 4. acre, area, plat 5. grave, tract 7. terrain

Plotinus . . . 11. philosopher (Alexandrian School)

plotted . . . 7. charted, hatched 8. lineated 9. conspired 10. delineated 11. prearranged

plotter . . . 5. Haman 7. Jacobin, planner, schemer 8. agitator 9. contriver 11. conspirator

ploughshare (plowshare) part . . . 6. colter (coulter)

plover . . . 4. dupe 5. piper, sandy 7. lapwing 9. courtesan, sandpiper, shorebird

plover (pert to) . . .
crab . . 5. drome
crested . . 7. lapwing
egg . . 11. darning ball
genus . . 12. Charadriidae

Old World.. 8. dotterel, killdeer
page.. 6. dunlin 9. sandpiper
quail.. 13. plain wanderer
ring.. 5. pandy
plow... 4. rove, till 5. break, miner, scaut 6. furrow, turn up 7. break up 8. reinvest 9. cultivate
plow (pert to)...
fish.. 3. ray
gang.. 6. oxgang 7. measure
light.. 10. Plow Monday 13. hoggler's light
man.. 6. rustic 10. countryman, husbandman
part.. 4. buck, chip, hale 5. share, slade, stilt 6. clevis, colter
type.. 5. sulky 8. mole plow
plowed land... 5. arada, arado
pluck... 3. pug, rob, tug 4. grab, jerk, pick, pull 5. nerve, spunk, steal, strip, strum 6. avulse, divest, fleece, gather, twitch 7. courage, harvest, pick off, plunder, strip of, swindle 10. resolution, straighten (wool)
plucky... 4. game 5. brave, nervy 6. spunky, sticky 8. adhesive, resolute, spirited 10. courageous
plug... 3. peg, tap, top 4. blow, bung 5. horse, knock, punch, shoot, spile, wedge 7. commend, hydrant, stopper, stopple, tobacco 9. persevere, publicity, publicize 12. commendation
plug (pert to)...
board.. 11. switchboard
cannon muzzle.. 7. tampion (tampeon, tampoon)
dentristy.. 7. filling
hat.. 4. tile 5. gibus 6. topper
medical.. 4. clot 6. fibrin, tampon 7. embolus
slender.. 5. spill
up.. 4. calk (caulk)
plum... 5. drupe, money, prune 6. Prunus 8. dividend 9. good thing, sugarplum
plum (pert to)...
beetle.. 8. curculio
bitter.. 4. sloe
California (wild).. 5. islay
coco.. 5. icaco
England.. 6. damson
Europe.. 7. bullace
hybrid.. 7. plumcot
India.. 7. hog plum
Java.. 7. jambool (jambul) 8. jambolan
type.. 4. gage 6. damson 9. greengage, wild–goose 11. Reine Claude
plumage... 4. down 6. hackle 7. floccus (first down) 8. feathers, ornament
plumb... 4. seal, true 5. delve, gauge, sound, utter 6. adjust, fathom, sinker, weight (lead) 7. examine, measure, plummet 8. absolute, complete, vertical 9. downright 13. perpendicular
plumbage... 8. leadwork
plumbog... 9. raspberry (dwarf)
plumcot... 6. hybrid 11. plum apricot

plume... 5. crest, egret, preen, pride 6. plumet 7. feather, panache 8. decorate, plumelet
plummet... 4. dive, drop, fall, lead, plop, test 5. pitch, sound, swoop 6. fathom, plunge, weight 9. criterion
plump... 3. fat 4. drop, dull, fall, plop, rude, sink, tidy 5. blunt, buxom, flock, fubsy, obese 6. chubby, dilate, fatten, flatly 7. distend 8. blurt out, straight 9. corpulent, filled out 10. vertically 11. well–rounded
plumpness of person... 9. stoutness 10. embonpoint
plunder... 3. rob 4. boot, loot, pelf, prey, raid, rape, sack 5. booty, poach, raven, reave, rifle, strip 6. boodle, fleece, maraud, profit, rapine, ravage, spoils 7. despoil, pillage 8. spoliate 9. depredate
plundered... 4. reft 6. looted, robbed
plunderer... 5. thief 6. looter, pirate, preyer, raider, robber 7. spoiler, stealer 8. pillager 10. freebooter
plunge... 3. bet, dip 4. dash, dive, fall, pool, risk, sink 5. douse, drive, lunge, plumb, souse 6. gamble, thrust 7. baptize, immerse 8. flounder 9. gravitate, overwhelm, speculate
plunge (into)... 4. clap, dive 5. begin 7. immerge, immerse 9. set to work, undertake
plunger... 5. diver 6. risker 7. gambler 10. speculator
plunk... 4. blow, drop, pull, push, sink, thud 5. drive, plump, strum, throw 7. a dollar 10. play truant
plurality... 8. majority 9. multitude 11. greater part, large number
plural marriage... 8. polygamy
Plutarch (Gr)... 10. biographer
Pluto (pert to)...
Astron.. 6. planet (most remote)
god of.. 10. lower world
Greek name.. 5. Hades
kingdom.. 5. Hades
Roman name.. 3. Dis 5. Orcus
wife.. 10. Proserpina
plutocracy... 13. rule by wealthy 17. dominion of the rich
Plutus (pert to)...
god of.. 6. wealth
son of.. 6. lasion 7. Demeter
pluvia... 4. rain 9. pluviosus
pluviometer, pluvioscope... 9. rain gauge
pluvious... 5. rainy 7. pluvial
ply... 4. bend, fold, mold, sail, urge 5. exert, plait, wield 6. employ, handle, lamina 8. navigate 9. importune, thickness
pneuma... 4. soul 5. neume 6. breath, spirit 9. breathing, life force, vital soul
pneumology *(science of)*... 5. lungs 17. respiratory organs
poach... 3. mix, ram 4. poke, push, sock, stir 5. drive, force, shirr (egg), steal 6. thrust 7. trample 8. encroach, trespass

poacher... 7. lurcher, stalker, widgeon
Poblacht... 8. Republic
Pocahontas (pert to)...
father.. 8. Powhatan (Chief)
husband.. 9. John Rolfe
Indian title.. 8. Princess
name.. 12. Rebecca Rolfe
rescuer of.. 9. John Smith (Capt)
pocket... 3. bag, bin, cly, fob, sac
4. poke, sack, take 5. money,
pouch, purse 6. cavity, hollow
7. conceal, confine, enclose
8. envelope
pocketbook... 3. bag, lil 5. pouch,
purse 6. income, wallet 8. notebook
9. resources
pod... 3. bag, kid, sac 4. aril, boll
5. belly, carob, chili, pouch, shuck
6. legume
poem... 3. dit, lay, ode 4. Edda, epic,
epos, hymn, rune, saga 5. elegy,
epode, idyll, psalm, verse 6. ballad
(ballade), jingle, rondel (roundelle),
sonnet 7. eclogue, erotics, rondeau
8. limerick, rondelet 9. dithyramb
10. villanelle 11. acatalectic
poem (pert to)...
division.. 5. canto, epode, verse
6. stanza 7. refrain
eight lines.. 7. triolet
famed.. 5. Iliad 7. Odyssey
foot.. 6. iambic 7. anapest, pyrrhic
imitation.. 6. parody
line.. 5. stich 6. octave, septet,
sestet, tercet 7. couplet, triplet
8. cinquain, quatrain
meter.. 6. iambic 8. spondaic,
trochaic 9. dactyllic, hexameter
10. anaepestic (anapestic),
pentameter
ref to.. 5. meter, rhyme, verse
7. cadence, helicon 8. feminine,
scansion 9. masculine
religious.. 4. hymn 5. psalm
rhythmic break.. 7. caesura
satirical.. 3. dit 6. parody
poem, famed...
Homer.. 5. Iliad 7. Odyssey
Khayyám.. 8. Rubáiyát
Milton.. 12. Paradise Lost
Ovid.. 13. Metamorphoses
Poe.. 8. The Raven
Poem in Marble.. 8. Taj Mahal
poem of declaration.. 8. Invictus
Shakespeare.. 7. Macbeth
Spenser.. 12. Faerie Queene
poems... 5. poesy, sylva 6. poetry
poet... 4. bard 5. odist, rimer 6. lyrist
7. dreamer 8. laureate 9. poetaster,
rhymester, versifier
poet (famed)...
German.. 5. Heine
mythology.. 6. Ossian
Negro.. 11. Braithwaite
Persian.. 7. Khayyám
Sierra.. 13. Joaquin Miller
Poet Laureate (a few)... 6. Dryden
7. Spenser 8. Tennyson 9. Ben
Jonson, Masefield 10. Wordsworth
poetry (pert to)...
Muse of.. 5. Erato 6. Thalia
8. Calliope

Norse god of.. 5. Bragi
School of (anc).. 9. Parnassus
type.. 4. epic 5. lyric 6. ballad
8. didactic 9. free verse, narrative
10. blank verse
pogoniate... 7. bearded
pogonip... 3. fog (Sierras)
pogonology *(study of)*... 6. beards
pogrom... 8. massacre
poi... 4. food, taro, then (Mus)
poignant... 4. keen 5. acute 6. biting,
bitter 7. cutting, pungent
point... 3. aim, dot, jab, jot, neb, nib,
pin 4. apex, barb, cape, gaff, gist,
node, peak, stop, tack 5. focus,
prong, quill, spike 6. bodkin, direct,
needle, period, summit, zenith
7. apicula, punctum 10. breakwater,
promontory
point (pert to)...
antler, branch.. 4. snag
astronomy.. 5. apsis 6. syzygy
central, pivotal.. 4. crux
farthest from earth.. 6. apogee
focal.. 9. epicenter
geometry.. 6. acnode 7. crunode
highest.. 4. acme, apex, peak
6. summit, zenith 8. meridian,
pinnacle
lace.. 10. petit point 11. needlepoint
law.. 3. res 5. locus
lowest.. 5. nadir 6. bottom
mathematics.. 5. unode
nearest earth.. 7. perigee
of contact.. 5. focus
of debate.. 5. issue, topic
of honor.. 7. scruple
of view.. 5. angle, slant 8. attitude
opposite zenith.. 5. nadir
reference to.. 6. apical
salient.. 7. feature
starting, golf.. 3. tee
strong.. 5. forte
utmost.. 7. extreme
weak.. 4. flaw 5. fault 6. foible
pointed... 5. aimed, noded, piked,
sharp, terse 6. acuate, marked,
peaked 7. angular, concise, conical
8. aculeate, piercing, poignant
spicated, stinging 9. acuminate,
pertinate, spiculate 10. emphasized
11. conspicuous, significant
12. epigrammatic
pointed (pert to)...
architecture.. 5. ogive 6. Gothic
end.. 4. cusp
fox.. 3. red
instrument.. 3. awl, gad 4. prod
6. gimlet, stylet
rod.. 4. goad
pointer... 3. arm, dog, tip 4. sign
5. index 6. fescue, gnomon
pointless... 4. dull 5. blunt, inane,
silly, vapid 6. stupid 7. insipid,
witless
poise... 6. aplomb 7. balance, ballast
8. carriage 9. composure, equipoise,
stability
poison (pert to)...
arrow.. 4. inee, upas 5. urari
6. curare (curari)
deadly.. 4. bane, upas 5. arrow

7. arsenic, cyanide, hemlock
10. strychnine
study of .. 10. toxicology
poissarde ... 8. fishwife, low woman
poisson ... 4. fish
poisson bleu ... 7. catfish 8. bluefish,
grayling
poitrel ... 5. armor, plate 9. stomacher
11. breastplate
poke ... 3. bag, jab, jog, pry 4. bore,
goad, prod, root, sack 5. grope,
nudge, probe, purse 6. dawdle,
potter, search, thrust, wallet
7. project, tobacco
poker ... 3. rod 6. beadle 7. bugbear,
pochard 9. hobgoblin
poker (pert to) ...
face .. 8. immobile
form of .. 4. draw, stud
painting .. 10. pyrography
picture .. 11. pyrogravure
stake .. 3. pot 4. ante 6. roodle
poky, pokey ... 4. dull, mean, slow
5. dowdy, small 6. bonnet, narrow,
shabby 7. cramped, tedious
Poland ... see also *Polish*
ancestors .. 5. Lakha, Slavs
ancient name .. 7. Polonia
capital .. 6. Warsaw
city .. 4. Lodz 6. Gdynia, Krakow,
Lublin
river .. 7. Dnieper, Vistula
Poland China ... 5. swine
polar ... 5. curve 6. Arctic 7. guiding
8. opposite 9. Antarctic, magnetism
Polar base (exploration) ... 4. Etah
Polaris ... 5. Alpha 9. North Star
11. guiding star
pole ... 3. bar, oar, pew, poy, rod, xat
4. axle, beam, mast, prop, spar
5. shaft, sprit, staff, stool, totem
pole (pert to) ...
bad end .. 7. raw deal
burn .. 7. disease (tobacco)
cat .. 5. skunk, zoril 6. ferret, musang
7. fitchew 8. Putorius 9. scoundrel
cat weed .. 12. skunk cabbage
electric .. 5. anode, pitch 7. cathode
8. magnetic 9. electrode
Gaelic .. 5. caber
head .. 7. tadpole
Spanish .. 4. pale, palo
star .. 5. guide 7. polaris 8. lodestar
9. North Star 13. l'Etoile du Nord
vehicle .. 4. cope, crab 5. thill
well .. 5. sweep
polemic ... 9. disputant 11. contentious
13. argumentative, controversial
polenta ... 8. porridge
poles of cold ... 7. Siberia
(Verkhoyansk) 12. Grinnell Land (Fort
Conger)
police (pert to) ...
badge .. 6. buzzer, shield
club .. 8. spontoon
man .. 3. cop 5. guard 6. bobbie,
copper, peeler, Ranger 7. officer,
sheriff, trooper 8. constable,
detective, N W Mounted
11. carabinière (carabineer)
station .. 5. thana 6. lockup
8. bargello

policy ... 3. wit 4. plan 6. wisdom
8. regulate, sagacity 9. insurance
10. government, management,
shrewdness 11. contrivance
13. judiciousness 14. administration
policy of segregation ... 9. apartheid
polish ... 3. rub 4. buff 5. glaze, gloss,
rabat, scour, shine 6. finish, luster,
smooth 7. burnish, culture, furbish
8. brighten, civilize, elegance,
lapidate, levigate, urbanity
10. refinement
Polish (pert to) ...
Bull .. 13. Constellation
cake .. 4. baba
carriage .. 7. britska
composer, pianist .. 6. Chopin
10. Paderewski
dance .. 7. mazurka 9. polonaise
11. cracovienne (krakowiak)
nobleman .. 7. starost
premier .. 10. Paderewski (pianist)
president (1st) .. 10. Philsudski
scientist .. 5. Curie (Madame)
polishing material ... 5. emery, rabat,
rouge 6. pumice 11. rottenstone
polite ... 4. neat, tidy 5. civil, suave,
urban 6. gentle, smooth, urbane
7. gallant, genteel, refined
8. polished 9. courteous, debonaire
(debonair, debonnaire) 10. cultivated
11. complaisant
politesse ... 10. politeness (formal)
11. cleanliness, courtliness
12. decorousness
politic ... 4. wary 7. cunning, tactful
8. cautious, discreet 9. judicious,
political, politique, provident
10. diplomatic
political (pert to) ...
boss .. 7. cacique
district .. 4. city, ward 5. State
6. canton, county, parish 7. borough
10. palatinate
economy .. 9. economics
faction .. 4. bloc, ring 5. junta, party
7. machine
hanger-on .. 6. heeler 10. ward heeler
influence .. 5. lobby, rally 6. caucus
party (old) .. 4. Tory, Whig 9. Politique
politician ... 7. schemer 9. intriguer,
statesman 11. gerrymander
12. politicaster
politics ... 7. cunning 8. scheming
10. government, profession
15. partisan rivalry 16. political
affairs
Polizei ... 9. the police
poll ... 3. cut, tax 4. clip, head, roll,
vote 5. shear, skull 6. fleece, survey
7. despoil 8. election, schedule
pollan ... 9. whitefish
polled ... 5. shorn 6. shaved
8. hornless
pollen ... 4. seed 6. anther 8. fine
dust 11. microspores 13. fertilization
pollen brush (bee's) .. 6. scopa
pollenization ... 5. xenia 13. fertilization
pollent ... 6. strong 8. powerful
poller ... 5. voter 6. barber
9. plunderer 11. extortioner,
taxgatherer

pollex... 5. thumb 11. bastard wing (bird) 13. dactylopodite
pollex impression... 10. thumbprint
polliwog... 7. tadpole
pollute... 4. soil 5. taint 6. befoul, defile, ravish 7. corrupt, debauch, profane 9. desecrate, inebriate 11. contaminate
pollution... 8. impurity 9. infection 10. corruption, defilement 13. contamination
Pollux (pert to)...
  brother (twin).. 6. Castor
  father.. 4. Zeus
  mother.. 4. Leda
  protector of.. 7. sailors
  star.. 13. Beta Geminorum
Polonius... 8. courtier (Shak)
polony... 7. sausage
poltergeist (folklore)... 5. ghost 6. spirit
poltfoot... 8. clubfoot
poltroon... 4. idle, lazy 6. coward, craven, wretch 7. buffoon, dastard 8. cowardly 9. dastardly 10. ne'er–do–well, scaramouch
polverine... 6. potash (of Levant) 8. pearlash
polyandrium (Gr)... 8. cemetery
polyandry... 8. polygamy 14. plural husbands (Tibet)
polychromatic... 10. variegated
polyglot... 6. jargon 9. languages (confusion of) 10. dictionary 11. philologist 21. Complutensian Polyglot (Bib)
polygon... 6. isagon 7. decagon, hexagon, nonagon, octagon 8. heptagon 9. dodecagon
polygyny... 8. polygamy 11. plural wives
polyhedron... 5. solid 6. figure 14. trisoctahedron 17. triakisoctahedron
polymny... 10. sacred song
Polynesia...
  native.. 5. Maori 6. Kanaka 8. Hawaiian 10. Melanesian
  ocean.. 7. Pacific
  origin (probable).. 7. Savaiki (Isl)
  South Sea Island group.. 5. Samoa 6. Hawaii, Tahiti 7. Savaiki 10. New Zealand
Polynesian (pert to)...
  butterfly.. 2. io
  chestnut.. 4. rata
  cloth.. 4. tapa
  demon.. 4. atua
  dragon.. 3. ati
  goddess of volcanoes.. 4. Pele
  god of forests.. 4. Tane
  hero.. 4. Maui
  homeland (fabled).. 7. Havaiki
  loincloth.. 5. pareu
  memorial.. 3. ahu
  oven.. 3. umu
  social tradition.. 6. tattoo
  tribe.. 3. Ati
  wages, reward.. 3. utu
polyp... 5. coral, Hydra, tumor 10. sea anemone 12. invertebrate
polyphone... 4. lute

polytropic... 9. versatile
pomade... 6. anoint 7. pomatum, unguent 8. ointment
pome... 4. pear 5. apple, fruit 6. quince 11. pomegranate
pomelo... 8. shaddock 10. grapefruit
Pomerania (pert to)...
  animal.. 3. dog
  capital.. 7. Stettin
  formerly.. 5. duchy (Prussia)
  river.. 4. Oder
pomme de terre... 6. potato
Pomona... 4. city (Calif) 7. college, goddess (of fruit)
pomp... 5. pride, state 6. parade 7. cortege, display, pageant 8. grandeur 9. pageantry, spectacle 10. ceremonial 11. ostentation 12. magnificence
pompano... 7. alewife
Pompeii, Italy (pert to)... 10. earthquake, excavation, Mt Vesuvius (site)
pompous... 5. budge 6. august, stilty 7. Podsnap (Dickens), stilted 9. bombastic, grandiose 11. ceremonious 12. high–sounding, ostentatious, stuffed shirt
Ponce de Leon (pert to)...
  discoverer of.. 7. Florida 15. Fountain of Youth
  famed as.. 8. explorer
  landing site, America.. 11. St Augustine
pond... 4. pool 5. ocean (humorous) 6. lagoon 7. lakelet
pond (pert to)...
  apple.. 9. evergreen
  crow, hen.. 4. coot
  dogwood.. 10. buttonbush
  duck.. 7. mallard
  fish.. 7. sunfish
  frog.. 8. ranarium
  glass.. 8. aquarium
ponder... 4. mull, muse, pore 5. brood, opine, weigh 7. perpend, reflect 8. appraise, cogitate, consider, evaluate, meditate, ruminate
ponderous... 4. dull, huge 5. bulky, heavy 7. weighty 8. ungainly 9. important, momentous 11. elephantine
pongee... 4. silk 6. tussah 8. shantung
poniard... 4. dirk, kill 5. sword 6. dagger, pierce
ponica... 8. gardener
pont... 5. ferry, float 6. bridge 7. caisson, pontoon 9. ferryboat
Pontiac... 4. city (Mich) 5. Chief (Ottawa Indian) 6. Indian
pontiff... 4. pope 6. bishop 8. pontifex
pony... 3. cab, nag 4. crib 5. glass, horse, pinto 6. bronco 7. Express (mail, 1860), piebald 8. Shetland 11. translation
pooch... 3. dog 5. pouch
pooka... 6. goblin 7. specter
pool... 3. lin, pot 4. carr, fund, game, linn, mere, pond, tank, tarn 5. kitty, stake 6. cartel, lagoon, league, puddle

7. alberca, plashet 9. billiards, reservoir, resources 10. natatorium 11. aggregation
pool ball... 3. cue 4. spot 6. ringer
poon tree... 5. domba, keena
poor... 3. bad 4. mean, thin 5. needy 6. feeble, humble, meager, paltry, shabby, sickly 7. hapless, unlucky 8. indigent, inferior 9. destitute, illogical, imperfect, infertile 10. unskillful (unskilful) 11. impecunious, unfavorable, unfortunate 12. impoverished, inauspicious, insufficient 14. unsatisfactory
poor (pert to)...
creature.. 9. pilgarlic
joe.. 5. heron
John.. 3. cod 4. hake 8. mean fare
man's remedy.. 8. valerian
Richard.. 8. Saunders (Richard)
section of city.. 4. slum 6. ghetto 7. skid row 10. shantytown
soldier.. 9. friarbird
poorly... 3. ill 5. badly 8. abjectly, meagerly, shabbily 10. indisposed 11. defectively 13. disparagingly
pop... 4. bang, snap, soda 5. bulge, burst, crack 6. bubble 7. concert 8. beverage
popadam... 5. wafer (fried) 10. popper cake
popdock... 8. foxglove
pope... 3. fin 4. ruff 6. bishop, puffin, shrike, weevil 8. beverage 9. bullfinch 14. painted bunting
Pope (pert to)...
cathedral.. 7. Lateran
collar.. 5. orale
court officer.. 6. datary
crown.. 5. tiara 6. triple
first.. 5. Peter
headdress.. 5. miter (mitre)
name.. 4. Pius 5. Ratti 7. Gregory
palace.. 7. Vatican
poetry.. 10. Essay on Man
scarf.. 5. fanon
popeler... 7. sea gull 9. spoonbill
popinac... 8. huisache
popinjay... 6. parrot
poplar... 5. abele, alamo, aspen, bahan, white 10. cottonwood 12. balm of Gilead
poplar (pert to)...
Arabic.. 5. bahan, garab
balsam.. 9. tacamahac
Fr black.. 4. liar 10. cottonwood
N American.. 7. Populus 8. Lombardy
white.. 5. abele, bolle
poppy... 3. maw 4. Papaver (opium), ponceau 8. foxglove
poppycock... 3. rot 4. bosh 8. nonsense
populace... 3. mob 4. mass 5. demos, plebs 6. people 11. inhabitants 12. common people
popular... 3. lay, pop 5. cheap, liked, usual 6. famous, simple, vulgar 7. crowded, demotic, secular 8. accepted, epidemic, favorite, populous 9. prevalent, well-known, well-liked 11. fashionable, proletarian

12. nontechnical
popular belief... 4. lore 7. opinion 9. tradition 12. old wives' tale, superstition
popularity... 4. fame 5. vogue 10. reputation 15. fashionableness
popular success... 3. hit
population study... 10. larithmics
porcelain... 4. frit 5. china 6. kaolin 7. ramekin (mold)
porcelain (kind)... 5. Spode 6. Sèvres 7. celadon, Dresden, Limoges 8. Haviland
porch... 4. door, stoa 5. stoop 6. harbor, loggia 7. galilee, gallery, portico, veranda 8. entrance 9. colonnade
porcine animal... 3. hog, pig, sow 5. shoat, swine 6. porker 7. peccary 8. babirusa (babiroussa) 9. razorback
porcupine (pert to)...
anteater.. 7. echidna
Canada.. 5. urson 7. cawquaw
disease.. 10. ichthyosis
grass.. 5. stipa
species.. 6. rodent, tenrec (tendrac) 8. hedgehog, quill pig
pore... 3. con 4. duct, gaze, vent 5. stare, stoma, study 6. ponder 7. eporose (without), opening, orifice, ostiole 8. lenticel
porgy... 4. fish, scup 5. bream, pargo 6. pagrus, red tai
pork (pert to)...
barrel.. 4. fund (Polit) 6. boodle
chop.. 7. griskin
fish.. 4. sisi
porker... 3. hog, pig 5. swine, sword (obs)
porpoise... 4. Inia 6. seahog 7. dolphin, pellock 8. cetacean, Phocaena
porr... 4. cram, kick, poke, push, stir 5. poker 6. thrust
porrect... 6. tender 7. present
porridge... 3. pob 4. pobs, samp 5. atole, brose, grout, gruel 6. cereal 7. oatmeal, polenta, pottage 9. stirabout
port... 4. gate, left, mien, wine 5. armor, haven 6. harbor, portal 7. airport, bearing, opening, posture 8. carriage, demeanor, larboard, porthole, portside 10. deportment 11. destruction
portable... 6. mobile 7. movable
portable altar... 10. altar stone, superaltar (Hist)
portal... 4. door, gate 5. porch 7. gateway 8. entrance 9. vestibule 12. porte-cochere
portcullis... 3. bar 4. shut 5. herse 7. barrier, grating, lattice (Her) 13. fortification
Porte... 12. Ottoman court (anc), Sublime Porte
porte-bonheur... 5. charm 6. amulet
porte-cochere... 5. porch (carriage) 7. gateway
portefeuille... 9. portfolio
portend... 4. bode 5. augur 7. betoken, predict, presage

8. forebode, foreshow, foretell,
prophecy 9. foretoken
portent... 4. omen, sign 6. marvel,
ostent 7. prodigy 11. forewarning
portentous... 4. dire 5. fatal, grave
6. solemn 7. fateful, ominous
8. sinister 9. monstrous, wonderful
10. impressive 13. extraordinary
porter... 3. ale 4. beer 5. hamal
(hammal), stout (drink) 6. bearer
7. carrier, janitor 9. attendant
10. doorkeeper
Porter's pseudonym... 6. O Henry
Portia (pert to)...
character (Merchant of Venice)..
7. heiress
husband.. 8. Bassanio
husband's friend.. 7. Antonio
maid.. 7. Nerissa
portico... 4. stoa 6. atrium, xystus
(xyst) 7. pteroma, veranda
9. colonnade, peristyle, vestibule
portion... 3. bit, cut, dab, lot 4. dole,
dose, dunt, fate, half, mete, part,
some 5. piece, share, whack
6. moiety, parcel 7. section,
segment 8. quantity 9. allotment,
apportion, partition
portion (pert to)...
curve.. 3. arc 7. segment
detached.. 6. coupon
inheritance.. 7. legitim 9. dead's part
marriage.. 5. dowry
sectional.. 5. curve
widow's.. 5. dower
Portland (pert to)...
arrowroot, sago.. 4. arum
beds (Eng).. 11. Upper Oolite
13. Upper Jurassic
city of.. 5. Maine 6. Oregon
stone.. 6. cement 8. concrete
vase.. 9. Barberini (Rom palace)
10. cameo glass
portmanteau... 3. bag 4. word
(blended) 5. cloak 6. mantle, valise
portoise... 7. gunwale 8. portlast
Porto Rico... see *Puerto Rico*
portrait... 4. copy 5. image 7. picture
8. likeness, painting 10. similitude
11. description, portraiture
12. lifelikeness 14. representation
portrait on dollars...
fifty.. 5. Grant
five.. 7. Lincoln
five hundred.. 8. McKinley
five thousand.. 7. Madison
one.. 10. Washington
one hundred.. 8. Franklin
one hundred thousand.. 6. Wilson
one thousand.. 9. Cleveland
ten.. 8. Hamilton
ten thousand.. 5. Chase
twenty.. 7. Jackson
two.. 9. Jefferson
portray... 3. act 4. draw, form, limn
5. enact, frame, image, paint
6. depict 7. fashion, picture
8. describe 9. delineate, represent
portrayal... 3. act 5. drama
7. process 8. portrait 9. depiction
11. delineation, description
portreeve... 5. mayor 7. bailiff

Port Royal.... 15. Cistercian abbey
(Versailles)
Portugal... see also *Portuguese*
bridge.. 7. Salazar
capital.. 6. Lisbon
city.. 5. Braga 6. Aveiro, Guarda,
Oporto 7. Granada
island.. 6. Azores 7. Madeira
8. Principe
mountain.. 15. Serra da Estrella
peninsula.. 7. Iberian
port.. 6. Aveiro
province.. 3. Goa 5. Macao, Timor
9. Cape Verde 10. Mozambique
resort.. 7. Estoril
river.. 5. Tagus (Tajo)
Portuguese (pert to)...
author.. 9. de Lobeira
bird, fish.. 8. man–of–war
ceremonial (Inquisition).. 8. auto de fe
coin (gold).. 6. escudo 7. milreis (old)
lady.. 4. dona
legislature.. 6. Cortes 12. Cortes
Geraes
money of account.. 4. reis
navigator.. 6. da Gama 8. Magellan
wine.. 5. porto
Portunus (Rom Relig)... 10. god of
gates
posada... 3. inn 5. hotel
Posaune... 8. trombone 9. organ stop
posca... 5. drink (Hist)
pose... 3. put, sit 5. model 6. baffle,
puzzle, stance 7. nonplus, posture,
pretend, propose 8. attitude,
position, pretense, propound
9. postulate 11. affectation,
impersonate
Poseidon (pert to)...
attributes.. 5. horse 7. dolphin,
trident
cult site.. 7. Corinth
father.. 6. Cronus
god of.. 3. sea 6. waters
mother.. 4. Rhea
wife.. 10. Amphitrite
poser... 5. facer 6. puzzle 7. problem,
sticker 14. attitudinarian
posh... 5. smart 6. spruce 7. elegant
9. luxurious
position... 3. job, lie 4. pose, rank,
seat, site 5. coign (coigne), place,
situs, stand, state 6. manner, stance,
ubiety 7. opinion, posture, premise
8. attitude, location, prestige,
proposal 9. viewpoint 11. affirmation,
supposition
position (pert to)...
anchorlike.. 5. apeak
fencing.. 7. septime
finder (gun).. 13. triangulation
golf.. 6. stance
inescapable.. 7. impasse
of affairs.. 6. status
relative.. 8. standing
secure.. 7. footing
with no responsibility.. 8. sinecure
positive... 4. plus, sure 5. exact
6. actual, thetic 7. certain
8. dogmatic, emphatic 9. assertive,
convinced, downright 11. dictatorial
positive (pert to)...

charge (Elec).. **8.** positron
evidence.. **7.** constat
pole.. **5.** anode
saying.. **6.** dictum
school, criminology.. **10.** Lombrosian (by Lombroso)
positivism... **7.** Comtism **9.** certainty, dogmatism **10.** confidence **11.** materialism
positure... **7.** posture **11.** arrangement, disposition **13.** configuration
posnet... **3.** pot (3–footed) **8.** saucepan
poss... **4.** beat, dash, push **5.** drive, knock, pound, stamp **6.** thrust
posse... **5.** crowd **6.** throng **7.** company **9.** armed band **10.** detachment (police)
possess... **3.** own **4.** have, know, take **5.** haunt **6.** inform, occupy **7.** bewitch, inhabit **8.** convince, demonize, persuade
possessed... **5.** hadst, owned **6.** insane **7.** haunted **8.** demoniac, obsessed **9.** bewitched
possessing (pert to)...
feeling.. **6.** souled
flavor.. **5.** sapid, tasty
land.. **5.** acred
pincer claws.. **8.** chelated
power.. **11.** plenipotent
sensation.. **8.** sentient
special ability.. **6.** gifted **8.** talented
possession... **4.** hold **5.** asset **6.** taking, wealth **7.** control, country, mastery **8.** dominion, property **9.** obsession, ownership **10.** equanimity **11.** bewitchment
possession (pert to)...
again.. **6.** revest
law.. **6.** seizin (seisin)
not in (possession).. **6.** devoid
suffix.. **3.** ose
possessions... **6.** assets, estate, wealth **7.** effects **8.** property
posset... **4.** turn **6.** curdle, pamper **8.** beverage, infusion **9.** coagulate
possibility... **4.** bare **7.** latency **9.** liability, potential **10.** good chance, likelihood **11.** contingency **13.** improbability **16.** prospective value
possible... **6.** latent, liable, likely **8.** feasible **9.** plausible, potential **11.** practicable
possibly... **5.** maybe **7.** perhaps **9.** perchance **11.** conceivably
post... **3.** bet, dak (dawk), xat **4.** bitt, fort, list, mail, trot **5.** enter, newel, opium, place, stake, totem **6.** alette, assign, hasten, inform, marker, office, pillar, pledge **7.** bollard, placard, station, upright **8.** dispatch, position **9.** messenger, sternpost **12.** enter account
post (pert to)...
adverb.. **5.** after, later **9.** afterward
boat.. **4.** mail **5.** stage **6.** packet
boy.. **7.** courier **9.** postilion (postillion)
dance (army sl).. **8.** struggle
goal (anc).. **4.** meta
Indian memorial.. **3.** xat **5.** totem

meridian.. **9.** afternoon
mortem.. **7.** autopsy **8.** necropsy **10.** after death
office.. **6.** correo
prefix.. **5.** after **6.** behind **10.** subsequent
stair.. **5.** newel
postage stamp paper (pert to)...
design.. **8.** spandrel
paper.. **6.** pelure
pattern.. **6.** burele **8.** burelage
poster... **4.** bill, card **7.** placard, sticker **8.** bulletin **9.** messenger **10.** billposter
posthumous... **5.** after **10.** after death, post–mortem
postiche... **9.** false hair **10.** artificial **11.** counterfeit
postilion... **5.** guide **7.** postboy **9.** postrider
postimpressionist... **6.** cubist, Derain **7.** Cezanne, Matisse
postpone... **4.** wait **5.** defer, delay, remit, table **6.** put off, shelve **7.** adjourn, reserve, suspend **8.** hold over, prorogue **10.** pigeonhole **11.** subordinate **13.** procrastinate
postponement... **7.** remanet, respite **8.** deferral, reprieve **9.** deferment **11.** prorogation
postprandial... **11.** after dinner
postulate... **6.** assume **7.** prelude, premise **9.** condition, predicate, stipulate **10.** hypothesis **11.** stipulation, supposition
posture... **4.** pose **6.** stance **8.** attitude, position, pretense **9.** viewpoint **11.** frame of mind
pot... **3.** jug, pan **4.** olla **5.** belly, crock, cruse **6.** aludel, kettle, liquor, teapot **7.** amphora (anc), caldron **9.** flowerpot **10.** jardiniere
potash... **6.** potass, saline **7.** potassa **8.** pearlash **18.** potassium carbonate
potassium (pert to)...
bitartrate.. **13.** cream of tartar
bromide.. **8.** sedative
carbonate.. **6.** potash
compound.. **4.** alum
dichromatic.. **6.** chrome
iodide.. **8.** medicine
nitrate.. **5.** niter **9.** saltpeter
permanganate.. **8.** oxidizer **12.** disinfectant
sulphate.. **4.** alum
potate... **9.** liquefied
potation... **5.** draft, drink **6.** liquor **8.** beverage, tippling **12.** drinking bout
potato... **3.** oca, yam **4.** papa, spud **5.** tuber
potato (pert to)...
beetle.. **8.** hardback
bogle.. **9.** scarecrow
French.. **12.** pomme de terre
French style.. **9.** lyonnaise
genus.. **10.** Solanaceae
Indian.. **4.** yamp
moss.. **9.** pondgrass
S Am.. **7.** Uruguay
sweet.. **6.** patata
potator... **5.** poter **7.** tippler

potboiler... 4. book 6. writer
8. painting (for quick money)
9. potwaller
potdar... 7. assayer, cashier, weigher
potence, potency... 3. vis 4. élan
5. cross, power 6. energy, gibbet
7. gallows 8. virility 9. authority,
influence
potent... 4. able 6. cogent, mighty,
strong, virile 7. dynamic, warrant
(Mil) 8. forcible, heraldry, powerful,
puissant, virulent 9. effective, efficient
11. efficacious, influential
13. authoritative
potentate... 4. amir (ameer), emir
(emeer) 5. mogul, ruler 6. dynast,
prince 7. emperor, monarch
8. syzerain 9. sovereign
potential... 4. mood (Gram) 5. ergal
6. latent, mighty 8. possible
11. influential, in the making,
possibility, undeveloped
potentiality... 5. power 7. latency
11. possibility
poter... 5. toper 7. drinker
potgun... 5. rumor 6. cannon, mortar,
pistol 8. braggart
pothead... 7. dullard 8. terminal (Elec)
9. blackfish
pother... 3. ado, row 4. fuss, stir
5. worry 6. bother, bustle, harass
7. fluster, perplex, trouble
9. commotion 10. excitement,
perplexity 11. disturbance
12. perturbation
potherb... 4. mint 6. greens
7. spinach
pothook... 3. rod 4. hook (S–shaped)
5. crook 6. scrawl, stroke (S–like)
9. pot lifter 10. iron collar (penalty)
pothouse... 3. bar, low 6. saloon,
tavern, vulgar 7. barroom
8. alehouse, grogshop, mughouse
11. public house
potiche... 4. vase 7. ceramic
potion... 4. dose, dram, drug 5. draft,
drink 7. draught, philter 8. nepenthe
potlatch... 4. gift 5. feast 8. Festival
potomania... 10. dipsomania
15. delirium tremens
potong... 5. crown 6. wreath 9. head
cloth
potoroo... 11. rat kangaroo
potpourri... 4. olio, stew 6. medley
7. mixture, perfume 9. anthology
11. olla–podrida, salamagundi
potrero... 4. farm 7. pasture
10. cattle farm
pottage... 4. soup 6. brewis
8. porridge
pottah... 5. lease 6. tenure 9. title
deed
potter... 3. pry 4. mess, poke, push
6. dawdle, doodle, meddle, putter,
tamper, trifle 7. saunter 8. ceramist
potter's clay, earth... 4. slip 5. argil
6. galena, kaolin 8. alquifou
10. terra cotta
potter's wheel... 4. disk 5. lathe,
throw 6. jigger, pallet (palet)
pottery... 5. Delft 6. Samian
7. celadon (Chin), keramos (Gr)

8. Arretine (It), ceramics, Majolica (It)
9. delftware (Holland), keramikos (Gr)
11. earthenware 14. terra sigillata
(anc)
pottery (pert to)...
black.. 6. basalt
broken.. 5. shard (sherd)
decorate.. 6. stamps 9. sigillate
decoration.. 11. sigillation
firing box.. 6. sagger
glasslike.. 8. vitreous
glaze.. 6. enamel
mineral.. 8. feldspar
paste.. 9. barbotine
red.. 7. aretine
pottle... 3. pot 6. basket, vessel
7. tankard
potty... 3. pot 5. crazy 7. foolish,
haughty 8. trifling 12. supercilious
13. insignificant
pot–valiant... 10. courageous (when
drunk)
pouch... 3. bag, pod, sac 4. cyst,
poke, sack 5. bulge, bursa, purse
6. gipser (Hist), pocket 7. bladder,
mailbag, silicle, sporran (sporan)
10. pocketbook
pouch bone... 9. marsupial
pouched (pert to)...
dog.. 9. thylacine 13. Tasmanian wolf
frog.. 9. marsupial
gopher.. 6. pocket
mouse.. 9. marsupial
rat.. 8. kangaroo
rodent (cheek–pouched)..
11. spermophile
stork.. 8. adjutant
poultry... 4. fowl, hens 5. cocks,
ducks, geese 6. capons 7. Bantams,
peahens, pigeons, turkeys
8. chickens, peacocks, roosters,
volaile 9. cockerels, pheasants
10. guinea fowl
poultry (breeds)... 6. Ancona, Bantam,
Brahma 7. Cornish, Dorking,
Hamburg, Leghorn, Minorca
9. Wyandotte 12. Plymouth Rock
14. Rhode Island Red
poultry (pert to)...
disease.. 3. pip 4. roup, tick
dish.. 9. galantine
farm.. 7. hennery
pounamu... 4. jade 6. weapon
8. nephrite 10. greenstone
pound... 3. hit, ram 4. beat, ding,
drum, maul, pond, tamp 5. money,
pen up, thump 6. bruise, hammer,
kennel, prison 7. impound
9. enclosure, pulverize
pounding instrument... 6. hammer,
pestle
pounds (100)... 6. cental
13. hundredweight
pour... 4. flow, gush, rain, teem, vent,
well 5. flood 6. abound, effuse,
stream 7. niagara, radiate, torrent
8. downpour 9. discharge
11. extravasate
pour (pert to)...
molten glass.. 7. dagrade
molten steel.. 4. teem
off.. 5. drain 6. decant

oil upon.. **6.** anoint, pacify
out.. **11.** extravasate
sacrificial liquid.. **6.** libate
pouring hole (mold)... **5.** sprue
pout... **3.** bib, mop **4.** fish, moue, sulk
  5. pique **7.** catfish, eelpout, grimace
  9. sulkiness
poverty... **4.** lack, need, want **5.** illth
  (opp of wealth) **6.** dearth, penury
  8. leanness, poorness, scarcity
  9. indigence, pearlweed
  11. destitution
powder... **4.** dust, talc **5.** boral
  6. pollen, yttria **7.** crumble
  8. cosmetic, sprinkle **9.** explosive,
  pulverize
powder (pert to)...
antiseptic.. **6.** formin **7.** aristol
bag.. **6.** sachet
festival (Ind).. **4.** abir (perfumed)
goa.. **7.** araroba
heater, melter.. **6.** sinter
insecticide.. **9.** hellebore
medical.. **8.** tannigen
perfumed.. **6.** empasm
polishing.. **5.** emery **7.** tripoli
smokeless.. **6.** poudre **8.** amberite
stamping.. **6.** pounce
powdered (Her)... **4.** semé
power... **3.** arm, art, can, jet, vis
  4. dint, gift, iron, sway, will
  5. force, magic, might, steam, vigor
  6. degree, energy **7.** control, faculty,
  magnate, potency **8.** capacity,
  efficacy, strength **9.** authority,
  eloquence, influence, magnetism,
  puissance **10.** efficiency, government
  11. mathematics (term)
power (pert to)...
creative.. **6.** Shakti
device.. **9.** telemotor
hammer.. **4.** trip
inherent.. **6.** energy
of attorney.. **5.** agent **10.** procurator
of feeling.. **7.** sensate
of mind.. **4.** wits
of resistance.. **7.** stamina
persuasive.. **8.** rhetoric **9.** political
sovereign.. **6.** throne
spiritual.. **8.** divinity
superior.. **10.** prepotency
under one's.. **10.** subjugated
unit.. **3.** erg **4.** dyne **8.** kilowatt
powerful... **4.** loud **5.** great **6.** cogent,
  mighty, potent, strong **7.** drastic,
  intense, leonine, skookum
  8. eloquent, forcible, puissant
  9. effective, effectual, efficient
  10. armipotent, convincing
  11. efficacious, influential
  13. authoritative
powerful force... **6.** libido
powerful man, businessman...
  5. titan **6.** tycoon **7.** magnate
powerless... **4.** weak **8.** impotent
pownie... **7.** peacock
powwow... **6.** frolic, priest **7.** meeting
  8. assembly, ceremony, congress,
  conjurer **9.** gathering **10.** conference,
  convention
poyou... **9.** armadillo
prabble... **7.** chatter, quarrel

  8. squabble
practic... **6.** artful, shrews **7.** cunning,
  skilled **9.** difficult, practical, practiced
  11. experienced
practicable, practical... **5.** utile
  6. usable, useful **7.** virtual, working
  8. feasible, possible, workable
  9. available, expedient, operative,
  pragmatic, realistic **11.** pragmatical,
  utilitarian
practical (pert to)...
Christianity.. **10.** New Thought
example.. **6.** praxis
joke.. **4.** hoax **5.** trick **6.** humbug
judgment.. **7.** ethical (Kant)
practically... **9.** virtually **11.** essentially
  13. approximately
practice, practise... **2.** do **3.** ply, ure,
  use **4.** plot, rite **5.** drill, habit, train,
  usage **6.** action, addict, custom,
  scheme, tryout **7.** perform
  8. ceremony, exercise, intrigue,
  rehearse, training, vocation
  9. procedure **10.** experience,
  experiment, observance
practice (pert to)...
corrupt.. **5.** abuse
established.. **5.** canon **6.** custom
fraud.. **5.** cheat, shark **8.** trickery
specific.. **6.** praxis
voice.. **8.** intonate
witchcraft.. **3.** hex
practicer of evasions...
  13. tergiversator
practicer of palmistry...
  11. chiromancer
prad... **5.** horse
pragmatic... **7.** meddler, skilled
  8. busybody, dogmatic, meddling
  9. conceited, officious, practical
  10. systematic **11.** opinionated
pragmatical... **8.** dogmatic **9.** officious,
  practical **10.** meddlesome
  11. commonplace
Prague, Praha...
capital of.. **14.** Czechoslovakia
famed bldg.. **10.** University (1st in
  Cent Eur, 1348)
famed teachers (anc).. **4.** Huss
  6. Jerome
founder.. **14.** Duchess Libussa (722)
prairie... **3.** bay **5.** llano, plain
  6. camass (camas, cammas),
  meadow, steppe **7.** quamash
  (camass) **9.** grassland **10.** prairillon
prairie (pert to)...
anemone, crocus.. **12.** pasque flower
antelope.. **9.** pronghorn
apple.. **9.** breadroot
artichoke.. **9.** sunflower
berry.. **9.** trompillo
chicken.. **6.** grouse
dog.. **6.** marmot
mud.. **5.** gumbo
pigeon.. **6.** plover **9.** sandpiper
rose.. **14.** Baltimore belle
schooner.. **12.** covered wagon
squirrel.. **11.** spermophile
tree (clump).. **5.** motte
weed.. **10.** cinquefoil
wolf.. **6.** coyote
Prairie State... **8.** Illinois

praise... 4. laud 5. bless, extol, honor, kudos 6. eulogy 7. acclaim, applaud, commend, glorify, magnify, plaudit 8. applause, encomium, eulogize, macarize 9. adulation, celebrate, panegyric 11. approbation 12. commendation

praise (pert to)...
continual.. 5. chant
high.. 5. extol 8. encomium
hymn of.. 8. doxology
insincere.. 4. bull 7. flatter 8. flattery
of another's blessing.. 8. macarism 9. Beatitude
to God.. 7. Laus Deo
Ye The Lord.. 8. Alleluia (Alleluiah) 10. Hallelujah (Halleluiah)

praiseworthy... 8. laudable 11. commendable, meritorious

prana (Hind)... 6. spirit 9. life force 10. life breath

prance... 4. gait 5. caper, dance 6. cavort, spring 7. swagger

prank... 3. jig 4. fold, joke, prat 5. antic, caper, pleat, shine, trick 6. frolic, prance 7. caprice, dress up 8. escapade 11. monkeyshine

prankish... 9. facetious 10. frolicsome 11. mischievous

prate... 3. gab 4. chat, talk 5. gossip 7. chatter, twaddle 8. nonsense

prattle... 3. gab 4. chat, talk 5. clack, prate 6. babble 7. blather 12. impudent talk, trifling talk

prawn... 6. shrimp 10. crustacean, shrimp pink

pray... 3. ask, beg, sue 7. entreat, implore, request, worship 8. devotion 10. supplicate

praya... 4. bund, road 5. beach 6. strand

prayer... 3. ave 4. bead, bene, plea, suit 5. credo, grace, matin 6. litany, orison, vesper 7. request, worship 8. petition 12. intercession, supplication

prayer (pert to)...
book.. 4. ordo 6. missal 7. portass (portas) 8. breviary
call (Moham).. 4. azan (adan)
call tower.. 7. minaret
cloak.. 6. zizith (fringed) 7. tallith
evening.. 7. complin (compline) 9. night song
figure.. 5. orant
Incarnation.. 7. Angelus 11. Angelus Bell
liturgical.. 6. litany 7. complin
Lord's (prayer).. 11. Paternoster
morning.. 5. matin
nine days' devotional.. 6. novena
response.. 8. antiphon
short.. 5. grace
stick.. 4. paho

praying... 8. entreaty 9. precation 12. supplication

praying cricket... 6. mantis

praying figure... 5. orant

preach... 6. exhort 7. expound, lecture 8. advocate, homilize 9. discourse, sermonize

preacher... 6. parson, rector

7. evangel, teacher 8. homilist, lecturer, minister 9. clergyman, pulpiteer

preaching... 6. sermon 7. kerygma (kerugma) 10. preachment 11. exhortation

preaching friar... 9. Dominican

Preaching of Peter... 9. Apocrypha

preamble... 5. proem 7. preface, prelude 11. preliminary 12. introduction

prebellum... 7. antewar 12. before the war

prebend... 7. stipend 8. benefice 9. allowance

precarious... 7. assumed, dubious 8. insecure, unstable 9. hazardous, uncertain, unsettled 10. unreliable

preceded... 3. led 8. prefaced, was prior 9. anteceded, antedated 10. introduced, went before 13. had precedence, occurred first

precedence... 3. pas 4. lead, rank 8. priority 12. anteposition

precedent... 4. sign 5. model, usage 7. example, leading 8. anterior, decision, standard 10. antecedent, forerunner 11. going before

preceding others... 5. first 7. leading, ternary (by threes) 10. antecedent

precept... 4. rule, writ 5. adage, axiom, maxim, order, sutra (sutta), torah (tora) 6. belief 7. command 8. doctrine 9. direction 11. commandment, instruction

preceptor... 4. guru 5. guide, tutor 6. master, mentor, mullah, pundit 7. teacher 8. educator 10. instructor

precinct... 5. ambit, space 6. region 8. boundary, district, environs

precious... 4. dear, rare 5. great 6. costly, valued 7. beloved, elegant, perfect 8. complete, esteemed, overnice, valuable 9. downright 10. beloved one, fastidious, particular

precious (pert to)...
Blood (RCCh).. 5. Feast (July 1)
garnet.. 6. pyrope
stone.. 3. gem 4. opal, ruby 5. pearl, topaz 6. garnet, ligure 7. diamond, emerald, jacinth (Bib) 8. hyacinth, sapphire
stone, sometimes.. 7. cat's-eye 11. alexandrite

precipice... 4. crag, linn, pali 5. bluff, cliff 9. declivity

precipitancy... 5. haste 8. rashness

precipitation... 3. gel 4. fall, hail, mist, rain, snow 5. haste, sleet 8. downpour 9. hastening 11. prematurity 12. acceleration, condensation, recklessness

precipitous... 4. rash 5. hasty, steep 6. abrupt, sudden 7. rushing (headlong) 9. very rapid 11. precipitate

précis... 6. sketch 7. epitome, pandect, summary 8. abstract, synopsis 9. summarize

precise... 4. prim 5. exact 7. correct, literal, special 8. accurate, definite, detailed, overnice 10. meticulous,

overminute, particular, scrupulous
11. ceremonious, punctilious
preciseness... 9. exactness
10. strictness 12. definiteness
14. fastidiousness
precision... 6. nicety 8. accuracy
9. exactness, formality
11. preciseness 12. definiteness
preclude... 3. bar 4. omit, stop
5. avert, debar, estop 6. hinder,
impede 7. head off, prevent, shut
out 8. prohibit
precocious... 7. forward 8. advanced
9. premature
preconceive... 6. ideate, precox
7. presume 8. foreknow, prejudge
9. predecide 10. presuppose
predatory... 7. looting 9. marauding,
pillaging, piratical 10. plundering,
predaceous (predacious)
11. destructive
predatory bird... 3. owl 4. hawk, kite
6. falcon
predatory raid... 5. foray
predestine... 4. doom, fate 6. decree,
ordain 7. appoint 9. determine,
foretoken 10. foreordain
predetermine... 4. bias 7. destine
8. prejudge 9. prejudice, preordain
10. prepossess 11. premeditate
predicament... 3. fix 4. pass 5. state
6. plight, scrape 7. dilemma,
impasse 8. quandary 9. condition,
situation
predicator... 4. seer 5. friar
7. prophet 8. preacher 9. predicter
predict... 4. bode, dope, omen
7. foresee, portend, presage
8. forecast, foretell, prophecy
13. prognosticate
prediction... 6. augury 8. prophecy
9. foresight 10. foreboding
11. foretelling 15. prognostication
predilection... 4. bias 6. desire
8. tendency 9. prejudice
10. favoritism, partiality, preference,
propensity 11. disposition
13. preconception 14. predisposition
predominant... 5. chief 6. ruling
8. reigning, superior 9. hegemonic
11. controlling, influential,
outstanding
predominate... 5. excel 7. prevail
8. dominate 10. be superior
12. preponderate
pre-eminent... 3. top 4. only, star
5. chief 7. palmary, ranking
8. superior 9. excellent, principal
11. outstanding
pre-emption... 8. monopoly, purchase
10. prior right 13. appropriation
preen... 3. pin, sew 4. perk 5. clasp,
dress, groom, plume, primp
6. bodkin, brooch, stitch 9. make
sleek
preface... 5. front, proem 6. herald,
prayer 7. prelude, problem
8. exordium, foreword, preamble,
prologue 10. paraphrase
12. introduction
prefect, praefect... 4. dean (Jesuit)
6. chih fu 7. monitor, officer

8. director, minister, official
9. president 10. magistrate
prefecture... 7. eparchy
prefer... 5. elect, offer 6. choose,
select 7. outrank, present, proffer,
promote 9. be partial 12. give
priority
preference... 6. choice 8. favorite,
priority 9. advantage 10. favoritism
11. alternative, prior choice
12. predilection
prefiguration... 4. omen 9. foretoken,
prototype 12. typification
13. preindication
prefigure... 7. imagine, suggest
8. foretell 10. foreshadow
prefix for...
about.. 3. amb 4. peri
above.. 3. epi, sur 5. hyper, super,
supra
across.. 3. dia 4. tran 5. trans
again.. 2. re
against.. 4. anti
ahead.. 3. pre
all.. 4. omni
alongside.. 3. par 4. para
an.. 2. al
apart.. 2. se 3. dia, dis
appearing to.. 5. quasi
around.. 4. peri
away.. 3. aph, apo
back.. 2. re 3. ana
backward.. 5. retro
bad.. 3. dys, mal
badly.. 3. mis
beauty.. 5. calli (kalli)
before.. 2. ob 3. pre, pro 4. ante,
prae
beside.. 3. par 4. para
between.. 3. dia 4. meta 5. inter
black.. 4. atra
blood.. 4. haem, hemo
bone.. 4. oste 5. osteo
both.. 4. ambi
Chinese.. 4. sino 5. chino
clear.. 4. delo
dawn.. 2. eo
difficult.. 3. dys
distant.. 3. tel 4. tele
double.. 2. di
down.. 2. de 4. cata
earnest.. 5. serio
earth.. 3. geo
eight.. 3. oct 4. octa, octo
equal.. 3. iso
equally.. 4. equi
evil.. 3. mal
far.. 3. tel 4. tele
faulty.. 3. mis
fictitious.. 6. pseudo
fire.. 3. pyr
for.. 3. pro
former.. 2. ex
four.. 4. tetra
from.. 2. ab, de, ec
from away.. 3. apo
gas.. 4. aero
good.. 2. eu
half.. 4. demi, hemi, semi
hard.. 3. dys 6. stereo
ill.. 3. mal, mis
in, into.. 2. en

lizard.. 5. saura, sauro
many.. 4. mult, poly 5. multi
modern.. 3. neo
mountain.. 3. oro
nail.. 4. helo
negative.. 2. il, ir, un 3. mon
new.. 3. neo
not.. 2. il, im, ir, un 3. non
numerical.. 3. uni
one.. 3. uni 4. mono
out of, outer.. 2. ec, ex 3. ect, exo
   4. ecto
over.. 3. epi, sur 5. super, supra
possession.. 3. ose
pray.. 3. ora
priority.. 3. pre
recent.. 3. neo
release.. 2. un
reversed.. 2. di
same, equal.. 3. iso 4. equi, homo
separation.. 2. di 3. dis
shoulder.. 6. humero
single.. 4. mono
son of.. 3. Mac
ten.. 3. dec 4. deca
this side of.. 3. cis
three, thrice.. 3. ter, tri 4. tris
through.. 3. dia, per
to.. 2. ap
together.. 3. com, con, cor, syn
toward.. 2. ob, oc
turning.. 4. roto
twice.. 2. bi, di
twofold.. 2. bi, di 3. dua
under.. 3. sub
upon.. 2. ep 3. epi
upward.. 3. ana, ano
very much.. 3. eri
well.. 2. eu
with.. 3. col, com, pro, syl, syn
within.. 3. eso 4. endo 5. intra
without.. 2. se 3. ect 4. ecto
wood.. 4. xylo
wrong.. 3. mis
pregnancy... 6. cyesis 10. cyesiology
prehistoric (pert to)...
  animal.. 7. reptile 8. dinosaur,
    mastodon 9. phytosaur
  continent.. 8. Atlantis (Atalantis)
  man.. 4. cave, Dawn 11. lake dweller
  ref to.. 9. primitive
  tool.. 6. eolith
prejudiced... 6. biased 7. partial
   8. partisan 11. opinionated
   12. prepossessed
prejudicial... 9. injurious
   11. detrimental 15. disadvantageous
prelate... 4. head, pope 5. abbot,
   chief 6. bishop, priest 7. primate,
   red–blue 8. minister, superior
   9. Monsignor (Monsignore)
prelector, praelector... 6. reader
   7. teacher 8. lecturer 9. professor
preliminary... 5. prior 7. preface,
   prelude 8. entrance, previous,
   proemial 9. precedent, prefatory,
   threshold 10. antecedent
   11. preparatory 12. introduction,
   introductory
preliminary memo... 8. protocol
preliminary plan... 4. idea
prelude... 5. proem 6. verset

   7. preface 8. overture, ritornel
(ritornelle)
premature... 6. infant 8. too early,
   untimely 10. precocious
premier... 3. bet (gambling) 5. chief
   7. leading 8. earliest 9. principal
   13. prime minister
premiere... 4. show 10. first night
   12. presentation 16. first
   performance
premium... 4. agio 5. bonus, prize,
   stake 6. reward 8. gratuity, interest
   10. recompense
premonition... 5. hunch 6. notice
   7. warning 8. forecast
   10. foreboding 11. forewarning,
   information 12. presentiment
preoccupied... 4. lost 6. absent, filled
   8. absorbed, observed 9. engrossed
   10. abstracted, pre–engaged 13. lost
   in thought
preparation... 8. training 9. equipment,
   study hour 10. groundwork
   11. making ready 12. introduction
preparation (pert to)...
  of a dress.. 7. fitting
  place.. 10. laboratory, paratorium
  sugar, for candy.. 7. fondant
  without.. 5. ad lib 9. impromptu
prepare... 3. fit, fix, get 4. cook, gird,
   make, pave, yark 5. adapt, equip,
   ready, train 6. adjust 7. arrange
prepare (pert to)...
  by boiling.. 6. decoct
  for golf game.. 3. tee
  for melting glass.. 4. frit
  for publication.. 4. edit
  for seasoning.. 8. marinate
  skins.. 3. taw
prepared... 5. armed, ready
   7. adapted, groomed, skilled, trained
   8. equipped, provided
prepared instruction...
   13. propaedeutics
preponderance... 6. weight
   8. dominion, majority 9. influence
   11. outweighing, superiority
prepose... 6. prefix 7. preface
   11. place before
preposition... 2. at, by, ex, in, of, on,
   to, up 3. off, out, tae 4. into, onto,
   over, unto, upon, with
prepossession... 4. bent, bias
   9. obsession, prejudice
   10. preference 11. inclination
   12. predilection 13. appropriation,
   preconception 14. predisposition
presage... 4. bode, omen, osse, sign
   5. token 6. augury, betide, divine
   7. portend, predict 8. forebode,
   foretell 10. prediction, prognostic
   11. preindicate 13. foreknowledge
presager... 7. prophet 9. foreboder
presbytery... 6. church, clergy
   7. council 8. ministry 9. parsonage
   10. presbyters
prescribe... 3. set 5. allot, guide,
   limit, order 6. advise, bestow, direct,
   ordain 7. control, dictate
   9. designate
presence... 4. mien, port 7. bearing,
   posture, specter 8. phantasm

9. existence, proximity
10. apparition, appearance,
attendance 11. personality
present ... 3. now 4. boon, gift, give
5. grant, nonce, offer 6. bestow,
bounty, donate 7. largess (largesse)
8. donation, gratuity 9. introduce
10. contribute 11. benefaction
present (pert to) ...
for acceptance .. 6. tender
pupil to teacher .. 8. minerval
time .. 3. now 5. nonce, today
7. current 8. juncture
to customers .. 7. freebie, premium
8. giveaway 9. lagniappe (lagnappe)
to foreign ambassador .. 6. xenium
presentation ... 4. gift, plan 5. debut,
offer 7. present 8. bestowal,
donation, offering 10. appearance,
exhibition 12. introduction
presently .. 4. anon, soon 6. at once
7. shortly 8. nowadays 9. forthwith
10. before long 11. immediately
preservation ... 6. saving 9. retention,
safeguard 10. protection
11. maintenance, safekeeping
12. conservation, perpetuation
preservative ... 4. salt 5. spice
7. alcohol, vinegar 10. protective
14. sodium benzoate
preserve ... 3. can, jam, tin 4. corn,
cure, keep, salt, save 5. guard, jelly,
spare, store 6. defend, pickle, retain,
secure, shield, uphold 7. compote,
protect, sustain 8. conserve, maintain
9. freeze–dry, safeguard
preserve (pert to) ...
by drying .. 9. desiccate
fruit .. 7. compote 9. marmalade
grape .. 5. uvate (conserve)
in brine .. 4. corn, cure, salt
in oil .. 8. marinate
president ... 4. head 5. ruler
8. governor 14. chief executive
President (US) ... 4. Ford, Polk, Taft
5. Adams (John), Adams (John Q),
Grant, Hayes, Nixon, Tyler 6. Arthur
(Chester), Carter, Hoover, Monroe,
Pierce, Reagan, Taylor, Truman,
Wilson 7. Harding, Jackson, Johnson
(Andrew), Johnson (L B), Kennedy,
Lincoln, Madison 8. Buchanan,
Coolidge, Fillmore, Garfield, Harrison
(Benj), Harrison (Wm Henry), McKinley,
Van Buren 9. Cleveland, Jefferson,
Roosevelt (Theo), Roosevelt (F D)
10. Eisenhower, Washington
President (pert to) ...
place .. 10. Oval Office, White House
power .. 4. veto
press ... 3. dun 4. cram, iron, urge
5. crowd, force, wedge 6. compel,
hasten, smooth, throng, thrust
7. impress, squeeze 8. compress,
condense, insist on 9. extractor,
importune 10. compulsion, journalism,
newspapers 12. conscription
press (pert to) ...
ancient .. 6. Aldine
bookbinder .. 7. smasher
corrector .. 11. proofreader

critic .. 6. censor 8. reviewer
ranks .. 5. serry
pressed (pert to) ...
amber .. 8. amberoid
cheese .. 7. cheddar
grapes, residue .. 4. marc (mark)
into a mass .. 7. kneaded
together .. 5. dense 6. mashed
7. compact, crowded, serried
pressing .. 6. urgent, urging
7. exigent 9. insistent
10. compelling, extraction, motivating
11. importunity
pressure ... 4. urge 5. force
6. compel, stress, weight 7. squeeze,
urgency 8. exigency, instancy
9. authority, influence
10. compulsion, constraint,
harassment 11. compression
pressure (pert to) ...
barometer .. 7. mesobar
boiler, cooker .. 9. autoclave
instrument (for liquids) .. 9. manometer
10. piezometer 11. Bourdon tube
of necessity .. 7. urgency
resisting .. 8. renitent
unit .. 5. barad
prestidigitation ... 8. juggling
11. legerdemain 13. sleight of hand
prestige ... 4. bias, face, sway 5. clout,
éclat 6. renown, repute 7. sorcery
8. illusion 9. authority, deception,
influence 10. importance
11. superiority
presto ... 5. magic 7. command,
passing, quickly 8. suddenly
9. instantly 10. rapid tempo
11. immediately 13. instantaneous
presumably ... 7. no doubt 8. probably
10. ostensibly, supposedly
presume ... 4. dare, hope 5. imply,
judge, think 6. assure, impose
7. suppose, venture 10. presuppose
11. preconceive 14. take for granted
presumption ... 4. hope 6. daring
7. opinion 8. audacity 9. arrogance,
impudence, insolence 10. effrontery
11. implication, probability,
supposition
presumptive ... 5. brash 7. assumed,
Icarian 8. arrogant, inferred, probable
10. evidential
presumptuous ... 5. undue 7. forward,
haughty 8. arrogant, insolent
9. foolhardy 11. venturesome
pretend ... 3. act, aim 4. fake, sham
5. claim, feign, feint 6. affect, allege,
assume, pose as 7. presume, pretext,
profess 8. disguise, simulate
11. impersonate, make believe
pretended ... 4. sham 7. alleged
8. affected, intended, proposed,
so–called 10. ostensible
pretended omission (Rhet) ...
9. apophasis 11. paraleipsis
(paralepsis)
pretender ... 4. idol, snob 5. cowan,
quack 6. seemer 7. Aeolist (Eolist)
8. claimant, impostor 9. charlatan
10. mountebank 11. fourflusher
pretense, pretence ... 3. act 4. flam,

ruse, sham, show 5. claim, cloak,
cover, feint, horse, study 6. excuse,
tinsel 7. pretext 8. artifice, stalking
10. appearance, masquerade,
subterfuge 11. affectation, fabrication,
ostentation
pretentious... 4. arty 5. showy
  6. rococo 7. elegant, pompous
  8. affected, boastful 9. high–flown
  12. ostentatious 13. grandiloquent
pretentious words, use of...
  9. bombastic 10. lexiphanic
pretermit... 4. omit 6. pass by
  7. neglect, suspend 8. intermit, pass
  over 9. interrupt
pretext... 4. flam, plea 5. cloak, cover,
  trick 6. excuse 8. pretense (pretence)
  9. deception, semblance
pretty... 3. toy 4. cute, fair, joli, very
  5. bonny (bonnie) 6. clever, comely,
  lovely, rather 7. dollish, finical,
  foppish 8. handsome 9. ingenious,
  tolerably 10. attractive, knickknack
  11. good–looking, interesting
  15. pulchritudinous
prevail... 3. win 5. exist 6. induce,
  subdue 7. succeed, triumph
  8. dominate, frequent 9. prevalent
  11. predominate
prevailed... 3. got, won 5. urged
  9. succeeded, triumphed
prevailing... 4. rife 5. chief, usual
  6. common 7. current, general
  8. abundant, dominant 9. prevalent
  10. widespread 11. predominant
prevail upon... 4. urge 6. induce
  8. persuade
prevalent... 4. rife 6. potent
  7. current 8. dominant, powerful
  9. extensive 10. prevailing,
  successful, victorious, widespread
  11. efficacious, influential
prevaricate... 3. lie 5. evade
  7. deviate, quibble, shuffle
prevene... 7. prevent 9. forestall
  10. anticipate
prevent... 4. warn 5. avert, debar,
  deter, estop 7. ward off 8. preclude
  9. forestall, frustrate 10. circumvent
preventative, preventive... 8. antidote
  9. deterrent 12. prophylactic
previous... 4. past 5. prior 6. before,
  former 7. earlier 8. untimely
  9. foregoing, preceding, premature
  11. unwarranted
previously... 4. erst 6. before
  7. earlier 8. formerly 9. aforesaid
  10. heretofore
prey... 3. rob 5. booty, spoil
  6. quarry, victim 7. plunder
prey (to seize)... 9. raptorial
prey upon... 3. eat 4. feed 5. ravin
  (raven) 7. plunder, torment
  9. predacity
Priam (pert to)...
  daughter.. 8. Polyxena 9. Cassandra
  grandfather.. 4. Ilus
  King of.. 4. Troy
  servant.. 7. Agelaus
  son.. 5. Paris 6. Hector 7. Troilus
  wife.. 6. Hecuba
price... 3. sum 4. cost, fare, odds,

rate 5. offer, value, worth 6. charge
7. expense 10. estimation,
excellence, recompense
12. preciousness
priceless... 7. amusing 8. precious
  10. high–priced, invaluable, not
  salable
prick... 4. goad, pain, pang 5. sting,
  wound 6. pierce 7. prickle, remorse
  8. distress
pricked... 6. dotted, pinked 7. pointed
  9. punctured
prickle... 4. burr, prod, seta 5. spike,
  thorn 6. pierce, tingle 7. acantha
  8. stinging
prickly... 6. tingly 7. pointed
  8. echinate
prickly (pert to)...
  flower.. 4. burr
  pear.. 4. tuna 5. nopal 6. cactus
    7. Opuntia
  plant.. 3. ash 5. briar, elder 6. teasel
    7. juniper, lettuce, thistle
    12. Hercules'–club
pride... 6. vanity 7. conceit, egotism
  9. arrogance, proudness
  11. self–respect
priest... 3. Eli, fra 4. abbé, curé,
  lama, père 5. clerk, druid, padre
  6. cleric, father 7. prester
  9. oratorian
priest (pert to)...
  assistant.. 7. acolyte
  Brit order (anc).. 5. Druid
  cap.. 5. miter (mitre) 7. biretta
  collar.. 5. amice, stole
  fish.. 8. rockfish
  mantle.. 4. cope
  newly ordained.. 9. priesteen
  priest–in–the–pulpit.. 10. cuckoopint
  relating to.. 10. sacerdotal
  tribe (Israel).. 4. Levi
  vestment.. 3. alb 5. ephod
    8. scapular
priestly caste... 4. Magi 7. wise men
prig... 3. beg, fog, pan 4. buck, snob
  5. dandy, filch, plead, prink, prude,
  steal, thief 6. haggle, pilfer, purist,
  tinker 7. bargain, entreat, pitcher
  8. pilferer
priggish, prim... 7. prudish
  8. snobbish, thievish
prim... 4. fish, neat, smug 5. primp,
  smelt 6. demure, formal 7. precise,
  prudish 8. decorous
prima donna... 4. diva 6. singer
prima facie... 7. at sight 9. first view
  10. apparently
primal... 5. basic, chief, first
  7. primary 8. original 9. elemental,
  primitive
primary... 5. basic, color, first
  6. primal 7. initial 8. election,
  primeval, pristine 9. elemental,
  essential, firsthand, primitive, principal
  10. elementary 11. fundamental
primary (pert to)...
  armament.. 6. cannon
  circles.. 7. equator, horizon
    8. ecliptic, galactic
  colors.. 3. red 4. blue 6. yellow
primate, bishop... 10. Archbishop

Primates (Order of)... 3. ape, man
  5. lemur 6. mammal, monkey
  8. marmoset 9. orangutan
  (orangoutang)
prime... 4. best, dawn 5. first, paint
  7. primary, the best 8. original,
  primeval 9. primitive
prime minister... 7. premier
primer... 5. paint 8. hornbook,
  textbook, type size 9. detonator
  10. battledore
primeval... 6. primal 7. primary
  8. original, pristine
primeval deity... 5. Titan
primitive... 5. basic, first 6. embryo,
  native, quaint 7. ancient, priscan
  8. pristine 10. aboriginal, antiquated
  11. fundamental
primitive (pert to)...
  area.. 5. Idaho 8. Colorado
  art objects.. 9. artifacts
  group.. 6. ethnos
  self.. 2. id 8. instinct
primness... 8. neatness, niceness
  9. stiffness 11. preciseness
primo... 5. chief, first 12. leading
  tenor
primordial... 7. primary 8. original
  9. elemental, primitive 10. prototypal
  11. rudimentary 12. first created
primrose (pert to)...
  called.. 10. an innocent 13. flower of
  youth
  color.. 6. yellow 10. snapdragon
  genus.. 7. Primula 11. Primulaceae
  green.. 5. color
  League.. 13. Conservatives (Eng)
  path.. 7. sensual
prince... 4. knez 5. prinz 7. dynasty,
  monarch 8. archduke 9. potentate,
  princekin, sovereign 10. princeling
prince (pert to)...
  Albert.. 9. frock coat
  allowance.. 8. appenage
  petty.. 6. satrap
princely... 5. noble, regal, royal
  6. kingly 10. munificent
  11. magnificent
princely Italian family... 4. Este
Prince of...
  Afghanistan.. 4. amir
  apostate angels.. 5. Eblis
  Apostles.. 6. St Paul 7. St Peter
  darkness.. 5. devil, Satan 7. Ahriman
  demons.. 5. devil 9. Beelzebub
  destruction.. 9. Tamerlane
  evil spirits.. 7. Sammael
  liars.. 5. Pinto
  Peace.. 7. Messiah 11. Jesus Christ
  Spanish poetry.. 4. Vega
  the Church.. 8. cardinal
  the ode.. 7. Ronsard
  the sonnet.. 6. Bellay 15. Joachim du
  Bellay
  this world (Bib).. 5. Satan
  Tunis.. 3. bey
princess (pert to)...
  literally.. 5. Sarah
  loved by Cupid.. 6. Psyche
  loved by Zeus.. 6. Europa
  Mohammed.. 5. begum
  mythical.. 5. Danae 8. Atalanta

royal.. 14. eldest daughter
Tyrian.. 4. Dido (Elissa)
principal... 3. top 4. arch, head, main
  5. chief, major, prime 6. Führer,
  leader, master, origin, source
  7. captain, leading, palmary, primary
  8. foremost 9. important, organ
  stop, preceptor 10. capital sum
  11. outstanding
principality... 6. Monaco
principal meal (Rom)... 4. cena
principle... 4. rule 5. axiom, canon,
  prana, tenet 6. dictum 7. precept,
  theorem 9. essential 10. foundation
principle (pert to)...
  active in tobacco.. 8. nicotine
  distance.. 11. perspective
  Hindu.. 5. Sakti
  life, theosophy.. 5. prana, tenet
  musical.. 8. tonality
  vital.. 4. soul 5. anima
principles... 5. creed 9. generalia
  10. essentials 12. generalities
princox, princock... 7. coxcomb
  9. pert youth
prink... 4. deck, wink 5. adorn, preen,
  primp 6. bedeck, glance 7. dress up
print... 5. stamp 7. edition, engrave,
  impress, picture, publish
  11. indentation
printed (pert to)...
  defamation.. 5. libel
  fabric.. 4. silk 6. calico 7. percale
  sheets.. 8. pamphlet
printer... 8. pressman 9. publisher
  11. typographer 12. lithographer
printer (pert to)...
  aid.. 5. devil 10. apprentice
  dauber.. 5. biron
  direction.. 4. stet
  hand ink roller.. 6. brayer
  ink pad.. 6. dabber
  manuscript.. 4. copy
  mark.. 4. dash, stet 5. caret, serif,
  tilde 8. asterisk
  measure.. 2. em, en 4. pica
  type, mixed.. 3. pie (pi)
printing (pert to)...
  blur.. 6. mackle, macule
  cylinder.. 6. rounce
  error.. 7. erratum
  form.. 3. die
  for the blind.. 7. braille
  mark.. 4. dele 6. diesis 8. ellipsis
  measure.. 2. em, en 5. agate
  metal block.. 4. quad
  press part.. 6. platen, rounce
  7. frisket
prion... 6. petrel 7. sea bird
prior... 3. ere 4. fore, past 6. before,
  former 8. previous, priorate
  9. preceding 10. antecedent
priority... 10. precedence 11. order of
  time
priory... 5. abbey 8. cloister
priscan... 9. primitive
Priscian... 7. grammar 10. grammarian
Priscilla (pert to)...
  Bib.. 16. Christian convert
  color.. 7. fog blue
  Hist.. 7. Puritan
  husband.. 9. John Alden

tale .. 24. Courtship of Myles Standish
prism (optical device)... 5. Porro
prismatic... 10. iridescent, variegated
prison... 3. jug 4. brig, gaol, jail, keep,
　quod 5. clink 6. carcer
　10. guardhouse 12. penitentiary
prison (pert to)...
　courtyard .. 4. quad
　English (old) .. 7. Newgate 9. Bridewell
　French .. 8. Bastille
　guarded .. 10. panopticon
　keeper .. 5. guard 6. gaoler, jailer,
　　keeper, warden 7. turnkey
　Russian .. 5. gulag
　slang .. 3. jug 4. quod, rock 5. clink,
　　limbo 6. cooler 7. slammer 8. big
　　house, hoosegow
　spy .. 6. canary, mouton
Prisoner of...
　Chillon .. 16. Francois Bonivard
　Vatican .. 4. Pope
prisoner's release... 6. parole
pristine... 7. primary 8. original
　9. primitive
prittle–prattle... 7. chatter, prattle
　8. chitchat 9. chatterer, empty talk
privacy... 7. privity, retreat, secrecy
　8. solitude 9. seclusion
private... 5. privy 6. covert, secret
　7. one's own 8. esoteric, eyes–only,
　hush–hush, personal, secluded,
　separate, solitary 11. sequestered
　12. confidential
　15. uncommunicative
privateer... 4. Kidd (Capt) 5. caper
　6. pirate 7. corsair, soldier (not
　enlisted) 9. freelance
privately... 5. aside 6. secret 8. in
　secret 10. personally, unofficial
　12. unofficially
privation... 4. loss, want 6. misery
　7. poverty 8. hardship
　10. divestment 11. destitution
privilege... 3. soc, use 5. favor, right
　7. charter 8. easement 9. advantage
　10. concession 12. carte blanche
privileged... 6. exempt 8. licensed
prix... 5. prize
prize... 3. cup 5. award, booty, Detur
　(Harvard), medal, plate, price, purse,
　stake, value 6. assess, esteem, ribbon,
　trophy 7. premium, respect
　8. treasure
prize fight... 2. go, KO 3. TKO
　4. bout, spar 6. boxing 7. contest
　8. knockout, pugilism 10. fisticuffs
pro... 3. aye, for 6. before 8. behalf
　of 9. in front of 12. professional
probability... 4. odds 6. chance,
　shoo–in (sl) 7. vantage 9. liability
　10. conclusion, good chance,
　likelihood, likeliness 11. credibility
probe... 3. dig 4. prod, tent 5. sound
　6. feeler, pierce, search, stylet
　7. examine, explore, feel out, inquiry
　10. instrument, scrutinize
probity... 6. virtue 7. honesty
　9. integrity, rectitude 11. uprightness
problem... 3. nut 4. crux, knot
　6. enigma, riddle 7. theorem
　8. question 9. situation

pro bono publico... 16. for the public
good
proboscis... 4. nose 5. snout, trunk
procaccia... 4. cart (carrier's)
　7. carrier
procacious... 4. pert 8. insolent,
petulant
procacity... 8. pertness 9. insolence,
petulance
Procavis... 4. cony 5. hyrax 6. rabbit
procedure... 4. step 5. order
　6. custom, method, policy, system
　7. process 8. behavior
　11. continuance
proceed... 2. go 4. fare, move, pass,
　wend 5. arise, issue 6. derive
　7. emanate 8. continue, progress
　9. originate
proceed (pert to)...
　hastily .. 5. speed
　leisurely .. 5. amble, mosey (mosy)
　on one's way .. 4. wend
　rapidly .. 4. zoom 6. gallop
proceeding... 4. step 5. actum
　6. course 7. conduct, measure,
　process 8. activity, behavior
　9. procedure 11. transaction
proceeding (pert to)...
　by threes .. 7. ternary
　from earth .. 8. telluric
　from the sun .. 5. polar
proceedings... 4. acta 5. trial
　6. doings 7. affairs, lawsuit, minutes
　8. activity
proceeds... 4. gain, goes 6. income
　7. marches, profits, returns
procerity... 6. height 8. tallness
process... 4. cook, writ 5. lapse (of
　time), order 6. course, notice
　7. advance, mandate, summons
　8. progress 9. emanation, operation,
　outgrowth, procedure, sterilize
process (pert to)...
　beak (small) .. 9. rostrulum
　electroplating, steeling .. 8. acierage
　fabric coloring .. 5. batik
　fish (winglike) .. 3. fin
　in organisms .. 6. moisis
　of development .. 7. nascent
　pointed .. 3. awn
　steel making .. 8. Bessemer
　　11. cementation
　surveying .. 13. triangulation
　transferring pictures .. 5. decal
　　12. decalcomania
procession... 4. file 5. train 6. parade
　7. cortege 8. sequence 9. formation
prochein, prochain... 4. next
　7. nearest
proclaim... 4. hype (sl), tout 5. blaze,
　voice 6. herald 7. declare, enounce,
　presage, publish 8. announce
　10. promulgate
proclamation... 4. fiat 5. bando,
　banns (bans), blaze, edict, ukase
　6. decree, notice 9. manifesto
　12. announcement, promulgation
proclivity... 4. bent 6. desire
　7. leaning 8. tendency
　10. propensity 11. disposition,
inclination

procrastinate... 5. defer, delay, stall
  7. soldier 8. postpone
procrastination... 5. delay, stall
  7. laxness 10. hesitation
  11. vacillation 12. dilatoriness
procrastinator... 7. delayer, trifler
  8. deferrer
procreant... 8. fruitful 9. producing
  10. generating 11. propagative
Procrustes (Gr legend)...
  10. highwayman (Attica)
  14. Procrustean bed
procurator... 5. agent 6. lawyer
  7. proctor, steward
procure... 3. get 4. gain 5. bring,
  fetch 6. effect, elicit, induce, obtain
  7. acquire 8. contrive, purchase
prod... 3. egg, jab 4. goad, poke,
  urge 6. thrust
prodigal... 4. cloy 6. lavish 7. spender
  9. plentiful 10. squanderer
  11. extravagant, intemperate,
  spendthrift, squandering
prodigality... 5. waste 9. abundance
  12. extravagance, intemperance
  13. superabundant
prodigious... 4. huge 5. great
  7. amazing, immense 8. enormous
  9. marvelous, monstrous, wonderful
  10. miraculous, portentous,
  tremendous 11. astonishing
  13. extraordinary
prodigy... 4. omen, sign 6. genius,
  marvel, oddity, wonder 7. miracle
prodition... 7. treason 8. betrayal
produce... 2. do 4. bear, make, show,
  wage 5. carry, cause, stage, yield
  6. author, create, effect 7. exhibit,
  product 8. engender, generate,
  receipts 9. originate 10. accomplish
  11. merchandise
produce (pert to)...
  copy of.. 4. type
  effect.. 3. act
  ideas.. 6. ideate
  noise.. 5. sound
produced... 8. extended 9. elongated,
  prolonged
produced (pert to)...
  by heat.. 7. igneous 8. volcanic
  by kitchen gardens.. 7. olitory
  8. potherbs
  by wind.. 7. aeolian
  regularly.. 6. staple
producer... 4. doer 6. farmer, parent
  7. creator 10. theaterman
  12. manufacturer
producing (pert to)...
  cold.. 7. algific
  fire.. 8. sparking
  illusions.. 15. phantasmagorial
  poison.. 6. septic
product... 3. sum 4. crop 5. fruit
  6. result 7. hormone 8. artifact,
  creation 9. commodity, outgrowth
production... 3. hit 4. book, work
  5. fruit 7. produce 8. creation
  9. execution, extension
  14. accomplishment
productive... 4. rich 7. fertile, gainful
  8. creative, fruitful 9. inventive
  10. generative

proem... 7. preface, prelude
  8. foreword, preamble
  12. introduction
profane... 6. misuse, unholy, wicked
  7. godless, impious, ungodly, worldly
  8. temporal 9. desecrate
  10. unhallowed 11. blasphemous,
  unspiritual 12. unsanctified
profess... 4. avow 5. claim, feign
  6. affirm, allege 7. declare
  11. acknowledge
profession... 5. claim, faith, trade
  6. avowal, career, metier 7. calling,
  pretext 8. vocation 9. testimony
  10. occupation 11. affirmation
  14. acknowledgment
professional... 4. paid 5. hired
  6. expert 7. skilled, trained
  8. finished
professional, non... 3. lay 4. laic
  7. amateur 9. unskilled
proffer... 3. bid 4. give 5. offer
  6. tender
proficient... 3. apt 5. adept 6. expert,
  versed 7. skilled 12. accomplished
profile... 4. draw, form 7. contour,
  diagram, outline, picture 9. biography
  14. representation
profit... 3. net 4. boot, gain, good,
  mend 5. avail 6. return 7. benefit,
  rake–off, results 8. interest
  9. advantage 11. share of gain
  12. remuneration
profitable... 6. paying, useful
  7. helpful 8. repaying 9. expedient,
  lucrative 10. beneficial
  12. remunerative
profligate... 6. wicked 7. corrupt,
  spender, vicious 8. depraved,
  prodigal, wasteful 9. abandoned,
  dissolute, reprobate 10. overthrown
  11. extravagant
profound... 4. deep, wise 5. heavy
  7. abysmal, intense, learned
  8. abstruse, complete, deep–felt,
  poignant 9. downright, recondite,
  sagacious 11. far–reaching
  12. encompassing, unfathomable
  13. thoroughgoing
profundity... 5. depth 6. wisdom
  8. deepness 12. abstruseness
profuse... 6. galore, lavish 7. diffuse,
  liberal, palaver 8. abundant,
  generous, numerous, prodigal,
  wasteful 9. bountiful 10. munificent
  11. extravagant, overflowing
profusion... 6. plenty 9. abundance
  11. diffuseness, prodigality
  12. extravagance, lavish supply
progenitor... 4. sire 6. parent
  8. ancestor 9. precursor
  10. forefather
progenitor of giants (Norse Myth)...
  4. Ymir 8. rime–cold
progeny... 3. son 4. race 5. issue
  6. family 7. outcome 8. children,
  daughter, outbirth 9. offspring,
  parentage, resultant 11. descendants
prognosis... 7. outlook 8. forecast
  9. diagnosis 10. prediction
  14. interpretation
prognosticate... 4. bode, omen

7. betoken, predict, presage
8. forebode, foreshow, foretell,
prophecy 9. foretoken
program, programme... 4. bill
(printed), card, plan 5. edict
6. notice, policy 7. outline
8. bulletin, platform, schedule,
syllabus 9. broadcast, catalogue,
programma 10. prospectus
12. proclamation, prolegomenon
13. advertisement
programma... 5. edict 6. decree,
notice 7. preface 12. prolegomenon
progress... 4. fare, tour, wend
5. march 6. course, travel
7. advance, journey 10. expedition
11. progression
progress (pert to)...
chart.. 5. Gantt
clumsily.. 8. scramble
intelligently.. 6. egress 7. telesis
(telesia)
laborious.. 4. plod, wade
outward.. 6. egress
weakly.. 6. feebly
progressive... 6. modern, onward
7. forward, gradual, liberal
9. advancing, improving
11. consecutive 12. enterprising
prohibit... 3. ban, bar, bid 5. debar,
estop, taboo (tabu) 6. enjoin, forbid,
hinder 7. prevent 9. interdict
prohibited... 7. illegal, illicit
8. unlawful
prohibition... 3. ban 7. embargo
8. estoppel 9. exclusion
10. prevention, temperance
11. forbiddance 12. interdicting
project... 3. jet, jut 4. abut, cast,
idea, plan 5. shoot 6. beetle,
design, device, scheme 7. pattern,
problem 8. contrive, proposal,
protrude 9. intention 10. conception
11. undertaking
projectile... 4. bomb 5. shell 6. bullet,
rocket 7. missile, torpedo
8. parabola 9. cartridge
projection... 3. arm, ear, fin, jag, toe
4. barb, cape, lobe, ness, prop,
snag 5. apsis, bulge, ledge, prong,
redan, socle, tenon 6. lobule, tappet
8. headland
projet... 4. plan 6. design
prolific... 6. fecund 7. fertile, teeming
8. fruitful 9. inventive 10. generative
11. propagative 12. reproductive
prolix... 5. wordy 7. diffuse, verbose
8. tiresome 9. prolonged, rigmarole,
wearisome 10. long–winded,
pleonastic, protracted
prolocutor... 6. orator 7. speaker,
teacher 8. chairman 9. spokesman
10. mouthpiece 11. Lord Speaker
(Eng)
prolong... 4. spin 7. draw out
8. continue, lengthen, postpone,
protract
prolonged... 7. chronic, delayed
8. extended 9. continued, postponed
10. lengthened, protracted
promenade... 4. mall, walk 6. airing,
marina, pasear 7. alameda, gallery

Prometheus (pert to)...
famed as.. 5. Titan (a)
poem (Shelley).. 17. Prometheus
Unbound
tale, tragedy.. 15. Prometheus Bound
16. Prometheus Loosed
24. Prometheus the Fire Bringer
prominence... 4. cusp 6. height
8. eminence, prestige, salience
9. greatness 10. famousness,
importance 11. distinction,
obviousness, prosiliency
12. distinctness, protuberance
prominent... 4. high, star 5. great
6. famous, marked 7. obvious,
salient 8. distinct, manifest
9. important 10. celebrated,
noticeable, prosilient, protruding
11. conspicuous, distinctive,
outstanding 13. distinguished
promiscuous... 5. mixed 8. careless
9. haphazard, orderless
14. indiscriminate
promise... 3. vow 4. hope, oath
5. swear 6. engage, parole, pledge,
plight, votive (by vow) 7. betroth,
predict 8. affiance, contract, give
hope 9. assurance, ray of hope
11. declaration
Promised Land... 6. heaven, utopia
8. Paradise 9. millenium, Shangri–La
11. Happy Valley 13. Celestial City
promontory... 3. tor 4. cape, naze
(nase), ness, scaw 5. mount, point
8. headland 10. projection
promote... 4. help 5. exalt, nurse
6. extend, prefer 7. actuate,
advance, dignify, elevate, finance,
further, improve 8. increase
9. advertise, encourage, patronize
promoter... 5. agent 6. backer
7. planner 8. lobbyist 9. financier,
publicist
promotion... 6. brevet 7. advance
10. preferment 11. advertising,
furtherance, improvement
prompt... 3. cue 4. easy, hint, soon,
tell, yare (anc) 5. alert, early, quick,
ready 6. advise, remind 7. animate,
suggest 8. punctual 11. expeditious
prompter... 3. aid 4. cuer 6. pit man,
reader 7. inducer, reciter 8. reminder
promptly... 4. tite (anc) 6. at once
7. quickly 9. willingly
promulgate... 7. declare, publish
8. proclaim 9. make known
prone... 3. apt 4. bent, flat 5. apish
6. supine 7. willing 8. downward
9. prostrate, recumbent
13. ventricumbent
prone to sin... 8. peccable
prong... 3. nib, peg 4. fang, fork, tine
5. spike, tooth 6. branch
pronghorn... 6. cabree (cabrie)
9. prong buck, springbok
prong key... 7. spanner
pronoun... 2. he, it, me, my, us, we,
ye 3. her, him, one, she, thy, who,
you 4. that, thee, them, they, thou,
what, your 5. these, those 6. itself,
myself 7. herself, himself, oneself,
ourself 8. one's self, yourself

9. ourselves 10. themselves
pronoun (possessive)... 2. my 3. her,
his, its, our 4. hers, mine, one's,
ours, your 5. their, yours 6. theirs
pronounce... 3. say 5. bless (holy),
speak, utter 6. affirm, assert
7. adjudge, declare, deliver
8. announce 9. enunciate
10. adjudicate, articulate, assibilate
pronouncement... 6. decree
8. judgment 9. manifesto
11. affirmation, declaration
12. announcement
pronto... 5. quick 7. quickly
8. promptly 11. immediately
pronunciation... 4. burr 8. orthoepy
9. utterance (clear) 11. enunciation
pronunciation mark... 5. tilde
7. cedilla 8. dieresis
proof... 4. test 5. trial 6. result
7. outcome 8. evidence 9. testimony
11. galley proof 12. confirmation,
verification 13. certification
proofreader's mark... 4. dele, stet
5. caret, space
prop... 3. beg, gib, nog 5. brace,
shore, sprag, staff, stell 6. shorer
7. fulcrum, support 9. stanchion
propagate... 5. breed 6. extend,
spread 7. diffuse, publish
8. disperse, engender, generate,
increase, multiply, transmit
propel... 3. row 4. pole, push, urge
5. drive, impel 7. project
propeller... 3. fan, gun, oar 4. vane
5. screw 6. driver 9. plane part
propensity... 4. bent 6. desire
7. leaning 8. aptitude, tendency
9. proneness 10. proclivity
11. disposition, inclination
proper... 3. fit 4. fine, just, meet,
prim, smug 5. exact, right 6. chaste,
decent, goodly, honest, kilter
7. correct 8. decorous, inherent,
orthodox, suitable 9. excellent,
expedient 11. appropriate,
grammatical, respectable
12. conventional
properly... 5. fitly 7. rightly, utterly
8. decently, strictly, suitably
9. correctly 11. expediently
14. conventionally
proper sense of worth... 5. pride
property... 3. res 4. bona, gear
5. asset, goods, trait 6. estate,
nature, realty, wealth 8. holdings
9. attribute, copyright, ownership
10. real estate 11. peculiarity,
possessions 14. characteristic
property (pert to)...
act to regain.. 8. replevin (repleven)
destruction of.. 8. sabotage
9. vandalism
landed property.. 9. cadastral
light without heat..
15. phosphorescence
movable.. 4. gear 8. chattels
no private ownership..
11. aspheterism
of matter.. 7. inertia
one's own.. 7. alodium
right.. 4. lien

stolen.. 4. loot, pelf 5. lucre, spoil
suit for recovery.. 6. trover
transferrer.. 7. alienor, grantor
wife to husband.. 3. dos
woman's (Hindu).. 9. stridhana
(stridhan)
prophecy... 6. oracle 9. utterance
10. prediction 11. foretelling
prophesy... 4. osse 5. augur
7. predict, presage 8. forecast,
foreshow, foretell 10. vaticinate
11. preindicate 13. prognosticate
prophet... 4. seer 6. medium, oracle
7. psychic 8. Mohammed, preacher,
presager 9. John Smith, predictor
10. soothsayer 11. Joseph Smith
(Mormon)
prophet (Bib)... 4. Amos 5. Cyrus,
Hosea 6. Elijah (Elias) 7. Malachi,
Obadiah
prophet, murder of... 8. vaticide
prophetess... 5. sibyl 7. seeress
9. Cassandra (of evil)
prophetic, prophetical... 5. vatic
6. mantic 7. fateful, vatical
8. oracular 9. vaticinal
10. divinatory, presageful
11. predicative
propinquity... 7. kinship 8. nearness
9. proximity 12. neighborhood,
relationship 13. consanguinity
propitiate... 5. atone 6. pacify
8. atone for 10. conciliate
propitiation... 9. atonement, expiation
12. pacification, satisfaction
14. reconciliation
propitious... 4. rosy 5. happy, lucky
6. benign, timely 7. helpful
9. favorable, opportune, promising
10. auspicious, benevolent,
prosperous 12. advantageous,
well–disposed
proponent... 8. advocate
10. propounder
proportion... 4. part, rate 5. quota,
ratio, share 6. adjust, extent
7. analogy, compare, euphony,
prorate 8. equalize, symmetry
9. apportion
proportional... 4. rate 8. relative
10. comparable, respective
11. dimensional
proportionate... 5. equal 8. adequate,
relative 9. analogous 10. respective
11. comparative 13. corresponding
proposal... 3. bid 4. plan 5. offer
6. feeler, motion 8. marriage
9. intention 10. nomination,
suggestion 11. proposition,
supposition
propose... 5. image, offer, state, toast
6. intend, submit 7. purpose
8. nominate, propound 9. postulate
proposed (pert to)...
for consideration.. 9. suggested
for debate.. 6. mooted
international language.. 2. Ro 3. Ido
9. Esperanto
proposition... 4. plan 5. axiom, lemma
6. porism, thesis 7. project
8. empirema, proposal 9. corollary
11. supposition, undertaking

proposition, proof of ... 18. reductio ad absurdum
propound ... 6. submit 7. propose 8. set forth 9. postulate
proprietary ... 5. owner, title 8. interest, medicine (secret) 9. ownership 10. proprietor 12. landed estate
propriety ... 7. decency, decorum, fitness 8. standard 9. ownership 10. convention, expedience, properness 11. correctness, suitability 12. tastefulness 13. possessorship
propugnaculum ... 7. bulwark, defense 8. fortress
prorogue ... 5. defer 6. extend 7. adjourn, prolong 8. postpone, protract
prosaic ... 4. drab, dull, flat 5. plain, prosy 6. prolix, stupid 7. humdrum, insipid, tedious 8. ordinary, tiresome 10. unexciting 11. commonplace 12. matter-of-fact 13. unimaginative
proscribe ... 3. ban 6. forbid, outlaw 7. condemn (to death) 8. prohibit, restrain 9. interdict, ostracize
proscription ... 5. exile 8. outlawry 11. prohibition 12. interdiction
prosecute ... 3. sue 4. urge 5. chase 6. intend (law), pursue 7. carry on, enforce, execute
prosecutor ... 6. lawyer 7. accuser, relator 8. attorney
proselyte ... 3. ger (to Judaism) 7. convert
proseuche, proseucha ... 7. oratory 9. synagogue 13. place of prayer
prosody ... 13. versification
prospect ... 4. view 5. buyer, scene, vista 6. survey 7. explore, foresee, outlook 8. customer 9. applicant, candidate, foresight, intention 10. contestant 11. probability 12. anticipation
prosper ... 4. fare 5. cheve, speed 6. thrive 7. succeed 8. flourish
prosperity ... 3. hap, ups 4. boom, weal 6. thrift 7. success, welfare 9. well-being 11. good fortune
Prospero (pert to) ...
character .. 9. Ferdinand
daughter .. 7. Miranda
servant .. 5. Ariel
slave .. 7. Caliban
The Tempest .. 11. Duke of Milan
prosperous ... 4. weal 5. lucky, palmy, sonsy (sonsie) 7. wealthy 8. thriving 9. favorable, fortunate 10. auspicious, successful 11. flourishing
prostitute ... 4. drab 5. venal 6. harlot 7. corrupt 8. infamous 12. street walker
prostrate ... 4. flat, raze 5. abase, prone 6. fallen, grieve, supine 7. exhaust 8. helpless, supinate 9. flattened, recumbent 10. obsequious, submissive
prosy ... 3. dry 4. dull 6. jejune 7. prosaic, tedious 11. commonplace 13. plain-speaking
protagonist ... 4. hero, lead (theater) 5. actor 6. leader 8. advocate, champion, defender 9. contender, principal, spokesman 11. participant
Protagorus (Gr) ... 7. Sophist, teacher 11. philosopher
protasis ... 5. maxim 9. drama part 11. proposition 12. introduction
protect ... 3. arm 4. save 5. guard 6. defend, insure, police, screen, sheath, shield 7. cherish, shelter 8. enshield, preserve 9. safeguard
protected ... 5. armed 6. shaded 7. aproned, guarded 8. shielded 12. invulnerable
protection ... 3. bib, lee 4. coat, fort, moat 5. aegis (egis), apron, armor, guard, shade, shell, smock 6. glacis, refuge, safety 7. defense, parapet, shelter 8. havelock, passport, security 11. safekeeping 12. preservation
protector ... 6. patron, regent 8. defender, guardian 10. safekeeper
protector of vineyards (Gr) ... 7. Priapus
protégé ... 4. ward 6. charge 9. dependent
Proteida ... 7. Proteus 10. amphibians 11. salamanders
protein ... 6. casein 7. albumin, mucedin, peptone 8. globulin, lecithin, nutrient 9. protamine 11. chlorophyll
protein (pert to) ...
blood .. 6. fibrin 8. globulin
castor oil bean .. 5. ricin (poison)
egg .. 7. albumin
milk .. 6. casein
muscles .. 8. creatine
seeds .. 7. edestin 8. aleurone, prolamin
Proteles ... 8. aardwolf
protest ... 4. aver, beef, deny 6. assert 7. declare 9. objection, stipulate 10. asseverate 11. expostulate 13. expostulation
protestation ... 6. avowal (public) 7. protest 11. affirmation, obtestation 12. asseveration, supplication
Proteus (pert to) ...
biology .. 3. olm 6. amoeba 8. bacteria 10. salamander
Gr Myth .. 6. sea god
Shakespeare .. 17. Gentleman of Verona
protocol ... 5. rules (official) 7. compact 8. schedule 9. agreement, etiquette 10. memorandum (diplomatic) 12. original copy
protograph ... 9. holograph 12. illustration (of species)
protoplasm ... 5. spore 7. nucleus 9. archetype, cytoplasm 10. primordium 11. basis of life
protoplasmic (pert to) ...
body .. 8. ectosark 9. ectoplasm, endoplasm
cell .. 6. amoeba (ameba)
cell contents .. 9. metaplasm
substance .. 3. gel
Protozoa ... 6. amoeba (ameba), Lobosa, phylum 11. unicellular
protract ... 4. spin 5. defer, delay

6. extend 7. prolong, stretch
8. continue, elongate, lengthen,
postpone, protrude 9. expatiate
protrude... 3. jut 5. bulge 6. exsert
7. project 9. thrust out
protuberance... 3. jag, nub, wen
4. boss, bump, cere, hump, knob,
knot, lobe, lump, node, snag, wart
5. bulge, caput, inion, knurl, torus
8. eminence, swelling 9. extrusion
10. projection
proud... 4. vain 5. grand, lofty, noble
6. elated, lordly 7. haughty, pleased,
stately, valiant 8. arrogant, boastful,
imposing, splendid 9. conceited,
gratified 10. impressive
11. independent, magisterial,
magnificent 12. presumptuous,
supercilious
prove... 3. try 4. test 5. check, nurse
6. evince, try out, verify 7. confirm,
justify, probate 8. identify, manifest
9. ascertain, establish
11. corroborate, demonstrate
prove false... 6. refute
Provençal dialect... 9. langue d'oc
provender... 3. hay 4. food 5. grain
6. fodder 8. ensilage
proverb... 3. saw 5. adage, axiom
6. byword, enigma, saying
8. aphorism, link verb, paroemia
proverbial... 10. aphoristic
11. sententious 12. epigrammatic
provide... 4. give 5. cater, endow,
endue, equip, stock, treat, yield
6. afford, ration, supply 7. care for,
finance 9. make ready 10. contribute
provided... 2. if, so 5. boden
6. sobeit 8. afforded, equipped,
prepared, supplied 11. on condition
13. conditionally
Providence founder... 13. Roger
Williams (1636)
provident... 4. wise 6. frugal, saving
7. prudent, thrifty 9. judicious
10. economical 11. precautious,
preparatory
providential... 5. lucky 7. prudent
9. opportune, provident
10. miraculous 11. foresighted
province... 4. area, beat, nome
5. arena, range, shire, tract
6. colony, domain, empire, eparch,
region, sphere 7. circuit, diocese,
kingdom 8. district 9. territory
10. palatinate (royal) 12. jurisdiction
provincial... 4. rude 5. crude, local,
rural 6. narrow 7. insular, limited
8. suburban 10. restricted,
uncultured 11. countrified
12. narrow–minded
15. unsophisticated
provincialism (diction)... 6. patois
10. patavinity
provision... 4. fare, food 5. board,
stock, store 6. vivres 7. proviso
9. condition 11. preparation
provisional... 9. makeshift, temporary,
tentative 10. promissory, substitute
11. conditional, preparatory
12. experimental 14. circumstantial
provision seller (Mil)... 6. sutler

proviso... 5. salvo 6. clause
provocative... 9. desirable, provoking
10. appetizing, stirring up, suggestive
11. interesting
provoke... 3. ire, vex 4. bate, goad,
move, rile, spur, stir 5. anger,
annoy, start 6. arouse, incite, induce,
invite, invoke, nettle, offend, stir up,
summon 7. incense 8. irritate
9. challenge 10. antagonize,
exasperate
provoking... 8. annoying, exciting
10. suggestive 11. interesting
12. antagonizing
provoking laughter... 7. risible
prow... 3. bow 4. beak, duty, good,
proa, stem 5. brave, honor, prore
6. steven 7. courage, gallant, gun
deck
prowess... 5. valor 9. gallantry
proximal... 9. immediate (opp of distal)
proximate... 4. next 6. direct
7. closest, nearest 9. immediate
10. succeeding
proximity... 8. nearness, nighness,
relation, vicinity 9. adjacence,
closeness 11. propinquity
proxy... 5. agent, power 6. agency,
ballot, deputy 7. proctor 9. authority
10. procurator, substitute
prudence... 6. virtue, wisdom
7. caution, economy 8. sagacity
9. foresight 11. calculation,
forethought 13. judiciousness
14. circumspection
prudent... 4. wary, wise 5. canny
6. frugal 8. cautious, discreet
9. judicious, penny–wise, provident
10. economical 11. circumspect,
considerate
prudish... 4. prim 8. priggish
prune... 3. cut, lop 4. clip, food, frog,
plum, trim, weed 5. dress, plume,
preen, purge, shape 6. anoint 7. cut
down, tonsure 9. simpleton
prunelike fruit... 9. myrobalan
pruning knife... 8. serpette
prurient... 7. itching, longing, lustful
10. lascivious
Prussia...
 bay.. 4. Kiel 6. Danzig
 10. Pomeranian
 cathedral city.. 5. Essen 7. Cologne
 10. Düsseldorf
 city.. 6. Aachen
 color.. 4. blue 12. gold pheasant
 Knight.. 8. Noachite
 lagoon.. 4. haff 12. Frisches Haff
 lancer.. 5. Uhlan
 land aristocracy.. 6. Junker
 legislature.. 7. Landtag
 mountain.. 4. Harz
 resort.. 3. Ems
 river.. 3. Ems 4. Elbe, Oder, Saar
 seaport.. 4. Kiel 5. Emden 7. Stettin
 State.. 6. German
pry... 4. nose, peek 5. lever, mouse,
snoop 6. meddle, search
prying... 7. curious, peeking, peeping,
peering 8. snooping 9. searching
10. meddlesome 11. inquisitive
psalm (pert to)...

book.. 7. Psalter
Fiftieth, Vulgate.. 8. Miserere
Mass opening.. 7. introit
Ninety–fourth, Vulgate.. 6. Venite
Psalms (Old Test)... 7. Psalter
psalterium... 4. lyra 6. omasum
   7. stomach 9. manyplies
psammite... 4. rock 9. sandstone
psephology... 7. pebbles (study of)
psephomancy... 19. divination by
   pebbles
pseudatoll... 9. coral reef
pseudo... 4. sham 5. bogus, false
   6. untrue 7. feigned 8. spurious
   9. deceptive, imitation, pretender
pseudologist... 4. liar (humorous)
pseudology... 5. lying 9. falsehood
pseudonym... 5. alias 6. anonym
   7. pen name 10. nom de plume
pseudonym (famed)...
   C L Dodgson.. 12. Lewis Carroll
   Mary Ann Evans.. 11. George Eliot
   Samuel Clemens.. 9. Mark Twain
   W S Porter.. 6. O Henry
psychagogic... 9. inspiring
   10. attractive, persuasive
psyche... 4. mind, self, soul 6. spirit
psychic... 6. mental 9. spiritual
   10. Gnosticism 11. incorporeal
   12. spiritualist, supernatural
   13. psychological
psychic (pert to)...
   emanation.. 4. aura
   devotion.. 6. autism
   monism.. 10. one reality
psychotic... 3. mad 6. insane
   8. neurotic 12. psychopathic
Ptah (pert to)...
   Egypt Relig.. 8. chief god (of
   Memphis)
   father of.. 3. men 4. gods
   representation.. 5. mummy
   symbolic of.. 4. life 8. strength
ptarmigan... 4. rype 6. grouse
pterodactyl... 7. reptile (extinct)
   9. pterosaur 11. ornithosaur
pterography *(description of)*...
   8. feathers
pteroid... 8. fernlike, winglike
pteropod... 6. Clione (Arctic)
   7. mollusk
ptilosis... 7. plumage 9. madarosis
   10. loss of hair 15. loss of
   eyelashes
ptisan... 3. tea 5. drink 6. coddle
   9. decoction
Ptolemy (pert to)...
   author of.. 8. Almagest
   birthplace.. 5. Egypt (130 AD)
   famed as.. 10. astronomer,
   geographer
public... 3. inn 4. open 5. state
   6. people, vulgar 8. communal
   9. clientele, community
public (pert to)...
   assembly.. 4. Diet
   conveyance.. 3. bus, cab, car 4. taxi,
   tram 5. train 10. jinrikisha (jinricksha)
   display.. 10. exhibition
   13. exhibitionism
   edict.. 3. ban 12. proclamation

entertainment.. 7. ridotto
hangman (Eng).. 9. Jack Ketch
lands.. 4. ager (Hist) 6. domain
official.. 6. notary
position.. 8. official
storehouse.. 5. étape
walk.. 4. mall 7. alameda
   9. esplanade, promenade
publication... 4. book 8. pamphlet,
   printing 12. notification, proclamation,
   promulgation
publication (pert to)...
   article.. 7. feature
   condensed.. 7. tabloid
   make–up.. 6. format
   prelim.. 9. prodromus
publicist... 5. solon 6. Gallup, lawyer,
   writer 10. journalist, publicizer
   11. commentator
publish... 4. edit, vent 5. issue, print
   6. blazon, delate 7. divulge
   8. proclaim 10. promulgate
   11. disseminate
publish (pert to)...
   abroad.. 8. promulge
   after death.. 10. posthumous
   banns.. 7. betroth 8. marriage
   far and wide.. 6. blazon
   without authority.. 6. pirate
   10. plagiarize
publisher's description (book)...
   5. blurb 13. advertisement
publisher's inscription (book)...
   5. facts 8. colophon
Puccini heroine... 4. Mimi
pucker... 4. fold 5. bulge, purse
   6. crease 7. anxiety, fluster, wrinkle
   8. contract
puckered... 7. bullate 8. wrinkled
   10. contracted
puckish... 6. impish 8. Pucklike
   10. mysterious 11. mischievous
pud... 3. paw 4. hand 8. forefoot
pudding... 4. duff, mush, plum, sago
   6. junket 7. custard, dessert, tapioca
   8. roly–poly, softness, stuffing (game)
   9. Yorkshire
puddle... 3. mud 4. mess, pond, pool
   5. plash, swamp 6. muddle
   7. plashet, pollute
puddle duck... 7. mallard
puddock... 4. kite, toad 7. buzzard
   9. enclosure (paddock)
pueblo... 4. town 7. village
Pueblo (pert to)...
   ceremonial chamber.. 4. kiva
   Indian (American).. 4. Hopi, Piro,
   Tano, Zuni 5. Acoma 7. Keresan
   12. cliff dweller
   water jar.. 4. olla
puerile... 4. weak 5. young
   7. babyish, trivial 8. childish,
   juvenile, youthful 12. simple–minded
Puerto Rican (pert to)...
   bark, beverage.. 4. mabi
   dove.. 4. rola
   fish.. 4. sama, sisi 8. porkfish
Puerto Rico... see also *Puerto Rican*
   capital.. 7. San Juan
   city.. 5. Ponce 7. Arecibo
   discoverer.. 8. Columbus
   first settlement.. 7. Caparra

government.. 12. Commonwealth
Indian name.. 9. Borinquen
island (off shore).. 4. Mona
  7. Culebra
island group.. 15. Greater Antilles
politically.. 12. Commonwealth
program (Polit).. 18. Operation
  Bootstrap
sea.. 9. Caribbean
puff... 4. blow, blub, chug, flam, pant,
  pegh (Scot), pouf, waff 5. elate
  7. efflate
puffbird... 6. barbet 8. barbacou
pug... 3. dog, elf 4. moth, puck, snub
  5. chaff, dwarf 6. harlot, refuse
  (grain), sprite 8. bargeman, mistress,
  pugilist 9. footprint, hobgoblin
pugging... 8. grasping, thieving
pugilistic... 6. fistic 10. pugnacious
pugnacious... 9. combative
  11. belligerent, quarrelsome
pugnacious man... 12. fighting cock
pug–nosed... 5. camus (camuse)
puisne... 4. puny 5. judge, later, petty
  6. feeble, junior 9. associate,
  unskilled 10. law student, subsequent
  11. subordinate
puissance... 5. force, might, power
  8. strength 9. authority
puissant... 6. mighty, potent
  7. mastery 8. forcible, powerful
  13. authoritative
pulchritude... 5. grace 6. beauty
  10. comeliness, loveliness
pule... 4. peep 5. cheep, whine
  7. ululate, whimper
pulicat... 8. bandanna (bandana)
puling... 6. sickly 7. babyish, howling,
  whining 8. childish, delicate
Pulitzer prizes... 6. awards
  10. journalism, literature
pull... 2. pu 3. lug, tow, tug 4. drag,
  draw, haul, yank 5. bouse, drink,
  tweak 6. effort, strain 7. attract,
  extract 9. influence 10. attraction
pull (pert to)...
apart.. 4. rend, tear 7. destroy
  8. demolish, enfeeble, separate
back.. 5. demur 6. recoil 7. retract
  8. withdraw
down.. 4. fell, raze 9. dismantle
off.. 3. pug 6. avulse, commit
  8. carry out 10. accomplish
one's leg.. 4. hoax, joke 7. deceive,
  flatter 8. hoodwink 9. make fun of
out.. 5. leave 6. secede 7. extract
  9. eradicate
up.. 4. stop 5. elate 6. aviate
  7. arraign, extract
pullet... 4. fowl 5. child 7. bivalve
  8. poullard
pulley (pert to)...
groove.. 5. gorge
grooved.. 5. fusee (fuzee)
part.. 4. arse
wheel.. 6. sheave (grooved)
pulp... 3. pap 4. marc, mash, mass
  5. chyme 8. magazine 10. fleshy
  part
pulpit... 4. ambo, bema, dais, desk
  5. stage 6. clergy 7. rostrum
  8. platform, scaffold

pulpy... 5. mushy 7. squashy
pulpy (pert to)...
dregs.. 5. magma
fruit.. 3. uva 4. pome 6. sidder
  (siddow)
state.. 4. mash, soft 6. fleshy
pulsate... 4. beat, drum 5. throb
  7. vibrate
pulsation... 5. ictus 6. moving, rhythm
  7. impulse, systole 8. acrotism
  (failure), vitality 9. throbbing, vibrating
pulsatory... 8. rhythmic, systolic
  9. throbbing
pulse... 3. dal (split) 5. seeds (edible),
  throb 6. rhythm 7. beating
  8. resonate 9. pulsation, throbbing
pulse family... 3. pea 8. Fabaceae
pulverize... 4. bray, mull 5. crush,
  grind 6. abrade, powder 7. atomize
  8. levigate 9. triturate
  12. disintegrate
pulverulent... 5. dusty 7. crumbly
  8. powdered
puma... 6. cougar 7. Quechua
  (Kochua)
pummel... 4. beat, maul 5. thump
  6. batter, buffet, hammer, pommel,
  strike
pump... 3. gin, ram 4. draw, emit,
  quiz 5. eject 6. elicit, propel
  7. extract 10. pulsometer
  11. interrogate
pumpernickel... 5. bread (Westphalian)
pump handle... 5. sweep, swipe
pumpkin (pert to)...
head.. 4. dolt 7. Puritan
  9. blockhead, Roundhead
seed.. 7. sunfish 8. sailboat
yam.. 11. sweet potato
pun... 4. yoke 8. paragram
  9. assonance, equivoque (equivoke),
  witticism 11. paronomasia
punch... 3. die 4. blow, poke, prod,
  tool 5. douse, drink, negus, paste
  6. liquor, pierce 7. mattoir (etcher's)
  8. beverage, puncture 9. perforate
  11. punch cattle
Punch and Judy dog... 4. Toby
Punch Bowl... 6. crater 9. graveyard
  (Honolulu), hot spring (Yellowstone)
puncheon... 3. die 4. cask 5. punch,
  stamp 6. dagger
puncher... 6. cowboy 10. cowpuncher,
  perforator
punching... 8. piercing 9. pertusion
punctilious... 4. nice 5. exact
  6. formal, strict 7. correct, precise
  8. exacting 9. observant
  10. meticulous, scrupulous
punctuation mark... 3. dot 4. dash,
  star 5. brace, breve, colon, comma,
  tilde 6. dagger, hyphen, period, tittle,
  umlaut 8. brackets, ellipsis
  9. ampersand, semicolon
  10. apostrophe, circumflex
  11. exclamation 12. question mark
pundit... 6. nestor, savant 7. Brahmin,
  scholar, teacher 10. learned man
pung... 4. sled 6. sleigh
pungent... 4. keen, racy, sour, tart
  5. acrid, acute, sharp, smart, snell
  6. biting, bitter 7. caustic, odorous,

painful, peppery, piquant 8. piercing, poignant, stabbing 11. stimulating
pungent herb... 6. Asarum
punish... 4. fine 5. mulct, spank, wreak 6. amerce 7. chasten, correct 8. chastise, penalize 9. castigate 10. discipline
punishment (pert to)...
  Brehon law.. 4. eric
  by torture.. 9. strappado
  church.. 15. excommunication
  condign.. 11. retributive
  law.. 5. peine
  term.. 5. penal 7. penalty, revenge 8. punitive
  Turk, Chin.. 9. bastinade
  Welsh law (anc).. 3. cro 7. galanas
punitive... 5. penal 10. revengeful, vindictive 11. castigatory
Punjab, India...
  capital.. 6. Lahore (West) 8. Amritsar (East)
  language.. 7. Panjabi
  name meaning.. 10. Five Rivers
  soldier.. 4. Sikh
  summer capital.. 5. Simla
punk... 3. bad 5. child 6. amadou 7. lighter 8. inferior 9. touchwood
punto... 3. hit 5. joint (fencing) 6. stitch (needle)
puny... 4. weak 5. frail, petty 6. little, meager, puisne, sickly 8. delicate 14. inconsiderable
pupa... 5. shell 9. chrysalis
pupil... 3. eye, son 4. tyro 5. élève, youth 7. écolier, learner, scholar 8. disciple, neophyte
puppet... 3. guy 4. doll 5. image 6. maumet 9. miniature, nonentity 10. figurehead, marionette
puppeteer, famed... 4. Sarg
puppy... 3. dog, fop 5. shark, whelp
purblind... 10. dim–sighted 11. partly blind 12. narrow–minded, undiscerning
purchasable... 5. venal 8. bribable, hireling 9. mercenary 11. corruptible
purchase... 3. buy, win 4. earn, hold 5. bribe 6. buying, obtain 7. acquire, bribery, procure 8. barratry, foothold, leverage
purchaser... 5. buyer 6. patron, vendee 8. customer 9. acquéreur 13. adjudicataire
purdah (Ind)... 4. veil 6. screen 7. curtain
pure... 4. neat, real 5. clean, fresh, godly, sheer, utter 6. candid, chaste, simple, vestal 7. genuine, perfect, refined, unmixed 8. absolute, filtered, innocent 9. downright, faultless, inviolate, stainless, undefiled, unsullied 11. pure–blooded, uncorrupted, unqualified 13. unadulterated
purga (Russ)... 8. blizzard 9. snowstorm
purgative... 5. jalap 6. physic 8. absterge 9. catharsis, cathartic, cleansing
purgatory... 4. hell 5. limbo 6. erebus 7. torment
purified... 10. elutriated

purified wool fat... 7. lanolin (lanoline)
purify... 5. clean, purge 6. filter, refine, spurge 7. cleanse, epurate 8. lustrate, renovate, sanctify 9. elutriate
purifying... 7. smectic 8. depurant 9. cathartic, cleansing 10. distilling
Purim... 7. holiday 8. festival (Jew) 11. Feast of Lots
puritan... 5. prude 7. ascetic 9. precisian 10. Separatist
puritan clergyman... 10. Cartwright
puritanical... 6. strict 7. ascetic 11. strait–laced 13. hyperorthodox
purity... 8. chastity 9. innocence
purl... 4. eddy 5. frill 6. murmur, ripple 7. trickle
purloin... 5. filch, steal, swipe 6. finger 11. appropriate
purple... 4. bice, lake, plum, puce 5. lilac, mauve, pansy, regal, showy 6. damson, orchid, ornate, Tyrian, violet 7. Cassius, magenta, mollusk, pigment 8. amaranth, Burgundy, imperial, mulberry 9. brilliant, cathedral 11. sovereignty
purple (pert to)...
  bottle.. 4. moss
  cactus.. 8. Missouri
  death adder.. 10. black snake
  emperor.. 9. butterfly
  Forbidden City.. 5. Lhasa
  granadilla.. 13. passion flower
  haw.. 7. capulin (Mex) 8. bluewood
  Heart, Order of.. 5. medal (Mil) (est by Washington, re–est.1932)
  laurel.. 12. rhododendron
  lily.. 8. Turk's cap
  martin.. 7. swallow
  navy.. 10. marine blue
  nightshade.. 9. trompillo
purport... 4. feck, gist, mean 5. sense, tenor 6. allege, import, intent 7. meaning 9. substance
purpose... 3. aim, end 4. goal, idly, main, plan, sake 5. avail 6. design, intend, intent, motive 7. meaning, resolve 8. function 9. determine, discourse, intention, objective, predesign
purposive... 5. telic
purse... 3. bag, cly 5. pouch 6. pucker, wallet 7. wrinkle 8. crumenal (obs) 10. pocketbook 12. porte–monnaie
purser... 5. clerk (ship's) 6. bursar 7. boucher, cashier 9. paymaster
purse rat... 12. pocket gopher
pursue... 3. run 4. hunt, seek, tack 5. chase, court 6. follow 7. carry on, proceed 9. persecute 10. specialize
pursuit... 5. chase, quest, scent 9. objective 10. occupation
purvey... 5. cater 6. supply 7. foresee, provide
purveyor of untruth (Bib)... 7. Ananias
purview... 4. body (statute) 5. field (law), range, scope 7. compass 8. province
push... 2. go 4. bunt, butt, gang,

ping, pole, prod, urge 5. crowd, elbow, impel, nudge, press, shove 6. attack, energy, propel, thrust 9. importune, offensive (Mil) 10. forge ahead, propulsion 12. press forward

pusillanimous . . . 4. base, weak 5. timid 6. craven 8. cowardly 12. fainthearted, mean–spirited

put . . . 3. set 4. butt, dupe, fool, sail 5. place, throw 6. impose, option, phrase, repose, rustic 7. deposit 8. invest in 9. attribute

put (pert to) . . .
an end to . . 5. quash (law)
away . . 4. kill 5. store 6. murder
back . . 6. demote 7. replace, restore
before . . 6. appose
down . . 6. humble 7. degrade, deposit, depress 8. suppress
forth . . 5. exert 7. propose 9. circulate
off . . 4. doff, haft, sail 5. defer, delay, evade 8. postpone
on alert . . 5. alarm 6. alarum
out . . 3. vex 4. oust 5. eject 9. ostracize 10. expatriate
over . . 4. bilk 5. cheat, trick 7. deceive

put in, into . . .
action . . 6. excite
holy place . . 8. enshrine
motion . . 6. arouse
opposition . . 3. pit
order . . 4. trim 5. mense 6. settle 7. arrange 8. organize 11. systematize
rapture . . 8. entrance
relation to . . 9. correlate 10. coordinate, co–ordinate
rhythm . . 5. meter
scabbard . . 7. sheathe

putrefaction . . . 3. rot 5. decay 13. decomposition 14. disintegration

puttee . . . 6. gaiter 7. legging

put to . . .
flight . . 4. rout
strain . . 3. tax
trouble . . 10. discommode
use . . 5. apply
wrong use . . 8. misapply

put up . . . 3. pay 4. ante, hang 5. build, offer 6. pledge 7. install 8. nominate 9. construct

put up with . . . 4. bear 5. stand 6. endure, permit 7. stomach 8. tolerate

puzzle . . . 3. cap 4. crux, pose 5. griph (griphus), poser, rebus 6. enigma, riddle 7. anagram, confuse, mystify, nonplus, paradox, perplex, problem 8. entangle 9. conundrum 10. complicate, disconcert

puzzle (pert to) . . .
monkey . . 5. piñon
picture . . 5. rebus
word . . 7. charade 9. crossword 10. anacrostic

puzzling . . . 6. knotty 10. perplexing 11. enigmatical, paradoxical

pygarg, pygargus . . . 5. addax 8. sea eagle 9. quadruped (Bib)

Pygmalion (pert to) . . .

color . . 5. brown
endowed with life . . 7. Galatea (statue)
king of . . 6. Cyprus
sister . . 4. Dido
talented as . . 8. sculptor

pygmy, pigmy . . . 3. elf 4. Akka, Doko, pixy 5. atomy, Batwa, dwarf, gnome, minim, short 6. Abongo, Achuas 7. manikin 9. dandiprat

pygmy (pert to) . . .
hog . . 7. Porcula
musk deer . . 10. chevrotain
owl . . 8. gnome owl
rattlesnake . . 10. massasauga
squirrel (smallest known) . . 9. Sciuridae

pyic . . . 8. purulent, virulent

pyknic . . . 3. fat 5. round, stout

pylon . . . 4. post 5. tower 6. marker 7. gateway 14. monumental mass

pyosis . . . 3. pus 4. boil 11. suppuration

pyramid . . . 4. cone, heap, pile, tomb 5. tower 8. monument 9. speculate

pyramid (pert to) . . .
builder, largest . . 6. Cheops (khufu)
Egypt . . 9. The Sphinx 12. Great Pyramid, Tomb of Cheops
group . . 5. Gizeh 7. Menkare 8. Chephren 9. Mycerinus
kidney (Anat) . . 7. Perrein 10. Malpighian
Mexico . . 7. Benares
site of Cheops . . 4. Giza (Gizeh)
texts . . 12. inscriptions 13. Book of the Dead
world wonder . . 12. Great Pyramid, Tomb of Cheops

pyramidal . . . 4. huge 7. angular, conical 8. enormous, imposing

pyre . . . 4. bier, heap, pile 9. cremation, death fire

Pyrenees (pert to) . . .
bandit . . 8. Miquelet
mountain chain . . 11. France–Spain
peak . . 9. Pic d'Aneto 11. Pic de Méthou
resort . . 3. Pau
State . . 7. Andorra (Fr)

pyriform . . . 10. pear–shaped

pyrology (study of) . . . 4. heat

pyromaniac . . . 7. firebug 8. arsonist 10. incendiary

pyrope . . . 3. red 6. garnet 7. mineral

pyrophobia . . . 11. dread of fire

pyrotechnics . . . 7. oratory, science 9. fireworks

pyrrhic . . . 4. foot (Pros) 5. dance

Pyrrhic victory . . . 11. at great cost

pyrrho (comb form) . . . 3. red 5. tawny

Pyrrho (Gr) . . . 7. teacher (Pyrrhonism)

pyrrhotist . . . 7. redhead

Pyrrhulexia . . . 5. finch 8. grosbeak

Pythagorus (Gr) . . .
birthplace . . 5. Samos
daughter . . 4. Camo
famed as . . 11. philosopher
friend . . 5. Damon
teacher of . . 8. theorems 18. influence of numbers

Pythian (pert to) . . .
contests . . 6. Delphi
Festival . . 11. Panhellenic

patron.. 6. Apollo
term.. 8. ecstatic 9. phrenetic
python... 3. boa 8. anaconda
Python (pert to)...
  home.. 11. Mt Parnassus
  myth.. 14. monster serpent
  slaver.. 6. Apollo
  survivor of.. 10. muddy earth (anc)
pythonic... 4. huge 6. Pythia (Delphi),

python 8. oracular 9. monstrous
pythonism, art of... 8. prophecy
  10. divination
pyx, pix... 3. box 4. test, veil
  5. chest 6. coffer, vessel (Eccl)
  8. binnacle, ciborium 10. tabernacle
pyxie... 5. shrub 9. evergreen
pyxis... 3. box 4. Argo (Astron), vase
  9. jewel case

Q

Q... 5. queue 6. letter (17th)
QED... 21. Quod Erat Demonstrandum
Q–ship (Eng)... 11. mystery ship
qua, quabird... 10. night heron
quachil... 12. pocket gopher
quack... 3. cry (duck) 5. faker
  7. empiric 8. impostor 9. charlatan,
  pretender 10. medicaster,
  mountebank
quack medicine... 6. patent
  7. nostrum
quad (pert to)...
  printing.. 5. crown 7. quadrat
  school.. 4. yard 6. campus
  10. quadrangle
  slang (Brit).. 5. horse
quadra... 6. fillet, listel, plinth
quadragenarian... 12. forty–year–old
  (person)
Quadragesima... 4. Fast, Lent
  6. Sunday (1st in Lent) 7. Holy Day
  9. Forty Days
quadrangle... 5. plane (four–angles)
  6. square 7. rhombus 8. tetragon
quadrant... 4. gill 6. fourth
  7. measure, quarter 8. farthing, six
  hours 10. instrument, semicircle
quadrate... 4. suit 5. adapt, agree,
  ideal 6. square 7. conform, perfect,
  squared 8. balanced 10. correspond
  13. correspondent
quadriga... 3. car 7. chariot (4–horse)
  10. four horses
quadrumane... 3. ape 6. mammal
  7. gorilla, Primate (except Man)
  10. chimpanzee 13. feetlike hands
quadruped... 3. ass, cat, cow, dog
  4. bull, calf, colt, foal, lion, mule
  5. burro, horse, jenny, panda, tiger
  6. badger, donkey, mammal
  7. bullock 10. four–footed
quaff... 5. draft, drink 6. tipple
quag... 5. quake 6. quiver 8. quagmire
quagga... 5. zebra 7. wild ass
quaggy... 5. boggy, fenny 6. spongy
  7. queachy 8. yielding
quagmire... 3. bay, fen 4. lair
  5. marsh, swamp 6. morass
  11. predicament
quahog... 4. clam
quail... 3. cow 4. bird 5. colin, cower,

quake, shake 6. blench, curdle,
flinch, shrink, tremor, Turnix
  7. massena, tremble 8. bobwhite,
  Coturnix 9. coagulate, courtesan,
  eddish hen
quail (pert to)...
  button.. 6. Turnix
  call.. 4. pipe
  color.. 9. hair brown
  flock.. 4. bevy
  French.. 6. caille
  hawk.. 6. falcon
  quailhead.. 11. lark sparrow
  snipe.. 9. dowitcher
quaint... 3. odd 4. wise 5. proud
  6. expert, pretty, proper 7. curious,
  prudent, refined, strange, uncouth
  8. fanciful, peculiar
quake... 5. shake 6. quiver, shiver,
  tremor 7. shudder, tremble, vibrate
  10. earthquake
Quaker (pert to)...
  bird.. 9. albatross (sooty)
  city.. 12. Philadelphia
  colonizer.. 4. Penn (Wm)
  color.. 4. drab, gray 5. acier
  poet.. 6. Barton 8. Whittier
  sect.. 16. Society of Friends
  sect founder.. 9. George Fox
  State.. 12. Pennsylvania
qualified... 3. fit 4. able 6. fitted
  7. adapted, capable, enabled, limited
  8. eligible, entitled, equipped,
  modified, prepared, tempered
  9. competent 10. restrained,
  restricted 11. conditional
qualify... 3. fit 4. name 5. abate,
  adapt, be fit, equip, limit, train
  6. enable, modify, soften, temper
  7. assuage, prepare 8. diminish,
  mitigate, modulate, quantify, regulate,
  restrain, restrict
quality... 5. prime, trait, value
  6. nature, pathos, strain 7. caliber,
  texture 8. accident, capacity, inferior,
  nobility, property 9. attribute,
  character, specialty 10. difference,
  excellence 14. characteristic
quality of heredity... 9. lineality
qualm... 4. pall 5. demur, doubt,
  spasm 6. nausea, regret 7. scruple

9. faintness, misgiving
11. compunction 12. apprehension
quandary... 3. fix 6. pickle, plight,
strait 7. dilemma 10. perplexity
11. predicament
quandy... 9. squaw duck
quant... 11. punting pole
quantity... 3. ace, any, gob, lot, sea,
sum 4. bulk, dose, drop, mass, much,
raff, raft, scad, size, some 5. batch,
scads, store 6. amount, cupful,
degree, extent, hatful, number, oceans
7. handful
quantity (pert to)...
fixed.. 5. quota 8. constant
mathematics.. 4. surd 5. graph
6. scalar, vector
minute.. 4. atom, dram, iota, mill
standard.. 4. unit 9. allotment
time unit.. 4. rate
quantum... 4. body 5. share
6. amount, energy, theory 7. atomics,
portion 8. quantity
quap... 5. heave, throb 6. quaver
9. palpitate
Quapaw... 5. Sioux 8. Arkansas
11. Indian tribe
quarantine... 7. confine, isolate
8. pratique (marine) 9. forty days
(law), isolation, segregate
11. confinement
quarantine flag... 6. yellow
7. warning 10. yellow jack
quarenden... 5. apple (deep red)
quarentene... 4. rood 7. furlong
quark... 3. caw 5. croak, quawk
quarl, quarle... 4. sour, tile 5. brick
6. cundle, medusa 9. jellyfish
quarred... 6. soured 7. curdled (beer)
quarrel... 3. row 4. spat, tiff, tile
5. arrow, brawl, broil, cavil, flite
(flyte), gnarr, scene, scrap 6. affray,
bicker, chisel, dustup, hassle
7. diamond, wrangle 8. argument,
squabble 9. complaint
10. accusation, Donnybrook,
free–for–all 11. altercation
12. disagreement
16. misunderstanding
quarrel (pert to)...
hereditary.. 4. feud 8. vendetta
noisy.. 6. fracas, jangle, uproar
over.. 6. bicker 7. contend, dispute
petty.. 4. miff, spat, tiff
quarrelsome... 8. choleric, petulant
9. irascible, irritable, litigious
10. discordant, pugnacious
11. belliferent, contentious
13. argumentative
quarry... 4. delf, game, heap, mine,
prey 6. victim 8. entrails, excavate
12. object hunted
quart... 5. gills (eight) 6. fourth
7. measure 8. schooner
quarter... 4. coin, side 5. house
6. fourth, region 7. measure, two bits
8. insignia, semester 9. direction,
dismember 10. quadrature (Astron),
quadrisect
quarter (pert to)...
acre.. 4. rood
animal.. 5. horse

astronomy.. 10. quadrature
fathom.. 6. fourth
military.. 8. clemency (to enemy)
music.. 4. note 8. crotchet
nautical.. 4. deck, lift 6. galley
pint.. 4. gill
sports.. 4. back 11. quarterback
quartered... 8. billeted
12. quartersawed (wood)
quarters (living)... 4. camp, room
5. abode 7. housing, lodging, shelter
8. barracks, diggings, lodgings,
lodgment 9. dormitory
Quartodeciman... 10. paschalist
quartz... 4. onyx, sard 5. flint 6. silica
7. mineral
quartz (pert to)...
banded, spotted.. 4. onyx 5. agate
6. jasper 8. sardonyx
blue–red,. 10. bloodstone, heliotrope
brown.. 5. smoky 9. cairngorm
brownish–red.. 7. sinople
chalcedony.. 4. sard 9. carnelian
11. chrysoprase
flint.. 9. hornstone 10. touchstone
glass.. 6. silica
green.. 5. prase (dull) 6. plasma
(bright) 11. chrysoprase
hard.. 5. flint
opaque.. 6. jasper
purple.. 8. amethyst
red.. 4. sard 9. carnelian
ruby–red.. 7. rubasse
silica.. 5. silex
transparent.. 11. rock crystal
violet.. 8. amethyst
yellow.. 5. topaz (false) 7. citrine
quash... 4. cass, void 5. abate, annul,
crush, quell, shake 6. hush up,
subdue 7. shatter 8. suppress
9. overthrow 10. extinguish
quasi... 4. as if 6. pseudo 8. as it
were, as though 9. seemingly
Quasimodo... 9. Low Sunday (1st
after Easter)
quatern... 8. fourfold 10. quadrangle
12. four quarters (having)
quaver... 5. shake, trill 6. quiver
7. tremble, tremolo, vibrate
11. trepidation 13. tremulousness
quawk... 3. caw 5. heron (night)
7. screech 8. quagmire
quay, key... 4. pier 5. levee, wharf
7. landing
queachy... 5. boggy, bushy, fenny
6. marshy, swampy
quean... 4. girl, jade, slut 5. vixen,
wench 6. harlot
queasy... 4. sick 8. delicate, qualmish,
ticklish, troubled 9. hazardous, ill at
ease, nauseated, squeamish, uncertain,
unsettled
Quebec...
battle site.. 15. Plains of Abraham
capital.. 6. Quebec (province)
city.. 6. Verdun 8. Montreal
11. Three Rivers
founder.. 9. Champlain (1608)
river.. 10. St Lawrence
vehicle.. 7. calèche (2–wheeled)
quebrada... 3. gap 5. brook, gorge
7. fissure

qued, quede... 3. bad 4. evil 8. The Devil

queen... 3. ant, bee, cat 7. empress, goddess, monarch 8. chessman, honeybee 9. sovereign 10. chess piece 11. playing card

queen (pert to)...
bee.. 8. honeybee
cactus.. 7. Mexican 10. ornamental
conch.. 5. shell
fern.. 5. royal
pigeon.. 7. crowned

Queen (pert to)...
Bernice's Hair (Astron).. 13. Coma Berenices
City of the Lakes.. 7. Buffalo
City of the West.. 10. Cincinnati
Mab.. 11. Fairie Queen (Rom/Juliet)
Victoria.. 14. Widow of Windsor (nickname by Kipling)

Queen Anne's...
lace.. 6. carrot (wild)
melon.. 6. dudaim
War.. 17. Spanish Succession
War treaty.. 14. Peace of Utrecht

queen of...
chess.. 4. fers
fairies.. 3. Mab 7. Titania 8. Gloriana
gods.. 4. Hera (Gr), Juno (Rom)
Hearts.. 9. Elizabeth
heaven.. 10. Virgin Mary
Isles (Brit).. 6. Albion
night.. 4. moon
Sheba.. 6. Balkis (Koran)
Spades (solo).. 5. basta
the Adriatic.. 6. Venice
the Antilles.. 4. Cuba
the East.. 7. Antioch (Syria), Batavia (Java), Zenobia
the tides.. 7. the moon
the underworld.. 3. Hel

queen's (pert to)...
arm.. 6. musket
flower.. 9. bloodwood
hub.. 7. tobacco
July flower.. 8. damewort
ware.. 9. Wedgewood

Queensland (Austral)...
animal.. 8. kangaroo 9. koala bear (teddy bear)
bean.. 8. snuffbox
capital.. 8. Brisbane
fire tree.. 5. tulip
fish.. 9. trumpeter
hemp.. 4. sida 6. lucern 9. jellyleaf 11. paddy lucern
plum.. 8. Burdekin
tree (timber).. 3. box 4. pine 5. beech, ebony 10. sandalwood 12. Dundathu pine

queer... 3. odd, rum 4. sham 5. false, funny 6. insane, thwart 7. strange 8. peculiar, singular, spurious 9. eccentric, fantastic, interfere 10. disconcert, suspicious 11. counterfeit 12. questionable

queer fellow... 4. coot, goop 6. galoot, geezer 9. character

queersome... 3. odd 7. strange 8. abnormal

Queer Street... 9. imaginary

queest... 8. ringdove

queet... 4. coot 5. ankle

quell... 3. end 4. calm 5. allay, crush, quash, quiet 6. pacify, reduce, soothe, stifle, subdue 7. destroy, repress 8. suppress 9. overpower 10. extinguish

quench... 4. cool, damp, sate 5. allay, check, slake, still 6. stifle, subdue 7. assuage, gratify 8. suppress 10. discourage, extinguish 11. clamp down on

quenelle... 8. meatball

Quercus... 4. oaks

queriman... 4. fish 6. mullet

quern... 4. mill (grain)

quernal... 5. crown (oak leaves)

querulous... 7. fretful, peevish 9. plaintive 11. complaining 12. faultfinding

query... 5. doubt 6. murmur 7. inquire, inquiry, whining 8. question

quest... 3. bay (dog's) 4. hunt, seek 6. desire, pursue, search 7. inquest, request 8. seek alms 9. adventure 12. solicitation

question... 3. ask 4. quiz 5. cavil, doubt, grill, poser, query, scout, topic 6. riddle 7. dispute, inquire, inquiry, problem 8. erotesis 9. catechize (catechise) 11. interrogate, uncertainty 12. interpellate (formally) 13. interrogation

question, out of the... 6. absurd 7. refused 8. hopeless, rejected 10. impossible, prohibited 11. unthinkable

questionable... 4. moot 7. dubious 8. doubtful 9. debatable, dishonest, uncertain 10. disputable, improbable 12. unbelievable 13. problematical

questioning (prolonged)...
11. inquisition

question mark... 7. erotema, eroteme 9. guillemot

quet... 3. auk 5. murre 9. guillemot

quethe... 3. say 4. call, tell, will 5. quoth, speak 6. clamor 8. bequeath 9. testament

quetzal, quezal... 6. trogon 14. national emblem (Guatemala)

Quetzalcoatl... 10. god of winds (Aztec)

queue... 3. cue 4. hair, line (waiting), tail 7. pigtail 9. lance rest

quey... 6. heifer

quia–quia... 9. cigarfish

quib, quibble... 3. pun 4. carp, quip 5. argue, cavil, cheta, evade 7. shuffle

Quiche, Indian... 5. Mayan

quick... 3. apt 4. deft, fast, yare 5. agile, alert, brisk, fiery, fleet, hasty, rapid, ready, smart, swift 6. lively, nimble, presto, prompt, pronto, speedy, sudden 7. animate 9. dexterous, impatient, impulsive, sprightly, vital part 10. passionate 11. expeditious, hot–tempered

quicken... 5. hurry, rouse, speed 6. excite, hasten, incite, revive, vivify 7. animate, further, refresh, sharpen

8. energize, expedite 9. stimulate
10. accelerate 11. resuscitate
12. reinvigorate
quickly... 4. cito, fast, soon 5. apace
6. presto, pronto 7. briefly, hastily,
rapidly 8. promptly, speedily, vigorous
quickness... 4. nous (humor) 5. haste
6. acumen 7. acidity, agility
8. alacrity, celerity, dispatch,
pungency, rapidity 9. acuteness,
briskness, fleetness, sharpness,
smartness 10. expedition, promptness
13. impulsiveness
quicksand... 3. bog 4. syrt 6. Syrtis
quickset... 5. hedge 7. thicket
8. hawthorn
quicksilver... 5. metal 7. mercury
quid... 4. cud, fid 6. guinea
7. essence, tobacco 9. sovereign
quidam... 8. somebody 10. one
unknown
quidnunc... 6. gossip 7. what now
11. inquisitive
quid pro quo... 9. tit for tat
10. equivalent, substitute
11. interchange
quiescent... 5. quiet, still 6. at rest,
latent, silent, static 8. sleeping
10. motionless
quiet... 2. sh 3. pet 4. calm, ease,
hush, lull, mild 5. peace, sober, still
6. gentle, hushed, modest, placid,
smooth, soothe 7. halcyon, restful,
silence 8. peaceful, tranquil
9. contented, peaceable, quiescent,
reposeful, unruffled 10. unmolested
11. undisturbed
quietist... 6. mystic (Quietism)
quietive... 8. sedative
quietly... 6. calmly, gently, simply
8. modestly, silently 9. patiently,
peaceably, privately 10. composedly
11. noiselessly 16. unostentatiously
quietude... 4. rest 5. peace 6. repose
7. silence 10. quiescence
12. tranquillity (tranquility)
quietus... 4. mort, obit 5. death
6. defeat 7. release 9. acquittal,
deathblow, discharge (of debt)
quiff... 4. coif, puff 5. whiff
quilkin... 4. frog, toad
quill... 3. cop, pen 5. remex
6. bobbin 7. spindle
quilt... 3. pad 4. flog, gulp 5. duvet
6. caddow 7. swallow 8. coverlet
9. patchwork 11. comfortable,
counterpane
quin... 7. scallop
quincentenary... 11. anniversary
13. commemoration 16. five hundred
years
quindecemvir (Rom)... 10. custodians
(Sibylline Books), fifteen men
quink... 5. brant, goose
quinoa... 6. cereal 7. pigweed
Quinquagesima Sunday... 10. before
Lent 12. Shrove Sunday
quinque (comb form)... 4. five
quinsy... 10. sore throat 11. tonsillitis
quint... 3. tax (one 5th) 7. E string
8. interval, schooner (5–masted)
9. organ stop

quintal... 13. hundredweight
quintessence... 3. col 5. elite 6. elixir
7. essence, the best 10. perfection
quip... 3. mot 4. gibe, jest 5. sally,
taunt 6. oddity 7. caprice, quibble
8. gimcrack 9. witticism
12. equivocation
quires, twenty... 4. ream 6. sheets
(20)
quirk... 4. quip, turn 5. clock, shift,
twist 7. caprice, evasion, quibble
8. flourish 9. deviation, mannerism,
witticism 12. eccentricity
quirt... 4. whip 5. romal
quis... 8. woodcock
quisby... 5. idler, queer 8. bankrupt
10. down and out
quit... 3. rid 4. free, stop 5. cease,
clear, leave, pay up, repay, yield
6. depart, resign 7. abandon,
discard, forsake, release, relieve,
require 8. abdicate, liberate,
renounce 9. surrender 10. relinquish
11. discontinue
quitclaim... 6. acquit 7. release
12. convey a claim 13. deed of
release 14. relinquishment
quite... 3. all, yes 4. very 5. stark,
truly 6. really, wholly 7. totally
8. entirely, somewhat 10. absolutely,
completely, positively
quite so... 8. that is so, very true,
very well
quite some... 12. considerable
quittance... 5. repay 6. return
7. requite 8. reprisal, requital
9. atonement, departure, repayment
10. recompense 11. acquittance
quitter... 5. piker 6. coward, truant
7. shirker, welsher
quiver... 4. case 5. quake, shake
6. quaver, sheath, shiver, tremor
7. flicker, tremble, tremolo, vibrate
11. trepidation
quiver leaf... 5. aspen
Quivira (pert to)...
famous for.. 6. wealth
sought by.. 8. Coronado (1541)
town site.. 6. Kansas
Quivira, Gran... 12. mission ruins
16. National Monument (N Mex)
qui vive... 5. alert 7. excited
9. challenge 12. who goes there
quixotic... 7. utopian 9. visionary
10. Don Quixote (like)
11. impractical
quiz... 4. hoax, jest, joke, mock
5. coach 6. banter 8. ridicule
11. examination, inquisitive,
interrogate, questioning
quizzical... 3. odd 7. amusing, teasing
9. bantering, eccentric, inquiring,
perplexed
quizzing... 6. banter 11. questioning
quizzing glass... 7. monocle
8. eyeglass
quod... 3. jug 6. prison 8. imprison
quoddies... 7. herring
quod erat demonstrandum... 3. QED
24. which was to be demonstrated
quodlibet... 6. medley 8. fantasia,
subtlety 13. what you please

quoit... 4. disc 6. discus
quoit pin... 3. hob
quoits... 4. game 8. cromlech
   10. stone cover
quo modo... 5. means 6. manner,
   method
quondam... 6. former 8. formerly,
   sometime
quorum... 7. council 8. majority
   10. select body
quota... 4. part 5. share 6. ration
   10. proportion
quotable... 7. citable
quotation... 5. chria, cital, motto,
   price, stock 7. passage 8. citation

   10. memorandum, repetition
quotation mark... 9. guillemet
quote... 4. cite, name 5. price
   6. adduce, repeat 7. extract
   9. quotation, reference
quoth... 4. said 5. spoke
quotha... 6. indeed 8. forsooth
quotidian... 5. daily 8. day by day,
   every day, ordinary 9. recurring
   11. commonplace
quotient... 6. number, result
quotity... 5. group, quota 7. integer
   10. collection
quotum... 5. quota, ratio
quo vadis... 16. whither goest thou
Quo Vadis tyrant... 4. Nero

R

R... 3. rho (Gr) 6. letter (18th)
Ra, Egypt Relig (pert to)...
   atmosphere.. 3. Shu
   god of.. 3. sun
   morning sun.. 7. Chepera, Khepera
   night sun.. 7. Sokaris
   representation.. 3. cat 4. lion
      5. Bacis (bull) 6. falcon 9. solar disk
   rising sun.. 5. Horus 9. Marmachis
   setting sun.. 3. Tem
   solar disk.. 4. Aten
   son.. 6. Khonsu
   son of.. 3. Nut (the sky)
   wife.. 3. Mut
raad... 15. electric catfish
raad... 7. council (S Afr) 9. volksraad
raadzaal... 11. council hall (S Afr)
rab... 5. mixer (mortar) 6. beater
Rab... 5. title 6. master, rabban
   7. teacher 8. Gamaliel
rabato, rebato... 4. ruff 6. collar
   9. piccadill
rabbet... 4. weld 5. miter 6. groove,
   recess 7. channel 8. dovetail
rabbi... 4. lord 5. rabat, title
   6. master 7. teacher 9. clergyman
   11. breastpiece
rabbi (pert to)...
   examiners.. 8. sabaraim (saboraim)
   interpreters.. 7. amoraim
   teachers.. 7. tannaim
rabbit... 4. cony (coney), hare, tyro
   5. bunny, lapin 6. animal, novice,
   rodent 10. cottontail 11. Belgian
   hare
rabbit (pert to)...
   breeding ground.. 6. warren
      8. rabbitry
   ear.. 7. antenna 8. toadflax
   female.. 3. doe
   fever.. 9. tularemia
   fiction.. 6. Harvey
   fish.. 8. chimaera 9. globefish,
      porcupine

   foot.. 5. charm 8. talisman
   fur.. 4. cony (coney) 5. lapin
   genus.. 5. Lepus
   male.. 4. buck
   mouthed.. 10. harelipped
   rat.. 9. bandicoot
   S America.. 6. tapeti
   shelter.. 5. hutch
   stew.. 12. hasenpfeffer
   tail.. 3. fud 4. scut
rabbitry... 5. hutch 6. warren
rabble... 3. mob 4. herd, raff, rout,
   skim, stir 5. crowd 6. ragtag, tumult
   7. bobtail 8. canaille, riffraff
   9. confusion, rigmarole, the masses
   12. accumulation (chaotic)
rabble rouser... 6. ragtag
Rabelais (Fr)... 6. author 8. satirist
   9. Gargantua (1st work)
rabid... 3. mad 6. raging 7. frantic,
   furious, rampant, violent 8. frenzied
   9. fanatical 10. infuriated
rabies... 5. lyssa 11. hydrophobia
raccoon, ally of... 5. coati, panda
race... 3. cut, hie, run 4. flow, lane,
   line, rush, slit, sort, stem 5. breed,
   caste, flume, relay, speed 6. course,
   family, nation, people, strain
   7. contest, regatta, running, scratch
   10. passageway 11. competition,
   watercourse
race (pert to ethnos)...
   ancient.. 4. Mede 6. Belgae, Sabine
      7. Hittite, Iberian, Walloon
   comb form.. 4. geno
   family.. 3. ilk 6. stirpo
   human.. 3. Man
   mythical.. 7. centaur
   prehistoric.. 5. Aryan, Brunn
   rule by.. 10. ethnocracy
   science of.. 9. ethnology
   undivided.. 9. holethnos
   wandering.. 5. gypsy (gipsy)
race (pert to horses)...

R
S

chariot .. 13. Circus Maximus
gait .. 4. lope, pace, trot
horse .. 4. pony 5. racer 6. maiden, mantis, plater 8. bangtail
handicap .. 6. impost
open .. 10. Donnybrook, free–for–all
racecourse, racetrack (pert to) ...
   3. lap 4. heat, oval, tout, turf 5. track 6. circus (anc), colors 7. raceway, tipster 8. dopester
Rachel (pert to) ...
daughter of .. 5. Laban
mother of .. 6. Joseph 8. Benjamin
sister of .. 4. Leah
wife of .. 5. Jacob
racing colors ... 5. silks
rack ... 3. gin 4. gait, gear, pain, ruin 5. agony, frame 6. punish, strain, wrench 7. agonize, support, torment, torture 9. framework 10. excruciate
rack (pert to) ...
barrel .. 3. job
comb .. 9. toothcomb
corn .. 4. crib
floating .. 5. vapor
plate .. 5. creel
skin of .. 6. rabbit
racket ... 3. bat, din 5. fraud, noise, revel 6. bustle, clamor, crosse, outcry, scheme 8. vocation 9. commotion 15. illicit business
rackety ... 5. noisy 8. clattery, exciting 9. turbulent 10. boisterous
racy ... 5. brisk, fresh, naive, smart, spicy 6. lively, risqué 7. piquant, pungent, zestful 8. eloquent, spirited, stirring 11. interesting 12. exhilarating, full–flavored
rad ... 4. unit 5. eager, quick, ready 6. afraid, elated 11. exhilarated
radar (pert to) ...
beacon .. 4. buoy 5. racon 6. ramark
navigation .. 5. navar
range (Navig) .. 5. loran 6. shoran
sight .. 5. scope 6. radome, screen 7. display
signal .. 3. pip 4. beam, blip 5. pulse 11. transceiver, transponder
sounding .. 5. rawin 9. ionosonde
television .. 7. teleran
raddle ... 3. rod 4. beat, twig 5. cheat, color, fence, hedge 6. branch, hurdle, ruddle, thrash 7. wheedle 10. interweave
radeau ... 4. raft 5. gloat
radial ... 3. ray 8. quadrant 9. diverging
radiance ... 5. beamy, glare, light, nitor, sheen 6. beauty, luster 7. beaming, glitter, glowing, lambent, shining 8. splendor 9. brilliant, radiation 10. brilliancy, effulgence 12. cheerfulness
radiant ... 5. aglow, beamy, sheen 7. beaming, glowing, lambent, shining 8. glorious 9. beautiful, diverging, effulgent 11. resplendent
radiate ... 4. beam, emit, shed 5. gleam, shine 7. diffuse, diverge, emanate 9. irradiate 10. illuminate
radiation ... 5. alpha (particle), light,

polar (point) 10. divergence 12. illumination 13. radiant energy
radiation unit ... 3. rad, rem 8. roentgen
radical ... 3. red 4. atom, left, root, surd 5. basic, radix, ultra, vital 7. capital, drastic, extreme 8. cardinal, reformer 9. extremist 10. foundation 11. fundamental
radicated ... 6. rooted 11. established
radicle ... 4. root 5. radix 6. etymon 7. rootlet
radio (pert to) ...
activity .. 7. fallout 9. radiation
antenna .. 6. aerial
detector .. 5. radar 11. transceiver
frequency .. 5. audio
interference .. 6. static
operator .. 2. CB 3. ham (amateur) 11. dit–da–artist 12. citizens' band
rays .. 5. beams
receiver, interfering .. 7. blooper
tube .. 4. grid 5. diode
radium (pert to) ...
discoverer .. 5. Curie (1898)
emanation .. 5. niton, radon
paint .. 8. luminous
source of .. 7. uranite 9. carnotite
radius ... 4. area, bone 5. spoke 6. circle, extent 8. diameter
radix ... 4. root 6. etymon, source 7. radical, radicle
raff ... 4. heap, rake, scum 5. sweep, trash 6. jumble, litter 7. rubbish 8. leavings, riffraff
raffia ... 4. palm 5. fiber 6. jupati
raffish ... 3. low 6. common, flashy, frowsy 7. unkempt 9. worthless 12. disreputable
raffle ... 6. chance, rabble, tangle 7. confuse, crumple, lottery, perplex, serrate 8. entangle, plucking, riffraff 9. stripping 10. plundering
raft ... 3. lot 4. spar 5. balsa, float 6. rafter 7. to flock 10. collection (large)
raft–breasted (Ornith) ... 6. ratite
raft duck ... 5. scoup 7. redhead 8. bluebill
rag ... 3. fog 4. mist, sail 5. cloth, scold, shred 6. berate, catkin, lichen, tatter 7. ragtime, remnant 8. farthing 9. hoarfrost 11. syncopation
rag (pert to) ...
bag .. 10. depository
doll .. 3. toy 6. moppet, puppet 10. marionette
fish .. 10. Icosteidae
rag picker .. 5. tramp
weed .. 3. Iva
wool .. 5. mungo 6. shoddy
ragamuffin ... 8. titmouse 9. ragged boy 14. tatterdemalion
rage ... 3. fad 4. fume, fury, gret, ramp, rant, tear 5. anger, chafe, craze, furor (furore), storm, wrath 6. fervor, frenzy 7. bluster, passion 8. violence 9. vehemence 10. excitement
ragged ... 5. harsh, rough 6. jagged, raguly (Her), scoury, shabby, uneven

7. shreddy 9. defective, dissonant, irregular 10. straggling 11. dilapidated

raging... 4. grim 5. rabid 7. acharne 8. storming 9. ferocious, turbulent 10. blustering, infuriated 11. overwrought

raglan... 8. overcoat 11. sleeve style

Ragnarok, Norse (pert to)...
leader.. 4. Loki
meaning.. 16. world destruction
repeopler of the world.. 3. Lif 10. Lifthrasir

ragout... 4. beef 5. civet, salmi 6. mutton 7. goulash, haricot

rahdar... 14. tollroad keeper

raid... 4. tata 5. foray, seize 6. inroad 8. invasion 9. incursion

rail... 3. bar, jaw 4. coot, jest, rant, sora 5. cloak, crake, dress, scoff, scold 6. banter, revile, septum (altar) 7. courlan, garment, inveigh, limpkin, ortolan 8. reproach

railbird... 4. bird, weka 5. crake 7. clocker, wood hen 9. spectator 12. horse watcher

railing... 5. fence, rails 7. barrier, parapet 10. balustrade

raillery... 5. chaff, sport 6. banter 7. asteism (Rhet) 8. badinage, ridicule 10. persiflage

railroad (pert to)...
flare.. 5. fusee
signal.. 9. semaphore
sleeper.. 3. tie 7. pullman
switch.. 4. frog
torpedo.. 9. detonator
worker.. 6. dinger 8. strapper 11. gandy dancer

Rail Splitter... 14. Abraham Lincoln

raiment... 4. garb 5. amice, dress 7. apparel, clothes, vesture 8. clothing, garments

rain (pert to)...
cloud.. 6. nimbus
coat.. 4. mino 6. poncho 7. slicker
comb form.. 5. hyeto, ombro 6. pluvio
fine.. 4. mist 6. serein
fowl.. 6. cuckoo 10. woodpecker 11. channelbill
gauge.. 8. udometer 10. hyetometer
glass.. 9. barometer
icy.. 4. hail 5. sleet
protection.. 9. ombrifuge
short.. 6. shower
storm.. 5. spate 13. precipitation
study.. 9. hyetology, ombrology
sudden.. 5. plash, spate 6. deluge 7. torrent 8. downpour

rainbow... 3. arc 4. arch, iris, omen

rainbow (pert to)...
bridge (Norse Myth).. 7. Bifrost (to Asgarth)
chaser.. 9. visionary 11. doctrinaire
flower.. 4. iris
goddess.. 4. Iris
term.. 6. iridal
tree.. 5. saman 8. genisaro
unit.. 4. inch
worm.. 8. nematode 9. earthworm

rainy... 3. wet 7. showery

rais, reis (Moslem)... 5. chief, title 7. captain (ship's)

Rais... 10. Mongoloids

raise... 3. end 4. grow, levy, lift, rear, stir 5. boost, breed, erect, exalt, heave, hoist, rouse 6. awaken, excite, gather, leaven, muster, remove, uplift 7. collect, elevate, enhance, lighten, present, produce, provoke, recruit 8. heighten, increase 9. construct, cultivate, promotion, propagate 10. aggrandize

raise (pert to)...
a nap.. 5. tease 6. teasel
Cain.. 3. Ned 4. hell 5. cut up 7. be noisy 10. vociferate
the dead.. 13. lift the anchor
vegetables.. 12. olericulture

raised... 4. bred, hove 6. buoyed, enlève, hefted, lifted, reared 7. hoisted 8. elevated, leavened, produced, promoted

raised (pert to)...
spirits.. 6. elated
to 3rd power.. 5. cubed
troops.. 6. levied 7. drafted 11. conscripted
type.. 7. braille
uproar.. 6. rioted
with a bar.. 7. levered

raisin... 4. pasa 5. grape, lexia

raja, rajah... 4. king, rana 5. title 6. prince 9. dignitary

raja's consort... 4. rani (ranee) 8. princess

Rajmahal hemp... 5. fiber 9. jiti fiber

Rajput... 5. caste 9. Kshatriya

rake... 3. rut 4. comb, path, raff, roué 5. slope, teeth, track 6. lecher 7. debauch, seducer 8. enfilade, Lothario 9. cultivate, implement, libertine

rakehell... 4. free, rake 9. debauched, debauchee, dissolute 10. dissipated, licentious, profligate

rakh... 3. hay 8. hayfield 9. grassland

raki, rakee... 7. spirits (distilled)

rale... 6. rattle 8. rhonchus 11. morbid sound

rallentando... 9. direction (Mus) 10. ritardando, slackening

Rallidae... 5. birds, coots, rails, wekas 6. crakes 10. gallinules

rally... 6. banter 7. recover, reunite 8. assemble, recovery, ridicule 10. assemblage, call to arms

rallying cry... 4. call 6. slogan 9. battle cry, bugle call

ralph... 5. raven

ram... 3. hit, pun, tup 4. buck, butt, tamp 5. Aries, crash, sheep 6. rancid, wether 7. collide

Rama... 11. Ramachandra (7th of fame) 19. incarnation of Vishnu

ramada... 5. arbor 7. pergola

Ramadan (Moham)... 7. fasting 10. ninth month (for fasting)

ramage... 4. wild 5. rough 6. branch (tree), unruly 7. untamed 8. frenzied

ramage hawk... 8. brancher

ramass... 6. gather 7. collect

ramberge... 6. galley (swift)

ramble... 3. gad 4. roam, rove, walk
  5. jaunt, prowl, range 6. stroll,
  wander 7. deviate, digress, saunter
  8. straggle
rambling... 7. devious 9. desultory,
  deviation, deviative, wandering
  10. circuitous, discursive, distracted
  14. discursiveness
rambunctious... 4. wild 6. unruly
  10. rampageous 12. obstreperous
  14. uncontrollable
ramentum... 5. palea (palet) 6. scales
  8. a shaving, particle (minute)
Rameses Dynasties (pert to)...
  famed for.. 5. ruins 7. papyrus
  kings.. 6. twelve
  site.. 5. Egypt
ramex... 6. hernia 10. varicocele
ram–headed goat... 5. Ammon
ramie... 4. hemp, rhea 5. plant (fiber)
  7. garment 9. Boehmeria 10. China
  grass
ramification... 3. arm 5. ramus
  6. branch 8. offshoot 9. branching
  10. divergence 12. embranchment
rammack... 4. gawk, romp 5. scamp
rammel... 4. hard 6. coarse 7. new
  milk, raw milk 9. brushwood
  11. undergrowth
Ramona (pert to)...
  heroine.. 9. half–breed (Ind)
  novel by.. 7. Jackson (Helen Hunt)
  shrub.. 4. mint
ramp... 3. rob 4. rage, romp, walk
  5. bound, climb, crawl, creep, storm
  6. dupery, unruly 7. incline,
  rampage, swindle 8. gradient,
  platform 9. heli016line, impetuous
  10. cuckoopint
rampant... 6. fierce, unruly, vallum
  (anc) 7. ramping 8. abundant, reared
  up (Her) 9. exuberant, prevalent,
  unchecked 10. rampageous
  12. high–spirited, unrestrained
  13. perpendicular
rampart... 4. wall 5. agger, mound,
  redan 6. escarp 7. barrier, bulwark,
  defense, parapet, ravelin 8. buttress
  9. earthwork 10. embankment
  13. fortification
ram's horn (Heb)... 7. shophar (shofar)
ran... 4. fled, sped 6. flowed
  7. coursed, managed, trotted
  8. operated
ran (pert to)...
  aground.. 8. decamped, levanted,
  stranded
  away.. 4. fled 6. eloped
  9. absconded
  out.. 5. spilt 7. petered, spilled
rana (Ind)... 5. title 6. prince
Rana... 5. frogs 10. amphibians
  (tailless)
ranarium... 8. frog pond
rance... 4. prop 6. marble 7. support
ranch... 4. casa, farm 6. estate
  8. estancia, hacienda
ranchero... 6. cowman 7. vaquero
  8. herdsman 9. cattleman
rancid... 4. rank 5. musty, stale
  6. reechy 9. obnoxious, offensive

10. unpleasant
rancor, rancour... 3. ire 4. gall
  5. spite 6. enmity, hatred, malice,
  rankle 7. ill will 9. animosity
  10. resentment
rand... 4. edge, rant 5. ridge, storm
  6. border, margin
random... 5. stray 6. casual, chance
  7. aimless 8. casually 9. at liberty,
  haphazard, orderless 10. accidental,
  fortuitous 11. haphazardly
randy... 4. wild 5. revel, spree
  6. beggar, coarse, frolic, virago
  7. canvass 8. carousal 9. festivity
  10. disorderly 11. ill–mannered
  12. unmanageable
rang (pert to)... see also *ring*
  loudly.. 7. clanged
  mournfully.. 6. tolled 7. knelled
  slowly.. 6. tolled
range... 3. row 4. ally, area, line,
  rank, roam, size 5. align, gamut,
  orbit, scope 6. limits, ramble, region,
  series, wander 7. arrange, compass,
  earshot, habitat, pasture 8. classify,
  mountain 9. cookstove
range (pert to)...
  finder.. 9. mekometer, telemeter
  10. trekometer
  man.. 5. rider 6. warden
  of hills.. 5. ridge
  of knowledge.. 3. ken
  of stables.. 4. mews
rangle... 5. stray 6. wander
  8. entangle, straggle
rani, ranee (Hind)... 4. wife 5. queen
  7. empress 8. princess
rani (Romany)... 4. lady, wife
Ranier, Mt... 10. Washington (State)
ranine... 5. frogs 7. Raninae 8. mink
  frog
rank... 3. bad, row 4. file, foul, line,
  rate, size, tier 5. caste, class, grade,
  gross, order, range 6. degree,
  estate, rancid, status, wicked
  7. arrange, glaring, tainted
  8. absolute, abundant, classify,
  eminence, flagrant, indecent,
  infamous, nobility, palpable, position,
  prestige, unsavory 9. downright,
  formation, luxuriant, plentiful
  10. malodorous 11. distinction
rank (pert to)...
  and file.. 4. army 8. regulars
  10. commonalty 11. third estate
  celestial.. 9. hierarchy
  exalted.. 8. eminence
  military (old).. 8. banneret
  noble.. 10. patriciate
  rider.. 8. reckless 10. highwayman
  social.. 5. caste
rankle... 5. chafe 6. fester 7. putrefy
  8. make sore 9. suppurate 10. be
  inflamed
rann... 5. verse 6. stanza, strain
ransack... 4. rake, sack 5. rifle
  6. search 7. plunder, rummage
ransom... 4. fine 6. redeem, rescue
  7. expiate 8. recovery
ranstead... 8. toadflax (yellow)
  13. butter–and–eggs
rant... 4. rage, rail, rave 5. boast

6. steven 7. bluster, bombast,
declaim 9. gay frolic 10. get excited

rantipole... 4. wild 6. rakish, unruly
9. termagant

ranula... 4. cyst

Ranunculaceae... 7. anemone
8. aconitum, clematis, crowfoot
10. delphinium, ranunculus

rap... 3. bop, hit 4. bang, blow, gibe,
grab, knap, tirl 5. knock, steal
6. rascal, snatch, trifle 8. betrayal,
sentence (prison) 9. criticism,
reprimand 10. punishment 11. skein
of yarn

rapacious... 6. greedy, rapine
8. grasping, ravenous 9. devouring,
voracious 10. avaricious, predacious

rapacity... 5. greed, ravin (raven)
6. rapine 8. appetite 9. predacity

rapid... 4. fast 5. fleet, quick, swift
7. stretto (stretta)

rapidity... 5. haste, speed 8. celerity,
velocity 9. fleetness, quickness

rapidly... 5. amain, apace 7. quickly,
swiftly 8. snappily

rapids... 5. rifts 6. dalles

rapier... 5. bilbo, sword 6. verdun
7. ricasso (part)

rapine... 7. pillage, plunder 8. spoiling
10. ravishment, spoliation

rapport... 6. accord 7. empathy,
harmony 8. relation 9. agreement
11. co-operation (hypnotism)

rapt... 8. absorbed, ecstatic
10. enraptured, interested
11. preoccupied, transported

rapture... 3. joy 4. love 5. bliss
6. trance 7. delight, ecstasy
8. rhapsody 9. transport
10. exultation

rapturous... 8. ecstatic

rare... 3. odd, raw 4. thin 6. scarce,
seldom, sparse 7. notable, unusual
8. rarefied, uncommon 10. infrequent
11. undercooked

rare (pert to)...
bird.. 8. rara avis
earth.. 6. cerium 7. terbium, yttrium
metallic element.. 7. yttrium
object.. 5. curio 6. oddity 7. antique

Rare Ben, inscription... 15. tomb of
Ben Jonson (Westminster Abbey)

rarebit... 10. cheese dish 11. Welsh
rabbit

rarefy... 4. thin 6. dilute, expand
9. attenuate

rarely... 6. finely, seldom 8. not often,
scarcely 9. extremely, unusually
11. beautifully 12. infrequently

rarity... 6. oddity 7. fewness, tenuity
8. scarcity, thinness 11. infrequency

ras... 4. cape 6. prince
11. short-napped 13. Fascist leader

rasa... 3. sap (tree) 5. fluid, taste
6. amrita, flavor 7. essence
11. living water

rascal... 3. cad, imp 5. knave, rogue,
scamp 6. varlet 9. miscreant

rascally... 4. mean 6. impish
7. knavish, roguish 8. scampish
11. mischievous

rase... 3. cut, rub 4. tear 5. graze,

level 6. scrape 7. scratch

rash... 3. mad 4. wild 5. giddy, hasty,
heady, hives, scamp 6. unwary,
wanton 7. Icarian 8. careless,
eruption, heedless 9. desperate,
exanthema, impetuous
10. headstrong, incautious, indiscreet
11. temerarious, thoughtless

rasher... 5. piece, slice 7. portion
9. thin slice

rashness... 6. acrisy 7. acrisia
8. temerity 9. hastiness

rasion... 6. filing 7. erasing, rasping,
shaving 8. scraping

Rasores... 4. fowl 5. birds 6. quails
7. turkeys 8. Columbae, Gallinae
9. pheasants 10. partridges

rasp... 3. rub 4. file 5. belch, chafe,
erupt, grate 6. abrade, offend,
scrape 8. irritate 9. raspberry

raspberry... 3. red 5. apple, Rubus
6. raspis 7. plumbog 8. blackcap

rasping... 5. harsh 7. chafing, grating,
raucous 8. grinding, scraping, very
fast 9. offensive 10. irritating

raspings... 6. refuse 7. filings, remains

rasse... 5. civet

rasure... 3. cut 5. shave 7. erasure,
polling, scratch, tonsure 8. scraping
12. obliteration

rat... 3. rut 4. scab, snob, wart
5. track 6. desert, ratton, rodent
7. scratch, traitor 8. deserter
9. hairpiece, scoundrel

rat (pert to)...
fish.. 8. chimaera
goose.. 11. common brant
hare.. 4. pika
kangaroo.. 7. Potorus 9. marsupial
pineapple.. 7. pinguin
poison.. 8. ratsbane
ratlike.. 4. vole
rhyme.. 6. jargon 13. doggerel verse

ratafia... 7. biscuit (almond), curacao,
liqueur (Danzig)

ratchet... 4. pawl 5. click 6. bobbin,
detent

rate... 4. fare, pace 5. price, ratio,
style, tempo, value 6. assess, berate,
charge, reckon, regard 7. account,
deserve, premium, reprove
8. appraise, classify, estimate,
evaluate, interest

rate (of exchange)... 4. agio 5. batta

rath (anc)... 4. hill, home (walled)

rath, ratha... 3. car 6. temple (Seven
Pagodas, Madras) 7. chariot

Rathaus... 8. town hall

rathe, rath... 4. soon 5. eager, quick,
speed 7. betimes, quickly 8. speedily

rather... 3. ere, yes 6. before
7. earlier, however, instead
8. somewhat 9. more truly, tolerably
10. especially, preferably
11. immediately 14. on the other
hand

ratification... 4. amen 5. logic
8. sanction 9. reasoning
11. endorsement 12. confirmation

ratify... 4. amen, pass, seal 6. enseal,
verify 7. approve, confirm, consent,
endorse 8. roborate, sanction

9. authorize

ratio... 2. pi 4. rate, sine 5. share
6. cosine, ration 7. portion
10. proportion

ratiocination... 5. logic 7. thought
9. reasoning

ration... 5. share 6. budget 8. relation
9. allotment, allowance, provision
11. calculation

rational... 4. sane, wise 5. sober
7. logical 8. sensible 9. reasoning
10. reasonable 11. philosophic

rationale... 6. reason 11. explanation
12. the how and why

ratio scripta... 13. written reason

ratite... (opp of carinate) 7. Ratitae
8. unkeeled 14. flat breastbone

ratite bird... 3. emu (emeu), moa
7. ostrich 9. cassowary

ratoon... 5. shoot, stalk 6. spring,
sprout

rattan, ratan... 4. cane, palm, sega,
whip 6. switch 7. calamus

ratteen... 8. mahogany

rattle... 3. toy 4. herb, rale, rick, tirl
5. annoy, clack 6. assail, prison
(Nav), racket, uproar 7. agitate,
chatter, clapper, clatter, confuse,
fluster, maracas, prattle 8. nonsense
9. chatterer, rapid talk
10. disconcert, noisemaker

rattle (pert to)...
  bones.. 8. clappers, snappers
    9. castanets
  headed.. 8. confused
    11. empty–headed 13. rattlebrained
  mouse.. 3. bat
  nut.. 10. chinquapin
  pate.. 3. ass
  root.. 7. bugbane

rattlesnake... 7. rattler 8. belltail,
Crotalus, pit viper 9. Sistrurus

rattlesnake (pert to)...
  bean.. 6. cedron
  bite.. 9. meadow rue
  fern.. 9. chain fern, sporangia
  flag (Maine).. 13. Don't Tread on Me
    (Hist)
  herb.. 9. baneberry
  leaf.. 8. plantain
  pilot.. 10. copperhead
  plantain.. 6. orchid
  variety.. 3. red 6. banded, timber
    7. prairie 11. diamondback
  venom.. 8. crotalus

rattletrap... 6. gewgaw 7. rickety
8. claptrap, the mouth
10. knickknack, ramshackle

ratton... 3. rat

ratwa... 7. muntjac

raucous... 3. dry 4. bray, loud
5. harsh, noisy 6. hoarse, raucid,
rauque 8. strident 11. cacophonous

rauk, roke... 4. poke, stir 5. vapor
7. scratch

raun... 3. roe 4. fish 5. spawn

ravage... 4. loot, ruin, sack 5. havoc,
spoil, waste 6. damage, infest
7. debauch, destroy, overrun, pillage,
plunder 9. devastate 10. desolation
11. despoilment, devastation,
infestation

ravages of time... 13. deterioration
14. disintegration

rave... 4. rage, rant 5. crush, storm
7. bluster, declaim, enthuse 8. be
insane, harangue

ravel... 4. fray 6. runner, slough,
unwind 7. involve, unravel, untwist,
unweave 8. entangle, separate
11. disentangle, loose thread

ravelin... 7. railing 8. demilune,
half–moon 13. fortification

raven... 4. bird, crow 6. Corvus
8. standard (vikings) 10. raven–black
11. Corvus corax

Raven (The)... 4. poem (Edgar Allen
Poe)

ravening... 3. mad 5. rabid 6. greedy,
prying 8. desirous 9. rapacious,
turbulent

ravenous... 6. greedy 8. edacious
9. rapacious, voracious
10. gluttonous 11. catawampous

ravine... 3. gap 4. dell, linn (lin), wadi
(wady) 5. chine, gorge, gulch, slade,
strid 6. arroyo, clough, gulley, nullah
8. barranca

ravish... 3. rob 4. rape 5. seize
7. corrupt, debauch, delight, despoil,
plunder, violate 8. deflower, entrance
9. enrapture, transport

raw... 4. cold, sore 5. bleak, crude,
naked 6. chilly, unripe, vulgar
7. natural, not spun, untried
8. immature, indecent, uncooked
9. inclement, unskilled, wind–swept
10. unprepared 11. undeveloped,
unprocessed 13. inexperienced

rawboned... 4. lank 5. gaunt
7. angular 8. skeletal

rawbones... 5. Death 8. skeleton

raw–flesh–eating... 9. omophagia

rawhide... 4. skin (untanned), whip

rawhide whip... 5. knout, quirt, thong
7. sjambok

raw sugar... 9. cassonade

rax... 5. reach 6. become, strain
7. stretch

ray... 4. beam, dorn, soil, X–ray
5. array, dress, gamma, order, skate
(fish) 6. defile, radius, stripe, vision
7. besmear, raiment 8. particle,
radiance, stingray 11. arrangement,
irradiation

raya... 9. broadbill

rayless... 4. dark 5. blind

rayon... 3. ray 5. fiber 6. radius
14. postal district (Switz)

raze, rase... 3. cut 4. fell, ruin
5. erase, graze, level, shave
6. efface, scrape 7. destroy
8. demolish 9. dismantle, prostrate
10. obliterate

razee... 3. cut (Naut) 5. prune
7. abridge

razor (pert to)...
  back.. 3. hog 4. boar 5. ridge
    10. roustabout (circus)
  bill.. 3. auk 7. skimmer
  billed auk.. 4. falk 5. murre, noddy
  clam.. 5. Solen 11. chopa blanca
  grinder.. 10. goatsucker
  sharpen.. 4. hone 5. strop

stone.. 9. whetstone 10. novaculite
strap.. 5. strop
type.. 6. safety 7. rattler
razz... 5. chaff, tease 6. banter, deride
   8. ridicule 9. raspberry
razzle–dazzle... 5. cinch (game), spree
   6. dazzle 7. confuse 8. bewilder
   9. commotion 10. noisemaker
re... 4. back (pref) 5. about, again,
   anent, tone D (Mus) 8. syllable
   (Mus) 10. concerning
Re... 2. Ra (Egypt) see also *Ra*
reach... 4. come, gain, hawk, ryke,
   spar, spit 5. equal, retch 6. advene,
   arrive, attain, extend, length
   7. achieve, compass, earshot,
   expanse, possess, stretch
   8. distance, overtake 9. influence
   10. understand
reach (pert to)...
  across.. 4. span
  for applause.. 9. captation
  high point.. 9. culminate
  out.. 6. extend 7. stretch
  under.. 7. subtend
  up.. 6. aspire
reaction... 4. kick 6. change (Chem)
   7. tropism 8. response 9. influence
   10. opposition
reactionary... 4. Tory 10. malcontent
   12. conservative, recalcitrant
read... 3. con 4. pore, scan, skim, tell
   5. guess, solve 6. advise, browse,
   peruse, recite, relate 7. counsel,
   declare, discern, foresee, prelect
   (praelect), stomach 8. decipher,
   describe, foretell 9. interpret
   10. understand
readable... 7. legible 12. decipherable
reader... 6. lector, lister, primer
   (McGuffey) 7. browser, license,
   reciter, speaker, teacher 8. anagnost
   (anagnostes), literate, textbook
   9. churchman, prelector (praelector)
   10. pocketbook 11. proofreader
   12. elocutionist
readily... 6. at once, easily 7. quickly
   8. probably 9. willingly 10. very
   likely
readjust... 7. readapt, restore
   9. rearrange 11. reconstruct
   12. rehabilitate
ready... 3. apt, fit, fix 4. bain, free,
   here, ripe, yare 5. alert, apert,
   eager, handy, point, quick 6. facile,
   fitted, prompt 7. willing 8. cheerful,
   disposed, inclined, prepared, skillful
   9. dexterous 12. unhesitating
ready acceptance... 11. embracement
ready for... 6. awaits 8. liable to
   10. in store for 11. prepared for
ready–to–wear... 12. haute couture
real... 4. true, very 5. pucka (pukka)
   6. actual 7. factual, genuine, sincere
   8. absolute, existent, handmade,
   tangible 9. authentic, veritable
   10. unaffected 11. substantial
real (pert to)...
  being.. 6. entity
  estate.. 5. lands 6. domain, houses,
  realty 7. demesne 8. easement,

freehold, property 9. tenements
   13. hereditaments
  map.. 4. plot
  name (backwards).. 6. ananym
  school.. 10. Realschule
realistic... 5. vivid 8. lifelike
   9. practical 11. descriptive
reality... 5. truth 7. realism
   11. genuineness
reality, non–existent... 8. nihilism
realize... 3. get, win 4. gain, know
   5. sense 7. convert 8. conceive
   10. accomplish
realm... 6. domain, empire, region,
   sphere 7. country, demesne, kingdom
   8. division, province 10. department
   12. jurisdiction
realm (of)...
  darkness (Myth).. 2. po
  Jamshid.. 6. Persia
  perfection.. 6. Utopia
ream... 4. bore, foam, scum 5. widen
   6. bundle 7. enlarge 8. bevel out
   11. countersink 14. enormous
   amount
reanimate... 5. rally 6. revive
   7. refresh 11. resuscitate
   12. reinvigorate
rear... 3. aft 4. back, grow, lift, loom,
   rise, rump 5. breed, build, erect,
   raise, stern, train 6. behind, foster
   7. arriere, educate, elevate, produce
   8. instruct 9. construct, establish,
   posterior 10. background
rear (pert to)...
  admiral.. 7. two bars (silver)
  commodore, yacht club.. 7. officer
  end.. 6. breech 7. hind end
   9. afterpart, posterior
  horse (insect).. 6. mantis
  most.. 4. last
  toward.. 3. aft 5. abaft 6. astern
   8. backward, rearward
rearing up (horse)... 5. stend
   6. pesade
rearrange... 4. sort 8. readjust
   10. reordinate, reorganize
reason... 5. argue, cause, logic, sense,
   think 6. deduce, ground, motive,
   sanity 7. discuss 8. argument,
   conclude, judgment, question,
   solution 9. discourse, intellect
   11. explanation, ratiocinate, rationalize
   13. justification, understanding
reason (pert to)...
  discursively.. 11. ratiocinate
  doctrine of, author.. 10. Anaxagoras
  higher.. 4. mind, nous 5. logic
  Latin.. 5. causa
  ostensible.. 7. pretext
  pert to.. 6. noetic
  proof of.. 8. argument
  want of.. 7. amentia
  why.. 5. cause 6. motive
reasonable... 4. fair, just, sane
   6. proper 7. logical 8. rational
   9. equitable, plausible, practical
   10. fair–minded 11. inexpensive,
   intelligent, justifiable
reasoning (pert to)...
  basis of.. 7. premise
  delusive.. 7. fallacy

exact.. 5. logic
harmonize.. 11. rationalize
plausible.. 8. specious
reassure ... 6. assure, solace
   7. comfort, console, hearten
   8. embolden, give hope
reata ... 4. rope 5. lasso, riata 6. lariat
reave ... 3. rob 4. rend, tear 5. break,
   burst, seize, split 7. plunder
reb ... 5. rebel
rebate ... 5. check 6. reduce, weaken
   8. diminish, discount 9. abatement,
   deduction, remission
rebato (Hist) ... 4. ruff 6. collar, rabato
   9. piccadill
Rebekah (pert to) ...
   husband.. 5. Isaac
   sister.. 5. Laban
   son.. 4. Esau 5. Jacob
rebel ... 3. reb 4. rise 6. resist, revolt
   8. renounce, turncoat 9. insurgent
   13. revolutionist
rebellion ... 5. Great (Eng 1642–49)
   6. mutiny, revolt 8. American (Civil
   War 1861–65) 10. resistance,
   revolution 12. insurrection,
   renunciation
rebellious ... 8. mutinous 9. insurgent
   10. refractory 12. contumacious
   13. insubordinate, revolutionary
rebirth ... 7. revival 9. salvation
   10. conversion 11. renaissance
   13. reincarnation
rebound ... 4. stot 5. carom
   6. bounce, recoil, re–echo, spring
   7. resound 8. rebounce, ricochet
   11. reverberate
rebuff ... 4. slap, snub 5. chide, scold
   6. defeat, lesson, recoil, refuse,
   reject, resist 7. censure, refusal
   (brusque), reprove, repulse
   9. reprimand
rebuke ... 3. nip 4. slap 5. check,
   chide 6. rebuff 7. repress, reproof,
   reprove 8. admonish, reproach,
   restrain 9. criticize, reprehend,
   reprimand 11. comeuppance
recalcitrant ... 5. rebel 8. renitent
   9. obstinate, recoiling, resistant
   10. rebellious, refractory
   11. disobedient 12. ungovernable
recall ... 5. annul 6. encore, recant,
   remind, repeal, revoke, summon
   7. retract 8. remember, withdraw
   9. recollect, reminisce
   11. recantation 12. recollection
recant ... 6. abjure, revoke 7. disavow,
   retract 8. renounce, withdraw
   9. repudiate 10. contradict
recapitulate ... 5. essay, sum up
   6. repeat, review 7. restate
   8. argument 9. reiterate, summarize
recapture ... 6. recall, regain, retake
   7. recover
recede ... 3. ebb 4. wane 6. depart,
   retire 7. deviate, regress, retreat
   8. withdraw 10. retrograde
receipt ... 5. axiom 6. acquit, answer,
   recipe 7. formula 12. prescription
   14. acknowledgment
receipts ... 7. the take

receive ... 3. get 4. hold, take
   5. admit, greet, learn, reset
   6. accept, assent, derive, obtain,
   take in 7. acquire, contain, procure
   9. apprehend
receive (pert to) ...
   a confession.. 6. shrive
   a reward.. 4. reap
   stolen property.. 5. reset
receiver ... 5. donee, fence 7. catcher
   8. believer 9. recipient, treasurer
   10. receptacle
receiver (pert to) ...
   fixed income.. 7. rentier
   profits (law).. 6. pernor
   property in trust.. 6. bailee
   stolen property.. 5. fence
recension ... 6. review 8. revising,
   revision 9. reviewing
   11. enumeration, examination
recent ... 3. new 4. late, past 5. fresh
   6. former, modern 7. current,
   newborn 8. neonatal, neoteric
receptacle ... 3. bag, bin, box, can,
   cup, pan 4. case, cask, cyst (anc),
   etui, pail, tank, tray, vase 5. basin,
   crock 6. basket, bottle, bucket,
   carton, holder, hopper 7. compote,
   hanaper, platter 8. canister, catchall
   9. container 10. repository
receptacle (pert to) ...
   assayer's, stonecutter's.. 7. sebilla
   botany.. 5. torus
   coal.. 3. bin
   corporal (RCCh).. 5. burse
   grain.. 3. bin 8. elevator
   holy water.. 5. stoup
   vote.. 6. situla
reception ... 3. tea 5. levee, salon
   6. infare, soiree 7. accueil, ovation,
   receipt, welcome 8. ceremony,
   sociable 9. admission, interview,
   intuition 12. housewarming
   13. entertainment
reception hall, room ... 5. salon
   6. atrium, parlor 9. vestibule
receptionist ... 4. host 7. hostess
   8. landlord
receptive ... 6. pliant 8. sensible
   9. acceptant, admissive, teachable
   10. hospitable, open–minded
   11. persuasible
receptor ... 5. basin 8. receiver
   10. dispositor (Astron), sense organ
recess ... 3. ala, bay, pan (leaf)
   4. apse, nook, rest 5. crypt, niche,
   pause, sinus, space 7. adjourn,
   respite, retreat 9. recession, seclusion
   11. indentation 12. intermission
recipe ... 5. axiom 7. formula, receipt
   12. prescription
recipient ... 4. heir 5. donee 7. legatee
   8. receiver
reciprocal ... 5. joint 6. mutual, shared
   8. exchange 9. alternate
   11. convertible, correlative, retaliatory
   15. interchangeable
reciprocate ... 5. bandy 6. accord,
   concur 8. exchange 9. alternate,
   retaliate 10. correspond
   11. interchange
recision ... 6. repeal 7. pruning

9. canceling (cancelling)
10. rescinding
recital . . . 4. tale 5. story 6. lesson,
speech 7. account, concert
(exhibition) 8. musicale 9. narration,
narrative, rehearsal 10. recitation,
repetition 11. enumeration, reiteration
recitation . . . 6. lesson, speech
7. reading 10. exhibition
recite . . . 4. tell 5. quote, speak, state
6. relate, repeat 7. declaim, narrate,
recount 8. rehearse, tell over
9. enumerate, pronounce
12. recapitulate
recite (pert to) . . .
in monotone . . 6. intone
metrically . . 4. scan
rhetorically . . 7. declaim
to music . . 5. chant 10. cantillate
reciter . . . 4. book (of extracts) 5. roter
7. relator, speaker 8. narrator
reck . . . 4. care, deem, heed, mind
6. regard 7. concern 8. estimate
reckless . . . 4. rash 5. perdu (perdue)
6. madcap 7. hotspur 8. careless,
heedless 9. desperate, hotheaded,
imprudent 10. neglectful, regardless
11. indifferent, thoughtless,
unconcerned 13. inconsiderate
reckon . . . 4. aret (arette), date, deem,
tell 5. class, count, judge, tally, think
6. impute, number, regard, repute
7. account, compute, include,
suppose 8. consider, estimate,
evaluate 9. calculate, enumerate
reckoning . . . 3. sum 4. bill, shot
5. score, tally 6. esteem 7. account,
verdict 8. counting 9. summation
10. estimation 11. calculation
reckoning instrument . . . 6. abacus
9. tabulator 10. calculator
reclaim . . . 4. tame 5. renew, train
6. ransom, recall, redeem, revoke
7. convert, recover, restore 8. civilize
10. regenerate 12. rehabilitate
recline . . . 3. lay, lie, sit 4. lean, loll,
rest 6. repose 7. incline, lie down
reclining . . . 4. flat 5. prone 6. supine
7. lolling 8. couchant, reposing
9. prostrate, recumbent
recluse . . . 3. fra, nun 4. monk
6. hermit, hidden, secret, shut up
7. ascetic, eremite, retired (from
world) 8. anchoret, isolated, solitary
9. anchorite 10. cloistered
11. sequestered
recognition . . . 4. fame 6. recall
9. detection 10. cognizance
11. discernment
14. acknowledgment
recognize . . . 3. see 4. know 5. admit
6. detect 7. consent 8. identify,
perceive 10. appreciate, recognosce
11. acknowledge
recoil . . . 3. shy 4. funk 5. quail
6. flinch, resile, shrink 7. rebound,
retreat 8. reaction, withdraw
recollect . . . 6. recall, revive 7. think of
8. remember 10. call to mind
recollection . . . 4. mind 6. memory
9. anamnesis 11. remembrance
12. reminiscence

recommence . . . 5. renew 6. resume
8. return to 9. begin anew
recommend . . . 4. tout, urge 6. advise,
commit, denote, praise 7. commend,
consign, entrust 8. advocate
recompense . . . 3. fee, pay 4. meed
5. repay 6. reward 8. requital
9. indemnify, reimburse
10. compensate, remunerate
11. reciprocate
recompense (pert to) . . .
Brehon Law . . 4. eric
Germanic law . . 7. wergild
Scot law . . 3. cro
Welsh law . . 7. galanas
reconcile . . . 4. suit, wean 5. atone
6. adjust, pacify, settle 7. cleanse
(Eccl), conform, reunite 9. harmonize
10. conciliate, propitiate
reconciliation . . . 7. harmony, reunion
10. adjustment, conformity
12. pacification 13. reconcilement
reconciliator . . . 10. arbitrator,
reconciler 13. intermediator
recondite . . . 4. dark, deep 6. hidden,
mystic, occult 7. cryptic 8. abstract,
abstruse, esoteric 9. concealed
reconnaissance . . . 6. survey
8. scouting 11. examination
reconnoiter . . . 5. scout 6. survey
reconstruct . . . 6. recast, remake
7. rebuild, remodel 9. reproduce
11. reestablish
record . . . 3. log, tab 4. disc, file, list,
memo 5. annal, diary, enter, entry,
score 6. agenda, legend, memoir,
postea 7. archive, estreat, history
8. memorial, register 9. chronicle
10. chronology, transcribe, transcript
record (pert to) . . .
criminal investigation . . 7. dossier
document . . 8. protocol
earth tremor . . 11. seismograph
formal . . 4. vita 8. register
historic . . 6. annals 7. rotulet
keeper . . 9. registrar 10. chartulary
of events . . 5. annal, fasti 7. history
official . . 5. actum
pictorial . . 5. graph
ship's voyage . . 3. log
year's . . 5. diary 8. calendar
recording terms . . . 2. LP 4. reel, tape
5. album, Dolby 6. needle, stereo,
stylus 7. capstan 8. cassette
9. cartridge, videotape
recount . . . 3. min 4. tell 5. sum up
6. reckon, relate, repeat, retail
7. narrate 8. rehearse 9. enumerate,
reiterate 12. recapitulate
recoup . . . 4. gain 7. recover
8. retrieve 9. indemnity, reimburse
10. compensate
recourse . . . 3. use 5. recur 6. access,
betake, refuge, resort, return, revert
7. retreat
recover . . . 3. get 4. cure, gain, heal
5. rally, reach, upset 6. obtain,
recoup, redeem, regain, rescue,
resume 7. get well, reclaim, recruit
8. overcome, retrieve 9. repossess
10. convalesce, recuperate
recovery . . . 6. return 7. salvage

9. retrieval 11. reclamation,
reformation, restoration
recreant... 6. coward, wretch
7. dastard, knavish 8. apostate,
betrayer, cowardly, deserter
9. reprobate 10. unfaithful
recreation... 4. food, game, meal, play
5. sport 7. holiday, renewal
8. vacation 9. amusement, diversion
11. refreshment 12. reproduction
14. reconstruction
recrement... 5. dross 6. refuse, scoria
recruit... 5. raise 6. enlist, gather,
muster, novice, revive, rookie
7. recover, refresh, restore
8. assemble, inductee, newcomer
9. conscript, reinforce, replenish
12. reinvigorate
rectangle... 10. quadrangle
13. parallelogram
rectangular... 6. oblong
12. quadrangular
rectify... 5. amend, emend, right
6. adjust, better, reform, remedy
7. correct, justify 8. emendate,
regulate, set right 10. straighten
rector... 5. chief 6. leader, master
(Oxford), pastor 8. director, governor
9. churchman, clergyman
10. headmaster
rectory... 8. benefice 9. personage
recumbent... 4. idle 5. lying, prone
7. leaning, resting 8. inactive,
reposing 9. reclining
recuperate... 4. rest 6. recoup, regain
7. improve, recover, restore 9. get
better, reimburse
recur... 5. again 6. repeat, return
7. persist, reoccur 8. reappear
recurrent... 10. repetitive
recurring (pert to)...
continually.. 8. constant
10. habitually, repeatedly
ninth day.. 5. nonan
seventh day.. 6. septan
third day.. 7. tertian
red... 4. rosy 5. color, ruddy 7. radical
8. blushing, inflamed, rutilant,
sanguine 9. bloodshot
12. bloodstained 13. revolutionary
red (color)... 4. fire, lake, pink, puce,
rose, ruby, tile, wine 5. blood, brick,
canna, coral, flame, flesh, henna,
poppy 6. auburn, cerise, cherry,
claret, damask, maroon, minium,
raddle, salmon, titian, Turkey
7. anemone, annatto, carmine,
Chinese, crimson, lobster, magenta,
nacarat, scarlet, stammel 8. cardinal,
cinnabar 9. carnation, carnelian,
vermilion
red (pert to)...
cap (Turk).. 8. tarboosh
cell.. 11. erythrocite
corpuscle.. 10. hemoglobin (source of)
dog.. 4. game 8. banknote
dye.. 3. aal, lac 4. chay (choy)
5. aurin (aurine), eosin (eosine)
8. morindin
gum.. 10. strophulus
hair.. 6. titian
herring.. 4. ruse 9. diversion

minded.. 7. radical
planet.. 4. Mars
race.. 7. Indians
robbin.. 14. scarlet tanager
truffle.. 12. melanogaster
viper.. 10. copperhead
Red (pert to)...
Book.. 7. Austria 13. Royal Kalendar
Crescent.. 8. Red Cross (Turk)
Cross.. 9. St George's (Eng)
Friar.. 13. Knight Templar
Guard.. 4. Army 7. Russian
Hand.. 13. Badge of Ulster
Horse.. 10. Kentuckian
Planet.. 4. Mars
Polled.. 6. cattle (hornless)
Prince.. 7. Russian (Frederick Charles)
Ribbon.. 14. Order of the Bath
Rose.. 16. House of Lancaster
Russian.. 9. Bolshevik
Sea.. 14. Erythraean main
Sea city.. 9. Leningrad
Sea colony.. 7. Eritrea
Sea gulf.. 5. Aqaba
Square.. 6. Moscow
The Red.. 4. Eric (Scand)
Triangle.. 4. YMCA (symbol)
redact... 4. edit 5. draft, frame
6. revise
redactor... 6. editor 7. reviser
9. redacteur
reddish (pert to)...
blue.. 5. smalt 9. damascene
brown.. 3. bay 4. roan 5. henna
6. auburn, russet, sorrel 8. chestnut
dye.. 7. annatto
yellow.. 5. amber 6. orange
rede... 6. advice, relate 7. counsel,
explain, predict 9. interpret
redeem... 3. pay 6. ransom, regain,
rescue 7. convert, fulfill, reclaim,
recover 8. liberate 10. repurchase,
substitute
redeemer... 4. goel (Heb) 7. saviour
(savior) 9. deliverer, liberator
11. emancipator
Redeemer, The... 8. Son of God
10. The Messiah, The Saviour
11. Jesus Christ
redintegrate... 5. renew, unite
7. restore 9. reconcile
11. re–establish
redness... 4. glow 8. blushing
10. erubescent, rubescence
redolence... 4. odor 5. aroma, scent
9. fragrance, sweetness
redolent... 5. balmy 7. odorous,
scented 8. aromatic, fragrant
11. impregnated, reminiscent
redouble... 6. re–echo, repeat
7. reflect, reprise (fencing)
9. intensify 10. ingeminate, repetition
11. reduplicate
redoubt... 4. fear 5. doubt 6. reduit
7. defense, ravelin
redound... 5. surge 6. abound, return
7. conduce, resound 8. flow back,
overflow 10. contribute (to)
11. reverberate
redpoll... 5. finch 6. linnet 7. warbler
Red Polled cattle... 8. hornless
redress... 4. help 5. amend, emend

6. reform, remedy 7. correct, relieve
8. atone for, reprisal 9. atonement
10. correction, recompense,
reparation 11. reformation, restitution
reduce ... 3. cut 4. bant, bate, pare,
thin 5. abase, abate, lower, razee
6. demote, derate, humble, lessen,
subdue, weaken 7. abridge, analyze,
cheapen, conquer, curtail, deplete,
qualify, relieve, shorten 8. decrease,
diminish, discount, minimize,
moderate 9. subjugate
10. impoverish, slenderize
reduce in flesh ... 8. emaciate
reduce in rank ... 6. demote
reduce to ...
ashes.. 7. cremate
average.. 4. mean 6. equate
bondage.. 7. enslave
common measure.. 12. commensurate
half.. 9. dimidiate
lower grade.. 6. demote 7. degrade
mean time.. 6. equate
spray.. 7. atomize
reduction ... 6. rebate 7. subdual
8. decrease, demotion, discount,
lowering 9. weakening
10. abridgment, cheapening,
conversion, moderation
reduction (pert to) ...
in value.. 12. depreciation
to absurdity.. 18. reductio ad
absurdum
to common level.. 15. standardization
to compactness.. 12. condensation
to standard.. 15. standardization
redundancy ... 6. excess 7. profuse
8. pleonasm, verbiage 9. prolixity,
talkative, tautology, verbosity
10. repetition 11. periphrasis
13. diffusiveness 14. circumlocution
redundant ... 6. lavish 7. copious,
diffuse, verbose 9. excessive,
exuberant, plethoric 10. pleonastic
11. overflowing, repetitious,
superfluous 13. superabundant
ree ... 3. dam 4. sift, wild 5. crazy,
drunk, river 6. harbor, riddle
7. channel, fuddled 8. coalyard
9. enclosure, sheepfold
re—echo ... 7. resound 11. reverberate
reechy ... 5. fetid 6. rancid
reed ... 4. stem, tube 5. arrow, straw
6. thatch 10. instrument
reed (pert to) ...
bird.. 4. wren 7. babbler, warbler
8. bobolink
buck.. 5. bohor, nagar 8. antelope
bunting.. 7. sparrow 8. reedling
loom.. 4. sley
mace.. 7. cattail, matreed
measure (Jew).. 9. six cubits
pipe.. 5. kazoo 8. mirliton
reef ... 3. bar, cay (cayo), key (quay)
4. itch, lode, sail, vein 5. islet,
mange, shoal 6. island 7. shorten
8. eruption
reef (pert to) ...
coral.. 3. key
knot.. 6. square
mining.. 4. lode, vein
nautical.. 5. sails

sand.. 3. bar
reefer ... 5. miner 6. jacket, oyster
9. cigarette 10. midshipman
reek ... 3. fug, rig 4. fume 5. equip,
exude, smell, smoke, steam
7. malodor, seaweed 8. fetid air,
smell bad, vaporize 10. exhalation
reel ... 4. eddy, pirn, rock, sail, sway,
wind 5. dance, lurch, spool, swift
(yarn), swing, waver, wince 6. tatter
7. scrieve, stagger 8. flounder,
titubate, windlass 12. Virginia reel
reeling ... 5. drunk 7. swaying, winding
8. rotating
reem (Bib) ... 6. animal (horned), wild
ox 11. unicorn
re—embody ... 7. combine, reshape
10. reorganize 11. reincarnate
13. reincorporate
reeve ... 3. pen 4. ruff 5. strip
6. thread 8. official (Eng Hist)
9. enclosure, sheepfold
refect ... 7. refresh, restore
refectory ... 6. frater (monastery)
8. mess hall 10. dining hall
refer ... 4. cite 5. apply, recur
6. allude, appeal, charge, impute,
relate, return 7. ascribe 9. appertain,
attribute
refer (to) ... 4. harp 6. advert
7. consult, mention
referee ... 5. judge 6. umpire 7. arbiter
8. attorney 9. moderator
10. arbitrator
reference ... 6. regard 7. respect
8. allusion, relation 9. character,
relevance 10. connection, pertinence
14. recommendation
reference (pert to) ...
book.. 5. atlas 8. handbook, syllabus
9. thesaurus 10. dictionary
12. encyclopedia
referendum ... 4. vote 7. mandate
8. politics 10. plebiscite
refine ... 5. smelt 6. rarefy 7. clarify,
elevate, improve, sublime
9. elaborate, sensitize, sublimate
refined ... 4. fine, nice, pure, rare
5. urban 6. chaste 7. elegant,
smelted 8. cleansed, highbred,
purified, well—bred 9. clarified,
courteous, perfected 10. cultivated,
fastidious, meticulous
refined spirit ... 5. grace 6. elixir
refinement ... 5. taste 6. polish
7. finesse 8. delicacy, elegance,
fineness 9. gentility 11. cultivation,
rarefaction 13. clarification
refinery (ore) ... 7. smelter
refining cup ... 5. cupel
reflect ... 3. say 4. muse, pore
5. radar, think 6. divert, mirror,
ponder 7. deflect 8. cogitate,
consider, meditate, ruminate, turn
back 9. reproduce 11. reverberate
reflecting ... 6. musing 9. judicious
10. reflective, ruminating, thoughtful
11. insinuating 13. reverberatory
15. casting reproach
reflection ... 4. idea 5. image, light
6. musing 7. bending, thought
8. reaction, thinking 10. cogitation,

meditation, rumination
12. afterthought, recollection
13. consideration, contemplation

reflex... 4. bent 6. turned 8. allusion, reaction, reversed 9. duplicate, reflected 13. introspection

reflux... 3. ebb 6. ebbing, reflow 8. backflow, reaction 9. refluence, returning

reform... 4. mend 5. amend, emend, renew 6. better, remake, remass, repair 7. convert, rebuild, reclaim, rectify, restore 9. amendment 10. regenerate 11. reformation

reformation... 7. rebirth 10. conversion, emendation 12. regeneration, reproduction 15. re–establishment

Reformation leaders (Hist)... 4. Knox 6. Calvin, Luther, Ridley 7. Cranmer, Latimer, Zwingli 8. Campbell 11. Melanchthon

reformer... 7. amender, reviser 9. reformado, reformist 10. politician

refraction... 7. rebound 9. dioptrics 10. deflection, dispersion 11. anaclastics

refractor... 5. prism 9. telescope

refractory... 7. restive 8. indocile, stubborn 11. disobedient 12. ungovernable

refrain... 4. curb, shun 5. avoid, cease, derry, epode 6. chorus, govern 7. abstain, forbear 8. response, restrain

refrain from using... 5. spare 7. boycott

refresco... 4. food 5. drink 11. refreshment

refresh... 3. air, dew 4. cool 5. cheer, renew, slake 6. repose, revive 7. freshen, relieve 8. recreate, renovate 9. reanimate, replenish 10. invigorate, strengthen 11. refreshment 12. reinvigorate

refreshing... 5. balmy 7. bracing 8. regaling 10. heartening 11. stimulating 12. exhilarating

refrigerant... 3. ice 6. cooler 7. ammonia, coolant, cryogen

refrigeration... 7. cooling 8. cryogeny 10. anesthetic, cryogenics 12. preservation

refuge... 3. ark 4. plea 5. haven 6. asylum, covert, excuse 7. retreat, shelter 8. hospital, recourse 9. sanctuary 10. protection, safety zone

refugee... 5. exile, fleer 6. émigré 7. escapee, evacuee 8. fugitive, renegade

refulgence... 6. luster 8. radiance, splendor 10. brilliancy

refund... 5. repay 6. rebate 9. reimburse

refurbish... 4. vamp 5. renew 8. brighten, renovate 11. recondition

refusal... 3. nay 6. denial 9. rejection 11. declination

refuse... 3. cot (wool), ort 4. balk, coom (coomb), culm, deny, junk, marc, scum 5. attle, chaff, dregs,

dross, repel, scrap, trash, waste, weeds 6. debris, give up, litter, midden, naysay, reject, renege, scoria, scraps 7. abandon, bagasse, cast off, decline, garbage, hogwash, repulse 8. disclaim, leavings, oddments, renounce, withhold 9. excrement, repudiate 11. odds and ends

refuse to...
accept.. 6. reject
acknowledge.. 7. disavow 9. repudiate
comply.. 12. recalcitrant
proceed.. 4. balk

refutation... 6. answer 8. disproof, elenchus, rebuttal 11. confutation

refute... 4. deny, meet 5. rebut, refel 6. assoil 8. disprove, elenctic, redargue 9. overthrow 10. contradict

regain... 6. recoup 7. get back, recover 8. retrieve 9. get back to 10. reach again

regal... 5. royal 6. groove, kingly 7. channel, stately 8. imperial, majestic, splendid 9. dignified, sovereign

regale... 4. dine, fete 5. amuse, feast, treat 7. gratify, refresh 9. entertain 11. refreshment

regalia... 6. finery 7. costume, emblems, symbols 8. insignia 11. decorations 12. special dress 13. paraphernalia

regard... 3. air, awe 4. care, deem, gaze, heed, hold, look, love, mind, obey (law), rate, sake, view 5. honor, judge, think, treat 6. aspect, behold, esteem, remark, repute 8. attitude, consider, estimate, hold dear, listen to 9. attention, relevance, viewpoint 10. appearance, estimation 11. contemplate, observation 13. consideration

regard (pert to)...
for others.. 8. altruism
for other's wish.. 9. deference
highly.. 6. admire 7. lionize
with approval.. 6. admire
with deference.. 5. honor 7. respect
with veneration.. 6. revere

regardful... 7. careful, mindful 8. cautious 9. attentive, observant 10. altruistic, respectful, thoughtful 11. considerate

regarding... 2. re 5. anent 10. concerning, respecting

regardless... 6. anyhow 8. careless, heedless, slighted 9. negligent 10. neglectful 11. inattentive, indifferent, unconcerned, unobservant 15. notwithstanding

regards... 8. respects 9. greetings 11. compliments

regatta cup... 5. Platt 8. Carnegie, Grimoldi

regency... 4. rule 8. dominion 10. government

regenerate... 5. shape 6. redeem, reform, revive 7. convert, restore 8. re–create 9. reproduce 11. fashion anew

regeneration... 7. renewal, revival

9. reversion 10. re–creation
11. reformation 12. reproduction
14. divine function

regent... 5. ruler 6. deputy, ruling
7. regnant 8. governor

Regent diamond, 137 carats (pert
to)...
included in.. 11. State jewels (France)
named for.. 14. Regent of France
placed in.. 6. Louvre
sold (1717) to.. 4. Pitt (Gov of
Madras, Ind)

regime, regimen... 4. diet, rule
6. system 7. therapy
10. government, regulation
14. administration

regiment... 4. unit, wing 6. outfit
8. organize 11. systematize

regiment, framework of... 5. cadre

regina... 5. queen

region... 4. area, belt, zone 5. clime,
place, realm, space, tract 6. sphere
7. climate, cockpit, country,
demesne, kingdom, section
8. district, province

region (pert to)...
beyond Jordan.. 5. Perea 6. Basham
blissful.. 4. Eden
comb form.. 5. nesia
desert.. 3. erg 5. waste
indefinite.. 5. tract
infernal.. 7. Avernal 8. Tartarus
meteorological.. 6. pleion
wooded.. 4. wold
woodless.. 5. weald

region of...
contentment.. 6. Arcady
dead (Egypt Myth).. 6. Amenti
fabled wealth.. 8. Eldorado
nether darkness.. 6. Erebus
opposite side earth.. 9. Antipodes
Solomon's gold (Bib).. 5. Ophir

register... 3. act 4. list, roll 5. annal,
entry, index 6. docket, enlist, enroll,
record 7. rotulet 8. archives,
recorder, schedule 9. catalogue,
chronicle, necrology, registrar
11. account book, matriculate

registrar... 8. recorder 9. accounter

regius... 5. royal 13. professorship

regret... 3. rue 4. ruth 5. grief, sorry
6. repent, repine, sorrow 7. deplore,
remorse 9. penitence 10. repentance
11. compunction 12. self–reproach

regretful... 5. sorry 8. repining
9. repentant

regular... 4. even 5. usual 6. formal,
normal, smooth, stated 7. correct,
orderly, typical, uniform 8. constant,
habitual, ordinary, ordinate, rhythmic,
standard 9. isometric 10. systematic

regularity... 5. order 8. symmetry
9. constancy 10. smoothness,
uniformity

regularly... 6. always 7. usually
8. properly, smoothly 9. correctly
10. constantly, habitually
12. methodically, periodically
13. symmetrically

regulate... 3. set 4. rule 6. adjust,
direct, govern, manage, ordain,
remedy 7. arrange, control, dispose

8. organize 9. influence, methodize
11. standardize

regulation... 3. law 4. rule 5. bylaw,
order 6. system 7. control, precept
9. direction, principle

regulator... 7. control 8. governor,
rheostat 9. rheometer

Regulus... 4. king, star 5. Alpha
8. warblers 9. Cor Leonis (star)

rehabilitate... 7. restore 9. reeducate,
reinstall

rehash... 7. restate 9. réchauffé

rehearse... 3. say 4. tell 5. speak,
sum up, train 6. detail, recite, relate,
repeat, try out 7. mention, narrate,
recount 8. describe 9. enumerate,
reiterate 12. recapitulate

rehoboam... 3. hat 4. bowl 6. flagon
8. jeroboam

Rehoboam (Bib)... 11. King of Judah
(1st) 12. King of Israel (last)

reif... 7. plunder, robbery

reign... 3. raj 4. rule, sway 5. guide,
realm 6. empire 7. kingdom, prevail
8. dominion, flourish 11. sovereignty
12. supreme power

Reign of Terror (Fr Hist)... 7. anarchy
9. bloodshed, despotism
12. confiscation

reimburse... 3. pay 5. repay 6. refund
7. pay back, replace 9. indemnify
10. recompense

Reims, Rheims (pert to)...
capital (anc).. 4. Remi
famed building.. 9. Cathedral (Gothic)
famed site.. 15. crowning of kings
(Fr)

rein... 4. curb, stop 5. check, leash
6. direct, retard 7. control
8. reindeer, restrain 9. hindrance
10. bridle part

reina... 8. rockfish

reindeer... 6. tarand 7. caribou
13. constellation

reindeer (pert to)...
age, epoch.. 11. Paleolithic
flower.. 9. buttercup (white)
genus.. 8. Rangifer

reinforce... 4. back 5. add to, brace,
reman 6. restore, support
9. intensify, replenish 10. strengthen

reinforcement... 7. adjunct, support
8. addition 13. replenishment,
strengthening

reins... 5. loins 7. harness, kidneys
9. restraint

reis... 6. escudo 7. milreis 14. money
of account

reit... 5. sedge 7. seaweed

reiterate... 4. drum, harp 6. repeat
8. rehearse 12. recapitulate

reject... 5. repel, spurn 6. disown,
recuse (law), refuse 7. decline,
discard, dismiss 8. athetize, disallow
9. repudiate

rejectamenta... 5. wrack 6. refuse,
reject 7. rubbish 9. excrement

rejection... 6. heresy 7. discard,
refusal 8. ejection 9. exclusion,
objection 11. disapproval, repudiation

rejoice... 5. cheer, elate 7. delight,
gladden 8. jubilate

rejoinder . . . **5.** reply (law) **6.** answer, retort, return **8.** comeback

rejuvenate . . . **6.** revive **7.** restore **9.** stimulate **12.** reinvigorate

relâche . . . **10.** relaxation **12.** intermission **13.** no performance (Theat)

relapse . . . **4.** sink **5.** lapse **7.** subside **8.** slip back **9.** backslide, reversion **10.** recurrence, regression **11.** falling back **12.** recidivation

relate . . . **4.** tell **5.** state **6.** assert, detail, recite, report **7.** narrate, pertain, recount **8.** describe, rehearse **9.** appertain, associate

related (pert to) . . .
by blood . . **3.** sib **4.** akin **7.** cognate
on father's side . . **6.** agnate **7.** cognate **8.** agnation
on mother's side . . **5.** enate **6.** enatic **7.** cognate, enation **9.** umbilical
to land . . **8.** praedial (predial)

relating to . . .
bread . . **6.** panary
Chinese . . **7.** Sinitic
dancing . . **6.** gestic **13.** choreographic
fruit jelly . . **7.** pectous
grandparents . . **4.** aval
Hindu literature . . **5.** Vedic
life . . **5.** vital
morn . . **7.** matinal **8.** forenoon
motion . . **7.** kinetic **9.** kinematic
realities . . **7.** factual **9.** entelechy
soft palate . . **5.** velar
vascular fluid . . **5.** hemic

relation . . . **3.** kin **4.** mode, tale **6.** status, ubiety **7.** account, analogy, kinship, kinsman, recital, telling **8.** relative **9.** character, narration, reference, rehearsal, rishtadar (Hind law) **10.** connection **13.** consanguinity

relationship . . . **4.** outs **7.** kinship, kinsman, metochy **8.** affinity, relative **13.** consanguinity

relative . . . **3.** eme, kin, sib, son **4.** aunt **5.** niece, uncle **6.** allied, cousin, father, mother, nephew, sister **7.** brother, kindred **8.** apposite, daughter, kinsfolk **9.** pertinent **11.** comparative, correlative **13.** corresponding, proportionate

relative (pert to) . . .
favor to . . **8.** nepotism
rank . . **6.** degree
to . . **7.** apropos **12.** in proportion

relax . . . **4.** ease, open, rest **5.** abate, loose, remit **6.** divert, loosen, soften, unbend **7.** detente, slacken **8.** mitigate, slow down

relaxed . . . **4.** calm, cool **5.** casual **8.** laid–back **9.** easygoing

relay . . . **3.** dak (dawk) **4.** race **5.** shift **6.** remuda **7.** relieve **8.** avantlay **10.** television (station)

release . . . **4.** drop, free, trip, undo **5.** death, let go, loose, undam, unpen, untie **6.** acquit, escape, exempt, loosen, parole, remise **7.** deliver, freedom, manumit, receipt, relieve, unleash, unloose **8.** liberate **9.** discharge **10.** liberation, relinquish

11. acquittance, deliverance

relegate . . . **5.** exile, refer **6.** assign, banish, commit, deport, depute, remove **7.** ascribe, consign, discard, dismiss, exclude **8.** delegate

relent . . . **5.** abate, yield **6.** regret, soften, submit **7.** slacken

relentless . . . **6.** strict **9.** merciless **10.** inflexible, unyielding **11.** persevering, unremitting

relevant . . . **7.** germane **9.** pertinent **10.** sufficient **11.** referential

reliable . . . **4.** safe, sure **5.** tried **6.** stable, trusty **7.** solvent **8.** true–blue **11.** trustworthy

reliance . . . **4.** hope **5.** trust **6.** belief **8.** mainstay **10.** confidence, conviction, dependence

relic . . . **5.** curio, huaca, huaco, ruins **7.** antique, memento, remains **8.** artifact, fragment, memorial, souvenir, survival **9.** antiquity

relic cabinet . . . **7.** étagère, whatnot

relict . . . **5.** widow **7.** widower **8.** survivor

relied . . . **6.** banked **7.** counted, reposed, trusted **8.** confided, depended, reckoned

relief . . . **3.** aid **4.** bote (bot), dole, ease, fret (Arch), help **5.** spell **6.** remedy, succor **7.** comfort, outline, redress, relieve, welfare **8.** easement **10.** assistance, embossment, mitigation, substitute, sustenance **11.** alleviation, deliverance **15.** indemnification

relieve . . . **3.** aid **4.** cure, ease, free, help **5.** abate, allay, clear, raise, spell **6.** assist, remedy, remove, succor **7.** assuage, lighten, redress, refresh, support, sustain, unloose **8.** diminish **10.** substitute

religion (pert to) . . . **4.** sect **5.** creed, deism, faith, piety, trust **6.** belief, hermit, schism, theism, voodoo **8.** monastic, theology **9.** solipsism **10.** conformity, persuasion

religion, type . . . **5.** Islam **6.** Taoism **7.** Jainism, Judaism **8.** Buddhism, Hinduism **9.** Mormonism, Moslemism, Muslimism, Shintoism **11.** Anglicanism, Catholicism **12.** Christianity, Confucianism **13.** Mohammedanism, Protestantism

religious . . . **4.** holy **5.** exact, godly, pious, rigid **6.** devout, sacred **7.** devoted, fervent, zealous **9.** born–again, pharasaic, spiritual **10.** devotional, meticulous, scrupulous **11.** theological **13.** conscientious

religious (pert to) . . .
assembly . . **12.** congregation
belief . . **5.** deism **6.** omnist **10.** monotheism
brotherhood . . **8.** sodality **9.** ecumenism **10.** fellowship **11.** ecumenicism
center . . **7.** Lambeth (Eng)
composition . . **5.** motet
cult, sect . . **5.** fakir **6.** Shaker, Shinto **7.** Pietism, Sikhism **8.** cenobite **9.** anchorite **11.** Hare Krishna

devotee.. **5**. fakir
devotion.. **6**. novena
division.. **6**. schism
expedition (Mil).. **7**. crusade
fasting.. **4**. Lent **9**. Ember Days
 10. Ember Weeks
festival.. **4**. mela (Ind) **5**. Purim (Jew)
madness, mania.. **9**. theomania
metaphysics.. **7**. gnostic
musical.. **6**. anthem
offering.. **7**. deodate **8**. oblation
Order member.. **6**. Marist **7**. Templar
poem.. **5**. psalm
primitive.. **6**. voodoo
psalm.. **4**. hymn, poem, song
publication (RCCh).. **4**. ordo
relinquish.. **3**. let **4**. cede, quit
 5. forgo, leave, waive, yield
 6. desert, desist, forego, give up,
 remise, resign **7**. abandon, forsake,
 release **8**. abdicate, renounce
 9. surrender **11**. leave behind
 12. withdraw from
relinquishment... **9**. surrender
 11. abandonment **12**. renunciation
reliquary, reliquiae (pl)... **3**. box
 4. arca, tomb **5**. chest **6**. casket,
 chasse, shrine **8**. monument
relish... **4**. gust, tang, zest **5**. achar,
 enjoy, gusto, sauce, taste **6**. canape,
 caviar, degust, flavor, liking
 8. pleasure **9**. condiment, degustate,
 enjoyment, flavoring, seasoning
 11. hors d'oeuvre **13**. gratification
relucent... **5**. lucid **6**. lucent
 7. radiant, shining **8**. lightish
 9. refulgent
reluctance... **8**. aversion
 10. repugnance **13**. indisposition,
 unwillingness **14**. disinclination
reluctance unit (Elec)... **3**. rel
reluctant... **5**. chary, loath **6**. averse
 8. hesitant, not ready **9**. resisting,
 unwilling **11**. disinclined
reluctate... **5**. repel **6**. oppose
 9. repudiate
rely... **4**. hold, lean, rest **5**. count,
 trust **6**. cleave, depend, reckon,
 repose **7**. confide
rely on, upon... **4**. hope **5**. trust
 6. depend, lippen **7**. believe
remain... **3**. lie **4**. bide, last, rest, stay
 5. abide, tarry **6**. endure, reside
 8. continue
remainder... **4**. rest, stub **5**. relic,
 stump **6**. estate **7**. balance, remnant,
 residue, surplus **8**. fragment,
 leavings, residual, residuum
remaining... **4**. left, over **6**. ledger
 (leger) **7**. durable, remnant, staying,
 surplus **8**. residual **9**. permanent
remaining stationary... **6**. static
 7. waiting **8**. awaiting
remains... **5**. ashes, ruins, stays
 6. corpse, relics **7**. cadaver, fossils
 9. remainder
remanent... **4**. left **7**. further, lasting,
 remains, remnant, residue
 8. enduring, leftover, residual
 9. permanent, remainder
 10. additional **13**. supplementary
remark... **3**. say, see **4**. heed, note

 5. gloss, state **6**. notice, regard
 7. comment, observe **8**. perceive,
 point out **9**. statement
 10. annotation, commentary,
 indication **11**. observation
 12. interjection
remark (pert to)...
amusing, witty.. **3**. gag **4**. quip
clever.. **3**. mot
commonplace.. **9**. platitude
smarting.. **7**. sarcasm, stinger
upon.. **7**. explain
witless.. **5**. boner
remarkable... **5**. great **7**. notable,
 strange, unusual **8**. uncommon
 9. wonderful **10**. noteworthy,
 noticeable, observable
 11. conspicuous **13**. extraordinary
Rembrandt (pert to)...
birthplace.. **6**. Leyden (Neth)
color.. **5**. brown
famed as.. **6**. etcher (Dutch)
 7. painter
style.. **14**. Rembrandtesque
remedial... **6**. remedy (pert to)
 7. healing **8**. curative, panacean
 10. corrective **11**. therapeutic
remedy... **3**. aid, fix **4**. bote (bot),
 cure, gain, help **5**. amend **6**. doctor,
 relief **8**. antidote, medicine
 10. assistance, reparation
remedy (pert to)...
cure–all.. **6**. elixir
mysterious (of Paracelsus)..
 7. arcanum
quack.. **7**. nostrum
soothing.. **4**. balm **6**. balsam
universal.. **7**. panacea
remember... **3**. min **9**. recollect,
 reminisce **10**. keep in mind
remembrance... **4**. fame **5**. token
 6. memory, Minnie, trophy
 7. memento **8**. allusion, memorial,
 reminder, souvenir **12**. recollection
 13. commemoration
remex... **12**. quill feather
remind... **6**. prompt, recall
 8. remember **13**. call attention
reminder... **4**. memo, twit **7**. memento
 8. souvenir **10**. memorandum
 11. remembrance
reminiscence... **3**. act **4**. fact
 5. power **6**. memory **8**. anecdote
 10. experience **11**. memorabilia
 12. recollection
remise... **6**. giving, return **7**. release,
 replace, respite **8**. granting
 9. remission, surrender
remiss... **3**. lax **5**. slack **7**. lenient
 8. careless, dilatory, heedless
 9. negligent **10**. neglectful
 11. inattentive, thoughtless
remissness... **7**. neglect **9**. indolence
 10. negligence **12**. improvidence
remit... **3**. pay **5**. relax **6**. acquit,
 assign, cancel, excuse, pardon,
 reduce, resign **7**. absolve, forgive,
 release, restore, suspend **8**. abrogate,
 liberate, mitigate, recommit
 9. surrender
remnant... **3**. ash, end, ort, rag
 4. dreg, left, rest, stub **5**. piece,

relic, scrap, shred, trace 7. oddment, remains, yet left 8. fragment 9. remainder, remaining 10. suggestion

remolade ... 5. sauce 8. dressing, ointment

remonstrate ... 5. plead 7. protest 8. point out 11. expostulate

remontant ... 14. flowering again

remora ... 4. fish, pega (pegora)

remord ... 5. taint 6. ponder, rebuke 7. afflict, censure, remorse

remorse ... 4. pity 6. regret, sorrow 8. distress 9. penitence, repentent 10. compassion 11. compunction

remorseful ... 5. sorry 7. pitiful 8. contrite, merciful, penitent, pitiable 9. regretful 13. compassionate

remorseless ... 8. pitiless 9. merciless, unpitying 10. implacable, inflexible, relentless, unmerciful 11. unregretful

remote ... 3. far, off 5. alien, vague 6. elenge, forane, ultima 7. distant, foreign 8. abstruse, reserved, secluded, ulterior 10. farfetched, unsociable 11. out–of–the–way

remote control ... 10. pushbutton, tele–action

remote region ... 5. Thule (Greenland)

remotest ... 7. endmost, very end 8. farthest 14. ghost of a chance

removal ... 8. ejection 9. deduction 10. divestment, evacuation, extraction 11. elimination 12. transference

remove ... 3. rid 4. dele, doff, move, void, weed 5. erase, evict, expel, strip 6. change, debunk, delete, depose, divest, eloign (law) 7. dismiss, extract, relieve 8. abstract, displace, evacuate, put aside, transfer 9. eliminate, eradicate, translate 11. assassinate

remove (pert to) ...
cover .. 5. uncap
from office .. 4. oust 6. depose, recall
moisture .. 3. dry 5. wring 9. dehydrate
point of origin .. 6. distal
seed from flax .. 6. ribble
seeds .. 3. gin, pit
stalk .. 5. strig
to another place .. 8. transfer 9. translate
whole blubber .. 6. flense

removed ... 4. took 5. apart 6. betook, remote 7. distant, far away 8. reserved, secluded 9. separated, unrelated 10. unsociable

remover ... 6. porter 7. carrier, drayman, solvent 9. scavenger 10. contractor, eradicator

remunerate ... 3. pay 5. repay 6. reward 7. requite, satisfy 9. reimburse 10. compensate, recompense

remuneration ... 3. pay 6. reward 7. payment 8. pittance, requital 9. emolument 10. recompense 12. compensation, satisfaction 13. reimbursement

Remus (pert to) ...
brother .. 7. Romulus

father .. 4. Mars
legendary founder of .. 4. Rome (with brother)
slayer .. 7. Romulus

renable ... 4. glib 5. ready 6. fluent 8. eloquent

renaissance ... 7. rebirth, revival

Renaissance (pert to) ...
Archit .. 12. Roman classic
art .. 10. neoclassic
associated with .. 8. Petrarch
furniture .. 6. carved 7. English, Flemish
Italian reference .. 12. Resorgimento (new arising)
lace .. 10. Battenburg

renal ... 6. kidney 7. nephric

renascence ... 7. rebirth, revival 14. The Renaissance

rencounter ... 4. duel 5. clash 6. action, combat, flight 7. contest, meeting 8. conflict 9. collision

rend ... 3. rip 4. rive, tear 5. break, burst, sever, split, wrest 7. extract, rupture 8. fracture

render ... 3. pay, put 4. give, make, melt 6. return 7. clarify, convert, deliver, execute, extract, narrate, present, requite 8. transmit 9. translate 10. understand 11. communicate

render (pert to) ...
accessible .. 4. open
agreeable .. 7. dulcify
angry, choleric .. 6. enrage
conformable to Eng .. 7. Anglify 9. Anglicize
divine .. 5. deify
dull .. 8. hebetate
enduring .. 6. anneal
fat .. 3. try 6. try out
fertile .. 6. enrich
free from bacteria .. 9. sterilize
ineffective .. 4. void 5. annul 10. invalidate
intelligible .. 9. elucidate
less pliant .. 7. stiffen
muddy, turgid .. 4. roil
oblique .. 5. splay
obscure .. 6. darkle 9. obfuscate
sharp .. 9. acuminate
unconscious .. 4. stun

rendezvous ... 5. tryst 6. refuge 7. meeting, retreat 11. appointment

rendition ... 7. account 8. delivery 9. surrender 10. extraction 11. performance, translation 14. interpretation

renegade ... 3. rat 5. rebel 7. pervert, traitor 8. apostate, deserter, fugitive, turncoat

renege ... 4. deny 6. desert, revoke 7. decline 8. renounce

renew ... 6. resume, revamp, revive 7. convert, refresh, restore 8. renovate 10. invigorate, regenerate 12. redintegrate

renewal ... 10. conversion, renovation, resumption 11. restoration

renitent ... 7. opposed 9. reluctant, resistant 12. recalcitrant

rennet ... 3. lab 5. apple 6. curdle,

rennin 7. extract 9. coagulate
rennin... 6. enzyme
renommé... 8. renowned
  10. celebrated
Renommist... 8. braggart, renowner
  9. swaggerer
renounce... 4. cede, deny 5. forgo
  (forego), waive 6. abjure, desert,
  disown, recant, reject, renege, resign
  7. abandon, forsake, retract
  8. abnegate, forswear, swear off
  9. repudiate, surrender 10. relinquish
  12. abrenunciate
renouncement... 9. rejection
  10. temperance 11. abandonment,
  recantation
renovate... 5. renew 6. repair, resume,
  revive 7. restore 10. regenerate
renown... 4. fame, note 5. éclat, glory
  10. reputation
renowned... 5. famed, noted
  6. famous 10. celebrated
  11. illustrious 13. distinguished
rent... 3. let, pay 4. dues, hire, hole,
  slit, tear, toll, tore, torn 5. break,
  cleft, lease, share, split 6. reward
  7. revenue, rupture, slitted, tribute
  8. tattered
rent (pert to)...
  asunder.. 5. rived
  harvest.. 7. onstand
  in oats.. 7. avenage
  paid.. 3. tac
renter... 6. lessee, lodger, tenant
renunciation... 6. denial 9. disavowal,
  rejection, surrender 10. abjuration,
  disclaimer, temperance
  11. abandonment, recantation
  14. relinquishment
repaid in kind... 10. retaliated
repair... 3. fix 4. darn, heal, mend
  5. amend, patch, renew 6. doctor,
  remedy, resort 7. correct, rebuild,
  restore 8. atone for 9. condition
  13. betake oneself
reparation... 6. amende, amends,
  remedy, repair, reward 7. damages,
  redress 8. reprisal, requital
  9. atonement, indemnity
  10. recompense 11. restitution
  12. compensation, satisfaction
repartee... 3. wit 5. reply 6. retort
  7. riposte
repast... 3. tea 4. feed, meal 5. feast,
  lunch, treat 6. tiffin 8. mealtime,
  prandial 9. collation
repatriate... 5. exile 6. banish
  10. expatriate
repay... 4. meed 6. answer, avenge,
  refund, return 7. requite, restore
  9. reimburse, retaliate
  10. compensate, recompense,
  remunerate
repeal... 5. annul, emend, forgo
  (forego) 6. appeal, cancel, recall
  7. abandon, abolish, rescind, retract,
  reverse 8. abrogate, renounce,
  withdraw
repeat... 4. copy, echo, rame 5. recur
  7. iterate, restate 8. remember
  9. duplicate, reiterate
repeat (pert to)...

mathematics.. 8. repetend
mechanically.. 6. parrot
noisily.. 3. din
performance.. 6. encore
twice (pref).. 3. bis
repeating... 4. rote 10. repetitive
  11. repetitious
repel... 5. avert, check 6. offend,
  oppose, rebuff, refuse, reject, resist,
  revolt 7. disgust, repulse 9. drive
  back, force back
repellent... 5. harsh 6. odious
  9. repulsive, resistant, revolting
repent... 3. rue 6. reform, regret
  9. do penance
repentance... 4. ruth 5. shame
  6. regret 9. penitence 10. contrition
  11. compunction
repercussion... 4. blow 6. impact
  9. afterclap, aftermath 10. reflection
repertory... 4. list 5. index, store
  8. calendar, magazine, treasure
  9. catalogue 10. collection,
  repertoire, storehouse
repetition... 4. rote 5. troll 6. encore
  8. iterance 9. iteration 11. reiteration
  14. recapitulation
repetition (pert to)...
  biology.. 6. merism
  music.. 5. rondo 7. tremolo
  rhetoric.. 8. anaphora 9. tautology
  sound.. 4. echo
  sounds (slight).. 6. patter
repetitive... 8. habitual 9. redundant
  11. repetitious
repine... 4. fret 6. lament, regret
  7. grumble 8. complain
replace... 4. stet 5. reset, stead
  6. repone 7. restore 8. supplant
  9. discharge, supersede
  10. substitute
replaceable... 10. expendable
replenish... 4. feed, fill 5. store
  6. refill 7. perfect, provide
  8. complete
replete... 3. fat 4. full 5. sated
  6. filled, gorged 7. bloated
  8. abundant 9. surfeited
replevin... 4. bail, writ 8. recovery
replica... 3. bis 4. copy 6. repeat
  9. duplicate, facsimile
reply... 4. echo 5. rebut 6. answer,
  oracle, rejoin, retort 7. defense,
  epistle, respond 8. reaction, repartee,
  response 9. rejoinder 11. retaliation
report... 3. cry, pop 4. bang, note
  5. bruit, rumor, sound, state, story
  6. delate, recite, relate, repute
  7. account, hearsay, recital, verdict
  8. describe 9. narration, narrative,
  statement 10. accounting,
  commentary, responsory
  11. information, publication
report (pert to)...
  common.. 6. gossip
  false, absurd.. 5. rumor 6. canard
  7. slander
  following lightning.. 7. thunder
  for duty.. 14. present oneself
  official.. 7. hansard
  of proceedings.. 6. cahier
reporter... 3. cub 6. legman, pistol

7. newsman 8. newshawk
9. informant 12. newspaperman
reporter's rounds... 8. newsbeat
reporter's sign off... 6. thirty
repose... 3. lie, sit 4. ease, rely, rest
5. peace, place, sleep 7. deposit,
recline 9. quiescent, quietness
10. quiescence, relaxation
repository... 3. ark 4. file 5. vault
6. chapel (RCCh), museum
8. treasury 9. confidant, sepulcher
10. depository, storehouse
11. auction room
reposoir... 5. altar
repoussé... 7. art work
reprehensible... 8. blamable, culpable
9. accusable, obnoxious
10. censurable, reprovable
11. blameworthy
reprehension... 5. blame 7. censure,
reproof 9. reprimand 11. reprobation
12. condemnation, denunciation
represent... 5. enact 6. denote,
depict, typify 7. betoken, exhibit,
portray, produce 8. describe
9. delineate
representation... 3. art 4. copy, icon,
idea, idol, show 5. drama 6. avowal,
symbol 7. picture 9. depiction,
enactment, portrayal, spectacle
10. exhibition, profession
11. delineation, description,
portraiture 12. reproduction
representation (pert to)...
by characters (Mus).. 8. notation
graphic.. 5. chart
Medusa's head.. 9. gorgoneum
mental.. 5. image 7. eidolon,
phantom
of scene.. 7. tableau
of solar system.. 6. orrery
of star.. 7. estoile
small.. 5. model 9. miniature
representative... 4. heir, type
5. agent, envoy 6. deputy, legate
7. example, tribune, typical
8. delegate, exponent, symbolic
9. successor 10. ambassador,
legislator, lieutenant, substitute
12. illustrative
repress... 4. curb, rein, stop 5. check,
crush, quell 6. hush up, muffle, stifle
7. put down 8. restrain, suppress
9. overpower
reprieve... 5. delay 6. pardon, relief
7. relieve, respite 8. postpone
reprimand... 5. chide, scold, slate
6. rebuke 7. censure, reprove
reprisal... 7. revenge, revenue
8. requital 11. retaliation
reproach... 4. taca, twit 5. abuse,
blame, chide, shend, taunt
6. accuse, revile, vilify 7. censure,
condemn, reproof, sarcasm, upbraid
8. disgrace, dishonor 9. disrepute,
invective 10. accusation, opprobrium
12. vilification
reproach, free of... 9. blameless
reprobate... 6. disown, reject, wicked
7. abandon, corrupt, knavish, vicious
8. depraved, hardened, recreant
9. condemned, miscreant, reprehend,

scoundrel 10. black sheep
12. unprincipled 13. reprehensible
reproduce... 4. copy 6. recite, remake,
repeat 8. multiply 9. duplicate,
propagate
reproduction... 4. copy 6. ectype,
recall 7. picture, replica 8. likeness
10. repetition 11. counterpart,
duplication 14. representation
reproductive... 5. gamic, spore
10. recreative 12. regenerative
reproof... 5. roast 6. rebuke
7. chiding 8. disgrace, reproach
9. reprimand 10. admonition,
censurable, refutation
11. blameworthy, confutation
12. reprehension 13. reprehensible
reprove... 4. rate 5. blame, chide,
scold 6. berate, rebuke 7. censure,
correct, upbraid 8. admonish,
reproach 9. objurgate, reprehend,
reprimand
reproving... 10. admonitive
reptile... 4. toad, worm 5. snake,
viper 6. dragon, iguana, lizard, turtle
7. monitor, serpent 8. creeping,
Reptilia 9. scoundrel
reptile (pert to)...
class.. 8. Reptilia
crocodile.. 6. mugger
extinct.. 9. pterosaur 10. diplodocus
11. pterodactyl, Pterosauria
group.. 6. Sauria
hard-shelled.. 6. iguana, turtle
8. terrapin, tortoise
iguanalike.. 7. tuatara
large.. 3. boa 9. alligator, crocodile
10. salamander
lizard.. 3. eft 4. adda, newt, seps
5. skink (scink) 6. Anolis, iguana,
moloch 7. monitor 9. chameleon
10. chuckwalla 11. Gila monster
Mesozoic.. 8. dinosaur
myth.. 6. dragon 8. basilisk
10. cockatrice, salamander
oldest.. 9. sea turtle
salamander.. 3. eft 4. newt
scale.. 5. scute
snake.. 3. asp 5. adder, cobra, krait
6. garter, python 8. anaconda,
Squamata 10. copperhead
reptilian... 7. saurian
Reptilian Age... 8. Mesozoic
Republic... 5. State 6. France
7. Andorra (Andorre) 9. San Marino
10. commonweal, government
12. United States
Republican Party... 3. GOP
7. mugwump (bolter 1884)
Republic of Plato... 4. Book (famed)
8. dialogue 10. ideal State
repudiate... 4. deny 6. abjure, disown,
recant, reject 7. disavow, discard,
exclude 8. renounce
repugnance... 4. hate 5. odium
6. nausea 7. disgust, opposed
8. aversion, loathing 9. antipathy,
hostility 10. abhorrence, antagonism,
opposition, reluctance
12. disagreement
repugnant... 6. odious 7. adverse,
hostile, opposed 8. inimical

9. offensive, repellent, repulsive
10. refractory 11. distasteful
12. incompatible 14. irreconcilable
repulse... 5. repel 6. denial, rebuff
7. refusal 9. rejection
repulsive... 4. ugly, vile 5. nasty
6. odious 7. fulsome 9. offensive,
repellent, resistant, revolting
10. disgusting, forbidding,
malodorous
repurchase... 6. redeem
reputable... 6. worthy 9. estimable,
honorable 10. creditable
11. respectable
reputation... 4. fame, name, note
5. glory, honor 9. celebrity, notoriety
11. distinction 13. consideration
repute... 4. hold, word 5. éclat, honor
6. credit, esteem, regard, report,
revere 8. prestige 9. reputable
10. popularity, reputation
reputed... 6. deemed 7. assumed
8. accepted, presumed, putative,
supposed 10. understood
request... 3. ask, beg 4. plea, pray,
suit 6. appeal, behest, demand
7. entreat, solicit 8. entreaty,
petition, rogation 12. supplication
requiescat in pace... 11. rest in
peace
requiescence... 6. repose
requin... 5. shark 8. man–eater
require... 3. ask 4. need 5. claim,
exact, force 6. charge, compel,
demand, enjoin, entail, oblige
8. obligate 11. necessitate
requisition... 5. order 6. demand
11. application, requirement
requital... 7. payment, revenge
8. reprisal 10. recompense
11. retaliation, retribution
12. compensation
requite... 3. pay 5. atone, repay
6. avenge, return, reward
7. revenge, satisfy 9. retaliate
10. compensate, recompense
11. interchange
reredos... 4. wall 6. screen
9. back–plate (armor), partition
reremouse... 3. bat
res... 5. point, thing 6. matter
rescind... 5. annul 6. cancel, recall,
recant; repeal, revoke 7. abolish
8. abrogate
rescue... 3. aid 4. free, save
6. ransom, redeem, regain 7. deliver,
reclaim, recover, release 8. delivery,
liberate 9. extricate 11. deliverance
rese... 4. rage, rush 5. hurry, onset,
quake, shake 7. impulse, tremble
8. rashness
resemblance... 6. ringer 7. analogy
8. affinity, likeness 9. agreement,
semblance 10. similarity, similitude
resembling (pert to)...
bark.. 11. corticiform
comb.. 8. pectinal
goose.. 8. anserine
gypsum.. 11. alabastrine
horse.. 6. equoid
man.. 7. android
minute animals.. 11. animalcular

rind.. 8. cortical
salt.. 6. haloid
seed.. 6. ovular
snakes.. 7. elapine 8. viperine
star.. 7. stellar 8. stellate 9. stellated
turf.. 5. soddy
wall.. 5. mural
resentment... 3. ire 5. pique, spite
6. choler, enmity, hatred, malice,
rancor 7. dudgeon, umbrage
9. animosity, malignity
11. displeasure, indignation
reservation... 5. tract 8. preserve
9. reticence 10. engagement,
limitation 11. withholding
13. qualification
reserve... 4. bank, fund, keep, save
5. allot, spare, stock, store
6. engage, refuge 7. backlog,
modesty, shyness 8. coldness,
distance, postpone, withhold
9. exception, restraint, retention,
reticence, sanctuary 10. constraint,
diffidence, limitation, substitute
11. self–control, taciturnity
reserved... 3. coy 4. cool, kept, unco
5. aloof, saved, staid, taken
6. modest, sedate 7. distant
8. reticent 15. uncommunicative
reservoir... 4. font, pool, sump
5. store 6. cavity, cenote, supply
7. piscina, reserve 8. fountain
reservoir of Pecquet (Anat)...
12. lymph channel 13. cisterna chyli
res gestae... 5. deeds, facts
8. exploits 10. things done
resiant... 7. present 8. resident
reside... 4. bide, live, room, stay
5. abide, dwell, lodge 6. remain
7. sojourn 8. habitate
residence... 4. home, seat, stay
5. abode 6. palace 7. deanery
8. domicile, dwelling 9. consulate,
residency 10. habitation
residencia... 5. court, trial
resident... 3. cit 6. intern, tenant
7. burgess, citizen 8. diplomat,
occupant 10. inhabitant
residual... 7. remnant 8. residuum
9. remainder
residue... 3. ash, ort 4. coke, dreg,
marc, rest, silt, slag 5. ashes
6. pomace, relics 7. balance,
remains, remnant 8. leavings,
sediment 9. remainder
residuum... 7. residue 8. hangover,
leavings 9. remainder
resign... 4. cede, quit 5. demit, waive,
yield 6. give up, submit 7. abandon,
consign 8. abdicate, renounce
9. surrender 10. relinquish
resignation... 5. demit 8. patience
9. demission, endurance
10. abdication, submission
12. renunciation 14. relinquishment
resigned... 9. contented
10. submissive 11. acquiescent
13. uncomplaining
resilient... 7. buoyant, elastic
8. cheerful 9. recoiling
10. rebounding 11. returning to
12. recuperative

resin... 3. gum, lac 4. aloe, tolu
  5. amber, anime, copal, jalap, rosin
  6. dammar, mastic
resin (pert to)...
  aromatic.. 4. balm 5. elemi, myrrh
    6. balsam 7. acouchi, camphor,
    copaiba 8. sandarac 12. frankincense
  Bib.. 8. bdellium
  bitter.. 8. labdanum (ladanum)
  brown (mineral).. 9. elaterite
  Chian turpentine.. 3. alk
  fossil.. 5. amber 8. retinite
  gum.. 5. gugal (googul)
  hard.. 5. rosin
  medicinal.. 7. aroeira 9. asafetida
    (asafoetida)
  narcotic.. 6. charas
  pine.. 7. galipot
  soft.. 5. animé, copal, elemi
  translucent.. 8. sandarac
  tropical.. 5. copal
  varnish ingredient.. 6. dammar
  yellowish.. 5. amber 7. gamboge
resinous substance... 3. gum, lac
  5. copal 7. shellac
resist... 4. fend, stem 5. rebel, repel
  6. defeat, oppose 7. prevent, ward
  off 8. outstand 9. withstand
  10. counteract
resistance... 6. rebuff 7. defense
  8. rheostat 9. hostility 10. opposition
resistant... 5. tough 8. obdurate
  9. resisting 10. unyielding
  13. counteractive
resisting... 7. hostile 8. opposing
  9. oppugnant, tenacious
  12. antagonistic
resisting (pert to)...
  description.. 11. indefinable
  power.. 4. wiry
  pressure.. 8. renitent
  pressure bar.. 5. strut
resolute... 4. bold, firm 5. fixed, stern
  6. gritty, steady 7. decided
  8. constant, positive, resolved,
  unshaken 9. desperado, obstinate,
  steadfast 10. determined, inflexible,
  unyielding 11. perseverant,
  persevering
resolution... 4. firm 5. nerve
  6. motion, steady 7. courage,
  purpose, resolve, verdict 8. analysis,
  decision, resolved, strength
  9. assurance, constancy, fortitude
  10. conversion, conviction, relaxation,
  separation 11. persevering
  12. perseverance 13. determination,
  steadfastness 15. disentanglement
resolve... 4. melt 5. lapse (law),
  parse, relax, solve 6. assure, decide,
  dispel, inform, reduce, settle
  7. analyze, explain, purpose, unravel
  8. convince, dissolve, separate
  9. determine, transform
  13. disentangle
resonance... 8. sonority, vibrance
  10. resounding
resonant... 7. echoing, ringing, vibrant
  8. sonorous, sounding
  10. resounding 11. reverberant
resort... 3. spa 4. dive 5. haunt
  6. betake, casino, refuge 7. finagle,

purlieu 8. frequent, recourse,
resource 9. expedient, fainaigue,
honky–tonk
resound... 4. echo, peal, ring 6. be
loud, re–echo 8. proclaim
  11. reverberate
resounding... 4. loud 13. reverberating
resource... 5. means, skill 6. refuge,
resort, supply 9. expedient
  10. capability 11. contrivance
resourceful... 5. sharp 9. Daedalian,
ingenious
resources... 5. funds, means, money
  6. assets, supply 7. resorts
  10. expedients 12. contrivances
respect... 3. awe 4. heed 5. defer,
favor, honor 6. aspect, detail,
esteem, homage, regard, repute,
revere 7. concern, observe, regards
8. attitude, venerate 9. attention,
deference, relevance, reverence,
viewpoint 10. politeness
13. consideration
respectable... 6. decent 9. estimable,
honorable, reputable, tolerable
  11. presentable
respectful... 5. civil 6. polite
  7. careful, duteous, heedful
  8. reverent 11. deferential
respective... 6. mutual 7. careful,
heedful, several, special 9. attentive,
regardful 10. particular
  12. distributive
respiration... 4. rale, sigh 7. eupnoea
9. breathing
respire... 7. breathe
respite... 4. rest 5. delay, frist, pause
  6. breath 7. leisure 8. postpone,
reprieve 9. extension (time)
  10. suspension 11. opportunity,
short shrift 12. intermission
resplendent... 5. grand 7. aureate,
radiant, shining 8. lustrous, splendid
9. beautiful, brilliant, refulgent
  10. epiphanous 11. illustrious
respond... 4. echo 5. react, reply
  6. accord, answer, retort 8. response
  10. correspond 11. reciprocate
response... 4. echo 5. reply
  6. answer, anthem, chorus
  7. rapport, refrain 8. antiphon (Mus),
reaction
responsibility... 4. care, duty, onus
  6. charge 8. solvency 11. reliability
  14. accountability 15. trustworthiness
responsible... 6. liable 7. solvent
  8. amenable, reliable 10. answerable
  11. accountable, respectable,
trustworthy
responsive... 6. pliant 7. elastic
  8. reactive 9. answering, sensitive,
teachable 10. open–minded
  11. persuasible, sympathetic
res publica... 5. state 8. republic
  10. commonweal 12. commonwealth
rest... 3. lay, set, sit 4. base, calm,
ease, lair, lean, prop, seat, slip, stay,
stop 5. cease, death, found, pause,
peace, quiet, relax, renew 6. depend,
desist, ground, repose, settle
7. balance, leisure, recline, refresh,
remains, remnant, reposal, respite,

silence, support, surplus **8.** at anchor, interval, lodgment, residuum
9. cessation, quietness, remainder, stillness **10.** quiescence, remain idle
12. intermission, peacefulness, tranquillity
rest (pert to) . . .
assured . . **9.** be certain, believe me
at rest . . **4.** abed, dead **6.** otiose
11. comfortable
day . . **7.** Sabbath
foot . . **4.** rail **7.** hassock, ottoman
house (Orient) . . **5.** serai
reading . . **7.** caesura (cesura)
restaurant . . . **4.** café, deli (sl) **5.** diner
6. eatery **7.** automat, beanery, tearoom **8.** fast–food, pizzeria, snack bar **9.** cafeteria **10.** coffee shop
11. rathskeller **12.** luncheonette
resting . . . **4.** abed **7.** dormant
8. drowsing **9.** quiescent
resting place . . . **4.** tomb **5.** étape, roost **6.** hearth **7.** lairage, landing, support **8.** quarters
restitution . . . **6.** return **9.** atonement, repayment **10.** recompense, reparation **12.** compensation
13. reinstatement
restless . . . **5.** antsy, hyper, itchy
6. roving, uneasy **7.** agitato, fidgety, fretful, unquiet, restive, wakeful
8. agitated **9.** impatient, sleepless, unceasing, unrestful, unsettled, wandering **10.** changeable, reposeless
12. discontented
restoration . . . **6.** repair, return
7. renewal, revival **8.** recovery
10. renovation, reparation
11. improvement, restitution
14. redintegration
15. reestablishment
restorative . . . **6.** acopon **7.** anodyne
8. remedial **10.** reparative
restore . . . **4.** cure, heal **5.** renew, repay **6.** redeem, refund, repone, revive **7.** rebuild, recover, replace
8. renovate **9.** reinstate
11. reconstruct, reestablish
12. redintegrate, rehabilitate
restore (pert to) . . .
after cancelling . . **4.** stet
certainty, confidence . . **8.** reassure
to former position . . **9.** reinstate
to original condition . . **9.** refurbish
to proper position . . **5.** right
restrain . . . **3.** dam **4.** bate, bind, curb, rein, stay **5.** check, cramp, deter, limit, stint **6.** arrest, bridle, fetter, halter, hinder, tether **7.** abridge, confine, control, inhibit, overawe, qualify, repress **8.** restrict, suppress, withhold **9.** constrain, detention
restraint . . . **3.** bit **4.** curb, stop
5. check, force **7.** durance, modesty, reserve **9.** condition, hindrance, reticence **10.** abridgment, constraint, inhibition, limitation, moderation, repression, temperance
11. confinement, deprivation, self–control **12.** tastefulness
restraint, lack of . . . **9.** looseness
restrict . . . **3.** tie **4.** bind, curb

5. bound, cramp, limit, scant, stint
6. censor, coerce, modify **7.** confine, qualify, repress **10.** specialize
12. circumscribe
restricted . . . **5.** local **6.** narrow
7. limited, topical **9.** exclusive
10. restrained **11.** specialized
restriction . . . **5.** stint **9.** restraint
10. limitation, narrowness, regulation, tightening **11.** reservation
12. constriction **13.** qualification
resty . . . **5.** quiet **7.** restive **8.** sluggish
result . . . **3.** end, sum **4.** rise **5.** arise, ensue, event, fruit, issue, total
6. accrue, answer, effect, follow, sequel, spring, upshot **7.** proceed, product **8.** solution **9.** aftermath, deduction, eventuate, terminate
10. conclusion **11.** achievement, consequence, termination
resume . . . **5.** recur, renew **6.** reopen
7. recover **8.** reoccupy **9.** epitomize, reiterate, summarize **10.** recommence
résumé . . . **8.** abstract
10. compendium **11.** work history
resurrection . . . **6.** rising **7.** revival
10. apotheosis **11.** restoration
resuscitate . . . **6.** revive **7.** restore
8. revivify
ret . . . **3.** rot **4.** soak **5.** steep
6. expose, impute **7.** ascribe
retable . . . **5.** ledge, shelf **6.** gradin
(gradine) **8.** predella
retail . . . **4.** sale, sell **6.** repeat
8. dispense, disperse
retain . . . **4.** hold, keep, save, stet
6. employ **8.** maintain, preserve, remember **9.** recollect
retainer . . . **3.** fee **4.** cage **6.** menial, minion, vassal, yeoman **7.** servant
9. attendant, bodyguard
retaining wall . . . **9.** revetment
retaliate . . . **5.** repay **6.** avenge
7. requite **12.** make requital
retaliation . . . **6.** talion (Mosaic law, eye for eye, tooth for tooth) **7.** revenge
8. reprisal, requital **10.** punishment
11. comeuppance, retribution
retard . . . **4.** clog, drag, slow **5.** defer, delay, laten **6.** belate, deaden, detain, hinder, impede **8.** keep back, obstruct, postpone, slow down
retardant . . . **4.** clog, drag **6.** remora
8. obstacle
retardate . . . **6.** impede **8.** retarded
retch . . . **3.** gag **4.** barf (sl), hawk, spit
5. reach, vomit **6.** expand, extend, strain **7.** stretch, upchuck
rete . . . **3.** net **6.** plexus **7.** network
retention . . . **6.** memory **7.** custody, holding, keeping **8.** tenacity
11. maintenance, self–control
retentive . . . **6.** memory **7.** keeping
9. tenacious **12.** recollective
retenue . . . **7.** reserve **10.** discretion
11. self–control **13.** self–restraint
rethe . . . **5.** cruel **6.** ardent, fierce, severe
retiary . . . **6.** spider **7.** netlike
9. gladiator, retiarius
reticence . . . **7.** reserve, silence
9. restraint **13.** secretiveness

reticulated... 3. web 6. meshed, netted 7. network 12. intercrossed

reticule... 3. bag 4. etui 5. cabas (caba) 7. handbag, reticle, workbag

reticulum... 7. network, stomach (2nd) 9. neuroglia

retinue... 4. crew 5. harem, suite, train 6. escort 7. cortege, service 8. equipage 9. entourage, retainers 10. attendants

retire... 6. depart, depose, pay off, recede, vanish 7. go to bed, retreat 8. withdraw 9. disappear, discharge

retired... 4. abed, left, lone, paid 7. receded 8. departed, emeritus, recessed, resigned, secluded, solitary, vanished, withdrew 9. pensioned 10. disengaged 11. disappeared, sequestered

retirement... 7. deposal, payment, privacy, retreat 8. solitude 9. departure, recession, reticence 10. withdrawal 11. resignation 13. disemployment

retiring... 3. shy 6. modest 8. reserved, reticent 9. diffident 10. not forward, retreating 11. unobtrusive

retort... 3. mot 4. quip 5. reply 6. answer 7. riposte (ripost) 8. repartee 9. retaliate 11. retaliation

retract... 6. abjure, disown, draw in, recent, repeal 7. disavow, rescind, swallow 8. take back 9. repudiate

retraction... 6. repeal 8. palinode 10. revocation, withdrawal 11. recantation

retrad... 8. backward 11. posteriorly

retral... 8. backward 9. posterior 10. retrograde

retreat... 3. den 4. abri, lair, nest, nook, rout 6. asylum, recede, recoil, refuge, retire 7. privacy, retiral, sanctum, shelter 8. fallback, solitude 9. departure, katabasis, seclusion 10. retirement, withdrawal

retrench... 6. cut off, excise, lessen, reduce 7. abridge, curtail, cut down 8. decrease, diminish 9. economize, intercept

retrenchment... 3. cut 8. excision 9. lessening, reduction 10. abridgment 11. curtailment, economizing

retribution... 3. pay 6. return, reward 7. nemesis 8. reprisal, requital 9. vengeance 10. punishment 11. restitution 12. Last Judgment

retrieve... 5. fetch 6. redeem, regain, rescue, revive 8. make good

retrograde... 4. slow 6. recede, retral, revert 7. regress 8. backward, decadent, rearward 10. regressive 11. deteriorate 12. reversionary

retroussé... 6. pugged (nose) 8. turned up

retund... 4. beat, dull 5. blunt 6. refute, subdue 9. attenuate, drive back 10. render weak

return... 5. recur, repay, reply 6. answer, render, repeat, report, revert 7. regress, relapse, requiet,

respond, restore 9. repayment 11. restitution, retaliation

return (pert to)... *day*.. 12. answer to writ *evil for evil*.. 7. revenge 9. retaliate *tennis term*.. 3. lob *thrust (fencing)*.. 7. riposte (ripost) *to*.. 6. resume 7. relapse, revisit *to 1st theme (Mus)*.. 7. reprise

returns... 5. gains, polls 8. receipts

reune... 4. join 7. reunite 10. reassemble

reunion... 7. joining 8. sociable 14. reconciliation

re–up... 8. re–enlist

reus... 9. defendant

Reuter's News Agency... 6. London

reveal... 3. bid 4. bare, jamb, open, tell, wray 6. impart, unveil 7. divulge, exhibit, uncover 8. disclose, discover, evidence, indicate, manifest 11. communicate

reveal (in trust)... 7. confide

reveal intentionally... 4. tell 6. betray, expose 7. divulge, mislead

reveille... 4. call 5. levet 6. signal (sunrise)

revel... 3. joy 4. orgy, riot, wake 5. feast, spree, watch 6. frolic 7. carouse, delight, rejoice, revelry, wassail 8. carousal, festival 11. celebration, merrymaking 12. conviviality

revelant... 5. clear 8. manifest 12. intelligible

revelation... 6. oracle, vision 8. The Bible 9. discovery 10. appearance, disclosure 13. communication, manifestation

Revelation (Bib)... 10. Apocalypse

revelry... 3. joy 4. evoe, orgy, riot 6. revels 8. carnival, carousal 9. revelment, revelrout 11. merrymaking

revenant... 5. ghost 7. eidolon, specter (spectre) 9. recurring 10. apparition

revendicate... 7. reclaim, recover 10. real action

revenge... 6. avenge 7. requite 8. reprisal, requital 9. retaliate, vengeance 10. punishment 11. retribution

revenue... 3. tax 5. yield 6. income, profit 7. annates

reverberate... 4. echo, ring 5. repel, reply 6. return 7. rebound, reflect, resound

reverberation... 4. echo 9. reboation 10. reflection, resounding

revere... 4. love 5. adore, honor 6. esteem, regard, repute 7. respect, worship 8. venerate

reverence... 3. awe 5. dread, honor, piety 7. respect, worship 8. venerate 9. adoration, deference 10. veneration

reverent... 5. pious 6. devout 7. dutiful 10. respectful, worshipful

reverie... 4. muse 5. dream 6. notion, trance, vision 7. fantasy

reversal... 6. defeat, repeal

9. inversion, reversion
14. tergiversation
reverse . . . 4. back 5. upset 6. back up, defeat, invert, repeal, revert, revoke 7. relapse 8. contrary, converse, opposite, overturn 9. transpose 10. misfortune
reversion . . . 6. estate 7. revival 8. transfer 9. inversion 10. regression 11. inheritance
reversion (pert to) . . .
ancestral . . 7. atavism 9. atavistic
insurance . . 7. annuity
land . . 7. escheat
revert . . . 5. react, recur 6. advert, return 7. regress, relapse 11. antistrophe
revest . . . 4. robe 5. dress 6. attire, clothe 8. reinvest 9. reinstate
review . . . 4. edit 6. parade, relate, survey 8. critique, remember 9. criticism, criticize, re–examine 10. certiorati, commentary, compendium, discussion, inspection, periodical, reconsider 11. examination, reiteration 12. recollection 15. reconsideration
reviewer . . . 6. critic, writer 11. commentator
revile . . . 4. rail 5. abuse, curse 6. berate, debase, vilify 7. asperse 8. reproach, ridicule
revise . . . 4. edit 5. amend, emend 6. redact 7. correct, rewrite 8. readjust
revision . . . 7. revisal 10. correction, emendation 11. rebeholding 13. re–examination
revival . . . 7. rebirth, renewal 10. quickening 11. reanimation, renaissance, restoration 12. resurrection
revive . . . 4. stum (wine) 5. rally, renew, rouse 6. come to 7. enliven, recover, refresh, respire, restore 8. rekindle, remember 11. resuscitate
revocate . . . 6. recall, revoke 7. repress
revocation . . . 6. repeal 8. reversal 10. retraction, withdrawal 11. recantation
revoke . . . 5. adeem, annul 6. abjure, cancel, recall, recant, renege, repeal, revive 7. abolish, retract 8. abrogate 9. fainaigue 11. countermand
revolt . . . 5. rebel 6. mutiny, offend, strike 8. nauseate, sedition, uprising 9. rebellion 10. revolution 12. insurrection
revolting . . . 4. ugly 7. hideous 8. shocking 9. offensive, repellent 10. disgusting, nauseating
revolution . . . 4. gyre, turn 5. cycle, epoch, round 6. revolt 7. circuit 8. disorder, rotation 9. rebellion
revolutionary . . . 3. new 7. radical 12. catastrophic 15. insurrectionary
Revolutionary hero . . . 5. Allen (Ethan), Gates 6. Revere 8. Burgoyne 10. Cornwallis, Washington 15. Lighthorse Harry (Gen Lee)
revolve . . . 4. pirl, roll, spin, turn 5. recur, wheel, whirl 6. circle,

gyrate, ponder, rotate 7. trundle 8. meditate 9. circulate 10. deliberate
revolver . . . 3. gat, gun, rod 6. pistol 7. firearm 10. six–shooter
revolving . . . 3. orb 4. cowl (metal cap) 6. rotary
revolving (pert to) . . .
in thought . . 8. perusing
light . . 10. lighthouse
part . . 3. cam 5. rotor
storm . . 7. cyclone
revue . . . 6. medley, review 9. burlesque 13. musical comedy
reward . . . 3. pay, utu 4. meed 5. award, bonus, merit, Oscar, yield 6. hallow (to hounds) 7. guerdon 8. reprisal 10. recompense, remunerate 11. retribution 12. compensation, remuneration
reword . . . 5. alter 7. restate 8. rephrase 9. reiterate 10. paraphrase
rex . . . 4. king
rey . . . 4. king
Reynard . . . 3. fox (epic character)
rezai . . . 8. coverlet (quilted)
rhamn . . . 7. Rhamnus 9. buckthorn
rhapontic . . . 7. rhubarb 8. knapweed, pieplant
rhapsodic . . . 6. poetic 8. ecstatic
rhapsodist . . . 4. poet 8. minstrel 9. visionary 10. enthusiast
rhapsody . . . 6. jumble, medley 9. utterance (ecstatic) 10. recitation 11. composition
rhea . . . 3. emu (emeu) 5. nandu 7. ostrich
Rhea (pert to) . . .
called . . 15. Mother of the Gods
father . . 6. Uranus
home . . 5. Mt Ida (Crete)
mother . . 4. Gaea
mother of . . 4. Hera, Zeus 5. Hades 8. Poseidon
wife of . . 6. Cronus
rhebok . . . 5. peele 8. antelope
Rheims . . . see *Reims*
rhema . . . 4. term, verb, word
rheophile . . . 15. living in streams
rhetoric . . . 7. diction, oratory 9. eloquence 11. composition
rhetorical term . . . 6. aporia, simile 10. antithesis, oratorical 11. catachresis
rhetoric digression . . . 6. ecbole
rheumatism root . . . 7. wild yam
rheumatism weed . . . 10. Indian hemp, pepsissewa
rhexis . . . 7. rupture
rhinal . . . 5. nasal 6. narial
rhine . . . 5. ditch, drain 6. runnel
Rhine (pert to) . . .
breed . . 7. rabbits
native . . 11. Rhinelander
nymph . . 7. Lorelei
ref to . . 7. Rhenish
tributary . . 4. Ruhr 6. Neckar
wine . . 7. Moselle
rhino . . . 4. cash, nose (comb form) 5. money 10. rhinoceros
rhinoceros (pert to) . . .

Bib .. **4.** reem
bird .. **8.** hornbill **9.** beefeater
black .. **6.** borele **7.** keitlos
Malay .. **5.** abada
viper .. **5.** snake (poisonous)
rhizopod ... **6.** amoeba **8.** Protozoa
Rhoda ... **4.** rose
Rhode Island ...
bay .. **12.** Narragansett
capital .. **10.** Providence
city .. **7.** Newport **9.** Pawtucket
   10. Woonsocket
famed cotton mill .. **6.** Slater
first U.S. synagogue .. **5.** Touro
founder .. **13.** Roger Williams (1636)
Rebellion .. **5.** Dorr's (1842)
resort .. **7.** Newport **11.** Block Island
river .. **9.** Pawtucket **10.** Blackstone
settlers .. **8.** Puritans
State admission .. **10.** Thirteenth
State motto .. **4.** Hope
State nickname .. **11.** Little Rhody
Rhode Island Red ... **4.** fowl
Rhodesia ... see *Zimbabwe*
rhododaphne ... **8.** oleander
Rhoeadales ... **5.** poppy
   11. Papaverales
rhomb ... **7.** rhombus **10.** magic wheel
   11. spinning top
rhomboid ... **13.** parallelogram
rhombus ... **5.** rhomb
   13. parallelogram (equilateral)
Rhone tributary ... **5.** Isere
rhubarb ... **5.** clash, Rheum **6.** hassle
   7. citrine, dispute, yawweed
   8. argument, pieplant **9.** rhapontic
   10. discussion
Rhus ... **5.** sumac **7.** wax tree
rhyme, rime ... **4.** poem **6.** poetry,
   rhythm **7.** measure **9.** assonance
rhythm ... **4.** beat, lilt **5.** meter, pulse,
   swing, tempo **6.** poetry **7.** cadence,
   euphony, measure, pattern
   8. movement, rhythmus, symmetry
rhythmical break ... **7.** caesura
ria ... **5.** creek, inlet
rial ... **4.** coin, king **5.** great, noble,
   royal **6.** prince **8.** splendid
   9. excellent, stag's horn
   11. magnificent
rialto ... **4.** mart **6.** Bridge (Venice),
   market **7.** theater **8.** exchange
riant ... **3.** gay **6.** blithe, bright
   7. smiling **8.** laughing
riata ... **4.** rope **5.** lasso **6.** lariat
rib ... **4.** bone, meat, vein **5.** costa,
   ridge **6.** lierne
ribald ... **3.** low **4.** lewd. **6.** coarse,
   erotic, harlot, risqué, vulgar
   7. obscene **10.** scurrilous
   11. blasphemous **12.** ribble–rabble
riband ... **6.** ribbon
ribbed ... **3.** rep **5.** piqué **6.** corded,
   ridged **7.** costate
ribble–rabble ... **6.** gabble, rabble,
   ribald **7.** chatter **10.** incoherent
ribbon ... **3.** bow **4.** band, sash
   5. strip **6.** cestus, fillet, riband
   10. decoration
ribbon (pert to) ...
badge .. **6.** cordon
band .. **5.** corse **9.** banderole

fish .. **7.** oarfish **8.** dealfish
inked .. **10.** typewriter
knot .. **7.** rosette
ribbonlike .. **8.** taenioid
snake .. **6.** garter
Society .. **7.** Ireland
worm .. **8.** tapeworm **9.** nemertine
ribwort ... **8.** plantain
rice (pert to) ...
bird .. **4.** rail, sora **8.** bobolink
dish .. **5.** pilaf (pilau, pilaw) **7.** risotto
   8. kedgeree **9.** jambalaya, ricetable
drink .. **5.** bubud
feeding on .. **11.** oryzivorous
field .. **5.** paddy
hen .. **9.** gallinule
inferior .. **4.** chit, pago
paste .. **3.** ame
rat .. **8.** Oryzomys
refuse .. **5.** shood (shud)
Spanish .. **5.** arroz
wild .. **4.** reed
wine .. **4.** sake
rich ... **3.** fat **5.** opime **6.** creamy,
   fecund, fruity, mighty, ornate, potent
   7. copious, fertile, moneyed, opulent,
   wealthy **8.** abundant, affluent,
   colorful, powerful, resonant, valuable
   9. bountiful, expensive, luxuriant,
   sumptuous **10.** in the chips
   13. grandiloquent
rich (pert to) ...
English slang .. **4.** oofy **6.** oofier
man .. **5.** Dives (Bib), Midas, nabob
   7. Croesus **9.** plutocrat **10.** capitalist
   11. millionaire
richard ... **9.** plutocrat
riches ... **5.** lucre, means **6.** mammon
   (Bib), wealth **7.** bonanza, big bucks (sl)
   8. opulence **9.** affluence, megabucks
   (sl) **10.** prosperity
riches, demon of ... **6.** Mammon
rick ... **4.** heap, pile **5.** noise, scold,
   stack, twist **6.** pile up, rattle, sprain,
   wrench **7.** chatter
rickets ... **7.** disease **8.** rachitis
rickety ... **4.** weak **5.** crazy, shaky
   6. senile **7.** unsound **8.** unstable,
   unsteady **9.** tottering **10.** ramshackle
rickle ... **4.** heap, pile, rick **5.** stack
   6. jingle, rattle
rickrack ... **5.** braid **6.** edging
   9. insertion
ricksha, rickshaw ... **10.** jinrikisha
ricochet ... **5.** carom **7.** rebound
   10. bounce back
rid ... **4.** doff, free, kill **5.** clear, empty
   6. remove, rescue **7.** deliver, destroy,
   discard **9.** dispose of, drive away,
   eliminate **11.** disencumber
riddance ... **6.** escape **7.** discard
   11. elimination **14.** relinquishment
riddle ... **3.** ree **4.** crux, sift **5.** rebus,
   sieve **6.** enigma, pierce **7.** perplex
   8. separate **9.** conundrum, perforate
ride ... **4.** twit **5.** drive, float **6.** pester,
   travel **7.** be borne, journey, overlap
   8. domineer, ridicule **9.** carrousel
   (carousel), cavalcade, excursion
   10. forest road **12.** merry–go–round
   13. roller coaster
ride (pert to) ...

herd .. 9. guard over
off .. 4. polo (term)
roughshod over .. 9. tyrannize
shank's mare .. 4. walk
to hog, pig .. 11. boar hunting
to line .. 4. herd
rident ... 5. riant 7. smiling 8. laughing
rider ... 5. ryder 6. clause, knight
7. allonge, codicil 8. addition,
horseman 9. performer
10. freebooter, highwayman
11. endorsement, mosstrooper
Rider Haggard's novel ... 3. She
ridge ... 3. aas, rib 4. hill, rand, wale,
weal, welt 5. arête, bulge, chine,
crest 7. wrinkle
ridge (pert to) ...
anatomy .. 4. ruga 6. carina
barrier .. 5. parma
between furrows .. 7. porcate
8. porcated
coral .. 4. reef
glacial .. 2. os 5. esker (eskar)
military .. 6. rideau
mountain .. 4. loma 5. arête 6. sierra
narrow, raised .. 4. wale
oak .. 9. blackjack
raised by stroke .. 5. wheal, whelk
short .. 4. kame
sloping .. 6. cuesta
steep .. 7. hogback
stony .. 4. rand
zoology term .. 5. varix
ridicule ... 3. guy, pan 4. butt, gibe,
jeer, mock, quiz, twit 5. chaff, irony,
sneer, taunt 6. banter, deride, satire
7. asteism, mockery, sarcasm
8. derision, raillery 9. burlesque
ridiculous ... 5. funny 6. absurd
7. amusing 8. farcical 9. grotesque,
laughable, ludicrous 10. impossible,
outrageous 12. preposterous,
unbelievable
ridiculous failure ... 6. fiasco
riding (pert to) ...
bitts .. 11. anchor cable
breeches .. 8. jodhpurs
dress, costume .. 5. habit
knot .. 8. slipknot
rhyme .. 7. couplet
school .. 6. manège
whip .. 4. crop 5. quirt
rife ... 7. replete, rumored 8. abundant
9. abounding, plentiful, prevalent
10. prevailing, widespread
riff ... 6. rapids, riffle, ripple 7. midriff
9. diaphragm 13. improvisation
riffle ... 7. shallow, shuffle, wavelet
riffraff ... 3. mob 4. mean 5. offal
6. rabble, refuse, trashy 7. rubbish
9. sweepings
rifle ... 3. rob 5. reeve, steal, strip
6. Mauser, search, snider 7. carbine,
despoil, firearm, pillage, plunder,
ransack
rifle (pert to) ...
accessory .. 6. ramrod
ball .. 5. Minié 6. bullet
bird .. 14. bird of paradise
bomb .. 7. grenade
French .. 9. chassepot
old form .. 4. tige

rifler ... 4. hawk 6. robber
rift ... 3. gap, lag 4. rima, rive
5. break, cleft, split 6. cleave, divide
10. falling out
rig ... 3. fit 4. gear, suit 5. dress,
equip 6. lateen 7. bedizen, costume,
rigging, vehicle 9. Bermudian (Naut)
Riga (pert to) ...
balsam .. 5. resin (Swiss pine)
capital of .. 6. Latvia
native .. 4. Lett 7. Latvian
rine .. 4. hemp
rigging (ship) ... 4. gear, rope, spar
6. tackle 9. equipment
right ... 3. fit, pat 4. fair, true
6. adjust, dexter, proper, remedy
7. correct, justice, upright
8. becoming, suitable 9. equitable,
faultless, franchise, privilege, propriety
10. put in order 11. appropriate,
prerogative 13. justification
right (pert to) ...
angled .. 10. orthogonal
comb form .. 6. dextro
exclusive .. 6. patent 10. concession
hand .. 6. dexter
hand page .. 5. recto
law .. 5. droit
neither right nor wrong ..
11. adiaphorous
of belligerent (Naut) .. 6. angary
of ownership .. 5. title
of procedure .. 3. pas
real estate .. 8. easement
royal .. 7. regalia
time .. 3. tid
to choice .. 6. option
to pasture .. 6. eatage
turn .. 3. gee
righteous ... 4. holy, just 5. godly,
moral, pious 6. worthy 7. upright
8. virtuous 9. believers, blameless,
equitable, guiltless
righteousness ... 6. equity, virtue
8. holiness 9. godliness, rectitude
11. uprightness
rightful ... 4. just, true 5. legal, right
6. honest, lawful, proper 7. fitting,
genuine 9. equitable 11. appropriate
rigid ... 3. set 4. firm, hard 5. exact,
stern, stiff, tense 6. formal, narrow,
not lax, severe, strict 7. ascetic,
austere 8. rigorous 9. obstinate,
stringent, unbending 10. inflexible,
meticulous, unyielding
rigidity ... 7. tensity 8. hardness,
severity 9. exactness, obstinacy,
stiffness
rigol ... 4. ring 6. circle, groove
7. channel
Rigoletto ... 5. dance, opera (Verdi)
rigor, rigour ... 4. cold, fury 7. cruelty
8. asperity, rigidity, severity, violence
9. exactness, harshness, rigidness
10. shuddering, strictness
13. inflexibility
rigor mortis ... 10. stiffening (death)
12. rigor of death
rigorous ... 4. cold 5. exact, harsh,
rigid, stern, stiff 6. severe, strict
7. austere, drastic, violent
8. accurate 9. inclement, obstinate,

puritanic 10. inexorable, inflexible, relentless

rikk . . . 10. tambourine

rile . . . 3. vex 4. roil 5. anger, muddy 6. offend 7. agitate 8. irritate 9. turbidity

rill . . . 5. brook 6. course, runnel 7. rillock, rivulet 9. streamlet

rim . . . 3. lip, web 4. band, brim, edge, orle, tire 5. bezel, brink, felly (felloe), verge 6. border, flange, margin, shield 7. enclose, horizon, rimrock 8. boundary 9. perimeter

rima . . . 5. cleft 7. fissure 8. aperture 10. breadfruit

rima oris . . . 16. space between lips

rim ash . . . 9. hackberry

rimate . . . 8. fissured

rime . . . 4. hoar, poem, rent 5. chink, cleft, crack, frost, rhyme 6. poetry 7. fissure 8. aperture 9. assonance, hoarfrost 10. ladder step

rime–cold giant (Norse) . . . 4. Ymir (Ymer)

rimple . . . 4. fold 6. ripple, rumple 7. wrinkle

rimption . . . 3. lot 9. abundance

Rinaldo's steed . . . 6. Bayard

rind . . . 4. bark, husk, peel, skin 5. crust 6. cortex 7. epicarp 9. hoarfrost

rindle . . . 5. brook 6. runnel 7. rivulet

ring . . . 3. rim, set 4. band, halo, hoop, peal, toll 5. arena, bague, chime, group, knell 6. circle, clique, collar 7. annulus, circlet, coterie, resound 8. encircle, insignia, ornament, surround 9. encompass 11. association

ring (pert to) . . .
around . . 7. environ
around the sun . . 6. corona
barrel . . 4. hoop
bill . . 4. duck
bird . . 11. reed bunting
comb form . . 4. gyro
dove . . 6. cushat
finger . . 5. third
fruit jar . . 4. lute
gem crown . . 5. bezel
gem setting . . 6. chaton
gun carriage . . 7. lunette (lunet)
harness part . . 6. terret
horse training . . 5. longe
Latin . . 7. annulus
leader . . 6. rouser 9. demagogue 12. rabble–rouser
little . . 7. annulet, circlet
ornament (metal) . . 3. bee (angling)
ouzel . . 6. thrush
rope . . 7. grommet
sail . . 4. hank 8. ringtail
tail . . 3. cat 4. coon 5. lemur 6. godwit, marlin 10. cacomistle 11. golden eagle (young)

ringed boa . . . 5. aboma

ringed worm . . . 7. annelid

ringhals . . . 5. snake (spitting)

ringing . . . 7. clangor, orotund, pealing, tolling 8. clanging, resonant 10. resounding

ringle–eye . . . 7. walleye

ringlet . . . 4. curl, lock 5. tress 6. circle 7. circlet 9. fairy ring

ringworm . . . 5. tinea 6. tetter 7. disease, serpigo 9. millepede

rink . . . 4. hero, race, ring 6. circle, course 7. warrior 8. encircle, ice sheet (skating) 9. encounter

rinse . . . 4. lave, sind, wash 5. flush 6. sluice 7. cleanse 8. absterge

rinthereout, rintherout (Scot) . . . 5. tramp 7. vagrant 8. vagabond

rio . . . 5. river 6. coffee, stream

Rio de Janeiro . . . 7. capital (old, Braz)

Rio Grande . . . 5. river 7. disease (lettuce)

riot . . . 3. din 5. brawl, melee 6. clamor, excess, pogrom, revolt, tumult, uproar 7. dispute, quarrel, revelry 8. carousal, disorder, violence 9. commotion

riotous . . . 4. raid 5. aroar 6. wanton 7. violent 9. dissolute, luxuriant, seditious 10. profligate, tumultuous 12. unrestrained

riotous jollity . . . 9. dissolute 11. saturnalian

rip . . . 3. cut 4. rend, rent, tear 5. break, horse (old) 7. riptide 9. debauchee, libertine, reprobate 10. fish basket, laceration

ripe . . . 3. fit 5. ready, rifle 6. mature, mellow 7. plunder 8. finished, prepared, rareripe 9. developed, full–grown, perfected 10. consummate

ripen . . . 3. age 5. addle 6. digest, mellow, nature 7. develop, perfect, prepare 8. complete, grow ripe

riposte, ripost . . . 5. reply 6. answer, retort, thrust 8. repartee

ripping . . . 5. bully, grand, swell 9. admirable, hunky–dory 12. fine and dandy

rippit . . . 9. fist fight

ripple . . . 3. cut, lap 4. fret, purl, riff, tear, wave 5. acker, eagre, graze 6. dimple, murmur 7. crinkle, disturb, scratch, trickle, wavelet 11. corrugation

ripple grass plantain . . . 7. ribwort

ris de veau . . . 10. sweetbread

rise . . . 4. grow, soar, well 5. arise, begin, climb, get up, mount, raise, reach, rebel, start, surge, tower 6. ascend, ascent, attain, be high, emerge, growth, height, revolt, spring, thrive 7. succeed 8. eminence, flourish, increase, levitate, reaction 9. acclivity, ascension, beginning, elevation, originate 11. development

rise (pert to) . . .
above . . 4. loom 8. surmount 11. triumph over
again . . 7. resurge 11. resurrected
and fall of the sea . . 5. scend, tidal 6. welter
by buoyancy . . 8. levitate
gradually . . 4. loom
hawk's . . 6. mounty
high . . 5. tower

risible . . . 5. funny 6. absurd

9. laughable

rising... 6. ascent, ortive, revolt
7. growing, montant, sloping, surgent
8. elevated, emergent, gradient (by
degrees), swelling 9. acclivity,
advancing, ascending, ascension

rising and falling... 5. tidal 7. surging
8. undulant

risk... 4. dare 5. peril 6. chance,
danger, expose, gamble, hazard,
injury, plight 7. venture 8. endanger
10. investment 12. disadvantage

risky... 6. risqué 9. hazardous
11. venturesome

risp... 3. rub 4. file, rasp, tirl 5. stalk
7. bulrush, scratch

risper... 11. caterpillar

risqué... 4. racy 5. risky, salty
8. off–color 9. hazardous
10. suggestive

rissle... 4. pole 5. staff, stick

risus... 5. laugh 8. laughter

rit (rare)... 3. cut, rip 4. slit, tear
5. split 6. pierce 7. scratch

ritardando... 9. direction, retarding
10. slackening 11. rallentando

rite... 4. cult, form 6. ritual, sacrum
7. formula, liturgy, tonsure
8. ceremony 9. solemnity
10. ceremonial, initiation, observance
12. patriarchate

ritratto... 7. picture 8. portrait

Ritter... 6. knight

ritual... 4. book, code, cult, form, rite
5. feast, salat 6. novena, prayer
7. liturgy 8. ceremony
10. ceremonial

ritus... 5. usage 6. custom

ritzy... 5. smart (vulgarly), swank
6. swanky 11. pretentious
16. ultra–fashionable

rivage... 4. bank, duty 5. coast, green,
shore

rival... 3. foe, vie 4. even, peer
5. excel, match 7. compete, emulate
8. emulator, opponent
10. antagonist, competitor
11. compete with

rivalry... 4. feud 9. emulation
11. competition

rive... 3. rip 4. bank, open, rent, rift,
tear 5. cleft, sever, shore, split
6. cleave 8. lacerate

rive droite... 9. Right Bank (Seine)

rive gauche... 8. Left Bank (Seine,
Paris, including Latin Qtr)

rivel... 6. shrink 7. shrivel, wrinkle

river... 2. ea 3. ria, rio, run 4. ilog
5. amnis, brook, creek 6. stream
7. rivulet, torrent 8. riverlet
9. streamlet

river (pert to)...
arm (of sea).. 7. estuary
bank.. 4. ripa 5. levee
bank, pert to.. 8. riparian
bed.. 4. holm 6. alveus, bottom
7. channel
bend.. 5. oxbow
boat.. 3. ark
delta branch.. 5. bayou
dog.. 10. hellbender
dragon.. 9. crocodile

duck.. 4. teal
fish (spawning, from sea)..
10. anadromous
horse.. 5. hippo 12. hippopotamus
inlet.. 4. slew 5. fiord (fjord)
6. slough
islet.. 3. ait 4. holm
mouth.. 4. lade 5. delta 7. estuary
mussel.. 4. unio
Near East.. 4. wadi (wady)
Nile measure.. 9. Nilometer
nymph.. 4. nais 5. naiad
rat.. 5. thief
ref to.. 5. amnic
region (near).. 8. riverine
siren.. 7. Lorelei
thief.. 3. rat 6. ackman
winding.. 3. ess

river in...
Africa.. 4. Nile, Tana 5. Niger
Austria.. 4. Iser 5. Drava
Bavaria.. 4. Eger, Isar
Belgium.. 4. Yser
Bohemia.. 4. Elbe, Iser
Brazil.. 3. Rio
Bulgaria.. 5. Mesta
China.. 3. Wei 6. Yellow 7. Hwang
Ho
England.. 4. Isis 6. Thames
France.. 5. Seine
Germany.. 6. Danube
Italy.. 4. Arno 5. Tiber
Netherlands.. 3. Eem 4. Maas
(Meuse)
S America.. 6. Amazon
Siberia.. 2. Ob 4. Lena
Switzerland.. 3. Aar 5. Reuss

river of...
Annie Laurie.. 4. Nith
Caesar.. 7. Rubicon
lower regions.. 4. Styx 5. Lethe
7. Acheron
woe.. 7. Acheron

rixy... 4. tern

road... 3. via, way 4. iter, path, raid
5. agger 7. estrada, highway,
journey, passage 8. pavement
9. incursion, roadstead
10. expedition

road (pert to)...
block.. 3. dam 4. weir
goose.. 5. brant
hog.. 8. motorist 10. monopolist
horse.. 6. saddle (horse)
impassable.. 7. impasse
man.. 7. drummer, peddler
8. salesman 9. canvasser
map.. 5. chart, globe 9. directory
master.. 10. supervisor
11. trackmaster
nautical.. 9. roadstead
no outlet.. 8. cul–de–sac
paving.. 6. Tarmac 7. ballast,
macadam
runner.. 6. cuckoo
scraper.. 4. harl
weed.. 8. plantain

roam... 2. go 3. err, gad 4. rove
5. prowl, range 6. ramble, stroll,
wander 7. meander 9. gallivant

roan... 5. horse (bay, gray, chestnut)
8. antelope 9. sheepskin, yellow–red

roanoke... 6. wampum
Roanoke...
  city.. 8. Virginia
  famed as.. 11. First Colony (1584)
  famed for.. 12. Virginia Dare (1st
    white child, 1587)
  settler.. 16. Sir Walter Raleigh
    19. Sir Richard Grenville
roar... 4. bell, blow, boom, rote (surf)
  5. brool, laugh, shout 6. bellow,
  steven 7. ululate 8. cry aloud
  9. loud sound
roaring... 5. aroar, great 7. booming,
  riotous 10. disorderly
Roaring (pert to)...
  Forties.. 8. Broadway (NYC)
  game.. 7. curling (Scot)
  Twenties.. 14. Golden Twenties
    16. Age of Red Hot Mamas
roast... 4. beef, cook 5. cabob, parch
  6. assate, banter 7. torrefy
  8. ridicule 9. criticize
roasting (pert to)...
  ear.. 4. corn
  jack.. 9. smokejack
  stick.. 4. spit
rob... 4. loot, pelf 5. pinch (sl), reave,
  rifle, steal, touch 6. pilfer, ravish,
  snatch, snitch 7. despoil, pillage,
  plunder 10. plagiarize
robbed... 5. stole 6. rubato (Mus)
  8. snatched, snitched
robber... 4. yegg 5. crook (sl), thief
  6. bandit, reaver, rifler 7. brigand,
  burglar, yeggman 8. pillager
  9. despoiler, embezzler, larcenist,
  peculator 10. depredator,
  highwayman, shoplifter
robber (pert to)...
  grave.. 5. ghoul
  high seas.. 6. pirate 7. corsair
    9. privateer
  highway.. 7. footpad, ladrone
  Indian.. 6. dacoit
robbery... 4. reif 5. theft 6. burgle,
  piracy 7. larceny, pillage, plunder
  8. burglary 10. spoliation
  11. depredation
robe... 5. array, cover, dress, tunic
  6. invest, mantle 7. costume,
  garment 8. clerical, vestment
robe (pert to)...
  bishop's.. 6. chimer
  camel's hair.. 3. aba
  long.. 5. talar
  loose.. 5. cymar (symar)
  royal.. 6. ermine, purple
robin... 4. bird, lout, tody 6. thrush
  7. bumpkin 8. trimming 9. redbreast
  10. toxalbumin
robin (pert to)...
  dipper.. 14. bufflehead duck
  runaway.. 7. dewdrop
  sandpiper.. 4. knot 5. snipe
    9. dowitcher
  songbird.. 8. accentor
Robin Bluestring... 13. Robert
  Walpole
robinet... 6. cannon 9. chaffinch
Robin Goodfellow... 4. Puck 6. sprite
  9. hobgoblin
Robin Hood (pert to)...

famed as.. 6. archer, outlaw, yeoman
  followers.. 9. Friar Tuck 10. Little
  John, Maid Marian
  forest.. 8. Sherwood (Eng)
  habit.. 11. robbing rich (for the poor)
Robinson Crusoe's man... 6. Friday
roborant... 4. drug 5. tonic 6. bracer
  8. pick–me–up 9. stimulant
roborean... 5. oaken, stout 6. strong
robot... 9. automaton
Rob Roy... 5. canoe 6. outlaw (Scot)
  15. Robert MacGregor
robust... 4. hale 5. hardy, lusty,
  rough, sound, stout, wally 6. hearty,
  sinewy, strong, sturdy 7. healthy
  8. muscular, vigorous
roc... 4. bird (Arabian Nights)
  7. simurgh (simurg)
rocca... 4. hold 6. donjon 8. fortress
rock... 3. orc 4. lull, peak, sway, trap,
  tufa, tuff 5. agate, chert, cliff, quiet,
  shake, slate, stone 6. basalt, egeran,
  gneiss, refuge, schist, teeter
  7. diamond, missile 8. dolomite,
  porphyry, strength 9. whinstone
  10. promontory
rock (pert to)...
  black.. 6. basalt
  brittle.. 5. shale
  broken.. 4. sand 5. attle
  cavity.. 5. druse
  chain.. 4. reef
  coarse.. 8. psammite, psephite
  crystal.. 6. silica
  crystalline.. 6. gneiss, schist
  decomposed.. 6. gossan
  fluid.. 4. lava
  fragments.. 5. scree 8. detritus,
    xenolith
  geyser deposit.. 6. sinter
  glacial.. 7. moraine
  granitelike.. 6. gneiss
  granular.. 6. oolite, quartz 7. diorite
    10. rockallite
  gray.. 5. slate 8. andesite
  igneous.. 4. boss, trap 6. basalt
    7. peridot
  jutting.. 3. tor 4. crag
  nodule.. 5. geode
  pinnacle.. 4. scar 6. needle
  porous.. 4. tufa, tuff
  rounded.. 6. rognon
  science.. 9. petrology
  Sicilian.. 6. Scylla (opp Charybdis)
  stratified.. 5. shale
  suffix.. 3. ite, yte
  volcanic.. 4. tufa 6. basalt, domite,
    latite
rock, animal...
  badger.. 4. cony
  cavy.. 6. rodent
  dassie.. 6. rabbit
  goat.. 4. ibex
  kangaroo.. 7. wallaby
  squirrel.. 11. spermophile
rock, bird...
  blackbird.. 9. ring ouzel
  dove.. 9. guillemot 10. rockpigeon
  duck.. 9. harlequin
  goose.. 9. kelp goose
  grouse.. 9. ptarmigan
  hawk.. 6. falcon, merlin

hopper.. 7. penguin
lark.. 5. pipit
pigeon.. 10. sand grouse
sandpiper.. 5. pipit, snipe
shrike.. 10. rock thrush
starling.. 5. ouzel
swallow.. 10. rock martin
rock, fish...
bass.. 5. black 7. striped
clam.. 5. borer
cod.. 7. grouper
cook.. 6. wrasse 7. whiting
eel.. 6. gunnel
gurnet.. 9. fortescue
hind.. 7. grouper (spotted)
lobster.. 8. crayfish
salmon.. 7. codfish 9. amberfish
sucker.. 7. lamprey
trout.. 9. greenling
rock, flora...
bell.. 9. columbine
brake.. 8. polypody
candytuft.. 8. gold-dust
cedar.. 7. juniper
cranberry.. 8. mountain
elm.. 11. slippery elm
garden.. 6. alpine
geranium.. 8. alumroot
hair.. 6. lichen
lily.. 9. columbine 12. pasqueflower
maple.. 5. sugar
melon.. 10. cantaloupe
shrub.. 9. buckthorn
rocket... 5. lance 6. ascend, ascent,
fire at 8. aircraft, firework
9. skyrocket, spaceship
rocket (famed)... 5. Titan 6. Apollo,
Gemini, Saturn 7. Jupiter, Mercury
8. Redstone
Rock of Chickamauga... 6. Thomas
(Gen), (Civil War)
rocks... 5. money
rocks, on the... 7. aground
8. bankrupt, stranded 10. saxicoline
rocky.. 4. hard 5. stony 6. rugged
7. sickish 8. obdurate, unsteady
9. unfeeling
Rocky Ford... 9. muskmelon
Rocky Mountain...
group.. 5. Coast 8. Cascades
12. Sierra Nevada
park.. 5. Estes
peak.. 6. Elbert 8. McKinley
popular name.. 7. Rockies
range.. 5. Teton, Uinta
rococo... 6. florid 7. baroque, bizarre
9. fantastic, grotesque
13. ornamentation
rod... 3. gat, gun 4. pole, wand, whip
5. baton, perch, power, scion, staff
7. measure, scepter
rod (pert to)...
comb form.. 5. rhabd 6. rhabdo
fibrous.. 5. lytta
flat.. 6. ferula, ferule
grooved.. 4. came (stained glass)
knitting.. 6. needle
meat-holding.. 4. spit
mechanical.. 6. piston
metal.. 7. stemmer
mixing.. 3. rab
pointed.. 4. goat, spit

rodlike.. 9. vergiform
rotating.. 7. spindle
short.. 6. toggle
spinning.. 7. spindle
rodd... 8. crossbow, stonebow
rodent... 4. cony, hare, paca 5. hutia
(jutia), mouse, stoat 6. agouti
(agouty), beaver, gerbil, gopher,
marmot, murine 7. lemming, leveret
8. chipmunk, hedgehog, mongoose,
squirrel 9. guinea pig, porcupine
rodent (pert to)...
Andes.. 8. abrocome
aquatic.. 6. beaver 7. muskrat
Belgian.. 8. leporide
burrowing.. 6. marmot 8. sewellel
disease.. 9. tularemia
European.. 4. cony 5. lerot
fur-bearing.. 6. beaver
genus.. 3. Mus 5. Lepus
gnawing.. 3. rat 4. mole
hare.. 6. rabbit
jumping.. 6. jerboa
largest.. 8. capybara (capibara)
migrating.. 7. lemming
Mongoloid.. 3. rat 6. gopher
12. pocket gopher
mouselike.. 4. vole
rabbitlike.. 4. pika
reference to.. 7. gnawing 8. rosorial
S American.. 4. degu 5. coypu
6. agouti 8. capybara 10. chinchilla
spiny.. 9. porcupine
rodeo... 4. show 7. roundup
9. spectacle 11. performance (public)
rodomontade... 4. brag, rant 5. boast
7. bluster 8. boastful, boasting,
braggart, bragging
roe... 2. ra 3. doe 4. deer, hind, raun
5. coral (lobster) 8. fish eggs
Roentgen, Röntgen (Wilhelm)...
famed as.. 9. physicist
famed for.. 5. X-rays 10. Nobel Prize
(1901) 12. Roentgen rays
rogan... 4. bowl (wooden)
10. receptacle (maple sap)
Roger's plane (Will)... 9. Winnie May
rogue... 3. imp, wag 4. kite 5. cheat,
knave, scamp, shark, tramp
6. beggar, pirate, rascal 7. corsair,
vagrant, villain 8. elephant, picaroon,
vagabond 13. mischief-maker
roguish... 3. sly 4. arch 5. pawky
7. knavish 8. espiegle, rascally
10. frolicsome, picaresque
11. mischievous
roguishly... 5. slyly 8. impishly, trickily
10. prankishly
roid... 5. rough 6. severe 7. riotous
10. frolicsome 12. unmanageable
roil... 3. vex 4. foul, roam, romp
5. anger, annoy, horse (Flemish),
muddy 6. fidget, ruffle, wander
7. agitate, disturb 8. irritate
roister... 4. brag, rude 5. bully
7. bluster, boorish, swagger, violent
9. gilravage
roisterer (Hist)... 3. mun
rojo... 3. Red 6. Indian (Mex)
7. Redskin
roke... 3. fog 4. stir 5. moist, smoke,
steam, vapor 8. moisture

roker ... 3. ray 8. rockling 9. thornback
roky ... 4. damp 5. foggy, misty, smoky 6. hoarse
role ... 4. duty, part 6. office 8. capacity, function 9. character 13. impersonation
roll ... 3. bun, rob 4. coil, film, food, furl, list, pell, rota, sway, wind, wrap 5. trill, troll 6. billow, bundle, rotate, rumble, scroll 8. bankroll, cylinder, rotation
roll (pert to) ...
along.. 7. trundle
back.. 6. reduce 8. retrench
bread.. 3. bap
butter.. 3. pat
cloth.. 4. bolt
coins.. 7. rouleau
fish.. 7. rissole
hair.. 3. rat 7. chignon
military.. 5. cadre 6. roster
the bones.. 4. dice 10. shoot craps
tobacco.. 5. cigar
to one side.. 5. lurch
up.. 4. furl 6. bundle 10. accumulate
roller ... 4. wave 5. inker, skate, towel 6. canary, caster, fillet, pigeon, platen 7. bandage, rotator, sirgang 8. cylinder 10. Holy Roller, pulverizer
rolling (pert to) ...
movement.. 6. welter
pin.. 6. roller 8. cylinder
stock.. 7. coaches, engines 8. cabooses, Pullmans 9. motor cars 11. locomotives
stone.. 8. wanderer
weed.. 10. tumbleweed
rollix ... 4. play 6. frolic 7. rollick
romaine ... 10. cos lettuce
romal ... 5. quirt, thong
Roman ... 5. brave, Latin 6. frugal, honest, simple 7. Italian
Roman (pert to) ... see also *Rome*
afterpiece (theater).. 5. exode, farce 8. travesty
alcove.. 8. tablinum
apostle (Bib).. 4. Neri
assembly.. 5. forum 7. comitia
augur.. 6. auspex
awning.. 8. velarium
barrack, hut.. 6. canaba (cannaba)
basilica.. 7. Lateran
booth, shelter.. 7. taberna
bowl.. 6. patina
boxing glove.. 6. cestus
breastplate.. 6. lorica
bronze.. 3. aes
building.. 5. aedes (worship)
case.. 5. bulla (for amulets)
cathedral.. 7. Lateran
chariot.. 5. essed (esseda)
chest.. 4. cist
circus post.. 4. meta
circus wall.. 5. spina
cistern.. 9. impluvium
citadel.. 3. arx
citizen (nonvoting).. 8. aerarian
clan.. 4. gens
cloak.. 5. sagum (Mil) 6. abolla 7. planeta
concert hall.. 5. odeum
court (Pope's).. 5. Curia

cuirass.. 6. lorica
Curia office.. 6. datary 7. dataria
date.. 4. ides 5. nones 7. calends
dish.. 6. patera
division (Polit).. 5. curia
earthwork (Mil).. 5. agger
Empire district.. 5. Pagus
era.. 5. Varro
farce.. 5. exode
festival days.. 5. feria 10. feriae Jovi (festivals of Jupiter)
fish sauce.. 4. alec 5. garum
foot coverage, sock.. 3. udo
galley.. 6. bireme 7. trireme
garment.. 4. toga 5. palla, stole, tunic
general's cloak.. 12. paludamentum (paludament)
Govt of two men.. 10. duumvirate
Hades.. 5. Orcus 10. lower world
hairpin.. 4. acus
hall (concert).. 5. odeum
helmet.. 5. galea
highway.. 3. via 4. iter
highway, famed.. 9. Appian Way
hills.. 7. Viminal 8. Aventine, Palatine, Quirinal 9. Esquiline 10. Capitoline
javelin.. 5. pilum
land (public).. 4. ager
language.. 5. Latin
law.. 3. jus 4. cern
law, divine.. 3. fas
market day.. 7. nundine
marriage.. 13. confarreation
matron's garment.. 5. stola, stole
meal (chief).. 4. cena (coena)
military cloak.. 5. sagum
military machine.. 7. terebra
military unit.. 6. legion 7. maniple
money.. 3. aes
ornament (neck).. 5. bulla
palace.. 7. Lateran
peace.. 3. pax
provisions (free).. 6. annona
ram (battery).. 5. aries
religious law.. 3. fas
religious rite.. 5. sacra
road.. 4. iter 6. Appian (paved)
robe.. 4. toga
room.. 3. ala 6. atrium 8. tablinum
seat.. 5. sella
shelter, shop.. 7. taberna
shield.. 6. scutum
soldier's protection.. 7. testudo
spirits (group).. 5. manes 7. lemures
tablet (writing).. 7. diptych
temple.. 4. naos 5. cella
tent.. 7. taberna
theater.. 5. odeum
travesty.. 5. exode
vase.. 7. amphora (wine) 8. murrhine
warship.. 6. bireme 7. trireme
Way (famed).. 6. Appian
wine shop.. 7. taberna
romance ... 5. fancy, novel, story 7. fantasy, fiction, romanza, romaunt 8. idealize 9. falsehood, sentiment 11. imagination
romance (pert to) ...
language.. 6. French 7. Catalan, Italian, Spanish 9. Provençal 10. Portuguese

ref to.. **8.** knightly **10.** chivalrous
verse.. **7.** sestina
Roman god (of)...
chief.. **4.** Jove **7.** Jupiter
dead.. **5.** Orcus
fire.. **6.** Vulcan
Hades.. **3.** Dis **5.** Pluto **8.** Dispater
households.. **5.** Lares **7.** Penates
husbandry, animals.. **6.** Faunus
love.. **4.** Amor **5.** Cupid
mirth.. **5.** Comus
sun.. **3.** Sol
Supreme.. **4.** Jove **7.** Jupiter
two–faced.. **5.** Janus
underworld.. **3.** Dis **5.** Pluto
    8. Dispater
war.. **4.** Mars **8.** Quirinus
Roman goddess (of)...
agriculture.. **3.** Ops **5.** Ceres
beauty.. **5.** Venus
burials.. **8.** Libitina
childbirth.. **6.** Lucina
crops.. **6.** Annona
dawn.. **6.** Aurora
earth.. **6.** Tellus
fertility.. **6.** Annona
handicrafts.. **7.** Minerva
harvests.. **3.** Ops
health.. **7.** Minerva
hearth.. **5.** Vesta
horses.. **5.** Epona
love.. **5.** Venus
moon.. **4.** Luna **7.** Phoebus
mothers, nursing.. **6.** Rumina
night.. **3.** Nox
peace.. **3.** Pax **5.** Irene
religion.. **4.** Maia
strife.. **9.** Discordia
victory (war).. **6.** Vacuna
womanhood.. **4.** Juno
Roman people...
author.. **5.** Pliny, Varro
biographer.. **5.** Nepos
Bishop.. **4.** Pope
boy (free birth).. **8.** camillus
Catholic priest.. **8.** sacerdos
Catholic Society.. **6.** Jesuit
consul.. **6.** Scipio
Cupid.. **4.** Eros
deity.. **4.** faun
Diana.. **7.** Artemis
dictator.. **5.** Sulla **11.** Cincinnatus
diviner.. **5.** augur **6.** auspex
divinity (chief).. **4.** Jove
Emperor.. **4.** Nero, Otto **5.** Titus
    7. Maximus **8.** Tiberius
    11. Constantine **12.** Heliogabalus
Eros.. **5.** Cupid
farmer.. **7.** colonus
Fates.. **4.** Nona **5.** Morta **6.** Decuma
General.. **5.** Sulla, Titus **6.** Antony,
    Marius, Scipio
ghosts.. **7.** lemures
gladiator.. **7.** Samnite **9.** retiarius
gladiator trainer.. **7.** lanista
governor.. **9.** proconsul
guard.. **6.** lictor
historian.. **4.** Livy **5.** Nepos **7.** Sallust
    8. Appianus (Appian)
judge.. **6.** aedile (edile)
king (1st).. **7.** Romulus
king's adviser (Myth).. **6.** Egeria

magistrate, official.. **5.** augur **6.** aedile
    (edile), censor, consul **7.** praetor
    (pretor), tribune
maiden, betrayer to Sabrines..
    7. Tarpeia
military officer.. **9.** proconsul
Naturalist.. **5.** Pliny
nun.. **6.** vestal
nymph (fountain).. **6.** Egeria
officer.. **6.** lictor **8.** triumvir (one of
    three)
official of public games.. **7.** Asiarch
orator.. **5.** Pliny **6.** Cicero
palace officer.. **8.** palatine
patriot.. **4.** Cato
people (anc).. **7.** Sabines **8.** Samnites
    9. plebeians **10.** patricians
philosopher.. **4.** Cato **6.** Seneca
    7. Rosmini
physician.. **11.** Aesculapius
poet.. **4.** Ovid **5.** Lucan **6.** Horace,
    Vergil **7.** Juvenal (satirical)
politician, courtier.. **7.** Sejanus
priest.. **5.** epulo **8.** tresviri (10 in all)
    9. decemviri **10.** septemviri
priest, serving a god.. **6.** flamen
priestess.. **6.** vestal
priests of Faunus.. **7.** Luperci
race (conquered).. **6.** Sabine
saint.. **4.** Neri
scholar.. **5.** Varro
serf.. **6.** colona (fem) **7.** colonus
    (male)
slave (befriended lion).. **9.** Androcles
soldiers (body of).. **6.** cohort
statesman.. **4.** Cato **6.** Caesar, Cicero,
    Seneca
Tarquin rulers.. **9.** Etruscans
tenant farmer.. **7.** colonus
triumvirate, first.. **6.** Caesar, Pompey
    7. Crassus
triumvirate, second.. **6.** Antony
    7. Lepidus **8.** Octavius
troops.. **6.** alares
tyrant.. **4.** Nero
virgin.. **6.** vestal
writer (comic).. **7.** Terence
Romany, Rommany... **5.** gypsy
    10. mascot blue
Rome...
cathedral (world's largest).. **8.** St
    Peter's
churches.. **7.** Lateran **8.** Castello,
    Gandolfo
conqueror.. **6.** Alaric
founder (legendary).. **7.** Romulus
hills.. **5.** Seven **6.** Sabine **7.** Viminal
    8. Aventine, Palatine, Quirinal
lake.. **4.** Nemi
original city.. **12.** Roma Quadrata
palace (world's largest).. **7.** Vatican
peak (Capitoline).. **8.** Tarpeian
port (anc).. **5.** Ostia
prairie.. **8.** Campagna
river.. **5.** Tiber
seat of.. **7.** Holy See **11.** Vatican City
site, ancient.. **13.** Campus Martius
site, founding.. **12.** Palatine Hill
street (famed).. **5.** Corso
Romulus (pert to)...
brother.. **5.** Remus
city site.. **12.** Palatine Hill

father.. 4. Mars
founder (Myth).. 4. Rome
king (1st).. 4. Rome
mother.. 6. Sylvia
rescued from.. 5. Tiber
suckled by.. 7. she–wolf
ronde... 6. script (heavy) 9. round
hand
rondeau... 4. game, poem 5. rondo
6. rondel
rondel, rondelle... 4. poem 5. tower
(Fort) 8. round gem
rondure... 9. plumpness, roundness
ronier... 7. palmyra
ronin... 6. outlaw 7. outcast, samurai
rood... 5. cross (holy), goose
7. measure 8. crucifix
roodebok... 6. impala 9. duikerbok
roof... 3. hip 4. dome, eave, flat,
nave, tile 5. cover, gable, slate, spire
6. cupola, lean–to 7. chopper,
gambrel, mansard, pitched, shingle
8. housetop, thatched 9. penthouse
10. jerkinhead
roof (pert to)...
boards (thin).. 4. sark
brain cover.. 4. tela 14. telachorioidea
frame (raised).. 7. coaming
material.. 3. tin 4. tile 5. paper, slate
6. copper, shakes 7. roofage
8. shingles
mouth.. 6. palate
ornament.. 3. epi
tile.. 7. pantile
timber.. 6. rafter
tin (coating).. 5. terne
tool.. 3. zax
Roof of the World, Asia... 6. Pamirs
(The) 9. Bam i Dunya
rook... 4. bird, crow, dupe 5. cheat
6. castle 7. defraud, sharper
8. chessman 9. ruddy duck
rookery... 4. slum 9. confusion
13. breeding place (rooks, herons,
penguins) 14. breeding ground (seals)
rookie, rooky... 6. novice 7. recruit
8. beginner, newcomer
rooky... 4. roky 5. foggy
room... 3. ala (anc), den 4. aula, cell,
hall, sala, seat, shed 5. attic, lodge,
place, salon, scope, space 6. cellar,
leeway, pantry, parlor, reside
7. chamber, drawing, laundry,
nursery, quarter 8. capacity
9. apartment, storeroom
11. opportunity
room (pert to)...
church (bishop's).. 4. apse
convent.. 9. parlatory
dining.. 7. cenacle, dinette
9. refectory
harem.. 3. oda
household.. 5. ewery
inner.. 3. ben
large.. 4. aula, hall 7. rotunda,
theater 10. auditorium
monastery.. 4. cell
outer.. 3. but
pantry.. 6. larder 8. cupboard
prayer.. 7. oratory
Pueblo Ind ceremonial.. 4. kiva
Roman.. 6. atrium

ship's.. 4. brig 5. cabin, salon
sleeping.. 5. lodge 6. dormer
7. barrack, bedroom, chamber
9. dormitory
tower (bell).. 6. belfry
roomy... 4. airy 5. ample 8. spacious
9. capacious, expansive
10. commodious 11. large–framed
roon... 5. shred 6. border 7. darling
8. treasure
roorback, roorbach... 3. lie 6. canard
7. lampoon 9. falsehood
roose... 5. boast, vaunt 6. praise
Roosevelt...
president, 26th.. 8. Theodore
president, 32nd.. 8. Franklin
roost... 3. bed, sit 4. jouk, pole, rest
5. perch 6. settle 7. lodging,
support
rooster... 4. cock, male (animal)
5. gallo 7. percher 11. chanticleer
12. fighting cock
root... 4. bulb, word 5. cheer, plant,
radix, tuber 6. source 7. radical
8. take root 9. establish
root (pert to)...
aromatic.. 9. sassafras
edible.. 3. oca, yam 4. beet, eddo,
taro 6. carrot, potato, radish, turnip
7. parsnip 8. rutabaga
food (Maori).. 3. roi
medicinal.. 4. atis 5. jalep 6. ipecac,
senega 7. Senegal
out.. 4. seek 7. extract 9. eliminate,
eradicate
perfume.. 5. orris
pungent.. 6. ginger
starch.. 7. cassava
stock.. 7. rhizome
stringy.. 5. watap (watape)
taro.. 4. eddo
word.. 4. etym 6. etymon
rooted... 8. habitual 9. implanted
10. deep–seated 11. established,
traditional
rootlet... 7. radicel, rhizoid, taproot
rope... 3. tew, tie, tye 4. bind, cord,
line, rood 5. cable, cigar, lasso,
longe, noose, reata, wanty 6. fasten,
halter, hawser, lariat, string, tether
7. cordage, lanyard, measure
8. hangman's, inveigle
rope (pert to)...
boat's.. 4. rode 6. hawser 7. painter
chain.. 3. tye 9. stern fast
dancer, walker.. 8. balancer
11. equilibrist, funambulist
flag raising.. 7. halyard
gun carriage.. 8. prolonge
guy.. 4. stay, vang
nautical.. 3. tye 4. vang, wapp
6. parrel (parral) 7. snotter
of onions.. 5. reeve
security device.. 4. butt 5. cleat
ship's.. 3. tye 4. stay, vang
6. hawser, shroud 7. painter, ratline,
snotter
splicer's tool.. 3. fid
straw, twisted.. 5. sugan (soogan)
two strand.. 7. marline
walker.. 11. funambulist
ropery... 6. banter 7. roguery

roral... 4. dewy, rory 5. roric
rorqual... 5. whale 7. finback
Ros... 10. Slav rulers (Russ),
    Varangians
rosary... 4. aves 5. beads (prayer)
    7. chaplet (of roses), garland
    8. devotion
rose... 3. cut (jewelry) 5. color, flush,
    Rhoda 6. emblem, flower, nozzle,
    symbol, window 7. fixture
rose (pert to)...
    apple.. 4. plum 6. cherry 7. jambool
       8. poma rosa
    beetle.. 6. chafer, weevil
    City.. 8. Portland (Oreg)
    colored.. 8. alluring 10. auspicious,
       optimistic
    cross.. 6. symbol 11. Rosicrucian
       14. cross in a circle
    genus.. 4. Rosa 6. Acaena
       8. Rosaceae
    hiller.. 7. rosella 8. parakeet
    moss.. 9. portulaca
    of Sharon.. 6. Althea
    petal oil.. 4. otto 5. attar
    rash.. 7. roseola
    under the rose.. 6. secret 7. sub
       rosa
    wild.. 9. eglantine
Rosetta Stone (pert to)...
    decipherer.. 11. Champollion
    famed for.. 11. inscription
       13. hieroglyphics
    site found.. 4. Nile (1799)
    type.. 11. black basalt
roster... 4. list, roll, rota 5. slate
    8. schedule
rostrum... 4. beak, dais, prow
    5. snout, stage 6. pulpit 8. platform
    9. proboscis
rosy... 3. red 4. pink 7. flushed,
    roseate 8. blooming, blushing
    9. rosaceous 10. auspicious,
    optimistic
rot... 3. die 5. decay, spoil 6. blight
    7. corrupt, disease, putrefy
    8. nonsense 9. decompose
    10. degenerate 12. putrefaction
    13. decomposition
rota... 4. Club (Eng), list, roll 5. court,
    round (Mus) 6. roster 15. Sacra
    Romana Rota
rotate... 4. roll, spin, turn, whiz
    5. recur, wheel 6. gyrate 7. rabatte,
    revolve, trundle 8. rotiform
rotation... 4. spin, turn 5. round
    7. turning 8. sequence
    10. revolution, succession
rotator... 5. rotor 6. muscle 7. whirler
    9. carrousel 12. merry–go–round
rotche, rotch... 5. goose, rotge
    7. dovekie
rote... 6. course, custom, system
    7. by heart, routine 8. par coeur,
    practice 9. condition
roti... 5. roast 7. roasted
rotor... 5. wheel 6. roller, stator
    7. rotator, turbine 8. impeller
rotten... 3. bad 4. foul, punk
    5. doted, fetid 6. putrid, wicked
    7. decayed, tainted, unsound
    8. depraved, unstable 9. dishonest,

offensive, putrefied 10. putrescent,
    undermined 13. disintegrated
Rotten Row (Hyde Park, London)...
    12. thoroughfare (equestrian)
rottenstone... 6. polish 7. tripoli
rotter... 3. cad 7. bounder, shirker,
    slacker 10. blackguard
rottgoose... 5. brant
rotund... 5. plump, round, stout
    6. chubby 7. rounded 8. roly–poly
    9. corpulent, spherical
Rotwelsch... 5. argot, slang 6. jargon
    14. secret language
roué... 4. rake, wolf 7. rounder
    9. debauchee, libertine
rouge... 5. blush, flush 6. polish,
    redden 7. radical 8. cosmetic
rough... 4. hard, rude 5. crude, draft,
    harsh, raspy, rowdy, seamy, stern
    6. broken, choppy, coarse, hoarse,
    rugged, severe, shaggy 7. boorish,
    inexact, jarring, jolting, ruffled
    8. scabrous, unsmooth 9. imperfect,
    turbulent 10. incomplete, tumultuous,
    unfinished 11. approximate
rough (pert to)...
    avens.. 6. bennet (herb)
    cloth.. 5. terry
    footed (bird).. 9. feathered
    hair.. 4. shag
    hewn.. 6. brutal 10. unpolished
       12. uncultivated
    house.. 5. cut up 9. rowdiness
       10. disorderly, noisy sport
    jest (Mus).. 9. charivari
    neck.. 4. boor 5. rowdy, tough
    rider.. 9. Roosevelt (Teddy)
       10. cavalryman
    rock.. 4. crag
    shod (to ride).. 7. trample
       8. dominate 9. tyrannize
rough and...
    hoarse.. 7. raucous
    lean.. 6. craggy
    ready.. 4. rude 10. unpolished
    Ready.. 6. Taylor (Gen Zachary)
roughen... 4. chap, shag 8. asperate
roughly... 6. rudely 7. harshly
    8. coarsely, severely, unevenly,
    vulgarly 9. brusquely 10. unsmoothly
    13. approximately
roughness... 6. lipper (of the sea)
    8. acrimony, asperity, pungency,
    unfinish 9. gruffness, harshness,
    vulgarity 10. hoarseness
roughsome... 5. rough 6. rustic
    7. uncouth
roulade... 3. run 8. arpeggio, division,
    flourish 13. vocal flourish
roulette... 3. bas (bet) 4. disk, game
    5. wheel 6. roller 8. wagering
rounceval... 5. giant, large 6. strong,
    virago 9. termagant
round... 4. beat, bout, rota, rung, turn
    5. cycle, orbed, rondo 6. circle,
    curved, rotate, rotund, series, sphere
    7. circuit, routine 8. circular, globular
    9. in a circle, spherical
    11. cylindrical
round (pert to)...
    bone.. 3. hip
    building.. 7. rotunda

clam.. 6. quahog
fish.. 9. whitefish
head.. 5. Swede 7. Puritan
house.. 5. cabin, coach 6. lockup,
  prison 10. watch house
of applause.. 7. plaudit
regular.. 4. beat
robin.. 6. angler, letter 7. pancake,
  request 9. cigarfish
worm.. 4. nema 7. ascarid, Ascaris,
  eelworm
roundabout... 5. about, dance
  6. detour, jacket 7. ambient, devious
  8. indirect 10. circuitous
  13. approximately 14. circumlocution
rounded (pert to)...
heap of stone.. 5. cairn
irregularly.. 7. gibbous
leaf.. 6. retuse
molding.. 5. ovolo
projection.. 4. lobe 5. tooth
scalloped.. 7. crenate
Round Table (pert to)...
knight.. 7. Galahad 8. Lancelot
seating.. 7. knights (King Arthur's)
site.. 7. Camelot
type.. 6. marble
roundup... 5. rodeo
roup... 4. cold 6. clamor 7. auction
  8. shouting 10. hoarseness
rouse... 3. hie 4. stir, wake 5. alarm,
  raise, start, upset, waken 6. awaken,
  bestir, elicit, excite, kindle 7. disturb
  9. stimulate
rouser... 7. stirrer 8. surprise
  9. demagogue (demagog)
  10. instigator
roussette... 5. shark 7. dogfish 8. fruit
  bat
roust... 4. roar, stir 5. rouse
  6. bellow, tumult 7. current (tidal),
  roaring 9. bellowing
roustabout... 6. lumper 7. laborer
  8. handy man 12. longshoreman
rout... 3. low, mob 4. bray, roar
  5. crowd, snort 6. bellow, defeat,
  rabble 7. debacle, scatter
  8. disperse, stampede, vanquish
  9. agitation, discomfit, overpower,
  overthrow 11. put to flight
route... 3. way 4. line, path 5. march
  6. detour 7. circuit
routh... 6. plenty 8. abundant
  9. abundance, plentiful
routier... 6. robber 7. brigand 9. free
  lance, plunderer
routine... 3. rut 5. grind, habit, order,
  round, troll 6. course, system
  7. regular 8. everyday 9. treadmill
rove... 3. gad 4. flit, part, roam
  5. range, stray 6. maraud, ramble,
  stroll, swerve, wander, washer
  7. deviate 8. straggle
rover... 5. nomad 6. bandit, pirate,
  viking 7. corsair, pilgrim, vagrant
  8. marauder, wanderer
roving... 8. errantry 9. desultory,
  deviative 10. discursive
row... 3. air, oar 4. file, fuss, live,
  spat, tier 5. align, brawl, broil
  6. lineup, paddle, propel, series
  7. quarrel, ruction 9. commotion

rowboat... 3. cog, gig 4. dory
  5. canoe, coble, skiff 6. randan
rowdy... 5. cutup, rough, tough
  7. boorish, ruffian 8. larrikin,
  plug–ugly 10. boisterous, disorderly
rowdy contention... 10. donnybrook
rowel... 4. spur 5. wheel
rowen... 4. crop (secondary) 5. field
  7. stubble 9. aftermath
rowing... 5. sport 6. randan 7. regatta
  8. sculling
rox... 3. rot 5. decay
royal... 4. real, rial, stag, true 5. basil,
  noble, regal 6. august, kingly
  7. stately 8. imperial, majestic,
  princely, splendid 9. dignified,
  sovereign 11. magnificent
royal (pert to)...
agaric.. 8. mushroom
bay.. 6. laurel
color.. 4. blue 5. smalt
court.. 5. aulic 6. ermine
crest.. 10. fleur–de–lis (Fr)
deer's antler.. 8. tres–tine
fur.. 6. ermine
mace.. 7. scepter (sceptre)
martyr.. 8. Charles I (Eng, 1649)
maundy.. 4. alms
officer.. 7. naperer
rights.. 7. regalia
rock snake.. 6. python
stables.. 4. mews
stars (Astrol).. 7. Antares, Regulus
  9. Aldebaran, Fomalhaut
Royal (pert to)...
Academy.. 4. Arts (1768)
Arcanum.. 7. Society (1877)
Canadian Mounted Police..
  8. Mounties 16. Northwest Mounted
Castle.. 8. Balmoral
Crown.. 5. tiara
Highlanders.. 10. Black Watch
Highness.. 5. title 6. prince
  8. princess
House.. 5. Tudor 6. Stuart, Valois
  7. Bourbon, Hanover, Windsor
Oak (Eng Hist).. 7. lottery
  10. Shropshire
Psalmist.. 9. King David
Scot.. 16. Lothian Regiments
royet... 4. wild 6. unruly 7. romping
  11. mischievous
rub... 4. crux, fret, wipe 6. abrade,
  polish, scrape, smooth, stroke
  7. burnish, massage 8. friction,
  irritate 9. hindrance, triturate
rub (pert to)...
away.. 6. abrade
down.. 4. comb 5. curry, groom
  7. massage
elbows.. 9. associate 10. fraternize
off.. 5. erase 6. abrade, remove
  10. obliterate
out.. 4. kill 5. erase 6. cancel,
  efface, excise 7. expunge, wipe out
  10. obliterate
wrong way.. 6. ruffle 8. irritate
  9. displease 10. antagonize
rub–a–dub... 6. clamor 7. clatter,
  pit–a–pat, rat–a–tat 8. rattatoo
  9. drumbeats
Rubáiyát (pert to)...

author.. 11. Omar Khayyám
stanza form.. 8. quatrain
translator.. 10. Fitzgerald (1859)
rubber... 4. para 5. stare 6. eraser
7. ebonite, elastic 8. massager,
sight–see 10. caoutchouc
rubber (pert to)...
city.. 5. Akron
hard.. 7. ebonite
India (pure).. 10. caoutchouc
plant.. 5. Ficus
ring.. 4. lute 6. gasket
sap.. 5. latex
shoe.. 6. galosh (galoshe)
tree.. 3. ule 7. guayule
wild.. 5. Ceara 6. caucho
rubbish... 4. junk, ross 5. attle, dross,
stent, trash, waste 6. debris, refuse,
rubble, trashy 8. nonsense, riffraff,
trumpery 9. worthless
rubble... 5. brash, chalk, stone, trash
7. rubbish 8. nonsense
11. foolishness
rube... 4. dolt 6. rustic 7. hayseed
rubedity... 7. redness 9. ruddiness
rubella... 7. measles, rubeola
rubescent... 3. red 8. flushing
9. reddening 10. erubescent
rubiator... 4. rake 5. bully 6. rascal
Rubicon... 5. river (Caesar's)
9. Fiumicino (modern)
rubicund... 3. red 4. ruby 5. ruddy
6. florid 7. redness
rubric... 3. rod 6. paraph, ritual
8. category, red chalk 14. title page
in red
rubrics (book of)... 4. ordo
ruby (pert to)...
bird.. 11. hummingbird
heraldry.. 5. gules
stained quartz (red).. 6. Ancona
7. rubasse 9. Mont Blanc
stone.. 3. gem 5. balas 6. spinel
type.. 4. size
ruck... 3. rut, sit (on eggs) 4. heap,
pile, rick 5. cower, crowd, squat,
stack 6. crease, crouch, furrow,
horses (race), pucker 7. wrinkle
9. multitude 10. generality
ruckus... 3. ado, row 5. fight
6. rumpus, uproar 7. quarrel, ruction
8. outbreak 9. commotion
rudd... 3. hue 4. carp, fish 6. redden
7. azurine, redness 10. complexion
rudder... 4. helm 5. guide
rudder part... 8. bearding 9. whipstaff
rude... 3. raw 4. curt 5. rough, rowdy
6. clumsy, coarse, rugged, simple,
vulgar 7. boorish, uncouth
8. ignorant, insolent 9. barbarous,
inclement, makeshift, turbulent,
unlearned, unskilled, untrained
10. boisterous, unpolished
11. impertinent, uncivilized
12. discourteous
rudeness... 6. ferity 8. curtness
9. impudence, insolence, vulgarity
11. raucousness 12. impertinence
rudiment... 5. first 6. anlage, embryo,
origin 7. element 9. first step
rudimentary... 5. basic 7. initial

8. original 9. beginning, elemental,
embryonic, vestigial 11. undeveloped
rudimentary digit... 7. dewclaw
rue... 4. rake, Ruta 6. grieve, regret,
repent, sorrow 7. afflict, deplore
10. bitterness, compassion,
repentance 14. disappointment
ruff... 3. ree 5. pride, reeve, ruche,
trump 6. collar, fringe, rebato
7. sunfish 8. drumbeat 9. sandpiper,
vainglory
ruffian... 4. fish, pimp, thug 5. rowdy,
tough 6. brutal, cuttle, pander
8. assassin, paramour, the Devil
9. cutthroat, desperado, murderous,
vulgarian
ruffle... 3. vex 4. fret, roil 5. anger,
annoy, frill, jabot 6. edging, muddle,
nettle, rumple, tousle 7. agitate,
disturb, flounce, fluster, shuffle
8. dishevel, disorder, drumbeat,
irritate 9. balayeuse 10. disarrange,
discompose
ruffler... 5. bully 7. boaster, ruffian
8. braggart 9. swaggerer
10. attachment (sewing)
rug... 3. mat 4. maud, shag
5. Senna, throw 6. carpet, hooked,
petate 7. Chinese, drugget, steamer
8. coverlet, Oriental 9. Samarkand
ruga... 4. fold 7. wrinkle 8. membrane
Rugby... 5. Fives 6. Rugger, school
(Eng) 8. football
Rugby term... 9. scrum half,
scrummage
rugged... 4. rude 5. asper, hardy,
harsh, rough, surly 6. craggy, fierce,
robust, seamed, shaggy, strong,
sturdy 7. austere, crabbed, healthy,
uncivil 8. vigorous, wrinkled
9. irregular, not smooth, turbulent
11. substantial
rugged mountain crest... 5. arête
ruin... 4. bane, doom, fate, loss
5. blast, havoc, spoil, wrack, wreck
6. defeat 7. debauch, destroy,
subvert 8. bankrupt, demolish,
downfall 9. perdition 10. desolation,
subversion 11. destruction,
devastation
ruined... 4. gone 7. spoiled, wrecked
8. bankrupt, defeated 9. destroyed
11. dilapidated 12. irremediable
ruinous... 6. deadly 7. baneful,
decayed 10. demolished, disastrous,
pernicious, submersive, tumbledown
11. destructive
ruins... 5. relic, wreck 7. remains
rukh... 6. forest, jungle
rule... 3. law 4. norm, sway 5. axiom,
guide, habit, order, regle, reign
6. decree, govern, manage, method,
regime, screed 7. counsel, measure,
precept, prevail, regency, regimen
8. dominate, persuade, standard
9. criterion, direction, influence,
principle 12. jurisdiction
15. totalitarianism
rule by...
children.. 9. paedarchy
ecclesiasts.. 9. hierarchy
one.. 8. monarchy

race.. 10. ethnocracy
ten.. 8. decarchy
the mob.. 9. mobocracy
the people.. 9. democracy
tribes.. 9. phylarchy
rule out... 6. cancel, excise 7. obviate
ruler... 3. min 4. amir (ameer), czar,
emir, lord 5. queen 6. despot,
dynast, ferule, gerent, prince, regent,
satrap, sultan, tyrant 7. emperor,
monarch 8. autocrat, governor,
hierarch, measurer 9. potentate
ruling... 3. law 6. decree 7. average,
regnant, statute, verdict 8. decision,
reigning 9. governing, prevalent
11. predominant 12. drawing lines
rullion... 4. shoe 6. sandal
rum... 3. dye (blue), odd 4. good
5. queer, tafia (taffia) 6. liquor
8. Demon rum
rumal... 6. fabric 8. kerchief (man's)
Rumania...
capital.. 9. Bucharest
city.. 4. Cluj, Iasi 7. Ploesti
king.. 5. Carol (former)
mountains.. 10. Carpathian
port.. 6. Galati (Galatz)
privileged class.. 5. boyar (boyard)
river.. 6. Danube
rumble... 4. boom, seat (back)
5. rumor 6. murmur, ripple, stir up
9. complaint 11. rolling tone
rumen... 3. cud 5. tripe 6. gullet,
paunch 7. stomach (1st)
ruminant... 2. ox 3. cow, yak 4. bull,
deer, gaur, goat, oryx, zebu
5. bison, camel, eland, gayal, llama,
moose, okapi, sheep, steer
6. alpaca, nilgai, vicuna, wapiti
7. banteng, buffalo, caribou,
chamois, gemsbok, giraffe
8. antelope, elephant, reindeer,
seladang 9. dromedary, nannygoat,
pronghorn 10. cud–chewing,
hartebeest, meditative, rhinoceros,
thoughtful
ruminant (pert to)...
division.. 8. Ungulata 10. Ruminantia
first stomach.. 5. rumen 6. paunch
fourth stomach.. 8. abomasum
9. rennet bag
second stomach.. 9. reticulum
third stomach.. 6. omasum
9. manyplies 10. psalterium
ruminate... 4. chew, muse 6. ponder
7. reflect 8. consider, meditate
rummage... 4. junk 6. litter, search
7. collect (by search), ransack
rumor, rumour... 4. Fama, talk
5. bruit, noise, story 6. norate,
report 7. hearsay, tidings
11. scuttlebutt
rump... 4. bone 6. breech, sacrum
7. meat cut 8. bankrupt, buttocks
9. remainder
rumpade... 3. rob 6. hold up
rumple... 4. muss 5. touse 6. crease,
ruffle, tousle 7. crinkle, crumple,
wrinkle 8. dishevel 10. disarrange
rumpus... 3. row 6. fracas, hubbub,
uproar 9. commotion, confusion
11. disturbance

rumtytoo... 8. ordinary
11. commonplace
run... 2. go 3. fly, gad, hie 4. dart,
flee, flow, lope, melt, race, scud,
tend, trot 5. blend, hurry, speed,
trend 6. charge, course, elapse,
endure, extend, manage, pursue,
sprint, stream 7. average, liquefy,
operate, proceed, roulade, routine,
smuggle, stretch, trickle 8. continue
9. discharge, suppurate
run (pert to)...
about.. 5. wagon 6. gadder
8. roadster, runagate, vagabond
after.. 5. chase, fetch, toady
6. pursue 7. lionize
aground.. 6. strand 7. founder
along the edge.. 5. skirt
away.. 4. bolt, flee 5. elope
6. decamp, escape 8. stampede
before the wind.. 4. scud
between ports.. 3. ply
down.. 3. hit 4. find 5. trace 7. run
over 9. exhausted 11. dilapidated
12. deteriorated
out.. 3. end 5. lapse, waste
6. elapse, emerge, escape
7. exhaust 8. squander
over.. 6. browse, exceed, ponder
7. trample 8. overflow 9. reiterate
quickly, swiftly.. 4. dart, race, scud
5. scoot 6. gallop, sprint 7. scuttle
stocking.. 6. ladder
through.. 4. stab 6. pierce 7. inspect,
pervade 8. rehearse, squander,
transfix 11. superabound
up against.. 4. find 9. encounter,
stumble on 10. experience
runagate... 7. runaway 8. apostate,
fugitive, renegade, vagabond,
wanderer
rundle... 4. ball, coil, rung, step
5. round 6. circle, roller, sphere,
stream
rune... 5. magic 6. secret, symbol
7. mystery 9. character (anc)
rung... 4. step 5. round, spoke, stair,
tread 6. degree, rundle 7. girdled,
ratline
runic... 5. verse 6. poetic 7. writing
8. alphabet (anc), Norsemen
runner... 3. ski (skee) 4. sled 5. miler,
racer, stolo 6. stolon 7. tendril
8. operator, procurer, salesman,
smuggler, sprinter 9. messenger,
solicitor
running... 7. current, cursive, fleeing,
flowing, melting 9. advancing,
prevalent, smuggling 10. continuous
running knot... 5. noose
running race... 5. relay 6. sprint
running toad... 10. natterjack
runt... 3. elf 4. chit (letter), wrig
5. dwarf, pygmy 6. pigeon
10. diminutive
runway... 4. file, ramp 8. airstrip
rupa... 4. body, form (visual)
rupee... 4. anna, coin 14. money of
account
rupestrian... 14. composed of rock
15. inscribed on rock
ruption... 7. ruction, rupture

8. bursting
rupture... 4. rent 5. break, burst
  6. hernia, injury, rhexis 7. quarrel
  9. hostility 10. disruption, falling out,
  separating
rural... 6. rustic 7. bucolic 8. agrestic,
  pastoral 12. agricultural
rural (pert to)...
  deity.. 3. Pan 6. Faunus
  genus.. 6. potato
  life.. 8. pastoral
  poem.. 7. eclogue, georgic
  Spanish.. 9. policeman
  term.. 8. agrestic
Rusa... 4. deer 6. sambar
ruse... 4. fall, slip, wile 5. fraud, trick
  6. deceit 8. artifice 9. stratagem
  10. subterfuge
rush... 3. jet 4. dart, dash, flow, scud
  5. brook, haste, hurry, plant, press,
  scoot, spate, speed, surge 6. charge,
  course, defeat, demand, hasten,
  runlet, sortie 7. cattail, repulse
  8. outburst, reed mace, stampede
  9. attention, thronging
rush (pert to)...
  forth.. 5. sally
  hour.. 4. peak
  light.. 6. candle, feeble
  nut.. 5. chufa
  Scot.. 5. sprat (herb) 6. Juncus
  toad.. 10. natterjack
  wheat.. 10. couch grass
rusk... 5. bread 7. biscuit
rusma... 9. quicklime 10. depilatory
Russia... see also *Russian*
  capital.. 6. Moscow 9. Petrograd (old)
  citadel.. 7. Kremlin
  city.. 4. Baku, Kiev, Omsk 5. Minsk
  6. Rostov 7. Kharkov 8. Smolensk
  9. Leningrad (St Petersburg),
  Petrograd 10. Sevastopol (Sebastopol)
  11. Vladivostok
  coal fields.. 6. Donets (Ukraine)
  fleet base.. 10. Sevastopol, Stalingrad
  former name.. 7. Muscovy
  founder.. 4. Ivan 15. Ivan the Terrible
  gulf.. 4. Azov
  isthmus.. 7. Karelia
  lake.. 5. Onega 6. Baykal 7. Aral Sea
  10. Caspian Sea
  mountains.. 4. Ural 8. Caucasus
  peninsula.. 4. Kola 6. Crimea
  resort.. 5. Yalta 6. Crimea
  river.. 2. Ob 4. Amur, Lena, Neva,
  Ural 5. Volga 6. Donets 7. Dneiper,
  Yenisei
  sea.. 4. Azov 5. Black, White
  6. Baltic 7. Caspian
  strait.. 6. Bering
Russian (pert to)...
  antelope.. 5. saiga
  aristocratic order.. 4. knez 5. Boyar
  assembly.. 4. duma, rada 7. zemstoo
  association, guild.. 5. artel
  bank.. 4. game
  beer, beverage.. 5. kvass, vodka
  boat.. 6. baidak (baydak)
  braid (trim).. 8. soutache
  calendar (to 1918).. 6. Julian
  cap (peasant).. 4. aska
  carriage.. 6. drosky, troika

9. tarantass (tarantas)
cart, wagon.. 6. telega
cathedral.. 5. sober
cloak (fur).. 5. shuba
council.. 4. duma, rada 6. soviet
dance (rustic).. 7. ziganka
decree.. 5. ukase
dog (wolfhound).. 6. borzoi
  7. owtchah
dress (peasant).. 7. sarafan
duke, prince.. 4. knez (kniaz)
edict.. 5. ukase
fur (lamb).. 7. karakul (karakule)
  9. astrakhan
guild.. 5. artel
hemp.. 4. rine
hut.. 4. isba
leather.. 5. jufti (jufts) 6. Bulgar
  8. shagreen
marsh, lagoon.. 5. liman
massacre.. 6. pogrom
musical instrument.. 5. gudok, gusla
  9. balalaika
naval academy.. 6. Frunze
news agency.. 4. Tass
parliament.. 4. duma
peasant.. 4. Slav 5. kulak 6. muzhik
  (muzjik)
plain (treeless).. 6. steppe, tundra
police (secret).. 5. Cheka
pound.. 4. pood
prince, duke.. 4. knez (kniaz)
satellite.. 7. sputnik
soup (cabbage).. 5. stchi (shchi)
  6. borsch
stockade.. 5. etape
synod.. 5. sobor
tea urn.. 7. samovar
turnip.. 8. rutabaga
villa.. 5. dacha
wagon (springless).. 6. telega
wheat.. 5. emmer
whip.. 4. plet (plete) 5. knout
wolfhound.. 6. borzoi
yes.. 2. da
Russian people...
  chess champ (1892).. 8. Alekhine
  composer.. 3. Cui 10. Rubenstein,
  Stravinsky 12. Tschaikovsky
  14. Rimsky–Korsakov
  conqueror.. 6. Tatars 7. Mongols
  Cossack.. 5. Tatar
  czar.. 4. Ivan 13. Peter the Great
  duke.. 5. kniaz (knez, knyoz)
  empress.. 7. Czarina, Tsarina
  General.. 10. Timoshenko
  grand duke.. 8. Nicholas
  language deviser.. 8. Zamenhof
  9. Esperanto (pseudonym)
  leader.. 5. Lenin 6. Stalin 7. Molotov
  8. Brezhnev
  little Russian.. 7. Russene (Ruthene)
  monk.. 8. Rasputin
  novelist.. 7. Tolstoy
  people.. 4. Lett, Slav 7. Cossack
  8. Russniak 9. Muscovite, Ruthenian
  poet.. 7. Pushkin, Yesenin
  9. Pasternak
  premier.. 5. Lenin 7. Kosygin,
  Molotov 8. Bulganin 10. Kruschchev
  saint.. 4. Olga
  teacher, monk.. 7. starets

Youth Union.. 8. Comsomol
rust... 3. eat 5. erode 6. aerugo, patina 7. erosion, oxidize 9. corrosion
rustic... 4. boor, carl, rube, rude 5. churl, clown, Damon, rough, rural, swain, yokel 6. coarse, simple, sturdy, sylvan 7. artless, awkward, boorish, bucolic, Corydon, plowboy 8. agrestic, pastoral 9. agrestian 10. clodhopper, countryman, unpolished
rustic (pert to)...
lover.. 5. swain
maiden.. 9. Thestylis
peasant.. 4. boor
pipe.. 4. reed
poetic.. 4. carl
verse.. 4. idyl (idyll)

rustle... 4. flow 5. steal, swish, whisk 7. crinkle 11. sound softly
rut... 5. ditch, track 6. furrow, groove, strake 7. routine, wrinkle
Ruth (pert to)...
Book.. 12. Old Testament
country.. 4. Moab
husband.. 4. Boaz
mother–in–law.. 5. Naomi
ruthless... 5. cruel 8. pitiless 9. merciless 10. ironfisted
rye... 5. bread, grain, grass 6. cereal, whisky 9. gentleman (gypsy)
rye bread... 5. black 10. knackebrod 12. pumpernickel
ryot... 6. farmer, tenant 7. peasant
Rytina... 6. dugong, sea cow 7. manatee 12. Hydrodamalis 14. Steller's sea cow
Ryukyu Islands... 7. Okinawa

S

S (pert to)...
curve.. 4. ogee
letter.. 10. nineteenth
shaped.. 7. sigmate, sigmoid
suffix.. 6. plural
Saal... 4. hall, room (large)
sabalo... 6. tarpon 8. milkfish
sabana... 5. plain 7. plateau, savanna (savannah)
sabbat... 8. assembly (demons), festival (orgies)
Sabbatarian... 9. ritualist 11. Russian sect
Sabbath... 6. Sunday 7. holy day
sabbatical year... 7. seventh 8. vacation 14. leave of absence
sabbatism... 4. rest 9. ritualism 12. intermission (labor)
Sabbatist (pert to)...
devotee of.. 4. cult (Oriental)
member.. 6. Semite
named for.. 5. Sabbe (goddess) 8. Sambathe
saber, sabre (pert to)...
bean.. 4. jack
bill.. 6. curlew
fish.. 7. cutlass
knot.. 8. military
legged (horse).. 12. sickle–hocked
Mohammedan.. 8. yataghan (yatagan)
oriental.. 8. scimiter
toothed.. 3. cat 5. tiger 12. machairodont
wing.. 11. hummingbird
sabino... 9. ahuehuete, rock cedar
sabio... 4. sage 6. priest 7. wise man
sable... 4. ebon, pelt 5. black, brush 6. mammal, marten 8. antelope 10. mysterious, Russia iron
sabotage... 6. damage, mayhem

9. undermine 11. destruction (malicious)
Sabrina... 10. river nymph 11. River Severn
sabuline, sabulous... 5. sandy 6. gritty 8. psammous 10. arenaceous
sabutan... 5. fibre, straw
sac... 3. bag 4. cyst, sack 5. ascus, bursa, pouch, purse, theca 6. cavity, pocket, saccus 7. saccule, vesicle 8. sacculus
Sac, Sauk... 11. Indian tribe
sacalait... 7. crappie 8. warmouth 9. killifish
saccadic... 5. jerky 9. twitching 11. eye movement
saccharine... 5. sweet 7. honeyed 10. sweetening
saccos... 7. tunicle 8. vestment
sacerdocy... 10. priesthood 13. priestly order
sacerdos... 6. priest
sachem... 5. chief (Indian) 8. governor (Tammany)
sachet... 3. bag 5. pouch 6. powder 7. perfume 8. reticule 11. perfumed pad
sack... 3. bag 4. loot, poke, wine 5. ascus, bursa, catch, pouch, purse 6. defeat, ravage, secure 7. pillage, plunder 8. desolate 9. discharge, dismissal
sack (pert to)...
baseball.. 3. bag 4. base
Bible.. 8. mourning
but.. 4. butt, cask 8. trombone (anc)
cloth.. 7. penance, sacking 15. garb of penitence
dress.. 4. robe 6. jacket, sacque

sacrament... 3. act 4. oath 5. token
6. pledge, symbol 7. mystery
8. ceremony, covenant, practice
9. communion, Eucharist
10. intinction (to administer)
Sacramento (pert to)...
capital, river.. 10. California
cat.. 10. horned pout
pike.. 9. squawfish
salmon.. 7. quinnat
sacrarium (anc)... 6. chapel, shrine
7. oratory 8. sacristy 9. sanctuary,
synsacrum
sacred... 4. holy 6. divine 7. blessed
8. hallowed, reverend 9. dedicated,
inviolate, religious, venerable
10. inviolable, sacrosanct
11. consecrated 13. sanctimonious
sacred (pert to)...
bark.. 7. cascara 14. cascara sagrada
bean.. 11. Indian lotus
beetle.. 10. scarabaeus
bird.. 4. ibis
book.. 5. Bible, Koran
bo tree.. 3. fig 5. pipal
bull.. 4. apis, zebu
chest.. 4. arca 9. reliquary
comb form.. 5. hagio, hiero
dialect (Buddh writings).. 4. Pali
grove.. 5. Altis (Olympia)
image.. 4. icon (ikon) 5. Pietà
instrument.. 4. Urim 7. Thummim
malady.. 8. epilepsy
monkey.. 6. baboon, rhesus
8. entellus
most.. 10. sacrosanct
music.. 4. hymn 5. chant, motet
8. oratorio
river (Ind).. 6. Ganges (Ganga)
room.. 8. sacristy
traffic (in sacred things).. 6. simony
weed.. 7. vervain
wine vessel.. 3. ama
writ.. 10. Scriptures
sacrifice... 4. lose, loss 5. offer
6. give up, victim 8. chiliomb
(1,000 oxen), hecatomb (100 oxen),
immolate, libation, oblation, offering
9. atonement, holocaust, martyrdom,
privation, surrender 11. crucifixion,
destruction
sacrificer... 6. martyr
sacrificial fire... 5. ignis
sacrilege... 7. robbery (church)
9. blasphemy 11. desecration,
profanation
sacrilegious... 7. impious
10. irreverent 11. blasphemous,
irreligious
sacrosanct... 4. holy 6. sacred
8. ironical, most holy
sad... 3. bad 4. blue, dark, dire, dull
5. dusky, sorry 6. solemn, somber,
triste, wicked 7. doleful, pensive,
unhappy 8. dejected, downcast,
grievous, pathetic, shameful, terrible
9. cheerless, depressed, sorrowful
10. calamitous, deplorable,
depressing, melancholy
11. distressing, unfortunate
saddle... 4. meat (cut of), ride, seat
5. ridge 6. burden 7. harness (part)

8. encumber, straddle
saddle (pert to)...
back.. 4. hill 5. ridge
bag.. 7. alforja, pannier
blanket.. 6. corona, tilpah
boot.. 7. gambado
cloth.. 5. cover 7. housing
8. shabrack 9. appendage
10. horsecloth
elephant.. 6. howdah
girth.. 5. cinch
horse.. 5. mount 6. remuda 7. palfrey
light.. 5. pilch 7. pillion
pack.. 7. aparejo
part.. 6. cantle, crutch, pommel
8. tapadera (tapadero) 9. saddlebow
place behind.. 5. croup
rock.. 6. oyster
strap.. 5. girth 6. latigo
saddler... 4. seal 5. horse 6. cozier
7. cobbler, lorimer 8. merchant
9. shoemaker
sadness... 5. dolor 6. pathos, sorrow
9. dejection 10. gloominess,
melancholy 11. unhappiness
13. sorrowfulness
sad tree... 10. hursinghar (dye yield)
safari... 4. tour, trip 6. junket
7. caravan, journey 10. expedition,
pilgrimage
safe... 4. pete (thieves' sl), sane, sure
5. chest, vault 6. closet, secure,
unhurt 8. cautious, cupboard,
unharmed 9. protected, strongbox
11. trustworthy
safeblower... 7. burglar, peteman
8. peterman
safe conduct... 4. pass 5. cowle
guard 6. convoy, escort 8. passport
10. precaution, protection
safekeeping... 4. care 7. custody,
storage 10. protection
12. preservation
safety lamp (miner's)... 4. Davy
safety rail... 9. guardrail
saffron... 6. crocus, yellow
10. colchicine
sag... 4. bend, hang, reed, rush, sink,
wilt 5. drift, droop, sedge, slump
6. weaken 10. depreciate
saga... 4. Edda, epic, tale 5. story,
witch 6. legend 7. recital, sagaman
9. narrative
Saga... 7. goddess, seeress
sagacious... 4. sage, wise 5. aware,
witty 6. argute, astute, shrewd
7. politic, sapient 9. judicious
10. discerning, farsighted
11. penetrative 13. perspicacious
sagacity... 3. ken 6. acumen, wisdom
9. acuteness, quickness
10. shrewdness 11. discernment,
penetration 13. judiciousness
sage... 4. mint, wise 5. solon
6. astute, Salvia, shrewd 7. sapient
9. counselor, judicious, sagebrush
10. discerning 11. philosopher
Sage (of)...
Chelsea.. 7. Carlyle (Thomas)
Concord.. 7. Emerson (Ralph W)
Emporia.. 5. White (Wm Allen)
Ferney.. 8. Voltaire

Monticello .. 9. Jefferson (Thomas)
Pylos .. 6. Nestor
sage (pert to) . . .
Bethlehem .. 9. spearmint
cheese .. 7. Cheddar
chippy .. 14. Brewer's sparrow
cock, hen .. 6. grouse
family .. 4. mint
rose .. 5. alder (yellow)
tea .. 5. tonic
Sagebrush State ... 6. Nevada
sagene ... 5. seine 7. measure,
network
sagitta ... 7. otolith 8. keystone (Arch),
The Arrow
Sagittarius ... 6. bowman 9. The
Archer 13. constellation
sago (pert to) . . .
palm .. 6. gebang, gomuti
plant .. 10. cuckoopint
product .. 6. starch
tree .. 7. coontie
sagoin ... 8. marmoset
saguaro ... 6. cactus, flower
saguing ... 6. banana
Sahara ... 5. cocoa (color), leste (wind)
6. desert
sahib ... 5. title 6. master
9. gentleman
sai ... 6. monkey 8. capuchin
said ... 6. stated 7. uttered
9. aforesaid 15. before–mentioned
said to be ... 7. reputed, rumored
8. reported
saiga ... 8. antelope
Saigon nickname ... 14. Paris of the
East
sail ... 3. jib, lug 4. luff, tack 5. craft,
float 6. vessel, voyage 8. navigate
sail (pert to) . . .
around .. 14. circumnavigate
close to wind .. 4. luff
end .. 7. yardarm
fish .. 12. basking shark 15. quillback
sucker
fore and aft .. 7. spanker
foresail .. 9. spinnaker
part .. 4. clew, yard 5. leech
rope .. 5. sheet 6. earing
secure, lash .. 7. trice up
strings .. 10. reef points
type .. 3. jib, lug, top, try 4. main,
reef, stay 6. lateen, mizzen, square
7. topsail 8. mainsail, save–alls
12. mutton–legger
sailboat ... 4. yawl 5. ketch, skiff,
sloop, yacht 7. caravel (caravelle)
sailing term ... 3. leg, run 4. asea,
beat, jibe, scud, tack 5. hoist (sail),
point, reach 7. gliding
sailing vessel ... 4. bark (barque), brig,
saic, yawl 5. sloop 7. frigate
8. schooner 10. barkentine
(barquentine), windjammer
sailor ... 3. gob, tar 4. salt, wave
5. middy 6. lascar, matlow
7. mariner, voyager 8. seafarer
10. bluejacket, lobscouser (sl)
sailor (pert to) . . .
associate at meals .. 8. messmate
clothes .. 11. bell–bottoms
kit .. 8. ditty bag 9. housewife

knot .. 8. geranium
mess tub .. 3. kid
patron saint .. 4. Elmo
song .. 7. chantey 9. barcarole
Saimiri ... 4. titi 6. monkey 8. squirrel
sain doux ... 4. lard 6. grease
saint ... 3. Ste 5. angel 7. apostle,
pietist 8. canonize, enshrine, sanctify
10. holy person 11. godly person
Saint (pert to) . . .
Anthony's fire .. 10. erysipelas
Buddhist .. 5. arhat
Elmo's fire (or light) .. 6. corona,
Helena 9. corposant
Esprit .. 9. holy ghost
Francis of Assisi .. 11. il Poverello
13. little poor man
Gaudens .. 8. sculptor
George's flag .. 14. national emblem
Helena's hemlock .. 7. jellica
John Lateran .. 12. Mother Church
John's bread .. 5. carob 9. algarroba
Leger (Eng) .. 9. horse race
Luke's summer .. 12. Indian summer
Martin .. 13. Bishop of Tours
Martin's feast .. 9. Martinmas
Mary–le–Bow .. 15. Cheapside Church
(Cockney area)
Mohammedan .. 3. pir
Patrick's breastplate .. 6. lorica
Paul .. 12. Saul of Tarsus
Paul's Church (London), designer . .
18. Sir Christopher Wren
Peter's dome architect . .
12. Michelangelo
Vitus' dance .. 6. chorea
Saint, patron . . .
children's .. 8. Nicholas (Santa Claus)
English .. 6. George
French .. 5. Denis
hospitals .. 9. John of God 10. Juan
Ciudad
Irish .. 7. Patrick
Italian .. 7. Anthony
lawyer's .. 4. Ives
lover's .. 9. Valentine
sailor's .. 4. Elmo
Scottish .. 6. Andrew
Spanish .. 5. James
Welsh .. 5. David
saints (pert to) . . .
biography .. 9. hagiology
11. hagiography
tomb .. 6. shrine
worship of .. 10. hagiolatry
sajou ... 6. monkey 7. sapajou
sake ... 4. beer 6. motive, reason
7. purpose 8. beverage (rice)
salacious ... 4. lewd 5. horny (sl)
7. lustful, obscene 8. unchaste
9. lecherous
salad plant, vegetable ... 4. bibb
5. cress 6. celery, endive
7. cabbage, lettuce, romaine
10. watercress
salamander ... 3. eft 4. newt 5. poker
6. triton 7. axolotl, Caudata, urodela
9. fire–eater 10. hellbender
12. pocket gopher
salary ... 3. fee, pay 4. hire, wage
5. wages 6. reward 7. stipend
8. pittance 9. allowance, emolument,

salt money (anc) **10.** honorarium
   12. compensation, remuneration
salat... **6.** prayer (facing Mecca)
sale... **4.** deal, vend **6.** barter,
   demand, market **7.** auction, handsel
   (1st in morning) **8.** contract
   11. black market
salesman... **5.** agent **6.** vendor
   7. drummer **9.** solicitor
   14. representative **18.** commercial
   traveler
salient... **4.** bold **6.** trench **7.** eminent,
   jetting, jumping, leaping, obvious
   8. bounding, extended **9.** prominent
   10. noticeable, protruding
   11. conspicuous
salient angle... **5.** arris, Doric
Salientia... **5.** Anura, frogs, toads
   8. Amphibia (tailless)
salient point... **7.** feature (detail)
saline... **5.** salty **6.** salina **8.** solution
   10. saliferous
saliva... **7.** spittle **8.** digester, ptyalism
salivary gland... **8.** racemose
sallow... **3.** wan **4.** gray, pale
   5. muddy, pasty **6.** pallid
   9. yellowish
sally... **4.** jest, leap, trip **5.** issue,
   jaunt, start **6.** sortie **7.** journey
   8. escapade, outburst **9.** witticism
salmagundi... **4.** hash, olio, stew
   6. medley **7.** mixture **9.** potpourri
   10. periodical (old)
salmon... **4.** fish **5.** color **6.** orlean,
   sauqui **7.** annatto, saumont
salmon (pert to)...
   adult.. **7.** gilling
   after spawning.. **4.** kelt
   cured.. **6.** kipper
   dog.. **4.** keta
   family.. **10.** Salmonidae
   female.. **4.** raun **6.** baggit
   genus.. **12.** Oncorhynchus
   herring.. **8.** milkfish
   humpbacked.. **5.** haddo, holia
   kind.. **7.** quinnat
   landlocked.. **7.** kokanee
   male.. **3.** gib **6.** kipper
   newly hatched.. **4.** pink
   second year.. **6.** hepper
   silver.. **4.** coho
   small.. **4.** peal **6.** grilse
   third year.. **4.** mort
   trout.. **5.** sewen
   young.. **3.** fog **4.** parr **5.** smolt
      6. grilse, samlet **7.** essling
Salome (pert to)...
   Bib... **6.** dancer
   father.. **8.** Herodias
   grandfather.. **5.** Herod
   opera, by.. **7.** Strauss
salon... **7.** gallery **8.** New Salon
   (Paris), Old Salon **9.** reception
   10. assemblage, exhibition
   11. drawing room
Salon del Prado (Madrid)...
   9. promenade
saloon... **3.** bar **4.** deck **6.** tavern
   7. barroom, cantina, gallery
   8. dramshop, groggery **11.** drawing
   room
saloop... **8.** hot drink **9.** sassafras

salt... **3.** sal **4.** cure **5.** brine, taste
   6. flavor, halite, sailor, saline
   8. piquancy **9.** seasoning
   10. antiseptic, corrective **14.** sodium
   chloride
salt (pert to)...
   acetic acid.. **7.** acetate
   alkaline.. **5.** borax
   astringent.. **4.** alum
   block, rock.. **3.** pig
   boric acid.. **6.** borate
   cat.. **4.** lump **10.** pigeon food
   comb form.. **4.** sali
   cracker.. **7.** saltine
   dish for.. **10.** saltcellar
   ethereal.. **5.** ester
   flat.. **5.** playa
   lake.. **5.** shott (chott)
   marsh, pond.. **6.** salina
   native.. **6.** halite
   nature of, like.. **6.** haloid
   of the earth.. **7.** the best
      10. commonalty
   peter, petre.. **5.** niter
   rock, block.. **3.** pig
   spring.. **4.** lick
   tax.. **7.** gabelle
   tree.. **4.** atle (atlee) **5.** cedar
      7. tamarix **8.** tamarisk
   working.. **7.** halurgy
   works.. **7.** saltern, saltery **9.** salthouse
saltant... **7.** dancing, jumping, leaping
   8. bouncing, bounding
salted... **5.** briny, cured **6.** corned
   7. treated **8.** brackish, hardened,
   seasoned **11.** experienced
salty... **3.** reh **5.** briny, salic, witty
   6. risqué, saline
salubrious... **4.** good **8.** salutary
   9. healthful, wholesome
   10. beneficial
salutary... **7.** healthy **8.** curative
   9. medicinal **10.** salubrious
   11. restorative
salutation... **2.** hi **3.** ave **4.** hail
   5. aloha, hello, howdy, skoal
   6. curtsy, homage, kowtow, Mizpah
   (Mizpeh), prosit, salaam (salam)
   7. Dear Sir **8.** greeting, serenade
salute... **4.** hail, kiss **5.** greet
   6. homage, signal **7.** address
salvage... **4.** save **6.** redeem, rescue
   10. redemption **11.** reclamation
salvation... **8.** soterial **10.** liberation,
   redemption **11.** deliverance,
   soteriology **12.** preservation
salve... **3.** tip **4.** balm, cure **5.** allay,
   quiet **6.** anoint, cerate **7.** assuage,
   relieve **8.** flattery, medicate, ointment
   9. gloss over, lubricate, mitigator
   10. medication
salver... **4.** tray **9.** flatterer **11.** serving
   dish
salvo... **6.** excuse **7.** gunfire, pretext,
   proviso, quibble, rockets **8.** applause
   9. discharge, exception
   11. projectiles, reservation
Samaria (pert to)...
   capital (anc).. **6.** Israel
   deity.. **6.** Nibhaz
   destroyer.. **6.** Romans
   founder.. **4.** Omri (925 BC)

people.. 9. Assyrians
province of.. 9. Palestine
rebuilder.. 5. Herod (the Great)
Samaritan, good... 5. aider 6. helper
  10. befriender, benefactor
  11. helping hand
Sambal (Zambal) language... 4. Tino
sambar (sambur)... 4. deer, maha,
rusa
same... 2. id 3. ilk, one 4. ibid, idem,
self 5. alike, ditto 7. cognate, identic
  8. selfsame 9. identical
  10. equivalent
sameness... 6. parity, tedium
  7. analogy, oneness 8. identity,
monotony 9. alikeness 10. similarity,
uniformity 11. equivalence
  14. correspondence
Samian (pert to)...
island.. 5. Samos
Sage.. 10. Pythagoras
sea.. 6. Aegean
ware.. 8. Arretine
samlet... 4. parr 6. salmon (young)
Samoa...
capital.. 4. Apia
councilor.. 7. faipule
islands.. 8. American
islands, main.. 5. Manua, Upolu
  6. Savaii 7. Tutuila
natives.. 10. Polynesian
owl (barn).. 4. lulu
political council.. 4. fono
town.. 8. Pago Pago
warrior.. 3. toa
samovar... 3. urn 6. teapot
Samoyed, Samoyede... 3. dog (Arctic)
  8. Siberian
sample... 4. test 5. model, taste
  6. swatch 7. example, pattern
  8. specimen
sampler... 8. original 9. archetype
  10. needlework
Samson (pert to)...
Bib.. 5. judge (Israelite)
death site.. 4. Gaza (Syria)
famed as.. 9. strong man
opera.. 16. Samson and Delilah
tribe.. 3. Dan
wife.. 7. Delilah (betrayer)
Samuel... 4. Book (Old Test) 5. judge
  7. prophet
samurai... 6. vassal 7. officer
Sana native... 8. Yemenite
San Andreas rift... 15. earthquake
fault (Calif)
San Antonio mission... 5. Alamo
sanative... 7. healing 8. curative,
sanatory
Sancta Sanctis... 20. Holy things for
the holy
sanctify... 5. honor 6. hallow
  10. consecrate 11. free from sin
sanctimonious... 4. holy 6. sacred
  7. saintly 8. affected 12. hypocritical
sanction... 4. abet, amen, fiat
  6. assent, permit, ratify 7. approve,
endorse, support 8. approval
  9. approbate, authority, authorize
  11. countenance, endorsement
  12. ratification 13. authorization
sanctity... 8. holiness 9. godliness,

solemnity 10. sacredness
  11. saintliness 13. inviolability
sanctuary... 4. bema, fane, holy, naos
  5. abbey, bamah, cella, haven
  6. priory, refuge, temple 7. Alsatia,
convent, retreat, shelter 8. cloister
  9. monastery 10. penetralia
sanctum... 3. den 5. study 6. adytum,
office 7. retreat
sand... 4. grit 5. arena, nerve, pluck,
stone
sand (pert to)...
applied to body.. 9. arenation
bog.. 4. syrt 9. quicksand
eel.. 4. grig 6. launce
flea.. 6. chigoe, red bug 7. chigger,
sandboy
fluke.. 7. sand dab 8. flounder
hill, mound.. 4. dene, dune
hog.. 7. laborer (in compressed air)
  8. tunneler (tunneller)
inhabiting.. 11. arenicolous
like (sand).. 9. arenulous
  10. arenaceous
man.. 5. genie
mixture (clay).. 4. loam 9. sandstone
pear.. 5. Pyrus
submerged bank.. 3. bar 5. hurst,
shoal
sugar.. 5. niter
widgeon.. 7. gadwall
sandal... 4. boat, shoe, sock 7. talaria
sandpiper... 3. ree 4. knot, pume,
ruff, stib 5. stint (long–toed)
  6. dunlin 8. pectoral, triddler
sandstone... 7. sarsens 8. ganister
Sandwich Islands... 6. Hawaii
  8. Hawaiian
sandy... 6. desert, gritty 7. arenose
  8. granular, sabulous, Scotsman
  9. sandpiper 10. arenaceous, ring
plover
sane... 5. lucid, sound 7. logical
  8. rational, sensible 9. practical
  10. reasonable
San Francisco Mil Post... 8. Presidio
sang... 5. blood, sheng 7. chanted,
ginseng, Society
sang–froid... 8. coolness 9. cold
blood, composure 11. insouciance
sanguinary... 3. ant (slave) 4. gory
  5. cruel 6. bloody, yarrow
  8. sanguine 9. bloodroot, murderous
  12. bloodthirsty
sanguine... 4. warm 5. ruddy
  6. ardent 7. hopeful 8. blood–red
  9. confident 10. optimistic
  12. bloodthirsty
sanity... 6. reason 8. lucidity, saneness
  9. soundness 13. wholesomeness
San Juan Hill... 4. Cuba (Battle,
1898)
San Juan Indian... 4. Tewa
San Kuo... 13. Three Kingdoms (Shu,
Wei, Wu)
San Marino, Europe (pert to)...
famed as.. 11. oldest State (Eur)
government.. 8. Republic (smallest)
mountains.. 8. Appenine
site.. 8. Mt Titano
sannup... 6. Indian (married male) (opp
of squaw)

Sanskrit (pert to) . . .
college . . 3. tol
dialect . . 4. Pali
drama . . 9. Sakuntala (Shakuntala)
epic . . 8. Ramayana
god . . 4. Kama (Cupid), Vayu (wind)
   5. Indra (Great) 6. Aditya
goddess . . 3. Uma (Splendor) 4. Devi
   (Mother) 5. Aditi, Gauri
human spirit . . 7. jivatma
literature . . 5. sruti (shruti)
period . . 5. Vedic
Phonet (sounds) . . 6. sandhi
poem (epic) . . 11. Race of Raghu,
   Raghuvamsha
poet . . 8. Kalidasa
sacred books . . 4. Veda
soul . . 5. atman
treatise . . 9. Upanishad
Santo Domingo . . . 7. capital
   (Dominican Republic)
sap . . . 3. gum 4. boob, dupe, fool,
   mine, seve, upas 5. drain, fluid,
   lymph, sapor 6. juices, trench,
   weaken 7. essence, schnook
   8. unsettle 9. simpleton, undermine
sapid . . . 5. tasty 7. zestful 8. flavored
   9. palatable, toothsome
sapient . . . 4. sage, wise 6. shrewd
   7. knowing 8. profound 9. sagacious
   10. discerning
sapiutan . . . 4. anoa 6. wild ox
sapodilla . . . 5. chico 6. chicle, zapote
   7. nispero 9. naseberry
sapor . . . 5. savor, taste 6. flavor, relish
sapper . . . 5. miner 6. digger
   9. excavator
Saracen . . . 4. Arab 5. nomad, pagan
   6. Muslim (Moslem) 7. heathen,
   infidel, ragwort 9. Moor's head (Her)
Saracen Knight . . . 8. Ruggiero
Sarah (pert to) . . .
bird . . 9. wake–robin
husband . . 7. Abraham
mother of . . 5. Isaac
slave of . . 5. Hagar
sarcasm . . . 4. gibe 5. irony, taunt
   6. satire 8. ironical, ridicule
sarcastic . . . 3. dry 6. biting, ironic
   7. caustic, cutting, satiric 8. ironical,
   sardonic 9. malicious 10. mordacious
sarcophagic . . . 10. sarcophagy
   11. flesh–eating 13. sarcophageous
sarcophagus . . . 5. chest 6. coffin
   9. limestone 11. Assian stone, lapis
   Assius
sardine . . . 4. bang 7. alewife, anchovy,
   herring (young) 8. pilchard
Sardinia, Italy . . .
capital . . 8. Cagliari
island . . 13. Mediterranean
sheep . . 7. mouflon (moufflon)
tower (Prehist) . . 6. nuragh
sardonic . . . 3. dry 6. ironic, morose
   7. cynical, satiric 8. derisive
   9. sarcastic 11. Rabelaisian
sartor . . . 6. tailor
sash . . . 3. obi 4. band, belt, benn, tobe
   6. girdle 8. casement
   10. cummerbund
sash pulley weight . . . 5. mouse

Saskatchewan, Canada . . .
capital . . 6. Regina
city . . 8. Moose Jaw 9. Saskatoon
sassaby . . . 8. antelope
sassafras (pert to) . . .
nut . . 8. pichurim
oil of (part) . . 6. safrol
tea . . 6. saloop
tree . . 4. ague
Satan . . . 5. Demon, Devil, Eblis, fiend
   6. Belial 7. Lucifer, Tempter
   9. archfiend 14. Mephistopheles
   16. Prince of Darkness
Satan (pert to) . . .
angel (bottomless pit) . . 8. Apollyon
associate . . 6. Azazel 9. Beelzebub
before his fall . . 7. Lucifer
Jewish . . 8. Asmodeus
Scottish . . 4. deil
son . . 3. Imp (jocular)
satanic . . . 5. cruel 6. wicked
   8. devilish, infernal 10. diabolical
satchel . . . 3. bag 4. case, etui, grip,
   sack 5. cabas 6. valise
sate . . . 4. cloy, glut 5. gorge
   7. gratify, satiate, satisfy, surfeit
   8. saturate
sated . . . 4. full 5. blasé 6. gorged
satellite . . . 4. Echo, luna, moon
   5. Atlas 6. comsat, planet
   7. aerosat, Landsat, Sputnik, Telstar
   8. Explorer, follower, Vanguard
   9. companion, dependent
satellite of Jupiter . . . 2. Io (1st)
   6. Europa (2nd) 8. Callisto,
   Ganymede
satellite of Saturn . . . 4. Rhea
   5. Dione, Mimas, Titan 6. Phoebe,
   Tethys 8. Hyperion 9. Enceladus
satellite of Uranus . . . 5. Ariel
   6. Oberon 7. Titania, Umbriel
satellite's orbit . . . 4. path
   14. geosynchronous
Sati (Egypt) . . . 5. Queen
satiate . . . 4. cloy, glut, pall, sate
   5. gorge 7. gratify, satisfy, surfeit
satin . . . 4. silk 6. étoile, fabric,
   sateen, satiny 9. satinette
   10. smoothness
satire . . . 3. wit 5. irony, spoof
   6. parody 7. lampoon
satiric, satirical . . . 3. dry 6. bitter,
   ironic 7. abusive, caustic, cutting
   8. ironical, poignant 9. burlesque,
   sarcastic 11. reproachful
satisfaction . . . 3. cro 4. duel
   6. amends 7. comfort, content,
   payment, satiety 8. adequacy,
   pleasure, reprisal 9. atonement
   10. recompense, reparation
   11. contentment, fulfillment
   12. compensation, propitiation,
   remuneration 15. indemnification
satisfied . . . 5. proud, sated 7. content,
   pleased 8. satiated 9. contented,
   convinced, gratified 10. paid in full
satisfy . . . 2. do 3. pay 4. fill, sate,
   suit 5. atone, solve 6. pay off,
   please, supply 7. assuage, content,
   fulfill, gratify; indulge, requite, satiate
   8. atone for, convince

satrap (anc) ... 5. ruler 6. despot,
  prince 8. governor, overlord
saturate ... 3. ret, sop, wet 4. fill, soak
  5. imbue, souse, steep 6. drench,
  seethe 7. satiate 8. overfill, permeate
  10. impregnate
saturated ... 4. full 6. soaked, sodden
Saturday ... 6. Samedi 9. sabbatine
  13. Jewish Sabbath
Saturn (pert to) ...
  Astron .. 6. planet
  consort .. 3. Ops
  god of .. 4. seed
  Latin .. 8. Saturnus
  rings .. 7. moonlet 9. particles
  rings, part .. 4. ansa
  satellite .. 4. Rhea 5. Dione, Titan
  7. Iapetus 8. Hyperion
  Temple treasury (State) .. 8. aerarium
saturnalia ... 4. orgy 7. debauch
  8. Festival (of Saturn)
  11. pandemonium
saturnine ... 6. dismal, gloomy, somber
  8. funereal
satyr ... 4. faun 5. deity 7. demigod,
  silenus 9. butterfly, capripede,
  orangutan
sauce ... 3. soy 4. alec, pulp 5. caper,
  curry, garum, gravy, pesto 6. gansel,
  tahini 7. catchup (catsup), soubise,
  Tabasco, veloute 8. amandine,
  dressing, marinara 9. espagnole,
  insolence, seasoning 11. beurre blanc
  12. impertinence
saucy ... 4. bold, pert, vain 5. brash,
  cocky, sassy, smart 7. forward
  8. impudent, malapert 9. officious
  11. impertinent 13. disrespectful
Saudi Arabia ...
  city .. 5. Islam
  founder .. 7. Ibn Saud (1913)
  gulf .. 7. Persian
  Mohammed's tomb .. 6. Medina
  mosque .. 5. Kaaba
  peninsula .. 7. Arabian
  provinces .. 4. Asir, Nejd 5. Hejaz
  6. El Hasa
  sea .. 3. Red
  sect .. 6. Wahabi (Wahabee, Wahhabi)
sauerbraten ... 8. pot roast
sauger ... 9. pike perch
Saul (pert to) ...
  concubine .. 6. Rizpah
  daughter .. 6. Michal
  father .. 4. Kish
  herdsman .. 4. Doeg
  of Tarsus .. 4. Paul
  uncle .. 3. Ner
  wife .. 3. Ahinoam
  witch of .. 5. Endor
Sault Ste Marie ... 3. Soo 6. rapids
  9. ship canal
saumont ... 6. salmon
sauna ... 4. bath (Finnish)
saunter ... 3. jog, lag, mog 4. roam,
  rove, walk 5. range, stray 6. dawdle,
  loiter, lounge, potter, ramble, stroll,
  wander 8. ruminate
sauqui ... 6. salmon
saurian ... 6. lizard, Sauria 7. reptile,
  crocodile

sausage ... 6. banger, salami
  7. bologna, chorizo, saveloy
  8. kielbasa (kolbasi), rolliche
  9. bratwurst, pepperoni
  10. knackwurst
sausage–shaped ... 9. allantoid
  10. botuliform
savage ... 3. att 4. rude, wild 5. brute,
  cruel, feral, yahoo 6. ferine, fierce,
  Indian 7. brutish, howling 8. cannibal,
  pitiless 9. atrocious, barbarian,
  ferocious, merciless, primitive
  11. uncivilized 12. uncultivated
savanna, savannah ... 5. plain
  9. grassland 11. level region
savant ... 4. sage 6. pundit 7. scholar
  9. scientist 10. classicist
  12. intellectual, man of letters
save ... 3. but 4. keep 5. catch,
  hoard, lay by 6. except, redeem,
  rescue, scrimp 7. prevent, protect,
  reserve, salvage 8. conserve
  9. economize, excepting, safeguard
  10. accumulate
savin, savine ... 5. cedar 7. juniper
  9. evergreen
savior, Saviour ... 8. Redeemer
  9. deliverer, liberator
  11. emancipator, Jesus Christ
savoir–faire ... 4. tact 5. poise, savvy
  (sl) 7. culture 9. gentility 12. ease of
  manner, mannerliness
savor, savour ... 4. odor, zest 5. nidor,
  sapor, scent, smack, smell, taste
  6. flavor, relish 9. degustate
savory, savoury ... 5. sapid, tasty
  7. piquant 8. gustable 9. agreeable
  10. appetizing, delightful
saw ... 3. cut 4. dict 5. adage, maxim
  6. cliché, saying, truism 7. noticed,
  proverb 9. platitude, serration
saw (kind) ... 3. jig, rip 4. band, buzz,
  hack, whip 5. crown, power
  7. keyhole 8. crosscut
saw (pert to) ...
  back .. 6. sierra
  bill .. 6. motmot 9. merganser
  buck .. 8. sawhorse 13. ten–dollar bill
  crosscut .. 5. briar
  fish .. 3. ray
  grass .. 5. sedge
  horse .. 4. buck, rack 7. sawbuck
  log .. 5. edger
  of sawfish .. 5. serra
  surgeon's .. 6. trepan (trephine)
  teeth .. 5. tines
  two–bladed .. 6. stadda
sawmill gate ... 4. sash
saw–whet ... 10. Acadian owl
saxhorn ... 4. tuba 7. althorn 8. bass
  tuba 9. saxcornet
saxifrage ... 6. Seseli
Saxon (pert to) ...
  color .. 5. smalt 8. Saxe blue
  10. Bremen blue 13. indigo carmine
  king .. 6. Egbert 8. Ethelred
  14. Alfred the Great
  language .. 10. Anglo–Saxon
  12. Plattdeutsch
  people .. 7. English 9. Sassenach
  10. Anglo–Saxon 11. Lowland Scot

serf.. 4. esne
swineherd.. 5. Gurth (Ivanhoe)
warrior.. 5. thane
Saxony capital ... 7. Dresden
   10. Wittenburg (anc)
say... 4. aver, cite, tell 5. gnome,
   speak, state, utter 6. affirm, answer,
   assert, assume, recite, remark,
   speech 9. authority 11. declaration
   12. conversation
say (pert to)...
   a blessing.. 5. bensh
   again.. 6. repeat 7. restate
      9. reiterate
   further.. 3. add
   no (to).. 6. negate, refuse 8. prohibit
      10. disapprove
   one thing, mean another.. 6. palter
      7. falsify 9. fluctuate 10. equivocate
      12. be capricious
   uncle.. 4. cede 6. surrender
      10. capitulate 15. throw in the
      towel
saying... 3. dit, mot, saw 4. quip
   5. adage, axiom, maxim 6. byword,
   enigma, phrase, remark 7. proverb
   8. aphorism, apothegm
   11. declaration
saying, sayings (pert to)...
   collection of.. 9. gnomology
   criterion, party cry.. 10. shibboleth
   dogmatic.. 6. dictum
   religious.. 5. logia
scab... 3. rat 4. sore 5. crust, mange
   6. rotter 7. blemish 8. deserter
   9. scoundrel 12. incrustation
   13. strikebreaker
scabbard... 6. sheath 7. holster,
   pilcher 13. emblem of peace
scabbard fish... 7. cutlass 9. frostfish
scaddle... 5. cruel, timid 6. fierce
   7. nervous 8. skittish, thievish
   11. mischievous
scads... 4. gobs, wads 5. heaps,
   money, piles 6. oodles 11. great
   number 12. considerable
scaffold, scaffolding... 5. easel, stage
   7. staging, support 8. platform
   9. grain loft
scalawag, scallawag... 5. scamp
   6. rascal 7. sculpin 10. scapegrace
scale... 3. hut 4. husk, peel, rate,
   shed, size 5. climb, crust, flake,
   gamut 6. ascend, degree, ladder,
   lamina, rustre (anc armor), series,
   weight 7. compare, measure
   12. incrustation
scale (pert to)...
   botany.. 5. palea
   color.. 10. tintometer
   comb form.. 4. cten 5. cteno, lepis
   duck.. 9. merganser, sheldrake
   fish.. 6. ganoid 8. scabbard
   grand.. 4. epic
   music.. 3. E la (highest note)
      5. gamut, minor 9. chromatic,
      hexachord 10. tetrachord
   slide.. 7. vernier
   tail.. 6. rodent
   Zool.. 6. scutum
scallop... 4. quin 5. crena, notch
   7. mollusk 9. serration, shellfish

12. summer squash
scalloped... 6. cooked 7. notched
   8. invected (Her) 9. crenulate
scalpel... 5. knife 6. lancet 7. dissect
   8. bistoury
scaly... 5. flaky 6. crusty, scabby,
   scurfy 7. leprose 8. squamous
scamp... 3. imp 5. cheat, knave,
   rogue 6. rascal, slight 7. bacalao,
   codfish 8. scalawag, spalpeen
   9. scoundrel 15. worthless fellow
scamper... 3. hie, run 4. dash, race,
   scud 5. haste 6. hasten 7. brattle
   9. hasten off, skedaddle 11. hasty
   flight
scan... 3. eye 6. browse, peruse
   7. examine 10. scrutinize
   11. contemplate 16. recite metrically
scance... 5. blame, shine 6. glance
   7. comment, glitter
scandal... 5. odium, shame 6. gossip
   7. calumny, offense, slander
   8. disgrace, ignominy
   10. defamation, detraction,
   opprobrium 11. abomination
scandalous... 6. wicked 8. libelous,
   terrible 10. defamatory, slanderous
   11. disgraceful, opprobrious
Scandinavia, countries... see also
   Scandinavian 6. Norway, Sweden
   7. Denmark, Iceland
Scandinavian (pert to)...
   alphabetical character.. 4. rune
   ash tree.. 10. Yggdrasill
   author.. 8. Andersen (Hans C)
   bay.. 5. fjord
   explorer.. 4. Eric
   goblin, brownie.. 5. nisse 6. kobold
   god.. 4. Lake, Thor
   goose.. 5. nisse
   hall of Odin (heroes' souls)..
      8. Valhalla
   legend.. 4. Edda, saga
   maiden of Odin.. 8. Valkyrie
   navigator.. 4. Eric
   people.. 4. Dane, Lapp 5. Swede
      8. Norseman 9. Norwegian
   people, type.. 8. Teutonic
   pert to.. 5. runic
   plateau.. 5. fjeld
   rulers.. 10. Varangians
   saga narrator.. 7. sagaman
   sea monster (fabled).. 6. kraken
   supernatural being (dwarf or giant)..
      5. troll
scant... 3. few 5. chary 6. meager,
   narrow, scarce, slight, sparse
   7. slender, sparing 12. parsimonious
scanty... 4. rare 6. meager (meagre),
   narrow, scarce, sparse 7. scrimpy
   12. insufficient 14. inconsiderable
scapegoat... 4. goat (Bib) 9. sacrifice
   10. substitute
scapegrace... 5. scamp 8. scalawag
   (scallawag) 9. reprobate
   10. profligate 12. incorrigible
scar... 3. arr, shy 4. seam, sear
   5. cliff, mound 7. blemish 8. cicatrix
scarce... 4. rare 5. short 6. scanty
   7. sparing 8. uncommon 9. deficient
   10. infrequent
scarcely... 6. barely, hardly 7. but just

12. infrequently

scarcity... 4. lack, want 6. dearth, famine, rarity 7. paucity 8. rareness 11. infrequency 13. insufficiency

scare... 3. cow 5. alarm, panic 7. startle, terrify 8. affright, frighten

scarecrow... 4. ogre 5. bogle 6. effigy, goblin, malkin, shewel (sewel) 9. jackstraw 10. frightener 11. hide–and–seek

scarf... 3. boa, tie 4. sash 5. ascot, cloud, nubia 6. tippet 7. muffler 9. rigolette 10. fascinator

scarf (pert to)...
bird.. 9. cormorant
broad.. 5. shawl
clerical.. 5. fanon, orale, rabat, stole
feather.. 3. boa
head.. 10. fascinator
Hindu.. 4. sari
India.. 7. dopatta
Mexico.. 6. tapalo
skin.. 7. cuticle 9. epidermis

Scarlet Letter... 5. novel (Hawthorne)

Scarlet O'Hara's home... 4. Tara

scarp... 5. cliff, pitch 7. descent, incline 9. declivity

scary... 5. eerie, timid, weird 7. ghostly, uncanny 8. alarming 12. easily scared

scat... 4. hiss 5. burst, smash 6. buffet 7. scatter

scat, scatt (Orkney Isls)... 3. tax 7. tribute

scathe... 4. flay, harm, hurt 6. assail, damage, injury, scorch 7. scarify 9. excoriate 10. misfortune

scatter... 3. sow, ted 4. deal, rout 5. spray, strew 6. dispel, litter, shower, splash, spread 7. bestrew, diffuse, radiate 8. disperse, separate, squander 9. circulate, dissipate 10. disarrange, strew about

scattered... 4. semé 5. dealt 6. sparse, strewn 8. confused, sparsile, sporadic 9. broadcast, dispersed, separated, sprinkled 10. widespread 11. distributed

scattering... 3. few 8. Diaspora 10. dispersion, separating 13. dissemination

scatty... 7. showery

scaup... 4. duck 8. bluebill 9. blackhead, broadbill

scavenger... 4. bird 8. organism 10. saprophyte 16. garbage collector

scaw... 8. headland 10. promontory

scene... 4. site, view 5. anger, sight, vista 6. locale 7. diorama, picture, tableau

scene (pert to)...
behind the.. 8. secretly 9. backstage, invisible
inside.. 7. neorama
last.. 6. finale
of action.. 5. arena, stage 6. sphere
of confusion.. 5. babel
of miracle (Bib).. 4. Cana
opera.. 5. scena
wright.. 6. artist 8. designer (scenery), stageman

scenic... 8. dramatic 9. panoramic

11. picturesque

scenic (pert to)...
enigma.. 7. charade
pert to.. 5. stage 7. episode, scenery
representation.. 7. diorama
13. motion picture

scent... 4. aura, clue, nose, odor 5. aroma, flair, nairn, nidar, smell, spoor 6. detect 7. perfume 9. fragrance

scented... 5. olent 6. odored 8. perfumed, smelling 11. odoriferous

scepter, sceptre... 3. rod 4. mace 5. baton, staff 6. emblem (royal) 8. insignia 11. sovereignty

schedule... 4. card, list 5. slate 7. program 8. calendar, document 9. catalogue, inventory

scheme... 3. aim 4. lark, plan, plot 5. cabal 6. device, devise, racket, system 7. complot, concoct, diagram, epitome, outline, project, purpose 8. artifice, contrive 9. boomerang 10. conspiracy, enterprise 11. machination

schemer... 7. plotter 8. conniver, finagler 9. intriguer

schism... 4. rent, sect 5. split 6. breach 7. dissent, faction 8. division 10. falling–out, separation

schismatic... 7. heretic, sectary 8. apostate 9. dissenter, sectarian 10. factionist

schist... 4. mica, rock 5. slate 10. hornblende

scholar... 6. pedant, savant 7. learner, student 8. disciple 11. philologist

scholarly... 7. erudite, learned 8. academic, studious 9. philomath 10. scholastic

scholarship... 5. burse 8. learning 9. education, erudition, knowledge 10. foundation 11. instruction

school... 4. cult, sect 5. class, drill, flock, order, teach, train 7. convent, educate, seminar 8. instruct, seminary 9. institute

school (pert to)...
book.. 6. primer, reader 7. speller
English.. 4. Eton 6. Oxford 9. Cambridge
French.. 5. école, lycée
German.. 6. schule
head, inspector.. 9. scholarch
master.. 7. dominie 9. pedagogue (pedagog)
ref to.. 10. scholastic
riding.. 6. manège
teacher.. 4. marm
term.. 8. semester
wrestling.. 9. gymnasium, palaestra (palestra)

school of...
art.. 4. Dada
Fine Arts.. 9. Wagnerian
fishes.. 5. shoal
philosophers.. 7. Eleatic
philosophy.. 7. Gnostic
seals.. 3. pod
thieves.. 4. gang
whales.. 3. gam, pod

schooner... 4. boat, brig, tern 5. glass

6. vessel 7. measure, prairie (Hist)
schuit, schuyt... 5. sloop 6. vessel
7. eelboat
science... 3. art 5. ology, skill
9. knowledge 11. proficiency
science of...
agriculture.. 8. agronomy
better living.. 9. euthenics
breeding.. 8. eugenics
character.. 8. ethology
children's diseases.. 10. pediatrics
(paediatrics)
controversy.. 8. polemics
creatures.. 10. entomology
dining.. 10. aristology
doctrines.. 9. esoterics
ears.. 7. otology
family symbols.. 8. heraldry
forest trees.. 7. silvics (sylvics)
good.. 6. ethics 9. euthenics
10. agathology
government.. 8. politics
happiness.. 11. eudaemonics
healing.. 9. iatrology
health.. 7. hygiene
kissing.. 13. philematology
language.. 9. philology, semantics
11. linguistics
life.. 7. biology 10. entomology
light.. 6. optics
mind.. 10. psychology
moral conduct.. 6. ethics
organism behavior.. 7. ecology
(oecology) 9. bionomics
philosophy.. 6. noesia
reality.. 10. philosophy
reasoning.. 5. logic
rocks.. 9. petrology
sea (the).. 12. oceanography
self-defense.. 4. judo 7. jujitsu
sound.. 9. acoustics
theology interpretation.. 8. exegesis
12. hermeneutics
verse.. 7. prosody
virtue.. 8. aretaics
words.. 9. semantics
scientific... 5. exact 9. realistic,
technical 16. precise knowledge
scimitar, scimiter... 4. snee 5. saber
8. billhook
scintilla... 4. atom, iota, whit
5. spark, trace 7. modicum
scintillate... 5. flash, gleam, spark
7. be witty, glitter, twinkle
9. coruscate 10. be eloquent
scion, cion... 3. son 4. slip 5. graft,
shoot 10. descendant
scold... 3. jaw, nag 4. carp, rail, rate
5. chide, shrew 6. berate, chider,
rebuke 7. reprove, upbraid
8. admonish 9. reprimand
scolding... 7. froward 8. reproach,
shrewish 10. upbraiding
12. admonishment, reprimanding
sconce... 3. top 4. head 5. brain,
mulct, skull 6. screen 7. bulwark,
lantern, redoubt, skelter
11. candlestick, counterfort
scoop... 4. bail, beat, lade, news
5. empty, ladle, spoon 6. bucket,
hollow, shovel 8. excavate, gather in

scoop out... 3. dig 5. gouge
6. chisel, hollow 7. fashion
scope... 4. area, room 5. ambit,
arena, range, reach 6. degree,
domain 7. compass, freedom, liberty
8. latitude 9. gyroscope, intention,
periscope, telescope 10. microscope
11. stethoscope 12. kaleidoscope,
spectroscope
scorch... 4. burn, char, sear, sere
5. parch, singe, speed 7. shrivel
9. criticize
scordato... 9. out of tune 14. made
discordant
score... 3. peg, run, sum, tab 4. debt,
gain, goal, rate 5. corge, judge,
notch, scold, slash, tally 6. berate,
furrow, groove, points, reason, twenty
7. account, arrange, scratch
8. incision 9. calculate, tally mark
10. obligation 11. arrangement,
composition, orchestrate
12. indebtedness
scoria (volcano)... 4. lava, slag
5. dross 6. refuse 7. residue
scorn... 4. defy, geck, mock 5. spurn
6. deride, reject 7. contemn,
despise, disdain 8. contempt,
derision, disgrace 9. contumely
scornful... 8. derisive, insolent
10. disdainful 12. contemptuous,
contumelious
Scorpio (pert to)...
constellation in.. 8. Milky Way
genus.. 8. Scorpius
night mansion of.. 4. Mars
pictured as.. 8. scorpion
star (brightest).. 7. Antares
zodiac sign.. 6. eighth
scorpion... 4. nepa 7. alacran, scourge
(Bib) 8. arachnid, catapult 10. pine
lizard, vinaigrier 11. vinegarroon
(vinagron) 15. blue–tailed skink
Scot... 3. Mac 4. Celt, Gael 5. Saxon
6. Sawney 7. bluecap 8. Scotsman
10. Caledonian, Highlander
Scotland... see also *Scottish*
capital.. 9. Edinburgh
city.. 3. Ayr 5. Perth 6. Atholl
(Athole), Dundee 7. Glasgow
(largest), Renfrew 8. Aberdeen
9. Inverness
congress (musical).. 3. Mod
district.. 6. Argyll, Atholl
10. Midlothian
famed site.. 9. Trossachs (Lady of the
Lake) 10. Loch Lomond 11. Loch
Katrine
firth.. 3. Tay 4. Loch 5. Clyde, Forth,
Moray, Tweed
islands.. 6. Orkney 8. Hebrides,
Shetland
Latin name (anc).. 9. Caledonia
moors.. 10. Lochar Moss
mountain.. 9. Grampians
poetic name.. 6. Scotia 9. Caledonia
resort.. 4. Oban
river.. 3. Ayr, Dee, Tay 5. Afton,
Clyde, North, Tweed 6. Teviot
7. Deveron
seaport.. 4. Leth 6. Dundee
Scotland Yard headquarters...

6. London 18. Metropolitan Police
Scott, Sir Walter (pert to)...
estate.. 10. Abbotsford (Scot)
famed as.. 4. poet 8. novelist
novel.. 7. Ivanhoe
poem.. 13. Lady of the Lake
Scottish (pert to)...
accent.. 4. birr
alder.. 3. arn
attendant (hunter's).. 6. gillie (gilly)
bagpipe music.. 7. pibroch
beret.. 3. tam 11. tam–o'–shanter
bird.. 3. gae (blue) 6. grouse
   7. snabbie (snabby) 9. swinepipe
blessing.. 6. rebuke 8. scolding
blood money.. 3. cro 7. galanas
blue.. 6. homage 8. infernal
   11. reddish–blue
bluebell.. 8. harebell
boat.. 4. zulu 7. coracle, skaffie
bonnets.. 8. mushroom
brandy.. 6. Athole
breeches.. 5. trews
brier, briar.. 4. rose
broth.. 5. brose
bull, ox.. 4. stot
cake (tea).. 5. scone
cap.. 3. tam 8. Balmoral 9. Glengarry
   11. tam–o'–shanter
carpet.. 13. Kidderminster
cattle.. 8. Aberdeen 9. Ayrshire
celebration.. 4. kirn (harvest)
child.. 5. bairn 6. scuddy (naked)
church.. 4. kirk
cloth.. 4. kelt 6. tartan
coalfish.. 7. glashan, sillock
court officer.. 5. macer
cup.. 4. tass
dagger (anc).. 4. dirk
dagger, knife.. 8. skean dhu
dance.. 4. reel 5. fling 9. ecossaise
   10. strathspey 13. Highland fling
devil.. 4. deil 6. Hornie
dirge.. 8. coronach (as on bagpipes)
duck.. 4. coot 6. scoter
earth.. 4. eard
elder.. 7. tobacco
elm.. 7. wych–elm
excuse.. 6. sunyie
eye.. 2. ee
family (same).. 3. ilk
festival.. 3. Mod 7. uphelya (Epiphany)
fish.. 4. sile 7. sillock 8. spalding
fog.. 4. haar
Gaelic.. 4. Erse
ghost.. 6. taisch
girl.. 4. lass 6. lassie, towdie
   7. winklot
goblin.. 8. barghest
godmother.. 6. cummer (kimmer)
grandchild.. 2. oy (oye)
grandfather.. 8. gudesire
hill, hillside.. 4. brae 6. strone
icicle.. 7. shoggle
kilt.. 7. filibeg
kiss (stolen).. 8. smoorich
lake.. 4. loch
language.. 4. Erse 6. Lallan (Lalland)
liquor.. 5. scour 6. Athole 7. whitter
lovage.. 10. sea parsley
money, silver.. 6. siller
nephew.. 6. nepote

New Year's Day.. 7. Cake Day
   8. hogmanay
nightingale.. 7. warbler
ox, bullock.. 4. nowt
plaid.. 4. maud 6. tartan
porridge.. 5. brose
pouch, purse (kilt front).. 7. sporran
pudding.. 6. haggis
reel (fishing).. 4. pirn
rod, over the door.. 10. willow wand
sausage.. 9. whitehass (whitehawse)
schoolmaster.. 3. dux
shawl (plaid).. 4. maud
stream, brook.. 4. sike
sweetheart.. 2. jo
sword.. 8. claymore
toad.. 3. ted 4. taed
tobacco.. 5. elder
topaz.. 9. cairngorm
townhall.. 8. tolbooth (tollbooth)
uncle.. 3. eme
village.. 3. rew
waistcoat (under).. 6. fecket
whirlpool.. 7. swilkie
whisky.. 9. Glenlivet (Glenlivat)
   10. usquebaugh
window.. 7. winnock
youth.. 6. chield (chiel) 7. callant
   (callan)
scoundrel... 3. cad 5. cheat, knave,
   scamp 6. varlet 7. villain
   8. scalawag 9. miscreant
   10. blackguard 11. rapscallion
scoup... 3. run 4. leap, skip
   7. scamper
scourge... 4. bane, flog, lash, whip
   6. punish, swinge, switch 8. chastise
   10. affliction, infliction, punishment
Scourge of God... 6. Attila (King of
   Huns)
Scourge of Princes... 7. Aretino (It
   satirist)
scout... 3. spy 5. flout, scoff
   7. lookout, servant 8. emissary,
   watchman 9. guillemot
   11. reconnoiter 14. razor–billed auk
scow... 4. acon 6. garvey 7. lighter
scowl... 5. frown, lower 6. aspect
   (gloomy), glower 7. wrinkle (brow)
   10. sullen look
scraggly... 5. rough 6. ragged
   7. unkempt 9. irregular
scraggy... 4. bony 5. rough
   6. meager, rugged, skinny
   7. knotted, scrawny, stunted
scram... 6. begone, benumb, decamp
   7. vamoose
scramble... 4. push 5. climb, crowd,
   crush 6. jostle, strive 7. clamber,
   scatter 8. struggle
scrap... 3. bit, end, ort, rag 4. chip,
   junk 5. fight, melee, piece, waste
   6. morsel, refuse 7. cutting, discard,
   excerpt, extract, quarrel, remnant
   8. fragment, ramentum
scrape... 3. row, rub 4. rake, rasp
   5. grate, graze, shave 6. abrade, eke
   out, injure, sclaff 7. collect, scratch
   9. economize, obeisance 10. difficulty
   11. predicament
scraper... 4. harl (wool), tool
   6. barber, rasper 7. abrader, fiddler,

strigil 8. grattoir
scrappy... 9. irregular 10. pugnacious
11. contentious, fragmentary,
quarrelsome
scratch... 3. mar, rit, rub 4. claw,
draw, itch, mark, rake, rist, tear
5. erase 6. cancel, injury, scrape
7. blemish, roughen, scarify
8. scribble, withdraw
scrawl... 6. doodle 7. scratch
8. scribble
scrawny... 4. lean, poor, thin 5. spare
6. skinny 7. scranny 8. rawboned
scream... 3. cry 4. wail, yell 6. shriek,
squeal 7. screech
screamer... 5. swift (bird) 7. blunder
8. headline
scree... 5. stone, talus 6. debris,
pebble
screech... 3. cry, say 6. outcry,
scream, shriek, squeal 7. ululate
screech (pert to)...
  hawk.. 10. goatsucker
  martin.. 5. swift
  owl.. 4. barn 5. Scops
screed... 4. list, rend, tear 5. shred
6. tirade 7. lecture 8. fragment
12. dissertation
screen... 3. net 4. hide, laun, mask,
sift, sort, veil 5. arras, blind, cloak,
pavis, shade, sieve, spier 6. defend,
grille, riddle, sifter, sorter 7. conceal,
curtain, protect, reredos, shelter
8. parclose 9. partition, safeguard
10. protection 12. discriminate
screw... 3. key 4. coil, turn 5. horse,
twist 6. fasten, gimlet, rotate, spiral
7. contort, distort, tighten, turnkey
9. bargainer, propeller, skinflint
10. contortion, thumbscrew
screwlike... 6. spiral 7. spiroid
scribble... 6. doodle, scrawl 7. scratch
8. scrabble
scribe... 5. clerk 6. author, jurist,
lawyer, penman, writer 8. recorder
10. amanuensis, cuttlefish, journalist
13. bibliographer
scriggle... 5. twist 6. squirm
7. wriggle 8. curlicue
scrimmage... 3. row 5. fight 6. tussle
8. football (term), practice, skirmish,
struggle
scrimp... 4. save 5. scant, stint
6. scanty, scrape, sparse 7. sparing
9. economize
scrip... 3. bag 4. list 5. money
6. wallet 7. writing 8. document,
schedule
script... 5. ronde 6. letter 7. writing
8. scenario 10. manuscript,
typescript 11. handwriting
scriptural... 7. written 8. Biblical,
orthodox
scriptural interpreter... 7. exegete
scripture... 4. writ 5. motto, truth
7. passage, writing 8. document
10. manuscript 11. inscription
13. sacred writing
Scripture, Scriptures... 4. text
5. Bible 6. lesson 7. Oracles,
passage, Vulgate
Scripture interpretation... 8. exegesis

12. hermeneutics
scrivello... 4. tusk (elephant's)
scrivener... 6. notary, scribe, writer
8. recorder 10. amanuensis
scroll... 4. list, roll 5. draft 6. record,
spiral, volute 7. engross, writing
8. document, inscribe, schedule,
streamer 9. parchment
scroll roll... 8. makimono
scrub... 3. mop, rub 4. mean, runt,
tree, wash 5. clean, dwarf, scour
6. drudge, paltry 7. cleanse
8. inferior 10. undersized
scrubby... 4. base 6. paltry, shabby,
stubby 7. bristly, shrubby, stunted
10. underbrush 13. insignificant
scruff... 4. nape, scum, slur 5. crust,
dross, scuff 6. refuse 7. surface
8. dandruff
scruple... 4. coin 5. demur, qualm
6. object, weight 9. small part
10. hesitation 13. unwillingness
scrupulous... 4. nice 5. exact
6. formal, proper, strict 8. qualmish
10. fastidious, meticulous
11. punctilious 13. conscientious
scrutinize... 3. eye, pry 4. scan
5. probe 7. examine, inspect,
observe
scud... 4. dash, foam, gust, rain, sail,
skim 5. speed 6. clouds, shower
scuffle... 4. fray 5. melee 6. strive,
tussle 7. contend, contest, shamble,
shuffle 8. struggle
sculduddery... 9. grossness, obscenity
scull... 3. oar 4. gull 5. shoal, skate
6. basket, paddle, propel 7. rowboat
scullion... 4. base 6. menial
7. servant 10. dishwasher,
kitchenman
scullog, scullogue... 6. farmer, rustic
7. laborer
sculp... 5. carve 7. engrave 8. seal
skin 9. engraving, sculpture
sculptor... 6. artist, carver, imager,
molder 8. chiseler 13. constellation
19. Apparatus Sculptoris
(constellation)
sculptor (famed)... 5. Rodin 7. Cellini,
Phidias 10. Praxiteles
12. Michelangelo, Saint Gaudens
sculptor's tool... 6. chisel, graver
9. ébauchoir
sculpture... 4. form 5. carve, model
6. figure, statue 9. engraving
11. alto–relievo
scum... 4. film, foam 5. cover, dross,
froth, scurf, spume 6. refuse, scoria
7. coating 8. riffraff 10. impurities
scup... 5. bream, porgy
scurrility... 5. abuse 9. indignity,
obscenity
scurrilous... 3. low 4. vile 5. gross
6. vulgar 7. abusive 8. indecent,
scurrile 9. insulting 11. foulmouthed,
opprobrious
scurry... 3. hie 4. dash 5. scoot,
speed 6. flurry, hasten 7. scamper,
scuttle 9. skedaddle
scurvy... 4. base, mean 7. disease
12. contemptible, discourteous
scuttle... 3. hod, run 4. dish, sink

5. haste, scoot 6. basket, hasten, scurry, shovel 7. octopus, platter 8. hatchway 10. cuttlefish

scutum... 5. scute 6. shield
   13. constellation (Milky Way)
   15. Scutum Sobieskii

Scylla (pert to)...
  father.. 5. Nisus
  home.. 4. rock (coast of Italy)
  lover.. 5. Minos
  menace to.. 9. seafarers
  Myth.. 7. monster
  transformed to.. 7. sea bird

scythe... 2. sy (sye) 5. swath

scythe handle... 5. snath, snead

sea... 3. Red 4. Aral, Azov, Ross, wave 5. Black, brine, China, ocean, swell, water 6. aequor 7. Caspian 8. seashore 9. Caribbean

sea (pert to)...
  adder.. 8. pipefish 11. stickleback
  anemone.. 5. polyp
  Antarctic.. 4. Ross
  arm.. 4. gulf, meer, mere 5. bayou, firth 7. estuary
  bird.. 3. auk 4. erne (ern), gull, smew, tern 5. booby, cahow, solan 6. gannet, petrel, puffin 9. albatross 10. shearwater
  comb form.. 3. mer
  cow.. 6. dugong, rytina (Steller's), walrus 7. manatee 8. sirenian 12. hippopotamus
  cucumber.. 7. trepang
  devil.. 9. angelfish, devilfish
  dog.. 4. seal (Her) 6. fogdog, sailor
  dragon.. 8. dragonet, sea horse
  dread of.. 14. thalassophobia
  duck.. 5. eider, scaup 6. scoter
  eagle.. 4. erne (ern) 6. osprey
  ear.. 7. abalone
  eel.. 6. conger
  farer.. 3. tar 6. sailor, seaman 7. mariner
  foam.. 5. froth 9. sepiolite 10. meerschaum
  fowl.. 3. auk 4. gull, tern 6. gannet, petrel
  fox.. 5. shark
  god, deity.. 3. Lar 5. Aegir 6. Triton 7. Neptune, Phorcus, Proteus 8. Poseidon
  goddess.. 4. Nina 5. Doris 10. Amphitrite
  gull.. 3. cob, mew 9. kittiwake
  hare.. 7. mollusk
  hen.. 4. skua 9. guillemot
  hog.. 8. porpoise
  holly root.. 6. eryngo (eringo)
  ladder.. 6. Jacob's
  lion.. 4. seal
  mammal.. 4. seal 5. whale 6. dugong 7. manatee 11. bladdernose
  mouse.. 4. duck (harlequin) 6. dunlin 7. annelid
  nymph.. 5. naiad, siren 6. nereid 7. oceanid
  onion.. 6. squill
  otter.. 5. kalan
  owl.. 6. puffin 8. lumpfish
  pig.. 6. dugong 7. dolphin

8. porpoise
  pumpkin.. 8. cucumber
  quail.. 6. auklet 9. turnstone
  raven.. 7. sculpin 9. cormorant 10. squaretail
  reference to.. 5. naval 6. marine 7. oceanic, pelagic 8. maritime 9. Neptunian, thalassic
  robber.. 6. jaeger, pirate 7. corsair 9. buccaneer, privateer
  serpent.. 5. Hydra 8. snake eel
  shell.. 5. conch
  sickness.. 8. mal de mer 9. naupathia
  spider.. 10. spider crab
  turtle.. 5. green 9. hawksbill 10. loggerhead, thalassian 11. leatherback
  unicorn.. 7. narwhal
  urchin.. 5. heart 10. echinoderm, Spatangina 13. cushionflower
  wolf.. 4. seal 6. pirate 9. privateer, submarine

sea king... 3. Ler 5. chief 6. pirate, Viking 7. Neptune

seal (pert to)...
  bearded.. 5. ursuk 6. makluk
  breeding ground.. 7. rookery
  eared.. 5. otary
  flock.. 3. pod
  fur (fem).. 5. matka (matkah)
  harp (male).. 7. saddler
  leather.. 3. pin
  limb.. 7. flipper
  skin.. 5. sculp
  type.. 3. fur 7. sea lion 8. elephant, pinniped
  young.. 3. pup

sealed instrument... 6. escrow

seam... 4. line, load, scar 5. joint, ridge, strip 6. burden, groove, stitch, streak, suture 7. crevice, stratum 9. horseload 10. interstice, packsaddle

seaman... 3. gob, tar 6. sailor, Seabee 7. mariner

seaman's chapel... 6. bethel, church

seamark... 6. beacon 10. lighthouse

seamy... 5. rough 8. wrinkled 12. disreputable

séance... 7. session, sitting 9. treatment

séance holder... 6. medium

sear, sere... 3. dry 4. burn, cook 5. parch 6. braise, scorch, wither 7. dried up, shrivel 8. deadened, withered 9. cauterize 10. threadbare 11. deteriorate

search... 4. comb, fish, hunt, look, seek 5. frisk, ghoom, grope, probe, quest 6. ferret, forage, survey 7. inquire, ransack, rummage, zetetic 9. expiscate 10. scrutinize 11. investigate

searchlight... 4. beam 10. flashlight

seashell... 4. clam 5. conch, snail 7. scallop

season... 3. age 4. fall, salt, tide, time 5. devil, inure, spice 6. flavor, mature 7. qualify 8. accustom, preserve 11. acclimatize

season (pert to)...

Astron.. 5. Aries, Libra 6. Cancer
   11. Capricornus
Eccl.. 4. Lent 6. Advent, Easter
   7. Trinity 8. Epiphany 9. Christmas
   11. Whitsuntide
Lent.. 6. carême
Scot.. 4. sele
yearly.. 6. Autumn, Spring, Summer,
   Winter
seasonable ... 6. timely 7. apropos
seasoning ... 4. sage, salt 5. spice,
   thyme 6. cloves, garlic, pepper
   7. mustard, paprika 8. allspice,
   estragon, marjoram, rosemary,
   turmeric 9. condiment
Seasons, goddesses of ...
justice.. 4. Dike
order (Universe).. 5. Horae
peace.. 6. Eirene
wise laws.. 7. Eunomia
seat ... 3. pew 4. root, site 5. bench,
   chair, embed, sella, stool 6. settee,
   settle 7. install 9. establish
seat (pert to) ...
church.. 3. pew 6. sedile
of justice.. 4. banc
of self.. 3. ego
on elephant.. 6. howdah
outdoor.. 6. exedra
privileged.. 6. curule
series (one of).. 6. gradin (gradine)
seaweed ... 4. kelp 5. algae, dulse,
   laver, varec, wrack 6. Alaria
   8. agar–agar
secco ... 3. dry
secern ... 7. secrete 8. separate
   11. distinguish 12. discriminate
Secessionist (S Carolina) ... 5. Rhett
secluded ... 5. aloof, apart 6. hidden,
   lonely, remote, secret 7. private,
   retired 8. debarred, expelled, isolated,
   recessed, retiring, screened, solitary
   9. cloistral, concealed
seclusion ... 7. privacy, retreat
   8. solitude 9. aloofness, exclusion
   10. quarantine, retirement, separation
second ... 3. aid 4. abet, back, echo,
   time 5. jiffy, trice 6. assist, attend,
   backer, double, moment 7. instant,
   support, sustain 8. inferior
   9. assistant, encourage, imperfect,
   prototype, reinforce 11. corroborate,
   subordinate
second (pert to) ...
childhood.. 6. dotage, dotard
   8. senility
crop.. 5. rowen
lieutenant.. 9. shavetail
number.. 6. addend
rate.. 8. inferior, mediocre
Republic.. 6. French (1848–52)
sight.. 6. myopia 7. psychic
   9. intuition 12. clairvoyance
team.. 5. scrub 9. Yannigans
thought.. 6. sequel 12. afterthought
   15. reconsideration
secondary ... 4. less 5. minor
   6. deputy 8. inferior, offshoot
   9. auxiliary, dependent, satellite
   10. contingent, derivative,
   second–rate, subsequent, substitute
   11. subordinate, unessential

   12. nonessential, quill feather
secondary color ... 5. green 6. orange,
   purple
secondary school ... 4. prep 5. lycée
   7. academy 10. Realschule
secrecy ... 4. tile 6. hiding 7. mystery,
   privacy, privity 8. velation
   9. reticence, seclusion
   10. confidence 11. concealment
secret ... 3. key 4. dern 5. close,
   inner, privy 6. arcane, covert, hidden,
   mystic, occult 7. arcanum, cryptic,
   mystery, private, unknown 8. esoteric,
   intimate (armor), reticent, secluded,
   skullcap 9. concealed, recondite,
   secretive, underhand 10. confidence,
   mysterious 11. clandestine
   12. confidential 13. surreptitious
secret (pert to) ...
agent.. 3. spy 5. scout 6. espier
   7. spotter 8. emissary
   13. undercover man
council.. 5. by–end, junto 7. purpose
language.. 5. argot 7. dialect
meeting.. 5. tryst
movement.. 7. stealth
name.. 9. cryptonym
place.. 5. cache 6. adytum
   7. sanctum 9. sanctuary
society.. 3. hui (Chin) 4. tong
   7. Camorra (It)
secretary ... 4. bird, desk 5. agent
   6. scribe 7. officer 8. recorder
   9. confidant 10. amanuensis,
   escritoire
secrete ... 4. bury, hide, stow 5. exude
   7. conceal
secretion (pert to) ...
gland.. 7. hormone
inflammation.. 3. pus
liver.. 4. bile
mammal gland.. 9. lactation
mouth.. 6. saliva
nasal.. 10. secernment
scale, insect.. 3. lac
shrubs.. 4. lerp
whale.. 9. ambergris
secretly ... 5. aside, slyly 7. sub rosa
   8. covertly 9. not openly
   13. clandestinely
sect ... 4. clan, cult, part 5. Alogi
   (Hist), class, group, order, party
   6. essene, school, Yezidi (Kurdish)
   9. following, Mennonite
   10. shibboleth (Bib)
   12. denomination
sectarian ... 7. heretic 8. partisan
   9. dissenter, heterodox
   13. nonconformist
   14. denominational
section ... 4. area, part, plot 5. panel,
   piece, slice, tmema, torso 6. region
   7. portion, segment, ternion
   8. parabola, surgical 9. paragraph,
   signature 11. subdivision
secular ... 3. lay 4. laic 5. civil
   6. laical 7. earthly, profane, worldly
   8. temporal 9. centuried, temporary
secure ... 3. fix, get, pin 4. bind, easy,
   fast, firm, moor, nail, safe, tape
   5. fetch, spike, trice (sail) 6. elicit,
   ensure, fasten, obtain, stable

7. acquire, assured, certain, procure, receive 8. make fast 9. confident, guarantee 10. dependable 11. undisturbed

security... 4. bail, gage 5. guard 6. pledge, safety, vadium 7. defense, shelter 8. guaranty 9. guarantee, insurance, stability 10. protection

sedate... 4. calm 5. douce, quiet, sober, staid 6. demure, proper, serene, solemn 7. serious, settled 8. composed, decorous 9. dignified, unruffled 11. unobtrusive 13. contemplative, dispassionate

sedative... 6. remedy 7. anodyne, bromide, chloral, veronal 8. atropine, barbital, lenitive, soothing 9. calmative, mitigator, paregoric 10. palliative, phenacetin 12. tranquilizer (tranquilizer) 13. phenobarbital

sedent... 7. sitting (statue)

sediment... 4. lees, silt 5. dregs 7. deposit, grounds, siltage 9. settlings

sedition... 6. revolt, strife, tumult 7. treason 9. commotion 10. dissension, turbulence

seditious... 7. riotous 8. factious 9. turbulent 11. treasonable 15. insurrectionary

seduce... 4. lure 5. decoy, tempt 6. allure, enamor, entice 7. corrupt, mislead 8. inveigle

seducer... 7. enticer, tempter 8. Lothario 9. debaucher

seduction... 5. charm 10. allurement, corruption, temptation 11. debauchment

sedulous... 4. busy 6. steady 8. diligent, untiring 9. assiduous, laborious, unwearied 10. persistent 11. persevering, unremitting

see... 3. spy 4. espy, heed, know, look, scry, seat, view 5. visit 6. behold, descry, detect 7. diocese, discern, witness 8. discover, perceive 9. apprehend, interview, visualize 10. comprehend, understand 11. contemplate

seed... 3. egg, pip, pit, sow 4. germ 5. grain, ovule, plant, sperm, spore 6. kernel, origin 7. lineage, progeny 8. rudiment 9. beginning 11. descendants

seed (pert to)...
apple.. 3. pip
aromatic.. 5. anise 7. aniseed, caraway
coat.. 3. pod 4. aril, burr, husk 5. testa 6. carpel 8. pericarp
container, envelope.. 3. bur (burr), pod 6. loment, vessel 7. capsule
edible.. 3. pea 4. bean 5. grain 6. lentil
enclosing soft fruit.. 5. drupe
flower.. 6. pistil
immature.. 5. ovule
lemon, orange, apple.. 3. pip
licorice.. 9. jequerity
medicinal.. 8. flaxseed
Moringa, tropical.. 3. ben

naked (one–seeded fruit).. 6. achene (akene)
oak.. 5. acorn
one–celled.. 6. carpel
part.. 6. tunica
poppy, opium.. 3. maw
underground.. 6. peanut
winged.. 6. samara

seeds (pert to)...
cocoa.. 5. cacao
feeding on.. 11. granivorous
perfume.. 8. abelmosk
rudiments.. 3. ova 4. eggs, pips, pits 6. ovules, sperms

seedy... 5. dingy, lousy, tacky 6. shabby 7. worn out 8. slovenly 10. spiritless 11. spawn–filled 12. bearing seeds

seek... 3. beg 4. hunt 5. essay 6. pursue, search 7. explore, solicit 8. endeavor 9. neologize (new words) 11. investigate

seeker... 6. prober, tracer 7. pursuer, zetetic 8. aspirant, searcher 9. applicant 10. petitioner

seeker of...
knowledge.. 10. philonoist
new words.. 9. neologist
pleasure.. 7. epicure 8. hedonist

seem... 4. look 6. appear 7. pretend 8. resemble

seeming... 5. guise, quasi 8. apparent, illusion, illusory, pretense, specious 9. befitting

seeming contradiction... 7. paradox

seeming truth... 14. verisimilitude

seemly... 3. fit 4. meet 6. comely, decent, proper, suited 7. elegant, fitting 8. decorous, tasteful 9. expedient

seep... 4. leak, ooze 5. exude 6. filter 8. transude 9. percolate

seer, seeress... 5. sibyl 6. oracle, scryer 7. Phoebad, prophet 9. predictor, visionary 10. forecaster, prophetess, soothsayer 11. Nostradamus 14. prognosticator

seesaw... 6. teeter, tilter 7. pastime 9. alternate, crossruff, fluctuate, vacillate 11. oscillation 12. teeter–totter

seethe... 4. boil, stew, teem 5. be hot, steep 6. bubble 7. be angry

segment... 3. pip 4. part 5. tmema 6. cantle 7. portion, section 8. fragment 12. cross section

segment (pert to)...
botany.. 5. tmema 7. lacinia
corresponding part.. 7. isomere
curve.. 3. arc
shaped.. 5. toric
Zool.. 6. somite, telson 8. metamere, somatome

seine... 3. net 5. trawl 6. sagene 7. dragnet, network

seism... 10. earthquake

seize... 3. bag, cly, cop, nab, net 4. bind, bite, grab, grip, take, trap 5. annex, catch, grasp, ravin, reave, usurp, wrest 6. arrest, clutch, collar, fasten, ravish, snatch 7. capture, embargo, grapple 8. distrain

9. apprehend, lay hold of
10. confiscate, understand
11. appropriate
seizin ... 9. occupancy 10. possession
seizing ... 4. cord 7. lashing
9. arresting, raptorial
seizure ... 3. fit 4. grip, hold 5. spasm
6. arrest, attack, frenzy, seizin
9. ownership 10. convulsion,
occupation 11. manucapture
seladang ... 4. gaur 7. buffalo
selah (Bib) ... 4. sign 5. pause
select ... 4. cull, name, pick, take
5. elect, elite 6. choice, choose,
picked 7. appoint, pick out, specify
9. exclusive, segregate 10. registrate
11. distinguish, outstanding
selection ... 5. piece 6. choice
7. analect, excerpt, passage
10. collection 11. appointment
selective ... 5. draft 8. eclectic
9. exclusive 10. particular
14. discriminative
self ... 3. ego, own 4. same 5. being
6. person, psyche 7. oneself
10. individual 11. personality
self (pert to) ...
acting .. 9. automatic, voluntary
assertion .. 6. egoism, vanity
centered .. 7. selfish 9. egotistic
10. egocentric 11. independent
12. self-absorbed
comb form .. 4. auto
complacent .. 13. self-satisfied
confidence .. 5. poise 6. aplomb
9. assurance 11. self-reliant
contained .. 8. reserved 10. controlled,
sufficient (in itself) 11. independent
15. uncommunicative
control .. 8. stoicism 9. restraint
10. automation, discipline,
equanimity, temperance
defense .. 6. karate, jung fu 7. jujitsu
determination .. 8. autonomy
12. independence
enjoyment .. 13. gratification
esteem .. 5. pride 6. vanity
7. concept, ego-trip
evident .. 5. clear 9. axiomatic
examination .. 13. introspection,
introspective
French .. 3. soi
love of .. 6. egoism
ref to .. 8. personal
reproach .. 7. remorse
righteous .. 5. pious 9. Pharisaic
13. sanctimonious
14. holier-than-thou
same .. 9. identical
satisfied .. 4. smug 6. jaunty
Scottish .. 3. sel (sell)
worship .. 8. idolatry 9. autolatry
selfish ... 5. grabby (sl) 11. egotistical,
self-seeking 12. self-centered
sell ... 4. vend 5. scalp, trade
6. barter, market, retail 7. auction,
bargain 8. convince, exchange,
persuade 9. negotiate
sell (out) ... 6. betray, desert 8. inform
on 9. victimize
seller ... 6. dealer, vender, vendor

7. peddler 8. merchant, salesman
9. tradesman 10. saleswoman
semantics ... 8. meanings
11. semasiology
semblable ... 4. like 5. alike
7. seeming, similar 8. apparent,
suitable 10. ostensible, resembling
11. conformable
semblance ... 4. copy, face, form
5. guise, image 6. aspect, figure
7. pretext, umbrage 8. illusion
10. appearance, similarity
11. countenance, presumption,
resemblance
semeiology, semeiotics ... 5. signs
(signaling) 11. diagnostics
14. interpretation, symptomatology
semester ... 4. term 6. course, period
Seminole chief ... 7. Osceola
(1804-38)
Semitic (pert to) ...
deity .. 4. Baal
dialect .. 4. Geez
god (evil) .. 6. Moloch
language .. 5. Iraqi 6. Syrian
7. Arabian, Aramaic 8. Egyptian
11. Palestinian
people .. 6. Harari 8. Moabites
tribe (nomadic) .. 6. Shagia (Shaikiyeh)
semper eadem ... 13. always the same
(motto of Queen Elizabeth)
semper fidelis ... 13. always faithful
semper idem ... 13. always the same
semper paratus ... 11. always ready
senate ... 5. boule 7. council (Rom)
8. assembly 11. legislature
18. administrative body
send ... 4. mail, ship 5. drive, grant,
issue, speed 6. bestow, convey,
export, launch, propel 7. forward
8. dispatch, transmit 10. commission
send (pert to) ...
back .. 5. remit 6. remand, return
11. reverberate
by different person .. 5. relay
off .. 5. start 6. launch 7. impulse
8. dispatch 11. consignment
13. demonstration
out .. 4. emit, spew 5. shoot
out rays .. 7. radiate
payment .. 5. remit
to an address .. 7. deliver
Seneca ... 6. Indian 9. Iroquoian
Senegal, Africa ...
capital .. 5. Dakar
ebony .. 9. blackwood
gazell .. 5. korin
gum .. 9. gum arabic
mahogany .. 9. cailcedra
native .. 10. Senegalese
senescence ... 5. aging 10. growing
old
senicide ... 13. killing old men (tribal)
senility ... 6. dotage, old age
8. caducity, dementia 10. feebleness
senior ... 4. aine, dean 5. chief, elder
7. ancient, student 8. superior
sensation ... 5. sense 7. thrill, uproar,
wonder 7. emotion 8. rhigosis (cold)
10. perception 12. great success
sensational ... 5. lurid 6. superb

8. dramatic, exciting 9. emotional
12. melodramatic
sense... 4. feel, mind, sane 5. flair,
sight, smell 7. feeling, meaning
8. sapience 9. awareness, intuition,
sensation, sentience 10. perception,
understand 11. discernment,
recognition 12. intelligence
senseless... 5. inept 6. insane, stupid,
unwise 7. fatuous, foolish, idiotic,
inanity 9. illogical, inanimate,
insensate, unfeeling 10. irrational
11. meaningless, purposeless,
unconscious 12. unreasonable
13. unintelligent
sense of...
beauty.. 8. aesthete (esthete), tasteful
9. aesthetic
dignity.. 5. pride
distance.. 11. telesthetic
hearing.. 8. audition 12. auscultation
humor.. 10. risibility
sight.. 6. vision
smell.. 7. osmatic 9. olfaction
taste.. 6. palate
sense organ... 3. ear, eye 4. nose,
skin 6. tongue 8. receptor, sensilla
senses... 4. wits 6. sanity 7. sensory
9. sensation
sensible... 4. sane 5. aware, privy,
sound 7. logical, prudent 8. rational
9. cognizant, practical, sensitive
10. reasonable, responsive
11. intelligent, susceptible
sensitive... 4. nice, sore 5. acute
6. pliant, tender, touchy 7. sensory
8. sensible 9. receptive
10. responsive 11. susceptible
14. discriminating, impressionable
sensitivity... 9. emotional, hebetated
(blunted) 11. sensibility 12. irritability
14. discrimination
sentence... 4. doom 5. maxim, motto
6. phrase, remark, saying
7. condemn, passage, thought,
verdict 8. decision, judgment,
proposal 9. statement
12. condemnation
sentence (pert to)...
balance.. 7. parison
clause (concluding).. 8. apodosis
concluding.. 8. epilogue (epilog)
construction.. 6. syntax
difficult articulation.. 13. tongue
twister
introductory.. 8. protasis
judicial.. 5. futwa
pithy.. 5. motto 8. aphorism
punishment.. 11. year and a day
subordinate part.. 6. clause, phrase
sententious... 5. pithy, terse
7. concise, laconic 10. aphoristic
13. grandiloquent
sentient... 4. mind 5. aware 7. feeling
8. sensible 9. conscious, sensitive
10. perceptive 13. consciousness
sentiment... 5. toast 7. emotion,
feeling, opinion 8. attitude
10. perception, sentimento
11. sensibility 14. sentimentality
sentimental... 6. loving 7. maudlin,
mawkish 8. romantic 9. emotional

13. lackadaisical
sentimental song... 11. strephonade
sentinel... 5. guard 6. picket, sentry
7. vedette (mounted) 8. watchman
10. lookout man, watchtower
sepad... 5. think 7. believe, suppose
sepal... 4. leaf 5. petal
separate... 4. open, part, shed, sift,
sort 5. alone, apart, sever, space
6. cleave, detach, divide, secern,
single, sleave, sunder, winnow
7. disband, diverge, diverse, divided,
divorce, isolate 8. alienate, discrete,
distinct, peculiar, secluded
9. disjoined, partition, segregate,
sequester, unrelated 10. dissociate,
particular, respective
11. disembodied, unconnected
separate (pert to)...
Chem.. 11. fractionate
from others.. 5. aloof 8. isolated
metal from ore.. 5. smelt
thread.. 6. sleave
separation... 6. tmesis 7. divorce
8. autotomy 9. partition, secession,
seclusion 10. alienation
11. disjunction, segregation
13. sequestration 14. discontinuance,
discrimination
separatist... 7. heretic, seceder
8. apostate 9. dissenter
12. secessionist 13. nonconformist
sepia... 3. dun, ink 5. color
7. pigment 10. cuttlebone, cuttlefish
sepiment... 5. hedge 7. defense
9. enclosure
Sepiola... 10. cuttlefish
sepiolite... 10. meerschaum
sepoy... 7. soldier 9. policeman
seps... 6. lizard 7. serpent
sept... 4. clan 5. class, seven, tribe
7. lineage
septic... 6. morbid, pyemia (pyaemia)
8. diseased, infected, poisoned
9. gangrened, mortified, poisonous
10. septicemia (blood poison)
sepulcher, sepulchre... 4. bury, tomb
5. crypt, grave, vault 6. entomb
9. sepulture 10. repository
sepulchral... 5. urnal 6. gloomy,
hollow 7. charnel 8. funereal
9. deep-toned
sepulchral (pert to)...
chest.. 4. cist
mound.. 7. tumulus
vault.. 6. burial 8. catacomb,
monument 9. interview
sequel... 5. issue 6. effect, series,
upshot 7. outcome 8. follow up,
sequence, sequitur 9. posterity
10. succession
sequela... 7. disease (resulting)
8. adherent 9. inference
10. conclusion 11. concomitant,
consequence 15. morbid condition
sequence... 5. gamut 6. course
(usual), series, tierce (three cards)
8. straight 10. succession
sequential... 9. deducible, resultant
10. continuous, succeeding
11. consecutive
sequestered... 6. lonely, secret

7. private, recluse, retired
8. isolated, secluded, solitary,
withdraw 9. concealed, separated
12. unfrequented
sequitur... 9. inference, influence, it
follows 14. natural sequent
sequoia, Sequoia... 4. Park (Calif)
6. Indian (famed for alphabet) 7. big
tree, conifer, redwood
seraglio... 5. harem, serai 6. zenana
9. enclosure
serape... 5. shawl 7. blanket
seraph... 5. angel 6. cherub
seraphic... 7. angelic, sublime
8. cherubic 9. unworldly
Serb... 4. Slav 7. Serbian (Servian)
Serbia, Yugoslavia...
church.. 8. Orthodox
conqueror.. 5. Turks
hero.. 6. Dushan, Nemaya (1159)
queen.. 7. Natalie
Revolutionary.. 7. Chetnik
sere... 4. claw, sear, worn 5. talon
6. effete, yellow 8. withered
10. desiccated
serenade... 4. sing 5. music
8. serenata 9. charivari, entertain
10. callithump 11. celebration
serene... 4. calm, cool 5. clear, quiet
6. placid 8. peaceful, serenity,
tranquil 9. collected, unruffled
11. undisturbed 12. tranquillity
(tranquility)
serenity... 5. peace 6. repose
8. calmness, coolness 9. composure
10. quiescence
serf... 4. esne, neif (fem), peon
5. helot, slave 6. thrall, vassal
7. captive, villein
series... 3. set 4. nest 5. class,
gamut, group 8. sequence
9. seriation 10. succession
series, connected... 5. chain, suite
6. catena
series of...
discussions.. 9. symposium
heroic events.. 4. epos
meetings.. 7. session
pictures.. 8. panorama
races.. 7. regatta
rings.. 4. coil
six.. 5. hexad
steps.. 5. scale
syllogisms.. 7. sorites
travels.. 7. odyssey
serious... 4. keen 5. grave, serio
(comb form), sober, staid 6. demure,
sedate, solemn 7. capital, earnest,
weighty, zealous 8. resolute
9. important 10. thoughtful
seriousness... 4. zeal 7. gravity
10. importance 11. earnestness
sermon... 4. talk, text 5. psalm
6. homily, lesson, preach 7. address,
lecture, reproof 8. harangue
9. discourse, preaching
10. admonition
seron... 5. crate 6. hamper
7. boxwood, spanner
serotine... 3. bat 4. adda 9. late
bloom
serpent... 3. asp 4. seps (anc)

5. cobra, krait, racer, snake
serpent (pert to)...
deity, of good.. 12. agathodaemon
13. agathos daemon
fabulous.. 5. Hydra 6. dragon
8. basilisk 11. amphisbaena
large.. 3. boa 5. aboma 6. python
8. jararaca
monster.. 6. ellops
Old.. 5. Satan
semihuman (Hind Myth).. 4. Naga
sky (Vedic Myth).. 3. Ahi
worshipers (Gnostic).. 7. Ophites
serpentine... 4. wily 5. snaky
6. subtle, zigzag 7. sinuous, winding
8. diabolic, tempting 9. snakelike
10. circuitous, meandering
serpigo... 8. ringworm 11. skin disease
serrano... 12. squirrelfish
serrate... 7. notched, toothed
8. indented 10. saw–toothed
serried... 5. dense 7. compact,
concise, crowded
serum... 4. whey 5. blood, fluid
6. serous 9. antitoxin
servant... 3. gyp 4. bata, cook, maid,
maty, mozo, serf, syce 5. agent,
boots, chela, nurse, slave, valet
6. bildar, butler, flunky, garçon, gillie
(gilly), menial, servus, vassal, wallah
(walla) 7. equerry (nobleman's)
8. coistrel, domestic, handmaid
9. assistant 11. chamberlain
servant of God... 6. bishop
serve... 2. do 3. act, aid 4. deal,
help, wait 5. avail, cater 6. assist,
succor 7. advance, bestead, forward,
further, suffice, work for 8. bear
arms, fight for 9. officiate
10. administer, distribute
serve (pert to)...
as accomplice.. 4. abet
as escort.. 6. squire
food.. 4. wait 5. cater 7. dish out
religion.. 4. obey 7. worship
tennis.. 7. deliver
server... 4. tray 6. player, salver
7. acolyte
Servia... see *Serbia*
service... 3. aid, use 4. help, mail,
Mass, rite 5. favor, matin 6. employ,
ritual 7. benefit, nocturn, utility
8. ceremony, evensong, kindness,
ministry 9. servitude 10. attendance,
employment 12. ministration
service tree... 4. sorb 5. rowan
servile... 4. mean 6. abject, menial,
minion 7. fawning, slavish
8. cringing, faithful 9. dependent,
parasitic, truckling 10. obsequious,
submissive 11. subservient,
sycophantic
Servite... 9. mendicant 13. Order of
Friars (1233)
servitude... 7. bondage, serfdom,
service, slavery 8. servitus
9. vassalage 14. apprenticeship
sesame... 3. oil 4. herb 5. benne
7. gingili (seed), teel oil 8. ajonjoli,
sesamine
Sesame, Open... 10. magical key
12. magic command (Arab Nights)

sess... 4. heap, pile 9. soap frame
session... 5. court 6. séance
　　8. assembly 11. legislature
set... 3. lay 4. form, heal, laid, pose,
　　post 5. brood, class, fixed, group,
　　place, posit, ready, staid, stand
　　6. adjust, clique, define, fasten,
　　formal, ossify, series, settle
　　7. confirm, congeal, coterie, station,
　　stiffen 8. regulate, solidify
　　9. coagulate, designate, direction,
　　obstinate, stabilize 10. collection,
　　determined, solidified 11. established,
　　prepared for
set (pert to)...
afloat.. 6. launch
against.. 6. oppose 10. antagonize
apart.. 5. allot, elect, taboo
　　6. exempt 7. isolate, reserve,
　　seclude 8. allocate, separate
　　9. segregate, sequester
　　11. distinguish 13. differentiate
aside.. 4. void 5. annul 6. except,
　　reject 7. abolish, discard, dismiss,
　　earmark, exclude 8. overrule,
　　postpone
at an angle.. 4. cant
back.. 4. loss 5. check 6. demote,
　　hinder, recess 7. relapse 8. restrain,
　　slow down
exclusive.. 5. elect, taboo 6. clique
fire to.. 6. ignite, kindle 7. emblaze,
　　inflame 8. irritate
firmly.. 5. embed, plant, posit
　　6. cement, ossify
forth.. 5. adorn 6. depart, expose, lay
　　out 7. arrange, commend, display,
　　enounce, exhibit, explain, expound,
　　present, promote, propone, publish
　　8. announce, decorate, indicate,
　　manifest 9. translate 10. promulgate
　　11. demonstrate
free.. 6. acquit 7. absolve, release,
　　unloose 8. liberate 10. emancipate
　　11. disillusion
off.. 6. incite, offset 7. measure
　　8. beautify, detonate 9. demarcate,
　　embellish 11. distinguish
on firm basis.. 9. establish
out.. 4. plot 5. allot, begin
　　7. arrange
right.. 5. teach 6. adjust, direct,
　　remedy 11. disillusion
up.. 3. rig 4. plan 5. build, cause,
　　erect, exalt, hoist, print, raise
　　7. elevate, finance, install
　　9. construct, establish
　　10. inaugurate, prearrange
set (pert to in)...
a groove.. 5. dadoe
a row.. 4. tier 5. align, aline, range
columns.. 7. tabular 8. tabulate
from margin.. 6. indent
operation.. 4. move 5. start 6. launch
opposition.. 3. pit
order.. 5. align 6. adjust 7. arrange
set (pert to of)...
eight.. 6. ogdoad
friends.. 7. coterie
jeweled ornaments.. 6. parure
laws.. 4. code 8. statutes
on end.. 5. upend 10. topsy–turvy

opinions.. 5. credo
organ pipes.. 5. stops
rules.. 4. code
sheets (paper).. 5. quire
seta... 4. hair 5. spine 7. bristle,
　　feather
Seth (pert to)...
brother.. 4. Abel, Cain
father.. 4. Adam
son.. 4. Enos
wife.. 8. Nephthys
setting... 5. scene 6. locale
　　8. mounting, planting
　　10. background
settle... 3. fix, pay 4. nest, root, seat,
　　sink 5. agree, clear, lodge, order,
　　prove, quiet, solve 6. assign, assure,
　　decide, locate, pay off, purify, secure,
　　soothe 7. arrange, clarify, confirm,
　　mediate, resolve 8. colonize,
　　ensconce, regulate 9. designate,
　　determine, establish, reconcile
　　10. strengthen 11. tranquilize
settled... 4. paid 5. ended, fixed
　　6. proved, sedate 7. assured,
　　decided, located 9. steadfast
　　10. unchanging 11. established
settled in advance...
　　13. predetermined
settled in mind... 10. equanimity
settlement... 3. dos 4. camp
　　6. colony, hamlet 7. payment
　　8. fixation, sediment, showdown
　　9. community, endowment
　　10. adjustment 12. colonization,
　　conciliation, satisfaction
　　13. determination, establishment
Settlement House... 9. Hull House
　　(Chicago) 10. University (NY)
　　11. Toynbee Hall (London)
settler... 6. Sooner (Okla) 7. pioneer,
　　planter, Puritan 8. colonist
　　9. immigrant
settlings... 4. lees 5. dregs
　　8. sediment 10. settlement
　　12. precipitates
seven (pert to)...
angles.. 8. heptagon 9. septangle
arts.. 5. logic, music 7. grammar
　　8. geometry, rhetoric 9. astronomy
　　10. arithmetic
comb form.. 5. hepta, septi
days and nights.. 8. sennight
fold.. 8. septuple
gods of happiness.. 5. Ebisu, Hotei
　　6. Benten 7. Daikoku, Jurojin
　　8. Bishamon 10. Fuku–roku–ju
group.. 6. heptad, septet 8. septuple
　　12. septemvirate
Hills.. 4. Rome
languages.. 9. heptaglot
Latin.. 6. septum
number.. 8. hebdomad 9. septenary
Old Test Books (1st seven)..
　　10. Heptateuch
Seas.. 11. world oceans
Stars.. 8. Pleiades
tones.. 10. heptachord, heptatonic
seventy... 12. septuagenary
seventy–day period...
　　12. septuagesima
seventy–year–old... 14. septuagenarian

sever . . . **3.** cut, lop **4.** part, rend
5. break **6.** behead, cleave, detach,
divide, except, exempt **7.** disjoin
8. accurate, disunite, separate
9. interpose, segregate
10. decapitate, disconnect, dissociate
12. disassociate
several . . . **4.** many **6.** divers, sundry
7. diverse, various **8.** distinct
9. different **10.** respective
severe . . . **3.** bad **4.** dure, hard, keen,
sore, tart **5.** acute, cruel, exact, grave,
harsh, rigid, snell, sober, stern
6. biting, bitter, chaste, sedate,
simple, solemn, strict, taxing, trying
7. arduous, austere, condign, drastic,
extreme, intense, painful, serious,
violent **8.** accurate, rigorous
9. draconian, strenuous, stringent
10. censorious, restrained
severe critic (of Alexandria) . . .
9. Aristarch
severity . . . **5.** rigor **7.** cruelty
8. hardness, pungency, violence
9. austerity, exactness, gruffness,
harshness, solemnity, sternness,
stiffness **10.** bitterness, difficulty,
inclemency, simplicity, strictness
12. rigorousness
Seville cathedral tower . . . **7.** Giralda
Seville orange . . . **9.** red–yellow
12. bitter orange
Sèvres blue . . . **5.** color **9.** bleu de
roi, porcelain **11.** bleu céleste
sew . . . **4.** mend **5.** baste, unite
6. fasten, needle, secure, stitch
sewan . . . **5.** beads, money **6.** wampum
sewing . . . **6.** sutile **8.** suturing
9. stitching **10.** needlework
sewing case . . . **4.** etui
sewing machine inventor . . . **9.** Elias
Howe
sexagenarian . . . **13.** a sixty–year–old
sexagesimal . . . **5.** sixty
sexes, common to both . . . **6.** unisex
7. epicene
sexless . . . **6.** neuter **7.** epicene
sextet, sextette . . . **6.** sestet **8.** six
parts **10.** group of six **13.** six–line
stanza
sexton . . . **6.** beetle **7.** sacrist
9. sacristan **12.** underofficer
sextuplet . . . **7.** sestole (sestolet) **8.** six
notes
sha . . . **5.** sheep, urial (oorial)
shabbash . . . **5.** bravo **8.** well done
Shabbath . . . **7.** Sabbath (Jew)
shabbiness . . . **8.** baseness, slovenry
9. seediness
shabby . . . **4.** base, mean, worn
5. dowdy, faded, ratty, seedy, tacky,
yucky **6.** grungy, paltry, ragged,
scurvy, scuzzy, sleazy **7.** outworn,
shagrag, squalid **10.** despicable,
ragamuffin, threadbare
12. contemptible
shack . . . **3.** coe, hut **4.** husk, plug
5. chase, hutch, tramp **6.** shanty
7. stubble **8.** vagabond **9.** hibernate
shackle . . . **3.** tie **4.** band, bind, bond,
gyve, iron, ring **5.** chain **6.** fetter,

hobble, hogtie, impede, pinion
7. manacle, trammel **8.** restrain
shackled . . . **4.** tied **5.** bound, gyved
6. curbed, ironed **7.** hobbled
8. fettered, hampered, hindered,
manacled **10.** restrained
shad . . . **4.** fish **5.** Alosa **7.** crappie,
mojarra
shade . . . **3.** hue **4.** dull, roof, tint, tone,
veil **5.** ghost, tinge, visor **6.** awning,
canopy, darken, degree, follow,
nuance, screen, shadow, shield, sprite
7. eclipse, foliage, parasol, protect,
shelter, umbrage **10.** overshadow,
protection **11.** adumbration
shade, affording . . . **9.** umbratile
shadow . . . **3.** dim, dog, spy **4.** hide,
tail **5.** cloud, image, umbra **6.** attend,
screen **7.** blacken, conceal, protect,
remains **8.** follower, hanger–on,
illusion, penumbra **9.** adumbrate,
detective **10.** protection
shadow fighting . . . **9.** sciamachy
shadowless . . . **6.** ascian
Shadrach (pert to) . . .
enemy . . **14.** Nebuchadnezzar
name once . . **7.** Ananias **9.** Hannaniah
one of three Hebrew youths . .
  7. Meshach **8.** Abednago, Shadrach
shady . . . **4.** dark **5.** faint, fishy
6. umbral **7.** shadowy **9.** deceitful,
dishonest, underhand **10.** indistinct,
unreliable **12.** questionable
shaft . . . **3.** pit, rod **4.** axle, fust, mine,
orlo (part), stem, tige, tole **5.** arrow,
scape, shank, spire, stalk, thill, tower,
trunk **6.** column, tongue **7.** feather,
missile, obelisk **8.** monument
9. flagstaff
shag . . . **3.** nap **4.** hair, mane, pile
5. chase, dance **6.** follow, rascal
7. tobacco **9.** cormorant, make rough
10. blackguard
shaggy . . . **5.** bushy, furry, nappy, rough
6. ragged **7.** hirsute, unkempt, villous
8. confused (of thought), uncombed
10. unpolished
shagrag . . . **6.** ragged, tagrag
7. unkempt **8.** rascally
shake . . . **3.** jar, jog, wag **4.** jolt, rock,
stir, sway, toze **5.** swing, trill
6. dither, dodder, quiver, shimmy,
shiner, weaken **7.** agitate, flutter,
shingle, shudder, tremble, tremolo
8. enfeeble **10.** earthquake
Shakespeare (pert to) . . .
actor . . **4.** Ward **7.** Gielgud, Olivier,
Sothern **8.** Modjeska
called . . **10.** Bard of Avon
character, female . . **6.** Juliet, Portia
7. Ophelia **9.** Cleopatra
character, male . . **5.** Romeo, Timon
6. Antony, Hamlet **7.** Macbeth,
Othello **8.** Falstaff
forest . . **5.** Arden
river . . **4.** Avon
site . . **6.** Verona **8.** Elsinore
villain . . **4.** Iago
wife . . **11.** Anne Hathaway
shaky . . . **6.** infirm, wabbly, wobbly
7. fearful, nervous, unsound

8. agitated, unsecure 9. tottering,
trembling, uncertain, unsettled
10. precarious, unreliable
12. questionable
shale ... 4. rock 5. flake, scale
8. dandruff
Shalimar Gardens ... 6. Lahore
shallow ... 5. shoal 6. lagoon (lagune)
7. cursory, trivial 9. depthless,
frivolous, insincere 11. superficial
sham ... 3. ape 4. fake, hoax, mock
5. dummy, false, fraud, trick
6. deceit, humbug 7. feigned
8. pretense 9. imitation, imposture,
pretended
Shamash (pert to) ...
centers of worship .. 5. Larsa
6. Sippar
consort .. 3. Aya (Ai)
deity (Babylon) .. 6. sun god
messenger .. 6. Bunene
Sumerian equivalent .. 3. Utu (Utug)
6. Babbar
shame ... 5. abash 7. mortify
8. disgrace, dishonor 9. humiliate
11. abomination, humiliation,
impropriety
shameful ... 4. mean, vile 5. gross
6. wicked 8. flagrant, improper,
indecent, infamous, terrible
9. degrading 10. outrageous,
scandalous 11. disgraceful,
ignominious 12. dishonorable,
disreputable, vituperative
shameless ... 6. arrant, brazen
8. immodest, impudent 9. audacious
10. unblushing 11. brazenfaced
shammer ... 8. impostor
shanghai ... 6. abduct, to drug
9. slingshot
shank ... 3. leg 4. crus, gamb (gambe)
7. meat col 12. travel on foot
shape ... 4. bend, form, mold (mould),
plan 5. frame, model 6. adjust,
create, cut out, design, devise, figure
7. arrange, conform, contour,
develop, fashion, incline 8. phantasm
10. appearance, figuration
11. arrangement
shaped like a ...
comb .. 9. pectinate
shield .. 7. peltate, scutate
strap, thong .. 6. lorate
urn .. 9. urceolate
shapeless ... 7. lumpish 8. deformed,
formless 9. amorphous, contorted,
distorted, unshapely
shapely ... 3. fit 4. neat, trim
6. comely, gainly 10. well–formed
11. symmetrical
16. well–proportioned
shapes (ornamental, garden) ... 5. topia
7. topiary
share ... 3. cut, lot 4. dole, part
5. enter, quota 6. ration 7. partake,
portion 8. take part 9. allowance,
apportion 11. co–operative,
participate
sharecropper ... 7. metayer
shark ... 5. fraud 6. lawyer 8. parasite,
swindler 9. trickster
shark (fish) ... 4. gata, mako, tope

5. lamia (cub), Rhina 6. Galeos,
Galeus, requin 7. dogfish, tiburon
8. man–eater, Mustelus, Selachii,
sharklet, Squatina 9. porbeagle
10. Carcharias, hammerhead
11. Carcharodon, Galeorhinus
shark–clinger ... 4. pega 6. remora
sharp ... 4. acid, curt, edgy, keen, tart
5. acerb, acrid, acute, alert, brisk,
crisp, edged, harsh, quick, smart,
steep, witty 6. abrupt, astute, bitter,
crafty, shrill 7. angular, caustic,
cutting, nipping, painful, pointed,
pungent, sharper 8. incisive, poignant
9. penetrant, sagacious, sarcastic,
trenchant 10. discerning, proficient
11. acrimonious, penetrating,
well–dressed
sharp (pert to) ...
answer .. 6. retort
blow .. 4. slap
cornered .. 7. angular
edged .. 5. arris
flavor .. 4. tang
make .. 10. cacuminate
pointed .. 5. acute
saw .. 8. titmouse
Scot .. 5. snell 6. snelly
sighted .. 4. keen 6. astute 7. lyncean
sound .. 4. ping
Tuesday .. 13. Shrove Tuesday
witted .. 6. shrewd 10. discerning
11. intelligent
sharpen ... 3. nib, ted 4. edge, hone,
whet 5. grind, point, strop 6. acuate
7. enhance, quicken 9. intensify
10. cacuminate
sharper ... 5. cheat, knave, rogue
6. keener 8. deceiver, swindler
9. trickster
shatter ... 5. blast, break, crash,
smash, split 8. splinter
shave ... 3. cut 4. pare 5. cheat, strip
6. cut off 7. swindle, tonsure 9. cut
prices, thin slice
shaver ... 3. boy, lad 4. tool 5. cheat
6. barber 8. swindler 9. youngster
11. extortioner
shavetail ... 4. mule 6. ensign
10. lieutenant
shawl ... 5. manta 6. serape 7. paisley
8. cashmere
Shawnee (pert to) ...
chief .. 8. Tecumseh
Indian tribe .. 9. Algonquin
location (present) .. 8. Oklahoma
sheaf ... 4. kern, omer 6. bundle
7. cluster 11. hyperpencil
shear ... 3. cut 4. clip, snip, trim
5. sever 6. fleece, remove
7. scissor, whittle
shears ... 5. lewis 6. forfex 8. secateur
sheatfish ... 4. wels 7. catfish
sheath ... 4. case 5. forel (book),
glove, ocrea, theca 6. sleeve, spathe
7. stipule 8. scabbard
sheathe ... 4. wrap 5. cover, drape
6. encase 7. envelop 8. enshroud
sheave ... 5. wheel 6. pulley 9. back
water, eccentric
shebang ... 6. affair, boodle, outfit
7. concern 11. contrivance

13. establishment 14. kit and
caboodle

she–cat... 4. elle 9. grimalkin

shed... 3. hut 4. abri, cote, lair, molt
5. hovel, scale, spill 6. effuse,
hangar, lean–to, slough 7. cottage,
diffuse, radiate, shelter

shed (light)... 4. glow 7. explain,
radiate 10. illuminate

shedding... 7. ecdysis (Zool), molting

sheen... 5. glint, gloss, shine 6. luster
7. glitter, shimmer 8. splendor
9. shininess 10. brightness

sheep... 3. ewe, ram, sha, teg, tup
4. buck, lamb, Ovis, zenu 5. bidet,
dumba, oudad 6. argali, cosset,
gimmer, hogget, mutton, sheder,
wether 8. ruminant, shearhog,
yeanling 9. blackface

sheep (pert to)...
cry.. 3. baa 5. bleat
disease.. 3. coe, gid, rot 4. bane
5. braxy 7. anthrax
faced.. 3. shy 7. bashful 8. sheepish
female.. 3. ewe, teg 6. sheder
flock leader.. 10. bellwether
fold.. 3. ree 4. cote 5. kraal, reeve,
stell 6. church
head.. 5. jimmy 8. powsowdy
headed.. 5. silly 6. stupid
12. simple–minded
kidney extract.. 5. renes
laurel.. 6. Kalmia
leg wool.. 4. gare
male.. 3. ram, tup 4. buck 5. heder
6. wether
owner's mark.. 4. smit 6. ruddle
pet.. 6. cosset
sheeplike.. 5. ovine 9. tractable
skin, leather.. 4. pelt, roan 5. basil
7. chamois, diploma 8. woolfell
stealing.. 7. abigest
tick.. 3. ked
wild.. 3. sha 4. Ovis 5. urial
6. aoudad, argali, bharal, nayaur
7. mouflon (moufflon) 9. Thian Shan
(Marco Polo's)

sheep, breeds... 6. Merino, Romney
7. Cheviot, Delaine, Dishley, Karakul,
Suffolk, Targhee 8. Cotswold,
Dartmoor 9. Kerry Hill, Leicester,
Southdown, Teeswater
10. Corriedale, Dorset Horn, Oxford
Down, Shropshire 13. Hampshire
Down

sheer... 4. mere, pure, thin, turn
5. brant, steep, utter 6. abrupt,
swerve 7. deviate, unmixed
8. absolute 9. deviation, downright,
undiluted 10. completely, diaphonous
11. transparent 13. perpendicular

sheet... 4. leaf, rope, sail 5. paper
6. shroud 9. cover with, duodecimo
(12–fold), newspaper, sheathing

sheik, sheikh... 4. Arab 5. chief
6. prince

shelf... 4. berm (berme), reef, sell
5. ledge, shoal 6. mantel 7. stratum
8. postpone, put aside

shell... 3. pod 4. boat, bomb, husk
5. conch, crust, shard, shuck
6. cowrie (cowry) 7. bombard,

capsule, grenade, missile 8. carapace,
exterior, shrapnel 9. cartridge
10. projectile

shell (pert to)...
button source.. 5. troca 6. lorica,
mucket
cone.. 7. admiral
ear.. 7. abalone
explosive.. 3. dud 4. bomb
7. grenade
fish.. 4. clam, pipi 6. cockle, limpet,
mussel, oyster 7. abalone, lobster,
mollusk, scallop 8. barnacle
9. trunkfish
fossil.. 8. ammonite
game.. 10. thimblerig 13. sleight of
hand
marine.. 6. cowrie (cowry)
money.. 5. hawok, sewan, uhllo (ulo)
6. cowrie, wampum
out.. 4. give 6. expend, pay out
protective.. 6. lorica
ridge.. 4. lira 5. varix
seaweed.. 8. frustule
spiral.. 5. chank, whelk 8. caracole
trumpet (Triton's).. 5. conch

shelter... 3. lee, pad 4. abri, camp,
cote, digs, port, roof, shed, skug, tent
5. condo, cover, haven, house, hutch,
shack, shade 6. asylum, burrow,
dugout, hangar, harbor, refuge, screen,
shield 7. defense, hospice, pillbox,
protect, retreat 8. mantelet (mantlet),
quarters, security 9. coverture,
sanctuary 10. protection

sheltered side... 3. lee 4. alee
7. leeward

shelve... 5. slope, table, waive
6. retire 7. dismiss, incline
8. postpone, put aside
10. pigeonhole

Shem (pert to)...
brother.. 3. Ham
descendant.. 6. Semite
father.. 4. Noah
son.. 3. Lud 4. Aram, Elam

shenanigan... 7. foolery 8. trickery,
zaniness 9. horseplay
10. hanky–panky 11. monkeyshine

shend... 3. mar 4. harm, ruin 5. spoil
6. injure, revile 7. destroy, stupefy
8. confound, disgrace, reproach

Sheol... 4. Hell 5. Aralu, grave, Hades
6. the pit, Toppet 7. Abaddon,
Gehenna 10. underworld 11. nether
world 14. abode of the dead

shepherd... 5. guide 6. direct, escort,
feeder, herder, pastor, shadow
8. guardian, herdsman 9. clergyman

shepherd, shepherds (pert to)...
band of.. 10. pastoureau
dog.. 5. sheep 6. collie
flute.. 7. musette 9. flageolet
god.. 3. Pan
pipe.. 3. oat 4. reed 7. larigot
spider.. 13. daddy longlegs
staff.. 4. Kent 5. crook

sheriff (pert to)...
aide.. 5. posse
deputy.. 6. elisor 7. bailiff
jurisdiction.. 9. bailiwick
sheriffdom.. 10. shrievalty

sherry . . . 5. jerez, Xeres 7. oloroso
  8. montilla
Shetland Islands (pert to) . . .
  fishing grounds (deep–sea) . . 4. haaf
  kingdom of . . 8. Scotland
  land, fee simple . . 4. udal
  promontory . . 4. noup
  Supreme Court Pres . . 4. foud
  viol . . 3. gue
shewbread, showbread (Bib) . . .
  6. ritual 10. unleavened
shibboleth (Bib) . . . 4. mode 5. habit
  6. saying, slogan 9. criterion,
  watchword 11. peculiarity (speech)
shield . . . 3. écu 4. boss, umbo
  5. aegis (egis), armor, cover, pavis,
  pelta, scute, shade, shell, targe (anc)
  6. defend, scutum, target
  7. defense, protect, shelter
  8. insignia 9. protector
  10. escutcheon, protection
shield (pert to) . . .
  Athena's . . 5. aegis (egis)
  bearer . . 8. escudero
  border . . 4. orle 7. bordure
  emblem . . 7. impresa
  French (anc) . . 8. rondache
  heraldry . . 4. enté 6. points
  part . . 4. enté, orle, umbo
  Roman . . 6. scutum
  sacred . . 6. ancile (Rom)
  shaped . . 7. peltate, scutate
  8. aspidate
shift . . . 4. eddy, fend, jibe, move, ruse,
  stir, tack, veer 5. shunt, smock, trick
  6. baffle, change, device, rustle
  7. deviate, pretext, quibble 8. artifice,
  mutation, transfer 9. deviation,
  expedient, fluctuate, vacillate
  10. conversion, subterfuge
  12. redistribute 13. transposition
shifty . . . 6. crafty, tricky 7. devious,
  evasive, furtive 9. deceitful, makeshift
  10. changeable 11. treacherous
shill, shillaber (circus term) . . . 5. decoy
  8. employer, hanger–on
  10. accomplice
shillalagh, shillalah . . . 4. club
  6. cudgel 7. sapling
shilly–shally . . . 8. hesitate 9. vacillate
  10. hestation, indecision
  11. vacillation
Shiloh . . . 4. town (anc) 6. Seilun
  (modern) 9. sanctuary (the ark)
  10. battle site (Tenn)
shimmy . . . 5. quake 6. quiver
  7. chemise, tremble, vibrate 9. jazz
  dance, vibration
shin . . . 5. climb, tibia 6. cnemis
  7. foreleg
shindy . . . 3. row 4. lark, orgy, riot,
  romp 5. dance, party, revel, spree,
  wince 6. frolic, uproar 7. wassail
  8. carousal 9. commotion, festivity
  11. merrymaking
shine . . . 3. ray 4. beam, beek, star
  5. excel, gloss, prank 6. polish
  7. furbish, glisten, glister, glitter,
  radiate, splurge 8. rutilate 9. irradiate
shiner . . . 6. bruise 8. black eye
  9. bootblack 10. dollarfish
shingle . . . 4. sign, wood 6. hairdo

  7. haircut, overlap 8. chastise,
  coiffure, detritus 9. signboard
shining . . . 5. aglow, lucid, nitid, shiny
  6. glossy, lucent 7. beaming,
  glowing, radiant 8. luminous, lustrous,
  nitidous, rutilant, splendid 9. refulgent
  10. glistening, glittering
  11. illustrious, irradiating, resplendent
Shinto (pert to) . . .
  adherent . . 9. Shintoist
  cult . . 8. Japanese
  deity . . 8. Hachiman
  temple . . 3. sha 5. jinja (jinsha)
  7. yashiro
  temple gateway . . 5. torii
  temple deity . . 5. Jinja (Jinsha)
shiny . . . 5. nitid, sleek 6. bright
  7. radiant, shining 8. luminous,
  nitidous 9. unclouded
ship . . . 3. ark 4. lade, load, send
  5. liner, tramp 6. argosy, vessel
  7. freight, steamer 9. freighter,
  transport 10. watercraft
ship (pert to) . . .
  abandoned . . 8. derelict
  apparatus . . 5. crane, davit, winch
  7. bollard, capstan 8. windlass
  Argonaut's . . 4. Argo
  armored . . 7. carrack, cruiser
  9. destroyer, submarine
  attendant . . 7. steward
  auxiliary . . 4. dory, life 6. dinghy
  (dingy), tender
  biscuit . . 8. hardtack 10. pilot bread
  cabin . . 6. saloon 9. stateroom
  cargo . . 5. oiler 6. tanker 7. oreboat
  11. supertanker
  deck . . 4. main, poop 5. orlop, upper
  deck, cut down . . 5. razee
  deserter . . 3. rat
  duck shooting . . 4. skag
  flat bottom . . 4. keel 5. barge
  fleet . . 6. armada
  invoice . . 8. manifest
  jail . . 4. brig
  kitchen . . 6. galley 7. caboose
  Levantine . . 4. saic
  loader . . 9. stevedore
  12. longshoreman
  Mediterranean . . 5. xebec 6. galiot
  (galliot) 7. polacre
  officer . . 4. mate 6. purser 7. steward
  9. boatswain (bosun)
  one–masted . . 5. sloop
  part . . 4. brig, keel, skeg 5. stern,
  waist 6. bridge, rudder 8. binnacle,
  taffrail
  permit to enter . . 8. pratique
  platform (boarding) . . 9. gangplank
  privateer . . 10. brigantine
  prow . . 5. prore (Poet)
  quarters . . 5. berth 8. steerage
  10. forecastle (fo'c's'le)
  record . . 3. log
  rope . . 4. line 6. hawser 7. halyard,
  lanyard, painter, ratline
  sailing . . 4. bark (barque), dhow, proa,
  saic 5. ketch, sloop, xebec 6. caique,
  cutter, galley, lugger 7. Geordie,
  pinnace, polacre
  side . . 3. lee 4. port 9. starboard
  three–oar bank . . 7. trireme

twin–hulled .. 9. catamaran
two–oar bank .. 6. bireme
Venetian .. 9. frigatoon
voyage record .. 3. log
war .. 3. sub 7. cruiser, flattop
　9. destroyer, submarine
　11. dreadnaught
window .. 4. port 8. porthole
worm .. 5. borer 6. teredo
ship, famed ... 4. Nina 5. Maine, Pinta
　6. Bounty 7. Monitor, Titanic
　8. Clermont, Half Moon, Merrimac
　9. Mayflower 10. Golden Hind, Santa
　Maria 12. Constitution (Old Ironsides)
　15. Bonhomme Richard
shipment ... 5. cargo 7. carload
shippage ... 3. fee 4. levy 8. shipping
shipshape ... 3. nef (clock) 4. neat,
　tidy, trim 7. orderly
shipwreck, cargo overboard ...
　6. jetsam 7. flotsam
shire ... 5. horse 6. county 8. district,
　province 11. subdivision
shirk ... 4. duck, pike 5. avoid, dodge,
　evade, slink 7. goof off 9. fainaigue
　(finagle)
shirker ... 5. piker 6. truant 7. quitter,
　slacker 8. embusqué 10. malingerer
shirt ... 4. polo, sark 6. blouse,
　camisa, cilice, skivvy, T–shirt
　8. pullover
shiver ... 5. quake, shake 6. be cold
　7. shatter, shudder, tremble, vibrate
　8. fragment 11. trepidation
shivering ... 4. cold 6. creepy
　7. nervous, shaking 8. fragment
　9. agitation, twitching 10. chilliness
shoal ... 3. bar 4. bank, reef, spit
　5. crowd, flock 6. throng 8. sand
　bank (shallow) 9. multitude
shock ... 3. jar 4. blow, heap (grain),
　jolt, stun 5. appal, brunt, bushy
　(hair), shake, stack, start 6. appall,
　impact, offend, stroke, trauma
　7. disgust, horrify, startle, terrify
　8. calamity, frighten, paralyze
　9. collision, electrify 10. concussion
shock absorber ... 7. cushion, snubber
shocking ... 3. bad 5. awful, lurid
　6. horrid 7. ghastly, hideous
　8. horrible, terrible 9. appalling,
　frightful, offensive, revolting, startling
　10. abominable
shoe (pert to) ... 4. boot, clog, geta,
　mule, pump 5. horse, moyle, sabot,
　scuff 6. ballet, bootee, brogan,
　buskin, gillie, loafer, Oxford, patten,
　planch (planche), sandal, secque
　7. chopine, rullion, slipper, sneaker,
　talaria 8. moccasin, sabotine, solleret
　10. clodhopper
shoe (pert to) ...
form .. 4. last, tree
grip .. 5. cleat
lace .. 3. tie 5. aglet (aiglet), lacet
　6. lacing 7. latchet 8. bootlace
　10. shoestring
maker .. 5. sutor 7. cobbler, Crispin
　(patron saint) 8. zapatero
part .. 3. cap 4. rand, vamp, welt
　6. insole 7. counter 9. inner sole
shoebill, shoebird ... 5. stork

shoemaker's patron saint ... 7. Crispin
shogun ... 5. chief, title (Jap) 6. tycoon
　7. shikken
shoneen ... 4. snob 5. toady
shoot ... 3. rod 4. bine, dart, film, fine,
　hunt, kill, plug, twig, weft 5. bough,
　craps, eject, gemma, plant, scion,
　snipe, spear, sprig, throw, tuber,
　vimen 6. branch, sprout, stolon
　7. execute, project 9. discharge
　10. descendant, photograph
shooting (pert to) ...
fish .. 10. archer fish
iron .. 6. pistol 7. firearm 8. revolver
match .. 3. tir 5. skeet
objective .. 6. target
star .. 5. comet 6. meteor 7. cowslip
shop ... 4. mart 5. burse, store
　6. market, saloon 7. atelier
　8. boutique, emporium
shopping mania ... 9. oniomania
shore ... 4. bank, prop 5. beach, coast,
　marge, playa 6. rivage, strand
　7. support 9. foreshore, waterside
　10. run aground, waterfront
shore (pert to) ...
bird .. 3. ree 5. snipe 6. avocet,
　curlew, plover, wading 9. Limicolae
inhabiting .. 8. littoral
pine .. 4. sand 8. tamarack
　9. lodgepole 10. hack–me–tack
recess .. 3. bay 4. cove 5. bayou,
　inlet
short ... 4. curt, rude 5. brief, brusk,
　scant, terse 6. abrupt, scanty
　7. curtate, friable, summary
　8. abridged, succinct 12. insufficient
short (pert to) ...
and pointed .. 5. terse
and stout .. 5. dumpy 6. stocky,
　stodgy 8. roly–poly, thickset
essay .. 5. tract
legged .. 8. breviped
letter .. 4. chit
lived .. 9. ephemeral
stop .. 5. delay, pause 7. respite
　8. interval 9. cessation
shortage ... 4. want 6. ullage
　10. deficiency 13. insufficiency
shorten ... 3. bob, cut, lop 4. clip,
　dele, dock 5. elide 6. lessen,
　reduce, reef in 7. abridge, curtail
　8. condense, contract, decrease, hold
　back 9. decurtate 10. abbreviate
shortening a syllable ... 7. systole
shorthand ... 5. Gregg 6. Pitman
　8. Tironian (Rom) 11. stenography
　12. brachygraphy, speed writing
shortly ... 4. soon 6. curtly, not far
　7. harshly, quickly 8. abruptly
　9. presently
shortsighted ... 4. dull 6. myopic,
　obtuse 8. purblind 11. nearsighted
Shoshone Indian ... 3. Ute 4. Hopi
　5. Piute 7. Bannock 8. Comanche
shot ... 4. dram 5. carom, speed
　6. birdie, bullet, gamble, pellet,
　ruined 7. gunfire, missile, worn out
　8. marksman, unnerved 9. discharge
　10. detonation, photograph, projectile
　11. dilapidated, vaccination
shoulder ... 5. carry, shelf 6. épaule

7. meat cut, scapula, support
8. buttress, omoplate
shoulder (pert to) . . .
  armor . . 9. épaulière
  badge, ornament . . 7. epaulet
  blade . . 7. scapula 8. omoplate
  comb form . . 3. omo 6. humero
  inflammation . . 6. omitis 7. omalgia
  of a road . . 4. berm (berme)
  reference . . 7. humeral 8. scapular
shout . . . 3. cry 4. call, hoop, hoot,
  root, yell 5. cheer 7. acclaim
  8. applause, laughter
shouting . . . 6. clamor, crying 7. calling,
  hooting, yelling 9. bellowing
shove . . . 4. push 5. drive, eject, elbow
  6. propel, thrust
shovel . . . 4. peel, spud 5. scoop,
  skeet, spade 7. scooper 8. strockle
  10. antler part
show . . . 4. lead 5. movie, prove, revue,
  teach 6. cinema, escort, evince,
  reveal 7. betoken, display, divulge,
  exhibit 8. evidence, indicate, instruct,
  manifest 11. demonstrate
  13. demonstration
show (pert to) . . .
  case (glass) . . 7. vitrine
  deference . . 3. bow 6. salaam
  disapproval . . 3. boo 4. hiss, pout
  house . . 4. hall 5. odeum, opera
  6. circus 8. coliseum, showboat
  musical . . 5. revue
  off . . 6. flaunt 10. grandstand
  of learning . . 6. pedant
  pompous . . 6. parade 7. display,
  pageant 9. cavalcade 10. exhibition
  to a seat . . 5. guide, usher 6. escort
  7. conduct
  up . . 6. appear, arrive, attend, expose
shower . . . 4. bath, give, rain 6. abound
  8. sprinkle
shower of meteorites . . . 6. Leonid
  (from Leo) 9. Andromede
showing . . .
  animal remains . . 6. zootic
  care . . 9. attentive, regardful
  11. considerate
  display . . 10. exhibition
  12. presentation
  envy . . 9. invidious
  first . . 8. premiere
  good judgment . . 6. astute 8. sensible
showy . . . 3. gay 4. arty, loud 5. gaudy
  6. flashy, garish, sporty, tinsel
  7. pompous 8. gorgeous, splendid,
  striking 9. sumptuous
  12. ostentatious 13. grandiloquent
shred . . . 3. rag 4. snip 5. piece, strip
  6. sliver, tatter 7. vestige
  8. fragment, particle
shrew . . . 3. erd 4. tana 5. satan,
  scold, Sorex, vixen 6. mammal,
  migale, tartar 7. Blarina, outcast,
  villain 9. scoundrel, termagant,
  Xanthippe
shrewd . . . 3. sly 4. cagy, foxy, sage,
  wily 5. acute, canny, harsh, sharp,
  smart, stern 6. artful, astute, biting,
  clever, crafty 7. cunning, knowing,
  practic, sapient, subtile 8. shrewish

9. sagacious 10. discerning
11. penetrating, sharp–witted
13. perspicacious
shrewdness . . . 6. acumen 9. smartness
  10. craftiness
shriek . . . 3. cry, yip 4. yell 5. laugh
  6. holler, outcry, scream 7. screech
shrievalty . . . 7. sheriff (office of)
shrill . . . 4. keen, pipy 5. acute, clear,
  sharp 6. biting, squeak 7. screech
  8. piercing, strident
  11. high–pitched, penetrating
shrimp . . . 4. pink 5. dwarf, prawn
  7. artemia 8. crevette
  10. crustacean
shrine . . . 3. box 4. case, tomb
  5. altar, chest 6. chapel, temple
  8. monument 9. holy place, reliquary
  10. receptacle
shrine (pert to) . . .
  ancient . . 4. naos
  Buddhist . . 4. tope 5. stupa
  9. Amaravati
  India . . 6. dagoba (dagaba) 7. chaitya
  Mecca . . 5. Kaaba (Caaba) 11. Great
  Mosque
  secret, of goddesses . . 9. anaktoron
shrink . . . 5. cower, parch, quail, rivel,
  wince 6. blench, cringe, flinch,
  huddle, recoil 7. dwindle, shrivel
  8. contract, draw back 9. constrict
  10. depreciate
shrinking . . . 3. coy, shy 5. timid
  6. afraid 9. recoiling, sensitive
  10. withdrawal 11. contraction
shrivel . . . 3. age, dry 5. parch, wizen
  6. shrink, wither 11. deteriorate
shroud . . . 4. cowl, hide, mask, veil,
  wrap 5. cloak, cover, sheet
  6. clothe, screen 7. conceal, curtain,
  foliage, protect 8. cerement
  9. cerecloth 12. graveclothes
Shrove (pert to) . . .
  cake . . 7. pancake
  Sunday . . 13. Quinquagesima
  tide . . 9. pre–Lenten (3 days)
  Tuesday . . 9. Mardi gras 10. Pancake
  Day
shrub . . . 4. bush 5. plant (woody)
  6. frutex 8. beverage
shrub (pert to) . . .
  Adam's needle . . 5. yucca 9. lady's
  comb
  Arabian tea, narcotic . . 3. kat
  aromatic . . 3. tea 4. mint, sage
  5. thyme 6. Aralia 7. jasmine
  (jasmin) 8. lavender, rosemary
  Asian . . 5. musky 8. abelmosk
  cherry . . 4. Prunus 7. Cerasus
  12. laurocerasus
  Chinese . . 6. Kerria
  climbing . . 5. grape, liana, Vitis
  8. Bignonia, clematis 14. trumpet
  creeper
  creeping . . 5. pyxie
  dogwood . . 6. aucuba, Cornus
  evergreen . . 3. box, yew 4. ilex, moss,
  titi 5. erica, heath, pyxie, salal, savin
  6. laurel, myrtle 7. jasmine, juniper
  8. camellia, oleander 9. mistletoe
  flowering . . 5. lilac 6. azalea, laurel
  7. spiraea, syringa 10. mignonette

fragrant .. see *aromatic* (above)
Hawaiian .. 5. akala
Mexican .. 7. guayule 9. coyotillo
New Zealand .. 4. tutu 6. myrtle
   8. ramarama
ornamental .. 8. hawthorn
parasitic .. 9. mistletoe
pea .. 5. broom
pepper .. 4. kava 8. kavakava
poisonous .. 4. tutu 5. sumac
prickly .. 5. Rubus 6. smilax
   8. barberry, dewberry 9. raspberry
   10. blackberry
S America .. 5. ceibo
tropical .. 4. sida, titi 5. henna
   7. lantana 8. Oacaceae, tamarisk
   10. frangipani (frangipane)
shrunken ... 4. lank, thin 5. dried
   6. shrunk, wasted 8. puckered,
   withered 9. atrophied, shriveled
shudder ... 4. grue 5. abhor, dread,
   quake 6. agrise, loathe, quiver, shiver,
   tremor 7. frisson, tremble
shuffle ... 3. mix 5. scuff, shift
   6. huddle, juggle, riffle 7. confuse,
   evasion, quibble, scuffle
   10. equivocate 12. walk slovenly
shuffle off ... 5. evade, shirk 6. put
   off 7. push off 10. mosey along (sl)
shun ... 5. avoid, evade, evite
   6. eschew 10. escape from
   11. keep clear of 12. cold shoulder
shut ... 3. bar 4. stop 5. close
   7. close in, exclude 8. prohibit
shut (pert to) ...
   in .. 3. hem 5. embar 6. fenced,
   hemmed 7. bottled, confine, impound,
   invalid, recluse 8. confined, enclosed
   10. surrounded
   out .. 3. ban, bar 6. defeat
   7. exclude, lockout, occlude
   8. obstruct, preclude, prohibit
   up .. 3. dam, end 4. cage, pent
   5. close, mewed, pen in 6. refute
   7. confine, enclose 8. conclude,
   imprison 9. terminate
shutter ... 3. lid 4. gate 5. blind
   6. screen 7. seclude 8. jalousie
   9. diaphragm
shuttle ... 5. train 6. looper, weaver
   7. type bar 9. alternate, vacillate
   10. oscillator 11. money drawer
shy ... 3. coy, mim 4. wary 5. aloof,
   dodge, throw, timid 6. demure,
   modest, recoil, shrink 7. bashful,
   evasive, fearful, quibble, rabbity
   8. hesitant, reserved, retiring,
   secluded, sheepish, skittish
   9. diffident, reluctant, shrinking
   10. shamefaced, unassuming
   11. distrustful, unobtrusive
Shylock (pert to) ...
   character in .. 16. Merchant of Venice
   coin .. 5. ducat
   daughter .. 7. Jessica
   famed as .. 6. usurer 11. money
   lender 12. extortionist
   friend .. 5. Tubal
shyness ... 7. coyness, reserve
   8. timidity 10. diffidence
   11. bashfulness
Siam ... 8. Thailand

Siamese (pert to) ...
   group .. 3. Kui, Lao
   temple .. 3. wat
   twins .. 9. pygopagus (joined at spine)
   11. Chang and Eng
sib ... 4. akin 6. allied 7. kinsman,
   related (by blood)
Siberia ... see also *Siberian*
   city .. 7. Irkutsk 11. Novosibirsk
   conqueror .. 9. Timafeyev 11. Genghis
   Khan
   government .. 7. Russian
   gulf .. 2. Ob (Arctic)
   Mongoloid .. 6. Tartar
   mountains .. 4. Ural 5. Altai
   people .. 5. Yakut 6. Tartar (Tatar)
   9. Mongolian
   plain .. 6. steppe, tundra
   river .. 2. Ob, Om 4. Lena 5. Vitim
   6. Abakan 7. Yenisei
   squirrel .. 7. miniver
   storm .. 5. buran
Siberian (pert to) ...
   antelope .. 5. saiga
   hunters, fishers (tribe) .. 6. Giliak
   (Gilyak)
   mammal .. 5. sable
   squirrel fur .. 7. calaber (calabar)
   swamp .. 5. urman
   tent .. 4. yurt (yurta)
   windstorm .. 5. buran (bura)
sibilate ... 4. hiss, lisp 8. aspirate
sibling ... 5. child
Sibyl (Gr) ... 6. oracle 7. seeress
   10. prophetess 13. fortuneteller
Sibylline Books (3) ... 7. oracles
   16. prophetic sayings (BC)
sic ... 4. thus
siccity ... 7. aridity, drought, dryness
sice ... 3. six (dice) 8. sixpence
Sicilian Vespers (pert to) ...
   Bull (anc) .. 8. Phalaris
   massacre of .. 6. French (1282)
Sicily ...
   aborigines .. 6. Sicani
   anc name .. 9. Trinacria
   capital .. 7. Palermo 8. Syracuse (anc)
   composer .. 7. Bellini
   harbor .. 7. Palermo
   island .. 6. Lipari (group)
   11. Pantelleria
   river .. 4. Acis
   secret society .. 5. Mafia
   volcano .. 4. Etna 7. Vulcano
   9. Stromboli
   whirlpool .. 9. Charybdis
sick ... 3. ill, sad, wan 4. pale
   5. weary 6. sickly, unwell
   9. disgusted, nauseated
   10. indisposed
sick (pert to) ...
   be .. 3. ail
   deathly .. 5. amort 7. à la mort,
   fatally 10. terminally
   flag .. 6. yellow 10. quarantine
   headache .. 8. migraine
   of .. 7. tired of 8. satiated
   9. disgusted
   person .. 7. patient 9. aegrotant
   terms .. 3. bay 7. hospice
   8. syndrome 9. infirmary
   10. dispensary 13. intensive care

worker.. 5. nurse 11. nursekeeper
sicken... 4. tire 5. weary 6. impair,
  weaken 7. afflict, depress, surfeit
  8. languish 10. impoverish
sickly... 4. pale, sick, weak 5. faint
  6. ailing, feeble, infirm, weakly
  7. languid, mawkish 8. diseased
  9. unhealthy
Siddhartha, Siddhattha... 6. Buddha
side... 4. face, team, wall 6. behalf,
  border, region 7. faction, lateral,
  support, surface 9. declivity
side (pert to)...
  board.. 5. table 6. buffet 8. dressoir,
  whiskers
  by side.. 8. parallel
  ditch.. 6. escarp
  drum.. 5. snare
  hog (salted).. 6. flitch
  kick.. 3. pal 7. comrade, partner
  9. assistant 11. confederate
  left.. 4. port 8. larboard
  long.. 7. lateral, oblique, sloping
  8. indirect, slanting
  meat.. 5. bacon 8. salt pork
  of head.. 6. temple
  of triangle.. 3. leg
  on the side.. 5. apart
  sheltered.. 3. lee 4. alee 8. windless
  sidewalk salesman.. 8. pitchman
  step.. 4. duck 5. dodge, evade,
  hedge 6. astral, starry 7. quibble
  view.. 7. profile
  ways, wise.. 7. athwart, lateral
  9. laterally, obliquely
  whiskers.. 9. sideburns 10. sideboards
  windy.. 4. port 9. starboard
sidereal... 6. astral, starry 7. stellar
  9. celestial
sidero (comb form)... 4. iron
siderography... 14. steel engraving
siderology *(science of)*... 4. iron
sides, unequal... 7. scalene
sidle... 4. cant, edge, skew, tilt
  7. advance (furtive)
siècle... 3. age 7. century
siècle d'or... 9. Golden Age
siege... 7. besiege 8. assieger
  9. besetting 11. besiegement
  12. wearying time 13. beleaguerment
Siegfried (pert to)...
  hero of.. 5. opera (Wagner's)
  slayer.. 5. Hagen
  sword.. 7. Balmung
  wife.. 9. Kriemhild
Sierra Nevada fog... 7. pogonip
Sierra poet... 13. Joaquin Miller
siesta... 3. nap 4. lull, rest 6. cat
  nap, midday, snooze 10. forty winks
sieve... 3. lue 4. bolt, sift, sile
  5. purée 6. bolter, filter, riddle,
  semmet, sifter, sorter, strain
  7. dilluer 8. strainer 9. segregate,
  separator
sievelike... 8. cribrate
Sif (Norse), (pert to)...
  goddess of.. 4. home
  wife of.. 4. Thor
sift... 3. lue 4. bolt 5. sieve
  6. dredge, filter, riddle, screen,
  sorter, winnow 7. refiner 8. cribrate
sigh... 3. sob 5. mourn, sithe, yearn

6. bemoan, bewail, exhale, grieve,
  lament 7. deplore 10. lament over
  11. suspiration
sight... 3. see 4. espy, gaze, view
  5. scene, sense 6. behold, descry,
  vision 7. discern, display 8. aperture
  10. exhibition 11. observation
sight (pert to)...
  acuteness of.. 7. oxyopia
  come into.. 4. loom 5. issue
  disorder.. 7. anopsia 8. paropsis
  imaginary.. 6. vision
  offensive.. 7. eyesore
  out of.. 5. range 6. absent
  8. vanished 9. invisible
  10. exorbitant 11. disappeared
  second.. 3. ESP 7. psychic
sigil... 4. seal 5. image (magic), stamp
  8. sigillum 9. signature
  11. endorsement
sigmoid... 3. ess 5. curve 9. intestine
sign... 3. cue, nod 4. code, hire,
  mark, neon, omen 5. token, trace
  6. emblem, engage, intone, motion,
  notice, signal, symbol 7. endorse,
  execute, insigne, portent, presage,
  symptom, vestige, warning
  8. evidence, password 9. semaphore,
  subscribe, watchword 10. forerunner,
  indication, underwrite 11. countersign
  13. advertisement, constellation
sign (pert to)...
  astrological.. 5. Aries 6. Gemini,
  Pisces, Taurus 8. Aquarius
  9. Capricorn 11. Sagittarius
  briefly.. 7. initial
  by the same.. 8. likewise, moreover
  11. accordingly
  diacritical.. 5. tilde 7. cedilla
  language.. 11. dactylology
  music.. 5. presa
  off.. 8. withdraw 10. Yours truly
  11. discontinue
  ref to.. 5. semic 7. semeion
  representing a word.. 8. logogram
  spiritual.. 9. sacrament
  up.. 4. join 6. enlist
  zodiac.. see *astrological* (above)
signal... 3. cue 4. code, fire, flag,
  sign 5. alarm, flare, token
  6. beacon, emblem, notify, wigwag
  7. eminent, lantern, notable, warning
  8. striking 9. memorable, prominent,
  semaphore, watchword
  10. lighthouse, remarkable
  11. communicate, conspicuous
  13. extraordinary
signal (pert to)...
  aviator's.. 5. roger
  danger, warning.. 4. bell 5. alert,
  fusee
  flag.. 6. ensign, wigwag
  night.. 6. beacon, curlew, pharos
  10. lighthouse
  preceding taps.. 6. tattoo
  railroad.. 5. fusee 9. semaphore
signature... 4. mark, sign, visa (vise)
  5. prima, sigil, stamp 6. signum
  9. autograph 11. endorsement
signed by writer... 9. onomatous (opp
  of anonymous)
signet... 4. mark, seal 5. sigil, stamp

9. signature 10. impression
11. endorsement
significance... 6. import, moment,
weight 7. anagoge, meaning
significant... 4. sign 5. token
6. symbol 7. ominous 8. sinister
9. important, momentous
10. expressive, indicative, meaningful,
portentous, suggestive
13. consequential
signification... 6. import 7. meaning
10. indication 11. consequence
12. notification 13. comprehension,
specification
signify... 4. hint, mean, sign 5. imply,
utter 6. denote, import, matter,
signal 7. betoken, connote, declare,
specify 8. announce, evidence,
foreshow, indicate, intimate, manifest
11. communicate
signum... 4. bell (tower), mark, sign
5. cross 9. signature
sika... 4. deer
sike... 4. rill 5. brook, ditch, gully
6. ravine, stream, trench
sikhara, sikhra... 5. tower (pyramidal)
silage... 4. feed 6. fodder
9. pasturage, provender
Silas (pert to)...
  Bib.. 7. prophet 8. Silvanus
  character.. 4. Wegg
  companion of.. 4. Paul (Bib)
  novel.. 11. Silas Marner
sile... 3. fry 4. beam, drip, drop, fall,
flow, pass, pour, sink, skim 5. cheat,
cover, glide, sieve, spawn 6. betray,
filter, strain, stream 7. conceal,
deceive, herring (young), subside
8. strainer
silence... 3. gag 4. hush, kill, lull,
mute, rest 5. quiet, shush, still,
tacet 6. defeat, muffle 7. confute,
repress, secrecy 8. oblivion, preclude,
restrain, suppress 9. eliminate,
stillness 10. silentness 11. taciturnity
13. noiselessness, tacit omission
silent... 3. mum 4. mute, tace
5. quiet, still, tacet, tacit
8. reserved, reticent, taciturn
9. soundless 10. speechless
11. unexpressed
15. uncommunicative
silhouette... 6. shadow 7. contour,
outline, picture, profile 9. delineate,
hourglass
silica... 4. opal 5. silex
silicate... 4. mica 8. calamine, wellsite
silk (pert to)...
  ancient.. 6. Mantua, sendal
  artificial.. 5. nylon, rayon
  Assam.. 4. eria
  black.. 5. crape (mourning), crepe
  brown.. 4. muga 6. tussah
  corded.. 6. faille 7. Ottoman
  embroidery thread.. 5. floss
    8. arrasene
  fiber.. 5. floss
  gland.. 9. serictery
  gland of.. 7. spiders 9. silkworms
    11. insect larva 12. caterpillars
  gold.. 4. tash 6. samite 7. brocade
  heavy.. 4. crin

  kind of.. 5. China, crepe, moiré,
    ninon, satin, surah, tabby, tulle
    6. pongee, tobine, tussah 7. taffeta
  lining.. 8. sarcenet (sarsenet)
  muslin.. 16. mousseline de soie
  raw.. 8. marabout
  rustle of.. 6. scroop
  source.. 6. cocoon
  thin, glossy.. 7. alamode
  thread (for velvets).. 4. tram (trame)
  unspun.. 6. sleave
  upholstery.. 7. tabaret
  waste.. 4. noil 6. strass
  watered.. 5. moiré
  yarn.. 4. tram 7. schappe
  yarn size.. 6. denier
silken... 5. seric, silby, sleek, suave
6. gentle, smooth, tender 7. elegant
8. delicate, lustrous, silklike
9. luxurious 10. effeminate
12. ingratiating
silkworm (pert to)...
  Assam.. 3. eri 4. eria
  China.. 6. pernyi 9. Ailanthus
  cocoon.. 4. clew
  disease.. 7. pebrine
  genus (moth).. 6. Bombyx
  India.. 6. tussah
  Japan.. 7. yamamai
silky... 4. soft 5. quiet 6. glossy,
smooth 8. delicate 9. sericeous
11. filamentary 12. ingratiating
silky fabric... 6. barège
sill... 4. base, beam, seat, sile
5. basis 6. timber 9. threshold
10. foundation
silly... 3. mad 4. daft, fond 5. anile,
apish, dazed, dense, inane 6. dottle,
simple 7. asinine, fatuous, foolish,
shallow, trivial 9. brainless
10. indiscreet 12. simple–minded
silver... 2. Ag 4. gray 5. metal,
money, plate, white 6. argent
7. bullion 8. argentum, eloquent,
metallic, sterling
silver (pert to)...
  alchemy.. 4. luna 6. occamy
  alloy.. 6. billon
  ball.. 4. pome
  coin.. 6. tester
  containing.. 5. lunar
  German.. 6. albata
  gilded.. 7. vermeil
  ingots.. 5. sycee
  jackal.. 9. silver fox
  lace (with gold).. 5. orris 8. filigree
  leaf.. 4. foil 8. hardhack
    9. hydrangea, jewelweed 12. buffalo
    berry
  oak.. 11. flannelbush
  tongued.. 7. musical 8. eloquent
  uncoined.. 7. bullion
silversides... 5. smelt 6. minnow
12. silver salmon
Silver State... 6. Nevada
silverware... 5. vases 6. dishes
8. flatware 9. ornaments, tableware
silvery... 7. frosted, musical
8. lustrous, metallic 9. argentine
simian... 3. ape 6. monkey 7. apelike
similar... 4. akin, like, such 5. alike
7. uniform 8. analogic 9. analogous

11. homogeneous
similarity . . . 7. analogy 8. likeness
11. homogeneity, resemblance
13. approximation
simile . . . 8. allegory, metaphor
simper . . . 5. smirk 10. silly smile
13. affected smile
simple . . . 4. easy, mere 5. naive
6. dorian, oafish 7. artless
8. innocent 9. ingenuous
10. elementary 11. open and shut
15. unsophisticated
simpleton . . . 3. ass, daw, oaf 4. boob,
dolt, dupe, fool, gaby, gawk, gump,
simp, zang 5. dunce, goose, idiot,
ikona, moron, Simon, yokel, zombi
6. dawkin, gander, nitwit 7. half–wit
8. Abderite 9. greenhorn
10. nincompoop 11. Simple Simon
simplicity . . . 6. purity 7. modesty,
naiveté 9. clearness, ignorance,
innocence, plainness, rusticity
10. homeliness, humbleness,
simpleness 11. gullibility, informality
13. ingenuousness
14. unaffectedness
simplify . . . 7. clarify, explain, expound
9. elucidate, interpret
simply . . . 5. alone, truly 6. barely,
easily, merely, purely, really, solely
7. plainly 10. informally
simulate . . . 3. act, ape 4. sham
5. feign 6. affect, assume 7. imitate
11. counterfeit
simulated . . . 4. aped, sham 5. acted
7. assumed, feigned, shammed
9. pretended 10. fictitious
simurgh, simurg (Myth) . . . 3. roc
12. gigantic bird
sin . . . 3. err 4. evil, vice 5. crime,
error, guilt, wrong 6. felony, heresy
7. offense 8. iniquity, peccancy
9. deviation 10. immorality,
wickedness 11. misdemeanor
13. transgression
Sinai (pert to) . . .
famed for . . 5. Moses 15. Ten
Commandments
location . . 6. Red Sea 11. Gulf of
Aqaba (Akaba)
mountain (Bib) . . 5. Horeb 6. Serbal
9. Catharine, Umm Shomer
sinapis . . . 7. mustard
sinawa . . . 10. Ceylon hemp
sinay bean . . . 8. rice bean
since . . . 2. as 3. ago, for 4. ergo,
gone, past, syne 5. hence, later
7. already, because, whereas
8. inasmuch, until now 9. therefore,
thereupon 10. seeing that
11. considering 12. subsequently
sincere . . . 4. open, pure 5. frank
6. candid 7. correct, earnest,
genuine, intense, unmixed, upright,
zealous 9. authentic, unfeigned,
veracious 10. unaffected
11. unvarnished 13. unadulterated
15. straightforward
sincerity . . . 4. zeal 6. candor
7. honesty 10. heartiness
11. genuineness, sincereness
sincerity symbol . . . 8. amethyst

sind . . . 5. rinse 6. drench, quench
7. rinsing
Sind (Ind) . . .
capital . . 7. Karachi
ibex . . 8. wild goat
prince . . 5. ameer
Sindbad's bird . . . 3. roc
Sindbad the Sailor . . . 9. character
(Arabian Nights)
sindico . . . 7. trustee 8. assignee,
receiver
sine . . . 7. without
sinew . . . 4. thew 5. nerve, power
6. muscle, string, tendon
sinewy . . . 4. firm, wiry 5. thewy, tough
6. brawny, strong 7. fibrose, stringy
8. powerful, vigorous
sinful . . . 3. bad 4. evil 5. wrong
6. wicked 7. vicious 10. iniquitous
11. unrighteous
sing . . . 3. hum, say 4. hymn, lilt
5. carol, chant, croon, yodel
6. intone, warble 7. rejoice
8. proclaim, vocalize 9. celebrate
sing (pert to) . . .
exultantly . . 4. lilt 7. chortle
10. cheerfully
jovially . . 5. troll
off key . . 4. flat
or whistle . . 7. tweedle
shrilly . . 4. pipe
softly . . 5. croon
sorrowfully . . 7. despond 8. complain
Swisslike . . 5. yodel
with trills . . 6. warble 7. roulade
singe . . . 4. burn, sear 6. scorch
8. discolor
singer . . . 4. bard, bird, diva, poet
5. blues, siren, tenor, torch
6. cantor, hymner 7. caroler,
crooner, warbler, yodeler 8. minstrel,
songster, vocalist 9. chanteuse,
descanter 10. cantatrice, prima
donna 11. minnesinger
Singhalese tree . . . 4. poon 5. domba
singing (pert to) . . .
birds . . 6. Oscine
canary . . 10. white whale
fish . . 8. toadfish
group . . 5. choir 6. chorus
Memnon . . 9. Amenhotep (statue)
ref to . . 5. melic
single . . . 3. ace, odd, one 4. lone,
only, sole, unit 6. simple, unique
8. sporadic 9. unmarried
single (pert to) . . .
algebra . . 6. nomial
comb form . . 3. uni
odd . . 7. azygous
racing term . . 4. heat
tones (one of two) . . 10. monotonous
singleness . . . 5. unity 8. celibacy
9. sincerity, unmarried
singly . . . 4. once, only, solo 5. alone,
apart 6. simply 8. uniquely
9. severally 12. individually,
particularly, single–handed
singular . . . 3. odd 4. each, rare, sole,
unit 5. queer 6. unique 7. eminent,
special, strange, unusual 8. peculiar,
separate, uncommon 9. eccentric,
fantastic, whimsical 10. individual,

remarkable, unexampled
11. exceptional 12. unparalleled
13. extraordinary, unprecedented
14. characteristic
singularity... 6. oddity 7. oddness,
oneness 8. peculiar 11. peculiarity
12. eccentricity 13. individuality
15. distinctiveness
Sinic... 7. Chinese, Sinitic
sinister... 4. evil, grim, left 7. adverse,
corrupt, ominous 9. dishonest,
injurious, malicious, underhand
10. disastrous, portentous
11. unfortunate
sinistral... 7. baneful 10. left–handed
12. illegitimate, inauspicious (opp of
dextral)
sink... 3. age, bog, dip, ebb, sag
4. cave, drop, fall, mire, sump
5. drain, droop, lapse, lower, quail
6. cavity, deject, engulf, go down,
recede, settle, sicken, weaken
7. decline, depress, descend,
despond 8. decrease, diminish,
submerge 10. degenerate
sinuous... 4. wavy 7. winding
9. deviating, intricate 10. circuitous
Sioux (pert to)...
division.. 5. Teton 6. Santee
famed as.. 8. warriors
tribe.. 3. Oto (Otoe) 4. Crow, Iowa
5. Omaha, Osage 6. Dakota, Plains
9. Winnebago
sip... 3. lap, sup 4. gulp 5. drink,
quaff, taste 6. tipple
sircar... 5. ruler 6. master 7. servant
8. province (Mogul) 10. government
siren... 5. alarm, Circe, deity, lurer,
vixen 7. charmer, enticer, foghorn,
Lorelei, mermaid 9. bewitcher,
Cleopatra, temptress
Sirenia... 6. dugong, mammal
7. manatee 14. Steller's sea cow
siriasis... 9. sunstroke
Sirius... 4. star 7. Dog Star 10. Canis
Major, dog of Orion (Gr Myth)
sissy... 5. softy 6. prissy, sister
10. effeminate, pantywaist
11. mollycoddle
sister... 3. kin, nun, sib 5. nurse,
soror
sisterhood... 4. nuns 8. sorority
Sistrurus... 11. rattlesnake
sit... 3. fit 4. isle, loll, pose, rest
5. brood, perch, press, roost, squat
6. repose 7. convene 8. incubate
site... 4. ruin, seat 5. place, scene,
venue 6. locale, locate 8. location,
position
site of Taj Mahal... 4. Agra (Ind)
sitting... 4. seat 6. séance, sedent
7. posture, sessile, session
10. incubation 11. convocation
situated... 3. lie, set 4. case, seat
5. fixed 6. clutch, placed, plight
9. ensconced, stationed
11. established
situated (pert to)...
at back.. 6. astern 7. postern
9. posterior
at base.. 5. basal
between folds.. 11. interplical

in middle.. 6. medial, median
on left hand.. 9. sinistrad
on right hand.. 6. dexter
situation... 3. job 4. case, post
5. place, situs, state 6. office, plight
7. station 8. locality, location,
position 9. condition, placement
situation (pert to)...
approximate.. 11. whereabouts
difficult.. 6. scrape 7. dilemma
8. quandary 9. imbroglio
11. predicament 12. circumstance
doomed.. 7. rattrap
favorable.. 7. vantage
Latin.. 5. situs
perplexing.. 6. strait
three choices.. 8. trilemma
Siva, Shiva (pert to)...
consort.. 3. Uma 4. Devi
dancer.. 8. Natajara
god, deity.. 8. Hinduism 9. Destroyer
title.. 8. Mahadeva
trident.. 6. trisul (trisula)
six (pert to)...
balls (Medici).. 5. palle
dice number.. 4. sice
eyed.. 9. senocular
feet of earth.. 5. grave
fold.. 8. sextuple
footed.. 7. hexaped 9. hexapodal
group.. 5. hexad
lines.. 6. sestet 7. sextain
pence.. 6. bender 7. fiddler
pert to.. 6. senary
pointed figure.. 4. star
square.. 9. hexagonal
sixty, sixties... 5. cycle, saros
7. numeral
size... 3. cap 4. area, bulk, pica,
pope, pott 5. agate, grade 6. adjust
7. arrange, measure, portion
8. classify 9. magnitude
10. gargantuan 11. measurement
sizzle... 3. fry 4. hiss 5. speed 7. be
angry 10. effervesce
sjambok... 4. flog, whip
skate... 3. jag, ray (fish) 4. plug, skim
5. glide, horse, scull, spree
skean... 4. dirk 6. dagger
skedaddle... 4. bolt, flee, flit 6. scurry
7. run away, scamper
skein... 3. rap (120 yds), web
4. hank, yarn 6. thread 7. spireme
12. flight of fowl
skelder... 5. cheat 7. vagrant
9. panhandle
skeleton... 4. cage 5. bones, frame,
mummy 6. sketch 7. contour,
diagram, outline 8. thinness
9. framework
skeleton (pert to)...
at the feast.. 7. kill–joy 10. wet
blanket 11. crapehanger
English dialect.. 4. reme
framework.. 5. cadre
in the closet.. 4. evil 6. secret
13. mortification
key.. 6. master
marine animal.. 6. sponge
polyp.. 5. coral
skeptic, sceptic... 7. doubter, infidel
8. aporetic 10. Pyrrhonist, unbeliever

11. freethinker, irreligious, nullifidian

skeptical, sceptical ... 8. doubtful, doubting 11. incredulous, unbelieving

sketch ... 3. jap, jot 4. draw, idea, limn, plan, skit 5. draft, trace 6. aperçu, design 7. diagram, drawing, outline 8. esquisse, treatise 9. delineate 11. delineation, description

sketchy ... 5. rough, vague 10. unfinished

skewer ... 3. pin, rod 5. truss 6. fasten, pierce 9. brochette

skid ... 4. clog, shoe, slip, trig 5. brake, check, slide 7. travois 8. sideslip

skiff ... 4. boat, skim 5. canoe, glide, graze 6. caique 7. rowboat 11. slight touch

skill ... 3. art 5. craft, knack 6. gifted, talent 7. ability, address, aptness, cunning, finesse, mastery 8. aptitude, deftness, facility 9. adeptness, dexterity, expertise, readiness, smartness 10. adroitness, cleverness, proficient 11. proficiency

skilled ... 5. adept 6. expert 7. endowed, trained 8. talented 10. conversant, proficient

skilled (pert to) ...
  in government .. 9. statesman
  in mechanics .. 5. sloyd
  in strategy .. 7. finesse

skillful, skilful ... 3. apt 4. able, deft, fine 6. adroit, clever, crafty, daedal, expert 7. capable 8. artistic, dextrous, tactical 9. daedalian, dexterous, ingenious 10. proficient, well–versed 12. accomplished

skim ... 4. flit, sail, scan, scud 5. glide, graze, scoon, skirr 6. slight 8. pass over

skin ... 4. bark, derm, fell, flay, hide, pare, peel, pelt, rind, scum 5. cheat, cutis, derma, fraud, scalp 6. fleece, lamina, scrape 7. callous, cuticle, defraud, swindle 8. covering, tegument 9. epidermis 10. integument 11. decorticate

skin (pert to) ...
  animal .. 4. coat, hide, pelt 7. pellage
  animal's neck fold .. 6. dewlap
  beaver .. 4. plew
  comb form .. 4. derm 5. derma
  decoration .. 6. tattoo
  destitute of .. 8. apellous
  disease .. 4. acne 5. hives, mange, uredo 6. eczema, herpes, tetter 8. ringworm 9. urticaria
  drying frame .. 5. herse
  dryness .. 7. xerosis
  fawnskin (of Dionysus) .. 6. nebris
  fold .. 5. plica 6. dewlap
  fruit .. 7. epicarp
  gobbler's throat .. 3. tar
  layer .. 5. cutis, derma
  layer, outer .. 7. epicarp
  opening .. 4. pore
  pert to .. 6. dermal 7. dermoid
  piece .. 5. blype
  pigment, excess .. 8. melanism
  protuberance .. 4. mole, wart

salting bin .. 5. kench
squirrel .. 4. vair
tan .. 3. taw
tanned .. 5. suede
unsheared .. 8. woolfell

skinflint ... 5. cheat, miser 9. bargainer

skink ... 4. adda 6. lizard

skinned ... 6. bested 7. euchred, fleeced

skinned (pert to) ...
  dark .. 7. melanic, swarthy
  pert to .. 5. bared 7. denuded 8. stripped
  slang .. 7. euchred, fleeced
  thick .. 9. pachyderm 11. pachydermic

skinny ... 4. lean, thin 5. scant 6. stingy 8. skinlike 9. emaciated, niggardly

skip ... 3. dap 4. gait, jump, leap, omit 5. bound, caper, elide, frisk, salto, vault 6. gambol, lackey, spring 7. abscond 8. ricochet

skipjack ... 3. fop 4. pike 5. saury 6. bonito 7. bounder, parvenu, upstart 8. bluefish, sailboat 9. stripling (conceited) 10. butterfish 14. snapping beetle

skipper ... 5. saury 6. locust, maggot, master, serang 8. skipjack 9. butterfly 11. grasshopper

ski race (obstacle) ... 6. slalom

skirling ... 5. trout 6. salmon

skirmish ... 4. fray 5. brush, clash, melee 6. combat 8. conflict, flourish 9. encounter 10. velitation

skirt ... 5. dress, evade, woman 6. border, edging, fringe 9. appendage, baseboard, periphery, petticoat 10. pass around, saddle part

skirt (pert to) ...
  armor .. 5. tasse (tace) 7. lamboys
  attached to blouse .. 6. peplum
  chaser .. 9. libertine 11. philanderer
  dance .. 6. ballet
  short .. 4. kilt

skit ... 4. joke, play 5. caper 6. parody, shower, sketch

skittish ... 3. coy, shy 5. jumpy 6. fickle, frisky, tricky 7. bashful 8. unstable, volatile 9. excitable 10. capricious 13. irresponsible

skittles ... 4. game, play 8. ninepins 9. enjoyment (not all beer and skittles)

skoal ... 5. toast 10. salutation 11. exclamation 14. pledge of health

skulk ... 4. lurk 5. cower, dodge, hedge, sneak 8. malinger

skull ... 4. bean, head, mind 5. brain 7. cranium, harnpan 8. brain box

skull (pert to) ...
  cap .. 6. beanie 7. calotte 9. zucchetto 10. berrettino
  cavity .. 5. fossa
  measure .. 11. craniometer
  monk's .. 6. pileus
  operation .. 4. trepan
  part .. 5. inion 6. bregma 7. calotte, occiput
  ref to .. 5. inial 6. cranic 7. cranial
  science of .. 10. craniology

skull and crossbones... 5. death (symb) 10. danger sign
skunk... 5. zoril 6. defeat 7. fitchew, polecat, stinker 8. conepate (conepati), zorrillo 9. scoundrel
sky... 4. blue 5. ether, vault 6. caelum, canopy, heaven, welkin 7. heavens, the blue 8. empyrean 9. firmament 10. blue yonder
sky (pert to)...
  color.. 4. blue 5. azure 7. celeste 8. cerulean
  god.. 3. Anu
  lark.. 5. pipit 6. Alauda, frolic 7. titlark
  light.. 6. window 8. abatjour
  lure.. 7. horizon
  parlor.. 5. attic 6. garret
  pilot.. 8. chaplain 9. clergyman 10. missionary
  serpent.. 3. Ahi
slab... 3. mud 4. tile 5. board, dalle, plank, slime 6. lamina, ledger, pillar (stone), puddle 7. portion 8. monument 9. flagstone
slab (pert to)...
  grave.. 5. stele (stela)
  marble.. 5. dalle 6. tablet
  slablike.. 6. stelar
slack... 3. lax 4. lull, slow 5. chaff, inert, let up, loose, shirk, tardy 6. abated, remiss 7. relaxed 8. careless, dilatory, inactive, indolent, sluggish 9. reluctant, secondary 10. diminished, inadequate 11. inattentive
slacken... 5. abate, delay, relax 6. loosen, reduce, repose, retard 7. let down, relieve 8. hold back
slackening of strained relations... 7. detente (Internat)
slag... 4. lava 5. dross 6. cinder, scoria 7. residue 9. recrement 11. agglomerate
slain... 4. dead 6. fallen, killed 8. murdered 12. assassinated
slake... 4. cool, sate 5. abate, allay, slack 6. quench 7. assuage, crumble, hydrate, refresh, relieve, satisfy, slacken 8. decrease, mitigate, moderate 10. extinguish 12. disintegrate
slam... 4. bang, blow, give, shut, vole 5. abuse, score 6. impact 9. criticism, criticize
slander... 5. belie, libel 6. defame, malign, vilify 7. asperse, blacken, distort, traduce 8. derogate, disgrace, reproach 10. defamation, scandalize 12. misrepresent
slang... 4. cant 5. argot 6. jargon, patois 7. hep talk 10. vernacular
slant... 4. bend, cant, skew 5. angle, bevel, slope 6. aslant, aspect, biased, glance 7. incline, opinion 8. attitude, occasion 9. obliquely, viewpoint 10. hypotenuse 11. inclination, opportunity
slap... 3. hit 4. blow, clap, cuff, snub 5. crack, skelp, sound, twank 6. buffet, rebuff, slight, strike 8. chastise 12. chastisement

slash... 3. cut 4. gash, lash, slit 5. marsh, sever 6. attack, reduce, stripe 7. censure, scourge 8. price cut 9. criticize, reduction
slate... 4. list, rock 5. color, scold, sculp 6. ballot, enroll, record, roster, tablet, thrash 7. censure, roofing, writing 8. register, schedule, slattern 9. criticize, reprimand
slate (pert to)...
  ax.. 7. mattock
  black.. 4. gray
  blue.. 9. Swiss blue
  gray.. 7. Russian 9. red–yellow 10. sandy beige 13. oriental pearl
  roof.. 3. rag
  tool.. 3. zax 7. scantle
slater... 6. critic 7. hellier
slattern... 4. slut 5. frump, idler, mopsy 6. sloppy 7. trifler, trollop 8. careless, slovenly 10. litterbug
slaughter... 4. kill, slay 6. battue, murder, pogrom 7. butcher, carnage, killing 8. butchery, hecatomb, massacre, occision 9. bloodshed 10. butchering 11. destruction
slaughterhouse... 8. abattoir, Aceldama, butchery, matadero, shambles 9. stockyard 12. field of blood
Slav... 4. Pole, Slav, Sorb, Wend 5. Croat, Czech 6. Slovak 7. Russian, Serbian, Servian 8. Bohemian, Croatian, Moravian 9. Bulgarian
slave... 4. boor, esne, peon, serf 5. chela, helot, thane 6. drudge, lascar, minion, thrall, vassal 7. bondman, captive, chattel, enslave, odalisk, servant 8. slave ant 9. bondslave
slave (pert to)...
  block (selling).. 7. catasta
  born.. 4. neif
  comedy (stock name).. 5. Davus
  dealer.. 5. bichy, mango (obs)
  Eleusinian (Gr Relig).. 5. Baubo, lambe
  female.. 9. concubine, odalisque (odalisk)
  free.. 5. thane (thegn)
  fugitive.. 8. marooner
  Indian.. 10. Athapascan
  The Tempest.. 7. Caliban
slavery... 4. bond 7. bondage, service 8. drudgery 9. captivity, servitude, thralldom, vassalage 11. enslavement 12. enthrallment
Slave States... 5. Texas 7. Alabama, Florida, Georgia 8. Arkansas, Delaware, Kentucky, Maryland, Missouri, Virginia 9. Louisiana, Tennessee 11. Mississippi 13. North Carolina, South Carolina
slay... 4. kill 5. amuse, burke, knock, lynch, smite 6. murder, strike 7. butcher, destroy 9. slaughter 10. annihilate 11. assassinate, destroy life, exterminate
slayer... 6. killer 8. criminal, murderer, regicide, vaticide 9. matricide, patricide 10. fratricide, sororicide

sleave... 4. sley 5. floss 6. tangle
8. separate 9. floss silk
11. disentangle 13. untwisted silk
sled... 4. pung 6. sledge, sleigh,
travoy, troika 8. toboggan
sledge... 4. sled 6. hammer, sleigh,
strike 7. seven–up (game), vehicle
sleep... 3. nap, nod 4. dorm, doss,
doze, wink 5. death, sopor
6. drowse, snooze, somnus
7. slumber 10. narcolepsy,
somnipathy 11. hibernation
sleep (pert to)...
  comb form.. 5. somni
  deep.. 6. stupor 8. lethargy
  10. narcolepsy
  hypnotic.. 10. somnipathy
  inducing.. 5. dwale 6. opiate, potion
  8. sedative 9. soporific
  10. anesthesia, belladonna
  insensible.. 4. coma
  midday.. 6. siesta
  prolonged.. 5. sopor
  upon.. 8. consider, postpone
sleeper... 3. tie 4. beam 6. rafter,
rester, timber 7. Pullman, reposer,
support 8. dormouse 9. slumberer
10. slow seller 11. sleeping car
sleeping... 4. dead 5. inert 6. asleep,
latent 7. dormant 8. dormient,
inactive 9. quiescent 10. quiescence
11. inattentive
sleeping (pert to)...
  pill.. 9. soporific
  place.. 3. bed, cot 4. bunk, doss
  5. berth, couch 6. pallet 7. cubicle
  9. dormitory
  sickness.. 6. nagana, tsetse
  9. lethargus
sleepwalking... 8. neurosis
12. nightwalking, somnambulism
sleepy... 4. dull 5. tired 6. drowsy
8. soporose 9. lethargic, somnolent
11. somniferous
sleeve... 3. arm 5. gigot
(leg–o'–mutton) 10. copper tube
14. British channel
sleigh... 4. pung 6. cutter
sleight of hand performer... 4. mage
8. magician 14. legerdemainist
15. prestidigitator
slender... 4. lank, lean, slim, thin
5. gaunt, lanky, leger, reedy
6. lissom, narrow, svelte 7. gracile,
tenuous, trivial, willowy 9. elongated
slender pinnacle... 3. epi
sleuth... 6. tracer 8. hawkshaw
9. detective, sleuthdog
11. sleuthhound 12. investigator
slice... 3. cut, saw 4. gash, slab
5. piece, share, shave 6. rasher,
sliver, stroke 7. portion 8. golf term,
splinter 12. cross section
slick... 4. neat, tidy 5. alert, sleek
smart 6. clever, smooth 8. slippery,
unctuous 9. first–rate, lubricate
10. glistening 12. accomplished
slide... 3. ski 4. rule, skid, slip, slue
5. chute, clasp, glide, plane
(sloping), scoot, skate 6. elapse
7. lantern, slither 8. toboggan
9. avalanche 11. deteriorate

slight... 3. cut 4. defy, rare, snub,
thin 5. faint, frail, leger, minor, oligo
(comb form), scorn, small 6. flimsy,
ignore, little, meager 7. disdain,
fragile, neglect, nominal, scantly,
shallow, trivial 8. contempt, delicate
9. disregard, indignity 10. immaterial
11. unimportant 13. imperceptible,
unsubstantial 14. inconsiderable
slight (pert to)...
  convexity.. 6. camber
  sound.. 4. peep
  variation.. 6. nuance 7. shading
slightest... 5. least 6. barest
slightly (pert to)...
  damaged paper.. 6. retree
  sour.. 8. acescent
  tapering.. 6. terete
slim... 3. sly 4. lean, mean, thin
5. small, spare 6. adroit, scanty,
sparse, svelte 7. slender, tenuous
9. worthless
slime... 3. mud 4. ooze 5. filth, gleet
6. mucous
slip... 3. err, pew, sin 4. dock, fail,
pier, skid, slue 5. boner, cover,
error, fault, glide, lapse, slide, strip
6. bungle, elapse 7. blunder, cutting,
failure, faux pas, misdeed, mistake,
slither 9. youngling 10. pillowslip
12. undergarment 13. transgression
slipknot... 5. noose
slipper... 4. mule, neap, shoe
5. apron, moyle, Romeo 6. pinson,
sandal 7. scuffer 8. babouche
(baboosh), covering
slippery... 3. sly 4. eely, glib 5. slick
6. crafty, fickle, shifty, tricky, wanton
7. cunning, elusive, evasive
8. unctuous, unstable 9. deceitful,
uncertain 10. intangible, precarious,
unreliable 11. treacherous
13. untrustworthy
slit... 4. kerf 5. cleft, slash, split
6. furrow 7. severed
slither... 5. crawl, glide, sidle, slide
sliver... 3. cut 4. shred, slice, split
8. fragment, splinter
sloe... 3. haw 4. plum
sloe (pert to)...
  berry.. 7. juniper
  bush.. 10. blackthorn
  color.. 9. blue–black
  fruit (blackthorn).. 3. haw 4. sloe
  gin.. 12. sloe–flavored
slogan... 3. cry 5. motto 6. phrase
9. catchword, watchword
10. shibboleth (Bib)
sloop... 5. yacht 6. cutter, schuit
(schuyt) 7. eelboat
slope... 3. dip, lie 4. bank, hade,
ramp 5. bevel, scarp, slant, talus
6. calade, decamp, escarp, glacis
7. terrace 9. declivity 10. declension
11. inclination
sloping bank... 4. brae 7. terrace
sloth... 2. ai 4. pack (bears), pazy,
unau 6. acedia, mammal 7. inertia
8. idleness, slowness 9. indolence
slothful... 4. lazy 8. inactive, indolent,
sluggish
sloth monkey... 5. lemur, loris

slough . . . 3. bog 4. husk, mire, molt,
   shed, skin 5. bayou, swamp
   7. channel, discard
sloughing . . . 7. ecdysis, molting
   8. shedding 10. discarding
slovenly . . . 5. dowdy, messy, tacky
   6. frowzy, sloppy, untidy 8. careless,
   slattern, slipshod 9. negligent
   10. disheveled, disorderly, slatternly
slow . . . 4. dull, late, poky 5. delay,
   inert, relax 6. boring, hinder, retard,
   stupid 7. slacken 8. boresome,
   dilatory, inactive, moderate
   9. lingering 20. inch by inch
   phlegmatic 13. unprogressive
slow (pert to) . . .
   action . . 6. dawdle 10. deliberate
   adverb . . 10. behindhand
   down . . 4. idle 6. retard 8. wind
      down 10. decelerate
   music . . 5. largo, lento, molto, tardo
      6. adagio 7. andante 8. lentando
      10. lentamento
   poke . . 5. snail 7. dawdler
   up . . 3. lag 6. retard 7. decline
   witted . . 4. dull 6. stupid
sludge . . . 3. mud 4. gunk, mire, ooze
   5. slime 8. sediment
slug . . . 3. hit 4. blow, dose 5. Arion,
   drink, drone, idler, Limax, space, token
   6. bullet, loiter, nugget 7. trepang
   8. sluggard 9. gastropod
sluggish . . . 4. logy, slow 5. dopey,
   inert 6. drowsy, stupid, supine
   7. dronish, languid 8. dilatory,
   inactive, indolent, listless, stagnant
   9. stagnancy, stupidity, torpidity
sluice . . . 4. race 5. flush 6. drench,
   stream 7. channel 9. floodgate
slumber . . . 4. doze 5. sleep 6. catnap,
   drowse, repose, snooze, somnus
   14. arms of Morpheus
slump . . . 4. drop, fall 7. decline,
   descend, dessert, sinkage 9. fall short
   10. depreciate, depression
slur . . . 4. blur 5. elide 6. defame,
   insult, mackle, slight, stigma
   7. calumny, traduce 8. disgrace,
   innuendo, reproach, skim over
   9. aspersion, disparage
   10. calumniate, stigmatize
slush . . . 3. mud 4. mire, snow
   5. slime 14. sentimentality
sly . . . 4. arch, foxy, wary, wily, wink
   5. cagey, catty, snaky 6. covert,
   crafty, feline, shrewd, sneaky, subtle
   7. cunning, furtive 8. craftily
   9. underhand 11. mischievous,
   underhanded 15. surreptitiously
smack . . . 3. bit, bop 4. bang, belt,
   buss, glow, kiss, tang 5. clout, taste
   6. strike, vessel, wallop 8. chastise,
   sailboat
smacking . . . 5. brisk 6. lively
   7. dashing 8. spanking, vigorous
   9. energetic
small . . . 3. tot, wee 4. thin, tiny, wisp
   5. dwarf, petty 6. humble, little,
   meager, minute, modest, petite
   7. faintly, trivial 8. picayune, trifling
   9. miniature, minuscule, thumbnail
   10. diminutive, undersized

11. unimportant 13. insignificant
14. contemptuously, inconsiderable
small (pert to) . . .
   amount . . 3. dab 4. dram 5. minim
      6. morsel 7. modicum 8. pittance
   anvil . . 5. teest
   area . . 6. areola (areole)
   armadillo . . 4. peba
   arms . . 3. bow 5. rifle, sword 6. pistol
      7. carbine, grenade
   attractive . . 4. cute 6. dainty
   bomb . . 6. petard 7. grenade
   bottle . . 4. vial 5. phial
   case, handbag . . 4. etui
   comb form . . 5. lepto, micro
   dab . . 3. pat, wad 5. chunk
   deer . . 4. fawn, napu
   delicately . . 6. mignon
   distance . . 3. hop 4. step
   drink . . 3. nip 4. pony, swig
   drum . . 5. bongo, tabor
   field . . 5. croft
   fish . . 3. ide
   flag . . 6. fanion
   fruits . . 10. low growing
   fry . . 4. fish, kids, tots 8. children
      10. youngsters
   insect . . 4. flea 5. midge
   island . . 3. ait 4. isle
   lake . . 4. mere, pond
   law . . 5. petit
   minded . . 4. mean 5. petty 6. biased
      10. prejudiced, vindictive
   neat . . 6. dapper
   number . . 3. few 7. paucity
   opening . . 4. pore 5. stoma 7. orifice
   ox . . 4. anoa
   part . . 4. iota 6. detail 7. snippet
   particle . . 4. atom, mote 8. molecule
   people . . 5. elves 6. common
      7. fairies, midgets, Pygmies
   piece . . 3. mot 4. chip, tate 5. speck
      7. driblet, morceau
   post . . 9. paper size
   quantity . . 4. drop, mite 5. trace
      7. handful
   rope (Naut) . . 7. marline (marling)
   Scot . . 3. sma, wee
   shield . . 3. écu 9. scutellum
   stream . . 3. run 4. rill 6. rillet
   surface . . 5. facet
   talk . . 6. babble 7. prattle 8. chitchat
   task . . 5. chore 6. odd job
   things . . 3. fry
   tower . . 6. turret 7. minaret
   very . . 3. wee 8. picayune
      11. Lilliputian
   world . . 9. microcosm
smallpox . . . 7. variola
smaragd . . . 7. emerald
smart . . . 3. apt 4. chic, perk, posh,
   trig, trim, wise 5. acute, alert, natty,
   nifty, quick, sting 6. astute, clever,
   shrewd, spruce, trendy 7. dashing,
   painful, pungent, stylish 8. impudent,
   poignant, pricking 9. competent,
   ingenious 10. precocious
   11. fashionable, intelligent
smash . . . 4. blow, mash, pulp, ruin
   5. break, crush, drink (spirits), stave,
   wreck 6. defeat 7. collide, debacle,
   destroy, failure, shatter, success

8. accident, beverage 9. collision, pulverize

smear... 3. dab, rub 4. daub, gaum 5. slake, stain, sully 6. anoint, bedaub, defame, defile, grease, malign, smirch, smudge 7. besmear, plaster, pollute, slander 8. besmirch

smear with...
egg white.. 5. glair 8. meringue
mud.. 5. slime
ointment.. 6. anoint

smell... 4. odor, olid, reek 5. aroma, fetor, scent, sense, sniff, stink 6. detect 7. perfume 9. fragrance, redolence 10. atmosphere

smell (pert to)...
acute.. 8. oxyrhine
loss of sense of.. 7. anosmia
offensive.. 3. bad 4. foul, olid 5. fetor 6. stench
sense of.. 6. osmics 7. osmesis 9. olfaction

smelling salts... 9. hartshorn 17. ammonium carbonate

smelt... 4. fish, fuse, melt 6. tomcod 7. scorify 10. silverside

smilax... 8. catbrier 10. greenbrier

smile... 4. grin 5. laugh, smirk, sneer 6. simper 8. greeting

smiling... 5. agrin, merry, riant 6. rident 8. gleaming, grinning

smirch... 4. blot 5. smear, stain, sully, taint 6. blotch, smutch, stigma, vilify 7. begrime, blacken, blemish, tarnish 8. discolor 10. blackening

smirk... 4. grin, leer 6. simper

smite... 4. kill, slap 6. lay low, strike 7. chasten, impress, inflict, trouble 8. chastise

smithy... 6. forger, stithy 7. farrier 8. smithery 10. blacksmith

smock... 5. kamis, shift, tunic, woman (obs) 7. chemise 9. philander 11. overgarment

smoke... 4. burn, cure, floc, fume, pipe 5. cigar, cloud, cubeb, flume, smook, vapor 6. smudge 7. incense, tobacco 8. fumigate, preserve 9. cigarette

smokestack... 6. funnel 7. chimney 8. fumiduct

smoking apparatus (Orient)... 7. tabagie 8. narghile (nargile)

smolder, smoulder.. 4. burn 5. choke, smoke 6. smudge 7. smother 9. suffocate

smooth... 4. comb, ease, even, iron, lene, pave 5. bland, clear, level, plane, press, sleek, slick, suave 6. glossy, mangle, pacify, urbane 7. uniform 8. hairless, unctuous 10. facilitate, flattering 12. frictionless, ingratiating

smooth (pert to)...
breathing.. 13. spiritus lenis
comb form.. 3. lio
feathers, hair.. 5. preen
hard, transparent.. 6. glassy
phonetically.. 4. lene
tare.. 12. slender vetch
tongued.. 4. glib 5. suave 12. hypocritical

smooth and...
soft.. 5. furry, silky, soapy 7. velvety
soothing.. 5. bland
sweet.. 11. mellifluent
white.. 11. alabastrine

smother... 4. daub, kill 5. befog, choke, cover 6. deaden, hush up, muffle, stifle, welter 7. overlie, smolder 8. suppress 9. suffocate, to blanket 11. exterminate

smudge... 4. blot, smut, soil, spot 5. smear, smoke, stain 6. smutch 7. begrime, smolder

smug... 4. neat, tidy, trim 5. smart, suave 6. pilfer 7. correct 9. confident 10. complacent 13. self-satisfied

smuggler... 6. runner 9. rumrunner 13. contrabandist

smur... 4. mist 5. cloud, smurr 7. drizzle

Smyrna... 5. Izmir (present name)

Smyrna fig... 5. eleme (elemi)

Smyrna melon... 6. casaba

snail... 4. slug 5. drone, Helix, Mitra, whelk 6. Nerita, Triton 7. mollusk 9. gastropod 10. periwinkle

snake... 3. asp, ess 4. tree, worm 5. adder, cobra, coral, racer, viper 6. garter, gopher 7. hognose, rattler, reptile 8. Micrurus, moccasin 9. Heterodon 10. bushmaster, copperhead, sidewinder 11. cottonmouth, diamondback, rattlesnake 12. schaapsteker

snake (pert to)...
African.. 5. mamba
bird.. 6. darter
black.. 5. racer
cobra.. 3. nag (naga)
comb form.. 5. ophio, ophis 6. herpes
crusher.. 6. python 8. anaconda 14. boa constrictor
dance.. 4. Hopi 6. ophism
division (serpents).. 7. Ophidia 9. Serpentes
expert.. 13. herpetologist
fear of.. 13. herpetophobia
Florida.. 8. moccasin
front-fanged.. 5. cobra, mamba 6. elapid 8. Elapinne
garter.. 5. Elaps
genus.. 7. Ophidia
heraldic.. 5. bisse
horned.. 8. cerastes
India.. 5. krait 6. bongar
killer.. 8. mongoose
like.. 7. ophioid 9. colubrine
mouth.. 6. orchid
movement.. 4. coil, drag, wind 5. crawl, sneak, twist
mythical.. 6. Python (on Mt Parnassus)
nonpoisonous.. 4. king 6. garter, gopher 9. Colubrina
pert to.. 5. ophic 7. anguine 8. viperine 9. colubrine, scoundrel
poisonous.. 3. asp 5. adder, coral 7. rattler 8. moccasin 10. copperhead 11. cottonmouth 13. thanatophidia

python.. **8.** anaconda
python deity.. **5.** zombi (zombie)
reptilelike.. **9.** herpetoid
Russell's viper.. **6.** daboia, jessur
sacred.. **6.** Shesha
S America.. **5.** aboma
sand snake.. **4.** Eryx
semihuman, race of.. **4.** Naga
shaped.. **9.** anguiform
skin.. **6.** exuvia
spitting.. **8.** ringhals
snaky... **3.** sly **4.** wavy **7.** anguine,
sinuous, wriggly **8.** spiteful, twisting,
venomous **9.** snakelike **10.** perfidious,
serpentine **11.** treacherous
snaky sisters... **6.** Erinys
17. snaky–haired Furies
snap... **3.** bit **4.** bite, flip **5.** break,
crack, flick, quick, snarl, thump
6. energy, fasten, fillip (fingers)
7. bargain, crackle **8.** easy task,
handcuff, snapshot **9.** crispness,
fastening, smartness **10.** gingersnap,
photograph, resilience **11.** sharp
retort
snapper... **4.** bean, sesi **5.** error,
pargo **6.** beetle, bonbon, tamure,
turtle **7.** cracker, grouper **8.** fastener,
rosefish **9.** countfish **10.** stitchwort,
stringbean, woodpecker
11. firecracker
snappy... **4.** cold, fast **5.** quick
6. lively, sudden **7.** pungent
8. snappish **9.** crackling, energetic
snare... **3.** beg, gin, net, web **4.** lure,
mesh, trap **5.** benet, catch, noose,
steal **6.** entoil, trepan **7.** pitfall
9. deception
snark... **3.** nag **5.** snort **6.** boojum
8. creature (fabled)
snarl... **4.** gnar, knot **5.** gnarr, growl,
scold, snare **6.** tangle **7.** confuse,
ensnare, grumble, quarrel
8. complain, entangle **9.** confusion
10. complicate **12.** complication
snatch... **4.** grab, jerk, take **5.** catch,
erept, grasp, gripe, pluck, seize,
steal, wrest **6.** clutch, kidnap, rescue
7. seizure
sneak... **4.** lead (game), lurk **5.** cower,
creep, knave, slink, snoop **6.** coward,
cringe, tattle **7.** smuggle **11.** furtive
move
sneaking... **3.** sly **4.** mean, poor
6. craven, hidden, paltry, secret
7. furtive **8.** cowardly, stealthy
9. dastardly, niggardly, underhand
12. contemptible **13.** surreptitious
sneer... **4.** gibe, jeer, mock **5.** fleer,
flout, laugh, scoff, scorn
sneer, expressive... **8.** sardonic
snell... **4.** keen **5.** acute, eager, quick,
sharp, snood, swift **6.** active, biting,
severe **7.** caustic, pungent
8. piercing
snicker... **5.** laugh, neigh, sneer
6. giggle, nicker, tittle, whinny
7. snigger **8.** laughter
sniff... **4.** nose **5.** scent, smell, snuff
6. detect, inhale **7.** sniffle **8.** sibilate,
smell out **14.** show of contempt
snifter... **3.** nip **4.** dram, good

5. drink, sniff, snort **6.** snivel
9. excellent
snip... **3.** bit, cut **4.** clip, snap
5. notch, piece, shred **8.** fragment,
particle
snipe (pert to)...
eel.. **6.** thread
flock.. **4.** wisp
game.. **6.** godwit
hawk.. **7.** harrier
verb.. **7.** shoot at **10.** sharpshoot
snippy... **4.** curt, tart **5.** brief, sharp
8. snippety, snobbish
11. fragmentary **12.** supercilious
snirl... **5.** gnarl, snare **6.** tangle
7. wrinkle
snitch... **5.** pinch, steal **6.** betray,
inform, pilfer, snatch, tattle
8. informer, particle
snob... **4.** prig **7.** cobbler, parvenu
8. bluenose, commoner, courtier
9. sycophant
snobby, snobbish... **5.** proud
6. uppish **7.** haughty **8.** arrogant
9. exclusive **11.** overbearing
snood... **5.** snell **6.** fillet **7.** hairnet
snook... **4.** fish **5.** smell **6.** robalo,
search **9.** barracuda
snoop... **3.** pry **4.** nose **5.** prowl,
sneak **6.** meddle **7.** meddler
8. busybody **10.** sneak thief
snooze... **3.** nap **4.** doze **5.** sleep
6. cuddle, nuzzle, siesta **7.** snoozle,
snuggle
snore, snoring... **4.** rale **5.** sleep
7. stertor **8.** rhonchus, sibilate
10. sibilation, stertorous **15.** hoarse
breathing
snort... **5.** drink, grunt, laugh, snore
snotty... **5.** dirty, nasty **6.** offish,
snooty **7.** high–hat **9.** offensive
12. contemptible, supercilious
snow... **4.** firn, neve **5.** opium
8. narcotic **12.** interference
snow (pert to)...
bunting.. **5.** finch **9.** snowflake
glacial.. **4.** firn, neve
grouse, quail.. **9.** ptarmigan
house.. **5.** igloo
leopard.. **5.** ounce
lily.. **6.** violet (white)
living in.. **5.** nival
mouse.. **4.** vole **7.** lemming
ref to.. **5.** nival
ridges.. **8.** sastrugi (zastrugi)
runner.. **3.** ski **4.** sled
shoe.. **3.** pac **7.** webfoot
sliding.. **9.** avalanche
slope.. **8.** glissade
snub... **3.** cut **5.** check, quell, scold
6. cut off, ignore, rebuff, rebuke,
slight **7.** neglect, shorten **8.** restrain
9. reprimand **10.** inhalation
snuff... **5.** scent, smell, sniff **6.** draw
in, inhale, snoose **7.** tobacco
(pulverized), umbrage **10.** extinguish,
inhalation
snuff (pert to)...
a candle.. **4.** snot
box.. **4.** mull **9.** tabatière
color.. **10.** mummy brown
type.. **6.** rappee **8.** Maccaboy

10. Copenhagen

snug... 4. cozy, neat, safe, trim
5. close, tight 6. secure 7. compact
8. homelike, reticent 9. concealed,
secretive 10. prosperous
11. comfortable

snuggle... 6. cuddle, nestle

sny (shipbuilding)... 5. curve (of plank)

so... 2. as 3. how 4. ergo, thus, very
5. hence 6. if only 7. because
8. likewise, provided 9. therefore
11. accordingly, in order that
12. consequently

so (pert to)...
far.. 3. yet 7. thus far 8. until now
Latin.. 3. sic
so be it.. 4. Amen
to speak.. 8. as it were
12. figuratively

soak... 3. dip, sog, sop, wet 4. sock
5. souse, steep 6. drench, imbrue,
strike, tipple 7. extract, immerse
8. drunkard, macerate, marinate,
permeate, saturate 9. percolate
10. overcharge

soap... 4. sapo, suds, wash 5. bribe
6. lather 7. bribery 8. cleanser,
flattery 9. slush fund

soap (pert to)...
box.. 4. dais 5. stage 8. platform
convert to.. 8. saponify
fish.. 10. lizard fish
frame bar.. 4. sess
ingredient.. 3. lye
liniment (camphorated).. 9. opodeldoc
making.. 14. saponification
mottled.. 8. Eschwege (Eschweg)
opera.. 6. serial 9. broadcast
13. network serial
plant.. 5. amole
soft.. 8. flattery

soar... 3. fly 4. flit, rise, wing 5. float,
plane 6. ascend, aspire, be high
9. transcend

soaring... 6. flight 7. gliding, planing,
winging 8. essorant 9. skyriding
10. ballooning

sob... 3. cry 4. bawl, weep
6. boohoo, simper 7. whimper
9. shed tears

sobeit... 4. amen 8. provided

sober... 4. calm, cool, dark, sane
5. grave, quiet, staid 6. gentle,
sedate, solemn, somber, subdue,
temper 7. chasten, earnest, regular,
serious 8. composed, moderate,
sensible 9. abstinent, collected,
dignified, temperate 10. abstemious,
thoughtful 11. impassioned
13. unintoxicated

sobriety... 6. sanity 9. composure,
restraint, soberness 10. abstinence,
moderation, temperance
11. seriousness

sobriquet... 5. alias, title 6. byname
7. epithet 8. cognomen, nickname
11. appellation

sociable... 5. party 7. affable
8. familiar, friendly, informal
9. reception 10. accessible,
gregarious 13. communicative,
companionable

social... 3. tea 5. party 6. smoker
9. convivial, gathering
13. companionable

social (pert to)...
career.. 5. debut
class.. 4. clan, sept 5. caste
6. estate
ethics.. 6. morals 9. standards
10. principles
function.. 3. bee, tea 4. ball 5. party
6. soiree 7. reunion 9. reception
gathering, men.. 4. stag 6. smoker
group.. 4. sept 5. tribe 6. ethnos
8. smart set 10. upper crust
11. cafe society 13. kaffeeklatsch
insect.. 3. ant, bee
outcast.. 5. leper 6. pariah
standing.. 6. estate
system.. 6. regime

socialist... 3. Red 8. Nihilist
9. anarchist, communist
10. Bolshevist 12. collectivist

society... 5. union 7. company
8. alliance, populace 9. community
10. fellowship 11. association,
partnership 13. companionship,
confederation, participation

society (pert to)...
bud.. 3. deb
Chinese.. 4. Tong
German.. 6. Verein
high.. 5. elite 10. upper crust
Italian.. 6. maffia (mafia)
of Friends.. 7. Quakers
secret.. 5. lodge, Order

Society Islands...
capital.. 7. Papeete
chief island.. 6. Tahiti
site.. 12. South Pacific

Socrates (pert to)...
birthplace.. 6. Athens
disciple of.. 5. Plato
famed as.. 7. teacher 11. Grecian
sage
wife.. 9. Xanthippe (Xantippe)

sod... 4. soil, turf 5. divot, glebe,
sward 7. stratum 10. greensward

soda... 3. sal 8. beverage 9. saleratus,
saltpeter

sodden... 5. drunk, moist, soggy
6. soaked, stewed, stupid
7. drunken, steeped 9. saturated
11. intoxicated

sodium (pert to)...
carbonate.. 4. soda 5. borax, trona
7. sal soda, saltcat
chloride.. 3. sal, tar 4. NaCl, salt
nitrate.. 5. niter
salicylate.. 8. medicine
symbol.. 2. Na

sofa... 5. couch, divan 6. lounge,
settee 7. dos–à–dos 8. causeuse,
love seat 9. davenport, tête–à–tête
12. chesterfield

soft... 4. easy, limp, weak 5. bland,
downy, mushy, pulpy 6. dreamy,
gentle, placid, silken, supple, tender
7. clement, ductile, lenient, lightly,
quietly, squashy, velvety 8. flexible,
gullible, merciful, tranquil
9. temperate, tractable
10. effeminate, peacefully

11. comfortable, sentimental,
   sympathetic 13. compassionate
soft (pert to)...
   cancer.. 11. encephaloma
   coal.. 10. bituminous
   food.. 3. pap
   head.. 9. simpleton
   job.. 4. snap 8. sinecure
   mass.. 4. pulp
   music.. 5. dulce, piano
   palate.. 4. cion 5. uvula, velum
   pedal.. 3. ban 4. curb 6. subdue
    8. tone down
   soap.. 7. blarney 8. blandish, flattery
    9. wheedling
   spoken.. 4. mild 5. suave
soften... 4. melt, thaw 5. allay, malax,
   relax 6. affect, lenify, pacify, relent,
   soothe, temper, weaken 7. appease,
   assuage, cushion, mollify, relieve
   8. emoliate, enervate, enfeeble,
   macerate, mitigate, modulate
   9. alleviate, meliorate 11. tranquilize
soften (pert to)...
   by kneading.. 5. malax
   by soaking.. 8. macerate
   leather.. 5. sammy (sam)
   skins.. 3. taw
   temper.. 6. relent
softening... 7. lenient 8. emulsive
   9. relenting, relieving, tempering
   10. lightening, mitigating
softening of the brain... 8. dementia
softhearted... 4. kind 6. tender
   8. merciful
softly... 3. low 5. sotto 6. easily,
   gently 10. delicately
   13. unobtrusively
soggy... 3. wet 4. damp 5. heavy
   6. soaked, sodden, watery
   9. saturated
soil... 4. clay, daub, dirt, land, loam,
   sand, spot 5. adobe, dirty, earth,
   glebe, gumbo, humus, stain, sully
   6. bedaub, bemire, ground, region,
   smirch, vilify 7. begrime, besmear,
   corrupt, debauch, pollute, tarnish
   8. alluvium 9. bedraggle, bespatter
   11. contaminate 12. fuller's earth
soil (pert to)...
   barren.. 4. arid, gall 8. lifeless
   goddess of.. 7. Demeter
   kind of.. 4. clay, lair, loam, malm
    5. adobe, humus
   oneself.. 4. moil
   poetic.. 5. glebe
sojourn... 4. bide, stay, stop 5. abide
   6. reside 8. abidance, stop over
   11. peregrinate
solace... 5. allay, amuse, cheer
   6. soothe 7. assuage, comfort,
   console 9. alleviate, entertain
   10. relaxation 11. consolation
solan... 5. goose 6. gannet
solar (pert to)...
   deity.. 2. Ra 3. Shu (Su) 6. Helios
   disk.. 4. aten
   exposure.. 9. sunstroke 10. heatstroke
   halo.. 6. nimbus 7. aureole
    12. vesica piscis
   plexus.. 10. stomach pit
   system.. 6. bodies, planet

15. celestial bodies
system apparatus.. 6. orrery
year.. 5. epact
soldier... 3. ant 5. cadet, poilu
   6. galoot 7. fighter, private, regular,
   trooper, veteran, warrior
   8. gendarme, servitor 9. combatant,
   grenadier, musketeer 11. enlisted
   man
soldier (pert to)...
   Algeria.. 6. Zouave
   cavalryman.. 6. lancer 7. dragoon,
    trooper
   Croatian.. 5. Croat
   field worker.. 6. sapper
   flask.. 7. canteen
   French.. 5. poilu
   Gaelic.. 4. Kern
   girl.. 3. WAC (Army)
   Gr Myth.. 8. Myrmidon
   hireling.. 9. mercenary
   Ind (Brit).. 5. sepoy
   Ind (Brit), with own horse.. 8. silladar
   Moroccan.. 5. askar
   of fortune.. 7. Hessian 10. adventurer
   Prussian.. 5. uhlan
   slang.. 6. galoot 7. chicken
    8. shackman
soldiers, soldier's...
   body of.. 5. troop 6. cohort
    7. brigade, company, platoon
   captured, wounded.. 6. losses
   flask.. 7. canteen
   Maryland (Rev War).. 10. macaronies
   overcoat.. 6. capote
   quarters.. 7. billets 8. barracks
   Three.. 5. tales (by Kipling)
   vacation.. 4. pass 5. leave
    8. furlough
sole... 3. one 4. base, fish, only
   5. alone, slade 6. entire, lonely,
   single, unique 8. desolate, isolated,
   solitary, unshared 9. exclusive,
   unmarried, unmatched
   10. underframe
sole (pert to)...
   cookery.. 8. Marguéry
   foot.. 4. vola 6. planta
   hand (palm).. 4. vola
   pert to.. 7. plantar
   plow.. 5. slade
   toward the sole.. 7. plantad
solecism... 5. error 7. blunder
   9. barbarism, deviation
   11. impropriety
solemn... 3. sad 5. grave, pious,
   sober 6. august, devout, formal,
   gloomy, ritual, silent 7. earnest,
   serious, stately, sublime 8. funereal
   9. dignified 10. ceremonial,
   devotional 11. ceremonious,
   reverential 12. awe–inspiring
solemnity... 4. pomp 7. dignity,
   sadness 8. ceremony 9. formality
   10. importance
solicit... 3. ask, beg 4. lure, seek,
   tout 5. claim, court, crave, plead
   6. accost, demand, invite, obtain
   7. beseech, canvass, entreat,
   implore, request 8. campaign,
   petition 9. challenge, importune,
   panhandle, prosecute 10. supplicate

solicitor... 6. barker, lawyer
   8. attorney 9. canvasser
   10. petitioner
solicitude... 4. care, coda, heed
   7. anxiety, caution, concern
   9. attention 11. carefulness
   12. apprehension
   15. considerateness
solid... 4. cone, cube, firm, full, good,
   hard 5. dense, level, sound, stiff
   6. stable, strong 7. uniform
   8. complete, resolute, sensible,
   sterling 9. estimable, unanimous
   10. dependable, inflexible
   11. homogeneous, responsible,
   substantial, trustworthy
solid (pert to)...
   comb form .. 6. stereo
   geometrical .. 5. prism
   seven–faced .. 11. heptahedron
   six–faced .. 4. cube
   tapering .. 4. cone 7. pyramid
solidarity... 5. unity 10. correality
   11. nationality 12. completeness
solidity... 4. unity 6. volume
   7. density 8. firmness, hardness,
   solvency, strength 9. solidness,
   stability 11. compactness
   12. completeness 13. dependability
   14. substantiality
solidum... 4. dado 9. entire sum
soliloquy... 4. poem 9. discourse,
   monologue 16. talking to oneself
solitaire... 8. Canfield
solitary... 3. one 4. lone, only, sole
   5. alone, eremo (comb form)
   6. hermit, lonely, single 7. recluse
   8. deserted, desolate, lonesome
   10. individual 12. unfrequented
solitude... 6. desert 7. privacy, retreat
   9. aloneness, isolation, seclusion
   10. loneliness, wilderness
solo accompaniment... 9. obbligato
Solomon (pert to)...
   author of (reputed) .. 8. Proverbs
   9. Canticles 12. Ecclesiastes
   15. Wisdom of Solomon
   called also .. 8. Koheleth 11. The
   Preacher
   famed as .. 4. sage 7. wise man
   12. King of Israel
   father .. 5. David
   literally .. 9. peaceable
   mother .. 9. Bathsheba
Solomon Islands site... 9. South Seas
solon... 4. sage 8. lawmaker
   9. statesman
solstice... 5. limit 13. farthest point
   (from equator)
solution... 3. key 6. answer 7. solving
   8. analysis 10. denouement,
   resolution 11. explanation
   15. disentanglement
solution (pert to)...
   alkaline .. 3. lye
   saline .. 5. brine
   strength .. 5. titer (titre)
Somalia...
   capital .. 9. Mogadishu
   people .. 6. Somali 7. Hamitic
   port .. 5. Zeila 6. Bulhar

somber, sombre... 3. sad 4. dark
   5. grave 6. solemn 7. austere
   9. depressed 10. depressing,
   foreboding, lackluster, melancholy
   11. dark–colored, dispiriting
some... 3. any, one 5. about
   6. plural, suffix 7. several
   10. indefinite, more or less
   13. approximately
somebody... 6. person 7. big name
   8. luminary 9. celebrity, personage
somersault... 4. flip, leap 8. somerset
   9. cartwheel 10. end over end
something... 6. object 8. somewhat
   9. personage 12. in some degree
something (pert to)...
   abnormal .. 5. freak 6. mutant
   11. monstrosity 12. malformation
   else .. 10. irrelevant
   extra .. 5. bonus 6. bounty
   7. premium 9. lagniappe
   found .. 5. cache, trove
   11. serendipity 13. treasure–trove
   frightening .. 7. bugbear
   heavy .. 4. onus 9. ponderant
   illogical .. 7. alogism
   imagined .. 5. story 7. figment
   inserted .. 4. gore 5. inset, wedge
   like .. 7. related, similar 8. somewhat
   similar .. 8. analogue 11. counterpart
   small .. 3. dot, jot 4. atom, iota, whit
   5. speck 6. sliver, tittle
   soothing .. 7. unction
   superfluous .. 5. luxus 6. luxury
   unexplained .. 5. poser 7. mystery
   unfinished .. 4. quab
somewhat... 4. part 6. little, partly,
   rather 12. in some degree
somnifacient... 4. drug 8. hypnotic,
   sedative 9. soporific
somniloquy... 12. sleep talking
somnolence... 8. dormancy
   10. drowsiness, sleepiness
somnus... 5. sleep
Somnus (pert to)...
   brother .. 4. Mors (Death)
   known also as .. 6. Hypnos
   son of .. 3. Nox (Night)
son, son of (pert to)...
   a gun .. 5. rogue 6. fellow, wretch
   Anak .. 5. giant
   a Scot .. 3. Mac
   God .. 11. Jesus Christ
   Heaven (China) .. 7. Emperor
   in–law .. 5. gener
   in Trinity .. 6. second (person)
   Jacob .. 4. Levi
   man .. 4. male 6. mortal
   Odin .. 2. Ve
   Odysseus .. 9. Telegonus
   Priam .. 5. Paris
   reference to .. 3. ben 4. fils 5. scion
   6. filial 9. offspring 10. descendant
   Seth .. 4. Enos
   the soil .. 6. farmer 7. peasant
   youngest .. 5. cadet
sonance... 4. tune 5. sound
   7. sonancy
sonant... 5. sound, tonic, vocal
   6. voiced 8. sounding 9. intonated
song... 3. air, lay, ode 4. aria, leed,

lilt, noel, poem, tune 5. carol, chant, ditty, melos, troll, verse 6. ballad, melody, strain, trifle 7. chantey (chanty), descant 8. canticle, pittance 9. cabaletta

song (pert to)...
after.. 5. epode
Bib.. 8. canticle 11. Song of Songs 13. Song of Solomon
boat, gondolier.. 7. chantey (chanty)
choral Muse.. 11. Terpsichore
collection.. 9. anthology 10. cancionero
college.. 4. glee
depressing.. 5. blues
evening.. 6. vesper 8. evensong, serenade
French.. 7. chanson
funeral.. 5. dirge, elegy 6. lament 8. threnody 9. epicedium
gay.. 4. lilt
German.. 4. lied 9. Kunstlied
gypsy.. 10. zingaresca
Italian.. 7. canzone
lament.. 8. threnody
love.. 5. lyric 6. ballad 8. madrigal, serenade
merry.. 4. lilt
morning.. 5. matin
mountaineer.. 5. yodel
pert to.. 5. melic
praise.. 5. carol, paean (pean)
sacred.. 4. hymn 5. chant, motet, psalm 6. anthem
sailor's.. 7. chantey (chanty) 9. barcarole
short.. 7. arietta
simple.. 6. ballad
words.. 6. lyrics

songbird... 4. lark 5. mavis, robin, veery 6. canary, oriole, thrush 8. throstle 11. mockingbird

sonic recorder... 9. echograph

sonnet... 4. poem, song 5. verse

sonnet (pert to)...
first eight lines.. 5. octet
last six lines.. 6. sestet
two quatrains.. 7. Petrarchan

sonorous... 4. loud 6. tonous 7. ringing 8. resonant 9. melodious 10. impressive, resounding

sonsy, sonsie... 5. buxom, happy 6. comely 11. good–natured

sontag... 4. cape 6. jacket

soon... 3. ere 4. anon 5. early, later 6. at once 7. betimes, erelong, quickly, readily, shortly 8. promptly, speedily 9. certainly, presently 11. immediately

Sooner State... 8. Oklahoma

sooner than... 3. ere 6. before

soot... 4. smut, stup 5. black, grime, smoke 6. carbon, smudge 7. residue 9. lampblack

soothe... 3. pet 4. calm, lull 5. allay, quiet 6. pacify, please, solace 7. assuage, compose, mollify, relieve, satisfy 8. mitigate, palliate 9. alleviate 11. tranquilize

soother... 4. balm 6. luller 7. anodyne, placebo 8. lenitive, pacifier, sedative 9. flatterer

soothing... 5. balmy, sirup (syrup) 6. dulcet, gentle 7. calming 8. lenitive, sedative 9. appeasing, demulcent 13. tranquilizing

soothsayer... 4. seer 5. augur, vatis 6. mantis 7. diviner, prophet 8. Chaldean, haruspex 9. Cassandra 13. praying insect 14. prognosticator

sooty (pert to)...
brown.. 6. bister 8. teakwood
color.. 5. black
mangabey.. 6. monkey
pert to.. 9. albatross 10. fuliginous
petrel.. 7. skimmer 10. shearwater

sophistical... 8. captious 9. deceptive, sophistic

sophistication... 9. sophistry 10. corruption, experience 11. worldliness 13. ungullibility

soporific... 4. drug 6. drowsy, opiate 7. anodyne 8. hypnotic, narcotic, sedative 11. somniferous 12. sleep inducer, somnifacient

soprano (operatic)... 4. Alda, Bori, Lind, Pons 5. Calvé, Eames 6. Callas, Steber

sora... 4. rail 5. crake

sorcerer... 4. mage 5. Magus 6. wizard 7. diviner 8. conjurer, magician 11. necromancer

sorceress... 3. hex 5. Circe, lamia, Medea, witch 6. Gorgon 7. vampire 12. Witch of Endor

sorcery... 5. magic, obeah, spell 6. voodoo 8. pishogue 9. diablerie, diabolism 10. black magic, necromancy, witchcraft

sordid... 3. low 4. base, mean, vile 5. gross 6. filthy, menial 7. ignoble, servile, squalid 8. sluttish, wretched 10. despicable, slatternly 12. contemptible

sore... 4. pain, sair 5. angry, vexed, wound 6. tender 7. painful 8. abrasion, inflamed, offended 9. irritated, vexatious 11. distressing 12. inflammation

soreness... 4. ache 5. anger 8. vexation 10. bitterness, tenderness 11. painfulness 12. irritability

sorghum... 4. milo 5. durra (dari), grain, sorgo 6. imphee, shallu 8. feterita

sorority... 4. club 7. society 10. fellowship, sisterhood

sorrel... 3. oca 4. buck, herb 5. color (horse), Rumex 7. roselle

Sorrento, Italy (pert to)...
anc name.. 9. Sorrentum
famed as.. 6. resort
famed for.. 9. cathedral
site.. 11. Bay of Naples

sorrow... 3. rue, woe 4. sigh, teen, weal 5. dolor, grief, mourn 6. grieve, lament, misery, repent 7. remorse, trouble 8. calamity, distress, egrimony, mourning 9. adversity, penitence 10. affliction, contrition 11. lamentation, tribulation 12. disconsolate, wretchedness

sorrowful... 3. sad 4. blue 5. drear, sadly 6. dismal, dolent, dreary, rueful

7. doleful, grieved, tearful, unhappy
8. mournful **9.** plaintive
10. afflictive, melancholy
11. distressing **12.** disconsolate
sorry . . . **3.** sad **4.** hurt **5.** vexed
6. dismal, gloomy, rueful **7.** painful,
pitiful, unhappy **8.** contrite, grievous,
mournful, penitent, shameful, wretched
9. afflicted, chagrined, mortified,
regretful, repentant, worthless
10. displeased, melancholy
12. disappointed
sort . . . **3.** ilk, way **4.** cull, kind, rank
5. blend, class, grade, group
6. assort, manner, nature, strain
7. quality, species, variety **8.** classify,
separate **9.** character **11.** description
sortie . . . **4.** raid **5.** foray, onset, sally
6. attack, thrust
sottish . . . **4.** dull **6.** stupid **7.** doltish,
drunken, foolish **8.** bibulous
9. senseless
sotto (It) . . . **5.** below, under
sotto voce . . . **5.** aside **8.** secretly
9. privately, undertone **14.** under the
breath
soubrette . . . **9.** lady's maid
10. intrigante **11.** maidservant
soudagur . . . **8.** merchant
10. shopkeeper
soul . . . **2.** ba, ka **3.** ego, God **4.** life
5. anima **6.** pneuma, spirit
7. essence **8.** inspirer **9.** substance
10. embodiment **15.** exemplification,
personification
soul (pert to) . . .
beatified . . **5.** saint
destiny of . . **8.** theodicy
dwelling place . . **2.** Po **6.** heaven
Egypt . . **2.** Ba
Hindu . . **5.** atman **7.** jivatma
lost . . **9.** âme damnée, the damned
maligners . . **7.** Harpies
music . . **14.** rhythm and blues
personified . . **6.** Psyche
transmigration . . **7.** rebirth
13. reincarnation
sound . . . **3.** bam, cry, hum **4.** beep,
bong, hale, honk, rale, ring, sane, test,
tone, toot **5.** drone, noise, plumb,
probe, snore, valid, whole **6.** intact,
jingle, report, robust, stable, sturdy
7. feel out, perfect, resound
8. flawless, reliable, susurrus
9. undamaged **10.** scrutinize
11. trustworthy
sound (pert to) . . .
addition to word end . . **8.** paragoge
atonic . . **4.** surd
dashing . . **5.** swash **6.** splash
discordant . . **6.** jangle **9.** cacophony
drum, beating . . **8.** rataplan
explosion . . **4.** boom **6.** report
fixed . . **5.** toned
harsh . . **3.** caw **4.** bray **5.** creak,
twang **7.** stridor **9.** cacophony
insect's . . **5.** chirr
loud . . **4.** peal **5.** blare, clang
low . . **3.** hum **4.** moan **5.** drone
metallic . . **4.** ping, ting **5.** clank, clink,
twank **6.** tinkle
pert to . . **5.** tonal **6.** sonant

10. acoustical
prosody . . **4.** rime (rhyme)
reflected . . **4.** echo
sharp . . **3.** pop **7.** rat–a–tat, tapping
shrill . . **5.** reedy
sibilant . . **4.** hiss
similar . . **8.** assonant
small . . **4.** peep **6.** rustle
surf . . **4.** rote **5.** swish
throwing . . **8.** abat–sons
trumpet . . **7.** clarion
warning . . **5.** alarm, siren **6.** tocsin
whispering . . **8.** susurrus
with rhythm . . **5.** music
sounding . . . **5.** depth, rawin **6.** sonant
7. ringing **8.** sonation
10. resounding
soundness . . . **5.** truth **6.** sanity
8. solidity, solvency, strength
9. integrity, rectitude, stability
10. heartiness **11.** healthiness
soup . . . **3.** fog **5.** broth, chili, purée
6. bisque, potage, won ton
7. borscht, chowder, pottage
8. bouillon, consommé, gazpacho,
julienne **10.** oyster stew
11. vichyssoise **12.** mulligatawny
soupçon . . . **5.** taste **7.** portion
9. suspicion **10.** suggestion
soup dish . . . **6.** tureen
sour . . . **3.** wry **4.** acid, tart **5.** acerb,
acrid **6.** acetic, bitter, morose, off
key, rancid **7.** acetose, acidify,
crabbed, pungent, tainted
8. acescent, embitter **9.** acidulous
10. astringent, unpleasant
sour (pert to) . . .
apple . . **9.** crab apple
aspect . . **4.** dour, hard **6.** sullen
berry . . **9.** cranberry
bread . . **8.** leavened
cherry . . **7.** morello
stomach . . **4.** acor
turn sour . . **5.** prill **6.** bleeze
source . . . **4.** font, germ, mine, rise,
root, seed **5.** cause, fount **6.** origin,
parent, quarry **8.** fountain
9. beginning **10.** wellspring
12. fountainhead
source (pert to) . . .
income . . **7.** revenue
insecticides . . **9.** sabadilla
iodine . . **4.** kelp
ipecac . . **4.** evea
metal . . **3.** ore **7.** bonanza
opium . . **5.** poppy
rubber . . **3.** ule
South Africa . . . see also *South African*
capital . . **8.** Cape Town, Pretoria
city . . **6.** Durban **9.** Germiston
12. Johannesburg
division . . **5.** Natal **9.** Transvaal
14. Cape of Good Hope **15.** Orange
Free State
exports . . **4.** gold **8.** diamonds
legislature seat location . . **8.** Cape
Town
people . . **5.** Boers **7.** British, Kaffirs
10. Hottentots **11.** Afrikanders
(Dutch)
river . . **4.** Vaal **6.** Orange
South African (pert to) . . .

antelope .. **3.** gnu **5.** eland, oribi, peele
　6. rhebok **7.** sassaby
armadillo .. **4.** para
ass (wild) .. **6.** quagga
bird .. **4.** taha
camp .. **6.** laager
Cape ash .. **9.** essenhout
cocktail .. **9.** sundowner
cony .. **3.** das
council .. **4.** Raad
dialect .. **4.** Taal **9.** Afrikaans
diamond (blue–white) .. **5.** jager
fox .. **4.** asse **5.** caama
grass hut .. **8.** rondawel (rondavel)
grassland .. **4.** veld (veldt) **8.** bushveld
mountain, hill .. **3.** kop
snake .. **8.** eggeater
tableland .. **5.** karoo
tree (dogwood) .. **7.** assagai (assegai)
tribe .. **4.** Zulu **5.** Bantu
village .. **5.** kraal
war .. **4.** Boer
warrior .. **4.** impi
weaverbird .. **4.** taha
whip .. **7.** sjambok
South American (pert to) ...
animal .. **2.** ai **4.** paca **5.** llama, sloth,
　tapir **6.** jaguar, tapeti **7.** agouara
　(dog) **8.** anteater **9.** armadillo
armadillo .. **4.** apar (apara)
　10. pichiciago (burrowing)
arrow poison .. **6.** curare (curari)
balsam .. **4.** tolu
bellbird .. **8.** arapunga **9.** campanero
bird .. **4.** rara, taha **5.** agami, arara,
　chaja, macaw **6.** barbet **7.** oilbird,
　seriema, tinamou **8.** bellbird, boatbill,
　caracara, guacharo, puffbird
blanket .. **6.** serape
city section .. **6.** barrio
cloth .. **4.** crea
drink .. **5.** assai
fiber .. **6.** yachan
fish .. **4.** paru **7.** piranha, scalare
　8. arapaima
Indian .. **2.** Ge (Gesan) **3.** Ona **4.** Inca
　5. Carib **6.** Tapuya (50 tribes)
knife .. **7.** machete
leader .. **6.** Franko **7.** Pizarro
liberator .. **7.** Bolivar
mammal .. **5.** llama, tapir **6.** alpaca
　8. kinkajou **10.** chinchilla
marmoset .. **7.** tamarin
monkey .. **3.** sai **4.** saki, titi **5.** araba
　8. orabassu **9.** barrigudo
native .. **5.** Carib **6.** Arawak
ostrich .. **4.** rhea
palm .. **5.** assai **12.** chiquichiqui
parrot .. **5.** macaw
plains .. **6.** llanos, pampas
plainsman .. **7.** llanero
plant .. **6.** ipecac **11.** ipecacuanha
poison .. **6.** curare
river .. **3.** Apa **4.** Acre, Pará **5.** Plata
　6. Paraná
rodent .. **5.** coypu **6.** agouti (agouty)
　8. capibara, viscacha **10.** chinchilla
snake .. **4.** lora **5.** aboma **8.** anaconda
　10. bushmaster
stork .. **7.** maguari
tinamou .. **7.** tataupa
toucan .. **7.** aracari

trumpeter .. **5.** agami
tuber .. **3.** oca
vulture .. **6.** condor
weapon .. **4.** bola
wild cat .. **4.** eyra
wind .. **7.** pampero
South Carolina ...
capital .. **8.** Columbia
city .. **8.** Beaufort **10.** Charleston
　11. Spartanburg
monument .. **10.** Fort Sumter
mountain .. **10.** Blue Ridge, Sassafras
resort .. **11.** Myrtle Beach
State admission .. **6.** Eighth
State bird .. **4.** wren
State flower .. **9.** jessamine
State motto .. **8.** Dum Spiro, Spero
　(While I Breathe, I Hope)
State nickname .. **8.** Palmetto
State secession .. **5.** First (1860)
South Dakota ...
capital .. **6.** Pierre
city .. **5.** Huron **8.** Deadwood
　9. Rapid City **10.** Sioux Falls
Indians .. **5.** Brule, Sioux
mine (US largest) .. **9.** Homestake
monument .. **10.** Crazy Horse, Mt
　Rushmore
mountain .. **10.** Black Hills, Harney
　Peak
river .. **5.** White **8.** Cheyenne, Missouri
State admission .. **8.** Fortieth (or
　Thirty–ninth)
State bird .. **8.** pheasant
State flower .. **12.** pasqueflower
State motto .. **21.** Under God the
　People Rule
State nickname .. **6.** Coyote
　8. Sunshine
topography .. **8.** Bad Lands **10.** Black
　Hills
southeast wind ... **5.** Eurus
southern ... **7.** austral
Southern (pert to) ...
Buddhism .. **8.** Hinayana
Cross .. **4.** Crux **12.** Stars and Bars
Crown .. **15.** Corona Australis
dish .. **3.** yam **4.** okra, pone **5.** gumbo
　7. catfish, hoecake **8.** chess pie, ham
　hocks **9.** cornbread **11.** hush puppies
　12. chitterlings, turnip greens
shrub .. **8.** magnolia, oleander
States .. **5.** Dixie **7.** Sunbelt
southernmost city ... **12.** Puerto
　Arenas (Chile)
South Pole bird ... **4.** skua **7.** penguin
South Pole constellation ... **4.** Pavo
South Sea ... **12.** Pacific Ocean
South Sea Bubble ... **6.** scheme
　(1720) **10.** stock fraud (Eng)
South Wales people ... **7.** Silures
southwest wind ... **4.** afer
south wind ... **5.** Notus
souvenir ... **5.** relic, token **6.** memory,
　trophy **7.** memento **8.** keepsake,
　memorial, reminder **11.** remembrance
　12. recollection, remembrancer
sovereign ... **5.** chief, liege, regal, ruler
　6. divine, prince, ruling **7.** empress,
　monarch, supreme **8.** princely,
　superior, suzerain **9.** effectual, gold
　piece, paramount, potentate

11. controlling, independent
sovereign (pert to) . . .
claim . . 11. seigniorage
coin . . 4. skiv
decree . . 5. arrêt
pardon . . 7. amnesty
petty . . 8. tetrarch
power . . 6. throne
sovereignty . . . 5. realm 6. diadem,
empery, empire 7. dynasty, scepter
(sceptre) 8. dominion 9. supremacy
Soviet, Russian (pert to) . . .
committee . . 9. presidium
farm . . 7. sovkhoz (sovkhose)
government . . 9. Communism,
Sovietism 10. Bolshevism
hero . . 5. Lenin
newspaper . . 6. Pravda 8. Izvestia
police, secret service . . 3. KGB
sow . . . 3. pig 4. gilt, seed 5. plant
7. implant, scatter 8. disperse,
squander 9. broadcast
10. salamander 11. disseminate
sow bug . . . 6. slater
sow thistle . . . 7. Sonchus
soybean . . . 4. Soja 8. soya bean
soybean enzyme . . . 6. urease
spa . . . 3. Ems 4. Bath 5. Baden
6. Bilina (Bilin), hot tub 7. Jacuzzi (tm)
space . . . 3. gap 4. area, rank, room,
time, void 5. blank, inane, niche,
place, range 6. areola, areole, degree,
extent, vacuum 7. arrange, expanse
8. capacity, distance, interval
9. concourse, elbow room
space (pert to) . . .
architectural . . 6. metope 8. pediment
blank . . 5. chasm 6. hiatus, lacuna
botany (leaves) . . 6. areola
environment . . 5. ambit 8. ambiance
larynx . . 7. glottis
occupied . . 6. volume
ref to . . 5. areal, outer 6. cosmos,
galaxy, pulsar 7. heavens, lacunal,
spatial 8. galactic, infinity 9. black
hole, deep space
storage . . 4. shed 5. attic, depot
6. cellar, garage 9. storeroom,
warehouse
theory . . 7. plenism
time . . 8. interval
travel . . 4. NASA 7. reentry, swingby
8. time warp
traveler . . 5. alien 6. cyborg
8. aeronaut 9. astronaut, cosmonaut
vehicle . . 6. rocket, Skylab 7. shuttle,
sputnik
void . . 5. chasm 7. inanity
wall . . 5. niche
spacious . . . 5. ample, broad, roomy
9. capacious, expansive, extensive
10. commodious, far and wide,
widespread 13. comprehensive
spadassin . . . 5. bravo 7. duelist
9. swordsman
spade . . . 3. dig, loy 4. spud, stag (3–yr
old), suit (cards) 5. slade 6. shovel
11. playing card
spade (pert to) . . .
bone . . 13. shoulder blade
fish . . 5. porgy 10. paddlefish
foot . . 4. toad

grass . . 4. rush
Irish . . 5. slane
money . . 7. Chinese (early)
peat . . 5. slade
triangular . . 5. didle
spae . . . 6. divine 8. foretell
Spain . . . see also *Spanish*
cape . . 9. Trafalgar
capital . . 6. Madrid
city . . 4. Irun 5. Cadiz, Lorca
6. Malaga 7. Cordoba, Granada,
Seville 8. Valencia
city cathedral . . 9. Saragossa
islands . . 5. Ceuta 6. Canary 7. Melilla
8. Balearic
mountain . . 8. Asturias, Pyrenees
old name . . 6. Iberia
palace . . 8. Escorial
river . . 4. Ebro, Muga 5. Tagus
span . . . 3. two 4. arch, join, pair, team
6. bridge, extend, length, period (time)
7. breadth, measure, stretch
8. overarch 9. encompass
spangle . . . 6. aiglet, sequin 7. glitter,
sparkle 8. ornament, zecchino
spaniel . . . 5. trasy 6. cocker
8. Brittany, springer
Spanish (pert to) . . .
arbor . . 6. ramada
battle . . 6. Armada (1588)
bayonet . . 5. yucca
boat . . 5. aviso 7. galleon (ship)
Christmas . . 7. Navidad
cloak . . 4. capa 5. manta 6. mantle
7. zamarra (zamarro)
corral . . 5. atajo
dance . . 5. tango 6. bolero, gitano
8. fandango, saraband
fabric . . 4. crea (cotton) 5. tiraz (silk)
fortress chief . . 4. caid 7. alcaide
friend . . 5. amigo
fruit . . 8. pimiento
game . . 6. pelota 7. jai alai
garment . . 6. serape 8. mantilla
gift holder . . 6. piñata
gold . . 3. oro 8. El Dorado
governor . . 10. gobernador
grass . . 5. spart 7. esparto
gruel . . 5. atole
gypsy . . 7. zincalo
holiday . . 6. fiesta
horse . . 5. genet 6. jennet 7. caballo
hotel . . 6. posada
house . . 4. casa 6. casita
jar . . 4. olla, tina 6. tinaja
knight . . 8. cavalier 9. caballero
lake . . 4. lago
language . . 6. Basque 7. Catalan,
Spanish 8. Galician 9. Castilian
mausoleum . . 8. Escorial
musical instrument . . 6. atabel, guitar
8. castanet
plant . . 3. aji 8. capsicum
porridge . . 5. atole
promenade . . 5. paseo
raisin . . 4. pasa
river . . 3. ria, rio
road . . 6. camino
room . . 4. sala
shawl . . 5. manta 6. serape
sheep . . 6. merino
sherry . . 5. Xeres 7. oloroso

sorcerer.. **5**. brujo
street.. **5**. calle
three.. **4**. tres
title.. **3**. don **5**. señor **6**. señora
 7. hidalgo **8**. señorita
trail.. **6**. camino
vehicle.. **7**. tartana
watch.. **5**. reloj
watchtower.. **7**. atalaya
watchword.. **6**. alerta
watercourse.. **6**. arroyo
wind.. **6**. solano
window.. **7**. ventana
witchcraft.. **8**. brujeria
year.. **3**. ano
Spanish people...
chaperone.. **6**. duenna
conqueror.. **7**. Pizarro
dramatist.. **9**. Echegaray (Nobel Prize
 1904)
explorer.. **7**. Mendoza
gentleman.. **5**. señor **8**. cavalier
 9. caballero
God.. **4**. Dios
herdsman.. **7**. llanero **8**. ranchero
hero.. **3**. Cid
justice of the peace.. **7**. entrada
king.. **6**. Aragon **8**. Alphonso
lady.. **4**. doña **6**. señora **8**. señorita
letter carrier.. **6**. correo
man.. **3**. don **6**. hombre
monk.. **5**. padre
painter.. **4**. Dali, Goya **9**. Velasquez
peasant.. **7**. paisano
people.. **5**. genta
pianist.. **6**. Iturbi
soldier.. **8**. miquelet
soprano.. **4**. Bori (Lucrezia)
spar... **3**. box **4**. beam, boom, gaff,
 mast, rung, yard **5**. sprit, steve
 6. timber **7**. dispute, quarrel,
 topmast, yardarm
spare... **4**. lean, thin **5**. chary, lanky
 6. afford, exempt, frugal, meager,
 scanty **7**. sparing, surplus
 8. preserve **9**. duplicate, parsimony
 10. economical, occasional
 11. superfluous **12**. parsimonious
spare time... **7**. leisure
sparing... **5**. chary **6**. frugal, meager,
 saving, scanty **7**. scrimpy, thrifty
 8. merciful, reticent, stinting
 9. scrimping **12**. parsimonious
spark... **4**. beau, fire, funk **5**. aizle,
 court, dandy, lover **6**. incite
 7. diamond, gallant, glitter, modicum,
 sparkle **8**. humorist **10**. sweetheart
 11. scintillate
sparkle... **5**. flash, gleam, glint, shine,
 trace **7**. be smart, be witty, glisten,
 glister, glitter, radiate, reflect,
 spangle, twinkle **8**. be lively
 9. coruscate **10**. effervesce,
 illuminate **11**. scintillate
 13. scintillation
sparkling... **4**. dewy **5**. crisp, witty
 6. bright, starry **7**. shining
 8. cheerful, eloquent, glittery,
 gorgeous, mousseux (wine)
 9. twinkling **10**. glittering, reflecting
 12. effervescent
sparoid fish... **4**. scup **5**. porgy

 8. sea bream **10**. sheepshead
Sparta, Greece... see also *Spartan*
 capital.. **7**. Laconia (anc)
 kingdom.. **12**. Peloponnesus
 river.. **7**. Eurotas
spartan... **5**. hardy, stoic
 10. courageous **13**. uncomplaining
Spartan (pert to)...
 army division.. **4**. mora **6**. lochus
 cipher writing.. **7**. scytale
 class (anc).. **8**. perioeci
 commander.. **7**. lochage
 dog.. **10**. bloodhound
 festival.. **6**. Carnea **7**. Carneia
 king.. **8**. Leonidas, Menelaus
 lawgiver.. **8**. Lycurgus
 magistrate.. **5**. ephor
 native.. **8**. Laconian **9**. Spartiate
 serf.. **5**. helot
spasmodic... **6**. fitful **7**. snatchy
 9. excitable, irregular **10**. convulsive
 12. intermittent **13**. highly wrought
spasmodic (pert to)...
 disease.. **5**. croup **7**. tetanus
 inspiration.. **8**. hiccough
 twitch.. **3**. tic
spat... **3**. row **4**. slap, tiff **5**. spawn
 6. gaiter, oyster, strike **7**. dispute,
 legging, quarrel **10**. oysterseed
spate... **4**. gush **5**. flood **7**. freshet,
 torrent **10**. overwhelm, rainstorm
 10. waterspout
spatial... **5**. areal **8**. sterical
 11. dimensional
spatter... **3**. wet **4**. soil, spot **5**. spurt
 6. dabble, splash **7**. sputter
 8. splutter, sprinkle
spawn... **3**. ova, roe **4**. eggs, germ,
 seed **7**. lay eggs **8**. generate
 13. numerous issue
speak... **3**. say **4**. chat, lisp, talk, tell
 5. orate, utter **6**. reveal **7**. address,
 chatter, declaim, sputter **8**. converse,
 proclaim **9**. discourse, pronounce
 10. articulate **11**. tell in words
speak (pert to)...
 affectedly.. **4**. mime **5**. mince
 against.. **6**. oppose
 boastfully.. **4**. brag **5**. vaunt
 7. enlarge **10**. exaggerate
 from memory.. **6**. recite
 ill of.. **5**. decry **8**. backbite
 9. disparage
 noisily.. **4**. rant, rime **8**. harangue
 offhand.. **11**. extemporize
 slowly.. **5**. drawl
 softly.. **7**. whisper
 under breath.. **5**. mouth **6**. mumble,
 murmur, mutter **7**. grumble
speaker... **5**. sayer **6**. lisper, orator,
 proser **8**. lecturer **9**. demagogue
 10. mouthpiece, prolocutor
 11. spellbinder
speaker of languages... **8**. linguist,
 polyglot
speaking (pert to)...
 generally.. **7**. as a rule, roughly
 12. in the long run
 13. approximately
 of.. **7**. apropos **12**. incidentally
 offhand.. **13**. extemporizing
 privately.. **7**. whisper **9**. in one's ear

11. into one's ear
publicly.. 7. oratory 11. declamation
style.. 8. fluently
spear... 4. dart, pike, stab 5. catch,
lance 6. pierce, weapon 7. javelin,
missile 9. penetrate
spear (pert to)...
anc Teutons.. 6. framea (fram)
fish.. 3. gig 4. gaff
iron–tipped.. 7. assagai
shaped.. 7. hastate
three–pronged.. 7. trident
two–pronged.. 6. bident
spearfish... 6. marlin 9. quillback
special... 4. rare 5. extra 6. unique
7. notable, unusual 8. concrete,
detailed, favorite, specific, uncommon
10. individual, noteworthy, particular,
restricted 11. distinctive, exceptional
13. extraordinary
special (pert to)...
ability.. 5. forte 6. talent 7. charism
8. charisma
commodity.. 6. leader 7. feature
10. best seller
edition.. 5. extra
favor.. 9. influence, privilege
train.. 5. flier 7. express
10. cannonball
specialist (pert to)...
atomic.. 9. physicist
ear.. 6. aurist 9. otologist
eye.. 7. oculist 15. ophthalmologist
medical.. 6. doctor 7. surgeon
money.. 9. economist
specialty... 5. skill 8. aptitude,
contract 13. particularity
14. characteristic
specie... 4. cash, coin 5. money (hard)
species... 4. kind, sort, type 5. class,
genre, genus, group 7. general,
isotope, mankind, variety 8. category,
humanity 11. Homo sapiens
12. nomenclature
specific... 5. exact, virus 6. remedy
7. limited, precise, special
8. definite, detailed, explicit, peculiar
specificity... 9. haecceity
specify... 4. name 5. limit, state
6. define, detail 8. indicate 9. be
precise, designate, enumerate,
stipulate
specimen... 4. copy 5. model, piece,
taste, token 6. person, sample,
swatch 7. example, pattern
14. representative
specious... 4. fair 5. showy 7. alleged
8. illusory, pleasing 9. plausible
10. ostensible 12. hypocritical
speck... 3. bit, dot, jot, nit 4. blot,
iota, mark, mite, mote, spot, whit
5. fleck, stain 7. blemish 8. particle
10. sand darter
speckled... 6. menald 7. mottled
9. sprinkled 10. variegated
spectacle... 4. show, view 5. scene,
sight 6. wonder 7. diorama, display,
pageant 8. panorama, spyglass
10. exhibition 14. representation
spectacles... 7. glasses
spectator... 6. espier, viewer
7. watcher, witness 8. audience,

beholder, kibitzer, looker–on, observer,
onlooker 9. bystander
specter, spectre... 4. bogy (bogey,
bogie) 5. ghost, shade, spook
6. idolum, spirit, wraith 7. eidolon,
phantom 8. illusion, phantasm,
revenant 10. apparition
spectral... 5. eerie (eery) 6. ghosty,
spooky 7. ghostly, phantom
12. apparitional
speculate... 5. guess, think 6. gamble,
ponder, wonder 8. consider,
meditate, ruminate, theorize
10. deliberate, doctrinize, philosophy
11. contemplate
speculative... 5. risky 9. uncertain
10. thoughtful 11. inquisitive,
theoretical 12. experimental
13. contemplative
speculator... 7. lookout, scalper
8. explorer, observer, theorist
12. investigator
speculum... 7. diopter 9. reflector
sped... 4. hied 5. raced 6. darted,
dashed, let fly 8. galloped, hastened
10. discharged
speech... 5. spiel 6. dilogy, orison
7. address, chatter, diction, oration
8. colloquy, harangue, language
9. elocution, utterance
12. conversation
speech (pert to)...
abusive.. 6. tirade
blunder.. 8. improper, solecism
comb form.. 4. logo
conclusion.. 10. peroration
conversational.. 13. colloquialism
defective.. 10. disphrasia
difficulty.. 9. baryphony
10. baryphonia
famous.. 9. Philippic (Demosthenes)
goddess.. 3. Vac
hasty.. 7. stammer, stumble, stutter
impediment.. 4. lisp 8. betacism,
mytacism
intemperate.. 6. tirade
loss of.. 6. alalia 7. aphasia
movements.. 9. vocimotor
parts.. 4. verb 6. adverb 9. adjective
11. conjunction, preposition
12. interjection
pompous.. 12. magniloquent
provincial.. 6. patois 7. dialect
set speech (drama).. 6. rhesis
term.. 6. zeugma 9. syllepsis
understatement.. 7. litotes
vitriolic.. 6. tirade
voiceless.. 7. spirate
without.. 4. mute 6. alogia
world.. 7. Volapük 9. Esperanto
speechless... 4. dumb, mute 6. silent
7. aphasic 8. taciturn 9. voiceless
speed... 3. fly, hie, run 4. flit, race,
zoom 5. haste, hurry, spurt 6. assist,
go fast, hasten 8. celerity, dispatch,
expedite, promptly, rapidity, velocity
9. posthaste, quickness, swiftness
10. accelerate, expedition, facilitate
12. precipitance
speedily... 4. soon 5. apace 6. presto
7. betimes, quickly, rapidly, swiftly
8. promptly 13. expeditiously

speedy... 4. fast 5. apace, fleet, hasty, quick, rapid, swift 6. prompt, racing, sudden

spell... 4. bout, mean, snap, tell, turn 5. charm, magic, relay, shift 6. glamor, relate, relief, trance 7. explain, relieve, sorcery, syncope 9. take turns 11. abracadabra 12. entrancement 13. substitute for

spell (pert to)...
binder.. 6. orator 7. charmer, spieler
bound.. 10. astonished, interested 11. under a spell
brief.. 4. snap
in another alphabet.. 13. transliterate
out.. 7. explain, itemize
pretended.. 11. abracadabra
under a spell.. 9. in a trance 10. hypnotized, mesmerized
with loss of letter.. 7. syncope

spend... 3. use 4. pass 5. waste 6. employ, expend, lavish, weaken 7. consume, exhaust 8. disburse, squander 9. dissipate, sacrifice 10. distribute

spend the summer... 8. estivate (aestivate)

spendthrift... 4. daft 6. waster 7. spender, wastrel 8. prodigal 10. profligate, squanderer

Spenser, Edmund (pert to)...
character.. 3. Una
famed as.. 4. poet
famed work.. 12. Faerie Queene
poetic stanza.. 10. Spenserian

Spenser's Ireland personified... 5. Irene

spent... 4. paid 5. weary 6. effete, used up, wasted 7. worn out 8. consumed, lavished, tired out 9. exhausted 10. squandered

speos... 4. cave, tomb 6. grotto

sphenoid... 11. wedge–shaped

sphere... 3. orb 4. ball, star 5. arena, earth, field, glove, orbit, realm, scope 6. extent, planet 7. circuit, heavens 8. terrible 10. atmosphere 12. jurisdiction

sphere of...
action.. 6. domain
life.. 5. world
making.. 7. orbific

spherical (pert to)...
aberration, free from.. 9. aplanatic
geometry.. 10. magnitudes
lune.. 7. portion
magnet.. 8. terrella (terella)
nearly.. 8. obrotund
reference to.. 6. rotund 7. globose 9. orbicular 15. celestial bodies
ungula.. 5. wedge

sphericity... 9. globosity, rotundity, roundness

sphinx (pert to)...
builder (Great Sphinx).. 6. Khafre (IV Dynasty)
Great Sphinx site.. 4. Gaza (Egypt)
Greek myth.. 7. monster (sphinxlike)
reference to.. 9. enigmatic 11. inscrutable
Zool.. 8. hawk moth

spice... 4. dill, herb, mace, sage

5. chili, clove 6. cassia, nutmeg, pepper, season, stacte 7. mustard 8. marjoram, pungency 9. condiment, flavoring, fragrance, seasoning

spicy... 3. hot 4. keen, racy, sexy 5. balmy, natty, smart 6. risque 7. gingery, peppery, piquant, pungent 8. aromatic, fragrant, spirited

spider... 3. cob, pan 5. arain 6. Epeira, katipo, tripod, trivet 7. pokomoo, retiary, skillet, spinner 8. arachnid, attercop, telarian 9. tarantula 10. black widow

spider (pert to)...
comb form.. 7. arachno
crab.. 4. Maia (genus)
fly.. 4. tick
genus.. 4. Maia 6. Aranea 7. Agalena, Attidae, Pholcus 9. Drassidae
Gr Myth.. 7. Arachne (Lydian girl)
Latin.. 6. aranea
leaping.. 10. saltigrade
monkey.. 6. ateles, coaita
nest.. 5. nidus
scorpion.. 8. pedipalp
scorpion appendage.. 10. pedipalpus
study of.. 10. araneology
web (anc).. 8. attercop
weblike.. 9. arachnoid
web–spinning organ.. 9. spinneret

spieler... 5. crier 6. barker, talker 7. sharper, speaker 8. lecturer 9. solicitor 10. ballyhooer

spiffy... 4. fine, neat 5. smart 8. splendid 9. excellent

spigot... 3. peg, tap 5. spile, spout 6. dossil, faucet 7. stopper

spike... 3. cob, ear 4. brob, stab, tine, umbo 5. ament, prong, thorn 6. antler, flower, pierce, spadix 7. amentum, disable, spinule, trenail 10. adulterate 12. tenpenny nail

spikenard... 3. phu (Cretan) 4. herb, nard 8. ointment

spile... 3. pin, rod 4. plug, tube 5. spill, spout, stake 6. Aralia, spigot

spill... 4. blab, fall, shed, slop 5. flosh, waste 6. let out, splash, tumble 7. divulge, scatter 8. downpour, overflow, overture 11. tell secrets

spin... 4. birl, fish, reel, ride, turn 5. swirl, twirl, twist, whirl 6. extend, gyrate, rotate 7. prolong, revolve

spinach (wrinkled)... 5. savoy

spinal (pert to)...
column.. 9. vertebrae
cord.. 4. alba 6. myelon (marrow) 16. medulla oblongata
disease.. 8. myelitis 10. meningitis
muscle (attached).. 5. psoas

spindle... 3. pin, rod 4. axis, axle, hasp 5. pivot, xeres 6. swivel 7. mandrel

spindle–legged... 4. lean 5. lanky 14. spindle–shanked

spindling... 4. long 5. gawky, leggy 6. skinny 7. slender 11. ineffectual

spine... 3. awn 4. axis, seta 5. chine, ridge, thorn 6. spirit 7. acicula,

courage, process 8. backbone,
spiculum 9. scoliosis (curvature)
12. spinal column

spinel . . . 5. balas (ruby) 7. mineral
8. spinelle

spineless . . . 4. limp, weak 5. frail
10. weak–willed 12. invertebrate

spinet . . . 5. piano 7. giraffe 8. virginal
10. clavichord 11. couched harp,
harpsichord

spinnaker . . . 4. sail

spinner . . . 3. top 4. liar 6. spider,
weaver 8. narrator 9. nighthawk
10. goatsucker 11. storyteller
12. whippoorwill

spinning . . . 6. rotary 7. strobic
8. telarian, whirling 9. revolving

spinning device . . . 5. jenny 7. distaff,
spindle 8. throstle

spiracle . . . 4. pore, vent 7. orifice
8. aperture, blowhole

spiral . . . 4. coil, curl 5. helix 6. galaxy,
volute 7. helical, winding 8. circling,
helicoid 9. corkscrew

spire . . . 4. coil, surl 5. tower, twist,
whorl 6. ascend, finial, summit
7. steeple

spire finial . . . 3. épi

spirit . . . 3. imp, pep, vim 4. dash,
élan, fire, life, mood, pixy, soul
5. demon, devil, fairy, genie, ghost,
heart, metal, pluck, Satan, shade,
spook, verve 6. animus, breath,
energy, fervor, goblin, intent, morale,
pneuma, sprite 7. bravery, courage,
essence, extract, gremlin, specter
8. spiritus 9. animation
10. enterprise, individual 11. real
meaning 12. cheerfulness
13. consciousness

spirit, spirit of (pert to) . . .
avarice . . 6. Mammon
bad . . 6. afreet 7. Amaimon
(Amaymon)
Egypt . . 2. ba, ka 3. akh
English folklore . . 2. po
evil . . 4. jinn 5. Aecto, jinni (jinnel)
6. Azazel, Belial, Erinys 7. Tempter
(The) 9. Beelzebub
female . . 6. undine 7. banshee
good . . 8. Eudaemon
household . . 5. Lares 15. Lares and
Penates
infatuation . . 3. Ate
knights . . 8. errantry
malignant . . 3. Ker
mockery . . 5. Momus
people . . 5. ethos
refined . . 6. elixir
tapping (theory) . . 9. typtology
the air . . 5. Ariel
the sea . . 5. siren 6. Triton
7. mermaid, Neptune 9. Davy Jones

spirited . . . 3. gay 4. gamy, racy
5. brisk, eager, fiery 6. lively, plucky,
spunky 7. dashing, fervent
8. eloquent, generous, vigorous
9. audacious, energetic, spiritoso,
sprightly 10. mettlesome

spiritless . . . 4. dead, dull, meek
5. amort, vapid 6. gloomy
8. dejected, lifeless, listless

9. depressed, heartless
10. despondent, dispirited

spirits (pert to) . . .
Babylonian . . 5. Igigi
dwelling . . 2. po 5. Hades 7. Elysium
low . . 5. blues, dumps, gloom
8. doldrums
of the dead . . 5. Manes (Rom)
7. lemures 9. chthonian (Gr)

spiritual . . . 4. holy, pure, song
5. pious 6. devout, divine, sacred
7. psychic 8. churchly, internal,
platonic, spectral 9. unworldly
10. immaterial 11. disembodied,
incorporeal 12. supernatural
14. ecclesiastical, heavenly minded

spiritual (pert to) . . .
affinity . . 8. soul mate
apathy . . 6. acedia
being . . 3. ens 5. angel 6. seraph
darkness . . 4. Hell 5. tamas
director . . 9. confessor
meaning of words . . 7. anagoge
meeting . . 6. séance
shrine . . 6. adytum 7. sanctum

spirt . . . 3. jet 4. gush 5. flare, spurt
6. squirt

spit . . . 3. rod 4. rain 5. eject, image,
stick 6. impale, pierce, saliva,
skewer, sputum 7. hissing, spindle,
sputter 8. likeness, sprinkle, turnspit
9. exsputory 11. expectorate

spite . . . 3. vex 4. hate 5. pique,
shame, venom 6. enmity, malice,
offend, thwart 7. dislike, ill will
8. disgrace, dishonor 9. animosity,
cattiness, humiliate 10. resentment
11. malevolence 12. spitefulness

spiteful . . . 4. mean 5. catty 7. cattish
8. annoying 9. malicious, malignant
10. irritating, vindictive

spittoon . . . 6. pigdan 8. crachoir,
cuspidor

splash . . . 3. lap, wet 4. spot 5. spray,
swash 6. blotch, flouse (floush),
ripple 7. scatter, spatter, splurge
8. cut a dash, splatter 9. dashingly
14. ostentatiously

splashboard . . . 4. gate (false) 5. plank
6. fender, screen 9. dashboard
10. flashboard, flushboard

splay . . . 3. hem 4. turn 5. adorn,
carve, slant, slope 6. clumsy,
expand, spread 7. awkward, display
9. dislocate, displayed, expansion

spleen . . . 3. fit 4. fire, mood, whim
5. anger, ardor, freak, gland
6. malice, temper 7. impulse 8. ill
humor 10. low spirits, melancholy,
resentment 11. impetuosity

spleen (pert to) . . .
amarinth . . 4. weed
excision . . 13. splenectomize
reference to . . 6. lienal 7. splenic

splendid . . . 4. braw, fine 5. grand,
regal, showy 6. costly, superb
7. gallant, shining, sublime
8. glorious, gorgeous 9. beautiful,
brilliant, excellent, sumptuous
10. brilliance, effulgence
11. illustrious, magnificent

splendor . . . 4. gite, pomp 5. éclat,

glory **6.** beauty, luster **7.** display
8. grandeur, radiance, richness
9. pageantry, showiness **10.** brilliance
12. gorgeousness, magnificence,
resplendence
splint ... **4.** scob, tace **5.** brace, plate,
strip **6.** fasten, tasset **7.** confine
splinter ... **4.** chip **5.** break, broom
6. shiver, sliver **7.** shatter
8. fragment **9.** matchwood
split ... **3.** cut, rit **4.** chap, open, rend,
rent, rive, tear **5.** break, burst, cleft,
crack, laugh, leave (sl), riven, wedge
6. bisect, cleave, cloven, depart (sl),
divide, sunder **7.** dispart, divided,
rupture, shatter **8.** separate
9. apportion, partition **10.** separation
split (pert to) ...
 hairs .. **7.** quibble **12.** discriminate
  13. differentiate
 into two parts .. **5.** bifid **6.** cloven
 pea .. **3.** dal **5.** dahll
 the difference .. **5.** share **7.** average
  10. compromise **12.** go fifty–fifty
 up .. **5.** cleft **7.** disband, divorce
  8. separate **9.** apportion, partition
spoil ... **3.** mar, rot **4.** loot, prey, ruin,
sack **5.** botch, decay, harry
6. coddle, impair, injure, pamper
7. destroy, estrepe, louse up (sl),
pillage, plunder, vitiate **9.** frustrate
spoilation ... **6.** rapine **7.** pillage
10. plundering, spoliation
spoiled ... **3.** bad **5.** moldy, musty
6. addled, marred, molded, preyed,
wasted **7.** botched, bungled, decayed,
tainted **8.** pampered, pillaged
9. plundered **12.** deteriorated
spoiler ... **6.** robber **7.** marplot
8. pillager **9.** despoiler, plunderer
spoils ... **4.** loot, prey, swag **5.** booty,
perks (sl) **11.** perquisites
spoilsport ... **7.** marplot **10.** wet
blanket **11.** party–pooper
spoke ... **3.** bar, pin, ray, rod **4.** rung,
said **5.** check, round, spake, stake
6. radius, speech **7.** uttered
9. hindrance **10.** impediment
spoke monotonously ... **6.** droned
spoken ... **4.** oral **5.** parol
9. declaimed, ideophone (word)
spoliation ... **6.** rapine **7.** pillage
8. ravaging **10.** spoilation
sponge ... **3.** dry, wet **4.** bath, swab
5. erase, mooch **6.** absorb, animal,
efface, eraser, extort **7.** badiaga,
cleanse, sponger, zimocca
8. drunkard, parasite **9.** absorbent,
sycophant **10.** obliterate, porousness
sponge (pert to) ...
 Europe .. **7.** badiaga
 fruit .. **5.** luffa (loofah)
 Mediterranean .. **7.** zimocca
 opening .. **7.** apopyle
 orifice .. **7.** osculum
 young .. **5.** ascon **6.** rhagon
sponger ... **4.** sorn **5.** leech **6.** cadger
7. moocher **8.** parasite **9.** scrounger
10. freeloader
sponsor ... **5.** angel **6.** backer, patron
7. finance **9.** financier, godparent,
guarantee, guarantor, patronize

sponsorship ... **5.** aegis (egis)
7. subsidy **8.** auspices
spontaneous ... **4.** free **6.** native
8. untaught **9.** automatic, voluntary
10. self–acting **11.** instinctive,
involuntary
spontoon ... **4.** club, pike **7.** halberd,
pantoon **9.** espantoon, truncheon
spoof ... **3.** guy **4.** fool, hoax, joke
5. trick **7.** deceive, swindle
8. nonsense **9.** deception
spook ... **5.** ghost **6.** spirit, zombie
(zombi) **7.** specter **8.** frighten
9. hobgoblin **10.** apparition
spooky ... **5.** eerie, weird **7.** ghostly,
haunted, uncanny **8.** spectral
spool ... **4.** reel, wind **6.** bobbin
7. spindle **8.** cylinder
spoon ... **4.** club **5.** labis, ladle
6. shovel **7.** fish for **8.** cochlear,
make love, runcible
spoonbill ... **5.** ajaja (ayaya)
9. sandpiper
Spoon River poet ... **7.** Masters (E L)
spore (pert to) ...
 capsule, sac .. **5.** ascus, theca
  10. sporangium
 cluster .. **5.** sorus
 formation .. **6.** tetrad
 fruit .. **7.** asocarp
sport ... **3.** fun, toy **4.** game, hunt, jest,
joke, play, romp, wear **5.** dandy,
mirth **6.** banter, flaunt, frolic, gamble,
racing, skiing **7.** contest, gambler,
jesting, mockery, pastime **8.** raillery
9. amusement, bon vivant, diversion,
good loser, plaything, sportsman
10. pleasantry, recreation
13. entertainment
sport (pert to) ...
 art of (contests) .. **10.** agonistics
 cheap .. **5.** piker
 of kings .. **6.** racing **7.** the turf
sportive ... **3.** gay **5.** merry **7.** jocular,
playful **8.** frolicky, playsome
9. facetious **10.** frolicsome
sports ... **5.** Rugby, track **6.** hockey, jai
lai, soccer, squash, tennis **7.** cricket
8. baseball, football, la crosse, softball
9. athletics, palaestra **10.** acrobatics,
gymnastics **11.** racquetball
sports attendance ... **4.** gate
sports official ... **5.** coach, judge
6. umpire **7.** referee **8.** linesman
10. timekeeper
sporty ... **5.** rorty, showy **6.** dressy,
flashy
spot ... **3.** dot **4.** blet, blot, espy, flaw,
mark, site, soil **5.** fleck, place, point,
speck, stain, taint **6.** detect, locate,
macula, macule, stigma **7.** asperse,
blemish, freckle, observe, speckle,
splotch **8.** discolor, disgrace, locality,
location, position **9.** bespatter,
limelight, recognize **11.** predicament,
small amount
spot (pert to) ...
 cards .. **3.** pip
 fertile .. **5.** oasis
 fish .. **7.** pinfish
 high .. **4.** apex **5.** climax
 mineral .. **5.** macle

on the spot.. 3. now 4. here
   7. imperil, present 8. promptly
payment.. 4. cash
secluded.. 6. alcove
sun.. 6. lucule 7. granule
wood.. 3. wem
spotless... 4. pure 5. clean 6. chaste
   8. innocent 9. blameless, faultless,
   unsullied 10. immaculate
   11. unblemished, untarnished
   14. irreproachable
spotted... 6. espied, marked, soiled
   7. dappled, guttate (droplike),
   mottled, stained, sullied 8. speckled
   9. blemished, sprinkled, tarnished
   11. diversified
spouse... 4. mate, wife 5. bride
   7. consort, partner 9. companion
   10. better half
spout... 3. jet, jut, lip 4. dale, gush,
   pawn, rant, spew 5. erupt, spile,
   spurt 6. pledge, recite, spigot, squirt,
   trough 7. chatter, conduit, declaim
   8. downpour, gargoyle (carved)
   9. discharge, waterfall
   10. waterspout
spouter... 5. whale 6. geyser 7. oil
   well, speaker 9. declaimer
   11. speechifier
sprat... 6. garvie 7. herring
   8. sixpence
spray... 3. jet 4. foam 5. stour, water
   6. squirt 7. atomize, flowers, gunfire
   8. perfumer, sprinkle 9. spindrift
   10. spoondrift
spread... 3. ted 4. meal 5. bruit,
   feast, flare, strew, widen 6. expand,
   extent, sprawl, unfurl 7. divulge,
   radiate, scatter 8. disperse
   9. broadcast 11. disseminate
   13. advertisement
spread (pert to)...
by defamation.. 5. libel
by report.. 6. norate
by rumor.. 5. noise
eagle.. 8. boastful, insignia
   9. patriotic 12. exaggeration
out.. 3. fan 4. open, span 5. flare
   6. deploy
over.. 5. cover, smear
thickly.. 7. slather
thin.. 4. bray
spree... 4. lark, orgy, romp 5. binge,
   revel 6. bender, frolic, shindy
   7. wassail 8. carousal
sprig... 4. trim, twig 5. scion, shoot,
   smart 6. active, spruce 8. ornament
   9. youngling
sprightly... 3. gay 4. airy, pert
   5. alive, brisk, peart 6. blithe, lively
   7. briskly, ghostly 8. vigorous
   10. enlivening, spiritedly
   11. incorporeal
spring... 3. fly, hop, spa 4. dart, font,
   jump, leap, well 5. shoot, spurt,
   vault, vigor 6. bounce, energy,
   geyser, origin, season, source
   9. saltation 10. elasticity, resilience
spring (pert to)...
back.. 6. recoil, resile 7. rebound
of the Muses.. 7. Pierian
ref to.. 6. vernal

up.. 4. grow 5. arise, occur
   6. appear, ascend 9. originate
springing into being... 9. renascent
springs... 4. spas 5. baths, fonts
   6. resort (health) 7. thermae
sprinkle... 3. deg, dot, wet 4. rain
   5. bedew, spray, strew, water
   6. bedrop, sparge, spreng 7. baptize,
   scatter 9. bespatter
sprinkler... 11. aspergillum (Eccl)
sprinkle with...
flour.. 6. dredge
grit.. 4. sand
heraldic.. 4. semé
powder.. 4. dust
water.. 3. deg
sprint... 3. run 4. dash, race
sprite... 3. elf, fay, hob, imp, nix
   4. peri 5. fairy, ghost, gnome, pixie,
   sylph 6. goblin, spirit 7. brownie
   9. hobgoblin 10. apparition
sprite (pert to)...
fiction.. 5. Ariel
Irish.. 10. leprechaun
mischievous.. 4. Puck
ref to.. 6. elfish
sprocket... 5. tooth, wheel 8. cylinder
   (toothed) 10. projection
sprout... 3. bud, son 4. cion, grow
   5. scion, shoot, spire, sprit
   6. branch, ratoon, tiller 7. burgeon,
   upstart 8. offshoot 9. germinate
   10. descendant
spruce... 4. chic, neat, posh, smug,
   tree, trig, trim 5. adorn, natty, smart
   6. dapper 7. finical, smarten
   8. titivate
spruce (pert to)...
beverage.. 4. beer
black.. 7. yew pine
fir.. 6. Norway
genus.. 5. Abies, Picea
Japanese.. 6. Alcock
type.. 7. Douglas, hemlock
white.. 8. épinette
sprue... 3. dross, waste 6. thrush
   7. disease 8. psilosis 9. asparagus
spry... 5. agile, brisk, quick, smart
   6. active, nimble 8. vigorous
   9. sprightly
spud... 5. drill, knife, spade 6. dagger,
   paddle, potato, reamer, shovel
spume... 4. foam, scum 5. froth
spunky... 4. game 5. quick 6. plucky,
   touchy 8. spirited 10. courageous,
   mettlesome 13. quick-tempered
spur... 3. egg 4. goad, move, urge
   5. drive, press, ridge, rowel, spine
   6. calcar, excite, griffe, incite, needle
   7. provoke 8. stimulus 9. instigate,
   stimulate 10. incitement
spur (pert to)...
badge.. 10. knighthood
fowl.. 5. quail 9. partridge
gamecock's.. 4. gaff 7. gablock
mountain.. 5. arête
pert to.. 7. spicate
railroad.. 5. track
wheel.. 5. rowel
spurious... 4. fake, sham 5. false
   6. pseudo 7. bastard 10. adulterate,
   apocryphal, artificial, fictitious,

fraudulent 11. counterfeit
12. illegitimate 14. supposititious
spurious (pert to) . . .
fruit . . 10. pseudocarp
olive . . 9. heartwood
rainbow . . 8. faint arc
wing . . 7. bastard
spurn . . . 4. defy 5. scorn 6. reject,
strike 7. contemn, disdain
spurt . . . 3. jet, jut 4. dash, gush, spew
5. burst, spout 7. outpour, upsurge
8. outbreak
spy . . . 3. pry, see 4. espy, note, tout
5. scout, sneak, snoop, watch
6. behold, descry, detect, search
7. examine, snooper 8. discover,
emissary, informer, perceive
10. scrutinize 11. reconnoiter
spy (pert to) . . .
city . . 7. Belgium
in clothing circles . . 4. keek
Man of . . 14. paleolithic man
prison . . 6. mouton
squab . . . 3. fat 4. fowl, sofa 5. piper,
plump 6. fat man, pigeon 7. cushion
8. nestling 9. fledgling
squabble . . . 5. brawl 6. bicker, jangle
7. contend, quarrel, wrangle
10. disarrange (Print)
13. collieshangie
squad . . . 4. team, unit 5. posse
7. company
squalid . . . 4. foul, mean, poor 5. dirty
6. filthy, sordid 7. unclean
8. slovenly 9. repellent, repulsive
11. squalidness 15. poverty–stricken
squall . . . 3. cry, row 4. blow, gale,
gust, wail, wind, yell 6. squawk,
squeal 9. commotion 11. disturbance
squalor . . . 4. dirt, mire 5. filth
8. slovenry 9. dirtiness 10. filthiness
11. squalidness 16. unkempt
condition
squander . . . 5. waste 6. lavish
7. scatter 8. disperse, misspend
9. dissipate, throw away 10. run
through
squanderer . . . 5. loser 7. wastrel
square . . . 4. even, meal 5. bribe, plaza
6. common, honest, settle 7. exactly,
obelisk, old fogy 8. absolute, cube
face, directly, equalize, quadrate
9. city block, divergent
11. unequivocal 13. parallelogram
14. unsophisticate
15. straightforward
squash . . . 4. mash, pepo, pulp
5. crush, gourd, press 6. cushaw,
refute, simlin, simnel, soften
7. cymling (cymbling), Hubbard,
squeeze 8. pattypan, suppress
9. crookneck 10. extinguish
11. calabazilla
squat . . . 3. low 5. dumpy, pudgy,
quash, stoop 6. crouch, hunker,
settle, stubby 7. sit down
8. squatter, thickset
squatter . . . 6. nester (illegal) 7. pioneer
9. sandpiper 11. homesteader
Squatter State . . . 6. Kansas
squaw . . . 6. coween, Indian, mahala
(mahaly)

squeal . . . 6. betray, inform 7. protest,
quarrel
squealer . . . 4. fink 6. grouse, pigeon,
plover 7. traitor 8. informer
squeamish . . . 4. nice 5. dizzy
6. dainty, queasy 7. prudish
8. overnice, qualmish 9. nauseated
10. fastidious, scrupulous
squeeze . . . 3. hug, jam, nip 4. cram,
crux 5. crowd, crush, pinch, press,
wring 6. crisis, extort 7. embrace
8. compress 9. constrict, influence
10. constraint 11. compression
squeezer, fruit . . . 6. juicer, reamer
squelch . . . 5. crush, quash, quell
6. rebuke, refute, subdue 7. repress,
silence 8. suppress 10. disconcert
squib . . . 4. bomb, fuse, pipe, skit, tube
6. speech, squirt 7. explode,
lampoon, writing 9. bespatter
10. pasquinade 11. firecracker
squire . . . 4. beau 5. court, lover
6. escort 7. gallant 8. henchman,
nobleman 9. attendant, gentleman,
landowner
squirm . . . 5. twist 6. wiggle, writhe
7. wriggle
squirrel (pert to) . . .
African . . 5. xerus
American . . 5. bunny 7. assapan
8. chipmunk 9. chickaree
American, flying . . 7. assapan
Asian . . 5. sisel 6. suslik
Austral, flying . . 9. phalanger
burrowing . . 6. gopher
cage . . 9. treadmill
color . . 4. lead
E Ind, flying . . 6. taguan
fish . . 7. serrano
fur (Her) . . 4. vair
genus . . 6. Tamias 7. Sciurus
Java . . 8. jelerang
like . . 8. sciuroid
nest . . 4. dray, drey
shrew . . 4. tana 6. Tupaia
skin . . 4. vair
Spanish . . 7. ardilla
squirrellike mammal . . . 8. banxring,
dormouse
stab . . . 4. gore, pang, pink 5. knife,
knive, lunge, wound 6. attack, injury,
pierce, thrust 7. poniard, slander
8. puncture, stoccado
stability . . . 5. poise 7. balance
8. firmness, strength 9. constancy
10. permanence, stableness,
steadiness 11. reliability
12. immovability, immutability
13. steadfastness
stabilize . . . 3. set 5. poise 6. steady
7. ballast 8. regulate
stable . . . 3. mew (Royal) 4. barn, byre,
firm, safe 5. fixed, solid, sound, stall
6. steady, strong 7. durable, lasting,
paddock, support 8. constant, reliable
9. confirmed, permanent, steadfast
10. stationary, unwavering
11. established, trustworthy
stableman . . . 5. groom 7. hostler
(ostler)
staccato . . . 7. détaché 8. ricochet
12. disconnected

stack ... 4. heap, load, pile, rick
5. mound, shock 6. pile up
7. chimney, conduit 8. quantity
stacked ... 11. accumulated,
prearranged
stacked pack, cards ... 8. cold deck
stadium ... 5. stage 6. course, dromos
8. foot race (anc)
stadium race, start ... 7. aphesis
staff ... 3. rod 4. club, mace, pole
5. baton, music, stave 7. scepter,
support 8. caduceus, insignia,
pastoral 9. personnel 10. assistants,
associates
staff (pert to) ...
Bacchus .. 7. thyrsus
bearer .. 5. macer
magician's .. 7. rhabdos
marshal's .. 5. baton
member, officer .. 4. aide 7. attaché
mountain climbing .. 10. alpenstock
pastoral .. 5. pedum 7. baculus,
crosier (crozier)
shepherd's .. 5. crook, pedum
sovereign's .. 7. scepter (sceptre)
stag ... 4. colt, deer (red), hart
5. party, royal, spade 7. male fox,
pollard 8. gamecock, informer
stage ... 4. dais, tier 5. arena, phase,
scene 6. degree 7. display, estrade,
perform, rostrum 8. platform, scaffold
9. dramatize, gradation
10. proscenium, stagecoach
stage (pert to) ...
call (trumpet) .. 6. sennet
direction .. 5. aside, manet 6. sennet
of disease .. 9. catabasis
of insects .. 5. imago, larva
part .. 5. stair 8. dutchman (patch)
10. proscenium
scene (side) .. 8. coulisse
scenery .. 3. set
stagger ... 4. reel, stot, stun, sway,
walk 5. lurch 6. excite, totter, zigzag
7. be drunk, tremble, vibrate
8. astonish, flounder, frighten,
titubate, unsettle 9. alternate,
fluctuate
staggering ... 5. areel 9. startling
10. astounding 11. the staggers
12. unbelievable
Stagirite, The ... 9. Aristotle
stagnant ... 4. dull, foul 5. inert, stale,
still 8. inactive, sluggish, standing
10. motionless, not flowing
13. unprogressive
stagnate ... 3. rot 4. dull 5. inert
8. stagnant, vegetate 10. motionless
staid ... 5. grave, sober 6. demure,
sedate, solemn 7. serious, settled
8. composed, decorous, sensible
9. steadfast
stain ... 3. dye 4. blot, soil, spot, tint
5. color, paint, smear, sully
6. infamy, smudge, stigma
7. blemish, corrupt, pigment, tarnish
8. discolor, disgrace, dishonor,
maculate 9. pollution 10. stigmatize
11. contaminate 13. discoloration
stained by decay ... 4. doty
stained glass rod (lead) ... 4. came
stair ... 4. step 5. riser, stage, tread

6. degree, flight (series)
staircase (pert to) ...
French .. 8. escalier
moving .. 9. escalator
outdoor .. 6. perron
post .. 5. newel
ship's .. 12. companionway
spiral .. 8. caracole
stairs to bath (Ind) ... 4. ghat (ghaut)
stake ... 3. bet, peg, pel, pin 4. ante,
pale, pile, post, risk, spit 5. sowel,
teest, wager 6. chance, estate,
gamble, hazard, picket, pledge
7. finance, venture
stale ... 3. old 5. banal, fusty, trite,
vapid 7. insipid, spoiled
9. hackneyed, tasteless 10. flavorless
11. commonplace
stalemate ... 6. corner 7. impasse
8. cul–de–sac, deadlock 10. blind
alley, standstill
stalk ... 4. axis, hunt, risp, stem, walk
6. pursue, stride 7. pedicel
8. peduncle 11. reconnoiter
stalk (pert to) ...
cotton, sugar cane .. 6. ratoon
dry .. 3. hay, kex 5. haulm (halm)
flower .. 7. petiole
grain, grass .. 4. culm 5. straw
6. ressum
strawberry .. 4. risp
stalkless ... 7. sessile
stall ... 3. cot, pew 4. crib, fail, loge,
mire, stop 5. booth, check, choir,
stick 6. hinder, manger, stable
7. disgust 9. temporize 10. dillydally
11. compartment 12. parking space
13. procrastinate
stalwart ... 5. brave, stout 6. strong,
sturdy 7. valiant 8. partisan, resolute
9. corpulent 10. courageous,
unyielding
stamina ... 5. pluck, vigor 7. courage
8. backbone, strength 9. endurance,
fortitude 12. staying power
stammer ... 3. haw, hem 4. mant
6. falter 7. stumble, stutter
8. hesitate
stammering ... 8. psellism
stamp ... 3. die 4. date, dink, form,
mark, seal, sign, tool 5. brand, infix,
label 6. signet 7. engrave, impress,
imprint, postage, trading 8. tressure
(tressour) 11. endorsement
14. characteristic
stamp (pert to) ...
border .. 8. tressure (tressour)
collecting .. 9. philately
collector .. 11. philatelist
madness .. 11. timbromania
paper .. 6. pelure
postage .. 6. timbre
space .. 8. spandrel
stampede ... 3. run 4. rout, rush
5. panic 6. flight 7. debacle
11. wild scamper
stance ... 4. pose 7. posture, station
8. position
stanch ... 5. allay, check, quell
6. steady, strong 7. zealous
8. faithful 9. steadfast 10. extinguish
11. substantial

stanchion ... 3. bar 4. post, prop
  5. brace, piton 6. secure 7. support,
  upright
stand ... 4. bear, bier, halt, rack, stop,
  zarf 5. abide, arise, booth, easel,
  store, table 6. endure, tripod
  7. coaster, étagère, footing, impasse,
  sustain, taboret 8. attitude, foothold,
  pedestal, position, tolerate
  9. withstand 10. standstill
stand (pert to) ...
  against .. 6. resist
  by .. 3. aid 6. defend 7. support
    9. be present
  cost of .. 5. treat
  Eccl .. 4. ambo
  for .. 6. permit, typify 9. represent,
    symbolize
  for candles .. 7. epergne
    10. candelabra
  in .. 6. deputy 10. substitute
  it .. 4. bear 5. brook 6. suffer
  offish .. 4. cold 5. aloof 8. reserved
    10. not cordial
  opposite .. 4. face
  three–legged .. 6. teapoy, tripod, trivot
  up to .. 5. brave 6. resist
standard ... 3. par 4. flag, norm
  5. grade, model, usual 6. ensign
  7. average, classic, paragon, precept
  8. orthodox 9. customary, principle
  13. authoritative
standard (pert to) ...
  battle .. 9. oriflamme (oriflamb)
  bearer .. 6. leader 7. officer
    10. politician
  chem test .. 5. titer (titre)
  ensign .. 8. gonfalon, gonfanon
  flag (Rom) .. 8. vexillum
  of excellence .. 4. idea
  of intelligence .. 5. Binet
  of light .. 6. carcel
  of quantity .. 4. unit
  Ottoman Emp .. 4. alem
standardize ... 9. calibrate, normalize
standing ... 4. rank 5. fixed, state
  6. at rest, status 7. footing, settled,
  station, upright 8. duration, prestige
  9. permanent 10. durability,
  reputation
standing (pert to) ...
  long .. 7. durable 8. duration
    11. traditional
  mode of .. 6. stance
  out .. 7. eminent, salient
  room only .. 3. SRO
  social .. 6. estate, status 8. prestige
  upright .. 11. orthostatic
stannum ... 2. Sn 3. tin
stanza ... 4. rann, unit 5. stave, verse
  6. octave, sestet 7. strophe, triolet
  (8–lined)
stanza scheme ... 6. ballad 10. Gray's
  Elegy, Spenserian
star ... 3. sun 4. hero, lead 5. actor,
  shine 6. étoile 7. destiny, fortune
  8. asterisk, insignia, ornament
  9. emphasize, principal
  11. hummingbird 12. heavenly body,
  luminous body
star (pert to) ... see also *Stars*
  brightest .. 3. Cor, sun 5. Deneb

  6. Altair, Lucida, Sirius
Bull's Eye .. 9. Aldebaran
divination .. 9. astrology
Dog .. 4. Sept 6. Sirius 8. Canicula
  12. Canis Majoris
evening .. 5. Venus 6. Hesper, Vesper
  7. evestar 8. Hesperus
feather .. 9. comatulid
five–pointed .. 9. pentagram, pentalpha
French .. 6. étoile
gazer .. 4. fish 10. astronomer
giant .. 10. Betelgeuse (Betelgeux)
group (fixed) .. 13. constellation
guiding .. 5. Alpha, North 7. Polaris
  8. Cynosure, loadstar, lodestar,
  polestar
large .. 5. Rigel
morning .. 4. Mars 5. Venus 6. Saturn
  7. daystar, Jupiter, Mercury
  8. Phosphor
new .. 4. Nova
North .. 7. Polaris 8. loadstar, lodestar
of Africa .. 15. Cullinan diamond
of Bethlehem (Bib) .. 11. guide of
  Magi
of the sea .. 11. Maris Stella (Stella
  Maris)
ornament .. 4. semé
path .. 5. orbit
ref to .. 6. astral, starry 7. sideral,
  stellar 8. sidereal 9. planatoid
representation .. 6. étoile
shooting .. 5. comet 6. Leonid, meteor
starch ... 3. vim 4. sago 5. hilum,
  vigor 6. amidin, energy, farina, fecula
  7. cassava 8. glycogen 9. arrowroot,
  formality, stiffness
starchy ... 5. stiff 6. formal, viscid
  7. amyloid, precise 9. unbending
stare ... 4. gape, gawk, gaze, look,
  ogle, peer 5. glare 6. glower,
  goggle, wonder
starfish ... 7. asteria 10. echinoderm
stark ... 4. bare, mere 5. rigid, tense
  6. barren, wholly 7. violent
  8. absolute, complete, entirely
  9. downright, unadorned
  10. absolutely
starling ... 4. myna, sali 6. pastor
Stars (pert to) ...
  and Bars .. 15. Confederate flag
  belt, tract (luminous) .. 6. Galaxy
    8. Milky Way
  circumpolar group .. 5. Draco
    6. Dragon
  four (famed) .. 4. Crux 13. Southern
    Cross
  North Pole group .. 9. Great Bear
    10. Little Bear 11. Septentrion
  Ursa Major .. 9. Big Dipper, Great
    Bear
  Ursa Minor .. 10. Little Bear 12. Little
    Dipper
start ... 4. dart, dash, jerk, rush
  5. begin, enter, sally 6. broach,
  origin, twitch 7. get away, startle
  8. commence 9. advantage,
  beginning, departure, originate
  10. inaugurate
starting point ... 4. text (sermon)
  7. scratch 9. departure
startle ... 5. alarm, rouse, scare, shock

6. excite, fright 8. astonish
9. electrify
starve . . . 3. die 4. kill 5. crave
6. famish, perish, scrimp 7. atrophy,
destroy 10. be indigent
starved . . . 4. thin 5. empty 6. frozen,
hungry 8. famished, ravenous
starwort . . . 5. aster 9. colicroot
stash . . . 5. cache, plant, store 7. lay
away 8. hide away
state . . . 3. say 4. aver, case, état,
mode, tell 5. utter 6. affirm, allege,
assert, plight, recite, remark, report
7. country, declare, expound,
express, narrate 8. announce,
propound 9. condition, enunciate,
postulate, pronounce, territory
10. government, possession
11. body politic 12. circumstance,
commonwealth
state (pert to) . . .
a fact . . 4. aver 5. posit 6. avouch
7. declare
agitated . . 9. disturbed, perturbed
disordered . . 9. cluttered
formally . . 8. propound 9. enunciate,
pronounce
French . . 4. état
hypnotic . . 6. trance
ideal . . 6. Utopia
office . . 8. governor 11. secretariat
on oath . . 6. depose
police . . 7. trooper
reference . . 6. statal
secret . . 7. arcanum
specifically . . 6. define 7. itemize
13. particularize
treasury . . 4. fisc 6. fiscus
ultimate . . 3. end
under foreign control . .
12. protectorate
without proof . . 6. allege
stately . . . 5. grand, largo, lofty, regal,
royal 6. august, coldly, kingly
7. haughty, queenly, togated
8. eloquent, imperial, imposing,
majestic 9. dignified, grandiose
11. magnificent
statement . . . 4. bill, list 5. audit, dixit
6. dictum, remark, report, resumé
7. account, invoice, premise
8. abstract, proposal, schedule
9. affidavit, assertion, manifesto
10. accounting, expression, recitation
11. declaration 12. announcement,
presentation
statement (pert to) . . .
abridged . . 6. précis, resumé
7. summary 10. abridgment
11. abridgement
assumed true . . 7. premise
contradictory . . 7. paradox
defamatory . . 5. libel
detailed . . 8. schedule
dogmatic . . 6. dictum
introductory . . 5. proem 7. preface,
prelude 8. foreword, prologue
legal . . 11. declaration
mathematical . . 7. theorem
of belief . . 5. credo, creed
of introduction . . 8. prologue
precise . . 8. aphorism

self–evident . . 6. truism
sworn . . 9. affidavit
State nicknames . . .
Alabama . . 6. Cotton 12. Heart of
Dixie, Yellowhammer
Alaska . . (no official)
Arizona . . 11. Grand Canyon
Arkansas . . 17. Land of Opportunity
California . . 6. Golden
Colorado . . 10. Centennial
Connecticut . . 6. Nutmeg
Delaware . . 5. First
Florida . . 8. Sunshine
Georgia . . 5. Peach
Hawaii . . 5. Aloha
Idaho . . 3. Gem
Illinois . . 7. Prairie
Indiana . . 7. Hoosier
Iowa . . 7. Hawkeye
Kansas . . 9. Sunflower
Kentucky . . 9. Bluegrass
Louisiana . . 7. Pelican
Maine . . 8. Pine Tree
Maryland . . 4. Free 7. Old Line
Massachusetts . . 3. Bay 9. Old Colony
Michigan . . 9. Wolverine
Minnesota . . 6. Gopher 9. North Star
Mississippi . . 8. Magnolia
Missouri . . 6. Show Me
Montana . . 8. Treasure
Nebraska . . 4. Beef 10. Cornhusker
Nevada . . 6. Silver 9. Sagebrush
New Hampshire . . 7. Granite
New Jersey . . 6. Garden
New Mexico . . 17. Land of
Enchantment
New York . . 6. Empire
North Carolina . . 7. Tarheel 8. Old
North
North Dakota . . 5. Sioux 11. Flickertail
Ohio . . 7. Buckeye
Oklahoma . . 6. Sooner
Oregon . . 6. Beaver
Pennsylvania . . 8. Keystone
Rhode Island . . 11. Little Rhody
South Carolina . . 8. Palmetto
South Dakota . . 6. Coyote 8. Sunshine
Tennessee . . 9. Volunteer
Texas . . 8. Lone Star
Utah . . 7. Beehive
Vermont . . 13. Green Mountain
Virginia . . 11. Old Dominion
Washington . . 9. Evergreen
West Virginia . . 8. Mountain
Wisconsin . . 6. Badger
Wyoming . . 8. Equality
state of . . .
dissension . . 8. scission
disuse . . 9. desuetude
ecstasy . . 6. trance 7. rapture
8. paradise
hostility . . 6. feudal
mind . . 4. mood 5. humor 6. morale
8. attitude
unconsciousness . . 4. coma 5. faint
state of being . . .
a layman . . 9. laicality
artless . . 7. naiveté
a son . . 7. sonship
a woman . . 10. muliebrity
behindhand . . 9. in arrears
beyond natural laws . . 12. supernatural

complete.. 9. plenitude
confined.. 10. internment
free from error.. 9. inerrancy
married twice, illegally.. 6. bigamy
married twice, legally.. 6. digamy
overfull.. 8. plethora
passive.. 9. stolidity
poison.. 5. toxic 8. toxicity
voiced.. 7. sonancy
worse.. 8. pejority
wrong.. 7. errancy
static... 5. inert, noise 6. stable
  7. resting 8. electric, inactive
  9. quiescent 10. stationary
  12. atmospherics, interference
station... 4. fire, post, rank, seat, stop
  5. berth, depot, place, radio, serai
  6. health, police 7. calling, dignity
  8. location, position, prestige
  9. situation 11. institution
stationary... 3. set 5. fixed, still
  6. stable, static, stator 8. immobile
  9. immovable 10. motionless,
  unchanging
stationery... 3. pen 5. paper 6. pencil
  9. onionskin, papeterie 12. writing
  paper
statue... 4. bust 5. image 8. acrolith,
  figurine, monument 9. sculpture,
  statuette
statue (pert to)...
at Thebes.. 6. Memnon
gigantic.. 8. Colossus
Guildhall (London).. 3. Gog 5. Magog
holy.. 4. icon (ikon)
male figure (support).. 7. telamon
part.. 5. socle, trunk 6. plinth
primitive.. 6. xoanon
Pygmalion's.. 7. Galatea
world wonder.. 6. Helios (Rhodes)
status... 4. rank 5. class, state
  7. station 8. position, prestige,
  standing
status symbol... 11. swivel chair
statute... 3. act, jus, law, lex
  5. bylaw, canon, edict, title
  6. decree, rubric, treaty 8. statutum
  9. enactment, ordinance
  10. regulation 11. legislation
staunch, stanch... 4. firm, true
  6. hearty 7. devoted 8. faithful,
  resolute 9. steadfast 10. dependable
  11. trustworthy
stave... 3. bar, leg 4. fend, pole,
  rung, slat 5. staff, stick 6. cudgel,
  lathee, letter, stanza 7. baculus,
  support, ward off 8. overcome
  11. set of verses
stave off... 4. fend 7. prevent
  8. postpone
staves, bundle of... 5. shook
stay... 3. guy, leg, rib 4. prop, rely,
  stop, wait 5. abide, brace, cease,
  check, pause, tarry 6. adhere, arrest,
  linger, remain, retard, status
  7. prevent, respite 8. postpone,
  restrain 9. cessation, hindrance
  10. impediment 12. postponement
stead... 4. help, lieu 5. place
  6. assist, behalf 7. replace, service,
  support 9. advantage, farmstead,
  homestead

steadfast... 4. firm, true 5. fixed
  6. stable 7. durable, staunch
  8. constant, faithful, reliable
  9. unwinking 10. unchanging,
  unswerving 11. unalterable
steadiness... 5. nerve 7. balance
  9. constancy, stability 10. uniformity
  11. reliability
steady... 4. firm 5. fixed, grave, sober,
  staid 6. stable, sturdy 7. assured,
  equable, regular, uniform 8. constant,
  resolute 9. incessant, steadfast
  10. invariable, unswerving
  11. unfaltering, unmitigated
  13. uninterrupted
steal... 3. cly, cop, gyp, nim, rap, rob
  4. crib, lift, loot 5. filch, pinch,
  poach, swipe 6. finger, kidnap, pilfer,
  snitch 7. purloin 8. embezzle,
  peculate 10. plagiarize
  11. appropriate
steal (pert to)...
a march on.. 5. evade 7. precede
  10. anticipate 13. gain advantage
away.. 5. creep, slink, sneak
cattle.. 6. rustle
feloniously.. 6. ratten
game.. 5. poach 8. trespass
insane desire to.. 11. kleptomania
nautical.. 7. manavel
stealer... 5. crook, thief 6. lifter, pirate
  7. abactor, abigens, filcher, rustler
  8. pilferer 9. embezzler, peculator,
  purloiner 10. pickpocket, plagiarist
  11. biblioklept 12. kleptomaniac
stealthy... 3. sly 6. artful, feline,
  secret 7. catlike, cunning, furtive
  11. clandestine
steam... 4. boil, fume, heat, mist, reek
  5. force, power, smoke, stufa, vapor
  6. energy, pother (puther) 8. vaporize
  9. evaporate
steam (pert to)...
boat.. 5. liner 7. steamer
  9. steamship 11. side–wheeler
jet of.. 5. stufa 8. suffione
organ.. 8. calliope
steamboat cabin (officer's)... 5. texas
steamy... 5. misty 7. excited
  8. vaporous 9. steamed up
steatite... 4. talc 9. soapstone
steed... 3. nag 5. horse 7. charger,
  courser, Pegasus (winged)
steel... 5. inure 6. harden, smooth
  10. strengthen
steel (pert to)...
armor plate.. 4. tace 5. tasse
color.. 4. gray 9. steel blue
  12. Prussian blue
conversion to.. 10. acieration
India.. 5. wootz 10. wootz steel
metallurgy of.. 9. siderurgy
process.. 8. Bessemer
  11. cementation
type.. 6. damask, Toledo
  8. Damascus
steep... 3. ret, sop 4. brae, buck,
  high, soak, stew, tall 5. cleve
  (cleeve), hilly, lofty, scarp, sharp,
  sheer 6. abrupt, clifty, escarp,
  imbrue, infuse, seethe 7. extract,
  extreme 8. elevated, headlong,

macerate 9. difficult, excessive,
expensive, precipice 10. exorbitant
11. precipitous 13. perpendicular
steeple . . . 5. spire, tower 6. flèche
7. minaret 8. pinnacle
steer . . . 2. ox 3. cow, ply, yaw
4. helm, luff, stot 5. guide, pilot
6. bovina, direct, govern, manage
7. bullock, control, operate
steer clear of . . . 4. snub 5. avert,
avoid 9. sidetrack, step aside 14. be
inhospitable
steer close to wind . . . 4. luff
steeve . . . 4. lade, pack, spar (a)
5. store, stuff 6. freeze
stein . . . 3. mug 4. Toby
stellar . . . 6. astral, starry 7. leading,
starlit 8. starlike, stellate
10. theatrical
Steller's sea cow . . . 6. Rytina
stem . . . 3. dam 4. axis, base, cion,
corm, prow, root, stop, tige
5. check, shaft, stalk, tuber
6. branch, breast, oppose, scapel,
stanch 7. lineage, petiole
8. ancestry, peduncle 9. originate
stem (pert to) . . .
bulblike . . 4. corm, drub
cylinder . . 5. stele
grass . . 4. culm
joint . . 4. cane, node
mushroom . . 5. stipe
plant . . 4. bine
seedling . . 7. tigella (tigelle)
9. hypocotyl
strawberry . . 4. risp
twining . . 7. tendril
underground . . 5. tuber
stemless herb (evergreen) . . . 5. Galax
11. acaulescent
stench . . . 4. odor 5. fetor, smell, stink
stenographer of Cicero . . . 4. Tiro
step . . . 3. pas, way 4. gait, pace, rung
5. dance, grise, phase, riser, stair,
stalk, strut, tread 6. degree, stride
7. advance, imprint, measure,
process 8. distance, footstep
9. footprint, gradation 10. stepladder
step (pert to) . . .
arrangement of troops . . 7. echelon
clumsy . . 5. stamp
dance . . 3. pas 6. chassé
mincingly . . 6. sashay
mother . . 7. noverca
stately . . 5. stalk
up . . 8. approach 9. intensify
10. accelerate
steppe . . . 5. plain 9. grassland
steps (outdoor flight) . . . 6. perron
stereotyped . . . 5. banal, corny, trite
6. common, old hat 9. hackneyed
11. cut and dried
sterile . . . 4. arid 6. barren 7. useless
8. impotent 9. fruitless 10. unfruitful
11. ineffective, ineffectual
12. unproductive
stern . . . 4. dour, grim, hard, rear, rump
5. harsh 6. gloomy, severe, strict,
sullen, unkind 7. austere 8. buttocks,
hind part, rigorous 9. harshness,
unfeeling 10. strictness, unyielding
11. hardhearted 14. uncompromising

sternutation . . . 8. sneezing
sternutative . . . 7. errhine
stertorous . . . 7. snoring 15. hoarse
breathing
stevedore . . . 5. lader 6. loader, stower
7. carrier 8. unloader
12. longshoreman
stew . . . 3. pot 4. boil, cook, food, fret,
fume, mess, olio, olla 5. anger,
imbue, steep, worry 6. bustle,
ragout, seethe, simmer 7. haricot,
swelter 8. meat dish 9. Brunswick
10. excitement, hodgepodge
11. predicament
steward . . . 5. agent, reeve 6. seaman,
waiter 7. dapifer, erenach, foreman,
granger, manager, servant
8. manciple 9. custodian,
major–domo, seneschal, treasurer
10. magistrate 11. chamberlain,
fiscal agent
Stewart, Stuart sovereigns (last) . . .
4. Anne 5. Henry
stewed fruit . . . 7. compote
stick . . . 3. bar, bat, bow, gad, gum,
rod 4. cane, dolt, glue, mast, pogo,
ship, stab, wand, wood 5. baton,
cling, fagot, paste, shaft, staff, stall,
stave, stilt 6. adhere, baffle, ballow,
cleave, cohere, mallet, pierce, puzzle,
thrust 7. defraud 8. chatwood,
revolver, transfix 9. drumstick,
persevere 10. matchstick, overcharge
13. stick–in–the–mud
stick (pert to) . . .
bamboo . . 6. lathee (lathi)
bundle . . 5. fagot 6. fasces
crooked . . 5. caman 7. cammock,
gambrel
insects . . 5. Emesa
mountain climbing . . 10. alpenstock
sticker . . . 4. burr 5. label, poser, thorn
6. poster, puzzle, weapon 7. bramble
8. adherent
sticky . . . 3. goo 5. gluey, humid,
moist, woody 6. clammy, slushy,
viscid 7. viscous 8. adhesive
9. difficult, glutinous, tenacious
10. saccharine
stiff . . . 4. dead, hard, hobo, limp, taut
5. harsh, horse, idler, rigid, stark,
tense 6. corpse, formal, proper,
severe, strict 7. awkward, cadaver,
starchy 8. resolute, rigorous, starched
9. dead–drunk, obstinate, unbending
14. uncompromising
stiff–necked . . . 8. stubborn
9. ankylotic, obstinate
11. strait–laced 12. contumacious
stiffness . . . 8. rigidity 9. formality,
toughness 10. strictness
11. starchiness
stifle . . . 3. gag 4. stop 5. choke
6. deaden, muffle, quench
7. repress, smother 8. strangle,
throttle 9. suffocate 10. extinguish
stigma . . . 4. blot, mark, scar, slur
5. brand, odium, stain, stamp, taint
6. defect 7. blemish 8. disgrace,
reproach
stigmatism . . . 7. blemish 10. refraction
(eye)

stigmatize . . . 5. brand 6. defame
8. denounce
still . . . 3. but, mum, yet 4. calm,
even, lull, moot 5. allay, check, inert,
quiet 6. always, hushed, pacify,
silent, soothe, subdue 7. silence,
subdued 8. inactive, restrain,
suppress, tranquil, until now
9. quiescent 10. distillery,
motionless, photograph
11. continually 12. nevertheless
15. notwithstanding
still water . . . 4. pond, pool 6. lagoon
stilt . . . 6. crutch 7. yeguita
(black–necked)
stilted . . . 6. formal 7. pompous
8. elevated, inflated, on stilts
9. bombastic, inelegant
stimulant . . . 3. tea 5. salts, tonic
6. bracer, coffee 7. alcohol
8. caffeine, stimulus 9. digitalis,
sassafras 10. adrenaline, strychnine
11. epinephrine
stimulate . . . 3. jog, pep 4. goad, stir,
urge, whet 5. elate, impel, rouse,
sting 6. excite, fillip (filip), incite,
spur on 7. animate, enliven, quicken,
refresh 8. energize, motivate
9. encourage, instigate, sensitize
10. exhilarate, invigorate
stimulating . . . 4. cool 7. piquant
8. exciting 10. energizing, refreshing
stimulus . . . 4. spur 5. sting 6. motive
7. impetus 9. incentive, stimulant
sting . . . 4. bite, pain 5. smart
6. offend, tingle 8. irritate
sting of conscience . . . 5. pangs, voice
6. qualms, twinge 11. compunction
sting organ . . . 10. nematocyst
stingy . . . 4. dree, mean, near 5. close
6. scanty 7. miserly, selfish
8. covetous 9. niggardly
10. avaricious 11. closefisted
12. parsimonious
stinkbird . . . 7. hoatzin
stint . . . 4. duty, task 5. limit 6. scrimp
7. confine 8. be frugal, restrict
9. be sparing
stipend . . . 3. ann, fee, pay 5. annat,
wages 6. salary 7. annates, pension,
subsidy 9. allowance
12. compensation, remuneration
stipulate . . . 5. agree 6. demand
7. bargain, specify 8. contract,
indicate 9. designate, guarantee,
postulate
stipulation . . . 4. bond 6. clause,
demand, detail 7. compact, proviso
8. contract, covenant 9. agreement,
condition 11. arrangement
13. specification
stir . . . 3. ado, mix 4. fuss, jail, move,
poke, roil, to–do 5. budge, churn,
rally, rouse, shake, stoke, waken
6. arouse, awaken, bestir, bustle,
excite, flurry, hubbub, pother, prison,
rustle, tumult 7. agitate, animate,
disturb, inflame, provoke 8. activity,
movement 9. commotion
12. penitentiary
stir (pert to) . . .
colors (calico) . . 4. teer

fire . . 5. stoke
together . . 3. mix 6. stodge
up . . 3. mix 4. rile, roil 5. anger,
awake, rouse 6. arouse, foment,
incite
stirring . . . 6. moving 7. rousing
8. bustling, eventful, exciting
9. animating, inspiring
11. stimulating
stirrup . . . 4. ring 5. strap 6. saddle
(part), stapes 7. support 8. footrest,
tapadera
stitch . . . 3. bit, hem, sew 4. mend,
pain 5. baste, piece, ridge 6. suture,
tailor 8. particle 9. embroider
stitch (type) . . . 3. hem 5. chain, coral,
cross 6. carpet, damask, suture
7. glover's 11. needlepoint,
over–and–over
stitchbird . . . 3. ihi 10. honey eater
stithy . . . 5. anvil, forge 6. smithy
8. smithery
stoa . . . 7. portico 9. colonnade
stoat . . . 6. ermine, weasel
stob . . . 4. post, stab, stub 5. stake
6. gibbet, pierce
stoccado, stoccata . . . 4. stab 6. thrust
(rapier)
stock . . . 4. fund, line, race, stem
5. breed, broth, hoard, store, trunk
6. assets, cravat, pillar, strain, supply
7. capital, lineage, provide, rhizome
8. credence, original 9. livestock,
provision, replenish 10. progenitor
stock (pert to) . . .
book . . 6. ledger
breeding . . 5. brood
certificate . . 5. scrip 8. document
flower . . 11. gillyflower
hawk . . 15. peregrine falcon
in trade . . 6. assets, supply
11. merchandise
market . . 6. Bourse 8. Exchange
10. Wall Street
of goods . . 4. line
owl . . 8. eagle owl
pile . . 7. reserve 12. accumulation
theater . . 5. plays
stockade . . . 3. pen 5. étape, pound
6. corral, kennel, laager 7. barrier,
bulwark, parapet, rampart, redoubt
8. palisade 9. barricade, earthwork,
enclosure
stocking . . . 4. hose, sock 6. anklet,
argyle 7. bandage, fortune, hosiery
8. seamless 9. livestock
12. bluestocking 15. Leatherstocking
(Natty Bumppo)
stocks . . . 7. pillory, shackle
10. securities
stoic, stoical . . . 7. passive, Spartan
8. enduring 9. impassive
11. unflinching
Stoic School founder . . . 4. Zeno
stoker . . . 5. firer 6. seaman, teaser
7. fireman, greaser 8. trainman
stolen (pert to) . . .
goods receiver . . 5. fence 7. smasher,
swagman
property . . 4. pelf 5. booty, spoil
stolid . . . 4. dull, slow 5. beefy
6. stupid 7. adamant, passive

9. impassive, inanimate
11. inexcitable, unexcitable
stoma... 4. pore 5. mouth 7. opening,
orifice
stomach... 3. gut, maw 4. craw, crop,
vell 5. belly, rumen, taste 6. desire,
endure, gaster, paunch 7. abdomen,
gizzard 8. tolerate 10. resentment
stomach (pert to)...
ache.. 5. colic, cramp 7. gullion
8. rumbling 11. borborygmus
acidity.. 4. acor
animal.. 3. maw
bird.. 4. craw, crop
comb form.. 6. gaster 7. gastero
ref to.. 7. gastric, pyloric
ruminant.. 5. rumen 6. omasum
8. abomasum, roddikin 9. manyplies,
reticulum 10. psalterium
stone... 3. gem, pit 4. kill, pelt, rock,
seed 5. agate, block, geode, jewel,
lapis, shale, slate, spall 6. attack,
pebble 7. diamond, peridot, sharpen
8. monument, pavement 9. hailstone,
sculpture, whetstone 10. gravestone,
grindstone 12. philosopher's
stone (pert to)...
abrasive.. 5. emery
Age.. 8. Eolithic 9. Neolithic
11. Paleolithic
alchemy.. 6. carmot 12. philosopher's
arch (top stone).. 8. keystone
Bib.. 4. ezel
broke.. 4. flat 8. strapped
broken.. 6. rubble
carved.. 5. cameo 8. intaglio
chisel.. 4. celt
cutters' disease.. 9. silicosis
10. chalicosis
famed.. 4. Hope, Pitt 5. Mogul,
Sancy 6. Jonker, Orloff, Regent
7. Blarney, Rosetta 8. Cullinan,
Kohinoor (Kohinur) 9. Excelsior
10. Great Mogul 12. Plymouth Rock,
Star of Africa
flat.. 4. flag, slab 5. slate
fruit.. 3. pip 4. paip, seed 5. cling
7. putamen 8. endocarp
gem.. 4. jade, opal, ruby, sard
5. agate, pearl, topaz 6. garnet,
ligure, spinel 7. diamond, emerald,
peridot 8. amethyst, sapphire
9. turquoise 11. alexandrite
gem cutting.. 6. adamas
hammer.. 5. kevel
hard.. 7. adamant 9. chatoyant
(cat's-eye)
heap.. 5. cairn
instrument.. 8. lapideon
masonry.. 6. ashlar
medical.. 4. gall 5. renal 7. biliary,
otolith 8. calculus
oil.. 4. hone
ornamental.. 9. scagliola
pert to.. 7. lithoid
pillar.. 8. monolith
pyramid.. 6. benben
quarry.. 6. latomy
small.. 6. pebble 8. lapillus
special.. 3. key, lap, oil, rub 4. curb,
flag, head, lime, lode, mile, tomb,
whet 5. birth, flint, grave, grind

6. cobble, corner 8. stepping
statue (part wood).. 8. acrolith
to dress.. 3. nig
uncut.. 4. naif
woman turned to stone by Zeus..
5. Niobe
stonecutter (pert to)...
disease of.. 9. silicosis 10. chalicosis
receptacle.. 7. sebilla
tool.. 6. eolith
type.. 6. jadder 7. jeweler 8. lapidary
worker.. 5. mason
stonecutting art... 10. stereotomy
stoning, death by... 10. lapidation
stony... 4. cold, hard 5. rigid, rocky
6. rugged 7. adamant 8. lapidose,
obdurate, pitiless 9. petrified
10. inflexible, relentless, unyielding
15. uncompassionate
stooge... 4. foil 5. toady 6. flunky
7. cat's-paw 8. henchman
stool... 4. seat 5. bench 6. pigeon,
tripod 7. taboret 8. informer
stop... 2. ho 3. bar, dam, end
4. balk, foil, halt, kill, quit, stay,
stem, whoa 5. avast, block, cease,
check, choke, close, delay 6. arrest,
desist, detain 7. impasse, prevent,
silence 8. preclude, swear off
10. standstill 11. discontinue,
obstruction, punctuation 12. lower
the boom
stop (pert to)...
close.. 8. obturate
debate.. 7. cloture
fermentation.. 4. stum
gap.. 7. stopper 9. expedient,
makeshift
momentarily.. 5. pause
nautical.. 5. avast
organ.. 5. viola 7. gemsbok
8. dulsiana
seams (boat).. 4. calk
short.. 5. pause 7. respite 8. interval
12. intermission
unintentional.. 5. stall
watch.. 5. timer
with clay.. 3. pug
stopper... 4. bung, cork, plug 5. spile
7. bouchon
storage (pert to)...
bin.. 3. mow 4. loft, shed, silo
7. granary 8. elevator
fodder (in silo).. 6. ensile
hidden.. 5. cache
place.. 3. bin 4. barn 5. attic, depot,
étape 6. cellar, closet 7. arsenal,
granary 8. cupboard, elevator,
magazine 10. promptuary, repository
stork... 4. ibis 6. jabiru 7. Maguari,
marabou 8. adjutant
storklike... 8. pelargic
storm... 4. blow, fume, fury, rage,
rain, rave, snow, wind 5. orage
6. attack, shower, simoom (simoon),
tumult 7. bluster, disturb, tempest,
trouble 8. calamity, eruption,
outbreak, upheaval, violence
9. agitation 11. disturbance
storm (pert to)...
cold.. 11. northeaster
evil storm god.. 2. Zu 9. blackbird

(symb), Hlorrithi
extreme.. 4. gale 7. cyclone,
monsoon, tempest, tornado
9. hurricane
occidental.. 6. wester
recorder (thunder).. 11. brontometer
sand.. 6. tebbad
snow.. 5. buran
stormy... 5. rainy 7. furious, riotous,
violent 8. agitated 9. inclement,
turbulent 10. tumultuous
11. tempestuous
story... 3. fib, lie 4. hoax, joke, lore,
saga, tale, tier, yarn 5. fable, floor
6. gossip, legend, serial 7. mystery,
narrate, parable, romance
8. anecdote 9. chronicle, falsehood,
tradition
story (pert to)...
absurd.. 4. hoax, yarn 6. canard
doleful.. 8. jeremiad
exclusive.. 4. beat, news 5. scoop
part.. 6. serial
short.. 5. conte 7. novella
storyteller... 4. liar 5. Aesop 6. fibber
7. relater 9. raconteur
stot... 2. ox 4. bull 5. steer
6. bounce 7. paunchy, stammer,
stumble, stutter
stout... 3. fat 4. bold 5. brave, bulky,
burly, hardy, obese, plump 6. fleshy,
rotund, stocky, strong 7. haughty,
violent 8. forcible, powerful, resolute,
thickset 9. corpulent, undaunted
10. courageous, persistent
stoutness... 7. courage 8. strength
10. corpulence, embonpoint
stove... 4. etna, kiln, oven 5. grate,
plate, range 6. heater 7. Coleman,
furnace, smelter
stove part... 4. oven, pipe 6. burner
7. firebox, griddle
stow... 4. cram, hide, mass, pack
5. crowd, lodge, store, stuff
6. steeve 7. arrange, secrete
straddle... 5. salvo 6. option
7. astride 8. bestride 9. be neutral,
go halfway
straggle... 4. rove 6. wander
7. deviate, meander
straight... 5. cards, erect, exact, rigid,
stern 6. candid, direct, honest
7. correct, exactly, unmixed
8. directly, reliable, sequence,
unbroken, vertical 9. authentic
10. horizontal, racing term
11. straightway, undeviating
13. uninterrupted 15. straightforward
straight (pert to)...
baseball.. 5. liner
course.. 7. beeline
edge.. 5. ruler
line.. 6. secant 8. enfilade
9. asymptote
Math.. 8. vinculum
out.. 6. candid 9. downright
11. unqualified 13. thoroughgoing
14. uncompromising
shooter.. 11. on the square
way.. 4. anon 8. directly 9. forthwith
11. immediately
straighten... 5. align, aline, level,

order, plumb 6. tidy up 7. rectify,
unravel 11. disentangle
straightforward... 5. frank 6. candid,
direct, honest 7. sincere 8. outright
9. outspoken 10. forthright
11. undeviating
straightway... 4. anon 8. directly
9. downright, forthwith 10. forthright
11. immediately
strain... 3. sye, tax, try, tug 4. bend,
dash, kind, mood, ooze, race, sort,
tone, vein 5. breed, shade, stock,
tense, touch 6. filter, melody,
overdo, poetry, refine, sprain, streak,
stress, strive 7. descent, fatigue,
lineage, progeny, stretch, tension,
variety 8. ancestry, endeavor, exertion
9. constrain, overheave, percolate
10. generation
strained... 4. taut 5. tense 6. forced
7. intense, labored 8. wrenched
9. stretched 10. farfetched
strainer... 4. sile 5. sieve, tamis
6. filter, screen, sifter 8. colander,
filterer 17. Hippocrates' sleeve
strait... 3. gut 4. neck, need 5. inlet
6. angust, narrow, strict 7. channel,
limited 8. rigorous 9. difficult
10. restricted, scrupulous
11. distressful, predicament
Strait... 6. Bering 7. Surigao
8. Bosporus 9. Belleisle
Strait of Gibraltar... 17. Pillars of
Hercules
Straits Settlements...
capital, Penang.. 10. Georgetown
capital, Singapore.. 9. Singapore
city.. 7. Malacca
peninsula.. 5. Malay
port.. 4. Prai
strand... 3. sea 4. bank, quay
5. beach, shore 6. maroon, thread
7. channel, current 8. filament
strange... 3. coy, new, odd, shy
4. rare, xeno (comb form) 5. alien,
eerie, novel, queer, timid 6. exotic,
quaint 7. curious, erratic, unknown,
unusual 8. peculiar, singular,
uncommon 9. eccentric, unrelated
10. extraneous, outlandish,
tramontane, unfamiliar
12. unaccustomed, unacquainted
13. extraordinary, preternatural
stranger... 3. ger 5. alien, guest
7. visitor 8. intruder 9. foreigner,
outlander
strangle... 5. choke 6. stifle
7. execute, garrote, repress, squeeze
8. suppress, throttle 9. suffocate
strap... 3. tie 4. belt, bind, hang,
jess, rein, riem, whip 5. leash, strop,
thong 6. enarme, latigo, oxreim
7. lanyard (laniard) 8. chastise
strap–shaped... 6. lorate 8. ligulate
strass... 5. glass, paste 10. silk refuse
strata... 6. layers 7. classes
10. formations
stratagem... 4. coup, ruse, trap, wile
5. trick 6. device 7. finesse
8. artifice
strategy... 7. tactics 8. artifice,
intrigue, maneuver

stratum... 3. bed 4. coat 5. layer
straw... 4. stem 5. mulch 6. fodder,
sennit, trifle 7. remains, sabutan
straw (pert to)...
bid.. 5. fraud 7. auction 9. worthless
coat (Jap peasant).. 4. mino
color.. 6. flaxen
flower.. 11. everlasting
hat.. 4. baku 5. milan 6. panama
like.. 6. chaffy 11. stramineous
vote.. 5. Roper 6. Gallup
stray... 3. err, gad, sin 4. cavy, roam,
rove, waif 5. range 6. swerve,
wander 7. deviate, digress
8. aberrant, aberrate, go astray
9. wandering 10. occasional
streak... 3. roe 4. line, seam, vein
5. fleck, layer, stria 6. groove, strain,
strake, stripe
streaked... 4. liny 6. banded
7. brindle, striped 8. brindled,
striated
stream... 3. run 4. burn, flow, rill, sike
(syke) 5. brook, creek, river
6. abound, course, rillet, runlet,
runnel, throng 7. current, rivulet,
torrent 9. streamlet 11. watercourse
stream (pert to)...
dry.. 6. arroyo, spruit
gold.. 6. placer
of consciousness.. 8. thoughts
10. psychology 11. abstraction
of forgetfulness.. 5. Lethe
underground.. 3. aar
street... 4. road 5. calle 6. avenue
7. highway, roadway 8. chaussée
9. boulevard 12. thoroughfare
street (pert to)...
car.. 4. tram
famed.. 4. Beal, Main, Wall 5. Canal
6. Beacon 7. Downing 8. Broadway
9. Peachtree 12. Threadneedle
French.. 3. rue
narrow.. 4. lane 5. alley
show.. 4. peep 5. raree
Spanish.. 5. calle
urchin.. 4. Arab 5. gamin 7. outcast
8. vagabond 11. guttersnipe
Street called Straight (Bib)...
8. Damascus
strength... 3. vis 4. iron, thew
5. brawn, force, might, nerve, power,
rally, sinew, titer, vigor 6. energy,
health 7. potency, stamina, sthenia,
support 8. firmness 9. endurance,
lustiness, stoutness, toughness,
vehemence, willpower 10. robustness,
stronghold
strengthen... 4. grow, prop 5. brace,
nerve 6. deepen 7. confirm, fortify,
nourish, toughen 8. increase,
roborate 9. encourage, intensify,
reinforce 10. invigorate
11. consolidate
strengthening... 7. bracing 8. roborant
12. invigorating, invigoration
strenuous... 6. ardent, severe
7. zealous 8. vigorous 9. difficult,
energetic, laborious 11. industrious
strepent... 4. loud 5. noisy
streperous... 4. loud 5. harsh
7. noisily 9. turbulent 10. boisterous

strepor... 5. noise
stress... 5. arsis, ictus, labor
6. accent, insist, strain, weight
7. urgency 8. emphasis, exigency,
pressure 9. emphasize 10. elasticity,
exaggerate 12. exaggeration
stretcher... 3. bar, lie 6. litter, racker
9. falsehood
stretch out... 6. be long, extend
9. expatiate
strew... 3. ted 6. spread 7. diffuse,
overlay, scatter 8. disperse
10. distribute 11. disseminate
strewn... 4. semé 8. littered
9. scattered 12. disseminated
stria... 4. line 5. ridge, strip 6. fillet,
furrow, groove, hollow, streak, stripe
7. channel 9. striation
stricken... 7. smitten, worn out,
wounded 8. unnerved
13. incapacitated
strickle... 5. rifle 7. pattern
8. template 10. sweepboard
13. striking board
strict... 4. hard 5. exact, harsh, rigid,
stern 6. severe 7. ascetic, austere,
precise 8. accurate, rigorous
9. puritanic, stringent 10. forbidding,
inexorable, inflexible, meticulous,
relentless, scrupulous
11. strait-laced, undeviating
13. conscientious
14. uncompromising
strict disciplinarian... 8. martinet
strict discipline... 13. regimentation
stricture... 7. binding, censure
9. criticism, narrowing
11. contraction 12. constriction
stride... 4. gait, pace, step, walk
8. bestride, progress, straddle,
velocity
strident... 6. shrill 7. grating, raucous
11. cacophonous
strife... 3. war 4. feud 5. fight
6. battle, combat, stasis 7. contest,
quarrel 8. conflict, exertion, struggle
9. logomachy 11. altercation
strike... 3. hit, pat, rap 4. bump,
bunt, slap, swat 5. clout, labor,
smite, whack 6. attack, revolt
7. impinge 9. discovery
strike (pert to)...
a balance.. 5. weigh 7. average
8. equalize 10. compromise
against.. 7. collide 8. illision
and rebound.. 5. carom (carrom)
9. carambole
breaker.. 4. fink, scab
dumb.. 4. stun
heavily.. 3. lam, ram 4. bash, slam,
slog, sock, wham 5. punch, smite
obliquely.. 5. carom 6. glance
out.. 3. fan 4. dele 5. elide, erase
6. cancel, delete 9. eliminate
to and fro.. 6. bandy
with beak.. 4. peck
with fist.. 5. pound, punch
with head.. 4. butt
with weapon.. 5. crunt
with wonder.. 3. awe 7. astound
striking... 7. salient 8. dramatic,
eloquent, exciting 9. arresting,

wonderful 10. noticeable, remarkable, surprising
striking effect . . . 5. éclat
striking part . . . 7. clapper
string . . . 3. ran, set 4. bind, cord 5. lacet, snare, twine 6. fasten, series, thread 10. succession
string (pert to) . . .
alphabet . . 5. knots (for blind)
of beads . . 6. rosary 8. necklace
of horses . . 6. stable
out . . 6. line up 8. lengthen 9. expatiate
pottery . . 13. Schnurkeramik (neolithic)
stringed instrument . . . 4. harp, lute, lyre 5. banjo, piano, recta, viola 6. fiddle, guitar, violin, zither 7. bandore, mandore, ukulele 8. mandolin, psaltery 9. mandolute 11. harpsichord
stringed instrument bridge . . . 5. magas
stringent . . . 4. ropy 5. rigid, tight 6. cogent, severe, strict 10. convincing 11. acrimonious, restrictive
stringy . . . 4. ropy 5. gluey, tough 6. sinewy, viscid 7. fibrous 10. threadlike 11. filamentous
strip . . . 4. bare, belt, live, pare, peel, skin, slat 5. cleat, shred, unrig 6. denude, divest, remove, strake 7. deprive, plunder, pull off, uncloak, uncover, undress 9. dismantle 10. dispossess, impoverish 11. decorticate
strip (pert to) . . .
blubber . . 6. flense
curved . . 5. stave
lead (stained glass) . . 4. came
leather . . 4. welt 5. thong 6. latido 7. belting
narrow . . 4. lath, slat, tape, welt 5. reeve, stave, strap
off skin . . 4. flay
of possessions . . 4. milk 5. bleed, bunko (bunco), shear 6. fleece 7. despoil, swindle 10. dispossess
raised . . 5. ridge
tease dancer . . 8. stripper 9. ecdysiast
wood . . 5. stave 6. reglet, spline
stripe . . . 3. bar, pin 4. band, beat, line, mark, sort, type, wale, weal, welt, whip 5. chalk, strip, vitta 6. streak 7. chevron 8. insignia 9. striation
striped (pert to) . . .
alder . . 11. winterberry
antelope . . 5. bongo
gillyflower . . 9. carnation
longitudinally . . 7. vittate
stripling . . . 3. boy, lad 5. youth 8. juvenile 9. youngster
strive . . . 3. aim, try, tug 4. toil 5. labor 6. battle, buffet, strain 7. compete, contend, emulate 8. endeavor, struggle
strive (pert to) . . .
for . . 3. aim 4. seek
to equal . . 5. rival 6. strain 7. emulate
to overtake . . 5. ensue

with . . 3. vie 7. compete
strobile . . . 4. cone 8. pine cone
strockle . . . 6. shovel
stroke . . . 3. fit, pat, pet, rub 4. beat, blow, coup, flip, line, putt, shot 5. ictus, serif, spasm, trait, whisk 6. caress, fondle 7. illness, solidus
stroll . . . 4. roam, walk 5. range, stray 6. go slow, ramble, wander 7. meander, saunter 8. ambulate 9. promenade 11. perambulate
stroller . . . 5. actor, tramp 6. beggar 7. peddler, vagrant 8. wanderer 9. saunterer 12. perambulator
strolling . . . 7. nomadic 8. rambling 10. meandering 13. perambulation
strong . . . 3. fit, hot 4. able, firm, hale, hard, wiry 5. fetid, hardy, lusty, solid, sound, stout, tough 6. potent, robust, sinewy, stable, sturdy, virile 7. healthy, intense, odorous, tainted 8. accented, forceful, forcible, muscular, resonant, stalwart, vigorous 9. effective, energetic 10. outrageous, persuasive, pronounced, remarkable 11. substantial 12. concentrated
strong (pert to) . . .
drink . . 6. liquor 7. spirits 9. distilled
flavor . . 4. racy 5. acrid 7. pungent
hold . . 4. fort 7. citadel 8. fastness, Fort Knox, fortress, muniment, treasury
man . . 5. Atlas 6. Samson (Sampson)
muscles . . 5. brawn, thewy
music . . 4. loud 5. forte 7. saccade
willed . . 8. resolute 9. obstinate 10. determined
wind . . 7. pampero
stroygood . . . 7. wastrel 11. spendthrift
strubbly . . . 6. untidy 7. unkempt
struck . . . 4. smit 5. smote 7. smitten, swatted 8. shutdown (see also *strike*)
struck (pert to) . . .
an attitude . . 5. posed
out . . 5. deled 6. elided, erased, fanned 7. deleted
with fear . . 6. aghast 7. alarmed
with missiles . . 6. pelted
structure . . . 3. dam 4. dais, form, pier 5. frame, house, jetty, kiosk, stage, tower 6. bridge, make–up, pagoda 7. edifice 8. building, platform 9. formation 10. tabernacle 11. composition 12. constitution, construction
structure (pert to) . . .
calcareous . . 5. coral
conical . . 7. pyramid
crownlike . . 6. corona
filamentous . . 4. hair
human . . 8. physique
monumental . . 5. pylon
roof . . 6. cupola, dormer
tall . . 5. tower 7. steeple 9. campanile
tentlike . . 10. tabernacle
struggle . . . 3. tug, vie 4. cope, wade 5. labor 6. effort, Peniel (Bib) strife, strike, strive, tussle 7. contend, contest, scuffle, wrestle 8. endeavor, flounder, scramble 10. contention, difficulty

strumpet ... 5. belie 6. harlot
8. harridan 10. prostitute
stub ... 3. end 4. dock, tail 5. squat,
stump 6. coupon, stocky 7. remnant
8. thickset 11. counterfoil
stubble ... 5. beard, stump 6. arrish
7. bristle 8. eelgrass
stubborn ... 3. set 4. rude 5. fixed,
hardy, rough, tough 6. coarse, mulish,
sturdy 7. restive 8. perverse,
resolute, starkish, vigorous
9. obstinate, pigheaded
10. determined, headstrong, inflexible,
refractory, unyielding 11. intractable
12. recalcitrant
stuck ... 4. fast 7. baffled, cohered
8. coherent, stranded (see also *stick*)
stuck-up ... 4. vain 8. arrogant
9. conceited 10. egocentric
12. supercilious 13. self–important
stud ... 3. dot, pin 4. boss, knob
5. haras 6. enstar 7. hobnail
8. ornament, stallion 9. studhorse
student ... 4. co–ed 5. cadet, eleve,
plebe, pupil 6. tosher 7. learner,
scholar 8. disciple 9. collegian
student of ...
behavior (human) .. 12. psychologist
birds .. 13. ornithologist
birds' eggs .. 8. oologist
Eton .. 7. Etonian
law .. 8. stagiary
medical .. 6. intern (interne)
military .. 5. cadet, plebe
natural history .. 10. naturalist
navy .. 5. cadet 12. midshipman
Oxford .. 8. commoner
proverbs .. 14. paroemiologist
punishment .. 10. penologist
reptiles .. 13. herpetologist
spiders .. 13. arachnologist
students, advanced group ...
7. seminar 13. upperclassmen
studied ... 5. boned, pored 6. formal
7. learned, planned, weighed
8. designed, measured, reasoned
10. well–versed 11. intentional
12. premeditated
studio ... 4. shop 7. atelier, bottega
8. workshop 11. working room
study ... 3. con, den 4. bone, muse,
pore, scan 5. étude, grind, learn,
weigh 7. discuss 6. peruse, ponder
7. analyze, examine, pegging,
reverie, science, subject, thought
8. endeavor, learning, treatise
10. discussion, inspection
11. contemplate 13. contemplation
study of ...
animals .. 7. zoology 9. zoography
bees .. 8. apiology
birds' eggs .. 6. oology
disease .. 8. nosology
fingerprints .. 13. dactylography
handwriting .. 10. graphology
insects .. 10. entomology
man .. 12. anthropology
mountains .. 7. orology
old age .. 9. nostology 10. geriatrics
11. gerontology
population .. 10. demography,
larithmics 12. demographics

punishment .. 8. penology
sacred images .. 9. iconology
temples .. 7. naology
words .. 9. etymology
12. lexicography
stuff ... 3. goo, pad, ram, wad
4. cram, fill, stow 5. gorge, trash
6. fabric, matter, potion 7. content,
element, rubbish, satiate 8. marinate,
material, nonsense, overfill, trumpery
9. principle, substance 10. gluttonize
stuffiness ... 7. prudery 8. dullness
9. obstinacy 10. sullenness, sultriness
11. pompousness
stuffing ... 6. lining 7. padding
8. contents, dressing 9. forcemeat
stuffy ... 3. fat 4. dull, prim 5. close,
stout 6. stodgy, sullen, sultry
7. airless, pompous, prudish
8. resolute 9. bombastic, obstinate
10. old–fogyish 11. strait–laced
12. conservative 13. ill–ventilated
stulm ... 4. adit 7. passage
8. entrance
stumble ... 3. err 4. fall, trip 5. lurch
6. boggle, bungle, chance, falter,
happen 7. blunder, perplex, stagger,
stammer 8. confound, flounder
stump ... 4. butt, dare, skeg, snag,
stab, stub 5. clump, scrab 6. baffle,
trudge 7. declaim, nonplus
8. platform 9. challenge, remainder,
tortillon 11. electioneer
stun ... 4. bowl, daze 5. amaze, daunt
6. benumb, bruise, deaden
7. astound, stupefy, terrify
8. astonish, bewilder 9. overpower,
overwhelm
stunning ... 8. striking 9. beautiful
10. astounding, stupefying, terrifying
stunt ... 4. feat 5. blunt, check, cramp,
crowl, dwarf, whale (2–yr) 6. hinder
7. curtail, exploit, shorten
10. tomfoolery
stunted ... 7. blunted, checked,
dwarfed 9. curtailed, shortened
stupa ... 4. tomb 5. mound, tower
6. shrine 8. monument
stupefied ... 5. doped 6. aghast,
sotted 7. drugged, shocked, stunned
8. benumbed 9. petrified
stupefy ... 4. daze, dope, drug, numb,
pall, stun 5. besot, blunt, shock
6. bedaze, bemuse, muddle
7. astound, confuse, petrify, terrify
8. bewilder, confound 10. incrassate,
make stupid 11. flabbergast (sl)
stupid ... 4. clod, dull, dumb 5. blunt,
crass, dense, inane 6. oafish, obtuse,
simple, stolid 7. asinine, doltish,
foolish, witless 8. blockish, Boeotian,
gullible 9. brainless, senseless
11. heavywitted 13. unintelligent
stupid (pert to) ...
grossly .. 7. asinine 9. imbecilic
person .. 3. ass, oaf 4. clod, coot,
dolt, loon, lout, nerd 5. goose, klutz,
stirk 7. tomfool 11. gillygaupus
render .. 8. hebetate
stupidity ... 7. fatuity 8. dullness,
hebetude 11. foolishness
12. indifference 13. foolish remark

stupor ... 4. coma, daze 5. sleep,
sopor 6. apathy, torpor, trance
8. lethargy, neurosis, numbness
9. lassitude 15. unconsciousness
sturdy ... 4. firm 5. burly, hardy, lusty,
stout 6. robust, stable, steady, strong
8. resolute, stalwart, stubborn,
vigorous 10. courageous, determined,
unyielding 11. substantial
sturgeon ... 6. beluga, caviar 7. sterlet
9. Acipenser 10. hackleback
stutter ... 6. falter 7. stammer
sty ... 3. pen 4. boil 5. hovel, stair,
steps, stile 6. ladder, pimple
7. pustule 8. swelling 9. enclosure
style ... 3. air, pen, way 4. form, kind,
mode, name 5. get–up, gusto, trend,
vogue 6. gnomon, graver, phrase,
stylus 7. alamode, diction, fashion
8. elegance 9. execution
10. appearance 12. characterize,
presentation
style (pert to) ...
architecture .. 5. Doric, Greek, Ionic,
Roman 6. Gothic, Norman 7. Italian
8. Colonial, Georgian 9. Byzantine
10. Corinthian, Romanesque
11. Renaissance
painting .. 5. genre 11. Renaissance
type .. 5. roman, runic 6. italic
styled ... 5. named 6. called, termed,
y–clept (y–cleped) 7. phrased
stylet ... 5. probe 6. trocar 7. poniard
8. stiletto 9. specillum
stylish ... 3. mod 4. chic, cool, neat,
tony 5. nifty, ritzy, sharp, smart,
swank 6. chi–chi, dressy, jaunty,
modish, preppy, snazzy, trendy
7. alamode, voguish 11. fashionable
styptic ... 4. alum 10. astringent,
tannic acid 12. constringent
Styx (pert to) ...
ferryman .. 6. Charon
suant ... 4. even 6. demure, smooth,
steady 7. equable, regular
suave ... 4. oily, smug 5. bland
6. urbane 7. fulsome 8. unctuous
9. agreeable 12. ingratiating,
mealy–mouthed 13. smooth–talking
suavity ... 7. amenity 8. civility,
courtesy, urbanity 9. gentleness
subdue ... 3. cow 4. calm, tame
5. allay, crush, lower, quash, quell,
sober 6. disarm, muffle, reduce,
soften 7. conquer, repress, squelch
8. mitigate, overcome, suppress,
surmount, vanquish 9. overpower,
subjugate 11. subordinate
subdued ... 4. meek, soft 7. muffled,
quelled 8. disarmed, relieved,
tempered 9. conquered, toned down
10. made gentle, subjugated 11. soft
colored, unperturbed
subject ... 4. text, word 5. cause,
prone, theme, topic 6. matter, motive,
submit, vassal 7. citizen, servant
8. inferior 9. subjugate, substance
10. predispose 11. subordinate
12. part of speech
subjective ... 6. mental 7. topical
8. fanciful, illusory 9. of the mind

10. nominative 11. introverted
subject of ...
discourse .. 5. theme, topic
disease .. 4. case 7. patient
lawsuit .. 3. res 7. grounds
sentence .. 4. noun
subject to ...
abuse .. 6. revile
analysis .. 7. titrate
argument .. 4. moot
change .. 7. mutable 8. amenable
choice .. 8. elective
control .. 7. rulable
death .. 6. mortal
depression .. 5. moody
dislike .. 8. aversion
mistakes .. 7. erratic
outbursts .. 9. irritable
tension .. 8. strained
vassalage .. 5. feoff
sublimation ... 9. underling
12. underscoring
sublime ... 4. high 5. grand, great,
lofty, noble, proud 6. refine
7. exalted, haughty 8. elevated,
eloquent, empyreal, majestic, splendid,
upraised, vaporize 9. beautiful,
expletive 11. magnanimous
Sublime Porte ... 12. Ottoman Court
17. Turkish government
sublimity ... 4. acme 5. glory
6. beauty 7. majesty 8. grandeur
9. greatness 10. excellence
11. distinction 12. magnificence
submarine ... 3. sub 4. boat, ship
8. Nautilus, Scorpion, Thresher
11. submersible
submarine eye ... 9. periscope
submission ... 5. kneel 6. fatalism,
meekness, patience, yielding
9. deference, obedience, surrender
10. compliance, confession
11. resignation 13. nonresistance
submissive ... 4. meek, tame
6. humble 7. dutiful, patient
8. obedient, resigned, uxorious (to
wife), yielding 9. compliant
11. acquiescent, conformable
submit ... 3. bow 4. obey 5. defer,
remit, stoop, yield 6. soften, temper
7. succumb 8. moderate
9. acquiesce, postulate, surrender
10. condescend
submit to ... 4. obey 6. endure
11. acknowledge
subordinate ... 4. exon 5. minor
6. subdue 7. servant, subject
8. inferior, parergon 9. appendage,
assistant, dependent, secondary
10. collateral, incidental, submissive
11. subservient
subsequent ... 5. later 7. ensuing
9. following, postnatal
10. succeeding 11. consecutive
subservient ... 6. vassal 7. servile,
subject 9. assistant, truckling
10. obsequious, submissive
11. subordinate 12. instrumental
subside ... 3. ebb 4. bate, fall, lull,
sink, wane 5. abate 6. settle
7. descend, relapse 8. decrease,

languish 9. gravitate 11. deteriorate
subsidiary... 8. inferior 9. assistant,
auxiliary, extrinsic, tributary
10. collateral 11. stipendiary
12. nonessential 13. supplementary
subsist... 2. be 4. live 5. abide, exist
6. endure, remain 7. prevail, survive
8. continue
subsist on prey... 9. rapacious
substance... 3. sum 4. gist, meat
5. stuff 6. import, matter, wealth
7. aliment, element, essence,
meaning, purport, summary
8. hardness, material 9. actuality,
affluence, solidness 11. consistency
substance (pert to)...
absorbent.. 5. fomes
aeriform.. 3. gas 5. argon
amorphous.. 7. ferrite
antitoxic.. 5. serum
aromatic.. 5. myrrh, spice 6. balsam
basic.. 7. element
bitter.. 5. aloes, aloin, linin
7. amarine, emetine 8. elaterin
brittle.. 5. glass
cleansing, purifying.. 8. depurant
10. abstergent, clarifiant
corrosive.. 4. acid 7. caustic
dissolved.. 6. solute
dissolving.. 9. resolvent
electrical.. 3. ion
elemental.. 5. metal
expanding.. 8. dilatant
fatty.. 5. lipin, suint
ferment.. 9. activator
flocculent.. 4. wool
food.. 7. protein
fruit jellying.. 6. pectin
gelatinous.. 4. agar
hard.. 4. bone 5. ivory 7. adamant
hypnotic.. 4. ural
inflammable.. 6. tinder 7. bitumen
inorganic.. 7. mineral
ipecac root.. 7. emetine
light.. 4. cork
milk curdling.. 6. rennet
moss (Ceylon).. 4. agar 8. agar–agar
neutralizing.. 6. alkali
resinous.. 3. gum, lac 5. copal
7. shellac
rubberlike.. 5. gutta
soapmaking.. 3. lye
stabilizing.. 7. ballast
sulphur.. 5. hepar
tar.. 6. cresol
unctuous.. 3. fat, oil 7. pinguid
vegetable.. 5. resin, rosin
wax, waxy.. 5. cerin 7. suberin
8. paraffin
whale (perfume).. 9. ambergris
wood ash.. 6. potash
substantial... 4. firm, real, true
5. pucka (pukka), solid, stout
6. actual, bodily, hearty, stable,
strong, sturdy 7. genuine
8. abundant, tangible 9. corporeal,
essential, important 10. nourishing
12. considerable
substantiate... 6. embody, verify
7. confirm, justify 8. underpin
9. establish 11. corroborate
substantive... 4. firm, noun 5. sound

6. actual, entity 7. pronoun
9. essential 11. substantial
13. self–contained
substitute... 5. proxy, vicar 6. deputy,
ersatz 7. apology, replace
8. exchange, nominate 9. alternate,
surrogate 10. understudy, viceregent
11. replacement
subterfuge... 4. ruse 5. blind, trick
6. refuge 7. evasion, pretext
8. artifice, pretense 9. expedient
13. prevarication
subterranean... 6. hidden, secret
8. hypogeal, plutonic 10. in the
earth 11. underground
subtile... 3. sly 4. rare, wily 6. crafty,
subtle 7. cunning, elusive
9. beguiling
subtle... 3. sly 4. fine, nice, rare, thin
6. artful, clever, crafty, shrewd
7. cunning, refined, subtile
8. analytic, delicate 9. beguiling,
designing, ingenious 10. mysterious
14. discriminating
subtle (pert to)...
emanation (invisible).. 4. aura
10. atmosphere
sarcasm.. 5. irony
variation.. 6. nuance
subtlety... 5. guile 7. cunning, finesse,
slyness 8. delicacy, fineness
9. quodlibet 10. shrewdness
subtraction, terms... 7. minuend
9. deduction 10. difference,
subtrahend
subversion... 4. ruin (utter)
9. overthrow 10. corruption,
revolution 11. destruction
subvert... 4. ruin 5. evert, upset
6. refute, uproot 7. corrupt, destroy,
pervert 8. alienate, overturn
9. overthrow, undermine
subvertive... 8. eversive
subway... 4. tube 5. train 6. tunnel
11. underground 18. underground
railway
succade... 8. preserve 10. confection
succeed... 5. ensue, occur 6. attain,
follow, thrive 7. achieve, devolve,
prosper, replace, triumph 8. come
next, flourish, supplant
10. accomplish
succeeding... 4. next 7. ensuing,
sequent 9. following 10. subsequent,
successful 11. in the wake of
success... 2. go 3. hit 4. luck
5. elate 7. fortune, outcome
8. accolade, smash hit 10. prosperity
11. consequence
successful... 5. lucky 8. thriving
9. fortunate 10. prosperous,
succeeding, triumphant
11. flourishing
succession... 3. row, run 5. music
(rhythmic) 6. series 7. dynasty,
lineage 8. sequence 9. posterity
succin... 5. amber
succinct... 4. curt 5. brief, hasty,
short, terse 7. compact, concise,
laconic, summary 10. compressed
11. compendious, sententious
succor, succour... 3. aid 4. abet, help

6. brandy (Alpine), relief, rescue
7. comfort, deliver, relieve, sustain
8. befriend, mitigate 10. assistance
succulent . . . 3. uva 4. lush 5. juicy,
pappy, tasty 6. cactus, tender
succumb . . . 3. die 5. faint, yield
6. perish, submit 7. give way 8. get
tired
such (as) . . . 3. sic 4. like 7. certain,
similar 8. analogue 9. analogous
suction (as in clicks of Bantu) . . .
9. implosive
Sudan, Africa . . .
capital . . 8. Khartoum
desert . . 6. Libyan, Nubian
export . . 9. gum arabic
gazelle . . 4. dama
gum forests . . 8. Kordofan
lake . . 4. Chad
language . . 2. Ga 6. Arabic
people . . 4. Arab, Sere 5. Fulah
(Fula), Negro 6. Nubian
Plain . . 6. Gezira
river . . 8. Blue Nile 9. White Nile
town . . 5. Segou
sudden . . . 4. rash 5. hasty, swift
6. abrupt, prompt, speedy 7. violent
8. headlong 9. impetuous,
impromptu, impulsive
10. unexpected, unforeseen
11. precipitate, precipitous
sudden (pert to) . . .
all of a . . 5. short 6. presto
8. suddenly
and brilliant . . 8. meteoric
fear . . 13. consternation
sally . . 6. sortie
shock . . 4. jolt
stroke . . 4. coup, dash
thrust . . 3. jab 5. lunge
sudor . . . 5. sweat 8. sudation
9. exudation 12. perspiration
Sudra caste . . . 3. mal (low) 5. palli
sue . . . 3. beg, woo 4. plea, urge
5. court, plead 6. appeal, pursue
7. entreat, request 8. continue,
petition 9. prosecute, seek after
suet . . . 6. tallow 8. leaf lard
Suez Canal builder . . . 9. de Lesseps
(Ferdinand)
suffer . . . 3. let 4. bear, dree 5. admit,
allow 6. endure, permit, submit
7. undergo 8. tolerate
10. experience
suffer (pert to) . . .
distress . . 5. gripe, groan, smart
6. starve
from heat . . 7. swelter
remorse . . 3. rue
ruin . . 5. wreck
sufferance . . . 4. pain 6. misery
9. endurance, passivity
10. permission 11. forbearance
suffering, scene of . . . 10. Gethsemane
suffice . . . 2. do 5. avail, serve
6. answer 7. appease, content,
satisfy 11. sufficiency
sufficiency . . . 4. fill 7. ability, conceit
8. adequacy, capacity, validity
9. abundance 10. competency
14. self–confidence
sufficient . . . 3. due, fit 4. enow, full,

good 5. ample, valid 6. enough,
plenty 7. suffice 8. adequate
9. qualified 11. responsible
12. satisfactory
suffix, for or denoting . . .
abounding in . . 5. ulent
abundant . . 3. ose
act of . . 3. ure 4. ance, tion
advocate . . 3. ite
alcohol . . 2. ol
being . . 3. ure
capable of . . 3. ile
chemical . . 2. ac 3. ane, ene, ile, ine,
iol, ole, ose 4. alic, idin, itol
diminutive . . 2. el 3. cle, ole, ule
4. ette
disease . . 4. itis
doer . . 4. ator
enzyme . . 3. ase
feminine . . 3. ess
follower . . 3. ist, ite
full of . . 3. ose
geological age . . 4. cene
inflammation . . 4. itis
inhabitants of . . 3. ese 4. ites
jurisdiction . . 3. ric
law . . 2. ee
medicine . . 2. ia 3. oma 4. itis
profession . . 3. eer
suffocate . . . 5. burke, choke 6. stifle
7. smother 8. strangle, suppress,
throttle 10. asphyxiate, extinguish
12. deprive of air
suffrage . . . 4. vote 5. voice 6. assent,
ballot, prayer 7. witness 8. petition
9. franchise 10. assistance 11. right
to vote 12. intercession, supplication
sugar . . . 4. cane 5. biose, bribe,
candy, maple, money 6. doctor,
season 7. sucrose, sweeten
9. sugarcoat 10. endearment,
saccharose, sweetening
12. carbohydrate 13. dissaccharide
14. monosaccharide
sugar (pert to) . . .
and molasses . . 6. melada
burnt . . 7. caramel
chemical . . 4. acrose 7. osamine,
sucrose 8. fructose 10. saccharose
crude . . 3. gur 5. maple
10. massecuite, piloncillo
fruit, honey . . 8. levulose
plant . . 7. sorghum
raw . . 9. cassonade, muscovado
sand . . 5. niter
simple . . 6. ketose, triose 7. glucide
substitute . . 5. honey
syrup . . 7. treacle 8. molasses
tree . . 5. maple
without . . 3. sec
wood . . 6. xylose
sugar cane (pert to) . . .
disease . . 5. sereh
pulp, refuse . . 4. marc 7. bagasse
stalk . . 6. ratoon
sugared . . . 5. sweet 7. honeyed
9. sweetened 11. mellifluous,
sugarcoated
suggest . . . 4. hint, mean, move
5. imply 6. advise, allude, prompt
7. connote, inspire, propose
8. indicate, intimate 9. insinuate

suggestion... 4. clue, hint, idea, plan
5. tinge, trace 6. advice, symbol
7. soupçon 8. proposal 9. hypnotism
10. indication, intimation 11. small
amount, supposition
Suidae... 5. swine
suit... 3. fit 4. plea 5. befit, cards,
dress, habit, match, serve, tally
6. adjust, answer, attire, become,
prayer, wooing 7. clothes, comport,
conform, costume, lawsuit, retinue
8. petition, sequence 9. courtship
10. litigation 11. accommodate
suit (pert to)...
at law.. 10. litigation
for property.. 6. trover
maker.. 6. sartor, tailor
starter.. 7. relator
the occasion.. 6. timely
suitability... 7. fitness 9. propriety
10. expedience, timeliness
11. eligibility 13. qualification
suitable... 3. apt, due, fit, pat
4. meet 6. proper, timely
8. adequate, apposite, eligible,
idoneous 9. accordant, agreeable,
competent, congruent, congruous,
consonant, expedient 10. compatible,
consistent 11. appropriate
12. commensurate 13. correspondent
suitably proportioned...
13. commensurable
suite... 3. set 5. music, staff
7. retinue 8. sequence 9. apartment
10. attendance, succession
11. consequence
suitor... 5. swain, wooer 7. amoroso
10. petitioner 12. party to a suit
sulk... 3. pet 4. mope, plow, pout
6. furrow
sulky... 3. gig 4. dull, glum, plow
5. moody, pouty, surly 6. gloomy,
go–cart, sullen 8. carriage
9. obstinate
sullen... 4. dour, glum, grim, sour
5. cross, gruff, harsh, moody, pouty,
sulky, surly 6. crusty, gloomy,
morose 7. austere, cynical, fretful,
peevish, pettish 8. chumpish,
churlish, petulant, spiteful
9. obstinate, saturnine
sully... 4. foul 5. dirty, smear, stain,
taint 6. defile, smirch, vilify
7. blemish, corrupt, debauch,
disdain, pollute 9. bespatter,
denigrate 10. stigmatize
11. contaminate
sulphur (pert to)...
alchemy.. 7. chibrit
alloy.. 6. niello
butterfly.. 7. clouded 9. cloudless
color.. 6. yellow
comb form.. 5. thion
element.. 11. nonmetallic
reference to.. 7. thionic 9. brimstone
sultan (pert to)...
decree.. 5. irade
fowls.. 5. breed
home.. 5. serai
Mohammedan State.. 5. ruler
6. prince 9. sovereign
Turkish ruler.. 6. Caliph 8. Padishah

13. Grand Seignior
wife.. 7. sultana
sultana... 4. roll (dessert), wife
5. grape 8. mistress 9. gallinule
sultry... 3. hot 5. humid, lurid
6. torrid 7. dog days, sensual
10. oppressive, sweltering
sum... 3. add, tot 4. loot 5. count,
gross, total, whole 6. amount,
number, result 7. summary
8. addition, quantity 9. aggregate,
summarize, summation
12. recapitulate
sum (pert to)...
forfeited.. 5. dédit
of money.. 6. budget
total.. 8. entirety
unexpended.. 7. savings
up.. 3. tot 5. count 8. perorate
sumac... 5. Rheus 7. dogwood
8. shadbush 9. squawbush
13. Toxicodendron 14. buckthorn
brown
Sumatra...
harbor.. 6. Padang 9. Palembang
island of.. 16. Malay Archipelago
kingdom.. 5. Achin, Jambi
mountain.. 12. Bukit Barisan
raft (bamboo).. 5. rakit
river.. 4. Musi 5. Jambi, Rokan
6. Asahan
squirrel shrew.. 4. tana
wildcat.. 4. balu
sumless... 11. inestimable
12. incalculable 13. unaccountable
summary... 5. brief, short 6. digest,
prompt, resume 7. epitome
8. abstract 10. compendium
11. abridgement, enumeration,
reiteration 14. recapitulation
summary (pert to)...
book.. 5. blurb
concise.. 6. précis
of facts.. 7. roundup
of knowledge.. 12. encyclopedia
(encyclopaedia)
of principles.. 5. creed
of speech.. 5. notes
summer... 3. été 6. season
summer (pert to)...
bird.. 7. cuckold, sparrow, tanager,
wryneck
coot.. 9. gallinule
house.. 6. gazebo 9. belvedere
lilac.. 8. damewort
pert to.. 7. estival
rash.. 11. prickly heat
resort.. 4. camp
squash.. 7. cymling, scallop
9. crookneck
summit... 3. top 4. acme, apex, knap,
peak 5. crest, crown, knoll, spire
6. height 7. Everest 8. pinnacle
9. fastigium 10. perfection
11. culmination, mountaintop
summon... 4. call, cite, page, sist
5. evoke 6. call up, demand, elicit,
invite, muster 7. conjure, evocate
8. remember 9. conscript
sumpter... 4. mule 9. pack horse
sun... 3. orb, Sol 4. bask 6. Helios
7. Phoebus 12. heavenly body

13. celestial body

sun (pert to)...
clock.. 6. gnomon (part) 7. sundial
comb form.. 5. helio
crossing the equator.. 7. equinox
disk.. 4. aten
down.. 3. eve 8. twilight
farthest from.. 8. aphelion
fish.. 4. mola, opah 5. bream
god.. 2. Ra 4. Amen, Baal, Lier
  (Llew) 6. Apollo, Helios 7. Khepera
  (Chepera), Shamash, Sokaris
  8. Hyperion
mock.. 9. parhelion
nearest to.. 10. perihelion
outer layer.. 6. corona
over the equator.. 7. equinox
path.. 4. halo 6. circle 8. ecliptic
pert to.. 5. solar 6. heliac
  9. heliology
poetic.. 5. glory, power 6. sunset
  7. daystar, sunrise 8. splendor
satellite.. 6. planet
spot.. 6. facula 7. freckle
squall.. 9. jellyfish
stroke.. 8. siriasis 9. calenture
sundang... 4. bolo 5. knife
sunder... 4. part, rend, rive 5. sever,
  split 6. cleave, divide 7. divorce
  8. dissever, disunite, sejugate
sundry... 6. divers 7. several, various
  8. frequent, manifold, numerous
  9. different 10. multiplied
  12. multifarious 13. miscellaneous
sunflower... 8. marigold, rockrose
  10. heliotrope
Sunflower State... 6. Kansas
sunk... 4. turf 7. baffled, concave,
  lowered 8. dejected, overcome
  9. depressed (see also *sink*)
sunk fence... 4. ha-ha (haw-haw)
sunny... 4. warm 5. clear, merry
  6. bright, sunlit 8. cheerful
  9. sparkling, vivacious
sunrise... 4. dawn
sunset... 3. eve 4. dusk 7. evening,
  sundown 8. twilight
Sunset State... 6. Oregon 7. Arizona
Sunshine State... 9. New Mexico
  11. South Dakota
supawn... 4. mush 12. hasty pudding
superabundance... 5. flood 6. excess,
  plenty 7. surplus 8. plethora
  10. exuberance 11. superfluity
superabundant... 4. rank 6. lavish
  7. profuse 9. excessive, exuberant,
  luxuriant, plentiful 11. overflowing
  14. oversufficient
superannuate... 6. retire 9. antiquate
  10. pension off 13. prove obsolete
superb... 4. rich 5. grand, noble
  6. lordly 7. elegant, stately
  8. majestic, splendid 9. sumptuous
  11. magnificent 13. extraordinary
  14. superexcellent
supercilious... 5. proud 7. haughty
  8. arrogant 9. arbitrary
  11. overbearing 12. contemptuous
  13. hypercritical
supercilious person... 4. snob
superficial... 4. glib 6. slight, square
  7. cursory, shallow, smatter, surface,

trivial 8. apparent, external
  9. frivolous, insincere
superfluity... 6. excess, luxury, wealth
  7. overset 8. frippery 10. redundancy
  11. prodigality 14. superabundance
superfluous... 4. over 5. luxus, spare
  6. excess 7. surplus, useless
  8. needless, wasteful 9. redundant
  10. inordinate 11. extravagant
  12. nonessential 13. superabundant
  14. supererogatory
superhuman... 6. divine 9. Herculean
  12. supernatural 13. extraordinary
superimposed... 4. over, upon
  5. above 7. covered, layered
  8. overlaid 9. overlying
superintend... 4. boss 5. guide
  6. direct, manage 7. oversee
  8. overlook 9. look after, supervise
  10. administer, have charge
superintendent... 4. boss 7. curator,
  manager 8. director, overseer
  9. inspector, straw boss
  10. supervisor 11. chamberlain
superior... 4. over, peer 5. above,
  chief, upper 6. higher, senior
  7. exalted, mastery, ranking
  8. goodness, priority 9. advantage,
  paramount, seniority 10. ascendancy,
  excellence, pre-eminent, surpassing
  11. pre-eminence 12. predominancy
superlative... 4. acme, best, peak
  6. utmost 7. elative, extreme,
  supreme, the best 8. peerless
  9. hyperbole 12. exaggeration
supernatural... 5. eerie, magic
  6. divine 10. miraculous,
  superhuman 13. hyperphysical,
  preternatural
supernatural (pert to)...
being.. 3. God 4. atua 5. jinni
  (jinnee) 7. banshee (banshie), specter
  (spectre)
event.. 7. miracle
power.. 4. ngai 5. fetish 8. talisman
  11. incantation
superscribe... 6. direct 7. address (a
  letter), engrave 8. inscribe
supersede... 4. omit 7. replace,
  succeed 8. displace, make void,
  supplant
superstition... 6. notion, voodoo
  8. folklore, idolatry 9. tradition
  10. Aberglaube 12. old wives' tale
superstitious... 6. goetic 7. magical
  10. idolatrous 11. fetishistic
  (fetichistic)
supervene... 5. occur 6. accrue,
  happen 7. be added 12. be
  subsequent
supervise... 4. boss, read, scan
  5. check 6. direct, govern, peruse,
  revise 7. inspect, oversee
  11. superintend
supervisor... 4. boss 7. foreman,
  proctor 9. inspector, straw boss
supine... 5. inert, prone 6. abject,
  drowsy 7. servile, unalert 8. careless,
  inclined, indolent, listless, sluggish
  9. apathetic, lethargic, recumbent
  11. inattentive, indifferent,
  thoughtless

supplant... 5. upset, usurp 6. remove, uproot 7. replace 8. displace, drive out 9. eradicate, extirpate, overthrow, supersede

supple... 3. sly 4. bent 5. agile, lithe 6. limber, nimble, pliant 7. fawning, lissome 8. flexible, yielding 9. compliant, resilient 10. obsequious, responsive 11. complaisant

supplement... 3. add, eke 5. add to 6. sequel 7. ripieno 8. addition, appendix, complete 9. accessory 10. complement 12. nonessential 13. reinforcement

supplementary, music... 7. ripieno

supplicate... 3. beg 4. pray 5. crave, plead 6. appeal, obtest 7. beseech, conjure, entreat, implore, solicit 8. petition 9. importune, obsecrate

supplication... 4. plea 6. litany, prayer 7. craving 8. entreaty, petition, rogative 11. obtestation 12. solicitation

supplies... 6. hoards, relays, stocks, stores 8. estovers, ordnance 9. provender

supply... 4. fund, give 5. cache, cater, hoard, relay, stock, store, yield 6. purvey, remuda 7. provide, reserve 9. provision, reservoir 10. administer, contribute

supply (pert to)...
food.. 4. feed 5. cater 9. alimental
fuel.. 5. stoke
funds.. 5. endow
horses.. 5. relay
provisions.. 6. purvey

support... 3. aid, arm, fid, guy, leg, peg, rib 4. abet, ally, back, base, buoy, limb, mast, prop 5. brace, cleat, shore, spile, stell, strut, tenon 6. backer, pillar, second, uphold 7. bolster, fulcrum, trestle 8. buttress, underlie 9. auxiliary, encourage, reinforce, stanchion 10. assistance, foundation 11. corroborate 12. substantiate 13. corroboration

support (pert to)...
anatomy.. 3. rib 5. spine
cannon.. 8. trunnion
coffin.. 4. bier
mast.. 4. bibb
resilient.. 6. spring
three–legged.. 5. easel 6. tripod, trivot
upright.. 8. baluster 9. stanchion
wedge–shaped.. 5. cleat

supporters... 6. allies, braces 7. backers, bracers, garters 10. suspenders 15. ministerialists

suppose... 3. wis 4. deem, trow 5. allow, imply, judge, opine, think 6. assume, expect, repute 7. presume 8. conclude, consider 9. apprehend, intention 10. conjecture 11. supposition

supposed... 8. putative

supposition... 2. if 6. theory 7. surmise 8. supposed 9. postulate 10. assumption, conjecture,

hypothesis 11. connotation, implication

suppress... 4. kill, stop 5. check, crush, elide, quash, quell 6. hush up, muffle, retard, stifle 7. abolish, exclude, oppress, smother 8. hold back, prohibit, restrain, withhold 9. interdict, overpower 10. extinguish

suppression... 6. hush up 7. reserve 8. hush–hush 9. overthrow, restraint 10. inhibition

supremacy... 5. power 7. control, mastery, primacy 8. dominion 9. influence 10. ascendancy, domination, first place 11. sovereignty 12. championship

supreme... 3. top 4. last 5. chief, final 6. divine, ruling 7. crucial, highest 8. foremost, greatest, peerless 9. paramount 10. preeminent

supreme being... 3. God 4. Lord 5. Allah, Deity, monad 6. Brahma, Buddha 7. Creator, Jehovah 8. autocrat

surcease... 3. end 4. rest, stop 5. defer, delay 6. desist, relief 7. respite 8. drop work, postpone 9. cessation

surd... 4. deaf, mute 7. aphonic, radical 9. voiceless

sure... 3. yes 4. fast, firm, safe, true 5. bound 6. indeed, secure, stable, steady, strong 7. assured, certain 8. positive, reliable 9. confident, steadfast, unfailing 10. guaranteed, inevitable, infallible 11. trustworthy 12. indisputable 13. incontestable 14. unquestionable

surety... 4. bail, bond, fact 6. backer, pledge, safety 7. sponsor 8. security, sureness 9. certainty 10. confidence, engagement

surf... 4. foam, rote, wave 5. bathe, spray, surge, swell 7. breaker

surface... 4. area, face, orlo, pave, plat, skin 5. facet, meros 6. facing, patina 7. outside 8. exterior 9. periphery

surface (pert to)...
artificial.. 4. rink
front (coin).. 7. obverse
gem.. 5. facet
geometric.. 6. toroid
medical.. 7. acrotic
toward.. 5. ectad
under.. 6. latent 10. internally
water.. 4. ryme

surfeit... 4. cloy, feed, glut, jade, sate 6. excess 7. replete, satiate, satisfy 9. satiation 11. overindulge, superfluity

surge... 4. eddy, flow, rush, wave 5. swarm, swell, whirl 6. billow, thrill 7. estuate 9. gurgitate 11. rise and fall

surgeon (pert to)...
ancient.. 10. chirurgeon
case (instrument).. 6. tweeze (tweese)
slang.. 8. sawbones

surgery... 7. aciurgy 8. medicine 9. operation, resection

surgery (pert to)...
chin .. 11. mentoplasty
ears .. 9. otoplasty
face lift .. 13. rhytidoplasty
   14. blepharoplasty (eyelids)
fractures .. 10. agmatology
mouth, lip .. 12. cheiloplasty
   (chiloplasty)
nose .. 7. nose job 11. rhinoplasty
organ .. 10. transplant
skin .. 12. dermabrasion
vein .. 10. phlebotomy
vertebra .. 11. laminectomy
surgical (pert to)...
compress .. 4. swab 5. stupe
counterirritant .. 5. seton
equpment .. 4. X–ray 6. splint 7. CAT
   scan, scanner 8. iron lung
   10. respirator, tomography, tourniquet
   11. stethoscope 12. resuscitator
hook .. 9. tenaculum
instrument .. 3. saw 5. fleam, lance,
   probe 6. catlin, lancet, stylet, trepan,
   xyster 7. forceps 8. hemostat,
   keratome, speculum, tweezers
knife .. 7. scalpel
puncture .. 8. centesis
saw .. 6. trepan
stitch .. 5. seton 6. suture
Suriname (pert to)...
capital .. 10. Paramaribo
former name .. 11. Dutch Guiana
mountain .. 10. Tumuc–Humac
toad .. 4. pipa
surly ... 4. glum, grum, rude 5. gruff
   6. abrupt, grumpy, morose, sullen
   7. crabbed 8. arrogant, growling
   10. ill–natured 11. intractable
surmise ... 4. deem 5. fancy, guess,
   judge, opine, think 7. imagine,
   presume 8. mistrust 9. suspicion
   10. assumption, conclusion,
   conjecture 11. supposition
surmount ... 3. top 4. pass, rise
   5. climb, excel, mount 6. subdue
   7. conquer, surpass 8. overcome
   9. transcend
surname ... 6. eponym, family, maiden
   7. agnomen 8. cognomen
   10. patronymic 11. appellation
surpass ... 3. cap, top 4. best
   5. excel, outdo 6. better, exceed,
   outvie, outwit 7. outrank, outride
   8. go beyond, outrange, outreach,
   outshine, outsmart, outstrip, surmount
   9. transcend
surpassing ... 12. transcendent
surplice ... 3. fee 5. cotta, ephod
   6. collar 7. pelisse
surplus ... 4. over, rest 5. epact
   6. excess 7. overage, reserve
   8. overplus 9. remaining
   10. additional, redundancy
   11. superfluous
surprise ... 3. awe 5. alarm, amaze,
   seize, shock 6. wonder 7. astound,
   capture, perplex, startle 8. astonish,
   bewilder, confound, dumfound
   9. amazement, dumbfound,
   overwhelm, surprisal 10. wonderment
   11. flabbergast 12. astonishment
surprising ... 7. amazing 8. striking

   9. startling 10. unexpected
   11. astonishing, unlooked for
   13. extraordinary
surrender ... 4. cede, give 5. yield
   6. give up, remise, resign
   7. abandon, cession, deliver
   8. dedition, remittal 9. extradite
   10. relinquish, submission
   11. abandonment, divestiture
   12. cancellation 14. relinquishment
surreptitious ... 3. sly 6. hidden,
   secret 8. stealthy 9. concealed,
   deceitful 10. fraudulent
   11. clandestine
surround ... 4. gird, isle, wrap
   5. beset, hem in, inarm 6. circle,
   encase, incase, invest 7. besiege,
   enclave, enclose, envelop, environ
   8. encircle, inundate, overflow
   9. encompass 12. circumscribe
   14. circumnavigate
surrounding ... 5. about, beset, midst
   7. ambient, setting 9. hemming in,
   perioptic 10. encircling, enveloping
   11. circumpolar 12. circumjacent
survey ... 4. plan, poll, scan 5. study,
   vista 6. regard, review 7. examine,
   inspect, oversee 8. traverse
   9. delineate, determine 10. scrutinize
   11. examination, reconnoiter,
   superintend 14. reconnaissance
surveying (pert to)...
instrument .. 7. alidade (alidad), transit
   9. stadia rod 10. throdolite
mathematics .. 7. geodesy
process .. 13. triangulation
surveyor (pert to)...
helper .. 6. rodman 7. lineman,
   poleman
land .. 8. measurer, overseer
   9. arpenteur
measure .. 5. chain
mine .. 6. dialer
survival ... 5. relic 9. endurance,
   outliving 10. durability
survivor ... 6. relict 8. outliver,
   remainer, survival 11. joint tenant
susceptibility ... 5. sense 7. emotion,
   feeling, pliancy 11. sensibility
   12. teachability 13. affectibility,
   vulnerability 14. sentimentality
susceptible ... 4. easy 6. liable, pliant
   7. exposed, subject 8. sensible
   9. receptive, sensitive, teachable
   10. responsive, vulnerable
   11. softhearted 13. tenderhearted
   14. impressionable
suslik ... 5. sisel 8. squirrel
   11. spermophile
suspect ... 4. fear 5. doubt, fancy,
   guess 7. imagine, presume, suppose
   8. distrust, mistrust 9. discredit
   10. disbelieve, suspicious
suspecting ... 4. wary 8. doubtful,
   doubting 11. incredulous, mistrusting
suspend ... 4. hang, oust, stay, stop
   5. cease, debar, defer, expel, remit
   6. dangle, depose, recess 7. adjourn,
   pensile 8. intermit, postpone, set
   aside, withhold 9. pretermit
suspended ... 4. hung 5. inert
   6. barred, latent 7. abeyant, pendent

8. inactive 9. pendulous
11. inoperative, interrupted
suspenders... 4. pegs 5. belts, hooks,
rings 6. braces, straps 7. gallows,
garters 8. galluses 9. bretelles
10. supporters 11. clothespins
suspense... 5. pause 7. anxiety
10. expectancy 11. uncertainty
12. apprehension, irresolution
14. indecisiveness
suspension... 4. stop 5. delay
7. deposal, failure, hanging, respite
8. abeyance, buoyancy
11. withholding 12. intermission,
interruption
suspicious... 4. fear, hint 5. doubt,
hunch, trace 7. askance, inkling,
soupçon 8. distrust, jealousy,
mistrust, wariness 9. mere trace,
misgiving 10. diffidence, intimation,
skepticism, suggestion 11. incredulity,
supposition 12. apprehension
Sussex (pert to)...
breed (Eng).. 4. fowl 6. cattle
kingdom (anc).. 7. English
land measure.. 4. wist
land tract (Downs).. 5. laine
man.. 8. Piltdown (Prehist)
spaniel.. 6. gun dog
sustain... 4. bear, buoy, feed, prop
5. abide, carry 6. endure, foster,
keep up, uphold 7. confirm, justify,
nourish, prolong, support, undergo
8. continue, maintain, preserve
9. encourage, establish
10. strengthen 11. corroborate
sustained... 6. tenuto, upheld
9. permanent, prolonged, supported
10. unflagging
Susu... 5. tribe (Afr)
suttee... 5. widow 9. cremation,
sacrifice 14. self–immolation
suture... 5. unite 6. stitch 7. pterion
12. synarthrosis
swagger... 4. brag, gait, walk 5. bluff,
boast, bully, strut, swell 6. prance
7. bluster, dashing, roister, stagger,
stylish 8. domineer 11. braggadocio,
ostentation 16. ultrafashionable
swain... 3. boy, lad 4. beau 5. lover
6. suitor 7. admirer, gallant, peasant
8. shepherd 10. countryman
swallow... 3. sip 4. gulp 5. drink
6. absorb, englut, engulf, imbibe,
ingest, recant 7. consume, engorge,
retract 8. tolerate 10. bear meekly
swallow (pert to)...
chimney.. 5. swift
European.. 6. martin
hawk.. 4. kite
plover.. 10. pratincole
sea.. 4. tern
tail.. 4. coat 9. butterfly
the anchor.. 10. quit the sea
swamp... 3. bog, fen 4. mire, muck,
sink, slue, sump 5. flood, marsh
6. deluge, engulf, morass, slough
7. cienaga, pocosin 8. quagmire,
submerge 9. everglade, overwhelm
swamp (pert to)...
boggy.. 7. queachy 8. muskeggy
earth.. 4. muck

gas.. 6. miasma
grass.. 5. sedge
marsh.. 5. slash 8. paludine
tract.. 10. Everglades
swan... 3. cob, pen 4. Olor 5. swear
6. cygnet, cygnus 7. declare
9. trumpeter
swan (pert to)...
astronomy.. 6. Cygnus
flower.. 6. orchid
goose.. 7. Bewick's, Chinese
myth (Hind).. 5. hansa
poem.. 12. Swan of Thames (Pope)
15. Sweet Swan of Avon (Jonson)
star (brightest).. 5. Deneb
trumpeter.. 4. wild
type.. 4. mute 5. black 8. whooping
11. black–necked
swap... 4. beat 5. trade 6. barter,
thrash 8. exchange
11. give–and–take
sward... 3. sod 4. lawn, turf 5. grass
10. greensward
swarm... 3. fry 5. crowd, flock, horde
6. abound, infest, throng 7. pervade
9. migration, multitude
10. congregate 11. aggregation
swarthy... 3. dun 4. dark 5. dusky
8. bistered (bistred), blackish
swashbuckler... 5. bravo 6. gascon
7. ruffian 8. Almanzor 9. blusterer,
daredevil, swaggerer 10. Drawcansir
swastika (swastica)... 6. fylfot, symbol
(since 1918) 9. gammadion
10. hakenkreuz
swat... 3. bat, hit 5. clout 6. strike
7. hit hard
swathe... 4. band, bind, wrap
6. enfold 7. envelop, swaddle
sway... 4. bend, bias, rock, rule, veer,
wave 5. lurch, power, shake, swing,
waver, wield 6. direct, empire,
govern, induce, totter, waddle
7. command, control, deflect, incline
8. flounder 9. fluctuate, influence,
oscillate, vacillate 10. ascendancy
11. fluctuation
swayback... 8. lordosis
swaying... 7. pensile, sagging
8. swinging, waddling 11. influential,
oscillating
swear... 3. vow 4. oath 5. curse,
vouch 6. adjure, pledge (sacred)
7. confirm, declare, promise
10. asseverate, deposition 11. bear
witness
swear (pert to)...
at.. 5. clash (colors), curse
8. disagree
by.. 5. bet on 7. count on 8. take
oath
falsely.. 7. perjure
off.. 4. stop 6. eschew, give up
7. abandon 8. renounce
sweat... 4. work 5. exude, grill, sudor
6. drudge 7. excrete, ferment
8. perspire, transude 9. exudation
10. impatience 11. nervousness
Sweden... see also *Swedish*
capital.. 9. Stockholm
city.. 7. Uppsala (Upsala)
dynasty (1st).. 8. Ynglings

gulf .. **7.** Bothnia
lake .. **6.** Vanern **7.** Vattern
mountain .. **5.** Kölen (Kjölen)
parliament .. **7.** Riksdag
peninsula .. **11.** Scandinavia
port .. **8.** Göteborg **9.** Stockholm
river .. **4.** Klar **7.** Götaalv
sea .. **6.** Baltic
university (oldest) .. **7.** Uppsula (Upsula, 1477)
Swedish (pert to) . . .
artist .. **4.** Zorn
bread .. **10.** knäckebröd
clover .. **6.** alsike
dance .. **6.** polska
explorer .. **5.** Hedin
fir .. **10.** Scotch pine
idiom .. **7.** Suecism
manual training .. **5.** sloyd (slojd)
novelist .. **8.** Lagerlöf (Pulitzer prize, 1909)
philosopher .. **10.** Swedenborg
religion (State) .. **8.** Lutheran
soprano .. **10.** Jennie Lind
18. Swedish Nightingale
turnip .. **8.** rutabaga
sweep . . . **3.** oar **4.** scan **5.** clean, clear, cover, curve, glide, strip, surge, swish, trail **6.** course, vision **7.** contour **8.** traverse
sweeping . . . **8.** complete, thorough **9.** extensive **12.** all–embracing **13.** comprehensive
sweet . . . **5.** bonny, candy **10.** dolce douce **5.** fresh, spicy **6.** dulcet, gentle, sugary, syrupy **7.** caramel, honeyed, lovable **8.** aromatic, fragrant, luscious, pleasant, preserve **9.** agreeable, ambrosial, melodious, nectarine **10.** confection, saccharine **11.** mellifluous, mellisonant
sweet (pert to) . . .
and fair .. **5.** bonny
bread .. **4.** food **6.** thymus **8.** pancreas **9.** ris de veau
brier .. **4.** rose **9.** eglantine
drink .. **6.** nectar
meat .. **4.** cake **5.** candy **6.** comfit, éclair, pastry **7.** caramel, dessert **8.** marzipan **10.** confection
potato .. **3.** yam **6.** batata
potato, musical .. **7.** ocarina
sop .. **4.** ates, atta **6.** Annone **14.** Annona squamosa
sounding .. **11.** mellisonant
wine .. **4.** port **5.** Lunel
sweetheart . . . **2.** jo **3.** gra **4.** beau, lass **5.** flame, leman, lover, spark, swain **7.** darling **8.** dowsabel, honeybun (sl), ladylove **9.** Amaryllis, inamorata, valentine
swell . . . **3.** fob, nob **4.** grow, rise, surf, wave **5.** bulge, dandy, grand, heave, mound, surge **6.** billow, dilate, expand, growth, puff up, tiptop **7.** distend, inflate, stylish **8.** increase, protrude **9.** sumptuous **10.** aristocrat, prominence **11.** enlargement **12.** augmentation
swell (pert to) . . .
ocean .. **4.** surf **6.** billow, expand, roller

rolling .. **7.** seagate
slang .. **3.** nob **5.** dandy, grand **9.** first–rate
swelled (pert to) . . .
head .. **3.** ego **7.** conceit **9.** cockiness **14.** self–importance
out .. **4.** lump, node **5.** tumid **6.** bulged, podded, turgid **9.** grandiose
swelling . . . **4.** sore **5.** bulge, edema **6.** dropsy **9.** bombastic **10.** distention, increasing **12.** protuberance
swelter . . . **4.** fret **5.** exude, roast, sweat **8.** perspire **10.** sultry heat
swerve . . . **4.** veer **5.** dodge, sheer, shift **6.** recoil **7.** deflect, deviate **9.** deviation, turn aside
swift . . . **4.** bird, fast, racy, reel **5.** alert, fleet, hasty, quick, rapid, ready **6.** lizard, prompt, speedy, sudden, winged **8.** headlong
swift (pert to) . . .
astronomer .. **5.** Lewis (Swift)
bird .. **4.** crin **7.** chimney
boat .. **7.** flyboat **10.** Hovercraft
footed .. **5.** ariel (gazelle) **7.** Mercury
satirist .. **8.** Jonathan (Swift)
swiftness . . . **5.** haste, speed **8.** celerity, velocity **9.** quickness **10.** promptness
swimmer . . . **5.** diver **6.** bather **7.** Cloelia (Tiber Riv), Leander (Hellespont), natator
swimming . . . **5.** crawl **6.** natant **7.** vertigo **9.** dizziness, freestyle, skinny–dip **10.** sidestroke **12.** breast stroke
swimming (pert to) . . .
birds .. **9.** natatores
bladder .. **10.** air bladder (fish)
pert to .. **5.** dizzy **7.** aquatic **8.** natatory
pool .. **4.** hole, tank **10.** natatorium
sandpiper .. **9.** phalarope
swindle . . . **3.** con, gyp **4.** dupe, fake, sell **5.** bunco, cheat **6.** trepan **7.** defraud **8.** flimflam **9.** gold brick
swindler . . . **3.** gyp **5.** biter, cheat, crook, knave, rogue, shark **6.** gypper **7.** sharper **9.** defrauder
swindling . . . **6.** estafa
swine . . . **3.** hog, pig, sow, Sus **4.** boar **7.** Anthony (smallest), peccary **8.** slattern **9.** scoundrel
swine, breed of . . . **8.** Cheshire, Tamworth **9.** Berkshire, Hampshire, razorback, Yorkshire **11.** Duroc–Jersey, Poland China **12.** Chester–White
swineherd (pert to) . . .
patron saint .. **7.** Anthony
reference to .. **7.** sybotic
swinelike . . . **7.** porcine
swing . . . **4.** hang, jazz, jive, lilt, sway **5.** shake, trend, waver, wield **6.** dangle, manage, rhythm, totter **7.** suspend, trapeze, vibrate **8.** pendulum, undulate **9.** fluctuate, oscillate
swingtree . . . **11.** whippletree
swinish . . . **5.** gross **6.** carnal, filthy,

greedy 7. beastly, porcine, sensual
  8. gluttony
swipe . . . 4. gulp 5. draft, drink, lever,
  steal, swape, swath, sweep
  6. handle, pilfer, snatch 7. purloin
swipes . . . 4. beer (Eng sl)
swirl . . . 4. curl, eddy 5. curve, gurge,
  surge, twist, whirl, whorl
swirly . . . 7. knotted, tangled, twisted
Swiss (pert to) . . . see also *Switzerland*
  ax (ice) . . 6. piolet
  bell . . 9. alpenhorn (alphorn)
  cabin . . 6. chalet
  composer . . 4. Raff
  flower, emblem . . 9. edelweiss
  herdsman . . 4. senn
  hero . . 11. William Tell
  language . . 6. French, German
    7. Italian 8. Romansch
  legislature . . 9. Bundesrat (Bundesrath),
    Grosse Rat (Grossrat)
  mathematician . . 5. Euler
  pine . . 6. arolla
  scientist . . 6. Haller (von)
  surgeon . . 6. Kocher (Nobel Prize)
  theologian . . 5. Vinet
  warble . . 5. yodel
  warbler . . 7. yodeler (yodeller)
  wind . . 4. bise
  wine . . 7. Dezaley
Switzerland (pert to) . . .
  ancient . . 8. Helvetia
  canton . . 5. Aarau
  capital . . 5. Berne (Bern)
  city . . 5. Basel 6. Geneva, Zurich
    7. Locarno, Lucerne 8. Lausanne
    9. Constance
  famed for . . 5. banks (Finan)
  lake . . 3. Uri 6. Brienz, Geneva, Zurich
    7. Lucerne 8. Maggiore
    9. Constance, Neuchâtel
    10. Stattersee
  mountain . . 4. Alps, Jura 5. Blanc
    8. Jungfrau 9. Monte Rosa (peak)
    10. Matterhorn
  resort . . 7. Urseren, Yverdon
  river . . 3. Aar 5. Reuss, Rhine, Rhone
  tunnel . . 5. Cenis 7. Gothard, Simplon
    11. Loetschberg
  university (oldest) . . 5. Basel
  valley . . 3. Aar
swollen . . . 5. pursy, tumid 6. turgid
    7. bloated, bulbous, bulging,
    pompous 8. enlarged, inflated, puffed
    up, varicose 9. bombastic, distended,
    plethoric, tumescent 11. protuberant
swoon . . . 3. fit 5. faint, spell
    7. ecstasy, syncope 8. languish
    10. heavy sleep
swoop . . . 5. seize, sweep 6. attack,
    pounce 7. descend
sword (pert to) . . .
  ancient . . 5. estoc 6. glaive
  cavalry . . 5. saber (sabre)
  curved . . 7. cutlass, Ferrara
    8. Claymore, scimitar
  fencing . . 4. foil, epee 6. rapier
  fine . . 6. Toledo 8. Damascus
  handle . . 4. haft, hilt
  India . . 5. kukri
  like . . 7. xiphoid

  Mohammedan's . . 8. scimitar
  part . . 5. forte, talon 6. foible
  practice . . 5. fence
  scabbard tip . . 7. crampit
  Scot Highlander's . . 4. dirk
  seaman's . . 6. hanger
  shaped . . 6. ensate 7. xiphoid
    (xyphoid) 8. ensiform, gladiate
  sheik's . . 4. pata
  Siegfried's . . 4. Gram 7. Balmung
  Sir Bevis' . . 7. Morglay
  Spanish . . 5. bilbo
  support . . 7. baldric
  two–handed . . 7. espadon
  type . . 4. epee, pata 5. blade, degen,
    estoc, gully, saber 6. barong, creese,
    parang, rapier 7. cutlass 9. gladiolus
swordfish . . . 6. dorado, Dorado
    (constellation), espada 7. espadon,
    Xiphias 9. broadbill
sword of . . .
  Damocles . . 12. fateful thing
  God . . 6. Khaled (Moslem hero)
  mercy . . 7. Curtana (pointless)
  Sir Bevis . . 7. Morglay (death)
  St George . . 7. Askelon
  the Cid . . 6. Colada
swordsman . . . 6. fencer 7. duelist,
    epeeist, saberer, sabreur 9. gladiator
    11. Beau Sabreur
sworn statement . . . 9. affidavit
sworn to secrecy . . . 5. tiled
sybarite . . . 7. epicure 10. voluptuary
    11. luxury lover
sybil (sibil) . . . 4. seer 5. witch
    7. seeress 10. prophetess
    13. fortuneteller
syce . . . 5. groom
sycophant . . . 5. toady 7. fawning,
    spaniel 8. hanger–on, informer,
    parasite 9. charlatan, flatterer,
    toadeater 10. talebearer
sycophantic . . . 7. fawning, servile,
    slavish 8. obedient, toadying
    10. obsequious 11. bootlicking
syllable . . .
  accented . . 5. arsis
  by syllable . . 11. syllabation
  charm . . 2. om 6. mantra
  last . . 6. ultima
  last, omission of . . 7. apocope
  last but one . . 6. penult
  last but two . . 10. antepenult
  lengthening of . . 7. ectasis
  ref to . . 5. affix 6. prefix, suffix
    8. dactylic, syllabic
  short . . 4. mora
  shortening . . 7. systole
  stress . . 5. ictus
  table . . 9. syllabary
  unaccented . . 4. lene 6. thesis
syllabled, three . . . 7. triseme (3
    moras) 11. trisyllabic
syllabus . . . 6. aperçu, digest
    8. abstract, synopsis
    10. compendium, conspectus
syllogism . . . 7. premise, sorites
    9. deduction, reasoning
    11. epicheirema (epichirema)
    18. deductive reasoning
sylvan, silvan . . . 5. woody 6. groved,
    rustic, wooded 8. forested

10. forestlike
sylvan deity... 3. Pan 4. faun
   5. Satyr, Vidar 6. Faunus
symbol... 2. om 4. icon, palm, sign,
   type 5. badge, crest, cross, image,
   token, totem 6. emblem, ensign,
   figure, letter, number 9. character
   (graphic), prototype, trademark
   12. abbreviation
symbol (pert to)...
  authority.. 4. mace
  bondage.. 4. yoke
  ecclesiastic.. 4. ring
  England.. 4. lion
  France.. 4. lily
  mathematics.. 7. operand
  military.. 3. bar 4. star 5. eagle,
   wings 6. stripe 7. chevron, epaulet
   (epaulette) 8. caduceus
  peace.. 4. dove
  power.. 4. mace
  prayer figure (anc).. 5. orant
  royal.. 3. rod 5. crown, tiara
   6. corona 7. scepter (sceptre)
  Tammany Hall.. 5. tiger
  tribal.. 5. totem (pole)
  victory.. 4. palm
symbol for...
  arsenic.. 2. As
  calcium.. 2. Ca
  chromium.. 2. Cr
  copper.. 2. Cu
  gold.. 2. Au
  iron.. 2. Fe
  lead.. 2. Pb
  neon.. 2. Ne
  nickel.. 2. Ni
  radium.. 2. Ra
  silver.. 2. Ag, Ar
  sodium.. 2. Na
  tin.. 2. Sn
symbolic, symbolical... 7. typical
   9. imagerial 10. figurative, relational
   11. allegorical, significant
   12. emblematical 14. representative
symbolism... 7. mystery, writing
   9. mysticism, ritualism, symbolics
   10. figuration 11. hieroglyphy
   14. representation
symmetric, symmetrical... 7. orderly,
   regular, spheral, uniform 8. balanced
   10. euphonious
symmetry... 5. order 7. balance,
   euphony, harmony 8. equality
   9. congruity 10. conformity,
   proportion 11. consistency
sympathetic... 4. kind 6. humane,
   tender 7. empathy, pitying
   8. dewy–eyed 10. responsive
   13. compassionate, understanding
sympathy... 4. pity 5. favor
   7. consent, harmony, support
   8. affinity, interest 9. agreeable,
   agreement, tolerance 11. sensitivity
   13. commiseration, understanding
sympathy, lack of... 8. dyspathy
   9. antipathy
symphony... 6. accord 7. concert,
   harmony 8. ritornel 9. orchestra
   10. consonance 11. composition
symposium... 4. book, talk 7. banquet
   8. dialogue, tippling 10. collection,

discussion 11. compotation
symptom... 4. mark, note, omen, sign
   5. alarm, token 7. warning
   10. indication
synagogue... 6. temple 10. tabernacle
   12. congregation
synagogue (pert to)...
  founder (anc).. 4. Ezra
  platform.. 7. almemar
  singer.. 6. cantor, chazan (chazzan)
synchronize... 5. agree 6. concur
   8. coincide 9. harmonize
   12. contemporize
syncopation... 5. tempo 7. ragtime,
   syncope
syncope... 5. faint, swoon 7. elision
   8. fainting, swooning 9. haplology
   11. contraction, hyphaeresis
syndicate... 5. chain (journalistic),
   group, trust 6. cartel, school
   7. combine, council 9. committee
   10. underworld 11. association
   12. organization
synonym... 7. antonym, homonym,
   metonym 8. identity 9. heteronym
synonymous... 4. like 5. alike
   7. similar 10. equivalent,
   homonymous
synopsis... 6. digest, manual
   7. epitome, summary 8. abstract,
   syllabus 9. statement 10. abridgment
   (abridgement), compendium,
   conspectus, tabulation
synthesis... 5. logic 11. combination,
   composition 13. incorporation
   14. identification
Syracuse (pert to)...
  ancient name.. 8. Siracusa
  city of.. 6. Sicily
  famed for.. 6. battle (BC)
  founded by.. 6. Greeks
  tyrant of.. 9. Dionysius
Syria, Arab Republic... see also
  Syrian
  ancient name.. 4. Aram
  capital.. 8. Damascus
  city.. 4. Hama, Homs 6. Aleppo,
   Beirut 7. Antioch, Latakia
   8. Damascus
  language.. 6. Arabic
  organization, party.. 5. Baath
  river.. 6. Barada, Jordan 7. Orontes
   9. Euphrates
Syrian (pert to)...
  antiquarian.. 11. Syriologist
  deity.. 2. El 4. Baal 6. Mammon
   7. Resheph
  goat.. 6. Angora
  grass.. 7. Johnson
  mallow.. 4. okra
  script.. 8. Peshitta (Peshito)
   10. estrangelo 11. Syro–Chaldee
  sect.. 5. Druse
  tribe.. 7. Ansarie (Ansarieh)
  wind (hot).. 6. simoom (simoon)
syrinx... 4. tomb 6. larynx 7. Panpipe
   10. mouthpiece (anc lute)
   13. Arcadian nymph
syrup, sirup... 4. Karo, sapa 5. maple
   6. orgeat 7. dhebbus, glucose,
   sorghum, treacle 8. molasses
   9. grenadine

system... 3. ism, way 4. code, plan
  5. order 6. regime, theory
  8. religion, universe 9. procedure
  10. hypothesis, regularity
  11. arrangement, orderliness
system (pert to)...
  conduct.. 4. code
  eating.. 4. diet 7. dietary
  geological.. 5. Trias
  management.. 6. regime
  manual training.. 5. sloyd
  mystic.. 6. cabala
  numbering.. 7. decimal
  pitch (Mus).. 5. neume
  religious.. 4. cult 6. cultus
  solar.. 6. planet
  weights.. 4. long, troy 5. cubic
  6. liquid 11. avoirdupois
  12. apothecaries'
systematic... 4. neat 6. formal
  7. orderly, regular 9. organized,

schematic 10. methodical
systematics... 8. taxonomy
  14. classification
systematize... 4. code 6. codify
  7. arrange 8. classify, organize,
  regiment 9. catalogue (catalog),
  formulate
systematized knowledge... 7. science
systole (pert to)...
  correlative.. 8. diastole
  medical.. 11. contraction (heart)
  14. coming and going
  rhyme.. 10. shortening (syllable)
syzygy (pert to)...
  astronomy.. 7. appulse
  11. conjunction
  Gnosticism.. 5. aeons (pair)
  rhyme.. 11. coupled feet (group)
  zoology.. 5. union 7. segment
szlachta... 8. nobility (Poland)
szopelka... 4. oboe (Russ)

T

T... 3. tau (Gr) 6. letter (20th)
taa... 6. pagoda
Taal... 8. language 9. Afrikaans
taar... 10. tambourine
Taaroa... 3. God
tab... 3. pan, tag 4. bill, cost, flap,
  loop 5. aglet (aiglet), label, strip
  6. eartab, record 7. account, latchet,
  pendant (pendent) 8. afterpart,
  appendage, reckoning 10. accounting
tabac... 5. brown, snuff 7. tobacco
tabard... 4. cape 5. cloak 6. chimer,
  jacket, mantle
Tabard... 3. Inn (Canterbury Tales)
tabatière... 8. snuffbox
tabby... 3. cat 4. gown, silk 5. dress
  6. fabric, gossip 7. old maid, taffeta
tabernacle... 4. tent 5. abode, niche
  6. church, temple 7. shelter, support
  8. enshrine 9. sanctuary
  10. habitation
table... 4. fare, list, slab 5. board,
  panel, plate, stand 6. lamina, repast,
  tablet, teapoy 7. console, plateau,
  weights 8. postpone, put aside,
  synopsis, tabulate 9. reference
  10. collection 14. multiplication
table (pert to)...
  calculating.. 6. abacus
  centerpiece.. 7. epergne
  communion.. 5. altar 8. credence,
  credenza
  contents.. 5. index
  cover.. 5. baize, tapis
  dish.. 6. tureen
  land.. 4. mesa 6. karroo (karoo),
  plains 7. plateau
  linen.. 6. napery
  philosophy.. 13. deipnosophism

talk (versed in).. 13. deipnosophist
type.. 3. tea 4. turn 6. coffee,
  gaming 7. dinette, dresser, gate–leg,
  kitchen, taboret 8. captain's,
  drop–leaf
tableau... 5. drama, scene 7. picture
  8. schedule 14. representation
tablet... 3. pad 4. pill, slab 5. facia,
  slate, stele 6. troche 7. lozenge
  8. monument, notebook
taboo, tabu... 3. ban 4. deny
  5. debar 6. forbid 7. embargo
  8. disallow, prohibit 9. forbidden,
  interdict, proscribe 11. prohibition
  12. interdiction
tabulate... 4. list 6. record 7. tabular
  8. classify, schedule
tabulation... 7. listing 8. calendar,
  paradigm 12. registration
taccada... 9. fanflower
tacit... 6. silent 7. implied
  8. unspoken, wordless 9. indicated,
  noiseless 10. understood
taciturn... 6. silent 8. reserved,
  reticent 9. saturnine
tack... 4. brad, gear, jibe, join, rope,
  sail, trip 5. baste, lease, route
  6. course, fasten, secure, staple,
  tackle 7. clothes 9. fastening
  10. supplement
tackle... 3. cat, rig 4. gear, tack
  5. davit, seize 6. burton, collar,
  garnet 7. cordage, grapple, harness,
  rigging 8. football (term)
  9. encounter, equipment, undertake
tacky... 5. crude, dowdy, seedy
  6. shabby, sticky, untidy 8. adhesive,
  slovenly
tact... 5. grace, poise, taste

7. address, finesse 8. delicacy
9. diplomacy 10. adroitness,
cleverness, discretion
11. discernment, savoir–faire
14. discrimination

tadpole . . . 4. frog, toad 8. polliwog,
porwigle 9. youngling

tag . . . 3. add, end, rag, tab 4. flap,
game, loop, name 5. aglet (aiglet),
label, sheep, strip 6. fasten, follow
7. earmark, frazzle, pendant, taglock
9. appendage 11. aiguillette
(ornamental)

Tagalog, Tagal (pert to) . . .
child, servant . . 4. anac, bata
deity . . 6. Batala
game (gambling) . . 10. panguingui
native of . . 5. Luzon 11. Philippines
peasant . . 3. tao
race . . 4. Aeta (dwarf) 7. Malayan

Tahiti . . .
arrowroot . . 3. pia
boat . . 4. pahi
capital . . 7. Papeete (of all Society
Isles)
food plant . . 4. taro
god . . 3. oro 6. Taaroa (Supreme)
old name . . 8. Otaheite
robe (coronation) . . 4. malo
woman . . 6. wahine (vahine)

Tai, Thai tribes . . . 4. Laos, Shan
7. Siamese

tail . . . 3. bun, cue, end 4. arse, back,
hair, last, rear 5. cauda, stern
6. follow, shadow 7. pendant
8. entailed, streamer 9. afterpart,
appendage, extremity

tail (pert to) . . .
aircraft's . . 9. empennage
boar's . . 6. wreath
coin . . 5. verso 7. reverse
dog's . . 5. plume, stern, twist
having a . . 7. caudate
peacock's . . 5. train
pert to . . 6. caudal 9. coccygeal
rabbit's . . 4. scut
rudimentary . . 6. coccyx
tailrace . . 5. flume 7. channel

tailing . . . 5. chaff, waste 6. refuse

tailless . . . 6. tenrec (mammal)
7. acaudal, anurous, Ranidae
8. acaudate, ecaudate

tailor . . . 3. cut, fit 4. form 6. darzee,
draper, sartor 7. fashion 8. tailleur

tailor (pert to) . . .
goose . . 4. iron 12. pressing iron
made . . 6. fitted 9. fashioned
reference to . . 9. sartorial
twist . . 10. silk thread (stout)

taint . . . 3. due, hue 5. color, imbue,
spoil, stain, sully, tinge 6. defile,
infect, poison, stigma 7. blemish,
corrupt, deprave, pollute, vitiate
8. disgrace 9. denigrate, infection
10. corruption, stigmatize
11. contaminate

tainted . . . 3. bad 6. soiled 7. stained
8. diseased 9. corrupted

taintless . . . 4. good 5. clean
6. chaste 8. flawless, innocent

Taiwan . . .
capital . . 6. Taipai

Taj Mahal (pert to) . . .
architecture . . 9. Saracenic
builder . . 9. Shah–Jahan
mausolem site . . 4. Agra
named for . . 4. wife

take . . . 2. go 3. get, win 4. deem,
doff, gain, shut 5. atone, booty, carry,
catch, seize, snare, steal, usurp
6. accept, borrow, deduce, endure,
obtain 7. capture, conduct, control,
detract, receive 8. proceeds, receipts,
subtract, tolerate 9. apprehend
11. appropriate

take (pert to) . . .
a chair . . 3. sit
a direction . . 5. steer
advantage of . . 5. abuse 6. misuse
apart . . 8. demolish 11. disassemble
as one's own . . 5. adopt 6. borrow
away . . 5. adeem, clear, reave, steal,
wrest 6. adempt, deduct, remove
7. deprive, detract, retract
8. derogate, subtract, withdraw
11. expropriate
back . . 6. recant, repeal, return
by storm . . 5. seize 6. attack
by stratagem . . 4. trap 8. outsmart
care of . . 4. mind 5. guard, nurse,
serve, watch 6. beware 7. support
10. provide for
charge of . . 8. attend to 9. look after
down . . 4. fell, raze 5. lower, write
6. humble, record 7. reprove,
swallow 8. emaciate
first . . 7. pre–empt
for granted . . 5. infer 6. assume,
expect 7. believe, presume, suppose
in . . 3. eat, see 4. hear 5. admit,
annex, learn 6. absorb, attend
7. embrace, include, involve, receive,
shorten 9. encompass
notice . . 2. NB 3. see
out . . 4. dele 5. elide 6. delete, efface
7. expunge
place of . . 8. supplant 9. supersede
the floor . . 5. speak 7. address
9. legislate
to flight . . 4. flee 7. run away,
scamper 9. skedaddle
up . . 4. fill, lift 5. adopt, begin, raise
6. absorb, assume, gather, occupy
8. engage in 9. undertake
without authority . . 5. usurp

talapoin . . . 6. monkey (guenon)
8. poonghie 12. Buddhist monk

talc . . . 6. powder, talcum 7. agalite
8. steatite 9. soapstone

tale . . . 3. lai, lay, lie 4. myth, saga,
yarn 5. conte, fable, story 6. gossip,
legend 7. romance 8. anecdote
9. discourse, falsehood, narration,
narrative 11. declaration
12. conversation

tale (pert to) . . .
adventure . . 4. gest
bearer . . 6. gossip 7. blabber, tattler
8. informer 13. scandalmonger
chivalry . . 7. romance
doleful . . 5. jeremiad
fatality . . 5. drama 7. tragedy
symbolic . . 8. allegory
traditional . . 4. saga 8. folktale

T
Z

talent... 4. gift 5. dower, flair, forte, money (anc), skill 6. genius 7. ability, faculty 8. aptitude, artistry 9. attribute 11. disposition 14. accomplishment
talesman... 5. juror 8. narrator
talisman... 4. juju, mojo, tara 5. charm, karma 6. amulet, fetish, grigri (greegree), scarab 7. periapt 12. antinganting
talk... 3. gab, gas, rap, yak, yap 4. blab, blat, chat, chin, harp, rant, rave 5. lingo, orate, parle, prate, rumor, speak, spiel, utter 6. babble, confab, confer, gabble, gossip, jargon, lesson, speech 7. address, blabber, chatter, declaim, discuss 8. causerie, chitchat, colloquy, converse, language, parlance 9. dalliance, discourse 11. communicate 12. conversation
talk (pert to)...
about.. 5. rumor 6. gossip
affected, pretentious.. 4. cant, rant
ancient.. 5. parle
back.. 4. sass 6. retort 7. riposte 8. feedback, repartee
flattering.. 7. palaver
fluent.. 7. verbose, voluble
idiotically.. 6. drivel
long.. 9. gibberish, rigmarole
loud.. 5. blate
promoting.. 4. hype 8. ballyhoo
running.. 6. patter
silly.. 5. drool 6. drivel, footle 7. blather, prattle, twaddle
slang.. 3. gab, gas 4. sass 5. spiel
slowly.. 5. drawl
small.. 3. gab 4. chat, chin 7. prattle 8. chitchat
Spanish.. 7. palabra
talkative... 4. glib 6. fluent 7. verbose, voluble 9. garrulous 10. loquacious 13. communicative
talker... 6. gasser, proser, ranter 7. speaker, spieler 9. chatterbox 17. conversationalist
tall... 4. high, long 5. lofty 6. seemly 7. procere, sky-high 8. towering, yielding 10. incredible, statuesque 11. exaggerated
tall (pert to)...
order.. 9. falsehood 10. difficulty
person.. 10. hypermeter
structure.. 7. steeple
talk.. 4. brag 12. exaggeration 14. grandiloquence
tallest known race... 10. Patagonian
tally... 3. run, sum, tab 4. goal, list, mark 5. agree, check, count, match, notch, score 6. accord, reckon, record 7. account, compare, count up 8. coincide, estimate 9. reckoning 10. bottom line, correspond
Talmud... 9. Jewish law
Talmud (pert to)...
academy.. 8. Yeshivah (Yeshiva)
commentary.. 6. Gemara
student.. 5. bahur
text.. 7. Mishnah
talon... 4. paw 5. claw, fang, nail 6. clutch, finger, pincer
talus... 5. ankle 8. clubfoot

tamarisk... 4. atle (atlee) 8. salt tree
tambo... 3. inn 6. corral, stable, tavern 10. tambourine
tambor... 6. puffer 8. rockfish
tambour... 4. desk, drum, lace 5. frame 6. stitch 7. drummer 8. ornament, stockade 9. embroider
tambourine... 4. dove, drum, taar 5. daira 7. timbrel 8. minstrel
tambourine effect (Mus)... 7. travale
tambreet... 8. duckbill
tamburone... 4. drum 8. bass drum
tame... 4. dull, meek, mild 5. inert 6. docile, gentle, humble, subdue 7. crushed, insipid, subdued 8. tone down 9. tractable 10. cultivated 11. domesticate 12. domesticated
Tamil... 5. Hindu 8. language (oldest Dravidian) 9. Dravidian
tamis... 5. sieve, tammy 8. strainer
Tammany (pert to)...
Hall.. 14. Democratic Club
man.. 10. politician
officer.. 8. Wiskinky (Wiskinkie)
scandal.. 9. Tweed Ring
Society site.. 11. New York City (1789)
symbol.. 5. tiger
tamper with... 4. plot 5. alter, bribe 6. meddle, monkey, scheme, tinker 7. falsify 9. influence, interfere
tampion, tampon... 4. plug 6. tympan 7. stopper, turnpin 9. rhynobyon
tan... 3. dun, taw 4. buff, ecru, tent, whip 5. beige, brown, color, tawny 6. rabbit, suntan, thrash 7. sunburn
tanager... 4. yeni 5. lindo 7. Piranga, redbird
tanbark... 3. oak 7. hemlock
Tancred... 6. leader (1st crusade)
Tanganyika... see *Tanzania*
tangible... 4. real 7. tactile 8. palpable 9. objective, touchable 11. perceptible, substantial
tangle... 3. mat, mop 4. kink, shag 5. ravel, snare, snarl, weave 6. entrap, medley, muddle, sleave, tousle 7. ensnare, involve 8. quandary 9. interlock 10. complicate, interweave
tank... 3. vat 4. lake, pond, pool 5. basin 6. hot tub 7. cistern, stomach 9. reservoir 11. army vehicle, hard drinker
tanker... 4. ship 5. oiler 8. fuel ship
tanning shrub... 5. alder, sumac (sumach)
tantalize... 3. vex 5. taunt, tease 6. harass, plague 7. torment
tantalum symbol... 2. Ta
Tantalus (pert to)...
father.. 4. Zeus
father of.. 5. Niobe 6. Pelops
genus of.. 4. ibis
king (rich).. 6. Greece
tantamount... 5. equal 9. identical 10. equivalent 13. corresponding
tantara... 7. fanfare 9. tantarara 12. trumpet blare
tantrum... 3. fit 4. rage 7. caprice 8. tirrivee (tirrivie) 10. conniption

Tanzania, Africa...
  capital.. 11. Dar es Salaam (Haven of
    Peace)
  famed Mt.. 11. Kilimanjaro
  famed plains.. 9. Serengeti
  famed town.. 5. Ujiji (Stanley found
    Livingstone, 1871)
  formerly.. 8. Zanzibar 10. Tanganyika
  language.. 7. Swahili
  natives.. 5. Bantu
Taoism, names... 6. Kwanti, Laotze
  7. Yu Hwang
tap... 3. dum, hit, hob, rap 4. plug,
  tamp 5. sound, spile 6. faucet,
  liquor, siphon, spigot, strike
  7. censure, petcock, reprove
tape... 3. gin, tie 4. band, wick
  5. strip 6. fillet, ribbon, secure
  7. bandage, measure 9. recording
taper... 4. ream, wick 5. point, snape,
  spire 6. candle, cierge, narrow
  7. conical 8. decrease, diminish
  9. acuminate 11. pyramidical
tapering (pert to)...
  blades.. 6. spires
  pert to.. 6. spired, terete 7. conical,
    pointed 8. fusiform 9. narrowing
  piece.. 4. gore 5. miter 6. gusset
  pillar.. 7. obelisk
  solid.. 4. cone
tapestry... 5. arras, tapis 6. Bayeux,
  dosser 7. Gobelin
tapeworm... 6. Taenia
tapeworm (pert to)...
  embryonic.. 10. oncosphere
  like.. 8. taenioid
  segment.. 8. strobila
tapioca, source... 5. salep 7. cassava
  (casava)
Tapirus... 6. tapirs
tapster... 7. barmaid, skinker
tar... 3. gob 4. brea, pave, salt
  5. black, pitch 6. cresol, maltha,
  sailor, seaman 7. mariner 8. telegram
  10. bluejacket
tarantula... 6. spider 7. mygalid
  10. wolf spider
tarboosh... 3. fez 6. red cap
tardy... 3. lag, lax 4. late, slow
  5. slack 6. remiss 7. belated,
  lagging, overdue 8. dilatory
  10. behindhand 11. cunctatious
tare... 4. weed (Bib) 5. vetch
  8. discount 9. allowance, deduction
target... 3. aim, tee 4. butt, goal,
  goat, mark, prey 5. sight 6. object,
  shield, tassel 8. bull's–eye, ridicule
  9. objective
tariff... 4. duty, list, rate 6. charge
  7. tribute 8. schedule
tariffist... 8. advocate
  13. protectionist
tarnish... 3. dim 4. dull, soil, spot
  5. cloud, stain, sully, taint 6. smirch,
  stigma, vilify 7. blemish, destroy,
  obscure 8. besmirch, discolor
  10. lose luster, stigmatize
taro... 3. poi 4. eddo, food, gabi
  (gabe) 5. cocco, tania (tanier)
  12. elephant's–ear
tarot... 14. fortunetelling (cards)
tarried... 6. waited 7. dallied

8. lingered, remained
tarry... 3. lag 4. bide, stay, wait
  5. abide, await, dally, delay, pause,
  stall 6. dawdle, linger, loiter, retard
  7. outstay
tarsus... 5. ankle 7. segment
tart... 4. acid, sour 5. acrid, sharp
  6. pastry, severe 7. caustic, pungent,
  waspish 8. poignant, turnover
  10. astringent 11. acrimonious
tartan... 4. wool 5. plaid 7. pattern
  (plaid) 10. Highlander
tartar... 5. argol (argal), shrew, valet
  12. incrustation
Tartar, Tatar... 4. Turk 6. Mongol
Tartar, Tatar (pert to)...
  domain.. 7. Khanate
  horseman.. 7. Cossack
  lancer.. 5. uhlan
  nobleman.. 5. murza
  people of.. 6. Turkey 8. Mongolia
  title.. 4. Khan
  tribe.. 2. Hu 3. Hun 6. Mongol
tartarean... 5. cruel 7. hellish
  8. infernal
Tartarus (Myth)... 4. hell 5. Hades
  15. infernal regions (Iliad)
task... 3. job 4. duty, snap, test, toil
  5. chore, labor, stent, stint 6. burden,
  dargue, impost, strain 10. assignment,
  employment 11. undertaking
Tasmania (pert to)...
  animal (burrowing).. 6. wombat
  discoverer.. 6. Tasman (1642)
  marsupial.. 9. phalanger
  mountain.. 6. Cradle 9. Ben Lomond
  strait.. 4. Bass
taste... 3. sip, sup 4. tang 5. flair,
  sapor, savor, sense, smack, style
  6. liking, palate, relish, sample
  7. soupçon 8. delicacy, elegance,
  fondness, judgment 9. gustation
  10. experience 14. discrimination
  15. aesthetic liking
taste (pert to)...
  bite.. 4. nosh 5. snack
  decided.. 8. fondness, penchant
  French.. 7. soupçon
  fundamental.. 4. acid, salt 5. sweet
    6. bitter
  lacking.. 4. rude 5. bland, gross, stale
    10. unpolished
  ref to.. 7. palatal 9. gustatory
  sharp.. 4. acid, tang
tasteless... 4. dull, flat 5. vapid
  6. vulgar, watery 7. insipid 8. lifeless
  9. savorless 10. inartistic
tasty... 6. savory 8. saporous, tasteful
  9. delicious, palatable, toothsome
Tatar... see *Tartar*
tatouay... 9. armadillo
tatter... 3. rag 4. tags, tear 5. patch,
  piece, shred 6. ribbon
tatterdemalion... 5. gamin
  9. ragpicker 10. ragamuffin
tattle... 4. blab, tell 5. prate 6. gossip
  7. chatter, divulge, prattle 8. idle
  talk, inform on
tattler... 6. gossip, willet 8. quidnunc,
  redshank, telltale 10. alarm clock,
  talebearer, yellowlegs
tattoo... 4. call (drum, bugle), pony,

scar 13. entertainment
tau... 4. ankh, crux, rood 5. cross
6. letter (Gr) 7. T-shaped
tau cross... 4. ankh 6. symbol
8. crucifix, insignia 10. St Anthony's
taunt... 4. gibe, jeer, mock, twit
5. sneer, tease 6. deride 7. provoke
8. reproach, ridicule 9. aggravate
Taurus... 4. bull 8. Pleiades
13. constellation
taut... 4. firm, snug, tidy 5. tense,
tight 6. severe, strict 7. nervous
9. distended
tautology... 8. pleonasm
10. redundancy, repetition
tavern... 3. inn, pub 5. hotel
7. barroom, cabaret, Gasthof, taberna
8. alehouse, Gasthaus, hostelry
taw... 4. game, whip 6. marble
7. tanning
tawdry... 4. loud 5. cheap, gaudy,
showy 6. garish 7. blatant
tawny, tawney... 3. tan 5. dusky,
olive, tenne 6. tanned 7. jacinth
8. brindled 9. bullfinch
tax... 4. cess, duty, geld, levy, scat
(scatt), task, toll 5. stent 6. assess,
burden, custom, excise, impose,
income, octroi, strain 7. doomage,
license, tribute 8. exaction, overtire
9. prescribe 10. assessment
tax (pert to)...
ancient.. 3. cro 4. geld 7. galanas
assessment.. 4. rate 5. ratal
7. doomage
church.. 5. tithe
commodity.. 6. octroi
French history.. 6. taille
kind.. 5. tithe 6. excise, surtax, taille
7. boscage 8. auxilium, carucage
9. surcharge
liquor.. 6. abkari (abkary)
pasturage (Shetland Isls).. 4. scat
(scatt)
tea... 5. dance, party, shrub 6. supper
8. beverage, function, sociable
9. collation, reception
tea (pert to)...
chemical content.. 6. tannin, theine
(thein) 8. caffeine
Chinese.. 5. black, hyson
Formosa.. 6. oolong
Ind Ceylon.. 5. pekoe
infusion.. 6. ptisan, tisane
Labrador.. 5. Ledum 8. gowiddie
Paraguay.. 5. yerba
receptacle.. 5. caddy 8. canister
table.. 6. teapoy (tepoy)
type.. 3. cha 4. tsia 5. Assam, black,
green, hyson, Ledum, oopak, pekoe
6. oolong 7. cambric 8. gowiddie
urn.. 3. pot 7. samovar
weak.. 7. cambric
teach... 4. show 5. coach, drill, edify,
guide, prime, train, tutor 6. direct,
impart, preach, school 7. educate,
show how 8. instruct 9. enlighten
11. demonstrate
teacher... 5. coach, guide, rabbi, tutor
6. doctor, mentor, pastor, pedant,
priest, pundit, reader, regent, rhetor,
scribe 7. edifier, starets 8. educator,

preacher 9. pedagogue, preceptor
10. instructor
teacher (pert to)...
Alexandrian.. 6. Origen
Indian.. 4. guru
Jewish.. 5. rabbi
Mohammedan.. 3. pir 4. imam
6. mullah
of the deaf.. 7. oralist
Russian.. 7. starets
teaching... 5. moral 6. docent
7. precept 8. doctrine 11. instruction
Teaching of the Twelve... 10. The
Didache
team... 3. two 4. haul, join, pain,
span, yoke 5. brood, chain, wagon
7. vehicle 8. carriage 9. yannigans
teamster... 6. carter, driver 7. carrier
Teapot Dome (pert to)...
known as.. 8. Scandals (Teapot
Dome)
leased by.. 4. Fall (Sec'y of Interior)
lease of.. 8. oil field
site.. 8. Elk Hills (Wyo)
tear... 3. rip 4. rend, rent, rive
5. revel, sever, speed, split, spree
6. cleave, hasten 7. destroy, shatter,
torment 8. lacerate, separate
10. dilacerate
tear (pert to)...
apart.. 7. disjoin 8. demolish
asunder.. 10. dilacerate
down.. 4. rase, raze
limb from limb.. 6. punish
9. dismember
to shreds.. 6. tatter
up.. 3. rip 6. damage
up the roots.. 6. arache
teardrop lace design... 5. larme
tearful... 3. sad 7. maudlin, weeping
9. lachrymal (lacrimal)
tears... 5. drops (lachrymal), grief,
rheum 6. lament 9. teardrops
tease... 3. guy, nag, rag, vex 4. twit
5. annoy, devil, taunt 6. bother,
harass, heckle, needle, pester, plague
7. provoke, torment 8. irritate
9. aggravate, tantalize
teaser... 4. gull 6. carder, curler,
sniper, stoker 7. curtain, fireman,
problem 8. pesterer, willower
9. tormentor 13. advertisement
technical... 7. skilled, trained
8. specific 11. specialized
12. professional
technocracy... 12. organization
17. rule by technicians
technology... 3. art 7. science
9. technique 10. agrotechny,
virtuosity 11. terminology
12. nomenclature 13. ethnotechnics
techy... 6. touchy, vexing 7. fretful,
peevish 9. irascible, irritable, sensitive
tedious... 3. dry 4. dull 5. bored,
prosy 6. boring, prolix 7. irksome,
noxious 11. displeasing, repetitious
13. uninteresting
tedium... 5. ennui 7. boredom
10. melancholy 11. tediousness
teeming... 4. full 6. aswarm
7. pouring, replete 8. crowding,
numerous, prolific 9. abounding

10. productive 11. overflowing
teeter ... 4. rock 5. waver 6. jiggle,
seesaw 9. alternate, fluctuate,
sandpiper, vacillate 12. teeter–totter
teeth ... 5. bucks, fangs 6. molars,
tushes 7. canines, ivories 8. grinders,
incisors
teeth (pert to) ...
all alike .. 7. isodont
cleaning .. 5. brush, floss
10. dentrifice, toothpaste
covering .. 6. enamel
crustation .. 6. tartar
destitute of .. 5. morné (Her)
8. edentate 10. edentulous
elephant's .. 9. scrivello 11. scrivelloes
false .. 8. choppers (sl), dentures
few .. 12. oligodontous
large .. 8. megadont 9. macrodont
pointed .. 5. fangs, tusks 6. tushes
ref to .. 4. pulp 5. molar 6. dental
7. dentine 8. odontoid
science .. 10. odontology
teething ... 6. growth 9. dentition,
odontosis 10. odontogeny
teetotaller ... 3. dry 7. non–user
9. abstainer, nephalist, Rechabite (Bib)
11. teetotalist
teg, tag ... 3. doe 5. sheep (young),
woman 6. fleece (sheep's)
teguexin ... 4. teju 6. lizard
tegument ... 4. bark, coat, skin
5. cover 6. cortex 10. integument
tekke ... 3. rug 6. carpet 7. convent
9. monastery
tela ... 6. tissue 8. membrane
Telamon (Gr Myth, pert to) ...
brother .. 6. Peleus
companion .. 8. Hercules
expedition .. 8. boar hunt
10. Argonautic
male figure .. 6. column 7. support
son .. 4. Ajax 6. Teucer
telegraph (pert to) ...
code, inventor .. 5. Morse (Samuel F)
key .. 6. tapper
service .. 5. cable 8. dispatch
telephone (pert to) ...
inventor .. 4. Bell (Alexander)
term .. 3. PBX 4. buzz, call, dial, hold,
horn (sl), ring, toll 5. trunk 6. call up
7. collect, hotline 8. exchange,
intercom 10. videophone
11. push–button, switchboard
12. speakerphone 14. radiotelephone
telescope ... 4. Lick 6. Yerkes
7. Palomar 8. Galilean (1609)
9. Gregorian (Scot 1663)
telescopic ... 9. farseeing
television ... 2. TV 3. box, set 4. tube
5. telly (Brit) 8. boob tube, idiot box
11. small screen
television (pert to) ...
person .. 6. anchor, viewer 7. sponsor
9. superstar 10. newscaster
program .. 4. show 6. sitcom
7. variety 8. newscast 9. docudrama,
soap opera
term .. 3. air 5. audio, bleep, cable,
rerun 7. channel, minicam 8. telecast
10. commercial, laugh track
tell ... 3. say 4. talk 5. count, peach,

utter 6. assail, impart, inform, recite,
reckon, relate, repeat, report, reveal
7. divulge, narrate, recount
8. acquaint, disclose, rehearse
9. recognize 11. communicate
teller ... 6. banker 8. informer, narrator
9. describer, informant
telling ... 6. cogent, potent 8. forceful,
striking 9. affective, narration,
pertinent 11. influential, significant
telltale ... 4. blab, clue, hint 6. bearer,
device, gossip 7. tattler 8. informer
9. indicator, informing 10. indication,
talebearer
tellurian ... 2. Te 7. earthly
11. terrestrial 12. earth dweller
temeritous, temerarious ... 4. rash
8. heedless, reckless 10. headstrong
temerity ... 4. gall 5. cheek, nerve
8. audacity, rashness 10. effrontery
12. recklessness
temper ... 4. mood 5. humor
6. adjust, animus, anneal, attune,
dander, harden, nature, season, soften
7. assuage, mollify, tantrum
8. hardness, mitigate, moderate
9. composure 10. equanimity,
irritation 11. disposition, temperament
temper (pert to) ...
bad .. 5. angry, rabid 6. fuming,
savage 7. furious, ranting
clay .. 6. puddle
even .. 4. calm 5. staid 6. sedate
heat of .. 6. choler
in a .. 4. huff, rage, stew 5. tizzy
metal .. 6. anneal, harden 7. toughen
temperament ... 4. mood 6. crasis,
nature 8. artistic 11. disposition
temperance ... 6. virtue 8. calmness,
sobriety 10. abstinence, moderation
11. self–control 13. self–restraint
14. abstemiousness
temperate ... 4. calm, cool 5. sober
8. moderate 10. abstemious,
restrained 14. self–controlled
tempered ... 5. angry 6. sedate
8. annealed, disposed, moderate
9. moderated, mollified, qualified
tempest ... 4. gale, wind 5. blast,
orage, storm 6. tumult 7. turmoil
9. agitation, commotion, windstorm
10. excitement 12. thunderstorm
Tempest (pert to) ...
Cuban .. 6. bayamo
in a teapot .. 10. triviality
12. exaggeration
The (character) .. 5. Ariel (spirit)
7. Caliban, Miranda 8. Prospero
tempestuous ... 5. windy 6. stormy
7. excited, violent 9. turbulent
temple ... 4. fane, naos 5. cella, ratha,
speos 6. aedile, church, pagoda
7. edifice
temple (pert to) ...
Anglo–Ind .. 5. kovil (covil)
approach .. 5. toran (torana)
Assyrian .. 8. ziggurat (anc)
Aztec temple site .. 12. Tenochtitlan
Chinese .. 6. pagoda
Hawaiian .. 5. heiau
Mexico .. 8. teocalli
Mohammedan .. 6. mosque

part.. 4. naos 5. cella 6. adytum
  7. narthex, sanctum 10. penetralia
ref to.. 6. hieron
sanctuary.. 10. penetralia
Shinto.. 3. Sha 5. jinja (jinsha)
  7. yashiro
Temple Bar (London)... 7. gateway
Temple Butte site... 11. Grand
Canyon
Temple of Heaven... 7. Peiping
Temple of Onias... 5. Egypt
Temple of Reason... 9. Notre Dame
Temple of the Sphinx... 5. Egypt
tempo... 4. pace, time 5. grave, largo,
speed 6. adagio, presto, rhythm
  7. allegro, andante 8. moderato
  11. synchronism
temporal... 4. bene, laic 5. civil
  7. earthly, secular, worldly
  9. ephemeral, temporary
  10. transitory 11. present time
  13. chronological
temporize... 5. delay 6. demand,
parley 9. negotiate 13. procrastinate
tempt... 4. lead, lure 5. decoy
  6. allure, entice, induce, seduce
  7. attract 8. persuade 9. seduction
  10. inducement
Tempter, The... 5. Devil, Satan 7. Evil
One 10. Evil Spirit, Old Serpent
  14. Prince of Devils
temptress... 5. siren 7. Delilah (Bib),
mermaid 11. enchantress
ten (pert to)...
ace.. 10. bridge game
Commandments.. 9. Decalogue
dollars.. 7. sawbuck
fold.. 6. denary 7. decuple
footed.. 7. decapod
gallon hat.. 7. Stetson 8. sombrero
geometric figure.. 7. decagon
  10. decahedron
measure.. 4. acre, bath 6. decare
number.. 5. decad 7. several
physics.. 3. bel
poetic.. 9. decameter (decametre)
prefix.. 4. deca (deka)
stringed.. 9. decachord
thousand.. 6. myriad
year period.. 6. decade 9. decenniad,
decennium
tenable... 10. defensible
  12. maintainable
tenacious... 5. tough 6. dogged, viscid
  7. viscous 8. adhesive, cohesive,
sticking, stubborn 9. glutinous,
obstinate, retentive 10. persistent
  12. pertinacious
tenant... 4. saer 5. ceile, dreng
(drengh) 6. holder, leaser, lessee,
renter, vassal 7. cottier, dweller,
villein 8. occupant 10. inhabitant
tenant's tribute... 4. cens
tend... 4. care, heed, lean, mind, wait
  5. nurse, offer, serve, watch
  6. attend, manage 7. incline, oversee
  8. converge, minister 9. cultivate,
gravitate, look after
tendency... 4. bent, bias, tide 5. drift,
drive, trend 6. course, object
  7. bearing, leaning 8. aptitude,
relation 9. direction, proneness

  10. proclivity, propensity
  11. disposition, inclination
tender... 3. bed, pay 4. boat, fond,
gift, give, kind, soft, sore 5. offer,
young 6. extend, gentle, humane,
waiter 7. pitiful, present, rail car
  8. delicate, merciful 9. attendant,
sensitive 10. effeminate
  11. softhearted, sympathetic,
warmhearted 12. affectionate
  13. compassionate
tender (pert to)...
animal.. 6. cowboy, herder
farm.. 10. husbandman
feeling.. 9. sentiment
foot.. 4. dude 6. novice 8. newcomer
  10. raw recruit
hearted.. 4. kind 8. merciful
horse.. 5. groom 6. ostler 7. hostler
regard.. 4. love 6. tendre
ship.. 7. pinnace
style.. 7. amoroso
tenderloin... 4. meat 7. brothel
  12. city district, vice district
tenderness... 4. love, pity 8. sympathy
  9. affection 10. compassion,
gentleness
tending to...
arouse.. 7. emotive
assist memory.. 8. mnemonic
check.. 10. repressive
clear of guilt.. 11. exculpatory
control.. 10. regulating
drive away.. 9. repellant
evade.. 7. elusory
lateness.. 7. tardive
separate.. 8. divisive
tear.. 10. lacerative
wear away.. 8. abrasive
tendon... 4. cord, thew 5. sinew
  8. ligament 11. aponeurosis
tendril... 4. coil, curl 5. shoot, sprig
  6. branch, cirrus 7. stipule
  8. filament
tenet... 3. ism 4. rule 5. canon,
creed, dogma, maxim 6. belief
  7. precept 8. doctrine 9. principle
tenne... 5. brown, color
Tennessee...
battle.. 11. Chattanooga 14. Above
the Clouds
capital.. 9. Nashville (Athens of the
South)
city.. 7. Memphis 8. Oak Ridge
  9. Knoxville 11. Chattanooga
first State.. 8. Franklin
Mts.. 7. Lookout 10. Cumberland,
Great Smoky 13. Clingman's Dome
museum.. 9. Hermitage, Parthenon
  12. Atomic Energy (Oak Ridge)
  13. Ancestral Home (Pres Polk)
park.. 6. Shiloh
river.. 9. Tennessee
State admission.. 9. Sixteenth
State motto.. 16. America At Its Best
State nickname.. 9. Volunteer
tennis (pert to)...
four persons.. 7. doubles
player.. 6. netman
score.. 3. ace 4. love 5. deuce
series.. 3. set
site.. 5. court

stroke.. 3. cut, lob
term.. 3. ace, lob, net, set 5. serve
  6. hazard 7. receive
two persons.. 7. singles
tenon... 3. cog 4. tusk 5. tooth
  7. mortise
tenor... 4. alto (violin), copy, mode,
  tone 5. drift, trend 6. course, intent,
  singer 7. meaning, purport
  8. tenoreno 9. male voice, procedure
  10. transcript
tense... 4. rapt, taut 5. rigid, tight
  6. intent 7. intense, nervous, stretch
  8. strained 9. stretched
  10. breathless
tense (grammar)... 4. past 6. future
  7. perfect, present 9. preterite
  10. pluperfect 11. past perfect,
  progressive
tensile... 6. pliant 7. ductile
  8. tensible
tension... 6. strain, stress 7. detente,
  nervous 9. disaccord, stiffness
tent... 3. hut 4. camp, show 5. cover,
  lodge 6. dossil 7. marquee
  8. pavilion
tent (pert to)...
  covering.. 4. tilt
  Eskimo.. 5. tubik (skin)
  general's.. 10. praetorium (pretorium)
  India.. 4. pawl
  Indian.. 5. tepee 6. teepee, wigwam
  occupant.. 5. nomad 6. camper
  7. tourist
  Russian.. 7. kibitka
  Scottish.. 6. pulpit
  surgical.. 6. screen
  tribe (Arab).. 5. Kedar
  type.. 3. fly, pup 4. bell, wall
  6. Sibley 8. pavilion
tentacle... 4. hair, palp 6. feeler
  7. tendril
tentative... 7. feeling, testing
  9. makeshift, temporary
  10. substitute 11. making trial,
  provisional 12. experimental
tenterhooks... 6. strain 8. suspense
  10. uneasiness
tenth... 5. decim, tithe 6. decima
  9. organ stop
tenth Muse... 6. Sappho
Tent Maker... 4. Omar
tenuity... 6. rarity 7. poverty
  8. delicacy, subtlety, thinness
  9. indigence, unreality
tenuous... 4. rare, thin 7. slender,
  subtile 8. delicate, ethereal
  13. unsubstantial
tenure... 4. term 5. lease 6. socage
  7. holding 10. possession
tepee, teepee... 4. tent 6. wigwam
tepid... 4. mild, warm 8. lukewarm
tequila... 6. liquor 12. century plant
teraphim... 5. idols 6. images
teras... 7. monster
tergiversate... 3. lie 5. evade, shift
  10. apostasize, equivocate
term... 3. age, end, era 4. date,
  name, time, word 5. epoch, limit,
  style 6. estate, period, tenure
  7. premise 8. duration, semester,
  terminus 12. nomenclature

term (pert to)...
  connotation.. 6. intent 11. designation
  death.. 4. doom, mort
  for years.. 10. real estate
  glacial.. 5. stoss
  golf.. 4. hook 5. bogey (bogie), divot,
  eagle, slice 6. birdie
  grammar.. 6. phrase, syntax
  11. phraseology
  logic.. 4. mode 5. major, minor
  of life.. 3. age 5. sands (hourglass)
  Rugby.. 5. scrum
  sea.. 4. ahoy 5. avast, belay
  tennis.. 4. love 5. deuce, serve
termagant... 5. scold, shrew, vixen
  6. Amazon, virigo 7. furious
  8. scolding 9. turbulent
  10. boisterous, tumultuous
  11. quarrelsome
Termagant... 5. deity 14. imaginary
  being
terminal... 3. end 4. goal 5. anode,
  depot, final, limit 6. finish 7. limital,
  station 8. desinent, terminus,
  ultimate 9. end of life, extremity
  10. concluding 11. desinential,
  destination, termination
terminal (pert to)...
  battery.. 5. anode 7. cathode
  9. electrode
  leaf.. 8. apiculus
  ornament.. 6. finial
  town (end of line).. 8. terminus
terminate... 3. end 4. halt 5. cease,
  close, limit 6. expire, result 7. end
  with 8. complete, conclude .
termination... 3. end 4. amen
  5. close, limit 6. ending, result
  7. outcome 8. terminus 9. desinence
  10. completion, conclusion, expiration
termite... 3. ant (white) 4. anay (anai)
  8. Isoptera (Order)
tern... 4. darr (black), gull 6. Sterna
  (genus) 8. schooner (Naut)
  9. threefold 10. sea swallow
ternary... 5. three, triad 6. tercet
  (Poet), triple 7. ternion, trinity
  9. threefold
ternate... 4. tern 9. threefold
  12. trifoliolate
terpsichore... 5. dance 6. dancer
  7. dancing
Terpsichore (Myth)... 13. Muse of
  dancing
terra... 5. earth 10. terra firma
terrace... 4. flaw (marble), mesa, step
  7. balcony, gallery, plateau, portico
  8. platform (earth) 9. colonnade
terrain, terrane... 4. land 5. tract
  6. region 11. environment
terrapin... 4. Emys 6. turtle
  8. Chelonia, Emydinae, tortoise
  9. cheloniid
terrapin, turtle (pert to)...
  color.. 9. grapenuts
  type.. 6. potter, slider 10. red–bellied
  11. diamondback 13. yellow–bellied
  War.. 14. Eighteen Twelve (1812)
terrene, terrestrial... 4. land 5. earth,
  realm 6. earthy, mortal 7. earthly,
  mundane, worldly
terrestrial planets... 4. Mars 5. Venus

7. Mercury

terrible . . . 3. bad 4. dire 5. awful
6. tragic 7. fearful, ghastly, hideous, painful 8. dreadful, horrible, terrific 9. appalling, frightful 10. formidable, terrifying, unpleasant

Terrible, The . . . 4. Ivan (Russ Czar)

terrier . . . 3. fox 4. bull, Skye 5. Cairn, Irish, Welsh 6. Boston 8. Airedale, Scottish, Sealyham 9. Kerry blue, schnauzer 10. Bedlington, Clydesdale 13. Dandie Dinmont

terrific . . . 5. great 6. superb 7. extreme 8. dreadful, exciting, terrible 9. appalling, excessive, frightful 10. tremendous

terrify . . . 3. awe, cow 4. stun 5. alarm, appal, haunt, scare, shock 6. appall, freeze 7. horrify, petrify 8. affright, frighten

territory . . . 4. area, land 5. banat, field 6. canton, region 7. country 8. district, environs, Pashalic (Pasha's), province 10. palatinate

terror . . . 3. awe 4. fear 5. alarm, dread, panic 6. fright, horror 7. hellion, Reign of (Hist) 13. consternation

terrorism . . . 11. subjugation 12. intimidation

terse . . . 4. curt, neat 5. pithy 6. smooth 7. compact, concise, laconic, pointed, refined 8. succinct 11. sententious 12. accomplished, epigrammatic

Tertiary period . . . 6. Eocene 7. Miocene 8. Pliocene 9. Oligocene 12. Age of Mammals

tertium quid . . . 12. third someone 13. third somewhat

tertulia . . . 4. club 5. party 7. meeting

tessellated . . . 6. mosaic 9. checkered

tessera . . . 3. die 4. cube, tile 5. token 6. marble, ticket 8. password 11. certificate

test . . . 3. try 4. exam, feel 5. assay, proof, prove, taste, tempt, trial 6. ordeal, sample 7. examine, witness 8. evidence, standard 9. criterion, testimony 10. experience, experiment 11. examination, performance 12. authenticate

test (pert to) . . .
fineness . . 3. pyx
orally . . 7. examine
ore, value . . 5. assay
pot . . 8. crucible
severe . . 6. ordeal

testa . . . 7. coating 8. covering, tegument

testament . . . 3. New, Old 4. will 8. covenant

testator . . . 7. legator, witness 9. testatrix

tester . . . 6. canopy, helmet, prover, taster 7. assayer, candler, sampler

testify . . . 4. avow 5. affirm, depone, depose 7. declare, profess, protest 8. indicate, manifest 11. bear witness

testimonial . . . 5. token 7. tribute,

warrant 8. evidence 9. reference 10. compliment 11. certificate

testimony . . . 7. witness 8. evidence 10. Scriptures 11. affirmation, attestation, declaration

testy, tetchy . . . 6. touchy 7. fretful, peevish 8. petulant, snappish 9. irascible, obstinate 10. headstrong

tetched in the head . . . 9. pixilated

tetrad . . . 4. four 7. quartet (quartette), quatern 8. foursome 10. quaternion

tetragon . . . 4. park 6. square 7. rhombus 9. courtyard 10. quadrangle

Tetragrammaton . . . 7. Jehovah 12. Supreme Being 14. four consonants (unpronounced)

Teuton . . . 4. Goth 6. German

Teutonic (pert to) . . .
alphabet character . . 4. rune
deity . . 2. Er 3. Tiu (Tiwaz), Tyr 4. Frea, Odin, Thor 5. Aesir, Bragi, Wodin 6. Balder, Frigga 7. Forseti 8. Heimdall
demon . . 3. alp
giantess . . 4. Norn 11. demigoddess
goddess . . 3. Eir, Hel, Ran 4. Norn, Urth (Urthr), Wyrd
homicide (tribal) . . 5. morth
land . . 4. odal
law . . 5. Salic
nymph (water) . . 3. nis
race . . 5. Goths, Jutes 6. Franks, Saxons 7. Vandals 8. Lombards 10. Norwegians 13. Scandinavians
supernatural being . . 5. troll

Teutonic goddess of . . .
death . . 3. Hel, Ran
healing . . 3. Eir
peace . . 7. Nerthus

Teutonic god of . . .
justice . . 7. Forseti (Forsete)
pantheon . . 5. Aesir (group)
peace . . 6. Balder
sea . . 5. Aegir
skill . . 3. Ull (Ullr)
sky . . 2. Er 3. Tiu (Tiwaz), Tyr
thunder . . 4. Thor 5. Donar
war . . 3. Tiu (Tiwaz), Tyr

Texas . . .
birthplace of Pres . . 10. Eisenhower
capital . . 6. Austin
cattle . . 8. longhorn
city . . 4. Waco 6. Dallas, El Paso 7. Abilene, Denison, Houston 9. Fort Worth, Galveston 10. San Antonio
flags (six) . . 5. Spain 6. France, Mexico 8. Republic (of Texas) 11. Confederate 12. United States
flower . . 10. bluebonnet, yellow rose
Indian tribe . . 5. Caddo
monument (Battle) . . 10. San Jacinto
police . . 7. Rangers
river . . 3. Red 5. Pecos 9. Rio Grande
shrine, mission . . 5. Alamo
State admission . . 12. Twenty–eighth
State motto . . 5. Tejas 10. Friendship
State nickname . . 8. Lone Star

text . . . 4. book 5. topic, verse 7. passage 8. libretto, textbook 11. letterpress

textile screw pine . . . 3. ara

textile shop... 7. mercery
texture... 3. web 4. wale, warp, wooz
    5. grain, weave 6. cobweb, fabric
    7. textile 9. roughness, structure
    10. smoothness
Thailand (Siam), capital... 7. Bangkok
Thames River town... 4. Eton
thana... 13. police station
thanador... 7. officer (Hind)
thanatology doctrine... 5. death
thane... 5. baron (anc) 7. servant,
    warrior 9. Scots peer
thankless... 7. ingrate 10. ungrateful
    13. unappreciated
thanks... 5. grace 6. prayer
    8. gramercy 9. gratitude
    12. appreciation 14. acknowledgment
Thanks to God... 10. Deo gratias
that (pert to)...
    is.. 2. ie 5. id est
    is to say.. 3. viz 5. to wit 6. namely
    9. videlicit
    pronoun.. 3. who 4. what
thatch (pert to)...
    grass.. 4. rope 6. slough
    hair.. 3. mop 4. crop, mane
    palm.. 5. Sabal 7. Thrinax
    roofing.. 5. reeds, straw 6. rushes
    support.. 6. wattle
thatcher... 7. hellier
thaumaturgy... 5. magic 7. sorcery
    8. wizardry 11. legerdemain
the (pert to)...
    end.. 5. omega 6. thirty
    French.. 2. la, le 3. les
    German.. 3. das, der, die
    Italian.. 2. il, la, le 4. ella
    same.. 4. idem 5. ditto
    Spanish.. 2. el, la 3. las, los
theater, theatre... 5. arena, drama,
    odeum, stage 6. lyceum 8. coliseum
    9. playhouse 12. amphitheater
theater (pert to)...
    actress.. 7. heroine, ingénue
    box.. 4. loge
    curtain.. 4. drop 6. teaser
    district.. 6. Rialto 8. Broadway
    floor (lower).. 7. parquet
    full house.. 3. SRO
    Greek.. 5. odeum (odeon)
    part.. 3. box, pit 4. loge 5. foyer,
    stage 7. balcony, gallery, parquet
    8. parterre 9. orchestra
    10. proscenium
theatrical... 5. showy, stagy
    8. affected, dramatic 10. artificial,
    histrionic 12. melodramatic
theatrical (pert to)...
    art.. 10. histrionic
    company.. 6. troupe
    machine.. 9. eccyclema
    spectacle.. 5. revue 7. pageant
    star.. 4. hero, lead 7. heroine
Theban (pert to)...
    bard.. 6. Pindar
    deity.. 4. Amen (Amon) 6. Amen–Ra
    god.. 5. Ammon (Zeus)
    king.. 5. Laius 7. Amphion, Oedipus
    8. Pentheus
    queen.. 5. Niobe 7. Jocasta
    soothsayer (blind).. 8. Tiresias
    triad.. 3. Mut 6. Amen–Ra, Khonsu

Thebes...
    capital of.. 10. Upper Egypt (anc)
    famed avenue.. 8. Sphinxes
    famed for.. 5. ruins
    location.. 4. Nile
    ruined temple.. 5. Ammon 6. Karnak
    Seven against (one of).. 6. Tydeus
theca... 3. pod 4. case, cell
    7. capsule
theft... 6. holdup, piracy 7. larceny,
    robbery 8. burglary, stealing
    10. plagiarism 12. embezzlement
theftlike... 7. piratic 9. piratical
theme... 4. text 5. essay, lemma,
    motif, thema, topic 6. matter, thesis
    7. subject 9. discourse, leitmotiv
then... 3. poi (Mus) 4. also, next,
    when 5. hence 7. besides
    8. formerly 9. therefore
    12. subsequently
thence... 4. away 5. hence 9. after
    that, elsewhere, therefore
    10. henceforth, thereafter
theogamy... 14. marriage of gods
theologian... 5. Arius (Bib) 6. Luther
    7. a divine 8. canonist
theology... 7. irenics 8. canonics,
    religion 9. depositum 10. doctrinism
theorem... 3. law 4. rule 5. axiom,
    topic 7. premise 9. principle,
    statement 11. proposition
theoretical... 5. ideal 8. academic,
    platonic 11. conjectural, impractical,
    speculative 12. hypothetical, not
    practical
theorize... 6. reason 9. postulate,
    speculate
theory... 3. ism 4. plan 6. scheme
    7. formula, opinion 8. analysis,
    doctrine 10. hypothesis
    11. speculation, supposition
    13. contemplation
theory of...
    evolution.. 9. Darwinism
    10. Lamarckism 13. Spencerianism
    knowledge.. 12. epistemology
    language.. 6. bowwow 8. ding–dong,
    pooh–pooh
    philosophy.. 13. phenomenalism
    relativity.. 8. Einstein
theosophist... 7. Mahatma
theosophy... 4. yoga 6. cabala
    7. Nirvana 8. kamarupa (Kama)
therapeutic... 7. healing 8. curative,
    remedies
therapy... 4. cure 5. faith 9. dietetics,
    medicines, treatment
    12. hydrotherapy, therapeutics
    13. psychotherapy
there... 3. yon 5. ready 6. yonder
    7. thereat, thither 11. at that place
therefore... 2. as, so 4. ergo
    5. hence, since 6. thence
    9. thereupon, to that end, wherefore
    11. accordingly 12. consequently
thermometer... 5. Hydra 7. Reaumur
    10. Centigrade, Fahrenheit
Thesaurus compiler... 5. Roget
thesis... 5. essay, theme, topic
    6. accent 7. premise 8. treatise
    9. postulate 10. assumption
    11. affirmation 12. dissertation

thespian... 3. art 5. actor 6. player,
tragic 7. actress, Thespis (founder)
8. dramatic
Thessaly, Greece...
ancient name.. 9. Thessalia
famed for.. 6. horses 8. horsemen
mountain.. 4. Ossa 6. Pelion
native.. 5. Greek 10. Thessalian
town.. 7. Larissa
thew... 5. brawn, sinew 6. manner,
muscle, virtue 8. strength
they go out... 6. exeunt
thick... 4. burr, dull, hazy 5. broad,
bushy, close, crass, dense, gross,
husky, plump, solid, squat 6. coarse,
espeso, stodgy, stupid 7. crowded,
grumous, muffled 8. familiar, friendly,
intimate, numerous, thickset
9. luxuriant 10. indistinct
11. inspissated 12. impenetrable
thicken... 3. gel 4. clot, curd
5. cloud, flock 6. curdle, deepen,
harden 7. congeal, stiffen
8. increase, solidify 9. intensify
10. incrassate, inspissate, strengthen
thicket... 4. bosk, rone 5. copse,
grove, hedge, shola 6. bosket
(bosquet) 7. boscage, coppice,
spinney 9. brushwood, chaparral
10. underbrush
thickheaded... 4. dull 5. dense
6. stupid 7. doltish
thickness... 3. ply 5. layer 7. density
8. diameter, intimacy
10. opaqueness 11. consistency,
measurement
thickset... 5. squat, stout 6. stocky,
stodgy, stubby 14. closely planted
thick-skinned... 7. callous
11. hardhearted, insensitive,
pachydermic 14. pachydermatous
thick soup... 5. purée
thief... 5. scamp 6. ackman, bandit,
looter, pirate, rascal, robber
7. burglar, filcher, rustler, stealer
8. gangster, larcener 9. larcenist,
scoundrel 10. freebooter, pickpocket,
plagiarist
thieves (famed)... 5. Fagin 9. Robin
Hood 10. Dick Turpin, Jesse James
11. Claude Duval 12. Jonathan Wild
13. Thief of Bagdad
thieves' Latin... 4. cant 5. slang
12. secret jargon
thigh (pert to)...
animal's.. 3. ham 4. hock 5. flank
armor plate.. 6. cuisse (cuish)
bone.. 5. femur, ilium
ref to.. 5. groin, meros (merus)
6. crural
thimble... 3. cap 4. ring 5. cover,
watch
thimble (pert to)...
berry.. 9. raspberry 10. blackberry
eye.. 12. chub mackerel
flower.. 8. foxglove
rig.. 5. cheat 7. swindle 13. sleight
of hand
weed.. 6. clover
thin... 4. bony, lank, lean, poor, rare,
slim, weak 5. gaunt, lanky, lathy,
reedy, sheer, spare, washy 6. dilute,

meager, rarefy, shrill, sleazy, slinky,
sparse, watery 7. haggard, insipid,
scraggy, scrawny, slender
8. araneous, rarefied 10. attenuated,
diaphanous 11. transparent
thin (pert to)...
air.. 5. smoke, vapor 6. bubble
and delicate.. 8. araneous
10. diaphanous
and haggard.. 5. gaunt
and withered.. 7. wizened 9. shriveled
fabric.. 8. gossamer
out.. 5. peter
plate, bone.. 6. tegmen
plate, metal.. 4. leaf
plate, Zool.. 6. lamina 7. lamella
skinned.. 6. gentle, tender, touchy
Thin Man's dog.. 4. Asta
thine... 4. tuum
thing... 3. act, res 4. deed, fact, idea,
unit 5. being, event 6. affair, entity,
gadget, object 7. article, reality
8. anything, creature 9. happening,
situation, something
thing (pert to)...
added.. 6. insert 8. addendum
9. insertion 10. supplement
assumed.. 7. premise 11. implication
complete.. 4. unit
cursed.. 8. anathema
done.. 5. actum
following.. 6. sequel
found.. 5. trove
hard to classify.. 11. nondescript
huge.. 7. monster
indefinite.. 7. so—and—so
10. thingumbob (thingumabob)
12. what's—its—name
nonexisting.. 9. nonentity
of little worth.. 6. stiver, trifle
7. trinket
the (thing).. 7. the rage
unique.. 4. sole
things (pert to)...
added.. 7. addenda 11. additaments
brought into being.. 9. creations
found, surprise.. 11. serendipity
intricate.. 9. involutes
little.. 16. inconsequentials
moving to and fro.. 7. wigwags
of like nature.. 8. cognates
suitable to eat.. 9. esculents
theoretical.. 7. noumena
to be done.. 6. agenda
to be learned.. 7. lessons
to follow.. 7. sequels 8. sequelae
to sharpen.. 10. whetstones
widely separated.. 8. extremes
think... 3. wis 4. deem, muse, trow
5. opine 6. reason 7. believe,
imagine, reflect, suppose 8. cogitate,
conceive, meditate 11. contemplate
think (pert to)...
better of.. 6. repent 10. reconsider
bring to mind.. 6. recall 7. imagine
10. conjecture
logically.. 6. reason
of.. 5. judge 6. intend, recall
8. consider, remember 9. recollect
10. call to mind
over.. 3. wis 4. mull, muse 5. brood
6. ponder 8. meditate

up.. 6. devise, scheme 7. concoct
thinker, Relig freedom...
  14. latitudinarian
thinness... 6. rarity 7. tenuity
  8. rareness 11. slenderness
third (pert to)...
  comb form.. 3. tri 4. trit
  day (Quakers).. 7. Tuesday
  estate.. 6. people
  figure.. 7. ferison
  in number.. 8. tertiary
  music.. 6. tierce
  ordinal of.. 5. three
  person.. 6. escort 7. grammar
  8. chaperon
  power.. 4. cube
  Republic.. 6. French (1871)
thirst... 6. desire, hunger 7. craving,
  dryness, longing
this... 4. near 9. the nearer
Thisbe's lover (Bab)... 7. Paramus
thisness... 9. haecceity
thistle (pert to)...
  bird.. 9. goldfinch
  color.. 6. violet (cobalt)
  emblem.. 8. Scotland
  genus.. 6. Arnica, Cosmos 7. Carlina
  star.. 7. caltrop (caltrap)
thistledown... 6. pappus
  12. thistlebeard
thither... 3. yon 5. hence 6. yonder
thong... 4. lash, riem, whip 5. knout,
  lorum, quirt, romal, strap 6. lorate
  7. amentum, lanyard (laniard)
Thor (pert to)...
  father.. 4. Odin
  German.. 5. Donar
  god of.. 7. thunder
  other name.. 9. Hlorrithi
  stepson.. 3. Ull (Ullr)
  wife.. 3. Sif
thorax... 5. chest 6. cavity 7. cuirass
  8. pectoral 11. breastplate
thorn... 4. bane 5. briar (brier), spine
  7. acantha, bramble, prickle
thorn (pert to)...
  apple.. 3. haw 6. Datura
  back.. 3. ray 4. dorn 5. skate
  10. spider crab 11. stickleback
  bill.. 11. hummingbird
  comb form.. 5. spini
  full of.. 6. briary
  letters.. 2. th 3. edh
  lizard.. 6. moloch
  pert to.. 6. spinal
  small.. 7. spinule
thornless... 5. inerm 8. inermous
thorny... 5. sharp, spiny 7. brambly,
  prickly 9. acanthoid, bristling, difficult
thorough... 4. full 8. absolute,
  complete 9. downright, intensive
  10. exhaustive 11. painstaking
thoroughfare... 4. road 6. artery,
  street 7. highway, parkway, passage,
  roadway, thruway 8. arterial,
  autobahn, highroad, pent road,
  turnpike, waterway 9. boulevard,
  concourse 10. autostrada
thoroughgoing... 4. zeal 7. extreme
  9. downright 11. painstaking
thoroughly... 3. all 9. intensive,
  out-and-out 11. intensively

  13. letter-perfect
thorp, thorpe... 4. dorp, town
  6. hamlet 7. village
those (pert to)...
  adept at table talk..
  14. deipnosophists
  brought to terms.. 11. transigents
  in office.. 3. ins
  in the stock market.. 5. bears, bulls
  7. traders 9. investors
  of a habit.. 7. addicts
  of the same goal.. 6. rivals
  outside a profession.. 5. laity
those who...
  read and write.. 9. literates
  ridicule.. 8. deriders
  verify.. 13. corroborators
  work together.. 13. collaborators
thou... 3. tha 7. pronoun 8. thousand
thought... 4. care, heed, idea, view
  5. logic 6. deemed, opined
  7. anxiety, opinion 9. attention,
  cogitated, reasoning 10. cogitation,
  meditation, reflection 11. cerebration
  12. deliberation, recollection
  13. consideration, ratiocination
thought (pert to)...
  continuous.. 10. meditation
  deep in.. 10. cogitabund
  form.. 6. ideate
  laws of.. 7. noetics
  reader.. 11. telepathist
thoughtful... 4. kind 5. moody
  7. mindful, museful, pensive,
  prudent, serious 9. attentive
  10. cogitative, meditative, reflective,
  ruminative, solicitous
  11. circumspect, considerate
  13. contemplative
thoughtless... 4. rash 6. stupid
  7. foolish 8. careless, heedless,
  reckless 9. brainless, impulsive
  11. harum-scarum, inattentive,
  thought-free 12. unreflecting
  13. inconsiderate
thousand... 3. mil 5. mille 7. chiliad
  10. ten hundred
Thousand and One Nights...
  13. Arabian Nights
thousand men, command of...
  11. chiliarchia
thousandth... 9. chiliadal
  10. millesimal
thousand years... 7. chiliad
  9. millenary 10. millennium
thrall... 4. esne, serf 5. slave
  7. bondage, bondman, captive,
  slavery 9. thralldom 10. oppression
thrash... 3. lam, tan 4. beat, cave,
  drub, flog, whip 5. flail, pound, twist
  6. defeat, punish, strike, swinge,
  thresh 7. belabor, trounce
  8. urticate, vanquish 9. pulverize,
  toss about
thrashing... 7. beating, milling
  8. drubbing, flogging, whipping
  10. punishment
thread... 4. flax, jute, line, silk, vein,
  wire, yarn 5. fiber, floss, linen, lisle,
  rayon 6. cotton, dacron, sleave
  8. arrasene, filament
thread (pert to)...

ancient.. 4. byss
a needle.. 5. reeve
ball.. 4. clew (clue)
cell.. 5. cnida
coiled.. 3. cop
comb form.. 3. nem 4. nema
  5. nemat 6. nemato
fish.. 7. cutlass 9. threadfin
  11. cobblerfish
herring.. 11. gizzard shad
like.. 5. filar 6. filose
loose.. 4. lint 7. raveled
medical.. 5. seton
metal.. 4. wire
mystery lead.. 4. clue
shoemaker's (obs).. 6. lingel (lingle)
silk.. 5. floss 9. filoselle
tangle.. 6. sleave
tape, braid (thread).. 5. inkle
tester.. 9. serimeter
weaving term.. 4. warp, weft, woof
  5. leash
threadbare... 4. sere, worn 5. trite
  6. shabby
threaten... 4. warn 5. curse
  6. menace 7. portend 8. forebode
  9. comminate 10. intimidate
  12. anathematize
threatening... 4. dark 7. ominous
  8. imminent, lowering, menacing
three (pert to)...
banded armadillo.. 4. apar 5. apara
comb form.. 3. ter
dimensional.. 5. bruit, cubic
  12. stereoscopic
fold.. 4. tern 6. ternal, treble, triple
  7. ternate
group of.. 4. trio 5. triad 7. triplet
  8. triplets
hundredth anniversary..
  13. tercentennial
in one.. 6. triune 7. trinity 10. The
  Godhead
legged stand.. 6. teapoy, tripod, trivet
lined.. 9. trilinear
masted vessel.. 5. xebec 7. frigate
  8. schooner
math term.. 2. pi (3.1416)
prefix.. 3. tri
R's.. 7. reading, writing
  10. arithmetic
seeded.. 11. trispermous
sided figure.. 6. trigon 8. triangle
spot.. 4. trey
styled.. 10. trystylous
toed sloth.. 2. ai
Three Kingdoms (Chin)... 2. Wu
  3. Shu, Wei
Three Kings of Cologne... 6. Gaspar
  8. Melchior 9. Balthasar 12. Three
  Wise Men
Three Musketeers... 5. Athos
  6. Aramis 7. Porthos 9. D'Artagnan
  (friend)
Three Sisters (Myth)... 5. Fates
  6. Clotho 7. Atropos 8. Lachesis
Three Wise Men (Kings of Cologne)...
  6. Gaspar 8. Melchior 9. Balthasar
threnody... 5. dirge 7. requiem
  8. coronach
threshold... 3. eve 4. gate, sill
  5. limen 6. portal 8. doorsill

threw... see also *throw* 4. cast
  5. flung, slung 6. bunged, heaved,
  hurled, pelted, tossed 7. pitched
thrice... 3. ter, tri 5. fully 6. highly
  10. repeatedly, three times
thrift... 7. economy 8. prudence
  9. husbandry 10. providence
  11. thriftiness
thriftless... 6. lavish 8. prodigal,
  wasteful 11. extravagant, improvident
thrifty... 6. frugal, saving 7. careful,
  prudent, sparing 9. provident
  10. economical, forehanded,
  prosperous 11. flourishing
thrill... 4. tirl 6. dindle, thrush, tingle,
  tremor 7. delight 9. electrify
  10. excitement
thrive... 4. grow 5. moise (Eng)
  6. batten 7. prosper, succeed
  8. flourish, increase
throat... 3. maw 4. crop, neck
  5. gular, halse, mouth, voice
  6. groove, gullet, larynx, mutter
  7. channel, glottis, jugular, orifice,
  pharynx, trachea 9. esophagus
  10. passageway 12. constriction
throb... 4. ache, beat, drum, pant
  5. pulse 7. pulsate, vibrate
  9. palpitate
throe... 4. pang 5. agony 7. anguish
  8. struggle
Throgmorton Street... 13. Stock
Exchange (London)
throne... 3. see 4. apse 5. exalt
  8. enthrone 9. royal seat
  11. sovereignty, supreme rank
  12. Chair of State
throng... 4. crew, host, push
  5. crowd, horde, press, swarm
  6. bustle, stress 7. hurried
  9. confusion, multitude
throttle... 5. choke, lever, seize
  6. throat 7. garrote 8. strangle,
  suppress, windpipe
through... 2. by 3. dia, per 4. into,
  thru 5. ended 7. perpend 8. finished
  9. because of, by means of,
  completed
throughout... 5. about 6. during
  8. thorough 10. completely,
  everywhere
throw... 3. cob, don, lob, peg, shy
  4. bear, cast, hurl, kist, pelt, toss,
  yerk 5. chuck, fling, heave, pitch,
  sling, twist, whirl 6. baffle, strike,
  thwart 7. discard, project
  9. prostrate
throw (pert to)...
a scare.. 7. terrify
away.. 7. discard 8. handbill,
  squander
back.. 5. repel 6. reject, revert
dice (term).. 4. sise 7. ambsace
in the towel.. 4. cede, quit
  9. surrender
into confusion.. 7. disturb, perturb,
  trouble 8. stampede 10. demoralize
into ecstasy.. 7. enrapture
into shade.. 7. eclipse
off.. 4. cast, shed 6. derail, reject
  7. abandon, discard
out.. 4. emit, lade 5. egest, eject,

expel 6. bounce 7. discard, project
9. eliminate
over.. 4. jilt 5. build 6. give up,
refute 7. abandon, discard
9. eliminate
overboard.. 8. jettison
water upon.. 5. douse
throwback... 7. setback 9. reversion
10. misfortune, regression
throwing (pert to)...
rope.. 5. lasso, reata, riata 6. lariat
science.. 10. ballistics
stick (anc).. 6. womera (woomera)
thrum... 3. bit, hum 4. drum, tuft
5. strum 6. fringe, repeat
thrush... 5. brown, mavis, robin, veery
7. disease 8. shagbark, songbird
9. blackbird
thrush (pert to)...
American.. 5. robin, veery 12. hermit
thrush
European.. 5. ouzel (ousel) 6. missel
7. redwing 11. nightingale
golden.. 6. oriole
Hawaiian.. 4. omao
Ind.. 5. shama
Scot.. 8. throstle
thrust... 3. dig, jab 4. gird, poke,
push, stab 5. lunge 6. extend,
pierce 7. intrude, obtrude, riposte
8. protrude 9. interject, interpose
thrust (pert to)...
aside.. 5. shove 7. dismiss 8. brush
off
down.. 7. detrude
fencing term.. 5. lunge 7. allonge,
riposte 8. estocade
one's self in.. 5. enter 7. intrude
out.. 5. eject 6. extend 8. protrude
thug... 4. goon, yegg 6. cuttle,
gunman 7. ruffian 8. assassin
9. cutthroat, roughneck
thumb... 6. pollex, thenar
thumb (pert to)...
a ride.. 9. hitchhike
bird.. 9. goldcrest
lady's (herb).. 9. peachwort, persicary
mark.. 4. soil 10. impression
11. fingerprint 14. identification
nail.. 5. small 8. complete
over.. 4. skim 6. browse
part.. 6. thenar
thump... 4. bang, beat, blow, drum,
thud, whip, yerk 5. knock, pound
6. hammer, pummel, strike, thrash
8. chastise 10. pound along
thunder... 4. boom, peal, roar
5. storm 9. fulminate
thunder (pert to)...
bolt.. 5. speed 6. Caesar 8. surprise
9. lightning 11. fulmination
fish.. 4. raad 5. loach 7. catfish
(electric)
god.. 4. Thor 6. Manito
of applause.. 5. cheer 7. ovation
peal.. 4. clap 5. crash
smitten goddess.. 6. Semele
8. Keraunia
thurible... 6. censer
thurifer... 12. censer bearer
Thursday... 4. Thor 8. fifth day
12. god of thunder

thus... 2. so 3. sic 5. hence 7. this
way 9. therefore 11. for instance
12. consequently
thwack... 3. rap 4. bang, blow, club
5. crush, knock, whack 6. defeat,
pommel, strike, thrash 7. belabor
thwart... 4. balk, foil 5. block, clash,
cross, parry, spite 6. defeat, gaffle,
oppose, outwit 7. oblique, prevent
8. obstruct, stubborn 9. frustrate,
interpose 10. across from, disappoint
thymus... 5. gland 10. sweetbread
(lambs, calves)
tiara... 5. crown 6. diadem 7. coronet
8. ornament
Tibbett opera... 12. Emperor Jones
(1932)
tibert... 3. cat
Tibet, Asia... see also *Tibetan*
animal.. 3. goa, sus 5. panda
capital.. 5. Lhasa
dialect.. 9. Bhutanese
kingdom.. 5. Nepal
Mts.. 8. Himalaya 9. Karakoram
religion.. 7. Lamaism
river.. 5. Hwang, Indus 7. Yangtze
11. Brahmaputra
ruler.. 9. Dalai Lama
Tibetan (pert to)...
beer (barley).. 5. chang
deer.. 4. shou
food (barley).. 6. tsamba
gazelle.. 3. goa
monk, priest.. 4. lama
ox.. 3. yak
sheep.. 3. sha 5. urial 6. bharal,
nahoor, nayaur
wild ass.. 5. kiang
wildcat.. 5. manul
tibia... 4. bone, shin 5. flute
6. cnemis
Tibur (anc)... 6. Tivoli
tiburon... 5. shark
Tiburtine... 12. Sibyl of Tibur
tick... 3. ked, tap 4. beat, mark, mite,
pest 5. Argas 6. acarid, Ixodes
7. instant 8. carapato, function,
ticktock 10. pajahuello (pajaroello)
ticket... 3. tag 4. note, pass, slip
5. check, ducat, label, token
6. ballot, billet, permit, record
7. license, voucher 8. document
11. certificate
ticket dealer... 7. scalper
tickle... 5. amuse 6. thrill, tingle
7. delight 9. titillate, vellicate
ticklish... 5. risky 6. fickle, queasy,
touchy 7. comical 8. unstable,
unsteady 9. uncertain 10. precarious,
unreliable
tidal (pert to)...
creek.. 6. estero 7. estuary
current.. 8. tiderace
flood.. 5. eagre
flow.. 3. ebb 4. bore, neap 5. surge
tidbit, titbit... 5. goody 6. morsel
7. saynete 8. delicacy
tide... 3. ebb, rip 4. high, neap, time
5. drift 6. period, stream 7. current
8. low water 9. be carried
tide (pert to)...
gate.. 9. floodgate

go with.. 5. drift, float 7. proceed
13. be fashionable
out with.. 3. ebb 6. recede
8. diminish, fade away
over.. 6. endure 8. surmount 11. live
through
tidings... 4. news, word 6. gospel,
report, rumors 7. message
10. evangelist 11. information
tidy... 4. neat, trig, trim 5. groom,
natty, plump 6. spruce 7. orderly
9. shipshape 10. put in order
12. antimacassar, considerable
tie... 4. bind, bond, draw, even, knot,
lash, link 5. ascot, equal, nexus,
noose, trice, truss 6. cravat, enlace,
fasten, relate, tether 7. confine,
necktie, sleeper 8. equality, fastener,
restrain, shoelace 10. allegiance,
obligation
tie (pert to)...
off.. 5. belay
ornament.. 3. pin
ready–made.. 4. teck
securely.. 7. trammel
sports.. 8. dead heat
uniting.. 4. bond 5. tache
up.. 4. bind, wrap 5. truss 6. fasten
8. restrain
tier... 3. row 5. grade, layer 6. series
Tiergarten... 4. park 16. Zoological
Garden
tiff... 3. sip 4. huff, spat 5. drink
7. dudgeon, quarrel 8. outburst
10. fit of anger
tiffin... 3. tea 5. brown, lunch
6. repast 8. luncheon
tiger... 5. bully 6. emblem, savage
9. swaggerer
tiger (pert to)...
American.. 6. jaguar
bird.. 5. finch 8. amadavat
family.. 3. cat 6. mammal 11. Felis
tigris
hunting dog.. 5. dhole
S African.. 7. leopard
Tasmania.. 9. thylacine 13. Tasmanian
wolf
wolf.. 5. hyena
young.. 3. cub
tight... 4. fast, snug, taut, trim
5. alert, close, drunk, tense
6. narrow, stingy 7. exactly, shapely
9. condensed 11. closefisted
12. close–fitting, parsimonious
tight (pert to)...
fisted.. 6. stingy 12. parsimonious
lipped.. 5. terse 9. secretive
wad.. 5. miser 10. curmudgeon
tighten... 4. frap, lace 5. brace, tense
6. fasten, tauten 7. squeeze
9. constrict
Tigris River city of ruins...
7. Nineveh (anc)
til... 4. tree 6. sesame
tilde... 4. dash, mark, sign 6. accent,
tittle 15. diacritical mark
tile... 3. red 5. slate 6. domino,
mosaic, pament (pamment), tegula
7. ceramic, pantile, tessera
8. pavement
tiler... 5. thief 6. slater 7. hellier

10. doorkeeper
till... 3. box 4. farm, plow, tray, when
5. labor, while 6. before, casket,
drawer, whilst 7. develop 9. cultivate
tillable... 6. arable
tiller... 4. helm 5. stalk 6. farmer,
sprout 7. plowman, rancher
8. harrower 10. cultivator,
husbandman
tilt... 3. tip 4. cant, heel, list 5. joust,
pitch, slant, slope 6. careen, oliver
(hammer), seesaw, unload 7. incline
8. log house 10. tournament
11. altercation
timber... 3. log 4. beam, tree, wood
6. forest, lumber 7. support
9. underpier
timber (pert to)...
bend.. 3. sny
building.. 4. sill, stud 5. joist
6. purlin, rafter 8. stringer
convex.. 6. camber
cribs (logging).. 4. dram
cut.. 6. lumber 7. fallage
decay.. 4. doty (doaty)
end.. 5. tenon
hard, heartwood.. 7. duramen
Naut.. 3. rib 4. bitt, keel, mast, spar,
wale 8. sternson
support.. 6. corbel
upright.. 8. puncheon
wolf.. 4. lobo
timbre... 4. tone 5. clang, crest (Her),
miter 7. coronet 9. resonance, tone
color
timbrel... 4. drum 5. tabor 7. sistrum
10. tambourine
time... 3. age, day, eon, era 4. aeon,
date, hour, term, turn, week, year
5. clock, epoch, shift, tempo
6. decade, minute, moment, period,
season, second 7. century
8. duration, occasion, schedule
9. fortnight
time (pert to)...
accurate.. 10. isochronon
equal.. 10. isochronal
Fast.. 4. Lent
geologic.. 5. azoic
granted.. 4. stay 5. delay 8. reprieve
legal.. 6. usance 11. year and a day
long ago.. 4. once, yore 8. formerly
medical.. 4. tid 8. ter in die (three
times a day)
of vigor.. 6. heyday
one.. 4. once
present.. 5. nonce 12. contemporary
prior.. 9. antedated 11. retroactive
right.. 3. tid
same.. 7. however 9. meanwhile
10. concurrent 11. synchronous
14. simultaneously
spare.. 7. leisure
waste.. 4. idle, loaf 5. dally 6. loiter
wrong.. 11. anachronism
13. anachronistic
timeless... 7. ageless, eternal, undated
8. dateless, unending, untimely
9. premature 11. everlasting
12. interminable
timely... 3. apt, pat 4. soon 5. early
6. prompt 9. opportune

10. seasonably 11. opportunity
timepiece... 4. dial 5. clock, watch
6. gnomon 8. egg glass, horologe
9. clepsydra, hourglass, metronome
10. isochronon, wristwatch
11. chronometer
times... 3. ago, eld 4. yore 5. often
10. frequently, yesterdays 11. ups
and downs
timid... 3. shy 5. eerie, henny, mousy,
pavid, scary 6. afraid, trepid
7. bashful, fearful, nervous, not bold
8. cowardly, retiring, timorous
9. diffident, shrinking 12. fainthearted
13. pusillanimous
timocracy (pert to)...
defined by.. 5. Plato
principle.. 11. love of honor
State.. 6. Sparta (anc)
Timon of Athens... 5. Cynic (The)
11. misanthrope
timorous... 5. timid 6. afraid
7. bashful, fearful 8. hesitant
9. shrinking
Timothy (pert to)...
Bib.. 7. convert 8. Epistles
grass.. 3. hay 10. herd's grass
timpani... 11. kettledrums
tin... 3. can, pan 5. money, plate
7. element, stannum 8. preserve
10. not genuine
tin (pert to)...
alloy (copper).. 6. pewter
box.. 7. trummel
coat with.. 5. terne 10. terneplate
comb form.. 6. stanni
extract.. 8. prillion
foil, plate.. 4. tain
mine.. 8. stannary
ref to.. 7. stannic
sheet.. 6. latten
symbol.. 2. Sn
tinamou... 4. yutu 7. tataupa
9. partridge
tincture... 4. dash 5. color, imbue,
myrrh, tinge, trace 6. iodine
7. extract, vestige 8. solution
9. paregoric, suspicion 10. extraction
tinder... 4. punk 5. spunk 6. amadou
9. touchwood
tine... 3. nib 5. prong, spike, tooth
tinea... 7. sycosis 8. ringworm
tinge... 3. dye 4. tint 5. color, imbue,
shade, stain, taint 6. flavor
8. coloring, tincture 10. suggestion
tingle... 4. ring 5. sting 6. dingle,
thrill 7. prickle 9. sensation,
stimulate
tinkle... 5. clink 6. dingle, tingle
tint... 3. due, hue 4. tone 5. blush,
color, tinge 6. nuance
tintinnabulum... 4. bell 6. tinkle
9. rhymester
tintype... 9. ferrotype
12. old–fashioned
tiny... 3. wee 5. small, teeny
6. atomic, infant, minute, petite
9. miniature 10. diminutive
13. infinitesimal
tip... 3. cue, end, fee, neb, top
4. apex, cant, heel, hint, lean, list,
tilt 5. crown, point, slant, spire,

upset 6. careen, inform, summit,
tiptop 7. cumshaw, incline
8. bonamano, gratuity, overturn
9. extremity, overthrow
tip (pert to)...
end.. 3. neb
French.. 9. pourboire
Italian.. 8. bonamano
near.. 6. apical
Near East.. 9. baksheesh (bakshish)
scabbard.. 5. chape 7. crampet
(crampette)
slender.. 6. arista
to one side.. 4. list, tile 5. alist
6. careen
up and over.. 4. cant
tippet... 4. cape, hood 5. amice, scarf
6. almuce 7. muffler 8. liripipe,
palatine 9. comforter
tipple... 3. bib, nip, pot, sip 4. suck
5. drink, quaff 6. fuddle, guzzle,
liquor, tumble 7. spirits 8. beverage,
overturn
tippler... 3. sot 5. souse, toper
7. drinker 9. draftsman
tipster... 4. tout 8. dopester
9. informant, predictor
10. forecaster, speculator
tipsy... 4. awry 5. drunk, shaky
6. groggy 7. fuddled, muddled
10. staggering 11. intoxicated
tiptoe... 5. alert 6. warily 7. eagerly,
quietly 8. cautious, stealthy
10. cautiously
tirade... 6. screed, speech 8. berating
9. philippic
tire... 3. fag, lag, rim 4. bore, jade
5. dress, weary 6. attire 7. exhaust,
fatigue
tired... 5. bored, jaded, spent, weary
6. aweary
tireless... 8. untiring 9. unwearied
10. unwearying 13. indefatigable
tiresome... 3. dry 4. dull, tame
6. boring, prolix 7. irksome, tedious
8. annoying 9. fatiguing, vexatious,
wearisome 10. irritating
tissue... 3. web 4. bast, tela 5. fiber,
paper 6. fabric 7. culture
8. meshwork
tissue (pert to)...
Biol.. 4. bone 5. nerve 6. muscle
8. ganglion 10. epithelium
cell.. 8. meristem
cellular.. 10. epithelium
connecting.. 6. stroma, tendon
8. ligament
decay.. 6. caries
fatty.. 3. fat 4. suet
hardening of.. 9. sclerosis
horny.. 7. keratin
layer.. 7. stratum
lymphoid.. 7. tonsils
nerve.. 8. ganglion
ref to.. 4. tela 5. telar
spinal.. 4. alba
vegetable.. 4. bast 7. endarch
8. meristem
wood.. 6. lignin, lignum
Titan... 4. Rhea, Thea 5. Coeus,
Creus, deity, Dione, giant, Theia
6. Phoebe, Tethys, Themis

7. Cronius, Iapetus, Oceanus
8. Hyperion 9. Mnemosyne
titanic... 4. huge 5. great 7. immense
8. colossal, enormous, gigantic
Titan War (Thessaly)...
11. Titanomachy
tithe... 3. tax 4. part 5. teind, tenth
11. frank pledge
titi... 6. monkey 7. sea bird
8. ironwood 9. buckwheat
Titian... 3. red 6. artist 7. red hair
9. red–haired
titillate... 5. amuse 6. thrill, tickle
7. delight 8. interest
titlark... 5. pipit
title... 3. sir 4. dame, deed, earl, lord,
name, sire, term, type 5. claim, right
6. knight, madame, squire
7. caption, epithet, esquire, heading
8. muniment 9. designate
11. appellation, designation
titled member, Stock Exchange...
6. orchid (sl)
titmouse... 3. mag, tit 4. wren
5. Parus 6. parine, tomtit 7. jacksaw
9. mumruffin
titter... 5. laugh, te–hee 6. giggle,
tee–hee 7. snicker
tittle... 3. dot, jot 4. iota, mark, whit
5. tilde 6. gossip, tattle 8. particle
tittle–tattle... 6. gossip 8. idle talk
16. scandalmongering
tittupy... 3. gay 5. shaky 6. lively
8. prancing, unsteady
titubate... 4. reel 6. totter 7. stagger,
stammer
titular... 7. nominal 9. incumbent (of a
title)
Tlingit... 6. Indian (Alaska)
TNT... 6. trotol 9. explosive
15. trinitrotoluene
to... 2. at 4. into, till, unto 5. until
6. toward 7. as far as, thither
11. preposition
to (pert to)...
to be.. 4. esse, être
to–do.. 3. ado 4. fuss, stir 6. bustle
9. commotion
to each his own.. 10. suum cuique
to which.. 7. whereto
to wit.. 3. viz 6. namely 8. scilicet
9. videlicet
toad... 4. agua, Bufo, frog, pipa
6. anuran, peeper 7. crapaud
9. amphibian, Batrachia, spadefoot
10. natterjack
toad (pert to)...
eater.. 5. toady 8. hanger–on,
parasite
fish.. 6. puffer, slimer 8. frogfish
head.. 6. plover (golden)
lily.. 9. waterlily
stabber.. 9. jackknife
tree.. 4. Hyla
toadflax... 8. flaxweed, ranstead
13. butter–and–eggs
toadstool... 5. morel 6. fungus
8. mushroom, puffball
toady... 4. ugly 8. parasite, truckler
9. repulsive, sycophant, toadeater
toast... 3. tan 4. cook, leep 5. bread,
brede, brown, parch, roast, skoal

6. pledge, sippet 7. drink to
8. cinnamon
tobacco (pert to)...
ash.. 6. dottle (dottel)
Cuban.. 4. capa 6. Vuelta (leaf)
disease.. 6. calico, mosaic 7. walloon
English.. 8. bird's–eye
epithet.. 12. Lady Nicotine
French.. 7. caporal
Greek.. 7. Knaster
hookah smoking.. 7. goracco
Indian.. 7. uppowoc
introduced by.. 7. Raleigh (Sir Walter)
Kentucky.. 6. Burley
kind.. 4. capa, shag 5. tabac
6. Burley, Vuelta 7. caporal,
henbane, Latakia, perique, Turkish
8. Virginia 9. salvadora
paste.. 7. goracco
Persian.. 6. tumbak (tumbaki)
pipe.. 7. calumet, chibouk (chibouque)
principle (active).. 8. nicotine
receptacle.. 4. pipe 7. humidor
S American.. 8. canaster
small cut.. 3. cud 4. plug, quid
6. dottle (dottel) 7. carotte
Turkish.. 7. Latakia
wrapping.. 9. broadleaf
toboggan... 4. sled 5. coast, glide
7. coaster 12. sharp decline
14. downhill course
toby... 3. dog (Punch's), jug, mug, rob
5. cigar 7. highway, pitcher
tocsin... 5. alarm 9. alarm bell
13. warning signal
toe... 3. tae, tip 5. digit 6. dactyl,
hallux 7. minimus
toehold... 7. footing 8. foothold,
purchase
toes, odd–numbered...
13. perissodactyl
together... 3. com, con, syn 4. mass,
with 5. union 10. conjointly
11. unanimously 12. coincidently,
concurrently, continuously
toggery... 3. set 4. garb, togs
5. dress 7. clothes, harness
9. trappings 12. haberdashery
tolerable... 4. so–so 8. bearable,
passable 9. endurable
10. acceptable, fairly well, sufferable
11. supportable
tolerance... 8. patience
10. indulgence, permission
tolerant... 7. lenient, patient
9. indulgent 10. forbearing,
permissive
tolerate... 4. bear, bide 5. abide,
allow, brook, stand 6. endure,
permit, suffer 9. put up with
toll... 3. due, tax 4. call, duty, peal,
ring 5. knell 6. allure, charge,
custom, entice, impost, invite, strike
7. ringing 8. exaction
10. assessment 12. compensation
Tolypeutes... 4. apar 9. armadillo
Tom, Dick and Harry... 8. everyone,
humanity 15. persons at random
tomahawk... 3. axe 4. kill 6. attack
7. hatchet
tomb... 4. cist, lair 5. crypt, grave,
speos, vault 6. shrine 7. mastaba

(mastabah), orruary, tritaph
8. catacomb, cenotaph
9. mausoleum, sepulcher
tombé... 4. drum
tomboy... 3. meg 4. romp 5. rowdy
6. hoyden (hoiden), tomrig
tomcat... 3. gib
tomcod... 8. bocaccio
tome... 4. book, opus 5. atlas
6. volume 11. papal letter,
publication
tomorrow... 5. later 6. mañana 9. the
morrow
tonant... 7. blatant 10. thundering
tone... 4. mode, mood, note, tang,
tune 5. pitch, reedy, sound, trend,
twang, vigor 6. accent, energy,
melody, nuance, timbre 7. cadence
8. modulate, monotone, tonology
9. harmonize 10. inflection,
intonation, modulation
tone (pert to)...
down.. 3. dim 6. mellow, modify,
soften 8. moderate
lacking.. 5. atony 6. atonal
quality, color.. 6. timbre
series.. 5. scale
single.. 8. monotone
succession.. 5. melos
thin.. 7. sfogato
vibrant.. 7. twang
toneless... 4. weal 5. stony 6. silent
9. colorless
tonga... 7. vehicle (2–wheeled)
Tonga... 15. Friendly Islands
tongue... 3. gab 4. meat 5. lingo,
speak 6. speech 7. clapper, lingula
8. language, lorriker, parlance
9. utterance
tongue (pert to)...
classical.. 5. Greek, Latin 6. Hebrew
fish.. 4. sole
Jesus.. 7. Aramaic
lash.. 5. scold 8. scolding
pivoted.. 4. pawl
reference to.. 7. glossal, lingual
sacred.. 4. Pali
shaped.. 9. lingulate
tied.. 4. mute 8. taciturn
wagon.. 4. neap, pole
tongueless... 4. dumb, mute
10. speechless
tonic... 6. bracer, catnip, liquor
7. bracing 8. medicine, remedial,
roborant 9. stimulant 10. refreshing
11. corroborant 12. invigorating
tonsil... 8. amygdala
tonsorialist... 6. barber
tonsured... 4. bald 5. shorn 6. shaven
7. clipped 10. baldheaded
too... 3. and 4. also, over, very
6. overly 7. besides 8. likewise
9. extremely 11. excessively
12. additionally
too (pert to)...
bad.. 4. alas
much.. 4. trop 6. excess 7. nimiety
small.. 13. unappreciable
soon.. 9. premature
tool... 3. axe, saw 4. dupe, file
5. agent 6. device, gadget, puppet
7. engrave, gimmick, utensil, utility

9. appliance 11. contrivance
tool (type)... 2. ax (axe) 3. adz (adze),
awl, bit, hob, hoe, saw, sax, tap
4. file, jack, pick, tong, vise
5. brush, burin, drill, knife, lathe,
level, plane, punch, razor, spade
6. chisel, gimlet, hammer, lifter,
peavey (peavy), pliers, reamer, shears,
slater, slicer, square, trepan, wrench
7. cleaver, mattock, mattoir, scalpel,
spatula 11. screwdriver
tools (pert to)...
category.. 5. power, speed 7. cutlery,
machine, medical 9. precision
11. labor–saving 12. straightedge
prehistoric.. 4. celt 6. eolith
9. paleolith
stone.. 6. banner
theft of.. 6. ratten
toosh... 4. gown (short), robe
9. nightgown
toot... 3. pry, spy 4. fool, gaze, peep
5. blare, drink, revel, shout, spree
6. sprout 7. whistle 8. carousal,
eminence, proclaim 9. blow a horn,
elevation
tooth... 3. cog 4. dent, fang, snag,
tine, tusk 5. ivory, molar, point,
prong, taste 6. canine, cuspid,
wisdom 7. grinder, incisor
8. bicuspid, eyetooth 10. projection
tooth, teeth (pert to)...
ache.. 8. dentagra 9. dentalgia
comb form.. 5. denti, odont
6. odonto 7. odontia
cutting of.. 8. teething 9. dentition
decay.. 6. caries, cavity
11. saprodontia
destitute of.. 8. edentate
irregularity.. 11. odontoloxia
molar.. 4. wang
ref to.. 6. dental 7. odontic
science.. 10. odontology
Scot.. 3. gam
socket.. 8. alveolus
toothlike.. 8. odontoid 9. dentiform
toothless... 8. decrepid, edentate
toothsome... 5. tasty 9. delicious,
palatable
top... 3. cap, fid, lid, tip, toy
4. acme, apex, pate, roof 5. crest,
criss, crown, excel, mensa, outdo,
ridge, scalp 6. finial, summit, vertex,
zenith 7. highest, supreme, surpass,
topmost 8. dominate, pinnacle,
teetotum 9. uppermost
topaz... 3. gem 5. color 7. mineral
11. hummingbird 13. precious stone
tope... 4. tomb, wren 5. drink, grove,
shark, stupa, tower 6. guzzle, shrine
7. dogfish
toper... 3. sot 4. tope 5. shark
6. barfly, boozer 7. guzzler, tippler,
tosspot 8. drunkard 9. alcoholic,
inebriate 12. bacchanalian
tophet, topheth... 4. hell 5. chaos
8. darkness
topi, topee... 3. cap, hat 8. antelope
topiary... 6. garden 9. gardening
topic... 4. plot, text 5. theme
6. reason, remedy 7. subject
8. argument 11. application

topical... 5. local 9. temporary
10. thematical
topknot... 5. crest, onkos 6. pigeon
8. flounder 9. headdress
topmost... 6. apical 7. highest,
supreme 8. foremost 9. uppermost
topnotcher... 3. ace 4. hero, star
6. tiptop 7. supreme 9. first–rate
11. unsurpassed
topography... 7. mapping 8. location
9. surveying 11. description
15. regional anatomy
topple... 3. tip 4. fall, tilt 5. pitch,
upset 6. totter, tumble 8. overturn
9. overthrow 10. somersault
topsail... 5. raffe (raffee)
topsy–turvy... 8. confused
10. contrarily, disordered
11. withershins
toque... 3. hat 6. monkey (bonnet)
9. headdress
tor... 4. crag, peak 5. mound
8. pinnacle
torah, tora... 3. law 7. precept
10. Law of Moses, Pentateuch,
revelation
torch... 4. lamp 5. blaze, flare, fusee
(fuzee), light 7. lighter, lucigen
8. flambeau 10. flashlight
torero... 11. bullfighter
torment... 3. rib, vex 4. bait, pain,
rack 5. agony, devil, harry, tease,
worry 6. badger, harass, harrow,
hector, pester, plague, stir up
7. afflict, anguish, bedevil, torture
8. distress, vexation 9. suffering,
tantalize 10. punishment
11. persecution
torn... 4. rent 5. riven, split 6. ripped
7. severed 8. tattered 9. alienated,
lacerated (see also *tear*)
tornado... 4. wind 7. cyclone, twister
8. blizzard, outburst 9. hurricane,
whirlwind, windstorm
12. thunderstorm
toro... 4. bull 7. cavalla, cowfish
torpedo... 3. ray 4. boat, mine
5. shoot 6. attack, gunman
7. explode 8. fire upon, firework,
numbfish 9. crampfish, detonator,
submarine
torpid... 4. dull, numb 5. inert
6. stupid 7. dormant 8. benumbed,
inactive, lifeless, listless, sluggish
9. apathetic, lethargic
torpor... 4. coma 6. acedia, apathy,
stupor 7. languor 8. dormancy,
lethargy 9. inertness 10. inactivity
12. sluggishness 13. insensibility
torque... 5. chain 6. collar 7. torsion
8. necklace, ornament
torrefy... 5. parch, roast 6. scorch
torrent... 5. flood, spate 6. stream
7. current, roaring 8. downpour,
outburst
torrential... 12. overwhelming
torrid... 3. hot 4. arid 7. burning,
parched 8. scorched, tropical
10. oppressive, passionate
tortilla cooking dish... 5. comal
tortoise... 4. emyd, Emys 6. gopher,
turtle 7. hicatee 8. Chelonia,

matamata 9. ellachick
tortuous... 6. spiral 7. devious,
sinuous, winding 8. twisting
10. circuitous, roundabout
12. labyrinthine
torture... 4. flay, pain, rack 5. agony,
twist 6. impale, punish, wrench
7. crucify, distort, torment
10. punishment
tory, Tory... 6. bandit, outlaw, Papist
8. loyalist, marauder, partisan,
Royalist 11. reactionary
12. Conservative
toss... 3. lob 4. cast, flip, hurl
5. bandy, chuck, fling, flirt, heave,
pitch, throw 6. billow, thrash
7. disturb 8. flounder, scramble
9. commotion 10. excitement
toss (pert to)...
a coin.. 4. flip
and turn.. 6. thrash 8. flounder
9. vacillate
off.. 5. drink 6. tipple 9. dispose of,
improvise
out.. 5. eject 8. trick out
together.. 8. scramble
tosspot... 3. sot 5. drunk, toper
6. flagon 8. drunkard
tossup... 6. gamble 10. even chance
11. uncertainty
tota... 6. grivet, monkey
total... 3. add, all, sum, tot 5. gross,
utter, whole 6. amount, entire
7. perfect, summary 8. absolute,
complete, entirety 9. aggregate
totally... 5. quite 6. wholly 8. entirely
10. completely
totem... 4. pole, post 6. fetish, pillar,
symbol
totem pole... 3. xat
toto... 3. all 4. baby 5. totum
totter... 4. reel, rock, sway 5. pitch,
shake, waver 6. falter, seesaw
7. stagger 8. titubate 9. fluctuate,
vacillate
toucan... 4. toco 7. aracari 8. hornbill
13. constellation (opp Southern
Cross)
touch... 3. dab, tag, tap, tig 4. abut,
feel, meet 5. taste, trait 6. adjoin,
border 7. contact 9. acuteness
touch (pert to)...
acuteness of.. 8. oxyaphia
bound.. 4. abut
closely.. 7. impinge 8. osculate
examine.. 7. palpate
light, lightly.. 3. pat 5. brush
7. attinge, lambent
off.. 4. fire 6. incite
ref to.. 7. tactile, tactual
stone.. 8. basanite 9. criterion
11. Lydian stone
wood.. 4. punk 6. amadou, tinder
touching... 6. moving 7. contact,
feeling, tangent 8. pathetic
9. affecting, attingent 10. concerning
11. interesting
touchy... 4. sore 5. cross, testy
7. peevish 8. ticklish 9. irascible,
irritable, sensitive 10. precarious
13. oversensitive
tough... 4. hard, wiry 5. hardy, rowdy,

stiff **6.** robust, sinewy, strong
7. ruffian **8.** adhesive, hardened,
leathery, stubborn **9.** difficult,
obstinate, resistant, tenacious
10. unyielding
toupee... **3.** wig **6.** peruke **7.** periwig
9. false hair
tour... **4.** trip **5.** shift **6.** travel
7. circuit, journey **9.** barnstorm,
excursion
tourmaline... **3.** gem **6.** schorl
9. rubellite **10.** indicolite
tournament... **4.** tilt **5.** games, joust,
trial **6.** battle **7.** contest, regatta,
tourney **8.** Olympics **9.** encounter
11. Turnierfest
tourniquet... **6.** binder, garrot
7. bandage
tousle, tousel... **4.** pull, tear
6. rumple, tussle **8.** dishevel
tout... **3.** spy **5.** scout, watch
6. praise **7.** canvass, lookout, tipster
8. give a tip, informer, smuggler
9. predictor, solicitor
tow... **3.** tew, tug **4.** drag, draw, haul,
pull, rope **5.** chain **6.** hawser
8. cordelle
toward... **2.** ad, at, to **4.** near
5. anent **6.** facing **7.** forward,
towards, willing **8.** imminent
9. compliant, headed for
11. approaching
toward (pert to)...
blood vessels.. **5.** hemad (haemad)
center.. **5.** entad **6.** inward
direction.. **7.** leeward, seaward
8. homeward, landward, windward
9. earthward **10.** heavenward
exterior.. **5.** ectad
front.. **8.** anterior
left.. **3.** haw **5.** aport **9.** sinistrad,
sinistral
mouth.. **4.** orad
right.. **7.** dextrad **9.** dextrally
stern.. **3.** aft **5.** abaft **6.** astern
towards... **7.** ynesche
tower... **3.** tor **4.** boom, silo, soar
5. exalt, pylon, spire, stupa **6.** belfry,
height, turret, uplift **7.** bulwark,
defense, elevate, steeple, surpass
8. domineer, fortress **9.** campanile
10. stronghold, watchtower
tower (pert to)...
astrology.. **7.** mansion **14.** planetary
house
bell.. **9.** campanile
chess.. **6.** castle
church.. **5.** spire **6.** belfry, cupola
glacial.. **5.** serac
India.. **5.** minar **7.** sikhara
marker.. **5.** pylon
of.. **4.** Pisa **5.** Babel, Minar **6.** Eiffel,
Hunger, London **7.** silence (dakhma)
10. Kutab Minar
Oriental.. **7.** minaret
watch.. **7.** mirador
towering... **4.** high, huge, tall
5. great, lofty **6.** Alpine **7.** eminent,
soaring **10.** overweening
towhee... **5.** finch **7.** bunting, chewink
town... **4.** burg, deme **6.** ciudad,
hamlet, Podunk, suburb **7.** borough,

commune, village **8.** boom town,
township **9.** ghost town
townsman... **3.** cit **7.** citizen, oppidan
(Eton student) **8.** resident
9. selectman
toxic... **7.** noxious **8.** poisoned,
venomous, virulent **9.** poisonous
toxicology (*science of*)... **7.** poisons
9. antidotes
toxology... **7.** archery
toxophilite... **6.** archer
toy... **3.** pet, top **4.** doll, hoop, play,
whim **5.** dally, fancy, flirt **6.** bauble,
gewgaw, hoople, rattle, trifle **7.** cat's
paw, trinket **8.** flirting **9.** plaything
10. knickknack
trace... **4.** clew (clue), copy, find, hint,
mark, nose, seek, sign **5.** refer,
shade, tinge, track, trail **6.** deduce,
derive, detect, follow, sketch
7. glimpse, outline, thought, vestige
8. evidence, traverse **9.** delineate,
footprint **11.** investigate, small
amount
trachea... **4.** duct **8.** windpipe
tracing... **4.** copy **6.** record
8. ergogram **10.** cardiogram
12. reproduction
track... **3.** rut, way **4.** path, rail, slot,
spur, wake **5.** route, spoor, trail,
tread **6.** follow, pursue **7.** nereite
(worm), vestige **8.** traverse
9. footprint, spectacle
tract... **4.** area, plot, zone **5.** essay,
range **6.** estate, region **7.** booklet,
country, expanse, leaflet, quarter,
stretch **8.** brochure, district,
pamphlet, treatise **9.** territory
10. exposition **11.** subdivision
12. dissertation
tract (pert to)...
arid.. **4.** dene **6.** desert
boggy, swampy.. **6.** morass
10. Everglades
grassland.. **7.** prairie
lava.. **8.** pedregal
treeless.. **5.** llano **6.** steppe **7.** prairie
tractable... **4.** easy **6.** docile, gentle,
pliant **7.** ductile **8.** amenable, flexible
9. adaptable, compliant, malleable
10. governable **11.** conformable
trade... **3.** buy **4.** deal, sell, swap,
wind **5.** craft **6.** barter, merger,
metier **7.** bargain, calling, dealing,
pursuit, traffic **8.** business,
commerce, exchange, practice,
purchase, vocation **10.** handicraft,
occupation, profession **11.** intercourse
trade—mark, trademark... **5.** brand,
label
trader... **6.** dealer, monger, sutler
8. merchant **9.** tradesman
10. shopkeeper
trading association... **5.** hanse (hansa)
trading station (Mil)... **2.** PX **4.** fort,
post
tradition... **4.** lore, myth **5.** usage
6. custom, legend **7.** culture
8. folklore **10.** convention
(established) **12.** superstition
traditional... **3.** old **9.** legendary
10. historical **12.** conventional,

long–standing 15. long–established

traditional tale... 4. saga 6. legend

traduce... 4. slur 5. abuse, belie
6. debase, defame, malign, vilify
7. asperse, pervert, slander
8. disgrace 10. calumniate

traffic... 3. buy 4. sell 5. trade
6. barter, simony (sacred)
8. business, carriage, commerce,
dealings 11. familiarity, intercourse

tragedy... 6. misery 4. calamity,
disaster 10. misfortune

tragic... 3. sad 4. dire 5. fatal
8. dramatic, pathetic 10. calamitous,
disastrous, fatal event

tragopan... 8. pheasant

trail... 3. lag 4. drag, hunt, path, slot,
spur 5. blaze, piste, route, scent,
spoor, trace, track 6. camino, follow
7. draggle 8. be behind, footpath
9. lag behind

Trail (famed)... 6. Mormon, Oregon
7. Santa Fe, Spanish 8. Chisholm, El
Camino, Heritage 10. Lewis–Clark,
Wilderness 11. Appalachian
12. Natchez Trace, Pacific Crest

trail (pert to)...
blazer.. 7. pioneer
deer.. 4. slot
mark a.. 5. blaze
marker.. 5. cairn
mountain.. 4. pass
Spanish.. 6. camino

train... 2. el 4. line, load, tail
5. breed, chain, coach, drill, flier,
focus, shape, suite 6. direct, school,
series 7. caravan, cortege, educate,
retinue 8. accustom, instruct,
railroad, rehearse 9. afterpart,
entourage, following 10. attendants,
conveyance, discipline, line of cars,
procession 11. progression,
streamliner 13. accommodation

trained mechanic... 7. artisan

trainee... 6. rookie 7. recruit, student
8. enrollee

traipse... 3. gad 5. trail, tramp
6. trudge, wander 8. gadabout

trait... 5. habit, touch 6. streak
7. feature, quality 9. lineament,
mannerism 11. peculiarity
13. individuality 14. characteristic

traitor... 3. rat 8. informer, Quisling,
turncoat 10. treasonist
13. double–crosser, Judas Iscariot
14. Benedict Arnold

traject... 3. way 4. sage 5. ferry,
route 6. course 7. passage
8. crossing

trajectory... 5. route 6. rocket
9. celestial 10. fixed orbit

tram... 3. car 4. limb 5. wagon
7. carrier, railway, tramcar, trolley,
vehicle 9. streetcar 10. conveyance

tramontane... 5. alien 8. polestar
9. foreigner, North Star
11. transalpine

tramp... 3. bum 4. hike, hobo, hoof,
step, walk 5. jaunt, nomad, tread
6. beggar, trudge, wander
7. sponger, traipse, trample, vagrant
8. vagabond 9. sundowner

10. landlouper (landloper), pedestrian
11. bindle stiff 12. foot traveler

trample... 5. crush, tread 6. bruise,
subdue 7. conquer, destroy, run over
9. press down

trance... 4. coma, doze 5. dream,
spell, swoon 6. raptus, stupor
7. amentia, ecstasy, rapture
8. hypnosis 9. catalepsy, enrapture,
hypnotize, spellbind

tranchant... 5. sharp 7. cutting
9. trenchant

tranquil... 4. calm, cool, easy, mild
5. quiet, still 6. gentle, placid,
serene 7. pacific, restful
8. composed, peaceful 9. quiescent
11. undisturbed 13. imperturbable

tranquility... 3. keg 5. peace, quiet
8. calmness, serenity 9. composure
10. quiescence 12. peacefulness

tranquilize... 4. calm, lull 5. allay,
quiet, still 6. pacify, settle, soothe
7. appease, assuage, compose

transaction... 4. deal, sale 6. action,
affair 7. bargain 8. business
9. discharge, execution
10. proceeding 11. negotiation,
performance, proposition 16. buying
and selling

transcend... 3. cap 5. excel, mount
6. ascend, exceed 7. surpass 8. go
beyond, outstrip, surmount

transcendent... 5. above 8. ethereal,
heavenly, superior 9. recondite
10. superhuman, surpassing
12. metaphysical, supernatural,
transmundane 13. extraordinary
14. transcendental 15. beyond
knowledge

transcribe... 4. copy 5. write
6. record 9. reproduce, translate
10. paraphrase

transcript... 4. copy 6. record
8. apograph 9. duplicate, imitation
12. reproduction

transfer... 4. cede, deed, pass, sale
5. grant, shift 6. assign, attorn,
change, convey, depute, remove
7. removal 8. alienate, delivery
9. transport 10. conveyance,
transcript

transfer (pert to)...
conveyance (estate).. 5. lease
6. demise
crown to successor.. 6. demise
design.. 5. decal 12. decalcomania
medical.. 10. transplant
of ownership.. 6. attorn
10. abalienate, alienation, conveyance
of property.. 8. disposal

transfigure... 5. exalt 6. change
7. glorify 8. idealize 9. irradiate,
transform, transmute
12. metamorphose

transfix... 3. pin 4. hold 5. spear
6. fasten, impale, pierce 9. hold
fixed 11. transpierce 14. hold
motionless

transform... 4. turn 5. alter
6. change, revamp 7. convert
9. transmute 10. assimilate
11. transfigure 12. metamorphose,

transmogrify 16. transubstantiate
transformation... 3. wig 6. change
8. mutation 10. conversion, false
front 13. metamorphosis,
transmutation 17. anthropomorphosis
transgress... 3. err, sin 5. cross
6. exceed, offend, thwart 7. disobey,
infract, violate 8. overstep, trespass
9. break a law
transgression... 3. sin 5. crime, fault
7. misdeed, offense 8. trespass
9. violation 10. effrontery, infraction
11. lawbreaking 12. infringement
13. nonconformity
transgressor... 6. sinner 8. offender
9. wrongdoer 10. delinquent,
malefactor
transient... 5. brief 6. lodger 7. flighty
8. fleeting, fugitive, traveler
9. ephemeral, migratory, momentary
10. evanescent, short–lived, transitory
transit... 6. travel 7. passage
9. metabasis 10. conveyance
12. transference
transition... 5. shift 7. passage
9. anabolism, evolution, metabasis
10. catabolism (katabolism),
conversion, metabolism, modulation
11. transfusion
transitory... 5. brief, fleet 8. fleeting,
temporal 9. ephemeral, temporary,
transient 10. evanescent 11. not
enduring
transitory things... 8. ephemera
translate... 4. read, rede 6. decode,
render 7. convert 8. construe,
transfer 9. interpret 10. paraphrase
translation... 4. pony, trot 7. version
9. rendition 10. paraphrase
12. transference 14. interpretation
15. transliteration
translucent... 6. limpid 8. luminous
11. transparent 14. shining through
transmit... 4. send 6. convey, render
7. devolve, forward 8. bequeath,
hand down, transfer
11. communicate
transmutation... 9. evolution
transmute... 6. change 7. convert,
resolve 9. transform 11. transfigure
12. metamorphose
16. transubstantiate
transparent... 4. open 5. clear, gauzy,
lucid, sheer 6. bright, candid, glassy,
lucent 7. crystal, pelucid, shining
8. luminous, lustrous 9. guileless
10. diaphanous 11. crystalline,
perspicuous, translucent, unconcealed
transparent thing... 4. mica, silk, veil
5. beryl, water 6. quartz, tissue
7. crystal, diamond 8. gossamer
9. isinglass
transport... 3. dak 4. boat, move, raft,
send, ship 5. bring, carry, truck
6. banish, convey, deport, vessel
7. ecstasy, freight, passion, rapture,
smuggle 8. carriage, emigrate,
entrance, palander, transfer
9. enrapture, troopship
transpose... 5. shift 6. change,
convey, invert 7. convert, reverse
8. transfer 9. rearrange, translate,

transmute 11. interchange
transposition of sounds, words...
10. metathesis, spoonerism
Transvaal (pert to)...
capital.. 8. Pretoria
city.. 12. Johannesburg
daisy.. 7. gerbera
discovery.. 4. gold, Rand (The)
famed emigration.. 9. great trek
(1836)
legislature.. 4. raad
policeman.. 4. zarp
settlers.. 5. Boers
War.. 4. Boer (1899–1902)
transverse... 6. across 7. oblique,
transom 8. diagonal 9. crosswise
10. crosspiece
trap... 3. gin, net, pat, web 4. cage,
door, lure, rock, tipe, tree, weir
5. catch, creel, mouth, snare
6. ambush, corner, device, eelpot,
enmesh, recess 7. dragnet, ensnare,
pitfall, springe 8. carriage, deadfall,
trapping, trickery 9. caparison, road
block, stratagem
trapper... 5. lurer 6. hunter, netter,
snarer 7. decoyer
trappings... 4. gear, tack 5. props
7. scenery 8. wardrobe 9. apparatus,
caparison, ornaments 10. horse cloth
13. paraphernalia
trash... 4. bosh, dirt, junk 5. waste
6. debris, refuse, rubble 7. rubbish
8. nonsense, riffraff, trumpery
10. balderdash
trashy... 5. cheap, toshy 6. paltry
7. useless 8. rubbishy 9. worthless
11. nonsensical
trauma... 5. shock, wound 6. injury
travail... 4. pain, toil 5. agony, labor
7. journey, trouble 9. suffering
11. parturition
trave... 9. crossbeam
travel... 2. go 4. fare, move, mush,
post, ride, taxi, tour, trek, wend
5. coast 6. motion 7. commute,
journey, migrate, sojourn 8. progress,
traverse 9. gallivant 11. peregrinate
travel (pert to)...
equipment.. 7. baggage 9. viaticals
expense.. 8. viaticum
group.. 7. caravan
over obstacles.. 9. roughshod
pert to.. 6. viatic
place to place.. 9. itinerate
traveler, travelers... 5. farer 6. viator
7. caravan, tourist 8. salesman,
wayfarer 9. journeyer
travels... 7. odyssey 8. journeys
14. peregrinations
traverse... 4. deny, pass 5. cross
6. refute, thwart 7. athwart, oblique,
parados 8. navigate 10. counteract
travesty... 5. drama 6. parody, satire
7. lampoon 8. disguise 9. burlesque
10. caricature 11. incongruity
tray... 6. salver, server 7. ashtray,
coaster
treacherous... 5. false, Judas, punic,
snaky 8. disloyal, plotting, unstable
9. deceitful, faithless, insidious
10. perfidious, traitorous, unreliable

11. disaffected 13. Machiavellian
(Machiavelian), untrustworthy
treachery... 5. guile 6. deceit
7. perfidy, treason 8. betrayal
10. disloyalty
treacle... 4. cure 6. remedy
7. claggum, sweeten 8. molasses
10. sweetening
treacle water... 7. cordial
tread... 3. rut 4. gait, mark, pace,
step, volt, walk 5. crush, stair
6. course 7. conquer, set foot,
trample 8. footstep, shoe sole
9. footprint
treadle... 5. lever, pedal 7. chalaza
tread underfoot... 5. crush 6. subdue
7. oppress, run over 8. domineer
9. tyrannize
treason... 7. perfidy 8. betrayal,
sedition 9. treachery
treasonable, treasonous...
10. perfidious, traitorous
11. treacherous
treasure... 4. fisc (fisk), fund, roon
5. cache, chest, hoard, prize, purse,
store, trove, value 6. coffer, fiscus,
riches, wealth 7. cherish 8. hold
dear 9. exchequer, thesaurus
10. appreciate, depository, repository,
storehouse
treasurer... 6. bursar, purser
7. cashier, curator, officer 8. receiver
9. paymaster 11. chamberlain
Treasure State... 7. Montana
treasure–trove... 5. money (hidden)
7. bullion 9. discovery 14. buried
treasure
treat... 4. dose 5. Dutch, feast
6. doctor, handle, regale, repast
7. delight, discuss, process
8. consider 9. discourse, entertain,
negotiate 10. manipulate
treat (pert to)...
improperly.. 4. snub 5. flout, spite
6. insult, misuse, offend 9. humiliate
maliciously.. 5. frame, spite
of morals.. 6. ethics
royally.. 6. regale 9. with honor
silk (for rustle).. 6. scroop
snobbishly.. 7. high hat, high–hat
surgically.. 7. operate
tenderly.. 6. coddle, pamper
with contempt.. 5. flout, scorn, scout,
spurn 7. contemn
with deference.. 7. respect
treatise... 5. essay, study, tract
6. thesis 7. article 9. discourse
10. discussion 12. dissertation
treatise on...
forests.. 5. silva
fruit trees.. 6. pomona
language.. 7. grammar
pines.. 7. pinetum
treatment (pert to)...
application (Med).. 5. stupe
compassionate.. 5. mercy
harsh.. 5. abuse 8. misusage, severity
ill.. 5. abuse
preparatory.. 8. training 10. ground
work, processing
term.. 5. usage 8. addition (to soil),
handling

treaty... 4. mise, pact 6. cartel
7. compact, entente 8. contract
9. agreement 10. convention
11. arrangement, negotiation
12. capitulation 13. understanding
treaty (pert to)...
bound nations.. 6. allies
Elm.. 12. Philadelphia (1682)
first draft.. 8. protocol
peace.. 5. truce 6. Pax Dei
9. armistice 10. pax in bella
secret.. 13. the Engagement (1647)
treble... 5. three, voice 6. latten, triple
7. soprano 9. threefold
11. high–pitched
treble clef... 3. Gee 5. G clef, staff
(G clef)
tree... 5. plant 6. corner, timber
7. gallows 9. genealogy
tree (pert to)... see also *trees*
antidote for snakebite.. 6. cedron
aromatic.. 9. sassafras
bear.. 7. raccoon
cactus.. 7. saguaro
camphor.. 5. kapur
cat.. 9. palm civet
cobra.. 6. mambra
cone–bearing.. 3. fir, yew 5. alder,
cedar, larch 7. conifer
evergreen fruit.. 5. lemon 6. orange
exudation.. 3. gum, lac, sap
India.. 4. dita 10. devil's tree
lotus.. 4. sadr
mineral (formed on).. 8. dendrite
of Buddha.. 2. bo
of chastity.. 11. agnus castus
of life.. 10. arbor vitae
of strength.. 3. oak
rain.. 5. saman (zaman) 8. genisaro
resin.. 3. fir 4. pine 6. balsam
sacred (Bib).. 7. asherah
salt.. 4. atle (atlee) 8. tamarisk
snake.. 4. gimp, lora
sprout.. 5. copse, sprig 7. coppice
sugar.. 5. maple
Texas.. 5. alamo 6. poplar
tiger.. 7. leopard
toad.. 4. hyla
trunk.. 4. bole 5. caber, stock
umbrella.. 5. wahoo
victor's crown.. 6. laurel
worshiper.. 5. dryad, nymph (wood)
trees (pert to)...
grove.. 5. copse
plantation.. 6. forest 7. orchard,
pinetum
poem.. 6. Kilmer (Joyce)
ref to.. 8. arboreal 9. cacuminal
science.. 7. silvics 12. silviculture
service (rowan).. 5. sorbs
trefoil... 6. clover 8. shamrock
10. black medic, clover leaf (Her)
tregetour (anc)... 7. juggler
8. magician
trek... 6. travel 7. journey, migrate
10. expedition
trellis... 5. arbor 7. lattice, pergola
8. espalier 11. latticework
tremble... 5. quake, shake 6. doddle,
falter, quaver, quiver, shiver, tatter,
thrill, tremor 7. shudder, tremolo,
twitter, vibrate 8. be afraid 9. be

excited, trepidate
trembling... **5**. aspen **6**. dither, trepid
7. fearful, nervous, quaking, quavery,
shaking **9**. vibrating
tremendous... **3**. big **4**. huge
5. awful, giant, great **6**. superb
8. horrible, powerful, terrific
9. frightful, momentous, monstrous
10. terrifying **13**. extraordinary
tremolo... **6**. quaver **10**. fluttering
tremor... **5**. palsy, quake, shake
6. quiver, thrill **7**. tremble
9. vibration
tremulous... **5**. aspen, quaky, timid
7. excited, fearful, nervous, palsied,
shaking, shivery **9**. quavering,
sensitive, trembling, vibratory
11. palpitating
trench... **3**. gaw **4**. bury, gash, leat,
moat **5**. canal, carve, ditch, drain,
fosse **6**. furrow, groove, gutter
7. acequia, intrude **8**. aqueduct,
encroach, entrench, infringe, trespass
10. excavation **12**. entrenchment
trenchant... **4**. keen **5**. acute, sharp
6. biting **7**. cutting **8**. clear–cut,
incisive **11**. penetrating
trencherman... **5**. eater **7**. sponger
8. gourmand **9**. chowhound
11. gormandizer
trend... **4**. tone, turn, vein **5**. drift,
skirt, swing, tenor **6**. strike
7. deviate, revolve **8**. movement,
tendency **9**. direction **11**. inclination
trepan... **3**. saw **4**. lure, tool **5**. snare,
trick **6**. entrap **7**. deceive, swindle
8. deceiver, trephine **9**. stratagem,
trickster
trepang... **10**. bêche–de–mer **11**. sea
cucumber **14**. sea caterpillar
trepid... **7**. quaking **8**. timorous
9. trembling
trepidation... **4**. fear **5**. alarm
6. dismay **7**. quaking **9**. agitation,
confusion **10**. excitement
11. disturbance, oscillation
12. perturbation **13**. consternation
trespass... **3**. sin **4**. tort **5**. poach
6. breach, invade, trench **7**. intrude,
offense **8**. encroach, entrench,
infringe, overstep **10**. infraction,
transgress **11**. misfeasance
12. infringement **13**. transgression
tress... **4**. curl, hair **5**. braid, plait
7. ringlet **10**. lock of hair
tressure... **4**. band **6**. border, fillet,
ribbon **9**. headdress
trestle... **5**. bench **7**. support, viaduct
tret... **9**. allowance
triad... **5**. chord, three, trine **7**. trinary,
trinity **9**. trivalent **12**. ternary group
trial... **2**. go **4**. bout, case, test
5. venue **6**. assize, ordeal
7. attempt, contest, empiric
8. evidence, hardship **9**. prolusion,
trying out **10**. experiment
11. examination, tribulation
triangle... **6**. trigon **8**. virginal
13. constellation
triangle (pert to)...
connection.. **5**. delta

draw circle within.. **7**. escribe
military.. **10**. punishment
music instrument.. **10**. percussion,
triquetrum (anc)
side.. **3**. leg
three acute angles.. **6**. oxygon
two equal sides.. **9**. isosceles
unequal sides.. **7**. scalene
triangular (pert to)...
decoration.. **8**. pediment, triqueta
muscle.. **7**. deltoid
pert to.. **10**. trilateral
piece.. **4**. gore **5**. miter, wedge
6. gusset
sail.. **6**. lateen **9**. spinnaker
shaped.. **7**. deltoid **8**. oxygonal
tribal custom... **7**. couvade (childbirth)
tribal symbol... **5**. totem **9**. totem
pole
tribe... **4**. clan, kind, race, sept
5. class, group **6**. family **7**. company
11. aggregation **14**. classification
tribe (pert to)...
birds.. **5**. flock
head of.. **5**. chief **6**. sachem
9. patriarch
Israel.. **3**. Dan **4**. Levi **6**. Reuben
migrated.. **5**. Aryan
New Zealand.. **3**. ati
of Ben.. **5**. poets (Ben Jonson)
Tribes, Five Civilized... **5**. Creek
7. Choctaw **8**. Cherokee, Seminole
9. Chickasaw
Tribes, Five Nations (Iroquois)...
6. Cayuga, Mohawk, Oneida, Seneca
8. Onondaga
tribulation... **5**. trial **6**. ordeal, sorrow
8. distress **9**. suffering
tribunal... **3**. bar **4**. banc, seat
5. bench, court, curia, forum
9. Areopagus (anc)
tributary... **4**. fork, vein **6**. branch,
feeder **8**. affluent, effluent, influent
9. auxiliary **11**. subordinate
12. contributary
tribute... **3**. fee, pay, tax **4**. cain,
duty, levy, scat **5**. allow, grant
6. assign, bestow, homage, impost,
praise, rental **7**. chevage (Hist),
ovation, payment, pension, respect
8. encomium **9**. attribute, gratitude
10. allegiance, contribute, obligation
11. retribution
tricar... **8**. tricycle **10**. motorcycle (with
extra car)
trice... **5**. jiffy **6**. moment **7**. instant
9. twinkling
trick... **3**. fob, gag **4**. dido, dupe,
feat, flam, gull, jest, ruse, wile
5. cheat, child, dodge, fraud, guile,
knack, prank, shift, stunt **6**. deceit,
delude **7**. deceive, defraud, finesse,
pretext **8**. artifice, delusion, flimflam,
illusion **9**. chicanery, deception,
imposture **10**. subterfuge
11. contrivance, legerdemain
trickery... **5**. fraud, hocus **6**. deceit
7. roguery **8**. artifice, cheating,
trumpery **9**. chicanery, deception,
duplicity **10**. hanky–panky
11. amenability, legerdemain
trickle... **4**. drip, drop, flow, leak

7. distill (distil), dribble, dripple, leakage

tricks... 4. shab 5. ruses 7. roguery 10. deceptions

trickster... 3. fox 5. cheat, rogue 6. rascal 7. slicker 8. deceiver 12. Artful Dodger

tricky... 3. sly 5. snide 6. artful, clever, crafty, shrewd 7. cunning, devious 8. rascally 9. deceitful 13. Machiavellian

trident... 5. curve, spear 6. symbol 7. leister

tried... 4. true 6. proved, tested 7. devoted 8. faithful, reliable 11. trustworthy

tries... 5. tests 6. assays 8. attempts, contests

trifle... 3. ace, bit, fig, toy 4. doit, fico, fool, jest 5. dally, fable, straw 6. bauble, dabble, dawdle, doodle, fiddle, gewgaw, palter, pewter, potter, wanton 7. dessert, nothing, traneen 8. flimflam, gimcrack, make love 9. bagatelle 10. knickknack, peccadillo, triviality 11. small amount 12. treat lightly

trifler... 7. dallier, flaneur 8. palterer, putterer 10. dilettante

trifles... 4. toys 6. trivia 7. gewgaws, palters 8. minutiae, trumpery

trifling... 4. idle, mere 5. inane, petty 6. little 7. trivial 8. badinage, frippery 9. nugacious 10. immaterial 13. insignificant

trifolium... 6. clover 8. shamrock

trig... 4. chic, neat, prim, tidy, trim 5. natty, smart 6. lively, spruce 7. precise 10. methodical

trigo... 5. wheat

trigon... 4. game, harp, lyre (anc) 8. triangle

trigonometry term... 4. sine 6. cosine, secant 7. tangent 8. spherics 10. goniometry

trihoral... 11. three–hourly 15. every three hours

trill... 4. move, sing 5. shake, twirl 6. quaver, ripple, warble 7. mordent, tremolo, trickle, vibrate 8. grupetto 12. pralltriller

trillion... 5. trega (comb form) 14. million million

trim... 3. bob, cut, lop 4. chic, clip, crop, neat, perk, snod, tidy, whip 5. adorn, natty, nifty, panel, preen, prune, shear, shrag 6. border, dapper, defeat, punish, reduce 7. compact, orderly 8. decorate, ornament 9. embellish, shipshape 10. decoration

trimming... 4. gimp, lace 5. braid, jabot, ruche 6. edging, frieze, fringe, piping 7. falbala, ruching 8. furbelow, ornament 9. chicanery, garniture 10. decoration 11. accessories 13. passementerie

trinity... 5. three, triad 6. triune

Trinity (Eccl)... 7. Godhead (Father, Son, Holy Ghost) 8. Trimurti

trinket... 3. toy 4. gaud, tali (tahli) 5. bijou, jewel 6. bangle, gewgaw,

trifle 7. bibelot 8. ornament 10. knickknack

trip... 3. err, run 4. halt, skip, slip, trap 5. caper, dance, jaunt, speed 6. bungle, cruise, errand, flight, frolic, voyage 7. journey, misstep, stumble 8. obstruct 9. excursion 10. expedition

triple... 3. tri 5. trine 6. tercet, treble 9. intensify, threefold 12. three–base hit

triple crown... 5. tiara (Pope's)

triplet (one of)... 4. trin

tripletail... 4. fish, sama 9. berrugate, spadefish

tripod... 3. cat (6–legged) 5. easel, stand, three 6. trivet

Tripoli, Libya...
capital of.. 12. Tripolitania
caravan route to.. 5. Wadai 8. Lake Chad, Timbuktu
famed arch to.. 14. Marcus Aurelius
people.. 4. Arab, Turk 5. Negro 6. Berber
ruler.. 3. bey, dey

triptych... 5. volet (part) 10. altarpiece, writing pad 13. writing tablet (3–part)

trismus... 7. lockjaw, tetanus 16. gnashing the teeth

trist... see *tryst*

Tristan and Isolde... 5. opera (Wagner)

triste... 3. sad 4. full 6. dismal 10. depressing

tristful... 3. sad 10. melancholy

tristich group... 10. three lines 11. three verses (stanza)

Tristram & Iseult... 4. poem (Arnold)

trite... 5. banal, corny, petty, stale, vapid 6. betide, cliché, common, jejune 7. bromide 9. hackneyed, well–known 10. threadbare, unoriginal 11. commonplace, stereotyped 13. platitudinous

triton... 3. eft 4. newt 5. shell, snail 10. salamander

Triton (pert to)...
art figure.. 7. demigod
Gr Myth.. 10. sea demigod
symbol.. 7. trumpet

triumph... 3. win 5. exult, glory 6. defeat 8. ceremony (anc), conquest 10. exultation 11. achievement

trivia... 5. trash 7. trifles 8. trumpery

trivial... 5. banal, petty, small, trite 6. common, paltry, slight 7. nominal, piperly, shallow 8. doggerel, ordinary, trifling 9. frivolous, nugacious 11. commonplace, unimportant 13. insignificant

triviality... 3. toy 6. bauble, gewgaw, trifle 8. falderal, nugacity 9. bagatelle, frivolity 10. knickknack 14. insignificance

troche... 4. pill 6. button, rotula, tablet 7. lozenge 8. pastille (pastil) 9. cough drop 10. deer's tines

trochee... 4. foot (2–syllable) 5. meter 7. choreus

trod... see *tread*

trogger ... 7. peddler, vagrant
trogon ... 7. quetzal
Troilus (pert to) ...
  butterfly genus .. 7. Papilio
  legendary hero of .. 7. Chaucer
  son of .. 5. Priam
Trojan (pert to) ...
  astronomy .. 9. asteroids
  epic .. 5. Iliad 6. Aeneid 7. Odyssey
  expedition hero .. 4. Ajax 8. Achilles
  founder of .. 4. Troy
  hero .. 5. Paris 6. Hector
    9. Palamedes
  horse .. 6. wooden
  horse builder .. 5. Epeus
  king .. 5. Priam
  native .. 6. Dardan
  soothsayer .. 7. Helenus
  war cause .. 5. Helen (of Troy)
  war leader .. 9. Agamemnon
  warrior .. 6. Agenor
troll (Myth) ... 5. dwarf, giant, gnome
troll ... 4. bowl, fish, roll, sing 5. angle
  (fishing), rondo 6. allure, entice,
  propel 7. revolve, trundle 9. circulate
trolley ... 4. cart, tram 5. truck
  6. barrow, sledge 7. tramcar
  8. handcart 9. streetcar
trolley, off his ... 4. nuts 5. balmy,
  batty, daffy, dippy, dotty, goofy
  6. cuckoo
trollop ... 5. slump 6. slouch
  8. slattern
trombone (pert to) ...
  ancient .. 7. sackbut, sambuke
  instrument .. 5. brass
  mouthpiece .. 5. bocal
  popular size .. 5. tenor
troop ... 4. army, band, unit 5. crowd
  7. company, march on, ressala
  8. quantity, soldiers 9. go forward
  10. armed force
troop (pert to) ...
  arrangement .. 7. echelon
  encampment .. 5. étape
  formation .. 4. line
  one of .. 7. peltast 8. chasseur
  ship .. 9. transport
troops (pert to) ...
  assemble .. 6. muster
  German .. 6. Panzer
  hidden .. 6. ambush
  Hungary .. 7. Hussars
  mounted .. 7. cavalry
  sally .. 6. sortie
  term for .. 4. army 5. squad 6. forces
    7. battery, militia, phalanx
    9. commandos 11. armed forces
trophy ... 3. cup 4. palm 5. award,
  medal, Oscar, prize 6. reward
  7. laurels, memento 8. memorial
tropical (pert to) ...
  animal .. 4. eyra 5. araba, coati, potto
    6. agouti 7. peccary
  bird .. 3. ani 4. tody 5. jalap
    6. motmot 7. jacamar
  dolphin .. 4. inia
  fish .. 4. toro 6. remora, salema
  fruit .. 3. fig 4. date 5. guava,
    mango, papaw 6. banana, papaya
  lizard .. 5. agama
  rodent .. 6. agouti

tree .. 4. coco, palm 5. balsa, seron
  6. sapota 8. tamarind
vine .. 7. cowhage, lantana
  14. trumpet creeper
trot ... 3. jog, run 4. gait, pony
  5. hurry 7. routine 11. translation
trotting horse ... 6. Morgan
  7. Hackney 12. Hambletonian
trottoir (rare) ... 8. footpath, pavement,
  sidewalk
troubadour ... 4. bard, poet
  8. jongleur, minstrel, musician
  9. trovatore
trouble ... 3. ado, ail, irk 4. fuss,
  harm, stir 5. annoy, grief, worry
  6. bother, effort, grieve, harass,
  pester, plague, sorrow 7. agitate,
  anxiety, concern, disturb, perturb,
  torment 8. calamity, disorder,
  disquiet, distress, mischief
  9. adversity, annoyance, commotion
  10. affliction, difficulty, misfortune
  11. disturbance 13. inconvenience,
  interfere with
troubled ... 6. queasy 7. annoyed,
  anxious 8. agitated 9. disturbed
  10. distressed
troublemaker ... 8. agitator, gossiper
  13. mischief–maker
troublesome ... 5. pesky 8. annoying,
  perverse 9. difficult, laborious,
  turbulent, vexatious, wearisome
  10. bothersome, burdensome,
  disturbing, oppressing 11. distressing
  12. inconvenient
trough ... 3. bin 4. bosh, bowl, dale,
  tank 5. basin, chute, drain, toper
  6. coffin, gutter, manger, sluice,
  trench 7. channel, conduit
trounce ... 4. beat, flog 5. scald
  6. indict, punish, thrash 7. censure,
  journey
trout ... 4. char, peal 7. oquassa
  9. namaycush 11. Dolly Varden
trout (pert to) ...
  genus .. 5. Salmo 6. Trutta
  lake .. 9. namaycush
  Maine .. 7. oquassa
  parasite (external) .. 3. sug
  ref to .. 11. truttaceous
  type .. 3. sea 4. rock 5. brook,
    brown, river 7. oquassa, rainbow
    8. speckled 9. cutthroat
trovatore ... 10. troubadour
trove ... 4. find 8. treasure (buried)
  9. discovery 10. thing found
  13. treasure–trove
trow ... 4. boat, hope 5. barge, think,
  trust 6. expect 7. believe, suppose
  9. catamaran
trowing ... 5. creed 6. belief 7. opinion
Troy, or Ilium ...
  capital of .. 5. Troad (anc)
  defender .. 6. Aeneas
  famed for .. 5. ruins
  founder (Myth) .. 4. Ilus (son of Tros),
    Tros
  king .. 5. Priam 9. Agamemnon
  king's wife .. 5. Helen
  mountain .. 3. Ida
  name, present .. 9. Hissarlik
  pert to .. 5. Iliac 6. Trojan

site.. 9. Asia Minor
troy weight... 5. grain, ounce, pound
  11. pennyweight
truant... 4. idle 7. shirker, trivant,
  vagrant 8. absentee
truant, to play... 5. miche
truce... 5. pause, peace, trêve
  9. armistice, cessation 10. brief
  quiet 12. intermission
truck... 3. van 4. deal, dray, haul
  5. bogie, dance, lorry, trade
  6. barter, peddle 7. flatcar, traffic
  8. commerce, exchange, nonsense
  9. groceries
truckle... 4. fawn 5. toady 6. cringe,
  submit 7. knuckle
truculent... 4. base, mean 5. cruel
  6. fierce, savage 8. ruthless,
  scathing 9. barbarous, ferocious
  11. destructive
trudge... 4. pace, plod, slog, walk
  5. tramp 6. go slow 7. traipse
true... 2. so 4. fact, leal, pure, real
  6. gospel, honest, lawful 7. certain,
  devoted, germane, precise, sincere,
  upright 8. faithful, orthodox, reliable,
  straight, unerring 9. authentic,
  steadfast, veracious, veritable
  10. legitimate 11. trustworthy,
  unfaltering
true (pert to)...
blue.. 5. loyal 8. faithful, orthodox
  10. man of honor
copy.. 7. estreat
not.. 5. false 10. figurative
poetic.. 4. leal
skin.. 4. derm (suff) 5. derma
to fact.. 7. literal
to life.. 8. lifelike 11. descriptive
truffle... 5. fungi, tuber 8. earthnut
  10. ascus fruit
truism... 5. axiom, truth 9. platitude
  11. commonplace
trull... 4. girl, lass 5. demon, fiend,
  giant, wench 7. trollop 8. strumpet
truly... 3. yea 4. amen 5. sooth
  6. indeed, justly, verily 7. exactly,
  rightly 8. properly 9. certainly
  10. accurately, positively, truthfully
trump... 3. pam 4. card, ruff (cards),
  suit 7. surpass 10. good fellow
  12. masterstroke
trumpery... 5. fraud, trash 6. deceit
  7. rubbish 8. nonsense
trumpet... 4. horn 5. blare
  6. summon 7. clarion 8. proclaim
  9. organ stop 10. elephant's cry
  14. wind instrument
trumpet (pert to)...
blare.. 7. fanfare, tantara
call (stage).. 6. sennet
creeper.. 6. tecoma
fish.. 7. bellows 10. flutemouth
lily.. 5. calla 7. Bermuda
trumpeter... 4. bird, fish, swan
  5. agami, perch 6. pigeon 7. whiting
  8. musician 9. messenger
truncheon... 4. club 5. baton, staff
  6. cudgel 8. splinter
trunk... 3. box, log 4. body, bole,
  pool, soma, tank 5. chest, stalk,
  torso 6. coffer 7. railway 8. main

stem 9. proboscis 10. lobster pot
trunkfish... 4. toro 7. cowfish
truss... 3. tie 4. bind, gird, pack
  6. bundle, fasten 7. support
  10. strengthen
trust... 4. hope, rely, task 5. faith
  6. belief, commit, credit, dartle,
  depend, estate 7. believe, confide,
  consign, custody, entrust, loyalty
  8. credence, reliance, security
  9. assurance, syndicate
  10. confidence, dependence, give
  credit, investment 12. organization
trustee... 6. bailee 7. sindico
  9. fiduciary, treasurer 10. depository
  13. administrator
trustful... 5. liege 7. reliant 8. trusting
  9. confiding, credulous
  13. unquestioning
trustworthiness... 9. axiopisty
  12. trustability 13. dependability
trustworthy... 4. safe 5. solid
  6. honest 7. certain 8. reliable
  9. authentic 10. dependable
trusty... 7. convict 8. faithful, prisoner
  10. dependable 11. trustworthy
truth... 3. tao 4. fact, real 5. sooth
  (anc) 6. verity 7. honesty, reality
  8. fidelity, veracity 9. constancy,
  exactness, orthodoxy, sincerity
  11. correctness 14. verisimilitude
truth (pert to)...
ancient term.. 5. sooth 6. certes
Chinese Philos.. 3. tao
goddess.. 4. Maat
personified.. 3. Una 4. Maat
ref to.. 6. verily 11. verisimilar
  14. verisimilitude
self-evident.. 5. axiom 6. truism
truthful... 6. honest 7. veridic
  9. veracious, veridical
truthfulness... 5. truth 7. honesty
  8. accuracy, veracity
  13. veraciousness
try... 2. do 3. say 4. test 5. annoy,
  assay, ettle, prove, taste, trial
  6. purify, refine, render, sample,
  strive 7. attempt, contest, torment
  8. audition, endeavor, irritate
  9. prosecute, undertake
  10. experiment 11. demonstrate,
  investigate
trying... 7. irksome, painful, tasting
  8. annoying, sampling 10. attempting
  12. exasperating 13. experimenting
tryst... 6. invite, market 7. beguile,
  meeting 9. agreement, betrothal
  10. engagement, rendezvous
  11. appointment 12. meeting place
tsamba... 5. flour 6. barley
tsar... 4. czar, tzar 6. despot
  8. autocrat
tsetse, tsetse fly... 4. kivu
  8. Glossina, parasite
tsetse fly disease... 6. nagana
  16. sleeping sickness
T-shaped... 3. tau
tsine... 6. wild ox 7. banteng
tuatara, tuatera... 7. reptile
  (iguanalike)
tub... 3. hod, keg, kid, soe, tun, vat
  4. cask, ship, wash 5. barge, bathe,

bowie, keeve 6. barrel, firkin, piggin,
vessel 7. bathtub, cistern, washtub
9. container, fat person
tuba... 6. liquor (palm) 7. helicon,
trumpet (anc) 9. bombardon
10. contrabass 11. bass saxhorn
12. mythical tree
Tubal–cain's father... 6. Lamech
Tubal's father... 7. Japheth
tube... 3. cop 4. bulb, duct, hose,
pipe 5. auget, chute, diode
6. siphon, tunnel 7. burette, cannula,
conduit, fistula, matrass, railway,
salpinx 8. cylinder, electron, stenosis
9. spaghetti, telescope
tuber... 3. oca, yam 4. beet, bulb,
eddo, root, taro 5. jalap, salep
6. potato 12. protuberance
tubular... 4. pipy 5. round 6. tubate
8. cannular, fistular, tubiform
11. cylindrical
tuck... 3. eat, nip 4. cram, fold, poke
5. feast, pinch, pleat, press
7. shorten, tighten 9. appendage
tucker... 3. bib 4. food, meal
5. board 6. ration
Tuesday (pert to)...
French.. 5. Mardi
Norse god.. 3. Tyr (Tiu)
Shrove.. 9. Mardi gras
Teutonic.. 10. Martis dies
tufa... 4. rock, toph, tuff 5. trass
tuft... 4. coma, doss, hair 5. beard,
bunch, clump, crest 6. button,
goatee, pompon, tassel 7. cluster,
fetlock 8. aigrette, feathers
tug... 3. tow 4. drag, draw, haul, pull,
toil 5. labor 6. drudge, effort, strain,
tussle 7. contend, contest, wrestle
8. struggle
tulip (pert to)...
center (World).. 7. Holland
color.. 6. auburn 9. tulipwood
genus.. 6. Tulipa
Mexican.. 6. orchid
military slang.. 9. explosive
tree.. 6. timber 7. majagua, waratah
type.. 6. Darwin, parrot 7. breeder,
cottage
tumble... 4. fall, flop, trip, veer
5. pitch, spill 6. jumble, rumple,
topple, tousle, wallow 7. stumble
8. collapse, disorder, flounder, roll
over 9. break down, confusing
10. handspring, somersault
11. precipitate
tumbler... 3. dog 4. cart, drum
5. glass 6. Dunker, pigeon, vessel
7. acrobat, gymnast, tippler, tumbrel
8. lock part 13. contortionist
tumbleweed... 6. indigo 7. bugseed,
pigweed, thistle 10. amaranthus
tumbrel, tumbril... 4. cart 5. wagon
8. dumpcart 12. cucking stool (Hist)
tumescent, tumid... 6. turgid
7. bloated, bulging, pompous
8. inflated 9. bombastic, disturbed,
plethoric 11. protuberant
tumor... 3. wen 4. cyst, wart
6. cancer, goiter, growth, lipoma,
struma 7. adenoma, sarcoma
8. ganglion, swelling 11. excrescence

12. protuberance
tumor, eyelid... 9. pladaroma
tumult... 3. din, mob 4. fray, riot
5. Babel, brawl, noise 6. affray,
babble, bustle, émeute, hubbub,
uproar 7. bluster, ferment, turmoil
8. disorder, outbreak, uprising
9. agitation, commotion, confusion
10. excitement, turbulence
11. disturbance
tumultuous... 4. wild 5. noisy, rough
7. lawless, riotous, violent
8. agitated, confused 9. disturbed,
turbulent 10. boisterous, disorderly,
hurly–burly
tumulus... 5. mound, stump 6. barrow
7. hillock
tun... 3. cup (anc), jar, tub, vat
4. cask, year (Mayan, 360–day)
5. drink 6. guzzle, vessel 7. measure
tuna... 5. tunny 8. albacore
tune... 3. air, key 4. aria, lilt, port,
song 5. pitch 6. adjust, melody
7. chorale, harmony, sonance
9. harmonize 10. adjustment,
intonation
tune (pert to)...
correctly.. 3. key
down.. 6. reduce, soften 8. moderate
musical instrument.. 6. string
out of.. 9. dissonant 11. inaccordant
12. unconforming
tungsten... 7. wolfram
Tunisia...
cape.. 3. Bon
capital.. 5. Tunis
famed ruins.. 8. Carthage
gulf.. 5. Gabes
oasis.. 5. Gafsa
people.. 5. Arabs 7. Berbers
resort island.. 6. Djerba
river.. 7. Medjerda
ruler.. 3. dey 5. pasha
seaport.. 4. Sfax 7. Bizorte
tunnel... 4. adit, bore, cave, tube
5. drift 6. burrow, dig out, funnel,
subway 10. excavation, smokestack
tunny... 4. tuna 8. albacore
tup... 3. ram 4. beat, butt 5. sheep
6. mallet 7. cuckold
turban... 6. entrée, fillet, Moslem,
mundil, squash 8. bandanna,
seerband 9. headdress
turbid... 4. dark, dull 5. dense,
muddy, roily 6. cloudy, impure,
opaque 7. clouded, muddled
8. confused, feculent, polluted
turbot... 5. brill 8. flatfish
turbulence... 4. fury 6. tumult, uproar
7. bluster, rioting, turmoil
9. agitation, commotion
10. excitement, unruliness
11. disturbance, impetuosity
14. tumultuousness
turbulent... 4. loud, wild 5. noisy,
rough 6. stormy 7. excited, furious
8. virulent 10. tumultuous
turf... 3. sod 4. peat, slab 5. divot,
glebe, grass, sward, track 10. race
course
turgid... 5. tumid 7. bloated,
pompous, swollen 8. inflated

9. bombastic, distended, grandiose,
redundant 12. magniloquent,
ostentatious 13. grandiloquent
Turk... 5. Tatar 6. Tartar 7. Osmanli,
Ottoman 9. Kizilbash
Turkestan people... 5. Uzbek (Uzbeg)
turkey... 4. fowl 5. poult 7. bustard,
gobbler, vulture
Turkey... see also *Turkish*
capital.. 6. Angora (anc), Ankara
city.. 5. Adana, Izmir (Smyrna)
6. Edessa, Samsun 7. Scutari
8. Istanbul (Constantinople)
10. Adrianople
founder.. 6. Othman
mountain.. 6. Ararat
peninsula.. 9. Anatolian
river.. 5. Mesta 6. Seyhan
Turkish (pert to)...
army corps.. 4. ordu 8. seraglio
commander, ruler.. 3. aga (agha), bey
4. wali 5. pasha 6. atabeg (atabek)
court (Ottoman).. 5. Porte
12. Sublime Porte
dignitary.. 5. pasha
dish (food).. 5. cabob 6. pilaff (pilau)
drink.. 4. boza (bozah), raki 5. airan
6. mastic 9. lion's milk
dynasty.. 6. seljuk
emblem.. 8. crescent
Empire.. 7. Ottoman
flag.. 4. alem, toug (former)
harem girl.. 6. kadein (kadine)
hat, cap.. 3. fez 6. calpac (calpack)
hospice, inn.. 6. imaret
infidel.. 6. giaour
javelin.. 6. jereed (jerid)
judge.. 4. cadi (kadi)
minister of state.. 6. vizier
money of account.. 5. asper
mosque.. 4. jami
music.. 8. janizary
native.. 6. Edesan (anc)
palace.. 5. serai
pavilion.. 5. kiosk
pipe (long–stemmed).. 7. chibouk
(chibouque)
regiment.. 4. alai
religious war.. 5. jihad (jehad)
rug.. 5. Melas, Tekke, Yomud, Yuruk
6. Afghan 8. Turkoman 9. Kurdistan
ruler.. 3. bey, dey 4. khan 6. sultan
7. chambul
sailing vessel.. 4. saic 6. mahone
sailor.. 9. galiongee (galionji)
soldier.. 5. nizan, redif 6. Arnaut
(Arnaout) 8. Janizary
11. bashi–bazouk
statute.. 8. Tanzimat (1839)
sultan.. 5. Ahmed, Selim 7. Ilderim,
Saladin
sultan's title.. 6. caliph (calif)
sword.. 8. yataghan (yatagan)
tambourine.. 5. daira
tax (from Christians).. 6. avania
title.. 3. aga (agha), ali 4. amir
(ameer)
tobacco.. 7. chibouk (chibouque),
Latakia
tribe.. 5. Ersar, Tatar 7. Bashkir,
Viddhal
Turkoman.. 11. tribal group

veil (double).. 7. yashmak (yashmac)
vest.. 6. jelick
whip, lash.. 7. kurbash
turmeric... 3. rea 4. ango, herb
5. olena 8. curcumin
turmoil... 3. ado, din 5. upset, worry
6. tumult, unrest 7. ferment,
tempest, trouble 8. disquiet
9. agitation, commotion, confusion
10. excitement, turbulence
12. perturbation
turn... 3. bow, lap 4. bend, deed,
gyre, roll, slew, slue, spin, tour,
veer, vert 5. curve, lathe, pivot,
quirk, round, shift, spell, wheel,
whirl, whorl 6. abvert, change, crisis,
gyrate, rotate, swivel, zigzag
7. deflect, deviate, reverse, revolve
8. aptitude, circuity, maneuver,
persuade, rotation, tendency
9. deviation, pirouette, reversion
11. convolution 12. metamorphose
turn (pert to)...
about.. 9. alternate
aside, away.. 4. slew, slue 5. avert,
deter, repel, shunt 6. divert, swerve
7. deflect, deviate, digress, diverge
back.. 5. repel 6. coward, revert
7. evolute, head off, reflect
coat.. 7. traitor 8. apostate, deserter,
renegade
comb form.. 5. tropo
down.. 4. veto 6. refuse, reject
7. decline
gate.. 5. stile 9. turnstile
inside out.. 5. evert 6. invert
7. ransack
inward.. 8. introrse 9. introvert
left.. 3. haw 4. port
of duty.. 5. spell, trick
off.. 5. shunt 7. dismiss, execute
10. extinguish
on axis.. 6. obvert, rotate
one's back upon.. 4. flee, snub
5. avoid 6. ignore, oppose, refuse,
reject
on pivot.. 6. swivel
out.. 4. fare, oust 5. array, evert,
expel, track 6. detour, output, siding
7. dismiss 8. assemble, clearing
9. eventuate, gathering
10. accomplish, extinguish
outward.. 5. evert, splay 8. extrorse
9. extrovert
over.. 3. pie 4. keel, tart 5. sales,
shift, spill 6. assign, pastry
7. capsize 8. hand over, overturn
over a new leaf.. 6. change, reform
over pages.. 4. leaf 5. thumb
over to others.. 4. farm 7. farm out
to left.. 3. haw 4. port
to right.. 3. gee 9. starboard
up.. 4. find, keel 5. occur 6. appear,
arrive 7. be found
upside down.. 4. roll 6. invert, whelve
7. ransack 8. overturn
turned up (nose)... 9. retroussé
turning... 6. rotary 7. bending,
crooked, winding 8. rotation,
twisting, whirling 9. deviating,
deviation 10. circuitous, revolution
11. convolution, sinistrorse

turning (pert to)...
left to right.. **9**. dextrorse
machine.. **5**. lathe
point.. **6**. crisis **8**. decision, landmark
  11. climacteric **13**. crucial period
right to left.. **11**. sinistrorse
turnip... **4**. neep, rape, root
  8. rutabaga
turnip (pert to)...
large.. **7**. Russian, Swedish
  8. rutabaga
shaped.. **8**. napiform
wild.. **5**. navew
Turnix... **4**. bird (3-toed) **5**. quail
  10. Hemipodius
Turpentine State... **13**. North Carolina
turpentine tree... **4**. pine **6**. tarata
  9. terebinth
turpid... **3**. low **4**. base, vile
  8. cowardly
turpitude... **6**. fedity **8**. baseness,
  vileness **9**. decadence, depravity
  10. corruption
turquoise... **3**. gem **4**. blue
  7. mineral, Turkish
turret... **4**. loom, soar **5**. tower
  6. cupola (revolving), height
  9. structure **10**. stronghold,
  watchtower
turtle (pert to)...
edible.. **8**. terrapin
freshwater.. **4**. emyd **8**. tortoise
genus.. **4**. Emys
hawklike.. **5**. carat **9**. hawk's-bill
large.. **5**. arrau **6**. jurara, mamata
largest.. **11**. leatherback
ref to.. **9**. chelonian
sea.. **10**. thalassian
shell.. **8**. carapace
snapping.. **6**. cooter **8**. shagtail
Tuscany...
birthplace of.. **7**. Galileo (Astronomer)
capital.. **8**. Florence
city.. **4**. Pisa **7**. Leghorn
color.. **9**. colcothar
famed tower.. **4**. Pisa (1174)
island.. **4**. Elba (1st exile, Napoleon)
native.. **6**. Tuscan
marble.. **7**. Carrara
province.. **4**. Pisa
river.. **4**. Arno **6**. Cecina **7**. Ombrone
wine.. **7**. chianti
tusk... **4**. fang **5**. ivory, tooth
  6. canine **7**. incisor **9**. scrivello
  (elephant's)
Tussaud, Madame's London district...
  8. Waxworks (Museum)
  10. Marylebone
tussis... **5**. cough
tussle... **7**. contend, contest, scuffle,
  wrestle **8**. struggle
tutelage... **7**. nurture **8**. teaching,
  tutorage **9**. oversight, tutorship
  11. instruction **12**. guardianship
tutelary gods (Rom)... **5**. lares
  7. penates
tutor... **5**. coach, teach **6**. docent,
  ground, mentor, school **7**. teacher
  8. instruct **9**. pedagogue (pedagog),
  preceptor
twaddle... **3**. rot **6**. drivel, gabble
  7. chatter, fustian, prattle

  8. claptrap, nonsense **9**. absurdity,
  silly talk **10**. flapdoodle **16**. trash
  and nonsense
twang... **4**. tang **5**. strum **6**. accent
  7. dialect **8**. pungency
tweak... **4**. jerk, pain **5**. pinch
  6. snatch, twitch
tweeg... **10**. hellbender, salamander
tweezers... **7**. pincers **10**. instrument
twelfth... **5**. twait, uncia **8**. duodenal
  9. duodenary
Twelfth Night character... **5**. Viola
  6. Olivia, Orsino **7**. Sir Toby
  8. Malvolio **12**. Sir Toby Belch
Twelfthtide... **8**. Epiphany
  10. Twelfth-day
twelve (pert to)...
amount.. **5**. dozen
angles.. **9**. dodecagon
prefix.. **5**. dodec **6**. dodeca
rule of.. **9**. dodecarch
series.. **8**. dodecade
Twelve, The... **8**. Apostles
twenty (pert to)...
Anglo–Ind.. **5**. carge, score
comb form.. **4**. icos **5**. icosa, icosi
faces.. **11**. icosahedron
pert to.. **7**. icosian **8**. vicenary
quires.. **4**. ream
symbol.. **2**. XX
years.. **9**. vicennial
twenty-fourth part (gold alloy)...
  5. carat (karat)
twibil (twibill)... **2**. ax (axe) **6**. pickax
  (pickaxe) **7**. mattock **8**. battle-ax
  (battle-axe)
twice... **2**. bi, di **6**. doubly **7**. twofold
  8. two times
twig... **4**. reis **5**. besom, birch, bough
  6. branch, sallow, switch, twitch,
  wattle
twigs, bundle of... **5**. fagot **6**. barsom
  (sacred)
twilight... **3**. dim **4**. blue, dusk
  6. shaded **7**. obscure **8**. foredawn,
  gloaming **9**. cocklight **10**. crepuscule
Twilight of the Gods... **8**. Ragnarok
twill... **3**. rib **5**. flute, weave **6**. fabric
  9. tricotine
twilled... **3**. rep **5**. reedy, ridgy, sedgy,
  serge **6**. corded, fluted
twin... **3**. two **4**. dual, mate, pair
  5. gemel, macle **6**. couple, double
  7. didymus, Siamese **8**. didymous,
  matching **9**. duplicate, identical
  11. counterpart **12**. accompanying
Twin Cities (Minn)... **6**. St Paul
  11. Minneapolis
twine... **4**. bend, coil, turn, wind, wrap
  5. braid, snarl, twist, weave
  6. enfold, enlace, tangle **7**. embrace,
  enclasp, entwine, wreathe
  8. convolve, encircle **9**. interlace
  10. intertwine, interweave
  11. intermingle
twine (pert to)...
color.. **4**. dune **7**. anamite
hank of.. **3**. ran
left to right.. **9**. dextrorse
right to left.. **11**. sinistrorse
Scot.. **4**. part
twinge... **4**. ache, pain, pang

5. pinch, qualm 6. twitch
twin stars... 6. Castor, Pollux
twin stock... 4. bees 7. beehive (two
colonies)
twirl... 4. coil, eddy, gyre, spin
5. pitch, querl, twist, whirl 6. gyrate,
writhe 7. revolve 8. flourish, rotation
11. convolution
twist... 3. cue, ply 4. coil, curl, slew,
slub, slue, spin, turn, warp, wind
5. braid, quirk, tweak, wrest
7. contort, deflect, distort, falsify,
meander, pervert, wreathe, wriggle
8. convolve 9. insinuate, interlace,
prejudice 10. distortion
12. eccentricity, misrepresent
twisted... 3. wry 4. awry, cued
5. askew, kinky, torse, wrung
6. warped 7. complex, torqued,
tortile, wrested, writhed
twisted cord... 7. torsade
twister... 3. lie 7. cruller, tornado
8. doughnut 9. dust whirl 10. sand
column, somersault, waterspout
twit... 4. gibe, josh 5. blame, taunt,
tease, tweet 6. banter 7. upbraid
8. reproach, ridicule
twitch... 3. nip, tic, tug 4. hurt, jerk,
yank 5. pluck, shake, tweak
6. snatch 9. be excited, quick pull,
vellicate 11. contraction
twitter... 5. chirp 6. giggle, titter
7. chatter, tremble 9. agitation
two (pert to)...
chambered.. 9. bicameral
colored.. 9. dichromic
edged.. 9. ancipital
faced.. 5. false 6. double 9. deceitful
11. treacherous 12. falsehearted
fisted.. 6. virile
fold.. 4. dual, twin 6. binary, double,
duplex 8. didymous
forked.. 6. bident 9. bifurcate
11. dichotomous
handed.. 7. bimanal 8. bimanous
10. secondhand 12. ambidextrous
headed.. 9. ancipital 11. dicephalous
masted ship.. 4. yawl, zulu
parts.. 3. duo 4. duad, dyad
7. duality
poetic.. 5. twain
prefix.. 2. bi, di
Scot.. 3. twa
Spanish.. 3. dos
spot.. 5. deuce
time.. 7. deceive
wheeled carriage, chariot.. 3. gig
6. esseda 10. jinrikisha (jinriksha)
Tyche... 7. Fortuna 16. goddess of
Fortune
tycoon... 6. shogun 7. magnate
9. financier 13. industrialist
tylopod... 5. camel
tympanum... 7. eardrum 9. middle ear
10. water wheel
tympany... 6. tympan 7. bombast
9. inflation 10. distention
typal... 7. typical 8. symbolic
type... 2. pi 4. font, form, kind, norm,
sign, sort 5. genre, genus, model,
print, Roman, token 6. emblem,
italic, minion, symbol 7. measure,

pattern, species 8. boldface, classify,
standard 9. archetype, character
10. transcribe 11. Baskerville
14. characteristic, representative
type (pert to)...
assortment.. 4. font, kern
block of.. 4. quad 7. quadrat
bold style.. 4. text
bridge.. 7. bascule
classic.. 5. Roman 6. italic 11. black
letter (Gothic)
line.. 4. slug
measure.. 2. em, en
mixed.. 2. pi
mold.. 6. matrix
perfection.. 7. paragon
set.. 7. compose
setter.. 8. linotype, monotype
10. compositor
size.. 4. norm, pica, ruby 5. agate,
canon, pearl 6. minion 7. diamond
stroke.. 5. serif
tray.. 6. galley
typewriter (pert to)...
bar.. 6. spacer
cylinder.. 6. platen, spacer
type.. 4. pica 5. elite
type of.. 6. ticker 8. teletype
9. stenotype
typhoon... 4. wind 5. storm
7. cyclone
typhus fever... 10. tabardillo
typical... 4. norm 5. typal 6. normal
7. regular 10. conforming,
emblematic, figurative 11. precedental
14. characteristic, representative
typify... 6. embody 9. prefigure,
represent, symbolize
Tyr (Norse)... 3. Tiu 6. sky–god,
war–god
tyrannical... 5. cruel 6. lordly
8. despotic 9. imperious
10. oppressive 11. domineering
tyrannize... 7. oppress 8. domineer
tyranny... 8. severity 9. despotism
tyrant... 4. czar, Ivan, Nero, tsar, tzar
6. despot 7. monarch
Tyre... see also *Tyrian*
capital of.. 9. Phoenicia (anc)
famed for.. 9. purple dye
seaport of.. 7. Lebanon
site.. 9. peninsula 13. Mediterranean
Tyrian (pert to)...
alphabet.. 7. Moabite
Cynosure.. 9. Ursa Minor
god (Teut).. 2. Er
king.. 5. Hiram
princess.. 4. Dido (Elissa)
tyro, tiro... 5. pupil 6. novice
7. amateur 8. beginner, neophyte
9. commencer, fledgling, greenhorn
10. apprentice 11. abecedarian
Tyrol...
capital.. 9. Innsbruck
dialect.. 5. Ladin
district.. 8. Trentino
mountain.. 4. Alps 9. Dolomites
province of.. 7. Austria
river.. 4. Isar
tzar, tsar, czar... 4. king 5. ruler
6. tyrant
tzigane... 5. gypsy

U

U... 6. letter (21st)
uang... 6. beetle
uberous... 7. copious 8. abundant, fruitful 9. plentiful
uberty... 6. plenty 12. fruitfulness
ubiety... 8. location, position, relation 9. whereness
ubiquity... 8. doctrine (Luther) 10. everywhere 12. omnipresence
U–boat... 3. sub 9. submarine
  base.. 4. Kiel
Uca... 11. fiddler crab
Uchean Indian... 5. Yuchi (Uchee)
udometer... 9. rain gauge
Uffizi Gallery... 8. Florence
Uganda (pert to)...
  capital.. 7. Kampala
  Falls.. 4. Owen 9. Murchison
  lake.. 8. Victoria
  lake explorer.. 7. Stanley
  mountain.. 9. Ruwenzori
    18. Mountains of the Moon
  tribe.. 5. pygmy
ugly... 5. cross, surly 6. cranky, homely 7. crabbed, hideous, vicious 8. gruesome, uncomely, unlovely 9. frightful, loathsome, offensive, repulsive, unsightly 10. ill–favored, ill–natured, unpleasant 11. ill–tempered, quarrelsome 12. disagreeable
uhlan... 6. lancer 7. militia, soldier 10. cavalryman
uhllo... 6. wampum 8. currency (shell)
uitlander... 9. foreigner, outlander
ukase... 5. edict, order 12. proclamation
Ukraine (pert to)...
  capital.. 4. Kiev 7. Kharkov
  legislature.. 4. rada
  official name.. 12. Ukrainian SSR
  Relig.. 9. Ruthenian 13. Little Russian
  scientist.. 10. Bogomolets
  sea.. 5. Black
  seaport.. 6. Odessa
  statesman.. 7. Mazeppa
  writer.. 6. Franko
ullage... 5. dregs 7. deficit, wantage 8. shortage 9. shrinkage 10. deficiency
Ulmas... 3. elm
ulna... 4. bone 5. elbow 7. cubitus
ulster... 8. overcoat
ulterior... 6. future 7. further, remoter, thither 10. additional, extraneous, subsequent, succeeding 11. undisclosed
ultima... 4. last 5. final 8. farthest 10. most remote 12. last syllable
ultimate... 3. end 4. dire, last

5. final, telus 6. future, latest, result 7. extreme, maximum 8. eventful, eventual, farthest, terminal 9. elemental 10. conclusive, end product
ultimatum... 5. offer 6. demand 13. ultimate point 14. final objective
ultimo... 3. ult 9. past month (opp of proximo)
ultra... 6. beyond 7. extreme, radical 9. excessive, extremist, fanatical 11. extravagant 14. uncompromising
ultramarine... 11. blue pigment, lapis lazuli 12. beyond the sea
ultramontane... 5. alien 6. beyond 9. foreigner 10. tramontane 13. beyond the Alps, Roman Catholic
ulu (Esk)... 5. knife
ululate... 4. hoot, howl, wail, yelp 6. bellow, lament
Ulysses (pert to)...
  antagonist.. 4. Irus
  dog.. 5. Argos
  enchantress.. 5. Circe
  father.. 7. Laertes
  Greek name.. 8. Odysseus
  hero.. 7. Odyssey (Homer's)
  literally.. 5. hater
  son.. 9. Telegonus
  wife.. 8. Penelope
umber... 3. raw 5. brown, burnt 6. shadow, Turkey 8. grayling, umbrette 10. brown earth
umbilicus (pert to)...
  anatomy.. 5. navel
  botany.. 5. hilum
  geometry.. 5. focus
  paleology.. 5. stick (papyrus)
  zoology.. 3. pit 10. depression
umbra... 4. fish 5. ghost, shade 6. shadow 7. phantom, vestige
umbrage... 5. doubt, pique, shade, trace 6. offend, resent 7. foliage, offense, shelter 8. disfavor 9. semblance, suspicion 10. overshadow, resentment 11. displeasure
umbrella... 4. gamp 5. cover, guard, shade 6. chatta, payong, pileus (of a jellyfish) 7. parasol, shelter 9. parachute, sea anchor 11. bumbershoot
umbrella tree... 5. bendy 7. dogwood, ginseng 8. magnolia
umbrette... 4. bird, fish 5. omber (ombre) 9. hammerkop
umpire... 5. judge 7. arbiter, referee 8. mediator 9. moderator 10. arbitrator, negotiator
Umpqua... 6. Indian 10. Athapascan

607

unable... 6. cannot 8. helpless,
impotent 9. incapable
11. incompetent, inefficient,
unqualified 13. incapacitated
Una boat... 7. catboat
unabridged... 8. complete
11. uncondensed
unaccented... 4. lene 6. atonic
unaccountable... 7. lawless, strange
9. fantastic 10. mysterious
12. inexplicable, unfathomable
13. irresponsible, unpredictable
unacknowledged... 9. anonymous,
forgotten, unthanked 10. unrewarded
unadorned... 4. bald, bare, form
5. grace, naked, stark 7. austere
13. plain–speaking
unadulterated... 4. pure 5. naked
6. honest 7. unmixed 9. unalloyed,
undiluted 11. uncorrupted
unaffected... 4. naif, real 5. naive,
plain 6. simple 7. artless, genuine,
natural, sincere 8. informal
9. unaltered, untouched
12. uninfluenced 13. plain–speaking
Unalaska... 5. Aleut, tribe
9. Eskimauan
unanimous... 5. solid 6. agreed,
mutual, united 8. agreeing 9. of one
mind 10. concordant 11. consentient
12. with one voice
unanimously... 7. una voce 12. with
one voice
unapproachable... 8. reserved
10. unsociable 12. inaccessible
unapt... 4. dull, slow 5. inapt
8. backward 10. unskillful, unsuitable
13. inappropriate
unaroused... 6. latent 7. dormant
8. inactive 9. unstirred
unaspirated... 4. lene 6. smooth
unassuming... 3. shy 6. modest
7. genuine, natural 8. informal,
retiring 9. diffident 11. undeceptive
14. unostentatious
unau... 5. sloth (2–toed)
unavailing... 6. futile 8. gainless
unbalanced... 6. insane, uneven,
unjust 7. unequal 8. deranged,
lopsided, one–sided 9. off center
10. disordered
unbecoming... 4. rude 5. inept
8. unseemly 10. indecorous,
unsuitable 12. unattractive
unbelievable... 9. fantastic, untenable
10. incredible, unreliable
11. implausible, unthinkable
13. inconceivable
unbeliever... 5. pagan 6. Kaffir (Kafir)
7. atheist, doubter, heretic, infidel,
skeptic 8. agnostic
unbend... 4. rest, thaw 5. frese, relax,
yield 6. loosen 7. slacken 8. be
pliant, unfasten 10. condescend,
straighten
unbending... 5. rigid, stern, stiff
8. resolute 10. inexorable, inflexible,
unyielding
unbiased... 4. fair, just 9. impartial
12. free from bias, unprejudiced
unbind... 4. free, undo 5. loose, untie
6. loosen 7. absolve, deliver, release

8. dissolve, unfasten
unbound... 4. free 5. loose
10. unconfined
unbounded... 8. infinite 9. limitless,
unchecked, unlimited 10. unconfined
11. measureless 12. uncontrolled,
unrestrained
unbridled... 4. free 5. loose
7. lawless, violent 10. licentious
12. uncontrolled, unrestrained
unbroken... 4. even 5. undug, whole
6. direct, entire, intact, smooth
7. untamed 8. constant, straight,
unplowed 10. continuous
13. uninterrupted
uncanny... 5. eerie (eery), weird
6. spooky 7. ghostly, strange
8. careless 9. unnatural
10. mysterious
unceasing... 6. eterne 7. endless,
eternal 9. continual, incessant
11. everlasting
unceremonious... 4. curt 5. blunt
6. abrupt, casual 7. offhand
8. informal 14. unconventional
uncertain... 4. hazy 5. vague
6. chancy, fickle, fitful, shifty, unsure
7. dubious 8. doubtful, unsteady,
variable 9. ambiguous, irregular,
undecided 10. changeable, indefinite,
irresolute, precarious 11. unequivocal
12. questionable 13. indeterminate,
problematical, untrustworthy
uncertainty... 5. doubt 6. wonder
7. dubiety 8. suspense 9. dubiosity
10. fickleness, skepticism
12. irresolution 14. precariousness
unchanging... 7. eternal, settled,
uniform 9. immutable, unvarying
10. invariable, stationary
unchaste... 4. lewd 5. bawdy
6. impure 7. obscene 8. immodest
unchecked... 4. free 5. loose
7. rampant 9. permanent, unbridled
unchristian... 5. pagan 7. heathen,
infidel, ungodly 9. barbarous,
excessive 11. irreligious, uncivilized
uncivil... 4. rude 6. savage 7. ill–bred
8. impolite 9. barbarous
10. indecorous, ungracious
11. ill–mannered, uncivilized
12. discourteous 13. disrespectful
uncivilized... 4. rude, wild 5. feral
6. brutal, ferine, savage 8. barbaric
9. primitive, unrefined
uncle... 3. eme (yeme), oom
unclean... 4. foul, tref, vile 5. dirty
6. filthy, immund, impure
8. polluted, unchaste
11. unwholesome
Uncle Tom's Cabin (pert to)...
author.. 5. Stowe (Harriet Beecher)
character.. 5. Topsy 6. Legree
8. Uncle Tom 9. Little Eva
subject.. 7. slavery
unclose... 3. ope 4. open 6. reveal
7. expound 8. disclose
uncolored... 7. genuine 9. colorless
10. achromatic
uncommon... 3. odd 4. nice, rare
5. novel 6. scarce, unique
7. special, strange, unusual

8. unwonted 10. infrequent, remarkable 11. exceptional 12. unaccustomed 13. extraordinary

uncommunicative ... 6. silent 8. reserved, reticent 9. secretive 10. unsociable

uncomplaining ... 5. stoic 7. stoical

uncompromising ... 4. firm 5. rigid 6. strict 9. obstinate, unbending 10. inflexible, unyielding 12. conservative, intransigent

unconcerned ... 4. cool, free 8. careless 9. apathetic 10. insouciant 11. indifferent, not involved 13. disinterested

unconditional ... 4. free 8. absolute, explicit 10. unreserved

unconfined ... 5. loose 9. boundless, limitless, unlimited 12. unrestrained

unconscious ... 3. out 6. asleep 7. unaware 8. heedless, ignorant, mindless 9. inanimate, senseless, unfeeling 10. abstracted, insensible 11. involuntary 12. subconscious

unconstrained ... 4. easy, free 6. candid 7. natural 8. informal 11. spontaneous 12. unrestrained

uncontrolled ... 4. free, wild 5. loose 7. lawless 9. impulsive, irregular, unmanaged 10. capricious, changeable, licentious, ungoverned 11. not governed, unregulated 12. unrestrained

unconventional ... 4. easy 5. outré 6. casual 7. devious, offbeat 8. Bohemian, informal 10. unorthodox 13. unceremonious

uncorrupted ... 8. pristine

uncouth ... 3. odd 4. rude 5. crude 6. clumsy, rustic 7. awkward, boorish, strange 9. inelegant, unrefined, untrained 10. outlandish, uncultured, unpolished

uncover ... 4. bare, open 6. detect, divest, expose, remove, reveal, unveil 7. divulge, lay bare, take off, undrape 8. disclose, discover

uncovered ... 4. bald, bare, nude, open 7. exposed 8. divested, revealed, stripped, unveiled 9. décolleté 10. bareheaded 11. unprotected

unction ... 4. balm, rite 6. fervor 7. lanolin, unguent 8. flattery, function (divine), ointment 10. anointment

unctuous ... 4. oily, smug 5. bland, fatty, salvy, suave 6. fervid, greasy 7. gushing, pinguid, plastic 10. flattering, oleaginous 12. hypocritical 13. sanctimonious

uncultured ... 7. artless, boorish, uncouth 8. Bohemian 9. unlearned, unrefined 10. Philistine 11. countrified, undeveloped

undaunted ... 4. bold 5. brave 7. Spartan, untamed 8. fearless, intrepid, unafraid 9. confident, dauntless 10. courageous, undismayed 11. persevering, unconquered

undecided ... 4. moot 7. pending 8. doubtful, wavering 9. uncertain,

unsettled 10. inconstant, irresolute, unresolved 13. problematical

undependable ... 6. fickle 7. erratic 9. uncertain 13. irresponsible, untrustworthy

under ... 3. sub 4. alow 5. below, least, neath, sotto 6. nether 7. beneath 8. guidance 9. lower than 10. subjection, underneath 11. subordinate

undercover ... 6. secret 7. furtive 11. clandestine, underground 13. surreptitious

underestimate ... 8. belittle, minimize 9. set too low, underrate 10. undervalue

underfong ... 6. entrap 7. ensnare, receive, sustain 9. undertake 10. circumvent

undergo ... 4. bear, dree, pass 5. shirt 6. endure, suffer 7. sustain 9. undermine 10. experience

underhanded ... 3. sly 4. dern, mean 5. shady 6. covert, crafty, secret, sneaky 8. sneaking, unfairly 9. deceitful, dishonest 10. fraudulent 11. clandestine, short-handed 13. unobtrusively 15. surreptitiously

underling ... 6. menial, minion 7. servant 8. inferior 11. subordinate

underlying ... 5. basic 8. cardinal 11. fundamental

undermine ... 3. sap 4. ruin 5. drain, erode 6. weaken 7. subvert 8. enfeeble, excavate

understand ... 3. ken, see 4. know 5. grasp, infer, savvy, sense 6. follow, reason 7. discern, explain, realize, signify 8. conceive, perceive 9. apprehend, interpret 10. comprehend

understandable ... 5. clear, lucid 12. intelligible

understanding ... 5. amity, sense 6. accord, reason, treaty 7. compact, concept, entente, knowing 8. sympathy, Verstand 9. agreement, intellect, knowledge, tolerance, unanimity 10. acceptance, accordance, perception 11. discernment, penetration 12. intelligence 13. comprehension

understatement ... 7. litotes

understood ... 5. clear, known, lucid, tacit 7. assumed, implied, settled 8. implicit 11. traditional

undertake ... 3. try 4. dare 6. accept, assume, pledge 7. attempt, promise, reprove 8. contract, covenant, endeavor, engage in, set about 9. guarantee, underfong

undertaker ... 5. cerer 6. surety 7. manager, rebuker, sponsor 8. embalmer 9. godfather, mortician 12. entrepreneur

undertaking ... 3. act 4. task 6. cautio 7. calling, project, promise, venture 8. business 9. adventure, guarantee 10. enterprise

undertone ... 4. tone (low) 5. aside 6. murmur 12. subdued color

undertow ... 7. riptide

underworld... 3. Dis 4. hell 5. Hades, limbo, Mafia, Orcus, Sheol 6. Erebus, Tophet 7. Abaddon, Xibalba 8. Dis pater, gangland 9. Black Hand, chthonian, perdition, purgatory

underwrite... 6. assure, insure 7. finance, sponsor 8. submit to

underwriter... 7. insurer 8. endorser 9. financier 10. underclerk 13. Stock Exchange 14. Lloyd's of London

undesirable condition... 6. malady

undetermined... 5. vague 7. dubious 8. not fixed, unproved 9. uncertain, undecided 10. irresolute

undeveloped... 5. crude 6. embryo, latent 8. immature 10. unprepared 11. rudimentary

undignified... 6. vulgar 8. informal, infra dig, unworthy 9. inelegant

undine... 3. nix 5. gnome, sylph 6. vessel (glass) 9. planetoid 10. salamander

undivided... 3. one 5. total, whole 6. entire, intact, joined 7. unitary 8. unbroken 9. not shared 10. continuous

undo... 4. open 5. annul, loose 6. cancel, defeat, foredo, unlash, unwrap 7. destroy, disjoin, nullify, release, uncover, unravel 8. unfasten 10. disconnect, invalidate

undoing... 4. ruin 6. defeat 8. downfall 9. annulment, overthrow 11. destruction, disassembly

undomesticated... 4. wild 5. feral 6. ferine

undone... 3. raw 9. neglected 10. defeasible

undue... 5. wrong 6. unjust 7. extreme 8. improper, not owing 9. excessive 10. exorbitant, immoderate, inordinate, undeserved, unsuitable 11. unwarranted 13. inappropriate

undulating... 4. wavy 6. waving 7. aripple, rolling 8. rippling 11. fluctuating 16. rising and falling

undulation... 4. beat, wave 5. heave, surge, swell 6. motion, waving 7. tremolo, vibrato 8. waviness 9. pulsation 11. convolution

undying... 6. eterne 7. ageless, endless, eternal 8. immortal, unending 9. deathless 11. amaranthine 12. imperishable 14. indestructible

unearth... 4. find 5. dig up 6. exhume, expose 7. uncover 8. disclose, discover, disinter 12. bring to light

unearthly... 5. eerie (eery), godly, weird 7. awesome, ghostly, strange, uncanny 8. heavenly, terrific 9. appalling, deathlike 10. mysterious, outlandish 12. preposterous, supernatural 13. preternatural

uneasiness... 5. worry 6. unrest 7. anxiety, malaise 8. disquiet 10. impatience 11. displeasure, disquietude, disturbance

12. apprehension

uneasy... 5. stiff 7. anxious, awkward, inquiet, restive, worried 8. agitated, cramping, restless 9. difficult, impatient, perturbed 10. disquieted, distressed 11. constrained, troublesome

unemotional... 4. cold 5. stoic 7. stoical 10. phlegmatic

unemployed... 4. idle, lazy 6. otiose, unused 7. not used 8. inactive, leisured 11. not invested

unencumbered... 4. free

unending... 7. endless, eternal 8. termless, timeless 9. boundless, perpetual 10. continuous 12. interminable

unequal... 3. odd 4. odds 5. aniso (comb form) 6. uneven, unfair, unjust 8. variable 9. disparate, irregular 11. fluctuating, not adequate 12. asymmetrical 16. disproportionate

unequaled... 7. supreme 8. peerless 9. matchless, nonpareil, unmatched, unrivaled 10. inimitable, surpassing, unbeatable, unexcelled 12. unparalleled

unequivocal... 5. clear, plain 6. candid 7. sincere 8. explicit 9. downright 11. categorical, indubitable

unerring... 4. sure, true 5. exact 7. certain 8. accurate, virtuous 9. unfailing 10. infallible

unessential... 8. needless 9. extrinsic 10. irrelevant 11. superfluous, unimportant 13. insignificant, void of essence

unethical... 6. amoral

uneven... 3. odd 5. erose, rough 6. rugged, unfair, unjust 7. erratic, unequal, varying 8. not level 10. ill-matched 11. fluctuating

unexamined... 7. a priori

unexampled... 8. peerless 10. unimitated 12. unparalleled 13. extraordinary, unprecedented

unexpected... 6. abrupt, sudden 7. unusual 9. inopinate 10. unforeseen 14. not anticipated

unfair... 4. foul 5. wrong 6. biased, uneven, unjust 8. unseemly 9. dishonest, unethical 10. not cricket, unsporting 11. inequitable, unfavorable 12. disingenuous, not equitable

unfaithful... 6. betray 7. infidel, traitor 8. apostate, recreant, turncoat 9. faithless 10. inaccurate 12. nonobservant 13. untrustworthy

unfamiliar... 3. new 7. strange, unknown 8. not known 12. unaccustomed, unconversant

unfasten... 4. free, open, undo 5. unbar, unfix, unpin, untie 6. detach, loosen, unhook, unlock 7. unloose 8. unbutton 9. disengage

unfavorable... 3. bad, ill 6. averse 7. adverse, opposed 8. contrary, untimely 9. repulsive 12. inauspicious

unfeeling... 4. dull 5. cruel, stoic, stony 6. brutal, steely, stolid, unkind 7. callous 8. numbness, obdurate

9. apathetic, bloodless, heartless, inanimate, insensate 10. insensible 11. hardhearted 13. unsusceptible 16. unimpressionable

unfeigned... 4. real 7. genuine, natural, sincere 11. undeceptive 14. not counterfeit 15. not hypocritical

unfermented grape juice... 4. stum

unfertile... 4. arid 6. barren

unfettered... 4. free 5. broad 9. liberated, unchained 10. unshackled

unfinished... 5. crude, rough 7. sketchy 9. imperfect 10. incomplete 11. uncompleted

unfit... 5. inept 6. faulty, not fit, unable 8. disabled 9. untenable 11. handicapped, incompetent, unqualified 12. disqualified

unfledged... 4. eyas 5. green 6. callow 8. immature 11. undeveloped 12. not feathered

unflinching... 7. staunch 8. resolute, unafraid 9. steadfast 10. unwavering, unyielding 12. not shrinking

unfold... 3. ope 4. open 6. evolve, expand, flower, reveal, spread, unfurl 7. develop, display, divulge, evolute, explain, release 8. disclose

unfortunate... 3. ill 4. poor 6. wretch 7. hapless, unlucky 8. luckless, untimely 10. calamitous 12. inauspicious, unsuccessful

unfounded... 4. idle, vain 8. baseless 9. untenable 10. chimerical 11. unsupported, unwarranted

unfriendly... 3. icy 4. cool 7. asocial, hostile, not kind, opposed 8. inimical, unsocial 10. unsociable 12. inhospitable

unfruitful... 6. barren, wasted 7. sterile, useless 9. fruitless, infertile 12. unproductive, unprofitable 13. not productive

unfurl... 4. open 6. expand, spread, unfold, unroll

ungainly... 5. gawky, lanky 6. clumsy, gauche 7. awkward, uncouth 8. bungling 10. cumbersome, ungraceful

ungenteel... 6. vulgar 7. ill–bred 8. plebeian 9. inelegant 10. unmannerly

ungentle... 4. rude 5. harsh, rough 7. ill–bred 12. discourteous

ungodly... 6. sinful, wicked 7. impious 9. atheistic 11. unbelieving

ungovernable... 4. wild 6. unruly 9. unbridled 10. disorderly, licentious, rebellious, refractory 12. incorrigible, obstreperous, recalcitrant 13. irrepressible 14. uncontrollable

unguent... 4. balm 5. salve 6. cerate, chrism, pomade 7. unction 8. ointment 9. lubricant, unguentum

ungula... 4. claw, hoof, nail 6. unguis

ungulate... 3. pig 4. deer 5. horse, swine, tapir 6. hoofed 8. elephant, Ungulata 10. rhinoceros 15. hoofed quadruped

unhallowed... 6. unholy, wicked 10. desecrated

unhappy... 3. sad 6. dismal, woeful 8. dejected, ill–fated, wretched 9. miserable, sorrowful 10. calamitous, displeased 11. melancholic, unfortunate 12. discontented, unsuccessful

unhealthy... 3. ill 4. sick 6. sickly, unsafe 11. unwholesome

unhesitating... 4. sure 5. ready 8. implicit, resolute 10. undoubting

unholy... 6. wicked 7. impious, profane 8. shocking 10. scandalous, unhallowed

unicorn... 4. reem (Bib), unie 7. monster 8. narwhale 9. monoceros, spike team 10. pursuivant (Her), rhinoceros (one–horned)

uniform... 4. even 5. equal 6. livery, outfit, simple, smooth 7. equable, orderly, regular 8. constant, equiform 9. unvarying 10. consistent, invariable, unchanging 11. symmetrical

uniformity... 5. order 8. equality, evenness, sameness, symmetry 10. compliance, conformity, smoothness 11. consistency, homogeneity 13. invariability

unify... 5. merge, unite 7. combine, make one 8. coalesce 9. integrate 11. consolidate

unimaginative... 4. dull 7. literal, prosaic 10. unfanciful

unimpaired... 4. free 6. entire, intact 8. unmarred 9. undamaged, unspoiled

unimpressed... 6. unawed 7. unmoved 9. unstirred 10. unaffected, uninspired

uninformed... 8. ignorant, nescient 9. unknowing 10. unapprized 13. unenlightened, unintelligent

uninhabited... 5. empty 6. vacant 8. deserted, desolate, forsaken 9. abandoned, unpeopled 10. unoccupied, untenanted

uninspired... 4. dull 6. stodgy 9. uninhaled

unintelligent... 4. dumb 5. brute 6. stupid, unwise 7. foolish 8. ignorant 9. senseless

unintentional... 7. unmeant 9. unwitting 10. accidental, unintended 11. inadvertent, involuntary, unmeditated 14. unpremeditated

uninterested... 5. bored 9. apathetic, impartial, incurious 11. unconcerned 13. disinterested

uninteresting... 3. dry 4. arid, drab, dull 6. boring, prolix, stupid 7. humdrum, insipid, prosaic, tedious 8. tiresome 9. colorless 10. unexciting

union... 3. one 4. bond 5. joint, unity 6. accord, fusion, league, merger 7. amalgam, entente, liaison, oneness 8. alliance, junction, marriage 9. coalition 10. federation

11. affiliation, association,
combination, concurrence,
confederacy, conjunction
13. juxtaposition
Union (pert to)...
ensign, British.. 12. three crosses (St
Andrew, St George, St Patrick)
General.. 7. Sherman (Civil War)
of States.. 6. Empire 12. United
States
of workers.. 5. artel, guild
Union of So Africa...
capital.. 8. Cape Town (Legis),
Pretoria (Admin)
city.. 6. Durban 9. Germiston
12. Johannesburg
famed Park.. 6. Kruger
**Union of Soviet Socialist
Republics**... see also *Russia*
anc citadel.. 7. Kremlin
capital.. 6. Moscow
city.. 9. Leningrad
Republics (number).. 7. fifteen
resort.. 5. Yalta 6. Crimea
river.. 2. Ob 3. Don 4. Lena, Neva,
Ural 5. Volga 7. Dnieper
sea.. 4. Aral, Azov 5. Black, White
6. Baltic 7. Caspian
strait.. 6. Bering
unique... 3. odd, one 4. rare, sole
5. alone, novel 6. single 7. notable,
special, unusual 8. original, peculiar,
peerless, singular 9. matchless
12. single–valued 13. extraordinary
unison... 5. union 6. accord, assent
7. concord, harmony 9. agreement,
unanimity 10. concordant,
consonance
unit... 3. ace, ane, one 4. item, word
5. digit, group 6. entity 7. measure
8. syllable
unit (pert to)...
astronomy.. 6. parsec
biology.. 5. idant
electrical.. 3. amp, mho, ohm, rel
4. volt, watt 5. farad, henry, joule
6. ampere, proton 7. coulomb
energy.. 3. erg, rad 5. ergon 6. kilerg
7. quantum
fluidity.. 3. rhe
force.. 4. dyne 5. tonal 7. kinetic
heat.. 5. therm (therme) 7. calorie
(calory)
induction.. 5. henry
light.. 3. lux, pyr, rad 5. lumen
6. Hefner
linear.. 3. ell 4. foot, inch, mile, yard
7. furlong
magnetic.. 5. gauss, weber
7. maxwell, oersted
matter.. 5. monad
measure.. 3. are, rod 4. pint
5. maund, meter, stere
military.. 7. brigade, platoon
8. regiment
power.. 2. HP 3. bel 5. dynam,
horse
pressure.. 5. barad, barie
reluctance.. 3. rel
resistance.. 3. ohm
speed.. 4. velo

telegraphic.. 4. baud
thermal.. 7. calorie (calory)
velocity.. 4. velo
volume.. 3. ton 4. cord, peck, pint
5. ounce, pound 6. barrel, bushel,
gallon 8. hogshead
weight.. 3. ton 5. carat (karat),
ounce, pound
wire.. 3. mil
work.. 3. erg 5. ergon, joule 6. kilerg
yarn.. 6. denier
unite... 3. fay, tie, wed 4. ally, bind,
fuse, join, knit, link, meld, weld
5. annex, graft, marry, merge
6. adhere, cement, concur, mingle,
solder 7. combine, connect
8. coalesce, condense, converge,
federate, side with 9. affiliate,
associate 10. amalgamate, federalize
11. consolidate, incorporate
unite (pert to)...
by freezing.. 8. regelate
by interweaving.. 5. plash 6. pleach,
splice
by joints.. 10. articulate
closely.. 11. concentrate
in concordance.. 9. harmonize
timbers.. 6. rabbet
united... 3. one, wed 4. knit, tied
5. added 6. allied, banded, joined,
linked, merged, welded 7. cohered,
grafted, rallied, spliced 8. cemented,
clannish 9. concerted, corporate
10. concurrent, corporated
United Provinces... 11. (The)
Netherlands 13. Dutch Republic
United States... 9. Etats–Unis
United States... see also *American*
artist.. 4. Pyle, Wood 5. Flagg,
Moses (Grandma), Peale, Ryder,
Sloan 6. Eakins, Stuart
author.. 3. Ade, Poe 4. Pyle, Ward
5. Alger, Barth, Beach, Davis, Field,
Harte, James, Lewis, Stowe
6. Alcott, Bryant, Cooper, Ferber,
Hersey, Holmes, Irving, London,
Lowell, O'Henry, Porter 7. Clemens,
Dreiser, Emerson, Stewart, Thoreau,
Whitman 8. Faulkner, Sinclair,
Whittier 9. Hawthorne, Hemingway
10. Longfellow, Tarkington
canal.. 4. Erie 6. Panama
capital.. see separate States
composer.. 4. Kern 5. Foote, Nevin
6. Berlin, Foster 7. Rodgers
8. Gershwin 9. Bernstein
emblem.. 5. eagle
explorer.. 4. Byrd, Long, Pike
5. Boone, Clark, Lewis, Logan, Perry
Falls.. 7. Niagara 8. Yosemite
9. Multnomah
Indian.. see under *Indian (Am)*
inventor.. 3. Hoe 4. Bell, Howe
5. Fiske, Fitch, Morse 6. Edison,
Fulton 7. Whitney
mountain.. 4. Hood 6. Elbert, Helena,
Shasta 7. Rainier, Whitney
8. Katahdin, McKinley
naturalist.. 4. Muir 5. Beebe, Seton
7. Thoreau
ornithologist.. 7. Audubon

philosopher.. **5.** James
pirate.. **4.** Kidd
poet.. **3.** Poe **4.** Nash **5.** Benét,
Field, Moore, Wylie **6.** Bryant,
Holmes, Kilmer, Lanier, Lowell, Millay
7. Whitman **8.** Whittier
10. Longfellow
unity... **3.** one **5.** union **6.** accord
7. concord, harmony, oneness
8. alliance **9.** agreement
10. singleness, uniformity
11. conjunction, unification
12. completeness
universal... **3.** all **5.** local, total, usual,
whole **6.** cosmic, entire, public
7. general **8.** catholic **9.** prevalent,
unlimited, well–known **11.** widely
known
universal (pert to)...
knowledge.. **9.** pantology
language.. **2.** Ro **3.** Ido **9.** Esperanto
language, written.. **10.** pasigraphy
remedy.. **7.** panacea
solvent.. **8.** alkahest
successor, heir.. **5.** heres (haeres)
universe... **4.** olam **5.** world
6. cosmos, system **9.** macrocosm
10. Great World
universe, controlling principle...
5. logos
unkempt... **5.** messy, rough **6.** frowsy,
shaggy, untidy **7.** ruffled, squalid,
tousled, uncouth **9.** unrefined
10. disarrayed, disheveled, unpolished
unkind... **3.** ill **5.** cruel, harsh, stern
6. brutal, severe **8.** ungenial
9. inclement **10.** ungracious,
ungrateful **13.** unsympathetic
15. uncompassionate
unknowable... **6.** mystic **8.** mystical,
noumenon **9.** enigmatic
13. indiscernible **14.** unintelligible
15. absolute reality (Kant), ultimate
reality (Spencer)
unknowable object... **3.** God **7.** the
soul **8.** noumenon
unknown... **7.** inconnu, strange
8. stranger **9.** anonymous, hereafter,
incognito, unheard of **10.** unfamiliar,
unrenowned **12.** incalculable
unlawful... **7.** bastard, illegal, illicit,
lawless **9.** irregular **10.** contraband
11. unwarranted **12.** illegitimate,
unauthorized
unlearned... **4.** lewd **5.** gross
8. ignorant, untaught **10.** illiterate,
uneducated **11.** instinctive
unleashed... **4.** free **5.** loose **6.** untied
8. released **10.** unfettered,
unshackled, untethered
unleavened... **7.** azymous
unleavened bread... **4.** azym **5.** azyme
7. matzoth
unless... **4.** nisi, save **6.** except
7. without **9.** except for, excepting
10. except that
unlettered... **8.** ignorant **10.** illiterate,
uneducated
unlike... **6.** sundry, uneven **7.** dislike,
diverse **9.** different, irregular
10. dissimilar, improbable
11. unpromising **12.** disagreeable

13. heterogeneous
unlikelihood... **11.** small chance
13. improbability
unlikeness... **8.** contrast
13. dissimilarity
unlimited... **4.** vast **9.** boundless,
unbounded, universal **10.** unconfined
11. illimitable **12.** immeasurable,
unrestricted **13.** indeterminate
unload... **3.** rid **4.** dump, sell
5. empty **7.** discard, lighten
9. disburden, discharge, liquidate
unlucky... **3.** bad, fey, ill **7.** infaust
8. ill–fated, untimely **9.** ill–omened
11. unfortunate **12.** inauspicious, not
favorable
unmannerly... **4.** rude **7.** boorish,
uncivil **8.** impolite **10.** mannerless
12. discourteous
unmelodious... **9.** dissonant
11. cacophonous
unmerciful... **5.** cruel **6.** unkind
7. extreme, inhuman **8.** pitiless,
ruthless **9.** heartless, merciless
10. relentless
unmistakable... **4.** open **5.** clear, plain
6. patent **7.** certain, evident, obvious
8. apparent, distinct, manifest
11. unqualified
unmitigated... **4.** mere **5.** sheer
6. arrant **8.** clear–cut, thorough
9. downright **11.** not softened,
unqualified
unmoved... **4.** calm, dead, firm
5. inert **6.** serene **8.** obdurate,
unshaken **9.** apathetic
unnatural... **5.** eerie (eery) **7.** labored,
strange, uncanny **8.** abnormal,
affected **9.** eccentric, irregular
10. artificial, factitious
unnecessary... **4.** fuss **7.** useless
8. needless **11.** not required,
superfluous, uncalled–for
12. nonessential
unobtrusive... **6.** modest **8.** retiring
11. clandestine
unoccupied... **4.** idle, void **5.** empty
7. not busy **8.** deserted
10. unemployed, untenanted
11. empty–headed, uninhabited
unorthodox... **9.** heretical
10. fallacious, left–handed
14. unconventional
unostentatious... **5.** quiet **6.** lenten,
modest **10.** restrained
unparalleled... **5.** alone **6.** unique
8. peerless **9.** matchless, unequaled,
unmatched **10.** inimitable
13. extraordinary
unpleasant... **8.** unsavory **9.** offensive
10. not amiable, ungracious
11. displeasing, distasteful
12. disagreeable
unpolished... **5.** bruit, crude, rough
6. coarse, rugged **7.** uncouth
8. agrestic, unpolite **9.** inelegant
10. agrestical **11.** countrified
unprecedented... **3.** new **5.** novel
10. unexampled, unimitated
13. extraordinary
unprejudiced... **4.** fair **7.** neutral
8. unbiased **9.** impartial

10. impersonal 13. dispassionate

unprepared ... 3. raw 5. unfit
6. unwary 7. unready 9. premature,
unskilled

unprepossessing ... 4. grim, ugly
9. grim–faced 10. ill–looking

unpretentious ... 6. humble, modest,
simple 7. natural 10. unaffected
11. in good taste

unprincipled ... 7. corrupt 9. dishonest
10. fraudulent, perfidious
12. dishonorable, unscrupulous

unprofessional ... 3. lay 6. laical
7. amateur 9. unskilled
10. amateurish 14. unbusinesslike

unprofitable ... 6. barren 7. useless
8. gainless 9. fruitless 10. unfruitful

unpropitious ... 7. adverse, ominous,
opposed 8. untimely 10. disastrous
12. inauspicious

unqualified ... 5. unfit 6. unable
7. genuine, plenary 8. absolute,
complete, unfitted 9. incapable
10. ineligible 11. incompetent
12. not qualified 13. unconditional

unquestionable ... 7. certain, decided,
evident 8. positive 10. undeniable
11. indubitable, irrefutable
12. indisputable, unimpeachable

unravel ... 4. undo 5. feaze, solve
6. unfold, unlace 8. separate
9. disengage 10. disinvolve
11. disentangle

unreal ... 5. false, ideal 7. fancied
8. fanciful, illusory, spurious
9. fantastic, imaginary, visionary
10. artificial, fictitious 11. imaginative
13. unsubstantial

unreasonable ... 3. mad 6. absurd,
unwise 9. excessive, fanatical,
illogical, senseless 10. capricious,
exorbitant, immoderate, irrational
11. extravagant, impractical
13. unjustifiable

unrecognizable ... 3. dim 5. vague
7. blurred, obscure, unclear
9. undefined 10. indistinct
14. unintelligible

unrecognized ... 6. unsung 7. unknown
13. unappreciated

unrefined ... 3. raw 4. loud, rude
5. crass, crude, gross, rough
6. coarse, common, earthy, vulgar
7. uncouth 9. inelegant
11. countrified 12. uncultivated

unrefuted ... 4. true 6. proved
8. undenied 10. unanswered

unrelaxed ... 4. taut 5. rigid, tense
7. nervous

unrelenting ... 4. grim, hard, iron
5. stern 6. severe, strict 8. rigorous
9. merciless 10. inexorable,
relentless, unyielding

unreliable ... 6. fickle, unsafe
9. uncertain 10. capricious,
changeable 12. undependable
13. irresponsible, untrustworthy
14. tergiversating

unremitting ... 4. busy 8. constant
9. continual, incessant, perpetual
10. continuous, persistent
11. persevering

unrequited ... 6. unpaid 9. forgotten,
unthanked 10. ungrateful, unrewarded

unreserved, unreservedly ... 4. free,
open 5. frank 6. openly 7. frankly
8. candidly, outright, thorough
9. outspoken 12. unrestricted

unrest ... 6. bustle 8. disquiet
9. commotion 12. restlessness

unrestrained ... 3. lax 4. free, wild
5. loose 6. candid, wanton
7. lawless, riotous 9. unbridled,
unlimited 10. capricious

unrestricted ... 4. free, open
9. unlimited 11. extravagant
12. undiminished 13. communicative

unruffled ... 4. calm, cool 5. still
6. placid, poised, sedate, serene,
smooth 9. quiescent, unexcited
10. unaffected 11. undisturbed

unruly ... 7. lawless 9. fractious,
obstinate, turbulent 10. disorderly,
licentious, refractory 11. disobedient
12. recalcitrant, ungovernable,
unmanageable

unsafe ... 7. dubious, exposed, unsound
8. insecure, perilous 9. dangerous
10. unreliable 12. undependable

unsatisfactory ... 8. inferior
10. inadequate, unbearable
11. intolerable 12. insufficient,
ungratiating 13. disheartening,
unsupportable

unsavory ... 7. insipid 9. offensive,
tasteless 10. unpleasant
11. unpalatable 12. disagreeable

unscrupulous ... 7. devious
9. dishonest 12. unparticular,
unprincipled 13. untrustworthy
16. indiscriminating

unseasonable ... 8. untimely
9. premature 11. inopportune

unseemly ... 5. inapt, wrong 6. vulgar
8. improper, indecent 9. inelegant
10. indecorous, solecistic,
unbecoming 11. undignified
13. ungrammatical

unseen ... 6. hidden 8. unheeded,
viewless 9. invisible, unnoticed
12. undiscovered

unsettled ... 4. moot 6. fickle, queasy
8. confused, deranged, restless,
unplaced, unproved, unstable
9. ambiguous, disturbed, irregular,
uncertain, unquieted 10. irresolute,
unoccupied, up in the air
11. unpopulated

unshorn ... 5. hairy, whole 6. shaggy

unshorn sheep (2nd year) ... 3. tag,
teg

unsightly ... 4. ugly 8. uncomely,
unlovely 9. inelegant, not comely
12. unattractive

unskilled ... 5. green 6. puisne
8. ignorant, malapert

unskillful ... 5. inept 7. artless,
awkward 9. maladroit
12. unproficient 13. inexperienced

unsophisticated ... 4. naif, pure, soft
5. green, naive 6. simple 7. artless,
genuine 8. gullible, innocent
9. ingenuous 11. uncorrupted

unsound ... 4. weak 5. crazy, dotty,

risky, shaky 6. addled, fickle
8. impaired, insecure 9. defective,
imperfect
unspoken... 5. tacit 6. silent
7. implied 9. ineffable, unuttered
unstable... 4. weak 6. fickle, fitful,
labile, scanty 7. astatic, erratic,
flighty, plastic 8. insecure, not solid,
ticklish, unsteady 9. ephemeral,
irregular, unsettled 10. inconstant,
precarious, unreliable 11. fluctuating,
vacillating
unsteady... 5. dizzy, shaky 6. groggy,
wobbly 7. quavery, rickety, unsound
8. titubate, unstable, wavering
9. irregular, uncertain 10. capricious,
changeable, flickering, inconstant,
precarious 11. fluctuating,
ill-balanced, lightheaded, vacillating
unsubstantial... 4. airy, rare, slim
5. filmy, light 6. aerial, flimsy,
papery 8. illusory 9. illogical,
visionary 10. immaterial, intangible,
unreliable
unsuitable... 5. inept, undue, unfit
8. untimely 10. unbecoming
11. inexpedient 13. inappropriate
14. unsatisfactory
unsullied... 4. pure 5. clean 6. chaste
8. innocent, spotless, virginal
10. immaculate
unsure... 4. weak 5. timid 6. infirm
8. doubtful 10. precarious
11. vacillating
unsweetened... 3. dry, sec 4. sour,
tart 10. unpleasant
unsympathetic... 6. unkind 7. hostile
8. pitiless 9. heartless 10. intolerant
11. hardhearted 12. unresponsive
untamed... 4. wild 5. feral 6. savage
9. unsubdued 11. uncivilized
untangle... 4. free 5. loose, solve
6. sleave 9. extricate 11. disentangle
untenable... 10. incredible
11. implausible 12. unbelievable,
unreasonable 13. inconceivable
unthinking... 4. rash 7. puerile
8. careless, heedless 9. impetuous,
impulsive 11. injudicious, instinctive,
involuntary, thoughtless
13. inconsiderate
untidy... 5. dowdy, messy 6. frowzy,
shabby 8. careless, frumpish,
slipshod, slovenly, unsuited, untimely
10. disheveled
untie... 4. free 5. loose 6. loosen,
unbind, unknot, unlash 8. unfasten
9. disengage
until now... 8. hitherto
untiring... 8. sedulous, tireless
9. unwearied 10. unflagging
13. indefatigable
untold... 4. vast 8. infinite
9. boundless, countless
10. uninformed, unrevealed
11. innumerable, unexpressed
12. immeasurable, incalculable,
undetermined
untouched... 3. new 4. pure 6. intact,
unused 8. pristine, virginal
10. impenitent, unaffected
untoward... 6. unruly 7. unlucky

8. perverse, stubborn, unseemly
10. indecorous, ungraceful
11. unfavorable, unfortunate
12. unpropitious
untrained... 4. soft, wild 5. green
8. indocile 9. unskilled, untutored
10. amateurish 11. unpracticed
14. unaccomplished
untrammeled... 4. free 5. loose 8. not
bound 9. unimpeded, unlimited
10. unfettered, unhampered,
unhindered
untransferable... 11. inalienable
untried... 3. new 5. fresh, green
8. unproved 9. unhandled
13. inexperienced
untrue... 5. false, wrong 8. disloyal
9. dishonest, erroneous, incorrect,
not honest 10. fallacious, unfaithful
untrustworthy... 6. tricky, unsafe
8. slippery 9. deceitful, dishonest,
uncertain 10. perfidious
untruth... 3. lie 5. error, fable
7. falsity 9. falsehood, treachery
10. disloyalty 11. fabrication
13. faithlessness
unusual... 3. odd 4. rare 5. novel,
queer 6. exotic, quaint, unique
7. strange 8. terrific, uncommon
9. anomalous 10. infrequent,
remarkable 11. exceptional
13. extraordinary
unutterable... 6. sacred, secret
9. ineffable, wonderful
11. unspeakable 13. inexpressible
unvarnished... 5. plain 6. simple
7. genuine 9. unadorned, unglossed
11. undeceptive 13. unembellished
unvarying... 7. uniform 8. constant
9. permanent 10. monotonous
unwarranted... 4. idle, vain 5. undue
7. illegal 8. baseless 9. excessive,
unfounded, untenable 10. exorbitant,
unentitled 11. unjustified
unwary... 4. rash 7. unaware
8. heedless, off guard 9. unguarded
10. unwatchful
unwavering... 4. firm, sure 5. solid
8. constant 9. steadfast
10. unweakened 11. not yielding,
persevering
unwelcome... 8. non grata, unwanted
9. intrusive, uninvited
unwholesome... 4. evil, sick 6. impure
7. corrupt, immoral, noisome,
noxious 9. unhealthy 12. insalubrious
unwieldy... 5. bulky 6. clumsy
7. awkward, restive 8. ungainly
9. ponderous 10. cumbersome
12. unmanageable 13. insubordinate
unwilling... 5. loath (loth) 6. averse
9. reluctant 11. disinclined,
involuntary
unwilling to prosecute... 7. nol-pros
13. nolle prosequi
unwise... 7. foolish 9. impolitic,
imprudent, senseless 10. irrational
11. inexpedient, injudicious
unwonted... 4. rare 6. unused
7. unusual 8. uncommon 9. not
wonted 10. infrequent
12. unaccustomed

unworldly ... 5. eerie (eery), godly,
naive, weird 8. heavenly 9. spiritual,
unearthly 10. immaterial
12. supernatural
unyielding ... 3. set 4. firm, hard, iron
5. rigid, stern, stiff 6. strict
7. adamant 8. obdurate, stubborn
9. immovable, obstinate
10. adamantine, determined,
inexorable, inflexible
14. uncompromising
up (pert to) ...
and coming .. 7. go–ahead 8. hustling
and down .. 6. seesaw, uneven
8. vertical 10. undulating
13. perpendicular
in arms .. 6. at odds 8. prepared
9. resistant
ref to .. 10. at the plate (game)
to .. 4. able, till, unto 5. until
9. cognizant, competent
to date .. 3. new 6. modern 7. stylish
11. fashionable
upas tree, arrow poison ... 6. antiar
upbraid ... 4. twit 5. blame, chide,
scold, score 6. rebuke 7. reprove
8. admonish, reproach 9. reprimand
10. put to shame
upheaval ... 5. storm 6. revolt
9. agitation, cataclysm, elevation
10. convulsion
upheld ... 5. aided 6. backed
7. abetted 8. defended 9. supported,
sustained 10. encouraged, maintained
uphill ... 6. upward 7. upgrade
9. ascending, difficult, laborious
10. slantingly
uphold ... 3. aid 4. abet, back, buoy
5. favor, raise 6. defend 7. confirm,
support, sustain 8. maintain, preserve
9. encourage 11. corroborate,
countenance, lend support
upkeep ... 4. cost 6. repair 7. support
11. maintenance
upland ... 4. wold 5. weald 6. coteau,
inland 7. country, plateau 8. highland
uplands ... 7. country 9. highlands
10. the country
uplift ... 5. elate, erect, raise
7. elevate, ennoble, glorify, improve
8. upheaval 9. elevation
11. inspiration
upon ... 2. on 3. sur 4. atop, onto
5. about, above 7. against 9. by
means of 10. after which
upon (pert to) ...
law .. 3. sur
prefix .. 3. epi, sur
that .. 7. whereat 9. whereupon
which .. 7. whereat
upper ... 6. higher 8. superior
upper (pert to) ...
bed .. 4. bunk
crust .. 7. society 11. aristocracy
13. highest circle
end .. 3. tip 4. apex, head
hand .. 7. mastery 8. dominion
9. advantage, influence
10. preference
House of Congress .. 6. Senate
shoe part .. 4. vamp
uppermost ... 3. top 6. upmost

7. highest, supreme, topmost
8. farthest, foremost 9. outermost
uppish ... 5. drunk, proud 6. uppity
7. haughty, peevish, stuck–up
8. arrogant, assuming, snobbish
9. high–flown
upright ... 4. good, just, true 5. erect,
moral, piano 6. honest, square
7. endwise, sincere 8. vertical,
virtuous 9. equitable, honorable,
righteous 13. perpendicular
upright (pert to) ...
chair part .. 4. slat
comb form .. 5. ortho
posture .. 8. orthotic 11. orthostatic
slab .. 5. stela
timber .. 4. jamb, stud
uprising ... 4. riot 6. ascent, mutiny,
revolt 7. sloping 9. acclivity,
ascending, rebellion 12. insurrection
uproar ... 3. din 4. riot, rout 5. noise
6. bedlam, bustle, clamor, fracas,
hubbub, outcry, tumult 7. turmoil
8. outbreak 9. commotion, confusion
10. donnybrook, hurly–burly,
tintamarre, turbulence
11. pandemonium 12. insurrection
upset ... 3. irk 4. rile, ruin, stir
6. defeat, refute, topple 7. agitate,
capsize, confuse, disturb, fluster,
startle, subvert, unnerve 8. distress,
overturn, startled, unnerved
9. embarrass, overthrow
10. discompose, disconcert,
distressed, frustrated, overturned,
refutation, revolution 11. frustration,
overwrought
upshot ... 3. end 5. fruit, issue
6. result, sequel 7. outcome
10. conclusion 11. consequence,
eventuality, termination
12. consummation
upside down ... 8. confused, disorder
9. confusion 10. resupinate,
topsy–turvy
upsilon (Gr) ... 5. hyoid, vowel
7. Y–shaped
upstart ... 4. snob 7. bounder, parvenu
13. social climber
up–to–date ... 6. modern 7. alamode,
topical 8. informed 11. fashionable
upward ... 2. up 3. ano (comb form)
4. over 5. above, aloft 6. onward
7. skyward 8. upstream 9. ascending
upward movement of vessels ...
5. scend
uraeus (Egypt Relig) ... 3. asp
6. symbol 8. symbolic
Ural ... 5. river 9. mountains
Urania (pert to) ...
blue .. 12. independence
epithet of .. 9. Aphrodite
genus of .. 5. moths
Gr Myth .. 4. Muse (Astron)
uranology *(study of)* ... 7. heavens
15. celestial bodies
Uranus (pert to) ...
astronomy .. 6. planet
daughter .. 5. Rhea
father of .. 9. The Titans (12)
personification of .. 6. heaven
satellite .. 5. Ariel 6. Oberon

7. Titania, Umbriel
son.. 6. Cronus
urare, urari... 6. curare
urban... 5. civic 6. ghetto, polite,
uptown 7. oppidan, refined
8. downtown, polished 9. courteous,
municipal 12. metropolitan
13. sophisticated
urbane... 5. civil, suave 6. polish,
polite 7. affable 8. gracious
9. courteous 11. deferential
urbanity... 7. amenity 8. civility,
courtesy 9. deference
urchin... 3. boy, elf, imp, tad 4. arab,
brat 5. gamin 6. elfish 8. hedgehog
9. dandiprat, sea urchin, youngster
urge... 3. dun, egg, hie, ply, yen
4. abet, coax, goad, prod, push,
spur 5. drive, egg on, impel, press
6. advise, compel, dehort, desire,
exhort, fillip, hasten, incite, induce
7. animate, entreat, solicit
8. persuade 9. constrain, importune,
influence, instigate 10. inducement
urgent... 3. hot 5. grave 7. clamant,
exigent, instant 8. critical, pressing
9. impelling, important, insistent,
necessary 11. importunate
urial... 3. sha 5. sheep 6. oorial
Uriel... 9. archangel 10. flame of God
(Bib)
Urim and Thummim (Bib)...
11. instruments 12. interpreters
(Mormon)
urn... 3. jar 4. ewer, urna (anc), vase
5. grave, steen 6. vessel 7. pitcher,
samovar, vaselet 10. jardiniere
urn–shaped... 8. urceolus 9. urceolate
Ursa... 4. bear 9. Ursa Major (Great
Bear), Ursa Minor (Little Bear)
ursal... 7. fur seal
ursuk... 11. bearded seal
Ursula... 5. Saint 7. she–bear
9. butterfly 15. British princess
(legend)
urubu... 7. vulture
Uruguay...
capital.. 10. Montevideo
city.. 4. Melo 5. Minar 9. Maldonado
estuary.. 5. Plata 12. Rio de la Plata
lake.. 5. Merim
river.. 7. Uruguay
settler.. 5. Cabot (Sebastian, 1527)
university.. 10. Montevideo (1849)
windstorm.. 7. pampero
urus... 2. ox 3. tur 7. aurochs
usable... 3. fit 9. practical
10. functional 11. serviceable,
utilitarian
usage... 3. use 4. wont 5. habit, ritus
6. custom, method 7. utility
8. behavior, practice 9. treatment
10. convention
use... 3. try 5. apply, avail, exert,
spend, treat, wield 6. employ,
expend, occupy 7. consume, exploit,
utilize 8. function 10. manipulate
11. consumption, utilization
use (pert to)...
abusive language.. 4. rail
divining rod.. 5. dowse
frugally.. 5. stint

pert to words.. 7. neology, verbose
8. enallage, pleonasm 9. verbosity
poetry.. 4. vail
refrain from.. 7. boycott
subterfuge.. 7. chicane
up.. 3. eat 7. consume, deplete,
exhaust, fatigue
useful... 4. good 5. utile 7. helpful
9. practical 10. beneficial,
commodious 11. serviceable,
subservient 12. advantageous,
instrumental
usefulness... 5. avail, value 6. profit
7. utility 13. conduciveness
useless... 4. idle, null, vain 6. futile,
otiose 7. of no use 8. bootless,
hopeless 9. fruitless, worthless
10. fifth wheel 11. ineffectual,
superfluous 12. unprofitable
13. unserviceable 14. good for
nothing
uselessness... 8. futility 9. inutility
10. inefficacy
usher... 4. lead, page 5. guide
6. escort 7. chobdar, teacher
9. attendant, harbinger, precursor
10. doorkeeper, forerunner,
inaugurate
usquebaugh... 6. whisky 7. cordial
ustion... 7. burning 13. cauterization
ustulate... 8. scorched 10. discolored
usual... 7. average, typical, usitate
8. everyday, frequent 11. status in
quo
usuer... 5. shark 6. loaner 7. Shylock
11. moneylender
usurp... 4. take 5. seize 6. assume
8. arrogate 11. appropriate
Utah...
capital.. 12. Salt Lake City
city.. 5. Logan, Ogden, Provo
7. Bingham
dam.. 10. Glen Canyon 12. Flaming
Gorge
lake.. 6. Powell 9. Great Salt
mountain.. 5. Uinta 7. Wasatch
9. King's Peak
name desired.. 7. Deseret
natural wonder.. 4. Zion 5. Bryce
13. Rainbow Bridge
settled by.. 7. Mormons 12. Brigham
Young 15. Latter–day Saints
State admission.. 10. Forty–fifth
State motto.. 8. Industry
State nickname.. 7. Beehive
utensil... 3. mop, pan, pot 4. tool
5. broom, brush 6. device, ramrod
7. skillet, sweeper 9. apparatus,
appliance, implement 10. instrument
utilitarian... 5. plain 6. useful
8. economic 9. practical
10. functional 12. matter–of–fact
utility... 3. use 4. tool 5. avail
6. profit 7. benefit, service
9. appliance, happiness, implement
10. usefulness
utmost... 4. best, last 5. final
7. extreme, maximum, supreme
8. farthest, greatest 9. uttermost
11. most distant
Utopia... 4. Eden 6. heaven, island
(imaginary) 7. Erewhon 8. paradise

9. fairyland, Shangri–La
10. millennium
utopian... 5. ideal 6. Edenic
8. Quixotic, romantic 9. visionary
10. chimerical, idealistic, millennial
utter... 3. say 4. emit, pass, tell, vent
5. issue, sheer, speak, total, voice
6. assert, entire, mumble, reveal
7. deliver, divulge, express, extreme,
publish, unusual 8. abnormal,
absolute, complete, disclose,
disperse, intonate 9. downright,
enunciate, out–and–out, pronounce
10. peremptory 11. unqualified
13. unconditional
utter (pert to)...
harshly.. 3. rap 4. bray
heedlessly.. 4. blat
in devotion.. 4. pray
in slow tone.. 5. drawl
musically.. 6. warble
publicly.. 4. tell 5. voice 7. enounce
softly.. 6. murmur 7. whisper
want.. 9. indigency 11. destitution

with effort.. 5. heave
with impulse.. 9. ejaculate
without voice.. 4. surd 7. spirate
utterance (pert to)...
dogmatic.. 6. dictum
gushing.. 8. effusion
rhythmic.. 7. cadence
voice.. 8. phonesis, speaking
9. phonation 12. articulation
wise.. 6. oracle
utterer of pithy remarks... 8. aphorist
utterly... 5. fully, stark 7. totally
8. entirely 10. absolutely, completely
17. straightforwardly
uttermost... 5. final 6. utmost
7. extreme
utu... 6. reward 12. compensation,
satisfaction
uva... 5. fruit, grape
uvate... 8. conserve (grape)
uvea... 4. iris
uxor... 4. wife
uxoricide... 10. wife murder
Uz (Bib)... 8. Job's home
Uzziel... 5. angel (Paradise Lost)

V

V... 5. notch 6. letter (22nd), symbol
14. five–dollar bill
vaagmer... 8. dealfish (mare of the
sea)
Vac (Hind)... 7. goddess (of speech)
vacant... 4. free, idle, void 5. blank,
empty, inane 6. barren, devoid
7. leisure, vacuous 8. unfilled
10. disengaged, untenanted
11. thoughtless 12. unencumbered
14. expressionless
vacate... 4. free, quit, void 5. annul,
empty, leave 6. depart 7. abandon
8. abdicate, abrogate, evacuate,
withdraw
vacation... 4. rest 5. leave 6. outing,
recess, repeal 7. nonterm, respite
8. furlough, justitum 10. recreation
12. intermission 14. leave of
absence
vacation place... 3. spa 4. lake, park
5. beach 6. forest, resort
9. mountains
vaccination... 11. inoculation
vaccine (pert to)...
discoverer.. 4. Salk 6. Jenner
protection for.. 5. virus 6. cowpox
term.. 5. lymph, serum, virus
vacillate... 4. sway 5. waver 6. dacker
(daiker), seesaw, teeter, totter
7. flutter, stagger 8. hesitate,
titubate 9. fluctuate, oscillate
13. procrastinate
vacillation... 5. doubt 8. wavering
9. faltering, hesitancy 10. fickleness,

indecision, titubation 11. oscillation,
uncertainty 12. irresolution
14. changeableness
15. procrastination
vacuate... 5. empty 8. evacuate
vacuous... 4. dull, void 5. blank,
empty 6. stupid 8. unfilled
9. senseless 11. empty–headed,
thoughtless 13. unintelligent
vacuum... 3. gap 4. void 9. emptiness
11. rarefaction
vagabond... 3. bum, vag 4. hobo
5. lorel, scamp, tramp 6. beggar,
picaro, rascal, rodney 7. vagrant,
wastrel 8. Bohemian, brodyaga,
wanderer 10. ne'er–do–well
vagary... 4. whim 5. caper, fancy,
jaunt, prank, trick 6. notion, ramble
7. caprice, whimsey (whimsy)
9. excursion, wandering
10. digression 13. manifestation
vagrant... 3. bum 4. hobo 5. rogue,
tramp 6. roving, truant 7. nomadic,
prowler, wayward 8. brodyaga,
vagabond, wanderer 9. desultory,
deviative, itinerant 10. capricious
vague... 3. dim 4. dark, hazy 5. loose,
misty 6. dreamy 7. obscure,
shadowy, unfixed 8. confused,
formless, nebulous, not clear
9. ambiguous, unsettled, wandering
10. indefinite, indistinct, intangible
13. indeterminate
vail... 3. tip 4. doff (a hat), dole
5. avail, bribe, yield 6. humble,

submit 7. descend 8. gratuity
10. beneficial 12. advantageous
vain... 4. idle 5. empty, proud
6. devoid, futile, otiose, snooty
7. foolish, trivial, useless 8. arrogant,
boastful, nugatory 9. conceited,
fruitless, worthless 10. unavailing,
unrewarded 11. empty–headed,
overweening, unimportant
12. vainglorious
vain boasting... 11. fanfaronade
vainglorious... 4. vain 7. heroics
8. boastful 9. gasconade
vair... 3. fur
vajra (Buddh)... 7. diamond, trident
(Indra's) 10. adamantine
11. thunderbolt
valance... 5. drape 6. border, pelmet,
ruffle 7. curtain, drapery, hanging
vale... 4. dale, dell, glen 5. earth,
glade, world 6. valley
valediction... 5. adieu 7. address
8. farewell 11. valedictory
valedictory... 7. address, oration
10. apopemptic 11. leave–taking,
valediction
Valentine (pert to)...
romance.. 5. Orson 8. love song
Saint.. 6. martyr (Rom) 7. holiday
8. feast day
State.. 7. Arizona (adm 2/14/1912)
sweetheart.. 11. one's beloved
valerian... 4. drug 5. plant 7. panacea
valet... 3. man 7. Crispin
9. attendant, cameriere, chamberer
10. manservant 11. body servant
14. valet de chambre
valetudinarian... 6. infirm, shut–in,
sickly, weakly 7. invalid
11. languishing
Valhalla (Valhall)... 8. Pantheon
(Bavaria) 10. hall of Odin (Norse
Myth)
valiant... 4. bold, fine 5. brave
6. heroic, strong, sturdy 7. doughty
8. intrepid, stalwart, vigorous,
virtuous 9. steadfast 10. chivalrous,
courageous 11. meritorious
12. stouthearted
valid... 4. good, just, true 5. legal,
sound 6. cogent, lawful, proved
7. binding, weighty 9. authentic,
effective 10. sufficient 11. efficacious
12. well–grounded
validate... 6. affirm, attest 7. confirm
8. legalize 12. substantiate
validity... 5. force 6. cogency
9. authority, soundness
14. substantiality
Valjean (pert to)...
discoverer.. 6. Javert
friend.. 6. Marius
hero of.. 13. Les Miserables (Victor
Hugo)
protégé.. 7. Cosette
valley... 4. dale, dell, dene, glen, vale,
wady 5. glade, gully 6. coulee,
dingle, ravine, trough 10. depression
valley (pert to)...
anatomy.. 9. vallecula
circular.. 6. rincon
deep.. 6. canyon

geology.. 5. atrio
India.. 5. dhoon
Jerusalem (near).. 6. Hinnom
7. Gehenna, Rephaim
moon.. 5. rille
open.. 6. canada
where David killed Goliath.. 4. Elah
(Bib)
valonia oak... 6. camata (fruit)
9. evergreen
valor... 5. merit, worth 6. virtue
7. bravery, courage, heroism,
prowess 8. boldness, chivalry
9. gallantry 11. distinction
12. fearlessness
valuable... 4. dear 5. asset 6. prized,
useful, worthy 8. precious
9. estimable, treasured
10. worthwhile
value... 3. par, use 4. rate 5. price,
prize, worth 6. assess, esteem,
parity, status 7. apprize (apprise),
cherish, compute, meaning, respect,
utility 8. appraise, estimate, evaluate
9. valuation 10. estimation,
excellence, importance
value (pert to)...
equal.. 6. parity
least possible.. 5. plack
nominal.. 3. par
reduction.. 12. depreciation
valueless... 4. baff 9. worthless
10. threepenny 14. good–for–nothing
valve... 3. tap 4. cock, door, gate
6. faucet, piston, spigot 7. petcock
vamoose... 2. go 4. blow, scat
5. leave, scram 6. beat it, decamp
7. skiddoo 9. skedaddle
vamp... 4. hose, sock 5. flirt, patch,
upper 6. recoct, repair, seduce
7. beguile, bewitch, concoct, touch
up 9. improvise, temptress, transform
vampire... 3. bat 5. fiend, ghost,
lamia, witch 6. Alukah 9. bewitcher,
sorceress, temptress 11. bloodsucker,
extortioner 12. extortionist
van... 4. lead, wing 5. front, wagon
6. shovel, summit, winnow 7. vehicle
9. forefront 10. baggage car
12. advance guard
vandal... 3. Hun 7. wrecker
9. destroyer, mutilator, plunderer
10. iconoclast
vandalize... 3. mar 5. wreck 6. deface
Vandyke... 5. beard, brown 6. artist,
collar 7. picture
vane... 4. cock 11. weathercock,
weathervane
vanish... 3. die 4. fade, flee, melt,
pass 6. perish 8. evanesce 9. cease
to be, disappear
vanity... 5. pride 6. egoism
7. conceit, egotism, falsity 8. futility
9. arrogance, emptiness, vainglory
10. hollowness 11. fatuousness,
self–conceit 12. boastfulness
13. dressing table
vanity case... 4. etui 6. make–up
7. compact 9. cosmetics
vanquish... 3. win 4. beat, best, rout
5. expel 6. defeat, subdue
7. conquer 8. confound, overcome,

suppress, surmount 9. overthrow
vantage... 4. gain 9. advantage
10. perquisite 11. opportunity,
superiority
vapid... 3. dry 4. dead, dull, flat
5. inane, stale 7. insipid, prosaic
8. lifeless 9. pointless, tasteless
10. spiritless, unanimated
11. indifferent 13. uninteresting
vapor... 3. air, fog, gas 4. fume, haze,
mist 5. brume, cloud, fancy, humor,
smoke, steam 6. breath, bubble
7. halitus 8. humidity, illusion,
phantasm 9. evaporate 10. exhalation
vaporous... 4. vain 5. foggy, misty
6. cloudy, steamy 7. gaseous
8. ethereal, fanciful, fleeting
13. unsubstantial
variable... 6. fickle, fitful, mobile
7. protean, unequal 8. shifting,
unstable, unsteady 10. capricious,
changeable, inconstant
variance... 3. out 7. dissent
9. deviation, disaccord
10. contention, difference
11. discrepancy 12. disagreement
varied... 5. mixed 6. daedal, motley
7. changed, dappled, diverse,
mottled, piebald, several, various
8. speckled 9. different
10. variegated 11. diversified
variegated... 5. pinto 6. daedal,
motley, varied 7. dappled, diverse,
mottled, painted 9. different
11. diversified, many–colored
variegation... 7. variety 9. diversity
10. multicolor
variety... 4. kind, mode, sort 5. class
6. change 7. species 9. diversity,
variation 10. assortment, difference
13. entertainment
variola... 6. cowpox 8. smallpox
various... 4. many 6. divers, sundry
7. diverse, several 8. manifold,
variable 9. different, many–sided,
uncertain 10. changeable, inconstant,
variegated 11. diversified
varnish... 4. spar 5. adorn, gloss,
japan, paint 7. distort, falsify, furbish,
lacquer, pretext 8. coat over
9. embellish
Varuna (pert to)...
art consorts.. 5. Jumna 6. Ganges
deity.. 6. cosmic (supreme)
god.. 3. sea
Vedic equiv.. 13. Avestan Ormazd
Vedic Relig.. 5. Aditi (fem deity)
vary... 5. alter, range, shift 6. change,
differ, modify 7. deviate, dissent,
diverge 8. disagree 9. alternate,
diversify, fluctuate, vacillate, variegate
13. differentiate
vas... 4. duct 6. pledge, surety, vessel
vascular (pert to)... 5. hemic (haemic)
6. vessel (blood, lymph) 7. tubular
9. vesicular 10. hot–blooded
vase... 3. jar, urn 4. bowl 5. ascus
6. vessel 8. ornament
10. cassolette, jardiniere
vase (pert to)...
covered.. 7. potiche
Etruscan.. 7. canopic

Greek.. 5. askos, diota 6. deinos
(dinos) 7. amphora
Roman.. 8. murrhine
vassal... 3. man 4. esne, serf
5. helot, liege, slave 6. varlet
7. bondman, servant, servile, subject
9. dependent, feudatory
11. subordinate, subservient
12. feudal tenant
vassalage... 5. valor 6. fealty
7. courage, enfeoff, prowess, slavery
8. dominion 9. servitude
10. subjection
vast... 4. huge 5. broad, great, large
6. cosmic, mighty, untold
7. immense, mammoth 8. colossal,
enormous, gigantic, spacious
9. cyclopean, extensive
11. far–reaching
vast (pert to)...
expanse.. 5. ocean 6. desert, empire,
region
numbers.. 6. myriad
period.. 3. eon, era 5. cycle
space.. 5. waste 9. boundless,
immensity, limitless
vastness... 6. extent 7. expanse
9. greatness, magnitude
vat... 3. bac, pit, tub, tun 4. cask,
gyle, kier, tank 6. barrel, vessel
7. caldron (cauldron), chessel,
cistern, measure, salt pit 8. chessart
Vatican (pert to)...
chapel.. 7. Sistine
church.. 8. St Peter's
city.. 10. Papal State (Rome)
palace of.. 4. Pope
statuary group.. 7. Laocoon
vaticination... 8. prophecy
10. prediction 11. prophesying
vault... 3. sky 4. arch, dome, leap,
over, tomb 5. bound, crypt, enbow,
groin 6. canopy (of heaven), coffer,
curvet, grotto, welkin 10. depository
11. testudinate
vaunt... 4. brag 5. boast
Vauxhall... 6. resort 13. London
Quarter (Thames) 14. Lambeth
Gardens
Veda (pert to)...
hymns.. 8. Sama–Veda
language.. 13. Vedic Sanskrit
literature.. 6. sacred (most anc)
oldest.. 7. Rig–Veda
prose, poetry (popular)..
11. Atharva–Veda
ritualistic.. 9. Yajur–Veda
Vedic (pert to)...
cosmic order.. 4. Rita
dialect.. 4. Pali
god.. 4. Agni 5. Dyaus 6. Aditya,
Varuna 7. Savitar
goddess.. 5. Aditi
hymn.. 6. mantra
language.. 4. Pali 8. Sanskrit
sky serpent.. 3. Ahi
text, treatise.. 6. shakha (sakha)
9. Upanishad
veer... 3. shy, yaw 4. slue, sway, turn
5. alter, shift, sidle 6. career,
change, swerve 7. deviate, digress
9. fluctuate

veery . . . 6. thrush 13. Wilson's thrush
vegetable . . . 3. pea, yam 4. bean,
beet, corn, leek, okra 5. onion
6. carrot, celery, lentil, potato, radish,
squash, tomato, turnip 7. cabbage,
lettuce, parsnip, rhubarb, shallot,
spinach (spinage) 8. broccoli,
eggplant, rutabaga, scallion
9. artichoke 11. cauliflower
vegetable (pert to) . . .
and meat dish . . 4. stew 6. ragout
caterpillar . . 5. aweto
dealer . . 8. huckster 11. greengrocer
12. costermonger
green . . 5. sabzi
herb . . 7. salsify
leafy, salad . . 5. chard 6. endive
7. lettuce, romaine, spinach
oil . . 7. soybean 8. macassar
poison . . 5. abrin
stew . . 11. ratatouille
sugar yielding . . 4. beet
vegetate . . . 4. grow, rest 5. exist
vegetation, goddess of . . . 5. Ceres
vehemence . . . 3. ire 4. fire, fury, rage,
zeal 5. anger, ardor 8. violence
9. eloquence 11. impetuosity
vehement . . . 3. hot 5. angry, eager,
fiery 6. ardent, fervid, heated
7. animose, furious, intense, violent,
zealous 8. forceful, vigorous
9. impetuous 10. passionate
vehicle . . . 3. ark, bus, cab, car, van,
wag 4. auto, cart, dray, hack, jeep,
limo (sl), semi, shay, sled, tank
5. buggy, coach, lorry, moped, sulky,
tonga, truck, wagon 6. go–cart,
hansom, hot rod, jalopy, landau,
sleigh, travoy, troika, wheels (sl)
7. caleche, caravan, chariot, clunker
(sl), kibitka, minibus, omnibus, phaeton,
scooter 8. brougham, carriage,
dragster 9. buckboard, dune buggy,
limousine 10. automobile,
conveyance, jinrikisha (jinriksha),
motorcycle 11. convertible
vehicle for oil colors . . . 6. megilp
(meguilp)
veil . . . 3. dim 4. caul, film, mask
5. cloak, cover, orale, shade, velum,
volet 6. fannel, masque, screen,
shroud, soften 7. conceal, curtain,
garment, pretext, secrecy 8. disguise
9. incognito 11. superimpose
veiled . . . 5. vague 6. masked, shaded,
velate 7. covered 8. shrouded
9. curtained
veiling . . . 5. tulle, voile 7. curtain
8. covering 10. obvelation
vein . . . 3. rib 4. dash, hilo, lode, mood,
tang, vena, wave 5. costa, shade,
smack, spice, tinge, touch 6. cavity,
streak 7. bonanza, channel, crevice,
fissure, mineral, stratum
vein (pert to) . . .
arrangement . . 9. neuration
inflammation . . 9. phlebitis
leaf . . 3. rib
ref to . . 5. veiny 6. veinal, venous
7. marbled 8. venulose
small . . 6. venule 7. veinlet
stone . . 6. gangue, matrix 9. lodestuff

without a . . 7. avenous
velar . . . 7. palatal, throaty 8. gutteral
veld, veldt . . . 6. meadow 8. bushveld
9. grassland, grassveld
velleity . . . 4. hope 6. desire
8. volition 9. faint hope 10. slight
wish
vellicate . . . 3. nip 5. pinch 6. tickle,
twitch 9. titillate
vellum . . . 9. parchment 10. manuscript
(on parchment)
velocity . . . 4. pace 5. speed
8. celerity, rapidity 9. quickness,
swiftness 10. speediness
velocity measure . . . 4. velo
velum . . . 6. palate (soft) 8. membrane
velvet (pert to) . . .
breast . . 9. merganser
cotton . . 9. velveteen
fabric . . 5. panne 6. velure
Japanese . . 6. birodo
knife . . 6. trevet
leaf . . 6. mallow 7. mullein
return . . 4. gain 6. profit
texture . . 4. soft 5. nappy 6. smooth
venal . . . 5. hired 6. venous 7. corrupt,
salable (saleable), vedible 8. hireling,
vendible 9. mercenary
11. corruptible
vend . . . 4. hawk, sell 5. trade
6. market, peddle 8. dispense
13. publish abroad
vender, vendor . . . 6. seller 7. alienor
vendetta . . . 4. feud 8. bad blood
vendue . . . 4. sale 7. auction
venerable . . . 3. old 4. aged, hoar,
sage 5. hoary, olden, title 6. august,
sacred 7. ancient, antique, classic,
elderly, revered 9. dignified
11. reverential
venerate . . . 4. love 5. adore 6. revere
7. worship
veneration . . . 3. awe 4. fear 5. dulia,
piety 6. esteem, latria 7. respect,
worship 8. devotion 9. adoration,
reverence
Venetian (pert to) . . .
barge . . 9. bucentaur
beach, resort . . 4. Lido
boat . . 4. topo (toppo) 7. gondola
bridge (famed) . . 6. Rialto
magistrate . . 4. doge 7. podesta
medal (New Year's) . . 5. osela (osella)
painter . . 6. Titian 7. Bellini (family),
Vecchio 10. Tintoretto
school of . . 8. painting
song . . 9. barcarole
window (Arch) . . 9. Palladian
Venezuela . . .
anc name . . 12. Little Venice
capital . . 7. Caracas
city . . 8. LaGuaira, Valencia
9. Maracaibo 6. Ciudad, Guyana
13. Cuidad Bolivar
copper center . . 4. Aroa
Falls (world's tallest) . . 5. Angel (found
1937)
hero, liberator . . 7. Bolivar
lake . . 9. Maracaibo, Tacarigua
Mt . . 5. Andes 6. Concha, Parima,
Sierra 9. Pacaraima
plains . . 6. llanos

river.. 6. Caroni 7. Orinoco
sea.. 9. Caribbean
snake.. 4. Iora
vengeance... 4. harm 7. revenge
  8. reprisal, requital 10. avengement,
  punishment 11. retaliation, retribution
Vengeance, goddess of (Gr)... 3. Ara,
  Ate 7. Nemesis
Vengeance, god of (Gr)... 6. Erinys
  7. Alastor
veni, vidi, vici... 19. I came, I saw, I
  conquered (Caesar)
venial... 7. trivial 9. excusable,
  tolerable 10. pardonable
  13. insignificant
Venice... see also *Venetian*
  beach.. 4. Lido
  bridge.. 6. Rialto
  canal.. 5. Grand 8. Merceria, San
  Marco
  capital of.. 7. Venetia (province)
  color.. 4. blue
  island.. 6. Rialto
  landmark.. 9. Campanile 12. Doges'
  Palaces 13. Bridge of Sighs
  of the North.. 9. Stockholm
  river.. 6. Brenta
venison... 8. pemmican (pemican)
vennel... 4. lane 5. alley, sewer
  6. gutter
venom... 4. gall 5. spite, virus
  6. malice, poison 9. animosity,
  malignity, virulence
venomous... 5. toxic 6. deadly
  7. baneful, noxious 8. spiteful,
  virulent 9. envenomed, malicious,
  malignant, poisonous, rancorous
vent... 3. say 4. exit, hole, slit
  5. eject, utter 6. egress, escape,
  outlet 7. air hole, fissure, opening,
  publish, release, ventage, volcano
  8. aperture, let loose
  10. escapement
venta... 3. inn
ventilate... 3. air, fan 5. utter
  6. aerate 7. discuss, publish, refresh
  9. oxygenate
ventose... 5. windy 9. flatulent
  12. cupping glass
ventral... 7. sternal 9. abdominal
venture... 3. hap, try 4. dare, risk,
  wage 5. brave, guess, stake 6. be
  bold, chance, danger, gamble, hazard
  7. attempt, presume 8. run a risk
  9. adventure, haphazard, speculate
  10. enterprise, investment
  11. speculation, undertaking
venturesome... 4. bold, rash 5. brave,
  risky 6. daring, heroic 8. fearless,
  reckless 9. dangerous, foolhardy,
  venturous 11. adventurous,
  temerarious 12. enterprising
venturous... 4. bold, rash 5. hardy,
  risky 6. daring 8. fearless
  9. dangerous, hazardous
  11. temerarious, venturesome
venue... 4. bout, site 5. match, onset
  6. thrust 7. arrival, assault
  9. encounter
Venus (pert to)...
  astronomy.. 6. planet
  church.. 11. Verticordia

goddess.. 7. Victrix 9. Aphrodite
goddess of (Rom).. 6. Beauty
son.. 5. Cupid
sweetheart.. 6. Adonis
zoology.. 7. mollusk
Venus statue (marble)...
  Florence.. 8. de Medici
  Louvre.. 7. of Arles 8. Genetrix
  Melos.. 6. de Milo
  Naples.. 7. of Capua
  Rome.. 8. Borghese 12. of the
  Capitol
veracity... 5. truth 7. honesty
  8. accuracy, trueness 11. correctness
  12. truthfulness
veranda, verandah... 4. pyal, stoa
  5. lanai, porch, stoep 6. loggia,
  piazza 7. gallery, portico
verb (Gram)... 5. rhema 6. action
verbal... 4. oral 5. wordy 7. literal,
  verbose 8. verbatim 9. talkative,
  vocabular
verbal noun... 6. gerund
verbatim... 6. orally 7. literal
  8. verbally 11. word for word
verbiage... 4. talk 7. chatter, diction,
  fustian, wording 8. claptrap
  9. prolixity, verbosity, wordiness
  10. redundancy
verbose... 5. wordy 6. prolix 7. diffuse
  9. redundant
verbosity... 10. redundancy
verboten... 5. taboo (tabu)
  9. forbidden 10. prohibited
verdant... 3. raw 5. color, green
  6. unripe 9. evergreen
  13. inexperienced 15. unsophisticated
verdelho... 4. wine (white)
verdict... 4. word 7. finding, opinion
  8. decision, judgment
  13. consideration
verdigris... 4. drug 5. green 6. aerugo
  7. deposit (on copper)
verecund... 6. modest 7. bashful
verge... 3. lip, rim, top 4. edge, tend,
  wand 5. brink, limit, marge, range,
  scope 6. border, emblem, extend,
  margin 7. incline 9. extremity
  10. contiguous 13. circumference
Vergil (pert to)...
  birthplace.. 6. Mantua (It)
  called.. 10. Roman Homer
  famed as.. 4. poet
  friend.. 8. Maecenas
  name (last).. 4. Maro
  poem.. 6. Aeneid 8. Eclogues,
  Georgics
  poetic form.. 4. epic 15. heroic
  hexameter (Aeneid)
verification... 4. oath, test
  8. averment 9. collation
  12. confirmation 13. ascertainment
verify... 4. back, test 5. check, prove
  6. affirm, attest, second 7. confirm,
  support 8. maintain 12. authenticate,
  substantiate
verily... 3. yea 4. amen 5. truly
  6. certes, indeed, in fact, really
  9. certainly 10. positively
  11. confidently
verisimilitude... 5. truth 10. likelihood
  11. probability, verisimilar

veritable... 4. real, true 6. actual,
gospel, honest 7. genuine
9. authentic
verity... 4. fact 5. truth 7. honesty,
reality 8. veracity
vermilion... 3. dye, red 7. pigment,
vermeil 8. cinnabar
vermin... 4. lice, mice, rats 5. filth,
fleas, flies, moths, worms
7. bedbugs, beetles, insects, spiders,
weasels, weevils 8. riffraff, termites
9. parasites 10. centipedes,
mosquitoes 11. cockroaches
Vermont...
capital.. 10. Montpelier
city.. 5. Barre 7. Rutland
10. Burlington 11. Brattleboro
first town.. 10. Fort Dummer
hero.. 10. Ethan Allen
historic group.. 17. Green Mountain
Boys
lake.. 9. Champlain
mountain.. 5. Green 7. Taconic
9. Mansfield
museum.. 9. Shelburne
10. Bennington
product.. 6. marble 10. maple sugar
river.. 5. Otter 11. Connecticut
State admission.. 10. Fourteenth
State motto.. 15. Freedom and Unity
State nickname.. 13. Green Mountain
vernacular... 5. lingo, local
6. common, jargon, native, patois,
vulgar 7. dialect 10. colloquial,
indigenous
vernal... 4. mild, warm 5. fresh
10. springlike
verse... 4. epic, poem, rime 5. canto,
lyric, rhyme, stave, stich 6. poetry,
rondel, sonnet, stanza 7. measure,
strophe, triolet, trochee 8. limerick
verse (pert to)...
art.. 10. orthometry
book of.. 5. poesy 9. anthology
devotion.. 8. antiphon
form.. 7. virelay 10. villanelle
Homeric.. 4. epic 6. epopee
Irish.. 4. rann
pause.. 6. cesura 9. diaeresis
(dieresis)
romantic.. 7. sestina
satiric.. 6. iambic
scripture.. 4. text
stress.. 5. ictus
term.. 5. ictic, meter 6. accent,
poetic, rhythm, scheme 7. cadence
8. eye rhyme, scansion
10. synaeresis (syneresis)
12. alliteration
trivial.. 6. jingle 8. doggerel, limerick
verse (pert to feet)...
eight.. 9. octameter
four.. 10. tetrameter
one.. 9. monometer
three.. 7. tripody
two.. 7. dimeter
versed... 5. adept 7. erudite, learned,
skilled 8. familiar 9. practiced
10. acquainted, conversant, proficient
versification... 7. prosody
10. orthometry
versifier... 4. bard, muse, poet

5. rimer 6. rhymer 7. poetess
8. ballader, eulogist 9. poetaster,
rhymester
version... 7. edition 9. rendition
10. paraphrase 11. translation
version, Bible... 5. Douay, Greek,
Latin 6. Coptic, Geneva, Gothic, Italic
(Itala) 7. Aramaic, Bishops', Luther's,
Revised, Targums, Vulgate
8. Cranmer's, Georgian, Matthew's,
Peshitta, Slavonic 9. Apocrypha, King
James, Serampore 10. Pentateuch,
Septuagint 11. Alexandrian
vers libra... 9. free verse
verso (opp of recto)... 7. reverse
9. back cover 12. left–hand side
versus... 3. con 7. against 8. contrast,
opposite 11. alternative
vertebra, vertebrae... 4. axis
8. backbone 12. spinal column
vertebrate... 6. linked 8. well–knit
9. backboned
vertebrates (pert to)...
division.. 6. somite 10. Vertebrata
feathered.. 5. birds
group.. 4. Aves 7. Amniota
vertex... 3. top 4. apex 6. summit
11. culmination
vertical... 5. apeak, erect, plumb,
sheer 6. height 7. upright
10. upstanding 13. perpendicular
vertical panel... 5. stile
verticil... 5. whorl 6. circle
vertigo... 5. dinus 6. megrim
9. confusion, dizziness, giddiness
11. disturbance 12. bewilderment
verve... 3. pep 4. dash, élan 5. vigor
6. energy, fervor, spirit 8. vivacity
9. animation 10. liveliness
vervet... 6. monkey
very... 3. eri (comb form) 4. much,
real, très, true 5. truly, utter
6. actual, in fact, really 7. exactly,
genuine 8. absolute, especial,
peculiar, truthful 9. extremely,
precisely, veracious, veritable
10. legitimate 11. exceedingly
Very light... 5. flare 6. signal (Very
system)
vesica... 7. bladder
vesicate... 7. blister
vesicle... 3. sac 4. cyst 5. bulla
6. bubble, cavity, vessel 7. bladder,
blemish, blister
Vespa... 4. wasp 6. hornet
vespers... 6. prayer 7. service
8. ceremony, evensong
vessel... 3. ark, can, cup, jar, jug,
mug, pod, pot, tub, urn, vas, vat
4. boat, bowl, dhow, drum, duct,
ewer, junk, olla, olpe, proa, said,
seed, ship, tank, vase, yawl 5. bocal,
craft, crock, cupel, glass, gourd,
jorum, ketch, stein 6. aftaba, aludel,
ampule, barrel, bottle, bucket, caster,
cutter, dipper, firkin, goblet, kettle,
picard, retort, trader, trough
7. catboat, cistern, coracle, cruiser,
frigate, pitcher, psykter, steamer,
tankard, utensil 8. aiguière, ciborium,
decanter, demijohn, hogshead,
schooner 9. alcarraza, catamaran,

privateer, washbasin 10. receptacle
11. earthenware
vessel (pert to)...
anc.. 3. nef 5. yanky 6. bireme
7. caravel, galleon, trireme
Arab.. 4. dhow
baptismal.. 4. font 7. piscina
chemist.. 4. etna 6. aludel, beaker,
retort
Columbus.. 7. caravel
cooking.. 9. autoclave
druggist.. 4. vial 5. phial 8. gallipot
Dutch.. 4. koff 5. yanky 6. galiot
(galliot)
Eccl.. 3. ama, pyx 4. wine 5. amula
7. stamnos
Hebrides.. 7. birlinn (birling)
heraldry.. 7. lymphad
India.. 6. shibar
Mediterranean.. 5. xebec 6. settee
(setee), tartan 7. polacre
merchant.. 6. argosy 7. baggala
Nile houseboat.. 8. dahabeah
oil—burning.. 7. cresset
part.. 4. deck, keel, prow, skeg
5. brail 8. steerage
sacred.. 3. ama
Scottish.. 6. pourie
Thames (fishing).. 6. bawley
Venice.. 9. bucentaur
war.. 3. sub 5. Maine 6. corvet
7. cruiser, felucca, flattop,
Monitor 9. submarine
11. dreadnaught 12. Old Ironsides
vessel (sailing)... 3. hoy 4. bark, brig,
koff, proa, saic, ship, yawl 5. ketch,
sloop, smack, xebec
vest... 4. robe 5. endow, gilet
6. invest, jerkin, linder, weskit
7. furnish, garment 9. waistcoat
vesta... 5. match
Vesta (Rom)... 7. goddess (Hearth)
8. asteroid
vestal... 4. pure 6. chaste 8. virginal
vestige... 4. mark, sign 5. relic, shred,
tinge, trace, track 7. remains
8. footstep 9. vestigium
vestiture... 4. garb 5. dress
8. clothing, covering
vestment... 3. alb 4. cope, garb,
gown, hood, robe 5. amice, cotta,
dress, ephod, miter, orale, tunic
6. saccos, tippet 7. cassock,
garment, maniple 8. chasuble,
crucifix, dalmatic, scapular, surplice
10. habiliment, omophorion
vestry... 4. room 5. group (Eccl)
8. sacristy, wardrobe 10. repository
Vesuvius (pert to)...
Great Eruption (79 AD).. 6. buried
city.. 7. Pompeii 11. Herculaneum
mountain.. 7. volcanic
site.. 6. Naples
veteran... 4. long 7. old hand, soldier
8. seasoned 9. practiced
11. experienced
veterinarian... 7. farrier, surgeon
veto... 6. forbid 8. negative, prohibit
10. disapprove 12. interdiction
vex... 3. irk 4. cark, fret, fuss, gall,
miff, rile, roil 5. anger, annoy, harry,
spite, tease, worry 6. bother, harass,

nettle, plague, pother, ruffle
7. agitate, chagrin, despite, dispute,
disturb, pervert, provoke, torment
8. disquiet, irritate 9. displease
vexation... 7. anxiety, chagrin, fatigue,
trouble 8. disquiet, irritate
9. annoyance, weariness
10. affliction, foreboding, harassment,
irritation 11. disturbance
13. mortification
vexatious... 5. pesky 6. thorny
7. irksome 8. annoying 9. disturbed,
pestilent, provoking, worrisome
10. afflictive 11. troublesome
vexillum... 3. web 4. flag 5. cross
6. banner, colors, ensign 7. labarum,
pennant 8. standard 10. Jolly Roger
via... 2. by 3. way 4. away, road
6. begone 7. by way of, passage,
through
viaduct... 4. span 6. bridge 7. trestle
vial... 5. cruet, phial 6. bottle, caster,
castor, vessel 7. ampoule (ampul),
ampulla 9. container
viameter... 7. measure 8. odometer
12. perambulator
viander... 4. host 6. vendor
viands... 4. cate, fare, food 7. viandry
8. victuals 10. provisions
viaticum... 5. money 8. supplies
9. allowance, last rites 10. provisions
14. Extreme Unction
viator... 8. traveler, wayfarer
vibrant... 5. alive 7. pulsing, travale
8. resonant, sonorous, vigorous
9. energetic, thrilling, vibrating
10. resounding
vibrate... 4. beat, rock, tirl, whir
5. pulse, quake, swing, throb, waver
6. dindle, quaver, quiver, shimmy,
shiver, thrill 7. agitate, resound,
tremble 8. brandish, flichter, resonate
9. fluctuate, oscillate
vibration... 6. quiver, thrill, tremor
7. flutter, pulsing 9. resonance,
throbbing 11. oscillation
vibration, music... 5. trill 7. sonance,
tremolo, vibrato
vibration measure... 9. tonometer
vicar... 5. proxy 6. curate, deputy,
priest 9. churchman, clergyman
10. substitute, vicegerent
vice... 3. sin 4. evil 5. crime, fault,
taint 6. defect 7. blemish, stopper
8. iniquity 9. depravity, in place of,
instead of 10. corruption, substitute,
succeeding, wickedness, wrongdoing
11. viciousness
viceroy... 5. nabob 6. satrap
8. governor 9. butterfly
vicinity... 6. region 9. proximity
11. propinquity 12. neighborhood
vicious... 3. bad, ill 4. evil, foul, lewd,
mean, ugly, vile 6. faulty, impure,
wicked 7. corrupt, immoral, noxious
8. depraved, spiteful 9. dangerous,
malicious, nefarious, obstinate,
perverted 10. iniquitous, profligate
11. ill—tempered
vicissitude... 6. change 8. mutation,
shifting 9. variation 10. revolution
11. fluctuation

victim... 4. dupe, gull, prey 5. cully
6. sucker 7. patient 8. sufferer
victor... 6. captor, master, winner
8. unbeaten 9. conqueror
10. vanquisher
victor fish... 3. aku 6. bonito
Victoria, victoria... 4. plum 5. cross
(Maltese) 7. goddess 8. asteroid,
carriage 10. automobile
Victorian... 3. era 4. prim 6. stuffy
7. antique, archaic, prudish
10. antiquated 11. puritanical,
strait—laced
victorious... 7. winning 8. unbeaten
9. defeating 10. conquering,
triumphant
victory... 7. mastery, success, triumph
8. conquest 9. supremacy
victory (pert to)...
 at too great cost.. 7. Pyrrhic
 Day.. 9. Armistice
 goddess.. 4. Nike
 hymn.. 9. epinicion (epinikion)
 memorial.. 6. trophy
 symbol.. 4. palm
Victrola dog (symbol)... 6. Nipper
victuals... 4. food, grub 6. viands
8. supplies 11. nourishment
videlicet... 3. viz 5. to wit 6. namely
8. scilicet
vie... 3. bet 4. cope, life 5. bandy,
stake, wager 6. endure, oppose,
strive 7. compare, compete, contend,
contest, emulate 8. struggle
9. challenge
Vienna...
 artist.. 4. Lieb, Pilz 6. Makart, Zauner
 7. Kisling
 boulevard (famed).. 11. Ringstrasse
 capital of.. 7. Austria
 Ger name.. 4. Wien
 musician.. 5. Gluck, Haydn 6. Czerny,
 Mozart 7. Strauss 8. Schubert,
 Schumann 9. Beethoven
 palace.. 10. Schönbrunn
 park.. 6. Prater
 river.. 6. Danube
Vietnam road... 14. Ho Chi Minh Trail
view... 3. aim, end, eye, ken, see
4. look, scan 5. scene, vista
6. aperçu, aspect, object, regard,
survey 7. examine, glimpse, opinion,
outlook, picture 8. attitude,
judgment, panorama, prospect
9. intention 10. appearance,
perception, scrutinize
11. contemplate, expectation
13. contemplation
vigil... 3. eve 4. wake 5. guard,
watch 6. patrol 8. watchman
9. keep guard 11. wakefulness
13. sleeplessness
vigilant... 4. agog, wary 5. alert,
awake, aware 6. awatch 7. wakeful
8. cautious, open—eyed, watchful
9. attentive, observant, sleepless
11. circumspect
vigilantes... 5. posse 9. committee
(vigilance)
vigor, vigour... 3. pep, vim, vir
4. life, zeal 5. force, power, verve
6. energy, health 7. potency,

stamina, sthenia 8. strength, validity,
virility 9. animation, fraîcheur,
vehemence 10. liveliness
vigorous... 4. able, hale, racy, spry
5. eager, frank, fresh, hardy, lusty,
tough 6. potent, robust, strong
7. healthy, zealous 8. athletic,
forceful, spirited, vehement
9. effective, energetic, sprightly,
strenuous 11. efficacious, flourishing
Viking... 4. Eric 5. rover 6. pirate
8. Norseman, Northman, sea rover
9. plunderer 12. Scandinavian
vile... 3. bad 4. base, evil, foul, mean
5. cheap, lowly, nasty 6. coarse,
filthy, impure, odious, sinful, sordid,
wicked 7. corrupt, debased, ignoble,
obscene, unclean, vicious
8. depraved, infamous 9. degrading,
loathsome, nefarious, repulsive
10. abominable, disgusting
12. contaminated
vilify... 5. abuse, curse, libel
6. debase, defame, malign, revile
7. asperse, cheapen, degrade,
slander, traduce 8. belittle, disgrace,
reproach, vilipend 9. blaspheme,
disparage 10. calumniate, stigmatize
vilipend... 6. slight 7. despise
8. belittle 9. disparage
10. depreciate, slanderous
12. calumniatory
villa... 5. aldea, dacha 9. residence,
villaette 10. villanette
village... 3. mir 4. dorp, stad 5. thorp
(thorpe), tract 6. aldeia, castle,
hamlet, pueblo
Village Blacksmith author...
10. Longfellow
villain... 4. boor, lout, ogre, serf
5. demon, heavy, knave, rogue
6. rascal 7. caitiff 9. miscreant,
scoundrel
villainous... 3. bad, low 4. base, evil,
mean, vile 6. vulgar, wicked
7. boorish, knavish 8. criminal,
rascally, terrible, wretched
9. dastardly 10. detestable, iniquitous
11. scoundrelly 13. objectionable
villous... 5. nappy 6. napped, shaggy
vim... 3. pep, zip 4. dash, élan, fire,
gimp, kick 5. drive, force, verve,
vigor 6. energy, esprit, spirit
8. strength
vinaigre... 7. vinegar
vindicate... 4. free 5. claim, clear
6. acquit, assert, avenge, defend,
excuse, uphold 7. absolve, justify,
support, sustain 8. maintain
9. exculpate, exonerate
vindication... 7. defense
vindictive... 7. hostile 8. punitive,
spiteful, vengeful 10. revengeful
11. retaliatory, retributive
vine... 3. hop, ivy 4. bine, odal
5. betel, grape, liana (liane), Vitis
7. cupseed, trailer 8. clematis,
wisteria 9. grapevine 10. chilicothe
11. honeysuckle 12. morning glory
vinegar... 4. acid, sour 6. acetum,
alegar 8. vinaigre
vinegar (pert to)...

acid.. 6. acetic
comb form.. 5. aceto
dregs.. 6. mother
eel.. 4. worm
ester.. 7. acetate
fly.. 5. fruit
preserve in.. 6. pickle 8. marinate
salt.. 7. acetate
spice.. 8. tarragon
tree.. 13. staghorn sumac
Vinegar Joe (Army)... 9. Stillwell (Gen)
vinegarroon... 8. scorpion, vinagron
vinegary... 4. sour, tart 7. acetose,
  crabbed, pungent 9. unamiable
vineyard... 3. cru 7. Priapus (god of)
  10. plantation
vinology (science of)... 5. vines
  10. grapevines
vinous... 4. winy 5. color
vintner... 8. merchant (wine)
viol... 3. gue 4. rope 5. rebec, ruana
  6. vielle 7. quinton, sarinda 9. organ
  stop
viola... 5. gamba 7. sarangi 9. organ
  stop 11. tenor violin
violate... 5. abuse, break, wrong
  6. defile, invade, ravage, ravish
  7. debauch, outrage, pollute, profane
  8. deflower, dishonor, mistreat
  9. desecrate 10. transgress
violation... 7. offense 10. infraction
  11. anacoluthon, disturbance,
  profanation 12. infringement,
  interruption 13. nonobservance,
  transgression
violence... 5. anger, force 6. unjust
  7. assault, cruelty, outrage
  8. coercion 9. vehemence
  10. roughhouse 11. profanation
  12. infringement
violent... 4. loud 5. acute, great,
  rabid, sharp, vivid 6. fierce, savage,
  stormy 7. extreme, furious, intense
  8. coercive, vehement 9. turbulent
  10. passionate 11. tempestuous
violent (pert to)...
Norse folklore.. 8. warriors
  9. beserkers
outbreak.. 4. riot 6. tumult, uproar
  8. eruption
pain.. 4. pang 5. throe 6. fierce
violet (pert to)...
color.. 5. mauve 6. purple
  7. blue–red
dye.. 6. archil (orchil)
emblem of.. 7. gravity 8. chastity
genus.. 9. Violaceae
perfume.. 5. irone 6. ionone
  9. orrisroot
tip.. 9. butterfly
violin (pert to)...
ancient.. 5. rebab, rebec, rocta
  12. viola de gamba
bar.. 4. fret
bass.. 11. violoncello
bow.. 5. arcus
city (famed).. 7. Cremona (It)
make.. 5. Amati 7. Cremona
  10. Guarnerius 12. Stradivarius
maker.. 5. Amati 9. Guarnieri
  10. Stradivari
reference to.. 4. pins 5. belly

Scot.. 6. fiddle
small.. 3. kit
tenor.. 4. alto
violinist (famed)... 5. Elman, Stern
  7. Heifitz, Menuhin
violinist, first... 13. concertmaster
viper... 3. asp 5. adder, Echis, snake
  6. kupper 7. serpent 8. cerastes,
  ophidian 9. scoundrel
  10. bushmaster
vir... 5. vigor
virage... 5. scold, shrew, vixen, woman
  7. beldame, rullion 9. termagant
Virgil... see Vergil
virgin... 3. new 4. maid, pure
  6. chaste, maiden, vestal 8. spinster
  9. undefiled, unsullied, untouched
  13. unadulterated
virginal... 3. new 5. piano (spinet)
  6. chaste, ritual 7. natural
  8. maidenly 9. unmarried, unsullied
Virginia...
bay.. 10. Chesapeake
capital.. 8. Richmond
city.. 7. Norfolk, Roanoke
  9. Arlington, Lexington, Lynchburg
  11. Newport News 12. Hampton
  Roads
famed sites.. 8. Mt Vernon
  10. Monticello 12. Williamsburg
  13. Stratford Hall
first white child born.. 12. Virginia
  Dare
historic town.. 8. Yorktown
  9. Jamestown 10. Appomattox
Indian sachem.. 8. Powhatan
mountain.. 9. Blue Ridge
  11. Alleghenies
resort.. 13. Virginia Beach
river.. 4. York 5. James 7. Potomac,
  Rapidan 12. Rappahannock
settlement (first).. 9. Jamestown
State admission.. 5. Tenth
State motto.. 17. Sic Semper
  Tyrannis 19. Thus Always to Tyrants
State nickname.. 11. Old Dominion
Virgin Islands, British...
capital.. 8. Road Town
crop.. 9. sugar cane
group.. 7. Leeward
number islands.. 6. thirty
Virgin Islands, United States...
capital.. 8. St Thomas 15. Charlotte
  Amalia (former)
discoverer.. 8. Columbus (1493)
largest.. 6. St John 7. St Croix 8. St
  Thomas
virginity... 8. celibacy, chastity
  10. maidenhood 12. spinsterhood
Virgin Mary... 5. Pietà (image) 7. Our
  Lady 11. Maris Stella, Mother of
  God 12. Star of the Sea 13. Mother
  of Jesus
viridity... 5. youth 7. verdure
  9. freshness, greenness 10. grass
  color
virile... 4. male 5. manly 8. forceful,
  powerful, vigorous 9. masculine,
  masterful
virose... 5. fetid 8. virulent
  9. poisonous 10. malodorous
virtu... 5. curio 7. antique 8. artistry

12. love of curios 15. artistic quality, study of fine arts
virtual... 9. essential, potential 10. energizing 12. constructive
virtually... 7. morally 11. potentially, practically
virtue... 5. valor, value, worth 6. energy, purity 7. potency, probity 8. chastity, efficacy, goodness, morality 9. godliness, innocence, integrity, rectitude 11. uprightness 13. righteousness
virtue, logic... 8. aretaics
virtues, cardinal... 4. hope 5. faith 7. charity
virtuoso... 6. expert 7. scholar 11. connoisseur, philosopher
virtuous... 4. good, pure 5. brave, godly, moral 6. chaste, honest, potent 7. upright, valiant 8. valorous 9. righteous 11. efficacious
virulent... 5. acrid, rabid 6. deadly, potent 7. noxious 8. venomous 9. animosity, malignant, poisonous 10. infectious, resentment 11. acrimonious
visa, visé... 7. endorse 9. signature 11. certificate, endorsement (passport)
visage... 4. face, look 5. image 11. countenance 14. visible surface
vis-à-vis... 4. seat, sofa 8. carriage, opposite 9. encounter 10. face to face
viscera... 4. guts 6. bowels, vitals 7. insides 8. entrails 10. intestines 11. inside parts
visceral... 7. enteric 10. intestinal, splanchnic
viscid... 4. ropy, waxy 5. slimy 6. sticky 7. viscous 8. adhering, adhesive 9. glutinous
viscosity... 8. tenacity 10. stickiness
viscous... 4. ropy, sizy 5. gluey, gummy, tarry 6. mucous, sticky, viscid 7. stringy 9. glutinous 10. stickiness
vise... 3. jaw 4. tool 5. clamp, winch 6. device 7. squeeze
Vishnu (pert to)...
consort.. 3. Sri 7. Lakshim
deity (supreme).. 6. bhakti 9. preserver
eighth.. 7. Krishna
epithet.. 8. bhagavat
seventh.. 4. Rama
tenth, last incarnation.. 5. Kalki
vehicle.. 6. Garuda
visible... 4. open, seen 5. clear 6. extant, in view 7. evident, in sight, obvious 8. apparent, manifest 10. noticeable 11. discernible, perceivable, perceptible
Visigoth king... 6. Alaric
vision... 3. eye 5. dream, fancy, image, sight 6. glance, mirage 7. glimpse, imagine, specter 8. eyesight 10. apparition
vision (pert to)...
comb form.. 4. opto
daylight.. 8. photopia
defect.. 6. anopia, myopia

double.. 8. diplopia
illusory.. 5. image
lacking.. 8. purblind
measure.. 9. optometer
night.. 8. scotopia
science of.. 9. optometry
term.. 5. optic 6. ocular 9. binocular, monocular
visionary... 4. aery, airy, seer, wild 5. ideal 6. dreamy, unreal 7. dreamer, Laputan, utopian 8. delusive, idealist, quixotic, romantic 9. fantastic, imaginary 10. chimerical, rhapsodist 11. imaginative, impractical
visit... 3. see, vis 4. call, chat, go to, slum 5. haunt 6. attend, call on 10. inspection, visitation 12. conversation
visitor... 5. guest 6. caller 7. company 8. visitant
visne... 5. venue 8. neighbor, vicinage
vison... 4. mink
visor, vizor... 4. mask 6. vizard 8. disguise 10. camouflage
vista... 4. view 5. scene, visto 7. outlook 8. corridor, panorama, prospect
visual... 5. optic 6. ocular 11. perceptible
visualize... 7. imagine, picture 8. envisage, envision 9. objectify
vital... 4. live 5. basic 6. living, mortal, viable 7. animate, exigent, needful, organic 8. inherent, vigorous 9. essential, important, necessary, requisite 10. imperative 11. fundamental 13. indispensable
vital (pert to)...
air.. 6. oxygen
force.. 6. energy, spirit 7. neurism 8. bathmism, phrenism 9. theosophy
impulse.. 6. libido 8. instinct
organs.. 6. vitals 7. viscera
records.. 10. demography, statistics
strength.. 7. stamina
vitality... 3. sap, vim 4. life 5. vigor 8. strength 9. animation, lustiness 10. liveliness
vitals... 7. insides, viscera 9. internals 11. vital organs (heart, liver, lungs, brain)
vitamin... 6. biotin, niacin 7. carotin, thiamin 10. riboflavin 11. lactoflavin 12. ascorbic acid
vitellus... 4. yolk 7. egg yolk
vitiate... 5. spoil, taint 6. debase, impair, poison, weaken 7. corrupt, deprave, pervert, pollute 10. adulterate, demoralize, invalidate 11. contaminate
vitiated... 5. pical 6. wicked 7. corrupt, debased, spoiled 9. defective 11. ineffective, invalidated
vitiosity... 4. vice 6. defect 9. depravity 11. viciousness
vitium... 5. fault 6. defect
vitric... 9. glasslike
vitrics... 9. glassware, glasswork
vitrify... 5. glaze 13. make into glass
vitriolic... 4. acid 5. sharp 6. biting,

bitter 7. caustic 8. scathing, virulent
11. acrimonious

vituperate . . . 5. abuse, curse, scold
6. berate, revile 7. censure

vituperative . . . 7. abusive, railing
8. reviling, scolding 10. scurrilous
11. maledictory, opprobrious

vivacious . . . 3. gay 4. airy 5. merry
6. active, lively 8. animated,
gamesome, spirited, sportive
9. energetic 12. lighthearted

vivacity . . . 4. dash, élan, fire, keen,
zeal, zest 5. ardor, verve, vigor
6. energy, gaiety (gayety)
9. animation 10. liveliness

Viverra . . . 6. civets 9. civet cats

vivers . . . 4. food 8. victuals

vix . . . 8. scarcely

vixen . . . 3. cat, fox 5. scold, shrew,
witch 6. virago 9. termagant
12. female animal

viz . . . 5. to wit 6. namely 9. videlicet

vizard . . . 4. mask 5. guise, visor
8. disguise

vlei (vley) . . . 5. creek, marsh, swamp

voar . . . 6. spring (of the year)

vocabulary . . . 5. words 6. jargon
7. diction, lexicon 8. glossary,
wordbook 10. dictionary

vocabulist . . . 6. writer
13. lexicographer

vocal (pert to) . . .
chink . . 7. glottis
composition . . 4. aria, song 5. motet
7. cantata
expression . . 4. oral 9. utterance
flourish . . 7. roulade
handicap . . 4. lisp 7. stutter
sound . . 5. vowel 6. sonant
statue . . 6. Memnon

vocalist . . . 4. alto 5. basso, tenor
6. artist, cantor, singer 7. caroler,
crooner, soprano, yodeler 8. songster
10. coloratura, prima donna,
songstress

vocalization . . . 11. melismatics

vocalize . . . 4. sing 5. sound, utter
6. phrase

vocation . . . 4. call 5. trade 6. career
7. calling 8. business
10. employment, occupation,
profession

vociferous . . . 4. loud 5. noisy
7. blatant 8. brawling, strident
9. clamorous, turbulent
11. loudmouthed 12. obstreperous

vogue . . . 3. ton 4. mode 5. style
6. custom 7. fashion 8. practice
10. popularity

voice . . . 3. say, vox 4. alto, bass,
tone, vote, wish 5. rumor, tenor,
utter 7. divulge, opinion, soprano
8. announce, falsetto 9. utterance
10. expression 12. articulation

voice (pert to) . . .
box . . 6. larynx
Greek . . 9. phthongos
handicap . . 4. lisp 7. stammer, stutter
loss of . . 7. anaudia, aphonia
loud . . 12. megalophonic
phonetics . . 9. affricate

quality . . 6. timbre (timber)
quiet . . 5. sotto
raise . . 6. insist 10. supplicate
raise against . . 5. decry 6. accuse,
object
singing, above natural . . 8. falsetto
singing, natural . . 7. dipetto
stress . . 5. arsis
with one . . 9. unanimous
12. concurrently

voiced . . . 6. sonant, spoken 7. sounded
9. phthongal 11. articulated

voiceless . . . 4. dumb, mute, surd
6. atonic, silent 7. spirate 9. not
voiced 12. not expressed

void . . . 4. idle, lack, null, want
5. abyss, annul, egest, empty
6. devoid, hollow, vacant, vacuum
7. abolish, nothing, nullify, useless
8. evacuate 9. destitute, emptiness
10. unoccupied 11. ineffectual,
nonexistent

void of . . .
interest . . 6. jejune 7. insipid
sense . . 5. inane, silly
space . . 5. blank 6. vacuum

volaille . . . 4. fowl 7. poultry

volant . . . 5. agile, light, quick 6. flying,
nimble 7. current 8. volatile, volitant

volatile . . . 4. airy 5. light 6. fickle,
flying, lively, volant 7. alcohol,
ammonia, buoyant, flighty, gaseous
8. fleeting, vaporous 9. ephemeral,
mercurial 10. capricious, changeable,
transitory 11. vaporizable
12. lighthearted

volatile (pert to) . . .
alkali . . 7. ammonia
flux . . 5. smear
liquid . . 5. ether 7. alcohol
oil . . 7. essence, perfume

volcanic (pert to) . . .
glass . . 6. pumice 7. perlite
8. obsidian
matter . . 2. aa 4. lava, slag, tufa
5. trass 6. pumice 8. lapillus,
pahoehoe
mud . . 5. salse
orifice of gas issue . . 8. fumarole
ref to . . 9. excitable, explosive
11. hot–tempered
rock . . 5. trass 6. dacite 8. tephrite
saucer . . 6. crater

volcano (pert to) . . .
Africa . . 11. Kilimanjaro
Alaska . . 6. Katmai 8. Wrangell
Chile . . 6. Lascar
Ecuador . . 8. Cotopaxi
goddess . . 4. Pele (Hawaii)
Guatemala . . 5. Fuego 7. Atitlan
Hawaii . . 8. Mauna Loa
Iceland . . 5. Askja, Hekla
Italy . . 4. Etna 8. Vesuvius
9. Stromboli
Japan . . 4. Fuji 9. Asamayama
Java . . 4. Gede
Mexico . . 12. Popocatepetl
Philippines . . 3. Apo (Mindanao)
Sumatra . . 6. Merapi
United States (mainland) . . 6. Lassen,
Shasta 7. Rainier
West Indies . . 5. Pelée

vole . . . 6. craber, rodent 8. water rat
10. field mouse 11. meadow mouse
volée . . . 6. flight, volley
volery (volary) . . . 6. aviary 8. bird
cage
volition . . . 4. will 6. choice
11. voluntarily 13. determination
volley . . . 4. fire 5. blast, salvo, shots
Voltaire . . . 11. philosopher (of Ferney)
voluble . . . 4. glib 6. fluent 8. rotating,
unstable 9. garrulous, revolving,
talkative 10. loquacious
volume . . . 4. book, bulk, mass, size,
tome 6. amount 7. compass
8. capacity, fullness (fulness)
9. aggregate, Decameron
10. crassitude 14. fullness of tone
voluntary . . . 4. free 7. prelude, willing
8. elective, intended, purposed
9. volunteer, willingly 10. deliberate,
volitional 11. intentional, spontaneous
13. not accidental
volunteer . . . 5. offer 6. enlist 7. proffer
9. be willing, voluntary 11. be of
service
Volunteer State . . . 9. Tennessee
volute . . . 4. turn 5. whorl 6. cilery
(cillery) 8. rolled up 10. scroll–like
voodoo . . . 5. magic, obeah 6. fetish
8. sorcerer
voracious . . . 6. greedy, hungry
8. edacious, esurient, ravening,
ravenous 9. devouring, rapacious
10. gluttonous, immoderate,
unsatiable
voracity . . . 5. greed 7. edacity
8. gluttony, rapacity 9. esurience
vorago . . . 4. gulf 5. abyss
vortex . . . 4. apex, eddy 5. whirl
7. tornado 8. flatworm 9. whirlpool,
whirlwind 10. waterspout
votary . . . 6. zealot 7. devotee
8. adherent, aesthete, follower
9. supporter 10. enthusiast
vote . . . 3. vow 5. elect, straw
6. ballot, choice, ticket 7. declare
8. suffrage 9. designate
10. plebescite, referendum
vote (pert to) . . .
group . . 4. bloc
in . . 5. elect
of assent . . 6. placet
plump . . 14. straight ticket
receptacle . . 6. situla
voter . . . 6. poller 7. elector 8. balloter
11. constituent
voters . . . 10. electorate
votive . . . 7. devoted 11. consecrated
vouch . . . 4. back 6. affirm, attest,
depose 7. confirm, declare, promise,
sponsor, support 8. accredit
9. assertion 11. attestation, bear
witness
vouchsafe . . . 4. give 5. deign
6. accept, assure, bestow, permit
7. concede 9. guarantee
10. condescend
voussoir . . . 8. keystone
vow . . . 3. vum 4. oath 5. swear,
vouch 6. behest, devote, pledge
7. declare, promise 8. dedicate

9. assertion 10. consecrate,
obligation 11. asservation
12. supplication
vowel (pert to) . . .
change of . . 6. umlaut
contradiction . . 6. crasis 7. digraph
9. diphthong
loss of . . 7. aphesis
mark . . 6. macron
point (Heb) . . 4. sere (tsere)
separate syllables . . 9. diaeresis
(dieresis)
short . . 5. breve
two, contracted . . 6. crasis
two, group . . 6. digram 7. digraph
9. diphthong (dipthong)
unaspirated . . 4. lene
vowels, none . . . 6. syzygy
vowels in sequence . . . 8. caesious
vox (pert to) . . .
clandestina . . 7. whisper
Dei . . 10. Voice of God
Latin for . . 5. voice
populi . . 16. voice of the people
voyage . . . 4. trip 6. cruise, travel
7. journey, passage, passing (sea)
9. excursion 10. expedition,
pilgrimage 11. undertaking
Vulcan (pert to) . . .
consort . . 4. Maia
epithet . . 8. Mulciber
feast of . . 10. Vulcanalia
god of . . 4. fire
Greek . . 10. Hephaestus
work site . . 4. Etna
vulcanite . . . 7. ebonite
vulcanize . . . 9. rubberize
vulgar . . . 3. low 4. lewd 5. crude,
gross 6. coarse, common, garish,
public, ribald 7. boorish, general,
obscene, profane 8. indecent,
ordinary, plebeian 9. inelegant,
offensive, unrefined 10. boisterous, in
bad taste, rowdydowdy
vulgarian . . . 4. snob 9. pretender
Vulgate . . . 10. Scriptures
vulnerable . . . 6. liable 7. exposed
8. beatable 9. pregnable, subject to
10. expungable 11. conquerable,
defenseless, susceptible
vulpine . . . 4. foxy 6. artful, crafty,
tricky 7. cunning, foxlike 9. alopecoid
10. vulpecular
vult . . . 4. mien 6. aspect
10. expression 11. countenance
vulture (pert to) . . .
African . . 8. aasvogel
American . . 4. aura 5. urubu
6. condor 13. turkey buzzard
European . . 7. griffin 11. lammergeier
(lammergeir)
king . . 4. papa
large . . 6. condor 11. lammergeier
Mexican . . 8. zopilote
raven . . 9. Corvultur
Spanish . . 9. gallinazo
term . . 5. harpy 9. raptorial 10. bird
of prey, predacious
vulturous . . . 6. lupine 7. wolfish
8. ravenous 9. rapacious
vying . . . 7. emulous 8. rivaling
9. competing 11. competitive

W

W ... **6.** letter (23rd) **7.** double U
WAAC ... **24.** Women's Auxiliary Army Corps
waag ... **6.** grivet, monkey
waapa ... **5.** canoe
wabber ... **4.** cony **5.** daman
wabble ... see *wobble*
wabby ... **4.** loon (red–throated)
wabe, wabi ... **5.** shrub **8.** huisache
wachna ... **7.** codfish
wad ... **3.** pad, ram **4.** cram, lump, mass, plug, roll, tuft **5.** money, stuff, track **6.** bundle, pledge, wealth **7.** stopper **8.** bankroll
wadding ... **4.** wads **6.** lining **7.** padding **8.** compress, stopping, stuffing
waddle ... **4.** sway **5.** mince **6.** toddle, wabble, wamble, wobble **10.** clumsy gait
waddy, waddie ... **3.** peg **4.** beat, club **5.** stick **6.** attack, cowboy
wade ... **4.** ford, pass **5.** study **6.** attack, drudge, paddle, plodge **8.** struggle
wader ... **4.** coot, ibis, rail **5.** crane, heron, snipe, stork **6.** jaçana **9.** sandpiper, shore bird **11.** Grallatores
wadi, wady ... **5.** oasis, river **6.** ravine, valley **7.** channel **11.** watercourse
waeg ... **9.** kittiwake
wafer ... **4.** cake, disk, ring, seal, snap **5.** bread **7.** biscuit, cracker **10.** altar bread
waff ... **3.** wag **4.** flap, wave **5.** ghost **7.** lowborn, vagrant **8.** inferior **9.** worthless **12.** disreputable
waft ... **4.** gust, puff, wave **5.** carry, float, whiff **6.** beckon, convey, convoy, signal **7.** glimpse, pennant **9.** beckoning, transport
wag ... **3.** wit **4.** card, wave **5.** joker, rogue, shake **6.** signal, waddle, wiggle **7.** farceur, vibrate **8.** humorist, jokester **9.** oscillate
wagang ... **5.** death **9.** departure **11.** leave–taking
wage, wages ... **3.** bet, fee, pay, utu **4.** hire, levy, pawn, risk **5.** fight, incur, stake, yield **6.** employ, engage, pledge, reward, salary **7.** attempt, contend, hire out, stipend, venture **9.** emolument **10.** recompense **12.** compensation, remuneration
wage insurance ... **7.** chômage
wager ... **3.** bet, bid, vie **4.** risk **5.** sport, stake **6.** gamble, hazard, parlay, pledge **7.** venture
waggish ... **5.** droll, merry **7.** jesting,

jocular, parlous, roguish **8.** humorous, sportive **9.** facetious **10.** frolicsome **11.** mischievous
Wagnerian opera ... **6.** Rienzi **8.** Parsifal **9.** Lohengrin **10.** Tannhauser **15.** Gotterdammerung
wagon ... **3.** car, van **4.** cart, dray, tram, wain **5.** araba, coach, lorry, tonga **6.** telega **7.** caisson, chariot, vehicle **8.** carryall, schooner (prairie) **12.** perambulator
wagon (pert to) ...
canvas–covered .. **15.** prairie schooner
lit .. **7.** Pullman **11.** sleeping car
load .. **6.** fother
maker .. **10.** wagonsmith, wainwright
on the (wagon) .. **8.** sworn off, teetotal
part .. **4.** neap **5.** blade, thill
police .. **3.** van **10.** Black Maria
sideless .. **6.** rolley
wah ... **5.** panda
wahine ... **4.** wife **5.** woman **8.** mistress **10.** sweetheart
wahoo ... **4.** bark, fish, peto **5.** shrub **7.** rock elm **8.** nonsense, tommyrot **9.** buckthorn, guarapucu **12.** umbrella tree
waif ... **4.** Arab, flag **5.** gamin, stray **7.** vagrant, wastrel **8.** castaway, homeless, wanderer **9.** lost sheep
wail ... **3.** cry, sob **4.** howl, moan, weep **5.** mourn **6.** bemoan, grieve, lament **7.** deplore, screech, ululate **11.** lamentation **14.** mournful outcry
wainscot ... **4.** base, ceil, line **5.** panel **6.** lining **8.** paneling (panelling) **9.** partition
waist ... **4.** wasp **5.** shirt **6.** basque, blouse, bodice, dickey, middle, taille **7.** corsage, garment **9.** garibaldi **12.** undergarment
waistcoat ... **4.** vest **5.** benjy **6.** jacket, jerkin, weskit
wait ... **4.** bide, rest, stay, stop **5.** dally, defer, delay, hover, serve, tarry, watch **6.** attend, expect, linger, remain **7.** observe **8.** hesitate, postpone **11.** expectation **12.** watchfulness
waiter ... **4.** tray **6.** garçon, salver, server **7.** messboy, messman, servant, steward **8.** servitor **9.** attendant
wait on ... **4.** help **5.** await, cater, serve **6.** escort **7.** toady to **9.** accompany
waive ... **5.** defer, forgo (forego) **6.** desert, give up, reject, vacate **7.** abandon, cast off, forsake

630

8. postpone 9. disregard
10. condescend, relinquish
waka... 5. canoe
Wakashan Indian... 6. Nootka
8. Kwakiutl
wake... 4. call, stir 5. rouse, track,
vigil, waken, watch 6. arouse,
awaken, excite, revive 10. death
watch
wakeful... 5. alert 8. restless, vigilant,
watchful 9. sleepless, wide–awake
Wake Island... 6. Ottori (Jap name)
wake–robin... 4. Arum 8. Trillium
9. Anthurium 10. cuckoopint
12. philodendron
wale... 3. rib 4. welt 5. ridge, wheal
6. stripe
Wales... see also *Welsh*
anc.. 7. Cambria
city.. 7. Rhondda, Swansea
8. Hereford, Pembroke 9. Carnarvon
congress of literati.. 10. eisteddfod
deity.. 4. Bran
emblem (floral).. 4. leek
language.. 7. Cymraeg
mountain.. 7. Snowdon
native.. 5. Cymry (Kymry)
patron saint.. 5. David
port.. 7. Cardiff
river.. 3. Dee, Wye 6. Severn
sea.. 5. Irish
walk... 3. mog, pad 4. foot, gait,
hike, hoof, pace, path, plod, ramp,
step 5. allee, amble, scuff, strut,
tramp, tread 6. ramble, sphere,
stride, stroll, toddle, travel, trudge
7. conduct, shuffle, traipse
8. ambulate, behavior, frescade,
province, sidewalk 9. esplanade,
promenade, wandering
10. passageway 11. base on balls,
perambulate 13. peregrination
walk (pert to)...
a beat.. 6. patrol
about.. 11. perambulate
clumsily.. 5. mince 6. lumber, totter
health.. 14. constitutional
lime–bordered.. 9. tilicetum
proudly.. 5. strut 6. prance
public.. 4. mall 6. arcade 7. alameda
9. esplanade, promenade
wearily.. 4. limp, plod 5. tramp
6. hobble, trudge
with speed.. 10. heel and toe
walking (pert to)...
about.. 7. passant (Her)
11. peripatetic
bearlike.. 11. plantigrade
meter.. 9. pedometer
papers.. 7. deposal, the sack
8. mittimus, pink slip 9. discharge,
dismissal 10. retirement
wall... 4. dado, dike, ha–ha, mure,
pier 5. fence, levee, panel, redan
6. escarp, hinder, immure, paries,
podium, septum, shut in 7. barrier,
defense, enclose, fortify, parapet,
rampart 8. espalier, palisade, restrain,
stockade 9. barricade, enclosure,
encompass, partition, precipice,
revetment 13. fortification
wall (pert to)...

bracket.. 6. corbel, sconce
creeper.. 4. bird
go to the (wall).. 4. fail 10. go
bankrupt
lining.. 8. wainscot
lizard.. 4. newt 5. gecko
masonry.. 9. revetment
pert to.. 5. mural 8. parietal
recess.. 5. niche 6. alcove
Street.. 9. Manhattan 11. money
market, stock market
up.. 6. immure
wallaby... 8. kangaroo, Macropus,
wallaroo 10. paddymelon
wallah, walla... 5. agent 6. master,
person 7. servant
waller... 4. wels 9. saltmaker,
sheatfish
wallet... 3. bag 4. pack, poke, sack
5. purse 8. billfold, knapsack
10. pocketbook 12. porte–monnaie
walleye... 9. exotropia 10. strabismus
wallow... 4. fade, sail 5. surge
6. grovel, welter, wither 7. debauch,
founder, insipid 8. flounder,
kommetje, nauseous 9. tasteless
walnut... 6. bannut
walrus... 3. pod (group) 5. morse
6. mammal, sea cat 8. pinniped
9. rosmarine (fable) 10. pinnipedia
Waltonian... 6. angler 16. disciple of
Walton (Izaak)
wamble... 5. twist 6. quiver, ramble,
rumble, totter, writhe 7. revolve,
stagger, wriggle
wame... 4. room, womb 5. belly
7. stomach
wampum... 4. peag 5. beads, money,
uhllo 6. shells 7. jewelry, roanoke
8. ornament 10. wampumpeag
wan... 3. dim, sad 4. ashy, dark, pale,
sick 5. ashen, black, dusky, faint,
lurid 6. dismal, gloomy, pallid, sickly
7. ghastly, languid 9. deathlike,
sorrowful 10. lusterless
11. lead–colored
wand... 3. rod 4. mace, pole
5. baton, osier, staff, stick (magic)
6. switch, wattle 7. pointer, rhabdos
(magic), scepter (sceptre)
8. caduceus 9. horsewhip
wander... 3. err, gad 4. moon, rave,
roam, rove 5. drift, prowl, range,
stray 6. cruise, depart, ramble, stroll,
travel 7. digress, meander, saunter,
traipse 8. divagate, traverse
9. circulate, itinerate, scamander
11. peregrinate
wanderer... 4. Arab, waif 5. gypsy,
nomad, rover 6. ranger, roamer,
truant 7. migrant, pilgrim, vagrant
9. butterfly, itinerant, straggler
10. covenanter 12. peregrinator
wandering... 5. vague 6. astray,
errant, roving, vagary 8. aberrant,
delirium, straying 9. delirious,
deviating, deviation, itinerant
10. circuitous, discursive, journeying
11. noctivigant, perambulant
13. peregrination
wandering (pert to)...
bird.. 9. albatross

long.. 7. odyssey
minstrel.. 4. bard 10. troubadour
stars.. 12. seven planets
tattler.. 9. shore bird
votary.. 6. palmer
wanderoo... 6. langur, monkey
  7. macaque
wand–shaped... 7. virgate
wane... 3. age, ebb 4. fail, sink, want
  5. abate, peter 6. defect, lessen,
  recede, repine 7. decline, grow dim,
  subside 8. decrease, diminish
  10. defervesce 13. deterioration
wanga... 5. charm, spell 6. voodoo
  7. philter, sorcery
wangle... 4. fake, plot 6. adjust,
  juggle, obtain, totter, wiggle
  7. finagle (finaigue), wriggle
  8. contrive, maneuver (manoeuvre)
  9. extricate 10. manipulate
want... 4. lack, miss, need, wish
  5. crave 6. dearth, desire, hunger,
  penury 7. absence, craving, lacking,
  poverty 8. scarcity, shortage
  9. deficient, indigence, privation
  10. inadequacy 11. destitution,
  requirement
want (of)...
 appetite.. 6. asitia
 desire.. 11. inappetence
 lacking.. 4. sans 5. out of 7. empty
  of, scant of, short of 8. bereft of
  10. deprived of
 power.. 5. atony
 sense (good).. 5. folly
wanting... 4. void 5. minus, needy
  6. absent, bereft, devoid 7. lacking,
  missing, short of, without
  9. deficient, destitute, imperfect
wanting (pert to)...
 be found.. 9. fall short 10. be inferior
 confidence.. 11. distrustful
 in energy.. 6. atonic
 in firmness.. 7. flaccid
 in intelligence.. 12. feebleminded
wanton... 3. gay 4. lewd 5. merry
  6. frisky, harlot, unruly 7. immoral,
  lustful, wayward 8. flagrant, insolent,
  sportive, unchaste 9. dissolute,
  merciless 10. capricious, frolicsome,
  licentious 11. extravagant
  13. undisciplined
wapiti... 3. elk 4. deer, stag
war... 5. fight 6. attack, battle
  8. conflict
war (pert to)...
 agreement.. 6. cartel
 cause of.. 10. casus belli
 club.. 4. mace
 fleet.. 6. armada
 gas.. 8. adamsite
 German.. 5. krieg 10. blitzkrieg
 god.. 3. Ira, Tyr 4. Ares
 goddess.. 5. Bella 6. Ishtar
 hating.. 13. misopolemical
 hawk.. 5. jingo 7. bailiff
 horse.. 5. steed 7. charger
  8. partisan 10. campaigner, politician
 of words.. 9. logomachy
 religious.. 5. jihad (jehad)
 vessel, ship.. 3. sub 7. cruiser, frigate
  8. corvette (corvet) 9. destroyer,

submarine 11. dreadnought
  (dreadnaught)
war bird... 7. aviator, tanager (scarlet)
warble... 4. sing 5. carol, trill, yodel
  6. quaver 7. twitter, vibrate
warbler... 4. wren 6. singer
  8. blackcap, grosbeak, redstart,
  songster 9. beccafico 10. bluethroat
  11. whitethroat
ward... 4. jail, part, rule 5. watch
  6. govern, prison 7. custody, keeping
  8. district, garrison, guardian,
  watchman 9. dependent
  10. stronghold 12. guardianship
ward (pert to)...
 division.. 4. army, jail 6. forest
  8. hospital
 French.. 14. arrondissement
 heeler.. 8. henchman 10. politician
 off.. 4. fend 5. fence, parry, repel,
  stave 7. expiate, forfend, prevent
warden... 5. guard, nazir 6. dizdar
  (disdar), jailer, keeper, ranger, sexton
  7. alcaide (alcaid), turnkey
  8. director, guardian, official,
  watchman 9. concierge, custodian
  10. gatekeeper
warder... 6. warden 7. turnkey
wardrobe... 4. room 6. closet
  7. almirah, apparel, cabinet, clothes
  8. costumes 12. clothespress
ware... 4. sage, wary, wise 5. aware,
  china, goods, spend 6. shrewd
  7. careful, heedful, pottery, prudent,
  seaweed 8. cautious, vigilant
  9. cognizant, commodity, conscious,
  porcelain 11. commodities,
  earthenware, merchandise
warehouse... 4. silo 5. depot, étape
  6. fonduk (fondouk), godown
  7. storage 8. entrepôt
warfare... 7. contest 8. conflict,
  struggle 11. hostilities 12. armed
  contest
wariness... 7. stealth 8. distrust
  9. chariness, suspicion
warlock... 6. wizard 7. monster (Myth)
  8. conjuror, magician, sorcerer
warm... 3. red 4. heat, keen, mild
  5. angry, calid, eager, humid,
  muggy, tepid, toast 6. ardent, excite,
  genial, hearty, heated, torrid
  7. clement, cordial, fervent
  8. friendly, generous 10. responsive
  11. sympathetic 12. affectionate,
  enthusiastic 13. near discovery, near
  the object (see also *hot*)
warm (pert to)...
 bath.. 5. therm
 growing.. 9. calescent
 hearted.. 4. kind 6. hearty, kindly,
  tender 7. cordial 8. friendly,
  generous 11. sympathetic
  12. affectionate
 pert to.. 7. thermal
 praise.. 8. encomium
 room.. 10. tepidarium
 springs (Rom).. 7. thermae
warmblooded... 6. ardent 9. irascible
  13. homoiothermic, quick–tempered
  14. haematothermal (hematothermal)
warmed over... 5. stale, trite

8. rehashed, reheated 9. rechauffé, twice–told

warmth ... 4. élan, glow, heat, zeal 5. ardor 7. ardency, thermal 8. fervency 9. animation, eloquence, geniality, vehemence 10. enthusiasm, excitement 11. calefaction, earnestness

warn ... 4. flag 5. alarm, alert 6. advise, exhort, inform, notify, remind, signal 7. apprise (apprize), caution, counsel, previse 8. admonish, forebode, threaten 9. reprehend

warning ... 4. bell, omen 5. alarm, alert, radar, siren 6. alarum, beacon, beware, caveat, signal, threat, tocsin 7. blinker, sematic, summons 10. admonition, admonitive 12. caveat emptor

warp ... 4. bend, bias, hurl, sway, turn, woof 5. fling, throw, twist, weave 6. buckle, swerve 7. contort, deflect, distort, pervert 9. fabricate 10. aberration, distortion 12. misinterpret

warp (pert to) ...
cross threads.. 4. woof
threads.. 5. lease 6. stamen
yarn.. 3. abb

warragal, warrigal ... 5. dingo, horse, myall

warrant ... 4. earn, writ 5. order 6. attest, ensure, permit, secure 7. defense, justify, precept, promise, voucher 8. document, guaranty, sanction, security 9. authorize, guarantee, safeguard 10. credential, instrument, protection 11. acknowledge, certificate 13. authorization

warranty ... 4. writ 5. proof 7. promise, warrant 8. guaranty, sanction, security 13. authorization

warrior ... 4. hero, impi 5. brave 6. Amazon 7. fighter, martial, soldier 10. halberdier

warrior (pert to) ...
Bib.. 4. Ehud
female.. 6. Amazon
Indian.. 6. sannup
Roman.. 9. gladiator
Trojan.. 6. Agenor, Hector
Zulu.. 4. impi 7. Kaffirs

Warsaw (pert to) ...
capital.. 6. Poland
river.. 7. Vistula
suburb.. 5. Praga

wary ... 3. shy 5. alert, canny, chary, leery 7. careful, guarded, prudent 8. cautious, discreet, watchful 10. economical 11. circumspect

wash ... 3. lap, pan 4. lave 5. bathe, clean, elute, flush, leach, marsh, paint, purge, rinse, slosh, swash 6. debris, drench, dry bed (river), purify, splash 7. cleanse, immerse, launder, overlay, shampoo 8. ablution 9. lixiviate

wash (pert to) ...
basin.. 4. bowl 6. lavabo
bear.. 7. raccoon

dish.. 11. pied wagtail
for gold.. 3. pan
one's hands of.. 6. give up, refuse 10. relinquish
out.. 4. fade 5. elute, flunk 7. failure, freshet
sale (finance).. 10. fictitious

washing ... 7. coating 8. ablution 9. drenching

Washington, DC (famed sites) ...
7. Capitol (Bldg), The Mall 8. Pentagon, Treasury 10. Blair House, White House 11. Mount Vernon 12. Ford's Theater (Lincoln Museum), Supreme Court 14. cherry blossoms 15. Iwo Jima Monument, Lincoln Memorial 16. National Archives, Naval Observatory 17. Jefferson Memorial, Library of Congress 18. Walter Reed Hospital, Washington Monument 19. Unknown Soldier's Tomb 22. Smithsonian Institution 25. Arlington National Cemetery

Washington (State of) ...
capital.. 7. Olympia
city.. 6. Tacoma, Yakima 7. Everett, Seattle, Spokane 10. Bellingham, Walla Walla
dam.. 10. Bonneville 11. Grand Coulee
discoverer.. 4. Gray 9. Vancouver
explorer.. 5. Clark, Lewis 6. Wilkes 7. Fremont
Falls.. 10. Snoqualmie
Fort.. 5. Lewis
lake.. 5. Union 6. Chelan 8. Crescent
mountain.. 7. Rainier 8. Cascades, Olympics
river.. 5. Snake, White 7. Spokane 8. Columbia
Sound.. 5. Puget 7. Rosario
State admission.. 11. Forty–second
State motto.. 4. Al–Ki (By and By)
State nickname.. 9. Evergreen
wind (SW).. 7. chinook

wasp ... 5. Sphex, vespa, whamp 6. dauber, hornet, Tiphia, vespid 8. Vespidae 12. Hymenopteron, yellow jacket

waspish ... 4. mean 5. cross, testy 6. cranky 7. bearish, peevish, slender 8. choleric, churlish, petulant, snappish, spiteful 9. fractious, irascible, irritable 12. cantankerous

wasp's nest ... 8. vespiary

wassail ... 4. lark, orgy, romp 5. toast 6. frolic, shindy 7. carouse 8. beverage, carousal 9. festivity 10. salutation 11. celebration 12. drinking bout

waste ... 3. eat 4. idle, junk, loss, rind, ross, sack, slag, vain, wear, wild 5. chaff, chips, dross, havoc, spill, trash 6. barren, desert, expend, lavish, ravage, refuse 7. atrophy, exhaust, fritter, rubbish 8. clinkers, demolish, desolate, squander 9. dissipate 10. desolation, diminution 11. destruction, devastation, dissipation, prodigality, uninhabited 12. uncultivated,

unproductive 13. unserviceable
waste (pert to)...
   allowance.. 4. tret
   away.. 3. age 6. shrink, sicken
     7. decline 8. marasmus
     11. deteriorate
   lay waste.. 4. sack 6. ravage
     7. destroy 8. decimate
   matter.. 3. ort 4. slag 5. dross
     7. clinker
   mine.. 3. gob
   silk.. 4. knob, noil 6. frison
   time.. 4. idle, lazy 5. dally 6. daddle,
     footle, loiter 10. dillydally
wasted... 7. haggard 8. phthisic
wasteful... 6. lavish 10. thriftless
   11. extravagant, improvident
wasteland... 5. heath, marsh, swamp
   6. desert, morass 8. badlands
   10. barren land, everglades
wasting... 5. aging 6. awaste
   8. marasmic 10. enfeebling
   11. consumption, devastating
   13. deteriorating
wastrel... 4. waif 5. idler 8. vagabond
   10. profligate 11. spendthrift
watch... 3. eye, spy 4. espy, heed,
   mark, mind, tend, time, wake
   (funeral) 5. guard, vigil 6. ambush,
   patrol, police, sentry 7. bivouac,
   lookout, observe 8. horologe, sentinel
   9. ambuscade, timepiece, vigilance
   11. chronometer, observation,
   wakefulness
watch (pert to)...
   chain.. 3. fob 6. Albert
   face.. 5. bezel
   maker.. 10. horologist
   military.. 5. perdu (perdue) 6. sentry
     7. vedette
   stop.. 5. timer
   tower.. 6. beacon 7. atalaya, mirador
     10. lighthouse
   word.. 6. signal 10. shibboleth (Bib)
     11. countersign
   works.. 10. escapement
watchful... 3. Ira (Heb) 4. wary
   5. alert, aware 7. careful, heedful
   8. cautious, open–eyed, vigilant
   9. observant, regardful
   11. circumspect
watchman... 5. guard 6. sentry,
   warder 8. sentinel, watchdog
   10. gatekeeper
watchword... 4. hint, word 6. signal
   8. party cry 10. intimation,
   shibboleth (Bib) 11. countersign
watchworks... 10. escapement
water... 3. eau, ice, wet 4. aqua, rain
   5. fluid, flume, spray 6. dilute,
   lagoon, liquid 7. moisten
   8. beverage, calendar, irrigate,
   sprinkle 10. adulterate
water (pert to)...
   baptismal.. 5. laver
   bath.. 7. balneum
   bird.. 4. coot, loon 5. diver, ouzel
     6. dipper 7. pintail, swimmer
     9. merganser
   bottle.. 4. olla 6. carafe
   buffalo.. 2. ox 7. carabao
   channel.. 5. canal, flume 6. strait

     8. tailrace
   chart.. 10. hydrograph
   color (art).. 9. aquarelle
   comb form.. 5. hydro 6. hydato
   congealed.. 3. ice 4. snow 5. glacé
     6. icicle
   course.. 4. clow 5. bayou, gorge,
     gully 6. nullah, ravine, sluice
     9. watergate
   cow.. 6. sea cow 7. buffalo, manatee
   cure.. 10. hydropathy
     12. hydrotherapy
   deer.. 10. chevrotain
   destitute of.. 9. anhydrous
   divination by.. 10. hydromancy
   eagle.. 6. osprey
   element.. 6. oxygen 8. hydrogen
   elephant.. 12. hippopotamus
   exhibition.. 8. aquacade
   fowl.. 7. pelican
   gauge (rain).. 8. udometer
   goddess.. 4. Nina 7. Anahita, Anaitis
   hare.. 11. swamp rabbit
   heater.. 4. etna
   history.. 10. hydrognosy
   hog.. 8. capybara
   hole.. 5. oasis 6. tinaja 7. alberca
   jug.. 4. lota (lotah), olla 5. banga
     6. hydria, kalpis
   lava.. 12. hellgrammite
   lily.. 5. lotus 6. Nuphar 7. Nelumbo
     8. Nymphaea, Victoria
     11. spatterdock
   measure.. 10. hydrometer
   meter.. 7. Venturi
   mineral.. 5. Vichy 6. Shasta
     7. Seltzer
   monster.. 6. nicker (fabled)
   nymph.. 5. naiad 6. undine
     7. Oceanid
   of oblivion.. 5. Lethe 12. river of
     Hades
   opossum.. 5. yapok (yapock)
   pert to.. 7. aqueous 8. hydatoid
   plug.. 3. tap 4. cock, cork 6. faucet,
     spigot 7. hydrant
   pocket.. 6. tinaja
   rat.. 4. vole 8. vagabond
   reddish (with iron).. 6. riddam
   reservoir (underground).. 6. cenote
   rough.. 4. eddy 5. ocean 6. rapids
     7. riptide 8. undertow
   sapphire.. 6. iolite 10. saphir d'eau
   scorpion.. 4. Nepa 7. Ranatra
   search for.. 5. dowse
   sheet of.. 5. nappe
   spirit.. 3. Nix 5. Ariel, Nixie 6. kelpie,
     nicker, sprite
   spout.. 5. spate 8. gargoyle
   sprite.. 3. Nix 5. Nixie
   stratum.. 7. aquifer
   study, science of.. 9. hydrology
     11. hydrography
   surface.. 4. ryme
   swelling.. 5. edema
   turkey.. 9. snakebird
   vessel.. 3. jug 4. ewer, lota (lotah),
     pail 5. cruse, flask 6. bottle, bucket,
     tinaja 7. pitcher, stamnos
     8. decanter
   wheel.. 5. noria 6. sakieh (sakiyeh)
     7. turbine 8. tympanum

without.. 9. anhydrous
watery... 8. ichorous
Watling Street (London)... 6. Galaxy
   8. Milky Way 9. Roman road
wattle... 3. rod 4. beat, flog, plat,
   wand 5. fence, twist, weave, withe
   6. barbel, dewlap, hurdle, lappet
   8. caruncle 9. boobyalla, loose flap
   10. intertwine, interweave 11. skin
   process 12. native willow
wattlebird... 4. crow 10. honey eater
   11. brush turkey
Wattle Day... 7. holiday
wave... 3. ola, sea, wag 4. flap, tide
   5. crest, eagre, flood, ridge, surge,
   swell, tilde 6. beckon, billow,
   comber, flaunt, hairdo, marcel, ripple,
   roller, signal 7. breaker, decuman,
   flutter, tsunami, vibrate 8. brandish,
   coiffure, flourish, greeting, undulate
   9. fluctuate, vibration 10. undulation
waver... 4. reel, sway, veer 5. demur,
   quake 6. falter, quiver, totter
   7. flicker, flutter, stagger, tremble,
   vibrate 8. hesitate 9. fluctuate,
   oscillate, vacillate 12. be indecisive
wavering... 6. fickle 8. doubtful,
   unsteady 9. desultory 10. irresolute
wavy... 4. onde, undé (undee)
   5. curly, snaky 6. repand, undate
   7. billowy, rolling, sinuous
   8. undulant 9. undulated
   10. undulatory
wax... 4. cere, grow 6. candle, cerate,
   polish 7. beeswax, cerumen
   8. increase, paraffin 9. lubricant,
   lubricate 12. zietrisikite (mineral)
wax (pert to)...
beeswax cells.. 9. honeycomb
beeswax substitute.. 7. ceresin
candle.. 6. cierge
chemical.. 9. adipocere
Chinese.. 4. pela
molded in.. 7. fictile 9. ceroplast
ref to.. 5. ceral
substance.. 5. cerin
way... 3. via 4. lane, mode, path,
   plan, ramp, road 5. alley, habit,
   means, Milky, route, track 6. avenue,
   course, manner, method, street
   7. highway, passage 8. causeway,
   distance, sidewalk 9. banquette,
   direction, procedure
way (pert to)...
astronomy.. 6. Galaxy 8. Milky Way
give.. 5. break, yield 6. weaken
   7. despair 10. depreciate
god of.. 6. Hermes
in.. 7. ingress 8. entrance
in a way.. 8. as it were, somewhat
   13. theoretically
inclined.. 4. ramp
out.. 4. exit 6. egress, escape
roundabout.. 6. detour
waylay... 3. rob 5. await, seize
   6. ambush, lay for 8. surprise
   9. ambuscade
wayward... 6. unruly 7. erratic, willful
   8. perverse, stubborn, untoward
   10. capricious, headstrong, refractory
   11. disobedient, intractable
weak... 3. dim, lax, wan 4. pale,

puny, thin, worn 5. faint, frail, washy
   6. dotish, feeble, infirm, sickly,
   simple, unwise, watery 7. flaccid,
   foolish, fragile, insipid 8. cowardly,
   decrepit, fatigued, impotent, wavering
   9. enfeebled, exhausted, nerveless,
   powerless 10. effeminate
   11. debilitated, ineffective
   12. unconvincing
weak (pert to)...
fish.. 7. totuava 9. gray trout
   10. squeteague
hearted.. 6. afraid 7. fearful
   12. fainthearted
kneed.. 8. cowardly, yielding
   10. irresolute
sister.. 6. coward 8. weakling
   11. mollycoddle
weaken... 3. sap 4. tire 5. break
   6. dilute, impair, lessen, reduce
   7. cripple, disable, exhaust, unnerve
   8. enervate 9. undermine
   10. debilitate
weakness... 4. flaw 5. atony, fault
   6. defect, foible, liking 7. failing,
   fatigue, frailty 8. asthenia, debility
   9. cowardice, impotence, infirmity
   10. feebleness, infirmness
   11. decrepitude 12. imperfection
   13. powerlessness
weal... 4. mark, wale, welt 5. ridge,
   wheal 6. riches, wealth 7. welfare
   9. happiness, well-being
   10. commonweal
wealth... 4. good, weal 5. money
   6. assets, mammon, riches
   7. capital, fortune, welfare
   8. opulence, property, treasure
   9. abundance, affluence, well-being
   10. prosperity 11. possessions
wealth (pert to)...
god of.. 6. Plutus
person of.. 6. monied 7. magnate,
   opulent 9. plutocrat
pursuit of.. 10. plutomania
study of.. 9. economics, plutology
worship of.. 10. plutolatry
wealthy... 4. rich 5. ample
   8. abundant, affluent
wealthy (pert to)...
English slang.. 4. oofy
man.. 5. nabob 10. capitalist
rule by.. 10. plutocracy
wean... 6. detach 8. alienate, estrange
   9. reconcile
weapon... 3. arm, gat, gun 4. bola,
   bolo, celt, club, dart, epee, snee
   5. arrow, knife, lance, rifle, saber
   (sabre), spear, sword 6. dagger,
   musket, pistol, poleax (poleaxe),
   rapier 7. bayonet, bazooka, carbine,
   gisarme, halberd, machete, trident
   8. battle-ax (battle-axe), catapult,
   crossbow, revolver, stiletto, tomahawk
   9. derringer, Excalibur
   11. blunderbuss
wear... 3. use 4. bear, fray, fret, show
   5. chafe, weary 7. fatigue
   12. disintegrate
wear (pert to)...
away.. 3. eat, end 5. erode
   6. abrade 7. corrode, decline

down.. 4. tire 8. persuade
   9. influence
out.. 4. tire 5. waste 7. fatigue
weariness... 5. ennui 6. tedium
   7. boredom, fatigue 9. lassitude
wearisome... 4. hard 6. boring,
   dismal, dreary, tiring 7. irksome,
   tedious 8. tiresome, toilsome
   9. fatiguing, laborious, vexatious
   10. monotonous
weary... 3. fag, irk, sad 4. bore, jade,
   pall, tire, weak 5. bored, spent, tired
   6. plague 7. fatigue, languid
   9. forjesket
weasel... 4. stot, vare 5. ratel, stoat
   6. ermine, ferret
weasellike... 4. mink 5. otter, tayra
   9. musteline, musteloid
weather (pert to)...
  cock.. 4. vane
  glass.. 9. barometer, baroscope
  man.. 13. meteorologist
  map.. 6. isobar
weave... 3. mat 4. knit, lace, reel,
   spin, sway 5. plait, unite 6. devise,
   wattle 7. canelle, entwine, fashion
   8. contrive 9. fabricate, interlace,
   interwind 10. intertwine, intertwist
   11. push one's way
weaver bird... 4. baya, maya, taha
   5. Munia
weaving (pert to)...
  art of.. 4. loom
  fabric (rich).. 3. web 7. brocade,
   webbing
  French.. 5. lisse 8. Jacquard
  material.. 5. reeds, twigs 6. raffia
  term.. 4. beam, dent, loom, sley
   7. shuttle
  together.. 7. plexure
weazen (wizen)... 6. shrink, wither
   7. shrivel
web... 3. net, ply 4. caul, tela, trap,
   veil, warp 5. snare 6. tissue
   7. network, texture 8. filament,
   gossamer, membrane, vexillum
   12. entanglement
web (pert to)...
  footed.. 7. palmate
  like.. 4. lacy 5. telar 7. spidery
  spinning.. 6. telary 7. retiary
  term.. 5. telar
  toed.. 11. totipalmate
  winged.. 3. bat
  work.. 4. maze, mesh 6. tangle
   11. Gordian knot
wed... 4. join, mate 5. marry, mated,
   unite 6. joined 7. espouse, pledged,
   spliced 13. give in wedlock
wedding... 8. ceremony, espousal,
   marriage, nuptials
wedding (anniversary)...
  1st.. 5. paper
  2nd.. 5. straw
  3rd.. 5. candy
  4th.. 7. leather
  5th.. 6. wooden
  7th.. 6. floral
  10th.. 3. tin
  12th.. 5. linen
  13th.. 4. lace
  15th.. 7. crystal

  20th.. 5. china
  25th.. 6. silver
  30th.. 5. pearl
  35th.. 5. coral
  40th.. 7. emerald
  45th.. 4. ruby
  50th.. 6. golden
  75th.. 7. diamond
wedding (pert to)...
  flower.. 13. orange blossom
  proclamation.. 5. banns (bans)
  snow.. 4. rice
  term.. 7. marital, wedlock
   8. marriage, nuptials 9. matrimony
   11. espousement
wedge... 3. jam 4. club, shoe
   5. cleat, ingot, split 6. sector,
   wedgie 7. niblick 8. triangle, voussoir
   9. machinery
wedge–shaped... 7. cuneate
   9. cuneiform (cuniform)
Wednesday... 5. Woden (wise god)
   9. fourth day, Woden's Day
wee... 3. bit 4. dock, fine, tiny
   5. small, teeny 6. little, minute
   10. diminutive, teeny–weeny
weed... 3. bur (burr), hoe, rag 4. loco,
   milk, sida, tare 5. cigar, flesh, vetch
   6. darnel, excise, Jimson, knawel,
   spurge, tumble 7. allseed, mallows,
   mustard, ragweed, tobacco
   8. plantain, purslane, toadflax
   9. cultivate, dandelion
   11. undergrowth
weeds... 8. garments (mourning)
week... 8. hebdomad 9. seven days
week (pert to)...
  day.. 6. ferial
  Eccl.. 4. Holy 7. Passion
  of Sundays.. 5. seven 8. hebdomad
  of years.. 5. seven
  past.. 10. yesterweek
weekly... 5. aweek 10. hebdomadal,
   periodical 11. publication
weeks, two... 9. fortnight
weel... 4. pool, trap 6. basket 8. fish
   trap
ween... 5. think 6. expect 7. believe,
   imagine, suppose 8. conceive
weep... 3. cry, orp, sob 4. drip, rain,
   wail 5. exude, mourn 7. blubber,
   lapwing 9. percolate, shed tears
weeping... 6. crying 7. sobbing
   9. festering
weeping (pert to)...
  monkey.. 8. capuchin
  queen.. 5. Niobe
  tree.. 5. cedar 6. spruce, willow
Weeping Philosopher (anc)...
   10. Heraclitus
weevil (pert to)...
  cotton.. 4. boll
  malt.. 4. boud
  snout.. 8. curculio
  type (other).. 3. pea 4. palm, pine,
   rice, seed 5. flour
weigh... 4. tare, test 5. hoist, poise,
   scale 6. ponder, regard 7. balance,
   be heavy, compare, measure
   8. consider, encumber, estimate,
   ruminate 9. apportion, press hard
weigh down... 4. lade, load

6. burden, hamper 7. ballast,
depress, oppress 11. overbalance
weight... 4. load, mass 5. force,
power 6. burden, import, moment
7. gravity, tonnage 8. encumber,
pressure 9. authority, heaviness,
influence 10. importance
11. consequence 12. significance
weight (pert to)...
allowance.. 4. tare, tret 7. scalage
comb form.. 4. baro
gem.. 5. carat (karat)
light.. 6. suttle
system.. 3. net 4. troy 6. metric
10. apothecary 11. avoirdupois
total.. 5. gross
weighty... 3. fat 5. bulky, heavy, hefty,
large, obese 6. solemn 7. massive,
onerous, serious 8. forcible, powerful
9. corpulent, important, momentous,
ponderous 10. burdensome,
cumbersome, impressive, oppressive
11. influential 13. authoritative
weir... 3. dam, net 4. bank 5. fence,
levee, seine 7. barrier, milldam
9. floodgate
weird... 3. odd 4. omen, wild 5. eerie
(eery), queer, scary 6. creepy, spooky
7. awesome, curious, ghostly,
macabre, strange, uncanny 8. eldritch
9. deathlike, frightful 10. mysterious,
prediction
Weird Sisters (Scot)... 5. Fates
welcome... 4. hail 5. adopt, greet
7. acclaim, accueil 8. grateful,
greeting, pleasing 9. agreeable,
bienvenue, desirable 10. acceptable,
salutation
weld... 5. unite 11. consolidate
welfare... 4. good, weal 5. Salus
(goddess) 9. good cheer
10. prosperity 14. material plenty
welkin... 3. air, sky 6. heaven
10. atmosphere
well... 3. fit, gay, pit 4. gush, hale,
pool 5. aweel, fount, fully 6. easily,
gusher, hearty, justly, kindly, source
7. cistern, closely 8. artesian,
expertly, fountain, friendly 10. full
degree, intimately 11. excellently
12. satisfactory
well (pert to)...
being.. 4. weal 7. comfort 8. eucrasia
9. happiness
Bib.. 4. Esek
born.. 5. noble 7. eugenic
bred.. 6. polite 7. genteel, refined
8. cultured, wellborn 9. pedigreed
10. cultivated 11. gentlemanly
12. thoroughbred
comb form.. 4. mene
defined.. 8. distinct 11. distinctive
groomed.. 4. neat 5. sleek 6. soigné
(soignée)
grounded.. 5. valid 7. logical
9. plausible 11. established,
substantial 12. well–informed
gushing.. 8. artesian
heeled.. 4. rich 5. armed
7. moneyed, wealthy, well–off
8. well–to–do
known.. 6. famous 7. eminent

12. acknowledged
land drain.. 4. sump
lining.. 5. steen
off.. 5. lucky 10. prosperous
oil.. 6. gusher
pole.. 5. sweep
prefix.. 2. eu
timed.. 6. timely 9. opportune
versed.. 7. erudite
watered.. 9. irrigated, irriguous
welsh (welch)... 5. cheat 6. not pay,
renege 7. swindle 10. shirk out of
Welsh (pert to)... see also *Wales*
boat.. 7. coracle
congress of literati.. 10. eisteddfod
fine, for murder.. 7. galanas
god, underworld.. 4. Bran
instrument (reed).. 7. pibcorn
man.. 5. Taffy 8. Cambrian
onion.. 5. cibal
population.. 6. Cymric
rabbit.. 7. ramekin (ramequin), rarebit
romance collection.. 10. Mabinogion
(Mabinogi)
welt... 4. mark, wale 5. ridge
6. stripe, thrash
welter... 4. reel, roll, sail, toss
6. grovel, tumble, wallow 7. stagger
8. flounder, overturn 9. confusion
wen... 4. cyst, rune 5. tumor
7. blemish 11. excrescence
12. protuberance
wench... 4. doxy, gill, girl 5. child,
squaw, trull, woman 6. damsel,
maiden 7. consort, servant
8. strumpet 11. maidservant
wend... 2. go 4. fare, pass 6. depart,
direct, travel 7. circuit, proceed
8. progress
went (pert to)... see also *go*
astray.. 6. failed 10. miscarried
away.. 4. left 8. departed
before.. 3. led 8. preceded
9. anteceded
swiftly.. 3. ran 4. sped 6. darted
7. scooted, scudded 8. decamped
wenzel... 4. jack (card game) 5. knave
werewolf... 6. jaguar 8. uturuncu,
werefolk 11. lycanthrope
wergild... 3. cro 4. eric 7. galanas
9. Brehon Law
Wesleyan... 9. Methodist 14. Wesley
follower
West African (pert to)...
baboon.. 5. drill 8. mandrill
city.. 5. Accra, Dakar
gazelle.. 4. kudu, mohr (mhorr), oryx
lemur.. 5. potto 8. kinkajou
monkey.. 4. mona 6. guenon
native.. 7. Ashanti (Ashantee)
pepper.. 5. cubeb
tree.. 5. iroko, odoom
tribe.. 5. Igara
West End, London... 7. Mayfair
9. Belgravia 11. fashionable
12. aristocratic
Western... 9. Hesperian 10. Occidental
Westernmost US... 9. Aleutians
11. Attu Islands 12. Cape Wrangell
West Indies...
bird.. 4. tody 6. mucaro
boat.. 7. drogher (droger)

chief.. **7.** cacique
clingfish.. **6.** testar
crop.. **5.** sugar **7.** bananas
ebony.. **9.** cocuswood
fish.. **4.** cero, paru, sesi **6.** testar
flea.. **6.** chigoe
fruit.. **5.** papaw (pawpaw)
islands.. **4.** Cuba **5.** Haiti **6.** Cayman,
  Virgin **7.** Antigua, Bahamas, Leeward
  8. Antilles, Windward
liquor.. **5.** mobby (mobbie), tafia
  (taffia)
lizard.. **6.** arbalo
magic.. **5.** obeah
music.. **7.** calypso
owl.. **6.** mucaro
resident.. **9.** Antillean
rodent.. **6.** agouti (agouty)
snuff.. **8.** Maccaboy
tea.. **8.** goatweed
tortoise.. **7.** hicatee
tree.. **4.** ausu **5.** ebony, papaw
  6. bonduc **8.** bayberry **9.** sapodilla,
  satinwood
volcano.. **5.** Pelée
wood.. **9.** cocuswood, sapodilla
  10. granadilla
Westminster clock (London)... **6.** Big
  Ben
West Pointer... **5.** cadet, plebe
  8. yearling
West Point motto... **16.** Duty, Honor,
  Country
West Virginia...
capital.. **10.** Charleston
city.. **5.** Logan **8.** Wheeling
  11. Parkersburg
crop.. **4.** coal
mountain.. **10.** Spruce Knob
  11. Alleghenies
park (famed).. **12.** Harpers Ferry
river.. **4.** Ohio **7.** Kanawha
  11. Monongahela
Springs (resort).. **8.** Berkeley
  12. White Sulphur
State admission.. **11.** Thirty–fifth
State motto.. **19.** Montani Semper
  Liberi **22.** Mountaineers Always Free
State nickname.. **8.** Mountain
West wind... **8.** Favonius, Zephyrus
wet... **4.** asop, damp, dank, dewy, rain
  5. foggy, humid, leach, misty, moist,
  mushy, rainy, soggy, soppy
  6. dampen, drench, soaked, sodden,
  watery **7.** moisten **8.** sprinkle
wet blanket... **7.** kill–joy **8.** deadhead
  10. discourage, spoilsport
whale... **3.** orc **4.** cete, lash, whip
  5. whack **6.** beluga, blower, thrash
  7. grampus, ripsack **8.** hardhead
  9. zeuglodon **13.** sulphur–bottom
whale (pert to)...
Arctic.. **7.** narwhal
bird.. **4.** gull **6.** petrel **9.** phalarope
blubber pot.. **6.** try–pot
blue.. **9.** Sibbaldus
bone.. **6.** baleen
carcass.. **5.** kreng
constellation.. **5.** Cetus
fat.. **7.** blubber
food.. **4.** brit
gray.. **7.** ripsack **8.** hardhead

killer.. **4.** orca
killer of.. **8.** ceticide
legendary.. **9.** Mysticeti
monster.. **4.** Cete
mustache (legend).. **9.** Mysticeti
Order.. **7.** Cetacea
ref to.. **5.** cetic, sperm **6.** baleen
  7. blubber **8.** cetacean
school of.. **3.** gam, pod
secretion (perfume).. **9.** ambergris
small.. **7.** grampus
sperm type.. **8.** cachalot
study of.. **8.** cetology
toothed.. **10.** odontocete, zeuglodont
type.. **3.** orc **4.** blue, orca **5.** right,
  sperm **6.** killer **7.** dolphin, rorqual
  8. cachalot, humpback, porpoise
  9. whalebone
wax.. **10.** spermaceti
whalebone.. **6.** baleen **10.** stiffening
young.. **4.** calf **9.** shorthead
wharf... **4.** dock, pier, quay **5.** jetty
  6. staith **7.** landing
wharf (pert to)...
fish.. **6.** cunner
master.. **10.** wharfinger
worker.. **9.** stevedore
whatnot... **5.** thing **6.** object
  (nondescript) **7.** étagère
  10. miscellany
what's what... **4.** fact **5.** truth
  7. reality **10.** what's right
what wonders has God wrought
  (Arabic exclamation)... **9.** mashallah
whaup... **6.** curlew, outcry
  9. scoundrel
wheal... **4.** wale, weal, welt **5.** whelk
  6. stripe **7.** pustule
wheat (pert to)...
beard.. **3.** awn
beverage.. **6.** zythem
bird.. **4.** lark **8.** wheatear **9.** chaffinch
chaff.. **4.** bran
duck.. **7.** widgeon **8.** baldpate
Europe.. **5.** emmer, spelt (speltz)
flour.. **4.** atta **5.** Hovis
hard.. **5.** durum
India.. **4.** suji **8.** semolina
storage bin.. **4.** silo **8.** elevator
wheedle... **4.** coax, gain **5.** tease
  6. banter, cajole, entice **7.** blarney,
  flatter **8.** blandish, inveigle, persuade
  9. influence
wheel... **3.** cam, cog **4.** bike, disc,
  helm, ride, roll, rota **5.** drive, pivot,
  rotor, rowel, whirl **6.** caster, roller,
  rotate **7.** bicycle, revolve, rotator,
  torture, vehicle **8.** tricycle **10.** water
  wheel
wheel (pert to)...
gem–grinding.. **5.** skive
hub.. **4.** nave
man.. **5.** pilot **7.** cyclist **8.** helmsman,
  pedalist **9.** bicyclist
monkey.. **3.** gin
part.. **3.** rim **5.** felly (felloe), spoke
  6. hubcap
pulley.. **6.** sheave
shaped.. **8.** circular, rotiform
spoke.. **6.** radius
spur.. **5.** rowel
stopper.. **4.** grig **5.** sprag

swiveled .. **6.** caster
toothed .. **3.** cog **4.** gear **6.** pinion
turbine .. **5.** rotor
type .. **3.** cog, fly, pin **4.** cart, mill,
spur **5.** wagon **6.** Ferris, paddle
7. balance, potter's **9.** of fortune
water .. **5.** noria **6.** sakieh (sakiyeh)
wheels, logging ... **7.** katydid
wheen ... **3.** few **5.** group **7.** several
8. division, quantity
wheerikins ... **10.** posteriors
wheetle ... **5.** chirp **7.** whistle
wheeze ... **3.** gag **4.** joke **5.** hoose
(hooze) **6.** cliché, saying **7.** breathe
8. sibilate **9.** witticism **10.** sibilation
whelk ... **4.** acne **5.** snail **6.** papule,
pimple **7.** pustule
whelp ... **3.** boy, cub, pup **5.** child,
puppy, tiger, youth **9.** give birth,
youngling
when ... **2.** as **3.** tho **5.** until
6. though **7.** how soon, whereas
8. although, whenever **10.** how long
ago **11.** at which time
where ... **4.** here, spot **5.** place, there
7. whither **10.** inasmuch as **11.** at
what place, whereabouts
whereas ... **5.** since
whereby ... **7.** perquod
whereness ... **6.** ubiety
whereupon ... **4.** when **7.** on which
9. upon which **10.** after which
wherewithal ... **5.** means, money
9. resources
whet ... **4.** hone **5.** grind, point, rouse
6. excite **7.** quicken, sharpen
9. intensify, stimulate
whether ... **2.** if **6.** either
whey ... **4.** curd **5.** serum
whiff ... **4.** blow, fish, gust, odor, puff,
waft **6.** breath, exhale, stanch
7. puff out **8.** blow away
10. inhalation
while ... **2.** as **3.** yet **4.** time **5.** until
7. beguile, interim, whereas
11. space of time
whilom ... **4.** erst, once **5.** of old
6. former **8.** sometime **9.** erstwhile
whim ... **3.** fad, pun, toy **4.** idea
5. fancy, freak **6.** megrim, notion,
vagary **7.** boutade, caprice, whimsey
(whimsy) **8.** migraine
whimper ... **3.** cry, sob **4.** mewl,
moan, pule, weep **5.** whine **7.** sniffle
whimsey, whimsy ... **3.** wit **4.** whim
5. craze, fancy, freak **7.** caprice
whimsical ... **3.** fad, odd **4.** dish
5. droll, queer, witty **7.** amusing
8. fanciful, freakish, notional
9. crotchety, eccentric, fantastic,
grotesque **10.** capricious
whine ... **4.** moan, pule, wail **6.** snivel
7. screech, ululate, whimper
8. complain **12.** moaning sound
whinny ... **4.** bray **5.** neigh, whine
whip ... **3.** cat, tan **4.** beat, crop, flag,
flog, goad, lace, lash, wale **5.** birch,
froth, quirt, seize, spank, strap
6. defeat, incite, punish, strike,
swinge, thrash **7.** agitate, chabouk
(chabuk), conquer, scourge
8. emulsify, lambaste **9.** bullwhack

10. discipline **11.** congressman
whip (pert to) ...
hand .. **8.** dominion **9.** advantage,
influence
mark .. **4.** wale, weal, welt
political .. **5.** party **11.** floor leader
riding .. **4.** crop **5.** quirt
Russian .. **4.** plet (plete) **5.** knout
sewing .. **8.** overcast
socket .. **5.** snead
whir ... **3.** fly **4.** burr, buzz, whiz
5. hurry, swirl, whizz **6.** hurtle
7. revolve, vibrate **9.** commotion
whirl ... **4.** eddy, reel, spin, tirl, turn
5. twirl **6.** circle, gyrate, rotate
7. revelry, revolve **9.** commotion,
pirouette, turn about **10.** excitement
whirlpool ... **4.** eddy **6.** gurges (Her),
vortex **7.** sea puss (sea purse)
9. maelstrom
whirlwind ... **2.** oe (Faroes) **7.** cyclone,
tornado, twister, typhoon
9. hurricane, maelstrom
10. willy–willy
whisk ... **4.** tuft, whip, wist **5.** froth,
sweep, swish **6.** convey **7.** agitate
whiskers ... **4.** chin **5.** beard
8. vibrissa **9.** sideburns
whisky, whiskey ... **3.** rye **4.** corn
6. poteen, redeye **9.** moonshine
10. usquebaugh
whisky (pert to) ...
base .. **3.** rye **5.** wheat **6.** barley
drink .. **4.** soda, sour **5.** punch, smash
7. stinger
Insurrection .. **12.** Pennsylvania (1794)
Ring .. **10.** Conspiracy (1875)
term .. **6.** lively **7.** flighty
whisper ... **3.** tip **4.** blow, buzz
5. rumor **6.** breeze, murmur
7. divulge **14.** vox clandestina
whist, game ... **9.** Cavendish
10. Yarborough
whistle ... **4.** hiss, pipe, sing, toot
5. alarm **6.** rustle, warble, wheeze
12. interference
whistle (pert to) ...
duck .. **9.** goldeneye
fish .. **8.** rockling
pig .. **9.** woodchuck
stop .. **12.** one–horse town
tree (for boys' whistles) .. **5.** maple
6. willow
Whistler painting ... **15.** Little White
Girl, Whistler's Mother
whistling (pert to) ...
coot .. **6.** scoter
dick .. **6.** thrush
duck .. **6.** scoter **9.** goldeneye
hawk .. **5.** eagle
snipe .. **8.** woodcock
sound .. **7.** stridor
teal .. **6.** scoter **8.** tree duck
whit ... **3.** bit, jot **4.** atom, iota
5. bodle, speck **8.** particle
white ... **3.** wan **4.** milk, pale, snow
5. ashen, chalk, color, happy, ivory,
snowy **6.** albino, chalky, chaste,
honest, pallid **7.** ivorine, silvery
8. innocent, platinum **9.** alabaster,
albescent, Caucasian, favorable,
fortunate, honorable

11. snow–covered
white (pert to)...
admiral.. 9. butterfly
ant.. 4. anay (anai) 7. termite
belly.. 6. pigeon 7. widgeon
14. prairie chicken
cat.. 7. catfish
cell.. 9. leucocyte
chub.. 10. spawneater
cloud.. 6. cirrus 7. tendril
coal.. 10. water power
crow.. 7. vulture
curlew.. 4. ibis
devil.. 7. nailrod
elephant.. 6. burden 8. Oriental
ensign.. 12. British naval
fish.. 5. cisco 6. atinga, beluga
8. menhaden 9. Coregonus
10. white whale
grouse.. 9. ptarmigan
growing (hoary).. 9. canescent
head.. 6. pigeon 9. blue goose
10. surf scoter
heat.. 5. anger 13. incandescence
livered.. 6. feeble 8. cowardly
13. pusillanimous
matter (nerve).. 4. alba
merganser.. 4. smew
miller.. 11. clothes moth
monk.. 10. Cistercian
mule.. 5. gin 6. whisky (illicit)
9. moonshine
oak.. 5. roble
of egg.. 5. glair
partridge.. 9. ptarmigan
plague.. 7. disease 8. phthisis
11. consumption 12. tuberculosis
plantain.. 8. pussytoe
poplar.. 5. aspen
pot.. 7. pudding
pudding.. 7. sausage 9. whitehass
pyrite.. 5. marcasite
shark.. 8. man–eater
throat.. 6. muffet (Eng) 7. warbler
whale.. 6. beluga
White (pert to)...
Chapel (Jewish).. 13. London Quarter
Holland.. 6. turkey
Horse.. 6. emblem (Saxons) 7. carving
House designer.. 5. Hoban
Relig.. 6. Friars 7. Fathers, Sisters
8. Brethren
Rose (Eng).. 6. emblem (House of
York)
Sands (N Mex).. 13. proving ground
Squadron.. 4. Navy (US Navy 1883)
Tower.. 13. Tower of London
whiten... 6. blanch, bleach 8. etiolate
9. whitewash
whitewash... 5. paint 6. defeat,
whiten 7. conceal 9. disinfect,
exculpate, gloss over
whither... 5. where 7. whereto 11. to
what place, whereabouts
whiting... 4. fish 5. chalk 6. tomcod
10. butterfish
whitish... 4. pale 5. white
9. albescent
whitlow... 4. herb, sore 5. felon
6. agnail, fetlow 8. hangnail
9. saxifrage 10. paronychia
12. inflammation

Whitsunday... 9. Pentacost
Whittington, Dick... 9. Lord Mayor
(London)
whittle... 3. cut, hew 4. gash, hack,
pare, trim 5. knife 6. reduce
7. blanket
whiz, whizz... 3. hum 4. buzz, hiss,
pirr, whir, zizz 5. whirr 6. corker,
rotate 8. sibilate 10. speed along
12. clever person
who... 3. wer, wha 5. which
6. person 7. one that, pronoun
whole... 3. all, sum 4. pure, sole, unit
5. gross, total, uncut, unity
6. entire, intact, mostly, system
7. healthy, perfect 8. absolute,
complete, entirety, totality
9. aggregate, generally, unanimous,
undivided
whole (pert to)...
comb form.. 4. toti, toto
footed.. 5. frank 8. intimate
9. ingenuous 10. flat–footed
hearted.. 7. devoted, earnest, sincere
8. complete 10. unreserved
11. unmitigated
hog.. 8. whole way 12. all or nothing
note.. 9. semibreve
number.. 7. integer
skinned.. 6. unhurt 9. unscathed
souled.. 5. noble 7. devoted, sincere,
zealous 11. noble–minded
12. wholehearted
wholesome... 4. sane 5. sound
6. hearty, robust 7. healthy
8. salutary, vigorous 9. favorable,
healthful 10. beneficial, propitious,
salubrious
wholly... 3. all 4. toto (comb form)
5. fully, quite 6. solely 7. totally
8. entirely, entirety 9. perfectly
10. altogether, completely, thoroughly
11. exclusively
whoop... 4. call, hoot, urge, yell
5. cheer, shout 6. halloo, hoopee
10. enthusiasm
whooping cough... 9. pertussis
whoop it up... 7. be noisy 8. energize
9. make merry 12. create gaiety
whop... 4. bang, beat, bump, fall,
flop, whip 5. knock 6. strike, stroke
whopper... 3. lie (monstrous) 5. story
(false)
whorl... 4. curl 5. helix, spire
8. flywheel, verticil, volution (shell)
11. fingerprint
wicked... 3. bad, ill 4. evil, vile
6. guilty, sinful, unjust 7. heinous,
hellish, profane, roguish, ungodly,
vicious 8. criminal, depraved, devilish,
diabolic, flagrant 9. abandoned,
atrocious, malicious, nefarious,
perverted 10. diabolical, flagitious,
iniquitous, villainous 11. irreligious,
mischievous, unrighteous
wickedness... 3. sin 4. evil 6. Belial
(Bib) 7. badness 8. baseness, iniquity
10. sinfulness 13. maliciousness
wicked one... 5. Demon, Satan 7. Evil
One 8. The Devil
wicker (pert to)...
basket.. 5. cesta 6. hamper, kipsey

7. pannier
cradle .. 8. bassinet
material .. 5. twigs 6. osiers, willow, withes
ware .. 8. basketry, plaiting
wicket ... 4. arch, door, gate, hoop 6. grille, window 7. grating, guichet, lattice 8. loophole 12. grated window, ticket window
wickiup, wikiup ... 3. hut 7. shelter
Widal's, Widal reaction ... 16. typhoid fever test
widbin ... 7. dogwood 8. woodbine 11. honeysuckle
widdy ... 4. rope (twig) 5. noose, widow, withy 6. halter 7. gallows 11. gallows bird
wide ... 5. ample, broad, large, loose, roomy 6. opened 7. liberal 8. expanded, spacious 9. capacious, distended 13. comprehensive
wide–awake ... 3. hat 4. keen, tern (sooty) 5. alert 7. knowing 8. watchful
widemouthed ... 4. loud 5. noisy 6. greedy 7. barking 9. devouring
widen ... 4. ream 6. dilate, expand, extend, spread 7. amplify, broaden, enlarge
widespread ... 4. rife 5. broad 7. diffuse, general 8. not local, sweeping 9. dispersed, extensive, prevalent, scattered, universal 13. comprehensive
widgeon ... 4. duck, smee 5. goose 6. Mareca, zuisin 7. poacher 8. baldpate 9. simpleton
widow ... 6. relict 7. bereave, dowager, viduate
widow (pert to) ...
bird .. 5. finch, Vidua 6. whidah
cremated .. 6. suttee
fish .. 5. viuva
monkey .. 4. titi
suicide .. 6. suttee
widower ... 6. relict
widow's (pert to) ...
lock .. 8. hairline 10. widow's peak
mite .. 4. coin 6. lepton
portion .. 5. dower
right .. 5. terce
weeds .. 8. mourning 9. black veil, widowhood
width ... 5. girth 7. breadth 8. diameter, latitude, wideness
wield ... 3. ply, use 4. cope, deal, rule 5. power, swing 6. direct, employ, handle, manage 7. control 8. brandish 10. manipulate
wife ... 4. frau, mate, rani, uxor 5. bride, mujer 6. matron, spouse 7. consort 8. gudewife (guidwife), helpmate, helpmeet 10. better half 12. married woman
wife (pert to) ...
French .. 5. femme
killing .. 9. uxoricide
of a rajah .. 4. Rani (Ranee)
one .. 8. monogamy
pert to .. 7. uxorial
slave's .. 9. broadwife
wig ... 4. tête 5. jasey 6. peruke,

toupee 7. censure, periwig 8. seal hood 9. dignitary
wight ... 3. man 4. loud 5. brave, fairy, swift, witch 6. active, nimble 7. valiant 8. creature, powerful 11. living being
wigwag ... 6. signal 8. to and fro 11. oscillation
wigwam ... 4. tent 5. hogan, tepee 6. teepee
wild ... 3. mad 5. feral, myall, waste, weird 6. ferine, savage, stormy, unruly 7. bestial, howling, riotous 8. aberrant, desolate, dramatic, frenetic, reckless, untilled, wildwood 9. barbarian, barbarous, ferocious, imprudent, primitive, unbridled, uncertain 10. boisterous, chimerical, irrational, profligate, tumultuous, unexplored, wilderness 11. harum–scarum, uncivilized, uninhabited 12. obstreperous, uncontrolled, uncultivated 14. uncontrollable
wild (pert to) ...
alder .. 8. goutweed
animal .. 3. gnu 4. bear, deer, lion, lynx 5. kiang, moose, tiger 6. dragon, onager 7. polecat 8. antelope 10. wildebeest
banana .. 5. papaw (pawpaw)
beasts .. 4. ziim
buffalo .. 4. arna 5. arnee
carrot .. 8. hilltrot
cat .. 4. balm, eyra 6. ocelot 7. panther
coffee .. 9. feverroot
crocus .. 12. pasqueflower
fancy .. 6. vagary
fowl .. 4. duck 5. goose, quail 8. pheasant 9. partridge
garlic .. 4. moly
goat .. 3. tur 4. tahr 7. markhor (markhoor)
gourd .. 7. pumpkin 11. calabazilla
growing .. 8. agrarian
hog .. 4. boar 9. razorback 10. babiroussa
hop .. 6. bryony
horse .. 6. tarpan
ibex .. 5. Capra
Irishman (shrub) .. 10. tumatakuru
jalap .. 8. mayapple
mustard .. 8. charlock
ox .. 3. yak 4. anoa
pieplant .. 7. rhubarb
pineapple .. 7. pinguin
plum .. 4. sloe 5. islay
sheep .. 3. sha 5. urial (oorial) 6. argali
sweet potato .. 7. manroot
West show .. 5. rodeo
wildebeest ... 3. gnu
wilderness ... 5. waste, wilds 6. forest 8. wildwood 9. confusion 12. complication
wile ... 3. art, toy 4. lure, ruse 5. fraud, guile, trick 6. deceit 7. cunning 8. artifice, trickery 9. stratagem
will ... 4. wish 6. behest, choice, decree, demise, desire 7. bequest,

command **8.** volition **9.** intention,
testament **10.** resolution
11. disposition, inclination
13. determination
will (pert to)...
appendix.. **7.** codicil
convey.. **6.** demise **7.** bequest
having made.. **7.** testate
maker of.. **8.** testator
power.. **7.** purpose **10.** resolution
13. determination **14.** strength of
mind
proof of.. **7.** probate
to live (Buddh).. **5.** tanha
willful, wilful... **3.** mad **4.** rash
5. heady **7.** wayward **8.** perverse,
stubborn **9.** impetuous, obstinate,
voluntary **11.** intentional
14. self–determined
willing... **4.** free **5.** prone, ready
6. minded **8.** desirous, disposed,
unforced **9.** agreeable, voluntary
10. consenting, deliberate, ready to
act, volitional **11.** intentional
12. well–disposed
willingly... **4.** fain, lief **6.** freely, gladly
7. happily, readily **10.** cheerfully
12. with pleasure
willow... **3.** iva **4.** Itea **5.** osier, salix
6. sallow, teaser
willow (pert to)...
basket.. **7.** prickle
genus.. **5.** Salix
green.. **6.** reseda
lark.. **12.** sedge warbler
pattern.. **7.** Nanking **11.** earthenware
twig.. **5.** withe **6.** sallow
wren.. **10.** chiffchaff
willowy... **5.** lithe **6.** pliant, supple,
svelte **7.** slender **8.** flexible, graceful
15. tall and graceful
Will Rogers' plane... **9.** Winnie May
wilsome... **4.** wild **6.** astray, dreary
7. violent, willful (wilful) **8.** desolate
10. bewildered
wilt... **3.** sag **4.** flag, tire **5.** droop,
quail **6.** sicken, wither **8.** languish
11. deteriorate, lose courage, make
flaccid
Wilton... **3.** rug **6.** carpet
wily... **3.** sly **4.** foxy **5.** canny, smart
6. artful, astute, crafty, shrews,
subtle **7.** cunning **9.** cautelous
wimble... **3.** awl **4.** bore **5.** auger,
brace, scoop, twist **6.** gimlet, pierce
9. sprightly, whimsical
wimick... **3.** cry **7.** whimper
wimple... **4.** fold, veil **7.** meander
8. covering (head)
win... **3.** get **4.** earn, gain **5.** to get
6. attain, defeat, obtain, secure
7. achieve, acquire, succeed, triumph
8. be victor, endeavor, vanquish
9. captivate **10.** accomplish
win (pert to)...
all tricks (game).. **4.** slam
by guile.. **8.** inveigle
one's spurs.. **10.** knighthood
over.. **7.** convert **8.** convince
persuade.. **10.** conciliate
wince... **4.** reel **5.** start **6.** cringe,
flinch, recoil, shrink **8.** draw back,

windlass **10.** shrink from
wind... **2.** oe **3.** air **4.** bora, coil,
gale, gust, talk, turn, wrap **5.** blast,
buran, crank, trade **6.** boreal, breath,
breeze, simoom, zephyr **7.** chinook,
conceit, cyclone, deviate, etesian,
meander, monsoon, sinuate, sirocco,
tempest, tornado, typhoon
8. convolve, williwaw **9.** hurricane,
idle words, windstorm **10.** instrument
wind (pert to)...
action on land.. **8.** eolation
around.. **6.** master **8.** dominate
9. influence **13.** lead by the nose
cloud.. **4.** scud
comb form.. **5.** anemo
fall.. **7.** godsend **8.** buckshee, gratuity
flower.. **7.** anemone
gauge.. **4.** vane **10.** anemometer
god.. **4.** Adad **6.** Aeolus
god of north wind.. **6.** Boreas
god of SE wind.. **5.** Eurus
instrument.. **3.** sax **4.** fife, horn
5. flute, organ **6.** cornet **7.** bassoon,
hautboy, helicon, ocarina **8.** clarinet
9. harmonica, saxophone
in the (wind).. **5.** drunk **7.** sailing
8. imminent **9.** happening
into a ball.. **11.** agglomerate
personified.. **6.** Caurus **7.** Caecias
8. Favonius, Zephyrus
ref to.. **7.** Aeolian (Eolian)
rose.. **5.** poppy
science.. **9.** anemology
storm.. **5.** gale **7.** cyclone, typhoon
9. hurricane
up.. **3.** end **7.** prepare **8.** complete,
conclude
yarn.. **6.** windle
wind (type)...
Adriatic (cold).. **4.** bora
cold.. **4.** bise, bora, puna **7.** mistral
8. williwaw
desert.. **6.** simoom **7.** sirocco
dry.. **7.** harmattan
East.. **8.** levanter
Egypt.. **7.** khamsin (kamsin)
equator.. **5.** trade
fierce.. **4.** gale **6.** buster, squall
7. monsoon **8.** blizzard **9.** hurricane
gentle.. **4.** aura **6.** zephyr
Malta (cold).. **7.** gregale
Mediterranean.. **6.** solano **7.** etesian
8. levanter
North.. **6.** Boreas
Northwest.. **6.** Caurus **7.** etesian
Oriental.. **7.** monsoon
Peru.. **4.** puna
S America.. **4.** puna **7.** pampero
South.. **6.** Auster
Southeast.. **5.** Eurus
Southwest.. **7.** chinook
Spain.. **6.** solano
West (personified).. **8.** Favonius
whirl.. **2.** oe
windiness... **7.** conceit
12. boastfulness
winding... **5.** curve, snaky **6.** spiral
7. sinuous, twining **8.** rambling,
tortuous **9.** deviative, meandrous
10. circuitous
windjammer... **6.** bugler, talker, vessel

(sailing) 8. bandsman 9. trumpeter
windlass... 4. reel 5. winch 6. windle
   7. capstan, machine (hoisting)
windle... 4. reel 5. winch 6. basket
   7. measure, redwing
window (pert to)...
  arrangement.. 8. fanlight
   12. fenestration
  bay.. 5. oriel
  dormer, roof.. 5. gable 7. lucarne
   8. skylight
  frame.. 4. sash
  Latin.. 8. fenestra
  leading.. 4. came
  nautical.. 8. porthole
  oval.. 5. oxeye
  part.. 4. pane, sash, sill 5. glass
   7. shutter
  recess.. 6. exedra 9. embrasure
  ship's.. 4. port 8. porthole
  ticket.. 6. wicket 7. guichet
  type.. 4. port 5. gable, oriel
   7. eucarne 8. casement, skylight
windpipe... 6. gullet, throat
   7. trachea, weasand
windrow... 5. swath (swathe) 6. furrow
Winds, Father of (Gr)... 8. Astraeus
windward... 5. aloof 8. aweather
   9. weatherly
Windy City... 7. Chicago
wine (pert to)...
  and honey.. 5. clary, mulse
   7. oenomel
  Baden.. 8. Ruländer
  bag.. 8. wineskin
  bibber.. 3. sot 5. toper 7. tippler
   8. drunkard
  Bordeaux.. 6. claret
  bottle.. 6. magnum 8. decanter
  cask.. 3. tun
  cellar.. 6. bodega
  comb form.. 4. oeno
  cruet.. 7. burette
  cup.. 3. ama 6. goblet 7. chalice
  divination by.. 9. oenomancy
  dry.. 3. sec
  film.. 8. beeswing
  French.. 6. Masden, Pontac (Pontacq)
   8. muscatel 9. Hermitage
   10. Montrachet 12. Saint–Emilion,
   Saint–Estèphe
  glass.. 6. rummer (Rom)
  grower.. 8. vigneron
  hater of.. 11. oenophobist
  Italian.. 7. Orvieto 8. muscatel
  kind.. 4. port 5. Medoc, Rhine, tinta,
   Tokay 6. canary, claret, Malaga,
   sherry 7. Chablis, Madeira
   8. Burgundy, muscatel, sauterne,
   vermouth 9. champagne
  lover of.. 11. oenophilist
  maker.. 6. abkari (abkary)
  making.. 10. oenopoetic
  merchant.. 5. abkar
  miracle scene.. 4. Cana (Bib)
  palm.. 5. taree
  Persian.. 6. Shiraz
  pitcher.. 4. olpe 8. oenochoe
  reference to.. 5. vinic
  residue.. 4. marc
  sherry.. 5. Xeres 7. Catawba, Moselle,
   oloroso

  shop.. 3. bar 6. bistro, bodega
  Spain.. 6. Malaga
  sparkling.. 8. mousseux
  study of.. 8. oenology
  sweet.. 5. lunel
  taster.. 10. oenologist
  Tuscan.. 7. Chianti
  white.. 6. Malaga 8. Riesling,
   sauterne, verdelho 12. Marcobrunner
  year.. 7. vintage
wing... 3. ala, arm, fly 6. convey,
   flight, member, pinion 7. faction
   8. addition, dispatch
wing (pert to)...
  anterior.. 7. elytron
  comb form.. 7. pterygo
  false.. 5. alula
  fish.. 8. sea robin
  footed.. 6. aliped
  Greek.. 6. pteryx
  quill.. 7. remiges
  shaped.. 7. aliform
  tip.. 7. aileron
  winglike.. 4. alar 7. pteroid
   9. pterygoid
winged... 4. aile (Her), fast 5. alate,
   lofty, rapid, swift 7. pennate, sublime
   9. aliferous, aligerous
winged (pert to)...
  boots (of Hermes).. 7. talaria
  child.. 6. cherub
  fruit.. 6. samara
  monster.. 5. harpy
Winged Horse (Gr Myth)... 7. Pegasus
Winged Victory... 4. Nike
wingless... 7. apteral, Apteryx, exalate
   8. dealated (dealate)
wink... 3. nap, nod 4. hint 5. blink,
   flash 6. glance, signal, twitch
   7. flicker, instant, nictate, twinkle
   9. nictation, nictitate, twinkling
   10. palpebrate, periwinkle
winker... 3. eye 7. blinker, eyelash
   8. blinkard
winking... 13. blepharospasm
winks, forty... 3. nap 6. catnap
   10. light sleep
winner... 3. ace 6. earner, reaper,
   victor 7. sleeper 8. bangster
   9. conqueror 11. breadwinner
winning... 7. gaining, lovable, victory,
   winsome 8. alluring, charming
   10. attractive, successful, victorious
   11. acquisition, captivating
winninish, winnonish... 6. salmon
   (landlocked) 10. ouananiche
winnock... 6. window
winnow... 3. fan 4. sift, stir 6. assort,
   select, thresh 8. disperse, separate
   9. eliminate
winsome... 3. gay 5. bonny, merry
   7. lovable, winning 8. alluring,
   charming, cheerful, pleasant
   10. attractive 11. captivating
   12. lighthearted
winter... 4. bise, snow 5. hiems
   6. old age, season 8. coldness
winter (pert to)...
  beer.. 6. Schenk
  berry.. 4. Ilex 5. holly
  bloom.. 6. azalea 10. witch hazel
  bonnet.. 4. gull

duck.. 7. pintail 8. old squaw
fever.. 9. pneumonia
god.. 5. Hiems
lettuce.. 6. endive
mew.. 4. gull
pert to.. 6. brumal, hiemal
quarters.. 10. hibernacle
  12. hibernaculum
sleep.. 11. hibernation
teal.. 9. greenwing
Winter Palace (Leningrad)...
  6. museum
wipe... 3. dry, mop, rub 5. cheat,
  clean, erase 6. cancel, remove
  7. abolish, defraud 10. obliterate
  11. exterminate
wire... 4. coil, cord, line, whip
  5. cable, snare 6. thread 7. fencing,
  lametta (gold), netting, reticle
  8. telegram, wirework 9. cablegram,
  telegraph 10. pickpocket 14. knitting
  needle
wirepuller... 10. influencer, machinator,
  politician, strategist
wiry... 4. lean 5. hardy, stiff, tough
  6. sinewy, strong 7. stringy
  8. enduring, muscular
wis... 5. think 7. imagine, suppose
Wisconsin...
capital.. 7. Madison
city.. 6. Racine 7. Kenosha, Oshkosh
  8. Green Bay 9. Fond du Lac,
  Milwaukee
famed as.. 17. America's Dairyland
first white man.. 7. Nicolet (Jean)
lake.. 8. Michigan, Superior
  9. Winnebago
river.. 7. St Croix 11. Mississippi
State admission.. 9. Thirtieth
State motto.. 7. Forward
State nickname.. 6. Badger
wisdom... 5. logos 8. judgment,
  learning, sagacity, sapience
  9. erudition, knowledge
  10. discretion, profundity
wisdom god... 4. Nebo (Nabu)
  6. Ganesa (Ganesha)
wisdom goddess... 6. Athena
  7. Minerva (Gr)
wise... 3. hep 4. sage, sane, wary
  5. aware 6. shrewd, subtle, versed
  7. erudite, knowing, learned, politic,
  sapient 8. discreet, informed,
  profound 9. cognizant, expedient,
  judicious, provident 10. omniscient
  11. circumspect, enlightened,
  philosophic 13. sophisticated
wise (pert to)...
councilor.. 6. mentor, nestor
man.. 4. sage 5. solon, witan
  6. nestor, wizard 7. Solomon
saying.. 4. rede 5. adage
Wise Men (three)... 6. Gaspar
  8. Melchior 9. Balthasar
Wise Men of Greece... 5. Seven
Wise Men of the East... 19. Three
  Kings of Cologne
wish... 4. care, hope, will, wuss
  5. yearn 6. aspire, desire, invoke
  7. longing, request 8. optative,
  petition 10. aspiration
  11. imprecation

wishbone... 7. furcula 8. furculum
  10. fourchette 12. merry thought
wisp... 4. floc 5. brush, flock, shred
  6. bundle 7. handful 8. fragment
wistful... 7. longing, pensive
  8. desirous, yearning 9. nostalgic
  10. melancholy
wit... 3. pun, wag 5. humor, sense
  6. acumen, esprit, satire, wisdom
  7. punster 8. comedian, humorist,
  repartee 9. alertness 11. philosopher,
  savoir–faire 12. intelligence
  13. understanding
wit (to)... 3. viz 5. truly 6. indeed,
  namely, that is 8. scilicet 9. videlicet
witch... 3. hag, hex 4. baba 5. Circe,
  crone, lamia, shrew, vixen
  6. cummer, Hecate (Hekate), Lilith
  (Lilis), wizard 7. warlock 8. old
  woman 9. grimalkin, sorceress
  11. witch doctor 12. ugly old
  woman
witchcraft... 5. charm, magic, wanga
  7. cunning, hexerei, sorcery
  8. brujeria 9. sortilege, voodooism
  10. bewitchery, black magic
  11. enchantment 12. invultuation
witch doctor... 3. hex 6. shaman
  9. voodooist, wangateur
witchery... 5. charm, spell 7. sorcery
  8. wizardry 10. allurement,
  necromancy 11. enchantment,
  fascination
with (pref)... 2. co 3. com, con, cum,
  mit, syn 4. avec
with... 5. among 7. jointly 8. together
  9. alongside, including 10. hand in
  hand 11. association
  12. concurrently 13. co–operatively
withal... 5. still 9. thereupon 10. for
  all that
withdraw... 6. absent, deduct, recall,
  recant, recede, remove, repeal, retire,
  secede 7. abandon, detract, disavow,
  forsake, refrain, regress, retract,
  retreat, subside 8. alienate, evacuate,
  renounce 9. disengage 10. relinquish
withdrawal... 6. repeal 7. regress,
  retiral, retreat 8. escapism
  9. departure, recession, seclusion
  10. detachment, extraction,
  retraction, separation
  11. abandonment, recantation,
  resignation
withdrawn... 7. ingrown 8. detached,
  secluded
withe... 4. band, rope 5. snare
  6. halter, wattle, willow
wither... 3. age, die, dry 4. fade,
  sear, sere, wilt 5. decay, droop, dry
  up, wizen 6. blight, shrink 7. shrivel,
  wrinkle 8. languish 11. deteriorate
withered... 4. sere 8. shrunken
  9. shriveled
withering... 7. caustic 9. shrinking
  10. marcescent 12. contemptuous
  13. deteriorating
withhold... 4. curb, deny 5. check
  6. detain, refuse, retain 7. abstain,
  prevent, refrain, repress, reserve
  8. hold back, postpone, restrain
within... 6. at home, during, inside

7. indoors 8. inside of, inwardly
9. inner side
without ... 4. sans, sine 5. minus
6. beyond, except, lack of, unless
7. lacking, not with 9. absence of,
outwardly 10. externally, out–of–doors
without (pert to) ... see also *absence of*
action .. 8. deedless
animation .. 5. amort
appointment (of day) .. 7. sine die
beginning, or end .. 7. eternal
cause .. 10. unprovoked
connections .. 7. tieless
delay .. 9. summarily
doubt .. 9. sine dubio
ethics .. 6. amoral
exception .. 11. universally
feet .. 4. apod 6. apodal
foliage .. 8. aphylous
friends .. 4. lorn 7. forlorn 8. forsaken
knowledge .. 8. ignorant
mate .. 3. odd
prefix .. 4. ecto
rule .. 8. anarchic
substance .. 5. inane
support .. 7. legless 9. dependent
teeth .. 8. edentate 9. toothless
this .. 7. sine hoc
warning .. 12. out of the blue
wings .. 7. apteral
withstand ... 4. bear, bide, defy, last
5. abide 6. endure, oppose, resist
8. confront 10. contradict
witless ... 3. mad 5. crazy, dazed
6. stupid 7. foolish, unaware
8. heedless 9. brainless, unknowing
10. indiscreet 13. unintelligent
witness ... 3. eye, see 4. know
5. swear, teste, vouch 6. attend,
attest, beheld, behold, testor
7. observe, testify 8. beholder,
deponent, evidence, observer,
onlooker 9. informant, spectator,
subscribe, testimony 11. attestation
witticism ... 3. mot, pun 4. jest, joke,
quip 5. droll, sally, slent 8. repartee
9. wisecrack 10. pleasantry
11. gauloiserie, witty saying
wittingly ... 8. by design 9. knowingly
13. intentionally
witty ... 4. wise 5. comic, droll, sharp
6. clever, facete, jocose, jocund
7. amusing, comical, jocular, knowing
8. humorous 9. facetious, whimsical
wivern, wyvern (Her) ... 6. dragon
(2–legged)
wizard ... 4. mage, sage 6. expert,
genius, Merlin, pellar, shaman
7. magical, prodigy 8. conjurer,
magician, sorcerer 10. Wizard of Oz
11. necromancer, thaumaturge, witch
doctor 13. thaumaturgist
Wizard of the North ... 14. Sir Walter
Scott
wizen ... 3. age, dry 4. thin 6. gullet,
shrink, weazen, wither 7. shrivel
8. windpipe 11. deteriorate
wlo (obs) ... 3. hem 6. fringe
woad ... 3. dye 4. herb 5. tinge
8. dyestuff 10. pastel blue
wobble, wabble ... 4. walk 5. shake,

waver 7. stagger, tremble
8. hobbling 9. fluctuate, oscillate,
vacillate
Woden, Wodan (Myth) ... 3. god
(chief) 4. Odin 9. Wednesday (named
for Woden)
woe ... 4. bale, bane 5. grief
6. misery, sorrow 7. anguish, trouble
8. anathema, calamity 10. affliction,
melancholy, misfortune
woebegone ... 3. sad 6. woeful
7. unhappy 8. dejected, desolate
10. dispirited, melancholy
woeful ... 3. sad 6. paltry 7. direful,
pitiful 8. grievous, mournful, wretched
9. afflicted, miserable, sorrowful,
woebegone 10. deplorable
12. disconsolate
wold ... 3. lea 4. wood 5. downs,
plain, weald 6. forest, meadow
7. low hill
wolf ... 4. lobo 5. lupus 6. coyote,
mammal 7. Isegrim 8. werewolf
9. libertine 11. philanderer
wolf fish ... 6. blenny
wolfhound ... 6. borzoi
wolflike ... 6. lupine, thooid
wolverine ... 4. Gulo 11. Michigander,
Michiganite
Wolverine State ... 8. Michigan
woman ... 4. dame, girl, lady, rani, wife
5. adult, begum, gemme, madam,
squaw 6. female 7. distaff
8. feminine, paramour, senorita
9. weaker sex, womankind
10. sweetheart
woman (pert to) ...
adviser .. 6. Egeria (Rom Myth)
apartment of .. 3. oda (harem)
8. thalamus
beautiful .. 4. doll 5. filly, pin-up,
siren, sylph, Venus 7. charmer,
Zenobia 8. Musidora
bewitching .. 4. peri 5. siren, vixen
7. charmer
celibate .. 7. agapeta
chaser .. 9. libertine 11. philanderer
club (of women) .. 7. sorosis
8. sorority
comb form .. 3. gyn
dignified, elderly .. 7. dowager
dowdy .. 5. frump 6. untidy 8. slattern
gossipy .. 3. cat 15. flibbertigibbet
graceful .. 5. sylph 7. slender
gypsy .. 5. romni
hater .. 10. misogynist
hatred of .. 8. misogyny
kept .. 8. mistress 9. concubine
12. demimondaine
killer .. 8. femicide
learned .. 12. bluestocking
loose .. 4. drab 5. whore 6. harlot
7. trollop 10. prostitute
12. streetwalker
lover of .. 11. philogynist
modest (affectedly) .. 5. prude
mythical (ugly) .. 6. Gorgon
noisy .. 9. termagant
of rank .. 4. dame
old .. 5. crone, frump 6. granny
7. carline, dowager 8. grandame
9. cailleach

ruler.. 9. matriarch
scolding.. 5. shrew 6. virago
socialite.. 3. deb 6. subdeb
  9. debutante 13. fashion leader
stately.. 4. lady 6. matron
suffragist.. 8. feminist
vixenish.. 5. shrew 6. virago
  8. harridan
weeping.. 5. Niobe
will maker.. 9. testatrix
young, unmarried.. 4. lass 6. damsel
  8. spinster 10. demoiselle
womanhood... 4. Emer 10. femininity
woman's property (free)...
  10. parapherna
wonder... 3. awe 6. marvel, rarity
  7. miracle, prodigy 8. surprise
  9. amazement 10. admiration,
  wonderment 12. astonishment
wonderful... 6. superb, unique
  7. amazing, corking, mirific, strange
  8. wondrous 9. admirable,
  marvelous, mirifical 10. remarkable,
  surprising 11. astonishing
  13. extraordinary
wont... 3. use 5. habit, usage
  6. custom
woo... 3. sue 6. invite 7. beseech,
  entreat, solicit
wood... 4. tree 5. xylon 6. lignum,
  lumber, timber 8. firewood
wood (pert to)...
aromatic.. 5. aloes, cedar 8. agalloch
ash.. 6. potash
black.. 5. ebony
block.. 3. nog 4. dook
boring (of insects).. 8. xylotomy
bundles.. 6. fagots
carving.. 10. xyloglyphy
clearing.. 5. glade
color.. 7. biscuit
comb form.. 4. hylo, xylo 5. ligni,
  ligno, xylon
core.. 3. ame
curved strip.. 5. stave
dealer.. 10. xylopolist
deity.. 3. Pan 4. faun 5. Diana, Satyr
  7. Silenus 8. Silvanus
eating.. 11. xylophagous
goddess.. 5. Diana
growing on.. 6. fungus
  11. xylophilous
growth.. 7. boscage, coppice, thicket
hard.. 3. ash, elm 4. rate, teak
  5. ebony, maple 6. walnut
  8. mahogany
inlay.. 9. marquetry
nymph.. 4. moth 5. dryad
overlay.. 6. veneer
resembling.. 6. xyloid
stork.. 4. ibis
strip.. 4. lath, slat 5. sprag, stave
  6. batten
touch.. 4. punk 5. spunk (sponk)
  9. touchwood
tough, elastic.. 3. ash
tract.. 5. grove 6. forest
woodchuck... 6. marmot 9. ground
  hog
Woodchuck Day... 9. Candlemas
woodcock... 5. pewee 6. peewee,
  shrups 10. woodpecker

wooden (pert to)...
container.. 3. box 4. case 6. barrel
horse.. 6. Trojan
Indian.. 15. cigar–store brave
joint.. 5. tenon
made of.. 5. treen
pert to.. 4. dull 6. clumsy, stolid,
  stupid 8. lifeless 14. expressionless
pin.. 3. fid, nog, peg 5. dowel, spile
pole.. 4. palo
shoe.. 5. sabot 6. patten
stand.. 5. criss
tub.. 3. soe
woodpecker... 4. chab 5. Picus
  6. yaffle, yukkel (yuckle) 7. flicker,
  wryneck 8. hickwall 9. sapsucker
  10. carpintero, pickerwood
  11. woodknacker
woods (pert to)...
inhabiting.. 7. nemoral
lover of.. 11. nemophilist
pert to.. 6. sylvan (silvan)
  10. sylvestral
sacred (grove).. 10. Nemorensis
woodwind... 4. oboe 5. flute
  7. bassoon, piccolo 8. clarinet
  9. saxophone
woody... 6. sylvan, xyloid 8. ligneous
woof... 3. abb 4. weft 6. fabric
  7. filling, texture
wool... 3. fur 4. down, hair 5. cloth,
  llama, sheep 6. fleece 8. barragan
  (barragon)
wool (pert to)...
card.. 3. tum 4. comb 5. tease
clean.. 7. garnett
cloth.. 5. serge, tweed, yerga
  6. angora, duffel, kersey, satara,
  tartan, tricot, vicuña 7. doeskin,
  flannel, ratteen 8. cashmere
  10. broadcloth
comb form.. 4. lani
dead sheep's.. 8. mortling
dryer.. 5. fugal
fat.. 7. lanolin (lanoline)
fatty substance.. 5. suint
garment.. 6. alpaca, linder
implement.. 6. carder, shears, teaser
  7. distaff, spindle
inferior, dirty.. 7. cleamer
kind.. 6. alpaca, angora, merino
  8. picklock
leg.. 4. gare
reclaimed.. 5. mungo 6. shoddy
reference to.. 5. wooly 6. lanate,
  lanose 10. flocculent
spun.. 4. yarn
tuft.. 8. floccule 9. flocculus
undyed, natural.. 5. beige
waste.. 3. fud 4. noil
yarn.. 3. abb 7. eis wool
wooly (woolly)... 5. downy, fuzzy
  6. fleecy, lanate 7. blurred
  8. confused, floccose, peronate
word... 4. news, oath 5. adage,
  maxim, parol 6. avowal, remark,
  report 7. command, dispute,
  message, promise, tidings, vocable
  8. acrostic, password 9. discourse,
  statement 11. declaration, information
  13. communication
word, words (pert to)...

action .. **4.** verb
battle of .. **9.** logomachy
blindness .. **6.** alexia
book .. **6.** Gradus **7.** lexicon, speller
   8. glossary **9.** thesaurus
   10. dictionary
contraction .. **9.** haplology
deletion at end .. **7.** apocope
derivation .. **6.** etymon **9.** etymology
distinguishing (Bib) .. **10.** shibboleth
divine .. **5.** Logos
excessive interest .. **10.** verbomania
figurative use .. **5.** trope
figure of speech .. **7.** metonym,
   paronym
first on walls (Bib) .. **21.** mene, mene,
   tekel, upharsin
for word .. **8.** verbatim **9.** literally
hard to pronounce .. **10.** jawbreaker
inventor of .. **6.** coiner **9.** neologist
last syllable .. **6.** ultima
last syllable but one .. **6.** penult
last syllable omitted .. **7.** apocope
law .. **7.** by parol **11.** word of mouth
letter .. **8.** logogram **9.** logogriph
   11. grammalogue
longest in dictionary ..
   28. antidisestablishmentarianism
loss from middle .. **7.** syncope
magical .. **6.** presto, sesame
meaning .. **9.** semantics
misuse .. **11.** catachresis, heterophemy,
   malapropism
mysterious (Bib) .. **5.** selah
new .. **9.** neologism
new usage .. **7.** neology
of different name for same thing ..
   9. heteronym
of honor .. **6.** parole **7.** promise
of opposite meaning .. **7.** antonym
of same derivation .. **7.** paronym
of same meaning .. **7.** synonym
of same sound .. **7.** homonym
of imitation .. **6.** echoic **9.** onomatope
   12. onomatopoeia
popular .. **5.** cliché **8.** buzzword
pretentious use .. **10.** lexiphanic
puzzle .. **5.** rebus **7.** anagram
   8. acrostic **9.** crossword
repetition .. **5.** ploce
root .. **6.** etymon
same back to front .. **10.** palindrome
science .. **10.** lexicology
scrambled .. **7.** anagram
song hits .. **6.** lyrics
substitution .. **5.** trope **7.** metonym
theory .. **6.** bowwow **8.** pooh–pooh
The Word (Bib) .. **5.** Logos
with loss of vowel at beginning ..
   7. aphasia
without vowels .. **6.** rhythm, syzygy
with vowels (all) .. **7.** eulogia, miaoued,
   sequoia **12.** ambidextrous
with vowels in sequence .. **8.** caesious
wordiness ... **8.** pleonasm, verbiage
   9. prolixity, verbacity **10.** redundance
wording ... **8.** phrasing **10.** expression
wordless ... **5.** tacit **6.** silent
wordy ... **6.** prolix **7.** verbose
   9. garrulous **10.** long–winded
   12. long–drawn–out
work ... **3.** gig, job, mix **4.** book, deed,

duty, make, opus, plan, task, to–do,
   toil **5.** chore, ergon, labor, solve,
   trade **6.** action, Arbeit, create, effect,
   effort **7.** ferment, operate, perform,
   product, travail **8.** business, drudgery,
   endeavor, function, industry, struggle
   10. accomplish, employment,
   engagement, management,
   occupation, profession
   11. achievement, performance,
   undertaking
work (pert to) ...
agreement .. **4.** code, pact **8.** contract
bag .. **7.** tote bag **8.** reticule
carelessly .. **5.** scamp
clothes .. **8.** overalls **9.** blue jeans,
   coveralls, dungarees
comb form .. **3.** erg **4.** ergo
divine .. **7.** miracle, theurgy **9.** occult
   art
hard .. **3.** peg, tew **4.** char, moil, plug,
   toil **5.** labor, sweat **6.** drudge
   7. travail **9.** lucubrate **18.** burn the
   midnight oil
hate of .. **10.** ergophobia
helper .. **3.** aid (aide) **9.** assistant,
   paralegal, paramedic
horse .. **4.** mule **5.** burro
hours .. **9.** flexitime (flextime)
household .. **4.** char **5.** chare
incomplete art .. **7.** ébauche
inlay .. **6.** mosaic, niello
lover of .. **9.** ergophile
measure of .. **9.** ergometer
of excellence .. **4.** opus **7.** classic
out .. **5.** solve **7.** arrange, develop
   9. calculate
over .. **6.** recast, rehash, revamp
   9. brainwash, influence
shift .. **5.** swing **9.** graveyard,
   moonlight
slowly .. **6.** potter, putter **7.** ca'canny
study of .. **8.** ergology
together .. **4.** team **9.** cooperate
   11. collaborate
unit of .. **3.** erg **5.** ergon, joule
up .. **4.** plan **5.** rouse **6.** excite, incite
   7. advance, agitate, develop
   10. manipulate
workable ... **6.** pliant **7.** operant
   8. feasible, operable, solvable
   9. practical **11.** practicable
worker ... **3.** CPA **5.** diver, mason,
   miner **6.** barman, cooper, slater,
   smithy, tanner, warper, wright
   7. analyst, cobbler, glazier, plumber,
   riveter, sandhog, servant, spinner
   8. honeybee, mechanic, strapper
   9. carpenter, clinician, machinist,
   stevedore **10.** accountant
   11. breadwinner
worker (pert to) ...
fellow .. **5.** buddy **8.** confrere
group .. **4.** crew, gang, team **5.** corps,
   staff **9.** personnel
hard .. **6.** beaver, drudge, fagger
   10. workaholic
head .. **4.** boss **7.** foreman
   8. employer, overseer
   14. superintendent
indifferent .. **4.** scab **11.** scissorbill
migrant .. **4.** hobo **6.** boomer

7. floater, wetback
workhouse... 6. prison 9. almshouse, poorhouse
workman... 4. peon 6. coolie, earner 7. artisan, laborer 8. operator, opificer 9. artificer, craftsman, performer
workshop... 3. lab 4. mill 5. plant 6. studio 7. atelier, factory 10. laboratory 11. ergasterion
world... 5. globe, realm 6. cosmos, domain 7. kingdom, society 8. creation, humanity, universe 9. multitude, the public
world (pert to)...
  external.. 6. nonego
  great.. 9. macrocosm
  lower.. 5. Hades, Orcus
  miniature.. 9. microcosm
  of fairies.. 6. faerie (faery)
  precreation.. 10. premundane 11. antemundane
  reference to.. 7. mundane 11. terrestrial
worldly... 7. earthly, mundane, secular, terrene 11. terrestrial 13. materialistic, sophisticated
world's oldest city, still inhabited... 8. Damascus
world's speech... 7. Volapuk 9. universal
worm... 3. ess 4. coil, grub, wind 5. borer, tinea 6. blight, insect, maggot, vermin, wretch 8. helminth 9. trematode, vermicule 10. Nemertinea (Nemertina)
worm (pert to)...
  Africa.. 3. loa 6. Guinea
  aquatic, marine.. 7. eunicid, lugworm 8. flatworm 9. planarian 13. platyhelminth
  arrow.. 7. sagitta
  bait.. 9. angleworm, earthworm
  bloodsucking.. 5. leech
  caddie.. 5. cadew
  cotton.. 8. bollworm 10. boll weevil
  edible.. 6. palolo
  eye–infecting.. 3. loa
  genus.. 6. Virmes 7. Ascaris, Filaria 8. Annelida 10. Nemertinea (Nemertina)
  grublike.. 5. larva
  killer.. 9. vermicide
  larva.. 4. army, slug 5. cadew 6. caddis, looper 8. wireworm 11. caterpillar
  luminous.. 8. glowworm
  marine.. 7. eunicid
  measuring.. 6. looper 8. inchworm
  parasitic.. 7. Ascaris, Filaria 8. trichina, woodworm 9. trematode 10. Guinea worm 12. enthelmintha
  ref to.. 8. anneloid 9. nemertean, nemertine, nemertoid, trematoid
  ring.. 5. tinea 7. annelid
  round.. 7. ascarid, Ascaris
  segmented.. 8. Annelida
  ship.. 5. borer 6. teredo
  silk.. 4. eria
  soft.. 4. grub
  study of.. 10. vermeology 13. helminthology

tape.. 6. taenia
track.. 7. nereite 11. helminthite
wire.. 4. lava 9. millepede
worm (type)... 3. cut, dew, lug, pin 4. army, boll, eria, flat, glow, inch, ring, ship, silk, slug, tape, wire, wood 5. angle, earth, larva, leech, round, tinea 6. marine 9. measuring, parasitic
wormlike... 7. vermian 11. helminthoid
wormy... 6. earthy, humble, rotten 8. crawling 9. groveling
worn... 3. old 4. sere, used 5. stale, trite 7. abraded, haggard 8. attrited, tattered, weakened 9. exhausted, hackneyed 10. secondhand 11. commonplace
worn–out... 4. used 5. jaded, passé, seedy, spent, trite 6. shabby, used up 7. haggard 8. consumed, fatigued, impaired, tired out 9. enfeebled, exhausted 10. threadbare
worried... 5. cared, fazed 6. stewed 7. annoyed, anxious, fearful, fretted 8. troubled 9. perturbed
worry... 3. nag, rux, vex 4. care, cark, faze, fret, stew 5. annoy, brood, harry 6. bother, harass, pester, plague, pother 7. anxiety, bedevil, concern, perturb, torment, trouble 8. distress 9. annoyance 10. harassment, uneasiness
worship... 5. adore, honor, serve 6. bhakti, homage, revere 7. idolize, liturgy, respect 8. blessing, devotion, idolatry, venerate 9. adoration, deference, reverence 10. veneration
worship (pert to)...
  form of.. 6. preces, ritual 7. liturgy
  house of.. 6. chapel, church, mosque, shrine 9. cathedral, synagogue 10. tabernacle
  object of.. 4. icon, idol 5. totem 6. fetish
  place of.. 5. altar
  system of.. 4. cult 6. cultus, fetish, ritual 8. doctrine
worshiper... 6. adorer, bhakti, votary 8. disciple, idolater 10. ignicolist 12. iconomachist
worshipful... 6. devout 7. notable 8. esteemed 9. honorable, venerable 13. distinguished
worship of...
  a god.. 9. theolatry
  angels.. 5. dulia
  genii.. 10. geniolatry
  god.. 6. latria (RCCh)
  idols.. 8. idolatry
  images.. 10. iconolatry
  nature.. 11. physiolatry
  one god.. 9. monolatry
  snakes.. 10. ophiolatry
  soul.. 7. animism
  sun.. 10. heliolatry
  the mob.. 9. mobolatry
worst... 3. bad 4. beat, evil 6. defeat, wicked 7. harmful 8. inferior 10. calamitous, pernicious, unpleasant 12. disagreeable
worsted... 4. yarn 6. crewel

7. genappe
worth... 5. merit, price, value
6. desert, repute, riches, stiver,
wealth 8. eminence, meriting,
property 9. deserving 10. excellence,
importance, usefulness
worthless... 3. bad, ort 4. base, evil,
mean, raca (Bib), vile 6. futile,
nought (naught), paltry 7. fustian,
useless 8. nugatory, rubbishy,
unworthy 9. valueless
11. undeserving
14. good–for–nothing
worthwhile... 6. useful 7. gainful
9. expedient, well–spent
10. invaluable, profitable
worthy... 3. fit 7. merited 8. eligible,
valuable 9. celebrity, competent,
deserving, estimable, excellent,
honorable, qualified, reputable
11. meritorious
worthy of... 8. credible, meriting
9. deserving 10. entitled to
wound... 3. cut 4. gore, harm, hurt,
pain, rist, scar, sore, stab 5. sting
6. breach, damage, grieve, injury,
lesion, offend, trauma 8. distress
9. detriment
wound (pert to)...
 discharge.. 5. ichor 6. sanies
 dressing.. 7. bandage, pledget
 mark.. 4. scab, scar, welt 7. blister
woven... 4. spun 10. fabricated
wow... 4. howl, rave, wail 5. whine
wrack... 4. kelp, rack, ruin 5. tease,
trash, weeds, wreck 6. refuse
7. seaweed 8. eelgrass, wreckage
9. shipwreck 11. destruction
wraith... 4. food 5. ghost, spook
8. illusion 10. apparition
12. Doppelgänger, doubleganger
wrangle... 4. herd, spar 5. argue,
brawl 6. bicker, debate 7. contend,
dispute, quarrel 8. haggling
9. altercate, bickering 11. altercation,
controversy 12. disagreement
wrangler... 6. cowboy 7. debater,
student (Cambridge, Eng)
8. herdsman, opponent
9. combatant, disputant
10. antagonist
wrangling... 11. belligerent,
contentious
wrap... 3. rug 4. cape, cere, furl, roll,
wind 5. cloak, gange 6. afghan,
encowl, enfold, swathe 7. blanket,
conceal, package 8. covering,
enshroud, enswathe, envelope
9. encompass
wrapped up... 7. bound up, selfish
8. absorbed, included, involved
9. dependent, devoted to, engrossed
11. inseparable
wrapper... 4. gown 5. cerer 6. fardel,
kimono, tillot 7. garment, pelisse
8. envelope, peignoir
wrapping... 6. charta 7. wrapper
8. cerement, covering 9. parchment
wrasse... 4. fish 6. ballan, cunner,
Labrus 7. seawife 11. peacock fish
wrath... 3. ire 4. fury, grim, rage
5. anger 6. choler 7. passion

8. violence 10. turbulence
11. indignation 12. exasperation
wrathful... 3. mad 5. angry, irate
6. ireful, raging 7. angered
8. incensed 9. indignant, malignant
10. passionate
wreak... 4. do to 6. avenge 7. gratify,
indulge, inflict 13. bring down upon
wreath... 3. lei 4. band, orle
5. crown, torse (Her), whorl
6. anadem, circle, corona, laurel,
trophy 7. coronet, festoon, garland,
Iresine 8. encircle
wreathe... 4. coil, wind 5. crown,
twine, twist 7. entwine 8. decorate,
encircle 9. interlace 10. twist about
wreck... 4. raze, ruin, undo 5. crash,
smash 6. jalopy 7. destroy, disable
8. accident, demolish, derelict
9. shipwreck 10. broken form
11. disassemble, The Hesperus
wreckage... 5. ruins 6. jetsam
7. flotsam 8. driftage
wrench... 4. jerk, pipe, pull, tear
5. twist, wrest 6. sprain, twinge
7. distort 8. crescent, distress
wrench, type of... 3. box, pin
5. wramp 6. monkey 7. spanner
8. carriage, Stillson 9. alligator
wrest... 4. rend, turn 5. exact, force,
seize, twist, wring 6. elicit, extort,
wrench 7. distort, extract, pervert,
wrestle 8. misapply
wrestle... 3. tug 6. squirm, tussle
7. contend, grapple, scuffle, wriggle
8. struggle 9. throw down 10. twist
about 11. come to grips
wrestling school... 9. palaestra
(palestra)
wretch... 3. dog 5. miser, ronin
6. outlaw, pariah 7. caitiff, cullion,
outcast 8. derelict, sufferer
9. miscreant 10. base person
11. offscouring, rapscallion
14. good–for–nothing 16. pitiable
creature
wretched... 3. sad 4. base, mean
6. dismal, paltry, woeful 7. baleful,
forlorn, squalid, unhappy, very bad
8. grievous 9. execrable, miserable
10. despicable, distressed
12. contemptible, disreputable
wretchedness... 6. misery 8. distress,
meanness, poorness 10. paltriness
11. unhappiness 13. penuriousness
wriggle... 5. twist 6. squirm, writhe
7. meander
wriggle out of... 4. turn, wind
5. dodge, snake, twist 6. squirm,
writhe 8. slip away 10. crawl out of
11. squirm out of 13. find a
loophole
wring... 5. twist, wrest 6. extort,
wrench 7. extract, torture, wrestle
8. compress, convolve 9. cause pain
10. contortion, extraction
wrinkle... 3. fad 4. fold, idea, ruga,
seam 5. crimp, knack, ridge, rivel
6. crease, furrow, pucker, rimple,
ripple, rumple 7. crinkle, novelty
8. contract 9. corrugate
11. corrugation 12. clever notion

wrinkled... 4. aged 5. savoy
6. rugate, rugose, rugous 7. creased
8. crinkled, crumpled, furrowed,
puckered, rugulose 9. shriveled
10. contracted, corrugated
wrinkles... 5. rugae
wrist... 5. joint 6. carpal, carpus
8. os magnum 9. capitatum
writ... 5. breve, tales 6. capias, elegit,
venire 7. process 8. detainer,
document, mittimus, replevin,
subpoena 10. certiorari, instrument
11. fieri facias
writ (pert to)...
common law.. 11. fieri facias
court.. 7. summons 8. subpoena
execution.. 6. elegit
jury.. 5. tales 6. venire
law.. 4. capo, pone 5. breve, error
6. capias, elegit 7. mandate,
process, warrant 8. citation
10. certiorari
write... 3. pen 5. draft, trace
6. decree, depict, draw up, enroll,
indite, record, scrive 7. compose,
scriven 8. inscribe, scribble
11. communicate
write (pert to)...
carelessly.. 6. scrawl 8. scrabble,
scribble
in large hand.. 7. engross
off.. 4. drop 6. cancel, deduct, repeal
out.. 6. record 8. spill out 12. put in
writing
poetry.. 7. versify
up.. 6. record, report 7. article
9. publicize 11. press report
writer... 4. hack, poet 6. author,
penman, penner, scribe 7. elegist,
glosser, hymnist 8. annalist,
composer, lyricist, novelist, parodist,
scriptor 9. annotator, columnist,
scrivener 10. chronicler, journalist
13. correspondent
writer's afterthoughts... 7. addenda
writhe... 4. bend, coil, curl, wind
5. twist, wring 6. squirm 7. contort,
distort, wriggle
writing... 4. book, poem 6. script
7. article, epistle 8. covenant,
documertt, makimono 10. expression,
penmanship, profession
11. chirography, composition,
handwriting, inscription, publication
writing (pert to)...
alternate.. 13. boustrophedon
ancient characters.. 9. cuneiform
ancient manuscript.. 6. uncial
cipher.. 12. cryptography
instrument.. 3. pen 5. quill 6. stylus
italic.. 7. cursive
mania for.. 11. graphomania
material.. 3. pad 5. paper, slate
6. tablet 9. parchment 10. stationery
omission of a letter.. 8. lipogram
10. lipography
pert to.. 7. scribal
record.. 3. log 5. album, diary
script.. 5. ronde
scroll.. 8. makimono
scroll hanging.. 8. kakemono
secret.. 4. code 10. cryptogram

12. cryptography
unrhymed.. 5. prose
writings, sacred... 5. Bible, Koran
6. Psalms, Talmud 9. Testament
(Old, New) 10. Scriptures
written (pert to)...
agreement.. 6. cartel
characters.. 6. script
it is.. 8. it must be 10. in the
books, in the cards 12. the die is
cast
law.. 10. legislated
law, unwritten.. 6. common
memo.. 5. scrip
wrong... 3. bad, off, out, sin 4. awry,
evil, harm, side, tort, vice 5. amiss,
cheat, crime, false, malum, unfit
6. faulty, injure, injury, seduce,
sinful, unjust, wicked 7. defraud,
immoral, misdeed, offense
8. improper, iniquity, mistaken
9. erroneous, incorrect, injustice,
violation 10. inaccurate, iniquitous
11. impropriety, inexpedient,
malfeasance, misfeasance
12. illegitimate
wrong (pert to)...
go (wrong).. 3. err 4. fail 5. lapse
8. go astray, go to ruin 9. backslide
10. misbelieve 11. go to the dogs
in the.. 6. guilty 7. at fault, in error
8. mistaken 9. violation
law.. 4. tort 5. crime, malum
name.. 8. misnomer
nor right (neither).. 7. neutral
11. adiaphorous
prefix.. 3. mis
side of.. 5. shady
way.. 5. amiss 6. astray 10. out of
place
wrongdoer... 6. sinner 8. criminal,
evildoer, violator 10. malefactor,
trespasser 12. transgressor
wroth... 3. mad 5. angry, irate
7. violent 8. incensed, wrathful
9. turbulent, wrought up
11. exasperated
wrought... 4. made 6. formed,
shaped, worked 9. decorated,
fashioned, processed 10. elaborated,
ornamented 11. embroidered
12. manufactured
wrought up... 4. agog 5. angry, eager
7. excited 9. disturbed, stirred up
wry... 4. awry 6. biased, swerve,
turned 7. crooked, twisted
9. contorted
wryneck... 4. Jynx, weet 5. loxia
9. snakebird 11. torticollis
Württemberg, Germany...
capital.. 9. Stuttgart
city.. 3. Ulm 5. Esslingen, Heilbronn,
Hohenheim
lake.. 9. Constance
river.. 6. Danube, Neckar
Wyandot... 6. Indian (Iroquois)
Wyandotte... 4. cave, city, fowl
Wycliff (Wyclif), John (pert to)...
birthplace.. 9. Yorkshire (Eng)
disciple.. 4. Huss
remains cast into.. 10. Swift River
translator of.. 5. Bible

Wyoming...
capital.. **8.** Cheyenne
city.. **4.** Cody **6.** Casper **7.** Big Horn,
Laramie **8.** Cheyenne, Sheridan
historic site.. **11.** Fort Laramie
17. Buffalo Bill Center
mountain.. **6.** Tetons **7.** Rockies
11. Gannett Peak
park.. **10.** Grand Teton

11. Yellowstone
river.. **4.** Wind **6.** Platte **7.** Big Horn
river source.. **8.** Colorado, Columbia,
Missouri
State admission.. **11.** Forty–fourth
State bird.. **10.** meadowlark
State flower.. **16.** Indian paintbrush
State motto.. **11.** Equal Rights
Woman Suffrage.. **10.** First State

X

X... **3.** ten **5.** error **6.** letter (24th),
symbol **7.** unknown
xanthic... **6.** cyanic, yellow
Xanthippe, wife of... **8.** Socrates
xanthoma... **9.** xanthosis **11.** skin
disease **13.** yellow patches
xanthos... **6.** yellow
Xanthus (pert to)...
ancient site.. **7.** marbles (Xanthian)
placed now.. **13.** British Museum
xebec... **6.** vessel **7.** corsair
xen, xeno (comb form)... **7.** foreign
8. stranger
xenium... **4.** gift **7.** present (official)
Xenocrates (Gr)... **11.** philosopher
xenogamy... **18.** cross–fertilization
xenophobic... **9.** strangers (afraid of)
12. chauvinistic
Xenophon's historic tale...
8. Anabasis
xenophthalmia... **11.** foreign body
(eye) **14.** conjunctivitis
Xenopus... **5.** toads
Xenorhynchus... **6.** storks
Xenurus... **7.** tatouay **10.** armadillos
Xeres... **5.** jerez **6.** sherry
xerophagy... **4.** Fast (Lenten)
xerotes... **7.** dryness (body)
Xerox (tm)... **4.** copy **9.** duplicate,
replicate, reproduce
Xerus... **9.** squirrels
Xerxes (pert to)...

crossing of.. **10.** Hellespont
destroyer of.. **6.** Athens (BC)
king of.. **6.** Persia
xibalba... **10.** underworld
Xinca... **6.** Indian, Jincan
Xipe, Xipe–totec... **11.** god of sowing
Xiphias... **5.** comet (sword–shaped)
6. Dorado (constellation) **9.** swordfish
xiphoid... **4.** bone **8.** ensiform
9. swordlike **12.** xiphisternum
Xiphopagus... **7.** monster (twinlike)
Xiphosura... **8.** king crab
Xiuhtocutli... **7.** fire god (Aztec)
Xmas... **9.** Christmas
X ray (pert to)...
measure.. **3.** rad **11.** quantimeter
named.. **12.** Roentgen rays
type.. **7.** CAT scan **8.** tomogram
9. myelogram **11.** arteriogram
xyloglyphy... **11.** wood carving (art)
xylography... **13.** wood engraving
xyloid... **5.** woody **8.** ligneous,
woodlike
xylomancy, divination by... **4.** wood
10. wood pieces
xylophone... **5.** saron **7.** gambang,
marimba **8.** gamelang (gamelan),
gigelira, sticcado
xyrid... **4.** iris **5.** Xyris
xystus, xyst (Gr)... **16.** portico
colonnade

Y

Y... **4.** tube **5.** curve, track **6.** letter
(25th), prefix, suffix
yabber... **4.** talk **6.** jabber
yabby, yabbie... **8.** crayfish
yaboa... **10.** night heron
yabu, yaboo... **4.** pony
yacht... **4.** boat, race, sail, ship

yaffle... **6.** armful **7.** handful
10. woodpecker
yahoo... **4.** lout, rube **5.** brute
Yahoo (pert to)...
represented by.. **10.** Houyhnhnms
(horses of reason)
tale.. **16.** Gulliver's Travels

yakalo, yakattalo... 8. creature
10. crossbreed (yak, cattle)
yakka... 4. work 5. labor
yaksha... 4. ogre 5. demon, dryad,
fairy, gnome, jinni 6. Kubera (Chief),
spirit 7. tree–god 13. guardian angel
Yale (pert to)...
  college.. 8. New Haven
  color.. 4. blue 7. Rameses
  founded at.. 8. Saybrook
  founder.. 9. Elihu Yale
  graduate.. 9. Yalensian
Yalta Conference... 6. Crimea (1945)
yam (pert to)...
  Fiji.. 6. uviyam 8. white yam
  Hawaiian.. 3. hoi
  reference to.. 5. tuber 6. igname
  Scot.. 6. potato
  tropical.. 8. cush–cush
  US.. 11. sweet potato
yamstchik... 7. postboy 8. coachman
9. postilion
yang... 4. good, male 6. bright (opp
of yin)
yang–kin... 8. dulcimer
yank... 4. jerk, pull 6. Yankee
Yankee... 12. New Englander
Yannigans... 9. scrub team (baseball)
Yao... 6. Indian 9. aborigine
yap... 3. cur, dog, gab 4. bark, talk,
yell, yelp 6. jabber 7. bumpkin,
hoodlum 8. easy mark 9. greenhorn
yapok, yapock... 6. monkey
7. opossum
yapp... 11. bookbinding
yapster... 3. dog
Yaqui... 6. Indian
yard... 3. rae (sail) 4. lawn, spar,
wand 5. garth, stick, verge
6. campus 7. confine, enclose,
measure 9. courtyard, curtilage,
enclosure, yardstick 10. playground
yarn... 3. abb, cop 4. hank, joke, tale
5. fiber, skein, story 6. caddis,
crewel, spinel, thread 7. genappe
9. falsehood
yarn (pert to)...
  clew.. 4. ball
  holder.. 3. cop
  measure.. 4. hank, hasp 5. skein
  7. spangle
  size.. 6. denier
  winder.. 10. yarnwindle
yashiro... 3. sha 6. temple (Shinto)
yashmak... 4. veil (double)
yati... 7. ascetic, devotee
yaw... 4. sail, tack 5. steer, tumor
7. deviate 9. deviation
yawl... 4. boat, howl, wail, yell, yowl
5. ketch 9. jolly boat
yawn... 3. gap 4. gape 5. chasm,
mouth 7. opening, stretch 8. open
wide, oscitate 12. seek greedily
yaws... 9. frambesia
yawweed... 5. shrub 7. rhubarb
12. wild mulberry
Yazoo (pert to)...
  Fraud.. 9. land grant (1795)
  Indian.. 11. Mississippi
  river.. 11. Mississippi
yclept, ycleped... 5. named 6. called,
styled

year (pert to)...
  after year.. 10. constantly, repeatedly
  11. over and over
  book.. 7. almanac
  division of.. 6. season 8. semester
  9. trimester
  Latin.. 5. annus
  of mourning.. 11. annus luctus
  of our Lord.. 10. Anno Domini
  11. annus Domini, year of grace
  of thirteen months (384 days)..
  10. embolismic
  of travel.. 10. sabbatical, Wanderjahr
  14. leave of absence
  old (Zool).. 10. annotinous
  pert to.. 5. epact
  quarter.. 5. raith
  record.. 5. annal 8. calendar
yearly (pert to)...
  church income.. 7. annates
  payment.. 4. cens
  recurring.. 6. annual 7. etesian
  8. annually
yearn for... 3. yen 4. ache, hope,
itch, long, pine, sigh, wish 6. desire,
hanker
yearning... 3. yen 4. wish 5. eager
7. anxious, longing 9. hankering,
nostalgia 10. tenderness
11. languishing 12. homesickness
years (pert to)...
  adolescent.. 4. teen
  ago.. 4. ages 9. long since 10. days
  of yore, yesteryear
  eight.. 9. octennial
  fifteen.. 9. indiction
  five.. 6. pentad 7. lustrum
  hundred.. 9. centenary 10. centennial
  ten.. 9. decade 9. decennary
  thousand.. 7. chiliad 10. millennium
  two.. 8. biennial, biennium
yeast... 4. barm, foam, koji 5. froth
6. leaven 7. anamite, ferment
9. agitation
yeasty... 5. foamy, light, spumy
6. frothy 8. restless 9. frivolous,
leavening
yegg... 5. thief, tramp 6. robber
7. burglar, yeggman 8. criminal
10. safeblower 11. safebreaker,
safecracker
yell... 3. cry 4. howl, roar, wail, yowl
5. cheer, shout 6. outcry, scream,
shriek
yelling... 7. bawling 8. shouting,
strident 9. clamorous 11. full of yells
yellow... 3. dun, sil 4. buff, cuir,
deer, ecru, flax, gull, mean, nude,
yolk 5. amber, beige, color, cream,
grège, jaune, lemon, maize, ocher
(ochre), straw, taupe, topaz, twine
6. bisque, butter, canary, Cassel,
chrome, citron, creamy, flaxen,
golden, mimosa, sallow, Seasan
7. anamite, annatto, aureate, egg
yolk, envious, etiolin, jealous, jonquil,
saffron, sulphur, xanthic, xanthin
8. cowardly, ocherous, primrose,
recreant 9. champagne, dandelion,
flavicant, goldenrod, jaundiced,
lutescent, sunflower 10. flavescent,
melancholy 11. treacherous

yellow (pert to)...
brown.. 3. dun 5. straw 6. manila
coloring.. 7. xanthic 8. xanthine
comb form.. 5. luteo
dyestuff.. 5. morin 7. annatto
  8. luteolin
golden.. 2. or (Her) 4. gild, gilt
green.. 5. olive 8. tarragon
  10. chartreuse, serpentine
herb.. 3. iva
jacket.. 4. wasp
medical.. 7. icterus 8. jaundice
  11. xanthoderma
mustard.. 8. charlock
ocher, ochre.. 3. sil
pert to.. 7. xanthic
pigment.. 7. etiolin 8. orpiment
race.. 9. Mongolian
red.. 4. roan 5. aloma, sandy
  6. bisque, dorado, orange
  7. annatto, nacarat
sensational.. 5. press 7. journal
yellow fever mosquito... 12. Aëdes
  aegypti
yellowhammer... 4. yite 5. ammer,
  finch, skite 6. gladdy 7. flicker
  10. woodpecker 13. yellow bunting
Yellowhammer State... 7. Alabama
yellow jacket... 4. wasp 8. eucalypt
Yellowstone Park geyser... 11. Old
  Faithful
yelp... 3. cry, yip 4. bark, yell
  5. shout 6. outcry, shriek, squeal
  7. ululate 8. complain 9. criticize
yelper... 8. redshank 10. yellowlegs
  11. hunting call
yeme... 4. heed 5. guard 6. govern,
  regard
Yemen (pert to)...
archeology site.. 4. Sana 5. Marib
Bib kingdom.. 5. Sheba (Saba)
capital.. 4. Sana
citadel.. 5. Damar
division of.. 6. Arabia
plateau.. 7. El Jebel
port.. 5. Mocha 7. Hodeida, Loheiya
ruler.. 4. Imam
sea.. 3. Red
yemochik... see *yamstchik*
yen... 4. coin, urge 5. yearn 6. desire,
  hanker 7. longing
yeoman... 4. exon 5. clerk 6. butler,
  seaman 8. retainer 9. assistant,
  attendant 10. freeholder
  11. subordinate 12. petty officer
yep... 3. yes 4. bold 5. alert, smart
  6. active 8. vigorous
yerba... 4. herb, maté 5. plant
  11. Paraguay tea
yes...
English.. 3. aye, yea, yep 5. uh–huh
  6. assent 11. affirmation
French.. 3. oui
German.. 2. ja
Italian, Spanish.. 2. si
Russian.. 2. da
yesterday... 6. yester 7. the past
  10. days gone by, heretofore,
  yesteryear 11. bygone times
yet... 3. but 5. still 6. algate
  7. besides, however 10. eventually

  11. nonetheless 15. notwithstanding
yew... 5. green, Taxus 7. conifer,
  hemlock 9. evergreen
Yiddish... 6. Jewish
  12. Judaeo–German (Judeo–German)
yield... 3. bow, net 4. bear, bend,
  cede, crop, give, lose, obey, vail
  5. admit, allow, defer, grant, stoop,
  waive 6. accede, afford, comply, give
  up, relent, render, reward, soften,
  submit 7. concede, consent,
  produce, provide, requite, revenue,
  succumb 9. acquiesce, surrender
  10. capitulate, relinquish
  11. acknowledge
yielding... 4. meek, soft 6. pliant,
  supple 7. bearing 8. flexible
  9. compliant, deference, producing,
  tractable 10. compliance,
  manageable, submissive
Yigdal... 4. poem (Jew Relig)
yill–caup... 6. ale cup
yin... 4. dark, evil (opp of yang)
Ymir, Ymer (pert to)...
blood of.. 3. sea
bones of.. 9. mountains
brains of.. 6. clouds
flesh of.. 5. earth
killed by.. 2. Ve 4. Odin, Vili
Norse Myth.. 3. God 13. rime–cold
  giant (body–shaped world)
yodel, yodle... 4. call, sing (falsetto)
  5. carol, shout 6. warble
yoga (pert to)...
follower of.. 4. yogi (yogin) 5. fakir
  7. ascetic 9. occultist
objective.. 16. mental discipline
stages.. 5. jnana, karma 6. bhakti
trance.. 6. dhyana 7. dharana,
  samadhi
yoke... 3. two 4. join, link, pair, span,
  team 5. frame, marry 6. cangue,
  couple, inspan 7. bondage, enclave,
  harness, oppress, pillory, shackle,
  slavery 9. associate, servitude
yoked... 6. united 7. coupled
  9. conjugate
yokel... 3. oaf 4. boor, clod, hick,
  lout, rube 6. rustic 7. bumpkin,
  hayseed, plowboy 8. Abderite (anc),
  gullible 9. simpleton 10. countryman,
  slow–witted
yokemate... 4. mate 6. fellow, spouse
  7. partner 9. companion
yolked (egg)... 6. yellow 8. lecithal,
  vitellus
Yom Kippur (Jew)... 7. fast day
  14. Day of Atonement
Yom Teruah (Jew)... 15. Feast of
  Trumpets
Yom Tob, or Tov (Jew)... 8. festival
yon, yonder... 4. away 6. beyond
  7. distant, thither 11. at a distance
yore... 5. of old, olden 6. before 9. in
  old time, long since
young... 3. fry, new 4. tyro 5. brood,
  fresh, green 6. litter, novice, tender
  7. pliable 8. childish, immature,
  juvenile, youthful 9. offspring,
  succulent 13. inexperienced
young (pert to)...
bear, fox.. 3. cub

birds .. **5.** brood
calf (motherless) .. **5.** dogie
hare .. **7.** leveret
herring .. **4.** brit
horse .. **4.** colt, foal
oyster .. **4.** spat
pigeon .. **5.** piper
youngling ... **5.** youth **6.** novice
  8. beginner, neophyte
youngster ... **3.** boy, kid, lad, pup, tad
  4. baby, lass, tike **5.** child, youth
  6. filius, shaver, urchin **7.** Aladdin
  (Arab Nights) **8.** teenager **9.** fledgling,
  stripling
younker ... **5.** child, youth **6.** knight
  7. gallant **8.** nobleman **9.** stripling
youth goddess ... **4.** Hebe
yo–yo ... **3.** top, toy
Ypres, Belgium ...
  famed for .. **7.** Battles (WWI)
  lace .. **12.** Valenciennes
  province of .. **8.** Flanders
  ruins rebuilt .. **9.** Cloth Hall **15.** Gothic
  Cathedral (St Martin)
ypsiliform, shape of ... **7.** letter T (Gr)
yu (Chin) ... **4.** jade
Yucatan, Cent America ...
  anc domain of .. **5.** Mayas
  capital .. **6.** Mérida
  city .. **5.** Sisal
  peninsula of .. **6.** Mexico
yucca (pert to) ...
  called .. **11.** Adam's needle
  family .. **9.** Liliaceae
  native of .. **7.** America
  species .. **9.** bear grass

State flower of .. **9.** New Mexico
Yugoslavia ...
  capital .. **8.** Belgrade
  city .. **5.** Senta **7.** Skoplje
  former leader .. **4.** Tito (Communist)
  lead works (among world's largest) ..
  6. Trepca
  natives .. **5.** Serbs **6.** Croats
  8. Slovenes
  river .. **5.** Drava, Drina **6.** Danube
  sea .. **8.** Adriatic
  seaport .. **6.** Rijeka
yukkel ... **7.** flicker **10.** woodpecker
Yukon ...
  famed for .. **4.** gold (mining)
  ocean .. **6.** Arctic
  river .. **5.** Lewes, Yukon
  territory of .. **6.** Canada
  town .. **10.** Whitehorse
Yule ... **4.** Noel **8.** Nativity (Feast of
  the), yuletide **9.** Christmas
  13. Christmastide
Yule (pert to) ...
  plant .. **5.** holly **9.** mistletoe
  good cheer .. **11.** wassail bowl
Yuma (Ariz) ... **4.** city **9.** Talkepaia
  (Indian)
yun ... **9.** Laos tribe (tattooed)
Yunca ... **6.** Indian (Peru)
Yurma ... **6.** Indian (Brazil)
Yurok ... **6.** Indian (Calif)
yurt, yurta ... **4.** tent (Siberia)
Yuruk ... **10.** Turkish rug
yutu ... **7.** tinamou
Yuzen birodo ... **6.** velvet (designed)

Z

Z ... **3.** end, zed, zee **5.** omega
  6. izzard, letter (26th)
zac ... **4.** ibex
zacate ... **7.** herbage **9.** rice grass
Zacchaeus, Zaccheus ... **4.** pure
  8. innocent, publican (Bib)
Zachariah, Zacharias (Bib) ...
  father .. **9.** Barachias
  father of .. **14.** John the Baptist
  literally .. **21.** Jehovah hath
  remembered
Zadkiel (Jew) ... **5.** angel (of planet
  Jupiter)
zaftig ... **5.** buxom **7.** shapely
Zagreus ... **3.** god **8.** Dionysus
  (identified with)
Zaire, Africa ...
  capital .. **8.** Kinshasa
  formerly .. **12.** Belgian Congo
  river .. **5.** Kasai, Zaire (Congo)
zaman, zamang ... **8.** rain tree
Zambia, Africa ...
  capital .. **6.** Lusaka
  formerly .. **16.** Northern Rhodesia

  wealth .. **6.** copper (3rd largest)
Zamenhof, inventor of ...
  9. Esperanto
zampogna ... **7.** bagpipe, panpipe
zanja ... **5.** canal, gully **6.** arroyo
zany ... **3.** wag, wit **4.** dolt, fool
  5. clown, crazy, goofy, kooky, nutty
  6. madcap, sawney **7.** acrobat,
  bonkers, buffoon, idiotic **8.** clownish
  9. simpleton **10.** lieutenant,
  mountebank **11.** merry–andrew
Zanzibar, Africa ... see *Tanzania*
zap ... **4.** slay, stun **5.** smite **6.** strike
zapatero ... **7.** boxwood, cobbler,
  dogwood
zarf ... **9.** cup holder (Levant)
zati ... **6.** monkey (bonnet)
zeal ... **5.** ardor, piety **6.** desire, fervor
  7. passion **8.** devotion **9.** eagerness
  10. enthusiasm, fanaticism
zealot ... **4.** sect **5.** bigot, freak (sl)
  6. votary **7.** devotee, faddist, fanatic,
  pietist **8.** partisan **10.** enthusiast
zealous ... **5.** eager, pious **6.** ardent,

fervid 7. devoted, fervent
9. phrenetic 11. industrious
zebra (pert to) . . .
ally . . 6. quagga
Burchell's . . 4. dauw (nonstriped legs)
hybrid . . 8. zebrinny
insect . . 9. butterfly
ref to . . 7. zebrine, zebroid
zebrawood . . . 5. shrub 7. araroba
10. marblewood
zebu . . . 2. ox 5. zebus (group)
6. cattle 12. Brahmany bull (sacred)
zecchino . . . 6. sequin (chequeen)
Zechariah (Bib) . . . 7. prophet 12. King
of Israel
zed . . . 7. letter Z (Brit)
zeekoe . . . 12. hippopotamus
zeism . . . 8. pellagra 11. morbid state
zemi . . . 4. holy (Peru) 5. huaca (huaco)
6. fetish, sacred, spirit (magic)
Zemzem . . . 10. sacred well (Mecca)
Zen . . . 12. Buddhist sect
zenana . . . 5. harem, serai 7. mission
8. seraglio
Zenda, Prisoner of . . . 9. Ruritania
Zend-Avesta . . . 10. sacred text
(Zoroastrian)
zenith . . . 3. top 4. acme, apex, blue,
peak 6. apogee, climax, summit,
vertex 11. culmination 14. greatest
height (opp of nadir)
Zeno . . . 5. Stoic 11. philosopher (Gr)
zenography, study of . . . 7. Jupiter
(planet)
zenu . . . 5. sheep
zephyr . . . 3. shawl 6. breath, breeze
zero . . . 3. nil 4. hour 5. zilch
6. cipher, nought (naught) 7. nothing,
nullity 11. temperature
zest . . . 4. tang 5. gusto, savor
6. flavor, relish 8. membrane (fruit),
piquancy, pungency 9. eagerness
10. enthusiasm
Zeus (pert to) . . .
attendant . . 4. Nike
consort . . 6. Europa
brother of . . 5. Hades 8. Poseidon
deity . . 7. supreme 12. father of gods
father . . 6. Cronus
games in his honor . . 6. Nemean
8. Olympian
messenger . . 4. Iris 6. Hermes
mother . . 4. Rhea
oracle . . 6. Dodona
Roman . . 7. Jupiter
sister . . 4. Hera
son . . 4. Ares 5. Argus 6. Apollo,
Hermes 7. Perseus 8. Dionysus,
Hercules, Tantalus
temple (Athens) . . 8. Olympium
ziara, ziarat . . . 4. tomb (Moslem saint)
6. shrine
zibet, zibeth . . . 5. civet
ziganka . . . 5. dance (rustic)
zigeuner . . . 5. gypsy 7. czigany,
Zincalo, zingaro
ziggurat . . . 11. temple tower
12. Tower of Babel (Bib)
zigzag . . . 5. turns 6. angles 7. stagger
8. flexuous, wavering 9. alternate
zillion . . . 4. many 9. countless

Zimbabwe . . .
capital . . 6. Harare
Falls . . 8. Victoria
Falls discoverer . . 11. Livingstone
(1855)
formerly . . 8. Rhodesia
tribe . . 5. Bantu
zinc (pert to) . . .
alloy . . 5. bidri 7. paktong
alloy with copper . . 6. oroide
crude . . 7. tutenag (tutenague)
slabs . . 6. solder 7. spelter
symbol . . 2. Zn
zing . . . 3. pep, vim, zip 5. vigor
6. energy, spirit, thrill 10. enthusiasm
zingaresca (gypsy) . . . 4. song 5. dance
zingaro . . . 5. gypsy
Zion (pert to) . . . 4. hill (Jerusalem)
10. Israelites 12. chosen people
zip . . . 4. zing 5. close, speed
6. energy 8. pungency 10. sibilation
zizith . . . 7. fringes (Bib), tassels
zoanthropy . . . 9. monomania
15. changed to animal (belief)
zobo . . . 6. hybrid 10. zebu and yak
zodiac . . . 4. belt, zone 5. stars
7. circuit
zodiac signs (twelve) . . . 3. Leo
5. Aries, Libra, Virgo 6. Cancer,
Gemini, Pisces, Taurus 7. Scorpio
8. Aquarius 9. Capricorn
11. Capricornus, Sagittarius
zoetic . . . 5. vital 6. living 7. organic
zombi, zombie . . . 5. corpse 6. voodoo
zone . . . 4. area, band, belt, isle, path
5. Canal, clime, girth, tract 6. assise,
circle, course, Frigid, region, Torrid
7. stratum 8. cincture, latitude
9. Temperate
zoo . . . 9. menagerie 10. collection
12. animal garden
zoo, zo (comb form) . . . 6. animal
zoologist . . . 9. biologist, scientist
zoology, science of . . . 7. animals
zoology branches . . . 8. taxonomy
9. bionomics, phylogeny
10. embryology, entomology
11. herpetology, ornithology
zoom . . . 4. lens, rise 5. climb
zoopathology, science of . . .
8. diseases (animal) 11. zoonosology
zoophilist . . . 11. animal lover
zoophobia . . . 13. fear of animals
zoophyte . . . 5. coral 6. sponge
10. sea anemone
zootomy . . . 13. animal anatomy
16. animal dissection
zootrophy . . . 13. animal rearing
zoril, zorillo . . . 5. skunk 7. polecat
Zoroaster, Zarathustra . . . 7. Persian
8. reformer (Relig)
Zoroastrianism (pert to) . . .
adherence to . . 5. Parse (Parsee)
doctrine . . 7. dualism 11. good and
evil
evil spirit . . 4. deva 7. Ahriman
fire worshiper . . 6. Gheber
founder . . 9. Zoroaster
literature . . 8. Avesta
lord of creation . . 6. Ormazd
religion of . . 6. Persia (anc)

zoster... 4. zona 6. girdle 8. shingles (Med) 12. herpes zoster
Zouave... 4. Zu–Zu 8. chasseur 11. infantryman
Zu (Bab Myth)... 8. storm god (evil) 9. blackbird (symbol)
Zuider Zee (pert to)...
  gulf.. 8. North Sea
  Netherlands.. 4. dike 7. highway
  present name.. 9. Ijsel Lake, Ijselmeer
zuisin... 7. widgeon
Zulu (pert to)...
  army.. 4. impi 7. Kaffirs
  boy.. 6. umfaan
  conference.. 6. indaba
  marauders.. 4. Viti
  people.. 6. Santus 7. Kaffirs
  spear.. 7. assagai (assegai)

Zululand capital... 6. Eshowe
Zuñi (pert to)...
  famed for.. 19. Seven Cities of Cibola (Myth)
  Indian.. 4. Hopi 6. Ashivi
  kingdom of Cibola.. 16. gold–paved streets (Myth)
zwieback... 4. rusk 7. biscuit (toasted)
Zwinger... 6. palace (Dresden)
zygal... 7. H–shaped
zygodactyl (zygodactyle)... 8. yoke–toed 10. paired toes
zygon... 5. bench 6. thwart 9. brain part
zygous... 5. yoked 6. paired
zymology *(science of)*... 12. fermentation
zymosis... 12. fermentation
zythum... 4. beer (anc Egypt)